OFFICIAL BASEBALL REGISTER

PRESIDENT-CHIEF EXECUTIVE OFFICER
RICHARD WATERS

EDITOR
HOWARD M. BALZER

CONTRIBUTING EDITORS
JOHN DUXBURY
JOHN HADLEY

PUBLISHED BY

The Sporting News

1212 NORTH LINDBERGH BLVD.
P. O. BOX 56 • **ST. LOUIS, MISSOURI 63166**

Copyright © 1981
The Sporting News Publishing Company
a Times Mirror company

ISBN 0-89204-072-6
ISSN 0067-4281

Table
of
CONTENTS

⚔︎⊖⚔︎

Players included are those who played in at least one game in the majors in 1980, those part of a team's 1981 40-man roster and selected invitees to spring training.

⚔︎⊖⚔︎

On the cover: George Brett, THE SPORTING NEWS 1980 Man of the Year.

—Photograph by Malcolm Emmons

EXPLANATION OF ABBREVIATIONS

G—Games Played. Pos.—Position. AB—At-Bats. R—Runs. H—Hits. 2B—Two-Base Hits. 3B—Three-Base Hits. HR—Home Runs. RBI—Runs Batted In. B.A.—Batting Average. PO—Putouts. A—Assists. E—Errors. F.A.—Fielding Average. IP—Innings Pitched. W—Won. L—Lost. Pct.—Percentage. R—Runs. ER—Earned Runs. SO—Strikeouts. BB—Bases on Balls. ERA—Earned-Run Average.

Active Players

DONALD WILLIAM AASE

Name pronounced AH-see.

(Don)

Born September 8, 1954, at Orange, Calif.
Height, 6.03. Weight, 195.
Throws and bats righthanded.
Hobbies—Hunting and camping.
Attended California State University, Fullerton, Calif.

Led International League pitchers in games started with 29 in 1975.
Led Carolina League pitchers in games started with 30 and in complete games with 18 in 1974.
Tied for Carolina League lead in shutouts with 4 in 1974.
Named Carolina League Pitcher of the Year in 1974.

Year Club	League	G.	IP.	W.	L.	Pct.	H.	R.	ER.	SO.	BB.	ERA.
1972—Williamsport	NYP	12	62	0	*10	.000	60	48	40	40	34	5.81
1973—Winter Haven	Florida St.	29	170	12	●15	.444	153	82	68	127	73	3.60
1974—Winston-Salem	Carolina	32	*230	*17	8	.680	185	72	62	176	84	*2.43
1975—Pawtucket	Int'national	29	186	8	13	.381	173	85	75	125	88	3.63
1976—Rhode Island†	Int'national	10	54	5	2	.714	42	23	20	40	34	3.33
1977—Pawtucket	Int'national	18	109	6	6	.500	118	67	61	64	60	5.04
1977—Boston‡	American	13	92	6	2	.750	85	36	32	49	19	3.13
1978—California	American	29	179	11	8	.579	185	88	80	93	80	4.02
1979—California	American	37	185	9	10	.474	200	104	99	96	77	4.82
1980—California	American	40	175	8	13	.381	193	83	79	74	66	4.06
Major League Totals		119	631	34	33	.507	663	311	290	312	242	4.14

Selected by Boston Red Sox' organization in 6th round of free-agent draft, June 6, 1972.
†On disabled list, June 23 through remainder of season.
‡Traded with cash to California Angels for Second Baseman Jerry Remy, December 8, 1977.

CHAMPIONSHIP SERIES RECORD

Tied American League Championship Series record for most strikeouts by relief pitcher, game (4), October 5, 1979.

Year Club	League	G.	IP.	W.	L.	Pct.	H.	R.	ER.	SO.	BB.	ERA.
1979—California	American	2	5	1	0	1.000	4	1	1	6	2	1.80

WILLIAM GLENN ABBOTT

(Known by middle name.)

Born February 16, 1951, at Little Rock, Ark.
Height, 6.06. Weight, 200.
Throws and bats righthanded.
Hobbies—Hunting, fishing and golf.
Attended State College of Arkansas, Conway, Ark.

Year Club	League	G.	IP.	W.	L.	Pct.	H.	R.	ER.	SO.	BB.	ERA.
1970—Coos Bay-North Bend	Northwest	14	101	8	3	.727	106	55	43	92	40	3.83
1971—Burlington	Midwest	24	179	11	10	.524	166	67	54	195	52	2.72
1972—Birmingham	Southern	13	97	3	8	.273	84	38	27	78	31	2.51
1972—Iowa	Am. Assoc.	15	107	6	8	.429	90	42	40	62	35	3.36
1973—Tucson	P. Coast	29	206	*18	8	.692	219	97	80	120	67	3.50
1973—Oakland	American	5	19	1	0	1.000	16	8	8	6	7	3.79
1974—Tucson	P. Coast	11	85	6	2	.750	109	44	39	39	25	4.13
1974—Oakland	American	19	96	5	7	.417	89	38	32	38	34	3.00
1975—Tucson	P. Coast	4	30	2	2	.500	30	14	12	18	11	3.60
1975—Oakland	American	30	114	5	5	.500	109	61	54	51	50	4.26
1976—Oakland†	American	19	62	2	4	.333	87	41	38	27	16	5.52
1977—Seattle	American	36	204	12	13	.480	212	111	101	100	56	4.46
1978—Seattle‡	American	29	155	7	15	.318	191	99	91	67	44	5.28
1979—Seattle§	American	23	117	4	10	.286	138	78	67	25	38	5.15
1980—Seattle	American	31	215	12	12	.500	228	110	98	78	49	4.10
Major League Totals		192	982	48	66	.421	1070	546	489	392	294	4.48

Selected by Oakland A's organization in 15th round of free-agent draft, June 5, 1969.
†Selected by Seattle Mariners from Oakland A's in American League expansion draft, November 5, 1976.
‡On disabled list, April 21 to May 11, 1978.
§On disabled list, August 18 to September 7, 1979.

CHAMPIONSHIP SERIES RECORD

Year Club	League	G.	IP.	W.	L.	Pct.	H.	R.	ER.	SO.	BB.	ERA.
1975—Oakland	American	1	1	0	0	.000	0	0	0	0	0	0.00

GLENN CHARLES ADAMS

Born October 4, 1947, at Northbridge, Mass.
Height, 6.00. Weight, 188.
Throws right and bats lefthanded.
Hobbies—Hunting and playing scrabble.
Attended Springfield College, Springfield, Mass.

Year Club	League	Pos.	G.	AB.	R.	H.	2B.	3B.	HR.	RBI.	B.A.	PO.	A.	E.	F.A.
1968—Greensboro ......Carol.		OF	129	451	58	132	23	4	3	51	.293	139	11	12	.926
1969—Savannah ....South.		OF	36	121	13	27	6	1	1	12	.223	56	2	3	.951
1969—Peninsula ....Carol.		OF	71	247	32	69	5	0	4	23	.279	92	3	6	.941
1970—Columbus ....South.		OF	83	234	32	69	10	2	2	20	.295	74	6	5	.941
1971—Columbus ....South.		OF	24	81	13	31	7	0	2	10	.383	24	2	1	.963
1971—Okla. City† ......A.A.		OF	59	161	14	50	9	0	0	19	.311	61	2	2	.969
1972—						(Did not play)									
1973—Amarillo ....Tex.		OF	110	415	59	129	32	2	3	52	.311	88	1	4	.957
1974—Phoenix.............P.C.		OF	127	432	79	152	26	1	13	105	*.352	26	1	0	1.000
1975—Phoenix.............P.C.		DH	19	67	9	20	4	1	1	8	.299	0	0	0	.000
1975—San Francisco ....Nat.		OF	61	90	10	27	2	1	4	15	.300	31	1	2	.941
1976—San Francisco‡..Nat.		OF	69	74	2	18	4	0	0	3	.243	3	0	0	1.000
1977—Minnesota§.......Amer.		OF	95	269	32	91	17	0	6	49	.338	60	3	2	.969
1978—Minnesota ....Amer.		OF	116	310	27	80	18	1	7	35	.258	5	0	0	1.000
1979—Minnesota ....Amer.		OF	119	326	34	98	13	1	8	50	.301	66	2	3	.958
1980—Minnesota x......Amer.		OF	99	262	32	75	11	2	6	38	.286	18	0	1	.947
National League Totals..................			130	164	12	45	6	1	4	18	.274	34	1	2	.946
American League Totals.................			429	1167	125	344	59	4	27	172	.295	149	5	6	.963
Major League Totals			559	1331	137	389	65	5	31	190	.292	183	6	8	.959

Selected by Houston Astros' organization in 1st round of free-agent draft, January 28, 1968.
†Released by Houston Astros' organization, January 20, 1972; signed as a free agent by San Francisco Giants' organization, December 23, 1972.
‡Sold to Minnesota Twins, December 6, 1976.
§On disabled list, April 14 to May 16, 1977.
xOn supplemental disabled list, July 14 to July 29, 1980.

LUIS AGUAYO (MURIEL)

Born March 13, 1959, at Vega Baja, P.R.
Height, 5.09. Weight, 173.
Throws and bats righthanded

Led Carolina League second basemen in assists with 365, in errors with 30 and in fielding average with .953 in 1977.

Year Club	League	Pos.	G.	AB.	R.	H.	2B.	3B.	HR.	RBI.	B.A.	PO.	A.	E.	F.A.
1976—Spartanburg......W. Car.		2B	3	11	0	1	0	0	0	0	.091	5	2	1	.875
1976—Auburn ....NYP		2B-3B-SS	51	197	27	49	9	2	0	23	.249	79	99	10	.947
1977—Peninsula ....Carol.		2B-SS	130	497	73	127	28	2	9	41	.256	271	409	34	.952
1978—Reading ....East.		SS-2B	115	378	49	74	29	5	4	33	.196	198	341	25	.956
1979—Oklahoma City..A.A.		SS-2B	113	370	54	101	21	1	8	46	.273	191	320	27	.950
1980—Oklahoma City†.A.A.		SS	84	291	37	71	19	2	9	40	.244	154	268	*28	.938
1980—Philadelphia‡ ....Nat.		2B-SS	20	47	7	13	1	2	1	8	.277	44	44	3	.967
Major League Totals.......................			20	47	7	13	1	2	1	8	.277	44	44	3	.967

Signed as free agent by Philadelphia Phillies' organization, December 27, 1975.
†On disabled list, May 22 to June 6, 1980.
‡On supplemental disabled list, May 7 to May 22, 1980.

WILLIE MAYS AIKENS

Born October 14, 1954, at Seneca, S. C.
Height, 6.02. Weight, 220.
Throws right and bats lefthanded.
Attended South Carolina State College, Orangeburg, S.C.

Tied major league record for most consecutive games, home runs, bases filled (2), June 13 and 14, 1979.
Led Midwest League in sacrifice flies with 9 in 1975.
Led Texas League in total bases with 285 in 1976.

Year Club	League	Pos.	G.	AB.	R.	H.	2B.	3B.	HR.	RBI.	B.A.	PO.	A.	E.	F.A.
1975—Quad Cities ....Midw.		1B	125	443	69	126	17	1	17	*91	.284	1038	53	*26	.977
1976—El Paso ....Texas		1B	133	514	*99	163	24	4	*30	*117	.317	971	52	*20	.981
1977—Salt Lake City ...P.C.		1B-C	77	295	62	99	23	2	14	73	.336	700	48	10	.987
1977—California..........Amer.		1B	42	91	5	18	4	0	0	6	.198	94	8	3	.971
1978—Salt Lake City ...P.C.		*1B-OF	133	470	82	153	19	0	*29	110	.326	1030	*83	*25	.978
1979—California† ....Amer.		1B	116	379	59	106	18	0	21	81	.280	462	31	2	.996
1980—Kansas City ......Amer.		1B	151	543	70	151	24	0	20	98	.278	1081	65	*12	.990
Major League Totals			309	1013	134	275	46	0	41	185	.271	1637	104	17	.990

Selected by California Angels' organization in 1st round (second player selected) of free-agent draft, January 9, 1975.
†Traded with Shortstop Rance Mulliniks to Kansas City Royals for Outfielder Al Cowens, Shortstop Todd Cruz and a player to be named later, December 6, 1979; Pitcher Craig Eaton traded to California Angels' organization completing deal, April 1, 1980.

Year Club League	Pos.	G.	AB.	R.	H.	2B.	3B.	HR.	RBI.	B.A.	PO.	A.	E.	F.A.
1980—Kansas City ......Amer.	1B	3	11	0	4	0	0	0	2	.364	22	1	0	1.000

WORLD SERIES RECORD

Tied World Series record for most home runs, two consecutive innings (2), October 18, 1980 (first and second inning).

Year Club League	Pos.	G.	AB.	R.	H.	2B.	3B.	HR.	RBI.	B.A.	PO.	A.	E.	F.A.
1980—Kansas City ......Amer.	1B	6	20	5	8	0	1	4	8	.400	55	2	2	.966

DANIEL RAY AINGE

Name pronounced to rhyme with "strange"

(Danny)

Born March 17, 1959, at Eugene, Ore.
Height, 6.04. Weight, 175.
Throws and bats righthanded
Attending Brigham Young University, Provo, Utah

Year Club League	Pos.	G.	AB.	R.	H.	2B.	3B.	HR.	RBI.	B.A.	PO.	A.	E.	F.A.
1978—Syracuse...........Int.	SS-2B	119	389	33	89	10	1	4	30	.229	206	328	29	.948
1979—Syracuse...........Int.	2B	27	101	10	25	4	2	0	8	.248	56	77	4	.971
1979—Toronto† ....Amer.	2B	87	308	26	73	7	1	2	19	.237	198	261	10	.979
1980—Syracuse...........Int.	3-O-S	80	295	37	72	9	1	2	17	.244	111	140	3	.988
1980—Toronto‡ ....Amer.	OF-3-2	38	111	11	27	6	1	0	4	.243	69	12	1	.98F
Major League Totals......................		125	419	37	100	13	2	2	23	.239	267	273	12	.978

Selected by Toronto Blue Jays' organization in 15th round of free-agent draft, June 7, 1977.
†On restricted list, September 3 to October 3, 1979.
‡On restricted list, September 8 to October 8, 1980.

SANTO ALCALA

Name pronounced AL-kuh-luh.

Born December 23, 1952, at San Pedro de Macoris, Dominican Republic.
Height, 6.05. Weight, 195.
Throws and bats righthanded.

Tied for Eastern League lead in games started with 27 in 1973.

Year Club	League	G.	IP.	W.	L.	Pct.	H.	R.	ER.	SO.	BB.	ERA.
1970—Bradenton Reds ....Gulf Coast		11	72	4	6	.400	74	34	24	54	40	3.00
1971—Sioux Falls...........................Northern		20	41	0	2	.000	43	42	24	48	36	5.27
1972—Key West ....Florida St.		29	176	7	●14	.333	152	75	59	★176	59	3.02
1972—Three Rivers.......................Eastern		4	29	2	1	.667	14	3	2	18	7	0.62
1973—Three Rivers.......................Eastern		30	190	7	●13	.350	168	91	83	115	85	3.93
1974—Indianapolis ....Am. Assoc.		32	161	12	11	.522	152	84	75	113	74	4.19
1975—Indianapolis ....Am. Assoc.		27	173	13	12	.520	144	61	53	118	64	2.76
1976—Cincinnati ....National		30	132	11	4	.733	131	72	69	67	67	4.70
1977—Cinc.†-Mont.‡.......................National		38	117	3	7	.300	126	66	63	73	54	4.85
1978—Seattle§............................ American						Did not play						
1978—San Jose xy.......................P. Coast		15	57	5	2	.714	61	35	32	30	31	5.05
1979—Santo Domingo z................. Int.-Amer.						Did not play						
1979—Buffalo ab...........................Eastern		7	22	0	0	.000	24	20	15	16	11	6.14
1980—Chihuahua c.......................Mexican		15	113	5	9	.357	95	33	25	74	29	1.99
1980—Portland ....P. Coast		9	36	2	4	.333	40	23	19	18	16	4.75
Major League Totals................................		68	249	14	11	.560	257	138	132	140	121	4.77

†Traded to Montreal Expos for player to be named later, May 21, 1977; Pitchers Shane Rawley and Angel Torres traded to Cincinnati Reds' organization to complete deal, May 27, 1977.
‡Sold on waivers to Seattle Mariners, March 25, 1978.
§On disabled list, April 4 to April 29, 1978.
xOn disabled list, May 15 to May 26, 1978.
ySold to Santo Domingo, April 2, 1979.
zReleased, May 30, 1979; signed by Pittsburgh Pirates' organization, July 14, 1979.
aOn temporary inactive list, July 14 to July 26, 1979.
bSold to Chihuahua, April 9, 1980.
cSold to Pittsburgh Pirates' organization, July 16, 1980.

DOYLE LAFAYETTE ALEXANDER

Born September 4, 1950, at Cordova, Ala.
Height, 6.03. Weight, 200.
Throws and bats righthanded.
Hobbies—Hunting, fishing, golf and working on cars.
Attended Jefferson State Junior College, Pinson, Ala.

Year Club	League	G.	IP.	W.	L.	Pct.	H.	R.	ER.	SO.	BB.	ERA.
1968—Tri-City ....Northwest		13	70	3	●9	.250	66	47	32	58	47	4.11
1969—Daytona Beach...................Florida St.		30	185	13	9	.591	154	75	56	140	100	2.72
1969—Albuquerque ....Texas		3	15	0	3	.000	19	10	10	3	12	6.00
1970—Albuquerque ....Texas		10	80	4	3	.571	72	29	28	60	20	3.15
1970—Spokane ....P. Coast		19	137	9	7	.563	137	66	55	78	26	3.61
1971—Spokane ....P. Coast		15	110	6	3	.667	114	49	42	65	31	3.44

Year — Club	League	G.	IP.	W.	L.	Pct.	H.	R.	ER.	SO.	BB.	ERA.
1971—Los Angeles†	National	17	92	6	6	.500	105	45	39	30	18	3.82
1972—Baltimore	American	35	106	6	8	.429	78	36	29	49	30	2.46
1973—Baltimore‡	American	29	175	12	8	.600	169	85	75	63	52	3.86
1974—Baltimore	American	30	114	6	9	.400	127	65	51	40	43	4.03
1975—Baltimore	American	32	133	8	8	.500	127	47	45	46	47	3.05
1976—Balt.§-N.Y. x	American	30	201	13	9	.591	172	81	75	58	63	3.36
1977—Texas	American	34	237	17	11	.607	221	103	96	82	82	3.65
1978—Texas	American	31	191	9	10	.474	198	84	82	81	71	3.86
1979—Texas y	American	23	113	5	7	.417	114	65	56	50	69	4.46
1980—Atlanta z	National	35	232	14	11	.560	227	120	108	114	74	4.19
National League Totals		52	324	20	17	.541	332	165	147	144	92	4.08
American League Totals		244	1270	76	70	.521	1206	566	509	469	457	3.61
Major League Totals		296	1594	96	87	.525	1538	731	656	613	549	3.70

Selected by Los Angeles Dodgers' organization in 44th round of free-agent draft, June 7, 1968.

†Traded with Pitcher Bob O'Brien, Catcher Sergio Robles and First Baseman-Outfielder Royle Stillman to Baltimore Orioles for Pitcher Pete Richert and Outfielder Frank Robinson, December 2, 1971.

‡On disabled list, July 10 to August 6, 1973.

§Traded with Pitchers Kenny Holtzman and Grant Jackson, Catcher Elrod Hendricks and Pitcher Jimmy Freeman, latter assigned from Rochester to Syracuse, to New York Yankees for Pitchers Rudy May, Tippy Martinez, Dave Pagan, Scott McGregor and Catcher Rick Dempsey, June 15, 1976.

xPlayed out option year and granted free agency, November 1, 1976; signed as free agent by Texas Rangers, November 23, 1976.

yTraded with Shortstop Larvell Blanks to Atlanta Braves for Pitcher Adrian Devine, Shortstop Pepe Frias and a player to be named later, December 7, 1979; Braves received $50,000 to complete deal when Outfielder Jeff Burroughs exercised no-trade clause.

zTraded to San Francisco Giants for Pitcher John Montefusco and Outfielder Craig Landis, December 12, 1980.

CHAMPIONSHIP SERIES RECORD

Year — Club	League	G.	IP.	W.	L.	Pct.	H.	R.	ER.	SO.	BB.	ERA.
1973—Baltimore	American	1	3⅔	0	1	.000	5	3	2	1	0	4.91

WORLD SERIES RECORD

Year — Club	League	G.	IP.	W.	L.	Pct.	H.	R.	ER.	SO.	BB.	ERA.
1976—New York	American	1	6	0	1	.000	9	5	5	1	2	7.50

GARY WAYNE ALEXANDER

Born March 27, 1953, at Los Angeles, Calif.
Height, 6.02. Weight, 200.
Throws and bats righthanded.
Hobbies—Music, cars and clothes.
Attended Los Angeles Harbor Junior College, Wilmington, Calif.

Tied American League record for most home runs, consecutive plate appearances by pinch-hitter (2), July 5-6, 1980.

Led Midwest League batters in strikeouts with 126 in 1973.

Led American League batters in strikeouts with 166 in 1978.

Named California League Player of the Year in 1974.

Named Texas League Player of the Year in 1975.

Year — Club	League	Pos.	G.	AB.	R.	H.	2B.	3B.	HR.	RBI.	B.A.	PO.	A.	E.	F.A.
1972—Great Falls	Pion.	OF-C	55	136	14	28	6	1	2	14	.206	118	7	8	.940
1973—Decatur	Midw.	OF-C	123	406	68	106	16	5	17	66	.261	178	7	14	.930
1974—Fresno†	Calif.	*C-OF	103	356	84	106	15	3	*27	95	.298	475	54	*27	.951
1975—Phoenix	P.C.	OF	7	14	2	2	1	0	0	1	.143	0	0	0	.000
1975—Lafayette	Tex.	C-OF	103	346	80	114	24	1	•23	81	.329	275	22	11	.964
1975—San Francisco	Nat.	C	3	3	1	0	0	0	0	0	.000	2	0	0	1.000
1976—Phoenix	P.C.	C-1B	109	360	59	115	18	12	17	76	.319	398	63	13	.972
1976—San Francisco	Nat.	C	23	73	12	13	1	1	2	7	.178	92	16	4	.973
1977—Phoenix	P.C.	C-OF	59	211	54	72	11	3	7	55	.341	228	40	8	.971
1977—San Francisco‡	Nat.	C-OF	51	119	17	36	4	2	5	20	.303	174	8	6	.968
1978—Oak.§-Cleve.	Amer.	C-OF-1	148	498	57	112	20	4	27	84	.225	321	34	6	.983
1979—Cleveland	Amer.	*C-OF	110	358	54	82	9	2	15	54	.229	404	40	*18	.961
1980—Cleveland x	Amer.	C-OF	76	178	22	40	7	1	5	31	.225	34	2	1	.973
American League Totals			334	1034	133	234	36	7	47	169	.226	759	76	25	.971
National League Totals			77	195	30	49	5	3	7	27	.251	268	24	10	.967
Major League Totals			411	1229	163	283	41	10	54	196	.230	1027	100	35	.970

Selected by Montreal Expos' organization in 23rd round of free-agent draft, June 8, 1971.

Selected by San Francisco Giants' organization in secondary phase of free-agent draft, January 12, 1972.

†On disabled list after knee surgery, August 5 through remainder of season.

‡Traded with Outfielder Gary Thomasson, Pitchers Dave Heaverlo, Alan Wirth, John Johnson and Phillip Huffman, a player to be named later and cash estimated at $390,000 to Oakland A's for Pitcher Vida Blue, March 15, 1978 (Shortstop Mario Guerrero sent to A's to complete deal, April 7, 1978).

§Traded to Cleveland Indians for Outfielder Joe Wallis, June 15, 1978.

xTraded with Pitchers Victor Cruz, Rafael Vasquez and Bob Owchinko to Pittsburgh Pirates for Pitcher Bert Blyleven and Catcher Manny Sanguillen, December 9, 1980.

MATTHEW ALEXANDER, JR.
(Matt)

Born January 30, 1947, at Shreveport, La.
Height, 5.11. Weight, 170.
Throws right and bats right and lefthanded.
Hobbies—Billiards and cars.
Attended Grambling College, Grambling, La.

Major League stolen bases: 1973 (2), 1974 (8), 1975 (17), 1976 (20), 1977 (26), 1978 (4), 1979 (13), 1980 (10). Total—100.

Led Texas League in stolen bases with 38 and tied for lead in double plays by outfielders with 4 in 1972.

Year Club	League	Pos.	G.	AB.	R.	H.	2B.	3B.	HR.	RBI.	B.A.	PO.	A.	E.	F.A.
1968—Caldwell	Pion.	2-S-3	35	142	27	37	3	2	1	10	.261	55	75	8	.942
1969—Quincy	Midw.	3B	71	266	65	73	13	5	8	32	.274	●63	112	19	.902
1969—San Antonio	Tex.	3-1-SS	30	109	17	33	3	2	1	13	.303	81	42	8	.939
1970-71—Chicago	Nat.	(In Military Service)													
1972—Midland	Tex.	OF-2-3	124	460	78	124	18	2	5	45	.270	262	65	13	.962
1973—Wichita	A.A.	O-3-2	106	427	61	132	22	3	2	51	.309	114	60	14	.926
1973—Chicago	Nat.	OF	12	5	4	1	0	0	0	1	.200	2	0	0	1.000
1974—Wichita	A.A.	O-2-S	30	120	26	33	2	1	2	12	.275	68	27	3	.969
1974—Chicago	Nat.	3-O-2	45	54	15	11	2	1	0	0	.204	13	24	3	.925
1975—Wichita†	A.A.	OF	7	32	4	8	0	0	2	8	.250	25	1	0	1.000
1975—Oakland‡	Amer.	O-2-3	63	10	16	1	0	0	0	0	.100	7	2	1	.900
1976—Oakland	Amer.	OF	61	30	16	1	0	0	0	0	.033	23	0	0	1.000
1977—Oakland§	Amer.	O-S-2-3	90	42	24	10	1	0	0	2	.238	21	2	0	1.000
1978—Pittsburgh	Nat.	PR	7	0	2	0	0	0	0	0	.000	0	0	0	.000
1979—Buffalo	East.	2B-OF	32	134	26	42	10	0	5	16	.313	26	36	10	.861
1979—Pittsburgh	Nat.	OF-SS	44	13	16	7	0	1	0	1	.538	8	1	0	1.000
1980—Pittsburgh x	Nat.	OF-2B	37	3	13	1	1	0	0	0	.333	6	0	0	1.000
National League Totals			145	75	50	20	3	2	0	2	.267	29	25	3	.947
American League Totals			214	82	56	12	1	0	0	2	.146	51	4	1	.982
Major League Totals			359	157	106	32	4	2	0	4	.204	80	29	4	.965

Selected by Chicago Cubs' organization in 2nd round of free-agent draft, June 7, 1968.

†Traded by Chicago Cubs to Oakland Athletics for a player to be named later, April 28, 1975; Athletics sent Pitcher Howell (Buddy) Copeland to Cubs, May 2, 1975, to complete deal.

‡On disabled list, June 4 to July 4, 1975.

§Released, March 31, 1978; signed as free agent by Pittsburgh Pirates, September 1, 1978.

xOn supplemental disabled list, April 5 to April 24, 1980.

CHAMPIONSHIP SERIES RECORD

Year Club	League	Pos.	G.	AB.	R.	H.	2B.	3B.	HR.	RBI.	B.A.	PO.	A.	E.	F.A.
1979—Pittsburgh	Nat.	PR	1	0	1	0	0	0	0	0	.000	0	0	0	.000

WORLD SERIES RECORD

Year Club	League	Pos.	G.	AB.	R.	H.	2B.	3B.	HR.	RBI.	B.A.	PO.	A.	E.	F.A.
1979—Pittsburgh	Nat.	PR-OF	1	0	0	0	0	0	0	0	.000	0	0	0	.000

BRIAN MARSHALL ALLARD

Name pronounced AL-ard.

Born January 3, 1958, at Spring Valley, Ill.
Height, 6.02. Weight, 185.
Throws and bats righthanded
Attending Western Illinois University, Macomb, Ill.

Year Club	League	G.	IP.	W.	L.	Pct.	H.	R.	ER.	SO.	BB.	ERA.
1976—Sarasota Rangers	G. Coast	13	68	5	1	.833	46	25	18	35	33	2.38
1977—Asheville†	W. Carol.	26	166	8	9	.471	179	98	76	124	78	4.12
1978—Tulsa	Texas	26	155	7	10	.412	171	92	73	102	75	4.24
1979—Tucson	P. Coast	22	138	10	6	.625	159	81	69	70	54	4.50
1979—Texas	American	7	33	1	3	.250	36	17	16	14	13	4.36
1980—Charleston	Int'national	22	152	8	8	.500	146	62	53	68	43	3.14
1980—Texas‡	American	5	14	0	1	.000	13	13	9	10	10	5.79
Major League Totals		12	47	1	4	.200	49	30	25	24	23	4.79

Selected by Texas Rangers' organization in 4th round of free-agent draft, June 8, 1976.

†Played one game as outfielder.

‡Traded with Outfielder Richie Zisk, Pitchers Ken Clay, Steve Finch and Jerry Gleaton and Shortstop Rick Auerbach to Seattle Mariners for Catcher Larry Cox, Pitcher Rick Honeycutt, Outfielders Willie Horton and Leon Roberts and Shortstop Mario Mendoza, December 12, 1980.

KIM BRYANT ALLEN

Born April 5, 1952, at Fontana, Calif.
Height, 5.11. Weight, 175.
Throws and bats righthanded.
Attended University of California at Riverside, Riverside, Calif.

Led Pacific Coast League in stolen bases with 84 in 1980.

Year Club	League	Pos.	G.	AB.	R.	H.	2B.	3B.	HR.	RBI.	B.A.	PO.	A.	E.	F.A.
1975—Quad Cities .... Midw.		OF	49	138	33	37	11	0	1	11	.268	54	6	2	.968
1976—Salinas .... Calif.		OF	39	120	30	37	9	0	0	22	.308	58	2	1	.984
1976—Durango .... Mex.		OF	66	254	45	77	6	0	1	19	.303	156	8	3	.982
1977—Salinas .... Calif.		2B	20	87	25	29	7	1	1	13	.333	5	2	1	.875
1977—Salt Lake City ... P.C.		OF-3B	101	363	77	113	22	4	0	37	.311	139	13	2	.987
1978—Salt Lake City† .. P.C.		2B	15	46	2	10	3	1	0	9	.217	16	23	1	.975
1978—Col.‡-Roch.§ ...... Int.		3B-OF	68	208	46	60	11	2	2	14	.288	39	71	11	.909
1979—Maracaibo x ..... Int.-Am.		....	32	119	20	37	4	2	0	12	.311	....	....	....	....
1980—Spokane .... P.C.		OF-3B	118	436	71	128	22	3	1	41	.294	86	42	6	.955
1980—Seattle .... Amer.		2-O-SS	23	51	9	12	3	0	0	3	.235	26	42	2	.971
Major League Totals			23	51	9	12	3	0	0	3	.235	26	42	2	.971

Signed as free agent by California Angels' organization, June 30, 1975.
†Sold to Pittsburgh Pirates' organization, June 2, 1978.
‡Released, June 30, 1978; signed by Baltimore Orioles' organization, July 2, 1978.
§Sold to Maracaibo of Inter-American League, April 6, 1979.
xSigned as free agent by Seattle Mariners' organization, April 6, 1980.

NEIL PATRICK ALLEN

Born January 24, 1958, at Kansas City, Kan.
Height, 6.02. Weight, 185.
Throws and bats righthanded

Major League saves: 1979 (8), 1980 (22). Total—30.
Tied for Carolina League lead in complete games with 11 in 1977.

Year Club	League	G.	IP.	W.	L.	Pct.	H.	R.	ER.	SO.	BB.	ERA.
1976—Marion .... Ap'lachian		6	33	2	0	1.000	23	8	7	29	6	1.91
1976—Wausau............................... Midwest		6	48	4	2	.667	51	27	20	34	20	3.75
1977—Lynchburg† .... Carolina		20	142	10	2	.833	136	55	44	•126	43	2.79
1978—Jackson .... Texas		16	120	5	9	.357	88	38	28	111	38	•2.10
1978—Tidewater .... Int'national		10	57	2	7	.222	65	35	28	30	12	4.42
1979—New York‡ .... National		50	99	6	10	.375	100	46	39	65	47	3.55
1980—New York .... National		59	97	7	10	.412	87	43	40	79	40	3.71
Major League Totals.................................		109	196	13	20	.394	187	89	79	144	87	3.63

Selected by New York Mets' organization in 11th round of free-agent draft, June 8, 1976.
†On disabled list, July 26 to September 1, 1977.
‡On disabled list, June 1 to June 25, 1979.

RODERICK B. ALLEN

Born October 5, 1959, at Los Angeles, Calif.
Height, 6.01. Weight, 185.
Throws and bats righthanded.

Year Club	League	Pos.	G.	AB.	R.	H.	2B.	3B.	HR.	RBI.	B.A.	PO.	A.	E.	F.A.
1977—Sarasota W. Sox	Gulf C.	OF	43	176	21	54	5	2	1	23	.307	60	2	2	.969
1978—Appleton .... Midw.		OF	100	342	48	83	16	4	7	55	.243	134	7	8	.946
1979—Knoxville .... South.		OF	86	281	32	75	12	2	6	45	.267	98	6	5	.954
1980—Glens Falls† ...... East.		OF	31	121	26	43	5	4	3	27	.355	29	1	0	1.000
1980—Iowa‡ .... A.A.		OF	38	131	23	34	4	0	6	24	.260	42	0	0	1.000

Selected by Chicago White Sox' organization in 6th round of free-agent draft, June 7, 1977.
†On disabled list, August 1 to August 31, 1980.
‡On disabled list, July 8 to July 30, 1980.

GARY MARTIN ALLENSON

Born February 4, 1955, at Culver City, Calif.
Height, 5.11. Weight, 188.
Throws and bats righthanded
Attended Arizona State University, Tempe, Ariz.

Led International League catchers in putouts with 735 and in assists with 86 in 1978.
Named International League Most Valuable Player, 1978.

Year Club	League	Pos.	G.	AB.	R.	H.	2B.	3B.	HR.	RBI.	B.A.	PO.	A.	E.	F.A.
1976—Bristol .... East.		C	50	160	18	38	7	0	1	20	.238	190	36	6	.974
1977—Winter Haven .... Fla. St.		C	105	312	42	83	18	4	5	43	.266	474	•80	6	•.989
1977—Pawtucket .... Int.		C-1B	3	8	1	2	0	0	1	2	.250	4	1	0	1.000
1978—Pawtucket .... Int.		C-1B	133	445	82	133	31	3	20	76	.299	763	90	7	.992
1979—Boston .... Amer.		C-3B	108	241	27	49	10	2	3	22	.203	410	42	9	.980
1980—Boston .... Amer.		C-3B	36	70	9	25	6	0	0	10	.357	100	8	2	.982
Major League Totals......................			144	311	36	74	16	2	3	32	.238	510	50	11	.981

Selected by Boston Red Sox' organization in 9th round of free-agent draft, June 8, 1976.

WILLIAM FRANCIS ALMON
(Bill)

Born November 21, 1952, at Providence, R. I.
Height, 6.03. Weight, 170.
Throws and bats righthanded.
Attended Brown University, Providence, R. I.
Brother of John Almon, outfielder in San Diego Padres' organization.

Named College Player of the Year by THE SPORTING NEWS, 1974.
Led Pacific Coast League shortstops in chances accepted with 744 in 1975.
Tied for Pacific Coast League lead in stolen bases with 33 in 1975.
Led National League shortstops in total chances with 882 in 1977.
Led National League in sacrifice hits with 20 in 1977.
Received reported $100,000 bonus to sign with San Diego Padres, 1974.

Year Club	League	Pos.	G.	AB.	R.	H.	2B.	3B.	HR.	RBI.	B.A.	PO.	A.	E.	F.A.
1974—Hawaii ..............P.C.		SS	14	36	6	8	0	0	0	3	.222	16	33	7	.875
1974—Alexandria ....Tex.		SS	25	97	9	18	2	2	0	5	.186	48	70	8	.937
1974—San Diego..........Nat.		SS	16	38	4	12	1	0	0	3	.316	13	30	4	.915
1975—Hawaii ..............P.C.		SS ●144		496	76	113	22	0	1	47	.228	★288	456	★48	.939
1975—San Diego..........Nat.		SS	6	10	0	4	0	0	0	0	.400	6	5	0	1.000
1976—Hawaii ..............P.C.		SS	129	454	67	132	16	2	3	44	.291	★248	395	★36	.947
1976—San Diego..........Nat.		SS	14	57	6	14	3	0	1	6	.246	23	52	3	.962
1977—San Diego..........Nat.		SS	155	613	75	160	18	11	2	43	.261	★303	538	★41	.954
1978—San Diego ....Nat.		3B-S-2	138	405	39	102	19	2	0	21	.252	102	255	23	.939
1979—San Diego†........Nat.		2B-SS-O	100	198	20	45	3	0	1	8	.227	142	193	7	.980
1980—Mtl.‡-N.Y.§ ....Nat.		SS-2-3	66	150	15	29	4	3	0	7	.193	79	134	12	.947
Major League Totals			495	1471	159	366	48	16	4	88	.249	668	1207	90	.954

Selected by San Diego Padres' organization in 10th round of free-agent draft, June 8, 1971.
Selected by San Diego Padres' organization in 1st round (first player selected) of free-agent draft, June 5, 1974.
†Traded with First Baseman-Outfielder Dan Briggs to Montreal Expos for Second Baseman Dave Cash, November 27, 1979.
‡Became free agent after refusing option to Denver, July 7, 1980; signed by New York Mets, July 11, 1980.
§Released, December 19, 1980; signed by Chicago White Sox' organization, February 4, 1981.

WENDELL ALSTON
(Dell)

Born September 22, 1952, at White Plains, N.Y.
Height, 6.00. Weight, 180.
Throws right and bats lefthanded.
Hobby—Dancing.
Attended Concordia Junior College, Bronxville, N.Y., and Concordia Teachers College, River Forest, Ill., received Bachelor of Arts Degree in Elementary Education.

Year Club	League	Pos.	G.	AB.	R.	H.	2B.	3B.	HR.	RBI.	B.A.	PO.	A.	E.	F.A.
1973—Oneonta ....NYP		OF-2B	61	246	59	79	13	3	4	34	.321	96	43	12	.921
1974—Ft. Lauderdale ..Fla.St.		OF-3B	120	431	68	127	15	●12	2	52	.295	168	11	8	.957
1975—West Haven.......East.		OF	119	452	★77	139	18	7	6	47	.308	181	12	8	.960
1976—Syracuse ....Int.		OF	130	516	87	145	26	9	12	66	.281	183	6	11	.945
1977—Syracuse ....Int.		OF-1B	63	248	33	74	12	2	3	21	.298	177	6	4	.979
1977—New York.........Amer.		OF	22	40	10	13	4	0	1	4	.325	2	1	0	1.000
1978—Tac.-Vanc. ....P. C.		OF-1B	69	275	65	97	13	7	7	42	.353	317	16	1	.997
1978—N.Y.†-Oak.‡ ......Amer.		OF-1B	61	176	17	36	2	0	1	10	.205	106	0	4	.964
1979—Tacoma ....P. C.		OF-1B	75	310	58	83	13	5	1	33	.268	170	13	6	.968
1979—Cleveland.........Amer.		OF	54	62	10	18	0	2	1	12	.290	29	2	1	.969
1980—Tacoma ....P. C.		OF-1B	69	241	43	53	11	4	3	29	.220	208	11	6	.973
1980—Cleveland.........Amer.		OF	52	54	11	12	1	2	0	9	.222	35	1	2	.947
Major League Totals			189	332	48	79	7	4	3	35	.238	172	4	7	.962

Signed as free agent by New York Yankees' organization, August 21, 1972.
†Traded with Infielder Mickey Klutts and $50,000 to Oakland A's for Outfielder Gary Thomasson, June 15, 1978.
‡Released March 23, 1979; signed as free agent by Cleveland Indians' organization, April 5, 1979.

LARRY EUGENE ANDERSEN

Born May 6, 1953, at Portland, Ore.
Height, 6.03. Weight, 180.
Throws and bats righthanded.
Hobbies—Music and airplanes.
Attended Bellevue Community College, Bellevue, Wash.

Pitched 6-0 no-hit victory against Victoria, June 1, 1974.
Led Pacific Coast League in saves with 25 in 1978.

Year Club	League	G.	IP.	W.	L.	Pct.	H.	R.	ER.	SO.	BB.	ERA.
1971—Reno.....................California		7	24	1	0	1.000	37	20	18	10	9	6.75
1971—Sarasota Indians ....Gulf Coast		4	15	0	3	.000	15	7	5	10	7	3.00
1972—Reno.....................California		27	124	4	14	.222	166	102	90	79	57	6.53
1973—Reno.....................California		29	164	10	8	.556	173	91	72	115	67	3.95
1974—San Antonio ....Texas		25	169	10	6	.625	176	84	72	64	51	3.83
1975—Oklahoma City ....Am. Assoc.		25	156	10	11	.476	179	87	73	64	52	4.21

Year Club	League	G.	IP.	W.	L.	Pct.	H.	R.	ER.	SO.	BB.	ERA.
1975—Cleveland............................American		3	6	0	0	.000	4	3	3	4	2	4.50
1976—Toledo ....Int'national		6	23	0	2	.000	47	33	33	8	6	12.91
1976—Williamsport ....Eastern		21	133	9	6	.600	117	47	40	74	34	2.71
1977—Toledo ....Int'national		45	65	5	6	.455	52	20	14	40	37	1.94
1977—Cleveland............................American		11	14	0	1	.000	10	7	5	8	9	3.21
1978—Portland ....P. Coast		57	99	10	7	.588	92	42	38	65	45	3.45
1979—Portland ....P. Coast		27	112	10	6	.625	124	59	50	52	32	4.02
1979—Cleveland†...........................American		8	17	0	0	.000	25	14	14	7	4	7.41
1980—Portland‡.............................P. Coast		52	93	5	7	.417	78	24	18	65	16	1.74
Major League Totals		22	37	0	1	.000	39	24	22	19	15	5.35

Selected by Cleveland Indians' organization in 7th round of free-agent draft, June 8, 1971.

†Traded to Pittsburgh Pirates for Outfielder Larry Littleton and Pitcher John Burden, December 21, 1979.

‡Traded to Seattle Mariners, October 24, 1980, completing deal in which Pittsburgh acquired Pitcher Odell Jones, April 1, 1980.

JAMES LEA ANDERSON
(Jim)

Born February 23, 1957, at Los Angeles, Calif.
Height, 6.00. Weight, 170.
Throws and bats righthanded.
Hobbies—Hunting and all sports.

Led Texas League shortstops in double plays with 93 in 1977.

Year Club	League	Pos.	G.	AB.	R.	H.	2B.	3B.	HR.	RBI.	B.A.	PO.	A.	E.	F.A.
1975—Idaho Falls........Pion.		★SS-2B	71	253	42	73	3	6	0	27	.289	●94	★239	27	★.925
1976—Salinas..............Calif.		SS	136	469	67	124	14	4	4	51	.264	188	★406	★40	.937
1977—El Paso.............Texas		SS-2B	120	417	87	119	24	1	18	73	.285	243	381	27	.959
1978—Salt Lake City ...P. C.		SS-2B	72	248	36	64	13	1	5	32	.258	124	244	22	.944
1978—California ....Amer.		SS-2B	48	108	6	21	7	0	0	7	.194	72	99	8	.955
1979—California†........Amer.		S-3-2-C	96	234	33	58	13	1	3	23	.248	141	205	17	.953
1980—Seattle..............Amer.		SS-3-2-C	116	317	46	72	7	0	8	30	.227	120	264	22	.946
Major League Totals......................			260	659	85	151	27	1	11	60	.229	333	568	47	.950

Selected by California Angels' organization in 2nd round of free-agent draft, June 4, 1975.

†Traded to Seattle Mariners, December 2, 1979, completing deal in which California acquired Pitcher John Montague, August 29, 1979.

CHAMPIONSHIP SERIES RECORD

Year Club	League	Pos.	G.	AB.	R.	H.	2B.	3B.	HR.	RBI.	B.A.	PO.	A.	E.	F.A.
1979—California ....Amer.		SS	4	11	0	1	0	0	0	0	.091	4	11	0	1.000

RICHARD LEE ANDERSON
(Rick)

Born December 25, 1953, at Inglewood, Calif.
Height, 6.02. Weight, 210.
Throws and bats righthanded.
Attended Los Angeles Valley College, Van Nuys, Calif.

Led International League in saves with 21 and in wild pitches with 10 in 1979.
Tied for Florida State League lead in wild pitches with 10 in 1974.

Year Club	League	G.	IP.	W.	L.	Pct.	H.	R.	ER.	SO.	BB.	ERA.
1972—Fort Lauderdale...................Florida St.		15	71	3	7	.300	75	45	40	52	36	5.07
1972—Johnson City ....Ap'lachian		5	31	2	2	.500	22	13	11	40	13	3.19
1973—Oneonta†...........................N.Y.-Pa.		14	45	3	5	.375	45	36	23	56	23	4.60
1974—Fort Lauderdale...................Florida St.		24	173	13	8	.619	124	50	44	★179	65	2.29
1975—West Haven........................Eastern		21	143	11	9	.550	115	70	57	★138	81	3.59
1976—West Haven........................Eastern		19	124	10	4	.714	117	61	48	88	48	3.48
1976—Syracuse............................Int'national		6	9	0	0	.000	5	3	3	4	8	3.00
1977—West Haven‡.......................Eastern		29	98	7	7	.500	110	72	62	68	47	5.69
1978—West Haven........................Eastern		16	34	4	3	.571	33	14	12	35	17	3.18
1978—Tacoma ....P. Coast		26	63	4	4	.500	70	38	35	51	44	5.00
1979—Columbus ....Int'national		52	83	13	3	.813	53	21	15	72	39	1.63
1979—New York§..........................American		1	2	0	0	.000	1	1	1	0	4	4.50
1980—Spokane.............................P. Coast		49	80	6	0	1.000	70	35	29	65	49	3.26
1980—Seattle..............................American		5	10	0	0	.000	8	5	4	7	10	3.60
Major League Totals................................		6	12	0	0	.000	9	6	5	7	14	3.75

Selected by San Francisco Giants' organization in 4th round of free-agent draft, June 8, 1971.

Selected by New York Yankees' organization in secondary phase of free-agent draft, January 12, 1972.

†On Fort Lauderdale disabled list, April 17 to June 8, 1973.

‡On disabled list, May 31 to June 10, 1977.

§Traded with Pitcher Jim Beattie, Outfielder Juan Beniquez and Catcher Jerry Narron to Seattle Mariners for Outfielder Ruppert Jones and Pitcher Jim Lewis, November 1, 1979.

JOAQUIN ANDUJAR

Name pronounced Wah-Keen AHN-doo-hahr.

Born December 21, 1952, at San Pedro de Macoris, Dominican Republic.
Height, 5.11. Weight, 180.
Throws and bats righthanded.

Year Club	League	G.	IP.	W.	L.	Pct.	H.	R.	ER.	SO.	BB.	ERA.
1970—Bradenton Reds	Gulf Coast	12	82	3	5	.375	*86	*58	*38	88	56	4.17
1971—Sioux Falls	Northern	19	75	4	7	.364	61	67	53	82	63	6.36
1972—Three Rivers	Eastern	22	112	7	6	.538	87	59	44	73	73	3.54
1973—Indianapolis	Am. Assoc.	11	40	2	5	.286	42	45	40	23	45	9.00
1973—Three Rivers†	Eastern	10	59	5	2	.714	38	29	13	39	38	1.98
1974—Indianapolis	Am. Assoc.	33	111	8	8	.500	85	62	44	92	93	3.57
1975—Three Rivers‡§	Eastern	18	62	4	8	.333	57	36	28	44	40	4.06
1976—Houston	National	28	172	9	10	.474	163	74	69	59	75	3.61
1977—Houston	National	26	159	11	8	.579	149	80	65	69	64	3.68
1978—Houston x	National	35	111	5	7	.417	88	45	42	55	58	3.41
1979—Houston	National	46	194	12	12	.500	168	86	74	77	88	3.43
1980—Houston	National	35	122	3	8	.273	132	59	53	75	43	3.91
Major League Totals		170	758	40	45	.471	700	344	303	335	328	3.60

Signed as free agent by Cincinnati Reds' organization, November 14, 1969.
†On disabled list, August 5 to August 15, 1973.
‡On disabled list, May 11 to July 4, 1975.
§Traded by Cincinnati Reds to Houston Astros for two minor league players to be named later, October 24, 1975; Astros sent Pitchers Carlos Alfonso and Luis Sanchez to Reds, December 12, 1975, to complete deal.
xOn disabled list, July 8 to July 30, 1978.

CHAMPIONSHIP SERIES RECORD

Year Club	League	G.	IP.	W.	L.	Pct.	H.	R.	ER.	SO.	BB.	ERA.
1980—Houston	National	1	1	0	0	.000	0	0	0	0	1	0.00

ALL-STAR GAME RECORD

Year League	IP.	W.	L.	Pct.	H.	R.	ER.	SO.	BB.	ERA.
1979—National	2	0	0	.000	2	2	1	0	1	4.50

Member of National League All-Star Team in 1977; did not play.

LUIS E. APONTE (YURIPA)

Born June 14, 1954, at Lel Tigre, Venezuela.
Height, 6.00. Weight, 180.
Throws and bats righthanded.

Year Club	League	G.	IP.	W.	L.	Pct.	H.	R.	ER.	SO.	BB.	ERA.
1973—Winter Haven	Florida St.	4	9	0	0	.000	12	7	3	5	2	3.00
1973—Elmira	Eastern	16	84	2	7	.222	*113	55	45	47	22	4.82
1974—Winston-Salem	Carolina	28	56	3	1	.750	49	32	24	36	25	3.86
1975—Winston-Salem	Carolina	40	62	3	0	1.000	52	20	19	38	37	2.76
1976—Winter Haven	Florida St.	48	78	3	4	.429	83	42	30	45	23	3.46
1977—Bristol†‡	Eastern					Did not play						
1979—Maracaibo§	Inter.-Am.	11	44	3	5	.375	70	30	26	19	16	5.32
1980—Bristol	Eastern	29	54	9	1	.900	46	17	15	43	23	2.50
1980—Pawtucket	Int'national	31	49	6	2	.750	27	15	12	42	21	2.20

Signed as free agent by Boston Red Sox' organization, January 12, 1973.
†On suspended list, April 14 to May 3, 1977; on restricted list, May 3, 1977, to May 10, 1979.
‡Released May 10, 1979; signed by Maracaibo of Inter-American League, June 1, 1979.
§Signed as free agent by Boston Red Sox' organization, February 28, 1980.

ANTONIO RAFAEL ARMAS (MACHADO)
(Tony)

Born July 12, 1953, at Anzoategui, Venezuela.
Height, 6.01. Weight, 182.
Throws and bats righthanded.

Tied for American League lead in double plays by outfielders with 4 in 1977.
Tied major league record for fewest double plays by outfielder, season, for leader in most double plays (4), 1977.

Year Club	League	Pos.	G.	AB.	R.	H.	2B.	3B.	HR.	RBI.	B.A.	PO.	A.	E.	F.A.
1971—Monroe	W. Car.	OF	31	88	7	20	3	0	1	10	.227	37	3	6	.870
1971—Bradenton Pir	Gulf C.	OF	43	169	12	39	3	3	0	17	.231	*98	5	3	.972
1972—Gastonia	W. Car.	OF	117	399	50	106	18	4	9	51	.266	165	7	8	.956
1973—Sherbrooke†	East.	OF	84	302	46	91	15	5	11	45	.301	150	6	8	.951
1974—Thetford Mines	East.	OF	*137	476	64	132	26	3	15	81	.277	*329	18	10	.972
1975—Charleston	Int.	OF	128	450	65	135	28	4	12	72	.300	220	●14	3	.987
1976—Charleston	Int.	OF-1B	114	409	62	96	24	1	21	67	.235	210	8	7	.969
1976—Pittsburgh‡	Nat.	OF	4	6	0	2	0	0	0	1	.333	3	0	0	1.000
1977—Oakland§	Amer.	OF-SS	118	363	26	87	8	2	13	53	.240	294	9	6	.981
1978—Oakland x	Amer.	OF	91	239	17	51	6	1	2	13	.213	214	3	2	.991

Year Club League	Pos.	G.	AB.	R.	H.	2B.	3B.	HR.	RBI.	B.A.	PO.	A.	E.	F.A.
1979—Oakland y .... Amer.	OF	80	278	29	69	9	3	11	34	.248	194	7	5	.976
1980—Oakland .... Amer.	OF	158	628	87	175	18	8	35	109	.279	374	17	10	.975
National League Totals...................		4	6	0	2	0	0	0	1	.333	3	0	0	1.000
American League Totals.................		447	1508	159	382	41	14	61	209	.253	1076	36	23	.980
Major League Totals		451	1514	159	384	41	14	61	210	.254	1079	36	23	.980

Signed as free agent by Pittsburgh Pirates' organization, January 18, 1971.

†On disabled list, May 27 to July 12, 1973.

‡Traded with Pitchers Dave Giusti, Doc Medich, Doug Bair and Rick Langford and Outfielder Mitchell Page to Oakland Athletics for Infielders Tommy Helms and Phil Garner and Pitcher Chris Batton, March 15, 1977.

§On supplemental disabled list, August 5 to September 1, 1977.

xOn supplemental disabled list, April 28 to June 2, 1978.

yOn disabled list, April 15 to June 5, 1979.

MICHAEL DENNIS ARMSTRONG
(Mike)

Born March 7, 1954, at Glen Cove, N.Y.
Height, 6.03. Weight, 193.
Throws and bats righthanded.
Attended University of Miami, Coral Gables, Fla.

Led Eastern League in games started with 29 in 1977.

Year Club	League	G.	IP.	W.	L.	Pct.	H.	R.	ER.	SO.	BB.	ERA.
1974—Tampa ....Florida St.		6	16	0	2	.000	26	17	17	14	18	9.56
1974—Seattle ....Northwest		15	102	6	7	.462	85	45	30	86	47	2.65
1975—Three Rivers.......................Eastern		25	150	5	10	.333	116	55	45	86	44	2.70
1976—Three Rivers.......................Eastern		24	146	10	10	.500	143	77	57	91	52	3.51
1977—Three Rivers.......................Eastern		30	184	*16	10	.615	185	91	77	107	83	3.77
1978—Chattanooga.......................Southern		31	74	9	6	.600	61	34	25	54	37	3.04
1978—Indianapolis ....Am. Assoc.		16	23	1	2	.333	26	18	17	17	17	6.65
1979—Nashville† ....Southern		32	64	5	1	.833	58	30	24	53	29	3.38
1979—Amarillo ....Texas		7	31	2	3	.400	32	15	12	34	14	3.48
1979—Hawaii.................................P. Coast		3	7	0	0	.000	6	2	2	4	5	2.57
1980—Hawaii.................................P. Coast		42	74	4	4	.500	48	18	16	67	26	1.95
1980—San Diego ....National		11	14	0	0	.000	16	10	9	14	13	5.79
Major League Totals................................		11	14	0	0	.000	16	10	9	14	13	5.79

Selected by Cleveland Indians' organization in 9th round of free-agent draft, June 6, 1972.

Selected by Cincinnati Reds' organization in 1st round (24th player selected) of free-agent draft, January 9, 1974.

†Traded to San Diego Padres' organization for Third Baseman Paul O'Neil, July 25, 1979.

CARLOS RUBEN ARROYO (SALGADO)

Born November 21, 1958, at Vega Alta, Puerto Rico.
Height, 6.00. Weight, 155.
Throws and bats lefthanded.

Year Club	League	G.	IP.	W.	L.	Pct.	H.	R.	ER.	SO.	BB.	ERA.
1975—Pulaski ....Ap'lachian		10	46	3	5	.375	61	36	30	20	11	5.87
1976—Spartanburg.........................W. Carol.		37	102	7	4	.636	102	40	30	58	28	2.65
1977—Peninsula ....Carolina		32	106	7	7	.500	112	70	57	54	50	4.84
1978—Reading ....Eastern		20	126	11	4	.733	123	62	56	60	42	4.00
1979—Oklahoma City ....Am. Assoc.		38	74	3	5	.375	81	39	34	41	30	4.14
1980—Oklahoma City† ....Am. Assoc.		46	92	8	6	.571	87	39	33	33	42	3.23

Signed as free agent by Philadelphia Phillies' organization, December 29, 1974.

†Drafted by Chicago White Sox, December 8, 1980.

FERNANDO ARROYO

Born March 21, 1952, at Sacramento, Calif.
Height, 6.02. Weight, 190.
Throws and bats righthanded.
Hobbies—Music, fishing and sports in general.

Pitched seven-inning 5-0 perfect game against West Palm Beach, July 8, 1971.

Year Club	League	G.	IP.	W.	L.	Pct.	H.	R.	ER.	SO.	BB.	ERA.
1970—Bristol ....Appalachian		9	61	4	1	.800	45	28	14	53	21	2.07
1971—Lakeland ....Fla. State		25	193	11	11	.500	153	71	54	117	53	2.52
1972—Montgomery ....Southern		28	157	8	9	.471	142	81	67	82	55	3.84
1973—Montgomery ....Southern		23	159	9	8	.529	153	71	54	74	50	3.06
1974—Evansville............................Am. Assoc.		35	87	6	4	.600	93	50	41	45	45	4.24
1975—Evansville ....Am. Assoc.		11	86	5	4	.556	82	37	25	44	18	2.62
1975—Detroit ....American		14	53	2	1	.667	56	28	27	25	22	4.58
1976—Evansville ....Am. Assoc.		44	102	5	8	.385	120	74	54	56	41	4.76
1977—Detroit ....American		38	209	8	18	.308	227	102	97	60	52	4.18
1978—Evansville ....Am. Assoc.		20	105	4	10	.286	124	56	48	45	30	4.11
1978—Detroit† ....American		2	4	0	0	.000	8	4	4	1	0	9.00
1979—Evansville ....Am. Assoc.		19	114	7	4	.636	113	50	38	39	34	3.00
1979—Detroit‡ ....American		6	12	1	1	.500	17	11	11	7	4	8.25

Year Club	League	G.	IP.	W.	L.	Pct.	H.	R.	ER.	SO.	BB.	ERA.
1980—Toledo ....Int'national	9	72	6	1	.857	56	22	13	36	14	1.63
1980—Minnesota ....American	21	92	6	6	.500	97	55	48	27	32	4.70
Major League Totals	81	370	17	26	.395	405	200	187	120	110	4.55

Selected by Detroit Tigers' organization in 9th round of free-agent draft, June 4, 1970.
On disabled list, March 27 to May 3, 1978.
‡Traded to Minnesota Twins' organization for Pitcher Jeff Holly, December 5, 1979.

ALAN DEAN ASHBY

Born July 8, 1951, at Long Beach, Calif.
Height, 6.02. Weight, 190.
Throws right and bats left and righthanded.
Hobbies—Golf, basketball and football.
Attended Harbor Junior College, Wilmington, Calif.

Led California League catchers in double plays with 12 in 1971.
Led National League catchers in passed balls with 14 in 1980.

Year Club	League	Pos.	G.	AB.	R.	H.	2B.	3B.	HR.	RBI.	B.A.	PO.	A.	E.	F.A.
1969—Sara. Indians .....Gulf C.	C	48	117	10	28	3	1	0	14	.239	219	20	2	*.992
1970—Reno† ....Calif.	C	40	121	15	23	5	1	3	18	.190	321	27	7	.980
1971—Jacksonville ......South.	C	13	35	4	7	2	0	0	8	.200	76	6	1	.988
1971—Reno‡ ....Calif.	C-3B	77	239	52	70	14	1	18	60	.293	492	59	10	.982
1972—Portland...........P. C.	C	95	291	33	65	9	2	9	28	.223	601	50	8	.988
1973—Ok.C.§-Evan......A. A.	C-OF	41	124	20	28	8	0	3	16	.226	253	26	2	.993
1973—Cleveland.........Amer.	C	11	29	4	5	1	0	1	3	.172	45	0	1	.978
1974—Oklahoma City ..A. A.	C	66	211	26	60	19	1	2	24	.284	405	33	8	.982
1974—Cleveland.........Amer.	C	10	7	1	1	0	0	0	0	.143	12	0	0	1.000
1975—Cleveland.........Amer.	C-1-3	90	254	32	57	10	1	5	32	.224	450	43	6	.988
1976—Cleveland xy......Amer.	C-1-3	89	247	26	59	5	1	4	32	.239	476	52	7	.987
1977—Toronto............Amer.	C	124	396	25	83	16	3	2	29	.210	619	71	11	.984
1978—Toronto z ....Amer.	C	81	264	27	69	15	0	9	29	.261	399	38	6	.986
1979—Houston a ....Nat.	C	108	336	25	68	15	2	2	35	.202	548	57	8	.987
1980—Houston ....Nat.	C	116	352	30	90	19	2	3	48	.256	608	60	6	.991
American League Totals..................	405	1197	115	274	47	5	21	125	.229	2001	204	31	.986
National League Totals	224	688	55	158	34	4	5	83	.230	1156	117	14	.989
Major League Totals......................	629	1885	170	432	81	9	26	208	.229	3157	321	45	.987

Selected by Cleveland Indians' organization in 3rd round of free-agent draft, June 5, 1969.
†On military list, January 1 to May 23, 1970.
‡On temporary inactive list, August 27 to September 13, 1971.
§Loaned to Evansville, May 22, 1973.
xOn supplemental disabled list, August 9 to November 5, 1976.
yTraded with Outfielder-First Baseman Doug Howard (Toledo) to Toronto Blue Jays for Pitcher Al Fitzmorris, November 5, 1976.
zTraded to Houston Astros for Pitcher Mark Lemongello, Outfielder Joe Cannon and Shortstop Pedro Hernandez, November 27, 1978.
aOn supplemental disabled list, August 30 to September 17, 1979.

CHAMPIONSHIP SERIES RECORD

Year Club	League	Pos.	G.	AB.	R.	H.	2B.	3B.	HR.	RBI.	B.A.	PO.	A.	E.	F.A.
1980—Houston ....Nat.	C-PH	2	8	0	1	0	0	0	1	.125	11	2	0	1.000

THOMAS STEVEN ASHFORD
(Tucker)

Born December 4, 1954, at Memphis, Tenn.
Height, 6.01. Weight, 195.
Throws and bats righthanded.
Hobbies—Golf, basketball and billiards.
Attended University of Mississippi, University, Miss., and
Shelby State Community College, Memphis, Tenn.

Led Northwest League shortstops in double plays with 40 in 1974.
Led Texas League third basemen in double plays with 33 in 1976.
Led Pacific Coast League third basemen in putouts with 131, in assists with 314 and in double plays with 31 in 1979.
Led International League third basemen in assists with 250 and in double plays with 24 in 1980.

Year Club	League	Pos.	G.	AB.	R.	H.	2B.	3B.	HR.	RBI.	B.A.	PO.	A.	E.	F.A.
1974—Walla Walla.......N'west	S-O-3B	77	263	56	64	7	2	4	30	.243	123	159	26	.916
1975—Alexandria ....Texas	3B-S-O	120	376	33	89	12	1	3	38	.237	125	254	36	.913
1976—Amarillo ....Texas	3B-SS	132	519	91	141	29	0	12	67	.272	*112	288	*38	.913
1976—San Diego.........Nat.	3B	4	5	0	3	1	0	0	0	.600	1	2	0	1.000
1977—Hawaii ....P. C.	3B	73	281	53	79	21	4	7	45	.281	67	142	14	.937
1977—San Diego.........Nat.	3-S-2	81	249	25	54	18	0	3	24	.217	49	159	15	.933
1978—Hawaii ....P. C.	2B-3B	14	45	6	14	4	0	0	6	.311	20	36	3	.949
1978—San Diego ....Nat.	3B-2-1	75	155	11	38	11	0	3	26	.245	108	53	6	.946
1979—Hawaii† ....P. C.	3-S-1-2	146	509	70	130	25	6	13	62	.255	141	321	26	.947

Year Club	League	Pos.	G.	AB.	R.	H.	2B.	3B.	HR.	RBI.	B.A.	PO.	A.	E.	F.A.
1980—Charleston	Int.	3B-SS	107	366	50	102	18	3	8	38	.279	97	262	23	.940
1980—Texas‡	Amer.	3B-SS	15	32	2	4	0	0	0	3	.125	10	25	2	.946
National League Totals			160	409	36	95	30	0	6	50	.232	158	214	21	.947
American League Totals			15	32	2	4	0	0	0	3	.125	10	25	2	.946
Major League Totals			175	441	38	99	30	0	6	53	.224	168	239	23	.947

Selected by San Diego Padres' organization in 1st round (second player selected) of free-agent draft, January 9, 1974.

†Traded with Pitchers Gaylord Perry and Joe Carroll to Texas Rangers for First Baseman Willie Montanez, February 15, 1980.

‡Traded to New York Yankees' organization, December 8, 1980; completing deal in which Texas Rangers acquired infielder Roger Holt, October 24, 1980.

BRIAN HANLY ASSELSTINE

Name pronounced ASS-ul-styn.

Born September 23, 1953, at Santa Barbara, Calif.
Height, 6.01. Weight, 190.
Throws right and bats lefthanded.
Hobbies—Fishing, hunting, golf, water skiing and music.
Attended Allan Hancock College, Santa Maria, Calif.

Year Club	League	Pos.	G.	AB.	R.	H.	2B.	3B.	HR.	RBI.	B.A.	PO.	A.	E.	F.A.
1973—Savannah	South.	OF	15	47	5	7	1	0	1	3	.149	27	0	0	1.000
1973—Greenwood	W. Car.	OF	2	2	0	0	0	0	0	0	.000	0	0	0	.000
1974—Savannah	South.	OF	126	508	82	133	11	4	6	35	.262	294	9	10	.968
1975—Richmond†	Int.	●OF-SS	122	444	66	126	21	2	1	22	.284	284	6	●12	.960
1976—Richmond	Int.	OF-2B	122	458	73	134	23	5	5	58	.293	237	9	5	.980
1976—Atlanta..............	Nat.	OF	11	33	2	7	0	0	1	3	.212	19	0	0	1.000
1977—Richmond	Int.	OF	27	98	15	27	2	2	2	13	.276	64	2	1	.985
1977—Atlanta..............	Nat.	OF	83	124	12	26	6	0	4	17	.210	57	1	1	.983
1978—Atlanta‡...........	Nat.	OF	39	103	11	28	3	3	2	13	.272	60	1	2	.968
1979—Atlanta§...........	Nat.	OF	8	10	1	1	0	0	0	0	.100	1	0	0	1.000
1979—Richmond x	Int.	OF	21	63	3	17	5	0	0	4	.270	17	0	0	1.000
1980—Atlanta y	Nat.	OF	87	218	18	62	13	1	3	25	.284	102	0	4	.962
Major League Totals			228	488	44	124	22	4	10	58	.254	239	2	7	.972

Selected by San Francisco Giants' organization in 7th round of free-agent draft, June 6, 1972.
Selected by Atlanta Braves' organization in secondary phase of free-agent draft, January 10, 1973.
†On disabled list, July 1 to July 19, 1975.
‡On disabled list, June 1; transferred to emergency disabled list, July 26 to October 1, 1978.
§On disabled list, April 4 to May 25, 1979 and on emergency disabled list, July 28 to October 16, 1979.
xOn disabled list, July 18 to July 28, 1979.
yOn supplemental disabled list, August 24 to September 8, 1980.

KEITH ROWE ATHERTON

Born February 19, 1959, at Mathews, Va.
Height, 6.03. Weight, 190.
Throws and bats righthanded.

Tied for Northwest League lead in shutouts with 2 in 1978.
Led Eastern League in complete games with 13 in 1980.

Year Club	League	G.	IP.	W.	L.	Pct.	H.	R.	ER.	SO.	BB.	ERA.
1978—Bend....................................	Northwest	12	92	7	3	.700	86	44	35	81	40	3.42
1979—Waterbury	Eastern	4	21	0	3	.000	28	23	13	7	13	5.57
1979—Modesto	California	21	146	9	8	.529	190	107	97	103	51	5.98
1980—West Haven..........................	Eastern	27	190	11	12	.478	185	101	87	117	58	4.12

Selected by Oakland A's organization in third round of free-agent draft, June 6, 1978.

FREDERICK STEVEN AUERBACH

Name pronounced OWR-back.

(Rick)

Born February 15, 1950, at Woodland Hills, Calif.
Height, 6.00. Weight, 175.
Throws and bats righthanded.
Hobbies—Hunting, trapping and taxidermy.
Attended Pierce Junior College, Woodland Hills, Calif., and
Mesa Community College, Mesa, Ariz.

Year Club	League	Pos.	G.	AB.	R.	H.	2B.	3B.	HR.	RBI.	B.A.	PO.	A.	E.	F.A.
1969—Billings	Pion.	SS	12	49	12	14	4	0	3	9	.286	14	29	6	.878
1969—Clinton	Midw.	SS	63	203	37	46	8	3	1	20	.227	93	117	21	.909
1970—Clinton	Midw.	SS	28	117	26	38	5	1	1	5	.325	53	79	7	.950
1970—Portland............	P. C.	SS	80	300	52	90	15	2	3	19	.300	119	242	26	.933
1971—Evansville	A. A.	SS	63	227	41	56	10	5	3	18	.247	81	191	9	.968
1971—Milwaukee	Amer.	SS	79	236	22	48	10	0	1	9	.203	120	193	12	.963
1972—Milwaukee†	Amer.	SS	153	554	50	121	16	3	2	30	.218	256	452	30	.959
1973—Albuquerque‡	P. C.	SS-3B	74	255	45	64	7	3	1	26	.251	124	196	21	.938
1973—Milwaukee§	Amer.	SS	6	10	2	1	1	0	0	0	.100	4	6	2	.833
1974—Los Angeles.......	Nat.	S-2-3	45	73	12	25	0	0	1	4	.342	38	60	8	.925

— 14 —

Year Club League	Pos.	G.	AB.	R.	H.	2B.	3B.	HR.	RBI.	B.A.	PO.	A.	E.	F.A.
1975–Los Angeles x....Nat.	S-2-3	85	170	18	38	9	0	0	12	.224	82	137	9	.961
1976–Los Angeles y....Nat.	S-3-2	36	47	7	6	0	0	0	1	.128	41	50	6	.938
1977–Tidewater z a ....Int.	SS	22	81	8	19	4	0	0	7	.235	38	88	9	.933
1977–Cincinnati ....Nat.	2B-SS	33	45	5	7	2	0	0	3	.156	37	46	5	.943
1978–Cincinnati ....Nat.	SS-2-3	63	55	17	18	6	0	2	5	.327	29	47	3	.962
1979–Cincinnati ....Nat.	3B-SS-2B	62	100	17	21	8	1	1	12	.210	31	54	5	.944
1980–Cincinnati bcd...Nat.	SS-2-3	24	33	5	11	1	1	1	4	.333	4	14	1	.947
National League Totals..................		348	523	81	126	26	2	5	41	.241	262	408	37	.948
American League Totals.................		238	800	74	170	27	3	3	39	.213	380	651	44	.959
Major League Totals		586	1323	155	296	53	5	8	80	.224	642	1059	81	.955

Selected by California Angels' organization in 13th round of free-agent draft, June 7, 1968.
Selected by Seattle Pilots in secondary phase of free-agent draft, February 1, 1969.
†Traded to Los Angeles Dodgers for Infielder Tim Johnson, April 24, 1973.
‡On disabled list, June 22 to July 2, 1973; purchased by Milwaukee Brewers, September 4, 1973.
§Sold to Los Angeles Dodgers, October 27, 1973.
xOn supplemental disabled list, June 30 to July 17, 1975.
yTraded to New York Mets for Pitchers Rick Sander and Hank Webb, February 7, 1977.
zTraded to Texas Rangers May 20, 1977, completing deal in which New York Mets acquired Third Baseman Lenny Randle April 27, 1977.
aSold to Cincinnati Reds by Texas Rangers, June 15, 1977.
bTraded to Texas Rangers for a player to be named later, July 19, 1980.
cOn disqualified list, July 23 to December 12, 1980.
dTraded with Outfielder Richie Zisk and Pitchers Ken Clay, Brian Allard, Steve Finch and Jerry Gleaton to Seattle Mariners for Catcher Larry Cox, Pitcher Rick Honeycutt, Outfielders Willie Horton and Leon Roberts and Shortstop Mario Mendoza, December 12, 1980.

CHAMPIONSHIP SERIES RECORD

Year Club League	Pos.	G.	AB.	R.	H.	2B.	3B.	HR.	RBI.	B.A.	PO.	A.	E.	F.A.
1974–Los Angeles.......Nat.	PH	1	1	0	1	1	0	0	0	1.000	0	0	0	.000
1979–Cincinnati ....Nat.	PH	2	2	0	0	0	0	0	0	.000	0	0	0	.000
Championship Series Totals		3	3	0	1	1	0	0	0	.333	0	0	0	.000

WORLD SERIES RECORD

Year Club League	Pos.	G.	AB.	R.	H.	2B.	3B.	HR.	RBI.	B.A.	PO.	A.	E.	F.A.
1974–Los Angeles.......Nat.	PR	1	0	0	0	0	0	0	0	.000	0	0	0	.000

GERALD LEE AUGUSTINE
(Jerry)

Born July 24, 1952, at Green Bay, Wis.
Height, 6.00. Weight, 185.
Throws and bats lefthanded.
Hobbies—Reading, playing the guitar and outdoor activities.
Attended University of Wisconsin at La Crosse, La Crosse, Wis.;
received Bachelor of Science degree in Education.

Year Club	League	G.	IP.	W.	L.	Pct.	H.	R.	ER.	SO.	BB.	ERA.
1974–Danville............................Midwest		13	88	7	4	.636	81	34	25	52	34	2.56
1975–Sacramento†.......................P. Coast		15	79	4	3	.571	90	49	42	27	40	4.78
1975–Milwaukee ....American		5	27	2	0	1.000	26	9	9	8	12	3.00
1976–Milwaukee ....American		39	172	9	12	.429	167	69	63	59	56	3.30
1977–Milwaukee ....American		33	209	12	18	.400	222	119	104	68	72	4.48
1978–Milwaukee ....American		35	188	13	12	.520	204	100	95	59	61	4.55
1979–Milwaukee ....American		43	86	9	6	.600	95	38	33	41	30	3.45
1980–Milwaukee ....American		38	70	4	3	.571	83	37	35	22	36	4.50
Major League Totals		194	752	49	51	.490	797	372	339	257	267	4.06

Selected by Milwaukee Brewers' organization in 15th round of free-agent draft, June 5, 1974.
†On disabled list from beginning of season until June 28, 1975.

DOUGLAS REAGAN AULT
(Doug)

Born March 9, 1950, at Beaumont, Tex.
Height, 6.03. Weight, 200.
Throws left and bats righthanded.
Attended Panola Junior College, Carthage, Tex. and Texas Tech University, Lubbock, Tex.

Tied major league record for most home runs, opening game of season (2), April 7, 1977.
Led Pacific Coast League in total bases with 278 in 1976.
Led Pacific Coast League first basemen in double plays with 163 in 1976.
Tied for Western Carolinas League lead in sacrifice flies with 8 in 1973.

Year Club League	Pos.	G.	AB.	R.	H.	2B.	3B.	HR.	RBI.	B.A.	PO.	A.	E.	F.A.
1973–Gastonia ....W. Car.	OF-1B	•130	464	66	128	22	5	★19	★88	.276	179	9	6	.969
1974–Pittsfield ....East.	OF-1B	132	455	60	119	19	3	15	72	.262	586	30	10	.984
1975–Pittsfield ....East.	1B	75	277	42	78	13	3	11	56	.282	596	43	10	.985
1975–Spokane............P.C.	1B-OF	48	175	23	60	8	2	7	37	.343	403	41	13	.972
1976–Sacramento ......P.C.	1B	143	536	★112	168	25	5	25	83	.313	★1259	★99	13	.991
1976–Texas†..............Amer.	1B	9	20	0	6	1	0	0	0	.300	23	0	0	1.000

Year Club League	Pos.	G.	AB.	R.	H.	2B.	3B.	HR.	RBI.	B.A.	PO.	A.	E.	F.A.
1977—Toronto ....Amer.	1B	129	445	44	109	22	3	11	64	.245	1113	103	16	.987
1978—Toronto ....Amer.	1B-OF	54	104	10	25	1	1	3	7	.240	190	10	6	.971
1979—Syracuse...........Int.	OF-1B	121	444	53	112	25	6	12	71	.252	160	7	4	.977
1980—Syracuse...........Int.	OF-1B	53	203	24	61	11	1	10	51	.300	70	6	1	.987
1980—Toronto ....Amer.	1B-OF	64	144	12	28	5	1	3	15	.194	200	20	0	1.000
Major League Totals........................		256	713	66	168	29	5	17	86	.236	1526	133	22	.987

Selected by Pittsburgh Pirates' organization in 27th round of free-agent draft, June 5, 1969.
Selected by San Diego Padres' organization in secondary phase of free-agent draft, January 17, 1970.
Selected by Cleveland Indians' organization in secondary phase of free-agent draft, June 4, 1970.
Signed as free agent by Texas Rangers' organization, April 8, 1973.
†Selected by Toronto Blue Jays from Texas Rangers in American League expansion draft, November 5, 1976.

RAMON ANTONIO AVILES (MIRANDA)

Born January 22, 1952, at Manati, Puerto Rico.
Height, 5.09. Weight, 155.
Throws and bats righthanded.
Hobby—Music.
Attended University of Puerto Rico, Arecibo, Puerto Rico.
Led Western Carolinas League shortstops in double plays with 56 in 1971.

Year Club League	Pos.	G.	AB.	R.	H.	2B.	3B.	HR.	RBI.	B.A.	PO.	A.	E.	F.A.
1970—Greenville.........W.Car.	SS-2B	94	304	47	90	9	2	0	38	.296	136	245	32	.923
1973—Bristol ....East.	S-2-3-O	109	353	39	79	13	1	0	28	.224	179	316	19	.963
1974—Bristol ....East.	S-2-3	118	373	48	92	12	3	0	33	.247	196	297	35	.934
1975—Pawtucket ....Int.	S-2-OF	123	287	20	63	6	1	1	22	.220	180	337	23	.957
1976—Rhode Island.....Int.	SS	134	421	50	108	17	3	2	42	.257	238	452	35	★.952
1977—Pawtucket ....Int.	S-2-3-C	78	239	32	52	8	1	1	30	.218	101	219	18	.947
1977—Boston ....Amer.	2B	1	0	0	0	0	0	0	0	.000	0	1	0	1.000
1978—Oklahoma City ..A. A.	2B-SS	90	341	41	92	20	2	3	29	.270	196	230	12	.973
1979—Oklahoma City ..A. A.	2B-SS	72	252	37	63	7	1	0	18	.250	142	202	16	.956
1979—Philadelphia......Nat.	2B	27	61	7	17	2	0	0	12	.279	40	44	2	.977
1980—Oklahoma City ..A. A.		11	43	13	12	1	0	1	2	.279	16	35	1	.981
1980—Philadelphia......Nat.	SS-2B	51	101	12	28	6	0	2	9	.277	60	74	8	.944
American League Totals		1	0	0	0	0	0	0	0	.000	0	1	0	1.000
National League Totals		78	162	19	45	8	0	2	21	.278	100	118	10	.956
Major League Totals		79	162	19	45	8	0	2	21	.278	100	119	10	.956

CHAMPIONSHIP SERIES RECORD

Year Club League	Pos.	G.	AB.	R.	H.	2B.	3B.	HR.	RBI.	B.A.	PO.	A.	E.	F.A.
1980—Philadelphia......Nat.	PR	1	0	1	0	0	0	0	0	.000	0	0	0	.000

Signed as free agent by Boston Red Sox' organization, November 7, 1969.
†Sold to Philadelphia Phillies, April 5, 1978.

BENIGNO FELIX AYALA

Name pronounced eye-AL-uh.

(Benny)

Born February 7, 1951, at Yauco, Puerto Rico.
Height, 6.01. Weight, 195.
Throws and bats righthanded.
Attended Puerto Rico Junior College, Rio Piedras, P. R.
Hit home run in first major league at bat, August 27, 1974.

Year Club League	Pos.	G.	AB.	R.	H.	2B.	3B.	HR.	RBI.	B.A.	PO.	A.	E.	F.A.
1971—Visalia ....Calif.	3B	21	46	3	10	0	1	1	8	.217	8	16	7	.774
1971—Pompano Beach.Fla. St.	3B-OF	53	208	38	58	7	4	8	34	.279	57	59	17	.872
1972—Visalia ....Calif.	1B-OF	113	348	68	79	15	2	19	66	.227	442	38	22	.956
1973—Memphis ....Texas	OF	136	462	69	119	17	6	17	68	.258	44	5	3	.942
1974—Tidewater ....Int.	OF	92	288	41	79	21	1	11	40	.274	125	4	★16	.890
1974—New York..........Nat.	OF	23	68	9	16	1	0	2	8	.235	37	1	3	.927
1975—Tidewater†........Int.	OF	65	177	24	49	13	0	6	28	.277	66	1	4	.944
1976—Tidewater ....Int.	OF-1B	87	293	41	66	9	2	12	48	.225	47	2	3	.942
1976—New York..........Nat.	OF	22	26	2	3	0	0	1	2	.115	7	1	1	.889
1977—New Orleans .....A. A.	OF	126	450	71	134	27	5	18	73	.298	199	8	5	.976
1977—St. Louis ....Nat.	OF	1	3	0	1	0	0	0	0	.333	6	1	0	1.000
1978—Springfield§ ....A. A.	OF	47	165	16	41	2	0	5	21	.248	70	1	3	.959
1978—Columbus xy .....Int.	OF	59	203	30	69	11	4	6	35	.340	62	3	4	.942
1979—Rochester ....Int.	OF	17	62	10	22	1	3	1	7	.355	37	0	2	.949
1979—Baltimore ....Amer.	OF	42	86	15	22	5	0	6	13	.256	38	0	1	.974
1980—Baltimore ....Amer.	OF	76	170	28	45	8	1	10	33	.265	20	2	0	1.000
American League Totals		118	256	43	67	13	1	16	46	.262	58	2	1	.984
National League Totals		46	97	11	20	1	0	3	10	.206	50	3	4	.930
Major League Totals		164	353	54	87	14	1	19	56	.246	108	5	5	.958

Signed as free agent by New York Mets' organization, January 28, 1971.
†On disabled list, April 22 to May 29, 1975.
‡Traded to St. Louis Cardinals' organization for Infielder Doug Clarey, March 30, 1977.
§Loaned to Columbus (Pittsburgh Pirates' organization), June 21, 1978.
xOn suspended list, August 27 to September 5, 1978.

WORLD SERIES RECORD

Year	Club	League	Pos.	G.	AB.	R.	H.	2B.	3B.	HR.	RBI.	B.A.	PO.	A.	E.	F.A.
1979—Baltimore		Amer.	OF-PH	4	6	1	2	0	0	1	2	.333	4	0	0	1.000

ROBERT ERNEST BABCOCK
(Bob)

Born August 25, 1949, at New Castle, Pa.
Height, 6.05. Weight, 190.
Throws and bats righthanded.
Hobbies—Hunting and fishing.
Attended Beaver County Community College, Monaca, Pa.

Led Eastern League in wild pitches with 17 in 1971.
Led International League in saves with 14 in 1980.

Year	Club	League	G.	IP.	W.	L.	Pct.	H.	R.	ER.	SO.	BB.	ERA.
1968—Bradenton Pirates†‡		Gulf Coast	9	27	0	5	.000	32	31	21	19	21	7.00
1969—Bradenton Expos		Gulf Coast	9	39	2	1	.667	34	19	16	32	25	3.69
1970—West Palm Beach§		Florida St.	19	126	10	7	.588	89	41	28	70	59	2.00
1971—Quebec City		Eastern	27	132	7	9	.438	99	64	43	88	71	2.93
1972—Peninsula		Int'national	12	30	0	2	.000	33	23	22	17	19	6.60
1972—Quebec City		Eastern	16	97	7	5	.583	59	43	33	66	52	3.06
1973—Peninsula		Int'national	35	154	9	12	.429	152	75	57	71	98	3.33
1974—Quebec City		Eastern	22	43	1	5	.167	32	22	15	31	30	3.14
1974—Memphis x-Rochester		Int'national	16	31	0	5	.000	34	26	23	23	33	6.68
1975—Asheville		Southern	28	92	9	5	.643	73	29	25	49	36	2.45
1975—Rochester		Int'national	10	26	2	2	.500	27	16	14	11	12	4.85
1976—Rochester y		Int'national	34	91	7	6	.538	107	63	51	53	47	5.04
1977—Tucson		P. Coast	*56	128	6	5	.545	125	84	65	84	84	4.57
1978—Tucson		P. Coast	10	19	1	0	1.000	15	9	8	18	9	3.79
1979—Tucson		P. Coast	41	64	5	3	.625	53	27	23	54	33	3.23
1979—Texas		American	4	5	0	0	.000	7	7	6	6	7	10.80
1980—Charleston		Int'national	39	65	6	3	.667	38	13	11	59	26	1.52
1980—Texas		American	19	23	1	2	.333	20	13	12	15	8	4.70
Major League Totals			23	28	1	2	.333	27	20	18	21	15	5.79

Signed as free agent by Pittsburgh Pirates' organization, August 15, 1967.
†On restricted list, April 3 to July 1, 1968.
‡Released, June 16, 1969; signed as free agent by Montreal Expos' organization, June 29, 1969.
§On disabled list, June 15 to July 3, 1970.
xReleased, July 31, 1974; signed as free agent by Baltimore Orioles' organization, August 7, 1974.
yTraded to Texas Rangers' organization for Catcher Dave Criscione, December 15, 1976.

WALTER WAYNE BACKMAN
(Wally)

Born September 22, 1959, at Hillsboro, Ore.
Height, 5.09. Weight, 160.
Throws right and bats right and lefthanded.

Led International League batters in walks with 87 in 1980.

Year	Club	League	Pos.	G.	AB.	R.	H.	2B.	3B.	HR.	RBI.	B.A.	PO.	A.	E.	F.A.
1977—Little Falls		NY-P	SS-3B	69	255	44	83	10	2	6	30	.325	96	185	19	.937
1978—Lynchburg		Carol.	SS	132	494	86	149	19	•9	3	38	.302	*202	*329	30	*.947
1979—Jackson		Texas	SS-2B	110	404	63	114	11	5	2	19	.282	184	259	31	.935
1980—Tidewater		Int.	2B-SS	125	400	53	117	15	5	1	51	.293	237	320	22	.962
1980—New York		Nat.	2B-SS	27	93	12	30	1	1	0	9	.323	62	55	1	.992
Major League Totals				27	93	12	30	1	1	0	9	.323	62	55	1	.992

Selected by New York Mets' organization in 1st round (16th player selected) of free-agent draft, June 7, 1977.

MICHAEL JAMES BACSIK

Named pronounced Bassik.

(Mike)

Born April 1, 1952, at Dallas, Tex.
Height, 6.02. Weight, 188.
Throws and bats righthanded.
Hobbies—Golf and tennis.
Attended Trinity University, San Antonio, Tex.; received Bachelor of Arts degree
in Business Administration and Marketing

Year	Club	League	G.	IP.	W.	L.	Pct.	H.	R.	ER.	SO.	BB.	ERA.
1973—Sarasota Rangers		Gulf Coast	8	23	2	0	1.000	13	13	10	31	14	3.91
1974—Gastonia		W. Carol.	25	170	*15	5	*.750	*183	93	*80	121	59	4.24
1975—Spokane		P. Coast	19	110	6	10	.375	135	82	67	48	38	5.48
1975—Texas		American	7	21	1	2	.333	28	17	11	13	9	3.67
1976—Sacramento		P. Coast	12	77	4	3	.571	101	51	39	43	31	4.56
1976—Texas		American	23	55	3	2	.600	66	31	26	21	26	4.25

Year Club	League	G.	IP.	W.	L.	Pct.	H.	R.	ER.	SO.	BB.	ERA.
1977—Tucson	P. Coast	30	115	4	8	.333	161	117	96	67	61	7.51
1977—Texas	American	2	2	0	0	.000	9	5	5	1	0	22.50
1978—Tucson†	P. Coast	18	101	5	8	.385	116	75	60	50	40	5.35
1979—Toledo	Int'national	7	21	1	1	.500	19	3	3	16	3	1.29
1979—Minnesota	American	31	66	4	2	.667	61	39	32	33	29	4.36
1980—Toledo	Int'national	26	45	7	2	.778	45	19	18	30	29	3.60
1980—Minnesota‡	American	10	23	0	0	.000	26	12	11	9	11	4.30
Major League Totals		73	173	8	6	.571	190	104	85	77	75	4.42

Selected by Baltimore Orioles' organization in 55th round of free-agent draft, June 4, 1970.
Signed as free agent by Texas Rangers' organization, July 23, 1973.
†Traded to Minnesota Twins' organization for Pitcher Mac Scarce, December 13, 1978.
‡Traded to Seattle Mariners' organization for Outfielder Steve Stroughter, December 19, 1980.

STANLEY RAYMOND BAHNSEN

Name pronounced BONN-sun.

(Stan)

Born December 15, 1944, at Council Bluffs, Ia.
Height, 6.02. Weight, 198.
Throws and bats righthanded.
Hobbies—Fishing, hunting and pocket billiards.
Attended University of Nebraska, Lincoln, Neb.

Established major league record for most games taken out as starting pitcher, season (36), 1972.
Tied National League record for most consecutive home runs allowed, inning (3), September 30, 1977 (second inning).
Pitched seven-inning, 1-0 no-hit victory against Richmond, July 17, 1966.
Pitched seven-inning, 8-0 perfect game against Buffalo, July 9, 1967.
Named THE SPORTING NEWS American League Rookie Pitcher of the Year, 1968.
Named American League Rookie of the Year by the Baseball Writers' Association of America, 1968.
Received reported $30,000 bonus to sign with New York Yankees, 1965.

Year Club	League	G.	IP.	W.	L.	Pct.	H.	R.	ER.	SO.	BB.	ERA.
1965—Columbus	Southern	11	53	2	2	.500	47	21	16	39	29	2.72
1966—Toledo	Int'national	26	170	10	7	.588	141	67	55	151	71	2.91
1966—New York	American	4	23	1	1	.500	15	9	9	16	7	3.52
1967—Syracuse	Int'national	26	138	9	11	.450	122	64	54	115	41	3.52
1968—New York	American	37	267	17	12	.586	216	72	61	162	68	2.06
1969—New York	American	40	221	9	16	.360	222	102	36	2130	90	3.83
1970—New York	American	36	233	14	11	.560	227	100	86	116	75	3.32
1971—New York†	American	36	242	14	12	.538	221	99	90	110	72	3.35
1972—Chicago	American	43	252	21	16	.568	263	107	101	157	73	3.61
1973—Chicago	American	42	282	18	*21	.462	290	128	112	120	117	3.57
1974—Chicago	American	38	216	12	15	.444	230	128	113	102	110	4.71
1975—Chicago‡-Oakland	American	33	167	10	13	.435	166	91	81	80	77	4.37
1976—Oakland	American	35	143	8	7	.533	124	55	53	82	43	3.34
1977—Oakland§	American	11	22	1	2	.333	24	16	15	21	13	6.14
1977—Montreal	National	23	127	8	9	.471	142	76	68	58	38	4.82
1978—Montreal x	National	44	75	1	5	.167	74	35	32	44	31	3.84
1979—Montreal	National	55	94	3	1	.750	80	34	33	71	42	3.16
1980—Montreal y	National	57	91	7	6	.538	80	40	31	48	33	3.07
American League Totals		355	2068	125	126	.498	1998	907	815	1096	745	3.55
National League Totals		179	387	19	21	.475	376	185	164	221	144	3.81
Major League Totals		534	2455	144	147	.495	2374	1092	979	1317	889	3.59

Selected by New York Yankees' organization in 3rd round of free-agent draft, June 21, 1965.
†Traded to Chicago White Sox for Infielder-Outfielder Rich McKinney, December 2, 1971.
‡Traded with Pitcher Lee (Skip) Pitlock to Oakland Athletics for Pitcher Dave Hamilton and Infielder-Outfielder Chet Lemon, June 15, 1975.
§Traded to Montreal Expos for First Baseman-Outfielder Mike Jorgensen, May 22, 1977.
xOn disabled list, June 5 to June 27, 1978.
yGranted free agency, October 27, 1980; re-signed by Expos, January 6, 1981.

ROBERT MICHAEL BAILOR

(Bob)

Born July 10, 1951, at Connellsville, Pa.
Height, 5.10. Weight, 160.
Throws and bats righthanded.
Hobbies—Hunting and fishing.
Attended California State College, California, Pa.

Led California League in stolen bases with 63 in 1972.
Led Southern League shortstops in double plays with 85 in 1973 and tied for International League lead with 64 in 1975.
Led American League outfielders in double plays with 7 in 1978.

Year Club	League	Pos.	G.	AB.	R.	H.	2B.	3B.	HR.	RBI.	B.A.	PO.	A.	E.	F.A.
1970—Bluefield	Appal.	2-O-3-S-P	46	121	18	33	3	0	0	8	.273	53	43	6	.941
1971—Aberdeen	North.	S-3-O-2	68	268	*71	*91	11	2	2	50	*.340	92	140	32	.879
1972—Lodi	Calif.	*S-O-2	129	528	95	153	16	3	2	34	.290	*241	330	*54	.914

Year Club	League	Pos.	G.	AB.	R.	H.	2B.	3B.	HR.	RBI.	B.A.	PO.	A.	E.	F.A.
1973—Asheville	South.	SS	115	468	77	137	23	3	0	29	.293	*222	386	22	*.965
1973—Rochester	Int.	SS	17	47	5	13	1	0	1	4	.277	30	34	4	.941
1974—Rochester	Int.	S-O-3-2	96	330	45	76	13	3	1	25	.230	174	160	13	.963
1975—Rochester	Int.	SS	129	*501	68	147	19	6	5	39	.293	198	*386	*32	.948
1975—Baltimore	Amer.	SS-2B	5	7	0	1	0	0	0	0	.143	5	9	0	1.000
1976—Rochester†	Int.	3-SS-OF	36	103	21	32	10	1	1	12	.311	10	24	0	1.000
1976—Baltimore‡	Amer.	SS	9	6	2	2	0	1	0	0	.333	0	0	0	.000
1977—Toronto	Amer.	OF-SS	122	496	62	154	21	5	5	32	.310	235	165	12	.971
1978—Toronto	Amer.	OF-3B-S	154	621	74	164	29	7	1	52	.264	329	82	15	.965
1979—Toronto	Amer.	OF-3B	130	414	50	95	11	5	1	38	.229	217	32	3	.988
1980—Toronto§x	Amer.	O-S-2-3	117	347	44	82	14	2	1	16	.236	233	61	2	.933
Major League Totals			537	1891	232	498	75	20	8	138	.263	1019	349	32	.977

Signed as free agent by Baltimore Orioles' organization, August 13, 1969.

†On supplemental disabled list, April 14 to June 7; on disabled list, June 8 to June 18 and August 1 to August 16, 1976.

‡Selected by Toronto Blue Jays from Baltimore Orioles in American League expansion draft, November 5, 1976.

§On supplemental disabled list, June 12 to July 3, 1980.

xTraded to New York Mets for Pitcher Roy Lee Jackson, December 12, 1980.

PITCHING RECORD

Year Club	League	G.	IP.	W.	L.	Pct.	H.	R.	ER.	SO.	BB.	ERA.
1970—Bluefield	Appal.	1	1	0	0	.000	7	8	8	1	2	72.00
1980—Toronto	American	3	2	0	0	.000	4	2	2	0	1	9.00

HAROLD DOUGLASS BAINES

Born March 15, 1959, at St. Michaels, Md.
Height, 6.02. Weight, 175.
Throws and bats lefthanded.

Tied for American Association lead in double plays by outfielders with 4 in 1979.

Year Club	League	Pos.	G.	AB.	R.	H.	2B.	3B.	HR.	RBI.	B.A.	PO.	A.	E.	F.A.
1977—Appleton	Midw.	OF	69	222	37	58	11	2	5	29	.261	94	10	7	.937
1978—Knoxville	South.	OF-1B	137	502	70	138	16	6	13	72	.275	291	22	13	.960
1979—Iowa	A. A.	OF	125	466	87	139	25	8	22	87	.298	222	●16	11	.956
1980—Chicago	Amer.	OF	141	491	55	125	23	6	13	49	.255	229	6	9	.963
Major League Totals			141	491	55	125	23	6	13	49	.255	229	6	9	.963

Selected by Chicago White Sox' organization in 1st round (first player selected) of free-agent draft, June 7, 1977.

CHARLES DOUGLAS BAIR
(Doug)

Born August 22, 1949, at Defiance, O.
Height, 6.00. Weight, 185.
Throws and bats righthanded.
Hobbies—Hunting and fishing.
Attended Bowling Green State University, Bowling Green, O.; received
Bachelor of Science degree in Industrial Education.

Major League saves: 1976 (0), 1977 (8), 1978 (28), 1979 (16), 1980 (6). Total—58.
Led Carolina League pitchers in complete games with 15 in 1972.
Named Carolina League Pitcher of the Year in 1972.

Year Club	League	G.	IP.	W.	L.	Pct.	H.	R.	ER.	SO.	BB.	ERA.
1971—Salem†	Carolina	6	29	2	3	.400	35	22	19	18	26	5.90
1971—Waterbury	Eastern	1	7	1	0	1.000	5	0	0	2	0	0.00
1972—Salem	Carolina	24	180	15	7	.682	170	●86	57	186	*95	2.85
1972—Charleston	Int'national	1	4	0	1	.000	5	3	3	5	0	6.75
1973—Charleston	Int'national	26	158	7	11	.389	173	103	77	94	87	4.39
1974—Charleston‡	Int'national	26	170	7	*16	.304	166	87	77	117	91	4.08
1975—Charleston	Int'national	26	167	9	12	.429	157	72	56	113	58	3.02
1976—Charleston	Int'national	45	122	7	10	.412	102	48	43	108	57	3.17
1976—Pittsburgh§	National	4	6	0	0	.000	4	4	4	4	5	6.00
1977—San Jose	P. Coast	20	33	5	2	.714	24	8	8	49	17	2.18
1977—Oakland x	American	45	83	4	6	.400	78	39	32	68	57	3.47
1978—Cincinnati	National	70	100	7	6	.538	87	23	22	91	38	1.98
1979—Cincinnati	National	65	94	11	7	.611	93	47	45	86	51	4.31
1980—Cincinnati	National	61	85	3	6	.333	91	42	40	62	39	4.24
National League Totals		200	285	21	19	.525	275	116	111	243	133	3.51
American League Totals		45	83	4	6	.400	78	39	32	68	57	3.47
Major League Totals		245	368	25	25	.500	353	155	143	311	190	3.50

Selected by Pittsburgh Pirates' organization in 2nd round of free-agent draft, June 8, 1971.

†On temporary inactive list, June 23 to July 22, 1971.

‡Conditionally released by Pittsburgh Pirates' organziation to Detroit Tigers' organization, December 17, 1974; returned by Tigers to Pirates, March 28, 1975.

§Traded with Pitchers Doc Medich, Dave Giusti and Rick Langford, Outfielders Mitchell Page and Tony Armas to Oakland A's for Infielders Phil Garner and Tommy Helms, and Pitcher Chris Batton, March 15, 1977.

xTraded to Cincinnati Reds for First Baseman Dave Revering and cash, February 25, 1978.

Year Club	League	G.	IP.	W.	L.	Pct.	H.	R.	ER.	SO.	BB.	ERA.
1979—Cincinnati	National	1	1	0	1	.000	2	1	1	0	1	9.00

CHARLES JOSEPH BAKER
(Chuck)

Born December 6, 1952, at Seattle, Wash.
Height, 5.11. Weight, 175.
Throws and bats righthanded.
Attended Santa Ana Junior College, Santa Ana, Calif., Loyola Marymount University, Los Angeles, Calif.;
received Bachelor of Science degree in Engineering.

Tied for Texas League lead in double plays by shortstops with 58 in 1976.

Year Club	League	Pos.	G.	AB.	R.	H.	2B.	3B.	HR.	RBI.	B.A.	PO.	A.	E.	F.A.
1975—Reno	Calif.	SS	81	305	44	75	14	4	9	47	.246	126	247	39	.905
1976—Amarillo	Texas	*S-2-O-3	109	385	44	104	19	1	4	64	.270	163	*352	36	.935
1977—Hawaii†	P. C.	*SS-OF	130	490	60	119	27	2	11	68	.243	*259	*476	23	*.970
1978—San Diego	Nat.	2B-SS	44	58	8	12	1	0	0	3	.207	42	70	6	.949
1979—Hawaii	P. C.	SS	131	414	35	91	15	2	0	30	.220	216	396	29	.955
1980—Hawaii	P. C.	SS	114	472	69	129	21	6	9	45	.273	170	378	20	*.965
1980—San Diego‡	Nat.	SS	9	22	0	3	1	0	0	0	.136	3	23	1	.963
Major League Totals			53	80	8	15	2	0	0	3	.188	45	93	7	.952

Selected by Minnesota Twins' organization in 37th round of free-agent draft, June 8, 1971.
Selected by Kansas City Royals' organization in 26th round of free-agent draft, June 5, 1973.
Selected by Houston Astros' organization in secondary phase of free-agent draft, June 5, 1974.
Selected by San Diego Padres' organization in secondary phase of free-agent draft, January 9, 1975.
†On disabled list, July 4 to July 17, 1977.
‡Traded to Minnesota Twins for Outfielder Dave Edwards, December 8, 1980.

PITCHING RECORD

Year Club	League	G.	IP.	W.	L.	Pct.	H.	R.	ER.	SO.	BB.	ERA.
1976—Amarillo	Texas	1	1	0	0	.000	0	0	0	1	0	0.00

JOHNNIE B. BAKER, JR.
(Dusty)

Born June 15, 1949, at Riverside, Calif.
Height, 6.02. Weight, 187.
Throws and bats righthanded.
Hobbies—Fishing and hunting.
Attended American River Junior College, Sacramento, Calif.

Tied major league records for most plate appearances, most at bats and most times faced pitcher as batsman, inning (3), September 20, 1972 (second game of doubleheader).
Established National League record for fewest chances accepted by outfielder, season, 150 or more games (235), 1977.
Named as outfielder on THE SPORTING NEWS National League All-Star Team, 1980.
Named as outfielder on THE SPORTING NEWS Silver Bat Team, 1980.

Year Club	League	Pos.	G.	AB.	R.	H.	2B.	3B.	HR.	RBI.	B.A.	PO.	A.	E.	F.A.
1967—Austin	Texas	OF	9	39	6	9	1	0	0	1	.231	17	0	1	.944
1968—W. Palm B'ch†	Fla. St.	OF	6	21	2	4	0	0	0	2	.190	6	2	0	1.000
1968—Greenwood	W. Car.	OF	52	199	45	68	11	3	6	39	.342	82	1	3	.965
1968—Atlanta	Nat.	OF	6	5	0	2	0	0	0	0	.400	0	0	0	.000
1969—Shreveport	Texas	OF	73	265	40	68	5	1	9	31	.257	135	10	3	.980
1969—Richmond	Int.	OF-3B	25	89	7	22	4	0	0	8	.247	40	9	4	.925
1969—Atlanta	Nat.	OF	3	7	0	0	0	0	0	0	.000	2	0	0	1.000
1970—Richmond	Int.	OF	118	461	97	150	29	3	11	51	.325	236	10	7	.972
1970—Atlanta	Nat.	OF	13	24	3	7	0	0	0	4	.292	11	1	3	.800
1971—Richmond	Int.	OF-3B	80	341	62	106	23	2	11	41	.311	136	13	4	.974
1971—Atlanta	Nat.	OF	29	62	2	14	2	0	0	4	.226	29	1	0	1.000
1972—Atlanta‡	Nat.	OF	127	446	62	143	27	2	17	76	.321	344	8	4	.989
1973—Atlanta	Nat.	OF	159	604	101	174	29	4	21	99	.288	*390	10	7	.983
1974—Atlanta	Nat.	OF	149	574	80	147	35	0	20	69	.256	359	10	7	.981
1975—Atlanta§	Nat.	OF	142	494	63	129	18	2	19	72	.261	287	10	3	.990
1976—Los Angeles	Nat.	OF	112	384	36	93	13	0	4	39	.242	254	3	1	.996
1977—Los Angeles	Nat.	OF	153	533	86	155	26	1	30	86	.291	227	8	3	.987
1978—Los Angeles	Nat.	OF	149	522	62	137	24	1	11	66	.262	250	13	4	.985
1979—Los Angeles	Nat.	OF	151	554	86	152	29	1	23	88	.274	289	14	3	.990
1980—Los Angeles x	Nat.	OF	153	579	80	170	26	4	29	97	.294	308	5	3	.991
Major League Totals			1346	4788	661	1323	229	15	174	700	.276	2750	83	38	.987

Selected by Atlanta Braves' organization in 26th round of free-agent draft, June 6, 1967.
†On restricted list from beginning of season until June 13, 1968.
‡On Military List, June 17 to July 3, 1972.
§Traded with First Baseman-Third Baseman Ed Goodson to Los Angeles Dodgers for Outfielder Jimmy Wynn, Second Baseman Lee Lacy, First Baseman-Outfielder Tom Paciorek and Infielder Jerry Royster, November 17, 1975.

xGranted free agency, November 4, 1980; re-signed by Dodgers before re-entry draft, November 10, 1980.

Established Championship Series records for highest batting average, four-game Series (.467), 1978; most runs batted in, four-game Series (8), 1977.

Tied Championship Series records for most home runs with bases filled, game (1), October 5, 1977; most runs batted in, inning (4), October 5, 1977 (fourth inning).

Tied National League Championship Series record for most consecutive hits, one Series (4), 1978; most hits, game (4), October 7, 1978.

Year Club	League	Pos.	G.	AB.	R.	H.	2B.	3B.	HR.	RBI.	B.A.	PO.	A.	E.	F.A.
1977–Los Angeles.......Nat.		OF	4	14	4	5	1	0	2	8	.357	3	0	0	1.000
1978–Los Angeles ......Nat.		OF	4	15	1	7	2	0	0	1	.467	5	0	0	1.000
Championship Series Totals			8	29	5	12	3	0	2	9	.414	8	0	0	1.000

WORLD SERIES RECORD

Year Club	League	Pos.	G.	AB.	R.	H.	2B.	3B.	HR.	RBI.	B.A.	PO.	A.	E.	F.A.
1977–Los Angeles.......Nat.		OF	6	24	4	7	0	0	1	5	.292	11	0	1	.917
1978–Los Angeles ......Nat.		OF	6	21	2	5	0	0	1	1	.238	12	0	0	1.000
World Series Totals........................			12	45	6	12	0	0	2	6	.267	23	0	1	.958

STEPHEN CHARLES BALBONI
(Steve)

Born January 16, 1957, at Brockton, Mass.
Height, 6.03. Weight, 225.
Throws and bats righthanded.

Named Florida State League Most Valuable Player, 1979.
Named Southern League Player of the Year, 1980.
Led Florida State League batters in strikeouts with 154 in 1979.
Led Southern League in total bases with 288 in 1980.
Led Florida State League first basemen in double plays with 106 in 1979 and Southern League first basemen with 125 in 1980.

Year Club	League	Pos.	G.	AB.	R.	H.	2B.	3B.	HR.	RBI.	B.A.	PO.	A.	E.	F.A.
1978–West Haven.......	East.	DH	2	2	0	0	0	0	0	0	.000	0	0	0	.000
1978–Ft. Lauderdale ..	Fla. St.	1B	60	176	19	36	5	0	1	19	.205	475	19	4	.992
1979–Ft. Lauderdale ..	Fla. St.	1B	∗140	∗504	69	127	19	2	∗26	∗91	.252	∗1297	∗97	11	∗.992
1980–Nashville	South.	1B	141	521	∗101	157	25	2	∗34	∗122	.301	∗1218	76	13	∗.990

Selected by New York Yankees' organization in 4th round of free-agent draft, June 6, 1978.

CHRISTOPHER MICHAEL BANDO
(Chris)

Born February 4, 1956, at Cleveland, O.
Height, 6.00. Weight, 195.
Throws right and bats left and righthanded
Attended Arizona State University, Tempe, Ariz.
Brother of Sal Bando, Milwaukee Brewers' infielder.

Year Club	League	Pos.	G.	AB.	R.	H.	2B.	3B.	HR.	RBI.	B.A.	PO.	A.	E.	F.A.
1978–Chattanooga......	South.	C	76	241	30	55	12	0	4	21	.228	285	51	10	.971
1979–Chattanooga†	South.	C-3B	21	62	5	15	4	1	0	7	.242	61	13	0	1.000
1980–Chattanooga‡	South.	C-3B	121	404	78	141	31	3	12	73	∗.349	480	97	12	.980

Selected by Milwaukee Brewers' organization in 22nd round of free-agent draft, June 7, 1977.
Selected by Cleveland Indians' organization in 2nd round of free-agent draft, June 6, 1978.
†On disabled list, April 16 to August 9, 1979.
‡On disabled list, April 24 to May 6, 1980.

SALVATORE LEONARD BANDO
(Sal)

Born February 13, 1944, at Cleveland, O.
Height, 6.00. Weight, 200.
Throws and bats righthanded.
Hobby–Sports.
Attended Arizona State University, Tempe, Ariz.
Brother of Chris Bando, catcher in Cleveland Indians' organization.

Tied major league record for fewest doubles, season, for leader in doubles, 32, in 1973.
Led American League third basemen in double plays with 36 in 1975.
Led American League in sacrifice flies with 13 in 1974.
Tied for American League lead in total bases with 295 in 1973.
Named third baseman on THE SPORTING NEWS American League All-Star Team, 1973 and 1974.
Received reported $30,000 bonus to sign with Kansas City Athletics, 1965.

Year Club	League	Pos.	G.	AB.	R.	H.	2B.	3B.	HR.	RBI.	B.A.	PO.	A.	E.	F.A.
1965–Burlington.........	Midw.	3B	60	221	28	58	10	2	6	35	.262	39	127	11	.938
1966–Mobile...............	South.	3B	119	393	55	109	11	4	12	50	.277	65	179	18	.931
1966–Kansas City.......	Amer.	3B	11	24	1	7	1	1	0	1	.292	5	23	2	.933
1967–Vancouver.........	P.C.	3B	116	371	39	108	14	2	9	55	.291	85	231	19	.943
1967–Kansas City.......	Amer.	3B	47	130	11	25	3	2	0	6	.192	43	96	6	.959
1968–Oakland	Amer.	∗3B-OF	●162	605	67	152	25	5	9	67	.251	∗188	272	17	.964

Year Club League	Pos.	G.	AB.	R.	H.	2B.	3B.	HR.	RBI.	B.A.	PO.	A.	E.	F.A.
1969—Oakland ....Amer.	3B	•162	609	106	171	25	3	31	113	.281	178	321	•24	.954
1970—Oakland ....Amer.	3B	155	502	93	132	20	2	20	75	.263	*158	258	20	.954
1971—Oakland ....Amer.	3B	153	538	75	146	23	1	24	94	.271	141	267	12	.971
1972—Oakland ....Amer.	3B-2B	152	535	64	126	20	3	15	77	.236	124	337	20	.958
1973—Oakland ....Amer.	3B	•162	592	97	170	•32	3	29	98	.287	126	281	22	.949
1974—Oakland ....Amer.	3B	146	498	84	121	21	2	22	103	.243	113	287	23	.946
1975—Oakland ....Amer.	3B	•160	562	64	129	24	1	15	78	.230	122	314	15	.967
1976—Oakland† ....Amer.	3B-SS	158	550	75	132	18	2	27	84	.240	127	310	17	.963
1977—Milwaukee ....Amer.	3-2-SS	159	580	65	145	27	3	17	82	.250	98	283	13	.967
1978—Milwaukee ....Amer.	3B-1B	152	540	85	154	20	6	17	78	.285	132	332	15	.969
1979—Milwaukee ....Amer.	3-1-2-P	130	476	57	117	14	3	9	43	.246	106	225	12	.965
1980—Milwaukee ....Amer.	3B-1B	78	254	28	50	12	1	5	31	.197	62	112	12	.935
Major League Totals		1987	6995	972	1777	285	38	240	1030	.254	1723	3718	230	.959

Selected by Kansas City A's organization in 6th round of free-agent draft, June 19, 1965.

†Played out option year and granted free agency, November 1, 1976; signed as free agent by Milwaukee Brewers, November 19, 1976.

RECORD AS PITCHER

Year Club	League	G.	IP.	W.	L.	Pct.	H.	R.	ER.	SO.	BB.	ERA.
1979—Milwaukee ....American		1	3	0	0	.000	3	2	2	0	0	6.00

CHAMPIONSHIP SERIES RECORD

Tied Championship Series records for most hits, two consecutive games, one series (6), October 5 and 7, 1975; most consecutive hits, one series (5), 1975.

Tied American League Championship Series records for most consecutive hits, total Series (5); most Series, one or more home runs (3); most home runs, five-game Series (2), 1973; most strikeouts, five-game Series (6), 1973; most consecutive strikeouts, one Series, consecutive at bats (4), 1973.

Year Club League	Pos.	G.	AB.	R.	H.	2B.	3B.	HR.	RBI.	B.A.	PO.	A.	E.	F.A.
1971—Oakland ....Amer.	3B	3	11	3	4	2	0	1	1	.364	6	2	0	1.000
1972—Oakland ....Amer.	3B	5	20	0	4	0	0	0	0	.200	6	16	0	1.000
1973—Oakland ....Amer.	3B	5	18	2	3	0	0	2	3	.167	7	10	0	1.000
1974—Oakland ....Amer.	3B	4	13	4	3	0	0	2	2	.231	3	8	0	1.000
1975—Oakland ....Amer.	3B	3	12	1	6	2	0	0	2	.500	3	11	1	.933
Championship Series Totals.............		20	74	10	20	4	0	5	8	.270	25	47	1	.986

WORLD SERIES RECORD

Tied World Series record for most assists, third baseman, inning (3), October 16, 1974 (sixth inning).

Year Club League	Pos.	G.	AB.	R.	H.	2B.	3B.	HR.	RBI.	B.A.	PO.	A.	E.	F.A.
1972—Oakland ....Amer.	3B	7	26	2	7	1	0	0	1	.269	3	12	1	.938
1973—Oakland ....Amer.	3B	7	26	5	6	1	1	0	1	.231	6	14	1	.952
1974—Oakland ....Amer.	3B	5	16	3	1	0	0	0	2	.063	2	10	0	1.000
World Series Totals		19	68	10	14	2	1	0	4	.206	11	36	2	.959

ALL-STAR GAME RECORD

Year League	Pos.	AB.	R.	H.	2B.	3B.	HR.	RBI.	B.A.	PO.	A.	E.	F.A.
1969—American.............................	3B	3	0	1	0	0	0	0	.333	0	1	0	1.000
1972—American.............................	3B	2	0	0	0	0	0	0	.000	1	1	0	1.000
1973—American.............................	3B	1	0	0	0	0	0	0	.000	0	1	0	1.000
All-Star Game Totals		6	0	1	0	0	0	0	.167	1	3	0	1.000

Named to American League All-Star Team for 1974 game; replaced due to injury.

ALAN BANNISTER

Born September 3, 1951, at Montebello, Calif.
Height, 5.11. Weight, 175
Throws and bats righthanded.
Hobbies—Movies, cars and all sports.
Attended Arizona State University, Tempe, Ariz., and California State University
at Long Beach, Long Beach, Calif.

Major League stolen bases: 1974 (0), 1975 (2), 1976 (12), 1977 (4), 1978 (3), 1979 (22), 1980 (14). Total—57.

Tied for American League lead in sacrifice flies with 11 in 1977.

Received reported $85,000 bonus to sign with Philadelphia Phillies, 1973.

Year Club League	Pos.	G.	AB.	R.	H.	2B.	3B.	HR.	RBI.	B.A.	PO.	A.	E.	F.A.
1973—Eugene .............P.C.	2-3-S-O	130	460	72	105	17	2	4	46	.228	207	342	27	.953
1974—Toledo..............Int.	*SS-OF	94	343	56	99	17	7	4	40	.289	164	173	*27	.926
1974—Philadelphia ......Nat.	OF-SS	26	25	4	3	0	0	0	1	.120	10	0	0	1.000
1975—Toledo..............Int.	OF	101	335	50	74	7	3	5	27	.221	209	3	6	.972
1975—Philadelphia† ....Nat.	O-S-2	24	61	10	16	3	1	0	0	.262	54	4	2	.967
1976—Iowa ....A. A.	SS	32	118	24	29	6	0	3	12	.246	64	106	9	.950
1976—Chicago............Amer.	O-S-2-3	73	145	19	36	6	2	0	8	.248	92	36	5	.962
1977—Chicago............Amer.	*S-2-O	139	560	87	154	20	3	3	57	.275	265	331	*40	.937
1978—Chicago‡..........Amer.	OF-SS-2	49	107	16	24	3	2	0	8	.224	34	16	2	.962
1979—Chicago ....Amer.	2-O-3-1	136	506	71	144	28	8	2	55	.285	250	187	21	.954
1980—Chi.§-Clev. ....Amer.	O-2-3-S	126	392	57	111	23	4	1	41	.283	189	153	14	.961
American League Totals...................		523	1710	250	469	80	19	6	169	.274	830	723	82	.950
National League Totals...................		50	86	14	19	3	1	0	1	.221	64	4	2	.971
Major League Totals		573	1796	264	488	83	20	6	170	.272	894	727	84	.951

Selected by California Angels' organization in 1st round of free-agent draft, June 5, 1969.

Selected by Philadelphia Phillies' organization in 1st round (first player selected) of free-agent draft, January 10, 1973.

†Traded with Pitchers Dick Ruthven and Roy Thomas to Chicago White Sox for Pitcher Jim Kaat and Shortstop Mike Buskey, December 10, 1975.

‡On emergency disabled list July 29 through remainder of 1978 season.

§Traded to Cleveland Indians for Catcher-Outfielder Ron Pruitt, June 14, 1980.

FLOYD FRANKLIN BANNISTER

Born June 10, 1955, at Pierre, S. Dakota.
Height, 6.01. Weight, 190.
Throws and bats lefthanded.
Attended Arizona State University, Tempe, Ariz.
Brother-in-law of Greg Cochran, pitcher in New York Yankees' organization.
Named College Player of the Year by THE SPORTING NEWS, 1976.

Year Club	League	G.	IP.	W.	L.	Pct.	H.	R.	ER.	SO.	BB.	ERA.
1976—Covington	Ap'lachian	3	13	0	0	.000	3	0	0	27	2	0.00
1976—Columbus	Southern	3	24	1	0	1.000	16	4	4	20	14	1.50
1976—Memphis	Int'national	1	6	1	0	1.000	7	1	1	6	3	1.50
1977—Houston†	National	24	143	8	9	.471	138	70	64	112	68	4.03
1978—Houston‡	National	28	110	3	9	.250	120	59	59	94	63	4.83
1979—Seattle	American	30	182	10	15	.400	185	92	82	115	68	4.05
1980—Seattle	American	32	218	9	13	.409	200	96	84	155	66	3.47
National League Totals		52	253	11	18	.379	258	129	123	206	131	4.38
American League Totals		62	400	19	28	.404	385	188	166	270	134	3.74
Major League Totals		114	653	30	46	.395	643	317	289	476	265	3.98

Selected by Oakland A's organization in 3rd round of free-agent draft, June 5, 1973.

Selected by Houston Astros' organization in 1st round (first player selected) of free-agent draft, June 8, 1976.

†On disabled list, July 26 to August 22, 1977.

‡Traded to Seattle Mariners for Shortstop Craig Reynolds, December 8, 1978.

ANGEL SANTIAGO BAREZ (DIAZ)

Born September 15, 1960, at Santurce, Puerto Rico.
Height, 6.01. Weight, 180.
Throws and bats righthanded.
Tied for Gulf Coast League lead in games started with 10 in 1978.
Led Carolina League in wild pitches with 22 in 1980.

Year Club	League	G.	IP.	W.	L.	Pct.	H.	R.	ER.	SO.	BB.	ERA.
1978—Bradenton Pirates	G. Coast	10	58	3	5	.375	41	34	29	53	45	4.50
1978—Charleston	W. Carol.	2	9	0	1	.000	12	15	13	8	10	13.00
1979—Salem	Carolina	2	6	0	2	.000	12	11	8	2	6	12.00
1979—Shelby	W. Carol.	16	104	5	9	.357	93	52	43	88	49	3.72
1980—Salem†	Carolina	24	126	11	5	.688	126	75	58	67	78	4.14

Signed as free agent by Pittsburgh Pirates' organization, March 22, 1978.

†On disabled list, April 11 to April 25, 1980.

JESSE LEE BARFIELD

Born October 29, 1959, at Joliet, Ill.
Height, 6.01. Weight, 170.
Throws and bats righthanded.
Led Florida State League batters in strikeouts with 125 in 1978.

Year Club	League	Pos.	G.	AB.	R.	H.	2B.	3B.	HR.	RBI.	B.A.	PO.	A.	E.	F.A.
1977—Utica	NY-P	OF	70	234	37	53	9	3	5	35	.226	122	6	●13	.908
1978—Dunedin	Fla. St.	OF	133	441	40	91	12	3	2	34	.206	229	∗22	∗15	.944
1979—Kinston	Carol.	OF	136	477	66	126	24	5	8	71	.264	284	19	17	.947
1980—Knoxville†	South.	OF	124	433	63	104	12	8	14	65	.240	309	14	12	.964

Selected by Toronto Blue Jays' organization in 9th round of free-agent draft, June 7, 1977.

†On disabled list, August 15 to August 29, 1980.

LEONARD HAROLD BARKER, II
(Len)

Born July 7, 1955, at Ft. Knox, Ky.
Height, 6.04. Weight, 215.
Throws and bats righthanded.
Hobbies—Hunting and fishing.
Led Western Carolinas League in shutouts with 5 in 1974.

Year Club	League	G.	IP.	W.	L.	Pct.	H.	R.	ER.	SO.	BB.	ERA.
1973—Sarasota Rangers	Gulf Coast	11	59	●7	1	●.875	34	13	9	54	27	1.37
1974—Gastonia	W. Carol.	20	124	11	7	.611	101	57	46	140	53	3.34
1975—Pittsfield	Eastern	24	159	7	12	.368	117	72	51	133	109	2.89
1976—Sacramento	P. Coast	27	141	11	10	.524	140	103	87	92	96	5.55
1976—Texas	American	2	15	1	0	1.000	7	4	4	7	6	2.40
1977—Tucson	P. Coast	20	109	9	7	.563	114	77	69	93	77	5.70

Year Club	League	G.	IP.	W.	L.	Pct.	H.	R.	ER.	SO.	BB.	ERA.
1977—Texas	American	15	47	4	1	.800	36	15	14	51	24	2.68
1978—Tucson	P. Coast	8	26	4	0	1.000	22	8	3	16	16	1.04
1978—Texas†	American	29	52	1	5	.167	63	31	28	33	29	4.85
1979—Cleveland	American	29	137	6	6	.500	146	79	75	93	70	4.93
1980—Cleveland	American	36	246	19	12	.613	237	127	114	*187	92	4.17
Major League Totals		111	497	31	24	.564	489	256	235	371	221	4.26

Selected by Texas Rangers' organization in 3rd round of free-agent draft, June 5, 1973.
†Traded with outfielder Bobby Bonds to Cleveland Indians for Infielder Larvell Blanks and Pitcher Jim Kern, October 3, 1978.

MICHAEL ROSWELL BARLOW
(Mike)

Born April 30, 1948, at Stamford, N. Y.
Height, 6.05. Weight, 215.
Throws right and bats lefthanded.
Hobbies—Music, carpentry, reading and horses.
Attended Syracuse University, Syracuse, N.Y.; received
Bachelor of Arts degree in Economics.

Year Club	League	G.	IP.	W.	L.	Pct.	H.	R.	ER.	SO.	BB.	ERA.
1970—Coos Bay-North Bend	Northwest	16	74	4	3	.571	72	47	36	58	33	4.38
1971—Burlington	Midwest	26	80	5	3	.625	74	39	30	62	33	3.38
1972—Key West	Florida St.	19	124	10	8	.556	114	50	40	97	48	2.90
1972—Birmingham	Southern	18	53	2	4	.333	49	30	22	52	22	3.74
1973—Birmingham	Southern	28	109	5	4	.556	101	66	48	75	53	3.96
1974—Tucson	P. Coast	55	82	4	7	.364	81	30	24	68	44	2.63
1975—Tucson†	P. Coast	16	45	4	1	.800	29	16	13	43	26	2.60
1975—Tulsa	Am. Assoc.	20	73	4	4	.500	62	32	32	56	47	3.95
1975—St. Louis‡	National	9	8	0	0	.000	11	6	4	2	3	4.50
1976—Memphis	Int'national	9	11	2	0	1.000	10	6	6	8	6	4.91
1976—Houston§	National	16	22	2	2	.500	27	13	11	11	17	4.50
1976—Salt Lake City	P. Coast	25	50	5	1	.833	52	23	20	40	19	3.60
1977—Salt Lake City	P. Coast	26	51	3	5	.375	56	43	38	38	37	6.71
1977—California	American	20	59	4	2	.667	53	33	30	25	27	4.58
1978—Salt Lake City	P. Coast	44	77	6	5	.545	81	42	27	38	38	3.16
1978—California	American	1	2	0	0	.000	3	1	1	1	0	4.50
1979—California x	American	35	86	1	1	.500	106	54	49	33	30	5.13
1980—Syracuse	Int'national	20	51	3	2	.600	55	29	26	26	20	4.59
1980—Toronto	American	40	55	3	1	.750	57	29	25	19	21	4.09
National League Totals		25	30	2	2	.500	38	19	15	13	20	4.50
American League Totals		96	202	8	4	.667	219	117	105	78	78	4.68
Major League Totals		121	232	10	6	.625	257	136	120	91	98	4.66

Selected by Baltimore Orioles' organization in 26th round of free-agent draft, June 5, 1969.
Selected by Los Angeles Dodgers' organization in secondary phase of free-agent draft, January 17, 1970.
Signed as free agent by Oakland A's organization, June 17, 1970.
†Traded by Oakland Athletics to St. Louis Cardinals, May 23, 1975, to complete deal in which Athletics obtained Infielder Ted Martinez from Cardinals for Pitcher Steve Staniland and a player to be named later, May 18, 1975.
‡Traded to Houston Astros for Outfielder Mike Easler, September 30, 1975.
§Traded with Catcher Terry Humphrey to California Angels' organization for Catcher Ed Herrmann, June 6, 1976.
xOn disabled list, April 1 to April 28, 1979.

CHAMPIONSHIP SERIES RECORD

Year Club	League	G.	IP.	W.	L.	Pct.	H.	R.	ER.	SO.	BB.	ERA.
1979—California	American	1	1	0	0	.000	0	0	0	0	0	0.00

RICHARD MONROE BARNES
(Rich)

Born July 21, 1959, at Palm Beach, Fla.
Height, 6.04. Weight, 180.
Throws left and bats left and righthanded.
Tied for Gulf Coast League lead in games started with 12 in 1977.

Year Club	League	G.	IP.	W.	L.	Pct.	H.	R.	ER.	SO.	BB.	ERA.
1977—Sarasota White Sox	Gulf Coast	13	73	*8	1	.889	46	22	13	*61	37	1.60
1977—Knoxville	Southern	3	13	0	1	.000	11	5	3	9	7	2.08
1978—Knoxville	Southern	25	146	8	6	.571	144	72	53	69	75	3.27
1979—Knoxville	Southern	22	131	8	8	.500	136	79	61	91	86	4.19
1979—Iowa	Am. Assoc.	3	10	0	1	.000	12	6	5	5	7	4.50
1980—Iowa	Am. Assoc.	26	123	3	9	.250	131	73	63	59	93	4.61

Selected by Chicago White Sox' organization in 2nd round of free-agent draft, June 7, 1977.

DID YOU KNOW—
That the Royals have led the American League in triples the last six years?

THEODORE MICHAEL BARNICLE
(Ted)

Born November 20, 1953, at Boston, Mass.
Height, 6.00. Weight, 175.
Throws and bats lefthanded.
Attended Jacksonville State University, Jacksonville, Ala.;
received Bachelor of Science degree in Geography.

Pitched 5-0 no-hit victory against Dubuque, June 29, 1976.
Tied for California League lead in shutouts with 3 in 1977.

Year Club	League	G.	IP.	W.	L.	Pct.	H.	R.	ER.	SO.	BB.	ERA.
1975—Fresno	California	5	27	0	4	.000	24	28	25	20	28	8.33
1975—Great Falls	Pioneer	8	47	2	5	.286	46	27	24	60	38	4.60
1976—Cedar Rapids	Midwest	24	163	9	10	.474	132	94	73	*160	*142	4.03
1977—Fresno†	California	26	173	11	•13	.458	188	105	86	*779	91	4.47
1978—Albuquerque‡	P. Coast					Did not play						
1979—Knoxville§	Southern	20	89	3	11	.214	95	64	56	46	50	5.66
1980—Glens Falls x	Eastern	20	70	5	2	.714	75	37	33	42	47	4.24
1980—Iowa	Am. Assoc.	6	37	5	0	1.000	37	26	14	34	24	3.41

Selected by San Francisco Giants' organization in 1st round (8th player selected) of free-agent draft, June 4, 1975.

†Drafted by Los Angeles Dodgers' organization, December 6, 1977.
‡Released, April 5, 1978; signed by Chicago White Sox' organization, January 12, 1979.
§On disabled list, April 16 to May 2, 1979.
xOn disabled list, April 14 to May 7, 1980.

JAMES LELAND BARR
(Jim)

Born February 10, 1948, at Lynwood, Calif.
Height, 6.03. Weight, 215.
Throws and bats righthanded.
Hobbies—Woodworking and water skiing.
Attended University of Southern California, Los Angeles, Calif.;
received Bachelor of Arts degree in Business Administration.
Brother of Mark Barr, former pitcher in Boston Red Sox' organization.

Established major league record for most batters retired, consecutive, season, 41, August 23-29, 1972.

Year Club	League	G.	IP.	W.	L.	Pct.	H.	R.	ER.	SO.	BB.	ERA.
1970—Amarillo	Texas	14	98	6	5	.545	107	51	36	48	23	3.31
1971—Phoenix	P. Coast	47	79	6	3	.667	72	36	33	71	26	3.76
1971—San Francisco	National	17	35	1	1	.500	33	15	14	16	5	3.60
1972—San Francisco	National	44	179	8	10	.444	166	66	57	86	41	2.87
1973—San Francisco	National	41	231	11	17	.393	240	105	98	88	49	3.82
1974—San Francisco	National	44	240	13	9	.591	223	81	73	84	47	2.74
1975—San Francisco	National	35	244	13	14	.481	244	94	83	77	58	3.06
1976—San Francisco	National	37	252	15	12	.556	260	104	81	75	60	2.89
1977—San Francisco†	National	38	234	12	16	.429	286	130	124	97	56	4.77
1978—San Francisco‡	National	32	163	8	11	.421	180	69	64	44	35	3.53
1979—California	American	36	197	10	12	.455	217	100	92	69	55	4.20
1980—California§	American	24	68	1	4	.200	90	43	42	22	23	5.56
American League Totals		60	265	11	16	.407	307	143	134	91	78	4.55
National League Totals		288	1578	81	90	.474	1632	664	594	567	351	3.39
Major League Totals		348	1843	92	106	.465	1939	807	728	658	429	3.56

Selected by California Angels' organization in 13th round of free-agent draft, June 6, 1966.
Selected by Philadelphia Phillies' organization in 3rd round of free-agent draft, June 7, 1968.
Selected by New York Yankees' organization in secondary phase of free-agent draft, February 1, 1969.
Selected by Pittsburgh Pirates' organization in secondary phase of free-agent draft, June 5, 1969.
Selected by Minnesota Twins' organization in secondary phase of free-agent draft, January 17, 1970.
Selected by San Francisco Giants' organization in secondary phase of free-agent draft, June 4, 1970.
†On suspended list, June 1 to June 4, 1977.
‡Granted free agency, November 2, 1978; signed by California Angels, December 3, 1978.
§On disabled list, June 26 to August 5, 1980.

CHAMPIONSHIP SERIES RECORD

Year Club	League	G.	IP.	W.	L.	Pct.	H.	R.	ER.	SO.	BB.	ERA.
1971—San Francisco	National	1	1	0	0	.000	3	1	1	2	0	9.00

GERMAN BARRANCA (COSTALES)
Name pronounced Bah-RAHNK-a.

Born October 19, 1956, at Veracruz, Mexico.
Height, 6.00. Weight, 175.
Throws right and bats lefthanded.
Attended Veracruz Technical Institute, Veracruz, Mexico.
Cousin of Guillermo Barranca, former minor league pitcher.

Led American Association in stolen bases with 75 in 1979.

Year Club League	Pos.	G.	AB.	R.	H.	2B.	3B.	HR.	RBI.	B.A.	PO.	A.	E.	F.A.
1975–Sar. Royals ....Gulf C.	SS	22	64	14	17	2	0	0	4	.266	21	47	3	.958
1975–Waterloo ....Midw.	SS	65	190	26	43	5	3	0	22	.226	74	197	27	.909
1976–Waterloo ....Midw.	SS	92	319	69	89	14	3	0	27	.279	117	265	37	.912
1977–Jacksonville ......South.	2B	118	409	47	106	9	4	0	36	.259	199	349	19	.966
1978–Jacksonville .....South.	2B	49	182	22	44	3	2	2	13	.242	97	112	7	.968
1978–Omaha.............A.A.	2B	61	229	23	54	5	0	0	17	.236	126	167	13	.958
1979–Omaha.............A.A.	2B-SS-1B	122	472	79	120	18	7	8	49	.254	79	115	5	.975
1979–Kansas City ......Amer.	2B-3B	5	5	3	3	1	0	0	0	.600	4	7	0	1.000
1980–Omaha.............A.A.	OF-2B	93	305	39	69	10	3	3	26	.226	85	10	4	.960
1980–Kansas City†.....Amer.	PR	7	0	3	0	0	0	0	0	.000	0	0	0	.000
Major League Totals....................		12	5	6	3	1	0	0	0	.600	4	7	0	1.000

Signed as free agent by Ebano of Mexican Center League, October 8, 1973.

Sold to Mexico City of Mexican League, August 25, 1974; sold to Kansas City Royals' organization, August 26, 1974.

†Traded to Cincinnati Reds for Outfielder Cesar Geronimo, January 21, 1981.

FRANCISCO JAVIER BARRIOS (JIMENEZ)

Name pronounced BAR-ree-os

Born June 10, 1953, at Hermosillo, Mexico.
Height, 6.03. Weight, 195.
Throws and bats righthanded.

Named Mexican League Rookie of the Year, 1973.

Year Club League	G.	IP.	W.	L.	Pct.	H.	R.	ER.	SO.	BB.	ERA.
1971–San Luis Potosi ....Mex. Cent.	18	90	6	4	.600	76	45	32	43	32	3.20
1971–Mexicali ....Mex. North.	22	113	7	4	.636	103	38	34	71	44	2.71
1972–Zacatecas ....Mex. Cent.	19	97	5	•9	.357	102	*70	*60	55	41	5.57
1972–Jalisco ....Mexican	8	23	1	1	.500	23	15	12	11	14	4.70
1973–Jalisco† ....Mexican	33	198	10	12	.455	157	70	52	158	98	2.36
1973–Phoenix‡§ ....P. Coast	6	30	2	1	.667	36	18	15	9	10	4.50
1974–Knoxville ....Southern	26	124	9	5	.643	112	60	54	84	58	3.92
1974–Chicago ....American	2	2	0	0	.000	7	6	6	2	2	27.00
1975–Jalisco ....Mexican	31	183	10	12	.455	169	77	55	138	85	2.70
1975–Denver ....Am. Assoc.	3	23	2	0	1.000	21	10	10	12	9	3.91
1976–Chicago ....American	35	142	5	9	.357	136	72	68	81	46	4.31
1977–Chicago ....American	33	231	14	7	.667	241	117	106	119	58	4.13
1978–Chicago ....American	33	196	9	15	.375	180	93	88	79	85	4.04
1979–Chicago xy ....American	15	95	8	3	.727	88	49	38	28	33	3.60
1980–Appleton z ....Midwest	2	13	2	0	1.000	5	2	1	5	4	0.69
1980–Iowa a ....Am. Assoc.	1	3	0	0	.000	7	5	5	1	1	15.00
1980–Chicago ....American	3	16	1	1	.500	21	9	9	9	2	8	5.06
Major League Totals	121	682	37	35	.514	673	346	315	311	232	4.16

Signed as free agent by San Luis Potosi, February 28, 1971.

†Conditionally released to Phoenix (San Francisco Giants' organization), August 9, 1973.

‡Returned to Jalisco, September 6, 1973.

§Traded with Pitcher Manuel Lugo by Jalisco to Chicago White Sox for Infielder Rudy Hernandez, December 4, 1973.

xOn disabled list, July 13 to October 5, 1979.

yOn disabled list, March 31 to May 13, 1980.

zOn rehabilitation assignment, May 20 to June 4, 1980.

aOn disabled list, July 10 to August 27, 1980.

JOSE MANUEL BARRIOS

Born June 26, 1957, at New York, N. Y.
Height, 6.04. Weight, 195.
Throws and bats righthanded.
Attended Miami-Dade Community College South, Miami, Fla.

Led Eastern League first basemen in double plays with 98 in 1978.

Led Texas League first basemen in double plays with 113 in 1979.

Year Club League	Pos.	G.	AB.	R.	H.	2B.	3B.	HR.	RBI.	B.A.	PO.	A.	E.	F.A.
1975–Great Falls ....Pion.	OF-1B	47	166	21	46	7	2	2	26	.277	141	11	7	.956
1976–Cedar Rapids†...Midw.	OF	86	293	38	83	12	2	6	36	.283	76	3	2	.975
1977–Fresno.............Calif.	1B	123	469	73	132	28	1	12	79	.281	926	48	17	.983
1978–Waterbury ....East.	1B	*139	478	54	109	22	6	13	56	.228	*1207	*114	*15	.989
1979–Shreveport........Texas	1B	118	410	56	133	18	4	17	84	.324	1071	62	*15	.987
1980–Phoenix ...........P.C.	1B-OF	145	563	70	158	22	10	11	97	.281	1081	76	14	.988

Selected by San Francisco Giants' organization in 3rd round of free-agent draft, June 4, 1975.

†On disabled list, June 25 to July 29, 1976.

KEVIN CHARLES BASS

Born May 12, 1959, at Menlo Park, Calif.
Height, 6.00. Weight, 180.
Throws right and bats right and lefthanded.
Brother of Richard Bass, former outfielder in Chicago
Cubs' organization.

Led Eastern League outfielders in double plays with 7 in 1980.

Year Club	League	Pos.	G.	AB.	R.	H.	2B.	3B.	HR.	RBI.	B.A.	PO.	A.	E.	F.A.
1977—Newark ....NY-P	OF	48	189	30	56	11	•7	1	33	.296	56	2	3	.951
1978—Burlington ....Midw.	OF	129	499	81	132	27	5	18	69	.265	*281	14	11	.964
1979—Holyoke ....East.	OF	135	490	69	129	15	4	8	54	.263	280	•16	*17	.946
1980—Holyoke ....East.	OF	136	490	79	147	*31	7	4	51	.300	305	14	*18	.947

Selected by Milwaukee Brewers' organization in 2nd round of free-agent draft, June 7, 1977.

RANDY WILLIAM BASS

Born March 13, 1954, at Lawton, Okla.
Height, 6.01. Weight, 210.
Throws right and bats lefthanded.
Hobbies—Hunting, fishing and golf.

Led Florida East Coast League in total bases with 106 and in walks with 59 in 1972.
Led Carolina League first basemen in double plays with 107 in 1974.
Led American Association in slugging percentage with .644 in 1980.
Tied for American Association lead in sacrifice flies with 9 in 1980.

Year Club	League	Pos.	G.	AB.	R.	H.	2B.	3B.	HR.	RBI.	B.A.	PO.	A.	E.	F.A.
1972—Melb'ne Twins...Fla.E.C.	1B	59	199	*47	61	*15	0	*10	*41	.307	*527	14	•11	*.980
1973—Wis. Rapids ....Midw.	1B	114	388	83	112	23	1	*21	86	.289	*988	59	19	.982
1974—Lynchburg ....Carol.	1B	133	461	89	118	17	1	*30	*112	.256	*1237	*84	17	.987
1975—Tacoma.............P.C.	1B	120	397	64	102	14	5	18	80	.257	795	74	6	.993
1976—Tacoma.............P.C.	1B	141	451	73	126	15	3	21	76	.279	569	51	3	.995
1977—Tacoma.............P.C.	1B	134	455	79	146	26	4	25	117	.321	988	82	*14	.987
1977—Minnesota†........Amer.	DH-PH	9	19	0	2	0	0	0	0	.105	0	0	0	.000
1978—Omaha..............A. A.	1B	127	423	78	118	26	0	22	78	.279	*1142	*92	10	.992
1978—Kansas City‡.....Amer.	PH	2	2	0	0	0	0	0	0	.000	0	0	0	.000
1979—Denver§............A. A.	1B	122	421	91	140	28	1	36	105	.333	885	*92	7	*.993
1979—Montreal...........Nat.	1B	2	1	0	0	0	0	0	0	.000	1	0	0	1.000
1980—Denver x...........A.A.	1B	123	450	*106	150	25	2	*37	*143	.333	81	0	0	1.000
1980—San Diego ....Nat.	1B	19	49	5	14	0	1	3	8	.286	127	6	2	.985
National League Totals		21	50	5	14	0	1	3	8	.280	128	6	2	.985
American League Totals		11	21	0	2	0	0	0	0	.095	0	0	0	.000
Major League Totals......................		32	71	5	16	0	1	3	8	.225	128	6	2	.985

Selected by Minnesota Twins' organization in 7th round of free-agent draft, June 6, 1972.
†Sold to Kansas City Royals' organization, April 4, 1978.
‡Sold to Montreal Expos' organization, April 6, 1979.
§On disabled list, June 16 to June 26, 1979.
xTraded to San Diego Padres, September 5, 1980, completing deal in which Montreal acquired Pitcher John D'Acquisto and cash, August 11, 1980.

ROSS BAUMGARTEN

Born May 27, 1955, at Highland Park, Ill.
Height, 6.01. Weight, 180.
Throws and bats lefthanded.
Attended Florida Southern College, Lakeland, Fla., Palm Beach Junior College, Lake Worth, Fla. and
University of Florida, Gainesville, Fla.

Year Club	League	G.	IP.	W.	L.	Pct.	H.	R.	ER.	SO.	BB.	ERA.
1977—Appleton ....Midwest	17	84	3	6	.333	82	48	35	65	37	3.75
1978—Appleton ....Midwest	10	74	9	1	.900	49	19	15	73	18	1.82
1978—Knoxville ....Southern	4	25	2	1	.667	22	9	9	14	7	3.24
1978—Iowa ....Am. Assoc.	9	66	5	4	.556	57	30	24	54	23	3.27
1978—Chicago ....American	7	23	2	2	.500	29	15	15	15	9	5.87
1979—Chicago ....American	28	191	13	8	.619	175	82	75	72	83	3.53
1980—Chicago† ....American	24	136	2	12	.143	127	60	52	66	52	3.44
Major League Totals...............................	59	350	17	22	.436	331	157	142	153	144	3.65

Selected by Chicago White Sox' organization in 20th round of free-agent draft, June 7, 1977.
†On disabled list, July 24 to August 24, 1980.

DONALD EDWARD BAYLOR
(Don)

Born June 28, 1949, at Austin, Tex.
Height, 6.01. Weight, 195.
Throws and bats righthanded.
Hobbies—Fishing and reading poetry.
Attended Miami-Dade Junior College, Miami, Fla., and Blinn Junior
College, Brenham, Tex.

Established major league record for most times caught stealing, inning, 2, June 15, 1974 (9th inning).
Tied major league records for most long hits, opening game of season (4), April 6, 1973 (2 doubles, 1 triple, 1 home run); most consecutive home runs, two consecutive games (4), July 1 and 2, 1975 (bases on balls included).
Tied modern major league record for most at bats, game (7), August 25, 1979.
Tied American League record for most hits, two consecutive games (9), August 13 and 14, 1973.
Major League stolen bases: 1970 (1), 1971 (0), 1972 (24), 1973 (32), 1974 (29), 1975 (32), 1976 (52), 1977 (26), 1978 (22), 1979 (22), 1980 (6). Total—246.
Hit three home runs in one game, vs. Detroit Tigers, July 2, 1975.
Led Appalachian League in stolen bases with 26 and total bases with 135 in 1967.

Led International League in total bases with 296 in 1970.
Led American League in sacrifice flies with 12 in 1978.
Named Appalachian League Player of the Year, 1967.
Named by THE SPORTING NEWS as Minor League Player of the Year, 1970.
Named American League Most Valuable Player by Baseball Writers' Association of America, 1979.
Named American League Player of the Year by THE SPORTING NEWS, 1979.
Named as designated hitter on THE SPORTING NEWS American League All-Star Team, 1979.

Year	Club	League	Pos.	G.	AB.	R.	H.	2B.	3B.	HR.	RBI.	B.A.	PO.	A.	E.	F.A.
1967—Bluefield	Appal.	OF	•67	246	50	*85	10	*8	8	47	*.346	106	5	5	.957
1968—Stockton	Calif.	OF	68	244	52	90	6	3	7	40	.369	135	3	7	.952
1968—Elmira	East.	OF	6	24	4	8	1	1	1	3	.333	10	1	0	1.000
1968—Rochester	Int.	OF	15	46	4	10	2	0	0	4	.217	29	1	4	.882
1969—Miami	Fla.St.	OF	17	56	13	21	5	4	3	24	.375	30	2	3	.914
1969—Dal.-Ft. Worth	Texas	OF	109	406	71	122	17	•10	11	57	.300	241	7	*13	.950
1970—Rochester	Int.	OF	•140	508	*127	166	*34	*15	22	107	.327	286	5	7	.977
1970—Baltimore	Amer.	OF	8	17	4	4	0	0	0	4	.235	15	0	0	1.000
1971—Rochester	Int.	OF	136	492	104	154	•31	10	20	95	.313	210	4	9	.960
1971—Baltimore	Amer.	OF	1	2	0	0	0	0	0	1	.000	4	0	0	1.000
1972—Baltimore	Amer.	OF-1B	102	320	33	81	13	3	11	38	.253	206	4	5	.977
1973—Baltimore	Amer.	OF-1B	118	405	64	116	20	4	11	51	.286	228	10	6	.975
1974—Baltimore	Amer.	OF-1B	137	489	66	133	22	1	10	59	.272	260	2	5	.981
1975—Baltimore†	Amer.	OF-1B	145	524	79	148	21	6	25	76	.282	286	8	5	.983
1976—Oakland‡	Amer.	OF-1B	157	595	85	147	25	1	15	68	.247	781	45	12	.986
1977—California	Amer.	OF-1B	154	561	87	141	27	0	25	75	.251	280	16	7	.977
1978—California	Amer.	OF-1B	158	591	103	151	26	0	34	99	.255	194	9	6	.971
1979—California	Amer.	OF-1B	•162	628	*120	186	33	3	36	*139	.296	203	3	5	.976
1980—California§	Amer.	OF	90	340	39	85	12	2	5	51	.250	119	4	4	.969
Major League Totals			1232	4472	680	1192	199	20	172	661	.267	2576	101	55	.980

Selected by Baltimore Orioles' organization in 2nd round of free-agent draft, June 6, 1967.

†Traded with Pitchers Mike Torrez and Paul Mitchell to Oakland Athletics for Outfielder Reggie Jackson and Pitchers Ken Holtzman and Bill Van Bommel, April 2, 1976.

‡Played out option year and granted free agency, November 1, 1976; signed as free agent by California Angels, November 16, 1976.

§On disabled list, May 11 to June 26, 1980.

CHAMPIONSHIP SERIES RECORD

Year	Club	League	Pos.	G.	AB.	R.	H.	2B.	3B.	HR.	RBI.	B.A.	PO.	A.	E.	F.A.
1973—Baltimore	Amer.	OF-PH	4	11	3	3	0	0	0	1	.273	7	0	0	1.000
1974—Baltimore	Amer.	OF	4	15	0	4	0	0	0	0	.267	9	0	0	1.000
1979—California	Amer.	DH-OF	4	16	2	3	0	0	1	2	.188	4	0	0	1.000
Championship Series Totals			12	42	5	10	0	0	1	3	.238	20	0	0	1.000

ALL-STAR GAME RECORD

Year	League	Pos.	AB.	R.	H.	2B.	3B.	HR.	RBI.	B.A.	PO.	A.	E.	F.A.
1979—American		OF	4	2	2	1	0	0	1	.500	1	0	0	1.000

ROBERT BROOKS BEALL
(Bob)

Born April 24, 1948, at Portland, Ore.
Height, 5.11. Weight, 180.
Throws left and bats left and righthanded.
Hobbies—Poetry, classical music and books.
Attended Oregon State University, Corvallis, Ore.; received
Bachelor of Science degree in Mathematics.

Led Northwest League batters in bases on balls with 95 in 1970, Carolina League with 110 in 1971, Eastern League with 132 in 1972 and International League with 136 in 1974, with 135 in 1976 and with 133 in 1977.

Led Carolina League first basemen in double plays with 113 in 1971 and led Eastern League with 96 in 1972; tied for Northwest League lead with 47 in 1970.

Named Northwest League Player of the Year in 1970.

Year	Club	League	Pos.	G.	AB.	R.	H.	2B.	3B.	HR.	RBI.	B.A.	PO.	A.	E.	F.A.
1970—Walla Walla	N'west	1B	•80	262	*81	*102	17	3	8	55	*.389	*715	40	17	.978
1971—Peninsula	Carol.	1B	•138	452	78	142	*31	8	5	63	.314	*1179	*91	13	*.990
1972—Reading	East.	*1B-OF	139	421	82	119	24	5	5	53	.283	*1064	*67	11	.990
1973—Eugene†‡	P.C.	OF-1B	114	354	71	83	20	1	5	50	.234	603	62	10	.985
1974—Richmond	Int.	*1-O-3-P	139	447	*105	128	14	1	9	59	.286	*1047	53	9	.992
1975—Richmond	Int.	O-1-P	78	238	30	56	11	2	5	27	.235	208	14	3	.987
1975—Atlanta	Nat.	1B	20	31	2	7	2	0	0	1	.226	57	4	1	.984
1976—Richmond§	Int.	OF-1B	109	350	85	107	19	5	9	55	.306	372	25	4	.990
1977—Richmond	Int.	OF-1B	138	463	89	130	29	1	9	45	.281	593	55	5	.992
1978—Atlanta	Nat.	1B-OF	108	185	29	45	8	0	1	16	.243	282	24	4	.987
1979—Atlanta x	Nat.	1B	17	15	1	2	2	0	0	1	.133	9	1	0	1.000
1979—Richmond	Int.	1B-OF-P	32	104	27	38	5	1	4	17	.365	191	10	2	.990
1980—Richmond y	Int.	1-O-P	57	129	15	32	6	0	0	12	.248	71	10	0	1.000
1980—Portland	P.C.	1B-OF	45	157	29	34	12	0	1	11	.217	124	10	1	.993
1980—Pittsburgh	Nat.	PH	3	3	0	0	0	0	0	0	.000	0	0	0	.000
Major League Totals			148	234	32	54	12	0	1	18	.231	348	29	5	.987

Selected by Philadelphia Phillies' organization in 27th round of free-agent draft, June 4, 1970.

†On disabled list from beginning of season until May 9, 1973.

‡Traded by Philadelphia Phillies to Atlanta Braves for Infielder Gil Garrido, December 10, 1973, to complete deal in which Phillies obtained Pitcher Ron Schueler from Braves for Shortstop Craig Robinson and Pitcher Barry Lersch, December 3, 1973.

§On disabled list, June 24 to July 13, 1976.

xOn disabled list, April 25 to August 1, 1979.

yTraded to Pittsburgh Pirates' organization for Second Baseman Jerry McDonald, July 16, 1980.

PITCHING RECORD

Year Club	League	G.	IP.	W.	L.	Pct.	H.	R.	ER.	SO.	BB.	ERA.
1974—Richmond	Int'national	1	⅔	0	0	.000	1	0	0	1	0	0.00
1975—Richmond	Int'national	1	⅓	0	0	.000	0	0	0	0	0	0.00
1979—Richmond	Int'national	1	2	0	0	.000	2	0	0	1	0	0.00
1980—Richmond	Int'national	5	14	0	0	.000	21	16	16	7	7	10.29

CHARLES DAVID BEARD
(Dave)

Born October 2, 1959, at Chamblee, Ga.
Height, 6.05. Weight, 190.
Throws right and bats lefthanded

Led Eastern League in complete games with 20 in 1979.
Tied for California League lead in shutouts with 5 in 1978.

Year Club	League	G.	IP.	W.	L.	Pct.	H.	R.	ER.	SO.	BB.	ERA.
1977—Medicine Hat	Pioneer	11	71	4	5	.444	79	50	36	30	31	4.56
1978—Modesto	California	25	185	12	6	.667	161	94	60	142	64	2.42
1979—Waterbury	Eastern	25	★191	10	●14	.417	192	87	64	111	63	3.02
1980—Ogden†	P. Coast	16	97	7	8	.467	110	76	69	70	44	6.40
1980—Oakland	American	13	16	0	1	.000	12	6	6	12	7	3.38
Major League Totals		13	16	0	1	.000	12	6	6	12	7	3.38

Selected by Oakland A's organization in 6th round of free-agent draft, June 7, 1977.
†On disabled list, April 20 to May 2, 1980.

JAMES LOUIS BEATTIE

Name pronounced BEE-tee.

Born July 4, 1954, at Langeley AFB, Hampton, Va.
Height, 6.06. Weight, 205.
Throws and bats righthanded.
Hobbies—Painting and mountain climbing.
Attended Dartmouth College, Hanover, N. H.; received Business Administration degree
and attending Northeastern University graduate school of Business, Boston, Mass.

Tied major league records for most putouts by pitcher, inning (3), September 13, 1978 (second inning); most putouts by pitcher, nine-inning game (5), September 13, 1978.
Pitched seven-inning, 2-0 no-hit victory against Spokane, July 9, 1978.

Year Club	League	G.	IP.	W.	L.	Pct.	H.	R.	ER.	SO.	BB.	ERA.
1975—Oneonta†	NYP	5	24	2	0	1.000	15	11	5	22	7	1.88
1975—Syracuse	Int'national	5	33	2	2	.500	25	14	12	30	21	3.27
1976—Syracuse	Int'national	17	100	5	5	.500	106	67	67	74	80	6.03
1976—West Haven	Eastern	8	60	5	2	.714	47	19	15	48	33	2.25
1977—West Haven‡	Eastern	3	27	2	0	1.000	14	5	1	22	8	0.33
1977—Ft. Lauderdale	Fla. State	9	38	1	3	.250	52	27	25	28	17	5.92
1977—Syracuse	Int'national	12	80	6	5	.545	70	41	37	53	43	4.16
1978—Tacoma	P. Coast	4	23	3	0	1.000	17	5	4	15	12	1.57
1978—New York	American	25	128	6	9	.400	123	60	53	65	51	3.73
1979—Columbus	Int'national	8	53	5	1	.833	31	9	8	47	25	1.36
1979—New York§x	American	15	76	3	6	.333	85	45	44	32	41	5.21
1980—Seattle	American	33	187	5	15	.250	205	115	101	67	98	4.86
Major League Totals		73	391	14	30	.318	413	220	198	164	190	4.56

Selected by New York Yankees' organization in 4th round of free-agent draft, June 4, 1975.
†On disabled list, July 13 to July 29, 1975.
‡On disabled list, April 15 to May 2, 1977.
§On disabled list, June 25 to July 22, 1979.

xTraded with Outfielder Juan Beniquez, Catcher Jerry Narron and Pitcher Rick Anderson to Seattle Mariners for Outfielder Ruppert Jones and Pitcher Jim Lewis, November 1, 1979.

CHAMPIONSHIP SERIES RECORD

Year Club	League	G.	IP.	W.	L.	Pct.	H.	R.	ER.	SO.	BB.	ERA.
1978—New York	American	1	5⅓	1	0	1.000	2	1	1	3	5	1.69

WORLD SERIES RECORD

Year Club	League	G.	IP.	W.	L.	Pct.	H.	R.	ER.	SO.	BB.	ERA.
1978—New York	American	1	9	1	0	1.000	9	2	2	8	4	2.00

DID YOU KNOW—
That the Seattle Mariners had six pitchers who lost 10 or more games in 1980?

THOMAS JOSEPH BECKWITH
(Joe)

Born January 28, 1955, at Auburn, Ala.
Height, 6.03. Weight, 185.
Throws right and bats lefthanded.
Attended Auburn University, Auburn, Ala.

Year	Club	League	G.	IP.	W.	L.	Pct.	H.	R.	ER.	SO.	BB.	ERA.
1977—San Antonio	Texas		12	78	5	5	.500	88	40	29	31	20	3.35
1978—Albuquerque	P. Coast		28	150	8	9	.471	186	118	97	59	80	5.82
1979—Albuquerque	P. Coast		27	113	8	8	.500	119	74	58	64	46	4.62
1979—Los Angeles	National		17	37	1	2	.333	42	18	18	28	15	4.38
1980—Albuquerque	P. Coast		7	14	2	1	.667	15	8	4	12	5	2.57
1980—Los Angeles	National		38	60	3	3	.500	60	17	13	40	23	1.95
Major League Totals			55	97	4	5	.444	102	35	31	68	38	2.88

Selected by Cleveland Indians' organization in 12th round of free-agent draft, June 8, 1976.
Selected by Los Angeles Dodgers' organization in 2nd round of free-agent draft, June 7, 1977.

STEPHEN WAYNE BEDROSIAN
(Steve)

Born December 6, 1957, at Methuen, Mass.
Height, 6.03. Weight, 200.
Throws and bats righthanded.
Attended North Essex Community College, Haverhill, Mass., and
New Haven University, New Haven, Conn.

Tied for Southern League lead in games started with 29 in 1980.

Year	Club	League	G.	IP.	W.	L.	Pct.	H.	R.	ER.	SO.	BB.	ERA.
1978—Kingsport	Appal.		6	38	2	2	.500	38	18	13	29	25	3.08
1978—Greenwood	W. Carol.		8	55	5	1	.833	45	17	13	58	34	2.13
1979—Savannah†	Southern		13	89	5	5	.500	71	36	30	73	58	3.03
1980—Savannah	Southern		29	∗203	14	10	.583	167	91	72	∗161	96	3.19

Selected by Atlanta Braves' organization in 3rd round of free-agent draft, June 6, 1978.
†On disabled list, June 24 to September 18, 1979.

MARK HENRY BELANGER

Name pronounced Bel-LAN-ger.

Born June 8, 1944, at Pittsfield, Mass.
Height, 6.02. Weight, 170.
Throws and bats righthanded.
Hobbies—Announcing on radio station in home city and
coaching basketball.
Attended University of Tampa, Tampa, Fla.

Tied major league record for most doubles, inning, 2, August 18, 1969, 2nd inning.
Established American League record for highest fielding percentage, shortstop, lifetime (minimum 1,000 games) (.977).
Tied American League record for most years leading league in fewest grounded into double plays (2).
Led American League shortstops in total chances with 794 in 1973 and 808 in 1974.
Led American League in sacrifice hits with 15 in 1973 and 23 in 1975.
Tied for American League lead in double plays by shortstops with 105 in 1975.
Led Northern League shortstops in double plays with 76 in 1964.
Led Eastern League in stolen bases with 29 in 1965.
Named Rookie of the Year in Northern League, 1964.
Named shortstop on THE SPORTING NEWS American League All-Star Team, 1976.
Named shortstop on THE SPORTING NEWS American League All-Star fielding teams, 1969, 1971 and 1973 through 1978.
Received reported $35,000 bonus to sign with Baltimore Orioles, 1962.

Year	Club	League	Pos.	G.	AB.	R.	H.	2B.	3B.	HR.	RBI.	B.A.	PO.	A.	E.	F.A.
1962—Bluefield	Appal.		SS	47	151	44	45	7	1	3	23	.298	58	123	20	.900
1962—Elmira	East.		SS	8	22	0	1	0	0	0	0	.045	10	16	3	.897
1963—Baltimore†	Amer.							(In Military Service)								
1964—Aberdeen	North.		SS	117	∗465	79	105	21	6	4	28	.226	∗186	335	23	∗.958
1965—Elmira	East.		SS	125	481	84	110	16	5	2	33	.229	∗217	428	21	∗.968
1965—Baltimore	Amer.		SS	11	3	1	1	0	0	0	0	.333	1	1	0	1.000
1966—Rochester	Int.		SS	139	504	80	132	12	6	6	38	.262	242	387	17	∗.974
1966—Baltimore	Amer.		SS	8	19	2	3	1	0	0	0	.158	9	20	0	1.000
1967—Baltimore‡	Amer.		S-2-3B	69	184	19	32	5	0	1	10	.174	100	138	9	.964
1968—Baltimore§	Amer.		SS	145	472	40	98	13	0	2	21	.208	248	444	22	.969
1969—Baltimore	Amer.		SS	150	530	76	152	17	4	2	50	.287	251	449	23	.968
1970—Baltimore	Amer.		SS	145	459	53	100	6	5	1	36	.218	212	412	19	.970
1971—Baltimore	Amer.		SS	150	500	67	133	19	4	0	35	.266	280	443	16	.978
1972—Baltimore	Amer.		SS	113	285	36	53	9	1	2	16	.186	180	285	12	.975
1973—Baltimore	Amer.		SS	154	470	60	106	15	1	0	27	.226	241	∗530	23	.971
1974—Baltimore	Amer.		SS	155	493	54	111	14	4	5	36	.225	243	∗552	13	∗.984
1975—Baltimore	Amer.		SS	152	442	44	100	11	1	3	27	.226	259	508	17	.978
1976—Baltimore	Amer.		SS	153	522	66	141	22	2	1	40	.270	239	∗545	14	.982
1977—Baltimore	Amer.		SS	144	402	39	83	13	4	2	30	.206	244	417	10	∗.985
1978—Baltimore	Amer.		SS	134	348	39	74	13	0	0	16	.213	184	409	9	∗.985

Year Club League	Pos.	G.	AB.	R.	H.	2B.	3B.	HR.	RBI.	B.A.	PO.	A.	E.	F.A.
1979—Baltimore x ......Amer.	SS	101	198	28	33	6	2	0	9	.167	110	195	3	.990
1980—Baltimore ....Amer.	SS	113	268	37	61	7	3	0	22	.228	133	258	10	.975
Major League Totals		1897	5595	661	1281	171	31	19	375	.229	2934	5606	200	.977

Signed as free agent by Baltimore Orioles' organization, June 19, 1962.
†On military list, April 11, 1963 to March 6, 1964.
‡On military list, July 1 to July 17, 1967.
§On military list, June 16 to June 25, 1968.
xOn supplemental disabled list, June 10 to July 13, 1979.

CHAMPIONSHIP SERIES RECORD

Established Championship Series record for most runs, three-game Series (5), 1970.
Tied Championship Series record for most series played, one club (6); most at bats, three-game Series (15), 1969.
Established American League Championship Series record for most games, total Series, one club (21).
Tied American League Championship Series record for most runs, game (3), October 6, 1969.

Year Club League	Pos.	G.	AB.	R.	H.	2B.	3B.	HR.	RBI.	B.A.	PO.	A.	E.	F.A.
1969—Baltimore..........Amer.	SS	3	15	4	4	0	1	1	1	.267	4	9	0	1.000
1970—Baltimore..........Amer.	SS	3	12	5	4	0	0	0	1	.333	6	14	0	1.000
1971—Baltimore..........Amer.	SS	3	8	1	2	0	0	0	1	.250	6	11	0	1.000
1973—Baltimore..........Amer.	SS	5	16	0	2	0	0	0	1	.125	8	17	0	1.000
1974—Baltimore..........Amer.	SS	4	9	0	0	0	0	0	0	.000	7	12	1	.950
1979—Baltimore ....Amer.	SS-PR	3	5	0	1	0	0	0	1	.200	0	6	0	1.000
Championship Series Totals.............		21	65	10	13	0	1	1	5	.200	31	69	1	.990

WORLD SERIES RECORD

Tied World Series record for most assists by shortstop, inning (3), October 16, 1971.

Year Club League	Pos.	G.	AB.	R.	H.	2B.	3B.	HR.	RBI.	B.A.	PO.	A.	E.	F.A.
1969—Baltimore..........Amer.	SS	5	15	2	3	0	0	0	1	.200	7	14	0	1.000
1970—Baltimore..........Amer.	SS	5	19	0	2	0	0	0	1	.105	11	14	1	.962
1971—Baltimore..........Amer.	SS	7	21	4	5	0	1	0	0	.238	10	20	3	.909
1979—Baltimore ....Amer.	SS-PR	5	6	1	0	0	0	0	0	.000	3	7	1	.909
World Series Totals		22	61	7	10	0	1	0	2	.164	31	55	5	.945

ALL-STAR GAME RECORD

Year League	Pos.	AB.	R.	H.	2B.	3B.	HR.	RBI.	B.A.	PO.	A.	E.	F.A.
1976—American............................	SS	1	0	0	0	0	0	0	.000	1	1	0	1.000

DAVID GUS BELL
(Buddy)

Born August 27, 1951, at Pittsburgh, Pa.
Height, 6.02. Weight, 185.
Throws and bats righthanded.
Hobby—Sports in general.
Attended Xavier University, Cincinnati, O., and Miami University, Oxford, O.
Son of Gus Bell, outfielder with Pittsburgh Pirates, Cincinnati Reds, New York Mets and Milwaukee Braves, 1950 through 1964.

Tied major league record for first home run in majors, bases filled, April 22, 1972.
Led American League third basemen in double plays with 44 in 1973.
Led American League third basemen in assists with 364 in 1979.
Tied for American League lead among third basemen in double plays with 30 in 1978.
Led Gulf Coast League second basemen in double plays with 26 in 1969.
Named Rookie of the Year in American Association, 1971.
Named third baseman on THE SPORTING NEWS American League All-Star fielding team, 1979 and 1980.

Year Club League	Pos.	G.	AB.	R.	H.	2B.	3B.	HR.	RBI.	B.A.	PO.	A.	E.	F.A.
1969—Sarasota Ind......Gulf C.	2B	51	170	18	39	4	•3	3	24	.229	119	108	7	•.970
1970—Sumter..............W. Car.	3-2-S	121	442	81	117	19	3	12	75	.265	116	189	27	.919
1971—Wichita .............A.A.	*3-2-S-O	129	470	65	136	23	1	11	59	.289	*139	203	16	.955
1972—Cleveland ....Amer.	OF-3B	132	466	49	119	21	1	9	36	.255	284	23	3	.990
1973—Cleveland ....Amer.	*3B-OF	156	631	86	169	23	7	14	59	.268	*146	363	22	.959
1974—Cleveland† ....Amer.	3B	116	423	51	111	15	1	7	46	.262	112	274	15	.963
1975—Cleveland ....Amer.	3B	153	553	66	150	20	4	10	59	.271	144	330	25	.950
1976—Cleveland ....Amer.	3B-1B	159	604	75	170	26	2	7	60	.281	109	331	20	.957
1977—Cleveland ....Amer.	3B-OF	129	479	64	140	23	4	11	64	.292	134	253	16	.960
1978—Cleveland‡ ....Amer.	3B	142	556	71	157	27	8	6	62	.282	125	*355	15	.970
1979—Texas ....Amer.	3B-SS	•162	*670	89	200	42	3	18	101	.299	147	429	17	.971
1980—Texas§..............Amer.	*3B-SS	129	490	76	161	24	4	17	83	.329	125	282	8	*.981
Major League Totals		1278	4872	627	1377	221	34	99	570	.283	1323	2639	141	.966

Selected by Cleveland Indians' organization in 16th round of free-agent draft, June 5, 1969.
†On disabled list, May 27 to June 17 and August 8 to September 1, 1974.
‡Traded to Texas Rangers for Third Baseman Toby Harrah, December 8, 1978.
§On supplemental disabled list, June 9 to June 24, 1980.

ALL-STAR GAME RECORD

Year League	Pos.	AB.	R.	H.	2B.	3B.	HR.	RBI.	B.A.	PO.	A.	E.	F.A.
1973—American	PH	1	0	1	0	1	0	0	1.000	0	0	0	.000
1980—American	3B	2	0	0	0	0	0	0	.000	0	2	0	1.000
All-Star Game Totals		3	0	1	0	1	0	0	.333	0	2	0	1.000

JORGE BELL (MATHY)

Born October 21, 1959, at San Pedro de Macoris, Dominican Republic
Height, 6.01. Weight, 190.
Throws and bats righthanded.

Led Western Carolinas League in total bases with 270 in 1979.

Year Club	League	Pos.	G.	AB.	R.	H.	2B.	3B.	HR.	RBI.	B.A.	PO.	A.	E.	F.A.
1978—Helena..............	Pion.	OF	33	106	20	33	6	1	0	14	.311	39	4	4	.915
1979—Spartanburg......	W. Car.	OF	130	491	78	150	24	•15	22	•102	.305	206	14	8	.965
1980—Reading†‡.........	East.	OF	22	55	11	17	5	2	0	11	.309	24	0	1	.960

Signed as free agent by Philadelphia Phillies' organization, June 23, 1978.
†On disabled list, June 22 to October 20, 1980.
‡Drafted by Toronto Blue Jays, December 8, 1980.

KEVIN ROBERT BELL

Born July 13, 1955, at Los Angeles, Calif.
Height, 6.00. Weight, 195.
Throws and bats righthanded.
Attended Mount San Antonio Junior College, Walnut, Calif.
Son of Donald Robert Bell, former shortstop in Cleveland Indians' organization.

Year Club	League	Pos.	G.	AB.	R.	H.	2B.	3B.	HR.	RBI.	B.A.	PO.	A.	E.	F.A.
1974—Appleton	Midw.	3B	77	283	46	78	11	1	15	59	.276	59	151	18	.921
1975—Appleton	Midw.	3B	67	239	32	68	16	4	8	42	.285	57	137	25	.886
1975—Knoxville	South.	3B	66	224	31	68	15	1	11	41	.304	68	117	7	.9(
1976—Iowa	A.A.	3B	51	165	24	47	12	0	4	24	.285	39	100	16	.897
1976—Chicago.............	Amer.	3B	68	230	24	57	7	6	5	20	.248	70	124	6	.970
1977—Iowa	A.A.	S-3-O	49	183	39	56	9	1	14	39	.306	80	145	18	.926
1977—Chicago†	Amer.	S-3-O	9	28	4	5	1	0	1	6	.179	12	21	2	.943
1978—Iowa	A.A.	3B	89	305	48	65	12	1	2	40	.213	67	224	21	.933
1978—Chicago	Amer.	3B	54	68	9	13	0	0	2	5	.191	23	64	5	.946
1979—Iowa‡	A.A.	3B	55	191	28	45	4	1	11	37	.236	39	137	18	.907
1979—Chicago	Amer.	3B-SS	70	200	20	49	8	1	4	22	.245	51	154	17	.923
1980—Chicago§	Amer.	3B-SS	92	191	16	34	5	2	1	11	.178	36	153	16	.922
Major League Totals			293	717	73	158	21	9	13	64	.220	192	516	46	.939

Selected by Chicago White Sox' organization in 1st round (seventh player selected) of free-agent draft, January 9, 1974.
†On supplemental disabled list with knee injury, June 25 to July 16; transferred to emergency disabled list, July 16 through remainder of season.
‡On disabled list, May 27 to June 7, 1979.
§Released, December 2, 1980; signed by San Diego Padres' organization, January 15, 1981.

SERGIO A. BELTRE

Born October 22, 1958, at Azua, Dominican Republic
Height, 6.02. Weight, 175
Throws and bats righthanded.

Year Club	League	Pos.	G.	AB.	R.	H.	2B.	3B.	HR.	RBI.	B.A.	PO.	A.	E.	F.A.
1976—Marion	Appal.	OF	25	67	7	12	2	1	1	5	.179	39	1	2	.952
1977—Little Falls........	NYP	OF	69	214	32	43	7	0	1	29	.201	133	4	•13	.913
1978—Lynchburg	Carol.	OF	122	424	53	106	9	8	4	48	.250	285	6	7	.977
1979—Jackson	Texas	OF	125	374	38	91	19	2	9	50	.243	235	7	12	.953
1980—Jackson†	Texas	OF	45	148	17	46	8	2	3	19	.311	65	4	2	.972

Signed as free agent by New York Mets' organization, October 7, 1975.
†On disabled list, May 18 to August 5, 1980.

JOHNNY LEE BENCH

Born December 7, 1947, at Oklahoma City, Okla.
Height, 6.01. Weight, 215.
Throws and bats righthanded.
Hobbies—Golf, bowling, singing and playing cards.

Established major league records for most games, catcher, rookie season (154), 1968; most home runs by catcher, lifetime (323).
Tied major league records for most consecutive seasons leading league in sacrifice flies (2); fewest passed balls, season, 100 or more games (0), 1975; most bases on balls, game (5), July 22, 1979; most years and most consecutive years by catcher, with 100 or more games (13).
Established National League records for most doubles by catcher, season (40), 1968; most putouts by catcher, lifetime (9,083); most chances accepted by catcher, lifetime (9,920).
Tied National League records for most home runs, five consecutive games (7), May 30 through June 3, 1972; most home runs through July 31 (36), 1970; most seasons leading league in sacrifice flies (3); most home runs, bases filled, month (2), May, 1975.
Hit three home runs in a game, July 26, 1970, May 9, 1973 and May 29, 1980.
Hit home runs in all 12 National League parks, 1972.
Led National League in total bases with 315 in 1974.
Led National League catchers in double plays with 16 in 1974.
Led National League in passed balls with 18 in 1968 and tied for lead with 10 in 1973.
Led National League in sacrifice flies with 11 in 1970 and 12 in 1972.
Named Minor League Player of the Year by THE SPORTING NEWS, 1967.

Named THE SPORTING NEWS National League Rookie Player of the Year, 1968.
Named catcher on THE SPORTING NEWS National League All-Star fielding teams, 1968, 1969, 1970, 1971, 1972 1973, 1974, 1975, 1976 and 1977.
Named catcher on THE SPORTING NEWS National League All-Star Teams, 1968, 1969, 1970, 1972, 1973, 1974 and 1975.
Named National League Rookie of the Year by the Baseball Writers' Association of America, 1968.
Most Valuable Player in National League, 1970 and 1972.
Named by THE SPORTING NEWS as Major League Player of the Year, 1970.
Named by THE SPORTING NEWS as National League Player of the Year, 1970.
Named Player of the Year in Carolina League, 1966.

Year	Club	League	Pos.	G.	AB.	R.	H.	2B.	3B.	HR.	RBI.	B.A.	PO.	A.	E.	F.A.
1965—Tampa		Fla. St.	C-OF	68	214	29	53	13	1	2	35	.248	415	40	6	.987
1966—Peninsula		Carol.	C	98	350	59	103	16	0	22	68	.294	692	•87	•17	.979
1966—Buffalo†		Int.	C	1	0	0	0	0	0	0	0	.000	2	0	0	1.000
1967—Buffalo‡		Int.	•C-3-O-1	98	344	39	89	17	2	23	68	.259	577	•82	13	.981
1967—Cincinnati		Nat.	C	26	86	7	14	3	1	1	6	.163	175	16	1	.995
1968—Cincinnati		Nat.	C	154	564	67	155	40	2	15	82	.275	•942	•102	9	.991
1969—Cincinnati§		Nat.	C	148	532	83	156	23	1	26	90	.293	793	76	7	.992
1970—Cincinnati x		Nat.	C-O-1-3	158	605	97	177	35	4	•45	•148	.293	854	78	15	.984
1971—Cincinnati x		Nat.	C-O-1-3	149	562	80	134	19	2	27	61	.238	735	67	10	.988
1972—Cincinnati		Nat.	C-O-1-3	147	538	87	145	22	2	•40	•125	.270	791	63	10	.988
1973—Cincinnati		Nat.	C-O-1-3	152	557	83	141	17	3	25	104	.253	757	63	6	.993
1974—Cincinnati		Nat.	C-3-1	160	621	108	174	38	2	33	•129	.280	794	123	9	.990
1975—Cincinnati		Nat.	C-O-1	142	530	83	150	39	1	28	110	.283	646	52	8	.989
1976—Cincinnati		Nat.	•C-O-1	135	465	62	109	24	1	16	74	.234	•655	60	4	•.994
1977—Cincinnati		Nat.	C-O-1-3	142	494	67	136	34	2	31	109	.275	735	69	11	.987
1978—Cincinnati		Nat.	C-1B-O	120	393	52	102	17	1	23	73	.260	680	53	9	.988
1979—Cincinnati		Nat.	C-1B	130	464	73	128	19	0	22	80	.276	632	69	10	.986
1980—Cincinnati		Nat.	C	114	360	52	90	12	0	24	68	.250	505	39	5	.991
Major League Totals				1877	6771	1001	1811	342	22	356	1259	.267	9694	930	114	.989

Selected by Cincinnati Reds' organization in 2nd round of free-agent draft, June 21, 1965.
†On disabled list, July 31 to September 6, 1966. On military list, November 7, 1966 to April 9, 1967.
‡On temporary inactive list, July 29 to August 14, 1967.
§On military list, July 11 to July 18, 1969.
xOn military list, June 13 to June 17, 1971.

CHAMPIONSHIP SERIES RECORD

Established Championship Series record for most Series, one or more home runs (5).
Tied Championship Series records for most series played, one club (6); most games, total Series, one club (22).
Established National League Championship Series record for most long hits, total Series (11).
Tied National League Championship Series records for most series, played all games (6); most three-base hits, total Series (2); most stolen bases, five-game Series (2), 1972.

Year	Club	League	Pos.	G.	AB.	R.	H.	2B.	3B.	HR.	RBI.	B.A.	PO.	A.	E.	F.A.
1970—Cincinnati		Nat.	C	3	9	2	2	0	0	1	1	.222	20	3	0	1.000
1972—Cincinnati		Nat.	C	5	18	3	6	1	1	1	2	.333	28	3	1	.969
1973—Cincinnati		Nat.	C	5	19	1	5	2	0	1	1	.263	31	2	0	1.000
1975—Cincinnati		Nat.	C	3	13	1	1	0	0	0	0	.077	18	4	0	1.000
1976—Cincinnati		Nat.	C	3	12	3	4	1	0	1	1	.333	11	4	0	1.000
1979—Cincinnati		Nat.	C	3	12	1	3	0	1	1	1	.250	17	2	0	1.000
Championship Series Totals				22	83	11	21	4	2	5	6	.253	125	18	1	.993

WORLD SERIES RECORD

Tied World Series records for most double plays by catcher, total Series (6); most double plays by catcher, Series (3), 1975; one or more hits, each game, four-game Series, 1976.

Year	Club	League	Pos.	G.	AB.	R.	H.	2B.	3B.	HR.	RBI.	B.A.	PO.	A.	E.	F.A.
1970—Cincinnati		Nat.	C	5	19	3	4	0	0	1	3	.211	36	3	0	1.000
1972—Cincinnati		Nat.	C	7	23	4	6	1	0	1	1	.261	41	7	1	.980
1975—Cincinnati		Nat.	C	7	29	5	6	2	0	1	4	.207	44	6	0	1.000
1976—Cincinnati		Nat.	C	4	15	4	8	1	1	2	6	.533	18	2	0	1.000
World Series Totals				23	86	16	24	4	1	5	14	.279	139	18	1	.994

ALL-STAR GAME RECORD

Tied All-Star Game records for most strikeouts, nine-inning game (3), July 14, 1970; most putouts by catcher, game (10), July 15, 1975; most chances accepted by catcher, game (11), July 15, 1975.

Year	League	Pos.	AB.	R.	H.	2B.	3B.	HR.	RBI.	B.A.	PO.	A.	E.	F.A.
1968—National		C	0	0	0	0	0	0	0	.000	2	0	0	1.000
1969—National		C	3	2	2	0	0	1	2	.667	4	0	0	1.000
1970—National		C	3	0	0	0	0	0	0	.000	5	1	0	1.000
1971—National		C	4	1	2	0	0	1	2	.500	5	0	0	1.000
1972—National		C	2	0	1	0	0	0	0	.500	3	0	0	1.000
1973—National		C	3	1	1	0	0	1	1	.333	3	0	0	1.000
1974—National		C	3	1	2	0	0	0	0	.667	7	0	1	.875
1975—National		C	4	0	1	0	0	0	1	.250	10	1	0	1.000
1976—National		C	2	0	1	0	0	0	0	.500	1	0	0	1.000
1977—National		C	2	0	0	0	0	0	0	.000	4	0	0	1.000
1980—National		C	1	0	0	0	0	0	0	.000	5	0	0	1.000
All-Star Game Totals			27	5	10	0	0	3	6	.370	49	2	1	.981

Named to National League All-Star Team for 1978 game; replaced due to injury by Biff Pocoroba.
Named to National League All-Star Team for 1979 game; replaced due to injury by John Stearns.

— 33 —

BRUCE EDWIN BENEDICT

Born August 18, 1955, at Birmingham, Ala.
Height, 6.01. Weight, 185.
Throws and bats righthanded.
Attended University of Nebraska at Omaha.
Son of David Benedict, pitcher in New York Yankees', Washington Senators'
and St. Louis Cardinals' organizations, 1947 through 1959.

Year Club	League	Pos.	G.	AB.	R.	H.	2B.	3B.	HR.	RBI.	B.A.	PO.	A.	E.	F.A.
1976—Kingsport	Appal.	C	17	63	10	18	1	0	0	4	.286	98	25	3	.976
1976—Greenwood	W. Car.	C	21	54	7	13	1	0	1	10	.241	93	12	5	.955
1976—Savannah	South.	C	24	73	10	21	1	0	0	7	.288	107	12	2	.983
1977—Savannah	South.	C	124	395	55	104	15	0	7	40	.263	★770	★112	13	.985
1978—Richmond	Int.	C	111	348	41	97	13	0	2	34	.279	592	56	4	★.994
1978—Atlanta	Nat.	C	22	52	3	13	2	0	0	1	.250	81	14	1	.990
1979—Atlanta	Nat.	C	76	204	14	46	11	0	0	15	.225	344	35	6	.984
1980—Richmond	Int.	C	3	10	0	3	0	0	0	0	.300	10	5	0	1.000
1980—Atlanta	Nat.	C	120	359	18	91	14	1	2	34	.253	502	76	7	.988
Major League Totals			218	615	35	150	27	1	2	50	.244	927	125	14	.987

Selected by Atlanta Braves' organization in 5th round of free-agent draft, June 8, 1976.

JUAN JOSE BENIQUEZ (TORRES)

Name pronounced Be-NEE-Kez.

Born May 13, 1950, at San Sebastian, Puerto Rico.
Height, 5.11. Weight, 160.
Throws and bats righthanded.

Established modern major league record for most errors, shortstop, two consecutive games, 6, July 13-14, 1972.

Major league stolen bases: 1971 (3), 1972 (2), 1973 (0), 1974 (19), 1975 (7), 1976 (17), 1977 (26), 1978 (10), 1979 (3), 1980 (2). Total—89.

Led Florida State League shortstops in double plays with 51 in 1969.

Led International League in sacrifice hits with 11 in 1971.

Named as outfielder on THE SPORTING NEWS American League All-Star fielding team, 1977.

Year Club	League	Pos.	G.	AB.	R.	H.	2B.	3B.	HR.	RBI.	B.A.	PO.	A.	E.	F.A.
1969—Winter Haven	Fla. St.	★S-2	120	426	59	111	15	★14	2	59	.261	175	★373	★49	.918
1969—Winston-Salem	Carol.	SS	2	10	0	2	0	0	0	0	.200	2	6	0	1.000
1970—Winston-Salem	Carol.	SS	92	335	53	91	12	2	9	37	.272	144	275	35	.923
1970—Pawtucket	East.	SS	56	233	29	58	5	3	4	25	.249	105	167	29	.904
1971—Louisville	Int.	SS	132	534	82	149	12	★16	4	51	.279	205	364	★55	.912
1971—Boston	Amer.	SS	16	57	8	17	2	0	0	4	.298	24	27	6	.895
1972—Louisville	Int.	SS	66	277	40	82	10	7	5	32	.296	114	172	21	.932
1972—Boston	Amer.	SS	33	99	10	24	4	1	1	8	.242	38	88	14	.900
1973—Pawtucket	Int.	O-S-2	131	440	80	131	24	4	13	52	★.298	196	176	26	.934
1974—Boston†	Amer.	OF	106	389	60	104	14	3	5	33	.267	264	4	6	.978
1975—Boston†§	Amer.	OF-3B	78	254	43	74	14	4	2	17	.291	110	17	1	.992
1976—Texas	Amer.	OF-2B	145	478	49	122	14	4	0	33	.255	★411	★18	7	.984
1977—Texas x	Amer.	OF	123	424	56	114	19	6	10	50	.269	311	10	4	.988
1978—Texas yz	Amer.	OF	127	473	61	123	17	3	11	50	.260	309	8	9	.972
1979—New York ab	Amer.	OF-3B	62	142	19	36	6	1	4	17	.254	100	15	2	.983
1980—Seattle cdef	Amer.	OF	70	237	26	54	10	0	6	21	.228	176	3	8	.957
Major League Totals			760	2553	332	668	100	22	39	233	.262	1743	190	58	.971

Signed as free agent by Boston Red Sox' organization, October 1, 1968.

†On disabled list, July 3 to July 28, 1974.

‡On supplemental disabled list, July 2 to July 18, 1975.

§Traded with Pitcher Steve Barr, a minor league player to be named later and an estimated $200,000 to Texas Rangers for Pitcher Ferguson Jenkins, November 17, 1975; Red Sox sent Pitcher Craig Skok to Rangers, December 12, 1975, to complete deal.

xOn supplemental disabled list, July 31 through August 15, 1977.

yOn disabled list, June 13 to July 13, 1978.

zTraded with Pitchers Paul Mirabella, Mike Griffin and Dave Righetti and Outfielder Greg Jemison to New York Yankees for Pitchers Sparky Lyle, Larry McCall and Dave Rajsich, Catcher Mike Heath, Shortstop Domingo Ramos and cash, November 10, 1978.

aOn disabled list, July 9 to July 30, 1979; on supplemental disabled list, July 31 to September 1, 1979.

bTraded with Catcher Jerry Narron and Pitchers Jim Beattie and Rick Anderson to Seattle Mariners for Outfielder Ruppert Jones and Pitcher Jim Lewis, November 1, 1979.

cOn disabled list, April 9 to June 2, 1980.

dOn supplemental disabled list, July 19 to August 8, 1980.

eOn suspended list, September 2 to September 7, 1980.

fGranted free agency, October 24, 1980; signed by California Angels, December 29, 1980.

CHAMPIONSHIP SERIES RECORD

Year Club	League	Pos.	G.	AB.	R.	H.	2B.	3B.	HR.	RBI.	B.A.	PO.	A.	E.	F.A.
1975—Boston	Amer.	DH	3	12	2	3	0	0	0	1	.250	0	0	0	.000

WORLD SERIES RECORD

Year Club	League	Pos.	G.	AB.	R.	H.	2B.	3B.	HR.	RBI.	B.A.	PO.	A.	E.	F.A.
1975—Boston	Amer.	OF-PH	3	8	0	1	0	0	0	1	.125	6	1	0	1.000

ALFRED LEE BENTON
(Butch)

Born August 24, 1957, at Tampa, Fla.
Height, 6.01. Weight, 193.
Throws and bats righthanded.
Hobbies—Fishing, diving and hunting.

Led Midwest League in passed balls with 36 in 1976.
Led Texas League catchers in passed balls with 19 in 1978.
Tied for Carolina League lead in passed balls with 16 in 1977.
Tied for International League lead in passed balls with 15 in 1979.

Year Club League	Pos.	G.	AB.	R.	H.	2B.	3B.	HR.	RBI.	B.A.	PO.	A.	E.	F.A.
1975—Marion.............Appal.	C	45	145	25	36	11	1	2	18	.248	284	27	12	.963
1976—Wausau.............Midw.	C-1B	120	431	43	105	14	1	8	63	.244	552	70	30	.954
1977—Lynchburg ....Carol.	C	59	233	40	80	18	4	3	46	.343	277	36	9	.972
1977—Jackson...........Texas	C	60	181	18	52	13	0	3	18	.287	264	47	5	.984
1977—Tidewater ....Int.	PH	1	1	0	0	0	0	0	0	.000	0	0	0	.000
1978—Jackson ....Texas	C	106	360	49	99	31	2	6	44	.275	∗672	∗91	19	.976
1978—New York ....Nat.	C	4	4	1	2	0	0	0	2	.500	4	0	0	1.000
1979—Tidewater† .... Int.	C	94	313	39	62	9	1	3	25	.198	406	38	9	.981
1980—Tidewater ....Int.	C-O-1	67	240	36	63	15	2	5	34	.263	259	26	7	.976
1980—New York ....Nat.	C	12	21	0	1	0	0	0	0	.048	27	2	2	.935
Major League Totals......................		16	25	1	3	0	0	0	2	.120	31	2	2	.943

Selected by New York Mets' organization in 1st round (sixth player selected) of free-agent draft, June 4, 1975.

†On disabled list, July 9 to August 2, 1979.

JUAN BAUTISTA BERENGUER

Name pronounced BAIR-en-gair.

Born November 30, 1954, at Aguadulce, Panama
Height, 5.11. Weight, 186.
Throws and bats righthanded.

Tied for Midwest League lead in hit batsmen with 8 in 1975.
Led Carolina League in games started with 28 and in hit batsmen with 13 in 1976.
Tied for Texas League lead in games started with 26 in 1977.
Named International League Pitcher of the Year, 1978.

Year Club League	G.	IP.	W.	L.	Pct.	H.	R.	ER.	SO.	BB.	ERA.
1975—Wausau..............................Midwest	18	95	5	4	.556	83	41	31	58	50	2.94
1976—Lynchburg ....Carolina	28	187	10	13	.435	∗175	89	∗75	114	∗118	3.61
1977—Jackson ....Texas	26	181	9	8	.529	143	89	69	∗160	∗126	3.43
1978—Tidewater ....Int'national	24	147	10	7	.588	117	60	60	130	91	3.67
1978—New York†..........................National	5	13	0	2	.000	17	12	12	8	11	8.31
1979—Tacoma ....P. Coast	26	166	8	8	.500	128	101	90	∗220	129	4.88
1979—New York ....National	5	31	1	1	.500	28	13	10	25	12	2.90
1980—Tidewater ....Int'national	27	157	9	∗15	.375	122	78	67	∗178	76	3.84
1980—New York ....National	6	9	0	1	.000	9	9	6	7	10	6.00
Major League Totals.................................	16	53	1	4	.200	54	34	28	40	33	4.75

Signed as free agent by New York Mets' organization, February 22, 1975.

†Loaned to Cleveland Indians' organization, March 24, 1979; returned to New York Mets, August 29, 1979.

BRUCE MICHAEL BERENYI

Name pronounced Ber-ENN-yee.

Born August 21, 1954, at Bryan, O.
Height, 6.03. Weight, 215.
Throws and bats righthanded.
Attended Glen Oaks Community College, Centerville, Mich. and
Northeast Missouri State University, Kirksville, Mo.
Nephew of Ned Garver, pitcher with St. Louis Browns, Detroit Tigers,
Kansas City A's and Los Angeles Angels, 1948 through 1961.

Led American Association in shutouts with 3 and in wild pitches with 11 in 1979.
Named Southern League Pitcher of the Year, 1978.

Year Club League	G.	IP.	W.	L.	Pct.	H.	R.	ER.	SO.	BB.	ERA.
1976—Eugene ....Northwest	12	49	3	1	.750	50	37	26	39	55	4.78
1977—Shelby ....W. Caro.	25	145	10	8	.556	102	55	37	120	75	∗2.30
1978—Nashville†............................Southern	23	135	10	5	.667	107	44	37	103	63	2.47
1979—Indianapolis ....Am. Assoc.	25	166	9	9	.500	134	64	52	∗136	98	∗2.82
1980—Indianapolis ....Am. Assoc.	20	123	5	8	.385	111	66	59	∗121	●100	4.32
1980—Cincinnati ....National	6	28	2	2	.500	34	26	24	19	23	7.71
Major League Totals..............................	6	28	2	2	.500	34	26	24	19	23	7.71

Selected by Detroit Tigers' organization in 19th round of free-agent draft, June 4, 1975.
Selected by Cincinnati Reds' organization in secondary phase of free-agent draft, June 8, 1976.
†On disabled list, June 30 to July 27, 1978.

DAVID BRUCE BERGMAN
(Dave)

Born June 6, 1953, at Evanston, Ill.
Height, 6.02. Weight, 185.
Throws and bats lefthanded.
Attended Illinois State University, Normal, Ill.

Led International League in bases on balls with 95 in 1979.
Named Eastern League Player of the Year in 1975.
Named New York-Pennsylvania League Player of the Year in 1974.

Year—Club	League	Pos.	G.	AB.	R.	H.	2B.	3B.	HR.	RBI.	B.A.	PO.	A.	E.	F.A.
1974—Oneonta	NYP	1B	56	201	60	70	6	•7	10	48	*.348	494	*29	8	*.985
1975—West Haven	East.	1B-OF	124	399	76	124	15	6	11	60	*.311	610	61	5	.993
1975—New York	Amer.	OF	7	17	0	0	0	0	0	0	.000	10	1	1	.917
1976—Syracuse	Int.	*1B-OF	134	455	68	134	23	2	7	65	.295	*1201	82	10	.992
1977—Syracuse	Int.	OF-1B	132	468	88	146	29	4	16	59	.312	534	39	8	.986
1977—New York†	Amer.	OF-1B	5	4	1	1	0	0	0	1	.250	8	0	0	1.000
1978—Houston	Nat.	1B-OF	104	186	15	43	5	1	0	12	.231	328	16	4	.989
1979—Charleston	Int.	1B-OF	138	461	78	129	23	3	6	58	.280	910	61	11	.989
1979—Houston	Nat.	1B	13	15	4	6	0	0	1	2	.400	8	0	0	1.000
1980—Houston	Nat.	1B-OF	90	78	12	20	6	1	0	3	.256	187	16	1	.995
National League Totals			207	279	31	69	11	2	1	17	.247	523	32	5	.991
American League Totals			12	21	1	1	0	0	0	1	.048	18	1	1	.950
Major League Totals			219	300	32	70	11	2	1	18	.233	541	33	6	.990

Selected by Chicago Cubs' organization in 12th round of free-agent draft, June 8, 1971.
Selected by New York Yankees' organization in 2nd round of free-agent draft, June 5, 1974.
†Traded to Houston Astros, November 23, 1977, as completion of deal where New York Yankees obtained Cliff Johnson, June 15, 1977.

CHAMPIONSHIP SERIES RECORD

Year—Club	League	Pos.	G.	AB.	R.	H.	2B.	3B.	HR.	RBI.	B.A.	PO.	A.	E.	F.A.
1980—Houston	Nat.	PR-1B	4	3	0	1	0	1	0	2	.333	8	2	1	.909

DWIGHT VERN BERNARD

Born May 31, 1952, at Mt. Vernon, Ill.
Height, 6.02. Weight, 170.
Throws and bats righthanded.
Hobbies—Hunting and fishing.
Attended Free Will Baptist Bible College, Nashville, Tenn., and Belmont College, Nashville, Tenn; received Bachelor of Science degree in Physical Education.

Year—Club	League	G.	IP.	W.	L.	Pct.	H.	R.	ER.	SO.	BB.	ERA.
1974—Victoria†	Texas	14	103	7	4	.636	85	43	35	60	58	3.06
1975—Tidewater‡	Int'national	27	126	9	9	.500	96	51	46	70	77	3.29
1976—Tidewater	Int'national	15	90	1	9	.100	109	74	64	47	61	6.40
1976—Jackson	Texas	9	54	2	5	.286	48	28	25	33	32	4.17
1977—Tidewater	Int'national	29	173	9	13	.409	181	98	83	88	79	4.32
1978—Tidewater	Int'national	25	44	5	3	.625	36	13	8	21	15	1.64
1978—New York	National	30	48	1	4	.200	54	25	23	26	27	4.31
1979—Tidewater	Int'national	33	61	1	3	.250	39	12	12	49	29	1.77
1979—New York§	National	32	44	0	3	.000	59	26	23	20	26	4.70
1980—Vancouver x	P. Coast	12	19	0	1	.000	34	16	15	5	14	7.11
1980—Holyoke y	Eastern	9	14	1	0	1.000	20	17	12	11	12	7.71
Major League Totals		62	92	1	7	.125	113	51	46	46	53	4.50

Selected by New York Mets' organization in 2nd round of free-agent draft, June 5, 1974.
†Played one game as outfielder.
‡On disabled list, July 20 to August 4, 1975.
§Traded to Milwaukee Brewers for Pitcher Mark Bomback, October 26, 1979.
xOn suspended list, May 22 to June 6, 1980.
yOn disabled list, June 18 to August 1, 1980.

ANTONIO BERNAZARD (GARCIA)
(Tony)

Born August 24, 1956, at Caguas, P.R.
Height, 5.09. Weight, 164.
Throws right and bats right and lefthanded.
Attended Humacao College, Humacao, P.R.

Led Florida State League second basemen in assists with 386 in 1975.
Led Eastern League second basemen in double plays with 70 in 1976.
Led American Association second basemen in putouts with 297 and in assists with 386 in 1978.

Year—Club	League	Pos.	G.	AB.	R.	H.	2B.	3B.	HR.	RBI.	B.A.	PO.	A.	E.	F.A.
1974—Kinston†	Carol.	2B	56	225	22	45	3	1	0	16	.200	129	142	19	.934
1974—Sara. Expos‡	G.C.	2B	34	109	11	18	2	1	1	6	.165	95	71	7	.960
1975—W. Palm Beach	Fla. St.	2B-SS	*134	*509	65	121	16	2	6	50	.238	282	389	28	.960
1976—Quebec City	East.	2B	106	334	35	72	8	3	1	26	.216	227	257	18	.964
1977—Quebec City	East.	2B	125	425	68	119	11	6	1	34	.280	273	379	25	.963
1978—Denver	A.A.	*2B-3-O	128	479	*107	137	30	9	9	65	.286	302	390	*32	.956

Year	Club	League	Pos.	G.	AB.	R.	H.	2B.	3B.	HR.	RBI.	B.A.	PO.	A.	E.	F.A.
1979—Denver ..............A.A.			2B	82	273	58	82	15	2	3	29	.300	178	275	•19	.960
1979—Montreal...........Nat.			2B	22	40	11	12	2	0	1	8	.300	22	34	1	.982
1980—Montreal§ ....Nat.			2B-SS	82	183	26	41	7	1	5	18	.224	82	151	9	.963
Major League Totals......................				104	223	37	53	9	1	6	26	.238	104	185	10	.967

Signed as free agent by Montreal Expos' organization, November 13, 1973.
†On disabled list, June 10 to June 17, 1974.
‡On temporary inactive list, August 15 to September 25, 1974.
§Traded to Chicago White Sox for Pitcher Richard Wortham, December 12, 1980.

DALE ANTHONY BERRA

Born December 13, 1956, at Ridgewood, N. J.
Height, 6.00. Weight, 190.
Throws and bats righthanded.
Son of Yogi Berra, coach with New York Yankees; brother of Larry Berra Jr., former catcher in New York Mets' organization and Tim Berra, former wide receiver with New York Giants and Baltimore Colts.

Led New York-Pennsylvania League in sacrifice flies with 8 in 1975.
Tied for New York-Pennsylvania League lead in double plays by third basemen with 13 in 1975.
Led Western Carolinas League third basemen in double plays with 27 in 1976.

Year	Club	League	Pos.	G.	AB.	R.	H.	2B.	3B.	HR.	RBI.	B.A.	PO.	A.	E.	F.A.
1975—Niagara Falls ....NYP			3B	67	*269	36	69	6	4	3	*49	.257	67	137	24	.895
1976—Charleston ....W. Car.			3B	*139	527	78	157	28	5	16	89	.298	129	*269	*41	.907
1977—Columbus..........Int.			3B-SS	125	438	68	127	18	7	18	54	.290	97	252	29	.923
1977—Pittsburgh........Nat.			3B	17	40	0	7	1	0	0	3	.175	14	22	1	.973
1978—Columbus ....Int.			SS-3B	99	361	58	101	18	5	18	63	.280	142	280	22	.950
1978—Pittsburgh ....Nat.			3B-SS	56	135	16	28	2	0	6	14	.207	31	84	11	.905
1979—Portland ..........P.C.			SS-3B	56	210	37	68	13	2	6	32	.324	68	158	8	.966
1979—Pittsburgh ....Nat.			SS-2B	44	123	11	26	5	0	3	15	.211	43	86	12	.915
1980—Pittsburgh ....Nat.			3-S-2	93	245	21	54	8	2	6	31	.220	88	171	11	.959
Major League Totals				210	543	48	115	16	2	15	63	.212	176	363	35	.939

Selected by Pittsburgh Pirates' organization in 1st round (20th player selected) of free-agent draft, June 4, 1975.

JEFFREY PAUL BERTONI
(Jeff)

Born August 3, 1955, at Bakersfield, Calif.
Height 6.02. Weight, 180.
Throws and bats righthanded.
Attended California Lutheran College, Thousand Oaks, Calif.;
received Bachelor of Arts degree in Physical Education.

Led Midwest League shortstops in double plays with 81 in 1978.
Led Texas League shortstops in double plays with 103 in 1979.
Led Texas League in sacrifice flies with 14 in 1979.

Year	Club	League	Pos.	G.	AB.	R.	H.	2B.	3B.	HR.	RBI.	B.A.	PO.	A.	E.	F.A.
1977—Idaho Falls ....Pioneer			SS	55	171	38	52	8	1	2	19	.304	90	137	19	*.923
1978—Quad Cities ....Midw.			SS	138	504	97	134	22	7	4	45	.266	188	*500	34	*.953
1979—El Paso.............Texas			SS	•136	502	83	147	27	5	8	66	.293	*250	*424	27	.961
1980—Salt Lake City†..P.C.			SS-2B-3B	90	296	48	85	19	6	4	43	.287	150	265	30	.933

Signed as free agent by California Angels' organization, July 5, 1977.
†On disabled list, July 27 to August 20, 1980.

JAMES WILLIAM BESWICK
(Jim)

Born February 12, 1958, at Wilkinsburg, Pa.
Height, 6.01. Weight, 175.
Throws right and bats right and lefthanded.

Led Pacific Coast League outfielders in double plays with 6 in 1979.

Year	Club	League	Pos.	G.	AB.	R.	H.	2B.	3B.	HR.	RBI.	B.A.	PO.	A.	E.	F.A.
1976—Walla Walla ......N'west			OF-1B	42	112	13	24	2	1	2	8	.214	54	2	2	.966
1977—Reno................Calif.			OF	122	412	94	120	24	5	18	79	.291	188	16	7	.967
1978—Amarillo ....Texas			OF	103	367	61	112	28	5	17	69	.305	152	16	8	.955
1978—San Diego ....Nat.			OF	17	20	2	1	0	0	0	0	.050	8	0	0	1.000
1979—Hawaii..............P.C.			OF	144	459	41	98	15	5	7	57	.214	278	17	5	.983
1980—Hawaii..............P.C.			OF	128	443	67	118	25	4	3	54	.266	285	14	7	.977
Major League Totals......................				17	20	2	1	0	0	0	0	.050	8	0	0	1.000

Selected by San Diego Padres' organization in 5th round of free-agent draft, June 8, 1976.

DID YOU KNOW—

That the Astros started only one game in 1980 with a lefthanded pitcher? It was Randy Niemann on September 23.

KURT ANTHONY BEVACQUA
Name pronounced Buh-VAHK-wuh.

Born January 23, 1947, at Miami Beach, Fla.
Height, 6.02. Weight, 195.
Throws and bats righthanded.
Hobbies—Hunting, fishing, golf and billiards.
Attended Miami-Dade (North) Community College, Miami, Fla.

Led American Association third basemen in double plays with 26 in 1970.
Tied for Southern League lead in double plays by third basemen with 24 in 1969.

Year Club	League	Pos.	G.	AB.	R.	H.	2B.	3B.	HR.	RBI.	B.A.	PO.	A.	E.	F.A.
1967—Tampa ....Fla. St.		2B	65	217	13	48	2	1	0	11	.221	119	143	10	.963
1968—Tampa ....Fla. St.		2-1B	91	219	18	55	11	2	2	26	.251	264	74	7	.980
1969—Asheville ....South.		3B	133	490	72	155	26	6	16	91	.316	*129	245	29	.928
1970—Indianapolis ......A.A.		*O-INF	135	482	62	126	26	5	15	67	.261	*157	*216	21	*.947
1971—Ind.†-Wichita ....A.A.		3-S-2-O	60	235	36	71	16	1	9	38	.302	107	130	11	.956
1971—Cleveland.........Amer.		2-O-3-S	55	137	9	28	3	1	3	13	.204	77	72	5	.968
1972—Portland ...........P.C.		3-2-O-S	145	537	57	168	27	7	9	72	.313	223	252	30	.941
1972—Cleveland‡ ....Amer.		OF-3	19	35	2	4	0	0	1	1	.114	11	5	1	.941
1973—Kansas City§ .....Amer.		3-2-O-1	99	276	39	71	8	3	2	40	.257	120	90	9	.959
1974—Pittsburgh x .....Nat.		3B-OF	18	35	1	4	1	0	0	0	.114	8	13	1	.955
1974—Kansas City y ....Amer.		1-3-2-S	39	90	10	19	0	0	0	3	.211	90	29	5	.960
1975—Milwaukee ....Amer.		3-2-S-1	104	258	30	59	14	0	2	24	.229	157	168	13	.962
1976—Milwaukee ....Amer.		2B	12	7	3	1	0	0	0	0	.143	0	6	0	1.000
1976—Spokane z a ......P.C.		3-S-2-O	95	356	70	120	24	0	12	49	.337	116	197	22	.934
1977—Tucson.............P.C.		3B-SS	94	358	75	126	29	4	9	76	.352	74	231	23	.930
1977—Texas ....Amer.		O-3-1-2	39	96	13	32	7	2	5	28	.333	42	31	1	.986
1978—Texas b............Amer.		3B-2-1	90	248	21	55	12	0	6	30	.222	62	116	18	.908
1979—San Diego ....Nat.		3-2-1-O	114	297	23	75	12	4	1	34	.253	115	156	11	.961
1980—S.D.c-Pitt..........Nat.		3-O-1-2	84	114	5	26	7	1	0	16	.228	32	31	2	.969
National League Totals...................			216	446	29	105	20	5	1	50	.235	155	200	14	.962
American League Totals.................			457	1247	127	269	44	6	19	139	.216	559	517	52	.954
Major League Totals			673	1593	156	374	64	11	20	189	.235	714	717	66	.956

Selected by New York Mets' organization in 36th round of free-agent draft, June 6, 1966.
Selected by Atlanta Braves' organization in 6th round of free-agent draft, January 28, 1967.
Selected by Cincinnati Reds' organization in secondary phase of free-agent draft, June 7, 1967.
†Traded by Cincinnati Reds to Cleveland Indians for Outfielder Charles Bradford, May 8, 1971.
‡Traded to Kansas City Royals for Pitcher Mike Hedlund, November 2, 1972.
§Traded with Catcher-Outfielder Ed Kirkpatrick and First Baseman Winston Cole to Pittsburgh Pirates for Pitcher Nelson Briles and Infielder Fernando Gonzalez, December 4, 1973.
xTraded to Kansas City Royals for cash and Infielder Cal Meier, July 8, 1974.
ySold to Milwaukee Brewers for an undisclosed amount of cash, March 6, 1975.
zSold by Milwaukee Brewers to Seattle Mariners for an undisclosed amount of cash, October 22, 1976; released, March 28, 1977.
aSigned as free agent by Tucson (Texas Rangers' organization), April 8, 1977.
bTraded with Catcher Bill Fahey and First Baseman Mike Hargrove to San Diego Padres for Outfielder Oscar Gamble, Catcher Dave Roberts and cash estimated at $300,000, October 25, 1978.
cTraded with a player to be named later to Pittsburgh Pirates for Outfielders Rick Lancellotti and Luis Salazar, August 5, 1980; Pitcher Mark Lee traded to Pirates completing deal, August 12, 1980.

JAMES BLAIR BIBBY
(Jim)

Born October 10, 1944, at Franklinton, N. C.
Height, 6.05. Weight, 230.
Throws and bats righthanded.
Attended Fayetteville State College, Fayetteville, N. C., and Lynchburg College, Lynchburg, Va.
Brother of Henry Bibby, guard for Philadelphia 76ers.

Pitched 6-0 no-hit victory against Oakland Athletics, July 30, 1973.
Led International League in wild pitches with 20 in 1971.
Named righthanded pitcher on THE SPORTING NEWS National League All-Star Team, 1980.

Year Club	League	G.	IP.	W.	L.	Pct.	H.	R.	ER.	SO.	BB.	ERA.
1965—Marion....................Ap'lachian		13	24	2	3	.400	30	35	30	24	27	11.25
1966—Greenville...........................Carolina						(In Military Service)						
1967—Jacksonville.......................Int'national						(In Military Service)						
1968—Raleigh-Durham..................Carolina		23	131	7	7	.500	79	49	41	118	74	2.82
1969—Memphis.............................Texas		17	122	10	6	.625	94	58	45	115	57	3.32
1969—Tidewater ....Int'national		11	75	4	4	.500	64	33	29	65	34	3.48
1970—Tidewater ....Int'national						(On disabled list)						
1971—Tidewater†..........................Int'national		27	76	●15	6	.174	145	87	79	150	109	4.04
1972—Tulsa ....Am. Assoc.		27	195	13	9	.591	155	76	67	208	76	3.09
1972—St. Louis ....National		6	40	1	3	.250	29	18	15	28	19	3.38
1973—St. Louis‡...........................National		6	16	0	2	.000	19	17	17	12	17	9.56
1973—Texas ....American		26	180	9	10	.474	121	73	65	155	106	3.25
1974—Texas ....American		41	264	19	19	.500	255	146	*139	149	113	4.74
1975—Texas§-Cleveland ....American		36	181	7	15	.318	172	89	78	93	78	3.88
1976—Cleveland...........................American		34	163	13	7	.650	162	61	58	84	56	3.20
1977—Cleveland x.........................American		37	207	12	13	.480	197	100	82	141	73	3.57
1978—Pittsburgh ....National		34	107	8	7	.533	100	52	42	72	39	3.53

Year Club	League	G.	IP.	W.	L.	Pct.	H.	R.	ER.	SO.	BB.	ERA.
1979—Pittsburgh ....National		34	138	12	4	*.750	110	51	43	103	47	2.80
1980—Pittsburgh ....National		35	238	19	6	*.760	210	95	88	144	88	3.33
National League Totals............................		115	539	40	22	.645	468	233	205	359	210	3.42
American League Totals..........................		174	995	60	64	.484	907	469	422	622	426	3.82
Major League Totals		289	1534	100	86	.538	1375	702	627	981	636	3.68

Signed as free agent by New York Mets' organization, July 19, 1965.

†Traded by New York Mets with Pitchers Rich Folkers and Charlie Hudson and Outfielder-First Baseman Art Shamsky to St. Louis Cardinals for Pitchers Chuck Taylor and Harry Parker, Infielder Tom Coulter and Outfielder Jim Beauchamp, October 18, 1971.

‡Traded to Texas Rangers for Pitcher Mike Nagy and Catcher John Wockenfuss (both assigned from Spokane to Tulsa), June 6, 1973.

§Traded with Pitchers Jackie Brown and Rick Waits and an estimated $100,000 to Cleveland Indians for Pitcher Gaylord Perry, June 12, 1975.

xDeclared free agent in arbitration, March 6, 1978; signed by Pittsburgh Pirates, March 15, 1978.

CHAMPIONSHIP SERIES RECORD

Year Club	League	G.	IP.	W.	L.	Pct.	H.	R.	ER.	SO.	BB.	ERA.
1979—Pittsburgh ....National		1	7	0	0	.000	4	1	1	5	4	1.29

WORLD SERIES RECORD

Year Club	League	G.	IP.	W.	L.	Pct.	H.	R.	ER.	SO.	BB.	ERA.
1979—Pittsburgh ....National		2	10⅓	0	0	.000	10	4	3	10	2	2.61

ALL-STAR GAME RECORD

Year League	IP.	W.	L.	Pct.	H.	R.	ER.	SO.	BB.	ERA.
1980—National..	1	0	0	.000	1	0	0	0	0	0.00

GREGORY PETER BIERCEVICZ
(Greg)

Born October 21, 1955, at Derby, Conn.
Weight, 6.01. Weight, 185.
Throws and bats righthanded.
Attended University of Connecticut, Storrs, Conn.
Brother of Joe Biercevicz, former pitcher in Chicago Cubs' organization.

Led Northwest League in complete games with 9 and in shutouts with 3 in 1977.

Year Club	League	G.	IP.	W.	L.	Pct.	H.	R.	ER.	SO.	BB.	ERA.
1977—Bellingham ....Northwest		14	●110	*11	1	*.917	75	18	11	*97	35	*0.90
1978—Stockton ....California		6	39	2	2	.500	41	29	26	25	13	6.00
1978—San Jose† ....P. Coast		14	88	5	5	.500	91	48	42	57	44	4.30
1979—Spokane‡ ....P. Coast		24	141	10	10	.500	166	91	74	66	41	4.72
1980—Spokane§ ....P. Coast		20	126	10	9	.526	145	77	69	60	40	4.93

Selected by Seattle Mariners' organization in 15th round of free-agent draft, June 7, 1977.

†On disabled list, May 16 to June 5, 1978.

‡On disabled list, July 8 to July 19, 1979.

§On disabled list, April 10 to May 5 and May 12 to May 26, 1980.

LAWRENCE DAVID BIITTNER
(Larry)

Born July 27, 1947, at Pocahontas, Ia.
Height, 6.02. Weight, 205.
Throws and bats lefthanded.
Hobbies—Hunting and fishing.
Attended Drake University, Des Moines, Iowa and Buena Vista College, Storm Lake, Ia.;
received Bachelor of Arts degree in Physical Education.

Led International League in sacrifice flies with 9 in 1974.

Year Club	League	Pos.	G.	AB.	R.	H.	2B.	3B.	HR.	RBI.	B.A.	PO.	A.	E.	F.A.
1968—Savannah ....South.		OF-1B	58	199	24	57	12	2	1	21	.286	160	6	3	.982
1969—Savannah†.........South.		OF	14	44	4	9	2	0	0	2	.205	13	2	1	.938
1970—Pittsfield...........East.		1B-OF	102	388	51	126	27	6	9	62	.325	658	46	6	.992
1970—Washington ....Amer.		PH	2	2	0	0	0	0	0	0	.000	0	0	0	.000
1971—Denver..............A.A.		1B	25	101	20	36	10	2	2	18	.356	223	28	3	.988
1971—Washington‡......Amer.		OF-1B	66	171	12	44	4	1	0	16	.257	83	7	6	.938
1972—Texas................Amer.		1B-OF	137	382	34	99	18	1	3	31	.259	503	41	8	.986
1973—Texas§..............Amer.		OF-1B	83	258	19	65	8	2	1	12	.252	234	20	2	.992
1974—Memphis...........Int.		1B-OF	94	303	53	99	16	1	3	48	.327	413	36	6	.987
1974—Montreal ....Nat.		OF	18	26	2	7	1	0	0	3	.269	7	1	0	1.000
1975—Montreal ....Nat.		OF	121	346	34	109	13	5	3	28	.315	166	8	5	.972
1976—Mont.y-Chi.z......Nat.		1B-OF	89	224	23	53	14	1	0	18	.237	283	35	5	.984
1977—Chicago............Nat.		1B-OF-P	138	493	74	147	28	1	12	62	.298	792	65	11	.987
1978—Chicago ....Nat.		1B-OF	120	343	32	88	15	1	4	50	.257	601	53	9	.986
1979—Chicago ....Nat.		OF-1B	111	272	35	79	13	3	3	50	.290	282	23	6	.981
1980—Chicago a..........Nat.		1B-OF	127	273	21	68	12	2	1	34	.249	305	23	2	.994
American League Totals..................			288	813	65	208	30	4	4	59	.256	820	68	16	.982
National League Totals....................			724	1977	221	551	96	13	23	245	.279	2436	218	38	.986
Major League Totals			1012	2790	286	759	126	17	27	304	.272	3256	286	54	.985

Selected by Washington Senators' organization in 16th round of free-agent draft, June 7, 1968.
†On military list, February 2, 1969, to August 8, 1969.
‡On military list, August 3 to August 24, 1971.
§Traded to Montreal Expos for Pitcher Pat Jarvis, December 20, 1973.
yTraded with Pitcher Steve Renko to Chicago Cubs for First Baseman Andy Thornton, May 17, 1976.
zOn supplemental disabled list, July 26 to August 10, 1976.
aGranted free agency, October 23, 1980; signed by Cincinnati Reds, January 12, 1981.

PITCHING RECORD

Year Club	League	G.	IP.	W.	L.	Pct.	H.	R.	ER.	SO.	BB.	ERA.
1977—Chicago ....National		1	1	0	0	.000	5	6	6	3	1	54.00

JOHN EUGENE BILLINGHAM
(Jack)

Born February 21, 1943, at Orlando, Fla.
Height, 6.04½. Weight, 210.
Throws and bats righthanded.
Hobbies—Fishing, bowling and golf.
Distant cousin of Hall of Fame pitcher Christy Mathewson.

Led National League in shutouts with 7 in 1973.
Tied for National League lead in games started by pitchers with 40 in 1973.

Year Club	League	G.	IP.	W.	L.	Pct.	H.	R.	ER.	SO.	BB.	ERA.
1961—Orlando† ....Florida St.		12	56	1	6	.143	53	37	28	30	37	4.50
1962—St. Petersburg‡ ....Florida St.		22	68	1	5	.167	74	52	39	58	39	5.16
1963—Salisbury§ ....W. Carol.		31	142	9	6	.600	124	72	55	136	53	3.49
1964—Santa Barbara.....................California		16	22	1	1	.500	17	12	12	31	10	4.91
1964—St. Petersburg.....................Florida St.		32	105	7	3	.700	63	21	12	126	27	1.03
1965—Spokane.............................P. Coast		6	20	0	0	.000	17	9	8	20	10	3.60
1965—Albuquerque ....Texas		39	86	7	3	.700	68	29	17	67	27	1.78
1966—Spokane.............................P. Coast		50	106	6	9	.400	107	47	45	84	41	3.82
1967—Spokane.............................P. Coast		51	123	7	4	.636	98	46	41	108	46	3.00
1968—Los Angeles xy....................National		50	71	3	0	1.000	54	18	17	46	30	2.15
1969—Houston ....National		52	83	6	7	.462	92	45	39	71	29	4.23
1970—Houston ....National		46	188	13	9	.591	190	102	83	134	63	3.97
1971—Houston z............................National		33	228	10	16	.385	205	98	86	139	68	3.39
1972—Cincinnati...........................National		36	218	12	12	.500	197	83	77	137	64	3.18
1973—Cincinnati...........................National		40	•293	19	10	.655	257	112	99	155	95	3.04
1974—Cincinnati...........................National		36	212	19	11	.633	233	105	93	103	64	3.95
1975—Cincinnati...........................National		33	208	15	10	.600	222	100	95	79	76	4.11
1976—Cincinnati...........................National		34	177	12	10	.545	190	96	85	76	62	4.32
1977—Cincinnati a ....National		36	162	10	10	.500	195	105	94	76	56	5.22
1978—Detroit................................American		30	202	15	8	.652	218	95	87	59	65	3.88
1979—Detroit................................American		35	158	10	7	.588	163	74	58	59	60	3.30
1980—Detroit b-Boston c ....American		15	32	1	3	.250	56	36	36	7	18	10.13
American League Totals		80	392	26	18	.591	437	205	181	125	143	4.16
National League Totals		396	1840	119	95	.556	1835	864	768	1016	607	3.76
Major League Totals		476	2232	145	113	.562	2272	1069	949	1141	750	3.83

Signed as free agent by Los Angeles Dodgers' organization, June 12, 1961.
†On temporary inactive list, June 12 through June 23, 1961.
‡On disabled list, June 2 through June 4, and from July 24 through August 5, 1962.
§On disabled list, May 26 through June 5, 1963.
xSelected by Montreal Expos from Los Angeles Dodgers in expansion draft, October 5, 1968.
ySent with Pitcher Drannon (Skip) Guinn and cash by Montreal Expos to Houston Astros to complete earlier deal in which Donn Clendenon refused to report to Houston, April 8, 1969.
zTraded with Second Baseman Joe Morgan, Infielder Denis Menke and Outfielders Cesar Geronimo and Ed Armbrister to Cincinnati Reds for First Baseman Lee May, Second Baseman Tommy Helms and Outfielder Jim Stewart, November 29, 1971.
aTraded to Detroit Tigers for Pitcher George Cappuzzello and Outfielder John Valle, March 7, 1978.
bTraded to Boston Red Sox for player to be named later, May 12, 1980.
cReleased, June 21, 1980.

CHAMPIONSHIP SERIES RECORD

Year Club	League	G.	IP.	W.	L.	Pct.	H.	R.	ER.	SO.	BB.	ERA.
1972—Cincinnati..........................National		1	4⅔	0	0	.000	5	2	2	4	2	3.86
1973—Cincinnati..........................National		2	12	0	1	.000	9	6	6	9	4	4.50
Championship Series Totals		3	16⅔	0	1	.000	14	8	8	13	6	4.32

WORLD SERIES RECORD

Year Club	League	G.	IP.	W.	L.	Pct.	H.	R.	ER.	SO.	BB.	ERA.
1972—Cincinnati ....National		3	13⅔	1	0	1.000	6	1	0	11	4	0.00
1975—Cincinnati ....National		3	9	0	0	.000	8	2	1	7	5	1.00
1976—Cincinnati ....National		1	2⅔	1	0	1.000	0	0	0	1	0	0.00
World Series Totals		7	25⅓	2	0	1.000	14	3	1	19	9	0.36

ALL-STAR GAME RECORD

Member of National League All-Star Team for the 1973 game; did not play.

JAMES DOUGLAS BIRD
(Doug)

Born March 5, 1950, at Corona, Calif.
Height, 6.04. Weight, 180.
Throws and bats righthanded.
Hobbies—Hunting and fishing.
Attended Mesa Community College, Mesa, Ariz., and Mount San Antonio Junior College,
Walnut, Calif.

Major league saves: 1973 (20), 1974 (10), 1975 (11), 1976 (2), 1977 (14), 1978 (1), 1979 (0), 1980 (1). Total—59.
Tied for California League lead in games started with 27 and in shutouts with 3 in 1971.

Year Club	League	G.	IP.	W.	L.	Pct.	H.	R.	ER.	SO.	BB.	ERA.
1969—Winnipeg	Northern	16	99	6	2	.750	105	45	38	88	17	3.45
1970—San Jose	California	3	10	0	2	.000	10	10	7	14	3	6.30
1970—Waterloo	Midwest	22	147	11	9	.550	122	49	30	149	32	*1.84
1971—San Jose	California	29	*182	*15	9	.625	175	84	69	143	48	3.41
1972—Jacksonville	Southern	24	122	10	7	.588	117	43	33	72	32	2.43
1972—Omaha	Am. Assoc.	7	9	1	1	.500	9	4	3	13	5	3.00
1973—Omaha	Am. Assoc.	4	6	1	0	1.000	5	0	0	3	1	0.00
1973—Kansas City	American	54	102	4	4	.500	81	37	34	83	30	3.00
1974—Kansas City	American	55	92	7	6	.538	100	31	28	62	27	2.74
1975—Kansas City	American	51	105	9	6	.600	100	42	38	81	40	3.26
1976—Kansas City	American	39	198	12	10	.545	191	90	74	107	31	3.36
1977—Kansas City	American	53	118	11	4	.733	120	52	51	83	29	3.89
1978—Kansas City†	American	40	99	6	6	.500	110	63	58	48	31	5.27
1979—Philadelphia‡§	National	32	61	2	0	1.000	73	35	35	33	16	5.16
1980—Columbus	Int'national	15	48	6	0	1.000	33	15	12	36	13	2.25
1980—New York x	American	22	51	3	0	1.000	47	16	15	17	14	2.65
American League Totals		314	765	52	36	.591	749	331	298	481	202	3.51
National League Totals		32	61	2	0	1.000	73	35	35	33	16	5.16
Major League Totals		346	826	54	36	.600	822	366	333	514	218	3.63

Selected by Cleveland Indians' organization in 29th round of free-agent draft, June 7, 1968.
Selected by Seattle Pilots' organization in secondary phase of free-agent draft, February 1, 1969.
Selected by Kansas City Royals' organization in secondary phase of free-agent draft, June 5, 1969.
†Traded to Philadelphia Phillies for Shortstop Todd Cruz, April 3, 1979.
‡On disabled list, June 14 to July 5, 1979.
§Released, April 9, 1980; signed by New York Yankees' organization, April 29, 1980.
xGranted free agency, October 30, 1980; re-signed by Yankees before re-entry draft, November 8, 1980.

CHAMPIONSHIP SERIES RECORD

Year Club	League	G.	IP.	W.	L.	Pct.	H.	R.	ER.	SO.	BB.	ERA.
1976—Kansas City	American	1	4⅔	1	0	1.000	4	1	1	1	0	1.93
1977—Kansas City	American	3	2	0	0	.000	4	0	0	1	0	0.00
1978—Kansas City	American	2	1	0	1	.000	2	1	1	1	0	9.00
Championship Series Totals		6	7⅔	1	1	.500	10	2	2	3	0	2.35

MICHAEL DAVID BISHOP
(Mike)

Born November 5, 1958, at Santa Maria, Calif.
Height, 6.02. Weight, 188.
Throws and bats righthanded.
Led Texas League in slugging percentage with .603 in 1980.

Year Club	League	Pos.	G.	AB.	R.	H.	2B.	3B.	HR.	RBI.	B.A.	PO.	A.	E.	F.A.
1976—Idaho Falls	Pion.	3-0-1-S	68	231	45	67	8	9	3	40	.290	107	62	20	.894
1977—Quad Cities	Midw.	3B-SS	137	474	57	112	23	4	7	61	.236	95	243	26	.929
1978—Salinas†	Calif.	3B	7	22	1	2	0	0	0	1	.091	1	9	2	.833
1978—Quad Cities	Midw.	3B	80	279	56	75	15	1	19	64	.269	49	164	20	.914
1979—Salinas	Calif.	1B-3B	62	218	47	67	11	1	13	45	.307	375	49	6	.986
1979—El Paso	Texas	1B	75	276	51	89	15	3	15	51	.322	653	44	11	.984
1980—El Paso	Texas	OF-1B	126	489	96	159	27	5	*33	*104	.325	402	25	16	.964
1980—Salt Lake City	P. C.	1B	9	32	8	11	3	1	1	7	.344	18	1	1	.950

Selected by California Angels' organization in 12th round of free-agent draft, June 8, 1976.
†On disabled list, April 19 to May 16, 1978.

GEORGE ANTON BJORKMAN

Named pronounced Buh-JORK-man.

Born August 26, 1956, at Upland, Calif.
Height, 6.02. Weight, 190.
Throws and bats righthanded.
Attended Oral Roberts University, Tulsa, Okla.

Year Club	League	Pos.	G.	AB.	R.	H.	2B.	3B.	HR.	RBI.	B.A.	PO.	A.	E.	F.A.
1978—Johnson City	Appal.	C	12	41	8	11	0	1	4	8	.268	78	10	0	1.000
1978—Gastonia	W. Car.	C	46	152	20	39	11	0	6	22	.257	208	38	8	.969
1979—St. Petersburg	Fla. St.	C-1B	118	384	56	95	21	2	9	53	.247	563	68	14	.978
1980—Arkansas†‡	Texas	C-OF	70	196	20	47	14	1	4	18	.240	298	30	10	.970

Selected by St. Louis Cardinals' organization in 4th round of free-agent draft, June 6, 1978.
†On disabled list, April 25 to June 12, 1980.
‡Drafted by San Francisco Giants, December 8, 1980.

TIMOTHY P. BLACKWELL
(Tim)

Born August 19, 1952, at San Diego, Calif.
Height, 5.11. Weight, 185.
Throws right and bats left and righthanded.
Hobbies—Tennis, golf and basketball.
Attended Grossmont College, El Cajon, Calif.

Led National League catchers in double plays with 16 in 1980.
Tied for Eastern League lead in double plays by catchers with 12 in 1973.
Led National League catchers in double plays with 16 in 1980.

Year Club	League	Pos.	G.	AB.	R.	H.	2B.	3B.	HR.	RBI.	B.A.	PO.	A.	E.	F.A.
1970—Jamestown........	NYP	3B-C	28	81	8	19	3	2	0	10	.235	33	30	5	.926
1971—Greenville	W. Car.	C-0-3	55	140	18	25	6	0	0	10	.179	230	24	5	.981
1972—Winston-Salem†	.Carol.	C	60	177	25	44	14	3	3	26	.249	357	15	9	.976
1973—Bristol	East.	C-OF	102	318	39	90	15	0	5	38	.283	502	63	5	.991
1974—Pawtucket........	Int.	C	50	140	12	29	8	0	0	17	.207	302	24	6	.982
1974—Boston	Amer.	C	44	122	9	30	1	1	0	8	.246	182	21	6	.971
1975—Boston	Amer.	C	59	132	15	26	3	2	0	6	.197	230	23	4	.984
1976—Rhode Island‡ ..	Int.	C	2	3	0	0	0	0	0	0	.000	3	1	0	1.000
1976—Philadelphia	Nat.	C	4	8	0	2	0	0	0	1	.250	17	0	0	1.000
1976—Reading	East.	*C-OF	91	299	29	74	10	2	2	25	.247	427	•64	10	.980
1977—Reading	East.	C	5	14	2	7	3	0	0	2	.500	27	3	0	1.000
1977—Phila.§-Mont. x.	.Nat.	C	17	22	4	2	1	0	0	0	.091	37	2	3	.929
1978—Wichita.............	A.A.	C	64	184	32	54	7	0	8	33	.293	351	24	8	.979
1978—Chicago	Nat.	C	49	103	8	23	3	0	0	7	.223	213	20	3	.987
1979—Chicago	Nat.	C	63	122	8	20	3	1	0	12	.164	245	28	7	.975
1980—Chicago	Nat.	C	103	320	24	87	16	4	5	30	.272	572	93	12	.982
American League Totals.................			103	254	24	56	4	3	0	14	.220	412	44	10	.979
National League Totals...................			236	575	44	134	23	5	5	50	.233	1084	143	25	.980
Major League Totals			339	829	68	190	27	8	5	64	.229	1496	187	35	.980

Selected by Boston Red Sox' organization in 13th round of free-agent draft, June 4, 1970.
†On disabled list, May 24 to June 16, 1972.
‡Sold to Philadelphia Phillies, April 19, 1976.
§Traded to Montreal Expos with Pitcher Wayne Twitchell for Catcher Barry Foote and Pitcher Dan Warthen, June 15, 1977.
xReleased, January 14, 1978; signed by Wichita (Chicago Cubs' organization), February 10, 1978.

DENNIS HERMAN BLAIR

Born June 5, 1954, at Middletown, O.
Height, 6.04. Weight, 185.
Throws and bats righthanded.
Hobbies—Hiking, cycling and music.
Attended California State University, San Bernardino, Calif.

Year Club	League	G.	IP.	W.	L.	Pct.	H.	R.	ER.	SO.	BB.	ERA.
1972—Jamestown	NYP	1	4	0	0	.000	6	5	3	0	1	6.75
1972—Cocoa Expos	Fla. E. C't	5	33	1	0	1.000	29	20	9	21	23	2.45
1972—West Palm Beach	Florida St.	6	31	1	3	.250	34	18	16	13	9	4.65
1973—West Palm Beach	Florida St.	10	64	4	3	.571	45	27	16	55	24	2.25
1973—Quebec City	Eastern	15	86	3	9	.250	78	38	31	45	39	3.24
1974—Memphis.............................	Int'national	9	54	5	0	1.000	37	11	11	47	24	1.83
1974—Montreal............................	National	22	146	11	7	.611	113	61	53	76	72	3.27
1975—Montreal............................	National	30	163	8	15	.348	150	77	69	82	106	3.81
1976—Denver	Am. Assoc.	25	122	9	4	.692	131	73	61	91	84	4.50
1976—Montreal............................	National	5	16	0	2	.000	21	11	7	9	11	3.94
1977—Denver†	Am. Assoc.	15	76	5	4	.556	84	49	43	50	31	5.09
1977—Rochester	Int'national	9	67	4	3	.571	76	32	27	24	24	3.63
1978—Charlotte	Southern	14	100	6	4	.600	95	40	27	62	37	2.43
1978—Rochester	Int'national	9	38	0	6	.000	50	37	34	17	19	8.05
1979—Rochester‡	Int'national	7	35	2	2	.500	47	25	25	21	11	6.43
1979—Hawaii...............................	P. Coast	16	102	6	6	.500	99	58	55	64	52	4.85
1980—Hawaii...............................	P. Coast	23	146	6	12	.333	137	78	69	82	52	4.25
1980—San Diego	National	5	14	0	1	.000	18	10	10	11	3	6.43
Major League Totals...............................		62	339	19	25	.432	302	159	139	178	192	3.69

Selected by Montreal Expos' organization in 5th round of free-agent draft, June 6, 1972.
†Traded to Baltimore Orioles' organization, September 6, 1977, to complete deal in which Montreal obtained Pitcher Fred Holdsworth, July 14, 1977.
‡Traded to San Diego Padres' organization for Pitcher Randy Fierbaugh, June 6, 1979.

PAUL L. D. BLAIR

Born February 1, 1944, at Cushing, Okla.
Height, 6.00. Weight, 172.
Throws and bats righthanded.
Attended East Los Angeles Junior College, Los Angeles, Calif.

Tied major league record for fewest sacrifices, season, for leader in sacrifices (no sacrifice flies), 13, in 1969.

Hit three home runs in a game, April 29, 1970 against Chicago White Sox.
Tied for American League lead in sacrifice hits with 13 in 1969.
Led California League outfielders in double plays with 7 in 1962.
Led Eastern League in stolen bases with 34 in 1964.
Named outfielder on THE SPORTING NEWS American League All-Star fielding teams, 1967 and 1969 through 1975.
Named as center fielder on THE SPORTING NEWS American League All-Star Team, 1969 and 1974.

Year	Club	League	Pos.	G.	AB.	R.	H.	2B.	3B.	HR.	RBI.	B.A.	PO.	A.	E.	F.A.
1962—Santa Barbara†	..Calif.	O-3-S	122	417	69	95	11	3	17	63	.228	191	37	14	.942
1963—Stockton	...........Calif.	OF-INF	139	540	126	175	30	10	16	77	.324	250	72	17	.950
1964—Rochester	.........Int.	OF	23	69	6	9	1	1	2	5	.130	35	2	1	.974
1964—Elmira	..............East.	*OF-3B	108	415	81	129	18	11	5	52	*.311	249	13	5	*.981
1964—Baltimore	.........Amer.	OF	8	1	0	0	0	0	0	0	.000	2	0	0	1.000
1965—Baltimore	.........Amer.	OF	119	364	49	85	19	2	5	25	.234	241	5	2	.992
1965—Rochester	.........Int.	OF	37	143	17	47	6	5	4	21	.329	81	2	3	.965
1966—Baltimore	.........Amer.	OF	133	303	35	84	20	2	6	33	.277	204	4	2	.990
1967—Baltimore	.........Amer.	OF	151	552	72	162	27	*12	11	64	.293	*369	13	6	.985
1968—Baltimore	.........Amer.	OF-3B	141	421	48	89	22	1	7	38	.211	272	11	3	.990
1969—Baltimore	.........Amer.	OF	150	625	102	178	32	5	26	76	.285	*407	14	5	.988
1970—Baltimore‡	.........Amer.	OF-3B	133	480	79	128	24	2	18	65	.267	368	10	5	.987
1971—Baltimore	.........Amer.	OF	141	516	75	135	24	8	10	44	.262	331	4	3	.991
1972—Baltimore	.........Amer.	OF	142	477	47	111	20	8	8	49	.233	337	10	3	.991
1973—Baltimore	.........Amer.	OF	146	500	73	140	25	3	10	64	.280	369	•14	4	.990
1974—Baltimore	.........Amer.	OF	151	552	77	144	27	4	17	62	.261	447	7	7	.985
1975—Baltimore	.........Amer.	OF-1B	140	440	51	96	13	4	5	31	.218	327	8	3	.991
1976—Baltimore§	.........Amer.	OF	145	375	29	74	16	0	3	16	.197	327	6	7	.979
1977—New York	.........Amer.	OF	83	164	20	43	4	3	4	25	.262	125	1	4	.969
1978—New York	........Amer.	OF-2-S-3	74	125	10	22	5	0	2	13	.176	90	5	2	.979
1979—New York x	..Amer.	OF	2	5	0	1	0	0	0	0	.200	6	0	0	1.000
1979—Cincinnati y	......Nat.	OF	75	140	7	21	4	1	2	15	.150	117	3	1	.992
1980—New York z	.......Amer.	OF	12	2	2	0	0	0	0	0	.000	8	0	0	1.000
National League Totals	....		75	140	7	21	4	1	2	15	.150	117	3	1	.992
American League Totals	....		1871	5902	769	1492	278	54	132	605	.253	4230	112	56	.987
Major League Totals	....		1946	6042	776	1513	282	55	134	620	.250	4347	115	57	.987

Signed as free agent by Baltimore Orioles' organization, July 20, 1961.
†Drafted by Baltimore Orioles from Syracuse (New York Mets' organization), November 26, 1962.
‡On disabled list, May 31 through June 21, 1970.
§Traded to New York Yankees for Outfielders Elliott Maddox and Rick Bladt, latter assigned to Rochester, January 20, 1977.
xReleased, April 12, 1979; signed as free agent by Cincinnati Reds, May 8, 1979.
yGranted free agency, November 1, 1979; signed as New York Yankee minor league instructor, February 19, 1980.
zActivated, May 28, 1980; reinstated as instructor, July 1, 1980.

CHAMPIONSHIP SERIES RECORD

Established Championship Series records for most hits, game (5), October 6, 1969; most at bats, game (6), October 6, 1969.
Tied Championship Series records for most times on winning club (5); most at bats, three-game Series (15); most runs batted in, game (6), October 6, 1969.
Tied American League Championship Series records for most runs batted in, three-game Series (6), 1969; most total bases, three-game Series (11), 1969; most long hits, game (3), October 6, 1969; most positions played, total Series (3).

Year	Club	League	Pos.	G.	AB.	R.	H.	2B.	3B.	HR.	RBI.	B.A.	PO.	A.	E.	F.A.
1969—Baltimore	.........Amer.	OF	3	15	1	6	2	0	1	6	.400	8	0	0	1.000
1970—Baltimore	.........Amer.	OF	3	13	0	1	0	0	0	0	.077	4	0	0	1.000
1971—Baltimore	.........Amer.	OF	3	9	1	3	1	0	0	2	.333	5	0	0	1.000
1973—Baltimore	.........Amer.	OF	5	18	2	3	0	0	0	0	.167	8	0	0	1.000
1974—Baltimore	.........Amer.	OF	4	14	3	4	0	0	1	2	.286	7	0	0	1.000
1977—New York	.........Amer.	OF	3	5	1	2	0	0	0	0	.400	2	0	0	1.000
1978—New York	........Amer.	PH-2-OF	4	6	1	0	0	0	0	0	.000	8	0	0	1.000
Championship Series Totals	....		25	80	9	19	3	0	2	10	.238	42	0	0	1.000

WORLD SERIES RECORD

Tied World Series record for most times home run won game 1-0 (1), October 8, 1966; most hits, five-game Series (9), 1970; most singles, five-game Series (8), 1970.

Year	Club	League	Pos.	G.	AB.	R.	H.	2B.	3B.	HR.	RBI.	B.A.	PO.	A.	E.	F.A.
1966—Baltimore	.........Amer.	OF	4	6	2	1	0	0	1	1	.167	9	0	0	1.000
1969—Baltimore	.........Amer.	OF	5	20	1	2	0	0	0	0	.100	7	0	0	1.000
1970—Baltimore	.........Amer.	OF	5	19	5	9	1	0	0	3	.474	18	0	1	.947
1971—Baltimore	.........Amer.	PR-OF	4	9	2	3	1	0	0	0	.333	6	2	1	.889
1977—New York	.........Amer.	OF-PH	4	4	0	1	0	0	0	1	.250	1	0	0	1.000
1978—New York	........Amer.	O-PH-PR	6	8	2	3	1	0	0	0	.375	5	0	0	1.000
World Series Totals	....		28	66	12	19	3	0	1	5	.288	46	2	2	.960

ALL-STAR GAME RECORD

Year	League	Pos.	AB.	R.	H.	2B.	3B.	HR.	RBI.	B.A.	PO.	A.	E.	F.A.
1969—American	....	OF	2	0	0	0	0	0	0	.000	2	0	0	1.000
1973—American	....	OF	0	0	0	0	0	0	0	.000	1	0	0	1.000
All-Star Game Totals	....		2	0	0	0	0	0	0	.000	3	0	0	1.000

LARVELL BLANKS

Born January 28, 1950, at Del Rio, Tex.
Height, 5.08. Weight, 164.
Throws and bats righthanded.
Attended Sul Ross State University, Alpine, Tex., and Mesa Community College, Mesa, Ariz.
Nephew of Sid Blanks, former halfback with Houston Oilers, Boston Patriots
and Houston Texans.

Year Club League	Pos.	G.	AB.	R.	H.	2B.	3B.	HR.	RBI.	B.A.	PO.	A.	E.	F.A.
1969—Magic Valley.....Pion.	S-2-3-O	●72	260	43	75	●15	4	9	●60	.283	97	179	24	.920
1970—Greenwood........W. Car.	3-2-S	116	437	79	121	16	3	15	69	.277	104	232	16	.955
1971—Savannah ....South.	2B	134	477	58	106	22	3	14	48	.222	295	333	17	.974
1972—Savannah ....South.	SS-2B	83	271	38	77	17	3	6	34	.284	108	230	13	.963
1972—Atlanta.............Nat.	2-SS-3	33	85	10	28	5	0	1	7	.329	49	74	0	1.000
1973—Richmond ....Int.	2-3-S	100	366	45	91	21	1	6	35	.249	185	247	17	.962
1973—Atlanta.............Nat.	3-2-S	17	18	1	4	0	0	0	0	.222	1	3	0	1.000
1974—Richmond ....Int.	★S-3-2	136	466	72	126	★29	4	14	47	.270	167	★414	22	.964
1974—Atlanta.............Nat.	SS	3	8	0	2	0	0	0	1	.250	1	7	1	.889
1975—Atlanta†...........Nat.	SS-2B	141	471	49	110	13	3	3	38	.234	212	438	27	.960
1976—Cleveland.........Amer.	3-S-2	104	328	45	92	8	7	5	41	.280	152	214	11	.971
1977—Cleveland.........Amer.	S-3-2	105	322	43	92	10	4	6	38	.286	100	181	11	.962
1978—Cleveland‡........Amer.	SS-2-3	70	193	19	49	10	0	2	20	.254	83	144	13	.946
1979—Texas§.............Amer.	SS-2B	68	120	13	24	5	0	1	15	.200	65	90	3	.981
1980—Atlanta x ....Nat.	S-3-2	88	221	23	45	6	0	2	12	.204	65	189	17	.937
National League Totals..................		282	803	83	189	24	3	6	58	.235	328	711	45	.958
American League Totals.................		347	963	120	257	33	11	14	114	.267	400	629	38	.964
Major League Totals		629	1766	203	446	57	14	20	172	.253	728	1340	83	.961

Selected by Atlanta Braves' organization in 3rd round of free-agent draft, June 5, 1969.
†Traded with Outfielder Ralph Garr to Chicago White Sox for Outfielder Ken Henderson and Pitchers Dick Ruthven and Danny Osborn, December 12, 1975. Traded by Chicago White Sox to Cleveland Indians for Second Baseman Jack Brohamer, December 12, 1975.
‡Traded with Pitcher Jim Kern to Texas Rangers for Outfielder Bobby Bonds and Pitcher Len Barker, October 3, 1978.
§Traded with Pitcher Doyle Alexander to Atlanta Braves for Pitcher Adrian Devine, Shortstop Pepe Frias and a player to be named later, December 7, 1979; Braves received $50,000 to complete deal when Outfielder Jeff Burroughs exercised no-trade clause.
xReleased, August 8, 1980; signed by Pittsburgh Pirates' organization, January 19, 1981.

VIDA ROCHELLE BLUE, JR.

Born July 28, 1949, at Mansfield, La.
Height, 6.00. Weight, 200.
Throws left and bats left and righthanded.
Hobbies—Hunting and fishing.
Attended Southern University, Baton Rouge, La.

Tied American League record for: most strikeouts by lefthanded pitcher, extra-inning game (17), July 9, 1971 (pitched 11 of 20 innings).
Pitched seven-inning, 4-0 no-hit victory against Appleton, June 19, 1968.
Pitched 6-0 no-hit victory against Minnesota Twins, September 21, 1970.
Led American League in shutouts with 8 in 1971.
Won American League Cy Young Memorial Award, 1971.
Named lefthanded pitcher on THE SPORTING NEWS American League All-Star Team, 1971.
Named lefthanded pitcher on THE SPORTING NEWS National League All-Star Team, 1978.
Named American League Pitcher of the Year by THE SPORTING NEWS, 1971.
Named National League Pitcher of the Year by THE SPORTING NEWS, 1978.
Named Most Valuable Player in American League, 1971.

Year Club League	G.	IP.	W.	L.	Pct.	H.	R.	ER.	SO.	BB.	ERA.
1968—Burlington ....Midwest	24	152	8	●11	.421	102	67	42	★231	80	2.49
1969—Birmingham ....Southern	15	104	10	3	.769	80	40	37	112	52	3.20
1969—Oakland.............................American	12	42	1	1	.500	49	34	31	24	18	6.64
1970—Iowa ....Am. Assoc.	17	133	12	3	★.800	88	40	32	★165	55	2.17
1970—Oakland.............................American	6	39	2	0	1.000	20	12	9	35	12	2.08
1971—Oakland.............................American	39	312	24	8	.750	209	73	63	301	88	★1.82
1972—Oakland†...........................American	25	151	6	10	.375	117	55	47	111	48	2.80
1973—Oakland.............................American	37	264	20	9	.690	214	108	96	158	105	3.27
1974—Oakland.............................American	40	282	17	15	.531	246	118	102	174	98	3.26
1975—Oakland.............................American	39	278	22	11	.667	243	103	93	189	99	3.01
1976—Oakland.............................American	37	298	18	13	.581	268	90	78	166	63	2.36
1977—Oakland‡ ....American	38	280	14	●19	.424	★284	138	●119	157	86	3.83
1978—San Francisco ....National	35	258	18	10	.643	233	87	80	171	70	2.79
1979—San Francisco ....National	34	237	14	14	.500	246	143	★132	138	111	5.01
1980—San Francisco§ ....National	31	224	14	10	.583	202	79	74	129	61	2.97
National League Totals	100	719	46	34	.575	681	309	286	438	242	3.58
American League Totals	273	1946	124	86	.590	1650	731	638	1315	617	2.95
Major League Totals	373	2665	170	120	.586	2331	1040	924	1753	859	3.12

Selected by Kansas City A's organization in 2nd round of free-agent draft, June 6, 1967.
†On restricted list, March 30 through April 27, 1972.
‡On disqualified list, April 5 through April 16, 1977. Traded to San Francisco Giants for Outfielder Gary Thomasson, Catcher Gary Alexander, Pitchers Dave Heaverlo, Alan Wirth, John Johnson and Phillip Huffman, a player to be named later and cash estimated at $390,000, March 15, 1978; Shortstop Mario Guerrero

traded to Oakland to complete deal, April 7, 1978.
  §On disabled list, June 28 to August 2, 1980.

CHAMPIONSHIP SERIES RECORD

Tied Championship Series records for fewest hits allowed, game (2), October 8, 1974; most runs allowed, five-game Series (8), 1973.
Established American League Championship Series record for most games pitched, five game Series (4), 1972.

Year Club	League	G.	IP.	W.	L.	Pct.	H.	R.	ER.	SO.	BB.	ERA.
1971—Oakland	American	1	7	0	1	.000	7	5	5	8	2	6.43
1972—Oakland	American	4	5⅓	0	0	.000	4	0	0	5	1	0.00
1973—Oakland	American	2	7	0	1	.000	8	8	8	3	5	10.29
1974—Oakland	American	1	9	1	0	1.000	2	0	0	7	0	0.00
1975—Oakland	American	1	3	0	0	.000	6	3	3	2	0	9.00
Championship Series Totals		9	31⅓	1	2	.333	27	16	16	25	8	4.60

WORLD SERIES RECORD

Year Club	League	G.	IP.	W.	L.	Pct.	H.	R.	ER.	SO.	BB.	ERA.
1972—Oakland	American	4	8⅔	0	1	.000	8	4	4	5	5	4.15
1973—Oakland	American	2	11	0	1	.000	10	6	6	8	3	4.91
1974—Oakland	American	2	13⅔	0	1	.000	10	5	5	9	7	3.29
World Series Totals		8	33⅓	0	3	.000	28	15	15	22	15	4.05

ALL-STAR GAME RECORD

Only pitcher in All-Star Game history to start in each league: American League, 1971; National League, 1978.
Tied All-Star Game records for most home runs allowed, total games (4); most home runs allowed, inning (2), July 15, 1975 (second inning).

Year League	IP.	W.	L.	Pct.	H.	R.	ER.	SO.	BB.	ERA.
1971—American	3	1	0	1.000	2	3	3	3	0	9.00
1975—American	2	0	0	.000	5	2	2	1	0	9.00
1978—National	3	0	0	.000	5	3	3	2	1	9.00
All-Star Game Totals	8	1	0	1.000	12	8	8	6	1	9.00

Named to American League All-Star Team in 1977; replaced due to injury.
Named to National League All-Star Team in 1980; replaced due to injury by Ed Whitson.

RIK AALBERT BLYLEVEN
(Bert)

Born April 6, 1951, at Zeist, The Netherlands.
Height, 6.03. Weight, 207.
Throws and bats righthanded.
Hobbies—Bowling, golf, basketball and pool.

Tied modern major league record for most consecutive strikeouts, start of game (6), September 16, 1970.
Tied American League record for longest one-hit complete game (10 innings), June 21, 1976.
Led American League in shutouts with 9 in 1973.
Named by The Sporting News as American League Rookie Pitcher of the Year for 1970.
Pitched 6-0 no-hit victory against California Angels, September 22, 1977.

Year Club	League	G.	IP.	W.	L.	Pct.	H.	R.	ER.	SO.	BB.	ERA.
1969—Sarasota Twins	Gulf Coast	7	32	2	2	.500	31	13	10	39	11	2.81
1969—Orlando	Florida St.	6	37	5	0	1.000	36	6	6	41	14	1.46
1970—Evansvill	Am. Assoc.	8	54	4	2	.667	48	18	15	63	12	2.50
1970—Minnesota	American	27	164	10	9	.526	143	66	58	135	47	3.18
1971—Minnesota	American	38	278	16	15	.516	267	95	87	224	59	2.82
1972—Minnesota	American	39	287	17	17	.500	247	93	87	228	69	2.73
1973—Minnesota	American	40	325	20	17	.541	296	109	91	258	67	2.52
1974—Minnesota	American	37	281	17	17	.500	244	99	83	249	77	2.66
1975—Minnesota	American	35	276	15	10	.600	219	104	92	233	84	3.00
1976—Minnesota†-Texas	American	36	298	13	16	.448	283	106	95	219	81	2.87
1977—Texas‡	American	30	235	14	12	.538	181	81	71	182	69	2.72
1978—Pittsburgh	National	34	244	14	10	.583	217	94	82	182	66	3.02
1979—Pittsburgh	National	37	237	12	5	.706	238	102	95	172	92	3.61
1980—Pittsburgh§	National	34	217	8	13	.381	219	102	92	168	59	3.82
National League Totals		105	698	34	28	.548	674	298	269	522	217	3.47
American League Totals		282	2144	122	113	.519	1880	753	664	1728	553	2.79
Major League Totals		387	2842	156	141	.525	2554	1051	933	2250	770	2.95

Selected by Minnesota Twins' organization in 3rd round of free-agent draft, June 5, 1969.
  †Traded with Shortstop Danny Thompson to Texas Rangers for Pitcher Bill Singer, Infielders Roy Smalley and Mike Cubbage and Pitcher Jim Gideon, assigned to Tacoma, and a reported $250,000 cash, June 1, 1976.
  ‡Traded with First Baseman-Outfielder John Milner to Pittsburgh Pirates for Outfielder-First Baseman Al Oliver and Infielder Nelson Norman, December 8, 1977.
  §Traded with Catcher Manny Sanguillen to Cleveland Indians for Pitchers Bob Owchinko, Rafael Vasquez and Victor Cruz and Catcher Gary Alexander, December 9, 1980.

Year	Club	League	G.	IP.	W.	L.	Pct.	H.	R.	ER.	SO.	BB.	ERA.
1970—Minnesota		American	1	2	0	0	.000	2	1	0	2	0	0.00
1979—Pittsburgh		National	1	9	1	0	1.000	8	1	1	9	0	1.00
Championship Series Totals			2	11	1	0	1.000	10	2	1	11	0	0.82

WORLD SERIES RECORD

Year	Club	League	G.	IP.	W.	L.	Pct.	H.	R.	ER.	SO.	BB.	ERA.
1979—Pittsburgh		National	2	10	1	0	1.000	8	2	2	4	3	1.80

ALL-STAR GAME RECORD

Year	League	IP.	W.	L.	Pct.	H.	R.	ER.	SO.	BB.	ERA.
1973—American		1	0	1	.000	2	2	2	0	2	18.00

BRUCE ANTON BOCHTE

Name pronounced Bock-tee.

Born November 12, 1950, at Pasadena, Calif.
Height, 6.03. Weight, 200.
Throws and bats lefthanded.
Hobbies—Reading, tennis and collecting tropical fish.
Attended University of Santa Clara, Santa Clara, Calif.;
received Bachelor of Science Degree in Commerce.

Year	Club	League	Pos.	G.	AB.	R.	H.	2B.	3B.	HR.	RBI.	B.A.	PO.	A.	E.	F.A.
1972—Stockton	Calif.	1B-OF	72	266	36	87	14	2	11	42	.327	470	27	9	.982
1973—El Paso	Texas	1B-OF	122	417	57	133	32	4	10	79	.319	775	41	11	.987
1974—Salt Lake City	P.C.	OF-1B	92	332	55	118	15	2	9	56	.355	218	12	6	.975
1974—California	Amer.	OF-1B	57	196	24	53	4	1	5	26	.270	248	9	5	.981
1975—California†	Amer.	1B	107	375	41	107	19	3	3	48	.285	850	51	12	.987
1976—California	Amer.	OF-1B	146	466	53	120	17	1	2	49	.258	651	42	7	.990
1977—Calif.‡-Cleve.§	Amer.	OF-1B	137	492	64	148	23	1	7	51	.301	486	33	9	.983
1978—Seattle	Amer.	1B	140	486	58	128	25	3	11	51	.263	180	7	3	.984
1979—Seattle	Amer.	1B	150	554	81	175	38	6	16	100	.316	1361	114	*14	.991
1980—Seattle	Amer.	1B	148	520	62	156	34	4	13	78	.300	1273	98	6	.996
Major League Totals				885	3089	383	887	160	19	57	403	.287	5049	354	56	.990

Selected by California Angels' organization in 2nd round of free-agent draft, June 6, 1972.
†On disabled list, June 24 to August 13, 1975.
‡Traded with Pitcher Sid Monge and cash estimated at $250,000 to Cleveland Indians for Pitchers Dave Schuler and Dave LaRoche, May 11, 1977.
§Granted free agency, November 2, 1977; signed by Seattle Mariners, December 20, 1977.

ALL-STAR GAME RECORD

Year	League	Pos.	AB.	R.	H.	2B.	3B.	HR.	RBI.	B.A.	PO.	A.	E.	F.A.
1979—American		PH-1B	1	0	1	0	0	0	1	1.000	2	0	0	1.000

BRUCE DOUGLAS BOCHY

Name pronounced BOW-chee.
Born April 16, 1955, At Landes de Bussac, France.
Height, 6.04. Weight, 215.
Throws and bats righthanded.
Attended Brevard Community College, Cocoa, Fla., and
Florida State University, Tallahassee, Fla.
Brother of Joe Bochy, former catcher in Minnesota Twins' organization,
1969 through 1974.

Tied for Florida State League lead in passed balls with 12 in 1977.

Year	Club	League	Pos.	G.	AB.	R.	H.	2B.	3B.	HR.	RBI.	B.A.	PO.	A.	E.	F.A.
1975—Covington	Appal.	C	37	145	31	49	9	0	4	34	.338	231	36	4	.985
1976—Columbus	South.	C	69	230	9	53	6	0	0	16	.230	266	45	6	.981
1976—Dubuque	Midw.	C-1B	30	103	9	25	4	0	1	8	.243	165	25	5	.974
1977—Cocoa	Fla. St.	C	128	430	40	109	18	2	3	35	.253	*492	67	12	.979
1978—Columbus	South.	C	79	261	25	70	10	2	7	34	.268	419	49	7	.985
1978—Houston	Nat.	C	54	154	8	41	8	0	3	15	.266	268	35	8	.974
1979—Houston	Nat.	C	56	129	11	28	4	0	1	6	.217	198	29	7	.970
1980—Houston†	Nat.	C-1B	22	22	0	4	1	0	0	0	.182	19	1	0	1.000
Major League Totals				132	305	19	73	13	0	4	21	.239	485	65	15	.973

Selected by Chicago White Sox' organization in 8th round of free-agent draft, January 9, 1975.
Selected by Houston Astros' organization in secondary phase of free-agent draft, June 4, 1975.
†Sold to New York Mets' organization, February 11, 1981.

CHAMPIONSHIP SERIES RECORD

Year	Club	League	Pos.	G.	AB.	R.	H.	2B.	3B.	HR.	RBI.	B.A.	PO.	A.	E.	F.A.
1980—Houston	Nat.	C	1	1	0	0	0	0	0	0	.000	5	1	0	1.000

DID YOU KNOW—

That Ron LeFlore is the only player to win stolen base titles in both the National and American League?

MICHAEL JAMES BODDICKER
(Mike)

Born August 23, 1957, at Cedar Rapids, Iowa.
Height, 5.11. Weight, 172.
Throws and bats righthanded.
Attended University of Iowa, Iowa City, Iowa.

Year Club	League	G.	IP.	W.	L.	Pct.	H.	R.	ER.	SO.	BB.	ERA.
1978—Bluefield	Ap'lachian	8	19	2	1	.667	9	2	1	28	10	0.47
1978—Charlotte	Southern	10	65	4	3	.571	42	15	14	48	17	1.94
1978—Rochester	Int'national	1	5	1	0	1.000	4	1	1	3	2	1.80
1979—Charlotte	Southern	14	102	9	3	.750	82	40	34	89	36	3.00
1979—Rochester	Int'national	15	72	4	6	.400	88	48	48	48	27	6.00
1980—Rochester	Int'national	25	190	12	9	.571	149	57	46	109	35	2.18
1980—Baltimore	American	1	7	0	1	.000	6	6	5	4	5	6.43
Major League Totals		1	7	0	1	.000	6	6	5	4	5	6.43

Selected by Montreal Expos' organization in 8th round of free-agent draft, June 4, 1975.
Selected by Baltimore Orioles' organization in 9th round of free-agent draft, June 6, 1978.

THOMAS WINTON BOGGS

Born October 25, 1955, at Poughkeepsie, N.Y.
Height, 6.02. Weight, 200.
Throws and bats righthanded.
Hobby—Water skiing.

Tied for Gulf Coast League lead in shutouts with 2 in 1974.
Led Pacific Coast League pitchers in double plays with 5 in 1976.
Led International League in games started with 33, in complete games with 16 and in wild pitches with 18 in 1979.

Year Club	League	G.	IP.	W.	L.	Pct.	H.	R.	ER.	SO.	BB.	ERA.
1974—Sarasota Rangers	Gulf Coast	10	64	5	2	.714	50	21	18	55	35	2.53
1975—Pittsfield	Eastern	24	162	10	11	.476	153	84	63	100	73	3.50
1976—Sacramento	P. Coast	18	115	6	11	.353	153	101	88	77	60	6.89
1976—Texas	American	13	90	1	7	.125	87	42	35	36	34	3.50
1977—Tucson	P. Coast	22	97	5	10	.333	131	107	92	70	83	8.54
1977—Texas†	American	6	27	0	3	.000	40	18	18	15	12	6.00
1978—Richmond	Int'national	8	54	5	1	.833	51	20	17	29	22	2.83
1978—Atlanta	National	16	59	2	8	.200	80	46	44	21	26	6.71
1979—Richmond	Int'national	33	*227	15	10	.600	*230	*108	91	*138	99	3.61
1979—Atlanta	National	3	13	0	2	.000	21	11	9	1	4	6.23
1980—Atlanta	National	32	192	12	9	.571	180	80	73	84	46	3.42
National League Totals		51	264	14	19	.424	281	137	126	106	76	4.30
American League Totals		19	117	1	10	.091	127	60	53	51	46	4.08
Major League Totals		70	381	15	29	.341	408	197	179	157	122	4.23

Selected by Texas Rangers' organization in 1st round (second player selected) of free-agent draft, June 5, 1974.

†Traded with Pitcher Adrian Devine and Outfielder Eddie Miller to Atlanta Braves for First Baseman Willie Montanez, December 8, 1977.

BRUCE ARMAND BOISCLAIR
Name pronounced BOH-clair.

Born December 9 1952, at Putnam, Conn.
Height, 6.03. Weight, 200.
Throws and bats lefthanded.
Hobbies—Bicycle riding and all sports.
Attended Thames Valley State Technical College and Mohegan Community College,
Norwich, Conn. and University of Connecticut, Storrs, Conn.

Year Club	League	Pos.	G.	AB.	R.	H.	2B.	3B.	HR.	RBI.	B.A.	PO.	A.	E.	F.A.
1970—Marion	Appal.	OF-P	40	117	15	33	5	2	0	10	.282	49	3	0	1.000
1971—Pompano Bch.	Fla. St.	OF-1B	129	401	64	108	18	4	0	47	.269	163	6	4	.977
1972—Visalia†	Calif.	1B-OF	88	328	64	114	19	4	4	32	.348	473	26	9	.982
1973—Memphis	Texas	OF-1B	19	63	10	13	2	0	1	7	.206	71	5	2	.974
1973—Tidewater	Int.	OF	80	243	31	62	11	0	2	23	.255	112	3	2	.983
1974—Tidewater‡	Int.	OF-1B	107	297	27	71	8	4	5	31	.239	181	8	4	.986
1974—New York	Nat.	OF	7	12	0	3	1	0	0	1	.250	10	2	1	.923
1975—Tidewater	Int.	OF	127	453	62	126	16	5	4	37	.278	264	9	4	.986
1976—New York	Nat.	OF	110	286	42	82	13	3	2	13	.287	156	3	3	.981
1977—New York	Nat.	OF-1B	127	307	41	90	21	1	4	44	.293	159	2	6	.964
1978—New York	Nat.	OF-1B	107	214	24	48	7	1	4	15	.224	115	3	2	.983
1979—New York§x	Nat.	OF-1B	59	98	7	18	5	1	0	4	.184	36	2	0	1.000
1980—Hanshin y	Central	..	80	177	..	44	..	..	8	26	.249	..	..	..	....
Major League Totals			410	917	114	241	47	6	10	77	.263	476	12	12	.976

Selected by New York Mets' organization in 20th round of free-agent draft, June 4, 1970.
†On military list from beginning of season to May 12.
‡On temporary inactive list, June 14 to June 29, 1974.
§On disabled list, July 9, 1979; transferred to emergency disabled list, July 11 to September 7, 1979.
xReleased, April 1, 1980; signed by Hanshin Tigers of Japanese baseball.
ySigned by Toronto Blue Jays' organization, February 4, 1981.

PITCHING RECORD

Year Club	League	G.	IP.	W.	L.	Pct.	H.	R.	ER.	SO.	BB.	ERA.
1970—Marion	Appal.	1	4	0	0	.000	7	5	5	1	2	11.25

DANNY JON BOITANO

Name pronounced boy-TAHN-oh.

Born March 22, 1953, at Sacramento, Calif.
Height, 6.00. Weight, 185.
Throws and bats righthanded.
Hobby—Hunting ducks.
Attended Fresno City College, Fresno, Calif.
Pitched 2-0 no-hit victory against Elmira, August 21, 1973.
Led Pacific Coast League in saves with 18 in 1979.

Year Club	League	G.	IP.	W.	L.	Pct.	H.	R.	ER.	SO.	BB.	ERA.
1973—Auburn	NYP	14	104	8	3	.727	73	41	24	95	47	2.08
1974—Rocky Mount	Carolina	17	94	3	10	.231	99	68	59	82	55	5.65
1974—Spartanburg	W. Carol.	5	21	0	1	.000	26	15	12	20	9	5.14
1975—Reading	Eastern	40	78	10	3	.769	59	31	29	63	32	3.35
1976—Oklahoma City	Am. Assoc.	50	70	3	5	.375	65	39	33	50	54	4.24
1977—Reading	Eastern	4	19	2	2	.500	21	12	6	7	11	2.84
1977—Oklahoma City	Am. Assoc.	29	102	4	8	.333	109	75	65	66	51	5.74
1978—Oklahoma City	Am. Assoc.	40	133	7	11	.389	152	88	59	71	67	3.99
1978—Philadelphia†	National	1	1	0	0	.000	0	0	0	0	1	0.00
1979—Vancouver	P. Coast	53	81	6	8	.429	78	34	33	48	42	3.67
1979—Milwaukee	American	5	6	0	0	.000	6	1	1	5	3	1.50
1980—Vancouver	P. Coast	44	54	6	4	.600	52	31	26	33	34	4.33
1980—Milwaukee	American	11	18	0	1	.000	26	17	16	11	6	8.00
National League Totals		1	1	0	0	.000	0	0	0	0	1	0.00
American League Totals		16	24	0	1	.000	32	18	17	16	9	6.38
Major League Totals		17	25	0	1	.000	32	18	17	16	10	6.12

Selected by Milwaukee Brewers' organization in 6th round of free-agent draft, June 8, 1971.
Selected by St. Louis Cardinals' organization in secondary phase of free-agent draft, January 12, 1972.
Selected by Philadelphia Phillies' organization in secondary phase of free-agent draft, June 6, 1972.
Selected by Montreal Expos' organization in secondary phase of free-agent draft, January 10, 1973.
Selected by Philadelphia Phillies' organization in secondary phase of free-agent draft, June 5, 1973.
†Traded to Milwaukee Brewers' organization for Pitcher Gary Beare, March 28, 1979.

MARK VINCENT BOMBACK

Born April 14, 1953, at Portsmouth, Va.
Height, 5.11. Weight, 170.
Throws and bats righthanded.
Pitched seven-inning, 1-0 no-hit victory against Orlando, June 20, 1972.
Led International League pitchers in games started with 30 in 1974.
Led Pacific Coast League in games started with 33, in complete games with 16 and in shutouts with 5 in 1979.
Named Minor League Player of the Year by THE SPORTING NEWS, 1979.

Year Club	League	G.	IP.	W.	L.	Pct.	H.	R.	ER.	SO.	BB.	ERA.
1971—Williamsport	NYP	16	62	3	3	.500	69	44	38	62	24	5.52
1972—Winter Haven	Florida St.	21	162	14	5	.737	112	48	37	149	44	2.06
1972—Pawtucket	Eastern	7	48	5	1	.833	33	16	15	45	29	2.81
1973—Pawtucket	Int'national	23	150	10	7	.588	123	65	56	105	73	3.36
1974—Pawtucket	Int'national	30	172	10	15	.400	*215	*114	*104	102	91	5.44
1975—Pawtucket	Int'national	7	39	0	4	.000	43	33	29	37	21	6.69
1975—Bristol	Eastern	21	163	12	6	.667	130	49	42	118	59	2.32
1976—Rhode Island††	Int'national	18	120	5	7	.417	130	60	54	63	60	4.05
1977—Holyoke	Eastern	23	145	12	6	.667	152	82	73	76	54	4.53
1978—Holyoke	Eastern	8	56	5	2	.714	36	17	14	50	18	2.25
1978—Spokane	P. Coast	20	132	7	5	.583	135	58	52	111	47	3.55
1978—Milwaukee	American	2	2	0	0	.000	5	3	3	1	1	13.50
1979—Vancouver§	P. Coast	33	*246	*22	7	*.759	225	87	70	151	67	*2.56
1980—New York	National	36	163	10	8	.556	191	80	74	68	49	4.09
Major League Totals		38	165	10	8	.556	196	83	77	69	50	4.20

Selected by Boston Red Sox' organization in 25th round of free-agent draft, June 8, 1971.
†On disabled list, July 30 to August 31, 1976.
‡Released, April 7, 1977; signed by Milwaukee Brewers' organization, May 7, 1977.
§Traded to New York Mets for Pitcher Dwight Bernard, October 26, 1979.

BOBBY LEE BONDS

Born March 15, 1946, at Riverside, Calif.
Height, 6.01. Weight, 190.
Throws and bats righthanded.
Hobbies—Singing, dancing and listening to records.
Attended Riverside City College, Riverside, Calif.
Brother of Robert V. Bonds, Jr., 13th round draft choice
of Kansas City Chiefs in 1965.

Established major league records for most strikeouts, batter, season (189), 1970; most home runs as leadoff batter of game, season (11), 1973; most home runs, first batter of game, lifetime (35), 1975.

Tied major league record for most unassisted double plays, game (1), May 31, 1972.

Tied modern major league record for most chances accepted, right fielder, game (10), May 28, 1976.

Major league stolen bases: 1968 (16), 1969 (45), 1970 (48), 1971 (26), 1972 (44), 1973 (43), 1974 (41), 1975 (30), 1976 (30), 1977 (41), 1978 (43), 1979 (34), 1980 (15). Total—456.

Led National League in total bases with 341 in 1973.

Led National League outfielders in double plays with 7 in 1970.

Led National League batters in strikeouts with 187 in 1969, 189 in 1970 and 148 in 1973.

Led California League batters in strikeouts with 146 in 1966.

Hit grand slam home run in first major league game; first rookie to do so in 20th century (in his third at bat), June 25, 1968.

Only player in major league history to hit 30 or more home runs and steal 30 or more bases in the same season on five occasions (32 home runs and 45 stolen bases in 1969; 39 home runs and 43 stolen bases in 1973; 32 home runs and 30 stolen bases in 1975, 37 home runs and 41 stolen bases in 1977 and 31 home runs and 43 stolen bases in 1978).

Tied for National League lead in double plays by outfielders with 5 in 1973.

Named by THE SPORTING NEWS as National League Player of the Year, 1973.

Named as outfielder on THE SPORTING NEWS National League All-Star Team, 1973.

Named as outfielder on THE SPORTING NEWS American League All-Star Team, 1977.

Named as outfielder on THE SPORTING NEWS National League All-Star fielding teams, 1971, 1973 and 1974.

Year Club	League	Pos.	G.	AB.	R.	H.	2B.	3B.	HR.	RBI.	B.A.	PO.	A.	E.	F.A.
1965—Lexington..........W. Car.	OF	112	418	*103	135	12	11	25	86	.323	200	14	12	.947
1965—Fresno ....Calif.	OF	7	32	6	7	0	0	1	2	.219	16	0	1	.941
1966—Fresno† ....Calif.	OF	117	455	93	119	12	6	26	91	.262	181	15	10	.951
1967—Waterbury ....East.	*OF-1B	137	476	65	124	19	8	15	68	.261	229	13	*11	.957
1968—Phoenix............P.C.	OF	60	219	47	81	16	7	8	47	.370	156	7	2	.988
1968—San Francisco ...Nat.	OF	81	307	55	78	10	5	9	35	.254	169	6	4	.978
1969—San Francisco ...Nat.	OF	158	622	●120	161	25	6	32	90	.259	339	9	8	.978
1970—San Francisco ...Nat.	OF	157	663	134	200	36	10	26	78	.302	326	14	11	.969
1971—San Francisco ...Nat.	OF	155	619	110	178	32	4	33	102	.288	329	10	2	*.994
1972—San Francisco ...Nat.	OF	153	626	118	162	29	5	26	80	.259	345	8	8	.978
1973—San Francisco ...Nat.	OF	160	643	*131	182	34	4	39	96	.283	346	12	11	.970
1974—San Francisco‡ ..Nat.	OF	150	567	97	145	22	8	21	71	.256	305	11	11	.966
1975—New York§ ....Amer.	OF	145	529	93	143	26	3	32	85	.270	287	12	4	.987
1976—California x.......Amer.	OF	99	378	48	100	10	3	10	54	.265	199	9	5	.977
1977—California y.......Amer.	OF	158	592	103	156	23	9	37	115	.264	272	5	4	.986
1978—Chi.z-Tex.a ......Amer.	OF	156	565	93	151	19	4	31	90	.267	253	16	9	.968
1979—Cleveland b......Amer.	OF	146	538	93	148	24	1	25	85	.275	267	9	6	.979
1980—St. Louis cd.......Nat.	OF	86	231	37	47	5	3	5	24	.203	114	5	4	.967
American League Totals..................		704	2602	430	698	102	20	135	429	.268	1278	51	28	.979
National League Totals...................		1100	4278	802	1153	193	45	191	576	.270	2273	75	59	.975
Major League Totals		1804	6880	1232	1851	295	65	326	1005	.269	3551	126	87	.977

Signed as free agent by San Francisco Giants' organization, August 4, 1964.

†On disabled list, April 28 to May 17, 1966.

‡Traded to New York Yankees for Outfielder Bobby Murcer, October 21, 1974.

§Traded to California Angels for Outfielder Mickey Rivers and Pitcher Ed Figueroa, December 11, 1975.

xOn supplemental disabled list, April 2 to April 19, 1976; on emergency disabled list, August 9 to October 14, 1976.

yTraded with Outfielder Thad Bosley and Pitcher Dick Dotson to Chicago White Sox for Pitchers Chris Knapp and Dave Frost and Catcher Brian Downing, December 5, 1977.

zTraded to Texas Rangers for Outfielders Claudell Washington and Rusty Torres (assigned to Iowa) and a player to be named later, May 16, 1978.

aTraded with Pitcher Len Barker to Cleveland Indians for Infielder Larvell Blanks and Pitcher Jim Kern, October 3, 1978.

bTraded to St. Louis Cardinals for Pitcher John Denny and Outfielder Jerry Mumprey, December 7, 1979.

cOn supplemental disabled list, July 21 to August 12, 1980.

dReleased, December 22, 1980.

CHAMPIONSHIP SERIES RECORD

Year Club	League	Pos.	G.	AB.	R.	H.	2B.	3B.	HR.	RBI.	B.A.	PO.	A.	E.	F.A.
1971—San Francisco ...Nat.	OF	3	8	0	2	0	0	0	0	.250	3	0	1	.750

ALL-STAR GAME RECORD

Year League	Pos.	AB.	R.	H.	2B.	3B.	HR.	RBI.	B.A.	PO.	A.	E.	F.A.
1971—National.............................	OF	1	0	0	0	0	0	0	.000	0	0	0	.000
1973—National.............................	OF	2	1	2	1	0	1	2	1.000	0	0	0	.000
1975—American............................	OF	3	0	0	0	0	0	0	.000	0	1	0	1.000
All-Star Game Totals		6	1	2	1	0	1	2	.333	0	1	0	1.000

WILLIAM GORDON BONHAM
(Bill)

Born October 1, 1948, at Glendale, Calif.
Height, 6.03. Weight, 195.
Throws and bats righthanded.
Hobby—Basketball.
Attended Los Angeles Valley College, Van Nuys, Calif. and University of California at Los Angeles; received Bachelor of Arts degree in Psychology.

Established major league record for most consecutive hits allowed, start of game (7), August 5, 1975.
Tied major league record for most strikeouts, inning (4), July 31, 1974 (first game, second inning).

Year Club	League	G	IP	W	L	Pct.	H	R	ER	SO	BB	ERA.
1970—Huron..................................	Northern	18	39	3	3	.500	27	20	13	69	24	3.00
1971—Tacoma	P. Coast	8	11	2	1	.667	9	4	3	12	2	2.45
1971—Chicago	National	33	60	2	1	.667	63	38	31	41	36	4.65
1972—Wichita................................	Am. Assoc.	18	125	10	4	.714	120	57	49	116	41	3.53
1972—Chicago	National	19	58	1	1	.500	56	22	20	49	25	3.10
1973—Chicago	National	44	152	7	5	.583	126	55	51	121	64	3.02
1974—Chicago	National	44	243	11	•22	.333	246	133	104	191	109	3.85
1975—Chicago	National	38	229	13	15	.464	254	*133	*120	165	109	4.72
1976—Chicago	National	32	196	9	13	.409	215	102	93	110	96	4.27
1977—Chicago†	National	34	215	10	13	.435	207	111	104	134	82	4.35
1978—Cincinnati	National	23	140	11	5	.688	151	59	55	83	50	3.54
1979—Cincinnati	National	29	176	9	7	.563	173	80	74	78	60	3.78
1980—Tampa‡	Florida St.	3	16	1	0	1.000	7	3	1	14	5	0.56
1980—Cincinnati§	National	4	19	2	1	.667	21	10	10	13	5	4.74
Major League Totals		300	1488	75	83	.475	1512	743	662	985	636	4.00

Selected by California Angels' organization in 33rd round of free-agent draft, June 6, 1966.
Selected by California Angels' organization in secondary phase of free-agent draft, January 28, 1967.
Selected by Baltimore Orioles' organization in 31st round of free-agent draft, January 28, 1967.
Signed as free agent by Chicago Cubs' organization, June 10, 1970.
†Traded to Cincinnati Reds for Pitchers Woodie Fryman and Bill Caudill, October 31, 1977.
‡On rehabilitation assignment, June 30 to July 24, 1980.
§On disabled list, May 21 to June 30 and August 5 to September 1, 1980.

JUAN GUILLERMO BONILLA

Born February 12, 1955, at Santurce, Puerto Rico
Height, 5.09. Weight, 170.
Throws and bats righthanded.
Attended Florida State University, Tallahassee. Fla.
Led Midwest League second basemen in double plays with 84 in 1978, Southern League second basemen with 104 in 1979 and Pacific Coast League second basemen with 110 in 1980.
Led Midwest League in sacrifice flies with 13 in 1978.

Year Club	League	Pos.	G	AB	R	H	2B.	3B.	HR.	RBI.	B.A.	PO.	A.	E.	F.A.
1978—Waterloo..........	Midw.	2B	130	470	81	137	32	1	13	78	.291	*285	*381	21	.969
1979—Chattanooga......	South.	2B	138	550	80	150	26	0	5	59	.273	332	360	18	.975
1980—Tacoma	P. C.	2B	139	502	66	152	27	2	4	55	.303	*366	*422	15	.981

Selected by New York Yankees' organization in 24th round of free-agent draft, June 7, 1977.
Signed as free agent by Cleveland Indians' organization, January 6, 1978.

ROBERT BARRY BONNELL

(Known by middle name.)

Born October 27, 1953, at Cincinnati, O.
Height, 6.03. Weight, 200.
Throws and bats righthanded.
Hobbies—Flying, photography and amateur radio.
Attended Ohio State University, Columbus, O.
Brother of Glenn Bonnell, former infielder in Cincinnati Reds' organization.

Year Club	League	Pos.	G	AB	R	H	2B.	3B.	HR.	RBI.	B.A.	PO.	A.	E.	F.A.
1975—Spart.†-Green....	W.C.	OF	124	457	86	148	20	6	12	80	*.324	276	19	12	.961
1976—Savannah	South.	OF	51	188	31	42	6	2	6	23	.223	117	6	5	.961
1976—Richmond	Int.	OF	66	227	36	64	13	2	5	31	.282	134	4	3	.979
1977—Richmond	Int.	OF	14	50	8	19	3	0	0	10	.380	42	2	1	.978
1977—Atlanta‡	Nat.	OF-3B	100	360	41	108	11	0	1	45	.300	203	65	8	.971
1978—Atlanta	Nat.	OF-3B	117	304	36	73	11	3	1	16	.240	187	35	6	.974
1979—Atlanta§	Nat.	OF-3B	127	375	47	97	20	3	12	45	.259	221	8	4	.983
1980—Toronto x..........	Amer.	OF	130	463	55	124	22	4	13	56	.268	271	15	8	.973
National League Totals			344	1039	124	278	42	6	14	106	.268	611	108	18	.976
American League Totals			130	463	55	124	22	4	13	56	.268	271	15	8	.973
Major League Totals......................			474	1502	179	402	64	10	27	162	.268	882	123	26	.975

Selected by Chicago White Sox' organization in 8th round of free-agent draft, June 8, 1971.
Selected by Philadelphia Phillies' organization in secondary phase of free-agent draft, January 9, 1975.
†Traded with Catcher Jim Essian and cash by Philadelphia Phillies to Atlanta Braves for First Baseman Dick Allen and Catcher Johnny Oates, May 7, 1975.
‡On supplemental disabled list, June 29 to July 21, 1977.
§Traded with Pitcher Joey McLaughlin to Toronto Blue Jays for First Baseman Chris Chambliss and Shortstop Luis Gomez, December 5, 1979.
xOn supplemental disabled list, August 13 to September 2, 1980.

DID YOU KNOW—

That Giants pitcher Ed Whitson had the best home run-allowed rate in the majors last season? Whitson gave up just seven circuit clouts in 212 innings, an average of one every 30.3 innings.

ROBERT AVERILL BONNER
(Bob)

Born August 12, 1956, at Uvalde, Tex.
Height, 6.00. Weight, 185.
Throws and bats righthanded.
Attended Texas A&M University, College Station, Tex.

Led International League shortstops in assists with 454, in errors with 31, in double plays with 73 and in fielding average with .956 in 1980.

Year	Club	League	Pos.	G.	AB.	R.	H.	2B.	3B.	HR.	RBI.	B.A.	PO.	A.	E.	F.A.
1978—Charlotte	South.	SS	35	107	8	25	2	0	0	10	.234	60	91	11	.932
1979—Charlotte	South.	S-2-O	119	460	55	134	29	3	7	67	.291	136	322	20	.947
1979—Rochester	Int.	2B-SS	4	11	1	3	0	0	0	0	.273	10	12	0	1.000
1980—Rochester	Int.	SS-2B	133	469	46	113	8	2	2	41	.241	230	467	31	.957
1980—Baltimore	Amer.	SS	4	4	1	0	0	0	0	1	.000	2	6	1	.889
Major League Totals			4	4	1	0	0	0	0	1	.000	2	6	1	.889

Selected by Montreal Expos' organization in 10th round of free-agent draft, June 5, 1974.
Selected by Kansas City Royals' organization in 9th round of free-agent draft, June 7, 1977.
Selected by Baltimore Orioles' organization in 6th round of free-agent draft, June 6, 1978.

ROBERT RAYMOND BOONE
(Bob)

Born November 19, 1947, at San Diego, Calif.
Height, 6.02. Weight, 202.
Throws and bats righthanded.
Hobbies—Fishing, golf and basketball.
Attended Stanford University, Palo Alto, Calif.; received Bachelor of Arts degree in Psychology.
Son of Raymond Otis Boone, former major league infielder and presently Boston Red Sox scout.
Brother of Rodney Alan Boone, catcher-outfielder in Kansas City Royals' and Houston Astros' organization, 1972 through 1975.

Led National League catchers in total chances with 924 in 1974.
Led National League catchers in fielding percentage with .991 in 1978.
Led Pacific Coast League catchers in passed balls with 18 and in double plays with 13 in 1972.
Tied for Carolina League lead in double plays by third basemen with 18 in 1969.
Named catcher on THE SPORTING NEWS National League All-Star Team, 1976.
Named catcher on THE SPORTING NEWS National League All-Star fielding team, 1978 and 1979.

Year	Club	League	Pos.	G.	AB.	R.	H.	2B.	3B.	HR.	RBI.	B.A.	PO.	A.	E.	F.A.
1969—Raleigh-Dur.	Carol.	3B	80	300	45	90	13	1	5	46	.300	71	160	20	.920
1970—Reading†	East.	3B	20	80	12	23	2	0	2	37	.288	28	38	7	.904
1971—Reading‡	East.	3B-C-S	92	328	41	87	14	3	4	37	.265	206	138	17	.953
1972—Eugene	P. C.	C	138	513	77	158	32	4	17	67	.308	*699	*77	*24	.970
1972—Philadelphia	Nat.	C	16	51	4	14	1	0	1	4	.275	66	7	5	.936
1973—Philadelphia	Nat.	C	145	521	42	136	20	2	10	61	.261	868	*89	10	.990
1974—Philadelphia	Nat.	C	146	488	41	118	24	3	3	52	.242	*825	77	*22	.976
1975—Philadelphia	Nat.	C-3B	97	289	28	71	14	2	2	20	.246	459	48	5	.990
1976—Philadelphia	Nat.	C-1B	121	361	40	98	18	2	4	54	.271	587	39	6	.990
1977—Philadelphia	Nat.	C-3B	132	440	55	125	26	4	11	66	.284	654	83	8	.989
1978—Philadelphia	Nat.	C-1B-O	132	435	48	123	18	4	12	62	.283	650	55	8	.989
1979—Philadelphia	Nat.	C-3B	119	398	38	114	21	3	9	58	.286	527	66	8	.987
1980—Philadelphia	Nat.	C	141	480	34	110	23	1	9	55	.229	741	88	*18	.979
Major League Totals			1049	3463	330	909	165	21	61	432	.262	5377	552	90	.985

Selected by Philadelphia Phillies' organization in 20th round of free-agent draft, June 5, 1969.
†On military list, May 26 through remainder of season.
‡On disabled list from beginning of season until June 4, 1971.

CHAMPIONSHIP SERIES RECORD

Year	Club	League	Pos.	G.	AB.	R.	H.	2B.	3B.	HR.	RBI.	B.A.	PO.	A.	E.	F.A.
1976—Philadelphia	Nat.	C	3	7	0	2	0	0	0	1	.286	8	2	0	1.000
1977—Philadelphia	Nat.	C	4	10	1	4	0	0	0	0	.400	18	2	0	1.000
1978—Philadelphia	Nat.	C	3	11	0	2	0	0	0	0	.182	16	2	1	.947
1980—Philadelphia	Nat.	C	5	18	1	4	0	0	0	2	.222	22	3	0	1.000
Championship Series Totals			15	46	2	12	0	0	0	3	.261	64	9	1	.986

WORLD SERIES RECORD

Year	Club	League	Pos.	G.	AB.	R.	H.	2B.	3B.	HR.	RBI.	B.A.	PO.	A.	E.	F.A.
1980—Philadelphia	Nat.	C	6	17	3	7	2	0	0	4	.412	49	3	0	1.000

ALL-STAR GAME RECORD

Year	League	Pos.	AB.	R.	H.	2B.	3B.	HR.	RBI.	B.A.	PO.	A.	E.	F.A.
1976—National		C	2	0	0	0	0	0	0	.000	5	0	0	1.000
1978—National		C	1	1	1	0	0	0	2	1.000	3	1	0	1.000
1979—National		C	2	1	1	0	0	0	0	.500	0	0	0	.000
All-Star Game Totals			5	2	2	0	0	0	2	.400	8	1	0	1.000

PEDRO BORBON (RODRIGUEZ)
Name pronounced bor-BOHN.

Born December 2, 1946, at Valverde Mao, Dominican Republic.
Height, 6.02. Weight, 185.
Throws and bats righthanded.
Hobby—Rooster fights.

Year Club	League	G.	IP.	W.	L.	Pct.	H.	R.	ER.	SO.	BB.	ERA.
1966—Cedar Rapids	Midwest	38	69	6	1	.857	53	22	15	58	16	1.96
1967—St. Petersburg	Florida St.	36	63	5	4	.556	52	22	16	50	17	2.29
1968—Modesto†	California	*65	100	8	5	.615	99	34	26	96	22	2.34
1969—California‡§	American	22	41	2	3	.400	55	31	28	20	11	6.15
1970—Indianapolis	Am. Assoc.	32	71	5	2	.714	81	27	26	53	29	3.30
1970—Cincinnati	National	12	17	0	2	.000	21	15	13	6	6	6.88
1971—Indianapolis	Am. Assoc.	56	97	12	6	.667	101	34	33	75	20	3.06
1971—Cincinnati	National	3	4	0	0	.000	3	3	2	4	1	4.50
1972—Cincinnati	National	62	122	8	3	.727	115	45	43	48	32	3.17
1973—Cincinnati	National	80	121	11	4	.733	137	33	29	60	35	2.16
1974—Cincinnati	National	73	139	10	7	.588	133	54	50	53	32	3.24
1975—Cincinnati	National	67	125	9	5	.643	145	47	41	29	21	2.95
1976—Cincinnati	National	69	121	4	3	.571	135	49	45	53	31	3.35
1977—Cincinnati	National	73	127	10	5	.667	131	48	45	48	24	3.19
1978—Cincinnati	National	62	99	8	2	.800	102	56	55	35	27	5.00
1979—Cin.x-San Fran.y	National	60	91	6	5	.545	104	45	42	49	21	4.15
1980—St. Louis z	National	10	19	1	0	1.000	17	10	8	4	10	3.79
American League Totals		22	41	2	3	.400	55	31	28	20	11	6.15
National League Totals		571	985	67	36	.650	1043	405	373	389	240	3.41
Major League Totals		593	1026	69	39	.639	1098	436	401	409	251	3.52

Signed as free agent by St. Louis Cardinals' organization, October 15, 1964.
†Drafted by California Angels from Tulsa (St. Louis Cardinals' organziation), December 2, 1968.
‡On disabled list, May 7 to June 5, 1969.
§Traded with Pitchers Jim McGlothlin and Vern Geishert to Cincinnati Reds for Outfielder Alex Johnson and Infielder Chico Ruiz, November 25, 1969. Completed transaction of October 24, 1969, in which California acquired Pitcher Mel Queen from Indianapolis, Reds' affiliate.
xTraded to San Francisco Giants for Outfielder Heity Cruz, June 28, 1979.
yReleased, April 3, 1980; signed by St. Louis Cardinals, April 30, 1980.
zReleased, May 27, 1980.

CHAMPIONSHIP SERIES RECORD

Year Club	League	G.	IP.	W.	L.	Pct.	H.	R.	ER.	SO.	BB.	ERA.
1972—Cincinnati	National	3	4⅓	0	0	.000	2	1	1	1	0	2.08
1973—Cincinnati	National	4	4⅔	1	0	1.000	3	0	0	3	0	0.00
1975—Cincinnati	National	1	1	0	0	.000	0	0	0	1	0	0.00
1976—Cincinnati	National	2	4⅓	0	0	.000	4	0	0	0	1	0.00
Championship Series Totals		10	14⅓	1	0	1.000	9	1	1	5	1	0.63

WORLD SERIES RECORD

Year Club	League	G.	IP.	W.	L.	Pct.	H.	R.	ER.	SO.	BB.	ERA.
1972—Cincinnati	National	6	7	0	1	.000	7	3	3	4	2	3.86
1975—Cincinnati	National	3	3	0	0	.000	3	3	2	1	2	6.00
1976—Cincinnati	National	1	1⅔	0	0	.000	0	0	0	0	0	0.00
World Series Totals		10	11⅔	0	1	.000	10	6	5	5	4	3.86

RICHARD ALBERT BORDI
(Rich)

Born April 18, 1959, at South San Francisco, Calif.
Height, 6.07. Weight, 210.
Throws and bats righthanded.

Year Club	League	G.	IP.	W.	L.	Pct.	H.	R.	ER.	SO.	BB.	ERA.
1980—West Haven	Eastern	11	76	4	6	.400	75	42	35	49	30	4.14
1980—Oakland	American	1	2	0	0	.000	4	1	1	0	0	4.50
Major League Totals		1	2	0	0	.000	4	1	1	0	0	4.50

Selected by Minnesota Twins' organization in 5th round of free-agent draft, June 7, 1977.
Selected by Oakland A's organization in 3rd round of free-agent draft, June 3, 1980.

WILLIAM CHARLES BORDLEY
(Bill)

Born January 9, 1958, at Los Angeles, Calif.
Height, 6.02. Weight, 200.
Throws and bats lefthanded.
Attended El Camino College, Torrance, Calif. and University of
Southern California, Los Angeles, Calif.
Brother of Art Bordley, pitcher in Baltimore Orioles' and
Oakland A's organizations, 1975 through 1977.

Led Pacific Coast League in wild pitches with 20 in 1979.
Received reported $90,000 bonus to sign with San Francisco Giants, 1979.

Year Club	League	G.	IP.	W.	L.	Pct.	H.	R.	ER.	SO.	BB.	ERA.
1979—Phoenix	P. Coast	27	156	8	11	.421	181	106	79	84	94	4.56
1980—Phoenix	P. Coast	19	111	4	8	.333	129	70	66	66	54	5.35
1980—San Francisco	National	8	31	2	3	.400	34	19	16	11	21	4.65
Major League Totals		8	31	2	3	.400	34	19	16	11	21	4.65

Selected by Milwaukee Brewers' organization in 1st round (fourth player selected) of free-agent draft, June 8, 1976.

Selected by Cincinnati Reds' organization in secondary phase of free-agent draft, January 9, 1979.

Note: California Angels were fined $15,000 and two draft choices for tampering by Commissioner Bowie Kuhn. Bordley chose five teams—the Los Angeles Dodgers, Kansas City Royals, Milwaukee Brewers, Seattle Mariners and San Francisco Giants—as teams he would go to and not return to college. The Giants were awarded his rights, February 24, 1979.

GLENN DENNIS BORGMANN

Name pronounced Board-mun.

Born May 25, 1950, at Paterson, N. J.

Height, 6.02. Weight, 210.

Throws and bats righthanded.

Hobbies—Fishing, hunting and playing cards.

Attended Miami-Dade (North) Community College, Miami, Fla., and
University of South Alabama, Mobile, Ala.

Year Club	League	Pos.	G.	AB.	R.	H.	2B.	3B.	HR.	RBI.	B.A.	PO.	A.	E.	F.A.
1971—Wis. Rapids	Midw.	C-1B	55	182	27	64	8	0	7	28	.352	348	45	6	.985
1971—Charlotte	South.	C-OF	22	70	10	18	4	1	3	15	.257	113	7	0	1.000
1972—Tacoma	P. C.	C-1B	66	235	37	79	13	0	12	39	.336	440	39	3	.994
1972—Minnesota	Amer.	C	56	175	11	41	4	0	3	14	.234	304	31	12	.965
1973—Tacoma	P. C.	C	136	485	69	133	18	3	8	71	.274	570	63	12	.981
1973—Minnesota	Amer.	C	12	34	7	9	2	0	0	9	.265	55	2	0	1.000
1974—Minnesota	Amer.	C	128	345	33	87	8	1	3	45	.252	652	52	2	*.997
1975—Minnesota	Amer.	C	125	352	34	73	15	2	2	33	.207	618	81	8	.989
1976—Minnesota	Amer.	C	24	65	10	16	3	0	1	6	.246	110	13	3	.976
1977—Minneota†	Amer.	C	17	43	12	11	1	0	2	7	.256	70	8	0	1.000
1978—Minnesota§	Amer.	C	49	123	16	26	4	1	3	15	.211	185	20	2	.990
1979—Minnesota‡§	Amer.	C	31	70	4	14	3	0	0	8	.200	129	11	1	.993
1980—Iowa x	A. A.	C	73	213	28	67	15	0	6	36	.315	290	28	4	.988
1980—Chicago y	Amer.	C	32	87	10	19	2	0	2	14	.218	134	18	0	1.000
Major League Totals			474	1294	137	296	42	4	16	151	.229	2257	236	28	.989

Selected by Pittsburgh Pirates' organization in special phase of free-agent draft, June 5, 1969.

Selected by Minnesota Twins' organization in secondary phase of free-agent draft, January 7, 1970.

Selected by Minnesota Twins' organization in secondary phase of free-agent draft, June 8, 1971.

†On disabled list, June 20 to September 1, 1977.

‡Granted free agency, November 1, 1979; signed by Chicago White Sox, February 3, 1980.

§Released, April 3, 1980; re-signed by White Sox' organization, April 8, 1980.

xOn disabled list, June 15 to June 25, 1980.

yGranted free agency, October 30, 1980.

RICHARD ALAN BOSETTI

Name pronounced boh-SET-ee.

(Rick)

Born August 5, 1953, at Redding, Calif.

Height, 5.11. Weight, 185.

Throws and bats righthanded.

Attended Shasta College, Redding, Calif.

Led New York-Pennsylvania League third basemen in double plays with 16 in 1973.

Led New York-Pennsylvania League in total bases with 125 and in stolen bases with 27 in 1973.

Led American Association in stolen bases with 42 in 1976.

Year Club	League	Pos.	G.	AB.	R.	H.	2B.	3B.	HR.	RBI.	B.A.	PO.	A.	E.	F.A.
1973—Spartanburg	W. Car.	3B	26	79	4	18	4	0	0	5	.228	14	25	11	.780
1973—Auburn	NYP	*3B-2B	67	*282	*68	94	13	3	4	34	.333	34	*158	*30	.881
1974—Rocky Mount	Carol.	3B	37	157	27	39	5	2	1	11	.248	26	73	15	.868
1974—Reading	East.	OF-3B	93	308	37	82	15	4	4	35	.266	82	92	12	.935
1975—Reading	East.	OF-3B	110	432	73	118	21	5	6	34	.273	233	18	6	.977
1976—Oklahoma City†	A.A.	OF	123	*504	82	*154	25	6	5	52	.306	*273	12	9	.969
1976—Philadelphia	Nat.	OF	13	18	6	5	1	0	0	0	.278	9	1	0	1.000
1977—Okla. City‡	N.O. A.A.	OF	81	323	61	100	17	5	7	21	.310	177	3	4	.978
1977—St. Louis§	Nat.	OF	41	69	12	16	0	0	0	3	.232	42	3	0	1.000
1978—Toronto x	Amer.	OF	136	568	61	147	25	5	5	42	.259	417	17	6	.986
1979—Toronto	Amer.	OF	*162	619	59	161	35	2	8	65	.260	*466	*18	*13	.974
1980—Toronto y	Amer.	OF	53	188	24	40	7	1	4	18	.213	124	4	2	.985
American League Totals			351	1375	144	348	67	8	17	125	.253	1007	39	21	.980
National League Totals			54	87	18	21	1	0	0	3	.241	51	4	0	1.000
Major League Totals			405	1462	162	369	68	8	17	128	.252	1058	43	21	.981

Selected by Philadelphia Phillies' organization in 7th round of free-agent draft, January 10, 1973.

†On disabled list, June 10 to June 20, 1976.

‡Traded by Philadelphia Phillies' organization to St. Louis Cardinals' organization with First Baseman

Dane Iorg and Pitcher Tom Underwood for Outfielder Bake McBride and Pitcher Steve Waterbury, June 15, 1977.

§Traded to Toronto Blue Jays for Pitcher Tom Bruno and cash, March 15, 1978.
xOn disabled list, June 12 to June 27, 1978.
yOn disabled list, June 23 to October 8, 1980.

THADDIS BOSLEY, JR.
Name pronounced BAHZ-lee.
(Thad)
Born September 17, 1956, at Oceanside, Calif.
Height, 6.03. Weight, 175.
Throws and bats lefthanded.
Hobby—Music; composing, playing and singing.
Attended Mira Costa Community College, Oceanside, Calif.
Led Pioneer League in base on balls with 71 in 1974.
Led California League in stolen bases with 90 in 1976.
Named California League Player of the Year, 1976.

Year	Club	League	Pos.	G.	AB.	R.	H.	2B.	3B.	HR.	RBI.	B.A.	PO.	A.	E.	F.A.
1974—Idaho Falls	Pion.		OF	68	223	55	54	3	4	0	14	.242	101	4	•11	.905
1975—Quad Cities†	Midw.		OF	108	379	67	113	12	3	1	50	.298	206	2	4	•.981
1976—Salinas	Calif.		OF	134	527	105	171	26	4	2	72	•.324	285	13	7	•.977
1977—Salt Lake City	P.C.		OF	69	298	55	97	22	2	2	38	.326	169	6	5	.972
1977—California‡§	Amer.		OF	58	212	19	63	10	2	0	19	.297	130	1	5	.963
1978—Iowa	A. A.		OF	47	179	27	52	3	0	3	15	.291	77	5	2	.976
1978—Chicago x	Amer.		OF	66	219	25	59	5	1	2	13	.269	155	3	4	.975
1979—Iowa y	A. A.		OF	95	382	62	101	14	5	1	24	.264	140	6	5	.967
1979—Chicago	Amer.		OF	36	77	13	24	1	1	1	8	.312	57	2	2	.967
1980—Chicago za	Amer.		OF	70	147	12	33	2	0	2	14	.224	91	1	4	.958
Major League Totals				230	655	69	179	18	4	5	54	.273	433	7	15	.967

Selected by California Angels' organization in 4th round of free-agent draft, June 5, 1974.
†On disabled list, April 19 to May 6, 1975.
‡On disabled list, June 29 to July 10, 1977.
§Traded with Outfielder Bobby Bonds and Pitcher Dick Dotson to Chicago White Sox for Pitchers Chris Knapp and Dave Frost and Catcher Brian Downing, December 5, 1977.
xOn supplemental disabled list, June 29 to July 17, 1978.
yOn disabled list, July 15 to July 25, 1979.
zOn supplemental disabled list, August 12 to October 3, 1980.
aOn emergency disabled list, October 3 to October 6, 1980.

RALPH WAYNE BOTTING
Name pronounced BAHT-ting.

Born May 12, 1955, at Houlton, Maine.
Height, 6.00. Weight, 195.
Throws and bats lefthanded.
Hobbies—Basketball and water skiing.
Pitched seven-inning, 3-0 no-hit victory against Wausau, July 26, 1976.

Year	Club	League	G.	IP.	W.	L.	Pct.	H.	R.	ER.	SO.	BB.	ERA.
1974—Idaho Falls	Pioneer		10	57	5	4	.556	48	32	26	64	45	4.11
1975—Quad Cities	Midwest		20	115	8	9	.471	91	48	33	125	55	2.58
1976—Salinas†	California		10	44	4	2	.667	55	35	28	39	36	5.73
1976—Quad Cities	Midwest		9	45	4	4	.500	39	23	20	38	28	4.00
1977—Salinas	California		8	53	8	0	1.000	41	13	12	63	27	2.04
1977—El Paso	Texas		19	101	5	7	.417	120	67	57	72	59	5.08
1978—El Paso‡	Texas		17	93	7	5	.583	115	80	73	74	52	7.06
1979—Salt Lake City	P. Coast		18	92	5	8	.385	110	51	49	42	50	4.79
1979—California	American		12	30	2	0	1.000	46	30	29	22	15	8.70
1980—Salt Lake City	P. Coast		28	173	•15	8	.652	202	117	•107	87	86	5.57
1980—California	American		6	26	0	3	.000	40	20	17	12	13	5.88
Major League Totals			18	56	2	3	.400	86	50	46	34	28	7.39

Selected by California Angels' organization in 7th round of free-agent draft, June 5, 1974.
†On disabled list, June 16 to July 12, 1976.
‡On disabled list, May 28 to June 12 and August 10 to September 11, 1978.

CHRISTOPHER BOURJOS
(Chris)
Born October 16, 1955, at Chicago, Ill.
Height, 6.00. Weight, 185.
Throws and bats righthanded.
Attended Mayfair Junior College, Chicago, Ill.
and Northern Illinois University, DeKalb, Ill.
Nephew of Otto Denning, former catcher with Cleveland Indians;
Cousin of Pat Denning, former catcher in New York Yankees' organization.

Year	Club	League	Pos.	G.	AB.	R.	H.	2B.	3B.	HR.	RBI.	B.A.	PO.	A.	E.	F.A.
1977—Cedar Rapids	Midw.		OF	65	261	53	86	15	4	12	42	.330	47	1	6	.889
1977—Fresno	Calif.		OF	57	215	53	67	7	2	15	62	.312	69	2	4	.947

— 54 —

Year Club League	Pos.	G.	AB.	R.	H.	2B.	3B.	HR.	RBI.	B.A.	PO.	A.	E.	F.A.
1978—Waterbury ....East.	OF	116	426	62	120	21	5	8	66	.282	181	7	6	.969
1979—Phoenix ....P. C.	OF	142	553	68	167	32	9	8	87	.302	276	*24	•10	.968
1980—Phoenix ....P. C.	OF	144	*577	90	170	30	13	9	86	.295	249	15	*13	.953
1980—San Francisco† .Nat.	OF	13	22	4	5	1	0	1	2	.227	5	0	0	1.000
Major League Totals......................		13	22	4	5	1	0	1	2	.227	5	0	0	1.000

Signed as free agent by San Francisco Giants' organization, April 26, 1977.
†Traded with Pitcher Bob Knepper to Houston Astros for Third Baseman Enos Cabell, December 8, 1980.

LAWRENCE ROBERT BOWA
(Larry)

Born December 6, 1945, at Sacramento, Calif.
Height, 5.10. Weight, 155.
Throws right and bats left and righthanded.
Hobbies—Golf and billiards.
Attended Sacramento City College, Sacramento, Calif.
Son of Paul Bowa, former minor league infielder and manager,
and nephew of Frank Bowa, former minor league infielder.

Established major league record for highest fielding percentage, shortstop, lifetime (1,000 or more games), .981; highest fielding percentage by shortstop, season (.991), 1979.
Tied modern major league record for most at bats, game (7), July 12, 1975.
Established National League record for fewest errors, season, 150 or more games, by shortstop, 9, 1972.
Tied National League record for most seasons leading league in fielding percentage by shortstop (5).
Major League stolen bases: 1970 (24), 1971 (28), 1972 (17), 1973 (10), 1974 (39), 1975 (24), 1976 (30), 1977 (32), 1978 (27), 1979 (20), 1980 (21). Total—272.
Led National League in sacrifice hits with 18 in 1972.
Led National League shortstops in total chances with 843 in 1971.
Tied for National League lead in double plays by shortstops with 97 in 1971.
Led Pacific Coast League in stolen bases with 48 in 1969.
Led Eastern League shortstops in double plays with 77 in 1968.
Named shortstop on THE SPORTING NEWS National League All-Star fielding team, 1972 and 1978.
Named shortstop on THE SPORTING NEWS National League All-Star Team, 1975 and 1978.

Year Club League	Pos.	G.	AB.	R.	H.	2B.	3B.	HR.	RBI.	B.A.	PO.	A.	E.	F.A.
1966—Spartanburg ......W. Car.	SS	97	429	70	134	14	4	2	36	.312	138	284	12	*.972
1966—San Diego..........P.C.	SS	5	19	0	6	0	1	0	1	.316	13	20	2	.943
1967—Bakersfield†......Calif.	SS-2B	7	32	4	6	2	0	0	3	.188	15	12	1	.964
1967—Reading ....East.	SS	22	89	11	25	4	0	0	9	.281	35	79	9	.927
1968—Reading ....East.	SS	133	480	47	116	14	2	3	36	.242	192	•395	24	.961
1969—Eugene ..............P.C.	*SS-2B	135	568	80	163	11	6	1	26	.287	*215	*469	18	*.974
1970—Philadelphia ......Nat.	SS-2B	145	547	50	137	17	6	0	34	.250	202	418	13	.979
1971—Philadelphia ......Nat.	SS	159	*650	74	162	18	5	0	25	.249	272	*560	11	*.987
1972—Philadelphia ......Nat.	SS	152	579	67	145	11	*13	1	31	.250	212	494	9	*.987
1973—Philadelphia‡ ....Nat.	SS	122	446	42	94	11	3	0	23	.211	191	361	12	.979
1974—Philadelphia ......Nat.	SS	162	669	97	184	19	10	1	36	.275	256	462	12	*.984
1975—Philadelphia§ ....Nat.	SS	136	583	79	178	18	9	2	38	.305	227	403	25	.962
1976—Philadelphia ......Nat.	SS	156	624	71	155	15	9	0	49	.248	180	492	17	.975
1977—Philadelphia ......Nat.	SS	154	624	93	175	19	3	4	41	.280	222	518	13	.983
1978—Philadelphia ......Nat.	SS	156	654	78	192	31	5	3	43	.294	224	502	10	*.986
1979—Philadelphia x...Nat.	SS	147	539	74	130	17	11	0	31	.241	229	448	6	*.991
1980—Philadelphia ......Nat.	SS	147	540	57	144	16	4	2	39	.267	225	449	17	.975
Major League Totals		1636	6455	782	1696	192	78	13	390	.263	2440	5107	145	.981

Signed as free agent by Philadelphia Phillies' organization, October 12, 1965.
†In military service from beginning of season to July 18.
‡On disabled list, July 26 to September 1, 1973.
§On supplemental disabled list, May 27 to June 23, 1975.
xOn supplemental disabled list, May 25 to June 9, 1979.

CHAMPIONSHIP SERIES RECORD

Year Club League	Pos.	G.	AB.	R.	H.	2B.	3B.	HR.	RBI.	B.A.	PO.	A.	E.	F.A.
1976—Philadelphia ......Nat.	SS	3	8	1	1	1	0	0	1	.125	2	11	0	1.000
1977—Philadelphia ......Nat.	SS	4	17	2	2	0	0	0	1	.118	0	17	0	1.000
1978—Philadelphia ......Nat.	SS	4	18	2	6	0	0	0	0	.333	5	16	0	1.000
1980—Philadelphia ......Nat.	SS	5	19	2	6	0	0	0	0	.316	4	11	1	.938
Championship Series Totals.............		16	62	7	15	1	0	0	2	.242	11	55	1	.985

WORLD SERIES RECORD

Established World Series record for most double plays started by shortstop, six-game Series (7), 1980.
Tied World Series records for most stolen bases, six-game Series (3), 1980; most double plays started by shortstop, nine-inning game (3), October 15, 1980.

Year Club League	Pos.	G.	AB.	R.	H.	2B.	3B.	HR.	RBI.	B.A.	PO.	A.	E.	F.A.
1980—Philadelphia ......Nat.	SS	6	24	3	9	1	0	0	2	.375	5	18	0	1.000

ALL-STAR GAME RECORD

Year League	Pos.	AB.	R.	H.	2B.	3B.	HR.	RBI.	B.A.	PO.	A.	E.	F.A.
1974—National..............................	SS	2	0	0	0	0	0	0	.000	2	0	0	1.000
1975—National..............................	SS	0	1	0	0	0	0	0	.000	2	0	0	1.000
1976—National..............................	SS	1	0	0	0	0	0	0	.000	2	1	0	1.000
1978—National..............................	SS	3	1	2	0	0	0	0	.667	2	4	0	1.000
1979—National..............................	SS	2	0	0	0	0	0	0	.000	1	3	0	1.000
All-Star Game Totals........................		8	2	2	0	0	0	0	.250	9	8	0	1.000

SAMUEL THOMAS BOWEN

Born September 18, 1952 at Brunswick, Ga.
Height, 5.09. Weight, 170.
Throws and bats righthanded.
Hobbies—Hunting and fishing.
Attended Brunswick Junior College, Brunswick, Ga. and Valdosta State College, Valdosta, Ga.;
received Bachelor of Science degree in Education.

Tied for Eastern League lead in sacrifice hits with 13 in 1976.

Year Club	League	Pos.	G.	AB.	R.	H.	2B.	3B.	HR.	RBI.	B.A.	PO.	A.	E.	F.A.
1974–Elmira	NYP	*O-2-1	62	217	57	66	13	3	11	51	.304	121	6	2	*.984
1975–Bristol	East.	OF	44	143	18	28	4	1	4	13	.196	78	7	1	.988
1975–Winter Haven	Fla. St.	OF	12	38	3	7	1	0	2	4	.184	26	0	1	.963
1976–Bristol†	East.	OF	127	433	60	92	20	3	6	44	.212	274	15	10	.967
1977–Pawtucket	Int.	O-3-1	115	362	58	96	18	3	15	49	.265	231	15	2	.992
1977–Boston	Amer.	OF	3	2	0	0	0	0	0	0	.000	3	0	0	1.000
1978–Pawtucket	Int.	OF	89	266	46	67	15	1	2	49	.252	194	9	4	.981
1978–Boston	Amer.	OF	6	7	3	1	0	0	1	1	.143	2	0	0	1.000
1979–Pawtucket	Int.	OF	125	456	68	107	16	4	*28	*75	.235	273	11	5	.983
1980–Pawtucket‡	Int.	OF	89	271	43	62	10	1	14	35	.229	168	10	4	.978
1980–Boston	Amer.	OF	7	13	0	2	0	0	0	0	.154	17	1	0	1.000
Major League Totals			16	22	3	3	0	0	1	1	.136	22	1	0	1.000

Selected by Cleveland Indians' organization in 25th round of free-agent draft, June 4, 1970.
Selected by Montreal Expos' organization in secondary phase of free-agent draft, June 8, 1971.
Selected by Atlanta Braves' organization in secondary phase of free-agent draft, January 12, 1972.
Selected by California Angels' organization in secondary phase of free-agent draft, June 6, 1972.
Selected by Boston Red Sox' organization in 7th round of free-agent draft, June 5, 1974.
†On disabled list, April 12 to April 27, 1976.
‡On disabled list, April 23 to May 9 and May 14 to June 11, 1980.

DORIAN SCOTT BOYLAND
(Doe)

Born January 5, 1955, at Chicago, Ill.
Height, 6.04. Weight, 204.
Throws and bats lefthanded.
Attended University of Wisconsin at Oshkosh, Oshkosh, Wis.

Year Club	League	Pos.	G.	AB.	R.	H.	2B.	3B.	HR.	RBI.	B.A.	PO.	A.	E.	F.A.
1976–Salem	Carol.	1B-OF	71	245	27	66	12	4	3	31	.269	311	8	31	.961
1977–Shreveport	Texas	1B	119	457	64	151	22	6	11	60	.330	991	42	*28	.974
1978–Columbus†	Int.	*1B-OF	113	405	64	118	19	6	12	61	.291	675	45	*14	.981
1978–Pittsburgh	Nat.	1B	6	8	1	2	0	0	0	1	.250	8	0	0	1.000
1979–Portland‡	P. C.	OF-1B	30	102	10	25	6	0	2	12	.245	30	2	2	.941
1979–Pittsburgh	Nat.	PH-PR	4	3	0	0	0	0	0	0	.000	0	0	0	.000
1980–Portland	P.C.	1B	120	413	77	116	22	6	14	67	.281	885	58	10	.990
Major League Totals			10	11	1	2	0	0	0	1	.182	8	0	0	1.000

Selected by Pittsburgh Pirates' organization in 2nd round of free-agent draft, June 8, 1976.
†On disabled list, June 5 to June 23, 1978.

LARRY BRADFORD

Born December 21, 1951, at Chicago, Illinois.
Height, 6.01. Weight, 205.
Throws left and bats righthanded.
Hobbies—Collecting music albums.
Attended Clark College, Atlanta, Ga.; received Bachelor of Arts degree.

Led Southern League in balks with 4 in 1977.

Year Club	League	G.	IP.	W.	L.	Pct.	H.	R.	ER.	SO.	BB.	ERA.
1973–Wytheville	Ap'lachian	21	63	4	3	.571	63	41	30	67	26	4.29
1974–Greenwood	W. Carol.	25	161	9	9	.500	154	76	60	116	68	3.35
1975–Lynchburg	Carolina	24	159	13	9	.591	145	61	46	84	64	2.60
1976–Savannah	Southern	23	136	7	7	.500	144	65	47	90	55	3.11
1977–Savannah	Southern	11	81	5	6	.455	83	31	27	45	25	3.00
1977–Richmond	Int'national	16	89	6	5	.545	101	43	33	54	32	3.34
1977–Atlanta	National	2	3	0	0	.000	3	1	1	1	0	3.00
1978–Richmond†	Int'national	22	107	7	9	.438	121	62	58	56	41	4.88
1979–Richmond‡	Int'national	18	34	3	1	.750	22	9	8	36	15	2.12
1979–Atlanta	National	21	19	1	0	1.000	11	5	2	11	10	0.95
1980–Atlanta	National	56	55	3	4	.429	49	20	15	32	22	2.45
Major League Totals		79	77	4	4	.500	63	26	18	44	32	2.10

Selected by Atlanta Braves' organization in 19th round of free-agent draft, June 5, 1973.
†On disabled list, July 18 to August 3, 1978.
‡On disabled list, July 9 to July 19, 1979.

MARK ALLEN BRADLEY

Born December 3, 1956, at Elizabethtown, Ky.
Height, 6.01. Weight, 180.
Throws and bats righthanded.

Led Texas League batters in walks with 97 in 1980.

Year Club	League	Pos.	G.	AB.	R.	H.	2B.	3B.	HR.	RBI.	B.A.	PO.	A.	E.	F.A.
1975—Bellingham	Northw.	S-O-2	76	239	27	61	7	2	2	33	.255	138	140	34	.891
1976—Danville	Midw.	*SS-OF	119	381	73	117	19	3	6	47	.307	197	343	*62	.897
1977—Lodi	Calif.	OF-3B	*140	486	104	160	35	6	16	87	.329	199	16	13	.943
1978—San Antonio	Texas	OF	92	277	49	56	14	1	3	30	.202	123	12	5	.964
1978—Lodi	Calif.	OF	29	109	23	27	2	0	2	11	.248	51	1	1	.981
1979—Lodi	Calif.	OF	31	101	24	28	5	1	1	14	.277	39	3	2	.955
1979—San Antonio	Texas	OF	98	328	46	95	18	4	8	55	.290	163	10	7	.961
1980—San Antonio	Texas	OF	•136	469	95	117	19	6	12	76	.249	241	17	8	.970

Selected by Los Angeles Dodgers' organization in 1st round (24th player selected) of free-agent draft, June 4, 1975.

MARSHALL LEE BRANT

Born September 17, 1955, at Garberville, Calif.
Height, 6.04. Weight, 215.
Throws and bats righthanded.
Attended Santa Rosa Junior College, Santa Rosa, Calif.

Tied for Appalachian League lead in double plays by first basemen with 38 in 1975.
Led Appalachian League in total bases with 144 in 1975.
Led Appalachian League first basemen in assists with 50 and in fielding average with .981 in 1975.
Led Carolina League first basemen in double plays with 101 in 1976.
Led Carolina League in total bases with 238 and in sacrifice flies with 11 in 1976.
Led International League in strikeouts with 119 in 1979.
Led International League first basemen in double plays with 124 in 1979.
Led International League in sacrifice flies with 11 in 1980.
Named Carolina League Most Valuable Player, 1976.

Year Club	League	Pos.	G.	AB.	R.	H.	2B.	3B.	HR.	RBI.	B.A.	PO.	A.	E.	F.A.
1975—Marion	Appal.	1B-C	64	245	49	80	15	5	*13	45	.327	529	51	12	.980
1976—Lynchburg	Carol.	1B	135	476	75	123	*32	7	*23	*93	.258	*1208	69	*15	*.988
1977—Jackson	Texas	*1B-OF	*130	496	71	143	26	6	17	84	.288	*1193	•82	8	.994
1978—Tidewater	Int.	1B	119	389	50	102	23	3	14	54	.262	736	51	10	.987
1979—Tidewater†	Int.	1B	138	488	58	123	21	2	22	65	.252	*1231	74	11	.992
1980—Columbus	Int.	1B	126	409	69	118	22	5	*23	*92	.289	1086	64	8	*.993
1980—New York‡	Amer.	1B	3	6	0	0	0	0	0	0	.000	9	1	0	1.000
Major League Totals			3	6	0	0	0	0	0	0	.000	9	1	0	1.000

Selected by New York Mets' organization in 4th round of free-agent draft, January 9, 1975.
†Sold to New York Yankees' organization, April 1, 1980.
‡Released, November 4, 1980; re-signed by Yankees' organization, January 23, 1981.

STEPHEN RUSSELL BRAUN, III
(Steve)

Born May 8, 1948, at Trenton, N. J.
Height, 5.10. Weight, 180.
Throws right and bats lefthanded.

Led Gulf Coast League second basemen in double plays with 47 in 1967.

Year Club	League	Pos.	G.	AB.	R.	H.	2B.	3B.	HR.	RBI.	B.A.	PO.	A.	E.	F.A.
1966—Sarasota Twins	Gulf C.	2B	45	152	23	35	5	*5	0	15	.230	70	85	*16	.906
1967—Wis. Rapids	Midw.	2B	10	9	1	2	1	0	0	2	.222	0	0	0	.000
1967—Sar. Twins†	Gulf C.	2B	54	184	37	45	6	*8	1	13	.245	*111	*153	*14	.950
1970—Lynchburg	Carol.	*3-2B	118	387	52	108	24	1	4	43	.279	109	253	29	*.926
1971—Minnesota	Amer.	3-2-S-O	128	343	51	87	12	2	5	35	.254	107	193	13	.958
1972—Minnesota	Amer.	3-2-S-O	121	402	40	116	21	0	2	50	.289	110	207	13	.961
1973—Minnesota	Amer.	3B-OF	115	361	46	102	28	5	6	42	.283	86	175	16	.942
1974—Minnesota	Amer.	OF-3B	129	453	53	127	12	1	8	40	.280	195	47	12	.953
1975—Minnesota	Amer.	O-1-3-2	136	453	70	137	18	3	11	45	.302	271	14	10	.966
1976—Minnesota‡	Amer.	OF-3B	122	417	73	120	12	3	3	61	.288	71	32	6	.954
1977—Seattle	Amer.	OF-3B	139	451	51	106	19	1	5	31	.235	186	11	5	.975
1978—Sea.§-Kan. City	Amer.	OF-3B	96	211	27	53	14	1	3	29	.251	68	9	4	.951
1979—Kansas City x	Amer.	OF-3B	58	116	15	31	2	0	4	10	.267	26	4	0	1.000
1980—K.C.y-Tor.z	Amer.	OF-3B	51	78	4	16	2	0	1	10	.205	2	1	0	1.000
1980—Syracuse	Int.	DH	19	61	11	20	3	1	2	11	.328	0	0	0	.000
Major League Totals			1095	3285	430	895	140	16	48	353	.272	1122	693	79	.958

Selected by Minnesota Twins' organization in 10th round of free-agent draft, June 22, 1966.
†On military list, September 6, 1967, to September 23, 1969.
‡Selected by Seattle Mariners in American League expansion draft, November 5, 1976.
§Traded to Kansas City Royals for Pitcher Jim Colborn, June 1, 1978.
xOn supplemental disabled list, July 29 to September 1, 1979.
yReleased, June 2, 1980; signed by Toronto Blue Jays' organization, July 10, 1980.
zGranted free agency, November 5, 1980.

CHAMPIONSHIP SERIES RECORD

Year Club	League	Pos.	G.	AB.	R.	H.	2B.	3B.	HR.	RBI.	B.A.	PO.	A.	E.	F.A.
1978—Kansas City	Amer.	OF-PH	2	5	0	0	0	0	0	0	.000	5	0	0	1.000

FRED LAWRENCE BREINING

Name pronounced BRYN-ing.
Born November 15, 1955, at San Francisco, Calif.
Height, 6.04. Weight, 185.
Throws and bats righthanded.
Hobbies—Cards, backgammon, dominoes and listening to music.
Attended College of San Mateo, San Mateo, Calif.

Year Club	League	G.	IP.	W.	L.	Pct.	H.	R.	ER.	SO.	BB.	ERA.
1974—Niagara Falls†-Auburn‡	NYP	11	38	3	2	.600	47	33	21	16	35	4.97
1975—Charleston	W. Carol.	35	92	3	8	.273	75	57	46	82	60	4.50
1976—Salem	Carolina	31	127	9	4	.692	127	70	49	106	58	3.47
1977—Shreveport	Texas	36	92	3	4	.429	77	37	26	79	41	2.54
1978—Shreveport	Texas	16	56	3	6	.333	53	35	23	50	21	3.70
1978—Columbus	Int'national	21	55	2	2	.500	54	45	39	34	33	6.38
1979—Buffalo§	Eastern	12	82	5	4	.556	77	39	24	73	41	2.63
1979—Shreveport	Texas	10	60	4	2	.667	50	12	8	50	17	1.20
1980—Phoenix	P. Coast	54	100	6	*13	.316	106	57	46	84	56	4.14
1980—San Francisco	National	5	7	0	0	.000	8	4	4	3	4	5.14
Major League Totals		5	7	0	0	.000	8	4	4	3	4	5.14

Selected by Pittsburgh Pirates' organization in 3rd round of free-agent draft, January 9, 1974.
†Loaned to Philadelphia Phillies' organization, July 25, 1974.
‡Returned to Pittsburgh Pirates' organization, September 30, 1974.
§Traded with Pitchers Eddie Whitson and Al Holland to San Francisco Giants for Third Basemen Bill Madlock and Lenny Randle and Pitcher Dave Roberts, June 28, 1979.

THOMAS MARTIN BRENNAN

Born October 30, 1952, at Chicago, Ill.
Height, 6.01. Weight, 180.
Throws and bats righthanded.
Attended Lewis University, Lockport, Ill.; received Bachelor of Arts degree in English.

Year Club	League	G.	IP.	W.	L.	Pct.	H.	R.	ER.	SO.	BB.	ERA.
1974—Oklahoma City	Am. Assoc.	13	50	3	5	.375	46	42	38	44	56	6.79
1975—Oklahoma City	Am. Assoc.	25	122	5	14	.263	149	103	96	52	98	7.08
1976—Williamsport	Eastern	11	61	3	4	.429	63	37	30	22	40	4.43
1976—San Jose	California	16	72	3	9	.250	95	64	46	28	37	5.75
1977—Waterloo	Midwest	9	58	4	3	.571	61	35	32	30	35	4.97
1977—Jersey City	Eastern	4	28	3	1	.750	33	10	8	13	13	2.57
1977—Toledo	Int'national	11	75	1	4	.200	79	36	29	17	31	3.48
1978—Portland	P. Coast	27	172	10	8	.556	202	108	87	82	32	4.55
1979—Tacoma	P. Coast	26	176	12	7	.632	176	70	62	102	38	3.17
1980—Tacoma	P. Coast	24	152	9	3	.750	167	48	42	77	29	2.49

Selected by Cleveland Indians' organization in 1st round (fourth player selected) of free-agent draft, June 5, 1974.

GEORGE HOWARD BRETT

Born May 15, 1953, at Wheeling, W. Va.
Height, 6.00. Weight, 200.
Throws right and bats lefthanded.
Hobbies—Horses and surfing.
Attended Longview Community College, Lee's Summit, Mo. and
El Camino College, Torrance, Calif.

Brother of Ken Brett, pitcher with Kansas City Royals, John Brett, former third baseman in Boston Red Sox' organization, and Bob Brett, former outfielder in Kansas City Royals' organization.

Established major league record for most consecutive games, three or more hits, season (6), May 8 through 13, 1976.

Tied major league record for most consecutive seasons leading major league in triples (2).

Established American League record for fewest putouts by third baseman for leader in most putouts, season (140), 1976.

Became sixth major-league player to collect 20 or more doubles, triples and home runs in one season, 1979.

Hit three home runs in one game, vs. Texas Rangers, July 22, 1979.

Hit for the cycle, vs. Baltimore Orioles, May 28, 1979.

Major League stolen bases: 1973 (0), 1974 (8), 1975 (13), 1976 (21), 1977 (14), 1978 (23), 1979 (17), 1980 (15). Total—111.

Led California League in sacrifice hits with 8 in 1972.

Led American League in total bases with 298 in 1976.

Led American League third baseman in putouts with 140 in 1976.

Led American League third basemen in errors with 30 in 1979.

Led American League in slugging percentage with .664 in 1980.

Named third baseman on THE SPORTING NEWS American League All-Star Team, 1976, 1979 and 1980.

Named third baseman on the THE SPORTING NEWS Silver Bat Team, 1980.

Named American League Player of the Year by THE SPORTING NEWS, 1980.

Named Major League Player of the Year by THE SPORTING NEWS, 1980.

Named American League Most Valuable Player by Baseball Writers' Association of America, 1980.

Named Man of the Year by THE SPORTING NEWS, 1980.

Year Club	League	Pos.	G.	AB.	R.	H.	2B.	3B.	HR.	RBI.	B.A.	PO.	A.	E.	F.A.
1971—Billings	Pion.	SS-3B	68	258	44	75	8	5	5	44	.291	87	140	28	.890
1972—San Jose†	Calif.	*3-S-2	117	431	66	118	13	5	10	68	.274	101	*213	*30	.913

Year Club League	Pos.	G.	AB.	R.	H.	2B.	3B.	HR.	RBI.	B.A.	PO.	A.	E.	F.A.
1973—Omaha..............A.A.	3B-OF	117	405	66	115	16	4	8	64	.284	92	219	26	.923
1973—Kansas City.......Amer.	3B	13	40	2	5	2	0	0	0	.125	9	28	1	.974
1974—Omaha..............A.A.	3B	16	64	9	17	2	0	2	14	.266	8	31	4	.907
1974—Kansas City.......Amer.	3B-SS	133	457	49	129	21	5	2	47	.282	102	279	21	.948
1975—Kansas City.......Amer.	•3B-SS	159	*634	84	*195	35	•13	11	89	.308	132	356	•26	.949
1976—Kansas City.......Amer.	3B-SS	159	*645	94	*215	34	*14	7	67	*.333	146	350	26	.950
1977—Kansas City.......Amer.	3B-SS	139	564	105	176	32	13	22	88	.312	115	325	21	.954
1978—Kansas City‡.....Amer.	3B-SS	128	510	79	150	*45	8	9	62	.294	104	289	16	.961
1979—Kansas City ......Amer.	3B-1B	154	645	119	*212	42	*20	23	107	.329	176	378	31	.947
1980—Kansas City§.....Amer.	3B-1B	117	449	87	175	33	9	24	118	*.390	107	256	17	.955
Major League Totals		1002	3944	619	1257	244	82	98	578	.319	891	2261	159	.952

Selected by Kansas City Royals' organization in 2nd round of free-agent draft, June 8, 1971.

†On disabled list, April 29 to May 11, 1972.

‡On supplemental disabled list, May 4 to May 19 and July 27 to August 14, 1978.

CHAMPIONSHIP SERIES RECORD

Established Championship Series records for most runs, total Series (16); most three-base hits, total Series (4); most three-base hits, Series (2), 1977; most runs, four-game Series (7), 1978; most long hits, total Series (13).

Tied Championship Series records for most home runs, game (3), October 6, 1978; most times home run as leadoff batter, start of game (1), October 6, 1978; most home runs, total Series (6); most Series, two or more home runs (2).

Established American League Championship Series records for highest slugging average, total Series, ten or more games and 30 or more at bats (.791); most home runs, four-game Series (3), 1978; highest slugging average, four-game Series (1.056), 1978; most hits, four-game Series (7), 1978; most total bases, four-game Series (19), 1978; most long hits, four-game Series (5), 1978; most long hits, two consecutive games, one series (4), October 6 and 7, 1978; most total bases, game (12), October 6, 1978; most total bases, total Series (53).

Tied American League Championship Series records for most at bats, four-game Series (18), 1978; most runs, game (3), October 6, 1978; most long hits, game (3), October 6, 1978; most consecutive games, one or more hits (9); most home runs, three-game Series (2), 1980; most Series, one or more home runs (3).

Year Club League	Pos.	G.	AB.	R.	H.	2B.	3B.	HR.	RBI.	B.A.	PO.	A.	E.	F.A.
1976—Kansas City.......Amer.	3B	5	18	4	8	1	1	1	5	.444	3	7	3	.769
1977—Kansas City.......Amer.	3B	5	20	2	6	0	2	0	2	.300	5	12	2	.895
1978—Kansas City.......Amer.	3B	4	18	7	7	1	1	3	3	.389	3	8	1	.917
1980—Kansas City ......Amer.	3B	3	11	3	3	1	0	2	4	.273	2	7	0	1.000
Championship Series Totals.............		17	67	16	24	3	4	6	14	.358	13	34	6	.887

WORLD SERIES RECORD

Year Club League	Pos.	G.	AB.	R.	H.	2B.	3B.	HR.	RBI.	B.A.	PO.	A.	E.	F.A.
1980—Kansas City ......Amer.	3B	6	24	3	9	2	1	1	3	.375	4	17	1	.955

ALL-STAR GAME RECORD

Year League	Pos.	AB.	R.	H.	2B.	3B.	HR.	RBI.	B.A.	PO.	A.	E.	F.A.
1976—American............................	3B	2	0	0	0	0	0	0	.000	0	1	0	1.000
1977—American	3B	2	0	0	0	0	0	0	.000	2	1	0	1.000
1978—American	3B	3	1	2	1	0	0	2	.667	0	2	0	1.000
1979—American	3B	3	1	0	0	0	0	0	.000	1	2	0	1.000
All-Star Game Totals		10	2	2	1	0	0	2	.200	3	6	0	1.000

Named to American League All-Star Team in 1980; replaced due to injury.

KENNETH ALVEN BRETT
(Ken)

Born September 18, 1948, at Brooklyn, N. Y.
Height, 5.11. Weight, 190.
Throws and bats lefthanded.
Hobbies—Golf and photography.
Attended Boston University, Boston, Mass.
Brother of George Brett, Kansas City Royals' third baseman, John Brett, former third baseman in Boston Red Sox' organization and Bob Brett, former outfielder in Kansas City Royals' organization.

Established major league record for most consecutive games, home runs by pitcher, 4, June 9-13-18-23, 1973.

Tied for International League lead in wild pitches with 12 in 1969.

Received reported $85,000 bonus to sign with Boston Red Sox, 1966.

Year Club	League	G.	IP.	W.	L.	Pct.	H.	R.	ER.	SO.	BB.	ERA.
1966—Oneonta..............................NYP	14	62	1	4	.200	75	49	40	53	39	5.81
1967—Winston-Salem ....Carolina	11	64	4	4	.500	42	19	16	77	38	2.25
1967—Pittsfield.............................Eastern	18	125	10	7	.588	87	30	25	142	59	1.80
1967—Boston ....American	1	2	0	0	.000	3	1	1	2	0	4.50
1968—Louisville†..........................Int'national	9	29	2	1	.667	25	12	10	20	13	3.10
1969—Louisville...........................Int'national	25	129	7	5	.583	122	58	47	81	56	3.28
1969—Boston ....American	8	39	2	3	.400	41	24	23	23	22	5.31
1970—Boston ....American	41	139	8	9	.471	118	71	63	155	79	4.08
1971—Boston‡..............................American	29	59	0	3	.000	57	38	35	57	35	5.34
1972—Milwaukee§.........................American	26	133	7	12	.368	121	76	67	74	49	4.53
1973—Philadelphia x ....National	31	212	13	9	.591	206	91	81	111	74	3.44

Year Club	League	G.	IP.	W.	L.	Pct.	H.	R.	ER.	SO.	BB.	ERA.
1974–Pittsburgh	National	27	191	13	9	.591	192	81	70	96	52	3.30
1975–Pittsburgh yz	National	23	118	9	5	.643	110	47	44	47	43	3.36
1976–N.Y. a-Chicago	American	29	203	10	12	.455	173	82	74	92	76	3.28
1977–Chi. b-Calif.	American	34	225	13	14	.481	258	120	113	80	53	4.52
1978–California c	American	31	100	3	5	.375	100	60	55	43	42	4.95
1979–Minnesota d	American	9	13	0	0	.000	16	7	7	3	6	4.85
1979–Los Angeles e	National	30	47	4	3	.571	52	20	18	12	13	3.45
1980–Omaha	Am. Assoc.	5	9	0	0	.000	11	5	4	2	4	4.00
1980–Kansas City	American	8	13	0	0	.000	8	0	0	4	5	0.00
American League Totals		216	926	43	58	.426	895	479	438	533	367	4.26
National League Totals		111	568	39	26	.600	560	239	213	267	181	3.38
Major League Totals		327	1494	82	84	.494	1455	718	651	800	548	4.26

Selected by Boston Red Sox' organization in 4th round of free-agent draft, June 22, 1966.

†On disabled list, May 16 to May 31 and June 13 to July 17, 1968.

‡Traded with Catcher Don Pavletich, Pitcher Jim Lonborg, First Baseman George Scott and Outfielders Billy Conigliaro and Joe Lahoud to Milwaukee Brewers for Pitchers Marty Pattin and Lew Krausse and Outfielders Tommy Harper and Pat Skrable, October 11, 1971.

§Traded with Pitchers Jim Lonborg, Ken Sanders and Earl Stephenson to Philadelphia Phillies for Infielders Don Money and John Vukovich and Pitcher Billy Champion, October 31, 1972.

xTraded to Pittsburgh Pirates for Infielder Dave Cash, September 18, 1973.

yOn disabled list, March 25 to April 16 and June 5 to June 26, 1975.

zTraded with Pitcher Dock Ellis and Second Baseman Willie Randolph to New York Yankees for Pitcher Doc Medich, December 11, 1975.

aTraded with Outfielder Rich Coggins to Chicago White Sox for Outfielder Carlos May, May 18, 1976.

bTraded to California Angels for Pitchers Don Kirkwood and John Verhoeven and Infielder John Flannery (latter assigned from Salinas to Iowa roster), June 15, 1977.

cReleased, April 2, 1979; signed by Minnesota Twins, April 30, 1979.

dReleased, June 4, 1979; signed by Los Angeles Dodgers, June 11, 1979.

eReleased, March 27, 1980; signed by Kansas City Royals' organization, August 11, 1980.

CHAMPIONSHIP SERIES RECORD

Year Club	League	G.	IP.	W.	L.	Pct.	H.	R.	ER.	SO.	BB.	ERA.
1974–Pittsburgh	National	1	2⅓	0	0	.000	3	2	2	1	2	7.71
1975–Pittsburgh	National	2	2⅓	0	0	.000	1	0	0	1	0	0.00
Championship Series Totals		3	4⅔	0	0	.000	4	2	2	2	2	3.86

WORLD SERIES RECORD

Youngest World Series pitcher (19 years, 20 days), October 8, 1967.

Year Club	League	G.	IP.	W.	L.	Pct.	H.	R.	ER.	SO.	BB.	ERA.
1967–Boston	American	2	1⅓	0	0	.000	0	0	0	1	1	0.00

ALL-STAR GAME RECORD

Year League		IP.	W.	L.	Pct.	H.	R.	ER.	SO.	BB.	ERA.
1974–National		2	1	0	1.000	1	0	0	0	1	0.00

DANIEL LEE BRIGGS
(Dan)

Born November 18, 1952, at Scotia, Calif.
Height, 6.00. Weight, 180.
Throws and bats lefthanded.
Attended University of California at Berkeley, Berkeley, Calif.

Tied major league record for most unassisted double plays by first baseman, game (2), April 16, 1977.
Led Pacific Coast League in total bases with 286 in 1978.

Year Club	League	Pos.	G.	AB.	R.	H.	2B.	3B.	HR.	RBI.	B.A.	PO.	A.	E.	F.A.
1970–Idaho Falls	Pion.	*1B-P	62	190	44	58	11	1	4	34	.305	389	31	*24	.946
1971–Quad Cities	Midw.	1B-P	29	82	8	14	2	0	0	5	.171	177	8	7	.964
1971–Idaho Falls	Pion.	1B	51	180	25	46	5	7	3	22	.256	401	26	*21	.953
1972–Stockton	Calif.	●OF-1B	131	449	66	104	14	3	18	56	.232	383	23	●27	.938
1973–Salinas	Calif.	1B	101	360	62	106	18	5	11	59	.294	854	55	13	.986
1973–El Paso	Tex.	1B-F	40	150	22	47	12	2	5	18	.313	306	20	9	.973
1974–El Paso	Tex.	1B	53	216	49	76	18	5	13	55	.352	454	31	12	.975
1974–Salt Lake C.	P.C.	1B	83	317	40	88	13	10	4	56	.278	726	49	15	.981
1975–Salt Lake C.†	P.C.	1B-OF	80	260	45	84	12	2	1	37	.323	352	36	7	.982
1975–California	Amer.	1B-OF	13	31	3	7	1	0	1	3	.226	49	1	2	.961
1976–Salt Lake C.	P.C.	1B-OF	56	219	41	66	14	3	7	42	.301	398	34	6	.986
1976–California	Amer.	1B-OF	77	248	19	53	13	2	1	14	.214	358	26	5	.987
1977–Salt Lake City‡	P.C.	1B-OF	26	92	20	31	8	1	4	18	.337	183	16	3	.985
1977–Indianapolis§	Int.	OF	26	90	11	24	3	2	0	16	.267	48	2	4	.926
1977–California x	Amer.	1B-OF	59	74	6	12	2	0	1	4	.162	154	14	2	.988
1978–Portland	P.C.	OF	134	509	101	168	*42	8	20	109	.330	313	11	10	.970
1978–Cleveland y	Amer.	OF	15	49	4	8	0	1	1	1	.163	38	1	0	1.000
1979–San Diego z	Nat.	OF-1B	104	227	34	47	4	3	8	30	.207	393	31	7	.984
1980–Denver	A.A.	OF-1B	110	427	59	135	25	3	13	74	.316	214	10	3	.987
American League Totals			164	402	32	80	16	3	4	22	.199	599	42	9	.986
National League Totals			104	227	34	47	4	3	8	30	.207	393	31	7	.984
Major League Totals			268	629	66	127	20	6	12	52	.202	992	73	16	.985

Selected by California Angels' organization in 2nd round of free-agent draft, June 4, 1970.
†On disabled list, June 2 to July 27, 1975.
‡Loaned to Indianapolis, June 16, 1977.
§Recalled, July 16, 1977.
xGranted free agency, November 2, 1977; signed by Cleveland Indians' organization, March 14, 1978.
yTraded to San Diego Padres for a player to be named later, March 30, 1979; Cleveland acquired Second Baseman Mike Champion to complete deal, April 3, 1979.
zTraded with Second Baseman Bill Almon to Montreal Expos for Second Baseman Dave Cash, November 27, 1979.

PITCHING RECORD

Year—Club	League	G.	IP.	W.	L.	Pct.	H.	R.	ER.	SO.	BB.	ERA.
1970—Idaho Falls	Pioneer	7	28	2	0	1.000	20	8	4	33	19	1.29
1971—Quad Cities	Midwest	1	2	0	0	.000	2	0	0	3	1	0.00
1978—Portland	P. Coast	2	3	0	0	.000	3	3	2	3	4	6.00

JOSE OSCAR BRITO

Born September 28, 1959, at Salcedo, Dominican Republic
Height, 6.02. Weight, 160.
Throws and bats righthanded.

Year—Club	League	G.	IP.	W.	L.	Pct.	H.	R.	ER.	SO.	BB.	ERA.
1977—Eugene	Northwest	15	90	6	6	.500	119	66	52	69	26	5.20
1978—Shelby	W. Carol.	30	155	10	8	.556	132	74	63	107	67	3.66
1979—Tampa	Florida St.	28	167	11	7	.611	126	57	45	154	82	2.43
1980—Waterbury	Eastern	25	172	12	6	.667	125	66	60	175	75	3.14

Signed as free agent by Cincinnati Reds' organization, March 2, 1977.

DOUGLAS RICHARD BRITT

Born November 2, 1957, at Orange, Calif.
Height, 6.05. Weight, 185.
Throws and bats lefthanded.

Year—Club	League	G.	IP.	W.	L.	Pct.	H.	R.	ER.	SO.	BB.	ERA.
1977—Brad. Braves-Sar. W. Sox	G. Coast	10	22	0	1	.000	25	10	9	13	13	3.68
1978—Charleston	W. Carol.	34	76	1	7	.125	69	76	56	54	63	6.63
1979—Salem	Carolina	35	78	3	8	.273	66	36	33	57	35	3.81
1980—Buffalo†	Eastern	8	11	1	0	1.000	11	5	4	3	11	3.27

Signed as free agent by Pittsburgh Pirates' organization, January 18, 1977.
†On disabled list, May 14 to September 29, 1980.

ANTHONY JOHN BRIZZOLARA
(Tony)

Born January 14, 1957, at Santa Monica, Calif.
Height, 6.05. Weight, 210.
Throws and bats righthanded.
Attended University of Texas, Austin, Tex.

Led International League in games started with 30 in 1980.

Year—Club	League	G.	IP.	W.	L.	Pct.	H.	R.	ER.	SO.	BB.	ERA.
1977—Kingsport	Ap'lachian	6	27	3	2	.600	21	8	7	27	10	2.33
1978—Greenwood	W. Carol.	3	20	3	0	1.000	9	3	2	21	8	0.90
1978—Savannah†	Southern	10	70	4	4	.500	57	19	15	55	21	1.93
1978—Richmond	Int'national	9	50	3	4	.429	57	34	33	40	18	5.94
1979—Richmond	Int'national	9	66	4	2	.667	47	15	14	42	28	1.91
1979—Atlanta	National	20	107	6	9	.400	133	70	63	64	33	5.30
1980—Richmond	Int'national	30	•206	10	•15	.400	198	102	85	128	56	3.71
Major League Totals		20	107	6	9	.400	133	70	63	64	33	5.30

Selected by Atlanta Braves' organization in 2nd round of free-agent draft, June 7, 1977.
†On disabled list, June 20 to June 29, 1978.

JOHN ANTHONY BROHAMER, JR.

Name pronounced Bro-hammer.

(Jack)

Born February 26, 1950, at Maywood, Calif.
Height, 5.09. Weight, 170.
Throws right and bats lefthanded.
Hobbies—Hunting, fishing and golf.
Attended Golden West College, Huntington Beach, Calif.

Tied for California League lead in sacrifice flies with 8 in 1969.

Year—Club	League	Pos.	G.	AB.	R.	H.	2B.	3B.	HR.	RBI.	B.A.	PO.	A.	E.	F.A.
1968—Rock Hill	W. Car.	SS	78	296	62	86	21	5	3	33	.291	138	206	23	.937
1968—Reno	Calif.	2B-SS	32	101	11	27	6	1	2	9	.267	49	50	8	.925
1969—Reno	Calif.	•SS-2	133	501	75	139	19	4	10	64	.277	161	•396	45	.925
1970—Savannah	South.	SS-2	75	269	31	63	17	5	4	22	.234	105	188	17	.945
1970—Wichita	A.A.	3-SS-2	40	146	24	34	7	1	2	17	.233	58	78	8	.944
1971—Wichita†	A.A.	2-3-SS	103	355	45	93	14	5	4	44	.262	172	245	8	.981

— 61 —

Year	Club	League	Pos.	G.	AB.	R.	H.	2B.	3B.	HR.	RBI.	B.A.	PO.	A.	E.	F.A.
1972—Cleveland..........Amer.			2B-3B	136	527	49	123	13	2	5	35	.233	285	395	16	.977
1973—Cleveland..........Amer.			2B	102	300	29	66	12	1	4	29	.220	215	279	15	.971
1974—Cleveland‡ ....Amer.			2B	101	315	33	85	11	1	2	30	.270	203	269	6	.987
1975—Cleveland§x.......Amer.			2B	69	217	15	53	5	0	6	16	.244	166	162	8	.976
1976—Chicago ....Amer.			2B-3B	119	354	33	89	12	2	7	40	.251	265	338	10	.984
1977—Chicago y ....Amer.			3B-2B	59	152	26	39	10	3	2	20	.257	54	100	8	.951
1978—Boston ....Amer.			3B-2B	81	244	34	57	14	1	1	25	.234	64	103	5	.971
1979—Boston z...........Amer.			2B-3B	64	192	25	51	7	1	1	11	.266	74	140	5	.977
1980—Bos.a-Clev. ....Amer.			2B-3B	74	199	18	50	7	1	2	21	.251	89	142	7	.971
Major League Totals				805	2500	262	613	91	12	30	227	.245	1415	1928	80	.977

Selected by Cleveland Indians' organization in 34th round of free-agent draft, June 6, 1967.
†On disabled list, May 17 to June 1, 1971.
‡On supplemental disabled list, July 31 to August 15 and August 19 to September 4, 1974.
§On supplemental disabled list, June 4 to July 4, 1975.
xTraded to Chicago White Sox for Infielder Larvell Blanks, December 12, 1975.
yGranted free agency, October 20, 1977; signed by Boston Red Sox, November 30, 1977.
zOn disabled list, August 27 to September 13, 1979.
aSold to Cleveland Indians, June 20, 1980.

THOMAS DALE BROOKENS

Born August 10, 1953, at Chambersburg, Pa.
Height, 5.10. Weight, 170.
Throws and bats righthanded.
Hobbies—Hunting and darts.
Attended Mansfield State College, Mansfield, Pa.

Twin brother of Tim Brookens, former infielder-outfielder in Detroit Tigers' organization; and cousin of Ike Brookens, former pitcher in Detroit Tigers' organization.

Tied American League record for most errors by third baseman, game (4), September 6, 1980.

Year	Club	League	Pos.	G.	AB.	R.	H.	2B.	3B.	HR.	RBI.	B.A.	PO.	A.	E.	F.A.
1975—Montgomery......South.			SS	100	329	37	73	11	2	7	36	.222	139	298	31	.934
1976—Montgomery......South.			2B	137	492	76	127	22	5	11	56	.258	310	*389	*25	.965
1977—Evansville ........A.A.			3B-2B	118	440	70	127	22	5	8	52	.289	132	250	25	.939
1978—Evansville† .......A.A.			3B-2B-1B	65	206	27	58	11	1	6	25	.282	76	100	20	.898
1979—Evansville ........A.A.			3B-2B	77	265	51	81	23	2	14	46	.306	71	166	16	.937
1979—Detroit.............Amer.			3B-2B	60	190	23	50	5	2	4	21	.263	76	141	11	.952
1980—Detroit.............Amer.			*3-2-S	151	509	64	140	25	9	10	66	.275	127	307	*29	.937
Major League Totals......................				211	699	87	190	30	11	14	87	.272	203	448	40	.942

Selected by Detroit Tigers' organization in 1st round (fourth player selected) of free-agent draft, January 9, 1975.
†On disabled list, April 14 to May 9 and June 4 to June 21, 1978.

HUBERT BROOKS JR.
(Hubie)

Born September 24, 1956, at Los Angeles, Calif.
Height, 6.00. Weight, 178.
Throws and bats righthanded.
Attended Mesa Community College, Mesa, Ariz., and Arizona State University,
Tempe, Ariz.; received Bachelor of Science degree.
Cousin of Donnie Moore, pitcher in St. Louis Cardinals' organization.

Year	Club	League	Pos.	G.	AB.	R.	H.	2B.	3B.	HR.	RBI.	B.A.	PO.	A.	E.	F.A.
1978—Jackson ....Texas			S-O-3	45	153	19	33	8	1	3	16	.216	49	84	14	.905
1979—Jackson ....Texas			3B-SS	112	406	68	124	21	2	3	28	.305	92	218	29	.942
1979—Tidewater ....Int.			SS-3B	5	15	1	6	1	0	1	3	.400	4	8	1	.923
1980—Tidewater ....Int.			O-3-S	113	417	50	124	18	5	3	50	.297	152	90	18	.931
1980—New York ....Nat.			3B	24	81	8	25	2	1	1	10	.309	16	40	2	.966
Major League Totals......................				24	81	8	25	2	1	1	10	.309	16	40	2	.966

Selected by Montreal Expos' organization in 19th round of free-agent draft, June 5, 1974.
Selected by Kansas City Royals' organization in secondary phase of free-agent draft, January 7, 1976.
Selected by Chicago White Sox' organization in secondary phase of free-agent draft, June 8, 1976.
Selected by Oakland A's organization in secondary phase of free-agent draft, January 11, 1977.
Selected by Chicago White Sox' organization in secondary phase of free-agent draft, June 7, 1977.
Selected by New York Mets' organization in 1st round (3rd player selected) of free-agent draft, June 6, 1978.

MARK STEVEN BROUHARD
Name pronounced BRO-hard

Born May 22, 1956, at Burbank, Calif.
Height, 6.01. Weight, 210.
Throws and bats righthanded.
Attended Pierce Junior College, Woodland Hills, Calif.

Led Texas League in total bases with 308 and in slugging percentage with .596 in 1979.
Named Texas League Player of the Year, 1979.

Year	Club	League	Pos.	G.	AB.	R.	H.	2B.	3B.	HR.	RBI.	B.A.	PO.	A.	E.	F.A.
1976—Idaho Falls ....Pion.			OF-1B	69	255	43	80	5	8	7	57	.314	46	2	5	.906
1977—Salinas ....Calif.			OF	136	507	85	141	27	3	16	87	.278	216	8	9	.961

Year	Club	League	Pos.	G.	AB.	R.	H.	2B.	3B.	HR.	RBI.	B.A.	PO.	A.	E.	F.A.
1978—Salinas	....	Calif.	OF-3B	133	532	86	165	29	5	21	91	.310	230	10	7	.972
1979—El Paso†	....	Texas	OF	132	517	97	181	29	7	*28	*107	.350	171	10	5	.973
1980—Milwaukee	....	Amer.	OF-1B	45	125	12	29	6	0	5	16	.232	77	4	1	.988
Major League Totals	....			45	125	17	29	6	0	5	16	.232	77	4	1	.988

Selected by California Angels' organization in 4th round of free-agent draft, January 7, 1976.
†Drafted by Milwaukee Brewers, December 3, 1979.

DARRELL WAYNE BROWN

Born October 29, 1955, at Oklahoma City, Okla.
Height, 6.00. Weight, 180.
Throws and bats righthanded.
Attended East Los Angeles Junior College, Monterey Park, Calif. and
California State University at Los Angeles, Los Angeles, Calif.

Year	Club	League	Pos.	G.	AB.	R.	H.	2B.	3B.	HR.	RBI.	B.A.	PO.	A.	E.	F.A.
1977—Lakeland	....	Fla. St.	OF	59	166	13	44	2	2	0	18	.265	84	4	3	.967
1978—Montgomery	.....	South.	OF	54	212	23	56	1	5	1	12	.264	94	4	6	.942
1978—Lakeland	....	Fla. St.	OF-SS	70	224	31	56	3	1	0	13	.250	138	53	12	.941
1979—Evansville	....	A.A.	OF	23	43	8	11	0	0	1	4	.256	33	0	1	.970
1979—Montgomery	.....	South.	OF	95	384	40	98	17	2	4	32	.255	232	7	6	.976
1980—Evansville	....	A.A.	OF	123	498	62	138	15	6	3	43	.277	288	5	8	.973

Selected by Houston Astros' organization in 1st round (13th player selected) of free-agent draft, January 9, 1975.
Selected by San Francisco Giants' organization in secondary phase of free-agent draft, June 4, 1975.
Selected by Milwaukee Brewers' organization in secondary phase of free-agent draft, June 8, 1976.
Selected by Detroit Tigers' organization in 3rd round of free-agent draft, June 7, 1977.

ROGERS LEE BROWN
(Bobby)

Born May 25, 1954, at Turbeville, Va.
Height, 6.01. Weight, 198.
Throws right and bats right and lefthanded.
Shared International League Player of the Year, 1979.

Year	Club	League	Pos.	G.	AB.	R.	H.	2B.	3B.	HR.	RBI.	B.A.	PO.	A.	E.	F.A.
1972—Bluefield	....	Appal.	OF	49	172	29	44	11	2	3	27	.256	53	4	8	.877
1973—Miami	....	Fla. St.	OF	100	279	35	79	8	3	3	17	.283	88	5	7	.930
1974—Miami	....	Fla. St.	OF	29	94	9	18	3	1	0	2	.191	50	1	4	.927
1974—Lodi	....	Calif.	OF-1B	95	359	44	108	7	6	8	58	.301	148	11	8	.952
1975—Lodi	....	Calif.	OF-1-3	133	491	77	146	15	8	6	64	.297	178	10	12	.940
1975—Asheville†	....	South.	OF	6	27	5	7	0	0	0	2	.259	13	2	0	1.000
1976—Peninsula	....	Carol.	O-3-1	102	393	68	137	18	*10	8	41	*.349	299	89	21	.949
1977—Reading	....	East.	OF	56	238	38	69	12	5	5	28	.290	151	2	5	.968
1977—Oklahoma City	..	A.A.	OF	79	312	53	98	12	5	4	22	.314	78	184	6	.969
1978—Oklahoma City‡	A.A.	OF-3B	50	216	31	62	10	6	4	18	.287	105	20	7	.947
1978—Tacoma§	....	P.C.	OF	66	261	51	81	11	4	10	39	.310	151	2	7	.956
1979—Tor.y-N.Y.x	.....	Amer.	OF	34	78	8	17	3	1	0	3	.218	64	0	3	.955
1979—San Juan	....	Int.-Am.	PR	10	0	1	0	0	0	0	1	.000	0	0	0	.000
1979—Columbus	....	Int.	OF	70	258	53	90	14	3	8	41	.349	166	7	3	.983
1980—New York	....	Amer.	OF	137	412	65	107	12	5	14	47	.260	303	7	9	.972
Major League Totals	....			171	490	73	124	15	6	14	50	.253	367	7	12	.969

Selected by Baltimore Orioles' organization in 11th round of free-agent draft, June 6, 1972.
†Released April 8, 1976. Signed by Peninsula (Philadelphia Phillies' organization), May 14, 1976.
‡Traded with Outfielder Jay Johnstone to New York Yankees for Pitcher Rawly Eastwick, June 14, 1978.
§Drafted from New York Yankees' organization by New York Mets, December 4, 1978.
xSold on waivers to Toronto Blue Jays, March 25, 1979.
ySold to New York Yankees' organization, April 19, 1979.
zLoaned to San Juan, April 20, 1979; returned, May 1, 1979.

CHAMPIONSHIP SERIES RECORD

Year	Club	League	Pos.	G.	AB.	R.	H.	2B.	3B.	HR.	RBI.	B.A.	PO.	A.	E.	F.A.
1980—New York	....	Amer.	OF	3	10	1	0	0	0	0	0	.000	7	0	0	1.000

SCOTT EDWARD BROWN

Born August 31, 1956, at DeQuincy, La.
Height, 6.06. Weight, 220.
Throws and bats righthanded.

Year	Club	League	G.	IP.	W.	L.	Pct.	H.	R.	ER.	SO.	BB.	ERA.
1975—Billings	....	Pioneer	10	18	0	1	.000	25	25	13	13	21	6.50
1976—Eugene	....	Northwest	16	102	6	5	.545	77	42	29	84	62	2.56
1977—Tampa	....	Florida St.	26	153	6	12	.333	157	85	65	82	65	3.82
1978—Tampa	....	Florida St.	17	117	7	6	.538	92	32	17	73	22	1.31
1978—Nashville	....	Southern	13	66	4	3	.571	82	36	33	47	29	4.50
1979—Nashville†	....	Southern	27	131	9	2	.818	103	40	35	109	43	*2.40
1980—Indianapolis	....	Am. Assoc.	40	123	6	7	.462	114	52	47	73	49	3.44

Selected by Cincinnati Reds' organization in 4th round of free-agent draft, June 4, 1975.
†On disabled list, July 17 to August 6, 1979.

STEVEN ELBERT BROWN
(Steve)

Born February 12, 1957, at San Francisco, Calif.
Height, 6.05. Weight, 200.
Throws and bats righthanded.
Attended University of California at Davis, Davis, Calif.
Tied for Texas League lead in complete games with 16 in 1980.

Year Club	League	G.	IP.	W.	L.	Pct.	H.	R.	ER.	SO.	BB.	ERA.
1978–Idaho Falls	Pioneer	14	99	7	3	.700	90	40	31	*95	31	2.82
1979–Salinas	California	17	123	10	5	.667	109	52	33	89	57	*2.41
1979–El Paso	Texas	10	73	4	4	.500	80	45	43	51	26	5.30
1980–El Paso	Texas	27	*209	14	•12	.538	215	103	85	103	81	3.66

Signed as free agent by California Angels' organization, June 9, 1978.

GLENN EDWARD BRUMMER

Born November 23, 1954, at Olney, Ill.
Height, 6.00. Weight, 185.
Throws and bats righthanded.
Attended Lake Land College, Mattoon, Ill.
Brother of Tom Brummer, infielder in Boston Red Sox' organization.
Led American Association catchers in passed balls with 13 in 1980.

Year Club	League	Pos.	G.	AB.	R.	H.	2B.	3B.	HR.	RBI.	B.A.	PO.	A.	E.	F.A.
1974–Sara. Cards	Gulf C.	C	24	69	7	20	4	1	0	7	.290	118	15	2	.985
1975–Johnson City	Appal.	C	50	183	27	47	7	1	5	23	.257	278	23	9	.971
1976–St. Petersburg	Fla. St.	C	113	367	41	96	14	1	0	41	.262	*644	*77	10	.986
1977–Arkansas	Texas	C	15	52	2	9	1	0	0	2	.173	97	6	6	.945
1977–St. Petersburg	Fla. St.	C	21	51	7	11	1	0	0	1	.216	113	5	1	.992
1977–Lynchburg	Carol.	C	40	137	16	45	3	2	0	16	.328	190	12	2	.990
1978–Arkansas	Texas	C	44	92	11	25	2	0	0	11	.272	135	14	3	.980
1979–Springfield†	A.A.	C	44	104	19	22	2	0	1	11	.212	196	12	4	.981
1980–Springfield	A.A.	C	110	323	36	83	12	0	1	40	.257	*562	55	12	.981

Signed as free agent by St. Louis Cardinals' organization, May 20, 1974.
†On disabled list, July 17 to September 1, 1979.

THOMAS ANDREW BRUNANSKY
(Tom)

Born August 20, 1960, at West Covina, Calif.
Height, 6.04. Weight, 205.
Throws and bats righthanded.
Tied for Texas League lead in double plays by outfielders with 4 in 1980.

Year Club	League	Pos.	G.	AB.	R.	H.	2B.	3B.	HR.	RBI.	B.A.	PO.	A.	E.	F.A.
1978–Idaho Falls	Pioneer	OF	48	190	55	63	14	4	6	45	.332	85	1	8	.915
1979–Salinas	Calif.	OF	*140	485	85	131	23	1	23	76	.270	279	11	6	.980
1980–El Paso	Texas	OF	128	495	103	160	24	8	24	97	.323	306	17	*14	.958
1980–Salt Lake City	P.C.	OF	9	32	7	11	2	2	1	8	.344	28	1	0	1.000

Selected by California Angels' organization in 1st round (13th player selected) of free-agent draft, June 6, 1978.

WARREN SCOTT BRUSSTAR

Name pronounced BROO-Stur.
Born February 2, 1952, at Oakland, Calif.
Height, 6.03. Weight, 200.
Throws and bats righthanded.
Hobbies–Sports and music.
Attended Napa Junior College, Napa, Calif., and Fresno State
University, Fresno, Calif.
Led Carolina League pitchers in wild pitches with 23 in 1975.
Led Eastern League pitchers in complete games with 19 in 1976.
Tied for Eastern League lead among pitchers in games started with 27 and in wild pitches with 13 in 1976.

Year Club	League	G.	IP.	W.	L.	Pct.	H.	R.	ER.	SO.	BB.	ERA.
1974–Spartanburg	W. Carol.	22	42	2	4	.333	39	23	9	34	24	1.93
1975–Rocky Mount†	Carolina	25	162	•14	8	.636	117	61	40	123	94	2.22
1976–Reading	Eastern	27	*199	10	*17	.370	167	83	60	119	*90	2.71
1977–Oklahoma City	Am. Assoc.	2	6	0	1	.000	3	3	1	5	5	1.50
1977–Philadelphia	National	46	71	7	2	.778	64	26	21	46	24	2.66
1978–Philadelphia	National	58	89	6	3	.667	74	25	23	60	30	2.33
1979–Philadelphia‡	National	13	14	1	0	1.000	23	12	11	3	2	7.07
1979–Reading	Eastern	1	2	0	0	.000	1	0	0	1	0	0.00
1980–Peninsula x	Carolina	7	14	1	1	.500	16	7	7	8	2	4.61
1980–Philadelphia§	National	26	39	2	2	.500	42	16	16	21	13	3.69
Major League Totals		143	213	16	7	.696	203	79	71	130	69	3.00

Selected by San Francisco Giants' organization in 27th round of free-agent draft, June 4, 1970.
Selected by San Francisco Giants' organization in secondary phase of free-agent draft, January 13, 1971.

Selected by New York Mets' organization in 33rd round of free-agent draft, June 5, 1973.
Selected by Philadelphia Phillies' organization in secondary phase of free-agent draft, January 9, 1974.
†On disabled list, May 29 to June 9, 1975.
‡On disabled list, March 29 to June 27, 1979.
§On disabled list, April 9 to June 16, 1980.
xOn rehabilitation assignment, June 16 to July 12, 1980.

CHAMPIONSHIP SERIES RECORD

Year Club	League	G.	IP.	W.	L.	Pct.	H.	R.	ER.	SO.	BB.	ERA.
1977–Philadelphia	National	2	2⅔	0	0	.000	2	1	1	2	1	3.38
1978–Philadelphia	National	3	2⅔	0	0	.000	2	0	0	0	1	0.00
1980–Philadelphia	National	2	2⅔	1	0	1.000	1	1	1	0	1	3.38
Championship Series Totals		4	8	1	0	1.000	5	2	2	2	3	2.25

WORLD SERIES RECORD

Year Club	League	G.	IP.	W.	L.	Pct.	H.	R.	ER.	SO.	BB.	ERA.
1980–Philadelphia	National	1	2⅓	0	0	.000	0	0	0	0	1	0.00

WILLIAM JOSEPH BUCKNER
(Bill)

Born December 14, 1949, at Vallejo, Calif.
Height, 6.01.   Weight, 185.
Throws and bats lefthanded.
Hobby–Hunting.
Attended University of Southern California, Los Angeles, Calif., and
Arizona State University, Tempe, Ariz.
Brother of Jim Buckner, outfielder in New York Mets' organization,
and Bob Buckner, scout for Chicago Cubs.

Led Pioneer League first basemen in double plays with 37 in 1968.

Year Club	League	Pos.	G.	AB.	R.	H.	2B.	3B.	HR.	RBI.	B.A.	PO.	A.	E.	F.A.
1968–Ogden	Pion.	1B	*64	*256	54	*88	10	*8	4	41	*.344	468	28	4	*.992
1969–Albuquerque	Texas	OF-1B	70	257	44	79	7	3	7	50	.307	220	15	3	.987
1969–Spokane	P.C.	OF-1B	36	143	21	45	1	1	2	27	.315	128	12	5	.966
1969–Los Angeles	Nat.	PH	1	1	0	0	0	0	0	0	.000	0	0	0	.000
1970–Spokane	P.C.	1B-OF	111	465	78	156	33	2	3	74	.335	582	22	7	.989
1970–Los Angeles	Nat.	OF-1B	28	68	6	13	3	1	0	4	.191	37	1	0	1.000
1971–Los Angeles	Nat.	OF-1B	108	358	37	99	15	1	5	41	.277	235	11	1	.996
1972–Los Angeles	Nat.	OF-1B	105	383	47	122	14	3	5	37	.319	434	22	4	.991
1973–Los Angeles	Nat.	1B-OF	140	575	68	158	20	0	8	46	.275	981	50	3	.997
1974–Los Angeles	Nat.	OF-1B	145	580	83	182	30	3	7	58	.314	284	5	7	.976
1975–Los Angeles†	Nat.	OF	92	288	30	70	11	2	6	31	.243	138	4	2	.986
1976–Los Angeles‡	Nat.	OF-1B	154	642	76	193	28	4	7	60	.301	315	7	5	.985
1977–Chicago§	Nat.	1B	122	426	40	121	27	0	11	60	.284	966	58	10	.990
1978–Chicago x	Nat.	1B	117	446	47	144	26	1	5	74	.323	1075	83	6	.995
1979–Chicago	Nat.	1B	149	591	72	168	34	7	14	66	.284	1258	124	7	.995
1980–Chicago	Nat.	1B-OF	145	578	69	187	41	3	10	68	*.324	916	78	8	.992
Major League Totals			1306	4936	575	1457	249	25	78	545	.295	6639	443	53	.993

Selected by Los Angeles Dodgers' organization in 9th round of free-agent draft, June 7, 1968.
†On supplemental disabled list, April 21 to May 12, 1975.
‡Traded with Infielder Ivan DeJesus and Pitcher Jeff Albert to Chicago Cubs for Outfielder Rick Monday and Pitcher Mike Garman, January 11, 1977.
§On disabled list with sprained ankle, March 28 to April 19, 1977.
xOn supplemental disabled list, June 22 to July 7, 1978.

CHAMPIONSHIP SERIES RECORD

Year Club	League	Pos.	G.	AB.	R.	H.	2B.	3B.	HR.	RBI.	B.A.	PO.	A.	E.	F.A.
1974–Los Angeles	Nat.	OF	4	18	0	3	1	0	0	0	.167	6	0	0	1.000

WORLD SERIES RECORD

Year Club	League	Pos.	G.	AB.	R.	H.	2B.	3B.	HR.	RBI.	B.A.	PO.	A.	E.	F.A.
1974–Los Angeles	Nat.	OF	5	20	1	5	1	0	1	1	.250	11	0	0	1.000

TERRY CHARLES BULLING

Born December 15, 1952, at Lynwood, Calif.
Height, 6.01. Weight, 200.
Throws and bats righthanded.
Hobbies–Fishing, bowling and golf.
Attended Golden West Junior College, Huntington Beach, Calif., and
California State University, Los Angeles, Calif.

Led Midwest League batters in walks with 102 in 1976.

Year Club	League	Pos.	G.	AB.	R.	H.	2B.	3B.	HR.	RBI.	B.A.	PO.	A.	E.	F.A.
1974–Wis. Rapids†	Midw.	C	4	12	1	3	0	0	0	3	.250	31	1	1	.970
1975–Wis. Rapids	Midw.	C	104	296	31	71	11	0	9	40	.240	*596	51	13	.980
1976–Wis. Rapids	Midw.	C	112	352	85	109	13	2	8	50	.310	*623	*105	17	.977
1977–Orlando	South.	C	67	253	36	72	13	2	5	36	.285	313	45	8	.978

Year	Club	League	Pos.	G.	AB.	R.	H.	2B.	3B.	HR.	RBI.	B.A.	PO.	A.	E.	F.A.
1977—Minnesota	....	Amer.	C	15	32	2	5	1	0	0	5	.156	37	3	2	.952
1978—Orlando‡	....	South.	C	110	373	43	92	19	1	3	36	.247	471	63	9	.983
1979—Spokane	....	P.C.	C	52	160	23	54	14	2	2	18	.338	218	31	4	.984
1980—Spokane	....	P.C.	C	109	323	44	90	14	3	4	40	.279	450	59	19	.964
Major League Totals	....			15	32	2	5	1	0	0	5	.156	37	3	2	.952

Selected by Minnesota Twins' organization in 14th round of free-agent draft, June 5, 1974.
†On temporary inactive list, July 8 to August 30, 1974.
‡Sold to Seattle Mariners' organization, March 29, 1979.

ALONZA BENJAMIN BUMBRY
(Al)

Born April 21, 1947, at Fredericksburg, Va.
Height, 5.08. Weight, 175.
Throws right and bats lefthanded.
Hobbies—Sports in general and corresponding.
Attended Virginia State College, Petersburg, Va.; received Bachelor of Science degree
in Physical Education.

Tied modern major league record for most triples, game, 3, September 22, 1973.
Major League stolen bases: 1972 (1), 1973 (23), 1974 (12), 1975 (16), 1976 (42), 1977 (18), 1978 (5), 1979 (37), 1980 (44). Total—198
Named American League Rookie Player of the Year by THE SPORTING NEWS, 1973.
Named American League Rookie of the Year by Baseball Writers' Association of America, 1973.
Named as outfielder on THE SPORTING NEWS American League All-Star Team, 1980.
Named Northern League Player of the Year in 1971.
Named International League Rookie of the Year in 1972.

Year	Club	League	Pos.	G.	AB.	R.	H.	2B.	3B.	HR.	RBI.	B.A.	PO.	A.	E.	F.A.
1969—Stockton†	....	Calif.	OF-1	35	73	19	13	4	0	0	3	.178	31	3	2	.944
1970—	....							(In Military Service.)								
1971—Aberdeen	....	North.	OF	66	247	68	83	14	6	6	53	.336	85	5	5	.947
1972—Asheville	....	South.	OF	26	121	26	42	4	4	4	10	.347	60	4	3	.955
1972—Rochester	....	Int.	OF	108	435	83	150	29	∗15	6	47	∗.345	198	14	0	∗1.000
1972—Baltimore	....	Amer.	OF	9	11	5	4	0	1	0	0	.364	4	0	0	1.000
1973—Baltimore	....	Amer.	OF	110	356	73	120	15	●11	7	34	.337	134	2	3	.978
1974—Baltimore	....	Amer.	OF	94	270	35	63	10	3	1	19	.233	115	7	6	.953
1975—Baltimore	....	Amer.	OF-3B	114	349	47	94	19	4	2	32	.269	70	2	0	1.000
1976—Baltimore	....	Amer.	OF	133	450	71	113	15	7	9	36	.251	251	9	3	.989
1977—Baltimore‡	....	Amer.	OF	133	518	74	164	31	3	4	41	.317	329	7	3	.991
1978—Baltimore§x	.....	Amer.	OF	33	114	21	27	5	2	2	6	.237	62	2	1	.985
1979—Baltimore	....	Amer.	OF	148	569	80	162	29	1	7	49	.285	367	7	7	.982
1980—Baltimore	....	Amer.	OF	160	645	118	205	29	9	9	53	.318	488	7	5	.990
Major League Totals	....			934	3282	524	952	153	41	41	270	.290	1820	43	28	.985

Selected by Baltimore Orioles' organization in 11th round of free-agent draft, June 7, 1968.
†On temporary inactive list, June 16, 1969. Transferred to military list, July 22, 1969 through June 3, 1971.
‡On supplemental disabled list, July 28 through August 12, 1977.
§On emergency disabled list, May 12 to September 1, 1978.
xGranted free agency, November 2, 1978; re-signed by Orioles, January 30, 1979.

CHAMPIONSHIP SERIES RECORD

Year	Club	League	Pos.	G.	AB.	R.	H.	2B.	3B.	HR.	RBI.	B.A.	PO.	A.	E.	F.A.
1973—Baltimore	....	Amer.	OF	2	7	1	0	0	0	0	0	.000	4	1	1	.833
1974—Baltimore	....	Amer.	PR-PH	2	1	0	0	0	0	0	0	.000	0	0	0	.000
1979—Baltimore	....	Amer.	OF	4	16	5	4	0	1	0	0	.250	10	0	1	.909
Championship Series Totals	....			8	24	6	4	0	1	0	0	.167	14	1	2	.882

WORLD SERIES RECORD

Year	Club	League	Pos.	G.	AB.	R.	H.	2B.	3B.	HR.	RBI.	B.A.	PO.	A.	E.	F.A.
1979—Baltimore	....	Amer.	OF-PH	7	21	3	3	0	0	0	1	.143	14	1	1	.938

ALL-STAR GAME RECORD

Year	League		Pos.	AB.	R.	H.	2B.	3B.	HR.	RBI.	B.A.	PO.	A.	E.	F.A.
1980—American	....		OF	1	0	0	0	0	0	0	.000	2	0	0	1.000

THOMAS HENRY BURGMEIER
(Tom)

Born August 2, 1943, at St. Paul, Minn.
Height, 5.11. Weight, 180.
Throws and bats lefthanded.
Hobbies—Fishing and hunting.

Major League saves: 1968 (4), 1969 (0), 1970 (1), 1971 (17), 1972 (9), 1973 (1), 1974 (4), 1975 (11), 1976 (1), 1977 (7), 1978 (4), 1979 (4), 1980 (24). Total—87.
Led Pacific Coast League pitchers in complete games with 15 in 1967.

Year	Club	League	G.	IP.	W.	L.	Pct.	H.	R.	ER.	SO.	BB.	ERA.
1962—Modesto	....	California	34	197	12	11	.522	204	122	95	210	100	4.34
1963—San Antonio	....	Texas	6	34	1	4	.200	46	27	24	19	14	6.35
1963—Durham	....	Carolina	15	76	3	9	.250	98	55	40	43	30	4.74

Year Club	League	G.	IP.	W.	L.	Pct.	H.	R.	ER.	SO.	BB.	ERA.
1964—Modesto†-San Jose ....California	California	22	122	8	7	.533	149	82	67	89	30	4.94
1965—Seattle.................................P. Coast	P. Coast	22	129	8	7	.533	114	57	46	94	32	3.21
1966—Seattle.................................P. Coast	P. Coast	12	41	2	5	.286	50	31	28	23	16	6.15
1966—El Paso.............................Texas	Texas	16	73	4	8	.333	87	52	40	40	28	4.93
1967—Seattle.................................P. Coast	P. Coast	32	230	11	14	.440	199	81	71	114	44	2.78
1968—California‡§ ....American	American	56	73	1	4	.200	65	41	35	33	24	4.32
1969—Kansas City‡ ....American	American	31	54	3	1	.750	67	31	25	23	21	4.17
1970—Omaha.................................Am. Assoc.	Am. Assoc.	10	22	3	1	.750	10	3	3	9	7	1.23
1970—Kansas City ....American	American	41	68	6	6	.500	59	31	24	43	23	3.18
1971—Kansas City ....American	American	67	88	9	7	.563	71	23	17	44	30	1.74
1972—Kansas City ....American	American	51	55	6	2	.750	67	32	26	18	33	4.25
1973—Omaha‡.............................Am. Assoc.	Am. Assoc.	24	61	2	4	.333	75	35	35	31	19	5.16
1973—Kansas City x.......................American	American	6	0	0	0	.000	13	6	6	4	4	5.40
1974—Minnesota...........................American	American	50	92	5	3	.625	92	46	46	34	26	4.50
1975—Minnesota...........................American	American	46	76	5	8	.385	76	32	26	41	23	3.08
1976—Minnesota...........................American	American	57	115	8	1	.889	95	36	32	45	29	2.50
1977—Minnesota y.........................American	American	61	97	6	4	.600	113	56	55	35	33	5.10
1978—Boston ....American	American	35	61	2	1	.667	74	33	30	24	23	4.43
1979—Boston ....American	American	44	89	3	2	.600	89	32	27	60	16	2.73
1980—Boston z.............................American	American	62	99	5	4	.556	87	30	22	54	20	2.00
Major League Totals		607	977	59	43	.578	968	429	371	458	305	3.42

Signed as free agent by Houston Colt .45's organization, September 24, 1961.

†Released by Houston Colt .45s' organization, June 10, 1964; signed as free agent by Los Angeles Angels' organization, July 22, 1964.

‡Appeared as outfielder in one game.

§Selected by Kansas City Royals from California Angels in expansion draft, October 15, 1968.

xTraded to Minnesota Twins for Pitcher Ken Gill, October 24, 1973.

yGranted free agency, November 2, 1977; signed by Boston Red Sox, February 17, 1978.

zPlayed one game in the outfield (no chances).

ALL-STAR GAME RECORD

Member of American League All-Star Team in 1980; did not play.

RICHARD PAUL BURLESON

(Rick)

Born April 29, 1951, at Lynwood, Calif.
Height, 5.10. Weight, 160.
Throws and bats righthanded.
Hobby—Sports in general.
Attended Cerritos Junior College, Norwalk, Calif.

Established major league record for most double plays by shortstop, season (147), 1980.
Led Eastern League shortstops in double plays with 80 in 1972.
Led American League shortstops in double plays with 147 in 1980.
Named shortstop on THE SPORTING NEWS American League All-Star Team, 1977.
Named shortstop on THE SPORTING NEWS American League All-Star fielding team, 1979.

Year Club	League	Pos.	G.	AB.	R.	H.	2B.	3B.	HR.	RBI.	B.A.	PO.	A.	E.	F.A.
1970—Winter Haven ....Fla. St.	Fla. St.	SS	118	419	42	92	13	4	1	29	.220	188	*400	38	.939
1971—Greenville ....W. Car.	W. Car.	SS	29	118	24	31	4	2	2	12	.263	32	68	11	.901
1971—Winston-Salem†.Carol.	Carol.	SS	77	299	35	82	14	2	4	30	.274	118	262	23	.943
1972—Pawtucket.........East.	East.	SS	136	488	59	115	26	0	9	51	.236	*191	380	23	*.961
1973—Pawtucket.........Int.	Int.	*SS-2B	*146	477	58	120	20	1	6	45	.252	241	431	25	*.964
1974—Pawtucket.........Int.	Int.	SS	10	41	7	14	4	0	1	4	.341	10	36	3	.939
1974—Boston ....Amer.	Amer.	S-2-3	114	384	36	109	22	0	4	44	.284	209	329	21	.962
1975—Boston ....Amer.	Amer.	SS	158	580	66	146	25	1	6	62	.252	267	498	29	.963
1976—Boston ....Amer.	Amer.	SS	152	540	75	157	27	1	7	42	.291	274	478	34	.957
1977—Boston ....Amer.	Amer.	SS	154	*663	80	194	36	7	3	52	.293	*285	482	24	.970
1978—Boston‡.............Amer.	Amer.	SS	145	626	75	155	32	5	5	49	.248	285	482	15	.981
1979—Boston ....Amer.	Amer.	SS	153	627	93	174	32	5	5	60	.278	272	523	16	*.980
1980—Boston§.............Amer.	Amer.	SS	155	644	89	179	29	2	9	53	.278	*301	*528	22	.974
Major League Totals			1031	4064	514	1114	203	21	39	362	.274	1893	3320	161	.970

Selected by Minnesota Twins' organization in 8th round of free-agent draft, June 5, 1969.

Selected by Boston Red Sox' organization in secondary phase of free-agent draft, January 17, 1970.

†On disabled list, June 1 to June 19, 1971.

‡On supplemental disabled list, July 14 to July 28, 1978.

§Traded with Third Baseman Butch Hobson to California Angels for Third Baseman Carney Lansford, Pitcher Mark Clear and Outfielder Rick Miller, December 10, 1980.

CHAMPIONSHIP SERIES RECORD

Year Club	League	Pos.	G.	AB.	R.	H.	2B.	3B.	HR.	RBI.	B.A.	PO.	A.	E.	F.A.
1975—Boston ....Amer.	Amer.	SS	3	9	2	4	2	0	0	1	.444	4	12	1	.941

WORLD SERIES RECORD

Year Club	League	Pos.	G.	AB.	R.	H.	2B.	3B.	HR.	RBI.	B.A.	PO.	A.	E.	F.A.
1975—Boston ....Amer.	Amer.	SS	7	24	1	7	1	0	0	2	.292	9	19	1	.966

Year League	Pos.	AB.	R.	H.	2B.	3B.	HR.	RBI.	B.A.	PO.	A.	E.	F.A.
1977—American	SS	2	0	0	0	0	0	0	.000	0	0	0	.000
1979—American	PR-SS	2	1	0	0	0	0	0	.000	0	1	0	1.000
All-Star Game Totals		4	1	0	0	0	0	0	.000	0	1	0	1.000

Named to American League All-Star Team for 1978 game; replaced due to injury by Jerry Remy.

ROBERT BRITT BURNS

(Known by middle name.)
Born June 8, 1959, at Houston, Tex.
Height, 6.05. Weight, 215.
Throws left and bats righthanded.
Named American League Rookie Pitcher of the Year by THE SPORTING NEWS, 1980.

Year Club	League	G.	IP.	W.	L.	Pct.	H.	R.	ER.	SO.	BB.	ERA.
1978—Appleton	Midwest	6	30	3	2	.600	25	8	8	28	2	2.40
1978—Knoxville	Southern	4	21	1	1	.500	24	16	10	17	4	4.29
1978—Chicago	American	2	8	0	2	.000	14	12	11	3	3	12.38
1979—Knoxville	Southern	20	110	6	10	.375	126	68	59	92	37	4.83
1979—Iowa	Am. Assoc.	7	41	2	3	.400	41	17	15	34	15	3.29
1979—Chicago	American	6	5	0	0	.000	10	5	3	2	1	5.40
1980—Chicago	American	34	238	15	13	.536	213	83	75	133	63	2.84
Major League Totals		42	251	15	15	.500	237	100	89	138	67	3.19

Selected by Chicago White Sox' organization in 3rd round of free-agent draft, June 6, 1978.

SHELDON JOHN BURNSIDE

Born December 22, 1954, at South Bend, Ind.
Height, 6.05. Weight, 200.
Throws left and bats righthanded.
Nephew of Robert Burnside, catcher in Detroit Tigers' organization, 1956-57.
Pitched seven-inning 8-0 no-hit victory against Charlotte, June 24, 1976.
Tied for Southern League lead in complete games with 16 in 1977.

Year Club	League	G.	IP.	W.	L.	Pct.	H.	R.	ER.	SO.	BB.	ERA.
1975—Bristol	Ap'lachian	21	78	4	6	.400	66	49	33	.65	48	3.81
1976—Lakeland	Florida St.	10	76	6	3	.667	61	30	22	54	25	2.61
1976—Montgomery	Southern	12	79	6	5	.545	62	31	24	43	20	2.73
1977—Montgomery	Southern	27	176	10	12	.455	154	80	65	100	86	3.32
1978—Evansville	Am. Assoc.	41	161	●14	5	.737	184	82	63	100	51	3.52
1978—Detroit	American	2	4	0	0	.000	4	4	4	3	2	9.00
1979—Detroit†‡	American	10	21	1	1	.500	28	16	15	13	8	6.43
1979—Indianapolis	Am. Assoc.	39	57	6	4	.600	50	22	19	48	33	3.00
1980—Indianapolis	Am. Assoc.	51	80	5	1	.833	89	30	27	46	31	3.04
1980—Cincinnati	National	7	5	1	0	1.000	6	1	1	2	1	1.80
American League Totals		12	25	1	1	.500	32	20	19	16	10	6.84
National League Totals		7	5	1	0	1.000	6	1	1	2	1	1.80
Major League Totals		19	30	2	1	667	38	21	20	18	11	6.00

Signed as free agent by Detroit Tigers' organization, July 26, 1974.
†Loaned to Indianapolis (Cincinnati Reds' organization), May 29, 1979; returned, August 27, 1979.
‡Traded to Cincinnati Reds, October 24, 1979, completing deal in which Detroit acquired Outfielder Champ Summers, May 25, 1979.

BERTRAM RAY BURRIS

(Known by middle name.)
Born August 22, 1950, at Idabel, Okla.
Height, 6.05. Weight, 200.
Throws and bats righthanded.
Hobby—Basketball.
Attended Southwestern State, Weatherford, Okla.; received Bachelor of Arts
degree in Recreational Leadership.

Year Club	League	G.	IP.	W.	L.	Pct.	H.	R.	ER.	SO.	BB.	ERA.
1972—Midland	Texas	14	95	7	5	.583	98	43	37	91	20	3.51
1973—Wichita	Am. Assoc.	8	59	4	3	.571	72	45	37	34	19	5.64
1973—Chicago	National	31	65	1	1	.500	65	22	21	57	27	2.91
1974—Wichita	Am. Assoc.	7	46	2	3	.400	52	33	26	34	23	5.09
1974—Chicago	National	40	75	3	5	.375	91	61	55	40	26	6.60
1975—Chicago	National	36	238	15	10	.600	259	121	109	108	73	4.12
1976—Chicago	National	37	249	15	13	.536	251	102	86	112	70	3.11
1977—Chicago	National	39	221	14	16	.467	270	132	116	105	67	4.72
1978—Chicago	National	40	199	7	13	.350	210	112	105	94	79	4.75
1979—Chicago†-New York§	National	18	43	0	2	.000	44	27	23	24	21	4.81
1979—New York‡	American	15	28	1	3	.250	40	22	19	19	10	6.11
1980—New York xy	National	29	170	7	13	.350	181	86	76	83	54	4.02
American League Totals		15	28	1	3	.250	40	22	19	19	10	6.11
National League Totals		270	1260	62	73	.459	1371	663	591	623	417	4.22
Major League Totals		285	1288	63	76	.453	1411	685	610	642	427	4.26

Selected by Chicago Cubs' organization in 17th round of free-agent draft, June 6, 1972.
†Traded to New York Yankees for Pitcher Dick Tidrow, May 23, 1979.
‡Sold on waivers to New York Mets, August 20, 1979.
§On emergency disabled list, September 15 to October 3, 1979.
xOn disabled list, July 3 to August 4, 1980.
yGranted free agency, October 27, 1980; signed by Montreal Expos, February 18, 1981.

JEFFREY ALAN BURROUGHS

Born March 7, 1951, at Long Beach, Calif.
Height, 6.00. Weight, 200.
Throws and bats righthanded.
Hobby—Fishing.
Attended Long Beach City College, Long Beach, Calif.

Tied major league record for fewest caught stealing, season, 150 or more games (0), 1976.
Led American League batters in strikeouts with 155 in 1975.
Led American League outfielders in double plays with 5 in 1974.
Led American League in sacrifice flies with 11 in 1973.
Led National League in bases on balls with 117 in 1978.
Named Most Valuable Player in American League, 1974.
Named American League Player of the Year by THE SPORTING NEWS, 1974.
Named as outfielder on THE SPORTING NEWS American League All-Star Team, 1974.
Received reported $88,000 bonus to sign with Washington Senators, 1969.

Year	Club	League	Pos.	G.	AB.	R.	H.	2B.	3B.	HR.	RBI.	B.A.	PO.	A.	E.	F.A.
1969—Wytheville	Appal.	1B-OF	52	183	41	65	16	4	6	48	.355	192	12	10	.953
1970—Denver	A.A.	O-3-1	115	390	64	105	17	6	17	71	.269	250	52	16	.950
1970—Washington	Amer.	OF	6	12	1	2	0	0	0	1	.167	5	0	0	1.000
1971—Denver	A.A.	OF	81	298	51	87	13	3	12	58	.292	108	7	10	.920
1971—Washington	Amer.	OF	59	181	20	42	9	0	5	25	.232	82	3	3	.966
1972—Denver†	A.A.	OF	84	307	60	93	13	2	24	59	.303	118	5	5	.961
1972—Texas	Amer.	OF-1B	22	65	4	12	1	0	1	3	.185	33	2	2	.946
1973—Texas	Amer.	OF-1B	151	526	71	147	17	1	30	85	.279	320	14	8	.977
1974—Texas	Amer.	OF-1B	152	554	84	167	33	2	25	*118	.301	242	11	8	.969
1975—Texas	Amer.	OF	152	585	81	132	20	0	29	94	.226	249	10	9	.966
1976—Texas‡	Amer.	OF	158	604	71	143	22	2	18	86	.237	289	12	4	.987
1977—Atlanta	Nat.	OF	154	579	91	157	19	1	41	114	.271	249	9	7	.974
1978—Atlanta	Nat.	OF	153	488	72	147	30	6	23	77	.301	224	13	6	.975
1979—Atlanta	Nat.	OF	116	397	49	89	14	1	11	47	.224	175	8	7	.963
1980—Atlanta	Nat.	OF	99	278	35	73	14	0	13	51	.263	129	0	3	.977
American League Totals			700	2527	332	645	102	5	108	412	.255	1220	52	34	.974
National League Totals			522	1742	247	466	77	8	88	289	.268	777	30	23	.972
Major League Totals			1222	4269	579	1111	179	13	196	701	.260	1997	82	57	.973

Selected by Washington Senators' organization in 1st round (first player selected) of free-agent draft, June 5, 1969.
†On supplemental disabled list, April 27 to May 16, 1972.
‡Traded to Atlanta Braves for Outfielders Ken Henderson and Dave May, Pitchers Carl Morton, Rogelio Moret and Adrian Devine, and cash estimated at $250,000, December 9, 1976.

ALL-STAR GAME RECORD

Year	League	Pos.	AB.	R.	H.	2B.	3B.	HR.	RBI.	B.A.	PO.	A.	E.	F.A.
1974—American		OF	0	0	0	0	0	0	0	.000	1	0	0	1.000

Member of National League All-Star Team for 1978 game; did not play.

STEVEN LEE BUSBY
(Steve)

Born September 29, 1949, at Burbank, Calif.
Height, 6.02. Weight, 205.
Throws and bats righthanded.
Hobbies—Golf and bowling.
Attended University of Southern California, Los Angeles, Calif.
Fourth-cousin of Jim Busby, former coach of Baltimore Orioles, Houston Astros,
Atlanta Braves, Chicago White Sox and Seattle Mariners.

Established American League record for most consecutive batsmen retired, season (33), June 19-24, 1974.
Pitched 2-0 no-hit victory against Milwaukee Brewers, June 19, 1974.
Pitched 3-0 no-hit victory against Detroit Tigers, April 27, 1973.
Led American Association pitchers in complete games with 17 in 1972.
Tied for American Association lead in games started by pitchers with 30 and in wild pitches with 13 in 1972.
Named American League Rookie Pitcher of the Year by THE SPORTING NEWS, 1973.

Year	Club	League	G.	IP.	W.	L.	Pct.	H.	R.	ER.	SO.	BB.	ERA.
1971—San Jose	California	8	40	4	1	.800	31	14	3	50	14	0.68
1972—Omaha	Am. Assoc.	30	*217	12	14	.462	197	87	77	*221	64	3.20
1972—Kansas City	American	5	40	3	1	.750	28	9	7	31	8	1.58
1973—Kansas City	American	37	238	16	15	.516	246	125	112	174	105	4.24
1974—Kansas City	American	38	292	22	14	.611	284	118	110	198	92	3.39
1975—Kansas City	American	34	260	18	12	.600	233	96	89	160	81	3.08
1976—Kansas City†	American	13	72	3	3	.500	58	42	35	29	49	4.38

Year Club	League	G.	IP.	W.	L.	Pct.	H.	R.	ER.	SO.	BB.	ERA.
1977—Daytona Beach‡	Fla. State	1	3	0	1	.000	11	5	5	2	1	15.00
1978—Omaha§	Am. Assoc.	12	66	3	7	.300	78	47	40	32	32	5.45
1978—Sarasota Royals	G. Coast	2	13	1	0	1.000	7	0	0	9	0	0.00
1978—Kansas City	American	7	21	1	0	1.000	24	18	18	10	15	7.71
1979—Kansas City	American	22	94	6	6	.500	71	45	38	45	64	3.64
1980—Omaha	Am. Assoc.	8	58	3	2	.600	45	19	16	29	28	2.48
1980—Kansas City x	American	11	42	1	3	.250	59	30	29	12	19	6.21
Major League Totals		167	1059	70	54	.565	1003	483	438	659	433	3.72

Selected by San Francisco Giants' organization in 4th round of free-agent draft, June 6, 1967.
Selected by Kansas City Royals' organization in 2nd round of free-agent draft, June 8, 1971.
†On disabled list, March 25 to April 17, 1976; and emergency disabled list July 10 to October 19, 1976.
‡On Kansas City disabled list, April 1 to May 4, 1977.
§On disabled list, July 14 to August 19, 1978.
xReleased, August 29, 1980; signed by St. Louis Cardinals' organization, January 27, 1981.

ALL-STAR GAME RECORD

Tied All-Star Game record for most balks, game (1), July 15, 1975.

Year League			IP.	W.	L.	Pct.	H.	R.	ER.	SO.	BB.	ERA.
1975—American			2	0	0	.000	4	1	1	0	0	4.50

Member of American League All-Star Team in 1974 game; did not play.

THOMAS WILLIAM BUSKEY
(Tom)

Born February 20, 1947, at Harrisburg, Pa.
Height, 6.03. Weight, 215.
Throws and bats righthanded.
Hobby—Bowling.
Attended University of North Carolina, Chapel Hill, N. C.; received Bachelor of Arts degree in Education.

Tied for Florida State League lead in shutouts with 5 in 1970.

Year Club	League	G.	IP.	W.	L.	Pct.	H.	R.	ER.	SO.	BB.	ERA.
1969—Johnson City	Ap'lachian	5	41	5	0	1.000	25	8	6	51	4	1.32
1969—Fort Lauderdale	Florida St.	7	48	3	3	.500	49	17	12	29	9	2.25
1970—Fort Lauderdale†	Florida St.	18	133	10	5	.667	98	37	29	81	19	1.96
1970—Kinston	Carolina	2	13	1	1	.500	7	2	2	5	3	1.38
1971—Manchester	Eastern	21	122	7	5	.583	104	46	37	76	28	2.73
1971—Syracuse	Int'national	9	21	0	3	.000	36	22	21	8	11	9.00
1972—West Haven	Eastern	24	137	9	5	.643	123	55	43	83	27	2.82
1973—Syracuse	Int'national	30	87	6	4	.600	76	34	28	52	28	2.90
1973—New York	American	8	17	0	1	.000	18	12	10	8	4	5.29
1974—New York‡-Cleveland	American	55	99	2	7	.222	103	40	37	43	36	3.36
1975—Cleveland§	American	50	77	5	3	.625	69	27	22	29	29	2.57
1976—Cleveland	American	39	94	5	4	.556	88	42	38	32	34	3.64
1977—Toledo	Int'national	10	30	1	3	.250	26	18	15	16	8	4.50
1977—Cleveland x	American	21	34	0	0	.000	45	24	20	15	8	5.29
1978—Texas y	American					(Did not play)						
1978—Syracuse	Int'national	45	119	7	13	.350	113	51	39	62	41	2.95
1978—Toronto z	American	8	13	0	1	.000	14	5	5	7	5	3.46
1979—Syracuse	Int'national	12	17	0	0	.000	15	5	4	11	8	2.12
1979—Toronto	American	44	79	6	10	.375	74	33	30	44	25	3.42
1980—Toronto a	American	33	67	3	1	.750	68	35	33	34	26	4.43
Major League Totals		258	480	21	27	.438	479	218	195	212	167	3.66

Signed as free agent by New York Yankees' organization, June 21, 1969.
†On temporary inactive list, April 17 to June 9, 1970.
‡Traded with Pitchers Fritz Peterson, Steve Kline and Fred Beene to Cleveland Indians for First Baseman Chris Chambliss and Pitchers Dick Tidrow and Cecil Upshaw, April 26, 1974.
§On disabled list, July 25 to September 1, 1975.
xTraded with First Baseman-Outfielder John Lowenstein to Texas Rangers for Outfielder-Designated Hitter Willie Horton and Pitcher David Clyde, February 28, 1978.
yReleased, April 1, 1978; signed by Syracuse (Toronto Blue Jays' organization), May 13, 1978.
zOn disabled list, March 21 to April 11, 1979.
aReleased, August 8, 1980.

JOHN DANIEL BUTCHER

Born March 8, 1957, at Glendale, Calif.
Height, 6.04. Weight, 185.
Throws and bats righthanded.
Attended Yavapai College, Prescott, Ariz.

Led International League in complete games with 14 in 1980.

Year Club	League	G.	IP.	W.	L.	Pct.	H.	R.	ER.	SO.	BB.	ERA.
1977—Sarasota Rangers	G. Coast	6	42	3	2	.600	28	10	6	23	11	1.29
1977—Asheville	W. Carol.	2	16	1	0	1.000	13	4	2	13	6	1.13
1978—Asheville	W. Carol.	24	154	10	9	.526	150	81	57	103	77	3.33
1979—Tulsa†	Texas	26	155	9	12	.429	197	106	88	82	53	5.11

Year Club	League	G.	IP.	W.	L.	Pct.	H.	R.	ER.	SO.	BB.	ERA.
1980—Charleston ....Int'national	22	152	10	7	.588	141	57	56	71	50	3.32
1980—Texas ....American	6	35	3	3	.500	34	19	16	27	13	4.11
Major League Totals................................	6	35	3	3	.500	34	19	16	27	13	4.11

Selected by St. Louis Cardinals' organization in 2nd round of free-agent draft, January 7, 1976.
Selected by Atlanta Braves' organization in secondary phase of free-agent draft, June 8, 1976.
Selected by Houston Astros' organization in secondary phase of free-agent draft, January 11, 1977.
Selected by Texas Rangers' organization in secondary phase of free-agent draft, June 7, 1977.

SALVATORE PHILIP BUTERA
(Sal)

Born September 25, 1952, at Richmond Hill, N.Y.
Height, 6.00. Weight, 189.
Throws and bats righthanded.
Attended Suffolk Community College, Selden, N.Y.

Led Carolina League catchers in passed balls with 20 in 1974.
Tied for Carolina League lead in double plays by catchers with 9 in 1974.

Year Club	League	Pos.	G.	AB.	R.	H.	2B.	3B.	HR.	RBI.	B.A.	PO.	A.	E.	F.A.
1972—Sara. W. Sox .....G. C.	C	36	114	18	28	7	0	0	16	.246	253	20	10	.965
1973—Ft. Lauderdale ..Fla. St.	C	99	319	21	76	12	1	1	32	.238	503	*86	10	.983
1974—Lynchburg ....Carol.	C	124	417	35	90	16	2	3	55	.216	589	*102	7	*.990
1975—Orlando ....South.	C	20	51	8	9	2	0	0	4	.176	61	14	0	1.000
1975—Tacoma ....P. C.	C	73	215	21	52	9	0	2	26	.242	376	36	6	.986
1976—Orlando ....South.	C	90	267	45	73	8	0	3	28	.273	326	41	6	.984
1977—Tacoma ....P. C.	C	87	252	27	70	13	0	4	45	.278	257	49	9	.971
1978—Toledo ....Int.	C	74	206	20	52	7	0	4	28	.252	334	32	5	.987
1979—Toledo ....Int.	C	78	236	20	70	13	0	2	29	.297	392	33	11	.975
1980—Minnesota.........Amer.	C	34	85	4	23	1	0	0	2	.271	106	9	6	.950
Major League Totals.......................	34	85	4	23	1	0	0	2	.271	106	9	6	.950

Signed as free agent by Minnesota Twins' organization, May 15, 1972; loaned to Sarasota White Sox, June 26, 1972.

MARTIN EUGENE BYSTROM
(Marty)

Born July 26, 1958, at Miami, Fla.
Height, 6.05. Weight, 200.
Throws and bats righthanded.
Attended Miami-Dade South Junior College, Miami, Fla.

Pitched 3-0 perfect game victory against Salem, August 12, 1978.
Led American Association in games started with 26 in 1979.
Tied for Western Carolinas League lead in games started with 27 in 1977.
Tied for Carolina League lead in complete games with 13 and in shutouts with 5 in 1978.

Year Club	League	G.	IP.	W.	L.	Pct.	H.	R.	ER.	SO.	BB.	ERA.
1977—Spartanburg.......................W. Carol.	27	184	13	11	.542	*199	83	69	99	49	3.38
1978—Peninsula ....Carolina	26	*197	●15	7	.682	170	71	62	*159	46	2.83
1979—Oklahoma City ....Am. Assoc.	26	172	9	5	.643	174	102	78	108	69	4.08
1980—Oklahoma City†....................Am. Assoc.	14	91	6	5	.545	89	49	37	68	27	3.66
1980—Philadelphia........................National	6	36	5	0	1.000	26	6	6	21	9	1.50
Major League Totals................................	6	36	5	0	1.000	26	6	6	21	9	1.50

Signed as free agent by Philadelphia Phillies' organization, December 15, 1976.
†On disabled list, April 14 to May 16 and May 27 to June 12, 1980.

CHAMPIONSHIP SERIES RECORD

Year Club	League	G.	IP.	W.	L.	Pct.	H.	R.	ER.	SO.	BB.	ERA.
1980—Philadelphia........................National	1	5⅓	0	0	.000	7	2	1	1	2	1.69

WORLD SERIES RECORD

Year Club	League	G.	IP.	W.	L.	Pct.	H.	R.	ER.	SO.	BB.	ERA.
1980—Philadelphia........................National	1	5	0	0	.000	10	3	3	4	1	5.40

ENOS MILTON CABELL, JR.
Name pronounced kuh-BELL.

Born October 8, 1949, at Fort Riley, Kan.
Height, 6.05. Weight, 185.
Throws and bats righthanded.
Hobby—Sports in general.
Attended Harbor Junior College, San Pedro, Calif.
Cousin of Dick Davis, outfielder with Philadelphia Phillies.

Led Appalachian League in total bases with 149 in 1969.
Major league stolen bases: 1972 (0), 1973 (1), 1974 (5), 1975 (12), 1976 (35), 1977 (42), 1978 (33), 1979 (37), 1980 (21). Total—186.
Led National League third basemen in putouts with 140 and in errors with 23 in 1977.
Named Appalachian League Player of the Year, 1969.
Named Player of the Year in Texas League, 1971.

Year	Club	League	Pos.	G.	AB.	R.	H.	2B.	3B.	HR.	RBI.	B.A.	PO.	A.	E.	F.A.
1969—Bluefield	Appal.	1B	●69	⋆270	⋆62	⋆101	14	2	10	43	.374	⋆471	30	9	.982
1970—Stockton	Calif.	⋆1B-OF	138	517	78	147	25	6	10	67	.284	844	⋆81	⋆33	.966
1971—Dall-Ft. Worth	Tex.	⋆1-3-O	140	521	65	⋆162	24	6	6	79	⋆.311	1135	⋆122	●20	.984
1972—Rochester	Int.	⋆1-0-3-S	141	●540	82	145	26	9	8	66	.269	893	⋆110	11	⋆.989
1972—Baltimore	Amer.	1B	3	5	0	0	0	0	0	1	.000	7	0	0	1.000
1973—Rochester	Int.	1-3-2	60	229	43	81	9	1	2	24	.354	510	47	10	.982
1973—Baltimore	Amer.	1B-3B	32	47	12	10	2	0	1	3	.213	111	4	1	.991
1974—Baltimore	Amer.	1-O-3-2	80	174	24	42	4	2	3	17	.241	223	45	4	.985
1975—Houston	Nat.	O-1-3	117	348	43	92	17	6	2	43	.264	197	58	6	.977
1976—Houston	Nat.	3B-1B	144	586	85	160	13	7	2	43	.273	131	263	17	.959
1977—Houston	Nat.	3-1B-SS	150	625	101	176	36	7	16	68	.282	176	288	24	.951
1978—Houston	Nat.	3B-1B	●162	⋆660	92	195	31	8	7	71	.295	211	277	18	.964
1979—Houston	Nat.	3B-1B	155	603	60	164	30	5	6	67	.272	396	199	14	.977
1980—Houston‡	Nat.	3B-1B	152	604	69	167	23	8	2	55	.276	118	250	⋆29	.927
American League Totals			115	226	36	52	6	2	4	21	.230	341	49	5	.987
National League Totals			880	3426	450	954	150	41	35	347	.278	1229	1335	108	.960
Major League Totals			995	3652	486	1006	156	43	39	368	.275	1570	1384	113	.963

Signed as free agent by Baltimore Orioles' organization, September 22, 1968.

†Traded with Second Baseman Rob Andrews to Houston Astros for First Baseman Lee May and Outfielder Jay Schlueter, December 3, 1974.

‡Traded to San Francisco Giants for Outfielder Chris Bourjos and Pitcher Bob Knepper, December 8, 1980.

CHAMPIONSHIP SERIES RECORD

Year	Club	League	Pos.	G.	AB.	R.	H.	2B.	3B.	HR.	RBI.	B.A.	PO.	A.	E.	F.A.
1974—Baltimore	Amer.	O-PH-PR	3	4	0	1	0	0	0	0	.250	2	0	0	1.000
1980—Houston	Nat.	3B	5	21	1	5	1	0	0	0	.238	1	9	0	1.000
Championship Series Totals			8	25	1	6	1	0	0	0	.240	3	9	0	1.000

WAYNE LEVELL CAGE

Born November 23, 1951, at Jonesboro, Louisiana.
Height, 6.04. Weight, 190.
Throws and bats lefthanded.
Hobby—Sports of all kinds.

Led Florida State League in total bases with 227 and in strikeouts with 103 in 1973.

Year	Club	League	Pos.	G.	AB.	R.	H.	2B.	3B.	HR.	RBI.	B.A.	PO.	A.	E.	F.A.
1971—Sara Indians	Gulf C.	PH-P	8	4	2	2	0	0	0	1	.500	3	2	0	1.000
1972—Reno	Calif.	P	9	6	0	1	0	0	0	0	.167	3	2	1	.833
1972—Sara Indians	Gulf C.	P-1B	19	25	2	7	1	0	0	6	.280	20	6	0	1.000
1973—Key West	Fla. St.	⋆1B-3B	128	440	77	133	30	5	⋆18	⋆82	.302	1029	56	⋆23	.979
1974—San Antonio	Texas	1B	30	111	11	21	2	0	0	13	.189	243	22	5	.982
1974—Reno	Calif.	1B	94	338	52	92	11	6	7	47	.272	791	30	14	.983
1975—San Jose	Calif.	1B	92	308	44	86	11	3	3	48	.279	708	68	18	.977
1975—San Antonio	Texas	1B	41	153	15	32	8	3	3	12	.209	390	27	5	.988
1976—Williamsport†	East.	1B	117	416	46	119	11	3	10	42	.286	1043	79	13	.989
1977—Toledo	Int.	1B	119	452	62	136	30	5	13	77	.301	1077	74	14	.988
1978—Portland	P.C.	1B	77	277	59	102	23	2	18	69	.368	633	46	7	.990
1978—Cleveland	Amer.	1B	36	98	11	24	6	1	4	13	.245	73	8	1	.988
1979—Tacoma	P.C.	1B	86	315	47	87	14	3	13	55	.276	660	73	9	.988
1979—Cleveland	Amer.	1B	29	56	6	13	2	0	1	6	.232	37	4	0	1.000
1980—Tacoma	P.C.	OF-1B	122	409	65	126	26	3	19	89	.308	386	24	6	.986
Major League Totals			65	154	17	37	8	1	5	19	.240	110	12	1	.992

Selected by Cleveland Indians' organization in 3rd round of free-agent draft, June 8, 1971.

†On disabled list, May 1 to May 14, 1976.

PITCHING RECORD

Year	Club	League	G.	IP.	W.	L.	Pct.	H.	R.	ER.	SO.	BB.	ERA.
1971—Sarasota Indians	Gulf Coast	3	6	1	0	1.000	2	2	1	7	5	1.50
1972—Reno	California	9	22	1	1	.500	19	13	9	28	17	3.68
1972—Sarasota Indians	Gulf Coast	9	24	1	2	.333	17	13	11	22	18	4.13

RALPH MICHAEL CALDWELL
(Mike)

Born January 22, 1949, at Tarboro, N. C.
Height, 6.00. Weight, 185.
Throws left and bats righthanded.
Hobby—Model airplanes.
Attended North Carolina State University, Raleigh, N. C.
Son of Ralph Franklin Caldwell, former minor league catcher.

Tied American League record for most home runs allowed, inning (4), May 31, 1980 (fourth inning).
Led American League in complete games with 23 in 1978.
Named American League Comeback Player of the Year by The Sporting News, 1978.

Year Club	League	G.	IP.	W.	L.	Pct.	H.	R.	ER.	SO.	BB.	ERA.
1971–Tri-City ....Northwest		2	11	2	0	1.000	9	2	2	19	5	1.64
1971–Lodi..California		17	32	4	1	.800	31	14	13	38	12	3.66
1971–San Diego ....National		6	7	1	0	1.000	4	0	0	5	3	0.00
1972–San Diego ....National		42	164	7	11	.389	183	92	73	102	49	4.01
1973–San Diego† ....National		55	149	5	14	.263	146	77	62	86	53	3.74
1974–San Francisco ....National		31	189	14	5	.737	176	80	62	83	63	2.95
1975–San Francisco ....National		38	163	7	13	.350	194	102	87	57	48	4.80
1976–San Francisco‡ ....National		50	107	1	7	.125	145	74	58	55	20	4.88
1977–Cincinnati§ ....National		14	25	0	0	.000	25	11	11	11	8	3.96
1977–Milwaukee ....American		21	94	5	8	.385	101	58	48	38	36	4.60
1978–Milwaukee ....American		37	293	22	9	.710	258	90	77	131	54	2.37
1979–Milwaukee ....American		30	235	16	6	.727	252	96	86	89	39	3.29
1980–Milwaukee ....American		34	225	13	11	.542	248	112	101	74	56	4.04
National League Totals...........................		236	804	35	50	.412	873	436	353	399	244	3.95
American League Totals..........................		122	847	56	34	.622	859	356	312	332	185	3.32
Major League Totals		358	1651	91	84	.520	1732	792	665	731	429	3.63

Selected by San Diego Padres' organization in 11th round of free-agent draft, June 8, 1971.

†Traded to San Francisco Giants for First Baseman Willie McCovey and Outfielder Bernie Williams (latter on Phoenix roster), October 25, 1973.

‡Traded with Pitcher John D'Acquisto and Catcher Dave Rader to St. Louis Cardinals for Outfielder Willie Crawford, Pitcher John Curtis, and Infielder-Outfielder Vic Harris, October 26, 1976. Traded to Cincinnati Reds' organization for Pitcher Pat Darcy, March 29, 1977.

§Traded to Milwaukee Brewers for Pitcher Richard O'Keeffe and Infielder Garry Pyka (both assigned from Holyoke to Three Rivers), June 15, 1977.

MICHAEL SALVATORE CALISE
(Mike)

Born March 16, 1957, at Westport, Conn.
Height, 6.02. Weight, 190.
Throws and bats righthanded.
Attended Mesa Community College, Mesa, Ariz.

Year Club	League	Pos.	G.	AB.	R.	H.	2B.	3B.	HR.	RBI.	B.A.	PO.	A.	E.	F.A.
1977–Gastonia ....W. Car.		OF-3B	115	398	64	112	16	4	21	95	.281	106	79	19	.907
1978–Arkansas ....Texas		3B-OF	28	98	23	29	7	1	8	24	.296	19	38	2	.966
1978–Springfield† ......A.A.		3B	12	36	5	7	1	1	1	2	.194	7	14	3	.875
1979–St. Petersburg‡ .Fla. St.		3B-OF	25	88	10	21	3	0	1	9	.239	15	20	0	1.000
1980–Arkansas§........Texas		3B	16	58	8	21	8	0	3	16	.362	9	35	6	.880
1980–Gastonia ....S. Atl.		DH	22	81	14	25	8	0	3	17	.391	0	0	0	.000

Selected by St. Louis Cardinals' organization in 24th round of free-agent draft, June 8, 1976.

†On disabled list, May 13 to June 8, 1978.

‡On disabled list, April 13 to April 25, May 29 to July 24 and August 7 to September 1, 1979.

§On disabled list, May 5 to August 8, 1980.

ERNIE CARLOS CAMACHO

Born February 1, 1956, at Salinas, Calif.
Height, 6.01. Weight, 180.
Throws and bats righthanded.
Attended Hartnell Junior College, Salinas, Calif.

Year Club	League	G.	IP.	W.	L.	Pct.	H.	R.	ER.	SO.	BB.	ERA.
1976–Modesto................................California		10	56	3	4	.429	69	47	35	29	39	5.63
1977–Modesto† ....California		5	32	2	1	.667	30	19	14	21	23	3.94
1977–Chattanooga........................Southern		11	60	3	8	.273	74	50	43	20	28	6.45
1978–Modesto‡ ....California		1	2	0	0	.000	0	0	0	2	2	0.00
1979–Ogden....................................P. Coast		21	97	7	9	.438	102	86	71	60	70	6.59
1980–Ogden....................................P. Coast		33	64	5	3	.625	60	29	28	58	26	3.94
1980–Oakland ....American		5	12	0	0	.000	20	9	9	9	5	6.75
Major League Totals................................		5	12	0	0	.000	20	9	9	9	5	6.75

Selected by Pittsburgh Pirates' organization in 12th round of free-agent draft, June 4, 1975.
Selected by California Angels' organization in secondary phase of free-agent draft, January 7, 1976.
Selected by Oakland A's organization in secondary phase of free-agent draft, June 8, 1976.

†On disabled list, April 23 to June 14, 1977.

‡On Jersey City temporary inactive list, April 14 to July 18, 1978; on Modesto temporary inactive list, July 18 to August 30, 1978.

RICK LAMAR CAMP

Born June 10, 1953, at Trion, Ga.
Height, 6.01. Weight, 198.
Throws and bats righthanded.
Attended West Georgia College, Carrollton, Ga.

Major League saves: 1976 (0), 1977 (10), 1978 (0), 1980 (22). Total–32.

Year Club	League	G.	IP.	W.	L.	Pct.	H.	R.	ER.	SO.	BB.	ERA.
1974–Kingsport............................Ap'lachian		7	43	3	2	.600	44	23	15	52	16	3.14
1975–Savannah ....Southern		25	176	12	10	.545	161	68	56	100	62	2.86

Year Club	League	G.	IP.	W.	L.	Pct.	H.	R.	ER.	SO.	BB.	ERA.
1976—Richmond	Int'national	49	164	10	11	.476	177	90	78	85	68	4.28
1976—Atlanta	National	5	11	0	1	.000	13	9	8	6	2	6.55
1977—Atlanta†	National	54	79	6	3	.667	89	47	35	51	47	3.99
1978—Atlanta	National	42	74	2	4	.333	99	42	31	23	32	3.77
1979—Richmond‡	Int'national	22	55	3	2	.600	59	31	26	33	12	4.25
1980—Atlanta	National	77	108	6	4	.600	92	26	23	33	29	1.92
Major League Totals		178	272	14	12	.538	293	124	97	113	110	3.21

Selected by Atlanta Braves' organization in 7th round of free-agent draft, June 5, 1974.
†On disabled list, July 28 to September 1, 1977.
‡On disabled list, April 13 to May 7 and August 7 to August 27, 1979.

DAGOBERTO BLANCO CAMPANERIS
(Bert and Campy)

Born March 9, 1942, at Pueblo Nuevo, Matanzas, Cuba.
Height, 5,10. Weight, 160.
Throws and bats righthanded.
Hobby—Fishing.
Cousin of Jose Cardenal, outfielder with Kansas City Royals in 1980.

Established major league record for most double plays, shortstop, extra-inning game (6), September 13, 1970, first game (11 innings).

Tied major league records for most home runs, first major league game (2), July 23, 1964; fewest caught stealing, season, 50 or more stolen bases (8), 1962; most stolen bases by pinch-runner, inning (2), October 4, 1972 (fourth inning); most bases on balls, inning (2), June 18, 1975 (seventh inning); most positions played, season (9), 1965; most positions played, game (9), September 8, 1965.

Tied modern major league record for most triples, game (3), August 29, 1967.

Established American League records for fewest hits, for leader in hits, season (177), 1968; most times caught stealing, lifetime (190).

Tied American League records for most home runs as leadoff batter, season (6), 1970; most home runs, first two major league games (2), July 23 and 24, 1964.

On August 13, 1962, pitching in relief for Daytona Beach against Ft. Lauderdale, Campaneris pitched righthanded to the righthanded batters and lefthanded to the lefthanded batters. In two innings he gave up one run and one hit while walking one and striking out four.

Major League stolen bases: 1964 (10), 1965 (51), 1966 (52), 1967 (55), 1968 (62), 1969 (62), 1970 (42), 1971 (34), 1972 (52), 1973 (34), 1974 (34), 1975 (24), 1976 (54), 1977 (27), 1978 (22), 1979 (13), 1980 (10). Total—638.

Led American League in stolen bases with 51 in 1965, 52 in 1966, 55 in 1967, 62 in 1968, 42 in 1970 and 52 in 1972.

Led American League in sacrifice hits with 20 in 1972 and with 40 in 1977.

Led American League shortstops in total chances with 795 in 1972.

Named shortstop on THE SPORTING NEWS American League All-Star Team, 1973 and 1974.

Year Club	League	Pos.	G.	AB.	R.	H.	2B.	3B.	HR.	RBI.	B.A.	PO.	A.	E.	F.A.
1962—Daytona Beach	Fl. St.	O-1-C-S	100	334	59	97	15	2	1	33	.290	384	68	24	.950
1962—Binghamton	Ea.	I-OF-P	13	44	11	16	3	0	0	3	.364	12	4	2	.889
1963—Lewiston	Northw.	PH	11	6	2	0	0	0	0	1	.000	0	0	0	.000
1963—Binghamton	Ea.	SS-C-1B	35	117	21	36	5	1	0	12	.308	99	49	12	.925
1964—Birmingham	South.	SS	86	354	69	115	18	•11	6	40	.325	163	229	12	.945
1964—Kansas City	Amer.	SS-O-3	67	269	27	69	14	3	4	22	.257	102	108	8	.963
1965—Kansas City	Amer.	SS-OF†	144	578	67	156	23	•12	6	42	.270	258	276	35	.938
1966—Kansas City	Amer.	SS	142	573	82	153	29	10	5	42	.267	283	350	19	.971
1967—Kansas City	Amer.	SS	147	601	85	149	29	6	3	32	.248	•259	365	•30	.954
1968—Oakland	Amer.	•SS-OF	159	•642	87	•177	25	9	4	38	.276	•283	458	•34	.956
1969—Oakland	Amer.	SS	135	547	71	142	15	2	2	25	.260	220	391	21	.967
1970—Oakland	Amer.	SS	147	603	97	168	28	4	22	64	.279	267	414	19	.973
1971—Oakland‡	Amer.	SS	134	569	80	143	18	4	5	47	.251	231	303	•26	.954
1972—Oakland	Amer.	SS	149	•625	85	150	25	2	8	32	.240	•283	494	18	.977
1973—Oakland	Amer.	SS	151	601	89	150	17	6	4	46	.250	228	496	23	.969
1974—Oakland§	Amer.	SS	134	527	77	153	18	8	2	41	.290	207	423	22	.966
1975—Oakland	Amer.	SS	137	509	69	135	15	3	4	46	.265	199	378	23	.962
1976—Oakland x	Amer.	SS	149	536	67	137	14	1	1	52	.256	231	490	23	.969
1977—Texas	Amer.	SS	150	552	77	140	19	7	5	46	.254	269	483	25	.968
1978—Texas y	Amer.	SS	98	269	30	50	5	3	1	17	.186	151	263	20	.954
1979—Tex. z-Calif.	Amer.	SS	93	248	29	57	4	4	0	15	.230	148	233	17	.957
1980—California	Amer.	SS-2B	77	210	32	53	8	1	2	18	.252	108	157	12	.957
Major League Totals			2213	8459	1151	2182	306	85	78	625	.258	3277	6082	375	.961

Signed as free agent by Kansas City A's organization, April 25, 1961.
†On September 8 against the California Angels, Campaneris played one inning at each of the nine positions.
‡On disabled list, July 3 to July 23, 1971.
§On supplemental disabled list, July 28 to August 12, 1974.
xPlayed out option year, and granted free agency, November 1, 1976; signed as free agent by Texas Rangers, November 17, 1976.
yOn supplemental disabled list, May 19 to June 6, 1978.
zTraded to California Angels for Third Baseman Dave Chalk, May 4, 1979

CHAMPIONSHIP SERIES RECORD

Tied Championship Series record for most times home run as leadoff batter, start of game (1), October 7, 1973.

Established American League Championship Series record for most consecutive hitless times at bat, total Series (24).

Tied American League Championship Series record for most home runs, five-game Series (2), 1973.

Year	Club	League	Pos.	G.	AB.	R.	H.	2B.	3B.	HR.	RBI.	B.A.	PO.	A.	E.	F.A.
1971—Oakland		Amer.	SS	3	12	0	2	1	0	0	0	.167	3	6	0	1.000
1972—Oakland		Amer.	SS	2	7	3	3	0	0	0	0	.429	3	7	0	1.000
1973—Oakland		Amer.	SS	5	21	3	7	1	0	2	3	.333	6	15	1	.955
1974—Oakland		Amer.	SS	4	17	0	3	0	0	0	3	.176	3	17	0	1.000
1975—Oakland		Amer.	SS	3	11	1	0	0	0	0	0	.000	2	10	0	1.000
1979—California		Amer.	SS	1	0	0	0	0	0	0	0	.000	0	0	0	.000
Championship Series Totals				18	68	7	15	2	0	2	6	.221	17	55	1	.986

WORLD SERIES RECORD

Tied World Series records for most times hit by pitch, total Series (3); fewest chances accepted by shortstop, game (0), October 18, 1972.

Year	Club	League	Pos.	G.	AB.	R.	H.	2B.	3B.	HR.	RBI.	B.A.	PO.	A.	E.	F.A.
1972—Oakland		Amer.	SS	7	28	1	5	0	0	0	0	.179	17	15	1	.970
1973—Oakland		Amer.	SS	7	31	6	9	0	1	1	3	.290	10	28	1	.974
1974—Oakland		Amer.	SS	5	17	1	6	2	0	0	2	.353	6	16	2	.917
World Series Totals				19	76	8	20	2	1	1	5	.263	33	59	4	.958

ALL-STAR GAME RECORD

Year	League	Pos.	AB.	R.	H.	2B.	3B.	HR.	RBI.	B.A.	PO.	A.	E.	F.A.
1968—American		SS	1	0	0	0	0	0	0	.000	1	0	0	1.000
1973—American		SS	3	0	0	0	0	0	0	.000	1	2	0	1.000
1974—American		SS	4	0	0	0	0	0	0	.000	2	3	0	1.000
1975—American		SS	2	0	2	0	0	0	0	1.000	3	2	0	1.000
1977—American		SS	1	1	0	0	0	0	0	.000	0	1	0	1.000
All-Star Game Totals			11	1	2	0	0	0	0	.182	7	8	0	1.000

Member of American League All-Star Team for the 1972 game; did not play.

PITCHING RECORD

Year	Club	League	G.	IP.	W.	L.	Pct.	H.	R.	ER.	SO.	BB.	ERA.
1962—Daytona Beach		Florida St.	3	6	0	0	.000	5	2	2	6	2	3.00
1962—Binghamton		Eastern	1	2	0	0	.000	2	5	1	0	4	4.50
1965—Kansas City		American	1	1	0	0	.000	1	1	1	1	2	9.00
Major League Totals			1	1	0	0	.000	1	1	1	1	2	9.00

WILLIAM RICHARD CAMPBELL
(Bill)

Born August 9, 1948, at Highland Park, Mich.
Height, 6.03. Weight, 190.
Throws and bats righthanded.
Hobby—Coaching girls' basketball team.
Attended Mount San Antonio Junior College, Walnut, Calif.

Established American League record for most innings pitched by relief pitcher, season (168), 1976.
Tied American League record for most games won, season, all as relief pitcher (17), 1976.
Major League saves: 1973 (7), 1974 (19), 1975 (5), 1976 (20), 1977 (31), 1978 (4), 1979 (9), 1980 (0). Total—95.
Led Southern League pitchers in complete games with 14 and tied for lead in games started with 29 in 1972.
Led American League in saves with 31 in 1977.
Named by THE SPORTING NEWS as American League Fireman of the Year, 1976 and 1977.

Year	Club	League	G.	IP.	W.	L.	Pct.	H.	R.	ER.	SO.	BB.	ERA.
1971—Wisconsin Rapids†		Midwest	9	63	5	3	.625	42	13	8	91	19	1.14
1972—Charlotte		Southern	29	219	13	10	.565	181	74	59	*204	69	2.42
1973—Tacoma		P. Coast	18	133	10	5	.667	123	63	54	110	46	3.65
1973—Minnesota		American	28	52	3	3	.500	44	20	18	42	20	3.12
1974—Minnesota		American	63	120	8	7	.533	109	37	35	89	55	2.63
1975—Minnesota‡		American	47	121	4	6	.400	119	58	51	76	46	3.79
1976—Minnesota		American	*78	168	17	5	*.773	145	63	56	115	62	3.00
1977—Boston		American	69	140	13	9	.591	112	48	46	114	60	2.96
1978—Boston		American	29	51	7	5	.583	62	25	22	47	17	3.88
1979—Boston		American	41	55	3	4	.429	55	28	26	25	23	4.25
1980—Boston§		American	23	41	4	0	1.000	44	26	22	17	22	4.83
Major League Totals			378	748	59	39	.602	690	305	276	525	305	3.32

Signed as free agent by Minnesota Twins' organization, September 25, 1970.
†On disabled list, June 14, 1971 through remainder of season.
‡Granted free agency, November 1, 1976; signed as free agent by Boston Red Sox, November 6, 1976.
§On emergency disabled list, March 25 to June 20, 1980.

ALL-STAR GAME RECORD

Year	League	IP.	W.	L.	Pct.	H.	R.	ER.	SO.	BB.	ERA
1977—American		1	0	0	.000	0	0	0	2	1	0.00

DID YOU KNOW—

That in the two last two seasons, Willie Wilson's stolen base percentage has been .880? The fleet Royal has been caught just 22 times in 184 attempts.

JOHN ROBERT CANDELARIA

Born November 6, 1953, at Brooklyn, N.Y.
Height, 6.07. Weight, 232.
Throws and bats lefthanded.
Hobbies—Records, fishing, hunting and basketball.
Pitched 2-0 no-hit victory against Los Angeles Dodgers, August 9, 1976.
Received reported $40,000 bonus to sign with Pittsburgh Pirates, 1973.

Year Club	League	G.	IP.	W.	L.	Pct.	H.	R.	ER.	SO.	BB.	ERA.
1973—Charleston	W. Carol.	18	95	10	2	*.833	84	45	40	60	38	3.79
1974—Salem	Carolina	25	154	11	8	.579	146	80	63	147	63	3.68
1974—Charleston	Int'national	1	11	0	0	.000	7	2	2	10	1	1.64
1975—Charleston	Int'national	10	61	7	1	.875	53	15	12	48	17	1.77
1975—Pittsburgh	National	18	121	8	6	.571	95	47	37	95	36	2.75
1976—Pittsburgh	National	32	220	16	7	.696	173	87	77	138	60	3.15
1977—Pittsburgh	National	33	231	20	5	*.800	197	64	60	133	52	*2.34
1978—Pittsburgh	National	30	189	12	11	.522	191	73	68	94	49	3.24
1979—Pittsburgh	National	33	207	14	9	.609	201	83	74	101	41	3.22
1980—Pittsburgh	National	35	233	11	14	.440	246	114	104	97	50	4.02
Major League Totals		181	1201	81	52	.609	1103	468	420	658	286	3.15

Selected by Pittsburgh Pirates' organization in 2nd round of free-agent draft, June 6, 1972.

CHAMPIONSHIP SERIES RECORD

Established Championship Series record for most strikeouts, three-game Series (14), 1975.
Tied Championship Series records for most strikeouts, game (14), October 7, 1975; most consecutive strikeouts, start of game (4), October 7, 1975.

Year Club	League	G.	IP.	W.	L.	Pct.	H.	R.	ER.	SO.	BB.	ERA.
1975—Pittsburgh	National	1	7⅔	0	0	.000	3	3	3	14	2	3.52
1979—Pittsburgh	National	1	7	0	0	.000	5	2	2	4	1	2.57
Championship Series Totals		2	14⅔	0	0	.000	8	5	5	18	3	3.07

WORLD SERIES TOTALS

Year Club	League	G.	IP.	W.	L.	Pct.	H.	R.	ER.	SO.	BB.	ERA.
1979—Pittsburgh	National	2	9	1	1	.500	14	6	5	4	2	5.00

ALL-STAR GAME RECORD

Member of National League All-Star Team in 1977; did not play.

JOSEPH JEROME CANNON
(J.J.)

Born July 13, 1953, at Camp Lejeune, N. C.
Height, 6.03. Weight, 193.
Throws right and bats lefthanded.
Hobbies—Golf, hunting and fishing.
Attended Pensacola Junior College, Pensacola, Fla.
Cousin of Willie Broughton, infielder with San Francisco Giants' organization,
and Pittsburgh Pirates' organization, 1957 through 1961.
Tied for International League lead among outfielders in double plays with 5 in 1978.

Year Club	League	Pos.	G.	AB.	R.	H.	2B.	3B.	HR.	RBI.	B.A.	PO.	A.	E.	F.A.
1974—Covington	Appal.	OF	66	*280	55	*84	13	*8	6	40	.300	66	136	6	.928
1974—Cedar Rapids	Midw.	OF	11	38	2	7	2	1	0	1	.184	20	0	0	1.000
1975—Dubuque	Midw.	OF	119	346	47	72	8	5	6	37	.208	160	17	12	.937
1976—Columbus	South.	OF	127	478	64	142	13	4	2	40	.297	238	12	8	.969
1977—Charleston	Int.	OF	113	431	67	132	22	6	10	60	.306	180	6	7	.964
1977—Houston	Nat.	OF	9	17	3	2	2	0	0	1	.118	7	0	0	1.000
1978—Charleston	Int.	OF	136	518	72	152	17	*18	8	75	.293	304	14	12	.964
1978—Houston†	Nat.	OF	8	18	1	4	0	0	0	1	.222	7	0	2	.778
1979—Syracuse	Int.	OF	59	231	41	67	14	7	6	24	.290	153	4	5	.969
1979—Toronto	Amer.	OF	61	142	14	30	1	1	1	5	.211	81	5	0	1.000
1980—Toronto	Amer.	OF	70	50	16	4	0	0	0	4	.080	29	1	1	.968
National League Totals			17	35	4	6	2	0	0	2	.171	14	0	2	.875
American League Totals			131	192	30	34	1	1	1	9	.177	110	6	1	.991
Major League Totals			148	227	34	40	3	1	1	11	.176	124	6	3	.977

Selected by Houston Astros' organization in 1st round (16th player selected) of free-agent draft, January 9, 1974.

†Traded with Pitcher Mark Lemongello and Shortstop Pedro Hernandez to Toronto Blue Jays for Catcher Alan Ashby, November 27, 1978.

DOUGLAS EDMUND CAPILLA

Name pronounced kuh-PILL-uh.

(Doug)

Born January 7, 1952, at Honolulu, Hawaii.
Height, 5.08. Weight, 175.
Throws and bats lefthanded.
Hobbies—Fishing, swimming and dancing.
Attended West Valley College, Saratoga, Calif.

Pitched seven-inning, 1-0 no-hit victory against Appleton, May 31, 1972.
Tied for Midwest League lead in hit batsmen with 12 and tied for lead in wild pitches with 25 in 1972.

Year—Club	League	G.	IP.	W.	L.	Pct.	H.	R.	ER.	SO.	BB.	ERA.
1970—Great Falls†	Pioneer	17	38	2	5	.286	24	37	28	69	57	6.63
1971—Fresno‡	California						Did not play.					
1972—Decatur	Midwest	26	161	6	12	.333	134	•100	•84	192	•125	4.70
1973—Fresno§	California	24	86	4	7	.364	86	67	42	112	74	4.40
1974—Arkansas	Texas	20	88	6	6	.500	87	72	60	78	84	6.14
1975—St. Petersburg	Florida St.	8	51	3	4	.429	38	20	12	45	39	2.12
1975—Arkansas	Texas	16	80	3	5	.375	91	51	41	48	34	4.61
1976—Tulsa	Am. Assoc.	49	57	4	4	.500	59	38	31	58	45	4.89
1976—St. Louis	National	7	8	1	0	1.000	8	5	5	5	4	5.63
1977—New Orleans	Am. Assoc.	13	58	3	4	.429	57	35	29	50	29	4.50
1977—St. Louis x-Cincinnati	National	24	109	7	8	.467	96	57	54	75	61	4.46
1978—Indianapolis	Am. Assoc.	22	132	10	6	.625	131	91	80	87	93	5.45
1978—Cincinnati	National	6	11	0	1	.000	14	12	12	9	11	9.82
1979—Cincinnati y-Chicago	National	18	24	1	1	.500	21	12	11	10	12	4.13
1979—Wichita	Am. Assoc.	28	83	6	8	.429	85	44	42	45	51	4.55
1980—Chicago	National	39	90	2	8	.200	82	46	41	51	51	4.10
Major League Totals		94	242	11	18	.379	221	132	123	150	139	4.57

Selected by San Francisco Giants' organization in 25th round of free-agent draft, June 4, 1970.
†Played in five games as an outfielder.
‡On suspended list, May 18, 1971 to March 2, 1972.
§Drafted from San Francisco Giants' organization by Arkansas (St. Louis Cardinals' organization), December 3, 1973.
xTraded to Cincinnati Reds for Pitcher Rawly Eastwick, June 15, 1977.
yTraded to Chicago Cubs for a player to be named later, May 3, 1979; Cincinnati acquired Pitcher Mark Gilbert to complete deal, October 12, 1979.

GEORGE ANGELO CAPPUZZELLO

Born January 15, 1954, at Youngstown, O.
Height, 6.00. Weight, 175.
Throws left and bats righthanded.
Attended Youngstown State University, Youngstown, O. and attending Florida State University, Tallahassee, Fla.
Led Southern League in shutouts with 6 in 1980.
Tied for Southern League lead in complete games with 12 in 1980.

Year—Club	League	G.	IP.	W.	L.	Pct.	H.	R.	ER.	SO.	BB.	ERA.
1973—Anderson	W. Carol.	25	117	9	5	.643	118	54	37	89	54	2.85
1974—Lakeland	Florida St.	4	4	0	0	.000	5	6	5	4	8	11.25
1974—Dubuque	Midwest	24	136	7	11	.389	120	70	44	137	69	2.91
1975—Lakeland	Florida St.	16	110	5	8	.385	92	46	31	89	64	2.54
1975—Montgomery	Southern	8	32	0	3	.000	27	17	13	23	20	3.66
1976—Montgomery	Southern	17	117	7	7	.500	102	57	46	105	65	3.54
1976—Evansville	Am. Assoc.	11	49	1	4	.200	50	22	15	37	20	2.76
1977—Evansville†	Am. Assoc.	39	123	5	3	.625	138	72	61	75	56	4.46
1978—Indianapolis‡	Am. Assoc.	40	56	3	1	.750	45	25	19	57	39	3.05
1979—Indianapolis	Am. Assoc.	19	17	1	1	.500	17	26	24	13	19	12.71
1979—Nashville§	Southern	44	82	8	4	.667	89	34	22	72	31	2.41
1980—Montgomery	Southern	27	152	9	9	.500	114	65	55	121	70	3.26
1980—Evansville	Am. Assoc.	3	14	0	1	.000	17	8	7	9	3	4.50

Selected by Detroit Tigers' organization in 27th round of free-agent draft, June 6, 1972.
†Traded with Outfielder John Valle to Cincinnati Reds for Pitcher Jack Billingham, March 7, 1978.
‡On disabled list, July 21 to August 4, 1978.
§Released, April 8, 1980; signed by Detroit Tigers' organization, April 28, 1980.

BERNARDO CARBO
(Bernie)

Born August 5, 1947, at Detroit, Mich.
Height, 6.00. Weight, 185.
Throws right and bats lefthanded.
Hobby—Sports.
Led Southern League batters in walks with 91 in 1968.
Led Carolina League batters in walks with 108 and third basemen in double plays with 27 in 1966.
Tied for Southern League lead in double plays by outfielders with 3 in 1968.
Named Most Valuable Player in American Association, 1969.
Named to THE SPORTING NEWS Minor League All-Star Team, 1969.
Named THE SPORTING NEWS National League Rookie Player of the Year, 1970.

Year—Club	League	Pos.	G.	AB.	R.	H.	2B.	3B.	HR.	RBI.	B.A.	PO.	A.	E.	F.A.
1965—Tampa	Fla. St.	3B	71	211	25	46	2	4	0	19	.218	66	124	16	.922
1966—Peninsula	Carol.	3B	132	402	66	108	•30	1	15	57	.269	80	•270	•41	.895
1967—Knoxville	So.	•3B-OF	93	279	23	56	5	7	2	27	.201	59	150	•31	.871
1968—Asheville	South.	•OF-3	127	417	87	117	20	7	20	66	.281	153	•34	9	.954
1969—Indianapolis	A. A.	OF	111	404	83	145	•37	2	21	76	•.359	191	16	6	.972
1969—Cincinnati	Nat.	PH-PR	4	3	0	0	0	0	0	0	.000	0	0	0	.000
1970—Cincinnati	Nat.	OF	125	365	54	113	19	3	21	63	.310	177	8	4	.979
1971—Cincinnati	Nat.	OF	106	310	33	68	20	1	5	20	.219	154	7	3	.982
1972—Cinn.†-St. L.	Nat.	•OF-3B	118	323	44	81	13	1	7	34	.251	171	•16	6	.969

— 77 —

Year	Club	League	Pos.	G.	AB.	R.	H.	2B.	3B.	HR.	RBI.	B.A.	PO.	A.	E.	F.A.
1973–St. Louis‡	...Nat.	OF	111	308	42	88	18	0	8	40	.286	171	11	4	.978
1974–Boston	...Amer.	OF	117	338	40	84	20	0	12	61	.249	164	5	1	.994
1975–Boston	...Amer.	OF	107	319	64	82	21	3	15	50	.257	157	7	4	.976
1976–Bos.§-Mil. x	...Amer.	OF	86	238	25	56	11	0	5	21	.235	72	5	0	1.000
1977–Boston	...Amer.	OF	86	228	36	66	6	1	15	34	.289	131	5	7	.951
1978–Bos. y-Cleve. z	...Amer.	OF	77	220	28	62	11	0	5	22	.282	27	0	0	1.000
1979–St. Louis	...Nat.	OF	52	64	6	18	1	0	3	12	.281	10	0	0	1.000
1980–St. L.a-Pitt.b	...Nat.	PH	21	17	0	4	0	0	0	1	.235	0	0	0	.000
American League Totals			473	1343	193	350	69	4	52	188	.261	551	22	12	.979
National League Totals			537	1390	179	372	71	5	44	170	.268	683	42	17	.977
Major League Totals			1010	2733	372	722	140	9	96	358	.264	1234	64	29	.978

Selected by Cincinnati Reds' organization in 1st round of free-agent draft, June 24, 1965.

†Traded to St. Louis Cardinals for First Baseman Joe Hague, May 18, 1972.

‡Traded with Pitcher Rick Wise to Boston Red Sox for Outfielder Reggie Smith and Pitcher Ken Tatum, October 26, 1973.

§Traded with undisclosed amount of cash to Milwaukee Brewers' for Outfielder Bobby Darwin and Pitcher Tom Murphy, June 3, 1976.

xTraded with First Baseman George Scott to Boston Red Sox for First Baseman Cecil Cooper, December 6, 1976.

ySold to Cleveland Indians, June 15, 1978.

zGranted free agency, November 2, 1978; signed by St. Louis Cardinals, March 10, 1979.

aReleased, May 27, 1980; signed by Pittsburgh Pirates, September 1, 1980.

bReleased, October 8, 1980.

CHAMPIONSHIP SERIES RECORD

Year	Club	League	Pos.	G.	AB.	R.	H.	2B.	3B.	HR.	RBI.	B.A.	PO.	A.	E.	F.A.
1970–Cincinnati	...Nat.	OF	2	6	0	0	0	0	0	0	.000	0	0	0	.000

WORLD SERIES RECORD

Tied World Series records for most home runs as pinch-hitter, Series (2), 1975; most total bases as pinch-hitter, Series (8), 1975; most home runs as pinch-hitter, game (1), October 14 and 21, 1975.

Year	Club	League	Pos.	G.	AB.	R.	H.	2B.	3B.	HR.	RBI.	B.A.	PO.	A.	E.	F.A.
1970–Cincinnati	...Nat.	OF-PH	4	8	0	0	0	0	0	0	.000	4	0	0	1.000
1975–Boston	...Amer.	PH-OF	4	7	3	3	1	0	2	4	.429	1	1	0	1.000
World Series Totals			8	15	3	3	1	0	2	4	.200	5	1	0	1.000

JOSE DOMEC CARDENAL

Name pronounced Car-duh-NAHL.

Born October 7, 1943, at Matanzas, Cuba.
Height, 5.10. Weight, 151.
Throws and bats righthanded.
Hobbies—Movies and sports cars.
Brother of Pedro Cardenal, infielder in St. Louis Cardinals' organization and Cousin of Dagoberto (Bert) Campaneris, Texas Rangers' shortstop.

Tied major league record for most unassisted double plays, outfielder, season (2), 1968.
Major League stolen bases: 1963 (0), 1964 (2), 1965 (37), 1966 (24), 1967 (10), 1968 (40), 1969 (36), 1970 (25), 1971 (21), 1972 (25), 1973 (19), 1974 (23), 1975 (34), 1976 (23), 1977 (5), 1978 (2), 1979 (0), 1980 (0). Total—329.
Made six hits in one game, May 2, 1976 (14 innings).
Led Sophomore League in total bases with 336 and stolen bases with 64 in 1961.
Led Pacific Coast League outfielders in double plays with 6 in 1962.
Tied for Pacific Coast League lead in stolen bases with 40 in 1964.

Year	Club	League	Pos.	G.	AB.	R.	H.	2B.	3B.	HR.	RBI.	B.A.	PO.	A.	E.	F.A.
1961–El Paso	...Soph.	O-IN-P	128	502	•159	178	•39	7	•35	108	.355	196	132	34	.906
1961–Eugene	...Northw.	OF	9	25	2	7	1	0	0	1	.280	12	1	1	.929
1962–Tacoma	...P. C.	O-3-1B	121	391	55	87	16	6	16	41	.223	208	22	9	.962
1963–San Francisco	...Nat.	OF	9	5	1	1	0	0	0	2	.200	0	0	0	.000
1963–El Paso	...Tex.	OF-3B	125	475	112	148	27	5	36	95	.312	258	47	21	.936
1964–Tacoma	...P. C.	OF-2B	132	464	70	134	18	3	12	54	.289	262	13	9	.968
1964–San Francisco†	...Nat.	OF	20	15	3	0	0	0	0	0	.000	8	2	1	.909
1965–California	...Amer.	•OF-3-2	134	512	58	128	23	2	11	57	.250	287	13	•11	.965
1966–California	...Amer.	OF	154	561	67	155	15	3	16	48	.276	351	10	3	.992
1967–California‡	...Amer.	OF	108	381	40	90	13	5	6	27	.236	195	10	3	.986
1968–Cleveland	...Amer.	OF	157	583	78	150	21	7	7	44	.257	367	12	10	.974
1969–Cleveland§	...Amer.	OF-3B	146	557	75	143	26	3	11	45	.257	329	12	6	.983
1970–St. Louis	...Nat.	OF	148	552	73	162	32	6	10	74	.293	276	6	9	.969
1971–St. Louis	...Nat.	OF	89	301	37	73	12	4	7	48	.243	181	9	6	.969
1971–Milwaukee y	...Amer.	OF	53	198	20	51	10	0	3	32	.258	133	6	3	.979
1972–Chicago	...Nat.	OF	143	533	96	155	24	6	17	70	.291	223	11	7	.971
1973–Chicago	...Nat.	OF	145	522	80	158	33	2	11	68	.303	234	13	5	.980
1974–Chicago	...Nat.	OF	143	542	75	159	35	3	13	72	.293	262	15	10	.965
1975–Chicago	...Nat.	OF	154	574	85	182	30	2	9	68	.317	313	14	8	.976
1976–Chicago	...Nat.	OF	136	521	64	156	25	2	8	47	.299	246	10	5	.981
1977–Chicago z	...Nat.	O-2-S	100	226	33	54	12	1	3	38	.239	85	1	2	.989
1978–Philadelphia	...Nat.	1B-OF	87	201	27	50	12	0	4	33	.249	365	17	5	.987
1979–Phila. a-N.Y. b	...Nat.	OF-1B	40	85	12	21	7	0	2	13	.247	49	0	0	1.000

Year	Club	League	Pos.	G.	AB.	R.	H.	2B.	3B.	HR.	RBI.	B.A.	PO.	A.	E.	F.A.
1980—New York c	Nat.	OF-1B	26	42	4	7	1	0	0	4	.167	30	1	0	1.000
1980—Kansas City d	Amer.	OF	25	53	8	18	2	0	0	5	.340	30	2	1	.970
National League Totals			1240	4119	590	1178	223	26	84	517	.286	2272	99	58	.976
American League Totals			777	2845	346	735	110	20	54	258	.258	1692	65	37	.979
Major League Totals			2017	6964	936	1913	333	46	138	775	.275	3964	164	95	.978

Signed as free agent by San Francisco Giants' organization, September 25, 1960.
†Traded to Los Angeles Angels for Catcher Jack Hiatt, November 21, 1964.
‡Traded to Cleveland Indians for Outfielder Chuck Hinton, November 29, 1967.
§Traded to St. Louis Cardinals for Outfielder Vada Pinson, November 20, 1969.
xTraded with Infielder Dick Schofield (latter on Tulsa roster) and Pitcher Bob Reynolds (assigned to Evansville) to Milwaukee Brewers for Shortstop Ted Kubiak and Pitcher Charlie Loseth (assigned from Raleigh-Durham to St. Petersburg), July 29, 1971.
yTraded to Chicago Cubs for Pitcher Jim Colborn, Outfielder Brock Davis and Pitcher Earl Stephenson, latter assigned to Evansville, December 3, 1971.
zOn supplemental disabled list, June 21 through July 9, 1977. Traded to Philadelphia Phillies for Pitcher Manny Seoane, October 25, 1977.
aSold to New York Mets, August 2, 1979.
bOn disabled list, August 18 to September 27, 1979.
cReleased, August 13, 1980; signed by Kansas City Royals, August 21, 1980.
dGranted free agency, November 13, 1980.

PITCHING RECORD

Year	Club	League	G.	IP.	W.	L.	Pct.	H.	R.	ER.	SO.	BB.	ERA.
1961—El Paso	Soph.		1	1	0	0	.000	1	0	0	1	2	0.00

CHAMPIONSHIP SERIES RECORD

Year	Club	League	Pos.	G.	AB.	R.	H.	2B.	3B.	HR.	RBI.	B.A.	PO.	A.	E.	F.A.
1978—Philadelphia	Nat.		1B	2	6	0	1	0	0	0	0	.167	21	0	0	1.000

WORLD SERIES RECORD

Year	Club	League	Pos.	G.	AB.	R.	H.	2B.	3B.	HR.	RBI.	B.A.	PO.	A.	E.	F.A.
1980—Kansas City	Amer.		PH-OF	4	10	0	2	0	0	0	0	.200	7	0	0	1.000

RODNEY CLINE CAREW
(Rod)

Born October 1, 1945, at Gatun, Panama.
Height, 6.00. Weight, 182.
Throws right and bats lefthanded.

Tied major league record for most times stealing home, season (7), 1969; most stolen bases, inning (3), May 18, 1969 (3rd inning); most home runs with bases filled by pinch-hitter, game (1), September 9, 1976.
Established American League record for most games, one or more hits, season (131), 1977.
Tied American League record for most double plays, first baseman, extra-inning game (6), August 29, 1977 (1st game, 10 innings); most seasons leading league, intentional bases on balls (3).
Led American League first basemen in double plays with 149 in 1976 and with 161 in 1977.
Led American League first basemen in assists with 121 in 1977.
Major league stolen bases: 1967 (5), 1968 (12), 1969 (19), 1970 (4), 1971 (6), 1972 (12), 1973 (41), 1974 (38), 1975 (35), 1976 (49), 1977 (23), 1978 (27), 1979 (18), 1980 (23). Total—312.
Named American League Rookie Player of the Year by THE SPORTING NEWS, 1967.
Named American League Rookie of the Year by the Baseball Writers' Association of America, 1967.
Named second baseman on THE SPORTING NEWS American League All-Star Team, 1967-68-69-72-73-74-75.
Named first baseman on THE SPORTING NEWS American League All-Star Team, 1977 and 1978.
Named American League Player of the Year by THE SPORTING NEWS, 1977.
Named Major League Player of the Year by THE SPORTING NEWS, 1977.
Named American League Most Valuable Player by the Baseball Writers' Association of America, 1977.

Year	Club	League	Pos.	G.	AB.	R.	H.	2B.	3B.	HR.	RBI.	B.A.	PO.	A.	E.	F.A.
1964—Melb'rne Twins	Coc. Rk.	2B	37	123	17	40	5	•3	0	21	.325	86	48	7	.950
1965—Orlando	Fla. St.	2B	125	439	57	133	20	8	1	52	.303	290	328	•28	.957
1966—Wilson	Carol.	2B	112	383	64	112	19	3	1	30	.292	248	275	21	.961
1967—Minnesota†	Amer.	2B	137	514	66	150	22	7	8	51	.292	289	314	15	.976
1968—Minnesota‡	Amer.	•2B-SS	127	461	46	126	27	2	1	42	.273	266	285	•18	.968
1969—Minnesota§	Amer.	2B	123	458	79	152	30	4	8	56	*.332	244	302	17	.970
1970—Minnesota x	Amer.	2B-1B	51	191	27	70	12	3	4	28	.366	79	122	8	.962
1971—Minnesota	Amer.	2B-3B	147	577	88	177	16	10	2	48	.307	324	331	16	.976
1972—Minnesota	Amer.	2B	142	535	61	170	21	6	0	51	*.318	331	378	16	.978
1973—Minnesota	Amer.	2B	149	580	98	*203	30	•11	6	62	*.350	383	413	13	.984
1974—Minnesota	Amer.	2B	153	599	86	*218	30	5	3	55	*.364	375	416	*33	.960
1975—Minnesota	Amer.	2B-1B	143	535	89	192	24	4	14	80	*.359	408	377	21	.974
1976—Minnesota	Amer.	1B-2B	156	605	97	200	29	12	9	90	.331	1398	110	16	.990
1977—Minnsota	Amer.	1B-2B	155	616	*128	*239	38	*16	14	100	*.388	1463	124	10	.994
1978—Minnesota y	Amer.	1B-2-OF	152	564	85	188	26	10	5	70	*.333	1363	105	16	.989
1979—California z	Amer.	1B	110	409	78	130	15	3	3	44	.318	804	55	10	.988
1980—California	Amer.	1B	144	540	74	179	34	7	3	59	.331	897	57	6	.994
Major League Totals			1889	7184	1102	2394	354	100	80	836	.333	8624	3389	215	.982

Signed as free agent by Minnesota Twins' organization, June 25, 1964.
†On military list, August 5 to August 21, 1967.
‡On military list, June 8 to June 24, 1968.

§On military list, August 17 to September 1, 1969.
xOn disabled list, June 24 to September 1, 1970.
yTraded to California Angels for Outfielder Ken Landreaux, Pitchers Paul Hartzell and Brad Havens and Third Baseman Dave Engle, February 3, 1979.
zOn supplemental disabled list, June 5 to July 19, 1979.

CHAMPIONSHIP SERIES RECORD

Tied Championship Series record for most two-base hits, four-game Series (3), 1979.
Tied American League Championship Series record for most hits, four-game Series (7), 1979.

Year Club	League	Pos.	G.	AB.	R.	H.	2B.	3B.	HR.	RBI.	B.A.	PO.	A.	E.	F.A.
1969—Minnesota	Amer.	2B	3	14	0	1	0	0	0	0	.071	6	3	1	.900
1970—Minnesota	Amer.	PH	2	2	0	0	0	0	0	0	.000	0	0	0	.000
1979—California	Amer.	1B	4	17	4	7	3	0	0	1	.412	34	1	0	1.000
Championship Series Totals			9	33	4	8	3	0	0	1	.242	40	4	1	.978

ALL-STAR GAME RECORD

Established All-Star Game record for most three-base hits, game (2), July 11, 1978.
Tied All-Star Game record for most at bats, nine-inning game (5), July 15, 1975.

Year League	Pos.	AB.	R.	H.	2B.	3B.	HR.	RBI.	B.A.	PO.	A.	E.	F.A.
1967—American	2B	3	0	0	0	0	0	0	.000	2	3	0	1.000
1968—American	2B	3	0	0	0	0	0	0	.000	2	2	0	1.000
1969—American	2B	3	0	0	0	0	0	0	.000	0	2	0	1.000
1971—American	2B	1	1	0	0	0	0	0	.000	1	2	0	1.000
1972—American	2B	2	0	1	0	0	0	1	.500	2	3	0	1.000
1973—American	2B	3	0	0	0	0	0	0	.000	5	1	0	1.000
1974—American	2B	1	1	0	0	0	0	0	.000	0	1	0	1.000
1975—American	2B	5	0	1	0	0	0	0	.200	3	1	0	1.000
1976—American	1B	3	0	0	0	0	0	0	.000	9	2	0	1.000
1977—American	1B	3	1	1	0	0	0	0	.333	7	0	0	1.000
1978—American	1B	4	2	2	0	2	0	0	.500	6	1	0	1.000
1980—American	1B	2	1	2	1	0	0	0	1.000	4	0	0	1.000
All-Star Game Totals		33	6	7	1	2	0	1	.212	41	18	0	1.000

Named to American League All-Star Team for 1970 and 1979 games; replaced due to injury.

BROOKS MICHAEL CAREY

Born March 18, 1956, at Key West, Fla.
Height, 6.01. Weight, 185.
Throws and bats lefthanded.

Year Club	League	G.	IP.	W.	L.	Pct.	H.	R.	ER.	SO.	BB.	ERA.
1978—Bluefield	Appal.	15	94	3	•8	.273	•98	55	35	58	32	3.35
1979—Miami	Florida St.	19	125	10	7	.588	118	44	34	116	23	2.45
1979—Charlotte	Southern	8	51	4	2	.667	49	24	21	34	13	3.71
1980—Charlotte	Southern	25	163	8	7	.533	158	74	67	78	39	3.70

Selected by Baltimore Orioles' organization in 15th round of free-agent draft, June 6, 1978.

STEVEN NORMAN CARLTON
(Steve)

Born December 22, 1944, at Miami, Fla.
Height, 6.05. Weight, 219.
Throws and bats lefthanded.
Hobbies—Hunting, pool and winter sports.
Attended Miami-Dade Community College, Miami, Fla.

Established major league records for most strikeouts, game by lefthanded pitcher and losing pitcher (19), September 15, 1969; most games, no relief appearances in between, career (364); most balks, season (11), 1979; most strikeouts, by lefthanded pitcher, career (2,969).
Tied major league record for most strikeouts, game (19), September 15, 1969.
Established modern National League record for most one-hit games, career (6).
Tied modern National League record for most games won, season, by lefthander (27), 1972.
Led National League pitchers in games started with 41 and in complete games with 30 in 1972.
Led National League in wild pitches with 17 and tied for lead in games started with 38 in 1980.
Tied for National League lead in games started with 40 and tied for lead in complete games with 18 in 1973.
Won National League Cy Young Memorial Award, 1972, 1977 and 1980.
Named lefthanded pitcher on THE SPORTING NEWS National League All-Star Team, 1969, 1971, 1972, 1977, 1979 and 1980.
Named THE SPORTING NEWS National League Pitcher of the Year, 1972, 1977 and 1980.

Year Club	League	G.	IP.	W.	L.	Pct.	H.	R.	ER.	SO.	BB.	ERA.
1964—Rock Hill	W. Carol.	11	79	10	1	.909	39	17	9	91	36	1.03
1964—Winnipeg	Northern	12	75	4	4	.500	63	40	28	79	48	3.36
1964—Tulsa	Texas	4	24	1	1	.500	16	13	7	21	18	2.63
1965—St. Louis	National	15	25	0	0	.000	27	7	7	21	8	2.52
1966—Tulsa	P. Coast	19	128	9	5	.643	110	65	51	108	54	3.59
1966—St. Louis	National	9	52	3	3	.500	56	22	18	25	18	3.12
1967—St. Louis	National	30	193	14	9	.609	173	71	64	168	62	2.98
1968—St. Louis	National	34	232	13	11	.542	214	87	77	162	61	2.99
1969—St. Louis	National	31	236	17	11	.607	185	66	57	210	93	2.17
1970—St. Louis	National	34	254	10	•19	.345	239	123	105	193	109	3.72
1971—St. Louis†	National	37	273	20	9	.690	275	120	108	172	98	3.56

Year Club	League	G.	IP.	W.	L.	Pct.	H.	R.	ER.	SO.	BB.	ERA.
1972–Philadelphia	National	41	*346	*27	10	.730	*257	84	76	*310	87	*1.98
1973–Philadelphia	National	40	●293	13	*20	.394	*293	*146	*127	223	113	3.90
1974–Philadelphia	National	39	291	16	13	.552	249	118	104	*240	*136	3.22
1975–Philadelphia	National	37	255	15	14	.517	217	116	101	192	104	3.56
1976–Philadelphia	National	35	253	20	7	*.741	224	94	88	195	72	3.13
1977–Philadelphia	National	36	283	*23	10	.697	229	99	83	198	89	2.64
1978–Philadelphia	National	34	247	16	13	.552	228	91	78	161	63	2.84
1979–Philadelphia	National	35	251	18	11	.621	202	112	101	213	89	3.62
1980–Philadelphia	National	38	*304	*24	9	.727	243	87	79	*286	90	2.34
Major League Totals		525	3788	249	169	.596	3311	1443	1273	2969	1292	3.02

Signed as free agent by St. Louis Cardinals' organization, October 8, 1963.
†Traded to Philadelphia Phillies for Pitcher Rick Wise, February 25, 1972.

CHAMPIONSHIP SERIES RECORD

Established Championship Series record for most bases on balls, total Series (23).
Tied Championship Series records for most home runs by pitcher, total Series (1); most bases on balls, four-game Series (8), 1977; most bases on balls, five-game series (8), 1980.
Established National League Championship Series records for most strikeouts, total Series (26); most games started, total Series (6); most innings pitched, total Series (40); most hits allowed, total Series (40); most runs allowed, total Series (21); most earned runs allowed, total Series (20).
Tied National League Championship Series record for most bases on balls, three-game Series (5), 1976.

Year Club	League	G.	IP.	W.	L.	Pct.	H.	R.	ER.	SO.	BB.	ERA.
1976–Philadelphia	National	1	7	0	1	.000	8	5	4	6	5	5.14
1977–Philadelphia	National	2	11⅔	0	1	.000	13	9	9	6	8	6.94
1978–Philadelphia	National	1	9	1	0	1.000	8	4	4	8	2	4.00
1980–Philadelphia	National	2	12⅓	1	0	1.000	11	3	3	6	8	2.19
Championship Series Totals		6	40	2	2	.500	40	21	20	26	23	4.50

WORLD SERIES RECORD

Tied World Series record for most games won, losing none, six-game Series (2), 1980.

Year Club	League	G.	IP.	W.	L.	Pct.	H.	R.	ER.	SO.	BB.	ERA.
1967–St. Louis	National	1	6	0	1	.000	3	1	0	5	2	0.00
1968–St. Louis	National	2	4	0	0	.000	7	3	3	3	1	6.75
1980–Philadelphia	National	2	15	2	0	1.000	14	5	4	17	9	2.40
World Series Totals		5	25	2	1	.667	24	9	7	25	12	2.52

ALL-STAR GAME RECORD

Year League	IP.	W.	L.	Pct.	H.	R.	ER.	SO.	BB.	ERA.
1968–National	1	0	0	.000	0	0	0	1	0	0.00
1969–National	3	1	0	1.000	2	2	2	2	1	6.00
1972–National	1	0	0	.000	0	0	0	0	1	0.00
1979–National	1	0	0	.000	2	3	3	0	1	27.00
All-Star Game Totals	6	1	0	1.000	4	5	5	3	3	7.50

Member of National League All-Star Team in 1971, 1974, 1977 and 1980; did not play.

GARY EDMUND CARTER

Born April 8, 1954, at Culver City, Calif.
Height, 6.02. Weight, 215.
Throws and bats righthanded.
Brother of Gordon Carter, outfielder in San Francisco Giants' organization, 1972 and 1973.

Established major league record for fewest passed balls, season, 150 or more games (1), 1978.
Led International League catchers in double plays with 15 in 1974.
Led National League catchers in putouts with 811 in 1977 and with 781 in 1978.
Led National League catchers in double plays with 9 in 1978 and with 12 in 1979.
Hit three home runs in one game, vs. Pittsburgh Pirates, April 20, 1977.
Named catcher on THE SPORTING NEWS National League All-Star Team, 1980.
Named catcher on THE SPORTING NEWS National League All-Star fielding team, 1980.
Named National League Rookie Player of the Year by THE SPORTING NEWS, 1975.

Year Club	League	Pos.	G.	AB.	R.	H.	2B.	3B.	HR.	RBI.	B.A.	PO.	A.	E.	F.A.
1972–Cocoa Expos	Fla.E.C.	C-1-3	18	71	6	17	3	0	2	9	.239	111	12	10	.925
1972–W. Palm Beach	Fla. St.	C	20	50	9	16	2	2	0	5	.320	84	12	2	.980
1973–Quebec City	East.	C-1-O	130	439	65	111	16	1	15	68	.253	823	75	20	.978
1973–Peninsula	Int.	C	8	25	2	7	2	0	0	1	.280	5	1	0	1.000
1974–Memphis	Int.	*C-1-3	135	441	62	118	14	7	23	83	.268	*908	*76	12	*.988
1974–Montreal	Nat.	C-OF	9	27	5	11	0	1	1	6	.407	28	4	0	1.000
1975–Montreal	Nat.	O-C-3	144	503	58	136	20	1	17	68	.270	430	38	9	.981
1976–Montreal†	Nat.	C-OF	91	311	31	68	8	1	6	38	.219	364	42	2	.995
1977–Montreal	Nat.	*C-OF	154	522	86	148	29	2	31	84	.284	813	*101	9	.990
1978–Montreal	Nat.	C-1B	157	533	76	136	27	1	20	72	.255	787	83	10	.989
1979–Montreal	Nat.	C	141	505	74	143	26	5	22	75	.283	*751	88	9	.989
1980–Montreal	Nat.	C	154	549	76	145	25	5	29	101	.264	*822	*108	7	*.993
Major League Totals			850	2950	406	787	135	16	126	444	.267	3995	464	46	.990

Selected by Montreal Expos' organization in 3rd round of free-agent draft, June 6, 1972.
†On disabled list, June 6 to July 22, 1976.

Year League	Pos.	AB.	R.	H.	2B.	3B.	HR.	RBI.	B.A.	PO.	A.	E.	F.A.
1975—National	OF	0	0	0	0	0	0	0	.000	1	0	0	1.000
1979—National	C	2	0	1	0	0	0	1	.500	6	1	0	1.000
1980—National	C	1	0	0	0	0	0	0	.000	1	0	0	1.000
All-Star Game Totals		3	0	1	0	0	0	1	.333	8	1	0	1.000

DAVID CASH, JR.
(Dave)

Born June 11, 1948, at Utica, N. Y.
Height, 5.11. Weight, 172.
Throws and bats righthanded.

Established major league records for most at bats, season (699), 1975; fewest sacrifice hits, most at bats, season (0 and 699), 1975.

Tied major league records for most consecutive seasons leading major leagues in at bats (3), 1974 through 1976; most at bats, extra-inning game (11), May 21, 1977 (21 innings); most consecutive seasons leading league in at bats (3), 1974 through 1976.

Established National League records for highest fielding average, second baseman, lifetime, 1,000 or more games (.983); most consecutive games, second baseman, lifetime (443).

Major League stolen bases: 1969 (2), 1970 (5), 1971 (13), 1972 (9), 1973 (2), 1974 (20), 1975 (13), 1976 (10), 1977 (21), 1978 (12), 1979 (7), 1980 (6). Total—120.

Led National League second basemen in double plays with 141 in 1974, 126 in 1975 and 110 in 1976.

Led National League second basemen in total chances with 937 in 1974 and 898 in 1975.

Year Club	League	Pos.	G.	AB.	R.	H.	2B.	3B.	HR.	RBI.	B.A.	PO.	A.	E.	F.A.
1966—Salem	Appal	2B-SS	58	192	23	51	7	2	2	25	.266	93	127	17	.928
1967—Gastonia	W. Car.	•S-2	114	442	80	•148	17	3	4	38	•.335	•203	274	29	.943
1968—Salem	Carol.	2B-SS	124	473	68	131	20	1	6	59	.277	307	343	21	.969
1969—Columbus	Int.	2B	115	426	57	124	17	•12	4	49	.291	262	342	10	•.984
1969—Pittsburgh	Nat.	2B	18	61	8	17	3	1	0	4	.279	37	60	1	.990
1970—Columbus	Int.	2B	35	128	20	40	3	2	1	16	.313	89	86	5	.972
1970—Pittsburgh†	Nat.	2B	64	210	30	66	7	6	1	28	.314	147	156	8	.974
1971—Pittsburgh‡	Nat.	2B-3-S	123	478	79	138	17	4	2	34	.289	254	333	10	.983
1972—Pittsburgh§	Nat.	2B	99	425	58	120	22	4	3	30	.282	260	342	5	.992
1973—Pittsburgh x	Nat.	2B-3B	116	436	59	118	21	2	2	31	.271	244	311	12	.979
1974—Philadelphia	Nat.	2B	162	•687	89	206	26	11	2	58	.300	396	•519	22	.977
1975—Philadelphia	Nat.	2B •162	162	•699	111	•213	40	3	4	57	.305	•400	481	17	.981
1976—Philadelphia y	Nat.	2B	160	•666	92	189	14	•12	1	56	.284	407	424	10	•.988
1977—Montreal	Nat.	2B	153	650	91	188	42	7	0	43	.289	343	443	11	.986
1978—Montreal	Nat.	2B	159	658	66	166	26	3	3	43	.252	•362	400	11	•.986
1979—Montreal z	Nat.	2B	76	187	24	60	11	1	2	19	.321	88	110	6	.971
1980—San Diego	Nat.	2B	130	397	25	90	14	2	1	23	.227	290	326	8	.987
Major League Totals			1422	5554	732	1571	243	56	21	426	.283	3228	3905	121	.983

Selected by Pittsburgh Pirates' organization in 5th round of free-agent draft, June 29, 1966.

†On military list, June 27 to July 13, 1970.

‡On military list, July 10 to July 26, 1971.

§On military list, July 8 to July 24, 1972.

xTraded to Philadelphia Phillies for Pitcher Ken Brett, October 18, 1973.

yGranted free agency, November 1, 1976; signed as free agent with Montreal Expos, November 17, 1976.

zTraded to San Diego Padres for Second Baseman Bill Almon and First Baseman- Outfielder Dan Briggs, November 27, 1979.

CHAMPIONSHIP SERIES RECORD

Established Championship Series record for most hits, four-game Series (8), 1971.

Tied Championship Series record for most at bats, four-game Series (19), 1971.

Year Club	League	Pos.	G.	AB.	R.	H.	2B.	3B.	HR.	RBI.	B.A.	PO.	A.	E.	F.A.
1970—Pittsburgh	Nat.	2B	2	8	1	1	1	0	0	0	.125	6	8	0	1.000
1971—Pittsburgh	Nat.	2B	4	19	5	8	2	0	0	1	.421	11	11	1	.957
1972—Pittsburgh	Nat.	2B	5	19	0	4	0	0	0	3	.211	5	10	1	.938
1976—Philadelphia	Nat.	2B	3	13	1	4	1	0	0	1	.308	8	8	0	1.000
Championship Series Totals			14	59	7	17	4	0	0	5	.288	30	37	2	.971

WORLD SERIES RECORD

Year Club	League	Pos.	G.	AB.	R.	H.	2B.	3B.	HR.	RBI.	B.A.	PO.	A.	E.	F.A.
1971—Pittsburgh	Nat.	2B	7	30	2	4	1	0	0	1	.133	20	23	0	1.000

ALL-STAR GAME RECORD

Year League	Pos.	AB.	R.	H.	2B.	3B.	HR.	RBI.	B.A.	PO.	A.	E.	F.A.
1974—National	PH-2B	1	0	0	0	0	0	0	.000	0	1	0	1.000
1975—National	2B	1	0	0	0	0	0	0	.000	0	0	0	.000
1976—National	2B	1	1	1	0	0	0	0	1.000	1	1	0	1.000
All-Star Game Totals		3	1	1	0	0	0	0	.333	1	2	0	1.000

DID YOU KNOW—
That there were 12 one-hitters in the majors in 1980?

ESTEBAN MANUEL ANTONIO CASTILLO
Name pronounced kuh-STEE-yoh.
(Manny)

Born April 1, 1957, at Santo Domingo, Dominican Republic.
Height, 5.09. Weight, 160.
Throws right and bats right and lefthanded.
Hobby—Horse racing.

Led Texas League second basemen in double plays with 83 in 1977.
Led American Association third basemen in double plays with 27 in 1980.

Year	Club	League	Pos.	G.	AB.	R.	H.	2B.	3B.	HR.	RBI.	B.A.	PO.	A.	E.	F.A.
1973—Marion	Appal.	3B-2B	10	19	1	2	0	0	0	1	.105	8	10	2	.900
1974—Marion	Appal.	3B-2B	42	144	19	42	6	1	1	21	.292	41	55	9	.914
1975—Wausau†	Midw.	3B-OF	68	212	28	69	9	4	1	34	.325	39	110	19	.887
1976—Arkansas	Texas	3-2-1B	116	355	36	99	11	2	0	35	.279	130	194	15	.956
1977—Arkansas	Texas	SS	115	430	39	128	20	5	0	43	.298	239	★357	21	.966
1977—New Orleans	A. A.	2B-SS	13	48	3	8	1	0	0	6	.167	28	49	2	.975
1978—Springfield	A. A.	2B-3B-OF	108	382	39	96	21	1	2	39	.251	145	220	16	.958
1979—Springfield‡	A. A.	3B-2B-SS	127	★524	75	★169	29	4	2	57	.323	120	231	20	.946
1980—Omaha	A. A.	★3B-O-P	★137	★599	86	★173	20	●11	6	70	.289	★139	★272	20	★.954
1980—Kansas City	Amer.	3B-2B	7	10	1	2	0	0	0	0	.200	2	8	0	1.000
Major League Totals			7	10	1	2	0	0	0	0	.200	2	8	0	1.000

RECORD AS PITCHER

Year	Club	League	G.	IP.	W.	L.	Pct.	H.	R.	ER.	SO.	BB.	ERA.
1980—Omaha	Am. Assoc.	1	1	0	0	.000	0	3	3	1	6	27.00

Signed as free agent by New York Mets' organization, March 3, 1973.
†Drafted by St. Louis Cardinals' organization, December 9, 1975.
‡Drafted by Kansas City Royals, December 3, 1979.

MARTIN HORACE CASTILLO
(Marty)

Born January 16, 1957, at Long Beach, Calif.
Height, 6.01. Weight, 190.
Throws and bats righthanded.
Attended Chapman College, Orange, Calif.
Brother of Art Castillo, former outfielder in Minnesota Twins' organization.

Year	Club	League	Pos.	G.	AB.	R.	H.	2B.	3B.	HR.	RBI.	B.A.	PO.	A.	E.	F.A.
1978—Lakeland	Fla. St.	3B	67	205	24	53	4	2	5	25	.259	73	95	9	.949
1979—Montgomery†	South.	3B	74	274	47	84	17	1	9	47	.307	70	174	22	.917
1979—Evansville‡	A. A.	3B	31	103	11	24	4	1	1	6	.233	27	66	3	.969
1980—Evansville	A. A.	★3B-C-1	132	455	59	114	28	4	12	62	.251	137	268	★26	.940

Selected by Minnesota Twins' organization in 21st round of free-agent draft, June 4, 1975.
Selected by California Angels' organization in 8th round of free-agent draft, January 11, 1977.
Selected by Detroit Tigers' organization in 5th round of free-agent draft, June 6, 1978.
†On disabled list, April 21 to May 1, 1979.
‡On disabled list, July 30 to August 11, 1979.

ROBERT ERNIE CASTILLO JR.

Born April 18, 1955, at Los Angeles, Calif.
Height, 5.10. Weight, 170.
Throws and bats righthanded.
Attended Los Angeles Valley Junior College, Van Nuys, Calif.

Year	Club	League	G.	IP.	W.	L.	Pct.	H.	R.	ER.	SO.	BB.	ERA.
1976—Reynosa†	Mexican	13	72	5	5	.500	52	16	14	56	36	1.75
1977—Monterrey‡	Mexican	34	255	19	11	.633	216	72	63	199	110	2.22
1977—Los Angeles	National	6	11	1	0	1.000	12	5	5	7	2	4.09
1978—Albuquerque	P. Coast	15	82	5	3	.625	81	54	49	65	51	5.38
1978—Los Angeles	National	18	34	0	4	.000	28	19	15	30	33	3.97
1979—Albuquerque§	P. Coast	16	45	4	3	.571	49	34	28	42	31	5.60
1979—Los Angeles	National	19	24	2	0	1.000	26	5	3	25	13	1.13
1980—Los Angeles	National	61	98	8	6	.571	70	31	30	60	45	2.76
Major League Totals		104	167	11	10	.524	136	60	53	122	93	2.86

†Appeared in one game as third baseman with two assists and two errors.
‡Sold to Los Angeles Dodgers, June 16, 1977.

RECORD AS INFIELDER-OUTFIELDER

Year	Club	League	Pos.	G.	AB.	R.	H.	2B.	3B.	HR.	RBI.	B.A.	PO.	A.	E.	F.A.
1974—Sara. Royals†	G. C.	●3B-OF	47	150	15	38	7	4	3	21	.253	31	70	●13	.886

Selected by Kansas City Royals' organization in 6th round of free-agent draft, January 9, 1974.
†Released, April 7, 1975; signed by Reynosa, May 1, 1976.

JOHN ANTHONY CASTINO

Born October 23, 1954, at Evanston, Ill.
Height, 5.11. Weight, 169.
Throws and bats righthanded.
Attended Rollins College, Winter Park, Fla.

Led American League third basemen in double plays with 31 in 1979.
Tied for American League lead in assists by third basemen with 340 in 1980.
Named American League Co-Rookie of the Year by the Baseball Writer's Association of America, 1979.

Year Club	League	Pos.	G.	AB.	R.	H.	2B.	3B.	HR.	RBI.	B.A.	PO.	A.	E.	F.A.
1976—Wis. Rapids	Midw.	3B	65	252	42	72	15	2	6	41	.286	60	155	16	.931
1977—Orlando	South.	3B	36	111	8	21	2	1	2	7	.189	28	89	11	.914
1977—Visalia	Calif.	3B	72	275	54	90	14	5	16	54	.327	68	152	13	.944
1978—Orlando	South.	3B	137	494	59	136	21	7	11	63	.275	*122	312	15	*.967
1979—Minnesota	Amer.	3B-SS	148	393	49	112	13	8	5	52	.285	91	286	15	.962
1980—Minnsota	Amer.	3B-SS	150	546	67	165	17	7	13	64	.302	128	395	22	.960
Major League Totals			298	939	116	277	30	15	18	116	.295	219	681	37	.961

Selected by Minnesota Twins' organization in 3rd round of free-agent draft, June 8, 1976.

WILLIAM RADHAMES CASTRO (CHECO)
(Bill)

Born December 13, 1953, at Barrero, Santiago, Dominican Republic.
Height, 6.00. Weight, 175.
Throws and bats righthanded.
Hobbies—Hunting, music and volleyball.

Major league saves: 1974 (0), 1975 (1), 1976 (8), 1977 (13), 1978 (8), 1979 (6), 1980 (8). Total—44.
Led Midwest League in saves with 17 in 1972.

Year Club	League	G.	IP.	W.	L.	Pct.	H.	R.	ER.	SO.	BB.	ERA.
1971—Newark	NYP	9	13	0	1	.000	20	7	6	10	6	4.15
1972—Danville	Midwest	45	74	10	9	.526	59	31	25	66	26	3.04
1973—Danville	Midwest	46	114	11	4	●.733	96	33	23	104	24	1.82
1974—Sacramento	P. Coast	50	105	9	5	.643	133	68	55	52	35	4.71
1974—Milwaukee	American	8	18	0	0	.000	19	10	9	10	5	4.50
1975—Milwaukee†	American	18	75	3	2	.600	78	28	21	25	17	2.52
1976—Milwaukee‡	American	39	70	4	6	.400	70	29	27	23	19	3.47
1977—Milwaukee	American	51	69	8	6	.571	76	34	32	28	23	4.17
1978—Milwaukee	American	42	50	5	4	.556	43	14	10	17	14	1.80
1979—Milwaukee	American	39	44	3	1	.750	40	14	10	10	13	2.05
1980—Milwaukee§	American	56	84	2	4	.333	89	35	26	32	17	2.79
Major League Totals		253	410	25	23	.521	415	164	135	145	108	2.96

Signed as free agent by Milwaukee Brewers' organization, October 24, 1970.
†On disabled list, July 23 to September 1, 1975.
‡On disabled list, May 19 to June 9, 1976.
§Granted free agency, October 22, 1980; signed by New York Yankees, February 17, 1981.

WILLIAM HOLLAND CAUDILL
(Bill)

Born July 13, 1956, at Santa Monica, Calif.
Height, 6.01. Weight, 175.
Throws and bats righthanded.
Hobbies—Hunting and fishing.

Pitched six-inning, 4-0 no-hit victory against Winter Haven, May 14, 1975.
Led Florida State League in complete games with 12 in 1975.

Year Club	League	G.	IP.	W.	L.	Pct.	H.	R.	ER.	SO.	BB.	ERA.
1974—Sarasota Cardinals	Gulf Coast	8	30	1	0	1.000	18	9	6	35	13	1.80
1975—St. Petersburg	Fla. St.	25	163	●14	8	.636	123	63	57	*153	87	3.15
1976—Arkansas†	Texas	27	140	6	15	.286	128	79	69	*140	84	4.44
1977—Indianapolis	Am. Assoc.	8	44	2	2	.500	31	20	18	25	31	3.68
1977—Three Rivers‡	Eastern	19	114	13	4	*.765	97	56	53	93	72	4.18
1978—Wichita	Am. Assoc.	29	158	8	9	.471	151	103	97	124	105	5.53
1979—Wichita	Am. Assoc.	6	36	3	1	.750	27	11	11	36	17	2.75
1979—Chicago	National	29	90	1	7	.125	89	57	48	104	41	4.80
1980—Chicago	National	72	128	4	6	.400	100	37	31	112	59	2.18
Major League Totals		101	218	5	13	.278	189	94	79	216	100	3.26

Selected by St. Louis Cardinals' organization in 8th round of free-agent draft, June 5, 1974.
†Traded from St. Louis Cardinals' organization to Cincinnati Reds' organization for Infielder-Outfielder Joel Youngblood, March 28, 1977.
‡Traded with Pitcher Woodie Fryman by Cincinnati Reds' organization to Chicago Cubs for Pitcher Bill Bonham, October 31, 1977.

CESAR CEDENO

Name pronounced Suh-DAYN-yo.

Born February 25, 1951, at Santo Domingo, Dominican Republic.
Height, 6.02. Weight, 195.
Throw and bats righthanded.

Tied major league record for most doubles, inning (2), April 9, 1973 (1st game, 6th inning).
Led National League outfielders in double plays with 5 in 1976.
Tied for National League lead in sacrifice flies with 9 in 1979.
One of two players in major league history to steal 50 or more bases and hit 20 or more home runs in the same season on three occasions (55 stolen bases and 22 home runs in 1972; 56 stolen bases and 25 home runs in 1973; 57 stolen bases and 26 home runs in 1974).
Hit for cycle, August 9, 1976.
Major league stolen bases: 1970 (17), 1971 (20), 1972 (55), 1973 (56), 1974 (57), 1975 (50), 1976 (58), 1977 (61), 1978 (23), 1979 (30), 1980 (48). Total—475.
Named outfielder on THE SPORTING NEWS National League All-Star fielding team, 1972, 1973, 1974, 1975 and 1976.
Named outfielder on THE SPORTING NEWS National League All-Star Team, 1972, 1976 and 1980.

Year	Club	League	Pos.	G.	AB.	R.	H.	2B.	3B.	HR.	RBI.	B.A.	PO.	A.	E.	F.A.
1968—Covington	Appal.		OF	36	131	23	49	5	6	0	21	.374	49	•8	7	.891
1968—Cocoa	Fla. St.		OF	69	180	19	46	8	2	0	16	.256	70	4	7	.914
1969—Peninsula	Carol.		1-OF	142	497	62	136	*32	3	5	39	.274	761	52	17	.980
1970—Okla. City	A. A.		OF	54	233	47	87	14	9	14	61	.373	113	6	4	.967
1970—Houston	Nat.		OF	90	355	46	110	21	4	7	42	.310	211	1	7	.968
1971—Houston	Nat.		OF-1B	161	611	85	161	*40	6	10	81	.264	348	6	4	.989
1972—Houston	Nat.		OF	139	559	103	179	●39	8	22	82	.320	345	9	7	.981
1973—Houston	Nat.		OF	139	525	86	168	35	2	25	70	.320	357	10	7	.981
1974—Houston	Nat.		OF	160	610	95	164	29	5	26	102	.269	*446	11	3	.993
1975—Houston†	Nat.		OF	131	500	93	144	31	3	13	63	.288	322	8	6	.982
1976—Houston	Nat.		OF	150	575	89	171	26	5	18	83	.297	377	11	8	.980
1977—Houston‡	Nat.		OF	141	530	92	148	36	8	14	71	.279	335	14	1	*.997
1978—Houston§	Nat.		OF	50	192	31	54	8	2	7	23	.281	149	2	2	.987
1979—Houston	Nat.		*1B-OF	132	470	57	123	27	4	6	54	.262	948	35	*17	.983
1980—Houston	Nat.		OF	137	499	71	154	32	8	10	73	.309	338	9	8	.977
Major League Totals				1430	5426	848	1576	324	55	158	744	.290	4176	116	70	.984

Signed as free agent by Houston Astros' organization, October 25, 1967.
†On supplemental disabled list, July 20 to August 8, 1975.
‡On disabled list, March 23 to April 13, 1977.
§On disabled list, June 17 to September 29, 1978.

CHAMPIONSHIP SERIES RECORD

Year	Club	League	Pos.	G.	AB.	R.	H.	2B.	3B.	HR.	RBI.	B.A.	PO.	A.	E.	F.A.
1980—Houston	Nat.		OF	3	11	1	2	0	0	1	.182	5	0	0	1.000

ALL-STAR GAME RECORD

Year	League	Pos.	AB.	R.	H.	2B.	3B.	HR.	RBI.	B.A.	PO.	A.	E.	F.A.
1972—National		OF	2	1	1	0	0	0	0	.500	0	0	0	.000
1973—National		OF	3	0	1	0	0	0	1	.333	3	0	0	1.000
1974—National		OF	2	0	0	0	0	0	0	.000	2	0	0	1.000
1976—National		OF	2	1	1	0	0	1	2	.500	1	0	0	1.000
All-Star Game Totals			9	2	3	0	0	1	3	.333	6	0	0	1.000

RICHARD ALDO CERONE

Name pronounced ce-RONE.

(Rick)

Born May 19, 1954, at Newark, N. J.
Height, 5.11. Weight, 185.
Throws and bats righthanded.
Hobbies—Golf, swimming and tennis.
Attended Seton Hall University, South Orange, N. J.; received Bachelor of Science degree in Physical Education.

Named catcher on THE SPORTING NEWS American League All-Star Team, 1980
Received reported $60,000 bonus to sign with Cleveland Indians, 1975.

Year	Club	League	Pos.	G.	AB.	R.	H.	2B.	3B.	HR.	RBI.	B.A.	PO.	A.	E.	F.A.
1975—Okla. City	A.A.		C-OF	46	140	22	35	6	1	2	13	.250	178	30	3	.986
1975—Cleveland	Amer.		C	7	12	1	3	1	0	0	0	.250	18	1	0	1.000
1976—Toledo†	Int.		C	96	339	38	86	19	0	11	49	.254	351	50	18	.957
1976—Cleveland‡	Amer.		C	7	16	1	2	0	0	0	1	.125	25	1	1	.963
1977—Charleston	Int.		C-OF	70	231	30	54	10	1	6	40	.234	254	32	5	.983
1977—Toronto	Amer.		C	31	100	7	20	4	0	1	10	.200	146	15	1	.944
1978—Toronto	Amer.		C	88	282	25	63	8	2	3	20	.223	426	44	4	.992
1979—Toronto§	Amer.		C	136	469	47	112	27	4	7	61	.239	560	68	13	.980
1980—New York	Amer.		C	147	519	70	144	30	4	14	85	.277	800	73	9	.990
Major League Totals				416	1398	151	344	70	10	25	177	.246	1975	202	28	.987

Selected by Cleveland Indians' organization in 1st round (seventh player selected) of free-agent draft, June 4, 1975.
†On disabled list May 13 to May 24, 1976.

‡Traded with Infielder-Outfielder John Lowenstein to Toronto Blue Jays for Outfielder Rico Carty, December 6, 1976.

§Traded with Pitcher Tom Underwood and Outfielder Ted Wilborn to New York Yankees for First Baseman Chris Chambliss, Infielder Damaso Garcia and Pitcher Paul Mirabella, November 1, 1979.

CHAMPIONSHIP SERIES RECORD

Tied Championsip Series record for hitting home run in first Series at-bat, October 8, 1980 (first inning).

Year Club	League	Pos.	G.	AB.	R.	H.	2B.	3B.	HR.	RBI.	B.A.	PO.	A.	E.	F.A.
1980—New York	Amer.	C	3	12	1	4	0	0	1	2	.333	14	4	0	1.000

RONALD CHARLES CEY

Name pronounced Say.

(Ron)

Born February 15, 1948, at Tacoma, Wash.
Height, 5.09. Weight, 180.
Throws and bats righthanded.
Attended Washington State University, Pullman, Wash., and Western
Washington State College, Bellingham, Wash.

Led National League third basemen in double plays with 39 in 1973.
Led Pacific Coast League batters in bases on balls with 117 in 1972.
Led California League third basemen in double plays with 22 in 1969.
Led Northwest League in sacrifice flies with 7 in 1968.
Tied for Pacific Coast League lead in double plays by third basemen with 24 in 1972.

Year	Club	League	Pos.	G.	AB.	R.	H.	2B.	3B.	HR.	RBI.	B.A.	PO.	A.	E.	F.A.
1968—Tri-City		Northw.	3B	74	254	50	76	11	4	9	*62	.299	46	*175	10	*.957
1969—Albuquerque		Texas	3B	13	32	8	5	1	0	0	2	.156	13	19	1	.970
1969—Bakersfield		Calif.	3B	98	353	68	117	16	1	22	56	.331	82	197	22	.927
1970—Albuquerque		Texas	3B	71	239	31	79	22	1	4	56	.331	44	132	10	.946
1971—Spokane		P. C.	3B	137	500	85	164	26	4	32	*123	.328	95	283	24	*.940
1971—Los Angeles		Nat.	PH	2	2	0	0	0	0	0	0	.000	0	0	0	.000
1972—Albuquerque		P. C.	3B-2B	142	496	99	163	25	7	23	103	.329	*108	*279	21	.949
1972—Los Angeles		Nat.	3B	11	37	3	10	1	0	1	3	.270	7	20	3	.900
1973—Los Angeles		Nat.	3B	152	507	60	124	18	4	15	80	.245	111	*328	18	.961
1974—Los Angeles		Nat.	3B	159	577	88	151	20	2	18	97	.262	155	365	22	.959
1975—Los Angeles		Nat.	3B	158	566	72	160	29	2	25	101	.283	144	309	19	.960
1976—Los Angeles		Nat.	3B	145	502	69	139	18	3	23	80	.277	111	334	16	.965
1977—Los Angeles		Nat.	3B	153	564	77	136	22	3	30	110	.241	138	346	18	.964
1978—Los Angeles		Nat.	3B	159	555	84	150	32	0	23	84	.270	116	336	16	.966
1979—Los Angeles		Nat.	3B	150	487	77	137	20	1	28	81	.281	123	265	9	*.977
1980—Los Angeles		Nat.	3B	157	551	81	140	25	0	28	77	.254	*127	317	13	.972
Major League Totals				1246	4348	611	1147	185	15	191	713	.264	1032	2620	134	.965

Selected by New York Mets' organization in 24th round of free-agent draft, June 6, 1966.
Selected by Los Angeles Dodgers' organization in 3rd round of free-agent draft, June 7, 1968.

CHAMPIONSHIP SERIES RECORD

Tied Championship Series records for most home runs with bases filled, game (1), October 4, 1977; most runs batted in, inning (4), October 4, 1977 (seventh inning); most two-base hits, four-game Series (3), 1974.
Tied National League Championship records for most consecutive hits, one Series (4); most hits, game (4), October 6, 1974.

Year	Club	League	Pos.	G.	AB.	R.	H.	2B.	3B.	HR.	RBI.	B.A.	PO.	A.	E.	F.A.
1974—Los Angeles		Nat.	3B	4	16	2	5	3	0	1	1	.313	2	4	2	.750
1977—Los Angeles		Nat.	3B	4	13	4	4	1	0	1	4	.308	7	14	1	.955
1978—Los Angeles		Nat.	3B	4	16	4	5	1	0	1	3	.313	2	13	0	1.000
Championship Series Totals				12	45	10	14	5	0	3	8	.311	11	31	3	.933

WORLD SERIES RECORD

Tied World Series record for batting in all club's runs, game, most (4), October 11, 1978.

Year	Club	League	Pos.	G.	AB.	R.	H.	2B.	3B.	HR.	RBI.	B.A.	PO.	A.	E.	F.A.
1974—Los Angeles		Nat.	3B	5	17	1	3	0	0	0	0	.176	5	9	1	.933
1977—Los Angeles		Nat.	3B	6	21	2	4	1	0	1	3	.190	5	7	0	1.000
1978—Los Angeles		Nat.	3B	6	21	2	6	0	0	1	4	.286	2	12	0	1.000
World Series Totals				17	59	5	13	1	0	2	7	.220	12	28	1	.976

ALL-STAR GAME RECORD

Year	League	Pos.	AB.	R.	H.	2B.	3B.	HR.	RBI.	B.A.	PO.	A.	E.	F.A.
1974—National		3B	2	1	1	0	0	0	2	.500	0	0	0	.000
1975—National		3B	3	0	1	0	0	0	0	.333	0	1	0	1.000
1976—National		3B	0	0	0	0	0	0	0	.000	0	0	0	.000
1977—National		3B	2	0	0	0	0	0	0	.000	0	0	0	.000
1978—National		3B	1	0	0	0	0	0	0	.000	1	0	0	1.000
1979—National		3B	1	0	0	0	0	0	0	.000	2	1	0	1.000
All-Star Game Totals			9	0	2	1	0	0	2	.222	3	2	0	1.000

DAVID LEE CHALK
(Dave)

Born August 30, 1950, at Del Rio, Tex.
Height, 5.10. Weight, 170.
Throws and bats righthanded.
Hobby—Sports in general.
Attended University of Texas, Austin, Tex.

Year Club	League	Pos.	G.	AB.	R.	H.	2B.	3B.	HR.	RBI.	B.A.	PO.	A.	E.	F.A.
1972—Shreveport	Tex.	3B-2B	76	265	31	67	11	0	3	25	.253	63	155	15	.936
1973—El Paso	Tex.	SS-2B	48	174	34	51	6	1	4	18	.293	85	183	10	.964
1973—Salt Lake City ...	P.C.	SS	92	330	46	78	8	2	5	38	.236	118	290	21	.951
1973—California.........	Amer.	SS	24	69	14	16	2	0	0	6	.232	36	66	4	.962
1974—California.........	Amer.	●SS-3B	133	465	44	117	9	3	5	31	.252	200	350	●34	.942
1975—California.........	Amer.	3B	149	513	59	140	24	2	3	56	.273	108	333	11	.976
1976—California.........	Amer.	SS-3B	142	438	39	95	14	1	0	33	.217	176	387	17	.971
1977—California.........	Amer.	3-2-S	149	519	58	144	27	2	3	45	.277	147	287	25	.946
1978—California†‡......	Amer.	SS-2B-3B	135	470	42	119	12	0	1	34	.253	216	339	23	.960
1979—Tex.§-Oak. x	Amer.	2B-SS-3B	75	220	15	49	6	0	2	13	.223	123	154	11	.962
1980—Kansas City y....	Amer.	3-2-S	69	167	19	42	10	1	1	20	.251	57	88	6	.960
Major League Totals			876	2861	290	722	104	9	15	238	.252	1063	2004	131	.959

Selected by California Angels' organization in 1st round (10th player selected) of free-agent draft, June 6, 1972.

†On disabled list, March 20 to May 4, 1979.

‡Traded to Texas Rangers for Shortstop Bert Campaneris, May 4, 1979.

§Traded with Catcher Mike Heath and cash to Oakland A's for Pitcher John Henry Johnson, June 15, 1979.

xGranted free agency, November 1, 1979; signed by Kansas City Royals, March 28, 1980.

yGranted free agency, October 24, 1980; re-signed by Royals before re-entry draft, November 11, 1980.

WORLD SERIES RECORD

Year Club	League	Pos.	G.	AB.	R.	H.	2B.	3B.	HR.	RBI.	B.A.	PO.	A.	E.	F.A.
1980—Kansas City	Amer.	3B	1	0	1	0	0	0	0	0	.000	0	1	0	1.000

ALL-STAR GAME RECORD

Year League	Pos.	AB.	R.	H.	2B.	3B.	HR.	RBI.	B.A.	PO.	A.	E.	F.A.
1974—American.............................	3B	1	0	0	0	0	0	0	.000	0	0	0	.000

Member of American League All-Star Team for 1975 game; did not play.

CRAIG PHILIP CHAMBERLAIN

Born February 2, 1957, at Hollywood, Calif.
Height, 6.01. Weight, 190.
Throws and bats righthanded.
Attended University of Arizona, Tucson, Ariz.

Year Club	League	G.	IP.	W.	L.	Pct.	H.	R.	ER.	SO.	BB.	ERA.
1979—Jacksonville.........................	Southern	22	160	12	9	.571	142	57	46	117	45	2.59
1979—Kansas City	American	10	70	4	4	.500	68	31	29	30	18	3.73
1980—Omaha................................	Am. Assoc.	27	170	11	10	.524	184	105	●90	81	81	4.76
1980—Kansas City	American	5	9	0	1	.000	10	8	7	3	5	7.00
Major League Totals.............................		15	79	4	5	.444	78	39	36	33	23	4.10

Selected by New York Mets' organization in 19th round of free-agent draft, June 7, 1977.

Selected by Kansas City Royals' organization in secondary phase of free-agent draft, June 6, 1978.

Did not pitch in 1978 because of broken ankle.

CARROLL CHRISTOPHER CHAMBLISS
(Chris)

Born December 26, 1948, at Dayton, O.
Height, 6.01. Weight, 215.
Throws right and bats lefthanded.
Hobby—Collecting phonograph records.
Attended Mira Costa Junior College, Oceanside, Calif., and University of California
at Los Angeles, Los Angeles, Calif.; attending Montclair State College
Upper Montclair, N.J., for degree in Recreation.
Cousin of Jo Jo White, guard with Golden State Warriors.

Tied major league record for fewest caught stealing, season, 150 or more games (0), 1976 and 1977.

Led American League first basemen in total chances with 1,565 in 1973.

Named by THE SPORTING NEWS as American League Rookie Player of the Year, 1971.

Named by the Baseball Writers' Association as American League Rookie of the Year, 1971.

Named American Association Rookie of the Year in 1970.

Named first baseman on THE SPORTING NEWS American League All-Star Team, 1976.

Named first baseman on THE SPORTING NEWS American League All-Star Fielding Team, 1978.

Year Club	League	Pos.	G.	AB.	R.	H.	2B.	3B.	HR.	RBI.	B.A.	PO.	A.	E.	F.A.
1970—Wichita†	A. A.	OF-1B	105	383	60	131	17	8	7	52	*342	413	21	13	.971
1971—Wichita	A.A.	OF-1B	13	42	8	12	3	0	2	6	.286	42	3	0	1.000
1971—Cleveland	Amer.	1B	111	415	49	114	20	4	9	48	.275	943	55	8	.992
1972—Cleveland‡	Amer.	1B	121	466	51	136	27	2	6	44	.292	1109	56	8	.993

Year Club League	Pos.	G.	AB.	R.	H.	2B.	3B.	HR.	RBI.	B.A.	PO.	A.	E.	F.A.
1973—Cleveland..........Amer.	1B	155	572	70	156	30	2	11	53	.273	1437	114	*14	.991
1974—Cleve.§-N. Y. .....Amer.	1B	127	467	46	119	20	3	6	50	.255	1035	84	11	.990
1975—New York..........Amer.	1B	150	562	66	171	38	4	9	72	.304	1222	106	12	.991
1976—New York..........Amer.	1B	156	641	79	188	32	6	17	96	.293	1440	109	9	.994
1977—New York..........Amer.	1B	157	600	90	172	32	6	17	90	.287	1368	98	16	.989
1978—New York ....Amer.	1B	162	625	81	171	26	3	12	90	.274	1366	111	4	*.997
1979—New York xy.....Amer.	1B	149	554	61	155	27	3	18	63	.280	1299	95	7	.995
1980—Atlanta ....Nat.	1B	158	602	83	170	37	2	18	72	.282	*1626	101	12	.993
American League Totals..................		1288	4902	593	1382	252	33	105	606	.282	11219	828	89	.993
National League Totals....................		158	602	83	170	37	2	18	72	.282	1626	101	12	.993
Major League Totals.......................		1446	5504	676	1552	289	35	123	678	.282	12845	929	101	.993

Selected by Cincinnati Reds' organization in 31st round of free-agent draft, June 6, 1967.
Selected by Cincinnati Reds' organization in secondary phase of free-agent draft, January 27, 1968.
Selected by Cleveland Indians' organization in 1st round of free-agent draft, January 17, 1970.
†On disabled list, May 25 to June 16, 1970.
‡On military list, June 23 to June 30, 1972.
§Traded with Pitchers Dick Tidrow and Cecil Upshaw to New York Yankees for Fritz Peterson, Steve Kline, Fred Beene and Tom Buskey, April 26, 1974.
xTraded with Infielder Damaso Garcia and Pitcher Paul Mirabella to Toronto Blue Jays for Catcher Rick Cerone, Pitcher Tom Underwood and Outfielder Ted Wilborn, November 1, 1979.
yTraded with Shortstop Luis Gomez to Atlanta Braves for Outfielder Barry Bonnell and Pitcher Joey McLaughlin, December 5, 1979.

CHAMPIONSHIP SERIES RECORD

Established Championship Series records for highest slugging average, five-game Series (.952), 1976; most hits, five-game Series (11), 1976; most total bases, five-game Series (20), 1976; most runs batted in, five-game Series (8), 1976.
Tied Championship Series records for most hits, two consecutive games, one Series (6), October 3 and 4, 1978; most consecutive hits, one Series (5), 1978.
Established American League Championship Series records for most one-base hits, four-game Series (6), 1978; highest batting average, five-game Series (.524), 1976.
Tied American League Championship Series records for most consecutive hits, total Series (5); most home runs, five-game Series (2), 1976.

Year Club League	Pos.	G.	AB.	R.	H.	2B.	3B.	HR.	RBI.	B.A.	PO.	A.	E.	F.A.
1976—New York..........Amer.	1B	5	21	5	11	1	1	2	8	.524	50	3	1	.981
1977—New York..........Amer.	1B	5	17	0	1	0	0	0	0	.059	35	7	0	1.000
1978—New York ....Amer.	1B	4	15	1	6	0	0	0	2	.400	28	1	0	1.000
Championship Series Totals....................		14	53	6	18	1	1	2	10	.340	113	11	1	.992

WORLD SERIES RECORD

Tied World Series records for most errors by first baseman, four-game Series (1), 1976; one or more hits, each game, four-game Series, 1976.

Year Club League	Pos.	G.	AB.	R.	H.	2B.	3B.	HR.	RBI.	B.A.	PO.	A.	E.	F.A.
1976—New York..........Amer.	1B	4	16	1	5	1	0	0	1	.313	26	3	1	.967
1977—New York..........Amer.	1B	6	24	4	7	2	0	1	4	.292	55	5	0	1.000
1978—New York ....Amer.	1B	3	11	1	2	0	0	0	0	.182	17	1	0	1.000
World Series Totals		13	51	10	14	3	0	1	5	.275	98	9	1	.991

ALL-STAR GAME RECORD

Year League	Pos.	AB.	R.	H.	2B.	3B.	HR.	RBI.	B.A.	PO.	A.	E.	F.A.
1976—American.............................	PH	1	0	0	0	0	0	0	.000	0	0	0	.000

HARRY PERRY CHAPPAS

Born October 26, 1957, at Mt. Rainier, Md.
Height, 5.07. Weight, 155.
Throws right and bats right and lefthanded.
Attended Miami-Dade (North) Community College, Miami, Fla.

Led Midwest League in stolen bases with 60 in 1978.

Year Club League	Pos.	G.	AB.	R.	H.	2B.	3B.	HR.	RBI.	B.A.	PO.	A.	E.	F.A.
1976—Appleton ....Midw.	SS	102	378	61	99	9	8	4	38	.262	125	304	43	.909
1977—Knoxville ....South.	SS-2B	123	386	51	89	10	4	2	18	.231	191	335	29	.948
1978—Appleton ....Midw.	SS	130	493	91	149	23	14	1	62	.302	180	379	35	.941
1978—Chicago ....Amer.	SS	20	75	11	20	1	0	0	6	.267	28	64	0	1.000
1979—Iowa ....A. A.	SS	77	259	36	79	6	3	5	32	.305	134	222	17	.954
1979—Chicago ....Amer.	SS	26	59	9	17	1	0	1	4	.288	28	63	7	.929
1980—Iowa ....A. A.	SS	76	248	33	51	7	0	2	22	.206	90	182	13	.954
1980—Chicago ....Amer.	SS-2B	26	50	6	8	2	0	0	2	.160	18	36	1	.982
Major League Totals.......................		72	184	26	45	4	0	1	12	.245	75	163	8	.967

Selected by Chicago White Sox' organization in 21st round of free-agent draft, June 4, 1975.
Selected by Chicago White Sox' organization in secondary phase of free-agent draft, January 7, 1976.

DID YOU KNOW—

That Atlanta's Bob Horner has hit 91 homers in 1,273 at-bats in his three major league seasons? That's an average of one home run for every 13.99 at-bats.

JOSEPH CHARBONEAU
(Joe)

Born June 17, 1955, at Belvidere, Ill.
Height, 6.02. Weight, 200.
Throws and bats righthanded.
Attended West Valley Junior College, Saratoga, Calif.

Named American League Rookie Player of the Year by THE SPORTING NEWS, 1980.
Named American League Rookie of the Year by Baseball Writers' Association of America, 1980.

Year	Club	League	Pos.	G.	AB.	R.	H.	2B.	3B.	HR.	RBI.	B.A.	PO.	A.	E.	F.A.
1976—Spartanburg		W. Car.	OF	43	121	20	36	3	0	4	18	.298	67	3	0	1.000
1977—Peninsula†‡		Carol.	OF	12	29	4	5	0	0	1	2	.172	12	1	4	.765
1978—Visalia§		Calif.	OF	130	497	119	174	35	5	18	116	*.350	244	10	7	.973
1979—Chattanooga		South.	OF	109	372	70	131	24	2	21	78	*.352	187	7	5	.975
1980—Cleveland		Amer.	OF	131	453	76	131	17	2	23	87	.289	125	6	5	.963
Major League Totals				131	453	76	131	17	2	23	87	.289	125	6	5	.963

Selected by Minnesota Twins' organization in 6th round of free-agent draft, January 7, 1976.
Selected by Philadelphia Phillies' organization in secondary phase of free-agent draft, June 8, 1976.
†On suspended list, May 19, 1977, to February 25, 1978.
‡Loaned to Minnesota Twins' organization, April 2, 1978; returned, September 18, 1978.
§Traded to Cleveland Indians' organization for Pitcher Cardell Camper, December 6, 1978.

MICHAEL CHRIS
(Mike)

Born October 8, 1957, at Santa Monica, Calif.
Height, 6.02. Weight, 175.
Throws and bats lefthanded.
Attended Pierce Junior College, Woodland Hills, Calif. and
West Los Angeles Junior College, Culver City, Calif.

Pitched 1-0 no-hit victory against St. Petersburg, May 6, 1977.

Year	Club	League	G.	IP.	W.	L.	Pct.	H.	R.	ER.	SO.	BB.	ERA.
1977—Lakeland		Florida St.	26	188	●18	5	*.783	150	53	42	99	67	*2.01
1978—Montgomery		Southern	16	105	9	6	.600	80	44	34	85	48	2.91
1978—Evansville		Am. Assoc.	8	41	3	3	.500	38	23	14	21	23	3.07
1979—Evansville		Am. Assoc.	19	105	7	8	.467	113	78	65	71	67	5.57
1979—Detroit		American	13	39	3	3	.500	46	30	30	31	21	6.92
1980—Evansville		Am. Assoc.	28	140	7	*14	.333	148	82	71	85	90	4.56
Major League Totals			13	39	3	3	.500	46	30	30	31	21	6.92

Selected by Oakland A's organization in 24th round of free-agent draft, June 4, 1975.
Selected by California Angels' organization in secondary phase of free-agent draft, January 7, 1976.
Selected by Oakland A's organization in secondary phase of free-agent draft, June 8, 1976.
Selected by Detroit Tigers' organization in secondary phase of free-agent draft, January 11, 1977.

GARY RICHARD CHRISTENSON

Born May 5, 1953, at Mineola, N. Y.
Height, 6.05. Weight, 212.
Throws and bats lefthanded.
Hobbies—Golf and bowling.
Attended Montclair State College, Montclair, N. J.

Led Florida State League pitchers in complete games with 17 in 1974.

Year	Club	League	G.	IP.	W.	L.	Pct.	H.	R.	ER.	SO.	BB.	ERA.
1971—Bristol		Ap'lachian	21	28	1	0	1.000	31	7	7	24	12	2.25
1972—Lakeland		Florida St.	10	15	0	0	.000	21	14	11	13	8	6.60
1972—Clinton†		Midwest	24	53	2	2	.500	47	30	24	35	41	4.08
1973—Lakeland		Florida St.	26	47	1	1	.500	35	15	14	34	26	2.68
1974—Lakeland		Florida St.	28	*209	15	10	.600	168	65	51	93	85	2.20
1975—Evansville‡		Am. Assoc.	2	5	1	0	1.000	6	3	3	1	5	5.40
1975—Montgomery§		Southern	15	93	8	4	.667	77	38	34	67	46	3.29
1976—Montgomery		Southern	12	66	4	2	.667	70	29	24	24	25	3.27
1976—Evansville		Am. Assoc.	16	50	3	4	.429	60	40	38	29	33	6.84
1977—Montgomery		Southern	21	146	13	4	.765	127	62	51	93	47	3.14
1977—Evansville x		Am. Assoc.	4	11	0	0	.000	19	17	10	5	3	8.18
1978—Jacksonville		Southern	9	60	5	3	.625	50	18	12	32	20	1.80
1978—Omaha		Am. Assoc.	18	110	8	5	.615	109	63	52	61	37	4.25
1979—Omaha		Am. Assoc.	51	91	4	3	.571	69	33	26	63	43	2.57
1979—Kansas City		American	6	11	0	0	.000	10	5	4	4	2	3.27
1980—Omaha		Am. Assoc.	25	41	2	4	.333	29	18	11	37	21	2.41
1980—Kansas City		American	24	31	3	0	1.000	35	23	18	16	18	5.23
Major League Totals			30	42	3	0	1.000	45	28	22	20	20	4.71

Selected by Detroit Tigers' organization in 13th round of free-agent draft, June 8, 1971.
†On disabled list, June 16 to June 27, 1972.
‡On disabled list, July 9 to July 30, 1975.
§On disabled list, August 15 to September 1, 1975.
xSold to Kansas City Royals' organization, January 12, 1978.

LARRY RICHARD CHRISTENSON

Born November 10, 1953, at Everett, Wash.
Height, 6.04. Weight, 213.
Throws and bats righthanded.
Hobbies—Fishing and hunting.

Year	Club	League	G.	IP.	W.	L.	Pct.	H.	R.	ER.	SO.	BB.	ERA.
1972—Pulaski	Ap'lachian	8	38	4	2	.667	27	26	12	42	14	2.84
1973—Eugene	P. Coast	16	100	7	6	.538	109	65	57	64	54	5.13
1973—Philadelphia	National	10	34	1	4	.200	53	25	25	11	20	6.62
1974—Toledo	Int'national	27	172	11	9	.550	131	77	63	137	82	3.30
1974—Philadelphia	National	10	23	1	1	.500	20	11	11	18	15	4.30
1975—Toledo†	Int'national	2	12	2	0	1.000	5	0	0	10	3	0.00
1975—Philadelphia	National	29	172	11	6	.647	149	73	70	88	45	3.66
1976—Philadelphia	National	32	169	13	8	.619	199	77	69	54	42	3.67
1977—Philadelphia	National	34	219	19	6	.760	229	113	99	118	69	4.07
1978—Philadelphia	National	33	228	13	14	.481	209	90	82	131	47	3.24
1979—Philadelphia‡	National	19	106	5	10	.333	118	56	53	53	30	4.50
1980—Philadelphia§	National	14	74	5	1	.833	62	35	33	49	27	4.01
Major League Totals		181	1025	68	50	.576	1039	480	442	522	295	3.88

Selected by Philadelphia Phillies' organization in 1st round (third player selected) of free-agent draft, June 6, 1972.

†On disabled list, April 11 to April 30, 1975.
‡On disabled list, March 29 to May 11 and July 4 to August 3, 1979.
§On emergency disabled list, May 26 to August 11, 1980.

CHAMPIONSHIP SERIES RECORD

Year	Club	League	G.	IP.	W.	L.	Pct.	H.	R.	ER.	SO.	BB.	ERA.
1977—Philadelphia	National	1	3⅓	0	0	.000	7	3	3	2	0	8.10
1978—Philadelphia	National	1	4⅓	0	1	.000	7	7	6	3	1	12.46
1980—Philadelphia	National	2	6⅔	0	0	.000	5	3	3	2	5	4.05
Championship Series Totals		4	14⅓	0	1	.000	19	13	12	7	6	7.53

WORLD SERIES RECORD

Year	Club	League	G.	IP.	W.	L.	Pct.	H.	R.	ER.	SO.	BB.	ERA.
1980—Philadelphia	National	1	⅓	0	1	.000	5	4	4	0	0	108.00

STEPHEN RANDALL CHRISTMAS
(Steve)

Born December 9, 1957, at Orlando, Fla.
Height, 6.00. Weight, 190.
Throws right and bats lefthanded.
Attended Oklahoma City Southwestern Junior College, Oklahoma City, Okla.

Led Florida State League catchers in putouts with 646 and in assists with 113 in 1979.
Led Eastern League catchers in fielding average with .984 in 1980.
Tied for Florida State League lead in passed balls with 17 in 1979.

Year	Club	League	Pos.	G.	AB.	R.	H.	2B.	3B.	HR.	RBI.	B.A.	PO.	A.	E.	F.A.
1977—Eugene	N'west	C-3B-1B	46	173	30	53	13	1	6	30	.306	214	24	7	.971
1978—Shelby	W. Car.	C	106	352	53	88	10	0	9	40	.250	∗532	∗77	18	.971
1979—Tampa	Fla. St.	●C-1B	122	377	50	99	18	2	6	39	.263	684	119	●17	.979
1980—Waterbury	East.	C-1B	115	347	44	84	15	2	7	44	.242	621	81	11	.985

Selected by Minnesota Twins' organization in 33rd round of free-agent draft, June 4, 1975.
Signed as free agent by Cincinnati Reds' organization, February 13, 1977.

NORMAN JAMES CHURCHILL
(Norm)

Born April 16, 1958, at Hempstead, N. Y.
Height, 6.04. Weight, 205.
Throws and bats lefthanded.
Attended Hillsborough Community College, Tampa, Fla.

Tied for New York-Pennsylvania League lead in games started with 14 in 1977.
Tied for Florida State League lead in shutouts with 5 in 1978.

Year	Club	League	G.	IP.	W.	L.	Pct.	H.	R.	ER.	SO.	BB.	ERA.
1977—Waterloo	Midwest	4	5	0	1	.000	8	5	4	5	5	7.20
1977—Batavia†	NYP	14	82	8	4	.667	74	35	24	60	32	2.63
1978—Pompano Beach	Florida St.	26	159	8	13	.381	159	87	66	88	70	3.74
1979—Quad Cities	Midwest	20	48	4	3	.571	55	35	24	39	21	4.50
1979—Wichita	Am. Assoc.	11	53	4	1	.800	54	20	20	21	26	3.40
1980—Wichita	Am. Assoc.	9	24	3	1	.750	33	13	12	15	10	4.50
1980—Quad Cities	Midwest	7	36	2	3	.400	29	18	9	29	13	2.25
1980—Midland	Texas	16	65	3	2	.600	74	29	28	50	33	3.88

Selected by Cleveland Indians' organization in 4th round of free-agent draft, January 11, 1977.
†Traded with Outfielder Bruce Compton to Chicago Cubs' organization for Infielder Dave Rosello, December 5, 1977.

JAMES CLANCY
(Jim)

Born December 18, 1955, at Chicago, Ill.
Height, 6.04. Weight, 202.
Throws and bats righthanded.
Hobby—Playing guitar.

Tied for Gulf Coast League lead in shutouts with 2 in 1974.

Year	Club	League	G.	IP.	W.	L.	Pct.	H.	R.	ER.	SO.	BB.	ERA.
1974—Sarasota Rangers	Gulf Coast	9	53	3	3	.500	40	21	16	58	28	2.72
1975—Anderson	W. Carol.	23	148	6	13	.316	139	85	63	109	91	3.83
1976—San Antonio†‡	Texas	23	125	6	8	.429	133	94	89	77	98	6.41
1977—Jersey City	Eastern	20	118	5	13	.278	116	87	64	99	75	4.88
1977—Toronto	American	13	77	4	9	.308	80	47	43	44	47	5.03
1978—Toronto	American	31	194	10	12	.455	199	96	88	106	91	4.08
1979—Toronto§	American	12	64	2	7	.222	65	44	39	33	31	5.48
1980—Toronto	American	34	251	13	16	.448	217	108	92	152	128	3.30
Major League Totals		90	586	29	44	.397	561	295	262	335	297	4.02

Selected by Texas Rangers' organization in 4th round of free-agent draft, June 5, 1974.
†On disabled list, June 15 to June 26, 1976.
‡Selected by Toronto Blue Jays from Texas Rangers in American League expansion draft, November 5, 1976.
§On disabled list, May 12 to July 4 and August 5 to October 3, 1979.

BRYAN DONALD CLARK

Born July 12, 1956, at Madera, Calif.
Height, 6.02. Weight, 185.
Throws and bats lefthanded.

Led New York-Pennsylvania League in wild pitches with 24 in 1975.
Led Western Carolinas League in wild pitches with 31 in 1976.
Led Carolina League in wild pitches with 24 in 1977 and with 27 in 1979.
Tied for Gulf Coast League lead in shutouts with 2 in 1974.
Tied for Carolina League lead in shutouts with 3 in 1979.

Year	Club	League	G.	IP.	W.	L.	Pct.	H.	R.	ER.	SO.	BB.	ERA.
1974—Bradenton Pirates	Gulf Coast	11	62	4	6	.400	49	35	23	47	•40	3.34
1975—Charleston	W. Carol.	12	57	4	7	.364	56	48	34	38	67	5.37
1975—Niagara Falls	N.Y.-Pa.	13	74	3	•10	.231	47	49	37	59	•71	4.50
1976—Charleston	W. Carol.	22	103	1	13	.071	97	87	70	79	104	6.12
1977—Salem	Carolina	26	125	5	•13	.278	135	105	66	108	105	4.75
1978—Charleston†	W. Carol.	12	56	1	6	.143	55	53	38	44	55	6.11
1978—Bellingham	Northwest	2	4	0	0	.000	4	1	1	6	3	2.25
1978—Stockton	California	11	27	0	4	.000	30	32	22	18	39	7.33
1979—Alexandria	Carolina	23	167	•14	5	.737	124	57	49	116	•112	2.64
1980—Spokane	P. Coast	8	41	2	5	.286	43	35	24	19	37	5.27
1980—Lynn	Eastern	16	116	9	5	.643	102	49	40	93	50	3.10

Selected by Pittsburgh Pirates' organization in 10th round of free-agent draft, June 5, 1974.
†Sold to Seattle Mariners' organization, June 12, 1978.

JACK ANTHONY CLARK

Born November 10, 1955, at New Brighton, Pa.
Height, 6.03. Weight, 205.
Throws and bats righthanded.
Hobby—Music.

Led Texas League third basemen in double plays with 29 in 1975.
Led California League in total bases with 254 in 1974 and Texas League with 239 in 1975.
Named California League Rookie of the Year, 1974.
Tied for National League in double plays by outfielders with 7 in 1979.
Named outfielder on THE SPORTING NEWS National League All-Star Team, 1978.

Year	Club	League	Pos.	G.	AB.	R.	H.	2B.	3B.	HR.	RBI.	B.A.	PO.	A.	E.	F.A.
1973—Great Falls	Pion.	O-P-3	65	234	46	75	20	1	9	54	.321	73	9	1	.988
1974—Fresno	Calif.	3B	131	495	88	156	23	9	19	•117	.315	100	204	•53	.852
1975—Lafayette	Texas	•3B-OF	126	466	94	141	25	2	•23	77	.303	•107	•279	•56	•.873
1975—San Francisco	Nat.	OF-3B	8	17	3	4	0	0	0	2	.235	8	1	0	1.000
1976—Phoenix	P.C.	OF-3B	131	470	111	152	29	•16	17	86	.323	188	23	9	.959
1976—San Francisco	Nat.	OF	26	102	14	23	6	2	2	10	.225	71	3	1	.987
1977—San Francisco	Nat.	OF	136	413	64	104	17	4	13	51	.252	226	11	6	.975
1978—San Francisco	Nat.	OF	156	592	90	181	46	8	25	98	.306	320	16	6	.982
1979—San Francisco	Nat.	OF-3B	143	527	84	144	25	2	26	86	.273	262	13	5	.971
1980—San Francisco†	Nat.	OF	127	437	77	124	20	8	22	82	.284	229	7	8	.967
Major League Totals			596	2088	332	580	114	24	88	329	.278	1116	51	26	.978

Selected by San Francisco Giants' organization in 13th round of free-agent draft, June 5, 1973.

PITCHING RECORD

Year	Club	League	G.	IP.	W.	L.	Pct.	H.	R.	ER.	SO.	BB.	ERA.
1973—Great Falls	Pioneer	5	15	0	2	.000	24	24	10	17	19	6.00

Year	League	Pos.	AB.	R.	H.	2B.	3B.	HR.	RBI.	B.A.	PO.	A.	E.	F.A.
1978—National		OF	1	0	0	0	0	0	0	.000	0	0	0	.000
1979—National		PH	1	0	0	0	0	0	0	.000	0	0	0	.000
All-Star Game Totals			2	0	0	0	0	0	0	.000	0	0	0	.000

ROBERT CALE CLARK
(Bobby)

Born June 13, 1955, at North Highland, Calif.
Height, 6.00. Weight, 190.
Throws and bats righthanded.
Hobbies—Backgammon, cards and sports in general.
Attended Riverside City Junior College, Riverside, Calif. and University of California, Riverside, Calif.

Led Midwest League outfielders in double plays with 9 in 1977.
Led Texas League in total bases with 297 in 1978.
Named Texas League Most Valuable Player, 1978.

Year	Club	League	Pos.	G.	AB.	R.	H.	2B.	3B.	HR.	RBI.	B.A.	PO.	A.	E.	F.A.
1975—Idaho Falls		Pion.	*OF-1-3	*72	253	43	64	7	*9	4	38	.253	154	10	6	*.965
1976—Quad Cities		Midwest	*OF-1B	*129	477	82	139	19	8	10	77	.291	365	*28	10	.975
1977—Salinas		Calif.	*O-C-1	137	524	107	149	19	10	23	88	.284	311	11	7	*.979
1978—El Paso		Texas	OF	129	491	108	155	35	7	*31	*111	.316	261	*23	9	.969
1979—Salt Lake City		P.C.	OF	129	474	85	144	30	9	15	91	.304	*328	12	7	.980
1979—California		Amer.	OF	19	54	8	16	2	2	1	5	.296	41	4	1	.978
1980—Salt Lake City		P.C.	OF	33	113	18	39	6	4	4	21	.345	57	2	1	.983
1980—California		Amer.	OF	78	261	26	60	10	1	5	23	.230	213	6	4	.982
Major League Totals				97	315	34	76	12	3	6	28	.241	254	10	5	.981

Selected by Houston Astros' organization in 14th round of free-agent draft, June 5, 1973.
Selected by California Angels' organization in secondary phase of free-agent draft, January 9, 1975.

CHAMPIONSHIP SERIES RECORD

Year	Club	League	Pos.	G.	AB.	R.	H.	2B.	3B.	HR.	RBI.	B.A.	PO.	A.	E.	F.A.
1979—California		Amer.	OF	1	3	0	0	0	0	0	0	.000	3	0	0	1.000

KENNETH EARL CLAY
(Ken)

Born April 6, 1954, at Lynchburg, Va.
Height, 6.02. Weight, 195.
Throws and bats righthanded.

Led Florida State League in hit batsmen with 13 and tied for lead in complete games with 11 in 1973.
Tied for Appalachian League lead in games started with 13 and in shutouts with 2 in 1972.

Year	Club	League	G.	IP.	W.	L.	Pct.	H.	R.	ER.	SO.	BB.	ERA.
1972—Johnson City		Ap'lachian	13	91	7	2	.778	69	32	30	66	53	2.97
1973—Fort Lauderdale		Florida St.	24	158	10	10	.500	129	61	40	97	80	2.28
1974—West Haven†		Eastern	31	155	5	●13	.278	160	●103	*84	99	77	4.88
1975—West Haven		Eastern	15	106	10	2	.833	83	39	31	77	44	2.63
1975—Syracuse		Int'national	9	48	3	5	.375	60	34	32	32	27	6.00
1976—Syracuse		Int'national	30	168	11	8	.579	202	94	77	87	67	4.13
1977—Syracuse		Int'national	10	75	5	1	.833	48	18	14	32	33	1.68
1977—New York		American	21	56	2	3	.400	53	32	27	20	24	4.34
1978—New York‡		American	28	76	3	4	.429	89	41	36	32	21	4.26
1979—New York		American	32	78	1	7	.125	88	49	47	28	25	5.42
1980—Columbus§		Int'national	20	138	9	4	.692	106	40	30	78	50	*1.96
1980—Texas x		American	8	43	2	3	.400	43	24	22	17	29	4.60
Major League Totals			89	253	8	17	.320	273	146	132	97	99	4.70

Selected by New York Yankees' organization in 2nd round of free-agent draft, June 6, 1972.
†Played in one game as an outfielder.
‡On disabled list, July 2 to July 23, 1978.
§Traded with a player to be named later to Texas Rangers for Pitcher Gaylord Perry, August 14, 1980; Outfielder Marvin Thompson traded to Rangers completing deal, October 1, 1980.
xTraded with Outfielder Richie Zisk, Shortstop Rick Auerbach and Pitchers Steve Finch, Jerry Gleaton and Brian Allard to Seattle Mariners for Catcher Larry Cox, Pitcher Rick Honeycutt, Shortstop Mario Mendoza and Outfielders Willie Horton and Leon Roberts, December 12, 1980.

CHAMPIONSHIP SERIES RECORD

Year	Club	League	G.	IP.	W.	L.	Pct.	H.	R.	ER.	SO.	BB.	ERA.
1978—New York		American	1	3⅔	0	0	.000	0	0	0	2	3	0.00

WORLD SERIES RECORD

Year	Club	League	G.	IP.	W.	L.	Pct.	H.	R.	ER.	SO.	BB.	ERA.
1977—New York		American	2	3⅔	0	0	.000	2	1	1	0	1	2.45
1978—New York		American	1	2⅓	0	0	.000	4	4	3	2	2	11.57
World Series Totals			3	6	0	0	.000	6	5	4	2	3	6.00

MARK ALAN CLEAR

Born May 27, 1956, at Los Angeles, Calif.
Height, 6.04. Weight, 200.
Throws and bats righthanded.
Attended Mount San Antonio College, Walnut, Calif.
Nephew of Bob Clear, coach with California Angels.

Major League saves: 1979 (14), 1980 (9). Total—23.
Named American League Rookie Pitcher of the Year by THE SPORTING NEWS, 1979.

Year Club	League	G.	IP.	W.	L.	Pct.	H.	R.	ER.	SO.	BB.	ERA.
1974—Pulaski†	Ap'lachian	14	51	0	7	.000	73	•69	49	38	43	8.65
1975—Idaho Falls	Pioneer	13	28	1	2	.333	24	14	6	29	30	1.93
1976—Quad Cities	Midwest	30	144	8	10	.444	135	84	63	109	111	3.94
1977—Quad Cities	Midwest	13	74	6	3	.667	64	47	40	48	50	4.86
1977—Salinas	California	13	44	1	4	.200	49	36	32	26	45	6.55
1978—Salinas	California	10	53	3	5	.375	51	38	32	55	40	5.43
1978—El Paso	Texas	31	52	4	2	.667	28	14	14	80	32	2.42
1979—California	American	52	109	11	5	.688	87	48	44	98	68	3.63
1980—California‡	American	58	106	11	11	.500	82	51	39	105	65	3.31
Major League Totals		110	215	22	16	.579	169	99	83	203	133	3.47

Selected by Philadelphia Phillies' organization in 8th round of free-agent draft, June 5, 1974.
†Released by Philadelphia Phillies' organization, April 2, 1975; signed by California Angels' organization, June 16, 1975.
‡Traded with Third Baseman Carney Lansford and Outfielder Rick Miller to Boston Red Sox for Shortstop Rick Burleson and Third Baseman Butch Hobson, December 10, 1980.

CHAMPIONSHIP SERIES RECORD

Year Club	League	G.	IP.	W.	L.	Pct.	H.	R.	ER.	SO.	BB.	ERA.
1979—California	American	1	5⅔	0	0	.000	4	3	3	3	2	4.76

ALL-STAR GAME RECORD

Year League	IP.	W.	L.	Pct.	H.	R.	ER.	SO.	BB.	ERA.
1979—American	2	0	0	.000	2	1	1	0	1	4.50

REGINALD LESLIE CLEVELAND
(Reggie)

Born May 23, 1948, at Swift Current, Saskatchewan, Canada.
Height, 6.01. Weight, 200.
Throws and bats righthanded.
Hobbies—Reading and skin diving.

Led Northwest League pitchers in games started with 19 in 1967.
Tied for Northwest League lead in complete games with 11 in 1967 and tied for Texas League lead with 13 in 1969.
Named THE SPORTING NEWS National League Rookie Pitcher of the Year, 1971.

Year Club	League	G.	IP.	W.	L.	Pct.	H.	R.	ER.	SO.	BB.	ERA.
1966—St. Petersburg	Florida St.	3	5	0	0	.000	3	0	0	2	2	0.00
1966—Eugene	Northwest	11	18	0	1	.000	16	11	11	16	16	5.50
1967—St. Petersburg	Florida St.	2	11	0	2	.000	9	6	6	4	3	4.91
1967—Lewiston	Northwest	20	•146	8	10	.444	•125	75	47	82	64	2.90
1968—St. Petersburg	Florida St.	27	185	•15	10	.600	152	71	57	135	68	2.77
1969—Arkansas	Texas	23	170	15	6	.714	156	75	64	103	62	3.39
1969—Tulsa	Am. Assoc.	6	48	3	3	.500	39	19	15	30	23	2.81
1969—St. Louis	National	1	4	0	0	.000	7	4	4	3	1	9.00
1970—Tulsa	Am. Assoc.	24	155	12	8	.600	165	78	69	106	49	4.01
1970—St. Louis	National	16	26	0	4	.000	31	27	22	22	18	7.62
1971—St. Louis	National	34	222	12	12	.500	238	107	99	148	53	4.01
1972—St. Louis	National	33	231	14	15	.483	229	•120	101	153	60	3.94
1973—St. Louis†	National	32	224	14	10	.583	211	88	75	122	61	3.01
1974—Boston	American	41	221	12	14	.462	234	121	106	103	69	4.32
1975—Boston	American	31	171	13	9	.591	173	90	84	78	52	4.42
1976—Boston	American	41	170	10	9	.526	159	73	58	76	61	3.07
1977—Boston	American	36	190	11	8	.579	211	97	90	85	43	4.26
1978—Boston‡-Texas§	American	54	76	5	8	.385	66	34	26	46	23	3.08
1979—Milwaukee	American	29	55	1	5	.167	77	44	41	22	23	6.71
1980—Milwaukee	American	45	154	11	9	.550	150	73	64	54	49	3.74
American League Totals		277	1037	63	62	.504	1070	532	469	464	320	4.07
National League Totals		116	707	40	41	.494	716	346	301	448	193	3.83
Major League Totals		393	1744	103	103	.500	1786	878	770	912	513	3.97

Signed as free agent by St. Louis Cardinals' organization, August 28, 1965.
†Traded with Pitcher Diego Segui and Infielder Terry Hughes to Boston Red Sox for Pitchers Lynn McGlothen, John Curtis and Mike Garman, December 7, 1973.
‡Sold to Texas Rangers, April 18, 1978.
§Traded to Milwaukee Brewers for Pitcher Ed Farmer, First Baseman Gary Holle and cash, December 15, 1978.

CHAMPIONSHIP SERIES RECORD

Year Club	League	G.	IP.	W.	L.	Pct.	H.	R.	ER.	SO.	BB.	ERA.
1975—Boston	American	1	5	0	0	.000	7	3	3	2	1	5.40

WORLD SERIES RECORD

Year Club	League	G.	IP.	W.	L.	Pct.	H.	R.	ER.	SO.	BB.	ERA.
1975—Boston	American	3	6⅔	0	1	.000	7	5	5	5	3	6.75

STANLEY GENE CLIBURN

Born December 19, 1956, at Jackson, Miss.
Height, 6.00. Weight, 195.
Throws and bats righthanded.
Hobbies—Golf, basketball, hunting and fishing.
Attended Hinds Junior College, Raymond, Miss. and
Southern Mississippi University, Hattiesburg, Miss.
Brother of Stewart Cliburn, pitcher in Pittsburgh Pirates' organization.

Led Pioneer League catchers in double plays with 3 in 1975.

Year Club	League	Pos.	G.	AB.	R.	H.	2B.	3B.	HR.	RBI.	B.A.	PO.	A.	E.	F.A.
1974—Idaho Falls........	Pion.	C-1B	64	214	30	61	11	0	4	35	.285	211	25	9	.963
1975—Idaho Falls........	Pion.	*C-1-3-O	57	179	33	45	10	0	0	25	.251	367	34	3	*.993
1975—Quad Cities	Midw.	C	27	80	9	16	2	0	0	7	.200	149	11	7	.958
1976—Quad Cities	Midw.	C-1B	76	262	39	80	15	0	5	44	.305	358	41	7	.983
1977—Salinas..............	Calif.	C	104	380	65	118	28	1	7	54	.311	612	54	8	*.988
1978—El Paso.............	Texas	C	30	93	13	18	4	1	4	16	.194	162	17	5	.973
1978—Salt Lake City†..	P. C.	C	47	148	18	31	4	1	3	16	.209	225	28	3	.988
1979—Salt Lake City‡..	P.C.	C	62	206	15	49	12	1	4	26	.238	257	33	7	.976
1980—Salt Lake City ...	P.C.	C	7	24	2	3	1	0	0	3	.125	28	5	0	1.000
1980—California	Amer.	C	78	261	26	60	10	1	5	23	.230	127	9	4	.971
Major League Totals......................			78	261	26	60	10	1	5	23	.230	127	9	4	.971

Selected by California Angels' organization in 16th round of free-agent draft, June 5, 1974.
†On disabled list, July 1 to July 19, 1978.
‡On disabled list, June 20 to August 2, 1979.

JAMES STANLEY COCANOWER
(Jaime)

Born February 14, 1957, at Balboa Heights, Canal Zone
Height, 6.04. Weight, 200.
Throws and bats righthanded.

Named California League co-Most Valuable Player, 1980.

Year Club	League	G.	IP.	W.	L.	Pct.	H.	R.	ER.	SO.	BB.	ERA.
1978—Burlington†..........................	Midwest					(Did not play)						
1979—Stockton‡............................	California	20	78	2	4	.333	73	42	36	36	45	4.15
1980—Stockton	California	27	●198	17	5	.773	143	74	48	132	105	2.18

Signed as free agent by Milwaukee Brewers' organization, June 7, 1978.
†On disabled list, June 17 to September 27, 1978.
‡On temporary inactive list, August 16 to September 8, 1979.

GREGORY MAHLON COCHRAN
(Greg)

Born November 15, 1953, at Whittier, Calif.
Height, 6.02. Weight, 195.
Throws and bats righthanded.
Attended Arizona State University, Tempe, Ariz.; received Bachelor of Science degree in marketing.
Brother-in-law of Floyd Bannister, pitcher with Seattle Mariners.

Year Club	League	G.	IP.	W.	L.	Pct.	H.	R.	ER.	SO.	BB.	ERA.
1975—Modesto	California	12	70	3	7	.300	78	49	40	51	39	5.14
1976—Modesto†	California	21	133	9	8	.529	170	76	55	86	55	3.72
1977—Chattanooga........................	Southern	12	76	4	2	.667	66	29	25	56	30	2.96
1977—San Jose	P. Coast	14	68	3	9	.250	93	68	47	44	28	6.22
1978—Jersey City‡........................	Eastern	28	192	10	13	.435	184	●104	74	121	54	3.47
1979—Columbus	Int'national	24	89	3	2	.600	78	41	35	60	43	3.54
1979—West Haven..........................	Eastern	3	25	2	1	.667	17	7	6	16	5	2.16
1980—Columbus	Int'national	24	165	12	7	.632	129	51	47	106	56	2.56

Selected by Philadelphia Phillies' organization in 4th round of free-agent draft, June 8, 1971.
Selected by Oakland A's organization in 2nd round of free-agent draft, June 4, 1975.
†On disabled list, May 11 to June 8, 1976.
‡Sold to New York Yankees' organization for reported $100,000, February 3, 1979.

MICHAEL MALLOY COLBERN
(Mike)

Born April 19, 1955, at Santa Monica, Calif.
Height, 6.03. Weight, 205.
Throws and bats righthanded.
Attending Arizona State University, Tempe, Ariz.
Son of Louis M. Colbern, former minor league player.

Year Club	League	Pos.	G.	AB.	R.	H.	2B.	3B.	HR.	RBI.	B.A.	PO.	A.	E.	F.A.
1976—Sara. W. Sox......	G. C.	C	26	103	7	25	3	4	0	16	.243	142	15	6	.963
1977—Knoxville	South.	C-OF	119	407	39	116	23	2	11	55	.285	579	94	16	.977
1978—Iowa	A. A.	C-OF	75	251	32	71	11	0	12	44	.283	339	39	13	.967
1978—Chicago	Amer.	C	48	141	11	38	5	1	2	20	.270	203	19	7	.969
1979—Iowa	A. A.	C-OF	57	214	29	56	15	1	8	43	.262	262	33	5	.983

Year Club	League	Pos.	G.	AB.	R.	H.	2B.	3B.	HR.	RBI.	B.A.	PO.	A.	E.	F.A.
1979—Chicago†	Amer.	C	32	83	5	20	5	1	0	8	.241	121	12	4	.971
1980—Iowa‡	A. A.	C-OF	84	268	30	66	12	1	8	34	.246	344	44	9	.977
Major League Totals			80	224	16	58	10	2	2	28	.259	324	31	11	.970

Selected by Kansas City Royals' organization in 5th round of free-agent draft, June 5, 1973.
Selected by Chicago White Sox' organization in 2nd round of free-agent draft, June 8, 1976.
†On supplemental disabled list, July 28 to August 27, 1979.
‡On league suspended list, April 25 to May 9, 1980.

TIMOTHY ALAN COLE

Born May 1, 1959, at Saugerties, N.Y.
Height, 6.00. Weight, 189.
Throws and bats lefthanded.

Year Club	League	G.	IP.	W.	L.	Pct.	H.	R.	ER.	SO.	BB.	ERA.
1977—Kingsport	Ap'lachian	7	37	3	1	.750	29	20	17	31	31	4.14
1978—Greenwood	W. Carol.	22	106	5	8	.385	85	85	66	68	99	5.60
1979—Savannah	Southern	24	137	6	11	.353	141	110	90	74	98	5.91
1980—Savannah	Southern	27	154	10	13	.435	145	98	80	108	105	4.68

Selected by Atlanta Braves' organization in 1st round (fourth player selected) of free-agent draft, June 7, 1977.

DAVID S. COLLINS
(Dave)

Born October 20, 1952, at Rapid City, S. D.
Height, 5.10. Weight, 175.
Throws left and bats left and righthanded.
Hobbies—Weight lifting, basketball and hunting.
Attended Mesa Community College, Mesa, Ariz.

Major league stolen bases: 1975 (24), 1976 (32), 1977 (25), 1978 (7), 1979 (16), 1980 (79). Total—183.
Led Pioneer League outfielders in double plays with 3 in 1972.
Named Most Valuable Player in Pioneer League, 1972.

Year Club	League	Pos.	G.	AB.	R.	H.	2B.	3B.	HR.	RBI.	B.A.	PO.	A.	E.	F.A.
1972—Idaho Falls	Pion.	*OF-1B	68	252	40	69	8	*8	1	27	.274	101	*11	3	.974
1973—Quad Cities†	Midw.	OF	110	387	61	100	15	7	4	49	.258	229	10	11	.956
1974—Salinas	Calif.	OF-1B	39	143	30	49	3	5	1	21	.343	109	0	5	.956
1974—El Paso	Texas	1B-OF	82	324	64	114	15	4	4	49	*.352	381	14	12	.971
1975—Salt Lake City	P.C.	OF	51	193	41	60	7	6	0	24	.311	58	2	1	.984
1975—California	Amer.	OF	93	319	41	85	13	4	3	29	.266	159	3	2	.988
1976—Salt Lake City	P.C.	OF	35	136	28	49	13	4	0	12	.360	50	3	2	.964
1976—California‡	Amer.	OF	99	365	45	96	12	1	4	28	.263	160	3	1	.994
1977—Seattle§	Amer.	OF	120	402	46	96	9	3	5	28	.239	124	6	2	.985
1978—Cincinnati	Nat.	OF	102	102	13	22	1	0	0	7	.216	30	1	1	.969
1979—Cincinnati	Nat.	OF-1B	122	396	59	126	16	4	3	35	.318	223	3	4	.983
1980—Cincinnati	Nat.	OF	144	551	94	167	20	4	3	35	.303	337	5	5	.986
National League Totals			368	1049	166	315	37	8	6	77	.300	590	9	10	.984
American League Totals			312	1086	132	277	34	8	12	85	.255	443	12	5	.989
Major League Totals			680	2135	298	592	71	16	18	162	.277	1033	21	15	.986

Selected by Cincinnati Reds' organization in 23rd round of free-agent draft, June 8, 1971.
Selected by Kansas City Royals' organization in secondary phase of free-agent draft, January 12, 1972.
Selected by California Angels' organization in secondary phase of free-agent draft, June 6, 1972.
†On disabled list, May 21 to May 31, 1973.
‡Selected by Seattle Mariners in special American League expansion draft, November 5, 1976.
§Traded to Cincinnati Reds for Pitcher Shane Rawley, December 9, 1977.

CHAMPIONSHIP SERIES RECORD

Year Club	League	Pos.	G.	AB.	R.	H.	2B.	3B.	HR.	RBI.	B.A.	PO.	A.	E.	F.A.
1970—Cincinnati	National	OF	3	14	0	5	1	0	0	1	.357	5	0	0	1.000

DONALD EDWARD COLLINS
(Don)

Born September 15, 1952, at Lyons, Ga.
Height 6.02. Weight, 195.
Throws left and bats righthanded.
Hobbies—Reading, music and watching television.
Attended South Georgia College, Douglas, Ga.

Year Club	League	G.	IP.	W.	L.	Pct.	H.	R.	ER.	SO.	BB.	ERA.
1972—Wytheville	Ap'lachian	8	50	5	1	.833	34	19	16	57	19	2.88
1973—Greenwood	W. Carol.	22	114	4	10	.286	117	54	41	107	83	3.24
1974—Savannah	Southern	22	110	6	8	.429	116	77	59	65	83	4.83
1975—Savannah	Southern	24	157	8	7	.533	153	66	55	79	69	3.15
1976—Richmond†	Int'national	23	88	4	6	.400	109	58	49	40	50	5.01
1977—Richmond‡	Int'national	3	19	1	0	1.000	14	9	7	7	7	3.32

Year Club	League	G.	IP.	W.	L.	Pct.	H.	R.	ER.	SO.	BB.	ERA.
1977–Atlanta ....National		40	71	3	9	.250	82	43	40	27	41	5.07
1978–Richmond ....Int'national		10	58	1	5	.167	69	42	39	39	29	6.05
1978–Savannah§ ....Southern		12	60	2	1	.667	54	24	13	51	28	1.95
1979–Richmond x ....Int'national		34	187	12	7	.632	203	84	72	119	64	3.47
1980–Tacoma ....P. Coast		25	158	10	8	.556	175	99	77	74	78	4.39
1980–Cleveland............................American		4	6	0	0	.000	9	5	5	0	7	7.50
National League Totals............................		40	71	3	9	.250	82	43	40	27	41	5.07
American League Totals...........................		4	6	0	0	.000	9	5	5	0	7	7.50
Major League Totals................................		44	77	3	9	.250	91	48	45	27	48	5.26

Selected by Milwaukee Brewers' organization in 1st round (fifth player selected) of free-agent draft, January 13, 1971.
Selected by New York Mets' organization in secondary phase of free-agent draft, June 8, 1971.
Selected by Cleveland Indians' organization in secondary phase of free-agent draft, January 12, 1972.
Selected by Atlanta Braves' organization in secondary phase of free-agent draft, June 6, 1972.
†On disabled list August 20 to September 2, 1976.
‡On disabled list, July 11 to July 21, 1977.
§On disabled list, June 20 to July 7, 1978.
xTraded to Cleveland Indians for pitcher Gary Melson, February 15, 1980.

GEOFFREY WADE COMBE
(Geoff)

Born February 1, 1956, at Melrose, Mass.
Height, 6.01. Weight, 185.
Throws and bats righthanded

Led Florida State League in saves with 13 in 1976.
Led Southern League in saves with 27 in 1979.
Led American Association in saves with 23 in 1980.
Named Southern League Pitcher of the Year, 1979.

Year Club	League	G.	IP.	W.	L.	Pct.	H.	R.	ER.	SO.	BB.	ERA.
1975–Eugene ....Northwest		19	*102	9	3	.750	99	40	31	40	41	2.74
1976–Tampa..................................Florida St.		47	102	9	2	.818	78	31	24	63	39	2.12
1977–Three Rivers........................Eastern		46	82	6	6	.500	72	24	22	68	34	2.41
1978–Nashville ....Southern		*66	100	12	6	.667	84	31	21	68	38	1.89
1979–Indianapolis ....Am. Assoc.		14	22	1	0	1.000	28	12	11	7	16	4.50
1979–Nashville ....Southern		54	87	5	5	.500	66	29	20	84	30	2.07
1980–Indianapolis ....Am. Assoc.		*60	77	2	2	.500	50	20	19	72	35	2.22
1980–Cincinnati ....National		4	7	0	0	.000	9	8	8	10	4	10.29
Major League Totals................................		4	7	0	0	.000	9	8	8	10	4	10.29

Signed as free agent by Cincinnati Reds' organization, September 2, 1974.

STEVEN MICHAEL COMER
(Steve)

Born January 13, 1954, at Minneapolis, Minn.
Height, 6.03. Weight, 207.
Throws right and bats right and lefthanded.
Attended University of Minnesota, Minneapolis, Minn.

Tied for Gulf Coast League lead in shutouts with 2 in 1976.

Year Club	League	G.	IP.	W.	L.	Pct.	H.	R.	ER.	SO.	BB.	ERA.
1976–Sarasota Rangers.................Gulf Coast		9	60	7	2	.778	35	9	6	40	18	*0.90
1977–Tulsa....................................Texas		14	105	7	6	.538	102	50	37	53	28	3.17
1977–Tucson.................................P. Coast		14	84	6	4	.600	101	45	39	32	33	4.18
1978–Texas ....American		30	117	11	5	.688	107	36	30	65	37	2.31
1979–Texas ....American		36	242	17	12	.586	230	114	99	86	84	3.68
1980–Texas†.................................American		12	42	2	4	.333	65	41	37	9	22	7.93
Major League Totals................................		78	401	30	21	.588	402	191	166	160	143	3.73

Signed as free agent by Texas Rangers' organization, July 10, 1976.
†On disabled list, May 25 to June 28 and August 15 to September 11, 1980.

DAVID ISMAEL CONCEPCION (BONITEZ)
Name pronounced con-sep-see-OHN.

(Dave)

Born June 17, 1948, at Ocumare de la Costa, Aragua, Venezuela.
Height, 6.01. Weight, 180.
Throws and bats righthanded.
Hobby–Hunting.
Attended College Augustin Codazzi, Aragua, Venezuela.

Tied major league records for most stolen bases, pinch-runner, inning, 2, July 7, 1974 (1st game, 7th inning); and most double plays, shortstop, game, 5, June 25, 1975.
Major league stolen bases: 1970 (10), 1971 (9), 1972 (13), 1973 (22), 1974 (41), 1975 (33), 1976 (21), 1977 (29), 1978 (23), 1979 (19), 1980 (12). Total–232.
Led Southern League shortstops in double plays with 64 in 1969.
Tied for National League lead in double plays by shortstops with 102 in 1979.

Named shortstop on THE SPORTING NEWS National League All-Star fielding team, 1974 through 1977 and 1979.

Named shortstop on THE SPORTING NEWS National League All-Star Team, 1974, 1976 and 1977.

Year Club League	Pos.	G.	AB.	R.	H.	2B.	3B.	HR.	RBI.	B.A.	PO.	A.	E.	F.A.
1968—Tampa ....Fla. St.	*S-2B	120	329	47	77	11	1	0	22	.234	151	239	20	*.951
1969—Asheville ....South.	SS	96	340	47	100	11	5	1	37	.294	*157	*292	*29	*.939
1969—Indianapolis ......A.A.	S-2-3-O	42	167	29	57	7	1	0	17	.341	76	128	9	.958
1970—Cincinnati ....Nat.	SS-2B	101	265	38	69	6	3	1	19	.260	144	247	22	.947
1971—Cincinnati† ....Nat.	S-2-3-O	130	327	24	67	4	4	1	20	.205	182	310	13	.974
1972—Cincinnati ....Nat.	SS-3-2	119	378	40	79	13	2	2	29	.209	197	372	19	.968
1973—Cincinnati‡........Nat.	SS-OF	89	328	39	94	18	3	8	46	.287	167	292	12	.975
1974—Cincinnati ....Nat.	*SS-OF	160	594	70	167	25	1	14	82	.281	239	*536	30	.963
1975—Cincinnati ....Nat.	SS-3B	140	507	62	139	23	1	5	49	.274	241	446	16	.977
1976—Cincinnati ....Nat.	SS	152	576	74	162	28	7	9	69	.281	304	506	27	.968
1977—Cincinnati ....Nat.	SS	156	572	59	155	26	3	8	64	.271	280	490	11	*.986
1978—Cincinnati ....Nat.	SS	153	565	75	170	33	4	6	67	.301	255	459	23	.969
1979—Cincinnati ....Nat.	SS	149	590	91	166	25	3	16	84	.281	284	495	27	.967
1980—Cincinnati ....Nat.	SS-2B	156	622	72	162	31	8	5	77	.260	265	451	16	.978
Major League Totals		1505	5324	644	1430	232	39	75	606	.269	2558	4604	216	.971

Signed as free agent by Cincinnati Reds' organization, September 12, 1967.
†On disabled list March 21 to April 20, 1971.
‡On disabled list July 22 through remainder of season.

CHAMPIONSHIP SERIES RECORD

Tied World Series records for most sacrifice flies, total Series (3); fewest chances accepted by shortstop, game (0), October 16, 1975; one or more hits, each game, four-game Series, 1976

Year Club League	Pos.	G.	AB.	R.	H.	2B.	3B.	HR.	RBI.	B.A.	PO.	A.	E.	F.A.
1970—Cincinnati ....Nat.	PR-SS	3	0	0	0	0	0	0	0	.000	1	1	0	1.000
1972—Cincinnati ....Nat.	PH-S-PR	3	2	0	0	0	0	0	0	.000	0	0	0	.000
1975—Cincinnati ....Nat.	SS	3	11	2	5	0	0	1	1	.455	6	8	1	.933
1976—Cincinnati ....Nat.	SS	3	10	4	2	1	0	0	0	.200	2	12	0	1.000
1979—Cincinnati ....Nat.	SS	3	14	1	6	1	0	0	0	.429	3	14	0	1.000
Championship Series Totals.............		15	37	7	13	2	0	1	1	.351	12	35	1	.979

WORLD SERIES RECORD

Tied World Series records for most sacrifice flies, total Series (3); fewest chances accepted by shortstop, game (0), October 16, 1975; one or more hits, each game, four-game Series, 1976.

Year Club League	Pos.	G.	AB.	R.	H.	2B.	3B.	HR.	RBI.	B.A.	PO.	A.	E.	F.A.
1970—Cincinnati ....Nat.	SS	3	9	0	3	0	1	0	3	.333	2	2	0	1.000
1972—Cincinnati ....Nat.	S-PR-PH	6	13	2	4	0	0	0	2	.308	4	11	1	.938
1975—Cincinnati ....Nat.	SS	7	28	3	5	1	0	1	4	.179	12	22	1	.971
1976—Cincinnati ....Nat.	SS	4	14	1	5	1	1	0	3	.357	6	11	1	.944
World Series Totals		20	64	6	17	2	3	1	12	.266	24	46	3	.959

ALL STAR GAME RECORD

Year League	Pos.	AB.	R.	H.	2B.	3B.	HR.	RBI.	B.A.	PO.	A.	E.	F.A.
1975—National..............................	SS	2	0	1	0	0	0	0	.500	1	1	1	.667
1976—National..............................	SS	2	0	1	0	0	0	0	.500	2	3	0	1.000
1977—National..............................	SS	1	0	0	0	0	0	0	.000	1	1	0	1.000
1978—National..............................	SS	0	1	0	0	0	0	0	.000	2	0	0	1.000
1980—National..............................	SS	1	1	0	0	0	0	0	.000	0	2	0	1.000
All-Star Game Totals		6	2	2	0	0	0	0	.333	6	7	1	.929

Named to National League All-Star Team for 1973 game; replaced due to an ankle injury.
Named to National League All-Star Team for 1979 game; replaced due to injury by Larry Parrish.

ONIX CONCEPCION (CARDONA)

Born October 5, 1957, at Dorado, Puerto Rico
Height, 5.06. Weight, 160.
Throws and bats righthanded.

Led California League shortstops in double plays with 85 in 1979.

Year Club League	Pos.	G.	AB.	R.	H.	2B.	3B.	HR.	RBI.	B.A.	PO.	A.	E.	F.A.
1976—Jacksonville......South.	2B-SS	5	13	1	4	0	0	0	4	.308	10	18	2	.933
1976—Sara. Royals .....G. C.	SS	18	47	13	11	3	0	0	4	.234	16	40	8	.875
1977—Sara. Royals .....G. C.	2B-SS-1B	28	59	7	11	1	0	0	4	.186	45	37	5	.943
1978—Fort Myers ....Fla. St.	SS-2B	79	213	29	50	7	0	0	13	.235	120	223	24	.935
1979—Bakersfield ....Calif.	SS	127	504	88	151	25	3	14	75	.300	*227	*454	*55	.925
1980—Jacksonville......South.	SS	74	273	48	88	13	3	12	44	.322	117	249	16	.958
1980—Omaha..............A.A.	SS	58	210	22	59	9	3	4	34	.281	74	135	11	.950
1980—Kansas City ......Amer.	SS	12	15	1	2	0	0	0	2	.133	5	10	3	.833
Major League Totals......................		12	15	1	2	0	0	0	2	.133	5	10	3	.833

Signed as free agent by Kansas City Royals' organization, March 10, 1976.

WORLD SERIES RECORD

Year Club League	Pos.	G.	AB.	R.	H.	2B.	3B.	HR.	RBI.	B.A.	PO.	A.	E.	F.A.
1980—Kansas City ......Amer.	PR	3	0	0	0	0	0	0	0	.000	0	0	0	.000

TIMOTHY JAMES CONROY
(Tim)

Born April 3, 1960, at Monroeville, Pa.
Height, 6.00. Weight, 180.
Throws and bats lefthanded.

Led Eastern League in wild pitches with 22 in 1979.
Tied for Eastern League lead in wild pitches with 16 in 1980.

Year Club	League	G.	IP.	W.	L.	Pct.	H.	R.	ER.	SO.	BB.	ERA.
1978—Oakland	American	2	5	0	0	.000	3	6	4	0	9	7.20
1978—Vancouver†	P. Coast	3	9	0	1	.000	13	16	16	3	10	16.00
1979—Waterbury	Eastern	25	138	7	●14	.333	115	95	80	106	★119	5.22
1980—West Haven	Eastern	25	147	8	14	.364	160	119	101	72	93	6.18
Major League Totals		2	5	0	0	.000	3	6	4	0	9	7.20

Selected by Oakland A's organization in 2nd round of free-agent draft, June 6, 1978.
†On disabled list, July 16 to September 1, 1978.

ARNALDO JUAN CONTRERAS
(Nardi)

Born September 19, 1951, at Tampa, Fla.
Height, 6.02. Weight, 190.
Throws right and bats right and lefthanded.
Attended Hillsborough Community College, Tampa, Fla.

Year Club	League	G.	IP.	W.	L.	Pct.	H.	R.	ER.	SO.	BB.	ERA.
1969—Sioux Falls	Northern	12	70	5	1	.833	68	38	33	68	36	4.24
1970—Tampa†	Florida St.	22	108	3	10	.231	89	56	46	75	59	3.83
1971—Raleigh-Durham	Carolina	7	22	1	2	.333	30	17	13	23	21	5.32
1971—Tampa	Florida St.	3	17	0	3	.000	17	12	10	7	15	5.29
1971—Sioux Falls	Northern	12	56	2	4	.333	52	38	29	71	41	4.66
1972—Key West‡	Florida St.	30	140	9	7	.563	89	63	54	166	83	3.47
1973—Visalia	California	25	177	10	11	.476	158	83	60	170	66	3.05
1974—Victoria§	Texas	17	88	7	6	.538	82	43	35	69	37	3.58
1975—Tidewater x	Int'national	36	60	3	4	.429	49	18	13	40	35	1.96
1976—Reading	Eastern	12	29	2	1	.667	19	14	12	22	20	3.72
1976—Oklahoma City	Am. Assoc.	25	27	1	2	.333	26	9	8	17	18	2.67
1977—Reading	Eastern	31	103	6	5	.545	101	45	37	85	37	3.23
1977—Oklahoma City	Am. Assoc.	6	7	0	0	.000	6	0	0	5	3	0.00
1978—Oklahoma City y	Am. Assoc.	44	70	7	5	.583	71	42	33	55	57	4.24
1979—Iowa z	Am. Assoc.	20	95	7	6	.538	117	69	63	66	41	5.97
1980—Iowa	Am. Assoc.	20	118	9	7	.563	124	66	55	58	26	4.19
1980—Chicago	American	8	14	0	0	.000	18	10	9	8	7	5.79
Major League Totals		8	14	0	0	.000	18	10	9	8	7	5.79

Selected by Cincinnati Reds' organization in 12th round of free-agent draft, June 5, 1969.
†On disabled list, May 1 to May 18, 1970.
‡Drafted by New York Mets' organization, November 27, 1972.
§On disabled list, May 16 to May 26 and July 31 to August 15, 1974.
xReleased, April 7, 1976; signed by Philadelphia Phillies' organization April 17, 1976.
yReleased, March 29, 1979; signed by Chicago White Sox' organization, May 16, 1979.
zOn disabled list, August 24 to August 31, 1979.

CECIL CELESTER COOPER

Born December 20, 1949, at Brenham, Tex.
Height, 6.02. Weight, 190.
Throws and bats lefthanded.
Attended Prairie View A&M College, Prairie View, Tex.

Tied major league record for most strikeouts, extra-inning game (6), June 14, 1974 (15 innings).
Hit three home runs in one game, vs. New York Yankees, July 27, 1979.
Led American League in total bases with 335 in 1980.
Led American League first basemen in double plays with 160 in 1980.
Named Midwest League Player of the Year in 1970.
Named first baseman on THE SPORTING NEWS American League All-Star Team, 1979 and 1980.
Named first baseman on THE SPORTING NEWS American League All-Star fielding team, 1979 and 1980.
Named first baseman on THE SPORTING NEWS American League Silver Bat Team, 1980.

Year Club	League	Pos.	G.	AB.	R.	H.	2B.	3B.	HR.	RBI.	B.A.	PO.	A.	E.	F.A.
1968—Jamestown	NYP	1B	26	84	16	38	6	0	0	6	.452	130	0	1	.992
1969—Greenville†	W. Car.	1-O	62	212	27	63	12	2	1	18	.297	434	32	8	.983
1970—Danville‡	Midw.	1-OF	114	420	86	141	16	8	3	39	★336	535	33	12	.979
1971—Winston-Salem	Carol.	1B	42	153	31	58	6	3	6	26	.379	359	21	5	.987
1971—Pawtucket	East.	1B-OF	98	367	55	126	21	2	10	60	.343	740	35	12	.985
1971—Boston	Amer.	1B	14	42	9	13	4	1	0	3	.310	82	3	1	.988
1972—Louisville	Int.	1B	134	515	86	★162	★31	9	10	78	.315	1102	78	★17	.986
1972—Boston	Amer.	1B	12	17	0	4	1	0	0	2	.235	19	0	0	1.000
1973—Pawtucket	Int.	1B	128	450	68	132	27	1	15	77	.293	1082	84	12	.990
1973—Boston	Amer.	1B	30	101	12	24	2	0	3	11	.238	227	17	4	.984
1974—Boston	Amer.	1B	121	414	55	114	24	1	8	43	.275	637	40	12	.983

Year Club	League	Pos.	G.	AB.	R.	H.	2B.	3B.	HR.	RBI.	B.A.	PO.	A.	E.	F.A.
1975—Boston ....Amer.		1B	106	305	49	95	17	6	14	44	.311	197	20	1	.995
1976—Boston§............Amer.		1B	123	451	66	127	22	6	15	78	.282	600	42	4	.994
1977—Milwaukee ....Amer.		1B	160	643	86	193	31	7	20	78	.300	1386	118	12	.992
1978—Milwaukee x .....Amer.		1B	107	407	60	127	23	2	13	54	.312	842	66	11	.988
1979—Milwaukee ....Amer.		1B	150	590	83	182	•44	1	24	106	.308	1323	78	10	.993
1980—Milwaukee ....Amer.		1B	153	622	96	219	33	4	25	*122	.352	1336	*106	5	*.997
Major League Totals			976	3592	516	1098	201	28	122	541	.306	6649	490	60	.992

Selected by Boston Red Sox' organization in 27th round of free-agent draft, June 7, 1968.

†On temporary inactive list, April 13 through June 4.

‡Drafted by St. Louis Cardinals from Louisville (Boston Red Sox' organization), November 30, 1970. Returned to Boston organization, April 5, 1971.

§Traded to Milwaukee Brewers' for First Baseman George Scott and Outfielder Bernie Carbo, December 6, 1976.

xOn supplemental disabled list, June 9 to July 21, 1978.

CHAMPIONSHIP SERIES RECORD

Year Club	League	Pos.	G.	AB.	R.	H.	2B.	3B.	HR.	RBI.	B.A.	PO.	A.	E.	F.A.
1975—Boston ....Amer.		1B	3	10	0	4	2	0	0	1	.400	24	1	1	.962

WORLD SERIES RECORD

Year Club	League	Pos.	G.	AB.	R.	H.	2B.	3B.	HR.	RBI.	B.A.	PO.	A.	E.	F.A.
1975—Boston ....Amer.		1B-PH	5	19	0	1	1	0	0	1	.053	40	1	0	1.000

ALL-STAR GAME RECORD

Year League	Pos.	AB.	R.	H.	2B.	3B.	HR.	RBI.	B.A.	PO.	A.	E.	F.A.
1979—American	PH	0	0	0	0	0	0	0	.000	0	0	0	.000
1980—American	1B	1	0	0	0	0	0	0	.000	6	0	0	1.000
All-Star Game Totals		1	0	0	0	0	0	0	.000	6	0	0	1.000

DONALD JAMES COOPER
(Don)

Born February 15, 1957, at New York, N.Y.
Height, 6.01. Weight, 185.
Throws and bats righthanded.
Attended New York Institute of Technology, Old Westbury, N.Y.

Year Club	League	G.	IP.	W.	L.	Pct.	H.	R.	ER.	SO.	BB.	ERA.
1978—Oneonta...........................NY-Penn.		5	20	1	2	.333	18	12	8	22	10	3.60
1978—Ft. Lauderdale ....Florida St.		10	52	2	3	.400	41	22	13	34	20	2.25
1979—West Haven.........................Eastern		28	54	6	4	.600	49	31	26	44	30	4.33
1979—Columbus ....Int'national		8	18	0	0	.000	19	11	11	14	11	5.50
1980—Nashville ....Southern		32	60	9	5	.643	43	18	12	62	29	1.80
1980—Columbus† ....Int'national		12	38	3	2	.600	30	11	9	29	16	2.13

Selected by New York Yankees' organization in 17th round of free-agent draft, June 6, 1978.

†Drafted by Minnesota Twins, December 8, 1980.

GARY NATHANIEL COOPER

Born December 22, 1956, at Savannah, Ga.
Height, 6.00. Weight, 175.
Throws right and bats left and righthanded.
Hobbies—Basketball, dancing, swimming and bowling.

Year Club	League	Pos.	G.	AB.	R.	H.	2B.	3B.	HR.	RBI.	B.A.	PO.	A.	E.	F.A.
1975—Kingsport ....Appal.		OF	51	163	26	39	8	1	1	19	.239	76	10	6	.935
1976—Greenwood ....W. Car.		OF	129	459	97	109	17	1	1	29	.237	208	17	11	.953
1977—Greenwood........W. Car.		OF	125	493	90	135	13	*9	12	64	.274	162	13	12	.936
1978—Savannah ....South.		OF	107	377	50	83	11	9	4	30	.220	206	8	7	.968
1979—Savannah ....South.		OF	107	390	49	90	8	2	2	32	.231	218	12	6	.975
1980—Savannah† ....South.		OF	109	400	58	90	10	3	2	29	.225	235	14	7	.973
1980—Atlanta ....Nat.		OF	21	2	3	0	0	0	0	0	.000	5	1	0	1.000
Major League Totals......................			21	2	3	0	0	0	0	0	.000	5	1	0	1.000

Selected by Atlanta Braves' organization in 3rd round of free-agent draft, June 4, 1975.

†On disabled list, May 8 to May 28, 1980.

DOUGLAS MITCHELL CORBETT
(Doug)

Born November 4, 1952, at Sarasota, Fla.
Height, 6.01. Weight, 192.
Throws and bats righthanded.
Attended University of Florida, Gainesville Fla.; received
Bachelor of Science degree in Physical Education.

Established American League record for most games by pitcher, rookie season (73), 1980.

Major League saves: 1980 (23).

Led American Association in saves with 12 in 1979.

Year Club	League	G.	IP.	W.	L.	Pct.	H.	R.	ER.	SO.	BB.	ERA.
1974—Sarasota Royals†..................Gulf Coast		11	42	4	2	.667	36	22	14	32	18	3.00

Year Club	League	G.	IP.	W.	L.	Pct.	H.	R.	ER.	SO.	BB.	ERA.
1975–Tampa	Florida St.	27	61	2	3	.400	42	11	10	48	21	1.48
1976–Tampa	Florida St.	45	85	10	5	.667	86	25	21	37	22	2.22
1977–Three Rivers	Eastern	39	88	4	5	.444	72	35	27	65	40	2.76
1978–Nashville	Southern	15	25	2	1	.667	18	11	7	33	7	2.52
1978–Indianapolis	Am. Assoc.	38	68	4	4	.500	54	22	15	46	17	1.99
1979–Indianapolis‡	Am. Assoc.	*69	110	3	6	.333	94	38	36	77	39	2.95
1980–Minnesota	American	73	136	8	6	.571	102	31	30	89	42	1.99
Major League Totals		73	136	8	6	.571	102	31	30	89	42	1.99

Signed as free agent by Kansas City Royals' organization, June 11, 1974.
†Released, April 10, 1975; signed as free agent by Cincinnati Reds' organization, May 6, 1975.
‡Drafted by Minnesota Twins, December 3, 1979.

TIMOTHY MICHAEL CORCORAN
(Tim)

Born March 19, 1953, at Glendale, Calif.
Height, 5.11. Weight, 175.
Throws and bats lefthanded.
Hobbies—Fishing and crossword puzzles.
Attended Mount San Antonio Junior College, Walnut, Calif. and California
State University at Los Angeles, Calif.
Brother of Pat Corcoran, former infielder in Cleveland Indians' organization.

Year Club	League	Pos.	G.	AB.	R.	H.	2B.	3B.	HR.	RBI.	B.A.	PO.	A.	E.	F.A.
1974–Bristol	Appal.	OF	27	92	20	34	6	0	3	25	.370	32	0	0	1.000
1974–Lakeland	Fla. St.	OF	36	126	15	34	1	3	1	16	.270	71	3	1	.987
1975–Montgomery	South.	OF-1B	122	388	42	95	20	3	3	36	.245	283	21	4	.987
1976–Montgomery	South.	OF-1B	129	437	66	135	25	5	5	60	.309	607	49	5	.992
1977–Evansville	A. A.	1B-OF	39	136	27	47	11	3	7	33	.346	303	21	8	.976
1977–Detroit	Amer.	OF	55	103	13	29	3	0	3	15	.282	38	0	0	1.000
1978–Detroit	Amer.	OF	116	324	37	86	13	1	1	27	.265	186	6	3	.985
1979–Evansville	A. A.	OF-1B	87	287	40	97	15	0	4	50	.338	292	23	2	.994
1979–Detroit	Amer.	OF-1B	18	22	4	5	1	0	0	6	.227	45	2	0	1.000
1980–Detroit	Amer.	1B-OF	84	153	20	44	7	1	3	18	.288	274	19	5	.983
Major League Totals			273	602	74	164	24	2	7	66	.272	543	27	8	.986

Signed as free agent by Detroit Tigers' organization, June 10, 1974.

PITCHING RECORD

Year Club	League	G.	IP.	W.	L.	Pct.	H.	R.	ER.	SO.	BB.	ERA.
1977–Evansville	Am. Assoc.	1	3	0	0	.000	2	2	2	2	1	6.00

MARK MUNDELL COREY

Born November 3, 1955, at Tucumcari, N. M.
Height, 6.02. Weight, 205.
Throws and bats righthanded.
Attended Central Arizona Junior College, Coolidge, Ariz.

Led Appalachian League in total bases with 191 in 1976.
Led Southern League in total bases with 233 in 1977.
Tied for Southern League lead in double plays by outfielders with 4 in 1977.
Named Appalachian League Player of the Year, 1976.

Year Club	League	Pos.	G.	AB.	R.	H.	2B.	3B.	HR.	RBI.	B.A.	PO.	A.	E.	F.A.
1976–Bluefield	Appa.	OF	*70	*285	*62	*114	10	*8	*17	*59	*.400	97	5	3	.971
1977–Charlotte	South.	OF	133	490	76	*152	26	5	15	76	*.310	221	12	6	.975
1978–Rochester†	Int.	OF	74	250	47	81	15	3	5	40	.324	66	4	3	.959
1979–Rochester	Int.	OF-1B	92	317	38	79	21	1	10	30	.249	150	7	3	.981
1979–Baltimore	Amer.	OF	13	13	1	2	0	0	0	1	.154	10	0	0	1.000
1980–Rochester	Int.	OF-1B	82	265	34	61	14	2	3	25	.230	149	5	4	.975
1980–Baltimore	Amer.	OF	36	36	7	10	2	0	1	2	.278	20	0	0	1.000
Major League Totals			49	49	8	12	2	0	1	3	.245	30	0	0	1.000

Selected by Pittsburgh Pirates' organization in 6th round of free agent draft, January 9, 1975.
Selected by Baltimore Orioles' organization in 2nd round of free agent draft, January 7, 1976.
†On disabled list, April 14 to May 31, 1978.

VICTOR CROSBY CORRELL, JR.
(Vic)

Born February 5, 1946, at Florence, S. C.
Height, 5.10. Weight, 185.
Throws and bats righthanded.
Hobbies—Golf, hunting, fishing and other outdoor sports.
Attended Georgia Southern, Statesboro, Ga.; received Bachelor of Science degree in Recreation.

Led International League catchers in passed balls with 17 and in total chances with 972 in 1972.
Led Western Carolinas League catchers in double plays with 8 in 1968.
Tied for Western Carolinas League lead in sacrifice flies with 8 in 1968.

Year Club	League	Pos.	G.	AB.	R.	H.	2B.	3B.	HR.	RBI.	B.A.	PO.	A.	E.	F.A.
1967–Rock Hill	W. Car.	C	60	180	23	43	3	3	4	15	.239	360	31	11	.973
1968–Rock Hill	W. Car.	*C-1	105	301	47	86	17	2	16	66	.286	643	*73	14	.981
1969–Waterbury	East.	C-OF	94	271	20	57	4	0	6	33	.210	405	45	17	.964
1970–Savannah†	South.	C	116	371	31	85	15	3	8	41	.229	647	71	*17	.977
1971–Asheville‡	South.	C-OF	113	337	52	92	20	0	22	58	.273	440	38	6	.988
1972–Louisville	Int.	*C-OF	137	491	64	133	25	0	10	65	.271	*894	*68	10	.990
1972–Boston	Amer.	C	1	4	1	2	0	0	0	1	.500	9	1	0	1.000
1973–Pawtucket§	Int.	C	95	284	30	52	11	0	10	41	.183	415	33	5	.989
1974–Atlanta	Nat.	C	73	202	20	48	15	1	4	29	.238	282	40	4	.988
1975–Atlanta	Nat.	C	103	325	37	70	12	1	11	39	.215	413	63	13	.973
1976–Atlanta	Nat.	C	69	200	26	45	6	2	5	16	.225	319	36	7	.981
1977–Atlanta x	Nat.	C	54	144	16	30	7	0	7	16	.208	247	38	8	.973
1978–Indianapolis	A. A.	C-2B	33	104	15	27	2	0	6	19	.260	163	19	4	.978
1978–Cincinnati	Nat.	C	52	105	9	25	7	0	1	6	.238	180	18	4	.980
1979–Cincinnati y	Nat.	C	48	133	14	31	12	0	1	15	.233	221	19	2	.992
1980–Tampa z	Fla. St.	C	14	35	5	12	2	0	0	8	.343	45	4	0	1.000
1980–Cincinnati a	National	C	10	19	1	8	1	0	0	3	.421	33	1	3	.919
American League Totals			1	4	1	2	0	0	0	1	.500	9	1	0	1.000
National League Totals			409	1128	123	257	60	4	29	124	.228	1695	215	41	.979
Major League Totals			410	1132	124	259	60	4	29	125	.229	1704	216	41	.979

Selected by Cleveland Indians' organization in 9th round of free agent draft, June 6, 1967.

†Released by Cleveland Indians' organization, April 5, 1971; signed as free agent by Chicago White Sox' organization, April 11, 1971.

‡Drafted from Asheville (Chicago White Sox' organization) by Louisville (Boston Red Sox' organization), November 29, 1971.

§On disabled list, April 13 to April 25, 1973. Traded by Boston Red Sox to Atlanta Braves for Infielder Chuck Goggin, March 26, 1974.

xReleased, March 30, 1978; signed by Indianapolis (Cincinnati Reds' organization), April 9, 1978 as coach; named player-coach, April 18, 1978.

yOn emergency disabled list, March 21 to August 5, 1980.

zOn rehabilitation assignment, August 5 to August 24, 1980.

aReleased, October 24, 1980.

DONALD RAY COSEY

(Known by middle name).

Born February 15, 1956, at San Rafael, Calif.
Height, 5.10. Weight, 185.
Throws and bats lefthanded.
Hobbies–Bicycling and cards.

Led Northwest League in strikeouts with 64 in 1974.

Year Club	League	Pos.	G.	AB.	R.	H.	2B.	3B.	HR.	RBI.	B.A.	PO.	A.	E.	F.A.
1973–Lewiston†	Northw.	OF	47	114	9	15	2	0	0	10	.132	28	0	3	.903
1974–Lewiston	Northw.	OF	80	292	39	76	9	3	7	33	.260	*192	8	7	.966
1975–Modesto	Calif.	OF	106	397	69	108	17	2	13	49	.272	177	9	3	.984
1976–Modesto‡	Calif.	OF	91	373	73	114	19	3	25	69	.306	195	6	12	.944
1976–Chattanooga	South.	OF	8	38	6	11	3	1	0	2	.289	16	1	1	.944
1977–Chattanooga	South.	OF	118	396	42	101	14	5	8	49	.255	169	4	13	.930
1978–Jersey City	East.	OF	127	477	62	127	25	8	11	87	.266	202	6	10	.954
1979–Ogden	P. C.	OF	144	*566	80	178	21	11	12	91	.314	203	7	6	.972
1980–Ogden	P. C.	OF	95	331	52	98	17	5	7	52	.296	144	4	4	.974
1980–Oakland	Amer.	PH	9	9	0	1	0	0	0	0	.111	0	0	0	.000
Major League Totals			9	9	0	1	0	0	0	0	.111	0	0	0	.000

Signed as free agent by Oakland A's organization, June 13, 1973.

†On disabled list, July 12 to July 22, 1973.

‡On disabled list, August 3 to September 2, 1976.

ALFRED EDWARD COWENS, JR.

(Al)

Born October 25, 1951, at Los Angeles, Calif.
Height, 6.02. Weight, 200.
Throws and bats righthanded.
Hobbies–Hunting and fishing.

Named Southern League Player of the Year, 1973.
Named as outfielder on The Sporting News American League All-Star fielding team, 1977.

Year Club	League	Pos.	G.	AB.	R.	H.	2B.	3B.	HR.	RBI.	B.A.	PO.	A.	E.	F.A.
1969–Kingsport	Appal.	3-S-O	51	180	30	53	6	1	2	30	.294	48	85	16	.893
1970–Billings	Pion.	OF-SS	62	237	45	67	9	5	7	47	.283	82	20	5	.953
1971–Waterloo	Midw.	3-1-O	16	48	5	14	5	0	0	5	.292	37	12	3	.942
1971–San Jose	Calif.	OF	99	380	60	108	14	5	8	66	.284	138	14	3	*.981
1972–Waterloo	Midw.	3B	8	31	5	7	1	0	0	3	.226	5	17	2	.917
1972–San Jose	Calif.	O-3-1	83	307	36	86	17	2	5	53	.280	134	53	10	.949
1972–Jacksonville	South.	OF	35	120	17	24	2	1	4	9	.200	48	5	2	.964
1973–Jacksonville	South.	O-1-3	135	491	91	142	25	7	16	81	.289	444	52	18	.965
1974–Kansas City	Amer.	OF-3B	110	269	28	65	7	1	1	25	.242	151	14	3	.982
1975–Kansas City	Amer.	OF	120	328	44	91	13	8	4	42	.277	214	4	5	.978

Year Club League	Pos.	G.	AB.	R.	H.	2B.	3B.	HR.	RBI.	B.A.	PO.	A.	E.	F.A.
1976–Kansas City......Amer.	OF	152	581	71	154	23	6	3	59	.265	329	13	5	.986
1977–Kansas City......Amer.	OF	•162	606	98	189	32	14	23	112	.312	307	14	6	.982
1978–Kansas City†.....Amer.	OF-3B	132	485	63	133	24	8	5	63	.274	280	20	4	.987
1979–Kansas City‡§ ...Amer.	OF	136	516	69	152	18	7	9	73	.295	288	3	4	.986
1980–Calif.x-Det........Amer.	OF	142	522	69	140	20	3	6	59	.268	263	11	3	.989
Major League Totals		955	3307	442	924	137	47	51	433	.279	1832	79	30	.985

Selected by Kansas City Royals' organization in 84th round of free agent draft, June 5, 1969.
†On supplemental disabled list, June 29 to July 24, 1978.
‡On disabled list, May 9 to May 30, 1979.
§Traded with Shortstop Todd Cruz and a player to be named later to California Angels for First Baseman Willie Mays Aikens and Shortstop Rance Mulliniks, December 6, 1979; pitcher Craig Eaton traded to California Angels' organization completing deal, April 1, 1980.
xTraded to Detroit Tigers for First Baseman Jason Thompson, May 27, 1980.

CHAMPIONSHIP SERIES RECORD

Year Club League	Pos.	G.	AB.	R.	H.	2B.	3B.	HR.	RBI.	B.A.	PO.	A.	E.	F.A.
1976–Kansas City......Amer.	OF	5	21	3	4	0	1	0	0	.190	15	0	0	1.000
1977–Kansas City......Amer.	OF	5	19	2	5	0	0	1	5	.263	14	0	0	1.000
1978–Kansas City ......Amer.	OF	4	15	2	2	0	0	0	1	.133	5	0	0	1.000
Championship Series Totals.............		14	55	7	11	0	1	1	6	.200	34	0	0	1.000

JEFFREY LINDON COX
(Jeff)

Born November 9, 1955, at Los Angeles, Calif.
Height, 5.11. Weight, 170.
Throws and bats righthanded.
Attended Manatee Junior College, Bradenton, Fla., Mount San Antonio Junior College,
Walnut, Calif. and attending California State Poly University, Pomona, Calif.

Led Southern League in stolen bases with 68 in 1977.

Year Club League	Pos.	G.	AB.	R.	H.	2B.	3B.	HR.	RBI.	B.A.	PO.	A.	E.	F.A.
1974–S. K.C.-Acad.†... G.C.						(Did not play)								
1974–N.West.‡-Port.§. N'west.	O-3-S-2	49	144	23	25	2	1	0	7	.174	56	68	11	.919
1975–Boise ....N'west.	3-2-1-S	54	161	33	38	7	0	0	12	.236	88	75	17	.906
1976–Modesto ....Calif.	2B-SS-3B	70	241	55	75	11	2	3	29	.311	119	194	15	.954
1976–Chattanooga......South.	SS-2B	36	131	20	38	3	2	1	14	.290	76	114	7	.964
1977–Chattanooga......South.	2B-3B	133	476	78	127	15	3	0	39	.267	230	291	24	.956
1977–San Jose ....P. C.	2B	8	29	3	6	0	0	0	0	.207	19	22	2	.953
1978–Vancouver x .....P. C.	2B-SS	47	131	21	33	2	0	0	12	.252	76	107	9	.953
1978–Jersey City ....East.	2B	28	107	14	19	1	0	0	7	.178	65	72	6	.958
1979–Ogden ....P. C.	2B	139	520	102	148	10	1	1	37	.285	302	•501	25	.970
1980–Ogden ....P. C.	2-S-3	74	274	55	79	7	1	0	21	.288	152	217	17	.956
1980–Oakland ....Amer.	2B	59	169	20	36	3	0	0	9	.213	107	167	6	.979
Major League Totals......................		59	169	20	36	3	0	0	9	.213	107	167	6	.979

Signed as free agent by Kansas City Royals' organization, August 23, 1973.
†Released, April 23, 1974; signed as free agent by New Westminster, June 9, 1974.
‡Sold to Portland, June 24, 1974.
§Released, June 13, 1975; signed as free agent by Oakland A's organization, June 16, 1975.
xOn disabled list, April 14 to May 22 and July 3 to July 15, 1978.

LARRY EUGENE COX

Born September 11, 1947, At Bluffton, O.
Height, 5.11 Weight, 190.
Throws and bats righthanded.
Hobbies–Basketball, football, billiards, hunting and fishing.

Led Northern League catchers in double plays with 5 in 1966.
Led Pacific Coast League catchers in double plays with 15 in 1976.

Year Club League	Pos.	G.	AB.	R.	H.	2B.	3B.	HR.	RBI.	B.A.	PO.	A.	E.	F.A.
1966–Huron ....North.	C	54	155	21	34	9	0	0	15	.219	497	45	•12	.978
1967–Tidewater ....Carol.	PH	2	0	0	0	0	0	0	0	.000	0	0	0	.000
1968–Huron ....North.	P	4	9	0	2	0	0	0	1	.222	2	4	0	1.000
1968–Spartanburg .....W.Car.	P-C	11	15	1	3	1	0	1	2	.200	26	4	2	.938
1969–Raleigh-Dur. .....Carol.	C-P	73	240	19	46	9	0	0	16	.192	458	43	7	.986
1970–Reading‡...........East.	C	59	189	22	41	3	0	5	27	.217	289	25	7	.978
1970–Eugene ..............P.C.	C	16	40	4	5	0	0	2	2	.125	62	6	1	.986
1971–Eugene ..............P.C.	C	6	18	2	4	0	0	0	1	.222	33	5	0	1.000
1971–Reading ....East.	C-OF	75	238	17	54	7	1	2	29	.227	390	42	7	.984
1972–Hawaii ..............P.C.	C	110	363	34	83	12	6	7	38	.229	604	64	15	.978
1973–Reading ....East.	C	28	59	7	17	3	1	1	8	.288	143	16	1	.994
1973–Eugene ..............P.C.	C	60	185	30	43	9	1	2	20	.232	336	41	6	.984
1973–Philadelphia ......Nat.	C	1	0	0	0	0	0	0	0	.000	1	0	0	1.000
1974–Toledo..............Int.	C	32	90	14	23	2	1	3	16	.256	192	25	4	.982
1974–Philadelphia§ .....Nat.	C	30	53	5	9	2	0	0	4	.170	90	9	1	.990
1975–Toledo..............Int.	C	32	80	5	10	2	0	0	1	.125	168	19	4	.979
1975–Philadelphia x ...Nat.	C	11	5	0	1	0	0	0	1	.200	10	0	0	1.000

Year	Club	League	Pos.	G.	AB.	R.	H.	2B.	3B.	HR.	RBI.	B.A.	PO.	A.	E.	F.A.
1976—Tacoma y	....	P.C.	C	135	457	61	121	22	5	12	66	.265	*641	*104	*23	.970
1977—Seattle z a	....	Amer.	C	35	93	6	23	6	0	2	6	.247	138	26	5	.970
1978—Chicago bc	....	Nat.	C	59	121	10	34	5	0	2	18	.281	178	26	7	.967
1979—Seattle	....	Amer.	C	100	293	32	63	11	3	4	36	.215	408	49	9	.981
1980—Seattle d	....	Amer.	C	105	243	18	49	6	2	4	20	.202	412	45	3	*.993
National League Totals	....			101	179	15	44	7	0	2	23	.246	279	35	8	.975
American League Totals	....			240	629	56	135	23	5	10	62	.215	958	120	17	.984
Major League Totals	....			341	808	71	179	30	5	12	85	.222	1237	155	25	.982

Signed as free agent by Philadelphia Phillies' organization, February 8, 1966.

†On disabled list, July 19 to July 29, 1967; on temporary inactive list, August 1 to August 4, 1967.

‡On disabled list, July 24 to August 10, 1970.

§On supplemental disabled list, August 14 to September 11, 1974.

xTraded to Minnesota Twins for Shortstop Sergio Ferrer, October 24, 1975.

ySold to Seattle Mariners, October 22, 1976.

zOn disabled list, March 28 through April 19, 1977.

aTraded with Pitcher Jim Todd to Chicago Cubs for Pitcher Steve Hamrick, October 25, 1977 (completing deal in which Cubs acquired Pete Broberg, April 20, 1977).

bOn disabled list, July 24 to September 1, 1978.

cTraded to Seattle Mariners for Outfielder Luis Delgado, March 20, 1979.

dTraded with Pitcher Rick Honeycutt, Shortstop Mario Mendoza and Outfielders Willie Horton and Leon Roberts to Texas Rangers for Outfielder Richie Zisk, Shortstop Rick Auerbach and Pitchers Brian Allard, Ken Clay, Steve Finch and Jerry Gleaton, December 12, 1980.

PITCHING RECORD

Year	Club	League	G.	IP.	W.	L.	Pct.	H.	R.	ER.	SO.	BB.	ERA.
1967—Spartanburg	....	W. Carol.	1	1	0	0	.000	1	0	0	0	1	0.00
1968—Spartanburg	....	W. Carol.	7	21	2	0	1.000	15	6	5	20	18	2.14
1968—Huron†	....	Northern	4	27	1	2	.333	25	16	10	22	12	3.33
1969—Raleigh-Durham	....	Carolina	1	4	0	0	.000	1	0	0	3	8	0.00

†On temporary inactive list, July 12 to September 3, 1968.

WILLIAM TED COX

(Known by middle name.)

Born January 24, 1955, at Midwest City, Okla.
Height, 6.03. Weight, 195.
Throws and bats righthanded.
Hobbies—Golf and racquet ball.

Established major league record for most consecutive hits, start of career (6), September 18 and 19, 1977.

Tied major league records for most hits, first major league game (4), September 18, 1977; most consecutive hits, first major league game (4), September 18, 1977.

Tied for New York-Pennsylvania League lead in double plays by shortstops with 34 in 1973.

Named International League Most Valuable Player, 1977.

Year	Club	League	Pos.	G.	AB.	R.	H.	2B.	3B.	HR.	RBI.	B.A.	PO.	A.	E.	F.A.
1973—Elmira	....	NYP	SS	58	205	28	60	8	5	0	24	.293	105	166	18	*.938
1974—Winter Haven	....	Fla. St.	SS-3B	103	340	39	83	11	2	6	39	.244	103	233	22	.939
1975—Winston-Salem	..	Carol.	3B	137	505	63	*154	23	5	10	80	*.305	*125	287	25	.943
1976—Bristol	....	East.	3B	110	399	39	111	13	3	3	53	.278	73	208	14	.952
1977—Pawtucket	....	Int.	3-1-O-S	95	341	63	114	17	4	14	81	.334	114	144	22	.921
1977—Boston†	....	Amer.	DH	13	58	11	21	3	1	1	6	.362	0	0	0	.000
1978—Cleveland	....	Amer.	O-3-1-S	82	227	14	53	7	0	1	19	.233	100	42	4	.973
1979—Cleveland‡	....	Amer.	3B-O-2	78	189	17	40	6	0	4	22	.212	57	81	6	.958
1980—Seattle	....	Amer.	3B	83	247	17	60	9	0	2	23	.243	47	142	11	.945
Major League Totals	....			256	721	59	174	25	1	8	70	.241	204	265	21	.977

Selected by Boston Red Sox' organization in 1st round (17th player selected) of free agent draft, June 5, 1973.

†Traded with Pitchers Rick Wise and Mike Paxton and Catcher Bo Diaz to Cleveland Indians for Pitcher Dennis Eckersley and Catcher Fred Kendall, March 30, 1978.

‡Traded to Seattle Mariners for Pitchers Rob Pietroburgo and Rafael Vasquez and a player to be named later, December 6, 1979; Pitcher Bud Anderson traded to Cleveland Indians' organization completing deal, March 29, 1980.

RODNEY PAUL CRAIG

Born January 12, 1958, at Los Angeles, Calif.
Height, 6.01. Weight, 195.
Throws right and bats right and lefthanded.
Attended San Jacinto College, Pasadena, Tex

Year	Club	League	Pos.	G.	AB.	R.	H.	2B.	3B.	HR.	RBI.	B.A.	PO.	A.	E.	F.A.
1977—Bellingham	....	N'west.	OF-3B	54	208	29	59	11	2	4	22	.284	63	6	5	.932
1978—Stockton	....	Calif.	OF	90	342	58	93	12	0	1	21	.272	121	10	7	.949
1979—Spokane	....	P. C.	OF	46	181	36	57	8	2	2	13	.315	113	2	1	.991
1979—San Jose	....	Calif.	OF	64	238	51	75	7	5	3	27	.315	54	1	2	.965
1979—Seattle	....	Amer.	OF	16	52	9	20	8	1	0	6	.385	24	0	2	.923

Year Club League	Pos.	G.	AB.	R.	H.	2B.	3B.	HR.	RBI.	B.A.	PO.	A.	E.	F.A.
1980–Seattle† ....Amer.	OF	70	240	30	57	15	1	3	20	.238	155	2	2	.987
1980–Spokane‡ ....P. C.	OF	36	131	19	39	5	5	1	15	.298	58	1	1	.983
Major League Totals......................		86	292	39	77	23	2	3	26	.264	179	2	4	.978

Signed as free agent by Seattle Mariners' organization, May 20, 1977.
†On supplemental disabled list, June 12 to June 27, 1980.
‡On disabled list, July 10 to August 3, 1980.

STEVE RAY CRAWFORD

Born April 29, 1958, at Pryor, Okla.
Height, 6.05. Weight, 225.
Throws and bats righthanded.
Attended Claremore Junior College, Claremore, Okla. and
Northeastern Oklahoma State University, Tahlequah, Okla.
Led Carolina League in games started with 28 and in complete games with 15 in 1979.
Tied for Carolina League lead in shutouts with 3 in 1979.

Year Club League	G.	IP.	W.	L.	Pct.	H.	R.	ER.	SO.	BB.	ERA.
1978–Winston-Salem ....Carolina	19	110	9	5	.643	109	53	42	60	48	3.44
1979–Winston-Salem ....Carolina	29	∗211	11	11	.500	∗208	88	●69	127	67	2.94
1980–Bristol† ....Eastern	24	177	9	7	.563	170	68	52	97	64	2.64
1980–Boston ....American	6	32	2	0	1.000	41	14	13	10	8	3.66
Major League Totals..................................	6	32	2	0	1.000	41	14	13	10	8	3.66

Signed as free agent by Boston Red Sox' organization, May 6, 1978.
†On disabled list, April 14 to May 2, 1980.

WARREN LIVINGSTON CROMARTIE

Name pronounced Kroh-MART-ee.

Born September 29, 1953, at Miami Beach, Fla.
Height, 6.00. Weight, 200.
Throws and bats lefthanded.
Hobbies—Listening to rock music and playing drums.
Attended Miami-Dade (North) Community College, Miami, Fla.

Led Eastern League in total bases with 235 in 1974.
Tied for National League lead among outfielders in double plays with 5 in 1978.

Year Club League	Pos.	G.	AB.	R.	H.	2B.	3B.	HR.	RBI.	B.A.	PO.	A.	E.	F.A.
1974–Quebec City.......East.	OF-1B	129	482	94	∗164	20	7	13	61	.336	389	22	9	.979
1974–Montreal ....Nat.	OF	8	17	2	3	0	0	0	0	.176	8	0	0	1.000
1975–Memphis ....Int.	OF-1B	119	400	42	107	16	6	3	38	.268	478	35	15	.972
1976–Denver† ............A.A.	OF-1B	107	415	69	140	12	5	8	60	.337	274	13	6	.980
1976–Montreal ....Nat.	OF	33	81	8	17	1	0	0	2	.210	61	1	2	.969
1977–Montreal ....Nat.	OF	155	620	64	175	41	7	5	50	.282	319	10	8	.976
1978–Montreal ....Nat.	●OF-1B	159	607	77	180	32	6	10	56	.297	351	●24	8	.979
1979–Montreal ....Nat.	OF	158	659	84	181	46	5	8	46	.275	343	16	9	.976
1980–Montreal ....Nat.	∗1B-OF	162	597	74	172	33	5	14	70	.288	1459	93	∗14	.991
Major League Totals		675	2581	309	728	153	23	37	224	.282	2541	144	∗41	.985

Selected by Chicago White Sox' organization in 7th round of free-agent draft, June 8, 1971.
Selected by Minnesota Twins' organization in secondary phase of free-agent draft, January 12, 1972.
Selected by San Diego Padres' organization in secondary phase of free-agent draft, June 6, 1972.
Selected by Oakland A's organization in secondary phase of free-agent draft, January 10, 1973.
Selected by Montreal Expos' organization in secondary phase of free-agent draft, June 5, 1973.
†On suspended list, May 19 to May 21, 1976.

TERRENCE MICHAEL CROWLEY
(Terry)

Born February 16, 1947, at Staten Island, N. Y.
Height, 6.00. Weight, 182.
Throws and bats lefthanded.
Hobby—Basketball.
Attended Long Island University, Brooklyn, N. Y.

Led International League in total bases with 246 in 1969.
Led International League in slugging percentage with .600 in 1977.

Year Club League	Pos.	G.	AB.	R.	H.	2B.	3B.	HR.	RBI.	B.A.	PO.	A.	E.	F.A.
1966–Miami ....Fla. St.	OF	19	51	5	13	1	0	0	3	.255	15	0	1	.938
1967–Miami ....Fla. St.	1-O	135	497	50	130	∗24	10	3	49	.262	1057	56	23	.980
1968–Elmira ....East.	OF-1B	55	181	19	49	8	1	0	22	.271	132	5	3	.979
1968–Rochester ....Int.	OF-1B	75	271	37	71	13	3	8	34	.262	274	18	6	.980
1969–Rochester ....Int.	OF-1B	132	475	78	134	24	2	28	83	.282	247	4	6	.977
1969–Baltimore.........Amer.	1B-OF	7	18	2	6	0	0	0	3	.333	23	2	0	1.000
1970–Baltimore.........Amer.	OF-1B	83	152	25	39	5	0	5	20	.257	138	6	2	.986
1971–Rochester ....Int.	1B-OF	78	259	56	73	9	4	19	63	.282	591	47	5	.992
1971–Baltimore.........Amer.	OF-1B	18	23	2	4	0	0	0	1	.174	7	0	0	1.000
1972–Baltimore.........Amer.	OF-1B	97	247	30	57	10	0	11	29	.231	170	8	1	.994
1973–Baltimore† ....Amer.	OF-1B	54	131	16	27	4	0	3	15	.206	33	5	3	.927
1974–Cincinnati ....Nat.	OF-1B	84	125	11	30	12	0	1	20	.240	58	5	2	.969

Year Club League	Pos.	G.	AB.	R.	H.	2B.	3B.	HR.	RBI.	B.A.	PO.	A.	E.	F.A.
1975—Cincinnati‡........Nat.	1B-OF	66	71	8	19	6	0	1	11	.268	43	4	0	1.000
1976—Atlanta§............Nat.	PH	7	6	0	0	0	0	0	1	.000	0	0	0	.000
1976—Rochester ....Int.	1B	20	69	4	18	7	0	2	7	.261	14	1	0	1.000
1976—Baltimore x.......Amer.	1B	33	61	5	15	1	0	0	5	.246	13	2	0	1.000
1977—Rochester ....Int.	1B-OF	108	403	69	124	24	2	*30	80	.308	407	28	7	.984
1977—Baltimore.........Amer.	1B	18	22	3	8	1	0	1	9	.364	3	0	0	1.000
1978—Baltimore ....Amer.	OF-1B	62	95	9	24	2	0	0	12	.253	1	1	0	1.000
1979—Baltimore ....Amer.	1B	61	63	8	20	5	1	1	8	.317	5	0	0	1.000
1980—Baltimore ....Amer.	1B	92	233	36	67	8	0	12	50	.288	19	5	0	1.000
American League Totals..................		525	1045	136	267	36	1	33	152	.256	412	29	6	.987
National League Totals....................		157	202	19	49	18	0	2	32	.242	101	9	2	.982
Major League Totals		682	1247	155	316	54	1	35	184	.253	513	38	8	.986

Selected by Baltimore Orioles' organization in 15th round of free-agent draft, June 10, 1966.

†Sold to Texas Rangers for an estimated $100,000, December 6, 1973. Sold by Texas Rangers to Cincinnati Reds, March 19, 1974.

‡Traded to Atlanta Braves for Pitcher Mike Thompson, April 6, 1976.

§Unconditionally released, May 6, 1976; signed as free agent with Baltimore Orioles' organization, May 26, 1976.

xReleased, March 26, 1977; signed as free agent by Rochester (Baltimore Orioles' organization), April 12, 1977.

CHAMPIONSHIP SERIES RECORD

Year Club League	Pos.	G.	AB.	R.	H.	2B.	3B.	HR.	RBI.	B.A.	PO.	A.	E.	F.A.
1973—Baltimore..........Amer.	PH-OF	2	2	0	0	0	0	0	0	.000	1	0	0	1.000
1975—Cincinnati ....Nat.	PH	1	0	0	0	0	0	0	0	.000	0	0	0	.000
1979—Baltimore..........Amer.	PH	2	2	0	1	0	0	0	1	.500	0	0	0	.000
Championship Series Totals.............		5	4	0	1	0	0	0	1	.250	1	0	0	1.000

WORLD SERIES RECORD

Tied World Series record for most games as pinch-hitter, series (5), 1979.

Year Club League	Pos.	G.	AB.	R.	H.	2B.	3B.	HR.	RBI.	B.A.	PO.	A.	E.	F.A.
1970—Baltimore..........Amer.	PH	1	1	0	0	0	0	0	0	.000	0	0	0	.000
1975—Cincinnati ....Nat.	PH	2	2	0	1	0	0	0	0	.500	0	0	0	.000
1979—Baltimore..........Amer.	PH	5	4	0	1	1	0	0	2	.250	0	0	0	.000
World Series Totals		8	7	0	2	1	0	0	2	.286	0	0	0	.000

HECTOR CRUZ (DILAN)

(Heity)

Born April 2, 1953, at Arroyo, Puerto Rico.
Height, 5.11. Weight, 180.
Throws and bats righthanded.
Hobbies—Music, swimming, fishing, and reading.
Brother of Jose Cruz, outfielder for Houston Astros, and Cirilo (Tommy) Cruz, outfielder with Nippon Ham Fighters in Japanese baseball.

Tied major league record for fewest caught stealing, season, 150 or more games (0), 1976.
Led Texas League in total bases with 249 in 1973.
Named Texas League Most Valuable Player, 1973.
Named Player of the Year in American Association, 1975.
Named Minor League Player of the Year by THE SPORTING NEWS, 1975.

Year Club League	Pos.	G.	AB.	R.	H.	2B.	3B.	HR.	RBI.	B.A.	PO.	A.	E.	F.A.
1970—Sarasota Cards ..Gulf C.	OF	3	9	3	4	0	1	0	2	.444	4	0	0	1.000
1970—Cedar Rapids.....Midw.	OF	24	41	8	6	0	1	0	1	.146	35	2	0	1.000
1971—Cedar Rapids.....Midw.	OF	111	406	71	112	21	4	23	68	.276	*236	10	11	.957
1972—Modesto ....Calif.	OF	83	314	58	88	11	2	22	77	.280	164	4	5	.971
1972—Cedar Rapids.....Midw.	OF	40	141	22	47	10	2	5	24	.333	93	5	2	.980
1973—Arkansas...........Texas	OF	114	403	*94	132	21	3	*30	*105	.328	228	12	6	.976
1973—St. Louis ....Nat.	OF	11	11	1	0	0	0	0	0	.000	7	0	0	1.000
1974—Tulsa ....A. A.	OF	134	459	70	117	17	8	11	72	.255	236	*15	9	.965
1975—Tulsa ....A. A.	3B-OF	115	435	84	133	30	1	*29	*116	.306	93	197	17	.945
1975—St. Louis ....Nat.	3B-OF	23	48	7	7	2	2	0	6	.146	20	4	3	.889
1976—St. Louis ....Nat.	3B	151	526	54	120	17	1	13	71	.228	100	270	*26	.934
1977—St. Louis†.........Nat.	OF-3B	118	339	50	80	19	2	6	42	.236	154	10	7	.959
1978—Chi.‡-San Fran..Nat.	OF-3B	109	273	27	62	13	1	8	33	.227	117	32	2	.987
1979—S.F.§-Cinci..Nat.	OF-3B	90	207	26	47	10	2	4	28	.227	127	10	3	.979
1980—Cincinnati x ......Nat.	OF	52	75	5	16	4	1	1	5	.213	42	0	2	.955
Major League Totals		554	1479	170	332	65	9	32	185	.224	567	326	43	.954

Signed as free agent by St. Louis Cardinals' organization, January 22, 1970.

†Traded with Catcher Dave Rader to Chicago Cubs for Outfielder Jerry Morales, Catcher Steve Swisher and a player to be named later, December 8, 1977.

‡Traded to San Francisco Giants for Pitcher Lynn McGlothen, June 15, 1978.

§Traded to Cincinnati Reds for Pitcher Pedro Borbon, June 28, 1979.

xTraded to Chicago Cubs for Outfielder Mike Vail, December 12, 1980.

CHAMPIONSHIP SERIES RECORD

Year Club League	Pos.	G.	AB.	R.	H.	2B.	3B.	HR.	RBI.	B.A.	PO.	A.	E.	F.A.
1979—Cincinnati ....Nat.	OF-PH	2	5	1	1	1	0	0	0	.200	3	0	0	1.000

JOSE CRUZ (DILAN)

Born August 8, 1947, at Arroyo, Puerto Rico.
Height, 6.00. Weight, 175.
Throws and bats lefthanded.
Hobbies—Swimming and fishing.
Brother of Hector Cruz, third baseman-outfielder with Chicago Cubs,
and Cirilo (Tommy) Cruz, outfielder with Nippon Ham Fighters in Japanese baseball

Tied major league record for fewest double plays by outfielder, season, 150 or more games (0), 1978.
Major league stolen bases: 1970 (0), 1971 (6), 1972 (9), 1973 (10), 1974 (4), 1975 (6), 1976 (28), 1977 (44), 1978 (37), 1979 (36), 1980 (36). Total—216.
Led National League outfielders in double plays with 5 in 1972.
Led Texas League in total bases with 254 in 1970.
Tied for National League lead in sacrifice flies with 10 in 1977.
Tied for National League lead in errors by outfielders with 11 in 1980.

Year—Club	League	Pos.	G.	AB.	R.	H.	2B.	3B.	HR.	RBI.	B.A.	PO.	A.	E.	F.A.
1967—St. Petersburg	Fla. St.	OF-1B	78	205	33	57	8	9	1	20	.278	113	5	7	.944
1968—Modesto	Calif.	OF-SS	133	504	101	144	24	10	13	53	.286	219	10	11	.954
1969—Arkansas†	Texas	OF	102	400	56	109	18	9	6	49	.273	235	16	9	.965
1970—Arkansas	Texas	OF	133	493	89	148	★29	7	21	90	.300	★276	10	12	.960
1970—St. Louis	Nat.	OF	6	17	2	6	1	0	0	1	.353	16	0	0	1.000
1971—Tulsa	A. A.	OF	67	254	56	83	15	7	15	49	.327	146	1	7	.955
1971—St. Louis	Nat.	OF	83	292	46	80	13	2	9	27	.274	197	2	5	.975
1972—St. Louis	Nat.	OF	117	332	33	78	14	4	2	23	.235	220	9	5	.979
1973—St. Louis	Nat.	OF	132	406	51	92	22	5	10	57	.227	276	2	6	.979
1974—St. Louis‡	Nat.	OF-1B	107	161	24	42	4	3	5	20	.261	81	2	2	.976
1975—Houston	Nat.	OF	120	315	44	81	15	2	9	49	.257	187	6	4	.980
1976—Houston	Nat.	OF	133	439	49	133	21	5	4	61	.303	265	10	8	.972
1977—Houston	Nat.	OF	157	579	87	173	31	10	17	87	.299	311	11	9	.973
1978—Houston	Nat.	OF-1B	153	565	79	178	34	9	10	83	.315	328	5	8	.977
1979—Houston	Nat.	OF	157	558	73	161	33	7	9	72	.289	320	7	14	.959
1980—Houston	Nat.	OF	160	612	79	185	29	7	11	91	.302	323	16	11	.969
Major League Totals			1325	4276	567	1209	217	54	86	571	.283	2524	70	72	.973

Signed as free agent by St. Louis Cardinals' organization, October 27, 1966.
†On disabled list, April 8 to May 12, 1969.
‡Sold to Houston Astros, October 24, 1974.

CHAMPIONSHIP SERIES RECORD

Established Championship Series record for most walks, five-game series (8), 1980.

Year—Club	League	Pos.	G.	AB.	R.	H.	2B.	3B.	HR.	RBI.	B.A.	PO.	A.	E.	F.A.
1980—Houston	Nat.	OF	5	15	3	6	1	1	0	4	.400	19	0	0	1.000

ALL-STAR GAME RECORD

Member of National League All-Star Team in 1980; did not play.

JULIO LUIS CRUZ

Born December 2, 1954, at Brooklyn, N. Y.
Height, 5.09. Weight, 160.
Throws right and bats right and lefthanded.
Hobby—Working on cars.
Attended San Bernardino Valley College, San Bernardino, Calif.; received Associate of Arts degree.

Major League stolen bases: 1977 (15), 1978 (59), 1979 (49), 1980 (45). Total—168.
Led American League second basemen in fielding average with .987 in 1978.
Led Pioneer League in stolen bases with 34 in 1974.
Tied for Midwest League in sacrifice hits with 11 in 1975.
Tied for Pacific Coast League lead in sacrifice hits with 9 in 1977.

Year—Club	League	Pos.	G.	AB.	R.	H.	2B.	3B.	HR.	RBI.	B.A.	PO.	A.	E.	F.A.
1974—Idaho Falls	Pioneer	2B-S-3	72	237	44	57	4	1	0	27	.241	137	185	22	.936
1975—Quad Cities	Midw.	2B	108	368	79	96	6	6	0	35	.261	228	259	14	.972
1976—Salinas	Calif.	2B	96	348	92	107	12	3	1	45	.307	234	314	10	★.982
1976—El Paso	Texas	2B	13	49	9	16	4	1	0	9	.327	23	21	0	1.000
1976—Salt Lake C.†	P.C.	2-3-OF	20	69	11	17	2	2	0	6	.246	30	47	1	.987
1977—Hawaii	P.C.	2B	75	303	71	111	9	9	0	33	.366	189	237	7	.984
1977—Seattle	Amer.	2B	60	199	25	51	3	1	1	7	.256	114	171	5	.983
1978—Seattle	Amer.	2B-SS	147	550	77	129	14	1	1	25	.235	295	482	11	.986
1979—Seattle‡	Amer.	2B	107	414	70	112	16	2	1	29	.271	258	361	13	.979
1980—Seattle§	Amer.	2B	119	442	66	88	9	3	2	16	.209	269	355	11	.983
Major League Totals			433	1605	238	380	42	7	5	77	.237	936	1369	40	.983

Signed as free agent by California Angels' organization, May 7, 1974.
†Selected by Seattle Mariners from California Angels in American League expansion draft, November 5, 1976.
‡On disabled list, June 5 to August 3, 1979.
§On supplemental disabled list, April 24 to May 9, 1980.

DID YOU KNOW—

That Larry Bowa of the Phillies hit two inside-the-park homers in 1980?

TODD RUBEN CRUZ

Born November 23, 1955, at Highland Park, Mich.
Height, 6.00. Weight, 175.
Throws and bats righthanded.
Hobby—Karate.
Son of Robert, former member of Detroit Tigers' organization.

Led Carolina League shortstops in double plays with 68 in 1974 and 74 in 1975.
Led Carolina League in strikeouts by batters with 127 and in sacrifice flies with 10 in 1974.
Led Eastern League in total chances by shortstops with 714 in 1977.
Tied for Appalachian League in strikeouts by batters with 76 in 1973.
Tied for Eastern League lead in double plays by shortstops with 77 in 1977.

Year—Club	League	Pos.	G.	AB.	R.	H.	2B.	3B.	HR.	RBI.	B.A.	PO.	A.	E.	F.A.
1973—Pulaski	Appal.	SS	69	208	29	38	10	1	4	18	.183	95	174	*49	.846
1974—Rocky Mount	Carol.	SS	126	445	34	86	13	6	1	43	.193	*222	321	*49	.917
1974—Toledo	Int.	SS	4	10	1	1	1	0	0	1	.100	3	8	2	.846
1975—Rocky Mount	Carol.	SS	134	453	57	92	23	1	11	67	.203	*218	*457	41	*.943
1976—Reading	East.	SS	123	424	34	98	126	11	1	5	.231	203	388	53	.918
1977—Reading	East.	SS	131	464	42	100	23	3	2	51	.216	*228	*436	*50	.930
1978—Oklahoma City	A.A.	SS	121	459	58	120	22	2	11	69	.261	209	379	*40	.936
1978—Philadelphia†	Nat.	SS	3	4	0	2	0	0	0	2	.500	1	6	0	1.000
1979—Omaha	A.A.	SS	23	91	14	24	4	2	7	21	.264	47	86	5	.964
1979—Kansas City‡	Amer.	SS-3B	55	118	9	24	7	0	2	15	.203	54	118	7	.961
1980—Calif.§-Chi.	Amer.	S-3-2-O	108	333	28	79	14	1	3	23	.237	156	323	28	.956
National League Totals			3	4	0	2	0	0	0	2	.500	1	6	0	1.000
American League Totals			163	451	37	103	21	1	5	38	.228	210	441	35	.949
Major League Totals			166	455	37	105	21	1	5	40	.231	211	447	35	.949

Selected by Philadelphia Phillies' organization in 2nd round of free agent draft, June 5, 1973.
†Traded to Kansas City Royals' organization for Pitcher Doug Bird, April 3, 1979.
‡Traded with Outfielder Al Cowens and a player to be named later to California Angels for First Baseman Willie Mays Aikens and Shortstop Rance Mulliniks, December 6, 1979; pitcher Craig Eaton traded to California Angels' organization completing deal, April 1, 1980.
§Traded to Chicago White Sox for Pitcher Randy Scarbery, June 12, 1980.

VICTOR MANUEL CRUZ

Born December 24, 1957, at Rancho Viejo La Vega, Dominican Republic.
Height, 5.09. Weight, 215.
Throws and bats righthanded.

Led Appalachian League in shutouts with 3 in 1976.

Year—Club	League	G.	IP.	W.	L.	Pct.	H.	R.	ER.	SO.	BB.	ERA.
1976—Johnson City	Ap'lachian	12	80	6	3	.667	57	23	18	100	23	2.03
1977—Arkansas	Texas	18	83	3	8	.273	79	57	46	83	40	4.99
1977—St. Petersburg†	Florida St.	13	30	2	3	.400	14	12	11	48	13	3.30
1978—Syracuse	Int'national	25	42	3	2	.600	31	23	21	56	35	4.50
1978—Toronto‡	American	32	47	7	3	.700	28	10	9	51	35	1.72
1979—Cleveland	American	61	79	3	9	.250	70	41	37	63	44	4.22
1980—Cleveland§	American	55	86	6	7	.462	71	36	33	88	27	3.45
Major League Totals		148	212	16	19	.457	169	87	79	202	106	3.35

Signed as free agent by St. Louis Cardinals' organization, January 9, 1976.
†Traded with Pitcher Tom Underwood to Toronto Blue Jays for Pitcher Pete Vuckovich, December 6, 1977; Outfielder John Scott traded to St. Louis Cardinals' organization completing deal, December 16, 1977.
‡Traded to Cleveland Indians for Shortstop Alfredo Griffin and Third Baseman Phil Lansford, December 6, 1978.
§Traded with Pitchers Bob Owchinko and Rafael Vasquez and Catcher Gary Alexander to Pittsburgh Pirates for Pitcher Bert Blyleven and Catcher Manny Sanguillen, December 9, 1980.

MICHAEL LEE CUBBAGE

(Mike)

Born July 21, 1950, at Charlottesville, Va.
Height, 6.00. Weight, 180.
Throws right and bats lefthanded.
Hobbies—Golf and tennis.
Attended University of Virginia, Charlottesville, Va.

Year—Club	League	Pos.	G.	AB.	R.	H.	2B.	3B.	HR.	RBI.	B.A.	PO.	A.	E.	F.A.
1971—Geneva	NYP	2-3-S	56	174	42	60	15	0	8	46	.345	116	138	17	.937
1972—Burlington	Carol.	2-3-O	105	334	50	94	17	2	6	36	.281	152	240	19	.954
1973—Pittsfield	East.	2-3-O	109	346	81	108	16	3	13	65	.312	188	251	16	.965
1974—Spokane	P. C.	2B-3B	90	339	62	107	25	2	16	61	.316	180	224	13	.969
1974—Texas	Amer.	3B-2B	9	15	0	0	0	0	0	0	.000	7	9	1	.941
1975—Spokane	P. C.	2-3-1	56	217	50	68	18	2	10	34	.313	120	152	8	.971
1975—Texas	Amer.	2B-3B	58	143	12	32	6	0	4	21	.224	68	115	8	.958
1976—Texas†-Minn.	Amer.	3-2	118	374	42	96	19	5	3	49	.257	180	218	19	.954
1977—Minnesota	Amer.	3B	129	417	60	110	16	5	9	55	.264	90	266	18	.952
1978—Minnesota	Amer.	3B-2B	125	394	40	111	12	7	7	57	.282	69	237	9	.971
1979—Minnesota‡	Amer.	3B-1B-2B	94	243	26	67	10	1	2	23	.276	38	94	10	.930
1980—Minnesota§x	Amer.	1-3-2	103	285	29	70	9	0	8	42	.246	545	100	4	.994
Major League Totals			636	1871	209	486	72	18	33	247	.260	997	1039	69	.967

Selected by Washington Senators' organization in 5th round of free agent draft, June 7, 1968.
Selected by Washington Senators' organization in secondary phase of free agent draft, June 8, 1971.
†Traded with Pitcher Bill Singer, Infielder Roy Smalley and Pitcher Jim Gideon, latter assigned to Tacoma, and a reported $250,000 cash, to Minnesota Twins for Pitcher Bert Blyleven and Shortstop Danny Thompson, June 1, 1976.
‡On supplemental disabled list, May 28 to June 15, 1979.
§On supplemental disabled list, July 29 to August 13, 1980.
xGranted free agency, October 23, 1980; signed by New York Mets, December 19, 1980.

ROBERT CUELLAR
Name pronounced QUAY-yahr.
(Bobby)
Born August 20, 1952, at Alice, Tex.
Height, 5.11. Weight, 190.
Throws and bats righthanded.
Hobbies—Golf and Pool.
Attended University of Texas, Austin, Tex.
Led Carolina League in saves with 17 in 1975.

Year Club	League	G.	IP.	W.	L.	Pct.	H.	R.	ER.	SO.	BB.	ERA.
1974—Sarasota Rangers	Gulf Coast	5	8	0	0	.000	11	4	3	10	1	3.38
1974—Gastonia	W. Carol.	17	20	4	1	.800	15	11	8	22	10	3.60
1975—Lynchburg	Carolina	49	91	9	4	.692	70	32	26	73	55	2.57
1976—San Antonio†	Texas	48	85	9	5	.643	67	30	25	63	31	2.65
1977—Tucson	P. Coast	50	93	10	6	.625	106	39	36	66	34	3.48
1977—Texas	American	4	7	0	0	.000	4	1	1	3	2	1.29
1978—Tucson‡	P. Coast	39	76	4	8	.333	90	45	37	36	39	4.38
1979—Tacoma	P. Coast	37	127	3	7	.300	127	61	47	69	53	3.33
1980—Tacoma	P. Coast	51	90	8	3	.727	82	37	33	55	35	3.30
Major League Totals		4	7	0	0	.000	4	1	1	3	2	1.29

Selected by Texas Rangers' organization in 29th round of free-agent draft, June 5, 1974.
†Appeared in one game as an outfielder.
‡Traded with Outfielder David Rivera to Cleveland Indians for Outfielder Johnny Grubb, October 3, 1978.

WILFRED HILLARD CULMER
(Wil)
Born November 11, 1958, at Nassau, Bahamas.
Height, 6.04. Weight, 210.
Throws and bats righthanded.
Led Carolina League in total bases with 276 in 1980.

Year Club	League	Pos.	G.	AB.	R.	H.	2B.	3B.	HR.	RBI.	B.A.	PO.	A.	E.	F.A.
1978—Helena	Pion.	OF-1B	55	187	44	67	5	3	10	44	.358	50	4	4	.931
1979—Peninsula	Carol.	OF	33	107	10	16	1	0	0	7	.150	45	4	7	.875
1979—Spartanbrug	W. Car.	OF	68	228	35	70	17	3	6	46	.307	40	2	8	.840
1980—Peninsula	Carol.	OF-3B	139	498	*112	*184	28	5	18	93	*.369	140	65	27	.884

Signed as free agent by Philadelphia Phillies' organization, October 25, 1977.

ROBERT EMMETT CUMMINGS
(Bob)
Born September 8, 1960, at Chicago, Ill.
Height, 6.02. Weight, 185.
Throws and bats righthanded.
Tied for Pioneer League lead in passed balls with 27 in 1978.

Year Club	League	Pos.	G.	AB.	R.	H.	2B.	3B.	HR.	RBI.	B.A.	PO.	A.	E.	F.A.
1978—Great Falls	Pion.	C	41	141	22	33	7	2	0	10	.234	249	32	11	.962
1979—Cedar Rapids	Midw.	C	56	184	29	45	4	0	1	12	.207	263	45	7	.978
1979—Shreveport	South.	C	12	41	4	11	2	0	0	3	.268	68	6	1	.987
1979—Fresno	Calif.	C	17	59	6	12	0	0	1	7	.203	97	7	4	.963
1980—Clinton	Midw.	C-1B	116	365	50	103	15	3	13	79	.282	477	97	12	.980

Selected by San Francisco Giants' organization in 1st round (7th player selected) of free-agent draft, June 6, 1978.

JOHN DUFFIELD CURTIS, II
Born March 9, 1948, at Newton, Mass.
Height, 6.02. Weight, 185.
Throws and bats lefthanded.
Hobbies—Reading and amateur photography.
Attended Clemson University, Clemson, S. C.; received Bachelor of Arts degree in English.

Year Club	League	G.	IP.	W.	L.	Pct.	H.	R.	ER.	SO.	BB.	ERA.
1968—Winston-Salem	Carolina	16	103	6	8	.429	82	49	39	101	41	3.41
1969—Greenville	W. Carol.	25	149	6	*12	.333	141	*91	*74	*158	*97	4.47
1970—Pawtucket	Eastern	21	138	9	8	.529	113	65	57	114	75	3.72
1970—Boston	American	1	2	0	0	.000	4	4	3	1	1	13.50
1971—Louisville	Int'national	27	187	10	12	.455	167	99	71	165	*111	3.42

Year Club	League	G.	IP.	W.	L.	Pct.	H.	R.	ER.	SO.	BB.	ERA.
1971—Boston	American	5	26	2	2	.500	30	9	9	19	6	3.12
1972—Louisville	Int'national	8	67	4	3	.571	55	19	15	64	27	2.01
1972—Boston	American	26	154	11	8	.579	161	69	64	106	50	3.74
1973—Boston†	American	35	221	13	13	.500	225	103	88	101	83	3.58
1974—St. Louis	National	33	195	10	14	.417	199	91	82	89	83	3.78
1975—St. Louis	National	39	147	8	9	.471	151	70	56	67	65	3.43
1976—St. Louis‡	National	37	134	6	11	.353	139	68	67	52	65	4.50
1977—San Francisco	National	43	77	3	3	.500	95	48	47	47	48	5.49
1978—San Francisco	National	46	63	4	3	.571	60	31	26	38	29	3.71
1979—San Francisco§	National	27	121	10	9	.526	121	62	56	85	42	4.17
1980—San Diego	National	30	187	10	8	.556	184	84	73	71	67	3.51
American League Totals		67	403	26	23	.531	420	185	164	227	140	3.66
National League Totals		255	924	51	57	.472	949	454	407	449	399	3.96
Major League Totals		322	1327	77	80	.490	1369	639	571	676	539	3.87

Selected by Cleveland Indians' organization in 8th round of free-agent draft, June 6, 1966.
Selected by Boston Red Sox' organization in 1st round of free-agent draft, June 7, 1968.
†Traded with Pitchers Mike Garman and Lynn McGlothen to St. Louis Cardinals for Infielder Terry Hughes and Pitchers Reggie Cleveland and Diego Segui, December 7, 1973.
‡Traded with Outfielder Willie Crawford and Infielder-Outfielder Vic Harris to San Francisco Giants for Pitchers John D'Acquisto and Mike Caldwell and Catcher Dave Rader, October 20, 1976.
§Granted free agency, November 1, 1979; signed by San Diego Padres, November 26, 1979.

JOHN FRANCIS D'ACQUISTO

Name pronounced dee-uh-KWISS-toh.

Born December 24, 1951, at San Diego, Calif.
Height, 6.03. Weight, 205.
Throws and bats righthanded.
Hobbies—Hunting and fishing.
Cousin of Lou Marone, former pitcher with Pittsburgh Pirates.

Tied National League record for most wild pitches, inning (3), September 24, 1976 (seventh inning).
Pitched seven-inning, 7-0 no-hit victory against Tacoma, May 16, 1973.
Led Pacific Coast League pitchers in games started with 31 and hit batsmen with 11 in 1973.
Led California League in complete games with 17 and tied for lead in hit batsmen with 15 in 1972.
Led Midwest League pitchers in games started with 29 in 1971.
Tied for Pacific Coast League lead in shutouts with 4 and tied for lead in complete games with 14 in 1973.
Named National League Rookie Pitcher of the Year by THE SPORTING NEWS, 1974.

Year Club	League	G.	IP.	W.	L.	Pct.	H.	R.	ER.	SO.	BB.	ERA.
1970—Great Falls	Pioneer	12	55	2	5	.286	33	46	32	84	*74	5.24
1971—Decatur	Midwest	31	*233	10	●13	.435	*178	*98	*81	*244	*124	3.13
1972—Fresno	California	27	209	17	6	.739	184	94	77	*245	102	3.32
1973—Phoenix	P. Coast	31	*212	16	12	.571	186	97	84	185	*113	3.57
1973—San Francisco	National	7	28	1	1	.500	23	14	11	29	19	3.54
1974—San Francisco	National	38	215	12	14	.462	182	101	90	167	124	3.77
1975—San Francisco†	National	10	28	2	4	.333	29	35	32	22	34	10.29
1976—San Francisco‡	National	28	106	3	8	.273	93	69	63	53	102	5.35
1977—St. L.§x-S. D.	National	20	52	1	2	.333	54	45	38	54	57	6.58
1977—Hawaii	P. Coast	8	60	4	3	.571	44	27	25	47	40	3.75
1978—San Diego	National	45	93	4	3	.571	60	24	22	104	56	2.13
1979—San Diego	National	51	134	9	13	.409	140	83	73	97	86	4.90
1980—San Diego y-Montreal x	National	50	88	2	5	.286	81	36	33	59	45	3.38
Major League Totals		249	744	34	50	.405	662	407	362	585	523	4.38

Selected by San Francisco Giants' organization in 1st round (17th player selected) of free-agent draft, June 4, 1970.
†On disabled list, May 25 to September 2, 1975.
‡Traded with Pitcher Mike Caldwell and Catcher Dave Rader to St. Louis Cardinals for Outfielder Willie Crawford, Infielder-Outfielder Vic Harris and Pitcher John Curtis, October 20, 1976.
§On disabled list, April 9 to April 30, 1977.
xTraded with Infielder Pat Scanlon to San Diego Padres for Pitcher Butch Metzger, May 18, 1977.
yTraded to Montreal Expos for cash and a player to be named later, August 11, 1980; Padres acquired First Baseman Randy Bass completing deal, September 5, 1980.
zGranted free agency, November 3, 1980; signed by California Angels, December 11, 1980.

LONNIE PAUL DADE

(Known by middle name.)

Born December 7, 1951, at Seattle, Wash.
Height, 6.00. Weight, 195.
Throws and bats righthanded.
Hobbies—Sports, music and traveling.

Led Pacific Coast League in double plays by third basemen with 41 in 1974.

Year Club	League	Pos.	G.	AB.	R.	H.	2B.	3B.	HR.	RBI.	B.A.	PO.	A.	E.	F.A.
1970—Idaho Falls† ......Pion.		3B	46	158	28	48	7	5	1	35	.304	44	84	16	.889
1971—Shreveport ....Texas		3B	14	45	10	11	0	2	1	5	.244	10	21	3	.912
1971—Quad Cities ....Midw.		3B	101	355	57	114	21	2	2	51	.321	81	166	17	*.936
1972—Shreveport ....Texas		3-O-S-2	131	491	70	133	15	2	8	55	.271	145	209	29	.924

Year Club League	Pos.	G.	AB.	R.	H.	2B.	3B.	HR.	RBI.	B.A.	PO.	A.	E.	F.A.
1973—El Paso.............Texas	2B-SS	83	298	51	84	13	4	6	57	.282	175	185	21	.945
1973—Salt Lake City ...P. C.	3B-SS	41	119	18	34	7	1	1	17	.286	24	69	12	.886
1974—Salt Lake City ...P. C.	*3B-SS	134	504	71	149	21	7	3	53	.296	102	*275	27	.933
1975—El Paso†............Tex.	2B-3B	100	343	81	114	23	5	16	84	.332	155	268	26	.942
1975—Salt Lake City ...P. C.	3B-SS	9	33	12	18	5	1	3	14	.545	3	8	2	.846
1975—California........Amer.	OF-3B	11	30	5	6	4	0	0	1	.200	8	1	0	1.000
1976—Salt Lake City ...P. C.	3-2B-OF	91	320	66	116	18	4	4	65	*.363	59	133	12	.941
1976—California§........Amer.	O-2-3	13	9	2	1	0	0	0	1	.111	5	4	1	.900
1977—Cleveland.........Amer.	O-3-2	134	461	65	134	15	3	3	45	.291	192	51	7	.972
1978—Cleveland.........Amer.	OF	93	307	37	78	12	1	3	20	.254	171	6	7	.962
1979—Cleveland x.......Amer.	OF-3B	44	170	22	48	4	1	3	18	.282	73	4	3	.963
1979—San Diego ....Nat.	3B-OF	76	283	38	78	19	2	1	19	.276	47	163	11	.950
1980—Hawaii..............P. C.	OF-3B	4	14	1	5	0	0	0	2	.357	5	1	0	1.000
1980—San Diego y.......Nat.	3B-OF	68	53	17	10	0	0	0	3	.189	14	18	5	.865
National League Totals		144	336	55	88	19	2	1	22	.262	61	181	16	.938
American League Totals		295	977	131	267	35	5	9	85	.273	449	66	18	.966
Major League Totals		439	1313	186	355	54	7	10	107	.270	510	247	34	.957

Selected by California Angels' organization in 1st round (10th player selected) of free-agent draft, June 4, 1970.

†On temporary inactive list, June 25 to July 5, 1970.
‡On disabled list, May 7 to May 26, 1975.
§Granted free agency, November 1, 1976; signed by Cleveland Indians, February 10, 1977.
xTraded to San Diego Padres for First Baseman Mike Hargrove, June 14, 1979.
yOn supplemental disabled list, August 11 to September 2, 1980.

DANNY WAYNE DARWIN

Born October 25, 1955, at Bonham, Tex.
Height, 6.03. Weight, 195.
Throws and bats righthanded.
Attended Grayson County College, Denison, Tex.

Tied for Texas League lead in shutouts with 4 in 1977.

Year Club	League	G.	IP.	W.	L.	Pct.	H.	R.	ER.	SO.	BB.	ERA.
1976—Asheville ....W. Carol.		16	102	6	3	.667	96	54	41	76	48	3.62
1977—Tulsa† ....Texas		23	154	13	4	.765	130	53	43	129	72	2.51
1978—Tucson ....P. Coast		23	125	8	9	.471	147	100	87	126	83	6.26
1978—Texas ....American		3	9	1	0	1.000	11	4	4	8	1	4.00
1979—Tucson ....P. Coast		13	95	6	6	.500	89	43	38	65	42	3.60
1979—Texas ....American		20	78	4	4	.500	50	36	35	58	30	4.04
1980—Texas‡ ....American		53	110	13	4	.765	98	37	32	104	50	2.62
Major League Totals		76	197	18	8	.692	159	77	71	170	81	3.24

Signed as free agent by Texas Rangers' organization, May 18, 1976.
†On disabled list, April 25 to May 4 and May 22 to June 11, 1977.
‡On disabled list, June 5 to June 26, 1980.

RICHARD FREMONT DAUER
(Rich)

Born July 27, 1952, at San Bernardino, Calif.
Height, 6.00. Weight, 180.
Throws and bats righthanded.
Attended San Bernardino Valley College, San Bernardino, Calif., and
University of Southern California, Los Angeles, Calif.

Established major league records for most consecutive errorless games by second baseman, season (86), 1978; most consecutive errorless chances accepted by second baseman, season (425), 1978.
Named International League Rookie of the Year, 1976.
Shared International League Most Valuable Player, 1976.

Year Club League	Pos.	G.	AB.	R.	H.	2B.	3B.	HR.	RBI.	B.A.	PO.	A.	E.	F.A.
1974—Asheville...........South.	2B-3B	53	180	30	59	7	0	11	35	.328	72	104	3	.983
1975—Rochester ....Int.	2B-3B	18	47	2	8	1	0	0	0	.170	17	30	2	.959
1975—Asheville...........South.	3B-2B	106	374	51	94	13	0	6	44	.251	98	195	6	*.980
1976—Rochester ....Int.	*2B-SS-1	132	*524	84	*176	26	3	11	78	*.336	276	402	18	*.974
1976—Baltimore..........Amer.	2B	11	39	0	4	0	0	0	3	.103	22	22	0	1.000
1977—Baltimore ....Amer.	2B-3B	96	304	38	74	15	1	5	25	.243	182	233	7	.983
1978—Baltimore ....Amer.	2B-3B	133	459	57	121	23	0	6	46	.264	222	321	7	.987
1979—Baltimore ....Amer.	2B-3B	142	479	63	123	20	0	9	61	.257	234	355	17	.972
1980—Baltimore ....Amer.	2B-3B	152	557	71	158	32	0	2	63	.284	334	418	8	.989
Major League Totals		534	1838	229	480	90	1	22	198	.261	994	1349	39	.984

Selected by Oakland A's organization in 5th round of free agent draft, January 13, 1971.
Selected by Oakland A's organization in 9th round of free agent draft, January 12, 1972.
Selected by Cleveland Indians' organization in secondary phase of free agent draft, June 6, 1972.
Selected by Baltimore Orioles' organization in 1st round (24th player selected) of free agent draft, June 5, 1974.

CHAMPIONSHIP SERIES RECORD

Year Club League	Pos.	G.	AB.	R.	H.	2B.	3B.	HR.	RBI.	B.A.	PO.	A.	E.	F.A.
1979—Baltimore ....Amer.	2B	4	11	0	2	0	0	0	0	.182	10	12	0	1.000

Year Club	League	Pos.	G.	AB.	R.	H.	2B.	3B.	HR.	RBI.	B.A.	PO.	A.	E.	F.A.
1979—Baltimore ....Amer.		PH-2B	6	17	2	5	1	0	1	1	.294	10	10	0	1.000

VICTOR JOSE DAVALILLO
Name pronounced Dav-ah-LEE-oh.
(Vic)
Born July 31, 1939, at Cabimas, Zulia, Venezuela.
Height, 5.07. Weight, 155.
Throws and bats lefthanded.
Hobby—Movies.
Brother of Pompeyo Davalillo, former infielder with Washington Senators.

Led American League outfielders in double plays with 5 in 1964.
Led International League in total bases with 296 and stolen bases with 24 in 1962.
Named outfielder on THE SPORTING NEWS American League All-Star fielding team, 1964.

Year Club	League	Pos.	G.	AB.	R.	H.	2B.	3B.	HR.	RBI.	B.A.	PO.	A.	E.	F.A.
1958—Visalia† ....Calif.		P	19	15	4	5	0	0	1	2	.333	4	14	3	.857
1958—Palatka ....Fla. St.		P	15	6	3	1	0	0	0	1	.167	2	5	0	1.000
1959—Palatka‡ ....Fla. St.		P	73	79	16	23	3	2	2	10	.291	7	32	1	.975
1960—Topeka ...............I.I.I.		P-OF	84	155	19	42	5	3	3	23	.271	48	30	5	.940
1960—Jersey City........Int.		P	6	6	0	3	1	0	0	1	.500	0	1	0	1.000
1961—Columbia ....Sally		P	34	46	2	9	1	0	1	8	.196	4	13	2	.895
1961—Topeka ..............I.I.I.		P	14	21	5	6	1	0	1	3	.286	1	6	0	1.000
1961—Jersey City§ ......Int.		OF-P	33	59	7	15	3	1	0	1	.254	26	8	1	.971
1962—Jacksonville ......Int.		●OF-P	150	578	99	*200	27	*18	11	69	*.346	307	17	●13	.961
1963—Cleveland x ......Amer.		OF	90	370	44	108	18	5	7	36	.292	247	10	3	.988
1964—Cleveland ....Amer.		OF	150	577	64	156	26	2	6	51	.270	346	11	5	.986
1965—Cleveland ....Amer.		OF	142	505	67	152	19	1	5	40	.301	320	5	4	.988
1966—Cleveland ....Amer.		OF	121	344	42	86	6	4	3	19	.250	208	6	3	.986
1967—Cleveland ....Amer.		OF	139	359	47	103	17	5	2	22	.287	202	5	3	.986
1968—Cleve.y-Calif. ....Amer.		OF	144	519	49	144	17	7	3	31	.277	296	8	4	.987
1969—California z ......Amer.		OF-1B	33	71	10	11	1	1	0	1	.155	36	1	0	1.000
1969—St. Louis ....Nat.		OF-P	63	98	15	26	3	0	2	10	.265	37	0	0	1.000
1970—St. Louis a ......Nat.		OF	111	183	29	57	14	3	1	33	.311	67	3	2	.972
1971—Pittsburgh........Nat.		OF-1B	99	295	48	84	14	6	1	33	.285	256	15	5	.982
1972—Pittsburgh........Nat.		OF-1B	117	368	59	117	19	2	4	28	.318	200	6	4	.981
1973—Pittsburgh b ....Nat.		1B-OF	59	83	9	15	1	0	1	3	.181	89	8	2	.980
1973—Oakland ....Amer.		OF-1B	38	64	5	12	1	0	0	4	.188	44	2	1	.979
1974—Oakland c.........Amer.		OF	17	23	0	4	0	0	0	1	.174	3	0	0	1.000
1974—Cordoba ....Mex.		OF-1B	71	249	46	82	9	5	4	27	.329	161	6	8	.954
1975—Cordoba d ....Mex.		OF-1B	114	408	70	145	21	3	9	70	.355	246	7	8	.969
1976—Puebla e..........Mex.		OF-1B	123	501	84	167	23	1	8	63	.333	312	16	5	.985
1977—Aguascalientes f Mex.		OF-1B	135	516	87	198	30	8	6	78	*.384	344	38	6	.985
1977—Los Angeles......Nat.		OF	24	48	3	15	2	0	0	4	.313	13	0	0	1.000
1978—Los Angeles .....Nat.		OF-1B	75	77	15	24	1	1	1	11	.312	21	1	0	1.000
1979—Albuquerque ....P. C.		OF-P	51	139	27	44	6	0	3	19	.317	24	2	1	.963
1979—Los Angeles g ...Nat.		OF	29	27	2	7	1	0	0	2	.259	2	0	0	1.000
1980—Aguas'ientes h ..Mex.		OF-P	94	363	67	143	15	5	6	50	.394	66	2	2	.971
1980—Albuquerque .....P.C.		OF-P	36	108	13	31	7	1	2	19	.287	5	2	0	1.000
1980—Los Angeles i ....Nat.		1B	7	6	1	1	0	0	0	0	.167	2	0	0	1.000
National League Totals....................			584	1185	181	346	55	12	10	124	.292	687	34	13	.982
American League Totals..................			874	2832	328	776	105	25	26	205	.274	1702	48	23	.987
Major League Totals			1458	4017	509	1122	160	37	36	329	.279	2389	82	36	.986

Signed as free agent by Cincinnati Reds' organization, April 16, 1958.
†On disabled list, June 22 through July 12.
‡On disabled list, July 31 through August 9.
§Sold by Cincinnati Reds to Cleveland Indians, October, 1961.
xSuffered broken right wrist, on disabled list from June 12 through August 10.
yTraded to California Angels for Outfielder Jimmie Hall, June 15, 1968.
zTraded to St. Louis Cardinals for Outfielder Jim Hicks, May 30, 1969.
aTraded with Pitcher Nelson Briles to Pittsburgh Pirates for Outfielder Matty Alou and Pitcher George Brunet, January 29, 1971.
bSold to Oakland Athletics, August 1, 1973.
cReleased, May 3, 1974; signed by Cordoba, May 16, 1974.
dSold to Puebla, December 10, 1975.
eSold to Aguascalientes, August 26, 1976.
fSold to Los Angeles Dodgers, August 17, 1977.
gReleased, December 28, 1979; signed by Aguascalientes, January 28, 1980.
hSold to Los Angeles Dodgers' organization, July 8, 1980.
iReleased, October 16, 1980.

CHAMPIONSHIP SERIES RECORD
Tied Championship Series record for most clubs, total Series (3).

Year Club	League	Pos.	G.	AB.	R.	H.	2B.	3B.	HR.	RBI.	B.A.	PO.	A.	E.	F.A.
1971—Pittsburgh.........Nat.		PH	2	2	0	0	0	0	0	0	.000	0	0	0	.000
1972—Pittsburgh.........Nat.		PH	1	0	0	0	0	0	0	0	.000	0	0	0	.000
1973—Oakland ....Amer.		O-1-PH	4	8	2	5	1	1	0	1	.625	7	0	1	.875
1977—Los Angeles.......Nat.		PH	1	1	1	1	0	0	0	0	1.000	0	0	0	.000
Championship Series Totals.............			8	11	3	6	1	1	0	1	.545	7	0	1	.875

Tied World Series record for most clubs, total Series (3), 1977.

Year Club League	Pos.	G.	AB.	R.	H.	2B.	3B.	HR.	RBI.	B.A.	PO.	A.	E.	F.A.
1971—Pittsburgh.........Nat.	PH-OF	3	3	1	1	0	0	0	0	.333	2	0	0	1.000
1973—Oakland ....Amer.	PH-O-1	6	11	0	1	0	0	0	0	.091	15	0	0	1.000
1977—Los Angeles......Nat.	PH	3	3	0	1	0	0	0	1	.333	0	0	0	.000
1978—Los Angeles ......Nat.	PH-DH	2	3	0	1	0	0	0	0	.333	0	0	0	.000
World Series Totals		14	20	1	4	0	0	0	1	.200	17	0	0	1.000

ALL-STAR GAME RECORD

Year League	Pos.	AB.	R.	H.	2B.	3B.	HR.	RBI.	B.A.	PO.	A.	E.	F.A.
1965—American............................	OF	2	0	1	0	0	0	0	.500	1	0	0	1.000

PITCHING RECORD

Year Club League	G.	IP.	W.	L.	Pct.	H.	R.	ER.	SO.	BB.	ERA.
1958—Visalia.............................Calif.	17	48	2	4	.333	34	22	18	36	28	3.38
1958—Palatka............................Fla. State	13	25	4	2	.667	22	8	7	20	21	2.52
1959—Palatka............................Fla. State	*53	147	16	7	.696	114	49	40	150	65	*2.45
1960—Topeka ....I. I. I.	48	102	6	9	.400	89	45	34	111	57	3.00
1960—Jersey City ....Int'national	4	5	0	0	.000	2	0	0	1	4	0.00
1961—Columbia ....Sally	18	43	1	4	.200	45	28	20	27	29	4.19
1961—Topeka ....I. I. I.	11	25	3	0	1.000	22	12	12	23	11	4.32
1961—Jersey City ....Int'national	9	22	0	0	.000	25	13	12	22	12	4.91
1962—Jacksonville.....................Int'national	6	18	0	1	.000	13	7	6	13	15	3.00
1969—St. Louis ....National	2	0	0	0	.000	2	1	1	0	2	......
1974—Cordoba ....Mexican	4	3	1	0	1.000	1	1	1	0	0	3.00
1977—Aguascalientes...................Mexican	11	19	1	1	.500	14	3	2	13	12	0.95
1979—Albuquerque ....P. Coast	3	6	0	0	.000	3	1	0	3	1	0.00
1980—Aguascalientes...................Mexican	1	0	0	0	.000	0	0	0	0	0	...
1980—Albuquerque ....P. Coast	3	7	0	0	.000	10	4	4	0	5	5.14
Major League Totals	2	0	0	0	.000	2	1	1	0	2	......

CHARLES THEODORE DAVIS

Born January 17, 1960, at Kingston, Jamaica.
Height, 6.03. Weight, 195.
Throws right and bats left and righthanded.

Year Club League	Pos.	G.	AB.	R.	H.	2B.	3B.	HR.	RBI.	B.A.	PO.	A.	E.	F.A.
1978—Cedar Rapids ....Midw.	C-OF	124	424	63	119	18	5	16	73	.281	365	45	25	.943
1979—Fresno.............Calif.	OF-C	134	490	91	132	24	5	21	95	.269	339	43	20	.950
1980—Shreveport........Texas	OF-C	129	442	50	130	30	4	12	67	.294	184	20	12	.944

Selected by San Francisco Giants' organization in 11th round of free-agent draft, June 7, 1977.

JODY RICHARD DAVIS

Born November 12, 1956, at Gainesville, Ga.
Height, 6.04. Weight, 192.
Throws and bats righthanded.
Attended Middle Georgia College, Cochran, Ga.

Led Carolina League in sacrifice flies with 13 in 1978.
Led Carolina League catchers in double plays with 8 in 1978.

Year Club League	Pos.	G.	AB.	R.	H.	2B.	3B.	HR.	RBI.	B.A.	PO.	A.	E.	F.A.
1976—Marion ....Appal.	C	50	164	20	38	5	1	5	19	.232	290	30	*13	.961
1977—Little Falls........N.Y.-P.	C-1B	64	214	37	62	11	2	11	46	.290	369	50	12	.972
1978—Lynchburg ....Carol.	C-1-3	120	408	57	107	24	2	16	94	.262	595	79	15	.978
1979—Jackson†..........Texas	C-1B	132	433	57	128	23	4	21	91	.296	661	81	15	.980
1980—St. Petersburg...Fla. St.	C-1B	45	155	27	43	4	0	6	27	.277	171	20	5	.974
1980—Springfield‡§.....A. A.	C-1B	13	36	3	6	1	0	0	2	.167	59	7	1	.985

Selected by New York Mets' organization in 3rd round of free-agent draft, January 7, 1976.
†Traded to St. Louis Cardinals' organization for Pitcher Ray Searage, December 10, 1979.
‡On disabled list, April 14 to June 20, 1980.
§Drafted by Chicago Cubs, December 8, 1980.

MARK WILLIAM DAVIS

Born October 19, 1960, at Livermore, Calif.
Height, 6.03. Weight, 180.
Throws and bats lefthanded.
Attended Chabot College, Hayward, Calif.

Led Western Carolinas League in shutouts with 5 in 1979.
Tied for Eastern League lead in shutouts with 4 and in games started with 28 in 1980.
Named Most Valuable Player in Eastern League, 1980.

Year Club League	G.	IP.	W.	L.	Pct.	H.	R.	ER.	SO.	BB.	ERA.
1979—Spartanburg.........................W. Carol.	26	166	11	9	.550	147	76	59	135	49	3.20
1980—Reading ....Eastern	28	*193	*19	6	*.760	140	63	53	*185	75	*2.47

Selected by New York Mets' organization in 21st round of free-agent draft, June 6, 1978.
Selected by Philadelphia Phillies' organization in secondary phase of free-agent draft, January 9, 1979.

MICHAEL DWAYNE DAVIS
(Mike)

Born June 11, 1959, at San Diego, Calif.
Height, 6.02. Weight, 165.
Throws and bats lefthanded.
Attended Mesa College, Mesa, Ariz.
Cousin of Dave Grayson, former defensive back with Dallas Texans,
Kansas City Chiefs and Oakland Raiders.

Year Club	League	Pos.	G.	AB.	R.	H.	2B.	3B.	HR.	RBI.	B.A.	PO.	A.	E.	F.A.
1977—Medicine Hat	Pion.	*OF-1B	59	213	53	67	5	3	2	18	.315	82	6	*15	.854
1978—Modesto	Calif.	OF-1B	106	406	74	136	12	4	2	35	.335	201	10	13	.942
1979—Modesto	Calif.	OF	41	161	48	63	10	4	0	19	.391	76	3	7	.919
1979—Waterbury	East.	OF	97	351	51	77	9	5	6	39	.219	208	7	15	.935
1980—Ogden	P.C.	OF	19	69	14	21	7	2	1	14	.304	34	2	1	.973
1980—Oakland	Amer.	OF-1B	51	95	11	20	2	1	1	8	.211	76	7	1	.988
Major League Totals			51	95	11	20	2	1	1	8	.211	76	7	1	.988

Selected by Minnesota Twins' organization in 31st round of free agent draft, June 8, 1976.
Selected by Oakland A's organization in 3rd round of free agent draft, June 7, 1977.

ODIE ERNEST DAVIS

Born August 13, 1955, at San Antonio, Tex.
Height, 6.01. Weight, 178.
Throws and bats righthanded.
Attended Prairie View A&M University, Prairie View, Tex.

Year Club	League	Pos.	G.	AB.	R.	H.	2B.	3B.	HR.	RBI.	B.A.	PO.	A.	E.	F.A.
1977—Asheville	W. Car.	SS	37	86	13	14	5	1	2	8	.163	45	82	10	.927
1978—Tulsa	Texas	SS	113	366	63	112	21	9	6	60	.306	146	275	*42	.909
1979—Tucson	P.C.	*SS-2B	119	376	54	95	11	2	4	75	.253	220	360	*38	.939
1980—Charleston	Int.	S-3-2	110	341	30	83	11	2	2	29	.243	144	340	24	.953
1980—Texas	Amer.	SS-3B	17	8	0	1	0	0	0	0	.125	7	15	3	.880
Major League Totals			17	8	0	1	0	0	0	0	.125	7	15	3	.880

Selected by Chicago Cubs' organization in 7th round of free agent draft, June 8, 1976.
Selected by Texas Rangers' organization in 7th round of free agent draft, June 7, 1977.

RICHARD EARL DAVIS
(Dick)

Born September 25, 1953, at Long Beach, Calif.
Height, 6.03. Weight, 195.
Throws and bats righthanded.
Hobby—Music.
Attended Snow College, Ephraim, Utah.
Cousin of Enos Cabell, infielder with San Francisco Giants.

Year Club	League	Pos.	G.	AB.	R.	H.	2B.	3B.	HR.	RBI.	B.A.	PO.	A.	E.	F.A.
1972—Newark	NYP	OF	37	139	16	40	7	1	1	18	.288	41	1	2	.955
1973—Danville	Midw.	OF	101	365	57	100	13	6	8	43	.274	138	3	5	.966
1974—Danville	Midw.	OF	114	451	76	118	17	7	11	38	.262	161	10	9	.950
1975—Thetford Mines..	East	OF	132	455	66	115	23	1	*16	67	.253	124	4	10	.928
1976—Berkshire	East.	OF	126	470	70	136	24	1	16	69	.289	157	4	4	.976
1977—Spokane	P.C.	OF	114	476	94	169	25	8	13	74	.355	162	7	4	.977
1977—Milwaukee	Amer.	OF	22	51	7	14	2	0	0	6	.275	13	0	0	1.000
1978—Milwaukee	Amer.	OF	69	218	28	54	10	1	5	26	.248	54	2	0	1.000
1979—Milwaukee	Amer.	OF	91	335	51	89	13	1	12	41	.266	72	1	2	.973
1980—Milwaukee†	Amer.	OF	106	365	50	99	26	2	4	30	.271	63	3	2	.971
Major League Totals			288	969	136	256	51	4	21	103	.264	202	6	4	.981

Signed as free agent by Milwaukee Brewers' organization, July 10, 1972.
†Traded to Philadelphia Phillies for Pitcher Randy Lerch, March 1, 1981.

ROBERT JOHN EUGENE DAVIS
(Bob)

Born March 1, 1952, at Pryor, Okla.
Height, 6.00. Weight, 190.
Throws and bats righthanded.
Hobbies—Snake hunting and deer hunting.
Attended Northeastern State College, Tahlequah, Okla., and
Claremore Junior College, Claremore, Okla.

Tied for Northwest League lead in total bases with 159 and in sacrifice flies with 6 in 1971.

Year Club	League	Pos.	G.	AB.	R.	H.	2B.	3B.	HR.	RBI.	B.A.	PO.	A.	E.	F.A.
1970—Tri-City	N'west	*3-2	77	279	58	82	14	3	11	48	.294	*102	132	28	.893
1971—Lodi	Calif.	1-O-C	21	54	6	9	1	0	2	5	.167	96	3	1	.990
1971—Tri-City	N'west	C-O-2-3	75	296	54	97	12	4	●14	*83	.328	318	53	7	.981
1972—Alexandria†	Texas	2-C-1-3	54	165	16	35	5	0	4	21	.212	140	94	6	.975
1973—San Diego	Nat.	C	5	11	1	1	0	0	0	0	.091	32	0	2	.941
1973—Alexandria	Texas	C-1-O	118	421	58	119	16	2	12	58	.283	839	102	12	.987
1974—Hawaii‡	P.C.	C-O-1	77	244	32	56	6	2	5	30	.230	415	45	9	.981

— 113 —

Year Club	League	Pos.	G.	AB.	R.	H.	2B.	3B.	HR.	RBI.	B.A.	PO.	A.	E.	F.A.
1975—Hawaii ..............P.C.		C	94	331	45	109	19	4	6	69	.329	499	54	9	.984
1975—San Diego..........Nat.		C	43	128	6	30	3	2	0	7	.234	195	18	3	.986
1976—San Diego..........Nat.		C	51	83	7	17	0	1	0	5	.205	120	19	5	.965
1977—San Diego..........Nat.		C	48	94	9	17	2	0	1	10	.181	136	19	4	.975
1978—Hawaii ..............P.C.		C	90	311	49	92	8	4	10	42	.296	415	74	12	.976
1978—San Diego§ ....Nat.		C	19	40	3	8	1	0	0	2	.200	43	5	2	.960
1979—Toronto ....Amer.		C	32	89	6	11	2	0	1	8	.124	114	11	2	.984
1980—Toronto x ....Amer.		C	91	218	18	47	11	0	4	19	.216	317	28	6	.983
National League Totals...................			166	356	26	73	6	3	1	24	.205	526	61	16	.973
American League Totals			123	307	24	58	13	0	5	27	.189	431	39	8	.983
Major League Totals.......................			289	663	50	131	19	3	6	51	.198	957	100	24	.978

Selected by San Diego Padres' organization in 6th round of free agent draft, June 4, 1970.
†On disabled list, May 1 to June 10, 1972.
‡On disabled list, July 30 through remainder of season.
§Drafted from San Diego Padres' organization by Toronto Blue Jays, December 4, 1978.
xReleased, December 17, 1980; signed by California Angels' organization, January 15, 1981.

RONALD GENE DAVIS
(Ron)

Born August 6, 1955, at Houston Tex.
Height, 6.04. Weight, 198.
Throws and bats righthanded.
Attended Blinn Junior College, Brenham, Tex.

Established American League record for most wins by rookie relief pitcher, season (14), 1979.

Year Club	League	G.	IP.	W.	L.	Pct.	H.	R.	ER.	SO.	BB.	ERA.
1976—Pompano Beach ....Florida St.		18	115	8	8	.500	110	62	48	78	51	3.76
1977—Midland† ....Texas						(Did not play)						
1977—Pompano Beach ....Florida St.		21	111	8	7	.533	119	63	51	58	59	4.14
1978—Midland‡ ....Texas		12	68	3	3	.500	80	51	48	45	38	6.35
1978—West Haven...........................Eastern		21	60	9	2	.818	41	14	10	39	27	1.50
1978—New York ....American		4	2	0	0	.000	3	4	3	0	3	13.50
1979—Columbus ....Int'national		11	19	0	1	.000	13	9	9	10	15	4.26
1979—New York ....American		44	85	14	2	*.875	84	29	27	43	28	2.86
1980—New York ....American		53	131	9	3	.750	121	50	43	65	32	2.95
Major League Totals................................		101	218	23	5	.821	208	83	73	108	63	3.01

Selected by Chicago Cubs' organization in 3rd round of free-agent draft, January 7, 1976.
†On disabled list, April 9 to May 6, 1977.
‡Traded to New York Yankees' organization, June 12, 1978 (completing deal in which Cubs acquired Pitcher Ken Holtzman, June 10, 1978).

CHAMPIONSHIP SERIES RECORD

Year Club	League	G.	IP.	W.	L.	Pct.	H.	R.	ER.	SO.	BB.	ERA.
1980—New York ....American		1	4	0	0	.000	3	1	1	3	1	2.25

ANDRE FERNANDO DAWSON

Born July 10, 1954, at Miami, Fla.
Height, 6.03. Weight, 192.
Throws and bats righthanded.
Hobby—Fishing.
Attended Florida A&M University, Tallahassee, Fla.
Nephew of Theodore Taylor, who played in Pittsburgh Pirates' organization, 1967 through 1969.

Tied major league records for most total bases, inning (8) and most home runs, inning (2), July 30, 1978 (third inning).
Major league stolen bases: 1976 (1), 1977 (21), 1978 (28), 1979 (35), 1980 (34). Total—119.
Led Pioneer League in total bases with 168 and sacrifice flies with 5 in 1975.
Named National League Rookie Player of the Year by THE SPORTING NEWS, 1977.
Named National League Rookie of the Year by The Baseball Writers' Association of America, 1977.
Named outfielder on THE SPORTING NEWS National League Silver Bat team, 1980.
Named outfielder on THE SPORTING NEWS National League All-Star fielding team, 1980.

Year Club	League	Pos.	G.	AB.	R.	H.	2B.	3B.	HR.	RBI.	B.A.	PO.	A.	E.	F.A.
1975—Lethbridge ....Pion.		OF	72	*300	52	*99	14	7	*13	50	.330	*142	7	*10	.937
1976—Quebec City.......East.		OF	40	143	27	51	6	0	8	27	.357	89	3	6	.939
1976—Denver..............A.A.		OF	74	240	51	84	19	4	20	46	.350	97	2	2	.980
1976—Montreal ....Nat.		OF	24	85	9	20	4	1	0	7	.235	61	1	2	.969
1977—Montreal ....Nat.		OF	139	525	64	148	26	9	19	65	.282	352	9	4	.989
1978—Montreal...........Nat.		OF	157	609	84	154	24	8	25	72	.253	411	17	5	.988
1979—Montreal...........Nat.		OF	155	639	90	176	24	12	25	92	.275	394	7	5	.988
1980—Montreal...........Nat.		OF	151	577	96	178	41	7	17	87	.308	410	14	6	.986
Major League Totals			626	2428	343	676	119	37	86	323	.278	1628	48	22	.987

Selected by Montreal Expos' organization in 11th round of free-agent draft, June 4, 1975.

DID YOU KNOW—
That there were 23 inside-the-park homers in 1980? Fifteen were in the American League.

KENNETH GRANT DAYLEY
(Ken)

Born February 25, 1959, at Jerome, Idaho.
Height, 6.00. Weight, 178.
Throws and bats lefthanded.
Attended University of Portland, Portland, Ore.

Year Club	League	G.	IP.	W.	L.	Pct.	H.	R.	ER.	SO.	BB.	ERA.
1980—Savannah............................Southern		16	105	8	3	.727	86	38	30	104	54	2.57

Selected by Atlanta Braves' organization in 1st round (3rd player selected) of free-agent draft, June 3, 1980.

DOUGLAS VERNON DeCINCES
Name pronounced Duh-SIN-say.
(Doug)

Born August 29, 1950, at Burbank, Calif.
Height, 6.02. Weight, 195.
Throws and bats righthanded.
Hobbies—Golf, photography, breeding German shepherd dogs and refinishing antiques.
Attended Pierce Junior College, Woodland Hills, Calif., and University of
California at Los Angeles, Los Angeles, Calif.

Led American League third basemen in assists with 330 in 1977.
Led American League third basemen in double plays with 34 in 1977 and with 41 in 1980.

Year Club	League	Pos.	G.	AB.	R.	H.	2B.	3B.	HR.	RBI.	B.A.	PO.	A.	E.	F.A.
1970—Bluefield...........Appal.		INF-P	54	164	28	48	10	0	4	27	.293	105	98	18	.919
1970—Dallas-Ft. W......Texas		SS	11	35	3	6	1	0	0	2	.171	25	19	3	.936
1971—Dallas-Ft. W.† ...Texas		2B-SS	78	235	29	61	10	1	5	29	.260	154	164	12	.964
1972—Asheville...........So.		★2B-SS	123	396	71	104	23	7	10	60	.263	254	314	★28	.953
1973—Rochester ....Int.		★3B-S-2	131	438	79	117	25	3	19	79	.267	150	264	17	★.961
1973—Baltimore..........Amer.		3-2-S	10	18	2	2	0	0	0	3	.111	4	19	2	.920
1974—Rochester ....Int.		3B	132	444	70	125	17	4	11	66	.282	98	255	★32	.917
1974—Baltimore..........Amer.		3B	1	1	0	0	0	0	0	0	.000	0	2	0	1.000
1975—Baltimore..........Amer.		3-S-2-1	61	167	20	42	6	3	4	23	.251	92	115	7	.967
1976—Baltimore..........Amer.		3-2-1-S	129	440	36	103	17	2	11	42	.234	191	257	20	.957
1977—Baltimore..........Amer.		3-1-2	150	522	63	135	28	3	19	69	.259	125	331	20	.958
1978—Baltimore‡........Amer.		3B-2B	142	511	72	146	37	1	28	80	.286	138	308	14	.970
1979—Baltimore‡........Amer.		3B	120	422	67	97	27	1	16	61	.230	99	247	13	.964
1980—Baltimore..........Amer.		3B-1B	145	489	64	122	23	2	16	64	.249	122	●340	19	.960
Major League Totals			758	2570	324	647	138	12	94	342	.252	771	1619	95	.962

Selected by San Diego Padres' organization in 3rd round of free-agent draft, June 5, 1969.
Selected by Baltimore Orioles' organization in secondary phase of free-agent draft, January 17, 1970.
†On disabled list, June 25 to July 27, 1971.
‡On supplemental disabled list, April 27, 1979; transferred to disabled list, May 14 to June 5, 1979.

PITCHING RECORD

Year Club	League	G.	IP.	W.	L.	Pct.	H.	R.	ER.	SO.	BB.	ERA.
1970—Bluefield..............................Ap'lachian		1	2	0	1	.000	3	2	1	1	1	4.50

CHAMPIONSHIP SERIES RECORD

Year Club	League	Pos.	G.	AB.	R.	H.	2B.	3B.	HR.	RBI.	B.A.	PO.	A.	E.	F.A.
1979—Baltimore ....Amer.		3B	4	13	4	4	1	0	0	3	.308	5	8	0	1.000

WORLD SERIES RECORD

Tied World Series records for hitting home run in first series at bat, October 10, 1979; most errors by third baseman, inning (2), October 10, 1979 (sixth inning); most bases on balls, game (4), October 13, 1979.

Year Club	League	Pos.	G.	AB.	R.	H.	2B.	3B.	HR.	RBI.	B.A.	PO.	A.	E.	F.A.
1979—Baltimore ....Amer.		3B	7	25	2	5	0	0	1	3	.200	7	21	3	.903

IVAN DeJESUS (ALVAREZ)
Name pronounced day-HAY-soos.

Born January 9, 1953, at Santurce, Puerto Rico.
Height, 5.11. Weight, 175.
Throws and bats righthanded.
Hobbies—Music, swimming and basketball.
Attended University of Puerto Rico, Rio Piedras, Puerto Rico.

Established National League record for most assists by shortstop, season, 162-game schedule (595), 1977.
Major league stolen bases: 1974 (0), 1975 (1), 1976 (0), 1977 (24), 1978 (41), 1979 (24), 1980 (44). Total—134.
Hit for the cycle against St. Louis Cardinals, April 22, 1980.
Led Florida State League shortstops in double plays with 56 in 1970.
Led California League shortstops in double plays with 53 in 1971 and with 87 in 1973.
Led Pacific Coast League shortstops in double plays with 114 in 1974.

Year Club	League	Pos.	G.	AB.	R.	H.	2B.	3B.	HR.	RBI.	B.A.	PO.	A.	E.	F.A.
1970—Daytona Beach ..Fla. St.		SS	123	396	51	92	12	7	2	38	.232	164	361	38	.933
1971—Bakersfield ....Calif.		★SS-2B	126	462	77	108	16	2	6	30	.234	159	★323	★49	.908
1972—Daytona Beach ..Fla. St.		SS	131	442	56	108	15	4	7	39	.244	187	★452	37	.945

Year Club League	Pos.	G.	AB.	R.	H.	2B.	3B.	HR.	RBI.	B.A.	PO.	A.	E.	F.A.
1973—Bakersfield ....Calif.	SS	132	519	77	125	17	1	7	57	.241	221	★403	★47	.930
1974—Albuquerque......P.C.	SS	140	510	81	152	17	5	7	55	.298	★268	★479	38	.952
1974—Los Angeles.......Nat.	SS	3	3	1	1	0	0	0	0	.333	1	0	0	1.000
1975—Albuquerque......P.C.	SS	62	221	24	60	10	2	1	21	.271	97	265	24	.938
1975—Los Angeles.......Nat.	SS	63	87	10	16	2	1	0	2	.184	45	107	4	.974
1976—Albuquerque......P.C.	SS-3B	108	405	69	123	27	7	7	64	.304	161	341	35	.935
1976—Los Angeles† .....Nat.	SS-3B	22	41	4	7	2	1	0	2	.171	20	47	3	.957
1977—Chicago............Nat.	SS	155	624	91	166	31	7	3	40	.266	234	★595	33	.962
1978—Chicago ....Nat.	SS	160	619	★104	172	24	7	3	35	.278	232	★558	27	.967
1979—Chicago ....Nat.	SS	160	636	92	180	26	10	5	52	.283	235	507	32	.959
1980—Chicago ....Nat.	SS	157	618	78	160	26	3	3	33	.259	229	529	24	.969
Major League Totals		720	2628	380	702	111	29	14	164	.267	996	2343	123	.964

Signed as free agent by Los Angeles Dodgers' organization, May 23, 1969.

†Traded with First Baseman Bill Buckner and Pitcher Jeff Albert to Chicago Cubs for Outfielder Rick Monday and Pitcher Mike Garman, January 11, 1977.

JOHN RIKARD DEMPSEY
(Rick)

Born September 13, 1949, at Fayetteville, Tenn.
Height, 6.00. Weight, 184.
Throws and bats righthanded.
Hobbies—Hunting and fishing.
Attended Pierce Junior College, Woodland Hills, Calif.
Brother of Pat Dempsey, catcher in Oakland A's organization.

Tied major league record for most double plays by catcher, game (3), June 1, 1977.
Tied for American League lead among catchers in double plays with 14 in 1978.
Led International League in passed balls with 14 in 1973.
Tied for New York-Pennsylvania League lead in double plays by catchers with 4 in 1968.
Named New York-Pennsylvania League Rookie of the Year, 1968.

Year Club League	Pos.	G.	AB.	R.	H.	2B.	3B.	HR.	RBI.	B.A.	PO.	A.	E.	F.A.
1967—Sarasota Twins..Gulf C.	C-O-1	40	102	9	21	4	3	0	9	.206	133	16	2	.987
1968—Wis. Rapids.......Midw.	C	11	35	12	8	2	0	1	6	.229	68	2	1	.986
1968—Auburn ....NYP	★C-1-O	73	270	48	79	10	7	7	61	.293	★505	★38	7	★.987
1969—Wis. Rapids.......Midw.	C	50	151	35	55	11	2	6	31	.364	341	30	●13	.966
1969—Minnesota ....Amer.	C	5	6	1	3	1	0	0	0	.500	5	0	1	.833
1970—Charlotte..........South	C-OF-2	105	351	28	86	20	6	4	42	.245	506	76	18	.970
1971—Charlotte..........South	C-OF	105	338	39	82	16	2	8	47	.243	599	65	8	.988
1971—Minnesota ....Amer.	C	6	13	2	4	1	0	0	0	.308	30	4	2	.944
1972—Tacoma.............P. C.	C-OF	48	161	13	38	6	2	3	18	.236	284	33	5	.984
1972—Minnesota†........Amer.	C	25	40	0	8	1	0	0	0	.200	67	5	1	.986
1973—Syracuse ....Int.	C-OF-3	122	387	53	96	14	4	6	47	.248	585	69	9	.986
1973—New York.........Amer.	C	6	11	0	2	0	0	0	0	.182	9	0	2	.818
1974—New York.........Amer.	C-OF	43	109	12	26	3	0	2	12	.239	152	22	4	.978
1975—New York.........Amer.	C-O-3	71	145	18	38	8	0	1	11	.262	92	9	3	.971
1976—N.Y.‡-Balt. ....Amer.	C-OF	80	216	12	42	2	0	0	12	.194	302	39	4	.988
1977—Baltimore§........Amer.	C	91	270	27	61	7	4	3	34	.226	416	52	11	.977
1978—Baltimore ....Amer.	C	136	441	41	114	25	0	6	32	.259	636	79	11	.985
1979—Baltimore ....Amer.	C	124	368	48	88	23	0	6	41	.239	615	★81	7	.990
1980—Baltimore ....Amer.	C-OF-1	119	362	51	95	26	3	9	40	.262	544	55	8	.987
Major League Totals		711	1988	213	481	97	7	27	182	.242	2880	346	55	.983

Selected by Minnesota Twins' organization in 12th round of free-agent draft, June 6, 1967.

†Released to Syracuse (in trade which sent Outfielder Danny Walton from Syracuse to Minnesota), October 27, 1972.

‡Traded with Pitchers Rudy May, Tippy Martinez, Dave Pagan and Scott McGregor to New York Yankees for Pitchers Ken Holtzman, Doyle Alexander and Grant Jackson, Catcher Ellie Hendricks and Pitcher Jimmy Freeman, latter assigned from Rochester to Syracuse, June 15, 1976.

§On supplemental disabled list, July 9 to July 28; on disabled list, July 28 to August 21, 1977.

CHAMPIONSHIP SERIES RECORD

Year Club League	Pos.	G.	AB.	R.	H.	2B.	3B.	HR.	RBI.	B.A.	PO.	A.	E.	F.A.
1979—Baltimore ....Amer.	C	3	10	3	4	2	0	0	2	.400	10	1	0	1.000

WORLD SERIES RECORD

Year Club League	Pos.	G.	AB.	R.	H.	2B.	3B.	HR.	RBI.	B.A.	PO.	A.	E.	F.A.
1979—Baltimore ....Amer.	C-PR	7	21	3	6	2	0	0	0	.286	38	2	0	1.000

PATRICK ARCHER DEMPSEY
(Pat)

Born October 23, 1956, at Encino, Calif.
Height, 6.04. Weight, 185.
Throws and bats righthanded.
Attended Columbia State Community College, Columbia, Tenn.
Brother of Rick Dempsey, catcher with Baltimore Orioles.

Led California League catchers in double plays with 7 in 1977 and with 9 in 1978.
Led California League catchers in putouts with 652 and in errors with 26 in 1978.

Year	Club	League	Pos.	G.	AB.	R.	H.	2B.	3B.	HR.	RBI.	B.A.	PO.	A.	E.	F.A.
1977—Modesto	Calif.	C-1B	82	281	29	83	8	1	2	37	.295	438	48	14	.972
1977—Chattanooga	South.	C	4	6	0	0	0	0	0	0	.000	13	1	1	.933
1978—Modesto	Calif.	C-1B	106	388	50	98	12	1	2	40	.253	676	85	28	.965
1979—Modesto	Calif.	C	57	208	25	53	3	3	1	25	.255	307	42	11	.969
1979—Ogden	P.C.	C	44	149	14	42	3	0	2	20	.282	213	24	11	.956
1980—Ogden	P.C.	C-1B	111	377	59	120	21	5	2	41	.318	492	78	20	.966

Selected by Oakland A's organization in 2nd round of free-agent draft, January 11, 1977.

JOHN ALLEN DENNY

Born November 8, 1952, at Prescott, Ariz.
Height, 6.03. Weight, 190.
Throws and bats righthanded.
Hobbies—Building model ships and astronomy.
Attended Yavapai College, Prescott, Ariz., and Southern Illinois University, Edwardsville, Ill.

Pitched 8-1 no-hit victory against Midland, May 17, 1973.

Year	Club	League	G.	IP.	W.	L.	Pct.	H.	R.	ER.	SO.	BB.	ERA.
1970—Sarasota Cardinals	Gulf Coast	11	42	2	2	.500	32	14	6	43	9	1.29
1971—St. Petersburg	Florida St.	26	139	8	13	.381	123	58	47	62	3.04
1972—Modesto†	California	14	92	7	5	.583	95	54	45	65	39	4.40
1973—Arkansas‡	Texas	20	147	10	6	.625	128	57	51	81	52	3.11
1974—Tulsa	Am. Assoc.	21	132	9	8	.529	127	66	55	79	57	3.74
1974—St. Louis	National	2	2	0	0	.000	3	2	0	1	0	0.00
1975—Tulsa	Am. Assoc.	7	60	3	1	.750	47	12	12	44	32	1.80
1975—St. Louis	National	25	136	10	7	.588	149	73	60	72	51	3.97
1976—St. Louis	National	30	207	11	9	.550	189	71	58	74	74	*2.52
1977—St. Louis§	National	26	150	8	8	.500	165	85	75	60	62	4.50
1978—St. Louis	National	33	234	14	11	.560	200	81	77	103	74	2.96
1979—St. Louis x	National	31	206	8	11	.421	206	116	111	99	100	4.85
1980—Cleveland y	American	16	109	8	6	.571	116	54	53	59	47	4.38
National League Totals		147	935	51	46	.526	912	428	381	409	361	3.67
American League Totals		16	109	8	6	.571	116	54	53	59	47	4.38
Major League Totals		163	1044	59	52	.532	1028	482	434	468	408	3.74

Selected by St. Louis Cardinals' organization in 29th round of free-agent draft, June 4, 1970.
†On disabled list, July 17 through remainder of season.
‡On disabled list, August 11 through remainder of season.
§On disabled list, June 22 to July 29, 1977.
xTraded with Outfielder Jerry Mumphrey to Cleveland Indians for Outfielder Bobby Bonds, December 7, 1979.
yOn disabled list, July 15 to September 8, 1980.

RUSSELL EARL DENT
(Bucky)

(Nicknamed by grandmother; word means "small Indian boy.")

Born November 25, 1951, at Savannah, Ga.
Height, 5.11. Weight, 184.
Throws and bats righthanded.
Attended Miami-Dade (North) Community College, Miami, Fla.

Led American League shortstops in total chances with 838 and tied for lead in double plays with 105 in 1975.
Led Amercian League in sacrifice hits with 23 in 1974.
Tied for American League lead in double plays by shortstops with 108 in 1974.
Led Midwest League in sacrifice hits with 12 and led shortstops in double plays with 51 in 1971; led American Association in sacrifice hits with 12 in 1973.
Tied for Gulf Coast League lead in sacrifice flies with 5 in 1970.

Year	Club	League	Pos.	G.	AB.	R.	H.	2B.	3B.	HR.	RBI.	B.A.	PO.	A.	E.	F.A.
1970—Sarasota W. S.	G. C.	3-S-2	22	77	18	27	2	1	0	13	.351	30	55	11	.885
1970—Appleton	Midw.	SS-2	39	163	23	42	4	2	3	12	.258	53	116	17	.909
1971—Appleton†	Midw.	SS-3	83	294	34	68	16	0	1	29	.231	109	230	24	.934
1972—Knoxville	South.	SS	125	453	58	134	10	6	6	56	.296	167	437	31	.951
1973—Iowa	A. A.	*SS-3B	95	356	58	105	10	3	3	38	.295	137	308	*33	.931
1973—Chicago	Amer.	S-2-3	40	117	17	29	2	0	0	10	.248	55	134	7	.964
1974—Chicago	Amer.	SS	154	496	55	136	15	3	5	45	.274	251	499	22	.972
1975—Chicago	Amer.	SS	157	602	52	159	29	4	3	58	.264	*279	*543	16	*.981
1976—Chicago‡	Amer.	SS	158	562	44	138	18	4	2	52	.246	279	468	18	.976
1977—New York	Amer.	SS	158	477	54	118	18	4	8	49	.247	250	434	18	.974
1978—New York§	Amer.	SS	123	379	40	92	11	1	5	40	.243	178	341	10	.981
1979—New York	Amer.	SS	141	431	47	99	14	2	2	32	.230	219	512	17	.977
1980—New York x	Amer.	SS	141	489	57	128	26	2	5	52	.262	224	489	13	*.982
Major League Totals			1072	3553	366	899	133	20	30	338	.253	1735	3420	121	.977

Selected by St. Louis Cardinals' organization in 5th round of free-agent draft, June 5, 1969.
Selected by St. Louis Cardinals' organization in secondary phase of free-agent draft, January 17, 1970.
Selected by Chicago White Sox' organization in secondary phase of free-agent draft, June 4, 1970.
†On military list from beginning of season to May 14, 1971.
‡Traded to New York Yankees for Outfielder Oscar Gamble, Pitchers Bob Polinsky and Dewey Hoyt, and cash estimated at $200,000, April 5, 1977.
§On supplemental disabled list, July 9 to July 31, 1978.
xOn supplemental disabled list, June 15 to June 30, 1980.

CHAMPIONSHIP SERIES RECORD

Year	Club	League	Pos.	G.	AB.	R.	H.	2B.	3B.	HR.	RBI.	B.A.	PO.	A.	E.	F.A.
1977—New York	.........Amer.		SS	5	14	1	3	1	0	0	2	.214	10	14	1	.960
1978—New York	........Amer.		SS	4	15	0	3	0	0	0	4	.200	2	8	1	.909
1980—New York	........Amer.		SS	3	11	0	2	0	0	0	0	.182	9	12	0	1.000
Championship Series Totals				12	40	1	8	1	0	0	6	.200	21	34	2	.965

WORLD SERIES RECORD

Tied World Series record for one or more hits, each game, six-game Series, 1978.

Year	Club	League	Pos.	G.	AB.	R.	H.	2B.	3B.	HR.	RBI.	B.A.	PO.	A.	E.	F.A.
1977—New York	.........Amer.		SS	6	19	0	5	0	0	0	2	.263	2	15	1	.944
1978—New York	........Amer.		SS	6	24	3	10	1	0	0	7	.417	8	16	2	.923
World Series Totals	....			12	43	3	15	1	0	0	9	.349	10	31	3	.932

ALL-STAR GAME RECORD

Year	League	Pos.	AB.	R.	H.	2B.	3B.	HR.	RBI.	B.A.	PO.	A.	E.	F.A.
1975—American	....	SS	1	0	0	0	0	0	0	.000	0	1	0	1.000
1980—American	....	SS	2	0	1	0	0	0	0	.500	0	1	0	1.000
All-Star Game Totals	....		3	0	1	0	0	0	0	.333	0	2	0	1.000

ROBERT EUGENE DERNIER
(Bob)

Born January 5, 1957, at Kansas City, Mo.
Height, 6.00. Weight, 160.
Throws and bats righthanded.
Attended Longview Community College, Lee's Summit, Mo.

Tied for Pioneer League lead in double plays by third basemen with 9 in 1978.
Led Carolina League in stolen bases with 77 in 1979 and led Eastern League in stolen bases with 71 in 1980.
Led Carolina League outfielders in putouts with 315 in 1979.
Named Most Valuable Player in Carolina League, 1979.

Year	Club	League	Pos.	G.	AB.	R.	H.	2B.	3B.	HR.	RBI.	B.A.	PO.	A.	E.	F.A.
1978—Spartanburg	......W. Car.		SS	22	57	9	8	1	0	0	5	.140	23	61	16	.840
1978—Helena	.............Pioneer		3B	53	186	49	56	6	2	4	27	.301	38	104	22	.866
1979—Peninsula	.........Carol.		OF-3B	135	491	102	143	19	2	4	42	.291	331	23	10	.973
1980—Reading	............East.		OF	136	*536	*111	160	29	4	10	57	.299	*325	9	9	.974
1980—Philadelphia	......Nat.		OF	10	7	5	4	0	0	1	1	.571	9	0	0	1.000
Major League Totals	....			10	7	5	4	0	0	1	1	.571	9	0	0	1.000

Selected by Cincinnati Reds' organization in 12th round of free-agent draft, January 11, 1977.
Signed as free agent by Philadelphia Phillies' organization, August 5, 1977.

JOSEPH DE SA
(Joe)

Born July 27, 1959, at Honolulu, Hawaii.
Height, 5.11. Weight, 170.
Throws and bats lefthanded.

Led Pioneer League first basemen in double plays with 65 in 1977.

Year	Club	League	Pos.	G.	AB.	R.	H.	2B.	3B.	HR.	RBI.	B.A.	PO.	A.	E.	F.A.
1977—Calgary	............Pion.		1B	*70	279	65	76	13	1	3	55	.272	*607	37	10	.985
1978—Gastonia	...........W. Car.		1B	42	149	23	39	11	0	4	25	.262	326	17	4	.988
1978—St. Petersburg	...Fla. St.		1B	86	277	41	86	13	0	5	30	.310	722	53	1	.999
1979—Arkansas	.........Texas		1B	130	463	71	147	32	5	13	86	.317	*1129	*71	11	.991
1980—Springfield	......A. A.		1B	123	423	54	124	25	2	9	74	.293	1005	*86	6	*.995
1980—St. Louis	...........Nat.		1B-OF	7	11	0	3	0	0	0	0	.273	3	0	0	1.000
Major League Totals	....			7	11	0	3	0	0	0	0	.273	3	0	0	1.000

Selected by St. Louis Cardinals' organization in 3rd round of free-agent draft, June 7, 1977.

ROBERT WAYNE DETHERAGE
(Bob)

Born September 20, 1954, at Springfield, Mo.
Height, 6.00. Weight, 180.
Throws and bats righthanded.
Hobby—Car racing.

Tied for Pioneer League lead in double plays by outfielders with 1 in 1973.
Named Most Valuable Player in Pioneer League, 1973.

Year	Club	League	Pos.	G.	AB.	R.	H.	2B.	3B.	HR.	RBI.	B.A.	PO.	A.	E.	F.A.
1973—Daytona Beach	..Fla. St.		OF	9	19	1	2	1	0	0	2	.105	4	1	0	1.000
1973—Ogden	...............Pion.		OF-P	67	244	43	*85	14	*7	5	*55	.348	100	5	6	.946
1974—Bakersfield	.......Calif.		OF	137	483	95	150	17	7	14	77	.311	226	13	12	.952
1975—Waterbury	........East.		OF	127	433	53	109	21	1	4	35	.252	313	11	11	.967
1976—Waterbury†	........East.		OF	14	45	9	13	1	0	4	11	.289	38	2	1	.976
1976—Arkansas	.........Texas		OF	41	148	18	44	3	1	3	18	.297	74	3	4	.951
1976—Tulsa‡	..............A.A.		OF	21	71	13	15	4	0	1	1	.211	27	2	2	.935
1977—Columbus	.........South.		OF	81	283	49	76	11	4	6	28	.269	176	10	5	.974
1977—Charleston§x	.....Int.		OF	23	59	7	17	3	1	1	7	.288	36	3	3	.929

Year Club League	Pos.	G.	AB.	R.	H.	2B.	3B.	HR.	RBI.	B.A.	PO.	A.	E.	F.A.
1978—Albuquerque y... P.C.					Did not play									
1978—Omaha..............A.A.	OF	82	291	39	77	10	5	5	47	.265	153	3	3	.981
1979—Omaha..............A.A.	OF	97	267	30	63	8	5	5	34	.236	248	11	4	.985
1980—Omaha..............A.A.	OF	87	284	29	69	10	4	4	29	.243	241	5	7	.972
1980—Kansas City ......Amer.	OF	20	26	2	8	2	0	1	7	.308	16	0	0	1.000
Major League Totals......................		20	26	2	8	2	0	1	7	.308	16	0	0	1.000

Selected by Los Angeles Dodgers' organization in 3rd round of free-agent draft, June 6, 1972.

†Traded with Catcher-Outfielder Joe Ferguson and Infielder Freddie Tisdale, latter assigned from Lodi to St. Petersburg, to St. Louis Cardinals for Outfielder Reggie Smith, June 15, 1976.

‡Traded with Catcher-Outfielder Joe Ferguson to Houston Astros for Pitcher Larry Dierker and Infielder Jerry DaVanon, November 23, 1976.

§On disabled list, July 17 to August 3, 1977.

xSold to Los Angeles Dodgers' organization, September 16, 1977.

yReleased, April 14, 1978; signed by Kansas City Royals' organization, June 9, 1978.

RECORD AS PITCHER

Year Club	League	G.	IP.	W.	L.	Pct.	H.	R.	ER.	SO.	BB.	ERA.
1973—Ogden.................................Pioneer		1	1	0	0	.000	5	4	2	1	1	18.00

PAUL ADRIAN DEVINE
(Known by middle name.)

Born December 2, 1951, at Galveston, Tex.
Height, 6.04. Weight, 205.
Throws and bats righthanded.
Hobby—Photography.
Attended Sam Houston State University, Huntsville, Tex.

Major League saves: 1973 (4), 1974 (0), 1975 (0), 1976 (9), 1977 (15), 1978 (3), 1979 (0), 1980 (0). Total—31.

Year Club	League	G.	IP.	W.	L.	Pct.	H.	R.	ER.	SO.	BB.	ERA.
1970—Magic Valley......................Pioneer		14	66	5	6	.455	80	45	38	54	25	5.18
1971—Greenwood..........................W. Carol.		8	30	2	1	.667	23	8	8	24	8	2.40
1972—Savannah...........................Southern		25	130	12	8	.600	128	54	45	94	29	3.12
1973—Richmond ....Int'national		13	80	2	7	.222	87	43	39	62	41	4.39
1973—Atlanta ....National		24	32	2	3	.400	45	24	23	15	12	6.47
1974—Richmond†......................Int'national		4	14	0	1	.000	19	14	14	4	7	9.00
1975—Richmond ....Int'national		27	148	10	6	.625	148	55	49	82	51	2.98
1975—Atlanta ....National		5	16	1	0	1.000	19	8	8	8	7	4.50
1976—Atlanta‡...............................National		48	73	5	6	.455	72	30	26	48	26	3.21
1977—Texas§.................................American		56	106	11	6	.647	102	43	42	67	31	3.57
1978—Atlanta ....National		31	65	5	4	.556	84	45	43	26	25	5.95
1979—Atlanta x ....National		40	67	1	2	.333	84	28	24	22	25	3.22
1980—Texas y................................American		13	28	1	1	.500	49	22	15	8	9	4.82
National League Totals..............................		148	253	14	15	.483	304	135	124	119	95	4.41
American League Totals............................		69	134	12	7	.632	151	65	57	75	40	3.83
Major League Totals		217	387	26	22	.542	455	200	181	194	135	4.21

Selected by Atlanta Braves' organization in 2nd round of free-agent draft, June 4, 1970.

†On disabled list, April 19 to May 24 and June 9 to June 17, 1974.

‡On disabled list, June 16 to July 21, 1976. Traded with Outfielders Ken Henderson and Dave May, Pitchers Carl Morton and Roger Moret, and cash estimated at $250,000 to Texas Rangers for Outfielder Jeff Burroughs, December 9, 1976.

§Traded with Pitcher Tommy Boggs and Outfielder Eddie Miller to Atlanta Braves for First Baseman Willie Montanez, December 8, 1977.

xTraded with Shortstop Pepe Frias and a player to be named later to Texas Rangers for Shortstop Larvell Blanks and Pitcher Doyle Alexander, December 7, 1979; Braves received $50,000 to complete deal when Outfielder Jeff Burroughs exercised no-trade clause.

yOn disabled list, July 12, 1980; transferred to emergency disabled list, August 30 to October 24, 1980.

BAUDILIO JOSE DIAZ (SEIJAS)
Name pronounced DEE-az.

(Bo)

Born March 23, 1953, at Cua, Miranda, Venezuela.
Height, 5.11. Weight, 190.
Throws and bats righthanded.
Hobby—Music.

Tied for International League lead in double plays by catchers with 7 in 1977.

Year Club League	Pos.	G.	AB.	R.	H.	2B.	3B.	HR.	RBI.	B.A.	PO.	A.	E.	F.A.
1971—Williamsport .....NYP	PH-C	1	1	0	0	0	0	0	0	.000	0	0	0	.000
1971—Pawtucket.........East.	PH-C	1	2	0	0	0	0	0	0	.000	4	0	0	1.000
1971—Greenville.........W. Car.	C	10	25	2	5	1	0	0	0	.200	35	2	2	.949
1972—Winter Haven ....Fla. St.	C	14	44	3	7	1	0	0	0	.159	72	7	0	1.000
1973—Elmira..............NYP	C	25	69	3	17	3	0	0	9	.246	107	16	1	.992
1974—Winter Haven ....Fla. St.	C-3B	97	327	31	79	20	1	1	38	.242	476	75	14	.975
1975—Winston-Salem ..Carol.	C	59	179	22	47	8	1	6	29	.263	271	45	9	.972
1976—Rhode Island .....Int.	C-OF	62	117	10	29	42	1	0	18	.248	222	28	3	.988
1977—Pawtucket.........Int.	C-3B	105	308	37	81	14	1	7	54	.263	459	67	6	*.989

Year Club	League	Pos.	G.	AB.	R.	H.	2B.	3B.	HR.	RBI.	B.A.	PO.	A.	E.	F.A.
1977—Boston†	Amer.	C	2	1	0	0	0	0	0	0	.000	5	0	0	1.000
1978—Cleveland‡	Amer.	C	44	127	12	30	4	0	2	11	.236	183	18	6	.971
1979—Tacoma	P. C.	C	34	115	5	28	7	0	2	11	.243	223	24	5	.980
1979—Cleveland§	Amer.	C	15	32	0	5	2	0	0	1	.156	63	6	3	.958
1980—Cleveland	Amer.	C	76	207	15	47	11	2	3	32	.227	317	35	4	.989
Major League Totals			137	367	27	82	17	2	5	44	.223	568	59	13	.980

Signed as free agent by Boston Red Sox' organization, November 25, 1970.

†Traded with Pitchers Rick Wise and Mike Paxton and Third Baseman Ted Cox to Cleveland Indians for Pitcher Dennis Eckersley and Catcher Fred Kendall, March 30, 1978.

‡On emergency disabled list, April 16 to June 16, 1978.

§On supplemental disabled list, March 31 to April 17 and June 8 to July 20, 1979.

STEPHEN BRADLEY DILLARD
(Steve)

Born December 8, 1951, at Memphis, Tenn.
Height, 6.01. Weight, 180.
Throws and bats righthanded.
Hobby—Basketball.
Attended University of Mississippi, Oxford, Miss.

Year Club	League	Pos.	G.	AB.	R.	H.	2B.	3B.	HR.	RBI.	B.A.	PO.	A.	E.	F.A.
1972—Winston-Salem	Carol.	3-S-2	44	114	14	26	0	3	0	9	.228	30	56	4	.956
1973—Winston-Salem	Carol.	*SS-O	132	516	84	144	20	8	7	64	.279	*214	*428	43	*.937
1974—Bristol	East.	SS-2B	24	28	7	5	2	0	0	4	.179	10	23	2	.943
1974—Pawtucket	Int.	SS	90	338	50	89	11	1	1	14	.263	132	233	22	.943
1975—Pawtucket†	Int.	SS	57	155	20	30	4	0	0	4	.194	53	100	19	.890
1975—Bristol	East.	2B	68	261	34	73	5	2	1	20	.280	30	33	3	.955
1975—Boston	Amer.	2B	1	5	2	2	0	0	0	0	.400	5	4	0	1.000
1976—Boston	Amer.	3-2-S	57	167	22	46	14	0	1	15	.275	58	102	11	.936
1976—Rhode Island	Int.	2B	34	135	17	31	5	0	1	9	.230	87	107	13	.937
1977—Boston‡	Amer.	2B-SS	66	141	22	34	7	0	1	13	.241	90	122	6	.972
1978—Detroit§	Amer.	2B	56	130	21	29	5	2	0	7	.223	88	118	9	.958
1979—Chicago	Nat.	2B-3B	89	166	31	47	6	1	5	24	.283	114	138	4	.984
1980—Chicago	Nat.	3-2-S	100	244	31	55	8	1	4	27	.225	92	171	14	.949
American League Totals			180	443	67	111	26	2	3	35	.251	241	346	26	.958
National League Totals			189	410	62	102	14	2	9	51	.249	206	309	18	.966
Major League Totals			369	853	129	213	40	4	11	86	.250	447	655	44	.962

Selected by San Diego Padres' organization in 25th round of free-agent draft, June 4, 1970.

Selected by Boston Red Sox' organization in 2nd round of free-agent draft, June 6, 1972.

†On disabled list, May 1 to May 11, 1975.

‡Traded to Detroit Tigers for Pitchers Mike Burns and Frank Harris and cash, January 30, 1978.

§Sold to Chicago Cubs, March 20, 1979.

MIGUEL ANGEL DILONE (REYES)
Name pronounced De-lo-NAY.

Born November 1, 1954, at Santiago, Dominican Republic.
Height, 6.00. Weight, 160.
Throws right and bats left and righthanded.

Established National League record for most stolen bases with no caught stealing, season (12), 1977.

Major League stolen bases: 1974 (2), 1975 (2), 1976 (5), 1977 (12), 1978 (50), 1979 (21), 1980 (61). Total—153.

Led Western Carolinas League in stolen bases with 95 in 1973, Carolina League with 84 in 1974 and International League with 48 in 1975.

Named Player of the Year in Carolina League, 1974.

Year Club	League	Pos.	G.	AB.	R.	H.	2B.	3B.	HR.	RBI.	B.A.	PO.	A.	E.	F.A.
1972—Niagara Falls	NYP	OF	61	223	50	50	6	0	0	16	.224	83	4	5	.946
1973—Charleston	W. Car.	OF	115	438	*94	119	8	5	1	24	.272	228	11	7	.972
1974—Salem	Carol.	OF	132	532	106	*176	28	9	1	47	.331	271	8	13	.955
1974—Pittsburgh	Nat.	PR-OF	12	2	3	0	0	0	0	0	1.000	1	0	0	1.000
1975—Charleston	Int.	OF	125	471	61	102	12	5	1	26	.217	275	11	6	.978
1975—Pittsburgh	Nat.	OF	18	6	8	0	0	0	0	0	.000	3	0	0	1.000
1976—Charleston	Int.	OF-3B	100	408	63	137	7	6	1	17	.336	202	26	9	.962
1976—Pittsburgh	Nat.	OF	16	17	7	4	0	0	0	0	.235	11	0	0	1.000
1977—Columbus	Int.	OF	38	144	28	31	5	1	0	7	.215	101	2	1	.990
1977—Pittsburgh†	Nat.	OF	29	44	5	6	0	0	0	0	.136	21	1	0	1.000
1978—Oakland	Amer.	OF-3B	135	258	34	59	8	0	1	14	.229	196	4	5	.976
1979—Oakland‡	Amer.	OF	30	91	15	17	1	2	1	6	.187	47	0	2	.959
1979—Chicago	Nat.	OF	43	36	14	11	0	0	0	1	.306	27	0	0	1.000
1980—Wichita§	A.A.	OF	20	84	12	20	5	0	0	2	.238	48	0	1	.980
1980—Cleveland	Amer.	OF	132	528	82	180	30	9	0	40	.341	249	7	7	.973
American League Totals			297	877	131	256	39	11	2	60	.292	492	11	14	.973
National League Totals			118	105	37	21	0	0	0	1	.200	63	1	0	1.000
Major League Totals			415	982	168	277	39	11	2	61	.282	555	12	14	.976

Originally signed as a free agent by Pittsburgh Pirates but on a later date the St. Louis Cardinals also signed him not realizing that the Pittsburgh club had a valid contract. The National Association ruled in favor of the Pirates, April 20, 1972.

†On supplemental disabled list, May 16 through June 25, 1977. Traded with Pitcher Elias Sosa and a player

to be named later to Oakland A's for Catcher Manny Sanguillen, April 4, 1978; Infielder Mike Edwards sent to Oakland to complete deal, April 7, 1978.

‡Sold to Chicago Cubs, July 4, 1979.

§Sold to Cleveland Indians, May 7, 1980.

FRANK MICHAEL DiPINO

Born October 22, 1956, at Syracuse, N.Y.
Height, 5.10. Weight, 175.
Throws and bats lefthanded.
Attended St. Leo College, St. Leo, Fla.

Pitched seven-inning 6-0 no-hit victory against Reading, June 8, 1980.

Year	Club	League	G.	IP.	W.	L.	Pct.	H.	R.	ER.	SO.	BB.	ERA.
1977—Newark		NYP	14	29	1	3	.250	14	12	8	41	22	2.48
1978—Burlington		Midwest	15	88	5	4	.556	98	58	46	68	36	4.70
1979—Stockton†		California	16	99	5	3	.625	92	45	38	67	46	3.45
1980—Holyoke		Eastern	16	76	7	0	1.000	46	13	11	58	27	1.30
1980—Vancouver		P. Coast	24	28	3	1	.750	24	10	7	32	14	2.25

Signed as free agent by Milwaukee Brewers' organization, July 11, 1977.

†On disabled list, May 19 to June 11, 1979.

THOMAS JAMES DONOHUE
(Tom)

Born November 15, 1952, at Westbury, N. Y.
Height, 6.00. Weight, 195.
Throws and bats righthanded.
Hobbies—Golf and fishing.
Attended Idaho State University, Pocatello, Ida., and Nassau
Community College, Garden City, N. Y.

Led Pacific Coast League catchers in fielding average with .982, in putouts with 492 and in total chances with 562 in 1977.

Year	Club	League	Pos.	G.	AB.	R.	H.	2B.	3B.	HR.	RBI.	B.A.	PO.	A.	E.	F.A.
1972—Quad Cities	Midw.		OF	37	86	13	9	1	1	1	7	.105	46	2	3	.941
1972—Idaho Falls	Pion.		OF	55	204	18	47	7	4	1	10	.230	115	2	6	.951
1973—Quad Cities	Midw.		OF-C-3B	83	239	26	49	11	0	7	27	.205	180	15	7	.965
1974—Salinas	Calif.		C-OF	45	152	19	32	4	3	4	21	.211	182	27	4	.981
1974—Quad Cities	Midw.		OF-C	38	143	13	26	3	2	3	11	.182	144	12	4	.975
1974—El Paso	Texas		C	4	13	1	2	1	0	0	2	.154	14	4	0	1.000
1975—Salinas	Calif.		OF	8	20	3	6	2	0	1	6	.300	8	1	1	.900
1975—El Paso	Texas		C-OF	100	338	46	91	15	2	12	59	.269	340	36	7	.982
1976—El Paso†	Texas		C-OF	37	135	22	44	9	2	3	23	.326	146	22	4	.977
1977—Salt Lake City	P. C.		C-OF	110	395	53	108	22	8	15	67	.273	497	60	11	.981
1978—Salt Lake City	P. C.		C-3-2-O	98	313	51	91	19	4	10	57	.291	218	87	9	.971
1979—Salt Lake City	P. C.		C-OF	15	51	9	13	4	1	3	13	.255	54	8	0	1.000
1979—California	Amer.		C	38	107	13	24	3	1	3	14	.224	136	16	3	.981
1980—California‡	Amer.		C	84	218	18	41	4	1	2	14	.188	330	29	5	.986
Major League Totals				122	325	31	65	7	2	5	28	.200	466	45	8	.985

Selected by California Angels' organization in 1st round (ninth player selected) of free-agent draft, January 12, 1972.

†On disabled list, May 22 to August 19, 1976.

‡On supplemental disabled list, August 5 to August 20, 1980.

JAMES EDWARD DORSEY
(Jim)

Born August 2, 1955, at Chicago, Ill.
Height, 6.02. Weight, 190.
Throws and bats righthanded.
Attended Los Angeles Valley Junior College, Van Nuys, Calif.

Pitched 4-0, seven-inning no-hit victory against Clinton, May 20, 1975.

Year	Club	League	G.	IP.	W.	L.	Pct.	H.	R.	ER.	SO.	BB.	ERA.
1975—Quad Cities		Midwest	25	161	15	3	.833	114	49	38	161	56	2.12
1976—El Paso		Texas	26	164	9	9	.500	188	104	82	101	77	4.50
1977—El Paso		Texas	25	144	10	9	.526	167	*105	80	73	70	5.00
1978—El Paso		Texas	9	59	5	2	.714	62	42	38	56	33	5.80
1978—Salt Lake City		P. Coast	19	132	1	7	.611	118	57	49	83	77	3.34
1979—Salt Lake City		P. Coast	28	168	10	12	.455	176	113	*103	92	100	5.52
1980—Salt Lake City		P. Coast	27	173	14	7	.667	177	89	77	109	93	4.01
1980—California†		American	4	16	1	2	.333	25	16	16	8	8	9.00
Major League Total			4	16	1	2	.333	25	16	16	8	8	9.00

Selected by California Angels' organization in 21st round of free-agent draft, June 5, 1973.

Selected by Los Angeles Dodgers' organization in secondary phase of free-agent draft, January 9, 1974.

Selected by California Angels' organization in 2nd round of free-agent draft, January 9, 1975.

†Traded with Pitcher Frank Tanana and Outfielder Joe Rudi to Boston Red Sox for Outfielder Fred Lynn and Pitcher Steve Renko, January 23, 1981.

RICHARD ELLIOTT DOTSON

Born January 10, 1959, at Cincinnati, O.
Height, 6.00. Weight, 185.
Throws and bats righthanded.

Year	Club	League	G.	IP.	W.	L.	Pct.	H.	R.	ER.	SO.	BB.	ERA.
1977–Idaho Falls†	Pioneer	13	66	4	5	.444	65	61	42	83	63	5.73
1978–Knoxville	Southern	26	145	11	10	.524	128	85	69	152	*105	4.28
1979–Knoxville	Southern	25	163	9	9	.500	133	81	67	133	88	3.70
1979–Chicago	American	5	24	2	0	1.000	28	13	10	13	6	3.75
1980–Chicago	American	33	198	12	10	.545	195	105	94	109	87	4.27
Major League Totals		33	222	14	10	.583	223	118	104	122	93	4.22

Selected by California Angels' organization in 1st round (seventh player selected) of free-agent draft, June 7, 1977.

†Traded with Outfielders Bobby Bonds and Thad Bosley to Chicago White Sox for Catcher Brian Downing and Pitchers Chris Knapp and Dave Frost, December 6, 1977.

BRIAN JAY DOWNING

Born October 9, 1950, at Los Angeles, Calif.
Height, 5.10. Weight, 200.
Throws and bats righthanded.
Hobby–Music.
Attended Cypress Junior College, Cypress, Calif.

Year	Club	League	Pos.	G.	AB.	R.	H.	2B.	3B.	HR.	RBI.	B.A.	PO.	A.	E.	F.A.
1970–Sarasota W. S.	Gulf C.	C-OF	34	96	16	21	1	1	0	14	.219	167	11	1	.994
1971–Appleton	Midw.	3-C-O	99	333	51	82	6	3	3	22	.246	353	98	13	.972
1972–Knoxville	South.	O-3-C	135	442	75	123	24	7	15	67	.278	250	123	21	.947
1973–Iowa	A. A.	3-O-C	68	228	34	56	6	1	7	27	.246	84	90	8	.956
1973–Chicago†	Amer.	O-C-3	34	73	5	13	1	0	2	4	.178	72	17	5	.947
1974–Chicago	Amer.	C-OF	108	293	41	66	12	1	10	39	.225	337	30	2	.995
1975–Chicago	Amer.	C	138	420	58	101	12	1	7	41	.240	730	84	8	.990
1976–Chicago‡	Amer.	C	104	317	38	81	14	0	3	30	.256	450	38	6	.988
1977–Chicago§	Amer.	C-OF	69	169	28	48	4	2	4	25	.284	325	28	6	.983
1978–California	Amer.	C	133	412	42	105	15	0	7	46	.255	681	82	5	.993
1979–California	Amer.	C	148	509	87	166	27	3	12	75	.326	669	35	11	.985
1980–California x	Amer.	C	30	93	5	27	6	0	2	25	.290	69	6	0	1.000
Major League Totals			764	2286	304	607	91	7	47	285	.266	3333	338	43	.988

Signed as free-agent by Chicago White Sox' organization, August 19, 1969.

†On disabled list, June 1 to July 9, 1973.

‡On disabled list, July 30 to August 15, 1976.

§Traded with Pitchers Chris Knapp and Dave Frost to California Angels for Outfielders Bobby Bonds and Thad Bosley and Pitcher Dick Dotson, December 5, 1977.

xOn supplemental disabled list, April 20, 1980; transferred to emergency disabled list, May 14 to September 1, 1980.

CHAMPIONSHIP SERIES RECORD

Year	Club	League	Pos.	G.	AB.	R.	H.	2B.	3B.	HR.	RBI.	B.A.	PO.	A.	E.	F.A.
1979–California	Amer.	C	4	15	1	3	0	0	0	1	.200	27	0	0	1.000

ALL-STAR GAME RECORD

Year	League	Pos.	AB.	R.	H.	2B.	3B.	HR.	RBI.	B.A.	PO.	A.	E.	F.A.
1979–American		C	1	0	1	0	0	0	0	1.000	3	0	0	1.000

BRIAN REED DOYLE

Born January 26, 1954, at Glasgow, Ky.
Height, 5.10. Weight, 170.
Throws right and bats lefthanded.
Brother of Denny Doyle, former infielder with Philadelphia Phillies, California Angels and Boston Red Sox and Blake Doyle, infielder in Cincinnati Reds' organization.

Led New York-Pennsylvania League shortstops in double plays with 40 in 1972.

Year	Club	League	Pos.	G.	AB.	R.	H.	2B.	3B.	HR.	RBI.	B.A.	PO.	A.	E.	F.A.
1972–Geneva	NYP	SS-2B	62	215	37	55	5	3	4	20	.256	101	162	24	.916
1973–Gastonia	W. Car.	2-3B-SS	95	329	52	74	6	2	1	28	.225	214	219	21	.954
1974–Pittsfield	East.	3B-2B	65	115	11	29	4	0	0	8	.252	34	46	5	.941
1975–Lynchburg	Carol.	*2B-SS	107	369	41	88	4	3	1	37	.238	264	260	14	*.974
1976–San Antonio	Texas	3B-SS	25	86	15	30	2	1	1	7	.349	28	53	13	.862
1976–Sacramento†	P. C.	3B-2B	96	393	65	114	15	4	3	32	.290	77	185	18	.936
1977–Syracuse‡	Int.	2B-3B	107	358	35	88	19	2	3	37	.246	202	299	22	.958
1978–Tacoma	P. C.	2B-3-S	35	133	22	38	7	2	2	16	.286	49	84	2	.985
1978–New York	Amer.	2B-S-3	39	52	6	10	0	0	0	2	.192	39	65	1	.990
1979–Columbus	Int.	S-2-3-1-O	39	126	15	32	6	2	2	9	.254	51	104	5	.969
1979–New York	Amer.	2B-3B	20	32	2	4	2	0	0	5	.125	12	27	2	.951
1980–Columbus§	Int.	SS-2B	47	160	11	36	10	1	0	5	.225	71	131	16	.927
1980–New York x	Amer.	2-S-3	34	75	8	13	1	0	1	5	.173	40	77	5	.959
Major League Totals			93	159	16	27	3	0	1	10	.170	91	169	8	.970

Selected by Texas Rangers' organization in 4th round of free-agent draft, June 6, 1972.

†Traded with Infielder Greg Pryor and cash from Texas Rangers' organization to New York Yankees' organization for Infielder Sandy Alomar, February 17, 1977.

‡On disabled list, May 26 to June 11, 1977.

§On disabled list, July 14 to July 24, 1980.

xDrafted by Oakland A's, December 8, 1980.

CHAMPIONSHIP SERIES RECORD

Year Club	League	Pos.	G.	AB.	R.	H.	2B.	3B.	HR.	RBI.	B.A.	PO.	A.	E.	F.A.
1978—New York .... Amer.		2B	3	7	0	2	0	0	0	1	.286	3	6	0	1.000

WORLD SERIES RECORD

Year Club	League	Pos.	G.	AB.	R.	H.	2B.	3B.	HR.	RBI.	B.A.	PO.	A.	E.	F.A.
1978—New York .... Amer.		2B	6	16	4	7	1	0	0	2	.438	17	7	0	1.000

RICHARD ANTHONY DRAGO
(Dick)

Born June 25, 1945, at Toledo, O.
Height, 6.01. Weight, 200.
Throws and bats righthanded.
Hobbies—Golf, bowling, fishing.
Attended University of Detroit, Detroit, Mich., and University of Tampa, Tampa, Fla.

Tied major league record for most strikeouts, three consecutive games (10), September 5, 10 and 17, 1970.
Pitched seven-inning, 5-0 no-hit victory against Greensboro, May 15, 1966.
Major League saves: 1969 (1), 1970 (0), 1971 (0), 1972 (0), 1973 (0), 1974 (3), 1975 (15), 1976 (6), 1977 (5), 1978 (7), 1979 (13), 1980 (3). Total—53.
Led Carolina League in shutouts with 7 in 1966 and tied for Southern League lead in shutouts with 4 in 1967.
Tied for Southern League lead in complete games by pitchers with 12 in 1967.

Year Club	League	G.	IP.	W.	L.	Pct.	H.	R.	ER.	SO.	BB.	ERA.
1965—Daytona Beach .... Florida St.		14	80	4	7	.364	84	42	29	64	28	3.26
1965—Rocky Mount .... Carolina		13	62	1	7	.125	66	36	24	41	30	3.48
1966—Rocky Mount .... Carolina		29	186	15	9	.625	144	45	37	151	49	1.79
1967—Montgomery .... Southern		28	179	∗15	10	.600	171	65	48	∗134	54	2.41
1967—Toledo .... Int'national		1	3	0	0	.000	2	1	1	1	0	3.00
1968—Toledo† .... Int'national		27	182	15	8	.652	163	77	68	146	43	3.36
1969—Kansas City .... American		41	201	11	13	.458	190	95	84	108	65	3.76
1970—Kansas City .... American		35	240	9	15	.375	239	110	100	127	72	3.75
1971—Kansas City .... American		35	241	17	11	.607	251	84	80	109	46	2.99
1972—Kansas City .... American		34	239	12	17	.414	230	88	80	135	51	3.01
1973—Kansas City‡ .... American		37	213	12	14	.462	252	116	100	98	76	4.23
1974—Boston .... American		33	176	7	10	.412	165	71	68	90	56	3.48
1975—Boston§ .... American		40	73	2	2	.500	69	31	31	43	31	3.82
1976—California .... American		43	79	7	8	.467	80	42	39	43	31	4.44
1977—California x-Baltimore y .... American		49	61	6	4	.600	71	27	23	35	18	3.39
1978—Boston .... American		37	77	4	4	.500	71	30	26	42	32	3.04
1979—Boston .... American		53	89	10	6	.625	85	33	30	67	21	3.03
1980—Boston .... American		43	133	7	7	.500	127	67	61	63	44	4.13
Major League Totals		480	1822	104	111	.484	1830	794	722	960	543	3.57

Signed as free agent by Detroit Tigers' organization, September 16, 1964.

†Recalled by Detroit Tigers; selected by Kansas City Royals from Detroit in expansion draft, October 15, 1968.

‡Traded to Boston Red Sox for Pitcher Marty Pattin, October 24, 1973.

§Traded to California Angels for Outfielders John Balaz and Dick Sharon and Shortstop Dave Machemer, March 3, 1976.

xTraded to Baltimore Orioles for Pitcher Dyar Miller, June 13, 1977.

yGranted free agency, October 25, 1977; signed as free agent by Boston Red Sox, December 27, 1977.

CHAMPIONSHIP SERIES RECORD

Tied American League Championship Series record for most saves, total Series (2).

Year Club	League	G.	IP.	W.	L.	Pct.	H.	R.	ER.	SO.	BB.	ERA.
1975—Boston .... American		2	4⅔	0	0	.000	2	0	0	2	1	0.00

WORLD SERIES RECORD

Year Club	League	G.	IP.	W.	L.	Pct.	H.	R.	ER.	SO.	BB.	ERA.
1975—Boston .... American		2	4	0	1	.000	3	1	1	1	1	2.25

ROBERT ALAN DRESSLER
(Rob)

Born February 2, 1954, at Portland, Ore.
Height, 6.03. Weight, 195.
Throws and bats righthanded.
Hobbies—Camping and listening to classical music.
Attended Portland State University, Portland, Ore.

Led Texas League pitchers in games started with 30 in 1974.
Tied for Pacific Coast League lead in shutouts with 3 in 1975.

Year Club	League	G.	IP.	W.	L.	Pct.	H.	R.	ER.	SO.	BB.	ERA.
1972—Great Falls	Pioneer	14	92	5	7	.417	88	44	31	74	38	3.03
1973—Decatur	Midwest	25	182	11	10	.524	170	72	57	133	54	2.82
1974—Amarillo	Texas	30	*191	11	12	.478	*214	97	81	125	62	3.82
1975—Lafayette	Texas	6	46	5	1	.833	32	11	10	5	9	1.96
1975—Phoenix	P. Coast	25	169	8	14	.364	174	81	65	91	58	3.46
1975—San Francisco	National	3	16	1	0	1.000	17	3	2	6	4	1.13
1976—Phoenix	P. Coast	6	48	5	1	.833	46	7	6	18	11	1.13
1976—San Francisco	National	25	108	3	10	.231	125	68	53	33	35	4.42
1977—Phoenix	P. Coast	31	199	10	10	.500	231	128	117	75	85	5.29
1978—Phoenix†	P.Coast	20	140	9	8	.529	132	66	55	80	58	3.54
1978—Springfield	Am.Assoc.	7	41	1	4	.200	48	30	27	15	20	5.93
1978—St. Louis‡	National	3	13	0	1	.000	12	3	3	4	4	2.08
1979—Spokane	P. Coast	10	74	3	4	.429	76	36	31	39	24	3.77
1979—Seattle	American	21	104	3	2	.600	134	61	57	36	22	4.93
1980—Seattle	American	30	149	4	10	.286	161	75	66	50	33	3.99
National League Totals		31	137	4	11	.267	154	74	58	43	43	3.81
American League Totals		51	253	7	12	.368	295	136	123	86	55	4.38
Major League Totals		82	390	11	23	.324	449	210	181	129	98	4.18

Selected by San Francisco Giants' organization in 1st round (19th player selected) of free-agent draft, June 6, 1972.

†Traded by San Francisco Giants' organization to St. Louis Cardinals' organization, July 24, 1978; completing trade in which Giants received Catcher John Tamargo, July 18, 1978.

‡Loaned to Seattle Mariners' organization, April 4, 1979; sold to Seattle, June 7, 1979.

DANIEL DRIESSEN
(Dan)

Born July 29, 1951, at Hilton Head, S. C.
Height, 5.11. Weight, 190.
Throws right and bats lefthanded.

Major league stolen bases: 1973 (8), 1974 (10), 1975 (10), 1976 (14), 1977 (31), 1978 (28), 1979 (11), 1980 (19). Total—131.

Tied for National League lead in bases on balls with 93 in 1980.

Year Club	League	Pos.	G.	AB.	R.	H.	2B.	3B.	HR.	RBI.	B.A.	PO.	A.	E.	F.A.
1970—Tampa	Fla. St.	1B	93	242	28	54	2	1	0	20	.223	473	37	5	.990
1971—Tampa	Fla. St.	1B	136	468	72	153	27	9	4	62	.327	1064	86	15	.987
1972—Three Rivers	East.	*1B-3B	136	481	62	155	37	4	4	65	.322	805	138	9	*.991
1973—Indianapolis	A. A.	3B-1B	47	181	42	74	14	4	6	46	.409	50	97	6	.961
1973—Cincinnati	Nat.	3-1-O	102	366	49	110	15	2	4	47	.301	160	157	12	.964
1974—Cincinnati	Nat.	3-1-O	150	470	63	132	23	6	7	56	.281	186	206	26	.938
1975—Cincinnati†	Nat.	1B-OF	88	210	38	59	8	1	7	38	.281	309	20	5	.985
1976—Cincinnati	Nat.	1B-OF	98	219	32	54	11	1	7	44	.247	314	23	2	.994
1977—Cincinnati	Nat.	1B	151	536	75	161	31	4	17	91	.300	1182	75	7	.994
1978—Cincinnati	Nat.	1B	153	524	68	131	23	3	16	70	.250	1264	93	6	*.996
1979—Cincinnati	Nat.	1B	150	515	72	129	24	3	18	75	.250	1289	79	9	.993
1980—Cincinnati	Nat.	1B	154	524	81	139	36	1	14	74	.265	1349	85	7	.995
Major League Totals			946	3364	478	915	171	21	90	495	.272	6056	738	74	.989

Signed as free agent by Cincinnati Reds' organization, August 28, 1969.

†On disabled list, March 23 to April 15, 1975.

CHAMPIONSHIP SERIES RECORD

Year Club	League	Pos.	G.	AB.	R.	H.	2B.	3B.	HR.	RBI.	B.A.	PO.	A.	E.	F.A.
1973—Cincinnati	Nat.	3B-PR	4	12	0	2	1	0	0	1	.167	3	2	1	.833
1976—Cincinnati	Nat.	PH	1	1	0	0	0	0	0	0	.000	0	0	0	.000
1979—Cincinnati	Nat.	1B	3	12	1	1	0	0	0	0	.083	32	0	0	1.000
Championship Series Totals			8	25	1	3	1	0	0	1	.120	35	2	1	.974

WORLD SERIES RECORD

Year Club	League	Pos.	G.	AB.	R.	H.	2B.	3B.	HR.	RBI.	B.A.	PO.	A.	E.	F.A.
1975—Cincinnati	Nat.	PH	2	2	0	0	0	0	0	0	.000	0	0	0	.000
1976—Cincinnati	Nat.	DH	4	14	4	5	2	0	1	1	.357	0	0	0	.000
World Series Totals			6	16	4	5	2	0	1	1	.312	0	0	0	.000

HAL JOSEPH DUES

Born September 22, 1954, at LaMarque, Texas.
Height, 6.03. Weight, 185.
Throws and bats righthanded.
Hobbies—Hunting and fishing.
Attended Mary Hardin-Baylor College, Belton, Tex.

Pitched six-inning, 2-0 no-hit victory against Pompano Beach, August 1, 1976.

Year Club	League	G.	IP.	W.	L.	Pct.	H.	R.	ER.	SO.	BB.	ERA.
1974—Kinston	Carolina	18	110	4	7	.364	122	54	40	76	41	3.27
1975—Quebec City	Eastern	3	14	0	2	.000	23	19	12	2	10	7.71
1975—West Palm Beach	Florida St.	18	118	7	7	.500	99	49	39	65	61	2.97

Year Club	League	G.	IP.	W.	L.	Pct.	H.	R.	ER.	SO.	BB.	ERA.
1976—West Palm Beach ....Florida St.		24	162	12	10	.545	120	57	37	114	69	2.06
1977—Quebec City† ....Eastern		16	96	6	6	.500	100	46	40	56	35	3.75
1977—Montreal ....National		6	23	1	1	.500	26	14	11	9	9	4.30
1978—Montreal ....National		25	99	5	6	.455	85	29	26	36	42	2.36
1979—Memphis ....Southern		7	44	2	2	.500	51	24	20	12	19	4.09
1979—Denver‡ ....Am. Assoc.		5	20	1	3	.250	31	21	21	3	19	9.45
1980—Denver ....Am. Assoc.		16	98	7	4	.636	87	38	37	39	46	3.40
1980—Montreal ....National		6	12	0	1	.000	17	9	9	2	4	6.75
Major League Totals		37	134	6	8	.429	128	52	46	47	55	3.09

Signed as free agent by Montreal Expos' organization, May 20, 1974.
†On disabled list, April 13 to May 5 and May 6 to June 18, 1977.
‡On disabled list, June 14 to August 31, 1979.

DANIEL JAMES DURAN
(Dan)

Born March 16, 1954, at Palo Alto, Calif.
Height, 5.11. Weight, 190.
Throws and bats lefthanded.
Attended Foothill Junior College, Los Altos Hills, Calif.
Led Western Carolinas League first basemen in double plays with 88 in 1974.

Year Club	League	Pos.	G.	AB.	R.	H.	2B.	3B.	HR.	RBI.	B.A.	PO.	A.	E.	F.A.
1973—Sara. Rangers ...Gulf C.		1B	50	182	36	55	7	2	2	29	.302	361	16	5	.987
1974—Gastonia ....W. Car.		1B	133	480	79	129	22	5	22	*99	.269	*1146	63	16	.987
1975—Lynchburg ....Carol.		1B	68	258	36	63	9	2	4	41	.244	552	42	4	.993
1975—Pittsfield ....East.		1B	53	178	17	39	6	0	3	17	.219	457	33	3	.994
1976—San Antonio† .....Texas		1B	112	377	45	96	13	1	10	50	.225	907	68	10	.990
1977—Tulsa ....Texas		*1B-OF	115	368	64	101	19	3	16	70	.274	953	74	6	*.994
1978—Tulsa ....Texas		1B	60	200	38	66	13	2	7	40	.330	509	40	8	.986
1978—Tucson ....P. C.		1B-OF	73	257	54	84	15	2	10	55	.327	643	42	4	.994
1979—Tucson ....P. C.		1B-OF	113	388	65	106	26	3	7	59	.273	830	45	7	.992
1980—Charleston ....Int.		1B-OF	116	399	52	110	20	2	13	71	.276	759	79	8	.991

Selected by Texas Rangers' organization in 30th round of free-agent draft, June 5, 1973.
†On disabled list, June 20 to July 10, 1976.

LEON DURHAM

Born July 31, 1957, at Cincinnati, O.
Height, 6.01. Weight, 185.
Throws and bats lefthanded.
Led Texas League first basemen in double plays with 96 in 1978.

Year Club	League	Pos.	G.	AB.	R.	H.	2B.	3B.	HR.	RBI.	B.A.	PO.	A.	E.	F.A.
1976—Sara. Cardinals .Gulf C.		1B-OF	44	156	25	35	3	5	2	18	.224	296	5	12	.962
1977—Gastonia ....W. Car.		1B	63	239	45	88	18	3	4	44	.368	492	28	8	.985
1977—St. Petersburg...Fla. St.		1B	63	209	26	60	3	6	0	25	.287	533	27	9	.984
1978—Arkansas† ....Texas		1B	102	367	72	116	21	5	12	70	.316	931	42	8	*.992
1979—Springfield ....A. A.		OF-1B	127	449	84	139	33	4	23	88	.310	304	19	6	.982
1980—Springfield ....A. A.		OF-1B	32	128	20	33	5	5	5	23	.258	96	8	4	.963
1980—St. Louis‡ ....Nat.		OF-1B	96	303	42	82	15	4	8	42	.271	180	22	3	.985
Major League Totals			96	303	42	82	15	4	8	42	.271	180	22	3	.985

Selected by St. Louis Cardinals' organization in 1st round (15th player selected) of free-agent draft, June 8, 1976.
†On disabled list, April 23 to May 25, 1978.
‡Traded with Third Baseman Ken Reitz and a player to be named later to Chicago Cubs for Pitcher Bruce Sutter, December 9, 1980; Third Baseman Ty Waller traded to Cubs completing deal, December 22, 1980.

JAMES EDWARD DWYER
(Jimmy)

Born January 3, 1950, at Evergreen Park, Ill.
Height, 5.10. Weight, 175.
Throws and bats lefthanded.
Hobbies—Golf and listening to music.
Attended Southern Illinois University, Carbondale, Ill.; received
Bachelor of Arts degree in Accounting.
Nephew of Don Dwyer, former minor leaguer in New York Giants' organization.

Year Club	League	Pos.	G.	AB.	R.	H.	2B.	3B.	HR.	RBI.	B.A.	PO.	A.	E.	F.A.
1971—Cedar Rapids.....Midw.		OF	58	201	30	63	6	6	2	15	.313	73	3	3	.962
1972—Modesto ....Calif.		OF	92	354	87	115	15	*13	9	45	.325	149	8	4	.975
1972—Arkansas...........Texas		OF	44	162	16	41	1	0	2	14	.253	101	6	2	.982
1973—Tulsa ................A.A.		OF	87	349	63	135	22	8	1	40	*.387	127	8	5	.964
1973—St. Louis ....Nat.		OF	28	57	7	11	1	1	0	0	.193	32	0	0	1.000

Year Club	League	Pos.	G.	AB.	R.	H.	2B.	3B.	HR.	RBI.	B.A.	PO.	A.	E.	F.A.
1974—Tulsa ................A.A.	OF-1B	36	119	20	40	7	2	1	15	.336	120	13	3	.978
1974—St. Louis ....Nat.	OF-1B	74	86	13	24	1	0	2	11	.279	31	3	0	1.000
1975—Tulsa ................A.A.	OF	33	109	17	44	8	2	1	17	.404	49	2	2	.962
1975—St.L.†-Mont. ......Nat.	OF	81	206	26	56	8	1	3	21	.272	104	8	4	.966
1976—Mont.‡-N.Y. §....Nat.	OF-PH	61	105	9	19	3	1	0	5	.181	35	0	1	.972
1976—Tidewater ....Int.	OF	8	26	0	5	1	0	0	1	.192	14	0	1	.933
1977—Wichita x..........A.A.	OF	130	464	*113	*154	*38	12	18	70	*.332	245	6	8	.969
1977—St. Louis ....Nat.	OF	13	31	3	7	1	0	0	2	.226	16	0	0	1.000
1978—St.L. y-S.F. z.....Nat.	OF-1B	107	238	30	53	12	2	6	26	.223	216	15	3	.987
1979—Boston ....Amer.	1B-OF	76	113	19	30	7	0	2	14	.265	167	16	4	.979
1980—Boston a ....Amer.	OF-1B	93	260	41	74	11	1	9	38	.285	143	15	4	.975
National League Totals....................		364	723	88	170	26	5	11	65	.235	434	26	8	.983
American League Totals.................		169	373	60	104	18	1	11	52	.279	310	31	8	.977
Major League Totals.......................		533	1096	148	274	44	6	22	117	.250	744	57	16	.980

Selected by St. Louis Cardinals' organization in 11th round of free-agent draft, June 8, 1971.

†Traded to Montreal Expos for Infielder Larry Lintz, July 25, 1975.

‡Traded with Outfielder Jose (Pepe) Mangual to New York Mets for Outfielder Del Unser and Infielder Wayne Garrett, July 21, 1976.

§In three-club deal, Chicago Cubs traded Outfielder-First Baseman Pete LaCock to Kansas City Royals, the New York Mets sent Outfielder Jim Dwyer from Tidewater to Wichita (Cubs' affiliate), and Mets received a player to be named later, December 8, 1976; Royals sent Outfielder Sheldon Mallory to Tidewater to complete deal, December 13, 1976.

xReleased by Chicago Cubs, September 7, 1977. Signed by St. Louis Cardinals, September 13, 1977.

yTraded to San Francisco Giants, June 15, 1978; completing deal in which Cardinals acquired Pitcher Frank Riccelli, October 25, 1977.

zTraded to Boston Red Sox for a player to be named later, March 15, 1979; deal settled with cash, January 15, 1980.

aGranted free agency, October 22, 1980; signed by Baltimore Orioles, December 23, 1980.

JEROME DYBZINSKI
(Jerry)

Born July 7, 1955, at Cleveland, O.
Height, 6.02. Weight, 180.
Throws and bats righthanded.
Attended Cleveland State University, Cleveland, O.

Led New York-Pennsylvania League shortstops in double plays with 51 in 1977.

Year Club	League	Pos.	G.	AB.	R.	H.	2B.	3B.	HR.	RBI.	B.A.	PO.	A.	E.	F.A.
1977—Batavia.............NYP	SS	58	169	39	37	7	0	0	16	.219	*117	*198	19	*.943
1978—Waterloo...........Midw.	SS	134	508	96	144	15	2	12	63	.283	*191	412	*47	.928
1979—Tacoma ....P. C.	SS	132	469	58	119	16	3	1	25	.254	*269	409	30	.958
1980—Cleveland..........Amer.	S-2-3	114	248	32	57	11	1	1	23	.230	140	263	13	.969
Major League Totals.......................		114	248	32	57	11	1	1	23	.230	140	263	13	.969

Selected by Cleveland Indians' organization in 15th round of free-agent draft, June 7, 1977.

DON ROBERT DYER
(Duffy)

Born August 15, 1945, at Dayton, O.
Height, 6.00. Weight, 200.
Throws and bats righthanded.
Hobbies—Golf and billiards.
Attended Arizona State University, Tempe, Ariz.

Led National League catchers in double plays with 12 in 1972.
Led Eastern League catchers in double plays with 11 in 1967.

Year Club	League	Pos.	G.	AB.	R.	H.	2B.	3B.	HR.	RBI.	B.A.	PO.	A.	E.	F.A.
1966—Williamsport .....East.	C	22	52	3	9	2	0	0	1	.173	86	12	0	1.000
1966—Greenville ....W. Car.	C	19	57	7	14	0	1	0	2	.246	169	5	0	1.000
1967—Williamsport .....East.	C-OF	106	346	26	67	12	3	1	28	.194	689	73	10	.987
1968—Jacksonville ......Int.	●C-3B	111	339	39	78	10	4	16	43	.230	654	65	B11	.985
1968—New York.........Nat.	C	1	3	0	1	0	0	0	0	.333	8	0	0	1.000
1969—Tidewater ....Int.	C	35	112	22	35	6	1	5	26	.313	155	15	0	1.000
1969—New York.........Nat.	C	29	74	5	19	3	1	3	12	.257	105	10	1	.991
1970—New York.........Nat.	C	59	148	8	31	1	0	2	12	.209	294	20	3	.991
1971—New York.........Nat.	C	59	169	13	39	7	1	2	18	.231	336	21	3	.992
1972—New York.........Nat.	C-OF	94	325	33	75	17	3	8	36	.231	690	61	6	.992
1973—New York.........Nat.	C	70	189	9	35	6	1	1	9	.185	308	26	2	.994
1974—New York†.......Nat.	C	63	142	14	30	1	1	0	10	.211	196	19	4	.982
1975—Pittsburgh........Nat.	C	48	132	8	30	5	2	3	16	.227	187	14	2	.990
1976—Pittsburgh........Nat.	C	69	184	12	41	8	0	3	9	.223	279	37	2	.994
1977—Pittsburgh........Nat.	C	94	270	27	65	11	1	3	19	.241	502	41	2	*.996
1978—Pittsburgh ‡§ ....Nat.	C	58	175	7	37	8	1	0	13	.211	326	22	3	.991
1979—Montreal x ....Nat.	C	28	74	4	18	6	0	1	8	.243	141	10	1	.993
1980—Detroit.............Amer.	C	48	108	11	20	1	0	4	11	.185	129	10	2	.986
National League Totals....................		672	1885	140	421	73	11	26	162	.223	3372	281	29	.992
American League Totals.................		48	108	11	20	1	0	4	11	.185	129	10	2	.986
Major League Totals.......................		720	1993	151	441	74	11	30	173	.221	3501	291	31	.992

Selected by New York Mets' organization in 7th round of free-agent draft, July 2, 1966.
†Traded to Pittsburgh Pirates for Outfielder Gene Clines, October 21, 1974.
‡On supplemental disabled list, March 29 to April 22, 1978.
§Granted free agency, November 2, 1978; signed by Montreal Expos, November 28, 1978.
xTraded to Detroit Tigers for Infielder Jerry Manuel, March 14, 1980.

CHAMPIONSHIP SERIES RECORD

Year Club	League	Pos.	G.	AB.	R.	H.	2B.	3B.	HR.	RBI.	B.A.	PO.	A.	E.	F.A.
1975—Pittsburgh.........Nat.		PH	1	0	0	0	0	0	0	1	.000	0	0	0	.000

WORLD SERIES RECORD

Year Club	League	Pos.	G.	AB.	R.	H.	2B.	3B.	HR.	RBI.	B.A.	PO.	A.	E.	F.A.
1969—New York..........Nat.		PH	1	1	0	0	0	0	0	0	.000	0	0	0	.000

MICHAEL ANTHONY EASLER
(Mike)

Born November 29, 1950, at Cleveland, O.
Height, 6.01. Weight, 196.
Throws right and bats lefthanded.
Hobbies—Table tennis and bowling.
Attended Cleveland State University, Cleveland, O.
Brother-in-law of Cliff Johnson, catcher-first baseman with Oakland A's.

Year Club	League	Pos.	G.	AB.	R.	H.	2B.	3B.	HR.	RBI.	B.A.	PO.	A.	E.	F.A.
1969—Covington..........Appla.	OF-3B	33	113	21	36	7	2	0	11	.319	25	10	4	.897
1970—Cocoa† ....Fla. St.	OF	96	314	30	79	11	4	1	24	.252	142	5	7	.955
1971—Cocoa‡ ....Fla. St.	OF	109	392	61	115	15	5	11	68	.293	153	14	8	.954
1972—Columbus ....South.	OF	106	372	52	100	11	4	13	46	.269	149	7	8	.951
1973—Columbus ....South.	OF	48	168	27	52	11	1	6	32	.310	81	2	1	.988
1973—Denver.............A. A.	OF	48	176	24	50	11	2	7	26	.284	74	2	6	.927
1973—Houston.............Nat.	OF	6	7	1	0	0	0	0	0	.000	1	0	1	.500
1974—Denver.............A. A.	OF	100	367	75	104	18	8	19	63	.283	172	7	5	.973
1974—Houston.............Nat.	PH	15	15	0	1	0	0	0	0	.067	0	0	0	.000
1975—Iowa§-Tulsa.......A. A.	OF	113	415	69	130	31	6	15	69	.313	161	6	8	.954
1975—Houston x..........Nat.	PH	5	5	0	0	0	0	0	0	.000	0	0	0	.000
1976—Tulsa y.............A. A.	OF	118	378	75	133	31	2	26	77	*.352	172	*16	8	.959
1976—California z ....Amer.	DH	21	54	6	13	1	1	0	4	.241	0	0	0	.000
1977—Columbus ....Int.	OF	127	451	83	136	29	5	18	75	.302	171	7	3	.983
1977—Pittsburgh.........Nat.	OF	10	18	3	8	2	0	1	5	.444	7	0	0	1.000
1978—Columbus ab.......Int.	OF-1B	126	448	84	148	26	3	18	84	*.330	378	31	5	.988
1979—Pittsburgh ....Nat.	OF	55	54	8	15	1	1	2	11	.278	0	0	0	.000
1980—Pittsburgh ....Nat.	OF	132	393	66	133	27	3	21	74	.338	201	6	3	.986
National League Totals...................		223	492	78	157	30	4	24	90	.319	209	6	4	.982
American League Totals.................		21	54	6	13	1	1	0	4	.241	0	0	0	.000
Major League Totals		244	546	84	170	31	5	24	94	.311	209	6	4	.982

Selected by Houston Astros' organization in 6th round of free-agent draft, June 5, 1969.
†On temporary inactive list, May 13 to May 25, 1970.
‡On temporary inactive list, May 25 to June 14, 1971.
§Loaned by Houston Astros' organization to St. Louis Cardinals' organization, June 25, 1975.
xTraded to St. Louis Cardinals for Pitcher Mike Barlow, September 30, 1975.
yTraded to California Angels for a player to be named later, September 3, 1976 (Infielder Ron Farkas sent to St. Louis to complete deal, September 7, 1976).
zTraded to Pittsburgh Pirates for Pitcher Randy Sealy, April 4, 1977.
aSold to Boston Red Sox, October 27, 1978.
bTraded to Pittsburgh Pirates for Outfielder George Hill and Pitcher Martin Rivas, March 15, 1979.

CHAMPIONSHIP SERIES RECORD

Year Club	League	Pos.	G.	AB.	R.	H.	2B.	3B.	HR.	RBI.	B.A.	PO.	A.	E.	F.A.
1979—Pittsburgh ....Nat.		PH	1	1	0	0	0	0	0	0	.000	0	0	0	.000

WORLD SERIES RECORD

Year Club	League	Pos.	G.	AB.	R.	H.	2B.	3B.	HR.	RBI.	B.A.	PO.	A.	E.	F.A.
1979—Pittsburgh ....Nat.		PH	2	1	0	0	0	0	0	0	.000	0	0	0	.000

JAMES MORRIS EASTERLY
(Jamie)

Born February 17, 1953, at Houston, Tex.
Height, 5.10. Weight, 180.
Throws left and bats left and righthanded.
Hobbies—Golf and watching television.
Attended Sam Houston State University, Huntsville, Tex.

Pitched seven-inning, 10-0 perfect game victory against Iowa, July 14, 1979.

Year Club	League	G.	IP.	W.	L.	Pct.	H.	R.	ER.	SO.	BB.	ERA.
1971—Greenwood..........................W. Carol.	8	29	3	0	1.000	14	3	2	33	9	0.62
1972—Greenwood..........................W. Carol.	7	24	1	0	1.000	11	0	0	29	13	0.00

Year—Club	League	G.	IP.	W.	L.	Pct.	H.	R.	ER.	SO.	BB.	ERA.
1972—Savannah†	Southern	2	4	0	1	.000	7	2	2	4	4	4.50
1973—Savannah‡	Southern	15	67	5	3	.625	62	40	28	53	41	3.76
1974—Richmond	Int'national	26	138	9	6	.600	115	48	39	84	75	2.54
1974—Atlanta	National	3	3	0	0	.000	6	7	5	0	4	15.00
1975—Richmond	Int'national	2	10	1	1	.500	11	3	2	4	6	1.80
1975—Atlanta	National	21	69	2	9	.182	73	47	38	34	42	4.96
1976—Richmond	Int'national	33	137	7	6	.583	133	56	45	91	88	2.96
1976—Atlanta	National	4	22	1	1	.500	23	12	12	11	13	4.91
1977—Atlanta§	National	22	59	2	4	.333	72	46	40	37	30	6.10
1978—Atlanta	National	37	78	3	6	.333	91	52	49	42	45	5.67
1979—Richmond	Int'national	10	13	0	0	.000	5	0	0	12	7	0.00
1979—Atlanta xy	National	4	3	0	0	.000	7	6	4	3	3	12.00
1979—Denver	Am. Assoc.	20	88	5	6	.455	100	40	32	55	39	3.27
1980—Denver z	Am. Assoc.	56	134	9	8	.529	118	64	54	105	56	3.63
Major League Totals		91	234	8	20	.286	272	170	148	127	137	5.69

Selected by Atlanta Braves' organization in 2nd round of free-agent draft, June 8, 1971.

†On disabled list, April 11 to April 27, July 7 to July 28 and August 5 through remainder of season.

‡On disabled list, April 24 to May 12 and May 24 to July 9, 1973.

§On disabled list, June 6 to July 4 and July 21 to September 19, 1977.

xLoaned to Montreal Expos' organization, June 6, 1979.

yReturned, August 31, 1979; traded to Montreal Expos for cash and a player to be named later, October 17, 1979.

zSold to Milwaukee Brewers, September 22, 1980.

RAWLINS JACKSON EASTWICK, III
(Rawly)

Born October 24, 1950, at Camden, N. J.
Height, 6.03. Weight, 175.
Throws and bats righthanded.
Hobbies—Painting and drawing.

Tied major league records for most consecutive seasons and most seasons leading league in saves (2), 1975 (tied) and 1976.

Established National League record for most consecutive errorless games by pitcher, career (274).

Major League saves: 1974 (2), 1975 (22), 1976 (26), 1977 (11), 1978 (0), 1979 (6), 1980 (0). Total—67.

Tied for National League lead in saves with 22 in 1975.

Led National League in saves with 26 in 1976.

Led Eastern League in saves with 20 in 1972.

Named by THE SPORTING NEWS as National League Fireman of the Year, 1976.

Year—Club	League	G.	IP.	W.	L.	Pct.	H.	R.	ER.	SO.	BB.	ERA.
1969—Bradenton Reds	Gulf Coast	10	29	1	4	.200	41	23	16	15	10	4.97
1970—Tampa	Florida St.	37	101	2	9	.182	93	53	39	70	45	3.48
1971—Raleigh-Durham	Carolina	23	41	3	2	.600	35	19	19	41	24	4.17
1971—Three Rivers	Eastern	19	37	1	1	.500	32	22	22	30	14	5.35
1972—Three Rivers	Eastern	∗66	119	9	9	.500	86	37	31	90	37	2.34
1973—Indianapolis	Am. Assoc.	43	121	9	7	.563	116	58	52	83	34	3.87
1974—Indianapolis	Am. Assoc.	47	117	8	7	.533	115	62	52	79	39	4.00
1974—Cincinnati	National	8	18	0	0	.000	12	5	4	14	5	2.00
1975—Indianapolis	Am. Assoc.	13	20	1	0	1.000	11	8	3	14	4	1.35
1975—Cincinnati	National	58	90	5	3	.625	77	26	26	61	25	2.60
1976—Cincinnati	National	71	108	11	5	.688	93	30	25	70	27	2.08
1977—Cinc.†-St. L.‡	National	64	97	5	9	.357	114	48	42	47	29	3.90
1978—New York§	American	8	25	2	1	.667	22	9	9	13	4	3.24
1978—Philadelphia	National	22	40	2	1	.667	31	21	18	14	18	4.05
1979—Philadelphia x	National	51	83	3	6	.333	90	46	45	47	25	4.88
1980—Omaha	Am. Assoc.	17	28	2	2	.500	27	10	8	12	10	2.57
1980—Kansas City y	American	14	22	0	1	.000	37	14	13	5	8	5.32
National League Totals		274	436	26	24	.520	417	176	160	253	129	3.30
American League Totals		22	47	2	2	.500	59	23	22	18	12	4.21
Major League Totals		296	483	28	26	.519	476	199	182	271	141	3.39

Selected by Cincinnati Reds' organization in 3rd round of free-agent draft, June 5, 1969.

†Traded to St. Louis Cardinals for Pitcher Doug Capilla, June 15, 1977.

‡Granted free agency, November 2, 1977; signed by New York Yankees, December 12, 1977.

§Traded to Philadelphia Phillies for Outfielders Jay Johnstone and Bobby Brown, June 14, 1978.

xReleased, April 9, 1980; signed by Kansas City Royals, June 12, 1980.

yReleased, August 21, 1980; signed by Chicago Cubs' organization, January 15, 1981.

CHAMPIONSHIP SERIES RECORD

Year—Club	League	G.	IP.	W.	L.	Pct.	H.	R.	ER.	SO.	BB.	ERA.
1975—Cincinnati	National	2	3⅔	1	0	1.000	2	0	0	1	2	0.00
1976—Cincinnati	National	2	3	1	0	1.000	7	5	4	1	2	12.00
1978—Philadelphia	National	1	1	0	0	.000	3	1	1	1	0	9.00
Championship Series Totals		5	7⅔	2	0	1.000	12	6	5	3	4	5.87

WORLD SERIES RECORD

Tied World Series record for most games won as relief pitcher, Series (2), 1975 (seven-game Series).

Year—Club	League	G.	IP.	W.	L.	Pct.	H.	R.	ER.	SO.	BB.	ERA.
1975—Cincinnati	National	5	8	2	0	1.000	6	2	2	4	3	2.25

DENNIS LEE ECKERSLEY

Born October 3, 1954, at Oakland, Calif.
Height, 6.02. Weight, 190.
Throws and bats righthanded.
Hobby—Music.
Son-in-law of Al Jacinto, former infielder in Chicago White Sox' organization.

Tied American League record for most low-hit (no-hit and one-hit) games, season (3), 1977.
Led California League pitchers in games started with 31 and tied for lead in shutouts with 5 in 1973.
Led Texas League in hit batsmen with 10 in 1974.
Named American League Rookie Pitcher of the Year by THE SPORTING NEWS, 1975.
Received reported $32,000 bonus to sign with Cleveland Indians, 1972.
Pitched 1-0 no-hit victory against California Angels, May 30, 1977.

Year	Club	League	G.	IP.	W.	L.	Pct.	H.	R.	ER.	SO.	BB.	ERA.
1972—Reno		California	12	75	5	5	.500	87	46	40	56	33	4.80
1973—Reno		California	31	202	12	8	.600	182	97	82	218	91	3.65
1974—San Antonio		Texas	23	167	•14	3	*.842	141	66	63	•163	60	3.40
1975—Cleveland		American	34	187	13	7	.650	147	61	54	152	90	2.60
1976—Cleveland		American	36	199	13	12	.520	155	82	76	200	78	3.44
1977—Cleveland†		American	33	247	14	13	.519	214	100	97	191	54	3.53
1978—Boston		American	35	268	20	8	.714	258	99	89	162	71	2.99
1979—Boston		American	33	247	17	10	.630	234	89	82	150	59	2.99
1980—Boston		American	30	198	12	14	.462	188	101	94	121	44	4.27
Major League Totals			201	1346	89	64	.582	1196	532	492	976	396	3.29

Selected by Cleveland Indians' organization in 3rd round of free-agent draft, June 6, 1972.
†Traded with Catcher Fred Kendall to Boston Red Sox for Pitchers Rick Wise and Mike Paxton, Third Baseman Ted Cox and Catcher Bo Diaz, March 30, 1978.

ALL-STAR GAME RECORD

Year	League	IP.	W.	L.	Pct.	H.	R.	ER.	SO.	BB.	ERA.
1977—American		2	0	0	.000	0	0	0	1	0	0.00

BENNY JOE EDELEN

Name pronounced EE-duh-lun.
(Known by middle name)
Born September 16, 1955, at Durant, Okla.
Height, 6.00. Weight, 165.
Throws and bats righthanded.
Hobbies—Hunting, fishing, skiing, golf, and taxidermy.

Tied for Florida State League lead in double plays by third basemen with 32 in 1974.
Tied for Florida State League lead in shutouts with 4 in 1977.
Led Gulf Coast League batters in strikeouts with 60 in 1973.

Year	Club	League	G.	IP.	W.	L.	Pct.	H.	R.	ER.	SO.	BB.	ERA.
1975—St. Petersburg		Florida St.	5	10	0	1	.000	5	4	0	7	5	0.00
1976—St. Petersburg		Florida St.	15	79	5	6	.455	80	34	26	43	20	2.96
1977—Arkansas		Texas	13	80	6	3	.667	73	35	30	62	26	3.38
1977—St. Petersburg		Florida St.	13	97	6	3	.667	75	22	17	58	25	1.58
1978—Arkansas		Texas	9	53	5	1	.833	36	24	20	38	28	3.40
1978—Springfield		Am. Assoc.	15	62	2	5	.286	81	41	33	37	31	4.79
1979—Springfield		Am. Assoc.	13	67	4	7	.364	88	53	50	39	34	6.72
1979—Arkansas		Texas	12	71	4	4	.500	79	37	37	32	16	4.69
1980—Arkansas		Texas	26	161	13	5	.722	150	64	47	100	53	*2.63

Selected by St. Louis Cardinals' organization in 1st round (12th player selected) of free-agent draft, June 5, 1973.

RECORD AS INFIELDER-OUTFIELDER

Year	Club	League	Pos.	G.	AB.	R.	H.	2B.	3B.	HR.	RBI.	B.A.	PO.	A.	E.	F.A.
1973—Sarasota Cards		G.C.	3-O-S	49	165	19	36	8	0	5	25	.218	40	70	16	.873
1974—St. Petersburg		Fla. St.	3B	112	391	43	94	23	1	4	44	.240	113	258	*33	.918
1975—Arkansas		Texas	3B	69	193	18	36	8	0	5	22	.187	57	138	20	.907
1975—St. Petersburg		Fla. St.	3B	24	31	5	8	1	1	0	7	.258	5	21	1	.963
1976—Arkansas		Texas	3B-2B	39	109	13	25	4	0	2	12	.229	16	59	8	.904

DAVID DELMAR EDLER

(Dave)

Born August 5, 1956, at Sioux City, Iowa.
Height, 6.00. Weight, 185.
Throws and bats righthanded.
Attended Washington State University, Pullman, Wash.

Led California League in sacrifice flies with 12 in 1979.
Led California League third basemen in double plays with 26 in 1979.

Year	Club	League	Pos.	G.	AB.	R.	H.	2B.	3B.	HR.	RBI.	B.A.	PO.	A.	E.	F.A.
1978—Bellingham		Northw.	3B	69	248	42	67	12	4	6	46	.270	46	132	21	.894
1979—San Jose		Calif.	3B	138	508	101	152	28	7	14	104	.299	*111	*309	29	.935
1980—Spokane		P.C.	3B-SS-1B	140	458	79	132	25	6	10	72	.288	101	220	25	.928
1980—Seattle		Amer.	3B	28	89	11	20	1	0	3	9	.225	18	64	3	.965
Major League Totals				28	89	11	20	1	0	3	9	.225	18	64	3	.965

Selected by Seattle Mariners' organization in 22nd round of free-agent draft, June 6, 1978.

HECTOR LEONARDO EDUARDO

Born April 10, 1954, at San Pedro de Macoris, Dominican Republic.
Height, 6.06. Weight, 184.
Throws and bats righthanded.

Tied for Gulf Coast League lead in total bases with 87 in 1973.
Tied for Texas League lead in shutouts with 3 in 1979.

Year	Club	League	G.	IP.	W.	L.	Pct.	H.	R.	ER.	SO.	BB.	ERA.
1976—St. Petersburg	Florida St.	15	35	1	2	.333	21	23	18	29	26	4.63
1977—St. Petersburg	Florida St.	21	85	6	5	.545	69	47	33	64	57	3.49
1978—St. Petersburg	Florida St.	23	149	13	7	.650	113	59	44	97	83	2.66
1979—Arkansas	Texas	20	134	10	4	.714	102	50	39	90	70	2.62
1979—Springfield	Am. Assoc.	6	37	2	1	.667	33	18	17	29	20	4.14
1980—Springfield‡	Am. Assoc.	25	148	8	13	.381	140	97	88	108	•100	5.35

RECORD AS INFIELDER

Year	Club	League	Pos.	G.	AB.	R.	H.	2B.	3B.	HR.	RBI.	B.A.	PO.	A.	E.	F.A.
1972—Sara. Cardinals	G.C.	OF-1B	50	156	19	42	4	1	1	26	.269	87	7	7	.940
1973—Key West	Fla. St.	1B-3B	31	90	7	21	1	1	2	6	.233	115	21	9	.938
1973—Sara. Cardinals	G. C.	1B	48	169	26	54	9	3	*6	38	.320	333	27	*16	.957
1974—St. Petersburg†	Fla. St.	1B	82	288	28	64	12	2	4	25	.222	580	37	9	.986

Signed as free agent by St. Louis Cardinals' organization, November 25, 1971.
†On voluntarily retired list, April 10 to September 30, 1975.
‡Sold conditionally to Chicago White Sox, October 24, 1980.

DAVID LEONARD EDWARDS
(Dave)

Born February 24, 1954, at Los Angeles, Calif.
Height, 6.00. Weight, 170.
Throws and bats righthanded.
Hobbies—Golf, bowling, music and cars.
Attended Los Angeles City Community College, Los Angeles, Calif.
Brother of Mike Edwards, former infielder with Oakland A's and Marshall
Edwards, outfielder in Milwaukee Brewers' organization.

Led Florida State League outfielders in double plays with 6 in 1973.
Tied for International League lead among outfielders in double plays with 5 in 1978.

Year	Club	League	Pos.	G.	AB.	R.	H.	2B.	3B.	HR.	RBI.	B.A.	PO.	A.	E.	F.A.
1971—Sarasota Twins	Gulf C.	OF	29	96	11	19	1	2	0	10	.198	34	0	3	.919
1972—Orlando	Fla. St.	OF-SS	43	143	19	31	2	1	0	3	.217	81	5	4	.956
1972—Melb'rne Twins	Fla.E.C.	OF	53	192	40	60	6	2	4	33	*.313	86	5	5	.948
1973—Ft. Lauderdale	Fla. St.	OF	137	457	84	132	17	4	10	44	.289	215	12	8	.966
1974—Lynchburg	Carol.	OF	124	417	77	102	19	6	3	34	.245	274	9	9	.969
1975—Reno	Calif.	OF	137	481	103	147	21	9	7	75	.306	*320	13	7	.979
1976—Orlando†	South.	OF	55	209	32	61	10	5	3	26	.292	134	6	3	.979
1977—Tacoma	P.C.	OF	122	453	61	122	25	2	11	80	.269	289	12	8	.974
1978—Toledo	Int.	OF	139	458	66	120	22	6	16	70	.262	307	15	9	.973
1978—Minnesota	Amer.	OF	15	44	7	11	3	0	1	3	.250	35	3	2	.950
1979—Minnesota	Amer.	OF	96	229	42	57	8	0	8	34	.249	165	7	3	.983
1980—Minnesota‡§	Amer.	OF	81	200	26	50	9	1	2	20	.250	144	7	11	.932
Major League Totals			192	473	75	118	20	1	11	58	.249	344	17	16	.958

Selected by Minnesota Twins' organization in 7th round of free-agent draft, June 8, 1971.
†On disabled list, July 1 to July 11 and July 19 to September 24, 1976.
‡On supplemental disabled list, April 5 to April 29, 1980.
§Traded to San Diego Padres for Infielder Chuck Baker, December 8, 1980.

MARSHALL LYNN EDWARDS

Born August 27, 1952, at Fort Lewis, Wash.
Height, 5.09. Weight, 157.
Throws and bats lefthanded.
Attended Los Angeles City College, Los Angeles, Calif., and University
of California at Los Angeles, Los Angeles, Calif.
Brother of Dave Edwards, outfielder with San Diego Padres and
Mike Edwards, former infielder with Oakland A's.

Led Florida State League in stolen bases with 57 in 1977.

Year	Club	League	Pos.	G.	AB.	R.	H.	2B.	3B.	HR.	RBI.	B.A.	PO.	A.	E.	F.A.
1974—Ogden	Pion.	OF	72	234	37	68	6	5	0	15	.291	*124	8	8	.943
1975—Miami	Fla. St.	OF	124	459	62	128	8	3	0	31	.279	234	12	6	.976
1976—Miami	Fla. St.	OF	123	449	69	133	7	1	0	34	.296	240	14	5	.981
1977—Charlotte	South.	OF	36	129	15	22	3	1	0	9	.171	66	4	1	.986
1977—Miami†	Fla. St.	OF	94	344	62	115	12	4	0	27	*.334	137	7	3	.980
1978—Holyoke	East.	OF	136	*515	63	147	20	•11	1	56	.285	*354	5	*16	.957
1979—Vancouver	P.C.	OF	111	385	39	105	10	1	2	44	.273	200	11	6	.972
1980—Vancouver	P.C.	OF	134	478	70	139	14	*17	2	68	.291	234	13	7	.972

Signed as free agent by Baltimore Orioles' organization, June 24, 1974.
†Drafted by Milwaukee Brewers' organization, December 6, 1977.

MICHAEL LEWIS EDWARDS
(Mike)

Born August 27, 1952, at Fort Lewis, Wash.
Height, 5.10. Weight, 152.
Throws and bats righthanded.
Hobbies—Golf, bowling, and playing various musical instruments.
Attended Los Angeles City College, Los Angeles, Calif., and University of
California at Los Angeles, Los Angeles, Calif.
Brother of Dave Edwards, outfielder with Minnesota Twins and Marshall Edwards,
outfielder in Milwaukee Brewers' organization.

Established major league record for most times caught stealing, rookie season (21), 1978.
Tied major league record for most unassisted double plays by second baseman, game (2), August 10, 1978.
Led American League second basemen in errors with 20 in 1978.
Led New York-Pennsylvania League second basemen in double plays with 60 in 1974.
Led International League in stolen bases with 62, in double plays by second basemen with 94, and in total chances by second basemen with 723 in 1977.

Year Club	League	Pos.	G.	AB.	R.	H.	2B.	3B.	HR.	RBI.	B.A.	PO.	A.	E.	F.A.
1974—Niagara Falls ....NYP		2B	69	*275	43	86	11	*7	3	28	.313	*196	166	12	*.968
1975—Shreveport ....Texas		2B-SS	93	368	57	112	26	3	3	41	.304	194	221	13	*.970
1975—Charleston ....Int.		2B	31	132	11	37	6	1	1	15	.280	48	84	4	.971
1976—Charleston ....Int.		2B-SS	62	223	24	46	3	2	3	21	.206	133	146	7	.975
1976—Shreveport ....Texas		2B-SS	53	209	28	67	12	2	4	23	.321	103	157	18	.935
1977—Columbus..........Int.		*2-3-S	133	*531	77	*157	13	7	4	61	.296	*280	*426	18	.975
1977—Pittsburgh† ......Nat.		2B	7	6	1	0	0	0	0	0	.000	7	8	0	1.000
1978—Oakland............Amer.		2B-SS	142	414	48	113	16	2	1	23	.273	233	318	22	.962
1979—Oakland............Amer.		*2B-SS	122	400	35	93	12	2	1	23	.233	246	318	*22	.962
1980—Oakland‡ ....Amer.		2B-OF	46	59	10	14	0	0	0	3	.237	19	48	2	.971
American League Totals			310	873	93	220	28	4	2	49	.252	498	684	46	.963
National League Totals			7	6	1	0	0	0	0	0	.000	7	8	0	1.000
Major League Totals			317	879	94	220	28	4	2	49	.250	505	692	46	.963

Selected by California Angels' organization in 18th round of free-agent draft, June 4, 1970.
Selected by California Angels' organization in secondary phase of free-agent draft, January 13, 1971.
Selected by Montreal Expos' organization in 5th round of free-agent draft, January 12, 1972.
Selected by Pittsburgh Pirates' organization in 7th round of free-agent draft, June 5, 1974.
†Traded to Oakland A's, April 7, 1978, to complete deal in which Pirates obtained Manny Sanguillen, April 4, 1978.
‡Released, December 12, 1980.

JUAN TYRONE EICHELBERGER

Name pronounced EYE-kul-burg-ur.

Born October 21, 1953, at St. Louis, Mo.
Height, 6.02. Weight, 195.
Throws and bats righthanded.
Attended University of California, Berkeley, Calif.

Tied major league record for most consecutive strikeouts as batter, season (14), 1980.

Year Club	League	G.	IP.	W.	L.	Pct.	H.	R.	ER.	SO.	BB.	ERA.
1975—Reno....................California		16	117	10	4	.714	105	52	36	92	54	2.77
1975—Alexandria.....................Texas		8	50	3	4	.429	52	31	24	31	21	4.32
1976—Amarillo ....Texas		11	66	2	6	.250	77	50	41	41	45	5.59
1976—Reno....................................California		13	89	6	1	.857	71	48	35	77	63	3.54
1977—Amarillo† ....Texas		25	162	12	7	.632	177	90	74	92	77	4.11
1978—Hawaii................................P. Coast		26	156	8	13	.381	143	95	78	106	*113	4.50
1978—San Diego ....National		3	3	0	0	.000	4	4	4	2	2	12.00
1979—Hawaii................................P. Coast		28	195	13	9	.591	151	79	73	159	*137	3.37
1979—San Diego ....National		3	21	1	1	.500	15	10	8	12	11	3.43
1980—Hawaii................................P. Coast		11	77	7	3	.700	56	35	30	62	49	3.51
1980—San Diego‡.............................National		15	89	4	2	.667	73	41	36	43	55	3.64
Major League Totals.................................		21	113	5	3	.625	92	55	48	57	68	3.82

Selected by San Francisco Giants' organization in 36th round of free-agent draft, June 8, 1971.
Selected by San Diego Padres' organization in secondary phase of free-agent draft, January 9, 1975.
†Played two games in outfield.
‡On disabled list, July 18 to August 8, 1980.

RANDY LEE ELLIOTT

Born June 5, 1951, at Camarillo, Calif.
Height, 6;02. Weight, 195.
Throws and bats righthanded.

Led Texas League in slugging percentage with .544 and in total bases with 258 in 1972.
Led Pioneer League first basemen in double plays with 42 in 1969
Tied for Pioneer League lead in sacrifice flies with 5 in 1969.
Tied for California League lead in double plays by outfielders with 3 in 1970.
Tied for California League lead in sacrifice flies with 10 in 1971.
Named Texas League Most Valuable Player, 1972.

Year Club	League	Pos.	G.	AB.	R.	H.	2B.	3B.	HR.	RBI.	B.A.	PO.	A.	E.	F.A.
1969—Salt Lake City ... Pion.		1B	63	225	42	68	8	*9	4	50	.302	*459	*29	9	*.982
1970—Lodi..................Calif.		*OF-1	132	481	68	135	20	6	14	51	.281	241	*21	10	.963

Year Club League	Pos.	G.	AB.	R.	H.	2B.	3B.	HR.	RBI.	B.A.	PO.	A.	E.	F.A.
1971—Lodi..................Calif.	OF	126	481	89	126	25	4	14	75	.262	194	•16	12	.946
1972—Alexandria.......Texas	OF-1B	138	474	84	159	*32	5	19	*85	*.335	208	16	7	.970
1972—San Diego ....Nat.	OF	14	49	5	10	3	1	0	6	.204	29	0	0	1.000
1973—Hawaii† ..........P.C.	OF	29	99	14	28	6	0	2	15	.283	53	3	0	1.000
1974—Hawaii.............P.C.	OF-1B	112	392	70	126	22	7	11	69	.321	265	30	4	.987
1974—San Diego ....Nat.	OF-1B	13	33	5	7	1	0	1	2	.212	10	0	0	1.000
1975—Hawaii‡ ..........P.C.	OF	95	338	63	93	22	3	12	60	.275	140	9	7	.955
1976—S.L.C. y-Pho...... P.C.						(Did not play)								
1977—San Fran.z ....Nat.	OF	73	167	17	40	5	1	7	26	.240	68	5	2	.973
1978—Portland a.........P.C.						(Did not play)								
1979—Tacoma b.........P.C.						(Did not play)								
1980—Ogden c .........P.C.	OF	8	28	6	12	3	0	2	6	.429	8	1	0	1.000
1980—Oakland d ....Amer.	DH	14	39	4	5	3	0	0	1	.128	0	0	0	.000
National League Totals		100	249	27	57	9	2	8	34	.229	107	5	2	.982
American League Totals		14	39	4	5	3	0	0	1	.128	0	0	0	.000
Major League Totals.......................		114	288	31	62	12	2	8	35	.215	107	5	2	.982

†On disabled list, May 28 through September 7, 1973.
‡On disabled list, August 1 through September 24, 1975; released, February 26, 1976; signed as free agent with Salt Lake City (California Angels' organization) March 4, 1976.
yOn inactive list, April 17 through May 6, 1976; released, May 6, 1976; signed as free agent with Phoenix (San Francisco Giants' organizaton), September 3, 1976.
zReleased, March 27, 1978; signed by Cleveland Indians' organization, April 11, 1978.
aOn voluntarily retired list, April 28 to December 11, 1978.
bReleased, March 25, 1979; signed by Oakland A's organization, April 10, 1980.
cOn suspended list, April 20 to May 20 and July 3 to August 18, 1980.
dReleased, October 23, 1980.

JOHN CHARLES ELLIS

Born August 21, 1948, at New London, Conn.
Height, 6.02. Weight, 210.
Throws and bats righthanded.
Hobbies—Fishing and hunting.
Attended Mitchell College, New London, Conn.

Year Club League	Pos.	G.	AB.	R.	H.	2B.	3B.	HR.	RBI.	B.A.	PO.	A.	E.	F.A.
1967—Ft. Laud† ....Fla. St.	C	34	107	17	30	6	0	3	20	.280	167	11	5	.973
1968—Ft. Laud† ....Fla. St.	C	70	207	28	51	10	3	6	22	.246	327	32	6	.984
1968—Syracuse ....Int.	C	13	46	7	16	2	0	1	7	.348	83	12	0	1.000
1969—Kinston ....Carol.	C	24	97	17	35	5	1	6	28	.361	160	12	1	.994
1969—Syracuse§..........Int.	C-OF	38	123	24	41	8	3	8	31	.333	56	5	2	.968
1969—New York..........Amer.	C	22	62	2	18	4	0	1	8	.290	83	7	2	.978
1970—New York..........Amer.	1B-3-C	78	226	24	56	12	1	7	29	.248	461	41	5	.990
1971—New York..........Amer.	1B-C	83	238	16	58	12	1	3	34	.244	625	35	7	.990
1972—New York x ....Amer.	C-1B	52	136	13	40	5	1	5	25	.294	190	12	6	.971
1973—Cleveland..........Amer.	C-1B	127	437	59	118	12	2	14	68	.270	487	31	10	.981
1974—Cleveland y ....Amer.	1B-C	128	477	58	136	23	6	10	64	.285	823	55	9	.990
1975—Cleveland z a .....Amer.	C-1B	92	296	22	68	11	1	7	32	.230	413	45	13	.972
1976—Texas b ....Amer.	C	11	31	4	13	2	0	1	8	.419	21	2	0	1.000
1977—Texas...............Amer.	C-1B	49	119	7	28	7	0	4	15	.235	89	5	0	1.000
1978—Texas ....Amer.	C	34	94	7	23	4	0	3	17	.245	81	10	4	.958
1979—Texas ....Amer.	1B-C	111	316	33	90	12	0	12	61	.285	232	12	5	.980
1980—Texas c............Amer.	1B-C	73	182	12	43	9	1	1	23	.236	244	12	2	.992
Major League Totals		860	2614	257	691	113	13	68	384	.264	3749	267	63	.985

Signed as free agent by New York Yankees' organization, August 15, 1966.
†On temporary inactive list, May 26 through May 29. On temporary inactive list, June 2, 1967. Transferred to the military list, June 5 through October 3.
‡On temporary inactive list, April 26 through April 29, May 24 through May 27, June 21 through June 24, July 11 through 28, and August 2 through August 6.
§On temporary inactive list, April 25 through April 28. On military list, June 17 through July 7.
xTraded with Infielder Jerry Kenney, Outfielders Charlie Spikes and Rosendo Torres to Cleveland Indians for Third Baseman Graig Nettles and Catcher Jerry Moses, November 27, 1972.
yOn disabled list, June 1 to June 30, 1974.
zOn supplemental disabled list, August 15 to September 1, 1975.
aTraded to Texas Rangers for Pitcher Stan Thomas and Utilityman Ron Pruitt, December 9, 1975.
bOn disabled list, May 9 to October 6, 1976.
cOn disabled list, June 9 to June 30, 1980.

RALPH DAVID ENGLE
(Dave)

Born November 30, 1956, at San Diego, Calif.
Height, 6.03. Weight, 210.
Throws and bats righthanded.
Attended University of Southern California, Los Angeles, Calif.

Year Club League	Pos.	G.	AB.	R.	H.	2B.	3B.	HR.	RBI.	B.A.	PO.	A.	E.	F.A.
1978—Salinas† ....Calif.	3B	53	203	34	62	11	0	6	40	.305	20	65	10	.895
1979—Toledo ....Int.	3B	106	363	46	104	17	1	7	51	.287	72	197	23	.921
1980—Toledo ....Int.	OF	133	489	74	150	27	3	7	73	*.307	225	16	5	.980

Selected by California Angels' organization in 2nd round of free-agent draft, June 6, 1978.
†Traded with Outfielder Ken Landreaux and Pitchers Paul Hartzell and Brad Havens to Minnesota Twins for First Baseman Rod Carew, February 3, 1979.

RICHARD DOUGLAS ENGLE
(Rick)

Born April 7, 1957, at Corbin, Ky.
Height, 5.11. Weight, 180.
Throws and bats lefthanded.

Tied for Florida State League lead in shutouts with 5 in 1978.
Tied for American Association lead in games started with 28 in 1980.

Year Club	League	G.	IP.	W.	L.	Pct.	H.	R.	ER.	SO.	BB.	ERA.
1977—West Palm Beach	Florida St.	24	86	6	5	.545	77	62	47	56	82	4.92
1978—West Palm Beach†	Florida St.	21	108	7	8	.467	85	54	32	92	69	2.67
1979—Memphis	Southern	27	161	6	8	.429	162	95	84	103	68	4.70
1980—Denver	Am. Assoc.	28	168	12	7	.632	160	90	84	90	96	4.50

Signed as free agent by Montreal Expos' organization, March 17, 1977.
†On temporary inactive list, May 10 to May 21, 1978.

ROGER FARRELL ERICKSON

Born August 30, 1956, at Springfield, Ill.
Height, 6.03. Weight, 199.
Throws and bats righthanded.
Attended Springfield College of Illinois, Springfield, Ill.; and
Unviersity of New Orleans, New Orleans, La.

Year Club	League	G.	IP.	W.	L.	Pct.	H.	R.	ER.	SO.	BB.	ERA.
1977—Orlando	Southern	16	109	8	4	.667	99	34	24	72	27	1.98
1978—Minnesota	American	37	266	14	13	.519	268	129	117	121	79	3.96
1979—Toledo†	Int'national	5	33	3	1	.750	30	8	6	19	10	1.59
1979—Minnesota	American	24	123	3	10	.231	154	86	77	47	48	5.63
1980—Minnesota	American	32	191	7	13	.350	198	83	69	97	56	3.25
Major League Totals		93	580	24	36	.400	620	298	263	265	183	4.08

Selected by Minnesota Twins' organization in 3rd round of free-agent draft, June 7, 1977.
†On disabled list, July 4 to July 24, 1979.

NICHOLAS ANDREW ESASKY
(Nick)

Born February 24, 1960, at Hialeah, Fla.
Height, 6.03. Weight, 190.
Throws and bats righthanded.

Led Eastern League batters in strikeouts with 131 in 1980.

Year Club	League	Pos.	G.	AB.	R.	H.	2B.	3B.	HR.	RBI.	B.A.	PO.	A.	E.	F.A.
1978—Billings	Pion.	3B	64	213	38	65	10	5	4	48	.305	*62	88	22	.872
1979—Tampa	Fla. St.	3B	124	439	52	118	16	3	10	66	.269	91	234	27	.923
1980—Waterbury	East.	3B	135	425	79	115	18	4	*30	79	.271	98	241	23	.936

Selected by Cincinnati Reds' organization in 1st round (17th player selected) of free-agent draft, June 6, 1978.

JUAN ESPINO (REYES)

Born March 16, 1956, at Bonao, Dominican Republic.
Height, 6.00. Weight, 185.
Throws and bats righthanded.

Led New York-Pennsylvania League batters in strikeouts with 61 in 1975.

Year Club	League	Pos.	G.	AB.	R.	H.	2B.	3B.	HR.	RBI.	B.A.	PO.	A.	E.	F.A.
1975—Oneonta	NYP	C-OF	48	157	24	36	5	5	2	23	.229	26	3	2	.935
1976—Ft. Lauderdale†	Fla. St.	C	39	118	18	30	5	3	4	20	.254	170	20	3	.984
1977—Ft. Lauderdale	Fla. St.	C	52	141	8	28	8	0	0	16	.199	266	40	9	.971
1978—West Haven	East.	C	82	261	32	73	14	0	6	37	.280	426	44	6	*.987
1979—West Haven	East.	C	95	296	40	70	11	1	8	44	.236	509	57	13	.978
1980—Nashville	South.	C	17	56	3	9	1	0	0	9	.161	115	6	2	.984
1980—Columbus	Int.	C	48	129	11	27	7	1	1	16	.209	238	29	5	.982

Signed as free agent by New York Yankees' organization, December 26, 1974.
†On disabled list, May 26 to June 9, 1976.

ARNULFO ACEVEDO ESPINOSA
Name pronounced es-puh-NOH-suh.

(Nino)

Born August 15, 1953, at Villa Altagracia, Dominican Republic.
Height, 6.01. Weight, 186.
Throws and bats righthanded.
Brother of Juan Acevedo, pitcher in St. Louis Cardinals' organization, 1963.

Year Club	League	G.	IP.	W.	L.	Pct.	H.	R.	ER.	SO.	BB.	ERA.
1971—Key West	Florida St.	41	115	6	12	.333	116	53	44	70	32	3.44
1972—Pompano Beach†	Florida St.	40	89	8	6	.571	115	51	41	64	12	4.15
1973—Visalia	California	24	174	10	10	.500	184	99	81	109	54	4.19
1974—Victoria‡	Texas	25	137	9	8	.529	137	66	52	63	26	3.42
1974—New York	National	2	9	0	0	.000	12	5	5	2	0	5.00
1975—Tidewater§	Int'national	24	141	8	5	.615	127	48	41	83	38	2.62
1975—New York	National	2	3	0	1	.000	8	6	6	2	1	18.00
1976—Tidewater	Int'national	14	108	7	3	.700	106	40	35	66	34	2.92
1976—New York	National	12	42	4	4	.500	41	21	17	30	13	3.64
1977—New York	National	32	200	10	13	.435	188	82	76	105	55	3.42
1978—New York x	National	32	204	11	15	.423	230	117	•107	76	75	4.72
1979—Philadelphia	National	33	212	14	12	.538	211	94	86	88	65	3.65
1980—Philadelphia y	National	12	76	3	5	.375	73	36	32	13	19	3.79
1980—Spartanburg z	So. Atlantic	3	17	1	1	.500	15	6	5	11	2	2.65
Major League Totals		125	746	42	50	.457	763	361	329	316	228	3.97

Signed as free agent by New York Mets' organization, September 30, 1970.
†On temporary inactive list from beginning of season until April 25, 1972.
‡Played one game at third base.
§On disabled list, April 22 to May 2, 1975.
xTraded to Philadelphia Phillies for Third Baseman Richie Hebner and Second Baseman Jose Moreno, March 27, 1979.
yOn disabled list, April 2 to June 16, 1980.
zOn rehabilitation assignment, June 16 to July 1, 1980.

JAMES SARKIS ESSIAN JR.

Name pronounced Ess-ee-en.

(Jim)

Born January 2, 1951, at Detroit, Mich.
Height, 6.01. Weight, 187.
Throws and bats righthanded.
Hobbies—Music and chess.
Attended Arizona State University, Tempe, Ariz.

Led Carolina League catchers in double plays with 13 in 1971.

Year Club	League	Pos.	G.	AB.	R.	H.	2B.	3B.	HR.	RBI.	B.A.	PO.	A.	E.	F.A.
1970—Pulaski	Appal.	*C-3B	36	119	17	36	9	0	5	30	.303	243	21	2	*.992
1970—Spartanburg	W. Car.	C	35	119	19	35	8	2	6	20	.294	204	21	5	.978
1971—Peninsula	Carol.	C	131	429	54	107	20	0	12	46	.249	*856	68	*22	.977
1972—Reading	East.	C	96	312	45	79	14	1	4	33	.253	512	60	20	.966
1973—Reading	East.	*C-1-3-O	105	315	58	92	15	5	10	55	.292	609	57	*22	.968
1973—Philadelphia	Nat.	C	2	3	0	0	0	0	0	0	.000	0	0	0	.000
1974—Toledo	Int.	1-C-3B	58	181	24	51	4	0	5	24	.282	372	50	11	.975
1974—Philadelphia	Nat.	C-1-3	17	20	1	2	0	0	0	0	.100	38	4	1	.977
1975—Reading	East.	C-3B	12	36	5	7	2	0	1	2	.194	61	12	1	.986
1975—Philadelphia†	Nat.	C	2	1	1	1	0	0	0	1	1.000	1	1	0	1.000
1975—Hawaii	P. C.	C	40	129	14	27	2	0	2	9	.209	228	22	2	.992
1976—Chicago	Amer.	C-1B-3B	78	199	20	49	7	0	0	21	.246	320	53	10	.974
1977—Chicago‡	Amer.	C-3B	114	322	50	88	18	2	10	44	.273	593	62	9	.986
1978—Oakland	Amer.	C-1-2	126	278	21	62	9	1	3	26	.223	452	79	10	.982
1979—Oakland§	Amer.	C-3-1-O	98	313	34	76	16	0	8	40	.243	400	79	9	.982
1980—Oakland x	Amer.	C-1B	87	285	19	66	11	0	5	29	.232	339	46	5	.987
National League Totals			21	24	2	3	0	0	0	1	.125	39	5	1	.978
American League Totals			503	1397	144	341	61	3	26	160	.244	2104	319	43	.983
Major League Totals			524	1421	146	344	61	3	26	161	.242	2143	324	44	.982

Signed as free agent by Philadelphia Phillies' organization, August 29, 1969.
†Traded with Outfielder Barry Bonnell and cash to Atlanta Braves for First Baseman Dick Allen and Catcher Johnny Oates, May 7, 1975. Sent by Atlanta Braves to Chicago White Sox, May 15, 1975, to complete deal in which Braves acquired First Baseman Dick Allen from White Sox for $5,000 and a player to be named later, December 3, 1974.
‡Traded with Pitcher Steve Renko to Oakland A's for Pitcher Pablo Torrealba, March 30, 1978.
§On supplemental disabled list, June 13 to June 28, 1979.
xGranted free agency, October 31, 1980; signed by Chicago White Sox, November 20, 1980.

BARRY STEVEN EVANS

Born November 30, 1956, at Atlanta, Ga.
Height, 6.01. Weight, 180.
Throws and bats righthanded.
Attended West Georgia College, Carrollton, Ga.

Led Northwest League in total bases with 146 in 1977.
Led Texas League third basemen in fielding average with .957 in 1978.

Year Club	League	Pos.	G.	AB.	R.	H.	2B.	3B.	HR.	RBI.	B.A.	PO.	A.	E.	F.A.
1977—Walla Walla	N'west	2B-3B-S	67	271	47	*97	12	2	11	*64	.358	92	165	13	.952
1978—Amarillo	Texas	3B-SS-O	128	514	69	157	24	2	10	67	.305	138	350	23	.955
1978—San Diego	Nat.	3B	24	90	7	24	1	1	0	4	.267	13	59	4	.947
1979—San Diego†	Nat.	3B-SS-2B	56	162	9	35	5	0	1	14	.216	30	110	7	.952

Year	Club	League	Pos.	G.	AB.	R.	H.	2B.	3B.	HR.	RBI.	B.A.	PO.	A.	E.	F.A.
1980—Hawaii		P.C.	2B	28	104	13	26	8	1	2	15	.250	57	95	3	.981
1980—San Diego		Nat.	3-2-S-1	73	125	11	29	3	2	1	14	.232	52	87	2	.986
Major League Totals				153	377	27	88	9	3	2	32	.233	95	256	13	.964

Selected by New York Mets' organization in 8th round of free-agent draft, June 8, 1976.
Selected by San Diego Padres' organization in 2nd round of free-agent draft, June 7, 1977.
†Placed on suspended list, June 26 to September 4, 1979, when he did not report to Amarillo (Texas), June 22, 1979.

DARRELL WAYNE EVANS

Born May 26, 1947, at Pasadena, Calif.
Height, 6.02. Weight, 205.
Throws right and bats lefthanded.
Hobbies—Sports and stamp collecting.
Attended Pasadena City College, Pasadena, Calif. and
California State Univeristy at Los Angeles.
Grandson of Dale Salazar, former minor league player.

Established National League records for most double plays, third baseman, (45), 1974; most games, consecutive, one or more bases on balls (15), April 9-27, 1976.
Led National League batters in walks with 124 in 1973 and 126 in 1974.
Led National League third basemen in double plays with 45 in 1974 and 41 in 1975.
Led National League third basemen in total chances with 471 in 1973, 578 in 1974 and 578 in 1975.
Named third baseman on THE SPORTING NEWS National League All-Star Team, 1973.
Named Player of the Year in Gulf Coast League, 1967.

Year	Club	League	Pos.	G.	AB.	R.	H.	2B.	3B.	HR.	RBI.	B.A.	PO.	A.	E.	F.A.
1967—Peninsula		Carol.	3B	8	28	4	11	1	1	0	6	.393	6	13	2	.905
1967—Bradenton A's		Gulf C.	3B-SS	14	45	13	22	3	3	2	11	.489	25	30	2	.965
1967—Leesburg		Fla. St.	3-SS	39	142	18	37	4	2	0	12	.261	49	81	11	.922
1968—Birmingham†		South.	3-1-2B	56	187	18	45	6	3	3	25	.241	103	101	10	.953
1969—Richmond		Int.	3B	59	211	43	76	12	4	7	45	.360	51	103	19	.890
1969—Shreveport		Texas	3-S-O	24	79	14	22	5	4	2	14	.278	25	40	3	.956
1969—Atlanta		Nat.	3B	12	26	3	6	0	0	0	1	.231	4	7	1	.917
1970—Richmond		Int.	*3-1-O	120	447	92	134	20	7	20	83	.300	99	220	16	*.952
1970—Atlanta		Nat.	3B	12	44	4	14	1	1	0	9	.318	6	26	2	.941
1971—Richmond		Int.	OF-3B	31	101	20	31	2	2	6	30	.307	59	11	1	.986
1971—Atlanta		Nat.	3B-OF	89	260	42	63	11	1	12	38	.242	77	138	14	.939
1972—Atlanta‡		Nat.	3B	125	418	67	106	12	0	19	71	.254	126	273	25	.941
1973—Atlanta		Nat.	3B-1B	161	595	114	167	25	8	41	104	.281	266	335	24	.962
1974—Atlanta		Nat.	3B	160	571	99	137	21	3	25	79	.240	*185	367	26	.955
1975—Atlanta		Nat.	*3B-1B	156	567	82	138	22	2	22	73	.243	*164	*382	*36	.938
1976—Atl.§-S.F.		Nat.	1B-3B	136	396	53	81	9	1	11	46	.205	978	110	10	.991
1977—San Francisco		Nat.	0-1-3	144	461	64	117	18	3	17	72	.254	324	83	13	.969
1978—San Francisco x		Nat.	3B	159	547	82	133	24	2	20	78	.243	*147	*348	*25	.952
1979—San Francisco		Nat.	3B	160	562	68	142	23	2	17	70	.253	*129	*369	*30	.943
1980—San Francisco		Nat.	3B-1B	154	556	69	147	23	0	20	78	.264	232	340	27	.955
Major League Totals				1468	5003	747	1251	189	23	204	719	.250	2638	2778	233	.959

Selected by Chicago Cubs' organization in 8th round of free-agent draft, June 22, 1965.
Selected by New York Yankees' organization in secondary phase of free-agent draft, January 29, 1966.
Selected by Detroit Tigers' organization in 5th round of free-agent draft, June 6, 1966.
Selected by Philadelphia Phillies' organization in 3rd round of free-agent draft, January 28, 1967.
Selected by Kansas City A's organization in secondary phase of free-agent draft, June 7, 1967.
†Drafted by Atlanta Braves from Vancouver (Oakland Athletics' organization), December 2, 1968.
‡On military list, June 17 through July 3, 1972.
§Traded with Shortstop Marty Perez to San Francisco Giants for First Baseman-Outfielder Willie Montanez, Shortstop Craig Robinson, Infielder Mike Eden (assigned to Richmond) and Outfielder Jake Brown (assigned to Savannah), June 13, 1976.
xGranted free agency, November 2, 1978; re-signed with Giants, December 5, 1978.

ALL-STAR GAME RECORD

Year	League	Pos.	AB.	R.	H.	2B.	3B.	HR.	RBI.	B.A.	PO.	A.	E.	F.A.
1973—National		PH	0	0	0	0	0	0	0	.000	0	0	0	.000

DWIGHT MICHAEL EVANS

Born November 3, 1951, at Santa Monica, Calif.
Height, 6.03. Weight, 205.
Throws and bats righthanded.

Tied major league record for most putouts and chances accepted by right fielder, extra-inning game (10), September 10, 1974.
Led American League outfielders in double plays with 8 in 1975.
Led Western Carolinas League in sacrifice flies with 8 in 1970.
Tied for Carolina League lead in double plays by outfielders with 3 in 1971.
Named Most Valuable Player in International League, 1972.
Named as outfielder on THE SPORTING NEWS American League All-Star fielding team, 1976, 1978 and 1979.

Year	Club	League	Pos.	G.	AB.	R.	H.	2B.	3B.	HR.	RBI.	B.A.	PO.	A.	E.	F.A.
1969—Jamestown		NYP	OF-3B	34	100	13	28	3	2	1	12	.280	44	10	3	.947
1970—Greenville		W. Car.	O-3	108	355	69	98	14	*11	7	68	.276	130	11	7	.953
1971—Winston-Salem		Carol.	O-1	118	402	63	115	20	4	12	63	.286	219	17	10	.959

Year Club League	Pos.	G.	AB.	R.	H.	2B.	3B.	HR.	RBI.	B.A.	PO.	A.	E.	F.A.
1972—Louisville ....Int.	OF	•144	496	90	149	23	8	17	*95	.300	270	12	6	.979
1972—Boston ....Amer.	OF	18	57	2	15	3	1	1	6	.263	25	3	0	1.000
1973—Boston ....Amer.	OF	119	282	46	63	13	1	10	32	.223	178	4	1	.995
1974—Boston ....Amer.	OF	133	463	60	130	19	8	10	70	.281	294	8	3	.990
1975—Boston ....Amer.	OF	128	412	61	113	24	6	13	56	.274	281	15	4	.987
1976—Boston ....Amer.	OF	146	501	61	121	34	5	17	62	.242	324	15	2	*.994
1977—Boston† ....Amer.	OF	73	230	39	66	9	2	14	36	.287	126	2	1	.992
1978—Boston ....Amer.	OF	147	497	75	123	24	2	24	63	.247	305	14	6	.982
1979—Boston ....Amer.	OF	152	489	69	134	24	1	21	58	.274	307	15	4	.988
1980—Boston ....Amer.	OF	148	463	72	123	37	5	18	60	.266	268	11	5	.982
Major League Totals		1064	3394	485	888	187	31	128	443	.262	2108	87	26	.988

Selected by Boston Red Sox' organization in 5th round of free-agent draft, June 5, 1969.

†On supplemental disabled list, June 21 to July 8, and August 25 to September 21, 1977.

CHAMPIONSHIP SERIES RECORD

Year Club League	Pos.	G.	AB.	R.	H.	2B.	3B.	HR.	RBI.	B.A.	PO.	A.	E.	F.A.
1975—Boston ....Amer.	OF	3	10	1	1	0	0	0	0	.100	7	0	0	1.000

WORLD SERIES RECORD

Tied World Series record for highest fielding average by outfielder, seven-game Series (1.000 with 24 chances), 1975.

Year Club League	Pos.	G.	AB.	R.	H.	2B.	3B.	HR.	RBI.	B.A.	PO.	A.	E.	F.A.
1975—Boston ....Amer.	OF	7	24	3	7	1	1	1	5	.292	23	1	0	1.000

ALL-STAR GAME RECORD

Year League	Pos.	AB.	R.	H.	2B.	3B.	HR.	RBI.	B.A.	PO.	A.	E.	F.A.
1978—American	OF	1	0	0	0	0	0	0	.000	3	0	0	1.000

LEONARDO LAGO FAEDO

Name pronounced Fah-A-doh

(Lenny)

Born May 13, 1960, at Tampa, Fla.
Height, 6.00. Weight, 170.
Throws and bats righthanded.

Year Club League	Pos.	G.	AB.	R.	H.	2B.	3B.	HR.	RBI.	B.A.	PO.	A.	E.	F.A.
1978—Elizabethton .....Appal.	SS	55	232	29	65	8	1	2	35	.280	77	166	22	.917
1979—Orlando† ....South.	SS	103	336	35	91	13	3	3	34	.271	153	352	30	.944
1980—Orlando‡ ....South.	SS-3B	114	437	47	105	13	1	6	26	.240	187	365	21	.963
1980—Minnesota ....Amer.	SS	5	8	1	2	1	0	0	0	.250	4	5	2	.818
Major League Totals......................		5	8	1	2	1	0	0	0	.250	4	5	2	.818

Selected by Minnesota Twins' organization in 1st round (16th player selected) of free-agent draft, June 6, 1978.

†On disabled list, April 27 to May 24, 1979.

‡On disabled list, April 11 to May 3, 1980.

WILLIAM ROGER FAHEY

(Bill)

Born June 14, 1950, at Detroit, Mich.
Height, 6.00. Weight, 200.
Throws right and bats lefthanded.
Hobbies—Hunting and music.
Attended University of Detroit, Detroit, Mich., St. Clair County Community College,
Port Huron, Mich., and University of Tampa, Tampa, Fla.

Led Pacific Coast League in passed balls with 15 in 1973.

Year Club League	Pos.	G.	AB.	R.	H.	2B.	3B.	HR.	RBI.	B.A.	PO.	A.	E.	F.A.
1970—Burlington.........Carol.	C	118	377	49	92	10	2	3	36	.244	*724	76	10	.988
1971—Pittsfield...........East.	C	99	325	44	93	13	4	6	38	.286	536	54	6	*.990
1971—Denver..............A. A.	C	4	15	1	4	0	0	1	2	.267	19	2	0	1.000
1971—Washington ....Amer.	C	2	8	0	0	0	0	0	0	.000	8	2	1	.909
1972—Denver..............A. A.	C	75	226	28	61	5	4	1	25	.270	421	43	6	.987
1972—Texas...............Amer.	C	39	119	8	20	2	0	1	10	.168	236	26	2	.992
1973—Spokane ....P. C.	C	104	370	45	103	15	2	1	44	.278	535	52	8	*.987
1974—Spokane ....P. C.	C	92	317	39	82	9	2	3	39	.259	553	43	3	*.995
1974—Texas...............Amer.	C	6	16	1	4	0	0	0	0	.250	21	2	0	1.000
1975—Texas† ....Amer.	C	21	37	3	11	1	1	0	3	.297	54	5	1	.983
1976—Texas...............Amer.	C	38	80	12	20	2	0	1	9	.250	126	19	1	.993
1977—Texas...............Amer.	C	37	68	3	15	4	0	0	5	.221	104	5	0	1.000
1978—Tucson ....P. C.	C-OF	66	212	35	53	7	0	2	19	.250	333	44	5	.987
1978—Texas‡§.............						Did not play								
1979—San Diego ....Nat.	C	73	209	14	60	8	1	3	19	.287	277	33	2	.994
1980—San Diego ....Nat.	C	93	241	18	62	4	0	1	22	.257	309	34	8	.977
American League Totals		143	328	27	70	9	1	2	27	.213	549	59	5	.992
National League Totals		166	450	32	122	12	1	4	41	.271	586	67	10	.985
Major League Totals......................		309	778	59	192	21	2	6	68	.247	1135	126	15	.988

Selected by Baltimore Orioles' organization in 13th round of free-agent draft, June 7, 1968.

Selected by Washington Senators' organization in secondary phase of free-agent draft, January 17, 1970.

†On disabled list, June 22 to August 14, 1975.
‡On emergency disabled list, August 22 to October 23, 1978.
§Traded with Third Baseman Kurt Bevacqua and First Baseman Mike Hargrove to San Diego Padres for Outfielder Oscar Gamble, Catcher Dave Roberts and cash estimated at $300,000, October 25, 1978.

PETER FALCONE

Name pronounced fowl-KOHN.

(Pete)

Born October 1, 1953, at Brooklyn, N. Y.
Height, 6.02. Weight, 185.
Throws and bats lefthanded.
Attended Kingsborough Community College, Brooklyn, N. Y.
Second cousin of Joe Pignatano, coach with New York Mets.

Year Club	League	G.	IP.	W.	L.	Pct.	H.	R.	ER.	SO.	BB.	ERA.
1973—Great Falls	Pioneer	12	72	8	1	*.889	49	19	12	102	53	*1.50
1974—Fresno	California	17	137	10	4	.714	116	61	46	172	61	3.02
1974—Amarillo	Texas	7	37	2	4	.333	41	14	11	35	18	2.68
1975—San Francisco†	National	34	190	12	11	.522	171	97	88	131	111	4.17
1976—St. Louis	National	32	212	12	16	.429	173	87	76	138	93	3.23
1977—St. Louis	National	27	124	4	8	.333	130	79	75	75	61	5.44
1977—New Orleans	Am. Assoc.	7	44	2	5	.286	45	107	99	32	22	4.91
1978—St. Louis‡	National	19	75	2	7	.222	94	52	48	28	48	5.76
1979—New York	National	33	184	6	14	.300	194	91	85	113	76	4.16
1980—New York	National	37	157	7	10	.412	163	89	79	109	58	4.53
Major League Totals		182	942	43	66	.394	925	495	451	494	447	4.31

Selected by Minnesota Twins' organziation in 13th round of free-agent draft, June 6, 1972.
Selected by Atlanta Braves' organization in secondary phase of free-agent draft, January 10, 1973.
Selected by San Francisco Giants' organization in secondary phase of free-agent draft, June 5, 1973.
†Traded to St. Louis Cardinals for Third Baseman Ken Reitz, December 8, 1975.
‡Traded to New York Mets for Outfielder Tom Grieve and Pitcher Kim Seaman, December 5, 1978.

EDWARD JOSEPH FARMER

(Ed)

Born October 18, 1949, at Evergreen Park, Ill.
Height, 6.05. Weight, 205.
Throws and bats righthanded.
Hobbies—Basketball and reading.
Attended Chicago State College, Chicago, Ill.

Major League saves: 1971 (4), 1972 (7), 1973 (3), 1974 (0), 1977 (0), 1978 (1), 1979 (14), 1980 (30). Total—59.
Led International League in wild pitches with 13 in 1977.

Year Club	League	G.	IP.	W.	L.	Pct.	H.	R.	ER.	SO.	BB.	ERA.
1967—Sarasota Indians	Gulf Coast	7	32	3	0	1.000	12	13	7	29	30	1.97
1968—Waterbury	Eastern	4	14	0	3	.000	12	15	11	9	13	7.07
1968—Reno	California	23	125	8	5	.615	132	74	65	122	69	4.68
1969—Waterbury	Eastern	7	26	0	4	.000	36	26	20	12	19	6.92
1969—Monroe	W. Carol.	10	46	3	5	.375	44	39	30	30	43	5.87
1970—Wichita†	Am. Assoc.	23	121	5	7	.417	114	64	54	69	70	4.02
1971—Wichita	Am. Assoc.	7	40	2	2	.500	35	22	20	19	15	4.50
1971—Cleveland	American	43	79	5	4	.556	77	42	38	48	41	4.33
1972—Cleveland	American	46	61	2	5	.286	51	32	30	33	27	4.43
1973—Cleveland-Detroit‡§x	American	40	62	3	2	.600	77	38	34	38	32	4.94
1974—Toledo	Int'national	7	47	2	3	.400	33	18	14	34	23	2.68
1974—Philadelphia y	National	14	31	2	1	.667	41	32	29	20	27	8.42
1975—Sacramento	P. Coast	14	61	2	8	.200	69	59	53	53	67	7.82
1975—Union Laguna	Mexican	2	1	0	1	.000	1	4	3	0	4	27.00
1976—Salt Lake City z	P. Coast					(Did not play)						
1977—Rochester	Int'national	24	131	11	5	.688	127	72	65	96	89	4.47
1977—Baltimore a	American	1	0	0	0	.000	1	1	1	0	1	.....
1978—Spokane	P.Coast	55	90	9	7	.563	103	73	60	50	53	6.00
1978—Milwaukee b	American	3	11	1	0	1.000	7	1	1	6	4	0.82
1979—Texas c-Chicago	American	53	114	5	7	.417	96	57	38	73	53	3.00
1980—Chicago	American	64	100	7	9	.438	92	37	37	54	56	3.33
American League Totals		250	427	23	27	.460	401	208	179	252	214	3.77
National League Totals		14	31	2	1	.667	41	32	29	20	27	8.42
Major League Totals		264	458	25	28	.472	442	240	208	272	241	4.09

Selected by Cleveland Indians' organization in 5th round of free-agent draft, June 6, 1967.
†On disabled list July 23 through August 21.
‡Traded to Detroit Tigers for Pitcher Tom Timmerman and Infielder Kevin Collins (latter transferred from Toledo to Oklahoma City), June 15, 1973.
§Traded to New York Yankees for Catcher Jerry Moses in three-team deal in which Cleveland Indians acquired Pitcher Jim Perry from Detroit and Indians sent Outfielder Walt Williams and Pitcher Rick Sawyer to Yankees, March 19, 1973.
xSold by New York Yankees to Philadelphia Phillies, March 21, 1974.
yTraded to Milwaukee Brewers for Infielder-Outfielder Steve McCartney, December 3, 1974.
zReleased, April 4, 1976; signed by Rochester (Baltimore Orioles' organization), March 2, 1977.
aReleased, March 28, 1978; signed by Milwaukee Brewers' organization, April 1, 1978.

bTraded with First Baseman Gary Holle and cash to Texas Rangers for Pitcher Reggie Cleveland, December 15, 1978.

cTraded with First Baseman Gary Holle to Chicago White Sox for Third Baseman Eric Soderholm, June 15, 1979.

ALL-STAR GAME RECORD

Year League	IP.	W.	L.	Pct.	H.	R.	ER.	SO.	BB.	ERA.
1980—American	⅔	0	0	.000	1	0	0	0	0	0.00

TERRY LANE FELTON

Born October 29, 1957, at Texarkana, Tex.
Height, 6.02. Weight, 185.
Throws and bats righthanded.

Year Club	League	G.	IP.	W.	L.	Pct.	H.	R.	ER.	SO.	BB.	ERA.
1976—Elizabethton	Ap'lachian	14	87	2	6	.250	89	54	37	91	27	3.83
1977—Orlando	Southern	23	154	8	9	.471	145	72	58	88	82	3.39
1978—Toledo	Int'national	26	162	9	9	.500	147	75	63	80	58	3.50
1979—Toledo	Int'national	28	184	7	10	.412	156	89	70	127	74	3.42
1979—Minnesota	American	1	2	0	0	.000	0	0	0	1	0	0.00
1980—Toledo	Int'national	25	146	7	8	.467	129	73	65	100	81	4.01
1980—Minnesota	American	5	18	0	3	.000	20	18	14	14	9	7.00
Major League Totals		6	20	0	3	.000	20	18	14	15	9	6.30

Selected by Minnesota Twins' organization in 2nd round of free-agent draft, June 8, 1976.

JOSEPH VANCE FERGUSON

(Joe)

Born September 19, 1946, at San Francisco, Calif.
Height, 6.02. Weight, 215.
Throws and bats righthanded.
Hobbies—Golf and art (sketching).
Attended University of the Pacific, Stockton, Calif.

Established major league record for fewest errors, season, catcher (700 or more chances), 3, 1973.
Led National League catchers in passed balls with 16 in 1977.
Led National League catchers in double plays with 17 in 1973.
Tied for National League lead in sacrifice flies with 10 in 1973.
Led Northwest League batters in walks with 54 and strikeouts with 77 in 1968.
Led Florida State League catchers in passed balls with 44 in 1969.

Year Club	League	Pos.	G.	AB.	R.	H.	2B.	3B.	HR.	RBI.	B.A.	PO.	A.	E.	F.A.
1968—Tri-City	Northw.	OF	70	226	44	65	9	4	*12	52	.288	101	6	2	.982
1969—Daytona Beach	F.S.	*C-O-1	123	391	66	112	21	4	9	58	.286	*728	*90	*26	.969
1970—Albuquerque	Tex.	*C-O-3	109	364	72	111	20	4	16	65	.305	606	83	8	*.989
1970—Los Angeles	Nat.	C	5	4	0	1	0	0	0	1	.250	9	0	0	1.000
1971—Spokane	P.C.	C-OF	60	213	27	54	10	1	10	43	.254	345	31	7	.982
1971—Los Angeles	Nat.	C	36	102	13	22	3	0	2	7	.216	167	9	3	.983
1972—Albuquerque	P.C.	C-OF	123	380	68	99	21	4	10	67	.292	516	40	10	.982
1972—Los Angeles	Nat.	C-OF	8	24	2	7	3	0	1	5	.292	42	1	0	1.000
1973—Los Angeles†	Nat.	*C-OF	136	487	84	128	26	0	25	88	.263	786	57	5	*.994
1974—Los Angeles	Nat.	C-OF	111	349	54	88	14	1	16	57	.252	486	40	7	.987
1975—Los Angeles‡	Nat.	C-OF	66	202	15	42	2	1	5	23	.208	215	20	2	.992
1976—L.A.§St.L.x	Nat.	C-OF	125	374	46	79	15	4	10	39	.211	409	46	14	.970
1977—Houston	Nat.	C-1B	132	421	59	108	21	3	16	61	.257	644	80	11	.985
1978—Hous. y-L.A.	Nat.	C-OF	118	348	40	78	16	0	14	50	.224	573	52	7	.989
1979—Los Angeles	Nat.	C-OF	122	363	54	95	14	0	20	69	.262	414	37	9	.980
1980—Los Angeles z	Nat.	C-OF	77	172	20	41	3	2	9	29	.238	297	23	7	.979
Major League Totals			936	2846	387	689	117	11	118	429	.242	4069	365	65	.986

Selected by Los Angeles Dodgers' organization in 13th round of free-agent draft, June 7, 1968.
†On supplemental disabled list, June 21 to July 10, 1973.
‡On disabled list, July 2 to September 29, 1975.
§Traded with Outfielder Bobby Detherage and Infielder Freddie Tisdale, latter assigned from Lodi to St. Petersburg, to St. Louis Cardinals for Outfielder Reggie Smith, June 15, 1976.
xTraded with Outfielder Bobby Detherage, assigned to Memphis, to Houston Astros for Pitcher Larry Dierker and Infielder Jerry DaVanon, November 23, 1976.
yTraded to Los Angeles Dodgers for two players to be named later, July 1, 1978; Outfielder Rafael Landestoy sent to Houston, July 7, 1978 and Outfielder Jeff Leonard sent to Houston, September 11, 1978 to complete deal.
zOn disabled list, April 16 to May 9, 1980.

CHAMPIONSHIP SERIES RECORD

Year Club	League	Pos.	G.	AB.	R.	H.	2B.	3B.	HR.	RBI.	B.A.	PO.	A.	E.	F.A.
1974—Los Angeles	Nat.	OF-C	4	13	3	3	0	0	0	2	.231	9	0	1	.900
1978—Los Angeles	Nat.	PH	2	2	0	0	0	0	0	0	.000	0	0	0	.000
Championship Series Totals			6	15	3	3	0	0	0	2	.200	9	0	1	.900

WORLD SERIES RECORD

Tied World Series records for most errors, catcher, 5-game series, 2, in 1974, and most errors, catcher, game, 2, October 15, 1974.

Year Club	League	Pos.	G.	AB.	R.	H.	2B.	3B.	HR.	RBI.	B.A.	PO.	A.	E.	F.A.
1974—Los Angeles	Nat.	OF-C	5	16	2	2	0	0	1	2	.125	14	1	2	.882
1978—Los Angeles	Nat.	C	2	4	1	2	2	0	0	0	.500	11	0	1	.917
World Series Totals			7	20	3	4	2	0	1	2	.200	25	1	3	.897

ROBERT EUGENE FERRIS
(Bob)

Born May 7, 1955, at Arlington, Va.
Height, 6.06. Weight, 225.
Throws and bats righthanded.
Attended University of Maryland, College Park, Md.

Year Club	League	G.	IP.	W.	L.	Pct.	H.	R.	ER.	SO.	BB.	ERA.
1976—Quad Cities	Midwest	6	19	1	0	1.000	17	7	7	7	9	3.32
1977—El Paso	Texas	17	102	8	3	.727	103	50	42	72	40	3.71
1977—Salt Lake City	P. Coast	7	34	2	4	.333	46	29	21	28	23	5.56
1978—Salt Lake City†	P. Coast	22	118	8	10	.444	136	92	75	71	70	5.72
1979—Salt Lake City	P. Coast	30	166	14	7	.667	161	92	83	98	71	4.50
1979—California	American	2	6	0	0	.000	5	2	1	2	3	1.50
1980—Salt Lake City	P. Coast	26	167	14	8	.636	196	89	76	88	68	4.10
1980—California	American	5	15	0	2	.000	23	13	10	4	9	6.00
Major League Totals		7	21	0	2	.000	28	15	11	6	12	4.71

Selected by California Angels' organization in 2nd round of free-agent draft, June 8, 1976.
†On disabled list, May 20 to May 30, 1978.

NEIL STEPHEN FIALA

Born August 24, 1956, at St. Louis, Mo.
Height, 6.01. Weight, 185.
Throws right and bats lefthanded.
Attended Meramec Community College, Kirkwood, Mo. and
Southern Illinois University, Carbondale, Ill.
Son of Neil Fiala, minor league second baseman in Cleveland Indians'
and St. Louis Cardinals' organization, 1952-53.

Led American Association second basemen in fielding average with .977 in 1980.

Year Club	League	Pos.	G.	AB.	R.	H.	2B.	3B.	HR.	RBI.	B.A.	PO.	A.	E.	F.A.
1977—Gastonia	W. Car.	2B-SS	68	233	47	61	9	3	4	45	.262	154	196	2	.994
1978—St. Petersburg	Fla. St.	2B	92	326	44	106	15	3	1	27	.325	200	257	4	.991
1978—Arkansas	Texas	2B	43	162	19	44	3	0	0	13	.272	109	142	3	.988
1979—Arkansas	Texas	2B	105	369	51	107	11	4	2	36	.290	217	301	12	.977
1979—Springfield	A.A.	2B	58	58	5	18	4	1	1	8	.310	41	44	1	.988
1980—Springfield	A.A.	2-3-S	126	385	58	114	17	4	2	40	.296	223	334	6	.989

Selected by St. Louis Cardinals' organization in 22nd round of free-agent draft, June 5, 1974.
Selected by St. Louis Cardinals' organization in 32nd round of free-agent draft, June 7, 1977.

MARK STEVEN FIDRYCH

Born August 14, 1954, at Worcester, Mass.
Height, 6.03. Weight, 175.
Throws and bats righthanded.

Led American League in complete games with 24 in 1976.
Named American League Rookie of the Year by Baseball Writers' Association of America, 1976.
Named American League Rookie Pitcher of the Year by THE SPORTING NEWS, 1976.

Year Club	League	G.	IP.	W.	L.	Pct.	H.	R.	ER.	SO.	BB.	ERA.
1974—Bristol	Ap'lachian	23	34	3	0	1.000	24	13	9	40	16	2.38
1975—Lakeland	Florida St.	17	117	5	9	.357	111	58	49	73	50	3.77
1975—Montgomery	Southern	7	14	2	0	1.000	15	6	5	11	3	3.21
1975—Evansville	Am. Assoc.	6	40	4	1	.800	27	8	7	29	9	1.58
1976—Detroit	American	31	250	19	9	.679	217	76	65	97	53	•2.34
1977—Detroit†	American	11	81	6	4	.600	82	29	26	42	12	2.89
1978—Detroit‡	American	3	22	2	0	1.000	17	6	6	10	5	2.45
1978—Lakeland	Florida St.	4	13	1	1	.500	6	5	5	6	6	3.46
1979—Detroit§	American	4	15	0	3	.000	23	17	17	5	9	10.20
1980—Evansville	Am. Assoc.	24	117	6	7	.462	123	56	51	62	54	3.92
1980—Detroit	American	9	44	2	3	.400	58	35	28	16	20	5.73
Major League Totals		58	412	29	19	.604	397	163	142	170	99	3.10

Selected by Detroit Tigers' organization in 10th round of free-agent draft, June 5, 1974.
†On disabled list, March 31 to May 24, and July 25 through the remainder of 1977 season.
‡On disabled list, May 1 to July 20 and on emergency disabled list, August 8 through remainder of 1978 season.
§On disabled list, April 1 to May 1 and May 24 to October 10, 1979.

ALL-STAR GAME RECORD

Year League	IP.	W.	L.	Pct.	H.	R.	ER.	SO.	BB.	ERA.
1976—American	2	0	1	.000	4	2	2	1	0	9.00

Named to American League All-Star Team in 1977; replaced due to injury.

EDUARDO FIGUEROA (PADILLA)

Name pronounced fee-gur-OH-uh.

(Ed)

Born October 14, 1948, at Ciales, Puerto Rico.
Height, 6.00. Weight, 187.
Throws and bats righthanded.
Hobbies—Music, fishing and basketball.

Tied for Midwest League lead in shutouts with 3 in 1970.

Year	Club	League	G.	IP.	W.	L.	Pct.	H.	R.	ER.	SO.	BB.	ERA.
1966—Marion	Appal'chian		2	10	1	1	.500	16	8	6	6	4	5.40
1966—Greenville	W. Carol.		2	12	1	1	.500	13	3	3	10	1	2.25
1967—Winter Haven	Florida St.		26	176	12	5	.706	140	50	40	123	44	2.05
1968—Raleigh-Dur.†	Carolina		7	13	0	2	.000	14	10	9	11	7	6.23
1969—		(In Military Service)											
1970—Decatur	Midwest		13	102	8	3	.727	86	33	22	85	23	1.94
1970—Fresno	California		14	51	1	5	.167	55	27	25	47	18	4.41
1971—Fresno‡	California		14	101	10	4	.714	94	52	41	111	37	3.65
1971—Amarillo	Texas		14	104	8	5	.615	85	28	24	91	25	2.08
1972—Phoenix	P. Coast		29	139	10	2	.833	163	77	66	105	45	4.27
1973—Phoenix§-S.L.C.	P. Coast		29	150	6	8	.429	189	94	69	87	46	4.14
1974—Salt Lake C.	P. Coast		4	30	3	0	1.000	27	14	8	20	9	2.40
1974—California	American		25	105	2	8	.200	119	46	43	49	36	3.69
1975—Salt Lake C.	P. Coast		2	15	2	0	1.000	13	5	3	6	3	1.80
1975—California x	American		33	245	16	13	.552	213	96	79	139	84	2.90
1976—New York	American		34	257	19	10	.655	237	101	86	119	94	3.01
1977—New York	American		32	239	16	11	.593	228	102	95	104	75	3.58
1978—New York	American		35	253	20	9	.690	233	96	84	92	77	2.99
1979—New York y	American		16	105	4	6	.400	109	49	48	42	35	4.11
1980—New York z-Texas a	American		23	98	3	10	.231	152	76	71	25	36	6.52
Major League Totals			198	1302	80	67	.544	1291	566	506	570	437	3.50

Signed as free agent by New York Mets' organization, July 12, 1966.
†Released by New York Mets' organization, June 30, 1968; signed as free agent by San Francisco Giants' organization, February 21, 1970.
‡Appeared as outfielder in one game.
§Traded by San Francisco Giants to California Angels for Pitcher Don Rose and Infielder Bruce Christensen, July 6, 1973.
xTraded with Outfielder Mickey Rivers to New York Yankees for Outfielder Bobby Bonds, December 11, 1975.
yOn disabled list, June 25 to July 23 and August 2 to October 5, 1979.
zSold to Texas Rangers, July 28, 1980.
aGranted free agency, October 22, 1980.

CHAMPIONSHIP SERIES RECORD

Tied Championship Series record for most runs allowed, five-game Series (8), 1976.

Year	Club	League	G.	IP.	W.	L.	Pct.	H.	R.	ER.	SO.	BB.	ERA.
1976—New York	American		2	12⅓	0	1	.000	14	8	8	5	2	5.84
1977—New York	American		1	3⅓	0	0	.000	5	4	4	3	2	10.80
1978—New York	American		1	1	0	1	.000	5	5	3	0	0	27.00
Championship Series Totals			4	16⅔	0	2	.000	24	17	15	8	4	8.10

WORLD SERIES RECORD

Year	Club	League	G.	IP.	W.	L.	Pct.	H.	R.	ER.	SO.	BB.	ERA.
1976—New York	American		1	8	0	1	.000	6	5	5	2	5	5.63
1978—New York	American		2	6⅔	0	1	.000	9	6	6	2	5	8.10
World Series Totals			3	14⅔	0	2	.000	15	11	11	4	10	6.75

JESUS MARIA FIGUEROA (FIGUEROA)

Born February 20, 1957, at Santo Domingo, Dominican Republic.
Height, 5.10. Weight, 160.
Throws and bats lefthanded.

Year	Club	League	Pos.	G.	AB.	R.	H.	2B.	3B.	HR.	RBI.	B.A.	PO.	A.	E.	F.A.
1975—Fort Lauderdale	Fla. St.		OF	94	343	49	86	7	0	0	12	.251	215	13	7	.970
1976—Fort Lauderdale	Fla. St.		OF	108	385	50	95	7	2	0	30	.247	226	11	6	.975
1977—West Haven‡§	East.		OF	79	304	61	82	13	1	5	39	.270	121	5	10	.926
1978—Wichita	A.A.		OF	69	201	23	51	4	0	2	14	.254	82	7	7	.927
1979—Wichita	A.A.		OF	116	426	58	124	15	0	1	27	.291	211	14	4	.983
1980—Wichita	A.A.		OF	11	39	5	4	0	0	1	3	.103	29	1	1	.968
1980—Chicago x	Nat.		OF	115	198	20	50	5	0	1	11	.253	89	6	2	.979
Major League Totals				115	198	20	50	5	0	1	11	.253	89	6	2	.979

Signed as free agent by New York Yankees' organization, September 29, 1974.
†On disabled list, May 6 to May 26, 1976.
‡On disabled list, August 10 to August 19, 1977.
§Drafted by Chicago Cubs' organization, December 6, 1977.
xTraded with Outfielder Jerry Martin to San Francisco Giants for Pitcher Phil Nastu and Second Baseman Joe Strain, December 12, 1980.

THOMAS CARSON FILER
(Tom)

Born December 1, 1956, at Philadelphia, Pa.
Height, 6.01. Weight, 195.
Throws and bats righthanded.

Year Club	League	G.	IP.	W.	L.	Pct.	H.	R.	ER.	SO.	BB.	ERA.
1978—Oneonta	N.Y.-Penn.	9	43	2	3	.400	30	14	8	34	14	1.67
1979—West Haven	Eastern	24	154	12	8	.600	132	73	62	80	53	3.62
1980—Nashville†	Southern	27	187	13	9	.591	168	94	61	112	86	2.94

Signed as free agent by New York Yankees' organization, June 28, 1978.
†Drafted by Oakland A's, December 8, 1980.

LESLIE WILLIAM FILKINS
(Les)

Born September 14, 1956, at Chicago, Ill.
Height, 5.11. Weight, 185.
Throws and bats lefthanded.

Led Florida State League outfielders in double plays with 6 in 1976.

Year Club	League	Pos.	G.	AB.	R.	H.	2B.	3B.	HR.	RBI.	B.A.	PO.	A.	E.	F.A.
1975—Bristol	Appal.	OF	32	108	19	32	5	0	5	26	.296	52	1	4	.930
1975—Clinton	Midw.	OF	26	98	15	19	3	1	2	7	.194	45	3	0	1.000
1976—Lakeland	Fla.St.	OF	132	472	54	111	17	3	3	46	.235	220	14	4	.983
1977—Lakeland	Fla.St.	OF	113	389	56	86	13	4	1	37	.221	213	5	4	.982
1978—Montgomery	South.	OF	136	478	46	111	22	5	5	39	.232	207	10	5	.977
1979—Montgomery†	South.	OF	109	357	51	99	17	1	9	43	.277	146	11	6	.963
1980—Montgomery	South.	OF	49	174	22	50	10	1	6	31	.287	82	4	3	.966
1980—Evansville	A.A.	OF	83	273	41	123	19	1	7	38	.297	110	8	3	.975

Selected by Detroit Tigers' organization in 1st round (3rd player selected) of free-agent draft, June 4, 1975.
†On disabled list, April 12 to May 10, 1979.

STEVEN HARRY FINCH
(Steve)

Born March 9, 1955, at Escondido, Calif.
Height, 6.03. Weight, 160.
Throws and bats righthanded.
Attended American River College, Sacramento, Calif.

Year Club	League	G.	IP.	W.	L.	Pct.	H.	R.	ER.	SO.	BB.	ERA.
1976—Sarasota Rangers	G. Coast	10	59	4	1	.800	41	21	17	53	36	2.59
1977—Asheville	W. Carol.	25	191	15	5	.750	165	79	62	193	55	2.92
1978—Tulsa†	Texas	7	29	1	2	.333	28	19	16	24	17	4.97
1979—Tulsa‡	Texas	12	68	2	7	.222	70	35	27	50	20	3.57
1980—Charleston§	Int'national	22	116	7	6	.538	125	59	54	52	30	4.19

Selected by Texas Rangers' organization in 2nd round of free-agent draft, June 8, 1976.
†On disabled list, April 11 to April 21, May 17 to June 20 and June 29 to September 29, 1978.
‡On disabled list, May 15 to July 2, 1979.
§Traded with Outfielder Richie Zisk, Shortstop Rick Auerbach and Pitchers Brian Allard, Ken Clay and Jerry Gleaton to Seattle Mariners for Catcher Larry Cox, Pitcher Rick Honeycutt, Shortstop Mario Mendoza and Outfielders Leon Roberts and Willie Horton, December 12, 1980.

ROLAND GLEN FINGERS
(Rollie)

Born August 25, 1946, at Steubenville, O.
Height, 6.04. Weight, 195.
Throws and bats righthanded.
Hobby—Golf.
Attended Chaffey Junior College, Alta Loma, Calif.
Son of George M. Fingers, who spent four years in the St. Louis Cardinals' organization, and brother of Gordon Fingers, former pitcher in Oakland Athletics' organization.

Established major league records for most seasons and most consecutive seasons leading major leagues in saves (2); most saves, lifetime (244).
Tied major league records for most seasons and most consecutive seasons leading league in saves (2).
Tied National League record for most saves, season (37).
Major league saves: 1968 (0), 1969 (12), 1970 (2), 1971 (17), 1972 (21), 1973 (22), 1974 (18), 1975 (24), 1976 (20), 1977 (35), 1978 (37), 1979 (13), 1980 (23). Total—244.
Led National League in saves with 35 in 1977 and with 37 in 1978.
Tied for Southern League lead in shutouts with 3 in 1968.
Named National League Fireman of the Year by THE SPORTING NEWS, 1977 and 1978.
Named National League co-Fireman of the Year by THE SPORTING NEWS, 1980.

Year Club	League	G.	IP.	W.	L.	Pct.	H.	R.	ER.	SO.	BB.	ERA.
1965—Leesburg	Florida St.	25	175	8	15	.348	148	83	58	108	69	2.98
1966—Modesto	California	22	159	11	6	.647	120	61	49	152	43	2.77
1967—Birmingham†‡	Southern	18	102	6	5	.545	75	34	25	61	36	2.21
1968—Birmingham	Southern	18	108	10	4	.714	94	38	36	93	28	3.00
1968—Oakland	American	1	1	0	0	.000	4	4	4	0	1	36.00

Year Club	League	G.	IP.	W.	L.	Pct.	H.	R.	ER.	SO.	BB.	ERA.
1969—Oakland	American	60	119	6	7	.462	116	60	49	61	41	3.71
1970—Oakland	American	45	148	7	9	.438	137	65	60	79	48	3.65
1971—Oakland	American	48	129	4	6	.400	94	46	43	98	30	3.00
1972—Oakland	American	65	111	11	9	.550	85	35	31	113	32	2.51
1973—Oakland	American	62	127	7	8	.467	107	41	27	110	39	1.91
1974—Oakland	American	*76	119	9	5	.643	104	41	35	95	29	2.65
1975—Oakland	American	*75	127	10	6	.625	95	43	42	115	33	2.98
1976—Oakland§	American	70	135	13	11	.542	118	40	37	113	40	2.47
1977—San Diego	National	*78	132	8	9	.471	123	47	44	113	36	3.00
1978—San Diego	National	67	107	6	13	.316	84	33	30	72	29	2.52
1979—San Diego	National	54	84	9	9	.500	91	47	42	65	37	4.50
1980—San Diego xy	National	66	103	11	9	.550	101	35	32	69	32	2.80
American League Totals		502	1016	67	61	.523	860	375	328	784	293	2.91
National League Totals		265	426	34	40	.459	399	162	148	319	134	3.13
Major League Totals		767	1442	101	101	.500	1259	537	476	1103	427	2.97

Signed as free agent by Kansas City A's organization, December 24, 1964.

†On disabled list, April 18 to June 1, 1967.

‡On military list, December 29, 1967, to May 12, 1968.

§Played out option year and granted free agency, November 1, 1976; signed as free agent with San Diego Padres, December 14, 1976.

xTraded with Pitcher Bob Shirley, Catcher-First Baseman Gene Tenace and a player to be named later to St. Louis Cardinals for Catchers Terry Kennedy and Steve Swisher, Pitchers John Littlefield, Al Olmsted, Kim Seaman and John Urrea and Infielder Mike Phillips, December 8, 1980; Cardinals acquired Catcher Bob Geren completing deal, December 10, 1980.

yTraded with Catcher Ted Simmons and Pitcher Pete Vuckovich to Milwaukee Brewers for Outfielders Sixto Lezcano and David Green and Pitchers Lary Sorensen and Dave PaPoint, December 12, 1980.

CHAMPIONSHIP SERIES RECORD

Established American League Championship Series record for most games pitched, total Series (11).
Tied American League Championship Series record for most saves, total Series (2).

Year Club	League	G.	IP.	W.	L.	Pct.	H.	R.	ER.	SO.	BB.	ERA.
1971—Oakland	American	2	2⅓	0	0	.000	2	2	2	2	1	7.71
1972—Oakland	American	3	5⅓	1	0	1.000	4	1	1	3	1	1.69
1973—Oakland	American	3	4⅔	0	1	.000	4	1	1	4	2	1.93
1974—Oakland	American	2	3	0	0	.000	3	1	1	3	1	3.00
1975—Oakland	American	1	4	0	1	.000	5	3	3	3	1	6.75
Championship Series Totals		11	19⅓	1	2	.333	18	8	8	15	6	3.72

WORLD SERIES RECORD

Established World Series record for most saves, total Series (6); most games as relief pitcher, total Series (16); most saves, five-game Series (2), 1974.

Year Club	League	G.	IP.	W.	L.	Pct.	H.	R.	ER.	SO.	BB.	ERA.
1972—Oakland	American	6	10⅓	1	1	.500	4	2	2	11	4	1.74
1973—Oakland	American	6	13⅔	0	1	.000	13	5	1	8	4	0.66
1974—Oakland	American	4	9⅓	1	0	1.000	8	2	2	6	2	1.93
World Series Totals		16	33⅓	2	2	.500	25	9	5	25	10	1.35

ALL-STAR GAME RECORD

Year League	IP.	W.	L.	Pct.	H.	R.	ER.	SO.	BB.	ERA.
1973—American	1	0	0	.000	0	0	0	0	0	0.00
1974—American	1	0	0	.000	1	2	2	0	1	18.00
1978—National	2	0	0	.000	1	0	0	1	0	0.00
All-Star Game Totals	4	0	0	.000	2	2	2	1	1	4.50

Member of American League All-Star Team in 1975 and 1976; did not play.

STEPHEN JOHN FIREOVID
(Steve)

Born June 6, 1957, at Bryan, O.
Height, 6.02. Weight, 195.
Throws right and bats left and righthanded.
Attended Miami University, Oxford, O.

Year Club	League	G.	IP.	W.	L.	Pct.	H.	R.	ER.	SO.	BB.	ERA.
1978—Walla Walla	Northwest	14	106	9	2	.818	82	45	29	99	52	2.46
1979—Reno	California	26	168	13	9	.591	182	92	76	135	65	4.07
1980—Amarillo	Texas	27	164	12	6	.667	196	100	86	106	52	4.72

Selected by San Diego Padres' organization in 7th round of free-agent draft, June 6, 1978.

MICHAEL THOMAS FISCHLIN

Born September 13, 1955, at Sacramento, Calif.
Height, 6.01. Weight, 165.
Throws and bats righthanded.
Hobbies—Fishing, camping and the outdoors.
Attended Cosumnes River Junior College, Sacramento, Calif.,
and Sacramento State University, Sacramento, Calif.

Tied National League record for fewest chances offered by shortstop, two consecutive games (1), June 18 and 20, 1978.

Led Pacific Coast league shortstops in putouts with 200 and in double plays with 88 in 1980.

Year	Club	League	Pos.	G.	AB.	R.	H.	2B.	3B.	HR.	RBI.	B.A.	PO.	A.	E.	F.A.
1975—Oneonta	...........NYP		SS	35	135	22	31	4	3	0	6	.230	34	128	15	.915
1975—Ft. Lauderdale	..Fla. St.		SS	29	104	7	19	4	0	0	7	.183	54	90	10	.935
1976—West Haven	.......East.		S-3-2	91	248	16	38	7	1	2	20	.153	149	243	27	.936
1976—Oneonta	...........NYP		SS	14	55	13	14	3	0	0	5	.255	36	48	7	.923
1977—Ft. Lauderdale†	.Fla. St.		SS-2B	53	201	28	59	6	4	0	20	.294	84	188	16	.944
1977—Columbus	.........South.		SS	66	223	23	54	5	0	1	16	.242	104	204	16	.951
1977—Houston	...........Nat.		SS	13	15	0	3	0	0	0	0	.200	3	17	0	1.000
1978—Charleston	........Int.		SS	82	280	38	59	10	2	0	19	.211	141	279	13	.970
1978—Houston	...........Nat.		SS	44	86	3	10	1	0	0	6	.116	49	67	9	.928
1979—Charleston‡	.......Int.		SS	44	138	13	31	4	1	0	8	.225	73	134	8	.963
1980—Tucson	.............P.C.		*SS-OF	131	417	65	117	24	7	3	49	.281	201	*437	*40	.941
1980—Houston	...........Nat.		SS	1	1	0	0	0	0	0	0	.000	0	0	0	.000
Major League Totals	....			58	102	3	13	1	0	0	0	.127	52	84	9	.938

Selected by New York Yankees' organization in 7th round of free-agent draft, June 4, 1975.

†Traded with Pitcher Randy Niemann (assigned from West Haven to Columbus, Ga.) and a player to be named later by New York Yankees' organziation to Houston Astros' organization for Outfielder Cliff Johnson, June 15, 1977. Dave Bergman was assigned to Houston to complete deal, November 23, 1977.

‡On disabled list, June 18 to August 28, 1979.

CARLTON ERNEST FISK

Born December 26, 1947, at Bellows Falls, Vt.
Height, 6.02. Weight, 220.
Throws and bats righthanded.
Hobbies—Sports, reading and woodworking.
Attended University of New Hampshire, Durham, N. H.
Brother of Calvin Fisk, former catcher in Baltimore Orioles' organization.
Brother-in-law of Rick Miller, outfielder with California Angels. Cousin of
Dave Jennings, punter with New York Giants.

Tied major league record for most home runs, opening game of season (2), April 6, 1973.
Tied modern major league record for most long hits, inning (2), May 15, 1975 (eighth inning) and June 30, 1977 (eighth inning).
Tied American League record for fewest passed balls, season, 150 or more games (4), 1977.
Led American League catchers in errors with 10 in 1980.
Led International League catchers in double plays with 12 in 1971.
Named American League Rookie of the Year by the Baseball Writers' Association of America, 1972.
Named THE SPORTING NEWS American League Rookie Player of the Year, 1972.
Named catcher on THE SPORTING NEWS American League All-Star Team, 1972 and 1977.
Named catcher on THE SPORTING NEWS American League All-Star fielding team, 1972.

Year	Club	League	Pos.	G.	AB.	R.	H.	2B.	3B.	HR.	RBI.	B.A.	PO.	A.	E.	F.A.
1967—Greenville†	........W. Car.			(In Military Service)												
1968—Waterloo‡	.........Midw.		C	62	195	31	66	11	2	12	34	.338	385	42	8	.982
1969—Boston	.............Amer.		C	2	5	0	0	0	0	0	0	.000	2	0	0	1.000
1970—Pawtucket	.........East.		C-O-1	93	284	43	65	18	1	12	44	.229	482	50	7	.987
1971—Louisville	.........Int.		C-O-3	94	308	45	81	10	4	10	43	.263	588	51	13	.980
1971—Boston	.............Amer.		C	14	48	7	15	2	1	2	6	.313	72	6	2	.975
1972—Boston	...........Amer.		C	131	457	74	134	28	•9	22	61	.293	*846	*72	•15	.984
1973—Boston	...........Amer.		C	135	508	65	125	21	0	26	71	.246	*739	50	*14	.983
1974—Boston§	...........Amer.		C	52	187	36	56	12	1	11	26	.299	267	26	6	.980
1975—Boston x	...........Amer.		C	79	263	47	87	14	4	10	52	.331	347	30	8	.979
1976—Boston	.............Amer.		C	134	487	76	124	17	5	17	58	.255	649	73	12	.984
1977—Boston	.............Amer.		C	152	536	106	169	26	3	26	102	.315	779	69	11	.987
1978—Boston	.............Amer.		*C-OF	157	571	94	162	39	5	20	88	.284	734	90	*17	.980
1979—Boston y	.........Amer.		C-OF	91	320	49	87	23	2	10	42	.272	155	8	3	.982
1980—Boston z	...........Amer.		C-1-3-O	131	478	73	138	25	3	18	62	.289	543	56	11	.982
Major League Totals	....			1078	3860	627	1097	207	33	162	568	.284	5133	480	99	.983

Selected by Baltimore Orioles' organization in 36th round of free-agent draft, June, 1965.

Selected by Boston Red Sox' organization in 1st round (second player selected) of free-agent draft, January, 1967.

†On temporary inactive list, April 17, 1967. Transferred to the military list, May 18, 1967 through April 9, 1968.

‡On temporary inactive list, August 5 through August 20.

§On disabled list from beginning of season until April 26 and from June 28 through remainder of season.

xOn disabled list from beginning of season until June 23, 1975.

yOn supplemental disabled list, April 14 to May 21, 1979.

zGranted free agency by arbitrator's ruling, February 12, 1981.

CHAMPIONSHIP SERIES RECORD

Year	Club	League	Pos.	G.	AB.	R.	H.	2B.	3B.	HR.	RBI.	B.A.	PO.	A.	E.	F.A.
1975—Boston	.............Amer.		C	3	12	4	5	1	0	0	2	.417	15	0	0	1.000

WORLD SERIES RECORD

Tied World Series records for most at bats inning and most times faced pitcher inning (2), October 15, 1975 (fourth inning); most errors by catcher, game (2), October 14, 1975.

Year	Club	League	Pos.	G.	AB.	R.	H.	2B.	3B.	HR.	RBI.	B.A.	PO.	A.	E.	F.A.
1975—Boston	.............Amer.		C	7	25	5	6	0	0	2	4	.240	37	3	2	.952

Year League	Pos.	AB.	R.	H.	2B.	3B.	HR.	RBI.	B.A.	PO.	A.	E.	F.A.
1972—American	C	2	1	1	0	0	0	0	.500	2	0	0	1.000
1973—American	C	2	0	0	0	0	0	0	.000	3	0	0	1.000
1976—American	C	1	0	0	0	0	0	0	.000	1	0	0	1.000
1977—American	C	2	0	0	0	0	0	0	.000	6	1	0	1.000
1978—American	C	2	0	0	0	0	0	1	.000	4	0	0	1.000
1980—American	C	2	0	0	0	0	0	0	.000	5	0	0	1.000
All-Star Game Totals		11	1	1	0	0	0	1	.091	21	1	0	1.000

Named to American League All-Star Team for 1974 game; replaced due to injury.

MICHAEL KENDALL FLANAGAN
(Mike)

Born December 16, 1951, at Manchester, N. H.
Height, 6.00. Weight, 195.
Throws and bats lefthanded.
Hobbies—Hunting and fishing.
Attended University of Massachusetts, Amherst, Mass.
Son of Ed Flanagan, Jr., former pitcher in Boston Red Sox' organization.

Tied for American League lead in games started with 40 in 1978.
Tied for Southern League lead in shutouts with 3 in 1974.
Tied for American League lead in shuouts with 5 in 1979.
Named lefthanded pitcher on THE SPORTING NEWS American League All-Star Team, 1979.
Won American League Cy Young Memorial Award, 1979.

Year—Club	League	G.	IP.	W.	L.	Pct.	H.	R.	ER.	SO.	BB.	ERA.
1973—Miami	Florida St.	11	61	4	1	.800	39	21	15	61	25	2.21
1974—Miami	Florida St.	14	103	6	6	.500	67	32	24	119	48	2.10
1974—Asheville	Southern	11	84	6	4	.600	61	19	17	62	18	1.82
1975—Rochester	Int'national	27	173	13	4	*.765	155	58	48	135	56	2.50
1975—Baltimore	American	2	10	0	1	.000	9	4	3	7	6	2.70
1976—Baltimore	American	20	85	3	5	.375	83	41	39	56	33	4.13
1976—Rochester	Int'national	7	51	6	1	.857	40	16	12	24	14	2.12
1977—Baltimore	American	36	235	15	10	.600	235	100	95	149	70	3.64
1978—Baltimore	American	40	281	19	15	.559	271	128	126	167	87	4.04
1979—Baltimore	American	39	266	*23	9	.719	245	107	91	190	70	3.08
1980—Baltimore	American	37	251	16	13	.552	*278	121	115	128	71	4.12
Major League Totals		174	1128	76	53	.589	1121	501	469	697	337	3.74

Selected by Houston Astros' organization in 15th round of free-agent draft, June 8, 1971.
Selected by Baltimore Orioles' organization in 7th round of free-agent draft, June 5, 1973.

CHAMPIONSHIP SERIES RECORD

Year Club	League	G.	IP.	W.	L.	Pct.	H.	R.	ER.	SO.	BB.	ERA.
1979—Baltimore	American	1	7	1	0	1.000	6	6	4	2	1	5.14

WORLD SERIES RECORD

Year Club	League	G.	IP.	W.	L.	Pct.	H.	R.	ER.	SO.	BB.	ERA.
1979—Baltimore	American	3	15	1	1	.500	18	7	5	13	2	3.00

ALL-STAR GAME RECORD
Named to American League All-Star Team for 1978 game; did not play.

TIMOTHY EARL FLANNERY
(Tim)

Born September 29, 1957, at Tulsa, Okla.
Height, 5.11. Weight, 170.
Throws right and bats lefthanded.
Attended Chapman College, Orange, Calif.
Nephew of Hal Smith, former catcher with Pittsburgh Pirates;
currently scout with St. Louis Cardinals.

Year Club	League	Pos.	G.	AB.	R.	H.	2B.	3B.	HR.	RBI.	B.A.	PO.	A.	E.	F.A.
1978—Reno	Calif.	2B-P	84	340	65	119	11	5	2	49	.350	213	269	11	.962
1979—Amarillo	Texas	2B-SS	125	524	88	*181	23	6	6	71	.345	287	374	28	.959
1979—San Diego	Nat.	2B	22	65	2	10	0	1	0	4	.154	45	60	1	.991
1980—Hawaii	P. C.	2B	47	182	27	63	10	3	1	16	.346	102	146	5	.980
1980—San Diego	Nat.	2B-3B	95	292	15	70	12	0	0	25	.240	140	204	8	.977
Major League Totals			117	357	17	80	12	1	0	29	.224	185	264	9	.980

Selected by San Diego Padres' organization in 6th round of free-agent draft, June 6, 1978.

PITCHING RECORD

Year Club	League	G.	IP.	W.	L.	Pct.	H.	R.	ER.	SO.	BB.	ERA.
1978—Reno	California	1	1/3	0	1	.000	3	6	5	0	1	135.00

JOHN RICHARD FLINN

Born September 2, 1954, at Merced, Calif.
Height, 6.01. Weight, 180.
Throws and bats righthanded.
Hobbies—Fishing, hunting and furniture making.
Attended Los Angeles Valley Junior College, Van Nuys, Calif.

Led Florida State League in shutouts with 6 in 1974.

Year Club	League	G.	IP.	W.	L.	Pct.	H.	R.	ER.	SO.	BB.	ERA.
1973—Bluefield	Ap'lachian	23	42	4	2	.667	29	15	10	51	22	2.14
1974—Miami	Florida St.	33	181	12	10	.545	137	46	35	151	63	1.74
1974—Asheville	Southern	4	4	2	1	.667	8	4	4	2	3	9.00
1975—Asheville	Southern	20	85	0	9	.000	99	58	50	53	37	5.29
1975—Miami	Florida St.	4	13	1	2	.333	15	8	8	14	9	5.54
1976—Charlotte	Southern	24	148	9	8	.529	151	62	47	76	28	2.86
1977—Rochester	Int'national	48	119	10	7	.588	110	63	47	80	54	3.55
1978—Rochester†	Int'national	24	38	1	0	1.000	42	25	22	36	14	5.21
1978—Baltimore	American	13	16	1	1	.500	24	18	14	8	13	7.88
1979—Rochester	Int'national	26	100	6	6	.500	92	36	30	71	22	2.70
1979—Baltimore‡	American	4	3	0	0	.000	2	0	0	0	1	0.00
1980—Vancouver	P. Coast	17	43	2	3	.400	24	24	21	28	15	4.40
1980—Milwaukee	American	20	37	2	1	.667	31	20	16	15	20	3.89
Major League Totals		37	56	3	2	.600	57	38	30	23	34	4.82

Selected by Baltimore Orioles' organization in 28th round of free-agent draft, June 6, 1972.
Selected by Baltimore Orioles' organization in secondary phase of free-agent draft, January 10, 1973.
†On disabled list, August 3 to September 1, 1978.
‡Traded to Milwaukee Brewers for Second Baseman Lenn Sakata, December 6, 1979.

ROBERT DOUGLAS FLYNN, JR.

(Doug)

Born April 18, 1951, at Lexington, Ky.
Height, 5.11. Weight, 160.
Throws and bats righthanded.
Hobbies—Golf and fishing.
Attended University of Kentucky, Lexington, Ky., and Somerset
Community College, Somerset, Ky.
Son of Robert Douglas Flynn, Sr., former player in Brooklyn Dodgers' organization.

Tied modern major league record for most three-base hits, game (3), August 5, 1980.
Led Eastern League shortstops in double plays with 97 and tied for league lead in sacrifice flies with 9 in 1973.
Led American Association shortstops in double plays with 91 in 1974.
Led National League second basemen in putouts with 369 and in double plays with 98 in 1979.
Named second baseman on THE SPORTING NEWS National League All-Star fielding team, 1980.

Year Club	League	Pos.	G.	AB.	R.	H.	2B.	3B.	HR.	RBI.	B.A.	PO.	A.	E.	F.A.
1972—Tampa	Fla. St.	3-S-2-P	98	313	32	66	12	2	1	37	.211	109	240	18	.951
1973—Three Rivers	East.	SS	*139	*500	52	129	11	0	3	42	.258	*231	*453	34	.953
1974—Indianapolis	A.A.	SS	134	458	57	116	13	6	2	34	.253	213	*392	16	.948
1975—Cincinnati	Nat.	3-2-S	89	127	17	34	7	0	1	20	.268	57	118	2	.989
1976—Cincinnati	Nat.	2-3-S	93	219	20	62	15	2	1	20	.283	107	152	4	.985
1977—Cinc.†-N.Y.	Nat.	S-2-3	126	314	14	62	7	2	0	19	.197	171	235	14	.967
1978—New York	Nat.	2B-SS	156	532	37	126	12	8	0	36	.237	332	426	15	.981
1979—New York	Nat.	2B-SS	157	555	35	135	19	5	4	61	.243	402	421	16	.981
1980—New York‡	Nat.	*2B-SS	128	443	46	113	9	8	0	24	.255	284	374	6	*.991
Major League Totals			749	2190	169	532	69	25	6	180	.243	1353	1726	57	.982

Signed as free agent by Cincinnati Reds' organization, August 25, 1971.
†Traded with Outfielders Dan Norman and Steve Henderson and Pitcher Pat Zachry to New York Mets for Pitcher Tom Seaver, June 15, 1977.
‡On supplemental disabled list, August 20 to September 6, 1980.

PITCHING RECORD

Year Club	League	G.	IP.	W.	L.	Pct.	H.	R.	ER.	SO.	BB.	ERA.
1972—Tampa	Florida St.	1	3	0	0	.000	3	1	1	3	1	3.00

CHAMPIONSHIP SERIES RECORD

Year Club	League	Pos.	G.	AB.	R.	H.	2B.	3B.	HR.	RBI.	B.A.	PO.	A.	E.	F.A.
1976—Cincinnati	National	2B	1	0	0	0	0	0	0	0	.000	0	0	0	.000

MARVIS EDWIN FOLEY

Born August 29, 1953, at Stanford, Ky.
Height, 6.00. Weight, 195.
Throws right and bats lefthanded.
Hobbies—Hunting and fishing.
Attended University of Kentucky, Lexington, Ky.; received Bachelor of General Studies degree.

Led Southern League catchers in double plays with 12 in 1978.

Year Club	League	Pos.	G.	AB.	R.	H.	2B.	3B.	HR.	RBI.	B.A.	PO.	A.	E.	F.A.
1975—Appleton	Midw.	1B-OF	6	13	1	4	0	0	0	1	.308	16	1	0	1.000
1975—Knoxville	South.	C-1B	51	150	22	44	9	0	1	27	.293	74	6	4	.952

Year Club	League	Pos.	G.	AB.	R.	H.	2B.	3B.	HR.	RBI.	B.A.	PO.	A.	E.	F.A.
1976—Knoxville ....South.		1B-C-3	126	414	44	104	12	2	2	36	.251	755	86	13	.985
1977—Appleton ....Midw.		1-C-3	48	162	24	44	6	2	3	21	.272	404	48	6	.987
1977—Iowa ................A.A.		1-C-3	10	27	1	5	3	0	1	4	.185	66	5	2	.973
1977—Knoxville ....South.		1B-C	66	226	33	68	13	3	6	42	.301	410	39	2	.996
1978—Knoxville† ....South.		C-1B	103	338	52	93	20	5	1	44	.275	584	69	7	.989
1978—Chicago ....Amer.		C	11	34	3	12	0	0	0	6	.353	41	4	3	.938
1979—Iowa ....A. A.		C-1B	77	250	32	70	15	1	2	25	.280	387	40	8	.982
1979—Chicago ....Amer.		C	34	97	6	24	3	0	2	10	.247	128	11	1	.993
1980—Glens Falls ....East.		C	21	68	10	22	5	0	1	9	.324	59	10	1	.986
1980—Iowa ....A. A.		C-OF	25	76	20	16	4	0	3	9	.211	112	9	2	.984
1980—Chicago ....Amer.		C-1B	68	137	14	29	5	0	4	15	.212	220	17	2	.992
Major League Totals......................			113	268	23	65	8	0	6	31	.243	389	32	6	.986

Selected by Chicago White Sox' organization in 17th round of free-agent draft, June 4, 1975.
†On disabled list, June 4 to June 29, 1978.

THOMAS MICHAEL FOLEY
(Tom)

Born September 9, 1959, at Columbus, Ga.
Height, 6.01. Weight, 160.
Throws right and bats lefthanded.
Attended Miami-Dade Community College South, Miami, Fla.

Led Western Carolinas League shortstops in double plays with 98 in 1978.
Led Florida State League shortstops in double plays with 71 in 1979.

Year Club	League	Pos.	G.	AB.	R.	H.	2B.	3B.	HR.	RBI.	B.A.	PO.	A.	E.	F.A.
1977—Billings.............Pion.		3B-SS	59	209	37	53	7	1	2	21	.254	53	109	24	.871
1978—Shelby ....W. Car.		SS	124	424	55	98	19	1	2	41	.231	*217	●352	30	*.950
1979—Tampa ....Fla. St.		SS	125	414	38	95	12	6	0	37	.229	223	*394	35	.946
1980—Waterbury ....East.		2B	131	477	49	119	16	4	4	41	.249	*222	329	31	.947

Selected by Cincinnati Reds' organization in 7th round of free-agent draft, June 7, 1977.

WILLIAM EDWARD FOLEY
(Bill)

Born September 2, 1956, at Flushing, N.Y.
Height, 6.02. Weight, 210.
Throws and bats righthanded.
Attended Clemson University, Clemson, S.C.

Led Midwest League in total bases with 265 in 1978.
Named Most Valuable Player in Midwest League, 1978.

Year Club	League	Pos.	G.	AB.	R.	H.	2B.	3B.	HR.	RBI.	B.A.	PO.	A.	E.	F.A.
1977—Newark ....NYP		C	52	188	38	53	11	1	13	42	.282	271	35	2	.994
1978—Burlington ....Midw.		C	118	409	84	130	31	1	*34	93	.318	424	52	9	.981
1979—Holyoke ....East.		C-3B	96	333	46	90	16	2	18	74	.270	339	58	9	.978
1979—Vancouver ....P. C.		1B	28	102	15	26	2	1	5	21	.255	7	0	1	.875
1980—Vancouver† ....P. C.		C	100	277	29	74	14	0	4	38	.267	292	39	8	.976

Selected by Minnesota Twins' organization in 25th round of free-agent draft, June 5, 1974.
Selected by Milwaukee Brewers' organization in 6th round of free-agent draft, June 7, 1977.
†On disabled list, May 21 to June 8, 1980.

TIMOTHY JOHN FOLI
(Tim)

Born December 8, 1950, at Culver City, Calif.
Height, 6.00. Weight, 175.
Throws and bats righthanded.
Hobbies—Singing, golfing and fishing.
Brother of Ernie Foli, former infielder-outfielder in California Angel, St. Louis Cardinal,
Houston Astro and Kansas City Athletic organizations.

Led National League shortstops in total chances with 795 in 1972 and 778 in 1975.
Led National League shortstops in double plays with 104 in 1975 and with 102 in 1976.
Led Appalachian League shortstops in double plays with 29 in 1968.
Led California League shortstops in double plays with 72 in 1969.
Received reported $75,000 bonus to sign with New York Mets, 1968.

Year Club	League	Pos.	G.	AB.	R.	H.	2B.	3B.	HR.	RBI.	B.A.	PO.	A.	E.	F.A.
1968—Marion..............Appal.		*S-1	63	235	38	66	10	3	4	36	.281	*105	*167	23	*.922
1968—Memphis† ....Texas		SS	5	20	4	5	0	0	0	1	.250	8	10	2	.900
1969—Visalia ....Calif.		SS	95	383	60	116	10	0	15	62	.303	154	280	36	.923
1970—Tidewater ....Int.		SS-2B	103	375	63	98	10	4	6	30	.261	181	289	20	.959
1970—New York..........Nat.		SS-3B	5	11	0	4	0	0	0	1	.364	4	10	0	1.000
1971—New York‡ ....Nat.		2-3-S-O	97	288	32	65	12	2	0	24	.226	150	199	12	.967
1972—Montreal ....Nat.		*SS-2B	149	540	45	130	12	2	2	35	.241	*281	487	27	.966
1973—Montreal§ ....Nat.		S-2-O	126	458	37	110	11	0	2	36	.240	248	399	27	.960
1974—Montreal x ....Nat.		SS-3B	121	441	41	112	10	3	0	39	.254	220	412	19	.971
1975—Montreal ....Nat.		*SS-2B	152	572	64	136	25	2	1	29	.238	*261	*497	21	.973

Year Club League	Pos.	G.	AB.	R.	H.	2B.	3B.	HR.	RBI.	B.A.	PO.	A.	E.	F.A.
1976—Montreal...........Nat.	SS-3B	149	546	41	144	36	1	6	54	.264	249	470	18	.976
1977—Mont. yz-S.F. a..Nat.	S-2-3-O	117	425	32	94	22	4	4	30	.221	217	345	13	.977
1978—New York b......Nat.	SS	113	413	37	106	21	1	1	27	.257	190	314	18	.966
1979—N.Y. c-Pitts.......Nat.	SS	136	532	70	153	23	1	1	65	.288	259	410	15	.978
1980—Pittsburgh d......Nat.	SS	127	495	61	131	22	0	3	38	.265	212	402	12	*.981
Major League Totals		1292	4721	460	1185	194	16	20	378	.251	2291	3945	182	.972

Selected by New York Mets' organization in 1st round (first player selected) of free-agent draft, June 7, 1968.

†On military list, January 13 to May 24, 1969.

‡On military list, August 16 through September 1, 1971. Traded with Outfielder Ken Singleton and First Baseman Mike Jorgensen to the Montreal Expos for Outfielder Rusty Staub, April 5, 1972.

§On supplemental disabled list, July 9 to August 7, 1973.

xOn supplemental disabled list, May 13 to May 29, 1974

yTraded to San Francisco Giants for Shortstop Chris Speier, April 27, 1977.

zOn supplemental disabled list, June 21 through July 21, 1977.

aTraded to New York Mets for cash and a player to be named later, December 7, 1977.

bOn disabled list, April 26 to May 22, 1978.

cTraded with Pitcher Greg Field to Pittsburgh Pirates for Shortstop Frank Taveras, April 19, 1979.

dOn supplemental disabled list, May 29 to June 13, 1980.

CHAMPIONSHIP SERIES RECORD

Year Club League	Pos.	G.	AB.	R.	H.	2B.	3B.	HR.	RBI.	B.A.	PO.	A.	E.	F.A.
1979—Pittsburgh ....Nat.	SS	3	12	1	4	1	0	0	3	.333	3	9	0	1.000

WORLD SERIES RECORD

Established World Series records for fewest strikeouts, most at bats, Series (0 and 30), 1979; most assists by shortstop, seven-game Series (32), 1979.

Tied World Series records for most double plays by shortstop, seven-game Series (7), 1979; most double plays started by shortstop, seven-game Series (4), 1979; most assists by shortstop, inning (3), October 12, 1979 (second inning).

Year Club League	Pos.	G.	AB.	R.	H.	2B.	3B.	HR.	RBI.	B.A.	PO.	A.	E	F.A.
1979—Pittsburgh ....Nat.	SS	7	30	6	10	1	1	0	3	.333	8	32	3	.930

BARRY CLIFTON FOOTE

Born February 16, 1952, at Smithfield, N. C.
Height, 6.03. Weight, 215.
Throws and bats righthanded.
Attended North Carolina State University, Raleigh, N. C.
Son of Amby Foote, former third baseman-pitcher in Brooklyn Dodger and
Pittsburgh Pirate organizations.

Led National League in sacrifice flies with 12 in 1974.
Tied for National League lead in double plays by catchers with 10 in 1975.
Led Florida State League catchers in double plays with 11 and in passed balls with 31 in 1971.
Led Eastern League catchers in double plays with 21 in 1972.

Year Club League	Pos.	G.	AB.	R.	H.	2B.	3B.	HR.	RBI.	B.A.	PO.	A.	E.	F.A.
1970—B'denton Expos .Gulf C.	C	46	143	26	38	7	0	3	29	.266	268	21	7	.976
1971—W. Palm Beach..Fla. St.	*C-1B	115	366	45	84	14	5	8	42	.230	●677	*89	*28	.965
1972—Quebec City.......East.	*C-OF	124	427	62	108	23	0	16	75	.253	658	58	*25	.966
1973—Peninsula...........Int.	C-3-O	137	465	63	122	22	2	19	65	.262	452	94	12	.978
1973—Montreal ....Nat.	PH	6	6	0	4	0	1	0	1	.667	0	0	0	.000
1974—Montreal ....Nat.	C	125	420	44	110	23	4	11	60	.262	640	*83	12	.984
1975—Montreal ....Nat.	C	118	387	25	75	16	1	7	30	.194	590	50	10	.985
1976—Montreal†.........Nat.	C-3-1	105	350	32	82	12	2	7	27	.234	487	61	6	.989
1977—Mont.‡-Phila......Nat.	C	33	81	7	19	4	1	3	11	.235	121	11	2	.985
1978—Philadelphia§ ....Nat.	C	39	57	4	9	0	0	1	4	.158	78	5	0	1.000
1979—Chicago ....Nat.	C	132	429	47	109	26	0	16	56	.254	713	63	*17	.979
1980—Chicago x..........Nat.	C	63	202	16	48	13	1	6	28	.238	317	36	3	.992
Major League Totals		621	1932	175	456	94	10	51	217	.236	2946	309	50	.985

Selected by Montreal Expos' organization in 1st round (third player selected) of free-agent draft, June 4, 1970.

†On disabled list, August 7 through August 23, 1976.

‡Traded with Pitcher Dan Warthen to Philadelphia Phillies for Pitcher Wayne Twitchell and Catcher Tim Blackwell, June 15, 1977.

§Traded with Outfielder Jerry Martin, Second Baseman Ted Sizemore and Pitchers Derek Botelho and Henry Mack to Chicago Cubs for Second Baseman Manny Trillo, Outfielder Greg Gross and Catcher Dave Rader, February 23, 1979.

xOn supplemental disabled list, May 25 to June 13 and August 18 to September 2, 1980.

CHAMPIONSHIP SERIES RECORD

Year Club League	Pos.	G.	AB.	R.	H.	2B.	3B.	HR.	RBI.	B.A.	PO.	A.	E.	F.A.
1978—Philadelphia......Nat.	PH	1	1	0	0	0	0	0	0	.000	0	0	0	.000

DID YOU KNOW—
That the National League won its ninth straight All-Star Game in 1980?

DARNELL GLENN FORD, SR.
(Dan)

Born May 19, 1952, at Los Angeles, Calif.
Height, 6.01. Weight, 185.
Throws and bats righthanded.
Hobbies—Hunting, fishing, horse riding and motor cycles.
Attended Southwestern College, Chula Vista, Calif., and Mesa Community College, Mesa, Ariz.

Hit for the cycle against Seattle Mariners, August 10, 1979.
Led Pacific Coast League outfielders in double plays with 7 in 1973.
Tied for American League lead in sacrifice flies with 13 in 1979.

Year Club League	Pos.	G.	AB.	R.	H.	2B.	3B.	HR.	RBI.	B.A.	PO.	A.	E.	F.A.
1971—Burlington.........Midw.	OF	107	397	75	106	21	4	14	80	.267	186	11	10	.952
1972—Burlington† ....Midw.	OF	72	246	55	87	15	4	18	61	.354	137	4	8	.946
1973—Tucson‡ ....P. C.	OF	128	465	80	136	21	12	14	70	.292	310	•16	11	.967
1974—Tucson§x..........P. C.	OF	115	428	62	117	11	9	12	65	.273	263	11	14	.951
1975—Minnesota ....Amer.	OF	130	440	72	123	21	1	15	59	.280	246	3	3	.988
1976—Minnesota ....Amer.	OF	145	514	87	137	24	7	20	86	.267	267	6	9	.968
1977—Minnesota ....Amer.	OF	144	453	66	121	25	7	11	60	.267	205	9	8	.964
1978—Minnesota y ......Amer.	OF	151	592	78	162	36	10	11	82	.274	376	6	9	.977
1979—California ....Amer.	OF	142	569	100	165	26	5	21	101	.290	332	10	8	.977
1980—California z.......Amer.	OF	65	226	22	63	11	0	7	26	.279	75	3	5	.940
Major League Totals		777	2794	425	771	143	30	85	414	.276	1501	37	42	.973

Selected by Oakland A's organization in 1st round (16th player selected) of free-agent draft, June 4, 1970.
†On temporary inactive list, April 15 to May 20, 1972.
‡On temporary inactive list, April 13 to April 16, 1973.
§On temporary inactive list, July 12 to August 2, 1974.
xTraded with Pitcher Dennis Myers by Oakland Athletics to Minnesota Twins for First Baseman Pat Bourque, October 23, 1974.
yTraded to California Angels for Third Baseman Ron Jackson and Catcher Danny Goodwin, December 4, 1978.
zOn supplemental disabled list, June 3 to August 5, 1980.

CHAMPIONSHIP SERIES RECORD

Tied Championship Series record by hitting home run in first Series at bat, October 3, 1979.

Year Club League	Pos.	G.	AB.	R.	H.	2B.	3B.	HR.	RBI.	B.A.	PO.	A.	E.	F.A.
1979—California ....Amer.	OF	4	17	2	5	1	0	2	4	.294	6	0	1	.857

DAVID ALAN FORD

Born December 29, 1956, at Cleveland, O.
Height, 6.04. Weight, 200.
Throws and bats righthanded.
Hobbies—Listening to music and playing cards.

Led Southern League in complete games with 19 and tied for lead in shutouts with 4 in 1976.
Named Southern League Pitcher of the Year, 1976.

Year Club	League	G.	IP.	W.	L.	Pct.	H.	R.	ER.	SO.	BB.	ERA.
1975—Bluefield ....Ap'lachian		7	52	3	3	.500	50	23	18	33	16	3.12
1975—Miami...............................Florida St.		2	12	1	0	1.000	8	3	3	7	4	2.25
1976—Charlotte ....Southern		27	*212	*17	7	.708	•188	76	59	*121	31	2.50
1977—Rochester ....Int'national		30	176	9	*14	.391	206	104	94	96	43	4.81
1978—Rochester ....Int'national		25	156	11	6	.647	173	81	66	74	30	3.81
1978—Baltimore ....American		2	15	1	0	1.000	10	0	0	5	2	0.00
1979—Rochester † ....Int'national		15	109	6	5	.545	110	55	43	63	25	3.55
1979—Baltimore ....American		9	30	2	1	.667	23	7	7	7	7	2.10
1980—Baltimore ....American		25	70	1	3	.250	66	34	33	22	13	4.24
Major League Totals................................		36	115	4	4	.500	99	41	40	34	22	3.13

Selected by Baltimore Orioles' organization in 1st round (23rd player selected) of free-agent draft, June 4, 1975.
†On disabled list, July 11 to July 22, 1979.

KENNETH ROTH FORSCH
(Ken)

Born September 8, 1946, at Sacramento, Calif.
Height, 6.04. Weight, 205.
Throws and bats righthanded.
Hobbies—Hunting and fishing.
Attended Sacramento City College, Sacramento, Calif., and Oregon State University, Corvallis, Ore.
Brother of Bob Forsch, pitcher with St. Louis Cardinals.

Pitched 6-0 no-hit victory against Atlanta Braves, April 7, 1979.
Major League saves: 1970 (0), 1971 (0), 1972 (0), 1973 (4), 1974 (10), 1975 (2), 1976 (19), 1977 (8), 1978 (7), 1979 (0), 1980 (0). Total—50.
Led Southern League in shutouts with 5 in 1970.

Year Club	League	G.	IP.	W.	L.	Pct.	H.	R.	ER.	SO.	BB.	ERA.
1968—Greensboro ....Carolina		3	6	0	0	.000	6	2	2	6	3	3.00
1968—Williamsport ....NYP		4	26	1	2	.333	14	6	4	40	9	1.38

Year Club	League	G	IP	W	L	Pct.	H	R	ER	SO	BB	ERA.
1969—Peninsula†	Carolina	17	94	6	5	.545	67	40	33	100	53	3.16
1970—Columbus	Southern	22	167	•13	8	.619	135	48	38	152	39	2.05
1970—Oklahoma City	Am. Assoc.	5	40	4	0	1.000	25	7	7	37	10	1.58
1970—Houston	National	4	24	1	2	.333	28	15	15	13	5	5.63
1971—Houston	National	33	188	8	8	.500	162	60	53	131	53	2.54
1972—Houston	National	30	156	6	8	.429	163	75	68	113	62	3.92
1973—Houston	National	46	201	9	12	.429	197	101	94	149	74	4.21
1974—Houston	National	70	103	8	7	.533	98	38	32	48	37	2.80
1975—Houston‡	National	34	109	4	8	.333	114	42	39	54	30	3.22
1976—Houston	National	52	92	4	3	.571	76	23	22	49	26	2.15
1977—Houston	National	42	86	5	8	.385	80	32	26	45	28	2.72
1978—Houston	National	52	133	10	6	.625	136	44	40	71	37	2.71
1979—Houston§	National	26	178	11	6	.647	155	67	60	58	35	3.03
1980—Houston	National	32	222	12	13	.480	230	90	79	84	41	3.20
Major League Totals		421	1492	78	81	.491	1439	587	528	815	428	3.18

Selected by California Angels' organization in 13th round of free-agent draft, June, 1966.
Selected by Chicago Cubs' organization in secondary phase of free-agent draft, June 7, 1967.
†On disabled list, June 11 to July 11, 1969.
‡On disabled list, July 31 to September 22, 1975.
§On disabled list, May 23 to June 26, 1979.

CHAMPIONSHIP SERIES RECORD

Year Club	League	G	IP	W	L	Pct.	H	R	ER	SO	BB	ERA.
1980—Houston	National	2	8⅔	0	1	.000	10	4	4	6	1	4.15

ALL-STAR GAME RECORD

Year League	IP	W	L	Pct.	H	R	ER	SO	BB	ERA.
1976—National	1	0	0	.000	0	0	0	1	0	0.00

ROBERT HERBERT FORSCH
(Bob)

Born January 13, 1950, at Sacramento, Calif.
Height, 6.04. Weight, 200.
Throws and bats righthanded.
Hobbies—Hunting and fishing.
Attended Sacramento City College, Sacramento, Calif.
Brother of Ken Forsch, pitcher with Houston Astros.

Pitched 5-0 no-hit victory against Philadelphia Phillies, April 16, 1978.
Pitched 5-0 no-hit victory against Denver, May 25, 1973.
Pitched seven-inning, 4-0 no-hit victory against Memphis, May 13, 1972.
Received reported $25,000 bonus to sign with St. Louis Cardinals, 1968.

Year Club	League	G	IP	W	L	Pct.	H	R	ER	SO	BB	ERA.
1970—Cedar Rapids	Midwest	1	3	0	0	.000	6	4	4	1	2	12.00
1970—Lewiston	Northwest	7	28	2	3	.400	32	22	13	15	17	4.18
1971—Cedar Rapids	Midwest	23	158	11	7	.611	140	74	55	134	41	3.13
1972—Arkansas	Texas	24	153	8	10	.444	158	85	*74	109	47	4.35
1973—Tulsa	Am. Assoc.	27	166	12	12	.500	169	91	81	124	66	4.36
1974—Tulsa	Am. Assoc.	15	103	8	5	.615	95	49	42	71	33	3.67
1974—St. Louis	National	19	100	7	4	.636	84	38	33	39	34	2.97
1975—St. Louis	National	34	230	15	10	.600	213	89	73	108	70	2.86
1976—St. Louis	National	33	194	8	10	.444	209	112	85	76	71	3.94
1977—St. Louis	National	35	217	20	7	.741	210	97	84	95	69	3.48
1978—St. Louis	National	34	234	11	17	.393	205	110	96	114	97	3.69
1979—St. Louis	National	33	219	11	11	.500	215	102	93	92	52	3.82
1980—St. Louis	National	31	215	11	10	.524	225	102	90	87	33	3.77
Major League Totals		219	1409	83	69	.546	1361	650	554	611	426	3.54

Selected by St. Louis Cardinals' organization in 38th round of free-agent draft, June 7, 1968.

RECORD AS INFIELDER

Year Club	League	Pos.	G.	AB.	R.	H.	2B.	3B.	HR.	RBI.	B.A.	PO.	A.	E.	F.A.
1968—Sarasota Cards	Gulf C.	3B	44	143	17	32	5	0	0	16	.224	29	80	12	*.901
1969—Lewiston	Northw.	3-O-2	26	74	11	15	3	0	3	10	.203	12	45	13	.814
1969—Modesto	Calif.	3B-OF	33	119	8	28	2	0	1	7	.235	33	58	6	.938
1970—Modesto	Calif.	3B-OF	20	47	4	7	3	0	1	1	.149	19	20	3	.929
1970—Cedar Rapids	Midw.	3-1-P	19	34	2	3	2	0	0	1	.088	9	19	3	.903
1970—Lewiston	Northw.	P-S-2-3	18	30	5	4	0	1	0	3	.133	9	13	6	.786

TERRY JAY FORSTER

Born January 14, 1952, at Sioux Falls, S. D.
Height, 6.03. Weight, 210.
Throws and bats lefthanded.
Hobbies—Skiing, music, painting and golf.
Attended Grossmont College, El Cajon, Calif.

Major League saves: 1971 (1), 1972 (29), 1973 (16), 1974 (24), 1975 (4), 1976 (1), 1977 (1), 1978 (22), 1979 (2), 1980 (0). Total—100.

Led American League in saves with 24 in 1974.
Named American League Fireman of the Year by THE SPORTING NEWS, 1974.

Year	Club	League	G.	IP.	W.	L.	Pct.	H.	R.	ER.	SO.	BB.	ERA.
1970–Appleton		Midwest	10	54	6	1	.857	30	11	8	42	29	1.33
1971–Chicago		American	45	50	2	3	.400	46	23	22	48	23	3.96
1972–Chicago		American	62	100	6	5	.545	75	31	25	104	44	2.25
1973–Chicago		American	51	173	6	11	.353	174	69	62	120	78	3.23
1974–Chicago		American	59	134	7	8	.467	120	57	54	105	48	3.63
1975–Chicago†		American	17	37	3	3	.500	30	12	9	32	24	2.19
1976–Chicago‡		American	29	111	2	12	.143	126	61	54	70	41	4.38
1977–Pittsburgh§		National	33	87	6	4	.600	90	47	43	58	32	4.45
1978–Los Angeles		National	47	65	5	4	.556	56	19	14	46	23	1.94
1979–Los Angeles x		National	17	16	1	2	.333	18	11	10	8	11	5.63
1980–Los Angeles y		National	9	12	0	0	.000	10	4	4	2	4	3.00
American League Totals			263	605	26	42	.382	571	253	226	479	258	3.36
National League Totals			106	180	12	10	.545	174	81	71	114	70	3.55
Major League Totals			369	785	38	52	.422	745	334	297	593	328	3.41

Selected by Chicago White Sox' organization in 2nd round of free-agent draft, June 4, 1970.
†On disabled list, May 25 to July 1, July 26 to August 17 and August 18 to September 29, 1975.
‡Traded with Pitcher Rich Gossage to Pittsburgh Pirates for Outfielder Richie Zisk and Pitcher Silvio Martinez, December 10, 1976.
§Granted free agency, October 20, 1977; signed by Los Angeles Dodgers, November 22, 1977.
xOn disabled list, March 21 to May 25, 1979; on emergency disabled list, August 13 to October 26, 1979.
yOn disabled list, April 2 to July 14 and August 5 to September 15, 1980.

CHAMPIONSHIP SERIES RECORD

Year	Club	League	G.	IP.	W.	L.	Pct.	H.	R.	ER.	SO.	BB.	ERA.
1978–Los Angeles		National	1	1	1	0	1.000	1	0	0	2	0	0.00

WORLD SERIES RECORD

Year	Club	League	G.	IP.	W.	L.	Pct.	H.	R.	ER.	SO.	BB.	ERA.
1978–Los Angeles		National	3	4	0	0	.000	5	0	0	6	1	0.00

GEORGE ARTHUR FOSTER

Born December 1, 1948, at Tuscaloosa, Ala.
Height, 6.01. Weight, 195.
Throws and bats righthanded.
Hobbies–Records and sports in general.
Attended El Camino College, Torrance, Calif.

Established major league record for most home runs, righthanded batter on road (31), 1977.
Tied major league record for most consecutive seasons leading league in runs batted in (3).
Hit three home runs in one game, vs. Atlanta Braves, July 14, 1977.
Led Northwest League outfielders in double plays with 4 in 1968.
Led California League outfielders in chances accepted with 281 in 1969.
Led National League in total bases with 388 and in slugging percentage with .631 in 1977.
Named National League Player of the Year by THE SPORTING NEWS, 1976 and 1977.
Named as outfielder on THE SPORTING NEWS National League All-Star Team, 1976 through 1978.
Named Most Valuable Player in National League by the Baseball Writers' Association of America, 1977.

Year	Club	League	Pos.	G.	AB.	R.	H.	2B.	3B.	HR.	RBI.	B.A.	PO.	A.	E.	F.A.
1968–Medford		Northw.	OF	72	253	47	70	9	5	3	30	.277	*142	6	5	.967
1969–Fresno		Calif.	OF	121	449	68	144	5	8	14	85	.321	*267	14	4	*.986
1969–San Francisco		Nat.	OF	9	5	1	2	0	0	0	1	.400	3	0	0	1.000
1970–Phoenix†		P.C.	OF	114	403	54	124	18	6	8	66	.308	202	5	9	.958
1970–San Francisco		Nat.	OF	9	19	2	6	1	1	1	4	.316	10	0	0	1.000
1971–S.F.‡–Cin.		Nat.	OF	140	473	50	114	23	4	13	58	.241	315	9	5	.985
1972–Cincinnati		Nat.	OF	59	145	15	29	4	1	2	12	.200	71	1	2	.973
1973–Indianapolis		A.A.	OF	134	496	77	130	26	1	15	60	.262	*332	7	10	.971
1973–Cincinnati		Nat.	OF	17	39	6	11	3	0	4	9	.282	19	1	0	1.000
1974–Cincinnati		Nat.	OF	106	276	31	73	18	0	7	41	.264	172	2	2	.989
1975–Cincinnati		Nat.	OF-1B	134	463	71	139	24	4	23	78	.300	299	11	3	.990
1976–Cincinnati		Nat.	OF-1B	144	562	86	172	21	9	29	*121	.306	322	9	2	*.994
1977–Cincinnati		Nat.	OF	158	615	*124	197	31	2	*52	*149	.320	352	12	3	.992
1978–Cincinnati		Nat.	OF	158	604	97	170	26	7	40	*120	.281	319	10	10	.971
1979–Cincinnati§		Nat.	OF	121	440	68	133	18	3	30	98	.302	214	7	4	.982
1980–Cincinnati		Nat.	OF	144	528	79	144	21	5	25	93	.273	295	6	1	.997
Major League Totals				1199	4169	630	1190	190	36	226	784	.285	2391	68	32	.987

Selected by San Francisco Giants' organization in 3rd round of free-agent draft, January 27, 1968.
†On disabled list June 10 to June 30, 1970.
‡Traded to Cincinnati Reds for Shortstop Frank Duffy and Pitcher Vern Geishert (latter assigned from Indianapolis to Phoenix), May 29, 1971.
§On supplemental disabled list, July 22 to August 12, 1979.

CHAMPIONSHIP SERIES RECORD

Tied Championship Series record for most consecutive games, one or more runs batted in (4).

Year	Club	League	Pos.	G.	AB.	R.	H.	2B.	3B.	HR.	RBI.	B.A.	PO.	A.	E.	F.A.
1972–Cincinnati		Nat.	PR	1	0	1	0	0	0	0	0	.000	0	0	0	.000
1975–Cincinnati		Nat.	OF	3	11	3	4	0	0	0	0	.364	7	0	0	1.000

Year	Club	League	Pos.	G.	AB.	R.	H.	2B.	3B.	HR.	RBI.	B.A.	PO.	A.	E.	F.A.
1976–Cincinnati	........Nat.	OF	3	12	2	2	0	0	2	4	.167	7	0	0	1.000
1979–Cincinnati	........Nat.	OF	3	10	1	2	0	0	1	2	.200	6	2	0	1.000
Championship Series Totals............			10	33	7	8	0	0	3	6	.242	20	2	0	1.000

WORLD SERIES RECORD

Established World Series records for most putouts by left fielder, game (8), October 21, 1976; most chances accepted by left fielder, game (8), October 21, 1976.

Tied World Series record for most times caught stealing, four-game Series (2), 1976; one or more hits, each game, four-game Series, 1976; most putouts by outfielder, game (8), October 21, 1976.

Year	Club	League	Pos.	G.	AB.	R.	H.	2B.	3B.	HR.	RBI.	B.A.	PO.	A.	E.	F.A.
1972–Cincinnati	........Nat.	PR-OF	2	0	0	0	0	0	0	0	.000	0	0	0	.000
1975–Cincinnati	........Nat.	OF	7	29	1	8	1	0	0	2	.276	13	1	0	1.000
1976–Cincinnati	........Nat.	OF	4	14	3	6	1	0	0	4	.429	14	0	0	1.000
World Series Totals........................			13	43	4	14	2	0	0	6	.326	27	1	0	1.000

ALL-STAR GAME RECORD

Year	League	Pos.	AB.	R.	H.	2B.	3B.	HR.	RBI.	B.A.	PO.	A.	E.	F.A.
1976–National...............................		OF	3	1	1	0	0	1	3	.333	0	0	0	.000
1977–National...............................		OF	3	1	1	1	0	0	1	.333	2	0	0	1.000
1978–National...............................		OF	2	1	0	0	0	0	0	.000	2	0	0	1.000
1979–National...............................		OF	1	0	1	1	0	0	1	1.000	0	0	0	.000
All-Star Game Totals........................			9	3	3	2	0	1	5	.333	4	0	0	1.000

JULIO CESAR FRANCO

Born August 23, 1958, at San Pedro de Macoris, Dominican Republic
Height, 5.11. Weight, 155.
Throws right and bats left and righthanded

Led Northwest League in total bases with 98 in 1979.
Led Northwest League shortstops in double plays with 45 in 1979.
Led Carolina League shortstops in double plays with 73 in 1980.

Year	Club	League	Pos.	G.	AB.	R.	H.	2B.	3B.	HR.	RBI.	B.A.	PO.	A.	E.	F.A.
1978–Butte	................Appal.	SS	47	141	34	43	5	2	3	28	.305	37	52	25	.781
1979–Central Ore.	.........Northw.	SS	•71	299	57	•98	15	5	•10	45	.328	103	•256	31	.921
1980–Peninsula	.........Carol.	SS	140	•555	105	178	25	6	11	•99	.321	179	•412	42	.934

Signed as free agent by Philadelphia Phillies' organization, June 23, 1978.

TERRY JON FRANCONA

Born April 22, 1959, at Aberdeen, S. D.
Height, 6.01. Weight, 190.
Throws and bats lefthanded.
Attended University of Arizona, Tucson, Ariz.
Son of John (Tito) Francona, major league outfielder-first baseman, 1956-70.

Named THE SPORTING NEWS College Player of the Year, 1980.

Year	Club	League	Pos.	G.	AB.	R.	H.	2B.	3B.	HR.	RBI.	B.A.	PO.	A.	E.	F.A.
1980–Memphis	...........South.	OF	60	210	20	63	13	2	1	23	.300	59	4	4	.940

Selected by Chicago Cubs' organization in 2nd round of free-agent draft, June 7, 1977.
Selected by Montreal Expos' organization in 1st round (22nd player selected) of free-agent draft, June 3, 1980.

GEORGE ALLEN FRAZIER

Born October 13, 1954, at Oklahoma City, Okla.
Height, 6.05. Weight, 205.
Throws and bats righthanded.
Attended University of Oklahoma, Norman, Okla.

Year	Club	League	G.	IP.	W.	L.	Pct.	H.	R.	ER.	SO.	BB.	ERA.
1976–Newark	...............................NY-P	6	15	2	1	.667	11	3	3	17	4	1.80
1976–Burlington	..........................Midwest	20	36	7	2	.778	30	9	7	28	14	1.75
1977–Spokane	............................P. Coast	7	11	2	2	.500	9	5	5	9	5	4.09
1977–Holyoke†	...........................Eastern	45	98	12	7	.632	94	44	36	71	29	3.31
1978–Springfield	.......................Am. Assoc.	32	69	6	5	.545	59	33	26	52	25	3.39
1978–St. Louis	............................National	14	22	0	3	.000	22	14	10	8	6	4.09
1979–Springfield	.......................Am. Assoc.	24	56	1	2	.333	40	17	15	56	23	2.41
1979–St. Louis	............................National	25	32	2	4	.333	35	19	16	14	12	4.50
1980–Springfield	.......................Am. Assoc.	35	60	1	3	.250	44	22	20	55	23	3.00
1980–St. Louis	............................National	22	23	1	4	.200	24	10	7	11	3	2.74
Major League Totals................................			61	77	3	11	.214	81	43	33	33	21	3.86

Selected by Texas Rangers' organization in 13th round of free-agent draft, June 6, 1972.
Selected by Milwaukee Brewers' organization in 9th round of free-agent draft, June 8, 1976.
†Traded by Milwaukee Brewers' organization to St. Louis Cardinals' organization for Catcher Buck Martinez, December 9, 1977.

JESUS MARIA FRIAS (ANDUJAR)

Name pronounced FREE-uhs.

(Pepe)

Born July 14, 1948, at San Pedro de Macoris, Dominican Republic.
Height, 5.10. Weight, 165.
Throws and bats righthanded.
Hobby—Music.

Led Southern League shortstops in double plays with 68 in 1970.
Led Eastern League in sacrifice hits with 15 in 1971.
Tied for American Association lead in double plays by shortstops with 88 in 1972.

Year Club	League	Pos.	G.	AB.	R.	H.	2B.	3B.	HR.	RBI.	B.A.	PO.	A.	E.	F.A.
1967—Decatur†	Midw.	2B	15	44	5	8	0	0	0	1	.182	19	39	6	.906
1967—Salt Lake City‡	Pion.	2B	4	8	0	1	0	0	0	0	.125	4	4	1	.889
1968—Daytona Beach§	Fla. St.					(Did not play)									
1969—Decatur x	Midw.	SS-3B	44	128	10	24	5	1	0	12	.188	42	95	21	.867
1970—Jacksonville	South.	SS	136	492	42	125	13	2	0	44	.254	*204	*432	*32	*.952
1971—Winnipeg	Int.	SS	12	40	5	7	0	0	0	2	.175	19	25	2	.957
1971—Quebec City	East.	SS	126	463	50	111	20	5	1	29	.240	179	*425	25	.960
1972—Evansville	A. A.	SS	132	424	53	93	14	3	2	41	.219	•215	401	34	.948
1973—Montreal	Nat.	S-2-3-O	100	225	19	52	10	1	0	22	.231	122	215	15	.957
1974—Montreal	Nat.	S-3-2-O	75	112	12	24	4	1	0	7	.214	64	115	5	.973
1975—Montreal	Nat.	S-3-2	51	64	4	8	2	0	0	4	.125	55	67	7	.946
1976—Montreal	Nat.	S-2-3-O	76	113	7	28	5	0	0	8	.248	81	116	11	.947
1977—Montreal	Nat.	2-S-3	53	70	10	18	1	0	0	5	.257	27	50	1	.987
1978—Montreal y	Nat.	2B-SS	73	15	5	4	2	1	0	5	.267	17	28	0	1.000
1979—Atlanta z	Nat.	SS	140	475	41	123	18	4	1	44	.259	229	432	32	.954
1980—Texas a	Amer.	SS-3-2	116	227	27	55	5	1	0	10	.242	124	182	17	.947
1980—Los Angeles	Nat.	SS	14	9	1	2	1	0	0	0	.222	5	9	1	.933
American League Totals			116	227	27	55	5	1	0	10	.242	124	182	17	.947
National League Totals			582	1083	99	259	43	7	1	95	.239	600	1032	72	.958
Major League Totals			698	1310	126	314	48	8	1	105	.240	724	1214	89	.956

Signed as free agent by San Francisco Giants' organization, September 18, 1966.
†On disabled list, May 18 through June 10, 1967.
‡Released by San Francisco Giants' organization, July 1, 1967; signed as free agent by Los Angeles Dodgers' organization, November 13, 1967.
§Released by Los Angeles Dodgers' organization, April 1, 1968; signed as free agent by San Francisco Giants' organization, October 22, 1968.
xReleased by San Francisco Giants' organization, July 1, 1969; signed as free agent by Montreal Expos' organization, August 27, 1969.
yTraded to Atlanta Braves for Pitcher Dave Campbell, March 31, 1979.
zTraded with Pitcher Adrian Devine and a player to be named later to Texas Rangers for Pitcher Doyle Alexander and Shortstop Larvell Blanks, December 7, 1979; Braves received $50,000 to complete deal when Outfielder Jeff Burroughs exercised no-trade clause.
aTraded to Los Angeles Dodgers for Pitcher Dennis Lewallyn and cash, September 13, 1980.

DOUGLAS STEVEN FROBEL

(Doug)

Born June 6, 1959, at Ottawa, Ont.
Height, 6.03. Weight, 190.
Throws right and bats lefthanded.

Year Club	League	Pos.	G.	AB.	R.	H.	2B.	3B.	HR.	RBI.	B.A.	PO.	A.	E.	F.A.
1978—Charleston	W. Car.	OF-1B	93	287	30	68	15	1	2	33	.237	80	12	9	.911
1979—Shelby	W. Car.	OF-1-3	48	130	11	24	3	0	3	13	.185	153	33	3	.984
1979—Auburn	NYP	3B-1B	35	118	16	34	4	2	4	31	.288	18	30	11	.814
1980—Shelby†	S. Atl.	1B-3B	67	246	42	80	14	1	13	41	.325	220	56	13	.955
1980—Salem	Carol.	1-3-OF	40	144	21	34	8	1	7	18	.236	294	29	8	.976

Signed as free agent by Pittsburgh Pirates' organization, August 18, 1977.
†On disabled list, May 19 to June 4, 1980.

CARL DAVID FROST

(Dave)

Born November 17, 1952, at Long Beach Calif.
Height, 6.06. Weight, 235.
Throws and bats righthanded.
Hobbies—Fishing and skin diving.
Attended Long Beach City College, Long Beach, Calif. and
Stanford University, Stanford, Calif., received
Bachelor of Arts degree in Political Science.

Year Club	League	G.	IP.	W.	L.	Pct.	H.	R.	ER.	SO.	BB.	ERA.
1974—Sarasota White Sox	Gulf Coast	10	45	2	3	.400	35	14	9	33	18	1.80
1974—Knoxville	Southern	1	3	0	0	.000	2	1	1	1	3	3.00
1975—Knoxville	Southern	28	171	5	14	.263	157	73	61	100	68	3.21
1976—Knoxville	Southern	20	136	8	7	.533	121	43	36	88	32	2.38
1977—Iowa	Am. Assoc.	23	136	9	8	.529	138	69	61	99	41	4.04

Year Club	League	G.	IP.	W.	L.	Pct.	H.	R.	ER.	SO.	BB.	ERA.
1977—Chicago‡	American	4	24	1	1	.500	30	9	8	15	3	3.00
1978—Salt Lake City	P. Coast	13	91	6	4	.600	100	50	40	53	32	3.96
1978—California	American	11	80	5	4	.556	71	24	23	30	24	2.59
1979—California	American	36	239	16	10	.615	226	108	95	107	77	3.58
1980—California§	American	15	78	4	8	.333	97	53	46	28	21	5.31
Major League Totals		66	421	26	23	.531	424	194	172	180	125	3.68

Selected by Chicago White Sox' organization in 18th round of free-agent draft, June 5, 1974.

†On disabled list, April 13 to May 24, 1976.

‡Traded with Pitcher Chris Knapp and Catcher Brian Downing to California Angels for Outfielders Bobby Bonds and Thad Bosley and Pitcher Dick Dotson, December 5, 1977.

§On disabled list, July 5 to September 1, 1980.

CHAMPIONSHIP SERIES RECORD

Year Club	League	G.	IP.	W.	L.	Pct.	H.	R.	ER.	SO.	BB.	ERA.
1979—California	American	2	4⅓	0	1	.000	8	10	9	1	5	18.69

WOODROW THOMPSON FRYMAN
(Woodie)

Born April 12, 1940, at Ewing, Ky.
Height, 6.02. Weight, 215.
Throws left and bats righthanded.
Hobbies—Hunting and fishing.

Major league saves: 1969 (0), 1970 (0), 1971 (2), 1972 (1), 1973 (0), 1974 (0), 1975 (3), 1976 (2), 1977 (1), 1978 (1), 1979 (10), 1980 (17). Total—37.

Year Club	League	G.	IP.	W.	L.	Pct.	H.	R.	ER.	SO.	BB.	ERA.
1965—Batavia	NYP	6	30	3	1	.750	13	5	5	45	14	1.50
1965—Columbus	Int'national	6	34	0	3	.000	32	15	14	29	15	3.71
1966—Pittsburgh	National	36	182	12	9	.571	182	86	77	105	47	3.81
1967—Pittsburgh†	National	28	113	3	8	.273	121	67	51	74	44	4.06
1968—Philadelphia	National	34	214	12	14	.462	198	78	66	151	64	2.78
1969—Philadelphia	National	36	228	12	15	.444	243	123	112	150	89	4.42
1970—Philadelphia‡	National	27	128	8	6	.571	122	61	58	97	43	4.08
1971—Philadelphia	National	37	149	10	7	.588	133	61	56	104	46	3.38
1972—Philadelphia§	National	23	120	4	10	.286	131	64	58	69	39	4.35
1972—Detroit	American	16	114	10	3	.769	93	31	26	72	31	2.05
1973—Detroit	American	34	170	6	13	.316	200	106	101	119	64	5.35
1974—Detroit x	American	27	142	6	9	.400	120	73	68	92	67	4.31
1975—Montreal	National	38	157	9	12	.429	141	69	58	118	68	3.32
1976—Montreal y	National	34	216	13	13	.500	218	89	81	123	76	3.38
1977—Cincinnati za	National	17	75	5	5	.500	83	45	45	57	45	5.40
1978—Chicago b-Montreal	National	32	150	7	11	.389	157	76	70	81	74	4.20
1979—Montreal	National	44	58	3	6	.333	52	25	18	44	22	2.79
1980—Montreal	National	61	80	7	4	.636	61	23	20	59	30	2.25
National League Totals		447	1870	105	120	.467	1842	867	770	1232	687	3.71
American League Totals		77	426	22	25	.468	413	210	195	283	162	4.12
Major League Totals		524	2296	127	145	.467	2255	1077	965	1515	849	3.78

Signed as free agent by Pittsburgh Pirates' organization, July 6, 1965.

†Traded with Pitchers Harold Clem and Bill Laxton and Infielder Don Money to Philadelphia Phillies for Pitcher Jim Bunning, December 15, 1967.

‡On disabled list July 29 through August 31.

§Released on waivers to Detroit Tigers, August 2, 1972.

xTraded to Montreal Expos for Pitcher Tom Walker and Catcher Terry Humphrey, December 4, 1974.

yTraded with Pitcher Dale Murray to Cincinnati Reds for First Baseman Tony Perez and Pitcher Will McEnaney, December 16, 1976.

zPlaced on suspended list, July 12, 1977; transferred to disqualified list, July 13, 1977.

aTraded to Chicago Cubs with Pitcher Bill Caudill for Pitcher Bill Bonham, October 31, 1977.

bTraded to Montreal Expos for a player to be named later, June 9, 1978; Outfielder Jerry White sent to Chicago to complete deal, June 23, 1978.

CHAMPIONSHIP SERIES RECORD

Tied Championship Series record for most games lost, Series (2), 1972.

Year Club	League	G.	IP.	W.	L.	Pct.	H.	R.	ER.	SO.	BB.	ERA.
1972—Detroit	American	2	12⅓	0	2	.000	11	6	5	8	2	3.65

ALL-STAR GAME RECORD

Member of National League All-Star Team in 1968 and 1976; did not play.

JOHN THOMAS FULGHAM

Name pronounced Fuljum

Born June 9, 1956, at St. Louis, Mo.
Height, 6.02. Weight, 205.
Throws and bats righthanded.
Attended University of Miami, Coral Gables, Fla., Yavapai Junior College, Prescott, Ariz.
and attends Florida State University, Tallahassee, Fla.
Great grandson-in-law of Elisha Norton, pitcher with Washington Nationals, 1896 and 1897.

Led Florida State League in complete games with 17 in 1977.
Tied for Florida State League lead in shutouts with 4 in 1977.

Year Club	League	G.	IP.	W.	L.	Pct.	H.	R.	ER.	SO.	BB.	ERA.
1976–Sarasota Cardinals	G. Coast	12	56	3	3	.500	54	29	21	41	22	3.38
1977–St. Petersburg.....................	Florida St.	26	•202	•18	6	.750	157	54	46	•130	64	2.05
1978–Arkansas	Texas	27	154	9	7	.563	160	84	69	119	64	4.03
1979–Springfield	Am. Assoc.	11	77	6	3	.667	61	31	27	50	25	3.16
1979–St. Louis	National	20	146	10	6	.625	123	47	41	75	26	2.53
1980–St. Louis†	National	15	85	4	6	.400	66	33	32	48	32	3.39
1980–Arkansas‡..........................	Texas	1	5	0	0	.000	1	0	0	5	1	0.00
Major League Totals.................................		35	231	14	12	.538	189	80	73	123	58	2.84

Selected by New York Yankees' organization in 1st round (15th player selected) of free-agent draft, January 7, 1976.
Selected by St. Louis Cardinals' organization in secondary phase of free-agent draft, June 8, 1976.
†On disabled list, June 15 to July 24, 1980.
‡On rehabilitation assignment, July 24 to July 30, 1980.

MARK CLIFFORD FUNDERBURK

Born May 16, 1957, at Charlotte, N. C.
Height, 6.04. Weight, 226.
Throws and bats righthanded.
Attended Louisburg College, Louisburg, N. C.

Led Midwest League batters in strikeouts with 129 in 1978.

Year Club	League	Pos.	G.	AB.	R.	H.	2B.	3B.	HR.	RBI.	B.A.	PO.	A.	E.	F.A.
1976–Elizabethton	Appal.	OF	61	225	25	53	7	4	7	33	.236	82	8	4	.957
1977–Wisc. Rapids	Midw.	OF	38	124	14	33	4	2	3	17	.266	32	1	2	.943
1977–Elizabethton	Appal.	OF	47	177	23	49	5	2	7	31	.277	61	2	6	.913
1978–Wisc. Rapids	Midw.	•1B-OF	132	497	76	128	19	1	25	78	.258	1022	46	•20	.982
1979–Visalia..............	Calif.	1B-OF	128	484	106	150	20	1	•31	109	.310	1038	77	21	.982
1980–Orlando	South.	OF-1B	139	525	70	131	21	2	26	87	.250	223	15	6	.975

Selected by Minnesota Twins' organization in 16th round of free-agent draft, June 8, 1976.

RICHARD BLACKWELL GALE

Born January 19, 1954, at Littleton, N. H.
Height, 6.07. Weight, 225.
Throws and bats righthanded.
Hobby–Avid outdoorsman.
Attended University of New Hampshire, Durham, N. H.

Namd American League Rookie Pitcher of the Year by THE SPORTING NEWS, 1978.

Year Club	League	G.	IP.	W.	L.	Pct.	H.	R.	ER.	SO.	BB.	ERA.
1975–Sarasota Royals	G. Coast	9	33	3	1	.750	23	11	10	18	16	2.73
1976–Waterloo.............................	Midwest	23	148	11	6	.647	118	64	57	88	76	3.47
1977–Jacksonville........................	Southern	12	80	6	5	.545	64	32	32	68	24	3.60
1977–Omaha...............................	Am. Assoc.	12	71	6	2	.750	60	31	29	62	31	3.68
1978–Omaha...............................	Am. Assoc.	3	21	1	1	.500	17	13	10	24	8	4.29
1978–Kansas City	American	31	192	14	8	.636	171	78	66	88	100	3.09
1979–Kansas City	American	34	182	9	10	.474	197	131	114	103	99	5.64
1980–Kansas City	American	32	191	13	9	.591	169	90	83	97	78	3.91
Major League Totals.................................		97	565	36	27	.571	537	299	263	288	277	4.19

Selected by Kansas City Royals' organization in 5th round of free-agent draft, June 4, 1975.

WORLD SERIES RECORD

Year Club	League	G.	IP.	W.	L.	Pct.	H.	R.	ER.	SO.	BB.	ERA.
1980–Kansas City	American	2	6⅓	0	1	.000	11	4	3	4	4	4.26

OSCAR CHARLES GAMBLE

Born December 20, 1949, at Ramer, Ala.
Height, 5.11. Weight, 187.
Throws right and bats lefthanded.
Hobbies–Hunting, fishing and dancing.

Year Club	League	Pos.	G.	AB.	R.	H.	2B.	3B.	HR.	RBI.	B.A.	PO.	A.	E.	F.A.
1968–Caldwell............	Pion.	OF	34	94	18	25	2	0	2	12	.266	42	4	4	.920
1969–San Antonio.......	Texas	OF	119	477	62	142	•32	3	7	32	.298	247	10	8	.970
1969–Chicago†..........	Nat.	OF	24	71	6	16	1	1	1	5	.225	41	1	4	.913
1970–Eugene	P.C.	OF	28	108	26	32	7	2	1	8	.296	54	3	0	1.000
1970–Philadelphia......	Nat.	OF	88	275	31	72	12	4	1	19	.262	148	4	7	.956
1971–Eugene	P.C.	OF	39	138	30	40	5	2	4	20	.290	65	4	3	.958
1971–Philadelphia......	Nat.	OF	92	280	24	62	11	1	6	23	.221	125	4	4	.970
1972–Eugene	P.C.	OF	42	144	30	42	8	1	8	20	.292	67	8	1	.987
1972–Philadelphia‡	Nat.	OF-1B	74	135	17	32	5	2	1	13	.237	54	2	0	1.000
1973–Cleveland.........	Amer.	OF	113	390	56	104	11	3	20	44	.267	67	1	2	.971
1974–Cleveland.........	Amer.	OF	135	454	74	132	16	4	19	59	.291	19	1	0	1.000
1975–Cleveland§	Amer.	OF	121	348	60	91	16	3	15	45	.261	146	8	2	.987
1976–New York x.......	Amer.	OF	110	340	43	79	13	1	17	57	.232	199	10	4	.981
1977–Chicago y........	Amer.	OF	137	408	75	121	22	2	31	83	.297	73	1	1	.987
1978–San Diego z.......	Nat.	OF	126	375	46	103	15	3	7	47	.275	172	12	4	.979

Year	Club	League	Pos.	G.	AB.	R.	H.	2B.	3B.	HR.	RBI.	B.A.	PO.	A.	E.	F.A.
1979—Tex.a-N.Y.	....	Amer.	OF	100	274	48	98	10	1	19	64	.358	88	5	3	.969
1980—New York b	....	Amer.	OF	78	194	40	54	10	2	14	50	.278	65	2	0	1.000
National League Totals	....			404	1136	124	285	44	11	16	107	.251	540	23	19	.967
American League Totals	....			794	2408	396	679	98	16	135	402	.282	657	28	12	.983
Major League Totals	....			1198	3544	520	964	142	27	151	509	.272	1197	51	31	.976

Selected by Chicago Cubs' organization in 16th round of free-agent draft, June 7, 1968.

†Traded with Pitcher Dick Selma to Philadelphia Phillies for Outfielder Johnny Callison, November 17, 1969.

‡Traded with Outfielder Roger Freed to Cleveland Indians for Outfielder Del Unser and Infielder Terry Wedgewood, November 30, 1972.

§Traded to New York Yankees for Pitcher Pat Dobson, November 22, 1975.

xTraded with Pitchers Bob Polinsky and Dewey Hoyt, and cash estimated at $250,000 to Chicago White Sox for Shortstop Bucky Dent, April 5, 1977.

yGranted free agency, October 28, 1977; signed by San Diego Padres, November 29, 1977.

zTraded with Catcher Dave Roberts to Texas Rangers for Third Baseman Kurt Bevacqua, Catcher Bill Fahey, First Baseman Mike Hargrove and cash estimated at $300,000, October 25, 1978.

aTraded with Third Baseman Amos Lewis and two players to be named later to New York Yankees for Outfielder Mickey Rivers and three players to be named later, August 1, 1979; New York sent Pitchers Bob Polinsky, Neal Mersch and Mark Softy and Texas sent Pitchers Gene Nelson and Ray Fontenot to complete deal, October 8, 1979.

bOn supplemental disabled list, May 14, 1980; transferred to disabled list, June 15 to June 23, 1980.

CHAMPIONSHIP SERIES RECORD

Year	Club	League	Pos.	G.	AB.	R.	H.	2B.	3B.	HR.	RBI.	B.A.	PO.	A.	E.	F.A.
1976—New York	....	Amer.	OF-PH	3	8	1	2	1	0	0	1	.250	4	0	2	.667
1980—New York	....	Amer.	O-D, PH	2	5	1	1	0	0	0	0	.200	1	0	0	1.000
Championship Series Totals	....			5	13	2	3	1	0	0	1	.231	5	0	2	.714

WORLD SERIES RECORD

Year	Club	League	Pos.	G.	AB.	R.	H.	2B.	3B.	HR.	RBI.	B.A.	PO.	A.	E.	F.A.
1976—New York	....	Am.	PH-OF	3	8	0	1	0	0	0	1	.125	3	0	0	1.000

JAMES ELMER GANTNER
(Jim)

Born January 5, 1954, at Fond du Lac, Wis.
Height, 5.11. Weight, 175.
Throws right and bats lefthanded.
Hobbies—Hunting and fishing.
Attended University of Wisconsin (Oshkosh), Oshkosh, Wis.

Led Pacific Coast League third basemen in putouts with 136 and in fielding average with .936 in 1977.

Year	Club	League	Pos.	G.	AB.	R.	H.	2B.	3B.	HR.	RBI.	B.A.	PO.	A.	E.	F.A.
1974—Newark	....	NYP	SS-3B	62	177	35	54	6	2	5	21	.305	64	134	14	.934
1975—Thetford Mines	..East.		3B-SS	138	456	61	117	17	0	12	48	.257	129	317	33	.931
1976—Berkshire	....	East.	3B-SS	126	403	56	118	21	1	6	53	.293	120	294	20	*.954
1976—Milwaukee	....	Amer.	3B	26	69	6	17	1	0	0	7	.246	17	37	1	.982
1977—Spokane	....	P.C.	*3B-OF	143	541	98	152	35	5	15	80	.281	137	*321	31	.937
1977—Milwaukee	....	Amer.	3B	14	47	4	14	1	0	1	2	.298	8	29	4	.902
1978—Milwaukee	....	Amer.	2-3-S-1	43	97	14	21	1	0	1	8	.216	46	82	5	.962
1979—Milwaukee	....	Amer.	3-2-S-P	70	208	29	59	10	3	2	22	.284	80	161	7	.972
1980—Milwaukee	....	Amer.	3-2-S	132	415	47	117	21	3	4	40	.282	159	335	15	.971
Major League Totals	....			285	836	100	228	34	6	8	79	.273	310	644	32	.968

Selected by Milwaukee Brewers' organization in 12th round of free-agent draft, June 5, 1974.

PITCHING RECORD

Year	Club	League	G.	IP.	W.	L.	Pct.	H.	R.	ER.	SO.	BB.	ERA.
1979—Milwaukee	....	American	1	1	0	0	.000	2	0	0	0	0	0.00

HENRY EUGENE GARBER
(Gene)

Born November 13, 1947, at Lancaster, Pa.
Height, 5.10. Weight, 175.
Throws and bats righthanded.
Hobbies—Basketball and football.
Attended Elizabethtown College, Elizabethtown, Pa.; received Bachelor's degree
in History and Political Science.

Established major league record for most games lost by relief pitcher, season (16), 1979.

Tied major league record for most consecutive games won by relief pitcher, three consecutive games (3), May 15 through 17, 1975.

Tied for International League lead in complete games with 13 in 1972.

Named International League Pitcher of the Year, 1972.

Major League Saves: 1969 (0), 1970 (0), 1972 (0), 1973 (11), 1974 (5), 1975 (14), 1976 (11), 1977 (19), 1978 (25), 1979 (25), 1980 (7). Total—117.

Year	Club	League	G.	IP.	W.	L.	Pct.	H.	R.	ER.	SO.	BB.	ERA.
1965—Salem	....	Ap'lachian	1	⅔	0	0	.000	0	0	0	2	2	0.00
1965—Batavia	....	NYP	11	72	4	3	.571	71	42	28	40	31	3.50

Year Club	League	G.	IP.	W.	L.	Pct.	H.	R.	ER.	SO.	BB.	ERA.
1966–Raleigh	Carolina	16	94	4	4	.500	106	53	48	76	28	4.60
1967–Raleigh	Carolina	18	138	8	6	.571	103	41	29	68	47	1.89
1968–York	Eastern	16	118	7	2	.778	79	33	21	86	30	1.60
1968–Columbus	Int'national	23	59	5	1	.833	62	21	16	32	17	2.44
1969–York	Eastern	11	73	5	3	.625	61	40	25	57	40	3.08
1969–Pittsburgh	National	2	5	0	0	.000	6	3	3	3	1	5.40
1969–Columbus†	Int'national	17	123	7	6	.538	116	51	42	74	37	3.07
1970–Columbus	Int'national	30	95	5	2	.714	96	57	50	75	38	4.74
1970–Pittsburgh	National	14	22	0	3	.000	22	13	13	7	10	5.32
1971–Charleston‡	Int'national	24	170	14	6	.700	•184	85	79	105	54	4.18
1972–Charleston	Int'national	20	163	14	3	•.824	131	49	41	103	45	•2.26
1972–Pittsburgh§	National	4	6	0	0	.000	7	5	5	3	3	7.50
1973–Kansas City	American	48	153	9	9	.500	164	78	72	60	49	4.24
1974–Kansas City x	American	17	28	1	2	.333	35	21	15	14	13	4.82
1974–Toledo	Int'national	3	22	2	1	.667	19	7	1	17	3	0.41
1974–Philadelphia	National	34	48	4	0	1.000	39	15	11	27	31	2.06
1975–Philadelphia	National	•71	110	10	12	.455	104	48	44	69	27	3.60
1976–Philadelphia	National	59	93	9	3	.750	78	33	29	92	30	2.81
1977–Philadelphia	National	64	103	8	6	.571	82	30	27	78	23	2.36
1978–Philadelphia y-Atlanta	National	65	117	6	5	.545	84	32	28	85	24	2.15
1979–Atlanta	National	68	106	6	16	.273	121	66	51	56	24	4.33
1980–Atlanta	National	68	82	5	5	.500	95	42	35	51	24	3.84
American League Totals		65	181	10	11	.476	199	99	87	74	62	4.33
National League Totals		449	692	48	50	.490	638	287	246	471	197	3.20
Major League Totals		514	873	58	61	.487	837	386	333	545	259	3.43

Selected by Pittsburgh Pirates' organization in 13th round of free-agent draft, June 14, 1965.

†On military list, September 2, 1969, through February 18, 1970.

‡On temporary inactive list, June 24, 1971 through July 12, 1971.

§Released to Kansas City Royals (in trade which sent Pitcher Jim Rooker from Omaha to Pittsburgh Pirates), October 25, 1972.

xSold to Philadelphia Phillies, July 12, 1974.

yTraded to Atlanta Braves for Pitcher Dick Ruthven, June 15, 1978.

CHAMPIONSHIP SERIES RECORD

Year Club	League	G.	IP.	W.	L.	Pct.	H.	R.	ER.	SO.	BB.	ERA.
1976–Philadelphia	National	2	⅔	0	1	.000	2	2	1	0	1	13.50
1977–Philadelphia	National	3	5⅓	1	1	.500	4	3	2	3	0	3.38
Championship Series Totals		5	6	1	2	.333	6	5	3	3	1	4.50

ALFONSO RAFAEL GARCIA
(Kiko)
(Nicknamed by grandparents.)

Born October 14, 1953, at Martinez, Calif.
Height, 5.11. Weight, 178.
Throws and bats righthanded.

Led Southern League shortstops in double plays with 105 in 1974.
Led International League second basemen in double plays with 71 in 1975.
Led International League shortstops in double plays with 112 in 1976.

Year Club	League	Pos.	G.	AB.	R.	H.	2B.	3B.	HR.	RBI.	B.A.	PO.	A.	E.	F.A.
1971–Bluefield	Appal.	SS	56	203	35	51	3	•5	2	23	.251	95	128	24	.503
1971–Stockton	Calif.	SS	4	14	1	4	0	1	0	2	.286	8	13	2	.913
1972–Miami	Fla.St.	SS-3B	126	445	51	112	15	6	2	39	.252	176	416	40	.937
1973–Lodi	Calif.	SS	129	494	89	128	15	10	3	36	.259	•237	361	43	.933
1974–Asheville	South.	SS	135	511	68	140	18	5	7	53	.274	•250	•510	48	.941
1975–Rochester	Int.	2B-SS	122	405	34	99	11	1	3	32	.244	260	255	25	.953
1976–Rochester	Int.	SS	130	450	75	124	11	•10	3	44	.276	•241	•473	•38	.949
1976–Baltimore	Amer.	SS	11	32	2	7	1	1	1	4	.219	15	27	0	1.000
1977–Baltimore	Amer.	SS-2B	65	131	20	29	6	0	2	10	.221	78	152	8	.966
1978–Baltimore	Amer.	SS-2B	79	186	17	49	6	4	0	13	.263	87	175	16	.942
1979–Baltimore	Amer.	S-2-O-3	126	417	54	103	15	9	5	24	.247	209	321	27	.952
1980–Baltimore†	Amer.	3-2-OF	111	311	27	62	8	0	1	27	.199	177	292	11	.977
Major League Totals			392	1077	120	250	36	14	9	78	.232	566	967	62	.961

Selected by Baltimore Orioles' organization in 3rd round of free-agent draft, June 8, 1971.

†On supplemental disabled list, May 23 to June 7, 1980.

CHAMPIONSHIP SERIES RECORD

Year Club	League	Pos.	G.	AB.	R.	H.	2B.	3B.	HR.	RBI.	B.A.	PO.	A.	E.	F.A.
1979–Baltimore	Amer.	SS	3	11	1	3	0	0	0	2	.273	6	16	2	.917

WORLD SERIES RECORD

Tied World Series records for most hits, game (4), October 12, 1979; most times reached first base safely, game (5), October 12, 1979; most at bats and most times faced pitcher, inning (2), October 13, 1979 (eighth inning); most three-base hits, game, batting in three runs (1), October 12, 1979.

Year Club	League	Pos.	G.	AB.	R.	H.	2B.	3B.	HR.	RBI.	B.A.	PO.	A.	E.	F.A.
1979–Baltimore	Amer.	SS	6	20	4	8	2	1	0	6	.400	10	17	1	.964

DAMASO DOMINGO GARCIA

Born February 7, 1957, at Moca, Dominican Republic.
Height, 6.00. Weight, 170.
Throws and bats righthanded.
Hobbies—Music and soccer.
Attended Madre y Maestra University, Santiago, Dominican Republic.

Led Florida State League second baseman in double plays with 83 in 1976.
Tied for New York-Pennsylvania League lead in double plays by second basemen with 33 in 1975.

Year	Club	League	Pos.	G.	AB.	R.	H.	2B.	3B.	HR.	RBI.	B.A.	PO.	A.	E.	F.A.
1975—Oneonta		NYP	2B	50	157	28	42	4	2	0	17	.268	103	118	*17	.929
1976—Ft. Lauderdale†	Fla.St.		2B	124	412	55	109	●22	4	1	41	.265	*273	353	21	*.968
1977—West Haven	East.		2B	129	445	62	118	13	9	0	53	.265	263	382	19	.971
1978—Tacoma	P. C.		2B-SS	102	385	51	103	18	6	1	53	.268	217	345	25	.957
1978—New York	Amer.		2B-SS	18	41	5	8	0	0	0	1	.195	36	35	4	.947
1979—Columbus ‡	Int.		SS-1B	39	118	18	32	1	0	1	3	.271	53	85	6	.958
1979—New York §	Amer.		SS-3B	11	38	3	10	1	0	0	4	.263	9	28	4	.902
1980—Toronto	Amer.		2B	140	543	50	151	30	7	4	46	.278	316	471	16	.980
Major League Totals				169	622	58	169	31	7	4	51	.272	361	534	24	.974

Signed as free agent by New York Yankees' organization, March 10, 1975.
†On suspended list, June 4 to June 7, 1977.
‡On disabled list, May 14 to July 24 and July 31 to August 13, 1979.
§Traded with First Baseman Chris Chambliss and Pitcher Paul Mirabella to Toronto Blue Jays for Catcher Rick Cerone, Pitcher Tom Underwood and Outfielder Ted Wilborn, November 1, 1979.

DANIEL RAPHAEL GARCIA
(Danny)

Born April 29, 1954, at Brooklyn, N. Y.
Height, 6.01. Weight, 182.
Throws and bats lefthanded.
Attended Baruch College, New York, N. Y.

Tied for Gulf Coast League lead in double plays by first baseman with 32 in 1975.

Year	Club	League	Pos.	G.	AB.	R.	H.	2B.	3B.	HR.	RBI.	B.A.	PO.	A.	E.	F.A.
1975—Sarasota Royals	Gulf C.		1B	48	171	25	43	4	2	0	24	.251	308	15	7	.979
1976—Waterloo	Midw.		1B-OF	123	422	73	123	12	0	2	44	.291	901	64	23	.977
1977—Jacksonville	South.		1B-OF	42	142	23	30	1	0	0	13	.211	404	28	3	.993
1977—Daytona Beach	Fla. St.		1B	94	361	46	93	4	2	0	23	.258	785	46	14	.983
1978—Ft. Myers	Fla. St.		OF-1B	117	439	77	125	11	3	0	48	.285	196	7	6	.971
1979—Jacksonville	South.		OF-1B	136	440	70	127	19	3	0	41	.289	256	13	8	.971
1980—Omaha	A.A.		OF-1B	120	406	61	130	11	6	1	49	.320	206	10	3	.986

Selected by Kansas City Royals' organization in 11th round of free-agent draft, June 4, 1975.

MARCUS WAYNE GARLAND
(Known by middle name.)

Born October 26, 1950, at Nashville, Tenn.
Height, 6.00. Weight, 190.
Throws and bats righthanded.
Attended Gulf Coast Junior College, Panama City, Fla.

Pitched 5-0 no-hit victory against Charleston, April 20, 1974.
Led Texas League pitchers in complete games with 20 and tied for lead in shutouts with 6 in 1971.
Named Texas League Pitcher of the Year, 1971.

Year	Club	League	G.	IP.	W.	L.	Pct.	H.	R.	ER.	SO.	BB.	ERA.
1969—Miami	Florida St.		9	63	4	3	.571	60	31	23	46	39	3.29
1970—Dallas-Ft. Worth	Texas		21	140	7	10	.412	122	63	55	107	63	3.54
1971—Dallas-Ft. Worth	Texas		26	211	*19	5	*.792	140	43	40	154	50	*1.71
1972—Rochester	Int'national		26	152	7	9	.438	159	69	64	136	49	3.79
1973—Rochester†	Int'national		25	164	10	11	.476	164	79	65	141	69	3.57
1973—Baltimore	American		4	16	0	1	.000	14	8	7	10	7	3.94
1974—Rochester	Int'national		6	35	2	2	.500	36	24	21	16	17	5.40
1974—Baltimore	American		20	91	5	5	.500	68	37	30	40	26	2.97
1975—Baltimore	American		29	87	2	5	.286	80	37	36	46	31	3.72
1976—Baltimore‡	American		38	232	20	7	.741	224	81	69	113	64	2.68
1977—Cleveland	American		38	283	13	●19	.406	281	130	113	118	88	3.59
1978—Cleveland§	American		6	30	2	3	.400	43	27	26	13	16	7.80
1979—Cleveland x	American		18	95	4	10	.286	120	70	55	40	34	5.21
1980—Cleveland	American		25	150	6	9	.400	163	85	77	55	48	4.62
Major League Totals			178	984	52	59	.468	993	475	413	435	314	3.78

Selected by Pittsburgh Pirates' organization in 14th round of free-agent draft, June 7, 1968.
Selected by St. Louis Cardinals' organization in secondary phase of free-agent draft, February 1, 1969.
Selected by Baltimore Orioles' organization in secondary phase of free-agent draft, June 5, 1969.
†On disabled list, May 6 to May 18 and June 18 to June 28, 1973.
‡Played out option year and granted free agency, November 1, 1976; signed as free agent with Cleveland Indians, November 19, 1976.
§On disabled list, May 2 through remainder of 1978 season.
xOn disabled list, March 28 to April 19 and June 30 to August 14, 1979.

Year Club	League	G.	IP.	W.	L.	Pct.	H.	R.	ER.	SO.	BB.	ERA.
1974–Baltimore ....American		1	⅔	0	0	.000	1	0	0	0	1	0.00

PHILIP MASON GARNER
(Phil)

Born April 30, 1949, at Jefferson City, Tenn.
Height, 5.10. Weight, 177.
Throws and bats righthanded.
Hobbies–Golf, leathercrafts and playing the guitar.
Attended University of Tennessee, Knoxville, Tenn.; received Bachelor
of Science degree in General Business.

Tied major league record for most home runs, bases filled, two consecutive games (2), September 14 and 15, 1978.

Tied National League record for most home runs, bases filled, month (2), September, 1978.

Major League stolen bases: 1973 (0), 1974 (1), 1975 (4), 1976 (35), 1977 (32), 1978 (27), 1979 (17), 1980 (32). Total–148.

Led Pacific Coast League third basemen in double plays with 23 in 1973.

Led National League second basemen in assists with 499 and in double plays with 116 in 1980.

Year Club	League	Pos.	G.	AB.	R.	H.	2B.	3B.	HR.	RBI.	B.A.	PO.	A.	E.	F.A.
1971–Burlington.........Midw.		3B	116	439	73	122	22	4	11	70	.278	*122	203	29	.918
1972–Birmingham......South.		3B	71	264	45	74	10	6	12	40	.280	74	116	13	.936
1972–Iowa ................A.A.		3B	70	247	33	60	18	4	9	22	.243	50	140	10	.950
1973–Tucson..............P.C.		*3B-2B	138	516	87	149	23	12	14	73	.289	*107	*270	*35	.915
1973–Oakland ....Amer.		3B	9	5	0	0	0	0	0	0	.000	2	3	0	1.000
1974–Tucson..............P.C.		3B-SS	96	388	78	128	29	10	11	51	.330	92	182	15	.948
1974–Oakland ....Amer.		3-S-2	30	28	4	5	1	0	0	1	.179	11	24	1	.972
1975–Oakland ....Amer.		*2B-SS	●160	488	46	120	21	5	6	54	.246	355	427	*26	.968
1976–Oakland† ....Amer.		2B	159	555	54	145	29	12	8	74	.261	378	*465	22	.975
1977–Pittsburgh.........Nat.		3-2-S	153	585	99	152	35	10	17	77	.260	223	351	17	.971
1978–Pittsburgh ....Nat.		3B-2B-S	154	528	66	138	25	9	10	66	.261	258	389	28	.959
1979–Pittsburgh ....Nat.		3B-2B-S	150	549	76	161	32	8	11	59	.293	234	396	22	.966
1980–Pittsburgh ....Nat.		*2B-SS	151	548	62	142	27	6	5	58	.259	349	500	*21	.976
American League Totals..................			358	1076	104	270	51	17	14	129	.251	746	919	49	.971
National League Totals....................			608	2210	303	593	119	33	43	260	.268	1064	1636	88	.968
Major League Totals			966	3286	407	863	170	50	57	389	.263	1810	2555	137	.970

Selected by Montreal Expos' organization in 8th round of free-agent draft, June 4, 1970.

Selected by Oakland A's organization in secondary phase of free-agent draft, January 13, 1971.

†Traded with Infielder Tommy Helms and Pitcher Chris Batton to Pittsburgh Pirates for Pitchers Doc Medich, Dave Giusti, Rick Langford and Doug Bair and Outfielders Mitchell Page and Tony Armas, March 15, 1977.

CHAMPIONSHIP SERIES RECORD

Year Club	League	Pos.	G.	AB.	R.	H.	2B.	3B.	HR.	RBI.	B.A.	PO.	A.	E.	F.A.
1975–Oakland ....Amer.		2B	3	5	0	0	0	0	0	0	.000	7	4	1	.917
1979–Pittsburgh ....Nat.		2B-SS	3	12	4	5	0	1	1	1	.417	8	9	0	1.000
Championship Series Totals			6	17	4	5	0	1	1	1	.294	15	13	1	.966

WORLD SERIES RECORD

Established World Series record for most double plays by second baseman, seven-game Series (9), 1979.

Tied World Series records for highest batting average, seven-game Series (.500), 1979; one or more hits, each game, seven-game Series, 1979; most assists by second baseman, inning (3), October 13, 1979 (ninth inning).

Year Club	League	Pos.	G.	AB.	R.	H.	2B.	3B.	HR.	RBI.	B.A.	PO.	A.	E.	F.A.
1979–Pittsburgh ....Nat.		2B	7	24	4	12	4	0	0	5	.500	21	23	2	.957

ALL-STAR GAME RECORD

Year League		Pos.	AB.	R.	H.	2B.	3B.	HR.	RBI.	B.A.	PO.	A.	E.	F.A.
1976–American.............................		2B	1	0	0	0	0	0	0	.000	1	1	0	1.000
1980–National.............................		2B	2	1	1	0	0	0	0	.500	1	3	0	1.000
All-Star Game Totals			3	1	1	0	0	0	0	.333	2	4	0	1.000

RALPH ALLEN GARR

Born December 12, 1945, at Monroe, La.
Height, 5.11. Weight, 185.
Throws right and bats lefthanded.
Attended Grambling College, Grambling, La.; received Bachelor of
Science degree in Physical Education.

Tied major league records for most at bats, extra-inning game (11), May 4, 1973 (20 innings); most home runs, game, in extra innings (2), May 17, 1971 (tenth and twelfth innings).

Major League stolen bases: 1968 (1), 1969 (1), 1970 (5), 1971 (30), 1972 (25), 1973 (35), 1974 (26), 1975 (14), 1976 (14), 1977 (12), 1978 (7), 1979 (2), 1980 (0). Total–172.

Led National League in sacrifice hits with 18 in 1971.

Led International League in stolen bases with 63 in 1969 and 39 in 1970.

Tied for Texas League lead in stolen bases with 32 and led outfielders in double plays with 6 in 1968.

Year Club	League	Pos.	G.	AB.	R.	H.	2B.	3B.	HR.	RBI.	B.A.	PO.	A.	E.	F.A.
1967—Austin...............Texas		2B-OF	58	234	37	64	9	3	3	18	.274	103	11	16	.930
1968—Shreveport ....Texas		OF	127	485	76	142	20	6	2	35	.293	222	11	12	.951
1968—Atlanta.............National		PH	11	7	3	2	0	0	0	0	.286	0	0	0	.000
1969—Richmond ....Int.		OF	106	438	64	144	12	5	2	25	*.329	197	10	9	.958
1969—Atlanta.............National		OF	22	27	6	6	1	0	0	2	.222	6	0	1	.857
1970—Richmond ....Int.		OF	98	391	83	151	26	3	7	51	*.386	182	7	6	.969
1970—Atlanta.............National		OF	37	96	18	27	3	0	0	8	.281	43	0	0	1.000
1971—Atlanta.............National		OF	154	639	101	219	24	6	9	44	.343	315	15	11	.968
1972—Atlanta.............National		OF	134	554	87	180	22	0	12	53	.325	246	8	10	.962
1973—Atlanta.............National		OF	148	668	94	200	32	6	11	55	.299	293	9	10	.968
1974—Atlanta.............National		OF	143	606	87	*214	24	*17	11	54	*.353	255	8	9	.967
1975—Atlanta†...........National		OF	151	625	74	174	26	*11	6	31	.278	298	12	*11	.966
1976—Chicago.............Amer.		OF	136	527	63	158	22	6	4	36	.300	254	7	6	.978
1977—Chicago.............Amer.		OF	134	543	78	163	29	7	10	54	.300	225	10	3	.987
1978—Chicago.............Amer.		OF	118	443	67	122	18	9	3	29	.275	205	5	9	.959
1979—Chi.‡-Calif........Amer.		OF	108	331	34	89	10	2	9	39	.269	94	3	5	.951
1980—California§........Amer.		OF	21	42	5	8	1	0	0	3	.190	3	0	1	.750
American League Totals..................			517	1886	247	540	80	24	26	161	.286	781	25	24	.971
National League Totals....................			800	3222	470	1022	132	40	49	247	.317	1456	52	52	.967
Major League Totals			1317	5108	717	1562	212	64	75	408	.306	2237	77	76	.968

Selected by Atlanta Braves' organization in 3rd round of free-agent draft, June 6, 1967.

†Traded with Infielder Larvell Blanks to Chicago White Sox for Outfielder Ken Henderson and Pitchers Dick Ruthven and Danny Osborn, December 12, 1975.

‡Sold to California Angels, September 20, 1979.

§Released, June 6, 1980.

ALL-STAR GAME RECORD

Year League	Pos.	AB.	R.	H.	2B.	3B.	HR.	RBI.	B.A.	PO.	A.	E.	F.A.
1974—National..............................PH-OF		3	0	0	0	0	0	0	.000	0	0	0	.000

STEVEN PATRICK GARVEY
(Steve)

Born December 22, 1948, at Tampa, Fla.
Height, 5.10. Weight, 190.
Throws and bats righthanded.
Hobby—Golf.
Attended Michigan State University, East Lansing, Mich.

Tied major league records for most games, first baseman, season (162), 1976, 1978 and 1979; most unassisted double plays, first baseman, game (2), August 31, 1976; most long hits, consecutive, game (5), August 28, 1977; most long hits, game (5), August 28, 1977.

Established National League records for fewest errors, first baseman, season, 1,500 or more total chances (3), 1976; highest fielding average by first baseman, season, 150 or more games (.998), 1976; most seasons leading league in games by first baseman (6).

Tied National League record for most long hits, consecutive, season (5), August 28, 1977.

Led National League first basemen in total chances with 1606 in 1974, 1585 in 1975 and 1669 in 1977.

Led Pioneer League in total bases with 151, led third basemen in double plays with 10 and tied for league lead in sacrifice flies with 4 in 1968.

Named Most Valuable Player in National League, 1974.

Named first baseman on THE SPORTING NEWS National League All-Star Team, 1974, 1975, 1977 and 1978.

Named first baseman on THE SPORTING NEWS National League All-Star fielding team, 1974, 1975, 1976 and 1977.

Year Club	League	Pos.	G.	AB.	R.	H.	2B.	3B.	HR.	RBI.	B.A.	PO.	A.	E.	F.A.
1968—Ogden ....Pion.		3B	62	216	49	73	12	3	*20	*59	.338	*51	*109	*23	.874
1969—Albuquerque......Texas		3B-1B	83	316	51	118	18	2	14	85	.373	348	86	20	.956
1969—Los Angeles.......Nat.		PH	3	3	0	1	0	0	0	0	.333	0	0	0	.000
1970—Spokane ...........P.C.		*3-2-O	95	376	71	120	26	5	15	87	.319	103	178	*26	.915
1970—Los Angeles.......Nat.		3B-2B	34	93	8	25	5	0	1	6	.269	23	59	5	.943
1971—Los Angeles†.....Nat.		3B	81	225	27	51	12	1	7	26	.227	53	161	14	.939
1972—Los Angeles......Nat.		*3B-1B	96	294	36	79	14	2	9	30	.269	104	189	*28	.913
1973—Los Angeles......Nat.		1B-OF	114	349	37	106	17	3	8	50	.304	731	27	7	.991
1974—Los Angeles......Nat.		1B	156	642	95	200	32	3	21	111	.312	*1536	62	8	.995
1975—Los Angeles.......Nat.		1B	160	659	85	210	38	6	18	95	.319	*1500	77	8	*.995
1976—Los Angeles.......Nat.		1B	162	631	85	200	37	4	13	80	.317	*1583	67	3	*.998
1977—Los Angeles.......Nat.		1B	●162	646	91	192	25	3	33	115	.297	*1606	55	8	*.995
1978—Los Angeles ......Nat.		1B	●162	639	89	*202	36	9	21	113	.316	*1546	74	9	.994
1979—Los Angeles ......Nat.		1B	162	648	92	204	32	1	28	110	.315	1402	93	7	.995
1980—Los Angeles ......Nat.		1B	●163	658	78	*200	27	1	26	106	.304	1502	112	6	.996
Major League Totals			1455	5487	723	1670	275	33	185	842	.304	11586	976	103	.992

Selected by Minnesota Twins' organization in 3rd round of free-agent draft, June, 1966.

Selected by Los Angeles Dodgers' organization in secondary phase of free-agent draft, June 7, 1968.

†On disabled list, June 23 to July 26, 1971.

CHAMPIONSHIP SERIES RECORD

Established Championship Series records for highest slugging average, total Series, 10 or more games and 30 or more at bats (.816); most consecutive hits, total Series (6); most long hits, Series (6), 1978; most total bases, four-game Series (22), 1978.

Tied Championship Series records for most home runs, four-game Series (4), 1978; most runs, game (4), October 9, 1974.

Established National League Championship Series record for most runs, four-game Series (6), 1978.

Tied National League Championship Series records for most consecutive hits, one Series (4); most hits, game (4), October 9, 1974.

Year Club League	Pos.	G.	AB.	R.	H.	2B.	3B.	HR.	RBI.	B.A.	PO.	A.	E.	F.A.
1974—Los Angeles.......Nat.	1B	4	18	4	7	1	0	2	5	.389	40	2	1	.977
1977—Los Angeles.......Nat.	1B	4	13	2	4	0	0	0	0	.308	40	1	0	1.000
1978—Los Angeles ......Nat.	1B	4	18	6	7	1	1	4	7	.389	44	5	0	1.000
Championship Series Totals.............		12	49	12	18	2	1	6	12	.367	124	8	1	.992

WORLD SERIES RECORD

Tied World Series record for most singles, five-game Series, (8), 1974; one or more hits, each game, five-game Series, 1974.

Year Club League	Pos.	G.	AB.	R.	H.	2B.	3B.	HR.	RBI.	B.A.	PO.	A.	E.	F.A.
1974—Los Angeles.......Nat.	1B	5	21	2	8	0	0	0	1	.381	34	3	0	1.000
1977—Los Angeles.......Nat.	1B	6	24	5	9	1	1	1	3	.375	59	6	0	1.000
1978—Los Angeles ......Nat.	1B	6	24	1	5	1	0	0	0	.208	58	3	1	.984
World Series Totals........................		17	69	8	22	2	1	1	4	.319	151	12	1	.994

ALL-STAR GAME RECORD

Year League	Pos.	AB.	R.	H.	2B.	3B.	HR.	RBI.	B.A.	PO.	A.	E.	F.A.
1974—National...............................	1B	4	1	2	1	0	0	1	.500	6	2	0	1.000
1975—National...............................	1B	3	1	2	0	0	1	1	.667	4	1	0	1.000
1976—National...............................	1B	3	1	1	0	1	0	1	.333	6	0	0	1.000
1977—National...............................	1B	3	1	1	0	0	1	1	.333	1	0	0	1.000
1978—National...............................	1B	3	1	2	0	1	0	2	.667	7	1	0	1.000
1979—National...............................	1B	2	1	0	0	0	0	0	.000	5	0	0	1.000
1980—National...............................	1B	2	0	0	0	0	0	0	.000	7	0	0	1.000
All-Star Game Totals........................		20	6	8	1	2	2	6	.400	36	4	0	1.000

THEODORE JARED GARVIN
(Jerry)

Born October 21, 1955, at Oakland, Calif.
Height, 6.03. Weight, 195.
Throws and bats lefthanded.
Hobbies—Swimming and Music.
Attended Merced College, Merced, Calif.

Pitched seven-inning, 2-0 no-hit victory against Waterloo, August 22, 1974.
Led California League in complete games with 17, and tied for lead in shutouts with 3 in 1975.

Year Club League	G.	IP.	W.	L.	Pct.	H.	R.	ER.	SO.	BB.	ERA.
1974—Wisconsin Rapids ....Midwest	27	163	14	7	.667	168	82	*68	138	44	3.75
1975—Reno....................................California	25	*201	*17	5	*.773	188	77	57	129	56	2.55
1976—Orlando ....Southern	23	178	11	9	.550	163	73	67	91	50	3.39
1976—Tacoma†.............................P. Coast	7	55	4	3	.571	52	27	25	36	22	4.09
1977—Toronto..............................American	34	245	10	18	.357	247	127	114	127	85	4.19
1978—Toronto ....American	26	145	4	12	.250	189	92	89	67	48	5.52
1979—Syracuse............................Int'national	8	9	1	0	1.000	6	3	2	5	4	2.00
1979—Toronto‡.............................American	8	23	0	1	.000	15	9	7	14	10	2.74
1980—Toronto ....American	61	83	4	7	.364	70	23	21	52	27	2.28
Major League Totals	129	496	18	38	.321	521	251	231	260	170	4.19

Selected by Baltimore Orioles' organization in 17th round of free-agent draft, June 5, 1973.
Selected by Minnesota Twins' organization in secondary phase of free-agent draft, January 9, 1974.
†Selected by Toronto Blue Jays from Minnesota Twins in expansion draft, November 5, 1976.
‡On disabled list, June 4 to September 1, 1979.

JAMES JENNINGS GAUDET
Name pronounced Go-DAY.
(Jim)

Born June 3, 1955, at New Orleans, La.
Height, 6.00. Weight, 185.
Throws and bats righthanded.
Attended Tulane University, New Orleans, La.

Year Club League	Pos.	G.	AB.	R.	H.	2B.	3B.	HR.	RBI.	B.A.	PO.	A.	E.	F.A.
1976—Sara. Royals .....G. C.	C	30	101	17	35	9	1	0	15	.347	119	21	9	.940
1976—Jacksonville......South.	C	15	50	5	15	4	0	0	4	.300	63	9	1	.986
1977—Jacksonville† ....South.	C	93	292	30	74	14	5	1	28	.253	532	69	10	.984
1978—Omaha..............A. A.	C	107	374	44	83	10	4	4	36	.222	489	53	*19	.966
1978—Kansas City ......Amer.	C	3	8	0	0	0	0	0	0	.000	14	1	1	.938
1979—Omaha..............A. A.	C	109	371	33	97	13	1	6	33	.261	474	51	●14	.974
1979—Kansas City ......Amer.	C	3	6	0	1	0	0	0	0	.167	13	0	0	1.000
1980—Oma.‡-Evans. ...A. A.	C	89	296	35	77	16	1	4	31	.260	427	45	7	.985
Major League Totals........................		6	14	0	1	0	0	0	0	.071	27	1	1	.966

Selected by Atlanta Braves' organization in 3rd round of free-agent draft, June 5, 1973.
Selected by Kansas City Royals' organization in 6th round of free-agent draft, June 8, 1976.
†On disabled list, August 13 to August 31, 1977.
‡Loaned to Detroit Tigers' organization, May 5, 1980; returned June 11, 1980.

RICHARD LEO GEDMAN
(Rich)

Born September 26, 1959, at Worcester, Mass.
Height, 6.00. Weight, 210.
Throws right and bats lefthanded.
Led International League catchers in double plays with 13 in 1980.

Year	Club	League	Pos.	G.	AB.	R.	H.	2B.	3B.	HR.	RBI.	B.A.	PO.	A.	E.	F.A.
1978—Winter Haven	....	Fla. St.	C	98	297	35	89	17	3	3	32	.300	377	39	2	*.995
1979—Bristol	....	East.	C	130	470	48	129	25	1	12	63	.274	497	58	11	*.981
1980—Pawtucket	....	Int.	C	111	347	43	82	18	2	11	29	.236	367	*65	7	.984
1980—Boston	....	Amer.	C	9	24	2	5	0	0	0	1	.208	13	0	2	.867
Major League Totals				9	24	2	5	0	0	0	1	.208	13	0	2	.867

Signed as free agent by Boston Red Sox' organization, August 5, 1977.

CESAR FRANCISCO GERONIMO

Name pronounced juh-RON-uh-moh.

Born March 11, 1948, at El Seibo, Dominican Republic.
Height, 6.02. Weight, 175.
Throws and bats lefthanded.

Major league stolen bases: 1969 (5), 1970 (0), 1971 (2), 1972 (2), 1973 (5), 1974 (9), 1975 (13), 1976 (22), 1977 (10), 1978 (8), 1979 (1), 1980 (2). Total—74.
Led National League outfielders in total chances with 423 and double plays with 5 in 1975.
Named as outfielder on THE SPORTING NEWS National League All-Star fielding team, 1974, 1975, 1976 and 1977.

Year	Club	League	Pos.	G.	AB.	R.	H.	2B.	3B.	HR.	RBI.	B.A.	PO.	A.	E.	F.A.
1967—Oneonta†	....	NYP	OF	4	10	1	1	0	0	0	1	.100	2	0	1	.667
1967—Johnson City	.....	Appal.	OF-P	18	14	1	1	0	0	0	0	.071	5	1	0	1.000
1968—Ft. Lauderdale‡	.	Fla. St.	OF	109	324	35	63	11	5	1	27	.194	186	17	4	.981
1969—Houston	....	Nat.	OF	28	8	8	2	1	0	0	0	.250	1	0	0	1.000
1970—Columbus	....	South.	OF	74	264	26	71	9	4	0	21	.269	113	8	2	.984
1970—Houston	....	Nat.	OF	47	37	5	9	0	0	0	2	.243	23	0	2	.920
1971—Houston§	....	Nat.	OF	94	82	13	18	2	2	1	6	.220	42	1	1	.977
1972—Cincinnati	....	Nat.	OF	120	255	32	70	9	7	4	29	.275	150	10	3	.982
1973—Cincinnati	....	Nat.	OF	139	324	35	68	14	3	4	33	.210	243	9	2	.992
1974—Cincinnati	....	Nat.	OF	150	474	73	133	17	8	7	54	.281	355	13	5	.987
1975—Cincinnati	....	Nat.	OF	148	501	69	129	25	5	6	53	.257	*408	12	3	.993
1976—Cincinnati	....	Nat.	OF	149	486	59	149	24	11	2	49	.307	386	4	6	.985
1977—Cincinnati	....	Nat.	OF	149	492	54	131	22	4	10	52	.266	375	9	3	.992
1978—Cincinnati	....	Nat.	OF	122	296	28	67	15	1	5	27	.226	259	4	5	.981
1979—Cincinnati	....	Nat.	OF	123	356	38	85	17	4	4	38	.239	291	11	2	.993
1980—Cincinnati x	.....	Nat.	OF	103	145	16	37	5	0	2	9	.255	110	2	0	1.000
Major League Totals				1372	3456	430	898	151	45	45	352	.260	2643	75	32	.988

Signed as free agent by New York Yankees' organization, February 23, 1967.
†On disabled list, April 17 through June 20.
‡Drafted by Houston Astros from Syracuse (New York Yankees' organization), December 2, 1968.
§Traded with Second Baseman Joe Morgan, Infielder Denis Menke, Pitcher Jack Billingham and Outfielder Ed Armbrister (latter assigned from Oklahoma City to Indianapolis) to Cincinnati Reds for First Baseman Lee May, Second Baseman Tommy Helms and Infielder Jim Stewart, November 29, 1971.
xTraded to Kansas City Royals for Infielder German Barranca, January 21, 1981.

PITCHING RECORD

Year	Club	League	G.	IP.	W.	L.	Pct.	H.	R.	ER.	SO.	BB.	ERA.
1967—Johnson City	....	Ap'lachian	1	2	0	0	.000	3	4	2	1	2	9.00

CHAMPIONSHIP SERIES RECORD

Established Championship Series records for most consecutive strikeouts, one Series, consecutive at bats (7), 1975; most consecutive strikeouts, one Series, consecutive plate appearances (5), 1975.
Tied Championship Series records for most strikeouts, three-game Series (7), 1975; most strikeouts, five-game Series (7), 1973.
Established National League Championship Series records for most consecutive hitless times at bat, total Series (30); most strikeouts, total Series (24).

Year	Club	League	Pos.	G.	AB.	R.	H.	2B.	3B.	HR.	RBI.	B.A.	PO.	A.	E.	F.A.
1972—Cincinnati	....	Nat.	OF	5	20	2	2	0	0	1	1	.100	11	1	0	1.000
1973—Cincinnati	....	Nat.	OF	4	15	0	1	0	0	0	0	.067	11	1	0	1.000
1975—Cincinnati	....	Nat.	OF	3	10	0	0	0	0	0	0	.000	13	0	0	1.000
1976—Cincinnati	....	Nat.	OF	3	11	0	2	0	1	0	2	.182	10	0	0	1.000
1979—Cincinnati	....	Nat.	OF	2	7	0	1	0	0	0	0	.143	8	0	1	.889
Championship Series Totals				17	63	2	6	0	1	1	4	.095	53	2	1	.982

Tied World Series record for highest fielding average by outfielder, seven-game Series (1.000, with 24 chances), 1975; most stolen bases, four-game Series (2), 1976.

Year Club	League	Pos.	G.	AB.	R.	H.	2B.	3B.	HR.	RBI.	B.A.	PO.	A.	E.	F.A.
1972—Cincinnati ....Nat.	OF	7	19	1	3	0	0	0	3	.158	9	0	0	1.000
1975—Cincinnati ....Nat.	OF	7	25	3	7	0	1	2	3	.280	23	1	0	1.000
1976—Cincinnati ....Nat.	OF	4	13	3	4	2	0	0	1	.308	12	0	1	.923
World Series Totals......................		18	57	7	14	2	1	2	7	.246	44	1	1	.978

KIRK HAROLD GIBSON

Born May 28, 1957, at Pontiac, Mich.
Height, 6.03. Weight, 210.
Throws and bats lefthanded.
Attended Michigan State University, East Lansing, Mich.

Named as wide receiver on THE SPORTING NEWS College Football All-America Team, 1978.
Selected by St. Louis Cardinals in 7th round of NFL draft, May, 1979.
Received reported $200,000 bonus to sign with Detroit Tigers, 1978.

Year Club	League	Pos.	G.	AB.	R.	H.	2B.	3B.	HR.	RBI.	B.A.	PO.	A.	E.	F.A.
1978—Lakeland† ....Fla. St.	OF	54	175	27	42	5	4	8	40	.240	115	2	6	.951
1979—Evansville‡ .......A.A.	OF	89	327	50	80	13	5	9	42	.245	100	5	9	.921
1979—Detroit.............Amer.	OF	12	38	3	9	3	0	1	4	.237	15	0	0	1.000
1980—Detroit§ ....Amer.	OF	51	175	23	46	2	1	9	16	.263	122	1	1	.992
Major League Totals......................		63	213	26	55	5	1	10	20	.258	137	1	1	.993

Selected by Detroit Tigers' organization in 1st round (12th player selected) of free-agent draft, June 6, 1978.

†On restricted list, August 15, 1978, to March 1, 1979.
‡On disabled list, April 13 to May 21. 1979.
§On supplemental disabled list, June 18 to October 6, 1980.

BRIAN JEFFREY GILES

Born April 27, 1960, at Manhattan, Kan.
Height, 6.01. Weight, 165.
Throws and bats righthanded.

Year Club	League	Pos.	G.	AB.	R.	H.	2B.	3B.	HR.	RBI.	B.A.	PO.	A.	E.	F.A.
1978—Little Falls........NYP	2B	61	195	36	44	5	5	4	21	.226	*135	144	16	.946
1979—Lynchburg† ....Carol.	2B	86	278	40	83	16	2	2	33	.299	180	271	13	.972
1980—Jackson ....Texas	2B	132	448	76	128	30	8	10	57	.286	291	325	26	.960

Selected by New York Mets' organization in 2nd round of free-agent draft, June 6, 1978.
†On disabled list, July 10 to August 11, 1979.

GERALD GORDON GLASER JR.
(Gordy)

Born November 19, 1957, at Baton Rouge, La.
Height, 6.03. Weight, 185.
Throws and bats righthanded.
Attended Louisiana College, Pineville, La.
Son of Gerald Gordon Glaser Sr., former minor league player, 1949-50.

Year Club	League	G.	IP.	W.	L.	Pct.	H.	R.	ER.	SO.	BB.	ERA.
1978—Batavia................................NYP	14	47	2	5	.286	56	42	34	42	24	6.51
1978—Chattanooga........................Southern	6	22	0	0	.000	16	4	4	11	9	1.64
1979—Chattanooga........................Southern	39	138	8	7	.533	163	84	75	62	45	4.89
1980—Chattanooga........................Southern	24	100	6	4	.600	88	40	29	41	21	2.61
1980—Tacoma ....P. Coast	8	50	4	3	.571	72	39	36	7	14	6.48

Selected by Cleveland Indians' organization in 11th round of free-agent draft, June 6, 1978.

JERRY DON GLEATON

Born September 14, 1957, at Brownwood, Tex.
Height, 6.03. Weight, 210.
Throws and bats lefthanded.
Attended University of Texas, Austin, Tex.

Year Club	League	G.	IP.	W.	L.	Pct.	H.	R.	ER.	SO.	BB.	ERA.
1979—Tulsa ....Texas	5	35	3	2	.600	37	19	19	21	15	4.89
1979—Texas ....American	5	10	0	1	.000	15	7	7	2	2	6.30
1980—Tulsa ....Texas	25	178	13	7	.650	179	83	72	138	68	3.64
1980—Texas† ....American	5	7	0	0	.000	5	2	2	2	4	2.57
Major League Totals...............................		10	17	0	1	.000	20	9	9	4	6	4.76

Selected by Baltimore Orioles' organization in 2nd round of free-agent draft, June 8, 1976.
Selected by Texas Rangers' organization in 1st round (17th player selected) of free-agent draft, June 5, 1979.

†Traded with Pitchers Brian Allard, Ken Clay and Steve Finch, Shortstop Rick Auerbach and Outfielder Richie Zisk to Seattle Mariners for Catcher Larry Cox, Pitcher Rick Honeycutt, Outfielders Willie Horton and Leon Roberts and Shortstop Mario Mendoza, December 12, 1980.

EDWARD PAUL GLYNN
(Ed)

Born June 3, 1953, at Flushing, N. Y.
Height, 6.02.   Weight, 180.
Throws left and bats righthanded.
Hobby—All sports.
Attended York College, Jamaica, N. Y.

Pitched seven-inning 3-0 no-hit victory against Iowa, July 15, 1976.

Year Club	League	G.	IP.	W.	L.	Pct.	H.	R.	ER.	SO.	BB.	ERA.
1972—Lakeland	Florida St.	15	57	1	4	.200	52	30	28	54	50	4.42
1972—Bristol	Ap'alachian	11	57	4	2	.667	38	35	30	67	46	4.74
1973—Clinton	Midwest	24	135	9	6	.600	109	71	68	130	84	4.53
1974—Clinton	Midwest	15	114	8	4	.667	104	46	38	104	46	3.00
1974—Montgomery	Southern	9	49	1	4	.200	60	44	30	31	29	5.51
1975—Montgomery	Southern	19	127	10	5	.667	116	50	44	66	72	3.12
1975—Evansville	Am. Assoc.	7	40	1	2	.333	40	18	11	23	19	2.48
1975—Detroit	American	3	15	0	2	.000	11	8	7	8	8	4.20
1976—Evansville	Am. Assoc.	24	148	9	7	.563	146	76	59	92	82	3.59
1976—Detroit	American	5	24	1	3	.250	22	18	16	17	20	6.00
1977—Evansville	Am. Assoc.	28	156	6	8	.429	163	97	86	125	71	4.96
1977—Detroit	American	8	27	2	1	.667	36	17	16	13	12	5.33
1978—Evansville	Am. Assoc.	27	38	3	2	.600	32	14	14	28	32	3.32
1978—Detroit †	American	10	15	0	0	.000	11	5	5	9	4	3.00
1979—Tidewater	Int'national	17	29	0	1	.000	22	10	7	16	9	2.17
1979—New York	National	46	60	1	4	.200	57	22	20	32	40	3.00
1980—New York‡	National	38	52	3	3	.500	49	26	24	32	23	4.15
American League Totals		26	81	3	6	.333	80	48	44	47	44	4.89
National League Totals		84	112	4	7	.364	106	48	44	64	63	3.54
Major League Totals		110	193	7	13	.350	186	96	88	111	107	4.10

Signed as free agent by Detroit Tigers' organization, September 25, 1971.
†Traded to New York Mets for Pitcher Mardie Cornejo, March 13, 1979.
‡On disabled list, August 16 to September 6, 1980.

DAVID ALLAN GOLTZ
(Dave)

Born June 23, 1949, at Pelican Rapids, Minn.
Height, 6.04.   Weight, 215.
Throws and bats righthanded.
Hobby—Hunting.
Attended Moorhead State College, Moorhead, Minn.

Pitched seven-inning, 5-0 no-hit victory against Burlington, August 26, 1971.
Led Northern League pitchers in complete games with 12 and tied for lead in games started with 16 in 1968.
Tied for American League lead in games started with 39 in 1977.

Year Club	League	G.	IP.	W.	L.	Pct.	H.	R.	ER.	SO.	BB.	ERA.
1967—Sarasota Twins	Gulf Coast	12	72	•6	2	•.750	63	23	16	51	14	*2.00
1968—St. Cloud	Northern	16	*123	10	3	.769	103	39	22	*122	29	1.61
1969—Minnesota	American					(In Military Service)						
1970—Charlotte†	Southern	1	2	0	1	.000	1	1	0	2	1	0.00
1970—Orlando	Florida St.	1	6	0	1	.000	3	4	4	2	6	6.00
1971—Orlando	Florida St.	7	53	7	0	1.000	49	16	13	34	16	2.21
1971—Lynchburg	Carolina	13	87	7	3	.700	76	37	32	64	32	3.31
1972—Tacoma	P. Coast	19	118	8	8	.500	131	65	51	99	42	3.89
1972—Minnesota	American	15	91	3	3	.500	75	30	27	38	26	2.67
1973—Minnesota	American	32	106	6	4	.600	138	68	62	65	32	5.26
1974—Tacoma	P. Coast	4	30	3	1	.750	25	13	11	26	15	3.30
1974—Minnesota	American	28	174	10	10	.500	192	81	63	89	45	3.26
1975—Minnesota	American	32	243	14	14	.500	235	112	99	128	72	3.67
1976—Minnesota	American	36	249	14	14	.500	239	113	93	133	91	3.36
1977—Minnesota	American	39	303	20	11	.645	•284	129	113	186	91	3.36
1978—Minnesota	American	29	220	15	10	.600	209	72	61	116	67	2.50
1979—Minnesota ‡	American	36	251	14	13	.519	*282	124	116	132	69	4.16
1980—Los Angeles	National	35	171	7	11	.389	198	91	82	91	59	4.32
American League Totals		247	1637	96	79	.549	1654	729	634	887	493	3.49
National League Totals		35	171	7	11	.389	198	91	82	91	59	4.32
Major League Totals		282	1808	103	90	.534	1852	820	716	978	552	3.56

Selected by Minnesota Twins' organization in 17th round of free-agent draft, June 6, 1967.
†On disabled list May 26 to June 6 and June 15 to July 13.
‡Granted free agency, November 1, 1979; signed by Los Angeles Dodgers, November 14, 1979.

LUIS GOMEZ

Born August 19, 1951, at Guadalajara, Mexico.
Height, 5.09.   Weight, 150.
Throws and bats righthanded.
Attended University of California at Los Angeles, Los Angeles, Calif.

Year	Club	League	Pos.	G.	AB.	R.	H.	2B.	3B.	HR.	RBI.	B.A.	PO.	A.	E.	F.A.
1973—Orlando	South.		SS	76	250	20	56	4	0	0	14	.224	105	222	11	.967
1974—Tacoma	P.C.		SS	12	35	7	8	0	0	0	3	.229	17	43	1	.984
1974—Minnesota	Amer.		SS-2B	82	168	18	35	1	0	0	3	.208	97	194	12	.960
1975—Minnesota	Amer.		SS-2B	89	72	7	10	0	0	0	5	.139	55	80	3	.978
1976—Minnesota	Amer.		2-S-3-O	38	57	5	11	1	0	0	3	.193	36	58	1	.989
1976—Tacoma	P.C.		SS-2B	12	32	3	6	1	0	0	0	.188	25	34	2	.967
1977—Tacoma	P.C.		SS	60	214	27	61	8	2	0	19	.285	94	202	11	.964
1977—Minnesota†	Amer.		2-S-3-O	32	65	6	16	4	2	0	11	.246	46	55	2	.981
1978—Toronto	Amer.		SS	153	413	39	92	7	3	0	32	.223	247	400	16	.976
1979—Toronto ‡	Amer.		3B-2B-SS	59	163	11	39	7	0	0	11	.239	70	116	3	.984
1980—Atlanta	Nat.		SS	121	278	18	53	6	0	0	24	.191	135	319	15	.968
American League Totals				453	938	86	203	20	5	0	65	.216	551	903	37	.975
National League Totals				121	278	18	53	6	0	0	24	.191	135	319	15	.968
Major League Totals				574	1216	104	256	26	5	0	89	.211	686	1222	52	.973

Selected by Minnesota Twins' organization in 7th round of free-agent draft, June 5, 1973.

†Granted free agency, November 2, 1977; signed by Toronto Blue Jays, November 11, 1977.

‡Traded with First Baseman Chris Chambliss to Atlanta Braves for Outfielder Barry Bonnell and Pitcher Joey McLaughlin, December 5, 1979.

DANIEL DAVID GONZALES
(Dan)

Born September 30, 1953, at Whittier, Calif.
Height, 6.01. Weight, 195.
Throws right and bats lefthanded.
Attended Fullerton Junior College, Fullerton, Calif.

Year	Club	League	Pos.	G.	AB.	R.	H.	2B.	3B.	HR.	RBI.	B.A.	PO.	A.	E.	F.A.
1972—Rocky Mount	Carol.		OF	65	215	15	51	4	0	0	26	.237	100	4	9	.920
1973—Anderson	W.C.		OF	102	376	39	109	11	2	2	51	.290	138	13	3	.981
1973—Lakeland	Fla. St.		OF	10	20	1	3	0	0	0	0	.150	8	0	0	1.000
1974—Lakeland†	Fla. St.		OF	101	358	35	93	9	2	4	46	.260	161	8	4	.977
1975—Montgomery	South.		OF	123	467	45	123	19	*11	10	54	.263	181	11	2	*.990
1975—Evansville	A.A.		OF	7	27	4	10	0	0	0	2	.370	12	0	0	1.000
1976—Montgomery	South.		OF	77	271	26	79	10	3	4	31	.292	98	8	2	.981
1976—Evansville	A.A.		OF	37	108	15	33	6	0	3	14	.306	40	1	4	.911
1977—Evansville	A.A.		OF	79	234	27	56	10	2	6	25	.239	71	3	2	.974
1978—Evansville‡	A.A.		OF	107	364	54	111	25	5	4	66	.305	157	2	3	.981
1979—Evansville§	A.A.		OF	40	151	23	51	10	1	2	20	.338	44	3	0	1.000
1979—Tucson	P.C.		OF	51	198	37	64	11	4	10	52	.323	76	4	2	.976
1979—Detroit	Amer.		OF	7	18	1	4	1	0	0	2	.222	3	0	0	1.000
1980—Detroit	Amer.		OF	2	7	1	1	0	0	0	0	.143	3	0	1	.750
1980—Evansville xy	A.A.		OF	15	49	7	10	2	1	2	5	.204	19	2	0	1.000
1980—Rochester	Int.		OF	59	194	25	57	11	0	6	31	.294	57	0	1	.983
Major League Totals				9	25	2	5	1	0	0	2	.200	6	0	1	.857

Selected by Detroit Tigers' organization in 2nd round of free-agent draft, January 12, 1972.

†On disabled list, July 1 to July 11, 1974.

‡On disabled list, May 9 to May 19, 1978.

§Loaned to Texas Rangers' organization, June 29, 1979; returned, August 28, 1979.

xOn disabled list, April 18 to May 11, 1980.

yTraded with Catcher Ed Putman to Baltimore Orioles' organization for Catcher Larry Doby Johnson and Pitchers Larry Anderson and Bill Presley, June 10, 1980.

JULIO CESAR GONZALEZ (HERNANDEZ)
(Cesar)

Born December 25, 1953, at Caguas, Puerto Rico.
Height, 5.11. Weight, 165.
Throws and bats righthanded.
Hobby—Reading.

Led Midwest League shortstops in double plays with 63 in 1973.

Year	Club	League	Pos.	G.	AB.	R.	H.	2B.	3B.	HR.	RBI.	B.A.	PO.	A.	E.	F.A.
1972—Quincy	Midw.		SS	96	346	39	82	14	7	7	37	.237	111	248	45	.889
1973—Quincy	Midw.		SS	•125	*492	81	146	16	8	5	39	.297	*190	*342	*61	.897
1974—Key West†	Fla. St.		SS-2B	87	333	26	74	12	2	1	20	.222	145	222	29	.926
1975—Midland	Texas		3-SS-2	81	324	37	88	13	2	2	27	.272	95	174	24	.918
1975—Wichita	A.A.		2B-3B	56	171	13	35	5	0	0	11	.205	90	128	10	.956
1976—Wichita‡	A.A.		2-SS-3	128	484	49	136	12	5	3	41	.281	264	372	38	.943
1977—Houston	Nat.		SS-2B	110	383	34	94	18	3	1	27	.245	154	293	27	.943
1978—Charleston	Int.		SS-3-2	8	30	3	11	1	0	0	2	.367	6	28	2	.944
1978—Houston	Nat.		2B-S-3	78	223	24	52	3	1	1	16	.233	83	139	7	.969
1979—Houston	Nat.		2B-SS-3B	68	181	16	45	5	2	0	10	.249	92	146	12	.952
1980—Tucson	P.C.		3B	38	149	21	44	9	2	2	25	.295	22	105	9	.934
1980—Houston	Nat.		S-2-3	40	52	5	6	1	0	0	1	.115	22	31	1	.981
Major League Totals				296	839	79	197	27	6	2	54	.235	351	609	47	.953

Signed as free agent by Chicago Cubs' organization, February 14, 1972.

†On Midland disabled list, April 10 to May 16, 1974.

‡Traded to Houston Astros for Outfielder Greg Gross, December 8, 1976.

ORLANDO EUGENE GONZALEZ

Born November 15, 1951, at Havana, Cuba.
Height, 6.02. Weight, 175.
Throws and bats righthanded.
Hobby—Music.
Attended Miami-Dade Junior College—South, Miami, Fla., and University of Miami,
Coral Gables, Fla.; received Bachelor of Science degree in Education.

Year—Club	League	Pos.	G.	AB.	R.	H.	2B.	3B.	HR.	RBI.	B.A.	PO.	A.	E.	F.A.
1974—San Antonio	Texas	1B	64	233	28	65	8	1	1	17	.279	538	40	4	.993
1975—San Antonio	Texas	1B	54	210	38	66	11	3	1	22	.314	517	37	8	.986
1975—Oklahoma City ..	A.A.	OF-1B	85	297	40	91	15	3	0	29	.306	231	16	3	.988
1976—Toledo	Int.	OF-1B	98	357	49	111	17	4	1	45	.311	494	47	9	.984
1976—Cleveland.........	Amer.	1B-OF	28	68	5	17	2	0	0	4	.250	123	8	1	.992
1977—Toledo†	Int.	OF-1B	132	474	75	145	21	4	1	43	.306	245	10	4	.985
1978—Oklahoma City ..	A.A.	OF-1B	74	260	49	77	14	2	1	36	.296	186	11	4	.980
1978—Philadelphia......	Nat.	OF-1B	26	26	1	5	0	0	0	0	.192	16	0	0	1.000
1979—Oklahoma City ..	A.A.	OF-1B	125	480	87	150	29	7	6	76	.313	258	6	6	.978
1980—Oklahoma City‡.	A.A.	OF-1B	97	370	60	131	22	7	2	55	.354	218	9	7	.970
1980—Oakland...........	Amer.	1B-OF	25	70	10	17	0	0	0	1	.243	95	8	1	.990
National League Totals			26	26	1	5	0	0	0	0	.192	16	0	0	1.000
American League Totals			53	138	15	34	2	0	0	5	.246	218	16	2	.992
Major League Totals			79	164	16	39	2	0	0	5	.238	234	16	2	.992

Selected by San Francisco Giants' organization in 13th round of free-agent draft, June 6, 1972.
Selected by Cleveland Indians' organization in 18th round of free-agent draft, June 5, 1974.
†Granted free agency, November 2, 1977; signed by Philadelphia Phillies' organization, February 11, 1978.
‡Sold to Oakland A's, July 25, 1980.

CHAMPIONSHIP SERIES RECORD

Year—Club	League	Pos.	G.	AB.	R.	H.	2B.	3B.	HR.	RBI.	B.A.	PO.	A.	E.	F.A.
1978—Philadelphia......	Nat.	PH	1	1	0	0	0	0	0	0	.000	0	0	0	.000

DANNY KAY GOODWIN

Born September 2, 1953, at St. Louis, Mo.
Height, 6.01. Weight, 203.
Throws right and bats lefthanded.
Attended Southern University, Baton Rouge, La.; received
Bachelor of Science degree in Zoology.

Named College Player of the Year by THE SPORTING NEWS, 1975.
Received reported $125,000 bonus to sign with California Angels, 1975.

Year—Club	League	Pos.	G.	AB.	R.	H.	2B.	3B.	HR.	RBI.	B.A.	PO.	A.	E.	F.A.
1975—El Paso	Texas	C-1-O	46	138	10	38	6	0	2	18	.275	224	10	3	.987
1975—California	Amer.	DH-PH	4	10	0	1	0	0	0	0	.100	0	0	0	.000
1976—Salinas	Calif.	C	38	139	24	43	7	2	2	30	.309	168	13	10	.948
1976—El Paso	Texas	C	63	220	43	67	17	0	6	39	.305	195	12	4	.981
1977—Salt Lake City ...	P.C.	C-OF	77	279	56	85	24	3	10	66	.305	146	9	9	.945
1977—California	Amer.	DH-PH	35	91	5	19	6	1	1	8	.209	0	0	0	.000
1978—El Paso	Texas	C-1B	101	361	90	130	17	4	25	89	*.360	193	13	12	.945
1978—California†‡	Amer.	DH-PH	24	58	9	16	5	0	2	10	.276	0	0	0	.000
1979—Ogden	P. C.	1B	100	370	66	129	22	7	20	94	.349	832	46	14	.984
1979—Minnesota	Amer.	1B	58	159	22	46	8	5	5	27	.289	40	2	0	1.000
1980—Minnesota	Amer.	1B	55	115	12	23	5	0	1	11	.200	87	6	0	1.000
Major League Totals			176	433	48	105	24	6	9	56	.242	127	8	0	1.000

Selected by Chicago White Sox' organization in 1st round (first player selected) of free-agent draft, June 8, 1971.
Selected by California Angels' organization in 1st round (first player selected) of free-agent draft, June 29, 1975.
†Traded with Third Baseman Ron Jackson to Minnesota Twins for Outfielder Dan Ford, December 4, 1978.
‡Loaned to Oakland A's organization, April 4, 1979; returned, July 16, 1979.

RICHARD MICHAEL GOSSAGE
(Rich)

Born July 5, 1951, at Colorado Springs, Colo.
Height, 6.03. Weight, 217.
Throws and bats righthanded.
Hobby—Hunting.
Attended Southern Colorado State College, Pueblo, Colo.

Tied major league record for most seasons leading league in saves (2).
Established National League record for most strikeouts by relief pitcher, season (151), 1977.
Major League saves: 1972 (2), 1973 (0), 1974 (1), 1975 (26), 1976 (1), 1977 (26), 1978 (27), 1979 (18), 1980 (33). Total—134.
Led American League in saves with 26 in 1975 and with 27 in 1978.
Tied for American League lead in saves with 33 in 1980.
Led Midwest League in complete games with 15 and shutouts with 7 in 1971.
Named American League Fireman of the Year by THE SPORTING NEWS, 1975.
Named Midwest League Player of the Year, 1971.
Named American League Fireman of the Year by THE SPORTING NEWS, 1978.

Year Club	League	G.	IP.	W.	L.	Pct.	H.	R.	ER.	SO.	BB.	ERA.
1970—Sarasota White Sox	Gulf Coast	3	16	0	0	.000	11	6	5	21	4	2.81
1970—Appleton	Midwest	10	35	0	3	.000	41	27	23	21	19	5.91
1971—Appleton	Midwest	25	187	*18	2	*.900	141	48	38	149	50	*1.83
1972—Chicago	American	36	80	7	1	.875	72	44	38	57	44	4.28
1973—Iowa	Am. Assoc.	12	71	5	4	.556	59	32	29	66	28	3.68
1973—Chicago	American	20	50	0	4	.000	57	44	41	33	37	7.38
1974—Appleton	Midwest	2	8	0	2	.000	8	6	3	5	4	3.38
1974—Chicago	American	39	89	4	6	.400	92	45	41	64	47	4.15
1975—Chicago	American	62	142	9	8	.529	99	32	29	130	70	1.84
1976—Chicago†	American	31	224	9	17	.346	214	104	98	135	90	3.94
1977—Pittsburgh‡	National	72	133	11	9	.550	78	27	24	151	49	1.62
1978—New York	American	63	134	10	11	.476	87	41	30	142	59	2.01
1979—New York§	American	36	58	5	3	.625	48	18	17	41	19	2.64
1980—New York	American	64	99	6	2	.750	74	29	25	103	37	2.27
National League Totals		72	133	11	9	.550	78	27	24	151	49	1.62
American League Totals		351	876	50	52	.490	743	357	319	685	403	3.28
Major League Totals		423	1009	61	61	.500	821	384	343	836	452	3.06

Selected by Chicago White Sox' organization in 9th round of free-agent draft, June 4, 1970.

†Traded with Pitcher Terry Forster to Pittsburgh Pirates for Outfielder Richie Zisk and Pitcher Silvio Martinez, December 10, 1976.

‡Granted free agency, October 28, 1977; signed by New York Yankees, November 23, 1977.

§On disabled list, April 21 to July 9, 1979.

CHAMPIONSHIP SERIES RECORD

Year Club	League	G.	IP.	W.	L.	Pct.	H.	R.	ER.	SO.	BB.	ERA.
1978—New York	American	2	4	1	0	1.000	3	2	2	3	0	4.50
1980—New York	American	1	⅓	0	1	.000	3	2	2	0	0	54.00
Championship Series Totals		3	4⅓	1	1	.500	6	4	4	3	0	8.31

WORLD SERIES RECORD

Year Club	League	G.	IP.	W.	L.	Pct.	H.	R.	ER.	SO.	BB.	ERA.
1978—New York	American	3	6	1	0	1.000	1	0	0	4	1	0.00

ALL-STAR GAME RECORD

Year League	IP.	W.	L.	Pct.	H.	R.	ER.	SO.	BB.	ERA.
1975—American	1	0	0	.000	1	1	1	0	0	9.00
1977—National	1	0	0	.000	1	2	2	2	1	18.00
1978—American	1	0	1	.000	4	4	4	1	1	36.00
1980—American	1	0	0	.000	0	0	0	0	0	0.00
All-Star Game Totals	4	0	1	.000	6	7	7	3	2	15.75

Member of American League All-Star Team in 1976; did not play.

DANIEL JAY GRAHAM
(Dan)

Born July 19, 1954, at Ray, Ariz.
Height, 6.01. Weight, 212.
Throws right and bats lefthanded.
Hobbies—Landscaping.
Attended LaVerne College, LaVerne, Calif., and Mesa Community College, Mesa, Ariz.
Son of Edward Graham, pitcher in Pittsburgh Pirates' organization, 1950-1953.

Led California League in total bases with 281 in 1976.

Year Club	League	Pos.	G.	AB.	R.	H.	2B.	3B.	HR.	RBI.	B.A.	PO.	A.	E.	F.A.
1975—Wis. Rapids	Midw.	C-3B	54	154	12	42	8	2	4	27	.273	175	71	6	.976
1976—Reno	Calif.	C-1B-3B	132	482	96	154	26	7	*29	*115	.320	506	71	17	.971
1977—Tacoma	P.C.	3B-1B	84	306	44	79	11	1	12	51	.258	59	164	25	.899
1977—Orlando	South.	3B	45	155	27	44	10	1	8	36	.284	43	85	5	.962
1978—Toledo	Int.	3B-1-O	135	458	67	127	20	2	23	85	.277	494	163	14	.979
1979—Toledo	Int.	3B-1B	119	403	48	86	19	2	9	55	.213	287	132	19	.957
1979—Minnesota†	Amer.	DH-PH	2	4	0	0	0	0	0	0	.000	0	0	0	.000
1980—Rochester	Int.	C	16	52	10	18	3	0	4	12	.346	60	7	3	.957
1980—Baltimore	Amer.	C-3-OF	86	266	32	74	7	1	15	54	.278	333	42	7	.982
Major League Totals			88	270	32	74	7	1	15	54	.274	333	42	7	.982

Selected by San Francisco Giants' organization in 21st round of free-agent draft, June 5, 1973.
Selected by Philadelphia Phillies' organization in secondary phase of free-agent draft, January 9, 1974.
Selected by Minnesota Twins' organization in 5th round of free-agent draft, June 4, 1975.

†Traded to Baltimore Orioles for First Baseman Tom Chism, December 7, 1979.

ROBERT GRANDAS
(Bob)

Born April 4, 1957, at Flint, Mich.
Height, 6.01. Weight, 190.
Throws and bats righthanded.
Attended Central Michigan University, Mt. Pleasant, Mich.

Year Club	League	Pos.	G.	AB.	R.	H.	2B.	3B.	HR.	RBI.	B.A.	PO.	A.	E.	F.A.
1978—Jersey City†	East.	OF	25	87	14	26	1	2	0	15	.299	34	0	2	.944

Year Club	League	Pos.	G.	AB.	R.	H.	2B.	3B.	HR.	RBI.	B.A.	PO.	A.	E.	F.A.
1979—Jersey City	East.	OF	59	221	44	55	4	4	4	24	.249	125	4	1	.992
1979—Ogden	P.C.	OF	56	204	29	60	9	3	1	28	.294	123	3	4	.969
1980—Ogden	P.C.	OF-SS	101	311	45	86	14	11	4	54	.277	184	6	9	.955

Selected by Detroit Tigers' organization in 3rd round of free-agent draft, June 4, 1975.
Selected by Oakland A's organization in 3rd round of free-agent draft, June 6, 1978.

GARY GEORGE GRAY

Born September 21, 1952, at New Orleans, La.
Height, 6.00. Weight, 187.
Throws and bats righthanded.
Hobbies—Hunting and playing checkers.
Attended Oklahoma City Southwestern Junior College, Oklahoma City, Okla., and
Southeastern Oklahoma State University, Durant, Okla.

Year Club	League	Pos.	G.	AB.	R.	H.	2B.	3B.	HR.	RBI.	B.A.	PO.	A.	E.	F.A.
1974—Sar. Rangers	Gulf C.	1B-3B	52	184	32	57	10	3	0	34	.310	257	29	13	.956
1975—Anderson	W. Car.	1B	135	487	79	147	•27	1	18	95	.302	1138	71	•27	.978
1976—San Antonio	Texas	1-OF-3	124	443	74	135	27	8	19	109	.305	222	13	6	.975
1977—Tucson	P. C.	1-OF-3	91	361	55	112	26	4	9	88	.310	561	46	16	.974
1977—Texas	Amer.	OF	1	2	0	0	0	0	0	0	.000	0	0	0	.000
1978—Tucson	P. C.	1B	95	399	66	126	22	4	13	98	.316	251	11	7	.974
1978—Texas	Amer.	DH-PH	17	50	4	12	1	0	2	6	.240	0	0	0	.000
1979—Tucson	P. C.	1B	87	315	58	96	22	3	17	67	.305	58	1	1	.983
1979—Texas†	Amer.	DH	16	42	4	10	0	0	1	.238	0	0	0	.000
1980—Tacoma	P.C.	1B-OF	96	355	65	119	22	2	20	73	.335	415	24	4	.991
1980—Cleveland‡	Amer.	1B-OF	28	54	4	8	1	0	2	4	.148	16	2	0	1.000
Major League Totals			62	148	12	30	2	0	4	11	.203	16	2	0	1.000

Selected by Texas Rangers' organization in 18th round of free-agent draft, June 5, 1974.
†Traded with Pitcher Larry McCall and Third Baseman-Outfielder Mike Bucci to Cleveland Indians for Pitcher David Clyde and Outfielder Jim Norris, January 4, 1980.
‡Drafted by Seattle Mariners, December 8, 1980.

DAVID ALEJANDRO GREEN (CASAYA)

Born December 4, 1960, at Managua, Nicaragua
Height, 6.03. Weight, 170.
Throws and bats righthanded.

Year Club	League	Pos.	G.	AB.	R.	H.	2B.	3B.	HR.	RBI.	B.A.	PO.	A.	E.	F.A.
1979—Stockton	Calif.	OF	136	500	68	131	16	9	8	70	.262	282	8	6	.980
1980—Holyoke†	East.	OF	129	446	71	130	13	•19	8	67	.291	261	18	13	.955

Signed as free agent by Milwaukee Brewers' organization, September 24, 1978.
†Traded with Outfielder Sixto Lezcano and Pitchers Lary Sorensen and Dave LaPoint to St. Louis Cardinals' organization for Catcher Ted Simmons and Pitchers Pete Vuckovich and Rollie Fingers, December 12, 1980.

ROBERT ANTHONY GRICH
(Bobby)

Born January 15, 1949, at Muskegon, Mich.
Height, 6.02. Weight, 190.
Throws and bats righthanded.
Hobby—Hunting.
Attended University of California at Los Angeles, Los Angeles, Calif., and
Fresno State University, Fresno, Calif.

Established major league records for highest fielding average by second baseman, career, 10 or more seasons (.985); most putouts, second baseman, season, 484, in 1974.
Tied major league record for fewest errors by second baseman (800 or more chances), season, 5, 1973.
Tied American League record for most games, second baseman, season, 162, 1973.
Hit three home runs in a game, June 18, 1974, against Minnesota Twins.
Led American League second basemen in double plays with 130 in 1973, 132 in 1974 and 122 in 1975.
Led American League second basemen in total chances with 945 in 1973, 957 in 1974 and 928 in 1975.
Major League stolen bases: 1970 (1), 1971 (1), 1972 (13), 1973 (17), 1974 (17), 1975 (14), 1976 (14), 1977 (6), 1978 (4), 1979 (1), 1980 (7). Total—95.
Led International League in total bases with 299 and led shortstops in double plays with 81 in 1971.
Named International League Most Valuable Player in 1971.
Shared Texas League Most Valuable Player Award, 1969.
Named by THE SPORTING NEWS as Minor League Player of the Year, 1971.
Named second baseman on THE SPORTING NEWS American League All-Star fielding team, 1973, 1974, 1975 and 1976.
Named second baseman on THE SPORTING NEWS American League All-Star Team, 1976 and 1979.
Received reported $40,000 bonus to sign with Baltimore Orioles, 1967.

Year Club	League	Pos.	G.	AB.	R.	H.	2B.	3B.	HR.	RBI.	B.A.	PO.	A.	E.	F.A.
1967—Bluefield	Appal.	SS	58	213	43	54	10	4	3	26	.254	74	126	24	.893
1968—Stockton	Calif.	SS	113	426	63	97	18	2	8	44	.228	205	•379	35	.943
1969—Dal.-Ft. Worth†	Texas	SS	121	413	60	128	16	8	2	50	.310	•199	368	29	.951
1970—Rochester	Int.	2B-SS	63	235	67	90	11	3	9	42	.383	144	199	9	.974
1970—Baltimore	Amer.	SS-2-3	30	95	11	20	1	3	0	8	.211	56	79	7	.951

— 167 —

Year Club	League	Pos.	G.	AB.	R.	H.	2B.	3B.	HR.	RBI.	B.A.	PO.	A.	E.	F.A.
1971—Rochester ....Int.		SS	130	473	*124	159	26	9	*32	83	*.336	*238	*394	17	*.974
1971—Baltimore..........Amer.		SS-2	7	30	7	9	0	0	1	6	.300	11	31	0	1.000
1972—Baltimore..........Amer.		S-2-1-3	133	460	66	128	21	3	12	50	.278	299	338	20	.970
1973—Baltimore..........Amer.		2B	•162	581	82	146	29	7	12	50	.251	*431	*509	5	.995
1974—Baltimore..........Amer.		2B	160	582	92	153	29	6	19	82	.263	*484	*453	20	.979
1975—Baltimore..........Amer.		2B	150	524	81	136	26	4	13	57	.260	*423	*484	21	.977
1976—Baltimore‡ ....Amer.		*2B-3B	144	518	93	138	31	4	13	54	.266	*389	400	12	.985
1977—California§ ....Amer.		SS	52	181	24	44	6	0	7	23	.243	88	141	4	.983
1978—California ....Amer.		2B	144	487	68	122	16	2	6	42	.251	325	419	13	.983
1979—California ....Amer.		2B	153	534	78	157	30	5	30	101	.294	340	438	13	.984
1980—California ....Amer.		2B-1B	150	498	60	135	22	2	14	62	.271	353	464	9	.989
Major League Totals			1285	4490	662	1188	211	36	127	535	.265	3199	3756	124	.982

Selected by Baltimore Orioles' organization in 1st round (18th player selected) of free-agent draft, June 6, 1967.

†On military list, September 2, 1969 to April 1, 1970.
‡Granted free agency, November 1, 1976; signed by California Angels, November 24, 1976.
§On supplemental disabled list, June 9 to June 26; disabled list, June 26 to July 5; and emergency disabled list, July 5 through remainder of season, 1977.

CHAMPIONSHIP SERIES RECORD

Year Club	League	Pos.	G.	AB.	R.	H.	2B.	3B.	HR.	RBI.	B.A.	PO.	A.	E.	F.A.
1973—Baltimore..........Amer.		2B	5	20	1	2	0	0	1	1	.100	16	9	0	1.000
1974—Baltimore..........Amer.		2B	4	16	2	4	1	0	1	2	.250	13	12	1	.962
1979—California ....Amer.		2B	4	13	0	2	1	0	0	2	.154	4	12	1	.941
Championship Series Totals.............			13	49	3	8	2	0	2	5	.163	33	33	2	.971

ALL-STAR GAME RECORD

Year League		Pos.	AB.	R.	H.	2B.	3B.	HR.	RBI.	B.A.	PO.	A.	E.	F.A.
1972—American............................		SS	4	0	0	0	0	0	0	.000	0	3	0	1.000
1974—American............................		2B	3	0	1	0	0	0	0	.333	0	2	0	1.000
1976—American............................		2B	2	0	0	0	0	0	0	.000	1	1	0	1.000
1979—American		2B	1	0	0	0	0	0	0	.000	2	0	0	1.000
1980—American		2B	0	0	0	0	0	0	0	.000	0	1	0	1.000
All-Star Game Totals			10	0	1	0	0	0	0	.100	3	7	0	1.000

GEORGE KENNETH GRIFFEY
(Ken)

Born April 10, 1950, at Donora, Pa.
Height, 6.00. Weight, 200.
Throws and bats lefthanded.
Hobby—Drawing cartoons.

Tied major league record for most at bats, game, since 1900, 7, June 13, 1975.
Major league stolen bases: 1973 (4), 1974 (9), 1975 (16), 1976 (34), 1977 (17), 1978 (23), 1979 (12), 1980 (23). Total—138.
Led American Association in stolen bases with 43 in 1973.
Tied for Eastern League lead in double plays by outfielders with 6 in 1972.
Named American Association Rookie of the Year, 1973.
Named as outfielder on THE SPORTING NEWS National League All-Star Team, 1976.

Year Club	League	Pos.	G.	AB.	R.	H.	2B.	3B.	HR.	RBI.	B.A.	PO.	A.	E.	F.A.
1969—Bradenton Reds.Gulf C.		*OF-1	49	153	22	43	*11	1	1	12	.281	57	4	*10	.859
1970—Sioux Falls ....North.		OF	51	164	20	40	2	1	2	24	.244	76	2	7	.918
1971—Tampa ....Fla. St.		OF	88	281	60	96	7	11	3	33	.342	137	13	8	.949
1971—Three Rivers.....East.		OF	9	32	1	13	1	2	0	4	.406	17	0	1	.944
1972—Three Rivers.....East.		•OF-SS	128	472	*96	150	21	3	14	52	.318	212	10	•15	.937
1973—Indianapolis ......A. A.		OF	107	397	88	130	18	5	10	58	.327	171	11	6	.968
1973—Cincinnati ....Nat.		OF	25	86	19	33	5	1	3	14	.384	25	1	0	1.000
1974—Indianapolis ......A. A.		OF	43	162	34	54	6	4	5	18	.333	70	4	1	.987
1974—Cincinnati ....Nat.		OF	88	227	24	57	9	5	2	19	.251	115	5	0	1.000
1975—Cincinnati ....Nat.		OF	132	463	95	141	15	9	4	46	.305	202	6	7	.967
1976—Cincinnati ....Nat.		OF	148	562	111	189	28	9	6	74	.336	270	10	6	.976
1977--Cincinnati ....Nat.		OF	154	585	117	186	35	8	12	57	.318	298	10	3	.990
1978—Cincinnati ....Nat.		OF	158	614	90	177	33	8	10	63	.288	296	13	10	.969
1979—Cincinnati† ....Nat.		OF	95	380	62	120	27	4	8	32	.316	175	8	3	.984
1980—Cincinnati ....Nat.		OF	146	544	89	160	28	10	13	85	.294	266	5	6	.978
Major League Totals			946	3461	607	1063	180	54	58	390	.307	1647	58	35	.980

Selected by Cincinnati Reds' organization in 29th round of free-agent draft, June 5, 1969.
†On disabled list, August 14 to September 7, 1979.

CHAMPIONSHIP SERIES RECORD

Tied Championship Series record for most stolen bases, game (3), October 5, 1975.

Year Club	League	Pos.	G.	AB.	R.	H.	2B.	3B.	HR.	RBI.	B.A.	PO.	A.	E.	F.A.
1973—Cincinnati ....Nat.		OF-PH	3	7	0	1	1	0	0	0	.143	2	0	0	1.000
1975—Cincinnati ....Nat.		OF	3	12	3	4	1	0	0	4	.333	4	1	0	1.000
1976—Cincinnati ....Nat.		OF	3	13	2	5	0	1	0	2	.385	11	0	0	1.000
Championship Series Totals.............			9	32	5	10	2	1	0	6	.312	17	1	0	1.000

Tied World Series record for fewest chances accepted by outfielder, extra-inning game (0), October 21, 1975 (12 innings); most at-bats, game, no hits (5), October 21, 1976.

Year	Club	League	Pos.	G.	AB.	R.	H.	2B.	3B.	HR.	RBI.	B.A.	PO.	A.	E.	F.A.
1975—Cincinnati		Nat.	OF	7	26	4	7	3	1	0	4	.269	10	1	0	1.000
1976—Cincinnati		Nat.	OF	4	17	2	1	0	0	0	1	.059	5	0	0	1.000
World Series Totals				11	43	6	8	3	1	0	5	.186	15	1	0	1.000

ALL-STAR GAME RECORD

Year	League	Pos.	AB.	R.	H.	2B.	3B.	HR.	RBI.	B.A.	PO.	A.	E.	F.A.
1976—National		OF	1	1	1	0	0	0	1	1.000	1	0	0	1.000
1980—National		OF	3	1	2	0	0	1	1	.667	0	0	0	.000
All-Star Game Totals			4	2	3	0	0	1	2	.750	1	0	0	1.000

Member of National League All-Star Team in 1977; did not play.

ALFREDO CLAUDINO GRIFFIN

Born March 6, 1957, at Dominican Republic City, Dominican Republic.
Height, 5.11. Weight, 165.
Throws right and bats left and righthanded.
Hobby—Music.

Tied American League record for most three-base hits by switch-hitter, season (15), 1980.
Major League stolen bases: 1976 (0), 1977 (2), 1978 (0), 1979 (21), 1980 (18). Total—41.
Named American League Co-Rookie of the Year by the Baseball Writers' Association of America, 1979.

Year	Club	League	Pos.	G.	AB.	R.	H.	2B.	3B.	HR.	RBI.	B.A.	PO.	A.	E.	F.A.
1974—Reno		Calif.	SS	11	35	4	9	0	0	0	1	.257	10	22	9	.780
1974—Sarasota Ind.		Gulf C.	SS	49	158	17	41	1	0	0	11	.259	67	133	*25	.889
1975—San Jose		Calif.	SS	124	358	42	82	4	3	0	25	.229	189	281	47	.909
1976—San Jose		Calif.	SS	64	224	40	58	3	1	0	17	.259	91	145	24	.908
1976—Williamsport		East.	SS	58	200	22	55	3	0	0	17	.275	86	172	17	.938
1976—Toledo		Int.	SS	22	88	5	19	7	1	0	6	.216	44	71	7	.943
1976—Cleveland		Amer.	SS	12	4	0	1	0	0	0	0	.250	1	2	1	.750
1977—Toledo		Int.	SS	125	457	60	114	14	5	1	32	.249	*223	398	*49	.927
1977—Cleveland		Amer.	SS	14	41	5	6	1	0	0	3	.146	17	30	3	.940
1978—Portland		P. C.	*SS-OF	133	474	82	138	22	10	5	48	.291	201	395	*40	.937
1978—Cleveland†		Amer.	SS	5	4	1	2	1	0	0	0	.500	4	7	1	.917
1979—Toronto		Amer.	SS	153	624	81	179	22	10	2	31	.287	272	501	*36	.956
1980—Toronto		Amer.	SS	155	653	63	166	26	•15	2	41	.254	295	489	*37	.955
Major League Totals				339	1326	150	354	50	25	4	75	.267	589	1029	78	.954

Signed as free agent by Cleveland Indians' organization, August 22, 1973.

†Traded with Third Baseman Phil Lansford to Toronto Blue Jays for Pitcher Victor Cruz, December 6, 1978.

MICHAEL LEROY GRIFFIN

(Mike)

Born June 26, 1957, at Colusa, Calif.
Height, 6.05. Weight, 195.
Throws and bats righthanded.
Attended American River College, Sacramento, Calif.

Led Western Carolinas League in complete games with 19 in 1977.
Led Texas League in wild pitches with 26 in 1978.
Tied for Western Carolinas League lead in games started with 27 in 1977.

Year	Club	League	G.	IP.	W.	L.	Pct.	H.	R.	ER.	SO.	BB.	ERA.
1976—Asheville		W. Caro.	11	65	6	3	.667	71	36	35	26	25	4.85
1977—Asheville		W. Caro.	27	*209	*17	9	.654	189	100	81	*201	75	3.49
1978—Tulsa†		Texas	27	169	6	*19	.240	*217	140	114	112	85	6.07
1979—West Haven		Eastern	17	125	8	7	.533	120	53	41	66	26	2.95
1979—Columbus		Int'national	6	41	3	1	.750	35	9	8	34	13	1.76
1979—New York		American	3	4	0	0	.000	5	2	2	5	2	4.50
1980—Columbus		Int'national	13	83	7	2	.778	88	37	32	47	22	3.47
1980—New York		American	13	54	2	4	.333	64	36	29	25	23	4.83
Major League Totals			16	58	2	4	.333	69	38	31	30	25	4.81

Selected by Texas Rangers' organization in 3rd round of free-agent draft, June 8, 1976.

†Traded with Outfielders Juan Beniquez and Greg Jemison and Pitchers Paul Mirabella and Dave Righetti to New York Yankees for Pitchers Sparky Lyle, Larry McCall and Dave Rajsich, Shortstop Domingo Ramos, Catcher Mike Heath and cash, November 10, 1978.

THOMAS JAMES GRIFFIN

(Tom)

Born February 22, 1948, at Los Angeles, Calif.
Height, 6.03. Weight, 210.
Throws and bats righthanded.
Attended Los Angeles Valley Junior College, Van Nuys, Calif., and
Pierce Junior College, Woodland Hills, Calif.

Named by THE SPORTING NEWS as National League Rookie Pitcher of the Year, 1969.

Year Club	League	G.	IP.	W.	L.	Pct.	H.	R.	ER.	SO.	BB.	ERA.
1966—Bismarck-Mandan ....Northern		11	46	3	5	.375	44	33	29	66	29	5.67
1966—Amarillo ....Texas		2	7	0	1	.000	9	4	4	6	7	5.14
1967—Oklahoma City ....P. Coast		8	34	0	5	.000	38	25	22	30	27	5.82
1967—Asheville† ....Carolina		12	58	3	4	.429	66	43	36	50	23	5.59
1968—Oklahoma City ....P. C.		29	168	7	14	.333	157	91	81	144	94	4.34
1969—Houston ....National		31	188	11	10	.524	156	80	74	200	93	3.54
1970—Oklahoma City ....Am. Assoc.		5	28	3	2	.600	23	14	4	27	16	1.29
1970—Houston ....National		23	111	3	13	.188	118	72	71	72	72	5.76
1971—Oklahoma City ....Am. Assoc.		16	107	6	8	.429	101	43	37	90	48	3.11
1971—Houston ....National		10	38	0	6	.000	44	22	20	29	20	4.74
1972—Houston ....National		39	94	5	4	.556	92	39	34	83	38	3.26
1973—Houston‡ ....National		25	100	4	6	.400	83	51	46	69	46	4.14
1974—Houston ....National		34	211	14	10	.583	202	97	83	110	89	3.54
1975—Houston§ ....National		17	79	3	8	.273	89	52	47	56	46	5.35
1976—Houston x-San Diego............National		31	112	9	6	.600	100	56	51	69	79	4.10
1977—San Diego y.........................National		38	151	6	9	.400	144	88	75	79	88	4.47
1978—California z ....American		24	56	3	4	.429	63	39	25	35	31	4.02
1979—San Francisco ....National		59	94	5	6	.455	83	46	41	82	46	3.93
1980—San Francisco ....National		42	108	5	1	.833	80	35	33	79	49	2.75
American League Totals		24	56	3	4	.429	63	39	25	35	31	4.02
National League Totals		349	1286	65	79	.451	1191	638	575	928	666	4.02
Major League Totals		373	1342	68	83	.450	1254	677	600	963	697	4.02

Signed as free agent by Houston Astros' organization, April 3, 1966.
†On disabled list, June 13 to July 27, 1967.
‡On disabled list, May 27 to June 21, 1973.
§On disabled list, July 2 to October 3, 1975.
xSold on waivers to San Diego Padres, August 3, 1976.
yGranted free agency, October 28, 1977; signed by California Angels, January 27, 1978.
zReleased, November 2, 1978; signed by San Francisco Giants, April 4, 1979.

ROSS ALBERT GRIMSLEY, II

Born January 7, 1950, at Topeka, Kan.
Height, 6.03. Weight, 200.
Throws and bats lefthanded.
Hobby—Hunting.
Attended Jackson State Community College, Jackson, Tenn.
Son of Ross Grimsley, pitcher for Chicago White Sox, 1951.

Year Club	League	G.	IP.	W.	L.	Pct.	H.	R.	ER.	SO.	BB.	ERA.
1969—Sioux Falls..........................Northern		18	103	9	4	.692	84	38	32	97	34	2.80
1970—Indianapolis ....Am. Assoc.		29	188	11	8	.579	140	65	57	162	59	*2.73
1978—Indianapolis ....Am. Assoc.		6	43	6	0	1.000	31	15	14	40	8	2.95
1971—Cincinnati ....National		26	161	10	7	.538	151	67	64	67	43	3.58
1972—Indianapolis ....Am. Assoc.		4	20	1	1	.500	26	9	9	9	15	4.05
1972—Cincinnati ....National		30	198	14	8	.636	194	73	67	79	50	3.05
1973—Cincinnati† ....National		38	242	13	10	.565	245	96	87	90	68	3.24
1974—Baltimore ....American		40	296	18	13	.581	267	111	101	158	76	3.07
1975—Baltimore ....American		35	197	10	13	.435	210	95	89	89	47	4.07
1976—Baltimore ‡.........................American		28	137	8	7	.533	143	66	60	41	35	3.94
1977—Baltimore‡..........................American		34	218	14	10	.583	230	105	96	53	74	3.96
1978—Montreal ....National		36	263	20	11	.645	237	103	89	84	67	3.05
1979—Montreal.............................National		32	151	10	9	.526	199	102	90	42	41	5.36
1980—Montreal§ ....National		11	41	2	4	.333	61	31	29	11	12	6.37
1980—Cleveland ....American		14	75	4	5	.444	103	63	56	18	24	6.72
National League Totals..........................		173	1056	69	49	.585	1087	472	426	373	281	3.63
American League Totals.........................		151	923	54	48	.529	953	440	402	359	256	3.92
Major League Totals		324	1979	123	97	.559	2040	912	828	732	537	3.77

Selected by Detroit Tigers' organization in 10th round of free-agent draft, June 7, 1968.
Selected by Cincinnati Reds' organization in secondary phase of free-agent draft, February 1, 1969.
†Traded with Catcher Wally Williams to Baltimore for Outfielder Merv Rettenmund, Infielder Junior Kennedy and Catcher Bill Wood, December 4, 1973.
‡Granted free agency, October 10, 1977; signed by Montreal Expos, December 21, 1977.
§Traded to Cleveland Indians for Infielder Dave Oliver and cash, July 11, 1980.

CHAMPIONSHIP SERIES RECORD

Tied Championship Series record for fewest hits allowed, game (2), October 10, 1972.

Year Club	League	G.	IP.	W.	L.	Pct.	H.	R.	ER.	SO.	BB.	ERA.
1972—Cincinnati ....National		1	9	1	0	1.000	2	1	1	5	0	1.00
1973—Cincinnati ....National		2	3⅔	0	1	.000	7	5	5	3	2	12.27
1974—Baltimore ....American		2	5⅓	0	0	.000	1	1	1	2	2	1.69
Championship Series Totals		5	18	1	1	.500	10	7	7	10	4	3.50

WORLD SERIES RECORD

Tied World Series record for most games won as relief pitcher, Series (2), 1972 (six-game Series).

Year Club	League	G.	IP.	W.	L.	Pct.	H.	R.	ER.	SO.	BB.	ERA.
1972—Cincinnati ....National		4	7	2	1	.667	7	2	2	2	3	2.57

ALL-STAR GAME RECORD

Member of National League All-Star Team for 1978 game; did not play.

GREGORY EUGENE GROSS
(Greg)

Born August 1, 1952, at York, Pa.
Height, 5.11. Weight, 175.
Throws and bats lefthanded.
Hobby—Golf.

Established major league record for most times caught stealing, rookie season, 20, 1974.
Tied for Appalachian League lead in double plays by outfielders with 3 in 1970.
Named National League Rookie Player of the Year by THE SPORTING NEWS, 1974.
Named Appalachian League Player of the Year, 1970.

Year	Club	League	Pos.	G.	AB.	R.	H.	2B.	3B.	HR.	RBI.	B.A.	PO.	A.	E.	F.A.
1970—Covington	Appal.	OF	54	211	40	*74	8	3	2	27	.351	93	*10	3	.972
1971—Columbus	South.	OF-1B	132	494	57	144	14	4	2	33	.291	244	13	9	.966
1972—Columbus	South.	OF	101	367	55	111	14	2	0	25	.302	172	9	3	.984
1972—Okla. City	A.A.	OF	28	109	15	27	4	0	0	8	.248	64	4	1	.986
1973—Denver	A.A.	OF	131	528	98	*174	25	6	0	55	.330	226	11	10	.960
1973—Houston	Nat.	OF	14	39	5	9	2	1	0	1	.231	13	2	0	1.000
1974—Houston†	Nat.	OF	156	589	78	185	21	8	0	36	.314	296	15	2	.994
1975—Houston†	Nat.	OF	132	483	67	142	14	10	0	41	.294	216	14	10	.958
1976—Houston‡	Nat.	OF	128	426	52	122	12	3	0	27	.286	208	13	5	.978
1977—Chicago	Nat.	OF	115	239	43	77	10	4	5	32	.322	109	3	1	.991
1978—Chicago§	Nat.	OF	124	347	34	92	12	7	1	39	.265	182	6	4	.979
1979—Philadelphia x	Nat.	OF	111	174	21	58	6	3	0	15	.333	82	5	2	.978
1980—Philadelphia	Nat.	OF-1B	127	154	19	37	7	2	0	12	.240	69	5	2	.974
Major League Totals				907	2451	319	722	84	38	6	203	.295	1175	63	26	.979

Selected by Houston Astros' organization in 4th round of free-agent draft, June 4, 1970.
†On supplemental disabled list, April 2 to April 24, 1975.
‡Traded to Chicago Cubs for Infielder Julio Gonzalez, December 8, 1976.
§Traded with Second Baseman Manny Trillo and Catcher Dave Rader to Philadelphia Phillies for Outfielder Jerry Martin, Catcher Barry Foote, Second Baseman Ted Sizemore and Pitchers Derek Botelho and Henry Mack, February 23, 1979.
xGranted free agency, November 1, 1979; re-signed by Phillies, December 13, 1979.

CHAMPIONSHIP SERIES RECORD

Year	Club	League	Pos.	G.	AB.	R.	H.	2B.	3B.	HR.	RBI.	B.A.	PO.	A.	E.	F.A.
1980—Philadelphia	Nat.	PH-OF	4	4	2	3	0	0	0	1	.750	1	0	0	1.000

WORLD SERIES RECORD

Year	Club	League	Pos.	G.	AB.	R.	H.	2B.	3B.	HR.	RBI.	B.A.	PO.	A.	E.	F.A.
1980—Philadelphia	Nat.	PH-OF	4	2	0	0	0	0	0	0	.000	1	0	0	1.000

WAYNE DALE GROSS

Born January 14, 1952, at Riverside, Calif.
Height, 6.02. Weight, 205.
Throws right and bats lefthanded.
Hobbies—Fishing and skiing.
Attended California Poly State University, Pomona, Calif.

Year	Club	League	Pos.	G.	AB.	R.	H.	2B.	3B.	HR.	RBI.	B.A.	PO.	A.	E.	F.A.
1973—Lewiston	Northw.	1B	8	29	4	7	2	0	1	1	.241	58	4	0	1.000
1973—Burlington	Midw.	1B-OF	56	187	27	44	8	3	4	36	.235	426	19	4	.991
1974—Birmingham	South.	1-OF-3	105	316	36	77	12	2	14	54	.244	503	42	15	.973
1975—Birmingham	South.	OF-1B	130	435	69	121	23	2	19	71	.278	193	16	13	.941
1976—Tucson	P.C.	3-1-OF	115	395	77	128	30	7	19	75	.324	164	16	6	.965
1976—Oakland	Amer.	1B-OF	10	18	0	4	0	0	0	1	.222	30	1	1	.969
1977—Oakland	Amer.	*3B-1B	146	485	66	113	21	1	22	63	.233	127	242	*27	.932
1978—Vancouver	P.C.	3B-1-O	17	56	20	23	5	0	3	10	.411	32	33	5	.929
1978—Oakland	Amer.	3B-1B	118	285	18	57	10	2	7	23	.200	120	150	22	.925
1979—Oakland	Amer.	3B-1B-OF	138	442	54	99	19	1	14	50	.224	252	225	21	.958
1980—Oakland	Amer.	3B-1B	113	366	45	103	20	3	14	61	.281	125	136	11	.960
Major League Totals				525	1596	183	376	70	7	57	198	.236	654	754	82	.945

Selected by Oakland A's organization in 9th round of free-agent draft, June 5, 1973.

ALL-STAR GAME RECORD

Member of American League All-Star Team in 1977; did not play.

GERALD WAYNE GROTE
(Jerry)

Born October 6, 1942, at San Antonio, Tex.
Height, 5.10. Weight, 185.
Throws and bats righthanded.
Hobbies—Bowling, hunting and fishing.
Attended Trinity University, San Antonio, Tex.

Established major league records for most putouts and most chances accepted by catcher, two consecutive games (31), April 21 and 22, 1970; most putouts by catcher, game (20), April 22, 1970; most consecutive putouts by catcher, game (10), April 22, 1970.

Tied major league records for most innings by catcher, game; most errorless innings by catcher, game and most innings by catcher, game, no passed balls (24), April 15, 1968.

Established modern major league record for most times reached first base on error, game (3), September 5, 1975.

Tied modern major league record for most chances accepted by catcher, game (20), April 22, 1970.

Led Texas League catchers in passed balls with 21 in 1963.

Year	Club	League	Pos.	G.	AB.	R.	H.	2B.	3B.	HR.	RBI.	B.A.	PO.	A.	E.	F.A.
1963—San Antonio		Texas	C	121	384	50	103	22	5	14	62	.268	*792	57	18	.979
1963—Houston		Nat.	C	3	5	0	1	0	0	0	1	.200	10	0	0	1.000
1964—Houston		Nat.	C	100	298	26	54	9	3	3	24	.181	522	52	9	.985
1965—Oklahoma City†		P.C.	3B-C	118	374	43	99	23	1	11	47	.265	402	126	16	.971
1966—New York		Nat.	C-3B	120	317	26	75	12	2	3	31	.237	519	55	11	.981
1967—New York		Nat.	C	120	344	25	67	8	0	4	23	.195	609	62	7	.990
1968—New York		Nat.	C	124	404	29	114	18	0	3	31	.282	754	60	5	.994
1969—New York		Nat.	C	113	365	38	92	12	3	6	40	.252	718	63	7	.991
1970—New York		Nat.	C	126	415	38	106	14	1	2	34	.255	*855	46	8	.991
1971—New York		Nat.	C	125	403	35	109	25	0	2	35	.270	*892	41	9	.990
1972—New York		Nat	C-3-O	64	205	15	43	5	1	3	21	.210	407	43	1	.998
1973—New York‡		Nat.	C-3B	84	285	17	73	10	2	1	32	.256	546	37	4	.993
1974—New York		Nat.	C	97	319	25	82	8	1	5	36	.257	549	36	7	.988
1975—New York		Nat.	C	119	386	28	114	14	5	2	39	.295	706	55	4	*.995
1976—New York		Nat.	C-OF	101	323	30	88	14	2	4	28	.272	622	49	5	.993
1977—N.Y.§-L.A.		Nat.	C-3B	60	142	11	38	3	1	0	11	.268	18	40	2	.991
1978—Los Angeles x		Nat.	C-3B	41	70	5	19	5	0	0	9	.271	125	21	3	.980
Major League Totals				1397	4281	348	1075	157	21	38	395	.251	8014	660	82	.991

†Sold to New York Mets, October 19, 1965; deal completed with sale of Pitcher Tom Parsons by Mets to Houston Astros, November 24, 1965.

‡On disabled list, May 12 to July 11, 1973.

§Traded to Los Angeles Dodgers for player to be named later and cash, August 31, 1977. (Infielder Randy Rogers sent to Mets completing deal, October 24, 1977).

xGranted free agency, November 2, 1978; signed by Kansas City Royals' organization, February 5, 1981.

CHAMPIONSHIP SERIES RECORD

Year	Club	League	Pos.	G.	AB.	R.	H.	2B.	3B.	HR.	RBI.	B.A.	PO.	A.	E.	F.A.
1969—New York		Nat.	C	3	12	3	2	1	0	0	1	.167	22	1	0	1.000
1973—New York		Nat.	C	5	19	2	4	0	0	0	2	.211	42	1	1	.977
1977—Los Angeles		Nat.	C-PH	2	0	0	0	0	0	0	0	.000	0	0	0	.000
1978—Los Angeles		Nat.	C	1	0	0	0	0	0	0	0	.000	2	0	0	1.000
Championship Series Totals				11	31	5	6	1	0	0	3	.194	66	2	1	.986

WORLD SERIES RECORD

Established World Series records for highest fielding average by catcher, seven-game Series (1.000 with 71 chances), 1973 (chances are most in any length Series with 1.000 average); most putouts by catcher, seven-game Series (67), 1973; most chances accepted by catcher, seven-game Series (71), 1973.

Year	Club	League	Pos.	G.	AB.	R.	H.	2B.	3B.	HR.	RBI.	B.A.	PO.	A.	E.	F.A.
1969—New York		Nat.	C	5	19	1	4	2	0	0	1	.211	29	2	0	1.000
1973—New York		Nat.	C	7	30	2	8	0	0	0	0	.267	67	5	0	1.000
1977—Los Angeles		Nat.	C	1	1	0	0	0	0	0	0	.000	3	3	0	1.000
1978—Los Angeles		Nat.	C	2	0	0	0	0	0	0	0	.000	3	0	0	1.000
World Series Totals				15	50	3	12	2	0	0	1	.240	102	10	0	1.000

ALL-STAR GAME RECORD

Year	League	Pos.	AB.	R.	H.	2B.	3B.	HR.	RBI.	B.A.	PO.	A.	E.	F.A.
1968—National		C	2	0	0	0	0	0	0	.000	3	0	0	1.000
1974—National		C	0	0	0	0	0	0	0	.000	1	0	0	1.000
All-Star Game Totals			2	0	0	0	0	0	0	.000	4	0	0	1.000

JOHN MAYWOOD GRUBB, JR.

Born August 4, 1948, at Richmond, Va.
Height, 6.03. Weight, 188.
Throws right and bats lefthanded.
Hobbies—Golf and playing guitar.
Attended Manatee Junior College, West Bradenton, Fla., and graduated from Florida State University, Tallahassee, Fla.

Tied for Texas League lead in double plays by outfielders with 4 in 1972.

Year	Club	League	Pos.	G.	AB.	R.	H.	2B.	3B.	HR.	RBI.	B.A.	PO.	A.	E.	F.A.
1971—Lodi		Calif.	O-3-2	116	409	69	126	23	5	12	56	.308	158	84	14	.945
1972—Alexandria		Texas	*OF-1B	126	446	66	132	25	2	10	61	.296	205	12	2	*.991
1972—San Diego		Nat.	OF	7	21	4	7	1	1	0	1	.333	16	0	0	1.000
1973—San Diego		Nat.	OF-3B	113	389	52	121	22	3	8	37	.311	229	11	3	.988
1974—San Diego		Nat.	OF-3B	140	444	53	127	20	4	8	42	.286	321	8	8	.976
1975—San Diego		Nat.	OF	144	553	72	149	36	2	4	38	.269	334	3	3	.991
1976—San Diego†		Nat.	O-1-2	109	384	54	109	22	1	5	27	.284	248	7	6	.977
1977—Cleveland‡		Amer.	OF	34	93	8	28	3	3	2	14	.301	47	2	0	1.000
1978—Clv.§-Tex.		Amer.	OF	134	411	62	113	19	6	15	67	.275	213	16	6	.974

Year Club	League	Pos.	G.	AB.	R.	H.	2B.	3B.	HR.	RBI.	B.A.	PO.	A.	E.	F.A
1979—Texas x.............	Amer.	OF	102	289	42	79	14	0	10	37	.273	135	8	2	.986
1980—Texas	Amer.	OF	110	274	40	76	12	1	9	32	.277	112	6	6	.952
National League Totals..................			513	1791	235	513	101	11	25	145	.286	1148	29	20	.983
American League Totals.................			380	1067	152	296	48	10	36	150	.277	507	32	14	.975
Major League Totals			893	2858	387	809	149	21	61	295	.283	1655	61	34	.981

Selected by Boston Red Sox' organization in 3rd round of free-agent draft, February 1, 1969.
Selected by Cincinnati Reds' organization in secondary phase of free-agent draft, June 5, 1969.
Selected by Atlanta Braves' organization in secondary phase of free-agent draft, June 4, 1970.
Selected by San Diego Padres' organization in secondary phase of free-agent draft, January 13, 1971.
†On disabled list, April 26 to May 28, 1976; traded with Catcher Fred Kendall and Shortstop Hector Torres to Cleveland Indians for Outfielder George Hendrick, December 8, 1976.
‡On disabled list, April 1 to April 23, 1977; on supplemental disabled list, July 8 through remainder of season, 1977.
§Traded to Texas Rangers for a player to be named later, August 31, 1978; Pitcher Bobby Cuellar and Outfielder David Rivera sent to Cleveland to complete deal, October 3, 1978.
xOn disabled list, August 6 to September 1, 1979.

ALL-STAR GAME RECORD

Year League	Pos.	AB.	R.	H.	2B.	3B.	HR.	RBI.	B.A.	PO.	A.	E.	F.A.
1974—National.............................	OF	1	0	0	0	0	0	0	.000	0	0	0	.000

MARIO MIGUEL GUERRERO (ABUD)
Name pronounced Gur-RARE-O.

Born September 28, 1950, at Santo Domingo, Dominican Republic.
Height, 5.10. Weight, 155.
Throws and bats righthanded.
Hobbies—Music and golf.
Attended LaSalle College, Santo Domingo, Dominican Republic.
Brother of Eppy Guerrero, scout for Toronto Blue Jays.

Tied major league record for most double plays, game, shortstop, 5, June 2, 1973.
Tied for Carolina League lead in double plays by shortstops with 58 in 1969.

Year Club	League	Pos.	G.	AB.	R.	H.	2B.	3B.	HR.	RBI.	B.A.	PO.	A.	E.	F.A.
1968—Ft. Lauderdale ..	Fla. St.	SS	91	317	28	72	5	1	1	14	.227	110	195	25	.924
1969—Kinston	Carol.	SS	132	496	61	140	22	1	3	46	.282	180	329	45	.919
1970—Manchester	East.	SS	139	*555	57	134	19	1	2	38	.241	*225	*355	*44	.929
1971—Syracuse	Int.	SS-3B	116	434	53	126	18	1	1	34	.290	144	237	27	.934
1972—Syra.†-Lou.........	Int.	S-3-2	131	452	50	132	10	4	2	49	.292	169	305	17	.965
1973—Boston	Amer.	SS-2B	66	219	19	51	5	2	0	11	.233	106	183	8	.973
1974—Boston‡	Amer.	SS	93	284	18	70	6	2	0	23	.246	136	266	13	.969
1975—Tulsa	A.A.	SS	31	115	11	32	6	1	0	15	.278	44	83	5	.962
1975—St. Louis	Nat.	SS	64	184	17	44	9	0	0	11	.239	76	198	13	.955
1976—Tulsa§	A.A.	2B-SS	29	81	7	19	2	0	2	4	.235	45	60	4	.963
1976—California..........	Amer.	2-SS	83	268	24	76	12	0	1	18	.284	129	172	14	.956
1977—California xyz....	Amer.	SS-2B	86	244	17	69	8	2	1	28	.283	61	105	2	.988
1978—Oakland	Amer.	SS	143	505	27	139	18	4	3	38	.275	258	330	26	.958
1979—Oakland	Amer.	SS	46	166	12	38	5	0	0	18	.229	68	129	10	.952
1980—Oakland a	Amer.	SS	116	381	32	91	16	2	2	23	.239	184	276	18	.962
American League Totals..................			633	2067	149	534	70	12	7	159	.258	942	1461	91	.964
National League Totals..................			64	184	17	44	9	0	0	11	.239	76	198	13	.955
Major League Totals			697	2251	166	578	79	12	7	170	.257	1018	1659	104	.963

Signed as free agent by New York Yankees' organization, April 27, 1968.
†Traded by New York Yankees to Boston Red Sox, June 30, 1972, to complete deal in which Yankees obtained Pitcher Sparky Lyle for Infielder Danny Cater, March 22, 1972.
‡Sold to St. Louis Cardinals and assigned to Tulsa, April 4, 1975; Pitcher Jim Willoughby was sent by Cardinals to Boston Red Sox, July 4, 1975, to complete deal.
§Traded to California Angels for Catcher Ed Jordan, assigned from El Paso to Arkansas, and a player to be named later, May 29, 1976; California assigned First Baseman-Outfielder Ed Kurpiel from Salt Lake City to Tulsa to complete deal, July 30, 1976.
xOn disabled list, April 2 to May 12, 1977.
yGranted free agency, November 2, 1977; signed by San Francisco Giants, December 15, 1977.
zTraded to Oakland A's, April 7, 1978, to complete deal in which San Francisco acquired Vida Blue, March 15, 1978.
aTraded to Seattle Mariners for a player to be named later, December 6, 1980.

PEDRO GUERRERO
Name pronounced guh-RAIR-oh.

Born June 29, 1956, at San Pedro de Macoris, Dominican Republic.
Height, 5.11. Weight, 176.
Throws right and bats left and righthanded.
Led Pacific Coast League in sacrifice flies with 15 in 1978.

Year Club	League	Pos.	G.	AB.	R.	H.	2B.	3B.	HR.	RBI.	B.A.	PO.	A.	E.	F.A.
1973—Sarasota Ind.† ...	Gulf C.	3B-SS	44	153	13	39	2	3	2	22	.255	32	82	11	.912
1974—Orangeburg.......	W. Car.	3B	19	55	3	8	1	0	0	1	.145	11	22	5	.868
1974—Bellingham........	Northw.	3B	82	297	49	94	*23	2	3	55	.316	69	124	23	.894
1975—Danville	Midw.	3B-OF	104	351	81	121	25	5	10	76	*.345	111	168	31	.900

Year Club League	Pos.	G.	AB.	R.	H.	2B.	3B.	HR.	RBI.	B.A.	PO.	A.	E.	F.A.
1976—Waterbury.........East.	1B	132	495	73	151	*30	•10	5	66	.305	1129	*96	*19	.985
1977—Albuquerque‡ ....P.C.	1B	32	129	30	52	11	4	4	39	.403	329	17	10	.972
1978—Albuquerque....P.C.	1B-3B	134	492	92	166	28	4	14	*116	.337	982	80	10	.991
1978—Los Angeles ......Nat.	1B	5	8	3	5	0	1	0	1	.625	25	1	0	1.000
1979—Albuquerque ....P.C.	OF-3-1	113	453	94	151	33	9	22	*103	.333	188	9	5	.975
1979—Los Angeles ......Nat.	OF-1-3	25	62	7	15	2	0	2	9	.242	53	4	1	.983
1980—Los Angeles§.....Nat.	O-2-3-1	75	183	27	59	9	1	7	31	.322	103	110	3	.986
Major League Totals......................		105	253	37	79	11	2	9	41	.312	181	115	4	.987

Signed as free agent by Cleveland Indians' organization, January 15, 1973.
†Traded to Los Angeles Dodgers for Pitcher Bruce Ellingsen, April 4, 1974.
‡On disabled list, May 19 to August 30, 1977.
§On disabled list, August 23 to September 15, 1980.

RONALD AMES GUIDRY

Name pronounced GID-ree.

(Ron)

Born August 28, 1950, at Lafayette, La.
Height, 5.11. Weight, 160.
Throws and bats lefthanded.
Hobbies—Hunting and raising German Shepherd dogs.
Attended University of Southwestern Louisiana, Lafayette, La.

Established major league record for highest winning percentage, season, 20 or more wins (.893), 1978.
Established American League record for most strikeouts by lefthanded pitcher, game (18), June 17, 1978.
Tied American League record for most shutouts by lefthanded pitcher, season (9), 1978.
Led American League in shutouts with 9 in 1978.
Named Man of the Year by THE SPORTING NEWS, 1978.
Named Major League Player of the Year by THE SPORTING NEWS, 1978.
Named American League Pitcher of the Year by THE SPORTING NEWS, 1978.
Won Cy Young Memorial Award, 1978.
Named lefthanded pitcher on THE SPORTING NEWS American League All-Star Team, 1978.

Year Club	League	G.	IP.	W.	L.	Pct.	H.	R.	ER.	SO.	BB.	ERA.
1971—Johnson City	Ap'lachian	7	47	2	2	.500	34	13	11	61	27	2.11
1972—Ft. Lauderdale†....................	Florida St.	15	66	2	4	.333	53	35	28	61	50	3.82
1973—Kinston‡	Carolina	20	101	7	6	.538	85	53	36	97	70	3.21
1974—West Haven§	Eastern	37	77	2	4	.333	80	48	45	79	53	5.26
1975—Syracuse..............................	Int'national	42	62	6	5	.545	46	24	20	76	37	2.90
1975—New York	American	10	16	0	1	.000	15	6	6	15	9	3.38
1976—New York	American	7	16	0	0	.000	20	12	10	12	4	5.63
1976—Syracuse..............................	Int'national	22	40	5	1	.833	16	5	3	50	13	0.68
1977—New York	American	31	211	16	7	.696	174	72	66	176	65	2.82
1978—New York	American	35	274	*25	3	*.893	187	61	53	248	72	*1.74
1979—New York†	American	33	236	18	8	.692	203	83	73	201	71	*2.78
1980—New York	American	37	220	17	10	.630	215	97	87	166	80	3.56
Major League Totals		153	973	76	29	.724	814	331	295	818	301	2.73

Selected by New York Yankees' organization in 3rd round of free-agent draft, June 8, 1971.
†Played in one game, as an outfielder.
‡On temporary inactive list, July 13 to August 3, 1973.
§Appeared as an outfielder.

CHAMPIONSHIP SERIES RECORD

Year Club	League	G.	IP.	W.	L.	Pct.	H.	R.	ER.	SO.	BB.	ERA.
1977—New York	American	2	11⅓	1	0	1.000	9	5	5	8	3	3.97
1978—New York	American	1	8	1	0	1.000	7	1	1	7	1	1.13
1980—New York	American	1	3	0	1	.000	5	4	4	2	4	12.00
Championship Series Totals		4	22⅓	2	1	.667	21	10	10	17	8	4.03

Appeared as pinch-runner for New York Yankees in one game of 1976 Championship Series.

WORLD SERIES RECORD

Year Club	League	G.	IP.	W.	L.	Pct.	H.	R.	ER.	SO.	BB.	ERA.
1977—New York	American	1	9	1	0	1.000	4	2	2	7	3	2.00
1978—New York	American	1	9	1	0	1.000	8	1	1	4	7	1.00
World Series Totals...................................		2	18	2	0	1.000	12	3	3	11	10	1.50

ALL-STAR GAME RECORD

Year League	IP.	W.	L.	Pct.	H.	R.	ER.	SO.	BB.	ERA.
1978—American	⅓	0	0	.000	0	0	0	0	0	0.00
1979—American	⅓	0	0	.000	0	0	0	0	1	0.00
All-Star Game Totals	⅔	0	0	.000	0	0	0	0	1	0.00

BRADLEY LEE GULDEN

Born June 10, 1956, at New Ulm, Minn.
Height, 5.11. Weight, 182.
Throws right and bats lefthanded.
Hobbies—Hunting and fishing.

Led Northwest League catchers in double plays with 9 and in passed balls with 23 in 1975.

Led California League catchers in passed balls with 18 in 1977.
Led Pacific Coast League in passed balls with 21 in 1978.

Year	Club	League	Pos.	G.	AB.	R.	H.	2B.	3B.	HR.	RBI.	B.A.	PO.	A.	E.	F.A.
1975—Bellingham	N'west		C	66	203	25	33	4	0	2	15	.163	*319	*70	*33	.922
1976—Danville	Midwest		*C-OF	103	334	42	95	20	2	3	51	.284	521	90	*40	.939
1977—Lodi	Calif.		C	118	423	76	127	23	2	15	86	.300	*704	*66	*24	.970
1978—Albuquerque	P. C.		C	125	436	69	128	21	4	8	72	.294	*610	*88	*23	.968
1978—Los Angeles†	Nat.		C	3	4	0	0	0	0	0	0	.000	8	1	0	1.000
1979—Columbus	Int.		C	80	230	28	57	10	0	6	34	.248	326	22	3	.991
1979—New York	Amer.		C	40	92	10	15	4	0	0	6	.163	178	24	1	.995
1980—Columbus	Int.		C	14	51	6	8	2	0	2	10	.157	54	13	4	.944
1980—Nashville‡	South.		C-OF	85	295	34	70	13	6	6	46	.237	543	80	12	.981
1980—New York§	Amer.		C	2	3	1	1	0	0	1	2	.333	3	0	0	1.000
National League Totals				3	4	0	0	0	0	0	0	.000	8	1	0	1.000
American League Totals				42	95	11	16	4	0	1	8	.168	181	24	1	.995
Major League Totals				45	99	11	16	4	0	1	8	.162	189	25	1	.995

Selected by Los Angeles Dodgers' organization in 17th round of free-agent draft, June 4, 1975.
†Traded to New York Yankees for Outfielder Gary Thomasson, February 15, 1979.
‡On disabled list, August 7 to August 17, 1980.
§Traded to Seattle Mariners for Infielder Larry Milbourne, November 18, 1980.

WILLIAM LEE GULLICKSON
(Bill)

Born February 20, 1959, at Marshall, Minn.
Height, 6.03. Weight, 210.
Throws and bats righthanded.
Named National League Rookie Pitcher of the Year by THE SPORTING NEWS, 1980.

Year	Club	League	G.	IP.	W.	L.	Pct.	H.	R.	ER.	SO.	BB.	ERA.
1977—West Palm Beach	Florida St.		10	56	3	3	.500	67	30	25	35	17	4.02
1978—West Palm Beach	Florida St.		20	148	9	9	.500	121	45	30	127	52	1.82
1978—Memphis	Southern		8	50	1	4	.200	44	19	17	43	19	3.06
1979—Denver	Am. Assoc.		11	54	3	3	.500	65	44	40	31	26	6.67
1979—Memphis	Southern		16	116	10	3	.769	110	52	47	115	42	3.65
1979—Montreal	National		1	1	0	0	.000	2	0	0	0	0	0.00
1980—Denver	Am. Assoc.		9	66	6	2	.750	47	14	14	64	29	1.91
1980—Montreal	National		24	141	10	5	.667	127	53	47	120	50	3.00
Major League Totals			25	142	10	5	.667	129	53	47	120	50	2.98

Selected by Montreal Expos' organization in 1st round (second player selected) of free-agent draft, June 7, 1977.

LAWRENCE CYRIL GURA
(Larry)

Born November 26, 1947, at Joliet, Ill.
Height, 6.01. Weight, 185.
Throws left and bats left and righthanded.
Hobbies—Hunting, trapping and fishing.
Attended Arizona State University, Tempe, Ariz.; received Bachelor of Arts degree.

Tied for International League lead in shutouts with 4 in 1974.
Received reported $50,000 bonus to sign with Chicago Cubs, 1969.

Year	Club	League	G.	IP.	W.	L.	Pct.	H.	R.	ER.	SO.	BB.	ERA.
1969—Tacoma	P. Coast		16	88	4	8	.333	79	39	31	47	24	3.17
1970—Tacoma	P. Coast		10	61	3	4	.429	55	32	27	32	17	3.98
1970—Chicago	National		20	38	1	3	.250	35	18	16	21	23	3.79
1971—Tacoma	P. Coast		30	190	11	8	.579	199	93	75	140	50	3.55
1971—Chicago	National		6	3	0	0	.000	6	3	2	2	1	6.00
1972—Wichita	Am. Assoc.		26	130	11	4	*.733	127	60	53	109	38	3.65
1972—Chicago	National		7	12	0	0	.000	11	5	5	13	3	3.75
1973—Wichita	Am. Assoc.		5	31	1	2	.333	38	18	16	29	11	4.65
1973—Chicago†	National		21	65	2	4	.333	79	39	35	43	11	4.85
1974—Spokane‡	P. Coast		7	29	1	1	.500	34	14	10	25	9	3.10
1974—Syracuse	Int'national		17	118	7	7	.500	89	32	28	97	19	*2.14
1974—New York	American		8	56	5	1	.833	54	17	15	17	12	2.41
1975—New York§	American		26	151	7	8	.467	173	65	59	65	41	3.52
1976—Kansas City x	American		20	63	4	0	1.000	47	20	16	22	20	2.29
1977—Kansas City y	American		52	106	8	5	.615	108	43	37	46	28	3.14
1978—Kansas City	American		26	222	16	4	.800	183	73	67	81	60	2.72
1979—Kansas City	American		39	234	13	12	.520	226	137	116	85	73	4.46
1980—Kansas City	American		36	283	18	10	.643	272	107	93	113	76	2.96
National League Totals			54	118	3	7	.300	131	65	58	79	38	4.42
American League Totals			207	1115	71	40	.640	1063	462	403	429	310	3.25
Major League Totals			261	1233	74	47	.612	1194	527	461	508	348	3.36

Selected by Chicago Cubs' organization in 2nd round of free-agent draft, June 5, 1969.
†Traded to Texas Rangers, November 14, 1973 (completion of deal in which Cubs obtained Pitcher Mike Paul, August 31, 1973).
‡Traded by Texas Rangers to New York Yankees for Catcher Duke Sims, May 8, 1974.

§Traded to Kansas City Royals for Catcher Fran Healy, May 15, 1976.
xOn disabled list, June 1 to June 23, 1976.
yGranted free agency, November 2, 1978; re-signed with Kansas City Royals, November 13, 1978.

CHAMPIONSHIP SERIES RECORD

Established Championship Series record for most hits allowed, game (12), October 9, 1976.
Established American League Championship Series record for most hits allowed, five-game Series (18), 1976.

Year Club	League	G.	IP.	W.	L.	Pct.	H.	R.	ER.	SO.	BB.	ERA.
1976—Kansas City	American	2	10⅔	0	1	.000	18	6	5	4	1	4.22
1977—Kansas City	American	2	2	0	1	.000	7	5	4	2	1	18.00
1978—Kansas City	American	1	6⅓	1	0	1.000	8	2	2	2	2	2.84
1980—Kansas City	American	1	9	1	0	1.000	10	2	2	4	1	2.00
Championship Series Totals		6	28	2	2	.500	43	15	13	12	5	4.18

WORLD SERIES RECORD

Tied World Series record for most double plays by pitcher, six-game Series (2), 1980.

Year Club	League	G.	IP.	W.	L.	Pct.	H.	R.	ER.	SO.	BB.	ERA.
1980—Kansas City	American	2	12⅓	0	0	.000	8	4	3	4	3	2.19

ALL-STAR GAME RECORD

Named to American League All-Star Team in 1980; did not play.

DOUGLAS WAYNE GWOSDZ

Name pronounced Goosh.

(Doug)

Born June 20, 1960, at Houston, Tex.
Height, 5.11. Weight, 180.
Throws and bats righthanded.

Year Club	League	Pos.	G.	AB.	R.	H.	2B.	3B.	HR.	RBI.	B.A.	PO.	A.	E.	F.A.
1978—Walla Walla	Northw.	C	48	170	25	42	6	0	5	26	.247	256	51	5	*.984
1979—Reno	Calif.	C	85	258	37	67	7	3	6	40	.260	583	51	8	.988
1980—Amarillo	Texas	C	97	286	40	70	18	2	7	43	.245	597	66	14	.979

Selected by San Diego Padres' organization in 2nd round of free-agent draft, June 6, 1978.

BRYAN EDMUND HAAS

(Moose)

Born April 22, 1956, at Baltimore, Md.
Height, 6.00. Weight, 170.
Throws and bats righthanded.
Hobby—Sports.
Attended Catonsville Junior College, Catonsville, Md.

Year Club	League	G.	IP.	W.	L.	Pct.	H.	R.	ER.	SO.	BB.	ERA.
1974—Newark	NYP	13	96	5	5	.500	91	43	34	89	41	3.19
1975—Burlington	Midwest	25	171	11	8	.579	149	66	39	146	49	2.05
1976—Spokane	P. Coast	30	172	13	9	.591	208	116	*106	130	86	5.55
1976—Milwaukee	American	5	16	0	1	.000	12	8	7	9	12	3.94
1977—Milwaukee	American	32	198	10	12	.455	195	104	95	113	84	4.32
1978—Milwaukee†	American	7	31	2	3	.400	33	22	21	32	8	6.10
1979—Milwaukee	American	29	185	11	11	.500	198	112	98	95	59	4.77
1980—Milwaukee	American	33	252	16	15	.516	246	96	87	146	56	3.11
Major League Totals		106	682	39	42	.481	684	342	308	395	219	4.06

Selected by Milwaukee Brewers' organization in 2nd round of free-agent draft, June 5, 1974.
†On disabled list, April 20 to June 21 and June 27 to September 15, 1978.

EDWARD LOUIS HALICKI

Name pronounced huh-LICK-ee.

(Ed)

Born October 4, 1950, at Kearny, N. J.
Height, 6.07. Weight, 225.
Throws and bats righthanded.
Attended Monmouth College, West Long Branch, N. J.; received Bachelor of Science degree.

Pitched 6-0 no-hit victory against New York Mets, August 24, 1975 (second game of doubleheader).

Year Club	League	G.	IP.	W.	L.	Pct.	H.	R.	ER.	SO.	BB.	ERA.
1972—Great Falls	Pioneer	12	21	0	2	.000	15	9	3	29	14	1.29
1972—Decatur	Midwest	7	48	4	2	.667	31	20	13	65	24	2.44
1973—Fresno	California	26	182	14	6	.700	142	66	54	162	63	2.67
1974—Phoenix	P. Coast	19	123	8	6	.571	124	65	59	72	34	4.32
1974—San Francisco	National	16	74	1	8	.111	84	49	35	40	31	4.26
1975—Phoenix	P. Coast	8	56	5	3	.625	46	26	24	55	21	3.86
1975—San Francisco	National	24	160	9	13	.409	143	76	62	153	59	3.49
1976—San Francisco	National	32	186	12	14	.462	171	86	75	130	61	3.63

Year Club	League	G.	IP.	W.	L.	Pct.	H.	R.	ER.	SO.	BB.	ERA.
1977–San Francisco	National	37	258	16	12	.571	241	105	95	168	70	3.31
1978–San Francisco†	National	29	199	9	10	.474	166	74	63	105	45	2.85
1979–San Francisco‡	National	33	126	5	8	.385	134	82	64	81	47	4.57
1980–San Francisco§	National	11	25	0	0	.000	29	15	15	14	10	5.40
1980–California xy	American	10	35	3	1	.750	39	22	19	16	11	4.89
American League Totals		10	35	3	1	.750	39	22	19	16	11	4.89
National League Totals		182	1028	52	65	.444	968	487	409	691	323	3.58
Major League Totals		192	1063	55	66	.455	1007	509	428	707	334	3.62

Selected by St. Louis Cardinals' organization in 12th round of free-agent draft, June 7, 1968.
Selected by San Francisco Giants' organization in 24th round of free-agent draft, June 6, 1972.
†On disabled list, April 16 to May 14, 1978.
‡On disabled list, May 28 to June 26, 1979.
§Sold on waivers to California Angels, June 20, 1980.
xOn disabled list, August 5 to September 8, 1980.
yReleased, October 24, 1980; invited to Philadelphia Phillies camp, 1981.

ALBERT HALL

Born March 7, 1959, at Birmingham, Ala.
Height, 5.11. Weight, 155.
Throws right and bats left and righthanded.
Led Gulf Coast League shortstops in double plays with 23 in 1978.
Led Western Carolinas League in stolen bases with 66 in 1979.
Led Carolina League in stolen bases with 100 in 1979.

Year Club	League	Pos.	G.	AB.	R.	H.	2B.	3B.	HR.	RBI.	B.A.	PO.	A.	E.	F.A.
1977–Kingsport	Appal.	SS	35	68	11	11	0	0	0	3	.162	10	28	10	.792
1978–Brad. Braves	G. C.	SS	34	123	15	36	4	2	0	14	.293	55	100	•15	.912
1979–Greenwood	W. Car.	SS	105	368	84	106	10	3	0	38	.288	120	288	•72	.850
1980–Durham	Carol.	OF-SS	125	491	95	139	16	7	4	41	.283	166	32	16	.925

Selected by Atlanta Braves' organization in 6th round of free-agent draft, June 7, 1977.

MELVIN HALL JR.
(Mel)

Born September 16, 1960, at Lyons, N.Y.
Height, 6.00. Weight, 185.
Throws and bats lefthanded.
Son of Melvin Hall, minor league player, 1949.

Year Club	League	Pos.	G.	AB.	R.	H.	2B.	3B.	HR.	RBI.	B.A.	PO.	A.	E.	F.A.
1978–Bradenton Cubs.	G. C.	OF	43	145	42	61	7	3	2	17	.290	•97	5	4	.962
1979–Geneva	NYP	OF	66	251	49	79	18	5	3	53	.315	113	5	7	.944
1980–Midland	Texas	OF	37	128	17	34	7	3	1	14	.266	58	3	3	.953
1980–Quad Cities	Midw.	OF	97	347	54	102	14	4	6	42	.294	171	9	5	.973

Selected by Chicago Cubs' organization in 2nd round of free-agent draft, June 6, 1978.

DAVID EDWARD HAMILTON
(Dave)

Born December 13, 1947, at Seattle, Wash.
Height, 6.00. Weight, 190.
Throws and bats lefthanded.
Attended Everett Community College, Everett, Wash.

Year Club	League	G.	IP.	W.	L.	Pct.	H.	R.	ER.	SO.	BB.	ERA.
1966–Lewiston	Northwest	16	90	6	6	.500	84	46	41	103	36	4.10
1967–Burlington	Midwest	15	60	3	5	.375	67	37	22	62	29	3.30
1968–Peninsula	Carolina	11	67	3	5	.375	64	44	33	44	33	4.43
1968–Leesburg†	Florida St.	10	63	0	7	.000	50	28	18	52	32	2.57
1969–Lodi	California	22	135	8	8	.500	127	67	62	131	58	4.13
1969–Birmingham	Southern	5	25	2	2	.500	13	3	3	24	6	1.08
1970–Birmingham	Southern	21	104	6	4	.600	88	39	28	86	32	2.42
1971–Iowa	Am. Assoc.	30	121	12	4	•.750	98	58	51	88	54	3.79
1972–Iowa	Am. Assoc.	8	59	5	1	.833	52	19	15	60	23	2.29
1972–Oakland	American	25	101	6	6	.500	94	34	33	55	31	2.94
1973–Tucson	P. Coast	15	105	8	5	.615	98	49	44	83	38	3.77
1973–Oakland	American	16	70	6	4	.600	74	37	34	34	24	4.37
1974–Oakland	American	29	117	7	4	.636	104	45	41	69	48	3.15
1975–Oakland‡-Chicago	American	41	105	7	7	.500	105	42	38	71	47	3.26
1976–Chicago	American	45	90	6	6	.500	81	38	36	62	45	3.60
1977–Chicago§	American	55	67	4	5	.444	71	33	27	45	33	3.63
1978–St.L. x-Pitt. y	National	29	40	0	2	.000	39	29	20	23	18	4.50
1979–Oakland z	American	40	83	3	4	.429	80	42	34	52	43	3.69
1980–Ogden	P. Coast	15	31	0	1	.000	32	19	12	25	22	3.48
1980–Oakland a	American	21	30	0	3	.000	44	39	38	23	28	11.40
American League Totals		272	663	39	39	.500	653	310	281	411	299	3.81
National League Totals		29	40	0	2	.000	39	29	20	23	18	4.50
Major League Totals		301	703	39	41	.488	692	339	301	434	317	3.85

Selected by Kansas City A's organization in free-agent draft, June 10, 1966.

†Appeared as first baseman in 5 games and as outfielder in one game.

‡Traded with Infielder-Outfielder Chet Lemon to Chicago White Sox for Pitchers Stan Bahnsen and Lee (Skip) Pitlock, June 15, 1975.

§Assigned to St. Louis Cardinals with Pitcher Silvio Martinez to complete deals in which Chicago White Sox obtained Infielder Don Kessinger and Pitcher Clay Carroll, November 28, 1977. Nyls Nyman was assigned to New Orleans (St. Louis organization), and Pitcher Steve Staniland was assigned to Iowa (White Sox organization).

xSold to Pittsburgh Pirates, May 28, 1978.

yGranted free agency, November 2, 1978; signed by Oakland A's, February 28, 1979.

zGranted free agency, November 1, 1979; signed by Oakland A's, February 20, 1980.

aReleased, December 12, 1980; re-signed by A's organization, January 10, 1981.

CHAMPIONSHIP SERIES RECORD

Year Club	League	G.	IP.	W.	L.	Pct.	H.	R.	ER.	SO.	BB.	ERA.
1972—Oakland	American	1	0*	0	0	.000	1	0	0	0	1	0.00

*Pitched to two batters in tenth inning of fourth game.

WORLD SERIES RECORD

Year Club	League	G.	IP.	W.	L.	Pct.	H.	R.	ER.	SO.	BB.	ERA.
1972—Oakland	American	2	1⅓	0	0	.000	3	4	4	1	1	27.00

TIMOTHY CRAIG HAMM
(Tim)

Born August 8, 1960, at Santa Cruz, Calif.
Height, 6.04. Weight, 200.
Throws and bats righthanded.

Year Club	League	G.	IP.	W.	L.	Pct.	H.	R.	ER.	SO.	BB.	ERA.
1978—Walla Walla	Northwest	3	13	0	1	.000	12	10	7	9	7	4.85
1979—Reno	California	6	13	0	0	.000	22	13	9	6	6	6.23
1979—Walla Walla	Northwest	14	94	8	6	.571	107	49	39	52	31	3.73
1980—Reno	California	25	179	15	7	.682	*203	82	62	122	42	3.12

Selected by San Diego Padres' organization in 9th round of free-agent draft, June 6, 1978.

RONALD GARRY HANCOCK

(Known by middle name)
Born January 23, 1954, at Tampa, Fla.
Height, 6.00. Weight, 175.
Throws and bats lefthanded.
Attended University of South Carolina, Columbia, S. C.

Year Club	League	Pos.	G.	AB.	R.	H.	2B.	3B.	HR.	RBI.	B.A.	PO.	A.	E.	F.A.
1976—San Jose	Calif.	OF-1B	135	526	56	162	22	5	5	77	.308	215	20	9	.963
1977—Jersey City†	East.	OF	63	240	22	77	9	9	1	34	.321	117	6	5	.961
1977—Toledo‡	Int.	OF	53	189	17	50	6	1	3	16	.265	103	7	4	.965
1978—Pawtucket	Int.	OF	84	310	41	94	15	4	8	44	.303	146	11	6	.963
1978—Boston	Amer.	OF	38	80	10	18	3	0	0	4	.225	29	3	0	1.000
1979—Pawtucket§	Int.	OF-1B	111	406	51	132	22	3	15	58	*.325	166	15	3	.983
1980—Pawtucket	Int.	OF-1B	60	216	24	52	6	2	6	19	.241	144	11	4	.975
1980—Boston	Amer.	OF	46	115	9	33	6	0	4	19	.287	49	3	2	.963
Major League Totals			84	195	19	51	9	0	4	23	.262	78	6	2	.977

Selected by Baltimore Orioles' organization in 25th round of free-agent draft, June 4, 1970.

Selected by Texas Rangers' organization in 22nd round of free-agent draft, June 6, 1972.

Selected by Cleveland Indians' organization in 10th round of free-agent draft, January 9, 1974.

Selected by Texas Rangers' organization in secondary phase of free-agent draft, June 5, 1974.

Selected by California Angels' organization in secondary phase of free-agent draft, June 4, 1975.

Selected by Cleveland Indians' organization in secondary phase of free-agent draft, January 7, 1976.

†On disabled list, May 15 to May 29, 1977.

‡Traded by Cleveland Indians' organization to Boston Red Sox' organization for First Baseman Jack Baker, December 7, 1977.

§On disabled list, June 3 to June 17, 1979.

PRESTON LEE HANNA

Born September 10, 1954, at Pensacola, Fla.
Height, 6.01. Weight, 185.
Throws and bats righthanded.
Hobbies—Hunting, fishing, tennis, yoga and sailing.
Attended Pensacola Junior College, Pensacola, Fla.

Year Club	League	G.	IP.	W.	L.	Pct.	H.	R.	ER.	SO.	BB.	ERA.
1972—Wytheville	Ap'lachian	8	36	3	2	.600	40	28	26	42	25	6.50
1973—Greenwood	W. Carol.	23	147	8	11	.421	138	69	58	130	80	3.55
1974—Savannah	Southern	27	167	11	6	.647	146	80	64	117	117	3.45
1975—Richmond†	Int'national	26	141	10	10	.500	125	73	52	101	92	3.32
1975—Atlanta	National	4	6	0	0	.000	7	1	1	2	5	1.50
1976—Richmond‡	Int'national	27	126	4	9	.308	126	81	74	47	84	5.29
1976—Atlanta	National	5	8	0	0	.000	11	5	4	3	4	4.50
1977—Richmond§	Int'national	12	62	2	6	.250	72	42	38	34	44	5.52
1977—Savannah	Southern	7	31	2	1	.667	26	5	4	20	14	1.16
1977—Atlanta	National	17	60	2	6	.250	69	40	33	37	34	4.95

Year Club	League	G.	IP.	W.	L.	Pct.	H.	R.	ER.	SO.	BB.	ERA.
1978—Atlanta ....National	National	29	140	7	13	.350	132	89	80	90	93	5.14
1979—Atlanta x ....National	National	6	24	1	1	.500	27	11	8	15	15	3.00
1980—Atlanta ....National	National	32	79	2	0	1.000	63	28	28	44	3.19
Major League Totals		93	317	12	20	.375	309	174	154	182	195	4.37

Selected by Atlanta Braves' organization in 1st round (11th player selected) of free-agent draft, June 6, 1972.

†Played in one game as an outfielder.
‡On temporary inactive list, April 16 to April 30, 1976.
§On disabled list, April 28 to May 8, 1977.
xOn emergency disabled list, April 4 to July 7, 1979.

GERALD ELLIS HANNAHS

Born March 6, 1953, at Binghamton, N.Y.
Height, 6.03. Weight, 210.
Throws and bats lefthanded.
Attended University of Arkansas, Fayetteville, Ark.; received Bachelor of Science degree in Finance.

Year Club	League	G.	IP.	W.	L.	Pct.	H.	R.	ER.	SO.	BB.	ERA.
1974—Sarasota Expos ....Gulf Coast	Gulf Coast	9	24	1	1	.500	16	9	7	24	12	2.63
1974—West Palm Beach ....Florida St.	Florida St.	4	19	2	1	.667	15	7	6	19	12	2.84
1975—West Palm Beach ....Florida St.	Florida St.	8	55	2	3	.400	38	17	12	46	27	1.96
1975—Quebec City ....Eastern	Eastern	19	121	8	3	.727	94	43	38	86	66	2.83
1976—Quebec City ....Eastern	Eastern	26	173	•20	6	.769	144	56	46	126	88	2.39
1976—Montreal.............................National	National	3	16	2	0	1.000	20	14	12	10	12	6.75
1977—Denver ....Am. Assoc.	Am. Assoc.	17	82	6	2	.750	80	39	35	60	64	3.84
1977—Montreal.............................National	National	8	37	1	5	.167	43	27	20	21	17	4.86
1978—Memphis†...........................Southern	Southern	6	35	1	3	.250	38	21	18	31	22	4.63
1978—San Antonio‡.......................Texas	Texas	21	109	9	5	.643	82	45	31	95	56	2.56
1978—Los Angeles ....National	National	1	2	0	0	.000	3	2	2	5	0	9.00
1979—Albuquerque ....P. Coast	P. Coast	26	136	11	8	.579	137	88	78	99	98	5.16
1979—Los Angeles ....National	National	4	16	0	2	.000	10	8	6	6	13	3.38
1980—Albuquerque§.......................P. Coast	P. Coast	28	189	•15	9	.625	178	82	67	93	108	3.19
Major League Totals		16	71	3	7	.300	76	51	40	42	42	5.07

Signed as free agent by Montreal Expos' organization, July 5, 1974.
†Traded to Los Angeles Dodgers' organization for Pitcher Mike Garman, May 20, 1978.
‡On suspended list, July 2 to July 7, 1978.
§Traded to Minnesota Twins' organization for Pitcher Dave Moore, February 6, 1981.

ALAN ROBERT HARGESHEIMER
(Al)

Born November 21, 1956, at Chicago, Ill.
Height, 6.03. Weight, 200.
Throws and bats righthanded.
Attended Mayfair Junior College, Chicago, Ill. and Northeastern Illinois University, Chicago, Ill.; received Bachelor of Arts degree in Physical Education.

Tied for California League lead in games started with 28 in 1978.

Year Club	League	G.	IP.	W.	L.	Pct.	H.	R.	ER.	SO.	BB.	ERA.
1978—Fresno.................................California	California	29	176	7	11	.389	•216	117	96	109	82	4.91
1979—Shreveport...........................Texas	Texas	24	141	6	10	.375	165	96	71	80	60	4.53
1980—Shreveport...........................Texas	Texas	12	81	2	6	.250	67	28	16	40	30	1.78
1980—Phoenix ....P. Coast	P. Coast	2	17	1	1	.500	18	8	8	13	13	4.24
1980—San Francisco ....National	National	15	75	4	6	.400	82	38	36	40	32	4.32
Major League Totals.................................		15	75	4	6	.400	82	38	36	40	32	4.32

Signed as free agent by San Francisco Giants' organization, March 21, 1978.

DUDLEY MICHAEL HARGROVE
(Mike)

Born October 26, 1949, at Perryton, Tex.
Height, 6.00. Weight, 195.
Throws and bats lefthanded.
Hobbies—Hunting and golf.
Attended Northwestern State University, Alva, Okla.; received
Bachelor of Science degree in Education.

Led American League batters in walks with 97 in 1976 and with 107 in 1978.
Led Western Carolinas League in total bases with 247 in 1973.
Led Western Carolinas League first basemen in double plays with 118 in 1973 and led New York-Pennsylvania League first basemen with 58 in 1972.
Named American League Rookie Player of the Year by THE SPORTING NEWS, 1974.
Named American League Rookie of the Year by Baseball Writers' Association of America, 1974.
Named Western Carolinas League Player of the Year in 1973.

Year Club	League	Pos.	G.	AB.	R.	H.	2B.	3B.	HR.	RBI.	B.A.	PO.	A.	E.	F.A.
1972—Geneva ....NYP	NYP	1B	•70	243	38	65	8	0	4	37	.267	•537	•40	10	•.983
1973—Gastonia ....W. Car.	W. Car.	1B	•130	456	88	•160	•35	8	12	82	•.351	•1121	•77	14	•.988
1974—Texas...............Amer.	Amer.	1B-OF	131	415	57	134	18	6	4	66	.323	638	72	9	.987

Year Club League	Pos.	G.	AB.	R.	H.	2B.	3B.	HR.	RBI.	B.A.	PO.	A.	E.	F.A.
1975—Texas..............Amer.	OF-1B	145	519	82	157	22	2	11	62	.303	513	45	13	.977
1976—Texas..............Amer.	1B	151	541	80	155	30	1	7	58	.287	1222	110	*21	.984
1977—Texas..............Amer.	1B	153	525	98	160	28	4	18	69	.305	1393	100	11	.993
1978—Texas†............Amer.	1B	146	494	63	124	24	1	7	40	.251	1221	*116	*17	.987
1979—San Diego‡........Nat.	1B	52	125	15	24	5	0	0	8	.192	323	17	5	.986
1979—Cleveland.........Amer.	OF-1B	100	338	60	110	21	4	10	56	.325	356	16	2	.995
1980—Cleveland.........Amer.	1B	160	589	86	179	22	2	11	85	.304	*1391	88	10	.993
American League Totals		986	3421	526	1019	165	20	68	436	.298	6734	547	83	.989
National League Totals		52	125	15	24	5	0	0	8	.192	323	17	5	.986
Major League Totals......................		1038	3546	541	1043	170	20	68	444	.294	7057	564	88	.989

Selected by Texas Rangers' organization in 25th round of free-agent draft, June 6, 1972.

†Traded with Third Baseman Kurt Bevacqua and Catcher Bill Fahey to San Diego Padres for Outfielder Oscar Gamble, Catcher Dave Roberts and cash estimated at $300,000, October 25, 1978.

‡Traded to Cleveland Indians for Outfielder Paul Dade, June 14, 1979.

ALL-STAR GAME RECORD

Year League	Pos.	AB.	R.	H.	2B.	3B.	HR.	RBI.	B.A.	PO.	A.	E.	F.A.
1975—American...........................	PH	1	0	0	0	0	0	0	.000	0	0	0	.000

LARRY DUANE HARLOW

Born November 13, 1951, at Colorado Springs, Colo.
Height, 6.02. Weight, 176.
Throws and bats lefthanded.
Attended Mesa Community College, Mesa, Ariz.

Led Southern League outfielders in double plays with 5 in 1974 and International League outfielders with 5 in 1975.

Tied for California League lead in double plays by outfielders with 3 in 1973.

Year Club League	Pos.	G.	AB.	R.	H.	2B.	3B.	HR.	RBI.	B.A.	PO.	A.	E.	F.A.
1971—Key West..........Fla. St.	OF-P	70	205	22	42	6	2	2	21	.205	95	9	7	.937
1971—Aberdeen ....North.	OF	57	217	50	66	8	6	3	34	.304	93	5	5	.951
1972—Lodi ....Calif.	OF	131	480	66	112	9	2	2	47	.233	*274	13	6	.980
1973—Lodi ....Calif.	OF	134	493	88	140	20	11	5	67	.284	*367	18	*18	.955
1974—Asheville..........South.	OF	134	529	86	147	21	2	4	42	.278	284	*18	14	.956
1974—Rochester ....Int.	OF	4	5	0	1	0	0	0	0	.200	5	1	0	1.000
1975—Rochester ....Int.	OF	132	424	65	108	11	4	2	31	.255	280	10	8	.972
1975—Baltimore..........Amer.	OF	4	3	1	1	0	0	0	0	.333	2	0	0	1.000
1976—Rochester ....Int.	OF	130	442	81	109	22	0	7	47	.247	*308	12	9	.973
1977—Rochester ....Int.	OF-1B	93	343	56	115	14	3	9	50	.335	216	8	4	.982
1977—Baltimore..........Amer.	OF	46	48	4	10	0	1	0	0	.208	47	0	6	.887
1978—Baltimore ....Amer.	OF-P	147	460	67	112	25	1	8	26	.243	313	7	7	.979
1979—Balt.†-Calif. ......Amer.	OF	100	200	27	48	9	2	0	15	.240	147	4	4	.974
1980—California ....Amer.	OF-1B	109	301	47	83	13	4	4	27	.276	235	11	6	.976
Major League Totals		406	1012	146	254	47	8	12	68	.251	744	22	23	.971

Signed as free agent by Baltimore Orioles' organization, August 24, 1970.

†Traded to California Angels for Infielder Floyd Rayford and cash, June 5, 1979.

PITCHING RECORD

Year Club League	G.	IP.	W.	L.	Pct.	H.	R.	ER.	SO.	BB.	ERA.
1971—Key West ....Florida St.	2	1	0	0	.000	3	4	0	2	1	0.00
1978—Baltimore ....American	1	1	0	0	.000	2	5	5	1	4	45.00

CHAMPIONSHIP SERIES RECORD

Year Club League	Pos.	G.	AB.	R.	H.	2B.	3B.	HR.	RBI.	B.A.	PO.	A.	E.	F.A.
1979—California ....Amer.	OF-PH	3	8	0	1	1	0	0	1	.125	6	0	0	1.000

BRIAN DAVID HARPER

Born October 16, 1959, at Los Angeles, Calif.
Height, 6.02. Weight, 195.
Throws and bats righthanded.

Led Texas League catchers in passed balls with 19 in 1979.

Year Club League	Pos.	G.	AB.	R.	H.	2B.	3B.	HR.	RBI.	B.A.	PO.	A.	E.	F.A.
1977—Idaho Falls ....Pion.	C	52	186	28	60	9	3	1	33	.323	352	36	13	.968
1978—Quad Cities ....Midw.	C	129	508	80	149	31	2	24	*101	.293	430	46	16	.967
1979—El Paso.............Texas	C	132	531	85	167	*37	3	14	90	.315	443	66	*29	.946
1979—California ....Amer.	DH	1	2	0	0	0	0	0	0	.000	0	0	0	.000
1980—El Paso†...........Texas	C	105	400	61	114	23	3	12	66	.285	214	30	7	.972
Major League Totals......................		1	2	0	0	0	0	0	0	.000	0	0	0	.000

Selected by California Angels' organization in 4th round of free-agent draft, June 7, 1977.

†On disabled list, July 1 to July 17, 1980.

TERRY JOE HARPER

Born August 19, 1955, at Douglasville, Ga.
Height, 6.01. Weight, 195.
Throws and bats righthanded.
Led International League outfielders in double plays with 5 in 1980.

Year Club League	Pos.	G.	AB.	R.	H.	2B.	3B.	HR.	RBI.	B.A.	PO.	A.	E.	F.A.
1973–Wytheville ....Appal.	P	13	17	3	4	0	0	0	2	.235	3	7	4	.714
1974–Greenwood†‡ ....W. Car.	P	15	15	0	4	0	1	0	1	.267	1	11	2	.857
1975–Greenwood§x ....W. Car.	P	14	0	0	0	0	0	0	0	.000	6	17	0	1.000
1976–Greenwood y.....W. Car.	P	2	0	0	0	0	0	0	0	.000	1	0	0	1.000
1976–Brad. Braves.....G. C.	OF-3-1	51	185	21	48	6	6	1	37	.259	87	8	6	.941
1977–Greenwood ....W. Car.	OF-3-1	70	251	45	74	12	3	4	43	.295	200	10	4	.981
1977–Savannah..........South.	OF	54	149	14	36	3	5	1	18	.242	94	8	2	.981
1978–Savannah..........South.	OF	47	174	17	46	9	1	4	21	.264	85	10	2	.979
1978–Richmond ....Int.	OF	73	205	21	52	5	3	0	24	.254	137	5	2	.896
1979–Richmond z......Int.	OF	108	327	49	99	18	3	10	58	.303	164	9	9	.951
1980–Richmond ....Int.	OF	*140	512	66	143	19	8	13	72	.279	315	19	6	.982
1980–Atlanta ....Nat.	OF	21	54	3	10	2	1	0	3	.185	30	0	1	.968
Major League Totals......................		21	54	3	10	2	1	0	3	.185	30	0	1	.968

Selected by Atlanta Braves' organization in 16th round of free-agent draft, June 5, 1973.
†On disabled list, May 5 to May 31, 1974.
‡On disabled list, June 24 to July 9, 1974.
§On disabled list, June 18 to July 7, 1975.
xOn disabled list, August 2 to August 16, 1975.
yOn disabled list, April 27 to June 25, 1976.
zOn disabled list, August 20 to August 30, 1979.

PITCHING RECORD

Year Club League	G.	IP.	W.	L.	Pct.	H.	R.	ER.	SO.	BB.	ERA.
1973–Wytheville ....Ap'lachian	12	58	3	3	.500	60	36	25	42	36	3.88
1974–Greenwood ....W. Carol.	15	43	4	2	.667	44	23	19	37	25	3.98
1975–Greenwood ....W. Carol.	14	69	1	5	.167	95	48	40	27	39	5.22
1976–Greenwood ....W. Carol.	2	8	1	1	.500	9	10	10	4	7	11.25

COLBERT DALE HARRAH
(Toby)

Born October 26, 1948, at Sissonville, W. Va.
Height, 6.00. Weight, 180.
Throws and bats righthanded.
Hobbies–Hunting, riding horses and motorcycles.
Attended Ohio Northern University, Ada, O.

Established major league records for most innings by third baseman, no assists, game (17), September 17, 1977; fewest chances offered by third baseman, doubleheader (0), June 25, 1976.
Tied major league record for fewest chances offered by third baseman, two consecutive games (0), June 25, 1976 (doubleheader).
Led American League in bases on balls with 109 in 1977.
Major League stolen bases: 1969 (0), 1971 (10), 1972 (16), 1973 (10), 1974 (15), 1975 (23), 1976 (8), 1977 (27), 1978 (31), 1979 (20), 1980 (17). Total–177.
Named shortstop on THE SPORTING NEWS American League All-Star Team, 1975.

Year Club League	Pos.	G.	AB.	R.	H.	2B.	3B.	HR.	RBI.	B.A.	PO.	A.	E.	F.A.
1967–Huron† ....North.	2B-SS	63	207	34	53	6	0	3	22	.256	136	163	23	.929
1968–Burlington..........Carol.	SS	135	468	73	112	16	3	6	39	.239	217	356	*50	.920
1969–Burlington‡ ....Car.	SS-2B	46	147	27	45	4	2	4	12	.306	76	152	10	.958
1969–Savannah ....South.	SS	28	80	8	19	2	0	2	7	.238	36	78	11	.912
1969–Washington ....Amer.	SS	8	1	4	0	0	0	0	0	.000	0	0	0	.000
1970–Pittsfield§ ....East.	SS-3B	95	359	57	99	18	1	3	37	.276	159	293	27	.944
1971–Washington ......Amer.	SS-3B	127	383	45	88	11	3	2	22	.230	187	321	24	.955
1972–Texas x ....Amer.	SS	116	374	47	97	14	3	1	31	.259	166	308	20	.960
1973–Texas y ....Amer.	SS-3B	118	461	64	120	16	1	10	50	.260	155	332	27	.947
1974–Texas.................Amer.	*SS-3B	161	573	79	149	23	2	21	74	.260	*283	474	●29	.963
1975–Texas.................Amer.	S-3-2	151	522	81	153	24	1	20	93	.293	253	481	29	.962
1976–Texas.................Amer.	SS-3B	155	584	64	152	21	1	15	67	.260	●294	481	*37	.954
1977–Texas.................Amer.	3B-SS	159	539	90	142	25	5	27	87	.263	108	278	15	.963
1978–Texas z ....Amer.	3B-SS	139	450	56	103	17	3	12	59	.229	129	330	11	.977
1979–Cleveland.........Amer.	3B-SS	149	527	99	147	25	1	20	77	.279	113	215	19	.947
1980–Cleveland.........Amer.	3B-SS	160	561	100	150	22	4	11	72	.267	121	319	13	.971
Major League Totals		1443	4975	729	1301	198	24	139	632	.262	1809	3539	224	.960

Signed as free agent by Philadelphia Phillies' organization, December 27, 1966.
†Drafted by Honolulu (Washington Senators' organization) from Reading (Philadelphia Phillies' organization), November 28, 1967.
‡On military list from beginning of season to June 2, 1969.
§On temporary inactive list, July 24 to August 11, 1970.
xOn disabled list, August 14 to September 6, 1972.
yOn supplemental disabled list, July 2 to August 7, 1973.
zTraded to Cleveland Indians for Third Baseman Buddy Bell, December 8, 1978.

Year League	Pos.	AB.	R.	H.	2B.	3B.	HR.	RBI.	B.A.	PO.	A.	E.	F.A.
1976—American.............................	SS	2	0	0	0	0	0	0	.000	0	0	0	.000

Named to American League All-Star Team for the 1972 game; replaced due to an injury.
Member of American League All-Star Team for 1975 game; did not play.

DERREL McKINLEY HARRELSON
(Bud)

(Named by brother, who couldn't say Derrel so called him "Bubba"
and it ended up "Bud".)

Born June 6, 1944, at Niles, Calif.
Height, 5.10½. Weight, 155.
Throws right and bats left and righthanded.
Hobby—Golf.
Attended San Francisco State College, San Francisco, Calif.

Tied major league record for most assists, shortstop, extra-inning game, 14, May 24, 1973 (19 innings).
Established National League record for fewest hits, season, 400 or more at bats, 90, in 1972; fewest assists by shortstop, season, 150 or more games (401), 1970.
Named shortstop on THE SPORTING NEWS National League All-Star Team, 1971.
Named shortstop on THE SPORTING NEWS National League All-Star fielding team, 1971.

Year Club League	Pos.	G.	AB.	R.	H.	2B.	3B.	HR.	RBI.	B.A.	PO.	A.	E.	F.A.
1963—Salinas† ....Calif.	SS	36	136	21	30	2	2	1	9	.221	41	99	18	.886
1964—Salinas..............Calif.	SS	135	441	65	102	12	5	3	48	.231	215	347	34	*.943
1965—Buffalo..............Int.	SS	131	446	37	112	15	1	2	36	.251	243	350	*31	.950
1965—New York..........Nat.	SS	19	37	3	4	1	1	0	0	.108	28	36	3	.955
1966—Jacksonville ......Int.	SS	117	389	56	86	8	5	1	26	.221	194	379	28	.953
1966—New York..........Nat.	SS	33	99	20	22	2	4	0	4	.222	52	91	1	.993
1967—New York..........Nat.	SS	151	540	59	137	16	4	1	28	.254	254	467	32	.958
1968—New York‡ ....Nat.	SS	111	402	38	88	7	3	0	14	.219	199	317	15	.972
1969—New York§ ....Nat.	SS	123	395	42	98	11	6	0	24	.248	243	347	19	.969
1970—New York..........Nat.	SS	157	564	72	137	18	8	1	42	.243	*305	401	21	.971
1971—New York..........Nat.	SS	142	547	55	138	16	6	0	32	.252	257	441	16	.978
1972—New York x.......Nat.	SS	115	418	54	90	10	4	1	24	.215	191	334	16	.970
1973—New York y.......Nat.	SS	106	356	35	92	12	3	0	20	.258	153	315	10	.979
1974—New York..........Nat.	SS	106	331	48	75	10	0	1	13	.227	196	325	17	.968
1975—New York z.......Nat.	SS	34	73	5	16	2	0	0	3	.219	44	67	7	.941
1976—New York..........Nat.	SS	118	359	34	84	12	4	1	26	.234	183	330	20	.962
1977—New York a.......Nat.	SS	107	269	25	48	6	2	1	12	.178	141	239	6	.984
1978—Philadelphia b...Nat.	2B-SS	71	103	16	22	1	0	0	9	.214	72	109	4	.978
1979—Philadelphia c...Nat.	2-S-3-O	53	71	7	20	6	0	0	7	.282	63	71	4	.971
1980—Texas de ....Amer.	SS-2B	87	180	26	49	6	0	1	9	.272	121	222	18	.950
National League Totals		1446	4564	513	1071	130	45	6	258	.235	2385	3890	191	.970
American League Totals		87	180	26	49	6	0	1	9	.272	121	222	18	.950
Major League Totals.......................		1533	4744	539	1120	136	45	7	267	.236	2502	4112	209	.969

Signed as free agent by New York Mets' organization, June 7, 1963.
†On disabled list, July 17 to September 8, 1963.
‡On military list, May 23 to June 12, 1968.
§On military list, June 25 to July 11, 1969.
xOn supplemental disabled list, August 3 to August 25, 1972.
yOn disabled list, June 5 to July 8, 1973; on supplemental disabled list, August 3 to August 18, 1973.
zOn emergency disabled list, May 27 to September 1, 1975.
aTraded to Philadelphia Phillies for Second Baseman Fred Andrews and cash, March 23, 1978.
bGranted free agency, November 2, 1978; signed by Philadelphia Phillies, May 25, 1979.
cReleased, April 4, 1980; signed by Texas Rangers, May 7, 1980.
dOn supplemental disabled list, July 17, 1980; transferred to disabled list, August 30 to September 1, 1980.
eGranted free agency, October 25, 1980.

CHAMPIONSHIP SERIES RECORD

Year Club League	Pos.	G.	AB.	R.	H.	2B.	3B.	HR.	RBI.	B.A.	PO.	A.	E.	F.A.
1969—New York..........Nat.	SS	3	11	2	2	1	1	0	3	.182	6	6	1	.923
1973—New York..........Nat.	SS	5	18	1	3	0	0	0	2	.167	12	14	0	1.000
Championship Series Totals.............		8	29	3	5	1	1	0	5	.172	18	20	1	.974

WORLD SERIES RECORD

Tied World Series records for highest fielding average by shortstop, five-game Series (1.000 with 29 chances), 1969; most assists by shortstop, inning (3), October 14, 1969 (fifth inning) and October 13, 1973 (seventh inning).

Year Club League	Pos.	G.	AB.	R.	H.	2B.	3B.	HR.	RBI.	B.A.	PO.	A.	E.	F.A.
1969—New York..........Nat.	SS	5	17	1	3	0	0	0	0	.176	12	17	0	1.000
1973—New York..........Nat.	SS	7	24	2	6	1	0	0	1	.250	11	24	0	1.000
World Series Totals		12	41	3	9	1	0	0	1	.220	23	41	0	1.000

ALL-STAR GAME RECORD

Year League	Pos.	AB.	R.	H.	2B.	3B.	HR.	RBI.	B.A.	PO.	A.	E.	F.A.
1970—National..............................	SS	3	2	2	0	0	0	0	.667	0	4	0	1.000
1971—National..............................	SS	2	0	0	0	0	0	0	.000	1	2	0	1.000
All-Star Game Totals		5	2	2	0	0	0	0	.400	1	6	0	1.000

GREG ALLEN HARRIS

Born November 2, 1955, at Lynwood, Calif.
Height, 6.00. Weight, 165.
Throws right and bats left and righthanded.
Attended Long Beach City College, Long Beach, Calif.

Year Club	League	G.	IP.	W.	L.	Pct.	H.	R.	ER.	SO.	BB.	ERA.
1977—Jackson	Texas	30	83	3	6	.333	96	63	50	56	36	5.42
1978—Lynchburg	Carolina	21	154	8	9	.471	114	52	37	102	74	2.16
1978—Jackson	Texas	6	33	2	3	.400	24	13	11	18	10	3.00
1979—Jackson	Texas	25	163	9	11	.450	125	58	41	89	81	*2.26
1980—Tidewater	Int'national	39	110	2	9	.182	99	45	33	92	40	2.70

Selected by California Angels' organization in 10th round of free-agent draft, June 5, 1974.
Selected by New York Mets' organization in secondary phase of free-agent draft, January 9, 1975.
Selected by New York Mets' organization in 7th round of free-agent draft, January 7, 1976.
Signed as free agent by New York Mets' organization, September 17, 1976.

JOHN THOMAS HARRIS JR.

Born September 13, 1954, at Portland, Ore.
Height, 6.03. Weight, 215.
Throws and bats lefthanded.
Attended Lubbock Christian College, Lubbock, Tex.

Led Pacific Coast League in total bases with 266 in 1980.
Tied for Midwest League lead in sacrifice flies with 9 in 1977.

Year Club	League	Pos.	G.	AB.	R.	H.	2B.	3B.	HR.	RBI.	B.A.	PO.	A.	E.	F.A.
1977—Quad Cities	Midw.	1B	131	472	76	150	*38	4	23	92	.318	1116	*78	9	*993
1978—Salinas	Calif.	1B	131	478	81	163	25	8	14	86	.341	958	71	8	*992
1979—Salt Lake City†	P. C.	1B	111	418	63	136	38	2	13	88	.325	1022	80	5	.995
1979—California	Amer.	1B	1	2	0	0	0	0	0	0	.000	6	0	0	1.000
1980—Salt Lake City	P. C.	1B	140	516	90	*172	35	4	17	98	.333	1145	82	4	.997
1980—California	Amer.	1B-OF	19	41	8	12	5	0	2	7	.293	63	3	0	1.000
Major League Totals			20	43	8	12	5	0	2	7	.279	69	3	0	1.000

Selected by California Angels' organization in 29th round of free-agent draft, June 8, 1976.
†On disabled list, May 17 to May 30 and June 4 to June 22, 1979.

VICTOR LANIER HARRIS
(Vic)

Born March 27, 1950, at Los Angeles, Calif.
Height, 6.00. Weight, 170.
Throws right and bats left and righthanded.
Hobbies—All sports, music and records.
Attended Los Angeles Valley Junior College, Van Nuys, Calif.

Led Midwest League in stolen bases with 39 and in sacrifice flies with 8 in 1971.

Year Club	League	Pos.	G.	AB.	R.	H.	2B.	3B.	HR.	RBI.	B.A.	PO.	A.	E.	F.A.
1970—Coos Bay-N.B'd	N'west	*2-S	75	288	63	94	12	0	7	53	.326	157	203	20	*.947
1971—Burlington	Midw.	2B	120	444	84	129	27	6	6	55	.291	256	298	27	.954
1972—Birmingham	South.	2B	32	126	17	37	6	1	0	12	.294	84	71	6	.963
1972—Iowa†	A.A.	2B	64	249	42	73	9	6	6	25	.293	148	161	6	.981
1972—Texas	Amer.	2-SS	61	186	8	26	5	1	0	10	.140	113	135	10	.961
1973—Texas‡	Amer.	O-3-2	152	555	71	138	14	7	8	44	.249	354	79	21	.954
1974—Chicago§	Nat.	2B	62	200	18	39	6	3	0	11	.195	122	144	16	.943
1975—Wichita	A.A.	OF	32	132	23	32	2	2	1	11	.242	63	7	1	.986
1975—Chicago x	Nat.	O-3-2	51	56	6	10	0	0	0	5	.179	15	14	2	.935
1976—St. Louis y	Nat.	2-O-3-S	97	259	21	59	12	3	1	19	.228	173	103	14	.952
1977—Phoenix	P.C.	O-2-S	36	139	26	37	8	3	1	18	.266	47	49	4	.960
1977—San Francisco	Nat.	2-S-3-O	69	165	28	43	12	0	2	14	.261	69	96	8	.954
1978—Phoenix	P.C.	SS-3-O	20	81	11	21	2	3	2	12	.259	9	20	6	.829
1978—San Fran.z	Nat.	SS-2B-O	53	100	8	15	4	0	1	11	.150	40	58	5	.951
1979—Vancouver	P.C.	O-2-3	142	509	82	140	25	7	9	66	.275	303	61	7	.981
1980—Vancouver	P.C.	OF-2B	69	238	29	65	12	2	3	37	.273	151	3	4	.975
1980—Milwaukee a	Amer.	O-3-2	34	89	8	19	4	1	1	7	.213	59	4	2	.969
American League Totals			247	830	87	183	23	9	9	61	.220	526	218	33	.958
National League Totals			332	780	81	166	34	6	4	60	.213	419	415	45	.949
Major League Totals			579	1610	168	349	57	15	13	67	.217	945	633	78	.953

Selected by New York Mets' organization in 25th round of free-agent draft, June 5, 1969.
Selected by Oakland A's organization in secondary phase of free-agent draft, January 17, 1970.
†Traded with Infielder Orlando Martinez and Pitcher Steve Lawson to Texas Rangers for First Baseman Don Mincher and Infielder Ted Kubiak, July 20, 1972.
‡Traded with Third Baseman Bill Madlock to Chicago Cubs for Pitcher Ferguson Jenkins, October 25, 1973.
§On disabled list, July 7 through remainder of season.
xTraded to St. Louis Cardinals for Shortstop Mick Kelleher, December 22, 1975.
yTraded with Outfielder Willie Crawford and Pitcher John Curtis to San Francisco Giants for Pitchers John D'Acquisto and Mike Caldwell, and Catcher Dave Rader, October 20, 1976.
zGranted free agency, November 2, 1978; signed by Milwaukee Brewers' organization, March 6, 1979.
aGranted free agency, October 28, 1980; signed by Kintetsu Buffaloes of Japanese baseball.

JAMES MICHAEL HART
(Mike)

Born December 20, 1951, at Portage, Mich.
Height, 6.02. Weight, 180.
Throws right and bats right and lefthanded.
Attended Alma College, Alma, Mich., and Kalamazoo Valley Community
College, Kalamazoo, Mich.

Led New York-Pennsylvania League in bases on balls with 106 in 1973.
Led Pacific Coast League in bases on balls with 122 in 1979.
Tied for Eastern League lead in sacrifice flies with 8 in 1976.

Year	Club	League	Pos.	G.	AB.	R.	H.	2B.	3B.	HR.	RBI.	B.A.	PO.	A.	E.	F.A.
1972—Jamestown	.......NYP		2B-3B	52	160	32	33	2	5	4	10	.206	105	95	4	.980
1973—W. Palm Beach	.Fla. St.		OF-2-1	131	394	79	105	18	4	12	56	.266	300	108	16	.962
1974—W. Palm Beach	.Fla. St.		OF	130	430	71	103	16	3	5	42	.240	221	7	5	.979
1975—Quebec City	......East.		OF	129	446	68	124	17	2	7	44	.278	181	12	10	.951
1976—Quebec City	......East.		OF	129	420	65	108	13	1	17	70	.257	166	4	10	.944
1977—Quebec City	......East.		OF	7	25	9	10	3	1	2	7	.400	14	1	2	.882
1977—Denver	.............A.A.		OF-2B	85	186	40	44	11	5	4	23	.237	100	13	1	.991
1978—Denver†	............A.A.		OF	125	444	94	142	23	10	19	98	.320	198	4	3	.985
1979—Tucson	..........P.C.		OF	139	466	98	141	23	11	8	72	.303	265	11	●10	.965
1980—Charleston‡	......Int.		OF	55	193	28	43	4	1	2	16	.223	107	1	1	.991
1980—Omaha§	...........A.A.		OF	49	155	30	52	5	4	4	30	.335	113	3	1	.991
1980—Texas	......Amer.		OF	5	4	1	1	0	0	0	0	.250	1	0	0	1.000
Major League Totals	....			5	4	1	1	0	0	0	0	.250	1	0	0	1.000

Selected by Montreal Expos' organization in 11th round of free-agent draft, June 6, 1972.
†Traded to Texas Rangers for Shortstop Jim Mason, December 8, 1978.
‡Loaned to Kansas City Royals' organization, July 6, 1980.
§Returned, August 29, 1980.

PAUL FRANKLIN HARTZELL JR.

Name pronounced HART-zull.

Born November 2, 1953, at Bloomsburg, Pa.
Height, 6.05. Weight, 200.
Throws and bats righthanded.
Attended University of California at Irvine, Irvine, Calif., and Lehigh University, Bethlehem, Pa.;
received Bachelor of Science degree in Mechanical Engineering.

Year	Club	League	G.	IP.	W.	L.	Pct.	H.	R.	ER.	SO.	BB.	ERA.
1975—Quad Cities	.........................Midwest		24	46	2	1	.667	28	14	7	37	12	1.37
1976—California	.............................American		37	166	7	4	.636	166	64	51	43	43	2.77
1977—California	...........................American		41	189	8	12	.400	200	92	75	79	38	3.57
1978—California†	...........................American		54	157	6	10	.375	168	67	60	55	41	3.44
1979—Minnesota‡§	.......................American		28	163	6	10	.375	193	102	97	44	44	5.36
1980—Rochester	........................Int'national		16	104	10	4	.714	112	42	37	43	20	3.20
1980—Baltimore x	.........................American		6	18	0	2	.000	22	14	13	5	9	6.50
Major League Totals	....		166	693	27	38	.415	749	339	296	234	175	3.84

Selected by California Angels' organization in 10th round of free-agent draft, June 4, 1975.
†Traded with Outfielder Ken Landreaux, Pitcher Brad Havens and Third Baseman Dave Engle to Minnesota Twins for First Baseman Rod Carew, February 3, 1979.
‡On disabled list, August 2 to August 27, 1979.
§Released, April 3, 1980; signed by Baltimore Orioles' organization, April 21, 1980.
xReleased, December 15, 1980.

RONALD WILLIAM HASSEY

Born February 27, 1953, at Tucson, Ariz.
Height, 6.02. Weight, 195.
Bats left and throws righthanded.
Attended University of Arizona, Tucson, Ariz.
Son of Bill Hassey, minor league outfielder, 1949 through 1952.

Year	Club	League	Pos.	G.	AB.	R.	H.	2B.	3B.	HR.	RBI.	B.A.	PO.	A.	E.	F.A.
1976—San Jose	...........Calif.		C-3B	22	62	7	19	4	0	1	7	.306	55	2	2	.966
1976—Williamsport	.....East.		C	21	68	6	19	3	0	0	8	.279	63	10	4	.948
1977—Toledo	..............Int.		C-3-1-O	129	446	50	132	21	1	10	57	.296	484	82	21	.964
1978—Portland	...........P.C.		C-3B	72	235	42	76	12	1	12	52	.323	312	32	7	.980
1978—Cleveland	.........Amer.		C	25	74	5	15	0	0	2	9	.203	130	15	1	.993
1979—Tacoma	............P.C.		C-3B	44	157	25	53	10	0	3	27	.338	282	44	2	.994
1979—Cleveland	.........Ameri.		C-1B	75	223	20	64	14	0	4	32	.287	368	29	3	.993
1980—Cleveland	.........Amer.		C-1B	130	390	43	124	18	4	8	65	.318	564	52	4	.994
Major League Totals	....			230	687	68	203	32	4	14	106	.295	1062	96	8	.993

Selected by Cincinnati Reds' organization in 23rd round of free-agent draft, June 6, 1972.
Selected by Kansas City Royals' organization in 22nd round of free-agent draft, June 4, 1975.
Selected by Cleveland Indians' organization in 18th round of free-agent draft, June 8, 1976.

ANDREW EARL HASSLER
(Andy)

Born October 18, 1951, at Texas City, Tex.
Height, 6.05 Weight, 215.
Throws and bats lefthanded.
Hobbies—Golf, billiards and tennis.

Tied for Pacific Coast League lead in games started with 31 and in wild pitches with 14 in 1972.

Year Club	League	G.	IP.	W.	L.	Pct.	H.	R.	ER.	SO.	BB.	ERA.
1970—El Paso†	Texas	22	144	10	7	.588	138	80	62	122	87	3.88
1971—Salt Lake City‡	P. Coast	9	51	5	1	.833	50	34	26	42	39	4.59
1971—California	American	6	19	0	3	.000	25	10	8	13	15	3.79
1972—Salt Lake City	P. Coast	32	174	9	10	.474	163	106	85	150	*114	4.40
1973—Salt Lake City	P. Coast	24	163	13	8	.619	166	93	76	127	81	4.20
1973—California	American	7	32	0	4	.000	33	23	13	19	19	3.66
1974—Salt Lake City	P. Coast	12	79	5	7	.417	98	61	52	52	48	5.92
1974—California	American	23	162	7	11	.389	132	64	47	76	79	2.61
1975—California	American	30	133	3	12	.200	158	94	88	82	53	5.95
1976—Calif.§-K. C.	American	33	147	5	12	.294	139	68	59	61	56	3.61
1977—Kansas City x	American	29	156	9	6	.600	166	88	73	83	75	4.21
1978—Kan. City y-Boston	American	24	88	3	5	.375	114	49	38	49	37	3.89
1979—Boston z	American	8	15	1	2	.333	23	17	15	7	7	9.00
1979—New York a	National	29	80	4	5	.444	74	35	33	53	42	3.71
1980—Pittsburgh b	National	6	12	0	0	.000	9	6	5	4	4	3.75
1980—California	American	41	83	5	1	.833	67	25	23	75	37	2.49
National League Totals		35	92	4	5	.444	83	41	38	57	46	3.72
American League Totals		201	835	33	56	.371	857	438	364	465	378	3.92
Major League Totals		236	927	37	61	.378	940	479	402	522	424	3.90

Selected by California Angels' organization in 25th round of free-agent draft, June 5, 1969.
†On disabled list, August 10 to September 6, 1970.
‡On disabled list April 27 to May 12 and June 28 to August 31, 1971.
§Sold to Kansas City Royals, July 5, 1976.
xOn disabled list, April 27 to May 25, 1977.
yTraded to Boston Red Sox for a player to be named later, July 24, 1978.
zSold to New York Mets, June 15, 1979.
aGranted free agency, November 1, 1979; signed by Pittsburgh Pirates, November 21, 1979.
bSold to California Angels, June 10, 1980.

CHAMPIONSHIP SERIES RECORD

Year Club	League	G.	IP.	W.	L.	Pct.	H.	R.	ER.	SO.	BB.	ERA.
1976—Kansas City	American	2	7⅓	0	1	.000	8	6	5	4	6	6.14
1977—Kansas City	American	1	5⅔	0	1	.000	5	3	3	3	0	4.76
Championship Series Totals		3	13	0	2	.000	13	9	8	7	6	5.54

MICHAEL VAUGHN HATCHER JR.
(Mickey)

Born March 15, 1955, at Cleveland, O.
Height, 6.02. Weight, 195.
Throws and bats righthanded.
Attended Mesa Community College, Mesa, Ariz., and
University of Oklahoma, Norman, Okla.

Year Club	League	Pos.	G.	AB.	R.	H.	2B.	3B.	HR.	RBI.	B.A.	PO.	A.	E.	F.A.
1977—Clinton	Midw.	OF	78	288	47	89	12	4	11	53	.309	126	9	4	.971
1978—San Antonio†	Tex.	3B	83	334	60	111	12	6	8	62	.332	55	124	22	.891
1978—Albuquerque	P. C.	3B	41	155	25	51	11	5	7	39	.329	24	63	8	.916
1979—Albuquerque	P. C.	3B-OF	103	420	88	156	29	12	10	93	*.371	127	156	12	.959
1979—Los Angeles	Nat.	OF-3B	33	93	9	25	4	1	1	5	.269	47	24	5	.934
1980—Albuquerque	P.C.	OF-3B	43	181	28	65	7	2	7	40	.359	52	32	9	.903
1980—Los Angeles	Nat.	3B-OF	57	84	4	19	2	0	1	5	.226	31	23	3	.947
Major League Totals			90	177	13	44	6	1	2	10	.376	78	47	8	.940

Selected by Houston Astros' organization in 14th round of free-agent draft, June 5, 1974.
Selected by New York Mets' organization in 2nd round of free-agent draft, January 7, 1976.
Selected by Los Angeles Dodgers' organization in 5th round of free-agent draft, June 7, 1977.
†On disabled list, July 13 to July 23, 1978.

THOMAS MATTHEW HAUSMAN
(Tom)

Born March 31, 1953, at Mobridge, S. D.
Height, 6.05. Weight, 200.
Throws and bats righthanded.
Hobbies—Hunting and riding dirt bikes.

Led Pacific Coast League in games started with 30 in 1977.
Tied for Pacific Coast League lead in complete games with 11 in 1974.

Year Club	League	G.	IP.	W.	L.	Pct.	H.	R.	ER.	SO.	BB.	ERA.
1971—Newark	NYP	13	74	7	1	*.875	54	30	22	54	30	2.68
1972—Danville†	Midwest	10	55	3	1	.750	53	18	13	32	17	2.13

Year Club	League	G.	IP.	W.	L.	Pct.	H.	R.	ER.	SO.	BB.	ERA.
1973—Shreveport	Texas	25	162	12	9	.571	*193	101	80	56	49	4.44
1974—Sacramento	P. Coast	26	180	12	9	.571	215	137	120	104	68	6.00
1975—Milwaukee	American	29	112	3	6	.333	110	57	51	46	47	4.10
1976—Spokane‡	P. Coast	22	111	4	10	.286	135	81	70	40	38	5.68
1976—Milwaukee	American	3	3	0	0	.000	3	2	2	1	3	6.00
1977—Spokane§	P. Coast	30	207	13	6	.684	251	113	97	88	55	4.22
1978—Tidewater x	Int'national	10	74	5	2	.714	64	18	10	42	23	1.22
1978—New York	National	10	52	3	3	.500	58	28	27	16	9	4.67
1979—Tidewater	Int'national	12	72	6	4	.600	75	41	36	27	23	4.50
1979—New York	National	19	79	2	6	.250	65	25	24	33	19	2.73
1980—New York	National	55	122	6	5	.545	125	63	54	53	26	3.98
American League Totals		32	115	3	6	.333	113	59	53	47	50	4.15
National League Totals		84	253	11	14	.440	248	116	105	102	54	3.74
Major League Totals		116	368	14	20	.412	361	175	158	149	104	3.86

Selected by Milwaukee Brewers' organization in 9th round of free-agent draft, June 8, 1971.
†On disabled list, June 13 to August 6, 1972.
‡On suspended list, August 14 to September 7, 1976.
§Granted free agency, November 2, 1977; signed by New York Mets, November 21, 1977.
xOn disabled list, May 25 to June 17, 1978.

BRADLEY DAVID HAVENS
(Brad)

Born November 17, 1959, at Highland Park, Mich.
Height, 6.01. Weight, 180.
Throws and bats lefthanded.

Led Midwest League in complete games with 17 in 1978.
Led California League in complete games with 12 in 1980.
Tied for California League lead in games started with 28 in 1980.

Year Club	League	G.	IP.	W.	L.	Pct.	H.	R.	ER.	SO.	BB.	ERA.
1978—Quad Cities†	Midwest	26	*200	13	10	.565	171	80	59	*197	74	2.66
1979—Orlando	Southern	19	94	4	10	.286	128	85	76	63	50	7.28
1979—Wisconsin Rapids	Midwest	10	73	6	1	.857	62	35	34	80	18	4.19
1980—Visalia	California	28	195	14	9	.609	186	90	72	*179	82	3.32

Selected by California Angels' organization in 8th round of free-agent draft, June 7, 1977.
†Traded with Outfielder Ken Landreaux, Pitcher Paul Hartzell and Third Baseman Dave Engle to Minnesota Twins for First Baseman Rod Carew, February 3, 1979.

MELTON ANDREW HAWKINS
(Andy)

Born January 21, 1960, at Waco, Tex.
Height, 6.03. Weight, 200.
Throws and bats righthanded.

Year Club	League	G.	IP.	W.	L.	Pct.	H.	R.	ER.	SO.	BB.	ERA.
1978—Walla Walla	Northwest	14	102	8	3	.727	95	52	24	73	45	2.12
1979—Reno	California	27	188	8	13	.381	*232	143	*117	130	97	5.60
1980—Reno	California	26	171	13	10	.565	183	108	81	124	79	4.26

Selected by San Diego Padres' organization in 1st round (5th player selected) of free-agent draft, June 6, 1978.

VON FRANCIS HAYES

Born August 31, 1958, at Stockton, Calif.
Height, 6.05. Weight, 185.
Throws right and bats lefthanded.
Attended St. Mary's College, Moraga, Calif.

Led Midwest League third basemen in fielding average with .930 in 1980.
Named Midwest League Most Valuable Player, 1980.

Year Club	League	Pos.	G.	AB.	R.	H.	2B.	3B.	HR.	RBI.	B.A.	PO.	A.	E.	F.A.
1980—Waterloo	Midw.	3B-SS	134	492	105	*162	*33	3	15	90	*.329	94	291	30	.928

Selected by Cleveland Indians' organization in 7th round of free-agent draft, June 5, 1979.

WILLIAM ERNEST HAYES
(Bill)

Born October 24, 1957, at Cheverly, Md.
Height, 6.00. Weight, 195.
Throws and bats righthanded.
Attended Indiana State University, Terre Haute, Ind.

Year Club	League	Pos.	G.	AB.	R.	H.	2B.	3B.	HR.	RBI.	B.A.	PO.	A.	E.	F.A.
1978—Pompano Beach	Fla. St.	C	64	208	24	44	2	1	2	21	.163	273	36	8	.975
1979—Midland	Texas	C	107	377	51	113	21	2	10	55	.300	*497	*80	10	.983
1980—Wichita	A.A.	*C-OF	111	367	29	84	14	1	8	48	.229	484	43	*15	.972
1980—Chicago	Nat.	C	4	9	0	2	1	0	0	0	.222	9	2	0	1.000
Major League Totals			4	9	0	2	1	0	0	0	.222	9	2	0	1.000

Selected by Chicago Cubs' organization in 1st round (13th player selected) of free-agent draft, June 6, 1978.

DRUNGO LARUE HAZEWOOD

Born September 2, 1959, at Mobile, Ala.
Height, 6.03. Weight, 210.
Throws and bats righthanded.

Led Southern League batters in strikeouts with 137 in 1979 and with 177 in 1980.

Year	Club	League	Pos.	G.	AB.	R.	H.	2B.	3B.	HR.	RBI.	B.A.	PO.	A.	E.	F.A.
1977—Bluefield		Appal.	OF	51	141	21	26	4	3	4	21	.184	65	2	10	.870
1978—Miami		Fla. St.	OF	111	372	41	90	14	3	8	46	.242	188	9	6	.970
1979—Charlotte		South.	OF	122	398	60	92	11	2	21	64	.231	187	11	4	.980
1980—Charlotte		South.	OF	142	499	80	130	16	6	28	80	.261	260	13	11	.961
1980—Baltimore		Amer.	OF	6	5	1	0	0	0	0	0	.000	1	0	0	1.000
Major League Totals				6	5	1	0	0	0	0	0	.000	1	0	0	1.000

Selected by Baltimore Orioles' organization in 1st round (19th player selected) of free-agent draft, June 7, 1977.

KELLY MARK HEATH

Born September 4, 1957, at Plattsburg, N.Y.
Height, 5.07. Weight, 155.
Throws and bats righthanded.
Attended Louisburg College, Louisburg, N. C.

Year	Club	League	Pos.	G.	AB.	R.	H.	2B.	3B.	HR.	RBI.	B.A.	PO.	A.	E.	F.A.
1977—Daytona Beach		Fla. St.	SS	59	181	13	42	4	4	2	30	.232	108	147	19	.931
1978—Jacksonville†		South.	SS	70	231	29	62	6	0	3	24	.268	115	217	31	.915
1979—Jacksonville		South.	SS-2B	129	422	67	115	26	3	7	61	.273	167	348	31	.943
1980—Omaha		A.A.	SS	56	182	22	46	10	1	3	22	.253	75	128	11	.949
1980—Jacksonville		South.	SS	55	205	26	63	10	2	5	27	.307	75	186	12	.956

Selected by Kansas City Royals' organization in 7th round of free-agent draft, June 7, 1977.
†On disabled list, May 8 to June 30, 1978.

MICHAEL THOMAS HEATH
(Mike)

Born February 5, 1955, at Tampa, Fla.
Height, 5.11. Weight, 176.
Throws and bats righthanded.
Hobbies—All sports.

Year	Club	League	Pos.	G.	AB.	R.	H.	2B.	3B.	HR.	RBI.	B.A.	PO.	A.	E.	F.A.
1973—Johnson City		Appal.	S-2-3B	48	166	17	29	5	2	0	10	.175	83	137	24	.902
1974—Oneonta		NYP	SS	65	234	51	66	6	3	3	34	.282	114	170	27	.913
1975—Ft. Lauderdale†		Fla. St.	SS	98	376	43	87	7	3	1	23	.231	184	256	31	.934
1976—Ft. Lauderdale‡		Fla. St.	SS-3B-C	80	267	28	71	16	3	2	30	.266	144	121	16	.943
1977—West Haven		East.	C-3B	98	352	58	94	13	5	8	42	.267	492	72	16	.972
1978—West Haven		East.	C-SS	66	217	43	64	16	1	8	27	.295	335	53	10	.975
1978—New York§		Amer.	C	33	92	6	21	3	1	0	8	.228	151	11	5	.970
1979—Tucson x		P. C.	C	54	196	21	53	8	2	1	28	.270	183	24	7	.967
1979—Oakland		Amer.	OF-C-3B	74	258	19	66	8	0	3	27	.256	167	32	5	.975
1980—Oakland		Amer.	C-OF	92	305	27	74	10	2	1	33	.243	292	20	4	.987
Major League Totals				199	655	52	161	21	3	4	68	.246	610	82	14	.980

Selected by New York Yankees' organization in 2nd round of free-agent draft, June 5, 1973.
†On Syracuse disabled list, August 2 to September 16, 1975.
‡On disabled list, June 29 to July 13, 1976.
§Traded with Pitchers Sparky Lyle, Larry McCall and Dave Rajsich, Shortstop Domingo Ramos and cash to Texas Rangers for Outfielders Juan Beniquez and Greg Jemison and Pitchers Mike Griffin, Paul Mirabella and Dave Righetti, November 10, 1978.
xTraded with Third Baseman Dave Chalk and cash to Oakland A's for Pitcher John Henry Johnson, June 15, 1979.

PITCHING RECORD

Year	Club	League	G.	IP.	W.	L.	Pct.	H.	R.	ER.	SO.	BB.	ERA.
1976—Ft. Lauderdale		Florida St.	1	1	0	0	.000	1	0	0	1	0	0.00

WORLD SERIES RECORD

Year	Club	League	Pos.	G.	AB.	R.	H.	2B.	3B.	HR.	RBI.	B.A.	PO.	A.	E.	F.A.
1978—New York		Amer.	C	1	0	0	0	0	0	0	0	.000	0	0	0	.000

DAVID WALLACE HEAVERLO

Name pronounced HAV-ur-low.

(Dave)

Born August 25, 1950, at Ellensburg, Wash.
Height, 6.01. Weight, 195.
Throws and bats righthanded.
Hobbies—Hunting, golf and fishing.
Attended Central Washington State College, Ellensburg, Wash.; received
Bachelor of Arts degree in Special Education.

Led California League in saves with 17 in 1973.

Year Club	League	G.	IP.	W.	L.	Pct.	H.	R.	ER.	SO.	BB.	ERA.
1973—Fresno	California	*63	98	7	5	.583	100	39	31	100	31	2.85
1974—Amarillo	Texas	*48	85	9	5	.643	94	32	25	77	28	2.65
1975—San Francisco	National	42	64	3	1	.750	62	18	17	35	31	2.39
1976—San Francisco	National	61	75	4	4	.500	85	45	37	40	15	4.44
1977—Phoenix	P. Coast	6	11	1	0	1.000	11	7	5	10	3	4.09
1977—San Francisco†	National	56	99	5	1	.833	92	36	28	58	21	2.55
1978—Oakland	American	69	130	3	6	.333	141	56	47	71	41	3.25
1979—Oakland‡	American	62	86	4	11	.267	97	42	39	40	42	4.08
1980—Seattle	American	60	79	6	3	.667	75	37	34	42	35	3.87
National League Totals		159	238	12	6	.667	239	99	82	133	67	3.10
American League Totals		191	295	13	20	.394	313	135	121	153	118	3.69
Major League Totals		350	533	25	26	.490	552	234	203	286	185	3.43

Selected by San Diego Padres' organization in 9th round of free-agent draft, June 6, 1972.

Selected by San Francisco Giants' organization in secondary phase of free-agent draft, January 10, 1973.

†Traded with Outfielder Gary Thomasson, Catcher Gary Alexander, Pitchers Alan Wirth, John Johnson and Phillip Huffman, a player to be named later and cash estimated at $390,000 to Oakland A's for Pitcher Vida Blue, March 15, 1978; Shortstop Mario Guerrero sent to Oakland to complete deal, April 7, 1978.

‡Sold on waivers to Seattle Mariners, April 9, 1980.

RICHARD JOSEPH HEBNER
(Richie)

Born November 26, 1947, at Norwood, Mass.
Height, 6.01. Weight, 195.
Throws right and bats lefthanded.
Hobbies—Hockey and hunting.
Brother of William Hebner, International League umpire.

Tied major league record for most bases on balls, inning (2), August 27, 1974 (third inning).
Tied modern major league record for most at bats, game (7), September 16, 1975.
Received reported $40,000 bonus to sign with Pittsburgh Pirates, 1966.

Year Club	League	Pos.	G.	AB.	R.	H.	2B.	3B.	HR.	RBI.	B.A.	PO.	A.	E.	F.A.
1966—Salem†	Appal.	1B	26	92	17	33	9	3	4	20	.359	167	10	2	.989
1967—Raleigh‡	Carol.	3B	78	274	45	92	15	6	2	33	.336	69	135	17	.923
1968—Columbus‡‡	Int.	*3B-SS	104	381	50	105	20	5	6	51	.276	77	224	*23	.929
1968—Pittsburgh	Nat.	PH	2	1	0	0	0	0	0	0	.000	0	0	0	.000
1969—Pittsburgh	Nat.	3B-1B	129	459	72	138	23	4	8	47	.301	81	240	19	.944
1970—Pittsburgh§	Nat.	3B	120	420	60	122	24	8	11	46	.290	64	235	19	.940
1971—Pittsburgh x	Nat.	3B	112	388	50	105	17	8	17	67	.271	89	172	14	.949
1972—Pittsburgh	Nat.	3B	124	427	63	128	24	4	19	72	.300	76	210	9	.969
1973—Pittsburgh	Nat.	3B	144	509	73	138	28	1	25	74	.271	92	260	23	.939
1974—Pittsburgh	Nat.	3B	146	550	97	160	21	6	18	68	.291	115	304	*28	.937
1975—Pittsburgh	Nat.	3B	128	472	65	116	16	4	15	57	.246	86	244	19	.946
1976—Pittsburgh y	Nat.	3B	132	434	60	108	21	3	8	51	.249	87	236	16	.953
1977—Philadelphia z	Nat.	1B-3B-2B	118	397	67	113	17	4	18	62	.285	933	85	11	.989
1978—Philadelphia a	Nat.	1B-3B-2B	137	435	61	123	22	3	17	71	.283	994	94	8	.993
1979—New York b	Nat.	3B-1B	136	473	54	127	25	2	10	79	.268	125	248	23	.942
1980—Detroit	Amer.	1B-3B	104	341	48	99	10	7	12	82	.290	485	84	4	.993
National League Totals			1428	4965	722	1378	238	47	166	694	.278	2742	2328	189	.964
American League Totals			104	341	48	99	10	7	12	82	.290	485	84	4	.993
Major League Totals			1532	5306	770	1477	248	54	178	776	.278	3227	2412	193	.967

Selected by Pittsburgh Pirates' organization in 1st round (15th player selected) of free-agent draft, June 28, 1966.

†On temporary inactive list, August 9. On military list, August 18, 1966 through April 6, 1967.

‡On temporary inactive list, May 13 through May 15, June 10 through June 24 and July 20 through August 16.

‡‡On temporary inactive list, July 13 through July 29.

§On military list, August 8 through August 24.

xOn military list, July 25 through August 9.

yPlayed out option year and granted free agency, November 1, 1976; signed as free agent by Philadelphia Phillies, December 15, 1976.

zOn disabled list, March 27 to April 29, 1977.

aTraded with Second Baseman Jose Moreno to New York Mets for Pitcher Nino Espinosa, March 27, 1979.

bTraded to Detroit Tigers for Third Baseman Phil Mankowski and Outfielder Jerry Morales, October 31, 1979.

CHAMPIONSHIP SERIES RECORD

Established Championship Series record for most times on losing club (6).
Tied Championship Series record for most two-base hits, total Series (7).
Established National League Championship Series records for most games, total Series (25); most Series played (7); most Series, one or more hits (7).

Year Club	League	Pos.	G.	AB.	R.	H.	2B.	3B.	HR.	RBI.	B.A.	PO.	A.	E.	F.A.
1970—Pittsburgh	Nat.	3B	2	6	0	4	2	0	0	0	.667	0	4	0	1.000
1971—Pittsburgh	Nat.	PH-3B	4	17	3	5	1	0	2	4	.294	4	3	1	.875
1972—Pittsburgh	Nat.	3B	5	16	2	3	1	0	0	1	.188	5	11	0	1.000
1974—Pittsburgh	Nat.	3B	4	13	1	3	0	0	1	4	.231	5	7	0	1.000
1975—Pittsburgh	Nat.	3B	3	12	2	4	1	0	0	2	.333	0	2	0	1.000

Year	Club	League	Pos.	G.	AB.	R.	H.	2B.	3B.	HR.	RBI.	B.A.	PO.	A.	E.	F.A.
1977—Philadelphia	Nat.	1B-PH	4	14	2	5	2	0	0	0	.357	32	0	0	1.000
1978—Philadelphia	Nat.	1B-PH	3	9	0	1	0	0	0	1	.111	21	0	0	1.000
Championship Series Totals				25	87	10	25	7	0	3	12	.287	67	27	1	.989

WORLD SERIES RECORD

Year	Club	League	Pos.	G.	AB.	R.	H.	2B.	3B.	HR.	RBI.	B.A.	PO.	A.	E.	F.A.
1971—Pittsburgh	Nat.	3B	3	12	2	2	0	0	1	3	.167	1	3	1	.800

DANIEL WILLIAM HEEP
(Danny)

Born July 3, 1957, at San Antonio, Tex.
Height, 5.11. Weight, 185.
Throws and bats lefthanded.
Attended St. Mary's University, San Antonio, Tex.

Led Southern League in total bases with 274 in 1979.
Named Southern League co-Most Valuable Player, 1979.

Year	Club	League	Pos.	G.	AB.	R.	H.	2B.	3B.	HR.	RBI.	B.A.	PO.	A.	E.	F.A.
1978—Daytona Beach	Fla. St.	OF	66	212	29	72	18	2	2	24	.340	89	9	2	.980
1979—Columbus	South.	OF	138	523	103	*171	30	5	21	84	.327	211	12	6	.974
1979—Houston	Nat.	OF	14	14	0	2	0	0	0	2	.143	7	0	0	1.000
1980—Tucson	P.C.	1B-OF	96	376	63	129	28	5	17	69	*.343	810	53	8	.991
1980—Houston	Nat.	1B	33	87	6	24	8	0	0	6	.276	188	8	2	.990
Major League Totals			47	101	6	26	8	0	0	8	.257	195	8	2	.990

Selected by Houston Astros' organization in 2nd round of free-agent draft, June 6, 1978.

CHAMPIONSHIP SERIES RECORD

Year	Club	League	Pos.	G.	AB.	R.	H.	2B.	3B.	HR.	RBI.	B.A.	PO.	A.	E.	F.A.
1980—Houston	Nat.	PH	1	1	0	0	0	0	0	0	.000	0	0	0	.000

DAVID LEE HENDERSON
(Dave)

Born July 21, 1958, at Dos Palos, Calif.
Height, 6.02. Weight, 210.
Throws and bats righthanded.
Hobby—Entomology.
Nephew of Joe Henderson, former pitcher with Chicago
White Sox and Cincinnati Reds.

Year	Club	League	Pos.	G.	AB.	R.	H.	2B.	3B.	HR.	RBI.	B.A.	PO.	A.	E.	F.A.
1977—Bellingham	N'west	OF	65	251	47	79	14	2	●16	63	.315	136	5	*11	.928
1978—Stockton	Calif.	OF	117	409	48	95	16	4	7	63	.232	204	12	14	.939
1979—San Jose	Calif.	OF	136	507	103	152	23	3	27	99	.300	264	18	4	.986
1980—Spokane†	P.C.	OF	109	341	48	95	26	1	7	50	.279	258	9	7	.974

Selected by Seattle Mariners' organization in 1st round (26th player selected) of free-agent draft, June 7, 1977.

†On disabled list, June 26 to July 22, 1980.

KENNETH JOSEPH HENDERSON
(Ken)

Born June 15, 1946, at Carroll, Ia.
Height, 6.02. Weight, 185.
Throws right and bats left and righthanded.
Hobbies—Golf and billiards.
Attended West Valley College, Campbell, Calif.
Distant cousin of Kerry Dineen, outfielder with Philadelphia Phillies organization.

Hit two home runs in one game, one righthanded and one lefthanded, August 29, 1975.

Year	Club	League	Pos.	G.	AB.	R.	H.	2B.	3B.	HR.	RBI.	B.A.	PO.	A.	E.	F.A.
1964—Fresno	Calif.	OF	14	40	5	9	1	0	1	6	.225	18	3	1	.955
1964—Magic Valley	Pion.	OF	31	104	22	19	4	3	0	20	.183	65	8	1	.986
1964—Tacoma	P. C.	OF	18	39	3	7	0	0	0	0	.179	27	0	3	.900
1965—San Francisco	Nat.	OF	63	73	10	14	1	1	0	7	.192	47	2	1	.980
1966—Phoenix	P. C.	OF	133	464	66	126	15	10	13	66	.272	286	10	8	.974
1966—San Francisco	Nat.	OF	11	29	4	9	1	1	1	1	.310	11	0	1	.917
1967—San Francisco	Nat.	OF	65	179	15	34	3	0	4	14	.190	86	3	5	.947
1967—Phoenix	P. C.	OF	41	143	18	38	12	1	3	13	.266	99	1	1	.990
1968—Phoenix	P. C.	OF	106	350	53	89	21	5	11	60	.254	178	6	4	.979
1968—San Francisco	Nat.	OF	3	3	1	1	0	0	0	0	.333	2	0	0	1.000
1969—San Francisco	Nat.	OF-3B	113	374	42	84	14	4	6	44	.225	175	12	6	.969
1970—San Francisco	Nat.	OF	148	554	104	163	35	3	17	88	.294	272	15	10	.966
1971—San Francisco	Nat.	OF-1B	141	504	80	133	26	6	15	65	.264	277	3	10	.966
1972—San Francisco†	Nat.	OF	130	439	60	113	21	2	18	51	.257	247	14	7	.974
1973—Chicago‡	Amer.	OF	73	262	32	68	13	0	6	32	.260	102	1	3	.972
1974—Chicago	Amer.	OF	*162	602	76	176	35	5	20	95	.292	*462	7	6	.987

Year	Club	League	Pos.	G.	AB.	R.	H.	2B.	3B.	HR.	RBI.	B.A.	PO.	A.	E.	F.A.
1975—Chicago§	...........Amer.		OF	140	513	65	129	20	3	9	53	.251	394	7	4	.990
1976—Atlanta x	...........Nat.		OF	133	435	52	114	19	0	13	61	.262	219	3	3	.987
1977—Texas y	.............Amer.		OF	75	244	23	63	14	0	5	23	.258	113	0	2	.983
1978—N.Y. za-Cin.	......Nat.		OF	71	166	12	29	8	1	4	23	.175	93	0	0	1.000
1979—Cin. bc-Chi.	.......Nat.		OF	72	94	12	22	3	0	2	10	.234	21	0	1	.955
1980—Chicago de	........Nat.		OF	44	82	7	16	3	0	2	9	.195	31	3	2	.944
National League Totals...................				994	2932	399	732	134	18	82	373	.250	1481	55	46	.971
American League Totals.................				450	1621	196	436	82	8	40	203	.269	1071	15	15	.986
Major League Totals				1444	4553	595	1168	216	26	122	576	.257	2552	70	61	.977

Signed as free agent by San Francisco Giants' organization, June 20, 1964.

†Traded with Pitcher Steve Stone to Chicago White Sox for Pitcher Tom Bradley, November 29, 1972.

‡On supplemental disabled list, May 26 to June 28, 1973; on disabled list, August 14 through remainder of season.

§Traded with Pitchers Dick Ruthven and Danny Osborn to Atlanta Braves for Outfielder Ralph Garr and Infielder Larvell Blanks, December 12, 1975.

xTraded with Outfielder Dave May, Pitchers Carl Morton, Roger Moret and Adrian Devine, and cash estimated at $250,000 to Texas Rangers for Outfielder Jeff Burroughs, December 9, 1976.

yOn supplemental disabled list, May 12 through May 27, 1977. On supplemental disabled list, July 25, transferred to regular disabled list, July 31; reinstated September 2, 1977. Sent to New York Mets, completing December 8 trade involving Willie Montanez, Tom Grieve, Jon Matlack and John Milner, March 15, 1978.

zOn supplemental disabled list, April 21 to May 19, 1978.

aTraded to Cincinnati Reds for Pitcher Dale Murray, May 19, 1978.

bOn supplemental disabled list, April 4 to May 25, 1979.

cSold to Chicago Cubs, June 28, 1979.

dOn supplemental disabled list, April 15 to May 18, 1980.

eReleased, July 20, 1980.

CHAMPIONSHIP SERIES RECORD

Year	Club	League	Pos.	G.	AB.	R.	H.	2B.	3B.	HR.	RBI.	B.A.	PO.	A.	E.	F.A.
1971—San Francisco	...Nat.		OF	4	16	3	5	1	0	0	2	.313	4	0	0	1.000

RICKEY HENLEY HENDERSON

Born December 25, 1958, at Chicago, Ill.
Height, 5.10. Weight, 180.
Throws left and bats righthanded.

Established American League record for most stolen bases, season (100), 1980.
Major League stolen bases: 1979 (33), 1980 (100). Total—133.
Led California League in stolen bases with 95 in 1977.
Led Eastern League in stolen bases with 81 in 1978.
Led Eastern League outfielders in double plays with 4 in 1978.
Led American League in stolen bases with 100 in 1980.

Year	Club	League	Pos.	G.	AB.	R.	H.	2B.	3B.	HR.	RBI.	B.A.	PO.	A.	E.	F.A.
1976—Boise	................N'west.		OF	46	140	34	47	13	2	3	23	.336	99	3	*12	.895
1977—Modesto	............Calif.		OF	134	481	120	166	18	4	11	69	.345	278	15	*20	.936
1978—Jersey City	.......East.		OF	133	455	81	141	14	4	0	34	.310	305	●15	7	.979
1979—Ogden	..............P. C.		OF	71	259	66	80	11	8	3	26	.309	149	6	6	.963
1979—Oakland	............Amer.		OF	89	351	49	96	13	3	1	26	.274	215	5	6	.973
1980—Oakland	............Amer.		OF	158	591	111	179	22	4	9	53	.303	407	15	7	.984
Major League Totals........................				247	942	160	275	35	7	10	79	.292	622	20	13	.980

Selected by Oakland A's organization in 4th round of free-agent draft, June 8, 1976.

ALL-STAR GAME RECORD

Year	League	Pos.	AB.	R.	H.	2B.	3B.	HR.	RBI.	B.A.	PO.	A.	E.	F.A.
1980—American	....	OF	1	0	0	0	0	0	0	.000	0	0	0	.000

STEPHEN CURTIS HENDERSON

(Steve)

Born November 18, 1952, at Houston, Tex.
Height, 6.01. Weight, 185.
Throws and bats righthanded.
Hobbies—Music, movies, and sports.
Attended Prairie View A & M University, Prairie View, Tex.

Led Eastern League in total bases with 255 in 1976.

Year	Club	League	Pos.	G.	AB.	R.	H.	2B.	3B.	HR.	RBI.	B.A.	PO.	A.	E.	F.A.
1974—Billings	.............Pion.		OF	72	249	*60	72	19	5	●8	●44	.289	114	6	6	*.952
1975—Tampa	............Fla. St.		OF-SS	123	413	59	115	9	*16	0	54	.278	263	7	8	.971
1976—Three Rivers	.....East.		OF	134	506	90	*158	24	*11	17	61	.312	260	12	8	.971
1977—Indianapolis†	.......A. A.		OF	60	233	35	76	12	6	7	25	.326	107	3	3	.973
1977—New York	..........Nat.		OF	99	350	67	104	16	6	12	65	.297	189	4	4	.980
1978—New York	............Nat.		OF	157	587	83	156	30	9	10	65	.266	315	18	11	.968
1979—New York‡	........Nat.		OF	98	350	42	107	16	8	5	39	.306	201	6	2	.990
1980—New York§	........Nat.		OF	143	513	75	149	17	8	8	58	.290	299	7	6	.981
Major League Totals				497	1800	267	516	79	31	35	227	.287	1004	35	23	.978

Selected by Cincinnati Reds' organization in 5th round of free-agent draft, June 5, 1974.

†Traded with Infielder Doug Flynn, Outfielder Dan Norman and Pitcher Pat Zachry to New York Mets for Pitcher Tom Seaver, June 15, 1977.

‡On disabled list, July 31 to September 17, 1979.

§Traded with cash to Chicago Cubs for Outfielder Dave Kingman, February 28, 1981.

GEORGE ANDREW HENDRICK, JR.

Born October 18, 1949, at Los Angeles, Calif.
Height, 6.03. Weight, 195.
Throws and bats righthanded.

Hit three home runs in a game, June 19, 1973 against Detroit Tigers.
Named as outfielder on THE SPORTING NEWS National League All-Star Team, 1980.
Named as outfielder on THE SPORTING NEWS National League Silver Bat team, 1980.

Year	Club	League	Pos.	G.	AB.	R.	H.	2B.	3B.	HR.	RBI.	B.A.	PO.	A.	E.	F.A.
1968	Burlington	Midw.	OF	103	364	58	119	•25	4	5	60	*.327	134	8	8	.947
1969	Lodi	Calif.	OF	86	316	47	97	13	2	4	28	.307	121	5	4	.969
1970	Burlington	Midw.	OF	54	198	37	61	9	3	12	43	.308	80	1	5	.942
1970	Birmingham	South.	OF	54	199	30	57	12	0	6	20	.286	115	4	5	.960
1971	Iowa	A. A.	OF	63	249	57	83	9	2	21	63	.333	113	5	3	.975
1971	Oakland	Amer.	OF	42	114	8	27	4	1	0	8	.237	52	1	1	.981
1972	Iowa	A. A.	OF	8	33	0	9	0	0	0	4	.273	14	2	0	1.000
1972	Oakland†	Amer.	OF	58	121	10	22	1	1	4	15	.182	68	0	0	1.000
1973	Cleveland‡	Amer.	OF	113	440	64	118	18	0	21	61	.268	242	7	3	.988
1974	Cleveland	Amer.	OF	139	495	65	138	23	1	19	67	.279	355	9	4	.989
1975	Cleveland	Amer.	OF	145	561	82	145	21	2	24	86	.258	338	4	6	.983
1976	Cleveland§	Amer.	OF	149	551	72	146	20	3	25	81	.265	288	13	4	.987
1977	San Diego	Nat.	OF	152	541	75	168	25	2	23	81	.311	386	11	7	.983
1978	S.D. x-St.L.	Nat.	OF	138	493	64	137	31	1	20	75	.278	313	6	2	.994
1979	St. Louis	Nat.	OF	140	493	67	148	27	1	16	75	.300	254	*20	2	.993
1980	St. Louis	Nat.	OF	150	572	73	173	33	2	25	109	.302	322	10	2	.994
American League Totals				646	2282	301	596	87	8	93	318	.261	1343	34	18	.987
National League Totals				580	2099	279	626	116	6	84	340	.298	1275	47	13	.990
Major League Totals				1226	4381	580	1222	203	14	177	658	.279	2618	81	31	.989

Selected by Oakland A's organization in 1st round (first player selected) of free-agent draft, January 27, 1968.

†Traded with Catcher Dave Duncan to Cleveland Indians for Catcher Ray Fosse and Infielder Jack Heidemann, March 24, 1973.

‡On supplemental disabled list, August 14 to September 29, 1973.

§Traded to San Diego Padres for Outfielder Johnny Grubb, Catcher Fred Kendall and Shortstop Hector Torres, December 8, 1976.

xTraded to St. Louis Cardinals for Pitcher Eric Rasmussen, May 26, 1978.

CHAMPIONSHIP SERIES RECORD

Year	Club	League	Pos.	G.	AB.	R.	H.	2B.	3B.	HR.	RBI.	B.A.	PO.	A.	E.	F.A.
1972	Oakland	Amer.	PH-OF	5	7	2	1	0	0	0	0	.143	1	0	0	1.000

WORLD SERIES RECORD

Year	Club	League	Pos.	G.	AB.	R.	H.	2B.	3B.	HR.	RBI.	B.A.	PO.	A.	E.	F.A.
1972	Oakland	Amer.	OF	5	15	3	2	0	0	0	0	.133	12	0	0	1.000

ALL-STAR GAME RECORD

Year	League	Pos.	AB.	R.	H.	2B.	3B.	HR.	RBI.	B.A.	PO.	A.	E.	F.A.
1974	American		2	0	1	0	0	0	0	.500	3	0	0	1.000
1975	American	PR-OF	1	1	1	0	0	0	0	1.000	0	0	0	.000
1980	National	OF	2	0	1	0	0	0	1	.500	0	0	0	.000
All-Star Game Totals			5	1	3	0	0	0	1	.600	3	0	0	1.000

GUILLERMO HERNANDEZ (VILLANUEVA)
(Willie)

Born November 14, 1955, at Aguada, Puerto Rico.
Height, 6.02. Weight, 180.
Throws and bats lefthanded.

Led Western Carolinas League in games started with 26 and in complete games with 13 in 1977.

Year	Club	League	G.	IP.	W.	L.	Pct.	H.	R.	ER.	SO.	BB.	ERA.
1974	Spartanburg	W. Carol.	26	*190	11	11	.500	169	82	58	*179	49	2.75
1975	Reading	Eastern	13	91	8	2	.800	79	32	30	46	25	2.97
1975	Toledo	Int'national	13	80	6	4	.600	86	43	29	46	26	3.26
1976	Oklahoma City†	Am. Assoc.	25	135	8	9	.471	154	82	68	88	30	4.53
1977	Chicago	National	67	110	8	7	.533	94	42	37	78	28	3.03
1978	Chicago	National	54	60	8	2	.800	57	26	25	38	35	3.75
1979	Chicago	National	51	79	4	4	.500	85	50	44	53	39	5.01
1980	Chicago	National	53	108	1	9	.100	115	58	53	75	45	4.42
Major League Totals			225	357	21	22	.488	351	176	159	244	147	4.01

Signed as free agent by Philadelphia Phillies' organization, September 11, 1973.

†Drafted by Chicago Cubs from Philadelphia Phillies' organization, December 6, 1976.

DID YOU KNOW—

That Tim Foli was the first Pirate to lead the league's shortstops in fielding average since Rabbit Maranville in 1923? Foli had a percentage of .981.

KEITH HERNANDEZ

Born October 20, 1953, at San Francisco, Calif.
Height, 6.00. Weight, 185.
Throws and bats lefthanded.
Attended College of San Mateo, San Mateo, Calif.
Son of John Hernandez, former minor league first baseman, and brother of Gary Hernandez,
former first baseman-outfielder in St. Louis Cardinals' organization.

Tied National League record for most home runs with bases filled, month (2), September, 1977.
Led National League first basemen in double plays with 146 in 1977, with 145 in 1979 and with 146 in 1980.
Led Texas League first basemen in double plays with 101 in 1973.
Named National League Player of the Year by THE SPORTING NEWS, 1979.
Named co-National League Most Valuable Player by Baseball Writers' Association of America, 1979.
Named first baseman on THE SPORTING NEWS National League All-Star Team, 1979 and 1980.
Named first baseman on THE SPORTING NEWS National League All-Star Fielding Team, 1978 through 1980.
Named first baseman on THE SPORTING NEWS National League Silver Bat team, 1980.

Year Club League	Pos.	G.	AB.	R.	H.	2B.	3B.	HR.	RBI.	B.A.	PO.	A.	E.	F.A.
1972–St. Petersburg†..Fla. St.	1B	84	309	38	79	16	5	5	41	.256	682	52	7	.991
1972–Tulsa ................A.A.	1B	11	29	5	7	1	0	0	1	.241	54	2	0	1.000
1973–Arkansas..........Tex.	1B	105	388	62	101	20	2	3	52	.260	960	61	9	*.991
1973–Tulsa ................A.A.	1B	31	120	20	40	6	1	5	25	.333	289	15	1	.997
1974–Tulsa‡..............A.A.	1B-OF	102	353	67	124	18	6	14	63	*.351	690	50	12	.984
1974–St. Louis ....Nat.	1B	14	34	3	10	1	2	0	2	.294	70	1	2	.973
1975–Tulsa ................A.A.	●1B-OF	85	324	70	107	29	3	10	48	.330	597	53	●13	.980
1975–St. Louis ....Nat.	1B	64	188	20	47	8	2	3	20	.250	469	36	2	.996
1976–St. Louis ....Nat.	1B	129	374	54	108	21	5	7	46	.289	862	●107	10	.990
1977–St. Louis ....Nat.	1B	161	560	90	163	41	4	15	91	.291	1453	106	12	.992
1978–St. Louis ....Nat.	1B	159	542	90	138	32	4	11	64	.255	1436	96	10	.994
1979–St. Louis ....Nat.	1B	161	610	*116	210	*48	11	11	105	*.344	*1489	*146	8	.995
1980–St. Louis ....Nat.	1B	159	595	*111	191	39	8	16	99	.321	1572	115	9	.995
Major League Totals		847	2903	484	867	190	36	63	427	.299	7351	607	53	.993

Selected by St. Louis Cardinals' organization in 42nd round of free-agent draft, June 8, 1971.
†On disabled list from beginning of season until May 30, 1972.
‡On disabled list, April 16 to May 20, 1974.

ALL-STAR GAME RECORD

Year League	Pos.	AB.	R.	H.	2B.	3B.	HR.	RBI.	B.A.	PO.	A.	E.	F.A.
1979–National..............................	PH	1	0	0	0	0	0	0	.000	0	0	0	.000
1980–National..............................	PH-1B	2	0	2	0	0	0	0	1.000	5	0	0	1.000
All-Star Game Totals		3	0	2	0	0	0	0	.667	5	0	0	1.000

PEDRO JULIO HERNANDEZ

Born April 4, 1959, at La Romana, Dominican Republic
Height, 6.01. Weight, 160.
Throws and bats righthanded.

Led Carolina League shortstops in errors with 46 in 1979.

Year Club League	Pos.	G.	AB.	R.	H.	2B.	3B.	HR.	RBI.	B.A.	PO.	A.	E.	F.A.
1976–Covington..........Appal.					(Did not play)									
1977–Sara. Astros......G. C.	SS-3B	35	115	16	25	3	0	0	16	.217	38	94	20	.868
1978–Daytona Beach..Fla. St.	SS-3B-2B	61	217	18	58	3	1	0	13	.267	71	168	29	.892
1978–Sara. Astros†....G. C.	SS	29	101	16	29	5	2	0	9	.287	29	85	8	.934
1979–Kinston.............Carol.	SS-3B	122	430	50	98	13	6	1	35	.228	149	289	48	.901
1979–Toronto ....Amer.	PR	3	0	1	0	0	0	0	0	.000	0	0	0	.000
1980–Knoxville ....South.	S-3-O	112	424	51	120	14	4	4	43	.283	121	233	43	.892
Major League Totals.......................		3	0	1	0	0	0	0	.000	0	0	0	.000

Signed as free agent by Houston Astros' organization, May 29, 1976.
†Traded with Pitcher Mark Lemongello and Outfielder Joe Cannon to Toronto Blue Jays for Catcher Alan Ashby, November 27, 1978.

LARRY DARNELL HERNDON

Born November 3, 1953, at Sunflower, Miss.
Height, 6.03. Weight, 195.
Throws and bats righthanded.
Hobby–Playing pool.
Attended Tennessee State University, Nashville, Tenn. and Skyline College, San Bruno, Calif.

Led Texas League in stolen bases with 50 in 1974.
Tied for Texas League lead in double plays by outfielders with 4 in 1974.
Tied for National League lead in errors by outfielders with 11 in 1980.
Named National League Rookie Player of the Year by THE SPORTING NEWS, 1976.

Year Club League	Pos.	G.	AB.	R.	H.	2B.	3B.	HR.	RBI.	B.A.	PO.	A.	E.	F.A.
1971–Sarasota Cards ..Gulf C.	OF	40	138	13	33	2	0	0	8	.239	68	4	3	.960
1972–St. Petersburg ..Fla. St.	OF	7	28	2	4	0	0	0	0	.143	12	1	2	.867
1972–Sarasota R. B. ...Gulf C.	OF	31	113	16	29	5	3	0	9	.257	50	5	3	.948
1972–Cedar Rapids† ...Midw.	OF	7	21	1	6	0	0	0	1	.286	10	0	0	1.000
1973–St. Petersburg ...Fla. St.	OF	141	485	83	139	9	5	3	41	.287	233	10	8	.968

Year	Club	League	Pos.	G.	AB.	R.	H.	2B.	3B.	HR.	RBI.	B.A.	PO.	A.	E.	F.A.
1974—Arkansas		Tex.	OF	132	498	74	142	16	●10	2	41	.285	325	∗24	16	.956
1974—St. Louis		Nat.	PR-OF	12	1	3	1	0	0	0	0	1.000	1	0	0	1.000
1975—Tulsa‡		A.A.	OF	22	96	13	23	5	0	1	5	.240	35	2	3	.925
1975—Phoenix		P.C.	OF	115	427	49	115	6	4	2	44	.269	287	10	10	.967
1976—Phoenix		P.C.	OF	14	57	8	14	2	1	1	5	.246	38	3	0	1.000
1976—San Francisco		Nat.	OF	115	337	42	97	11	3	2	23	.288	226	8	8	.967
1977—San Francisco§		Nat.	OF	49	109	13	26	4	3	1	5	.239	87	2	4	.957
1978—San Francisco		Nat.	OF	151	471	52	122	15	9	1	32	.259	369	3	10	.974
1979—San Francisco		Nat.	OF	132	354	35	91	14	5	7	36	.257	196	10	8	.963
1980—San Francisco		Nat.	OF	139	493	54	127	17	11	8	49	.258	247	8	11	.959
Major League Totals				598	1765	199	464	61	31	19	145	.263	1126	31	41	.966

Selected by St. Louis Cardinals' organization in 3rd round of free-agent draft, June 8, 1971.

†On disabled list August 11 through remainder of 1972 season.

‡Traded with Pitcher Tony Gonzalez to San Francisco Giants for for Pitcher Ron Bryant, May 9, 1975.

§On disabled list, June 19 to August 26, 1977; on disqualified list, August 26 through remainder of season.

THOMAS MITCHELL HERR
(Tom)

Born April 4, 1956, at Lancaster, Pa.
Height, 6.00. Weight, 175.
Throws right and bats left and righthanded.
Hobbies—Sports and reading.
Attends University of Delaware, Newark, Del.

Led Florida State League in stolen bases with 50 and in double plays by second basemen with 91 in 1977.

Year	Club	League	Pos.	G.	AB.	R.	H.	2B.	3B.	HR.	RBI.	B.A.	PO.	A.	E.	F.A.
1975—Johnson City		Appal.	2B-SS	42	133	29	41	8	1	0	15	.308	74	125	5	.975
1976—St. Petersburg		Fla. St.	SS-2B	82	275	47	74	6	1	0	21	.269	133	211	18	.950
1977—St. Petersburg		Fla. St.	2B	136	∗515	∗80	∗156	13	7	1	53	.303	∗348	∗430	21	∗.974
1978—Arkansas		Texas	2B	89	335	70	98	23	4	3	45	.293	207	280	13	.974
1978—Springfield		A. A.	2B	33	86	16	24	6	1	0	8	.279	45	63	7	.939
1979—Springfield		A. A.	2B	109	423	74	124	20	6	6	48	.293	225	324	10	∗.982
1979—St. Louis		Nat.	2B	14	10	4	2	0	0	0	1	.200	12	11	0	1.000
1980—Springfield		A. A.	2B-3B	37	141	29	44	6	2	1	16	.312	29	52	1	.988
1980—St. Louis		Nat.	2B-SS	76	222	29	55	2	5	0	15	.248	124	184	7	.978
Major League Totals				90	232	33	57	12	5	0	16	.246	136	195	7	.979

Signed as free agent by St. Louis Cardinals' organization, August 22, 1974.

JOHN CHARLES HESSLER

Born June 3, 1957, at Kansas City, Mo.
Height, 6.03. Weight, 200
Throws and bats righthanded.
Attended Crowder College, Neosho, Mo., and University of Tulsa, Tulsa, Okla.

Pitched eight-inning 2-1 no-hit victory against Sarasota Royals, July 28, 1978.
Led Florida State League in wild pitches with 28 in 1979.
Led Southern League in wild pitches with 17 in 1980.
Tied for Gulf Coast League lead in games started with 10 in 1978.

Year	Club	League	G.	IP.	W.	L.	Pct.	H.	R.	ER.	SO.	BB.	ERA.
1978—Sarasota Astros		G. Coast	10	53	2	4	.333	39	33	18	31	43	3.06
1978—Daytona Beach		Florida St.	3	10	0	3	.000	12	9	7	13	15	6.30
1979—Daytona Beach		Florida St.	25	130	8	11	.421	104	∗98	70	139	∗132	4.85
1980—Columbus		Southern	27	153	9	7	.563	127	87	75	121	∗135	4.41

Selected by New York Mets' organization in 5th round of free-agent draft, January 11, 1977.
Selected by Houston Astros' organization in 3rd round of free-agent draft, June 6, 1978.

KEVIN JOHN HICKEY

Born February 25, 1957, at Chicago, Ill.
Height, 6.01. Weight, 170.
Throws and bats lefthanded.

Year	Club	League	G.	IP.	W.	L.	Pct.	H.	R.	ER.	SO.	BB.	ERA.
1978—Paintsville		Appal.	9	36	2	4	.333	37	19	16	24	23	4.00
1979—Appleton		Midwest	29	121	5	10	.333	122	64	48	100	71	3.57
1980—Glens Falls		Eastern	26	169	9	7	.563	184	92	81	80	73	4.31

Signed as free agent by Chicago White Sox' organization, August 18, 1977.

MARC KEVIN HILL

Born February 18, 1952, at Louisiana, Mo.
Height, 6.03. Weight, 210.
Throws and bats righthanded.
Hobbies—Hunting and fishing.
Son of Edward Hill, former minor league outfielder.

Led American Association catchers in double plays with 18 in 1974.

Led Gulf Coast League catchers in double plays with 5 in 1970.
Led Florida State League catchers in total chances with 983, total chances accepted with 968 and in double plays with 14 in 1972.
Named American Association Rookie of the Year, 1974.

Year Club	League	Pos.	G.	AB.	R.	H.	2B.	3B.	HR.	RBI.	B.A.	PO.	A.	E.	F.A.
1970—Sarasota Cards..Gulf C		C	28	78	6	15	3	0	0	6	.192	176	24	2	.990
1971—Cedar Rapids.....Midw.		C	87	272	21	63	9	1	1	27	.232	572	57	8	.987
1972—St. Petersburg...Fla. St.		C	124	421	34	104	12	1	8	65	.247	*876	*92	15	.985
1972—Modesto ....Calif.		C-1B	7	24	2	8	2	0	0	4	.333	39	3	0	1.000
1973—Arkansas..........Texas		C	122	403	41	97	19	2	9	49	.241	*670	64	8	.989
1973—Tulsa .................A.A.		C	9	29	4	12	1	0	3	8	.414	61	5	0	1.000
1973—St. Louis ....Nat.		C	1	3	0	0	0	0	0	0	.000	5	0	0	1.000
1974—Tulsa ...............A.A.		C-1B	96	327	46	91	16	1	14	58	.278	553	61	9	.986
1974—St. Louis† ....Nat.		C	10	21	2	5	1	0	0	2	.238	41	5	0	1.000
1975—San Francisco ...Nat.		C-3B	72	182	14	39	4	0	5	23	.214	282	27	2	.994
1976—San Francisco‡..Nat.		C-1B	54	131	11	24	5	0	3	15	.183	186	24	1	.995
1977—San Francisco ...Nat.		C	108	320	28	80	10	0	9	50	.250	505	57	6	.989
1978—San Francisco ...Nat.		C-1B	117	358	20	87	15	1	3	36	.243	592	56	9	.986
1979—San Francisco§ .Nat.		C-1B	63	169	20	35	3	0	3	15	.207	285	31	3	.991
1980—San Francisco x Nat.		C	17	41	1	7	2	0	0	0	.171	61	8	2	.972
1980—Seattle y ....Amer.		C	29	70	8	16	2	1	2	9	.229	101	10	1	.991
National League Totals			442	1225	96	277	40	1	23	141	.226	1957	208	23	.989
American League Totals			29	70	8	16	2	1	2	9	.229	101	10	1	.991
Major League Totals........................			471	1295	104	293	42	2	25	150	.226	2058	218	24	.990

Selected by St. Louis Cardinals' organization in 10th round of free-agent draft, June 4, 1970.
†Traded to San Francisco Giants for Pitcher Elias Sosa and Catcher Ken Rudolph, October 14, 1974.
‡On disabled list, August 4 to October 5, 1976.
§On disabled list, July 25 to October 3, 1979.
xSold on waivers to Seattle Mariners, June 20, 1980.
yGranted free agency, October 28, 1980; signed by Chicago White Sox, February 12, 1981.

JOHN FREDERICK HILLER

Born April 8, 1943, at Toronto, Ontario, Canada.
Height, 6.01. Weight, 190.
Throws left and bats righthanded.
Hobby—Most sports.

Established major league record for most saves, season (38), 1973.
Tied modern major league record for most consecutive strikeouts, start of game (6), August 6, 1968.
Established American League record for most intentional bases on balls, season (19), 1974.
Tied American League records for most games won by relief pitcher, season (17), 1974; most games lost, relief pitcher, season (14), 1974.
Major League saves: 1965 (0), 1966 (0), 1967 (1), 1968 (5), 1969 (4), 1970 (3), 1972 (3), 1973 (38), 1974 (13), 1975 (14), 1976 (13), 1977 (7), 1978 (15), 1979 (9), 1980 (0). Total—125.
Named American League Comeback Player of the Year by THE SPORTING NEWS, 1973.
Named American League Fireman of the Year by THE SPORTING NEWS, 1973.

Year Club	League	G.	IP.	W.	L.	Pct.	H.	R.	ER.	SO.	BB.	ERA.
1963—Jamestown ....NYP		29	181	14	9	.609	178	89	81	172	78	4.03
1964—Duluth-Superior ....Northern		30	167	10	*13	.435	167	74	64	137	66	3.45
1964—Knoxville ....Southern		3	15	0	3	.000	19	13	6	15	4	3.60
1965—Montgomery ....Southern		47	103	5	7	.417	91	33	29	84	32	2.53
1965—Detroit................................American		5	6	0	0	.000	5	0	0	4	1	0.00
1966—Detroit................................American		1	2	0	0	.000	2	2	2	1	2	9.00
1966—Syracuse...........................Int'national		54	87	3	7	.300	71	46	43	69	33	4.45
1967—Toledo ....Int'national		13	45	5	1	.833	34	16	15	39	21	3.00
1967—Detroit................................American		23	65	4	3	.571	57	20	19	49	9	2.63
1968—Detroit................................American		39	128	9	6	.600	92	37	34	78	51	2.39
1969—Detroit................................American		40	99	4	4	.500	97	50	44	74	44	4.00
1970—Detroit................................American		47	104	6	6	.500	82	39	35	89	46	3.03
1971†						(Did not play)						
1972—Detroit‡ ....American		24	44	1	2	.333	39	13	10	26	13	2.05
1973—Detroit ....American		*65	125	10	5	.667	89	21	20	124	39	1.44
1974—Detroit ....American		59	150	17	14	.548	127	51	44	134	62	2.64
1975—Detroit§ ....American		36	71	2	3	.400	52	20	17	87	36	2.15
1976—Detroit ....American		56	121	12	8	.600	93	37	32	117	67	2.38
1977—Detroit ....American		45	124	8	14	.364	120	59	49	115	61	3.56
1978—Detroit x ....American		51	92	9	4	.692	64	27	24	74	35	2.35
1979—Detroit y ....American		43	79	4	7	.364	83	47	46	46	55	5.24
1980—Detroit z ....American		11	31	1	0	1.000	38	15	15	18	14	4.35
Major League Totals		545	1241	87	76	.534	1040	438	391	1036	535	2.84

Signed as free agent by Detroit Tigers' organization, June 16, 1962.
†Placed on voluntarily retired list, March 19. Released by Detroit Tigers, August 31, 1971. Signed by Detroit Tigers, September 9, and placed on voluntary retired list, September 30, 1971.
‡Signed by Detroit Tigers as batting practice pitcher, June 3, 1972. Reinstated as active player, July 8, 1972.
§On disabled list, July 26 to September 1, 1975.
xOn disabled list, July 13 to August 3, 1978.
yOn disabled list, August 27 to October 10, 1979.
zOn voluntarily retired list, May 30, 1980.

Year Club	League	G.	IP.	W.	L.	Pct.	H.	R.	ER.	SO.	BB.	ERA.
1972—Detroit..................................	American	3	3⅓	1	0	1.000	1	0	0	1	1	0.00

WORLD SERIES RECORD

Year Club	League	G.	IP.	W.	L.	Pct.	H.	R.	ER.	SO.	BB.	ERA.
1968—Detroit..................................	American	2	2	0	0	.000	6	4	3	1	3	13.50

ALL-STAR GAME RECORD

Member of American League All-Star Team in 1974 game; did not play.

LARRY EUGENE HISLE

Name pronounced HY-sul.

Born May 5, 1947, at Portsmouth, O.
Height, 6.02. Weight, 195.
Throws and bats righthanded.
Attended Ohio State University, Columbus, O.

Major league stolen bases: 1968 (0), 1969 (18), 1970 (5), 1971 (1), 1972 (0), 1973 (11), 1974 (12), 1975 (17), 1976 (31), 1977 (21), 1978 (10), 1979 (1), 1980 (1). Total—128.
Tied major league record for most times struck out rookie season, 152, 1969.
Led Carolina League in total bases with 251 in 1967.
Named outfielder on THE SPORTING NEWS American League All-Star Team, 1977 and 1978.

Year Club	League	Pos.	G.	AB.	R.	H.	2B.	3B.	HR.	RBI.	B.A.	PO.	A.	E.	F.A.
1966—Huron† ....North.	OF	21	60	12	26	5	0	3	13	.433	19	1	2	.909
1967—Portsmouth ....Carol.	OF	136	503	82	152	24	3	23	78	.302	274	13	11	.963
1968—San Diego .........P.C.	OF	69	267	37	81	10	5	6	26	.303	169	3	1	.994
1968—Philadelphia ......Nat.	OF	7	11	1	4	1	0	0	1	.364	8	0	0	1.000
1969—Philadelphia ......Nat.	OF	145	482	75	128	23	5	20	56	.266	324	11	8	.977
1970—Philadelphia ......Nat.	OF	126	405	52	83	22	4	10	44	.205	262	5	6	.978
1971—Eugene ....P. C.	OF	62	186	33	61	17	3	9	30	.328	97	4	1	.990
1971—Philadelphia§ ....Nat.	OF	36	76	7	15	3	0	0	3	.197	48	2	2	.962
1972—Albuquerque xy .P. C.	OF	131	456	87	148	21	9	23	91	.325	197	9	8	.963
1973—Minnesota ....Amer.	OF	143	545	88	148	25	6	15	64	.272	337	11	9	.975
1974—Minnesota ....Amer.	OF	143	510	68	146	20	7	19	79	.286	279	4	6	.979
1975—Minnesota z ....Amer.	OF	80	255	37	80	9	2	11	51	.314	118	2	3	.976
1976—Minnesota ....Amer.	OF	155	581	81	158	19	5	14	96	.272	361	16	6	.984
1977—Minnesota a .....Amer.	OF	141	546	95	165	36	3	28	•119	.302	287	11	8	.974
1978—Milwaukee ....Amer.	OF	142	520	96	151	24	0	34	115	.290	172	6	4	.978
1979—Milwaukee b .....Amer.	OF	26	96	18	27	7	0	3	14	.281	17	2	0	1.000
1980—Milwaukee c .....Amer.	DH	17	60	16	17	0	0	6	16	.283	0	0	0	.000
National League Totals..................		314	974	135	230	49	9	30	104	.236	642	18	16	.976
American League Totals.................		847	3113	499	892	140	23	130	554	.287	1571	52	36	.978
Major League Totals		1161	4087	634	1122	189	32	160	658	.275	2213	70	52	.978

Selected by Philadelphia Phillies' organization in free-agent draft, August 16, 1965.
†On restricted list, February 25 to June 11. On disabled list, August 12 to September 5.
‡On disabled list from July 2 to August 26 with hepatitis.
§Traded to Los Angeles Dodgers for First Baseman Tommy Hutton, October 22, 1971.
xReleased by Los Angeles Dodgers to St. Louis Cardinals (in trade which sent Pitcher Rudy Arroyo from St. Louis to Los Angeles and Pitcher Greg Millikan from Arkansas to Albuquerque), October 26, 1972.
yTraded by St. Louis Cardinals with Pitcher John Cumberland (latter assigned from Arkansas to Tacoma) to Minnesota Twins for Pitcher Wayne Granger, November 29, 1972.
zOn disabled list, June 27 to July 12 and July 25 to September 2, 1975.
aGranted free agency, November 2, 1977; signed by Milwaukee Brewers, November 17, 1977.
bOn supplemental disabled list, May 13 to September 1, 1979.
cOn supplemental disabled list, June 3, 1980; transferred to disabled list, June 24, 1980; transferred to emergency disabled list, July 21 to October 1, 1980.

ALL-STAR GAME RECORD

Year League	Pos.	AB.	R.	H.	2B.	3B.	HR.	RBI.	B.A.	PO.	A.	E.	F.A.
1977—American............................	PH	1	0	0	0	0	0	0	.000	0	0	0	.000
1978—American	PH	1	0	1	0	0	0	0	1.000	0	0	0	.000
All-Star Game Totals		2	0	1	0	0	0	0	.500	0	0	0	.000

RODNEY STEVON HOBBS
(Rod)

Born May 13, 1959, at Seattle, Wash.
Height, 6.03. Weight, 190.
Throws and bats righthanded.

Year Club	League	Pos.	G.	AB.	R.	H.	2B.	3B.	HR.	RBI.	B.A.	PO.	A.	E.	F.A.
1977—Bellingham ....N'west	OF	63	264	46	73	12	1	7	30	.277	98	2	6	.943
1978—Stockton† ....Calif.	OF	112	393	51	109	12	6	7	48	.277	198	13	6	.972
1979—Alexandria ....Carol.	OF	126	417	61	107	15	2	8	61	.257	207	9	16	.931
1980—Lynn................East.	OF	125	412	57	89	16	5	9	40	.216	265	•18	16	.946

Selected by Seattle Mariners' organization in 8th round of free-agent draft, June 7, 1977.
†On disabled list, June 13 to July 7, 1978.

CLELL LAVERN HOBSON, JR.
(Butch)

Born August 17, 1951, at Tuscaloosa, Ala.
Height, 6.01. Weight, 190.
Throws and bats righthanded.
Attended University of Alabama, University, Ala.
Son of Clell Hobson, infielder in Cleveland Indians' organization, 1953 through 1957.

Led Eastern League in total bases with 201 in 1975.
Led American League in strikeouts with 162 in 1977.

Year	Club	League	Pos.	G.	AB.	R.	H.	2B.	3B.	HR.	RBI.	B.A.	PO.	A.	E.	F.A.
1973—Winston-Salem	..Carol.		3B-OF	17	39	8	7	2	1	0	5	.179	10	10	1	.952
1974—Winston-Salem	..Carol.		O-3-1	119	423	66	120	18	8	14	74	.284	211	79	12	.960
1975—Bristol	..............East.		3B	•138	471	68	125	25	3	15	73	.265	102	309	28	.936
1975—Boston	..............Amer.		3B	2	4	0	1	0	0	0	0	.250	1	3	0	1.000
1976—Rhode Island	.....Int.		3B-SS	90	360	56	103	21	1	25	72	.286	91	204	15	.952
1976—Boston	..............Amer.		3B	76	269	34	63	7	5	8	34	.234	60	146	14	.936
1977—Boston	..............Amer.		3B	159	593	77	157	33	5	30	112	.265	128	272	23	.946
1978—Boston	..............Amer.		3B	147	512	65	128	26	2	17	80	.250	122	261	*43	.899
1979—Boston	..............Amer.		3B-2B	146	528	74	138	26	7	28	93	.261	110	251	25	.935
1980—Boston†‡	..............Amer.		3B	93	324	35	74	6	0	11	39	.228	52	109	16	.910
Major League Totals	....			623	2230	285	561	98	19	94	358	.252	473	1042	121	.926

Selected by Boston Red Sox' organization in 8th round of free-agent draft, June 5, 1973.
†On supplemental disabled list, July 27 to August 11 and August 23 to September 7, 1980.
‡Traded with Shortstop Rick Burleson to California Angels for Third Baseman Carney Lansford, Pitcher Mark Clear and Outfielder Rick Miller, December 10, 1980.

RONALD WRAY HODGES
(Ron)

Born June 22, 1949, at Rocky Mount, Va.
Height, 6.01. Weight, 185.
Throws right and bats lefthanded.
Hobby—Hunting.
Attended Appalachian State University, Boone, N. C.

Tied major league record for most double plays by catcher, extra-inning game (3), April 23, 1978.

Year	Club	League	Pos.	G.	AB.	R.	H.	2B.	3B.	HR.	RBI.	B.A.	PO.	A.	E.	F.A.
1972—Pompano Beach	.Fla. St.		•C-3-O	112	359	59	92	15	4	15	48	.256	684	71	•18	.977
1973—Memphis	...........Texas		C	47	139	12	24	4	0	1	11	.173	275	3	6	.980
1973—New York	..........Nat.		C	45	127	5	33	2	0	1	18	.260	241	13	2	.992
1974—New York	..........Nat.		C	59	136	16	30	4	0	4	14	.221	227	14	12	.953
1975—Tidewater	.........Int.		C-O-1	95	278	27	74	8	0	2	33	.266	431	45	7	.986
1975—New York	..........Nat.		C	9	34	3	7	1	0	2	4	.206	69	1	0	1.000
1976—New York†	........Nat.		C	56	155	21	35	6	0	4	24	.226	262	18	7	.976
1977—New York	..........Nat.		C	66	117	6	31	4	0	1	5	.265	112	19	1	.992
1978—New York	.........Nat.		C	47	102	4	26	4	1	0	7	.255	145	20	3	.982
1979—New York	..........Nat.		C	59	86	4	14	4	0	0	5	.163	82	16	2	.980
1980—New York‡	..........Nat.		C	36	42	4	10	2	0	0	5	.238	47	9	1	.982
Major League Totals	....			377	799	63	186	27	1	12	82	.233	1185	110	28	.979

Selected by Baltimore Orioles' organization in 6th round of free-agent draft, June 4, 1970.
Selected by Kansas City Royals' organization in secondary phase of free-agent draft, January 13, 1971.
Selected by Atlanta Braves' organization in secondary phase of free-agent draft, June 8, 1971.
Selected by New York Mets' organization in secondary phase of free-agent draft, January 12, 1972.
†On disabled list, June 13 to June 28, 1976.
‡On disabled list, July 5 to October 14, 1980.

WORLD SERIES RECORD

Year	Club	League	Pos.	G.	AB.	R.	H.	2B.	3B.	HR.	RBI.	B.A.	PO.	A.	E.	F.A.
1973—New York	..........Nat.		PH	1	0	0	0	0	0	0	0	.000	0	0	0	.000

PAUL JOSEPH DENIS HODGSON

Born April 14, 1960, at Montreal, Canada.
Height, 6.02. Weight, 190.
Throws and bats righthanded.

Year	Club	League	Pos.	G.	AB.	R.	H.	2B.	3B.	HR.	RBI.	B.A.	PO.	A.	E.	F.A.
1977—Utica	................NYP		3B	7	19	4	9	2	0	0	3	.474	0	2	1	.667
1978—Medicine Hat†	...Pion.		3B	11	43	8	12	0	2	0	4	.279	14	18	3	.914
1979—Dunedin	...........Fla. St.		OF	127	446	45	112	13	4	6	57	.251	215	14	9	.962
1980—Knoxville	.........South.		OF	59	187	22	44	8	6	5	26	.235	75	4	1	.988
1980—Kinston	............Carol.		OF	60	219	39	77	17	0	7	39	.352	86	4	2	.978
1980—Toronto	............Amer.		OF	20	41	5	9	0	1	1	5	.220	19	1	0	1.000
Major League Totals	....			20	41	5	9	0	1	1	5	.220	19	1	0	1.000

Signed as free agent by Toronto Blue Jays' organization, April 14, 1977.
†On temporary inactive list, July 12 to September 5, 1978.

GLENN EDWARD HOFFMAN

Born July 7, 1958, at Orange, Calif.
Height, 6.02. Weight, 170.
Throws and bats righthanded.

Led International League shortstops in double plays with 87 in 1978.
Tied for Florida State League lead among shortstops in putouts with 220 in 1977.

Year	Club	League	Pos.	G.	AB.	R.	H.	2B.	3B.	HR.	RBI.	B.A.	PO.	A.	E.	F.A.
1976—Elmira	NYP		SS	60	191	29	52	7	2	3	34	.272	*83	139	17	.925
1977—Winter Haven	Fla.St.		SS-3B-1B	126	425	51	123	17	2	3	61	.289	225	377	36	.944
1977—Pawtucket	Int.		SS	4	9	2	4	1	0	0	2	.444	4	10	1	.933
1978—Pawtucket	Int.		SS-P	131	411	27	116	17	1	2	48	.282	*211	*391	45	.930
1979—Pawtucket	Int.		3B-SS	139	520	70	148	13	3	11	54	.285	172	286	19	.960
1980—Boston	Amer.		3-S-2	114	312	37	89	15	4	4	42	.285	78	202	17	.943
Major League Totals				114	312	37	89	15	4	4	42	.285	78	202	17	.943

Selected by Boston Red Sox' organization in 2nd round of free-agent draft, June 8, 1976.

RECORD AS PITCHER

Year	Club	League	G.	IP.	W.	L.	Pct.	H.	R.	ER.	SO.	BB.	ERA.
1978—Pawtucket	Int'national		1	⅓	0	0	.000	0	0	0	0	0	0.00
1979—Pawtucket	Int'national		1	1	0	0	.000	1	1	1	0	1	9.00

GUY ALAN HOFFMAN

Born July 9, 1956, at Ottawa, Ill.
Height, 5.09. Weight, 175.
Throws and bats lefthanded.
Attended Bradley University, Peoria, Ill.

Year	Club	League	G.	IP.	W.	L.	Pct.	H.	R.	ER.	SO.	BB.	ERA.
1978—Appleton	Midwest		7	34	2	0	1.000	22	10	9	31	15	2.38
1979—Appleton	Midwest		2	5	0	0	.000	2	0	0	4	1	0.00
1979—Iowa	Am. Assoc.		13	70	6	0	1.000	62	30	26	34	40	3.34
1979—Chicago	American		24	30	0	5	.000	30	18	18	23	5.40
1980—Iowa	Am. Assoc.		15	75	6	3	.667	59	31	30	56	34	3.60
1980—Chicago	American		23	38	1	0	1.000	38	12	11	24	17	2.61
Major League Totals			47	68	1	5	.167	68	30	29	42	40	3.84

Signed as free agent by Chicago White Sox' organization, July 17, 1978.

FREDRICK WILLIAM HOLDSWORTH
(Fred)

Born May 29, 1952, at Detroit, Mich.
Height, 6.01. Weight, 190.
Throws and bats righthanded.
Attended University of Michigan, Ann Arbor, Mich.

Led International League pitchers in games started with 30 in 1973.

Year	Club	League	G.	IP.	W.	L.	Pct.	H.	R.	ER.	SO.	BB.	ERA.
1970—Bristol	Ap'lachian		8	62	5	1	.833	56	14	9	64	15	*1.31
1970—Lakeland	Florida St.		3	7	0	1	.000	7	5	2	5	3	2.57
1971—Lakeland	Florida St.		9	62	3	5	.375	56	22	13	50	14	1.89
1971—Rocky Mount	Carolina		18	119	8	4	.667	101	47	37	79	32	2.80
1971—Montgomery	Southern		3	23	2	1	.667	16	10	7	16	3	2.74
1972—Toledo†	Int'national		21	107	7	5	.583	119	55	46	83	38	3.87
1972—Detroit	American		2	7	0	1	.000	13	10	10	5	2	12.86
1973—Toledo	Int'national		30	*214	14	10	.583	*194	92	81	121	79	3.41
1973—Detroit	American		5	15	0	1	.000	13	11	11	9	6	6.60
1974—Evansville	Am. Assoc.		21	153	9	6	.600	150	72	55	114	38	3.24
1974—Detroit	American		8	36	0	3	.000	40	20	17	16	14	4.25
1975—Evansville‡	Am. Assoc.		7	46	2	4	.333	47	25	22	39	10	4.30
1975—Rochester	Int'national		19	111	4	9	.308	99	49	40	99	43	3.24
1976—Rochester	Int'national		14	98	5	4	.556	102	43	38	54	41	3.49
1976—Baltimore	American		16	40	4	1	.800	24	9	9	24	13	2.03
1977—Baltimore§x	American		12	14	0	1	.000	17	11	10	4	16	6.43
1977—Montreal	National		14	42	3	3	.500	35	17	15	21	18	3.21
1978—Denver	Am. Assoc.		9	41	2	3	.400	55	33	28	15	21	6.15
1978—Montreal yz	National		6	9	0	0	.000	16	10	7	3	8	7.00
1979—Montgomery	Southern		8	60	3	4	.429	55	24	21	46	31	3.15
1979—Evansville	Am. Assoc.		23	104	10	6	.625	113	59	48	62	58	4.15
1980—Vancouver b	P. Coast		20	118	5	5	.500	99	42	35	65	47	2.67
1980—Milwaukee c	American		9	20	0	0	.000	24	12	10	12	9	4.50
American League Totals			52	132	4	7	.364	121	73	67	70	60	4.57
National League Totals			20	51	3	3	.500	51	27	22	24	26	3.88
Major League Totals			72	183	7	10	.412	172	100	89	94	86	4.38

Selected by Detroit Tigers' organization in 16th round of free-agent draft, June 4, 1970.
†On disabled list, April 14 to May 1, 1972.
‡Traded to Baltimore Orioles for Pitcher Bob Reynolds, May 29, 1975.
§On disabled list, May 24 to June 24, 1977.

xTraded to Montreal Expos for player to be named later, July 14, 1977.
yOn disabled list, May 15 to July 9, 1978.
zReleased, January 17, 1979; signed by Detroit Tigers' organization, February 20, 1979.
aSold to Milwaukee Brewers' organization, December 4, 1979.
bOn disabled list, April 10 to April 20, 1980.
cGranted free agency when refused option to minors, December 19, 1980.

ALFRED WILLIS HOLLAND
(Al)
Born August 16, 1952, at Roanoke, Va.
Height, 5.11. Weight, 210.
Throws left and bats righthanded.
Hobby—Reading.
Attended North Carolina A&T University, Greensboro, N. C.;
received Bachelor of Science degree in Recreation.

Tied for New York-Pennsylvania League lead in shutouts with 2 in 1975.

Year Club	League	G.	IP.	W.	L.	Pct.	H.	R.	ER.	SO.	BB.	ERA.
1975—Bradenton Pirates	Gulf Coast	5	40	2	2	.500	24	6	5	39	20	1.13
1975—Niagara Falls	NYP	6	49	4	2	.667	44	20	14	50	14	2.57
1976—Salem	Carolina	39	76	4	2	.667	59	32	25	72	45	2.96
1977—Shreveport	Texas	21	36	4	1	.800	23	7	5	25	17	1.25
1977—Columbus	Int'national	27	86	6	4	.600	83	44	34	73	36	3.56
1977—Pittsburgh	National	2	2	0	0	.000	4	2	2	1	0	9.00
1978—Columbus†	Int'national	20	91	8	5	.615	102	59	54	65	34	5.34
1979—Portland‡-Phoenix	P. Coast	29	174	10	10	.500	173	99	87	140	87	4.50
1979—San Francisco	National	3	7	0	0	.000	3	0	0	7	5	0.00
1980—San Francisco	National	54	82	5	3	.625	71	21	16	65	34	1.76
Major League Totals		59	91	5	3	.625	78	23	18	73	39	1.78

Selected by Texas Rangers' organization in 30th round of free-agent draft, June 5, 1974.
Selected by San Diego Padres' organization in secondary phase of free-agent draft, January 9, 1975.
Signed as free agent by Pittsburgh Pirates' organization, June 28, 1975.
†On disabled list, April 14 to May 28 and July 20 to July 31, 1978.
‡Traded with Pitchers Ed Whitson and Fred Breining to San Francisco Giants for Third Basemen Bill Madlock and Lenny Randle and Pitcher Dave Roberts, June 28, 1979.

RANDY SCOTT HOLMAN
(Known by middle name.)
Born September 18, 1958, at Santa Paula, Calif.
Height, 6.00. Weight, 190.
Throws and bats righthanded.
Attended Ventura College, Ventura, Calif.

Led International League in shutouts with 4 in 1979.

Year Club	League	G.	IP.	W.	L.	Pct.	H.	R.	ER.	SO.	BB.	ERA.
1977—Wausau	Midwest	48	100	3	11	.214	96	51	39	83	37	3.51
1978—Jackson†	Texas	23	138	11	5	.688	128	57	50	68	66	3.26
1979—Tidewater	Int'national	24	149	13	7	.650	125	45	33	62	51	*1.99
1980—Tidewater‡	Int'national	11	48	3	3	.500	54	35	26	16	18	4.88
1980—New York	National	4	7	0	0	.000	6	2	1	3	1	1.29
Major League Totals		4	7	0	0	.000	6	2	1	3	1	1.29

Signed as free agent by New York Mets' organization, December 26, 1979.
†On disabled list, June 26 to July 6, 1978.
‡On disabled list, May 29 to July 31, 1980.

ROGER BOYD HOLT
Born April 8, 1956, at Daytona Beach, Fla.
Height, 5.11. Weight, 165.
Throws right and bats left and righthanded.
Attended University of Florida, Gainesville, Fla.

Led Eastern League second basemen in putouts with 282 and in double plays with 82 in 1978.
Tied for International League lead in double plays by second basemen with 74 in 1979.

Year Club	League	Pos.	G.	AB.	R.	H.	2B.	3B.	HR.	RBI.	B.A.	PO.	A.	E.	F.A.
1977—Fort Lauderdale	Fla. St.	SS-2B	76	271	46	66	6	2	0	20	.244	153	248	32	.926
1978—West Haven	East.	2B-SS	137	418	78	116	10	0	0	42	.278	283	347	29	.956
1979—Columbus	Int.	2B-O-S	130	454	72	127	16	3	1	33	.280	252	318	11	.981
1980—Columbus	Int.	2B	121	380	49	81	9	1	3	35	.213	207	332	9	.984
1980—New York†	Amer.	2B	2	6	0	1	0	0	0	1	.167	3	9	0	1.000
Major League Totals			2	6	0	1	0	0	0	1	.167	3	9	0	1.000

Selected by New York Yankees' organization in 4th round of free-agent draft, June 7, 1977.
†Traded to Texas Rangers for cash and a player to be named later, October 24, 1980; Infielder Tucker Ashford traded to Yankees' organization completing deal, December 8, 1980.

BRIAN JOHN HOLTON

Born November 29, 1959, at McKeesport, Pa.
Height, 6.01. Weight, 174.
Throws and bats righthanded.
Attended Louisburg College, Louisburg, N. C.

Tied for California League lead in shutouts with 2 in 1979.
Tied for Texas League lead in complete games with 16 in 1980.

Year	Club	League	G.	IP.	W.	L.	Pct.	H.	R.	ER.	SO.	BB.	ERA.
1978—Clinton†	Midwest	14	79	6	4	.600	94	51	38	54	23	4.33
1979—Lodi	California	10	72	7	0	1.000	47	26	21	72	32	2.63
1979—San Antonio	Texas	13	51	3	5	.375	50	24	21	40	25	3.71
1980—San Antonio	Texas	27	207	•15	10	.600	204	93	79	139	65	3.43

Selected by Los Angeles Dodgers' organization in 1st round (22nd player selected) of free-agent draft, January 10, 1978.

†On temporary inactive list, June 12 to July 7, 1978.

FREDERICK WAYNE HONEYCUTT
(Rick)

Born June 29, 1952, at Chattanooga, Tenn.
Height, 6.02. Weight, 190.
Throws and bats lefthanded.
Hobbies—Golf and racquetball
Attended University of Tennessee, Knoxville, Tenn.; received Bachelor
of Science degree in Health Education.

Tied for New York-Pennsylvania League lead in complete games with 7 in 1976.

Year	Club	League	G.	IP.	W.	L.	Pct.	H.	R.	ER.	SO.	BB.	ERA.
1976—Niagara Falls†	NYP	13	•97	5	3	.625	91	36	28	•98	20	2.60
1977—Shreveport‡§	Texas	21	135	10	6	.625	144	53	37	82	42	•2.47
1977—Seattle	American	10	29	0	1	.000	26	16	14	17	11	4.34
1978—Seattle x	American	26	134	5	11	.313	150	81	73	50	49	4.90
1979—Seattle	American	33	194	11	12	.478	201	103	87	83	67	4.04
1980—Seattle y	American	30	203	10	17	.370	221	99	89	79	60	3.95
Major League Totals		99	560	26	41	.388	598	299	263	229	187	4.23

Selected by Baltimore Orioles' organization in 14th round of free-agent draft, June 6, 1972.
Selected by Pittsburgh Pirates' organization in 17th round of free-agent draft, June 8, 1976.

†Played two games as first baseman and one game as shortstop.

‡Sent to Seattle by Pittsburgh Pirates' organization, August 22, 1977, to complete deal in which Pittsburgh obtained Pitcher Dave Pagan, July 27, 1977.

§Appeared as shortstop.

xOn disabled list, May 20 to June 26, 1978.

yTraded with Catcher Larry Cox, Outfielders Willie Horton and Leon Roberts and Shortstop Mario Mendoza to Texas Rangers for Pitchers Brian Allard, Ken Clay, Steve Finch and Jerry Gleaton, Shortstop Rick Auerbach and Outfielder Richie Zisk, December 12, 1980.

ALL-STAR GAME RECORD
Member of American League All-Star Team in 1980; did not play.

DONALD HARRIS HOOD
(Don)

Born October 16, 1949, at Florence, S. C.
Height, 6.03. Weight, 188.
Throws and bats lefthanded.
Hobbies—Hunting and fishing.
Attended St. Petersburg Junior College, St. Petersburg, Fla.

Tied for California League lead in shutouts with 5 in 1970.

Year	Club	League	G.	IP.	W.	L.	Pct.	H.	R.	ER.	SO.	BB.	ERA.
1969—Bluefield	Ap'lachian	9	48	5	1	.833	53	29	24	54	24	4.50
1970—Stockton	California	28	178	10	10	.500	165	78	57	196	66	2.88
1971—Dallas-Ft. Worth	Texas	26	167	11	9	.550	146	68	50	96	60	2.69
1972—Rochester	Int'national	27	150	9	10	.474	160	66	58	84	58	3.48
1973—Rochester	Int'national	15	91	4	7	.364	75	40	32	62	33	3.16
1973—Baltimore	American	8	32	3	2	.600	31	17	14	18	6	3.94
1974—Baltimore†‡	American	20	57	1	1	.500	47	26	22	26	20	3.47
1975—Cleveland	American	29	135	6	10	.375	136	76	66	51	57	4.40
1976—Cleveland	American	33	78	3	5	.375	89	46	42	32	41	4.85
1977—Cleveland	American	41	105	2	1	.667	87	42	35	62	49	3.00
1978—Cleveland	American	36	155	5	6	.455	166	82	77	73	77	4.47
1979—Cleveland§-New York x	American	40	89	4	1	.800	75	33	32	29	44	3.24
1980—St. Louis y	National	33	82	4	6	.400	90	39	31	35	34	3.40
American League Totals		207	651	24	26	.480	631	322	288	291	294	298
National League Totals		33	82	4	6	.400	90	39	31	35	34	3.40
Major League Totals		240	733	28	32	.467	721	361	319	326	328	3.92

Selected by Baltimore Orioles' organization in 1st round (17th player selected) of free-agent draft, June 5, 1969.

†On restricted list, May 26 to June 4, 1974.
‡Traded with First Baseman Boog Powell to Cleveland Indians for Catcher Dave Duncan and Outfielder Alvin McGrew (assigned to Rochester), February 25, 1974.
§Traded to New York Yankees for Catcher Cliff Johnson, June 15, 1979.
xGranted free agency, November 1, 1979; signed by St. Louis Cardinals, March 21, 1980.
yReleased, October 20, 1980.

CHAMPIONSHIP SERIES RECORD

Year Club	League	Pos.	G.	AB.	R.	H.	2B.	3B.	HR.	RBI.	B.A.	PO.	A.	E.	F.A.
1973—Baltimore	Amer.	PR	1	0	0	0	0	0	0	0	.000	0	0	0	.000

BURT CARLTON HOOTON

Born February 7, 1950, at Greenville, Tex.
Height, 6.01. Weight, 200.
Throws and bats righthanded.
Attended University of Texas, Austin, Tex.

Pitched 4-0 no-hit victory against Philadelphia Phillies, April 16, 1972.

Year Club	League	G.	IP.	W.	L.	Pct.	H.	R.	ER.	SO.	BB.	ERA.
1971—Tacoma	P. Coast	12	102	7	4	.636	73	26	19	135	19	1.68
1971—Chicago	National	3	21	2	0	1.000	8	5	5	22	10	2.14
1972—Chicago	National	33	218	11	14	.440	201	78	68	132	81	2.81
1973—Chicago	National	42	240	14	17	.452	248	107	98	134	73	3.68
1974—Chicago	National	48	176	7	11	.389	214	112	94	94	51	4.81
1975—Chicago†-Los Angeles	National	34	235	18	9	.667	190	88	80	153	68	3.06
1976—Los Angeles	National	33	227	11	15	.423	203	93	82	116	60	3.25
1977—Los Angeles	National	32	223	12	7	.632	184	74	65	153	60	2.62
1978—Los Angeles	National	32	236	19	10	.655	196	74	71	104	61	2.71
1979—Los Angeles	National	29	212	11	10	.524	191	85	70	129	63	2.97
1980—Los Angeles	National	34	207	14	8	.636	194	90	84	118	64	3.65
Major League Totals		320	1995	119	101	.541	1829	806	717	1155	591	3.23

Selected by New York Mets' organization in 5th round of free-agent draft, June 7, 1968.
Selected by Chicago Cubs' organization in secondary phase of free-agent draft, June 8, 1971.
†Traded to Los Angeles Dodgers for Pitchers Geoffrey Zahn and Eddie Solomon, May 2, 1975.

CHAMPIONSHIP SERIES RECORD

Tied Championship Series record for most bases on balls, inning (4), October 7, 1977 (second inning).
Tied National League Championship Series records for most hits allowed, game (10), October 4, 1978; most hits allowed, inning (5), October 4, 1978 (fifth inning).

Year Club	League	G.	IP.	W.	L.	Pct.	H.	R.	ER.	SO.	BB.	ERA.
1977—Los Angeles	National	1	1⅔	0	0	.000	2	3	3	1	4	16.20
1978—Los Angeles	National	1	4⅔	0	0	.000	10	4	4	5	0	7.71
Championship Series Totals		2	6⅓	0	0	.000	12	7	7	6	4	9.95

WORLD SERIES RECORD

Year Club	League	G.	IP.	W.	L.	Pct.	H.	R.	ER.	SO.	BB.	ERA.
1977—Los Angeles	National	2	12	1	1	.500	8	5	5	9	2	3.75
1978—Los Angeles	National	2	8⅓	1	1	.500	13	7	6	6	3	6.48
World Series Totals..................................		4	20⅓	2	2	.500	21	12	11	15	5	4.87

JAMES ROBERT HORNER
(Bob)

Born August 6, 1957, at Junction City, Kan.
Height, 6.01. Weight, 210.
Throws and bats righthanded.
Attended Arizona State University, Tempe, Ariz.

Named College Player of the Year by THE SPORTING NEWS, 1978.
Named National League Rookie Player of the Year by THE SPORTING NEWS, 1978.
Named National League Rookie of the Year by the Baseball Writers Association of America, 1978.
Received reported $175,000 bonus to sign with Atlanta Braves, 1978.

Year Club	League	Pos.	G.	AB.	R.	H.	2B.	3B.	HR.	RBI.	B.A.	PO.	A.	E.	F.A.
1978—Atlanta	Nat.	3B	89	323	50	86	17	1	23	63	.266	81	199	13	.956
1979—Atlanta †	Nat.	3B-1B	121	487	66	153	15	1	33	98	.314	470	167	22	.967
1980—Atlanta‡	Nat.	3B-1B	124	463	81	124	14	1	35	89	.268	80	253	23	.935
Major League Totals......................			334	1273	197	363	46	3	91	250	.285	631	619	58	.956

Selected by Oakland A's organization in 15th round of free-agent draft, June 4, 1975.
Selected by Atlanta Braves' organization in 1st round (first player selected) of free-agent draft, June 6, 1978.
†On supplemental disabled list, April 11 to April 26, 1979.
‡On disqualified list when refused option to Richmond, April 28, 1980; reinstated May 10, 1980.

WILLIE WATTISON HORTON

Born October 18, 1942, at Arno, Va.
Height, 5.10. Weight, 209.
Throws and bats righthanded.
Hobby—Collecting recordings.

Tied major league record for most putouts and most chances accepted by left fielder, game (11), July 18, 1969.

Hit three home runs in a game, vs. Milwaukee Brewers, June 9, 1970 and vs. Kansas City Royals, May 15, 1977.

Led American League designated hitters in strikeouts with 114 in 1977.
Led Northern League in total bases with 203 in 1962.
Named designated hitter on THE SPORTING NEWS American League All-Star Team, 1975.
Named outfielder on THE SPORTING NEWS American League All-Star Team, 1968.
Named American League Comeback Player of the Year by THE SPORTING NEWS, 1979.
Received reported $50,000 bonus to sign with Detroit Tigers, 1961.

Year	Club	League	Pos.	G.	AB.	R.	H.	2B.	3B.	HR.	RBI.	B.A.	PO.	A.	E.	F.A.
1962—Duluth-Superior	.North.		OF	123	441	68	130	20	4	15	72	.295	184	3	10	.949
1963—Syracuse	.Int.		OF	21	78	12	17	2	1	2	8	.218	40	2	1	.977
1963—Knoxville	.Sally		OF	118	442	77	147	20	9	14	70	.333	183	7	7	.964
1963—Detroit	.Amer.		OF	15	43	6	14	2	1	1	4	.326	13	0	0	1.000
1964—Syracuse	.Int.		OF-3B	135	490	73	141	16	9	28	99	.288	265	6	10	.964
1964—Detroit	.Amer.		OF	25	80	6	13	1	3	1	10	.163	33	0	2	.943
1965—Detroit	.Amer.		OF-3B	143	512	69	140	20	2	29	104	.273	249	9	3	.989
1966—Detroit	.Amer.		OF	146	526	72	138	22	6	27	100	.262	233	4	5	.979
1967—Detroit	.Amer.		OF	122	401	47	110	20	3	19	67	.274	165	5	5	.971
1968—Detroit	.Amer.		OF	143	512	68	146	20	2	36	85	.285	212	6	6	.973
1969—Detroit	.Amer.		OF	141	508	66	133	17	1	28	91	.262	272	8	8	.972
1970—Detroit†	.Amer.		OF	96	371	53	113	18	2	17	69	.305	154	10	3	.982
1971—Detroit	.Amer.		OF	119	450	64	130	25	1	22	72	.289	176	8	7	.963
1972—Detroit‡	.Amer.		OF	108	333	44	77	9	5	11	36	.231	131	6	0	1.000
1973—Detroit§	.Amer.		OF	111	411	42	130	19	3	17	53	.316	160	2	●10	.942
1974—Detroit x	.Amer.		OF	72	238	32	71	8	1	15	47	.298	106	2	6	.947
1975—Detroit	.Amer.		DH	159	615	62	169	13	1	25	92	.275	0	0	0	.000
1976—Detroit y	.Amer.		DH	114	401	40	105	17	0	14	56	.262	0	0	0	.000
1977—Det.z-Tex.a	.Amer.		OF	140	523	55	151	23	3	15	75	.289	16	0	1	.941
1978—Cl.b-Ok.c-Tr.d	.Amer.		OF	115	393	38	99	21	0	11	60	.252	1	0	2	.333
1979—Seattle e	.Amer.		DH	●162	646	77	180	19	5	29	106	.279	0	0	0	.000
1980—Seattle fg	.Amer.		DH	97	335	32	74	10	1	8	36	.221	0	0	0	.000
Major League Totals				2058	7298	873	1993	284	40	325	1163	.273	1921	60	58	.972

Signed as free agent by Detroit Tigers' organization, August 7, 1961.
†On disabled list, July 25 to November 8, 1970.
‡On supplemental disabled list, May 22 to June 6, 1972.
§On supplemental disabled list, May 11 to May 29, 1973.
xOn disabled list, July 12 through remainder of season.
yOn disabled list, June 6 to July 15, 1976.
zTraded to Texas Rangers for Pitcher Steve Foucault, April 12, 1977.
aTraded with Pitcher David Clyde to Cleveland Indians for First Baseman-Outfielder John Lowenstein and Pitcher Tom Buskey, February 28, 1978.
bReleased, July 3, 1978; signed by Oakland A's, July 13, 1978.
cTraded with Pitcher Phillip Huffman to Toronto Blue Jays for Designated Hitter Rico Carty, August 15, 1978.
dGranted free agency November 2, 1978; signed by Seattle Mariners, January 27, 1979.
eGranted free agency, November 1, 1979; re-signed by Mariners, December 20, 1979.
fOn disabled list, June 22 to July 16 and August 22 to September 15, 1980.
gTraded with Catcher Larry Cox, Pitcher Rick Honeycutt, Shortstop Mario Mendoza and Outfielder Leon Roberts to Texas Rangers for Pitchers Brian Allard, Ken Clay, Steve Finch and Jerry Gleaton, Shortstop Rick Auerbach and Outfielder Richie Zisk, December 12, 1980.

CHAMPIONSHIP SERIES RECORD

Year	Club	League	Pos.	G.	AB.	R.	H.	2B.	3B.	HR.	RBI.	B.A.	PO.	A.	E.	F.A.
1972—Detroit	.Amer.		O-PH	5	10	0	1	0	0	0	0	.100	6	0	0	1.000

WORLD SERIES RECORD

Year	Club	League	Pos.	G.	AB.	R.	H.	2B.	3B.	HR.	RBI.	B.A.	PO.	A.	E.	F.A.
1968—Detroit	.Amer.		OF	7	23	6	7	1	1	1	3	.304	5	1	1	.857

ALL-STAR GAME RECORD

Year	League	Pos.	AB.	R.	H.	2B.	3B.	HR.	RBI.	B.A.	PO.	A.	E.	F.A.
1965—American		OF	3	0	0	0	0	0	0	.000	2	0	0	1.000
1968—American		OF	2	0	0	0	0	0	0	.000	1	0	0	1.000
1970—American		OF	2	1	2	0	0	0	0	1.000	1	0	0	1.000
1973—American		PH	1	0	0	0	0	0	0	.000	0	0	0	.000
All-Star Game Totals			8	1	2	0	0	0	0	.250	4	0	0	1.000

DID YOU KNOW—

That there were five triple plays in the majors in 1980? Teams accomplishing it were Seattle, Chicago White Sox, Montreal, Detroit and San Francisco.

DAVID ALAN HOSTETLER
(Dave)

Born March 27, 1956, at Pasadena, Calif.
Height, 6.04. Weight, 215.
Throws and bats righthanded.
Attended Citrus College, Azusa, Calif., and University
of Southern California, Los Angeles, Calif.

Year Club League	Pos.	G.	AB.	R.	H.	2B.	3B.	HR.	RBI.	B.A.	PO.	A.	E.	F.A.
1978—West Palm B'ch Fla. St.	1B	75	249	27	67	12	0	5	29	.269	541	36	11	.981
1979—Memphis...........South.	1B •145	548	77	148	28	4	20	*114	.270	959	55	9	.991
1980—Denver .............A.A.	1B	126	453	62	122	17	1	9	58	.269	1039	63	*16	.986

Selected by San Francisco Giants' organization in 4th round of free-agent draft, January 9, 1975.
Selected by San Francisco Giants' organization in 4th round of free-agent draft, January 7, 1976.
Selected by Cleveland Indians' organization in secondary phase of free-agent draft, June 8, 1976.
Selected by San Francisco Giants' organization in secondary phase of free-agent draft, June 7, 1977.
Selected by Montreal Expos' organization in 3rd round of free-agent draft, June 6, 1978.

CHARLES OLIVER HOUGH
Name pronounced Huff.
(Charlie)

Born January 5, 1948, at Honolulu, Hawaii.
Height, 6.02. Weight, 190.
Throws and bats righthanded.
Hobby—Fishing.

Major league saves: 1970 (2), 1971 (0), 1972 (0), 1973 (5), 1974 (1), 1975 (4), 1976 (18), 1977 (22), 1978 (7), 1979 (0), 1980 (1). Total—60.
Led Pacific Coast League in saves with 18 in 1970.

Year Club League	G.	IP.	W.	L.	Pct.	H.	R.	ER.	SO.	BB.	ERA.
1966—Ogden.................................Pioneer	21	68	5	•7	.417	82	56	36	68	29	4.76
1967—Santa Barbara.....................California	20	165	14	4	*.778	129	50	41	138	43	2.24
1967—Albuquerque ....Texas	7	36	2	1	.667	57	31	28	25	10	7.00
1968—Albuquerque ....Texas	27	121	6	10	.375	145	72	53	74	26	3.94
1969—Albuquerque ....Texas	27	163	10	9	.526	190	87	74	113	42	4.09
1970—Spokane...............................P. Coast	49	134	12	8	.600	98	43	29	90	44	1.95
1970—Los Angeles ....National	8	17	0	0	.000	18	11	10	8	11	5.29
1971—Spokane‡ ....P. Coast	47	117	10	8	.556	95	56	51	104	52	3.92
1971—Los Angeles ....National	4	4	0	0	.000	3	3	2	4	3	4.50
1972—Albuquerque§.......................P. Coast	58	125	14	5	.737	109	47	33	95	60	2.38
1972—Los Angeles ....National	2	3	0	0	.000	2	1	1	4	2	3.00
1973—Los Angeles ....National	37	72	4	2	.667	52	24	22	70	45	2.75
1974—Los Angeles ....National	49	96	9	4	.692	65	45	40	63	40	3.75
1975—Los Angeles ....National	38	61	3	7	.300	43	25	20	34	34	2.95
1976—Los Angeles ....National	77	143	12	8	.600	102	43	35	81	77	2.20
1977—Los Angeles ....National	70	127	6	12	.333	98	53	47	105	70	3.33
1978—Los Angeles ....National	55	93	5	5	.500	69	38	34	66	48	3.29
1979—Los Angeles ....National	42	151	7	5	.583	152	88	80	76	66	4.77
1980—Los Angeles x ....National	19	32	1	3	.250	37	21	20	55	21	5.63
1980—Texas ....American	16	61	2	2	.500	54	30	27	47	37	3.98
National League Totals	401	799	47	46	.505	641	352	311	566	417	3.50
American League Totals	16	61	2	2	.500	54	30	27	47	37	3.98
Major League Totals................................	417	860	49	48	.505	695	382	338	613	454	3.54

Selected by Los Angeles Dodgers' organization in free-agent draft, June 9, 1966.
†On temporary inactive list, June 19 to July 1, 1968.
‡On temporary inactive list, July 10 to July 24, 1971.
§Placed on temporary inactive list three times: June 12 to June 15, July 22 to July 24 and August 7 to August 12, 1972.
xSold to Texas Rangers, July 11, 1980.

BATTING RECORD

Year Club League	Pos.	G.	AB.	R.	H.	2B.	3B.	HR.	RBI.	B.A.	PO.	A.	E.	F.A.
1967—Santa Barbara ...Calif.	P-1B	28	72	8	14	2	0	0	4	.194	15	25	2	.953
1968—Albuquerque......Tex.	P-1-3	56	83	10	21	4	0	0	6	.253	43	25	4	.944
1969—Albuquerque......Tex.	P-3B	31	57	10	12	0	0	1	9	.211	10	19	2	.935
1970—Spokane ....P. C.	P-O-1	49	33	1	6	0	0	1	3	.182	7	28	3	.921
1971—Spokane ....P. C.	P-OF	48	36	2	10	0	0	0	3	.278	6	20	1	.963
1972—Albuquerque......P. C.	P-OF	58	34	4	9	1	0	0	5	.265	3	27	0	1.000

CHAMPIONSHIP SERIES RECORD

Year Club League	G.	IP.	W.	L.	Pct.	H.	R.	ER.	SO.	BB.	ERA.
1974—Los Angeles ....National	1	2⅓	0	0	.000	4	2	2	2	0	7.71
1977—Los Angeles ....National	1	2	0	0	.000	2	1	1	3	0	4.50
1978—Los Angeles ....National	1	2	0	0	.000	1	1	1	1	0	4.50
Championship Series Totals	3	6⅓	0	0	.000	7	4	4	6	0	5.68

WORLD SERIES RECORD

Tied World Series record for most wild pitches, inning and game (2), October 15, 1978 (seventh inning).

Year Club	League	G.	IP.	W.	L.	Pct.	H.	R.	ER.	SO.	BB.	ERA.
1974—Los Angeles	National	1	2	0	0	.000	0	0	0	4	1	0.00
1977—Los Angeles	National	2	5	0	0	.000	3	1	1	5	0	1.80
1978—Los Angeles	National	2	5⅓	0	0	.000	10	5	5	5	2	8.44
World Series Totals		5	12⅓	0	0	.000	13	6	6	14	3	4.38

PAUL WESLEY HOUSEHOLDER

Born September 4, 1958, at Columbus, O.
Height, 6.00. Weight, 180.
Throws right and bats right and lefthanded.

Led Western Carolinas League in strikeouts with 130 in 1977.
Led Southern League outfielders in fielding percentage with .989 and in double plays with 5 in 1979.

Year Club	League	Pos.	G.	AB.	R.	H.	2B.	3B.	HR.	RBI.	B.A.	PO.	A.	E.	F.A.
1976—Billings	Pion.	OF-3B	50	149	23	38	3	2	2	19	.255	74	8	6	.932
1977—Shelby	W. Car.	OF	137	500	72	116	15	•9	10	63	.232	278	10	8	.973
1978—Tampa	Fla. St.	OF	123	415	59	103	8	10	10	42	.248	213	8	11	.953
1979—Nashville	South.	OF-3B	142	488	93	138	24	7	20	95	.283	247	18	4	.985
1980—Indianapolis	A.A.	OF-3B	125	464	74	137	26	5	9	50	.295	249	10	8	.970
1980—Cincinnati	Nat.	OF	20	45	3	11	1	1	0	7	.244	16	2	0	1.000
Major League Totals			20	45	3	11	1	1	0	7	.244	16	2	0	1.000

Selected by Cincinnati Reds' organization in 2nd round of free-agent draft, June 8, 1976.

FRED IRVING HOWARD, III

Born September 2, 1956, at Portland, Me.
Height, 6.03. Weight, 190.
Throws and bats righthanded.
Attended Miami-Dade South Community College, Miami, Fla. and University of Maine at Portland.
Brother of Mike Howard, pitcher in Boston Red Sox' organization.

Year Club	League	G.	IP.	W.	L.	Pct.	H.	R.	ER.	SO.	BB.	ERA.
1976—Appleton	Midwest	6	13	0	0	.000	17	10	7	4	6	4.85
1976—Sarasota White Sox	G. Coast	14	67	4	5	.444	51	28	14	•76	37	1.88
1977—Appleton	Midwest	9	63	2	5	.286	48	25	15	52	18	2.14
1977—Iowa	Am. Assoc.	18	97	4	7	.364	91	44	43	70	41	3.99
1978—Knoxville†	Southern	21	139	12	6	.667	111	52	43	109	48	2.78
1979—Iowa	Am. Assoc.	7	49	4	1	.800	34	13	9	45	20	1.65
1979—Chicago	American	28	68	1	5	.167	73	34	27	36	32	3.57
1980—Iowa‡	Am. Assoc.	19	113	6	10	.375	121	69	63	49	32	5.02
Major League Totals		28	68	1	5	.167	73	34	27	36	32	3.57

Selected by Chicago White Sox' organization in 6th round of free-agent draft, January 7, 1976.
†On disabled list, May 14 to June 23, 1978.
‡On disabled list, August 1 to August 27, 1980.

MICHAEL FREDRICK HOWARD
(Mike)

Born April 2, 1958, at Seattle, Wash.
Height, 6.02. Weight, 185.
Throws right and bats left and righthanded.

Led Pioneer League shortstops in double plays with 31 in 1977.

Year Club	League	Pos.	G.	AB.	R.	H.	2B.	3B.	HR.	RBI.	B.A.	PO.	A.	E.	F.A.
1976—Bellingham	Northw.	OF	50	119	17	23	3	2	0	17	.193	58	4	1	.984
1977—Clinton†	Midw.					Did not play									
1977—Lodi	Calif.	SS-3B	5	6	0	0	0	0	0	0	.000	2	4	1	.857
1977—Lethbridge	Pioneer	SS	51	170	35	44	8	3	0	15	.259	86	139	24	.904
1978—Clinton‡	Midw.	S-2-O-3	95	294	53	85	15	2	2	29	.289	167	159	25	.929
1979—Jackson	Texas	O-1-S-2	131	447	43	102	13	3	2	42	.228	586	55	9	.986
1980—Jackson	Texas	O-S-1-2	135	508	91	148	30	8	9	56	.291	260	43	9	.971

Selected by Los Angeles Dodgers' organization in 6th round of free-agent draft, June 8, 1976.
†On temporary inactive list, April 16 to May 12, 1977.
‡Drafted by New York Mets' organization, December 5, 1978.

MICHAEL STEVEN HOWARD
(Mike)

Born October 14, 1957, at Portland, Me.
Height, 6.03. Weight, 185.
Throws and bats righthanded.
Brother of Fred Howard, pitcher in Chicago White Sox' organization.

Year Club	League	G.	IP.	W.	L.	Pct.	H.	R.	ER.	SO.	BB.	ERA.
1975—Elmira	N.Y.-Pa.	13	33	1	2	.333	39	19	13	19	18	3.55
1976—Elmira	N.Y.-Pa.	14	71	•8	2	.800	67	37	32	30	34	4.06
1977—Winter Haven	Florida St.	26	89	3	6	.333	113	69	52	44	52	5.26
1978—Winter Haven	Florida St.	28	123	5	10	.333	117	64	45	59	43	3.29
1979—Winston-Salem	Carolina	33	149	12	3	•.800	107	49	38	•161	62	2.30

Year	Club	League	G.	IP.	W.	L.	Pct.	H.	R.	ER.	SO.	BB.	ERA.
1980–Bristol		Eastern	19	112	10	5	.667	109	51	47	99	48	3.78
1980–Pawtucket		Int'national	9	59	1	5	.167	49	34	30	35	32	4.58

Selected by Boston Red Sox' organization in 6th round of free-agent draft, June 4, 1975.

ARTHUR HENRY HOWE, JR.
(Art)

Born December 15, 1946, at Pittsburgh, Pa.
Height, 6.01. Weight, 185.
Throws and bats righthanded.
Hobbies—Golf, handball and tennis.
Attended University of Wyoming, Laramie, Wyo.; received Bachelor
of Science degree in Business Administration.

Led International League third basemen in double plays with 24 in 1972.

Year	Club	League	Pos.	G.	AB.	R.	H.	2B.	3B.	HR.	RBI.	B.A.	PO.	A.	E.	F.A.
1971–Salem		Carol.	●3B-SS	114	382	77	133	27	7	12	79	★.348	●110	221	21	.940
1972–Charleston†		Int.	★3-2-S	109	365	68	99	21	3	14	53	.271	105	248	★24	.936
1973–Charleston‡		Int.	3-2-S	119	372	50	85	20	1	8	44	.228	141	229	21	.946
1974–Charleston		Int.	3B	60	207	26	70	17	4	8	36	.338	35	90	9	.933
1974–Pittsburgh		Nat.	3B-SS	29	74	10	18	4	1	1	5	.243	11	49	4	.938
1975–Charleston		Int.	3B-2B	11	42	4	15	1	3	0	3	.357	15	23	1	.974
1975–Pittsburgh§		Nat.	3B-SS	63	146	13	25	9	0	1	10	.171	19	89	7	.939
1976–Memphis		Int.	3B-1B	74	259	50	92	21	3	12	59	.355	93	120	14	.934
1976–Houston		Nat.	3B-2B	21	29	0	4	1	0	0	0	.138	17	16	1	.970
1977–Houston		Nat.	2-3-S	125	413	44	109	23	7	8	58	.264	213	333	8	.986
1978–Houston		Nat.	2B-3B-1B	119	420	46	123	33	3	7	55	.293	240	302	13	.977
1979–Houston		Nat.	2B-3B-1B	118	355	32	88	15	2	6	33	.248	188	261	7	.985
1980–Houston		Nat.	1-3-2-S	110	321	34	91	12	5	10	46	.283	598	86	10	.986
Major League Totals				585	1758	179	458	97	18	33	207	.261	1286	1136	50	.980

Signed as free agent by Pittsburgh Pirates' organization, June, 1971.
†On disabled list, August 17 to September 2, 1972.
‡On disabled list from beginning of season until May 6, 1973.
§Traded to Houston Astros, January 6, 1976, to complete deal in which Pirates obtained Second Baseman
Tommy Helms from Astros for a player to be named later, December 12, 1975.

CHAMPIONSHIP SERIES RECORD

Year	Club	League	Pos.	G.	AB.	R.	H.	2B.	3B.	HR.	RBI.	B.A.	PO.	A.	E.	F.A.
1974–Pittsburgh		Nat.	PH	1	1	0	0	0	0	0	0	.000	0	0	0	.000
1980–Houston		Nat.	1B-PH	5	15	0	3	1	1	0	2	.200	29	3	0	1.000
Championship Series Totals				6	16	0	3	1	1	0	2	.188	29	3	0	1.000

STEVEN ROY HOWE
(Steve)

Born March 10, 1958, at Pontiac, Mich.
Height, 6.01. Weight, 180.
Throws and bats lefthanded.
Attended University of Michigan, Ann Arbor, Mich.

Major League saves: 1980 (17).
Named National League Rookie of the Year by Baseball Writers' Association of America, 1980.

Year	Club	League	G.	IP.	W.	L.	Pct.	H.	R.	ER.	SO.	BB.	ERA.
1979–San Antonio		Texas	13	95	6	2	.750	78	36	33	57	22	3.13
1980–Los Angeles		National	59	85	7	9	.438	83	33	25	39	22	2.65
Major League Totals			59	85	7	9	.438	83	33	25	39	22	2.65

Selected by Los Angeles Dodgers' organization in 1st round (16th player selected) of free-agent draft, June
5, 1979.

JAY CANFIELD HOWELL

Born November 26, 1955, at Miami, Fla.
Height, 6.03. Weight, 200.
Throws and bats righthanded.
Attended University of Colorado, Boulder, Colo.

Year	Club	League	G.	IP.	W.	L.	Pct.	H.	R.	ER.	SO.	BB.	ERA.
1976–Eugene		Northwest	13	73	5	4	.556	65	30	24	79	34	2.96
1977–Tampa		Florida St.	23	158	7	13	.350	141	60	52	99	52	2.96
1978–Nashville		Southern	28	166	9	14	.391	134	70	57	●173	55	3.09
1979–Indianapolis		Am. Assoc.	24	128	10	10	.500	121	82	73	79	84	5.13
1980–Indianapolis		Am. Assoc.	25	98	5	11	.313	95	70	55	73	71	5.05
1980–Cincinnati†		National	5	3	0	0	.000	8	5	5	1	0	15.00
Major League Totals			5	3	0	0	.000	8	5	5	1	0	15.00

Selected by Cincinnati Reds' organization in 12th round of free-agent draft, June 5, 1973.
Selected by Cincinnati Reds' organization in 31st round of free-agent draft, June 8, 1976.
†Traded to Chicago Cubs for Catcher Mike O'Berry, October 17, 1980.

ROY LEE HOWELL

Born December 18, 1953, at Lompoc, Calif.
Height, 6.01. Weight, 190.
Throws right and bats lefthanded.

Year Club League	Pos.	G.	AB.	R.	H.	2B.	3B.	HR.	RBI.	B.A.	PO.	A.	E.	F.A.
1972—Pittsfield..........East.	3B	48	116	12	29	3	0	2	9	.250	21	64	9	.904
1973—Pittsfield..........East.	3-S-O	96	277	44	67	12	2	15	47	.242	51	156	23	.900
1974—Spokane ....P. C.	3B	136	513	101	144	23	5	22	80	.281	98	247	25	.932
1974—Texas...............Amer.	3B	13	44	2	11	1	0	1	3	.250	5	24	3	.906
1975—Texas...............Amer.	3B	125	383	43	96	15	2	10	51	.251	80	214	21	.933
1976—Texas...............Amer.	3b	140	491	55	124	28	2	8	53	.253	103	245	*28	.926
1977—Tex.‡-Tor...........Amer.	3-O-1	103	381	41	115	17	1	10	44	.302	94	165	13	.952
1978—Toronto ....Amer.	3B-OF	140	551	67	149	28	3	8	61	.270	116	306	22	.950
1979—Toronto§...........Amer.	3B	138	513	60	126	28	4	15	72	.247	108	290	20	.952
1980—Toronto x.........Amer.	3B	142	528	51	142	28	9	10	57	.269	105	257	16	.958
Major League Totals		801	2889	319	763	145	21	62	341	.264	611	1501	123	.945

Selected by Texas Rangers' organization in 1st round (fourth player selected) of free-agent draft, June 6, 1972.

†On disabled list, July 29 to August 14, 1973.

‡Traded to Toronto Blue Jays for Infielder Jim Mason, Pitcher Steve Hargan, and cash estimated at $200,000, May 9, 1977.

§On supplemental disabled list, June 14 to June 30, 1979.

xGranted free agency, October 23, 1980; signed by Milwaukee Brewers, December 20, 1980.

ALL-STAR GAME RECORD

Year League	Pos.	AB.	R.	H.	2B.	3B.	HR.	RBI.	B.A.	PO.	A.	E.	F.A.
1978—American	PH	1	0	0	0	0	0	0	.000	0	0	0	.000

DEWEY LAMARR HOYT

(Known by middle name)
Born January 1, 1955, at Columbia, S. C.
Height, 6.03. Weight, 190.
Throws and bats righthanded.
Son of Dewey Hoyt, former minor league player, 1947 through 1950.

Led Midwest League in games started with 27 in 1978.
Tied for Midwest League lead in shutouts with 3 in 1978.

Year Club League	G.	IP.	W.	L.	Pct.	H.	R.	ER.	SO.	BB.	ERA.
1973—Johnson City ....Ap'lachian	12	76	6	6	.500	73	44	33	58	40	3.91
1974—Ft. Lauderdale ....Florida St.	23	161	13	4	.765	143	66	43	77	60	2.40
1975—Ft. Lauderdale†....................Florida St.	7	26	2	1	.667	24	14	13	12	8	4.50
1975—West Haven...................Eastern	8	44	2	4	.333	45	25	15	22	13	3.07
1976—West Haven‡.......................Eastern	25	180	15	8	.652	169	66	50	103	46	2.50
1977—Knoxville ....Southern	25	132	4	●13	.235	160	70	62	67	35	4.23
1977—Iowa ....Am. Assoc.	6	25	1	2	.333	30	20	20	14	9	7.20
1978—Appleton ....Midwest	28	189	*18	4	*.818	*187	74	61	115	60	2.90
1979—Iowa ....Am. Assoc.	9	43	1	4	.200	50	29	22	27	24	4.60
1979—Knoxville ....Southern	37	82	9	5	.643	80	29	27	60	35	2.96
1979—Chicago ....American	2	3	0	0	.000	2	0	0	0	0	0.00
1980—Iowa ....Am. Assoc.	18	62	5	2	.714	61	22	20	36	22	2.90
1980—Chicago ....American	24	112	9	3	.750	123	66	57	55	41	4.58
Major League Totals.................................	26	115	9	3	.750	125	66	57	55	41	4.46

Selected by New York Yankees' organization in 5th round of free-agent draft, June 5, 1973.

†On disabled list, April 16 to June 6, 1975.

‡Traded by New York Yankees with Outfielder Oscar Gamble, Pitcher Bob Polinsky and cash estimated at $250,000 to Chicago White Sox for Shortstop Bucky Dent, April 5, 1977.

ALAN THOMAS HRABOSKY

Name pronounced Ra-BAH-ski.

(The Mad Hungarian)

Born July 21, 1949, at Oakland, Calif.
Height, 5.10. Weight, 180.
Throws left and bats righthanded.
Hobbies—Surfing, camping and fishing.
Attended Fullerton Junior College, Fullerton, Calif.

Major League saves: 1970 (0), 1971 (0), 1972 (0), 1973 (5), 1974 (9), 1975 (22), 1976 (13), 1977 (10), 1978 (20), 1979 (11), 1980 (3). Total—93.

Tied for National League lead in saves with 22 in 1975.

Named National League Fireman of the Year by THE SPORTING NEWS, 1975.

Year Club League	G.	IP.	W.	L.	Pct.	H.	R.	ER.	SO.	BB.	ERA.
1969—Modesto..............................California	15	98	8	2	.800	86	34	27	112	43	2.48
1969—Arkansas ....Texas	2	10	1	0	1.000	11	8	7	8	4	6.30
1970—Arkansas ....Texas	15	91	8	1	.889	80	36	33	68	33	3.26
1970—St. Louis ....National	16	19	2	1	.667	22	10	10	12	7	4.74
1971—Tulsa† ....Am. Assoc.	9	14	1	1	.500	23	21	20	7	10	12.86

Year Club	League	G.	IP.	W.	L.	Pct.	H.	R.	ER.	SO.	BB.	ERA.
1971—Arkansas	Texas	8	27	1	0	1.000	31	9	9	31	10	3.00
1971—St. Louis	National	1	2	0	0	.000	2	0	0	2	0	0.00
1972—Arkansas	Texas	24	145	7	12	.368	134	71	55	142	64	3.41
1972—St. Louis	National	5	7	1	0	1.000	2	0	0	9	3	0.00
1973—Tulsa	Am. Assoc.	9	57	3	6	.333	60	40	28	56	24	4.42
1973—St. Louis	National	44	56	2	4	.333	45	15	13	57	21	2.09
1974—St. Louis	National	65	88	8	1	.889	71	34	29	82	38	2.97
1975—St. Louis	National	65	97	13	3	.813	72	27	18	82	33	1.67
1976—St. Louis	National	68	95	8	6	.571	89	42	35	73	39	3.32
1977—St. Louis‡§	National	65	86	6	5	.545	82	44	42	68	41	4.40
1978—Kansas City	American	58	75	8	7	.533	52	24	24	60	35	2.88
1979—Kansas City x	American	58	65	9	4	.692	67	31	27	39	41	3.74
1980—Atlanta	National	45	60	4	2	.667	50	27	24	31	31	3.60
National League Totals		374	510	44	22	.667	435	199	171	416	213	3.02
American League Totals		116	140	17	11	.607	119	55	51	99	76	3.28
Major League Totals		490	650	61	33	.649	554	254	222	515	289	3.07

Selected by Minnesota Twins' organization in 8th round of free-agent draft, June 6, 1967.
Selected by St. Louis Cardinals' organization in 1st round (19th player selected) of free-agent draft, February 1, 1969.
†On military list, January 11 through May 4, 1971.
‡On suspended list, May 21 through May 23, 1977.
§Traded to Kansas City Royals for Pitcher Mark Littell and Catcher Buck Martinez, December 8, 1977.
xGranted free agency, November 1, 1979; signed by Atlanta Braves, November 20, 1979.

CHAMPIONSHIP SERIES RECORD

Year Club	League	G.	IP.	W.	L.	Pct.	H.	R.	ER.	SO.	BB.	ERA.
1978—Kansas City	American	3	3	0	0	.000	3	1	1	2	0	3.00

GLENN DEE HUBBARD

Born September 25, 1957, at Hahn Air Force Base, Germany
Height, 5.08, Weight, 165.
Throws and bats righthanded.
Hobby—Hunting.

Named International League Rookie of the Year, 1978.

Year Club	League	Pos.	G.	AB.	R.	H.	2B.	3B.	HR.	RBI.	B.A.	PO.	A.	E.	F.A.
1975—Kingsport	Appal.	3-S-2	53	136	31	39	6	4	2	21	.287	44	88	9	.936
1976—Kingsport	Appal.	2B	37	136	29	40	8	0	2	15	.294	96	122	1	.995
1976—Greenwood†	W. Car.	2B	33	126	26	40	8	1	4	21	.317	62	83	6	.960
1977—Greenwood	W. Car.	2B	45	182	39	70	10	1	5	44	.385	114	133	4	.984
1977—Savannah	South.	2B	87	298	49	67	15	2	6	32	.225	209	239	10	.978
1978—Richmond	Int.	2B	80	301	58	101	12	3	14	36	.336	208	243	11	.976
1978—Atlanta‡	Nat.	2B	44	163	15	42	4	0	2	13	.258	102	130	5	.979
1979—Richmond	Int.	3B-2B	34	125	21	42	5	1	2	17	.336	83	109	7	.965
1979—Atlanta	Nat.	2B	97	325	34	75	12	0	3	29	.231	193	268	15	.968
1980—Richmond	Int.	2B	38	143	23	45	11	2	2	25	.315	89	127	4	.982
1980—Atlanta	Nat.	2B	117	431	55	107	21	3	9	43	.248	268	405	15	.978
Major League Totals			258	919	104	224	37	3	14	85	.244	563	803	35	.975

Selected by Atlanta Braves' organization in 20th round of free-agent draft, June 4, 1975.
†On temporary inactive list, May 17 to June 22, 1976.
‡On supplemental disabled list, July 22 to August 23, 1978.

PHILLIP LEE HUFFMAN
(Phil)

Born June 20, 1958, at Freeport, Tex.
Height, 6.02. Weight, 180.
Throws and bats righthanded.

Year Club	League	G.	IP.	W.	L.	Pct.	H.	R.	ER.	SO.	BB.	ERA.
1977—Great Falls†	Pioneer	10	67	7	3	.700	79	47	39	59	29	5.24
1978—Jersey City	Eastern	5	33	3	0	1.000	27	8	8	10	3	2.18
1978—Vancouver‡	P. Coast	17	123	7	6	.538	145	66	53	46	45	3.88
1978—Syracuse	Int'national	2	11	1	1	.500	14	6	6	7	6	4.91
1979—Toronto	American	31	173	6	•18	.250	220	130	111	56	68	5.77
1980—Syracuse§	Int'national	16	93	3	9	.250	98	45	41	47	35	3.97
Major League Totals		31	173	6	18	.250	220	130	111	56	68	5.77

Selected by San Francisco Giants' organization in 2nd round of free-agent draft, June 7, 1977.
†Traded with Outfielder Gary Thomasson, Catcher Gary Alexander, Pitchers Dave Heaverlo, Alan Wirth and John Johnson, a player to be named later and cash estimated at $390,000 to Oakland A's for Pitcher Vida Blue, March 15, 1978; Shortstop Mario Guerrero sent to Oakland to complete deal, April 7, 1978.
‡Traded with Outfielder-Designated Hitter Willie Horton to Toronto Blue Jays for Designated Hitter Rico Carty, August 15, 1978.
§On disabled list, July 9 to August 8, 1980.

THOMAS HUBERT HUME, JR.
Name pronounced YOOM.
(Tom)

Born March 29, 1953, at Cincinnati, O.
Height, 6.01. Weight, 185.
Throws and bats righthanded.
Hobbies—Hunting and fishing.
Attended Manatee Junior College, West Bradenton, Fla.

Major League saves: 1977 (0), 1978 (1), 1979 (17), 1980 (25). Total—43.
Tied for Eastern League lead in games started with 27 in 1973.
Named National League co-Fireman of the Year by THE SPORTING NEWS, 1980.

Year Club	League	G.	IP.	W.	L.	Pct.	H.	R.	ER.	SO.	BB.	ERA.
1972—Tampa†	Florida St.	23	141	7	11	.389	135	69	54	112	68	3.45
1973—Three Rivers	Eastern	27	170	7	8	.467	186	97	81	103	99	4.29
1974—Three Rivers	Eastern	26	157	7	12	.368	*167	91	77	109	90	4.41
1975—Three Rivers	Eastern	7	45	3	2	.600	43	20	15	19	15	3.00
1975—Indianapolis	Am. Assoc.	17	100	6	6	.500	106	49	45	56	36	4.05
1976—Indianapolis	Am. Assoc.	27	182	9	12	.429	178	91	83	111	62	4.10
1977—Indianapolis	Am. Assoc.	28	106	5	6	.455	99	40	30	76	37	2.55
1977—Cincinnati	National	14	43	3	3	.500	54	36	34	22	17	7.12
1978—Cincinnati	National	42	174	8	11	.421	198	89	80	90	50	4.41
1979—Cincinnati	National	57	163	10	9	.526	162	54	50	80	33	2.76
1980—Cincinnati	National	78	137	9	10	.474	121	44	39	68	38	2.56
Major League Totals		191	517	30	33	.476	535	223	203	260	138	3.53

Selected by Los Angeles Dodgers' organzation in 35th round of free-agent draft, June 8, 1971.
Selected by Cincinnati Reds' organization in secondary phase of free-agent draft, January 12, 1972.
†Played in one game as a third baseman and in one game as a second baseman.

CHAMPIONSHIP SERIES RECORD

Year Club	League	G.	IP.	W.	L.	Pct.	H.	R.	ER.	SO.	BB.	ERA.
1979—Cincinnati	National	3	4	0	1	.000	6	3	3	2	0	6.75

DAVID BLAIN HUPPERT
(Dave)

Born April 1, 1957, at Southgate, Calif.
Height, 6.01. Weight, 190.
Throws and bats righthanded.

Tied for Florida State League lead in double plays by catchers with 7 in 1978.

Year Club	League	Pos.	G.	AB.	R.	H.	2B.	3B.	HR.	RBI.	B.A.	PO.	A.	E.	F.A.
1977—Bluefield	Appal.	C	51	125	21	29	4	0	6	12	.232	*292	*46	6	.983
1978—Miami	Fla. St.	C	47	184	28	42	5	2	2	15	.228	375	56	7	.984
1978—Charlotte†	South.	C	24	63	9	15	1	0	0	4	.238	104	21	4	.969
1979—Charlotte	South.	C	102	300	37	67	12	2	5	37	.223	543	73	10	.984
1980—Charlotte	South.	C	107	319	43	70	15	2	3	23	.219	521	61	*20	.967

Signed as free agent by Baltimore Orioles' organization, May 22, 1977.
†On disabled list, August 2 to October 11, 1978.

CLINTON MERRICK HURDLE
(Clint)

Born July 30, 1957, at Big Rapids, Mich.
Height, 6.03. Weight, 195.
Throws right and bats lefthanded.
Hobbies—Music and pool.

Led American Association outfielders in double plays with 4 in 1977.
Tied for American Association lead in double plays by outfielders with 4 in 1979.
Named American Association Rookie of the Year, 1977.
Received reported $50,000 bonus to sign with Kansas City Royals, 1975.

Year Club	League	Pos.	G.	AB.	R.	H.	2B.	3B.	HR.	RBI.	B.A.	PO.	A.	E.	F.A.
1975—Sarasota Royals.	Gulf C.	OF	49	175	34	48	4	4	1	*31	.274	94	5	2	.980
1976—Waterloo	Midw.	OF	127	429	89	101	22	5	19	89	.235	179	12	7	.965
1977—Omaha	A.A.	OF	129	442	85	145	35	3	16	66	.328	198	*17	6	.973
1977—Kansas City	Amer.	OF	9	26	5	8	0	0	2	7	.308	17	0	0	1.000
1978—Kansas City	Amer.	OF-1B-3	133	417	48	110	25	5	7	56	.264	544	30	12	.980
1979—Omaha	A. A.	OF	68	220	30	52	13	0	6	29	.236	124	14	4	.972
1979—Kansas City	Amer.	OF-3B	59	171	16	41	10	3	3	30	.240	89	2	3	.968
1980—Kansas City	Amer.	OF	130	395	50	116	31	2	10	60	.294	233	8	10	.960
Major League Totals			331	1009	119	275	66	10	22	153	.273	883	40	25	.974

Selected by Kansas City Royals' organization in 1st round (ninth player selected) of free-agent draft, June 4, 1975.

Year	Club	League	Pos.	G.	AB.	R.	H.	2B.	3B.	HR.	RBI.	B.A.	PO.	A.	E.	F.A.
1978—Kansas City		Amer.	PH-OF	4	8	1	3	0	1	0	1	.375	6	1	0	1.000
1980—Kansas City		Amer.	OF	3	2	0	0	0	0	0	0	.000	1	0	0	1.000
Championship Series Totals				7	10	1	3	0	1	0	1	.300	7	1	0	1.000

WORLD SERIES RECORD

Year	Club	League	Pos.	G.	AB.	R.	H.	2B.	3B.	HR.	RBI.	B.A.	PO.	A.	E.	F.A.
1980—Kansas City		Amer.	OF	4	12	1	5	1	0	0	0	.417	8	0	0	1.000

BRUCE VEE HURST

Born March 24, 1958, at St. George, Utah.
Height, 6.03. Weight, 185.
Throws and bats lefthanded.
Attended Dixie College, St. George, Utah.

Year	Club	League	G.	IP.	W.	L.	Pct.	H.	R.	ER.	SO.	BB.	ERA.
1976—Elmira		NYP	9	42	3	2	.600	25	18	14	40	38	3.00
1977—Winter Haven†		Florida St.	13	91	5	4	.556	77	28	21	69	25	2.08
1978—Bristol‡		Eastern	6	33	1	3	.250	32	15	10	35	17	2.73
1979—Winter Haven		Florida St.	12	84	8	2	.800	57	22	18	64	20	1.93
1979—Bristol		Eastern	16	113	9	4	.692	108	56	45	91	49	3.58
1980—Pawtucket		Int'national	17	105	8	6	.571	101	52	46	54	54	3.94
1980—Boston		American	12	31	2	2	.500	39	33	31	16	16	9.00
Major League Totals			12	31	2	2	.500	39	33	31	16	16	9.00

Selected by Boston Red Sox' organization in 1st round (22nd player selected) of free-agent draft, June 8, 1976.

†On disabled list, August 8 to September 14, 1977.

‡On disabled list, May 23 to September 21, 1978.

THOMAS GEORGE HUTTON
(Tommy)

Born April 20, 1946, at Los Angeles, Calif.
Height, 5.11. Weight, 172.
Throws and bats lefthanded.
Hobbies—Basketball and golf.
Attended Pasadena City College, Pasadena, Calif.
Brother-in-law of Dick Ruthven, pitcher with Philadelphia Phillies.

Led California League first basemen in double plays with 102 in 1965.
Led Texas League in sacrifice flies with 9 in 1966.
Named Most Valuable Player in Pacific Coast League, 1971.
Named Player of the Year in Texas League, 1966.

Year	Club	League	Pos.	G.	AB.	R.	H.	2B.	3B.	HR.	RBI.	B.A.	PO.	A.	E.	F.A.
1965—Santa Barbara		Calif.	1B	132	494	86	145	24	5	20	63	.294	•991	•98	14	•.987
1966—Albuquerque		Texas	1B	103	385	58	131	24	4	9	•81	•.340	890	•81	7	•.993
1966—Spokane		P.C.	1B	38	144	18	40	5	2	3	19	.278	326	33	2	.994
1966—Los Angeles		Nat.	1B	3	2	0	0	0	0	0	0	.000	2	0	0	1.000
1967—Spokane		P.C.	•1B-OF	135	442	41	111	18	4	5	45	.251	999	82	1	•.999
1968—Spokane		P.C.	1B	132	439	57	121	26	4	6	64	.276	1081	75	4	•.997
1969—Spokane		P.C.	1-OF-3	91	225	33	66	10	2	3	28	.293	625	53	3	.996
1969—Los Angeles		Nat.	1B	16	48	2	13	0	0	0	4	.271	130	19	1	.993
1970—Spokane†		P.C.	1B	90	310	51	100	21	5	7	56	.323	768	57	8	.990
1971—Spokane‡		P.C.	1B	•145	540	•117	•190	•46	5	19	103	•.352	•1280	•114	3	•.998
1972—Philadelphia		Nat.	1B-OF	134	381	40	99	16	2	4	38	.260	648	38	6	.991
1973—Philadelphia		Nat.	1B	106	247	31	65	11	0	5	29	.263	527	43	1	.998
1974—Philadelphia		Nat.	1B-OF	96	208	32	50	6	3	4	33	.240	285	15	2	.993
1975—Philadelphia		Nat.	1B-OF	113	165	24	41	6	0	3	24	.248	316	33	3	.991
1976—Philadelphia		Nat.	1B-OF	95	124	15	25	5	1	1	13	.202	294	28	0	1.000
1977—Philadelphia§		Nat.	1B-OF	107	81	12	25	3	0	2	11	.309	143	15	1	.994
1978—Toronto x		Amer.	OF-1B	64	173	19	44	9	0	2	9	.254	123	4	1	.992
1978—Montreal		Nat.	1B-OF	39	59	4	12	3	0	0	5	.203	102	3	0	1.000
1979—Montreal		Nat.	1B-OF	86	83	14	21	2	1	1	13	.253	89	11	0	1.000
1980—Montreal		Nat.	1B-OF	62	55	2	12	2	0	0	5	.218	20	1	0	1.000
National League Totals				857	1453	176	363	54	7	20	175	.250	2556	206	14	.995
American League Totals				64	173	19	44	9	0	2	9	.254	123	4	1	.992
Major League Totals				921	1626	195	407	63	7	22	184	.250	2679	210	15	.995

Signed as free agent by Los Angeles Dodgers' organization, November 20, 1964.

†On disabled list, June 12 to August 1, 1970.

‡Traded by Los Angeles Dodgers to Philadelphia Phillies for Outfielder Larry Hisle and cash, October 22, 1971.

§Sold to Toronto Blue Jays, December 8, 1977.

xTraded to Montreal Expos for future considerations, July 20, 1978.

Year	Club	League	Pos.	G.	AB.	R.	H.	2B.	3B.	HR.	RBI.	B.A.	PO.	A.	E.	F.A.
1976—Philadelphia	......Nat.		PH	1	1	0	0	0	0	0	0	.000	0	0	0	.000
1977—Philadelphia	......Nat.		1B-PH	3	3	0	0	0	0	0	0	.000	5	0	0	1.000
Championship Series Totals				4	4	0	0	0	0	0	0	.000	5	0	0	1.000

RECORD AS PITCHER

Year	Club	League	G.	IP.	W.	L.	Pct.	H.	R.	ER.	SO.	BB.	ERA.
1968—Spokane	.....P. Coast		1	2	0	0	.000	2	1	0	0	0	0.00
1980—Montreal	.....National		1	1	0	0	.000	3	3	3	1	1	27.00

DANE CHARLES IORG
Name pronounced Orj.

Born May 11, 1950, at Eureka, Calif.
Height, 6.00. Weight, 180.
Throws right and bats lefthanded.
Attended Brigham Young University, Provo, Utah.
Brother of Garth Iorg, second baseman with Toronto Blue Jays and
Lee Iorg, former outfielder with New York Mets' organization.
Named Most Valuable Player in Northwest League in 1971.

Year	Club	League	Pos.	G.	AB.	R.	H.	2B.	3B.	HR.	RBI.	B.A.	PO.	A.	E.	F.A.
1971—Walla Walla	.......Northw.		OF	77	275	64	101	•15	6	7	65	*.367	135	10	6	.960
1972—Reading	............East.		OF	15	43	2	6	2	0	0	1	.140	18	0	1	.947
1972—Burlington	........Carol.		OF	92	324	61	104	20	3	8	37	.321	119	5	5	.961
1973—Reading	............East.		OF	116	386	64	119	21	6	7	49	.308	149	8	5	.969
1974—Toledo	...............Int.		*1B-OF	133	444	53	110	19	3	10	59	.248	947	*91	9	.991
1975—Toledo	...............Int.		1B-3B	13	36	7	7	2	0	0	2	.194	76	2	0	1.000
1975—Reading	............East.		1B	97	319	47	88	19	5	6	59	.276	827	44	9	.990
1976—Oklahoma City	..A. A.		1B-OF-C	120	396	65	129	25	11	11	68	.326	741	68	11	.987
1977—Okla. City-N.O.	..A.A.		OF-1B-3	75	273	47	90	14	4	9	48	.330	246	20	6	.978
1977—Phil.†-St.L.	........Nat.		1B-OF	42	62	5	15	2	0	0	6	.242	71	4	2	.974
1978—Springfield	........Int.		1B-OF-3	89	345	73	128	20	0	24	87	*.371	643	64	12	.983
1978—St. Louis	...........Nat.		OF	35	85	6	23	4	1	0	4	.271	33	5	0	1.000
1979—St. Louis	..........Nat.		OF-1B	79	179	12	52	11	1	1	21	.291	121	7	2	.985
1980—St. Louis	..........Nat.		OF-1B	105	251	33	76	23	1	3	36	.303	133	2	1	.993
Major League Totals				261	577	56	166	40	3	4	67	.288	358	18	5	.987

Selected by Kansas City Royals' organization in 13th round of free-agent draft, June 7, 1968.
Selected by Philadelphia Phillies' organization in secondary phase of free-agent draft, June 8, 1971.
†Traded with Outfielder Rick Bosetti and Pitcher Tom Underwood to St. Louis Cardinals for Outfielder Bake McBride and Pitcher Steve Waterbury, June 15, 1977.

PITCHING RECORD

Year	Club	League	G.	IP.	W.	L.	Pct.	H.	R.	ER.	SO.	BB.	ERA.
1972—Burlington	...........Carolina		1	1	0	0	.000	3	3	3	0	1	27.00

GARTH RAY IORG
Name pronounced Orj.

Born October 12, 1954, at Arcata, Calif.
Height, 5.11. Weight, 165.
Throws and bats righthanded.
Hobbies—Hunting and fishing.
Attended College of the Redwoods, Eureka, Calif.
Brother of Dane Iorg, first baseman-outfielder with St. Louis Cardinals, and Lee Iorg,
former outfielder with New York Mets' organization.

Year	Club	League	Pos.	G.	AB.	R.	H.	2B.	3B.	HR.	RBI.	B.A.	PO.	A.	E.	F.A.
1973—Johnson City	.....Appal.		SS-2B	51	169	20	40	3	0	3	13	.237	88	120	20	.912
1974—Ft. Lauderdale	..Fla. St.		SS-2-3	102	325	30	70	11	4	0	38	.215	134	245	28	.931
1975—Ft. Lauderdale	..Fla. St.		3-2-O-S	50	186	10	47	4	2	0	16	.253	67	78	11	.929
1975—West Haven	.......East.		Inf.	76	236	19	59	6	2	0	21	.250		246	35	.970
1976—West Haven†	.....East.		2B	78	273	31	75	17	1	1	24	.275	172	236	18	.958
1977—Charleston‡	.......Int.		2B-SS	70	262	35	77	8	3	1	34	.294	158	234	18	.956
1978—Syracuse§	.........Int.		3B-2B-SS	89	324	29	70	16	2	6	25	.216	141	204	11	.969
1978—Toronto	............Amer.		2B	19	49	3	8	0	0	0	3	.163	34	51	3	.966
1979—Syracuse	..........Int.		2-3-S-O	121	430	65	121	23	4	5	39	.281	150	250	20	.952
1980—Syracuse	..........Int.		2B-3B	32	134	17	40	6	3	1	14	.299	60	99	4	.975
1980—Toronto	............Amer.		2-3-O-1-S	80	222	24	55	10	1	2	14	.248	122	155	3	.989
Major League Totals				99	271	27	63	10	1	2	17	.232	156	206	6	.984

Selected by New York Yankees' organization in 8th round of free-agent draft, June 5, 1973.
†Selected by Toronto Blue Jays from New York Yankees in American League expansion draft, November 5, 1976.
‡On disabled list, June 29 to September 1, 1977.
§On disabled list, June 18 to June 28, 1978.

TIMOTHY NEAL IRELAND
(Tim)

Born March 14, 1953, at Oakland, Calif.
Height, 6.00. Weight, 180.
Throws right and bats left and righthanded.
Attended Chabot College, Hayward, Calif.

Led New York-Pennsylvania League second basemen in double plays with 41 in 1973.
Tied for American Association lead in errors by second basemen with 19 in 1979.

Year Club League	Pos.	G.	AB.	R.	H.	2B.	3B.	HR.	RBI.	B.A.	PO.	A.	E.	F.A.
1973–Jamestown ....NYP	2B	69	269	43	77	10	3	1	26	.286	*169	167	14	.960
1974–West Palm B.....Fla. St.	2B	92	337	51	82	11	1	1	33	.243	219	231	17	.964
1974–Quebec City......East.	2B	40	99	16	22	4	1	0	5	.222	71	89	6	.964
1975–Que. C†-TR‡§....East.	2B	42	118	14	23	5	1	0	7	.195	88	102	4	.979
1975–Miami xy.........Fla. St.	2B	41	139	28	33	5	1	0	13	.237	80	123	11	.949
1976–Pompano Beach Fla. St.	2B	126	402	56	98	10	3	3	39	.244	252	309	20	.966
1977–Pompano B z.....Fla. St.	2B	9	11	4	2	0	0	0	0	.182	13	8	0	1.000
1977–Jacksonville......South.	2-3-S	48	155	19	38	5	1	0	11	.245	50	94	6	.960
1978–Jacksonville......South.	3B-2B	66	250	35	62	10	4	2	31	.248	116	162	15	.949
1978–Omaha.............A.A.	2B	62	193	29	52	7	1	4	27	.269	156	207	11	.971
1979–Omaha.............A.A.	2-3-S	109	370	53	97	16	1	5	33	.262	233	299	20	.964
1980–Omaha.............A.A.	2-S-3-O	126	450	70	133	*32	2	12	63	.296	270	389	21	.969

Selected by Montreal Expos' organization in 25th round of free-agent draft, June 5, 1973.
†Released, April 30, 1975; signed by Cincinnati Reds' organization, May 1, 1975.
‡On disabled list, May 15 to June 15, 1975.
§Released, July 7, 1975; signed by Baltimore Orioles' organization, July 15, 1975.
xReleased, October 24, 1975; signed by Milwaukee Brewers' organization, March 20, 1976.
ySold to Chicago Cubs' organization, April 8, 1976.
zReleased, May 25, 1977; signed by Kansas City Royals' organization, May 27, 1977.

ORLANDO ISALES (PIZARRO)
Name pronounced ee-SAHL-ess.

Born December 22, 1959, at Santurce, Puerto Rico
Height, 5.09. Weight, 175
Throws and bats righthanded.

Year Club League	Pos.	G.	AB.	R.	H.	2B.	3B.	HR.	RBI.	B.A.	PO.	A.	E.	F.A.
1975–Auburn ....NYP	OF	43	111	17	23	1	2	0	9	.207	49	5	10	.844
1976–Spartanburg......W. Car.	OF	121	439	47	111	19	0	2	47	.253	202	*19	*21	.913
1977–Peninsula..........Carol.	OF	127	445	70	107	17	4	9	46	.240	235	*24	10	.963
1978–Reading ....East.	OF	112	383	53	101	22	3	7	48	.264	226	11	13	.948
1979–Oklahoma City..A. A.	OF	95	303	45	83	17	8	3	35	.274	169	6	*13	.931
1980–Oklahoma City†.A. A.	OF	94	336	43	88	19	2	8	51	.262	192	12	10	.953
1980–Philadelphia.......Nat.	OF	3	5	1	2	0	1	0	3	.400	3	0	0	1.000
Major League Totals		3	5	1	2	0	1	0	3	.400	3	0	0	1.000

Signed as free agent by Philadelphia Phillies' organization, February 4, 1975.
†On disabled list, June 7 to June 30, 1980.

MICHAEL WILSON IVIE
(Mike)

Born August 8, 1952, at Atlanta, Ga.
Height, 6.04. Weight, 215.
Throws and bats righthanded.
Hobbies—Hunting and fishing.

Tied major league records for most home runs with bases filled, season, pinch-hitter (2), 1978; most two-base hits, inning (2), May 30, 1977 (seventh inning).
Tied National League record for most two-base hits, doubleheader (5), May 30, 1977.
Led Northwest League in passed balls with 18 in 1970.
Received reported $80,000 bonus to sign with San Diego Padres, 1970.

Year Club League	Pos.	G.	AB.	R.	H.	2B.	3B.	HR.	RBI.	B.A.	PO.	A.	E.	F.A.
1970–Tri-City.............Northw.	*C-O	56	198	29	51	10	0	3	25	.258	*419	4	*15	.968
1971–Lodi ....Calif.	*C-3-1	102	367	69	112	22	2	15	62	.305	685	*83	22	.972
1971–San Diego..........Nat.	C	6	17	0	8	0	0	0	3	.471	22	2	0	1.000
1972–Alexandria ....Tex.	*1B-3B	133	461	81	134	23	1	24	77	.291	1013	*86	*18	.984
1973–Hawaii†............P. Coast	1B	59	226	33	61	8	3	5	21	.270	446	19	7	.985
1974–Alexandria ....Tex.	1-O-3	108	397	57	116	16	1	18	68	.292	586	45	18	.972
1974–San Diego.........Nat.	1B	12	34	1	3	0	0	1	3	.088	67	5	1	.986
1975–San Diego‡.......Nat.	1-3-C	111	377	36	94	16	2	8	46	.249	540	138	23	.967
1976–San Diego.........Nat.	1-C-3	140	405	51	118	19	5	7	70	.291	1032	71	7	.994
1977–San Diego§x ......Nat.	1B-3B	134	489	66	133	29	2	9	66	.272	886	93	11	.989
1978–San Francisco ...Nat.	1B-OF	117	318	34	98	14	3	11	55	.308	579	18	15	.975
1979–San Francisco ...Nat.	1-O-3-2	133	402	58	115	18	3	27	89	.286	752	47	4	.995
1980–San Fran. yz .....Nat.	1B	79	286	21	69	16	1	4	25	.241	669	32	5	.993
Major League Totals		732	2328	267	638	112	16	67	357	.274	4547	406	66	.987

Selected by San Diego Padres' organization in 1st round (first player selected) of free-agent draft, June 4, 1970.

†On suspended list, June 14 through remainder of season.

‡On supplemental disabled list, August 17 to September 1, 1975.
§On suspended list, May 2 to May 3, 1977.
xTraded to San Francisco Giants for Infielder Derrel Thomas, February 28, 1978.
yOn supplemental disabled list, June 3 to June 20, 1980.
zOn suspended list, June 25, 1980; transferred to disqualified list, June 27 to July 14, 1980.

DARRELL PRESTON JACKSON

Born April 3, 1956, at Los Angeles, Calif.
Height, 5.10. Weight, 143.
Throws and bats lefthanded.
Attended Arizona State University, Tempe, Ariz.

Year Club	League	G.	IP.	W.	L.	Pct.	H.	R.	ER.	SO.	BB.	ERA.
1978—Orlando	Southern	10	75	4	3	.571	52	19	15	68	32	1.80
1978—Minnesota	American	19	92	4	6	.400	89	53	46	54	48	4.50
1979—Toledo	Int'national	14	89	6	5	.545	80	41	36	78	40	3.64
1979—Minnesota	American	24	69	4	4	.500	89	36	33	43	26	4.30
1980—Minnesota	American	32	172	9	9	.500	161	81	74	90	69	3.87
Major League Totals		75	333	17	19	.472	339	170	153	187	143	4.14

Selected by Minnesota Twins' organization in 6th round of free-agent draft, June 5, 1973.
Selected by Minnesota Twins' organization in 9th round of free-agent draft, June 7, 1977.

GRANT DWIGHT JACKSON

Born September 28, 1942, at Fostoria, O.
Height, 6.00. Weight, 204.
Throws and bats lefthanded.
Hobbies—Listening to records and working on cars.
Attended Bowling Green State University, Bowling Green, O.

Tied major league record for most consecutive games won by relief pitcher, three consecutive games (3), September 29 and 30, and October 1, 1974.

Major League saves: 1965 (0), 1966 (0), 1967 (1), 1968 (1), 1969 (1), 1970 (0), 1971 (0), 1972 (8), 1973 (9), 1974 (12), 1975 (7), 1976 (4), 1977 (4), 1978 (5), 1979 (14), 1980 (9). Total—75.

Tied for Northwest League lead in wild pitches with 21 in 1964.

Year Club	League	G.	IP.	W.	L.	Pct.	H.	R.	ER.	SO.	BB.	ERA.
1962—Bakersfield	California	29	98	4	5	.444	92	75	63	86	71	5.79
1963—Bakersfield	California	28	176	12	8	.600	164	100	76	159	87	3.89
1964—Chattanooga	Southern	4	14	0	3	.000	19	19	15	17	8	9.64
1964—Eugene	Northwest	20	134	8	9	.471	126	65	55	162	85	3.69
1965—Arkansas	P. Coast	32	155	9	11	.450	151	80	68	158	60	3.95
1965—Philadelphia	National	6	14	1	1	.500	17	11	11	15	5	7.07
1966—Philadelphia	National	2	2	0	0	.000	2	1	1	0	3	4.50
1966—San Diego	P. Coast	23	134	10	8	.556	126	64	59	132	58	3.96
1967—Philadelphia	National	43	84	2	3	.400	86	40	36	83	43	3.86
1968—Philadelphia	National	33	61	1	6	.143	59	28	20	49	20	2.95
1969—Philadelphia	National	38	253	14	18	.438	237	114	94	180	92	3.34
1970—Philadelphia†	National	32	150	5	15	.250	170	94	88	104	61	5.28
1971—Baltimore	American	29	78	4	3	.571	72	31	27	51	20	3.12
1972—Baltimore	American	32	41	1	1	.500	33	14	12	34	9	2.63
1973—Baltimore	American	45	80	8	0	1.000	54	18	17	47	24	1.91
1974—Baltimore	American	49	67	6	4	.600	48	19	19	56	22	2.55
1975—Baltimore	American	41	48	4	3	.571	42	18	18	39	21	3.38
1976—Baltimore‡	American	13	19	1	1	.500	19	11	11	14	9	5.21
1976—New York§	American	21	59	6	0	1.000	38	11	11	25	16	1.68
1977—Pittsburgh	National	49	91	5	3	.625	81	44	39	41	39	3.86
1978—Pittsburgh	National	60	77	7	5	.583	89	32	28	45	32	3.27
1979—Pittsburgh	National	72	82	8	5	.615	67	32	27	39	35	2.96
1980—Pittsburgh	National	61	71	8	4	.667	71	24	23	31	20	2.92
National League Totals		396	885	51	60	.459	879	420	367	587	350	3.73
American League Totals		230	392	30	12	.714	306	122	115	266	121	2.64
Major League Totals		626	1277	81	72	.529	1185	542	482	853	471	3.40

Signed as free-agent by Philadelphia Phillies' organization, November 24, 1961.
†Traded with Outfielder Jim Hutto and Outfielder Sam Parrilla (latter two assigned to Rochester) to Baltimore Orioles for Outfielder Roger Freed, December 16, 1970.
‡Traded with Pitchers Ken Holtzman and Doyle Alexander, Catcher Ellie Hendricks, and Pitcher Jimmy Freeman (latter assigned to Syracuse), to New New York Yankees for Pitchers Rudy May, Tippy Martinez, Dave Pagan and Scott McGregor and Catcher Rick Dempsey, June 15, 1976.
§Selected by Seattle Mariners in American League expansion draft, November 5, 1976; traded to Pittsburgh Pirates for Infielders Craig Reynolds and Jim Sexton, December 7, 1976.

CHAMPIONSHIP SERIES RECORD

Tied Championship Series record for most clubs, total Series (3).

Year Club	League	G.	IP.	W.	L.	Pct.	H.	R.	ER.	SO.	BB.	ERA.
1973—Baltimore	American	2	3	1	0	1.000	0	0	0	0	1	0.00
1974—Baltimore	American	1	⅓	0	0	.000	1	2	0	1	0	0.00
1976—New York	American	2	3⅓	0	0	.000	4	3	3	3	1	8.10
1979—Pittsburgh	National	2	2	1	0	1.000	1	0	0	2	1	0.00
Championship Series Totals		7	8⅔	2	0	1.000	6	5	3	6	3	3.12

Tied World Series record for most clubs, total Series (3).

Year	Club	League	G.	IP.	W.	L.	Pct.	H.	R.	ER.	SO.	BB.	ERA.
1971–Baltimore	..........................American	1	⅔	0	0	.000	0	0	0	0	1	0.00
1976–New York	..........................American	1	3⅔	0	0	.000	4	2	2	3	0	4.91
1979–Pittsburgh	..........................National	4	4⅔	1	0	1.000	1	0	0	2	2	0.00
World Series Totals	....	6	9	1	0	1.000	5	2	2	5	3	2.00

ALL-STAR GAME RECORD

Member of 1969 National League All-Star Team; did not play.

REGINALD MARTINEZ JACKSON
(Reggie)

Born May 18, 1946, at Wyncote, Pa.
Height, 6.00. Weight, 206.
Throws and bats lefthanded.
Hobby–Cars.
Attended Arizona State University, Tempe, Ariz.

Established major league records for most strikeouts by lefthanded batter, season (171), 1968; most consecutive years, 100 or more strikeouts (13).

Tied major league records for most consecutive years leading league in strikeouts (4), 1968 through 1971; most strikeouts, nine-inning game (5), September 27, 1968; most years, 100 or more strikeouts (12).

Established American League record for most strikeouts, career (1,728).

Tied American League records for most times, four or more strikeouts, game, season (5), April 7 (second game)–April 21–May 18–June 4–September 21 (first game), 1971; most consecutive games, one or more home runs (6), July 18-23, 1976; most seasons leading league, errors, outfielder (5), 1968-70-72-75-76; fewest errors, season, for leader in most errors (9), 1972.

Major League stolen bases: 1967 (1), 1968 (14), 1969 (13), 1970 (26), 1971 (16), 1972 (9), 1973 (22), 1974 (25), 1975 (17), 1976 (28), 1977 (17), 1978 (14), 1979 (9), 1980 (1). Total–212.

Hit three home runs in a game, July 2, 1969.

Hit home runs in all 12 parks, 1975.

Led American League batters in strikeouts with 171 in 1968, 142 in 1969, 135 in 1970, 161 in 1971 and tied for lead with 133 in 1978.

Led American League in slugging percentage with .608 in 1969, .531 in 1973 and .502 in 1976.

Tied for American League lead in double plays by outfielders with 5 in 1972.

Led Southern League in total bases with 232 in 1967.

Named College Player of the Year by THE SPORTING NEWS, 1966.

Named Major League Player of the Year by THE SPORTING NEWS, 1973.

Named American League Player of the Year by THE SPORTING NEWS, 1973.

Named American League Most Valuable Player, 1973.

Named outfielder on THE SPORTING NEWS American League All-Star Team, 1969, 1973, 1975, 1976 and 1980.

Named as outfielder on THE SPORTING NEWS American League Silver Bat team, 1980.

Named Southern League Player of the Year in 1967.

Received reported $90,000 bonus to sign with Kansas City Athletics, 1966.

Year	Club	League	Pos.	G.	AB.	R.	H.	2B.	3B.	HR.	RBI.	B.A.	PO.	A.	E.	F.A.
1966–Lewiston	..........Northw.		OF	12	48	14	14	3	2	2	11	.292	23	0	1	.958
1966–Modesto	............Calif.		OF	56	221	50	66	6	0	21	60	.299	108	3	9	.925
1967–Birmingham	......South.		OF	114	413	•84	121	26	•17	17	58	.293	228	3	•18	.928
1967–Kansas City	.......Amer.		OF	35	118	13	21	4	4	1	6	.178	55	1	4	.933
1968–Oakland	...........Amer.		OF	154	553	82	138	13	6	29	74	.250	269	14	•12	.959
1969–Oakland	...........Amer.		OF	152	549	•123	151	36	3	47	118	.275	278	14	11	.964
1970–Oakland	...........Amer.		OF	149	426	57	101	21	2	23	66	.237	251	8	•12	.956
1971–Oakland	...........Amer.		OF	150	567	87	157	29	3	32	80	.277	285	15	7	.977
1972–Oakland†	..........Amer.		OF	135	499	72	132	25	2	25	75	.265	301	5	•9	.971
1973–Oakland	...........Amer.		OF	151	539	•99	158	28	2	•32	•117	.293	302	4	9	.971
1974–Oakland	...........Amer.		OF	148	506	90	146	25	1	29	93	.289	296	8	10	.968
1975–Oakland‡	..........Amer.		OF	157	593	91	150	39	3	•36	104	.253	315	13	•12	.965
1976–Baltimore§	.......Amer.		OF	134	498	84	138	27	2	27	91	.277	284	8	•11	.964
1977–New York	.........Amer.		OF	146	525	93	150	39	2	32	110	.286	236	7	13	.949
1978–New York	........Amer.		OF	139	511	82	140	13	5	27	97	.274	212	6	3	.986
1979–New York x	........Amer.		OF	131	465	78	138	24	2	29	89	.297	274	7	4	.986
1980–New York	........Amer.		OF	143	514	94	154	22	4	•41	111	.300	174	3	7	.962
Major League Totals	....			1924	6863	1145	1874	345	41	410	1231	.273	3532	113	124	.967

Selected by Kansas City A's organization in 1st round (second player selected) of free-agent draft, June 13, 1966.

†On supplemental disabled list, August 10 through August 25, 1972.

‡Traded with Pitchers Ken Holtzman and Bill Van Bommel to Baltimore Orioles for Outfielder Don Baylor and Pitchers Mike Torrez and Paul Mitchell, April 2, 1976.

§On disqualified list, April 9 to May 2, 1976. Played out option year and granted free agency, November 1, 1976; signed as free agent with New York Yankees, November 29, 1976.

xOn supplemental disabled list, June 3 to June 27, 1979.

CHAMPIONSHIP SERIES RECORD

Established Championship Series records for most Series played (8); most series, one or more hits (8); most strikeouts, total Series (27); most Series played all games (8); most games, total Series (32); most at bats, total Series (115); most runs batted in, total Series (15); most times, stealing home, game (1), October 12, 1972.

Tied Championship Series records for most times on winning club (5); most times reached first base safely, game (5), October 3, 1978.

Established American League Championship Series records for most hits, total Series (30); most one-base hits, total Series (20); highest batting average, four-game Series (.462), 1978; most runs batted in, four-game Series (6), 1978.

Tied American League Championship Series records for most Series, one or more home runs (3); most home runs, three-game Series (2), 1971; most total bases, three-game Series (11), 1971; highest slugging average, three-game Series (.917), 1971; most strikeouts, five-game Series (6), 1972 and 1973; most bases on balls, four-game Series (5), 1974.

Year	Club	League	Pos.	G.	AB.	R.	H.	2B.	3B.	HR.	RBI.	B.A.	PO.	A.	E.	F.A.
1971—Oakland		Amer.	OF	3	12	2	4	1	0	2	2	.333	9	1	0	1.000
1972—Oakland		Amer.	OF	5	18	1	5	1	0	0	2	.278	14	0	1	.933
1973—Oakland		Amer.	OF	5	21	0	3	0	0	0	0	.143	19	0	0	1.000
1974—Oakland		Amer.	DH-OF	4	12	0	2	1	0	0	1	.167	0	0	0	.000
1975—Oakland		Amer.	OF	3	12	1	5	0	0	1	3	.417	5	1	0	1.000
1977—New York		Amer.	O-D-PH	5	16	1	2	0	0	1	1	.125	10	1	0	1.000
1978—New York		Amer.	DH-OF	4	13	5	6	1	0	2	6	.462	4	0	0	1.000
1980—New York		Amer.	OF	3	11	1	3	1	0	0	0	.273	5	0	0	1.000
Championship Series Totals				32	115	11	30	5	0	5	15	.261	66	3	1	.986

WORLD SERIES RECORD

Established World Series records for most home runs, two consecutive Series, two consecutive years (7), 1977 and 1978; highest slugging percentage, six-game Series (1.250), 1977; most home runs, Series (5), 1977; most total bases, Series (25), 1977; most runs, Series (10), 1977; most long hits, six-game Series (6), 1977 (tied record for any length Series); most extra bases on long hits, Series (16), 1977; most home runs, three consecutive games, one Series (5), 1977; most home runs, two consecutive games, Series (4), October 16 and 18, 1977; most consecutive home runs, two consecutive games (4), October 16 and 18, 1977; most home runs, four consecutive games, one in each game (6); highest slugging average, total Series, 20 or more games (.767).

Tied World Series records for most home runs, game (3), October 18, 1977 (consecutive, each on first pitch); most hits game (4), October 14, 1973; most home runs, two consecutive innings (2), October 18, 1977 (fourth and fifth inning); most total bases, game (12), October 18, 1977; most runs, game (4), October 18, 1977; most consecutive games, one or more runs batted in (6); one or more hits, each game, six-game Series, 1978.

Year	Club	League	Pos.	G.	AB.	R.	H.	2B.	3B.	HR.	RBI.	B.A.	PO.	A.	E.	F.A.
1973—Oakland		Amer.	OF	7	29	3	9	3	1	1	6	.310	17	0	0	1.000
1974—Oakland		Amer.	OF	5	14	3	4	1	0	1	1	.286	6	1	1	.875
1977—New York		Amer.	OF	6	20	10	9	1	0	5	8	.450	9	0	0	1.000
1978—New York		Amer.	DH	6	23	2	9	1	0	2	8	.391	0	0	0	.000
World Series Totals				24	86	18	31	6	1	9	23	.360	32	1	1	.971

ALL-STAR GAME RECORD

Tied All-Star Game record for most home runs by pinch-hitter, game (1), July 13, 1971.

Year	League	Pos.	AB.	R.	H.	2B.	3B.	HR.	RBI.	B.A.	PO.	A.	E.	F.A.
1969—American		OF	2	0	0	0	0	0	0	.000	2	0	0	1.000
1971—American		PH	1	1	1	0	0	1	2	1.000	0	0	0	.000
1972—American		OF	4	0	2	1	0	0	0	.500	5	0	0	1.000
1973—American		OF	4	1	1	1	0	0	0	.250	0	0	0	.000
1974—American		OF	3	0	0	0	0	0	0	.000	3	0	0	1.000
1975—American		OF	3	0	1	0	0	0	0	.333	2	0	0	1.000
1977—American		OF	2	0	1	0	0	0	0	.500	0	0	0	.000
1979—American		PH-OF	1	0	0	0	0	0	0	.000	0	0	0	.000
1980—American		OF	2	0	1	0	0	0	0	.500	0	0	0	.000
All-Star Game Totals			22	2	7	2	0	1	2	.318	12	0	0	1.000

Named to American League All-Star Team for 1978 game; replaced due to injury by Graig Nettles.

RONNIE DAMIEN JACKSON
(Ron)

Born May 9, 1953, at Birmingham, Ala.
Height, 6.00. Weight, 217.
Throws and bats righthanded.
Attended Lawson State Junior College, Birmingham, Ala.
Brother of Lawrence Jackson, outfielder in Chicago White Sox'
organization, 1968 and 1969.

Led Pacific Coast League third basemen in double plays with 31 in 1975.
Led Pioneer League third basemen in double plays with 8 in 1971.
Tied for Texas League lead in double plays by third basemen with 26 in 1973.
Led American League first basemen in putouts with 1,447, in assists with 137 and in double plays with 175 in 1979.

Year	Club	League	Pos.	G.	AB.	R.	H.	2B.	3B.	HR.	RBI.	B.A.	PO.	A.	E.	F.A.
1971—Idaho Falls		Pion.	3B	•70	260	36	54	8	0	1	22	.208	•60	•111	•32	.842
1972—Quad Cities		Midw.	•3B-SS	•126	•489	62	134	•29	7	12	73	.274	•116	243	30	.923
1973—El Paso		Texas	•3B-SS	136	481	75	128	31	4	7	68	.266	•120	252	•36	.912
1974—El Paso		Texas	3B	133	519	84	170	36	8	11	74	.328	82	257	•33	.911
1975—Salt Lake City	...P.C.		•3-OF-1	•144	513	82	144	24	5	9	85	.281	•189	•269	•26	.946
1975—California		Amer.	OF-3B	13	39	2	9	2	0	0	2	.231	19	4	2	.920
1976—Salt Lake City	...P.C.		3B	10	33	9	12	2	0	2	10	.364	14	18	2	.941
1976—California		Amer.	3-2-OF	127	410	44	93	18	3	8	40	.227	91	225	16	.952

Year	Club	League	Pos.	G.	AB.	R.	H.	2B.	3B.	HR.	RBI.	B.A.	PO.	A.	E.	F.A.
1977—California	Amer.	1-3-O-S	106	292	38	71	15	2	8	28	.243	314	75	6	.985
1978—California†‡	Amer.	1-3B-OF	105	387	49	115	18	6	6	57	.297	606	88	8	.989
1979—Minnesota	Amer.	1-3-S-O	159	583	85	158	40	5	14	68	.271	1448	140	9	.994
1980—Minnesota	Amer.	1-OF-3	131	396	48	105	29	3	5	42	.265	1000	74	10	.991
Major League Totals			641	2107	266	551	122	19	41	237	.262	3478	606	51	.988

Selected by California Angels' organization in 2nd round of free-agent draft, June 8, 1971.

†On supplemental disabled list, July 31 to September 1, 1978.

‡Traded with Catcher Danny Goodwin to Minnesota Twins for Outfielder Dan Ford, December 4, 1978.

ROY LEE JACKSON

Born May 1, 1954, at Opelika, Ala.
Height, 6.02. Weight, 195.
Throws and bats righthanded.
Attended Tuskegee Institute, Tuskegee, Ala.

Year	Club	League	G.	IP.	W.	L.	Pct.	H.	R.	ER.	SO.	BB.	ERA.
1975—Marion	Appal.		8	50	4	2	.667	35	10	8	35	14	1.44
1975—Wausau	Midwest		5	38	1	3	.250	29	12	10	35	7	2.37
1976—Lynchburg	Carolina		7	55	2	3	.400	51	26	21	19	15	3.44
1976—Jackson	Texas		20	132	8	6	.571	136	51	44	82	39	3.00
1977—Tidewater	Int'national		28	168	13	7	.650	174	78	69	110	73	3.70
1977—New York	National		4	24	0	2	.000	25	16	16	13	15	6.00
1978—Tidewater	Int'national		27	176	11	10	.524	176	91	73	132	51	3.73
1978—New York	National		4	13	0	0	.000	21	13	13	6	9	9.00
1979—Tidewater	Int'national		33	137	12	7	.632	143	63	57	89	33	3.74
1979—New York	National		8	16	1	0	1.000	11	4	4	10	5	2.25
1980—Tidewater	Int'national		22	78	3	5	.375	63	33	20	56	51	2.31
1980—New York†	National		24	71	1	7	.125	78	37	33	58	20	4.18
Major League Totals			40	124	2	9	.182	135	70	66	87	46	4.79

Selected by Houston Astros' organization in 12th round of free-agent draft, June 6, 1972.

Signed as free-agent by New York Mets' organization, June 27, 1975.

†Traded to Toronto Blue Jays for Outfielder Bob Bailor, December 12, 1980.

ROBERT HARVEY JAMES
(Bob)

Born August 15, 1958, at Glendale, Calif.
Height, 6.04. Weight, 215.
Throws and bats righthanded.

Led Florida State League in wild pitches with 19 in 1978.
Tied for American Association lead in games started with 26 in 1979.

Year	Club	League	G.	IP.	W.	L.	Pct.	H.	R.	ER.	SO.	BB.	ERA.
1976—Lethbridge	Pioneer		3	8	0	1	.000	7	8	4	11	9	4.50
1977—West Palm Beach†	Florida St.		21	100	5	5	.500	99	51	37	83	76	3.33
1978—West Palm Beach‡	Florida St.		21	127	10	7	.588	99	53	44	139	86	3.11
1978—Memphis	Southern		3	20	2	1	.667	14	5	1	25	11	0.45
1978—Montreal	National		4	4	0	1	.000	4	4	4	3	4	9.00
1979—Denver	Am. Assoc.		26	132	8	13	.381	139	•112	•98	122	•123	6.68
1979—Montreal	National		2	2	0	0	.000	2	3	3	1	3	13.50
1980—Denver§	Am. Assoc.		17	87	9	2	.818	66	42	37	79	74	3.83
Major League Totals			6	6	0	1	.000	6	7	7	4	7	10.50

Selected by Montreal Expos' organization in 1st round (ninth player selected) of free-agent draft, June 8, 1976.

†On temporary inactive list, April 13 to May 6, 1977.

‡On disabled list, April 10 to April 21, 1978.

§On disabled list, July 13 to September 1, 1980.

JESSE HARRISON JEFFERSON, JR.

Born March 3, 1950, at Midlothian, Va.
Height, 6.03. Weight, 188.
Throws and bats righthanded.
Attended John Tyler Community College, Chester, Va.

Year	Club	League	G.	IP.	W.	L.	Pct.	H.	R.	ER.	SO.	BB.	ERA.
1968—Bluefield	Ap'alachian		16	69	3	7	.300	64	65	39	99	•66	5.09
1969—Miami	Florida St.		2	7	0	0	.000	1	2	1	9	8	1.29
1969—Bluefield	Ap'alachian		10	34	0	•7	.000	29	37	31	54	51	8.21
1970—Stockton	California		26	157	8	•16	.333	129	89	64	177	•123	3.67
1971—Dallas-Fort Worth	Texas		27	172	12	11	.522	144	84	66	150	•109	3.45
1972—Asheville	Southern		11	71	5	4	.556	70	37	26	55	33	3.30
1972—Rochester	Int'national		17	103	6	3	.667	79	35	28	66	68	2.45
1973—Rochester	Int'national		10	66	6	2	.750	52	29	25	39	53	3.41
1973—Baltimore	American		18	101	6	5	.545	104	53	46	52	46	4.10
1974—Baltimore	American		20	57	1	0	1.000	55	30	23	31	38	4.42

Year Club	League	G.	IP.	W.	L.	Pct.	H.	R.	ER.	SO.	BB.	ERA.
1975—Baltimore†-Chicago ....American		26	115	5	11	.313	105	72	63	71	102	4.93
1976—Chicago‡................................American		19	62	2	5	.286	86	62	59	30	42	8.56
1977—Toronto................................American		33	217	9	17	.346	224	123	104	114	83	4.31
1978—Toronto ....American		31	212	7	16	.304	214	109	103	97	86	4.37
1979—Toronto ....American		34	116	2	10	.167	150	75	71	43	45	5.51
1980—Toronto§ ....American		29	122	4	13	.235	130	78	74	53	52	5.46
1980—Pittsburgh x........................National		1	7	1	0	1.000	3	1	1	4	2	1.29
National League Totals		1	7	1	0	1.000	3	1	1	4	2	1.29
American League Totals		210	1002	36	77	.319	1068	602	548	491	494	4.92
Major League Totals		211	1009	37	77	.325	1071	603	549	495	496	4.90

Selected by Baltimore Orioles' organization in 4th round of free-agent draft, June 7, 1968.
†Traded to Chicago White Sox for First Baseman Tony Muser, June 15, 1975.
‡Selected by Toronto Blue Jays in American League expansion draft, November 5, 1976.
§Sold on waivers to Pittsburgh Pirates, September 11, 1980.
xGranted free agency, October 22, 1980; signed by California Angels, January 26, 1981.

FERGUSON ARTHUR JENKINS
(Fergie)

Born December 13, 1943, at Chatham, Ontario, Canada.
Height, 6.05. Weight, 210.
Throws and bats righthanded.

Tied major league record for most 1-0 games lost, season (5), 1968; most years leading league in home runs allowed (5).
Led American League pitchers in complete games with 29 in 1974.
Led National League pitchers in complete games with 20 in 1967, 24 in 1970 and 30 in 1971.
Led National League pitchers in games started with 40 in 1968 and 42 in 1969; tied for lead in games started with 39 in 1971.
Won National League Cy Young Memorial Award, 1971.
Named American League Comeback Player of the Year by THE SPORTING NEWS, 1974.
Named as pitcher on THE SPORTING NEWS National League All-Star Team, 1967.
Named righthanded pitcher on THE SPORTING NEWS National League All-Star Team, 1971-72.
Named National League Pitcher of the Year by THE SPORTING NEWS, 1971.

Year Club	League	G.	IP.	W.	L.	Pct.	H.	R.	ER.	SO.	BB.	ERA.
1962—Miami ....Florida St.		11	65	7	2	.778	34	10	7	69	19	0.97
1962—Buffalo ....Int'national		3	13	1	1	.500	18	9	8	6	5	5.54
1963—Arkansas ....Int'national		4	10	0	1	.000	13	7	7	13	3	6.30
1963—Miami ....Florida St.		20	140	12	5	.706	110	66	53	135	59	3.41
1964—Chattanooga........................Southern		21	139	10	6	.625	124	61	48	149	42	3.11
1964—Arkansas ....P. Coast		11	57	5	5	.500	40	27	20	49	34	3.16
1965—Arkansas ....P. Coast		32	122	8	6	.571	104	48	40	112	42	2.95
1965—Philadelphia........................National		7	12	2	1	.667	7	3	3	10	2	2.25
1966—Philadelphia†-Chicago ....National		61	184	6	8	.429	150	77	68	150	52	3.33
1967—Chicago ....National		38	289	20	13	.606	230	101	90	236	83	2.80
1968—Chicago ....National		40	308	20	15	.571	255	96	90	260	65	2.63
1969—Chicago ....National		43	311	21	15	.583	284	122	111	*273	71	3.21
1970—Chicago ....National		40	313	22	16	.579	265	128	●118	274	60	3.39
1971—Chicago ....National		39	*325	*24	13	.649	*304	114	100	263	37	2.77
1972—Chicago ....National		36	289	20	12	.625	253	111	*103	184	62	3.21
1973—Chicago‡..............................National		38	271	14	16	.467	267	133	117	170	57	3.89
1974—Texas ....American		41	328	●25	12	.676	286	117	103	225	45	2.83
1975—Texas§ ....American		37	270	17	18	.486	261	130	118	157	56	3.93
1976—Boston ....American		30	209	12	11	.522	201	85	76	142	43	3.27
1977—Boston x..............................American		28	193	10	10	.500	190	91	79	105	36	3.68
1978—Texas ....American		34	249	18	8	.692	228	92	84	157	41	3.04
1979—Texas ....American		37	259	16	14	.533	252	127	117	164	81	4.07
1980—Texas ....American		29	198	12	12	.500	190	90	83	129	52	3.77
National League Totals...........................		342	2302	149	109	.578	2015	885	800	1820	489	3.13
American League Totals		236	1706	110	85	.564	1608	732	660	1079	354	3.48
Major League Totals		578	4008	259	194	.572	3623	1617	1460	2899	843	3.28

Signed as free agent by Philadelphia Phillies' organization, June 15, 1962.
†Traded with Outfielder Adolfo Phillips and Outfielder-First Baseman John Herrnstein to Chicago Cubs for Pitchers Bob Buhl and Larry Jackson, April 21, 1966.
‡Traded to Texas Rangers for Infielders Bill Madlock and Vic Harris, October 25, 1973.
§Traded to Boston Red Sox for Outfielder Juan Beniquez, Pitcher Steve Barr, a minor league player to be

DID YOU KNOW—

That Oakland's Rickey Henderson became just the fourth active player to get on base at least 300 times (hits-walks-hit by pitch) in 1980? Henderson was on base 301 times. Other American Leaguers are Carl Yastrzemski (315 in 1970) and Rod Carew (311 in 1977). Pete Rose is the only active National Leaguer to do it and he's accomplished the feat five times (311-1969, 301-1973, 310-1975, 307-1976 and 305-1979).

named later and an estimated $200,000, November 17, 1975; Red Sox sent Pitcher Craig Skok to Rangers, December 12, 1975, to complete deal.

xTraded to Texas Rangers for Pitcher John Poloni and cash estimated at $20,000, December 14, 1977.

ALL-STAR GAME RECORD

Tied All-Star Game record for most strikeouts, game (6), July 11, 1967.

Year League	IP.	W.	L.	Pct.	H.	R.	ER.	SO.	BB.	ERA.
1967—National	3	0	0	.000	3	1	1	6	0	3.00
1971—National	1	0	0	.000	3	2	2	0	0	18.00
All-Star Game Totals	4	0	0	.000	6	3	3	6	0	6.75

Named to National League All-Star Team for 1972 game; did not play.

THOMAS EDWARD JOHN
(Tommy)

Born May 22, 1943, at Terre Haute, Ind.
Height, 6.03. Weight, 203.
Throws left and bats righthanded.
Hobbies—Golf, fishing and reading.
Attended Indiana State College, Terre Haute, Ind.

Tied American League record for most hit batsmen, game, nine-innings (4), June 15, 1968.
Led American League in shutouts with 6 in 1980.
Tied for American League lead in shutouts with 5 in 1966 and 6 in 1967.
Tied for American League lead in wild pitches with 17 in 1970.
Named National League Comeback Player of the Year by THE SPORTING NEWS, 1976.
Named lefthanded pitcher on THE SPORTING NEWS American League All-Star Team, 1980.
Received reported $40,000 bonus to sign with Cleveland Indians, 1961.

Year—Club	League	G.	IP.	W.	L.	Pct.	H.	R.	ER.	SO.	BB.	ERA.
1961—Dubuque	Midwest	14	88	10	4	.714	74	47	31	99	59	3.17
1962—Charleston	Eastern	21	128	6	8	.429	129	67	55	114	71	3.87
1962—Jacksonville	Int'national	8	34	2	2	.500	29	20	18	27	16	4.76
1963—Charleston	Eastern	12	95	9	2	.818	85	25	17	45	12	1.61
1963—Jacksonville	Int'national	18	102	6	8	.429	115	53	40	63	39	3.53
1963—Cleveland	American	6	20	0	2	.000	23	10	5	9	6	2.25
1964—Cleveland	American	25	94	2	9	.182	97	53	41	65	35	3.93
1964—Portland†	P. Coast	13	74	6	6	.500	75	38	35	72	24	4.26
1965—Chicago	American	39	184	14	7	.667	162	67	63	126	58	3.08
1966—Chicago	American	34	223	14	11	.560	195	76	65	138	57	2.62
1967—Chicago	American	31	178	10	13	.435	143	62	49	110	47	2.48
1968—Chicago‡	American	25	177	10	5	.667	135	45	39	117	49	1.98
1969—Chicago	American	33	232	9	11	.450	230	91	84	128	90	3.26
1970—Chicago	American	37	269	12	17	.414	253	117	98	138	101	3.28
1971—Chicago§	American	38	229	13	16	.448	244	115	92	131	58	3.62
1972—Los Angeles	National	29	187	11	5	.688	172	68	60	117	40	2.89
1973—Los Angeles	National	36	218	16	7	*.696	202	88	75	116	50	3.10
1974—Los Angeles x	National	22	153	13	3	.813	133	51	44	78	42	2.59
1975—Los Angeles y	National					(Did not play)						
1976—Los Angeles	National	31	207	10	10	.500	207	76	71	91	61	3.09
1977—Los Angeles	National	31	220	20	7	.741	225	82	68	123	50	2.78
1978—Los Angeles z	National	33	213	17	10	.630	230	95	78	124	53	3.30
1979—New York	American	37	276	21	9	.700	268	109	91	111	65	2.97
1980—New York	American	36	265	22	9	.710	270	115	101	78	56	3.43
American League Totals		341	2147	127	109	.538	2020	860	728	1151	622	3.05
National League Totals		182	1198	87	42	.674	1169	460	396	649	296	2.97
Major League Totals		523	3345	214	151	.586	3189	1320	1124	1800	918	3.02

Signed as free agent by Cleveland Indians' organization, June 12, 1961.

†Traded to Chicago White Sox with Catcher John Romano and Outfielder Tommie Agee for Catcher Camilo Carreon and Outfielder Rocky Colavito, January 20, 1965, as part of three-way deal which saw White Sox obtain Colavito from Kansas City Athletics earlier same day for Outfielders Jim Landis and Mike Hershberger and a pitcher to be named later; White Sox assigned Pitcher Fred Talbot to Athletics, February 10, 1965, to complete deal.

‡On disabled list with torn ligament in left shoulder from August 22 through end of season.

§Traded with Infielder Steve Huntz (latter assigned to Spokane) to Los Angeles Dodgers for Infielder-Outfielder Richie Allen, December 2, 1971.

xOn disabled list, July 17 through remainder of season.

yOn emergency disabled list the entire season.

zGranted free agency, November 2, 1978; signed by New York Yankees, November 21, 1978.

CHAMPIONSHIP SERIES RECORD

Tied National League Championship Series record for most complete games, total Series (2).

Year—Club	League	G.	IP.	W.	L.	Pct.	H.	R.	ER.	SO.	BB.	ERA.
1977—Los Angeles	National	2	13⅔	1	0	1.000	11	5	1	11	5	0.66
1978—Los Angeles	National	1	9	1	0	1.000	4	0	0	4	2	0.00
1980—New York	American	1	6⅔	0	0	.000	8	2	2	3	1	2.70
Championship Series Totals		4	29⅓	2	0	1.000	23	7	3	18	8	0.92

WORLD SERIES RECORD

Year	Club	League	G.	IP.	W.	L.	Pct.	H.	R.	ER.	SO.	BB.	ERA.
1977—Los Angeles		National	1	6	0	1	.000	9	5	4	7	3	6.00
1978—Los Angeles		National	2	14⅔	1	0	1.000	14	8	5	6	4	3.07
World Series Totals			3	20⅔	1	1	.500	23	13	9	13	7	3.92

ALL-STAR GAME RECORD

Year	League	IP.	W.	L.	Pct.	H.	R.	ER.	SO.	BB.	ERA.
1968—American		⅔	0	0	.000	1	0	0	0	0	0.00
1980—American		2⅓	0	1	.000	4	3	3	1	0	11.57
All-Star Game Totals		3	0	1	.000	5	3	3	1	0	9.00

Member of National League All-Star Team for 1978 game; did not play.
Member of American League All-Star Team for 1979 game; did not play.

ANTHONY CLAIR JOHNSON
(Tony)

Born June 23, 1956, at Memphis, Tenn.
Height, 6.03. Weight, 195.
Throws and bats righthanded.
Attended Le Moyne-Owen College, Memphis, Tenn.

Led Southern League in stolen bases with 60 in 1980.

Year	Club	League	Pos.	G.	AB.	R.	H.	2B.	3B.	HR.	RBI.	B.A.	PO.	A.	E.	F.A.
1977—Sarasota Expos	.G.C.		OF	26	87	16	28	2	3	2	11	.322	37	1	3	.927
1977—Jamestown	NYP		OF	36	125	26	42	7	6	1	30	.336	18	3	3	.875
1978—West Palm B'ch	Fla. St.		OF	122	393	73	114	14	4	7	45	.290	129	7	6	.958
1979—Memphis	South.		OF	141	504	82	147	28	9	14	85	.292	236	15	*17	.937
1980—Memphis	South.		OF	135	511	79	153	24	7	8	89	.299	224	19	12	.953

Selected by Houston Astros' organization in 13th round of free-agent draft, June 5, 1974.
Selected by Texas Rangers' organization in secondary phase of free-agent draft, January 9, 1975.
Selected by Montreal Expos' organization in 26th round of free-agent draft, June 7, 1977.

BOBBY EARL JOHNSON
(Bob)

Born July 31, 1959, at Dallas, Tex.
Height, 6.03. Weight, 195.
Throws and bats righthanded.
Nephew of Ernie Banks, former shortstop-first
baseman with Chicago Cubs.

Tied for Midwest League lead in double plays by catchers with 9 in 1979.

Year	Club	League	Pos.	G.	AB.	R.	H.	2B.	3B.	HR.	RBI.	B.A.	PO.	A.	E.	F.A.
1977—Sara. Rangers	Gulf C.		C	36	115	10	28	7	3	0	9	.243	165	30	9	.956
1978—Asheville	W. Car.		C	76	203	23	45	12	0	4	33	.222	427	48	15	.969
1979—Wausau	Midw.		C	124	433	89	131	20	0	24	79	.303	*666	*86	*18	.977
1980—Tulsa	Texas		C	115	382	64	93	25	3	13	70	.243	520	70	16	.974
1980—Charleston	Int.		C	12	34	5	5	2	0	0	3	.147	36	1	1	.974

Selected by Texas Rangers' organization in 9th round of free-agent draft, June 7, 1977.

CLIFFORD JOHNSON, JR.
(Cliff)

Born July 22, 1947, at San Antonio, Tex.
Height, 6.04. Weight, 225.
Throws and bats righthanded.
Hobbies—Horseback riding, basketball and tennis.

DID YOU KNOW—

That Houston's J. R. Richard allowed just 105 baserunners in 114 innings last season? Richard was the only 100-inning pitcher in the majors to allow less than one man on base per inning. Dodger Don Sutton, now an Astro, was second-best with 212 runners allowed in 212 innings while the Yankee's Rudy May led the American League with 183 in 175 frames.

Brother-in-law of Mike Easler, outfielder with Pittsburgh Pirates;
Cousin of Elijah Johnson, former infielder-outfielder in Houston Astro
and Baltimore Oriole organizations.

Tied major league records for most home runs, inning (2) and most total bases, inning (8), June 30, 1977 (eighth inning).

Tied modern major league record for most long hits, inning (2), May 31, 1975 (eighth inning) and June 30, 1977 (eighth inning).

Hit three home runs in one game, vs. Toronto Blue Jays, June 30, 1977.

Led American Association in total bases with 285 in 1973.

Led American Association in passed balls with 17 in 1972 and tied for Southern League lead with 15 in 1971.

Tied for Appalachian League lead in double plays by catchers with 3 in 1967.

Led National League catchers in passed balls with 12 in 1976.

Named American Association Player of the Year, 1973.

Named Carolina League Most Valuable Player, 1970.

Year	Club	League	Pos.	G.	AB.	R.	H.	2B.	3B.	HR.	RBI.	B.A.	PO.	A.	E.	F.A.
1967—Cocoa	Fla. St.	C-O	53	156	13	41	5	1	4	20	.263	168	13	10	.948
1967—Covington	Appal.	O-C-1	36	110	21	34	7	2	5	24	.309	103	10	6	.950
1968—Cocoa	Fla. St.	*C-O-1	117	353	60	102	17	3	10	61	.289	641	55	*26	.964
1969—Peninsula	Carol.	C	103	327	37	75	16	1	11	54	.229	615	68	21	.970
1970—Raleigh-Durham	Carol.	C-O	102	343	74	114	24	0	*27	*91	.332	474	40	9	.983
1970—Oklahoma City	A. A.	C-O-1	22	55	12	21	4	1	1	5	.382	63	9	2	.973
1971—Oklahoma City	A. A.	C-1B	31	105	16	26	5	2	5	15	.248	219	20	2	.992
1971—Columbus	South.	C-1B	58	164	16	30	10	0	4	21	.183	350	35	5	.987
1972—Columbus	South.	C-3-1	42	160	28	46	11	2	10	38	.288	235	36	8	.971
1972—Oklahoma City	A. A.	●C-1B	89	313	55	88	12	5	17	59	.281	600	59	●15	.978
1972—Houston	Nat.	C	5	4	0	1	0	0	0	0	.250	6	0	0	1.000
1973—Denver	A. A.	1B	133	490	*105	148	30	4	*33	*117	.302	132	15	4	.974
1973—Houston	Nat.	1B	7	20	6	6	2	0	2	6	.300	47	2	0	1.000
1974—Houston	Nat.	C-1B	83	171	26	39	4	1	10	29	.228	270	18	4	.986
1975—Houston	Nat.	1-C-O	122	340	52	94	16	1	20	65	.276	604	38	12	.982
1976—Houston	Nat.	C-O-1	108	318	36	72	21	2	10	49	.226	468	35	9	.982
1977—Houston†	Nat.	OF-1B	51	144	22	43	8	0	10	23	.299	113	11	3	.976
1977—New York	Amer.	C-1B	56	142	24	42	8	0	12	31	.296	145	14	1	.994
1978—New York	Amer.	C-1B	76	174	20	32	9	1	6	19	.184	71	10	2	.976
1979—N.Y.‡-Cleve	Amer.	C	100	304	48	82	16	0	20	67	.270	10	1	0	1.000
1980—Cleveland§	Amer.	DH	54	174	25	40	3	1	6	28	.230	0	0	0	.000
1980—Chicago x	Nat.	1B-C	68	196	28	46	8	0	10	34	.235	469	16	4	.992
National League Totals			444	1193	170	301	59	4	62	206	.252	1977	120	32	.985
American League Totals			286	794	117	196	36	2	44	145	.247	226	25	3	.988
Major League Totals			730	1987	287	497	95	6	106	351	.250	2203	145	35	.985

Selected by Houston Astros' organization in free-agent draft, August 22, 1966.

†Traded to New York Yankees for Infielder Mike Fischlin, Pitcher Randy Niemann and a player to be named later, June 15, 1977. Fischlin and Niemann were assigned to Columbus, Ga., and Dave Bergman was assigned to Houston to complete deal, November 23, 1977.

‡Traded to Cleveland Indians for Pitcher Don Hood, June 15, 1979.

§Traded to Chicago Cubs for two players to be named later, June 23, 1980; Outfielder-First Baseman Karl Pagel and cash sent to Indians completing deal, June 30, 1980.

xTraded with Infielder Keith Drumright to Oakland A's for Pitcher Mike King, December 11, 1980.

CHAMPIONSHIP SERIES RECORD

Year	Club	League	Pos.	G.	AB.	R.	H.	2B.	3B.	HR.	RBI.	B.A.	PO.	A.	E.	F.A.
1977—New York	Amer.	DH-PH	5	15	2	6	2	0	1	2	.400	0	0	0	.000
1978—New York	Amer.	PH	1	1	0	0	0	0	0	0	.000	0	0	0	.000
Championship Series Totals			6	16	2	6	2	0	1	2	.375	0	0	0	.000

WORLD SERIES RECORD

Year	Club	League	Pos.	G.	AB.	R.	H.	2B.	3B.	HR.	RBI.	B.A.	PO.	A.	E.	F.A.
1977—New York	Amer.	PH-C	2	1	0	0	0	0	0	0	.000	0	0	0	.000
1978—New York	Amer.	PH	2	2	0	0	0	0	0	0	.000	0	0	0	.000
World Series Totals			4	3	0	0	0	0	0	0	.000	0	0	0	.000

JOHN HENRY JOHNSON

Born August 21, 1956, at Houston, Tex.
Height, 6.02. Weight, 185.
Throws and bats lefthanded.
Hobbies—Fishing and hunting

DID YOU KNOW—

That when current Baltimore coach Jimmy Williams was a manager with Leesburg of the Florida State League in 1966, he defeated Sparky Anderson's St. Petersburg team in the playoff finals? Also managing in the league that season were Billy DeMars, now a Phillies' coach and Johnny Goryl, the Minnesota manager.

Year Club	League	G.	IP.	W.	L.	Pct.	H.	R.	ER.	SO.	BB.	ERA.
1974—Great Falls ....Pioneer		14	33	2	1	.667	25	12	10	33	25	2.73
1975—Cedar Rapids ....Midwest		22	127	4	12	.250	127	72	53	89	49	3.76
1976—Cedar Rapids ....Midwest		20	131	13	2	.867	93	42	28	94	50	1.92
1977—Fresno† ....California		23	149	14	2	*.875	142	79	56	155	64	*3.38
1978—Oakland ....American		30	186	11	10	.524	164	81	70	91	82	3.39
1979—Oakland‡-Texas....................American		31	167	4	14	.222	168	95	86	96	72	4.63
1980—Charleston ....Int'national		16	77	3	9	.250	84	49	33	55	35	3.86
1980—Texas ....American		33	39	2	2	.500	27	12	10	44	15	2.31
Major League Totals................................		94	392	17	26	.395	359	188	166	231	169	3.81

Selected by San Francisco Giants' organization in 15th round of free-agent draft, June 5, 1974.

†Traded with Outfielder Gary Thomasson, Catcher Gary Alexander, Pitchers Dave Heaverlo, Alan Wirth and Phillip Huffman, a player to be named later and cash estimated at $390,000 to Oakland A's for Pitcher Vida Blue, March 15, 1978; Shortstop Mario Guerrero sent to Oakland to complete deal, April 7, 1978.

‡Traded to Texas Rangers for Third Baseman Dave Chalk and Catcher Mike Heath, June 15, 1979.

LAMAR JOHNSON SR.

Born September 2, 1950, at Bessemer, Ala.
Height, 6.02. Weight, 225.
Throws and bats righthanded.
Attended Lawson State Junior College, Birmingham, Ala.

Led Midwest League in total bases with 227 in 1972 and led American Association with 262 in 1975.
Led Gulf Coast League in sacrifice flies with 5 in 1969.
Led Midwest League first basemen in double plays with 98 in 1971 and with 78 in 1972.
Led Northern League first basemen in double plays with 44 in 1970, led Southern League with 128 in 1973 and led American Association with 107 in 1975.

Year Club	League	Pos.	G.	AB.	R.	H.	2B.	3B.	HR.	RBI.	B.A.	PO.	A.	E.	F.A.
1968—Sarasota W. Sox.Gulf C.		C-1B	20	47	9	18	2	1	2	7	.383	94	9	6	.945
1969—Sarasota W. Sox.Gulf C.		O-1-C	45	109	8	25	5	2	1	16	.229	61	1	4	.939
1970—Appleton ....Midw.		1B	7	13	0	3	0	0	0	0	.231	11	4	1	.938
1970—Duluth-Superior.North.		1B	55	221	35	71	10	2	6	44	.321	411	27	12	.973
1971—Appleton ....Midw.		1B	119	442	80	119	22	4	18	*97	.269	966	41	•19	.981
1972—Knoxville ....South.		PH	2	2	0	0	0	0	0	0	.000	0	0	0	.000
1972—Appleton ....Midw.		1B	114	402	63	126	17	3	*26	*89	.313	900	46	*18	.981
1973—Knoxville ....South.		1B	138	491	74	144	24	1	16	93	.293	*1187	*69	16	.981
1974—Iowa ....A. A.		1B	122	455	81	137	23	0	20	*96	.301	*1036	68	*20	.982
1974—Chicago.............Amer.		1B	10	29	1	10	0	0	0	2	.345	40	2	0	1.000
1975—Denver..............A. A.		1B	129	485	73	*163	*35	2	20	101	*.336	939	71	•13	.987
1975—Chicago............Amer.		1B	8	30	2	6	3	0	1	1	.200	46	2	2	.960
1976—Chicago............Amer.		1B-OF	82	222	29	71	11	1	4	33	.320	210	18	4	.983
1977—Chicago............Amer.		1B	118	374	52	113	12	5	18	65	.302	346	32	4	.990
1978—Chicago............Amer.		1B	148	498	52	136	23	2	8	72	.273	887	71	8	.992
1979—Chicago ....Amer.		1B	133	479	60	148	29	1	12	74	.309	748	63	11	.987
1980—Chicago ....Amer.		1B	147	541	51	150	26	3	13	81	.277	671	56	7	.990
Major League Totals			646	2173	247	634	104	12	56	328	.292	2948	244	36	.989

Selected by Chicago White Sox' organization in 3rd round of free-agent draft, June 7, 1968.

LARRY DOBY JOHNSON

Born August 17, 1950, at Cleveland, O.
Height, 6.00. Weight, 184.
Throws and bats righthanded.
Hobbies—Dancing and reading.
Attended Manatee Junior College, West Bradenton, Fla., and Cleveland State University, Cleveland, O.

Led Southern League catchers in double plays with 11 and tied for lead in passed balls with 15 in 1971.
Led Western Carolinas League in passed balls with 34 in 1969.
Tied for California League lead in double plays by catchers with 8 and in passed balls with 25 in 1970.
Tied for Eastern League lead in passed balls with 24 in 1972.

Year Club	League	Pos.	G.	AB.	R.	H.	2B.	3B.	HR.	RBI.	B.A.	PO.	A.	E.	F.A.
1968—Sara. Indians ....G. C.		C-3B	29	72	11	25	3	2	0	10	.347	115	19	4	.971
1969—Waterbury ....East.		C	5	15	1	3	0	0	0	1	.200	27	4	2	.939
1969—Monroe.............W. Car.		*C-3	83	249	30	67	7	0	5	37	.269	450	57	10	*.981
1969—Sara. Indians ....G. C.		C	6	16	1	4	0	0	0	6	.250	24	3	0	1.000

DID YOU KNOW—

That Mets pitcher Pete Falcone was credited with a game-winning RBI in a 1980 game but was not credited with a victory? Falcone knocked in the first run in an eight-run second inning but did not last the five innings needed to register the win.

Year Club	League	Pos.	G.	AB.	R.	H.	2B.	3B.	HR.	RBI.	B.A.	PO.	A.	E.	F.A.
1970—Reno.................Calif.		C-OF	89	293	36	76	13	5	2	31	.259	747	63	14	.983
1971—Jacksonville......South.		*C-O-1	101	312	42	76	17	3	5	27	.244	577	60	5	*.939
1972—Elmira.............East.		C-OF	115	334	33	80	16	4	7	47	.240	531	54	10	.983
1972—Cleveland..........Amer.		C	1	2	0	1	0	0	0	0	.500	4	0	0	1.000
1973—San Antonio ......Texas		O-C-2	37	127	11	36	7	2	3	14	.283	37	6	0	1.000
1973—Oklahoma City ..A. A.		C-OF	54	151	27	48	11	2	7	27	.318	156	9	2	.988
1974—Cleveland.........Amer.		PR	1	0	1	0	0	0	0	0	.000	0	0	0	.000
1974—Oklahoma City†.A. A.		C-3B	74	236	35	58	10	0	9	39	.246	243	20	9	.967
1975—Memphis..........Int.		C-O-1	108	320	33	76	10	5	4	33	.238	408	41	10	.978
1975—Montreal..........Nat.		C	1	3	0	1	1	0	0	1	.333	4	1	0	1.000
1976—Denver ....A. A.		C-1B	84	235	37	68	14	1	14	43	.289	354	51	9	.978
1976—Montreal..........Nat.		C	6	13	0	2	1	0	0	0	.154	22	2	0	1.000
1977—Denver‡............A. A.		C-OF-1B	94	280	54	78	15	5	8	38	.279	395	37	5	.989
1978—Iowa ....A. A.		C-OF-3B	112	368	44	95	13	1	13	52	.258	337	38	5	.987
1978—Chicago§..........Amer.		C	3	8	0	1	0	0	0	0	.125	5	1	1	.857
1979—Miami x............Int.Am.		....	62	224	47	71	10	4	6	40	.317	....	....	....	....
1979—Rochester ....Int.		C-O-3	40	131	14	41	4	1	3	14	.313	117	7	2	.984
1980—Rochester y ......Int.		C	26	74	11	14	3	0	4	8	.189	36	2	0	1.000
1980—Evansville ....A. A.		C-O-1	65	196	28	53	7	0	7	35	.270	240	31	3	.989
American League Totals			5	10	1	2	0	0	0	0	.200	9	1	1	.909
National League Totals			7	16	0	3	2	0	0	1	.188	26	3	0	1.000
Major League Totals.......................			12	26	1	5	2	0	0	1	.192	35	4	1	.975

Selected by Cleveland Indians' organization in 9th round of free-agent draft, June 7, 1968.
†Traded to Montreal Expos for Pitcher Mike Baldwin, January 13, 1975.
‡Granted free agency, November 2, 1977; signed by Chicago White Sox' organization, November 24, 1977.
§Sold to Miami of Inter-American League, April 6, 1979.
xSigned by Baltimore Orioles' organization after Inter-American League folded, July 13, 1979.
yTraded with Pitchers Larry Anderson and Bill Presley to Detroit Tigers' organization for Outfielder Dan Gonzales and Catcher Ed Putman, June 10, 1980.

RANDALL STUART JOHNSON
(Randy)

Born August 15, 1958, at Miami, Fla.
Height, 6.02. Weight, 195.
Throws and bats lefthanded.
Attended Miami-Dade Community College South, Miami, Fla.

Year Club	League	Pos.	G.	AB.	R.	H.	2B.	3B.	HR.	RBI.	B.A.	PO.	A.	E.	F.A.
1979—Appleton ....Midw.		OF-1B	105	339	57	89	25	5	9	46	.263	338	17	8	.978
1980—Glens Falls ....East.		OF	78	280	59	79	15	0	25	70	.282	108	10	9	.929
1980—Chicago ....Amer.		OF-1B	12	20	0	4	0	0	0	3	.200	2	0	0	1.000
1980—Iowa .................A.A.		OF	18	60	5	14	1	0	1	8	.233	19	3	1	.957
Major League Totals.......................			12	20	0	4	0	0	0	3	.200	2	0	0	1.000

Selected by Chicago White Sox' organization in 3rd round of free-agent draft, January 9, 1979.

RONALD DAVID JOHNSON
(Ron)

Born March 23, 1956, at Long Beach, Calif.
Height, 6.02. Weight, 223.
Throws and bats righthanded.
Attended Fullerton College, Fullerton, Calif.,
and Fresno State University, Fresno, Calif.

Year Club	League	Pos.	G.	AB.	R.	H.	2B.	3B.	HR.	RBI.	B.A.	PO.	A.	E.	F.A.
1978—Sarasota Royals. G. C.		1B	14	49	10	16	1	0	0	13	.327	60	4	0	1.000
1978—Ft. Myers ....Fla. St.		1B	29	78	9	18	2	1	1	10	.231	7	0	1	.875
1979—Ft. Myers ....Fla. St.		1B	116	381	47	117	19	2	8	58	.307	104	6	1	.991
1979—Jacksonville......South.		1B-OF	17	61	8	15	6	0	2	10	.246	11	0	0	1.000
1980—Jacksonville......South.		1B	142	514	81	139	*40	0	23	104	.270	626	34	6	.991

Selected by California Angels' organization in 13th round of free-agent draft, January 7, 1976.
Selected by Kansas City Royals' organization in 24th round of free-agent draft, June 6, 1978.

DID YOU KNOW—

That Steve Carlton was 6-0 against the Cardinals in 1980, becoming the first major league pitcher since 1971 to defeat another club six times in one season? Since being traded by St. Louis to the Phillies in 1972, Carlton is 29-8 against his old team.

GREGORY BERNARD JOHNSTON
(Greg)

Born February 12, 1955, at Los Angeles, Calif.
Height, 6.00. Weight, 175.
Throws and bats lefthanded.
Attended Citrus Community College, Azusa, Calif.

Led Eastern League in stolen bases with 36 in 1977.
Led International League in total bases with 220 in 1980.

Year Club	League	Pos.	G.	AB.	R.	H.	2B.	3B.	HR.	RBI.	B.A.	PO.	A.	E.	F.A.
1976—Fresno..............Calif.		OF	139	*598	86	153	15	4	6	67	.256	*311	13	12	.964
1977—Waterbury........East.		OF	138	*549	89	143	30	3	12	54	.260	308	12	13	.961
1978—Phoenix............P. C.		OF	133	519	64	142	21	6	6	68	.274	279	8	8	.973
1979—Phoenix............P. C.		OF-1B	104	415	64	123	17	10	10	72	.296	283	10	6	.980
1979—San Francisco† .Nat.		OF	42	74	5	15	2	0	1	7	.203	27	1	1	.966
1980—Toledo ....Int.		OF	132	507	68	150	22	3	14	66	.296	297	10	5	.984
1980—Minnesota.........Amer.		OF	14	27	3	5	3	0	0	1	.185	25	0	0	1.000
National League Totals..................			42	74	5	15	2	0	1	7	.203	27	1	1	.966
American League Totals..................			14	27	3	5	3	0	0	1	.185	25	0	0	1.000
Major League Totals......................			56	101	8	20	5	0	1	8	.198	52	1	1	.981

Selected by San Francisco Giants' organization in 12th round of free-agent draft, June 4, 1975.
†Sold to Minnesota Twins' organization, April 3, 1980.

JOHN WILLIAM JOHNSTONE, JR.
(Jay)

Born November 20, 1945, at Manchester, Conn.
Height, 6.01. Weight, 190.
Throws right and bats lefthanded.
Hobbies—Hunting and fishing.
Attended Mount San Antonio Junior College, Walnut, Calif.

Year Club	League	Pos.	G.	AB.	R.	H.	2B.	3B.	HR.	RBI.	B.A.	PO.	A.	E.	F.A.
1963—San Jose............Calif.		OF-S-3	48	155	21	39	5	3	1	18	.252	51	31	9	.901
1964—San Jose............Calif.		OF	126	454	66	132	27	●11	4	48	.291	250	14	12	.957
1965—El Paso ....Texas		OF	35	137	21	39	9	2	1	21	.285	82	4	4	.956
1965—San Jose............Calif.		OF	97	356	53	107	17	6	6	60	.301	198	11	10	.954
1966—El Paso ....Texas		OF	7	25	5	9	2	0	1	1	.360	19	0	0	1.000
1966—Seattle ..............P.C.		OF	81	318	60	108	14	7	7	42	.340	170	7	4	.978
1966—California.........Amer.		OF	61	254	35	67	12	4	3	17	.264	114	2	3	.975
1967—California.........Amer.		OF	79	230	18	48	7	1	2	10	.209	141	3	4	.973
1967—Seattle ..............P.C.		OF	49	184	21	58	11	1	4	21	.315	117	3	4	.968
1968—California.........Amer.		OF	41	115	11	30	4	1	0	3	.261	58	4	1	.984
1968—Seattle ..............P.C.		OF	84	314	45	87	15	4	13	56	.277	203	11	9	.960
1969—California.........Amer.		OF	148	540	64	146	20	5	10	59	.270	331	12	6	.983
1970—California†........Amer.		OF	119	320	34	76	10	5	11	39	.238	200	7	4	.981
1971—Chicago............Amer.		OF	124	388	53	101	14	1	16	40	.260	232	9	8	.968
1972—Chicago‡ ....Amer.		OF	113	261	27	49	9	0	4	17	.188	154	5	2	.988
1973—Tucson..............P.C.		OF	69	242	58	84	15	5	9	44	.347	125	2	6	.955
1973—Oakland§..........Amer.		OF-2B	23	28	1	3	1	0	0	3	.107	7	0	0	1.000
1974—Toledo..............Int.		OF-1B	57	155	31	49	15	1	8	25	.316	77	6	3	.965
1974—Philadelphia......Nat.		OF	64	200	30	59	10	4	6	30	.295	88	4	3	.968
1975—Philadelphia......Nat.		OF	122	350	50	115	19	2	7	54	.329	152	10	4	.976
1976—Philadelphia......Nat.		OF-1B	129	440	62	140	38	4	5	53	.318	293	10	8	.974
1977—Philadelphia......Nat.		OF-1B	112	363	64	103	18	4	15	59	.284	294	15	1	.997
1978—Philadelphia x...Nat.		1B-OF	35	56	3	10	2	0	0	4	.179	77	7	1	.988
1978—New York ....Amer.		OF	36	65	6	17	0	0	1	6	.262	31	0	0	1.000
1979—New York y ......Amer.		OF	23	48	7	10	1	0	1	7	.208	32	0	0	1.000
1979—San Diego z.......Nat.		OF-1B	75	201	10	59	8	2	0	32	.294	185	18	4	.981
1980—Los Angeles .....Nat.		OF	109	251	31	77	15	2	2	20	.307	100	9	4	.965
National League Totals...................			646	1861	250	563	110	18	35	252	.303	1189	73	25	.981
American League Totals.................			767	2249	256	547	78	17	48	201	.243	1300	42	28	.980
Major League Totals			1413	4110	506	1110	188	35	83	453	.270	2489	115	53	.980

Signed as free agent by California Angels' organization, June 30, 1963.
†Traded with Pitcher Tom Bradley and Catcher Tom Egan to Chicago White Sox for Outfielder Ken Berry, Second Baseman Syd O'Brien and Pitcher Billy Wynne, November 30, 1970.
‡Released unconditionally, March 7, 1973; signed as free agent by Oakland Athletics, March 31, 1973.
§Conditionally released to St. Louis Cardinals, January 9, 1974; released by Cardinals, March 26, 1974.
Signed as free agent by Philadelphia Phillies (assigned to Toledo), April 3, 1974.
xTraded with Outfielder Bobby Brown to New York Yankees for Pitcher Rawly Eastwick, June 14, 1978.
yTraded to San Diego Padres for Pitcher Dave Wehrmeister, June 15, 1979.
zGranted free agency, November 1, 1979; signed by Los Angeles Dodgers, December 4, 1979.

CHAMPIONSHIP SERIES RECORD

Established Championship Series record for highest batting average, three-game Series (.778), 1976.
Tied Championship Series records for most hits, three-game Series (7), 1976; most hits, two consecutive games, one Series (6), October 10 and 12, 1976.

Year	Club	League	Pos.	G.	AB.	R.	H.	2B.	3B.	HR.	RBI.	B.A.	PO.	A.	E.	F.A.
1976—Philadelphia	......Nat.		PH-OF	3	9	1	7	1	1	0	2	.778	3	0	0	1.000
1977—Philadelphia	......Nat.		OF-PH	2	5	0	1	0	0	0	0	.200	4	0	0	1.000
Championship Series Totals				5	14	1	8	1	1	0	2	.571	7	0	0	1.000

WORLD SERIES RECORD

Year	Club	League	Pos.	G.	AB.	R.	H.	2B.	3B.	HR.	RBI.	B.A.	PO.	A.	E.	F.A.
1978—New York	.........Amer.		OF	2	0	0	0	0	0	0	0	.000	1	0	0	1.000

DOUGLAS REID JONES
(Doug)

Born June 24, 1957, at Lebanon, Ind.
Height, 6.02. Weight, 170.
Throws and bats righthanded.
Attended Central Arizona College, Coolidge, Ariz.

Led Midwest League in complete games with 16 and tied for lead in shutouts with 3 in 1979.

Year	Club	League	G.	IP.	W.	L.	Pct.	H.	R.	ER.	SO.	BB.	ERA.
1978—Newark†	NYP	15	38	2	4	.333	49	30	22	27	15	5.21
1979—Burlington	Midwest	28	*190	10	10	.500	144	63	37	115	73	*1.75
1980—Stockton	California	11	76	6	2	.750	63	32	24	54	31	2.84
1980—Vancouver	P. Coast	8	53	3	2	.600	52	19	19	28	15	3.23
1980—Holyoke	Eastern	8	62	5	3	.625	57	23	20	39	26	2.90

Selected by Milwaukee Brewers' organization in 3rd round of free-agent draft, January 10, 1978.
†On disabled list, June 20 to July 12, 1978.

JEFFREY ALLEN JONES
(Jeff)

Born July 29, 1956, at Detroit, Mich.
Height, 6.03. Weight, 210.
Throws and bats righthanded.
Attended St. Clair College, Port Huron, Mich., and
Bowling Green State University, Bowling Green, O.

Led Eastern League pitchers in games started with 29 in 1978.

Year	Club	League	G.	IP.	W.	L.	Pct.	H.	R.	ER.	SO.	BB.	ERA.
1977—Modesto	California	11	46	4	3	.571	35	28	26	41	32	5.09
1977—Chattanooga	Southern	7	9	0	0	.000	9	0	0	5	3	0.00
1978—Jersey City	Eastern	29	191	10	13	.435	187	102	79	121	84	3.72
1979—Ogden	P. Coast	28	175	13	7	.650	152	79	68	126	89	3.50
1980—Oakland	American	35	44	1	3	.250	32	21	14	34	26	2.86
Major League Totals			35	44	1	3	.250	32	21	14	34	26	2.86

Selected by Oakland A's organization in 13th round of free-agent draft, June 7, 1977.

LARRY KEITH JONES

Born February 6, 1955, at Richmond, Va.
Height, 6.02. Weight, 195.
Throws and bats righthanded.
Attended Florida State University, Tallahassee, Fla.; received Bachelor of
Science degree in Mass Communications.

Year	Club	League	G.	IP.	W.	L.	Pct.	H.	R.	ER.	SO.	BB.	ERA.
1977—Bluefield	Ap'lachian	1	5	0	1	.000	7	7	6	6	2	10.80
1977—Miami	Florida St.	12	76	7	4	.636	72	35	25	48	36	2.96
1978—Charlotte	Southern	4	13	0	2	.000	20	11	9	7	7	6.23
1978—Miami	Florida St.	24	183	13	10	.565	148	72	50	*143	87	2.46
1979—Charlotte	Southern	19	135	10	3	.769	127	63	59	100	77	3.93
1979—Rochester	Int'national	10	57	1	7	.125	63	21	19	39	20	3.00
1980—Rochester	Int'national	28	180	13	14	.481	168	*104	87	88	81	4.35

Selected by Pittsburgh Pirates' organization in 28th round of free-agent draft, June 5, 1973.
Selected by Boston Red Sox' organization in 4th round of free-agent draft, June 8, 1976.
Selected by Baltimore Orioles' organization in 5th round of free-agent draft, June 7, 1977.

LYNN MORRIS JONES

Born January 1, 1953, at Meadville, Pa.
Height, 5.09. Weight, 175.
Throws and bats righthanded.
Attended Thiel College, Greenville, Pa.; received Bachelor of Arts degree in Sociology.
Brother of Darryl Jones, outfielder in New York Yankees' organization.

Tied for Eastern League lead in sacrifice flies with 8 in 1976.

Year	Club	League	Pos.	G.	AB.	R.	H.	2B.	3B.	HR.	RBI.	B.A.	PO.	A.	E.	F.A.
1974—Seattle	N'west.		OF	76	282	53	74	15	2	2	37	.262	166	*13	4	.978
1975—Three Rivers	East.		OF-SS	53	141	12	29	3	1	1	14	.206	89	25	6	.950
1975—Eugene	N'west.		OF-3B	62	211	53	71	13	3	13	46	.336	90	9	6	.943
1976—Three Rivers	East.		OF	131	418	41	105	17	0	2	36	.251	196	5	8	.962
1977—Three Rivers†	East.		OF	94	324	49	87	14	2	5	32	.269	229	14	1	*.996

Year	Club	League	Pos.	G.	AB.	R.	H.	2B.	3B.	HR.	RBI.	B.A.	PO.	A.	E.	F.A.
1978—Indianapolis‡	.....A. A.		OF-2B	126	482	81	158	28	4	9	62	.328	246	14	3	.989
1979—Detroit	.............Amer.		OF	95	213	33	63	8	0	4	26	.296	142	3	3	.980
1980—Evansville	........A. A.		OF	34	121	10	33	4	0	0	11	.273	29	1	1	.968
1980—Detroit§	...........Amer.		OF	30	55	9	14	2	2	0	6	.255	31	0	0	1.000
Major League Totals				125	268	42	77	10	2	4	32	.287	173	3	3	.983

Selected by Cincinnati Reds' organization in 10th round of free-agent draft, June 5, 1974.
†On disabled list, July 8 to August 8, 1977.
‡Drafted by Detroit Tigers, December 4, 1978.
§On disabled list, April 30 to July 25, 1980.

MICHAEL CARL JONES
(Mike)

Born July 30, 1959, at Pittsford, N.Y.
Height, 6.05. Weight, 226.
Throws and bats lefthanded.
Nephew of Bert Jones, catcher in Baltimore Orioles' organization, 1966.

Tied for Gulf Coast League lead in complete games with 4 in 1977.
Led Southern League in wild pitches with 16 in 1979.

Year	Club	League	G.	IP.	W.	L.	Pct.	H.	R.	ER.	SO.	BB.	ERA.
1977—Sarasota Royals		Gulf Coast	8	55	5	1	.833	41	19	15	52	43	2.45
1977—Daytona Beach		Florida St.	1	7	1	0	1.000	6	2	2	5	3	2.57
1978—Ft. Myers		Florida St.	25	169	13	9	.591	150	80	69	118	*117	3.67
1979—Jacksonville		Southern	26	167	9	13	.409	142	92	76	116	*109	4.10
1980—Jacksonville		Southern	24	158	13	6	.684	152	79	68	116	83	3.87
1980—Kansas City		American	3	5	0	1	.000	6	7	6	2	5	10.80
Major League Totals			3	5	0	1	.000	6	7	6	2	5	10.80

Selected by Kansas City Royals' organization in 1st round (21st player selected) of free-agent draft, June 7, 1977.

RANDALL LEO JONES
(Randy)

Born January 12, 1950, at Fullerton, Calif.
Height, 6.00. Weight, 180.
Throws left and bats righthanded.
Attended Chapman College, Orange, Calif.; received Bachelor of Arts degree in Business.

Established major league record for most chances accepted, no errors, pitcher, season, 112, 1976.
Tied major league record for highest fielding percentage, pitcher, season (1.000), 1976; most assists by pitcher, inning (3), September 28, 1975 (third inning).
Tied following National League records: most double plays, pitcher, season, 12, 1976; most innings pitched, consecutive, no bases on balls allowed, 68, May 17-June 2, 1976.
Led National League pitchers in complete games with 25 in 1976.
Won National League Cy Young Memorial Award, 1976.
Named National League Comeback Player of the Year by THE SPORTING NEWS, 1975.
Named lefthanded pitcher on THE SPORTING NEWS National League All-Star Team, 1975 and 1976.
Named National League Pitcher of the Year by THE SPORTING NEWS, 1976.

Year	Club	League	G.	IP.	W.	L.	Pct.	H.	R.	ER.	SO.	BB.	ERA.
1972—Tri-City		Northwest	1	5	1	0	1.000	1	0	0	1	2	0.00
1972—Alexandria		Texas	12	68	3	5	.375	53	28	22	63	13	2.91
1973—Alexandria		Texas	10	67	8	1	.889	55	24	15	67	22	2.01
1973—San Diego		National	20	140	7	6	.538	129	58	49	77	37	3.15
1974—San Diego		National	40	208	8	•22	.267	217	118	103	124	78	4.46
1975—San Diego		National	37	285	20	12	.625	242	94	71	103	56	*2.24
1976—San Diego		National	*40	*315	*22	14	.611	*274	109	96	93	50	2.74
1977—San Diego†		National	27	147	6	12	.333	173	85	75	44	36	4.59
1978—San Diego		National	37	253	13	14	.481	263	104	81	71	64	2.88
1979—San Diego		National	39	263	11	12	.478	257	120	106	112	64	3.63
1980—San Diego‡		National	24	154	5	13	.278	165	71	67	53	29	3.92
Major League Totals			264	1765	92	105	.467	1720	759	648	677	414	3.30

Selected by San Diego Padres' organization in 5th round of free-agent draft, June 6, 1972.
†On disabled list, June 19 to July 30, 1977.
‡Traded to New York Mets for Second Baseman Jose Moreno and Pitcher John Pacella, December 15, 1980.

ALL-STAR GAME RECORD

Year	League	IP.	W.	L.	Pct.	H.	R.	ER.	SO.	BB.	ERA.
1975—National		1	0	0	.000	0	0	0	1	0	0.00
1976—National		3	1	0	1.000	2	2	0	1	1	0.00
All-Star Game Totals		4	1	0	1.000	2	2	0	2	1	0.00

DID YOU KNOW—

That 1980 was the tenth consecutive year that a lefthander won the American League batting title? The last righthander was Alex Johnson in 1970.

RUPPERT SANDERSON JONES

Born March 12, 1955, at Dallas, Tex.
Height, 5.10. Weight, 171.
Throws and bats lefthanded.

Tied major league record for most putouts by outfielder, extra-inning game (12), May 16, 1978.
Tied American League record for most chances accepted by outfielder, extra-inning game (12), May 16, 1978.
Tied for Pioneer League lead in double plays by outfielders with 1 in 1973.

Year Club	League	Pos.	G.	AB.	R.	H.	2B.	3B.	HR.	RBI.	B.A.	PO.	A.	E.	F.A.
1973—Billings	Pion.	OF	61	193	45	58	10	4	4	31	.301	55	5	5	.923
1974—Waterloo	Midw.	OF	68	249	44	88	15	0	13	43	.353	94	7	3	.971
1974—San Jose	Calif.	OF	53	191	29	53	7	3	8	45	.277	101	2	4	.963
1975—Omaha	A.A.	OF	119	403	62	98	25	5	13	54	.243	171	15	•13	.935
1976—Omaha	A.A.	OF	102	359	65	94	15	9	19	73	.262	243	2	8	.968
1976—Kansas City†	Amer.	OF	28	51	9	11	1	1	1	7	.216	21	0	0	1.000
1977—Seattle	Amer.	OF	160	597	85	157	26	8	24	76	.263	465	11	9	.981
1978—Seattle‡	Amer.	OF	129	472	48	111	24	3	6	46	.235	393	10	6	.985
1979—Seattle§	Amer.	OF	•162	622	109	166	29	9	21	78	.267	453	13	5	.989
1980—New York x	Amer.	OF	83	328	38	73	11	3	9	42	.223	246	4	3	.988
Major League Totals			562	2070	289	518	91	24	61	249	.250	1578	38	23	.986

Selected by Kansas City Royals' organization in 3rd round of free-agent draft, June 5, 1973.
†Selected by Seattle Mariners in American League expansion draft, November 5, 1976.
‡On disabled list, June 16 to July 20, 1978.
§Traded with Pitcher Jim Lewis to New York Yankees for Outfielder Juan Beniquez, Pitchers Jim Beattie and Rick Anderson and Catcher Jerry Narron, November 1, 1979.
xOn disabled list, May 27 to July 10 and August 26 to October 24, 1980.

ALL-STAR GAME RECORD

Year League	Pos.	AB.	R.	H.	2B.	3B.	HR.	RBI.	B.A.	PO.	A.	E.	F.A.
1977—American	PH	1	0	0	0	0	0	0	.000	0	0	0	.000

MICHAEL JORGENSEN
(Mike)

Born August 16, 1948, at Passaic, N. J.
Height, 6.00. Weight, 192.
Throws and bats lefthanded.
Hobbies—Golf and bridge.
Attended St. John's University, Jamaica, N. Y.

Tied for International League lead in sacrifice flies with 8 in 1969.
Named first baseman on THE SPORTING NEWS National League All-Star fielding team, 1973.

Year Club	League	Pos.	G.	AB.	R.	H.	2B.	3B.	HR.	RBI.	B.A.	PO.	A.	E.	F.A.
1966—Marion	Appal.	1B	46	150	30	47	0	0	8	37	.313	298	16	4	.987
1967—Winter Haven	Fla. St.	1-O	84	302	56	89	11	4	5	41	.295	639	29	7	.990
1968—New York	Nat.	1B	8	14	0	2	1	0	0	0	.143	32	1	0	1.000
1968—Memphis	Texas	1B	28	100	7	16	1	2	0	10	.160	211	11	0	1.000
1968—Raleigh-Dur.	Carol.	1B-OF	57	213	34	67	13	4	3	27	.315	311	25	3	.991
1969—Tidewater	Int.	1B	105	359	75	104	15	5	21	69	.290	882	50	5	•.995
1970—New York	Nat.	1B-OF	76	87	15	17	3	1	3	4	.195	145	12	3	.981
1971—Tidewater	Int.	1B-OF	65	228	50	78	12	1	15	41	.342	157	7	3	.982
1971—New York†	Nat.	OF-1B	45	118	16	26	1	1	5	11	.220	64	2	3	.957
1972—Montreal‡	Nat.	1B-OF	113	372	48	86	12	3	13	47	.231	801	57	6	.993
1973—Montreal	Nat.	•1B-OF	138	413	49	95	16	2	9	47	.230	1002	80	5	•.995
1974—Montreal	Nat.	1B-OF	131	287	45	89	16	1	11	59	.310	653	54	1	.999
1975—Montreal	Nat.	1B-OF	144	445	58	116	18	0	18	67	.261	1153	91	7	.994
1976—Montreal	Nat.	1B-OF	125	343	36	87	13	0	6	23	.254	651	58	8	.989
1977—Montreal§	Nat.	1B	19	20	3	4	1	0	0	0	.200	23	4	0	1.000
1977—Oakland xy	Amer.	1B-OF	66	203	18	50	4	1	8	32	.246	365	32	4	.990
1978—Texas	Amer.	1B-OF	96	97	20	19	3	0	1	9	.196	317	31	2	.994
1979—Texas za	Amer.	1B-OF	90	157	21	35	7	0	6	16	.223	320	31	4	.989
1980—New York	Nat.	1B-OF	119	321	43	82	11	0	7	43	.255	562	37	4	.993
National League Totals			918	2420	313	604	92	8	72	301	.250	5086	376	37	.993
American League Totals			252	457	59	104	14	1	15	57	.228	1002	94	10	.991
Major League Totals			1170	2877	372	708	106	9	87	358	.246	6088	470	47	.993

Selected by New York Mets' organization in free-agent draft, June 30, 1966.
†Traded with Infielder Tim Foli and Outfielder Ken Singleton to Montreal Expos for Outfielder Rusty Staub, April 6, 1972.
‡On military list, July 7 to July 10 and July 20 to August 6, 1972.
§Traded to Oakland Athletics for Pitcher Stan Bahnsen, May 22, 1977.
xOn disabled list, July 11 to August 31, 1977.
yGranted free agency, October 20, 1977; signed by Texas Rangers, January 21, 1978.
zOn supplemental disabled list, June 1 to July 1, 1979.
aTraded to New York Mets, October 23, 1979, completing deal in which Texas acquired First Baseman Willie Montanez, August 12, 1979.

VON EVERETT JOSHUA

Born May 1, 1948, at Oakland, Calif.
Height, 5.10. Weight, 170.
Throws and bats lefthanded.
Hobbies—Basketball and fishing.
Attended Laney College, Oakland, Calif., and California State College, Hayward, Calif.

Year	Club	League	Pos.	G.	AB.	R.	H.	2B.	3B.	HR.	RBI.	B.A.	PO.	A.	E.	F.A.
1967—Tri-City	....	Northw.	OF	66	267	57	•97	*17	*8	3	40	*.363	139	7	12	.924
1967—Santa Barbara	...	Calif.	OF	8	34	9	13	0	1	0	1	.382	18	2	0	1.000
1968—Albuquerque	......	Texas	OF-1B	74	295	47	88	12	6	5	32	.298	150	8	6	.963
1969—Spokane	....	P.C.	OF	107	386	55	107	21	10	2	30	.277	201	9	10	.955
1969—Los Angeles	....	Nat.	OF	14	8	2	2	0	0	0	0	.250	4	0	1	.800
1970—Spokane	....	P.C.	OF	16	53	7	19	4	1	1	9	.358	27	2	0	1.000
1970—Los Angeles	....	Nat.	OF	72	109	23	29	1	3	1	8	.266	47	1	3	.941
1971—Spokane	....	P.C.	OF	56	165	19	44	7	4	2	21	.267	82	1	2	.976
1971—Los Angeles†	....	Nat.	OF	11	7	2	0	0	0	0	0	.000	7	0	0	.000
1972—Albuquerque	.....	P.C.	OF	125	484	93	163	29	9	9	76	*.337	193	9	10	.953
1973—Los Angeles‡	.....	Nat.	OF	75	159	19	40	4	1	2	17	.252	61	2	1	.984
1974—Los Angeles§	....	Nat.	OF	81	124	11	29	5	1	1	16	.234	33	0	2	.943
1975—San Francisco	...	Nat.	OF	129	507	75	161	25	10	4	43	.318	279	10	2	*.993
1976—San Francisco x.		Nat.	OF	42	156	13	41	5	2	0	2	.263	70	3	4	.948
1976—Milwaukee	....	Amer.	OF	107	423	44	113	13	5	5	28	.267	268	10	5	.982
1977—Milwaukee y	......	Amer.	OF	144	536	58	140	25	7	9	49	.261	311	8	10	.970
1978—Tabasco z	....	Mex.	OF	107	406	59	124	20	12	6	53	.305	225	11	7	.971
1979—Los Angeles a	...	Nat.	OF	94	142	22	40	7	1	3	14	.282	56	2	2	.967
1980—San Diego bc	.....	Nat.	OF	53	63	8	15	2	1	2	7	.238	18	0	0	1.000
National League Totals	....			571	1275	175	357	49	19	16	107	.280	575	18	15	.975
American League Totals	....			251	959	102	253	38	12	14	77	.264	579	18	15	.975
Major League Totals	....			822	2234	277	610	87	31	30	184	.273	1154	36	30	.975

Signed as free agent by Los Angeles Dodgers' organization, June 28, 1967.
†On military list, June 19 through July 3, 1971.
‡On supplemental disabled list, April 17 to May 14, 1973.
§Released on waivers to San Francisco Giants, January 29, 1975.
xSold to Milwaukee Brewers, June 2, 1976.
yReleased, March 30, 1978; signed by Tabasco of Mexican League, April 9, 1978.
zSold to Los Angeles Dodgers, January 9, 1979.
aSold on waivers to San Diego Padres, December 3, 1979.
bOn supplemental disabled list, June 2 to June 20, 1980.
cReleased, August 11, 1980.

CHAMPIONSHIP SERIES RECORD

Year	Club	League	Pos.	G.	AB.	R.	H.	2B.	3B.	HR.	RBI.	B.A.	PO.	A.	E.	F.A.
1974—Los Angeles	....	Nat.	PH	1	0	0	0	0	0	0	0	.000	0	0	0	.000

WORLD SERIES RECORD

Year	Club	League	Pos.	G.	AB.	R.	H.	2B.	3B.	HR.	RBI.	B.A.	PO.	A.	E.	F.A.
1974—Los Angeles	....	Nat.	PH	4	4	0	0	0	0	0	0	.000	0	0	0	.000

JAMES LEE KAAT

Name pronounced Cott.

(Jim)

Born November 7, 1938, at Zeeland, Mich.
Height, 6.05. Weight, 195.
Throws and bats lefthanded.
Hobbies—Golf and music.
Attended Hope College, Holland, Mich.

Established major league records for most sacrifice flies allowed, lifetime (129); most games taken out as starting pitcher, season (35), 1965.
Tied major league record for most consecutive years by pitcher (22).
Established American League records for most games lost by lefthanded pitcher, career (191); most sacrifice flies allowed, career (108).
Led American League in hit batsmen with 11 in 1961 and 18 in 1962; tied for league lead in wild pitches with 10 in 1961 and led league with 13 in 1962; led league in games started with 42 in 1965 and 41 in 1966; tied for league lead in shutouts with 5 in 1962; led league in complete games with 19 in 1966.
Led Pioneer League in games started with 30, shutouts with 5, and tied for lead in complete games with 15 in 1958.
Named pitcher on The Sporting News American League All-Star fielding team, 1962 through 1975.
Named pitcher on The Sporting News National League All-Star fielding team, 1976 and 1977.
Named lefthanded pitcher on The Sporting News American League All-Star Team, 1975.
Named pitcher on The Sporting News American League All-Star Team, 1966.
Named American League Pitcher of the Year by The Sporting News, 1966.

Year	Club	League	G.	IP.	W.	L.	Pct.	H.	R.	ER.	SO.	BB.	ERA.
1957—Superior	....	Neb. St.	14	73	5	6	.455	65	45	30	95	35	3.70
1958—Missoula	....	Pioneer	39	*223	16	9	.640	189	108	74	*245	118	*2.99
1959—Chattanooga	....	Southern	24	134	8	8	.500	126	71	61	132	73	4.10
1959—Washington	....	American	3	5	0	2	.000	7	9	7	2	4	12.60

Year	Club	League	G.	IP.	W.	L.	Pct.	H.	R.	ER.	SO.	BB.	ERA.
1960—Washington		American	13	50	1	5	.167	48	39	31	25	31	5.58
1960—Charleston		Am. Assoc.	30	146	7	10	.412	154	80	62	106	51	3.82
1961—Minnesota		American	36	201	9	17	.346	188	105	87	122	82	3.90
1962—Minnesota		American	39	269	18	14	.563	243	106	94	173	75	3.14
1963—Minnesota		American	31	178	10	10	.500	195	96	83	105	38	4.20
1964—Minnesota		American	36	243	17	11	.607	231	100	87	171	60	3.22
1965—Minnesota		American	45	264	18	11	.621	*267	*121	83	154	63	2.83
1966—Minnesota		American	41	*305	*25	13	.658	*271	114	93	205	55	2.74
1967—Minnesota		American	42	263	16	13	.552	*269	110	89	211	42	3.05
1968—Minnesota		American	30	208	14	12	.538	192	78	68	130	40	2.94
1969—Minnesota		American	40	242	14	13	.519	252	114	94	139	75	3.50
1970—Minnesota		American	45	230	14	10	.583	244	110	91	120	58	3.56
1971—Minnesota		American	39	260	13	14	.481	275	104	96	137	47	3.32
1972—Minnesota†		American	15	113	10	2	.833	94	36	26	64	20	2.07
1973—Minnesota‡-Chicago		American	36	224	15	13	.536	250	124	109	109	43	4.38
1974—Chicago		American	42	277	21	13	.618	263	106	90	142	63	2.92
1975—Chicago§		American	43	304	20	14	.588	*321	121	105	142	77	3.11
1976—Philadelphia		National	38	228	12	14	.462	241	95	88	83	32	3.47
1977—Philadelphia		National	35	160	6	11	.353	211	100	96	55	40	5.40
1978—Philadelphia		National	26	140	8	5	.615	150	67	64	48	32	4.11
1979—Philadelphia x		National	3	8	1	0	1.000	9	4	4	2	5	4.50
1979—New York y		American	40	58	2	3	.400	64	29	25	23	14	3.88
1980—New York z		American	4	5	0	1	.000	8	5	4	1	4	7.20
1980—St. Louis		National	49	130	8	7	.533	140	61	55	36	33	3.81
American League Totals			620	3699	237	191	.554	3682	1627	1362	2175	891	3.31
National League Totals			151	666	35	37	.486	751	327	307	224	142	4.15
Major League Totals			771	4365	272	228	.544	4433	1954	1669	2399	1033	3.44

Signed as free agent by Washington Senators' organization, June 17, 1957.
†On disabled list, July 6 through September 27.
‡Sold via waivers to Chicago White Sox, August 15, 1973.
§Traded with Shortstop Mike Buskey to Philadelphia Phillies for Outfielder-Infielder Alan Bannister and Pitchers Dick Ruthven and Roy Thomas, December 10, 1975.
xSold to New York Yankees, May 11, 1979.
yGranted free agency, November 1, 1979; re-signed by Yankees, April 1, 1980.
zSold to St. Louis Cardinals, April 30, 1980.

CHAMPIONSHIP SERIES RECORD

Year	Club	League	G.	IP.	W.	L.	Pct.	H.	R.	ER.	SO.	BB.	ERA.
1970—Minnesota		American	1	2	0	1	.000	6	4	2	1	2	9.00
1976—Philadelphia		National	1	6	0	0	.000	2	2	2	1	2	3.00
Championship Series Totals			2	8	0	1	.000	8	6	4	2	4	4.50

WORLD SERIES RECORD

Holds World Series records for most putouts, pitcher, seven game Series (5), 1965 and most putouts, game, nine innings, pitcher (5), October 7, 1965.

Year	Club	League	G.	IP.	W.	L.	Pct.	H.	R.	ER.	SO.	BB.	ERA.
1965—Minnesota		American	3	14⅓	1	2	.333	18	7	6	6	2	3.77

ALL-STAR GAME RECORD

Year	League	IP.	W.	L.	Pct.	H.	R.	ER.	SO.	BB.	ERA.
1966—American		2	0	0	.000	3	1	1	1	0	4.50
1975—American		2	0	0	.000	0	0	0	0	0	0.00
All-Star Game Totals		4	0	0	.000	3	1	1	1	0	2.25

Member of American League All-Star Team in 1962 (second game); did not play.

DONALD WAYNE KAINER
Name pronounced KINER.

(Don)

Born September 3, 1955, at Houston, Tex.
Height, 6.02. Weight, 205.
Throws and bats righthanded.
Attended University of Texas, Austin, Tex.
Brother of Ronald Kainer, pitcher in Kansas City Royals' organization.

Year	Club	League	G.	IP.	W.	L.	Pct.	H.	R.	ER.	SO.	BB.	ERA.
1977—Tulsa†		Texas	6	24	1	2	.333	23	15	9	6	5	3.38
1978—Tulsa		Texas	17	119	9	5	.643	117	63	54	75	29	4.08
1978—Tucson		P. Coast	9	58	2	4	.333	75	39	37	29	29	5.74
1979—Tucson		P. Coast	28	167	6	13	.316	222	114	99	69	56	5.34
1980—Charleston		Int'national	22	138	9	7	.563	128	58	44	66	46	2.87
1980—Texas		American	4	20	0	0	.000	22	7	4	10	9	1.80
Major League Totals			4	20	0	0	.000	22	7	4	10	9	1.80

Selected by Houston Astros' organization in 7th round of free-agent draft, June 5, 1974.
Selected by Texas Rangers' organization in 13th round of free-agent draft, June 7, 1977.
†On temporary inactive list, June 17 to June 30, and disabled list, August 7 to August 18, 1977.

RICKEY KEETON

Born March 18, 1957, at Cincinnati, O.
Height, 6.02. Weight, 190.
Throws and bats righthanded.
Attended Southern Illinois University, Carbondale, Ill.

Year Club	League	G.	IP.	W.	L.	Pct.	H.	R.	ER.	SO.	BB.	ERA.
1978—Holyoke	Eastern	15	96	4	8	.333	111	63	52	51	33	4.88
1979—Vancouver	P. Coast	32	203	15	14	.517	187	102	85	96	82	3.77
1980—Vancouver	P. Coast	20	136	10	4	.714	131	58	50	51	54	3.31
1980—Milwaukee	American	5	28	2	2	.500	35	15	15	8	9	4.82
Major League Totals		5	28	2	2	.500	35	15	15	8	9	4.82

Selected by Montreal Expos' organization in 21st round of free-agent draft, June 4, 1975.
Selected by Milwaukee Brewers' organization in 2nd round of free-agent draft, June 6, 1978.

MICHAEL DENNIS KELLEHER
(Mick)

Born July 25, 1947, at Seattle, Wash.
Height, 5.09. Weight, 170.
Throws and bats righthanded.
Hobbies—Basketball, golf and studying the stock market.
Attended Wenatchee Valley College, Wenatchee, Wash., and University of
Puget Sound, Tacoma, Wash.; received Bachelor of Science degree in Political Science.

Led California League shortstops in double plays with 49 in 1971.

Year Club	League	Pos.	G.	AB.	R.	H.	2B.	3B.	HR.	RBI.	B.A.	PO.	A.	E.	F.A.
1969—Modesto	Calif.	SS	76	274	31	58	13	3	1	23	.212	119	210	33	.909
1970—Cedar Rapids†	Midw.	SS	59	188	23	50	10	3	0	27	.266	85	157	10	.960
1970—Arkansas	Texas	SS	21	83	12	18	3	1	0	3	.217	44	68	6	.949
1971—Modesto	Calif.	SS	114	429	66	109	20	1	1	45	.254	172	301	31	*.938
1972—Tulsa	A.A.	*S-2B	113	375	30	91	13	0	0	26	.243	166	338	11	*.979
1972—St. Louis	Nat.	SS	23	63	5	10	2	1	0	1	.159	60	61	2	.984
1973—Tulsa	A.A.	SS	25	89	9	20	2	0	0	13	.225	36	85	7	.945
1973—St. Louis‡	Nat.	SS	43	38	4	7	2	0	0	2	.184	30	55	4	.955
1974—Denver	A.A.	*SS-3B	105	347	36	82	10	4	0	28	.236	150	377	18	*.967
1974—Houston§	Nat.	SS	19	57	4	9	0	0	0	2	.158	23	62	5	.944
1975—Tulsa	A.A.	*SS-2B	127	420	48	100	17	0	0	27	.238	246	376	14	*.978
1975—St. Louis x	Nat.	SS	7	4	0	0	0	0	0	0	.000	3	7	1	.909
1976—Chicago	Nat.	S-3-2	124	337	28	77	12	1	0	22	.228	167	324	12	.976
1977—Chicago y	Nat.	2-S-3	63	122	14	28	5	2	0	11	.230	78	126	4	.981
1978—Chicago	Nat.	3B-2B-SS	68	95	8	24	1	0	0	6	.253	52	100	0	1.000
1979—Chicago z	Nat.	3B-2B-SS	73	142	14	36	4	1	0	10	.254	78	148	6	.974
1980—Chicago z	Nat.	2-3-S	105	96	12	14	1	1	0	4	.146	82	129	7	.978
Major League Totals			525	954	89	205	27	6	0	58	.215	573	1012	41	.975

Selected by St. Louis Cardinals' organization in 3rd round of free-agent draft, June 5, 1969.
†On temporary inactive list, April 17 to May 13, 1970.
‡Purchased by Houston Astros, October 23, 1973.
§Sold to St. Louis Cardinals, December 13, 1974.
xTraded to Chicago Cubs for Infielder-Outfielder Vic Harris, December 22, 1975.
yOn supplemental disabled list, August 17 to September 2, 1977.
zGranted free agency, October 23, 1980.

DALE PATRICK KELLY
(Pat)

Born August 27, 1955, at Santa Maria, Calif.
Height, 6.03. Weight, 210.
Throws and bats righthanded.
Brother of Mike Kelly, outfielder in Toronto Blue Jays' organization.

Led Pioneer League in passed balls with 17 in 1973.
Led Midwest League in passed balls with 22 in 1974.

Year Club	League	Pos.	G.	AB.	R.	H.	2B.	3B.	HR.	RBI.	B.A.	PO.	A.	E.	F.A.
1973—Idaho Falls	Pion.	C	31	105	13	23	4	1	0	4	.219	197	18	3	.986
1974—Quad Cities	Midw.	C	86	281	30	62	8	3	5	39	.221	564	59	14	.978
1975—Quad Cities	Midw.	C	40	115	14	38	1	0	1	8	.330	239	22	5	.981
1975—Salinas†	Calif.	C	13	36	4	8	1	0	0	0	.222	60	7	1	.985
1976—Salinas	Calif.	C	111	396	63	124	24	2	4	50	.313	612	60	19	.973
1977—El Paso‡	Texas	C	107	365	73	99	18	5	14	53	.271	505	55	*22	.962
1978—Syracuse§	Int.	C	55	168	8	27	6	0	0	12	.161	308	26	*15	.957
1979—Syracuse	Int.	C	6	17	0	3	1	0	0	0	.176	21	1	2	.917
1979—Kinston	Carol.	C-1B-OF	96	350	48	108	23	6	1	50	.309	606	63	12	.982
1980—Syracuse	Int.	C-OF	72	236	24	49	10	2	2	12	.208	296	34	8	.976
1980—Toronto	Amer.	C	3	7	0	2	0	0	0	0	.286	17	0	0	1.000
Major League Totals			3	7	0	2	0	0	0	0	.286	17	0	0	1.000

Selected by California Angels' organization in 3rd round of free-agent draft, June 5, 1973.
†On disabled list, August 12 to September 30, 1975.
‡Traded with First Baseman Butch Alberts (assigned from Salt Lake City to Syracuse) to Toronto Blue Jays for First Baseman-Outfielder Ron Fairly, December 8, 1977.
§On disabled list, July 1 to July 17, 1978.

HAROLD PATRICK KELLY
(Pat)

Born July 30, 1944, at Philadelphia, Pa.
Height, 6.01. Weight, 185.
Throws and bats lefthanded.
Hobby—Dancing.
Attended Morgan State College, Baltimore, Md.
Brother of Leroy Kelly, former halfback with Cleveland Browns,
Oakland Raiders and Chicago Fire.

Major League stolen bases: 1967 (0), 1968 (0), 1969 (40), 1970 (34), 1971 (14), 1972 (32), 1973 (22), 1974 (18), 1975 (18), 1976 (15), 1977 (25), 1978 (10), 1979 (4), 1980 (16). Total—248.

Led Carolina League batters in walks with 119 and tied for lead in double plays by outfielders with 3 in 1965.

Led Pacific Coast League in stolen bases with 38 in 1968.

Year	Club	League	Pos.	G.	AB.	R.	H.	2B.	3B.	HR.	RBI.	B.A.	PO.	A.	E.	F.A.
1963—Erie		NYP	OF	69	247	50	70	10	4	4	30	.283	137	4	9	.940
1963—Orlando		Fla. St.	OF	49	157	27	38	6	3	0	26	.242	77	3	0	1.000
1964—Wilson		Carol.	OF	18	49	8	12	3	2	0	8	.245	26	1	2	.931
1964—Wis. Rapids		Midw.	OF	104	387	79	138	•26	5	16	70	.357	144	10	13	.922
1965—Wilson		Carol.	OF	144	488	101	138	16	9	4	52	.283	•296	14	•22	.934
1966—Charlotte		South.	OF	113	392	74	126	23	6	3	55	.321	242	9	12	.954
1967—Minnesota†		Amer.	PH-PR	8	1	1	0	0	0	0	0	.000	0	0	0	.000
1967—Denver		P.C.	OF	65	245	42	70	3	2	0	15	.286	151	4	6	.963
1968—Denver		P.C.	OF	108	396	70	121	21	4	3	31	.306	276	14	9	.970
1968—Minnesota‡		Amer.	OF	12	35	2	4	2	0	1	2	.114	20	1	1	.955
1969—Kansas City		Amer.	OF	112	417	61	110	20	4	8	32	.264	237	12	5	.980
1970—Kansas City§		Amer.	OF	136	452	56	106	16	1	6	38	.235	254	8	10	.963
1971—Tucson		P.C.	OF	75	301	71	107	18	7	6	43	.355	159	4	3	.982
1971—Chicago		Amer.	OF	67	213	32	62	6	3	3	22	.291	100	7	1	.991
1972—Chicago		Amer.	OF	119	402	57	105	14	7	5	24	.261	173	8	6	.968
1973—Chicago		Amer.	OF	144	550	77	154	24	5	1	44	.280	254	9	6	.978
1974—Chicago		Amer.	OF	122	424	60	119	16	3	4	21	.281	79	2	2	.976
1975—Chicago		Amer.	OF	133	471	73	129	21	7	9	45	.274	222	4	2	•.991
1976—Chicago x		Amer.	OF	107	311	42	79	20	3	5	34	.254	37	1	2	.950
1977—Baltimore		Amer.	OF	120	360	50	92	13	0	10	49	.256	181	2	3	.984
1978—Baltimore		Amer.	OF	100	274	38	75	12	1	11	40	.274	123	3	4	.969
1979—Baltimore		Amer.	OF	68	153	25	44	11	0	9	25	.288	36	0	0	1.000
1980—Baltimore y		Amer.	OF	89	200	38	52	10	1	3	26	.260	48	4	0	1.000
Major League Totals				1337	4263	612	1131	185	35	75	402	.265	1764	61	42	.978

Signed as free agent by Minnesota Twins' organization, September 11, 1962.

†In military service from beginning of season through May 14.

‡Selected by Kansas City Royals from Minnesota Twins in expansion draft, October 15, 1968.

§Traded with Pitcher Don O'Riley to Chicago White Sox for First Baseman-Catcher Gail Hopkins and Outfielder-First Baseman John Matias, October 13, 1970.

xTraded to Baltimore Orioles for Catcher Dave Duncan, November 18, 1976.

yGranted free agency, October 23, 1980; signed by Cleveland Indians, December 29, 1980.

CHAMPIONSHIP SERIES RECORD

Year	Club	League	Pos.	G.	AB.	R.	H.	2B.	3B.	HR.	RBI.	B.A.	PO.	A.	E.	F.A.
1979—Baltimore		Amer.	OF-DH	3	11	3	4	0	0	1	4	.364	3	0	0	1.000

WORLD SERIES RECORD

Tied World Series record for most games, Series, pinch-hitter (5), 1979.

Year	Club	League	Pos.	G.	AB.	R.	H.	2B.	3B.	HR.	RBI.	B.A.	PO.	A.	E.	F.A.
1979—Baltimore		Amer.	PH	5	4	0	1	0	0	0	0	.250	0	0	0	.000

ALL-STAR GAME RECORD

Year	League	Pos.	AB.	R.	H.	2B.	3B.	HR.	RBI.	B.A.	PO.	A.	E.	F.A.
1973—American		PH	1	0	0	0	0	0	0	.000	0	0	0	.000

STEVEN F. KEMP
(Steve)

Born August 7, 1954, at San Angelo, Tex.
Height, 6.00. Weight, 190.
Throws and bats lefthanded.
Hobbies—Fishing, golf and most sports.
Attended University of Southern California, Los Angeles, Calif.

Received reported $50,000 bonus to sign with Detroit Tigers, 1976.

Year	Club	League	Pos.	G.	AB.	R.	H.	2B.	3B.	HR.	RBI.	B.A.	PO.	A.	E.	F.A.
1976—Montgomery		South.	OF-1B	73	256	41	74	17	2	8	43	.289	91	4	2	.979
1976—Evansville		A.A.	OF	52	171	37	66	14	3	11	38	.386	91	2	5	.945
1977—Detroit		Amer.	OF	151	552	75	142	29	4	18	88	.257	252	10	5	.981
1978—Detroit		Amer.	OF	159	582	75	161	18	4	15	79	.277	325	11	8	.977

Year	Club	League	Pos.	G.	AB.	R.	H.	2B.	3B.	HR.	RBI.	B.A.	PO.	A.	E.	F.A.
1979—Detroit	Amer.	OF	134	490	88	156	26	3	26	105	.318	229	12	6	.976
1980—Detroit	Amer.	OF	135	508	88	149	23	3	21	101	.293	197	4	1	.995
Major League Totals			579	2132	326	608	96	14	80	373	.285	1003	37	20	.981

Selected by Detroit Tigers' organization in 1st round (1st player selected) of free-agent draft, January 7, 1976.

ALL-STAR GAME RECORD

Year	League	Pos.	AB.	R.	H.	2B.	3B.	HR.	RBI.	B.A.	PO.	A.	E.	F.A.
1979—American	PH	1	0	0	0	0	0	0	.000	0	0	0	.000

FRED LYN KENDALL

Born January 31, 1949, at Torrance, Calif.
Height, 6.01. Weight, 185.
Throws and bats righthanded.
Hobby—Fishing.

Led Northern League in passed balls with 22 in 1967 and led Southern League with 21 in 1968.
Tied for Northern League lead in double plays by catchers with 6 in 1967 and tied for Eastern League lead with 8 in 1969.

Year	Club	League	Pos.	G.	AB.	R.	H.	2B.	3B.	HR.	RBI.	B.A.	PO.	A.	E.	F.A.
1967—Sioux Falls	North.	C	63	216	20	65	11	2	2	32	.301	*491	*46	8	*.985
1968—Asheville†	South	*C-O-1	117	395	38	115	13	2	7	50	.291	*726	57	6	.992
1969—Elmira	East.	*C-O-1	136	456	52	128	16	4	10	61	.281	*743	*82	10	*.988
1969—San Diego	Nat.	C	10	26	2	4	0	0	0	0	.154	37	5	0	1.000
1970—Salt Lake City	P.C.	C-1-3	115	391	49	120	14	2	9	48	.307	729	52	4	.995
1970—San Diego	Nat.	C-1-O	4	9	0	0	0	0	0	1	.000	7	1	0	1.000
1971—Hawaii	P.C.	C-1-O	11	34	6	11	3	1	1	6	.324	56	3	1	.983
1971—San Diego	Nat.	C-1-3	49	111	2	19	1	0	1	7	.171	184	14	0	1.000
1972—San Diego	Nat.	C-1B	91	273	18	59	3	4	6	18	.216	506	41	3	.995
1973—San Diego	Nat.	C	145	507	39	143	22	3	10	59	.282	749	64	13	.984
1974—San Diego	Nat.	C	141	424	32	98	15	2	8	45	.231	631	64	12	.983
1975—San Diego	Nat.	C	103	286	16	57	12	1	0	24	.199	337	38	9	.977
1976—San Diego‡	Nat.	C	146	456	30	112	17	0	2	39	.246	582	54	4	.994
1977—Cleveland§	Amer.	C	103	317	18	79	13	1	3	39	.249	506	35	5	.991
1978—Boston x	Amer.	1B-C	20	41	3	8	1	0	0	4	.195	107	11	2	.983
1979—San Diego	Nat.	C-1B	46	102	8	17	2	0	1	6	.167	162	19	4	.978
1980—San Diego y	Nat.	C-1B	19	24	2	7	0	0	0	2	.292	31	1	2	.941
National League Totals			754	2218	149	516	72	10	28	201	.233	3226	301	47	.987
American League Totals			123	358	21	87	14	1	3	43	.243	613	46	7	.989
Major League Totals			877	2576	170	603	86	11	31	244	.234	3839	347	54	.987

Selected by Cincinnati Reds' organization in 4th round of free-agent draft, June 6, 1967.
†Recalled by Cincinnati Reds; selected by San Diego Padres from Cincinnati in expansion draft, October 14, 1968.
‡Traded with Outfielder Johnny Grubb and Shortstop Hector Torres to Cleveland Indians for Outfielder George Hendrick, December 8, 1976.
§Traded with Pitcher Dennis Eckersley to Boston Red Sox for Pitchers Rick Wise and Mike Paxton, Third Baseman Ted Cox and Catcher Bo Diaz, March 30, 1978.
xGranted free agency, November 2, 1978; signed by San Diego Padres, February 22, 1979.
yReleased, August 11, 1980.

JUNIOR RAYMOND KENNEDY

Born August 9, 1950, at Fort Gibson, Okla.
Height, 6.00. Weight, 185.
Throws and bats righthanded.
Attended Bakersfield College, Bakersfield, Calif.
Brother of James Kennedy, former infielder in New York Yankees', St. Louis
Cardinals' and Minnesota Twins' organizations.

Led International League shortstops in double plays with 80 in 1972.
Led American Association second basemen in fielding average with .976 in 1976.
Received reported $50,000 bonus to sign with Baltimore Orioles, 1968.

Year	Club	League	Pos.	G.	AB.	R.	H.	2B.	3B.	HR.	RBI.	B.A.	PO.	A.	E.	F.A.
1968—Aberdeen	North.	SS	65	225	32	59	5	0	0	22	.262	68	186	*33	.885
1969—Stockton	Calif.	SS	115	375	38	99	16	1	2	34	.264	159	332	*47	.913
1970—Dallas-Ft. Wth†	Texas	2B	3	9	1	3	0	0	0	2	.333	7	14	0	1.000
1971—Dallas-Ft. Wth.	Texas	SS	118	420	58	95	12	1	2	29	.226	198	310	34	.937
1972—Rochester	Int.	SS	123	388	41	93	14	5	3	33	.240	178	343	33	.940
1973—Rochester‡	Int.	SS	58	196	40	43	7	1	1	15	.219	100	159	21	.925
1973—Indianapolis§	A.A.	SS	46	142	21	40	3	3	0	5	.282	64	140	4	.981
1974—Indianapolis	A.A.	2B-SS	84	271	50	77	9	4	1	22	.284	159	232	15	.963
1974—Cincinnati	Nat.	2B-3B	22	19	2	3	0	0	0	0	.158	15	13	2	.933
1975—Indianapolis x	A.A.	SS-2B	116	405	49	112	13	5	3	46	.277	234	278	18	.966
1976—Indianapolis	A.A.	2B-SS	122	348	53	87	15	4	2	44	.250	226	320	16	.975
1977—Phoenix	P.C.	S-2-3	135	481	88	152	16	9	0	76	.316	282	529	29	.965
1978—Cincinnati	Nat.	2B-3B	89	157	22	40	2	2	0	11	.255	94	142	5	.979
1979—Cincinnati	Nat.	2B-SS-3B	83	220	29	60	7	0	1	17	.273	105	162	5	.982
1980—Cincinnati	Nat.	2B	104	337	31	88	16	3	1	34	.261	200	303	6	.988
Major League Totals			298	733	84	191	25	5	2	62	.261	414	620	18	.983

Selected by Baltimore Orioles' organization in 1st round (10th player selected) of free-agent draft, June 7, 1968.

†On disabled list May 19 to September 7, 1970.

‡Option transferred to Indianapolis in exchange for Infielder Tim Nordbrook, June 14, 1973; traded with Outfielder Merv Rettenmund and Catcher Bill Wood by Baltimore Orioles to Cincinnati Reds for Pitcher Ross Grimsley and Catcher Wally Williams, December 4, 1973.

§On disabled list, July 5 to August 3, 1973.

xOn disabled list, June 8 to June 26, 1975

TERRENCE EDWARD KENNEDY
(Terry)

Born June 4, 1956, at Euclid, O.
Height, 6.04. Weight, 220.
Throws right and bats lefthanded.
Hobbies—Golf, reading and music.
Attended Florida State University, Tallahassee, Fla.

Son of Bob Kennedy, Vice-President of Baseball Operations with Chicago Cubs and former third baseman-outfielder with Chicago White Sox, Baltimore Orioles, Cleveland Indians, Detroit Tigers and Los Angeles Dodgers; brother of Bob Kennedy Jr., scout with Chicago Cubs and former pitcher in St. Louis Cardinals' organization.

Named College Player of the Year by THE SPORTING NEWS, 1977.
Received reported $100,000 bonus to sign with St. Louis Cardinals, 1977.

Year Club League	Pos.	G.	AB.	R.	H.	2B.	3B.	HR.	RBI.	B.A.	PO.	A.	E.	F.A.
1977—Johnson City .....Appal.	C-1B	12	39	14	23	7	2	3	15	.590	66	3	1	.986
1977—St. Petersburg ...Fla. St.	C	45	166	22	41	8	0	4	22	.247	168	22	6	.969
1978—Arkansas ....Texas	C-OF	69	239	55	69	14	0	10	54	.289	365	30	7	.983
1978—Springfield ........A.A.	C-1B	64	230	35	76	13	0	10	46	.330	331	26	7	.981
1978—St. Louis ....Nat.	C	10	29	0	5	0	0	0	2	.172	46	4	1	.980
1979—Springfield ........A.A.	C	84	294	35	86	18	1	13	64	.293	434	38	13	.973
1979—St. Louis ....Nat.	C	33	109	11	31	7	0	2	17	.284	135	7	1	.993
1980—St. Louis† ....Nat.	C-OF	84	248	28	63	12	3	4	34	.254	231	22	7	.973
Major League Totals..............		127	386	39	99	19	3	6	53	.256	412	33	9	.980

Selected by St. Louis Cardinals' organization in 1st round (sixth player selected) of free-agent draft, June 7, 1977.

†Traded with Catcher Steve Swisher, Pitchers John Littlefield, Al Olmsted, Kim Seaman and John Urrea and Infielder Mike Phillips to San Diego Padres for Pitchers Rollie Fingers and Bob Shirley, Catcher-First Baseman Gene Tenace and a player to be named later, December 8, 1980; Catcher Bob Geren traded to Cardinals completing deal, December 10, 1980.

MATTHEW LON KEOUGH
(Matt)

Born July 3, 1955, at Pomona, Calif.
Height, 6.02. Weight, 175.
Throws and bats righthanded.
Hobbies—Hunting and golfing.
Attended University of California Los Angeles, Los Angeles, Calif.

Son of Marty Keough, scout with St. Louis Cardinals and former outfielder with Boston Red Sox' and Cincinnati Reds' organizations, 1952-66, and former scout for San Diego Padres' organization, 1967-1976 and Los Angeles Dodgers' organization, 1977-79; nephew of Joe Keough, outfielder with Oakland A's and Kansas City Royals' organizations, 1966-72.

Tied major league record for most consecutive games lost, start of season (14), 1979.
Tied for California League lead in sacrifice flies with 9 in 1975.
Named American League Comeback Player of the Year by THE SPORTING NEWS, 1980.

Year Club League	G.	IP.	W.	L.	Pct.	H.	R.	ER.	SO.	BB.	ERA.
1976—Chattanooga........................Southern	2	2	0	0	.000	1	0	0	2	0	0.00
1977—Chattanooga........................Southern	26	175	9	12	.429	162	87	74	*153	67	3.81
1977—Oakland ....American	7	43	1	3	.250	39	25	23	23	22	4.81
1978—Oakland ....American	32	197	8	15	.348	178	90	71	108	85	3.24
1979—Oakland ....American	30	177	2	17	.105	220	115	99	95	78	5.03
1980—Oakland ....American	34	250	16	13	.552	218	94	81	121	94	2.92
Major League Totals	103	667	27	48	.360	655	324	274	347	279	3.70

RECORD AS INFIELDER

Year Club League	Pos.	G.	AB.	R.	H.	2B.	3B.	HR.	RBI.	B.A.	PO.	A.	E.	F.A.
1974—Burlington.........Midw.	SS-1B	98	323	31	64	14	2	4	24	.198	143	207	34	.911
1975—Modesto ....Calif.	*SS-3B	123	445	73	135	*34	2	13	81	.303	191	312	*57	.898
1976—Chattanooga ......South.	3-S-O-1-P	124	420	43	88	13	3	6	52	.210	*125	*274	25	.941

Selected by Oakland A's organization in 7th round of free-agent draft, June 5, 1973.

ALL-STAR GAME RECORD

Year League	IP.	W.	L.	Pct.	H.	R.	ER.	SO.	BB.	ERA.
1978—American	⅓	0	0	.000	1	0	0	0	0	0.00

JAMES LESTER KERN
(Jim)

Born March 15, 1949, at Gladwin, Mich.
Height, 6.05. Weight, 205.
Throws and bats righthanded.
Hobbies—Hunting, fishing and fly-tying.
Attended Delta Junior College, University Center, Mich., and
Michigan State University, East Lansing, Mich.

Major League saves: 1974 (0), 1975 (0), 1976 (15), 1977 (18), 1978 (13), 1979 (29), 1980 (2). Total—77.
Pitched seven-inning, 2-0 no-hit victory against San Jose, May 29, 1971.
Led Western Carolinas League in wild pitches with 25 in 1970 and tied for American Association lead with 17 in 1974.
Named American Association Pitcher of the Year, 1974.
Named righthander pitcher on THE SPORTING NEWS American League All-Star Team, 1979.

Year Club	League	G.	IP.	W.	L.	Pct.	H.	R.	ER.	SO.	BB.	ERA.
1968—Rock Hill	W. Carol.	12	28	0	3	.000	29	30	21	25	26	6.75
1968—Sarasota Indians	Gulf Coast	12	45	4	4	.500	44	32	19	48	32	3.80
1969—†						(In Military Service)						
1970—Reno	California	4	15	0	0	.000	9	12	10	20	20	6.00
1970—Sumter	W. Carol.	14	72	5	6	.455	57	47	39	71	70	4.88
1971—Reno	California	24	100	7	9	.438	99	91	73	109	100	6.57
1972—Elmira	Eastern	22	104	3	11	.214	87	55	50	90	73	4.33
1973—San Antonio	Texas	25	166	11	7	.611	130	76	55	182	★129	2.98
1974—Oklahoma City	Am. Assoc.	25	189	★17	7	.708	139	63	53	★220	104	2.52
1974—Cleveland	American	4	15	0	1	.000	16	9	8	11	14	4.80
1975—Oklahoma City	Am. Assoc.	3	14	1	1	.500	12	10	10	11	11	6.43
1975—Cleveland	American	13	72	1	2	.333	60	31	30	55	45	3.75
1976—Cleveland	American	50	118	10	7	.588	91	38	31	111	50	2.36
1977—Cleveland	American	60	92	8	10	.444	85	39	35	91	47	3.42
1978—Cleveland‡	American	58	99	10	10	.500	77	36	34	95	58	3.09
1979—Texas	American	71	143	13	5	.722	99	35	25	136	62	1.57
1980—Texas§	American	38	63	3	11	.214	65	38	34	40	45	4.86
Major League Totals		294	602	45	46	.495	493	226	197	539	321	2.95

Signed as free agent by Cleveland Indians' organization, September 4, 1967.
†On military list, May 11, 1969 to January 7, 1970.
‡Traded with Infielder Larvell Blanks to Texas Rangers for Outfielder Bobby Bonds and Pitcher Len Barker, October 3, 1978.
§On disabled list, August 19 to September 15, 1980.

ALL-STAR GAME RECORD

Year League	IP.	W.	L.	Pct.	H.	R.	ER.	SO.	BB.	ERA.
1977—American	1	0	0	.000	0	0	0	2	0	0.00
1978—American	⅔	0	0	.000	1	0	0	1	1	0.00
1979—American	2⅔	0	1	.000	2	2	2	3	3	6.75
All-Star Game Totals	4⅓	0	1	.000	3	2	2	6	4	4.15

JOSEPH THOMAS KERRIGAN
(Joe)

Born November 30, 1954, at Philadelphia, Pa.
Height, 6.05. Weight, 205.
Throws and bats righthanded.
Hobby—Baseball memorabilia.
Attended Temple University, Philadelphia, Pa.
Brother of Tom Kerrigan, catcher in Philadelphia Phillies' organization, 1963

Year Club	League	G.	IP.	W.	L.	Pct.	H.	R.	ER.	SO.	BB.	ERA.
1974—Kinston	Carolina	36	128	4	10	.286	166	97	66	83	52	4.64
1975—W. Palm Beach	Fla. St.	22	23	0	2	.000	24	7	7	24	11	2.74
1975—Quebec City	Eastern	27	53	6	2	.750	38	11	4	28	15	0.68
1976—Denver	Am. Assoc.	22	32	2	0	1.000	26	13	12	13	12	3.38
1976—Montreal	National	38	57	2	6	.250	63	27	24	22	23	3.79
1977—Montreal†	National	66	89	3	5	.375	80	37	32	43	33	3.24
1978—Baltimore	American	26	72	3	1	.750	75	44	38	41	36	4.75
1979—Rochester	Int'national	★64	95	10	6	.625	88	41	37	55	49	3.50
1980—Rochester	Int'national	39	55	3	3	.500	46	19	17	23	23	2.78
1980—Baltimore‡	American	1	2	0	0	.000	3	1	1	1	0	4.50
National League Totals		104	146	5	11	.313	143	64	56	65	56	3.45
American League Totals		27	74	3	1	.750	78	45	39	42	36	4.74
Major League Totals		131	220	8	12	.400	221	109	95	107	92	3.89

Selected by Montreal Expos' organization in 1st round (10th player selected) of free-agent draft, January 9, 1974.
†Traded with Pitcher Don Stanhouse and Outfielder Gary Roenicke to Baltimore Orioles for Pitchers Rudy May, Randy Miller and Bryn Smith, December 7, 1977.
‡Traded with Catcher John Buffamoyer to Cincinnati Reds' organization for Outfielder John Hale and Infielder Mike Grace, January 22, 1981.

BRUCE EDWARD KIMM

Born June 29, 1951, at Norway, Ia.
Height, 5.11. Weight, 175.
Throws and bats righthanded.
Attended University of Iowa, Iowa City, Ia.

Led Northern League catchers in double plays with 8 in 1970.
Led American Association catchers in putouts with 545 in 1979.

Year Club	League	Pos.	G.	AB.	R.	H.	2B.	3B.	HR.	RBI.	B.A.	PO.	A.	E.	F.A.
1969—Sarasota W.S.	....G.C.	C-OF	36	84	9	26	2	0	1	12	.310	145	17	5	.970
1970—Appleton	.........Midw.	C	3	8	0	1	0	0	0	0	.125	32	1	0	1.000
1970—Duluth-Superior	.North	C	64	238	50	64	12	1	3	43	.269	★571	★54	6	★.990
1971—Appleton†	.........Midw.	C	54	168	18	28	3	3	2	15	.167	440	23	10	.979
1972—Knoxville	.........South.	C	119	353	51	91	5	3	9	55	.258	683	56	15	.980
1972—Tucson‡§	.........P.C.	C	10	19	1	3	1	0	0	0	.158	27	2	1	.967
1973—Montgomery	......South.	C-O-2	74	220	33	56	13	4	1	36	.255	327	33	9	.976
1973—Toledo	..............Int.	C-1-3	24	62	6	14	2	0	1	7	.226	139	13	3	.981
1974—Montgomery	......South.	C	33	111	22	24	2	0	2	14	.216	198	16	2	.991
1974—Evansville	.........A.A.	C-OF	64	200	27	56	7	5	2	25	.280	291	37	4	.988
1975—Evansville	........A.A.	●C-O-1	92	268	35	63	11	2	1	21	.235	369	43	●14	.967
1975—Tucson	..............P.C.	C	5	15	3	2	0	0	0	0	.133	21	5	1	.963
1976—Evansville	..............A.A.	C	2	6	1	2	1	0	1	1	.333	21	0	0	1.000
1976—Detroit	..............Amer.	C	63	152	13	40	8	0	1	6	.263	256	33	9	.970
1977—Rochester	.........Int.	C	37	108	11	18	3	1	0	11	.167	166	15	4	.978
1977—Detroit	..............Amer.	C	14	25	2	2	1	0	0	1	.080	43	3	2	.958
1978—Evansville	........A.A.	★C-O-3	127	389	61	94	16	1	8	49	.242	★699	75	7	★.991
1979—Evansville y	......A.A.	★C-O-3	113	382	63	108	18	1	10	75	.283	548	★73	13	.979
1979—Chicago z	.........Nat.	C	9	11	0	1	0	0	0	0	.091	30	1	1	.969
1980—Chicago	...........Amer.	C	100	251	20	61	10	1	0	19	.243	375	26	6	.985
American League Totals			177	428	35	103	19	1	1	26	.241	674	62	17	.977
National League Totals			9	11	0	1	0	0	0	0	.091	30	1	1	.969
Major League Totals			186	439	35	104	19	1	1	26	.237	704	63	18	.977

Selected by Chicago White Sox' organization in 7th round of free-agent draft, June 5, 1969.
†On disabled list, April 25 to June 11, 1971.
‡Traded by Chicago White Sox to California Angels, September 1, 1972, to complete deal in which White Sox obtained Pitcher Eddie Fisher from Angels for Infielder Bruce Miller, August 17, 1972.
§Traded by California Angels' organization to Detroit Tigers' organization for Outfielder Robert Brooks, March 25, 1973.
xLoaned to Tucson (Texas Rangers' organization), June 2, 1975.
ySold to Chicago Cubs, August 30, 1979.
zDrafted by Chicago White Sox (from Wichita roster), December 3, 1979.

JEROME ANTHONY KING
(Jerry)

Born August 23, 1958, at San Diego, Calif.
Height, 6.03. Weight, 185.
Throws and bats righthanded.

Year Club	League	G.	IP.	W.	L.	Pct.	H.	R.	ER.	SO.	BB.	ERA.
1976—Elmira	NYP	3	8	1	1	.500	6	8	7	10	10	7.88
1977—Winston-Salem	Carolina	13	61	1	6	.143	81	59	50	45	39	7.38
1977—Elmira	NYP	14	84	8	3	.727	89	39	34	76	38	3.64
1978—Winter Haven	Florida St.	1	6	1	0	1.000	7	8	6	7	5	9.00
1978—Winston-Salem	Carolina	14	85	7	4	.636	66	39	22	57	48	2.33
1979—Bristol	Eastern	25	143	7	11	.389	122	81	71	110	111	4.47
1980—Bristol	Eastern	28	131	6	6	.500	123	72	58	119	91	3.98

Selected by Boston Red Sox' organization in 24th round of free-agent draft, June 8, 1976.

BRIAN PAUL KINGMAN

Born July 27, 1954, at Los Angeles, Calif.
Height, 6.01. Weight, 190.
Throws and bats righthanded.
Hobbies—Chess, backpacking, and photography.
Attended Santa Monica City College, Santa Monica, Calif. and University of California at Santa Barbara, Santa Barbara, Calif.; received Bachelor of Arts degree in Sociology.

Year Club	League	G.	IP.	W.	L.	Pct.	H.	R.	ER.	SO.	BB.	ERA.
1975—Boise	N'west	16	74	4	6	.400	73	46	32	70	32	3.89
1976—Chattanooga	Southern	26	184	14	11	.560	167	69	54	101	47	2.64
1977—San José†	P. Coast	16	60	3	6	.333	76	52	49	47	32	7.35
1978—Modesto	California	10	38	2	2	.500	27	13	10	43	29	2.37
1979—Ogden	P. Coast	13	83	7	2	.778	90	47	43	62	38	4.66
1979—Oakland	American	18	113	8	7	.533	113	59	54	59	33	4.30
1980—Oakland	American	32	211	8	★20	.286	209	105	90	116	82	3.84
Major League Totals		50	324	16	27	.372	322	164	144	174	115	4.00

Selected by California Angels' organization in 12th round of free-agent draft, June 5, 1973.
Signed as free agent by Oakland A's organization, June 18, 1975.
†On disabled list, May 6 to June 20, and August 27 to September 16, 1977.

DAVID ARTHUR KINGMAN
(Dave)

Born December 21, 1948, at Pendleton, Ore.
Height, 6.06. Weight, 210.
Throws and bats righthanded.
Hobbies—Hunting and fishing.
Attended Harper College, Palatine, Ill., and University of Southern
California, Los Angeles, Calif.

Tied major league records for most home runs, two consecutive games (5), July 27 and 28, 1979; most times, three or more home runs, game, season (2), May 17 and July 28, 1979.
Tied modern major league record for most clubs played on, season, major leagues (4), 1977.
Tied National League record for fewest errors by first baseman for leader in errors, season (13), 1974.
Hit three home runs in one game, vs. Los Angeles Dodgers, June 4, 1976.
Hit three home runs in one game, vs. Los Angeles Dodgers, June 14, 1978.
Hit three home runs in one game, vs. Philadelphia Phillies, May 17, 1979.
Hit three home runs in one game, vs. New York Mets, July 28, 1979.
Led National League in slugging percentage with .613 and in strikeouts with 131 in 1979.
Named left fielder on THE SPORTING NEWS National League All-Star Team, 1979.

Year	Club	League	Pos.	G.	AB.	R.	H.	2B.	3B.	HR.	RBI.	B.A.	PO.	A.	E.	F.A.
1970—Amarillo		Texas	1B-OF	60	210	41	62	9	1	15	41	.295	226	9	9	.963
1971—Phoenix		P. C.	OF-1B	105	392	89	109	29	5	26	99	.278	785	40	8	.990
1971—San Francisco		Nat.	1B-OF	41	115	17	32	10	2	6	24	.278	168	9	4	.978
1972—San Francisco		Nat.	3-1-OF	135	472	65	106	17	4	29	83	.225	496	159	22	.968
1973—San Francisco		Nat.	3-1-P	112	305	54	62	10	1	24	55	.203	313	146	22	.954
1974—San Francisco†		Nat.	*1-3-O	121	350	41	78	18	2	18	55	.223	696	98	*25	.969
1975—New York		Nat.	O-1-3	134	502	65	116	22	1	36	88	.231	526	69	14	.977
1976—New York‡		Nat.	OF-1B	123	474	70	113	14	1	37	86	.238	293	18	9	.972
1977—N.Y.§-S.D.x		Nat.	O-1-3	114	379	38	84	16	0	20	67	.222	333	24	7	.981
1977—Cal.y-N.Y.z		Amer.	1B-OF	18	60	9	13	4	0	6	11	.217	73	5	2	.975
1978—Chicago a		Nat.	OF-1B	119	395	65	105	17	4	28	79	.266	226	10	6	.975
1979—Chicago		Nat.	OF	145	532	97	153	19	5	*48	115	.288	240	11	12	.954
1980—Chicago bcd		Nat.	OF-1B	81	255	31	71	8	0	18	57	.278	119	10	8	.942
National League Totals				1125	3779	543	920	151	20	264	709	.243	3410	554	129	.969
American League Totals				18	60	9	13	4	0	6	11	.217	73	5	2	.975
Major League Totals				1143	3839	552	933	155	20	270	720	.243	3483	559	131	.969

Selected by California Angels' organization in 2nd round of free-agent draft, June 6, 1967.
Selected by Baltimore Orioles' organization in secondary phase of free-agent draft, January 27, 1968.
Selected by San Francisco Giants' organization in secondary phase of free-agent draft, June 4, 1970.
†Sold to New York Mets for an estimated $125,000, February 28, 1975.
‡On disabled list, July 20 to August 27, 1976.
§Traded to San Diego Padres for Third Baseman-Outfielder Bobby Valentine and Pitcher Paul Siebert (assigned to Tidewater), June 15, 1977.
xSold on waivers to California Angels, September 6, 1977.
ySold to New York Yankees, September 15, 1977.
zGranted free agency, November 2, 1977; signed by Chicago Cubs, November 30, 1977.
aOn disabled list, July 1 to July 26, 1978.
bOn supplemental disabled list, June 13 to June 28 and July 10 to August 6, 1980.
cOn disabled list, August 6 to August 12, 1980.
dTraded to New York Mets for Outfielder Steve Henderson and cash, February 28, 1981.

PITCHING RECORD

Year	Club	League	G.	IP.	W.	L.	Pct.	H.	R.	ER.	SO.	BB.	ERA.
1973—San Francisco		National	2	4	0	0	.000	3	4	4	4	6	9.00

CHAMPIONSHIP SERIES RECORD

Year	Club	League	Pos.	G.	AB.	R.	H.	2B.	3B.	HR.	RBI.	B.A.	PO.	A.	E.	F.A.
1971—San Francisco		Nat.	PH-OF	4	9	0	1	0	0	0	0	.111	5	0	0	1.000

ALL-STAR GAME RECORD

Year	League	Pos.	AB.	R.	H.	2B.	3B.	HR.	RBI.	B.A.	PO.	A.	E.	F.A.
1976—National		OF	2	0	0	0	0	0	0	.000	1	0	0	1.000
1980—National		OF	1	0	0	0	0	0	0	.000	0	0	0	.000
All-Star Game Totals			3	0	0	0	0	0	0	.000	1	0	0	1.000

Named to National League All-Star Team for 1979 game; replaced due to injury by Keith Hernandez.

DENNIS PAUL KINNEY

Born February 26, 1952, at Toledo, O.
Height, 6.01. Weight, 170.
Throws and bats lefthanded.
Attended Bowling Green State University, Bowling Green, O.

Year	Club	League	G.	IP.	W.	L.	Pct.	H.	R.	ER.	SO.	BB.	ERA.
1970—Sarasota		Gulf Coast	14	31	3	2	.600	21	11	6	35	18	1.74
1971—Reno		California	14	23	0	1	.000	23	23	19	28	27	7.43
1971—Sarasota		Gulf Coast	16	49	5	1	.833	25	14	11	47	21	2.02
1972—Reno		California	*56	88	3	9	.250	84	54	42	112	72	4.30
1973—Reno		California	51	76	4	1	.800	77	42	32	84	47	3.79
1974—San Antonio		Texas	33	75	1	6	.143	81	44	38	68	52	4.56

Year Club	League	G.	IP.	W.	L.	Pct.	H.	R.	ER.	SO.	BB.	ERA.
1975—San Antonio	Texas	52	104	5	8	.385	133	75	64	68	46	5.54
1976—Williamsport	Eastern	33	67	1	2	.333	76	31	27	59	28	3.63
1976—San Jose	California	11	22	4	1	.800	21	12	8	16	10	3.27
1976—Toledo	Int'national	3	3	0	0	.000	2	1	1	4	1	3.00
1977—Jersey City	Eastern	8	11	0	1	.000	16	9	4	13	6	3.27
1977—Toledo	Int'national	40	118	6	6	.500	123	57	49	91	42	3.74
1978—Cleveland†	American	18	39	0	2	.000	37	21	19	19	14	4.38
1978—Hawaii	P. Coast	8	42	3	3	.500	55	38	18	22	12	3.86
1978—San Diego	National	7	7	0	1	.000	6	5	5	2	4	6.43
1979—Hawaii	P. Coast	20	87	4	11	.267	106	54	46	50	31	4.76
1979—San Diego	National	13	18	0	0	.000	17	8	7	11	8	3.50
1980—San Diego‡	National	50	83	4	6	.400	79	45	39	40	37	4.23
National League Totals		70	108	4	7	.364	102	58	51	53	49	4.25
American League Totals		18	39	0	2	.000	37	21	19	19	14	4.38
Major League Totals		88	147	4	9	.308	139	79	70	72	63	4.29

Selected by Cleveland Indians' organization in 10th round of free-agent draft, June 4, 1970.

†Traded to San Diego Padres for Pitcher Dan Spillner, June 14, 1978.

‡Traded to Detroit Tigers for Outfielder Dave Stegman, December 12, 1980.

MICHAEL JOHN KINNUNEN
(Mike)

Born April 1, 1958, at Seattle, Wash.
Height, 6.01. Weight, 185.
Throws and bats lefthanded.
Attended Washington State University, Pullman, Wash.

Year Club	League	G.	IP.	W.	L.	Pct.	H.	R.	ER.	SO.	BB.	ERA.
1979—Orlando	Southern	17	118	6	6	.500	129	63	54	55	45	4.12
1980—Toledo	Int'national	15	14	2	2	.500	13	5	4	9	5	2.57
1980—Minnesota	American	21	25	0	0	.000	29	18	14	8	9	5.04
Major League Totals		21	25	0	0	.000	29	18	14	8	9	5.04

Selected by Minnesota Twins' organization in 10th round of free-agent draft, June 5, 1979.

BRUCE EUGENE KISON
Name pronounced Key-son.

Born February 18, 1950, at Pasco, Wash.
Height, 6.04. Weight, 173.
Throws and bats righthanded.
Hobbies—Hunting, fishing, basketball and philately.
Attended Columbia Basin Junior College, Pasco, Wash., Manatee Junior College,
West Bradenton, Fla., and Central Washington State
College, Ellensburgh, Wash.

Year Club	League	G.	IP.	W.	L.	Pct.	H.	R.	ER.	SO.	BB.	ERA.
1968—Bradenton Pirates	Gulf Coast	10	24	2	1	.667	24	9	6	9	6	2.25
1969—Geneva†	NYP	13	94	5	2	.714	84	48	33	77	39	3.16
1970—Salem	Carolina	5	33	3	1	.750	17	5	3	26	7	0.82
1970—Waterbury	Eastern	19	130	10	4	.714	93	42	33	82	54	2.28
1971—Charleston	Int'national	12	85	10	1	.909	53	29	27	57	38	2.86
1971—Pittsburgh	National	18	95	6	5	.545	93	40	36	60	36	3.41
1972—Pittsburgh‡§	National	32	152	9	7	.563	123	61	55	102	69	3.26
1973—Charleston x	Int'national	20	114	8	6	.571	94	59	50	70	82	3.95
1973—Pittsburgh	National	7	44	3	0	1.000	36	17	15	26	24	3.07
1974—Pittsburgh	National	40	129	9	8	.529	123	64	50	71	57	3.49
1975—Pittsburgh	National	33	192	12	11	.522	160	89	69	89	92	3.23
1976—Pittsburgh	National	31	193	14	9	.609	180	83	66	98	52	3.08
1977—Pittsburgh	National	33	193	9	10	.474	209	113	105	122	55	4.90
1978—Pittsburgh y	National	28	96	6	6	.500	81	40	34	62	39	3.19
1979—Pittsburgh z	National	33	172	13	7	.650	157	70	61	105	45	3.19
1980—California	American	13	73	3	6	.333	73	46	40	28	32	4.93
National League Totals		255	1266	81	63	.563	1162	577	491	735	469	3.49
American League Totals		13	73	3	6	.333	73	46	40	28	32	4.93
Major League Totals		268	1339	84	69	.549	1235	623	531	763	501	3.57

Selected by Pittsburgh Pirates' organization in 6th round of free-agent draft, June 7, 1968.

†On restricted list, March 13 to June 18, 1969.

‡On disabled list, March 29 to April 20, 1972.

§On disabled list, March 23 to April 21, 1973.

xOn disabled list, June 14 to July 5, 1973.

yOn disabled list, May 28 to July 6, 1978.

zGranted free agency, November 1, 1979; signed by California Angels, November 16, 1979.

aOn disabled list, June 11 to July 14, 1980.

bOn emergency disabled list, July 15 to October 6, 1980.

CHAMPIONSHIP SERIES RECORD

Established National League Championship Series record for most bases on balls, game (6), October 8, 1974.

Tied National League Championship Series record for most games won, total Series (3).

Year	Club	League	G.	IP.	W.	L.	Pct.	H.	R.	ER.	SO.	BB.	ERA.
1971—Pittsburgh	National	1	4⅔	1	0	1.000	2	0	0	3	2	0.00
1972—Pittsburgh	National	2	2⅓	1	0	1.000	1	0	0	3	0	0.00
1974—Pittsburgh	National	1	6⅔	1	0	1.000	2	0	0	5	6	0.00
1975—Pittsburgh	National	1	2	0	0	.000	2	1	1	1	1	4.50
Championship Series Totals		5	15⅔	3	0	1.000	7	1	1	12	9	0.57

WORLD SERIES RECORD

Established World Series record for most hit batsmen, game (3), October 13, 1971.
Tied World Series record for most hit batsmen, Series (3), 1971.

Year	Club	League	G.	IP.	W.	L.	Pct.	H.	R.	ER.	SO.	BB.	ERA.
1971—Pittsburgh	National	2	6⅓	1	0	1.000	1	0	0	3	3	0.00
1979—Pittsburgh	National	1	⅓	0	1	.000	3	5	4	0	2	108.00
World Series Totals		3	6⅔	1	1	.500	4	5	4	3	5	5.40

GENE ELLIS KLUTTS
(Mickey)

Born September 30, 1954, at Montebello, Calif.
Height, 5.11. Weight, 189.
Throws and bats righthanded.

Shared International League Most Valuable Player, 1976.

Year	Club	League	Pos.	G.	AB.	R.	H.	2B.	3B.	HR.	RBI.	B.A.	PO.	A.	E.	F.A.
1972—Johnson City	Appal.	SS-3B	54	182	25	46	7	3	3	22	.253	54	114	19	.898
1973—Ft. Lauderdale	Fla.St.	SS-3B	34	94	4	12	1	0	1	9	.128	31	57	7	.926
1973—Oneonta	NYP	SS-2B	37	135	28	43	7	5	2	22	.319	57	107	8	.953
1974—Ft. Lauderdale†	Fla.St.	3B-SS	85	268	24	61	9	2	5	30	.228	101	237	20	.944
1975—West Haven‡	East.	3B-SS-1B	69	221	26	48	10	1	2	23	.217	53	180	19	.875
1976—Syracuse	Int.	SS-3B	119	430	75	137	22	3	24	80	.319	191	293	28	.945
1976—New York	Amer.	SS	2	3	0	0	0	0	0	0	.000	4	3	1	.875
1977—Syracuse	Int.	3B-SS-2B	85	320	52	92	19	7	14	66	.288	72	171	17	.935
1977—New York§	Amer.	3B-SS	5	15	3	4	1	0	1	4	.267	5	15	0	1.000
1978—New York xy	Amer.	3B	1	2	1	2	1	0	0	0	1.000	1	2	1	.750
1978—Vancouver za	P. C.	3-OF-SS	11	41	7	12	2	0	4	14	.293	6	6	0	1.000
1979—Oakland b	Amer.	SS-2B-3B	24	73	3	14	2	1	1	4	.192	35	50	7	.924
1980—Oakland c	Amer.	3-S-2	75	197	20	53	14	0	4	21	.269	63	104	9	.949
Major League Totals			107	290	27	73	18	1	6	29	.252	108	174	18	.940

Selected by New York Yankees' organization in 4th round of free-agent draft, June 6, 1972.
†On disabled list, May 23 to June 6, 1974.
‡On disabled list, August 2 to September 16, 1975.
§On disabled list, March 23 to April 30, 1977.
xOn supplemental disabled list, April 22 to May 19, 1978.
yTraded with Outfielder Dell Alston and $50,000 to Oakland A's for Outfielder Gary Thomasson, June 15, 1978.
zOn Oakland supplemental disabled list, June 16 to July 7, 1978 (did not play for A's).
aOn disabled list, July 30 to September 1, 1978.
bOn disabled list, May 24 to July 12; on emergency disabled list, July 12 to October 10, 1979.
cOn supplemental disabled list, June 29 to September 1, 1980.

ROBERT CHRISTIAN KNAPP
(Chris)

Born September 16, 1953, at Cherry Point, N. C.
Height, 6.05. Weight, 200.
Throws and bats righthanded.
Hobby—Carpentry.
Attended Kalamazoo Valley Community College, Kalamazoo, Mich.
and Central Michigan University, Mt. Pleasant, Mich.

Pitched seven inning 3-0, no-hit victory against Evansville, June 13, 1976.

Year	Club	League	G.	IP.	W.	L.	Pct.	H.	R.	ER.	SO.	BB.	ERA.
1975—Appleton	Midwest	14	87	6	6	.500	49	23	19	99	45	1.97
1975—Chicago	American	2	2	0	0	.000	2	1	1	3	4	4.50
1976—Knoxville	Southern	11	83	7	3	.700	58	26	22	68	42	2.39
1976—Iowa	Am. Assoc.	11	81	7	2	.778	63	24	23	74	28	2.56
1976—Chicago	American	11	52	3	1	.750	54	31	28	41	32	4.85
1977—Iowa	Am. Assoc.	5	32	0	4	.000	20	12	7	24	13	1.97
1977—Chicago†	American	27	146	12	7	.632	166	90	78	103	61	4.81
1978—California‡	American	30	188	14	8	.636	178	94	88	126	67	4.21
1979—California§	American	20	98	5	5	.500	109	73	60	36	35	5.51
1980—California	American	32	117	2	11	.154	133	83	80	46	51	6.15
Major League Totals		122	603	36	32	.529	642	372	335	355	250	5.00

Selected by Chicago White Sox' organization in 1st round (11th player selected) of free-agent draft, June 4, 1975.
†Traded with Pitcher Dave Frost and Catcher Brian Downing to California Angels for Outfielders Bobby Bonds and Thad Bosley and Pitcher Dick Dotson, December 5, 1977.
‡On disqualified list, July 13 to July 31, 1978.
§On disabled list, June 19 to August 10, 1979.

Year Club	League	G.	IP.	W.	L.	Pct.	H.	R.	ER.	SO.	BB.	ERA.
1979—California	American	1	2⅓	0	1	.000	5	2	2	0	1	7.71

ROBERT WESLEY KNEPPER

Name pronounced NEPP-ur.

(Bob)

Born May 25, 1954, at Akron, O.
Height, 6.02. Weight, 200.
Throws and bats lefthanded.
Hobbies—Hunting, fishing, coin collecting, music and reading.

Led National League in shutouts with 6 in 1978.
Led California League pitchers in games started with 30 and tied for lead in complete games with 16 in 1974.
Tied for Pacific Coast League lead in shutouts with 3 in 1976.

Year Club	League	G.	IP.	W.	L.	Pct.	H.	R.	ER.	SO.	BB.	ERA.
1972—Great Falls	Pioneer	12	68	7	1	.875	53	20	11	75	19	1.46
1973—Decatur	Midwest	11	79	7	2	.778	65	28	17	68	23	1.94
1973—Fresno................................	California	13	71	2	8	.200	78	54	32	66	35	4.06
1974—Fresno................................	California	30	*238	*20	5	•.800	*239	103	84	*247	80	3.18
1975—Phoenix	P. Coast	26	155	11	11	.500	169	101	79	94	78	4.59
1976—Phoenix	P. Coast	29	205	14	10	.583	209	105	98	130	64	4.30
1976—San Francisco	National	4	25	1	2	.333	26	9	9	11	7	3.24
1977—Phoenix	P. Coast	10	51	3	6	.333	68	51	42	24	25	7.41
1977—San Francisco	National	27	166	11	9	.550	151	73	62	100	72	3.36
1978—San Francisco	National	36	260	17	11	.607	218	85	76	147	85	2.63
1979—San Francisco	National	34	207	9	12	.429	241	117	107	123	77	4.65
1980—San Francisco†	National	35	215	9	16	.360	242	114	98	103	61	4.10
Major League Totals		136	873	47	50	.485	878	398	352	484	302	3.63

Selected by San Francisco Giants' organization in 2nd round of free-agent draft, June 6, 1972.
†Traded with Outfielder Chris Bourjos to Houston Astros for Third Baseman Enos Cabell, December 8, 1980.

ALAN LEE KNICELY

Born May 19, 1955, at Harrisonburg, Va.
Height, 6.00. Weight, 194.
Throws and bats righthanded.
Nephew of James Knicely, former player in Philadelphia Phillies' organization;
brother of Harold Knicely, former outfielder in Houston Astros' organization.

Led Pacific Coast League catchers in passed balls with 16 in 1980.
Tied for Southern League lead in strikeouts by batters with 112 in 1978.
Tied for Pacific Coast League lead in double plays by catchers with 8 in 1980.
Named Southern League co-Most Valuable Player award, 1979.

Year Club	League	Pos.	G.	AB.	R.	H.	2B.	3B.	HR.	RBI.	B.A.	PO.	A.	E.	F.A.
1974—Covington	Appal.	P	15	41	5	9	2	1	0	6	.220	3	*19	3	.880
1975—Dubuque	Midw.	P	27	35	5	11	1	0	1	9	.314	11	15	1	.963
1976—Dubuque	Midw.	P-1B	77	156	23	45	9	1	4	20	.288	84	23	3	.973
1977—Columbus	South.	3B-P	99	277	28	73	10	3	6	35	.264	84	140	24	.903
1978—Columbus	South.	OF	140	427	97	159	13	2	15	50	.227	262	22	10	.966
1979—Columbus	South.	C	120	422	77	122	12	3	*33	76	.289	446	51	15	.971
1979—Houston	Nat.	C-3B	7	6	0	0	0	0	0	0	.000	2	0	0	1.000
1980—Tucson	P.C.	C	133	468	69	149	18	4	22	*105	.318	511	*93	•23	.963
1980—Houston	Nat.	PH	1	1	0	0	0	0	0	0	.000	0	0	0	.000
Major League Totals......................			8	7	0	0	0	0	0	0	.000	2	0	0	1.000

Selected by Houston Astros' organization in 3rd round of free-agent draft, June 5, 1974.

PITCHING RECORD

Year Club	League	G.	IP.	W.	L.	Pct.	H.	R.	ER.	SO.	BB.	ERA.
1974—Covington	Ap'lachian	12	81	7	3	.700	78	35	31	53	42	3.44
1975—Dubuque	Midwest	26	122	4	10	.286	113	59	49	87	62	3.61
1976—Dubuque	Midwest	24	107	7	3	.700	100	58	47	87	62	3.95
1977—Columbus	Southern	14	42	1	5	.167	40	32	24	25	25	5.14

CHARLES RAY KNIGHT

(Known by middle name.)

Born December 28, 1952, at Albany, Ga.
Height, 6.02. Weight, 190.
Throws and bats righthanded.
Hobbies—Hunting, fishing, golfing and chess.
Attended Albany Junior College, Albany, Ga.

Tied major league records for most home runs, inning (2) and most total bases, inning (8), May 13, 1980 (fifth inning).
Tied for American Association lead in double plays by third basemen with 24 in 1974.

Year Club	League	Pos.	G.	AB.	R.	H.	2B.	3B.	HR.	RBI.	B.A.	PO.	A.	E.	F.A.
1971—Sioux Falls	North.	O-INF-P	64	239	34	68	5	2	6	31	.285	69	79	17	.897

Year	Club	League	Pos.	G.	AB.	R.	H.	2B.	3B.	HR.	RBI.	B.A.	PO.	A.	E.	F.A.
1972—Three Rivers	....East.	O-INF-P	97	302	25	64	8	1	2	35	.212	102	142	20	.924
1973—Three Rivers	....East.	O-3-1-2	57	193	41	54	14	2	2	22	.280	76	57	7	.950
1973—Indianapolis	......A.A.	3-O-1-P	78	253	20	55	10	4	1	16	.217	72	126	11	.947
1974—Indianapolis	......A.A.	*3B-OF	107	352	36	80	13	4	5	37	.227	94	177	11	*.961
1974—Cincinnati	........Nat.	3B	14	11	1	2	1	0	0	2	.182	2	8	0	1.000
1975—Indianapolis	......A.A.	*3B-1B	123	434	58	118	16	5	4	48	.272	*116	227	17	.953
1976—Indianapolis†	......A.A.	3B-1B	110	396	47	106	24	3	10	41	.268	136	181	13	.961
1977—Cincinnati	........Nat.	3-2-OF-S	80	92	8	24	5	1	1	13	.261	45	45	4	.957
1978—Cincinnati‡	......Nat.	3-2-O-S-1	83	65	7	13	3	0	1	4	.200	13	41	7	.885
1979—Cincinnati	........Nat.	3B	150	551	64	175	37	4	10	79	.318	120	262	15	.962
1980—Cincinnati	........Nat.	3B	162	618	71	163	39	7	14	78	.264	120	291	13	.969
Major League Totals	....		489	1337	151	377	85	12	26	176	.282	300	647	39	.960

Selected by Cincinnati Reds' organization in 10th round of free-agent draft, June 4, 1970.

†On disabled list, June 21 to July 2, 1976.

‡On disabled list, April 17 to May 8, 1978.

PITCHING RECORD

Year	Club	League	G.	IP.	W.	L.	Pct.	H.	R.	ER.	SO.	BB.	ERA.
1971—Sioux Falls	...........................Northern	3	4	1	1	.500	5	6	5	4	5	11.25
1972—Three Rivers	........................Eastern	2	4	0	0	.000	3	1	1	2	4	2.25
1973—Indianapolis	........................Am. Assoc.	1	2	0	0	.000	2	1	1	0	4	4.50

CHAMPIONSHIP SERIES RECORD

Year	Club	League	Pos.	G.	AB.	R.	H.	2B.	3B.	HR.	RBI.	B.A.	PO.	A.	E.	F.A.
1979—Cincinnati	.........Nat.	3B	3	14	0	4	1	0	0	0	.286	0	5	0	1.000

ALL-STAR GAME RECORD

Year	League	Pos.	AB.	R.	H.	2B.	3B.	HR.	RBI.	B.A.	PO.	A.	E.	F.A.
1980—National	....	3B	1	1	1	0	0	0	0	1.000	0	1	0	1.000

DAROLD DUANE KNOWLES

Born December 9, 1941, at Brunswick, Mo.
Height, 6.00. Weight, 185.
Throws and bats lefthanded.
Hobbies—Golf and hunting.
Attended University of Missouri, Columbia, Mo.

Established major league record for most games by lefthanded pitcher, lifetime (763).

Tied American League record for most games lost by relief pitcher, season (14), 1970.

Pitched six-inning, 3-0 no-hit loss against San Jose, June 15, 1962.

Major League saves: 1965 (0), 1966 (13), 1967 (14), 1968 (4), 1969 (13), 1970 (27), 1971 (9), 1972 (11), 1973 (9), 1974 (3), 1975 (15), 1976 (9), 1977 (4), 1978 (6), 1979 (6), 1980 (0). Total—143.

Led Northern League in hit batsmen with 12 in 1961.

Year	Club	League	G.	IP.	W.	L.	Pct.	H.	R.	ER.	SO.	BB.	ERA.
1961—Aberdeen	....................Northern	23	164	11	5	.688	118	79	60	*183	106	3.29
1962—Elmira	................................Eastern	2	9	0	1	.000	6	5	4	5	6	4.00
1962—Charlotte	............................Sally	6	7	0	1	.000	9	7	1	4	9	1.29
1962—Stockton	...........................California	23	161	12	7	.632	117	60	41	202	80	*2.29
1963—Elmira	................................Eastern	30	*201	●16	7	.696	180	67	61	146	60	2.73
1964—Rochester	..........................Int'national	37	136	6	7	.462	130	58	46	104	61	3.04
1965—Baltimore	..........................American	5	15	0	1	.000	14	15	15	12	10	9.00
1965—Rochester†	..........................Int'national	32	174	11	5	.688	160	59	49	155	64	2.53
1966—Philadelphia‡	......................National	69	100	6	5	.545	98	38	34	88	46	3.06
1967—Washington	..........................American	61	113	6	8	.429	91	37	34	85	52	2.71
1968—Washington§	......................American	32	41	1	1	.500	38	11	10	37	12	2.20
1969—Washington	..........................American	53	84	9	2	.818	73	25	21	59	31	2.25
1970—Washington	..........................American	71	119	2	14	.125	100	36	27	71	58	2.04
1971—Wash. x-Oak	......................American	55	68	7	4	.636	57	28	27	56	22	3.57
1972—Oakland y	..........................American	54	66	5	1	.833	49	12	10	36	37	1.36
1973—Oakland	..........................American	52	99	6	8	.429	87	44	34	46	49	3.09
1974—Oakland z	..........................American	45	53	3	3	.500	61	29	25	18	35	4.25
1975—Chicago	..........................National	58	88	6	9	.400	107	61	57	63	36	5.83
1976—Chicago a	..........................National	58	72	5	7	.417	61	30	23	39	22	2.88
1977—Texas bc	..........................American	42	50	5	2	.714	50	22	18	14	23	3.24
1978—Montreal d	........................National	60	72	3	3	.500	63	20	19	34	30	2.38
1979—St. Louis	..........................National	48	49	2	5	.286	54	27	22	22	17	4.04
1980—St. Louis e	..........................National	2	2	0	1	.000	3	2	2	1	0	9.00
National League Totals	....	295	383	22	30	.423	386	178	157	247	151	3.69
American League Totals	....	470	708	44	44	.500	620	259	221	434	329	2.81
Major League Totals	....	765	1091	66	74	.471	1006	437	378	681	480	3.12

Signed as free agent by Baltimore Orioles' organization, February 9, 1961.

†Recalled by Baltimore Orioles and traded with Outfielder Jackie Brandt to Philadelphia Phillies for Pitcher Jack Baldschun, December 6, 1965.

‡Traded with cash to Washington Senators for Outfielder Don Lock, November 30, 1966.

§In Military service from July 14 through end of season.

xTraded with First Baseman Mike Epstein to Oakland A's for First Baseman Don Mincher, Catcher Frank Fernandez and Pitcher Paul Lindblad, May 8, 1971.

yOn disabled list from September 29 through the end of the season.
zTraded with Pitcher Bob Locker and Second Baseman Manny Trillo to Chicago Cubs for Outfielder-First Baseman Billy Williams, October 23, 1974.
aTraded to Texas Rangers for Outfielder Gene Clines and cash, February 5, 1977.
bOn disabled list, March 27 to April 17, 1977.
cSold to Montreal Expos, November 10, 1977.
dGranted free agency, November 2, 1978; signed by St. Louis Cardinals, January 16, 1979.
eReleased, May 9, 1980.
St. Louis minor league pitching instructor, 1981.

CHAMPIONSHIP SERIES RECORD

Year Club	League	G.	IP.	W.	L.	Pct.	H.	R.	ER.	SO.	BB.	ERA.
1971—Oakland	American	1	⅓	0	0	.000	1	0	0	0	0	0.00

WORLD SERIES RECORD

Established World Series records for consecutive games pitched, most games pitched, and most games pitched, relief pitcher, seven-game Series (7), 1973.

Year Club	League	G.	IP.	W.	L.	Pct.	H.	R.	ER.	SO.	BB.	ERA.
1973—Oakland	American	7	6⅓	0	0	.000	4	1	0	5	5	0.00

ALL-STAR GAME RECORD

Year League	IP.	W.	L.	Pct.	H.	R.	ER.	SO.	BB.	ERA.
1969—American	⅔	0	0	.000	0	0	0	0	0	0.00

KEVIN RICHARD KOBEL

Born October 2, 1953, at Buffalo, N. Y.
Height, 6.01. Weight, 195.
Throws left and bats righthanded.
Attended Mesa Community College, Mesa, Ariz.

Year Club	League	G.	IP.	W.	L.	Pct.	H.	R.	ER.	SO.	BB.	ERA.
1971—Newark	NYP	11	60	5	1	.833	44	21	17	63	36	2.55
1972—San Antonio	Texas	29	140	3	*15	.167	151	84	67	107	56	4.31
1973—Shreveport	Texas	26	167	12	8	.600	160	83	63	103	62	3.39
1973—Milwaukee	American	2	8	0	1	.000	9	8	8	4	8	9.00
1974—Milwaukee	American	34	169	6	14	.300	166	84	75	74	54	3.99
1975—Sacramento†	P. Coast	7	30	3	2	.600	29	11	8	9	7	2.40
1976—Spokane	P. Coast	32	131	7	12	.368	153	86	80	56	43	5.50
1976—Milwaukee	National	3	4	0	1	.000	6	5	5	1	3	11.25
1977—Spokane‡§	P. Coast	35	153	12	6	.667	175	100	84	75	59	4.94
1978—Tidewater	Int'national	13	26	2	1	.667	23	7	7	17	10	2.42
1978—New York	National	32	108	5	6	.455	95	42	35	51	30	2.92
1979—New York x	National	30	162	6	8	.429	169	74	63	67	46	3.50
1980—New York y	National	14	24	1	4	.200	36	21	19	8	11	7.13
1980—Omaha	Am. Assoc.	17	53	2	1	.667	62	38	33	21	24	5.60
American League Totals		39	181	6	16	.273	181	97	88	79	65	4.38
National League Totals		76	294	12	18	.400	300	137	117	126	87	3.58
Major League Totals		115	475	18	34	.346	481	234	205	205	152	3.88

Selected by Milwaukee Brewers' organization in 10th round of free-agent draft, June 8, 1971.
†On disabled list, April 10 to April 21 and May 28 through remainder of season.
‡On disabled list, July 23 to August 2, 1977.
§Sold to New York Mets' organization, December 6, 1977.
xOn disabled list, March 24 to April 28, 1979.
yTraded to Kansas City Royals' organization for a player to be named later, June 17, 1980; Pitcher Randy McGilberry traded to Mets' organization completing deal, June 23, 1980.

JERRY MARTIN KOOSMAN

Born December 23, 1943, at Appleton, Minn.
Height, 6.02. Weight, 225.
Throws left and bats righthanded.
Hobbies—Flying, golf and water skiing.
Attended University of Minnesota, Morris, Minn., and
State School of Science, Wahpeton, N. D.

Established National League record for most strikeouts, season, by pitcher as batter (62), 1968.
Tied modern National League record for most shutout games won or tied, rookie season (7), 1968.
Named THE SPORTING NEWS National League Rookie Pitcher of the Year, 1968.

Year Club	League	G.	IP.	W.	L.	Pct.	H.	R.	ER.	SO.	BB.	ERA.
1965—Greenville	W. Carol.	27	107	5	11	.313	101	70	56	128	56	4.71
1965—Williamsport	Eastern	2	12	0	2	.000	11	7	5	11	11	3.75
1966—Auburn	NYP	24	170	12	7	.632	109	43	26	174	43	*1.38
1967—New York	National	9	22	0	2	.000	22	17	15	11	19	6.14
1967—Jacksonville	Int'national	25	178	11	10	.524	137	60	48	*183	46	2.43
1968—New York	National	35	264	19	12	.613	221	72	61	178	69	2.08
1969—New York	National	32	241	17	9	.684	187	66	61	180	68	2.28
1970—New York	National	30	212	12	7	.632	189	87	74	118	71	3.14
1971—New York†	National	26	166	6	11	.353	160	66	56	96	51	3.04
1972—New York	National	34	163	11	12	.478	155	81	75	147	52	4.14
1973—New York	National	35	263	14	15	.483	234	93	83	156	76	2.84
1974—New York	National	35	265	15	11	.577	258	113	99	188	85	3.36

Year Club	League	G.	IP.	W.	L.	Pct.	H.	R.	ER.	SO.	BB.	ERA.
1975–New York	National	36	240	14	13	.519	234	106	91	173	98	3.41
1976–New York	National	34	247	21	10	.677	205	81	74	200	66	2.70
1977–New York	National	32	227	8	●20	.286	195	102	88	192	81	3.49
1978–New York‡	National	38	235	3	15	.167	221	110	98	160	84	3.75
1979–Minnesota	American	37	264	20	13	.606	268	108	99	157	83	3.38
1980–Minnesota	American	38	243	16	13	.552	252	119	109	149	69	4.04
National League Totals		376	2545	140	137	.505	2281	994	875	1799	820	3.09
American League Totals		75	507	36	26	.581	520	227	208	306	152	3.69
Major League Totals		451	3052	176	163	.519	2701	1221	1083	2105	972	3.19

Signed as free agent by New York Mets' organization, August 27, 1964.
†On disabled list July 7 to August 9, 1971.
‡Traded to Minnesota Twins for Pitcher Greg Field and a player to be named later, December 8, 1978; Pitcher Jesse Orosco sent to New York Mets to complete deal, February 7, 1979.

CHAMPIONSHIP SERIES RECORD

Established National League Championship Series record for most earned runs allowed, inning (5), October 5, 1969 (fifth inning).
Tied National League Championship Series record for most runs allowed, inning (5), October 5, 1969 (fifth inning).

Year Club	League	G.	IP.	W.	L.	Pct.	H.	R.	ER.	SO.	BB.	ERA.
1969–New York	National	1	4⅔	0	0	.000	7	6	6	5	4	11.57
1973–New York	National	1	9	1	0	1.000	8	2	2	9	0	2.00
Championship Series Totals		2	13⅔	1	0	1.000	15	8	8	14	4	5.27

WORLD SERIES RECORD

Year Club	League	G.	IP.	W.	L.	Pct.	H.	R.	ER.	SO.	BB.	ERA.
1969–New York	National	2	17⅔	2	0	1.000	7	4	4	9	4	2.04
1973–New York	National	2	8⅔	1	0	1.000	9	3	3	8	7	3.12
World Series Totals		4	26⅓	3	0	1.000	16	7	7	17	11	2.39

ALL-STAR GAME RECORD

Year League	IP.	W.	L.	Pct.	H.	R.	ER.	SO.	BB.	ERA.
1968–National	⅓	0	0	.000	0	0	0	1	0	0.00
1969–National	1⅔	0	0	.000	1	0	0	1	0	0.00
All-Star Game Totals	2	0	0	.000	1	0	0	2	0	0.00

KENNETH PETER KRAVEC
(Ken)

Born July 29, 1951, at Cleveland, O.
Height, 6.02. Weight, 185.
Throws and bats lefthanded.
Hobbies—Golf and listening to music.
Attended Ashland College, Ashland, O.; received Bachelor of Science
degree in Management and Marketing.

Named Pitcher of the Year in Southern League, 1975.

Year Club	League	G.	IP.	W.	L.	Pct.	H.	R.	ER.	SO.	BB.	ERA.
1973–Knoxville	Southern	13	64	2	8	.200	53	44	36	52	65	5.06
1974–Knoxville	Southern	27	132	6	6	.500	100	58	50	105	79	3.41
1975–Knoxville	Southern	28	168	●14	7	.667	138	52	45	119	78	2.41
1975–Chicago	American	2	4	0	1	.000	1	3	3	1	8	6.75
1976–Iowa	Am. Assoc.	24	131	8	5	.615	103	68	63	142	89	4.33
1976–Chicago	American	9	50	1	5	.167	49	28	27	38	32	4.86
1977–Iowa	Am. Assoc.	9	59	4	4	.500	46	21	17	62	33	2.59
1977–Chicago	American	26	167	11	8	.579	161	87	76	125	57	4.10
1978–Iowa	Am. Assoc.	2	12	1	1	.500	10	5	5	14	5	3.75
1978–Chicago	American	30	203	11	16	.407	188	104	92	154	95	4.08
1979–Chicago	American	36	250	15	13	.536	208	115	104	132	111	3.74
1980–Chicago	American	20	82	3	6	.333	100	71	63	37	44	6.91
Major League Totals		123	756	41	49	.456	707	408	365	487	347	4.35

Selected by Cleveland Indians' organization in 29th round of free-agent draft, June 5, 1969.
Selected by Chicago White Sox' organization in 3rd round of free-agent draft, June 5, 1973.

WAYNE RICHARD KRENCHICKI

Born September 17, 1954, at Trenton, N.J.
Height, 6.01. Weight, 175.
Throws right and bats lefthanded
Attended University of Miami, Miami, Fla.
Brother of Tom Krenchicki, former shortstop in Los Angeles Dodgers' organization.

Led Florida State League shortstops in assists with 378, in double plays with 60 and in fielding average with .968 in 1976.
Led Southern League second basemen in double plays with 114 in 1977.

Year Club	League	Pos.	G.	AB.	R.	H.	2B.	3B.	HR.	RBI.	B.A.	PO.	A.	E.	F.A.
1976–Miami	Fla. St.	SS-3B	133	459	38	109	14	1	0	35	.237	190	439	19	.971
1977–Charlotte	South.	2B	131	510	69	140	17	9	3	42	.275	★325	★455	25	.969

Year Club	League	Pos.	G.	AB.	R.	H.	2B.	3B.	HR.	RBI.	B.A.	PO.	A.	E.	F.A.
1978—Rochester	Int.	3B-2B-SS	*140	520	*93	154	26	1	12	71	.296	204	389	32	.949
1979—Rochester†	Int.	2B-SS-3B	66	249	21	65	7	2	0	22	.261	129	173	9	.971
1979—Baltimore	Amer.	3B-2B	16	21	1	4	1	0	0	0	.190	12	12	2	.923
1980—Rochester‡	Int.	2-3-S	87	311	42	82	13	3	2	39	.264	137	230	10	.973
1980—Baltimore	Amer.	SS-2B	9	14	1	2	0	0	0	0	.143	9	9	0	1.000
Major League Totals......................			25	35	2	6	1	0	0	0	.171	21	21	2	.955

Selected by Philadelphia Phillies' orᵧ nization in 8th round of free-agent draft, June 6, 1972.
Selected by Baltimore Orioles' organization in secondary phase of free-agent draft, January 7, 1976.
†On disabled list, May 10 to June 1 and August 5 to August 15, 1979.
‡On disabled list, July 12 to August 1, 1980.

TED WILLIAMS KROMY

Born July 2, 1959, at Tacoma, Wash.
Height, 6.02. Weight, 173.
Throws and bats righthanded.
Attended University of Minnesota, Minneapolis, Minn.
Son of Darwin Kromy, minor league pitcher, 1953-55.
Tied for California League lead in games started with 28 in 1980.

Year Club	League	G.	IP.	W.	L.	Pct.	H.	R.	ER.	SO.	BB.	ERA.
1978—Wisconsin Rapids	Midwest	7	23	2	2	.500	34	24	18	12	20	7.04
1978—Elizabethton	Appal.	13	78	3	4	.429	85	37	29	35	23	3.35
1979—Wisconsin Rapids	Midwest	29	159	8	11	.421	177	87	60	87	38	3.40
1980—Visalia	California	28	196	12	12	.500	200	108	75	113	68	3.44

Signed as free agent by Minnesota Twins' organization, August 18, 1977.

MICHAEL EDWARD KRUKOW

Name pronounced Kroo-koh.

(Mike)

Born January 21, 1952, at Long Beach, Calif.
Height, 6.04. Weight, 195.
Throws and bats righthanded.
Hobbies—Music, backpacking, golf and raising dogs.
Attended California Poly State University, San Luis Obispo, Calif.
Nephew of Tim Ryan, who played in Pittsburgh Pirates' organization, 1949.
Tied for Gulf Coast League lead in complete games by pitchers with 4 in 1973.

Year Club	League	G.	IP.	W.	L.	Pct.	H.	R.	ER.	SO.	BB.	ERA.
1973—Bradenton Cubs....................	Gulf Coast	13	77	4	3	.571	76	32	27	*80	28	3.16
1974—Midland	Texas	6	30	1	1	.500	42	24	17	21	19	5.10
1974—Key West	Florida St.	20	130	5	10	.333	121	66	46	94	47	3.18
1975—Midland†	Texas	24	153	13	6	.684	143	65	58	100	66	3.41
1976—Wichita	Am. Assoc.	26	144	7	9	.438	142	61	53	108	47	3.31
1976—Chicago	National	2	4	0	0	.000	6	4	4	1	2	9.00
1977—Chicago	National	34	172	8	14	.364	195	96	84	106	61	4.40
1978—Wichita	Am. Assoc.	7	53	2	3	.400	51	27	23	29	21	3.91
1978—Chicago	National	27	138	9	3	.750	125	62	60	81	53	3.91
1979—Chicago	National	28	165	9	9	.500	172	84	77	119	81	4.20
1980—Chicago	National	34	205	10	15	.400	200	117	100	130	80	4.39
Major League Totals		125	684	36	41	.468	698	363	325	437	277	4.28

Selected by California Angels' organization in 32nd round of free-agent draft, June 4, 1970.
Selected by Chicago Cubs' organization in 8th round of free-agent draft, June 5, 1973.
†On disabled list, May 19 to June 7, 1975.

GILBERT THOMAS KUBSKI

Name pronounced Cub-ski

(Gil)

Born October 12, 1954, at Longview, Tex.
Height, 6.03. Weight, 185.
Throws right and bats lefthanded.
Hobbies—Golf, fishing and old movies.
Attended California State University, Northridge, Calif.
Son of Albert Kubski, minor league manager in Pittsburgh Pirates' organization; Baltimore Orioles' scout,
1964-1972; California Angels' scout, 1972-1977 and currently Kansas City Royals' scout.

Year Club	League	Pos.	G.	AB.	R.	H.	2B.	3B.	HR.	RBI.	B.A.	PO.	A.	E.	F.A.
1975—Salinas†	Calif.	OF	118	433	64	133	15	6	5	47	.307	200	6	10	.954
1976—El Paso‡	Texas	OF	99	310	36	85	15	4	3	38	.274	126	12	7	.952
1977—El Paso	Texas	OF	123	*546	*114	*177	29	2	9	90	.324	195	*19	8	.964
1978—Salt Lake City ...	P. C.	OF-2B-P	97	306	57	81	9	4	4	42	.265	104	18	6	.953
1979—Salt Lake City§..	P. C.	OF-1B-P	128	498	83	147	33	4	12	54	.295	269	18	8	.973
1980—Salt Lake City ...	P. C.	OF	123	476	92	146	18	5	8	54	.307	309	13	6	.982
1980—California x.......	Amer.	OF	22	63	11	16	3	0	0	6	.254	36	2	0	1.000
Major League Totals......................			22	63	11	16	3	0	0	6	.254	36	2	0	1.000

Selected by Pittsburgh Pirates' organization in 40th round of free-agent draft, June 6, 1972.
Selected by California Angels' organization in secondary phase of free-agent draft, January 9, 1975.

†On disabled list, August 24 to September 30, 1975.
‡On disabled list, April 24 to May 5, 1976.
§On disabled list, May 21 to June 4, 1979.
xTraded to Toronto Blue Jays' organization for Outfielder Don Pisker, February 6, 1981.

PITCHING RECORD

Year Club	League	G.	IP.	W.	L.	Pct.	H.	R.	ER.	SO.	BB.	ERA.
1978—Salt Lake City ....P. Coast		2	2	0	0	.000	0	4	4	1	4	18.00
1979—Salt Lake City ....P. Coast		1	1	0	0	.000	0	0	0	0	0	0.00

JOHN ANDREW KUCEK
(Jack)

Born June 8, 1953, at Warren, O.
Height, 6.02. Weight, 200.
Throws and bats righthanded.
Hobbies—Poetry and music.
Attended Miami University, Oxford, O.

Pitched 6-1 no-hit victory against Oklahoma City, May 26, 1978.

Year Club	League	G.	IP.	W.	L.	Pct.	H.	R.	ER.	SO.	BB.	ERA.
1974—Appleton ....Midwest		9	51	5	2	.714	33	11	10	49	22	1.76
1974—Chicago ....American		9	38	1	4	.200	48	25	22	25	21	5.21
1975—Denver ....Am. Assoc.		6	17	1	2	.333	24	13	13	17	3	6.88
1975—Knoxville ....Southern		21	114	10	4	*.714	93	38	35	77	48	2.76
1975—Chicago ....American		2	4	0	0	.000	9	2	2	2	4	4.50
1976—Iowa ....Am. Assoc.		22	124	5	9	.357	130	68	58	78	55	4.21
1976—Chicago ....American		2	5	0	0	.000	9	5	5	2	4	9.00
1977—Iowa ....Am. Assoc.		16	117	6	8	.429	93	41	33	83	39	*2.54
1977—Chicago† ....American		8	35	0	1	.000	35	20	14	25	10	3.60
1978—Iowa ....Am. Assoc.		21	150	9	8	.529	131	55	41	115	68	*2.46
1978—Chicago ....American		10	52	2	3	.400	42	23	19	30	27	3.29
1979—Chicago ‡ ....American		1	1	0	0	.000	0	4	0	0	3	0.00
1979—Oklahoma City ....Am. Assoc.		34	83	7	8	.467	74	40	34	62	63	3.69
1979—Philadelphia § ....National		4	4	1	0	1.000	6	4	4	2	1	9.00
1980—Syracuse............................Int'national		13	62	3	3	.500	64	32	29	46	21	4.21
1980—Toronto ....American		23	68	3	8	.273	83	56	51	35	41	6.75
American League Totals............................		55	203	6	16	.273	226	135	113	119	110	5.01
National League Totals		4	14	1	0	1.000	6	4	4	2	1	9.00
Major League Totals.................................		59	217	7	16	.304	232	139	117	121	111	4.85

Selected by Chicago White Sox' organization in 6th round of free-agent draft, June 8, 1971.
Selected by Chicago White Sox' organization in 2nd round of free-agent draft, June 5, 1974.
†On disabled list, August 23 to September 13, 1977.
‡Traded to Philadelphia Phillies for a player to be named later, April 13, 1979; White Sox acquired Infielder Jim Morrison to complete deal, July 10, 1979.
§Released, December 18, 1979; signed by Toronto Blue Jays' organization, January 10, 1980.

DUANE EUGENE KUIPER
Name pronounced KIPE-er.

Born June 19, 1950, at Racine, Wis.
Height, 6.00. Weight, 175.
Throws right and bats lefthanded.
Hobbies—Music and reading.
Attended Indian Hills Community College, Centerville, Ia., and Southern
Illinois University, Carbondale, Ill.; received Bachelor of Arts degree.
Second cousin of Dick Bosman, former pitcher with Washington Senators,
Texas Rangers, Cleveland Indians and Oakland Athletics.

Tied major league record for most triples, bases filled, game (2), July 27, 1978.
Led American Association in stolen bases with 28 in 1974.

Year Club	League	Pos.	G.	AB.	R.	H.	2B.	3B.	HR.	RBI.	B.A.	PO.	A.	E.	F.A.
1972—Reno ....Calif.		2-S-3	124	496	89	149	20	3	2	53	.300	264	283	18	.968
1973—Okla. City..........A. A.		2B	18	56	6	9	1	1	0	6	.161	42	34	3	.962
1973—San Antonio.......Tex.		2B	107	395	46	113	11	2	1	42	.286	220	317	19	.966
1974—Okla. City..........A. A.		2B	•135	*554	83	172	27	5	3	53	.310	291	*365	11	.984
1974—Cleveland..........Amer.		2B	10	22	7	11	2	0	0	4	.500	16	19	0	1.000
1975—Okla. City..........A. A.		2B	40	164	18	40	5	0	1	12	.244	110	94	3	.986
1975—Cleveland† ....Amer.		2B	90	346	42	101	11	0	0	25	.292	192	230	12	.972
1976—Cleveland..........Amer.		*2B-1B	135	506	47	133	13	6	0	37	.263	321	367	11	*.984
1977—Cleveland..........Amer.		2B	148	610	62	169	15	8	1	50	.277	334	449	12	.985
1978—Cleveland..........Amer.		2B	149	547	52	155	18	6	0	43	.283	341	408	16	.979
1979—Cleveland..........Amer.		2B	140	479	46	122	9	5	0	39	.255	345	380	9	*.988
1980—Cleveland‡ ....Amer.		2B	42	149	10	42	5	0	0	9	.282	87	111	1	.995
Major League Totals			714	2659	266	733	73	26	1	207	.276	1636	1964	61	.983

Selected by New York Yankees' organization in 12th round of free-agent draft, June 7, 1968.
Selected by Seattle Pilots' organization in secondary phase of free-agent draft, February 1, 1969.
Selected by Chicago White Sox' organization in 1st round (fifth player selected) of free-agent draft, January 17, 1970.

Selected by Cincinnati Reds' organization in secondary phase of free-agent draft, June 4, 1970.
Selected by Boston Red Sox' organization in secondary phase of free-agent draft, June 8, 1971.
Selected by Cleveland Indians' organization in secondary phase of free-agent draft, January 12, 1972.
†On supplemental disabled list, July 22 to August 11, 1975.
‡On emergency disabled list, June 2 to October 13, 1980.

RUSSELL JAY KUNTZ
(Rusty)

Born February 4, 1955, at Orange, Calif.
Height, 6.03. Weight, 190.
Throws and bats righthanded.
Attended Cuesta College, San Luis Obispo, Calif.,
and California State University.

Led Gulf Coast League in sacrifice flies with 6 and in bases on balls with 40 in 1977.
Led American Association batters in strikeouts with 111 in 1979.

Year	Club	League	Pos.	G.	AB.	R.	H.	2B.	3B.	HR.	RBI.	B.A.	PO.	A.	E.	F.A.
1977—Sara. W. Sox		Gulf C.	OF	51	174	•49	50	9	5	3	33	.287	87	•9	3	.970
1978—Knoxville		South.	OF	113	395	68	104	25	7	10	57	.263	244	9	3	.988
1979—Iowa		A.A.	OF	122	394	67	116	27	5	15	57	.294	287	12	5	.984
1979—Chicago		Amer.	OF	5	11	0	1	0	0	0	0	.091	12	1	0	1.000
1980—Iowa†		A.A.	OF	91	339	47	99	20	2	11	54	.292	198	9	7	.967
1980—Chicago		Amer.	OF	36	62	5	14	4	0	0	3	.226	45	2	1	.979
Major League Totals				41	73	5	15	4	0	0	3	.205	57	3	1	.984

Selected by Chicago White Sox' organization in 11th round of free-agent draft, June 7, 1977.
†On disabled list, May 24 to June 17, 1980.

ROBERT JOSEPH LACEY, JR.
(Bob)

Born August 25, 1953, at Fredericksburg, Va.
Height, 6.04. Weight, 190.
Throws left and bats righthanded.
Hobbies—Watching cartoons, collecting comic books and albums.
Attended Central Arizona College, Coolidge, Ariz.

Year	Club	League	G.	IP.	W.	L.	Pct.	H.	R.	ER.	SO.	BB.	ERA.
1972—Coos Bay—North Bend†		Northwest	8	39	0	3	.000	43	30	25	22	30	5.77
1973—Key West		Florida St.	13	90	6	1	.857	85	23	13	57	17	1.30
1973—Burlington		Midwest	15	83	7	1	.875	86	35	30	63	25	3.25
1974—Birmingham		Southern	32	155	6	13	.316	203	*111	79	72	35	4.59
1975—Birmingham		Southern	33	68	3	6	.333	81	34	28	47	39	3.71
1975—Tucson		P. Coast	10	35	3	1	.750	35	14	12	17	9	3.09
1976—Tucson‡		P. Coast	29	105	3	9	.250	139	73	69	35	26	5.91
1977—San Jose		P. Coast	11	16	2	0	1.000	10	0	0	9	6	0.00
1977—Oakland		American	64	122	6	8	.429	100	46	41	69	43	3.02
1978—Oakland		American	•74	120	8	9	.471	126	52	40	60	35	3.00
1979—Oakland§		American	42	48	1	5	.167	66	34	31	33	24	5.81
1980—Oakland		American	47	80	3	2	.600	68	29	26	45	21	2.93
Major League Totals			227	370	18	24	.429	360	161	138	207	123	3.36

Selected by Oakland A's organization in 10th round of free-agent draft, January 12, 1972.
†On suspended list, July 31 through remainder of season.
‡On disabled list, June 5 to June 16 and August 4 to September 8, 1976.
§On disabled list, July 14 to September 18, 1979.

RALPH PIERRE LaCOCK, II
(Pete)

Born January 17, 1952, at Burbank, Calif.
Height, 6.03. Weight, 210.
Throws and bats lefthanded.
Hobbies—Automobiles and oceanography.
Son of television personality Peter Marshall, and nephew of actress Joanne Dru.

Led Texas League hitters in bases on balls with 93 in 1972 and 84 in 1971.
Named American Association Most Valuable Player, 1974.

Year	Club	League	Pos.	G.	AB.	R.	H.	2B.	3B.	HR.	RBI.	B.A.	PO.	A.	E.	F.A.
1970—Caldwell		Pion.	OF	69	231	43	65	13	3	4	49	.281	76	6	*10	.891
1970—Quincy		Midw.	OF	18	13	3	1	0	0	0	2	.077	5	0	0	1.000
1971—San Antonio		Texas	OF	131	446	64	119	19	5	7	58	.267	187	11	10	.952
1972—Midland		Texas	OF	129	444	88	136	16	*13	8	70	.306	216	10	5	.978
1972—Chicago		Nat.	OF	5	6	3	3	0	0	0	4	.500	2	0	0	1.000
1973—Wichita		A.A.	OF-1B	130	518	89	154	24	6	9	69	.297	238	17	8	.970
1973—Chciago		Nat.	OF	11	16	1	4	1	0	0	3	.250	5	1	0	1.000
1974—Wichita		A.A.	1B-OF	121	455	95	149	25	4	23	91	.327	841	66	11	.988
1974—Chicago		Nat.	OF-1B	35	110	9	20	4	1	1	8	.182	134	12	2	.986
1975—Chicago		Nat.	1B-OF	106	249	30	57	8	1	6	30	.229	479	45	6	.989
1976—Chicago†		Nat.	1B-OF	106	244	34	54	9	2	8	28	.221	454	33	13	.974
1977—Kansas City		Amer.	1B-OF	88	218	25	66	12	1	3	29	.303	203	19	2	.991
1978—Kansas City		Amer.	1B	118	322	44	95	21	2	5	48	.295	700	39	5	.993

Year Club League	Pos.	G.	AB.	R.	H.	2B.	3B.	HR.	RBI.	B.A.	PO.	A.	E.	F.A.
1979—Kansas City ......Amer.	1B	132	408	54	113	25	4	3	56	.277	829	68	3	*.997
1980—Kansas City‡ .....Amer.	1B-OF	114	156	14	32	6	0	1	18	.205	308	22	2	.994
National League Totals...................		263	625	77	138	22	4	15	73	.221	1074	91	21	.982
American League Totals.................		452	1104	137	306	64	7	12	151	.277	2040	148	12	.995
Major League Totals		715	1729	214	444	86	11	27	224	.257	3114	239	33	.990

Selected by Chicago Cubs' organization in 1st round (19th player selected) of free-agent draft, January 17, 1970.

†Traded, in three-club deal, to Kansas City Royals, the New York Mets sent Outfielder Jim Dwyer from Tidewater to Wichita, Cubs' affiliate, and the Mets were to receive a player to be named later from the Royals, December 8, 1976; Royals assigned Outfielder Sheldon Mallory to Tidewater, Mets' affiliate, to complete deal, December 13, 1976.

‡Granted free agency, October 24, 1980; signed by Taiyo Whales of Japanese baseball, February 11, 1981.

CHAMPIONSHIP SERIES RECORD

Year Club League	Pos.	G.	AB.	R.	H.	2B.	3B.	HR.	RBI.	B.A.	PO.	A.	E.	F.A.
1977—Kansas City......Amer.	1B-PH	1	1	0	0	0	0	0	0	.000	4	0	0	1.000
1978—Kansas City ......Amer.	1B-PH	4	11	1	4	2	1	0	1	.364	25	1	0	1.000
1980—Kansas City ......Amer.	1B	1	0	0	0	0	0	0	0	.000	0	0	0	.000
Championship Series Totals		6	12	1	4	2	1	0	1	.333	29	1	0	1.000

WORLD SERIES RECORD

Year Club League	Pos.	G.	AB.	R.	H.	2B.	3B.	HR.	RBI.	B.A.	PO.	A.	E.	F.A.
1980—Kansas City ......Amer.	1B	1	0	0	0	0	0	0	0	.000	2	0	0	1.000

FRANK JOSEPH LaCORTE JR.

Name pronounced luh-KORT-ee.

Born October 13, 1952, at San Jose, Calif.
Height, 6.01. Weight, 180.
Throws and bats righthanded.
Hobby—Hunting.
Attended Gavilan College, Gilroy, Calif.

Year Club	League	G.	IP.	W.	L.	Pct.	H.	R.	ER.	SO.	BB.	ERA.
1973—Greenwood...........................	W. Carol.	18	105	7	8	.467	70	44	30	109	51	2.57
1973—Savannah...........................	Southern	7	30	2	1	.667	19	14	12	34	22	3.60
1974—Savannah...........................	Southern	23	120	7	8	.467	106	76	63	106	89	4.73
1975—Richmond	Int'national	24	128	9	7	.563	121	65	61	108	71	4.29
1975—Atlanta	National	3	14	0	3	.000	13	10	8	10	6	5.14
1976—Richmond	Int'national	14	78	3	3	.500	91	55	46	77	47	5.31
1976—Atlanta	National	19	105	3	12	.200	97	58	55	79	53	4.71
1977—Richmond†	Int'national	8	37	2	3	.400	38	25	25	40	29	6.08
1977—Atlanta	National	14	37	1	8	.111	67	51	48	28	29	11.68
1978—Richmond‡	Int'national	23	130	6	7	.462	125	67	61	99	66	4.22
1978—Atlanta	National	2	15	0	1	.000	9	6	6	7	4	3.60
1979—Atlanta§-Houston..................	National	18	35	1	2	.333	30	23	22	30	15	5.66
1979—Charleston	Int'national	12	79	4	7	.364	68	32	24	57	31	2.73
1980—Houston	National	55	83	8	5	.615	61	29	26	66	43	2.82
Major League Totals		111	289	13	31	.295	277	177	165	220	150	5.14

Signed as free agent by Atlanta Braves' organization, September 5, 1972.
†On disabled list, July 31 to August 11, 1977.
‡On disabled list, August 2 to August 16, 1978.
§Traded to Houston Astros for Pitcher Bo McLaughlin, May 25, 1979.

CHAMPIONSHIP SERIES RECORD

Year Club	League	G.	IP.	W.	L.	Pct.	H.	R.	ER.	SO.	BB.	ERA.
1980—Houston ....National	National	2	3	1	1	.500	7	2	1	2	2	3.00

MICHAEL JAMES LaCOSS
(Mike)

Born May 30, 1956, at Glendale, Calif.
Height, 6.04. Weight, 190.
Throws and bats righthanded.
Hobbies—Hunting and fishing.

Tied for American Association lead in shutouts with 3 in 1978.

Year Club	League	G.	IP.	W.	L.	Pct.	H.	R.	ER.	SO.	BB.	ERA.
1974—Billings...............................	Pioneer	13	87	6	5	.545	81	40	27	58	38	2.79
1975—Tampa................................	Florida St.	23	151	4	7	.412	131	61	48	72	41	2.86
1976—Three Rivers........................	Eastern	25	162	12	10	.545	148	66	53	80	53	2.94
1977—Indianapolis	Am. Assoc.	27	186	11	*13	.458	181	93	80	104	65	3.87
1978—Indianapolis	Am. Assoc.	19	130	11	5	.688	129	62	50	67	49	3.46
1978—Cincinnati	National	16	96	4	8	.333	104	56	48	31	44	4.50
1979—Cincinnati	National	35	206	14	8	.636	202	92	80	73	79	3.50
1980—Cincinnati	National	34	169	10	12	.455	207	101	87	59	68	4.63
Major League Totals.................		85	471	28	28	.500	513	249	215	163	193	4.11

Selected by Cincinnati Reds' organization in 3rd round of free-agent draft, June 5, 1974.

CHAMPIONSHIP SERIES RECORD

Year Club	League	G.	IP.	W.	L.	Pct.	H.	R.	ER.	SO.	BB.	ERA.
1979—Cincinnati ....National		1	1⅔	0	1	.000	1	2	2	0	4	10.80

ALL-STAR GAME RECORD

Year League	IP.	W.	L.	Pct.	H.	R.	ER.	SO.	BB.	ERA.
1979—National..	1⅓	0	0	.000	1	0	0	0	0	0.00

LEONDAUS LACY
(Lee)

Born April 10, 1949, at Longview, Tex.
Height, 6.01. Weight, 175.
Throws and bats righthanded.
Hobbies—Fishing and hunting.
Attended Laney Junior College, Oakland, Calif.

Led Pioneer League third basemen in double plays with 9 in 1969.

Year Club	League	Pos.	G.	AB.	R.	H.	2B.	3B.	HR.	RBI.	B.A.	PO.	A.	E.	F.A.
1969—Ogden ....Pion		*3-S-2	71	239	43	70	6	7	1	38	.293	*54	*121	*27	.866
1970—Bakersfield ....Calif.		*SS-3B	124	502	96	151	19	5	4	49	.301	189	291	*66	.879
1971—Albuquerque......Texas		2-3-S-O	132	488	54	150	17	7	0	57	.307	263	358	31	.952
1972—El Paso ....Texas		2-SS	68	258	39	96	22	4	1	35	.372	123	191	7	.978
1972—Los Angeles.......Nat.		2B	60	243	34	63	7	3	0	12	.259	125	161	8	.973
1973—Los Angeles.......Nat.		2B	57	135	14	28	2	0	0	8	.207	80	85	6	.965
1974—Los Angeles.......Nat.		2B-3B	48	78	13	22	6	0	0	8	.282	38	53	3	.968
1975—Los Angeles†......Nat.		2-O-S	101	306	44	96	11	5	7	40	.314	152	75	13	.946
1976—Atl.‡-L.A. ....Nat.		2-O-3	103	338	42	91	11	3	3	34	.269	193	111	9	.971
1977—Los Angeles§......Nat.		O-2-3	75	169	28	45	7	0	6	21	.266	56	69	4	.969
1978—Los Angeles x ...Nat.		O-2-3-S	103	245	29	64	16	4	13	40	.261	114	64	9	.952
1979—Pittsburgh ....Nat.		OF-2B	84	182	17	45	9	3	5	15	.247	77	8	3	.966
1980—Pittsburgh ....Nat.		OF-3B	109	278	45	93	20	4	7	33	.335	175	11	3	.984
Major League Totals			740	1974	266	547	89	22	41	211	.277	1010	637	58	.966

Selected by Los Angeles Dodgers' organization in 2nd round of free-agent draft, February 1, 1969.

†Traded with Outfielder Jimmy Wynn, First Baseman-Outfielder Tom Paciorek and Infielder Jerry Royster to Atlanta Braves for Outfielder Dusty Baker and First Baseman-Third Baseman Ed Goodson, November 17, 1975.

‡Traded with Pitcher Elias Sosa to Los Angeles Dodgers for Pitcher Mike Marshall, June 23, 1976.

§On supplemental disabled list, June 20 to July 15, 1977.

xGranted free agency, November 2, 1978; signed by Pittsburgh Pirates, January 19, 1979.

CHAMPIONSHIP SERIES RECORD

Year Club	League	Pos.	G.	AB.	R.	H.	2B.	3B.	HR.	RBI.	B.A.	PO.	A.	E.	F.A.
1974—Los Angeles.......Nat.		PR	1	0	0	0	0	0	0	0	.000	0	0	0	.000
1977—Los Angeles.......Nat.		PH	1	1	1	1	0	0	0	0	1.000	0	0	0	.000
1978—Los Angeles ......Nat.		PH	2	2	0	0	0	0	0	0	.000	0	0	0	.000
Championship Series Totals.............			4	3	1	1	0	0	0	0	.333	0	0	0	.000

WORLD SERIES RECORD

Year Club	League	Pos.	G.	AB.	R.	H.	2B.	3B.	HR.	RBI.	B.A.	PO.	A.	E.	F.A.
1974—Los Angeles.......Nat.		PH	1	1	0	0	0	0	0	0	.000	0	0	0	.000
1977—Los Angeles.......Nat.		PH-OF	4	7	1	3	0	0	0	2	.429	2	0	0	1.000
1978—Los Angeles ......Nat.		DH	4	14	0	2	0	0	0	1	.143	0	0	0	.000
1979—Pittsburgh ....Nat.		PH	4	4	0	1	0	0	0	0	.250	0	0	0	.000
World Series Totals			13	26	1	6	0	0	0	3	.231	2	0	0	1.000

PETER LINWOOD LADD

Born July 17, 1956, at Portland, Me.
Height, 6.03. Weight, 240.
Throws and bats righthanded.
Attended University of Massachusetts, Amherst, Mass.

Led Florida State League in saves with 18 in 1978.

Year Club	League	G.	IP.	W.	L.	Pct.	H.	R.	ER.	SO.	BB.	ERA.
1977—Winter Haven......................Florida St.		19	27	4	1	.800	19	8	5	27	7	1.67
1978—Winter Haven......................Florida St.		44	85	8	2	.800	69	36	30	66	30	3.18
1979—Bristol†................................Eastern		18	29	3	1	.750	12	2	2	26	8	0.62
1979—Columbus‡...........................Southern		13	41	6	1	.857	24	13	12	31	23	2.63
1979—Houston ....National		10	12	1	1	.500	8	5	4	6	8	3.00
1980—Columbus ....Southern		33	55	6	5	.545	47	27	21	38	29	3.44
1980—Tucson ....P. Coast		18	21	1	2	.333	18	7	6	24	4	2.57
Major League Totals..................................		10	12	1	1	.500	8	5	4	6	8	3.00

Selected by Boston Red Sox' organization in 25th round of free-agent draft, June 7, 1977.

†Traded with cash and a player to be named later to Houston Astros' organization for First Baseman Bob Watson, June 13, 1979; Pitcher Bob Sprowl assigned to Houston to complete deal, June 19, 1979.

‡On disabled list, July 4 to July 18, 1979.

LERRIN HARRIS LaGROW

Born July 8, 1948, at Phoenix, Ariz.
Height, 6.05. Weight, 230.
Throws and bats righthanded.
Hobbies—Basketball and golf.
Attended Arizona State University, Tempe Ariz.

Named Southern League Player of the Year, 1970.

Year	Club	League	G.	IP.	W.	L.	Pct.	H.	R.	ER.	SO.	BB.	ERA.
1969—Montgomery		Southern	14	84	2	10	.167	79	41	34	59	40	3.64
1970—Montgomery		Southern	19	146	11	4	*.733	111	49	34	126	49	2.10
1970—Detroit		American	10	12	0	1	.000	16	11	10	7	6	7.50
1971—Toledo		Int'national	36	69	2	6	.250	73	63	46	65	60	6.00
1972—Toledo		Int'national	22	115	8	6	.571	94	43	31	92	59	2.43
1972—Detroit		American	16	27	0	1	.000	22	4	4	9	6	1.33
1973—Toledo		Int'national	10	56	5	1	.833	57	29	27	40	16	4.34
1973—Detroit†		American	21	54	1	5	.167	54	26	26	33	23	4.33
1974—Detroit		American	37	216	8	19	.296	245	132	112	85	80	4.67
1975—Detroit‡		American	32	164	7	14	.333	183	105	80	75	66	4.39
1976—Tulsa		Am. Assoc.	25	161	6	10	.375	171	81	74	108	45	4.14
1976—St. Louis§		National	8	24	0	1	.000	21	4	4	10	7	1.50
1977—Chicago		American	66	99	7	3	.700	81	32	27	63	35	2.45
1978—Chicago		American	52	88	6	5	.545	85	47	43	41	38	4.40
1979—Chicago x		American	11	18	0	3	.000	27	21	18	9	16	9.00
1979—Los Angeles yz		National	31	37	5	1	.833	38	16	14	22	18	3.41
1980—Philadelphia a		National	25	39	0	2	.000	42	22	18	21	17	4.15
American League Totals			245	678	29	51	.363	713	378	320	322	270	4.25
National League Totals			64	100	5	4	.556	101	42	36	53	42	3.24
Major League Totals			309	778	34	55	.382	814	420	356	375	312	4.12

Selected by Detroit Tigers' organization in 32nd round of free-agent draft, June 5, 1969.
†On disabled list, June 15 to July 10, 1973.
‡Sold to St. Louis Cardinals, April 2, 1976.
§Traded to Chicago White Sox for Pitcher Clay Carroll, March 23, 1977.
xSold to Los Angeles Dodgers, May 11, 1979.
yOn disabled list, July 30 to August 25, 1979.
zGranted free agency, November 1, 1979; signed by Philadelphia Phillies, January 31, 1980.
aReleased, July 17, 1980.

CHAMPIONSHIP SERIES RECORD

Year	Club	League	G.	IP.	W.	L.	Pct.	H.	R.	ER.	SO.	BB.	ERA.
1972—Detroit		American	1	1	0	0	.000	0	0	0	1	0	0.00

JEFFREY ALLEN LAHTI
(Jeff)

Born October 8, 1956, at Oregon City, Ore.
Height, 6.00. Weight, 180.
Throws and bats righthanded.
Attended Treasure Valley Community College, Ontario, Ore. and
Portland State University, Portland, Ore.

Tied for Western Carolinas League lead in saves with 13 in 1979.

Year	Club	League	G.	IP.	W.	L.	Pct.	H.	R.	ER.	SO.	BB.	ERA.
1978—Eugene		Northwest	16	53	1	5	.167	58	34	26	32	21	4.42
1979—Greensboro		W. Carol.	53	92	7	2	.778	83	43	29	89	33	2.84
1979—Nashville		Southern	6	16	2	0	1.000	10	4	3	12	5	1.69
1980—Waterbury		Eastern	55	91	7	8	.467	75	34	28	78	40	2.77

Selected by Philadelphia Phillies' organization in 12th round of free-agent draft, January 7, 1976.
Selected by San Francisco Giants' organization in 7th round of free-agent draft, January 11, 1977.
Selected by Cincinnati Reds' organization in 5th round of free-agent draft, June 6, 1978.

STEVEN MICHAEL LAKE
(Steve)

Born March 14, 1957, at Inglewood, Calif.
Height, 6.01. Weight, 180.
Throws and bats righthanded.
Hobbies—Outdoor sports and automobile refurbishing.
Cousin of Mike Lake, former pitcher in Los Angeles Dodgers' organization.

Led Appalachian League catchers in passed balls with 15 in 1975.

Year	Club	League	Pos.	G.	AB.	R.	H.	2B.	3B.	HR.	RBI.	B.A.	PO.	A.	E.	F.A.
1975—Bluefield	Appal.		C	49	162	17	45	12	0	3	24	.278	254	*39	9	.970
1976—Miami	Fla. St.		PH	1	1	0	1	0	0	0	1	1.000	0	0	0	.000
1977—Miami	Fla. St.		C	79	232	25	55	10	1	2	24	.237	357	47	6	.985
1978—Miami†‡	Fla. St.		C	69	223	19	57	10	0	2	26	.256	300	49	6	.983
1979—Stockton§	Calif.		C	94	329	36	93	12	3	6	40	.283	504	73	8	.986
1980—Holyoke	East.		C	102	325	26	84	9	2	2	44	.258	445	107	10	.982

Selected by Baltimore Orioles' organization in 3rd round of free-agent draft, June 4, 1975.
†On disabled list, April 17 to May 16, 1978.
‡Sold to Milwaukee Brewers' organization, December 21, 1978.
§On disabled list, June 20 to July 6, 1979.

DENNIS PATRICK LAMP

Born September 23, 1952, at Los Angeles, Calif.
Height, 6.03. Weight, 190.
Throws and bats righthanded.
Hobbies—Music and coaching basketball.
Established National League record for most games taken out as starting pitcher, season (35).

Year Club	League	G.	IP.	W.	L.	Pct.	H.	R.	ER.	SO.	BB.	ERA.
1971—Caldwell	Pioneer	14	46	1	2	.333	51	39	33	43	32	6.46
1972—Bradenton Cubs	Gulf Coast	14	70	7	2	.778	56	20	15	56	21	1.93
1973—Quincy	Midwest	13	89	6	4	.600	67	32	26	71	29	2.63
1973—Midland	Texas	9	48	2	4	.333	54	29	25	23	11	4.69
1974—Key West	Florida St.	8	49	1	5	.167	39	15	8	20	14	1.47
1974—Midland	Texas	24	60	1	1	.500	70	38	31	42	22	4.65
1975—Midland	Texas	37	127	7	5	.583	112	52	47	71	54	3.33
1976—Wichita	Am. Assoc.	30	153	8	*14	.364	182	94	69	98	52	4.06
1977—Wichita	Am. Assoc.	20	129	11	4	.733	116	54	42	52	23	2.93
1977—Chicago	National	11	30	0	2	.000	43	21	21	12	8	6.30
1978—Chicago	National	37	224	7	15	.318	221	96	82	73	56	3.29
1979—Chicago	National	38	200	11	10	.524	223	96	78	86	46	3.51
1980—Chicago	National	41	203	10	14	.417	259	*123	*117	83	82	5.19
Major League Totals		127	657	28	41	.406	746	336	298	254	192	4.08

Selected by Chicago Cubs' organization in 3rd round of free-agent draft, June 8, 1971.

RICHARD ANTHONY LANCELLOTTI
(Rick)

Born July 5, 1956, at Providence, R.I.
Height, 6.03. Weight, 195.
Throws and bats lefthanded.
Attended Glassboro State College, Glassboro, N. J.
Led Eastern League in total bases with 296 in 1979.
Named Eastern League Most Valuable Player, 1979.

Year Club	League	Pos.	G.	AB.	R.	H.	2B.	3B.	HR.	RBI.	B.A.	PO.	A.	E.	F.A.
1977—Charleston	W. Car.	OF	73	239	37	63	14	4	9	31	.264	103	5	7	.939
1978—Salem	Carol.	OF	133	439	67	106	15	3	15	60	.241	198	15	*13	.942
1979—Buffalo	East.	OF	138	506	95	145	14	7	*41	●107	.287	190	13	16	.927
1980—Portland	P. C.	OF	61	199	25	44	8	0	7	29	.221	62	3	1	.985
1980—Buffalo†	East.	OF	30	107	19	28	1	0	10	21	.262	61	3	3	.955
1980—Amarillo	Texas	OF	22	79	15	30	8	1	4	15	.380	24	0	0	1.000

Selected by Pittsburgh Pirates' organization in 11th round of free-agent draft, June 7, 1977.
†Traded with Outfielder Luis Salazar to San Diego Padres' organization for Infielder Kurt Bevacqua and a player to be named later, August 5, 1980; Pitcher Mark Lee traded to Pirates' organization completing deal, August 12, 1980.

RAFAEL SILVIALDO CAMILO LANDESTOY (SANTANA)

Born May 28, 1953, at Bani, Dominican Republic.
Height, 5.09. Weight, 163.
Throws and bats righthanded.
Hobby—Listening to music.
Led Eastern League shortstops in double plays with 73 in 1975.
Led Pacific Coast League in stolen bases with 56 in 1977.

Year Club	League	Pos.	G.	AB.	R.	H.	2B.	3B.	HR.	RBI.	B.A.	PO.	A.	E.	F.A.
1972—Ogden	Pion.	OF	49	119	13	29	4	2	0	14	.244	50	2	4	.929
1973—Daytona Beach	Fla. St.	OF	96	288	31	84	11	0	0	24	.292	145	11	3	.981
1974—Orangeburg	W. Car.	SS-O-2B	●134	492	71	135	13	5	2	49	.274	264	218	47	.911
1975—Waterbury	East.	*SS-OF	130	439	61	123	10	7	0	31	.280	*203	*388	*60	.908
1976—Albuquerque	P.C.	S-2-3-O	140	463	68	128	14	7	2	54	.276	226	399	38	.943
1977—Albuquerque	P.C.	2B-OF	130	558	113	154	21	10	0	41	.276	270	391	21	.969
1977—Los Angeles	Nat.	2B-SS	15	18	6	5	0	0	0	0	.278	8	18	0	1.000
1978—Albuquerque†	SS-O-2	2B	66	277	46	76	12	6	1	35	.274	148	198	18	.951
1978—Houston	Nat.	SS-OF-2	59	218	18	58	5	1	0	9	.266	70	132	4	.981
1979—Houston	Nat.	2B-3B	129	282	33	76	9	6	0	30	.270	168	237	12	.971
1980—Houston	Nat.	2-S-3	149	393	42	97	13	8	1	27	.247	185	295	9	.982
Major League Totals			352	911	99	236	27	15	1	66	.259	431	682	25	.978

Signed as free agent by Los Angeles Dodgers' organization, May 29, 1972.
†Sent to Houston Astros, July 7, 1978, as partial completion of deal in which Los Angeles Dodgers received Catcher Joe Ferguson, July 1, 1978; Outfielder Jeff Leonard sent to Astros to complete deal, September 11, 1978.

CHAMPIONSHIP SERIES RECORD

Year Club	League	Pos.	G.	AB.	R.	H.	2B.	3B.	HR.	RBI.	B.A.	PO.	A.	E.	F.A.
1980—Houston	Nat.	2-PR-S	5	9	3	2	0	0	0	2	.222	5	8	1	.929

WORLD SERIES RECORD

Year Club	League	Pos.	G.	AB.	R.	H.	2B.	3B.	HR.	RBI.	B.A.	PO.	A.	E.	F.A.
1977—Los Angeles	Nat.	PR	1	0	0	0	0	0	0	0	.000	0	0	0	.000

CRAIG STEVEN LANDIS

Born December 29, 1958, at Richmond, Calif.
Height, 6.02. Weight, 195.
Throws and bats righthanded.
Son of Jim Landis, former major league outfielder.

Led Pacific Coast League outfielders in double plays with 5 in 1980.
Received reported $60,000 bonus to sign with San Francisco Giants, 1977.

Year	Club	League	Pos.	G.	AB.	R.	H.	2B.	3B.	HR.	RBI.	B.A.	PO.	A.	E.	F.A.
1977—Great Falls	Pion.		3B-OF	59	235	46	79	7	5	2	37	.336	47	43	19	.826
1978—Cedar Rapids	Midw.		OF	131	442	79	125	22	4	5	52	.283	194	12	8	.963
1979—Shreveport	Texas		OF	126	436	66	132	24	1	9	59	.303	197	16	9	.959
1980—Phoenix†	P. C.		OF	142	476	59	134	15	3	7	49	.282	309	11	5	.985

Selected by San Francisco Giants' organization in 1st round (10th player selected) of free-agent draft, June 7, 1977.
†Traded with Pitcher John Montefusco to Atlanta Braves for Pitcher Doyle Alexander, December 12, 1980.

KENNETH FRANCIS LANDREAUX

Name pronounced LAN-droh.

(Ken)

Born December 22, 1954, at Los Angeles, Calif.
Height, 5.11. Weight, 164.
Throws right and bats lefthanded.
Attended Arizona State University, Tempe, Ariz.

Tied major league record for most two-base hits, inning (2), July 3, 1979 (seventh inning).
Tied modern major league record for most three-base hits, game (3), July 3, 1980.
Named Minor League Player of the Year by THE SPORTING NEWS, 1977.

Year	Club	League	Pos.	G.	AB.	R.	H.	2B.	3B.	HR.	RBI.	B.A.	PO.	A.	E.	F.A.
1976—El Paso†	Texas		OF	21	59	15	13	3	1	2	11	.220	32	4	0	1.000
1977—El Paso	Texas		OF	57	209	57	74	17	4	16	59	.354	117	6	6	.953
1977—Salt Lake City	P.C.		OF	62	256	67	92	16	4	11	57	.359	164	3	4	.977
1977—California	Amer.		OF	23	76	6	19	5	1	0	5	.250	59	5	2	.970
1978—California‡	Amer.		OF	93	260	37	58	7	5	5	23	.223	138	6	2	.986
1979—Minnesota	Amer.		OF	151	564	81	172	27	5	15	83	.305	292	10	6	.981
1980—Minnesota	Amer.		OF	129	484	56	136	23	11	7	62	.281	231	8	6	.976
Major League Totals				396	1384	180	385	62	22	27	173	.278	720	29	16	.979

Selected by Houston Astros' organization in 8th round of free-agent draft, June 5, 1973.
Selected by California Angels' organization in 1st round (sixth player selected) of free-agent draft, June 8, 1976.
†On disabled list, July 17 to August 4, 1976.
‡Traded with Pitchers Paul Hartzell and Brad Heavens and Third Baseman Dave Engle to Minnesota Twins for First Baseman Rod Carew, February 3, 1979.

ALL-STAR GAME RECORD

Year	League	Pos.	AB.	R.	H.	2B.	3B.	HR.	RBI.	B.A.	PO.	A.	E.	F.A.
1980—American		PH-OF	1	0	0	0	0	0	0	.000	1	0	0	1.000

TERRY LEE LANDRUM
(Tito)

Born October 25, 1954, at Joplin, Mo.
Height, 5.11. Weight, 175.
Throws and bats righthanded.

Led Florida State League in stolen bases with 68 in 1978.

Year	Club	League	Pos.	G.	AB.	R.	H.	2B.	3B.	HR.	RBI.	B.A.	PO.	A.	E.	F.A.
1973—Orangeburg	W. Car.		OF	70	262	30	73	7	3	1	27	.279	168	7	1	.994
1974—St. Petersburg†	Fla. St.		OF	87	309	38	73	5	9	3	39	.236	214	7	8	.965
1975—St. Petersburg	Fla. St.		OF	132	435	76	96	21	4	11	45	.221	*313	5	7	.978
1976—Arkansas‡	Texas		OF	99	359	49	99	13	3	7	45	.276	201	12	7	.968
1976—Tulsa	A. A.		OF	9	24	1	6	1	0	0	1	.250	17	0	0	1.000
1977—Arkansas	Texas		OF	26	84	11	18	3	1	2	13	.214	50	5	1	.982
1977—St. Petersburg	Fla. St.		OF	67	249	40	61	15	3	4	40	.245	157	7	1	.994
1978—St. Petersburg	Fla. St.		OF	117	434	66	129	*25	1	4	45	.297	*305	8	3	.991
1979—Arkansas	Texas		OF	71	265	44	71	20	5	3	33	.268	134	7	4	.972
1979—Springfield	A. A.		OF	61	193	28	50	8	2	6	34	.259	126	5	2	.985
1980—Springfield	A. A.		OF	93	350	55	106	23	6	12	46	.303	193	6	4	.980
1980—St. Louis	Nat.		OF	35	77	6	19	2	2	0	7	.247	40	1	1	.976
Major League Totals				35	77	6	19	2	2	0	7	.247	40	1	1	.976

Signed as free agent by St. Louis Cardinals' organization, October 10, 1972.
†On disabled list, July 19 to September 20, 1974.
‡On disabled list, April 24 to May 10, 1976.

DID YOU KNOW

That Bill Gullickson's 18 strikeouts in a game against the Cubs was the highest strikeout total for a pitcher in 1980?

JAMES RICK LANGFORD
(Known by middle name.)

Born March 20, 1952, at Farmville, Va.
Height, 6.00. Weight, 180.
Throws and bats righthanded.
Hobbies—Sailing and all water sports.
Attended Manatee Junior College, Bradenton, Fla., and
Florida State University, Tallahassee, Fla.

Pitched 11-0 no-hit victory against Memphis, May 30, 1976.
Led American League in wild pitches with 16 in 1979.
Led American League in complete games with 28 in 1980.

Year	Club	League	G.	IP.	W.	L.	Pct.	H.	R.	ER.	SO.	BB.	ERA.
1973—Bradenton Pirates†		Gulf C.	3	10	1	0	1.000	5	3	0	10	7	0.00
1974—Salem		Carolina	26	174	11	7	.611	143	63	52	125	74	2.69
1975—Shreveport		Texas	16	42	5	2	.714	40	25	17	39	22	3.64
1975—Charleston		Int'national	13	65	7	2	.778	55	26	24	41	20	3.32
1976—Charleston		Int'national	16	121	9	5	.643	106	51	43	95	48	3.20
1976—Pittsburgh‡		National	12	23	0	1	.000	27	17	16	17	14	6.26
1977—Oakland		American	37	208	8	•19	.296	223	107	93	141	73	4.02
1978—Oakland		American	37	176	7	13	.350	169	77	67	92	56	3.43
1979—Oakland		American	34	219	12	16	.429	233	114	104	101	57	4.27
1980—Oakland		American	35	•290	19	12	.613	276	119	105	102	64	3.26
National League Totals			12	23	0	1	.000	27	17	16	17	14	6.26
American League Totals			143	893	46	60	.434	901	417	369	436	250	3.72
Major League Totals			155	916	46	61	.430	928	434	385	453	264	3.78

Selected by St. Louis Cardinals' organization in 11th round of free-agent draft, January 13, 1971.
Selected by Cleveland Indians' organization in 36th round of free-agent draft, June 6, 1972.
Signed as free agent by Pittsburgh Pirates' organization, June 17, 1973.
†On suspended list, July 17 through remainder of season.
‡Traded with Pitchers Doc Medich, Dave Giusti and Doug Bair, and Outfielders Mitchell Page and Tony Armas to Oakland A's for Infielders Phil Garner and Tommy Helms, and Pitcher Chris Batton, March 15, 1977.

CARNEY RAY LANSFORD

Born February 7, 1957, at San Jose, Calif.
Height, 6.02. Weight, 195.
Throws and bats righthanded.
Brother of Phil Lansford, third baseman in Toronto Blue Jays' organization and Jody Lansford,
first baseman in San Diego Padres' organization.

Hit three home runs in one game, vs. Cleveland Indians, September 1, 1979.
Led Texas League third basemen in double plays with 16 in 1977.
Led American League in sacrifice flies with 11 in 1980.

Year	Club	League	Pos.	G.	AB.	R.	H.	2B.	3B.	HR.	RBI.	B.A.	PO.	A.	E.	F.A.
1975—Idaho Falls†		Pion.	3B-SS	8	27	5	6	2	0	1	1	.222	8	14	9	.710
1976—Quad Cities		Midw.	3-O-S	121	418	87	120	19	5	14	86	.287	130	215	36	.906
1977—El Paso		Texas	3B	120	443	98	147	17	3	18	94	.332	•110	•210	15	•.955
1978—California‡		Amer.	3B-SS	121	453	63	133	23	2	8	52	.294	94	186	18	.940
1979—California		Amer.	3B	157	654	114	188	30	5	19	79	.287	•135	263	7	•.983
1980—California§		Amer.	3B	151	602	87	157	27	3	15	80	.261	•151	250	19	.955
Major League Totals				429	1699	264	478	80	10	42	211	.281	380	699	44	.961

Selected by California Angels' organization in 3rd round of free-agent draft, June 4, 1975.
†On disabled list, July 21 to September 30, 1975.
†On supplemental disabled list, June 11 to July 7, 1978.
§Traded with Pitcher Mark Clear and Outfielder Rick Miller to Boston Red Sox for Shortstop Rick Burleson and Third Baseman Butch Hobson, December 10, 1980.

CHAMPIONSHIP SERIES RECORD

Year	Club	League	Pos.	G.	AB.	R.	H.	2B.	3B.	HR.	RBI.	B.A.	PO.	A.	E.	F.A.
1979—California		Amer.	3B	4	17	2	5	0	0	0	3	.294	4	8	0	1.000

JOSEPH DALE LANSFORD
(Jody)

Born January 15, 1961, at San Jose, Calif.
Height, 6.05. Weight, 225.
Throws and bats righthanded.
Brother of Carney Lansford, third baseman with Boston Red Sox, and Phil Lansford,
infielder in Toronto Blue Jays' organization.

Led California League first basemen in double plays with 101 in 1980.
Received reported $100,000 bonus to sign with San Diego Padres, 1979.

Year	Club	League	Pos.	G.	AB.	R.	H.	2B.	3B.	HR.	RBI.	B.A.	PO.	A.	E.	F.A.
1979—Walla Walla		Northw.	1B	44	146	17	21	2	0	6	31	.144	204	21	6	.974
1980—Reno†		Calif.	1B	112	410	80	108	21	2	24	95	.263	•1067	73	10	.991

Selected by San Diego Padres' organization in 1st round (14th player selected) of free-agent draft, June 5, 1979.
†On disabled list, April 10 to May 8, 1980.

DAVID JEFFREY LaPOINT
(Dave)

Born July 29, 1959, at Glens Falls, N. Y.
Height, 6.03. Weight, 205.
Throws and bats lefthanded.

Pitched 4-0 no-hit victory against Reno, July 25, 1979.
Tied for California League lead in shutouts with 3 and in complete games with 11 in 1979.

Year Club	League	G.	IP.	W.	L.	Pct.	H.	R.	ER.	SO.	BB.	ERA.
1977—Newark ....NYP	NYP	13	69	5	2	.714	73	40	36	60	22	4.70
1978—Burlington ....Midwest	Midwest	25	161	12	12	.500	177	98	72	134	41	4.02
1979—Stockton ....California	California	27	180	12	10	.545	144	74	63	*208	85	3.15
1980—Vancouver† ....P. Coast	P. Coast	17	93	7	4	.636	71	48	29	64	45	2.81
1980—Milwaukee‡ ....American	American	5	15	1	0	1.000	17	14	10	5	13	6.00
Major League Totals..................................		5	15	1	0	1.000	17	14	10	5	13	6.00

Selected by Milwaukee Brewers' organization in 10th round of free-agent draft, June 7, 1977.
†On disabled list, May 6 to May 17 and June 6 to July 15, 1980.
‡Traded with Pitcher Lary Sorensen and Outfielders Sixto Lezcano and David Green to St. Louis Cardinals for Pitchers Pete Vuckovich and Rollie Fingers and Catcher Ted Simmons, December 12, 1980.

DAVID EUGENE LaROCHE
(Dave)

Born May 14, 1948, at Colorado Springs, Colo.
Height, 6.02. Weight, 195.
Throws and bats lefthanded.
Hobbies—Golf and Basketball.
Attended University of Nevada at Las Vegas, Las Vegas, Nev.

Major league saves: 1970 (4), 1971 (9), 1972 (10), 1973 (4), 1974 (5), 1975 (17), 1976 (21), 1977 (17), 1978 (25), 1979 (10), 1980 (4). Total—126.

Year Club	League	G.	IP.	W.	L.	Pct.	H.	R.	ER.	SO.	BB.	ERA.
1968—Quad Cities ....Midwest	Midwest	33	84	5	7	.417	76	33	22	80	29	2.36
1969—San Jose ....California	California	11	21	2	1	.667	21	11	9	19	8	3.68
1969—El Paso...............................Texas	Texas	33	49	6	3	.667	43	16	16	46	25	2.94
1970—Hawaii................................P. Coast	P. Coast	22	58	6	0	1.000	31	11	8	67	19	1.24
1970—California ....American	American	38	50	4	1	.800	41	20	19	44	21	3.42
1971—California† ....American	American	56	72	5	1	.833	55	21	20	63	27	2.50
1972—Minnesota‡ ....American	American	62	95	5	7	.417	72	33	30	79	39	2.84
1973—Chicago§............................National	National	45	54	4	1	.800	55	37	35	34	29	5.83
1974—Wichita...............................Am. Assoc.	Am. Assoc.	6	32	1	3	.250	37	19	18	17	7	5.06
1974—Chicago x............................National	National	49	92	5	6	.455	103	54	49	49	47	4.79
1975—Cleveland............................American	American	61	82	5	3	.625	61	26	20	94	57	2.20
1976—Cleveland............................American	American	61	96	1	4	.200	57	25	24	104	49	2.25
1977—Cleveland y-California ....American	American	59	100	8	7	.533	79	44	39	79	44	3.51
1978—California ....American	American	59	96	10	9	.526	73	35	30	70	48	2.81
1979—California ....American	American	53	86	7	11	.389	107	54	53	59	32	5.55
1980—California ....American	American	52	128	3	5	.375	122	62	58	89	39	4.08
American League Totals...........................		501	805	48	48	.500	667	320	293	681	356	3.28
National League Totals...........................		94	146	9	7	.563	158	91	84	83	76	5.18
Major League Totals		595	951	57	55	.509	825	411	377	764	432	3.57

Signed as free agent by California Angels' organization, March 9, 1967.
†Traded to Minnesota Twins for Shortstop Leo Cardenas, November 30, 1971.
‡Traded to Chicago Cubs for Pitchers Bill Hands, George (Joe) Decker and Bob Maneely, November 30, 1972.
§On disabled list, March 25 to April 17, 1973.
xTraded with Outfielder Brock Davis to Cleveland Indians for Pitcher Milt Wilcox, February 28, 1975.
yTraded with Pitcher Dave Schuler to California Angels for First Baseman-Outfielder Bruce Bochte, Pitcher Sid Monge, and cash estimated at $250,000, May 11, 1977.

RECORD AS OUTFIELDER

Year Club	League	Pos.	G.	AB.	R.	H.	2B.	3B.	HR.	RBI.	B.A.	PO.	A.	E.	F.A.
1967—San Jose............Calif.	Calif.	OF	16	55	4	10	2	0	0	6	.182	18	1	0	1.000
1967—Quad Cities ....Midw.	Midw.	OF	95	342	39	80	17	0	6	40	.234	189	8	8	.961
1968—Quad Cities ....Midw.	Midw.	P-O-1	58	98	15	21	3	0	2	9	.214	51	18	3	.958

CHAMPIONSHIP SERIES RECORD

Year Club	League	G.	IP.	W.	L.	Pct.	H.	R.	ER.	SO.	BB.	ERA.
1979—California ....American	American	1	1⅓	0	0	.000	2	1	1	1	1	6.75

ALL-STAR GAME RECORD

Year League	IP.	W.	L.	Pct.	H.	R.	ER.	SO.	BB.	ERA.
1977—American	1	0	0	.000	1	0	0	0	1	0.00

Member of American League All-Star Team in 1976; did not play.

DID YOU KNOW—
That three of Mike Schmidt's four lifetime grand slams were hit off the Mets?

DANIEL JAMES LARSON
(Dan)

Born July 4, 1954, at Los Angeles, Calif.
Height, 6.00. Weight, 175.
Throws and bats righthanded.
Hobbies—Backpacking, camping and music.
Attended Whittier College, Whittier, Calif.

Year	Club	League	G.	IP.	W.	L.	Pct.	H.	R.	ER.	SO.	BB.	ERA.
1972—Sarasota Cards	Gulf Coast	10	57	3	2	.600	34	17	9	44	37	1.42
1973—Modesto	California	19	100	4	10	.286	114	83	63	105	58	5.67
1973—St. Petersburg	Florida St.	6	26	3	1	.750	22	14	10	17	12	3.46
1974—Modesto	California	22	142	12	6	.667	164	96	78	125	61	4.94
1974—Arkansas†	Texas	2	14	2	0	1.000	7	5	4	10	6	2.57
1975—Columbus	Southern	17	132	7	8	.467	118	42	32	76	46	*2.18
1975—Iowa	Am. Assoc.	12	83	4	6	.400	82	42	34	67	45	3.69
1976—Memphis	Int'national	17	118	7	4	.636	132	68	57	79	60	4.35
1976—Houston	National	13	92	5	8	.385	81	40	31	42	28	3.03
1977—Houston	National	32	98	1	7	.125	108	72	63	44	45	5.79
1978—Charleston‡	Int'national	29	*202	●14	6	.700	180	93	84	121	65	3.74
1978—Philadelphia	National	1	1	0	0	.000	1	1	1	2	1	9.00
1979—Oklahoma City	Am. Assoc.	24	146	9	8	.529	162	93	78	87	70	4.81
1979—Philadelphia	National	3	19	1	1	.500	17	9	9	9	9	4.26
1980—Reading	Eastern	4	14	3	0	1.000	13	5	5	11	9	3.21
1980—Oklahoma City	Am. Assoc.	8	48	4	2	.667	41	24	21	35	20	3.94
1980—Philadelphia	National	12	46	0	5	.000	46	24	16	17	24	3.13
Major League Totals		61	256	7	21	.250	253	146	120	114	107	4.22

Selected by St. Louis Cardinals' organization in 1st round (21st player selected) of free-agent draft, June 6, 1972.

†Assigned by St. Louis Cardinals to Houston Astros, October 14, 1974, to complete deal in which Cardinals obtained Pitcher Claude Osteen from Astros for Pitcher Ron Selak and a player to be named later, August 15, 1974.

‡Traded to Philadelphia Phillies for Pitcher Dan Warthen, September 9, 1978.

WILLIAM ALAN LASKEY
(Bill)

Born December 20, 1957, at Toledo, O.
Height, 6.05. Weight, 190.
Throws and bats righthanded.
Attended Monroe County Community College, Monroe, Mich., and
Kent State University, Kent, O.

Year	Club	League	G.	IP.	W.	L.	Pct.	H.	R.	ER.	SO.	BB.	ERA.
1978—Sarasota Royals	G. Coast	4	23	1	2	.333	13	7	5	9	11	1.96
1978—Jacksonville	Southern	7	27	3	2	.600	23	14	13	13	15	4.33
1979—Ft. Myers	Florida St.	13	93	7	4	.636	71	24	23	72	35	2.23
1979—Jacksonville	Southern	15	97	4	3	.571	78	44	38	53	46	3.53
1980—Omaha	Am. Assoc.	27	145	5	8	.385	155	81	67	77	72	4.16

Selected by Detroit Tigers' organization in 8th round of free-agent draft, January 11, 1977.
Selected by Detroit Tigers' organization in secondary phase of free-agent draft, June 7, 1977.
Selected by Kansas City Royals' organization in secondary phase of free-agent draft, June 6, 1978.

GARY ROBERT LAVELLE

Born January 3, 1949, at Scranton, Pa.
Height, 6.02. Weight, 205.
Throws left and bats right and lefthanded.
Hobby—All sports.

Major league saves: 1974 (0), 1975 (8), 1976 (12), 1977 (20), 1978 (14), 1979 (20), 1980 (9). Total—83.
Pitched seven-inning, 4-0 no-hit game against Clinton, August 15, 1969.
Tied for Pacific Coast League lead in shutouts with 3 in 1974.

Year	Club	League	G.	IP.	W.	L.	Pct.	H.	R.	ER.	SO.	BB.	ERA.
1967—Salt Lake City	Pioneer	17	37	3	2	.600	37	18	12	32	23	2.92
1968—Medford	Northwest	13	60	3	3	.500	53	33	23	67	42	3.45
1969—Decatur†	Midwest	7	48	4	2	.667	41	17	9	30	24	1.69
1970—Amarillo	Texas	21	100	6	12	.333	99	75	60	64	72	5.40
1971—Amarillo	Texas	23	136	11	8	.579	132	65	53	77	56	3.50
1972—Phoenix	P. Coast	37	147	11	14	.440	161	91	69	107	55	4.22
1973—Phoenix‡	P. Coast	36	101	5	7	.417	112	56	51	61	43	4.54
1974—Phoenix	P. Coast	35	182	8	●16	.333	228	119	106	105	76	5.24
1974—San Francisco	National	10	17	0	3	.000	14	7	4	12	10	2.12
1975—San Francisco	National	65	82	6	3	.667	80	30	27	51	48	2.96
1976—San Francisco	National	65	110	10	6	.625	102	37	33	71	52	2.70
1977—San Francisco	National	73	118	7	7	.500	106	35	27	93	37	2.06
1978—San Francisco	National	67	98	13	10	.565	96	41	36	63	44	3.31
1979—San Francisco	National	70	97	7	9	.438	86	31	27	80	42	2.51
1980—San Francisco	National	62	100	6	8	.429	106	43	38	66	36	3.42
Major League Totals		412	622	49	46	.516	590	224	192	436	269	2.78

Selected by San Francisco Giants' organization in 34th round of free-agent draft, June 6, 1967.
†On suspended list, April 11, 1969. Transferred to military list through July 5, 1969.
‡On temporary inactive list, June 2 to June 20, 1973.

ALL-STAR GAME RECORD

Year League	IP.	W.	L.	Pct.	H.	R.	ER.	SO.	BB.	ERA.
1977—National	2	0	0	.000	1	0	0	2	0	0.00

RUDY KARL LAW

Born October 7, 1956, at Waco, Tex.
Height, 6.01. Weight, 165.
Throws and bats lefthanded.

Year Club	League	Pos.	G.	AB.	R.	H.	2B.	3B.	HR.	RBI.	B.A.	PO.	A.	E.	F.A.
1976—Bellingham	N'west.	OF-1B	54	161	40	54	7	1	1	16	.335	58	2	4	.938
1977—Lodi	Calif.	OF	122	451	124	174	22	5	9	88	*.386	107	2	6	.948
1978—Albuquerque	P.C.	OF	138	*573	118	179	21	9	4	72	.312	236	10	10	.961
1978—Los Angeles	Nat.	OF	11	12	2	3	0	0	0	1	.250	3	0	0	1.000
1979—Albuquerque†	P. C.	OF	72	270	46	80	4	2	0	28	.296	142	2	3	.980
1980—Los Angeles	Nat.	OF	128	388	55	101	5	4	1	23	.260	233	6	3	.988
Major League Totals			139	400	57	104	5	4	1	24	.260	236	6	3	.988

Signed as free agent by Los Angeles Dodgers' organization, September 1, 1975.
†On disabled list, June 22 to August 31, 1979.

VANCE AARON LAW

Born October 1, 1956, at Boise, Ida.
Height, 6.02. Weight, 185.
Throws and bats righthanded.
Attended Brigham Young University, Provo, Utah.
Son of Vern Law, pitcher with Pittsburgh Pirates, 1950-67.
Led Pacific Coast League in sacrifice hits with 14 in 1979.

Year Club	League	Pos.	G.	AB.	R.	H.	2B.	3B.	HR.	RBI.	B.A.	PO.	A.	E.	F.A.
1978—Brad. Pirates	G.C.	SS	1	3	0	1	0	0	0	0	.333	2	5	0	1.000
1978—Salem	Carol.	SS	60	213	48	68	13	7	2	30	.319	96	180	22	.926
1979—Portland	P.C.	S-3-2	131	448	62	139	16	8	2	52	.310	201	308	22	.959
1980—Portland	P.C.	SS	96	339	59	100	23	5	5	54	.295	169	295	14	.971
1980—Pittsburgh	Nat.	2-S-3	25	74	11	17	2	2	0	3	.230	31	54	3	.966
Major League Totals			25	74	11	17	2	2	0	3	.230	31	54	3	.966

Selected by Pittsburgh Pirates' organization in 38th round of free-agent draft, June 6, 1978.

THOMAS JAMES LAWLESS
(Tom)

Born December 19, 1956, at Erie, Pa.
Height, 6.00. Weight, 165.
Throws and bats righthanded.
Attended Pennsylvania State University-Behrend, Erie, Pa.;
received Bachelor of Arts degree in Political Science.
Led Pioneer League shortstops in putouts with 116 in 1978.
Led Florida State League in sacrifice hits with 13 and in stolen bases with 60 in 1979.

Year Club	League	Pos.	G.	AB.	R.	H.	2B.	3B.	HR.	RBI.	B.A.	PO.	A.	E.	F.A.
1978—Billings	Pioneer	SS-2B	63	254	64	70	5	•7	5	35	.276	117	186	24	.927
1979—Tampa	Fla. St.	2B	131	469	66	126	9	5	1	39	.269	*296	376	17	*.975
1980—Waterbury	East.	2B	130	498	83	137	20	7	2	29	.275	*316	333	14	.979

Selected by Cincinnati Reds' organization in 17th round of free-agent draft, June 6, 1978.

CHARLES WILLIAM LEA
(Charlie)

Born December 25, 1956, at Orleans, France.
Height, 6.04. Weight, 194.
Throws and bats righthanded.
Attended University of Mississippi, Oxford, Miss., Shelby State Community College,
Memphis, Tenn., and Memphis State University, Memphis, Tenn.

Year Club	League	G.	IP.	W.	L.	Pct.	H.	R.	ER.	SO.	BB.	ERA.
1978—Memphis	Southern	12	68	3	3	.500	57	34	27	37	32	3.57
1979—Memphis	Southern	24	162	8	8	.500	161	88	79	81	71	4.39
1980—Memphis	Southern	9	75	9	0	1.000	34	10	7	54	21	0.84
1980—Denver	Am. Assoc.	2	12	0	0	.000	8	2	2	9	5	1.50
1980—Montreal	National	21	104	7	5	.583	103	51	43	56	55	3.72
Major League Totals		21	104	7	5	.583	103	51	43	56	55	3.72

Selected by New York Mets' organization in 15th round of free-agent draft, June 4, 1975.
Selected by St. Louis Cardinals' organization in secondary phase of free-agent draft, June 8, 1976.
Selected by Chicago White Sox' organization in secondary phase of free-agent draft, January 11, 1977.
Selected by Montreal Expos' organization in 8th round of free-agent draft, June 6, 1978.

RICHARD MAX LEACH
(Rick)

Born May 4, 1957, at Ann Arbor, Mich.
Height, 6.01. Weight, 180.
Throws and bats lefthanded.
Attended University of Michigan, Ann Arbor, Mich.

Selected by Denver Broncos in 5th round of 1979 NFL draft.
Received reported $200,000 bonus to sign with Detroit Tigers, 1979.

Year Club	League	Pos.	G.	AB.	R.	H.	2B.	3B.	HR.	RBI.	B.A.	PO.	A.	E.	F.A.
1979—Lakeland†	Fla. St.	OF	48	168	21	51	10	1	2	23	.304	104	8	3	.974
1980—Evansville	A.A.	1B-OF	126	430	69	117	14	1	5	58	.272	767	62	9	.989

Selected by Philadelphia Phillies' organization in 11th round of free-agent draft, June 4, 1975.
Selected by Philadelphia Phillies' organization in 24th round of free-agent draft, June 6, 1978.
Selected by Detroit Tigers' organization in 1st round (13th player selected) of free-agent draft, June 5, 1979.

†On disabled list, June 18 to June 29, 1979.

LUIS ENRIQUE LEAL

Born March 21, 1957, at Barquisimento, Venezuela.
Height, 6.03. Weight, 205.
Throws and bats righthanded.

Tied American League record for most consecutive hits allowed, start of game (5), June 2, 1980.
Pitched 2-0 no-hit victory against Tampa, May 11, 1979.

Year Club	League	G.	IP.	W.	L.	Pct.	H.	R.	ER.	SO.	BB.	ERA.
1979—Dunedin	Florida St.	21	150	12	2	.857	137	51	44	90	45	2.64
1979—Syracuse	Int'national	1	6	1	0	1.000	4	3	3	2	2	4.50
1980—Syracuse	Int'national	16	110	6	5	.545	102	44	40	76	31	3.27
1980—Toronto	American	13	60	3	4	.429	72	35	30	26	31	4.50
Major League Totals		13	60	3	4	.429	72	35	30	26	31	4.50

Signed as free agent by Toronto Blue Jays' organization, 1979.

TIMOTHY JAMES LEARY
(Tim)

Born December 23, 1958, at Santa Monica, Calif.
Height, 6.03. Weight, 195.
Throws and bats righthanded.
Attended University of California at Los Angeles.

Led Texas League in shutouts with 6 in 1980.

Year Club	League	G.	IP.	W.	L.	Pct.	H.	R.	ER.	SO.	BB.	ERA.
1979—Jackson†	Texas					Did not play						
1980—Jackson	Texas	26	173	●15	8	.652	150	67	53	138	62	2.76

Selected by New York Mets' organization in 1st round (second player selected) of free-agent draft, June 5, 1979.

†On disabled list, July 19 to October 1, 1979.

DELRICK JOHN LEATHERWOOD
(Del)

Born March 30, 1955, at Houston, Tex.
Height, 6.01. Weight, 185.
Throws and bats righthanded.
Attended Texas A&M University, College Station, Tex.;
received Bachelor of Science degree in Secondary Education.
Brother of Larry Stegent, former running back with St. Louis Cardinals.

Led Southern League in shutouts with 4 in 1979.

Year Club	League	G.	IP.	W.	L.	Pct.	H.	R.	ER.	SO.	BB.	ERA.
1977—Sarasota Astros	Gulf Coast	11	44	3	3	.500	41	32	23	29	42	4.70
1978—Daytona Beach†	Florida St.	18	77	4	5	.444	79	57	37	41	59	4.32
1979—Columbus	Southern	28	•202	•15	11	.577	180	82	69	95	103	3.07
1980—Columbus‡	Southern	17	107	7	5	.583	98	48	36	60	38	3.03

Signed as free agent by Houston Astros' organization, June 18, 1977.
†On disabled list, May 24 to June 26, 1978.
‡On disabled list, June 8 to July 30, 1980.

MARK LINDEN LEE

Born June 14, 1953, at Inglewood, Calif.
Height, 6.04. Weight, 225.
Throws and bats righthanded.
Attended El Camino Junior College, Torrance, Calif., and
Pepperdine University, Malibu, Calif.

Year Club	League	G.	IP.	W.	L.	Pct.	H.	R.	ER.	SO.	BB.	ERA.
1976—Walla Walla	Northwest	•28	54	5	3	.625	46	25	18	49	34	3.00
1977—Amarillo	Texas	•60	113	10	8	.556	121	57	47	59	70	3.74

Year Club	League	G.	IP.	W.	L.	Pct.	H.	R.	ER.	SO.	BB.	ERA.
1978—Hawaii	P.Coast	4	5	0	0	.000	3	0	0	1	4	0.00
1978—San Diego	National	56	85	5	1	.833	74	34	31	31	36	3.28
1979—Hawaii	P.Coast	21	41	4	1	.800	31	9	8	20	16	1.76
1979—San Diego	National	46	65	2	4	.333	88	34	31	25	25	4.29
1980—Hawaii†-Portland	P. Coast	43	66	6	6	.500	70	33	30	43	30	4.09
1980—Pittsburgh	National	4	6	0	1	.000	5	3	3	2	3	4.50
Major League Totals		106	156	7	6	.538	167	71	65	58	64	3.75

Selected by Baltimore Orioles' organization in 6th round of free-agent draft, January 10, 1973.
Selected by Baltimore Orioles' organization in 9th round of free-agent draft, January 9, 1974.
Selected by San Diego Padres' organization in 13th round of free-agent draft, June 8, 1976.
†Traded to Pittsburgh Pirates, August 12, 1980; completing deal in which San Diego Padres traded Infielder Kurt Bevacqua for Outfielders Luis Salazar and Rick Lancellotti, August 5, 1980.

WILLIAM FRANCIS LEE III
(Bill)

Born December 28, 1946, at Burbank, Calif.
Height, 6.03. Weight, 190.
Throws and bats lefthanded.
Hobbies—Fishing, hunting and golf.
Attended University of Southern California, Los Angeles, Calif., and University of Southern Mississippi, Hattiesburg, Miss.; received Bachelor of Arts degree in Physical Education and Geography from U.S.C.

Year Club	League	G.	IP.	W.	L.	Pct.	H.	R.	ER.	SO.	BB.	ERA.
1968—Waterloo	Midwest	8	27	1	1	.500	14	10	4	31	17	1.33
1968—Winston-Salem	Carolina	8	47	3	3	.500	36	23	9	38	19	1.72
1969—Pittsfield	Eastern	10	70	6	2	.750	48	25	16	48	32	2.06
1969—Boston	American	20	52	1	3	.250	56	27	26	45	28	4.50
1970—Boston†	American	11	37	2	2	.500	48	20	19	19	14	4.62
1971—Boston	American	47	102	9	2	.818	102	35	31	74	46	2.74
1972—Boston	American	47	84	7	4	.636	75	31	30	43	32	3.21
1973—Boston	American	38	285	17	11	.607	275	100	87	120	76	2.75
1974—Boston	American	38	282	17	15	.531	•320	123	110	95	67	3.51
1975—Boston	American	41	260	17	9	.654	274	123	114	78	69	3.95
1976—Boston‡	American	24	96	5	7	.417	124	68	60	29	28	5.63
1977—Boston	American	27	128	9	5	.643	155	67	63	31	29	4.43
1978—Boston§	American	28	177	10	10	.500	198	89	68	44	59	3.46
1979—Montreal	National	33	222	16	10	.615	230	91	75	59	46	3.04
1980—Montreal x	National	24	118	4	6	.400	156	71	65	34	22	4.96
American League Totals		321	1503	94	68	.580	1627	683	608	578	448	3.64
National League Totals		57	340	20	16	.556	386	162	140	93	68	3.71
Major League Totals		378	1843	114	84	.576	2013	845	748	671	516	3.65

Selected by Boston Red Sox' organization in 12th round of free-agent draft, June 7, 1968.
†On military list June 5 to October 2, 1970.
‡On disabled list, May 21 to July 12, 1976.
§Traded to Montreal Expos for Infielder Stan Papi, December 7, 1978.
xOn disabled list, June 7 to July 11 and August 7 to September 1, 1980.

WORLD SERIES RECORD

Year Club	League	G.	IP.	W.	L.	Pct.	H.	R.	ER.	SO.	BB.	ERA.
1975—Boston	American	2	14⅓	0	0	.000	12	5	5	7	3	3.14

ALL-STAR GAME RECORD
Member of American League All-Star Team in 1973 game; did not play.

JOSEPH HENRY LEFEBVRE
Name pronounced Luh-fay.
(Joe)

Born Feburary 22, 1956, at Penacook, N.H.
Height, 5.10. Weight, 170.
Throws right and bats lefthanded.
Attended Eckerd College, St. Petersburg, Fla.

Tied American League record for most home runs, first two major league games (2), May 22-23, 1980.
Tied for Eastern League lead in assists by outfielders with 16 in 1979.

Year Club	League	Pos.	G.	AB.	R.	H.	2B.	3B.	HR.	RBI.	B.A.	PO.	A.	E.	F.A.
1977—Ft. Lauderdale	Fla. St.	OF-P	48	172	20	53	6	9	2	29	.308	76	4	2	.976
1977—West Haven	East.	OF	6	22	8	8	2	0	0	3	.364	7	2	0	1.000
1978—West Haven	East.	OF-3B-C	134	459	•102	122	21	•11	19	70	.266	240	48	14	.954
1979—West Haven	East.	O-I-P-C	138	487	85	142	28	10	21	•107	.292	248	31	10	.965
1980—Columbus	Int.	OF-3B	56	198	37	55	11	3	10	26	.278	89	3	5	.948
1980—New York	Amer.	OF	74	150	26	34	1	1	8	21	.227	75	3	2	.975
Major League Totals			74	150	26	34	1	1	8	21	.227	75	3	2	.975

Selected by New York Yankees' organization in 3rd round of free-agent draft, June 7, 1977.

Year Club	League	G.	IP.	W.	L.	Pct.	H.	R.	ER.	SO.	BB.	ERA.
1977—Ft. Lauderdale ....Florida St.		1	1	0	0	.000	1	1	1	1	2	9.00
1979—West Haven.........................Eastern		2	5	0	0	.000	5	2	2	4	1	3.60

CHAMPIONSHIP SERIES RECORD

Year Club League	Pos.	G.	AB.	R.	H.	2B.	3B.	HR.	RBI.	B.A.	PO.	A.	E.	F.A.
1980—New York ....Amer.	OF	1	0	0	0	0	0	0	0	.000	0	0	0	.000

RONALD LeFLORE
(Ron)

Born June 16, 1948, at Detroit, Mich.
Height, 6.00. Weight, 200.
Throws and bats righthanded.
Hobbies—Reading, chess and woodworking.

Tied major league record for fewest double plays by outfielder, season, 150 or more games (0), 1977.
Major league stolen bases: 1974 (23), 1975 (28), 1976 (58), 1977 (39), 1978 (68), 1979 (78), 1980 (97).
Total—391.
Led American League in stolen bases with 68 in 1978.
Led National League in stolen bases with 97 in 1980.
Named Most Valuable Player in Florida State League, 1974.

Year Club League	Pos.	G.	AB.	R.	H.	2B.	3B.	HR.	RBI.	B.A.	PO.	A.	E.	F.A.
1973—Clinton ....Midw.	OF	32	65	10	18	1	0	1	8	.277	17	0	1	.944
1974—Lakeland ....Fla. St.	OF	93	386	*79	131	11	7	6	38	*.339	202	9	*12	.946
1974—Evansville ........A.A.	OF	9	34	5	8	1	0	1	3	.235	11	0	1	.917
1974—Detroit..............Amer.	OF	59	254	37	66	8	1	2	13	.260	151	8	*11	.935
1975—Detroit..............Amer.	OF	136	550	66	142	13	6	8	37	.258	317	13	9	.973
1976—Detroit†.............Amer.	OF	135	544	93	172	23	8	4	39	.316	381	14	*11	.973
1977—Detroit..............Amer.	OF	154	652	100	212	30	10	16	57	.325	365	12	11	.972
1978—Detroit..............Amer.	OF	155	666	*126	198	30	3	12	62	.297	*440	9	11	.976
1979—Detroit‡.............Amer.	OF	148	600	110	180	22	10	9	57	.300	293	6	3	.990
1980—Montreal..........Nat.	OF	139	521	95	134	21	11	4	39	.257	233	14	●11	.957
American League Totals		787	3266	532	970	126	38	51	265	.297	1947	62	56	.973
National League Totals		139	521	95	134	21	11	4	39	.257	233	14	11	.957
Major League Totals......................		926	3787	627	1104	147	49	55	304	.292	2180	76	67	.971

Signed as free agent by Detroit Tigers' organization, July 2, 1973.
†On disabled list, September 15 to October 4, 1976.
‡Traded to Montreal Expos for Pitcher Dan Schatzeder, December 7, 1979.
§Granted free agency, October 28, 1980; signed by Chicago White Sox, December 5, 1980.

ALL-STAR GAME RECORD

Year League	Pos.	AB.	R.	H.	2B.	3B.	HR.	RBI.	B.A.	PO.	A.	E.	F.A.
1976—American............................	OF	2	0	1	0	0	0	0	.500	2	0	0	1.000

CHARLES LOUIS LEIBRANDT JR.
(Charlie)

Born October 4, 1956, at Chicago, Ill.
Height, 6.04. Weight, 200.
Throws left and bats righthanded.
Attended Miami University, Oxford, O.; received Bachelor of Science degree in Management.

Tied for American Association lead in games started with 26 in 1979.

Year Club	League	G.	IP.	W.	L.	Pct.	H.	R.	ER.	SO.	BB.	ERA.
1978—Eugene ....Northwest		3	20	2	0	1.000	24	13	9	18	5	4.05
1978—Tampa..................................Florida St.		6	47	4	1	.800	26	4	4	40	17	0.77
1978—Indianapolis ....Am. Assoc.		4	29	2	1	.667	20	9	9	12	12	2.79
1979—Indianapolis ....Am. Assoc.		27	162	8	*14	.364	146	67	53	100	65	2.94
1979—Cincinnati ....National		3	4	0	0	.000	2	0	0	1	2	2.00
1980—Cincinnati ....National		36	174	10	9	.526	200	84	82	62	54	4.24
Major League Totals................................		39	178	10	9	.526	202	84	82	63	56	4.15

Selected by Cincinnati Reds' organization in 9th round of free-agent draft, June 6, 1978.

CHAMPIONSHIP SERIES RECORD

Year Club	League	G.	IP.	W.	L.	Pct.	H.	R.	ER.	SO.	BB.	ERA.
1979—Cincinnati ....National		1	⅓	0	0	.000	0	0	0	0	0	0.00

STANLEY JAY LELAND
(Stan)

Born May 17, 1959, at Wabash, Ind.
Height, 6.04. Weight, 190.
Throws and bats righthanded.
Attended Ball State University, Muncie, Ind.

Year Club	League	G.	IP.	W.	L.	Pct.	H.	R.	ER.	SO.	BB.	ERA.
1977—Sarasota Astros....................Gulf Coast		8	48	3	4	.429	42	23	16	27	20	3.00
1977—Cocoa ....Florida St.		3	12	0	2	.000	15	15	13	7	14	9.75

Year Club	League	G.	IP.	W.	L.	Pct.	H.	R.	ER.	SO.	BB.	ERA.
1978—Daytona Beach	Florida St.	12	57	1	9	.100	85	64	56	31	34	8.84
1978—Sarasota Astros	Gulf Coast	8	43	2	3	.400	44	24	18	23	17	3.77
1979—Daytona Beach	Florida St.	22	130	5	*13	.278	127	67	54	111	62	3.74
1979—Columbus	Southern	5	31	1	2	.333	30	17	14	13	14	4.06
1980—Columbus	Southern	28	201	8	11	.421	186	99	78	95	76	3.49

Selected by Houston Astros' organization in 2nd round of free-agent draft, June 7, 1977.

DAVID LAWRENCE LEMANCZYK
Name pronounced La-MAN-sick.
(Dave)
Born August 17, 1950, at Syracuse, N. Y.
Height, 6.04. Weight, 230.
Throws and bats righthanded.
Hobby—Furniture building and refinishing.
Attended Hartwick College, Oneonta, N. Y.; received Bachelor of Arts degree in History.

Pitched 3-0 no-hit victory against Asheville, August 8, 1973.

Year Club	League	G.	IP.	W.	L.	Pct.	H.	R.	ER.	SO.	BB.	ERA.
1972—Lakeland	Florida St.	8	66	7	1	.875	44	14	13	55	17	1.77
1972—Toledo	Int'national	12	60	5	2	.714	55	22	20	32	28	3.00
1973—Toledo	Int'national	20	113	6	8	.429	115	61	59	84	55	4.70
1973—Montgomery	Southern	4	31	3	1	.750	18	8	8	28	14	2.32
1973—Detroit	American	1	2	0	0	.000	4	3	3	0	0	13.50
1974—Evansville	Am. Assoc.	7	44	2	4	.333	45	24	18	38	20	3.68
1974—Detroit	American	22	79	2	1	.667	79	43	35	52	44	3.99
1975—Detroit†	American	26	109	2	7	.222	120	62	54	67	46	4.46
1976—Evansville	Am. Assoc.	7	48	5	2	.714	36	16	14	27	18	2.63
1976—Detroit‡	American	20	81	4	6	.400	86	47	46	51	34	5.11
1977—Toronto	American	34	252	13	16	.448	278	*143	●119	105	87	4.25
1978—Toronto§	American	29	137	4	14	.222	170	97	95	62	65	6.24
1979—Toronto x	American	22	143	8	10	.444	137	65	59	63	45	3.71
1980—Toronto y-California z	American	31	110	4	9	.308	138	69	58	29	42	4.75
Major League Totals		185	913	37	63	.370	1012	529	469	429	363	4.62

Selected by Detroit Tigers' organization in 16th round of free-agent draft, June 6, 1972.
†On disabled list, June 23 to July 17, 1975.
‡Selected by Toronto Blue Jays in American League expansion draft, November 5, 1976.
§On disabled list, August 16 to September 5, 1978.
xOn disabled list, August 9 to September 1, 1979.
yTraded to California Angels for a player to named later, June 3, 1980; Pitcher Ken Schrom traded to Toronto completing deal, June 10, 1980.
zReleased, October 24, 1980; invited to Chicago White Sox' camp, 1981.

ALL-STAR GAME RECORD
Member of American League All-Star Team for 1979 game; did not play.

JOHNNIE LEE LeMASTER
Born June 19, 1954, at Portsmouth, O.
Height, 6.02. Weight, 165.
Throws and bats righthanded.
Hobbies—Hunting, billiards and all sports.
First-cousin of Ron Salyer, former pitcher in Cleveland Indians' organization.

Tied major league record by hitting home run in first major league at bat, September 2, 1975 (inside the park).
Led Pacific Coast League shortstops in double plays with 107 in 1975.
Led Pioneer League batters in strikeouts with 71 in 1973.
Led Pioneer League shortstops in double plays with 32 in 1973.

Year Club	League	Pos.	G.	AB.	R.	H.	2B.	3B.	HR.	RBI.	B.A.	PO.	A.	E.	F.A.
1973—Great Falls	Pion.	SS	70	250	34	61	8	2	2	33	.244	*106	*178	*38	.882
1974—Decatur	Midw.	SS	104	399	51	103	14	4	3	28	.258	145	280	*48	.899
1974—Fresno	Calif.	SS	21	84	15	24	3	0	1	4	.286	30	68	8	.925
1975—Phoenix	P. C.	SS	143	520	75	152	26	8	4	58	.292	207	*489	33	.955
1975—San Francisco	Nat.	SS	22	74	4	14	4	0	2	9	.189	26	62	3	.967
1976—Phoenix	P. C.	SS	105	380	60	94	14	5	4	35	.247	151	349	26	.951
1976—San Francisco	Nat.	SS	33	100	9	21	3	2	0	9	.210	54	109	11	.937
1977—Phoenix	P. C.	SS-2B	22	70	12	22	7	2	0	13	.314	37	71	6	.947
1977—San Francisco	Nat.	SS-3B	68	134	13	20	5	1	0	8	.149	66	134	14	.935
1978—San Francisco	Nat.	SS-2B	101	272	23	64	18	3	1	14	.235	135	261	14	.966
1979—San Francisco	Nat.	SS	108	343	42	87	11	2	3	29	.254	160	303	20	.959
1980—San Francisco	Nat.	SS	135	405	33	87	16	6	3	31	.215	200	372	26	.957
Major League Totals			467	1328	124	293	57	14	9	100	.221	641	1241	88	.955

Selected by San Francisco Giants' organization in 1st round (sixth player selected) of free-agent draft, June 5, 1973.

CHESTER EARL LEMON
(Chet)

Born February 12, 1955, at Jackson, Miss.
Height, 6.00. Weight, 190.
Throws and bats righthanded.
Hobbies—Rock and shell collecting and Greek mythology.
Attended Pepperdine University, Malibu, Calif., and Cerritos College, Norwalk, Calif.

Established American League records for most chances accepted by outfielder, season (524), 1977; most putouts by outfielder, season (512), 1977.
Tied American League record for most years by outfielder, 500 or more putouts (1).

Year Club League	Pos.	G.	AB.	R.	H.	2B.	3B.	HR.	RBI.	B.A.	PO.	A.	E.	F.A.
1972—Coos Bay-N. B. ...Northw.	SS-3	38	140	33	40	8	1	2	16	.286	56	94	16	.904
1972—Burlington.........Midw.	3-SS	33	129	18	33	5	0	1	8	.256	24	62	13	.869
1973—Burlington.........Midw.	3-SS	113	392	73	121	21	1	19	*88	.309	102	215	36	.898
1974—Birmingham† ....South.	3-SS	79	272	52	79	22	2	10	61	.290	84	135	23	.905
1975—Tucson‡ ....P. C.	3B-OF	65	243	43	68	7	2	5	33	.280	60	70	19	.872
1975—Denver.............A. A.	3B-OF	70	254	40	78	15	6	8	49	.307	39	76	19	.858
1975—Chicago............Amer.	3B-OF	9	35	2	9	2	0	0	1	.257	5	7	1	.923
1976—Chicago............Amer.	OF	132	451	46	111	15	5	4	38	.246	353	12	3	.992
1977—Chicago............Amer.	OF	150	553	99	151	38	4	19	67	.273	*512	12	12	.978
1978—Chicago§.........Amer.	OF	105	357	51	107	24	6	13	55	.300	284	8	5	.983
1979—Chicago ....Amer.	OF	148	556	79	177	•44	2	17	86	.318	411	10	10	.977
1980—Chicago ....Amer.	OF	147	514	76	150	32	6	11	51	.292	347	11	7	.981
Major League Totals		691	2466	353	705	155	23	64	298	.286	1912	60	38	.981

Selected by Oakland A's organization in 1st round (20th player selected) of free-agent draft, June 6, 1972.
†On disabled list, July 16 to September 16, 1974.
‡Traded with Pitcher Dave Hamilton by Oakland Athletics to Chicago White Sox for Pitchers Stan Bahnsen and Lee (Skip) Pitlock, June 15, 1975.
§On supplemental disabled list, August 12 to August 27, 1978.

ALL—STAR GAME RECORD

Year League	Pos.	AB.	R.	H.	2B.	3B.	HR.	RBI.	B.A.	PO.	A.	E.	F.A.
1978—American	OF	0	0	0	0	0	0	0	.000	0	0	1	.000
1979—American	OF	2	1	0	0	0	0	0	.000	2	0	0	1.000
All-Star Game Totals		2	1	0	0	0	0	0	.000	2	0	1	.667

MARK LEMONGELLO

Born July 21, 1955, at Jersey City, N. J.
Height, 6.01. Weight, 180.
Throws and bats righthanded.
Cousin of Mike Lemongello, a professional bowler.

Tied major league record for most putouts by pitcher, nine-inning game (5), August 9, 1978.

Year Club League	G.	IP.	W.	L.	Pct.	H.	R.	ER.	SO.	BB.	ERA.
1974—Lakeland ....Florida St.	23	105	6	6	.500	94	37	32	59	23	2.74
1975—Montgomery ....Southern	14	93	6	3	.667	90	43	26	44	26	2.52
1975—Evansville†.........................Am. Assoc.	15	100	7	4	.636	111	49	43	63	25	3.87
1976—Memphis‡.........................Int'national	30	165	10	6	.625	*208	102	83	62	51	4.53
1976—Houston ....National	4	29	3	1	.750	26	12	9	9	7	2.79
1977—Houston ....National	34	215	9	14	.391	237	88	83	83	52	3.47
1978—Houston§.............................National	33	210	9	14	.391	204	100	92	77	66	3.94
1979—Syracuse.............................Int'national	4	23	3	0	1.000	20	5	5	13	7	1.80
1979—Toronto x............................American	18	83	1	9	.100	97	64	58	40	34	6.29
1980—Wichita................................Am. Assoc.	27	128	6	10	.375	158	85	73	42	34	5.13
National League Totals.....................	71	454	21	29	.420	467	200	184	169	125	3.65
American League Totals	18	83	1	9	.100	97	64	58	40	34	6.29
Major League Totals.................................	89	537	22	38	.367	564	264	242	209	159	4.06

Signed as free agent by Detroit Tigers' organization, July 11, 1973.
†Traded with Outfielder Leon Roberts, Catcher Terry Humphrey and Pitcher Gene Pentz to Houston Astros for Catcher Milt May and Pitchers Jim Crawford and Dave Roberts, December 6, 1975.
‡On temporary inactive list, April 16 to April 26 and July 4 to July 15, 1976.
§Traded with Outfielder Joe Cannon and Shortstop Pedro Hernandez to Toronto Blue Jays for Catcher Alan Ashby, November 27, 1978.
xSold to Chicago Cubs' organization, April 7, 1980.

JAMES MATTHEW LENTINE
(Jim)

Born July 16, 1954, at Los Angeles, Calif.
Height, 6.00. Weight, 175.
Throws and bats righthanded.
Attended Arizona State University, Tempe, Ariz.
and LaVerne College, LaVerne, Calif.
Brother of Gip Lentine, a professional bowler.

Named American Association Rookie of the Year, 1978.

Year Club League	Pos.	G	AB	R	H	2B	3B	HR	RBI	B.A.	PO	A	E	F.A.
1975—Sara. Cardinals . G. C.	OF	4	15	2	7	2	2	0	4	.467	6	1	0	1.000
1975—St. Petersburg... Fla. St.	OF	12	42	3	10	2	0	1	5	.238	16	2	0	1.000
1975—Johnson City ..... Appal.	OF	29	91	25	31	5	1	2	15	.341	35	2	2	.949
1976—St. Petersburg... Fla. St.	OF	113	389	58	107	14	2	2	58	.275	193	7	9	.957
1976—Arkansas .... Texas	OF	27	73	7	14	2	0	3	6	.192	59	2	5	.924
1977—Arkansas† .... Texas	OF	85	243	40	71	10	6	6	37	.292	115	8	1	.992
1978—Arkansas .... Texas	OF	30	117	18	34	4	1	1	13	.291	47	3	1	.980
1978—Springfield .... A. A.	OF	111	406	92	139	27	7	11	63	.342	230	4	5	.979
1978—St. Louis .... Nat.	OF	8	11	1	2	0	0	0	1	.182	4	0	0	1.000
1979—Springfield‡ ...... A.A.	OF	106	383	73	109	19	0	15	62	.285	210	11	4	.982
1979—St. Louis .... Nat.	OF	11	23	2	9	1	0	0	1	.391	12	1	0	1.000
1980—Springfield .... A.A.	OF	22	72	15	22	6	0	1	7	.306	51	1	2	.963
1980—St. Louis§ .... Nat.	OF	9	10	1	1	0	0	0	1	.100	4	0	0	1.000
1980—Detroit............. Amer.	OF	67	161	19	42	8	1	1	17	.261	98	5	4	.963
American League Totals		67	161	19	42	8	1	1	17	.261	98	5	4	.963
National League Totals		28	44	4	12	1	0	0	3	.273	20	1	0	1.000
Major League Totals......................		95	205	23	54	9	1	1	20	.263	118	6	4	.969

Selected by Chicago White Sox' organization in 24th round of free-agent draft, June 6, 1972.
Selected by St. Louis Cardinals' organization in 12th round of free-agent draft, June 4, 1975.
†On disabled list, June 25 to July 8, 1977.
‡On disabled list, June 24 to July 21, 1979.
§Traded to Detroit Tigers for Pitcher John Martin and a player to be named later, June 2, 1980; Outfielder Al Greene traded to St. Louis completing deal, June 9, 1980.

DENNIS PATRICK LEONARD

Born May 8, 1951, at Brooklyn, N. Y.
Height, 6.01. Weight, 190.
Throws and bats righthanded.
Hobbies—Fishing and bowling.
Attended Iona College, New Rochelle, N. Y.

Pitched seven-inning, 3-0 no-hit victory against Quincy, July 15, 1972.
Pitched 2-0 no-hit victory against Visalia, April 26, 1973.
Led American League in games started with 38 in 1980.
Tied for American League lead in games started with 40 in 1978.
Tied for American League lead in shutouts with 5 in 1979.
Led American Association in complete games with 18 and shutouts with 4; also tied for lead in games started with 29 in 1974.
Tied for California League lead in complete games with 16 and in shutouts with 5 in 1973.

Year Club	League	G	IP	W	L	Pct.	H	R	ER.	SO.	BB.	ERA.
1972—Kingsport............................Ap'lachian		4	22	2	1	.667	19	9	8	31	6	3.27
1972—Waterloo ....Midwest		10	67	4	3	.571	58	28	23	63	26	3.09
1973—San Jose ....California		29	206	•15	9	.625	152	70	59	212	81	2.58
1974—Omaha................................Am. Assoc.		29	•223	12	13	.480	178	96	86	193	91	3.47
1974—Kansas City ....American		5	22	0	4	.000	28	15	13	8	12	5.32
1975—Omaha................................Am. Assoc.		3	19	0	2	.000	19	11	9	14	10	4.26
1975—Kansas City ....American		32	212	15	7	.682	212	98	89	146	90	3.78
1976—Kansas City ....American		35	259	17	10	.630	247	113	101	150	70	3.51
1977—Kansas City ....American		38	293	•20	12	.625	246	117	99	244	79	3.04
1978—Kansas City ....American		40	295	21	17	.553	283	125	109	183	78	3.33
1979—Kansas City ....American		32	236	14	12	.538	226	117	107	126	56	4.08
1980—Kansas City ....American		38	280	20	11	.645	271	127	118	155	80	3.79
Major League Totals		220	1597	107	73	.594	1513	712	636	1012	465	3.58

Selected by Kansas City Royals' organization in 2nd round of free-agent draft, June 6, 1972.

CHAMPIONSHIP SERIES RECORD

Tied Championship Series records for most games lost, total Series (3); most games lost, Series (2), 1978.
Established American League Championship Series records for most strikeouts, four-game Series (11), 1978; most hits allowed, four-game Series (13), 1978.

Year Club	League	G	IP	W	L	Pct.	H	R	ER.	SO.	BB.	ERA.
1976—Kansas City ....American		2	2⅓	0	0	.000	9	5	5	0	2	19.29
1977—Kansas City ....American		2	9	1	1	.500	5	4	3	4	2	3.00
1978—Kansas City ....American		2	12	0	2	.000	13	5	5	11	2	3.75
1980—Kansas City ....American		1	8	1	0	1.000	7	2	2	8	1	2.25
Championship Series Totals		7	31⅓	2	3	.400	34	16	15	23	7	4.31

WORLD SERIES RECORD

Year Club	League	G	IP	W	L	Pct.	H	R	ER.	SO.	BB.	ERA.
1980—Kansas City ....American		2	10⅔	1	1	.500	15	9	8	5	2	6.75

JEFFREY N. LEONARD
(Jeff)

Born September 22, 1955, at Philadelphia, Pa.
Height, 6.04. Weight, 200.
Throws and bats righthanded.
Hobby—Playing drums.
Named National League Rookie Player of the Year by THE SPORTING NEWS, 1979.

Year Club League	Pos.	G.	AB.	R.	H.	2B.	3B.	HR.	RBI.	B.A.	PO.	A.	E.	F.A.
1973—Bellingham........N'west	OF	55	187	30	52	4	3	2	20	.278	46	2	5	.906
1974—Orangeburg.......W. Car.	OF	8	15	0	1	0	0	0	1	.067	5	1	1	.857
1974—Bellingham........N'west	OF	78	278	47	90	12	4	3	43	.324	115	7	6	.953
1975—Bakersfield ......Calif.	OF	106	320	44	89	11	3	4	37	.278	137	5	7	.953
1976—Lodi ....Calif.	OF	133	509	93	168	29	9	8	85	.330	214	●13	★15	.938
1976—Albuquerque....P.C.	OF	7	27	2	8	2	1	1	6	.296	14	0	0	1.000
1977—San Antonio......Texas	OF	122	468	75	147	17	10	12	70	.314	241	12	8	.969
1977—Los Angeles.......Nat.	OF	11	10	1	3	0	1	0	2	.300	7	0	0	1.000
1978—Albuquerque†.... P. C.	OF	133	502	111	★183	23	14	11	93	★.365	216	8	6	.974
1978—Houston ....Nat.	OF	8	26	2	10	2	0	0	4	.385	16	1	0	1.000
1979—Houston ....Nat.	OF	134	411	47	119	15	5	0	47	.290	227	6	10	.959
1980—Houston ....Nat.	OF	88	216	29	46	7	5	3	20	.213	161	9	3	.983
Major League Totals		241	663	79	178	24	11	3	73	.268	411	16	13	.970

Signed as free agent by Los Angeles Dodgers' organization, June 7, 1973.

†Sent to Houston Astros, September 11, 1978, completing deal in which Los Angeles Dodgers acquired Catcher Joe Ferguson, July 1, 1978; Shortstop Rafael Landestoy sent to Astros as partial completion of deal, July 7, 1978.

CHAMPIONSHIP SERIES RECORD

Year Club League	Pos.	G.	AB.	R.	H.	2B.	3B.	HR.	RBI.	B.A.	PO.	A.	E.	F.A.
1980—Houston ....Nat.	PH-OF	3	3	0	0	0	0	0	0	.000	2	1	0	1.000

RANDY LOUIS LERCH

Born October 9, 1954, at Sacramento, Calif.
Height, 6.03. Weight, 195.
Throws and bats lefthanded.
Hobbies—Hunting and fishing.

Tied major league record for most sacrifice flies allowed, season (15), 1979.
Tied for American Association lead in complete games with 11 in 1976.

Year Club	League	G.	IP.	W.	L.	Pct.	H.	R.	ER.	SO.	BB.	ERA.
1973—Auburn ....NYP		16	96	9	2	.818	88	41	31	75	29	2.91
1974—Rocky Mount......................Carolina		22	143	7	7	.500	150	73	58	114	54	3.65
1975—Reading ....Eastern		25	177	★16	6	.727	173	66	53	108	45	2.69
1975—Philadelphia.........................National		3	7	0	0	.000	6	5	5	8	1	6.43
1976—Oklahoma City ....Am. Assoc.		★29	★207	13	11	.542	★203	91	77	★152	47	3.35
1976—Philadelphia.........................National		1	3	0	0	.000	3	1	1	0	0	3.00
1977—Philadelphia.........................National		32	169	10	6	.625	207	102	95	81	75	5.06
1978—Philadelphia.........................National		33	184	11	8	.579	183	89	81	96	70	3.96
1979—Philadelphia.........................National		37	214	10	13	.435	228	98	89	92	60	3.74
1980—Philadelphia†.........................National		30	150	4	14	.222	178	98	86	57	55	5.16
Major League Totals		136	727	35	41	.461	805	393	357	334	261	4.42

Selected by Philadelphia Phillies' organization in 8th round of free-agent draft, June 5, 1973.
†Traded to Milwaukee Brewers for Outfielder Dick Davis, March 1, 1981.

CHAMPIONSHIP SERIES RECORD

Year Club	League	G.	IP.	W.	L.	Pct.	H.	R.	ER.	SO.	BB.	ERA.
1978—Philadelphia.........................National		1	5⅓	0	0	.000	7	3	3	0	0	5.06

DENNIS DALE LEWALLYN

Name pronounced loo-ELL-un.

Born August 11, 1953, at Pensacola, Fla.
Height, 6.04. Weight, 195.
Throws and bats righthanded.
Hobbies—Golf and reading.
Attended Chipola Junior College, Marianna, Fla.

Led Pacific Coast League in saves with 24 in 1980.
Tied for Pacific Coast League lead in shutouts with 3 in 1975.

Year Club	League	G.	IP.	W.	L.	Pct.	H.	R.	ER.	SO.	BB.	ERA.
1972—Daytona Beach.....................Florida St.		22	146	11	6	.647	120	65	60	122	75	3.70
1973—Bakersfield ....California		29	175	11	12	.478	167	95	75	102	76	3.86
1974—Waterbury ....Eastern		27	138	7	10	.412	140	76	66	75	43	4.30
1975—Albuquerque ....P. Coast		29	180	13	10	.565	207	102	78	81	49	3.90
1975—Los Angeles ....National		2	3	0	0	.000	1	0	0	0	0	0.00
1976—Albuquerque ....P. Coast		25	180	★15	10	.600	207	98	71	62	61	3.55
1976—Los Angeles ╉.......................National		4	17	1	1	.500	12	5	4	4	6	2.12
1977—Albuquerque ....P. Coast		28	175	13	12	.520	★252	★146	★121	59	60	6.22
1977—Los Angeles†.......................National		5	17	3	1	.750	22	8	8	8	4	4.24
1978—Albuquerque ....P. Coast		52	85	8	10	.444	96	56	50	52	39	5.29
1978—Los Angeles ....National		1	2	0	0	.000	2	0	0	0	0	0.00
1979—Albuquerque ....P. Coast		43	125	10	8	.556	139	66	52	71	36	3.74
1979—Los Angeles ....National		7	12	0	1	.000	19	8	7	1	5	5.25
1980—Albuquerque‡.........................P. Coast		55	127	●15	2	★.882	110	33	30	58	40	★2.13
1980—Texas ....American		4	6	0	0	.000	7	5	5	1	4	7.50
National League Totals		19	51	4	3	.571	56	21	19	13	15	3.35
American League Totals.............................		4	6	0	0	.000	7	5	5	1	4	7.50
Major League Totals		23	57	4	3	.571	63	26	24	14	19	3.79

Selected by Atlanta Braves' organization in 3rd round of free-agent draft, June 8, 1971.
Selected by Los Angeles Dodgers' organization in secondary phase of free-agent draft, January 12, 1972.
†Sold to Minnesota Twins, November 23, 1977. Returned to Los Angeles Dodgers, March 15, 1978.
‡Traded with cash to Texas Rangers for Shortstop Pepe Frias, September 13, 1980.

CARLOS MANUEL LEZCANO
Name pronounced Lezz-KAHN-oh.

Born September 30, 1955, at Arecibo, Puerto Rico.
Height, 6.02. Weight, 185.
Throws and bats righthanded.
Attended Florida State University, Tallahassee, Fla.
Cousin of Sixto Lezcano, outfielder with St. Louis Cardinals.

Year—Club	League	Pos.	G.	AB.	R.	H.	2B.	3B.	HR.	RBI.	B.A.	PO.	A.	E.	F.A.
1977—Midland	Texas	OF-3B	71	225	27	52	8	1	6	22	.231	93	16	3	.973
1978—Midland†	Texas						(Did not play)								
1979—Midland	Texas	OF	124	457	94	149	28	9	11	82	.326	*338	11	5	.986
1980—Wichita‡	A.A.	OF	77	293	46	68	9	7	19	56	.232	200	4	7	.967
1980—Chicago	Nat.	OF	42	88	15	18	4	1	3	1	.205	70	3	4	.948
Major League Totals			42	88	15	18	4	1	3	1	.205	70	3	4	.948

Signed as free agent by Chicago Cubs' organization, May 23, 1977.
†On temporary inactive list entire 1978 season.
‡On disabled list, May 30 to June 9, 1980.

SIXTO LEZCANO
Name pronounced Lezz-KAHN-oh.

Born November 28, 1953, at Arecibo, Puerto Rico.
Height, 5.10. Weight, 175.
Throws and bats righthanded.
Hobbies—Listening to music and reading books.
Cousin of Carlos Lezcano, outfielder in Chicago Cubs' organization.
Tied major league record for most putouts by right fielder, game (10), May 20, 1977.
Tied modern major league record for most chances accepted by right fielder, game (10), May 20, 1977.
Named outfielder on THE SPORTING NEWS American League All-Star fielding team, 1979.

Year—Club	League	Pos.	G.	AB.	R.	H.	2B.	3B.	HR.	RBI.	B.A.	PO.	A.	E.	F.A.
1971—Newark	NYP	OF-3B	53	152	24	44	5	1	7	23	.289	55	11	5	.930
1972—Danville	Midw.	OF	114	423	67	114	20	5	10	56	.270	147	13	10	.941
1973—Shreveport	Texas	OF	134	458	69	134	*35	*7	18	90	.293	264	*17	13	.956
1974—Sacramento	P.C.	OF	131	508	100	165	23	8	34	99	.325	245	24	3	.989
1974—Milwaukee	Amer.	OF	15	54	5	13	2	0	2	9	.241	32	3	1	.972
1975—Milwaukee	Amer.	OF	134	429	55	106	19	3	11	43	.247	240	10	6	.977
1976—Milwaukee	Amer.	OF	145	513	53	146	19	5	7	56	.285	345	10	10	.973
1977—Milwaukee†	Amer.	OF	109	400	50	109	21	4	21	49	.273	238	11	3	.988
1978—Milwaukee	Amer.	OF	132	442	62	129	21	4	15	61	.292	262	*18	6	.979
1979—Milwaukee	Amer.	OF	138	473	84	152	29	3	28	101	.321	281	10	4	.986
1980—Milwaukee‡	Amer.	OF	112	411	51	94	19	3	18	55	.229	228	8	4	.983
Major League Totals			785	2722	360	749	130	22	102	374	.275	1626	70	34	.980

Signed as free agent by Milwaukee Brewers' organization, October 1, 1970.
†On disabled list, July 23 to August 16, 1977.
‡Traded with Pitchers Lary Sorensen and Dave LaPoint and Outfielder David Green to St. Louis Cardinals for Catcher Ted Simmons and Pitchers Pete Vuckovich and Rollie Fingers, December 12, 1980.

JOHN WILBUR LICKERT

Born April 4, 1960, at Pittsburgh, Pa.
Height, 5.11. Weight, 175.
Throws and bats righthanded.
Led Carolina League catchers in passed balls with 19 in 1979.
Led Eastern League catchers in putouts with 660, in assists with 127, in errors with 20 and in double plays with 14 in 1980.

Year—Club	League	Pos.	G.	AB.	R.	H.	2B.	3B.	HR.	RBI.	B.A.	PO.	A.	E.	F.A.
1978—Elmira	NYP	C	41	113	8	29	1	0	0	7	.257	178	28	7	.967
1979—Winston-Salem	Carol.	C	112	356	42	97	14	3	3	43	.272	*707	77	10	*.987
1980—Bristol	East.	C-OF	124	436	47	112	27	1	3	52	.257	663	127	20	.975

Selected by Boston Red Sox' organization in 12th round of free-agent draft, June 6, 1978.

RUFINO LINARES

Born February 28, 1955, at San Pedro de Macoris, Dominican Republic.
Height 6.00. Weight, 170.
Throws and bats righthanded.

Year—Club	League	Pos.	G.	AB.	R.	H.	2B.	3B.	HR.	RBI.	B.A.	PO.	A.	E.	F.A.
1974—Kingsport	Appal.	OF	56	220	32	64	7	1	6	41	.291	106	5	6	.949
1975—Greenwood	W. Car.	OF	106	302	36	77	12	2	2	35	.255	178	6	10	.948
1976—Greenwood	W. Car.	OF-1B	109	389	57	127	20	4	3	54	.326	52	4	1	.982
1977—Savannah	South.	OF	85	262	32	76	12	5	2	29	.290	93	9	5	.953
1978—Savannah	South.	OF	116	400	49	121	15	5	8	51	.303	158	12	3	.983

Year Club	League	Pos.	G.	AB.	R.	H.	2B.	3B.	HR.	RBI.	B.A.	PO.	A.	E.	F.A.
1978—Richmond .... Int.		DH	4	9	1	1	0	1	0	3	.111	0	0	0	.000
1979—Savannah .... South.		OF	53	198	35	65	11	1	8	37	.328	40	1	2	.953
1979—Richmond† .... Int.		OF	36	104	9	31	4	1	1	13	.298	22	1	5	.821
1980—Richmond .... Int.		OF	63	234	31	77	12	4	3	41	.329	56	5	0	1.000
1980—Savannah .... South.		OF	51	200	37	85	18	6	2	38	.425	100	4	5	.954

Signed as free agent by Atlanta Braves' organization, December 30, 1973.
†On disabled list, August 3 to August 13, 1979.

RICCARDO P. E. LISI
(Rick)

Born March 17, 1956, at Halifax, Nova Scotia.
Height, 6.00. Weight, 175.
Throws and bats righthanded.

Led Gulf Coast League third basemen in putouts with 39 in 1974.
Led Western Carolinas League third basemen in double plays with 26 in 1975.

Year Club	League	Pos.	G.	AB.	R.	H.	2B.	3B.	HR.	RBI.	B.A.	PO.	A.	E.	F.A.
1974—Sara. Rangers ... G. C.		3B-C	51	170	16	37	8	1	2	29	.218	48	96	12	.923
1975—Anderson .... W. Car.		3B	135	436	74	102	21	3	12	67	.234	*123	*274	*42	*.904
1976—Asheville .... W. Car.		3B-1B	126	473	73	127	24	4	16	75	.268	88	127	26	.912
1977—Tulsa .... Texas		O-C-3-1	112	375	55	95	23	3	6	50	.253	264	62	18	.948
1978—Tulsa .... Texas		C-1-O-3	101	342	44	78	16	5	9	46	.228	429	49	16	.968
1979—Tulsa .... Texas		OF-1B	120	435	86	133	32	5	22	84	.306	453	28	8	.984
1979—Tucson .... P.C.		OF	6	13	1	2	1	0	0	0	.154	2	0	0	1.000
1980—Charleston .... Int.		OF	132	461	51	113	20	5	14	65	.245	278	16	8	.974

Selected by Texas Rangers' organization in 13th round of free-agent draft, June 5, 1974.

MARK ALAN LITTELL

Born January 17, 1953, at Gideon, Mo.
Height, 6.03. Weight, 210.
Throws right and bats lefthanded.
Hobbies—Hunting and fishing.
Attended Union University, Jackson, Tenn., University of Tampa, Tampa, Fla., Longview
Community College, Lee's Summit, Mo. and University of Missouri at Kansas City.

Major League saves: 1973 (0), 1975 (0), 1976 (16), 1977 (12), 1978 (11), 1979 (13), 1980 (2). Total—54.
Led American Association pitchers in complete games with 15 in 1973.
Named American Association Pitcher of the Year in 1973.

Year Club	League	G.	IP.	W.	L.	Pct.	H.	R.	ER.	SO.	BB.	ERA.
1971—Billings .... Pioneer		13	87	5	1	.833	76	41	28	69	54	2.90
1972—Waterloo .... Midwest		25	153	10	9	.526	134	78	59	*199	79	3.47
1973—Omaha .... Am. Assoc.		22	179	*16	6	.727	144	58	50	133	81	*2.51
1973—Kansas City .... American		8	38	1	3	.250	44	25	24	16	23	5.68
1974—Omaha† .... Am. Assoc.		16	89	3	9	.250	92	58	47	44	43	4.75
1975—Omaha .... Am. Assoc.		24	168	13	6	.684	160	81	65	128	74	3.48
1975—Kansas City .... American		7	24	1	2	.333	19	11	10	19	15	3.75
1976—Kansas City .... American		60	104	8	4	.667	68	26	24	92	60	2.08
1977—Kansas City‡ .... American		48	105	8	4	.667	73	49	42	106	55	3.60
1978—St. Louis .... National		72	106	4	8	.333	80	38	33	130	59	2.80
1979—St. Louis .... National		63	82	9	4	.692	60	22	20	67	39	2.20
1980—St. Louis§ .... National		14	11	0	2	.000	14	11	11	7	7	9.00
American League Totals...........................		123	271	18	13	.581	204	111	100	233	153	3.32
National League Totals		149	199	13	14	.481	154	71	64	204	105	2.89
Major League Totals		272	470	31	27	.534	358	182	164	437	258	3.14

Selected by Kansas City Royals' organization in 12th round of free-agent draft, June 8, 1971.
†On disabled list, June 12 to July 1, 1974.
‡Traded with Catcher Buck Martinez to St. Louis Cardinals for Pitcher Al Hrabosky, December 8, 1977.
§On disabled list, June 1, 1980; transferred to emergency disabled list, July 24 to September 24, 1980.

CHAMPIONSHIP SERIES RECORD

Year Club	League	G.	IP.	W.	L.	Pct.	H.	R.	ER.	SO.	BB.	ERA.
1976—Kansas City .... American		3	4⅔	0	1	.000	4	1	1	3	1	1.93
1977—Kansas City .... American		2	3	0	0	.000	5	3	1	1	3	3.00
Championship Series Totals		5	7⅔	0	1	.000	9	4	2	4	4	2.35

DONALD JEFFERY LITTLE
(Jeff)

Born December 25, 1954, at Woodville, O.
Height, 6.06. Weight, 220.
Throws left and bats righthanded.
Son of Donald Little, minor league pitcher, 1953-58.

Pitched seven-inning 1-0 no-hit victory against Dubuque, June 12, 1974.
Tied for Pacific Coast League lead in games started with 28 in 1978.

Year Club	League	G.	IP.	W.	L.	Pct.	H.	R.	ER.	SO.	BB.	ERA.
1973—Great Falls .... Pioneer		14	69	4	7	.364	81	39	29	62	42	3.78
1974—Decatur .... Midwest		23	153	7	*14	.333	153	85	58	129	59	3.41

Year	Club	League	G.	IP.	W.	L.	Pct.	H.	R.	ER.	SO.	BB.	ERA.
1975–Lafayette	Texas	26	115	5	12	.294	143	84	69	59	53	5.40
1976–Lafayette	Texas	29	110	4	9	.308	107	67	60	66	59	4.91
1977–Waterbury	Eastern	26	162	14	10	.583	146	86	78	111	96	4.33
1978–Phoenix	P. Coast	29	175	11	7	.611	189	96	80	74	77	4.11
1979–Phoenix†‡	P. Coast	28	140	7	13	.350	179	110	92	72	76	5.91
1980–Arkansas§	Texas	9	11	3	1	.750	13	7	6	9	7	4.91
1980–Springfield	Am. Assoc.	22	62	3	4	.429	60	32	31	46	28	4.50
1980–St. Louis	National	7	19	1	1	.500	18	9	8	17	9	3.79
Major League Totals		7	19	1	1	.500	18	9	8	17	9	3.79

Selected by San Francisco Giants' organization in 3rd round of free-agent draft, June 5, 1973.
†On disabled list, July 27 to August 7, 1979.
‡Released, April 2, 1980; signed by St. Louis Cardinals' organization, April 7, 1980.
§On disabled list, April 10 to May 5, 1980.

JOHN ANDREW LITTLEFIELD

Born Janaury 5, 1954, at Covina, Calif.
Height, 6.02. Weight, 200.
Throws and bats righthanded.
Attended Arizona State University, Tempe, Ariz.
and Azusa Pacific College, Azusa, Calif.

Led American Association in saves with 10 in 1979.

Year	Club	League	G.	IP.	W.	L.	Pct.	H.	R.	ER.	SO.	BB.	ERA.
1976–Sarasota Cards	Gulf Coast	3	7	1	0	1.000	5	3	2	10	3	2.57
1976–Johnson City	Ap'lachian	14	44	6	3	.667	37	10	7	24	6	1.43
1977–St. Petersburg	Florida St.	9	17	2	1	.667	13	5	5	5	4	2.65
1977–Arkansas	Texas	33	98	9	1	.900	85	24	13	61	23	1.19
1978–Arkansas	Texas	50	97	9	8	.529	106	50	47	54	36	4.36
1979–Arkansas	Texas	26	58	2	4	.333	52	17	14	31	11	2.17
1979–Springfield	Am. Assoc.	29	46	6	5	.545	41	15	15	25	8	2.93
1980–Springfield	Am. Assoc.	17	32	3	0	1.000	32	11	8	17	9	2.25
1980–St. Louis†	National	52	66	5	5	.500	71	31	23	22	20	3.14
Major League Totals		52	66	5	5	.500	71	31	23	22	20	3.14

Selected by Los Angeles Dodgers' organization in 20th round of free-agent draft, June 6, 1972.
Selected by St. Louis Cardinals' organization in 31st round of free-agent draft, June 8, 1976.
†Traded with Catchers Terry Kennedy and Steve Swisher, Pitchers Kim Seaman, Al Olmsted and John Urrea and Infielder Mike Phillips to San Diego Padres for Pitchers Rollie Fingers and Bob Shirley, Catcher-First Baseman Gene Tenace and a player to be named later, December 8, 1980; Catcher Bob Geren traded to St. Louis completing deal, December 10, 1980.

DENNIS GERALD LITTLEJOHN

Born October 4, 1954, at Santa Monica, Calif.
Height, 6.02. Weight, 210.
Throws and bats righthanded.
Attended University of Southern California, Los Angeles, Calif.

Led California League in bases on balls with 103 in 1976.
Led California League catchers in double plays with 10 in 1976.
Led Eastern League in strikeouts with 127 in 1977.

Year	Club	League	Pos.	G.	AB.	R.	H.	2B.	3B.	HR.	RBI.	B.A.	PO.	A.	E.	F.A.
1976–Fresno	Calif.	C	124	416	93	102	15	2	16	56	.245	★807	★127	★27	.972
1977–Waterbury	East.	C	134	411	63	101	19	1	12	64	.246	★751	79	8	★.990
1978–Phoenix	P. C.	C-1B	78	223	28	57	12	1	4	31	.256	326	61	6	.985
1978–San Francisco	Nat.	C	2	0	0	0	0	0	0	0	.000	0	0	0	.000
1979–Phoenix	P. C.	C	66	239	33	68	11	5	5	34	.285	299	48	2	.994
1979–San Francisco	Nat.	C	63	193	15	38	6	1	1	13	.197	366	43	6	.986
1980–Phoenix†	P. C.	C-1B	53	169	32	54	9	2	3	22	.320	221	42	6	.978
1980–San Francisco	Nat.	C	13	29	2	7	1	0	0	2	.241	51	8	1	.983
Major League Totals			78	222	17	45	7	1	1	15	.203	417	51	7	.985

Selected by Oakland A's organization in 9th round of free-agent draft, June 6, 1972.
Selected by San Francisco Giants' organization in secondary phase of free-agent draft, January 7, 1976.
†On disabled list, April 19 to May 4, 1980.

LARRY MARVIN LITTLETON

Born April 3, 1954, at Charlotte, N. C.
Height, 6.01. Weight, 185.
Throws and bats righthanded.
Attended Middle Georgia College, Cochran, Ga., and University of Georgia,
Athens, Ga.; received Bachelor of Business Administration degree.
Cousin of Gordy Coleman, first baseman with Cleveland Indians and Cincinnati Reds, 1959-67.

Year	Club	League	Pos.	G.	AB.	R.	H.	2B.	3B.	HR.	RBI.	B.A.	PO.	A.	E.	F.A.
1976–Salem†	Carol.	OF	82	284	50	76	10	4	13	59	.268	164	8	2	.989
1977–Shreveport	Texas	OF	121	369	65	88	7	3	18	52	.238	220	9	2	.991
1978–Shreveport	Texas	OF	134	459	79	121	24	7	19	76	.264	266	10	8	.972
1979–Portland‡	P.C.	OF	133	459	66	128	24	6	8	71	.279	317	10	5	.985
1980–Tacoma	P.C.	OF	148	501	79	136	30	8	17	80	.271	★362	6	1	★.997

Selected by Boston Red Sox' organization in 7th round of free-agent draft, June 4, 1975.
Selected by Pittsburgh Pirates' organization in secondary phase of free-agent draft, January 7, 1976.
†On temporary inactive list, May 23 to June 10, 1976.
‡Traded with Pitcher John Burden to Cleveland Indians' organization for Pitcher Larry Andersen, December 21, 1979.

CLAUDE EDWARD LOCKWOOD JR.
(Skip)

Born August 17, 1946, at Boston, Mass.
Height, 6.00. Weight, 200.
Throws and bats righthanded.
Hobby—All types of sports.
Attended Merrimack College, Andover, Mass., Boston College, Chestnut Hill, Mass.,
Bryant & Stratton Junior College, Boston, Mass., Marquette University,
Milwaukee, Wis., Emerson College, Boston, Mass., and Carroll College,
Waukesha, Wis.; received Bachelor of Science degree in Speech
from Emerson College.

Received reported $100,000 bonus to sign with Kansas City Athletics, 1964.

Year—Club	League	G.	IP.	W.	L.	Pct.	H.	R.	ER.	SO.	BB.	ERA.
1966—Modesto	California	1	1	1	0	1.000	0	0	0	1	0	0.00
1968—Birmingham	Southern	4	10	0	0	.000	13	6	6	8	6	5.40
1968—Peninsula§	Carolina	17	65	6	3	.667	58	27	24	40	16	3.32
1969—Elmira	Eastern	15	66	6	2	.750	66	33	30	53	45	4.09
1969—Seattle	American	6	23	0	1	.000	24	9	9	10	6	3.52
1970—Portland	P. Coast	5	34	4	1	.800	29	13	10	24	9	2.65
1970—Milwaukee	American	27	174	5	12	.294	173	91	83	93	79	4.29
1971—Milwaukee	American	33	208	10	15	.400	191	93	77	115	91	3.33
1972—Milwaukee	American	29	170	8	15	.348	148	75	68	106	71	3.60
1973—Milwaukee x	American	37	155	5	12	.294	164	75	67	87	59	3.89
1974—California yz	American	37	81	2	5	.286	81	42	39	39	32	4.33
1975—Tucson a	P. Coast	30	84	6	2	.750	99	49	41	84	32	4.39
1975—Tidewater	Int'national	3	5	1	0	1.000	0	0	0	5	1	0.00
1975—New York	National	24	48	1	3	.250	28	9	8	61	25	1.50
1976—New York	National	56	94	10	7	.588	62	31	28	108	34	2.68
1977—New York	National	63	104	4	8	.333	87	40	39	84	31	3.38
1978—New York	National	57	91	7	13	.350	78	36	36	73	31	3.56
1979—New York bc	National	27	42	2	5	.286	33	7	7	42	14	1.50
1980—Boston	American	24	46	3	1	.750	61	31	27	11	17	5.28
American League Totals		193	857	33	61	.351	842	416	370	461	355	3.89
National League Totals		227	379	24	36	.400	288	123	118	368	135	2.80
Major League Totals		420	1236	57	97	.370	1130	539	488	829	490	3.55

RECORD AS INFIELDER

Year—Club	League	Pos.	G.	AB.	R.	H.	2B.	3B.	HR.	RBI.	B.A.	PO.	A.	E.	F.A.
1964—Burlington	Midw.	3B	64	236	30	49	4	1	5	29	.208	47	82	23	.849
1965—Kansas City	Amer.	3B	42	33	4	4	0	0	0	0	.121	9	4	0	1.000
1966—Modesto	Calif.	OF-3B	106	382	53	101	16	3	6	43	.264	140	56	20	.907
1967—Burlington†‡	Midw.	3-1-S	58	204	30	50	9	1	5	26	.245	117	109	19	.922
Major League Totals			42	33	4	4	0	0	0	0	.121	9	4	0	1.000

Signed as free agent by Kansas City A's organization, June 10, 1964.
†On military list, January 26 through June 23.
‡Drafted by Houston Astros from Vancouver (Oakland Athletics' organization), November 28, 1967; returned to Vancouver, April 3, 1968.
§Recalled by Oakland Athletics; drafted by Seattle Pilots from Oakland in expansion draft, October 15, 1968.

xTraded with Outfielders Ollie Brown and Joe Lahoud, Pitcher Gary Ryerson and Catcher Ellie Rodriguez to California Angels for Pitchers Clyde Wright and Steve Barber, Outfielder Ken Berry, Catcher Art Kusnyer and a player to be named later, October 22, 1973.

yTraded to New York Yankees for Utilityman Bill Sudakis, December 3, 1974; Yankees sent Outfielder Mike Krizmanich to Angels, December 5, 1975, to complete deal.

zReleased by New York Yankees, April 7, 1975; signed as a free agent by Tucson (Oakland Athletics' organization), April 14, 1975.

aSold by Oakland Athletics' organization to New York Mets' organization, July 28, 1975.

bOn disabled list, June 20 to October 3, 1979.

cGranted free agency, November 1, 1979; signed by Boston Red Sox, November 27, 1979.

HINTON DANIEL LOGAN
(Dan)

Born July 17, 1956, at Trion, Ga.
Height, 6.06. Weight, 230.
Throws and bats lefthanded.
Attended West Georgia College, Carrollton, Ga.

Led Appalachian League in total bases with 140 and in double plays by first basemen with 46 in 1977.
Led Florida State League first basemen in double plays with 107 in 1978.
Led Southern League first basemen in double plays with 133 in 1979.

Year Club	League	Pos.	G.	AB.	R.	H.	2B.	3B.	HR.	RBI.	B.A.	PO.	A.	E.	F.A.
1977—Bluefield	Appal.	1B	69	258	40	78	16	2	●14	★56	.302	★565	21	2	★.997
1978—Miami	Fla. St.	1B	117	425	38	133	16	5	5	76	.313	995	73	10	★.991
1979—Charlotte	South.	1B	136	485	83	137	19	2	21	79	.282	1225	81	10	.992
1980—Charlotte	South.	1B	78	288	34	80	9	0	13	57	.278	671	51	5	.993
1980—Rochester	Int.	1B	62	195	21	38	7	0	2	16	.195	545	60	9	.985

Selected by Baltimore Orioles' organization in 2nd round of free-agent draft, June 7, 1977.

ANGELO MICHAEL LoGRANDE

Born December 4, 1957, at San Pedro, Calif.
Height, 6.03. Weight, 215.
Throws and bats righthanded.

Led California League batters in strikeouts with 153 in 1976.

Year Club	League	Pos.	G.	AB.	R.	H.	2B.	3B.	HR.	RBI.	B.A.	PO.	A.	E.	F.A.
1975—Sara. Indians	G.C.	1B	45	170	19	45	9	2	1	19	.265	324	18	14	.961
1976—San Jose	Calif.	1B	132	494	70	125	25	3	19	77	.253	878	41	19	.980
1977—Jersey City	East.	1B	41	132	10	25	4	0	2	11	.189	272	12	12	.959
1977—Waterloo	Midw.	1B-3B	80	268	48	68	14	0	17	57	.254	546	29	20	.966
1978—Waterloo†	Midw.	1B	82	278	42	76	16	0	12	49	.273	544	21	12	.979
1979—Chattanooga	South.	1B	127	439	60	108	20	1	20	76	.246	409	22	4	.991
1980—Chattanooga‡	South.	1B	125	469	71	137	31	0	25	81	.292	915	42	14	.986

Selected by Cleveland Indians' organization in 17th round of free-agent draft, June 4, 1975.
†On disabled list, June 15 to August 1, 1978.
‡On disabled list, April 11 to April 24, 1980.

WILLIAM TIMOTHY LOLLAR
(Tim)

Born March 17, 1956, at Poplar Bluff, Mo.
Height, 6.03. Weight, 200.
Throws and bats lefthanded.
Attended Mineral Area College, Poplar Bluff, Mo., and University of Arkansas, Fayetteville, Ark.

Year Club	League	G.	IP.	W.	L.	Pct.	H.	R.	ER.	SO.	BB.	ERA.
1978—West Haven†	Eastern	8	31	1	1	.500	40	24	20	20	14	5.81
1979—West Haven	Eastern	22	119	8	5	.615	122	55	42	60	36	3.18
1980—Columbus	Int'national	21	49	2	1	.667	29	15	14	50	27	2.57
1980—New York	American	14	32	1	0	1.000	33	14	12	13	20	3.38
Major League Totals		14	32	1	0	1.000	33	14	12	13	20	3.38

Selected by Cleveland Indians' organization in 5th round of free-agent draft, June 6, 1977.
Selected by New York Yankees' organization in 4th round of free-agent draft, June 6, 1978.
†On disabled list, August 2 to August 14, 1978.

RECORD AS INFIELDER

Year Club	League	Pos.	G.	AB.	R.	H.	2B.	3B.	HR.	RBI.	B.A.	PO.	A.	E.	F.A.
1978—West Haven	East.	P-1B	28	55	11	14	2	1	2	7	.255	16	3	0	1.000
1979—West Haven	East.	P-1B	65	122	16	28	3	0	5	15	.230	137	9	1	.993

ROBERT EARL LONG
(Bob)

Born November 11, 1954, at Jasper, Tenn.
Height, 6.03. Weight, 178.
Throws and bats righthanded.
Attended Carson-Newman College, Jefferson City, Tenn., and Shorter College, Rome, Ga.

Year Club	League	G.	IP.	W.	L.	Pct.	H.	R.	ER.	SO.	BB.	ERA.
1976—Niagara Falls	NYP	11	68	3	5	.375	74	44	31	32	35	4.10
1977—Charleston	W. Carol.	17	85	6	4	.600	78	42	32	57	43	3.39
1978—Salem	Carolina	33	93	8	4	.667	74	42	29	81	40	2.81
1979—Buffalo	Eastern	44	92	4	10	.286	98	52	35	73	54	3.42
1980—Portland†	P. Coast	33	93	4	4	.500	86	48	44	54	41	4.26

Selected by Pittsburgh Pirates' organization in 24th round of free-agent draft, June 8, 1976.
†On disabled list, July 31 to August 10, 1980.

DAVID EARL LOPES

Name pronounced as ROPES.

(Davey)

Born May 3, 1946, at East Providence, R. I.
Height, 5.09. Weight, 170.
Throws and bats righthanded.
Hobbies—Basketball and tennis.
Attended Washburn University, Topeka, Kan.;
received Bachelor of Science degree in Education.

Established major league record for most consecutive stolen bases, season, 38, June 10 through August 24, 1975; highest stolen base percentage, lifetime, minimum 300 attempts, .827.
Tied major league record for most errors, inning, second baseman, 3, June 2, 1973 (1st inning).

Tied National League records for most stolen bases, game, since 1900, 5, August 24, 1974; and most double plays, second baseman, game, 5, May 18, 1975.

Led National League in stolen bases with 77 in 1975 and 63 in 1976.

Led National League in fewest times grounded into double plays, minimum 502 plate appearances, with 3 in 1977.

Hit three home runs in a game, August 20, 1974, against Chicago Cubs.

Major league stolen bases: 1972 (4), 1973 (36), 1974 (59), 1975 (77), 1976 (63), 1977 (47), 1978 (45), 1979 (44), 1980 (23). Total—398.

Led Pacific Coast League in stolen bases with 48 in 1972.

Named second baseman on THE SPORTING NEWS National League All-Star Team, 1978 and 1979.

Named second baseman on THE SPORTING NEWS National League All-Star fielding team, 1978.

Year—Club	League	Pos.	G.	AB.	R.	H.	2B.	3B.	HR.	RBI.	B.A.	PO.	A.	E.	F.A.
1968—Daytona Beach†.Fla. St.		OF	82	271	39	67	6	6	5	33	.247	109	7	4	.967
1969—Daytona Bea.‡§..Fla. St.		OF	72	264	53	74	7	4	9	33	.280	138	16	7	.957
1970—Spokane x.........P. C.		•OF-2B	100	343	48	90	15	4	6	35	.262	202	19	•12	.948
1971—Spokane y.........P. C.		OF-2B	94	353	78	108	9	9	6	36	.306	157	103	11	.959
1972—Albuquerque z ...P. C.		★2-O-S	104	397	94	126	18	6	11	53	.317	213	270	★21	.958
1972—Los Angeles.......Nat.		2B	11	42	6	9	4	0	0	1	.214	27	27	2	.964
1973—Los Angeles.......Nat.		2-O-S-3	142	535	77	147	13	5	6	37	.275	323	380	11	.985
1974—Los Angeles.......Nat.		2B	145	530	95	141	26	3	10	35	.266	309	360	★24	.965
1975—Los Angeles.......Nat.		2-O-S	155	618	108	162	24	6	8	41	.262	360	386	16	.979
1976—Los Angeles a...Nat.		2B-OF	117	427	72	103	17	7	4	20	.241	254	268	19	.965
1977—Los Angeles.......Nat.		2B	134	502	85	142	19	5	11	53	.283	287	380	14	.979
1978—Los Angeles ......Nat.		★2B-OF	151	587	93	163	25	4	17	58	.278	340	424	★20	.974
1979—Los Angeles ......Nat.		2B	153	582	109	154	20	6	28	73	.265	341	★384	14	.981
1980—Los Angeles ......Nat.		2B	141	553	79	139	15	3	10	49	.251	304	416	15	.980
Major League Totals			1149	4376	724	1160	163	39	94	367	.265	2545	3025	135	.976

Selected by San Francisco Giants' organization in 28th round of free-agent draft, June 6, 1967.

Selected by Los Angeles Dodgers' organization in secondary phase of free-agent draft, January 27, 1968.

†On restricted list, April 11 to June 13, 1968.

‡On temporary inactive list, April 11 to April 27, 1969.

§On military list, July 22, 1969 to April 8, 1970.

xOn temporary inactive list, June 9 to June 30, 1970.

yOn temporary inactive list, April 26 to April 29 and June 8 to July 2, 1971.

zOn temporary inactive list, June 16 to June 30 and August 28 to September 1, 1972.

aOn supplemental disabled list, March 31 to May 3, 1976.

CHAMPIONSHIP SERIES RECORD

Tied Championship Series records for most consecutive games, one or more runs batted in, total Series (4); most hits, two consecutive games, one Series (6), October 4 and 5, 1978.

Tied National League Championship Series record for most three-base hits, total Series (2).

Year—Club	League	Pos.	G.	AB.	R.	H.	2B.	3B.	HR.	RBI.	B.A.	PO.	A.	E.	F.A.
1974—Los Angeles.......Nat.		2B	4	15	4	4	0	1	0	3	.267	9	18	1	.964
1977—Los Angeles.......Nat.		2B	4	17	2	4	0	0	0	3	.235	9	10	1	.950
1978—Los Angeles ......Nat.		2B	4	18	3	7	1	1	2	5	.389	10	10	2	.909
Championship Series Totals.............			12	50	9	15	1	2	2	11	.300	28	38	4	.943

WORLD SERIES RECORD

Tied World Series records for most stolen bases, inning (2), October 15, 1974 (first inning); most putouts by second baseman, game (8), October 16, 1974; most chances accepted by second baseman, game (13), October 16, 1974; most putouts by second baseman, inning (3), October 16, 1974; most times home run as leadoff batter, start of game (1), October 17, 1978.

Year—Club	League	Pos.	G.	AB.	R.	H.	2B.	3B.	HR.	RBI.	B.A.	PO.	A.	E.	F.A.
1974—Los Angeles.......Nat.		2B	5	18	2	2	0	0	0	0	.111	19	9	0	1.000
1977—Los Angeles.......Nat.		2B	6	24	3	4	0	1	1	2	.167	12	22	0	1.000
1978—Los Angeles ......Nat.		2B	6	26	7	8	0	0	3	7	.308	10	19	1	.967
World Series Totals			17	68	12	14	0	1	4	9	.206	41	50	1	.989

ALL-STAR GAME RECORD

Year—League	Pos.	AB.	R.	H.	2B.	3B.	HR.	RBI.	B.A.	PO.	A.	E.	F.A.
1978—National..........................	PH-2B	1	0	1	0	0	0	1	1.000	0	1	0	1.000
1979—National..........................	2B	3	0	1	0	0	0	0	.333	4	1	0	1.000
1980—National..........................	2B	1	0	0	0	0	0	0	.000	0	2	0	1.000
All-Star Game Totals		5	0	2	0	0	0	1	.400	4	4	0	1.000

AURELIO ALEJANDRO LOPEZ (RIOS)

Born October 5, 1948, at Tecamachalco, Puebla, Mexico.
Height, 6.00. Weight, 230.
Throws and bats righthanded.
Hobbies—Reading, movies, football and soccer.

Pitched 1-0 no-hit victory against Carmen, May 24, 1969.

Major League saves: 1974 (0), 1978 (0), 1979 (21), 1980 (21). Total—42.

Led Mexican League in wild pitches with 18 in 1975.

Led Mexican League in saves with 20 in 1974, with 23 in 1975 and with 16 in 1976.

Named Mexican League Most Valuable Player, 1977.

Year—Club	League	G.	IP.	W.	L.	Pct.	H.	R.	ER.	SO.	BB.	ERA.
1967—Las Choapas ....Mex. SE.		27	96	5	3	.625	93	62	46	80	66	4.31
1968—Mexico City Reds ....Mexican		31	162	10	10	.500	154	73	47	99	64	2.61

Year	Club	League	G	IP	W	L	Pct.	H	R	ER	SO	BB	ERA.
1969—Minatitlan	Mex. SE.	16	83	7	4	.636	56	29	18	64	40	1.95
1969—Mexico City Reds	Mexican	21	105	10	4	.714	131	53	45	76	49	3.86
1970—Mexico City Reds	Mexican	37	172	16	11	.593	153	64	57	127	100	2.98
1971—Mexico City Reds†	Mexican	21	83	4	7	.364	86	49	45	36	59	4.88
1972—Mexico City Reds	Mexican	46	121	5	7	.417	109	57	49	89	58	3.64
1973—Mexico City Reds	Mexican	53	127	12	10	.545	115	58	47	117	82	3.33
1974—Mexico City Reds‡	Mexican	*60	113	7	7	.500	94	50	32	134	70	2.55
1974—Kansas City§	American	8	16	0	0	.000	21	12	10	5	10	5.63
1975—Mexico City Reds	Mexican	*71	114	10	8	.556	97	46	36	114	68	2.84
1976—Mexico City Reds	Mexican	*59	98	4	11	.267	111	61	49	65	49	4.50
1977—Mexico City Reds x	Mexican	*73	157	19	8	.704	132	39	35	165	49	2.01
1978—Springfield	Am. Assoc.	34	76	6	6	.500	72	37	30	81	39	3.55
1978—St. Louis y	National	25	65	4	2	.667	52	35	31	46	32	4.29
1979—Detroit	American	61	127	10	5	.667	95	37	34	106	51	2.41
1980—Detroit	American	67	124	13	6	.684	125	56	52	97	45	3.77
American League Totals		136	267	23	11	.676	241	105	96	208	106	3.24
National League Totals		25	65	4	2	.667	52	35	31	46	32	4.29
Major League Totals		161	332	27	13	.675	293	140	127	254	138	3.44

Signed as free agent by Las Choapas, March 28, 1967.

†On disabled list, April 30 to May 27 and June 28 to July 12, 1971.

‡Sold to Kansas City Royals, August 29, 1974.

§Sold to Mexico City Reds, March 27, 1975.

xSold to St. Louis Cardinals, October 26, 1977.

yTraded with Outfielder Jerry Morales to Detroit Tigers for Pitchers Bob Sykes and Jack Murphy, December 4, 1978.

CARLOS ANTONIO LOPEZ (MORALES)

Born September 27, 1950, at Mazatlan, Sinaloa, Mexico.
Height, 6.01. Weight, 192.
Throws and bats righthanded.
Hobbies—Fishing and billiards.

Tied for Texas League lead in double plays by outfielders with 4 in 1974.

Year	Club	League	Pos.	G.	AB.	R.	H.	2B.	3B.	HR.	RBI.	B.A.	PO.	A.	E.	F.A.
1969—Aguascalientes†	Mex.Cn.	Of	116	471	75	126	15	5	1	39	.268	256	17	18	.938
1969—Mex. C. Tigers‡	Mex.	OF	4	4	1	1	0	0	0	1	.250	3	0	0	1.000
1970—Tabasco	Mex.SE	OF	79	296	29	84	6	0	1	13	.284	158	11	10	.944
1971—Aguascalientes	Mex.Cn.	OF	67	245	52	88	18	3	4	41	.359	118	3	2	.984
1971—Ensenada	Mx. Nr.	...	77	304	53	102	11	4	4	37	.336	....	....	....	....
1972—Puebla	Mex.	OF	92	169	29	40	5	1	1	13	.237	106	7	3	.974
1973—M.C. Tig-Sab.x	Mex.	OF	75	218	39	61	11	0	3	21	.280	92	4	3	.970
1974—El Paso	Texas	OF	128	461	73	136	21	7	14	75	.295	149	14	10	.942
1975—El Paso	Texas	OF	112	428	77	140	22	*10	9	78	.327	198	9	9	.958
1975—Salt Lake City	P.C.	OF	15	48	3	12	2	0	1	5	.250	27	3	4	.882
1976—Salt Lake City	P.C.	OF-1B	123	448	95	157	19	12	9	88	.350	131	17	5	.967
1976—California y	Amer.	OF	9	10	1	0	0	0	0	0	.000	4	0	0	1.000
1977—Seattle za	Amer.	OF	99	297	39	84	18	1	8	34	.283	160	11	5	.972
1978—Baltimore	Amer.	OF	129	193	21	46	6	0	4	20	.238	151	7	2	.988
1979—Rochester bc	Int.	OF	62	234	38	66	10	2	6	30	.282	97	4	2	.981
1980—M.C. Tig-Rey.d	Mex.	OF	86	321	54	106	15	9	8	50	.330	107	5	6	.949
Major League Totals		237	500	61	130	24	1	12	54	.260	315	18	7	.979

Signed as free agent by Ensenada, October 3, 1968.

Sold to Aguascalientes, March 15, 1969.

†Sold to Mexico City Tigers, October 7, 1969.

‡Sold to Tabasco, March 15, 1970.

§Released, February 15, 1971; signed by Aguascalientes, March 3, 1971.

xPurchased by California Angels' organization from Mexico City Tigers, December 8, 1973.

ySelected by Seattle Mariners from California Angels in expansion draft, November 5, 1976.

zOn disabled list, September 12 through remainder of season, 1977.

aTraded with Pitcher Tommy Moore to Baltimore Orioles for Pitcher Mike Parrott, December 7, 1977.

bOn disabled list, July 6 to September 2, 1979.

cSold to Mexico City Tigers, January 2, 1980.

dDrafted by St. Louis Cardinals, December 8, 1980.

SCOTT GREGORY LOUCKS

Born November 11, 1956, at Anchorage, Alaska.
Height, 6.00. Weight, 178.
Throws and bats righthanded.
Attended Southeastern Oklahoma State University, Durant, Okla.

Led Florida State League batters in walks with 77 in 1979.

Year	Club	League	Pos.	G.	AB.	R.	H.	2B.	3B.	HR.	RBI.	B.A.	PO.	A.	E.	F.A.
1977—Sara. Astros	G.C.	OF	46	142	41	38	2	7	1	20	.268	46	5	•4	.927
1978—Daytona Beach	Fla. St.	OF	43	128	21	26	3	2	0	9	.203	71	4	7	.915
1978—Columbus	South.	OF	76	232	38	45	4	4	3	17	.194	131	1	5	.964
1979—Daytona Beach	Fla. St.	OF	108	338	80	83	6	3	2	18	.246	164	13	3	.983
1979—Columbus	South.	OF	9	8	3	1	0	0	0	1	.125	6	0	1	.857

Year	Club	League	Pos.	G.	AB.	R.	H.	2B.	3B.	HR.	RBI.	B.A.	PO.	A.	E.	F.A.
1980—Columbus	....	South.	OF	137	515	90	125	13	6	10	45	.243	264	12	6	.979
1980—Houston	....	Nat.	OF	8	3	4	1	0	0	0	0	.333	1	0	0	1.000
Major League Totals				8	3	4	1	0	0	0	0	.333	1	0	0	1.000

Selected by Houston Astros' organization in 5th round of free-agent draft, June 7, 1977.

JOHN PAUL LOVIGLIO
(Jay)

Born May 30, 1956, at Freeport, N.Y.
Height, 5.09. Weight, 160.
Throws and bats righthanded.
Attended Suffolk County Community College, Selden, N. Y.

Led Eastern League in stolen bases with 55 in 1979.

Year	Club	League	Pos.	G.	AB.	R.	H.	2B.	3B.	HR.	RBI.	B.A.	PO.	A.	E.	F.A.
1977—Auburn	....	NYP	2B	29	84	9	18	1	0	2	11	.214	71	71	9	.940
1977—Spartanburg	......	W. Car.	2B	28	101	12	19	2	1	0	3	.188	65	86	6	.962
1978—Peninsula	....	Carol.	2B	130	*495	89	133	14	4	4	46	.269	270	325	20	.967
1979—Reading	....	East.	2B	131	504	92	148	21	4	4	52	.294	211	*451	15	*.978
1980—Oklahoma City	..A.A.		2B	123	498	98	138	13	6	6	39	.277	262	413	8	.988
1980—Philadelphia	......	Nat.	2B	16	5	7	0	0	0	0	0	.000	3	2	0	1.000
Major League Totals				16	5	7	0	0	0	0	0	.000	3	2	0	1.000

Signed as free agent by Philadelphia Phillies' organization, May 16, 1977.

JOHN LEE LOWENSTEIN
Name pronounced Low-in-stine.

Born January 27, 1947, at Wolf Point, Mont.
Height, 6.01. Weight, 180.
Throws right and bats lefthanded.
Hobbies—Golf, traveling and hunting.
Attended University of California, Riverside, Calif.; received Bachelor of Arts
degree in Anthropology.

Major League stolen bases: 1970 (1), 1971 (1), 1972 (2), 1973 (5), 1974 (36), 1975 (15), 1976 (11), 1977 (1), 1978 (16), 1979 (16), 1980 (7). Total—111.

Year	Club	League	Pos.	G.	AB.	R.	H.	2B.	3B.	HR.	RBI.	B.A.	PO.	A.	E.	F.A.
1968—Waterbury	....	East.	PH	3	2	0	0	0	0	0	0	.000	0	0	0	.000
1968—Reno	....	Calif.	2B-3B	48	164	22	53	8	2	7	38	.323	71	106	8	.957
1969—Reno†	....	Calif.	1B-OF	26	67	7	19	4	2	1	11	.284	93	5	2	.980
1970—Wichita		A.A.	3-S-O-2	108	369	69	109	15	6	18	52	.295	130	218	13	.964
1970—Cleveland	....	Amer.	2-3-O-S	17	43	5	11	3	1	1	6	.256	15	37	2	.963
1971—Wichita	....	A. A.	OF-3	37	125	27	40	8	0	8	24	.320	55	4	2	.967
1971—Cleveland		Amer.	2-O-S	58	140	15	26	5	0	4	9	.186	103	66	4	.977
1972—Cleveland	....	Amer.	OF-1B	68	151	16	32	8	1	6	21	.212	82	7	0	1.000
1973—Cleveland	....	Amer.	O-2-3-1	98	305	42	89	16	1	6	40	.292	124	85	7	.968
1974—Cleveland	....	Amer.	O-3-1-2	140	508	65	123	14	2	8	48	.242	314	84	6	.985
1975—Cleveland	....	Amer.	O-3-2	91	265	37	64	5	1	12	33	.242	61	16	2	.975
1976—Cleveland‡	....	Amer.	OF-1B	93	229	33	47	8	2	2	14	.205	178	10	7	.964
1977—Cleveland§		Amer.	OF-1B	81	149	24	36	6	1	4	12	.242	63	1	0	1.000
1978—Texas x	....	Amer.	3B-OF	77	176	28	39	8	3	5	21	.222	34	42	6	.927
1979—Baltimore y	....	Amer.	OF-1-3	97	197	33	50	8	2	11	34	.254	124	7	1	.992
1980—Baltimore z	....	Amer.	OF	104	196	38	61	8	0	4	27	.311	128	3	1	.992
Major League Totals				924	2359	336	578	89	14	63	265	.245	1226	358	36	.978

Selected by Cleveland Indians' organization in 18th round of free-agent draft, June 7, 1968.
†On military list, January 31 through August 2, 1969.
‡Traded with Catcher Rick Cerone to Toronto Blue Jays for Outfielder Rico Carty, December 6, 1976. Traded to Cleveland Indians for Infielder Hector Torres, March 29, 1977.
§Traded with Pitcher Tom Buskey to Texas Rangers for Outfielder-Designated Hitter Willie Horton and Pitcher David Clyde, February 28, 1978.
xSold on waivers to Baltimore Orioles, November 27, 1978.
yOn supplemental disabled list, August 9 to August 24, 1979.
zOn disabled list, May 19 to June 11, 1980.

CHAMPIONSHIP SERIES RECORD

Tied Championship Series records for hitting home run in first Series at bat, October 3, 1979; most home runs by pinch-hitter, game (1), October 3, 1979.

Year	Club	League	Pos.	G.	AB.	R.	H.	2B.	3B.	HR.	RBI.	B.A.	PO.	A.	E.	F.A.
1979—Baltimore	....	Amer.	PH-OF	4	6	2	1	0	0	1	3	.167	6	0	0	1.000

WORLD SERIES RECORD

Year	Club	League	Pos.	G.	AB.	R.	H.	2B.	3B.	HR.	RBI.	B.A.	PO.	A.	E.	F.A.
1979—Baltimore	....	Amer.	OF-PH	6	13	2	3	1	0	0	3	.231	6	0	1	.857

GARY PAUL LUCAS

Born November 8, 1954, at Riverside, Calif.
Height, 6.05. Weight, 200.
Throws and bats lefthanded.
Attended Chapman College, Orange, Calif.

Year Club	League	G.	IP.	W.	L.	Pct.	H.	R.	ER.	SO.	BB.	ERA.
1976—Walla Walla	Northwest	14	93	7	3	.700	91	40	32	49	30	3.10
1977—Reno	California	28	176	13	7	.650	205	114	90	98	48	4.60
1978—Amarillo	Texas	25	159	8	17	.320	182	104	86	115	26	4.87
1979—Hawaii†	P. Coast	24	178	10	7	.588	151	64	55	98	58	2.78
1980—San Diego	National	46	150	5	8	.385	138	59	54	85	43	3.24
Major League Totals		46	150	5	8	.385	138	59	54	85	43	3.24

Selected by Cincinnati Reds' organization in 1st round (21st player selected) of free-agent draft, January 10, 1973.
Selected by Cincinnati Reds' organization in secondary phase of free-agent draft, June 5, 1973.
Selected by San Diego Padres' organization in 19th round of free-agent draft, June 8, 1976.
†On disabled list, August 5 to August 30, 1979.

STEPHEN LEE LUEBBER
(Steve)

Born July 9, 1949, at Clinton, Mo.
Height, 6.03. Weight, 195.
Throws and bats righthanded.
Hobbies—Basketball, golf, tennis, billiards and bowling.
Attended Missouri Southern College, Joplin, Mo.

Led Pacific Coast League in complete games with 15 and tied for lead in shutouts with 3 in 1975.
Led New York-Pennsylvania League in shutouts with 3 in 1968.
Led Pacific Coast League in shutouts with 5 and tied for lead in games started with 31 in 1972.
Led Florida State League pitchers in games started with 30 in 1970.

Year Club	League	G.	IP.	W.	L.	Pct.	H.	R.	ER.	SO.	BB.	ERA.
1967—Sarasota Twins	Gulf Coast	11	58	4	5	.444	31	24	19	58	•41	2.95
1968—Auburn	NYP	18	106	8	2	•.800	86	30	21	109	48	1.78
1969—Orlando†	Florida St.	9	49	1	2	.333	60	19	19	22	20	3.49
1970—Orlando	Florida St.	34	•237	17	11	.607	184	70	47	•172	79	1.78
1971—Charlotte	Southern	12	96	9	1	.900	61	25	21	86	33	1.97
1971—Minnesota	American	18	68	2	5	.286	73	42	38	35	37	5.03
1972—Tacoma	P. Coast	•31	•215	13	13	.500	200	97	86	•199	90	3.60
1972—Minnesota	American	2	2	0	0	.000	3	0	0	1	2	0.00
1973—Tacoma	P. Coast	11	36	2	4	.333	54	34	25	29	21	6.25
1973—Orlando	Southern	8	41	4	3	.571	27	24	21	9	34	4.61
1974—Orlando	Southern	26	176	10	6	.625	170	87	71	130	90	3.63
1975—Orlando	Southern	6	47	2	2	.500	43	16	16	26	15	3.06
1975—Tacoma	P. Coast	24	177	14	7	.667	145	62	47	123	79	•2.39
1976—Minnesota	American	38	119	4	5	.444	109	57	53	45	62	4.01
1977—Tacoma‡	P. Coast	27	179	10	10	.500	193	102	92	80	69	4.63
1978—Iowa§	Am. Assoc.	27	147	8	9	.471	171	98	89	80	74	5.45
1979—Syracuse	Int'national	29	183	11	8	.579	157	78	69	128	78	3.39
1979—Toronto x	American	1	0	0	0	.000	2	1	1	0	1	
1980—Rochester	Int'national	27	188	13	8	.619	178	83	75	83	56	3.59
Major League Totals		59	189	6	10	.375	187	100	92	81	102	4.38

Selected by Minnesota Twins' organization in 10th round of free-agent draft, June 6, 1967.
†On restricted list, April 28 to June 20, 1969.
‡Released, October 3, 1977; signed by Chicago White Sox' organization, January 24, 1978.
§Released, October 27, 1978; signed by Toronto Blue Jays' organization, March 17, 1979.
xReleased, March 29, 1980; signed by Baltimore Orioles' organization, April 5, 1980.

MICHAEL KEN-WAI LUM
(Mike)

Born October 27, 1945, at Honolulu, Hawaii.
Height, 6.00. Weight, 185.
Throws and bats lefthanded.
Hobby—Horses.
Attended Brigham Young University, Provo, Utah.

Hit three homers in one game, July 3, 1970, first game of a doubleheader vs. San Diego.

Year Club	League	Pos.	G.	AB.	R.	H.	2B.	3B.	HR.	RBI.	B.A.	PO.	A.	E.	F.A.
1963—Waycross	Ga.-Fla.	OF	51	114	17	30	3	2	0	12	.263	47	2	4	.925
1964—Binghamton	NYP	OF	•127	531	102	163	19	7	18	68	.307	254	14	16	.944
1965—Yakima	Northw.	OF	•139	535	99	153	•28	7	7	54	.286	•340	13	6	•.983
1966—Austin	Texas	OF	139	•541	76	144	19	8	6	48	.266	•374	12	7	.982
1967—Richmond	Int.	OF	109	411	47	104	19	4	11	37	.253	219	5	3	.987
1967—Atlanta	Nat.	OF	9	26	1	6	0	0	0	1	.231	16	1	1	.944
1968—Atlanta	Nat.	OF	122	232	22	52	7	3	3	21	.224	115	7	3	.976
1969—Atlanta	Nat.	OF	121	168	20	45	8	0	1	22	.268	119	2	1	.992
1970—Atlanta	Nat.	OF	123	291	25	74	17	2	7	28	.254	168	3	2	.988
1971—Atlanta	Nat.	OF-1B	145	454	56	122	14	1	13	55	.269	287	11	3	.990
1972—Atlanta	Nat.	OF-1B	123	369	40	84	14	2	9	38	.228	247	6	6	.977

Year Club	League	Pos.	G.	AB.	R.	H.	2B.	3B.	HR.	RBI.	B.A.	PO.	A.	E.	F.A.
1973–Atlanta..............Nat.	1B-OF	138	513	74	151	26	6	16	82	.294	833	45	9	.990
1974–Atlanta†...........Nat.	1B-OF	106	361	50	84	11	2	11	50	.233	554	26	4	.993
1975–Atlanta‡...........Nat.	1B-OF	124	364	32	83	8	2	8	36	.228	657	34	5	.993
1976–Cincinnati ....Nat.	OF	84	136	15	31	5	1	3	20	.228	48	0	0	1.000
1977–Cincinnati ....Nat.	OF-1B	81	125	14	20	1	0	5	16	.160	83	2	1	.988
1978–Cincinnati§ ....Nat.	OF-1B	86	146	15	39	7	1	6	23	.267	100	8	2	.982
1979–Atlanta ....Nat.	1B-OF	111	217	27	54	6	0	6	27	.249	420	30	1	.998
1980–Atlanta ....Nat.	OF-1B	93	83	7	17	3	0	0	5	.205	58	4	0	1.000
Major League Totals		1466	3485	398	862	127	20	88	424	.247	3705	179	38	.990

Signed as free agent by Atlanta Braves' organization, June 21, 1963.
†On disabled list, April 29 to May 14 and July 2 to July 25, 1974.
‡Traded to Cincinnati Reds for Infielder Darrel Chaney, December 12, 1975.
§Granted free agency, November 2, 1978; signed by Atlanta Braves, February 15, 1979.

CHAMPIONSHIP SERIES RECORD

Year Club	League	Pos.	G.	AB.	R.	H.	2B.	3B.	HR.	RBI.	B.A.	PO.	A.	E.	F.A.
1969–Atlanta..............Nat.	OF	2	2	0	2	1	0	0	0	1.000	0	0	0	.000
1976–Cincinnati ....Nat.	PH	1	1	0	0	0	0	0	0	.000	0	0	0	.000
Championship Series Totals.............		3	3	0	2	1	0	0	0	.667	0	0	0	.000

GREGORY MICHAEL LUZINSKI
(Greg)

Born November 22, 1950, at Chicago, Ill.
Height, 6.01. Weight, 217.
Throws and bats righthanded.
Hobbies—Bowling and golf.
Brother of Richard Luzinski, outfielder in Philadelphia Phillies' organization.

Tied major league record for fewest double plays by outfielder, season, 150 or more games (0), 1975.
Tied modern National League record for most home runs, October (3), 1972.
Led National League in total bases with 322 in 1975.
Led National League hitters in strikeouts with 140 in 1977.
Led Carolina League hitters in strikeouts with 148 in 1969, Eastern League with 148 in 1970 and Pacific Coast League with 167 in 1971.
Led Carolina League in total bases with 255 in 1969, Eastern League with 287 in 1970 and Pacific Coast League with 319 in 1971.
Led Eastern League first basemen in double plays with 119 in 1970 and Pacific Coast League first basemen with 129 in 1971.
Named outfielder on THE SPORTING NEWS National League All-Star Team, 1975 and 1977.
Named Eastern League Player of the Year in 1970.

Year Club	League	Pos.	G.	AB.	R.	H.	2B.	3B.	HR.	RBI.	B.A.	PO.	A.	E.	F.A.
1968–Huron ....North.	*1B-3B	57	212	22	55	5	0	*13	•43	.250	417	26	13	*.971
1969–Raleigh-Durham Carol.	1B	129	464	75	134	22	3	*31	*92	.289	1067	67	•17	.985
1970–Reading ....East.	1B	*141	471	*94	153	25	5	33	*120	*.325	1122	65	*21	.983
1970–Philadelphia ......Nat.	1B	8	12	0	2	0	0	0	0	.167	20	3	0	1.000
1971–Eugene .............P.C.	1B	142	548	104	171	30	5	36	114	.312	1071	76	•19	.984
1971–Philadelphia ......Nat.	1B	28	100	13	30	8	0	3	15	.300	247	34	1	.996
1972–Philadelphia ......Nat.	OF-1B	150	563	66	158	33	5	18	68	.281	257	9	12	.957
1973–Philadelphia ......Nat.	OF	161	610	76	174	26	4	29	97	.285	262	7	2	*.993
1974–Philadelphia†....Nat.	OF	85	302	29	82	14	1	7	48	.272	146	10	3	.981
1975–Philadelphia ......Nat.	OF	161	596	85	179	35	3	34	*120	.300	248	10	9	.966
1976–Philadelphia ......Nat.	OF	149	533	74	162	28	1	21	95	.304	204	8	8	.964
1977–Philadelphia ......Nat.	OF	149	554	99	171	35	3	39	130	.309	205	11	8	.964
1978–Philadelphia ......Nat.	OF	155	540	85	143	32	2	35	101	.265	232	7	4	.984
1979–Philadelphia ......Nat.	OF	137	452	47	114	23	1	18	81	.252	156	3	9	.946
1980–Philadelphia‡ ....Nat.	OF	106	368	44	84	19	1	19	56	.228	137	2	1	.993
Major League Totals		1289	4630	618	1299	253	21	223	811	.281	2114	104	57	.975

Selected by Philadelphia Phillies' organization in 1st round (11th player selected) of free-agent draft, June 7, 1968.
†On disabled list, June 6 to August 26, 1974.
‡On supplemental disabled list, July 8 to August 24, 1980.

CHAMPIONSHIP SERIES RECORD

Tied Championship Series record for most consecutive games, one or more runs batted in, total Series (4).
Tied National League Championship Series record for most long hits, total Series (11).

Year Club	League	Pos.	G.	AB.	R.	H.	2B.	3B.	HR.	RBI.	B.A.	PO.	A.	E.	F.A.
1976–Philadelphia ......Nat.	OF	3	11	2	3	2	0	1	3	.273	6	0	0	1.000
1977–Philadelphia ......Nat.	OF	4	14	2	4	1	0	1	2	.286	4	1	0	1.000
1978–Philadelphia ......Nat.	OF	4	16	3	6	0	1	2	3	.375	5	1	0	1.000
1980–Philadelphia ......Nat.	OF-PH	5	17	3	5	2	0	1	4	.294	5	0	1	.833
Championship Series Totals.............		16	58	10	18	5	1	5	12	.310	20	2	1	.957

WORLD SERIES RECORD

Year Club	League	Pos.	G.	AB.	R.	H.	2B.	3B.	HR.	RBI.	B.A.	PO.	A.	E.	F.A.
1980–Philadelphia ......Nat.	DH-OF	3	9	0	0	0	0	0	0	.000	1	0	0	1.000

Year League	Pos.	AB.	R.	H.	2B.	3B.	HR.	RBI.	B.A.	PO.	A.	E.	F.A.
1975–National..............................	PH	1	0	0	0	0	0	0	.000	0	0	0	.000
1976–National..............................	OF	3	0	0	0	0	0	0	.000	0	0	0	.000
1977–National..............................	OF	2	1	1	0	0	1	2	.500	0	0	0	.000
1978–National..............................	OF	2	0	1	0	0	0	1	.500	0	0	0	.000
All-Star Game Totals........................		8	1	2	0	0	1	3	.250	0	0	0	.000

ALBERT WALTER LYLE
(Sparky)

Born July 22, 1944, at Reynoldsville, Pa.
Height, 6.01. Weight, 195.
Throws and bats lefthanded.

Established major league records for most innings pitched by relief pitcher, lifetime (1,253); most saves, lifetime (since 1969) (215); most games finished, lifetime (593); most games, relief pitcher, no games started, lifetime (806); most consecutive relief appearances, lifetime (806).

Tied major league record for most seasons leading league, saves (2); most consecutive games won by relief pitcher, three consecutive games (3), August 29 through 31, 1977.

Established American League records for most games, relief pitcher, lifetime (796); most games won, relief pitcher, lifetime (87).

Led American League in saves with 35 in 1972 and 23 in 1976.

Major League saves: 1967 (5), 1968 (11), 1969 (17), 1970 (20), 1971 (16), 1972 (35), 1973 (27), 1974 (15), 1975 (6), 1976 (23), 1977 (26), 1978 (9), 1979 (13), 1980 (10). Total–233.

Named THE SPORTING NEWS American League Fireman of the Year, 1972.

Won American League Cy Young Memorial Award, 1977.

Year Club	League	G.	IP.	W.	L.	Pct.	H.	R.	ER.	SO.	BB.	ERA.
1964–Bluefield............................Ap'lachian		7	33	3	2	.600	23	19	16	44	25	4.36
1964–Fox Cities†........................Midwest		6	35	3	1	.750	30	14	9	51	18	2.31
1965–Winston-Salem ....Carolina		37	87	5	5	.500	84	45	41	79	55	4.24
1966–Pittsfield ....Eastern		40	74	4	2	.667	62	35	30	72	43	3.65
1967–Toronto..............................Int'national		16	21	2	2	.500	13	5	4	17	14	1.71
1967–Boston ....American		27	43	1	2	.333	33	13	11	42	14	2.30
1968–Boston ....American		49	66	6	1	.857	67	25	20	52	14	2.73
1969–Boston ....American		71	103	8	3	.727	91	33	29	93	48	2.53
1970–Boston ....American		63	67	1	7	.125	62	37	29	51	34	3.90
1971–Boston‡..............................American		50	52	6	4	.600	41	16	16	37	23	2.77
1972–New York ....American		59	108	9	5	.643	84	25	23	75	29	1.92
1973–New York ....American		51	82	5	9	.357	66	30	23	63	18	2.52
1974–New York ....American		66	114	9	3	.750	93	30	21	89	43	1.66
1975–New York ....American		49	89	5	7	.417	94	34	31	65	36	3.13
1976–New York ....American		64	104	7	8	.467	82	33	26	61	42	2.25
1977–New York ....American		*72	137	13	5	.722	131	41	33	68	33	2.17
1978–New York§..........................American		59	112	9	3	.750	116	46	43	33	33	3.46
1979–Texas ....American		67	95	5	8	.385	78	37	33	48	28	3.13
1980–Texas x..............................American		49	81	3	2	.600	97	47	42	43	28	4.67
1980–Philadelphia ....National		10	14	0	0	.000	11	5	3	6	6	1.93
National League Totals		10	14	0	0	.000	11	5	3	6	6	1.93
American League Totals		796	1253	87	67	.565	1135	447	380	820	423	2.73
Major League Totals.................................		806	1267	87	67	.565	1146	452	383	826	429	2.72

Signed as free agent by Baltimore Orioles' organization, June 17, 1964.

†Drafted by Boston Red Sox from Rochester (Baltimore Orioles' organization), November 30, 1964.

‡Traded to New York Yankees for First Baseman-Outfielder Danny Cater, March 22, 1972; Yankees sent Infielder Mario Guerrero to Red Sox, June 30, 1972, to complete deal.

§Traded with Catcher Mike Heath, Pitchers Larry McCall and Dave Rajsich, Shortstop Domingo Ramos and cash to Texas Rangers for Outfielders Juan Beniquez and Greg Jemison, Pitchers Mike Griffin, Paul Mirabella and Dave Righetti, November 10, 1978.

xTraded to Philadelphia Phillies for a player to be named later, September 13, 1980; Pitcher Kevin Saucier traded to Texas completing deal, November 19, 1980.

CHAMPIONSHIP SERIES RECORD

Tied Championship Series record for most games won, Series (2), 1977.

Established American League Championship Series record for most games pitched, five-game Series (4), 1977.

Year Club	League	G.	IP.	W.	L.	Pct.	H.	R.	ER.	SO.	BB.	ERA.
1976–New York ....American		1	1	0	0	.000	0	0	0	0	1	0.00
1977–New York ....American		4	9⅓	2	0	1.000	7	1	1	3	0	0.96
1978–New York ....American		1	1⅓	0	0	.000	3	2	2	0	0	13.50
Championship Series Totals		6	11⅔	2	0	1.000	10	3	3	3	1	2.31

WORLD SERIES RECORD

Year Club	League	G.	IP.	W.	L.	Pct.	H.	R.	ER.	SO.	BB.	ERA.
1976–New York ....American		2	2⅔	0	0	.000	1	0	0	3	0	0.00
1977–New York ....American		2	4⅔	1	0	1.000	2	1	1	2	0	1.93
World Series Totals		4	7⅓	1	0	1.000	3	1	1	5	0	1.23

ALL-STAR GAME RECORD

Year League	IP.	W.	L.	Pct.	H.	R.	ER.	SO.	BB.	ERA.
1973—American	1	0	0	.000	1	0	0	1	0	0.00
1977—American	2	0	0	.000	3	2	2	1	0	9.00
All-Star Game Totals	3	0	0	.000	4	2	2	2	0	6.00

Member of American League All-Star Team in 1976; did not play.

EDWARD FRANCIS LYNCH
(Ed)

Born February 25, 1956, at Brooklyn, N.Y.
Height, 6.05. Weight, 210.
Throws and bats righthanded.
Attended University of South Carolina, Columbia, S.C.; received Bachelor of
Science degree in Finance and attending University of Miami, Coral Gables, Fla.,
for Master's degree in Business Administration.

Year Club	League	G.	IP.	W.	L.	Pct.	H.	R.	ER.	SO.	BB.	ERA.
1977—Sarasota Rangers	G. Coast	13	56	1	4	.200	61	31	23	36	15	3.70
1978—Asheville	W. Carol.	18	123	7	9	.438	122	55	45	79	33	3.29
1978—Tulsa	Texas	7	54	4	3	.571	61	25	16	44	14	2.67
1979—Tucson†	P. Coast	27	156	10	11	.476	184	96	84	65	37	4.85
1980—Tidewater	Int'national	24	163	13	6	.684	151	69	57	91	42	3.15
1980—New York	National	5	19	1	1	.500	24	12	11	9	5	5.21
Major League Totals		5	19	1	1	.500	24	12	11	9	5	5.21

Selected by Texas Rangers' organization in 22nd round of free-agent draft, June 7, 1977.
†Traded to New York Mets' organization, September 18, 1979, as one of the two players to be named later in the trade in which Rangers traded First Baseman Willie Montanez to New York Mets, August 12, 1979; First Baseman Mike Jorgensen sent by Rangers to Mets, October 23, 1979, to complete deal.

FREDRIC MICHAEL LYNN
(Fred)

Born February 3, 1952, at Chicago, Ill.
Height, 6.01. Weight, 190.
Throws and bats lefthanded.
Hobbies—Fishing and golfing.
Attended University of Southern California, Los Angeles, Calif.

Established American League record for most doubles, rookie season, 47, in 1975.
Tied American League record for most total bases, game, 16, June 18, 1975.
Led American League in slugging percentage with .566 in 1975 and with .637 in 1979.
Hit three home runs in one game, vs. Detroit Tigers, June 18, 1975.
Hit for cycle against Minnesota Twins, May 13, 1980.
Named Most Valuable Player in American League, 1975.
Named American League Rookie of the Year by Baseball Writers' Association of America, 1975.
Named American League Player of the Year and Rookie Player of the Year by THE SPORTING NEWS, 1975.
Named outfielder on THE SPORTING NEWS American League All-Star fielding team, 1975 and 1978 through 1980.
Named center fielder on THE SPORTING NEWS American League All-Star Team, 1975, 1978 and 1979.
Received reported $40,000 bonus to sign with Boston Red Sox, 1973.

Year Club	League	Pos.	G.	AB.	R.	H.	2B.	3B.	HR.	RBI.	B.A.	PO.	A.	E.	F.A.
1973—Bristol	East.	OF	53	162	26	42	9	4	6	36	.259	79	3	5	.943
1974—Pawtucket	Int.	OF	124	415	65	117	19	2	21	68	.282	247	12	7	.974
1974—Boston	Amer.	OF	15	43	5	18	2	2	2	10	.419	18	2	0	1.000
1975—Boston	Amer.	OF	145	528	*103	175	*47	7	21	105	.331	404	11	7	.983
1976—Boston	Amer.	OF	132	507	76	159	32	8	10	65	.314	367	13	6	.984
1977—Boston†	Amer.	OF	129	497	81	129	29	5	18	76	.260	333	7	2	.994
1978—Boston	Amer.	OF	150	541	75	161	33	3	22	82	.298	408	11	7	.984
1979—Boston	Amer.	OF	147	531	116	177	42	1	39	122	*.333	381	10	5	.987
1980—Boston‡	Amer.	OF	110	415	67	125	32	3	12	61	.301	302	11	2	.994
Major League Totals			828	3062	523	944	217	29	124	521	.308	2213	65	29	.987

Selected by New York Yankees' organization in 3rd round of free-agent draft, June 4, 1970.
Selected by Boston Red Sox' organization in 2nd round of free-agent draft, June 5, 1973.
†On disabled list, March 24 to May 6, 1977.
‡Traded with Pitcher Steve Renko to California Angels for Pitchers Frank Tanana and Jim Dorsey and Outfielder Joe Rudi, January 23, 1981.

CHAMPIONSHIP SERIES RECORD

Year Club	League	Pos.	G.	AB.	R.	H.	2B.	3B.	HR.	RBI.	B.A.	PO.	A.	E.	F.A.
1975—Boston	Amer.	OF	3	11	1	4	1	0	0	3	.364	12	1	1	.929

WORLD SERIES RECORD

Tied World Series record for highest fielding average by outfielder, seven-game Series (1.000 with 24 chances), 1975.

Year Club	League	Pos.	G.	AB.	R.	H.	2B.	3B.	HR.	RBI.	B.A.	PO.	A.	E.	F.A.
1975—Boston	Amer.	OF	7	25	3	7	1	0	1	5	.280	23	1	0	1.000

Year League	Pos.	AB.	R.	H.	2B.	3B.	HR.	RBI.	B.A.	PO.	A.	E.	F.A.
1975—American	PH-OF	2	0	0	0	0	0	0	.000	1	0	0	1.000
1976—American	OF	3	1	1	0	0	1	1	.333	0	0	0	1.000
1977—American	OF	1	1	0	0	0	0	0	.000	2	0	0	1.000
1978—American	OF	4	0	1	0	0	0	0	.250	3	0	0	1.000
1979—American	OF	1	1	1	0	0	1	2	1.000	0	0	0	.000
1980—American	OF	3	1	1	0	0	1	2	.333	2	0	0	1.000
All-Star Game Totals		14	4	4	0	0	3	5	.286	8	0	0	1.000

RICHARD EUGENE LYSANDER
(Rick)

Born February 21, 1953, at Huntington Park, Calif.
Height, 6.02. Weight, 190.
Throws and bats righthanded.
Attended Citrus Junior College, Azusa, Calif., and
California State University at Los Angeles.

Year Club	League	G.	IP.	W.	L.	Pct.	H.	R.	ER.	SO.	BB.	ERA.
1974—Lewiston	Northwest	11	58	5	3	.625	54	28	17	25	18	2.64
1975—Modesto	California	21	131	8	8	.500	152	92	70	82	38	4.81
1975—Birmingham	Southern	8	57	5	2	.714	58	24	21	25	20	3.32
1976—Tucson	P. Coast	17	28	2	2	.500	41	21	20	21	15	6.43
1976—Chattanooga	Southern	18	118	7	6	.538	108	47	46	31	34	3.20
1977—Chattanooga	Southern	14	84	4	5	.444	104	55	46	41	31	4.93
1977—San Jose	P. Coast	29	61	3	3	.500	68	38	29	38	26	4.28
1978—Vancouver	P. Coast	14	29	0	0	.000	42	26	26	12	12	8.07
1978—Jersey City	Eastern	17	127	9	6	.600	128	58	36	58	40	2.55
1979—Ogden	P. Coast	50	84	10	3	.769	94	54	41	60	46	4.39
1980—Ogden	P. Coast	35	81	4	5	.444	103	55	46	46	43	5.11
1980—Oakland	American	5	14	0	0	.000	24	13	12	5	4	7.71
Major League Totals		5	14	0	0	.000	24	13	12	5	4	7.71

Selected by Oakland A's organization in 19th round of free-agent draft, June 5, 1974.

KENNETH EDWARD MACHA

Name pronounced MOCK-uh.

(Ken)

Born September 29, 1950, at Monroeville, Pa.
Height, 6.02. Weight, 210.
Throws and bats righthanded.
Hobbies—Golf, bowling, fishing and music.
Attended University of Pittsburgh, Pittsburgh, Pa.; received
Bachelor of Science degree in Civil Engineering.
Cousin of Hal Newhouser, pitcher with Detroit Tigers and Cleveland Indians, 1939 through 1955.

Led Eastern League in passed balls with 32 in 1973.
Named Eastern League Player of the Year in 1974.

Year Club	League	Pos.	G.	AB.	R.	H.	2B.	3B.	HR.	RBI.	B.A.	PO.	A.	E.	F.A.
1972—Salem	Carol.	C-3B	62	197	20	50	7	2	8	33	.254	386	36	13	.970
1973—Sherbrooke	East.	C-1-O-3	106	322	40	86	15	0	12	52	.267	551	53	17	.973
1974—Charleston	Int.	C-3B	21	65	6	12	3	0	2	10	.185	100	13	4	.966
1974—Thetford Mines	East.	C-3-1-O	117	386	87	133	22	2	21	100	*.345	531	70	16	.974
1974—Pittsburgh	Nat.	C	5	5	1	3	1	0	0	1	.600	1	0	0	1.000
1975—Charleston	Int.	*1-3-O	138	478	63	128	21	1	14	63	.268	1051	*88	●22	.981
1976—Charleston	Int.	3-C-O-1	126	458	68	138	29	1	14	77	.301	232	116	26	.930
1977—Columbus	Int.	O-1-C-3	76	254	51	85	18	2	11	64	.335	187	25	9	.959
1977—Pittsburgh	Nat.	3-1-OF	35	95	2	26	4	0	0	11	.274	72	25	1	.990
1978—Columbus	Int.	3B-OF-C	65	233	34	61	10	1	6	34	.262	62	114	18	.907
1978—Pittsburgh	Nat.	3B	29	52	5	11	1	1	0	5	.212	11	21	1	.970
1979—Denver	A. A.	C-3-OF-1	31	102	12	27	1	0	1	10	.265	92	17	8	.932
1979—Montreal	Nat.	3-1-OF-C	25	36	8	10	3	1	0	4	.278	24	18	0	1.000
1980—Montreal‡	Nat.	3-1-O-C	49	107	10	31	5	1	1	8	.290	30	43	6	.924
Major League Totals			143	295	26	81	14	3	1	29	.275	138	107	8	.968

Selected by Pittsburgh Pirates' organization in 6th round of free-agent draft, June 6. 1972.
†Drafted by Montreal Expos, December 4, 1978.
‡Sold to Toronto Blue Jays, January 15, 1981.

MICHAEL WILLIAM MACHA

Name pronounced MAH-ha.

(Mike)

Born Feburary 17, 1954, at Victoria, Tex.
Height, 5.11. Weight, 180.
Throws and bats righthanded.
Attended Rice University, Houston, Tex.;
received Bachelor of Arts degree in Commerce.

Led International League outfielders in fielding average with .988 in 1978.

Year Club	League	Pos.	G.	AB.	R.	H.	2B.	3B.	HR.	RBI.	B.A.	PO.	A.	E.	F.A.
1976—Greenwood	W. Car.	3B-OF	92	303	34	75	7	0	9	52	.248	102	103	36	.851
1977—Savannah†	South.	3B	116	408	64	108	13	9	13	67	.265	*99	*211	*34	.901
1978—Richmond	Int.	OF-3B	137	491	80	128	21	7	17	69	.261	188	41	12	.950
1979—Richmond‡........	Int.	OF-3B-2B	73	254	36	74	17	5	5	25	.291	108	22	10	.929
1979—Atlanta§...........	Nat.	3B	6	13	2	2	0	0	0	1	.154	2	8	3	.769
1980—Toronto x.........	Amer.	3B-C	5	8	0	0	0	0	0	0	.000	2	5	2	.778
1980—Evansville	A.A.	OF-3B	88	278	42	70	8	1	11	41	.252	139	7	3	.980
National League Totals			6	13	2	2	0	0	0	1	.154	2	8	3	.769
American League Totals			5	8	0	0	0	0	0	0	.000	2	5	2	.778
Major League Totals......................			11	21	2	2	0	0	0	1	.095	4	13	5	.773

Selected by Cleveland Indians' organization in 5th round of free-agent draft, June 4, 1975.
Selected by Atlanta Braves' organization in secondary phase of free-agent draft, January 7, 1976.
†On disabled list, June 25 to July 8, 1977.
‡On disabled list, July 30 to August 13, 1979.
§Drafted by Toronto Blue Jays, December 3, 1979.
xSold to Detroit Tigers' organization, May 28, 1980.

HENRY ALLAN MACK

Born November 10, 1958, at Winchester, Ky.
Height, 6.02. Weight, 185.
Throws and bats righthanded.

Lost 3-2 no-hit game vs. Lynchburg, July 1, 1978.
Tied for New York-Pennsylvania League lead in games started with 13 and in wild pitches with 10 in 1976.
Led Western Carolinas League in wild pitches with 17 in 1977.
Named Carolina League Pitcher of the Year, 1978.

Year Club	League	G.	IP.	W.	L.	Pct.	H.	R.	ER.	SO.	BB.	ERA.
1976—Auburn	NYP	13	54	2	*9	.182	54	49	44	44	*67	7.33
1977—Spartanburg.......................	W. Carol.	24	141	5	10	.333	142	93	82	87	*112	5.23
1978—Peninsula†........................	Carolina	23	158	●15	4	.789	102	62	49	158	118	2.79
1979—Midland	Texas	27	144	10	4	.714	156	99	79	102	*116	4.94
1980—Midland	Texas	26	142	5	11	.313	176	99	99	115	*142	6.27

Selected by Philadelphia Phillies' organization in 13th round of free-agent draft, June 8, 1976.
†Traded with Outfielder Jerry Martin, Catcher Barry Foote, Second Baseman Ted Sizemore and Pitcher Derek Botelho to Chicago Cubs for Second Baseman Manny Trillo, Outfielder Greg Gross and Catcher Dave Rader, February 23, 1979.

PETER MACKANIN JR.

Name pronounced Mac-can-un.

(Pete)

Born August 1, 1951, at Chicago, Ill.
Height, 6.02. Weight, 196.
Throws and bats righthanded.
Hobby—Sports in general.
Attended University of Illinois, Chicago Circle Campus, Ill.

Year Club	League	Pos.	G.	AB.	R.	H.	2B.	3B.	HR.	RBI.	B.A.	PO.	A.	E.	F.A.
1969—Wytheville.........	Appal.	3B	45	102	22	39	7	1	6	31	.241	●52	84	11	.925
1970—Burlington.........	Carol.	SS-3B	105	361	39	73	9	1	4	42	.202	122	258	35	.916
1971—Burlington.........	Carol.	2B-SS	125	451	49	117	17	7	5	46	.259	304	328	26	.960
1972—Pittsfield..........	East.	2-S-3	87	336	47	83	18	1	1	22	.247	146	214	21	.945
1972—Denver.............	A. A.	2-S-3	29	90	7	19	3	0	0	5	.211	47	64	10	.917
1973—Spokane	P. C.	SS	100	384	57	116	25	5	7	55	.302	174	293	31	.938
1973—Texas..............	Amer.	SS-3B	44	90	3	9	2	0	0	2	.100	39	88	7	.948
1974—Montreal	P. C.	SS	140	573	103	167	28	5	28	103	.291	234	401	*45	.934
1974—Texas†............	Amer.	SS	2	6	0	1	0	1	0	0	.167	3	8	0	1.000
1975—Montreal	Nat.	2-3-S	130	448	59	101	19	6	12	44	.225	300	411	26	.965
1976—Montreal	Nat.	2-3-S-O	114	380	36	85	15	2	8	33	.224	203	307	19	.964
1977—Montreal	Nat.	2-S-3-O	55	85	9	19	2	2	1	6	.224	34	44	4	.951
1978—Denver‡...........	A.A.	S-3-O-2	131	515	92	142	30	10	17	112	.276	181	319	23	.956
1978—Philadelphia......	Nat.	3B-1B	5	8	0	2	0	0	0	1	.250	6	2	0	1.000
1979—Philadelphia§x ..	Nat.	2B-3B-SS	13	9	2	1	0	0	1	2	.111	1	9	0	1.000
1980—Minnesota.........	Amer.	2-S-1-3	108	319	31	85	18	0	4	35	.266	168	285	18	.962
American League Totals			154	415	34	95	20	1	4	37	.229	210	381	25	.959
National League Totals			317	930	106	208	36	10	22	86	.224	544	773	49	.964
Major League Totals......................			471	1345	140	303	56	11	26	123	.225	754	1154	74	.963

Selected by Washington Senators' organization in 4th round of free-agent draft, June 5, 1969.
†Traded with Pitcher Don Stanhouse to Montreal Expos for Outfielder Willie Davis, December 5, 1974.
‡Sold on waivers to Philadelphia Phillies, September 5, 1978.
§On supplemental disabled list, April 25 to May 25, 1979; on disabled list, May 25 through remainder of 1979 season.
xTraded to Minnesota Twins for Pitcher Paul Thormodsgard, December 7, 1979.

STEVEN JOSEPH MACKO
(Steve)

Born September 6, 1954, at Burlington, Ia.
Height, 5.10. Weight, 160.
Throws right and bats lefthanded.
Attended Panola Junior College, Carthage, Tex., and Baylor University, Waco, Tex.;
received Bachelor of Science degree in Physical Education.
Son of Joe Macko, minor league first baseman, 1948-64; manager, 1961-64,
general manager, 1967-71 and currently equipment manager for Texas Rangers;
nephew of Don Voigt, minor league first baseman, 1949-64.

Led Texas League shortstops in double plays with 98 in 1978.

Year Club	League	Pos.	G.	AB.	R.	H.	2B.	3B.	HR.	RBI.	B.A.	PO.	A.	E.	F.A.
1977—Brad. Cubs	Gulf C.	SS	5	13	6	4	2	0	0	2	.308	9	20	0	1.000
1977—Pomp. Beach†	Fla. St.	SS	40	144	23	43	6	4	1	14	.299	69	95	16	.911
1978—Midland	Texas	SS	133	*550	90	*166	30	6	5	76	.302	*244	*410	40	.942
1979—Wichita	A. A.	SS-2B	119	426	56	104	27	1	6	44	.244	247	352	17	.972
1979—Chicago	Nat.	2B-3B	19	40	2	9	1	0	0	3	.225	21	33	0	1.000
1980—Wichita	A.A.	SS-2B	89	317	46	80	14	4	9	42	.252	167	313	19	.962
1980—Chicago‡	Nat.	S-3-2	6	20	2	6	2	0	0	2	.300	11	14	0	1.000
Major League Totals			25	60	4	15	3	0	0	5	.250	32	47	0	1.000

Selected by San Francisco Giants' organization in 28th round of free-agent draft, June 8, 1976.
Selected by Chicago Cubs' organization in 5th round of free-agent draft, June 7, 1977.
†On disabled list, August 7 to August 21, 1977.
‡On supplemental disabled list, August 6, 1980; transferred to disabled list, August 18 to September 13, 1980.

KEITH MacWHORTER

Born December 30, 1955, at Worcester, Mass.
Height, 6.04. Weight, 185.
Throws and bats righthanded.
Attended Bryant College, Smithfield, R. I.; received Bachelor of
Science degree in Law Enforcement.

Year Club	League	G.	IP.	W.	L.	Pct.	H.	R.	ER.	SO.	BB.	ERA.
1976—Danville†	Midwest	13	79	1	7	.125	78	56	47	51	52	5.35
1978—Winter Haven‡	Florida St.	33	115	11	6	.647	87	39	28	109	44	2.19
1979—Bristol	Eastern	37	166	11	10	.524	165	76	57	101	72	3.09
1980—Pawtucket	Int'national	19	123	7	6	.538	107	43	35	53	41	2.56
1980—Boston	American	14	42	0	3	.000	46	27	26	21	18	5.57
Major League Totals		14	42	0	3	.000	46	27	26	21	18	5.57

Selected by Los Angeles Dodgers' organization in 15th round of free-agent draft, June 8, 1976.
†Released April 5, 1977; signed by Boston Red Sox' organization, September 12, 1977.
‡Drafted by San Jose (Seattle Mariners' organization), December 5, 1978; returned to Boston Red Sox'
organization, April 2, 1979.

ELLIOTT MADDOX

Born December 21, 1948, at East Orange, N. J.
Height, 5.11. Weight, 185.
Throws and bats righthanded.
Hobbies—Basketball, photography and collecting stereo tapes.
Attended University of Michigan, Ann Arbor, Mich.; received Bachelor of Science degree.

Tied for Carolina League lead in double plays by third basemen with 18 in 1969.
Received reported $40,000 bonus to sign with Detroit Tigers, 1968.

Year Club	League	Pos.	G.	AB.	R.	H.	2B.	3B.	HR.	RBI.	B.A.	PO.	A.	E.	F.A.
1968—Lakeland	Fla. St.	OF	40	118	13	37	3	3	1	19	.314	60	6	1	.985
1968—Rocky Mount	Carol.	OF-3	34	111	21	33	4	4	0	20	.297	60	14	3	.961
1969—Rocky Mount	Carol.	*3-O-2	118	412	60	124	19	8	4	56	.301	138	*185	12	.964
1970—Detroit†	Amer.	3-O-S-2	109	258	30	64	13	4	3	24	.248	104	100	14	.936
1971—Washington	Amer.	OF-3B	128	258	38	56	8	2	1	18	.217	201	21	3	.987
1972—Texas	Amer.	OF	98	294	40	74	7	2	0	10	.252	199	7	2	.990
1973—Texas‡	Amer.	OF-3B	100	172	24	41	1	0	1	17	.238	148	14	3	.982
1974—New York	Amer.	O-2-3	137	466	75	141	26	2	3	45	.303	336	19	5	.986
1975—New York§	Amer.	OF-2B	55	218	36	67	10	3	1	23	.307	158	5	0	1.000
1976—New York x	Amer.	OF	18	46	4	10	2	0	0	3	.217	21	2	0	1.000
1977—Baltimore yz	Amer.	OF-3B	49	107	14	28	7	0	2	9	.262	99	0	1	.990
1978—New York a	Nat.	OF-3-1	119	389	43	100	18	2	2	39	.257	196	80	9	.968
1979—New York b	Nat.	OF-3B	86	224	21	60	13	0	1	12	.268	131	22	3	.981
1980—New York c	Nat.	3-OF-1B	130	411	35	101	16	1	4	34	.246	111	211	14	.958
American League Totals			694	1819	261	481	74	13	11	149	.264	1266	168	28	.981
National League Totals			335	1024	99	261	47	3	7	85	.255	438	313	26	.967
Major League Totals			1029	2843	360	742	121	16	18	234	.261	1704	481	54	.976

Selected by Houston Astros' organization in 7th round of free-agent draft, June, 1966.
Selected by Detroit Tigers' organization in secondary phase of free-agent draft, June 7, 1968.
†Traded with Pitcher Denny McLain, Third Baseman Don Wert and Pitcher Norm McRae to Washington
Senators for Shortstop Ed Brinkman, Third Baseman Aurelio Rodriguez and Pitchers Joe Coleman and Jim
Hannan, October 9, 1970.

‡On supplemental disabled list, May 16 to May 31, 1973. Sold to New York Yankees for an estimated $35,000, March 23, 1974.

§On disabled list, June 17 to October 3, 1975.

xOn disabled list, April 1 to June 22 and July 1 to September 2, 1976; traded with Outfielder Rick Bladt (assigned from Syracuse to Rochester) to Baltimore Orioles for Outfielder Paul Blair, January 20, 1977.

yOn disabled list, March 23 through July 14, 1977.

zGranted free agency, October 24, 1977; signed by New York Mets, November 30, 1977.

aOn disabled list, March 22 to April 25, 1978.

bOn supplemental disabled list, July 27 to August 18, 1979.

cReleased, February 5, 1981; invited to New York Yankees' camp, 1981.

CHAMPIONSHIP SERIES RECORD

Year Club	League	Pos.	G.	AB.	R.	H.	2B.	3B.	HR.	RBI.	B.A.	PO.	A.	E.	F.A.
1976—New York..........Amer.		OF	3	9	0	2	1	0	0	1	.222	9	0	0	1.000

WORLD SERIES RECORD

Year Club	League	Pos.	G.	AB.	R.	H.	2B.	3B.	HR.	RBI.	B.A.	PO.	A.	E.	F.A.
1976—New York..........Amer.		OF-DH	2	5	0	1	0	1	0	0	.200	0	0	0	.000

GARRY LEE MADDOX

Born September 1, 1949, at Cincinnati, O.
Height, 6.03. Weight, 185.
Throws and bats righthanded.
Hobbies—Writing and all sports.
Attended Harbor College, Wilmington, Calif.

Major League stolen bases: 1972 (13), 1973 (24), 1974 (21), 1975 (25), 1976 (29), 1977 (22), 1978 (33), 1979 (26), 1980 (25). Total—218.

Led National League outfielders in total chances with 456 in 1976.

Led Pioneer League batters in strikeouts with 68 and outfielders in double plays with 2 in 1968.

Named outfielder on THE SPORTING NEWS National League All-Star fielding team, 1975 through 1980.

Year Club	League	Pos.	G.	AB.	R.	H.	2B.	3B.	HR.	RBI.	B.A.	PO.	A.	E.	F.A.
1968—Salt Lake City ...Pion.		OF	58	206	34	52	11	2	5	29	.252	98	6	•10	.912
1968—Fresno ....Calif.		OF	5	19	2	6	0	0	0	5	.316	7	0	0	1.000
1969-70—.............................						(In Military Service)									
1971—Fresno ....Calif.		OF	120	475	105	142	25	5	30	106	.299	215	13	0	.962
1972—Phoenix ....P. C.		OF	11	48	16	21	3	2	9	22	.438	22	1	2	.920
1972—San Francisco ...Nat.		OF	125	458	62	122	26	7	12	58	.266	279	7	6	.979
1973—San Francisco ...Nat.		OF	144	587	81	187	30	10	11	76	.319	370	4	•12	.969
1974—San Francisco ...Nat.		OF	135	538	74	153	31	3	8	50	.284	345	3	5	.986
1975—S.F.†-Phil.‡ ....Nat.		OF	116	426	54	116	26	8	5	50	.272	325	13	5	.985
1976—Philadelphia......Nat.		OF	146	531	75	175	37	6	6	68	.330	•441	10	5	.989
1977—Philadelphia§ ...Nat.		OF	139	571	85	167	27	10	14	74	.292	383	7	9	.977
1978—Philadelphia......Nat.		OF	155	598	62	172	34	3	11	68	.288	•444	7	8	.983
1979—Philadelphia......Nat.		OF	148	548	70	154	28	6	13	61	.281	•433	13	2	.996
1980—Philadelphia......Nat.		OF	143	549	59	142	31	3	11	73	.259	405	7	10	.976
Major League Totals			1251	4806	622	1388	270	56	91	578	.289	3425	71	62	.983

Selected by San Francisco Giants' organization in 2nd round of free-agent draft, January 27, 1968.

†Traded to Philadelphia Phillies for First Baseman Willie Montanez, May 4, 1975.

‡On disabled list, May 25 to June 30, 1975.

§On supplemental disabled list, August 13 to August 28, 1977.

CHAMPIONSHIP SERIES RECORD

Tied Championship Series records for most consecutive games, one or more runs batted in, total Series (4); most at bats, four-game Series (19), 1978.

Tied National League Championship Series record for most stolen bases, five-game Series (2), 1980.

Year Club	League	Pos.	G.	AB.	R.	H.	2B.	3B.	HR.	RBI.	B.A.	PO.	A.	E.	F.A.
1976—Philadelphia......Nat.		OF	3	13	2	3	1	0	0	1	.231	9	0	0	1.000
1977—Philadelphia......Nat.		OF	2	7	1	3	0	0	0	2	.429	6	0	0	1.000
1978—Philadelphia......Nat.		OF	4	19	1	5	0	0	0	2	.263	16	0	1	.941
1980—Philadelphia......Nat.		OF	5	20	2	6	2	0	0	3	.300	23	0	0	1.000
Championship Series Totals.............			14	59	6	17	3	0	0	8	.288	54	0	1	.982

WORLD SERIES RECORD

Year Club	League	Pos.	G.	AB.	R.	H.	2B.	3B.	HR.	RBI.	B.A.	PO.	A.	E.	F.A.
1980—Philadelphia......Nat.		OF	6	22	1	5	2	0	0	1	.227	11	1	0	1.000

BILL MADLOCK, JR.

Born January 12, 1951, at Memphis, Tenn.
Height, 5.11. Weight, 185.
Throws and bats righthanded.
Attended Southeastern Community College, Keokuk, Ia.

Major League stolen bases: 1973 (3), 1974 (11), 1975 (9), 1976 (15), 1977 (13), 1978 (16), 1979 (32), 1980 (16). Total—115.

Led Pacific Coast League in total bases with 268 in 1973.

Made six hits in one game, July 26, 1975 (10 innings).

Named third baseman on THE SPORTING NEWS National League All-Star Team, 1975.

Year	Club	League	Pos.	G.	AB.	R.	H.	2B.	3B.	HR.	RBI.	B.A.	PO.	A.	E.	F.A.
1970—Geneva	..............NYP		*SS-3B	66	234	44	63	5	1	6	29	.269	*123	132	25	.911
1971—Pittsfield	..........East.		*3-2-S-O	112	376	62	88	14	2	10	37	.234	100	214	*34	.902
1972—Pittsfield	..........East.		2B-3B	42	131	29	43	13	3	4	26	.328	81	88	7	.960
1972—Denver	..............A.A.		3B-2B	26	61	7	13	3	0	1	9	.213	10	30	2	.952
1973—Spokane	............P.C.		2-3-O	123	491	*119	166	22	7	22	90	.338	172	245	25	.943
1973—Texas†	............Amer.		3B	21	77	16	27	5	3	1	5	.351	13	32	4	.918
1974—Chicago‡	..........Nat.		3B	128	453	65	142	21	5	9	54	.313	84	229	18	.946
1975—Chicago	............Nat.		3B	130	514	77	182	29	7	7	64	*.354	79	250	20	.943
1976—Chicago§	..........Nat.		3B	142	514	68	174	36	1	15	84	*.339	107	234	14	.961
1977—San Francisco	...Nat.		3B-2B	140	533	70	161	28	1	12	46	.302	101	234	18	.949
1978—San Francisco	...Nat.		2B-1B	122	447	76	138	26	3	15	44	.309	234	300	14	.974
1979—S.F.x-Pitts.	.......Nat.		3B-2B-1B	154	560	85	167	26	5	14	85	.298	209	297	14	.973
1980—Pittsburgh y	...Nat.		3B-1B	137	494	62	137	22	4	10	53	.277	159	217	7	.982
American League Totals	....			21	77	16	27	5	3	1	5	.351	13	32	4	.918
National League Totals	....			953	3515	503	1101	188	26	82	430	.313	973	1761	105	.963
Major League Totals	....			974	3592	519	1128	193	29	83	435	.314	986	1793	109	.962

Selected by St. Louis Cardinals' organization in 14th round of free-agent draft, June 5, 1969.

Selected by Washington Senators' organization in secondary phase of free-agent draft, January 17, 1970.

†Traded with Infielder-Outfielder Vic Harris to Chicago Cubs for Pitcher Ferguson Jenkins, October 25, 1973.

‡On supplemental disabled list, May 4 to June 4, 1974.

§Traded with Infielder Rob Sperring to San Francisco Giants for Outfielder Bobby Murcer, Infielder Steve Ontiveros and Pitcher Andrew Muhlstock, February 11, 1977.

xTraded with Third Baseman Lenny Randle and Pitcher Dave Roberts to Pittsburgh Pirates for Pitchers Ed Whitson, Fred Breining and Al Holland, June 28, 1979.

yOn suspended list, June 5 to June 20, 1980.

ALL-STAR GAME RECORD

Year	League	Pos.	AB.	R.	H.	2B.	3B.	HR.	RBI.	B.A.	PO.	A.	E.	F.A.
1975—National	....	3B	2	1	1	0	0	0	2	.500	0	0	0	.000

CHAMPIONSHIP SERIES RECORD

Year	Club	League	Pos.	G.	AB.	R.	H.	2B.	3B.	HR.	RBI.	B.A.	PO.	A.	E.	F.A.
1979—Pittsburgh	........Nat.		3B	3	12	1	3	0	0	1	2	.250	1	7	0	1.000

WORLD SERIES RECORD

Tied World Series records for most hits, game (4), October 14, 1979; most singles, game (4), October 14, 1979; most double plays by third baseman, seven-game Series (4), 1979; fewest chances offered by third baseman, game (0), October 12, 1979.

Year	Club	League	Pos.	G.	AB.	R.	H.	2B.	3B.	HR.	RBI.	B.A.	PO.	A.	E.	F.A.
1979—Pittsburgh	........Nat.		3B	7	24	2	9	1	0	0	3	.375	3	10	1	.929

MICHAEL JAMES MAHLER

Name pronounced May-ler

(Mickey)

Born July 30, 1952, at Montgomery, Ala.
Height, 6.03. Weight, 190.
Throws left and bats right and lefthanded.
Hobby—Golf.
Attended Trinity University, San Antonio, Tex.
Brother of Richard Mahler, pitcher in Atlanta Braves' organization.

Pitched seven-inning 6-0 no-hit victory against Birmingham, July 25, 1974.
Pitched 7-0 no-hit victory against Toledo, July 1, 1977.
Led International League in games started with 31 in 1977
Led Pacific Coast League in complete games with 14 in 1980.

Year	Club	League	G.	IP.	W.	L.	Pct.	H.	R.	ER.	SO.	BB.	ERA.
1974—Savannah	...........................Southern		14	77	8	1	.889	38	13	11	62	35	1.29
1975—Richmond	..........................Int'national		27	166	6	14	.300	167	82	71	129	70	3.85
1976—Richmond	..........................Int'national		17	84	5	9	.357	95	63	54	52	40	5.79
1976—Savannah	...........................Southern		8	53	3	5	.375	44	21	19	38	20	3.23
1977—Richmond	..........................Int'national		31	*217	13	10	.565	202	101	85	145	80	3.53
1977—Atlanta	................................National		5	23	1	2	.333	31	19	16	14	9	6.26
1978—Atlanta	................................National		34	135	4	11	.267	130	82	70	92	66	4.67
1979—Atlanta†	...............................National		26	100	5	11	.313	123	72	65	71	47	5.85
1980—Portland	...............................P. Coast		25	173	14	8	.636	143	67	51	*140	85	2.65
1980—Pittsburgh	..........................National		2	1	0	0	.000	4	7	7	1	3	63.00
Major League Totals	....		67	259	10	24	.294	288	180	158	178	125	5.49

Selected by Atlanta Braves' organization in 10th round of free-agent draft, June 5, 1974.

†Released, March 29, 1980; signed by Pittsburgh Pirates' organization, April 10, 1980.

DID YOU KNOW—

That there were 1,839 stolen bases in the National League in 1980, more than either league totaled in one season during this century?

RICHARD KEITH MAHLER
(Rick)

Born August 5, 1953, at Austin, Tex.
Height, 6.01. Weight, 190.
Throws and bats righthanded.
Brother of Mickey Mahler, pitcher in Atlanta Braves' organization.

Year Club	League	G.	IP.	W.	L.	Pct.	H.	R.	ER.	SO.	BB.	ERA.
1975—Kingsport	Ap'lachian	26	64	2	2	.500	52	23	21	58	26	2.95
1976—Greenwood	W. Carol.	31	105	6	6	.500	96	49	34	68	49	2.91
1977—Savannah	Southern	17	86	6	2	.750	71	31	22	53	38	2.30
1977—Richmond	Int'national	14	40	0	2	.000	45	29	27	25	23	6.08
1978—Richmond	Int'national	32	126	9	5	.643	130	65	55	66	53	3.93
1979—Richmond	Int'national	24	54	4	6	.400	46	26	20	40	18	3.33
1979—Atlanta	National	15	22	0	0	.000	28	16	15	12	11	6.14
1980—Richmond	Int'national	29	188	12	6	.667	172	68	54	101	80	2.59
1980—Atlanta	National	2	4	0	0	.000	2	1	1	1	0	2.25
Major League Totals		17	26	0	0	.000	30	17	16	13	11	5.54

Signed as free agent by Atlanta Braves' organization, June 16, 1975.

CANDIDO MALDONADO (GUADARRAMA)
(Candy)

Born September 5, 1960, at Humacao, Puerto Rico.
Height, 6.00. Weight, 185.
Throws and bats righthanded.

Led California League in total bases with 247 in 1980.
Tied for Pioneer League lead in sacrifice flies with 6 in 1978.
Shared California League Most Valuable Player Award, 1980.

Year Club	League	Pos.	G.	AB.	R.	H.	2B.	3B.	HR.	RBI.	B.A.	PO.	A.	E.	F.A.
1978—Lethbridge	Pion.	OF	57	210	45	61	15	5	12	48	.290	112	6	8	.937
1979—Clinton	Midw.	OF	50	158	25	37	13	1	2	26	.234	81	5	2	.977
1979—Lethbridge	Pion.	OF	59	234	42	70	*20	3	5	33	.299	81	5	4	.956
1980—Lodi†	Calif.	OF	121	456	75	139	27	3	25	*102	.305	211	13	11	.953

Signed as free agent by Los Angeles Dodgers' organization, June 6, 1978.
†On disabled list, August 16 to September 16, 1980.

JAMES MICHAEL MALER
Name pronounced Male-are

(Jim)

Born August 16, 1958, at New York, N.Y.
Height, 6.04. Weight, 230.
Throws and bats righthanded.
Attended University of Miami, Coral Gables, Fla., and
Miami-Dade Community College South, Miami, Fla.

Led California League first basemen in double plays with 111 in 1979.
Led Pacific Coast League first basemen in double plays with 117 in 1980.
Received reported $50,000 bonus to sign with Seattle Mariners, 1978.

Year Club	League	Pos.	G.	AB.	R.	H.	2B.	3B.	HR.	RBI.	B.A.	PO.	A.	E.	F.A.
1978—Stockton†	Calif.	1B	32	121	20	37	6	3	3	26	.306	294	18	5	.984
1979—San Jose	Calif.	1B	139	523	89	162	30	5	24	100	.310	*1260	75	17	.987
1980—Spokane	P.C.	1B	130	455	60	122	26	3	9	59	.268	1056	122	*16	.985

Selected by Seattle Mariners' organization in 1st round (5th player selected) of free-agent draft, January 10, 1978.
†On disabled list, May 21 to September 6, 1978.

PHILIP ANTHONY MANKOWSKI
(Phil)

Born January 9, 1953, at Buffalo, N.Y.
Height, 6.00. Weight, 180.
Throws right and bats lefthanded.
Hobbies—Music and tennis.
Brother of Paul Mankowski, infielder in Minnesota Twins'
organization, 1966 through 1969.
Son of Ben Mankowski, first baseman in Brooklyn Dodgers' organization, 1940.

Year Club	League	Pos.	G.	AB.	R.	H.	2B.	3B.	HR.	RBI.	B.A.	PO.	A.	E.	F.A.
1971—Bristol	Appal.	3B	14	53	5	20	3	2	0	8	.377	17	26	4	.915
1971—Batavia	NYP	3B-1B	52	195	20	51	9	0	3	27	.262	38	103	14	.910
1972—Lakeland	Fla. St.	3B	110	403	38	110	8	2	2	34	.273	71	210	16	.946
1973—Clinton	Midw.	3B	121	454	43	105	23	4	2	36	.231	77	233	32	.906
1974—Lakeland†	Fla. St.	3B	64	234	30	60	10	3	5	38	.256	45	125	9	.950
1975—Montgomery	South.	3B	124	407	44	115	18	2	9	49	.283	81	257	13	.963
1976—Evansville	A.A.	3B	122	413	50	119	21	2	5	49	.288	75	217	25	.921
1976—Detroit	Amer.	3B	24	85	9	23	2	1	1	4	.271	20	47	2	.971
1977—Detroit	Amer.	3B-2B	94	286	21	79	7	3	3	27	.276	73	196	10	.964

Year	Club	League	Pos.	G.	AB.	R.	H.	2B.	3B.	HR.	RBI.	B.A.	PO.	A.	E.	F.A.
1978—Detroit		Amer.	3B	88	222	28	61	8	0	4	20	.275	42	129	5	.972
1979—Detroit‡§		Amer.	3B	42	99	11	22	4	0	0	8	.222	22	56	3	.963
1980—Tidewater y		Int.	3B	9	28	2	7	1	0	0	2	.250	3	3	0	1.000
1980—New York xz		Nat.	3B	8	12	1	2	1	0	0	1	.167	0	4	3	.571
American League Totals				248	692	69	185	21	4	8	59	.267	157	428	20	.967
National League Totals				8	12	1	2	1	0	0	1	.167	0	4	3	.571
Major League Totals				256	704	70	187	22	4	8	60	.266	157	432	23	.962

Selected by Detroit Tigers' organization in 8th round of free-agent draft, June 4, 1970.

†On disabled list, July 11 to September 15, 1974.

‡On supplemental disabled list, July 8 to September 1, 1979.

§Traded with Outfielder Jerry Morales to New York Mets for First Baseman-Third Baseman Richie Hebner, October 31, 1979.

xOn supplemental disabled list, April 29 to July 7, 1980.

yOn rehabilitation assignment, July 7 to July 25, 1980.

zOn emergency disabled list, July 25 to September 23, 1980.

RICHARD EUGENE MANNING
(Rick)

Born September 2, 1954, at Niagara Falls, N. Y.
Height, 6.01. Weight, 180.
Throws right and bats lefthanded.
Hobbies—Camping and music.

Tied major league record for most strikeouts, game (5), May 15, 1977.
Named outfielder on THE SPORTING NEWS American League All-Star fielding team, 1976.
Received reported $65,000 bonus to sign with Cleveland Indians, 1972.

Year	Club	League	Pos.	G.	AB.	R.	H.	2B.	3B.	HR.	RBI.	B.A.	PO.	A.	E.	F.A.
1972—Reno		Calif.	OF-SS	57	216	45	52	4	4	3	23	.241	71	45	19	.859
1973—Reno		Calif.	OF-SS	137	486	*101	136	40	*14	6	67	.280	184	8	7	.965
1974—Oklahoma City		A. A.	OF	122	402	58	108	16	5	5	39	.269	207	12	8	.965
1975—Oklahoma City		A. A.	OF	30	117	18	37	5	2	0	15	.316	62	4	0	1.000
1975—Cleveland		Amer.	OF	120	480	69	137	16	5	3	35	.285	331	12	9	.974
1976—Cleveland		Amer.	OF	138	552	73	161	24	7	6	43	.292	359	8	5	.987
1977—Cleveland†		Amer.	OF	68	252	33	57	7	3	5	18	.226	191	2	2	.990
1978—Cleveland		Amer.	OF	148	566	65	149	27	3	3	50	.263	377	7	2	.995
1979—Cleveland		Amer.	OF	144	560	67	145	12	2	3	51	.259	417	9	6	.986
1980—Cleveland		Amer.	OF	140	471	55	110	17	4	3	52	.234	379	7	4	.990
Major League Totals				758	2881	362	759	103	24	23	249	.263	2054	45	28	.987

Selected by Cleveland Indians' organization in 1st round (second player selected) of free-agent draft, June 6, 1972.

†On supplemental disabled list, June 21 to July 8, and disabled list, July 8 to September 1, 1977.

JERRY MANUEL

Born December 23, 1953, at Hahira, Ga.
Height, 6.00. Weight, 155.
Throws right and bats left and righthanded.

Led American Association second basemen in double plays with 81 in 1974 and with 108 in 1975.

Year	Club	League	Pos.	G.	AB.	R.	H.	2B.	3B.	HR.	RBI.	B.A.	PO.	A.	E.	F.A.
1972—Bristol		Appal.	SS	67	233	31	56	8	8	4	29	.240	*112	*176	15	*.950
1973—Lakeland		Fla. St.	SS	117	433	66	109	17	4	2	28	.252	167	349	29	.947
1973—Toledo		Int.	SS	27	72	8	20	0	0	0	2	.278	44	90	4	.971
1974—Evansville		A. A.	2B	127	384	44	81	5	5	1	24	.211	*315	356	17	.975
1975—Evansville		A. A.	2B	*137	501	63	115	10	4	4	43	.230	*348	*394	16	.979
1975—Detroit		Amer.	2B	6	18	0	1	0	0	0	0	.056	11	23	2	.944
1976—Detroit		Amer.	2B-SS	54	43	4	6	1	0	0	2	.140	40	64	8	.928
1976—Evansville		A. A.	2B	11	44	6	8	1	0	1	3	.182	25	29	1	.982
1977—Evansville		A. A.	2B-SS	110	375	52	102	19	7	1	38	.272	198	304	17	.967
1978—Evansville†		A. A.	2B-SS	114	430	65	113	18	5	7	50	.263	264	321	20	.967
1979—Evansville‡		A. A.	2B-SS	130	460	71	116	26	3	9	75	.252	265	434	22	.969
1980—Denver		A. A.	SS	128	491	105	136	23	2	3	61	.277	*233	*357	22	.964
1980—Montreal		Nat.	SS	7	6	0	0	0	0	0	0	.000	5	11	1	.941
National League Totals				7	6	0	0	0	0	0	0	.000	5	11	1	.941
American League Totals				60	61	4	7	1	0	0	2	.115	51	87	10	.932
Major League Totals				67	67	4	7	1	0	0	2	.104	56	98	11	.933

Selected by Detroit Tigers' organization in 1st round (20th player selected) of free-agent draft, June 6, 1972.

†On disabled list, August 18 to September 1, 1978.

‡Traded to Montreal Expos' organization for Catcher Duffy Dyer, March 14, 1980.

MICHAEL ALLEN MARSHALL
(Mike)

Born January 12, 1960, at Libertyville, Ill.
Height, 6.05. Weight, 215.
Throws and bats righthanded.

Named California League Most Valuable Player and Rookie of the Year, 1979.

Led California League in total bases with 301 in 1979.
Led Texas League first basemen in double plays with 120 in 1980.

Year—Club	League	Pos.	G.	AB.	R.	H.	2B.	3B.	HR.	RBI.	B.A.	PO.	A.	E.	F.A.
1978—Lethbridge	Pion.	1B-OF	65	256	48	83	15	2	12	70	.324	308	16	7	.979
1979—Lodi	Calif.	1B	137	525	101	*186	*37	3	24	116	*.354	1173	71	20	.984
1980—San Antonio	Texas	1B	134	470	95	151	21	6	16	82	.321	*1157	64	●16	.987

Selected by Los Angeles Dodgers' organization in 5th round of free-agent draft, June 6, 1978.

MICHAEL GRANT MARSHALL
(Mike)

Born January 15, 1943, at Adrian, Mich.
Height, 5.10. Weight, 180.
Throws and bats righthanded.
Hobby—Chess.
Attended Michigan State University, East Lansing, Mich.;
received Bachelor of Arts and Master's degrees in Education.

Established major league records for most seasons leading major leagues, games finished (4); most seasons leading league, saves (3); most games by any pitcher, season (106), 1974; most games, season, no games started (106), 1974; most innings pitched by relief pitcher, season (208), 1974; most consecutive seasons, leading major leagues, games finished (3), 1972 through 1974; most games finished, season (84), 1979; most consecutive games pitched, season (13), June 18 to July 3, 1974.

Tied major league records for most seasons leading league, games finished (5); most consecutive seasons leading league, games finished, (4), 1971 through 1974; most consecutive seasons, leading league, saves (2), 1973 and 1974; most consecutive games won by relief pitcher, three consecutive games (3), June 21 through 23, 1974.

Established American League records for most games by pitcher, season (90), 1979; most games relief pitcher, season (89), 1979.

Tied American League record for most games lost by relief pitcher, season (14), 1979.

Tied National League record for most seasons leading league, games finished (4).

Major League saves: 1969 (0), 1970 (3), 1971 (23), 1972 (18), 1973 (31), 1974 21), 1975 (13), 1976 (14), 1977 (11), 1978 (21), 1979 (32), 1980 (1). Total—188.

Led National League in saves with 31 in 1973 and 21 in 1974.

Led American League in saves with 32 in 1979.

Led International League pitchers in complete games with 16 in 1968.

Named National League Fireman of the Year by THE SPORTING NEWS, 1973 and 1974.

Named National League Pitcher of the Year by THE SPORTING NEWS, 1974.

Won National League Cy Young Memorial Award, 1974.

Year—Club	League	G.	IP.	W.	L.	Pct.	H.	R.	ER.	SO.	BB.	ERA.
1965—Chattanooga	Southern	8	26	2	4	.333	25	15	9	21	13	3.12
1965—Eugene†	Northw.	36	59	6	5	.545	53	33	23	63	30	3.51
1966—Montgomery	Southern	51	108	11	7	.611	84	37	28	81	44	2.33
1967—Toledo	Int'national	10	15	2	0	1.000	10	1	1	16	5	0.60
1967—Detroit	American	37	59	1	3	.250	51	15	13	41	20	1.98
1968—Toledo‡	Int'national	31	*211	15	9	.625	191	85	69	190	52	2.94
1969—Toledo§	Int'national	11	87	6	4	.600	79	37	30	60	27	3.10
1969—Seattle x	American	20	88	3	10	.231	99	54	50	47	35	5.11
1970—Oklahoma City	Am. Assoc.	16	45	4	3	.571	32	11	8	42	16	1.60
1970—Winnipeg	Int'national	9	41	2	1	.667	30	13	10	23	19	2.20
1970—Houston y-Montreal	National	28	70	3	8	.273	64	39	30	43	33	3.86
1971—Montreal	National	66	111	5	8	.385	100	56	53	85	50	4.30
1972—Montreal	National	●65	116	14	8	.636	82	26	23	95	47	1.78
1973—Montreal z	National	*92	179	14	11	.560	163	52	53	124	75	2.66
1974—Los Angeles	National	*106	208	15	12	.556	191	66	56	143	56	2.42
1975—Los Angeles a	National	57	109	9	14	.391	98	46	40	64	39	3.30
1976—L. A. b-Atlanta c	National	54	99	6	4	.600	99	48	44	56	39	4.00
1977—Atlanta d	National	4	6	1	0	1.000	12	6	6	6	2	9.00
1977—Texas ef	American	12	36	2	2	.500	42	19	16	18	13	4.00
1978—Minnesota g	American	54	99	10	12	.455	80	31	27	56	37	2.45
1979—Minnesota	American	*90	143	10	15	.400	132	47	42	81	48	2.64
1980—Minnesota h	American	18	32	1	3	.250	42	23	22	3	12	6.19
American League Totals		231	457	27	45	.375	446	189	170	256	165	3.35
National League Totals		472	898	67	65	.508	809	349	305	616	341	3.06
Major League Totals		703	1355	94	110	.461	1255	538	475	872	506	3.15

Signed as free agent by Philadelphia Phillies' organization, September 13, 1960.
†Sold by Philadelphia Phillies' organization to Detroit Tigers' organization, April 11, 1966.
‡Recalled by Detroit; selected by Seattle Pilots from Detroit in expansion draft, October 15, 1968.
§Appeared in one game as an outfielder.
xSold to Houston Astros' organization, November 21, 1969.
yTraded to Montreal Expos for Outfielder Don Bosch, June 23, 1970.
zTraded to Los Angeles Dodgers for Outfielder Willie Davis, December 5, 1973.
aOn disabled list, May 10 to June 6, 1975.
bTraded in waiver deal to Atlanta Braves for Pitcher Elias Sosa and Infielder Lee Lacy, June 23, 1976.
cOn disabled list, August 31 to October 4, 1976.
dTraded to Texas Rangers for cash and a player to be named later, April 30, 1977.
eOn disqualified list, May 4 to May 12; on disabled list, June 28 to October 5, 1977.
fGranted free agency, November 9, 1977; signed by Minnesota Twins, May 15, 1978.
gGranted free agency, November 2, 1978; re-signed by Twins, January 6, 1979.
hReleased, June 6, 1980.

RECORD AS SHORTSTOP

Year	Club	League	Pos.	G.	AB.	R.	H.	2B.	3B.	HR.	RBI.	B.A.	PO.	A.	E.	F.A.
1961—Dotham	....	Ala.-Fl.	SS	118	425	82	112	15	2	7	51	.264	*196	281	*53	.900
1962—Bakersfield	....	Calif.	SS	134	521	85	147	15	3	5	63	.282	169	*420	*68	.896
1963—Magic Valley	.....	Pion.	SS	107	385	84	117	17	5	14	76	.304	152	259	45	.901
1964—Chattanooga	......	South.	SS	133	495	64	136	19	8	5	62	.275	213	356	*41	.933

CHAMPIONSHIP SERIES RECORD

Year	Club	League	G.	IP.	W.	L.	Pct.	H.	R.	ER.	SO.	BB.	ERA.
1974—Los Angeles	....	National	2	3	0	0	.000	0	0	0	1	0	0.00

WORLD SERIES RECORD

Established World Series records for most games appeared in and most games finished, relief pitcher, 5-game series, 5 in 1974.

Year	Club	League	G.	IP.	W.	L.	Pct.	H.	R.	ER.	SO.	BB.	ERA.
1974—Los Angeles	....	National	5	9	0	1	.000	6	1	1	10	1	1.00

ALL-STAR GAME RECORD

Year	League	IP.	W.	L.	Pct.	H.	R.	ER.	SO.	BB.	ERA.
1974—National	....	2	0	0	.000	0	0	0	2	1	0.00

Member of National League All-Star Team for 1975 game; did not play.

DONALD RENIE MARTIN

Known by middle name.
Born August 30, 1955, at Dover, Del.
Height, 6.04. Weight, 185.
Throws and bats righthanded.
Attended University of Richmond, Richmond, Va.;
Received Bachelor of Science degree in Finance.

Tied for Gulf Coast League lead in shutouts with 1 in 1977.

Year	Club	League	G.	IP.	W.	L.	Pct.	H.	R.	ER.	SO.	BB.	ERA.
1977—Sarasota Royals	....	Gulf Coast	4	31	3	1	.750	35	13	12	19	12	3.48
1977—Daytona Beach	....	Florida St.	10	20	2	2	.500	16	6	6	12	7	2.70
1978—Ft. Myers	....	Florida St.	26	44	4	7	.429	27	19	10	29	18	2.05
1978—Omaha	....	Am. Assoc.	13	19	2	2	.500	16	9	7	10	9	3.32
1979—Jacksonville	....	Southern	8	18	3	1	.750	10	3	2	14	4	1.00
1979—Kansas City	....	American	25	35	0	3	.000	32	20	20	25	14	5.14
1979—Omaha	....	Am. Assoc.	33	63	6	2	.750	56	27	22	47	38	3.14
1980—Kansas City	....	American	32	137	10	10	.500	133	84	67	68	70	4.40
Major League Totals	....		57	172	10	13	.435	165	104	87	93	84	4.55

Selected by Kansas City Royals' organization in 19th round of free-agent draft, June 7, 1977.

WORLD SERIES RECORD

Year	Club	League	G.	IP.	W.	L.	Pct.	H.	R.	ER.	SO.	BB.	ERA.
1980—Kansas City	....	American	3	9⅔	0	0	.000	11	3	3	2	3	2.79

JERRY LINDSEY MARTIN

Born May 11, 1949, at Columbia, S. C.
Height, 6.01. Weight, 195.
Throws and bats righthanded.
Attended Spartanburg Junior College, Spartanburg, S. C., and
Furman University, Greenville, S. C.
Son of Barney Martin, Sr., former pitcher in Cincinnati Reds' and New York Giants' organizations, and brother of Mike Martin, pitcher in Philadelphia Phillies' organization.

Led Western Carolinas League in total bases with 240 and tied for lead in sacrifice flies with 7 in 1972.
Tied for Eastern League lead in sacrifice flies with 9 in 1973.
Named Western Carolinas League Most Valuable Player in 1972.

Year	Club	League	Pos.	G.	AB.	R.	H.	2B.	3B.	HR.	RBI.	B.A.	PO.	A.	E.	F.A.
1971—Pulaski	....	Appal.	OF	40	156	35	49	8	1	6	28	.314	54	1	6	.902
1972—Spartanburg	......	W. Car.	OF	*132	*513	86	*162	*30	6	12	*112	.316	186	*15	8	.962
1973—Reading	....	East.	OF-3B	135	460	73	138	23	5	17	86	.300	214	11	7	.970
1974—Toledo	....	Int.	OF	139	497	67	144	23	4	8	64	.290	285	6	3	.990
1974—Philadelphia	......	Nat.	OF	13	14	2	3	1	0	0	1	.214	5	0	0	1.000
1975—Toledo	....	Int.	OF	94	342	64	89	12	4	14	40	.260	205	7	3	.986
1975—Philadelphia	......	Nat.	OF	57	113	15	24	7	1	2	11	.212	90	3	2	.979
1976—Philadelphia	......	Nat.	OF-1B	130	121	30	30	7	0	2	15	.248	85	0	2	.977
1977—Philadelphia	......	Nat.	OF-1B	116	215	34	56	16	3	6	28	.260	117	4	2	.984
1978—Philadelphia†	.....	Nat.	OF	128	266	40	72	13	4	9	36	.271	148	8	2	.987
1979—Chicago	....	Nat.	OF	150	534	74	145	34	3	19	73	.272	297	11	6	.981
1980—Chicago‡	....	Nat.	OF	141	494	57	112	22	2	23	73	.227	262	8	6	.978
Major League Totals	....			735	1757	252	442	100	13	61	237	.252	1004	34	20	.981

Signed as free agent by Philadelphia Phillies' organization, July 17, 1971.

†Traded with Catcher Barry Foote, Second Baseman Ted Sizemore and Pitchers Derek Botelho and Henry Mack to Chicago Cubs for Second Baseman Manny Trillo, Outfielder Greg Gross and Catcher Dave Rader, February 23, 1979.

‡Traded with Outfielder Jesus Figueroa to San Francisco Giants for Pitcher Phil Nastu and Second Baseman Joe Strain, December 12, 1980.

CHAMPIONSHIP SERIES RECORD

Tied Championship Series records for most home runs by pinch hitter, game, Series and total Series (1), October 4, 1978.

Year Club	League	Pos.	G.	AB.	R.	H.	2B.	3B.	HR.	RBI.	B.A.	PO.	A.	E.	F.A.
1976—Philadelphia......Nat.		OF	1	1	1	0	0	0	0	0	.000	1	0	0	1.000
1977—Philadelphia......Nat.		O-PR-PH	3	4	0	0	0	0	0	0	.000	1	0	0	1.000
1978—Philadelphia......Nat.		PH-OF	4	9	1	2	1	0	1	2	.222	7	0	0	1.000
Championship Series Totals.............			8	14	2	2	1	0	1	2	.143	9	0	0	1.000

JOHN ROBERT MARTIN

Born April 11, 1956, at Wyandotte, Mich.
Height, 6.00. Weight, 190.
Throws left and bats left and righthanded.
Attended Eastern Michigan University, Ypsilanti, Mich.

Year Club	League	G.	IP.	W.	L.	Pct.	H.	R.	ER.	SO.	BB.	ERA.
1978—Bristol ....Appal.		2	5	0	1	.000	2	3	3	5	4	5.40
1978—Lakeland ....Florida St.		12	50	4	1	.800	54	11	10	22	9	1.80
1979—Montgomery ....Southern		11	27	2	0	1.000	15	8	6	18	9	2.00
1979—Evansville ....Am. Assoc.		37	59	7	1	.875	49	12	9	53	25	1.37
1980—Evansville†-Springfield‡ ....Am. Assoc.		20	38	2	2	.500	39	25	25	31	22	5.92
1980—Arkansas ....Texas		5	27	1	1	.500	23	7	5	19	7	1.67
1980—St. Louis ....National		9	42	2	3	.400	39	20	20	23	9	4.29
Major League Totals................................		9	42	2	3	.400	39	20	20	23	9	4.29

Selected by Detroit Tigers' organization in 27th round of free-agent draft, June 6, 1978.
†Traded with player to be named later to St. Louis Cardinals' organization for Outfielder Jim Lentine, June 2, 1980; outfielder Al Greene traded to Cardinals completing deal, June 9, 1980.
‡On disabled list, June 23 to July 31, 1980.

ALFREDO MARTINEZ
(Fred)

Born March 15, 1957, at Los Angeles, Calif.
Height, 6.03. Weight, 190.
Throws and bats righthanded.
Attended Whittier College, Whittier, Calif.; East Los Angeles Junior College,
Monterey Park, Calif., and California State University, Los Angeles, Calif.
Brother of Rudy Martinez, former player in Detroit Tigers' organization.

Year Club	League	G.	IP.	W.	L.	Pct.	H.	R.	ER.	SO.	BB.	ERA.
1977—Little Falls............................NYP		2	7	1	0	1.000	4	2	0	7	3	0.00
1977—Lynchburg ....Carolina		11	54	2	2	.500	58	32	30	36	35	5.00
1978—Lynchburg ....Carolina		24	151	11	7	.611	143	80	71	111	65	4.23
1979—Jackson†..............................Texas		24	157	11	8	.579	152	71	58	108	74	3.32
1980—California ....American		30	149	7	9	.438	150	81	75	57	59	4.53
Major League Totals.................................		30	149	7	9	.438	150	81	75	57	59	4.53

Selected by New York Mets' organization in 5th round of free-agent draft, June 7, 1977.
†Drafted by California Angels, December 3, 1979.

FELIX ANTHONY MARTINEZ
(Tippy)

Born May 31, 1950, at La Junta, Colo.
Height, 5.10. Weight, 175.
Throws and bats lefthanded.
Hobbies—Tennis, golf and water skiing.
Attended Colorado State University, Fort Collins, Colo.

Major League saves: 1975 (8), 1976 (10), 1977 (9), 1978 (5), 1979 (3), 1980 (10). Total—45.
Tied for Carolina League lead in saves with 15 and in wild pitches with 17 in 1973.

Year Club	League	G.	IP.	W.	L.	Pct.	H.	R.	ER.	SO.	BB.	ERA.
1972—Oneonta ....NYP		2	9	1	0	1.000	3	2	2	9	10	2.00
1972—Kinston ....Carolina		5	20	0	0	.000	22	10	10	18	13	4.50
1973—Kinston ....Carolina		54	105	13	8	.619	74	38	31	160	61	2.66
1974—Syracuse................................Int'national		36	64	7	5	.583	49	29	27	70	32	3.80
1974—New York ....American		10	13	0	0	.000	14	7	6	10	9	4.15
1975—Syracuse ....Int'national		14	110	8	2	.800	91	39	25	105	35	2.05
1975—New York ....American		23	37	1	2	.333	27	15	11	20	32	2.68
1976—New York† ....American		11	28	2	0	1.000	18	6	6	14	14	1.93
1976—Baltimore ....American		28	42	3	1	.750	32	13	12	31	28	2.57
1977—Baltimore ....American		41	50	5	1	.833	47	17	15	29	27	2.70
1978—Baltimore ....American		42	69	3	3	.500	77	41	37	57	40	4.83
1979—Baltimore ....American		39	78	10	3	.769	59	29	25	61	31	2.88
1980—Baltimore ....American		53	81	4	4	.500	69	30	27	68	34	3.00
Major League Totals		247	398	28	14	.667	343	158	139	290	215	3.14

Selected by Washington Senators' organization in 35th round of free-agent draft, June 5, 1969.
Signed as free agent by New York Yankees' organization, July 22, 1972.

†Traded with Pitchers Rudy May, Dave Pagan and Scott McGregor and Catcher Rick Dempsey to Baltimore Orioles for Pitchers Ken Holtzman, Doyle Alexander and Grant Jackson, Catcher Ellie Hendricks and Pitcher Jimmy Freeman, June 15, 1976.

WORLD SERIES RECORD

Year Club	League	G.	IP.	W.	L.	Pct.	H.	R.	ER.	SO.	BB.	ERA.
1979—Baltimore ....American		3	1⅓	0	0	.000	3	1	1	1	0	6.75

JOHN ALBERT MARTINEZ
(Buck)

Born November 7, 1948, at Redding, Calif.
Height, 5.11. Weight, 190.
Throws and bats righthanded.
Hobbies—Golf, hunting and fishing.
Attended Sacramento City College, Sacramento, Calif., and
Sacramento State College, Sacramento, Calif.

Year Club	League	Pos.	G.	AB.	R.	H.	2B.	3B.	HR.	RBI.	B.A.	PO.	A.	E.	F.A.
1967—Eugene ....Northw.		●C-O-3	77	269	53	96	16	4	2	46	.357	294	●48	8	.977
1968—Spartanburg ......W. Car.		C	8	28	6	11	4	0	0	11	.393	51	2	0	1.000
1968—Tidewater†‡ ......Carol.		C	36	110	10	31	12	1	1	14	.282	272	16	1	.997
1969—Kansas City§ .....Amer.		C-OF	72	205	14	47	6	1	4	23	.229	292	26	9	.972
1970—Kansas City x ....Amer.		C	6	9	1	1	0	0	0	0	.111	20	3	1	.958
1971—Omaha..............A. A.		C	75	269	34	77	23	1	5	39	.286	502	37	8	.985
1971—Kansas City.......Amer.		C	22	46	3	7	2	0	0	1	.152	84	6	3	.968
1972—Omaha y ....A. A.		C	67	195	23	34	9	0	4	12	.174	493	47	6	.989
1973—Omaha..............A. A.		★C-1B	82	254	24	69	13	0	5	38	.272	522	47	3	★.995
1973—Kansas City.......Amer.		C	14	32	2	8	1	0	1	6	.250	52	4	2	.966
1974—Kansas City.......Amer.		C	43	107	10	23	3	1	1	8	.215	151	16	4	.977
1975—Kansas City.......Amer.		C	80	226	15	51	9	2	3	23	.226	361	39	8	.980
1976—Kansas City z ....Amer.		C	95	267	24	61	13	3	5	34	.228	420	40	4	.991
1977—Kansas City a ....Amer.		C	29	80	3	18	4	0	1	9	.225	133	8	1	.993
1978—Milwaukee ....Amer.		C	89	256	26	56	10	1	1	20	.219	327	32	8	.978
1979—Milwaukee ....Amer.		C-P	69	196	17	53	8	0	4	26	.270	198	39	8	.967
1980—Milwaukee ....Amer.		C	76	219	16	49	9	0	3	17	.224	293	33	5	.985
Major League Totals			595	1643	131	374	65	8	23	167	.228	2331	246	53	.980

Selected by Philadelphia Phillies' organization in 7th round of free-agent draft, January 28, 1967.
†Drafted by Houston Astros from San Diego (Philadelphia Phillies' organization), December 2, 1968.
‡Traded with Infielder Mickey Sinnerud and Catcher Tommie Smith (latter two transferred from Oklahoma City to Omaha) by Houston Astros to Kansas City Royals for Catcher John Jones, December 16, 1968.
§On restricted list, April 7 to June 17, 1969.
xOn military list, April 2 to August 10, 1970.
yOn disabled list, July 9 to August 25, 1972.
zOn supplemental disabled list, May 20 to June 5, 1976.
aTraded with Pitcher Mark Littell to St. Louis Cardinals for Pitcher Al Hrabosky, December 8, 1977; traded by St. Louis to Milwaukee Brewers for Pitcher George Frazier, December 8, 1977.

PITCHING RECORD

Year Club	League	G.	IP.	W.	L.	Pct.	H.	R.	ER.	SO.	BB.	ERA.
1979—Milwaukee ....American		1	1	0	0	.000	1	1	1	0	1	9.00

CHAMPIONSHIP SERIES RECORD

Year Club	League	Pos.	G.	AB.	R.	H.	2B.	3B.	HR.	RBI.	B.A.	PO.	A.	E.	F.A.
1976—Kansas City.......Amer.		C	5	15	0	5	0	0	0	4	.333	15	4	0	1.000

JOSE DENNIS MARTINEZ
(Known by middle name)

Born May 14, 1955, at Granada, Nicaragua.
Height, 6.01. Weight, 183.
Throws and bats righthanded.
Hobby—Music.

Led International League in complete games with 16 in 1976.
Led American League in games started with 39 and in complete games with 18 in 1979.
Named International League Pitcher of the Year, 1976.

Year Club	League	G.	IP.	W.	L.	Pct.	H.	R.	ER.	SO.	BB.	ERA.
1974—Miami................Florida St.		25	179	15	6	.714	124	48	41	162	53	2.06
1975—Miami................Florida St.		20	145	12	4	.750	125	54	42	114	35	2.61
1975—Asheville ....Southern		6	45	4	1	.800	45	16	13	18	12	2.60
1975—Rochester ....Int'national		2	5	0	0	.000	7	4	3	4	2	5.40
1976—Rochester ....Int'national		25	180	★14	8	.636	148	64	50	★140	50	★2.50
1976—Baltimore ....American		4	28	1	2	.333	23	8	8	18	8	2.57
1977—Baltimore ....American		42	167	14	7	.667	157	86	76	107	64	4.10
1978—Baltimore ....American		40	276	16	11	.593	257	121	108	142	93	3.25
1979—Baltimore ....American		40	★292	15	16	.484	279	129	119	132	78	3.67
1980—Baltimore† ....American		25	100	6	4	.600	103	44	44	42	44	3.96
1980—Miami‡ ....Florida St.		2	12	0	0	.000	3	1	0	7	5	0.00
Major League Totals		151	863	52	40	.565	819	388	355	441	287	3.70

Signed as free agent by Baltimore Orioles' organization, December 10, 1973.
†On disabled list, March 28 to April 20 and June 3 to July 1, 1980.
‡On rehabilitation assignment, July 1 to July 10, 1980.

CHAMPIONSHIP SERIES RECORD

Year Club	League	G.	IP.	W.	L.	Pct.	H.	R.	ER.	SO.	BB.	ERA.
1979—Baltimore ....American		1	8⅓	0	0	.000	8	3	3	4	0	3.24

WORLD SERIES RECORD

Year Club	League	G.	IP.	W.	L.	Pct.	H.	R.	ER.	SO.	BB.	ERA.
1979—Baltimore ....American		2	2	0	0	.000	6	4	4	0	0	18.00

SILVIO RAMON MARTINEZ

Born August 31, 1955, at Santiago, Dominican Republic.
Height, 5.11. Weight, 160.
Throws and bats righthanded.
Hobby—Fishing.

Pitched 4-0 no-hit victory against Omaha, May 26, 1978.
Led Texas League in shutouts with 7 in 1976.

Year Club	League	G.	IP.	W.	L.	Pct.	H.	R.	ER.	SO.	BB.	ERA.
1974—Niagara Falls......................NYP	12	67	4	5	.444	48	36	24	54	42	3.22
1975—Charleston ....W. Carol.	19	133	6	9	.400	115	63	53	113	55	3.59
1975—Salem ....Carolina	4	29	2	1	.667	25	10	10	28	10	3.10
1976—Shreveport.......................Texas	16	104	8	4	.667	74	29	28	71	33	2.42
1976—Charleston†.........................Int'national	8	44	2	4	.333	59	30	29	31	18	5.93
1977—Iowa ....Am. Assoc.	26	152	10	7	.588	134	87	76	118	73	4.50
1977—Chicago‡..............................American	10	21	0	1	.000	28	14	13	10	12	5.57
1978—Springfield...........................Am. Assoc.	7	54	5	2	.714	39	15	13	42	24	2.17
1978—St. Louis ....National	22	138	9	8	.529	114	65	56	45	71	3.65
1979—St. Louis ....National	32	207	15	8	.652	204	92	75	102	67	3.26
1980—St. Louis§............................National	25	120	5	10	.333	127	75	64	39	48	4.80
1980—St. Petersburg x ....Florida St.	2	6	0	0	.000	7	1	1	15	7	1.50
American League Totals	10	21	0	1	.000	28	14	13	10	12	5.57
National League Totals	79	465	29	26	.527	445	232	195	186	186	3.77
Major League Totals	89	486	29	27	.518	473	246	208	196	198	3.85

Signed as free agent by Pittsburgh Pirates' organization, March 14, 1974.
†Traded by Pittsburgh Pirates' organization with Outfielder Richie Zisk to Chicago White Sox for Pitchers Terry Forster and Rich Gossage, December 10, 1976.
‡Traded to St. Louis Cardinals, November 28, 1977, to complete deal in which Chicago White Sox obtained Pitcher Clay Carroll, August 31, 1977.
§On disabled list, June 1 to June 18, 1980.
xOn rehabilitation assignment, June 18 to July 4, 1980.

RANDY CARL MARTZ

Born May 28, 1956, at Harrisburg, Pa.
Height, 6.04. Weight, 210.
Throws right and bats lefthanded.
Attended University of South Carolina, Columbia, S. C.

Tied for American Association lead in games started with 26 in 1979.

Year Club	League	G.	IP.	W.	L.	Pct.	H.	R.	ER.	SO.	BB.	ERA.
1977—Bradenton Cubs...................G. Coast	2	9	0	1	.000	4	1	0	8	2	0.00
1977—Midland ....Texas	12	85	5	3	.625	96	45	39	42	14	4.13
1978—Midland ....Texas	18	127	8	6	.571	126	53	44	74	44	3.12
1978—Wichita................................Am. Assoc.	11	59	3	7	.300	82	51	47	24	27	7.17
1979—Wichita................................Am. Assoc.	30	178	8	13	.381	196	96	81	66	47	4.10
1980—Wichita†..............................Am. Assoc.	16	107	8	6	.571	98	41	37	53	29	3.11
1980—Chicago ....National	6	30	1	2	.333	28	14	7	5	11	2.10
Major League Totals................................	6	30	1	2	.333	28	14	7	5	11	2.10

Selected by Chicago Cubs' organization in 1st round (12th player selected) of free-agent draft, June 7, 1977.
†On disabled list, May 12 to July 16, 1980.

JONATHAN TRUMPBOUR MATLACK
(Jon)

Born January 19, 1950, at West Chester, Pa.
Height, 6.03. Weight, 200.
Throws and bats lefthanded.
Hobby—All sports.
Attended University of Pittsburgh, Pittsburgh, Pa., and West
Chester State College, West Chester, Pa.

Led National League in shutouts with 7 in 1974.
Tied for National League lead in shutouts with 6 in 1976.
Named THE SPORTING NEWS National League Rookie Pitcher of the Year, 1972.
Named 1972 National League Rookie of the Year by Baseball Writers' Association of America.
Received reported $55,000 bonus to sign with New York Mets, 1967.

— 282 —

Year	Club	League	G.	IP.	W.	L.	Pct.	H.	R.	ER.	SO.	BB.	ERA.
1967–Williamsport	Eastern	2	5	0	1	.000	10	8	8	4	4	14.40
1968–Raleigh-Dur.	Carolina	24	173	13	6	.684	133	59	53	188	66	2.76
1969–Tidewater	Int'national	26	176	14	7	.667	176	83	81	99	66	4.14
1970–Tidewater	Int'national	26	183	12	11	.522	168	94	84	146	90	4.13
1971–Tidewater	Int'national	22	152	11	7	.611	141	82	67	145	55	3.97
1971–New York	National	7	37	0	3	.000	31	18	17	24	15	4.14
1972–New York	National	34	244	15	10	.600	215	79	63	169	71	2.32
1973–New York	National	34	242	14	16	.467	210	93	86	205	99	3.20
1974–New York	National	34	265	13	15	.464	221	82	71	195	76	2.41
1975–New York	National	33	229	16	12	.571	224	105	86	154	58	3.38
1976–New York	National	35	262	17	10	.630	236	94	86	153	57	2.95
1977–New York†	National	26	169	7	15	.318	175	86	79	123	43	4.21
1978–Texas	American	35	270	15	13	.536	252	93	68	157	51	2.27
1979–Texas‡	American	13	85	5	4	.556	98	43	39	35	15	4.13
1980–Texas	American	35	235	10	10	.500	265	111	96	142	48	3.68
National League Totals		203	1448	82	81	.503	1312	557	488	1023	419	3.03
American League Totals		83	590	30	27	.526	615	247	203	334	114	3.10
Major League Totals		286	2038	112	108	.509	1927	804	691	1357	533	3.05

Selected by New York Mets' organization in 1st round (fourth player selected) of free-agent draft, June 6, 1967.

†Traded with First Baseman-Outfielder John Milner to Texas Rangers for First Baseman Willie Montanez, Outfielder Tom Grieve, and a player to be named later, December 8, 1977. (Ken Henderson sent to Mets, completing trade, March 15, 1978).

‡On disabled list, April 8 to May 1 and July 10 to September 12, 1979.

CHAMPIONSHIP SERIES RECORD

Tied Championship Series record for fewest hits allowed, game (2), October 7, 1973.

Year	Club	League	G.	IP.	W.	L.	Pct.	H.	R.	ER.	SO.	BB.	ERA.
1973–New York	National	1	9	1	0	1.000	2	0	0	9	3	0.00

WORLD SERIES RECORD

Year	Club	League	G.	IP.	W.	L.	Pct.	H.	R.	ER.	SO.	BB.	ERA.
1973–New York	National	3	16⅔	1	2	.333	10	7	4	11	5	2.16

ALL-STAR GAME RECORD

Year	League	IP.	W.	L.	Pct.	H.	R.	ER.	SO.	BB.	ERA.
1974–National	1	0	0	.000	1	0	0	0	1	0.00
1975–National	2	1	0	1.000	2	0	0	4	1	0.00
All-Star Game Totals	3	1	0	1.000	3	0	0	4	1	0.00

Member of National League All-Star Team in 1976; did not play.

GARY NATHANIEL MATTHEWS

Born July 5, 1950, at San Fernando, Calif.
Height, 6.03. Weight, 190.
Throws and bats righthanded.
Hobbies—Hunting, fishing and dancing.

Led Texas League in total bases with 232 in 1971.
Tied for California League lead in double plays by outfielders with 3 in 1970.
Major League stolen bases: 1972 (0), 1973 (17), 1974 (11), 1975 (13), 1976 (12), 1977 (22), 1978 (8), 1979 (18), 1980 (11). Total—112.
Hit three home runs in one game, vs. Houston Astros, September 25, 1976.
Named National League Rookie Player of the Year by THE SPORTING NEWS, 1973.
Named National League Rookie of the Year by Baseball Writers' Association of America, 1973.

Year	Club	League	Pos.	G.	AB.	R.	H.	2B.	3B.	HR.	RBI.	B.A.	PO.	A.	E.	F.A.
1969–Decatur	Midw.	OF	53	174	31	56	11	2	8	30	.322	63	7	8	.897
1970–Fresno	Calif.	OF	117	380	77	106	11	5	23	74	.279	133	15	*15	.908
1971–Amarillo	Texas	OF	•142	493	82	138	*37	6	15	*86	.280	290	10	5	*.984
1972–Phoenix	P.C.	OF	136	480	101	150	27	8	21	108	.313	218	•16	*13	.947
1972–San Francisco	Nat.	OF	20	62	11	18	1	1	4	14	.290	34	0	1	.971
1973–San Francisco	Nat.	OF	148	540	74	162	22	10	12	58	.300	277	11	5	.983
1974–San Francisco	Nat.	OF	154	561	87	161	27	6	16	82	.287	281	9	9	.970
1975–San Francisco†	Nat.	OF	116	425	67	119	22	3	12	58	.280	225	11	8	.967
1976–San Francisco‡	Nat.	OF	156	587	79	164	28	4	20	84	.279	265	8	7	.975
1977–Atlanta	Nat.	OF	148	555	89	157	25	5	17	64	.283	262	11	10	.965
1978–Atlanta§	Nat.	OF	129	474	75	135	20	5	18	62	.285	238	10	8	.969
1979–Atlanta	Nat.	OF	156	631	97	192	34	5	27	90	.304	292	12	8	.974
1980–Atlanta	Nat.	OF	155	571	79	139	17	3	19	75	.278	258	8	•11	.960
Major League Totals			1182	4406	658	1247	196	42	145	587	.283	2132	80	67	.971

Selected by San Francisco Giants' organization in 1st round (17th player selected) of free-agent draft, June 7, 1968.

†On disabled list, June 5 to July 18, 1975.

‡Granted free agency, November 1, 1976; signed with Atlanta Braves, November 17, 1976.

§On disabled list, April 15 to May 2, 1978.

ALL-STAR GAME RECORD

Year	League	Pos.	AB.	R.	H.	2B.	3B.	HR.	RBI.	B.A.	PO.	A.	E.	F.A.
1979–National	OF	2	0	0	0	0	0	0	.000	2	0	0	1.000

RICHARD CARLTON MATULA
(Rick)

Born November 22, 1953, at Wharton, Tex.
Height, 6.00. Weight, 195.
Throws and bats righthanded.
Attended Sam Houston State University, Huntsville, Tex.

Year Club	League	G.	IP.	W.	L.	Pct.	H.	R.	ER.	SO.	BB.	ERA.
1976—Kingsport	Ap'lachian	20	48	3	5	.375	49	18	14	31	14	2.63
1976—Greenwood	W. Carol.	3	6	1	0	1.000	10	5	5	8	0	7.50
1977—Greenwood	W. Carol.	7	21	2	1	.667	19	8	5	15	4	2.14
1977—Savannah	Southern	22	100	8	5	.615	117	51	36	75	27	3.24
1978—Savannah	Southern	27	87	7	5	.583	82	39	30	48	30	3.10
1978—Richmond	Int'national	16	40	3	0	1.000	39	16	14	23	8	3.15
1979—Atlanta	National	28	171	8	10	.444	193	90	79	67	64	4.16
1980—Atlanta	National	33	177	11	13	.458	195	100	90	62	60	4.58
Major League Totals		61	348	19	23	.452	388	190	169	129	124	4.37

Selected by Montreal Expos' organization in 16th round of free-agent draft, June 6, 1972.
Selected by Atlanta Braves' organization in 14th round of free-agent draft, June 8, 1976.

LEONARD JAMES MATUSZEK

Named pronounced mu-tu-zek.

(Len)

Born September 27, 1954, at Toledo, O.
Height, 6.02. Weight, 190.
Throws right and bats lefthanded.
Attended University of Toledo, Toledo, O.

Year Club	League	Pos.	G.	AB.	R.	H.	2B.	3B.	HR.	RBI.	B.A.	PO.	A.	E.	F.A.
1976—Peninsula	Carol.	1B	47	166	23	46	9	1	3	21	.277	426	34	1	.998
1977—Peninsula	Carol.	1B	122	410	56	94	18	4	10	56	.229	1051	74	12	*.989
1978—Reading†	East.	1B-3B	92	294	41	80	16	4	5	36	.272	556	85	13	.980
1979—Reading	East.	1B-3B	32	108	19	31	9	4	3	16	.287	145	42	5	.974
1979—Oklahoma City	A.A.	1B-3B	72	228	31	60	9	3	4	31	.263	421	55	10	.979
1980—Oklahoma City‡	A.A.	1B-3B	67	256	38	78	16	5	7	35	.305	580	55	6	.991

Selected by Philadelphia Phillies' organization in 5th round of free-agent draft, June 8, 1976.
†On disabled list, June 23 to July 26, 1978.
‡On disabled list, April 14 to May 16 and May 17 to June 21, 1980.

LEE ANDREW MAY

Born March 23, 1943, at Birmingham, Ala.
Height, 6.03. Weight, 205.
Throws and bats righthanded.
Attended Miles College, Birmingham, Ala.
Brother of Carlos May, outfielder-first baseman with New York Yankees.

Tied following major league records: most home runs, three consecutive games, hitting homer in each game, 6, May 24 (2), May 25 (2), and May 28 (2), 1969; most total bases, inning, 8, and most home runs, inning, 2, April 29, 1974 (6th inning).
Hit three home runs in a game, June 21, 1973 against San Diego Padres.
Led National League batters in strikeouts with 145 in 1972.
Led National League first basemen in double plays with 128 in 1969 and 143 in 1970.
Led National League first basemen in total chances with 1,400 and in double plays with 133 in 1972.
Led American League first basemen in total chances with 1428 and in double plays with 138 in 1975.
Led American League designated hitters in strikeouts with 108 in 1978.
Led Carolina League first basemen in double plays with 125 in 1963.
Led Pacific Coast League in total bases with 327 in 1965.
Named National League Rookie Player of the Year by The Sporting News, 1967.
Named first baseman on The Sporting News National League All-Star Team, 1971.

Year Club	League	Pos.	G.	AB.	R.	H.	2B.	3B.	HR.	RBI.	B.A.	PO.	A.	E.	F.A.
1961—Tampa	Fla. St.	1-OF	26	77	10	20	2	0	9	9	.260	114	7	5	.960
1962—Tampa	Fla. St.	1B	89	339	45	88	10	3	10	65	.260	674	48	16	.978
1963—Rocky Mount	Carol.	1B	144	520	79	137	23	4	18	80	.263	*1288	74	*27	.981
1964—Macon	South.	1-OF	•140	515	91	156	22	5	25	*110	.303	1019	72	20	.982
1965—San Diego	P. C.	1B-OF	143	558	83	179	32	7	34	103	.321	1165	67	15	.988
1965—Cincinnati	Nat.	PH	5	4	1	0	0	0	0	0	.000	0	0	0	.000
1966—Cincinnati	Nat.	1B	25	75	14	25	5	1	2	10	.333	132	9	4	.972
1966—Buffalo	Int.	1B	128	471	74	146	25	5	16	78	.310	1006	86	*16	.986
1967—Cincinnati	Nat.	1B-OF	127	438	54	116	29	2	12	57	.265	703	46	6	.992
1968—Cincinnati	Nat.	1B-OF	146	559	78	162	32	1	22	80	.290	1094	73	5	.996
1969—Cincinnati	Nat.	1B-OF	158	607	85	169	32	3	38	110	.278	1395	102	11	.993
1970—Cincinnati	Nat.	1B	153	605	78	153	34	2	34	94	.253	1362	109	10	.993
1971—Cincinnati†	Nat.	1B	147	553	85	154	17	3	39	98	.278	1261	78	8	.994
1972—Houston	Nat.	1B	148	592	87	168	31	2	29	98	.284	*1318	76	6	.996
1973—Houston	Nat.	1B	148	545	65	147	24	3	28	105	.270	1220	78	9	.993
1974—Houston‡	Nat.	1B	152	556	59	149	26	0	24	85	.268	1253	88	8	.994
1975—Baltimore	Amer.	1B	146	580	67	152	28	3	20	99	.262	*1312	106	10	.993
1976—Baltimore	Amer.	1B	148	530	61	137	17	4	25	109	.258	722	62	3	.996
1977—Baltimore	Amer.	1B	150	585	75	148	16	2	27	99	.253	907	56	5	.995

Year Club League	Pos.	G.	AB.	R.	H.	2B.	3B.	HR.	RBI.	B.A.	PO.	A.	E.	F.A.
1978–Baltimore ....Amer.	1B	148	556	56	137	16	1	25	80	.246	34	2	1	.973
1979–Baltimore ....Amer.	1B	124	456	59	116	15	0	19	69	.254	21	0	2	.913
1980–Baltimore§........Amer.	1B	78	222	20	54	10	2	7	31	.243	57	3	0	1.000
National League Totals...................		1209	4534	606	1243	230	17	228	737	.274	9738	659	67	.994
American League Totals.................		794	2929	338	744	102	12	123	487	.254	3053	229	21	.994
Major League Totals		2003	7463	944	1987	332	29	351	1224	.266	12791	888	88	.994

Signed as free agent by Cincinnati Reds' organization, June 1, 1961.

†Traded with Second Baseman Tommy Helms and Outfielder Jim Stewart to Houston Astros for Infielder Denis Menke, Second Baseman Joe Morgan, Pitcher Jack Billingham and Outfielders Cesar Geronimo and Ed Armbrister, latter assigned from Oklahoma City to Indianapolis, November 29, 1971.

‡Traded with Outfielder Jay Schlueter to Baltimore Orioles for Second Baseman Rob Andrews and Infielder-Outfielder Enos Cabell, December 3, 1974.

§Granted free agency, October 23, 1980; signed by Kansas City Royals, December 12, 1980.

CHAMPIONSHIP SERIES RECORD

Year Club League	Pos.	G.	AB.	R.	H.	2B.	3B.	HR.	RBI.	B.A.	PO.	A.	E.	F.A.
1970–Cincinnati ....Nat.	1B	3	12	0	2	1	0	0	2	.167	31	1	0	1.000
1979–Baltimore ....Amer.	DH	2	7	0	1	0	0	0	1	.143	0	0	0	.000
Championship Series Totals		5	19	0	3	1	0	0	3	.158	31	1	0	1.000

WORLD SERIES RECORD

Established World Series record for most double plays started by first baseman, Series (2), 1970.

Tied World Series records for most runs scored, five-game Series (6); most runs batted in, five-game Series (8) and most long hits, five-game Series (4), 1970; one or more hits, each game, five-game Series, 1970.

Year Club League	Pos.	G.	AB.	R.	H.	2B.	3B.	HR.	RBI.	B.A.	PO.	A.	E.	F.A.
1970–Cincinnati ....Nat.	1B	5	18	6	7	2	0	2	8	.389	48	3	0	1.000
1979–Baltimore ....Amer.	PH	2	1	0	0	0	0	0	0	.000	0	0	0	.000
World Series Totals........................		7	19	6	7	2	0	2	8	.368	48	3	0	1.000

ALL-STAR GAME RECORD

Tied All-Star Game record for most unassisted double plays by first baseman, game (1), July 25, 1972.

Year League	Pos.	AB.	R.	H.	2B.	3B.	HR.	RBI.	B.A.	PO.	A.	E.	F.A.
1969–National..............................	1B	1	0	0	0	0	0	0	.000	3	0	0	1.000
1971–National..............................	1B	1	0	0	0	0	0	0	.000	6	0	0	1.000
1972–National..............................	1B	4	0	1	0	0	0	1	.250	13	2	0	1.000
All-Star Game Totals........................		6	0	1	0	0	0	1	.167	22	2	0	1.000

MILTON SCOTT MAY
(Milt)

Born August 1, 1950, at Gary, Ind.
Height, 6.00. Weight, 192.
Throws right and bats lefthanded.
Hobby–Hunting.
Attended Manatee Junior College, West Bradenton, Fla.
Son of Merrill (Pinky) May, third baseman for Philadelphia Phillies, 1939 through 1943.

Led Western Carolinas League catchers in double plays with 10 in 1969.
Tied for International League lead in passed balls with 10 in 1970.
Tied for American League lead in double plays by catchers with 12 in 1977.

Year Club League	Pos.	G.	AB.	R.	H.	2B.	3B.	HR.	RBI.	B.A.	PO.	A.	E.	F.A.
1968–Brade'n Pirates .Gulf C.	C	52	166	21	40	4	0	0	23	.241	*337	31	*13	.966
1969–Gastonia†..........W. Car.	*C-1	86	301	58	87	17	2	11	57	.289	485	*63	11	.980
1970–Columbus..........Int.	C	111	397	49	111	14	3	21	86	.280	688	*69	15	.981
1970–Pittsburgh........Nat.	PH	5	4	1	2	1	0	0	2	.500	0	0	0	.000
1971–Pittsburgh‡ ....Nat.	C	49	126	15	35	1	0	6	25	.278	168	12	0	1.000
1972–Pittsburgh§ ....Nat.	C	57	139	12	39	10	0	0	14	.281	179	21	3	.985
1973–Pittsburgh x ......Nat.	C	101	283	29	76	8	1	7	31	.269	402	36	12	.973
1974–Houston ....Nat.	C	127	405	47	117	17	4	7	54	.289	525	63	4	*.993
1975–Houston y.......Nat.	C	111	386	29	93	15	1	4	52	.241	568	*70	9	.986
1976–Detroit z ....Amer.	C	6	25	2	7	1	0	0	1	.280	33	5	0	1.000
1977–Detroit............Amer.	C	115	397	32	99	9	3	12	46	.249	551	78	9	.986
1978–Detroit............Amer.	C	105	352	24	88	9	0	10	37	.250	406	58	10	.979
1979–Det. a-Chi. b......Amer.	C	71	213	24	54	15	0	7	31	.254	296	28	6	.982
1980–San Fran. c.......Nat.	C	111	358	27	93	16	2	6	50	.260	500	59	8	.986
National League Totals...................		561	1701	160	455	68	8	30	228	.267	2342	261	36	.986
American League Totals.................		297	987	82	248	34	3	29	115	.251	1286	169	25	.983
Major League Totals		858	2688	242	703	102	11	59	343	.262	3628	430	61	.985

Selected by Pittsburgh Pirates' organization in 17th round of free-agent draft, June 7, 1968.

†On temporary inactive list, April 13 to April 25 and from August 16 to September 30, 1969.

‡On military list, July 25 to August 8, 1971.

§On military list, July 15 to July 29, 1972.

xTraded to Houston Astros for Pitcher Jerry Reuss, October 31, 1973.

yTraded with Pitchers Dave Roberts and Jim Crawford to Detroit Tigers for Outfielder Leon Roberts, Catcher Terry Humphrey and Pitchers Gene Pentz and Mark Lemongello, December 6, 1975.

zOn disabled list, April 21 to September 3, 1976.

aSold to Chicago White Sox, May 27, 1979.

bGranted free agency, November 1, 1979; signed by San Francisco Giants, December 12, 1979.
cOn supplemental disabled list, July 31 to August 16, 1980.

CHAMPIONSHIP SERIES RECORD

Year	Club	League	Pos.	G.	AB.	R.	H.	2B.	3B.	HR.	RBI.	B.A.	PO.	A.	E.	F.A.
1971–Pittsburgh		Nat.	PH	1	1	0	0	0	0	0	0	.000	0	0	0	.000
1972–Pittsburgh		Nat.	C	1	2	0	1	0	0	0	1	.500	8	1	0	1.000
Championship Series Totals				2	3	0	1	0	0	0	1	.333	8	1	0	1.000

WORLD SERIES RECORD

Year	Club	League	Pos.	G.	AB.	R.	H.	2B.	3B.	HR.	RBI.	B.A.	PO.	A.	E.	F.A.
1971–Pittsburgh		Nat.	PH	2	2	0	1	0	0	0	1	.500	0	0	0	.000

RUDOLPH MAY JR.
(Rudy)

Born July 18, 1944, at Coffeyville, Kan.
Height, 6.02. Weight, 195.
Throws and bats lefthanded.
Hobby–Playing dominoes.
Attended San Francisco State College, San Francisco, Calif.

Led Northern League in wild pitches with 25 in 1963.
Tied for Carolina League lead in shutouts with 4 in 1964.

Year	Club	League	G.	IP.	W.	L.	Pct.	H.	R.	ER.	SO.	BB.	ERA.
1963–Bismarck-Mandan†		Northern	24	168	11	11	.500	142	100	●80	173	*120	4.29
1964–Tidewater		Carolina	20	155	13	6	.684	107	52	44	187	98	2.55
1964–Indianapolis‡§		P. Coast	10	52	4	2	.667	39	20	16	48	38	2.77
1965–California		American	30	124	4	9	.308	111	59	54	76	78	3.92
1966–Seattle		P. Coast	7	30	3	1	.750	36	18	17	12	15	5.10
1966–El Paso x		Texas	2	5	0	0	.000	4	2	2	4	7	3.60
1967–San Jose		California	14	84	7	2	.778	62	33	29	51	40	3.11
1968–El Paso		Texas	22	129	8	7	.533	133	71	64	112	39	4.47
1969–California		American	43	180	10	13	.435	142	81	69	133	66	3.45
1970–California y		American	38	209	7	13	.350	190	102	93	164	81	4.00
1971–California z		American	32	208	11	12	.478	160	74	70	156	87	3.03
1972–California		American	35	205	12	11	.522	162	79	67	169	82	2.94
1973–California		American	34	185	7	17	.292	177	101	90	134	80	4.38
1974–Calif. a-N.Y. b		American	35	141	8	5	.615	104	60	50	102	58	3.19
1975–New York		American	32	212	14	12	.538	179	87	72	145	99	3.06
1976–New York c-Baltimore		American	35	220	15	10	.600	205	105	91	109	70	3.72
1977–Baltimore d		American	37	252	18	14	.563	243	114	101	105	78	3.61
1978–Montreal e		National	27	144	8	10	.444	141	73	62	87	42	3.88
1979–Montreal f		National	33	94	10	3	.769	88	30	24	67	31	2.30
1980–New York g		American	41	175	15	5	.750	144	56	48	133	39	*2.47
American League Totals			392	2111	121	121	.500	1817	918	805	1426	818	3.43
National League Totals			60	238	18	13	.581	229	103	86	154	73	3.25
Major League Totals			452	2349	139	134	.509	2046	1021	891	1580	891	3.41

Signed as free agent by Minnesota Twins' organization, November 5, 1962.
fGranted free agency, November 1, 1979; signed by New York Yankees, November 8, 1979.
†Drafted by Chicago White Sox from Dallas-Fort Worth (Minnesota Twins' organization), December 2, 1963.
‡Traded by Chicago White Sox to Philadelphia Phillies for Catcher Bill Heath and player to be named later, October 15, 1964; Pitcher Joel Gibson was assigned to White Sox, November 23, 1964, to complete deal.
§Traded by Philadelphia Phillies to Los Angeles Angels with First Baseman Costen Shockley for Pitcher Robert (Bo) Belinsky, December 3, 1964.
xOn disabled list June 4 through end of season.
yOn military list July 10 through July 27.
zOn disabled list May 25 through June 17.
aSold to New York Yankees, June 15, 1974.
bOn disabled list, July 11 to August 1, 1974.
cTraded with Pitchers Felix Martinez, Dave Pagan and Scott McGregor and Catcher Rick Dempsey to Baltimore Orioles for Pitchers Ken Holtzman, Doyle Alexander and Grant Jackson, Catcher Ellie Hendricks, and Pitcher Jimmy Freeman, latter assigned from Rochester to Syracuse, June 15, 1976.
dTraded with Pitchers Randy Miller and Bryn Smith (latter assigned from Rochester to Denver) to Montreal Expos for Pitchers Don Stanhouse and Joe Kerrigan and Outfielder Gary Roenicke, December 7, 1977.
eOn disabled list, July 20 to September 1, 1978.
fGranted free agency, November 1, 1979; signed by New York Yankees, November 8, 1979.
gOn disabled list, April 1 to April 22, 1980.

CHAMPIONSHIP SERIES RECORD

Year	Club	League	G.	IP.	W.	L.	Pct.	H.	R.	ER.	SO.	BB.	ERA.
1980–New York		American	1	8	0	1	.000	6	3	3	4	3	3.38

DID YOU KNOW–

That Enrique Romo was the only pitcher to hit a grand slam in the majors in 1980?

JOHN CLAIBORN MAYBERRY

Born February 18, 1950, at Detroit, Mich.
Height, 6.03. Weight, 225.
Throws and bats lefthanded.
Attended University of Michigan, Ann Arbor, Mich.

Tied major league record for most home runs, opening day of season (2), April 9, 1980.
Tied American League record for most double plays, first baseman, nine-inning game, 6, May 6, 1972.
Led American League first basemen in total chances with 1,427 in 1972 and with 1,596 in 1976; led in double plays with 141 in 1972 and with 156 in 1973.
Led American League in total bases on balls with 122 in 1973 and with 119 in 1975.
Led American Association first basemen in double plays with 89 in 1969.
Led American League in sacrifice flies with 12 in 1976.
Hit three home runs in one game, vs. Texas Rangers, July 1, 1975 and vs. Toronto Blue Jays, June 1, 1977.
Named first baseman on THE SPORTING NEWS American League All-Star Team, 1973 and 1975.
Received reported $40,000 bonus to sign with Houston Astros, 1967.

Year Club	League	Pos.	G.	AB.	R.	H.	2B.	3B.	HR.	RBI.	B.A.	PO.	A.	E.	F.A.
1967—Covington	Appal.	1B	50	155	23	39	7	0	4	21	.252	380	★29	★11	.974
1968—Cocoa	Fla. St.	1B	64	195	34	66	9	3	14	48	.338	479	22	7	.986
1968—Greensboro	Carol.	1B	43	158	31	52	14	1	8	29	.329	297	22	3	.991
1968—Oklahoma City	P.C.	1B	24	78	3	20	0	0	1	5	.256	196	12	4	.981
1968—Houston	Nat.	1B	4	9	0	0	0	0	0	0	.000	25	0	0	1.000
1969—Oklahoma City	A.A.	★1B-2B	123	458	95	139	29	4	21	78	.303	★1005	61	11	★.990
1969—Houston	Nat.	1B	5	4	0	0	0	0	0	0	.000	0	0	0	.000
1970—Oklahoma City	A.A.	1B	70	231	55	63	7	3	13	38	.273	536	30	8	.986
1970—Houston	Nat.	1B	50	148	23	32	3	2	5	14	.216	371	35	2	.995
1971—Oklahoma City	A.A.	1B	64	222	50	72	10	3	12	40	.324	445	39	4	.992
1971—Houston†	Nat.	1B	46	137	16	25	0	1	7	14	.182	317	15	1	.997
1972—Kansas City	Amer.	1B	149	503	65	150	24	3	25	100	.298	★1338	82	7	★.995
1973—Kansas City	Amer.	1B	152	510	87	142	20	2	26	100	.278	★1457	81	9	.994
1974—Kansas City	Amer.	1B	126	427	63	100	13	1	22	69	.234	963	61	10	.990
1975—Kansas City	Amer.	1B	156	554	95	161	38	1	34	106	.291	1199	100	★16	.988
1976—Kansas City	Amer.	1B	161	594	76	138	22	2	13	95	.232	★1484	105	7	.996
1977—Kansas City‡	Amer.	1B	153	543	73	125	22	1	23	82	.230	1296	81	7	★.995
1978—Toronto	Amer.	1B	152	515	51	129	15	2	22	70	.250	1143	52	8	.993
1979—Toronto	Amer.	1B	137	464	61	127	22	1	21	74	.274	1192	74	6	.995
1980—Toronto	Amer.	1B	149	501	62	124	19	2	30	82	.248	1243	79	8	.994
National League Totals			105	298	39	57	3	3	12	28	.191	713	50	3	.996
American League Totals			1335	4611	633	1196	195	15	216	778	.259	11315	715	78	.994
Major League Totals			1440	4909	672	1253	198	18	228	806	.272	12028	765	81	.994

Selected by Houston Astros' organization in 1st round (sixth player selected) of free-agent draft, June 6, 1967.

†Traded with Third Baseman Dave Grangaard (latter assigned to Evansville) to Kansas City Royals for Pitchers Jim York and Lance Clemons, December 2, 1971.

‡Traded to Toronto Blue Jays for a player to be named later, April 4, 1978; deal completed with undisclosed payment of cash.

ALL-STAR GAME RECORD

Year League	Pos.	AB.	R.	H.	2B.	3B.	HR.	RBI.	B.A.	PO.	A.	E.	F.A.
1973—American	1B	3	0	1	1	0	0	0	.333	8	0	0	1.000
1974—American	PH	1	0	0	0	0	0	0	.000	0	0	0	.000
All-Star Game Totals		4	0	1	1	0	0	0	.250	8	0	0	1.000

CHAMPIONSHIP SERIES RECORD

Year Club	League	Pos.	G.	AB.	R.	H.	2B.	3B.	HR.	RBI.	B.A.	PO.	A.	E.	F.A.
1976—Kansas City	Amer.	1B	5	18	4	4	0	0	1	3	.222	48	1	0	1.000
1977—Kansas City	Amer.	1B	4	12	1	2	1	0	1	3	.167	29	1	2	.938
Championship Series Totals			9	30	5	6	1	0	2	6	.200	17	2	2	.975

LEE LOUIS MAZZILLI

Born March 25, 1955, at Brooklyn, N.Y.
Height, 6.01. Weight, 180.
Throws right and bats left and righthanded.
Hobby—Speed skating.
Son of Libero Mazzilli, former professional welterweight boxer.

Received reported $50,000 bonus to sign with New York Mets, 1973.
Major League stolen bases: 1976 (5), 1977 (22), 1978 (20), 1979 (34), 1980 (41). Total—122.
Led Texas League in walks with 111 in 1976.

Year Club	League	Pos.	G.	AB.	R.	H.	2B.	3B.	HR.	RBI.	B.A.	PO.	A.	E.	F.A.
1974—Anderson	W. Car.	OF	132	472	82	127	24	3	11	48	.269	227	9	9	.963
1975—Visalia	Calif.	OF-1B	125	430	103	121	10	4	13	52	.281	185	9	9	.956
1976—Jackson	Texas	OF	131	439	91	128	21	6	13	43	.292	262	8	8	.971
1976—New York	Nat.	OF	24	77	9	15	2	0	2	7	.195	55	2	1	.983
1977—New York	Nat.	OF	159	537	66	134	24	3	6	46	.250	386	9	3	.992
1978—New York	Nat.	OF	148	542	78	148	28	5	16	61	.273	386	8	5	.987
1979—New York	Nat.	OF-1B	158	597	78	181	34	4	15	79	.303	480	24	5	.990
1980—New York	Nat.	1B-OF	152	578	82	162	31	4	16	76	.280	874	53	14	.985
Major League Totals			641	2331	313	640	119	16	55	269	.275	2181	96	28	.988

Selected by New York Mets' organization in 1st round (14th player selected) of free-agent draft, June 5, 1973.

Tied All-Star Game record for most home runs by pinch-hitter, game (1), July 17, 1979.

Year	League	Pos.	AB.	R.	H.	2B.	3B.	HR.	RBI.	B.A.	PO.	A.	E.	F.A.
1979—National		PH-OF	1	1	1	0	0	1	2	1.000	0	0	0	.000

ARNOLD RAY McBRIDE
(Bake)

Born February 3, 1949, at Fulton, Mo.
Height, 6.02. Weight, 184.
Throws right and bats lefthanded.
Hobbies—Hunting, fishing and being around kids.
Attended Westminster College, Fulton, Mo.; received Bachelor of Arts degree in Physical Education.

Tied major league record for most chances accepted by right fielder, game (10), September 8, 1978.
Major League stolen bases: 1973 (0), 1974 (30), 1975 (26), 1976 (5), 1977 (36), 1978 (28), 1979 (25), 1980 (13). Total—163.
Named National League Rookie of the Year by Baseball Writers' Association of America, 1974.

Year	Club	League	Pos.	G.	AB.	R.	H.	2B.	3B.	HR.	RBI.	B.A.	PO.	A.	E.	F.A.
1970—Sarasota Cards	..Gulf C.		OF	17	71	15	30	2	4	2	13	.423	27	1	0	1.000
1970—Modesto	...........Calif.		OF	26	85	17	25	4	2	0	7	.294	26	1	4	.871
1971—Modesto	...........Calif.		OF	118	468	85	142	19	5	8	54	.303	181	9	6	.969
1972—Arkansas	...........Texas		OF	67	286	51	94	10	4	12	34	.329	130	3	3	.978
1972—Tulsa	................A.A.		OF	60	232	41	73	14	5	5	24	.315	108	5	1	.991
1973—Tulsa	................A.A.		OF	58	225	45	65	15	2	6	34	.289	111	7	3	.975
1973—St. Louis	...........Nat.		OF	40	63	8	19	3	0	0	5	.302	39	1	1	.976
1974—St. Louis	...........Nat.		OF	150	559	81	173	19	5	6	56	.309	395	9	4	.990
1975—St. Louis	...........Nat.		OF	116	413	70	124	10	9	5	36	.300	289	4	3	.990
1976—St. Louis‡	........Nat.		OF	72	272	40	91	13	4	3	24	.335	201	5	4	.981
1977—St.L.§-Phil.	........Nat.		OF	128	402	76	127	25	6	15	61	.316	188	8	2	.990
1978—Philadelphia	.....Nat.		OF	122	472	68	127	20	4	10	49	.269	234	8	1	*.996
1979—Philadelphia	.....Nat.		OF	151	582	82	163	16	12	12	60	.280	341	12	4	.989
1980—Philadelphia	.....Nat.		OF	137	554	68	171	33	10	9	87	.309	282	6	3	.990
Major League Totals				916	3317	493	995	139	50	60	378	.300	1969	53	22	.989

Selected by St. Louis Cardinals' organization in 37th round of free-agent draft, June 4, 1970.
†On supplemental disabled list, May 13 to June 4, 1975.
‡On disabled list, May 9 to May 24 and August 7 through remainder of 1976 season.
§Traded to Philadelphia Phillies with Pitcher Steve Waterbury for Pitcher Tom Underwood, First Baseman Dane Iorg, and Outfielder Rick Bosetti, June 15, 1977.

CHAMPIONSHIP SERIES RECORD

Tied Championship Series records for most home runs by pinch hitter, game, Series and total Series (1), October 7, 1978.
Tied National League Championship Series record for most stolen bases, five-game Series (2), 1980.

Year	Club	League	Pos.	G.	AB.	R.	H.	2B.	3B.	HR.	RBI.	B.A.	PO.	A.	E.	F.A.
1977—Philadelphia	.....Nat.		OF	4	18	2	4	0	0	1	2	.222	6	2	0	1.000
1978—Philadelphia	.....Nat.		OF-PH	3	9	2	2	0	0	1	1	.222	1	0	0	1.000
1980—Philadelphia	.....Nat.		OF	5	21	0	5	0	0	0	0	.238	11	3	1	.933
Championship Series Totals				12	48	4	11	0	0	2	3	.229	18	5	1	.958

WORLD SERIES RECORD

Year	Club	League	Pos.	G.	AB.	R.	H.	2B.	3B.	HR.	RBI.	B.A.	PO.	A.	E.	F.A.
1980—Philadelphia	.....Nat.		OF	6	23	3	7	1	0	1	5	.304	13	1	0	1.000

ALL-STAR GAME RECORD

Member of National League All-Star Team in 1976; did not play.

JAMES TIMOTHY McCARVER
(Tim)

Born October 16, 1941, at Memphis, Tenn.
Height, 6.01. Weight, 198.
Throws right and bats lefthanded.
Hobbies—Dancing and collecting matchbooks.
Attended Christian Brothers College, Memphis, Tenn., and Memphis State University, Memphis, Tenn.

Tied for National League lead in passed balls with 16 in 1963 and led with 18 in 1965.
Named as catcher on THE SPORTING NEWS National League All-Star Team, 1967.
Received reported $75,000 bonus to sign with St. Louis Cardinals, 1959.

Year	Club	League	Pos.	G.	AB.	R.	H.	2B.	3B.	HR.	RBI.	B.A.	PO.	A.	E.	F.A.
1959—Keokuk	............Midw.		C	65	275	58	99	6	4	3	24	.360	422	37	14	.970
1959—Rochester	........Int.		C	17	70	10	25	1	1	0	8	.357	94	9	0	1.000
1959—St. Louis	...........Nat.		C	8	24	3	4	1	0	0	0	.167	32	2	1	.971
1960—Memphis	...........South.		C	85	303	45	105	11	2	3	34	.347	500	26	4	.992
1960—St. Louis	...........Nat.		C	10	10	3	2	0	0	0	0	.200	9	0	0	1.000
1961—S. Juan-Char.	....Int.		C	81	275	26	63	10	0	1	27	.229	429	*51	5	.990
1961—St. Louis	...........Nat.		C	22	67	5	16	2	1	1	6	.239	86	9	3	.969

Year Club	League	Pos.	G.	AB.	R.	H.	2B.	3B.	HR.	RBI.	B.A.	PO.	A.	E.	F.A.
1962—Atlanta..............Int.		C	122	382	65	105	17	1	11	57	.275	*685	48	*11	.985
1963—St. Louis ....Nat.		C	127	405	39	117	12	7	4	51	.289	722	55	5	.994
1964—St. Louis ....Nat.		C	143	465	53	134	19	3	9	52	.288	762	43	*11	.987
1965—St. Louis ....Nat.		C	113	409	48	113	17	2	11	48	.276	687	43	4	*.995
1966—St. Louis ....Nat.		C	150	543	50	149	19	*13	12	68	.274	841	62	7	.992
1967—St. Louis ....Nat.		C	138	471	68	139	26	3	14	69	.295	819	*67	3	*.997
1968—St. Louis ....Nat.		C	128	434	35	110	15	6	5	48	.253	708	54	11	.986
1969—St. Louis†..........Nat.		C	138	515	46	134	27	3	7	51	.260	925	66	14	.986
1970—Philadelphia‡...Nat.		C	44	164	16	47	11	1	4	14	.287	314	18	3	.991
1971—Philadelphia ......Nat.		C	134	474	51	132	20	5	8	46	.278	673	51	11	.985
1972—Phil.‡‡-Mont.§ ...Nat.		C-O-3	122	391	33	96	13	1	7	34	.246	561	47	8	.987
1973—St. Louis ....Nat.		1B-C	130	331	30	88	16	4	3	49	.266	608	34	9	.986
1974—St. Louis x........Nat.		C-1B	74	106	13	23	0	1	0	11	.217	126	11	4	.972
1974—Boston ....Amer.		C	11	28	3	7	1	0	0	1	.250	37	5	0	1.000
1975—Boston y...........Amer.		C-1B	12	21	1	8	2	1	0	3	.381	21	4	1	.962
1975—Philadelphia ......Nat.		C-1B	47	59	6	15	2	0	1	7	.254	62	5	1	.985
1976—Philadelphia .....Nat.		C-1B	90	155	26	43	11	2	3	29	.277	265	9	0	.967
1977—Philadelphia .....Nat.		C-1B	93	169	28	54	13	2	6	30	.320	238	14	3	.988
1978—Philadelphia .....Nat.		C-1B	90	146	18	36	9	1	1	14	.247	215	14	2	.991
1979—Philadelphia z ...Nat.		C-OF	79	137	13	33	5	1	1	12	.241	174	12	2	.989
1980—Philadelphia a ...Nat.		1B	6	5	2	1	1	0	0	2	.200	8	0	0	1.000
National League Totals.....................			1886	5480	586	1486	239	56	97	641	.271	8835	616	102	.989
American League Totals.................			23	49	4	15	3	1	0	4	.306	58	9	1	.985
Major League Totals			1909	5529	590	1501	242	57	97	645	.271	8893	625	103	.989

Signed as free agent by St. Louis Cardinals' organization, June 8, 1959.

†Traded with Outfielders Curt Flood and Byron Browne and Pitcher Joe Hoerner to Philadelphia Phillies for First Baseman Richie Allen, Infielder Cookie Rojas and Pitcher Jerry Johnson, October 7, 1969. Flood refused to report and the Cardinals sent First Baseman Guillermo Montanez and a player to be named later to Philadelphia to complete the deal, April 8, 1970. Pitcher James Robert Browning was sent from St. Louis to Philadelphia as "the player to be named later," August 30, 1970.

‡On disabled list May 2 through September 1.

‡‡Traded to Montreal Expos for Catcher John Bateman, June 14, 1972.

§Traded to St. Louis Cardinals for Outfielder Jorge Roque, November 6, 1972.

xSold to Boston Red Sox, September 1, 1974.

yReleased, June 23, 1975; signed as a free agent by Philadelphia Phillies, July 1, 1975.

zReleased, November 7, 1979; re-signed by Phillies, September 1, 1980.

aReleased, October 24, 1980.

CHAMPIONSHIP SERIES RECORD

Year Club	League	Pos.	G.	AB.	R.	H.	2B.	3B.	HR.	RBI.	B.A.	PO.	A.	E.	F.A.
1976—Philadelphia ......Nat.		C-PH	2	4	0	0	0	0	0	0	.000	6	0	0	1.000
1977—Philadelphia ......Nat.		C-PH	3	6	1	1	0	0	0	0	.167	7	0	0	1.000
1978—Philadelphia ......Nat.		PH-C	2	4	2	0	0	0	0	1	.000	8	0	0	1.000
Championship Series Totals.............			7	14	3	1	0	0	0	1	.071	21	0	0	1.000

WORLD SERIES RECORD

Established World Series record for most chances accepted by catcher, inning (4), October 9, 1967 (ninth inning).

Tied World Series records for one or more hits, each game, seven-game Series, 1964; most times stealing home, game (1), October 15, 1964; most chances, catcher, game (18), October 2, 1968; most putouts, catcher, inning (3), October 2, 1968, (second inning and ninth inning).

Year Club	League	Pos.	G.	AB.	R.	H.	2B.	3B.	HR.	RBI.	B.A.	PO.	A.	E.	F.A.
1964—St. Louis ....Nat.		C	7	23	4	11	1	1	1	5	.478	57	1	0	1.000
1967—St. Louis ....Nat.		C	7	24	3	3	1	0	0	2	.125	55	4	0	1.000
1968—St. Louis ....Nat.		C	7	27	3	9	0	2	1	4	.333	61	1	0	1.000
World Series Totals........................			21	74	10	23	2	3	2	11	.311	173	6	0	1.000

ALL-STAR GAME RECORD

Year League		Pos.	AB.	R.	H.	2B.	3B.	HR.	RBI.	B.A.	PO.	A.	E.	F.A.
1966—National..............................		C	1	1	1	0	0	0	0	1.000	1	0	0	1.000
1967—National..............................		C	2	0	2	1	0	0	0	1.000	7	1	0	1.000
All-Star Game Totals........................			3	1	3	1	0	0	0	1.000	8	1	0	1.000

STEVEN EARL McCATTY
(Steve)

Born March 20, 1954, at Detroit, Mich.
Height, 6.03. Weight, 205.
Throws and bats righthanded.
Hobbies—Hockey and basketball.
Attended Macomb Community College, Warren, Mich.

Year Club	League	G.	IP.	W.	L.	Pct.	H.	R.	ER.	SO.	BB.	ERA.
1973—Lewiston..............................Northwest		19	70	2	2	.500	83	48	37	49	31	4.76
1974—Lewiston..............................Northwest		15	96	8	3	.727	99	58	35	62	42	3.28
1975—Modesto..............................California		37	126	4	8	.333	138	80	64	75	54	4.57
1976—Chattanooga........................Southern		36	77	5	4	.556	73	44	27	40	31	3.16

Year	Club	League	G.	IP.	W.	L.	Pct.	H.	R.	ER.	SO.	BB.	ERA.
1976—Tucson	P. Coast	5	10	1	1	.500	13	8	7	5	7	6.30
1977—Chattanooga	Southern	14	56	4	2	.667	46	14	12	39	10	1.93
1977—San Jose	P. Coast	23	146	7	8	.467	175	105	93	78	69	5.73
1977—Oakland	American	4	14	0	0	.000	16	9	8	9	7	5.14
1978—Vancouver†	P. Coast	39	55	7	4	.636	53	23	19	51	23	3.11
1978—Oakland	American	9	20	0	0	.000	26	14	10	10	9	4.50
1979—Odgen	P. Coast	8	20	1	1	.500	12	7	7	16	18	3.15
1979—Oakland	American	31	186	11	12	.478	207	106	87	87	80	4.21
1980—Oakland	American	33	222	14	14	.500	202	104	95	114	99	3.85
Major League Totals		77	442	25	26	.490	451	233	200	220	195	4.07

Signed as free agent by Oakland A's organization, June 24, 1973.
†Appeared as outfielder.

ROBERT CRAIG McCLURE
(Bob)

Born April 29, 1952, at Oakland, Calif.
Height, 5.11. Weight, 170.
Throws left and bats righthanded.
Hobbies—Hunting, fishing and cards.
Attended College of San Mateo, San Mateo, Calif.

Tied for Pioneer League lead in shutouts with 3 in 1973.

Year	Club	League	G.	IP.	W.	L.	Pct.	H.	R.	ER.	SO.	BB.	ERA.
1973—Billings	Pioneer	14	94	•10	2	.833	64	41	22	110	67	2.11
1974—Omaha	Am. Assoc.	21	136	5	8	.385	140	71	58	88	65	3.84
1975—Jacksonville†	Southern	9	42	3	2	.600	31	18	11	39	23	2.36
1975—Kansas City	American	12	15	1	0	1.000	4	0	0	15	14	0.00
1976—Omaha	Am. Assoc.	21	133	9	8	.529	133	61	44	91	41	2.98
1976—Kansas City‡	American	8	4	0	0	.000	3	4	4	3	8	9.00
1977—Milwaukee	American	68	71	2	1	.667	64	25	20	57	34	2.54
1978—Milwaukee	American	44	65	2	6	.250	53	30	27	47	30	3.74
1979—Milwaukee	American	36	51	5	2	.714	53	29	22	37	24	3.88
1980—Milwaukee	American	52	91	5	8	.385	83	34	31	47	37	3.07
Major League Totals		220	297	15	17	.469	260	122	104	206	147	3.15

Selected by Los Angeles Dodgers' organization in 3rd round of free-agent draft, January 10, 1973.
Selected by Kansas City Royals' organization in secondary phase of free-agent draft, June 5, 1973.
†On disabled list, April 15 to May 13 and June 5 to July 25, 1975.
‡Assigned to Milwaukee Brewers, March 15, 1977, to complete deal which sent Infielder Jamie Quirk and Outfielder Jim Wohlford to Milwaukee for Pitcher Jim Colborn and Catcher Darrell Porter, December 6, 1976.

DONALD ROSS McCORMACK
(Don)

Born September 18, 1955, at Omak, Wash.
Height, 6.03. Weight, 205.
Throws and bats righthanded.
Son of Ross McCormack, former minor league outfielder.

Led Appalachian League catchers in passed balls with 23 in 1974.
Led Carolina League catchers in fielding average with .979 in 1977.
Led American Association catchers in double plays with 8 in 1980.

Year	Club	League	Pos.	G.	AB.	R.	H.	2B.	3B.	HR.	RBI.	B.A.	PO.	A.	E.	F.A.
1974—Pulaski	Appal.	C	48	161	20	32	5	0	1	17	.199	271	26	7	.977
1975—Bat.-Aub.	NYP	C-O-1-3	46	161	21	36	10	1	2	25	.224	163	18	7	.963
1975—Spartanburg	W. Car.	C-1B-3B	24	79	13	16	4	0	1	11	.203	54	4	0	1.000
1976—Peninsula	Carol.	C-3B-1B	94	291	29	68	9	5	6	36	.234	390	48	7	.984
1977—Peninsula	Carol.	C-1B	94	316	37	79	13	0	9	37	.250	470	39	13	.975
1978—Reading	East.	C	78	244	34	78	14	1	3	30	.320	338	44	11	.972
1978—Oklahoma City	A. A.	C	40	147	19	46	7	0	7	31	.313	88	6	5	.949
1979—Oklahoma City	A. A.	C	115	384	45	100	18	3	3	55	.260	347	32	13	.967
1980—Oklahoma City	A. A.	C	121	411	55	108	16	3	14	64	.263	545	•56	13	.979
1980—Philadelphia	Nat.	C	2	1	0	1	0	0	0	0	1.000	6	0	0	1.000
Major League Totals			2	1	0	1	0	0	0	0	1.000	6	0	0	1.000

Selected by Philadelphia Phillies' organization in 4th round of free-agent draft, June 5, 1974.

WILLIE LEE McCOVEY

Born January 10, 1938, at Mobile, Ala.
Height, 6.04. Weight, 225.
Throws and bats lefthanded.
Hobbies—Reading comic books and attending motion pictures.

Established major league records for most intentional bases on balls, season (45), 1969; most seasons 20 or more intentional bases on balls (5); most seasons by first baseman (22).

Tied major league records for most home runs, inning (2) and most total bases, inning (8), April 12, 1973 (fourth inning) and June 27, 1977 (sixth inning); most home runs with bases filled by pinch-hitter, lifetime (3); most triples, first major league game (2), July 30, 1959; most seasons leading league in intentional bases on balls (4), (tied in 1971); most years leading league in errors by first baseman (5), (tied in 1967).

Tied modern major league record for most long hits, inning (2), April 12, 1973 (fourth inning) and June 27, 1977 (sixth inning).

Established National League records for most home runs by lefthanded hitter, lifetime (521); most home runs by first baseman, lifetime (439); most home runs with bases filled, lifetime (18).

Tied National League records for fewest errors by first baseman for leader in errors, season (13), 1977; made four hits in first major league game, July 30, 1959; most consecutive seasons played (22).

Hit three consecutive home runs in a game, on two occasions—September 22, 1963, and April 22, 1964. Hit three home runs in game, September 17, 1966.

Hit home runs in all 12 National League parks, 1970.

Led National League in slugging percentage with .545 in 1968, .656 in 1969 and .612 in 1970.

Led National League batters in bases on balls with 137 in 1970.

Led Georgia State League first basemen in double plays with 73 in 1955.

Led Pacific Coast League first basemen in double plays with 119 in 1958.

Named National League Rookie of the Year by THE SPORTING NEWS and National League Rookie of the Year by Baseball Writers' Association, 1959.

Named first baseman on THE SPORTING NEWS National League All-Star Teams, 1965-68-69-70.

Named by THE SPORTING NEWS as Major League Player of the Year, 1969.

Named Most Valuable Player in National League, 1969.

Named THE SPORTING NEWS National League Comeback Player of the Year, 1977.

Year—Club	League	Pos.	G.	AB.	R.	H.	2B.	3B.	HR.	RBI.	B.A.	PO.	A.	E.	F.A.
1955—Sandersville	Ga.-St.	1B	107	410	82	125	24	1	19	*113	.305	*897	51	23	.976
1956—Danville	Carol.	1B	152	519	119	161	*38	8	29	89	.310	1273	87	*34	.976
1957—Dallas	Texas	1B	115	395	63	111	21	9	11	65	.281	960	80	10	.990
1958—Phoenix	P.C.	1B	146	527	91	168	37	10	14	89	.319	*1171	69	*18	.986
1959—Phoenix	P.C.	1B	95	349	84	130	26	11	*29	●92	.372	896	43	16	.983
1959—San Francisco	Nat.	1B	52	192	32	68	9	5	13	38	.354	424	29	5	.989
1960—San Francisco	Nat.	1B	101	260	37	62	15	3	13	51	.238	557	39	9	.985
1960—Tacoma	P.C.	1B	17	63	14	18	1	2	3	16	.286	149	4	3	.980
1961—San Francisco	Nat.	1B	106	328	59	89	12	3	18	50	.271	669	55	11	.985
1962—San Francisco	Nat.	OF-1B	91	229	41	67	6	1	20	54	.293	186	9	3	.985
1963—San Francisco	Nat.	*OF-1B	152	564	103	158	19	5	●44	102	.280	363	21	*15	.962
1964—San Francisco	Nat.	OF-1B	130	364	55	80	14	1	18	54	.220	273	19	14	.954
1965—San Francisco	Nat.	1B	160	540	93	149	17	4	39	92	.276	1310	87	13	.991
1966—San Francisco	Nat.	1B	150	502	85	148	26	6	36	96	.295	1287	81	22	.984
1967—San Francisco	Nat.	1B	135	456	73	126	17	4	31	91	.276	1221	81	●15	.989
1968—San Francisco	Nat.	1B	148	523	81	153	16	4	*36	*105	.293	1305	103	*21	.985
1969—San Francisco	Nat.	1B	149	491	101	157	26	2	*45	*126	.320	1392	79	12	.992
1970—San Francisco	Nat.	1B	152	495	98	143	39	2	39	126	.289	1217	*134	*15	.989
1971—San Francisco	Nat.	1B	105	329	45	91	13	0	18	70	.277	828	63	*15	.983
1972—San Francisco†	Nat.	1B	81	263	30	56	8	0	14	35	.213	617	32	9	.986
1973—San Francisco‡	Nat.	1B	130	383	52	102	14	3	29	75	.266	930	76	12	.988
1974—San Diego	Nat.	1B	128	344	53	87	19	1	22	63	.253	815	47	11	.987
1975—San Diego	Nat.	1B	122	413	43	104	17	0	23	68	.252	979	73	15	.986
1976—San Diego§	Nat.	1B	71	202	20	41	9	0	7	36	.203	420	44	4	.991
1976—Oakland x	Amer.	DH	11	24	0	5	0	0	0	0	.208	0	0	0	.000
1977—San Francisco	Nat.	1B	141	478	54	134	21	0	28	86	.280	1072	60	*13	.989
1978—San Francisco	Nat.	1B	108	351	32	80	19	2	12	64	.228	721	44	10	.987
1979—San Francisco	Nat.	1B	117	353	34	88	9	0	15	57	.249	740	48	10	.987
1980—San Francisco y	Nat.	1B	48	113	8	23	8	0	1	16	.204	241	12	2	.992
National League Totals			2577	8173	1229	2206	353	46	521	1555	.270	17567	1236	256	.987
American League Totals			11	24	0	5	0	0	0	0	.208	0	0	0	.000
Major League Totals			2588	8197	1229	2211	353	46	521	1555	.270	17567	1236	256	.987

Signed as free agent by San Francisco Giants' organization, March 12, 1955.

†Placed on regular disabled list, April 19 through June 2, 1972.

‡Traded with Outfielder Bernie Williams (on Phoenix roster) to San Diego Padres for Pitcher Mike Caldwell, October 25, 1973.

§Sold to Oakland A's, August 30, 1976.

xPlayed out option year and granted free agency; signed as free agent with San Francisco Giants, January 6, 1977.

yOn voluntarily retired list, July 10, 1980.

CHAMPIONSHIP SERIES RECORD

Year—Club	League	Pos.	G.	AB.	R.	H.	2B.	3B.	HR.	RBI.	B.A.	PO.	A.	E.	F.A.
1971—San Francisco	Nat.	1B	4	14	2	6	0	0	2	6	.429	34	3	1	.974

WORLD SERIES RECORD

Tied World Series record for most positions played, Series (3), 1962 (first base, right field and left field).

Year—Club	League	Pos.	G.	AB.	R.	H.	2B.	3B.	HR.	RBI.	B.A.	PO.	A.	E.	F.A.
1962—San Francisco	Nat.	1B-OF	4	15	2	3	0	1	1	1	.200	23	4	2	.931

ALL-STAR GAME RECORD

Tied All-Star Game records for most home runs, game (2), July 23, 1969; most strikeouts, nine-inning game (3), July 9, 1968.

Year—League	Pos.	AB.	R.	H.	2B.	3B.	HR.	RBI.	B.A.	PO.	A.	E.	F.A.
1963—National	PH	1	0	0	0	0	0	0	.000	0	0	0	.000
1966—National	1B	3	0	0	0	0	0	0	.000	10	1	0	1.000
1968—National	1B	4	0	0	0	0	0	0	.000	10	0	0	1.000
1969—National	1B	4	2	2	0	0	2	3	.500	2	0	0	1.000
1970—National	1B	2	0	1	0	0	0	1	.500	1	0	0	1.000
1971—National	1B	2	0	0	0	0	0	0	.000	4	0	0	1.000
All-Star Game Totals		16	2	3	0	0	2	4	.188	27	1	0	1.000

ANDREW JOSEPH McGAFFIGAN
(Andy)

Born October 25, 1956, at West Palm Beach, Fla.
Height, 6.03. Weight, 185.
Throws and bats righthanded.
Attended Palm Beach Junior College, Lake Worth, Fla., and
Florida Southern College, Lakeland, Fla.

Named Southern League Pitcher of the Year, 1980.

Year Club	League	G.	IP.	W.	L.	Pct.	H.	R.	ER.	SO.	BB.	ERA.
1978—Oneonta	NYP	2	12	0	1	.000	14	8	6	13	9	4.50
1978—Ft. Lauderdale	Florida St.	11	66	4	5	.444	45	28	21	36	20	2.86
1979—West Haven	Eastern	23	144	10	6	.625	136	75	61	113	54	3.81
1980—Nashville†	Southern	31	170	15	5	.750	139	62	45	125	62	*2.38

Selected by Cincinnati Reds' organization in 36th round of free-agent draft, June 5, 1974.
Selected by Chicago White Sox' organization in 5th round of free-agent draft, January 7, 1976.
Selected by New York Yankees' organization in 6th round of free-agent draft, June 6, 1978.
†On disabled list, September 1 to September 22, 1980.

WILLIE DEAN McGEE

Born November 2, 1958, at San Francisco, Calif.
Height, 6.01. Weight, 176.
Throws right and bats right and lefthanded.
Attended Diablo Valley College, Pleasant Hill, Calif.

Year Club	League	Pos.	G.	AB.	R.	H.	2B.	3B.	HR.	RBI.	B.A.	PO.	A.	E.	F.A.
1977—Oneonta	NYP	OF	65	225	31	53	4	3	2	22	.236	103	5	10	.915
1978—Ft. Lauderdale	Fla. St.	OF	124	423	62	106	6	6	0	37	.251	243	12	9	.966
1979—West Haven	East.	OF	49	115	21	28	3	1	1	8	.243	88	3	3	.968
1979—Ft. Lauderdale	Fla. St.	OF	46	176	25	56	8	3	1	18	.318	103	3	2	.981
1980—Nashville†	South.	OF	78	223	35	63	4	5	1	22	.283	127	6	6	.957

Selected by Chicago White Sox' organization in 7th round of free-agent draft, June 8, 1976.
Selected by New York Yankees' organization in secondary phase of free-agent draft, January 11, 1977.
†On disabled list, May 22 to June 7 and July 14 to August 7, 1980.

LYNN EVERRATT McGLOTHEN

Name pronounced Mc-LAW-then.

Born March 27, 1950, at Monroe, La.
Height, 6.02. Weight, 195.
Throws right and bats lefthanded.
Hobbies—Hunting, fishing and listening to music.
Attended Grambling College, Grambling, La.

Tied major league record for striking out side on nine pitches, August 19, 1975 (second inning).
Led International League pitchers in complete games with 13 in 1971.
Led Carolina League pitchers in complete games with 16 and tied for lead in games started with 29 and in shutouts with 5 in 1970.
Named Carolina League Pitcher of the Year in 1970.

Year Club	League	G.	IP.	W.	L.	Pct.	H.	R.	ER.	SO.	BB.	ERA.
1968—Waterloo	Midwest	17	46	3	2	.600	45	20	17	34	36	3.33
1969—Winter Haven	Florida St.	32	179	15	8	.652	161	93	*78	153	106	3.92
1970—Winston-Salem	Carol.	31	*229	*15	7	.682	166	63	57	*202	91	2.24
1971—Louisville	Int'national	27	179	10	10	.500	162	89	74	151	98	3.72
1972—Louisville	Int'national	14	108	9	2	.818	69	24	23	88	39	1.92
1972—Boston	American	22	145	8	7	.533	135	66	55	112	59	3.41
1973—Pawtucket†	Int'national	9	53	2	4	.333	56	26	23	39	18	3.91
1973—Boston‡	American	6	23	1	2	.333	39	23	21	16	8	8.22
1974—St. Louis	National	31	237	16	12	.571	212	80	71	142	89	2.70
1975—St. Louis	National	35	239	15	13	.536	231	110	104	146	97	3.92
1976—St. Louis§	National	33	205	13	15	.464	209	96	89	106	68	3.91
1977—San Francisco x	National	21	80	2	9	.182	94	62	50	42	52	5.63
1978—San Fran. y-Chicago	National	54	93	5	3	.625	92	42	34	69	43	3.29
1979—Chicago	National	42	212	13	14	.481	236	103	97	147	55	4.12
1980—Chicago	National	39	182	12	14	.462	211	105	98	119	64	4.80
American League Totals		28	168	9	9	.500	174	89	76	128	67	4.07
National League Totals		255	1248	76	80	.487	1285	598	542	771	468	3.91
Major League Totals		283	1416	85	89	.489	1459	687	618	899	535	3.93

Selected by Boston Red Sox' organization in 3rd round of free-agent draft, June 7, 1968.
†On disabled list, July 3 to August 7, 1973.
‡Traded with Pitchers John Curtis and Mike Garman to St. Louis Cardinals for Pitchers Reggie Cleveland and Diego Segui and Infielder Terry Hughes, December 7, 1973.
§Traded to San Francisco Giants for Third Baseman Ken Reitz, December 10, 1976.
xOn disabled list, June 22 to July 13, 1977.
yTraded to Chicago Cubs for Outfielder Heity Cruz, June 15, 1978.

ALL-STAR GAME RECORD

Year League		IP.	W.	L.	Pct.	H.	R.	ER.	SO.	BB.	ERA.
1974—National		1	0	0	.000	0	0	0	1	0	0.000

FRANK EDWIN McGRAW, JR.
(Tug)
(Named by parents because he tugged on so many things as a baby.)

Born August 30, 1944, at Martinez, Calif.
Height, 6.00. Weight, 180.
Throws left and bats righthanded.
Attended Vallejo Junior College, Vallejo, Calif.
Brother of Hank McGraw, former outfielder-catcher in New York Met, Chicago Cub,
Philadelphia Phillie and Atlanta Brave organizations.

Pitched seven-inning, 4-0 no-hit victory against Cocoa, July 3, 1964.
Tied major league record for most home runs allowed, bases filled, season (4), 1979.
Established National League record for most saves, lifetime (164).
Major League saves: 1969 (12), 1970 (10), 1971 (8), 1972 (27), 1973 (25), 1974 (3), 1975 (14), 1976 (11), 1977 (9), 1978 (9), 1979 (16), 1980 (20). Total—164.

Year—Club	League	G.	IP.	W.	L.	Pct.	H.	R.	ER.	SO.	BB.	ERA.
1964—Florida Mets	Cocoa Rook.	8	47	5	2	.714	12	11	8	37	52	1.53
1964—Auburn	NYP	3	19	1	2	.333	17	12	4	14	15	1.89
1965—New York	National	37	98	2	7	.222	88	47	36	57	48	3.31
1966—New York	National	15	62	2	9	.182	72	38	37	34	25	5.37
1966—Jacksonville†	Int'national	11	32	2	2	.500	34	16	15	38	9	4.22
1967—Jacksonville	Int'national	22	167	10	9	.526	111	39	37	161	55	•1.99
1967—New York	National	4	17	0	3	.000	13	16	15	18	13	7.94
1968—Jacksonville‡	Int'national	24	166	9	9	.500	149	70	63	132	61	3.42
1969—New York	National	42	100	9	3	.750	89	31	25	92	47	2.25
1970—New York	National	57	91	4	6	.400	77	40	33	81	49	3.26
1971—New York	National	51	111	11	4	.733	73	22	21	109	41	1.70
1972—New York	National	54	106	8	6	.571	71	26	20	92	40	1.70
1973—New York§	National	60	119	5	6	.455	106	53	51	81	55	3.86
1974—New York§	National	41	89	6	11	.353	96	43	41	54	32	4.15
1975—Philadelphia x	National	56	103	9	6	.600	84	38	34	55	36	2.97
1976—Philadelphia	National	58	97	7	6	.538	81	34	27	76	42	2.51
1977—Philadelphia y	National	45	79	7	3	.700	62	25	23	58	24	2.62
1978—Philadelphia	National	55	90	8	7	.533	82	39	32	63	23	3.20
1979—Philadelphia za	National	65	84	4	3	.571	83	56	48	57	29	5.14
1980—Philadelphia za	National	57	92	5	4	.556	62	16	15	75	23	1.47
Major League Totals		697	1338	87	84	.509	1139	524	458	1002	527	3.08

Signed as free agent by New York Mets' organization, June 12, 1964.

†On disabled list, May 18 to June 11 and June 28 to July 8, 1966.

‡On disabled list, April 20 to April 30, 1968. On temporary inactive list, May 17 to May 20 and July 10 to July 20, 1968.

§On disabled list, May 16 to June 10, 1974. Traded with Outfielders Don Hahn and Dave Schneck to Philadelphia Phillies for Outfielder Del Unser, Pitcher Mac Scarce and Catcher John Stearns, December 3, 1974.

xOn disabled list, March 23 to April 25, 1975.

yOn disabled list, April 20 to June 18, 1977.

zOn disabled list, June 26 to July 17, 1980.

aGranted free agency, November 5, 1980; re-signed by Phillies, December 6, 1980.

CHAMPIONSHIP SERIES RECORD

Established Championship Series records for most games pitched, total Series (15); most games as relief pitcher, total Series (15); most saves, total Series (5); most games pitched, five-game Series (5), 1980; most saves, five game Series (2), 1980.

Tied Championship Series records for most Series pitched (6); most games finished, total Series (9).

Year—Club	League	G.	IP.	W.	L.	Pct.	H.	R.	ER.	SO.	BB.	ERA.
1969—New York	National	1	3	0	0	.000	1	0	0	1	1	0.00
1973—New York	National	2	5	0	0	.000	4	0	0	3	3	0.00
1976—Philadelphia	National	2	2⅓	0	0	.000	4	3	3	5	1	11.57
1977—Philadelphia	National	2	3	0	0	.000	1	0	0	3	2	0.00
1978—Philadelphia	National	3	5⅔	0	1	.000	3	2	1	5	5	1.59
1980—Philadelphia	National	5	8	0	1	.000	8	4	4	5	4	4.50
Championship Series Totals		15	27	0	2	.000	21	9	8	22	16	2.67

WORLD SERIES RECORD

Established World Series record for most saves, six-game Series (2), 1980.

Year—Club	League	G.	IP.	W.	L.	Pct.	H.	R.	ER.	SO.	BB.	ERA.
1973—New York	National	5	13⅔	1	0	1.000	8	5	4	14	9	2.63
1980—Philadelphia	National	4	7⅔	1	1	.500	7	1	1	10	8	1.17
World Series Totals		9	21⅓	2	1	.667	15	6	5	24	17	2.11

ALL-STAR GAME RECORD

Year—League		IP.	W.	L.	Pct.	H.	R.	ER.	SO.	BB.	ERA.
1972—National		2	1	0	1.000	1	0	0	4	0	0.00

Member of National League All-Star Team for 1975 game; did not play.

DID YOU KNOW—
That the last A.L. no-hitter was by Bert Blyleven in 1977?

SCOTT HOUSTON McGREGOR

Born January 18, 1954, at Inglewood, Calif.
Height, 6.01. Weight, 190.
Throws left and bats right and lefthanded.
Hobby—Photography.
Attended El Camino Junior College, Torrance, Calif. and Loyola Marymount University, Los Angeles, Calif.

Led International League pitchers in complete games with 12 in 1974.
Led Eastern League pitchers in complete games with 14 and tied for lead in games started with 27 in 1973.
Led International League in shutouts with 6 in 1976.
Named International League Pitcher of the Year, 1974.
Received reported $80,000 bonus to sign with New York Yankees, 1972.

Year Club	League	G.	IP.	W.	L.	Pct.	H.	R.	ER.	SO.	BB.	ERA.
1972—Ft. Lauderdale ....Florida St.		11	79	7	3	.700	66	30	24	54	25	2.73
1973—West Haven........................Eastern		27	∗197	●12	●13	.480	∗197	95	72	126	63	3.29
1974—Syracuse..........................Int'national		27	∗199	13	10	.565	204	88	76	124	75	3.44
1975—Syracuse† ....Int'national		21	124	6	9	.400	134	73	55	72	60	3.99
1976—Syracuse‡-Rochester ....Int'national		24	162	12	6	.667	159	59	55	83	40	3.06
1976—Baltimore ....American		3	15	0	1	.000	17	7	6	6	5	3.60
1977—Baltimore ....American		29	114	3	5	.375	119	57	56	55	30	4.42
1978—Baltimore ....American		35	233	15	13	.536	217	98	86	94	47	3.32
1979—Baltimore ....American		27	175	13	6	.684	165	70	65	81	23	3.34
1980—Baltimore ....American		36	252	20	8	.714	254	101	93	119	58	3.32
Major League Totals		130	789	51	33	.607	772	333	306	355	163	3.49

Selected by New York Yankees' organization in 1st round (14th player selected) of free-agent draft, June 6, 1972.
†On disabled list, August 1 to August 29, 1975.
‡Traded with Pitchers Rudy May, Felix Martinez and Dave Pagan, and Catcher Rich Dempsey to Baltimore Orioles for Pitchers Ken Holtzman, Doyle Alexander and Grant Jackson, Catcher Ellie Hendricks and Pitcher Jimmy Freeman, June 15, 1976.

CHAMPIONSHIP SERIES RECORD

Year Club	League	G.	IP.	W.	L.	Pct.	H.	R.	ER.	SO.	BB.	ERA.
1979—Baltimore ....American		1	9	1	0	1.000	6	0	0	4	1	0.00

WORLD SERIES RECORD

Year Club	League	G.	IP.	W.	L.	Pct.	H.	R.	ER.	SO.	BB.	ERA.
1979—Baltimore ....American		2	17	1	1	.500	16	6	6	8	2	3.18

DAVID LAWRENCE McKAY
(Dave)

Born March 14, 1950, at Vancouver, British Columbia, Canada.
Height, 6.00 Weight, 195.
Throws right and bats right and lefthanded.
Attended Columbia Basin Junior College, Pasco, Wash., and
Creighton University, Omaha, Neb.

Tied major league record by hitting home run, first major league appearance, August 22, 1975.

Year Club	League	Pos.	G.	AB.	R.	H.	2B.	3B.	HR.	RBI.	B.A.	PO.	A.	E.	F.A.
1971—Wis. Rapids.......Midw.		SS	65	257	27	58	9	0	3	22	.226	126	221	26	.930
1972—Lynchburg†.......Carol.		2-3-S	90	299	39	64	11	1	5	33	.214	145	238	23	.943
1973—Lynchburg ....Carol.		3-S-2	107	355	47	79	14	2	10	47	.223	107	204	22	.934
1974—Orlando ....South.		3B	100	360	59	100	12	2	8	41	.278	96	184	15	.949
1975—Tacoma ....P. C.		SS-3B	109	370	56	95	12	2	7	39	.257	174	264	31	.934
1975—Minnesota........Amer.		3B	33	125	8	32	4	1	2	16	.256	38	70	9	.923
1976—Minnesota........Amer.		3B-SS	45	138	8	28	2	0	0	8	.203	27	77	10	.912
1976—Tacoma‡..........P. C.		3-2-S	63	211	31	52	6	1	3	22	.246	40	123	12	.931
1977—Toronto ....Amer.		2-3-S	95	274	18	54	4	3	3	22	.197	141	205	14	.961
1978—Toronto ....Amer.		2-S-3	145	504	59	120	20	8	7	45	.238	310	414	12	.984
1979—Syracuse..........Int.		2B-3B	96	353	54	95	14	3	7	53	.269	189	272	9	.981
1979—Toronto§ ....Amer.		2B-3B	47	156	19	34	9	0	0	12	.276	119	150	7	.975
1980—Oakland...........Amer.		2-3-S	123	295	29	72	16	1	1	29	.244	155	242	10	.975
Major League Totals......................			488	1492	141	340	55	13	13	132	.228	765	1158	62	.969

Signed as free agent by Minnesota Twins' organization, June 20, 1971.
†On disabled list, May 15 to June 1, 1972.
‡Selected by Toronto Blue Jays in American League expansion draft, November 5, 1976.
§Released, November 5, 1979; signed by Oakland A's, April 4, 1980.

BYRON SCOTT McLAUGHLIN

Born September 29, 1955, at Van Nuys, Calif.
Height, 6.01. Weight, 175.
Throws and bats righthanded.
Attended Los Angeles Valley College, Van Nuys, Calif.

Year Club	League	G.	IP.	W.	L.	Pct.	H.	R.	ER.	SO.	BB.	ERA.
1975—Lodi..................................California		12	27	0	1	.000	29	17	14	12	17	4.67
1975—Bluefield† ....Ap'lachian		14	35	1	2	.333	45	31	29	32	15	7.46
1976—Victoria‡§ ....Gulf States		15	115	∗10	4	.714	104	48	39	74	46	3.05

Year Club	League	G.	IP.	W.	L.	Pct.	H.	R.	ER.	SO.	BB.	ERA.
1977—Nuevo Laredo ....Mexican		33	244	18	13	.581	186	76	50	*221	63	1.84
1977—Seattle...........................American		1	1	0	0	.000	5	4	4	1	0	36.00
1978—San Jose ....P. Coast		8	54	5	2	.714	45	23	21	52	32	3.50
1978—Seattle...........................American		20	107	4	8	.333	97	58	52	87	39	4.37
1979—Seattle...........................American		47	124	7	7	.500	114	58	58	74	60	4.21
1980—Seattle x ....American		45	91	3	6	.333	124	74	69	41	50	6.82
Major League Totals		113	323	14	21	.400	340	194	183	203	149	5.10

†Released, March 31, 1976; signed by Victoria, May 28, 1976.
‡Released, December 21, 1976; signed by Seattle Mariners' organization January 8, 1977.
§Loaned to Nuevo Laredo, April 1, 1977; returned, September 11, 1977.
xTraded to Minnesota Twins for Outfielder Willie Norwood, December 12, 1980.

RECORD AS HITTER

Year Club	League	Pos.	G.	AB.	R.	H.	2B.	3B.	HR.	RBI.	B.A.	PO.	A.	E.	F.A.
1974—W. Palm Beach† Fla. St.		DH-PH	7	16	1	5	0	0	1	.313	0	0	0	.000

Signed as free agent by Montreal Expos' organization, December 24, 1973.
†Released, June 6, 1974; signed by Baltimore Orioles' organization, March 4, 1975.

JOEY RICHARD McLAUGHLIN

Born July 11, 1956, at Tulsa, Okla.
Height, 6.02. Weight, 205.
Throws and bats righthanded.

Year Club	League	G.	IP.	W.	L.	Pct.	H.	R.	ER.	SO.	BB.	ERA.
1974—Kingsport..........................Ap'lachian		8	34	2	5	.286	41	27	20	32	15	5.29
1975—Greenwood.........................W. Carol.		20	122	12	5	.706	112	47	35	59	49	*2.58
1975—Savannah...........................Southern		8	53	4	3	.571	41	21	20	29	16	3.40
1976—Savannah...........................Southern		24	169	12	8	.600	165	69	52	70	44	2.77
1976—Richmond ....Int'national		1	1	0	0	.000	1	1	1	1	1	9.00
1977—Richmond†.........................Int'national		26	179	9	10	.474	188	96	76	70	74	3.82
1977—Atlanta ....National		3	6	0	0	.000	10	10	10	0	3	15.00
1978—Richmond‡.........................Int'national		26	179	9	13	.409	199	86	79	84	51	3.97
1979—Richmond ....Int'national		18	42	2	2	.500	31	16	10	33	18	2.14
1979—Atlanta§............................National		37	69	5	3	.625	54	23	19	40	34	2.48
1980—Toronto ....American		55	136	6	9	.400	159	79	68	70	53	4.50
National League Totals		40	75	5	3	.625	64	33	29	40	37	3.48
American League Totals		55	136	6	9	.400	159	79	68	70	53	4.50
Major League Totals..................................		95	211	11	12	.478	223	112	97	110	90	4.14

Selected by Atlanta Braves' organization in 2nd round of free-agent draft, June 5, 1974.
†On disabled list, April 15 to April 28, 1977.
‡On disabled list, April 14 to May 1, 1978.
§Traded with Outfielder Barry Bonnell to Toronto Blue Jays for First Baseman Chris Chambliss and Shortstop Luis Gomez, December 5, 1979.

HAROLD ABRAHAM McRAE
(Hal)

Born July 10, 1946, at Avon Park, Fla.
Height, 5.11. Weight, 180.
Throws and bats righthanded.
Attended Florida A&M University, Tallahassee, Fla.

Tied major league record for most long hits, doubleheader, 6, August 27, 1974, 5 doubles, 1 home run.
Major League stolen bases: 1968 (1), 1970 (0), 1971 (3), 1972 (0), 1973 (2), 1974 (11), 1975 (11), 1976 (22), 1977 (18), 1978 (17), 1979 (5), 1980 (10). Total—100.
Named designated hitter on THE SPORTING NEWS American League All-Star Team, 1976 and 1977.
Led American League designated hitters in doubles with 41 in 1977 and with 39 in 1978.
Led American League designated hitters in runs with 88 in 1978.

Year Club	League	Pos.	G.	AB.	R.	H.	2B.	3B.	HR.	RBI.	B.A.	PO.	A.	E.	F.A.
1965—Tampa ....Fla. St.		OF	22	65	3	10	3	0	0	4	.154	19	0	0	1.000
1966—Peninsula† ....Carol.		2B	109	394	65	113	19	4	11	56	.287	252	226	*28	.945
1967—Buffalo† ....Int.		2B	73	259	30	65	14	3	10	34	.251	133	208	23	.937
1967—Knoxville ....South.		2B	51	186	26	54	10	3	6	25	.290	140	136	12	.958
1968—Indianapolis .....P.C.		2B-OF	119	444	64	131	31	11	16	65	.295	222	307	14	.974
1968—Cincinnati ....Nat.		2B	17	51	1	10	1	0	0	2	.196	33	30	5	.926
1969—Indianapolis‡‡ ...A.A.		OF	17	41	2	9	1	0	0	4	.220	0	0	0	.000
1970—Cincinnati ....Nat.		OF-3-2	70	165	18	41	6	1	8	23	.248	53	7	1	.984
1971—Cincinnati ....Nat.		OF	99	337	39	89	24	2	9	34	.264	167	6	6	.966
1972—Cincinnati§........Nat.		OF-3B	61	97	9	27	4	0	5	26	.278	16	14	6	.833
1973—Kansas City......Amer.		OF-3B	106	338	36	79	18	3	9	50	.234	101	6	5	.955
1974—Kansas City......Amer.		OF-3B	148	539	71	167	36	4	15	88	.310	132	3	7	.951
1975—Kansas City......Amer.		OF-3B	126	480	57	147	38	6	5	71	.306	207	7	3	.986
1976—Kansas City......Amer.		OF	149	527	75	175	34	5	8	73	.332	63	2	2	.970
1977—Kansas City......Amer.		OF	•162	641	104	191	*54	11	21	92	.298	81	8	4	.957
1978—Kansas City ......Amer.		OF	156	623	90	170	39	5	16	72	.273	3	1	0	1.000

Year Club League	Pos.	G.	AB.	R.	H.	2B.	3B.	HR.	RBI.	B.A.	PO.	A.	E.	F.A.
1979—Kansas City x....Amer.	DH	101	393	55	113	32	4	10	74	.288	0	0	0	.000
1980—Kansas City y....Amer.	OF	124	489	73	145	39	5	14	83	.297	17	0	0	1.000
National League Totals..............		247	650	67	167	35	3	22	85	.257	269	57	18	.948
American League Totals.............		1072	4030	562	1187	290	43	98	603	.295	604	27	21	.968
Major League Totals		1319	4680	629	1354	325	46	120	688	.289	873	84	39	.961

Selected by Cincinnati Reds' organization in 6th round of free-agent draft, June, 1965.

†On disabled list, June 23 through July 6.

‡On disabled list, April 26 through May 7.

‡‡On disabled list, April 18 through May 28 and from July 4 through August 5.

§Traded with Pitcher Wayne Simpson to Kansas City Royals for Pitcher Roger Nelson and Outfielder Richie Scheinblum, November 30, 1972.

xOn supplemental disabled list, June 11 to July 6, 1979; on disabled list, July 6 to August 2, 1979.

yOn supplemental disabled list, May 13 to June 2, 1980.

CHAMPIONSHIP SERIES RECORD

Established Championship Series record for most runs, five-game Series (6), 1977.

Year Club League	Pos.	G.	AB.	R.	H.	2B.	3B.	HR.	RBI.	B.A.	PO.	A.	E.	F.A.
1970—Cincinnati ....Nat.	PH-OF	2	4	0	0	0	0	0	0	.000	2	0	0	1.000
1972—Cincinnati ....Nat.	PH	1	0	0	0	0	0	0	0	.000	0	0	0	.000
1976—Kansas City.......Amer.	DH	5	17	2	2	1	1	0	1	.118	5	1	0	1.000
1977—Kansas City.......Amer.	OF-DH	5	18	6	8	3	0	1	2	.444	2	1	0	1.000
1978—Kansas City......Amer.	DH	4	14	0	3	0	0	0	2	.214	0	0	0	.000
1980—Kansas City .....Amer.	DH	3	10	0	2	0	0	0	0	.200	0	0	0	.000
Championship Series Totals.............		20	63	8	15	4	1	1	5	.238	9	2	1	1.000

WORLD SERIES RECORD

Year Club League	Pos.	G.	AB.	R.	H.	2B.	3B.	HR.	RBI.	B.A.	PO.	A.	E.	F.A.
1970—Cincinnati ....Nat.	OF	3	11	1	5	2	0	0	3	.455	2	1	0	1.000
1972—Cincinnati ....Nat.	PH-OF	5	9	1	4	1	0	0	2	.444	4	0	0	1.000
1980—Kansas City ......Amer.	DH	6	24	3	9	3	0	0	1	.375	0	0	0	.000
World Series Totals		14	44	5	18	6	0	0	6	.409	6	1	0	1.000

ALL-STAR GAME RECORD

Year League	Pos.	AB.	R.	H.	2B.	3B.	HR.	RBI.	B.A.	PO.	A.	E.	F.A.
1975—American..........................	PH	1	0	0	0	0	0	0	.000	0	0	0	.000
1976—American..........................	PH	1	0	0	0	0	0	0	.000	0	0	0	.000
All-Star Game Totals		2	0	0	0	0	0	0	.000	0	0	0	.000

LARRY DEAN McWILLIAMS

Born February 10, 1954, at Wichita, Kan.
Height, 6.05. Weight, 175.
Throws and bats lefthanded.
Hobbies—Motorcycles and guitar.
Attended Paris Junior College, Paris, Tex.

Tied major league record for most strikeouts by batter, inning (2), April 22, 1979 (fourth inning).

Year Club League	G.	IP.	W.	L.	Pct.	H.	R.	ER.	SO.	BB.	ERA.
1974—Greenwood†.........................W. Carol.	11	64	4	3	.571	64	26	20	61	23	2.81
1975—Greenwood‡.........................W. Carol.	17	93	8	4	.667	83	36	29	71	18	2.81
1976—Greenwood.........................W. Carol.	8	48	2	2	.500	40	19	14	44	13	2.63
1976—Savannah............................Southern	16	74	3	8	.273	82	41	38	37	33	4.62
1977—Savannah............................Southern	26	158	8	9	.471	153	70	59	139	64	3.36
1978—Richmond ....Int'national	15	108	6	5	.545	87	36	34	78	41	2.83
1978—Atlanta ....National	15	99	9	3	.750	84	38	31	42	35	2.82
1979—Atlanta§...............................National	13	66	3	2	.600	69	41	41	32	22	5.59
1980—Atlanta ....National	30	164	9	14	.391	188	97	90	77	39	4.94
Major League Totals...............................	58	329	21	19	.525	341	176	162	151	96	4.43

Selected by Atlanta Braves' organization in 1st round (sixth player selected) of free-agent draft, January 9, 1974.

†On disabled list, July 22 to September 25, 1974.

‡On disabled list, April 11 to June 3, 1975.

§On disabled list, May 18 to June 15 and July 7 to September 1, 1979.

GEORGE FRANCIS MEDICH

Name pronounced Med-itch.

(Doc)

Born December 9, 1948, at Aliquippa, Pa.
Height, 6.05. Weight, 227.
Throws and bats righthanded.
Hobby—Sports in general.
Attended University of Pittsburgh, Pittsburgh, Pa.; received Bachelor of Science degree in Chemistry; received medical degree from University of Pittsburgh.

Tied major league record for most sacrifice flies allowed, season (15), 1975.

Year Club	League	G.	IP.	W.	L.	Pct.	H.	R.	ER.	SO.	BB.	ERA.
1970—Oneonta	NYP	4	31	3	1	.750	16	10	5	32	14	1.45
1970—Manchester	Eastern	8	42	0	5	.000	47	28	23	18	21	4.93
1971—Kinston†	Carolina	12	74	7	4	.636	47	21	20	72	23	2.43
1972—West Haven‡	Eastern	17	119	11	3	*.786	89	28	19	70	40	1.44
1972—New York	American	1	0	0	0	.000	2	2	2	0	2	.....
1973—New York	American	34	235	14	9	.609	217	84	77	145	74	2.95
1974—New York	American	38	280	19	15	.559	275	122	112	154	91	3.60
1975—New York§	American	38	272	16	16	.500	271	115	106	132	72	3.51
1976—Pittsburgh x	National	29	179	8	11	.421	193	80	70	86	48	3.52
1977—Oakland y-Sea.z	American	29	170	12	6	.667	181	98	86	77	53	4.55
1977—New York a	National	1	7	0	0	.000	6	3	3	3	1	3.86
1978—Texas	American	28	171	9	8	.529	166	78	71	71	52	3.74
1979—Texas	American	29	149	10	7	.588	156	78	69	58	49	4.17
1980—Texas	American	34	204	14	11	.560	230	104	89	91	56	3.93
American League Totals		231	1481	94	72	.566	1498	681	612	728	449	3.72
National League Totals		30	186	8	12	.400	199	83	73	89	49	3.53
Major League Totals		261	1667	102	84	.548	1697	764	685	817	498	3.70

Selected by New York Yankees' organization in 29th round of free-agent draft, June 4, 1970.

†On temporary inactive list from beginning of season until June 22, 1971.

‡On temporary inactive list from beginning of season until May 22, 1972.

§Traded to Pittsburgh Pirates for Pitchers Ken Brett and Dock Ellis and Second Baseman Willie Randolph, December 11, 1975.

xTraded with Pitchers Dave Giusti, Rick Langford and Doug Bair and Outfielders Mitchell Page and Tony Armas to Oakland A's for Infielders Phil Garner and Tommy Helms, and Pitcher Chris Batton, March 15, 1977.

ySold to Seattle Mariners, September 13, 1977.

zSold on waivers to New York Mets, September 26, 1977.

aGranted free agency, November 2, 1977; signed by Texas Rangers, November 11, 1977.

SAMUEL ELIAS MEJIAS

Name pronounced muh-HEE-us.

(Sam)

Born May 9, 1953, at Santiago, Dominican Republic.
Height, 6.00. Weight, 170.
Throws and bats righthanded.
Hobbies—Ping pong and playing the guitar.
Brother of Marcos Mejias, former outfielder in Milwaukee Brewers' organization.

Tied for New York-Pennsylvania League lead in double plays by outfielders with 3 in 1972.

Year Club	League	Pos.	G.	AB.	R.	H.	2B.	3B.	HR.	RBI.	B.A.	PO.	A.	E.	F.A.
1971—Newark	NYP	OF	66	227	34	59	14	0	4	26	.260	98	9	6	.947
1972—Danville	Midw.	OF	39	107	13	18	2	0	4	4	.168	52	4	0	1.000
1972—Newark	NYP	OF	59	232	38	72	14	3	5	32	.310	118	5	1	*.992
1973—Danville	Midw.	OF	114	432	70	107	16	9	6	39	.248	214	14	4	*.983
1974—Shreveport	Tex.	*OF-P	134	486	75	128	25	7	12	60	.263	*326	21	8	.977
1975—Thetford Mines	East.	OF	134	455	56	103	18	3	9	50	.226	280	11	8	.973
1976—Spokane†	P.C.	OF	51	123	13	29	8	0	0	6	.236	80	3	5	.943
1976—Tulsa	A. A.	OF-SS	70	263	49	85	13	3	6	30	.323	191	11	7	.967
1976—St. Louis‡	Nat.	OF	18	21	1	3	1	0	0	0	.143	19	1	0	1.000
1977—Montreal	Nat.	OF	74	101	14	23	4	1	3	8	.228	55	2	2	.966
1978—Montreal§	Nat.	OF-P	67	56	9	13	1	0	0	6	.232	35	2	2	.949
1979—Chi. x-Cin.	Nat.	OF	38	13	5	3	0	0	0	0	.231	8	0	1	.889
1979—Indianapolis	A. A.	OF	47	178	21	50	15	1	4	25	.281	112	4	0	1.000
1980—Cincinnati	Nat.	OF	71	108	16	30	5	1	1	10	.278	89	4	1	.989
Major League Totals			268	299	45	72	11	12	4	24	.241	206	9	6	.973

Signed as free-agent by Milwaukee Brewers' organization, October 24, 1970.

†Assigned to Tulsa on June 23 to complete deal which sent Pitcher Danny Frisella to Milwaukee Brewers, June 7, 1976.

‡Traded with Pitchers Bill Greif and Angel Torres to Montreal Expos for Pitcher Steve Dunning, Infielder Pat Scanlon, and Outfielder Tony Scott, November 6, 1976.

§Traded to Chicago Cubs for Infielder-Outfielder Rodney Scott and Outfielder Jerry White, December 14, 1978.

xSold to Cincinnati Reds, July 4, 1979.

PITCHING RECORD

Year Club	League	G.	IP.	W.	L.	Pct.	H.	R.	ER.	SO.	BB.	ERA.
1974—Shreveport	Texas	1	1	0	0	.000	3	3	3	0	0	27.00
1978—Montreal	National	1	1	0	0	.000	0	0	0	0	0	0.00

GARY LEON MELSON

Born February 27, 1953, at New Albany, Ind.
Height, 6.01. Weight, 180.
Throws and bats righthanded.
Attended Middle Tennessee State University, Murfreesboro, Tenn.;
received Bachelor of Science degree in Chemistry and Biology.

Year Club	League	G.	IP.	W.	L.	Pct.	H.	R.	ER.	SO.	BB.	ERA.
1975—San Jose	California	15	94	7	8	.467	84	47	36	92	51	3.45
1976—San Jose	California	2	2	1	0	1.000	2	3	2	1	3	9.00

Year Club	League	G.	IP.	W.	L.	Pct.	H.	R.	ER.	SO.	BB.	ERA.
1977—Jersey City ....Eastern	13	79	6	4	.600	72	35	28	55	27	3.19
1977—Toledo ....Int'national	13	85	3	7	.300	91	59	51	43	46	5.40
1978—Chattanooga....................Southern	12	74	7	3	.700	76	36	32	49	31	3.89
1978—Portland ....P. Coast	14	63	4	5	.444	90	59	55	32	31	7.86
1979—Tacoma†‡ ....P. Coast	26	137	6	9	.400	134	69	54	105	68	3.55
1980—Richmond ....Int'national	28	139	7	10	.412	117	53	44	110	64	2.85

Selected by Cleveland Indians' organization in 15th round of free-agent draft, June 4, 1975.

†On disabled list, June 24 to July 11, 1979.

‡Traded to Atlanta Braves' organization for Pitcher Don Collins, February 15, 1980.

DONALD KEVIN MENDON

(Known by middle name.)

Born August 7, 1956, at Corona, Calif.
Height, 6.04. Weight, 175.
Throws and bats righthanded.
Attended Kansas City Community College, Kansas City, Kan., and
Emporia State University, Emporia, Kan.

Year Club	League	G.	IP.	W.	L.	Pct.	H.	R.	ER.	SO.	BB.	ERA.
1978—Jamestown ....NYP	12	85	6	3	.667	84	40	32	73	22	3.39
1979—West Palm Beach ....Florida St.	28	196	13	11	.542	188	79	53	143	69	2.43
1980—Memphis..............................Southern	14	95	7	2	.778	91	35	29	59	23	2.75
1980—Denver ....Am. Assoc.	13	74	7	1	.875	75	43	35	40	35	4.26

Selected by Montreal Expos' organization in 18th round of free-agent draft, June 6, 1978.

MARIO MENDOZA (AIZPURU)

Born December 26, 1950, at Chihuahua, Mexico.
Height, 5.11. Weight, 187.
Throws and bats righthanded.
Hobby—Billiards.

Led Carolina League shortstops in double plays with 79 in 1972.

Year Club	League	Pos.	G.	AB.	R.	H.	2B.	3B.	HR.	RBI.	B.A.	PO.	A.	E.	F.A.
1970—Brad'n Pirates† .Gulf C.	SS-2B	47	167	21	44	5	2	0	21	.263	60	126	10	.949
1971—Monroe ....W. Car.	S-3	106	364	45	85	11	1	7	36	.234	139	262	30	.980
1972—Salem ....Carol.	SS	136	461	48	102	10	4	3	46	.221	211	365	40	.935
1973—Sherbrooke........East.	SS	132	488	54	131	22	2	8	43	.268	227	407	•35	.948
1974—Charleston ....Int.	SS	2	7	0	0	0	0	0	1	.000	4	4	0	1.000
1974—Pittsburgh ....Nat.	SS	91	163	10	36	1	2	0	15	.221	77	187	10	.964
1975—Charleston ....Int.	SS	31	106	14	29	7	0	0	8	.274	54	68	7	.947
1975—Pittsburgh.........Nat.	SS-3B	56	50	8	9	1	0	0	2	.180	29	70	5	.952
1976—Pittsburgh.........Nat.	S-3-2	50	92	6	17	5	0	0	12	.185	42	105	5	.967
1976—Charleston ....Int.	SS-3B	7	29	3	6	0	0	2	4	.207	13	11	2	.923
1977—Pittsburgh.........Nat.	S-3-P	70	81	5	16	3	0	0	4	.198	41	87	10	.928
1978—Pittsburgh‡.......Nat.	2B-3B-SS	57	55	5	12	1	0	1	3	.218	28	61	5	.947
1979—Seattle ....Amer.	SS	148	373	26	74	10	3	1	29	.198	177	422	19	.969
1980—Seattle§ ....Amer.	SS	114	277	27	68	6	3	2	14	.245	149	290	19	.959
National League Totals...................		324	441	34	90	11	2	1	36	.204	217	510	35	.954
American League Totals		262	650	53	142	16	6	3	43	.218	326	712	39	.964
Major League Totals......................		586	1091	87	232	27	8	4	79	.213	543	1222	74	.960

Signed as free agent by Pittsburgh Pirates' organization, July 14, 1970.

†On temporary inactive list, April 6 to July 14, 1970.

‡Traded with Pitchers Odell Jones and Rafael Vasquez to Seattle Mariners for Pitchers Enrique Romo and Rick Jones and Shortstop Tom McMillan, December 5, 1978.

§Traded with Catcher Larry Cox, Pitcher Rick Honeycutt and Outfielders Willie Horton and Leon Roberts to Texas Rangers for Pitchers Brian Allard, Ken Clay, Steve Finch and Jerry Gleaton, Outfielder Richie Zisk and Shortstop Rick Auerbach, December 12, 1980.

CHAMPIONSHIP SERIES RECORD

Year Club	League	Pos.	G.	AB.	R.	H.	2B.	3B.	HR.	RBI.	B.A.	PO.	A.	E.	F.A.
1974—Pittsburgh.........Nat.	SS	3	5	0	1	0	0	0	1	.200	4	7	0	1.000

PITCHING RECORD

Year Club	League	G.	IP.	W.	L.	Pct.	H.	R.	ER.	SO.	BB.	ERA.
1977—Pittsburgh ....National	1	2	0	0	.000	3	3	3	0	2	13.50

ORLANDO MERCADO

Born November 7, 1961, at Arecibo, Puerto Rico.
Height, 6.00. Weight, 180.
Throws and bats righthanded.

Led California League catchers in passed balls with 24 in 1979.
Led Eastern League catchers in passed balls with 23 in 1980.

Year Club	League	Pos.	G.	AB.	R.	H.	2B.	3B.	HR.	RBI.	B.A.	PO.	A.	E.	F.A.
1978—Bellingham ....Northw.	C	38	49	7	6	2	0	0	5	.122	184	20	4	.981
1979—San Jose ....Calif.	C-1B	110	335	53	86	18	2	10	54	.257	629	71	17	.976
1980—Lynn.................East.	C-1B	117	396	55	101	25	6	11	71	.255	607	78	11	.984

Signed as free agent by Seattle Mariners' organization, January 6, 1978.

ROGER HENRY METZGER

Born October 10, 1947, at Fredericksburg, Tex.
Height, 6.00. Weight, 165.
Throws right and bats right and lefthanded.
Hobbies—Water skiing, golf, fishing and hunting.
Attended Arizona State University, Tempe, Ariz., and St. Edward's University, Austin, Tex.;
received degree in Mathematics.

Established major league record for most consecutive errorless games by shortstop, season, 59, June 8-August 15 (1st game), 1976.
Led National League shortstops in double plays with 101 in 1972.
Named shortstop on THE SPORTING NEWS National League All-Star fielding team, 1973.

Year	Club	League	Pos.	G.	AB.	R.	H.	2B.	3B.	HR.	RBI.	B.A.	PO.	A.	E.	F.A.
1969—Tacoma		P. C.	SS	80	250	34	58	3	2	0	15	.232	148	276	22	.951
1970—Tacoma		P. C.	SS	134	492	59	133	20	7	1	32	.270	212	*483	37	.949
1970—Chicago†		Nat.	SS	1	2	0	0	0	0	0	0	.000	1	4	1	.833
1971—Houston		Nat.	SS	150	562	64	132	14	●11	0	26	.235	*275	459	17	.977
1972—Houston		Nat.	SS	153	641	84	142	12	3	2	38	.222	238	504	22	.971
1973—Houston		Nat.	SS	154	580	67	145	11	*14	1	35	.250	231	429	12	*.982
1974—Houston‡		Nat.	SS	143	572	66	145	18	10	0	30	.253	238	451	17	.976
1975—Houston		Nat.	SS	127	450	54	102	7	9	2	26	.227	186	441	15	.977
1976—Houston		Nat.	*SS-2B	152	481	37	101	13	8	0	29	.210	258	468	10	*.986
1977—Houston§		Nat.	SS-2B	97	269	24	50	9	6	0	16	.186	130	260	11	.973
1978—Hous.x-S. F.		Nat.	SS-2B	120	358	28	88	10	2	0	23	.246	171	289	14	.970
1979—San Francisco		Nat.	SS-2B-3B	94	259	24	65	7	8	0	31	.251	122	237	15	.960
1980—San Francisco y		Nat.	SS-2B	28	27	5	2	0	0	0	0	.074	14	19	1	.971
Major League Totals				1219	4201	453	972	101	71	5	254	.231	1864	3561	135	.976

Selected by Chicago Cubs' organization in 1st round (16th player selected) of free-agent draft, June 5, 1969.
†Traded to Houston Astros for Shortstop Hector Torres, October 12, 1970.
‡On supplemental disabled list, April 29 to May 17, 1974.
§On disabled list, April 27 to June 16, 1977.
xTraded to San Francisco Giants for a player to be named later, June 15, 1978; deal completed with payment of cash, November 1, 1978.
yReleased, August 16, 1980.
Coach, San Francisco Giants, August 16, 1980 through remainder of season; scout, San Francisco Giants, 1981.

DANIEL THOMAS MEYER
(Dan)

Born August 3, 1952, at Hamilton, O.
Height, 5.11. Weight, 180.
Throws right and bats lefthanded.
Attended Santa Ana College, Santa Ana, Calif., and University
of Arizona, Tucson, Ariz.

Tied major league record for most times awarded first base on catcher's interference, game (2), May 3, 1977.
Led Appalachian League in total bases with 158 in 1972.
Led American Association in sacrifice flies with 9 in 1974.
Named Appalachian League Player of the Year in 1972.

Year	Club	League	Pos.	G.	AB.	R.	H.	2B.	3B.	HR.	RBI.	B.A.	PO.	A.	E.	F.A.
1972—Bristol		Appal.	*3-2-O	65	235	54	*93	11	6	14	46	*.396	69	*124	13	.937
1973—Lakeland		Fla. St.	2B	133	473	63	114	17	6	10	59	.241	295	297	21	.966
1974—Evansville		A. A.	3-O-1	129	484	75	146	26	7	9	57	.302	238	153	22	.947
1974—Detroit		Amer.	OF	13	50	5	10	1	1	3	7	.200	29	0	1	.967
1975—Detroit†		Amer.	OF-1B	122	470	56	111	17	3	8	47	.236	571	41	12	.981
1976—Detroit‡		Amer.	OF-1B	105	294	37	74	8	4	2	16	.252	244	14	2	.992
1977—Seattle		Amer.	1B	159	582	75	159	24	4	22	90	.273	1407	109	12	.992
1978—Seattle§		Amer.	1B-OF	123	444	38	101	18	1	8	56	.227	1107	79	13	.989
1979—Seattle		Amer.	3B-O-1B	144	525	72	146	21	7	20	74	.278	198	205	22	.948
1980—Seattle		Amer.	OF-3-1	146	531	56	146	25	6	11	71	.275	219	22	10	.960
Major League Totals				812	2896	339	747	114	26	74	361	.258	3775	470	72	.983

Selected by Detroit Tigers' organization in 4th round of free-agent draft, June 6, 1972.
†On supplemental disabled list, July 20 to August 6, 1975.
‡Selected by Seattle Mariners in American League expansion draft, November 5, 1976.
§On supplemental disabled list, May 24 to June 8, 1978.

SCOTT WILLIAM MEYER

Born August 19, 1957, at Evergreen Park, Ill.
Height, 6.01. Weight, 195.
Throws and bats righthanded.
Attended Western Michigan University, Kalamazoo, Mich.

Led Eastern League catchers in passed balls with 23 in 1978 and with 33 in 1979.

Year	Club	League	Pos.	G.	AB.	R.	H.	2B.	3B.	HR.	RBI.	B.A.	PO.	A.	E.	F.A.
1978—Jersey City		East.	C	48	169	18	44	10	0	5	24	.260	223	23	3	.988
1978—Oakland		Amer.	C	8	9	1	1	1	0	0	0	.111	11	0	0	1.000

Year	Club	League	Pos.	G.	AB.	R.	H.	2B.	3B.	HR.	RBI.	B.A.	PO.	A.	E.	F.A.
1979—Waterbury		East.	C-OF	129	465	37	99	26	3	6	57	.213	541	86	14	.978
1980—West Haven†		East.	C	101	362	47	88	21	1	7	45	.243	305	51	10	.973
Major League Totals				8	9	1	1	1	0	0	0	.111	11	0	0	1.000

Selected by Oakland A's organization in 6th round of free-agent draft, June 6, 1978.
†On disabled list, July 21 to August 22, 1980.

LAWRENCE WILLIAM MILBOURNE

Name pronounced MILL-born.

(Larry)

Born February 14, 1951, at Port Norris, N. J.
Height, 6.00. Weight, 165.
Throws right and bats left and righthanded.
Hobbies—Music and reading.
Attended Glassboro State College, Glassboro, N. J., and Cumberland
County Junior College, Vineland, N. J.
Brother of Monty Milbourne, former minor leaguer in Chicago White Sox' organization.

Year	Club	League	Pos.	G.	AB.	R.	H.	2B.	3B.	HR.	RBI.	B.A.	PO.	A.	E.	F.A.
1969—Bluefield†		Appal.	SS	•69	246	49	75	10	•6	4	35	.305	94	171	*28	.904
1970—								(Did not play)								
1971—Decatur‡		Texas	2B	122	416	50	110	14	5	2	36	.264	273	314	25	.959
1972—Shreveport§		Midw.	*2-S-3	*123	*518	69	*156	23	5	5	38	.301	267	256	27	*.951
1973—Tulsa x		A. A.	2-3-O-S	111	367	55	104	13	6	5	43	.283	158	197	16	.957
1974—Houston		Nat.	2-S-O	112	136	31	38	2	1	0	9	.279	102	148	7	.973
1975—Iowa		A. A.	2B	24	77	9	17	3	1	1	6	.221	33	47	8	.909
1975—Houston		Nat.	2B-SS	73	151	17	32	1	2	1	9	.212	95	136	10	.959
1976—Houston		Nat.	2B	59	145	22	36	4	0	0	7	.248	67	100	6	.965
1976—Memphis y		Int.	2B-SS	71	292	45	95	12	2	5	31	.325	132	245	13	.967
1977—Seattle		Amer.	2-S-3	86	242	24	53	10	0	2	21	.219	120	209	12	.965
1978—Seattle		Amer.	3-SS-2B	93	234	31	53	6	2	2	20	.226	92	169	9	.967
1979—Seattle		Amer.	SS-2B-3B	123	356	40	99	13	4	2	26	.278	144	265	12	.971
1980—Seattle z		Amer.	SS-3-2	106	258	31	68	6	6	0	26	.264	103	195	8	.987
National League Totals				244	432	70	106	7	3	1	25	.245	264	384	23	.966
American League Totals				408	1090	126	273	35	12	6	93	.250	459	838	41	.969
Major League Totals				652	1522	196	379	42	15	7	118	.249	723	1222	64	.968

Signed as free agent by Baltimore Orioles' organization, June 18, 1969.
†Released by Bluefield (Baltimore Orioles' organization), April 7, 1970; signed as free agent by Decatur (San Francisco Giants' organization), April 2, 1971.
‡Drafted from Amarillo (San Francisco Giants' organization) by Salt Lake City (California Angels' organization), November 29, 1971.
§Drafted from Shreveport (California Angels' organization) by Tulsa (St. Louis Cardinals' organization), November 27, 1972.
xDrafted from Tulsa (St. Louis Cardinals' organization) by Houston Astros, December 3, 1973.
yTraded to Seattle Mariners for Pitcher Roy Thomas, March 30, 1977.
zTraded to New York Yankees for Catcher Brad Gulden, November 18, 1980.

DYAR K. MILLER

Born May 29, 1946, at Batesville, Ind.
Height, 6.01. Weight, 202.
Throws and bats righthanded.
Attended Utah State University, Logan, Utah.
Pitched seven-inning, 10-0 no-hit victory against Amarillo, May 9, 1970.

Year	Club	League	G.	IP.	W.	L.	Pct.	H.	R.	ER.	SO.	BB.	ERA.
1968—Huron†		Northern	1	1	0	0	.000	2	4	3	0	3	27.00
1969—Stockton		California	25	116	4	4	.500	80	36	30	111	58	2.33
1970—Dallas-Fort Worth		Texas	26	170	12	10	.545	149	69	61	102	83	3.23
1971—Dallas-Fort Worth		Texas	25	88	3	8	.273	65	47	34	74	58	3.48
1972—Asheville‡		Southern	15	49	4	1	.800	50	25	24	46	27	4.41
1973—Rochester§		Int'national	15	72	6	3	.667	53	27	22	41	29	2.75
1974—Rochester		Int'national	28	190	12	8	.600	143	65	57	138	95	2.70
1975—Rochester		Int'national	19	41	5	0	1.000	24	10	10	38	25	2.20
1975—Baltimore		American	30	46	6	3	.667	32	14	14	33	16	2.74
1976—Baltimore		American	49	89	2	4	.333	79	31	29	37	36	2.93
1977—Baltimore x-California		American	53	115	6	6	.500	106	49	45	58	40	3.52
1978—California y		American	41	85	6	2	.750	85	29	25	34	41	2.65
1979—California z-Toronto ab		American	24	51	1	0	1.000	71	32	31	23	18	5.47
1979—Denver c		Am. Assoc.	15	25	2	0	1.000	20	6	5	18	12	1.80
1980—Tidewater		Int'national	29	52	4	2	.667	66	33	27	35	23	4.67
1980—New York		National	31	42	1	2	.333	37	9	9	28	11	1.93
American League Totals			197	386	21	15	.583	373	155	144	185	151	3.36
National League Totals			31	42	1	2	.333	37	9	9	28	11	1.93
Major League Totals			228	428	22	17	.564	410	164	153	213	162	3.22

Signed as free agent by Philadelphia Phillies' organization, July 7, 1968.
†Released by Philadelphia Phillies' organization, July 28, 1968; signed as free agent by Baltimore Orioles' organization, January 16, 1969.
‡On disabled list from beginning of season until April 24, 1972.

§On disabled list, June 11 to June 25, 1973. On temporary inactive list, August 18 to September 2, 1973.
xTraded to California Angels for Pitcher Dick Drago, June 13, 1977.
yOn disabled list, July 26 to August 18, 1978.
zSold to Toronto Blue Jays, June 6, 1979.
aLoaned to Montreal Expos' organization, July 30, 1979; returned, August 27, 1979.
bTraded to Montreal Expos, October 24, 1979, completing deal in which Toronto acquired First Baseman Tony Solaita, July 30, 1979.
cReleased, March 30, 1980; signed by New York Mets' organization, April 12, 1980.

RECORD AS CATCHER

Year Club	League	Pos.	G.	AB.	R.	H.	2B.	3B.	HR.	RBI.	B.A.	PO.	A.	E.	F.A.
1968—Huron†	North.	C	4	7	1	1	0	0	0	0	.143	18	3	2	.913

EDWARD LEE MILLER JR.
(Eddie)

Born June 29, 1957, at San Pablo, Calif.
Height, 5.09. Weight, 165.
Throws right and bats left and righthanded.

Led Gulf Coast League in walks with 51 and in stolen bases with 30 in 1975.
Led Western Carolinas League in stolen bases with 65 in 1976.
Led Texas League in stolen baes with 80 in 1977.
Led International League in stolen bases with 76 in 1979 and with 60 in 1980.

Year Club	League	Pos.	G.	AB.	R.	H.	2B.	3B.	HR.	RBI.	B.A.	PO.	A.	E.	F.A.
1975—Sara. Rangers ...	Gulf C.	OF	51	180	*47	46	5	3	0	21	.256	*125	2	5	.962
1976—Asheville..........	W. Car.	OF	116	443	100	117	14	3	1	39	.264	299	18	14	.958
1977—Tulsa	Texas	OF	100	374	74	110	11	9	1	37	.294	219	17	8	.967
1977—Texas†	Amer.	OF	17	6	7	2	0	0	0	1	.333	4	0	0	1.000
1978—Richmond	Int.	OF	130	497	64	124	19	4	2	38	.249	312	*16	5	.985
1978—Atlanta	Nat.	OF	6	21	5	3	1	0	0	2	.143	7	0	0	1.000
1979—Richmond	Int.	OF	135	517	73	121	18	*11	5	37	.234	*335	13	5	.986
1979—Atlanta	Nat.	OF	27	113	12	35	1	0	0	5	.310	79	1	1	.988
1980—Richmond	Int.	OF	110	411	57	86	11	1	0	22	.209	218	9	7	.970
1980—Atlanta	Nat.	OF	11	19	3	3	0	0	0	0	.158	6	0	0	1.000
American League Totals			17	6	7	2	0	0	0	1	.333	4	0	0	1.000
National League Totals			44	153	20	41	2	0	0	7	.268	92	1	1	.989
Major League Totals.......................			61	159	27	43	2	0	0	8	.270	96	1	1	.990

Selected by Texas Rangers' organization in 2nd round of free-agent draft, June 4, 1975.
†Traded with Pitchers Adrian Devine and Tommy Boggs to Atlanta Braves for First Baseman Willie Montanez, December 8, 1977.

RICHARD ALLAN MILLER
(Rick)

Born April 19, 1948, at Grand Rapids, Mich.
Height, 6.00. Weight, 185.
Throws and bats lefthanded.
Hobbies—paddle ball and most sports activities.
Attended Michigan State University, East Lansing, Mich.
Brother-in-law of Carlton Fisk, catcher for Boston Red Sox.

Led International League batters in bases on balls with 106 in 1971.
Named outfielder on THE SPORTING NEWS American League All-Star fielding team, 1978.

Year Club	League	Pos.	G.	AB.	R.	H.	2B.	3B.	HR.	RBI.	B.A.	PO.	A.	E.	F.A.
1969—Pittsfield..........	East.	OF	77	221	25	58	7	1	6	32	.262	150	8	3	.981
1970—Pawtucket........	East.	OF	113	381	69	94	16	4	12	56	.247	227	5	5	.979
1971—Louisville	Int.	OF	133	461	79	114	24	2	15	58	.247	267	21	6	.980
1971—Boston	Amer.	OF	15	33	9	11	5	0	1	7	.333	30	1	1	.969
1972—Boston	Amer.	OF	89	98	13	21	4	1	3	15	.214	80	7	3	.967
1973—Boston	Amer.	OF	143	441	65	115	17	7	6	43	.261	301	4	7	.978
1974—Boston	Amer.	OF	114	280	41	73	8	1	5	22	.261	253	7	3	.989
1975—Boston	Amer.	OF	77	108	21	21	2	1	0	15	.194	101	2	2	.981
1976—Boston	Amer.	OF	105	269	40	76	15	3	0	27	.283	220	4	2	.991
1977—Boston†‡	Amer.	OF	86	189	34	48	9	3	0	24	.254	118	5	1	.992
1978—California	Amer.	OF	132	475	66	125	25	4	1	37	.263	353	9	4	.989
1979—California§........	Amer.	OF	120	427	60	125	15	5	2	28	.293	349	3	4	.989
1980—California x.......	Amer.	OF	129	142	52	113	14	3	2	38	.274	299	11	5	.984
Major League Totals			1010	2462	401	728	114	28	20	256	.296	2104	53	32	.985

Selected by Boston Red Sox' organization in 2nd round of free-agent draft, June 5, 1969.
†On disabled list, May 3 to May 30, 1977.
‡Granted free agency, November 2, 1977; signed by California Angels, December 21, 1977.
§On disabled list, June 2 to July 9, 1979.
xTraded with Pitcher Mark Clear and Third Baseman Carney Lansford to Boston Red Sox for Shortstop Rick Burleson and Third Baseman Butch Hobson, December 10, 1980.

CHAMPIONSHIP SERIES RECORD

Year Club	League	Pos.	G.	AB.	R.	H.	2B.	3B.	HR.	RBI.	B.A.	PO.	A.	E.	F.A.
1979—California	Amer.	OF	4	16	2	4	0	0	0	0	.250	14	2	0	1.000

WORLD SERIES RECORD

Year Club	League	Pos.	G.	AB.	R.	H.	2B.	3B.	HR.	RBI.	B.A.	PO.	A.	E.	F.A.
1975—Boston	Amer.	OF-PH	3	2	0	0	0	0	0	0	.000	1	0	0	1.000

JAMES BRADLEY MILLS
(Brad)

Born January 19, 1957, at Exeter, Calif.
Height, 6.00. Weight, 195.
Throws right and bats lefthanded.
Attended College of the Sequoias, Visalia, Calif., and
University of Arizona, Tucson, Ariz.

Year Club	League	Pos.	G.	AB.	R.	H.	2B.	3B.	HR.	RBI.	B.A.	PO.	A.	E.	F.A.
1979—W. Palm Beach	Fla. St.	3B	78	258	43	70	12	1	5	30	.271	66	110	9	.951
1980—Memphis	South.	3B	55	190	32	56	18	2	6	44	.295	39	135	9	.951
1980—Montreal	Nat.	3B	21	60	1	18	1	0	0	8	.300	19	24	1	.977
1980—Denver	A.A.	3B-2B	52	201	43	58	10	3	2	27	.289	42	113	9	.945
Major League Totals			21	60	1	18	1	0	0	8	.300	19	24	1	.977

Selected by Minnesota Twins' organization in 16th round of free-agent draft, January 11, 1977.
Selected by Montreal Expos' organization in 16th round of free-agent draft, June 5, 1979.

BRIAN TATE MILNER

Born November 17, 1959, at Fort Worth, Tex.
Height, 6.02. Weight, 200.
Throws and bats righthanded.
Attending Texas Christian University, Fort Worth, Tex.
Led Carolina League catchers in passed balls with 24 in 1980.

Year Club	League	Pos.	G.	AB.	R.	H.	2B.	3B.	HR.	RBI.	B.A.	PO.	A.	E.	F.A.
1978—Medicine Hat	Pion.	C-1B	51	189	33	58	9	3	4	36	.307	229	20	6	.976
1978—Toronto	Amer.	C	2	9	3	4	0	1	0	2	.444	4	0	1	.800
1979—Dunedin†	Fla. St.	C	38	133	7	25	5	1	0	11	.188	16	4	1	.952
1980—Kinston	Carol.	C	124	452	57	116	18	3	6	71	.257	627	94	14	.981
Major League Totals			2	9	3	4	0	1	0	2	.444	4	0	1	.800

Selected by Toronto Blue Jays' organization in 7th round of free-agent draft, June 6, 1978.
†On disabled list, April 26 to May 29 and July 30 to August 31, 1979.

EDDIE JAMES MILNER

Born May 21, 1955, at Columbus, O.
Height, 5.11. Weight, 170.
Throws and bats lefthanded.
Attended Muskingum College, New Concord, O., and Central State University, Wilberforce, O.;
received Bachelor of Science degree in Business.
Cousin of John Milner, first baseman-outfielder with Pittsburgh Pirates.
Tied for Pioneer League lead among outfielders in double plays with 1 in 1976.
Named Florida State League Most Valuable Player, 1978.

Year Club	League	Pos.	G.	AB.	R.	H.	2B.	3B.	HR.	RBI.	B.A.	PO.	A.	E.	F.A.
1976—Billings	Pion.	OF	67	231	51	59	14	3	2	27	.255	*149	*12	7	.958
1977—Shelby	W. Car.	OF	110	414	62	111	15	8	3	30	.268	254	10	10	.964
1978—Tampa	Fla. St.	OF	133	497	79	141	16	*16	8	44	.284	283	7	6	.980
1979—Indianapolis	A.A.	OF	30	98	9	18	0	2	0	5	.184	49	2	2	.962
1979—Nashville	South.	OF	104	369	70	97	12	12	11	51	.263	259	9	5	.982
1980—Indianapolis	A.A.	OF	130	468	63	118	11	7	5	37	.252	*363	6	7	.981
1980—Cincinnati	Nat.	PH-PR	6	3	1	0	0	0	0	0	.000	0	0	0	.000
Major League Totals			6	3	1	0	0	0	0	0	.000	0	0	0	.000

Selected by Cincinnati Reds' organization in 21st round of free-agent draft, June 8, 1976.

JOHN DAVID MILNER

Born December 28, 1949, at Atlanta, Ga.
Height, 6.00. Weight, 185.
Throws and bats lefthanded.
Cousin of Eddie Milner, outfielder in Cincinnati Reds' organization.
Tied major league record for most plate appearances and most times faced pitcher as batter, extra-inning game (12), September 11, 1974 (25 innings).
Led Texas League batters in bases on balls with 100 in 1970.

Year Club	League	Pos.	G.	AB.	R.	H.	2B.	3B.	HR.	RBI.	B.A.	PO.	A.	E.	F.A.
1968—Marion	Appal.	OF	67	234	51	75	*18	1	1	28	.321	88	7	6	.941
1969—Pompano Beach	Fla. St.	1-O	17	65	12	23	3	2	3	18	.354	118	6	0	1.000
1969—Visalia	Calif.	OF-1B	111	393	90	128	20	4	15	63	.326	388	26	13	.970
1970—Memphis	Texas	1B-O	*136	461	98	137	19	8	20	71	.297	792	36	10	.988
1971—Tidewater	Int.	OF-1B	133	497	82	144	27	5	19	87	.290	309	12	8	.976
1971—New York	Nat.	OF	9	18	1	3	1	0	0	1	.167	8	1	0	1.000
1972—New York	Nat.	OF-1B	117	362	52	86	12	2	17	38	.238	233	13	6	.976
1973—New York†	Nat.	1B-OF	129	451	69	108	12	3	23	72	.239	804	51	11	.987
1974—New York	Nat.	1B	137	507	70	128	19	0	20	63	.252	1147	77	7	.994
1975—New York	Nat.	OF-1B	91	220	24	42	11	0	7	29	.191	267	27	3	.990
1976—New York	Nat.	OF-1B	127	443	56	120	25	4	15	78	.271	239	9	3	.988
1977—New York‡	Nat.	1B-OF	131	388	43	99	20	3	12	57	.255	700	50	5	.993
1978—Pittsburgh	Nat.	OF-1B	108	295	39	80	17	0	6	38	.271	287	14	3	.990

Year Club	League	Pos.	G.	AB.	R.	H.	2B.	3B.	HR.	RBI.	B.A.	PO.	A.	E.	F.A.
1979—Pittsburgh .... Nat.		OF-1B	128	326	52	90	9	4	16	60	.276	367	20	8	.980
1980—Pittsburgh§ .... Nat.		1B-OF	114	238	31	58	6	0	8	34	.244	510	32	6	.989
Major League Totals			1046	3248	437	814	132	16	124	470	.251	4562	294	52	.989

Selected by New York Mets' organization in 14th round of free-agent draft, June 7, 1968.

†On supplemental disabled list, April 28 to May 13, 1973.

‡Traded with Pitcher Jon Matlack to Texas Rangers for First Baseman Willie Montanez, Outfielder Tom Grieve and a player to be named later, December 8, 1977; traded by Texas with Pitcher Bert Blyleven to Pittsburgh Pirates for Outfielder Al Oliver and Infielder Nelson Norman, December 8, 1977. (Ken Henderson sent to Mets completing first trade, March 15, 1978).

§Granted free agency, October 22, 1980; re-signed by Pirates, January 23, 1981.

CHAMPIONSHIP SERIES RECORD

Tied Championship Series record for most bases on balls, five-game Series (5), 1973.

Year Club	League	Pos.	G.	AB.	R.	H.	2B.	3B.	HR.	RBI.	B.A.	PO.	A.	E.	F.A.
1973—New York......... Nat.		1B	5	17	2	3	0	0	0	1	.176	37	6	0	1.000
1979—Pittsburgh .... Nat.		OF	3	9	0	0	0	0	0	0	.000	1	0	0	1.000
Championship Series Totals			8	26	2	3	0	0	0	1	.115	38	6	0	1.000

WORLD SERIES RECORD

Year Club	League	Pos.	G.	AB.	R.	H.	2B.	3B.	HR.	RBI.	B.A.	PO.	A.	E.	F.A.
1973—New York......... Nat.		1B	7	27	2	8	0	0	0	2	.296	66	1	0	1.000
1979—Pittsburgh .... Nat.		OF	3	9	2	3	1	0	0	1	.333	5	0	0	1.000
World Series Totals........................			10	36	4	11	1	0	0	3	.306	71	1	0	1.000

CRAIG STEPHEN MINETTO

Born April 25, 1954, at Stockton, Calif.
Height, 6.00. Weight, 185.
Throws and bats lefthanded.
Attended San Joaquin Delta College, Stockton, Calif.

Year Club	League	G.	IP.	W.	L.	Pct.	H.	R.	ER.	SO.	BB.	ERA.
1974—Kinston...............................Carolina		4	5	0	0	.000	5	2	2	2	5	3.60
1974—Sarasota Expos†...................G. Coast		6	19	0	4	.000	32	28	18	16	16	8.53
1975—						(Played in Bologna, Italy)						
1976—						(Played semi-pro in Lodi, Calif.)						
1977—Modesto ....California		16	89	5	4	.556	91	54	49	85	43	4.96
1977—Chattanooga.........................Southern		12	75	5	4	.556	57	32	26	56	21	3.12
1977—San Jose ....P. Coast		2	8	0	1	.000	6	3	3	10	5	2.25
1978—Vancouver ....P. Coast		23	134	10	4	.714	142	79	64	78	51	4.30
1978—Oakland..............................American		4	12	0	0	.000	13	10	5	3	7	3.75
1979—Oakland...............................American		36	118	1	5	.167	131	85	73	64	58	5.57
1980—Ogden ....P. Coast		22	41	3	2	.600	50	34	21	35	24	4.61
1980—Oakland‡ ....American		7	8	0	2	.000	11	7	7	5	3	7.88
Major League Totals...............................		47	138	1	7	.125	155	102	85	72	68	5.54

Selected by Los Angeles Dodgers' organization in 35th round of free-agent draft, June 6, 1972.

Selected by Los Angeles Dodgers' organization in secondary phase of free-agent draft, January 10, 1973.

Signed as free agent by Montreal Expos' organization, May 19, 1974.

†Released, September 18, 1974; signed by Oakland A's organization, January 9, 1977.

‡On disabled list, September 11 to October 6, 1980.

GREGORY BRIAN MINTON
(Greg)

Born July 29, 1951, at Lubbock, Tex.
Height, 6.02. Weight, 191.
Throws right and bats left and righthanded.
Hobbies—Fishing, hunting, golf, racquetball and handball.
Attended San Diego Mesa College, San Diego, Calif.

Major League saves: 1975 (0), 1976 (0), 1977 (0), 1978 (0), 1979 (4), 1980 (19). Total—23.
Led Pacific Coast League in wild pitches with 18 in 1977.

Year Club	League	G.	IP.	W.	L.	Pct.	H.	R.	ER.	SO.	BB.	ERA.
1970—Billings† ....Pioneer		16	40	1	4	.200	37	23	14	36	16	3.15
1971—Waterloo.............................Midwest		27	124	11	6	.647	118	52	42	117	55	3.05
1972—San Jose‡............................California		28	178	12	12	.500	182	117	78	153	77	3.94
1973—Phoenix ....P. Coast		5	13	0	0	.000	11	6	6	4	8	4.15
1973—Amarillo ....Texas		38	122	5	11	.313	138	87	61	77	48	4.50
1974—Fresno................................California		13	96	10	1	.909	85	32	24	81	18	2.25
1974—Amarillo ....Texas		6	29	1	4	.200	42	26	19	21	10	5.90
1975—Phoenix ....P. Coast		42	177	10	6	.625	178	73	51	76	76	2.59
1975—San Francisco ....National		4	17	1	1	.500	19	14	13	6	11	6.88
1976—San Francisco ....National		10	26	0	3	.000	32	18	14	7	12	4.85
1976—Phoenix§.............................P. Coast		13	74	4	5	.444	91	57	46	31	32	5.59
1977—Phoenix ....P. Coast		29	161	14	6	*.700	188	93	87	77	70	4.86
1977—San Francisco ....National		2	14	1	1	.500	14	8	7	5	4	4.50
1978—Phoenix ....P. Coast		14	92	7	4	.636	97	54	46	32	38	4.50
1978—San Francisco ....National		11	16	0	1	.000	22	14	14	6	8	7.88

Year Club	League	G.	IP.	W.	L.	Pct.	H.	R.	ER.	SO.	BB.	ERA.
1979—San Francisco x	National	46	80	4	3	.571	59	25	16	33	27	1.80
1980—San Francisco	National	68	91	4	6	.400	81	28	25	42	34	2.47
Major League Totals		141	244	10	15	.400	227	107	89	99	96	3.28

Selected by Kansas City Royals' organization in 3rd round of free-agent draft, January 17, 1970.
†Played in two games as an outfielder.
‡Traded by Kansas City Royals to San Francisco Giants for Catcher Fran Healy, April 2, 1973.
§On disabled list, July 24 to August 5, 1976.
xOn disabled list, March 26 to May 31, 1979.

PAUL THOMAS MIRABELLA

Born March 20, 1954, at Bellville, N. J.
Height, 6.02. Weight, 196.
Throws and bats lefthanded.
Attended Montclair State University, Upper Montclair, N. J.

Tied for Texas League lead in shutouts with 4 and in games started with 26 in 1977.

Year Club	League	G.	IP.	W.	L.	Pct.	H.	R.	ER.	SO.	BB.	ERA.
1976—Asheville	W. Carolina	22	149	10	7	.588	149	77	66	*136	69	3.99
1977—Tulsa	Texas	26	176	12	7	.632	167	90	75	112	70	3.83
1978—Tucson	P. Coast	22	143	9	6	.600	158	77	63	85	68	3.97
1978—Texas†	American	10	28	3	2	.600	30	18	18	23	17	5.79
1979—Columbus	Int'national	22	144	11	7	.611	129	75	62	98	50	3.88
1979—New York‡	American	10	14	0	4	.000	16	15	14	4	10	9.00
1980—Syracuse	Int'national	4	31	1	2	.333	28	13	9	23	8	2.61
1980—Toronto	American	33	131	5	12	.294	151	73	63	53	66	4.33
Major League Totals		53	173	8	18	.308	197	106	95	80	93	4.94

Selected by Minnsota Twins' organization in 16th round of free-agent draft, June 4, 1975.
Selected by Texas Rangers' organization in secondary phase of free-agent draft, January 7, 1976.
†Traded with Pitchers Mike Griffin and Dave Righetti and Outfielders Juan Beniquez and Greg Jemison to New York Yankees for Pitchers Sparky Lyle, Larry McCall and Dave Rajsich, Catcher Mike Heath, Shortstop Domingo Ramos and cash, November 10, 1978.
‡Traded with First Baseman Chris Chambliss and Infielder Damaso Garcia to Toronto Blue Jays for Catcher Rick Cerone, Pitcher Tom Underwood and Outfielder Ted Wilborn, November 1, 1979.

PAUL MICHAEL MITCHELL

Born August 19, 1950, at Worcester, Mass.
Height, 6.01. Weight, 195.
Throws and bats righthanded.
Attended Old Dominion University, Norfolk, Va.; received
Bachelor of Science degree in Education.

Tied for International League lead in wild pitches with 18 in 1973.

Year Club	League	G.	IP.	W.	L.	Pct.	H.	R.	ER.	SO.	BB.	ERA.
1972—Asheville	Southern	26	178	*16	8	.667	168	73	64	149	53	3.24
1973—Rochester	Int'national	27	152	8	7	.533	151	83	70	93	83	4.14
1974—Rochester	Int'national	26	168	14	6	*.700	145	67	54	131	62	2.89
1975—Rochester	Int'national	14	96	10	1	.909	73	31	22	78	19	2.06
1975—Baltimore†	American	11	57	3	0	1.000	41	23	23	31	19	3.63
1976—Tucson	P. Coast	4	23	3	1	.750	22	7	6	17	8	2.35
1976—Oakland	American	26	142	9	7	.563	169	74	67	67	30	4.25
1977—Chattanooga	Southern	5	32	0	3	.000	30	13	13	23	13	3.66
1977—San Jose	P. Coast	10	63	2	5	.286	78	45	37	34	42	5.29
1977—Oakland‡-Seattle	American	14	53	3	6	.333	71	42	38	25	23	6.45
1978—Seattle	American	29	168	8	14	.364	173	86	78	75	79	4.18
1979—Seattle§-Milwaukee	American	28	112	4	7	.364	127	76	66	50	25	5.30
1980—Vancouver	P. Coast	8	49	5	3	.625	53	27	18	29	10	3.31
1980—Milwaukee	American	17	89	5	5	.500	92	40	35	29	15	3.54
Major League Totals		125	621	32	39	.451	673	341	307	277	191	4.45

Selected by Pittsburgh Pirates' organization in 32nd round of free-agent draft, June 7, 1968.
Selected by Baltimore Orioles' organization in secondary phase of free-agent draft, June 8, 1971.
†Traded with Outfielder Don Baylor and Pitcher Mike Torrez to Oakland Athletics for Outfielder Reggie Jackson and Pitchers Ken Holtzman and Bill Van Bommel, April 2, 1976.
‡Sold to Seattle Mariners, August 4, 1977.
§Traded to Milwaukee Brewers for Pitcher Randy Stein, June 7, 1979.

ROBERT VAN MITCHELL
(Bobby)

Born April 7, 1955, at Salt Lake City, Utah.
Height, 5.10. Weight, 170.
Throws and bats lefthanded.
Attended University of Southern California,
Los Angeles, Calif.

Year Club	League	Pos.	G.	AB.	R.	H.	2B.	3B.	HR.	RBI.	B.A.	PO.	A.	E.	F.A.
1977—Clinton	Midw.	OF	74	221	37	72	19	1	3	28	.326	145	9	3	.981
1978—San Antonio	Texas	OF	131	480	76	140	17	5	1	42	.292	*302	10	4	.987

Year	Club	League	Pos.	G.	AB.	R.	H.	2B.	3B.	HR.	RBI.	B.A.	PO.	A.	E.	F.A.
1979–Albuquerque	..... P. C.		OF	123	453	104	148	24	8	2	59	.327	279	21	7	.977
1980–Albuquerque	..... P. C.		OF	109	347	62	111	20	6	3	53	.320	292	11	2	.993
1980–Los Angeles	...... Nat.		OF	9	3	1	1	0	0	0	0	.333	5	0	0	1.000
Major League Totals	....			9	3	1	1	0	0	0	0	.333	5	0	0	1.000

Selected by San Francisco Giants' organization in 5th round of free-agent draft, June 5, 1973.
Selected by Los Angeles Dodgers' organization in 7th round of free-agent draft, June 7, 1977.

RANDALL JAMES MOFFITT
(Randy)

Born October 13, 1948, at Long Beach, Calif.
Height, 6.03. Weight, 195.
Throws and bats righthanded.
Hobby—Freshwater fishing.
Attended California State College, Long Beach, Calif.
Brother of tennis star Billie Jean King.

Major League saves: 1972 (4), 1973 (14), 1974 (15), 1975 (11), 1976 (14), 1977 (11), 1978 (12), 1979 (2), 1980 (0). Total—83.

Year	Club	League	G.	IP.	W.	L.	Pct.	H.	R.	ER.	SO.	BB.	ERA.
1970–Fresno†	....	California	18	135	9	6	.600	91	35	24	149	23	1.60
1971–Phoenix‡	....	P. Coast	42	121	6	7	.462	147	78	69	94	48	5.13
1972–Phoenix	....	P. Coast	19	24	1	3	.250	22	9	6	24	15	2.25
1972–San Francisco	....	National	40	71	1	5	.167	72	31	29	37	30	3.68
1973–San Francisco	....	National	60	100	4	4	.500	86	30	27	65	31	2.43
1974–San Francisco	....	National	61	102	5	7	.417	99	52	51	49	29	4.50
1975–San Francisco	....	National	55	74	4	5	.444	73	35	32	39	32	3.89
1976–San Francisco	....	National	58	103	6	6	.500	92	36	26	50	35	2.27
1977–San Francisco	....	National	64	88	4	9	.308	91	41	35	68	39	3.58
1978–San Francisco	....	National	70	82	8	4	.667	79	35	30	52	33	3.29
1979–San Francisco§	....	National	28	35	2	5	.286	53	33	30	16	14	7.71
1980–San Francisco x	....	National	13	17	1	1	.500	18	10	9	10	4	4.76
Major League Totals	....		449	672	35	46	.432	663	303	269	386	247	3.60

Selected by San Francisco Giants' organization in 1st round (18th player selected) of free-agent draft, January 17, 1970.
†On military list, February 16 to June 5, 1970.
‡On disabled list, August 22 to September 2, 1971.
§On disabled list, February 20 to April 20 and June 22 to August 12, 1979.
xOn disabled list, May 12 to August 14, 1980.

DALE ROBERT MOHORCIC

Born January 25, 1956, at Cleveland, O.
Height, 6.03. Weight, 205.
Throws and bats righthanded.

Tied for Northwest League lead in shutouts with 2 in 1978.

Year	Club	League	G.	IP.	W.	L.	Pct.	H.	R.	ER.	SO.	BB.	ERA.
1978–Victoria†	....	Northwest	14	98	6	5	.545	84	39	22	73	36	2.02
1979–Dunedin‡	....	Florida St.	23	106	4	7	.364	134	59	52	52	27	4.42
1980–Salem	....	Carolina	47	111	7	5	.583	91	38	27	85	32	2.18

Signed as free agent by Victoria, June 11, 1978.
†Sold to Toronto Blue Jays' organization, September 25, 1978.
‡Released, January 8, 1980; signed by Pittsburgh Pirates' organization, April 5, 1980.

ROBERT JOSEPH MOLINARO
Name pronounced MOLE-in-aro.
(Bobby)

Born May 21, 1950, at Newark, N. J.
Height, 6.00. Weight, 180.
Throws right and bats lefthanded.
Hobbies—All sports.

Tied for American Association league lead in double plays by outfielders with 4 in 1976.
Led American Association in sacrifice flies with 9 in 1977.

Year	Club	League	Pos.	G.	AB.	R.	H.	2B.	3B.	HR.	RBI.	B.A.	PO.	A.	E.	F.A.
1968–Sarasota Tigers	.Gulf C.		OF	55	176	32	57	5	4	0	13	.324	68	5	2	.973
1969–Rocky Mount	.....Carol.		OF	111	415	66	107	9	4	4	28	.258	194	9	5	.976
1970–Montgomery	.....South.		OF	96	335	30	82	15	4	1	35	.245	150	8	6	.963
1971–Montgomery†	....South.		OF	45	166	26	50	11	2	4	25	.301	71	7	6	.929
1972–Toledo	...............Int.		OF	106	349	41	92	15	1	4	39	.264	138	8	5	.967
1973–Montgomery	.....South.		OF	69	248	33	78	5	2	5	45	.315	73	8	2	.976
1973–Toledo	...............Int.		OF	49	183	19	44	14	0	4	30	.240	86	0	2	.977
1974–Evansville	.........A. A.		OF	118	393	56	106	14	2	11	51	.270	92	8	3	.971
1975–Evansville	.........A. A.		OF	126	471	69	135	20	4	13	75	.287	174	2	5	.972
1975–Detroit	..............Amer.		OF	6	19	2	5	0	1	0	1	.263	8	1	0	1.000

Year Club League	Pos.	G.	AB.	R.	H.	2B.	3B.	HR.	RBI.	B.A.	PO.	A.	E.	F.A.
1976—Evansville........A. A.	OF	135	491	72	142	27	9	6	67	.289	211	12	12	.949
1977—Evansville........A. A.	OF	125	455	85	138	25	2	17	91	.303	196	12	7	.967
1977—Det.‡-Chi..........Amer.	OF	5	6	0	2	1	0	0	0	.333	1	0	0	1.000
1978—Chicago ....Amer.	OF	105	286	39	75	5	5	6	27	.262	88	2	0	1.000
1979—Iowa§ ....A. A.	OF	133	475	90	156	23	5	13	93	.328	65	10	2	.974
1979—Baltimore x.......Amer.	OF	8	6	0	0	0	0	0	0	.000	7	0	0	1.000
1980—Chicago ....Amer.	OF	119	344	48	100	16	4	5	36	.291	85	3	4	.957
Major League Totals		243	661	89	182	22	10	11	64	.275	189	6	4	.980

Selected by Detroit Tigers' organization in 2nd round of free-agent draft, June 7, 1968.
†On disabled list, June 12 to August 29, 1971.
‡Sold on waivers to Chicago White Sox, September 22, 1977.
§Sold on waivers to Baltimore Orioles, August 31, 1979.
xSold on waivers to Chicago White Sox, October 3, 1979.

PAUL LEO MOLITOR

Born August 22, 1956, at St. Paul, Minn.
Height, 6.00. Weight, 175.
Throws and bats righthanded.
Attending University of Minnesota, Minneapolis, Minn.

Major League stolen bases: 1978 (30), 1979 (33), 1980 (34). Total—97.
Named Midwest League Player of the Year, 1977.
Named American League Rookie Player of the Year by THE SPORTING NEWS, 1978.
Received reported $100,000 bonus to sign with Milwaukee Brewers, 1977.

Year Club League	Pos.	G.	AB.	R.	H.	2B.	3B.	HR.	RBI.	B.A.	PO.	A.	E.	F.A.
1977—Burlington.........Midw.	SS	64	228	52	79	12	0	8	50	.346	83	207	28	.912
1978—Milwaukee ....Amer.	2B-SS-3B	125	521	73	142	26	4	6	45	.273	253	401	22	.967
1979—Milwaukee ....Amer.	2B-SS	140	584	88	188	27	16	9	62	.322	309	440	16	.979
1980—Milwaukee† ......Amer.	2-S-3	111	450	81	137	29	2	9	37	.304	260	336	20	.968
Major League Totals		376	1555	242	467	82	22	24	144	.300	822	1177	58	.972

Selected by St. Louis Cardinals' organization in 28th round of free-agent draft, June 5, 1974.
Selected by Milwaukee Brewers' organization in 1st round (third player selected) of free-agent draft, June 7, 1977.
†On supplemental disabled list, June 24 to July 18, 1980.

ALL-STAR GAME RECORD
Named to American League All-Star Team in 1980; replaced due to injury.

ROBERT JAMES MONDAY JR.
(Rick)

Born November 20, 1945, at Batesville, Ark.
Height, 6.03. Weight, 200.
Throws and bats lefthanded.
Hobbies—Golf and hunting.
Attended Arizona State University, Tempe, Ariz.

Tied major league records for most strikeouts, game (5), April 29, 1970; most at bats, doubleheader, more than 18 innings (14), June 17, 1967 (28 innings); most strikeouts, two consecutive games (8), April 28 and 29, 1970.
Hit three home runs in one game, May 16, 1972.
Tied for National League lead in double plays by outfielders with 5 in 1974.
Tied for American League lead in double plays by outfielders with 6 in 1967.
Led Southern League batters in strikeouts with 143 in 1966.
Named College Player of the Year by THE SPORTING NEWS, 1965.
Received reported $104,000 bonus to sign with Kansas City Athletics, 1965.

Year Club League	Pos.	G.	AB.	R.	H.	2B.	3B.	HR.	RBI.	B.A.	PO.	A.	E.	F.A.
1965—Lewiston ....Northw.	OF-1B	72	247	45	67	12	2	13	44	.271	205	6	8	.963
1966—Mobile...............South.	OF	127	469	86	125	16	10	23	72	.267	*287	10	13	.958
1966—Kansas City.......Amer.	OF	17	41	4	4	1	1	0	2	.098	26	1	1	.964
1967—Kansas City.......Amer.	OF	124	406	52	102	14	6	14	58	.251	260	14	8	.972
1968—Oakland ....Amer.	OF	148	482	56	132	24	7	8	49	.274	299	11	7	.978
1969—Oakland ....Amer.	OF	122	399	57	108	17	4	12	54	.271	262	3	10	.964
1970—Oakland†..........Amer.	OF	112	376	63	109	19	7	10	37	.290	257	3	5	.981
1971—Oakland‡..........Amer.	OF	116	355	53	87	9	3	18	56	.245	238	6	4	.984
1972—Chicago............Nat.	OF	138	434	68	108	22	5	11	42	.249	268	6	1	*.996
1973—Chicago............Nat.	OF	149	554	93	148	24	5	26	56	.267	317	9	9	.973
1974—Chicago............Nat.	OF	142	538	84	158	19	7	20	58	.294	302	10	5	.984
1975—Chicago............Nat.	OF	136	491	89	131	29	4	17	60	.267	315	6	9	.973
1976—Chicago§ ....Nat.	OF-1B	137	534	107	145	20	5	32	77	.272	587	26	5	.992
1977—Los Angeles......Nat.	OF-1B	118	392	47	90	13	1	15	48	.230	221	5	2	.991
1978—Los Angeles ......Nat.	OF-1B	119	342	54	87	14	1	19	57	.254	217	3	1	.995
1979—Los Angeles x ...Nat.	OF	12	33	2	10	0	0	0	2	.303	27	0	1	.964
1980—Los Angeles......Nat.	OF	96	194	35	52	7	1	10	25	.268	92	1	3	.969
American League Totals		639	2059	285	542	84	28	62	256	.263	1342	38	35	.975
National League Totals		1047	3512	579	929	148	29	150	425	.265	2346	66	36	.985
Major League Totals		1686	5571	864	1471	232	57	212	681	.264	3688	104	71	.982

Selected by Kansas City A's organization in 1st round (first player selected) of free-agent draft, June 15, 1965.

†On military list June 18 through July 8.
‡Traded to Chicago Cubs for Pitcher Ken Holtzman, November 29, 1971.
§Traded with Pitcher Mike Garman to Los Angeles Dodgers for First Baseman-Outfielder Bill Buckner, Shortstop Ivan DeJesus and Pitcher Jeff Albert, January 11, 1977.
xOn disabled list, May 8 to July 26, 1979; on emergency disabled list, July 26 to October 26, 1979.

PITCHING RECORD

Year Club	League	G.	IP.	W.	L.	Pct.	H.	R.	ER.	SO.	BB.	ERA.
1965—Lewiston	Northwest	1	1	0	0	.000	0	0	0	2	2	0.00

CHAMPIONSHIP SERIES RECORD

Year Club	League	Pos.	G.	AB.	R.	H.	2B.	3B.	HR.	RBI.	B.A.	PO.	A.	E.	F.A.
1971—Oakland	Amer.	OF	1	3	0	0	0	0	0	0	.000	4	0	0	1.000
1977—Los Angeles	Nat.	OF-PH	3	7	1	2	1	0	0	0	.286	6	0	0	1.000
1978—Los Angeles	Nat.	OF-PH	3	10	2	2	0	1	0	0	.200	6	0	0	1.000
Championship Series Totals			7	20	3	4	1	1	0	0	.200	16	0	0	1.000

WORLD SERIES RECORD

Year Club	League	Pos.	G.	AB.	R.	H.	2B.	3B.	HR.	RBI.	B.A.	PO.	A.	E.	F.A.
1977—Los Angeles	Nat.	OF	4	12	0	2	0	0	0	0	.167	5	0	0	1.000
1978—Los Angeles	Nat.	OF-DH	5	13	2	2	1	0	0	0	.154	5	0	0	1.000
World Series Totals			9	25	2	4	1	0	0	0	.160	10	0	0	1.000

ALL-STAR GAME RECORD

Year League	Pos.	AB.	R.	H.	2B.	3B.	HR.	RBI.	B.A.	PO.	A.	E.	F.A.
1968—American	OF	2	0	0	0	0	0	0	.000	0	0	0	.000
1978—National	OF	2	0	0	0	0	0	0	.000	1	0	0	1.000
All-Star Game Totals		4	0	0	0	0	0	0	.000	1	0	0	1.000

DONALD WAYNE MONEY
(Don)

Born June 7, 1947, at Washington, D. C.
Height, 6.01. Weight, 190.
Throws and bats righthanded.
Hobbies—Golf, bowling, hunting and fishing.

Established major league records for highest fielding average by third baseman, season (.9894), 1974; fewest errors by third baseman (150 or more games) (5), 1974; most consecutive errorless games by third baseman, season (86), April 5 to July 16, 1974; most consecutive errorless chances accepted by third baseman, lifetime (261), September 28, 1973 (1st game) to July 16, 1974; most consecutive errorless chances accepted by third baseman, season (257), April 5 to July 16, 1974.

Tied major league record for most assists by second baseman, game (12), June 24, 1977.

Established American League record for most consecutive errorless games, third baseman, lifetime, 88, September 28 (2nd game), 1973 to July 16, 1974.

Established National League record for most consecutive errorless chances accepted by third baseman, season (163), July 23-September 11, 1972.

Tied for National League lead in double plays by third basemen with 31 in 1972.

Led Appalachian League shortstops in double plays with 34 in 1965 and Carolina League shortstops with 87 in 1967.

Named Most Valuable Player in Carolina League, 1967.

Year Club	League	Pos.	G.	AB.	R.	H.	2B.	3B.	HR.	RBI.	B.A.	PO.	A.	E.	F.A.
1965—Salem	Appal.	SS	66	216	46	52	7	0	6	24	.241	*88	*171	24	.915
1966—Clinton	Midw.	SS-2	●125	458	40	108	17	5	7	61	.236	186	345	33	.941
1967—Raleigh†	Carol.	SS	136	480	66	149	*37	5	16	86	.310	*250	*418	33	.953
1968—Philadelphia	Nat.	SS	4	13	1	3	2	0	0	2	.231	6	8	0	1.000
1968—San Diego	P.C.	SS	127	482	63	146	26	4	9	59	.303	226	441	26	.962
1969—Philadelphia	Nat.	SS	127	450	41	103	22	2	6	42	.229	212	443	21	.969
1970—Philadelphia	Nat.	3B-SS	120	447	66	132	25	4	14	66	.295	133	236	15	.961
1971—Philadelphia‡	Nat.	3-O-2	121	439	40	98	22	8	7	38	.223	167	197	11	.970
1972—Philadelphia‡‡	Nat.	*3B-SS	152	536	54	119	16	2	15	52	.222	*140	316	10	*.978
1973—Milwaukee	Amer.	*3B-SS	145	556	75	158	28	2	11	61	.284	146	276	13	*.970
1974—Milwaukee§	Amer.	*3B-2B	159	*629	85	178	32	3	15	65	.283	131	336	5	*.989
1975—Milwaukee	Amer.	3B-SS	109	405	58	112	16	1	15	43	.277	109	194	15	.953
1976—Milwaukee	Amer.	3B-SS	117	439	51	117	18	4	12	62	.267	96	202	13	.958
1977—Milwaukee	Amer.	2-OF-3B	152	586	86	159	28	3	25	83	.279	306	390	16	.978
1978—Milwaukee	Amer.	1-2-3-S	137	518	88	152	30	2	14	54	.293	705	216	9	.990
1979—Milwaukee x	Amer.	3B-1B-2B	92	350	52	83	20	1	6	38	.237	240	117	2	.994
1980—Milwaukee	Amer.	3-2-1	86	289	39	74	17	1	17	46	.256	176	129	12	.962
National League Totals			524	1885	202	455	87	16	42	200	.241	658	1200	57	.970
American League Totals			997	3756	534	1033	189	17	115	452	.275	1909	1860	85	.978
Major League Totals			1521	5641	736	1488	276	33	157	652	.264	2567	3060	142	.975

Signed as free agent by Pittsburgh Pirates' organization, June 20, 1965.

†Recalled by Pittsburgh Pirates; traded with Pitchers Woodie Fryman, Bill Laxton and Harold Clem to Philadelphia Phillies for Pitcher Jim Bunning, December 15, 1967.

‡On military list June 12 through June 30.

‡‡Traded with Infielder John Vukovich and Pitcher Billy Champion to Milwaukee Brewers for Pitchers Ken Brett, Ken Sanders, Jim Lonborg and Earl Stephenson, October 31, 1972.
§On disabled list, May 28 to June 24, 1975.
xOn disabled list, May 2 to June 16, 1979.

ALL-STAR GAME RECORD

Year League	Pos.	AB.	R.	H.	2B.	3B.	HR.	RBI.	B.A.	PO.	A.	E.	F.A.
1976—American	3B	1	0	0	0	0	0	0	.000	0	1	0	1.000
1978—American	2B	2	0	0	0	0	0	0	.000	1	1	0	1.000
All-Star Game Totals		3	0	0	0	0	0	0	.000	1	2	0	1.000

Member of American League All-Star Team in 1974 game; did not play.
Named to American League All-Star Team in 1977; replaced due to injury.

ISIDRO PEDROZA MONGE
Name pronounced Mon-jee.

(Sid)

Born April 11, 1951, at Agua Prieta, Sonora, Mexico.
Height, 6.02. Weight, 195.
Throws left and bats left and righthanded.
Hobbies—Basketball, fishing and hunting.

Major League saves: 1975 (0), 1976 (0), 1977 (4), 1978 (6), 1979 (19), 1980 (14). Total—43.
Pitched 6-0, no-hit victory against Cedar Rapids, May 4, 1971.

Year Club	League	G.	IP.	W.	L.	Pct.	H.	R.	ER.	SO.	BB.	ERA.
1970—Idaho Falls	Pioneer	17	62	5	1	.833	60	35	29	54	42	4.21
1971—Quad Cities	Midwest	25	169	12	11	.522	120	62	45	158	83	2.40
1972—Shreveport†	Texas	24	135	5	10	.333	116	62	52	106	73	3.47
1973—El Paso	Texas	25	147	7	11	.389	173	100	75	90	72	4.59
1974—El Paso	Texas	25	163	●14	5	.737	182	99	84	111	67	4.64
1975—Salt Lake City	P. Coast	27	167	14	9	.609	175	98	86	106	93	4.63
1975—California	American	4	24	0	2	.000	22	12	11	17	10	4.13
1976—California	American	32	118	6	7	.462	108	50	44	53	49	3.36
1977—Calif.‡-Cleve.	American	37	51	1	3	.250	61	37	31	29	33	5.47
1978—Cleveland	American	48	85	4	3	.571	71	36	26	54	51	2.75
1979—Cleveland	American	76	131	12	10	.545	96	37	35	108	64	2.40
1980—Cleveland	American	67	94	3	5	.375	80	39	37	61	40	3.54
Major League Totals		264	503	26	30	.464	438	211	184	322	247	3.29

Selected by California Angels' organization in 24th round of free-agent draft, June 4, 1970.
†On temporary inactive list, August 10, 1972 through end of season.
‡Traded with First Baseman-Outfielder Bruce Bochte and cash estimated at $250,000 to Cleveland Indians for Pitchers Dave LaRoche and Dave Schuler, May 11, 1977.

ALL-STAR GAME RECORD
Member of American League All-Star Team for 1979 game; did not play.

JOHN EVANS MONTAGUE JR.

Born September 12, 1947, at Newport News, Va.
Height, 6.02. Weight, 205.
Throws and bats righthanded.
Hobby—Hunting.
Attended Old Dominion College, Norfolk, Va.

Tied American League record for most batsmen retired, consecutive, season (33), July 22 (last 13) and July 24 (first 20), 1977.
Pitched seven-inning 1-0 no-hit victory against Oklahoma City, May 25, 1976.
Led American Association pitchers in shutouts with 6, and tied for lead in complete games with 11 in 1976.
Tied for International League lead in complete games by pitchers with 16 in 1973.
Named American Association Pitcher of the Year, 1976.

Year Club	League	G.	IP.	W.	L.	Pct.	H.	R.	ER.	SO.	BB.	ERA.
1968—Aberdeen	Northern					(On temporary inactive list)						
1969—Miami	Florida St.	31	176	12	8	.600	130	39	30	166	54	*1.53
1970—Rochester	Int'national	26	139	6	9	.400	137	82	75	102	60	4.86
1971—Rochester†	Int'national	28	117	8	6	.571	121	62	58	92	36	4.46
1972—Peninsula	Int'national	29	*214	9	11	.450	*216	93	78	149	69	3.28
1973—Peninsula	Int'national	27	194	*15	9	.625	188	73	67	108	54	3.11
1973—Montreal	National	4	8	0	0	.000	8	3	3	7	2	3.38
1974—Montreal	National	46	83	3	4	.429	73	37	29	43	38	3.14
1975—Memphis	Int'national	18	135	7	8	.467	114	36	26	68	27	1.73
1975—Montreal‡-Philadelphia	National	15	23	0	1	.000	31	16	16	10	10	6.26
1976—Oklahoma City§	Am. Assoc.	28	194	●14	6	.700	183	72	57	120	51	2.64
1977—Seattle	American	47	182	8	12	.400	193	95	87	98	75	4.30
1978—Seattle x	American	19	44	1	3	.250	52	31	30	14	24	6.14
1979—Seattle y-California	American	55	134	8	4	.667	141	85	82	66	56	5.51
1980—California z	American	37	74	4	2	.667	97	47	42	22	21	5.11
National League Totals		65	114	3	5	.375	112	56	48	60	50	3.79
American League Totals		158	434	21	21	.500	483	258	241	200	176	5.00
Major League Totals		223	548	24	26	.480	595	314	289	260	226	4.75

Selected by Chicago White Sox' organization in 22nd round of free-agent draft, June, 1965.

Selected by Baltimore Orioles' organization in secondary phase of free-agent draft, January, 1967.

†Option transferred by Baltimore Orioles' organization to Peninsula (Montreal Expos' organization), April 4, 1972. Sold by Baltimore Orioles to Montreal Expos, April 13, 1973; Expos assigned Pitcher Mickey Scott to Rochester (Baltimore Orioles' organization), April 4, 1974, to complete deal.

‡Sold via waivers to Philadelphia Phillies, September 2, 1975.

§Sold by Philadelphia Phillies to Seattle Mariners, November 6, 1976.

xOn disabled list, April 16 to May 24 and July 28 to October 5, 1978.

yTraded to California Angels for a player to be named later, August 29, 1979; Shortstop Jim Anderson was acquired by Seattle to complete deal, December 6, 1979.

zReleased, February 10, 1981.

CHAMPIONSHIP SERIES RECORD

Year	Club	League	G.	IP.	W.	L.	Pct.	H.	R.	ER.	SO.	BB.	ERA.
1979—California		American	2	4	0	1	.000	4	4	4	2	2	9.00

GUILLERMO NARANJO MONTANEZ

Name pronounced Mon-TAN-yez.

(Willie)

Born April 1, 1948, at Catano, Puerto Rico.
Height, 6.01. Weight, 185.
Throws and bats lefthanded.

Established major league records for most sacrifice flies, rookie season (13), 1971; most intentional bases on balls, rookie season (14), 1971.

Established National League records for most sacrifice flies by lefthanded batter, season (13), 1971; most grounded into double plays by lefthanded batter, season (26), 1975.

Led National League first basemen in total chances with 1698 in 1976.

Led National League first basemen in double plays with 143 in 1975 and with 138 in 1978.

Led National League in sacrifice flies with 13 in 1971.

Led Florida State League first basemen in double plays with 101 in 1967.

Named first baseman on THE SPORTING NEWS National League All-Star Team, 1976.

Year	Club	League	Pos.	G.	AB.	R.	H.	2B.	3B.	HR.	RBI.	B.A.	PO.	A.	E.	F.A.
1965—Sarasota Cards†	.Sar. Rk.		1B	32	81	5	19	0	0	0	8	.234	166	9	7	.962
1966—California	.Amer.		1B	8	2	2	0	0	0	0	0	.000	1	0	0	1.000
1966—Rock Hill	W. Car.		O-1	93	306	48	86	18	7	11	49	.281	177	6	11	.943
1967—St. Petersburg	Fla. St.		*1B-O	134	479	58	129	15	*17	5	61	.269	*1171	*102	13	*.990
1968—Modesto	Calif.		1B	46	174	26	52	8	2	4	18	.299	334	33	8	.979
1969—Tulsa‡§	A. A.		1B	14	56	12	21	4	2	1	7	.375	115	12	1	.992
1970—Eugene x	P.C.		*1-OF	119	434	65	120	24	9	16	80	.276	842	*66	5	.995
1970—Philadelphia	Nat.		OF-1B	18	25	3	6	0	0	0	3	.240	15	3	0	1.000
1971—Philadelphia	Nat.		OF-1B	158	599	78	153	27	6	30	99	.255	377	12	11	.972
1972—Philadelphia	Nat.		●OF-1B	147	531	60	131	●39	3	13	64	.247	429	●22	6	.987
1973—Philadelphia	Nat.		1B-OF	146	552	69	145	16	5	11	65	.263	852	58	6	.993
1974—Philadelphia	Nat.		1B-OF	143	527	55	160	33	1	7	79	.304	1217	79	10	.992
1975—Phil.y-S.F.	Nat.		1B	156	602	61	182	34	2	10	101	.302	1333	*98	10	.993
1976—S.F.z-Atl.	Nat.		1B	*163	650	74	206	29	2	11	84	.317	1569	●107	*22	.987
1977—Atlanta ab	Nat.		1B	136	544	70	156	31	1	20	68	.287	1129	70	10	.992
1978—New York	Nat.		1B	159	609	66	156	32	0	17	96	.256	1350	*104	8	.995
1979—New York c	Nat.		1B	109	410	36	96	19	0	5	47	.234	905	76	11	.989
1979—Texas	Amer.		1B	38	144	19	46	6	0	8	24	.319	191	16	1	.995
1980—S.D.d-Mont.e	Nat.		1B	142	500	401	136	12	4	6	64	.272	1214	86	8	.994
	American League Totals			46	146	21	46	6	0	8	24	.315	192	16	1	.995
	National League Totals			1477	5549	973	1527	272	24	130	770	.275	10390	715	102	.991
	Major League Totals			1523	5695	994	1573	278	24	138	794	.276	10582	731	103	.991

Signed as free agent by St. Louis Cardinals' organization, March 1, 1965.

†Drafted by California Angels from Jacksonville (St. Louis Cardinals' organization), November 29, 1965; returned to St. Louis organization, May 5, 1966.

‡On disabled list, May 1 through August 25.

§Released to Philadelphia Phillies by St. Louis Cardinals (as partial compensation for Outfielder Curt Flood who refused to report after being traded), April 8, 1970; Cardinals assigned Pitcher Bob Browning to Philadelphia organization, August 31, 1970, to complete deal.

xOn temporary inactive list, May 12 through July 6.

yTraded to San Francisco Giants for Outfielder Garry Maddox, May 4, 1975.

zTraded with Shortstop Craig Robinson, Outfielder Jake Brown, and Infielder Mike Eden to Atlanta Braves for Third baseman-First Baseman Darrell Evans and Shortstop Marty Perez, June 13, 1976.

aOn supplemental disabled list, May 2 to May 26, 1977.

bTraded to Texas Rangers for Pitchers Adrian Devine and Tommy Boggs and Outfielder Eddie Miller, December 8, 1977; traded by Texas Rangers with Outfielder Tom Grieve and a player to be named later to New York Mets for First Baseman-Outfielder John Milner and Pitcher Jon Matlack, December 8, 1977 (Ken Henderson sent to Mets completing trade, March 15, 1978).

cTraded to Texas Rangers for two players to be named later, August 12, 1979; New York acquired Pitcher Ed Lynch, September 18, 1979, and First Baseman Mike Jorgensen, October 23, 1979, to complete deal.

dTraded to Montreal Expos for Infielder Tony Phillips and cash, August 31, 1980.

eGranted free agency, October 26, 1980; re-signed by Expos, December 12, 1980.

ALL-STAR GAME RECORD

Year	League	Pos.	AB.	R.	H.	2B.	3B.	HR.	RBI.	B.A.	PO.	A.	E.	F.A.
1977—National		1B	2	0	0	0	0	0	0	.000	6	1	0	1.000

JOHN JOSEPH MONTEFUSCO JR.

Name pronounced mon-tuh-fyoos-koh
Born May 25, 1950, at Long Branch, N. J.
Height, 6.01. Weight, 192.
Throws and bats righthanded.
Attended Brookdale Community College, Lincroft, N. J.

Pitched 9-0 no-hit victory against Atlanta Braves, September 29, 1976.
Hit home run on first official major league time at bat, September 3, 1974.
Struck out eight consecutive batters against Salt Lake City, August 11, 1974.
Tied for National League lead in shutouts by pitchers with 6 in 1976.
Led Texas League in shutouts with 4 in 1974.
Tied for Pacific Coast League lead in shutouts with 3 in 1974.
Named National League Rookie of the Year by Baseball Writers' Association of America, 1975.
Named National League Rookie Pitcher of the Year by THE SPORTING NEWS, 1975.

Year Club	League	G.	IP.	W.	L.	Pct.	H.	R.	ER.	SO.	BB.	ERA.
1973—Decatur	Midwest	24	120	9	2	.818	94	40	29	126	44	2.18
1974—Amarillo	Texas	19	144	8	9	.471	143	61	50	107	37	3.13
1974—Phoenix	P. Coast	11	77	7	3	.700	60	35	28	90	26	3.27
1974—San Francisco	National	7	39	3	2	.600	41	22	21	34	19	4.85
1975—San Francisco	National	35	244	15	9	.625	210	85	78	215	86	2.88
1976—San Francisco	National	37	253	16	14	.533	224	90	80	172	74	2.85
1977—San Francisco†	National	26	157	7	12	.368	170	82	61	110	46	3.50
1978—San Francisco	National	36	239	11	9	.550	233	110	101	177	68	3.80
1979—San Francisco‡	National	22	137	3	8	.273	145	64	60	76	51	3.94
1980—San Francisco§x	National	22	113	4	8	.333	120	61	55	85	39	4.38
Major League Totals		185	1182	59	62	.488	1143	514	456	869	383	3.47

Signed as free agent by San Francisco Giants' organization, October 6, 1972.
†On disabled list, May 27 to July 6, 1977.
‡On disabled list, April 26 to June 13, 1979.
§On disabled list, July 17 to August 24, 1980.
xTraded with Outfielder Craig Landis to Atlanta Braves for Pitcher Doyle Alexander, December 12, 1980.

ALL-STAR GAME RECORD

Year League	IP.	W.	L.	Pct.	H.	R.	ER.	SO.	BB.	ERA.
1976—National	2	0	0	.000	0	0	0	2	2	.000

ALVIN EARL MOORE
(Junior)

Born January 25, 1953, at Waskom, Tex.
Height, 5.11. Weight, 185.
Throws and bats righthanded.
Attended College of Alameda, Alameda, Calif.

Year Club	League	Pos.	G.	AB.	R.	H.	2B.	3B.	HR.	RBI.	B.A.	PO.	A.	E.	F.A.
1971—Wytheville	Appal.	SS-3B	60	210	39	65	7	1	6	37	.310	74	135	35	.857
1972—Greenwood	W. C.	3B	117	420	52	126	10	4	5	56	.300	91	229	31	.912
1973—Savannah	South.	*2B-3B	137	471	65	108	14	1	11	43	.229	*329	319	16	*.976
1974—Savannah	South.	3B-2B	135	460	61	119	20	3	9	59	.259	118	281	25	.941
1974—Richmond	Int.	3B-SS	4	11	0	3	0	0	0	0	.273	2	7	0	1.000
1975—Richmond	Int.	*2B-3B	128	460	60	138	18	5	14	65	.300	247	283	18	*.967
1976—Richmond	Int.	O-2-3	103	398	58	131	23	3	3	72	.329	161	41	7	.966
1976—Atlanta	Nat.	3-O-2	20	26	1	7	1	0	0	2	.269	7	10	1	.944
1977—Atlanta†	Nat.	3B-2B	112	361	41	94	9	3	5	34	.260	86	189	17	.942
1978—Iowa‡	A. A.	OF-3B	35	133	24	44	10	4	1	29	.331	30	5	4	.897
1978—Chicago	Amer.	3B-OF	24	65	8	19	0	1	0	4	.292	12	9	2	.913
1979—Chicago	Amer.	OF-2B	88	201	24	53	6	2	1	23	.264	83	5	3	.967
1980—Iowa§	A.A.	OF-3B	30	102	11	29	4	1	3	22	.284	30	20	1	.980
1980—Chicago x	Amer.	3-O-1	45	121	9	31	4	1	1	10	.256	30	65	7	.931
National League Totals			132	387	42	101	10	3	5	36	.261	93	199	18	.942
American League Totals			157	387	41	103	10	4	2	37	.266	125	79	12	.944
Major League Totals			289	774	83	204	20	7	7	73	.264	218	278	30	.943

Selected by Atlanta Braves' organization in 11th round of free-agent draft, June 8, 1971.
†Granted free agency, October 27, 1977; signed by Chicago White Sox, November 28, 1977.
‡On disabled list, August 1 to September 1, 1978.
§On disabled list, July 29 to August 27, 1980.
xReleased, December 19, 1980.

BALOR LILBON MOORE

Born January 25, 1951, at Smithville, Tex.
Height, 6.03. Weight, 185.
Throws and bats lefthanded.
Hobbies—Golf, scuba diving, handball, motorcycles and hunting.
Attended West Palm Beach Junior College, West Palm Beach, Fla.
and St. Petersburg Junior College, St. Petersburg, Fla.

Pitched seven inning, 1-0 no-hit victory against Key West, August 18, 1969.
Led Gulf Coast League pitchers in complete games with 5 in 1969.

Year Club	League	G.	IP.	W.	L.	Pct.	H.	R.	ER.	SO.	BB.	ERA.
1969—Bradenton Expos	Gulf Coast	9	67	7	0	*1.000	41	5	2	*91	21	*0.27
1969—West Palm Beach	Fla. State	3	21	2	1	.667	11	5	2	7	7	0.86
1970—West Palm Beach	Fla. State	3	25	3	0	1.000	12	3	2	31	9	0.72
1970—Winnipeg	Int'national	18	119	4	9	.309	107	67	59	100	99	4.46
1970—Montreal	National	6	10	0	2	.000	14	9	8	6	8	7.20
1971—Winnipeg†	Int'national	15	91	2	11	.154	91	70	64	78	62	6.33
1972—Quebec City	Eastern	9	71	5	3	.625	31	16	5	72	35	0.63
1972—Montreal	National	22	148	9	9	.500	122	61	57	161	59	3.47
1973—Peninsula	Int'national	3	25	0	2	.000	13	11	10	20	20	3.60
1973—Montreal	National	35	176	7	16	.304	151	98	88	151	109	4.50
1974—Memphis‡	Int'national	6	15	0	3	.000	12	20	17	14	24	10.20
1974—Montreal	National	8	14	0	2	.000	13	8	6	16	15	3.86
1975—Memphis§	Int'national	14	27	1	3	.250	17	14	12	19	45	4.00
1975—Salinas x	California	5	28	2	2	.500	24	8	3	15	10	0.96
1976—El Paso	Texas	25	141	6	12	.333	153	*110	87	86	*113	5.55
1977—Salinas	California	12	16	2	0	1.000	13	10	3	18	10	1.69
1977—Salt Lake City	P. Coast	33	71	4	4	.500	72	41	31	46	56	3.93
1977—California y	American	7	23	0	2	.000	28	19	10	14	10	3.91
1978—Toronto	American	37	144	6	9	.400	165	85	79	75	54	4.94
1979—Toronto	American	34	139	5	7	.417	135	85	75	51	79	4.86
1980—Syracuse	Int'national	8	9	0	3	.000	13	10	9	4	9	9.00
1980—Toronto z	American	31	65	1	1	.500	76	43	38	22	31	5.26
National League Totals		71	348	16	29	.356	300	176	159	334	191	4.11
American League Totals		109	371	12	19	.387	404	232	202	162	174	4.90
Major League Totals		180	719	28	48	.368	704	408	361	496	365	4.52

Selected by Montreal Expos' organization in 1st round (22nd player selected) of free-agent draft, June 5, 1969.

†On military list July 6, 1971 through January 11, 1972.

‡On disabled list, June 22 to September 1, 1974.

§Sold by Montreal Expos to California Angels, June 15, 1975.

xOn disabled list, August 4 through remainder of season.

ySold to Toronto Blue Jays, April 13, 1978.

zReleased, September 3, 1980; invited to Oakland A's camp, 1981.

CHARLES WILLIAM MOORE JR.
(Charlie)

Born June 21, 1953, at Birmingham, Ala.
Height, 5.11. Weight, 180.
Throws and bats righthanded.
Hobbies—Hunting, fishing and golf.
Attended Mesa Junior College, Mesa, Ariz., and University of Alabama, Birmingham, Ala.
Son of Charles William Moore, Sr., former minor league pitcher.

Hit for the cycle against California Angels, October 1, 1980.
Led Midwest League catchers in double plays with 12 in 1972.
Led New York-Pennsylvania League in passed balls with 16 in 1971 and tied for Midwest League lead with 30 in 1972.

Year Club	League	Pos.	G.	AB.	R.	H.	2B.	3B.	HR.	RBI.	B.A.	PO.	A.	E.	F.A.
1971—Newark	NYP	C	60	209	36	62	12	3	6	27	.297	*439	*34	5	.990
1972—Danville	Midw.	*C-1B	106	348	56	90	14	4	12	44	.259	*723	*92	*25	.970
1973—Shreveport	Texas	C	76	271	47	69	14	2	8	45	.255	402	46	14	.970
1973—Evansville	A. A.	C	50	178	27	52	9	1	7	25	.292	274	30	2	.993
1973—Milwaukee	Amer.	C	8	27	0	5	0	1	0	3	.185	48	5	1	.981
1974—Milwaukee	Amer.	C	72	204	17	50	10	4	0	19	.245	229	28	4	.985
1975—Milwaukee	Amer.	C-OF	73	241	26	70	20	1	1	29	.290	234	23	10	.963
1976—Milwaukee	Amer.	C-O-3	87	241	33	46	7	4	3	16	.191	249	45	9	.970
1977—Milwaukee	Amer.	C	138	375	42	93	15	6	5	45	.248	566	78	•13	.980
1978—Milwaukee	Amer.	C	96	268	30	72	7	1	5	31	.269	314	41	6	.983
1979—Milwaukee	Amer.	C	111	337	45	101	16	2	5	38	.300	414	58	10	.979
1980—Milwaukee	Amer.	C	111	320	42	93	13	2	2	30	.291	319	28	4	.989
Major League Totals			696	2013	235	530	88	21	21	211	.263	2373	306	57	.979

Selected by Milwaukee Brewers' organization in 4th round of free-agent draft, June 8, 1971.

DONNIE RAY MOORE

Born February 13, 1954, at Lubbock, Tex.
Height, 6.00. Weight, 175.
Throws right and bats lefthanded.
Hobbies—Hunting, fishing, golf and billiards.
Attended Ranger Junior College, Ranger, Tex.
Cousin of Hubie Brooks, third baseman in New York Mets' organization.

Led Texas League in games started with 27 and tied for lead in shutouts with 3 in 1975.
Received reported $50,000 bonus to sign with Chicago Cubs, 1973.

Year Club	League	G.	IP.	W.	L.	Pct.	H.	R.	ER.	SO.	BB.	ERA.
1973—Bradenton Cubs	Gulf Coast	4	10	0	1	.000	9	5	4	6	6	3.60
1974—Key West†	Florida St.	26	174	11	12	.478	167	73	54	97	69	2.79

Year Club	League	G.	IP.	W.	L.	Pct.	H.	R.	ER.	SO.	BB.	ERA.
1974–Midland	Texas	5	22	0	4	.000	32	18	17	9	5	6.95
1975–Midland	Texas	28	185	14	8	.636	191	79	61	123	67	2.97
1975–Chicago	National	4	9	0	0	.000	12	4	4	8	4	4.00
1976–Wichita	Am. Assoc.	24	152	7	11	.389	170	96	80	92	61	4.74
1977–Wichita	Am. Assoc.	11	66	4	4	.500	68	38	36	34	22	4.91
1977–Chicago	National	27	49	4	2	.667	51	27	22	34	18	4.04
1978–Chicago	National	71	103	9	7	.563	117	55	47	50	31	4.11
1979–Wichita	Am. Assoc.	5	29	1	3	.250	29	26	26	16	20	8.07
1979–Chicago‡	National	39	73	1	4	.200	95	46	42	43	25	5.18
1980–St. Louis	National	11	22	1	1	.500	25	15	15	10	5	6.14
1980–Springfield	Am. Assoc.	14	85	6	5	.545	74	32	29	49	32	3.07
Major League Totals		152	256	15	14	.517	300	147	130	145	83	4.57

Selected by Boston Red Sox' organization in 12th round of free-agent draft, June 6, 1972.
Signed as free agent by Chicago Cubs' organization, June 3, 1973.
†Appeared as an outfielder in two games.
‡Traded to St. Louis Cardinals for Second Baseman Mike Tyson, October 17, 1979.

KELVIN ORLANDO MOORE

Born September 26, 1957, at LeRoy, Ala.
Height, 6.01. Weight, 195.
Throws left and bats righthanded.
Attended Jackson State University, Jackson, Miss.

Led Pacific Coast League batters in strikeouts with 132 in 1980.

Year Club	League	Pos.	G.	AB.	R.	H.	2B.	3B.	HR.	RBI.	B.A.	PO.	A.	E.	F.A.
1978–Jersey City	East.	1B	59	214	23	58	5	6	2	28	.271	517	58	11	.981
1979–Modesto	Calif.	OF-1B	51	199	45	64	5	1	16	55	.322	116	3	14	.895
1979–Waterbury	East.	1B	83	317	46	106	19	3	14	56	.334	700	35	•13	.983
1980–Ogden	P.C.	1B	126	461	75	130	21	8	25	100	.282	1045	76	12	.989

Selected by Oakland A's organization in 6th round of free-agent draft, June 6, 1978.

ROBERT DEVELL MOORE
(Bob)

Born November 8, 1958, at Sweetwater, La.
Height, 6.04. Weight, 190.
Throws and bats righthanded.

Year Club	League	G.	IP.	W.	L.	Pct.	H.	R.	ER.	SO.	BB.	ERA.
1976–Boise	Northwest	14	22	0	0	.000	23	23	13	20	18	5.32
1977–Medicine Hat	Pioneer	9	45	0	6	.000	55	59	37	45	50	7.40
1977–Modesto†	California	10	23	0	1	.000	24	27	19	28	32	7.43
1978–Modesto	California	23	117	2	10	.167	102	104	87	123	136	6.69
1979–Waterbury	Eastern	17	85	5	7	.417	86	64	56	42	69	5.93
1980–West Haven	Eastern	5	23	0	4	.000	32	25	23	7	15	9.00
1980–Modesto	California	18	109	4	6	.400	107	72	56	72	84	4.62

Selected by Oakland A's organization in 11th round of free-agent draft, June 8, 1976.
†On disabled list, May 18 to May 28, 1977.

ANDRES MORA (IBARRA)

Born May 25, 1955, at Saltillo, Coahuila, Mexico.
Height, 6.00. Weight, 180.
Throws and bats righthanded.

Led Mexican League in total bases with 288 in 1975.
Led Mexican League in slugging percentage with .606 in 1979.

Year Club	League	Pos.	G.	AB.	R.	H.	2B.	3B.	HR.	RBI.	B.A.	PO.	A.	E.	F.A.
1971–Zacatecas	Mex. C.	OF	56	137	22	42	8	4	1	29	.307	62	3	6	.951
1972–Saltillo†	Mex.	OF	2	1	0	0	0	0	0	0	.000	0	0	0	.000
1973–W. Palm Beach‡	Fla. St.	OF	8	21	1	0	0	0	0	0	.000	4	0	0	1.000
1974–Saltillo	Mex.	•OF-2B	132	444	56	138	17	6	14	77	.311	195	31	7	•.970
1975–Saltillo§	Mex.	•OF-3-2	133	492	82	151	18	7	•35	•109	.307	183	84	9	•.967
1976–Baltimore	Amer.	OF	73	220	18	48	11	0	6	25	.218	55	3	3	.951
1976–Rochester	Int.	OF-2-3	18	67	17	22	6	0	6	15	.328	24	15	1	.975
1977–Rochester	Int.	OF	45	183	31	55	13	2	11	45	.301	63	2	2	.970
1977–Baltimore	Amer.	OF-3B	77	233	32	57	8	2	13	44	.245	66	2	0	1.000
1978–Rochester	Int.	OF	23	88	15	20	3	1	4	10	.227	29	2	0	1.000
1978–Baltimore xy	Amer.	OF	76	229	21	49	8	0	8	14	.214	129	4	3	.978
1979–Saltillo	Mex.	OF	114	421	79	145	31	5	23	102	.344	181	10	2	.990
1980–Cleveland z	Amer.	OF	9	18	0	2	0	0	0	0	.111	6	0	0	1.000
1980–Saltillo	Mex.	OF	45	160	25	48	8	0	8	42	.300	61	1	2	.969
Major League Totals		235	700	71	156	27	2	27	83	.223	256	9	6	.978

Signed as free agent by Zacatecas, March 18, 1971.
†Conditionally released to Montreal Expos' organization, February 28, 1973.
‡On disabled list, May 8 through remainder of season. Returned by Montreal Expos' organization to Mexican League, March 14, 1974.

§Sold to Baltimore Orioles' organization, August 11, 1975.
xLoaned to Saltillo, April 2, 1979; returned, August 31, 1979.
yDrafted by Cleveland Indians, December 3, 1979.
zLoaned to Saltillo, May 8, 1980; returned, September 2, 1980.

JOSE MANUEL MORALES

Name pronounced mor-AHL-ess.

Born December 30, 1944, at Frederiksted, St. Croix, Virgin Islands.
Height, 6.00. Weight, 195.
Throws and bats righthanded.
Hobbies—Swimming and fishing.

Established major league records for most at bats as pinch-hitter, season (78), 1976; most hits as pinch-hitter, season (25), 1976.
Led California League in passed balls with 29 in 1965 and American Association with 21 in 1969.
Led American League designated hitters in batting average with .323 in 1978.

Year	Club	League	Pos.	G.	AB.	R.	H.	2B.	3B.	HR.	RBI.	B.A.	PO.	A.	E.	F.A.
1964—Lexington†	....	W. Car.	C	73	233	29	56	11	1	3	34	.240	640	40	13	.981
1965—Fresno	....	Calif.	C	95	321	39	91	13	1	4	48	.283	602	61	•26	.962
1966—Waterbury‡	....	East.	C	64	215	18	54	9	1	7	26	.251	319	33	10	.972
1967—Waterbury	....	East.	C-OF	94	246	19	61	7	4	4	31	.248	421	36	14	.970
1968—Amarillo‡‡	....	Texas	C	105	307	35	88	22	4	8	41	.287	566	70	•19	.971
1969—Iowa	....	A.A.	•C-OF	98	363	54	102	11	3	16	61	.281	350	60	•18	.958
1970—Iowa	....	A.A.	C	93	229	36	70	14	0	12	31	.306	327	31	9	.975
1971—Iowa§	....	A.A.	C-OF	71	153	15	38	7	0	9	22	.248	212	18	7	.970
1972—Tidewater xy	.....	Int.	•C-OF-1	86	256	28	75	18	2	7	48	.293	380	15	•14	.966
1973—Tucson	....	P.C.	C-1B-3B	76	248	37	88	17	2	4	50	.355	20	4	5	.828
1973—Oakland z	....	Amer.	DH-PH	6	14	0	4	1	0	0	1	.286	0	0	0	.000
1973—Montreal	....	Nat.	PH	5	5	0	2	0	0	0	0	.400	0	0	0	.000
1974—Memphis	....	Int.	1B-C	66	216	20	60	13	0	6	32	.278	442	29	6	.987
1974—Montreal	....	Nat.	C	25	26	3	7	4	0	1	5	.269	3	1	1	.800
1975—Montreal	....	Nat.	1-OF-C	93	163	18	49	6	1	2	24	.301	234	28	4	.985
1976—Montreal	....	Nat.	1B-C	104	158	12	50	11	0	4	37	.316	137	21	3	.981
1977—Montreal a	....	Nat.	1B-C	65	74	3	15	4	1	1	9	.203	52	3	0	1.000
1978—Minnesota	....	Amer.	1B-OF-C	101	242	22	76	13	1	2	38	.314	1	2	0	1.000
1979—Minnesota	....	Amer.	1B	92	191	21	51	5	1	2	27	.267	2	0	0	1.000
1980—Minnesota bc	....	Amer.	1B-C	97	241	36	73	17	2	8	36	.303	19	0	0	1.000
American League Totals		....		296	688	79	204	36	4	12	102	.297	22	2	0	1.000
National League Totals		....		292	426	36	123	25	2	8	75	.289	426	53	8	.984
Major League Totals		....		588	1114	115	327	61	6	20	177	.294	448	55	8	.984

Signed as free agent by San Francisco Giants' organization, September 13, 1963.
†On disabled list, July 25 through remainder of season.
‡On disabled list, May 28 to June 18 and July 21 through remainder of season.
‡‡Drafted from San Francisco Giants' organization by Vancouver (Oakland Athletics' organization), December 2, 1968.
§Loaned by Oakland Athletics' organization to Tidewater (New York Mets' organization), April 14, 1972.
xOn disabled list, July 12 to July 28, 1972.
yReturned by New York Mets' organization to Oakland Athletics' organization, September 29, 1972.
zPurchased by Montreal Expos, September 18, 1973.
aSold to Minnesota Twins, March 28, 1978.
bOn supplemental disabled list, May 10 to May 16, 1980.
cGranted free agency, October 24, 1980; signed by Baltimore Orioles, December 17, 1980.

JULIO RUBEN MORALES

Name pronounced mor-AHL-ess.

(Jerry)

Born February 18, 1949, at Yabucoa, Puerto Rico.
Height, 5.10. Weight, 165.
Throws and bats righthanded.
Hobbies—Riding horses and listening to music.

Led Appalachian League outfielders in double plays with 2 in 1966 and tied for lead by Pacific Coast League outfielders with 3 in 1971.
Named Player of the Year in Appalachian League, 1966.

Year	Club	League	Pos.	G.	AB.	R.	H.	2B.	3B.	HR.	RBI.	B.A.	PO.	A.	E.	F.A.
1966—Marion	....	Appal.	OF	38	119	33	41	8	2	1	25	.345	78	6	3	.966
1967—Winter Haven	....	Fla.St.	OF-2-3	139	501	82	124	11	14	8	48	.248	308	56	16	.958
1968—Raleigh-Durham		Carol.	OF	43	129	18	29	9	1	1	15	.225	83	2	3	.966
1968—Visalia†	....	Calif.	OF	70	250	44	66	7	2	6	33	.264	143	9	4	.974
1969—Elmira	....	East.	•OF-SS	127	459	62	125	11	•12	15	63	.272	•349	8	7	.981
1969—San Diego	....	Nat.	OF	19	41	5	8	2	0	1	6	.195	27	2	0	1.000
1970—Salt Lake City	...	P.C.	OF	109	433	50	107	20	7	6	35	.247	237	7	4	•.984
1970—San Diego	....	Nat.	OF	28	58	6	9	0	1	1	4	.155	25	0	2	.926
1971—Hawaii	....	P.C.	OF	137	470	81	128	12	11	11	52	.272	285	14	2	•.993
1971—San Diego	....	Nat.	OF	12	17	1	2	0	0	0	1	.118	8	0	0	1.000
1972—San Diego	....	Nat.	OF-3B	115	347	38	83	15	7	4	18	.239	214	8	4	.982
1973—San Diego‡	....	Nat.	OF	122	388	47	109	23	2	9	34	.281	214	5	2	.991
1974—Chicago	....	Nat.	OF	151	534	70	146	21	7	15	82	.273	266	5	7	.975

Year	Club	League	Pos.	G.	AB.	R.	H.	2B.	3B.	HR.	RBI.	B.A.	PO.	A.	E.	F.A.
1975–Chicago	....	Nat.	OF	153	578	62	156	21	0	12	91	.270	273	11	6	.979
1976–Chicago	....	Nat.	OF	140	537	66	147	17	0	16	67	.274	273	12	5	.983
1977–Chicago§	....	Nat.	OF	136	490	56	142	34	5	11	69	.290	247	8	4	.985
1978–St. Louis x	....	Nat.	OF	130	457	44	109	19	8	4	46	.239	254	5	6	.977
1979–Detroit y	....	Amer.	OF	129	440	50	93	23	1	14	56	.211	206	6	3	.986
1980–New York z	....	Nat.	OF	94	193	19	49	7	1	3	30	.254	107	3	3	.973
National League Totals	....			1100	3640	414	960	159	31	76	448	.264	1908	59	39	.981
American League Totals	....			129	440	50	93	23	1	14	56	.211	206	6	3	.986
Major League Totals	....			1229	4080	464	1053	182	32	90	504	.258	2114	65	42	.981

Signed as free agent by New York Mets' organization, June 23, 1966.

†Recalled by New York Mets; selected by San Diego Padres from New York in expansion draft, October 14, 1968.

‡Traded to Chicago Cubs for Second Baseman Glenn Beckert and Infielder Bob Fenwick (latter assigned from Wichita to Hawaii), November 12, 1973.

§Traded with Catcher Steve Swisher and a player to be named later to St. Louis Cardinals for Catcher Dave Rader and Outfielder-Third Baseman Heity Cruz, December 8, 1977.

xTraded with Pitcher Aurelio Lopez to Detroit Tigers for Pitchers Jack Murphy and Bob Sykes, December 4, 1978.

yTraded with Third Baseman Phil Mankowski to New York Mets for Third Baseman-First Baseman Richie Hebner, October 31, 1979.

zGranted free agency, October 31, 1980; signed by Chicago Cubs' organization, February 17, 1981.

ALL-STAR GAME RECORD

Year	League	Pos.	AB.	R.	H.	2B.	3B.	HR.	RBI.	B.A.	PO.	A.	E.	F.A.
1977–National	....	OF	0	1	0	0	0	0	0	.000	1	0	0	1.000

BOBBY KEITH MORELAND
Known by middle name.

Born May 2, 1954, at Dallas, Tex.
Height, 6.00. Weight, 200.
Throws and bats righthanded.
Hobbies–Hunting and fishing.
Attended University of Texas, Austin, Texas.

Led American Association in sacrifice flies with 10 in 1978 and with 13 in 1979.
Led American Association catchers in double plays with 10 in 1978.
Tied for Carolina League lead in double plays by third basemen with 19 in 1976.
Tied for American Association lead among catchers in passed balls with 10 in 1978.

Year	Club	League	Pos.	G.	AB.	R.	H.	2B.	3B.	HR.	RBI.	B.A.	PO.	A.	E.	F.A.
1975–Spartanburg	......	W. Car.	3B	69	246	28	68	13	1	1	41	.276	52	128	17	.914
1976–Peninsula	....	Carol.	●3B-SS	78	294	38	83	12	2	4	47	.282	50	221	●26	.912
1976–Reading	....	East.	3B-2B	61	199	7	52	5	0	0	7	.261	62	99	13	.925
1977–Reading	....	East.	C-3B	104	401	61	131	19	1	8	55	.327	339	60	8	.980
1977–Oklahoma City	.. A. A.		C	7	13	3	1	0	0	0	1	.077	17	1	0	1.000
1978–Oklahoma City	.. A. A.		C-1-3-O	130	501	73	145	25	4	16	98	.289	641	75	13	.982
1978–Philadelphia	......	Nat.	C	1	2	0	0	0	0	0	0	.000	4	0	0	1.000
1979–Oklahoma City	.. A. A.		C-3B	130	494	86	149	●34	3	20	109	.302	397	44	13	.971
1979–Philadelphia	......	Nat.	C	14	48	3	18	3	2	0	8	.375	71	3	0	1.000
1980–Philadelphia	......	Nat.	C-OF	62	159	13	50	8	0	4	29	.314	186	22	7	.967
Major League Totals	....			77	209	16	68	11	2	4	37	.325	261	25	7	.976

Selected by Philadelphia Phillies' organization in 7th round of free-agent draft, June 4, 1975.

CHAMPIONSHIP SERIES RECORD

Year	Club	League	Pos.	G.	AB.	R.	H.	2B.	3B.	HR.	RBI.	B.A.	PO.	A.	E.	F.A.
1980–Philadelphia	......	Nat.	C-PH	2	1	0	0	0	0	0	1	.000	0	0	0	.000

WORLD SERIES RECORD

Year	Club	League	Pos.	G.	AB.	R.	H.	2B.	3B.	HR.	RBI.	B.A.	PO.	A.	E.	F.A.
1980–Philadelphia	......	Nat.	DH	3	12	1	4	0	0	0	1	.333	0	0	0	.000

JOSE MORENO (SANTOS)

Born November 2, 1957, at Santo Domingo, Dominican Republic.
Height, 6.00. Weight, 175.
Throws right and bats left and righthanded.

Led Western Carolinas League second basemen in double plays with 73 in 1976.

Year	Club	League	Pos.	G.	AB.	R.	H.	2B.	3B.	HR.	RBI.	B.A.	PO.	A.	E.	F.A.
1975–Auburn	....	NYP	2B	58	231	40	62	11	1	3	22	.268	132	●162	12	.961
1976–Spartanburg	......	W. Car.	2B	135	523	88	148	19	3	6	46	.283	∗311	∗391	∗36	.951
1977–Reading	....	East.	2B	132	514	80	138	18	11	5	52	.268	∗336	370	∗28	.962
1978–Reading	....	East.	2B	110	366	58	95	17	6	6	48	.260	241	244	18	.964
1978–Oklahoma City†	. A. A.		2B	16	67	14	16	1	0	3	9	.239	33	40	3	.961
1979–Tidewater	....	Int.	3B-2B	119	407	49	104	17	4	3	49	.256	76	151	16	.934
1980–Tidewater	....	Int.	O-3-2	68	236	39	66	10	2	5	39	.280	100	42	6	.959
1980–New York‡	....	Nat.	3B-2B	37	46	6	9	2	1	2	9	.196	11	11	3	.880
Major League Totals	....			37	46	6	9	2	1	2	9	.196	11	11	3	.880

Signed as free agent by Philadelphia Phillies' organization, January 30, 1975.

†Traded with First Baseman-Third Baseman Richie Hebner to New York Mets for Pitcher Nino Espinosa, March 27, 1979.

‡Traded with Pitcher John Pacella to San Diego Padres for Pitcher Randy Jones, December 15, 1980.

OMAR RENAN MORENO (QUINTERO)

Born October 24, 1953, at Puerto Armuelles, Panama.
Height, 6.03. Weight, 170.
Throws and bats lefthanded.
Hobbies—Fishing and playing the guitar.

Major league stolen bases: 1975 (1), 1976 (15), 1977 (53), 1978 (71), 1979 (77), 1980 (96). Total—313.
Led Carolina League in stolen bases with 77 in 1973 and Eastern League with 67 in 1974.
Led National League in stolen bases with 71 in 1978 and with 77 in 1979.
Named center fielder on THE SPORTING NEWS National League All-Star Team, 1979.

Year	Club	League	Pos.	G.	AB.	R.	H.	2B.	3B.	HR.	RBI.	B.A.	PO.	A.	E.	F.A.
1969—Brad. Pirates	Gulf C.	OF	25	62	7	18	1	0	0	4	.290	22	0	3	.880
1970—Brad. Pirates	Gulf C.	OF-1B	51	219	32	51	7	4	1	19	.233	129	9	8	.945
1970—Niagara Falls	NYP	OF	10	23	1	4	0	0	0	3	.174	10	0	0	1.000
1971—Brad. Pirates	Gulf C.	OF	38	101	11	33	5	2	0	9	.327	35	4	2	.951
1972—Gastonia	W. Car.	OF	51	144	18	31	5	2	1	17	.215	95	3	3	.970
1972—Niagara Falls	NYP	OF	68	259	52	75	11	6	2	34	.290	87	4	5	.948
1973—Salem	Carol.	OF	136	529	*112	150	22	8	9	56	.284	242	14	13	.952
1973—Charleston	Int.	OF	3	12	1	4	0	1	1	3	.333	4	0	0	1.000
1974—Thetford Mines	East.	OF	112	407	88	122	15	6	7	39	.300	193	13	9	.958
1974—Charleston	Int.	OF	23	82	16	18	3	0	0	4	.220	40	2	1	.977
1975—Charleston	Int.	OF	130	447	73	127	20	2	9	51	.284	*328	10	6	.983
1975—Pittsburgh	Nat.	OF	6	6	1	1	0	0	0	0	.167	0	0	1	.000
1976—Charleston	Int.	OF	94	330	70	104	11	7	3	36	.315	200	*17	1	*.955
1976—Pittsburgh	Nat.	OF	48	122	24	33	4	1	2	12	.270	93	3	4	.960
1977—Pittsburgh	Nat.	OF	150	492	69	118	19	9	7	34	.240	366	10	9	.977
1978—Pittsburgh	Nat.	OF	155	515	95	121	15	7	2	33	.235	409	9	7	.984
1979—Pittsburgh	Nat.	OF	162	*695	110	196	21	12	8	69	.282	490	11	13	.975
1980—Pittsburgh	Nat.	OF	162	*676	87	168	20	●13	2	36	.249	*479	15	5	.990
Major League Totals				683	2506	386	637	79	42	21	184	.254	1837	48	39	.980

Signed as free agent by Pittsburgh Pirates' organization, March 30, 1969.

CHAMPIONSHIP SERIES RECORD

Year	Club	League	Pos.	G.	AB.	R.	H.	2B.	3B.	HR.	RBI.	B.A.	PO.	A.	E.	F.A.
1979—Pittsburgh	Nat.	OF	3	12	3	3	0	1	0	0	.250	7	0	0	1.000

WORLD SERIES RECORD

Tied World Series record for most at bats, seven-game Series (33), 1979.

Year	Club	League	Pos.	G.	AB.	R.	H.	2B.	3B.	HR.	RBI.	B.A.	PO.	A.	E.	F.A.
1979—Pittsburgh	Nat.	OF	7	33	4	11	2	0	0	3	.333	20	1	0	1.000

JOE LEONARD MORGAN

Born September 19, 1943, at Bonham, Tex.
Height, 5.07. Weight, 155.
Throws right and bats lefthanded.
Hobbies—Golf and billiards.
Attended Oakland City College, Oakland, Calif., and California State University
at Hayward, Hayward, Calif.
First cousin of Marsh White, running back with Detroit Lions.

Established major league record for most consecutive errorless games by second baseman, lifetime (91).
Tied major league record for fewest errors by second baseman, season, 150 or more games (5), 1977.
Established National League record for most games by second baseman, career (2,103).
Tied National League records for most runs batted in, two consecutive innings (7), August 19, 1974 (second and third innings); most seasons by second baseman (19).
Tied modern National League record for most bases on balls, game (5), June 2, 1966.
Led National League batters in walks with 97 in 1965, 115 in 1972 and 132 in 1975.
Led National League second basemen in total chances with 814 in 1972.
Led National League in slugging percentage with .576 in 1976.
Led National League batters in sacrifice flies with 12 in 1976.
Tied for National League lead in double plays by second basemen with 106 in 1973.
Tied for National League lead in walks with 93 in 1980.
First player to steal 60 or more bases and hit 25 or more home runs in the same season, 1973 and 1976; and one of two players in major league history to steal 50 or more bases and hit 20 or more home runs in same season (67 stolen bases and 26 home runs in 1973, 58 stolen bases and 22 home runs in 1974, and 60 stolen bases and 27 home runs in 1976).
Made six hits in one game, July 8, 1965, 12 innings.
Major league stolen bases: 1963 (1), 1964 (0), 1965 (20), 1966 (11), 1967 (29), 1968 (3), 1969 (49), 1970 (42), 1971 (40), 1972 (58), 1973 (67), 1974 (58), 1975 (67), 1976 (60), 1977 (49), 1978 (19), 1979 (28), 1980 (24). Total—625.
Led Texas League second basemen in double plays with 106 in 1964.
Voted Most Valuable Player in Texas League, 1964.
Named National League Rookie Player of the Year by THE SPORTING NEWS, 1975.
Named Most Valuable Player in National League, 1975 and 1976.

Named National League Player of the Year by THE SPORTING NEWS, 1975.
Named Major League Player of the Year by THE SPORTING NEWS, 1975 and 1976.
Named second baseman on THE SPORTING NEWS National League All-Star Team, 1972, 1974, 1975, 1976 and 1977.
Named second baseman on THE SPORTING NEWS National League All-Star Fielding Team, 1973, 1974, 1975, 1976 and 1977.

Year—Club	League	Pos.	G.	AB.	R.	H.	2B.	3B.	HR.	RBI.	B.A.	PO.	A.	E.	F.A.
1963—Modesto	Calif.	2B	45	152	42	40	5	3	5	27	.263	81	104	15	.925
1963—Durham	Carol.	2B	95	322	74	107	20	2	13	43	.332	217	273	24	.953
1963—Houston	Nat.	2B	8	25	5	6	0	1	0	3	.240	15	15	3	.909
1964—San Antonio	Texas	2B	•140	496	113	160	★42	8	12	90	.323	319	405	25	★.967
1964—Houston	Nat.	2B	10	37	4	7	0	0	0	0	.189	31	25	3	.949
1965—Houston	Nat.	2B	157	601	100	163	22	12	14	40	.271	348	492	★27	.969
1966—Houston†	Nat.	2B	122	425	60	121	14	8	5	42	.285	256	316	21	.965
1967—Houston	Nat.	2B-OF	133	494	73	136	27	11	6	42	.275	299	344	14	.979
1968—Houston‡	Nat.	2B-OF	10	20	6	5	0	1	0	0	.250	10	6	2	.889
1969—Houston	Nat.	2B-OF	147	535	94	126	18	5	15	43	.236	315	328	18	.973
1970—Houston§	Nat.	2B	144	548	102	147	28	9	8	52	.268	349	430	17	.979
1971—Houston x	Nat.	2B	160	583	87	149	27	•11	13	56	.256	336	★482	12	.986
1972—Cincinnati	Nat.	2B	149	552	★122	161	23	4	16	73	.292	★370	436	8	★.990
1973—Cincinnati	Nat.	2B	157	576	116	167	35	2	26	82	.290	★417	440	9	.990
1974—Cincinnati	Nat.	2B	149	512	107	150	31	3	22	67	.293	344	385	13	.982
1975—Cincinnati	Nat.	2B	146	498	107	163	27	6	17	94	.327	356	425	11	★.986
1976—Cincinnati	Nat.	2B	141	472	113	151	30	5	27	111	.320	342	335	13	.981
1977—Cincinnati	Nat.	2B	153	521	113	150	21	6	22	78	.288	★351	359	5	★.993
1978—Cincinnati	Nat.	2B	132	441	68	104	27	0	13	75	.236	252	290	11	.980
1979—Cincinnati y	Nat.	2B	127	436	70	109	26	1	9	32	.250	259	329	12	.980
1980—Houston z	Nat.	2B	141	461	66	112	17	5	11	49	.243	244	348	7	.988
Major League Totals			2186	7737	1413	2127	373	90	224	939	.275	4894	5785	206	.981

Signed as free agent by Houston Colt .45s' organization, November 1, 1962.
†Fractured knee cap, June 25; on disabled list from June 26 through August 5.
‡On disabled list from May 18 through September 14 with strained ligament in left knee. On military list, April 27 through April 29.
§On military list, June 6 through June 20.
xTraded with Pitcher Jack Billingham, Infielder Denis Menke and Outfielders Cesar Geronimo and Ed Armbrister (latter on Columbus roster) to Cincinnati Reds for First Baseman Lee May, Second Baseman Tommy Helms and Outfielder Jim Stewart, November 29, 1971.
yGranted free agency, November 1, 1979; signed by Houston Astros, January 31, 1980.
zReleased, December 8, 1980; signed by San Francisco Giants, February 9, 1981.

CHAMPIONSHIP SERIES RECORD

Established Championship Series records for most stolen bases, total Series (8); most bases on balls, total Series (21).
Tied Championship Series records for hitting home run in first Series at bat, October 7, 1972; most bases on balls, three-game Series (6), 1976; most two-base hits, three-game Series (3), 1975; most stolen bases, game (3), October 4, 1975; most stolen bases, Series (4), 1975.
Tied National League Championship Series record for most runs, five-game Series (5), 1972.

Year—Club	League	Pos.	G.	AB.	R.	H.	2B.	3B.	HR.	RBI.	B.A.	PO.	A.	E.	F.A.
1972—Cincinnati	Nat.	2B	5	19	5	5	0	0	2	3	.263	11	18	0	1.000
1973—Cincinnati	Nat.	2B	5	20	1	2	1	0	0	1	.100	12	27	0	1.000
1975—Cincinnati	Nat.	2B	3	11	2	3	3	0	0	1	.273	2	9	0	1.000
1976—Cincinnati	Nat.	2B	3	7	2	0	0	0	0	0	.000	9	5	0	1.000
1979—Cincinnati	Nat.	2B	3	11	0	0	0	0	0	0	.000	12	11	0	1.000
1980—Houston	Nat.	2B	4	13	1	2	1	1	0	0	.154	9	8	0	1.000
Championship Series Totals			23	81	11	12	5	1	2	5	.148	55	78	0	1.000

WORLD SERIES RECORD

Tied World Series record for most stolen bases, four-game Series (2), 1976; most putouts by second baseman, four-game Series (13), 1976; most errors by second baseman, four-game Series (2), 1976; one or more hits, each game, four-game Series, 1976.

Year—Club	League	Pos.	G.	AB.	R.	H.	2B.	3B.	HR.	RBI.	B.A.	PO.	A.	E.	F.A.
1972—Cincinnati	Nat.	2B	7	24	4	3	2	0	0	1	.125	18	18	1	.973
1975—Cincinnati	Nat.	2B	7	27	4	7	1	0	0	3	.259	17	28	0	1.000
1976—Cincinnati	Nat.	2B	4	15	3	5	1	1	1	2	.333	13	10	2	.920
World Series Totals			18	66	11	15	4	1	1	6	.227	48	56	3	.972

ALL-STAR GAME RECORD

Tied All-Star Game records for most consecutive games batted safely (7); most times home run as leadoff batter, start of game (1), July 19, 1977.

Year—League	Pos.	AB.	R.	H.	2B.	3B.	HR.	RBI.	B.A.	PO.	A.	E.	F.A.
1970—National	2B	2	1	1	0	0	0	0	.500	1	2	0	1.000
1972—National	2B	4	0	1	0	0	0	1	.250	3	5	0	1.000
1973—National	2B	3	2	1	1	0	0	0	.333	2	2	0	1.000
1974—National	2B	2	0	1	1	0	0	1	.500	3	4	0	1.000
1975—National	2B	4	0	1	0	0	0	0	.250	0	1	0	1.000
1976—National	2B	3	1	1	0	0	0	0	.333	2	3	0	1.000
1977—National	2B	4	1	1	0	0	1	1	.250	1	0	0	1.000
1978—National	2B	3	1	0	0	0	0	0	.000	2	1	0	1.000
1979—National	PH-2B	1	1	0	0	0	0	0	.000	1	1	0	1.000
All-Star Game Totals		26	7	7	2	0	1	3	.269	15	19	0	1.000

Named to National League All-Star Team for the 1966 game; replaced due to injury.

MICHAEL THOMAS MORGAN
(Mike)

Born October 8, 1959, at Tulare, Calif.
Height, 6.03. Weight, 195.
Throws and bats righthanded.

Received reported $50,000 bonus to sign with Oakland A's, 1978.

Year Club	League	G.	IP.	W.	L.	Pct.	H.	R.	ER.	SO.	BB.	ERA.
1978—Oakland	American	3	12	0	3	.000	19	12	10	0	8	7.50
1978—Vancouver	P. Coast	14	92	5	6	.455	109	67	57	31	54	5.58
1979—Ogden	P. Coast	13	101	5	5	.500	93	48	39	42	49	3.48
1979—Oakland	American	13	77	2	10	.167	102	57	51	17	50	5.96
1980—Ogden†‡	P. Coast	20	115	6	9	.400	135	79	69	46	77	5.40
Major League Totals		16	89	2	13	.133	121	69	61	17	58	6.17

Selected by Oakland A's organizaton in 1st round (fourth player selected) of free-agent draft, June 6, 1978.
†On disabled list, May 14 to June 27, 1980.
‡Traded to New York Yankees for Shortstop Fred Stanley and a player to be named later, November 3, 1980; Second Baseman Brian Doyle traded to Oakland completing deal, November 17, 1980.

MICHAEL CHARLES MORLEY
(Mike)

Born January 18, 1959, at Lansing, Mich.
Height, 5.11. Weight, 181.
Throws and bats righthanded.
Attended Ferris State College, Big Rapids, Mich.

Tied for Florida State League lead in shutouts with 5 in 1978.

Year Club	League	G.	IP.	W.	L.	Pct.	H.	R.	ER.	SO.	BB.	ERA.
1977—Sarasota Royals	Gulf Coast	9	55	6	1	.857	55	31	18	44	24	2.95
1978—Ft. Myers	Florida St.	15	109	13	2	*.867	97	30	23	62	27	1.90
1978—Jacksonville	Southern	10	69	3	5	.375	69	27	20	21	22	2.61
1979—Jacksonville	Southern	16	100	8	4	.667	96	43	35	63	40	2.89
1979—Omaha	Am. Assoc.	10	58	3	2	.600	63	32	31	34	24	4.81
1980—Omaha†	Am. Assoc.	7	38	2	2	.500	43	16	13	14	17	3.08

Selected by Kansas City Royals' organization in 2nd round of free-agent draft, June 7, 1977.
†On disabled list, May 10 to June 23 and July 31 to August 29, 1980.

DANIEL JOSEPH MOROGIELLO
(Dan)

Born March 26, 1955, at Brooklyn, N.Y.
Height, 6.01. Weight, 200.
Throws and bats lefthanded.
Attended Seton Hall University, South Orange, N.J.

Year Club	League	G.	IP.	W.	L.	Pct.	H.	R.	ER.	SO.	BB.	ERA.
1976—Kingsport	Ap'lachian	5	25	1	2	.333	28	11	9	26	5	3.24
1976—Greenwood	W. Carol.	8	41	4	1	.800	41	18	15	24	23	3.29
1977—Savannah	Southern	26	169	13	12	.520	164	87	75	109	*99	3.99
1978—Savannah	Southern	27	180	8	14	.364	184	81	62	96	81	3.10
1979—Richmond	Int'national	31	200	12	13	.480	186	90	79	116	76	3.56
1980—Richmond	Int'national	29	196	11	12	.478	*206	102	*88	71	50	4.04

Selected by Detroit Tigers' organization in 8th round of free-agent draft, June 5, 1974.
Selected by Atlanta Braves' organization in 3rd round of free-agent draft, June 8, 1976.

JOHN SCOTT MORRIS
(Jack)

Born May 16, 1956, at St. Paul, Minn.
Height, 6.03. Weight, 190.
Throws and bats righthanded.
Attended Brigham Young University, Provo, Utah.

Year Club	League	G.	IP.	W.	L.	Pct.	H.	R.	ER.	SO.	BB.	ERA.
1976—Montgomery	Southern	12	36	2	3	.400	37	31	25	18	36	6.25
1977—Evansville	Am. Assoc.	20	135	6	7	.462	141	68	54	95	42	3.60
1977—Detroit	American	7	46	1	1	.500	38	20	19	28	23	3.72
1978—Detroit	American	28	106	3	5	.375	107	57	51	48	49	4.33
1979—Evansville	Am. Assoc.	5	34	2	2	.500	22	13	9	28	18	2.38
1979—Detroit	American	27	198	17	7	.708	179	76	72	113	59	3.27
1980—Detroit	American	36	250	16	15	.516	252	125	*116	112	87	4.18
Major League Totals		98	600	37	28	.569	576	275	258	301	218	3.87

Selected by Detroit Tigers' organization in 5th round of free-agent draft, June 8, 1976.

JAMES FORREST MORRISON
(Jim)

Born September 23, 1952, at Pensacola, Fla.
Height, 5.11. Weight, 178.
Throws and bats righthanded.
Attended Georgia Southern, Statesboro, Ga.; received degree.

Tied major league record for fewest three-base hits, most at-bats, season (0 and 604), 1980.
Led Carolina League in total bases with 239 in 1975.
Led Carolina League third basemen in double plays with 35 in 1975.
Led American Association third basemen in double plays with 22 in 1976.
Led American League second basemen in assists with 481 and in double plays with 117 in 1980.

Year Club	League	Pos.	G.	AB.	R.	H.	2B.	3B.	HR.	RBI.	B.A.	PO.	A.	E.	F.A.
1974–Spartanburg	W. Car.	3B	3	8	1	3	1	0	1	3	.375	4	5	1	.900
1974–Rocky Mount	Carol.	3B	72	266	30	68	10	1	4	24	.256	54	156	19	.917
1975–Rocky Mount	Carol.	∗3B-SS	140	497	∗98	143	24	6	∗20	88	.288	135	∗331	∗35	.930
1976–Oklahoma City	A.A.	3B-SS	126	422	79	122	17	6	18	71	.289	100	239	24	.934
1977–Oklahoma City	A.A.	3-2-OF	127	452	72	133	23	4	12	71	.294	99	272	25	.937
1977–Philadelphia	Nat.	3B	5	7	3	3	0	0	0	1	.429	0	7	1	.875
1978–Oklahoma City	A.A.	2-3B-1B	54	189	37	52	6	1	10	28	.275	111	134	10	.961
1978–Philadelphia	Nat.	2-3B-OF	53	108	12	17	1	1	3	10	.157	88	97	6	.969
1979–Oklahoma City†	A.A.	2B-3B	79	281	59	90	15	0	22	61	.320	129	226	17	.954
1979–Chicago	Amer.	2B-3B	67	240	38	66	14	0	14	35	.275	121	185	9	.971
1980–Chicago	Amer.	∗2B-SS	162	604	66	171	40	0	15	57	.283	∗422	482	∗29	.969
National League Totals			58	115	15	20	1	1	3	11	.174	88	104	7	.965
American League Totals			229	844	104	237	54	0	29	92	.281	543	667	38	.970
Major League Totals			287	959	119	257	55	1	32	103	.268	631	771	45	.969

Selected by Pittsburgh Pirates' organization in 5th round of free-agent draft, January 12, 1972.
Selected by Pittsburgh Pirates' organization in secondary phase of free-agent draft, June 6, 1972.
Selected by Philadelphia Phillies' organization in 5th round of free-agent draft, June 5, 1974.
†Traded to Chicago White Sox, July 10, 1979, completing deal in which Philadelphia acquired Pitcher Jack Kucek, April 13, 1979.

CHAMPIONSHIP SERIES RECORD

Year Club	League	Pos.	G.	AB.	R.	H.	2B.	3B.	HR.	RBI.	B.A.	PO.	A.	E.	F.A.
1978–Philadelphia	Nat.	PH	1	1	0	0	0	0	0	0	.000	0	0	0	.000

LLOYD ANTHONY MOSEBY

Born November 5, 1959, at Portland, Ark.
Height, 6.03. Weight, 200.
Throws right and bats lefthanded.

Led Florida State League in total bases with 237 in 1979.

Year Club	League	Pos.	G.	AB.	R.	H.	2B.	3B.	HR.	RBI.	B.A.	PO.	A.	E.	F.A.
1978–Medicine Hat	Pion.	OF	67	253	65	77	12	4	10	38	.304	76	3	6	.929
1979–Dunedin	Fla. St.	OF	129	446	∗89	∗148	23	6	18	84	.332	190	11	9	.957
1980–Syracuse	Int.	OF	37	146	28	47	8	6	3	19	.322	83	1	3	.966
1980–Toronto	Amer.	OF	114	389	44	89	24	1	9	46	.229	208	12	4	.982
Major League Totals			114	389	44	89	24	1	9	46	.229	208	12	4	.982

Selected by Toronto Blue Jays' organization in 1st round (2nd player selected) of free-agent draft, June 6, 1978.

PAUL RICHARD MOSKAU

Name pronounced Moss-koh.

Born December 20, 1953, at St. Joseph, Mo.
Height, 6.02. Weight, 205.
Throws and bats righthanded.
Hobbies—Fishing, hunting, golf and tennis.
Attended Arizona State University, Tempe, Ariz., and Azusa Pacific College, Azusa, Calif.

Led Eastern League pitchers in shutouts with 6 in 1976.

Year Club	League	G.	IP.	W.	L.	Pct.	H.	R.	ER.	SO.	BB.	ERA.
1975–Billings	Pioneer	1	4	0	1	.000	3	5	1	6	3	2.25
1975–Eugene	Northwest	13	84	∗10	1	∗.909	52	22	14	∗92	41	∗1.50
1976–Three Rivers	Eastern	26	180	13	6	.684	134	42	31	124	55	∗1.55
1977–Indianapolis	Am. Assoc.	12	81	7	1	.875	69	35	32	55	26	3.56
1977–Cincinnati	National	20	108	6	6	.500	116	51	48	71	40	4.00
1978–Indianapolis	Am. Assoc.	4	26	1	1	.500	21	14	9	27	15	3.12
1978–Cincinnati	National	26	145	6	4	.600	139	65	64	88	57	3.97
1979–Indianapolis	Am. Assoc.	2	5	0	0	.000	2	0	0	5	1	0.00
1979–Cincinnati	National	21	106	5	4	.556	107	53	46	58	51	3.91
1980–Cincinnati	National	33	153	9	7	.563	147	69	68	94	41	4.00
Major League Totals		100	512	26	21	.553	509	238	226	311	189	3.97

Selected by Cleveland Indians' organization in 5th round of free-agent draft, January 9, 1974.
Selected by Cincinnati Reds' organization in 3rd round of free-agent draft, June 4, 1975.

DARRYL DeWAYNE MOTLEY

Born January 21, 1960, at Muskogee, Okla.
Height, 5.09. Weight, 196.
Throws and bats righthanded.

Year—Club	League	Pos.	G.	AB.	R.	H.	2B.	3B.	HR.	RBI.	B.A.	PO.	A.	E.	F.A.
1978—Sarasota Royals	Gulf C.	OF	10	41	10	20	1	0	2	9	.488	23	1	1	.960
1978—Ft. Myers	Fla. St.	OF	49	151	13	36	3	2	0	12	.238	100	1	4	.962
1979—Ft. Myers	Fla. St.	3B	123	447	47	106	20	2	8	45	.237	•109	183	•29	.910
1980—Ft. Myers†	Fla. St.	3-O-S	32	119	20	36	7	0	4	24	.303	33	56	9	.908
1980—Jacksonville‡	South.	3B	51	182	30	58	15	1	5	31	.319	43	100	10	.935

Selected by Kansas City Royals' organization in 2nd round of free-agent draft, June 6, 1978.
†On disabled list, April 11 to May 18, 1980.
‡On disabled list, August 9 to October 23, 1980.

STEVEN RANCE MULLINIKS

Name pronounced MUL-in-iks.

(Known by middle name.)

Born January 15, 1956, at Tulare, Calif.
Height, 6.00. Weight, 170.
Throws right and bats lefthanded.
Hobbies—Sports.
Son of Harvey Mulliniks, minor leaguer in New York Yankees' organization, 1956-57.

Year—Club	League	Pos.	G.	AB.	R.	H.	2B.	3B.	HR.	RBI.	B.A.	PO.	A.	E.	F.A.
1974—Idaho Falls	Pion.	SS	66	202	28	44	8	3	0	24	.218	•110	•170	•33	.895
1975—Quad Cities	Midw.	SS	52	186	34	50	6	2	1	21	.269	82	136	17	.928
1975—Salinas	Calif.	SS-2B	59	209	38	54	8	0	0	10	.258	88	146	14	.944
1976—El Paso†	Texas	SS-2B	90	333	81	105	22	4	7	51	.315	140	247	20	.951
1977—Salt Lake City	P.C.	SS	58	220	48	68	17	3	11	51	.309	116	207	15	.956
1977—California	Amer.	SS	78	271	36	73	13	2	3	21	.269	112	229	13	.963
1978—Salt Lake City	P.C.	SS	34	127	34	39	6	2	3	21	.307	65	109	12	.935
1978—California	Amer.	SS	50	119	6	22	3	1	1	6	.185	68	93	8	.953
1979—Salt Lake City	P.C.	SS-2B	116	402	94	138	21	7	3	59	.343	204	331	17	.969
1979—California‡	Amer.	SS	22	68	7	10	0	0	1	8	.147	46	43	4	.957
1980—Kansas City	Amer.	SS-2B	36	54	8	14	3	0	0	6	.259	30	53	1	.988
Major League Totals			186	512	57	119	19	3	5	41	.232	256	418	26	.963

Selected by California Angels' organization in 3rd round of free-agent draft, June 5, 1974.
†On disabled list, May 4 to June 9 and September 2 to September 24, 1976.
‡Traded with First Baseman Willie Mays Aikens to Kansas City Royals for Outfielder Al Cowens, Shortstop Todd Cruz and a player to be named later, December 6, 1979; Pitcher Craig Eaton traded to California completing deal, April 1, 1980.

FRANCIS JOSEPH MULLINS
(Fran)

Born May 14, 1957, at Oakland, Calif.
Height, 6.00. Weight, 180.
Throws and bats righthanded.
Attended University of Santa Clara, Santa Clara, Calif.;
received Bachelor of Science degree in Accounting.

Year—Club	League	Pos.	G.	AB.	R.	H.	2B.	3B.	HR.	RBI.	B.A.	PO.	A.	E.	F.A.
1979—Knoxville	South.	SS	53	164	21	44	5	1	4	22	.268	57	150	17	.924
1980—Glens Falls	East.	SS-2B	59	212	46	64	7	2	12	39	.302	109	197	20	.939
1980—Iowa	A.A.	3-2-S	53	201	25	51	12	1	6	35	.254	41	88	8	.942
1980—Chicago	Amer.	3B	21	62	9	12	4	0	0	3	.194	15	36	1	.981
Major League Totals			21	62	9	12	4	0	0	3	.194	15	36	1	.981

Selected by Detroit Tigers' organization in 3rd round of free-agent draft, June 6, 1978.
Selected by Chicago White Sox' organization in 3rd round of free-agent draft, June 5, 1979.

JERRY WAYNE MUMPHREY

Born September 9, 1952, at Tyler, Tex.
Height, 6.02. Weight, 185.
Throws right and bats left and righthanded.
Hobbies—Hunting and fishing.

Major league stolen bases: 1976 (22), 1977 (22), 1978 (14), 1979 (8), 1980 (52). Total—118.
Led American Association in stolen bases with 44 in 1975.
Led Gulf Coast League batters in strikeouts with 45 in 1971.

Year—Club	League	Pos.	G.	AB.	R.	H.	2B.	3B.	HR.	RBI.	B.A.	PO.	A.	E.	F.A.
1971—Sarasota Cards	Gulf C.	OF	38	141	20	36	3	2	0	6	.255	52	1	3	.946
1972—Sarasota Cards	Gulf C.	OF	26	111	21	38	5	2	0	12	.342	63	2	0	1.000
1972—Cedar Rapids	Midw.	OF	11	33	6	6	2	0	0	1	.182	15	0	0	1.000
1972—St. Petersburg	Fla. St.	OF	17	44	7	15	2	1	0	1	.341	11	1	1	.923
1973—St. Petersburg	Fla. St.	OF	142	•556	•93	•159	20	•9	5	52	.286	210	6	4	.982
1974—Arkansas	Tex.	OF	130	507	87	147	21	6	10	54	.290	209	11	9	.961
1974—St. Louis	Nat.	OF	5	2	0	0	0	0	0	0	.000	0	0	0	.000
1975—Tulsa	A. A.	OF	127	495	87	141	19	6	8	59	.285	248	7	6	.977
1975—St. Louis	Nat.	OF	11	16	2	6	2	0	0	1	.375	9	0	0	1.000

Year Club	League	Pos.	G.	AB.	R.	H.	2B.	3B.	HR.	RBI.	B.A.	PO.	A.	E.	F.A.
1976–Tulsa ....A. A.		OF	19	68	14	23	9	1	1	8	.338	42	4	0	1.000
1976–St. Louis ....Nat.		OF	112	384	51	99	15	5	1	26	.258	261	6	2	.993
1977–St. Louis ....Nat.		OF	145	463	73	133	20	10	2	38	.287	291	8	9	.971
1978–St. Louis ....Nat.		OF	125	367	41	96	13	4	2	37	.262	178	10	1	.995
1979–St. Louis †‡§......Nat.		OF	124	339	53	100	10	3	3	32	.295	180	3	3	.984
1980–San Diego ....Nat.		OF	160	564	61	168	24	3	4	59	.298	398	10	●11	.974
Major League Totals			682	2135	283	602	84	25	12	193	.282	1317	37	26	.981

Selected by St. Louis Cardinals' organization in 4th round of free-agent draft, June 8, 1971.
†On disabled list, March 29 to April 20, 1979.
‡Traded with Pitcher John Denny to Cleveland Indians for Outfielder Bobby Bonds, December 7, 1979.
§Traded by Cleveland Indians to San Diego Padres for Pitcher Bob Owchinko and Outfielder Jim Wilhelm, February 15, 1980.

SCOTT ANDREW MUNNINGHOFF

Born December 5, 1958, at Cincinnati, O.
Height, 6.00. Weight, 180.
Throws and bats righthanded.

Led Western Carolinas League in complete games with 9 in 1978.
Led Eastern League in games started with 26 in 1979.
Tied for Western Carolinas League lead in games started with 26 and in shutouts with 3 in 1978.

Year Club	League	G.	IP.	W.	L.	Pct.	H.	R.	ER.	SO.	BB.	ERA.
1977–Auburn ....NYP		6	31	0	5	.000	29	28	19	13	35	5.52
1978–Spartanburg.......................W. Carol.		26	180	*17	7	.708	159	77	46	89	84	2.30
1979–Reading...............................Eastern		26	188	●14	9	.609	172	94	78	87	94	3.73
1980–Oklahoma City ....Am. Assoc.		22	92	4	9	.308	112	63	52	30	54	5.09
1980–Philadelphia.......................National		4	6	0	0	.000	8	3	3	2	5	4.50
Major League Totals................................		4	6	0	0	.000	8	3	3	2	5	4.50

Selected by Philadelphia Phillies' organization in 1st round (22nd player selected) of free-agent draft, June 7, 1977.

STEPHEN ANDREW MURA

Name pronounced MYUR-uh

(Steve)

Born February 12, 1955, at New Orleans, La.
Height, 6.02. Weight, 188.
Throws and bats righthanded.
Attended Tulane University, New Orleans, La.

Tied for Pacific Coast League lead in shutouts with 3 in 1977.
Led Pacific Coast League in complete games with 16 in 1978.

Year Club	League	G.	IP.	W.	L.	Pct.	H.	R.	ER.	SO.	BB.	ERA.
1976–Walla Walla ....Northwest		8	59	7	0	*1.000	41	14	9	68	18	*1.37
1976–Amarillo ....Texas		7	59	4	2	.667	48	22	17	50	27	2.59
1977–Hawaii................................P. Coast		28	165	12	10	.545	164	106	87	123	122	4.75
1978–Hawaii................................P. Coast		26	177	10	*16	.385	177	94	82	*158	90	4.17
1978–San Diego ....National		5	8	0	2	.000	15	10	10	5	5	11.25
1979–San Diego† ....National		38	73	4	4	.500	57	30	25	59	37	3.08
1980–San Diego ....National		37	169	8	7	.533	149	74	69	109	86	3.67
Major League Totals................................		80	250	12	13	.480	221	114	104	173	128	3.74

Selected by San Diego Padres' organization in 2nd round of free-agent draft, June 8, 1976.
†On disabled list, May 23 to June 28, 1979.

BOBBY RAY MURCER

Born May 20, 1946, at Oklahoma City, Okla.
Height, 5.11. Weight, 185.
Throws right and bats lefthanded.
Hobby–Sports.
Attended University of Oklahoma, Norman, Okla.

Tied the following major league records: Most consecutive home runs, two games (4), June 24, 1970; most home runs, consecutive appearances (4), June 24, 1970, doubleheader; hitting for the cycle, August 29 (1st game), 1972.
Tied American League record for most home runs, doubleheader (4), June 24, 1970.
Major League stolen bases: 1965 (0), 1966 (2), 1969 (7), 1970 (15), 1971 (14), 1972 (11), 1973 (6), 1974 (14), 1975 (9), 1976 (12), 1977 (16), 1978 (14), 1979 (3), 1980 (2). Total–125.
Hit three home runs in a game, July 13, 1973.
Led American League in total bases with 314 in 1972.
Led American League outfielders in total chances with 396 in 1972.
Led National League in sacrifice flies with 12 in 1975.
Tied for National League lead in sacrifice flies with 10 in 1977.
Led International League shortstops in double plays with 91 in 1966.
Named outfielder on THE SPORTING NEWS American League All-Star Team, 1971-72-73.
Named outfielder on THE SPORTING NEWS American League All-Star fielding team, 1972.
Named Player of the Year in Carolina League, 1965.
Received reported $20,000 bonus to sign with New York Yankees, 1964.

Year Club League	Pos.	G.	AB.	R.	H.	2B.	3B.	HR.	RBI.	B.A.	PO.	A.	E.	F.A.
1964—Johnson City .....Appal.	S-2B	32	126	34	46	7	4	2	29	.365	39	78	34	.775
1965—Greensboro†......Carol.	SS	12	478	95	154	30	5	16	90	.322	166	320	•55	.898
1965—New York.........Amer.	SS	11	37	2	9	0	1	1	4	.243	28	41	5	.932
1966—New York.........Amer.	SS	21	69	3	12	1	1	0	5	.174	31	50	6	.931
1966—Toledo..............Int.	SS	133	492	69	131	19	9	15	62	.266	207	349	•36	.939
1967-68—New York‡ ....Amer.					(In Military Service)									
1969—New York.........Amer.	OF-3B	152	564	82	146	24	4	26	82	.259	235	81	22	.935
1970—New York.........Amer.	OF	159	581	95	146	23	3	23	78	.251	375	•15	3	.992
1971—New York.........Amer.	OF	146	529	94	175	25	6	25	94	.331	317	10	5	.985
1972—New York.........Amer.	OF	153	585	*102	171	30	7	33	96	.292	*382	11	3	.992
1973—New York§.......Amer.	OF	160	616	83	187	29	2	22	95	.304	380	•14	6	.985
1974—New York§.......Amer.	OF	156	606	69	166	25	4	10	88	.274	297	*21	7	.978
1975—San Francisco ...Nat.	OF	147	526	80	157	29	4	11	91	.298	201	10	4	.981
1976—San Francisco x.Nat.	OF	147	533	73	138	20	2	23	90	.259	282	11	12	.961
1977—Chicago............Nat.	O-2-S	154	554	90	147	18	3	27	89	.265	238	11	5	.980
1978—Chicago ....Nat.	OF	146	499	66	140	22	6	9	64	.281	225	8	5	.979
1979—Chicago y.........Nat.	OF	58	190	22	49	4	1	7	22	.258	110	4	0	1.000
1979—New York ....Amer.	OF	74	264	42	72	12	0	8	33	.273	169	4	3	.983
1980—New York ....Amer.	OF	100	297	41	80	9	1	13	57	.269	82	2	4	.955
American League Totals..................		1132	4148	613	1164	178	29	161	632	.281	2296	249	64	.975
National League Totals....................		652	2302	331	631	93	16	77	356	.274	1056	44	26	.977
Major League Totals		1784	6450	944	1795	271	45	238	988	.278	3352	293	90	.976

Signed as free agent by New York Yankees' organization, June 2, 1964.
†On disabled list, May 3 through May 15, 1965.
‡On military list, March 6, 1967 through December 6, 1968.
§Traded to San Francisco Giants for Outfielder Bobby Bonds, October 21, 1974.
xTraded with Infielder Steve Ontiveros and Pitcher Andrew Muhlstock to Chicago Cubs for Third Baseman Bill Madlock and Infielder Rob Sperring, February 11, 1977.
yTraded to New York Yankees for Pitcher Paul Semall and cash, June 26, 1979.

CHAMPIONSHIP SERIES RECORD

Year Club League	Pos.	G.	AB.	R.	H.	2B.	3B.	HR.	RBI.	B.A.	PO.	A.	E.	F.A.
1980—New York ....Amer.	DH	1	4	0	0	0	0	0	0	.000	0	0	0	.000

ALL-STAR GAME RECORD

Year League	Pos.	AB.	R.	H.	2B.	3B.	HR.	RBI.	B.A.	PO.	A.	E.	F.A.
1971—American..............	OF	3	0	1	0	0	0	0	.333	1	0	0	1.000
1972—American..............	OF	3	0	0	0	0	0	0	.000	1	0	0	1.000
1973—American..............	OF	3	0	0	0	0	0	0	.000	0	1	0	1.000
1974—American..............	OF	2	0	0	0	0	0	0	.000	0	0	0	.000
1975—National................	OF	2	0	0	0	0	0	0	.000	1	0	0	1.000
All-Star Game Totals		13	0	1	0	0	0	0	.077	3	1	0	1.000

DALE BRYAN MURPHY

Born March 12, 1956, at Portland, Ore.
Height, 6.05. Weight, 215.
Throws and bats righthanded.
Hobbies—Music, art and reading.
Attended Portland Community College, Portland, Ore.

Hit three home runs in one game, vs. San Francisco Giants, May 18, 1979.
Tied for International League lead in total bases with 249 in 1977.
Led National League in strikeouts with 145 in 1978 and with 133 in 1980.
Led National League first basemen in errors with 20 in 1978.
Named International League Rookie of the Year, 1977.

Year Club League	Pos.	G.	AB.	R.	H.	2B.	3B.	HR.	RBI.	B.A.	PO.	A.	E.	F.A.
1974—Kingsport..........Appal.	C	54	181	28	46	7	0	5	31	.254	389	28	7	.983
1975—Greenwood.........W. Car.	C-1B	131	443	48	101	20	1	5	48	.228	723	81	18	.978
1976—Savannah ....South.	C	104	352	37	94	13	5	12	55	.267	444	40	10	.980
1976—Richmond ....Int.	C-OF	18	50	10	13	1	1	4	8	.260	60	9	4	.945
1976—Atlanta..............Nat.	C	19	65	3	17	6	0	0	9	.262	100	13	3	.974
1977—Richmond ....Int.	C-1B	127	466	71	142	•33	4	22	*90	.305	600	50	15	.977
1977—Atlanta..............Nat.	C	18	76	5	24	8	1	2	14	.316	114	11	6	.954
1978—Atlanta..............Nat.	1B-C	151	530	66	120	14	3	23	79	.226	1220	105	23	.983
1979—Atlanta†............Nat.	1B-C	104	384	53	106	7	2	21	57	.276	812	57	20	.978
1980—Atlanta ....Nat.	OF-1B	156	569	98	160	27	2	33	89	.281	384	15	6	.985
Major League Totals		448	1624	225	427	62	8	79	248	.263	2630	201	58	.980

Selected by Atlanta Braves' organization in 1st round (fifth player selected) of free-agent draft, June 5, 1974.
†On disabled list, May 25 to July 19, 1979.

ALL-STAR GAME RECORD

Year League	Pos.	AB.	R.	H.	2B.	3B.	HR.	RBI.	B.A.	PO.	A.	E.	F.A.
1980—National................	OF	1	0	0	0	0	0	0	.000	0	0	0	.000

DWAYNE KEITH MURPHY

Born March 18, 1955, at Merced, Calif.
Height, 6.01. Weight, 180.
Throws right and bats lefthanded.
Hobby—Automobiles.

Tied for Southern League lead in double plays by outfielders with 4 in 1977.
Named as outfielder on THE SPORTING NEWS American League All-Star fielding team, 1980.

Year Club	League	Pos.	G.	AB.	R.	H.	2B.	3B.	HR.	RBI.	B.A.	PO.	A.	E.	F.A.
1973—Lewiston	N'west	OF	68	215	25	50	7	2	3	19	.233	102	*13	6	.950
1974—Burlington†	Mid.	OF	53	150	16	33	6	2	2	10	.220	55	2	3	.959
1975—Modesto	Calif.	OF	126	429	81	125	20	7	8	71	.291	250	7	9	.966
1976—Chattanooga	South.	OF	68	200	32	52	6	0	1	23	.260	138	6	1	.993
1976—Tucson	P. C.	OF	52	179	32	42	7	2	3	11	.235	125	6	4	.970
1977—Chattanooga	South.	OF	132	406	53	104	11	9	5	53	.256	320	14	5	*.985
1978—Vancouver	P.C.	OF-SS	42	148	35	39	4	1	7	17	.264	125	9	3	.978
1978—Oakland	Amer.	OF	60	52	15	10	2	0	0	5	.192	49	1	0	1.000
1979—Oakland‡	Amer.	OF	121	388	57	99	10	4	11	40	.255	322	10	4	.988
1980—Oakland	Amer.	OF	159	573	86	157	18	2	13	68	.274	*507	13	5	.990
Major League Totals			340	1013	158	266	30	6	24	113	.263	878	24	9	.990

Selected by Oakland A's organization in 15th round of free-agent draft, June 5, 1973.
†On disabled list, July 16 to September 16, 1974.
‡On disabled list, June 21 to July 14, 1979.

DALE ALBERT MURRAY

Born February 2, 1950, at Cuero, Tex.
Height, 6.03. Weight, 205.
Throws and bats righthanded.
Hobbies—Hunting and working on cars.
Attended Blinn Junior College, Brenham, Tex., and Victoria College, Victoria, Tex.

Tied major league record for most intentional bases on balls allowed, season (23), 1978.
Major League saves: 1974 (10), 1975 (9), 1976 (13), 1977 (4), 1978 (7), 1979 (5), 1980 (0). Total—48.

Year Club	League	G.	IP.	W.	L.	Pct.	H.	R.	ER.	SO.	BB.	ERA.
1970—Watertown	Northern	22	51	4	6	.400	50	41	32	48	39	5.65
1971—West Palm Beach†	Florida St.	1	1	0	1	.000	4	4	4	2	2	36.00
1972—West Palm Beach	Florida St.	7	10	3	1	.750	10	6	6	8	7	5.40
1972—Quebec City	Eastern	39	108	11	5	.688	85	41	29	64	53	2.42
1973—Peninsula	Int'national	28	150	8	•13	.381	145	77	71	89	75	4.26
1974—Memphis	Int'national	30	43	4	2	.667	34	11	7	36	19	1.47
1974—Montreal	National	32	70	1	1	.500	46	12	8	31	23	1.03
1975—Montreal‡	National	63	111	15	8	.652	134	59	49	43	39	3.97
1976—Montreal§	National	81	113	4	9	.308	117	47	41	35	37	3.27
1977—Cincinnati	National	61	102	7	2	.778	125	60	56	42	46	4.94
1978—Cincinnati x-New York	National	68	119	9	6	.600	119	59	50	62	53	3.78
1979—New York y-Montreal	National	67	110	5	10	.333	119	62	56	41	55	4.58
1980—Denver	Am. Assoc.	16	44	4	1	.800	31	13	8	25	17	1.64
1980—Montreal z	National	16	29	0	1	.000	39	23	20	16	12	6.21
Major League Totals		388	654	41	37	.526	699	322	280	270	265	3.85

Selected by Montreal Expos' organization in 18th round of free-agent draft, June 4, 1970.
†On disabled list, April 16 to September 30, 1971.
‡On disabled list, May 12 to June 17, 1975.
§Traded with Pitcher Woodie Fryman to Cincinnati Reds for First Baseman Tony Perez and Pitcher Will McEnaney, December 16, 1976.
xTraded to New York Mets for Outfielder Ken Henderson, May 19, 1978.
ySold to Montreal Expos, August 30, 1979.
zReleased, August 28, 1980.

RECORD AS OUTFIELDER

Year Club	League	Pos.	G.	AB.	R.	H.	2B.	3B.	HR.	RBI.	B.A.	PO.	A.	E.	F.A.
1970—W. Palm Beach	Fla. St.	OF	4	3	0	1	0	0	0	0	.333	0	0	0	.000

EDDIE CLARENCE MURRAY

Born February 24, 1956, at Los Angeles, Calif.
Height, 6.02. Weight, 200.
Throws right and bats left and righthanded.
Hobby—Basketball.
Attended California State University at Los Angeles, Los Angeles, Calif.
Brother of Richard Murray, first baseman in San Francisco Giants' organization;
Leon Murray, first baseman in San Franciso Giants' organization, 1970;
Charles Murray, outfielder in Houston Colt .45s—Astros' organization,
1962 through 1966 and 1969; and Venice Murray, former first
baseman in San Francisco Giants' organization.

Hit three home runs in one game, vs. Minnesota Twins, August 29, 1979.
Hit three home runs in one game, vs. Toronto Blue Jays, September 14, 1980.
Switch-hit home runs (two righthanded and one lefthanded), vs. Minnesota Twins, August 29, 1979.
Led Florida State League first basemen in double plays with 113 in 1974.
Led American League first basemen in putouts with 1504 in 1978.
Named Appalachian League Player of the Year, 1973.
Named American League Rookie of the Year by The Baseball Writers' Association of America, 1977.

Year Club League	Pos.	G.	AB.	R.	H.	2B.	3B.	HR.	RBI.	B.A.	PO.	A.	E.	F.A.
1973—Bluefield ....Appal.	1B	50	188	34	54	6	0	11	32	.287	421	14	13	.971
1974—Miami ....Fla. St.	1B	131	460	64	133	29	7	12	63	.289	*1114	*51	*25	.979
1974—Asheville ....South.	1B	2	7	1	2	2	0	0	2	.286	17	0	0	1.000
1975—Asheville ....South.	1B-3B	124	436	66	115	13	5	17	68	.264	637	58	15	.979
1976—Charlotte ....South.	1B	88	299	46	89	15	2	12	46	.298	746	45	9	.989
1976—Rochester ....Int.	1B-O-3	54	168	35	46	6	2	11	40	.274	291	13	5	.984
1977—Baltimore ....Amer.	OF-1B	160	611	81	173	29	2	27	88	.283	482	20	4	.992
1978—Baltimore ....Amer.	1B-3B	161	610	85	174	32	3	27	95	.285	1507	112	6	.996
1979—Baltimore ....Amer.	1B	159	606	90	179	30	2	25	99	.295	1456	107	10	.994
1980—Baltimore ....Amer.	1B	158	621	100	186	36	2	32	116	.300	1369	77	9	.994
Major League Totals		638	2448	356	712	127	9	111	398	.291	4814	316	29	.994

Selected by Baltimore Orioles' organization in 3rd round of free-agent draft, June 5, 1973.

CHAMPIONSHIP SERIES RECORD
Tied American League Championship Series record for most bases on balls, four-game Series (5), 1979.

Year Club League	Pos.	G.	AB.	R.	H.	2B.	3B.	HR.	RBI.	B.A.	PO.	A.	E.	F.A.
1979—Baltimore ....Amer.	1B	4	12	3	5	0	0	1	5	.417	44	3	2	.959

WORLD SERIES RECORD
Established World Series record for most double plays started by first baseman, game (2), October 11, 1979.

Year Club League	Pos.	G.	AB.	R.	H.	2B.	3B.	HR.	RBI.	B.A.	PO.	A.	E.	F.A.
1979—Baltimore ....Amer.	1B	7	26	3	4	1	0	1	2	.154	60	7	0	1.000

ALL-STAR GAME RECORD
Named to American League All-Star Team for 1978 game; did not play.

RICHARD DALE MURRAY
(Rich)

Born July 6, 1957, at Los Angeles, Calif.
Height, 6.04. Weight, 205.
Throws and bats righthanded.
Brother of Eddie Murray, outfielder-first basemen with Baltimore Orioles;
Leon Murray, first baseman in San Francisco Giants' organization, 1970;
Charles Murray, outfielder in Houston Colt .45s and Astros' organization,
1962 through 1966 and 1969; and Venice Murray, former first
baseman in San Francisco Giants' organization.

Led Pacific Coast League first basemen in double plays with 155 in 1978.
Tied for Midwest League in double plays by first basemen with 105 in 1977.

Year Club League	Pos.	G.	AB.	R.	H.	2B.	3B.	HR.	RBI.	B.A.	PO.	A.	E.	F.A.
1975—Great Falls........Pion.	1B-OF	25	85	8	23	2	1	1	14	.271	128	3	7	.949
1976—Cedar Rapids†..Midw.	1B-OF	66	178	24	47	7	4	6	30	.264	213	11	8	.966
1977—Cedar Rapids.....Midw.	1B	129	494	72	136	27	0	21	94	.275	1149	54	16	.987
1978—Phoenix‡..........P. C.	1B	117	442	66	124	23	6	5	58	.281	*1109	64	13	.989
1979—Phoenix ....P. C.	*1B-OF	125	441	63	116	13	8	5	67	.263	1043	86	*26	.977
1980—Phoenix ...........P.C.	3B-1B	49	168	22	44	6	1	7	31	.262	53	87	19	.881
1980—San Francisco§ .Nat.	1B	53	194	19	42	8	2	4	24	.216	508	35	7	.987
Major League Totals.......................		53	194	19	42	8	2	4	24	.216	508	35	7	.987

Selected by San Francisco Giants' organization in 6th round of free-agent draft, June 4, 1975.
†On disabled list, June 21 to July 29, 1976.
‡On disabled list, June 9 to June 28, 1978.
§On emergency disabled list, July 11 to September 9, 1980.

ROBERT HOWARD MYRICK JR.
(Bob)

Born October 1, 1952, at Hattiesburg, Miss.
Height, 6.01. Weight, 195.
Throws left and bats righthanded.
Hobbies—Hunting, fishing and all outdoor activities.
Attended Mississippi State University, Starkville, Miss.
Grand nephew of Charles (Buddy) Myer, infielder with Boston Red Sox and
Washington Senators, 1925 through 1941.

Year Club	League	G.	IP.	W.	L.	Pct.	H.	R.	ER.	SO.	BB.	ERA.
1974—Batavia................................NYP		12	82	3	5	.375	88	53	41	62	39	4.50
1974—Tidewater ....Int'national		2	2	0	0	.000	1	0	0	1	2	0.00
1975—Jackson ....Texas		22	116	7	4	.636	98	54	42	70	49	3.26
1975—Tidewater ....Int'national		7	11	3	0	1.000	7	0	0	9	2	0.00
1976—Tidewater ....Int'national		13	24	2	0	1.000	22	10	7	22	10	2.63
1976—New York ....National		21	28	1	1	.500	34	13	10	11	13	3.21
1977—New York†.........................National		44	87	2	2	.500	86	39	35	49	33	3.62
1978—Tidewater ....Int'national		31	94	4	8	.333	107	48	40	63	40	3.83
1978—New York ....National		17	25	0	3	.000	18	10	9	13	13	3.24
1979—New York‡.........................National						Did not play						
1979—Tidewater§ ....Int'national		9	27	3	1	.750	21	10	10	21	9	3.33

Year Club	League	G.	IP.	W.	L.	Pct.	H.	R.	ER.	SO.	BB.	ERA.
1979–Tucson x	P. Coast	22	42	3	4	.429	48	24	23	31	31	4.93
1980–Tidewater y	Int'national	2	6	0	1	.000	7	3	1	3	4	1.50
1980–Wichita	Am. Assoc.	42	73	6	2	.750	63	23	21	45	35	2.59
Major League Totals		82	140	3	6	.333	138	62	54	73	59	3.47

Selected by Baltimore Orioles' organization in 29th round of free-agent draft, June 4, 1970.
Selected by New York Mets' organization in 20th round of free-agent draft, June 5, 1974.
†On disabled list, July 4 to July 28, 1977.
‡On disabled list, March 22 to May 7, 1979.
§Traded with Pitcher Mike Bruhert to Texas Rangers' organization for Pitcher Dock Ellis, June 15, 1979.
xReleased, January 25, 1980; signed by New York Mets' organization, February 29, 1980.
yTraded to Chicago Cubs' organization for Infielder Todd Winterfeldt, April 29, 1980.

WILLIAM GERARD NAHORODNY
Name pronounced Na-ha-rod-knee.
(Bill)
Born August 31, 1953, at Hamtramck, Mich.
Height, 6.02. Weight, 195.
Throws and bats righthanded.
Hobby–Music.
Attended St. Clair County Community College, Port Huron, Mich.

Led New York-Pennsylvania League catchers in passed balls with 13 and tied for lead in double plays with 6 in 1972.
Tied for New York-Pennsylvania League lead in sacrifice flies with 6 in 1972.
Tied for American Association lead in double plays by catchers with 8 in 1976.
Named New York-Pennsylvania League Rookie of the Year, 1972.

Year Club	League	Pos.	G.	AB.	R.	H.	2B.	3B.	HR.	RBI.	B.A.	PO.	A.	E.	F.A.
1972–Auburn	NYP	★C-3B	69	217	36	57	14	2	6	33	.263	★532	●40	13	★.978
1973–Rocky Mount	Carol.	★C-1-3	118	389	40	102	23	1	14	76	.262	798	64	10	★.989
1974–Reading	East.	C-1-3	110	388	58	93	17	2	19	77	.240	642	70	13	.982
1975–Toledo	Int.	★C-1B	125	411	51	105	17	4	★19	64	.255	691	71	7	★.991
1976–Oklahoma City	A.A.	★C-1B	114	391	74	114	22	3	23	78	.292	★606	50	7	.989
1976–Philadelphia	Nat.	C	3	5	0	1	1	0	0	0	.200	7	0	0	1.000
1977–Oklahoma City†	A.A.	1B-C	115	386	52	101	16	4	17	69	.262	878	57	6	.994
1977–Chicago	Amer.	C	7	23	3	6	1	0	1	4	.261	29	6	0	1.000
1978–Chicago	Amer.	C-1B	107	347	29	82	11	2	8	35	.236	509	55	11	.981
1979–Chicago‡§	Amer.	C	65	179	20	46	10	0	6	29	.257	223	25	7	.973
1980–Atlanta	Nat.	C-1B	59	157	14	38	12	0	5	18	.242	178	24	2	.990
National League Totals			62	162	14	39	13	0	5	18	.241	185	24	3	.986
American League Totals			179	549	52	134	22	2	15	68	.244	761	86	18	.979
Major League Totals			241	711	66	173	35	2	20	86	.243	946	110	21	.981

Selected by Philadelphia Phillies' organization in 6th round of free-agent draft, June 6, 1972.
†Sold on waivers to Chicago White Sox, September 8, 1977.
‡On supplemental disabled list, June 30 to July 23, 1979.
§Traded to Atlanta Braves for Pitcher Rick Wieters, December 3, 1979.

TITO ANGELO NANNI JR.
Born December 3, 1959, at Philadelphia, Pa.
Height, 6.04. Weight, 220.
Throws and bats lefthanded.

Led Carolina League batters in strikeouts with 132 in 1979.

Year Club	League	Pos.	G.	AB.	R.	H.	2B.	3B.	HR.	RBI.	B.A.	PO.	A.	E.	F.A.
1979–Alexandria	Carol.	OF	113	402	49	91	19	1	6	48	.226	150	5	11	.934
1980–San Jose	Calif.	OF	57	191	25	38	6	2	3	23	.199	98	3	3	.971
1980–Wausau	Midw.	OF	64	237	33	60	8	0	12	40	.253	129	11	6	.959

Selected by Seattle Mariners' organization in 1st round (6th player selected) of free-agent draft, June 6, 1978.

STEVEN CURTIS NARLESKI
(Steve)
Born September 12, 1955, at Camden, N.J.
Height, 6.03. Weight, 195.
Throws and bats righthanded.
Attended Camden County Community College, Blackwood, N.J.
Son of Ray Narleski, pitcher with Cleveland Indians and Detroit Tigers,
1954 through 1959 and grandson of William Narleski, infielder
with Boston Braves, 1929 and 1930.

Year Club	League	G.	IP.	W.	L.	Pct.	H.	R.	ER.	SO.	BB.	ERA.
1976–San Jose	California	16	37	0	2	.000	35	35	24	16	28	5.84
1976–Batavia	NYP	18	38	2	1	.667	36	21	14	31	23	3.32
1977–Waterloo	Midwest	3	4	0	1	.000	8	9	9	3	4	20.25
1977–Batavia	NYP	25	36	2	2	.500	30	21	18	29	22	4.50
1978–Waterloo	Midwest	29	55	9	2	.818	46	22	19	46	18	3.11

Year Club	League	G.	IP.	W.	L.	Pct.	H.	R.	ER.	SO.	BB.	ERA.
1978–Chattanooga	Southern	12	24	0	1	.000	27	13	13	15	5	4.88
1979–Chattanooga	Southern	39	78	11	6	.647	69	32	30	44	22	3.46
1979–Tacoma	P. Coast	4	11	1	1	.500	7	7	5	4	5	4.09
1980–Chattanooga	Southern	47	102	11	12	.478	102	52	45	68	42	3.97

Signed as free agent by Cleveland Indians' organization, January 13, 1976.

JERRY AUSTIN NARRON

Born January 15, 1956, at Goldsboro, N. C.
Height, 6.03. Weight, 205.
Throws right and bats lefthanded.
Attends East Carolina University, Greenville, N. C.
Brother of John Narron, Jr., who played in New York Yankees' and Chicago White
Sox' organizations, 1974-75; nephew of Sam Narron, former catcher with
St. Louis Cardinals and former coach for the Pittsburgh Pirates.

Led Florida State League catchers in double plays with 7 in 1976.

Year Club	League	Pos.	G.	AB.	R.	H.	2B.	3B.	HR.	RBI.	B.A.	PO.	A.	E.	F.A.
1974–Johnson City	Appal.	C-OF	66	226	43	68	15	3	7	49	.301	249	19	8	.971
1975–Ft. Lauderdale	Fla. St.	1B-C-OF	113	360	39	76	12	0	2	34	.211	425	33	2	.996
1976–Ft. Lauderdale	Fla. St.	*C-1B	119	412	35	101	17	0	6	56	.245	563	56	8	*.987
1977–West Haven	East.	C-1B	121	438	80	131	16	0	28	93	.299	625	40	7	.990
1978–Tacoma	P.C.	C-1B	120	435	67	121	25	1	15	84	.278	552	78	18	.972
1979–New York†	Amer.	C	61	123	17	21	3	1	4	18	.171	167	15	5	.973
1980–Spokane	P.C.	C-1B	67	233	40	66	14	2	9	39	.283	223	19	6	.976
1980–Seattle	Amer.	C	48	107	7	21	3	0	4	18	.196	115	11	1	.992
Major League Totals			109	230	24	42	6	1	8	36	.183	282	26	6	.981

Selected by New York Yankees' organization in 6th round of free-agent draft, June 5, 1974.
†Traded with Outfielder Juan Beniquez and Pitchers Jim Beattie and Rick Anderson to Seattle Mariners for Outfielder Ruppert Jones and Pitcher Jim Lewis, November 1, 1979.

PHILIP NASTU

Name pronounced NASS-too.

(Phil)

Born March 8, 1955, at Bridgeport, Conn.
Height, 6.02. Weight, 185.
Throws and bats lefthanded.
Attended University of Bridgeport, Bridgeport, Conn.

Year Club	League	G.	IP.	W.	L.	Pct.	H.	R.	ER.	SO.	BB.	ERA.
1977–Cedar Rapids	Midwest	16	115	10	2	.833	82	35	24	134	36	*1.88
1977–Waterbury	Eastern	11	95	6	2	.750	73	29	25	67	28	2.37
1978–Phoenix	P. Coast	26	160	9	8	.529	157	94	83	114	91	4.67
1978–San Francisco	National	3	8	0	1	.000	8	5	5	5	2	5.63
1979–Phoenix	P. Coast	7	38	1	1	.500	38	17	14	27	15	3.32
1979–San Francisco	National	25	100	3	4	.429	105	51	48	47	41	4.32
1980–Phoenix†	P. Coast	16	93	4	8	.333	105	63	56	39	63	5.42
1980–San Francisco‡	National	6	6	0	0	.000	10	9	4	1	5	6.00
Major League Totals		34	114	3	5	.375	123	65	57	53	48	4.50

Signed as free agent by San Francisco Giants' organization, December 22, 1976.
†Played one game as oufielder with two putouts.
‡Traded with Second Baseman Joe Strain to Chicago Cubs for Outfielders Jerry Martin and Jesus Figueroa, December 12, 1980.

WAYLAND EUGENE NELSON II
(Gene)

Born December 3, 1960, at Tampa, Fla.
Height, 6.00. Weight, 172.
Throws and bats righthanded.

Led Florida State League in shutouts with 5 and in complete games with 16 in 1980.

Year Club	League	G.	IP.	W.	L.	Pct.	H.	R.	ER.	SO.	BB.	ERA.
1978–Sarasota Rangers	G. Coast	14	52	5	0	●1.000	41	18	13	28	20	2.25
1979–Asheville†	W. Car.	33	155	13	5	*.722	149	77	62	96	44	3.60
1980–Ft. Lauderdale	Florida St.	27	196	*20	3	*.870	146	51	43	130	70	1.97

Selected by Texas Rangers' organization in 29th round of free-agent draft, June 6, 1978.
†Traded with Pitcher Ray Fontenot to New York Yankees' organization for Pitchers Bob Polinsky, Neal Mersch and Mark Softy, October 8, 1979, to complete deal of August 1, 1979, in which Yankees traded Outfielder Mickey Rivers and three players to be named later to Rangers for Third Baseman Amos Lewis and two players to be named later.

GRAIG NETTLES

Born August 20, 1944, at San Diego, Calif.
Height, 6.00. Weight, 187.
Throws right and bats lefthanded.
Attended San Diego State College, San Diego, Calif.
Brother of Jim Nettles, outfielder with Kansas City Royals' organization.

Established major league records for most assists by third baseman, season, 412, and most double plays by third baseman, season, 54, 1971.

Tied major league records for most home runs month of April, 11, in 1974; and fewest three-base hits, season, 150 or more games, 0, 1972 and 1973.

Established American League record for most home runs by third baseman, career (267).

Tied American League record for most home runs, doubleheader, 4, April 14, 1974.

Led American League third basemen in total chances with 545 in 1974.

Led American League in sacrifice flies with 11 in 1975.

Led Southern League third basemen in double plays with 34 in 1967 and led Pacific Coast League third basemen with 20 in 1968.

Led American League third basemen in total chances with 539 and double plays with 30 in 1976.

Named third baseman on THE SPORTING NEWS American League All-Star Team, 1975, 1977 and 1978.

Named third baseman on THE SPORTING NEWS American League All-Star Fielding Team, 1977 and 1978.

Year—Club	League	Pos.	G.	AB.	R.	H.	2B.	3B.	HR.	RBI.	B.A.	PO.	A.	E.	F.A.
1966—Wis. Rapids	Midw.	2B-3B	117	413	84	111	19	6	*28	75	.269	240	245	28	.945
1967—Charlotte	South.	3B	140	499	69	116	18	4	●19	86	.232	107	*318	24	.947
1967—Minnesota	Amer.	PH	3	3	0	1	1	0	0	0	.333	0	0	0	.000
1968—Denver	P.C.	3-OF-1B	130	451	84	134	17	●12	22	83	.297	125	266	17	.958
1968—Minnesota	Amer.	OF-3-1	22	76	13	17	2	1	5	8	.224	50	9	2	.967
1969—Minnesota†	Amer.	OF-3B	96	225	27	50	9	2	7	26	.222	88	44	2	.985
1970—Cleveland	Amer.	*3B-OF	157	549	81	129	13	1	26	62	.235	135	358	17	*.967
1971—Cleveland	Amer.	3B	158	598	78	156	18	1	28	86	.261	*159	*412	16	.973
1972—Cleveland‡	Amer.	3B	150	557	65	141	28	0	17	70	.253	114	*358	*21	.957
1973—New York	Amer.	3B	160	552	65	129	18	0	22	81	.234	117	*410	26	.953
1974—New York	Amer.	*3B-SS	155	566	74	139	21	1	22	75	.246	*147	377	21	.961
1975—New York	Amer.	3B	157	581	71	155	24	4	21	91	.267	135	*379	19	.964
1976—New York	Amer.	3B-SS	158	583	88	148	29	2	*32	93	.254	137	*384	19	.965
1977—New York	Amer.	3B	158	589	99	150	23	4	37	107	.255	132	321	12	.974
1978—New York	Amer.	3B-SS	159	587	81	162	23	2	27	93	.276	110	326	11	.975
1979—New York	Amer.	3B	145	521	71	132	15	1	20	73	.253	110	339	16	.966
1980—New York§	Amer.	3B-SS	89	324	52	79	14	0	16	45	.244	59	183	10	.960
Major League Totals			1767	6311	865	1588	238	19	280	910	.252	1493	3900	192	.966

Selected by Minnesota Twins' organization in 4th round of free-agent draft, June 9, 1965.

†Traded with Pitchers Dean Chance and Robert L. Miller and Outfielder Ted Uhlaender to Cleveland Indians for Pitchers Luis Tiant and Stan Williams, December 12, 1969.

‡Traded with Catcher Jerry Moses to New York Yankees for Catcher-First Baseman John Ellis, Infielder Jerry Kenney and Outfielders Charlie Spikes and Rosendo Torres, November 27, 1972.

§On supplemental disabled list, July 27, 1980; transferred to disabled list, August 21 to October 2, 1980.

CHAMPIONSHIP SERIES RECORD

Tied American League Championship Series record for most home runs, five-game Series (2), 1976.

Year—Club	League	Pos.	G.	AB.	R.	H.	2B.	3B.	HR.	RBI.	B.A.	PO.	A.	E.	F.A.
1969—Minnesota	Amer.	PH	1	1	0	1	0	0	0	0	1.000	0	0	0	.000
1976—New York	Amer.	3B	5	17	2	4	1	0	2	4	.235	5	14	0	1.000
1977—New York	Amer.	3B	5	20	1	3	0	0	0	1	.150	2	12	0	1.000
1978—New York	Amer.	3B	4	15	3	5	0	1	1	2	.333	6	7	0	1.000
1980—New York	Amer.	3B-PH	2	6	1	1	0	0	1	1	.167	0	2	0	1.000
Championship Series Totals			17	59	7	14	1	1	4	8	.237	13	35	0	1.000

WORLD SERIES RECORD

Established World Series records for most double plays by third baseman, four-game Series (3), 1976; most assists by third baseman, six-game Series (20), 1977; highest fielding average by third baseman, six-game Series, most chances accepted (1.000 and 26), 1978; most double plays by third baseman, total Series (6); most double plays and double plays started by third baseman, six-game Series (3), 1978.

Tied World Series records for most double plays started by third baseman, four-game Series (2), 1976; most double plays started, game (2), October 19, 1976; fewest chances accepted by third baseman, game (0), October 18, 1977.

Year—Club	League	Pos.	G.	AB.	R.	H.	2B.	3B.	HR.	RBI.	B.A.	PO.	A.	E.	F.A.
1976—New York	Amer.	3B	4	12	0	3	0	0	0	2	.250	8	8	0	1.000
1977—New York	Amer.	3B	6	21	1	4	1	0	0	2	.190	2	20	1	.957
1978—New York	Amer.	3B	6	25	2	4	0	0	0	1	.160	8	18	0	1.000
World Series Totals			16	58	3	11	1	0	0	5	.190	18	46	1	.985

ALL-STAR GAME RECORD

Year—League	Pos.	AB.	R.	H.	2B.	3B.	HR.	RBI.	B.A.	PO.	A.	E.	F.A.
1975—American	3B	4	0	1	0	0	0	0	.250	2	2	0	1.000
1977—American	3B	2	0	0	0	0	0	0	.000	0	1	0	1.000
1978—American	3B	0	0	0	0	0	0	0	.000	0	1	0	.000
1979—American	3B	1	0	1	0	0	0	0	1.000	1	2	0	1.000
1980—American	3B	2	0	0	0	0	0	0	.000	0	1	0	1.000
All-Star Game Totals		9	0	2	0	0	0	0	.222	3	7	0	1.000

Originally replaced due to injury by Larry Hisle, then re-named to replace Reggie Jackson in 1978.

JEFFREY LYNN NEWMAN
(Jeff)

Born September 11, 1948, at Fort Worth, Tex.
Height, 6.02. Weight, 215.
Throws and bats righthanded.
Hobbies—Golf and fishing.
Attended Texas Christian University, Fort Worth, Tex.; received
Bachelor of Science degree in Education.

Led Texas League catchers in double plays with 10 and in passed balls with 29 in 1973.
Led California League in passed balls with 51 in 1972.

Year	Club	League	Pos.	G.	AB.	R.	H.	2B.	3B.	HR.	RBI.	B.A.	PO.	A.	E.	F.A.
1970—Sara. Indians		Gulf C.	1-3-O	55	195	27	61	9	0	•6	★53	.313	302	33	15	.957
1971—Reno†		Calif.	O-1-3-C	67	234	35	63	11	3	16	53	.269	173	19	9	.955
1972—Reno		Calif.	★C-1-3	107	410	59	106	20	6	20	84	.259	718	81	29	.965
1973—San Antonio‡		Texas	C	112	394	50	97	29	0	13	63	.246	668	★72	10	.987
1974—Oklahoma City		A.A.	C-1B	57	188	19	46	3	1	7	28	.245	292	17	6	.981
1974—Salt Lake City		P.C.	C	28	109	15	33	8	0	4	21	.303	30	1	0	1.000
1975—Toledo§		Int.	C	32	64	7	12	4	0	2	5	.188	87	6	2	.976
1975—Salt Lake City		P.C.	C-1B	58	176	24	40	10	0	5	25	.227	267	22	12	.960
1976—Tucson		P.C.	C	68	231	23	62	11	1	5	38	.268	311	26	13	.963
1976—Oakland		Amer.	C	43	77	5	15	4	0	0	4	.195	140	18	3	.981
1977—Oakland		Amer.	C	94	162	17	36	9	0	4	15	.222	251	36	9	.970
1978—Oakland x		Amer.	C-1B	105	268	25	64	7	1	9	32	.239	399	41	12	.973
1979—Oakland		Amer.	C-1B-3B	143	516	53	119	17	2	22	71	.231	730	95	18	.979
1980—Oakland		Amer.	1-C-3-2	127	438	37	102	19	1	15	56	.233	675	54	15	.980
Major League Totals				512	1461	137	336	56	4	50	178	.230	2195	244	57	.977

Selected by Cleveland Indians' organization in 26th round of free-agent draft, June 4, 1970.
†On military list, December 24, 1970 to June 13, 1971.
‡On temporary inactive list, May 31 to June 17, 1973.
§Sold by Cleveland Indians' organization to Oakland A's, October 24, 1975.
xOn supplemental disabled list, August 17 to September 1, 1978.

RECORD AS PITCHER

Year	Club	League	G.	IP.	W.	L.	Pct.	H.	R.	ER.	SO.	BB.	ERA.
1977—Oakland		American	1	1	0	0	.000	1	0	0	0	0	0.00
Major League Totals			1	1	0	0	.000	1	0	0	0	0	0.00

ALL-STAR GAME RECORD

Member of American League All-Star Team for 1979 game; did not play.

THOMAS REID NICHOLS

Known by middle name.
Born August 5, 1958, at Ocala, Fla.
Height, 5.11. Weight, 165.
Throws and bats righthanded.

Led Carolina League in total bases with 227 and assists by outfielders with 23 in 1979.

Year	Club	League	Pos.	G.	AB.	R.	H.	2B.	3B.	HR.	RBI.	B.A.	PO.	A.	E.	F.A.
1976—Elmira		NYP	2B-3-O	23	53	8	18	1	0	0	9	.340	11	12	2	.920
1977—Winter Haven		Fla. St.	OF-2B	116	387	41	102	15	7	2	34	.264	166	41	7	.967
1978—Winter Haven		Fla. St.	OF-3B	125	413	52	102	20	1	5	34	.247	200	24	9	.961
1979—Winston-Salem		Carol.	OF-3B	134	★532	★107	★156	25	5	12	59	.293	240	23	10	.963
1980—Pawtucket		Int.	OF	134	511	68	141	27	5	4	42	.276	250	12	6	.978
1980—Boston		Amer.	OF	12	36	5	8	0	1	0	3	.222	24	1	1	.962
Major League Totals				12	36	5	8	0	1	0	3	.222	24	1	1	.962

Selected by Boston Red Sox' organization in 12th round of free-agent draft, June 8, 1976.

STEVEN RICHARD NICOSIA

Name pronounced nuh-KOH-see-uh.

(Steve)

Born August 6, 1955, at Paterson, N. J.
Height, 5.10. Weight, 185.
Throws and bats righthanded.
Hobbies—Fishing and golf.

Year	Club	League	Pos.	G.	AB.	R.	H.	2B.	3B.	HR.	RBI.	B.A.	PO.	A.	E.	F.A.
1973—Charleston		W. Car.	C-OF	54	165	22	38	8	2	2	21	.230	389	25	7	.983
1973—Sherbrooke		East.	C	3	9	1	1	0	0	0	0	.111	29	1	0	1.000
1974—Salem		Carol.	★C-1-O	118	413	63	126	16	9	15	92	.305	★860	89	★13	.986
1975—Shreveport		Tex.	★C-OF	110	370	52	99	15	6	6	39	.268	★527	45	8	.986
1976—Charleston†		Int.	OF-1B	117	378	29	99	20	0	8	49	.262	616	57	8	.988
1977—Columbus†		Int.	C	25	85	12	18	5	0	4	12	.212	132	16	2	.987
1978—Columbus		Int.	C-O-1-3	111	366	66	118	20	5	12	74	.322	486	38	9	.983
1978—Pittsburgh		Nat.	C	3	5	0	0	0	0	0	0	.000	8	1	0	1.000

Year Club	League	Pos.	G.	AB.	R.	H.	2B.	3B.	HR.	RBI.	B.A.	PO.	A.	E.	F.A.
1979—Pittsburgh	Nat.	C	70	191	22	55	16	0	4	13	.288	320	25	3	.991
1980—Pittsburgh	Nat.	C	60	176	16	38	8	0	1	22	.216	284	25	5	.984
Major League Totals......................			133	372	38	93	24	0	5	35	.250	612	51	8	.988

Selected by Pittsburgh Pirates' organization in 1st round (24th player selected) of free-agent draft, June 5, 1973.

†On disabled list, May 17 to August 23, 1977.

WORLD SERIES RECORD

Year Club	League	Pos.	G.	AB.	R.	H.	2B.	3B.	HR.	RBI.	B.A.	PO.	A.	E.	F.A.
1979—Pittsburgh	Nat.	C	4	16	1	1	0	0	0	0	.063	23	2	0	1.000

JOSEPH FRANKLIN NIEKRO
(Joe)

Born November 7, 1944, at Martins Ferry, O.
Height, 6.01. Weight, 190.
Throws and bats righthanded.
Hobbies—Fishing and hunting.
Attended West Liberty State College, West Liberty, W. Va.
Brother of Phil Niekro, pitcher with Atlanta Braves.

Pitched seven-inning, 2-0 perfect game against Tidewater, July 16, 1972 (second game).
Tied for National League lead in shutouts with 5 and in wild pitches with 19 in 1979.
Named righthanded pitcher on THE SPORTING NEWS National League All-Star Team, 1979.

Year Club	League	G.	IP.	W.	L.	Pct.	H.	R.	ER.	SO.	BB.	ERA.
1966—Treasure Valley	Pioneer	1	4	0	0	.000	4	0	0	7	1	0.00
1966—Quincy......................	Midwest	4	25	1	2	.333	17	7	3	14	6	1.08
1966—Dallas-Fort Worth	Texas	12	79	5	4	.556	71	28	22	50	15	2.51
1967—Chicago	National	36	170	10	7	.588	171	68	63	77	32	3.34
1968—Chicago	National	34	177	14	10	.583	204	93	85	65	59	4.32
1969—Chicago†-San Diego‡............	National	41	221	8	18	.308	237	100	91	62	51	3.71
1970—Detroit.................................	American	38	213	12	13	.480	221	107	96	101	72	4.06
1971—Detroit.................................	American	31	122	6	7	.462	136	62	61	43	49	4.28
1972—Toledo§...............................	Int'national	2	14	2	0	1.000	6	1	1	11	3	0.64
1972—Detroit.................................	American	18	47	3	2	.600	62	20	20	24	8	3.83
1973—Toledo x..............................	Int'national	26	143	7	10	.412	148	74	59	77	47	3.71
1973—Atlanta	National	20	24	2	4	.333	23	11	11	12	11	4.13
1974—Richmond	Int'national	30	52	8	1	.889	44	14	12	50	18	2.08
1974—Atlanta y.............................	National	27	43	3	2	.600	36	19	17	31	18	3.56
1975—Iowa	Am. Assoc.	7	9	1	0	1.000	7	6	5	9	7	5.00
1975—Houston	National	40	88	6	4	.600	79	32	30	54	39	3.07
1976—Houston	National	36	118	4	8	.333	107	60	44	77	56	3.36
1977—Houston	National	44	181	13	8	.619	155	66	61	101	64	3.03
1978—Houston	National	35	203	14	14	.500	190	97	87	97	73	3.86
1979—Houston	National	38	264	●21	11	.656	221	102	88	119	107	3.00
1980—Houston	National	37	256	20	12	.625	268	119	101	127	79	3.55
National League Totals.............................		388	1745	115	98	.540	1691	767	678	822	589	3.50
American League Totals.............................		87	382	21	22	.488	419	189	177	168	129	4.17
Major League Totals..................................		475	2127	136	120	.531	2110	956	855	990	718	3.62

Selected by Cleveland Indians' organization in 7th round of free-agent draft, January, 1966.
Selected by Chicago Cubs' organization in 3rd round of free-agent draft, June, 1966.
†Traded with Pitcher Gary Ross and Infielder Francisco Libran to San Diego Padres for Pitcher Dick Selma, April 24, 1969. Libran remained on Cubs' San Antonio farm team but became San Diego property.
‡Traded to Detroit Tigers for Pitcher Pat Dobson and Shortstop-Outfielder Dave Campbell, December 4, 1969.
§On disabled list, August 7 to September 1, 1972.
xPurchased via waivers from Detroit Tigers by Atlanta Braves, August 7, 1973.
ySold to Houston Astros, April 5, 1975.

CHAMPIONSHIP SERIES RECORD

Established National League Championship Series record for most innings pitched, game (10), October 10, 1980.

Year Club	League	G.	IP.	W.	L.	Pct.	H.	R.	ER.	SO.	BB.	ERA.
1980—Houston	National	1	10	0	0	.000	6	0	0	2	1	0.00

ALL-STAR GAME RECORD

Member of National League All-Star Team for 1979 game; did not play.

PHILIP HENRY NIEKRO

Name pronounced NEE-krow.

(Phil)

Born April 1, 1939, at Blaine, O.
Height, 6.02. Weight, 195.
Throws and bats righthanded.
Hobbies—Fishing, hunting and basketball.
Brother of Joe Niekro, pitcher with Houston Astros.

Established major league records for fewest sacrifice flies allowed, season, most innings (0 and 284), 1969; most seasons and most consecutive seasons leading major leagues, runs allowed (3); most wild pitches, lifetime (179).

Tied major league records for most strikeouts, inning (4), July 29, 1977 (sixth inning); most seasons and most consecutive seasons leading league, runs allowed (3); most wild pitches, inning (4), August 4, 1979, second game (fifth inning); most seasons and most consecutive seasons leading league, games lost (4).

Tied modern major league record for most wild pitches, game (6), August 4, 1979, second game.

Established National League record for most games started, no relief appearances, season (44), 1979.

Pitched 9-0 no-hit victory against San Diego Padres, August 5, 1973.

Led National League in complete games with 18 in 1974, with 20 in 1977, with 22 in 1978 and with 23 in 1979.

Led National League in wild pitches with 19 in 1967 and with 17 in 1977.

Led National League in sacrifice hits with 18 in 1968.

Led National League in games started with 43 in 1977, with 42 in 1978 and with 44 in 1979.

Tied for National League lead in games started with 38 in 1980.

Named pitcher on THE SPORTING NEWS National League All-Star fielding team, 1978 through 1980.

Year Club	League	G	IP	W	L	Pct.	H	R	ER.	SO.	BB.	ERA.
1959—Wellsville	NYP	10	35	2	1	.667	47	38	29	16	24	7.46
1959—McCook	Neb. State	*23	52	7	1	.875	35	20	18	48	29	3.12
1960—Jacksonville	Sally	38	84	6	4	.600	66	36	26	52	52	2.79
1960—Louisville	Am. Assoc.	6	10	1	0	1.000	11	5	4	2	9	3.60
1961—Austin	Texas	*51	110	4	4	.500	100	45	36	84	53	2.95
1962—Louisville	Am. Assoc.	49	98	9	6	.600	111	50	42	48	41	3.86
1963—Denver	P. Coast					(In Military Service)						
1964—Milwaukee	National	10	15	0	0	.000	15	10	8	8	7	4.80
1964—Denver	P. Coast	29	172	11	5	.688	172	79	66	119	45	3.45
1965—Milwaukee	National	41	75	2	3	.400	73	32	24	49	26	2.88
1966—Atlanta	National	28	50	4	3	.571	48	32	23	17	23	4.14
1966—Richmond	Int'national	17	54	3	4	.429	43	27	22	36	16	3.67
1967—Atlanta	National	46	207	11	9	.550	164	64	43	129	55	*1.87
1968—Atlanta	National	37	257	14	12	.538	228	83	74	140	45	2.59
1969—Atlanta	National	40	284	23	13	.639	235	93	81	193	57	2.57
1970—Atlanta	National	34	230	12	18	.400	222	124	109	168	68	4.27
1971—Atlanta	National	42	269	15	14	.517	248	112	89	173	70	2.98
1972—Atlanta	National	38	282	16	12	.571	254	112	96	164	53	3.06
1973—Atlanta	National	42	245	13	10	.565	214	103	90	131	89	3.31
1974—Atlanta	National	41	*302	•20	13	.606	249	91	80	195	88	2.38
1975—Atlanta	National	39	276	15	15	.500	285	115	98	144	72	3.20
1976—Atlanta	National	38	271	17	11	.607	249	116	99	173	101	3.29
1977—Atlanta	National	44	*330	16	•20	.444	*315	*166	*148	*262	*164	4.04
1978—Atlanta	National	44	*334	19	*18	.514	*295	*129	•107	248	102	2.88
1979—Atlanta	National	44	*342	*21	*20	.512	*311	*160	129	208	*113	3.39
1980—Atlanta	National	40	275	15	*18	.455	256	119	111	176	85	3.63
Major League Totals		648	4044	233	209	.527	3661	1661	1409	2578	1218	3.14

Signed as free agent by Atlanta Braves' organization, July 19, 1958.

CHAMPIONSHIP SERIES RECORD

Established Championship Series record for most runs allowed, game (9), October 4, 1969.

Tied Championship Series record for most runs allowed, three-game Series (9), 1969.

Tied National League Championship Series record for most runs allowed, inning (5), October 4, 1969 (fifth inning).

Year Club	League	G	IP	W	L	Pct.	H	R	ER.	SO.	BB.	ERA.
1969—Atlanta	National	1	8	0	1	.000	9	9	4	4	4	4.50

ALL-STAR GAME RECORD

Year League	IP.	W.	L.	Pct.	H.	R.	ER.	SO.	BB.	ERA.
1969—National	1	0	0	.000	0	0	0	2	0	0.00
1978—National	⅓	0	0	.000	0	0	0	0	0	0.00
All-Star Game Totals	1⅓	0	0	.000	0	0	0	2	0	0.00

Member of National League All-Star Team for 1975 game; did not play.

RANDY H. NIEMANN

Born November 15, 1955, at Fortuna, Calif.
Height, 6.04. Weight, 200.
Throws and bats lefthanded.
Attended College of the Redwoods, Eureka, Calif.

Year Club	League	G	IP	W	L	Pct.	H	R	ER.	SO.	BB.	ERA.
1975—Oneonta	NYP	8	55	3	3	.500	53	26	15	23	20	2.45
1976—Fort Lauderdale	Florida St.	25	190	9	10	.474	173	74	60	79	73	2.84
1977—West Haven†	Eastern	13	62	4	4	.500	73	44	38	18	26	5.52
1977—Columbus	Southern	15	34	0	3	.000	36	22	18	15	19	4.76
1978—Columbus	Southern	29	123	9	5	.643	125	44	28	53	39	2.05
1979—Charleston	Int'national	8	47	3	2	.600	49	25	21	17	10	4.02
1979—Houston	National	26	67	3	2	.600	68	32	28	24	22	3.76
1980—Tucson	P. Coast	9	52	4	1	.800	64	36	28	26	26	4.85
1980—Houston	National	22	33	0	1	.000	40	21	20	18	12	5.45
Major League Totals		48	100	3	3	.500	108	53	48	42	34	4.32

Selected by Montreal Expos' organization in 5th round of free-agent draft, January 9, 1974.
Selected by Minnesota Twins' organization in 3rd round of free-agent draft, January 9, 1975.
Selected by New York Yankees' organization in secondary phase of free-agent draft, June 4, 1975.
†Traded with Infielder Mike Fischlin and a player to be named later to Houston Astros for Catcher Cliff Johnson, June 15, 1977; Outfielder Dave Bergman sent to Astros to complete deal, November 23, 1977.

JOSEPH WILLIAM NOLAN JR.
(Joe)

Born May 12, 1951, at St. Louis, Mo.
Height, 6.00. Weight, 190.
Throws right and bats lefthanded.
Hobbies— Golf, hunting and fishing.

Led Texas League catchers in double plays with 10 in 1972.
Tied for Appalachian League lead in double plays by catchers with 3 in 1969.
Led National League catchers in passed balls with 14 in 1978.

Year Club	League	Pos.	G.	AB.	R.	H.	2B.	3B.	HR.	RBI.	B.A.	PO.	A.	E.	F.A.
1969—Marion..............Appal.		C	52	160	33	40	5	0	2	19	.250	312	30	6	.983
1970—Pompano Beach.Fla. St.		*C-O-3	95	281	38	65	6	4	0	30	.231	438	59	*18	.965
1971—Visalia ....Calif.		*C-3-O	120	393	76	109	17	3	13	75	.277	*746	95	17	.980
1972—Memphis...........Texas		C	130	418	51	90	13	3	4	41	.215	*868	67	12	.987
1972—New York..........Nat.		C	4	10	0	0	0	0	0	0	.000	12	3	1	.938
1973—Tidewater ....Int.		C	97	287	34	69	9	1	4	29	.240	526	43	10	.983
1974—Tidewater†........Int.		C	57	145	18	39	8	0	5	20	.269	274	24	8	.974
1975—Richmond ....Int.		C-3-O-2	111	342	41	92	13	0	6	53	.269	572	51	7	.989
1975—Atlanta..............Nat.		C	4	4	0	1	0	0	0	0	.250	2	0	0	1.000
1976—Richmond‡........Int.		C	32	87	9	25	6	1	0	9	.287	134	14	0	1.000
1977—Atlanta§............Nat.		C	62	82	13	23	3	0	3	9	.280	80	7	0	1.000
1978—Atlanta ....Nat.		C	95	213	22	49	7	3	4	22	.230	295	24	7	.979
1979—Atlanta ....Nat.		C	89	230	28	57	9	3	4	21	.248	328	27	6	.983
1980—Atl.x-Cinci. ....Nat.		C	70	176	16	54	8	0	3	26	.307	271	26	5	.983
Major League Totals			324	715	79	184	27	6	14	78	.257	988	87	19	.983

Selected by New York Mets' organization in 2nd round of free-agent draft, June 5, 1969.
†Traded by New York Mets to Atlanta Braves for Infielder Leo Foster, April 4, 1975.
‡On disabled list, April 21 to July 14, 1976.
§On disabled list, May 4 to May 19, 1977.
xGranted free agency when refused option to minors, June 12, 1980; signed by Cincinnati Reds, June 13, 1980.

DICKIE RAY NOLES

Born November 19, 1956, at Charlotte, N. C.
Height, 6.02. Weight, 178.
Throws and bats righthanded.

Led Carolina League in games started with 27 in 1977.

Year Club	League	G.	IP.	W.	L.	Pct.	H.	R.	ER.	SO.	BB.	ERA.
1975—Auburn ....NYP		9	50	2	2	.500	49	30	20	31	27	3.60
1976—Spartanburg........................W. Carol.		24	137	4	*16	.200	166	*110	*90	95	65	5.91
1977—Peninsula ....Carolina		27	*199	10	11	.476	188	103	81	114	78	3.66
1978—Reading ....Eastern		27	159	12	8	.600	177	100	75	78	72	4.25
1979—Oklahoma City†...................Am. Assoc.		12	76	6	4	.600	69	38	33	48	28	3.91
1979—Philadelphia.......................National		14	90	3	4	.429	80	40	38	42	38	3.80
1979—Reading ....Eastern		1	9	0	1	.000	7	5	4	2	4	4.00
1980—Philadelphia.......................National		48	81	1	4	.200	80	42	35	57	42	3.89
Major League Totals.................................		62	171	4	8	.333	160	82	73	99	80	3.84

Selected by Philadelphia Phillies' organization in 4th round of free-agent draft, June 4, 1975.
†On disabled list, April 13 to April 24, 1979.

CHAMPIONSHIP SERIES

Year Club	League	G.	IP.	W.	L.	Pct.	H.	R.	ER.	SO.	BB.	ERA.
1980—Philadelphia.......................National		2	2⅔	0	0	.000	1	0	0	0	3	0.00

WORLD SERIES RECORD

Year Club	League	G.	IP.	W.	L.	Pct.	H.	R.	ER.	SO.	BB.	ERA.
1980—Philadelphia.......................National		1	4⅔	0	0	.000	5	1	1	6	2	1.93

WAYNE OREN NORDHAGEN

Born July 4, 1948, at Thief River Falls, Minn.
Height, 6.02. Weight, 195.
Throws and bats righthanded.
Hobbies—Fishing, hunting and skin diving.
Attended Treasure Valley Community College, Ontario, Ore., and
Portland State University, Portland, Ore.

Year Club	League	Pos.	G.	AB.	R.	H.	2B.	3B.	HR.	RBI.	B.A.	PO.	A.	E.	F.A.
1968—Johnson City .....Appal.		OF	63	213	35	62	9	1	7	34	.291	*107	•8	4	.966
1969—Kinston†............Carol.		OF	25	90	17	21	1	0	4	9	.233	62	3	5	.929

Year Club League	Pos.	G.	AB.	R.	H.	2B.	3B.	HR.	RBI.	B.A.	PO.	A.	E.	F.A.
1970—Kinston ....Carol.	OF-1B	88	283	31	65	10	3	2	30	.230	175	9	10	.948
1971—Kinston ....Carol.	OF	114	412	65	121	25	3	14	76	.294	224	10	7	.971
1972—West Haven ....East.	OF	117	414	50	109	21	4	14	73	.263	204	14	●15	.936
1973—Syra.‡-Rich. ......Int.	OF	130	438	46	115	15	0	13	70	.263	222	9	8	.967
1974—Richmond ....Int.	OF	112	374	53	108	18	6	16	77	.289	192	6	7	.966
1975—Richmond§........Int.	OF-1-3	34	90	8	23	3	0	2	8	.256	50	2	0	1.000
1975—Tulsa x y ..........A.A.	OF	74	268	40	94	19	2	13	60	.351	102	7	5	.956
1976—Ok. City z-Iowa..A.A.	OF-C	99	350	56	106	30	6	11	78	.303	182	12	7	.965
1976—Chicago............Amer.	OF-C	22	53	6	10	2	0	0	5	.189	35	3	1	.974
1977—Chicago............Amer.	OF-C	52	124	16	39	7	3	4	22	.315	52	1	5	.914
1978—Chicago a..........Amer.	OF-C	68	206	28	62	16	0	5	35	.301	87	12	6	.943
1979—Chicago ....Amer.	OF-C	78	193	20	54	15	0	7	25	.280	28	4	3	.914
1980—Chicago ....Amer.	OF	123	415	45	115	22	4	15	59	.277	120	6	4	.969
Major League Totals		343	991	115	280	62	7	31	146	.283	322	26	19	.948

Selected by New York Yankees' organization in 7th round of free-agent draft, June 7, 1968.

†On temporary inactive list, May 10, 1969. Transferred to Military List, May 23, 1969 through remainder of season.

‡Traded with First Baseman Frank Tepedino and two players to be named later by New York Yankees to Atlanta Braves for Pitcher Pat Dobson, June 7, 1973; Braves received Pitcher Alan Closter, September 5, 1973, and Pitcher Dave Cheadle, September 10, 1973, to complete deal.

§Traded by Atlanta Braves to St. Louis Cardinals, June 2, 1975, to complete deal in which Braves obtained Pitchers Elias Sosa and Ray Sadecki from Cardinals for Pitcher Ron Reed and a player to be named later, May 28, 1975.

xOn disabled list, June 22 to July 2, 1975.

ySold by St. Louis Cardinals to Philadelphia Phillies, April 9, 1976.

zTraded by Philadelphia Phillies to Chicago White Sox for Outfielder Rich Coggins, July 14, 1976.

aOn supplemental disabled list, July 19 to August 12 and on disabled list, August 12 to September 1, 1978.

PITCHING RECORD

Year Club	League	G.	IP.	W.	L.	Pct.	H.	R.	ER.	SO.	BB.	ERA.
1979—Chicago ....American		2	2	0	0	.000	2	2	2	2	1	9.00

DANIEL EDMUND NORMAN
(Dan)

Born January 11, 1955, at Los Angeles, Calif.
Height, 6.02. Weight, 195.
Throws and bats righthanded.
Attended Barstow Junior College, Barstow, Calif.

Year Club League	Pos.	G.	AB.	R.	H.	2B.	3B.	HR.	RBI.	B.A.	PO.	A.	E.	F.A.
1974—Billings ....Pion.	OF-1B	68	236	34	70	12	5	4	41	.297	87	6	8	.921
1975—Tampa ....Fla. St.	OF	129	461	71	126	14	10	7	52	.273	192	9	5	.976
1976—Three Rivers .....East.	OF	134	491	64	134	20	9	17	63	.273	230	13	5	.980
1977—Indianapolis† ....A.A.	OF	60	209	26	52	9	5	5	33	.249	102	6	2	.982
1977—Tidewater ....Int.	OF	80	276	33	73	13	2	10	30	.264	141	4	1	.993
1977—New York..........Nat.	OF	7	16	2	4	1	0	0	0	.250	8	0	0	1.000
1978—Tidewater ....Int.	OF	132	473	69	133	31	5	18	66	.281	243	6	9	.965
1978—New York ....Nat.	OF	19	64	7	17	0	1	4	10	.266	33	1	0	1.000
1979—Tidewater ....Int.	OF	81	297	35	82	15	5	7	50	.276	141	13	4	.975
1979—New York ....Nat.	OF	44	110	9	27	3	1	3	11	.245	54	4	2	.967
1980—New York ....Nat.	OF	69	92	5	17	1	1	2	9	.185	19	1	0	1.000
Major League Totals		139	282	23	65	5	3	9	30	.230	114	6	2	.984

Selected by Cincinnati Reds' organization in 15th round of free-agent draft, June 5, 1974.

†Traded with Infielder Doug Flynn, Outfielder Steve Henderson and Pitcher Pat Zachry to New York Mets' organization for Pitcher Tom Seaver, June 15, 1977.

FREDIE HUBERT NORMAN
(Fred)

Born August 20, 1942, at San Antonio, Tex.
Height, 5.08. Weight, 172.
Throws and bats lefthanded.
Hobbies—Golf, fishing, swimming and automobiles.
Attended Muskegon Junior College, Muskegon, Mich.

Established major league record for most games started, no complete games, season (31), 1978.
Pitched 4-0 no-hit victory against Indianapolis, June 5, 1971.
Named Texas League Pitcher of the Year, 1966.
Received reported $40,000 bonus to sign with Kansas City Athletics, 1961.

Year Club	League	G.	IP.	W.	L.	Pct.	H.	R.	ER.	SO.	BB.	ERA.
1961—Shreveport.........................Southern		14	54	1	7	.125	45	43	34	46	64	5.70
1962—Binghamton ....Eastern		11	70	3	5	.375	61	41	38	81	53	4.89
1962—Lewiston............................Northwest		16	95	7	5	.583	66	46	43	147	79	4.07
1962—Kansas City ....American		2	4	0	0	.000	4	1	1	2	1	2.25
1963—Binghamton ....Eastern		30	198	13	14	.481	143	76	68	•258	104	3.09
1963—Kansas City†......................American		2	6	0	1	.000	9	9	8	6	7	12.00
1964—Ft. Worth............................Texas		13	57	1	8	.111	55	46	44	40	33	6.95

Year Club	League	G.	IP.	W.	L.	Pct.	H.	R.	ER.	SO.	BB.	ERA.
1964—Chicago	National	8	32	0	4	.000	34	25	23	20	21	6.47
1964—Salt Lake City	P. Coast	15	50	2	6	.250	62	50	41	50	30	7.38
1965—Dallas-Ft. Worth	Texas	4	7	0	1	.000	10	7	7	9	7	9.00
1965—Wenatchee	Northwest	25	106	4	4	.500	110	74	65	116	63	5.52
1966—Dallas-Ft. Worth	Texas	42	191	12	11	.522	147	71	58	•198	65	2.73
1966—Chicago	National	2	4	0	0	.000	5	2	2	6	2	4.50
1967—Chicago‡	National	1	1	0	0	.000	0	0	0	3	0	0.00
1967—Spokane	P. Coast	16	102	8	5	.615	91	46	42	77	43	3.71
1968—Albuquerque§	Texas	23	121	6	8	.429	124	70	59	86	49	4.39
1969—Spokane	P. Coast	34	151	•13	6	.684	128	68	44	134	61	2.62
1970—Los Ang. x-St. Louis	National	31	63	2	0	1.000	66	40	36	47	33	5.14
1971—Tulsa	Am. Assoc.	9	62	6	1	.857	44	16	15	72	22	2.17
1971—St. Louis y-San Diego	National	24	131	3	12	.200	121	53	52	81	63	3.57
1972—San Diego	National	42	212	9	11	.450	195	88	81	167	88	3.44
1973—San Diego z-Cincinnati	National	36	240	13	13	.500	208	102	96	161	101	3.60
1974—Cincinnati	National	35	186	13	12	.520	170	69	65	141	68	3.15
1975—Cincinnati	National	34	188	12	4	.750	163	85	78	119	84	3.73
1976—Cincinnati	National	33	180	12	7	.632	153	71	62	126	70	3.10
1977—Cincinnati	National	35	221	14	13	.519	200	97	83	160	98	3.38
1978—Cincinnati	National	36	177	11	9	.550	173	86	73	111	82	3.71
1979—Cincinnati a	National	34	195	11	13	.458	193	86	79	95	57	3.65
1980—Montreal	National	48	98	4	4	.500	96	50	45	58	40	4.13
American League Totals		4	10	0	1	.000	13	10	9	8	8	8.10
National League Totals		399	1928	104	102	.505	1777	854	775	1295	807	3.62
Major League Totals		403	1938	104	103	.502	1790	864	784	1303	815	3.64

Signed as free agent by Kansas City A's organization, June 19, 1961.

†Traded to Chicago Cubs for Outfielder Nelson Mathews, December 15, 1963.

‡Traded to Los Angeles Dodgers for Pitcher Dick Calmus, April 26, 1967.

§Appeared in one game as an outfielder.

xReleased on waiver claim to St. Louis Cardinals, September 28, 1970.

yTraded with Outfielder Leron Lee to San Diego Padres for Pitcher Al Santorini, June 1, 1971.

zTraded to Cincinnati Reds for Outfielder Gene Locklear and Pitcher Mike Johnson (latter assigned from Indianapolis to Alexandria), June 12, 1973.

aGranted free agency, November 1, 1979; signed by Montreal Expos, December 11, 1979.

CHAMPIONSHIP SERIES RECORD

Tied National League Championship Series record for most bases on balls allowed, three-game Series (5), 1975.

Year Club	League	G.	IP.	W.	L.	Pct.	H.	R.	ER.	SO.	BB.	ERA.
1973—Cincinnati	National	1	5	0	0	.000	1	1	1	3	3	1.80
1975—Cincinnati	National	1	6	1	0	1.000	4	1	1	4	5	1.50
1979—Cincinnati	National	1	2	0	0	.000	4	4	4	1	1	18.00
Championship Series Totals		3	13	1	0	1.000	9	6	6	8	9	4.15

WORLD SERIES RECORD

Year Club	League	G.	IP.	W.	L.	Pct.	H.	R.	ER.	SO.	BB.	ERA.
1975—Cincinnati	National	2	4	0	1	.000	8	4	4	2	3	9.00
1976—Cincinnati	National	1	6⅓	0	0	.000	9	3	3	2	2	4.26
World Series Totals		3	10⅓	0	1	.000	17	7	7	4	5	6.10

NELSON AUGUSTO NORMAN

Born May 23, 1958, at San Pedro de Macoris, Dominican Republic.
Height, 6.02. Weight, 160.
Throws and bats righthanded.
Hobby—Music.
Attended Liceo Union Dominicana, San Pedro de Macoris, Dominican Republic.

Tied major league record for most double plays by shortstop, game (5), April 23, 1979.
Led Gulf Coast League shortstops in double plays with 22 and in total chances with 260 in 1975.
Led Western Carolinas League shortstops in total chances with 613 in 1976.

Year Club	League	Pos.	G.	AB.	R.	H.	2B.	3B.	HR.	RBI.	B.A.	PO.	A.	E.	F.A.
1975—Bradenton Pir.	Gulf C.	SS	51	•202	19	•53	5	0	0	13	.262	•101	•137	•22	•.915
1976—Charleston	W. Car.	SS	128	•544	88	151	15	1	2	48	.278	193	•381	•39	.936
1977—Shreveport	Texas	SS	94	358	31	90	14	2	0	23	.251	170	278	30	.937
1977—Columbus†	Int.	SS	28	90	9	21	4	0	0	8	.233	49	84	5	.964
1978—Tucson	P.C.	SS	122	469	82	133	17	7	2	76	.284	200	376	39	.937
1978—Texas	Amer.	SS-3B	23	34	1	9	2	0	0	1	.265	16	50	1	.985
1979—Texas	Amer.	SS-2B	147	343	36	76	9	3	0	21	.222	177	302	24	.952
1980—Charleston‡	Int.	SS-2B	28	99	7	24	2	0	0	5	.242	50	81	3	.978
1980—Texas	Amer.	SS	17	32	4	7	0	0	0	1	.219	21	45	4	.943
Major League Totals			187	409	41	92	11	3	0	23	.225	214	397	29	.955

Signed as free agent by Pittsburgh Pirates' organization, January 6, 1975.

†Traded with Outfielder Al Oliver to Texas Rangers for Pitcher Bert Blyleven and First Baseman-Outfielder John Milner, December 8, 1977.

‡On disabled list, June 23 to August 29, 1980.

JAMES FRANCIS NORRIS
(Jim)

Born December 20, 1948, at Brooklyn, N.Y.
Height, 5.10. Weight, 175.
Throws and bats lefthanded.
Hobbies—Golf and tennis.
Attended University of Maryland, College Park, Md.;
received Bachelor of Science degree in Business Administration.

Major league stolen bases: 1977 (26), 1978 (12), 1979 (15). Total—53.
Led Gulf Coast League in total bases with 85 in 1971.
Named Gulf Coast League Player of Year in 1971.

Year Club	League	Pos.	G.	AB.	R.	H.	2B.	3B.	HR.	RBI.	B.A.	PO.	A.	E.	F.A.
1971—Sara. Indians	Gulf C.	OF-1B	47	165	•34	•63	7	•6	1	21	•.382	223	13	5	.979
1971—Jacksonville	South.	OF-1B	13	37	2	8	1	0	0	4	.216	25	2	0	1.000
1972—Elmira	East.	1B-OF	106	329	37	76	9	4	2	34	.231	794	44	11	.987
1973—San Antonio	Texas	OF-1B	116	346	57	94	21	3	6	47	.272	178	14	0	1.000
1974—San Antonio†	Texas	OF-1B	82	291	46	85	15	5	5	40	.292	214	10	6	.974
1975—Oklahoma City‡	A.A.	OF-1B	79	253	32	71	14	4	1	33	.281	185	13	4	.980
1976—Toledo	Int.	OF-1B	133	435	92	139	23	7	7	68	.320	233	7	5	.980
1977—Cleveland	Amer.	OF-1B	133	440	59	119	23	6	2	37	.270	326	9	6	.982
1978—Cleveland	Amer.	OF-1B	113	315	41	89	14	5	2	27	.283	196	8	2	.990
1979—Cleveland§	Amer.	OF	124	353	50	87	15	6	3	30	.246	214	2	4	.982
1980—Texas	Amer.	OF-1B	119	174	23	43	5	0	0	16	.247	96	4	0	1.000
Major League Totals			489	1282	173	338	57	17	7	110	.264	832	23	12	.986

Selected by Chicago White Sox' organization in 41st round of free-agent draft, June 6, 1967.
Selected by Cincinnati Reds' organization in secondary phase of free-agent draft, June 4, 1970.
Selected by Cleveland Indians' organization in secondary phase of free-agent draft, January 13, 1971.
†On disabled list, April 19 to April 30, 1974.
‡On disabled list, July 3 to August 15, 1975.
§Traded with Pitcher David Clyde to Texas Rangers for Pitcher Larry McCall, Third Baseman-Outfielder Mike Bucci and First Baseman Gary Gray, January 4, 1980.

MICHAEL KELVIN NORRIS
(Mike)

Born March 19, 1955, at San Francisco, Calif.
Height, 6.02. Weight, 172.
Throws and bats righthanded.
Attended City College of San Francisco, San Francisco, Calif.

Pitched shutout in first major league game, April 10, 1975.
Named pitcher on THE SPORTING NEWS American League All-Star fielding team, 1980.
Received reported $25,000 bonus to sign with Oakland Athletics, 1973.

Year Club	League	G.	IP.	W.	L.	Pct.	H.	R.	ER.	SO.	BB.	ERA.
1973—Burlington	Midwest	20	110	8	4	.667	81	38	27	130	40	2.21
1974—Birmingham†	Southern	21	109	7	8	.467	107	64	49	103	65	4.05
1975—Oakland‡	American	4	17	1	0	1.000	6	2	0	5	8	0.00
1976—Tucson	P. Coast	5	33	2	1	.667	28	15	14	19	23	3.82
1976—Oakland	American	24	96	4	5	.444	91	53	51	44	56	4.78
1977—San Jose§	P. Coast	6	46	3	2	.600	42	18	18	35	18	3.52
1977—Oakland	American	16	77	2	7	.222	77	45	41	35	31	4.79
1978—Vancouver	P. Coast	7	42	3	3	.500	42	28	27	32	27	5.79
1978—Jersey City x	Eastern	9	66	2	6	.250	58	35	25	51	36	3.41
1978—Oakland	American	14	49	0	5	.000	46	34	30	36	35	5.51
1979—Oakland y	American	29	146	5	8	.385	146	87	78	96	94	4.81
1980—Oakland	American	33	284	22	9	.710	215	88	80	180	83	2.54
Major League Totals		120	669	34	34	.500	581	309	280	396	307	3.77

Selected by Oakland A's organization in 1st round (24th player selected) of free-agent draft, January 10, 1973.
†On disabled list, June 14 to June 24, 1974.
‡On emergency disabled list, April 28 to September 19, 1975.
§On disabled list, August 27 to September 6, 1977.
xOn suspended list, May 19 to May 28, 1978.
yOn disabled list, July 12 to August 7, 1969.

WILLIAM ALEXANDER NORTH
(Bill)

Born May 15, 1948, at Seattle, Wash.
Height, 5.11. Weight, 185.
Throws right and bats left and righthanded.
Hobbies—Reading and playing pool.
Attended Central Washington State College, Ellensburg, Wash.

Tied major league record for most unassisted double plays by outfielder, game (1), July 28, 1974.
Major league stolen bases: 1971 (1), 1972 (6), 1973 (53), 1974 (54), 1975 (30), 1976 (75), 1977 (17), 1978 (30), 1979 (58), 1980 (45). Total—369.
Led American League in stolen bases with 54 in 1974 and 75 in 1976.
Led Texas League in stolen bases with 47 in 1971 and led Pioneer League with 42 in 1969.

Year Club	League	Pos.	G.	AB.	R.	H.	2B.	3B.	HR.	RBI.	B.A.	PO.	A.	E.	F.A.
1969—Caldwell............Pion.		OF	59	188	67	50	8	1	2	16	.266	110	7	9	.929
1970—Quincy ....Midw.		OF	42	144	31	42	6	3	4	10	.292	86	5	2	.978
1970—San Antonio.......Texas		OF	25	77	14	16	2	1	0	3	.208	50	2	3	.945
1971—San Antonio.......Texas		OF	125	457	*91	133	21	7	10	45	.291	295	10	9	.971
1971—Chicago.............Nat.		OF	8	16	3	6	0	0	0	0	.375	4	0	0	1.000
1972—Wichita ....A. A.		OF-2B	28	114	21	40	7	0	0	12	.351	81	8	5	.947
1972—Chicago† ....Nat.		OF	66	127	22	23	2	3	0	4	.181	61	3	3	.955
1973—Oakland ....Amer.		OF	146	554	98	158	10	5	5	34	.285	*429	•14	9	.980
1974—Oakland ....Amer.		OF	149	543	79	141	20	5	4	33	.260	437	9	4	.991
1975—Oakland ....Amer.		OF	140	524	74	143	17	5	1	43	.273	*420	10	11	.975
1976—Oakland ....Amer.		OF	154	590	91	163	20	5	2	31	.276	397	8	9	.978
1977—Oakland‡...........Amer.		OF	56	184	32	48	3	3	1	9	.261	112	1	2	.983
1978—Oakland§ ....Amer.		OF	24	52	5	11	4	0	0	5	.212	31	1	0	1.000
1978—Los Angeles x ...Nat.		OF	110	304	54	71	10	0	0	10	.234	232	2	6	.975
1979—San Francisco ...Nat.		OF	142	460	87	119	15	4	5	30	.259	300	8	4	.987
1980—San Francisco ...Nat.		OF	128	415	73	104	12	1	1	19	.251	313	6	6	.982
National League Totals....................			454	1322	239	323	39	8	6	63	.244	910	19	19	.980
American League Totals.................			669	2447	379	664	74	23	13	155	.271	1826	43	35	.982
Major League Totals			1123	3769	618	987	113	31	19	218	.262	2736	62	54	.981

Selected by Chicago Cubs' organization in 12th round of free-agent draft, June 5, 1969.

†Traded to Oakland Athletics for Pitcher Bob Locker, November 21, 1972.

‡On supplemental disabled list, May 18 to June 11, and June 27 to July 27, 1977; on regular disabled list, July 27 to August 23, 1977.

§Traded to Los Angeles Dodgers for Outfielder Glenn Burke, May 17, 1978.

xGranted free agency, November 2, 1978; signed as free agent by San Francisco Giants, March 10, 1979.

CHAMPIONSHIP SERIES RECORD

Established Championship Series record for most consecutive hitless times at bat, total Series (31).

Year Club	League	Pos.	G.	AB.	R.	H.	2B.	3B.	HR.	RBI.	B.A.	PO.	A.	E.	F.A.
1974—Oakland ....Amer.		OF	4	16	3	1	1	0	0	0	.063	14	0	0	1.000
1975—Oakland ....Amer.		OF	3	10	0	0	0	0	0	1	.000	6	1	1	.875
1978—Los Angeles ......Nat.		OF	4	8	0	0	0	0	0	0	.000	9	0	0	1.000
Championship Series Totals.............			11	34	3	1	1	0	0	1	.029	29	1	1	.968

WORLD SERIES RECORD

Year Club	League	Pos.	G.	AB.	R.	H.	2B.	3B.	HR.	RBI.	B.A.	PO.	A.	E.	F.A.
1974—Oakland ....Amer.		OF	5	17	3	1	0	0	0	0	.059	17	0	1	.944
1978—Los Angeles ......Nat.		PH-OF	4	8	2	1	1	0	0	2	.125	7	0	0	1.000
World Series Totals........................			9	25	5	2	1	0	0	2	.080	24	0	1	.960

WILLIE NORWOOD

Born November 7, 1950, at Green County, Ala.
Height, 6.00. Weight, 185.
Throws and bats righthanded.
Hobbies—Reading, hiking and music.
Attended Long Beach State University, Long Beach, Calif., and
La Verne College, La Verne, Calif.

Led Carolina League in strikeouts with 140 in 1973.
Tied for Carolina League lead in double plays by outfielder with 3 in 1973.

Year Club	League	Pos.	G.	AB.	R.	H.	2B.	3B.	HR.	RBI.	B.A.	PO.	A.	E.	F.A.
1972—Orlando.............Fla. St.		OF	49	204	26	59	6	2	5	22	.289	126	3	12	.915
1973—Lynchburg ....Carol.		OF	126	473	63	130	17	5	16	54	.275	240	*17	15	.945
1974—Lynchburg ....Carol.		OF	•138	502	93	155	25	8	10	91	.309	228	9	*15	.940
1975—Orlando.............South.		OF	128	443	55	115	13	5	11	55	.260	262	8	10	.964
1976—Tacoma.............P. C.		OF	128	439	84	133	21	2	15	68	.303	274	6	8	.972
1977—Tacoma.............P. C.		OF	53	199	45	82	15	1	8	33	.412	108	5	3	.974
1977—Minnesota ....Amer.		OF	39	83	15	19	3	0	3	9	.229	59	0	3	.952
1978—Minnesota.........Amer.		OF	125	428	56	109	22	3	8	46	.255	227	7	*14	.944
1979—Minnesota.........Amer.		OF	96	270	32	67	13	3	6	30	.248	147	4	4	.974
1980—Toledo ....Int.		OF	48	138	16	38	3	1	8	22	.275	43	3	3	.939
1980—Minnesota† ....Amer.		OF	34	73	6	12	2	0	1	8	.164	42	0	0	1.000
Major League Totals			294	854	109	207	40	6	18	93	.242	475	11	21	.959

Selected by Minnesota Twins' organization in 3rd round of free-agent draft, June 6, 1972.

†Traded to Seattle Mariners for Pitcher Byron McLaughlin, December 12, 1980.

JOHNNY LANE OATES

Born January 21, 1946, at Sylva, N. C.
Height, 5.11. Weight, 185.
Throws right and bats lefthanded.
Hobbies—Golf and bowling.
Attended Virginia Tech, Blacksburg, Va.; received Bachelor of Science
degree in Health and Physical Education.

Led National League in passed balls with 15 in 1974.
Tied for National League lead in double plays by catchers with 10 in 1975.

Year Club League	Pos.	G.	AB.	R.	H.	2B.	3B.	HR.	RBI.	B.A.	PO.	A.	E.	F.A.
1967—Bluefield ....Appal.	C	5	12	5	5	1	0	1	4	.417	23	5	0	1.000
1967—Miami ....Fla. St.	C-OF	48	156	22	45	5	2	3	19	.283	271	37	8	.975
1968—Miami ....Fla. St.	C-OF	70	194	24	51	9	3	0	23	.263	384	42	3	.993
1969—Dal.-Ft. W. ....Texas	C	66	191	24	55	12	2	1	18	.288	253	42	4	.987
1970—Rochester ....Int.	C	9	16	1	6	1	0	0	4	.375	24	2	0	1.000
1970—Baltimore† ....Amer.	C	5	18	2	5	0	1	9	2	.278	30	1	2	.939
1971—Rochester ....Int.	C	114	346	49	96	16	3	7	44	.277	*648	*73	6	.992
1972—Baltimore‡ ....Amer.	C	85	253	20	66	12	1	4	21	.261	391	31	2	*.995
1973—Atlanta§ ....Nat.	C	93	322	27	80	6	0	4	27	.248	409	57	9	.981
1974—Atlanta...............Nat.	C	100	291	22	65	10	0	1	21	.223	434	55	4	.992
1975—Atl.x-Phil. ....Nat.	C	98	287	28	81	15	0	1	25	.282	450	45	5	.990
1976—Philadelphia yz..Nat.	C	37	99	10	25	2	0	0	8	.253	155	15	1	.994
1977—Los Angeles......Nat.	C	60	156	18	42	4	0	3	11	.269	258	37	4	.987
1978—Los Angeles .....Nat.	C	40	75	5	23	1	0	0	6	.307	77	10	4	.956
1979—Los Angeles a ...Nat.	C	26	46	4	6	2	0	0	2	.130	64	13	2	.975
1980—New York b ......Amer.	C	39	64	6	12	3	0	1	3	.188	99	10	1	.991
American League Totals..................		129	335	28	83	15	2	5	26	.248	520	42	5	.991
National League Totals....................		454	1276	114	322	40	0	9	100	.252	1847	232	29	.986
Major League Totals		583	1611	142	405	55	2	14	126	.251	2367	274	34	.987

Selected by Chicago White Sox' organization in 2nd round of free-agent draft, June, 1966.
Selected by Baltimore Orioles' organization in secondary phase of free-agent draft, January 28, 1967.
†On military list, April 21 through August 22, 1970.
‡Traded with Pitchers Pat Dobson and Roric Harrison and Second Baseman Dave Johnston to Atlanta Braves for Catcher Earl Williams and Infielder Taylor Duncan, November 30, 1972.
§On disabled list, July 17 to September 2, 1973.
xTraded with First Baseman Dick Allen to Philadelphia Phillies for Catcher Jim Essian, Outfielder Barry Bonnell and cash, May 7, 1975.
yOn disabled list April 14 to June 1, 1976.
zTraded with Pitcher R. Quency Hill to Los Angeles Dodgers for Infielder Ted Sizemore, December 20, 1976.
aReleased, March 27, 1980; signed by New York Yankees, April 4, 1980.
bGranted free agency, November 13, 1980; re-signed by Yankees' organization, January 23, 1981.

CHAMPIONSHIP SERIES RECORD

Year Club League	Pos.	G.	AB.	R.	H.	2B.	3B.	HR.	RBI.	B.A.	PO.	A.	E.	F.A.
1976—Philadelphia ......Nat.	C	1	1	0	0	0	0	0	0	.000	1	0	0	1.000

WORLD SERIES RECORD

Year Club League	Pos.	G.	AB.	R.	H.	2B.	3B.	HR.	RBI.	B.A.	PO.	A.	E.	F.A.
1977—Los Angeles.......Nat.	PH-C	1	1	0	0	0	0	0	0	.000	1	0	0	1.000
1978—Los Angeles ......Nat.	PH-C	1	1	0	1	0	0	0	0	1.000	3	1	0	1.000
World Series Totals.........................		2	2	0	1	0	0	0	0	.500	4	1	0	1.000

KENNETH RAY OBERKFELL

Name pronounced OH-burk-fell.

(Ken)

Born May 4, 1956, at Maryville, Illinois.
Height, 6.01. Weight, 185.
Throws right and bats lefthanded.
Attended Belleville Area Junior College, Belleville, Ill.

Led National League second basemen in fielding percentage with .985 in 1979.

Year Club League	Pos.	G.	AB.	R.	H.	2B.	3B.	HR.	RBI.	B.A.	PO.	A.	E.	F.A.
1975—Johnson City .....Appal.	SS	17	54	15	19	3	0	1	8	.352	21	58	4	.952
1975—St. Petersburg ...Fla. St.	SS	41	134	14	47	6	1	0	22	.351	71	107	6	.967
1976—Arkansas...........Texas	2B-SS	128	456	64	131	19	2	3	47	.287	259	321	18	.970
1977—New Orleans .....A. A.	2B-SS	120	418	67	105	18	5	4	32	.251	205	325	17	.969
1977—St. Louis ....Nat.	2B	9	9	0	1	0	0	0	1	.111	3	4	0	1.000
1978—Springfield........Int.	3B-2B-SS	64	242	41	69	13	4	6	38	.285	77	113	6	.969
1978—St. Louis ....Nat.	2B-3B	24	50	7	6	1	0	0	0	.120	30	48	1	.987
1979—St. Louis ....Nat.	2B-3B-SS	135	369	53	111	19	5	1	35	.301	223	343	9	.984
1980—St. Louis† ....Nat.	2B-3B	116	422	58	128	27	6	3	46	.303	227	340	7	.988
Major League Totals		284	850	118	246	47	11	4	82	.289	483	735	17	.986

Signed as free agent by St. Louis Cardinals' organization, May 4, 1975.
†On disabled list, May 11 to June 20, 1980.

PRESTON MICHAEL O'BERRY

(Mike)

Born April 20, 1954, at Birmingham, Ala.
Height, 6.02. Weight, 190.
Throws and bats righthanded.
Attended University of South Alabama, Mobile, Ala.; received Bachelor
of Science degree in Education; attends University of Alabama
at Birmingham, Birmingham, Ala.

Led Carolina League catchers in double plays with 10 in 1976.
Led Eastern League catchers in double plays with 10 in 1977.

Year Club	League	Pos.	G.	AB.	R.	H.	2B.	3B.	HR.	RBI.	B.A.	PO.	A.	E.	F.A.
1975—Winter Haven....	Fla. St.	C	39	96	5	8	2	1	0	5	.083	120	24	11	.929
1976—Winston-Salem ..	Carol.	C	111	330	51	66	12	4	4	32	.200	*608	*69	*13	.981
1977—Bristol	East.	C	125	352	46	72	10	2	2	25	.205	682	*89	*16	.980
1978—Bristol	East.	C	114	339	41	80	12	1	6	41	.236	*648	*76	13	.982
1979—Pawtucket	Int.	C-1B	34	78	6	13	1	0	1	5	.167	168	16	8	.958
1979—Boston†	Amer.	C	43	59	8	10	1	0	1	4	.169	103	7	5	.957
1980—Midland	Texas	C	57	173	31	42	9	3	1	23	.243	337	39	11	.972
1980—Wichita.............	A.A.	C-OF	9	23	4	6	2	0	0	6	.261	26	5	2	.939
1980—Chicago‡	Nat.	C	19	48	7	10	1	0	0	5	.208	94	16	2	.982
American League Totals			43	59	8	10	1	0	1	4	.169	103	7	5	.957
National League Totals			19	48	7	10	1	0	0	5	.208	94	16	2	.982
Major League Totals.......................			62	107	15	20	2	0	1	9	.187	197	23	7	.969

Selected by Boston Red Sox' organization in 22nd round of free-agent draft, June 4, 1975.
†Traded to Chicago Cubs, October 23, 1979, completing deal in which Boston acquired Second Baseman Ted Sizemore, August 17, 1979.

DANIEL JOGUES O'BRIEN
(Dan)

Born April 22, 1954, at St. Petersburg, Fla.
Height, 6.03. Weight, 215.
Throws and bats righthanded.
Attended Florida State University, Tallahassee, Fla.
Brother-in-law of Bill Freehan, catcher with Detroit Tigers, 1961 through 1976.
Tied for Texas League lead in shutouts with 4 in 1977.

Year Club	League	G.	IP.	W.	L.	Pct.	H.	R.	ER.	SO.	BB.	ERA.
1976—St. Petersburg.....................	Florida St.	24	153	11	7	.611	147	74	55	99	43	3.24
1977—St. Petersburg.....................	Florida St.	6	23	0	3	.000	20	11	10	28	13	3.91
1977—Arkansas	Texas	23	133	9	8	.529	140	53	51	95	46	3.45
1978—Arkansas	Texas	17	118	12	3	.800	99	45	36	91	62	2.75
1978—Springfield	Am. Assoc.	12	55	4	1	.800	45	25	21	40	32	3.44
1978—St. Louis	National	7	18	0	2	.000	22	12	9	12	8	4.50
1979—Springfield	Am. Assoc.	22	142	10	5	.667	156	78	70	83	42	4.44
1979—St. Louis†‡	National	6	11	1	1	.500	21	10	10	5	3	8.18
1980—Richmond	Int'national	30	106	8	2	*.800	95	38	35	44	33	2.97
Major League Totals................................		13	29	1	3	.250	43	22	19	17	11	5.90

Selected by Cleveland Indians' organization in 27th round of free-agent draft, June 6, 1972.
Selected by Chicago White Sox' organization in 16th round of free-agent draft, June 4, 1975.
Selected by St. Louis Cardinals' organization in secondary phase of free-agent draft, January 7, 1976.
†Sold to Seattle Mariners, November 9, 1979.
‡Released by Seattle Mariners, March 29, 1980; signed by Atlanta Braves' organization, April 15, 1980.

JACK WILLIAM O'CONNOR

Born June 2, 1958, at Yucca Valley, Calif.
Height, 6.03. Weight, 215.
Throws and bats lefthanded.

Year Club	League	G.	IP.	W.	L.	Pct.	H.	R.	ER.	SO.	BB.	ERA.
1976—Lethbridge	Pioneer	5	21	2	3	.400	22	16	15	17	20	6.43
1977—Jamestown	NYP	13	77	6	6	.500	72	36	30	56	30	3.51
1978—West Palm Beach	Florida St.	29	76	4	6	.400	78	42	34	53	46	4.03
1979—West Palm Beach	Florida St.	24	146	9	7	.563	125	60	46	87	63	2.84
1980—Memphis...............................	Southern	7	29	1	2	.333	30	27	25	17	20	7.76
1980—West Palm Beach	Florida St.	17	139	9	6	.600	105	46	37	93	70	2.40
1980—Denver†	Am. Assoc.	2	5	0	0	.000	3	1	1	7	6	1.80

Selected by Montreal Expos' organization in 9th round of free-agent draft, June 8, 1976.
†Drafted by Minnesota Twins, December 8, 1980.

RONALD JOHN OESTER

Name pronounced O-ster.

(Ron)

Born May 5, 1956, at Cincinnati, O.
Height, 6.02. Weight, 185.
Throws right and bats left and righthanded.
Hobbies—Football, basketball and golf.
Led Pioneer League shortstops in double plays with 27 in 1974.
Led Eastern League shortstops in double plays with 84 in 1976.
Led American Association shortstops in double plays with 102 in 1978.

Year Club	League	Pos.	G.	AB.	R.	H.	2B.	3B.	HR.	RBI.	B.A.	PO.	A.	E.	F.A.
1974—Billings	Pion.	SS	53	167	23	52	11	1	0	21	.311	87	141	27	.894
1975—Tampa	Fla. St.	SS	117	375	40	82	3	4	0	25	.219	174	358	34	.940
1976—Three Rivers	East.	SS	138	447	57	110	14	4	0	44	.246	*233	*408	38	.944
1977—Indianapolis	A. A.	SS	134	455	60	116	16	5	3	33	.255	203	*386	39	.938
1978—Indianapolis	A. A.	SS	•135	514	78	133	21	4	7	49	.259	*300	*428	32	.958
1978—Cincinnati	Nat.	SS	6	8	1	3	0	0	0	1	.375	3	9	0	1.000
1979—Indianapolis	A. A.	SS	136	509	62	143	19	6	2	33	.281	*244	397	31	.954

Year	Club	League	Pos.	G.	AB.	R.	H.	2B.	3B.	HR.	RBI.	B.A.	PO.	A.	E.	F.A.
1979–Cincinnati	....	Nat.	SS	6	3	0	0	0	0	0	0	.000	1	2	0	1.000
1980–Cincinnati	....	Nat.	2-S-3	100	303	40	84	16	2	2	20	.277	161	224	10	.975
Major League Totals	....			112	314	41	87	16	2	2	21	.277	165	235	10	.976

Selected by Cincinnati Reds' organization in 9th round of free-agent draft, June 5, 1974.

ROWLAND JOHNIE OFFICE

Born October 25, 1952, at Sacramento, Calif.
Height, 6.00. Weight, 170.
Throws and bats lefthanded.
Hobbies—Fishing, music and dancing.
Attended Sacramento City College, Sacramento, Calif.

Year	Club	League	Pos.	G.	AB.	R.	H.	2B.	3B.	HR.	RBI.	B.A.	PO.	A.	E.	F.A.
1971–Greenwood	....	W. Car.	OF	117	394	68	119	23	3	12	68	.302	194	3	9	.956
1972–Savannah	....	South.	OF	128	416	71	112	19	6	8	52	.269	245	9	5	.981
1972–Atlanta	....	Nat.	OF	2	5	1	2	0	0	0	0	.400	3	0	0	1.000
1973–Richmond	....	Int.	OF-1B	139	461	53	109	17	4	10	43	.286	275	7	6	.979
1974–Atlanta	....	Nat.	OF	131	248	20	61	16	1	3	31	.246	171	0	1	.994
1975–Atlanta	....	Nat.	OF	126	355	30	103	14	1	3	30	.290	229	6	8	.967
1976–Atlanta	....	Nat.	OF	99	359	51	101	17	1	4	34	.281	204	3	3	.986
1977–Atlanta†	....	Nat.	OF-1B	124	428	42	103	13	1	5	39	.241	250	8	3	.989
1978–Atlanta	....	Nat.	OF	146	404	40	101	13	1	9	40	.250	291	4	3	.990
1979–Atlanta‡	....	Nat.	OF	124	277	35	69	14	2	2	37	.249	164	4	2	.988
1980–Montreal	....	Nat.	OF	116	292	36	78	13	4	6	30	.267	150	2	2	.987
Major League Totals	....			868	2368	255	618	100	11	32	241	.261	1462	27	22	.985

Selected by Atlanta Braves' organization in 4th round of free-agent draft, June 4, 1970.
†On supplemental disabled list, May 19 to June 6, 1977.
‡Granted free agency, November 1, 1979; signed by Montreal Expos, December 11, 1979.

BENJAMIN A. OGLIVIE
(Ben)

Born February 11, 1949, at Colon, Panama.
Height, 6.02. Weight, 170.
Throws and bats lefthanded.
Hobbies—Swimming, table tennis and electronics.
Attended Bronx Community College, Bronx, N. Y., Northeastern University, Boston, Mass.,
and Wayne State University, Detroit, Mich.

Hit three home runs in one game, vs. Detroit Tigers, July 8, 1979.
Led Eastern League outfielders in double plays with 5 in 1970.
Named as outfielder on THE SPORTING NEWS American League All-Star Team, 1980.
Named as outfielder on THE SPORTING NEWS American League Silver Bat team, 1980.

Year	Club	League	Pos.	G.	AB.	R.	H.	2B.	3B.	HR.	RBI.	B.A.	PO.	A.	E.	F.A.
1968–Jamestown	....	NYP	1B-OF	16	45	7	13	1	0	1	5	.289	66	2	2	.971
1969–Greenville	....	W. Car.	OF	106	363	48	115	15	•7	8	62	.317	128	6	12	.918
1969–Winter Haven	....	Fla. St.	OF	11	32	4	8	1	0	0	5	.250	13	1	1	.933
1970–Pawtucket	....	East.	OF	115	391	62	91	15	0	10	51	.233	172	14	5	.974
1971–Louisville	....	Int.	OF	134	474	82	144	27	7	17	86	.304	215	*26	12	.953
1971–Boston	....	Amer.	OF	14	38	2	10	3	0	0	4	.263	22	1	1	.958
1972–Boston	....	Amer.	OF	94	253	27	61	10	2	8	30	.241	98	5	2	.981
1973–Boston†	....	Amer.	OF	58	147	16	32	9	1	2	9	.218	56	2	1	.983
1974–Detroit	....	Amer.	OF-1B	92	252	28	68	11	3	4	29	.270	162	11	5	.972
1975–Detroit	....	Amer.	OF-1B	100	332	45	95	14	1	9	36	.286	232	8	5	.980
1976–Detroit	....	Amer.	OF-1B	115	305	36	87	12	3	15	47	.285	234	8	3	.988
1977–Detroit‡	....	Amer.	OF	132	450	63	118	24	2	21	61	.262	236	10	6	.976
1978–Milwaukee	....	Amer.	OF-1B	128	469	71	142	29	4	18	72	.303	275	8	6	.979
1979–Milwaukee	....	Amer.	OF-1B	139	514	88	145	30	4	29	81	.282	320	10	5	.985
1980–Milwaukee	....	Amer.	OF	156	592	94	180	26	2	•41	118	.304	384	18	9	.978
Major League Totals	....			1028	3352	470	938	168	22	147	487	.280	2019	81	43	.980

Selected by Boston Red Sox' organization in 7th round of free-agent draft, June 7, 1968.
†Traded to Detroit Tigers for Second Baseman Dick McAuliffe, October 23, 1973.
‡Traded to Milwaukee Brewers for Pitchers Jim Slaton and Rich Folkers, December 9, 1977.

ALL-STAR GAME RECORD

Year	League	Pos.	AB.	R.	H.	2B.	3B.	HR.	RBI.	B.A.	PO.	A.	E.	F.A.
1980–American	....	OF	2	0	0	0	0	0	0	.000	1	0	0	1.000

ROBERT MICHAEL OJEDA

Name pronounced O-he-da

(Bob)

Born December 17, 1957, at Los Angeles, Calif.
Height, 6.01. Weight, 185.
Throws and bats lefthanded.
Attended College of the Sequoias, Visalia, Calif.

Tied for Florida State League lead in games started with 29 in 1979.

Year Club	League	G.	IP.	W.	L.	Pct.	H.	R.	ER.	SO.	BB.	ERA.
1978—Elmira................................NYP	NYP	18	43	1	6	.143	45	32	23	35	43	4.81
1979—Winter Haven.....................Florida St.	Florida St.	29	200	15	7	.682	163	66	54	150	84	2.43
1980—Pawtucket ....Int'national	Int'national	19	123	6	7	.462	107	54	44	78	56	3.22
1980—Boston ....American	American	7	26	1	1	.500	39	20	20	12	14	6.92
Major League Totals................................		7	26	1	1	.500	39	20	20	12	14	6.92

Signed as free agent by Boston Red Sox' organization, May 20, 1978.

ALBERT OLIVER JR.

(Al)

Born October 14, 1946, at Portsmouth, O.
Height, 6.01. Weight, 203.
Throws and bats lefthanded.
Attended Kent State University, Kent, O.

Tied major league records for most errors by first baseman, inning (3), May 23, 1969 (fourth inning); most long hits, doubleheader (6), August 17, 1980; most extra bases on long hits, doubleheader (15), August 17, 1980.
Tied modern major league record for most at bats, game (7), September 16, 1975.
Established American League record for most total bases, doubleheader (21), August 17, 1980.
Tied American League record for most home runs, doubleheader, home run in each game (4), August 17, 1980.
Hit three home runs in one game, vs. Minnesota Twins, May 23, 1979.
Hit three home runs in one game, vs. Detroit Tigers, August 17, 1980.
Led Western Carolinas League first basemen in double plays with 93 in 1965.
Named center fielder on THE SPORTING NEWS National League All-Star Team, 1975.
Named as outfielder on THE SPORTING NEWS American League Silver Bat team, 1980.

Year Club	League	Pos.	G.	AB.	R.	H.	2B.	3B.	HR.	RBI.	B.A.	PO.	A.	E.	F.A.
1964—Salem† ....Appal.	Appal.					(On disabled list all season due to knee injury)									
1965—Gastonia ....W. Car.	W. Car.	1B	123	*515	77	*159	19	5	10	71	.309	*1031	*64	21	.981
1966—Raleigh‡............Carol.	Carol.	1B	117	458	66	137	25	4	10	57	.299	1035	*75	16	.986
1967—Macon‡‡...........South.	South.	1B-O	38	126	18	28	1	2	1	4	.222	267	21	6	.980
1967—Raleigh§...........Carol.	Carol.	1B	40	145	20	43	4	4	2	15	.297	365	17	0	1.000
1968—Columbus..........Int.	Int.	1B-OF	132	473	61	149	22	13	14	74	.315	968	28	16	.984
1968—Pittsburgh.........Nat.	Nat.	OF	4	8	1	1	0	0	0	0	.125	3	0	0	1.000
1969—Pittsburgh.........Nat.	Nat.	1B-OF	129	463	55	132	19	2	17	70	.285	911	50	9	.991
1970—Pittsburgh.........Nat.	Nat.	OF-1B	151	551	63	149	33	5	12	83	.270	718	52	9	.988
1971—Pittsburgh.........Nat.	Nat.	OF-1B	143	529	69	149	31	7	14	64	.282	497	15	6	.988
1972—Pittsburgh.........Nat.	Nat.	OF-1B	140	565	88	176	27	4	12	89	.312	353	4	5	.986
1973—Pittsburgh.........Nat.	Nat.	OF-1B	158	654	90	191	38	7	20	99	.292	692	36	13	.982
1974—Pittsburgh.........Nat.	Nat.	OF-1B	147	617	96	198	38	12	11	85	.321	702	26	7	.990
1975—Pittsburgh.........Nat.	Nat.	OF-1B	155	628	90	176	39	8	18	84	.280	409	6	5	.988
1976—Pittsburgh.........Nat.	Nat.	OF-1B	121	443	62	143	22	5	12	61	.323	327	4	5	.985
1977—Pittsburgh x ......Nat.	Nat.	OF	154	568	75	175	29	6	19	82	.308	305	6	6	.981
1978—Texas y.............Amer.	Amer.	OF	133	525	65	170	35	5	14	89	.324	219	8	3	.987
1979—Texas ....Amer.	Amer.	OF	136	492	69	159	28	4	12	76	.323	260	9	7	.975
1980—Texas ....Amer.	Amer.	OF-1B	*163	656	96	209	43	3	19	117	.319	315	9	9	.973
National League Totals..................			1302	5026	689	1490	276	56	135	717	.296	4917	199	65	.981
American League Totals			432	1673	230	538	106	12	45	282	.322	794	26	19	.977
Major League Totals..................			1734	6699	919	2028	382	68	180	999	.303	5711	225	84	.986

Signed as free agent by Pittsburgh Pirates' organization, June 13, 1964.
†On disabled list, June 23 to July 1, 1964 and July 16 to September 22, 1964.
‡On temporary inactive list, May 26 to June 15, 1966.
‡‡On military list, January 7 to May 7, 1967.
§On temporary inactive list, June 21 to July 15, 1967.
xTraded with infielder Nelson Norman to Texas Rangers for Pitcher Bert Blyleven and First Baseman-Outfielder John Milner, December 8, 1977.
yOn supplemental disabled list, June 15 to July 13, 1978.

CHAMPIONSHIP SERIES RECORD

Year Club	League	Pos.	G.	AB.	R.	H.	2B.	3B.	HR.	RBI.	B.A.	PO.	A.	E.	F.A.
1970—Pittsburgh.........Nat.	Nat.	1B	2	8	0	2	0	0	0	1	.250	22	1	0	1.000
1971—Pittsburgh.........Nat.	Nat.	PH-OF	4	12	2	3	0	0	1	5	.250	5	0	0	1.000
1972—Pittsburgh.........Nat.	Nat.	OF	5	20	3	5	2	1	1	3	.250	17	1	0	1.000
1974—Pittsburgh.........Nat.	Nat.	OF	4	14	1	2	0	0	0	1	.143	9	0	0	1.000
1975—Pittsburgh.........Nat.	Nat.	OF	3	11	1	2	0	0	1	2	.182	5	0	0	1.000
Championship Series Totals.............			18	65	7	14	2	1	3	12	.215	58	2	0	1.000

WORLD SERIES RECORD

Year Club	League	Pos.	G.	AB.	R.	H.	2B.	3B.	HR.	RBI.	B.A.	PO.	A.	E.	F.A.
1971—Pittsburgh.........Nat.	Nat.	PH-OF	5	19	1	4	2	0	0	2	.211	11	0	1	.917

ALL-STAR GAME RECORD

Year League	Pos.	AB.	R.	H.	2B.	3B.	HR.	RBI.	B.A.	PO.	A.	E.	F.A.
1972—National..............................	OF	1	0	0	0	0	0	0	.000	0	0	0	.000
1975—National..............................	PH-OF	1	1	1	1	0	0	0	1.000	0	0	0	.000
1976—National..............................	OF	1	0	0	0	0	0	0	.000	1	0	0	1.000
1980—American	OF	1	0	0	0	0	0	0	.000	0	0	0	.000
All-Star Game Totals.....................		4	1	1	1	0	0	0	.250	1	0	0	1.000

ALAN RAY OLMSTED
(Al)

Born March 18, 1957, at St. Louis, Mo.
Height, 6.02. Weight, 195.
Throws left and bats righthanded.

Tied for American Association lead in complete games with 8 and in shutouts with 3 in 1980.

Year Club	League	G.	IP.	W.	L.	Pct.	H.	R.	ER.	SO.	BB.	ERA.
1976—Johnson City	Appal.	14	90	8	3	.727	55	22	15	79	27	1.50
1977—Gastonia†	W. Carol.	2	8	1	0	1.000	14	9	8	5	5	9.00
1977—Johnson City	Appal.	5	4	1	0	1.000	8	4	4	1	1	9.00
1978—St. Petersburg‡	Florida St.					Did not play						
1978—Gastonia	W. Carol.	7	35	4	0	1.000	32	9	4	41	9	1.03
1978—Arkansas	Texas	14	82	5	4	.556	84	35	32	37	20	3.51
1979—St. Petersburg	Florida St.	23	101	8	5	.615	91	31	25	70	27	2.23
1979—Arkansas	Texas	12	71	3	4	.429	83	42	37	46	20	4.69
1980—Arkansas	Texas	8	55	3	4	.429	51	23	20	41	17	3.27
1980—Springfield	Am. Assoc.	17	117	10	5	.667	107	41	36	62	33	*2.77
1980—St. Louis§	National	5	35	1	1	.500	32	13	11	14	14	2.83
Major League Totals		5	35	1	1	.500	32	13	11	14	14	2.83

Selected by St. Louis Cardinals' organization in 13th round of free-agent draft, June 4, 1975.
†On disabled list, May 13 to July 28, 1977.
‡On disabled list, April 11 to May 11, 1978.
§Traded with Catchers Terry Kennedy and Steve Swisher, Infielder Mike Phillips and Pitchers Jim Seaman, John Littlefield and John Urrea to San Diego Padres for Catcher-First Baseman Gene Tenace. Pitchers Bob Shirley and Rollie Fingers and a player to be named later, December 8, 1980; Catcher Bob Geren traded to St. Louis completing trade, December 10, 1980.

RICHARD ROY OLSEN
(Rich)

Born June 1, 1957, at Honolulu, Hawaii.
Height, 6.00. Weight, 180.
Throws and bats righthanded.
Attended University of Hawaii, Honolulu, Hawaii.

Year Club	League	G.	IP.	W.	L.	Pct.	H.	R.	ER.	SO.	BB.	ERA.
1978—Newark†	NYP	5	30	2	1	.667	22	12	11	36	10	3.30
1979—Holyoke	Eastern	13	83	9	2	.818	72	32	23	61	35	2.49
1979—Vancouver	P. Coast	14	80	4	3	.571	84	35	33	53	38	3.71
1980—Vancouver	P. Coast	17	91	7	6	.538	93	46	40	64	42	3.96

Selected by Milwaukee Brewers' organization in 3rd round of free-agent draft, June 6, 1978.
†On temporary inactive list, July 28 to September 2, 1978.

STEVEN ROBERT ONTIVEROS

Name pronounced on-tuh-VAIR-us.

(Steve)

Born October 26, 1951, at Bakersfield, Calif.
Height, 6.00. Weight, 185.
Throws right and bats right and lefthanded.
Hobby—Working with young boys.
Attended Bakersfield College, Bakersfield, Calif.
Brother of Ed Ontiveros, former pitcher in Houston Astros' organization.

Led Midwest League third basemen in double plays with 18 in 1970.
Named Minor League Player of the Year by The Sporting News, 1973.

Year Club	League	Pos.	G.	AB.	R.	H.	2B.	3B.	HR.	RBI.	B.A.	PO.	A.	E.	F.A.
1969—Great Falls	Pion.	*3B-SS	61	162	36	45	7	2	2	27	.278	34	82	13	*.899
1970—Decatur	Midw.	*3-S-2	117	417	64	114	23	3	11	52	.273	*99	*226	29	*.918
1971—Fresno	Calif.	3B-SS	133	461	103	148	*33	*10	18	92	.321	127	241	36	.911
1972—Amarillo	Texas	O-1-3	138	498	67	143	25	3	12	75	.287	477	27	10	.981
1973—Phoenix	P. C.	OF-1B	113	401	83	143	*32	*16	10	84	*.357	248	15	9	.967
1973—San Francisco	Nat.	1B-OF	24	33	3	8	0	0	1	5	.242	36	6	0	1.000
1974—San Francisco	Nat.	3-1-O	120	343	45	91	15	1	4	33	.265	225	158	19	.953
1975—San Francisco	Nat.	3-O-1	108	325	21	94	16	0	3	31	.289	80	189	21	.928
1976—San Francisco†	Nat.	3-O-1	59	74	8	13	3	0	0	5	.176	18	8	2	.928
1977—Chicago	Nat.	3B	156	546	54	163	32	3	10	68	.299	100	324	20	.955
1978—Chicago‡	Nat.	3B-1B	82	276	34	67	14	4	1	22	.243	64	194	9	.966
1979—Chicago	Nat.	3B-1B	152	519	58	148	28	2	4	57	.285	105	269	23	.942
1980—Chicago§	Nat.	3B	31	77	7	16	3	0	1	3	.208	13	39	4	.929
1980—Seibu	Pac.	....	65	258	...	81	...	...	16	50	.314	...	...	...	....
Major League Totals			732	2193	230	600	111	10	24	224	.274	641	1187	98	.949

Selected by San Francisco Giants' organization in 24th round of free-agent draft, June 5, 1969.
†Traded with Outfielder Bobby Murcer and Pitcher Andrew Muhlstock to Chicago Cubs for Third Baseman Bill Madlock and Infielder Rob Sperring, February 11, 1977.
‡On emergency disabled list, July 26 to October 26, 1978.
§Released, June 24, 1980; signed by Seibu Lions of Japanese baseball.

JESSE OROSCO

Born April 21, 1957, at Santa Barbara, Calif.
Height, 6.02. Weight, 174.
Throws left and bats righthanded.
Attended Santa Barbara City College, Santa Barbara, Calif.

Year Club	League	G.	IP.	W.	L.	Pct.	H.	R.	ER.	SO.	BB.	ERA.
1978—Elizabethton†	Ap'lachian	20	40	4	4	.500	29	7	5	48	20	1.13
1979—Tidewater	Int'national	16	81	4	4	.500	82	45	35	55	43	3.89
1979—New York	National	18	35	1	2	.333	33	20	19	22	22	4.89
1980—Jackson	Texas	37	71	4	4	.500	52	36	29	85	62	3.68
Major League Totals		18	35	1	2	.333	33	20	19	22	22	4.89

Selected by St. Louis Cardinals' organization in 7th round of free-agent draft, January 11, 1977.
Selected by Minnesota Twins' organization in 2nd round of free-agent draft, January 10, 1978.
†Traded to New York Mets, February 7, 1979; completing deal in which Mets acquired Pitcher Greg Field for Pitcher Jerry Koosman, December 8, 1978.

JORGE ORTA (NUNEZ)

Named pronounced OR-ta.

Born November 26, 1950, at Mazatlan, Mexico.
Height, 5.10. Weight, 175.
Throws right and bats lefthanded.

Made six hits in one game against Minnesota Twins, June 15, 1980.

Year Club	League	Pos.	G.	AB.	R.	H.	2B.	3B.	HR.	RBI.	B.A.	PO.	A.	E.	F.A.
1968—Fresnillo	Mx. Cen.	2-S	20	68	8	18	6	0	0	1	.265	29	39	4	.944
1969—S. Luis Potosi	Mx. C.					(Did not play.)									
1970—Puerto Mex.	Mx. S.E.	2-S	18	43	6	13	1	0	0	3	.302	29	28	1	.983
1971—San Luis Potosi	Mx. Cen.	2B	59	182	55	77	17	*7	7	53	*.423	115	108	15	.937
1971—Mexicali†	Mx. No.		58	207	45	75	14	2	16	48	.362	figures unavailable			
1972—Knoxville	South.	2B	53	196	41	62	6	7	7	34	.316	113	142	9	.966
1972—Chicago	Amer.	S-2-3	51	124	20	25	3	1	3	11	.202	50	85	8	.944
1973—Chicago	Amer.	2B-SS	128	425	46	113	9	10	6	40	.266	255	301	18	.969
1974—Chicago	Amer.	2B-SS	139	525	73	166	31	2	10	67	.316	297	313	18	.971
1975—Chicago	Amer.	2B	140	542	64	165	26	10	11	83	.304	354	354	16	.978
1976—Chicago	Ameru	OF-3B	158	636	74	174	29	8	14	72	.274	187	111	15	.952
1977—Chicago	Amer.	2B	144	564	71	159	27	8	11	84	.282	287	335	19	.970
1978—Chicago	Amer.	2B	117	420	45	115	19	2	13	53	.274	295	290	9	.984
1979—Chicago‡	Amer.	2B	113	325	49	85	18	3	11	46	.262	57	75	3	.978
1980—Cleveland	Amer.	OF	129	481	78	140	18	3	10	64	.291	269	10	5	.982
Major League Totals			1119	4042	520	1142	180	47	89	520	.283	2133	1874	111	.973

Signed as free agent by Fresnillo, June 13, 1968.
†Sold to Appleton (Chicago White Sox' organization), November 30, 1971.
‡Granted free agency, November 1, 1979; signed by Cleveland Indians, December 19, 1979.

ALL-STAR GAME RECORD
Named to American League All-Star Team for 1975 game; replaced due to injury.
Member of American League All-Star Team in 1980; did not play.

ADALBERTO ORTIZ JR. (COLON)

Born October 24, 1959, at Humacao, Puerto Rico.
Height, 5.11. Weight, 174.
Throws and bats righthanded.

Led Carolina League catchers in assists with 84, in errors with 17, in double plays with 12 and in passed balls with 17 in 1979.

Year Club	League	Pos.	G.	AB.	R.	H.	2B.	3B.	HR.	RBI.	B.A.	PO.	A.	E.	F.A.
1977—Charleston†	W. Car.	C	21	53	2	14	3	0	0	10	.264	93	13	4	.964
1977—Brad. Pirates	G. C.	C	34	118	11	24	5	1	1	12	.203	76	14	4	.957
1978—Charleston‡	W. Car.	C	41	122	12	26	4	0	1	16	213	198	44	7	.972
1979—Salem	Caro.	C-1B	108	396	35	112	21	2	5	66	.283	632	84	17	.977
1980—Buffalo	East.	C	126	515	79	*178	25	1	12	78	*.346	497	91	16	.974
1980—Portland	P. C.	C	8	27	1	3	0	1	0	3	.111	42	10	0	1.000

Signed as free agent by Pittsburgh Pirates' organization, January 18, 1977.
†On temporary inactive list, June 18 to June 22, 1977.
‡On disabled list, June 16 to September 5, 1978.

AMOS JOSEPH OTIS

Born April 26, 1947, at Mobile, Ala.
Height, 5.11. Weight, 166.
Throws and bats righthanded.
Hobbies—Bowling, billiards, dancing and fishing.

Tied major league records for fewest times caught stealing, season, 50 or more stolen bases (8), 1971; fewest double plays by outfielder, season, for leader in most double plays (4), 1971.
Established American League records for highest stolen base percentage, lifetime, 300 or more attempts

(.805); most stolen bases, two consecutive games (7), April 30 and May 4, 1975.

Major league stolen bases: 1967 (0), 1969 (1), 1970 (33), 1971 (52), 1972 (28), 1973 (13), 1974 (18), 1975 (39), 1976 (26), 1977 (23), 1978 (32), 1979 (30), 1980 (16). Total—311.

Led American League in stolen bases with 52 in 1971.

Led American League outfielders in double plays with 6 in 1970 and tied for lead with 4 in 1971.

Led Appalachian League third basemen in double plays with 13 in 1965.

Named outfielder on THE SPORTING NEWS American League All-Star fielding teams, 1971, 1972 and 1974.

Named outfielder on THE SPORTING NEWS American League All-Star Team, 1973.

Year Club	League	Pos.	G.	AB.	R.	H.	2B.	3B.	HR.	RBI.	B.A.	PO.	A.	E.	F.A.
1965–Harlan ....Appal.		3B	67	252	55	83	11	5	9	39	.329	46	76	12	*.910
1966–Oneonta† ....NYP		*1-OF-3	116	419	54	113	17	7	3	46	.270	484	*74	22	.962
1967–Jacksonville ......Int.		O-3-1-2	126	407	62	109	11	7	3	39	.268	251	65	8	.975
1967–New York..........Nat.		OF-3B	19	59	6	13	2	0	0	1	.220	23	2	0	1.000
1968–Jacksonville‡.....Int.		OF-1B	139	500	76	143	29	4	15	70	.286	428	23	9	.980
1969–Tidewater ....Int.		OF	71	248	55	81	14	2	10	43	.327	157	9	1	.994
1969–New York§ ....Nat.		OF-3B	48	93	6	14	3	1	0	4	.151	49	6	1	.982
1970–Kansas City.......Amer.		OF	159	620	91	176	•36	9	11	58	.284	*388	•15	4	.990
1971–Kansas City.......Amer.		OF	147	555	80	167	26	4	15	79	.301	*404	10	4	.990
1972–Kansas City.......Amer.		OF	143	540	75	158	28	2	11	54	.293	351	6	3	.992
1973–Kansas City.......Amer.		OF	148	583	89	175	21	4	26	93	.300	330	10	5	.986
1974–Kansas City.......Amer.		OF	146	552	87	157	31	9	12	73	.284	425	8	6	.986
1975–Kansas City x ...Amer.		OF	132	470	87	116	26	6	9	46	.247	310	9	4	.988
1976–Kansas City.......Amer.		OF	153	592	93	165	*40	2	18	86	.279	373	5	3	.992
1977–Kansas City.......Amer.		OF	142	478	85	120	20	8	17	78	.251	326	10	3	.991
1978–Kansas City ......Amer.		OF	141	486	74	145	30	7	22	96	.298	382	9	2	*.995
1979–Kansas City.......Amer.		OF	151	577	100	170	28	2	18	90	.295	385	11	3	*.992
1980–Kansas City y....Amer.		OF	107	394	56	99	16	3	10	53	.251	310	6	4	.988
American League Totals..................			1569	5847	917	1648	302	56	169	806	.282	3984	99	41	.990
National League Totals....................			67	152	12	27	5	1	0	5	.178	72	8	1	.988
Major League Totals			1636	5999	929	1675	307	57	169	811	.279	4056	107	42	.990

Selected by Pittsburgh Pirates' organization in 5th round of free-agent draft, June 13, 1965.

†Drafted by Jacksonville (New York Mets' organization) from Pittsfield (Boston Red Sox' organization), November 28, 1966.

‡On suspended list, May 31 through June 3, 1968.

§Traded with Pitcher Robert D. Johnson to Kansas City Royals for Third baseman Joe Foy, December 3, 1969.

xOn supplemental disabled list, June 25 to July 14, 1975.

yOn disabled list, April 9 to May 22, 1980.

CHAMPIONSHIP SERIES RECORD

Tied Championship Series records for most stolen bases, Series (4), 1978; most stolen bases, total Series (8).

Established American League Championship Series record for most strikeouts, four-game Series (5), 1978.

Tied American League Championship Series record for most stolen bases, three-game Series (2), 1980.

Year Club	League	Pos.	G.	AB.	R.	H.	2B.	3B.	HR.	RBI.	B.A.	PO.	A.	E.	F.A.
1976–Kansas City.......Amer.		OF	1	1	0	0	0	0	0	0	.000	0	0	0	.000
1977–Kansas City.......Amer.		OF-PH	5	16	1	2	1	0	0	2	.125	11	1	0	1.000
1978–Kansas City.......Amer.		OF	4	14	2	6	2	0	1	.429	8	0	1	.889
1980–Kansas City ......Amer.		OF	3	12	2	4	1	0	0	0	.333	11	0	0	1.000
Championship Series Totals.............			13	43	5	12	4	0	'0	3	.279	30	1	1	.969

WORLD SERIES RECORD

Established World Series record for most putouts by outfielder, extra-inning game (9), October 17, 1980 (10 innings).

Tied World Series records for hitting home run in first Series at bat, October 14, 1980 (second inning); most chances accepted by center fielder, 10-inning game (9), October 17, 1980.

Year Club	League	Pos.	G.	AB.	R.	H.	2B.	3B.	HR.	RBI.	B.A.	PO.	A.	E.	F.A.
1980–Kansas City ......Amer.		OF	6	23	4	11	2	0	3	7	.478	21	0	0	1.000

ALL-STAR GAME RECORD

Year League	Pos.	AB.	R.	H.	2B.	3B.	HR.	RBI.	B.A.	PO.	A.	E.	F.A.
1970–American...........................	OF	3	0	0	0	0	0	0	.000	2	0	0	1.000
1971–American...........................	OF	1	0	0	0	0	0	0	.000	0	0	0	.000
1973–American...........................	OF	2	0	2	0	0	0	1	1.000	0	0	0	.000
1976–American...........................	OF	1	0	0	0	0	0	0	.000	0	0	0	.000
All-Star Game Totals		7	0	2	0	0	0	1	.286	2	0	0	1.000

Named to American League All-Star Team for the 1972 game; replaced due to injury.

NATHAN EDWARD OTT
(Ed)

Born July 11, 1951, at Muncy, Pa.
Height, 5.10. Weight, 190.
Throws right and bats lefthanded.
Hobbies—Hunting and coin collecting.

Led International League in passed balls with 20 in 1975.

Led Carolina League outfielders in double plays with 9 in 1972.
Tied for International League lead in double plays by outfielders with 4 in 1974.
Led National League catchers in errors with 15 in 1978.

Year	Club	League	Pos.	G.	AB.	R.	H.	2B.	3B.	HR.	RBI.	B.A.	PO.	A.	E.	F.A.
1970—Niagara Falls	....NYP		OF	61	206	38	60	9	5	0	24	.291	84	8	2	.979
1971—Monroe	..............W. Car.		OF	105	356	58	104	12	6	10	48	.292	146	*16	5	.970
1972—Salem	...............Carol.		OF	133	450	84	137	18	*10	7	63	.304	211	19	8	.966
1973—Charleston	........Int.		OF-C	126	440	56	115	18	3	6	52	.261	203	7	7	.968
1974—Charleston	........Int.		*OF-3B	121	423	57	112	13	7	14	49	.265	207	*31	10	.960
1974—Pittsburgh	.........Nat.		OF	7	5	1	0	0	0	0	0	.000	1	0	0	1.000
1975—Charleston	........Int.		*C-OF	121	425	66	121	21	5	10	5	.285	*697	59	*21	.973
1975—Pittsburgh	.........Nat.		C	5	5	0	1	0	0	0	0	.200	2	0	0	1.000
1976—Pittsburgh	.........Nat.		C	27	39	2	12	2	0	0	5	.308	20	6	0	1.000
1977—Pittsburgh	.........Nat.		C	104	311	40	82	14	3	7	38	.264	455	49	9	.982
1978—Pittsburgh	........Nat.		C-OF	112	379	49	102	18	4	9	38	.269	547	43	16	.974
1979—Pittsburgh	........Nat.		C	117	403	49	110	20	2	7	51	.273	612	53	4	.994
1980—Pittsburgh	........Nat.		C-OF	120	392	35	102	14	0	8	41	.260	571	73	11	.983
Major League Totals	....			492	1534	176	409	68	9	31	173	.267	2208	224	40	.984

Selected by Pittsburgh Pirates' organization in 23rd round of free-agent draft, June 4, 1970.
†On supplemental disabled list, August 10 to September 1, 1976.

CHAMPIONSHIP SERIES RECORD

Year	Club	League	Pos.	G.	AB.	R.	H.	2B.	3B.	HR.	RBI.	B.A.	PO.	A.	E.	F.A.
1979—Pittsburgh	........Nat.		C	3	13	0	3	0	0	0	0	.231	25	3	0	1.000

WORLD SERIES RECORD

Year	Club	League	Pos.	G.	AB.	R.	H.	2B.	3B.	HR.	RBI.	B.A.	PO.	A.	E.	F.A.
1979—Pittsburgh	........Nat.		C	3	12	2	4	1	0	0	3	.333	20	0	0	1.000

JAMES EDWARD OTTEN SR.
(Jim)

Born July 1, 1951, at Lewistown, Mont.
Height, 6.02. Weight, 195.
Throws and bats righthanded.
Hobbies—Hunting, fishing and golf.
Attended Mesa Community College, Mesa, Ariz., and Arizona State University, Tempe, Ariz.

Year	Club	League	G.	IP.	W.	L.	Pct.	H.	R.	ER.	SO.	BB.	ERA.
1973—Knoxville	...........................Southern		14	75	4	8	.333	90	50	40	50	43	4.80
1974—Knoxville	...........................Southern		15	75	6	3	.667	80	41	35	54	29	4.20
1974—Iowa	..............................Am. Assoc.		11	76	7	2	.778	52	23	19	66	33	2.25
1974—Chicago	..........................American		5	16	0	1	.000	22	11	10	11	12	5.63
1975—Denver	................................Am. Assoc.		28	151	9	9	.500	131	79	69	114	71	4.11
1975—Chicago	..........................American		2	5	0	0	.000	4	5	4	3	7	7.20
1976—Iowa	..............................Am. Assoc.		38	133	6	6	.500	140	51	43	79	45	2.91
1976—Chicago	..........................American		2	6	0	0	.000	9	6	3	3	2	4.50
1977—Iowa†	...........................Am. Assoc.		34	100	5	9	.357	114	60	52	70	48	4.68
1978—Springfield‡	......................Am. Assoc.		18	90	5	5	.500	90	56	47	65	50	4.68
1978—Arkansas	...........................Texas		3	19	2	0	1.000	20	5	4	19	13	1.89
1979—Springfield§	......................Am. Assoc.		33	77	5	5	.500	70	39	36	62	46	4.21
1979—St. Petersburg	................Florida St.		1	9	1	0	1.000	7	1	1	5	4	1.00
1980—Springfield	......................Am. Assoc.		7	48	6	0	1.000	31	11	9	40	19	1.69
1980—St. Louis	.............................National		31	55	0	5	.000	71	38	34	38	26	5.56
American League Totals	....		9	27	0	1	.000	35	22	17	17	21	5.67
National League Totals	....		31	55	0	5	.000	71	38	34	38	26	5.56
Major League Totals	....		40	82	0	6	.000	106	60	51	55	47	5.60

Selected by San Francisco Giants' organization in 5th round of free-agent draft, June 4, 1970.
Selected by Boston Red Sox' organization in secondary phase of free-agent draft, January 13, 1971.
Selected by Chicago Cubs' organization in secondary phase of free-agent draft, June 8, 1971.
Selected by Chicago White Sox' organization in 2nd round of free-agent draft, June 5, 1973.
†Traded to St. Louis Cardinals' organization for Pitcher Stan Butkus, December 5, 1977.
‡On disabled list, April 14 to May 15, 1978.
§On disabled list, April 13 to May 2, 1979.

ROBERT DENNIS OWCHINKO

Name pronounced Oh-CHINK-oh.

(Bob)

Born January 1, 1955, at Detroit, Mich.
Height, 6.02. Weight, 195.
Throws and bats lefthanded.
Attended Eastern Michigan University, Ypsilanti, Mich.
Named National League Rookie Pitcher of the Year by THE SPORTING NEWS, 1977.

Year	Club	League	G.	IP.	W.	L.	Pct.	H.	R.	ER.	SO.	BB.	ERA.
1976—Amarillo	...........................Texas		13	91	6	2	.750	86	36	33	69	38	3.26
1976—San Diego	...........................National		2	4	0	2	.000	11	8	8	4	3	18.00
1977—Hawaii	................................P. Coast		6	44	5	1	.833	36	7	7	30	20	1.43
1977—San Diego	...........................National		30	170	9	12	.429	191	93	84	101	67	4.45

Year Club	League	G.	IP.	W.	L.	Pct.	H.	R.	ER.	SO.	BB.	ERA.
1978—San Diego	National	36	202	10	13	.435	198	87	80	94	78	3.56
1979—San Diego†	National	42	149	6	12	.333	144	73	62	66	55	3.74
1980—Cleveland‡	American	29	114	2	9	.182	138	71	67	66	47	5.29
National League Totals		110	525	25	39	.391	544	261	238	265	203	4.08
American League Totals		29	114	2	9	.182	138	71	67	66	47	5.29
Major League Totals		139	639	27	48	.360	682	332	305	331	250	4.30

Selected by San Diego Padres' organization in 1st round (fifth player selected) of free-agent draft, June 8, 1976.

†Traded with Outfielder Jim Wilhelm to Cleveland Indians for Outfielder Jerry Mumphrey, February 15, 1980.

‡Traded with Pitchers Victor Cruz and Rafael Vasquez and Catcher Gary Alexander to Pittsburgh Pirates for Pitcher Bert Blyleven and Catcher Manny Sanguillen, December 9, 1980.

JOHN LEWIS PACELLA

Name pronounced puh-SELL-uh.
Born September 15, 1956, at Brooklyn, N.Y.
Height, 6.02. Weight, 184.
Throws and bats righthanded.
Hobbies—Fishing, boating and music.
Pitched 3-0 no-hit victory against Tulsa, April 15, 1977.

Year Club	League	G.	IP.	W.	L.	Pct.	H.	R.	ER.	SO.	BB.	ERA.
1974—Marion	Ap'lachian	12	43	1	7	.125	48	31	24	19	32	5.02
1975—Wausau	Midwest	19	132	9	8	.529	124	71	56	73	58	3.82
1976—Lynchburg	Carolina	26	185	12	11	.522	151	*97	67	119	83	3.26
1977—Tidewater	Int'national	17	93	7	5	.583	100	50	41	46	54	3.97
1977—Jackson	Texas	11	73	3	4	.429	75	47	33	49	39	4.07
1977—New York	National	3	4	0	0	.000	2	2	0	1	2	0.00
1978—Jackson	Texas	7	48	4	3	.571	31	16	14	44	16	2.63
1978—Tidewater	Int'national	19	102	4	11	.267	110	71	57	77	40	5.03
1979—Tidewater	Int'national	26	142	7	10	.412	129	65	65	95	61	3.61
1979—New York	National	4	16	0	2	.000	16	8	8	12	4	4.50
1980—New York†	National	32	84	3	4	.429	89	51	48	68	59	5.14
Major League Totals		39	104	3	6	.333	107	61	56	81	65	4.85

Selected by New York Mets' organization in 4th round of free-agent draft, June 5, 1974.
†Traded with Infielder Jose Moreno to San Diego Padres for Pitcher Randy Jones, December 15, 1980.

THOMAS MARIAN PACIOREK

Name pronounced puh-CHOR-eck.

(Tom)

Born November 2, 1946, at Detroit, Mich.
Height, 6.04. Weight, 210.
Throws and bats righthanded.
Hobbies—Basketball, golf and football.
Attended University of Houston, Houston, Tex.; received Bachelor of Science degree in Education.
Brother of Mike Paciorek, first baseman in Los Angeles Dodgers' organization.

Led Pacific Coast League in total bases with 310 and tied for lead in sacrifice flies with 12 in 1972.
Named Pacific Coast League Most Valuable Player, 1972.
Named THE SPORTING NEWS Minor League Player of the Year, 1972.

Year Club	League	Pos.	G.	AB.	R.	H.	2B.	3B.	HR.	RBI.	B.A.	PO.	A.	E.	F.A.
1968—Ogden	Pion.	OF-1B	29	101	25	39	6	3	5	23	.386	45	3	2	.960
1968—Bakersfield	Calif.	OF-1B	38	116	16	32	1	1	0	10	.276	44	1	0	1.000
1969—Bakersfield†	Calif.	OF-3B	91	359	59	114	20	3	15	53	.318	111	44	16	.906
1970—Spokane	P.C.	OF	•146	549	88	179	36	12	17	101	.326	262	5	6	.978
1970—Los Angeles	Nat.	OF	8	9	2	2	1	0	0	0	.222	1	0	0	1.000
1971—Spokane	P.C.	OF-3B	144	564	89	172	31	*14	15	105	.305	240	9	8	.969
1971—Los Angeles	Nat.	OF	2	2	0	1	0	0	0	1	.500	1	0	0	1.000
1972—Albuquerque	P.C.	1B	147	*605	*125	*186	*33	5	*27	107	.307	*1239	80	•13	.990
1972—Los Angeles	Nat.	1B-OF	11	47	4	12	4	0	1	6	.255	53	3	1	.982
1973—Los Angeles	Nat.	OF-1B	96	195	26	51	8	0	5	18	.262	117	3	2	.984
1974—Los Angeles	Nat.	OF-1B	85	175	23	42	8	6	1	24	.240	85	1	5	.945
1975—Los Angeles‡	Nat.	OF	62	145	14	28	8	0	1	5	.193	69	0	2	.972
1976—Atlanta	Nat.	OF-1-3	111	324	39	94	10	4	4	36	.290	216	10	3	.987
1977—Atlanta§	Nat.	1-OF-3	72	155	20	37	8	0	3	15	.239	248	16	5	.981
1978—Atlanta x	Nat.	1B	5	9	2	3	0	0	0	0	.333	21	0	0	1.000
1978—San Jose	P. C.	OF	16	57	7	16	1	2	3	17	.281	32	1	1	.971
1978—Seattle y	Amer.	OF-1B	70	251	32	75	20	3	4	30	.299	115	5	2	.984
1979—Seattle	Amer.	OF-1B	103	310	38	89	23	4	6	42	.287	237	12	1	.996
1980—Seattle	Amer.	OF-1B	126	418	44	114	19	1	15	59	.273	360	22	5	.987
American League Totals			299	979	114	278	62	8	25	131	.284	712	39	8	.989
National League Totals			452	1061	130	270	47	10	15	105	.254	811	33	18	.979
Major League Totals			751	2040	244	548	109	18	40	236	.269	1523	72	26	.984

Selected by Los Angeles Dodgers' organization in 42nd round of free-agent draft, June 7, 1968.
†On restricted list, April 3 through June 3, 1969.
‡Traded with Outfielder Jimmy Wynn, Second Baseman Lee Lacy and Infielder Jerry Royster to Atlanta

Braves for Outfielder Dusty Baker and First Baseman-Third Baseman Ed Goodson, November 17, 1975.
  §Released March 30, 1978; re-signed by Atlanta Braves, April 7, 1978.
  xReleased, May 23, 1978; signed by Seattle Mariners' organization, May 31, 1978.
  yGranted free agency, November 2, 1978; re-signed by Mariners, January 6, 1979.

CHAMPIONSHIP SERIES RECORD

Year Club	League	Pos.	G.	AB.	R.	H.	2B.	3B.	HR.	RBI.	B.A.	PO.	A.	E.	F.A.
1974—Los Angeles.......Nat.		PH-OF	1	1	0	1	0	0	0	0	1.000	0	0	0	.000

WORLD SERIES RECORD

Year Club	League	Pos.	G.	AB.	R.	H.	2B.	3B.	HR.	RBI.	B.A.	PO.	A.	E.	F.A.
1974—Los Angeles.......Nat.		PH-PR	3	2	1	1	1	0	0	0	.500	0	0	0	.000

MITCHELL OTIS PAGE

Born October 15, 1951, at Los Angeles, Calif.
Height, 6.02. Weight, 205.
Throws right and bats lefthanded.
Hobbies—Music and bowling.
Attended California Poly State University, Pomona, Calif.

Major League stolen bases: 1977 (42), 1978 (23), 1979 (17), 1980 (14). Total—96.
Named American League Rookie Player of the Year by THE SPORTING NEWS, 1977.

Year Club	League	Pos.	G.	AB.	R.	H.	2B.	3B.	HR.	RBI.	B.A.	PO.	A.	E.	F.A.
1973—Charleston ....W. Car.		OF	18	65	11	18	4	2	2	15	.277	31	1	5	.865
1973—Salem†..............Carol.		OF	6	16	1	2	0	0	0	0	.125	9	0	0	1.000
1974—Salem ....Carol.		OF	123	423	80	125	15	9	17	75	.296	165	15	12	.938
1975—Shreveport ....Texas		OF	122	413	73	120	24	3	*23	90	.291	191	8	●14	.934
1976—Charleston‡.......Int.		1B-OF	126	456	76	134	21	1	22	83	.294	1046	66	*20	.982
1977—Oakland...........Amer.		OF	145	501	85	154	28	8	21	75	.307	279	11	*14	.954
1978—Oakland§ ....Amer.		OF	147	516	62	147	25	7	17	70	.285	211	4	6	.973
1979—Oakland ....Amer.		OF	133	478	51	118	11	2	9	42	.247	6	0	0	1.000
1980—Oakland...........Amer.		DH	110	348	58	85	10	4	17	51	.244	0	0	0	.000
Major League Totals			535	1843	256	504	74	21	64	238	.273	496	15	20	.962

Selected by Pittsburgh Pirates' organization in 3rd round of free-agent draft, June 5, 1973.
  †On disabled list, July 16 to September 6, 1973.
  ‡Traded with Pitchers Doc Medich, Dave Giusti, Rick Langford and Doug Bair, and Outfielder Tony Armas to Oakland A's for Infielders Tommy Helms and Phil Garner, and Pitcher Chris Batton, March 15, 1977.
  §On supplemental disabled list, March 25 to April 21, 1978.

KARL DOUGLAS PAGEL

Name pronounced PAY-gul.
Born March 29, 1955, at Madison, Wis.
Height, 6.02. Weight, 185.
Throws and bats lefthanded
Attended Glendale College, Glendale, Ariz. and University of Texas, Austin, Tex.

Led Texas League in bases on balls with 88 and in strikeouts with 117 in 1978.
Led American Association in total bases with 291 and in walks with 100 in 1979.
Named Texas League Most Valuable Player, 1977.
Named American Association Most Valuable Player, 1979.

Year Club	League	Pos.	G.	AB.	R.	H.	2B.	3B.	HR.	RBI.	B.A.	PO.	A.	E.	F.A.
1976—Midland ....Texas		OF	15	43	3	8	0	0	1	2	.186	22	5	1	.964
1976—Pompano Beach Fla. St.		OF	41	134	21	34	6	2	2	12	.254	68	4	2	.973
1977—Midland ....Texas		OF	118	410	88	137	28	6	*28	104	.334	190	9	3	.985
1978—Wichita.............A. A.		OF-1B	134	462	81	124	27	5	23	86	.268	466	16	14	.972
1978—Chicago ....Nat.		PH	2	2	0	0	0	0	0	0	.000	0	0	0	.000
1979—Wichita.............A. A.		OF-1B	●136	472	96	149	25	0	*39	*123	.316	270	14	4	.986
1979—Chicago† ....Nat.		PH	1	1	0	0	0	0	0	0	.000	0	0	0	.000
1980—Wichita‡§ .........A.A.		1B	56	187	34	50	10	2	11	32	.267	448	37	4	.992
1980—Tacoma ...........P.C.		OF-1B	48	163	26	43	9	2	4	26	.264	138	18	3	.981
Major League Totals......................			3	3	0	0	0	0	0	0	.000	0	0	0	.000

Selected by New York Mets' organization in 6th round of free-agent draft, January 9, 1975.
Selected by St. Louis Cardinals' organization in secondary phase of free-agent draft, June 4, 1975.
Selected by Chicago Cubs' organization in secondary phase of free-agent draft, June 8, 1976.
  †On disabled list, September 12 to October 4, 1979.
  ‡On disabled list, April 24 to May 7, 1980.
  §Traded to Cleveland Indians' organization with cash, June 30, 1980, completing deal in which Chicago Cubs acquired Catcher-First Baseman Cliff Johnson, June 17, 1980.

DAVID WILLIAM PALMER JR.

Born October 19, 1957, at Glens Falls, N.Y.
Height, 6.01. Weight, 205.
Throws and bats righthanded.

Year Club	League	G.	IP.	W.	L.	Pct.	H.	R.	ER.	SO.	BB.	ERA.
1976—Lethbridge...........Pioneer		13	45	0	5	.000	58	49	36	44	28	7.20
1977—West Palm Beach ....Florida St.		25	119	6	8	.429	120	49	38	88	44	2.87
1978—West Palm Beach ....Florida St.		7	51	4	2	.667	44	23	11	58	4	1.94
1978—Memphis...............Southern		19	130	8	10	.444	107	57	44	78	44	3.05

Year Club	League	G.	IP.	W.	L.	Pct.	H.	R.	ER.	SO.	BB.	ERA.
1978—Montreal	National	5	10	0	1	.000	9	4	3	7	2	2.70
1979—Montreal	National	36	123	10	2	.833	110	41	36	72	30	2.63
1980—Montreal†	National	24	130	8	6	.571	124	53	43	73	30	2.98
Major League Totals		65	263	18	9	.667	243	98	82	152	62	2.81

Selected by Montreal Expos' organization in 21st round of free-agent draft, June 8, 1976.
†On disabled list, July 21 to August 27, 1980.

JAMES ALVIN PALMER
(Jim)

Born October 15, 1945, at New York City, N.Y.
Height, 6.03. Weight, 194.
Throws and bats righthanded.
Hobbies—Golf, billiards and basketball.
Attended Arizona State University, Tempe, Ariz., and
Towson State College, Towson, Md.

Pitched 8-0 no-hit victory against Duluth-Superior, June 19, 1964.
Pitched 8-0 no-hit victory against Oakland Athletics, August 13, 1969.
Led American League in shutouts with 10 in 1975 and tied for lead with 5 in 1970.
Led Northern League in wild pitches with 23 in 1964.
Led American League pitchers in games started with 40 in 1976.
Tied for American League lead in games started with 39 and in complete games with 22 in 1977.
Named righthanded pitcher on THE SPORTING NEWS American League All-Star Team, 1971, 1973, 1975, 1976 and 1978.
Named American League Pitcher of the Year by THE SPORTING NEWS, 1973, 1975 and 1976.
Named pitcher on THE SPORTING NEWS American League All-Star fielding team, 1976 through 1979.
Won American League Cy Young Memorial Award, 1973, 1975 and 1976.
Received reported $60,000 bonus to sign with Baltimore Orioles, 1963.

Year Club	League	G.	IP.	W.	L.	Pct.	H.	R.	ER.	SO.	BB.	ERA.
1964—Aberdeen	Northern	19	129	11	3	.786	75	42	36	107	•130	2.51
1965—Baltimore	American	27	92	5	4	.556	75	49	38	75	56	3.72
1966—Baltimore	American	30	208	15	10	.600	176	83	80	147	91	3.46
1967—Baltimore	American	9	49	3	1	.750	34	18	16	23	20	2.94
1967—Rochester†	Int'national	2	7	0	0	.000	12	9	9	6	5	11.57
1967—Miami	Florida St.	5	27	1	1	.500	20	6	6	16	10	2.00
1968—Miami	Florida St.	2	8	0	0	.000	4	2	0	5	9	0.00
1968—Rochester	Int'national	2	4	0	0	.000	4	6	6	6	8	13.50
1968—Elmira‡	Eastern	6	25	0	2	.000	18	13	12	26	19	4.32
1969—Baltimore§	American	26	181	16	4	*.800	131	48	47	123	64	2.34
1970—Baltimore	American	39	•305	20	10	.667	263	98	92	199	100	2.71
1971—Baltimore	American	37	282	20	9	.690	231	94	84	184	106	2.68
1972—Baltimore	American	36	274	21	10	.677	219	73	63	184	70	2.07
1973—Baltimore	American	38	296	22	9	.710	225	86	79	153	113	•2.40
1974—Baltimore x	American	26	179	7	12	.368	176	78	65	84	69	3.27
1975—Baltimore	American	39	323	•23	11	.676	253	87	75	193	80	*2.09
1976—Baltimore	American	40	*315	*22	13	.629	255	101	88	159	84	2.51
1977—Baltimore	American	39	*319	●20	11	.645	263	106	103	193	99	2.91
1978—Baltimore	American	38	*296	21	12	.636	246	94	81	138	97	2.46
1979—Baltimore y	American	23	156	10	6	.625	144	66	57	67	43	3.29
1980—Baltimore	American	34	224	16	10	.615	238	108	99	109	74	3.98
Major League Totals		481	3499	241	132	.646	2929	1189	1067	2036	1166	2.74

Signed as free agent by Baltimore Orioles' organization, August 16, 1963.
†On disabled list with bad right shoulder from July 3 through August 8.
‡Recalled by Baltimore Orioles and placed on disabled list for remainder of season, August 28.
§On disabled list, June 29 to August 9, 1969.
xOn disabled list, June 20 to August 13, 1974.
yOn disabled list, July 16 to August 11, 1979.

CHAMPIONSHIP SERIES RECORD

Established Championship Series records for most strikeouts, total Series (46); most complete games, total Series (5).
Tied Championship Series records for most series played, one club (6); most series pitched (6); most games won, total Series (4); most bases on balls, five-game Series (8), 1973.
Established American League Championship Series records for most strikeouts, five-game Series (15), 1973; most strikeouts, three-game Series (12), 1970; most bases on balls, total Series (19).

Year Club	League	G.	IP.	W.	L.	Pct.	H.	R.	ER.	SO.	BB.	ERA.
1969—Baltimore	American	1	9	1	0	1.000	10	2	2	4	2	2.00
1970—Baltimore	American	1	9	1	0	1.000	7	1	1	12	3	1.00
1971—Baltimore	American	1	9	1	0	1.000	7	3	3	8	3	3.00
1973—Baltimore	American	3	14⅔	1	0	1.000	11	3	3	15	8	1.84
1974—Baltimore	American	1	9	0	1	.000	4	1	1	4	1	1.00
1979—Baltimore	American	1	9	0	0	.000	7	3	3	3	2	3.00
Championship Series Totals		8	59⅔	4	1	.800	46	13	13	46	19	1.96

WORLD SERIES RECORD

Established World Series record for most bases on balls with bases loaded, game (2), October 11, 1971.
Youngest pitcher to win complete World Series shutout game (20 years, 11 months), October 6, 1966.

Year	Club	League	G.	IP.	W.	L.	Pct.	H.	R.	ER.	SO.	BB.	ERA.
1966—Baltimore		American	1	9	1	0	1.000	4	0	0	6	3	0.00
1969—Baltimore		American	1	6	0	1	.000	5	4	4	5	4	6.00
1970—Baltimore		American	2	15⅔	1	0	1.000	11	8	8	9	9	4.60
1971—Baltimore		American	2	17	1	0	1.000	15	5	5	15	9	2.65
1979—Baltimore		American	2	15	0	1	.000	18	6	6	8	5	3.60
World Series Totals			8	62⅔	3	2	.600	53	23	23	43	30	3.30

ALL-STAR GAME RECORD

Established All-Star Game records for most bases on balls, total games (7); most home runs allowed, game (3), July 19, 1977.

Tied All-Star Game records for most runs and earned runs allowed, game (5), July 19, 1977; most home runs allowed, inning (2), July 19, 1977 (first inning).

Year	League	IP.	W.	L.	Pct.	H.	R.	ER.	SO.	BB.	ERA.
1970—American		3	0	0	.000	1	0	0	3	1	0.00
1971—American		2	0	0	.000	1	0	0	2	0	0.00
1972—American		3	0	0	.000	1	0	0	2	1	0.00
1977—American		2	0	1	.000	5	5	5	3	1	22.50
1978—American		2⅔	0	0	.000	3	3	3	4	4	10.11
All-Star Game Totals		12⅔	0	1	.000	11	8	8	14	7	5.68

Member of American League All-Star Team for 1975 game; did not play.

STANLEY GERARD PAPI

Name pronounced Pappy.

(Stan)

Born February 4, 1951, at Fresno, Calif.
Height, 6.00. Weight, 180.
Throws and bats righthanded.
Hobby—Golf.
Attended Fresno State College, Fresno, Calif.

Led American Association shortstops in putouts with 227 and in double plays with 88 in 1977.
Received reported $40,000 bonus to sign with Houston Astros, 1969.

Year	Club	League	Pos.	G.	AB.	R.	H.	2B.	3B.	HR.	RBI.	B.A.	PO.	A.	E.	F.A.
1969—Covington		Appal.	SS	44	146	30	41	8	0	5	35	.281	66	92	23	.873
1970—Cocoa		Fla. St.	2-3-S	91	300	24	72	4	1	0	16	.240	144	216	24	.938
1971—Cocoa		Fla. St.	SS-2B	109	339	57	98	11	3	7	52	.289	145	285	23	.949
1972—Columbus†		South.	SS	83	299	27	82	15	0	4	28	.274	131	272	26	.939
1972—Oklahoma City		A.A.	SS	13	35	1	1	0	0	0	0	.029	13	31	3	.936
1973—Den.‡-Tul.		A.A.	SS-3B	90	306	44	89	18	2	3	27	.291	129	275	24	.944
1974—Tulsa		A.A.	SS-2B	90	266	27	50	8	0	3	22	.188	169	280	23	.951
1974—St. Louis§		Nat.	SS-2B	8	4	0	1	0	0	0	1	.250	6	3	0	1.000
1975—Memphis x		Int.					(Did not play)									
1976—Denver		A.A.	S-3-2	108	318	46	86	23	6	4	53	.270	111	203	14	.957
1977—Denver		A.A.	SS-3B	130	453	81	134	31	5	13	80	.296	228	327	39	.934
1977—Montreal		Nat.	3-S-2	13	43	5	10	2	1	0	4	.233	10	15	2	.926
1978—Montreal y		Nat.	SS-3-2	67	152	15	35	11	0	0	11	.230	56	88	6	.960
1979—Boston z		Amer.	2B-SS	50	117	9	22	8	0	1	6	.188	61	118	3	.984
1980—Oklahoma City bA.A.			SS-2B	8	30	5	10	2	1	0	3	.333	12	18	2	.938
1980—Bos. a-Det.		Amer.	2-3-S-1	47	114	12	27	3	4	3	17	.237	68	80	5	.967
National League Totals				88	199	20	46	13	1	0	16	.231	72	106	8	.957
American League Totals				97	231	21	49	11	4	4	23	.212	129	198	8	.976
Major League Totals				185	450	41	95	24	5	4	39	.211	201	304	16	.969

Selected by Houston Astros' organization in 2nd round of free-agent draft, June 5, 1969.
†On temporary inactive list, June 30 to July 14 and August 11 to August 14, 1972.
‡Traded by Houston Astros to St. Louis Cardinals for Shortstop Ray Busse, June 8, 1973.
§Traded to Montreal Expos for Pitcher Craig Caskey, February 14, 1975.
xOn temporary inactive list the entire season.
yTraded to Boston Red Sox for Pitcher Bill Lee, December 7, 1978.
zOn emergency disabled list, March 20 to May 21, 1979.
aTraded to Philadelphia Phillies' organization, May 13, 1980, completing deal in which Boston acquired Catcher Dave Rader, March 30, 1980.
bSold to Detroit Tigers' organization, May 29, 1980.

DAVID GENE PARKER

(Dave)

Born June 9, 1951, at Jackson, Miss.
Height, 6.05. Weight, 230.
Throws right and bats lefthanded.

Major league stolen bases: 1973 (1), 1974 (3), 1975 (8), 1976 (19), 1977 (17), 1978 (20), 1979 (20), 1980 (10). Total—98.

Led National League in slugging percentage with .541 in 1975.
Led National League in total bases with 340 in 1978.
Led Carolina League in total bases with 270 and stolen bases with 38 in 1972.
Led National League outfielders in double plays with 9 in 1977.
Tied for Gulf Coast League lead in total bases with 107 in 1970.

Tied for National League lead in sacrifice flies with 9 in 1979.
Named Carolina League Player of the Year in 1972.
Named outfielder on THE SPORTING NEWS National League All-Star Team, 1975, 1977 and 1978.
Named outfielder on THE SPORTING NEWS National League All-Star fielding team, 1977 through 1979.
Named National League Player of the Year by THE SPORTING NEWS, 1978.
Named National League Most Valuable Player by Baseball Writers Association of America, 1978.

Year	Club	League	Pos.	G.	AB.	R.	H.	2B.	3B.	HR.	RBI.	B.A.	PO.	A.	E.	F.A.
1970—Bradenton Pir.	..Gulf C.		●OF-P	61	239	34	75	8	3	●6	41	.314	92	11	●8	.928
1971—Waterbury	........East.		OF	30	114	10	26	4	1	0	7	.228	43	5	6	.889
1971—Monroe	.............W. Car.		OF	71	268	49	96	16	4	11	48	.358	104	8	10	.918
1972—Salem	...............Carol.		OF	135	★523	★91	★162	★30	6	22	★101	★.310	★250	★20	★20	.931
1973—Charleston	........Int.		OF	84	309	44	98	20	7	9	57	.317	144	11	7	.957
1973—Pittsburgh	........Nat.		OF	54	139	17	40	9	1	4	14	.288	77	3	3	.964
1974—Pittsburgh†	......Nat.		OF-1B	73	220	27	62	10	3	4	29	.282	154	8	4	.976
1975—Pittsburgh	........Nat.		OF	148	558	75	172	35	10	25	101	.308	311	7	9	.972
1976—Pittsburgh	........Nat.		OF	138	537	82	168	28	10	13	90	.313	294	13	★14	.956
1977—Pittsburgh	........Nat.		★OF-2B	159	637	107	★215	★44	8	21	88	★.338	★389	★26	★15	.965
1978—Pittsburgh‡	.......Nat.		OF	148	581	102	194	32	12	30	117	★.334	302	12	★13	.960
1979—Pittsburgh	.......Nat.		OF	158	622	109	193	45	7	25	94	.310	34	15	★15	.960
1980—Pittsburgh	.......Nat.		OF	139	518	71	153	31	1	17	79	.295	235	14	9	.965
Major League Totals		....		1017	3812	590	1197	234	52	139	612	.314	2103	97	82	.964

Selected by Pittsburgh Pirates' organization in 14th round of free-agent draft, June 4, 1970.
†On disabled list, June 7 to June 28 and July 5 to July 31, 1974.
‡On supplemental disabled list, July 1 to July 16, 1978.

PITCHING RECORD

Year	Club	League	G.	IP.	W.	L.	Pct.	H.	R.	ER.	SO.	BB.	ERA.
1970—Bradenton Pirates	...............Gulf Coast		1	4	0	0	.000	7	2	2	2	1	4.50

CHAMPIONSHIP SERIES RECORD

Year	Club	League	Pos.	G.	AB.	R.	H.	2B.	3B.	HR.	RBI.	B.A.	PO.	A.	E.	F.A.
1974—Pittsburgh	........Nat.		OF-PH	3	8	0	1	0	0	0	0	.125	4	1	0	1.000
1975—Pittsburgh	........Nat.		OF	3	10	2	0	0	0	0	0	.000	13	1	0	1.000
1979—Pittsburgh	........Nat.		OF	3	12	2	4	0	0	0	2	.333	9	0	0	1.000
Championship Series Totals		....		9	30	4	5	0	0	0	2	.167	26	2	0	1.000

WORLD SERIES RECORD

Tied World Series record for most hits, game (4), October 10, 1979.

Year	Club	League	Pos.	G.	AB.	R.	H.	2B.	3B.	HR.	RBI.	B.A.	PO.	A.	E.	F.A.
1979—Pittsburgh	........Nat.		OF	7	29	2	10	3	0	0	4	.345	13	1	1	.933

ALL-STAR GAME RECORD

Established All-Star Game record for most assists by outfielder, game (2), July 17, 1979.

Year	League	Pos.	AB.	R.	H.	2B.	3B.	HR.	RBI.	B.A.	PO.	A.	E.	F.A.
1977—National	....	OF	3	1	1	0	0	0	0	.333	2	0	0	1.000
1979—National	....	OF	3	0	1	0	0	0	1	.333	0	2	0	1.000
1980—National	....	OF	2	0	0	0	0	0	0	.000	0	0	0	.000
All-Star Game Totals	....		8	1	2	0	0	0	1	.250	2	2	0	1.000

MARK ALAN PARKER

Born June 12, 1956, at Huntington, Ind.
Height, 6.02. Weight, 175.
Throws right and bats lefthanded.
Attended Huntington College, Huntington, Ind.;
received Bachelor of Science degree in Accounting.

Led New York-Pennsylvania League in complete games with 11 in 1978.
Tied for American Association lead in games started with 28 in 1980.

Year	Club	League	G.	IP.	W.	L.	Pct.	H.	R.	ER.	SO.	BB.	ERA.
1978—Geneva	...............................NYP		14	★117	★13	1	★.929	86	39	31	90	27	2.38
1979—Wichita	...............................Am. Assoc.		2	6	0	1	.000	6	10	8	4	6	12.00
1979—Midland	...............................Texas		24	156	11	8	.579	205	111	90	71	29	5.19
1980—Wichita	...............................Am. Assoc.		28	157	7	11	.389	181	★107	89	70	66	5.10

Selected by Chicago Cubs' organization in 7th round of free-agent draft, June 6, 1978.

LANCE MICHAEL PARRISH

Born June 15, 1956, at McKeesport, Pa.
Height, 6.03. Weight, 210.
Throws and bats righthanded.
Hobbies—Golf and snow skiing.

Led Appalachian League in strikeouts with 92 in 1974.
Led American League catchers in passed balls with 21 in 1979.
Tied for American League lead in passed balls with 17 in 1980.
Named catcher on THE SPORTING NEWS American League Silver Bat team, 1980.

Year	Club	League	Pos.	G.	AB.	R.	H.	2B.	3B.	HR.	RBI.	B.A.	PO.	A.	E.	F.A.
1974—Bristol	.............Appal.		3B-OF	68	253	45	54	11	1	11	46	.213	36	83	22	.844
1975—Lakeland	...........Fla. St.		C	100	341	30	75	15	2	5	37	.220	460	50	7	.986

Year	Club	League	Pos.	G.	AB.	R.	H.	2B.	3B.	HR.	RBI.	B.A.	PO.	A.	E.	F.A.
1976—Montgomery		South.	C	107	340	46	75	9	2	14	55	.221	*600	*79	11	*.984
1977—Evansville		A. A.	C	115	416	74	116	21	2	25	90	.279	*722	*82	11	*.987
1977—Detroit		Amer.	C	12	46	10	9	2	0	3	7	.196	76	6	0	1.000
1978—Detroit		Amer.	C	85	288	37	63	11	3	14	41	.219	353	39	5	.987
1979—Detroit		Amer.	C	143	493	65	136	26	3	19	65	.276	707	*79	9	.989
1980—Detroit		Amer.	C-1-OF	144	553	79	158	34	6	24	82	.286	607	67	7	.990
Major League Totals				384	1380	191	366	73	12	60	195	.265	1743	191	21	.989

Selected by Detroit Tigers' organization in 1st round (16th player selected) of free-agent draft, June 5, 1974.

ALL-STAR GAME RECORD

Year	League	Pos.	AB.	R.	H.	2B.	3B.	HR.	RBI.	B.A.	PO.	A.	E.	F.A.
1980—American		C	1	0	0	0	0	0	0	.000	0	0	0	.000

LARRY ALTON PARRISH

Born November 10, 1953, at Winter Haven, Fla.
Height, 6.03. Weight, 215.
Throws and bats righthanded.
Attended Seminole Junior College, Sanford, Fla.

Led Eastern League third basemen in double plays with 32 in 1974.
Led Florida State League in sacrifice flies with 9 in 1973.
Hit three home runs in one game, vs. St. Louis Cardinals, May 29, 1977 and vs. Atlanta Braves, July 30, 1978 and April 25, 1980.
Tied for National League lead in double plays by third basemen with 35 in 1976.
Named Florida State League Most Valuable Player, 1973.

Year	Club	League	Pos.	G.	AB.	R.	H.	2B.	3B.	HR.	RBI.	B.A.	PO.	A.	E.	F.A.
1972—W. Palm B'ch		Fla. St.	OF	2	4	0	1	0	0	0	0	.250	2	0	0	1.000
1972—Jamestown		NYP	OF	62	223	32	58	4	3	4	28	.260	69	3	3	.960
1973—W. Palm B'ch		Fla. St.	*3B-SS	138	481	82	141	14	6	16	33	.293	*100	*292	32	*.925
1974—Quebec City		East.	3B	119	437	61	124	14	2	13	77	.284	*108	*277	*31	.925
1974—Montreal		Nat.	3B	25	69	9	14	5	0	0	4	.203	20	51	1	.986
1975—Montreal		Nat.	3-S-2	145	532	50	146	32	5	10	65	.274	105	291	35	.919
1976—Montreal		Nat.	3B	154	543	65	126	28	5	11	61	.232	122	310	25	.945
1977—Montreal		Nat.	3B	123	402	50	99	19	2	11	46	.246	81	225	21	.936
1978—Montreal		Nat.	3B	144	520	68	144	39	4	15	70	.277	122	288	23	.947
1979—Montreal		Nat.	3B	153	544	83	167	39	2	30	82	.307	119	290	23	.947
1980—Montreal†		Nat.	3B	126	452	55	115	27	3	15	72	.254	106	231	18	.949
Major League Totals				870	3062	380	811	189	21	92	400	.265	775	1686	146	.944

Signed as free agent by Montreal Expos' organization, May 21, 1972.
†On supplemental disabled list, June 2 to June 30, 1980.

ALL-STAR GAME RECORD

Year	League	Pos.	AB.	R.	H.	2B.	3B.	HR.	RBI.	B.A.	PO.	A.	E.	F.A.
1979—National		3B	0	0	0	0	0	0	0	.000	0	0	0	.000

MICHAEL EVERETT ARCH PARROTT
(Mike)

Born December 6, 1954, at Camarillo, Calif.
Height, 6.04. Weight, 205.
Throws and bats righthanded.
Hobbies—Basketball, dog raising and all outside activities.
Brother of Stephen John Parrott, former pitcher in Minnesota Twins' organization.

Led Southern League pitchers in complete games with 14 in 1975.
Led International League in complete games with 15 in 1977.
Tied for California League lead in complete games by pitchers with 16 in 1974.
Named Most Valuable Pitcher in International League in 1977.

Year	Club	League	G.	IP.	W.	L.	Pct.	H.	R.	ER.	SO.	BB.	ERA.
1973—Bluefield		Appal.	14	74	5	4	.556	61	46	30	89	40	3.65
1974—Lodi		California	25	194	11	11	.500	139	77	60	181	110	2.78
1975—Asheville		Southern	25	77	12	10	.545	168	79	67	107	70	3.41
1975—Rochester		Int'national	2	2	1	0	1.000	1	0	0	2	2	0.00
1976—Miami		Florida St.	5	25	3	0	1.000	20	10	7	23	15	2.52
1976—Charlotte†		Southern	5	17	0	2	.000	19	13	10	3	10	5.29
1977—Rochester‡		Int'national	25	184	15	7	.682	167	79	70	*146	52	3.42
1977—Baltimore§		American	3	4	0	0	.000	4	1	1	2	2	2.25
1978—Seattle x		American	27	82	1	5	.167	108	59	47	41	32	5.16
1979—Seattle		American	38	229	14	12	.538	231	104	96	127	86	3.77
1980—Spokane		P. Coast	4	22	1	2	.333	13	3	2	13	9	0.82
1980—Seattle y		American	27	94	1	16	.059	136	83	76	53	42	7.28
Major League Totals			95	409	16	33	.327	479	247	220	223	162	4.84

Selected by Baltimore Orioles' organization in 1st round (15th player selected) of free-agent draft, June 5, 1973.
†On disabled list, June 30 to August 30, 1976.
‡On disabled list, April 15 to April 25, 1977.
§Traded to Seattle Mariners for Outfielder Carlos Lopez and Pitcher Tommy Moore (latter assigned to Rochester), December 7, 1977.
xOn disabled list, March 27 to April 20 and May 3 to June 16, 1978.
yOn disabled list, May 3 to May 24, 1980.

FRANK ENRICO PASTORE

Name pronounced pass-TORR-ee

Born August 21, 1957, at Alhambra, Calif.
Height, 6.03. Weight, 210.
Throws and bats righthanded.
Hobbies—Reading, restoring cars and driving.
Attended Cal Poly Pomona State University, Pomona, Calif.; and Stanford University, Palo Alto, Calif.

Year Club	League	G.	IP.	W.	L.	Pct.	H.	R.	ER.	SO.	BB.	ERA.
1975—Billings	Pioneer	15	88	5	•7	.417	89	47	25	69	27	2.56
1976—Tampa	Florida St.	21	107	5	7	.417	101	50	37	54	34	3.11
1977—Tampa	Florida St.	14	95	4	5	.444	78	31	24	36	22	2.27
1977—Three Rivers	Eastern	15	94	6	6	.500	98	43	38	51	32	3.64
1978—Indianapolis	Am. Assoc.	4	12	0	2	.000	24	15	9	8	5	6.75
1978—Nashville†	Southern	22	129	6	8	.429	106	58	50	120	46	3.49
1979—Cincinnati	National	30	95	6	7	.462	102	47	45	63	23	4.26
1979—Indianapolis	Am. Assoc.	10	68	7	2	.778	51	21	21	69	17	2.78
1980—Cincinnati‡	National	27	185	13	7	.650	161	72	67	110	42	3.26
Major League Totals		57	280	19	14	.576	263	119	112	173	65	3.60

Selected by Cincinnati Reds' organization in 2nd round of free-agent draft, June 4, 1975.
†On disabled list, August 24 to August 31, 1978.
‡On disabled list, July 27 to August 22, 1980.

CHAMPIONSHIP SERIES RECORD

Year Club	League	G.	IP.	W.	L.	Pct.	H.	R.	ER.	SO.	BB.	ERA.
1979—Cincinnati	National	1	7	0	0	.000	7	2	2	1	3	2.57

ROBERT WAYNE PATE
(Bob)

Born December 3, 1953, at Los Angeles, Calif.
Height, 6.03. Weight, 196.
Throws and bats righthanded.
Attended Mesa Community College, Mesa, Ariz., and
Arizona State University, Tempe, Ariz.
Brother of Ed Pate, former pitcher in New York Mets' organization.

Year Club	League	Pos.	G.	AB.	R.	H.	2B.	3B.	HR.	RBI.	B.A.	PO.	A.	E.	F.A.
1977—Quebec City	East.	OF	125	454	57	121	10	5	10	47	.267	225	8	7	.971
1978—Denver	A. A.	OF	129	463	76	130	27	*11	16	78	.281	183	11	7	.965
1979—Denver	A. A.	OF	118	428	85	147	26	1	15	63	.343	177	10	7	.963
1980—Denver	A. A.	OF	67	266	49	86	15	2	8	65	.323	126	5	2	.985
1980—Montreal	Nat.	OF	23	39	3	10	2	0	0	5	.256	18	0	0	1.000
Major League Totals			23	39	3	10	2	0	0	5	.256	18	0	0	1.000

Selected by Oakland A's organization in 15th round of free-agent draft, June 6, 1972.
Selected by Boston Red Sox' organization in secondary phase of free-agent draft, January 10, 1973.
Selected by Baltimore Orioles' organization in secondary phase of free-agent draft, June 5, 1973.
Selected by Detroit Tigers' organization in secondary phase of free-agent draft, January 9, 1974.
Selected by Montreal Expos' organization in 4th round of free-agent draft, June 8, 1976.

FREDDIE JOE PATEK

Born October 9, 1944, at Oklahoma City, Okla.
Height, 5.06. Weight, 150.
Throws and bats righthanded.
Hobbies—Hunting and fishing.

Tied major league record for most double plays, shortstop, 9 innings, 5, May 6, 1972.
Major League stolen bases: 1968 (18), 1969 (15), 1970 (8), 1971 (49), 1972 (33), 1973 (36), 1974 (33), 1975 (32), 1976 (51), 1977 (53), 1978 (38), 1979 (11), 1980 (7). Total—384.
Hit three home runs in one game, vs. Boston Red Sox, June 20, 1980.
Led American League shortstops in double plays with 107 in 1971, 113 in 1972 and 115 in 1973; tied for lead with 108 in 1974.
Led American League in stolen bases with 53 in 1977.
Led International League in sacrifice hits with 10 and in stolen bases with 42 in 1967.

Year Club	League	Pos.	G.	AB.	R.	H.	2B.	3B.	HR.	RBI.	B.A.	PO.	A.	E.	F.A.
1966—Gastonia	W. Car.	2-S	75	294	68	91	8	5	3	20	.310	156	201	20	.947
1966—Columbus	Int.	SS-3B	17	36	3	5	1	0	0	1	.139	14	19	5	.868
1966—Asheville	Sout.	SS	26	64	11	13	0	0	1	5	.203	28	49	11	.875
1967—Columbus	Int.	SS-O-2	128	471	77	120	14	5	6	27	.255	221	335	27	.954
1968—Columbus	Int.	SS	33	138	21	42	7	1	0	10	.304	77	108	5	.974
1968—Pittsburgh†	Nat.	SS-O-3	61	208	31	53	4	2	2	18	.255	90	166	6	.977
1969—Pittsburgh	Nat.	SS	147	460	48	110	9	1	5	32	.239	227	399	30	.954
1970—Pittsburgh‡	Nat.	SS	84	237	42	58	10	5	1	19	.245	122	212	10	.971
1971—Kansas City	Amer.	SS	147	591	86	158	21	*11	6	36	.267	459	25	.968
1972—Kansas City§	Amer.	SS	136	518	59	110	25	4	0	32	.212	230	*510	22	.971
1973—Kansas City x	Amer.	SS	135	501	82	117	19	5	5	45	.234	242	503	26	.966
1974—Kansas City	Amer.	SS	149	537	72	120	18	6	3	38	.225	250	493	25	.967
1975—Kansas City	Amer.	SS	136	483	58	110	14	5	5	45	.228	231	405	27	.959
1976—Kansas City	Amer.	SS	144	432	58	104	19	3	1	43	.241	233	426	26	.962

Year Club League	Pos.	G.	AB.	R.	H.	2B.	3B.	HR.	RBI.	B.A.	PO.	A.	E.	F.A.
1977—Kansas City.......Amer.	SS	154	497	72	130	26	6	5	60	.262	252	413	29	.958
1978—Kansas City ......Amer.	SS	138	440	54	109	23	1	2	46	.248	240	350	•32	.949
1979—Kansas City yz ..Amer.	SS	106	306	30	77	17	0	1	37	.252	153	249	19	.955
1980—California ....Amer.	SS	86	273	41	72	10	5	5	34	.264	129	199	16	.953
American League Totals.................		1331	4578	612	1108	192	46	33	416	.242	2261	4007	247	.962
National League Totals...................		292	905	121	221	23	8	8	69	.244	439	777	46	.964
Major League Totals		1623	5483	733	1329	215	54	41	485	.242	2700	4784	293	.962

Selected by Pittsburgh Pirates' organization in 35th round of free-agent draft, June 18, 1965.

†On disabled list, July 11 to August 7, 1968.

‡Traded with Pitcher Bruce Dal Canton and Catcher Jerry May to Kansas City Royals for Pitcher Robert D. Johnson, Shortstop Jackie Hernandez and Catcher Jim Campanis (Latter transferred from Omaha to Columbus), December 2, 1970.

§On disabled list, March 23 to April 25, 1972.

xOn supplemental disabled list, June 11 to June 26, 1973.

yOn disabled list, August 23 to September 7, 1979.

zGranted free agency, November 1, 1979; signed by California Angels, December 5, 1979.

CHAMPIONSHIP SERIES RECORD

Tied Championship Series record for most consecutive games, one or more runs batted in, total Series (4).

Tied American League Championship Series record for most consecutive games, one or more hits, total Series (9).

Year Club League	Pos.	G.	AB.	R.	H.	2B.	3B.	HR.	RBI.	B.A.	PO.	A.	E.	F.A.
1970—Pittsburgh.........Nat.	SS	1	3	0	0	0	0	0	0	.000	1	2	0	1.000
1976—Kansas City......Amer.	SS	5	18	2	7	2	0	0	4	.389	13	18	0	1.000
1977—Kansas City......Amer.	SS	5	18	4	7	3	1	0	5	.389	8	18	1	.963
1978—Kansas City ......Amer.	SS	4	13	2	1	0	0	1	2	.077	9	8	2	.895
Championship Series Totals.............		15	52	8	15	5	1	1	11	.288	31	46	3	.963

ALL-STAR GAME RECORD

Year League	Pos.	AB.	R.	H.	2B.	3B.	HR.	RBI.	B.A.	PO.	A.	E.	F.A.
1976—American...........................	SS	0	0	0	0	0	0	0	.000	0	1	0	1.000
1978—American...........................	SS	3	0	1	0	0	0	0	.333	1	1	0	1.000
All-Star Game Totals		3	0	1	0	0	0	0	.333	1	2	0	1.000

Named to American League All-Star Team for 1972 game; replaced due to injury.

MICHAEL LEE PATTERSON
(Mike)

Born January 26, 1958, at Los Angeles, Calif.
Height, 5.10. Weight, 170.
Throws and bats lefthanded.

Year Club League	Pos.	G.	AB.	R.	H.	2B.	3B.	HR.	RBI.	B.A.	PO.	A.	E.	F.A.
1975—Boise ....N'west	OF	35	74	8	20	1	0	0	9	.270	24	0	5	.828
1976—Modesto ....Calif.	OF	80	236	42	62	7	3	6	33	.263	95	5	8	.926
1977—Modesto ....Calif.	OF	111	430	83	118	23	1	13	79	.274	141	11	10	.938
1978—Jersey City ....East.	OF	20	66	6	10	0	0	0	2	.152	31	1	0	1.000
1978—Modesto ....Calif.	OF	96	354	58	99	24	10	8	54	.280	161	6	7	.960
1979—Waterbury ....East.	OF-1B	84	286	42	78	12	5	10	40	.273	144	6	8	.950
1979—Ogden ..............P.C.	OF	47	179	28	58	6	5	7	34	.324	74	4	3	.963
1980—West Haven.......East.	OF	114	392	47	103	12	2	15	50	.263	200	9	9	.959
1980—Ogden ..............P.C.	OF	17	56	10	17	4	2	1	5	.304	25	1	0	1.000

Signed as free agent by Oakland A's organization, June 30, 1975.

MARTIN WILLIAM PATTIN
(Marty)

Born April 6, 1943, at Charleston, Ill.
Height, 5.11. Weight, 180
Throws and bats righthanded.
Hobbies—Hunting and fishing.
Attended Eastern Illinois University, Charleston, Ill.; received Bachelor of
Science and Master's degrees in Education.
Did graduate work at Arizona State University, Tempe, Ariz.

Year Club League	G.	IP.	W.	L.	Pct.	H.	R.	ER.	SO.	BB.	ERA.
1965—El Paso.............................Texas	13	67	0	6	.000	79	42	35	47	25	4.70
1966—Quad Cities ....Midwest	5	43	4	1	.800	23	7	6	52	11	1.26
1966—Seattle ....P. Coast	13	83	9	2	.818	75	39	34	62	29	3.69
1967—Seattle ....P. Coast	30	184	12	11	.522	169	70	55	140	52	2.69
1968—Seattle ....P. Coast	4	26	1	0	1.000	20	10	7	23	8	2.42
1968—California†.............................American	52	84	4	4	.500	67	27	26	66	37	2.79
1969—Seattle ....American	34	159	7	12	.368	166	104	99	126	71	5.60
1970—Milwaukee ....American	37	233	14	12	.538	204	91	88	161	71	3.40
1971—Milwaukee‡..........................American	36	265	14	14	.500	225	100	92	169	73	3.12
1972—Boston ....American	38	253	17	13	.567	232	102	91	168	65	3.24
1973—Boston§...............................American	34	219	15	15	.500	238	112	105	119	69	4.32

Year Club	League	G.	IP.	W.	L.	Pct.	H.	R.	ER.	SO.	BB.	ERA.
1974—Kansas City	American	25	117	3	7	.300	121	55	52	50	28	4.00
1975—Kansas City	American	44	177	10	10	.500	173	77	64	89	45	3.25
1976—Kansas City	American	44	141	8	14	.364	114	51	39	65	38	2.49
1977—Kansas City	American	31	128	10	3	.769	115	56	51	55	37	3.59
1978—Kansas City	American	32	79	3	3	.500	72	41	29	30	25	3.30
1979—Kansas City x	American	31	94	5	2	.714	109	50	48	41	21	4.60
1980—Kansas City y	American	37	89	4	0	1.000	97	39	36	40	23	3.64
Major League Totals		475	2038	114	109	.511	1933	905	820	1179	603	3.62

Selected by Los Angeles Angels' organization in 7th round of free-agent draft, June 17, 1965.

†Selected by Seattle Pilots from California Angels in expansion draft, October 15, 1968.

‡Traded with Pitcher Lew Krausse and Outfielders Tommy Harper and Pat Skrable to Boston Red Sox for Catcher Don Pavletich, Pitchers Ken Brett and Jim Lonborg, First Baseman George Scott and Outfielders Billy Conigliaro and Joe Lahoud, October 11, 1971.

§Traded to Kansas City Royals for Pitcher Dick Drago, October 23, 1973.

xOn disabled list, April 3 to April 24, 1979.

yGranted free agency, October 24, 1980.

CHAMPIONSHIP SERIES RECORD

Year Club	League	G.	IP.	W.	L.	Pct.	H.	R.	ER.	SO.	BB.	ERA.
1976—Kansas City	American	2	⅓	0	0	.000	0	1	1	0	1	27.00
1977—Kansas City	American	1	6	0	0	.000	6	2	1	0	0	1.50
1978—Kansas City	American	1	⅔	0	0	.000	2	2	2	0	0	27.00
Championship Series Totals		4	7	0	0	.000	8	5	4	0	1	5.14

WORLD SERIES RECORD

Year Club	League	G.	IP.	W.	L.	Pct.	H.	R.	ER.	SO.	BB.	ERA.
1980—Kansas City	American	1	1	0	0	.000	0	0	0	2	0	0.00

ALL-STAR GAME RECORD

Member of American League All-Star Team for 1971 game; did not play.

MICHAEL DeWAYNE PAXTON
(Mike)

Born September 3, 1953, at Memphis, Tenn.
Height, 5.11. Weight, 190.
Throws and bats righthanded.
Hobbies—Golf and bowling.
Attended Memphis State University, Memphis, Tenn.

Tied major league record for most strikeouts, inning (4), July 21, 1978 (fifth inning).
Tied for New York-Pennsylvania League lead in shutouts with 2 in 1975.

Year Club	League	G.	IP.	W.	L.	Pct.	H.	R.	ER.	SO.	BB.	ERA.
1975—Elmira	NYP	5	43	5	0	1.000	26	7	3	43	5	0.63
1975—Winston-Salem	Carolina	8	64	5	3	.625	46	16	10	55	24	1.41
1976—Bristol	Eastern	8	51	4	3	.571	38	15	14	36	16	2.47
1976—Pawtucket	Int'national	19	126	7	6	.538	108	64	58	92	61	4.15
1977—Pawtucket	Int'national	7	55	5	0	1.000	34	7	5	46	18	0.82
1977—Boston†	American	29	108	10	5	.667	134	53	46	58	25	3.83
1978—Cleveland	American	33	191	12	11	.522	179	89	82	96	63	3.86
1979—Cleveland	American	33	160	8	8	.500	210	118	105	70	52	5.91
1980—Tacoma	P. Coast	23	135	6	10	.375	155	82	75	46	53	5.00
1980—Cleveland	American	4	8	0	0	.000	13	11	11	6	6	12.38
Major League Totals		99	467	30	24	.556	536	271	244	230	146	4.70

Selected by New York Yankees' organization in 13th round of free-agent draft, June 8, 1971.

Selected by Boston Red Sox' organization in 23rd round of free-agent draft, June 4, 1975.

†Traded with Pitcher Rick Wise, Third Baseman Ted Cox and Catcher Bo Diaz to Cleveland Indians for Pitcher Dennis Eckersley and Catcher Fred Kendall, March 30, 1978.

ADALBERTO PENA (RIVERA)
(Bert)

Born July 11, 1959, at Santurce, Puerto Rico.
Height, 5.11. Weight, 165.
Throws right and bats left and righthanded.

Led Florida State League shortstops in double plays with 66 in 1977.
Led Southern League shortstops in double plays with 78 in 1980.

Year Club	League	Pos.	G.	AB.	R.	H.	2B.	3B.	HR.	RBI.	B.A.	PO.	A.	E.	F.A.
1977—Cocoa	Fla. St.	SS	93	285	28	65	9	2	1	21	.228	161	279	29	.938
1978—Columbus	South.	SS	141	410	24	66	10	0	2	24	.161	*229	352	39	.937
1979—Daytona Beach	Fla. St.	SS	113	341	26	66	11	1	1	23	.194	152	290	*45	.908
1980—Columbus	South.	SS	124	386	47	97	20	0	9	49	.251	193	363	26	.955

Signed as free agent by Houston Astros' organization, May 2, 1977.

ANTONIO FRANCISCO PENA (PADILLA)
(Tony)

Born June 4, 1957, at Monte Cristy, Dominican Republic.
Height, 6.00. Weight, 175.
Throws and bats righthanded.

Led Carolina League catchers in double plays with 9 in 1977.
Led Eastern League catchers in double plays with 14 in 1979.
Tied for Carolina League lead among catchers in passed balls with 16 in 1977.

Year Club League	Pos.	G.	AB.	R.	H.	2B.	3B.	HR.	RBI.	B.A.	PO.	A.	E.	F.A.
1976—Brad. Pirates ....G. C.	O-1-C-3	33	110	10	23	2	2	1	11	.209	108	14	4	.968
1976—Charleston ....W. Car.	C	14	49	4	11	2	0	1	8	.224	64	7	2	.973
1977—Charleston ....W. Car.	C	29	101	10	24	4	0	3	16	.238	172	19	6	.970
1977—Salem ....Carol.	C	84	319	36	88	15	3	7	46	.276	•470	•66	•17	.969
1978—Shreveport ....Texas	C	104	348	34	80	14	0	8	42	.230	637	54	•25	.965
1979—Buffalo ....East.	C	134	515	89	161	16	4	34	97	.313	•768	•120	•26	.972
1980—Portland ..........P.C.	C	124	452	57	148	24	13	9	77	.327	•639	85	•23	.969
1980—Pittsburgh ....Nat.	C	8	21	1	9	1	1	0	1	.429	38	2	2	.952
Major League Totals...........		8	21	1	9	1	1	0	1	.429	38	2	2	.952

Signed as free agent by Pittsburgh Pirates' organization, July 22, 1975.

DAVID RICHARD PENNIALL
(Dave)

Born September 26, 1954, at Coronado, Calif.
Height, 5.10. Weight, 175.
Throws and bats righthanded.
Attended Glendale College, Glendale, Calif., and University of California at Los Angeles,
Los Angeles, Calif.; received Bachelor of Arts degree in Political Science.

Year Club League	Pos.	G.	AB.	R.	H.	2B.	3B.	HR.	RBI.	B.A.	PO.	A.	E.	F.A.
1976—Sarasota Cards..G.C.	OF	6	22	8	9	1	1	1	8	.409	7	0	0	1.000
1976—Johnson City .....Appal.	OF	45	171	33	65	14	4	6	32	.380	24	1	1	.962
1977—St. Petersburg...Fla. St.	OF	117	396	68	127	18	7	9	76	.321	155	3	1	.994
1978—Arkansas†........Texas	OF	91	336	68	102	17	4	6	59	.304	124	6	1	.992
1979—Springfield........A.A.	OF	52	156	16	34	5	1	2	19	.218	67	3	3	.959
1979—Arkansas ....Texas	OF	55	197	32	48	6	1	3	26	.244	131	1	1	.992
1980—Arkansas ....Texas	OF	47	180	39	53	16	0	4	23	.294	62	1	1	.984
1980—Springfield........A.A.	OF	50	165	32	49	13	0	13	39	.297	69	0	1	.986

Signed as free agent by St. Louis Cardinals' organization, June 15, 1976.
†On disabled list, July 2 to August 14, 1978.

JOHN PATRICK PERCONTE
(Jack)

Born August 31, 1954, at Joliet, Ill.
Height, 5.10. Weight, 160.
Throws right and bats lefthanded.
Attended Murray State University, Murray, Ky.;
received Bachelor of Science degree in Sociology.

Year Club League	Pos.	G.	AB.	R.	H.	2B.	3B.	HR.	RBI.	B.A.	PO.	A.	E.	F.A.
1976—Lodi.................Calif.	2B	68	252	58	72	7	1	1	19	.286	141	223	12	.968
1977—Lodi.................Calif.	2B	131	515	•132	172	21	12	6	58	.334	292	390	22	.969
1978—San Antonio ......Texas	2B	134	538	90	148	20	8	2	52	.275	286	357	21	.968
1979—Albuquerque .....P.C.	2B	143	521	104	168	25	7	2	68	.322	278	403	•35	.951
1980—Albuquerque†....P.C.	2B	120	439	84	143	16	7	2	46	.326	291	320	15	.976
1980—Los Angeles ......Nat.	2B	14	17	2	4	0	0	0	2	.235	13	18	0	1.000
Major League Totals...........		14	17	2	4	0	0	0	2	.235	13	18	0	1.000

Selected by Los Angeles Dodgers' organization in 16th round of free-agent draft, June 8, 1976.
†On disabled list, May 18 to June 9, 1980.

ATANASIO RIGAL PEREZ

Name pronounced PER-ez.

(Tony)

Born May 14, 1942, at Ciego de Avila, Camaguey, Cuba.
Height, 6.02. Weight, 205.
Throws and bats righthanded.

Tied modern major league record for most at bats, game (7), June 13, 1975.
Tied National League records for most home runs through May 31 (18), 1970; fewest errors by first baseman for leader in errors, season (13), 1973.
Led National League first basemen in double plays with 131 in 1973.
Led National League third basemen in double plays with 35 in 1969 and tied for lead with 33 in 1968.
Led Carolina League third basemen in double plays with 23 in 1962.
Named Most Valuable Player in Pacific Coast League, 1964.
Named third baseman on THE SPORTING NEWS National League All-Star Team, 1970.
Named first baseman on THE SPORTING NEWS National League All-Star Team, 1973.

Year Club	League	Pos.	G.	AB.	R.	H.	2B.	3B.	HR.	RBI.	B.A.	PO.	A.	E.	F.A.
1960—Geneva†	NYP	IN-O	104	384	82	107	21	4	6	43	.279	199	197	31	.927
1961—Geneva	NYP	3B	121	460	110	•160	32	7	27	•132	•.348	107	•232	•42	.890
1962—Rocky Mount‡	Carol.	3B	100	384	72	112	20	8	18	74	.292	88	178	30	.899
1963—San Diego	P. C.	3B	8	29	4	11	3	1	1	5	.379	6	8	1	.933
1963—Macon§	Sally	3B	69	256	44	79	19	3	11	48	.309	57	100	18	.897
1964—San Diego	P. C.	1-3-OF	124	479	96	148	20	8	34	107	.309	816	104	19	.980
1964—Cincinnati	Nat.	1B	12	25	1	2	1	0	0	1	.080	51	0	1	.981
1965—Cincinnati	Nat.	1B	104	281	40	73	14	4	12	47	.260	525	40	6	.989
1966—Cincinnati	Nat.	1B	99	257	25	68	10	4	4	39	.265	530	23	6	.989
1967—Cincinnati	Nat.	3-1-2B	156	600	78	174	28	7	26	102	.290	249	234	13	.974
1968—Cincinnati	Nat.	3B	160	625	93	176	25	7	18	92	.282	•151	343	•25	.952
1969—Cincinnati	Nat.	3B	160	629	103	185	31	2	37	122	.294	136	•342	•32	.937
1970—Cincinnati	Nat.	•3B-1B	158	587	107	186	28	6	40	129	.317	167	292	•35	.929
1971—Cincinnati	Nat.	•3B-1B	158	609	72	164	22	3	25	91	.269	281	•308	20	.967
1972—Cincinnati	Nat.	1B	136	515	64	146	33	7	21	90	.283	1207	68	9	.993
1973—Cincinnati	Nat.	1B	151	564	73	177	33	3	27	101	.314	•1318	85	•13	.991
1974—Cincinnati	Nat.	1B	158	596	81	158	28	2	28	101	.265	1292	75	6	•.996
1975—Cincinnati	Nat.	1B	137	511	74	144	28	3	20	109	.282	1192	72	9	.993
1976—Cincinnati x	Nat.	1B	139	527	77	137	32	6	19	91	.260	1158	73	5	.996
1977—Montreal	Nat.	1B	154	559	71	158	32	6	19	91	.283	1312	110	11	.992
1978—Montreal	Nat.	1B	148	544	63	158	38	3	14	78	.290	1181	82	11	.991
1979—Montreal y	Nat.	1B	132	489	58	132	29	4	13	73	.270	1114	65	11	.991
1980—Boston	Amer.	1B	151	585	73	161	31	3	25	105	.275	1301	87	10	.993
National League Totals			2162	7917	1080	2238	412	67	323	1357	.283	11864	2212	213	.985
American League Totals			151	585	73	161	31	3	25	105	.275	1301	87	10	.993
Major League Totals			2313	8502	1153	2399	443	70	348	1462	.282	13165	2299	223	.986

Signed as free agent by Cincinnati Reds' organization, March 12, 1960.
†On disabled list, June 25 through July 5, 1960.
‡On suspended list, April 13 through April 16, 1962. On disabled list, July 30 through September 4, 1962.
§On suspended list, April 11, 1963. Placed on restricted list, April 23 through June 25, 1963.
xTraded with Pitcher Will McEnaney to Montreal Expos for Pitchers Woodie Fryman and Dale Murray, December 16, 1976.
yGranted free agency, November 1, 1979; signed by Boston Red Sox, November 16, 1979.

CHAMPIONSHIP SERIES RECORD

Tied Championship Series records for most consecutive games, one or more runs batted in, total Series (4); most at bats, extra-inning game (6), October 9, 1973 (12 innings); most strikeouts, five-game Series (7), 1972.
Established National League Championship Series record for most runs batted in, total Series (13).

Year Club	League	Pos.	G.	AB.	R.	H.	2B.	3B.	HR.	RBI.	B.A.	PO.	A.	E.	F.A.
1970—Cincinnati	Nat.	3B-1B	3	12	1	4	2	0	1	2	.333	6	6	1	.923
1972—Cincinnati	Nat.	1B	5	20	0	4	1	0	0	2	.200	45	3	0	1.000
1973—Cincinnati	Nat.	1B	5	22	1	2	0	0	1	2	.091	47	4	0	1.000
1975—Cincinnati	Nat.	1B	3	12	3	5	0	0	1	4	.417	27	5	0	1.000
1976—Cincinnati	Nat.	1B	3	10	1	2	0	0	0	3	.200	27	2	1	.967
Championship Series Totals			19	76	6	17	3	0	3	13	.224	152	20	2	.988

WORLD SERIES RECORD

Tied World Series record for one or more hits, each game, seven-game Series, 1972; most unassisted double plays by first baseman, game (1), October 11, 1975.

Year Club	League	Pos.	G.	AB.	R.	H.	2B.	3B.	HR.	RBI.	B.A.	PO.	A.	E.	F.A.
1970—Cincinnati	Nat.	3B	5	18	2	1	0	0	0	0	.056	3	13	1	.941
1972—Cincinnati	Nat.	1B	7	23	3	10	2	0	0	2	.435	73	3	1	.987
1975—Cincinnati	Nat.	1B	7	28	4	5	0	0	3	7	.179	66	5	1	.986
1976—Cincinnati	Nat.	1B	4	16	1	5	1	0	0	2	.313	32	4	0	1.000
World Series Totals			23	85	10	21	3	0	3	11	.247	174	25	3	.980

ALL-STAR GAME RECORD

Year League	Pos.	AB.	R.	H.	2B.	3B.	HR.	RBI.	B.A.	PO.	A.	E.	F.A.
1967—National	3B	2	1	1	0	0	1	1	.500	0	3	0	1.000
1968—National	3B	0	0	0	0	0	0	0	.000	0	1	0	1.000
1969—National	3B	1	0	0	0	0	0	0	.000	1	1	0	1.000
1970—National	3B	3	0	0	0	0	0	0	.000	1	1	0	1.000
1974—National	PH	1	0	0	0	0	0	0	.000	0	0	0	.000
1975—National	PH-1B	1	0	0	0	0	0	0	.000	1	1	0	1.000
1976—National	1B	0	0	0	0	0	0	0	.000	2	0	0	1.000
All-Star Game Totals		8	1	1	0	0	1	1	.125	5	7	0	1.000

PASCUAL PEREZ

Born May 17, 1957, at San Cristobal, Dominican Republic.
Height, 6.02. Weight, 162.
Throws and bats righthanded.

Tied for Carolina League lead in shutouts with 5 in 1978.

Year Club	League	G.	IP.	W.	L.	Pct.	H.	R.	ER.	SO.	BB.	ERA.
1976—Bradenton Pirates†	G. Coast	10	56	2	5	.286	51	41	29	34	35	4.66
1977—Charleston	W. Carol.	25	156	10	5	.667	153	80	69	96	60	3.98

Year	Club	League	G.	IP.	W.	L.	Pct.	H.	R.	ER.	SO.	BB.	ERA.
1978—Salem	....................Carolina		24	152	11	7	.611	133	70	44	126	51	2.61
1978—Columbus	.........................Int'national		1	5	0	0	.000	4	0	0	4	1	0.00
1979—Portland‡	...........................P. Coast		20	103	9	7	.563	121	70	63	51	47	5.50
1980—Portland	..........................P. Coast		24	160	12	10	.545	172	76	72	105	48	4.05
1980—Pittsburgh	.........................National		2	12	0	1	.000	15	6	5	7	2	3.75
Major League Totals	....		2	12	0	1	.000	15	6	5	7	2	3.75

Signed as free agent by Pittsburgh Pirates' organization, January 27, 1976.
†On suspended list, August 26 to 28, 1976.
‡On disabled list, July 16 to August 14, 1979.

BRODERICK PHILLIP PERKINS

Born November 23, 1954, at Pittsburg, Calif.
Height, 5.10. Weight, 180.
Throws and bats lefthanded.
Attended Diablo Valley College, Pleasant Hill, Calif., and
St. Mary's College, Moraga, Calif.

Led Northwest League in total bases with 128 in 1976.
Led Northwest League first basemen in double plays with 65 in 1976.

Year	Club	League	Pos.	G.	AB.	R.	H.	2B.	3B.	HR.	RBI.	B.A.	PO.	A.	E.	F.A.
1976—Walla Walla	......N'west.		1B	60	228	47	81	13	2	10	*63	.355	585	23	11	.982
1977—Amarillo†	.........Texas		1B-OF	116	438	71	151	30	1	4	66	.345	899	66	14	.986
1978—Hawaii	..............P. C.		1B	78	282	37	82	16	4	3	42	.291	641	35	6	.991
1978—San Diego	.....Nat.		1B	62	217	14	52	14	1	2	33	.240	538	41	4	.993
1979—San Diego‡	........Nat.		1B	57	87	8	23	0	0	0	8	.264	155	10	3	.982
1979—Hawaii	..............P. C.		1B	43	159	19	52	9	2	2	17	.327	385	33	5	.988
1980—Hawaii	..............P. C.		1B	118	436	53	136	29	7	6	65	.312	1168	79	8	.994
1980—San Diego	.........Nat.		1B-OF	43	100	18	37	9	0	2	14	.370	159	9	3	.994
Major League Totals	....			162	404	40	112	23	1	4	55	.277	852	60	10	.989

Selected by San Diego Padres' organization in 15th round of free-agent draft, June 8, 1976.
†On disabled list, July 16 to July 29, 1977.
‡On disabled list, July 2 to July 19, 1979.

GAYLORD JACKSON PERRY

Born September 15, 1938, at Williamston, N. C.
Height, 6.04. Weight, 215.
Throws and bats righthanded.
Hobbies—Golf, hunting and fishing.
Attended Campbell College, Buies Creek, N. C.
Brother of Jim Perry, pitcher with Cleveland Indians, Minnesota Twins,
Detroit Tigers and Oakland Athletics, 1959 through 1975.

Established major league record by winning Cy Young Memorial Award in both leagues.
Tied National League record for most putouts by pitcher, game (5), July 18, 1970.
Pitched 1-0 no-hit victory against St. Louis Cardinals, September 17, 1968.
Led National League in shutouts with 5 in 1970.
Led National League pitchers in games started with 41 in 1970.
Led American League pitchers in complete games with 29 in 1972 and 29 in 1973.
Led American League in wild pitches with 17 in 1973.
Won American League Cy Young Memorial Award, 1972.
Won National League Cy Young Memorial Award, 1978.
Named righthanded pitcher on THE SPORTING NEWS American League All-Star Team, 1972.
Named righthanded pitcher on THE SPORTING NEWS National League All-Star Team, 1978.
Named Pacific Coast League Pitcher of the Year in 1961.
Received reported $90,000 bonus to sign with San Francisco Giants, 1958.

Year	Club	League	G.	IP.	W.	L.	Pct.	H.	R.	ER.	SO.	BB.	ERA.
1958—St. Cloud	............................Northern		17	128	9	5	.643	97	40	34	111	48	2.39
1959—Corpus Christi	......................Texas		41	191	10	11	.476	*218	*120	86	119	69	4.05
1960—Tacoma	.....................P. Coast		1	1	0	0	.000	1	1	1	0	0	9.00
1960—Rio Grande Valley	................Texas		31	188	9	13	.409	164	68	59	120	77	*2.82
1961—Tacoma	.....................P. Coast		33	*219	●16	10	.615	208	79	62	95	61	2.55
1962—San Francisco	.....................National		13	43	3	1	.750	54	29	25	20	14	5.23
1962—Tacoma	.....................P. Coast		22	156	10	7	.588	128	56	43	136	56	*2.48
1963—San Francisco	.....................National		31	76	1	6	.143	84	41	34	52	29	4.03
1963—Tacoma	.....................P. Coast		1	9	1	0	1.000	3	1	1	7	1	1.00
1964—San Francisco	.....................National		44	206	12	11	.522	179	65	63	155	43	2.75
1965—San Francisco	.....................National		47	196	8	12	.400	194	105	91	170	70	4.18
1966—San Francisco	.....................National		36	256	21	8	.724	242	92	85	201	40	2.99
1967—San Francisco	.....................National		39	293	15	17	.469	231	98	85	230	84	2.61
1968—San Francisco	.....................National		39	291	16	15	.516	240	93	79	173	59	2.44
1969—San Francisco	.....................National		40	*325	19	14	.576	290	115	90	233	91	2.49
1970—San Francisco	.....................National		41	*329	●23	13	.639	*292	138	117	214	84	3.20
1971—San Francisco†	.....................National		37	280	16	12	.571	255	116	86	158	67	2.76
1972—Cleveland	............................American		41	343	●24	16	.600	253	79	73	234	82	1.92
1973—Cleveland	............................American		41	344	19	19	.500	315	143	129	238	115	3.38
1974—Cleveland	............................American		37	322	21	13	.618	230	99	90	216	99	2.52
1975—Cleveland‡-Texas	.................American		37	306	18	17	.514	277	127	110	233	70	3.24

Year Club	League	G.	IP.	W.	L.	Pct.	H.	R.	ER.	SO.	BB.	ERA.
1976—Texas	American	32	250	15	14	.517	232	93	90	143	52	3.24
1977—Texas§	American	34	238	15	12	.556	239	108	89	177	56	3.37
1978—San Diego	National	37	261	∗21	6	∗.778	241	96	79	154	66	2.72
1979—San Diego xy	National	32	233	12	11	.522	225	90	79	140	67	3.05
1980—Texas z-New York a	American	34	206	10	13	.435	224	107	84	135	64	3.67
National League Totals................		436	2789	167	126	.570	2527	1078	913	1900	714	2.95
American League Totals...............		256	2009	122	104	.540	1770	755	665	1376	538	2.98
Major League Totals		692	4798	289	230	.557	4297	1833	1578	3276	1252	2.96

Signed as free agent by San Francisco Giants' organization, June 3, 1958.
†Traded with Shortstop Frank Duffy to Cleveland Indians for Pitcher Sam McDowell, November 29, 1971.
‡Traded to Texas Rangers for Pitchers Jim Bibby, Jackie Brown and Rick Waits and an estimated $100,000, June 12, 1975.
§Traded to San Diego Padres for Pitcher Dave Tomlin and $125,000, February 15, 1978.
xOn suspended list, September 5 to October 3, 1979.
yTraded with Third Baseman Tucker Ashford and Pitcher Joe Carroll to Texas Rangers for First Baseman Willie Montanez, February 15, 1980.
zTraded to New York Yankees for Pitcher Ken Clay and a player to be named later, August 14, 1980; Outfielder Marvin Thompson traded to Texas Rangers' organization completing deal, October 1, 1980.
aGranted free agency, October 23, 1980; signed by Atlanta Braves, January 7, 1981.

CHAMPIONSHIP SERIES RECORD

Established Championship Series records for most runs allowed, four-game Series (11), 1971; most hits allowed, four-game Series (19), 1971.
Tied Championship Series record for most earned runs allowed, game (7), October 6, 1971.
Tied National League Championship Series record for most hits allowed, game (10), October 6, 1971.

Year Club	League	G.	IP.	W.	L.	Pct.	H.	R.	ER.	SO.	BB.	ERA.
1971—San Francisco	National	2	14⅔	1	1	.500	19	11	10	11	3	6.14

ALL-STAR GAME RECORD

Year League	IP.	W.	L.	Pct.	H.	R.	ER.	SO.	BB.	ERA.
1966—National	2	1	0	1.000	1	0	0	1	1	0.00
1970—National	2	0	0	.000	4	2	2	0	1	9.00
1972—American	2	0	0	.000	3	2	2	1	0	9.00
1974—American	3	0	0	.000	3	1	1	4	0	3.00
1979—National..	0	0	0	.000	3	1	1	0	0	......
All-Star Game Totals	9	1	0	1.000	14	6	6	6	2	6.00

GERALD JUNE PERRY

Born October 30, 1960, at Savannah, Ga.
Height, 5.11. Weight, 172.
Throws right and bats lefthanded.

Led Gulf Coast League first basemen in double plays with 46 in 1978.
Led Carolina League first basemen in double plays with 109 in 1980.

Year Club	League	Pos.	G.	AB.	R.	H.	2B.	3B.	HR.	RBI.	B.A.	PO.	A.	E.	F.A.
1978—Brad. Braves.....	G. C.	1B	∗55	191	32	51	∗12	3	1	26	.267	∗479	∗37	6	∗.989
1979—Greenwood	W. Car.	1B	109	400	69	133	17	4	9	71	∗.333	881	59	19	.980
1980—Durham	Carol.	1B	138	497	102	124	19	5	15	92	.249	∗1296	93	16	.989

Selected by Atlanta Braves' organization in 11th round of free-agent draft, June 6, 1978.

RICHARD DEVIN PETERS

(Rick)

Born November 21, 1955, at Lynwood, Calif.
Height, 5.10. Weight, 160.
Throws right and bats left and righthanded.
Attended Arizona State University, Tempe, Ariz.

Year Club	League	Pos.	G.	AB.	R.	H.	2B.	3B.	HR.	RBI.	B.A.	PO.	A.	E.	F.A.
1977—Montgomery	South.	OF	38	108	9	33	2	1	0	8	.306	70	3	1	.986
1978—Evansville	A. A.	OF-3B	●135	463	92	128	28	8	2	48	.276	199	5	8	.962
1979—Evansville	A. A.	OF-3B-2B	107	387	88	124	17	10	3	42	.320	125	17	5	.966
1979—Detroit.............	Amer.	3B-OF	12	19	3	5	0	0	0	2	.263	3	0	2	.600
1980—Detroit.............	Amer.	OF	133	477	79	139	19	7	2	42	.291	296	1	7	.977
Major League Totals.....................			145	496	82	144	19	7	2	44	.290	299	1	9	.971

Selected by Minnesota Twins' organization in 18th round of free-agent draft, June 5, 1973.
Selected by Atlanta Braves' organization in 12th round of free-agent draft, June 8, 1976.
Selected by Detroit Tigers' organization in 7th round of free-agent draft, June 7, 1977.

EUGENE JAMES PETRALLI JR.

(Gene)

Born September 25, 1959, at Sacramento, Calif.
Height, 6.01. Weight, 180.
Throws right and bats left and righthanded.
Attended Sacramento City College, Sacramento, Calif.
Son of Gene Petralli, minor league first baseman, 1948-54.

Tied for Pioneer League lead in passed balls with 27 in 1978.

Year	Club	League	Pos.	G.	AB.	R.	H.	2B.	3B.	HR.	RBI.	B.A.	PO.	A.	E.	F.A.
1978—Medicine Hat	....	Pion.	C-3B	65	242	42	68	14	5	2	40	.281	238	68	19	.942
1979—Dunedin†	....	Fla. St.	C-3B-OF	52	184	18	53	13	0	1	24	.288	206	42	5	.980
1979—Syracuse	....	Int.	C	18	56	6	13	0	1	0	7	.232	67	12	1	.988
1980—Knoxville	....	South.	C-1B-OF	116	382	42	109	20	2	3	38	.285	569	82	18	.973

Selected by Toronto Blue Jays' organization in 3rd round of free-agent draft, January 10, 1978.
†On suspended list, April 13 to April 27, 1979.

DANIEL JOSEPH PETRY

Name pronounced PEET-ree.

(Dan)

Born November 13, 1958, at Palo Alto, Calif.
Height, 6.04. Weight, 200.
Throws and bats righthanded.

Year	Club	League	G.	IP.	W.	L.	Pct.	H.	R.	ER.	SO.	BB.	ERA.
1976—Bristol	...............................Ap'lachian		14	79	2	3	.400	54	42	33	51	*56	3.76
1977—Lakeland	............................Florida St.		25	145	10	11	.476	139	68	55	68	68	3.41
1978—Montgomery	......................Southern		14	92	6	7	.462	70	38	25	69	41	2.45
1978—Evansville	..........................Am. Assoc.		13	71	4	3	.571	59	38	36	50	33	4.56
1979—Evansville	..........................Am. Assoc.		15	91	4	3	.571	92	60	49	55	37	4.85
1979—Detroit	...............................American		15	98	6	5	.545	90	46	43	43	33	3.95
1980—Evansville	..........................Am. Assoc.		4	30	2	0	1.000	21	11	9	16	12	2.70
1980—Detroit	...............................American		27	165	10	9	.526	156	82	72	88	83	3.93
Major League Totals	....		42	263	16	14	.533	246	128	115	131	116	3.94

Selected by Detroit Tigers' organization in 4th round of free-agent draft, June 8, 1976.

FELIX EARL PETTAWAY

Born February 9, 1955, at Mobile, Ala.
Height, 6.02. Weight, 200.
Throws and bats righthanded.

Year	Club	League	G.	IP.	W.	L.	Pct.	H.	R.	ER.	SO.	BB.	ERA.
1976—Kingsport	...........................Appal.		9	31	1	4	.200	32	24	22	15	32	6.39
1976—Greenwood†	.........................W. Carol.						Did not play						
1977—Greenwood‡	.........................W. Carol.		11	37	2	4	.333	46	37	26	20	34	6.32
1977—Kingsport	...........................Appal.		9	13	1	0	1.000	13	16	8	13	9	5.54
1978—Greenwood	...........................W. Carol.		17	87	4	7	.364	84	54	35	36	56	3.62
1978—Kinston	...............................Carolina		8	42	4	2	.667	37	23	16	24	20	3.43
1979—Visalia	...............................California		24	116	5	7	.417	137	82	66	76	56	5.12
1979—Savannah	...........................Southern		6	15	2	2	.500	18	17	16	12	10	9.60
1980—Durham	...............................Carolina		51	91	11	4	.733	65	32	21	95	48	2.08

Signed as free agent by Atlanta Braves' organization, March 25, 1976.
†On disabled list, June 6 to June 21, 1976.
‡On temporary inactive list, April 14 to April 27, 1977.

JOSEPH PAUL PETTINI

(Joe)

Born January 26, 1955, at Wheeling, W. Va.
Height, 5.09. Weight, 165.
Throws and bats righthanded.
Attended Mercer University, Macon, Ga.

Led American Association shortstops in assists with 413, in errors with 33 and in double plays with 87 in 1979.

Year	Club	League	Pos.	G.	AB.	R.	H.	2B.	3B.	HR.	RBI.	B.A.	PO.	A.	E.	F.A.
1977—Sarasota Expos	.Gulf C.		SS-3B	4	14	3	5	0	0	0	1	.357	4	9	4	.765
1977—Jamestown	.......NYP		3B-SS-2B	56	210	47	64	6	1	3	26	.305	57	96	11	.933
1977—W. Palm Beach	.Fla. St.		SS	1	3	0	0	0	0	0	0	.000	3	4	1	.875
1978—Memphis†	.........South.		2B-3B-SS	113	355	52	87	14	3	0	25	.245	178	307	21	.958
1979—Denver‡	............A.A.		SS-3B	132	446	70	131	21	6	4	46	.294	199	415	34	.948
1980—Phoenix	............P.C.		SS	85	344	52	97	16	4	2	32	.282	157	284	29	.938
1980—San Francisco	...Nat.		S-3-2	63	190	19	44	3	1	1	9	.232	66	147	8	.964
Major League Totals	....			63	190	19	44	3	1	1	9	.232	66	147	8	.964

Signed as free agent by Montreal Expos' organization, June 22, 1977.
†On disabled list, May 23 to June 13, 1978.
‡Traded to San Francisco Giants' organization, March 14, 1980; completing deal in which Montreal acquired Catcher John Tamargo, August 10, 1979.

DID YOU KNOW—

That Amos Otis became the 16th batter to hit a home run in his first World Series at-bat in 1980?

KENNETH ALLEN PHELPS
(Ken)

Born August 6, 1954, at Seattle, Wash.
Height, 6.01. Weight, 209.
Throws and bats lefthanded.
Attended Washington State University, Pullman, Wash.; Mesa Community College,
Mesa, Ariz., and Arizona State University, Tempe, Ariz.; received Bachelor of Science
degree in Physical Education.

Led Southern League batters in walks with 99 in 1978.
Led American Association first basemen in double plays with 111 in 1979 and with 103 in 1980.
Led American Association in walks with 128 in 1980.

Year Club League	Pos.	G.	AB.	R.	H.	2B.	3B.	HR.	RBI.	B.A.	PO.	A.	E.	F.A.
1976—Sara. Royals .....G.C.	1B	28	98	20	29	6	3	3	28	.296	166	16	2	.989
1976—Waterloo...........Midw.	1B	25	72	12	19	8	0	1	10	.264	205	12	3	.986
1977—Daytona Beach..Fla. St.	1B	40	145	22	50	7	0	5	32	.345	341	31	8	.979
1977—Jacksonville......South.	1B	81	262	30	51	6	3	5	40	.195	691	38	10	.986
1978—Jacksonville......South.	1B	124	381	65	94	20	0	16	61	.247	1028	66	16	.986
1979—Omaha.............A.A.	1B	130	430	71	114	26	3	20	77	.265	*1129	80	*13	.989
1980—Omaha.............A.A.	1B	133	442	80	130	30	3	23	72	.294	*1154	51	12	.990
1980—Kansas City......Amer.	1B	3	4	0	0	0	0	0	0	.000	14	0	0	1.000
Major League Totals		3	4	0	0	0	0	0	0	.000	14	0	0	1.000

Selected by Atlanta Braves' organization in 8th round of free-agent draft, June 6, 1972.
Selected by New York Yankees' organization in 1st round (11th player selected) of free-agent draft, January 9, 1974.
Selected by Philadelphia Phillies' organization in secondary phase of free-agent draft, June 5, 1974.
Selected by Kansas City Royals' organization in 15th round of free-agent draft, June 8, 1976.

MICHAEL DWAINE PHILLIPS
(Mike)

Born August 19, 1950, at Beaumont, Tex.
Height, 6.01. Weight, 185.
Throws right and bats right and lefthanded.
Hobby—Hunting.
Attended Phoenix College, Phoenix, Ariz.

Year Club League	Pos.	G.	AB.	R.	H.	2B.	3B.	HR.	RBI.	B.A.	PO.	A.	E.	F.A.
1969—Great Falls........Pion.	*SS-2	55	167	23	36	9	1	0	18	.216	58	125	13	*.934
1970—Fresno ....Calif.	SS-2B	94	318	26	79	7	3	3	21	.248	133	264	34	.921
1971—Amarillo ....Texas	SS	89	347	45	81	15	6	2	22	.233	116	290	30	.931
1972—Phoenix............P. C.	S-2-3	114	375	57	93	17	7	0	32	.248	148	342	41	.932
1973—Phoenix............P. C.	SS	1	4	1	1	0	0	0	1	.250	1	2	0	1.000
1973—San Francisco ...Nat.	3-S-2	63	104	18	25	3	4	1	9	.240	42	69	6	.949
1974—San Francisco ...Nat.	3-2-S	100	283	19	62	6	1	2	20	.219	125	195	19	.944
1975—S. F.†-N. Y. ......Nat.	*S-2-3	126	414	34	104	10	7	1	29	.251	203	364	*32	.947
1976—New York.........Nat.	S-3-2	87	262	30	67	4	6	4	29	.256	115	191	11	.965
1977—N.Y.‡St.L. ....Nat.	2-S-3	86	173	22	39	5	3	1	12	.225	90	126	7	.969
1978—St. Louis ....Nat.	2B-SS-3B	76	164	14	44	8	1	1	28	.268	107	135	7	.972
1979—St. Louis ....Nat.	SS-2B-3B	44	97	10	22	3	1	1	6	.227	53	107	4	.976
1980—St. Louis§.........Nat.	S-2-3	63	128	13	30	5	0	0	7	.234	63	130	9	.955
Major League Totals		655	1625	160	393	44	23	11	140	.242	798	1317	95	.957

Selected by San Francisco Giants' organization in 1st round (18th player selected) of free-agent draft, June 5, 1969.
†Sold on waivers to New York Mets, May 3, 1975.
‡Traded to St. Louis Cardinals for Infielder-Outfielder Joel Youngblood, June 15, 1977.
§Traded with Catchers Terry Kennedy and Steve Swisher and Pitchers John Littlefield, Kim Seaman, Al Olmsted and John Urrea to San Diego Padres for Pitchers Rollie Fingers and Bob Shirley, Catcher-First Baseman Gene Tenace and a player to be named later, December 8, 1980; Catcher Bob Geren traded to Cardinals' organization completing deal, December 10, 1980.

ROBERT MICHAEL PICCIOLO
Name pronounced PEACH-alo.

(Rob)

Born February 4, 1953, at Santa Monica, Calif.
Height, 6.02. Weight, 185.
Throws and bats righthanded.
Hobby—Music.
Attended Santa Monica City College, Santa Monica, Calif. and Pepperdine University,
Malibu, Calif.; received degree in Journalism.

Led Southern League shortstops in double plays with 91 in 1975.

Year Club League	Pos.	G.	AB.	R.	H.	2B.	3B.	HR.	RBI.	B.A.	PO.	A.	E.	F.A.
1975—Birmingham......South.	SS	133	488	55	135	23	6	3	62	.277	*278	*404	18	*.974
1976—Tucson ....P. C.	SS	139	*570	78	170	19	4	5	54	.298	220	429	22	*.967
1977—San Jose..........P. C.	SS	10	38	5	8	1	0	1	4	.211	23	25	0	1.000
1977—Oakland ....Amer.	SS	148	419	35	84	12	3	2	22	.200	213	381	21	.966
1978—Vancouver ....P. C.	SS	26	90	14	23	3	4	2	17	.256	53	87	3	.979

Year Club	League	Pos.	G.	AB.	R.	H.	2B.	3B.	HR.	RBI.	B.A.	PO.	A.	E.	F.A.
1978—Oakland............Amer.		SS-2B-3B	78	93	16	21	1	0	2	7	.226	74	90	7	.959
1979—Oakland............Amer.		S-2-3-O	115	348	37	88	16	2	2	27	.253	203	288	17	.967
1980—Oakland............Amer.		S-2B-O	95	271	32	65	9	2	5	18	.240	164	208	6	.984
Major League Totals 436				1131	120	258	38	7	11	74	.228	654	967	51	.969

Selected by San Francisco Giants' organization in 2nd round of free-agent draft, January 10, 1973.
Selected by Kansas City Royals' organization in secondary phase of free-agent draft, June 5, 1973.
Selected by Detroit Tigers' organization in secondary phase of free-agent draft, June 5, 1974.
Selected by Oakland A's organization in secondary phase of free-agent draft, January 9, 1975.

ROBERT ANTHONY PIETROBURGO
(Rob)

Born January 1, 1957, at Columbia, Mo.
Height, 6.02. Weight, 180.
Throws and bats lefthanded.
Attended University of Missouri, Columbia, Mo.

Led Northwest League in saves with 9 in 1978.

Year Club	League	G.	IP.	W.	L.	Pct.	H.	R.	ER.	SO.	BB.	ERA.
1978—Bellingham ....Northwest		*32	48	4	4	.500	37	17	8	53	21	1.50
1979—Spokane†‡...........................P. Coast		32	54	1	4	.200	62	40	37	33	17	6.17
1980—Tacoma ....P. Coast		46	70	5	5	.500	75	32	28	61	26	3.60

Selected by Montreal Expos' organization in 19th round of free-agent draft, June 7, 1977.
Selected by Seattle Mariners' organization in 14th round of free-agent draft, June 6, 1978.
†On disabled list, May 21 to July 13, 1979.
‡Traded with Pitcher Rafael Vasquez and a player to be named later to Cleveland Indians for Third Baseman-Outfielder Ted Cox, December 6, 1979; Pitcher Bud Anderson traded to Indians' organization completing deal, March 29, 1980.

LOUIS VICTOR PINIELLA
Name pronounced Pin-ELLA.
(Lou)

Born August 28, 1943, at Tampa, Fla.
Height, 6.02. Weight, 199.
Throws and bats righthanded.
Hobbies—Fishing and golf.
Attended University of Tampa, Tampa, Fla.

Tied major league record for most assists by outfielder, inning (2), May 27, 1974 (third inning).
Named Rookie of the Year in Carolina League, 1963.
Named by Baseball Writers Association as American League Rookie of the Year, 1969.

Year Club	League	Pos.	G.	AB.	R.	H.	2B.	3B.	HR.	RBI.	B.A.	PO.	A.	E.	F.A.
1962—Selma†..............Ala.-Fl.		OF	70	278	40	75	10	5	8	44	.270	94	6	9	.917
1963—Peninsula.........Carol.		OF	143	548	71	170	29	4	16	77	.310	271	*23	8	.974
1964—Aberdeen‡.........North.		OF	20	74	8	20	8	3	0	12	.270	37	1	1	.974
1964—Baltimore.........Amer.		PH	4	1	0	0	0	0	0	0	.000	0	0	0	.000
1965—Elmira§ ....East.		OF	126	490	64	122	29	6	11	64	.249	176	5	7	.963
1966—Portland...........P. C.		OF	133	457	47	132	22	3	7	52	.289	177	11	11	.945
1967—Portland...........P. C.		OF	113	396	49	122	20	1	8	56	.308	199	7	6	.972
1968—Portland...........P. C.		OF	88	331	49	105	15	3	13	62	.317	167	6	7	.961
1968—Cleveland xy......Amer.		OF	6	5	1	0	0	0	0	1	.000	1	0	0	1.000
1969—Kansas City.......Amer.		OF	135	493	43	139	21	6	11	68	.282	278	13	7	.977
1970—Kansas City......Amer.		OF-1B	144	542	54	163	24	5	11	88	.301	250	6	4	.985
1971—Kansas City z ....Amer.		OF	126	448	43	125	21	5	3	51	.279	201	6	3	.986
1972—Kansas City.......Amer.		OF	151	574	65	179	*33	4	11	72	.312	275	8	7	.976
1973—Kansas City a ....Amer.		OF	144	513	53	128	28	1	9	69	.250	196	9	3	.986
1974—New York.........Amer.		OF-1B	140	518	71	158	26	0	9	70	.305	270	16	3	.990
1975—New York b.......Amer.		OF	74	199	7	39	4	1	0	22	.196	65	5	1	.986
1976—New York.........Amer.		OF	100	327	36	92	16	6	3	38	.281	199	10	4	.981
1977—New York.........Amer.		OF-1B	103	339	47	112	19	3	12	45	.330	86	3	2	.978
1978—New York ....Amer.		OF	130	472	67	148	34	5	6	69	.314	213	4	7	.969
1979—New York ....Amer.		OF	130	461	49	137	22	2	11	69	.297	204	13	4	.982
1980—New York ....Amer.		OF	116	321	39	92	18	0	2	27	.287	157	8	5	.971
Major League Totals 1503				5213	575	1512	266	38	88	689	.290	2395	101	50	.980

Signed as free agent by Cleveland Indians' organization, June 9, 1962.
†Drafted by Washington Senators from Jacksonville (Cleveland Indians' organization), November 26, 1962.
‡Reinstated from Military List by Washington Senators, July 20, 1964 and assigned to Baltimore Orioles to complete deal for Pitcher Lester (Buster) Narum, August 4, 1964; Orioles optioned him to Aberdeen.
§Traded by Baltimore Orioles to Cleveland Indians' organization for Catcher Cam Carreon, March 10, 1966.
xSelected by Seattle Pilots from Cleveland Indians in expansion draft, October 15, 1968.
yTraded by Seattle Pilots to Kansas City Royals for Outfielder Steve Whitaker and Pitcher John Gelnar (latter assigned to Vancouver), April 1, 1969.
zOn disabled list May 5 through June 8.
aTraded with Pitcher Ken Wright to New York Yankees for Pitcher Lindy McDaniel, December 7, 1973.
bOn supplemental disabled list, June 17 to July 6, 1975.

CHAMPIONSHIP SERIES RECORD

Year	Club	League	Pos.	G.	AB.	R.	H.	2B.	3B.	HR.	RBI.	B.A.	PO.	A.	E.	F.A.
1976—New York		Amer.	DH-PH	4	11	1	3	1	0	0	0	.273	0	0	0	.000
1977—New York		Amer.	OF-DH	5	21	1	7	3	0	0	2	.333	9	1	0	1.000
1978—New York		Amer.	OF	4	17	2	4	0	0	0	0	.235	13	0	0	1.000
1980—New York		Amer.	OF	2	5	1	1	0	0	1	1	.200	5	0	0	1.000
Championship Series Totals				15	54	5	15	4	0	1	3	.278	27	1	0	1.000

WORLD SERIES RECORD

Tied World Series record for one or more hits, each game, six-game Series, 1978.

Year	Club	League	Pos.	G.	AB.	R.	H.	2B.	3B.	HR.	RBI.	B.A.	PO.	A.	E.	F.A.
1976—New York		Amer.	D-O-PH	4	9	1	3	1	0	0	0	.333	1	0	0	1.000
1977—New York		Amer.	OF	6	22	1	6	0	0	0	3	.273	16	1	1	.944
1978—New York		Amer.	OF	6	25	3	7	0	0	0	4	.280	14	1	0	1.000
World Series Totals				16	56	5	16	1	0	0	7	.286	31	2	1	.971

ALL-STAR GAME RECORD

Year	League	Pos.	AB.	R.	H.	2B.	3B.	HR.	RBI.	B.A.	PO.	A.	E.	F.A.
1972—American		PH	1	0	0	0	0	0	0	.000	0	0	0	.000

GORDON CECIL PLADSON
(Gordie)

Born July 31, 1956, at New Westminster, B.C.
Height, 6.04. Weight, 210.
Throws and bats righthanded.
Attended Douglas College, Surrey, B. C.

Led Southern League in complete games with 14 in 1978.

Year	Club	League	G.	IP.	W.	L.	Pct.	H.	R.	ER.	SO.	BB.	ERA.
1973—Covington		Ap'lachian	8	30	1	3	.250	34	26	17	15	31	5.10
1974—Covington		Ap'lachian	10	35	2	6	.250	29	30	24	29	33	6.17
1975—Dubuque		Midwest	17	33	1	5	.167	37	33	26	28	24	7.09
1976—Dubuque		Midwest	27	127	7	4	.636	129	88	66	63	90	4.68
1977—Cocoa		Florida St.	23	132	7	9	.438	147	78	61	49	62	4.16
1977—Columbus		Southern	5	38	2	2	.500	25	12	9	13	18	2.13
1978—Columbus		Southern	26	182	11	10	.524	177	88	74	117	77	3.66
1979—Charleston		Int'national	27	196	13	14	.481	181	76	65	101	52	2.98
1979—Houston		National	4	4	0	0	.000	9	2	2	2	2	4.50
1980—Tucson		P. Coast	17	128	10	5	.667	121	62	51	66	44	3.59
1980—Houston		National	12	41	0	4	.000	38	23	20	13	16	4.39
Major League Totals			16	45	0	4	.000	47	25	22	15	18	4.40

Signed as free agent by Houston Astros' organization, June 30, 1973.

BIFF POCOROBA

Name pronounced poh-koh-ROH-buh.

Born July 25, 1953, at Burbank, Calif.
Height, 5.10. Weight, 170.
Throws right and bats left and righthanded.
Hobbies—Hunting and golf.
Brother of Joseph Pocoroba, shortstop in Los Angeles Dodgers' organization.

Year	Club	League	Pos.	G.	AB.	R.	H.	2B.	3B.	HR.	RBI.	B.A.	PO.	A.	E.	F.A.
1971—Wytheville		Appal.	C	42	124	17	37	7	0	3	19	.298	262	13	3	.989
1972—Greenwood		W. Car.	C	75	212	25	55	5	0	7	29	.259	446	25	10	*.979
1972—Richmond		Int.	PH	1	1	0	0	0	0	0	0	.000	0	0	0	.000
1973—Savannah†		South.	C	114	368	46	86	13	0	12	46	.234	417	38	7	.985
1974—Savannah‡		South.	*C-1B	79	241	48	75	10	2	9	45	.311	435	25	2	*.996
1975—Atlanta		Nat.	C	67	188	15	48	7	1	1	22	.255	237	25	8	.970
1976—Atlanta§		Nat.	C	54	174	16	42	7	0	0	14	.241	273	39	7	.978
1977—Atlanta		Nat.	C	113	321	46	93	24	1	8	44	.290	542	78	7	.989
1978—Atlanta x		Nat.	C	92	289	21	70	8	0	6	34	.242	454	43	5	.990
1979—Atlanta y		Nat.	C	28	38	6	12	4	0	0	4	.316	7	39	3	.933
1980—Atlanta z		Nat.	C	70	83	7	22	4	0	2	8	.265	56	1	4	.934
Major League Totals				424	1093	111	287	54	2	17	126	.263	1569	225	34	.981

Selected by Atlanta Braves' organization in 17th round of free-agent draft, June 8, 1971.
†On disabled list, July 12 to July 22, 1973.
‡On disabled list, April 26 to June 7, 1974.
§On disabled list, June 2 to July 6 and August 9 to October 4, 1976.
xOn disabled list, August 15 to October 1, 1978.
yOn disabled list, April 4 to June 5 and July 19 to September 1, 1979.
zOn supplemental disabled list, April 20 to June 10, 1980.

ALL-STAR GAME RECORD

Year	League	Pos.	AB.	R.	H.	2B.	3B.	HR.	RBI.	B.A.	PO.	A.	E.	F.A.
1978—National		C	0	0	0	0	0	0	0	.000	0	0	0	.000

JOHN WILLIAM POFF

Born October 23, 1952, at Chillicothe, O.
Height, 6.02. Weight, 200.
Throws and bats lefthanded.
Hobbies—Gardening, cycling and camping.
Attended Duke University, Durham, N. C.; received Bachelor of Arts degree.

Led Appalachian League in total bases with 154 in 1974.
Led Carolina League first basemen in double plays with 104 in 1975.

Year Club	League	Pos.	G.	AB.	R.	H.	2B.	3B.	HR.	RBI.	B.A.	PO.	A.	E.	F.A.
1974—Pulaski	Appal.	1B	68	241	48	83	*19	2	16	61	.344	*616	22	9	.986
1975—Rocky Mount	Carol.	1B-OF	127	445	76	119	20	6	8	62	.267	1158	72	*16	.987
1976—Reading	East.	OF-1B	124	443	47	115	18	2	9	51	.260	180	16	9	.956
1977—Reading	East.	1B-OF	56	215	41	61	6	4	11	31	.284	359	37	5	.988
1977—Oklahoma City	A. A.	OF-1B	69	225	37	69	9	7	5	36	.307	144	10	3	.981
1978—Oklahoma City	A. A.	*1B-OF	125	436	79	131	30	8	20	79	.300	980	89	*15	.986
1979—Oklahoma City	A. A.	1B-OF	132	481	77	141	•34	5	20	90	.293	814	69	12	.987
1979—Philadelphia	Nat.	OF-1B	12	19	2	2	1	0	0	1	.105	8	0	1	.889
1980—Oklahoma City†	A. A.	1B-OF	133	496	80	140	25	10	13	90	.282	673	64	14	.981
1980—Milwaukee	Amer.	1B	19	68	7	17	1	2	1	7	.250	23	0	1	.958
National League Totals			12	19	2	2	1	0	0	1	.105	8	0	1	.889
American League Totals			19	68	7	17	1	2	1	7	.250	23	0	1	.958
Major League Totals			31	87	9	19	2	2	1	8	.218	31	0	2	.939

Signed as free agent by Philadelphia Phillies' organization, July 2, 1974.
†Sold on waivers to Milwaukee Brewers, September 1, 1980.

THOMAS ARTHUR POQUETTE

Name pronounced POE-kett.

(Tom)

Born October 30, 1951, at Eau Claire, Wis.
Height, 5.11. Weight, 175.
Throws right and bats lefthanded.
Hobbies—Fishing, hunting and reading.

Tied for Southern League and in double plays b outfielders with 3 in 1972.

Year Club	League	Pos.	G.	AB.	R.	H.	2B.	3B.	HR.	RBI.	B.A.	PO.	A.	E.	F.A.
1970—Kingsport	Appal.	OF	56	209	41	57	7	1	8	18	.273	81	5	7	.925
1971—Waterloo	Midw.	O-3	111	381	65	113	21	4	8	60	.297	135	41	9	.951
1972—Jacksonville	South.	OF	126	451	49	113	25	3	6	51	.251	159	13	12	.935
1973—Omaha	A. A.	OF	131	478	66	128	22	4	9	50	.268	230	*17	*14	.946
1973—Kansas City	Amer.	OF	21	28	4	6	1	0	0	3	.214	19	1	3	.870
1974—Omaha†	A. A.	OF	63	223	42	68	10	3	4	27	.305	107	7	7	.909
1975—Jacksonville‡	South.	OF	105	355	50	91	16	0	5	40	.256	179	16	3	.985
1976—Kansas City§	Amer.	OF	104	344	43	104	18	10	2	34	.302	188	1	4	.979
1977—Kansas City x	Amer.	OF	106	342	43	100	23	6	2	33	.292	177	4	0	1.000
1978—Kansas City	Amer.	OF	80	204	16	44	9	2	4	30	.216	144	5	7	.955
1979—K.C. y-Boston	Amer.	OF	84	180	15	56	9	0	2	26	.311	80	3	4	.954
1980—Boston z	Amer.					Did not play									
Major League Totals			395	1098	121	310	60	18	10	126	.282	608	14	18	.972

Selected by Kansas City Royals' organization in 4th round of free-agent draft, June 4, 1970.
†On disabled list, June 22 to September 1, 1974.
‡On disabled list from beginning of season until May 21, 1975.
§On disabled list, June 23 to July 15, 1976.
xOn disabled list, March 29 to April 19, 1977.
yTraded to Boston Red Sox for First Baseman George Scott, June 13, 1979.
zOn disabled list, March 25, 1980; transferred to emergency disabled list, July 7 to October 21, 1980.

CHAMPIONSHIP SERIES RECORD

Year Club	League	Pos.	G.	AB.	R.	H.	2B.	3B.	HR.	RBI.	B.A.	PO.	A.	E.	F.A.
1976—Kansas City	Amer.	OF	5	16	1	3	2	0	0	4	.188	13	0	0	1.000
1977—Kansas City	Amer.	OF	2	6	0	1	0	0	0	0	.167	3	0	0	1.000
1978—Kansas City	Amer.	PH	1	1	0	0	0	0	0	0	.000	0	0	0	.000
Championship Series Totals			8	23	1	4	2	0	0	4	.174	16	0	0	1.000

DARRELL RAY PORTER

Born January 17, 1952, at Joplin, Mo.
Height, 6.01. Weight, 195.
Throws right and bats lefthanded.
Hobbies—Hunting, fishing and golf.

Led Midwest League in passed balls with 19 in 1971.
Led American League in passed balls with 15 in 1975.
Led American League catchers in double plays with 15 in 1979.
Led American League batters in walks with 121 in 1979.
Tied for American League lead in sacrifice flies with 13 in 1979.
Named catcher on THE SPORTING NEWS American League All-Star team, 1979.
Received bonus reported in excess of $70,000 to sign with Milwaukee Brewers, 1970.

Year Club	League	Pos.	G.	AB.	R.	H.	2B.	3B.	HR.	RBI.	B.A.	PO.	A.	E.	F.A.
1970–Clinton	Midw.	C	62	185	24	37	11	0	4	21	.200	380	42	10	.977
1971–Danville	Midw.	C	101	332	75	90	9	7	24	70	.271	674	*69	*19	.975
1971–Milwaukee	Amer.	C	22	70	4	15	2	0	2	9	.214	108	18	3	.977
1972–Evansville	A. A.	C	88	255	37	55	7	2	13	45	.216	541	*56	7	.988
1972–Milwaukee	Amer.	C	18	56	2	7	1	0	1	2	.125	113	8	3	.976
1973–Milwaukee	Amer.	C	117	350	50	89	19	2	16	67	.254	372	47	10	.977
1974–Milwaukee	Amer.	C	131	432	59	104	15	4	12	56	.241	484	60	12	.978
1975–Milwaukee	Amer.	C	130	409	66	95	12	5	18	60	.232	532	82	13	.979
1976–Milwaukee†	Amer.	C	119	389	43	81	14	1	5	32	.208	491	52	4	.975
1977–Kansas City	Amer.	C	130	425	61	117	21	3	16	60	.275	663	61	●13	.982
1978–Kansas City	Amer.	C	150	520	77	138	27	6	18	78	.265	608	62	8	.988
1979–Kansas City	Amer.	C	157	533	101	155	23	10	20	112	.291	628	68	13	.982
1980–Kansas City‡§	Amer.	C	118	418	51	104	14	2	7	51	.249	322	37	8	.978
Major League Totals			1092	3602	514	905	148	33	115	527	.251	4321	495	97	.980

Selected by Milwaukee Brewers' organization in 1st round (fourth player selected) of free-agent draft, June 4, 1970.

†Traded with Pitcher Jim Colborn to Kansas City Royals for Outfielder Jim Wohlford, Infielder Jamie Quirk and a player to be named later, December 6, 1976; Pitcher Bob McClure was sent to Milwaukee to complete deal, March 15, 1976.

‡On supplemental disabled list, April 4 to May 2, 1980.

§Granted free agency, October 24, 1980; signed by St. Louis Cardinals, December 13, 1980.

CHAMPIONSHIP SERIES RECORD

Year Club	League	Pos.	G.	AB.	R.	H.	2B.	3B.	HR.	RBI.	B.A.	PO.	A.	E.	F.A.
1977–Kansas City	Amer.	C	5	15	3	5	0	0	0	0	.333	18	0	0	1.000
1978–Kansas City	Amer.	C	4	14	1	5	1	0	0	3	.357	21	1	0	1.000
1980–Kansas City	Amer.	C	3	10	2	1	0	0	0	0	.100	17	1	0	1.000
Championship Series Totals			12	39	6	11	1	0	0	3	.282	56	2	0	1.000

WORLD SERIES RECORD

Year Club	League	Pos.	G.	AB.	R.	H.	2B.	3B.	HR.	RBI.	B.A.	PO.	A.	E.	F.A.
1980–Kansas City	Amer.	PH-C	5	14	1	2	0	0	0	0	.143	13	2	0	1.000

ALL-STAR GAME RECORD

Year League	Pos.	AB.	R.	H.	2B.	3B.	HR.	RBI.	B.A.	PO.	A.	E.	F.A.
1978–American	PH	1	0	0	0	0	0	0	.000	0	0	0	.000
1979–American	C	3	0	1	1	0	0	0	.333	2	0	0	1.000
1980–American	C	1	0	0	0	0	0	0	.000	0	1	0	.000
All-Star Game Totals		5	0	1	1	0	0	0	.200	2	1	0	1.000

Member of American League All-Star Team in 1974 game; did not play.

HOSKEN POWELL

Born May 14, 1955, at Salem, Ala.
Height, 6.01. Weight, 185.
Throws and bats lefthanded.
Attended Chipola Junior College, Marianna, Fla.

Year Club	League	Pos.	G.	AB.	R.	H.	2B.	3B.	HR.	RBI.	B.A.	PO.	A.	E.	F.A.
1975–Elizabethton	Appal.	OF	64	249	45	82	*23	6	3	*58	.329	98	9	8	.930
1976–Reno	Calif.	OF	126	484	*118	167	22	9	7	73	.345	171	8	7	.962
1977–Tacoma	P. C.	OF	133	473	107	154	20	7	5	51	.326	190	8	9	.957
1978–Minnesota	Amer.	OF	121	381	55	94	20	2	3	31	.247	219	9	4	.983
1979–Minnesota†	Amer.	OF	104	338	49	99	17	3	2	36	.293	165	6	4	.977
1979–Toledo	Int.	OF	10	44	14	11	3	0	0	6	.250	15	1	1	.941
1980–Minnesota	Amer.	OF	137	485	58	127	17	5	6	35	.262	265	11	9	.968
Major League Totals			362	1204	162	320	54	10	11	102	.266	659	26	17	.976

Selected by Pittsburgh Pirates' organization in 1st round (19th player selected) of free-agent draft, January 9, 1975.

Selected by Minnesota Twins' organization in secondary phase of free-agent draft, June 4, 1975.

†On disabled list, April 2 to May 7, 1979.

TED HENRY POWER

Born January 31, 1955, at Guthrie, Okla.
Height, 6.04. Weight, 220.
Throws and bats righthanded.
Attended Kansas State University, Manhattan, Kan.

Year Club	League	G.	IP.	W.	L.	Pct.	H.	R.	ER.	SO.	BB.	ERA.
1976–Lodi	California	13	51	1	3	.250	46	34	26	58	44	4.59
1977–San Antonio†	Texas	12	72	5	3	.625	51	35	31	60	55	3.88
1978–San Antonio‡	Texas	25	101	6	5	.545	92	57	45	97	75	4.01
1979–San Antonio	Texas	10	64	5	1	.833	69	44	37	52	43	5.20
1979–Albuquerque	P. Coast	18	101	5	5	.500	95	59	52	69	82	4.63
1980–Albuquerque	P. Coast	26	155	13	7	.650	160	93	78	113	95	4.53

Selected by Los Angeles Dodgers' organization in 5th round of free-agent draft, June 8, 1976.

†On disabled list, July 18 to July 29 and August 20 to September 4, 1977.

‡On disabled list, July 5 to July 21, 1978.

JOSEPH WALTER PRICE
(Joe)

Born November 29, 1956, at Inglewood, Calif.
Height, 6.04. Weight, 220.
Throws left and bats righthanded.
Attended Oklahoma State University, Stillwater, Okla., and
University of Oklahoma, Norman, Okla.

Year Club	League	G.	IP.	W.	L.	Pct.	H.	R.	ER.	SO.	BB.	ERA.
1977—Billings	Pioneer	15	94	6	5	.545	83	50	39	97	42	3.73
1978—Tampa	Florida St.	23	165	10	4	.714	123	40	27	128	51	1.47
1978—Nashville	Southern	2	10	0	0	.000	7	3	3	10	3	2.70
1979—Nashville	Southern	22	109	6	6	.500	101	58	48	69	41	3.96
1980—Indianapolis	Am. Assoc.	11	79	4	4	.500	64	36	34	83	30	3.87
1980—Cincinnati	National	24	111	7	3	.700	95	45	44	44	37	3.57
Major League Totals		24	111	7	3	.700	95	45	44	44	37	3.57

Selected by Cincinnati Reds' organization in 4th round of free-agent draft, June 7, 1977.

MICHAEL JAMES PROLY
(Mike)

Born December 15, 1950, at Jamaica, N. Y.
Height, 5.10. Weight, 185.
Throws and bats righthanded.
Hobbies—Fishing, swimming and golf.
Attended St. John's University, Jamaica, N. Y.; received Bachelor
of Science degree in Marketing.

Year Club	League	G.	IP.	W.	L.	Pct.	H.	R.	ER.	SO.	BB.	ERA.
1972—St. Petersburg	Florida St.	12	46	3	1	.750	28	9	4	41	10	0.78
1972—Modesto	California	6	29	1	3	.250	41	29	23	16	15	7.14
1973—St. Petersburg	Florida St.	37	164	14	5	*.737	129	44	32	112	28	*1.76
1974—Arkansas	Texas	39	101	8	2	.800	101	37	31	51	34	2.76
1975—Tulsa	Am. Assoc.	55	86	7	10	.412	101	42	37	51	43	3.87
1976—St. Louis	National	14	17	1	0	1.000	21	9	7	4	6	3.71
1976—Tulsa†	Am. Assoc.	50	67	6	4	.600	71	28	20	28	13	2.69
1977—Tacoma‡	P. Coast	55	130	9	12	.429	159	82	66	61	43	4.57
1978—Iowa	Am. Assoc.	22	66	6	2	.750	52	22	19	41	13	2.59
1978—Chicago§	American	14	66	5	2	.714	63	24	20	19	12	2.73
1979—Chicago x	American	38	88	3	8	.273	89	43	38	32	40	3.89
1980—Chicago	American	62	147	5	10	.333	136	67	50	56	58	3.06
National League Totals		14	17	1	0	1.000	21	9	7	4	6	3.71
American League Totals		114	301	13	20	.394	288	134	108	107	110	3.23
Major League Totals		128	318	14	20	.412	309	143	115	111	116	3.25

Selected by St. Louis Cardinals' organization in 9th round of free-agent draft, June 6, 1972.
†Drafted by Tacoma (Minnesota Twins' organization), November 29, 1976.
‡Granted free agency November 2, 1977; signed by Chicago White Sox' organization, November 22, 1977.
§On disabled list, August 30 to October 13, 1978.
xOn disabled list, June 14 to July 28, 1979.

RONALD RALPH PRUITT
(Ron)

Born October 21, 1951, at Flint, Mich.
Height, 6.00. Weight, 185.
Throws and bats righthanded.
Hobbies—Fishing and listening to music.
Attended Michigan State University, East Lansing, Mich.

Led Eastern League catchers in double plays with 13 in 1974.

Year Club	League	Pos.	G.	AB.	R.	H.	2B.	3B.	HR.	RBI.	B.A.	PO.	A.	E.	F.A.
1972—Denver	A. A.	O-C-2	60	167	22	36	5	0	5	24	.216	117	10	4	.969
1973—Spokane	P. C.	O-C-3-1	112	372	68	103	22	7	8	55	.277	319	68	11	.972
1974—Pittsfield	East.	*C-O-1-3	129	415	74	111	28	2	15	77	.267	319	*91	●17	.979
1975—Spokane	P. C.	C-3-O	77	271	51	75	10	3	9	42	.277	183	62	14	.946
1975—Texas†	Amer.	C-OF	14	17	2	3	0	0	0	0	.176	21	5	0	1.000
1976—Cleveland	Amer.	O-C-2-1	47	86	7	23	1	1	0	5	.267	73	16	1	.989
1977—Toledo	Int.	O-1-C	15	48	5	12	2	0	1	3	.250	32	1	0	1.000
1977—Cleveland	Amer.	O-C-3	78	219	29	63	10	2	2	32	.288	113	6	3	.975
1978—Cleveland	Amer.	C-O-3	71	187	17	44	6	1	6	17	.235	199	15	4	.982
1979—Cleveland	Amer.	OF-C-3B	64	166	23	47	7	0	2	21	.283	66	5	2	.973
1980—Clev.‡-Chi.	Amer.	OF-C-3-1	56	106	9	32	3	0	2	15	.302	34	2	1	.971
Major League Totals			330	781	87	212	27	4	12	90	.271	506	49	11	.981

Selected by Texas Rangers' organization in 2nd round of free-agent draft, June 6, 1972.
†Traded with Pitcher Stan Thomas to Cleveland Indians for Catcher John Ellis, December 9, 1975.
‡Traded to Chicago White Sox for Infielder Alan Bannister, June 14, 1980.

GREGORY RUSSELL PRYOR
(Greg)

Born October 2, 1949, at Marietta, O.
Height, 6.00. Weight, 175.
Throws and bats righthanded.
Hobbies—Music, reading, photography and sailing.
Attended Florida Southern College, Lakeland, Fla.; received Bachelor of
Science Degree in Industrial Management.
Brother of Jeff Pryor, pitcher in California Angels' organization, 1968-72.

Led International League shortstops in assists with 417 and in double plays with 87 in 1977.
Tied for Pacific Coast League lead in double plays by shortstop with 90 in 1976.

Year Club	League	Pos.	G.	AB.	R.	H.	2B.	3B.	HR.	RBI.	B.A.	PO.	A.	E.	F.A.
1971—Geneva	NYP	3-2-S-O	60	226	40	64	10	4	4	28	.283	76	138	21	.911
1972—Pittsfield	East.	SS	65	208	23	43	10	2	1	16	.207	89	155	29	.894
1972—Burlington	Carol.	SS-OF	39	119	16	28	2	1	1	15	.235	49	110	11	.935
1973—Rocky Mount	Carol.	SS-2B	126	443	53	130	20	9	2	44	.293	203	349	50	.917
1974—Pittsfield	East.	3-S-2	122	441	61	104	20	1	5	37	.236	113	255	26	.934
1975—Spokane	P. C.	S-3-2	135	481	59	117	21	2	5	53	.243	184	411	33	.947
1976—Sacramento	P. C.	SS	122	495	71	136	21	3	9	51	.275	158	409	32	.947
1976—Texas†	Amer.	2-3-S	5	8	2	3	0	0	0	1	.375	4	8	0	1.000
1977—Syracuse‡	Int.	∗S-3-2	124	461	60	125	18	6	7	52	.271	∗420	21	∗.968
1978—Chicago	Amer.	2-3-S	82	222	27	58	11	0	2	15	.261	100	202	11	.965
1979—Chicago	Amer.	SS-2B-3B	143	476	60	131	23	3	3	34	.275	218	447	26	.962
1980—Chicago	Amer.	SS-3-2	122	338	32	81	18	4	1	29	.240	130	344	16	.967
Major League Totals			352	1044	121	273	52	7	6	79	.261	452	1001	53	.965

Selected by Washington Senators' organization in 6th round of free-agent draft, June 8, 1971.
†Traded with Infielder Brian Doyle and cash estimated at $25,000 to New York Yankees for Infielder Sandy Alomar, February 17, 1977.
‡Granted free agency, November 5, 1977; signed by Chicago White Sox, November 28, 1977.

TERRY STEPHEN PUHL

Name pronounced POOL.

Born July 8, 1956, at Melville, Saskatchewan, Canada.
Height, 6.02. Weight, 197.
Throws right and bats lefthanded.
Hobby—Crossword puzzles.

Tied major league records for highest fielding percentage by outfielder, season, 150 or more games (1.000), 1979; fewest errors by outfielder, season, 150 or more games (0), 1979.
Major League stolen bases: 1977 (10), 1978 (32), 1979 (30), 1980 (27). Total—99.

Year Club	League	Pos.	G.	AB.	R.	H.	2B.	3B.	HR.	RBI.	B.A.	PO.	A.	E.	F.A.
1974—Covington	Appal.	OF	59	211	42	60	11	0	0	21	.284	89	2	2	.978
1975—Dubuque	Midw.	OF-1B	104	346	57	115	10	2	0	28	.332	230	11	7	.971
1976—Columbus	South.	OF	28	98	13	28	5	0	1	14	.286	76	1	2	.975
1976—Memphis	Int.	OF	105	372	50	99	17	3	1	39	.266	191	5	3	.985
1977—Charleston	Int.	OF	78	285	53	87	12	6	4	33	.305	189	4	3	.985
1977—Houston	Nat.	OF	60	229	40	69	13	5	0	10	.301	119	3	1	.992
1978—Houston	Nat.	OF	149	585	87	169	25	6	3	35	.289	386	6	3	.992
1979—Houston	Nat.	OF	157	600	87	172	22	4	8	49	.287	352	7	0	∗1.000
1980—Houston	Nat.	OF	141	535	75	151	24	5	13	55	.282	311	14	3	.991
Major League Totals			507	1949	289	561	84	20	24	149	.288	1168	30	7	.994

Signed as free agent by Houston Astros' organization, September 19, 1973.

CHAMPIONSHIP SERIES RECORD

Established Championship Series record for highest batting average, five-game Series (.526), 1980.
Tied Championship Series records for most at bats, extra-inning game (6), October 8, 1980; most one-base hits, five-game Series (8), 1980.
Established National League Championship Series record for most hits, five-game Series (10), 1980.
Tied National League Championship Series records for most stolen bases, five-game Series (2), 1980; most hits, game (4), October 12, 1980.

Year Club	League	Pos.	G.	AB.	R.	H.	2B.	3B.	HR.	RBI.	B.A.	PO.	A.	E.	F.A.
1980—Houston	Nat.	PH-OF	5	19	4	10	2	0	0	3	.526	13	0	0	1.000

ALL-STAR GAME RECORD

Member of National League All-Star Team for 1978 game; did not play.

LUIS BIENVENIDO PUJOLS (TORIBIA)

Name pronounced POO-holds.

Born November 18, 1955, at Santiago Rodriguez, Dominican Republic
Height, 6.01. Weight, 195.
Throws and bats righthanded.
Hobby—Music.

Led Appalachian League catchers in double plays with 3 and tied for lead in passed balls with 24 in 1973.
Led Appalachian League in sacrifice flies with 9 in 1974.

Year Club	League	Pos.	G.	AB.	R.	H.	2B.	3B.	HR.	RBI.	B.A.	PO.	A.	E.	F.A.
1973—Covington..........Appal.	C	26	86	8	23	2	0	1	4	.267	187	21	6	.972
1974—Cedar Rapids.....Midw.	C	26	86	4	17	0	1	0	10	.198	186	19	2	.990
1974—Covington..........Appal.	C	60	218	26	58	7	1	1	27	.266	408	49	11	.976
1975—Dubuque ....Midw.	C-OF-1B	102	341	23	75	13	1	0	31	.220	598	62	9	.987
1976—Columbus† ....South.	C-3B-OF	53	142	12	28	2	0	2	16	.197	186	21	1	.995
1977—Charleston‡.......Int.	C	58	180	15	41	4	0	1	19	.228	239	26	4	.985
1977—Houston ....Nat.	C	6	15	0	1	0	0	0	0	.067	18	4	0	1.000
1978—Charleston ....Int.	C	61	196	22	43	6	1	2	24	.219	277	19	3	.990
1978—Houston ....Nat.	C-1B	56	153	11	20	8	1	1	11	.131	272	33	6	.981
1979—Charleston ....Int.	C	105	345	29	86	18	2	6	41	.249	487	41	6	.989
1979—Houston ....Nat.	C	26	75	7	17	2	1	0	8	.227	136	6	1	.993
1980—Houston ....Nat.	C-3B	78	221	15	44	6	1	0	20	.199	349	35	4	.990
Major League Totals			166	464	33	82	16	3	1	39	.177	775	78	11	.987

Signed as free agent by Houston Astros' organization, January 9, 1973.
†On disabled list, June 11 to June 25; July 28 to August 14; August 22 to September 15, 1976.
‡On disabled list, April 15 to April 25, 1977.

CHAMPIONSHIP SERIES RECORD

Year Club	League	Pos.	G.	AB.	R.	H.	2B.	3B.	HR.	RBI.	B.A.	PO.	A.	E.	F.A.
1980—Houston ....Nat.	C	4	10	1	1	0	1	0	0	.100	21	2	0	1.000

CHARLES MICHAEL PULEO
(Charlie)

Born February 7, 1955, at Glen Ridge, N. J.
Height, 6.03. Weight, 190.
Throws and bats righthanded.
Attended Seton Hall University, South Orange, N. J.; received Bachelor of Science degree.
Pitched seven-inning 3-0 no-hit victory against St. Petersburg, August 13, 1979 (second game).

Year Club	League	G.	IP.	W.	L.	Pct.	H.	R.	ER.	SO.	BB.	ERA.
1978—Utica ....NYP	16	104	10	3	.769	81	46	31	125	48	2.68
1979—Dunedin.............Florida St.	22	123	10	10	.500	126	72	61	77	61	4.46
1980—Knoxville†............................Southern	19	108	8	7	.533	87	51	34	97	66	2.83

Selected by Detroit Tigers' organization in 13th round of free-agent draft, June 5, 1973.
Signed as free agent by Toronto Blue Jays' organization, March 14, 1978.
†On disabled list, April 24 to June 14, 1980.

NATHANIEL McKINLEY PURYEAR JR.
(Nate)

Born July 30, 1954, at Biloxi, Miss.
Height, 6.04. Weight, 205.
Throws and bats righthanded.
Attended Stillman College, Tuscaloosa, Ala.
Cousin of Jim "Mudcat" Grant, pitcher with Cleveland Indians, Minnesota Twins,
Los Angeles Dodgers, Montreal Expos, St. Louis Cardinals, Oakland A's
and Pittsburgh Pirates, 1958 through 1971.
Tied for Midwest League in shutouts with 3 in 1977.

Year Club	League	G.	IP.	W.	L.	Pct.	H.	R.	ER.	SO.	BB.	ERA.
1976—Batavia................................NYP	14	52	3	3	.500	44	42	31	38	60	5.37
1977—Waterloo.........................Midwest	24	155	12	9	.571	148	93	69	102	84	4.01
1978—Chattanooga.......................Southern	20	129	5	13	.278	117	68	49	59	95	3.42
1978—Portland ....P. Coast	4	14	1	2	.333	17	13	10	9	14	6.43
1979—Tacoma†...............................P. Coast	19	115	7	10	.412	127	74	63	50	67	4.93
1980—Tacoma‡..............................P. Coast					(Did not play)						

Selected by Boston Red Sox' organization in 1st round (21st player selected) of free-agent draft, January 7, 1976.
Selected by Cleveland Indians' organization in secondary phase of free-agent draft, June 8, 1976.
†On disabled list, July 17 to August 29, 1979.
‡On disabled list, April 10 to August 27, 1980.

PATRICK EDWARD PUTNAM
(Pat)

Born December 3, 1953, at Bethel, Vt.
Height, 6.01. Weight, 214.
Throws right and bats lefthanded.
Attended Miami-Dade Community College North, Miami, Fla. and
University of South Alabama, Mobile, Ala.
Led Western Carolina League in total bases with 305, sacrifice flies with 12, and intentional walks with 15 in 1976.
Named Minor League Player of the Year by THE SPORTING NEWS, 1976.
Named American League Rookie Player of the Year by THE SPORTING NEWS, 1979.

Year Club	League	Pos.	G.	AB.	R.	H.	2B.	3B.	HR.	RBI.	B.A.	PO.	A.	E.	F.A.
1975—Sara. Rangers ...Gulf C.	1B-OF	18	73	13	21	4	1	2	17	.288	144	9	2	.981
1975—Lynchburg ....Carol.	1B-C-OF	44	158	15	35	7	0	5	22	.222	366	23	3	.992

Year Club	League	Pos.	G.	AB.	R.	H.	2B.	3B.	HR.	RBI.	B.A.	PO.	A.	E.	F.A.
1976—Asheville..........W. Car.		*1B-C	138	538	100	*194	●33	3	*24	*142	.361	1156	97	11	*.991
1977—Tucson.............P.C.		1B-OF	130	495	71	149	31	4	15	102	.301	759	53	11	.987
1977—Texas..............Amer.		1B	11	26	3	8	4	0	0	3	.308	35	1	0	1.000
1978—Tucson .............P.C.		1B-OF	114	447	81	138	25	2	21	96	.309	433	28	9	.981
1978—Texas ....Amer.		1B	20	46	4	7	1	0	1	2	.152	15	1	0	1.000
1979—Texas ....Amer.		1B	139	426	57	118	19	2	18	64	.277	832	62	5	.994
1980—Texas ....Amer.		1B-3B	147	410	42	108	16	2	13	55	.263	979	80	9	.992
Major League Totals			317	908	106	241	40	4	32	124	.265	1861	143	14	.993

Selected by New York Mets' organization in 12th round of free-agent draft, June 5, 1974.

Selected by Texas Rangers' organization in secondary phase of free-agent draft, June 4, 1975.

JEFFREY THOMAS PYBURN
(Jeff)

Born December 16, 1957, at Birmingham, Ala.
Height, 6.02. Weight, 205.
Throws and bats righthanded.
Attended University of Georgia, Athens, Ga.
Son of Jim Pyburn, third baseman-outfielder with Baltimore Orioles, 1955-57.

Selected by Buffalo Bills in 5th round of 1980 NFL draft.

Year Club	League	Pos.	G.	AB.	R.	H.	2B.	3B.	HR.	RBI.	B.A.	PO.	A.	E.	F.A.
1980—Reno.................Calif.		OF	78	283	64	95	21	2	3	54	.336	132	1	5	.964

Selected by San Diego Padres' organization in 1st round (5th player selected) of free-agent draft, June 3, 1980.

RENE QUINONES

Born February 19, 1957, at Florida, Puerto Rico.
Height, 6.00. Weight, 180.
Throws and bats righthanded.

Year Club	League	G.	IP.	W.	L.	Pct.	H.	R.	ER.	SO.	BB.	ERA.
1976—Newark ....NYP		17	73	6	5	.545	58	31	24	62	56	2.96
1977—Burlington†........................Midwest		27	93	8	6	.571	75	54	45	97	69	4.35
1978—Burlington‡.........................						(Did not play)						
1979—Holyoke ....Eastern		40	136	10	8	.556	111	60	53	94	70	3.51
1980—Vancouver ....P. Coast		43	103	7	7	.500	92	47	40	74	90	3.50

Signed as free agent by Milwaukee Brewers' organization, November 15, 1975.

†On disabled list, August 3 to August 15, 1977.

‡On suspended list, April 14 to July 14, 1978; on restricted list, July 14, 1978, to January 10, 1979.

JAMES PATRICK QUIRK
(Jamie)

Born October 22, 1954, at Whittier, Calif.
Height, 6.04. Weight, 200.
Throws right and bats lefthanded.
Hobby—Sports in general.
Attended Whittier College, Whittier, Calif.

Led American Association third basemen in double plays with 31 in 1975.
Led Pioneer League shortstops in double plays with 16 in 1972.

Year Club	League	Pos.	G.	AB.	R.	H.	2B.	3B.	HR.	RBI.	B.A.	PO.	A.	E.	F.A.
1972—Billings ....Pion.		SS	55	208	29	53	9	4	5	37	.255	*63	*162	*28	*.889
1973—San Jose............Calif.		SS	132	429	58	99	12	7	8	45	.231	160	330	39	.926
1974—Jacksonville ......South.		SS	46	163	16	37	7	2	3	21	.227	75	133	20	.912
1974—Omaha..............A. A.		S-3-2	53	203	27	57	10	2	10	31	.281	64	141	14	.936
1975—Omaha..............A. A.		3B	127	445	62	122	23	4	13	64	.274	109	*254	16	*.958
1975—Kansas City......Amer.		OF-3B	14	39	2	10	0	0	1	5	.256	19	3	2	.917
1976—Kansas City†.....Amer.		S-3-1	64	114	11	28	6	0	1	15	.246	9	14	2	.920
1977—Milwaukee ....Amer.		OF-3B	93	221	16	48	14	1	3	13	.217	19	4	2	.920
1978—Spokane‡ ....P. C.		3B-1B	97	343	58	100	20	2	12	63	.292	235	142	20	.950
1978—Kansas City§.....Amer.		3B-SS	17	29	3	6	2	0	0	2	.207	11	16	2	.931
1979—Kansas City ......Amer.		C-SS-3B	51	79	8	24	6	1	1	11	.304	16	9	1	.960
1980—Kansas City ......Amer.		C-3-O-1	62	163	13	45	5	0	5	21	.276	78	66	8	.947
Major League Totals			301	645	53	161	33	2	11	67	.250	152	112	17	.940

Selected by Kansas City Royals' organization in 1st round (18th player selected) of free-agent draft, June 6, 1972.

†Traded with Outfielder Jim Wohlford and a player to be named later to Milwaukee Brewers for Pitcher Jim Colborn and Catcher Darrell Porter, December 6, 1976; Pitcher Bob McClure was sent to Milwaukee' to complete deal, March 15, 1977.

‡Traded to Kansas City Royals for Pitcher Gerry Ako and cash, August 3, 1978.

§On supplemental disabled list, August 14 to September 5, 1978.

CHAMPIONSHIP SERIES RECORD

Year Club	League	Pos.	G.	AB.	R.	H.	2B.	3B.	HR.	RBI.	B.A.	PO.	A.	E.	F.A.
1976—Kansas City.......Amer.		PH-DH	4	7	1	1	0	1	0	2	.143	0	0	0	.000

DANIEL RAYMOND QUISENBERRY

Name pronounced Quiz-en-berry.

(Dan)

Born February 7, 1953, at Santa Monica, Calif.
Height, 6.02. Weight, 180.
Throws and bats righthanded.
Attended Orange Coast College, Costa Mesa, Calif., LaVerne College, LaVerne, Calif.,
and Pacific College, Fresno, Calif.

Major League saves: 1979 (5), 1980 (33). Total—38.
Tied for Southern League lead in saves with 15 in 1978.
Tied for American League lead in saves with 33 in 1980.
Named American League Fireman of the Year by THE SPORTING NEWS, 1980.

Year Club	League	G.	IP.	W.	L.	Pct.	H.	R.	ER.	SO.	BB.	ERA.
1975—Waterloo	Midwest	20	44	3	2	.600	40	16	12	31	6	2.45
1975—Jacksonville	Southern	6	8	0	1	.000	5	3	2	2	4	2.25
1976—Jacksonville	Southern	9	12	0	1	.000	8	6	3	6	2	2.25
1976—Waterloo	Midwest	34	42	2	1	.667	28	4	3	19	9	0.64
1977—Jacksonville	Southern	33	74	3	1	.750	61	18	11	33	11	1.34
1978—Jacksonville	Southern	48	64	4	2	.667	62	22	17	29	12	2.39
1979—Omaha	Am. Assoc.	26	35	2	1	.667	29	15	14	16	10	3.60
1979—Kansas City	American	32	40	3	2	.600	42	16	14	13	7	3.15
1980—Kansas City	American	•75	128	12	7	.632	129	47	44	37	27	3.09
Major League Totals		107	168	15	9	.625	171	63	58	50	34	3.11

Signed as free agent by Kansas City Royals' organization, June 7, 1975.

CHAMPIONSHIP SERIES RECORD

Year Club	League	G.	IP.	W.	L.	Pct.	H.	R.	ER.	SO.	BB.	ERA.
1980—Kansas City	American	2	4⅔	1	0	1.000	4	1	0	1	2	0.00

WORLD SERIES RECORD

Established World Series records for most games pitched in relief, six-game Series (6), 1980; most games
finished, six-game Series (6), 1980.
Tied World Series record for most games lost, six-game Series (2), 1980.

Year Club	League	G.	IP.	W.	L.	Pct.	H.	R.	ER.	SO.	BB.	ERA.
1980—Kansas City	American	6	10⅓	1	2	.333	10	6	6	0	3	5.23

JOHN ANDREW RABB

Born June 23, 1960, at Los Angeles, Calif.
Height, 6.01. Weight, 179.
Throws and bats righthanded.
Attended El Camino Junior College, Torrance, Calif.

Led California League catchers in putouts with 661 and tied for lead in passed balls with 17 in 1980.

Year Club	League	Pos.	G.	AB.	R.	H.	2B.	3B.	HR.	RBI.	B.A.	PO.	A.	E.	F.A.
1978—Great Falls	Pioneer	C-OF-3-1	54	184	32	52	5	3	8	32	.283	185	22	6	.972
1979—Cedar Rapids	Midwest	C-OF	125	447	63	118	19	1	19	90	.264	384	50	15	.967
1980—Fresno	Calif.	C-OF-3B	128	395	69	96	21	2	19	80	.243	661	70	11	.985

Selected by San Francisco Giants' organization in 11th round of free-agent draft, June 6, 1978.

DAVID MARTIN RADER

(Dave)

Born December 26, 1948, at Claremore, Okla.
Height, 5.11½. Weight, 165.
Throws right and bats lefthanded.
Attended Bakersfield College, Bakersfield, Calif.

Tied major league record for most unassisted double plays by catcher, game (1), April 18, 1973.
Tied for Texas League lead in double plays by catchers with 9 in 1970.
Named THE SPORTING NEWS National League Rookie Player of the Year, 1972.

Year Club	League	Pos.	G.	AB.	R.	H.	2B.	3B.	HR.	RBI.	B.A.	PO.	A.	E.	F.A.
1967—Salt Lake City	Pion.	•C-3B	43	137	23	44	7	3	0	18	.321	329	25	•13	.965
1967—Fresno	Calif.	C	15	46	4	11	3	0	0	3	.239	112	8	3	.976
1968—Fresno†	Calif.	C	76	269	34	66	9	2	5	19	.245	649	29	10	.985
1969—Amarillo	Texas	C-3B	78	236	27	48	13	0	6	31	.203	389	50	5	.989
1970—Amarillo	Texas	C	92	282	44	68	9	4	10	41	.241	519	63	•14	.977
1971—Phoenix	P. C.	C	85	293	41	92	20	5	8	47	.314	506	26	•14	.974
1971—San Francisco	Nat.	C	3	4	0	0	0	0	0	0	.000	1	0	0	1.000
1972—Phoenix	P. C.	PH	1	1	0	0	0	0	0	0	.000	0	0	0	.000
1972—San Francisco	Nat.	C	133	459	44	119	14	1	6	41	.259	661	45	11	.985
1973—San Francisco	Nat.	C	148	462	59	106	15	4	9	41	.229	701	48	7	.991
1974—San Francisco	Nat.	C	113	323	26	94	16	2	1	26	.291	461	38	8	.984
1975—San Francisco	Nat.	C	98	292	39	85	15	0	5	31	.291	457	37	8	.984
1976—San Francisco‡	Nat.	C	88	255	25	67	15	0	1	22	.263	349	32	6	.984
1977—St. Louis§	Nat.	C	66	114	15	30	7	1	1	16	.263	147	13	4	.976
1978—Chicago x	Nat.	C	116	305	29	62	13	3	3	36	.203	412	51	11	.977

Year Club League	Pos.	G.	AB.	R.	H.	2B.	3B.	HR.	RBI.	B.A.	PO.	A.	E.	F.A.
1979—Philadelphia y...Nat.	C	31	54	3	11	1	1	1	5	.204	62	6	5	.932
1980—Boston z...........Amer.	C	50	137	14	45	11	0	3	17	.328	140	15	3	.981
National League Totals..................		796	2268	240	574	96	12	27	218	.253	3251	270	60	.983
American League Totals................		50	137	14	45	11	0	3	17	.328	140	15	3	.981
Major League Totals......................		846	2405	254	619	107	12	30	235	.257	3391	285	63	.983

Selected by San Francisco Giants' organization in 1st round (18th player selected) of free-agent draft, June 6, 1967.

†On military list from July 25 through end of season.

‡Traded with Pitchers John D'Acquisto and Mike Caldwell to St. Louis Cardinals for Outfielder Willie Crawford, Infielder-Outfielder Vic Harris, and Pitcher John Curtis, October 20, 1976.

§Traded with Outfielder Heity Cruz to Chicago Cubs for Outfielder Jerry Morales, Catcher Steve Swisher and a player to be named later, December 8, 1977.

xTraded with Second Baseman Manny Trillo and Outfielder Greg Gross to Philadelphia Phillies for Outfielder Jerry Martin, Catcher Barry Foote, Second Baseman Ted Sizemore and Pitchers Derek Botelho and Henry Mack, February 23, 1979.

yTraded to Boston Red Sox for cash and a player to be named later, March 30, 1980; Infielder Stan Papi traded to Phillies' organization completing deal, May 13, 1980.

zGranted free agency, October 23, 1980; signed by California Angels, February 2, 1981.

TIMOTHY RAINES

(Tim)

Born September 16, 1959, at Sanford, Fla.
Height, 5.08. Weight, 170.
Throws right and bats left and righthanded.

Led American Association in stolen bases with 77 in 1980.
Named Minor League Player of the Year by THE SPORTING NEWS, 1980.

Year Club League	Pos.	G.	AB.	R.	H.	2B.	3B.	HR.	RBI.	B.A.	PO.	A.	E.	F.A.
1977—Sarasota Expos .G. C.	2-3B-OF	49	161	28	45	6	2	0	21	.280	79	72	13	.921
1978—W. Palm Beach† Fla. St.	2B-SS	100	359	67	103	10	0	0	23	.287	219	273	24	.953
1979—Memphis..........South.	2B	•145	552	•104	160	25	10	5	50	.290	•341	•413	•23	.970
1979—Montreal..........Nat.	PR	6	0	3	0	0	0	0	0	.000	0	0	0	.000
1980—Denver ....A. A.	2B	108	429	105	152	23	11	6	64	•.354	226	338	16	.972
1980—Montreal..........Nat.	2B-OF	15	20	5	1	0	0	0	0	.050	15	16	0	1.000
Major League Totals......................		21	20	8	1	0	0	0	0	.050	15	16	0	1.000

Selected by Montreal Expos' organization in 5th round of free-agent draft, June 7, 1977.

†On disabled list, May 23 to June 5, 1978.

CHARLES DAVID RAINEY

(Chuck)

Born July 14, 1954, at San Diego, Calif.
Height, 5.11. Weight, 195.
Throws and bats righthanded.
Hobby—Stereo equipment.
Attended San Diego Mesa Junior College, San Diego, Calif.

Year Club League	G.	IP.	W.	L.	Pct.	H.	R.	ER.	SO.	BB.	ERA.
1974—Elmira...............................NYP	16	77	4	5	.444	89	59	48	63	51	5.61
1975—Winston-Salem ....Carolina	20	109	4	9	.308	110	75	53	77	66	4.38
1976—Bristol ....Eastern	22	101	7	4	.636	109	67	49	31	63	4.37
1977—Bristol ....Eastern	7	59	4	3	.571	55	19	15	40	21	2.29
1977—Pawtucket ....Int'national	19	123	5	9	.357	114	65	42	60	51	3.07
1978—Pawtucket ....Int'national	24	170	13	7	.650	169	71	55	104	75	2.91
1979—Boston† ....American	20	104	8	5	.615	97	47	44	41	41	3.81
1979—Pawtucket ....Int'national	3	17	1	0	1.000	8	0	0	9	3	0.00
1980—Boston‡ ....American	16	87	8	3	.727	92	49	47	43	41	4.86
Major League Totals...............................	36	191	16	8	.667	189	96	91	84	82	4.29

Selected by Boston Red Sox' organization in 1st round (19th player selected) of free-agent draft, January 9, 1974.

†On disabled list, July 20 to August 11, 1979.

‡On disabled list, July 4 to October 21, 1980.

DAVID CHRISTOPHER RAJSICH

Name pronounced RAY-sich.

(Dave)

Born September 28, 1951, at Youngstown, O.
Height, 6.05. Weight, 180.
Throws and bats lefthanded.
Hobbies—Hunting, fishing and golf.
Attended Phoenix College, Phoenix, Ariz., and University of Arizona,
Tucson, Ariz.; received Bachelor of Science degree in Biology.
Brother of Gary Rajsich, outfielder in Houston Astros' organization and Tim Rajsich,
former infielder in Pittsburgh Pirates' and San Francisco Giants' organizations.

Year Club	League	G.	IP.	W.	L.	Pct.	H.	R.	ER.	SO.	BB.	ERA.
1975—Ft. Lauderdale ....Florida St.		23	125	5	9	.357	88	45	34	79	48	2.45
1975—Syracuse.............................Int'national		4	8	0	0	.000	22	15	12	6	3	13.50
1976—West Haven.........................Eastern		30	61	4	4	.500	57	36	28	45	25	4.13
1977—West Haven.........................Eastern		12	38	8	2	.800	34	12	12	38	15	2.84
1977—Syracuse ....Int'national		17	57	0	6	.000	62	41	37	32	26	5.84
1978—Tacoma ....P. Coast		36	81	8	4	.667	82	40	32	59	40	3.56
1978—New York† ....American		4	13	0	0	.000	16	6	6	9	6	4.15
1979—Tucson ....P. Coast		5	6	1	0	1.000	1	0	0	1	4	0.00
1979—Texas ....American		27	54	1	3	.250	56	25	21	32	18	3.50
1980—Charleston‡.........................Int'national		3	4	1	0	1.000	6	4	4	3	3	9.00
1980—Texas ....American		24	48	2	1	.667	56	34	32	35	22	6.00
Major League Totals...................................		55	115	3	4	.429	128	65	59	76	46	4.62

Signed as free agent by New York Yankees' organization, September 6, 1974.

†Traded with Pitchers Sparky Lyle and Larry McCall, Catcher Mike Heath, Shortstop Domingo Ramos and cash to Texas Rangers for Outfielders Juan Beniquez and Greg Jemison and Pitchers Mike Griffin, Paul Mirabella and Dave Righetti, November 10, 1978.

‡On suspended list, July 16 to July 20, 1980.

GARY LOUIS RAJSICH

Name pronounced RAY-sich.

Born October 28, 1954, at Youngstown, O.
Height, 6.02. Weight, 190.
Throws and bats lefthanded.
Attended Arizona State University, Tempe, Ariz.
Brother of Dave Rajsich, pitcher with Texas Rangers and Tim Rajsich,
former infielder in Pittsburgh Pirates' and San Francisco Giants' organizations.

Led Appalachian League first basemen in double plays with 58 in 1976.
Led Florida State League first basemen in assists with 119 and in double plays with 115 in 1977.

Year Club	League	Pos.	G.	AB.	R.	H.	2B.	3B.	HR.	RBI.	B.A.	PO.	A.	E.	F.A.
1976—Covington ....Appal.		1B	66	244	33	54	8	3	6	27	.221	*649	*75	*14	.981
1977—Cocoa ....Fla. St.		1B-OF	136	486	50	119	19	5	8	53	.245	1153	119	25	.981
1978—Columbus ....South.		OF-1B	80	286	37	69	12	5	7	34	.241	359	28	2	.995
1978—Charleston ....Int.		OF	46	126	19	29	4	1	2	13	.230	74	3	1	.987
1979—Columbus ....South.		OF-2B	66	232	43	68	25	4	14	53	.293	105	7	4	.966
1979—Charleston ....Int.		OF	65	218	27	45	8	2	6	28	.206	114	1	4	.966
1980—Tucson .............P.C.		OF	134	445	94	143	22	14	21	99	.321	205	10	1	.995

Selected by Houston Astros' organization in 11th round of free-agent draft, June 8, 1976.

MARIO RAMIREZ (TORRES)

Born September 12, 1957, at Yauco, Puerto Rico.
Height, 5.09. Weight, 155.
Throws and bats righthanded.

Led International League shortstops in fielding percentage with .983 in 1979.

Year Club	League	Pos.	G.	AB.	R.	H.	2B.	3B.	HR.	RBI.	B.A.	PO.	A.	E.	F.A.
1976—Wausau.............Midw.		SS	89	287	48	66	16	1	2	28	.230	145	253	46	.896
1977—Lynchburg ....Carol.		SS	72	272	41	62	11	3	8	36	.228	123	186	19	.942
1977—Jackson ....Texas		SS	60	206	23	52	5	1	6	21	.252	110	170	14	.952
1978—Tidewater ....Int.		SS	126	389	43	81	14	4	5	41	.208	176	382	*46	.924
1979—Tidewater ....Int.		SS-2B	132	376	42	82	10	2	6	31	.218	190	432	9	.986
1980—New York ....Nat.		SS-2B-3B	18	24	2	5	0	0	0	0	.208	13	21	0	1.000
1980—Tidewater† ....Int.		SS-2-OF	71	208	17	42	7	2	0	15	.202	129	173	17	.947
Major League Totals.......................			18	24	2	5	0	0	0	0	.208	13	21	0	1.000

Signed as free agent by New York Mets' organization, March 5, 1976.
†Drafted by San Diego Padres, December 8, 1980.

RAFAEL EMILIO RAMIREZ (PEGUERO)

Born February 18, 1959, at San Pedro de Macoris, Dominican Republic.
Height, 6.00. Weight, 170.
Throws and bats righthanded.

Year Club	League	Pos.	G.	AB.	R.	H.	2B.	3B.	HR.	RBI.	B.A.	PO.	A.	E.	F.A.
1977—Brad. Braves.....G. C.		SS-OF	49	175	20	31	2	1	4	19	.177	52	94	32	.820
1978—Greenwood ....W. Car.		SS	81	282	54	77	15	3	6	46	.273	119	229	*43	.890
1978—Savannah.........South.		SS	38	131	14	27	4	0	2	13	.206	61	123	15	.925
1979—Savannah† ....South.		SS	113	386	47	80	17	3	10	39	.207	134	282	*38	.916
1980—Richmond‡........Int.		SS	80	281	33	79	15	3	5	38	.281	117	294	23	.947
1980—Atlanta ....Nat.		SS	50	165	17	44	6	1	2	11	.267	63	140	11	.949
Major League Totals.......................			50	165	17	44	6	1	2	11	.267	63	140	11	.949

Signed as free agent by Atlanta Braves' organization, September 28, 1976.
†On disabled list, April 16 to April 27, 1979.
‡On disabled list, June 23 to July 17, 1980.

DOMINGO ANTONIO RAMOS

Born March 29, 1958, at Santiago, Dominican Republic.
Height, 5.10. Weight, 154.
Throws and bats righthanded.

Year Club League	Pos.	G.	AB.	R.	H.	2B.	3B.	HR.	RBI.	B.A.	PO.	A.	E.	F.A.
1975–Oneonta ....NYP	SS-3B	49	166	29	39	4	1	0	21	.235	60	143	14	.935
1976–Ft. Lauderdale ..Fla. St.	SS	103	328	34	79	11	3	0	29	.241	150	343	35	.934
1976–Syracuse ....Int.	SS	11	39	7	10	2	1	0	8	.256	13	20	2	.943
1977–West Haven ......East.	SS	129	431	55	106	18	6	2	50	.246	222	433	23	*.966
1978–Tacoma ....P. C.	SS	91	314	43	74	13	3	0	30	.236	155	290	28	.941
1978–West Haven ....East.	SS	40	134	16	34	2	2	1	13	.254	40	128	6	.966
1978–New York†‡ .....Amer.	SS	1	0	0	0	0	0	0	0	.000	0	0	0	.000
1979–Syr.§-Colum. x ..Int.	SS	115	376	38	92	11	4	1	28	.245	211	323	26	.954
1980–Syracuse ....Int.	SS	84	319	45	80	8	4	4	27	.251	160	240	28	.935
1980–Toronto ....Amer.	SS-2B	5	16	0	2	0	0	0	0	.125	5	10	0	1.000
Major League Totals......................		6	16	0	2	0	0	0	0	.125	5	10	0	1.000

Signed as free agent by New York Yankees' organization, May 27, 1975.

†Traded with Pitchers Sparky Lyle, Larry McCall and Dave Rajsich, Catcher Mike Heath and cash to Texas Rangers for Outfielders Juan Beniquez and Greg Jemison and Pitchers Mike Griffin, Paul Mirabella and Dave Righetti, November 10, 1978.

‡Loaned to Toronto Blue Jays' organization, April 5, 1979.

§Loaned to New York Yankees' organization, July 30, 1979; returned, September 28, 1979.

xSold to Toronto Blue Jays, November 5, 1979.

ROBERTO RAMOS
(Bobby)

Born November 5, 1955, at Havana, Cuba.
Height, 5.11. Weight, 208.
Throws and bats righthanded.

Year Club League	Pos.	G.	AB.	R.	H.	2B.	3B.	HR.	RBI.	B.A.	PO.	A.	E.	F.A.
1974–Sarasota Expos..G. C.	*C-OF	48	144	16	36	3	4	2	16	.250	245	48	*14	.954
1975–W. Palm Beach..Fla. St.	C	73	204	16	39	7	2	1	12	.191	374	49	13	.970
1976–W. Palm B'ch†...Fla. St.	C	101	297	29	81	9	2	3	39	.273	417	60	*15	.970
1977–W. Palm Beach..Fla. St.	C	104	320	45	99	18	4	5	58	.309	430	47	8	.984
1978–Denver ....A. A.	C	12	39	4	7	0	0	0	2	.179	56	15	1	.986
1978–Memphis ....South.	C	109	343	36	91	16	2	9	51	.265	457	60	9	.983
1978–Montreal...........Nat.	C	2	4	0	0	0	0	0	0	.000	3	1	0	1.000
1979–Denver‡§ ....A. A.	C	8	11	0	2	0	0	0	2	.182	14	3	1	.944
1979–Salt Lake City ...P. C.	C-1B	58	179	27	51	9	1	3	21	.285	112	14	7	.947
1980–Denver ....A. A.	C	74	244	36	72	6	1	4	30	.295	399	51	4	.991
1980–Montreal...........Nat.	C	13	32	5	5	2	0	0	2	.156	47	7	2	.964
Major League Totals......................		15	36	5	5	2	0	0	2	.139	50	8	2	.967

Selected by Montreal Expos' organization in 7th round of free-agent draft, June 5, 1974.

†On suspended list, July 6 to July 12, 1976.

‡On suspended list, May 4 to May 17, 1979.

§Loaned to California Angels' organization, May 25, 1979; returned, August 29, 1979.

MICHAEL JAMES RAMSEY
(Mike)

Born March 29, 1954, at Roanoke, Va.
Height, 6.01. Weight, 170.
Throws right and bats left and righthanded.
Attended Appalachian State University, Boone, N.C.

Led Appalachian League in sacrifice hits with 12 in 1975.
Led Appalachian League shortstops in fielding average with .937 in 1975.

Year Club League	Pos.	G.	AB.	R.	H.	2B.	3B.	HR.	RBI.	B.A.	PO.	A.	E.	F.A.
1975–Johnson City .....Appal.	SS-2B	65	*277	43	79	14	1	0	25	.285	98	183	17	.943
1976–Arkansas†........Texas	SS	84	288	26	79	6	1	0	24	.274	109	231	32	.914
1977–Arkansas ....Texas	SS	121	484	51	121	21	4	1	28	.250	166	317	*44	.917
1978–Springfield‡ ......A.A.	SS	99	382	53	92	8	4	2	30	.241	172	223	*41	.906
1978–St. Louis ....Nat.	SS	12	5	4	1	0	0	0	0	.200	4	6	1	.909
1979–Springfield........A.A.	SS	97	281	28	62	9	3	1	27	.221	134	198	24	.933
1980–Springfield........A.A.	SS-OF	21	69	7	18	1	0	0	6	.261	34	47	6	.931
1980–St. Louis ....Nat.	2-3-SS	59	126	11	33	8	1	0	8	.262	62	94	9	.945
Major League Totals......................		71	131	15	34	8	1	0	8	.260	66	100	10	.943

Selected by Chicago Cubs' organization in 26th round of free-agent draft, June 6, 1972.

Selected by St. Louis Cardinals' organization in 3rd round of free-agent draft, June 4, 1975.

†On disabled list, July 17 to September 7, 1976.

‡On disabled list, May 13 to May 25, 1978.

DID YOU KNOW–

That Minnesota and California were the only two major league teams to score 20 runs in a game in 1980?

ROBERT LEE RANDALL
(Bob)

Born June 10, 1949, at Norton, Kan.
Height, 6.02. Weight, 175.
Throws and bats righthanded.
Hobby—Hunting.
Attended Kansas State University, Manhattan, Kan.; received
Bachelor of Science degree in Business Administration.

Led Pioneer League shortstops in double plays with 34 in 1969.
Led Pacific Coast League second basemen in double plays with 115 in 1974.
Led American League second basemen in double plays with 124 in 1976.

Year—Club	League	Pos.	G.	AB.	R.	H.	2B.	3B.	HR.	RBI.	B.A.	PO.	A.	E.	F.A.
1969—Ogden	Pion.	*SS-2B	71	271	52	*90	12	5	1	39	.332	*123	*161	23	.925
1970—Bakersfield†	Calif.	*2B-SS	98	362	48	97	14	3	3	39	.268	176	274	15	*.968
1971—Albuquerque	Tex.	3-2-S-C	38	94	8	22	3	0	0	7	.234	24	40	7	.901
1971—Bakersfield	Calif.	2B	42	171	26	46	5	1	1	16	.269	103	127	13	.947
1971—Spokane	P. C.	2B-SS	6	2	0	0	0	0	0	0	.000	1	1	1	.667
1972—Bakersfield‡	Calif.	2B-SS	135	*544	97	*184	27	3	5	57	.338	258	421	44	.939
1973—Albuquerque	P. C.	2B	21	47	6	9	3	0	0	3	.191	32	36	4	.944
1973—Waterbury	East.	2B	86	331	60	102	22	1	1	25	.308	192	232	13	.970
1974—Albuquerque	P. C.	*2B-3B	140	536	77	*181	32	4	3	60	.338	*278	*427	*22	.970
1975—Albuquerque§	P. C.	2B	107	391	62	114	23	3	2	43	.292	253	323	19	.968
1976—Minnesota	Amer.	2B	153	475	55	127	18	4	1	34	.267	327	423	*24	.969
1977—Minnesota x	Amer.	2B-3B-1B	103	306	36	73	13	2	0	22	.239	222	297	8	.985
1978—Minnesota	Amer.	2B-3B	119	330	36	89	11	3	0	21	.270	231	345	10	.983
1979—Minnesota y	Amer.	2-3-S-O	80	199	25	49	7	0	0	14	.246	130	169	5	.984
1980—Minnesota z	Amer.	3B-2B	5	15	2	3	1	0	0	0	.200	1	10	1	.917
1980—Toledo a	Int.	2B-3B-S	52	146	17	32	5	0	3	14	.219	82	144	5	.978
Major League Totals			460	1325	154	341	50	9	1	91	.257	911	1244	48	.978

Selected by Los Angeles Dodgers' organization in 48th round of free-agent draft, June, 1966.
Selected by Los Angeles Dodgers' organization in 7th round of free-agent draft, June 7, 1968.
Selected by Los Angeles Dodgers' organization in secondary phase of free-agent draft, June 5, 1969.
†On restricted list from beginning of season until May 18, 1970.
‡Player-coach.
§Traded by Los Angeles Dodgers to Minnesota Twins for Outfielder-Catcher Danny Walton, December 23, 1975.
xOn supplemental disabled list, July 6 to July 22, 1977.
yReleased, April 3, 1980; signed as Minnesota Twins coach, April 9, 1980; activated as player, May 16, 1980.
zReleased, June 3, 1980; re-signed by Twins' organization, June 18, 1980.
aReleased, September 16, 1980.

LEONARD SHENOFF RANDLE
(Lenny)

Born February 12, 1949, at Long Beach, Calif.
Height, 5.10. Weight, 175.
Throws right and bats left and righthanded.
Hobbies—Photography and collecting wine labels.
Attended Arizona State University, Tempe, Ariz.; received Bachelor of
Science degree in Political Science.

Major league stolen bases: 1971 (1), 1972 (4), 1973 (0), 1974 (26), 1975 (16), 1976 (30), 1977 (33), 1978 (14), 1979 (0), 1980 (19). Total—143.

Year—Club	League	Pos.	G.	AB.	R.	H.	2B.	3B.	HR.	RBI.	B.A.	PO.	A.	E.	F.A.
1970—Denver	A.A.	2B-SS	46	101	14	21	3	0	0	5	.208	68	92	4	.976
1971—Denver	A.A.	2B-OF	47	170	32	49	8	2	4	26	.288	94	139	4	.983
1971—Washington	Amer.	2B	75	215	27	47	11	0	2	13	.219	178	178	12	.967
1972—Denver	A.A.	2-S-O	41	161	23	42	3	1	2	10	.261	74	149	13	.945
1972—Texas	Amer.	2-S-O	74	249	23	48	13	0	2	21	.193	161	177	20	.944
1973—Spokane	P.C.	2-O-3	140	*562	118	159	24	7	4	58	.283	345	293	17	.974
1973—Texas	Amer.	2B-OF	10	29	3	6	1	1	1	1	.207	19	9	2	.933
1974—Texas	Amer.	3-2-O-S	151	520	65	157	17	4	1	49	.302	218	285	23	.956
1975—Texas	Amer.	I-C-O	156	601	85	166	24	7	4	57	.276	376	270	16	.976
1976—Texas†‡	Amer.	2-3-OF	142	539	53	121	11	6	1	51	.224	354	324	20	.971
1977—New York	Nat.	3-2-O-S	136	513	78	156	22	7	5	27	.304	152	261	15	.965
1978—New York§	Nat.	3B-2B	132	437	53	102	16	8	2	35	.233	111	215	11	.967
1979—Phoenix-Port.y	P. C.	3B-O-2	66	243	42	67	13	3	1	25	.276	100	101	9	.957
1979—New York za	Amer.	OF	20	39	2	7	0	0	0	3	.179	19	2	0	1.000
1980—Chicago b	Nat.	3-2-O	130	489	67	135	19	6	5	39	.276	119	273	25	.940
American League Totals			628	2192	258	552	77	18	11	195	.252	1325	1245	93	.965
National League Totals			398	1439	198	393	57	21	12	101	.273	382	749	61	.949
Major League Totals			1026	3631	456	945	134	39	23	296	.260	1707	1994	144	.963

Selected by St. Louis Cardinals' organization in 32nd round of free-agent draft, June 6, 1967.
Selected by Washington Senators' organization in secondary phase of free-agent draft, June 4, 1970.
†On suspended list, April 5 to April 27, 1977.
‡Traded to New York Mets for cash and a player to be named later, April 27, 1977; Cincinnati acquired Infielder Rick Auerbach to complete deal, May 20, 1977.
§Released, March 29, 1979; signed by San Francisco Giants' organization, May 16, 1979.
xTraded with Pitcher Dave Roberts and Infielder Bill Madlock to Pittsburgh Pirates' organization for Pitchers Ed Whitson, Al Holland and Fred Breining, June 28, 1979.

ySold to New York Yankees, August 2, 1979.
zGranted free agency, November 1, 1979; signed by Seattle Mariners' organization, March 8, 1980.
aTraded by Seattle Mariners to Chicago Cubs for cash or a player to be named later, April 1, 1980; deal settled with cash.
bGranted free agency, October 24, 1980; signed by Seattle Mariners, February 17, 1981.

WILLIAM LARRY RANDOLPH JR.
(Willie)

Born July 6, 1954, at Holly Hill, S. C.
Height, 5.11. Weight, 163.
Throws and bats righthanded.
Hobbies—Bowling, movies and listening to jazz music.
Borther of Terry Randolph, defensive back for the Green Bay Packers, 1977.

Tied major league record for most assists by second baseman in extra-inning game since 1900 with 13, August 25, 1976 (19 innings).

Established American League record for most chances accepted by second baseman in extra-inning game with 20, August 25, 1976 (19 innings).

Major League stolen bases: 1975 (1), 1976 (37), 1977 (13), 1978 (36), 1979 (33), 1980 (30). Total—150.

Led Western Carolinas League batters in walks with 90 and tied for lead in sacrifice flies with 8 in 1973.
Led Eastern League batters in walks with 110 in 1974.
Led American League second basemen in double plays with 128 in 1979.
Led American League batters in walks with 119 in 1980.
Named second baseman on THE SPORTING NEWS American League All-Star Team, 1977 and 1980.
Named second baseman on THE SPORTING NEWS American League Silver Bat team, 1980.

Year	Club	League	Pos.	G.	AB.	R.	H.	2B.	3B.	HR.	RBI.	B.A.	PO.	A.	E.	F.A.
1972—Brad'n Pirates...	Gulf C.	SS-OF	44	167	21	53	6	5	0	10	.317	85	116	24	.893
1973—Charleston	W. Car.	2B	121	428	93	120	25	6	8	51	.280	*285	308	*24	.961
1974—Thetford Mines..	East.	2B	135	461	*103	117	28	6	12	53	.254	269	319	21	.966
1975—Charleston	Int.	2B	91	313	41	106	13	5	7	42	.339	189	250	16	.965
1975—Pittsburgh†	Nat.	2B-3B	30	61	9	10	1	0	0	3	.164	34	45	6	.929
1976—New York.........	Amer.	2B	125	430	59	115	15	4	1	40	.267	307	415	19	.974
1977—New York.........	Amer.	2B	147	551	91	151	28	11	4	40	.274	350	454	16	.980
1978—New York‡........	Amer.	2B	134	499	87	139	18	6	3	42	.279	296	400	16	.978
1979—New York	Amer.	2B	153	574	98	155	15	13	5	61	.270	*355	*478	13	.985
1980—New York	Amer.	2B	138	513	99	151	23	7	7	46	.294	361	401	19	.976
National League Totals...			30	61	9	10	1	0	0	3	.164	34	45	6	.929
American League Totals...			697	2567	434	711	99	41	20	229	.277	1669	2148	83	.979
Major League Totals ...			727	2628	443	721	100	41	20	232	.274	1703	2193	89	.978

Selected by Pittsburgh Pirates' organization in 7th round of free-agent draft, June 6, 1972.
†Traded with Pitchers Ken Brett and Dock Ellis to New York Yankees for Pitcher Doc Medich, December 11, 1975.
‡On disabled list, June 23 to July 14, 1978.

CHAMPIONSHIP SERIES RECORD

Year	Club	League	Pos.	G.	AB.	R.	H.	2B.	3B.	HR.	RBI.	B.A.	PO.	A.	E.	F.A.
1975—Pittsburgh.........	Nat.	PH-PR-2	2	2	1	0	0	0	0	0	.000	0	1	0	1.000
1976—New York.........	Amer.	2B	5	17	0	2	0	0	1	.118	8	14	0	1.000
1977—New York.........	Amer.	2B	5	18	4	5	1	0	0	2	.278	13	9	0	1.000
1980—New York	Amer.	2B	3	13	0	5	2	0	0	1	.385	2	9	0	1.000
Championship Series Totals.............			15	50	5	12	3	0	0	4	.240	23	33	0	1.000

WORLD SERIES RECORD

Year	Club	League	Pos.	G.	AB.	R.	H.	2B.	3B.	HR.	RBI.	B.A.	PO.	A.	E.	F.A.
1976—New York.........	Amer.	2B	4	14	1	1	0	0	0	0	.071	13	8	0	1.000
1977—New York.........	Amer.	2B	6	25	5	4	2	0	1	1	.160	13	14	0	1.000
World Series Totals........................			10	39	6	5	2	0	1	1	.128	26	22	0	1.000

ALL-STAR GAME RECORD

Established All-Star Game record for most assists by second baseman, nine-inning game (6), July 19, 1977.
Tied All-Star Game records for most at bats, nine-inning game (5), July 19, 1977; most errors, game (2), July 8, 1980.

Year	League	Pos.	AB.	R.	H.	2B.	3B.	HR.	RBI.	B.A.	PO.	A.	E.	F.A.
1977—American..................		2B	5	0	1	0	0	0	1	.200	2	6	0	1.000
1980—American		2B	4	0	2	0	0	0	0	.500	0	3	2	.600
All-Star Game Totals			9	0	3	0	0	0	1	.333	2	9	2	.846

Named to American League All-Star Team for 1976 game; replaced due to injury.

JEFFREY DEAN RANSOM
(Jeff)

Born November 11, 1960, at Fresno, Calif.
Height, 5.11. Weight, 185.
Throws right and bats left and righthanded.
Led Texas League catchers in double plays with 13 in 1980.

Year Club	League	Pos.	G.	AB.	R.	H.	2B.	3B.	HR.	RBI.	B.A.	PO.	A.	E.	F.A.
1978—Fresno.............Calif.		OF-C	26	72	13	18	3	1	2	13	.250	64	10	4	.949
1979—Fresno.............Calif.		C-OF	62	216	29	55	7	1	4	22	.255	374	41	14	.967
1979—Shreveport.......Texas		C	43	145	10	40	6	1	0	14	.276	140	16	3	.981
1980—Shreveport.......Texas		C	124	394	38	104	14	2	0	39	.264	∗618	90	∗18	.975

Selected by San Francisco Giants' organization in 5th round of free-agent draft, June 6, 1978.

ERIC RALPH RASMUSSEN

Name pronounced ras-MUSS-un.
(Formerly known as Harry)

Born March 22, 1952, at Racine, Wis.
Height, 6.03. Weight, 205.
Throws and bats righthanded.
Hobbies—Music, camping, skeet shooting and movies.
Attended Indian Hills Community College, Centerville, Ia., and
University of New Orleans, New Orleans, La.

Pitched shutout in first major league game, July 21, 1975.
Tied for Texas League lead in complete games by pitchers with 13 in 1974.

Year Club	League	G.	IP.	W.	L.	Pct.	H.	R.	ER.	SO.	BB.	ERA.
1973—Sarasota Cardinals ....Gulf C.		3	23	2	0	1.000	16	4	3	27	4	1.17
1973—St. Petersburg.....................Florida St.		8	52	3	3	.500	47	17	13	33	6	2.25
1974—Arkansas ....Texas		22	159	∗14	5	.737	154	65	55	121	32	3.11
1975—Tulsa ....Am. Assoc.		18	129	10	5	.667	133	56	53	89	36	3.70
1975—St. Louis ....National		14	81	5	5	.500	86	44	34	59	20	3.78
1976—St. Louis ....National		43	150	6	12	.333	139	67	59	76	54	3.54
1977—St. Louis ....National		34	233	11	17	.393	223	103	90	120	63	3.48
1978—St. Louis†-San Diego.............National		37	207	14	15	.483	215	104	94	91	63	4.09
1979—San Diego ....National		45	157	6	9	.400	142	59	57	54	42	3.27
1980—San Diego ....National		40	111	4	11	.267	130	60	54	50	33	4.38
Major League Totals		213	939	46	69	.400	935	437	388	450	275	3.72

Selected by Boston Red Sox' organization in 4th round of free-agent draft, January 13, 1971.
Selected by St. Louis Cardinals' organization in 32nd round of free-agent draft, June 5, 1973.
†Traded to San Diego Padres for Outfielder George Hendrick, May 26, 1978.

STEPHEN WAYNE RATZER
(Steve)

Born September 9, 1953, at Paterson, N.J.
Height, 6.01. Weight, 192.
Throws and bats righthanded.
Attended St. John's University, Jamaica, N.Y.; received
Bachelor of Science degree in Computer Science.

Year Club	League	G.	IP.	W.	L.	Pct.	H.	R.	ER.	SO.	BB.	ERA.
1975—Lethbridge...........................Pioneer		30	85	3	4	.429	85	42	22	58	16	2.33
1976—West Palm Beach ....Florida St.		∗57	100	8	8	.500	112	50	38	48	19	3.42
1977—West Palm Beach ....Florida St.		15	26	3	3	.500	25	13	8	21	9	2.77
1977—Quebec City ....Eastern		27	73	3	6	.333	63	24	12	38	17	1.48
1977—Denver ....Am. Assoc.		2	9	0	2	.000	15	11	11	4	1	11.00
1978—Denver ....Am. Assoc.		40	135	7	10	.412	163	90	75	70	31	5.00
1979—Denver ....Am. Assoc.		40	151	8	9	.471	197	88	76	50	22	4.53
1980—Denver ....Am. Assoc.		30	163	∗15	4	∗.789	166	76	65	50	29	3.59
1980—Montreal.............................National		1	4	0	0	.000	9	5	5	0	2	11.25
Major League Totals.................................		1	4	0	0	.000	9	5	5	0	2	11.25

Signed as free agent by Montreal Expos' organization, June 11, 1975.

SHANE WILLIAM RAWLEY

Born July 27, 1955, at Racine, Wis.
Height, 6.00. Weight, 155.
Throws and bats lefthanded.
Hobby—Airplanes.
Attended Indian Hills Communtiy College, Centerville, Ia.

Major league saves: 1978 (4), 1979 (11), 1980 (13). Total—28.

Year Club	League	G.	IP.	W.	L.	Pct.	H.	R.	ER.	SO.	BB.	ERA.
1974—Sarasota Expos ....Gulf Coast		2	12	0	1	.000	12	9	3	16	4	2.25
1974—Kinston ....Carolina		5	19	0	2	.000	22	15	13	11	12	6.16
1975—West Palm Beach ....Florida St.		24	165	8	12	.400	148	80	56	113	73	3.05
1976—Quebec City ....Eastern		25	164	11	7	.611	143	55	49	113	79	2.69
1977—Denver† ....Am. Assoc.		7	47	1	4	.200	54	31	27	30	19	5.21
1977—Indianapolis‡§ ....Am. Assoc.		19	105	5	6	.455	96	58	53	62	49	4.54
1978—Seattle ....American		52	111	4	9	.308	114	57	51	66	51	4.14
1979—Seattle x ....American		48	84	5	9	.357	88	40	36	48	40	3.86
1980—Seattle ....American		59	114	7	7	.500	103	44	42	68	63	3.32
Major League Totals...............................		159	309	16	25	.390	305	141	129	182	154	3.76

Selected by Los Angeles Dodgers' organization in 4th round of free-agent draft, January 9, 1974.
Selected by Montreal Expos' organization in secondary phase of free-agent draft, June 5, 1974.

†Sent to Cincinnati Reds' organization from Montreal Expos' organization with Pitcher Angel Torres, May 27, 1977, completing deal in which Montreal acquired Pitcher Santo Alcala, May 21, 1977.
‡Appeared in one game as an outfielder.
§Traded to Seattle Mariners for Outfielder Dave Collins, December 9, 1977.
xOn disabled list, June 30 to August 21, 1979.

FLOYD KINNARD RAYFORD

Born July 27, 1957, at Memphis, Tenn.
Height, 5.10. Weight, 195.
Throws and bats righthanded.

Led California League third basemen in double plays with 21 in 1976.
Led Texas League third basemen in putouts with 95 and in assists with 216 in 1978.
Led Pacific Coast League third basemen in fielding percentage with .957 in 1979.
Led International League third basemen in fielding average with .942 in 1980.
Tied for California League lead in double plays by third basemen with 21 in 1977.

Year	Club	League	Pos.	G.	AB.	R.	H.	2B.	3B.	HR.	RBI.	B.A.	PO.	A.	E.	F.A.
1975—Idaho Falls	Pioneer	3-C-1-O-S		*72	272	43	77	12	5	2	43	.283	244	100	21	.942
1976—Salinas	Calif.		*3-C-2	125	462	73	126	19	6	5	67	.273	162	*216	16	.959
1977—Salinas	Calif.		3B	51	205	37	53	7	3	6	39	.259	40	117	7	.957
1977—El Paso	Texas		1-2-3-S-O	79	320	65	95	17	3	11	60	.297	427	133	12	.979
1978—El Paso	Texas		3-2-1-S	126	483	78	151	36	2	17	87	.313	113	230	14	.961
1979—Salt Lake City†	P. C.		3-S-1-2	135	551	98	162	28	6	13	80	.294	134	316	20	.957
1980—Rochester	Int.		3-2-S	107	387	51	89	22	0	9	46	.230	86	213	19	.940
1980—Baltimore	Amer.		3B-2B	8	18	1	4	0	0	0	1	.222	3	11	2	.875
Major League Totals				8	18	1	4	0	0	0	1	.222	3	11	2	.875

Selected by California Angels' organization in 4th round of free-agent draft, June 4, 1975.

†Traded with cash to Baltimore Orioles' organization for outfielder Larry Harlow, June 5, 1979. (Remained on option to Salt Lake City.)

JEFFREY JAMES REARDON
(Jeff)

Born October 1, 1955, at Pittsfield, Mass.
Height, 6.01. Weight, 190.
Throws and bats righthanded.

Led Carolina League in shutouts with 3 in 1977.

Year	Club	League	G.	IP.	W.	L.	Pct.	H.	R.	ER.	SO.	BB.	ERA.
1977—Lynchburg	Carolina	16	101	8	3	.727	89	42	37	60	30	3.30
1978—Jackson	Texas	28	163	*17	4	.810	128	56	46	115	65	2.53
1979—Tidewater†	Int'national	30	69	5	2	.714	46	18	16	64	21	2.09
1979—New York	National	18	21	1	2	.333	12	7	4	10	9	1.71
1980—New York	National	61	110	8	7	.533	96	36	32	101	47	2.62
Major League Totals		79	131	9	9	.500	108	43	36	111	56	2.47

Selected by New York Mets' organization in 23rd round of free-agent draft, June 5, 1973.

†On disabled list, June 13 to June 24 and June 29 to July 26, 1979.

PETER IRVING REDFERN
(Pete)

Born August 25, 1954, at Glendale, Calif.
Height, 6.02. Weight, 190.
Throws and bats righthanded.
Hobbies—Music and water skiing.
Attended University of Southern California, Los Angeles, Calif.

Received reported $40,000 bonus to sign with Minnesota Twins, 1976.

Year	Club	League	G.	IP.	W.	L.	Pct.	H.	R.	ER.	SO.	BB.	ERA.
1976—Tacoma	P. Coast	4	27	2	1	.667	23	8	8	18	9	2.67
1976—Minnesota	American	23	118	8	8	.500	105	61	46	74	63	3.51
1977—Minnesota†	American	30	137	6	9	.400	164	89	79	73	66	5.19
1978—Toledo	Int'national	20	128	9	8	.529	105	58	53	81	59	3.73
1978—Minnesota	American	3	10	0	2	.000	10	12	7	4	6	6.30
1979—Minnesota	American	40	108	7	3	.700	106	45	42	85	35	3.50
1980—Minnesota‡	American	23	105	7	7	.500	117	58	53	73	33	4.54
Major League Totals		119	478	28	29	.491	502	265	227	309	203	4.27

Selected by Cleveland Indians' organization in 10th round of free-agent draft, June 6, 1972.
Selected by Minnesota Twins' organization in secondary phase of free-agent draft, January 7, 1976.

†On disabled list, June 15 to July 6, 1977.
‡On disabled list, July 21 to September 1, 1980.

GARY EUGENE REDUS

Born November 1, 1956, at Athens, Ala.
Height, 6.01. Weight, 180.
Throws and bats righthanded.
Attended Calhoun Junior College, Decatur, Ala., and Athens State College, Athens, Ala.

Led Pioneer League in total bases with 199 and in stolen bases with 42 and tied for lead in sacrifice flies with 6 in 1978.
    Led Florida State League in total bases with 220 in 1980.
    Tied for Western Carolinas League lead in double plays by second basemen with 20 in 1979.
    Named Pioneer League Player of the Year, 1978.

Year Club	League	Pos.	G.	AB.	R.	H.	2B.	3B.	HR.	RBI.	B.A.	PO.	A.	E.	F.A.
1978—Billings.............	Pion.	2B	68	253	*100	*117	19	6	17	62	*.462	124	*185	*28	.917
1979—Nashville	South.	OF	36	109	7	19	2	1	0	7	.174	74	3	3	.963
1979—Greensboro	W. Car.	2B-OF	83	309	79	86	17	1	16	52	.278	172	193	21	.946
1980—Tampa..............	Fla. St.	O-3-1	128	452	78	136	18	9	16	68	.301	213	84	27	.917

    Selected by Boston Red Sox' organization in 17th round of free-agent draft, June 7, 1977.
    Selected by Cincinnati Reds' organization in 15th round of free-agent draft, June 6, 1978.

RONALD LEE REED
(Ron)

Born November 2, 1942, at La Porte, Ind.
Height, 6.06. Weight, 225.
Throws and bats righthanded.
Attended University of Notre Dame, Notre Dame, Ind.
Played professional basketball with Detroit Pistons, 1965-66 and 1966-67.

    Tied National League record for fewest home runs allowed, season, 250 or more innings (5), 1975.
    Major League saves: 1973 (1), 1976 (14), 1977 (15), 1978 (17), 1979 (5), 1980 (9). Total—61.
    Led International League in complete games with 17 and tied for lead in shutouts with 5 in 1967.

Year Club	League	G.	IP.	W.	L.	Pct.	H.	R.	ER.	SO.	BB.	ERA.
1965—West Palm Beach	Florida St.	7	43	3	2	.600	27	7	7	35	9	1.47
1966—Kinston...............................	Carolina	8	51	5	2	.714	43	16	10	39	12	1.76
1966—Austin...............................	Texas	4	30	3	1	.750	19	4	4	22	7	1.20
1966—Richmond	Int'national	14	87	5	2	.714	74	36	34	68	26	3.52
1966—Atlanta	National	2	8	1	1	.500	7	2	2	6	4	2.25
1967—Richmond	Int'national	28	*222	14	10	.583	179	68	62	172	53	2.51
1967—Atlanta	National	3	21	1	1	.500	21	8	7	11	3	3.00
1968—Atlanta	National	35	202	11	10	.524	189	87	75	111	49	3.34
1969—Atlanta	National	36	241	18	10	.643	227	103	93	160	56	3.47
1970—Shreveport	Texas	2	7	0	0	.000	5	2	2	6	2	2.57
1970—Atlanta†	National	21	135	7	10	.412	140	69	66	68	39	4.40
1971—Atlanta	National	32	222	13	14	.481	221	105	92	129	54	3.73
1972—Atlanta	National	31	213	11	15	.423	222	109	93	111	60	3.93
1973—Atlanta‡	National	20	116	4	11	.267	133	71	57	64	31	4.42
1974—Atlanta§	National	28	186	10	11	.476	171	76	70	78	41	3.39
1975—Atlanta x-St. Louis y	National	34	250	13	13	.500	274	114	98	139	53	3.53
1976—Philadelphia	National	59	128	8	7	.533	88	39	35	96	32	2.46
1977—Philadelphia	National	60	124	7	5	.583	101	41	38	84	37	2.76
1978—Philadelphia	National	66	109	3	4	.429	87	32	27	85	23	2.23
1979—Philadelphia	National	61	102	13	8	.619	110	52	47	58	32	4.15
1980—Philadelphia	National	55	91	7	5	.583	88	45	41	54	30	4.05
Major League Totals		543	2148	127	125	.504	2079	957	841	1254	544	3.52

    Signed as free agent by Atlanta Braves' organization, July 17, 1965.
    †On disabled list, March 24 through June 3, 1970.
    ‡On disabled list, July 10 to September 11, 1973.
    §On disabled list, May 16 to June 25, 1974.
    xTraded with a player to be named later to St. Louis Cardinals for Pitchers Elias Sosa and Ray Sadecki, May 28, 1975; Braves sent Outfielder Wayne Nordhagen to Cardinals, June 2, 1975, to complete deal.
    yTraded to Philadelphia Phillies for Outfielder Mike Anderson, December 9, 1975.

CHAMPIONSHIP SERIES RECORD

Year Club	League	G.	IP.	W.	L.	Pct.	H.	R.	ER.	SO.	BB.	ERA.
1969—Atlanta	National	1	1⅔	0	1	.000	5	4	4	3	3	21.60
1976—Philadelphia..........	National	2	4⅔	0	0	.000	6	4	4	2	2	7.71
1977—Philadelphia..........	National	3	5	0	0	.000	3	1	1	5	2	1.80
1978—Philadelphia..........	National	2	4	0	0	.000	6	1	1	2	0	2.25
1980—Philadelphia..........	National	3	2	0	1	.000	3	4	4	1	1	18.00
Championship Series Totals		11	17⅓	0	2	.000	23	14	14	13	8	7.27

WORLD SERIES RECORD

Year Club	League	G.	IP.	W.	L.	Pct.	H.	R.	ER.	SO.	BB.	ERA.
1980—Philadelphia...........	National	2	2	0	0	.000	2	0	0	2	0	0.00

ALL-STAR GAME RECORD

Year League	IP.	W.	L.	Pct.	H.	R.	ER.	SO.	BB.	ERA.
1968—National	⅓	0	0	.000	0	0	0	1	0	0.00

DID YOU KNOW—

That the Mets' catchers were noteworthy in 1980? The group tied a major league record by allowing just two passed balls but none of the backstops managed to hit a home run.

JONATHAN GENE REELHORN
(Jon)

Born July 12, 1959, at Stockton, Calif.
Height, 6.05. Weight, 200.
Throws and bats righthanded.
Attended Fresno State University, Fresno, Calif.

Year	Club	League	G.	IP.	W.	L.	Pct.	H.	R.	ER.	SO.	BB.	ERA.
1980—Reading		Eastern	16	111	9	3	.750	102	40	34	72	37	2.76

Selected by San Francisco Giants' organization in 5th round of free-agent draft, June 7, 1977.
Selected by Philadelphia Phillies' organization in 4th round of free-agent draft, June 3, 1980.

KENNETH JOHN REITZ
(Ken)

Born June 24, 1951, at San Francisco, Calif.
Height, 6.00. Weight, 185.
Throws and bats righthanded.
Hobby—Raising horses.
Brother of Roy Reitz, outfielder-first baseman in San Francisco Giants'
organization, 1963 through 1966.

Tied major league record for fewest putouts by third baseman, season, 150 or more games (86), 1980.
Established National League records for highest fielding percentage by third baseman, lifetime, 1,000 or more games (.969); fewest errors by third baseman, season, 150 or more games (8), 1980.
Led National League third basemen in double plays with 35 in 1977.
Led American Association third basemen in double plays with 35 in 1972 and led Texas League third basemen with 33 in 1971.
Named third baseman on THE SPORTING NEWS National League All-Star fielding team, 1975.

Year	Club	League	Pos.	G.	AB.	R.	H.	2B.	3B.	HR.	RBI.	B.A.	PO.	A.	E.	F.A.
1969—Sarasota Cards		Gulf C.	2B-3	11	37	8	12	2	0	0	4	.324	17	20	2	.949
1969—Cedar Rapids		Midw.	1-2-3	35	136	7	38	8	0	2	15	.279	125	33	10	.940
1970—St. Petersburg		Fla. St.	3B-1	127	*513	51	149	*33	1	6	75	.290	150	241	27	.935
1971—Arkansas		Tex.	3B	131	505	48	137	29	0	7	53	.271	*116	*316	17	*.962
1972—Tulsa		A. A.	3B	118	462	52	129	26	1	15	66	.279	*106	*259	*25	.936
1972—St. Louis		Nat.	3B	21	78	5	28	4	0	0	10	.359	17	26	2	.956
1973—St. Louis		Nat.	*3B-SS	147	426	40	100	20	2	6	42	.235	88	213	8	*.974
1974—St. Louis		Nat.	*3B-S-2	154	579	48	157	28	2	7	54	.271	131	281	12	*.972
1975—St. Louis†		Nat.	3B	161	592	43	159	25	1	5	63	.269	124	279	23	.946
1976—San Francisco‡		Nat.	3B-SS	155	577	40	154	21	1	5	66	.267	141	304	19	.959
1977—St. Louis		Nat.	3B	157	587	58	153	36	1	17	79	.261	121	320	9	*.980
1978—St. Louis		Nat.	3B	150	540	41	133	26	2	10	75	.246	111	314	12	*.973
1979—St. Louis		Nat.	3B	159	605	42	162	41	2	8	73	.268	124	290	12	.972
1980—St. Louis§		Nat.	3B	151	523	39	141	33	0	8	58	.270	86	293	8	*.979
Major League Totals				1255	4507	356	1187	234	11	66	520	.263	943	2320	105	.969

Selected by St. Louis Cardinals' organization in 34th round of free-agent draft, June 5, 1969.
†Traded to San Francisco Giants for Pitcher Pete Falcone, December 8, 1975.
‡Traded to St. Louis Cardinals for Pitcher Lynn McGlothen, December 10, 1976.
§Traded with First Baseman-Outfielder Leon Durham and a player to be named later to Chicago Cubs for Pitcher Bruce Sutter, December 9, 1980; Third Baseman Ty Waller traded to Chicago completing deal, December 22, 1980.

ALL-STAR GAME RECORD

Year	League	Pos.	AB.	R.	H.	2B.	3B.	HR.	RBI.	B.A.	PO.	A.	E.	F.A.
1980—National		3B	2	0	0	0	0	0	0	.000	1	0	0	1.000

WILHELMUS ABRAHAM REMMERSWAAL
(Win)

Born March 8, 1954, at The Hague, Holland.
Height, 6.02. Weight, 160.
Throws and bats righthanded.
Attended Technical University, Delft, Holland.

Led Eastern League in shutouts with 4 in 1977.

Year	Club	League	G.	IP.	W.	L.	Pct.	H.	R.	ER.	SO.	BB.	ERA.
1975—Winter Haven		Florida St.	27	127	8	7	.533	136	60	38	65	33	2.69
1976—Winter Haven		Florida St.	39	119	7	6	.538	94	40	23	118	40	*1.74
1976—Bristol		Eastern	1	0	0	0	.000	3	3	2	0	1	....
1977—Bristol		Eastern	23	140	9	11	.450	132	66	54	108	46	3.47
1977—Pawtucket		Int'national	4	8	0	0	.000	6	4	4	5	7	4.50
1978—Pawtucket		Int'national	34	155	8	6	.571	149	82	77	108	96	4.47
1979—Pawtucket		Int'national	39	92	4	6	.400	66	22	21	93	35	2.05
1979—Boston		American	8	20	1	0	1.000	26	16	16	16	12	7.20
1980—Pawtucket		Int'national	24	48	5	5	.500	42	28	25	33	29	4.69
1980—Boston		American	14	35	2	1	.667	39	18	18	20	9	4.63
Major League Totals			22	55	3	1	.750	65	34	34	36	21	5.56

Signed as free agent by Boston Red Sox' organization, November 22, 1974.

GERALD PETER REMY
(Jerry)

Born November 8, 1952, at Fall Rivers, Mass.
Height, 5.09. Weight, 165.
Throws right and bats lefthanded.
Hobby—Reading.
Attended Roger Williams College, Bristol, R. I.

Major League stolen bases: 1975 (34), 1976 (35), 1977 (41), 1978 (30), 1979 (14), 1980 (14). Total—168.
Led Midwest League second basemen in double plays with 73 in 1973.
Led California League second basemen in double plays with 86 in 1972.
Led American League second basemen in double plays with 114 in 1978.
Named Most Valuable Player in Midwest League, 1973.

Year Club	League	Pos.	G.	AB.	R.	H.	2B.	3B.	HR.	RBI.	B.A.	PO.	A.	E.	F.A.
1971—Magic Valley†	Pion.	2B-OF	32	104	25	32	5	3	0	6	.308	61	54	5	.958
1972—Stockton	Calif.	*2B-SS	133	532	59	141	18	3	4	43	.265	275	*404	28	.960
1973—Quad Cities	Midw.	2B	117	478	66	*160	23	10	4	36	*.335	*277	*330	24	.962
1974—El Paso	Tex.	2B	91	394	74	133	34	5	4	46	.338	233	267	18	.965
1974—Salt Lake City	P. C.	2B	48	195	33	57	6	5	0	21	.292	108	135	7	.972
1975—California	Amer.	2B	147	569	82	147	17	5	1	46	.258	336	427	14	.982
1976—California	Amer.	2B	143	502	64	132	14	3	0	28	.263	279	406	16	.977
1977—California‡	Amer.	2B-3B	154	575	74	145	19	10	4	44	.252	307	420	19	.975
1978—Boston	Amer.	2B-SS	148	583	87	162	24	6	2	44	.278	328	446	13	.983
1979—Boston§	Amer.	2B	80	306	49	91	11	2	0	29	.297	147	205	11	.970
1980—Boston x	Amer.	2B-OF	63	230	24	72	7	2	0	9	.313	109	189	7	.977
Major League Totals			735	2765	380	749	92	28	7	200	.271	1506	2093	80	.978

Selected by Washington Senators' organization in 19th round of free-agent draft, June 4, 1970.
Selected by California Angels' organization in secondary phase of free-agent draft, January 13, 1971.
†On disabled list, August 12 through remainder of season.
‡Traded to Boston Red Sox for Pitcher Don Aase and cash, December 8, 1977.
§On disabled list, July 2 to August 8 and August 17 to September 1, 1979.
xOn emergency disabled list, July 15 to October 21, 1980.

ALL-STAR GAME RECORD
Named to American League All-Star Team for 1978 game to replace injured Rick Burleson; did not play.

STEVEN RENKO JR.
(Steve)

Born December 10, 1944, at Kansas City, Kan.
Height, 6.06. Weight, 225.
Throws and bats righthanded.
Hobbies—Golf and riding horses.
Attended University of Kansas, Lawrence, Kan.

Pitched seven-inning, 1-0 no-hit victory against Albuquerque, July 21, 1968.
Led National League in wild pitches with 19 in 1974.

Year Club	League	G.	IP.	W.	L.	Pct.	H.	R.	ER.	SO.	BB.	ERA.
1966—Williamsport	Eastern	1	2	0	0	.000	0	0	0	2	1	0.00
1967—Winter Haven†	Florida St.	11	84	8	1	.889	44	17	15	109	39	1.61
1968—Memphis	Texas	22	145	7	11	.389	116	63	53	106	73	3.29
1968—Jacksonville	Int'national	7	51	4	1	.800	35	20	17	41	17	3.00
1969—Tidewater‡	Int'national	12	66	3	6	.333	56	43	40	57	43	5.45
1969—Montreal	National	18	103	6	7	.462	94	54	46	68	50	4.02
1970—Montreal	National	41	223	13	11	.542	203	121	107	142	104	4.32
1971—Montreal	National	40	276	15	14	.517	256	128	*115	129	135	3.75
1972—Montreal	National	30	97	1	10	.091	96	60	56	66	67	5.20
1973—Montreal	National	36	250	15	11	.577	201	94	78	164	108	2.81
1974—Montreal	National	37	228	12	16	.429	222	115	102	138	81	4.03
1975—Montreal	National	31	170	6	12	.333	175	89	77	99	76	4.08
1976—Mont.§-Chi.	National	33	176	8	12	.400	179	87	78	116	46	3.99
1977—Chicago xy	National	13	51	2	2	.500	51	32	26	34	21	4.59
1977—Chicago z	American	8	53	5	0	1.000	55	23	21	36	17	3.57
1978—Oakland a	American	27	151	6	12	.333	152	77	72	89	67	4.29
1979—Boston	American	27	171	11	9	.550	174	86	78	99	53	4.11
1980—Boston b	American	32	165	9	9	.500	180	86	77	90	56	4.20
National League Totals		279	1574	78	95	.451	1477	780	685	956	688	3.92
American League Totals		94	540	31	30	.508	561	272	248	314	193	4.13
Major League Totals		373	2114	109	125	.466	2038	1052	933	1270	881	3.97

Selected by New York Mets' organization in 14th round of free-agent draft, June, 1965.
†On disabled list from July 30 through end of season with left shoulder separation.
‡Recalled by New York Mets and traded to Montreal Expos with Infielder Kevin Collins (recalled from Tidewater), Pitcher Jay Carden (on Memphis roster) and Pitcher Dave Colon (with Marion) for First Baseman Donn Clendenon, June 15, 1969.
§Traded with Outfielder-First Baseman Larry Biittner to Chicago Cubs for First Baseman Andy Thornton, May 17, 1976.
xOn disabled list, April 28 to June 21, 1977.
yTraded to Chicago White Sox for cash and Pitcher Larry Anderson (assigned from Iowa to Wichita), August 18, 1977.
zTraded with Catcher Jim Essian to Oakland A's for Pitcher Pablo Torrealba, March 30, 1978.

aGranted free agency, November 2, 1978; signed by Boston Red Sox, January 23, 1979.

bTraded with Outfielder Fred Lynn to California Angels for Pitchers Frank Tanana and Jim Dorsey and Outfielder Joe Rudi, January 23, 1981.

RECORD AS FIRST BASEMAN

Year Club League	Pos.	G.	AB.	R.	H.	2B.	3B.	HR.	RBI.	B.A.	PO.	A.	E.	F.A.
1965—Marion..............Appal.	1-OF	50	169	39	49	3	3	7	32	.290	199	11	11	.950
1966—Auburn ....NYP	1B	69	246	38	57	10	2	10	42	.232	516	33	12	.979
1966—Williamsport .....East.	●1B-P	59	195	20	33	3	0	7	18	.169	450	24	●11	.977
1967—Winter Haven ....Fla. St.	1-P-O	71	197	27	43	3	1	8	24	.218	355	36	8	.980
1969—Tidewater ....Int.	P-1B	18	16	3	5	1	0	1	5	.313	15	4	1	.950
1972—Montreal ....Nat.	P-1B	32	24	0	7	0	0	0	0	.292	9	17	1	.963

RICKY EUGENE REUSCHEL
Name pronounced RUSH-ul.

(Rick)

Born May 16, 1949, at Quincy, Ill.
Height, 6.03. Weight, 230.
Throws and bats righthanded.
Attended Western Illinois University, Macomb, Ill.
Brother of Paul Reuschel, former pitcher with Chicago Cubs and Cleveland Indians.

Tied major league record for most putouts, pitcher, inning, 3, April 25, 1975, 3rd inning.
Led Northern League pitchers in complete games with 7 and tied for lead in games started with 14 in 1970.
Tied for National League lead in games started with 38 in 1980.
Named righthanded pitcher on THE SPORTING NEWS National League All-Star Team, 1977.

Year Club League	G.	IP.	W.	L.	Pct.	H.	R.	ER.	SO.	BB.	ERA.
1970—Huron................................Northern	14	102	9	2	.818	96	52	40	88	22	3.52
1971—San Antonio†........................Texas	16	121	8	4	.667	105	40	31	81	15	2.31
1972—Wichita................Am. Assoc.	12	102	9	2	.818	78	30	15	72	30	1.32
1972—Chicago ....National	21	129	10	8	.556	127	46	42	87	29	2.93
1973—Chicago ....National	36	237	14	15	.483	244	95	79	168	62	3.00
1974—Chicago ....National	41	241	13	12	.520	262	130	115	160	83	4.29
1975—Chicago ....National	38	234	11	∗17	.393	244	116	97	155	67	3.73
1976—Chicago ....National	38	260	14	12	.538	260	∗117	100	146	64	3.46
1977—Chicago ....National	39	252	20	10	.667	233	84	78	166	74	2.79
1978—Chicago ....National	35	243	14	15	.483	235	98	92	115	54	3.41
1979—Chicago ....National	36	239	18	12	.600	251	104	96	125	75	3.62
1980—Chicago ....National	38	257	11	13	.458	∗281	111	97	140	76	3.40
Major League Totals	322	2092	125	114	.523	2137	901	796	1262	584	3.42

Selected by Chicago Cubs' organization in 3rd round of free-agent draft, June 4, 1970.

†On temporary inactive list, July 2, 1971. Transferred to military list, July 8, 1971 through April 10, 1972.

ALL-STAR GAME RECORD

Year League	IP.	W.	L.	Pct.	H.	R.	ER.	SO.	BB.	ERA.
1977—National	1	0	0	.000	1	0	0	0	0	0.00

JERRY REUSS
Name pronounced Royce.

Born June 19, 1949, at St. Louis, Mo.
Height, 6.05. Weight, 217.
Throws and bats lefthanded.
Attended Southern Illinois University, Carbondale, Ill., Central Missouri State College,
Warrensburg, Mo., and University of California at Santa Barbara, Santa Barbara, Calif.

Tied major league record for most home runs allowed, bases filled, lifetime (9).
Pitched 8-0 no-hit victory against San Francisco Giants, June 27, 1980.
Led National League in shutouts with 6 in 1980.
Tied for National League lead in games started with 40 in 1973.
Led American Association in games started with 29 in 1969.
Led Texas League in wild pitches with 16 in 1968.
Named National League Comeback Player of the Year by THE SPORTING NEWS, 1980.
Received reported $30,000 bonus to sign with St. Louis Cardinals, 1967.

Year Club League	G.	IP.	W.	L.	Pct.	H.	R.	ER.	SO.	BB.	ERA.
1967—Sarasota Cards....................Gulf Coast	2	7	0	0	.000	7	6	4	6	3	5.14
1967—Cedar Rapids ....Midwest	9	58	2	5	.286	44	20	12	63	19	1.86
1967—Tulsa................................P. Coast	1	1	0	0	.000	2	6	6	1	4	54.00
1968—Arkansas ....Texas	17	112	7	8	.467	75	43	27	86	45	2.17
1969—Tulsa.................................Am. Assoc.	30	∗186	●13	11	.542	188	●112	84	∗151	116	4.06
1969—St. Louis ....National	1	7	1	0	1.000	2	0	0	3	3	0.00
1970—Tulsa.................................Am. Assoc.	11	85	7	2	.778	69	26	20	69	28	2.12
1970—St. Louis ....National	20	127	7	8	.467	132	62	58	74	49	4.11
1971—St. Louis†............................National	36	211	14	14	.500	228	125	112	131	109	4.78
1972—Houston ....National	33	192	9	13	.409	177	101	89	174	83	4.17
1973—Houston‡..............................National	41	279	16	13	.552	271	123	116	177	∗117	3.74
1974—Pittsburgh ....National	35	260	16	11	.593	259	115	101	105	101	3.50
1975—Pittsburgh ....National	32	237	18	11	.621	224	73	67	131	78	2.54

Year	Club	League	G.	IP.	W.	L.	Pct.	H.	R.	ER.	SO.	BB.	ERA.
1976–Pittsburgh		National	31	209	14	9	.609	209	98	82	108	51	3.53
1977–Pittsburgh		National	33	208	10	13	.435	225	109	95	116	71	4.11
1978–Pittsburgh§		National	23	83	3	2	.600	97	48	45	42	23	4.88
1979–Los Angeles		National	39	160	7	14	.333	178	88	63	83	60	3.54
1980–Los Angeles		National	37	229	18	6	.750	193	74	64	111	40	2.52
Major League Totals			361	2202	133	114	.538	2195	1016	892	1255	785	3.65

Selected by St. Louis Cardinals' organization in 2nd round of free-agent draft, June 6, 1967.

†Traded to Houston Astros for Pitchers Scipio Spinks and Lance Clemons, April 15, 1972.

‡Traded to Pittsburgh Pirates for Catcher Milt May, October 31, 1972.

§Traded to Los Angeles Dodgers for Pitcher Rick Rhoden, April 9, 1979.

CHAMPIONSHIP SERIES RECORD

Tied Championship Series records for most games lost, total Series (3); most games lost, Series (2), 1974; most bases on balls, four-game Series (8), 1974.

Year	Club	League	G.	IP.	W.	L.	Pct.	H.	R.	ER.	SO.	BB.	ERA.
1974–Pittsburgh		National	2	9⅔	0	2	.000	7	4	4	3	8	3.72
1975–Pittsburgh		National	1	2⅔	0	1	.000	4	4	4	1	4	13.50
Championship Series Totals			3	12⅓	0	3	.000	11	8	8	4	12	5.84

ALL-STAR GAME RECORD

Year	League	IP.	W.	L.	Pct.	H.	R.	ER.	SO.	BB.	ERA.
1975–National		3	0	0	.000	3	0	0	2	0	0.00
1980–National		1	1	0	1.000	0	0	0	3	0	0.00
All-Star Game Totals		4	1	0	1.000	3	0	0	5	0	0.00

DAVID ALVIN REVERING
(Dave)

Born February 12, 1953, at Roseville, Calif.
Height, 6.04. Weight, 205.
Throws right and bats lefthanded.
Hobby–Cars.

Led Eastern League batters in walks with 100 and tied for lead in strikeouts with 110 in 1973.
Led Eastern League first basemen in double plays with 105 in 1973.

Year	Club	League	Pos.	G.	AB.	R.	H.	2B.	3B.	HR.	RBI.	B.A.	PO.	A.	E.	F.A.
1971–Brad'ton Reds	...Gulf C		1B	45	133	24	36	8	3	*8	*33	.271	*312	18	2	*.976
1972–Tampa	Fla. St.		1B-O	126	413	51	112	*28	5	8	70	.271	1000	70	24	.978
1973–Three Rivers	East.		1B	117	371	74	97	18	1	16	74	.261	958	68	17	.984
1974–Three Rivers	East.		1B	16	47	11	16	3	0	5	12	.340	126	10	3	.978
1974–Indianapolis	A. A.		1B	94	302	40	80	19	3	15	60	.265	707	43	4	*.995
1975–Indianapolis	A. A.		1B	120	382	53	97	15	5	21	71	.254	*959	*91	12	.989
1976–Indianapolis	A. A.		1B	123	407	63	118	20	2	27	77	.290	*1051	75	7	.994
1977–Indianapolis†	A. A.		1B-C	128	443	82	133	21	2	29	110	.300	1104	66	10	.992
1978–Oakland	Amer.		1B	152	521	49	141	21	3	16	46	.271	1013	110	13	.989
1979–Oakland‡	Amer.		1B	125	472	63	136	25	5	19	77	.288	828	80	13	.986
1980–Oakland	Amer.		1B	106	376	48	109	21	5	15	62	.290	724	67	9	.989
Major League Totals				383	1369	160	386	67	13	50	185	.282	2565	267	35	.988

Selected by Cincinnati Reds' organization in 7th round of free-agent draft, June 8, 1971.

†Traded to Oakland Athletics for Pitcher Vida Blue and cash estimated at more than $1,000,000, December 9, 1977; voided by Commissioner Bowie Kuhn, January 30, 1978. Traded to Oakland Athletics for Pitcher Doug Bair, February 25, 1978.

‡On disabled list, June 28 to July 13, 1979.

MICHAEL WILLIAM REX
(Mike)

Born August 8, 1954, at Lebanon, Ore.
Height, 5.10. Weight, 170.
Throws and bats righthanded.
Attended Linfield College, McMinnville, Ore.; received Bachelor of Arts degree
in Psychology and Physical Education.

Led California League shortstops in putouts with 152, in assists with 353 and in double plays with 74 in 1977.
Led Eastern League second basemen in fielding average with .976 in 1978.

Year	Club	League	Pos.	G.	AB.	R.	H.	2B.	3B.	HR.	RBI.	B.A.	PO.	A.	E.	F.A.
1976–Great Falls	Pion.		SS	4	17	3	6	1	1	0	4	.353	4	15	2	.905
1976–Cedar Rapids	Midw.		SS-3B-2B	39	94	18	23	4	1	0	4	.245	27	43	10	.875
1977–Fresno	Calif.		*SS-2B	127	458	105	143	27	3	11	77	.312	155	357	*44	.921
1978–Waterbury	East.		2B-SS	128	476	74	146	20	9	5	52	.307	263	329	15	.975
1979–Phoenix	P. C.		2B-3B-SS	126	443	51	103	17	3	2	49	.233	218	337	23	.960
1980–Phoenix	P. C.		2B	136	471	74	137	23	2	6	61	.291	316	342	15	.978

Selected by San Francisco Giants' organization in 18th round of free-agent draft, June 8, 1976.

GORDON CRAIG REYNOLDS
(Known by middle name.)

Born December 27, 1952, at Houston, Tex.
Height, 6.01. Weight, 175.
Throws right and bats lefthanded.
Hobbies—Golf and bowling.
Attended Houston Baptist College, Houston, Tex.

Led Carolina League shortstops in double plays with 81 in 1973 and tied for International League lead with 64 in 1975.

Led National League in sacrifice hits with 34 in 1979.

Tied for Gulf Coast League lead in sacrifice flies with 4 in 1971.

Year—Club	League	Pos.	G.	AB.	R.	H.	2B.	3B.	HR.	RBI.	B.A.	PO.	A.	E.	F.A.
1971—Bradenton Pir.	Gulf C.	SS	48	192	26	61	8	0	0	16	.318	*87	112	*25	.888
1972—Gastonia†	W. Car.	SS	41	146	18	35	4	1	0	9	.240	55	94	12	.925
1973—Salem	Carol.	SS-2B	138	*558	75	*160	18	5	13	86	.287	200	395	50	.922
1973—Charleston	Int.	SS-3B	4	14	2	3	0	0	0	0	.214	4	11	1	.938
1974—Thetford Mines	East.	SS	64	234	31	66	7	0	6	29	.282	76	170	13	.950
1974—Charleston‡	Int.	SS-2B	36	107	12	36	5	0	0	5	.336	40	71	3	.974
1975—Charleston	Int.	SS	108	425	51	131	22	3	6	42	.308	151	287	26	.944
1975—Pittsburgh	Nat.	SS	31	76	8	17	3	0	0	4	.224	43	82	4	.969
1976—Charleston	Int.	SS-2B	126	497	57	144	18	1	2	47	.290	198	262	31	.937
1976—Pittsburgh§	Nat.	SS-2B	7	4	1	1	0	0	1	1	.250	2	6	1	.889
1977—Seattle	Amer.	SS	135	420	41	104	12	3	4	28	.248	197	397	28	.955
1978—Seattle x	Amer.	SS	148	548	57	160	16	7	5	44	.292	243	461	29	.960
1979—Houston	Nat.	SS	146	555	63	147	20	9	0	39	.265	208	428	23	.965
1980—Houston	Nat.	SS	137	381	34	86	9	6	3	28	.226	162	362	17	.969
National League Totals			321	1016	106	251	32	15	4	72	.247	415	878	45	.966
American League Totals			283	968	98	264	28	10	9	72	.273	440	858	57	.958
Major League Totals			604	1984	204	515	60	25	13	144	.260	855	1736	102	.962

Selected by Pittsburgh Pirates' organization in 1st round (22nd player selected) of free-agent draft, June 8, 1971.

†On disabld ist, June 6 to August 30, 1972.

‡On disabldlist, July 31 to August 21, 1974.

§Traded with Infielder Jim Sexton to Seattle Mariners for Pitcher Grant Jackson, December 7, 1976.

xTraded to Houston Astros for Pitcher Floyd Bannister, December 8, 1978.

CHAMPIONSHIP SERIES RECORD

Year—Club	League	Pos.	G.	AB.	R.	H.	2B.	3B.	HR.	RBI.	B.A.	PO.	A.	E.	F.A.
1975—Pittsburgh	Nat.	SS	2	1	0	0	0	0	0	0	.000	0	0	1	.000
1980—Houston	Nat.	SS	4	13	2	2	1	0	0	0	.154	8	12	1	.952
Championship Series Totals			6	14	2	2	1	0	0	0	.143	8	12	2	.909

ALL-STAR GAME RECORD

Year—League	Pos.	AB.	R.	H.	2B.	3B.	HR.	RBI.	B.A.	PO.	A.	E.	F.A.
1979—National	SS	2	0	0	0	0	0	0	.000	0	1	0	1.000

Named to American League All-Star Team for 1978 game; did not play.

RICHARD ALAN RHODEN
Name pronounced ROH-dun.

(Rick)

Born May 16, 1953, at Boynton Beach, Fla.
Height, 6.03. Weight, 195.
Throws and bats righthanded.
Hobbies—Golf, fishing, hunting and ping pong.

Year—Club	League	G.	IP.	W.	L.	Pct.	H.	R.	ER.	SO.	BB.	ERA.
1971—Daytona Beach	Florida St.	11	61	4	6	.400	59	32	27	67	29	3.98
1972—El Paso	Texas	13	87	6	4	.600	70	36	32	89	30	3.31
1972—Albuquerque	P. Coast	13	80	7	1	.875	83	41	34	55	34	3.83
1973—Albuquerque†	P. Coast	20	116	4	9	.308	117	66	58	68	70	4.50
1974—Albuquerque	P. Coast	26	178	9	10	.474	197	103	87	106	65	4.40
1974—Los Angeles	National	4	9	1	0	1.000	5	2	2	7	4	2.00
1975—Los Angeles	National	26	99	3	3	.500	94	40	34	40	32	3.09
1976—Los Angeles	National	27	181	12	3	.800	165	66	60	77	53	2.98
1977—Los Angeles	National	31	216	16	10	.615	223	98	90	122	63	3.75
1978—Los Angeles‡	National	30	165	10	8	.556	160	77	67	79	51	3.65
1979—Pittsburgh§	National	1	5	0	1	.000	5	4	4	2	2	7.20
1980—Portland	P. Coast	10	52	6	3	.667	47	22	17	24	21	2.94
1980—Pittsburgh	National	20	127	7	5	.583	133	58	54	70	40	3.83
Major League Totals		139	802	49	30	.620	785	345	311	397	245	3.49

Selected by Los Angeles Dodgers' organization in 1st round (20th player selected) of free-agent draft, June 8, 1971.

†On disabled list, July 20 to August 15, 1973.

‡Traded to Pittsburgh Pirates for Pitcher Jerry Reuss, April 9, 1979.

§On disabled list, May 12 to October 4, 1979.

CHAMPIONSHIP SERIES RECORD

Year Club	League	G.	IP.	W.	L.	Pct.	H.	R.	ER.	SO.	BB.	ERA.
1977—Los Angeles ....National		1	4⅓	0	0	.000	2	0	0	0	2	0.00
1978—Los Angeles ....National		1	4	0	0	.000	2	1	1	3	1	2.25
Championship Series Totals		2	8⅓	0	0	.000	4	1	1	3	3	1.08

WORLD SERIES RECORD

Year Club	League	G.	IP.	W.	L.	Pct.	H.	R.	ER.	SO.	BB.	ERA.
1977—Los Angeles ....National		2	7	0	1	.000	4	2	2	5	1	2.57

ALL-STAR RECORD

Year League	IP.	W.	L.	Pct.	H.	R.	ER.	SO.	BB.	ERA.
1976—National	1	0	0	.000	1	0	0	0	0	.000

JAMES EDWARD RICE
(Jim)

Born March 8, 1953, at Anderson, S. C.
Height, 6.02. Weight, 205.
Throws and bats righthanded.

Tied major league record for most consecutive seasons leading major leagues, total bases (2).
Tied American League record for most consecutive seasons leading league, total bases (3).
Led American League batters in strikeouts with 123 in 1976.
Led American League in slugging percentage with .593 in 1977 and with .600 in 1978.
Led American League designated hitters in average with .316, in total bases with 287, in home runs with 31 and in triples with 13 in 1977.
Led American League in total bases with 382 in 1977, with 406 in 1978 and with 369 in 1979.
Hit three home runs in one game, vs. Oakland A's, August 29, 1977.
Led Florida State League in total bases with 240 in 1972.
Led International League in total bases with 249 in 1974.
Named outfielder on THE SPORTING NEWS American League All-Star Team, 1975, 1977, 1978 and 1979.
Named American League Player of the Year by THE SPORTING NEWS, 1978.
Named American League Most Valuable Player by Baseball Writers Association of America, 1978.
Named Minor League Player of the Year by THE SPORTING NEWS, 1974.
Named International League Most Valuable Player and Rookie of the Year, 1974.
Received reported $45,000 bonus to sign with Boston Red Sox, 1971.

Year Club	League	Pos.	G.	AB.	R.	H.	2B.	3B.	HR.	RBI.	B.A.	PO.	A.	E.	F.A.
1971—Williamsport .....NYP		OF	60	223	34	57	9	5	5	27	.256	86	2	6	.936
1972—Winter Haven ....Fla. St.		OF	130	•491	•80	•143	20	13	17	87	.291	190	10	9	.957
1973—Bristol ....East.		OF	119	423	66	134	25	4	27	93	•.317	169	13	12	.938
1973—Pawtucket.........Int.		OF	10	37	7	14	2	0	4	10	.378	21	0	0	1.000
1974—Pawtucket.........Int.		OF	117	430	69	145	21	4	•25	•93	•.337	181	10	11	.946
1974—Boston ....Amer.		OF	24	67	6	18	2	1	1	13	.269	4	0	1	.800
1975—Boston ....Amer.		OF	144	564	92	174	29	4	22	102	.309	162	6	0	1.000
1976—Boston ....Amer.		OF	153	581	75	164	25	8	25	85	.282	199	8	7	.967
1977—Boston ....Amer.		OF	160	644	104	206	29	15	•39	114	.320	83	4	4	.956
1978—Boston ....Amer.		OF	•163	•677	121	•213	25	•15	•46	•139	.315	245	13	3	.989
1979—Boston ....Amer.		OF	158	619	117	201	39	6	39	130	.325	241	8	4	.984
1980—Boston† ....Amer.		OF	124	504	81	148	22	6	24	86	.294	233	10	3	.988
Major League Totals			926	3656	596	1124	171	55	196	669	.307	1167	49	22	.982

Selected by Boston Red Sox' organization in 1st round (15th player selected) of free-agent draft, June 8, 1971.

†On supplemental disabled list, June 22 to July 27, 1980.

ALL-STAR GAME RECORD

Tied All-Star Game record for most at bats, game (5), July 17, 1979.

Year League	Pos.	AB.	R.	H.	2B.	3B.	HR.	RBI.	B.A.	PO.	A.	E.	F.A.
1977—American	OF	2	0	1	0	0	0	0	.500	1	0	0	1.000
1978—American	OF	4	0	0	0	0	0	0	.000	2	0	0	1.000
1979—American	OF	5	0	1	1	0	0	0	.200	3	0	0	1.000
All-Star Game Totals		11	0	2	1	0	0	0	.182	6	0	0	1.000

Named to American League All-Star Team in 1980; replaced due to injury.

JAMES RODNEY RICHARD
(J. R.)

Born March 7, 1950, at Vienna, La.
Height, 6.08. Weight, 237.
Throws and bats righthanded.
Hobbies—Pool, dancing, movies, art and outdoor sports.
Attended Arizona State University, Tempe, Ariz.

Tied major league record for most base on balls, shutout game through nine innings (10), July 6, 1976.
Tied modern major league records for most strikeouts, first major league game, 15, September 5, 1971 (second game of doubleheader); most wild pitches, game (6), April 10, 1979.
Established modern National League record for most strikeouts by righthanded pitcher, season (303), 1978.

Tied modern National League records for most consecutive seasons, 300 or more strikeouts (2), 1978 and 1979; most strikeouts, season (313), 1979.

Pitched seven-inning, 2-0 no-hit victory against Daytona Beach, August 28, 1970.

Led American Association in wild pitches with 18 and tied for lead in shutouts with 3 in 1971.

Tied for National League lead in wild pitches with 19 in 1979.

Received reported $75,000 bonus to sign with Houston Astros, 1969.

Year Club	League	G.	IP.	W.	L.	Pct.	H.	R.	ER.	SO.	BB.	ERA.
1969—Covington	Ap'alchian	12	56	5	4	.556	51	50	41	71	*52	6.59
1970—Cocoa	Florida St.	19	109	4	11	.267	67	53	29	138	68	2.39
1971—Houston	National	4	21	2	1	.667	17	9	8	29	16	3.43
1971—Oklahoma City	Am. Assoc.	24	173	12	7	.632	116	55	47	*202	*105	*2.45
1972—Oklahoma City	Am. Assoc.	19	128	10	8	.556	94	57	43	169	79	3.02
1972—Houston	National	4	6	1	0	1.000	10	9	9	8	8	13.50
1973—Denver	Am. Assoc.	8	52	2	4	.333	54	39	33	66	26	5.71
1973—Houston	National	16	72	6	2	.750	54	37	32	75	38	4.00
1974—Columbus	Southern	13	87	5	8	.385	103	65	52	77	61	5.38
1974—Denver	Am. Assoc.	4	33	4	0	1.000	15	2	0	26	12	0.00
1974—Houston	National	15	65	2	3	.400	58	31	30	42	36	4.15
1975—Houston	National	33	203	12	10	.545	178	107	99	176	*138	4.39
1976—Houston	National	39	291	20	15	.571	221	105	89	214	*151	2.75
1977—Houston	National	36	267	18	12	.600	212	94	88	214	104	2.97
1978—Houston	National	36	275	18	11	.621	192	104	95	*303	*141	3.11
1979—Houston	National	38	292	18	13	.581	220	98	88	*313	98	*2.71
1980—Houston†	National	17	114	10	4	.714	65	31	24	119	40	1.89
Major League Totals		238	1606	107	71	.601	1227	625	562	1493	770	3.15

Selected by Houston Astros' organization in 1st round (second player selected) of free-agent draft, June 5, 1969.

†On disabled list, July 16, 1980; transferred to emergency disabled list, August 25 to October 21, 1980.

ALL-STAR GAME RECORD

Year League	IP.	W.	L.	Pct.	H.	R.	ER.	SO.	BB.	ERA.
1980—National	2	0	0	.000	1	0	0	3	2	0.00

EUGENE RICHARDS JR.
(Gene)

Born September 29, 1953, at Monticello, S. C.
Height, 6.00. Weight, 175.
Throws and bats lefthanded.
Hobbies—Hunting, fishing and archery.
Attended South Carolina State College, Orangeburg, S. C.

Established modern major league record for most stolen bases, rookie season, 56, 1977.

Tied National League record for most hits, extra-inning game (6), July 26, 1977 (15 innings).

Major League stolen bases: 1977 (56), 1978 (37), 1979 (24), 1980 (61). Total—178.

Led California League in total bases with 276 and in stolen bases with 85 in 1975.

Named California League Most Valuable Player and Rookie of the Year, 1975.

Year Club	League	Pos.	G.	AB.	R.	H.	2B.	3B.	HR.	RBI.	B.A.	PO.	A.	E.	F.A.
1975—Reno	Calif.	OF	134	501	*148	*191	29	10	12	58	*.381	203	6	8	.963
1976—Hawaii	P.C.	OF	137	522	102	*173	24	9	8	59	.331	231	13	12	.953
1977—San Diego	Nat.	OF-1B	146	525	79	152	16	11	5	32	.290	416	35	13	.972
1978—San Diego	Nat.	OF-1B	154	555	90	171	26	12	4	45	.308	421	20	17	.963
1979—San Diego	Nat.	OF	150	545	77	152	17	9	4	41	.279	320	7	9	.973
1980—San Diego	Nat.	OF	158	642	91	193	26	8	4	41	.301	307	*21	7	.979
Major League Totals			608	2267	337	668	85	40	17	159	.295	1464	83	46	.971

Selected by San Diego Padres' organization in 1st round (first player selected) of free-agent draft, January 9, 1975.

MICHAEL ANTHONY RICHARDT
(Mike)

Born May 24, 1958, at Los Angeles, Calif.
Height, 6.00. Weight, 170.
Throws and bats righthanded.
Attended Fresno City College, Fresno, Calif.

Tied for Gulf Coast League lead in sacrifice hits with 6 in 1978.

Tied for Gulf Coast League lead in double plays by second basemen with 24 and led second basemen in fielding average with .982 in 1978.

Tied for International League lead in double plays by second basemen with 74 in 1980.

Year Club	League	Pos.	G.	AB.	R.	H.	2B.	3B.	HR.	RBI.	B.A.	PO.	A.	E.	F.A.
1978—Sara. Rangers	G.C	2B-3B	45	160	30	45	9	2	0	14	.281	90	94	7	.963
1979—Asheville	W. Car.	2B	75	283	61	88	15	3	4	41	.311	173	212	16	.960
1979—Tulsa	Texas	2B	68	272	50	89	17	5	5	24	.327	162	218	6	.984
1980—Charleston	Int.	2B	124	487	74	136	21	13	12	46	.279	*262	385	10	*.985
1980—Texas	Amer.	2B	22	71	2	16	2	0	0	8	.225	32	55	2	.978
Major League Totals			22	71	2	16	2	0	0	8	.225	32	55	2	.978

Selected by Toronto Blue Jays' organization in 2nd round of free-agent draft, January 10, 1978.

Selected by Texas Rangers' organization in secondary phase of free-agent draft, June 6, 1978.

DAVID ALLAN RIGHETTI
(Dave)

Born November 28, 1958, at San Jose, Calif.
Height, 6.03. Weight, 195.
Throws and bats lefthanded.
Attended San Jose City College, San Jose, Calif.
Son of Leo Righetti, former shortstop in New York Yankees' organization;
Brother of Steven Righetti, third baseman in Texas Rangers' organization.

Year Club	League	G.	IP.	W.	L.	Pct.	H.	R.	ER.	SO.	BB.	ERA.
1977–Asheville	W. Carol.	17	109	11	3	*.786	98	47	38	101	53	3.14
1978–Tulsa†‡	Texas	13	91	5	5	.500	66	40	32	127	49	3.16
1979–West Haven§	Eastern	11	69	4	3	.571	45	23	15	78	45	1.96
1979–Columbus x	Int'national	8	40	3	2	.600	22	13	13	44	19	2.93
1979–New York	American	3	17	0	1	.000	10	7	7	13	10	3.71
1980–Columbus	Int'national	24	142	6	10	.375	124	79	73	139	*101	4.63
Major League Totals		3	17	0	1	.000	10	7	7	13	10	3.71

Selected by Texas Rangers' organization in 1st round (ninth player selected) of free-agent draft, January 11, 1977.

†On disabled list, July 31 to September 2, 1978.

‡Traded with Pitchers Mike Griffin and Paul Mirabella and Outfielders Juan Beniquez and Greg Jemison to New York Yankees for Pitchers Sparky Lyle, Larry McCall and Dave Rajsich, Catcher Mike Heath, Shortstop Domingo Ramos and cash, November 10, 1978.

§On disabled list, May 21 to June 28, 1979.

xOn disabled list, June 28 to July 20, and August 2 to August 23, 1979.

GEORGE MICHAEL RILEY

Born October 6, 1956, at Philadelphia, Pa.
Height, 6.02. Weight, 200.
Throws and bats lefthanded.
Hobbies—Fishing and music.

Pitched 10-0, seven-inning no-hit victory against Fort Lauderdale, July 11, 1976.
Led Florida State League in games started with 26 in 1975.

Year Club	League	G.	IP.	W.	L.	Pct.	H.	R.	ER.	SO.	BB.	ERA.
1974–Bradenton Cubs	Gulf Coast	5	21	0	3	.000	18	14	8	16	8	3.43
1975–Key West	Florida St.	28	155	10	10	.500	141	75	62	84	81	3.60
1976–Pompano Beach	Florida St.	20	114	7	10	.412	122	73	49	76	47	3.87
1976–Midland	Texas	8	47	1	5	.167	61	37	34	29	36	6.51
1977–Midland	Texas	30	75	3	1	.750	79	41	36	57	36	4.32
1977–Wichita	Am. Assoc.	9	13	0	0	.000	15	7	7	11	8	4.85
1978–Wichita	Am. Assoc.	24	36	3	5	.375	47	31	29	17	23	7.25
1978–Midland	Texas	10	69	5	3	.625	77	37	34	50	39	4.43
1979–Wichita†	Am. Assoc.	38	74	3	8	.273	75	53	50	53	53	6.08
1979–Chicago	National	4	13	0	1	.000	16	9	8	5	6	5.54
1980–Wichita	Am. Assoc.	28	47	3	3	.500	60	23	23	32	19	4.40
1980–Chicago‡	National	22	36	0	4	.000	41	29	23	18	20	5.75
Major League Totals		26	49	0	5	.000	57	38	31	23	26	5.69

Selected by Chicago Cubs' organization in 4th round of free-agent draft, June 5, 1974.

†On disabled list, April 17 to April 27, 1979.

‡Released, February 27, 1981.

ANDREW JOHN RINCON
(Andy)

Born March 5, 1959, at Pico Rivera, Calif.
Height, 6.03. Weight, 195.
Throws and bats righthanded.

Year Club	League	G.	IP.	W.	L.	Pct.	H.	R.	ER.	SO.	BB.	ERA.
1977–Calgary	Pioneer	7	40	3	1	.750	36	17	13	23	20	2.93
1978–Gastonia	W. Carol.	24	150	8	10	.444	132	85	69	67	86	4.14
1979–St. Petersburg	Florida St.	25	158	10	9	.526	153	74	59	89	66	3.36
1979–Arkansas	Texas	3	16	1	2	.333	18	8	8	7	5	4.50
1980–Arkansas	Texas	26	172	10	7	.588	165	80	65	138	51	3.40
1980–St. Louis	National	4	31	3	1	.750	23	9	9	22	7	2.61
Major League Totals		4	31	3	1	.750	23	9	9	22	7	2.61

Selected by St. Louis Cardinals' organization in 5th round of free-agent draft, June 7, 1977.

CALVIN EDWIN RIPKEN JR.
(Cal)

Born August 24, 1960, at Havre de Grace, Md.
Height, 6.04. Weight, 200.
Throws and bats righthanded.
Son of Cal Ripken, Baltimore Orioles' coach, and nephew of Bill Ripken,
former outfielder in Brooklyn Dodgers' organization.

Tied for Appalachian League lead in double plays by shortstops with 31 in 1978.
Tied for Southern League lead in sacrifice flies with 9 in 1980.
Led Southern League second basemen in putouts with 119, in assists with 268, in double plays with 34 and in fielding average with .933 in 1980.

Year	Club	League	Pos.	G.	AB.	R.	H.	2B.	3B.	HR.	RBI.	B.A.	PO.	A.	E.	F.A.
1978—Bluefield	Appal.	SS	63	239	27	63	7	1	0	24	.264	∗92	204	∗33	.900
1979—Miami	Fla. St.	3-S-2	105	393	51	119	∗28	1	5	54	.303	149	260	30	.932
1979—Charlotte	South.	3B	17	61	6	11	0	1	3	8	.180	13	26	3	.929
1980—Charlotte	South.	2B-SS	●144	522	91	144	28	5	25	78	.276	151	341	35	.934

Selected by Baltimore Orioles' organization in 2nd round of free-agent draft, June 6, 1978.

ALLEN STEVENS RIPLEY

Born October 18, 1952, at Norwood, Mass.
Height, 6.03. Weight, 200.
Throws and bats righthanded.
Hobbies—Fishing and golfing.
Son of Walt Ripley, pitcher in Boston Red Sox organization, 1932-1945.

Year	Club	League	G.	IP.	W.	L.	Pct.	H.	R.	ER.	SO.	BB.	ERA.
1973—Elmira	NYP	14	79	5	6	.455	74	34	0	64	26	2.96
1974—Winston-Salem	Carolina	28	170	10	9	.526	166	87	66	114	73	3.49
1975—Winston-Salem	Carolina	25	∗186	●14	7	.667	150	70	57	120	75	2.76
1975—Bristol	Eastern	1	5	1	0	1.000	7	2	1	3	1	1.80
1976—Bristol	Eastern	21	161	10	10	.500	161	67	58	88	39	3.22
1976—Rhode Island	Int'national	5	39	3	2	.600	40	19	17	33	16	3.92
1977—Pawtucket	Int'national	34	144	15	4	.789	160	77	71	99	47	4.44
1978—Pawtucket	Int'national	11	37	2	2	.500	42	24	23	28	17	5.59
1978—Boston	American	15	73	2	5	.286	92	49	45	26	22	5.55
1979—Pawtucket	Int'national	23	77	7	1	.875	54	13	12	51	28	1.40
1979—Boston†	American	16	65	3	1	.750	77	42	37	34	25	5.12
1980—Phoenix	P. Coast	7	44	5	0	1.000	48	18	12	19	15	2.45
1980—San Francisco	National	23	113	9	10	.474	119	59	52	65	36	4.14
American League Totals		31	138	5	6	.455	169	91	82	60	47	5.35
National League Totals		23	113	9	10	.474	119	59	52	65	36	4.14
Major League Totals		54	251	14	16	.467	288	150	134	125	83	4.80

Signed as free agent by Boston Red Sox' organization, August 17, 1972.
†Traded to San Francisco Giants' organization for a player to be named later, April 5, 1980; deal settled with cash.

JESUS TORRES RIVERA JR.
(Bombo)

Born August 2, 1952, at Ponce, Puerto Rico.
Height, 5.10. Weight, 192.
Throws and bats righthanded.
Hobbies—Dancing and fishing.
Led Florida State League outfielders in double plays with 5 in 1972.

Year	Club	League	Pos.	G.	AB.	R.	H.	2B.	3B.	HR.	RBI.	B.A.	PO.	A.	E.	F.A.
1970—Brad'ton Expos	Gulf C.	OF	39	125	25	30	8	1	4	20	.240	45	5	7	.877
1971—Quebec City	East.	OF	37	83	7	15	3	0	1	10	.181	35	1	3	.923
1971—Jamestown	NYP	OF-1B	55	210	32	52	6	4	3	22	.248	102	2	4	.963
1972—W. Palm Beach	Fla. St.	OF	125	439	44	114	14	12	3	60	.260	186	7	8	.960
1973—Quebec City	East.	OF-3B	121	408	48	99	14	5	6	45	.243	113	84	28	.876
1974—Quebec City	East.	O-3-C	108	352	47	102	12	1	7	42	.290	180	37	11	.952
1975—Memphis†	Int.	OF	40	140	22	41	5	1	9	22	.293	57	7	4	.941
1975—Montreal	Nat.	OF	5	9	1	1	0	0	0	0	.111	8	0	1	.889
1976—Montreal	Nat.	OF	68	185	22	51	11	4	2	19	.276	89	7	5	.950
1977—Denver‡§	A.A.	OF	124	441	63	133	18	∗14	17	95	.302	204	14	7	.969
1978—Minnesota	Amer.	OF	101	251	35	68	8	2	3	23	.271	162	5	3	.982
1979—Minnesota	Amer.	OF	112	263	37	74	13	5	2	31	.281	169	12	2	.989
1980—Minnesota x	Amer.	OF	44	113	13	25	7	0	3	10	.221	58	1	5	.922
National League Totals		73	194	23	52	11	4	2	19	.268	97	7	6	.945
American League Totals		257	627	85	167	28	7	8	64	.266	389	18	10	.976
Major League Totals		330	821	108	219	39	11	10	83	.267	486	25	16	.970

Signed as free agent by Montreal Expos' organization, June 22, 1970.
†On disabled list, June 10 to August 27, 1975.
‡On disabled list, June 25 to July 6, 1977.
§Sold to Minnesota Twins, October 25, 1977.
xOn disabled list, April 29 to July 14, 1980.

DID YOU KNOW—
That Sixto Lezcano has hit grand slams on Opening Day twice in his career? Then with the Brewers, he hit one in 1978 and one in 1980.

JOHN MILTON RIVERS
(Mickey)

Born October 31, 1948, at Miami, Fla.
Height, 5.10. Weight, 162.
Throws and bats lefthanded.
Attended Miami-Dade (North) Community College, Miami, Fla.

Tied major league record for most seasons, consecutive, leading major leagues, fewest grounded into double plays (minimum 500 at bats) (2), 1977.

Major League stolen bases: 1970 (1), 1971 (13), 1972 (4), 1973 (8), 1974 (30), 1975 (70), 1976 (43), 1977 (22), 1978 (25), 1979 (10), 1980 (18). Total—244.

Led American League in stolen bases with 70 in 1975.
Led Pacific Coast League in stolen bases with 47 in 1973.
Led Pioneer League batters in bases on balls with 66 in 1969.
Tied for Pacific Coast League lead in double plays by outfielders with 3 in 1971.
Named Most Outstanding Player in Texas League, 1970.
Named as outfielder on THE SPORTING NEWS American League All-Star Team, 1976.

Year	Club	League	Pos.	G.	AB.	R.	H.	2B.	3B.	HR.	RBI.	B.A.	PO.	A.	E.	F.A.
1969—Magic Valley†	....Pion.		OF	67	225	75	69	13	6	7	41	.307	67	8	*11	.872
1970—El Paso	..........Texas		OF	114	449	*99	•154	25	10	14	56	*.343	235	13	12	.954
1970—California	..........Amer.		OF	17	25	6	8	2	0	0	3	.320	10	0	0	1.000
1971—Salt Lake City	...P.C.		OF	72	292	54	94	13	11	10	47	.322	153	11	8	.953
1971—California	..........Amer.		OF	78	268	31	71	12	2	1	12	.265	159	5	4	.976
1972—Salt Lake City	...P.C.		OF	59	241	50	81	14	3	3	16	.336	129	3	5	.964
1972—California	..........Amer.		OF	58	159	18	34	6	2	0	7	.214	105	0	2	.981
1973—Salt Lake City	...P.C.		OF	141	556	113	*187	18	14	9	71	.336	*327	12	7	.980
1973—California	..........Amer.		OF	30	129	26	45	6	4	0	16	.349	60	0	6	.909
1974—California‡	........Amer.		OF	118	466	69	133	19	*11	3	31	.285	309	9	2	.994
1975—California§	........Amer.		OF	155	616	70	175	17	•13	1	53	.284	371	13	9	.977
1976—New York	..........Amer.		OF	137	590	95	184	31	8	8	67	.312	407	6	6	.986
1977—New York	..........Amer.		OF	138	565	79	184	18	5	12	69	.326	380	11	7	.982
1978—New York x	......Amer.		OF	141	559	78	148	25	8	11	48	.265	384	8	8	.980
1979—N. Y. yz-Tex	......Amer.		OF	132	533	72	156	27	8	9	50	.293	300	8	7	.978
1980—Texas	..........Amer.		OF	147	630	96	210	32	6	7	60	.333	342	*19	8	.978
Major League Totals				1151	4540	640	1348	195	67	52	416	.297	2827	79	59	.980

Selected by Chicago White Sox' organization in 1st round (13th player selected) of free-agent draft, January 27, 1968.

Selected by New York Mets' organization in secondary phase of free-agent draft, June 7, 1968.

Selected by Washington Senators' organization in secondary phase of free-agent draft, February 1, 1969.

Selected by Atlanta Braves' organization in secondary phase of free-agent draft, June 5, 1969.

†Traded with Pitcher Clint Compton by Atlanta Braves to California Angels for Pitchers Hoyt Wilhelm and Bob Priddy, September 8, 1969.

‡On disabled list, August 21 through remainder of season.

§Traded with Pitcher Ed Figueroa to New York Yankees for Outfielder Bobby Bonds, December 11, 1975.

xOn supplemental disabled list, June 17 to July 2, 1978.

yOn disabled list, June 30 to July 20, 1979.

zTraded with three players to be named later to Texas Rangers for Outfielder Oscar Gamble, infielder Amos Lewis and two players to be named later, August 1, 1979; Yankees sent Pitchers Bob Polinsky, Neal Mersch and Mark Softy to Rangers for Pitchers Gene Nelson and Ray Fontenot to complete deal, October 8, 1979.

CHAMPIONSHIP SERIES RECORD

Established Championship Series record for highest batting average, total Series, 10 or more games and 30 or more at-bats (.386).

Tied Championship Series records for most consecutive hits, one Series (5), 1976; most hits, two consecutive games, one Series (6), October 8 and 9, 1977.

Tied American League Championship Series records for most consecutive hits, total Series (5); most hits, two consecutive Series (14), 1977 and 1978; most runs, game (3), October 14, 1976; most at bats, five-game Series (23), 1976 and 1977.

Year	Club	League	Pos.	G.	AB.	R.	H.	2B.	3B.	HR.	RBI.	B.A.	PO.	A.	E.	F.A.
1976—New York	..........Amer.		OF	5	23	5	8	0	1	0	0	.348	11	0	0	1.000
1977—New York	..........Amer.		OF	5	23	5	9	2	0	0	2	.391	19	0	0	1.000
1978—New York	........Amer.		OF	4	11	0	5	0	0	0	0	.455	8	1	0	1.000
Championship Series Totals				14	57	10	22	2	1	0	2	.386	38	1	0	1.000

WORLD SERIES RECORD

Established World Series records for highest fielding average by outfielder, six-game Series (1.000 with 25 chances), 1977 (most chances accepted for any length Series); most putouts by outfielder, six-game Series (24), 1977; most chances accepted by outfielder, six-game Series (25), 1977.

Tied World Series record for most at bats, extra-inning game, no hits (6), October 11, 1977 (12 innings).

Year	Club	League	Pos.	G.	AB.	R.	H.	2B.	3B.	HR.	RBI.	B.A.	PO.	A.	E.	F.A.
1976—New York	..........Amer.		OF	4	18	1	3	0	0	0	0	.167	14	0	0	1.000
1977—New York	..........Amer.		OF	6	27	1	6	2	0	1	1	.222	24	1	0	1.000
1978—New York	........Amer.		OF-PH	5	18	2	6	0	0	0	1	.333	7	0	0	1.000
World Series Totals				15	63	4	15	2	0	0	2	.238	45	1	0	1.000

ALL-STAR GAME RECORD

Year	League	Pos.	AB.	R.	H.	2B.	3B.	HR.	RBI.	B.A.	PO.	A.	E.	F.A.
1976—American		OF	2	0	1	0	0	0	0	.500	2	0	0	1.000

BRUCE DUANE ROBBINS

Born September 10, 1959, at Portland, Ind.
Height, 6.02. Weight, 190.
Throws and bats lefthanded.
Brother of LeRoy Robbins, outfielder in Oakland A's organization.

Year Club	League	G.	IP.	W.	L.	Pct.	H.	R.	ER.	SO.	BB.	ERA.
1977–Bristol	Ap'lachian	2	3	0	2	.000	5	5	4	2	2	12.00
1978–Lakeland	Florida St.	16	79	3	5	.375	92	43	33	34	50	3.76
1978–Bristol	Ap'lachian	12	65	3	5	.375	57	36	29	39	48	4.02
1979–Lakeland	Florida St.	7	49	1	4	.200	46	18	18	31	18	3.31
1979–Montgomery	Southern	13	88	7	1	.875	80	34	29	86	37	2.97
1979–Detroit	American	10	46	3	3	.500	45	21	20	22	21	3.91
1980–Evansville	Am. Assoc.	9	58	2	6	.250	59	34	27	44	22	4.19
1980–Detroit	American	15	52	4	2	.667	60	40	38	23	28	6.58
Major League Totals		25	98	7	5	.583	105	61	58	45	49	5.33

Selected by Detroit Tigers' organization in 14th round of free-agent draft, June 7, 1977.

BERTRAND ROLAND ROBERGE
(Bert)

Born October 3, 1954, at Lewiston, Me.
Height, 6.04. Weight, 190.
Throws and bats righthanded.
Attended University of Maine, Orono, Me.;
received Bachelor of Science degree in Zoology.

Year Club	League	G.	IP.	W.	L.	Pct.	H.	R.	ER.	SO.	BB.	ERA.
1976–Covington†	Ap'lachian	14	36	2	2	.500	33	21	13	40	12	3.25
1976–Memphis	Int'national	2	10	0	0	.000	11	5	3	8	3	2.70
1977–Columbus	Southern	6	7	0	0	.000	13	5	5	9	3	6.43
1977–Cocoa	Florida St.	33	60	4	5	.444	54	24	17	35	26	2.55
1978–Columbus	Southern	21	32	0	3	.000	37	15	12	24	10	3.38
1979–Columbus	Southern	13	88	7	1	.875	80	34	29	86	37	2.97
1979–Houston‡	National	26	32	3	0	1.000	20	6	6	13	17	1.69
1980–Tucson	P. Coast	34	49	5	3	.625	44	28	26	47	28	4.78
1980–Houston	National	14	24	2	0	1.000	24	16	16	9	10	6.00
Major League Totals		40	56	5	0	1.000	44	22	22	22	27	3.54

Selected by Houston Astros' organization in 17th round of free-agent draft, June 8, 1976.
†Appeared in one game as outfielder.
‡On disabled list, August 16 to September 6, 1979.

DAVID ARTHUR ROBERTS
(Dave)

Born September 11, 1944, at Gallipolis, O.
Height, 6.03. Weight, 192.
Throws and bats lefthanded.
Hobbies–Golf and fishing.

Led Southern League in complete games with 14 and shutouts with 4 in 1966.
Named International League Pitcher of the Year, 1968.

Year Club	League	G.	IP.	W.	L.	Pct.	H.	R.	ER.	SO.	BB.	ERA.
1963–Spartanburg†	W. Car.	18	126	9	3	.750	95	32	25	121	18	*1.79
1964–Asheville	Southern	11	59	3	3	.500	64	33	30	44	28	4.58
1964–Kinston	Carolina	16	100	5	7	.417	102	47	40	109	34	3.60
1965–Columbus	Int'national	4	16	0	2	.000	20	18	18	12	10	10.13
1965–Asheville	Southern	24	132	9	8	.529	108	60	43	114	63	2.93
1966–Asheville‡	Southern	31	190	14	5	.737	153	63	55	157	60	*2.61
1967–Columbus§	Int'national	10	62	5	1	.833	55	18	15	37	16	2.18
1968–Columbus x	Int'national	27	193	*18	5	*.783	189	74	68	133	45	3.17
1969–Elmira	Eastern	15	121	7	5	.583	117	55	47	76	43	3.50
1969–San Diego	National	22	49	0	3	.000	65	30	26	19	19	4.78
1970–San Diego	National	43	182	8	14	.364	182	80	77	102	43	3.81
1971–San Diego y	National	37	270	14	17	.452	238	79	63	135	61	2.10
1972–Houston	National	35	192	12	7	.632	227	100	96	111	57	4.50
1973–Houston	National	39	249	17	11	.607	264	92	79	119	62	2.86
1974–Houston	National	34	204	10	12	.455	216	83	77	72	65	3.40
1975–Houston z	National	32	198	8	14	.364	182	98	94	101	73	4.27
1976–Detroit	American	36	252	16	17	.485	254	122	112	79	63	4.00
1977–Detroit a	American	22	129	4	10	.286	143	88	74	46	41	5.16
1977–Chicago	National	17	53	1	1	.500	55	22	19	23	12	3.23
1978–Chicago bc	National	35	142	6	8	.429	159	87	83	54	56	5.26
1979–San Fran. d-Pittsburgh	National	47	81	5	4	.556	83	33	26	38	30	2.89
1980–Pittsburgh e	National	2	2	0	1	.000	2	1	1	1	1	4.50
1980–Seattle f	American	37	80	2	3	.400	86	46	39	47	27	4.39
National League Totals		343	1622	81	92	.468	1679	705	641	775	479	3.56
American League Totals		95	461	22	30	.423	483	256	225	172	131	4.39
Major League Totals		438	2083	103	122	.458	2162	961	866	947	610	3.74

Signed as free agent by Philadelphia Phillies' organization, June 11, 1963.
†Released on waivers by Philadelphia Phillies to Pittsburgh Pirates, April 6, 1964.

‡Drafted by Kansas City Athletics from Columbus (Pittsburgh Pirates' organization), November 28, 1966; returned to Columbus, April 7, 1967.

§On disabled list for three months of season.

xRecalled by Pittsburgh Pirates; selected by San Diego Padres from Pittsburgh in expansion draft, October 14, 1968.

yTraded to Houston Astros for Infielder Derrel Thomas and Pitchers Bill Greif and Mark Schaeffer, December 3, 1971.

zTraded with Catcher Milt May and Pitcher Jim Crawford to Detroit Tigers for Outfielder Leon Roberts, Catcher Terry Humphrey and Pitchers Gene Pentz and Mark Lemongello, December 6, 1975.

aTraded to Chicago Cubs for cash and a player to be named later, July 30, 1977.

bOn disabled list, March 25 to April 19, 1978.

cGranted free agency, November 2, 1978; signed by San Francisco Giants, February 22, 1979.

dTraded with Third Basemen Bill Madlock and Lenny Randle to Pittsburgh Pirates for pitchers Fred Breining, Al Holland and Eddie Whitson, June 28, 1979.

eSold to Seattle Mariners, April 24, 1980.

fGranted free agency, November 4, 1980; signed by New York Mets, January 5, 1981.

CHAMPIONSHIP SERIES RECORD

Year Club	League	G.	IP.	W.	L.	Pct.	H.	R.	ER.	SO.	BB.	ERA.
1979–Pittsburgh	National	1	0	0	0	.000	0	0	0	0	1	0.00

DAVID WAYNE ROBERTS
(Dave)

Born February 17, 1951, at Lebanon, Ore.
Height, 6.03. Weight, 205.
Throws and bats righthanded.
Hobbies—Hunting, fishing, scuba diving, water skiing and sandlot football.
Attended University of Oregon, Eugene, Ore., and San Diego State University, San Diego, Calif.
Named College Player of the Year by THE SPORTING NEWS, 1972.

Year Club	League	Pos.	G.	AB.	R.	H.	2B.	3B.	HR.	RBI.	B.A.	PO.	A.	E.	F.A.
1972–San Diego	Nat.	3-2-S-C	100	418	38	102	17	0	5	33	.244	92	198	21	.932
1973–Hawaii	P.C.	3B-2B	22	80	14	30	5	2	1	7	.375	13	37	2	.962
1973–San Diego	Nat.	3B-2B	127	479	56	137	20	3	21	64	.286	92	276	24	.939
1974–San Diego	Nat.	3-S-O	113	318	26	53	10	1	5	18	.167	88	180	13	.954
1975–Hawaii	P.C.	2-3-S	121	442	60	116	31	3	12	71	.262	205	314	20	.963
1975–San Diego	Nat.	3B-2B	33	113	7	32	2	0	2	12	.283	37	68	8	.929
1976–Hawaii†	P.C.	C-1-2	106	366	54	91	17	1	10	53	.249	579	62	16	.976
1977–San Diego	Nat.	C-2-3-S	82	186	15	41	14	1	1	23	.220	256	30	7	.976
1978–Hawaii	P.C.	C-3B-1B	36	120	21	32	8	1	5	31	.267	163	15	4	.978
1978–San Diego‡§	Nat.	C-1B-OF	54	97	7	21	4	1	1	7	.216	150	14	3	.982
1979–Texas x	Amer.	C-O-2-3-1	44	84	12	22	2	1	3	14	.262	82	30	1	.991
1979–Tucson	P. C.	1B	9	34	4	13	4	0	2	10	.382	9	11	16	1.000
1980–Texas y	Amer.	C-O-INF	101	235	27	56	4	0	10	30	.238	138	100	11	.956
National League Totals			509	1611	149	386	67	6	35	157	.240	715	766	76	.951
American League Totals			145	319	39	78	6	1	13	44	.245	220	130	12	.967
Major League Totals			654	1930	188	464	73	7	48	201	.240	935	896	88	.954

Selected by San Diego Padres' organization in 1st round (first player selected) of free-agent draft, June 6, 1972.

†Sold to Toronto Blue Jays, October 22, 1976. Traded to San Diego Padres for Pitcher Jerry Johnson, February 17, 1977.

‡On disabled list, September 18 to October 25, 1978.

§Traded with Outfielder Oscar Gamble to Texas Rangers for Third Baseman Kurt Bevacqua, First Baseman Mike Hargrove, Catcher Bill Fahey and cash estimated at $300,000, October 25, 1978.

xOn disabled list, August 11 to September 1, 1979.

yGranted free agency, November 4, 1980; signed by Houston Astros, December 30, 1980.

LEON KAUFFMAN ROBERTS

Born January 22, 1951, at Vicksburg, Mich.
Height, 6.03. Weight, 200.
Throws and bats righthanded.
Hobbies—Golf and swimming.
Attended University of Michigan, Ann Arbor, Mich.
Brother of Bill Roberts, outfielder in Houston Astros' organization.

Year Club	League	Pos.	G.	AB.	R.	H.	2B.	3B.	HR.	RBI.	B.A.	PO.	A.	E.	F.A.
1972–Lakeland	Fla. St.	OF	74	254	36	78	14	3	5	52	.307	162	8	5	.971
1972–Rocky Mount	Carol.	OF	6	22	4	6	1	0	0	2	.273	15	0	0	1.000
1973–Montgomery	South.	OF	133	489	87	144	●30	1	14	70	.294	276	10	6	.979
1974–Evansville	A.A.	OF	132	481	74	137	31	4	12	79	.285	264	9	9	.968
1974–Detroit	Amer.	OF	17	63	5	17	3	2	0	7	.270	25	0	2	.926
1975–Detroit†	Amer.	OF	129	447	51	115	17	5	10	38	.257	268	10	5	.982
1976–Houston	Nat.	OF	87	235	31	68	11	2	7	33	.289	99	1	2	.980
1977–Charleston	Int.	OF-1B	73	264	39	79	20	2	2	34	.299	266	14	2	.993
1977–Houston‡	Nat.	OF	19	27	1	2	0	0	0	2	.074	3	2	0	1.000
1978–Seattle	Amer.	OF	134	472	78	142	21	7	22	92	.301	296	10	8	.975
1979–Seattle§	Amer.	OF	140	450	61	122	24	6	15	54	.271	286	6	5	.983
1980–Seattle§	Amer.	OF	119	374	48	94	18	3	10	33	.251	238	6	4	.984
American League Totals			539	1806	243	490	83	23	57	224	.271	1113	32	24	.979
National League Totals			106	262	32	70	11	2	7	35	.267	102	3	2	.981
Major League Totals			645	2068	275	560	94	25	64	259	.271	1215	35	26	.980

Selected by Detroit Tigers' organization in 10th round of free-agent draft, June 6, 1972.

†Traded with Catcher Terry Humphrey and Pitchers Gene Pentz and Mark Lemongello to Houston Astros for Catcher Milt May and Pitchers Jim Crawford and Dave Roberts, December 6, 1975.

‡Traded to Seattle Mariners for Infielder Jimmy Sexton, December 5, 1977.

§Traded with Catcher Larry Cox, Pitcher Rick Honeycutt, Outfielder Willie Horton and Shortstop Mario Mendoza to Texas Rangers for Pitchers Brian Allard, Ken Clay, Steve Finch and Jerry Gleaton, Outfielder Richie Zisk and Shortstop Rick Auerbach, December 12, 1980.

BRUCE PHILIP ROBINSON

Born April 16, 1954, at LaJolla, California.
Height, 6.02. Weight, 194.
Throws right and bats lefthanded.
Hobbies—Racquetball, guitar and water skiing.
Attended Stanford University, Stanford, Calif.; received Bachelor of Arts Degree in Economics.
Brother of David Robinson, outfielder with San Diego Padres, 1970 and 1971.

Year Club	League	Pos.	G.	AB.	R.	H.	2B.	3B.	HR.	RBI.	B.A.	PO.	A.	E.	F.A.
1975—Modesto ....Calif.		C-1B	24	84	11	21	4	0	5	19	.250	106	11	2	.983
1976—Chattanooga†.....South.		C	76	230	23	46	3	2	5	29	.200	320	46	10	.973
1977—Chattanooga ......South.		C	64	193	14	53	9	3	3	24	.275	313	57	6	.984
1977—San Jose............P. C.		C-1-O	53	179	23	41	10	1	5	21	.229	242	29	11	.960
1978—Vancouver ....P. C.		C-3B-OF	102	365	59	109	17	3	10	73	.299	393	58	13	.972
1978—Oakland‡ ....Amer.		C	28	84	5	21	3	1	0	8	.250	150	16	6	.965
1979—Columbus ....Int.		C-1B	102	316	37	79	10	2	9	45	.250	454	28	7	.986
1979—New York ....Amer.		C	6	12	0	2	0	0	0	2	.167	33	0	2	.943
1980—Columbus ....Int.		C	104	334	40	80	14	1	12	48	.240	★532	56	8	.987
1980—New York ....Amer.		C	4	5	0	0	0	0	0	0	.000	5	0	0	1.000
Major League Totals......................			38	101	5	23	3	1	0	10	.228	188	16	8	.962

Selected by Chicago White Sox' organization in 4th round of free-agent draft, June 6, 1972.

Selected by Oakland A's organization in 1st round (21st player selected) of free-agent draft, June 4, 1975.

†On disabled list, May 6 to May 25, 1976.

‡Sold to New York Yankees for $400,000, February 3, 1979.

DEWEY EVERETT ROBINSON

Born April 28, 1955, at Evanston, Ill.
Height, 6.00. Weight, 180.
Throws and bats righthanded.
Attended Southern Illinois University, Carbondale, Ill.; received Bachelor of Science degree in Finance.
Led Midwest League in saves with 17 in 1978.

Year Club	League	G.	IP.	W.	L.	Pct.	H.	R.	ER.	SO.	BB.	ERA.
1977—Appleton ....Midwest		10	15	0	0	.000	10	5	4	19	7	2.40
1977—Knoxville ....Southern		10	21	0	3	.000	23	14	13	23	11	5.57
1978—Appleton ....Midwest		★50	89	10	3	.769	55	22	17	121	40	1.72
1979—Iowa ....Am. Assoc.		49	86	★13	7	.650	69	32	28	76	43	2.93
1979—Chicago ....American		11	14	0	1	.000	11	12	10	5	9	6.43
1980—Iowa ....Am. Assoc.		40	73	5	5	.500	60	26	23	58	30	2.84
1980—Chicago ....American		15	35	1	1	.500	26	13	12	28	16	3.09
Major League Totals.................................		26	49	1	2	.333	37	25	22	33	25	4.04

Selected by Chicago White Sox' organization in 19th round of free-agent draft, June 7, 1977.

DON ALLEN ROBINSON

Born June 8, 1957, at Ashland, Ky.
Height, 6.04. Weight, 231.
Throws and bats righthanded.
Led Western Carolinas League in complete games with 11 in 1976.
Named National League Rookie Pitcher of the Year by THE SPORTING NEWS, 1978.

Year Club	League	G.	IP.	W.	L.	Pct.	H.	R.	ER.	SO.	BB.	ERA.
1975—Bradenton Pirates ....G. Coast		10	66	2	3	.400	51	23	18	70	31	2.45
1976—Charleston ....W. Carol.		25	★172	12	9	.571	146	79	62	132	64	3.24
1977—Shreveport ....Texas		18	112	7	6	.538	113	58	51	103	41	4.06
1977—Columbus† ....Int'national		1	5	1	0	1.000	7	0	0	3	1	0.00
1978—Pittsburgh ....National		35	228	14	6	.700	203	98	88	135	57	3.47
1979—Pittsburgh ....National		29	161	8	8	.500	171	74	69	96	52	3.86
1980—Pittsburgh‡ ....National		29	160	7	10	.412	157	74	71	103	45	3.99
Major League Totals.................................		93	549	29	24	.547	531	246	228	334	154	3.74

Selected by Pittsburgh Pirates' organization in 3rd round of free-agent draft, June 4, 1975.

†On disabled list, July 28 to September 6, 1977.

‡On disabled list, March 31 to May 1, 1980.

CHAMPIONSHIP SERIES RECORD

Year Club	League	G.	IP.	W.	L.	Pct.	H.	R.	ER.	SO.	BB.	ERA.
1979—Pittsburgh ....National		2	2	1	0	1.000	0	0	0	3	1	0.00

WORLD SERIES RECORD

Year Club	League	G.	IP.	W.	L.	Pct.	H.	R.	ER.	SO.	BB.	ERA.
1979—Pittsburgh ....National		4	5	1	0	1.000	4	3	3	3	6	5.40

WILLIAM HENRY ROBINSON JR.
(Bill)

Born June 26, 1943, at McKeesport, Pa.
Height, 6.03. Weight, 197.
Throws and bats righthanded.
Hobbies—Fishing, basketball and reading.

Tied National League record for most home runs with bases filled, week (2), July 28 and 30, 1977.
Hit three home runs in one game, vs. San Diego Padres, June 5, 1976 (15 innings).

Year Club	League	Pos.	G.	AB.	R.	H.	2B.	3B.	HR.	RBI.	B.A.	PO.	A.	E.	F.A.
1961—Wellsville ....NYP		OF	67	251	37	60	15	4	2	25	.239	107	7	8	.934
1962—Eau Claire........North.		OF	23	63	3	9	1	1	0	3	.143	27	2	0	1.000
1962—Dublin..............Ga.-Fla.		OF	62	207	46	63	9	4	8	37	.304	71	1	5	.935
1963—Waycross ....Ga.-Fla.		OF	113	418	69	*132	18	*10	10	62	.316	*225	10	8	*.967
1964—Yakima.............Northw.		OF	104	400	81	139	24	5	18	81	*.348	*247	21	10	.964
1965—Atlanta.............Int.		OF	133	407	41	109	17	2	10	37	.268	228	8	12	.952
1966—Richmond ....Int.		OF-2-3	139	509	86	159	30	4	20	79	.312	283	14	2	.993
1966—Atlanta†	Nat.	OF	6	11	1	3	0	1	0	3	.273	4	0	1	.800
1967—New York.........Amer.		OF	116	342	31	67	6	1	7	29	.196	169	10	6	.968
1968—New York.........Amer.		OF	107	342	34	82	16	7	6	40	.240	195	3	3	.985
1969—New York.........Amer.		OF-1B	87	222	23	38	11	2	3	21	.171	103	5	4	.964
1970—Syracuse‡..........Int.		OF-3B	115	372	68	96	20	0	13	43	.258	166	6	2	.989
1971—Tucson§ ............P.C.		OF-3-1	133	495	75	136	33	6	14	81	.275	328	26	6	.983
1972—Eugene ............P.C.		OF	65	240	47	73	9	2	20	66	.304	140	3	3	.979
1972—Philadelphia......Nat.		OF	82	188	19	45	9	1	8	21	.239	109	2	2	.982
1973—Philadelphia x ...Nat.		OF-3B	124	452	62	130	32	1	25	65	.288	234	18	8	.969
1974—Philadelphia y ...Nat.		OF	100	280	32	66	14	1	5	29	.236	162	8	5	.971
1975—Pittsburgh........Nat.		OF	92	200	26	56	12	2	6	33	.280	107	3	1	.991
1976—Pittsburgh........Nat.		O-3-1	122	393	55	119	22	3	21	64	.303	185	53	8	.967
1977—Pittsburgh........Nat.		1-O-3	137	507	74	154	32	1	26	104	.304	58	59	13	.984
1978—Pittsburgh z......Nat.		O-3-1B	136	499	70	123	36	2	14	80	.246	268	51	8	.976
1979—Pittsburgh........Nat.		OF-1-3	148	421	59	111	17	6	24	75	.264	394	29	3	.993
1980—Pittsburgh a......Nat.		1B-OF	100	272	28	78	10	1	12	36	.287	427	22	7	.985
American League Totals..................			310	906	88	187	33	10	16	90	.206	467	18	13	.974
National League Totals....................			1047	3223	426	885	184	19	141	510	.275	2648	245	56	.981
Major League Totals			1357	4129	514	1072	217	29	157	600	.260	3115	263	69	.980

Signed as free agent by Atlanta Braves' organization, June 14, 1961.
†Traded with Pitcher Chi-Chi Olivo (transferred from Richmond to Syracuse) to New York Yankees for Third Baseman Clete Boyer and player to be named later, November 29, 1966.
‡Traded by New York Yankees to Chicago White Sox for Pitcher Barry Moore, December 3, 1970.
§Traded by Chicago White Sox to Philadelphia Phillies for Catcher Jerry Rodriguez, December 13, 1971.
xOn disabled list, June 2 to June 25, 1973.
yTraded to Pittsburgh Pirates for Pitcher Wayne Simpson, April 5, 1975.
zOn supplemental disabled list, May 14 to May 29, 1978.
aOn supplemental disabled list, July 29, 1980; transferred to disabled list, August 18 to August 21, 1980.

PITCHING RECORD

Year Club	League	G.	IP.	W.	L.	Pct.	H.	R.	ER.	SO.	BB.	ERA.
1962—Dublin ....Ga.-Fla.		1	3	0	0	.000	5	6	5	0	1	15.00

CHAMPIONSHIP SERIES RECORD

Year Club	League	Pos.	G.	AB.	R.	H.	2B.	3B.	HR.	RBI.	B.A.	PO.	A.	E.	F.A.
1975—Pittsburgh.........Nat.		PH	2	2	0	0	0	0	0	0	.000	0	0	0	.000
1979—Pittsburgh ....Nat.		OF	3	3	0	0	0	0	0	0	.000	3	0	0	1.000
Championship Series Totals			5	5	0	0	0	0	0	0	.000	3	0	0	1.000

WORLD SERIES RECORD

Year Club	League	Pos.	G.	AB.	R.	H.	2B.	3B.	HR.	RBI.	B.A.	PO.	A.	E.	F.A.
1979—Pittsburgh ....Nat.		OF-PH	7	19	2	5	1	0	0	2	.263	11	1	0	1.000

AURELIO RODRIGUEZ (ITUARTE)

Born December 28, 1947, at Cananea, Sonora, Mexico.
Height, 5.11. Weight, 180.
Throws and bats righthanded.
Brother of Francisco Rodriguez, former shortstop in St. Louis Cardinals' organization
and presently playing in Mexican League with Aquascalientes.

Established American League record for most games played with two clubs, season (159), California (17)—Washington (142), 1970.
Tied American League record for most long hits, inning (2), August 20, 1972 (sixth inning).
Led American League third basemen in double plays with 41 in 1970 and 42 in 1969.
Led Mexican League third basemen in double plays with 35 in 1966.
Named Mexican League Rookie of the Year, 1966.
Named third baseman on THE SPORTING NEWS American League All-Star fielding team, 1976.

Year Club	League	Pos.	G.	AB.	R.	H.	2B.	3B.	HR.	RBI.	B.A.	PO.	A.	E.	F.A.
1965—Fresnillo ....Mex. C		3-O-2	138	552	103	162	26	9	25	104	.293	197	263	31	.937
1965—Jalisco ....Mex.		3B	15	50	5	13	1	1	0	3	.260	7	23	5	.857
1966—Jalisco ....Mex.		*3B-SS	135	480	64	140	17	*16	3	53	.292	*115	*316	*30	.935
1966—Seattle .............P.C.		SS-3B	17	59	6	15	0	2	0	6	.254	23	34	5	.919

Year	Club	League	Pos.	G.	AB.	R.	H.	2B.	3B.	HR.	RBI.	B.A.	PO.	A.	E.	F.A.
1967—El Paso	Texas		3B	79	309	49	101	20	9	11	47	.327	*69	148	6	.973
1967—Seattle	P.C.		3B	51	185	18	57	12	0	2	17	.308	36	79	3	.975
1967—California	Amer.		3B	29	130	14	31	3	1	1	8	.238	19	75	1	.989
1968—California	Amer.		3B-2B	76	223	14	54	10	1	1	16	.242	65	116	15	.923
1968—Seattle	P.C.		S-3B-2B	46	181	21	45	8	0	3	15	.249	65	99	9	.948
1969—California	Amer.		3B	159	561	47	130	17	2	7	49	.232	145	352	•24	.954
1970—Cal.†-Wash.‡	Amer.		*3B-SS	159	610	70	152	33	7	19	83	.249	127	*398	18	.967
1971—Detroit	Amer.		3B-SS	154	604	68	153	30	7	15	39	.253	128	344	23	.954
1972—Detroit	Amer.		*3B-SS	153	601	65	142	23	5	13	56	.236	*150	350	17	.967
1973—Detroit	Amer.		3B-SS	160	555	46	123	27	3	9	58	.222	137	338	14	.971
1974—Detroit	Amer.		3B	159	571	54	127	23	5	5	49	.222	132	389	21	.961
1975—Detroit	Amer.		3B	151	507	47	124	20	6	13	60	.245	136	375	25	.953
1976—Detroit§	Amer.		3B	128	480	40	115	13	2	8	50	.240	120	280	9	*.978
1977—Detroit x	Amer.		3B-SS	96	306	30	67	14	1	10	32	.219	60	222	8	.972
1978—Detroit	Amer.		3B	134	385	40	102	25	2	7	43	.265	79	228	4	*.987
1979—Detroit y	Amer.		3B-1B	106	343	27	87	18	0	5	36	.254	72	211	13	.956
1980—San Diego z	Nat.		3B-SS	89	175	7	35	7	2	2	13	.200	38	130	6	.966
1980—New York	Amer.		3B-2B	52	164	14	36	6	1	3	14	.220	33	89	7	.946
National League Totals				89	175	7	35	7	2	2	13	.200	38	130	6	.966
American League Totals				1716	6040	576	1443	262	43	116	593	.239	1403	3767	199	.963
Major League Totals				1805	6215	583	1478	269	45	118	606	.238	1441	3897	205	.963

Signed as free agent by Fresnillo, January 25, 1965.

†Traded with Outfielder Rick Reichardt to Washington Senators for Third Baseman Ken McMullen, April 26, 1970.

‡Traded with Shortstop Ed Brinkman and Pitchers Joe Coleman and Jim Hannan to Detroit Tigers for Pitcher Denny McLain, Third Baseman Don Wert, Pitcher Norm McRae and Infielder-Outfielder Elliott Maddox, October 9, 1970.

§On disabled list, August 30 to October 4, 1976.

xOn supplemental disabled list, April 27 to May 31, 1977.

yTraded to San Diego Padres for a player to be named later, December 7, 1979; deal settled with reported payment of $200,000.

zSold to New York Yankees, August 4, 1980.

CHAMPIONSHIP SERIES RECORD

Year	Club	League	Pos.	G.	AB.	R.	H.	2B.	3B.	HR.	RBI.	B.A.	PO.	A.	E.	F.A.
1972—Detroit	Amer.		3B	5	16	0	0	0	0	0	0	.000	2	14	1	.941
1980—New York	Amer.		3B	2	6	0	2	1	0	0	0	.333	2	2	0	1.000
Championship Series Totals				7	22	0	2	1	0	0	0	.091	4	16	1	.952

JOSE RODRIGUEZ

Born February 25, 1959, at Santiago, Dominican Republic.
Height, 6.01. Weight, 173.
Throws and bats righthanded.
Tied for Western Carolinas League lead in double plays by outfielders with 6 in 1980.

Year	Club	League	Pos.	G.	AB.	R.	H.	2B.	3B.	HR.	RBI.	B.A.	PO.	A.	E.	F.A.
1977—Brad. Pirates	G.C.		3B-OF	39	139	21	49	11	4	1	17	.353	35	70	12	.897
1977—Charleston	W. Car.		3B	16	45	3	10	1	0	1	4	.222	14	15	5	.853
1978—Charleston	W. Car.		3B-OF	49	143	21	32	5	1	1	15	.224	38	34	4	.947
1978—Niagara Falls	NYP		OF	7	24	3	4	1	1	0	4	.167	12	0	2	.857
1978—Brad. Pirates	G.C.		O-3-S	32	112	17	40	8	4	1	19	.357	39	34	11	.869
1979—Shelby	W. Car.		OF-3B	117	357	48	85	12	4	5	29	.238	208	40	19	.929
1980—Salem	Carol.		OF	126	459	68	132	24	12	13	75	.288	241	*20	9	.967

Signed as free agent by Pittsburgh Pirates' organization, September 21, 1976.

GARY STEVEN ROENICKE

Name pronounced Reh-NICK-ee.

Born December 5, 1954, at Covina, Calif.
Height, 6.03. Weight, 200.
Throws and bats righthanded.
Hobbies—Water skiing and fishing.
Attended California Poly State University, Pomona, Calif., Whittier College, Whittier, Calif., and University of California at Los Angeles, Los Angeles, Calif.
Brother of Ron Roenicke, outfielder in Los Angeles Dodgers' organization.

Tied for Florida State League lead in double plays by third basemen with 32 in 1974.
Named Eastern League Most Valuable Player, 1975.

Year	Club	League	Pos.	G.	AB.	R.	H.	2B.	3B.	HR.	RBI.	B.A.	PO.	A.	E.	F.A.
1973—Jamestown	NYP		3B	68	255	48	76	17	6	3	40	.298	*71	92	11	*.937
1974—W. Palm Beach	Fla. St.		3-O-1	131	470	68	130	24	0	14	*82	.277	152	216	31	.922
1974—Quebec City	East.		3B	1	3	0	1	0	0	0	0	.333	1	2	0	1.000
1975—Quebec City	East.		OF	131	466	67	133	23	0	14	*74	.285		*22	10	.961
1976—Denver	A. A.		OF	77	252	56	73	11	5	12	44	.290	110	9	5	.960
1976—Montreal	Nat.		OF	29	90	9	20	3	1	2	5	.222	39	3	2	.955
1977—Denver†	A. A.		O-3-1	124	448	87	144	31	4	11	72	.321	174	113	17	.944
1978—Rochester	Int.		O-1-3	98	329	49	101	15	1	13	64	.307	219	25	2	.992
1978—Baltimore	Amer.		OF	27	58	5	15	3	0	3	15	.259	22	1	0	1.000

Year Club	League	Pos.	G.	AB.	R.	H.	2B.	3B.	HR.	RBI.	B.A.	PO.	A.	E.	F.A.
1979—Baltimore ....Amer.		OF	133	376	60	98	16	1	25	64	.261	246	10	5	.981
1980—Baltimore‡........Amer.		OF	118	297	40	71	13	0	10	28	.239	197	8	0	★1.000
American League Totals			278	731	105	184	32	1	38	107	.252	465	19	5	.990
National League Totals			29	90	9	20	3	1	2	5	.222	39	3	2	.955
Major League Totals......................			307	821	114	204	35	2	40	112	.248	504	22	7	.987

Selected by Montreal Expos' organization in 1st round (eighth player selected) of free-agent draft, June 5, 1973.

†Traded with Pitchers Joe Kerrigan and Don Stanhouse to Baltimore Orioles for Pitchers Rudy May, Randy Miller and Bryn Smith, December 7, 1977.

‡On disabled list, June 10 to July 15, 1980.

CHAMPIONSHIP SERIES RECORD

Year Club	League	Pos.	G.	AB.	R.	H.	2B.	3B.	HR.	RBI.	B.A.	PO.	A.	E.	F.A.
1979—Baltimore ....Amer.		OF-PH	2	5	1	1	0	0	0	1	.200	3	1	0	1.000

WORLD SERIES RECORD

Year Club	League	Pos.	G.	AB.	R.	H.	2B.	3B.	HR.	RBI.	B.A.	PO.	A.	E.	F.A.
1979—Baltimore ....Amer.		OF-PH	6	16	1	2	1	0	0	0	.125	14	1	0	1.000

RONALD JON ROENICKE

Name pronounced Reh-NICK-ee

(Ron)

Born August 19, 1956, at Covina, Calif.
Height, 6.00. Weight, 180.
Throws left and bats left and righthanded.
Attended Mount San Antonio College, Walnut, Calif., and
University of California at Los Angeles, Los Angeles, Calif.
Brother of Gary Roenicke, outfielder with Baltimore Orioles.

Led Texas League outfielders in fielding percentage with .993 in 1979.

Year Club	League	Pos.	G.	AB.	R.	H.	2B.	3B.	HR.	RBI.	B.A.	PO.	A.	E.	F.A.
1977—Clinton ....Midw.		OF-1B	76	250	35	64	12	0	5	25	.256	253	7	4	.985
1978—Lodi† ....Calif.		OF	61	215	61	78	13	5	9	51	.363	100	8	6	.947
1978—San Antonio ......Texas		OF	30	109	16	26	2	2	1	11	.239	51	4	2	.965
1979—San Antonio ......Texas		OF-1B	130	464	82	140	24	6	13	69	.302	426	18	4	.991
1980—Albuquerque‡....P.C.		OF-1B	77	270	60	80	18	3	7	47	.296	167	9	8	.957

Selected by Oakland A's organization in 7th round of free-agent draft, June 5, 1974.
Selected by Detroit Tigers' organization in secondary phase of free-agent draft, January 7, 1976.
Selected by Atlanta Braves' organization in secondary phase of free-agent draft, June 8, 1976.
Selected by Los Angeles Dodgers' organization in secondary phase of free agent draft, June 7, 1977.
†On disabled list, June 11 to July 17, 1978.
‡On disabled list, July 1 to August 27, 1980.

STEPHEN DOUGLAS ROGERS

(Steve)

Born October 26, 1949, at Jefferson City, Mo.
Height, 6.01. Weight, 175.
Throws and bats righthanded.
Hobbies—Golf and collecting coins, stamps and Indian arrowheads.
Attended Tulsa University, Tulsa, Okla.; received Bachelor of Science
degree in Petroleum Engineering.

Established major league record for fewest complete games for leader in complete games (14), 1980.
Named National League Rookie Pitcher of the Year by THE SPORTING NEWS, 1973.
Led National League in complete games with 14 in 1980.
Tied for National League lead in shutouts with 5 in 1979.

Year Club	League	G.	IP.	W.	L.	Pct.	H.	R.	ER.	SO.	BB.	ERA.
1971—Winnipeg ....Int'national		15	102	3	10	.231	109	51	45	67	40	3.97
1972—Peninsula† ....Int'national		13	64	2	6	.250	75	32	29	39	25	4.08
1973—Quebec City ....Eastern		11	77	4	5	.444	61	29	23	64	33	2.69
1973—Peninsula...........................Int'national		4	29	3	1	.750	18	6	6	22	8	1.86
1973—Montreal............................National		17	134	10	5	.667	93	28	23	64	49	1.54
1974—Montreal............................National		38	254	15	●22	.405	255	★139	★126	154	80	4.46
1975—Montreal............................National		35	252	11	12	.478	248	104	92	137	88	3.29
1976—Montreal‡ ....National		33	230	7	17	.292	212	93	82	150	69	3.21
1977—Montreal............................National		40	302	17	16	.515	272	122	104	206	81	3.10
1978—Montreal............................National		30	219	13	10	.565	186	64	60	126	64	2.47
1979—Montreal............................National		37	249	13	12	.520	232	97	83	143	78	3.00
1980—Montreal............................National		37	281	16	11	.593	247	101	93	147	85	2.98
Major League Totals		267	1921	102	105	.493	1745	748	663	1127	594	3.11

Selected by New York Yankees' organization in 60th round of free-agent draft, June 6, 1967.
Selected by Montreal Expos' organization in secondary phase of free-agent draft, June 8, 1971.
†On temporary inactive list, April 14 to June 9, 1972.
‡On disabled list, May 26 to June 28, 1976.

Year League	IP.	W.	L.	Pct.	H.	R.	ER.	SO.	BB.	ERA.
1978—National	2	0	0	.000	2	0	0	2	0	0.00
1979—National	2	0	0	.000	0	0	0	2	0	0.00
All-Star Game Totals	4	0	0	.000	2	0	0	4	0	0.00

Member of National League All-Star Team in 1974 game; did not play.

EDGARDO ROMERO
(Ed)

Born December 9, 1957, at Santurce, Puerto Rico.
Height, 5.11. Weight, 150.
Throws and bats righthanded.

Led Midwest League shortstops in total chances with 647 and in double plays with 64 in 1976.
Led Pacific Coast League shortstops in double plays with 97 in 1979.

Year—Club	League	Pos.	G.	AB.	R.	H.	2B.	3B.	HR.	RBI.	B.A.	PO.	A.	E.	F.A.
1976—Burlington	Midwest	SS	●129	462	58	101	23	1	1	32	.219	187	★419	41	.937
1977—Holyoke	East.	SS	121	457	63	118	19	6	1	38	.258	203	372	41	.933
1977—Milwaukee	Amer.	SS	10	25	4	7	1	0	0	2	.280	9	24	1	.971
1978—Spokane	P. C.	SS-3B	129	440	73	123	27	2	4	52	.280	221	349	32	.947
1979—Vancouver	P. C.	SS	139	515	65	134	26	6	0	39	.260	215	★414	26	.960
1980—Vancouver	P. C.	SS-2B	50	172	19	47	7	1	0	16	.273	72	153	6	.974
1980—Milwaukee	Amer.	S-2-3	42	104	20	27	7	0	1	10	.260	60	102	12	.931
Major League Totals			52	129	24	34	8	0	1	12	.264	69	126	13	.938

Signed as free agent by Milwaukee Brewers' organization, November 14, 1975.

ENRIQUE ROMO (NAVARRO)

Born July 15, 1947, at Santa Rosalia, Baja Calif., Mexico.
Height, 5.11. Weight, 185.
Throws and bats righthanded.
Brother of Vicente Romo, former pitcher with Cleveland Indians and Boston
Red Sox organization, and now pitcher with Cordoba in Mexican League.

Major league saves: 1977 (16), 1978 (10), 1979 (5), 1980 (11). Total—42.

Year—Club	League	G.	IP.	W.	L.	Pct.	H.	R.	ER.	SO.	BB.	ERA.
1966—Puerto Mexico	Mex. S.E.	22	61	1	2	.333	65	28	21	32	15	3.10
1967—Puerto Mexico	Mex. S.E.	18	82	4	5	.444	65	42	34	51	35	3.74
1968—Jalisco	Mexican	23	106	9	9	.500	94	44	33	48	25	2.80
1969—Jalisco†	Mexican	33	161	8	9	.471	180	73	63	95	47	3.52
1970—Jalisco	Mexican	36	155	10	9	.526	159	67	48	79	50	2.79
1971—Jalisco	Mexican	35	149	10	9	.526	148	54	50	89	48	3.02
1972—Gomez Palacio	Mexican	38	186	11	8	.579	133	65	42	104	52	2.03
1973—Mexico Reds‡	Mexican	36	163	11	9	.550	172	72	57	117	36	3.15
1974—Mexico Reds§	Mexican	32	193	17	9	.654	197	85	66	130	49	3.08
1975—Mexico Reds	Mexican	30	219	13	8	.619	194	71	57	146	52	2.34
1976—Mexico Reds x	Mexican	29	233	20	4	★.833	169	60	49	★239	56	1.89
1977—Seattle	American	58	114	8	10	.444	93	40	36	105	39	2.84
1978—Seattle z	American	56	107	11	7	.611	88	46	44	62	39	3.70
1979—Pittsburgh	National	84	129	10	5	.667	122	50	43	106	43	3.00
1980—Pittsburgh	National	74	124	5	5	.500	117	53	45	82	28	3.27
American League Totals		114	221	19	17	.528	181	86	80	167	78	3.26
National League Totals		158	253	15	10	.600	239	103	88	188	71	3.13
Major League Totals		272	474	34	27	.557	420	189	168	355	149	3.19

Signed as free agent by Puerto Mexico, March 9, 1966.

CHAMPIONSHIP SERIES RECORD

Year Club	League	G.	IP.	W.	L.	Pct.	H.	R.	ER.	SO.	BB.	ERA.
1979—Pittsburgh	National	2	⅓	0	0	.000	3	0	0	1	1	0.00

WORLD SERIES RECORD

Year Club	League	G.	IP.	W.	L.	Pct.	H.	R.	ER.	SO.	BB.	ERA.
1979—Pittsburgh	National	2	4⅔	0	0	.000	5	2	2	4	3	3.86

Signed as free agent by Puerto Mexico, March 9, 1966.
†Appeared in one game as an outfielder.
‡Appeared in one game as an outfielder.
§Appeared in four games as an outfielder.
xTraded to Seattle Mariners for cash estimated at $75,000 and a player to be named later, April 1, 1977.
yOn disabled list, April 19 to May 10, 1977.
zTraded with Pitcher Rick Jones and Shortstop Tom McMillan to Pittsburgh Pirates for Shortstop Mario Mendoza and Pitchers Odell Jones and Rafael Vasquez, December 5, 1978.

DID YOU KNOW—

That the Oakland A's stole home seven times in 1980? Here's the tally: Rickey Henderson (2), Wayne Gross (2), Dwayne Murphy (2) and Jeff Cox (1). In all, there were 20 steals of home in the majors in 1980, 12 in the American League.

EUGENE LAWRENCE ROOF
(Gene)

Born January 13, 1958, at Mayfield, Ky.
Height, 6.02. Weight, 180.
Throws right and bats left and righthanded.
Brother of Phil, Adrian, Paul and David Roof, former major league players.

Year	Club	League	Pos.	G.	AB.	R.	H.	2B.	3B.	HR.	RBI.	B.A.	PO.	A.	E.	F.A.
1976—Sarasota Cards	.G.C.	SS-2B-3B	5	21	0	5	0	0	0	2	.238	6	15	2	.913
1976—Johnson City	Appal.	3B-OF	53	174	21	39	4	0	2	28	.224	35	103	13	.914
1977—Johnson City	Appal.	1-O-3-S	59	219	43	79	11	2	5	33	*.361	243	25	8	.971
1977—Gastonia	W. Caro.	3B-OF	42	138	19	28	3	1	1	11	.203	41	62	5	.954
1978—St. Petersburg†	Fla. St.	OF	101	360	50	93	7	6	2	31	.258	181	6	5	.974
1979—Arkansas	Texas	OF	128	478	86	145	22	3	11	53	.303	217	12	7	.970
1980—Springfield	A.A.	*O-3-1	133	481	68	124	23	0	10	57	.258	226	8	1	*.996

Selected by St. Louis Cardinals' organization in 12th round of free-agent draft, June 8, 1976.
†On disabled list, May 12 to June 23, 1978.

JAMES PHILLIP ROOKER
(Jim)

Born September 23, 1942, at Lakeview, Ore.
Height, 6.00. Weight, 195.
Throws left and bats righthanded.
Hobbies—Golf, fishing, hunting and gun collecting.

Year	Club	League	G.	IP.	W.	L.	Pct.	H.	R.	ER.	SO.	BB.	ERA.
1960—Decatur	Midwest						(Did not play)					
1961—Jamestown	NYP						(Did not play)					
1962—Jamestown	NYP	3	10	0	0	.000	11	10	9	3	8	8.10
1963—Duluth-Superior†	Northern						(Did not play)					
1964—Duluth-Superior	Northern	11	63	3	4	.429	49	46	37	51	60	5.28
1965—Montgomery	Southern	13	47	1	4	.200	34	30	22	45	28	4.21
1965—Rocky Mount	Carolina	15	68	1	7	.125	58	39	31	50	42	4.10
1966—Montgomery	Southern	5	7	0	0	.000	12	11	8	8	6	10.29
1966—Rocky Mount	Carolina	23	145	12	5	.706	98	44	33	99	75	2.05
1967—Montgomery	Southern	8	56	5	2	.714	50	22	18	45	22	2.89
1967—Toledo	Int'national	19	100	5	5	.500	98	48	42	92	51	3.78
1968—Toledo	Int'national	25	190	14	8	.636	144	67	55	*206	72	2.61
1968—Detroit‡§	American	2	5	0	0	.000	4	2	2	4	1	3.60
1969—High Point	Carolina	2	18	2	0	1.000	11	4	0	27	3	0.00
1969—Omaha	Am. Assoc.	2	18	2	0	1.000	12	3	3	16	3	1.50
1969—Kansas City	American	28	158	4	16	.200	136	80	66	108	73	3.76
1970—Kansas City x	American	38	204	10	15	.400	190	99	80	117	102	3.53
1971—Omaha	Am. Assoc.	6	46	2	3	.400	52	22	14	38	13	2.74
1971—Kansas City	American	20	54	2	7	.222	59	35	32	31	24	5.33
1972—Omaha	Am. Assoc.	8	62	3	5	.375	57	18	12	53	12	1.73
1972—Kansas City y	American	18	72	5	6	.455	78	37	35	44	24	4.38
1973—Pittsburgh	National	41	170	10	6	.625	143	59	54	122	52	2.86
1974—Pittsburgh	National	33	263	15	11	.577	228	93	81	139	83	2.77
1975—Pittsburgh	National	28	197	13	11	.542	177	80	65	102	76	2.97
1976—Pittsburgh	National	30	199	15	8	.652	201	83	74	92	72	3.35
1977—Pittsburgh	National	30	204	14	9	.609	196	87	70	89	64	3.09
1978—Pittsburgh	National	28	163	9	11	.450	160	94	77	76	81	4.25
1979—Pittsburgh	National	19	104	4	7	.364	106	58	53	44	39	4.59
1980—Pittsburgh ab	National	4	18	2	2	.500	16	7	7	8	12	3.50
American League Totals		106	493	21	44	.323	467	253	215	304	224	3.92
National League Totals		213	1318	82	65	.558	1227	561	481	672	479	3.28
Major League Totals		319	1811	103	109	.486	1694	814	696	976	703	3.46

Signed as free agent by Detroit Tigers' organization, June 21, 1960.
†On suspended list, June 10 to June 15, 1963.
‡Sold to New York Yankees, September 30, 1968.
§Selected by Kansas City Royals from New York Yankees in expansion draft, October 15, 1968.
xPlayed one game in outfield.
yReleased to Pittsburgh Pirates (in trade which sent Pitcher Gene Garber from Charleston to Kansas City), October 25, 1972.
zOn disabled list, March 28 to May 17 and August 12 to September 2, 1979.
aOn disabled list, May 3 to October 8, 1980.
bReleased, October 10, 1980.

RECORD AS OUTFIELDER-FIRST BASEMAN

Led NYP League batters in strikeouts with 164 in 1961 and led Northern League with 127 in 1963.

Year	Club	League	Pos.	G.	AB.	R.	H.	2B.	3B.	HR.	RBI.	B.A.	PO.	A.	E.	F.A.
1960—Decatur	Midw.	OF	69	254	33	56	11	3	1	18	.220	133	11	7	.954
1961—Jamestown	NYP	OF	125	451	83	121	16	●13	10	88	.268	*283	*17	13	*.958
1962—Jamestown	NYP	OF-P	119	455	101	128	15	8	16	80	.281	*214	*23	10	.960
1963—Dul.-Sup.	North.	OF	115	412	82	112	12	*11	19	78	.272	276	*20	11	.964
1964—Knoxville	South.	OF	27	79	5	14	3	0	3	11	.177	40	4	4	.917
1964—Dul.-Sup.	North.	O-1-P	77	251	35	57	6	1	10	40	.227	249	25	8	.972
1967—Toledo	Int.	P-O-1B	31	52	3	9	1	0	1	2	.173	6	17	0	1.000
1968—Toledo	Int.	P-OF	34	77	8	16	1	1	3	11	.208	12	29	1	.976

Year	Club	League	G.	IP.	W.	L.	Pct.	H.	R.	ER.	SO.	BB.	ERA.
1974—Pittsburgh		National	1	7	0	0	.000	6	2	2	4	5	2.57
1975—Pittsburgh		National	1	4	0	1	.000	7	4	4	5	0	9.00
Championship Series Totals			2	11	0	1	.000	13	6	6	9	5	4.91

WORLD SERIES RECORD

Year	Club	League	G.	IP.	W.	L.	Pct.	H.	R.	ER.	SO.	BB.	ERA.
1979—Pittsburgh		National	2	8⅔	0	0	.000	5	1	1	4	3	1.04

PATRICK EUGENE ROONEY
(Pat)

Born November 28, 1957, at Chicago, Ill.
Height, 6.01. Weight, 190.
Throws and bats righthanded.
Attended Eastern Illinois University, Charleston, Ill.

Year	Club	League	Pos.	G.	AB.	R.	H.	2B.	3B.	HR.	RBI.	B.A.	PO.	A.	E.	F.A.
1978—Jamestown		NYP	OF	71	282	54	74	9	10	8	51	.262	94	5	4	.961
1979—Memphis		South.	OF	125	458	52	115	18	5	16	69	.251	253	9	5	.981
1980—Memphis		South.	OF	142	482	86	135	23	6	28	102	.280	296	13	7	.978

Selected by Montreal Expos' organization in 20th round of free-agent draft, June 6, 1978.

LUIS ROSADO (ROBLES)

Born December 6, 1955, at Santurce, Puerto Rico.
Height, 6.00. Weight, 180.
Throws and bats righthanded.

Led Appalachian League catchers in assists with 33 in 1973.
Led Western Carolinas League catchers in putouts with 698, in assists with 68 and in errors with 21 in 1974.
Led Western Carolinas League in sacrifice hits with 7 in 1974.
Led International League catchers in assists with 69 and tied for lead in double plays with 7 in 1977.
Led International League catchers in double plays with 12 in 1978.
Led International League catchers in fielding average with .990 in 1980.

Year	Club	League	Pos.	G.	AB.	R.	H.	2B.	3B.	HR.	RBI.	B.A.	PO.	A.	E.	F.A.
1972—Marion		Appal.	C-1B	37	93	8	18	3	0	0	7	.194	162	11	11	.940
1973—Marion		Appal.	C-1B	59	204	35	68	16	3	3	33	.333	402	45	16	.965
1974—Anderson		W. Car.	C-1B	116	437	49	121	24	3	6	61	.277	824	78	24	.974
1975—Jackson		Texas	C	24	82	7	19	2	0	0	13	.232	105	16	4	.968
1975—Visalia		Calif.	C-1B	80	267	31	78	13	0	7	50	.292	478	74	8	.986
1976—Jackson		Texas	∗1-C-3	110	386	39	106	22	3	9	49	.275	914	56	8	∗.992
1977—Tidewater		Int.	C-1B	116	411	39	112	21	5	8	59	.273	539	77	9	.986
1977—New York		Nat.	1B-C	9	24	1	5	1	0	0	3	.208	46	4	2	.962
1978—Tidewater†		Int.	C-1B	105	363	42	98	15	2	6	42	.270	505	54	11	.981
1979—Syr.‡-Tide		Int.	C-3B-1B	99	333	35	83	20	1	4	29	.249	436	52	3	.994
1980—Tidewater		Int.	C-1B-3B	104	348	34	91	20	1	4	37	.261	608	59	5	.993
1980—New York		Nat.	1B	2	4	0	0	0	0	0	0	.000	11	0	0	1.000
Major League Totals				11	28	1	5	1	0	0	3	.179	57	4	2	.968

Signed as free agent by New York Mets' organization, May 15, 1972.
†On disabled list, August 19 to September 4, 1978.
‡Loaned to Toronto Blue Jays' organization, April 1, 1979; returned, July 9, 1979.

PETER EDWARD ROSE
(Pete)

Born April 14, 1941, at Cincinnati, O.
Height, 5.11. Weight, 203.
Throws right and bats right and lefthanded.
Brother of David Rose, minor league pitcher in Cincinnati Reds' organization, 1967-1970.

Named THE SPORTING NEWS Player of the Decade for 1970-79.
Established major league records for most seasons, 200 or more hits (10); most seasons, 150 or more games (15); most consecutive seasons, 600 or more at bats (13); highest fielding average by outfielder, lifetime, 1,000 or more games (.992); most seasons, 600 or more at bats (16); most plate appearances, season (771), 1974; fewest stolen bases, season, most at bats (0 and 662), 1975.
Tied major league records for most consecutive seasons leading major leagues in runs scored (3), 1974 through 1976; most consecutive seasons leading major leagues in hits (2), 1972 and 1973; most consecutive seasons leading major leagues in games (2), 1974 and 1975; fewest sacrifice flies, season, most at bats (0 and 680), 1973; most doubles by switch-hitter, season (51), 1978; most hits by switch-hitter, season (230), 1973.
Established National League records for most singles, lifetime (2,631); most 20-game hitting streaks, lifetime (6); fewest chances accepted by third baseman, season, 150 or more games (366), 1977; most one-base hits by switch-hitter, season (181), 1975.
Established modern National League record for most seasons leading league, at bats (4).
Tied National League records for most consecutive games, one or more hits, season (44), 1978; most games, switch hit home runs, lifetime (2), August 30, 1966 and August 2, 1967.
Tied modern National League records for highest batting average, switch hitter, season, 100 or more

games (.348), 1969; most seasons leading league, hits (6); most years leading league in fielding average by outfielder, 100 or more games (3); most consecutive years leading league in fielding average by outfielder, 100 or more games (2), 1970 and 1971 (tied).

Major League stolen bases: 1963 (13), 1964 (4), 1965 (8), 1966 (4), 1967 (11) , 1968 (3), 1969 (7), 1970 (12), 1971 (13), 1972 (10), 1973 (10), 1974 (2), 1975 (0), 1976 (9), 1977 (16), 1978 (13), 1979 (20), 1980 (12). Total—167.

Hit three home runs in one game, vs. New York Mets, April 29, 1978.

Led Florida State League in total bases with 246 in 1961.

Named National League Rookie Player of the Year by THE SPORTING NEWS and National League Rookie of the Year by the Baseball Writers' Association, 1963.

Named THE SPORTING NEWS National League Player of the Year, 1968.

Named second baseman on THE SPORTING NEWS National League All-Star Team, 1965 and 66.

Named outfielder on THE SPORTING NEWS National League All-Star Team, 1968 and 1973.

Named third baseman on THE SPORTING NEWS National League All-Star Team, 1978.

Named outfielder on THE SPORTING NEWS National League All-Star fielding team, 1969 and 1970.

Named National League Most Valuable Player, 1973.

Year Club	League	Pos.	G.	AB.	R.	H.	2B.	3B.	HR.	RBI.	B.A.	PO.	A.	E.	F.A.
1960—Geneva	NYP	2B	85	321	60	89	8	5	1	43	.277	198	193	*36	.916
1961—Tampa	Fla. St.	2B	130	484	105	*160	20	*30	2	77	.331	256	294	21	.963
1962—Macon................	Sally	2B	139	540	*136	178	31	*17	9	71	.330	317	368	24	.966
1963—Cincinnati†........	Nat.	2B-OF	157	623	101	170	25	9	6	41	.273	360	366	22	.971
1964—Cincinnati	Nat.	2B	136	516	64	139	13	2	4	34	.269	263	301	12	.979
1965—Cincinnati	Nat.	2B	162	*670	117	*209	35	11	11	81	.312	*382	403	20	.975
1966—Cincinnati	Nat.	2B-3B	156	654	97	205	38	5	16	70	.313	409	374	18	.978
1967—Cincinnati	Nat.	OF-2B	148	585	86	176	32	8	12	76	.301	287	93	11	.972
1968—Cincinnati‡........	Nat.	●O-2-1	149	626	94	●210	42	6	10	49	*.335	270	*20	3	.990
1969—Cincinnati	Nat.	OF-2B	156	627	●120	218	33	11	16	82	*.348	317	10	4	.988
1970—Cincinnati	Nat.	OF	159	649	120	●205	37	9	15	52	.316	309	8	1	*.997
1971—Cincinnati	Nat.	OF	160	632	86	192	27	4	13	44	.304	306	13	2	●.994
1972—Cincinnati	Nat.	OF	*154	*645	107	*198	31	11	6	57	.307	330	●15	2	.994
1973—Cincinnati	Nat.	OF	160	*680	115	*230	36	8	5	64	*.338	343	15	3	.992
1974—Cincinnati	Nat.	OF	*163	652	*110	185	*45	7	3	51	.284	346	11	1	*.997
1975—Cincinnati	Nat.	3B-OF	●162	662	*112	210	*47	4	7	74	.317	161	230	14	.965
1976—Cincinnati	Nat.	*3B-OF	162	665	*130	*215	*42	6	10	63	.323	115	293	13	*.969
1977—Cincinnati	Nat.	3B	●162	*655	95	204	38	7	9	64	.311	98	268	16	.958
1978—Cincinnati§	Nat.	3-O-1	159	655	103	198	*51	3	7	52	.302	135	256	15	.963
1979—Philadelphia......	Nat.	1B-3B-2B	163	628	90	208	40	5	4	59	.331	1429	93	10	.993
1980—Philadelphia......	Nat.	1B	162	655	95	185	*42	1	1	64	.282	1427	*123	5	*.997
Major League Totals			2830	11479	1842	3557	654	117	155	1077	.310	7287	2892	172	.983

Signed as free agent by Cincinnati Reds' organization, July 8, 1960.

†On military list, October 1, 1963, to March 14, 1964.

‡On disabled list, July 6 to July 27, 1968.

§Granted free agency, November 2, 1978; signed by Philadelphia Phillies, December 5, 1978.

CHAMPIONSHIP SERIES RECORD

Established Championship Series records for most positions played, total Series (4); most consecutive games, one or more hits (14); most hits, total Series (39); most total bases, total Series (57); most one-base hits, total Series (28); most hits, two consecutive Series (17), 1972 and 1973.

Tied Championship Series records for most times on winning club (5); most one-base hits, five-game Series (8), 1980; most two-base hits, total Series (7); most two-base hits, five-game Series (4), 1972.

Established National League Championship Series records for highest batting average, total Series, 10 or more games and 30 or more at-bats (.382); most at-bats, total Series (102); most runs, total Series (14); most long hits, total Series (11); most total bases, five-game Series (15), 1973.

Tied National League Championship Series record for most Series, played all games (6).

Year Club	League	Pos.	G.	AB.	R.	H.	2B.	3B.	HR.	RBI.	B.A.	PO.	A.	E.	F.A.
1970—Cincinnati	Nat.	OF	3	13	1	3	0	0	0	1	.231	3	0	0	1.000
1972—Cincinnati	Nat.	OF	5	20	1	9	4	0	0	2	.450	10	0	0	1.000
1973—Cincinnati	Nat.	OF	5	21	3	8	1	0	2	2	.381	10	1	0	1.000
1975—Cincinnati	Nat.	3B	3	14	3	5	0	0	1	2	.357	2	1	0	1.000
1976—Cincinnati	Nat.	3B	3	14	3	6	2	1	0	2	.429	2	5	1	.875
1980—Philadelphia......	Nat.	1B	5	20	3	8	0	0	0	2	.400	53	0	0	1.000
Championship Series Totals.............			24	102	14	39	7	1	3	11	.382	80	14	1	.989

WORLD SERIES RECORD

Tied World Series records for most positions played, total Series (4); most double plays by first baseman, six-game Series (8), 1980; most double plays by first baseman, nine-inning game (4), October 15, 1980; most times awarded first base on catcher's interference, game (1), October 10, 1970; most times home run as leadoff batter in game (1), October 20, 1972.

Year Club	League	Pos.	G.	AB.	R.	H.	2B.	3B.	HR.	RBI.	B.A.	PO.	A.	E.	F.A.
1970—Cincinnati	Nat.	OF	5	20	2	5	1	0	1	2	.250	14	1	1	.938
1972—Cincinnati	Nat.	OF	7	28	3	6	0	0	1	2	.214	14	1	0	1.000
1975—Cincinnati	Nat.	3B	7	27	3	10	1	1	0	2	.370	7	9	0	1.000
1976—Cincinnati	Nat.	3B	4	16	1	3	1	0	0	1	.188	6	3	0	1.000
1980—Philadelphia......	Nat.	1B	6	23	2	6	1	0	0	1	.261	49	6	0	1.000
World Series Totals			29	114	11	30	4	1	2	8	.263	90	20	1	.991

ALL-STAR GAME RECORD

Established All-Star Game record for most positions played, total games (5).

Year League	Pos.	AB.	R.	H.	2B.	3B.	HR.	RBI.	B.A.	PO.	A.	E.	F.A.
1965—National..............................	2B	2	0	0	0	0	0	0	.000	2	4	0	1.000

Year League	Pos.	AB.	R.	H.	2B.	3B.	HR.	RBI.	B.A.	PO.	A.	E.	F.A.
1967—National	2B	1	0	0	0	0	0	0	.000	1	0	0	1.000
1969—National	OF	1	0	0	0	0	0	0	.000	2	0	0	1.000
1970—National	OF	3	1	1	0	0	0	0	.333	3	0	0	1.000
1971—National	OF	0	0	0	0	0	0	0	.000	0	0	0	.000
1973—National	OF	3	1	0	0	0	0	0	.000	1	0	0	1.000
1974—National	OF	2	0	0	0	0	0	0	.000	1	0	0	1.000
1975—National	OF	4	0	2	0	0	0	1	.500	4	0	0	1.000
1976—National	3B	3	1	2	0	1	0	0	.667	0	1	0	1.000
1977—National	PH-3B	2	0	0	0	0	0	0	.000	0	1	0	1.000
1978—National	3B	4	0	1	1	0	0	0	.250	1	0	0	1.000
1979—National	PH-1B	2	0	0	0	0	0	0	.000	2	0	0	1.000
1980—National	PH	1	0	0	0	0	0	0	.000	0	0	0	.000
All-Star Game Totals		28	3	6	1	1	0	1	.214	17	6	0	1.000

Named to National League All-Star Team for 1968 game; replaced due to injury.

DAVID ROSELLO (RODRIGUEZ)
(Dave)

Born June 26, 1950, at Mayaguez, Puerto Rico.
Height, 5.11. Weight, 160.
Throws and bats righthanded.

Led American Association shortstops in total chances with 686 in 1972.
Tied for American Association lead in double plays by shortstops with 88 in 1972.

Year Club	League	Pos.	G.	AB.	R.	H.	2B.	3B.	HR.	RBI.	B.A.	PO.	A.	E.	F.A.
1969—Quincy	Midw.	S-O	99	297	38	56	8	3	1	26	.189	151	234	37	.912
1970—Quincy	Midw.	SS	51	165	33	42	6	0	4	16	.255	78	172	23	.916
1970—San Antonio	Texas	SS	64	209	22	49	7	1	3	16	.234	101	192	18	.942
1971—San Antonio	Texas	SS	125	487	44	111	11	7	2	38	.228	187	384	40	.935
1972—Wichita	A. A.	SS	•137	451	52	122	22	4	2	46	.271	•215	•436	•35	.945
1972—Chicago	Nat.	SS	5	12	2	3	0	0	1	3	.250	11	11	4	.846
1973—Wichita	A. A.	SS-2B	99	367	54	115	15	3	8	51	.313	157	304	34	.931
1973—Chicago	Nat.	2B-SS	16	38	4	10	2	0	0	2	.263	30	29	3	.952
1974—Wichita	A. A.	SS-2B	22	92	18	33	7	1	0	15	.359	31	69	6	.943
1974—Chicago	Nat.	2B-SS	62	148	9	30	7	0	0	10	.203	97	114	8	.963
1975—Wichita	A. A.	SS	135	•522	100	134	29	2	7	46	.257	225	•435	32	.954
1975—Chicago	Nat.	SS	19	58	7	15	2	0	1	8	.259	27	53	4	.952
1976—Chicago	Nat.	SS-2B	91	227	27	55	5	1	1	11	.242	129	217	12	.966
1977—Chicago†	Nat.	3-S-2	56	82	18	18	2	1	1	9	.220	8	42	6	.893
1978—Portland	P. C.	3-2-S-O	123	436	87	123	19	9	9	71	.282	123	200	16	.953
1979—Cleveland	Amer.	2B-3B-SS	59	107	20	26	6	1	3	14	.243	43	98	5	.966
1980—Cleveland	Amer.	2-3-S	71	117	16	29	3	0	2	12	.248	76	91	4	.977
National League Totals			249	565	67	131	18	2	4	43	.232	302	466	37	.954
American League Totals			130	224	36	55	9	1	5	26	.246	119	189	9	.972
Major League Totals			379	789	103	186	27	3	9	69	.236	421	655	46	.959

Signed as free agent by Chicago Cubs' organization, November 11, 1968.
†Traded to Cleveland Indians for Pitcher Norm Churchill and Outfielder Bruce Compton, December 5, 1977.

BRIAN PHILLIP ROSINSKI

Born October 12, 1956, at Chicago, Ill.
Height, 6.02. Weight, 205.
Throws right and bats lefthanded.
Attended North Park College, Chicago, Ill.

Year Club	League	Pos.	G.	AB.	R.	H.	2B.	3B.	HR.	RBI.	B.A.	PO.	A.	E.	F.A.
1975—Bradenton Cubs	Gulf C.	OF	40	140	20	43	5	4	0	28	.307	55	4	0	•1.000
1976—Pompano Beach	Fla. St.	OF	32	123	12	32	4	2	0	21	.260	48	3	4	.927
1977—Pompano Beach	Fla. St.	OF	100	279	39	73	13	0	3	19	.262	127	6	8	.943
1978—Midland	Texas	OF	116	401	65	101	20	3	11	59	.252	126	11	3	.979
1979—Midland	Texas	OF-1B	118	381	70	126	22	2	7	74	.331	117	9	7	.947
1980—Wichita	A.A.	OF	117	391	66	123	20	5	19	79	.315	110	4	3	.974

Selected by Chicago Cubs' organization in 1st round (4th player selected) of free-agent draft, June 4, 1975.

LAWRENCE LEE ROTHSCHILD
(Larry)

Born March 12, 1954, at Chicago, Ill.
Height, 6.02. Weight, 180.
Throws right and bats lefthanded.
Attended Florida State University, Tallahassee, Fla.

Tied for Northwest League lead in saves with 6 in 1975.

Year Club	League	G.	IP.	W.	L.	Pct.	H.	R.	ER.	SO.	BB.	ERA.
1975—Billings	Pioneer	6	8	0	2	.000	14	11	7	12	7	7.88
1975—Eugene	Northwest	21	33	3	0	1.000	17	11	10	36	21	2.73
1976—Three Rivers	Eastern	30	123	11	3	•786	96	33	28	75	28	2.05
1977—Indianapolis	Am. Assoc.	29	92	4	4	.500	93	51	43	43	34	4.21
1978—Nashville†	Southern	5	12	0	0	.000	14	7	6	9	4	4.50
1978—Amarillo	Texas	12	82	5	5	.500	83	42	38	57	21	4.17

Year	Club	League	G.	IP.	W.	L.	Pct.	H.	R.	ER.	SO.	BB.	ERA.
1978—Indianapolis		Am. Assoc.	8	45	4	0	1.000	31	15	11	38	19	2.18
1979—Indianapolis		Am. Assoc.	33	82	1	6	.143	85	52	48	68	56	5.27
1980—Indianapolis‡		Am. Assoc.	33	113	8	7	.533	111	60	53	74	44	4.22

Signed as free agent by Cincinnati Reds' organization, June 10, 1975.
†Loaned to San Diego Padres' organization, May 11, 1978; returned, July 18, 1978.
‡Drafted by Detroit Tigers, December 8, 1980.

THOMAS ALLEN ROWE
(Tom)

Born October 16, 1957, at Bronx, N.Y.
Height, 6.03. Weight, 190.
Throws and bats righthanded.
Attended Rockland Community College, Suffern, N.Y.

Tied for Florida State League lead in games started with 28 in 1978.
Tied for Southern League lead in games started with 28 in 1979.

Year	Club	League	G.	IP.	W.	L.	Pct.	H.	R.	ER.	SO.	BB.	ERA.
1977—Miami		Florida St.	21	127	10	6	.625	137	63	46	55	64	3.26
1978—Miami		Florida St.	28	*199	10	11	.476	*188	91	51	110	69	2.31
1979—Charlotte		Southern	28	167	11	14	.440	200	113	93	90	76	5.01
1980—Rochester		Int'national	17	92	6	7	.462	104	58	47	39	31	4.60
1980—Charlotte		Southern	9	49	4	2	.667	58	22	15	35	18	2.76

Selected by Baltimore Orioles' organization in 2nd round of free-agent draft, January 11, 1977.

MICHAEL EVAN ROWLAND
(Mike)

Born January 31, 1953, at Chicago, Ill.
Height, 6.03. Weight, 205.
Throws and bats righthanded.
Attended Millikin University, Decatur, Ill.; received Bachelor of Science degree in Industrial Engineering.

Pitched seven-inning, 1-0 no-hit victory against Jackson, August 5, 1976.
Tied for Eastern League lead in complete games with 15 in 1977.

Year	Club	League	G.	IP.	W.	L.	Pct.	H.	R.	ER.	SO.	BB.	ERA.
1975—Great Falls		Pioneer	5	32	2	2	.500	19	9	8	26	10	2.25
1975—Fresno		California	9	57	3	1	.750	46	26	16	50	21	2.53
1976—Lafayette		Texas	26	161	5	14	.263	157	76	66	87	59	3.69
1977—Waterbury		Eastern	26	185	14	10	.583	169	88	78	148	61	3.79
1978—Phoenix		P. Coast	27	114	1	8	.111	141	99	95	63	66	7.50
1979—Phoenix		P. Coast	30	191	10	12	.455	209	98	77	102	59	3.63
1980—Phoenix		P. Coast	23	140	5	11	.313	180	81	71	58	28	4.56
1980—San Francisco		National	19	27	1	1	.500	20	8	7	8	8	2.33
Major League Totals			19	27	1	1	.500	20	8	7	8	8	2.33

Selected by San Francisco Giants' organization in 22nd round of free-agent draft, June 4, 1975.

JERON KENNIS ROYSTER
(Jerry)

Born October 18, 1952, at Sacramento, Calif.
Height, 6.00. Weight, 165.
Throws and bats righthanded.
Hobbies—Water skiing and swimming.
Attended Healds Business College, Sacramento, Calif.

Tied for National League lead in double plays by third basemen with 35 in 1976.
Led Texas League third basemen in double plays with 26 in 1972.
Major league stolen bases: 1973 (1), 1974 (0), 1975 (1), 1976 (24), 1977 (28), 1978 (27), 1979 (35), 1980 (22). Total—138.
Named Pacific Coast League Player of the Year in 1975.

Year	Club	League	Pos.	G.	AB.	R.	H.	2B.	3B.	HR.	RBI.	B.A.	PO.	A.	E.	F.A.
1971—Bakersfield	Calif.		3B	7	20	2	2	1	0	0	2	.100	1	5	1	.857
1971—Daytona Beach	Fla. St.		3-S-2	111	371	68	100	13	7	8	42	.270	90	265	29	.924
1972—El Paso	Texas		*3-S-O	127	479	*89	123	28	3	18	59	.257	103	209	*35	.899
1973—Albuquerque	P. C.		3-S-O	122	463	78	140	24	11	6	68	.302	167	222	24	.942
1973—Los Angeles	Nat.		3B-2B	10	19	1	4	0	0	0	2	.211	3	14	3	.850
1974—Albuquerque	P. C.		*3-2-S	125	458	69	126	19	1	10	65	.275	121	257	14	*.964
1974—Los Angeles	Nat.		2-O-3	6	0	2	0	0	0	0	0	.000	0	3	0	1.000
1975—Albuquerque	P. C.		SS-3B	133	487	*91	162	31	7	10	65	*.333	183	349	38	.933
1975—Los Angeles†	Nat.		O-2-3-S	13	36	2	9	2	1	0	1	.250	12	15	2	.931
1976—Atlanta	Nat.		*3B-SS	149	533	65	132	13	1	5	45	.248	*158	310	19	.961
1977—Atlanta	Nat.		3-S-2-O	140	445	64	96	10	2	6	28	.216	182	267	28	.941
1978—Atlanta	Nat.		SS-2B-3B	140	529	67	137	17	8	2	35	.259	284	376	23	.966
1979—Atlanta	Nat.		3B-2B	154	601	103	164	25	6	3	51	.273	261	405	22	.968
1980—Atlanta	Nat.		2-3-O	123	392	42	95	17	5	1	20	.242	195	166	18	.953
Major League Totals				735	2555	346	637	84	23	17	182	.249	1095	1556	115	.958

Signed as free agent by Los Angeles Dodgers' organization, August 21, 1970.

†Traded with Outfielder Jimmy Wynn, Second Baseman Lee Lacy and First Baseman-Outfielder Tom Paciorek to Atlanta Braves for Outfielder Dusty Baker and First Baseman-Third Baseman Ed Goodson, November 17, 1975.

DAVID SCOTT ROZEMA
(Dave)

Born August 5, 1956, at Grand Rapids, Mich.
Height, 6.04. Weight, 200.
Throws and bats righthanded.
Attended Grand Rapids Junior College, Grand Rapids, Mich.

Tied for Midwest League lead in shutouts with 5 in 1975.
Tied for Southern League lead in shutouts with 4 in 1976.
Named American League Rookie Pitcher of the Year, 1977.

Year	Club	League	G.	IP.	W.	L.	Pct.	H.	R.	ER.	SO.	BB.	ERA.
1975—Clinton		Midwest	27	164	14	5	.737	128	50	38	123	32	2.09
1976—Montgomery†		Southern	19	126	12	4	.750	98	29	22	96	15	*1.57
1977—Detroit		American	28	218	15	7	.682	222	87	75	92	34	3.10
1978—Detroit		American	28	209	9	12	.429	205	83	73	57	41	3.14
1979—Detroit‡		American	16	97	4	4	.500	101	52	38	33	30	3.53
1980—Detroit		American	42	145	6	9	.400	152	68	63	49	49	3.91
Major League Totals			114	669	34	32	.515	680	290	249	231	154	3.35

Selected by San Francisco Giants' organization in 22nd round of free-agent draft, June 5, 1974.
Selected by Detroit Tigers' organization in secondary phase of free-agent draft, January 9, 1975.
†On disabled list May 9 to June 21, 1976.
‡On disabled list, June 16 to August 27, 1979.

DAVID MICHAEL RUCKER
(Dave)

Born September 1, 1957, at San Bernardino, Calif.
Height, 6.01. Weight, 185.
Throws and bats lefthanded.
Attended University of California at Los Angeles, Los Angeles, Calif., and
LaVerne College, LaVerne, Calif.

Year	Club	League	G.	IP.	W.	L.	Pct.	H.	R.	ER.	SO.	BB.	ERA.
1978—Bristol		Appal.	3	7	1	0	1.000	10	5	4	7	2	5.14
1978—Lakeland		Florida St.	18	31	6	3	.667	26	13	11	18	13	3.19
1979—Montgomery		Southern	28	96	4	7	.364	97	56	49	64	66	4.59
1979—Evansville		Am. Assoc.	2	13	1	1	.500	11	4	4	8	1	2.77
1980—Evansville		Am. Assoc.	52	92	7	8	.467	94	53	35	53	52	3.42

Selected by Philadelphia Phillies' organization in 19th round of free-agent draft, June 4, 1975.
Selected by Detroit Tigers' organization in 16th round of free-agent draft, June 6, 1978.

JOSEPH ODEN RUDI
(Joe)

Born September 7, 1946, at Modesto, Calif.
Height, 6.02. Weight, 200.
Throws and bats righthanded.
Hobbies—Hunting and golf.
Attended Modesto Junior College, Modesto, Calif., and Chabot College, Hayward, Calif.

Established American League record for highest fielding average by outfielder, lifetime, 1,000 or more games (.991).
Led American League in total bases with 287 in 1974.
Named outfielder on THE SPORTING NEWS American League All-Star Team, 1972, 1974 and 1976.
Named as outfielder on THE SPORTING NEWS American League All-Star fielding team, 1974, 1975 and 1976.

Year	Club	League	Pos.	G.	AB.	R.	H.	2B.	3B.	HR.	RBI.	B.A.	PO.	A.	E.	F.A.
1964—Wytheville		Appal.	OF	8	28	10	12	3	0	1	15	.429	8	13	0	1.000
1964—Daytona Beach†		Fla. St.	3-O	48	166	20	37	9	0	5	26	.223	49	44	15	.861
1965—Dubuque‡		Midw	*3-O	110	374	55	95	21	2	16	58	.254	*123	145	*37	.879
1966—Modesto		Calif.	OF-3B	101	381	67	113	19	4	24	85	.297	161	18	4	.978
1967—Kansas City		Amer.	1-OF	19	43	4	8	2	0	0	1	.186	69	1	1	.986
1967—Birmingham		South.	1-OF	121	437	62	126	26		13	70	.288	921	60	17	.983
1968—Vancouver		P. C.	OF	16	60	9	19	3	0	3	7	.317	23	1	1	.960
1968—Oakland		Amer.	OF	68	181	16	32	5	1	1	12	.177	77	1	1	.987
1969—Des Moines		A. A.	OF-1-3B	57	240	42	85	15	2	11	65	.354	436	39	8	.983
1969—Oakland		Amer.	OF-1B	35	122	10	23	3	1	2	6	.189	134	9	3	.979
1970—Oakland		Amer.	OF-1B	106	350	40	108	23	2	11	42	.309	302	18	4	.988
1971—Oakland		Amer.	OF-1B	127	513	62	137	23	4	10	52	.267	280	7	2	.993
1972—Oakland		Amer.	OF-3B	147	593	94	*181	32	•9	19	75	.305	247	9	2	.992
1973—Oakland		Amer.	OF-1B	120	437	53	118	25	1	12	66	.270	231	6	2	.992
1974—Oakland		Amer.	OF-1B	158	593	73	174	*39	4	22	99	.293	416	18	5	.989
1975—Oakland§		Amer.	1B-OF	126	468	66	130	26	6	21	75	.278	804	37	7	.992
1976—Oakland x		Amer.	OF-1B	130	500	54	135	32	3	13	94	.270	270	7	3	.989
1977—California y		Amer.	OF	64	242	48	64	13	2	13	53	.264	131	3	0	1.000
1978—California		Amer.	OF-1B	133	497	58	127	27	1	17	79	.256	292	10	2	.993

Year Club League	Pos.	G.	AB.	R.	H.	2B.	3B.	HR.	RBI.	B.A.	PO.	A.	E.	F.A.
1979—California z.......Amer.	1B-OF	90	330	35	80	11	3	11	61	.242	207	7	2	.991
1980—California ab.....Amer.	OF-1B	104	372	42	88	11	1	16	53	.237	244	5	2	.992
Major League Totals		1427	5241	649	1405	278	38	168	768	.268	3704	138	36	.991

Signed as free agent by Kansas City A's organization, June 13, 1964.

†Sold by Kansas City Athletics to Cleveland Indians, May 3, 1965 (the deal was designed to protect Rudi and Jim Rittwage, an Indian farmhand, from the first-year bonus draft rules then in effect). Transaction included swap of Catcher Phil Roof of Indians to Athletics for Outfielder Jim Landis, December 1, 1965.

‡Returned by Cleveland Indians' organization to Kansas City Athletics' organization, December 2, 1965.

§On disabled list, August 11 to September 11, 1975.

xPlayed out option year and granted free agency, November 1, 1976; signed as free agent by California Angels, November 17, 1976.

yOn supplemental disabled list, June 26 through remainder of season.

zOn disabled list, August 16 to September 28, 1979.

aOn supplemental disabled list, August 20 to October 6, 1980.

bTraded with Pitchers Frank Tanana and Jim Dorsey to Boston Red Sox for Outfielder Fred Lynn and Pitcher Steve Renko, January 23, 1981.

CHAMPIONSHIP SERIES RECORD

Year Club League	Pos.	G.	AB.	R.	H.	2B.	3B.	HR.	RBI.	B.A.	PO.	A.	E.	F.A.
1971—Oakland ....Amer.	OF	2	7	0	1	1	0	0	0	.143	4	0	0	1.000
1972—Oakland ....Amer.	OF	5	20	1	5	1	0	0	2	.250	11	0	0	1.000
1973—Oakland ....Amer.	OF	5	18	1	4	0	0	1	3	.222	11	0	0	1.000
1974—Oakland ....Amer.	OF	4	13	0	2	0	1	0	1	.154	5	0	0	1.000
1975—Oakland ....Amer.	1B-OF	3	12	1	3	2	0	0	0	.250	22	2	0	1.000
Championship Series Totals.............		19	70	3	15	4	1	1	6	.214	53	2	0	1.000

WORLD SERIES RECORD

Established World Series records for most putouts and most chances accepted by left fielder, extra-inning game (7), October 16, 1973 (11 innings).

Tied World Series records for most putouts, first baseman, inning (3), October 16, 1974, (sixth inning).

Year Club League	Pos.	G.	AB.	R.	H.	2B.	3B	HR.	RBI.	B.A.	PO.	A.	E.	F.A.
1972—Oakland ....Amer.	OF	7	25	1	6	0	0	1	1	.240	20	0	0	1.000
1973—Oakland ....Amer.	OF	7	27	3	9	2	0	0	4	.333	20	2	0	1.000
1974—Oakland ....Amer.	OF-1B	5	18	1	6	0	0	1	4	.333	28	0	0	1.000
World Series Totals		19	70	5	21	2	0	2	9	.300	68	2	0	1.000

ALL-STAR GAME RECORD

Tied All-Star Game record for most putouts and chances accepted by left fielder, game (5), July 15, 1975.

Year League	Pos.	AB.	R.	H.	2B.	3B.	HR.	RBI.	B.A.	PO.	A.	E.	F.A.
1972—American............................	OF	1	0	1	1	0	0	0	1.000	0	0	0	.000
1974—American............................	OF	2	0	0	0	0	0	0	.000	1	0	0	1.000
1975—American............................	OF	3	0	1	0	0	0	0	.333	5	0	0	1.000
All-Star Game Totals		6	0	2	1	0	0	0	.333	6	0	0	1.000

VERNON GERALD RUHLE
(Vern)

Born January 25, 1951, at Coleman, Mich.
Height, 6.01. Weight, 187.
Throws and bats righthanded.
Attended Olivet College, Olivet, Mich.

Year Club League	G.	IP.	W.	L.	Pct.	H.	R.	ER.	SO.	BB.	ERA.
1972—Bristol ....Ap'lachian	4	28	0	2	.000	24	6	4	30	5	1.29
1972—Rocky Mount...................Carolina	13	72	5	8	.385	87	53	38	53	28	4.75
1973—Lakeland ....Florida St.	15	96	6	5	.545	81	27	22	67	24	2.06
1973—Montgomery ....Southern	10	81	6	2	.750	72	33	26	34	17	2.89
1974—Montgomery ....Southern	5	45	5	0	1.000	29	6	3	32	12	0.60
1974—Evansville ....Am. Assoc.	22	156	13	5	.722	178	80	70	94	42	4.04
1974—Detroit...............................American	5	33	2	0	1.000	35	13	10	10	6	2.73
1975—Detroit...............................American	32	190	11	12	.478	199	104	85	67	65	4.03
1976—Detroit...............................American	32	200	9	12	.429	227	99	87	88	59	3.92
1977—Evansville†........................Am. Assoc.	10	21	1	4	.200	31	19	16	15	9	6.86
1977—Detroit‡§...........................American	14	66	3	5	.375	83	44	42	27	15	5.73
1978—Columbus ....Southern	5	39	4	1	.800	32	9	8	25	8	1.85
1978—Charleston ....Int'national	13	94	4	4	.500	89	36	29	48	16	2.78
1978—Houston ....National	13	68	3	3	.500	57	17	16	27	20	2.12
1979—Houston x..........................National	13	66	2	4	.250	64	33	30	33	8	4.09
1980—Houston ....National	28	159	12	4	.750	148	51	42	55	29	2.38
American League Totals	83	489	25	29	.463	544	260	224	192	145	4.12
National League Totals	54	293	17	13	.567	269	101	88	115	57	2.70
Major League Totals................................	137	782	42	42	.500	813	361	312	307	202	3.59

Selected by Detroit Tigers' organization in 17th round of free-agent draft, June 6, 1972.

†On disabled list, July 24 to August 5, 1977.

‡On disabled list, May 21 to June 16, 1977.

§Released, March 27, 1978; signed by Houston Astros' organization, March 29, 1978.

xOn disabled list, May 14 to September 1, 1979.

Year Club	League	G.	IP.	W.	L.	Pct.	H.	R.	ER.	SO.	BB.	ERA.
1980—Houston ....National		1	7	0	0	.000	8	3	3	3	1	3.86

MANUEL RUIZ
(Chico)

Bron November 1, 1951, at Santurce, Puerto Rico.
Height, 5.11. Weight, 170.
Throws and bats righthanded.
Hobbies—Reading and movies.

Led Western Carolinas League in bases on balls with 85 and in stolen bases with 47 in 1971.
Led International League in sacrifice hits with 20 in 1976.
Led International League second basemen in putouts with 336, in assists with 458 and in double plays with 109 in 1976.

Year Club	League	Pos.	G.	AB.	R.	H.	2B.	3B.	HR.	RBI.	B.A.	PO.	A.	E.	F.A.
1970—Greenwood	W.Carol.	2B-3B	31	82	8	15	1	1	0	6	.183	29	48	5	.939
1970—Twin Falls	Pion.	OF-2B	63	225	47	71	12	3	4	24	.316	119	81	10	.952
1971—Greenwood	W.Carol.	2B	123	446	*104	121	23	1	9	44	.271	216	326	23	*.959
1972—Savannah..........	South.	2B	*139	*530	81	143	27	2	8	43	.270	*314	369	21	*.970
1973—Rich.†-Penin.†...	Int.	2-S-O-1	120	384	45	78	8	3	0	19	.203	245	292	26	.954
1974—Richmond	Int.	OF-SS	7	6	1	0	0	0	0	0	.000	1	2	1	.750
1974—Savannah	South.	*SS-2B	111	406	70	109	23	5	4	35	.268	178	340	32	*.942
1975—Savannah§	South.	3B-2B-SS	107	355	52	96	10	4	3	41	.270	163	274	16	.965
1976—Richmond	Int.	*2B-SS	135	447	58	121	17	5	1	55	.254	338	460	*23	.972
1977—Richmond	Int.	2B	108	347	33	86	8	2	2	35	.248	249	311	11	.981
1978—Richmond	Int.	3B-2B-SS	84	283	32	62	9	2	2	28	.219	94	163	6	.977
1978—Atlanta	Nat.	2B-3B	18	46	3	13	3	0	0	2	.283	31	32	1	.984
1979—Richmond	Int.	2-S-3	122	443	52	105	15	7	4	53	.237	219	372	18	.970
1980—Richmond	Int.	2-S-3	85	258	26	67	7	2	2	23	.260	162	246	12	.971
1980—Atlanta	Nat.	3-S-2	25	26	3	8	2	1	0	2	.308	9	17	3	.897
Major League Totals......................			43	72	6	21	5	1	0	4	.292	40	49	4	.957

Signed as free agent by Atlanta Braves' organization, September 11, 1969.
†Loaned to Montreal Expos' organization, July 16, 1973.
‡Returned, September 4, 1973.
§On disabled list, August 4 to August 15, 1975.

WILLIAM ELLIS RUSSELL
(Bill)

Born October 21, 1948, at Pittsburg, Kan.
Height, 6.00. Weight, 175.
Throws and bats righthanded.
Attended Kansas State College, Pittsburg, Kan.

Established major league record for fewest putouts by shortstop, season, 150 or more games (194), 1974.
Tied major league record for most strikeouts, game (5), June 9, 1971.
Established National League record for fewest double plays by shortstop, season, 150 or more games (68), 1974.
Led National League shortstops in total chances with 834 in 1973.
Led National League shortstops in double plays with 102 in 1977.
Tied for California League lead in double plays by outfielders with 4 in 1968.
Named shortstop on THE SPORTING NEWS National League All-Star Team, 1973.

Year Club	League	Pos.	G.	AB.	R.	H.	2B.	3B.	HR.	RBI.	B.A.	PO.	A.	E.	F.A.
1966—Ogden	Pion.	OF	39	87	19	31	5	1	3	21	.356	25	3	2	.933
1967—Dubuque	Midw.	OF	67	263	29	58	11	1	5	21	.221	98	11	10	.916
1968—Bakersfield	Calif.	OF	115	439	76	123	16	3	17	55	.280	255	*22	7	.975
1969—Los Angeles.......	Nat.	OF	98	212	35	48	6	2	5	15	.226	132	4	3	.978
1970—Spokane	P.C.	O-3-SS	55	237	48	86	13	5	3	30	.363	112	39	6	.962
1970—Los Angeles.......	Nat.	OF-SS	81	278	30	72	11	9	0	28	.259	167	10	3	.983
1971—Los Angeles.......	Nat.	2B-O-S	91	211	29	48	7	4	2	15	.227	131	124	8	.970
1972—Los Angeles.......	Nat.	*SS-OF	129	434	47	118	19	5	4	34	.272	202	439	*34	.950
1973—Los Angeles.......	Nat.	SS	●162	615	55	163	26	3	4	56	.265	243	*560	31	.963
1974—Los Angeles.......	Nat.	*SS-OF	160	553	61	149	17	6	5	65	.269	194	491	*39	.946
1975—Los Angeles†	Nat.	SS	84	252	24	52	9	2	0	14	.206	94	230	11	.967
1976—Los Angeles.......	Nat.	SS	149	554	53	152	17	3	5	65	.274	251	476	28	.963
1977—Los Angeles.......	Nat.	SS	153	634	84	176	28	6	4	51	.278	234	523	29	.963
1978—Los Angeles	Nat.	SS	155	625	72	179	32	4	3	46	.286	245	533	31	.962
1979—Los Angeles	Nat.	SS	153	627	72	170	26	4	7	56	.271	218	452	30	.957
1980—Los Angeles	Nat.	SS	130	466	38	123	23	2	3	34	.264	179	387	19	.968
Major League Totals			1545	5461	600	1450	222	50	42	479	.266	2290	4229	266	.961

Selected by Los Angeles Dodgers' organization in 37th round of free-agent draft, June 12, 1966.
†On disabled list, April 13 to May 6 and May 11 to June 30, 1975.

CHAMPIONSHIP SERIES RECORD

Established Championship Series record for most one-base hits, four-game Series (7), 1974.

Year Club League	Pos.	G.	AB.	R.	H.	2B.	3B.	HR.	RBI.	B.A.	PO.	A.	E.	F.A.
1974—Los Angeles.......Nat.	SS	4	18	1	7	0	0	0	3	.389	13	16	0	1.000
1977—Los Angeles.......Nat.	SS	4	18	3	5	1	0	0	2	.278	11	12	2	.920
1978—Los Angeles ......Nat.	SS	4	17	1	7	1	0	0	2	.412	4	14	0	1.000
Championship Series Totals............		12	53	5	19	2	0	0	7	.358	28	42	2	.972

WORLD SERIES RECORD

Tied World Series record for one or more hits, each game, six-game Series, 1978.

Year Club League	Pos.	G.	AB.	R.	H.	2B.	3B.	HR.	RBI.	B.A.	PO.	A.	E.	F.A.
1974—Los Angeles.......Nat.	SS	5	18	0	4	0	1	0	2	.222	4	11	1	.938
1977—Los Angeles.......Nat.	SS	6	26	3	4	0	1	0	2	.154	9	21	0	1.000
1978—Los Angeles ..... Nat.	SS	6	26	1	11	2	0	0	2	.423	11	20	3	.912
World Series Totals........................		17	70	4	19	2	2	0	6	.271	24	52	4	.950

ALL-STAR GAME RECORD

Year League	Pos.	AB.	R.	H.	2B.	3B.	HR.	RBI.	B.A.	PO.	A.	E.	F.A.
1973—National..............................	SS	2	0	0	0	0	0	0	.000	0	2	0	1.000
1976—National..............................	SS	1	0	0	0	0	0	0	.000	1	2	0	1.000
1980—National..............................	SS	2	0	0	0	0	0	0	.000	0	2	0	1.000
All-Star Game Totals........................		5	0	0	0	0	0	0	.000	1	6	0	1.000

RICHARD DAVID RUTHVEN
(Dick)

Born March 27, 1951, at Sacramento, Calif.
Height, 6.03. Weight, 190.
Throws and bats righthanded.
Hobbies—Reading, electronics, fishing, skiing and music.
Attended Fresno State University, Fresno, Calif.
Brother-in-law of Tommy Hutton, first baseman-outfielder with Montreal Expos.
Tied major league record for most putouts by pitcher, nine-inning game (5), April 19, 1978.

Year Club	League	G.	IP.	W.	L.	Pct.	H.	R.	ER.	SO.	BB.	ERA.
1973—Philadelphia†	National	25	128	6	9	.400	125	69	60	98	75	4.22
1974—Philadelphia........................	National	35	213	9	13	.409	182	106	95	153	116	4.01
1975—Toledo	Int'national	23	153	10	12	.455	148	72	54	114	69	3.18
1975—Philadelphia‡	National	11	41	2	2	.500	37	22	19	26	22	4.17
1976—Atlanta	National	36	240	14	17	.452	255	112	112	142	90	4.20
1977—Atlanta§...........................	National	25	151	7	13	.350	158	86	71	84	62	4.23
1978—Atlanta x-Philadelphia	National	33	232	15	11	.577	214	95	87	120	56	3.38
1979—Philadelphia y	National	20	122	7	5	.583	121	59	58	58	37	4.28
1980—Philadelphia........................	National	33	223	17	10	.630	241	99	88	86	74	3.55
Major League Totals		218	1350	77	80	.490	1333	648	590	777	532	3.93

Selected by Baltimore Orioles' organization in 20th round of free-agent draft, June 5, 1969.
Selected by Minnesota Twins' organization in 1st round (eighth player selected) of free-agent draft, June 6, 1972.
Selected by Philadelphia Phillies' organization in secondary phase of free-agent draft, January 10, 1973.
†On disabled list, August 3 to September 1, 1973.
‡Traded with Pitcher Roy Thomas and Infielder-Outfielder Alan Bannister to Chicago White Sox for Pitcher Jim Kaat and Shortstop Mike Buskey, December 10, 1975. Traded with Outfielder Ken Henderson and Pitcher Danny Osborn by Chicago White Sox to Atlanta Braves for Outfielder Ralph Garr and Infielder Larvell Blanks, December 12, 1975.
§On disabled list, May 2; transferred to emergency disabled list, May 3 to July 4, 1977.
xTraded to Philadelphia Phillies for Pitcher Gene Garber, June 15, 1978.
yOn disabled list, July 2 to July 25 and August 16 to October 4, 1979.

CHAMPIONSHIP SERIES RECORD

Year Club	League	G.	IP.	W.	L.	Pct.	H.	R.	ER.	SO.	BB.	ERA.
1978—Philadelphia........................	National	1	4⅔	0	1	.000	6	3	3	3	0	5.59
1980—Philadelphia........................	National	2	9	1	0	1.000	3	2	2	4	5	2.00
Championship Series Totals		3	13⅔	1	1	.500	9	5	5	7	5	3.29

WORLD SERIES RECORD

Year Club	League	G.	IP.	W.	L.	Pct.	H.	R.	ER.	SO.	BB.	ERA.
1980—Philadelphia........................	National	1	9	0	0	.000	9	3	3	7	0	3.00

ALL-STAR GAME RECORD

Member of National League All-Star Team in 1976; did not play.

LYNN NOLAN RYAN JR.
(Known by middle name.)

Born January 31, 1947, at Refugio, Tex.
Height, 6.02. Weight, 195.
Throws and bats righthanded.
Hobby—Hunting.
Attended Alvin Junior College, Alvin, Tex.

Established major league records for most games, 15 or more strikeouts, lifetime (21); most games, 10 or more strikeouts, lifetime (131); most seasons, 300 or more strikeouts (5); most games, 10 or more strikeouts, season (23), 1973; most strikeouts, three consecutive games (including extra innings—27⅓) (47), August 12, 16 and 20, 1974; 1974; most strikeouts by losing pitcher, extra-inning game (19), August 20, 1974 (11 innings); most seasons leading major leagues and league, bases on balls allowed (6).

Established modern major league records for most consecutive seasons, 300 or more strikeouts (3); most strikeouts, season (383), 1973.

Tied major league records for striking out side on nine pitches, April 19, 1968 (third inning) and July 9, 1972 (second inning); most no-hit games, season (2), 1973; most strikeouts game (19), August 12, 1974; most clubs shut out, season (8), 1972; most no-hit games, lifetime (4); most consecutive seasons leading major leagues, bases on balls allowed (3); most strikeouts, three consecutive nine-inning games (41), August 7, 12 and 16, 1974.

Established American League record for most games, 10 or more strikeouts, lifetime (114); most consecutive strikeouts, game (9), July 9, 1972 and July 15, 1973; most games, 15 or more strikeouts, lifetime (19).

Tied American League records for most seasons, 200 or more strikeouts (7); most low-hit (no-hit and one-hit) games, season (3), 1973; most wild pitches, season (21), 1977; most seasons leading league, errors by pitcher (4); most seasons leading league, wild pitches (3); most consecutive seasons leading league, wild pitches (2).

Pitched 3-0 no-hit victory against Kansas City Royals, May 15, 1973.
Pitched 6-0 no-hit victory against Detroit Tigers, July 15, 1973.
Pitched 4-0 no-hit victory against Minnesota Twins, September 28, 1974.
Pitched 1-0 no-hit victory against Baltimore Orioles, June 1, 1975.
Led American League in shutouts with 9 in 1972 and with 7 in 1976 and tied for lead with 5 in 1979.
Led American League in wild pitches with 18 in 1972, with 21 in 1977 and with 13 in 1978.
Led Western Carolinas League pitchers in games started with 28 in 1966.
Tied for American League lead in complete games with 22 in 1977.
Tied for Appalachian League lead in hit batsmen with 8 in 1965.
Named Outstanding Pitcher in Western Carolinas League, 1966.
Named righthanded pitcher on THE SPORTING NEWS American League All-Star Team, 1977.
Named American League Pitcher of the Year by THE SPORTING NEWS, 1977.

Year	Club	League	G.	IP.	W.	L.	Pct.	H.	R.	ER.	SO.	BB.	ERA.
1965—Marion	Ap'lachian	13	78	3	6	.333	61	47	38	115	56	4.38
1966—Greenville	W. Carol.	29	183	*17	2	.895	109	59	51	*272	*127	2.51
1966—Williamsport	Eastern	3	19	0	2	.000	9	6	2	35	12	0.95
1966—New York	National	2	3	0	1	.000	5	5	5	6	3	15.00
1967—Winter Haven†	Florida St.	1	4	0	0	.000	1	1	1	5	2	2.25
1967—Jacksonville‡	Int'national	3	7	1	0	1.000	3	1	0	18	3	0.00
1968—New York§	National	21	134	6	9	.400	93	50	46	133	75	3.09
1969—New York	National	25	89	6	3	.667	60	38	35	92	53	3.54
1970—New York	National	27	132	7	11	.389	86	59	50	125	97	3.41
1971—New York x	National	30	152	10	14	.417	125	78	67	137	116	3.97
1972—California	American	39	284	19	16	.543	166	80	72	*329	*157	2.28
1973—California	American	41	326	21	16	.568	238	113	104	*383	*162	2.87
1974—California	American	42	*333	22	16	.579	221	127	107	*367	*202	2.89
1975—California	American	28	198	14	12	.538	152	90	76	186	132	3.45
1976—California	American	39	284	17	18	.486	193	117	106	*327	183	3.36
1977—California	American	37	299	19	16	.543	198	110	92	*341	*204	2.77
1978—California y	American	31	235	10	13	.435	183	106	97	*260	*148	3.71
1979—California z	American	34	223	16	14	.533	169	104	89	*223	114	3.59
1980—Houston	National	35	234	11	10	.524	205	100	87	200	*98	3.35
National League Totals		140	744	40	48	.455	574	330	290	693	442	3.51
American League Totals		291	2182	138	121	.533	1520	847	743	2416	1302	3.06
Major League Totals		431	2926	178	169	.513	2094	1177	1033	3109	1744	3.18

Selected by New York Mets' organization in 8th round of free-agent draft, June, 1965.
†On military list from beginning of season through May 13.
‡Suffered elbow injury; on disabled list July 16 to August 30.
§On disabled list with blisters on pitching hand from July 30 to August 30.
xTraded with Pitcher Don Rose, Outfielder Leroy Stanton and Catcher Francisco Estrada to California Angels for Infielder Jim Fregosi, December 10, 1971.
yOn disabled list, June 14 to July 5, 1978.
zGranted free agency, November 1, 1979; signed by Houston Astros, November 19, 1979.

CHAMPIONSHIP SERIES RECORD

Established Championship Series record for most strikeouts by relief pitcher, game (7), October 6, 1969.
Tied Championship Series records for most clubs, total Series (3); most runs and earned runs allowed, five-game Series (8), 1980; most strikeouts, start of game (4), October 3, 1979.
Established National League Championship Series record for most hits allowed, five-game Series (16), 1980.

Year	Club	League	G.	IP.	W.	L.	Pct.	H.	R.	ER.	SO.	BB.	ERA.
1969—New York	National	1	7	1	0	1.000	3	2	2	7	2	2.57
1979—California	American	1	7	0	0	.000	4	3	1	8	3	1.29
1980—Houston	National	2	13⅓	0	0	.000	16	8	8	14	3	5.40
Championship Series Totals		4	27⅓	1	0	1.000	23	13	11	29	8	3.62

WORLD SERIES RECORD

Year	Club	League	G.	IP.	W.	L.	Pct.	H.	R.	ER.	SO.	BB.	ERA.
1969—New York	National	1	2⅓	0	0	.000	1	0	0	3	2	0.00

ALL-STAR GAME RECORD

Year League	IP.	W.	L.	Pct.	H.	R.	ER.	SO.	BB.	ERA.
1973—American	2	0	0	.000	2	2	2	2	2	9.00
1979—American	2	0	0	.000	5	3	3	2	1	13.50
All-Star Game Totals	4	0	0	.000	7	5	5	4	3	11.25

Member of American League All-Star Team for the 1972 and 1975 games; did not play.
Named to American League All-Star Team to replace Frank Tanana for 1977 game; declined.

BRIAN JOSEPH RYDER

Born February 13, 1960, at Worcester, Mass.
Height, 6.06. Weight, 175.
Throws and bats righthanded.

Led Florida State League in shutouts with 6 in 1979.

Year Club	League	G.	IP.	W.	L.	Pct.	H.	R.	ER.	SO.	BB.	ERA.
1978—Oneonta	NYP	11	66	5	3	.625	43	34	26	71	63	3.55
1979—Ft. Lauderdale	Florida St.	25	171	15	5	.750	135	49	44	*156	76	2.32
1980—Nashville	Southern	28	201	15	9	.625	170	83	68	134	83	3.04

Selected by New York Yankees' organization in 1st round (26th player selected) of free-agent draft, June 6, 1978.

MICHAEL GEORGE SADEK

Name pronounced SAY-deck.

(Mike)

Born May 30, 1946, at Minneapolis, Minn.
Height, 5.10. Weight, 170.
Throws and bats righthanded.
Hobby—Sports in general.
Attended University of Minnesota, Minneapolis, Minn., and St. Cloud
State College, St. Cloud, Minn.

Year Club	League	Pos.	G.	AB.	R.	H.	2B.	3B.	HR.	RBI.	B.A.	PO.	A.	E.	F.A.
1967—St. Cloud	North.	C	53	177	37	41	5	0	0	17	.232	401	32	*14	.969
1968—Orlando	Fla. St.	O-C-3-2	60	162	29	43	3	0	0	12	.265	107	21	5	.962
1969—Charlotte†	South.	C-2B	81	224	28	43	9	3	0	22	.192	384	41	5	.988
1970—Amarillo	Texas	C	17	46	6	9	2	0	0	3	.196	116	17	2	.985
1970—Phoenix	P.C.	•C-O-3	74	197	29	48	5	3	1	25	.244	354	37	•10	.975
1971—Phoenix	P.C.	C	76	220	30	68	8	4	1	32	.309	473	33	•14	.973
1972—Phoenix	P.C.	C-3-S-O-2	78	212	25	52	9	1	1	24	.245	409	42	7	.985
1973—San Francisco‡	Nat.	C	39	66	6	11	1	1	0	4	.167	146	7	3	.981
1974—Phoenix	P.C.	C	117	371	50	93	17	5	1	38	.251	615	*61	14	.980
1975—Phoenix	P.C.	C	50	160	29	43	8	6	2	28	.269	293	48	3	.991
1975—San Francisco	Nat.	C	42	106	14	25	5	2	0	9	.236	207	10	1	.995
1976—San Francisco	Nat.	C	55	93	8	19	2	0	0	7	.204	191	11	3	.985
1977—San Francisco	Nat.	C	61	126	12	29	7	0	1	15	.230	227	32	2	.992
1978—San Francisco§	Nat.	C	40	109	15	26	3	0	2	9	.239	182	15	5	.975
1979—San Francisco	Nat.	C-OF	63	126	14	30	5	0	1	11	.238	246	21	2	.993
1980—San Fran. xy	Nat.	C	64	151	14	38	4	1	1	16	.252	266	29	8	.974
Major League Totals			364	777	83	178	27	4	5	71	.229	1465	125	24	.985

Selected by San Francisco Giants' organization in 11th round of free-agent draft, June, 1966.
Selected by Minnesota Twins' organization in secondary phase of free-agent draft, June 7, 1967.
†Drafted by San Francisco Giants from Denver (Minnesota Twins' organization), December 1, 1969.
‡On supplemental disabled list, June 25 to July 10, 1973.
§On disabled list, July 19 to August 25, 1978.
xOn supplemental disabled list, July 16 to July 31, 1980.
yGranted free agency, October 24, 1980; re-signed by Giants, December 24, 1980.

LENN HARUKI SAKATA

Name pronounced Sa-COT-a.

Born June 8, 1954, at Honolulu, Hawaii
Height, 5.09. Weight, 160.
Throws and bats righthanded.
Hobbies—Golf, tennis and weightlifting.
Attended Treasure Valley Community College, Ontario, Ore. and
Gonzaga University, Spokane, Wash.

Year Club	League	Pos.	G.	AB.	R.	H.	2B.	3B.	HR.	RBI.	B.A.	PO.	A.	E.	F.A.
1975—Thetford Mines†	East.	2B	121	421	63	108	9	3	9	43	.257	243	304	16	.972
1976—Spokane	P.C.	2B	141	510	64	143	23	5	10	70	.280	327	428	22	.972
1977—Spokane	P.C.	2B	94	345	52	105	19	4	4	73	.304	221	352	13	*.978
1977—Milwaukee	Amer.	2B	53	154	13	25	2	0	2	12	.162	102	159	4	.985
1978—Spokane	P.C.	2B	45	156	24	42	14	3	0	20	.269	73	160	5	.979
1978—Milwaukee	Amer.	2B	30	78	8	15	4	0	0	3	.192	50	66	3	.975
1979—Vancouver‡	P. C.	2B-3B	118	454	59	136	21	3	6	64	.300	266	409	14	.980
1979—Milwaukee§	Amer.	2B	4	14	1	7	2	0	0	1	.500	10	13	0	1.000
1980—Rochester x	Int.	2B	26	93	19	32	6	1	3	8	.344	45	87	4	.971
1980—Baltimore	Amer.	2B-SS	43	83	12	16	3	2	1	9	.193	55	73	2	.985
Major League Totals			130	329	34	63	11	2	3	25	.191	217	311	9	.983

Selected by San Francisco Giants' organization in 14th round of free-agent draft, June 6, 1972.
Selected by San Diego Padres' organization in 5th round of free-agent draft, June 5, 1974.
Selected by Milwaukee Brewers' organization in secondary phase of free-agent draft, January 9, 1975.
†On disabled list, August 26 to September 5, 1975.
‡On disabled list, April 30 to May 18, 1979.
§Traded to Baltimore Orioles for Pitcher John Flinn, December 6, 1979.
xOn suspended list, April 16 to April 21, 1980.

LUIS ERNESTO SALAZAR

Born May 19, 1956, at Barcelona, Venezuela.
Height, 6.00. Weight, 185.
Throws and bats righthanded.

Led Eastern League outfielders in putouts with 312 and tied for lead in double plays with 3 in 1979.

Year	Club	League	Pos.	G.	AB.	R.	H.	2B.	3B.	HR.	RBI.	B.A.	PO.	A.	E.	F.A.
1974—Sara. Royals†	G.C.		SS	2	4	0	1	0	0	0	1	.250	0	2	0	1.000
1976—Niagara Falls	NYP		SS-OF	42	151	18	36	3	4	1	17	.238	71	49	17	.876
1977—Salem	Carol.		S-3-2	116	433	72	117	17	5	11	48	.270	157	294	45	.909
1978—Salem	Carol.		O-3-S	126	472	55	138	20	4	3	49	.292	160	77	19	.926
1979—Buffalo	East.		OF-3B	∗139	∗561	∗108	∗181	17	5	27	86	.323	321	42	13	.965
1980—Port.‡-Hawaii	P.C.		OF	127	497	91	157	23	15	9	64	.316	304	11	8	.975
1980—San Diego	Nat.		3B-OF	44	169	28	57	4	7	1	25	.337	39	88	7	.948
Major League Totals				44	169	28	57	4	7	1	25	.337	39	88	7	.948

Signed as free agent by Kansas City Royals' organization, November 29, 1973.
†Released, July 8, 1974; signed by Pittsburgh Pirates' organization, November 23, 1975.
‡Traded with Outfielder Rick Lancellotti to San Diego Padres' organization for Infielder Kurt Bevacqua and a player to be named later, August 4, 1980; Pitcher Mark Lee traded to Pirates' organization completing deal, August 12, 1980.

JOSEPH CHARLES SAMBITO

Name pronounced sam-BEET-oh.

(Joe)

Born June 28, 1952, at Brooklyn, N.Y.
Height, 6.01. Weight, 190.
Throws and bats lefthanded.
Hobbies—Fishing and all sports.
Attended Adelphi University, Garden City, N.Y.

Major League saves: 1976 (1), 1977 (7), 1978 (11), 1979 (22), 1980 (17). Total—58.
Led Southern League in wild pitches with 14 and tied for lead in games started with 28 in 1975.
Tied for Appalachian League lead in shutouts with 2 in 1973.

Year	Club	League	G.	IP.	W.	L.	Pct.	H.	R.	ER.	SO.	BB.	ERA.
1973—Columbus	Southern		1	2	0	0	.000	4	4	4	2	1	18.00
1973—Covington	Ap'lachian		11	55	4	2	.667	32	18	9	57	13	1.47
1974—Cedar Rapids	Midwest		23	156	11	8	.579	133	59	52	182	49	3.00
1975—Columbus	Southern		30	∗209	12	9	.571	∗200	85	70	∗140	85	3.01
1976—Memphis	Int'national		5	27	3	0	1.000	37	19	19	17	13	6.33
1976—Columbus	Southern		12	100	8	2	.800	77	27	20	61	23	1.80
1976—Houston	National		20	53	3	2	.600	45	21	21	26	14	3.57
1977—Houston	National		54	89	5	5	.500	77	34	23	67	24	2.33
1978—Houston	National		62	88	4	9	.308	85	32	30	96	32	3.07
1979—Houston	National		63	91	8	7	.533	80	20	18	83	23	1.78
1980—Houston	National		64	90	8	4	.667	65	26	22	75	22	2.20
Major League Totals			263	411	28	27	.509	352	133	114	347	115	2.50

Selected by Houston Astros' organization in 17th round of free-agent draft, June 5, 1973.

CHAMPIONSHIP SERIES RECORD

Year	Club	League	G.	IP.	W.	L.	Pct.	H.	R.	ER.	SO.	BB.	ERA.
1980—Houston	National		3	3⅔	0	1	.000	4	2	2	6	2	4.91

ALL-STAR GAME RECORD

Year	League	IP.	W.	L.	Pct.	H.	R.	ER.	SO.	BB.	ERA.
1979—National		⅔	0	0	.000	0	0	0	0	1	0.00

WILLIAM AMOS SAMPLE
(Billy)

Born April 2, 1955, at Roanoke, Va.
Height, 5.09. Weight, 175.
Throws and bats righthanded.
Attended James Madison University, Harrisonburg, Va.; received
Bachelor of Science degree in Psychology.

Tied major league records for highest fielding percentage by outfielder, season, 100 or more games (1.000), 1979; most assists by outfielder, inning (2), April 28, 1979 (fourth inning).
Led Gulf Coast League in total bases with 86 in 1976.
Led Texas League second basemen in errors with 23 in 1977.

Led Pacific Coast League in bases on balls with 109 in 1978.

Year Club	League	Pos.	G.	AB.	R.	H.	2B.	3B.	HR.	RBI.	B.A.	PO.	A.	E.	F.A.
1976—Sara. Rangers	G.C.	2B	45	152	35	58	7	*9	1	33	*.382	81	113	8	.960
1977—Tulsa	Texas	2-O-3	113	408	86	142	26	*13	7	72	.348	169	122	26	.918
1978—Tucson	P.C.	OF-2B	131	483	*141	170	27	13	18	99	.352	234	11	6	.976
1978—Texas	Amer.	OF	8	15	2	7	2	0	0	3	.467	0	0	0	.000
1979—Texas	Amer.	OF	128	325	60	95	21	2	5	35	.292	173	7	0	1.000
1980—Texas	Amer.	OF	99	204	29	53	10	0	4	19	.260	105	2	3	.973
Major League Totals			235	544	91	155	33	2	9	57	.285	278	9	3	.990

Selected by Texas Rangers' organization in 28th round of free-agent draft, June 5, 1973.
Selected by Texas Rangers' organization in 10th round of free-agent draft, June 8, 1976.

ALEJANDRO SANCHEZ (PIMENTEL)

Born February 26, 1959, at San Pedro, Dominican Republic.
Height, 6.00. Weight, 175.
Throws and bats righthanded.

Year Club	League	Pos.	G.	AB.	R.	H.	2B.	3B.	HR.	RBI.	B.A.	PO.	A.	E.	F.A.
1978—Helena	Pion.	OF	6	24	4	5	0	1	0	5	.208	2	1	0	1.000
1978—Auburn	NYP	OF	58	242	30	58	9	5	4	28	.240	120	6	*14	.900
1979—Cen. Oregon	Northw.	OF	54	204	31	55	10	2	3	38	.270	97	6	5	.954
1980—Spartanburg	S. Atl.	OF	127	490	84	140	26	8	15	76	.286	223	15	●16	.937

Signed as free agent by Philadelphia Phillies' organization, April 10, 1978.

LUIS MERCEDES SANCHEZ

Born August 24, 1953, at Cariaco, Sucre, Venezuela.
Height, 6.02. Weight, 170.
Throws and bats righthanded.

Led Florida East Coast League in complete games with 6 in 1972.

Year Club	League	G.	IP.	W.	L.	Pct.	H.	R.	ER.	SO.	BB.	ERA.
1972—Cocoa Astros	Fla. E.C.	11	71	6	3	.667	55	29	20	49	31	2.54
1973—Cedar Rapids	Midwest	26	130	5	9	.357	140	75	61	93	43	4.22
1974—Cedar Rapids	Midwest	25	147	9	4	.692	122	39	26	130	44	*1.59
1975—Columbus	Southern	21	132	6	12	.333	137	76	59	60	64	4.02
1975—Dubuque†	Midwest	6	31	2	3	.400	25	19	12	19	10	3.48
1976—Tampa‡§x	Florida St.	2	8	0	2	.000	11	4	4	5	5	4.50
1977-78							Did not play					
1979—Caracas y	Int.-Amer.	13	35	2	4	.333	39	25	19	25	19	4.89
1980—Aguila z	Mexican	24	177	14	9	.609	149	47	40	155	35	2.03
1980—Albuquerque a	P. Coast	5	22	2	1	.667	27	14	13	15	10	5.32

Signed as free agent by Houston Astros' organization, September 1, 1971.
†Traded with Pitcher Carlos Alfonso to Cincinnati Reds' organization, December 12, 1975, completing deal in which Houston acquired Pitcher Joaquin Andujar, October 24, 1975.
‡On disabled list, April 17 to May 18, 1976.
§On temporary inactive list, May 28 to July 28, 1976.
xOn disqualified list, July 28, 1976 to March 30, 1979; signed by Caracas of Inter-American League, March 30, 1979.
ySigned by Aguila, December 29, 1979.
zLoaned to Los Angeles Dodgers' organization, July 31, 1980; returned, October 15, 1980.
aSold to California Angels, February 10, 1981.

ORLANDO SANCHEZ

Born September 7, 1956, at Canovanas, Puerto Rico.
Height, 6.00. Weight, 185.
Throws right and bats lefthanded.

Year Club	League	Pos.	G.	AB.	R.	H.	2B.	3B.	HR.	RBI.	B.A.	PO.	A.	E.	F.A.
1974—Marion	Appal.	C	23	63	11	13	3	0	0	8	.206	131	15	1	.993
1975—Pulaski†	Appal.	1B-OF-P	52	167	34	44	11	0	7	46	.263	188	4	11	.946
1976—Spartanburg	W. Car.	1B-C	122	445	61	118	18	5	13	81	.265	803	34	22	.974
1977—Peninsula	Car.	OF-1B-C	109	390	61	108	18	3	6	48	.277	232	19	19	.930
1978—Reading‡	East.	OF	80	288	50	84	12	3	14	48	.292	121	2	10	.925
1979—Reading	East.	OF-1B	70	219	23	71	11	1	6	30	.324	65	2	4	.944
1979—Oklahoma City	A.A.	OF	31	92	14	27	5	2	1	9	.293	27	0	1	.964
1980—Okla. City§x	A.A.	OF	68	218	21	67	9	2	1	21	.307	35	3	3	.927

Signed as free agent by New York Mets' organization, February 18, 1974.
†Released, December 30, 1975; signed by Philadelphia Phillies' organization, April 16, 1976.
‡On disabled list, April 25 to May 4 and June 10 to July 7, 1978.
§On disabled list, May 3 to May 27 and July 5 to July 24, 1980.
xDrafted by St. Louis Cardinals, December 8, 1980.

RECORD AS PITCHER

Year Club	League	G.	IP.	W.	L.	Pct.	H.	R.	ER.	SO.	BB.	ERA.
1975—Pulaski	Appal.	1	2	0	0	.000	3	6	5	0	4	22.50

RYNE DEE SANDBERG

Born September 18, 1959, at Spokane, Wash.
Height, 6.01. Weight, 175.
Throws and bats righthanded.

Led Pioneer League shortstops in double plays with 38 in 1978.
Led Western Carolinas League shortstops in double plays with 80 in 1979.
Led Eastern League shortstops in assists with 386, in fielding average with .964 and in double plays with 81 in 1980.

Year Club	League	Pos.	G.	AB.	R.	H.	2B.	3B.	HR.	RBI.	B.A.	PO.	A.	E.	F.A.
1978—Helena..............	Pioneer	SS	56	190	34	59	6	6	1	23	.311	92	∗200	24	.924
1979—Spartanburg......	W. Car.	SS	∗138	∗539	83	133	21	7	4	47	.247	134	∗467	35	∗.945
1980—Reading...........	East.	SS-3B	129	490	95	152	21	12	11	79	.310	156	388	20	.965

Selected by Philadelphia Phillies' organization in 21st round of free-agent draft, June 6, 1978.

SCOTT DOUGLAS SANDERSON

Born July 22, 1956, at Dearborn, Mich.
Height, 6.05. Weight, 198.
Throws and bats righthanded.
Attended Vanderbilt University, Nashville, Tenn.

Year Club	League	G.	IP.	W.	L.	Pct.	H.	R.	ER.	SO.	BB.	ERA.
1977—West Palm Beach	Florida St.	10	57	5	2	.714	58	22	17	37	23	2.68
1978—Memphis..............................	Southern	9	58	5	3	.625	55	32	26	44	19	4.03
1978—Denver	Am. Assoc.	9	49	4	2	.667	47	35	33	36	30	6.06
1978—Montreal..............................	National	10	61	4	2	.667	52	20	17	50	21	2.51
1979—Montreal..............................	National	34	168	9	8	.529	148	69	64	138	54	3.43
1980—Montreal..............................	National	33	211	16	11	.593	206	76	73	125	56	3.11
Major League Totals...............................		77	440	29	21	.580	406	165	154	313	131	3.15

Selected by Kansas City Royals' organization in 11th round of free-agent draft, June 5, 1974.
Selected by Montreal Expos' organization in 3rd round of free-agent draft, June 7, 1977.

MANUEL deJESUS SANGUILLEN

Name pronounced San-GHEE-yen.

(Manny)

Born March 21, 1944, at Colon, Panama.
Height, 6.00. Weight, 193.
Throws and bats righthanded.
Hobbies—Fishing and playing guitar.

Tied major league record for most triples with bases filled, season, 3, 1971.
Tied for National League lead in double plays by catchers with 12 in 1971.
Led New York-Pennsylvania League catchers in double plays with 9 in 1965.
Led Carolina League in passed balls with 17 in 1966 and International League with 9 in 1968.
Named catcher on The Sporting News National League All-Star Team, 1971.

Year Club	League	Pos.	G.	AB.	R.	H.	2B.	3B.	HR.	RBI.	B.A.	PO.	A.	E.	F.A.
1965—Batavia.............	NYP	C	99	340	45	80	8	2	6	36	.235	689	∗69	10	.987
1966—Raleigh.............	Carol.	C	115	400	62	131	19	3	8	49	.328	683	●87	16	.980
1966—Columbus...........	Int.	C	9	26	1	6	0	0	0	0	.231	37	12	0	1.000
1967—Columbus..........	Int.	C	71	240	28	62	6	2	9	29	.258	409	48	●10	.979
1967—Pittsburgh........	Nat.	C	30	96	6	26	4	0	0	8	.271	133	11	2	.986
1968—Columbus..........	Int.	C-1B-O	105	377	45	119	16	5	8	60	.316	592	60	8	.988
1969—Pittsburgh........	Nat.	C	129	459	62	139	21	6	5	57	.303	825	71	∗17	.981
1970—Pittsburgh........	Nat.	C	128	486	63	158	19	9	7	61	.325	775	66	10	.988
1971—Pittsburgh........	Nat.	C	138	533	60	170	26	5	7	81	.319	712	∗72	5	.994
1972—Pittsburgh........	Nat.	C-OF	136	520	55	155	18	8	7	71	.298	724	50	9	.989
1973—Pittsburgh........	Nat.	C-OF	149	589	64	166	26	7	12	65	.282	632	41	17	.975
1974—Pittsburgh........	Nat.	C	151	596	77	171	21	4	7	68	.287	713	76	12	.985
1975—Pittsburgh........	Nat.	C	133	481	60	158	24	4	9	58	.328	650	53	9	.987
1976—Pittsburgh†	Nat.	C	114	389	52	113	16	6	2	36	.290	518	52	∗13	.978
1977—Oakland‡..........	Amer.	C-1B-OF	152	571	42	157	17	5	6	58	.275	419	54	7	.985
1978—Pittsburgh	Nat.	1B-C	85	220	15	58	5	1	3	16	.264	438	20	0	1.000
1979—Pittsburgh........	Nat.	C-1B	56	74	8	17	5	2	0	4	.230	67	6	2	.973
1980—Pittsburgh§x	Nat.	1B	47	48	2	12	3	0	0	2	.250	40	3	2	.956
American League Totals..................			152	571	42	157	17	5	6	58	.275	419	54	7	.985
National League Totals....................			1296	4491	524	1343	188	52	59	527	.299	6227	521	98	.986
Major League Totals			1448	5062	566	1500	205	57	65	585	.296	6646	575	105	.986

Signed as free agent by Pittsburgh Pirates' organization, October 2, 1964.

†Traded with cash estimated at $100,000 to Oakland A's for Manager Chuck Tanner, November 5, 1976.

‡Traded to Pittsburgh Pirates for Outfielder Miguel Dilone, Pitcher Elias Sosa and a player to be named later, April 4, 1978; Infielder Mike Edwards traded to Oakland to complete deal, April 7, 1978.

§Traded with Pitcher Bert Blyleven to Cleveland Indians for Pitchers Bob Owchinko, Rafael Vasquez and Victor Cruz and Catcher Gary Alexander, December 9, 1980.

xReleased, February 18, 1981.

CHAMPIONSHIP SERIES RECORD

Year Club	League	Pos.	G.	AB.	R.	H.	2B.	3B.	HR.	RBI.	B.A.	PO.	A.	E.	F.A.
1970—Pittsburgh.........	Nat.	C	3	12	0	2	0	0	0	0	.167	13	1	1	.983

Year Club League	Pos.	G.	AB.	R.	H.	2B.	3B.	HR.	RBI.	B.A.	PO.	A.	E.	F.A.
1971—Pittsburgh........Nat.	C	4	15	1	4	0	0	0	1	.267	30	1	0	1.000
1972—Pittsburgh........Nat.	C-PH	5	16	4	5	1	0	1	2	.313	22	0	1	.957
1974—Pittsburgh........Nat.	C	4	16	0	4	1	0	0	0	.250	19	2	2	.913
1975—Pittsburgh........Nat.	C	3	12	0	2	0	0	0	0	.167	29	1	1	.968
Championship Series Totals.............		19	71	5	17	2	0	1	3	.239	113	5	5	.959

WORLD SERIES RECORD

Year Club League	Pos.	G.	AB.	R.	H.	2B.	3B.	HR.	RBI.	B.A.	PO.	A.	E.	F.A.
1971—Pittsburgh........Nat.	C	7	29	3	11	1	0	0	0	.379	37	0	0	1.000
1979—Pittsburgh ....Nat.	PH	3	3	0	1	0	0	0	1	.333	0	0	0	.000
World Series Totals........................		10	32	3	12	1	0	0	1	.375	37	0	0	1.000

ALL-STAR GAME RECORD

Year League	Pos.	AB.	R.	H.	2B.	3B.	HR.	RBI.	B.A.	PO.	A.	E.	F.A.
1972—National...............................	C	2	0	1	0	0	0	0	.500	6	0	0	1.000

Member of National League All-Star Team for 1971 and 1975 games; did not play.

RAFAEL FRANCISCO SANTANA (DeLaCRUZ)

Born January 31, 1958, at La Romana, Dominican Republic.
Height, 6.01. Weight, 156.
Throws and bats righthanded.

Year Club League	Pos.	G.	AB.	R.	H.	2B.	3B.	HR.	RBI.	B.A.	PO.	A.	E.	F.A.
1977—Oneonta............NYP	SS	60	157	26	41	5	0	0	23	.261	62	162	•27	.892
1978—Ft. Lauderdale..Fla. St.	SS	131	431	37	111	8	5	0	35	.258	372	•48		.918
1979—Ft. Lauderdale..Fla. St.	S-3-2	133	472	62	124	9	6	0	41	.263	160	351	16	.970
1980—Nashville ....South.	SS	86	275	33	64	4	3	0	20	.233	125	247	25	.937
1980—Ft. Lauderdale† Fla. St.	SS	51	168	20	38	2	0	1	17	.226	81	158	9	.964

Signed as free agent by New York Yankees' organization, August 31, 1976.
†Sold conditionally to St. Louis Cardinals, February 16, 1981.

RAFAEL SANTANA (RIVERA)

Born March 4, 1958 at San Pedro de Macoris, Dominican Republic
Height, 6.01. Weight, 165.
Throws and bats righthanded.

Tied for Florida State League lead in games started with 28 in 1978.

Year Club League	G.	IP.	W.	L.	Pct.	H.	R.	ER.	SO.	BB.	ERA.
1978—Dunedin.............................Florida St.	28	165	11	12	.478	178	•94	76	73	73	4.15
1979—Kinston...............................Carolina	26	142	10	7	.588	143	65	55	102	57	3.49
1980—Knoxville ....Southern	45	83	0	8	.000	91	39	36	63	39	3.90

Signed as free agent by Toronto Blue Jays' organization, April 9, 1978.

MANUEL EDUARDO SARMIENTO (APONTE)

Name pronounced sar-mee-EN-toh.

(Manny)

Born February 2, 1956, at Cagua, Aragua, Venezuela.
Height, 5.11. Weight, 170.
Throws and bats righthanded.
Hobbies—Listening to music and playing basketball.

Led Northwest League in saves with 14 in 1973 and Eastern League with 15 in 1975.

Year Club League	G.	IP.	W.	L.	Pct.	H.	R.	ER.	SO.	BB.	ERA.
1972—Bradenton Reds....................G. Coast	18	40	2	6	.250	40	22	13	34	15	2.93
1973—Seattle ....Northwest	•36	67	2	6	.250	53	22	16	60	24	2.15
1974—Tampa ....Florida St.	39	126	10	9	.526	112	42	40	80	47	2.86
1975—Three Rivers.......................Eastern	•64	129	6	8	.429	104	41	37	114	51	2.58
1976—Indianapolis ....Am. Assoc.	43	65	11	5	.688	49	21	20	51	24	2.77
1976—Cincinnati ....National	22	44	5	1	.833	36	14	10	20	12	2.05
1977—Indianapolis† ....Am. Assoc.	25	35	3	4	.429	45	26	26	35	12	6.69
1977—Cincinnati ....National	24	40	0	0	.000	28	13	11	23	11	2.48
1978—Cincinnati ....National	63	127	9	7	.563	109	65	62	72	54	4.39
1979—Indianapolis ....Am. Assoc.	19	38	1	0	1.000	41	14	10	34	11	2.37
1979—Cincinnati‡ ....National	23	39	0	4	.000	47	21	20	23	7	4.62
1980—Spokane ....P. Coast	51	63	8	7	.533	57	27	21	66	20	3.00
1980—Seattle ....American	9	15	0	1	.000	14	7	6	15	6	3.60
National League Totals	132	250	14	12	.538	220	113	103	138	84	3.71
American League Totals	9	15	0	1	.000	14	7	6	15	6	3.60
Major League Totals................................	141	265	14	13	.519	234	120	109	153	90	3.70

Signed as free agent by Cincinnati Reds' organization, March 25, 1972.
†On disabled list, April 13 to May 4, and May 28 to June 17, 1977.
‡Released, April 2, 1980; signed by Seattle Mariners' organization, April 14, 1980.

CHAMPIONSHIP SERIES RECORD

Year Club League	G.	IP.	W.	L.	Pct.	H.	R.	ER.	SO.	BB.	ERA.
1976—Cincinnati ....National	1	1	0	0	.000	2	2	2	0	1	18.00

WALFREDO E. SARMIENTO
(Wally)

Born November 25, 1958, at Cabimas, Venezuela.
Height, 6.00. Weight, 160.
Throws and bats righthanded.

Year Club	League	G.	IP.	W.	L.	Pct.	H.	R.	ER.	SO.	BB.	ERA.
1977—Eugene ....Northwest	Northwest	17	39	2	1	.667	40	23	16	25	20	3.69
1978—Eugene† ....Northwest	Northwest	23	41	4	1	.800	35	18	17	36	18	3.73
1979—Maracaibo ....Int-Amer.	Int-Amer.	15	83	6	3	.667	86	35	27	32	16	2.92
1979—Orlando‡.............................Southern	Southern	6	41	4	2	.667	36	15	12	29	15	2.63
1980—Toledo ....Int'national	Int'national	42	85	6	6	.500	63	31	25	39	35	2.65

Signed as free agent by Cincinnati Reds' organization, February 27, 1977.
†Released, April 4, 1979; signed by Maracaibo, April 11, 1979.
‡Signed as free agent by Minnesota Twins' organization, July 19, 1979.

KEVIN ANDREW SAUCIER

Name pronounced SO-Shay.

Born August 9, 1956, at Pensacola, Fla.
Height, 6.01. Weight, 195.
Throws left and bats righthanded.
Attended Pensacola Junior College, Pensacola, Fla.

Tied for Western Carolinas League lead in shutouts with 4 in 1975.

Year Club	League	G.	IP.	W.	L.	Pct.	H.	R.	ER.	SO.	BB.	ERA.
1974—Pulaski ....Ap'lachian	Ap'lachian	12	80	4	7	.364	*95	63	48	57	33	5.40
1975—Spartanburg........................W. Carol.	W. Carol.	25	159	12	9	.571	138	72	59	90	61	3.34
1976—Peninsula† ....Carolina	Carolina	14	82	5	3	.625	73	32	24	35	25	2.63
1977—Reading ....Eastern	Eastern	26	158	7	•16	.304	*189	87	71	74	37	4.04
1978—Oklahoma City ....Am. Assoc.	Am. Assoc.	27	173	7	12	.368	200	108	88	99	57	4.58
1978—Philadelphia.........................National	National	1	2	0	1	.000	4	4	4	2	1	18.00
1979—Oklahoma City ....Am. Assoc.	Am. Assoc.	24	47	2	1	.667	40	16	11	20	24	2.11
1979—Philadelphia.........................National	National	29	62	1	4	.200	68	31	29	21	33	4.21
1980—Philadelphia‡§x...................National	National	40	50	7	3	.700	50	21	19	25	20	3.42
Major League Totals..................................		70	114	8	8	.500	122	56	52	48	54	4.11

Selected by Philadelphia Phillies' organization in 2nd round of free-agent draft, June 5, 1974.
†On disabled list, August 6 to August 30, 1976.
‡On disabled list, August 24 to September 11, 1980.
§Traded to Texas Rangers, November 19, 1980, completing deal in which Phillies acquired Pitcher Sparky Lyle, September 13, 1980.
xTraded by Texas Rangers to Detroit Tigers for Shortstop Mark Wagner, December 10, 1980.

CHAMPIONSHIP SERIES RECORD

Year Club	League	G.	IP.	W.	L.	Pct.	H.	R.	ER.	SO.	BB.	ERA.
1980—Philadelphia.........................National	National	2	⅔	0	0	.000	1	0	0	0	2	0.00

WORLD SERIES RECORD

Year Club	League	G.	IP.	W.	L.	Pct.	H.	R.	ER.	SO.	BB.	ERA.
1980—Philadelphia.........................National	National	1	⅔	0	0	.000	0	0	0	0	2	0.00

STEPHEN LOUIS SAX

Born January 20, 1960, at Sacramento, Calif.
Height, 5.11. Weight, 185.
Throws and bats righthanded.

Led Florida State League second basemen in putouts with 360, in assists with 438, in fielding average with .976 and in double plays with 91 in 1980.

Year Club League	Pos.	G.	AB.	R.	H.	2B.	3B.	HR.	RBI.	B.A.	PO.	A.	E.	F.A.
1978—Lethbridge........Pion.	SS	39	131	24	43	6	3	0	21	.328	21	40	9	.871
1979—Clinton ....Midw.	O-2-3	115	386	64	112	15	2	2	52	.290	111	75	18	.912
1980—Vero Beach.......Fla. St.	2B-OF	•139	530	78	150	18	8	3	61	.283	360	438	20	.976

Selected by Los Angeles Dodgers' organization in 9th round of free-agent draft, June 6, 1978.

RANDY JAMES SCARBERY

Born June 22, 1952, at Fresno, Calif.
Height, 6.01. Weight, 185.
Throws right and bats left and righthanded.
Hobbies—Golf and painting.
Attended University of Southern California, Los Angeles, Calif.; received Bachelor of Business degree.

Year Club	League	G.	IP.	W.	L.	Pct.	H.	R.	ER.	SO.	BB.	ERA.
1973—Birmingham ....Southern	Southern	7	43	1	6	.143	44	28	23	29	25	4.81
1973—Tucson...............................P. Coast	P. Coast	10	58	3	3	.500	74	39	33	39	26	5.12
1974—Tucson...............................P. Coast	P. Coast	32	189	11	13	.458	*247	*140	*122	104	74	5.81
1975—Tucson†..............................P. Coast	P. Coast	12	44	1	1	.500	56	39	28	18	17	5.73
1975—Birmingham ....Southern	Southern	17	116	6	10	.375	121	66	50	51	42	3.88

Year Club	League	G.	IP.	W.	L.	Pct.	H.	R.	ER.	SO.	BB.	ERA.
1976–Chattanooga	Southern	9	65	6	2	.750	55	18	17	29	12	2.35
1976–Tucson	P. Coast	18	69	4	8	.333	97	58	43	48	33	5.61
1977–San Jose‡	P. Coast	38	112	7	9	.438	96	61	53	72	50	4.26
1977–New Orleans§	Am. Assoc.	4	25	2	1	.667	23	14	12	19	12	4.32
1978–Iowa	Am. Assoc.	37	144	8	11	.421	140	71	63	86	59	3.94
1979–Chicago	American	45	101	2	8	.200	102	56	52	45	34	4.63
1980–Chicago	American	15	29	1	2	.333	24	14	13	18	7	4.03
1980–Iowa x	Am. Assoc.	2	5	0	0	.000	5	0	0	4	1	0.00
1980–Salt Lake City	P. Coast	20	34	3	1	.750	47	29	28	13	15	7.41
Major League Totals		60	130	3	10	.231	126	70	65	63	41	4.50

Selected by Houston Astros' organization in 1st round (seventh player selected) of free-agent draft, June 4, 1970.

Selected by Oakland A's organization in 1st round (23rd player selected) of free-agent draft, June 5, 1973.

†On disabled list, April 10 to April 29, 1975.

‡Traded to New Orleans (St. Louis Cardinals' organization) for Pitcher Steve Dunning, August 12, 1977.

§Granted free agency, October 20, 1977; signed by Chicago White Sox' organization, November 6, 1977.

xTraded to California Angels' organization for Shortstop Todd Cruz, June 12, 1980.

DANIEL ERNEST SCHATZEDER
(Dan)

Born December 1, 1954, at Elmhurst, Ill.
Height, 6.00. Weight, 195.
Throws and bats lefthanded.
Attended University of Denver, Denver, Colo., received degree in Business Administration.

Year Club	League	G.	IP.	W.	L.	Pct.	H.	R.	ER.	SO.	BB.	ERA.
1976–W. Palm Beach	Florida St.	10	64	5	3	.625	49	22	19	49	20	2.67
1976–Quebec City	Eastern	5	28	2	3	.400	38	16	14	19	10	4.50
1977–Quebec City	Eastern	8	62	5	3	.625	39	20	19	59	15	2.76
1977–Denver†	Am. Assoc.	9	36	2	2	.500	45	25	24	28	14	6.00
1977–Montreal	National	6	22	2	1	.667	16	6	6	14	13	2.45
1978–Denver	Am. Assoc.	4	28	3	0	1.000	24	11	9	19	11	2.89
1978–Montreal	National	29	144	7	7	.500	108	54	49	69	68	3.06
1979–Montreal‡	National	32	162	10	5	.667	136	57	51	106	59	2.83
1980–Detroit§	American	32	193	11	13	.458	178	88	86	94	58	4.01
National League Totals		67	328	19	13	.594	260	117	106	189	140	2.91
American League Totals		32	193	11	13	.458	178	88	86	94	58	4.01
Major League Totals		99	521	30	26	.536	438	205	192	283	198	3.32

Selected by Montreal Expos' organization in 3rd round of free-agent draft, June 8, 1976.

†On disabled list, July 5 to August 30, 1977.

‡Traded to Detroit Tigers for Outfielder Ron LeFlore, December 7, 1979.

§On disabled list, May 27 to June 17, 1980.

WILLIAM JOSEPH SCHERRER
(Bill)

Born January 20, 1958, at Tonawanda, N. Y.
Height, 6.04. Weight, 180.
Throws and bats lefthanded.
Attended University of Nevada, Las Vegas, Nev.
Tied for Northwest League lead in shutouts with 2 in 1978.

Year Club	League	G.	IP.	W.	L.	Pct.	H.	R.	ER.	SO.	BB.	ERA.
1977–Shelby	W. Carol.	27	158	9	9	.500	132	87	62	122	105	3.53
1978–Shelby	W. Carol.	10	31	0	2	.000	27	19	14	18	26	4.06
1978–Eugene	Northwest	13	84	6	4	.600	61	43	33	87	42	3.54
1979–Tampa	Florida St.	25	159	12	3	.800	126	43	32	140	65	1.81
1980–Waterbury	Eastern	25	151	7	8	.467	139	58	56	84	58	3.34

Selected by Cleveland Indians' organization in 6th round of free-agent draft, June 8, 1976.

Selected by Cincinnati Reds' organization in secondary phase of free-agent draft, January 11, 1977.

DAVID FREDERICK SCHMIDT
(Dave)

Born December 22, 1956, at Mesa, Ariz.
Height, 6.01. Weight, 190.
Throws and bats righthanded.
Attended Saddleback Community College, Mission Viejo, Calif.,
and California State University, Fullerton, Calif.
Brother of Eric Schmidt, pitcher in Los Angeles Dodgers' organization.

Year Club	League	Pos.	G.	AB.	R.	H.	2B.	3B.	HR.	RBI.	B.A.	PO.	A.	E.	F.A.
1975–Elmira	NYP	C	59	181	32	45	11	2	3	20	.249	303	•48	8	.978
1976–Winter Haven†	Fla. St.	C	69	217	29	48	8	0	4	28	.221	329	33	10	.973
1977–Winston-Salem	Carol.	C-1B	120	373	60	88	7	4	14	53	.236	530	52	12	.977
1978–Winston-Salem	Carol.	C-1B	105	324	60	87	17	2	14	48	.269	456	50	8	.984
1979–Bristol	East.	C-OF-1B	117	371	78	123	•32	0	19	73	•.332	312	42	10	.973
1980–Pawtucket†	Int.	C-1B-OF	50	144	17	33	5	1	5	16	.229	155	22	3	.983

Selected by Boston Red Sox' organization in 2nd round of free-agent draft, June 4, 1975.

†On disabled list, June 23 to July 23 and August 4 to August 26, 1980.

MICHAEL JACK SCHMIDT
(Mike)

Born September 27, 1949, at Dayton, O.
Height, 6.02. Weight, 203.
Throws and bats righthanded.
Hobby—Golf.
Attended Ohio University, Athens, O.; received Bachelor of Arts degree in Business Administration.

Established major league records for most total bases, extra-inning game (17), April 17, 1976 (10 innings); most home runs by third baseman, season (48), 1980.

Tied major league records for most home runs, extra-inning game (4), April 17, 1976 (10 innings); most consecutive home runs, extra-inning game (4), April 17, 1976 (10 innings); most home runs, consecutive plate appearances (4), April 17, 1976 and July 6 and 7, 1979; most extra bases on long hits, game (12), April 17, 1976 (10 innings); most home runs, two consecutive games (5), April 17 and 18, 1976; most home runs, three consecutive games (6), April 17-20, 1976; most home runs, April (11), 1976; most consecutive seasons leading major leagues in strikeouts (3), 1974 through 1976; most home runs, October (4), 1980.

Established National League record for most assists, third baseman, season (404), 1974; fewest singles, season, 150 or more games (65), 1975.

Tied National League records for most home runs, bases full, one month, 2, June, 1973; most home runs, June (14), 1977; most home runs through July 31 (36), 1979; most home runs, five consecutive games, one or more homer each game (7), July 6 through 10, 1979.

Major league stolen bases: 1972 (0), 1973 (8), 1974 (23), 1975 (29), 1976 (14), 1977 (15), 1978 (19), 1979 (9), 1980 (12). Total—129.

Hit three home runs in one game, vs. San Francisco Giants, July 7, 1979.

Hit home runs in all 12 National League parks, 1979.

Led National League in total bases with 306 in 1976 and with 342 in 1980.

Led National League in slugging percentage with .546 in 1974 and with .624 in 1980.

Led National League batters in strikeouts with 138 in 1974, 180 in 1975 and 149 in 1976.

Led National League third basemen in double plays with 34 in 1978, with 36 in 1979 and with 31 in 1980.

Led National League in bases on balls with 120 in 1979.

Led National League in sacrifice flies with 13 in 1980.

Led Pacific Coast League batters in strikeouts with 145 in 1972.

Tied for National League lead in sacrifice flies with 9 in 1979.

Named third baseman on THE SPORTING NEWS National League All-Star Team, 1974, 1976, 1977, 1979 and 1980.

Named third baseman on THE SPORTING NEWS National League All-Star fielding team, 1976 through 1980.

Named third baseman on THE SPORTING NEWS National League Silver Bat team, 1980.

Named National League Player of the Year by THE SPORTING NEWS, 1980.

Named National League Most Valuable Player by Baseball Writers' Association of America, 1980.

Year	Club	League	Pos.	G.	AB.	R.	H.	2B.	3B.	HR.	RBI.	B.A.	PO.	A.	E.	F.A.
1971—Reading		East.	SS-3B	74	237	27	50	7	1	8	31	.211	100	224	23	.934
1972—Eugene		P.C.	2-3-SS	131	436	80	127	23	6	26	91	.291	271	324	25	.960
1972—Philadelphia†		Nat.	3B-2B	13	34	2	7	0	0	1	3	.206	10	25	2	.946
1973—Philadelphia‡		Nat.	3-2-1-S	132	367	43	72	11	0	18	52	.196	119	256	18	.954
1974—Philadelphia		Nat.	3B	162	568	108	160	28	7	*36	116	.282	134	*404	26	.954
1975—Philadelphia		Nat.	3B-SS	158	562	93	140	34	3	*38	95	.249	139	390	26	.953
1976—Philadelphia		Nat.	3B	160	584	112	153	31	4	*38	107	.262	139	*377	21	.961
1977—Philadelphia		Nat.	3B-SS-2B	154	544	114	149	27	11	38	101	.274	109	401	20	.962
1978—Philadelphia		Nat.	3B-SS	145	513	93	129	27	2	21	78	.251	98	325	16	.964
1979—Philadelphia		Nat.	3B-SS	160	541	109	137	25	4	45	114	.253	115	363	23	.954
1980—Philadelphia		Nat.	3B	150	548	104	157	25	8	*48	*121	.286	98	*372	27	.946
Major League Totals				1234	4261	778	1104	208	39	283	787	.259	961	2913	179	.956

Selected by Philadelphia Phillies' organization in 2nd round of free-agent draft, June 8, 1971.
†On disabled list, August 21 to September 2, 1972.
‡On disabled list, March 28 to April 21, 1973.

CHAMPIONSHIP SERIES RECORD

Established Championship Series record for most at-bats, five-game Series (24), 1980.
Tied Championship Series record for most at-bats, extra-inning game (6), October 8, 1980.

Year	Club	League	Pos.	G.	AB.	R.	H.	2B.	3B.	HR.	RBI.	B.A.	PO.	A.	E.	F.A.
1976—Philadelphia		Nat.	3B	3	13	1	4	2	0	2	2	.308	4	9	1	.929
1977—Philadelphia		Nat.	3B	4	16	2	1	0	0	0	1	.063	4	15	0	1.000
1978—Philadelphia		Nat.	3B	4	15	1	3	2	0	0	1	.200	3	18	2	.913
1980—Philadelphia		Nat.	3B	5	24	1	5	1	0	0	1	.208	3	17	1	.952
Championship Series Totals				16	68	5	13	5	0	5	.191	14	59	4	.948

WORLD SERIES RECORD

Tied World Series Record for fewest chances accepted by third baseman, nine-inning game (0), October 21, 1980.

Year	Club	League	Pos.	G.	AB.	R.	H.	2B.	3B.	HR.	RBI.	B.A.	PO.	A.	E.	F.A.
1980—Philadelphia		Nat.	3B	6	21	6	8	1	0	2	7	.381	9	8	0	1.000

ALL-STAR GAME RECORD

Year	League	Pos.	AB.	R.	H.	2B.	3B.	HR.	RBI.	B.A.	PO.	A.	E.	F.A.
1974—National		PH-3B	0	1	0	0	0	0	0	.000	0	1	0	1.000
1976—National		3B	1	0	0	0	0	0	0	.000	0	0	0	.000
1977—National		PR	0	0	0	0	0	0	0	.000	0	0	0	.000
1979—National		3B	3	2	2	1	1	0	1	.667	1	1	1	.667
All-Star Game Totals			4	3	2	1	1	0	1	.500	1	2	1	.750

Named to National League All-Star Team in 1980; replaced due to injury by Ray Knight.

KENNETH MARVIN SCHROM
(Ken)

Born November 23, 1954, at Grangeville, Ida.
Height, 6.02. Weight, 195.
Throws and bats righthanded.
Attended University of Idaho, Moscow, Ida.

Year Club	League	G.	IP.	W.	L.	Pct.	H.	R.	ER.	SO.	BB.	ERA.
1976—Idaho Falls	Pioneer	16	48	1	5	.167	42	31	20	46	32	3.75
1977—Quad Cities	Midwest	16	44	3	1	.750	22	10	7	40	20	1.43
1977—Salinas	California	15	21	1	1	.500	22	8	8	22	11	3.43
1977—El Paso	Texas	10	18	1	0	1.000	14	4	4	7	8	2.00
1978—El Paso	Texas	33	165	9	6	.600	180	93	86	126	52	4.69
1979—El Paso	Texas	25	168	7	8	.467	204	111	97	107	75	5.20
1979—Salt Lake City	P. Coast	3	4	0	0	.000	3	0	0	3	3	0.00
1980—Salt Lake City†	P. Coast	14	23	0	1	.000	32	25	20	11	17	7.83
1980—Syracuse	Int'national	26	46	0	2	.000	41	19	17	32	20	3.33
1980—Toronto	American	17	31	1	0	1.000	32	18	18	13	19	5.23
Major League Totals		17	31	1	0	1.000	32	18	18	13	19	3.23

Selected by Minnesota Twins' organization in 10th round of free-agent draft, June 5, 1973.
Selected by California Angels' organization in 17th round of free-agent draft, June 8, 1976.
†Traded to Toronto Blue Jays' organization, June 10, 1980, completing deal in which California acquired Pitcher Dave Lemanczyk, June 3, 1980.

DAVID PAUL SCHULER
(Dave)

Born October 4, 1953, at Framingham, Mass.
Height, 6.04. Weight, 211.
Throws left and bats righthanded.
Attended University of New Haven, West Haven, Conn.;
received Bachelor of Science degree in General Business Management.

Year Club	League	G.	IP.	W.	L.	Pct.	H.	R.	ER.	SO.	BB.	ERA.
1976—San Jose	California	54	89	4	7	.364	126	82	47	62	38	4.75
1977—Waterloo†	Midwest	8	15	1	2	.333	23	11	10	8	2	6.00
1977—Salinas	California	8	55	5	1	.833	53	12	11	25	5	1.80
1977—El Paso	Texas	17	90	8	2	.800	88	42	37	46	21	3.70
1978—Salt Lake City‡	P. Coast	6	23	0	1	.000	41	28	24	4	8	9.39
1979—Salt Lake City§	P. Coast	26	118	10	4	.714	120	64	57	36	34	4.35
1979—California	American	1	2	0	0	.000	2	2	2	0	0	9.00
1980—Salt Lake City	P. Coast	45	71	11	4	.733	54	23	18	42	23	2.28
1980—California	American	8	13	0	1	.000	13	5	5	7	2	3.46
Major League Totals		9	15	0	1	.000	15	7	7	7	2	4.20

Selected by Cleveland Indians' organization in 10th round of free-agent draft, June 4, 1975.
†Traded with Pitcher Dave LaRoche to California Angels' organization for First Baseman-Outfielder Bruce Bochte, Pitcher Sid Monge and cash estimated at $250,000, May 11, 1977.
‡On disabled list, May 26 to October 5, 1978.
§On disabled list, April 11 to May 17, 1979.

CHARLES BUDD SCHULTZ
(Buddy)

Born September 19, 1950, at Cleveland, O.
Height, 6.00. Weight, 170.
Throws left and bats righthanded.
Hobby—Coin collecting.
Attended Miami University, Oxford, O.; received Bachelor of
Science degree in Education

Year Club	League	G.	IP.	W.	L.	Pct.	H.	R.	ER.	SO.	BB.	ERA.
1972—Bradenton Cubs	Gulf Coast	11	52	2	2	.500	52	22	19	75	18	3.29
1973—Quincy	Midwest	14	88	7	4	.636	82	41	30	104	28	3.07
1973—Midland	Texas	9	65	3	4	.429	67	26	24	39	15	3.32
1974—Midland	Texas	29	67	9	6	.600	71	36	27	58	19	3.63
1974—Wichita	Am. Assoc.	10	15	3	0	1.000	12	3	3	20	3	1.80
1975—Wichita	Am. Assoc.	47	60	2	8	.200	62	38	27	48	21	4.05
1975—Chicago	National	6	6	2	0	1.000	11	6	4	4	5	6.00
1976—Chicago	National	29	24	1	1	.500	37	19	16	15	9	6.00
1977—New Orleans	Am. Assoc.	2	15	1	0	1.000	7	5	5	25	4	3.00
1977—St. Louis‡	National	40	85	6	1	.857	76	26	22	66	24	2.33
1978—St. Louis	National	62	83	2	4	.333	68	36	35	70	36	3.80
1979—St. Louis§	National	31	42	4	3	.571	40	21	21	38	14	4.50
1980—Springfield x	Am. Assoc.	5	24	0	2	.000	21	12	10	11	12	3.75
Major League Totals		168	240	15	9	.625	232	108	98	193	88	3.68

Selected by Philadelphia Phillies' organization in 4th round of free-agent draft, June 7, 1968.
Selected by Chicago Cubs' organization in 6th round of free-agent draft, June 6, 1972.
†Traded to New Orleans (St. Louis Cardinals' organization) for Pitcher Mark Covert, February 28, 1977.
‡On disabled list, July 4 to July 25, 1977.
§On disabled list, July 5 to September 9, 1979.
xOn disabled list, May 24 to September 8, 1980.

MICHAEL LORRI SCIOSCIA
(Name pronounced SO-sha)
(Mike)

Born November 27, 1958, at Darby, Pa.
Height, 6.02. Weight, 200.
Throws right and bats lefthanded.
Attends Pennsylvania State University, University Park, Pa.

Led Midwest League catchers in errors with 20 and in double plays with 12 in 1978.
Led Pacific Coast League catchers in double plays with 19 and in passed balls with 22 in 1979.

Year Club	League	Pos.	G.	AB.	R.	H.	2B.	3B.	HR.	RBI.	B.A.	PO.	A.	E.	F.A.
1976—Bellingham	N'west.	C	46	151	25	42	6	0	7	26	.278	202	35	14	.944
1977—Clinton	Midw.	C-1B	121	364	58	92	20	1	7	44	.253	764	95	22	.975
1978—San Antonio†	Texas	C	58	204	29	61	16	0	2	34	.299	214	17	4	.983
1979—Albuquerque	P. C.	C	143	461	80	155	34	0	3	68	.336	*690	*86	*15	.981
1980—Albuquerque	P. C.	C	52	160	33	53	11	1	3	33	.331	207	19	5	.978
1980—Los Angeles‡	Nat.	C	54	134	8	34	5	1	1	8	.254	226	26	2	.992
Major League Totals			54	134	8	34	5	1	1	8	.254	226	26	2	.992

Selected by Los Angeles Dodgers' organization in 1st round (19th player selected) of free-agent draft, June 8, 1976.

†On disabled list, May 19 to August 4, 1978.
‡On disabled list, April 10 to April 20, 1980.

DARYL ANTHONY SCONIERS

Born October 3, 1958, at San Bernardino, Calif.
Height, 6.02. Weight, 185.
Throws and bats lefthanded.
Attended Orange Coast College, Costa Mesa, Calif.

Led Midwest League first basemen in double plays with 106 in 1978.
Led Texas League in total bases with 296 in 1980.

Year Club	League	Pos.	G.	AB.	R.	H.	2B.	3B.	HR.	RBI.	B.A.	PO.	A.	E.	F.A.
1977—Idaho Falls	Pioneer	1B	49	158	34	49	10	1	0	24	.310	343	19	7	.961
1978—Quad Cities	Midw.	1B	126	466	88	133	*35	7	19	86	.285	*1194	52	16	.987
1979—Salinas†	Calif.	1B	108	365	60	105	17	6	11	50	.288	804	42	7	*.992
1980—El Paso	Texas	1B	•136	506	95	*187	*48	8	15	87	*.370	887	46	16	.983

Selected by California Angels' organization in 3rd round of free-agent draft, January 11, 1977.
†On temporary inactive list, April 6 to May 9, 1979.

ANTHONY SCOTT
(Tony)

Born September 18, 1951, at Cincinnati, O.
Height, 6.00. Weight, 175.
Throws right and bats right and lefthanded.
Hobbies—Cards, music and racing cars.

Major League stolen bases: 1973 (0), 1974 (1), 1975 (5), 1977 (13), 1978 (5), 1979 (37), 1980 (22). Total—83.

Year Club	League	Pos.	G.	AB.	R.	H.	2B.	3B.	HR.	RBI.	B.A.	PO.	A.	E.	F.A.
1969—Braden. Expos	Gulf C.	OF	38	95	13	17	1	2	0	7	.179	53	6	5	.922
1970—W. Palm Beach	Fla. St.	OF	3	2	0	1	0	0	0	0	.500	1	0	0	1.000
1970—Watertown	North.	OF	63	243	41	61	9	2	10	46	.251	108	*12	9	.930
1971—W. Palm Beach	Fla. St.	OF	47	84	21	19	3	2	1	9	.226	28	2	1	.968
1971—Jamestown	NYP	OF	69	258	41	68	13	3	2	22	.264	*173	8	6	.968
1972—Quebec City	East.	OF	135	412	47	88	9	0	2	39	.214	296	15	14	.957
1973—Quebec City	East.	OF	128	379	48	97	14	4	5	38	.256	231	21	4	.984
1973—Montreal	Nat.	OF	11	1	2	0	0	0	0	0	.000	0	0	1	.000
1974—Quebec City	East.	OF	109	359	76	102	8	4	10	38	.284	193	5	4	*.980
1974—Memphis	Int.	OF	11	6	2	0	0	0	0	0	.000	0	0	0	.000
1974—Montreal	Nat.	OF	19	7	2	2	0	0	0	1	.286	7	0	0	1.000
1975—Montreal	Nat.	OF	92	143	19	26	4	2	0	11	.182	94	6	4	.962
1976—Denver	A. A.	OF	106	328	63	102	21	9	8	45	.311	162	7	0	1.000
1977—St. Louis‡	Nat.	OF	95	292	38	85	16	3	3	41	.291	223	5	1	.996
1978—St. Louis	Nat.	OF	96	219	28	50	5	2	1	14	.228	100	6	6	.946
1979—St. Louis	Nat.	OF	153	587	69	152	22	10	6	68	.259	427	14	7	.984
1980—St. Louis	Nat.	OF	143	415	51	104	19	3	0	28	.251	324	5	1	*.997
Major League Totals			609	1664	209	419	66	20	10	163	.252	1175	36	20	.984

Selected by Montreal Expos' organization in 48th round of free-agent draft, June 5, 1969.
†Traded with Pitcher Steve Dunning and Infielder Pat Scanlon by Montreal Expos to St. Louis Cardinals for Pitchers Bill Greif and Angel Torres, and Outfielder Sam Mejias, November 6, 1976.
‡On disabled list, August 19 to October 4, 1977.

MICHAEL WARREN SCOTT
(Mike)

Born April 26, 1955, at Santa Monica, Calif.
Height, 6.03. Weight, 215.
Throws and bats righthanded.
Attended Pepperdine University, Malibu, Calif.

Tied for International League lead in games started with 29 in 1978.

Year Club	League	G.	IP.	W.	L.	Pct.	H.	R.	ER.	SO.	BB.	ERA.
1976–Jackson	Texas	7	44	3	3	.500	34	20	14	19	14	2.86
1977–Jackson	Texas	25	*187	*14	10	.583	132	77	61	97	55	2.94
1977–Tidewater	Int'national	2	2	0	1	.000	4	5	4	0	3	18.00
1978–Tidewater	Int'national	29	192	10	10	.500	196	105	84	93	83	3.94
1979–Tidewater	Int'national	18	99	8	4	.667	103	37	35	40	27	3.18
1979–New York	National	18	52	1	3	.250	59	35	31	21	20	5.37
1980–Tidewater	Int'national	27	170	13	7	.650	165	69	56	88	64	2.96
1980–New York	National	6	29	1	1	.500	40	14	14	13	8	4.34
Major League Totals.................		24	81	2	4	.333	99	49	45	34	28	5.00

Selected by New York Mets' organization in 2nd round of free-agent draft, June 8, 1976.

RODNEY DARRELL SCOTT

Born October 16, 1953, at Indianapolis, Ind.
Height, 6.00. Weight, 155.
Throws right and bats right and lefthanded.

Major League stolen bases: 1975 (4), 1976 (2), 1977 (33), 1978 (27), 1979 (39), 1980 (63). Total—168.
Led Pioneer League in stolen bases with 26 in 1973.

Year Club	League	Pos.	G.	AB.	R.	H.	2B.	3B.	HR.	RBI.	B.A.	PO.	A.	E.	F.A.
1972–Sarasota Royals	Gulf C.	S-3-O-2	35	125	23	47	4	2	1	14	.376	51	64	8	.935
1973–San Jose	Calif.	2B	48	159	23	35	3	2	2	15	.220	90	102	12	.941
1973–Billings	Pion.	*SS-2B	64	236	51	70	10	2	0	21	.297	91	144	26	*.900
1974–Waterloo	Midw.	S-2-O	58	221	43	57	6	1	1	16	.258	86	169	22	.921
1974–San Jose	Calif.	SS	63	230	38	69	6	2	1	15	.300	108	205	27	.921
1975–Jacksonville	South.	SS	20	77	19	26	2	0	0	8	.338	34	49	7	.922
1975–Omaha	A.A.	2B-SS	12	37	6	10	1	1	0	1	.270	13	18	5	.861
1975–Kansas City†	Amer.	2B-SS	48	15	13	1	0	0	0	0	.067	8	12	2	.909
1976–Denver	A.A.	S-O-2-3	114	375	75	115	20	6	1	26	.307	165	286	29	.940
1976–Montreal‡	Nat.	2B-SS	7	10	3	4	0	0	0	0	.400	6	8	0	1.000
1977–Oakland§	Amer.	2-S-3-O	133	364	56	95	4	4	0	20	.261	200	273	21	.957
1978–Wichita	A.A.	O-2-3	63	256	48	67	8	3	4	17	.262	150	43	9	.955
1978–Chicago x	Nat.	3-O-2-S	78	227	41	64	5	1	0	15	.282	77	119	14	.933
1979–Montreal	Nat.	2B-SS	151	562	69	134	12	5	3	42	.238	362	421	21	.974
1980–Montreal	Nat.	2B-SS	154	567	84	127	13	●13	0	46	.224	339	432	18	.977
American League Totals.................			181	379	69	96	4	4	0	20	.253	208	285	23	.955
National League Totals...................			390	1366	197	329	30	19	3	103	.241	784	980	53	.971
Major League Totals......................			571	1745	266	425	34	23	3	123	.244	992	1265	76	.967

Selected by Kansas City Royals' organization in 11th round of free-agent draft, June 6, 1972.

†Sold to Montreal Expos, December 12, 1975, to complete deal in which Royals obtained Catcher Bob Stinson from Expos, March 31, 1975.

‡Traded to Texas Rangers for Pitcher Jeff Terpko, March 15, 1977; traded with Pitcher Jim Umbarger and cash estimated at $100,000 to Oakland A's for Outfielder Claudell Washington, March 26, 1977.

§Sent to Chicago Cubs, April 4, 1978, in completion of deal in which Oakland acquired Pitcher Pete Broberg, March 29, 1978.

xTraded with Outfielder Jerry White to Montreal Expos for Outfielder Sam Mejias, December 14, 1978.

RODNEY GRANT SCURRY

Name pronounced SKUR-ee.

(Rod)

Born March 17, 1956, at Sacramento, Calif.
Height, 6.02. Weight, 180.
Throws and bats lefthanded.
Hobbies—Golf and basketball.

Pitched seven-inning 2-0 no-hit victory against Richmond, July 25, 1977.

Year Club	League	G.	IP.	W.	L.	Pct.	H.	R.	ER.	SO.	BB.	ERA.
1974–Niagara Falls......................	NYP	14	89	5	6	.455	55	36	34	102	74	3.44
1975–Salem...............................	Carolina	*26	150	9	12	.429	128	79	61	143	118	3.66
1976–Shreveport..........................	Texas	24	123	8	8	.500	120	71	53	83	83	3.88
1977–Shreveport..........................	Texas	18	113	3	11	.214	97	54	36	111	48	2.87
1977–Columbus...........................	Int'national	8	37	3	2	.600	30	31	19	39	32	4.62
1978–Columbus†..........................	Int'national	16	63	3	3	.500	69	44	40	57	43	5.71
1978–Shreveport..........................	Texas	5	29	1	4	.200	27	19	15	38	24	4.66
1979–Portland‡...........................	P. Coast	35	122	5	5	.500	121	64	56	94	72	4.13
1980–Pittsburgh..........................	National	20	38	0	2	.000	23	12	9	28	17	2.13
Major League Totals......................		20	38	0	2	.000	23	12	9	28	17	2.13

Selected by Pittsburgh Pirates' organization in 1st round (11th player selected) of free-agent draft, June 5, 1974.

†On disabled list, June 12 to July 11, 1978.
‡On disabled list, August 4, to August 14, 1979.

DID YOU KNOW—

That George Brett's .390 batting average in 1980 was the highest mark attained by a major leaguer since Ted Williams hit .406 in 1941?

KIM MICHAEL SEAMAN

Born May 6, 1957, at Moss Point, Miss.
Height, 6.03. Weight, 205.
Throws and bats lefthanded.
Attended Mississippi Gulf Coast Junior College, Perkinston, Miss.

Year Club	League	G.	IP.	W.	L.	Pct.	H.	R.	ER.	SO.	BB.	ERA.
1976—Wausau	Midwest	15	52	4	5	.444	58	39	32	34	42	5.54
1977—Wausau	Midwest	27	161	8	8	.500	155	91	70	144	91	3.91
1978—Jackson†	Texas	42	97	10	4	.714	73	30	23	117	52	2.13
1979—Springfield	Am. Assoc.	31	85	7	4	.636	101	61	54	61	64	5.72
1979—St. Louis	National	1	2	0	0	.000	0	0	0	3	2	0.00
1980—Springfield	Am. Assoc.	22	37	2	3	.400	34	20	19	28	15	4.62
1980—St. Louis‡	National	26	24	3	2	.600	16	9	9	10	13	3.38
Major League Totals		27	26	3	2	.600	16	9	9	13	15	3.12

Selected by Houston Astros' organization in 23rd round of free-agent draft, June 4, 1975.
Selected by New York Mets' organization in secondary phase of free-agent draft, January 7, 1976.
†Traded with Outfielder Tom Grieve to St. Louis Cardinals for Pitcher Pete Falcone, December 5, 1978.
‡Traded with Pitchers John Littlefield, Al Olmsted and John Urrea, Catchers Terry Kennedy and Steve Swisher and Infielder Mike Phillips to San Diego Padres for Pitchers Rollie Fingers and Bob Shirley, Catcher-First Baseman Gene Tenace and a player to be named later, December 8, 1980; Catcher Bob Geren traded to Cardinals' organization completing deal, December 10, 1980.

GEORGE THOMAS SEAVER
(Tom)

Born November 17, 1944, at Fresno, Calif.
Height, 6.01. Weight, 210.
Throws and bats righthanded.
Hobbies—Golf, hunting and bridge.
Attended Fresno City College, Fresno, Calif., and University of Southern California,
Los Angeles, Calif.; received Bachelor of Science degree.

Established major league records for most seasons, 200 or more strikeouts (10); most consecutive seasons, 200 or more strikeouts (9), 1968 through 1976; most consecutive strikeouts, game (10), April 22, 1970.
Tied major league record for most strikeouts game (19), April 22, 1970.
Established National League record for lowest earned run average, 200 or more games won, lifetime (2.55).
Tied National League record for most season opening games won, lifetime (6).
Tied modern National League record for most one-hit games, lifetime (5).
Pitched 4-0 no-hit victory against St. Louis Cardinals, June 16, 1978.
Led National League in shutouts with 7 in 1977.
Tied for National League lead in complete games with 18 in 1973.
Tied for National League lead in shutouts with 5 in 1979.
Led International League in games started by pitchers with 32 in 1966.
Named National League Rookie of the Year by the Baseball Writers' Association of America, 1967.
Won National League Cy Young Memorial Award, 1969, 1973 and 1975.
Named righthanded pitcher on THE SPORTING NEWS National League All-Star Team, 1969, 1973 and 1975.
Named National League Pitcher of the Year by THE SPORTING NEWS, 1969, 1973 and 1975.

Year Club	League	G.	IP.	W.	L.	Pct.	H.	R.	ER.	SO.	BB.	ERA.
1966—Jacksonville	Int'national	34	210	12	12	.500	184	87	73	188	66	3.13
1967—New York	National	35	251	16	13	.552	224	85	77	170	78	2.76
1968—New York	National	36	278	16	12	.571	224	73	68	205	48	2.20
1969—New York	National	36	273	★25	7	.781	202	75	67	208	82	2.21
1970—New York	National	37	291	18	12	.600	230	103	91	★283	83	★2.81
1971—New York	National	36	286	20	10	.667	210	61	56	★289	61	★1.76
1972—New York	National	35	262	21	12	.636	215	92	85	249	77	2.92
1973—New York	National	36	290	19	10	.655	219	74	67	★251	64	★2.08
1974—New York	National	32	236	11	11	.500	199	89	84	201	75	3.20
1975—New York	National	36	280	★22	9	.710	217	81	74	★243	88	2.38
1976—New York	National	35	271	14	11	.560	211	83	78	★235	77	2.59
1977—New York†-Cincinnati	National	33	261	21	6	.778	199	78	75	196	66	2.59
1978—Cincinnati	National	36	260	16	14	.533	218	97	83	226	89	2.87
1979—Cincinnati	National	32	215	16	6	.727	187	85	75	131	61	3.14
1980—Cincinnati‡	National	26	168	10	8	.556	140	74	68	101	59	3.64
Major League Totals		481	3622	245	141	.635	2895	1150	1048	2988	1008	2.60

Selected by Los Angeles Dodgers' organization in 22nd round of free-agent draft, June, 1965.
Signed by Atlanta Braves to Richmond contract for reported $40,000 bonus, February, 1966; subsequently, Commissioner William Eckert nullified the contract because the signing violated the college rule. However, since the University of Southern California then declared Seaver ineligible, Eckert decreed that any club other than the Braves which was willing to match terms of his Richmond contract would be eligible to draw for negotiation rights. Cleveland Indians, Philadelphia Phillies and New York Mets expressed that willingness, and Eckert drew the name of the Mets in a special drawing, April 3, 1966; Mets then signed Seaver to Jacksonville contract for reported $50,000 bonus.
†Traded to Cincinnati Reds for Infielder Doug Flynn, Pitcher Pat Zachry and Outfielders Dan Norman and Steve Henderson, June 15, 1977.
‡On disabled list, July 1 to August 4, 1980.

CHAMPIONSHIP SERIES RECORD

Established Championship Series record for most strikeouts, five-game Series (17), 1973.

Established National League Championship Series record for most innings pitched, five-game Series (16⅔), 1973.

Year Club	League	G.	IP.	W.	L.	Pct.	H.	R.	ER.	SO.	BB.	ERA.
1969—New York	National	1	7	1	0	1.000	8	5	5	2	3	6.43
1973—New York	National	2	16⅔	1	1	.500	13	4	3	17	5	1.62
1979—Cincinnati	National	1	8	0	0	.000	5	2	2	5	2	2.25
Championship Series Totals		4	31⅔	2	1	.667	26	11	10	24	10	2.84

WORLD SERIES RECORD

Year Club	League	G.	IP.	W.	L.	Pct.	H.	R.	ER.	SO.	BB.	ERA.
1969—New York	National	2	15	1	1	.500	12	5	5	9	3	3.00
1973—New York	National	2	15	0	1	.000	13	4	4	18	3	2.40
World Series Totals		4	30	1	2	.333	25	9	9	27	6	2.70

ALL-STAR GAME RECORD

Year League	IP.	W.	L.	Pct.	H.	R.	ER.	SO.	BB.	ERA.
1967—National	1	0	0	.000	0	0	0	1	1	0.00
1968—National	2	0	0	.000	2	0	0	5	0	0.00
1970—National	3	0	0	.000	1	0	0	4	0	0.00
1973—National	1	0	0	.000	0	0	0	0	1	0.00
1975—National	1	0	0	.000	2	3	3	2	1	27.00
1976—National	2	0	0	.000	2	1	1	1	1	4.50
1977—National	2	0	0	.000	4	3	2	2	1	9.00
All-Star Game Totals	12	0	0	.000	11	7	6	15	5	4.50

Member of National League All-Star Team for 1969, 1971, 1972 and 1978 games; did not play.

HERMAN NEILS SEGELKE

Born April 24, 1958, at San Mateo, Calif.
Height, 6.04. Weight, 215.
Throws and bats righthanded.

Year Club	League	G.	IP.	W.	L.	Pct.	H.	R.	ER.	SO.	BB.	ERA.
1976—Bradenton Cubs	G. Coast	8	45	3	2	.600	33	16	11	31	26	2.20
1977—Pompano Beach†	Florida St.	24	117	13	8	.619	128	69	58	60	48	4.46
1978—Midland	Texas	24	143	8	8	.500	159	92	73	58	95	4.59
1979—Midland	Texas	29	*184	13	8	.619	227	116	107	81	83	5.23
1980—Midland	Texas	47	129	7	10	.412	155	92	68	88	63	4.74

Selected by Chicago Cubs' organization in 1st round (seventh player selected) of free-agent draft, June 8, 1976.

†On disabled list, April 14 to April 24, 1977.

RICKY ALLEN SEILHEIMER

Born August 30, 1960, at Brenham, Tex.
Height, 5.11. Weight, 185.
Throws right and bats lefthanded.

Year Club	League	Pos.	G.	AB.	R.	H.	2B.	3B.	HR.	RBI.	B.A.	PO.	A.	E.	F.A.
1979—Niagara Falls	NYP	C	24	89	10	16	3	3	1	13	.180	5	0	0	1.000
1980—Glens Falls	East.	C	67	231	35	60	11	3	9	46	.260	269	30	2	.961
1980—Chicago	Amer.	C	21	52	4	11	3	1	1	3	.212	62	8	4	.946
Major League Totals			21	52	4	11	3	1	1	3	.212	62	8	4	.946

Selected by Chicago White Sox' organization in 1st round (19th player selected) of free-agent draft, June 5, 1979.

GARY WAYNE SERUM

Born October 24, 1956, at Fargo, N. D.
Height, 6.01. Weight, 180.
Throws and bats righthanded.
Hobbies—All sports.
Attends St. Cloud State, St. Cloud, Minn. and Moorhead State, Moorhead, Minn.

Year Club	League	G.	IP.	W.	L.	Pct.	H.	R.	ER.	SO.	BB.	ERA.
1975—Elizabethton	Ap'lachian	7	10	0	0	.000	17	10	9	2	5	8.10
1976—Elizabethton	Ap'lachian	6	32	1	2	.333	24	11	9	24	10	2.53
1976—Wisconsin Rapids	Midwest	7	46	1	4	.200	52	30	18	30	18	3.52
1977—Orlando	Southern	22	33	2	3	.400	31	18	15	16	14	4.09
1977—Tacoma	P. Coast	13	30	4	0	1.000	22	7	6	18	10	1.80
1977—Minnesota	American	8	23	0	0	.000	22	11	11	14	10	4.30
1978—Minnesota	American	34	184	9	9	.500	188	88	84	80	44	4.11
1979—Toledo	Int'national	2	13	1	1	.500	15	9	6	5	4	4.15
1979—Minnesota	American	20	64	1	3	.250	93	47	47	31	20	6.61
1980—Toledo	Int'national	38	91	3	7	.300	96	47	37	48	27	3.66
Major League Totals		62	271	10	12	.455	303	146	142	125	74	4.72

Signed as free agent by Minnesota Twins' organization, June 30, 1975.

JIMMY DALE SEXTON

Born December 15, 1951, at Mobile, Ala.
Height, 5.10. Weight, 175.
Throws and bats righthanded.
Hobbies—Hunting and fishing.

Led Texas League in stolen bases with 48 in 1975.
Led Pacific Coast League second basemen in errors with 20 in 1980.

Year	Club	League	Pos.	G.	AB.	R.	H.	2B.	3B.	HR.	RBI.	B.A.	PO.	A.	E.	F.A.
1970—Braden. Pirates	.Gulf C	S-2-3	33	113	17	32	2	0	0	7	.283	40	68	12	.900
1971—Braden. Pirates	.Gulf C	3-2-S	35	119	23	29	2	1	0	11	.244	45	54	1	.990
1972—Niagara Falls	....NYP	SS	69	212	41	61	2	3	0	23	.288	86	178	13	*.953
1973—Salem	..............Carol.	*2B-SS	124	446	86	120	17	3	3	39	.269	240	323	*33	.945
1974—Thetford Mines	..East.	*3-S-2	115	350	53	87	14	1	3	32	.249	97	197	18	*.942
1975—Shreveport	........Tex.	SS	103	383	82	105	23	5	3	28	.274	148	279	34	.926
1976—Shreveport	........Tex.	SS	59	207	43	67	14	2	4	30	.324	76	159	21	.918
1976—Charleston†	......Int.	2B-SS	49	154	21	42	8	1	3	12	.273	85	109	6	.970
1977—San José‡	.........P. C.	SS-2B	89	305	63	78	13	5	2	23	.256	152	271	13	.970
1977—Seattle§	.............Amer.	SS	14	37	5	8	1	1	1	3	.216	12	40	4	.929
1978—Houston	............Nat.	SS-3B-2B	88	141	17	29	3	2	2	6	.206	62	104	5	.971
1979—Houston	............Nat.	SS-3B-2B	52	43	8	9	0	0	0	1	.209	11	24	2	.946
1980—Tucson x	..........P.C.	2B-SS	113	446	81	132	18	6	1	33	.296	237	390	24	.963
American League Totals			14	37	5	8	1	1	1	3	.216	12	40	4	.929
National League Totals			140	184	25	38	3	2	2	7	.207	73	128	7	.966
Major League Totals			154	221	30	46	4	3	3	10	.208	85	168	11	.958

Signed as free agent by Pittsburgh Pirates' organization, July 25, 1970.
†Traded with Infielder Craig Reynolds to Seattle Mariners for Pitcher Grant Jackson, December 7, 1976.
‡On temporary inactive list, May 10 through May 29, 1977; on disabled list, June 8 through June 22, 1977.
§Traded to Houston Astros for Outfielder Leon Roberts, December 5, 1977.
xTraded to Oakland A's organization for cash and a player to be named later, February 12, 1981.

JOHN T. SHELBY

Born February 23, 1958, at Lexington, Ky.
Height, 6.01. Weight, 175.
Throws and bats righthanded.
Attended Columbia State Community College, Columbia, Tenn.

Led Appalachian League outfielders in double plays with 3 in 1978.
Led Florida State League outfielders in double plays with 7 in 1979.

Year	Club	League	Pos.	G.	AB.	R.	H.	2B.	3B.	HR.	RBI.	B.A.	PO.	A.	E.	F.A.
1977—Bluefield	...........Appal.	OF	60	211	28	54	9	1	0	1	.256	90	●12	7	.936
1978—Miami	...............Fla. St.	OF	13	26	4	6	1	0	0	3	.231	14	2	2	.889
1978—Bluefield	...........Appal.	OF	64	248	49	70	9	1	6	25	.282	128	*11	6	.959
1979—Miami	...............Fla. St.	OF	132	478	50	96	11	6	3	38	.201	*252	●22	8	.972
1980—Charlotte	..........South.	OF	134	560	66	135	27	11	6	51	.241	*361	21	*16	.960

Selected by Baltimore Orioles' organization in 1st round (19th player selected) of free-agent draft, January 11, 1977.

DENNIS LEE SHERRILL

Born March 3, 1956, at Miami, Fla.
Height, 6.00. Weight, 165.
Throws and bats righthanded.
Hobbies—Fishing, golf, basketball and football.

Signed reported $50,000 bonus to sign with New York Yankees, 1974.

Year	Club	League	Pos.	G.	AB.	R.	H.	2B.	3B.	HR.	RBI.	B.A.	PO.	A.	E.	F.A.
1974—Ft. Lauderdale	..Fla. St.	SS	58	183	25	33	7	2	1	18	.180	114	155	21	.928
1975—West Haven	.......East.	SS	113	335	47	74	10	5	1	34	.221	159	332	39	.926
1976—Syracuse	..........Int.	SS	5	10	0	0	0	0	0	0	.000	8	11	0	1.000
1976—West Haven†	.....East.	SS	37	109	12	20	2	0	0	4	.183	64	115	13	.932
1977—Syracuse‡	.........Int.	3B-2B-SS	7	16	0	1	0	0	0	0	.063	4	9	1	.929
1978—West Haven	.......East.	SS-3B	135	486	75	142	19	2	14	61	.292	171	396	43	.930
1978—New York	.........Amer.	3B	2	1	1	0	0	0	0	0	.000	0	0	0	.000
1979—Columbus§	........Int.	3-S-2	57	158	17	39	8	0	3	10	.247	40	123	2	.988
1979—West Haven	.......East.	SS-3B	21	66	5	14	0	0	2	2	.212	37	56	3	.969
1980—Columbus x	.......Int.	S-3-2	68	183	25	39	6	3	1	17	.213	82	161	17	.935
1980—New York	.........Amer.	SS-2B	3	4	0	1	0	0	0	0	.250	5	1	0	1.000
Major League Totals			5	5	1	1	0	0	0	0	.200	5	1	0	1.000

Selected by New York Yankees' organization in 1st round (12th player selected) of free-agent draft, June 5, 1974.
†On disabled list, July 11 to September 10, 1976.
‡On suspended list (Fort Lauderdale), May 6 to August 31, 1977.
§On disabled list, May 4 to May 16, 1979.
xOn temporary inactive list, July 24 to August 11, 1980.

ROBERT CHARLES SHIRLEY
(Bob)

Born June 25, 1954, at Oklahoma City, Okla.
Height, 5.11. Weight, 180.
Throws left and bats righthanded.
Attended University of Oklahoma, Norman, Okla.

Year Club	League	G.	IP.	W.	L.	Pct.	H.	R.	ER.	SO.	BB.	ERA.
1976—Amarillo	Texas	16	111	9	5	.643	113	55	41	90	39	3.32
1976—Hawaii	P. Coast	13	81	5	5	.500	91	62	47	47	24	5.22
1977—San Diego	National	39	214	12	18	.400	215	107	88	146	100	3.70
1978—San Diego	National	50	166	8	11	.421	164	75	68	102	61	3.69
1979—San Diego	National	49	205	8	16	.333	196	89	77	117	59	3.38
1980—San Diego†	National	59	137	11	12	.478	143	58	54	67	54	3.55
Major League Totals		197	722	39	57	.406	718	329	287	432	274	3.58

Selected by Los Angeles Dodgers' organization in 38th round of free-agent draft, June 6, 1972.
Selected by San Francisco Giants' organization in 5th round of free-agent draft, June 4, 1975.
Selected by San Diego Padres' organization in secondary phase of free-agent draft, January 7, 1976.
†Traded with Pitcher Rollie Fingers, Catcher-First Baseman Gene Tenace and a player to be named later to St. Louis Cardinals for Catchers Terry Kennedy and Steve Swisher, Pitchers John Littlefield, Al Olmsted, John Urrea and Kim Seaman and Infielder Mike Phillips, December 8, 1980; Catcher Bob Geren traded to Cardinals' organization completing deal, December 10, 1980.

ERIC VAUGHN SHOW

Name pronounced to rhyme with CHOW.

Born May 19, 1956, at Riverside, Calif.
Height, 6.01. Weight, 185.
Throws and bats righthanded.
Attended University of California at Riverside, Riverside, Calif.

Year Club	League	G.	IP.	W.	L.	Pct.	H.	R.	ER.	SO.	BB.	ERA.
1978—Walla Walla	Northwest	11	60	5	2	.714	47	28	19	43	20	2.85
1979—Reno	California	28	169	13	9	.591	144	79	67	186	92	3.57
1980—Amarillo	Texas	26	166	12	6	.667	141	81	69	144	81	3.74

Selected by Minnesota Twins' organization in 36th round of free-agent draft, June 5, 1974.
Selected by San Diego Padres' organization in 18th round of free-agent draft, June 6, 1978.

TED LYLE SIMMONS

Born August 9, 1949, at Highland Park, Mich.
Height, 6.00. Weight, 200.
Throws right and bats left and righthanded.
Hobby—Collecting Antiques.
Attended Wayne State University, Detroit, Mich. and
University of Michigan, Ann Arbor, Mich.

Established major league record for most intentional bases on balls by switch-hitter, season, since 1955 (25), 1977.
Established National League records for most home runs by switch hitter, career (172); fewest errors by catcher, season, for leader in errors (15), 1975.
Tied National League record for most games, switch-hit home runs, season (1), April 17, 1975 and June 11, 1979; most games switch-hit home runs, league (2).
Led National League in passed balls with 25 in 1973, with 28 in 1975 and with 14 in 1979.
Named Rookie of the Year and Most Valuable Player in California League, 1968.
Named catcher on THE SPORTING NEWS National League All-Star Team, 1977 through 1979.
Named catcher on THE SPORTING NEWS National League Silver Bat team, 1980.
Named American Association Rookie of the Year, 1969.
Received reported $50,000 bonus to sign with St. Louis Cardinals, 1967.

Year Club	League	Pos.	G.	AB.	R.	H.	2B.	3B.	HR.	RBI.	B.A.	PO.	A.	E.	F.A.
1967—Sarasota Cards	Gulf C.	C	6	20	5	7	1	1	2	8	.350	33	0	0	1.000
1967—Cedar Rapids	Midw.	OF-C	47	171	15	46	11	2	4	34	.269	119	8	3	.977
1968—Modesto	Calif.	*C-O	136	493	86	163	30	2	28	*117	*.331	*989	79	*16	.985
1968—St. Louis	Nat.	C	2	3	0	1	0	0	0	0	.333	3	1	0	1.000
1969—Tulsa	A. A.	C-3-O-1	129	499	80	158	33	4	16	88	.317	463	92	19	.967
1969—St. Louis†	Nat.	C	5	14	0	3	0	1	0	3	.214	22	0	1	.957
1970—Tulsa	A. A.	C	15	51	10	19	4	1	1	8	.373	99	7	0	1.000
1970—St. Louis	Nat.	C	82	284	29	69	8	2	3	24	.243	466	37	5	.990
1971—St. Louis‡	Nat.	C	133	510	64	155	32	4	7	77	.304	747	52	9	.989
1972—St. Louis	Nat.	*C-1B	152	594	70	180	36	6	16	96	.303	*967	*93	13	.988
1973—St. Louis	Nat.	*C-1-O	161	619	62	192	36	2	13	91	.310	*932	78	14	.986
1974—St. Louis	Nat.	C-1B	152	599	66	163	33	6	20	103	.272	813	87	15	.984
1975—St. Louis	Nat.	*C-1-O	157	581	80	193	32	3	18	100	.332	818	64	*15	.983
1976—St. Louis	Nat.	C-1-O-3	150	546	60	159	35	3	5	75	.291	726	88	10	.988
1977—St. Louis	Nat.	C-OF	150	516	82	164	25	3	21	95	.318	683	75	10	.987
1978—St. Louis	Nat.	*C-OF	152	516	71	148	40	5	22	80	.287	703	*88	10	.988
1979—St. Louis§	Nat.	C	123	448	68	127	22	0	26	87	.283	606	69	10	.985
1980—St. Louis x	Nat.	C-OF	145	495	84	150	33	2	21	98	.303	528	71	10	.984
Major League Totals			1564	5725	736	1704	332	37	172	929	.298	8014	803	122	.986

Selected by St. Louis Cardinals' organization in 1st round (10th player selected) of free-agent draft, June 6, 1967.

†On military list, December 12, 1969 through May 9, 1970.
‡On military list, June 19 through July 4, 1971.
§On disabled list, June 25 to July 24, 1979.
xTraded with Pitchers Rollie Fingers and Pete Vuckovich to Milwaukee Brewers for Pitchers Lary Sorensen and Dave LaPoint and Outfielders Sixto Lezcano and David Green, December 12, 1980.

ALL-STAR GAME RECORD

Year League	Pos.	AB.	R.	H.	2B.	3B.	HR.	RBI.	B.A.	PO.	A.	E.	F.A.
1973—National................................	PH-C	1	0	0	0	0	0	0	.000	1	1	0	1.000
1977—National................................	C	3	0	0	0	0	0	0	.000	5	0	0	1.000
1978—National................................	C	3	0	1	0	0	0	0	.333	4	1	0	1.000
All-Star Game Totals.........................		7	0	1	0	0	0	0	.143	10	2	0	1.000

Member of National League All-Star Team for 1972 and 1974 games; did not play.
Named to National League All-Star Team for 1979 game; replaced due to injury.

JOE ALLEN SIMPSON

Born December 31, 1951, at Purcell, Okla.
Height, 6.03. Weight, 175.
Throws and bats lefthanded.
Hobbies—Photography, listening to music and other sports.
Attended University of Oklahoma, Norman, Okla.

Year Club League	Pos.	G.	AB.	R.	H.	2B.	3B.	HR.	RBI.	B.A.	PO.	A.	E.	F.A.
1973—Albuquerque......P. C.	OF	15	54	10	12	0	0	0	6	.222	40	1	4	.911
1973—Bakersfield ....Calif.	OF	61	227	37	69	4	1	1	24	.304	127	4	3	.978
1974—Waterbury.........East.	OF	117	406	59	121	18	6	1	30	0	256	16	14	.951
1974—Albuquerque......P. C.	OF	13	43	2	7	1	1	0	0	.163	29	2	0	1.000
1975—Albuquerque†....P. C.	OF	133	514	84	142	24	6	2	49	.276	289	8	5	.983
1975—Los Angeles.......Nat.	OF	9	6	3	2	0	0	0	0	.333	5	0	0	1.000
1976—Albuquerque......P. C.	OF-1B	108	419	77	131	19	7	4	60	.313	193	15	8	.961
1976—Los Angeles.......Nat.	OF	23	30	2	4	1	0	0	0	.133	24	0	0	1.000
1977—Albuquerque......P. C.	OF	112	436	80	152	24	11	2	74	.349	260	10	6	.978
1977—Los Angeles.......Nat.	OF-1B	29	23	2	4	0	0	0	1	.174	24	2	1	.963
1978—Albuquerque......P. C.	*OF-1B	140	528	110	163	24	10	5	73	.309	310	20	*12	.965
1978—Los Angeles‡.....Nat.	OF	10	5	1	2	0	0	0	1	.400	8	0	0	1.000
1979—Seattle ....Amer.	OF	120	265	29	75	11	0	2	27	.283	162	10	6	.966
1980—Seattle ....Amer.	OF	129	365	42	91	15	3	3	34	.249	220	2	7	.932
National League Totals..................		71	64	8	12	1	0	0	2	.188	61	2	1	.984
American League Totals.................		249	630	71	166	26	3	5	61	.263	382	22	13	.969
Major League Totals......................		320	694	79	178	27	3	5	63	.256	443	24	14	.971

Selected by Washington Senators' organization in 14th round of free-agent draft, June 4, 1970.
Selected by Los Angeles Dodgers' organization in 3rd round of free-agent draft, June 5, 1973.
†On disabled list, April 10 to April 20, 1975.
‡Sold to Seattle Mariners, April 2, 1979.

MATTHEW STEPHEN SINATRO
(Matt)

Born March 22, 1960, at West Hartford, Conn.
Height, 5.09. Weight, 174.
Throws and bats righthanded.
Led Southern League catchers in double plays with 10 in 1980.

Year Club League	Pos.	G.	AB.	R.	H.	2B.	3B.	HR.	RBI.	B.A.	PO.	A.	E.	F.A.
1978—Kingsport..........Appal.	C	35	112	15	23	7	0	0	6	.205	198	26	2	.991
1979—Greenwood ....W. Car.	C	120	385	54	97	16	4	7	57	.252	639	69	11	.985
1980—Savannah ....South.	C	122	449	76	125	16	1	11	50	.278	514	70	15	.975

Selected by Atlanta Braves' organization in 2nd round of free-agent draft, June 6, 1978.

KENNETH WAYNE SINGLETON
(Ken)

Born June 10, 1947, at New York, N. Y.
Height, 6.04. Weight, 212.
Throws right and bats left and righthanded.
Attended Hofstra University, Hempstead, N. Y.

Tied National League record for most home runs, switch-hitting, one month, 9, July, 1973.
Led Florida State League batters in walks with 87 in 1967.
Led California League in sacrifice flies with 6 in 1968.
Named right fielder on THE SPORTING NEWS American League All-Star Team, 1979.

Year Club League	Pos.	G.	AB.	R.	H.	2B.	3B.	HR.	RBI.	B.A.	PO.	A.	E.	F.A.
1967—Winter Haven ....Fla. St.	O-1B	102	278	49	77	17	1	4	41	.277	222	7	5	.979
1968—Raleigh-Durham Carol.	1B-OF	26	74	21	19	3	0	3	12	.257	176	8	5	.974
1968—Visalia ....Calif.	OF-1B	80	263	61	83	5	0	11	35	.316	187	12	7	.966
1968—Jacksonville ......Int.	OF-1B	29	78	12	16	5	1	2	10	.205	34	0	2	.944
1969—Memphis ....Tex.	OF-1B	115	366	65	113	16	6	10	65	.309	234	10	3	.988
1970—Tidewater ....Int.	OF	64	219	48	85	16	1	17	46	.388	92	4	2	.980
1970—New York..........Nat.	OF	69	198	22	52	8	0	5	26	.263	90	1	3	.968

Year Club League	Pos.	G.	AB.	R.	H.	2B.	3B.	HR.	RBI.	B.A.	PO.	A.	E.	F.A.
1971—New York† ....Nat.	OF	115	298	34	73	5	0	13	46	.245	143	5	4	.974
1972—Montreal ....Nat.	OF	142	507	77	139	23	2	14	50	.274	236	9	7	.972
1973—Montreal ....Nat.	OF	●162	560	100	169	26	2	23	103	.302	278	*20	5	.983
1974—Montreal‡.........Nat.	OF	148	511	68	141	20	2	9	74	.276	224	7	11	.955
1975—Baltimore.........Amer.	OF	155	586	88	176	37	4	15	55	.300	283	9	3	.990
1976—Baltimore.........Amer.	OF	154	544	62	151	25	2	13	70	.278	278	9	5	.983
1977—Baltimore.........Amer.	OF	152	536	90	176	24	0	24	99	.328	278	8	4	.986
1978—Baltimore.........Amer.	OF	149	502	67	147	21	2	20	81	.293	244	1	6	.976
1979—Baltimore.........Amer.	OF	159	570	93	168	29	1	35	111	.295	247	8	5	.981
1980—Baltimore ....Amer.	OF	156	583	85	177	28	3	24	104	.304	248	3	4	.984
National League Totals...		636	2074	301	574	82	6	64	299	.277	971	42	30	.971
American League Totals...		925	3321	485	995	164	12	131	520	.300	1578	38	27	.984
Major League Totals ...		1561	5395	786	1569	246	18	195	819	.291	2549	80	57	.979

Selected by New York Mets' organization in 1st round of free-agent draft, January, 1967.

†Traded with First Baseman Mike Jorgensen and Infielder Tim Foli To Montreal Expos for Outfielder Rusty Staub, April 6, 1972.

‡Traded with Pitcher Mike Torrez to Baltimore Orioles for Pitchers Dave McNally and Bill Kirkpatrick and Outfielder Rich Coggins, December 4, 1974.

CHAMPIONSHIP SERIES RECORD

Year Club League	Pos.	G.	AB.	R.	H.	2B.	3B.	HR.	RBI.	B.A.	PO.	A.	E.	F.A.
1979—Baltimore ....Amer.	OF	4	16	4	6	2	0	0	2	.375	5	1	0	1.000

WORLD SERIES RECORD

Year Club League	Pos.	G.	AB.	R.	H.	2B.	3B.	HR.	RBI.	B.A.	PO.	A.	E.	F.A.
1979—Baltimore ....Amer.	OF	7	28	1	10	1	0	0	2	.357	9	0	0	1.000

ALL-STAR GAME RECORD

Year League	Pos.	AB.	R.	H.	2B.	3B.	HR.	RBI.	B.A.	PO.	A.	E.	F.A.
1977—American..............	OF	0	0	0	0	0	0	0	.000	0	0	0	.000
1979—American	PH	1	0	0	0	0	0	0	.000	0	0	0	.000
All-Star Game Totals		1	0	0	0	0	0	0	.000	0	0	0	.000

TED CRAWFORD SIZEMORE

Born April 15, 1945, at Gadsden, Ala.
Height, 5.10. Weight, 170.
Throws and bats righthanded.
Hobbies—Golf, chess and cards.
Attended University of Michigan, Ann Arbor, Mich.; received Bachelor of Science
degrees in Education and Marketing.

Tied major league records for most triples with bases filled, season (3), 1969; most errors by second baseman, inning (3), April 17, 1975 (sixth inning); longest errorless game by second baseman (25 innings), September 11, 1974.
Led National League in sacrifice hits with 25 in 1973.
Led National League second basemen in double plays with 104 in 1977.
Tied for National League lead in most times grounded into double plays with 25 in 1977.
Led Texas League in sacrifice flies with 9 in 1967.
Selected by Baseball Writers' Association as National League Rookie of the Year, 1969.
Named Player of the Year in Northwest League, 1966.

Year Club League	Pos.	G.	AB.	R.	H.	2B.	3B.	HR.	RBI.	B.A.	PO.	A.	E.	F.A.
1966—Tri-City.............N'west	C	58	191	34	63	8	2	4	37	.330	393	38	7	*.984
1967—Albuquerque......Texas	C-O-IN	131	440	53	130	21	4	5	61	.295	693	58	11	.986
1968—Spokane ....P. C.	OF-C	81	258	35	81	11	4	0	34	.314	192	13	7	.967
1969—Los Angeles.......Nat.	2-S-O	159	590	69	160	20	5	4	46	.271	347	469	24	.971
1970—Los Angeles††....Nat.	2-O-S	96	340	40	104	10	1	1	34	.306	209	239	9	.980
1971—St. Louis ....Nat.	2-S-O-3	135	478	53	126	14	5	3	42	.264	277	379	18	.973
1972—St. Louis ....Nat.	2B	120	439	53	116	17	4	2	38	.264	222	342	14	.976
1973—St. Louis§.........Nat.	2B-3B	142	521	69	147	22	1	1	54	.282	313	463	15	.981
1974—St. Louis x........Nat.	2-S-O	129	504	68	126	17	0	2	47	.250	336	412	16	.979
1975—St. Louis y........Nat.	2B	153	562	56	135	23	1	3	49	.240	329	405	21	.972
1976—Los Angeles z....Nat.	2-3-C	84	266	18	64	8	1	0	18	.241	178	191	7	.981
1977—Philadelphia......Nat.	2B	152	519	64	146	20	3	4	47	.281	348	427	11	.986
1978—Philadelphia ab.Nat.	2B	108	351	38	77	12	0	0	25	.219	232	302	12	.978
1979—Chicago c.........Nat.	2B	98	330	36	82	17	0	2	24	.248	230	312	●15	.973
1979—Boston ....Amer.	2B-C	26	88	12	23	7	0	1	6	.261	55	85	1	.993
1980—Boston d ....Amer.	2B	9	23	1	5	1	0	0	0	.217	16	22	3	.927
American League Totals		35	111	13	28	8	0	1	6	.252	71	107	4	.978
National League Totals		1376	4900	564	1283	180	21	22	424	.262	3021	3941	162	.977
Major League Totals......................		1411	5011	577	1311	188	21	23	430	.262	3092	4048	166	.977

Selected by Los Angeles Dodgers' organization in 40th round of free-agent draft, June 12, 1966.

†On disabled list, June 12 through July 11, 1970.

‡Traded with Catcher Bob Stinson to St. Louis Cardinals for First Baseman Dick Allen, October 5, 1970.

§On supplemental disabled list, April 26 to May 15, 1973.

xOn supplemental disabled list, July 4 to July 20, 1974.

yTraded to Los Angeles Dodgers for Outfielder Willie Crawford, March 2, 1976.

zTraded to Philadelphia Phillies for Catcher Johnny Oates and a player to be named later, December 20, 1976; Pitcher Quency Hill was assigned to Albuquerque to complete deal, January 4, 1977.

aOn disabled list, April 29 to June 20, 1978.

bTraded with Outfielder Jerry Martin, Catcher Barry Foote and Pitchers Derek Botelho and Henry Mack to Chicago Cubs for Second Baseman Manny Trillo, Outfielder Greg Gross and Catcher Dave Rader, February 23, 1979.

cTraded to Boston Red Sox for cash and a player to be named later, August 17, 1979; Chicago acquired Catcher Mike O'Berry, October 23, 1979, to complete deal.

dReleased, May 30, 1980.

CHAMPIONSHIP SERIES RECORD

Year	Club	League	Pos.	G.	AB.	R.	H.	2B.	3B.	HR.	RBI.	B.A.	PO.	A.	E.	F.A.
1977—Philadelphia	Nat.		2B	4	13	1	3	0	0	0	0	.231	10	8	2	.900
1978—Philadelphia	Nat.		2B	4	13	3	5	0	1	0	1	.385	7	8	0	1.000
Championship Series Totals				8	26	4	8	0	1	0	1	.308	17	16	2	.943

DAVID LINDSEY SKAGGS
(Dave)

Born June 12, 1951, at Santa Monica, Calif.
Height, 6.02. Weight, 205.
Throws and bats righthanded.
Hobbies—Golf, bowling and horse racing.

Year	Club	League	Pos.	G.	AB.	R.	H.	2B.	3B.	HR.	RBI.	B.A.	PO.	A.	E.	F.A.
1969—Aberdeen	North.		C	62	220	21	69	11	1	4	31	.314	*506	44	11	.980
1970—Aberdeen	North.						(On Military List)									
1971—Stockton	Calif.		C-OF	77	184	23	35	2	0	3	13	.190	395	45	12	.973
1972—Miami	Fla. St.		C-O-3	72	239	25	50	3	1	3	23	.209	433	55	10	.980
1973—Lodi	Calif.		C-3-1-O	82	260	33	66	9	5	1	37	.254	419	48	15	.969
1974—Asheville	South.		C	110	363	41	91	16	2	5	38	.251	531	*66	4	.993
1975—Asheville	South.		C-1B	59	199	26	53	8	1	0	24	.266	297	40	5	.985
1975—Rochester	Int.		C-1B	41	99	4	22	8	0	0	10	.222	177	18	4	.980
1976—Rochester†	Int.		C	85	252	40	61	8	2	2	27	.242	408	50	5	.989
1977—Baltimore	Amer.		C	80	216	22	62	9	1	1	24	.287	344	34	2	.995
1978—Baltimore	Amer.		C	36	86	6	13	1	1	0	2	.151	149	17	2	.988
1979—Baltimore	Amer.		C	63	137	9	34	8	0	1	14	.248	222	24	4	.984
1980—Balt.‡-Calif.§x	Amer.		C	26	71	7	14	0	0	1	9	.197	94	6	3	.971
Major League Totals				205	510	44	123	18	2	3	49	.241	809	81	11	.988

Selected by Baltimore Orioles' organization in 6th round of free-agent draft, June 5, 1969.

†On disabled list, May 26 to June 24, 1976.

‡Sold to California Angels, May 13, 1980.

§On disabled list, May 19 to September 1, 1980.

xReleased, February 2, 1981; signed by Seattle Mariners' organization, February 17, 1981.

CHAMPIONSHIP SERIES RECORD

Year	Club	League	Pos.	G.	AB.	R.	H.	2B.	3B.	HR.	RBI.	B.A.	PO.	A.	E.	F.A.
1979—Baltimore	Amer.		C	1	4	0	0	0	0	0	0	.000	3	1	0	1.000

WORLD SERIES RECORD

Year	Club	League	Pos.	G.	AB.	R.	H.	2B.	3B.	HR.	RBI.	B.A.	PO.	A.	E.	F.A.
1979—Baltimore	Amer.		C	1	3	1	1	0	0	0	0	.333	2	2	0	1.000

JAMES MICHAEL SLATON
(Jim)

Born June 19, 1950, at Long Beach, Calif.
Height, 6.00. Weight, 185.
Throws and bats righthanded.
Hobby—Water skiing.
Attended Antelope Valley College, Lancaster, Calif.

Pitched 5-0 no-hit victory against Wichita, August 3, 1972.

Year	Club	League	G.	IP.	W.	L.	Pct.	H.	R.	ER.	SO.	BB.	ERA.
1969—Billings	Pioneer		2	8	1	0	1.000	1	0	0	16	0	0.00
1969—Clinton	Midwest		13	82	6	3	.667	65	27	26	83	34	2.85
1970—Clinton†	Midwest		2	18	1	1	.500	9	4	3	15	5	1.50
1971—Evansville	Am. Assoc.		4	32	1	0	1.000	22	9	5	26	9	1.39
1971—Milwaukee	American		26	148	10	8	.556	140	67	62	63	71	3.77
1972—Evansville	Am. Assoc.		16	114	11	2	.846	97	39	37	68	37	2.92
1972—Milwaukee	American		9	44	1	6	.143	50	31	27	17	21	5.52
1973—Milwaukee	American		38	276	13	15	.464	266	127	114	134	99	3.72
1974—Milwaukee	American		40	250	13	16	.448	255	117	109	126	102	3.92
1975—Milwaukee	American		37	217	11	18	.379	238	129	109	119	90	4.52
1976—Milwaukee	American		38	293	14	15	.483	287	126	112	138	94	3.44
1977—Milwaukee‡	American		32	221	10	14	.417	223	104	88	104	77	3.58
1978—Detroit§	American		35	234	17	11	.607	235	117	107	92	85	4.12
1979—Milwaukee	American		32	213	15	9	.625	229	95	86	80	54	3.63
1980—Milwaukee x	American		3	16	1	1	.500	17	10	8	4	5	4.50
Major League Totals			290	1912	105	113	.482	1940	923	822	877	698	3.87

Selected by Seattle Pilots' organization in 14th round of free-agent draft, June 5, 1969.

‡Traded with Pitcher Rich Folkers to Detroit Tigers for Outfielder Ben Oglivie, December 9, 1977.
§Granted free agency, November 2, 1978; signed by Milwaukee Brewers, November 28, 1978.
xOn disabled list, May 25 to October 1, 1980.

ALL-STAR GAME RECORD
Member of American League All-Star Team in 1977; did not play.

ROY FREDERICK SMALLEY III

Born October 25, 1952, at Los Angeles, Calif.
Height, 6.01. Weight, 182.
Throws right and bats left and righthanded.
Attended Los Angeles City Community College, Los Angeles, Calif., and
University of Southern California, Los Angeles, Calif.
Son on Roy Smalley, Jr., former infielder with Chicago Cubs, Milwaukee Braves and
Philadelphia Phillies. Nephew of Gene Mauch, manager of Minnesota Twins.

Tied major league record for most strikeouts, two consecutive games (8), August 28 and 29, 1976 (26 innings).

Established American League record for most assists by shortstop, season (572), 1979.

Led American League batters in sacrifice hits with 25 in 1976.

Led American League shortstops in double plays with 116 in 1977, with 121 in 1978 and with 144 in 1979.

Led American League shortstops in putouts with 296 in 1979.

Named shortstop on THE SPORTING NEWS American League All-Star Team, 1979.

Received reported $100,000 bonus to sign with Texas Rangers, 1974.

Year	Club	League	Pos.	G.	AB.	R.	H.	2B.	3B.	HR.	RBI.	B.A.	PO.	A.	E.	F.A.
1974—Pittsfield	..........East.		SS	125	406	74	102	22	5	14	42	.251	146	376	*42	.926
1975—Spokane	............P. C.		SS-2B	43	162	26	55	8	1	2	19	.340	88	151	10	.960
1975—Texas	...............Amer.		S-2-C	78	250	22	57	8	0	3	33	.228	108	232	20	.944
1976—Tex.†-Minn.	.......Amer.		SS-2B	144	513	61	133	18	3	3	44	.259	274	447	26	.965
1977—Minnesota	........Amer.		SS	150	584	93	135	21	5	6	56	.231	255	*504	33	.958
1978—Minnesota	........Amer.		SS	158	586	80	160	31	3	19	77	.273	*287	*527	25	.970
1979—Minnesota	........Amer.		*SS-1B	●162	621	94	168	28	3	24	95	.271	305	*572	29	.968
1980—Minnesota	........Amer.		SS-1B	133	486	64	135	24	1	12	63	.278	226	448	17	.990
Major League Totals	....			825	3040	414	788	130	15	67	368	.259	1455	2730	150	.965

Selected by Montreal Expos' organization in 35th round of free-agent draft, June 4, 1970.

Selected by Boston Red Sox' organization in secondary phase of free-agent draft, January 13, 1971.

Selected by St. Louis Cardinals' organization in secondary phase of free-agent draft, June 8, 1971.

Selected by Boston Red Sox' organization in secondary phase of free-agent draft, January 12, 1972.

Selected by Texas Rangers' organization in 1st round (first player selected) of free-agent draft, January 9, 1974.

†Traded with Pitchers Bill Singer and Jim Gideon, Infielder Mike Cubbage, and $250,000 cash to Minnesota Twins for Pitcher Bert Blyleven and Shortstop Danny Thompson, June 1, 1976.

ALL-STAR GAME RECORD

Year	League	Pos.	AB.	R.	H.	2B.	3B.	HR.	RBI.	B.A.	PO.	A.	E.	F.A.
1979—American	....	SS	3	0	0	0	0	0	0	.000	2	2	0	1.000

BILLY L. SMITH

Born September 13, 1956, at LaMarque, Tex.
Height, 6.07. Weight, 200.
Throws and bats righthanded.
Attended Sam Houston State University, Huntsville, Tex.; received degree.

Led Southern League in complete games with 19 in 1979.

Year	Club	League	G.	IP.	W.	L.	Pct.	H.	R.	ER.	SO.	BB.	ERA.
1977—Sarasota Astros	...................G. Coast		7	44	2	4	.333	49	22	17	22	7	3.48
1977—Cocoa	.................Florida St.		4	29	1	3	.250	35	16	9	15	10	2.79
1978—Daytona Beach	....................Florida St.		13	93	6	6	.500	97	44	21	53	29	2.03
1978—Columbus	............................Southern		15	67	4	3	.571	67	26	19	34	19	2.55
1979—Columbus	...........................Southern		27	201	14	9	.609	187	77	59	76	68	2.64
1980—Tucson†	...............................P. Coast		28	143	12	4	.750	169	77	59	47	41	3.71

Selected by Houston Astros' organization in 14th round of free-agent draft, June 7, 1977.

†Drafted by New York Mets, December 8, 1980.

CARL REGINALD SMITH
(Reggie)

Born April 2, 1945, at Shreveport, La.
Height, 6.00. Weight, 195.
Throws right and bats right and lefthanded.
Hobbies—Working with plastics and all sports.
Attended Compton Community College, Compton, Calif.

Established National League records for most home runs by switch-hitter, two consecutive seasons (61), 1977 and 1978; most home runs on road by switch-hitter, season (17), 1977; most sacrifice flies by switch-hitter, season (13), 1978.

Tied National League record for most games, switch-hit home runs, season (1), May 4, 1975 and May 22, 1976; most games, switch-hit home runs, league (2).

Hit three home runs in one game, vs. Philadelphia Phillies, May 22, 1976.

Switch-hit home runs in one game four times in American League: August 20, 1967, August 11, 1968, July 2, 1972 and April 16, 1973.

Led American League in total bases with 302 in 1971.

Led National League in sacrifice flies with 13 in 1978.

Named outfielder on THE SPORTING NEWS American League All-Star fielding team, 1968.

Named outfielder on THE SPORTING NEWS American League All-Star Team, 1970.

Year	Club	League	Pos.	G.	AB.	R.	H.	2B.	3B.	HR.	RBI.	B.A.	PO.	A.	E.	F.A.
1963—Wytheville†	Appal.	SS	66	•253	59	65	8	3	8	37	.257	88	*146	*41	.851
1964—Reading	East.	3B	17	47	6	6	1	0	0	4	.128	7	20	9	.750
1964—Waterloo	Midw.	3-OF	87	308	63	98	18	5	15	60	.318	84	67	19	.888
1965—Pittsfield	East.	OF-2-3	130	499	85	129	23	14	8	64	.259	263	107	21	.946
1966—Toronto	Int.	*OF-S-2	143	506	86	162	30	9	18	80	*.320	303	49	*17	.954
1966—Boston	Amer.	OF	6	26	1	4	1	0	0	0	.154	17	0	1	.944
1967—Boston	Amer.	OF-2B	158	565	78	139	24	6	15	61	.246	353	32	7	.982
1968—Boston	Amer.	OF	155	558	78	148	*37	5	15	69	.265	*390	8	6	.985
1969—Boston	Amer.	OF	143	543	87	168	29	7	25	93	.309	321	8	14	.959
1970—Boston	Amer.	OF	147	580	109	176	32	7	22	74	.303	361	•15	9	.977
1971—Boston	Amer.	OF	159	618	85	175	*33	2	30	96	.283	386	15	*14	.966
1972—Boston	Amer.	OF	131	467	75	126	25	4	21	74	.270	247	8	5	.981
1973—Boston‡	Amer.	OF-1B	115	423	79	128	23	2	21	69	.303	282	8	5	.983
1974—St. Louis	Nat.	OF-1B	143	517	79	160	26	9	23	100	.309	286	9	7	.977
1975—St. Louis	Nat.	O-1-3	135	477	67	144	26	3	19	76	.302	650	39	15	.979
1976—St. L.§-L.A.	Nat.	OF-1-3	112	395	55	100	15	5	18	49	.253	314	48	4	.989
1977—Los Angeles	Nat.	OF	148	488	104	150	27	4	32	87	.307	240	7	5	.980
1978—Los Angeles	Nat.	OF	128	447	82	132	27	2	29	93	.295	220	8	12	.950
1979—Los Angeles x	Nat.	OF	68	234	41	64	13	1	10	32	.274	159	5	2	.988
1980—Los Angeles y	Nat.	OF	92	311	47	100	13	0	15	55	.322	153	15	1	.994
National League Totals			826	2869	475	850	147	24	146	492	.296	2022	131	46	.978
American League Totals			1014	3780	592	1064	204	33	149	536	.281	2357	94	61	.976
Major League Totals			1840	6649	1067	1914	351	57	295	1028	.288	4379	225	107	.977

Signed as free agent by Minnesota Twins' organization, June 21, 1963.

†Drafted by Boston Red Sox from Dallas-Fort Worth (Minnesota Twins' organization), December 2, 1963.

‡Traded with Pitcher Ken Tatum to St. Louis Cardinals for Pitcher Rick Wise and Outfielder Bernie Carbo, October 26, 1973.

§Traded to Los Angeles Dodgers for Catcher-Outfielder Joe Ferguson, Outfielder Bob Detherage, and Infielder Freddie Tisdale (latter assigned from Lodi to St. Petersburg), June 15, 1976.

xOn supplemental disabled list, August 2 to September 13, 1979.

yOn supplemental disabled list, August 25 to October 22, 1980.

CHAMPIONSHIP SERIES RECORD

Year	Club	League	Pos.	G.	AB.	R.	H.	2B.	3B.	HR.	RBI.	B.A.	PO.	A.	E.	F.A.
1977—Los Angeles	Nat.	OF	4	16	2	3	0	1	0	1	.188	7	0	1	.875
1978—Los Angeles	Nat.	OF	4	16	2	3	1	0	0	1	.188	5	0	1	.833
Championship Series Totals			8	32	4	6	1	1	0	2	.188	12	0	2	.857

WORLD SERIES RECORD

Tied World Series record for most putouts, inning, centerfielder (3), October 11, 1967, seventh inning.

Year	Club	League	Pos.	G.	AB.	R.	H.	2B.	3B.	HR.	RBI.	B.A.	PO.	A.	E.	F.A.
1967—Boston	Amer.	OF	7	24	3	6	1	0	2	3	.250	14	2	0	1.000
1977—Los Angeles	Nat.	OF	6	22	7	6	1	0	3	5	.273	14	1	0	1.000
1978—Los Angeles	Nat.	OF	6	25	3	5	0	0	1	5	.200	11	1	1	.923
World Series Totals			19	71	13	17	2	0	6	13	.239	39	4	1	.977

ALL-STAR GAME RECORD

Year	League	Pos.	AB.	R.	H.	2B.	3B.	HR.	RBI.	B.A.	PO.	A.	E.	F.A.
1969—American		OF	2	1	0	0	0	0	0	.000	0	0	0	.000
1972—American		PH	1	0	0	0	0	0	0	.000	0	0	0	.000
1974—National		OF	2	1	1	0	0	1	1	.500	2	0	0	1.000
1975—National		OF	2	1	1	0	0	0	0	.500	0	0	0	.000
1977—National		PH	1	0	1	0	0	0	0	1.000	0	0	0	.000
1978—National		PH-OF	3	0	0	0	0	0	0	.000	1	0	0	1.000
1980—National		OF	2	0	0	0	0	0	0	.000	0	0	0	.000
All-Star Game Totals			13	3	3	0	0	1	1	.231	3	0	0	1.000

CHRISTOPHER WILLIAM SMITH
(Chris)

Born July 18, 1957, at Torrance, Calif.
Height, 6.00. Weight, 185.
Throws right and bats left and righthanded.
Attended University of Southern California, Los Angeles, Calif.; received Bachelor of Science degree.

Year	Club	League	Pos.	G.	AB.	R.	H.	2B.	3B.	HR.	RBI.	B.A.	PO.	A.	E.	F.A.
1978—Tucson	P.C.	3B	19	62	5	16	4	0	0	8	.258	2	13	4	.789
1979—Tulsa†‡	Texas	3-O-1	98	354	46	117	18	3	6	54	.331	26	28	6	.900
1980—Denver	A.A.	DH-PH	9	25	3	5	0	0	1	3	.200	0	0	0	.000
1980—Memphis	South.	3-1-O	89	336	51	102	16	1	12	70	.304	160	86	15	.943

Selected by Baltimore Orioles' organization in 30th round of free-agent draft, June 4, 1975.
Selected by Texas Rangers' organization in 11th round of free-agent draft, June 6, 1978.
†On disabled list, May 10 to June 10, 1979.
‡Traded with Infielder-Outfielder LaRue Washington to Montreal Expos' organization for First Baseman-Outfielder Rusty Staub, March 31, 1980.

DAVID S. SMITH JR.
(Dave)

Born January 21, 1955, at San Francisco, Calif.
Height, 6.01. Weight, 195.
Throws and bats righthanded.
Attended San Diego State University, San Diego, Calif.

Major League saves: 1980 (10).

Year Club	League	G.	IP.	W.	L.	Pct.	H.	R.	ER.	SO.	BB.	ERA.
1976–Covington	Ap'lachian	15	97	5	5	.500	80	40	29	71	28	2.69
1977–Cocoa	Florida St.	14	93	7	5	.583	97	40	32	81	31	3.10
1977–Columbus	Southern	9	54	3	5	.375	52	26	21	29	24	3.50
1978–Columbus	Southern	26	181	10	13	.435	170	89	70	114	88	3.48
1979–Charleston	Int'national	34	160	7	8	.467	159	80	65	90	44	3.66
1980–Houston	National	57	103	7	5	.583	90	24	22	85	32	1.92
Major League Totals		57	103	7	5	.583	90	24	22	85	32	1.92

Selected by Houston Astros' organization in 8th round of free-agent draft, June 8, 1976.

CHAMPIONSHIP SERIES RECORD

Year Club	League	G.	IP.	W.	L.	Pct.	H.	R.	ER.	SO.	BB.	ERA.
1980–Houston	National	3	2⅓	1	0	1.000	4	1	1	4	2	3.86

KEITH LAVARNE SMITH

Born May 3, 1953, at Palmetto, Fla.
Height, 5.09. Weight, 178.
Throws and bats righthanded.
Hobbies–Singing and playing the harmonica.
Attended Manatee Junior College, Bradenton, Fla.
Brother of Bobby Smith, former outfielder in New York Mets' organization.

Tied for New York-Pennsylvania League lead in sacrifice hits with 5 in 1972.

Year Club	League	Pos.	G.	AB.	R.	H.	2B.	3B.	HR.	RBI.	B.A.	PO.	A.	E.	F.A.
1972–Geneva	NYP	OF	69	288	50	78	6	4	1	26	.271	135	8	5	.961
1973–						(Did not play)									
1974–Gastonia	W.Car.	OF	131	★496	73	141	18	●7	6	73	.284	201	●15	●13	.943
1975–Pittsfield	East.	OF	101	338	31	84	10	7	2	30	.249	145	7	●15	.910
1976–Sacramento	P.C.	OF	111	403	71	131	20	0	23	73	.325	119	10	6	.956
1977–Tucson	P.C.	OF	104	421	94	136	24	5	19	77	.323	137	4	4	.972
1977–Texas	Amer.	OF	23	67	13	16	4	0	2	6	.239	38	1	1	.975
1978–Tucson†	P.C.	OF	120	466	78	144	24	8	10	69	.309	193	6	10	.952
1979–Springfield	A.A.	OF	119	448	77	157	17	4	9	61	★.350	135	3	3	.979
1979–St. Louis	Nat.	OF	6	13	1	3	0	0	0	0	.231	14	1	0	1.000
1980–Springfield	A.A.	OF	69	271	39	80	10	2	5	32	.295	72	0	0	1.000
1980–St. Louis	Nat.	OF	24	31	3	4	1	0	0	2	.129	10	0	0	1.000
American League Totals			23	67	13	16	4	0	2	6	.239	38	1	1	.975
National League Totals			30	44	4	7	1	0	0	2	.159	24	1	0	1.000
Major League Totals			53	111	17	23	5	0	2	8	.207	62	2	1	.985

Selected by St. Louis Cardinals' organization in 7th round of free-agent draft, January 12, 1972.
Selected by Texas Rangers' organization in secondary phase of free-agent draft, June 6, 1972.
†Traded to St. Louis Cardinals' organization for Pitcher Tommy Toms, February 12, 1979.

KENNETH EARL SMITH
(Ken)

Born Feburary 12, 1958, at Youngstown, O.
Height, 6.01. Weight, 195.
Throws right and bats lefthanded.
Attended Youngstown State University, Youngstown, O.

Led Southern League batters in walks with 102 in 1979.
Led International League batters in strikeouts with 106 in 1980.
Led International League first basemen in putouts with 1158, in assists with 84 and in double plays with 95 in 1980.

Year Club	League	Pos.	G.	AB.	R.	H.	2B.	3B.	HR.	RBI.	B.A.	PO.	A.	E.	F.A.
1976–Brad. Braves	Gulf C.	OF-1B	32	94	24	24	3	1	1	12	.255	78	6	4	.955
1977–Greenwood†	W. Car.	OF-1B	67	212	38	64	7	0	1	25	.302	89	5	4	.959
1978–Savannah	South.	OF	138	462	55	110	19	5	2	40	.238	225	10	10	.959
1979–Savannah	South.	1B-OF	141	449	71	112	12	4	10	51	.249	1188	85	7	.995
1980–Richmond	Int.	1B-OF	132	418	61	103	17	4	12	53	.246	1167	86	15	.988

Selected by Atlanta Braves' organization in 1st round (3rd player selected) of free-agent draft, June 8, 1976.
†On disabled list, April 27 to June 24, 1977.

LEE ARTHUR SMITH

Born December 4, 1957, at Jamestown, La.
Height, 6.05. Weight, 220.
Throws and bats righthanded.
Attended Northwestern State University, Natchitoches, La.

Tied for American Association lead in wild pitches with 16 in 1980.

Year	Club	League	G.	IP.	W.	L.	Pct.	H.	R.	ER.	SO.	BB.	ERA.
1975—Bradenton Cubs	G. Coast	10	62	3	5	.375	35	23	16	35	*49	2.32
1976—Pompano Beach	Florida St.	26	101	4	8	.333	120	76	60	52	74	5.35
1977—Pompano Beach	Florida St.	26	130	10	4	.714	131	67	62	82	85	4.29
1978—Midland	Texas	30	155	8	10	.444	161	122	103	71	*128	5.98
1979—Midland	Texas	35	104	9	5	.643	122	65	57	46	85	4.93
1980—Wichita	Am. Assoc.	50	90	4	7	.364	70	49	37	63	56	3.70
1980—Chicago	National	18	22	2	0	1.000	21	9	7	17	14	2.86
Major League Totals		18	22	2	0	1.000	21	9	7	17	14	2.86

Selected by Chicago Cubs' organization in 2nd round of free-agent draft, June 4, 1975.

LONNIE SMITH

Born December 22, 1955, at Chicago, Ill.
Height, 5.09. Weight, 170
Throws and bats righthanded.
Hobby—Fishing.

Major League stolen bases: 1979 (2), 1980 (33). Total—35.
Led Western Carolinas League in stolen bases with 56 in 1975.
Led American Association in stolen bases with 66 in 1978.
Led American Association outfielders in double plays with 5 in 1978.
Named National League Rookie Player of the Year by THE SPORTING NEWS, 1980.

Year	Club	League	Pos.	G.	AB.	R.	H.	2B.	3B.	HR.	RBI.	B.A.	PO.	A.	E.	F.A.
1974—Auburn	NYP	OF	61	210	48	60	10	4	5	27	.286	143	6	●9	.943
1975—Spartanburg	W. Car.	OF	131	465	*114	*150	23	4	7	40	.323	*317	9	11	.967
1976—Oklahoma City	A.A.	OF	134	483	*93	149	24	9	8	54	.308	200	4	*14	.936
1977—Oklahoma City	A.A.	OF	125	477	91	132	14	10	4	41	.277	231	8	*13	.948
1978—Oklahoma City†	A.A.	OF	125	480	103	151	20	5	7	43	.315	274	*21	*12	.961
1978—Philadelphia	Nat.	OF	17	4	6	0	0	0	0	0	.000	5	1	0	1.000
1979—Oklahoma City	A.A.	OF	110	451	*106	149	26	9	7	44	.330	268	13	*12	.959
1979—Philadelphia	Nat.	OF	17	30	4	5	2	0	0	3	.167	19	1	0	1.000
1980—Philadelphia	Nat.	OF	100	298	69	101	14	4	3	20	.339	121	2	4	.969
Major League Totals			134	332	79	106	16	4	3	23	.319	145	4	4	.974

Selected by Philadelphia Phillies' organization in 1st round (third player selected) of free-agent draft, June 5, 1974.

†On disabled list, April 14 to April 25, 1978.

CHAMPIONSHIP SERIES RECORD

Year	Club	League	Pos.	G.	AB.	R.	H.	2B.	3B.	HR.	RBI.	B.A.	PO.	A.	E.	F.A.
1980—Philadelphia	Nat.	PR-OF	3	5	2	3	0	0	0	0	.600	2	1	0	1.000

WORLD SERIES RECORD

Year	Club	League	Pos.	G.	AB.	R.	H.	2B.	3B.	HR.	RBI.	B.A.	PO.	A.	E.	F.A.
1980—Philadelphia	Nat.	PR-O-D	6	19	2	5	1	0	0	1	.263	4	1	0	1.000

OSBORNE EARL SMITH
(Ozzie)

Born December 26, 1954, at Mobile, Ala.
Height, 5.10. Weight, 150.
Throws right and bats left and righthanded.
Attended California Polytechnic State University, San Luis Obispo, Calif.

Established major league record for most putouts by shortstop, season (621), 1980.
Major League stolen bases: 1978 (40), 1979 (28), 1980 (57). Total—125.
Led Northwest League in stolen bases with 30 in 1977.
Led Northwest League shortstops in double plays with 40 in 1977.
Led National League in sacrifice hits with 28 in 1978.
Led National League shortstops in double plays with 113 in 1980.
Named shortstop on THE SPORTING NEWS National League All-Star fielding team, 1980.

Year	Club	League	Pos.	G.	AB.	R.	H.	2B.	3B.	HR.	RBI.	B.A.	PO.	A.	E.	F.A.
1977—Walla Walla	N'west	SS	●68	*287	*69	87	10	2	1	35	.303	130	*254	23	*.943
1978—San Diego	Nat.	SS	159	590	69	152	17	6	1	46	.258	264	548	25	.970
1979—San Diego	Nat.	SS	156	587	77	124	18	6	0	27	.211	256	*555	20	.976
1980—San Diego	Nat.	SS	158	609	67	140	18	5	0	35	.230	*288	*621	24	.974
Major League Totals			473	1786	213	416	53	17	1	108	.233	808	1724	69	.973

Selected by Detroit Tigers' organization in 7th round of free-agent draft, June 8, 1976.
Selected by San Diego Padres' organization in 4th round of free-agent draft, June 7, 1977.

RAYMOND EDWARD SMITH
(Ray)

Born September 18, 1955, at Glendale, Calif.
Height, 6.01. Weight, 185.
Throws and bats righthanded.
Attended Mira Costa College, Oceanside, Calif., and University of Oregon, Eugene, Ore.

Year Club	League	Pos.	G.	AB.	R.	H.	2B.	3B.	HR.	RBI.	B.A.	PO.	A.	E.	F.A.
1977—Visalia	Calif.	SS	33	120	23	43	6	0	1	20	.358	54	101	19	.891
1977—Elizabethton	Appal.	C-1-3-S	63	234	50	71	13	1	7	42	.303	371	39	4	.990
1978—Orlando†	South.	C	72	216	26	58	10	0	2	31	.269	310	23	13	.962
1979—Toledo	Int.	C	78	233	24	58	7	3	3	24	.249	358	28	11	.972
1980—Toledo	Int.	C	115	398	36	109	14	4	0	46	.274	461	64	7	.987

Signed as free agent by Minnesota Twins' organization, January 24, 1977.
†On disabled list, May 23 to June 3, 1978.

BILLY MIKE SMITHSON
(Known by middle name)

Born January 21, 1955, at Centerville, Tenn.
Height, 6.08. Weight, 200.
Throws right and bats lefthanded.
Attended University of Tennessee, Knoxville, Tenn.

Year Club	League	G.	IP.	W.	L.	Pct.	H.	R.	ER.	SO.	BB.	ERA.
1976—Winter Haven	Florida St.	11	64	4	3	.571	63	27	22	29	20	3.09
1977—Winter Haven	Florida St.	25	172	13	8	.619	170	56	53	92	41	2.77
1977—Bristol	Eastern	1	3	0	1	.000	8	7	7	1	0	21.00
1978—Bristol	Eastern	27	160	11	10	.524	178	92	81	86	76	4.56
1979—Bristol	Eastern	*48	132	8	12	.400	128	82	69	89	53	4.70
1980—Pawtucket	Int'national	*50	99	5	9	.357	95	50	32	73	45	2.91

Selected by Boston Red Sox' organization in 5th round of free-agent draft, June 8, 1976.

ERIC THANE SODERHOLM
Name pronounced Sod-er-holm.

Born September 24, 1948, Cortland, N. Y.
Height, 5.11. Weight, 202.
Throws and bats righthanded.
Hobbies—Bowling, golf and sports in general.
Attended South Georgia Junior College, Douglas, Ga., University of South Florida,
Tampa, Fla., and University of Tampa, Tampa, Fla.
Brother of Dale Soderholm, shortstop in Minnesota Twins' organization.

Tied American League record with Jay Johnstone for most home runs, game, both clubs, pinch-hitters, 2, October 4, 1972 (both in sixth inning).
Named Florida State League Player of the Year in 1968.
Named THE SPORTING NEWS American League Comeback Player of the Year, 1977.

Year Club	League	Pos.	G.	AB.	R.	H.	2B.	3B.	HR.	RBI.	B.A.	PO.	A.	E.	F.A.
1968—Orlando	Fla. St.	SS	84	293	51	80	12	4	12	39	.273	115	272	17	.958
1969—Orlando	Fla. St.	SS	51	192	39	53	9	2	6	43	.276	75	177	13	.951
1969—Red Springs	Carol.	SS	20	68	8	20	4	1	1	4	.294	38	66	7	.937
1969—Charlotte	South.	SS-3	48	145	26	33	10	1	3	23	.228	71	131	9	.959
1970—Orlando	Fla. St.	3B	25	90	17	20	4	1	1	9	.222	20	55	4	.949
1970—Evansville	A.A.	SS-3B	98	310	44	77	11	3	15	42	.248	168	279	18	.961
1971—Portland	P.C.	3B-1B	132	454	80	125	28	3	22	83	.275	91	286	26	.935
1971—Minnesota	Amer.	3B	21	64	9	10	4	0	1	4	.156	17	48	4	.942
1972—Minnesota	Amer.	3B	93	287	28	54	10	0	13	39	.188	66	163	14	.942
1973—Tacoma	P.C.	3B-SS	116	390	60	93	27	5	10	55	.238	113	252	20	.948
1973—Minnesota	Amer.	3B-SS	35	111	22	33	7	2	1	9	.297	26	67	8	.921
1974—Minnesota	Amer.	3B-SS	141	464	63	128	18	3	10	51	.276	101	273	17	.957
1975—Minnesota†	Amer.	3B	117	419	62	120	17	2	11	58	.286	94	277	12	.969
1976—Minnesota‡§	Amer.					(Did Not Play)									
1977—Chicago	Amer.	3B	130	460	77	129	20	3	25	67	.280	99	249	8	*.978
1978—Chicago	Amer.	*3B-2B	143	457	57	118	17	1	20	67	.258	*128	249	14	.964
1979—Chi.x-Tex.y	Amer.	3B-1B	119	357	46	93	14	2	10	53	.261	84	203	8	.973
1980—New York	Amer.	3B	95	275	38	79	13	1	11	35	.287	15	65	4	.952
Major League Totals			894	2894	402	764	120	14	102	383	.264	630	1594	89	.962

Selected by Kansas City Royals' organization in 11th round of free-agent draft, June 6, 1967.
Selected by Minnesota Twins' organization in secondary phase of free-agent draft, January 27, 1968.
†On supplemental disabled list, August 21 to November 20, 1975.
‡On disabled list, March 31 to October 4, 1976.
§Granted free agency, November 1, 1976; signed with Chicago White Sox, November 26, 1976.
xTraded to Texas Rangers for Pitcher Ed Farmer and First Baseman Gary Holle, June 15, 1979.
yTraded to New York Yankees for two players to be named later, November 14, 1979; Texas acquired Third Baseman Amos Lewis and Pitcher Ricky Burdette to complete deal, December 13, 1979.

CHAMPIONSHIP SERIES RECORD

Year Club	League	Pos.	G.	AB.	R.	H.	2B.	3B.	HR.	RBI.	B.A.	PO.	A.	E.	F.A.
1980—New York	Amer.	DH	2	6	0	1	0	0	0	0	.167	0	0	0	.000

RICHARD MICHAEL SOFIELD
(Rick)

Born December 16, 1956 at Cheyenne, Wyoming.
Height, 6.01. Weight, 193.
Throws right and bats lefthanded.
Hobbies—Racquetball, tennis and basketball officiating.

Year Club League	Pos.	G.	AB.	R.	H.	2B.	3B.	HR.	RBI.	B.A.	PO.	A.	E.	F.A.
1975—Elizabethton......Appal.	SS	61	208	37	43	9	3	2	29	.207	*103	154	28	.902
1976—Wis. Rapids.......Midw.	OF-3B	104	340	43	81	11	4	4	55	.238	161	86	21	.922
1977—Visalia ....Calif.	OF	108	403	106	132	22	8	27	107	.328	198	15	10	.955
1977—Tacoma.............P. C.	OF-3B	4	12	3	3	0	0	0	1	.250	6	1	0	1.000
1978—Toledo†.............Int.	OF	22	61	8	10	2	0	0	4	.164	31	4	0	1.000
1978—Orlando ....South.	OF	65	185	31	52	9	3	5	23	.281	97	3	4	.962
1979—Toledo ....Int.	OF	54	177	28	42	9	0	3	14	.237	89	4	6	.939
1979—Orlando ....South.	OF	30	101	9	27	4	2	1	13	.267	73	2	2	.974
1979—Minnesota ....Amer.	OF	35	93	8	28	5	0	0	12	.301	61	1	3	.954
1980—Minnesota ....Amer.	OF	131	417	52	103	18	4	9	49	.247	267	7	6	.979
Major League Totals......................		166	510	60	131	23	4	9	61	.257	328	8	9	.974

Selected by Minnesota Twins' organization in 1st round (13th player selected) of free-agent draft, June 4, 1975.

†On disabled list, May 19 to May 30 and June 4 to June 15, 1978.

EDDIE SOLOMON JR.
(Buddy)

Born February 9, 1951, at Perry, Ga.
Height, 6.03. Weight, 190.
Throws and bats righthanded.
Hobbies—Dancing, playing pool and reading.

Tied for Pacific Coast League lead in complete games by pitchers with 11 in 1974.

Year Club League	G.	IP.	W.	L.	Pct.	H.	R.	ER.	SO.	BB.	ERA.
1969—Ogden...................................Pioneer	5	21	2	0	1.000	26	18	14	21	14	6.00
1970—Daytona Beach....................Florida St.	22	156	11	7	.611	131	61	41	104	72	2.37
1971—Albuquerque ....Texas	26	182	11	9	.550	181	72	61	130	56	3.02
1972—Albuquerque ....P. Coast	14	53	1	5	.167	54	33	25	34	22	4.25
1972—El Paso† ....Texas	15	74	3	8	.273	90	59	51	61	24	6.23
1973—Albuquerque ....P. Coast	30	178	9	12	.429	199	110	84	134	87	4.25
1973—Los Angeles ....National	4	6	0	0	.000	10	5	5	6	4	7.50
1974—Albuquerque ....P. Coast	18	138	11	4	.733	145	75	69	105	42	4.50
1974—Los Angeles ....National	4	6	0	0	.000	5	1	1	2	2	1.50
1975—Albuquerque‡......................P. Coast	3	27	3	0	1.000	33	13	12	21	16	4.00
1975—Chicago ....National	6	7	0	0	.000	7	6	1	3	6	1.29
1975—Wichita§-Tulsa ....Am. Assoc.	15	90	8	5	.615	96	64	50	60	42	5.00
1976—Tulsa ....Int'national	8	56	5	2	.714	42	19	15	49	16	2.41
1976—St. Louis ....National	26	37	1	1	.500	45	24	20	19	16	4.86
1977—New Orleans x ....Am. Assoc.	8	45	4	2	.667	53	25	21	30	14	4.20
1977—Richmond ....Int'national	7	52	5	1	.833	47	17	16	34	7	2.77
1977—Atlanta ....National	18	89	6	6	.500	110	64	45	54	34	4.55
1978—Atlanta ....National	37	106	4	6	.400	98	52	48	64	50	4.08
1979—Atlanta y ....National	31	186	7	14	.333	184	98	87	96	51	4.21
1980—Pittsburgh ....National	26	100	7	3	.700	96	44	30	35	37	2.70
Major League Totals	152	537	25	30	.455	555	294	237	279	200	3.97

Signed as free agent by Los Angeles Dodgers' organization, July 1, 1969.

†Played two games in outfield.

‡Traded with Pitcher Geoffrey Zahn by Los Angeles Dodgers to Chicago Cubs for Pitcher Burt Hooton, May 2, 1975.

§Traded by Chicago Cubs to St. Louis Cardinals for Pitcher Ken Crosby, July 22, 1975.

xSold to Atlanta Braves' organization, May 24, 1977.

yTraded to Pittsburgh Pirates for a player to be named later, March 28, 1980; Pitcher Greg Field traded to Braves' organization completing deal, April 25, 1980.

CHAMPIONSHIP SERIES RECORD

Year Club League	G.	IP.	W.	L.	Pct.	H.	R.	ER.	SO.	BB.	ERA.
1974—Los Angeles ....Nat.	1	2	0	0	.000	2	0	0	1	1	0.00

LARY ALAN SORENSEN

Born October 4, 1955, at Detroit, Mich.
Height, 6.02. Weight, 200.
Throws and bats righthanded.
Hobbies—Music and all sports.
Attending University of Michigan, Ann Arbor, Mich.

Tied for New York-Pennsylvania league lead in complete games with 7 and shutouts with 2 in 1976.
Tied for Pacific Coast League lead in shutouts with 3 in 1977.

Year Club	League	G.	IP.	W.	L.	Pct.	H.	R.	ER.	SO.	BB. ERA.
1976—Newark................................	NYP	13	75	6	2	.750	58	22	19	65	27 2.28
1976—Berkshire	Eastern	7	41	0	3	.000	44	19	15	25	16 3.29
1977—Spokane.............................	P. Coast	12	72	5	5	.500	79	41	37	43	31 4.63
1977—Milwaukee	American	23	142	7	10	.412	147	72	69	57	36 4.37
1978—Milwaukee	American	37	281	18	12	.600	277	111	100	78	50 3.20
1979—Milwaukee	American	34	235	15	14	.517	250	113	104	63	42 3.98
1980—Milwaukee†	American	35	196	12	10	.545	242	91	80	54	45 3.67
Major League Totals		129	854	52	46	.531	916	387	353	252	173 3.72

Selected by Milwaukee Brewers' organization in 8th round of free-agent draft, June 8, 1976.

†Traded with Outfielders Sixto Lezcano and David Green and Pitcher Dave LaPoint to St. Louis Cardinals for Pitchers Rollie Fingers and Pete Vuckovich and Catcher Ted Simmons, December 12, 1980.

ALL-STAR GAME RECORD

Year League			IP.	W.	L.	Pct.	H.	R.	ER.	SO.	BB. ERA.
1978—American			3	0	0	.000	1	0	0	0	0 0.00

ELIAS SOSA (MARTINEZ)
First name pronounced E-lee-us.

Born June 10, 1950, at La Vega, Dominican Republic.
Height, 6.02. Weight, 205.
Throws and bats righthanded.

Major League saves: 1972 (3), 1973 (18), 1974 (6), 1975 (2), 1976 (4), 1977 (1), 1978 (14), 1979 (18), 1980 (9). Total—75.

Year Club	League	G.	IP.	W.	L.	Pct.	H.	R.	ER.	SO.	BB. ERA.
1968—Salt Lake City	Pioneer	8	18	0	5	.000	33	32	16	15	14 8.00
1969—Decatur	Midwest	9	22	0	1	.000	27	13	11	24	17 4.50
1969—Great Falls	Pioneer	14	27	0	2	.000	22	21	18	38	22 6.00
1970—Amarillo	Texas	3	5	0	0	.000	3	2	1	2	4 1.80
1970—Fresno.................................	California	21	102	6	8	.429	119	66	58	95	39 5.12
1971—Fresno.................................	California	31	152	12	9	.571	140	68	56	124	48 3.32
1972—Phoenix	P. Coast	55	120	10	2	.833	123	40	39	107	44 2.93
1972—San Francisco	National	8	16	0	1	.000	10	4	4	10	12 2.25
1973—San Francisco	National	71	107	10	4	.714	95	42	39	70	41 3.28
1974—San Francisco†	National	68	101	9	7	.563	94	54	39	48	45 3.48
1975—St. Louis‡-Atlanta	National	57	90	2	5	.286	92	49	43	46	43 4.30
1976—Atlanta§-Los Angeles............	National	45	69	6	8	.429	71	42	34	52	25 4.43
1977—Los Angeles x	National	44	64	2	2	.500	42	15	14	47	12 1.97
1978—Oakland y	American	68	109	8	2	.800	106	37	32	61	44 2.64
1979—Montreal..............................	National	62	97	8	7	.533	77	24	21	59	37 1.95
1980—Montreal..............................	National	67	94	9	6	.600	104	33	32	58	19 3.06
National League Totals..........................		422	638	46	40	.535	585	263	226	390	234 3.19
American League Totals		68	109	8	2	.800	106	37	32	61	44 2.64
Major League Totals................................		490	747	54	42	.563	691	300	258	451	278 3.11

Signed as free agent by San Francisco Giants' organization, March 4, 1968.

†Traded with Catcher Ken Rudolph to St. Louis Cardinals for Catcher Marc Hill, October 14, 1974.

‡Traded with Pitcher Ray Sadecki to Atlanta Braves for Pitcher Ron Reed and a player to be named later, May 28, 1975; Braves sent Outfielder Wayne Nordhagen to Cardinals, June 2, 1975, to complete deal.

§Traded (via waivers) with Infielder Lee Lacy to Los Angeles Dodgers for Pitcher Mike Marshall, June 23, 1976.

xSold on waivers to Pittsburgh Pirates, January 31, 1978. Traded from Pirates with Outfielder Miguel Dilone and a player to be named later to Oakland A's for Catcher Manny Sanguillen, April 4, 1978; Infielder Mike Edwards sent to A's to complete deal, April 7, 1978.

yGranted free agency, November 2, 1978; signed by Montreal Expos, January 8, 1979.

CHAMPIONSHIP SERIES RECORD

Year Club	League	G.	IP.	W.	L.	Pct.	H.	R.	ER.	SO.	BB. ERA.
1977—Los Angeles	Nat.	2	2⅔	0	1	.000	5	4	3	0	0 10.13

WORLD SERIES RECORD

Year Club	League	G.	IP.	W.	L.	Pct.	H.	R.	ER.	SO.	BB. ERA.
1977—Los Angeles	Nat.	2	2⅓	0	0	.000	3	3	3	1	1 11.57

MARIO MELVIN SOTO

Born July 12, 1956, Bani, Dominican Republic.
Height, 6.00. Weight, 185.
Throws and bats righthanded.

Year Club	League	G.	IP.	W.	L.	Pct.	H.	R.	ER.	SO.	BB. ERA.
1974—Billings†	Pioneer					(Did not play)					
1975—Eugene	Northwest	5	30	2	3	.400	33	21	14	11	18 4.20
1976—Tampa	Florida St.	26	*197	13	7	.650	142	54	41	*124	80 1.87
1977—Indianapolis	Am. Assoc.	18	123	11	5	.688	100	51	42	109	61 3.07
1977—Cincinnati	National	12	61	2	6	.250	60	38	36	44	26 5.31
1978—Indianapolis	Am. Assoc.	26	160	9	12	.429	129	102	89	121	95 5.01
1978—Cincinnati	National	5	18	1	0	1.000	13	5	5	13	2 2.50
1979—Indianapolis‡	Am. Assoc.	15	25	1	1	.500	20	11	11	38	18 3.96
1979—Cincinnati	National	25	37	3	2	.600	33	25	22	32	30 5.35
1980—Cincinnati	National	53	190	10	8	.556	126	72	65	182	84 3.08
Major League Totals................................		95	306	16	16	.500	132	140	128	271	153 3.76

Signed as free agent by Cincinnati Reds' organization, December 3, 1973.
†On disabled list, July 1 to September 17, 1974.
‡On disabled list, April 13 to May 21, 1979.

CHAMPIONSHIP SERIES RECORD

Year	Club	League	G.	IP.	W.	L.	Pct.	H.	R.	ER.	SO.	BB.	ERA.
1979—Cincinnati		National	1	2	0	0	.000	0	0	0	1	0	0.00

KENNETH MARK SOUZA

(Known by middle name.)

Born February 1, 1954, at Redwood City, Calif.
Height, 6.00. Weight, 180.
Throws and bats lefthanded.
Attended College of San Mateo, San Mateo, Calif.

Year	Club	League	G.	IP.	W.	L.	Pct.	H.	R.	ER.	SO.	BB.	ERA.
1974—Kansas City Academy		G. Coast	10	42	5	2	.714	42	23	20	31	18	4.29
1974—San Jose		California	5	23	0	3	.000	33	14	10	11	8	3.91
1975—Waterloo		Midwest	32	58	3	1	.750	61	35	30	64	25	4.66
1976—Waterloo†		Midwest	36	57	6	2	.750	45	22	18	64	31	2.84
1977—Orlando‡		Southern	28	81	5	4	.556	79	46	42	52	35	4.67
1979—Puerto Rico§		Inter-Am.	8	60	1	6	.143	52	20	16	24	13	2.40
1979—Ogden		P. Coast	15	41	3	2	.600	42	23	20	25	20	4.39
1980—Ogden		P. Coast	41	86	7	5	.583	89	44	32	47	42	3.35
1980—Oakland		American	5	7	0	0	.000	9	6	6	2	5	7.71
Major League Totals			5	7	0	0	.000	9	6	6	2	5	7.71

Selected by Kansas City Royals' organization in 1st round (17th player selected) of free-agent draft, January 9, 1974.

†Drafted by Minnesota Twins' organization, December 8, 1976.

‡Released, April 12, 1978; signed by Miami of Inter-American League, 1979; sold by Miami to Puerto Rico, April 2, 1979.

§Declared free agent when Inter-American League folded, June 15, 1979; signed by Oakland A's organization, July 11, 1979.

CHRIS EDWARD SPEIER

Name pronounced Spire.

Born June 28, 1950, at Alameda, Calif.
Height, 6.01. Weight, 175.
Throws and bats righthanded.
Attended University of Santa Barbara, Santa Barbara, Calif.

Named shortstop on THE SPORTING NEWS National League All-Star Team, 1972.

Year	Club	League	Pos.	G.	AB.	R.	H.	2B.	3B.	HR.	RBI.	B.A.	PO.	A.	E.	F.A.
1970—Amarillo		Tex.	*SS-3-O	129	460	44	130	20	5	6	66	.283	*224	*327	38	.935
1971—San Francisco		Nat.	SS	157	601	74	141	17	6	8	46	.235	239	517	•33	.953
1972—San Francisco		Nat.	SS	150	562	74	151	25	2	15	71	.269	243	*517	20	.974
1973—San Francisco		Nat.	•SS-2B	153	542	58	135	17	4	11	71	.249	255	471	•33	.957
1974—San Francisco		Nat.	SS-2B	141	501	55	125	19	5	9	53	.250	215	453	21	.970
1975—San Francisco		Nat.	SS-3B	141	487	60	132	30	5	10	69	.271	247	421	12	*.982
1976—San Francisco		Nat.	S-2-3-1	145	495	51	112	18	4	3	40	.226	241	464	19	.974
1977—S.F.†-Mont.		Nat.	SS	145	548	59	128	31	6	5	38	.234	239	455	23	.968
1978—Montreal		Nat.	SS	150	501	47	126	18	3	5	51	.251	245	467	18	.975
1979—Montreal‡		Nat.	SS	113	344	31	78	13	1	7	26	.227	194	355	17	.970
1980—Montreal		Nat.	SS-3B	128	388	35	103	14	4	1	32	.265	187	397	21	.965
Major League Totals				1423	4969	544	1231	202	40	74	497	.248	2305	4517	217	.969

Selected by Washington Senators' organization in 11th round of free-agent draft, June 7, 1968.
Selected by San Francisco Giants' organization in secondary phase of free-agent draft, January 17, 1970.
†Traded to Montreal Expos for Shortstop Tim Foli, April 27, 1977.
‡On supplemental disabled list, July 8 to July 27, 1979.

CHAMPIONSHIP SERIES RECORD

Year	Club	League	Pos.	G.	AB.	R.	H.	2B.	3B.	HR.	RBI.	B.A.	PO.	A.	E.	F.A.
1971—San Francisco		Nat.	SS	4	14	4	5	1	0	1	1	.357	3	14	1	.944

All-STAR GAME RECORD

Year	League	Pos.	AB.	R.	H.	2B.	3B.	HR.	RBI.	B.A.	PO.	A.	E.	F.A.
1972—National		SS	2	0	0	0	0	0	0	.000	1	5	0	1.000
1973—National		SS	2	0	0	0	0	0	0	.000	1	1	0	1.000
All-Star Game Totals			4	0	0	0	0	0	0	.000	2	6	0	1.000

Member of National League All-Star Team in 1974 game; did not play.

JAMES LLOYD SPENCER

(Jim)

Born July 30, 1947, at Hanover, Pa.
Height, 6.02. Weight, 205.
Throws and bats lefthanded.
Hobbies—Golf and hunting.
Grandson of L. Benjamin Spencer, outfielder in minor leagues
from 1911-29; played with Washington in 1913.

Established American League record for highest fielding percentage by first baseman, lifetime, 1,000 or more games (.995).

Led American League first basemen in double plays with 131 in 1970.

Led Texas League in total bases with 267, in sacrifice flies with 10 and led first basemen in double plays with 109 in 1968.

Named first baseman on THE SPORTING NEWS American League All-Star fielding team, 1970 and 1977.

Shared Texas League Most Valuable Player Award, 1968.

Received reported $20,000 bonus to sign with California Angels, 1965.

Year Club	League	Pos.	G.	AB.	R.	H.	2B.	3B.	HR.	RBI.	B.A.	PO.	A.	E.	F.A.
1965—Quad Cities ......Midw.		1B	76	269	25	60	10	4	2	25	.223	562	16	10	.983
1966—El Paso	Texas	1B	133	488	72	129	22	7	16	53	.264	*1174	62	12	.990
1967—El Paso	Texas	*1-O	134	480	75	134	27	5	19	73	.279	1042	81	7	*.994
1968—El Paso	Texas	*1B-O	135	493	●85	144	29	5	*28	*96	.292	*1170	*80	11	*.991
1968—California	Amer.	1B	19	68	2	13	1	0	0	5	.191	152	18	1	.994
1969—Hawaii	P.C.	1B	47	172	30	45	8	0	6	22	.262	433	39	4	.992
1969—California	Amer.	1B	113	386	39	98	14	3	10	31	.254	926	66	9	.991
1970—California	Amer.	1B	146	511	61	140	20	4	12	68	.274	*1212	85	7	*.995
1971—California	Amer.	1B	148	510	50	121	21	2	18	59	.237	*1296	*93	5	*.996
1972—California	Amer.	1B-OF	82	212	13	47	5	0	1	14	.222	289	23	3	.990
1973—Calif.†-Texas	Amer.	1B	131	439	45	115	16	5	6	54	.262	994	74	1	*.999
1974—Texas	Amer.	1B	118	352	36	98	11	4	7	44	.278	389	27	1	.998
1975—Texas‡	Amer.	1B	122	403	50	107	18	1	11	47	.266	844	70	5	.995
1976—Chicago	Amer.	1B	150	518	53	131	13	2	14	70	.253	1206	*112	2	*.998
1977—Chicago§	Amer.	1B	128	470	56	116	16	1	18	69	.247	977	90	10	.991
1978—New York x	Amer.	1B	71	150	12	34	9	1	7	24	.227	90	7	0	1.000
1979—New York	Amer.	1B	106	295	60	85	15	3	23	53	.288	232	17	2	.992
1980—New York	Amer.	1B	97	259	38	61	9	0	13	43	.236	567	41	6	.990
Major League Totals			1441	4573	515	1166	168	26	140	581	.255	9174	723	52	.995

Selected by Los Angeles Angels' organization in 1st round (11th player selected) of free-agent draft, June, 1965.

†Traded with Pitcher Lloyd Allen to Texas Rangers for First Baseman Mike Epstein, Pitcher Rich Hand and Catcher Rick Stelmaszek (latter assigned to Salt Lake City), May 20, 1973.

‡Traded with an estimated $100,000 to California Angels for Pitcher Bill Singer, December 10, 1975. Traded with Outfielder Morris Nettles by California Angels to Chicago White Sox for Third Baseman Bill Melton and Pitcher Steve Dunning, December 11, 1975.

§Traded to New York Yankees for Pitcher Stan Thomas and cash, December 12, 1977 (as part of deal Chicago released Outfielder Cirilo Cruz and Pitcher Bob Polinsky, both on Iowa roster, to Tacoma, and New York released Pitcher Ed Ricks to Iowa).

xOn supplemental disabled list, August 3 to August 19, 1978.

CHAMPIONSHIP SERIES RECORD

Year Club	League	Pos.	G.	AB.	R.	H.	2B.	3B.	HR.	RBI.	B.A.	PO.	A.	E.	F.A.
1980—New York	Amer.	PH	1	1	0	0	0	0	0	0	.000	0	0	0	.000

WORLD SERIES RECORD

Year Club	League	Pos.	G.	AB.	R.	H.	2B.	3B.	HR.	RBI.	B.A.	PO.	A.	E.	F.A.
1978—New York	Amer.	1B-PH	4	12	3	2	0	0	0	0	.167	23	2	0	1.000

ALL-STAR GAME RECORD

Year League	Pos.	AB.	R.	H.	2B.	3B.	HR.	RBI.	B.A.	PO.	A.	E.	F.A.
1973—American.............................	PH	1	0	0	0	0	0	0	.000	0	0	0	.000

LESLIE CHARLES SPIKES
(Charlie)

Born January 23, 1951, at Bogalusa, La.
Height, 6.03. Weight, 220.
Throws and bats righthanded.
Hobby—Basketball.
Attended Grambling College, Grambling, La.
Brother of William Spikes, former outfielder in Pittsburgh Pirates' organization.

Led Carolina League in strikeouts with 117 in 1971 and Florida State League with 157 in 1970.

Received reported $60,000 bonus to sign with New York Yankees, 1969.

Year Club	League	Pos.	G.	AB.	R.	H.	2B.	3B.	HR.	RBI.	B.A.	PO.	A.	E.	F.A.
1969—Johnson City .....Appal.		*3-OF	47	163	29	33	2	0	8	21	.202	33	65	*29	.772
1970—Ft. Lauderdale ..Fla. St.		3-O	127	422	71	100	12	2	19	62	.237	132	135	40	.870
1971—Kinston ....Carol.		OF	127	423	77	114	16	1	*22	79	.270	151	14	*15	.917
1972—West Haven ....East.		OF	126	427	83	132	27	5	26	83	.309	191	12	14	.935
1972—New York†	Amer.	OF	14	34	2	5	1	0	0	3	.147	14	1	0	1.000
1973—Cleveland	Amer.	OF	140	506	68	120	12	3	23	73	.237	202	13	8	.964
1974—Cleveland	Amer.	OF	155	568	63	154	23	1	22	80	.271	284	16	10	.968
1975—Cleveland	Amer.	OF	111	345	41	79	13	3	11	33	.229	176	13	5	.974
1976—Cleveland	Amer.	OF	101	334	34	79	11	5	3	31	.237	185	7	3	.985
1977—Toledo‡ ....Int.		OF	49	164	31	48	7	3	7	31	.293	46	1	1	.979
1977—Cleveland§	Amer.	OF	32	95	13	22	2	0	3	11	.232	34	1	1	.972
1978—Evansville x ......A. A.		OF	16	50	8	16	3	2	2	11	.320	15	0	0	1.000
1978—Detroit y ....Amer.		OF	10	28	1	7	1	0	0	2	.250	9	1	1	.909

Year Club League	Pos.	G.	AB.	R.	H.	2B.	3B.	HR.	RBI.	B.A.	PO.	A.	E.	F.A.
1979–Atlanta .... Nat.	OF	66	93	12	26	8	0	3	21	.280	16	0	3	.842
1980–Atlanta z........... Nat.	OF	41	36	6	10	1	0	0	2	.278	4	0	0	1.000
American League Totals.................		563	1910	222	466	63	12	62	233	.244	904	52	28	.972
National League Totals		107	129	18	36	9	0	3	23	.279	20	0	3	.870
Major League Totals.......................		670	2039	240	502	72	12	65	256	.246	924	52	31	.969

Selected by New York Yankees' organization in 1st round (11th player selected) of free-agent draft, June 5, 1969.

†Traded with Outfielder Rosendo Torres, Catcher-First Baseman John Ellis, and Infielder Jerry Kenney to Cleveland Indians for Catcher Jerry Moses and Third Baseman Graig Nettles, November 27, 1972.

‡On disabled list, April 27 to May 9, 1977.

§Traded to Detroit Tigers for Shortstop Tom Veryzer, December 9, 1977.

xOn disabled list, May 19 to June 5 and June 21 to September 1, 1978.

yReleased, September 25, 1978; signed by Atlanta Braves, April 5, 1979.

zGranted free agency, November 13, 1980.

DANIEL RAY SPILLNER
(Dan)

Born November 27, 1951, at Casper, Wyo.
Height, 6.01. Weight, 190.
Throws and bats righthanded.
Hobby–Hunting.
Attended Green River Community College, Auburn, Wash.

Year Club League	G.	IP.	W.	L.	Pct.	H.	R.	ER.	SO.	BB.	ERA.
1970–Tri-City .... Northwest	7	29	1	1	.500	37	21	18	21	15	5.59
1971–Lodi..................................... California	25	148	10	5	.667	177	102	87	96	55	5.29
1972–Alexandria .... Texas	27	180	16	7	.696	156	75	68	126	•85	3.41
1973–Hawaii................................. P. Coast	32	188	10	11	.476	188	105	86	124	85	4.12
1974–Hawaii................................. P. Coast	7	54	4	2	.667	49	24	22	47	18	3.67
1974–San Diego .... National	30	148	9	11	.450	153	78	66	95	70	4.01
1975–San Diego .... National	37	167	5	13	.278	194	93	79	104	63	4.26
1976–San Diego† .... National	32	107	2	11	.154	120	70	60	57	55	5.05
1977–Hawaii .... P. Coast	3	16	1	1	.500	21	6	6	8	4	3.38
1977–San Diego .... National	76	123	7	6	.538	130	61	51	74	60	3.73
1978–San Diego‡ .... National	17	26	1	0	1.000	32	15	13	16	7	4.50
1978–Cleveland............................ American	36	56	3	1	.750	54	26	23	48	21	3.70
1979–Cleveland............................ American	49	158	9	5	.643	153	82	81	97	64	4.61
1980–Cleveland§ .... American	34	194	16	11	.593	225	122	114	100	74	5.29
American League Totals	119	408	28	17	.622	432	230	218	245	159	4.81
National League Totals	192	571	24	41	.369	629	317	269	346	255	4.24
Major League Totals	311	979	52	58	.473	1061	547	487	591	414	4.48

Selected by San Diego Padres' organization in 2nd round of free-agent draft, June 4, 1970.

†On disabled list, August 3 through remainder of 1976 season.

‡Traded to Cleveland Indians for Pitcher Dennis Kinney, June 14, 1978.

§Granted free agency, October 24, 1980; re-signed by Indians, December 8, 1980.

WILLIAM HARRY SPILMAN
(Known by middle name).

Born July 18, 1954, at Albany, Ga.
Height, 6.01. Weight, 190.
Throws right and bats lefthanded.
Hobbies–Hunting, golf and basketball.
Son of Harry Spilman, former catcher in Los Angeles Dodgers' organization.

Named Eastern League Most Valuable Player in 1977.
Led Eastern League in total bases with 277 and intentional walks received with 19 in 1977.

Year Club League	Pos.	G.	AB.	R.	H.	2B.	3B.	HR.	RBI.	B.A.	PO.	A.	E.	F.A.
1974–Billings .... Pion.	1B-3B	54	178	29	55	12	2	2	30	.309	92	8	3	.971
1975–Tampa .... Fla. St.	1B	115	348	33	90	13	1	1	38	.259	946	56	•17	.983
1976–Tampa .... Fla. St.	1B	118	361	50	90	12	5	6	35	.249	986	70	16	.985
1977–Three Rivers ..... East.	1B	133	493	•94	•184	•39	3	16	78	•.373	1095	78	7	.994
1978–Indianapolis ...... A. A.	3B-1B	133	488	95	144	26	4	13	79	.295	262	184	23	.951
1978–Cincinnati .... Nat.	PH	4	4	1	1	0	0	0	0	.250	0	0	0	.000
1979–Indianapolis ...... A.A.	3B-1B	71	267	42	77	13	3	3	27	.288	154	92	8	.969
1979–Cincinnati .... Nat.	1B-3B	43	56	7	12	3	0	0	5	.214	64	11	0	1.000
1980–Cincinnati .... Nat.	1-O-3	65	101	14	27	4	0	4	19	.267	132	15	2	.987
Major League Totals.......................		112	161	22	40	7	0	4	24	.248	196	26	2	.991

Signed as free agent by Cincinnati Reds' organization, June 25, 1974.

CHAMPIONSHIP SERIES RECORD

Year Club League	Pos.	G.	AB.	R.	H.	2B.	3B.	HR.	RBI.	B.A.	PO.	A.	E.	F.A.
1979–Cincinnati .... Nat.	PH	2	2	0	0	0	0	0	0	.000	0	0	0	.000

PAUL WILLIAM SPLITTORFF JR.

Name pronounced split-orf.

Born October 8, 1946, at Evansville, Ind.
Height, 6.03. Weight, 210.
Throws and bats lefthanded.
Attended Morningside College, Sioux City, Ia.; received Bachelor of
Science degree in Business Administration.

Led New York-Pennsylvania League in wild pitches with 17 and complete games with 11 in 1968.
Tied for American Association lead in complete games with 11 in 1969.

Year Club	League	G.	IP.	W.	L.	Pct.	H.	R.	ER.	SO.	BB.	ERA.
1968–Corning	NYP	16	●120	8	5	.615	*127	56	46	●136	47	3.45
1969–Omaha...............................	Am. Assoc.	28	174	12	10	.545	201	101	88	101	63	4.55
1970–Omaha...............................	Am. assoc.	28	162	8	12	.400	192	87	69	91	55	3.83
1970–Kansas City	American	2	9	0	1	.000	16	9	7	10	5	7.00
1971–Omaha...............................	Am. Assoc.	8	61	5	2	.714	51	16	10	51	10	1.48
1971–KansasCity	American	22	144	8	9	.471	129	49	43	80	35	2.69
1972–Kansas City	American	35	216	12	12	.500	189	81	75	140	67	3.13
1973–Kansas City	American	38	262	20	11	.645	279	135	116	110	78	3.98
1974–Kansas City	American	36	226	13	19	.406	252	122	103	90	75	4.10
1975–Kansas City	American	35	159	9	10	.474	156	75	56	76	56	3.17
1976–Kansas City†	American	26	159	11	8	.579	169	79	70	59	59	3.96
1977–Kansas City	American	37	229	16	6	*.727	243	104	94	99	83	3.69
1978–Kansas City	American	39	262	19	13	.594	244	113	99	76	60	3.40
1979–Kansas City	American	36	240	15	17	.469	248	137	113	77	77	4.24
1980–Kansas City	American	34	204	14	11	.560	236	101	94	53	43	4.15
Major League Totals		340	2110	137	117	.539	2161	1005	870	870	638	3.71

Selected by Kansas City Royals' organization in 22nd round of free-agent draft, June 7, 1968.
†On disabled list, July 28 to September 4, 1976.

CHAMPIONSHIP SERIES RECORD

Year Club	League	G.	IP.	W.	L.	Pct.	H.	R.	ER.	SO.	BB.	ERA.
1976–Kansas City	American	2	9⅓	1	0	1.000	7	2	2	2	5	1.93
1977–Kansas City	American	2	15	1	0	1.000	14	4	4	4	3	2.40
1978–Kansas City	American	1	7⅓	0	0	.000	9	5	4	2	0	4.91
1980–Kansas City	American	1	5⅓	0	0	.000	5	1	1	3	2	1.69
Championship Series Totals		6	37	2	0	1.000	35	12	11	11	10	2.68

WORLD SERIES RECORD

Year Club	League	G.	IP.	W.	L.	Pct.	H.	R.	ER.	SO.	BB.	ERA.
1980–Kansas City	American	1	1⅔	0	0	.000	4	1	1	0	0	5.40

ROBERT JOHN SPROWL JR.
(Bobby)

Born April 14, 1956, at Sandusky, O.
Height, 6.02. Weight, 190.
Throws and bats lefthanded.
Attended University of Alabama, Tuscaloosa, Ala.

Year Club	League	G.	IP.	W.	L.	Pct.	H.	R.	ER.	SO.	BB.	ERA.
1977–Winter Haven......................	Florida St.	26	60	9	4	.692	38	18	14	64	33	2.10
1978–Bristol	Eastern	20	103	9	3	.750	67	38	31	102	33	2.71
1978–Pawtucket	Int'national	15	78	7	4	.636	72	38	36	69	38	4.15
1978–Boston	American	3	13	0	2	.000	12	10	9	10	10	6.23
1979–Winter Haven......................	Florida St.	13	76	3	6	.333	81	36	31	88	31	3.67
1979–Pawtucket†-Charleston.........	Int'national	17	112	5	9	.357	95	48	40	70	38	3.21
1979–Houston	National	3	4	0	0	.000	1	0	0	3	2	0.00
1980–Tucson	P. Coast	26	180	10	11	.476	211	102	87	89	79	4.35
1980–Houston	National	1	1	0	0	.000	1	0	0	3	1	0.00
American League Totals		3	13	0	2	.000	12	10	9	10	10	6.23
National League totals		4	5	0	0	.000	2	0	0	6	3	0.00
Major League Totals		7	18	0	2	.000	14	10	9	16	13	4.50

Selected by Boston Red Sox' organization in 2nd round of free-agent draft, June 7, 1977.
†Traded to Houston Astros, June 19, 1979, completing deal in which Boston acquired First Baseman Bob Watson, June 13, 1979.

MICHAEL LYNN SQUIRES
(Mike)

Born March 5, 1952, at Kalamazoo, Mich.
Height, 5.11. Weight, 185.
Throws and bats lefthanded.
Hobbies–Basketball officiating and refinishing old furniture.
Attended Kalamazoo Valley Community College, Kalamazoo, Mich.
and Western Michigan University, Kalamazoo, Mich.

Led American Association first basemen in fielding average with .995 in 1978.
Named Most Valuable Player in Southern League, 1975.

Year Club League	Pos.	G.	AB.	R.	H.	2B.	3B.	HR.	RBI.	B.A.	PO.	A.	E.	F.A.
1973–Appleton ....Midw.	1-O-P	68	228	42	68	7	3	3	37	.298	479	44	4	.992
1974–Knoxville ....South.	1B	136	481	74	138	23	5	6	69	.287	∗1173	∗80	5	∗.996
1975–Knoxville ....South.	1B	129	448	68	136	23	5	3	50	.304	1085	78	6	∗.995
1975–Chicago.............Amer.	1B	20	65	5	15	0	0	0	4	.231	155	12	2	.988
1976–Iowa ....A. A.	∗1B-P	124	336	37	85	18	1	2	40	.253	823	47	4	∗.995
1977–Iowa ....A. A.	1B-OF-P	126	415	67	134	29	4	1	45	.323	897	65	7	.993
1977–Chicago.............Amer.	1B	3	3	0	0	0	0	0	0	.000	8	1	0	1.000
1978–Iowa ....A. A.	1B-OF	115	449	70	140	24	3	5	48	.312	922	71	6	.994
1978–Chicago ....Amer.	1B	46	150	25	42	9	2	0	19	.280	361	20	1	.997
1979–Chicago ....Amer.	1B-OF	122	295	44	78	10	1	2	22	.264	744	60	4	.995
1980–Chicago ....Amer.	1B-C	131	343	38	97	11	3	2	33	.283	905	68	5	.995
Major League Totals		322	856	112	232	30	6	4	78	.271	2173	161	12	.995

Selected by Chicago White Sox' organization in 18th round of free-agent draft, June 5, 1973.

PITCHING RECORD

Year Club	League	G.	IP.	W.	L.	Pct.	H.	R.	ER.	SO.	BB.	ERA.
1973–Appleton ....Midwest	1	⅓	0	0	.000	0	0	0	1	1	0.00
1976–Iowa ....Am. Assoc.	1	2	0	0	.000	5	4	4	1	1	18.00
1977–Iowa ....Am. Assoc.	1	1	0	0	.000	1	0	0	1	0	0.00

GEORGE CHARLES STABLEIN

Born October 29, 1957, at Inglewood, Calif.
Height, 6.04. Weight, 185.
Throws and bats righthanded.
Attended California State University at Dominguez Hills, Carson, Calif.

Tied for Texas League lead in games started with 27 in 1979.

Year Club	League	G.	IP.	W.	L.	Pct.	H.	R.	ER.	SO.	BB.	ERA.
1978–Reno ....California	14	91	8	4	.667	104	54	45	42	47	4.45
1979–Amarillo ....Texas	27	168	8	∗15	.348	∗235	132	∗116	88	57	6.21
1980–Hawaii† ....P. Coast	23	153	12	7	.632	152	75	66	81	46	3.88
1980–San Diego ....National	4	12	0	1	.000	16	4	4	4	3	3.00
Major League Totals.................................	4	12	0	1	.000	16	4	4	4	3	3.00

Selected by San Diego Padres' organization in 3rd round of free-agent draft, June 6, 1978.

DONALD JOSEPH STANHOUSE
(Don)

Born February 12, 1951, at Du Quoin, Ill.
Height, 6.02. Weight, 198.
Throws and bats righthanded.
Hobby—Golf.
Attended Mesa Community College, Mesa, Ariz.

Major League saves: 1972 (0), 1973 (1), 1974 (0), 1975 (0), 1976 (1), 1977 (10), 1978 (24), 1979 (21), 1980 (7). Total—64.

Tied for Northwest League lead in shutouts with 2 in 1969.

Year Club	League	G.	IP.	W.	L.	Pct.	H.	R.	ER.	SO.	BB.	ERA.
1969–Tri-City ....Northwest	12	61	5	1	.833	50	25	21	∗88	31	3.10
1970–Birmingham ....Southern	16	84	7	5	.583	57	27	21	80	42	2.25
1971–Iowa† ....Am. Assoc.	22	154	7	4	.636	143	71	64	104	85	3.73
1972–Denver‡ ....Am. Assoc.	5	35	2	2	.500	28	17	15	32	27	3.86
1972–Texas ....American	24	105	2	9	.182	83	48	44	78	73	3.77
1973–Spokane...............................P. Coast	12	66	3	5	.375	80	56	54	55	42	7.36
1973–Texas ....American	21	70	1	7	.125	70	41	37	42	44	4.76
1974–Spokane...............................P. Coast	12	48	4	5	.444	38	16	13	40	27	2.44
1974–Texas§ ....American	18	31	1	1	.500	38	20	17	26	17	4.94
1975–Memphis x..........................Int'national	13	80	6	5	.545	67	27	17	47	30	1.91
1975–Montreal..............................National	4	13	0	0	.000	19	12	12	5	11	8.31
1976–Montreal..............................National	34	184	9	12	.429	182	84	77	79	92	3.77
1977–Montreal y ....National	47	158	10	10	.500	147	72	60	89	84	3.42
1978–Baltimore ....American	56	75	6	9	.400	60	28	24	42	52	2.88
1979–Baltimore z.........................American	52	73	7	3	.700	49	24	23	34	51	2.84
1980–Los Angeles a ....National	21	25	2	2	.500	30	14	14	5	16	5.04
American League Totals	171	354	17	29	.370	300	161	145	222	237	3.69
National League Totals	106	380	21	24	.467	378	182	163	178	203	3.86
Major League Totals.................................	277	734	38	53	.418	678	343	308	400	440	3.78

Selected by Oakland A's organization in 1st round (ninth player selected) of free-agent draft, June 5, 1969.
†Traded by Oakland A's with Pitcher Jim Panther to Texas Rangers for Pitcher Denny McLain, March 4, 1972.
‡On disabled list, April 30 to May 31, 1972.
§Traded with Infielder Pete Mackanin to Montreal Expos for Outfielder Willie Davis, December 5, 1974.
xOn disabled list, July 24 to August 3, 1975.
yTraded with Pitcher Joe Kerrigan and Outfielder Gary Roenicke to Baltimore Orioles for Pitchers Rudy May, Bryn Smith and Randy Miller, December 7, 1977.
zGranted free agency, November 1, 1979; signed by Los Angeles Dodgers, November 17, 1979.
aOn disabled list, April 23 to July 24, 1980.

RECORD AS INFIELDER

Year	Club	League	Pos.	G.	AB.	R.	H.	2B.	3B.	HR.	RBI.	B.A.	PO.	A.	E.	F.A.
1969–Tri-City		Northw.	3-P-S	53	165	19	44	10	0	2	36	.269	47	70	17	.873

CHAMPIONSHIP SERIES RECORD

Year	Club	League	G.	IP.	W.	L.	Pct.	H.	R.	ER.	SO.	BB.	ERA.
1979–Baltimore		American	3	3	1	1	.500	5	3	2	0	3	6.00

WORLD SERIES RECORD

Year	Club	League	G.	IP.	W.	L.	Pct.	H.	R.	ER.	SO.	BB.	ERA.
1979–Baltimore		American	3	2	0	1	.000	6	3	3	0	3	13.50

ALL-STAR GAME RECORD

Member of American League All-Star team for 1979 game; did not play.

FREDERICK BLAIR STANLEY
(Fred)

Born August 13, 1947, at Farnhamville, Ia.
Height, 5.11. Weight, 167.
Throws and bats righthanded.
Hobbies—Hunting and fishing.
Attended Rio Hondo Junior College, Whittier, Calif.
Tied major league record for most double plays started by shortstop, game (5), April 29, 1975.

Year	Club	League	Pos.	G.	AB.	R.	H.	2B.	3B.	HR.	RBI.	B.A.	PO.	A.	E.	F.A.
1966–Salisbury		W. Car.	SS	52	174	24	42	3	1	0	8	.241	92	131	24	.903
1966–Bism.-Mandan		North.	SS	12	46	5	12	0	0	0	0	.261	12	28	6	.870
1967–Covington		Appal.					(In Military Service)									
1968–Dallas-Ft. W.		Tex.	*SS-2B	106	337	26	66	8	4	1	26	.196	165	336	27	*.949
1969–Savannah		South.	SS	80	257	28	70	7	1	1	22	.272	129	194	28	.920
1969–Okla. City†		A. A.	2B-SS	24	81	14	25	2	1	0	8	.309	55	71	4	.969
1969–Seattle		Amer.	SS-2B	17	43	2	12	2	1	0	4	.279	22	29	2	.962
1970–Portland		P. C.	S-2-O	88	291	26	78	8	4	0	33	.268	148	223	13	.966
1970–Milwaukee‡		Amer.	2B	6	0	1	0	0	0	0	0	.000	1	1	0	1.000
1971–Wichita		A. A.	SS-2B	32	114	12	28	8	1	1	8	.246	56	101	10	.940
1971–Cleveland		Amer.	SS-2B	60	129	14	29	4	0	2	12	.225	61	145	6	.972
1972–Cleveland§		Amer.	SS-2	6	12	1	2	1	0	0	0	.167	5	7	1	.923
1972–San Diego x		Nat.	2-S-3	39	85	15	17	2	0	0	2	.200	63	68	2	.985
1973–Syracuse		Int.	SS-C	111	322	57	80	15	1	2	30	.248	190	344	23	.959
1973–New York		Amer.	SS-2B	26	66	6	14	0	1	1	5	.212	42	72	2	.983
1974–Syracuse y		Int.	SS	72	225	21	58	11	0	1	21	.258	101	196	9	.971
1974–New York		Amer.	SS-2B	33	38	2	7	0	0	0	3	.184	32	59	1	.989
1975–New York		Amer.	S-2-3	117	252	34	56	5	1	0	15	.222	161	249	9	.979
1976–New York		Amer.	SS-2B	110	260	32	62	2	2	1	20	.238	148	251	7	.983
1977–New York		Amer.	SS-2B	48	46	6	12	0	0	1	7	.261	36	48	3	.966
1978–New York		Amer.	SS-2B-3B	80	160	14	35	7	0	1	9	.219	88	152	9	.964
1979–New York		Amer.	S-3-2-1-O	57	100	9	20	1	0	2	14	.200	42	113	8	.951
1980–New York zab		Amer.	SS-2-3	49	86	13	18	3	0	0	5	.209	39	86	7	.947
American League Totals				609	1192	134	267	25	5	8	94	.224	678	1212	55	.972
National League Totals				39	85	15	17	2	0	0	2	.200	63	68	2	.985
Major League Totals				648	1277	149	284	27	5	8	96	.222	741	1280	57	.973

Selected by Houston Astros' organization in 8th round of free-agent draft, June, 1966.
†Recalled by Houston Astros and sold to Seattle Pilots, September 8, 1969.
‡Sold to Cleveland Indians' organization, March 26, 1971.
§Traded to San Diego Padres for Pitcher Mike Kilkenny, June 11, 1972.
xTraded to Syracuse (New York Yankees' organization) for Catcher George Pena, October 24, 1972.
yOn disabled list, April 23 to May 3, 1974.
zOn disabled list, June 18 to July 10, 1980.
aOn supplemental disabled list, August 21 to September 5, 1980.
bTraded with a player to be named later to Oakland A's for Pitcher Mike Morgan, November 3, 1980;
Second Baseman Brian Doyle traded to A's organization completing deal, November 17, 1980.

CHAMPIONSHIP SERIES RECORD

Year	Club	League	Pos.	G.	AB.	R.	H.	2B.	3B.	HR.	RBI.	B.A.	PO.	A.	E.	F.A.
1976–New York		Amer.	SS	5	15	1	5	2	0	0	0	.333	7	15	1	.957
1977–New York		Amer.	SS	2	0	0	0	0	0	0	0	.000	1	0	0	1.000
1978–New York		Amer.	2B	2	5	0	1	0	0	0	0	.200	3	3	0	1.000
Championship Series Totals				9	20	1	6	2	0	0	0	.300	11	18	1	.967

WORLD SERIES RECORD

Year	Club	League	Pos.	G.	AB.	R.	H.	2B.	3B.	HR.	RBI.	B.A.	PO.	A.	E.	F.A.
1976–New York		Amer.	SS	4	6	1	1	1	0	0	1	.167	4	7	1	.917
1977–New York		Amer.	SS	1	0	0	0	0	0	0	0	.000	1	0	0	1.000
1978–New York		Amer.	2B	3	5	0	1	1	0	0	0	.200	5	2	0	1.000
World Series Totals				8	11	1	2	2	0	0	1	.182	10	9	1	.950

ROBERT WILLIAM STANLEY
(Bob)

Born November 10, 1954, at Portland, Me.
Height, 6.04. Weight, 205.
Throws and bats righthanded.

Led New York-Pennsylvania League pitchers in games started with 15 in 1974.
Tied for Florida State League lead in games started with 26 in 1975.
Tied for Eastern League lead in games started with 27 in 1976.

Year Club	League	G.	IP.	W.	L.	Pct.	H.	R.	ER.	SO.	BB.	ERA.
1974—Elmira	NYP	15	86	6	6	.500	94	57	44	45	40	4.60
1975—Winter Haven	Florida St.	27	169	5	*17	.227	136	76	55	73	74	2.93
1976—Bristol†	Eastern	27	186	15	9	.625	176	76	55	78	83	2.66
1977—Boston	American	41	151	8	7	.533	176	74	67	44	43	3.99
1978—Boston	American	52	142	15	2	.882	142	50	41	38	34	2.60
1979—Boston	American	40	217	16	12	.571	250	110	96	56	44	3.98
1980—Boston	American	52	175	10	8	.556	186	75	66	71	52	3.39
Major League Totals		185	685	49	29	.628	754	309	270	209	173	3.55

Selected by Los Angeles Dodgers' organization in 9th round of free-agent draft, June 5, 1973.
Selected by Boston Red Sox' organization in secondary phase of free-agent draft, January 9, 1974.
†On disabled list, June 19 to June 24, 1976.

ALL-STAR GAME RECORD

Year League	IP.	W.	L.	Pct.	H.	R.	ER.	SO.	BB.	ERA.
1979—American	2	0	0	.000	1	1	1	0	0	4.50

MICHAEL THOMAS STANTON
(Mike)

Born September 25, 1952, at St. Louis, Mo.
Height, 6.02. Weight, 200.
Throws and bats righthanded.
Attended Miami-Dade Community College (South), Miami, Fla.

Tied for Southern League lead in games started with 27 in 1974.

Year Club	League	G.	IP.	W.	L.	Pct.	H.	R.	ER.	SO.	BB.	ERA.
1973—Covington	Appal.	7	51	2	3	.400	34	26	11	70	21	1.94
1973—Cedar Rapids	Midwest	7	53	3	2	.600	40	16	8	59	18	1.36
1974—Columbus	Southern	27	179	11	*15	.423	158	85	61	*146	*121	3.07
1975—Iowa	Am. Assoc.	18	107	5	11	.313	95	56	49	105	66	4.12
1975—Houston	National	7	17	0	2	.000	20	14	14	16	20	7.41
1975—Columbus	Southern	10	39	2	3	.400	31	13	10	41	19	2.31
1976—Memphis	Int'national	21	128	6	11	.353	135	88	69	101	67	4.85
1977—Charleston†‡	Int'national	20	116	8	7	.533	115	53	44	81	47	3.41
1978—Syracuse§	Int'national	31	143	6	12	.333	155	*110	87	116	105	5.48
1979—Maracaibo x	Inter-Amer.	5	30	3	2	.600	24	15	9	7	7	2.70
1979—Tacoma	P. Coast	8	45	3	3	.500	43	17	12	34	23	2.40
1980—Cleveland	American	51	86	1	3	.250	98	57	51	74	44	5.34
National League Totals		7	17	0	2	.000	20	14	14	16	20	7.41
American League Totals		51	86	1	3	.250	98	57	51	74	44	5.34
Major League Totals		58	103	1	5	.167	118	71	65	90	64	5.68

Selected by Atlanta Braves' organization in 9th round of free-agent draft, June 8, 1971.
Selected by Kansas City Royals' organization in secondary phase of free-agent draft, January 12, 1972.
Selected by Texas Rangers' organization in secondary phase of free-agent draft, June 6, 1972.
Selected by Houston Astros' organization in secondary phase of free-agent draft, January 10, 1973.
†On disabled list, June 19 to July 4, 1977.
‡Sold to Toronto Blue Jays' organization, March 29, 1978.
§Sold to Maracaibo of Inter-American League, April 7, 1979.
xSigned as free agent by Cleveland Indians' organization after Inter-American League folded, July 18, 1979.

DAVID LESLIE STAPLETON
(Dave)

Born January 16, 1954, at Fairhope, Ala.
Height, 6.01. Weight, 170.
Throws and bats righthanded.
Attended University of South Alabama, Mobile, Ala.;
received Bachelor of Science degree in Education.

Led International League in total bases with 249 in 1979.
Shared International League Most Valuable Player award, 1979.

Year Club	League	Pos.	G.	AB.	R.	H.	2B.	3B.	HR.	RBI.	B.A.	PO.	A.	E.	F.A.
1975—Winter Haven	Fla. St.	2B-SS-O	56	199	23	48	8	1	1	14	.241	106	143	14	.947
1976—Winter Haven	Fla. St.	3-2-1-S-O	118	400	67	115	13	2	4	38	.288	164	248	17	.960
1977—Bristol	East.	2B-3B	86	304	52	93	21	4	8	28	.306	147	174	14	.958
1977—Pawtucket	Int.	3B-1B-2B	25	74	9	18	5	0	1	9	.243	34	29	2	.969
1978—Pawtucket†	Int.	3-2-1-S	113	432	69	112	26	3	11	49	.259	155	224	21	.948
1979—Pawtucket	Int.	1-3-2-O-S	140	*553	*88	*169	*33	1	15	64	.306	651	231	9	.990

Year	Club	League	Pos.	G.	AB.	R.	H.	2B.	3B.	HR.	RBI.	B.A.	PO.	A.	E.	F.A.
1980—Pawtucket		Int.	1-2-3-O	37	150	25	51	3	1	3	19	.340	239	53	8	.973
1980—Boston		Amer.	2-1-O-3	106	449	61	144	33	5	7	45	.321	269	338	12	.981
Major League Totals				106	449	61	144	33	5	7	45	.321	269	338	12	.981

Selected by Boston Red Sox' organization in 10th round of free-agent draft, June 4, 1975.
†On disabled list, April 10 to May 5, 1978.

WILVER DORNEL STARGELL
(Willie)

Born March 6, 1941, at Earlsboro, Okla.
Height, 6.03. Weight, 225.
Throws and bats lefthanded.
Hobbies—Bowling and dancing.
Attended Santa Rosa Junior College, Santa Rosa, Calif.

Established major league records for most strikeouts, lifetime (1,903); most consecutive seasons 10 or more intentional bases on balls (10).

Tied major league records for most seasons, 100 or more strikeouts (13); most long hits, game (5), August 1, 1970; most times, three or more home runs in a game, season (2), April 10 and April 21, 1971; most home runs, April (11), 1971; most home runs, opening game of season (2), April 10, 1975.

Established National League records for most consecutive seasons, 100 or more strikeouts (13); most games, 4 or more long hits, lifetime (4), 1973; most home runs through June 30 (28), 1971; most strikeouts by lefthanded batter, season (154), 1971.

Tied National League records for most strikeouts, two consecutive games (7), September 24-25, 1964; most home runs through July 31 (36), 1971.

Hit three home runs in a game, June 24, 1965, May 22, 1968, April 10 and April 21, 1971.
Hit home runs in all 12 National League parks, 1970 (13 including both Pittsburgh parks).
Led National League in slugging percentage with .646 in 1973.
Led National League batters in strikeouts with 154 in 1971.
Named as outfielder on THE SPORTING NEWS National League All-Star Team, 1965, 1966 and 1971.
Named first baseman on THE SPORTING NEWS National League All-Star Team, 1972.
Named National League Comeback Player of the Year by THE SPORTING NEWS, 1978.
Named Man of Year by THE SPORTING NEWS, 1979.
Named Major League Player of the Year by THE SPORTING NEWS, 1979.
Named National League co-Most Valuable Player by Baseball Writer's Association of America, 1979.

Year	Club	League	Pos.	G.	AB.	R.	H.	2B.	3B.	HR.	RBI.	B.A.	PO.	A.	E.	F.A.
1959—S. A'gelo-R'well		Soph.	1B	118	431	66	118	28	6	7	87	.274	842	22	*37	.959
1960—Grand Forks		North.	OF	107	396	63	103	19	1	11	61	.260	224	12	13	.948
1961—Asheville		Sally	OF	130	453	78	131	21	8	22	89	.289	264	14	*19	.936
1962—Columbus		Int.	OF-1B	138	497	97	137	21	8	27	82	.276	354	18	13	.966
1962—Pittsburgh		Nat.	OF	10	31	1	9	3	1	0	4	.290	12	1	1	.929
1963—Pittsburgh		Nat.	OF-1B	108	304	34	74	11	6	11	47	.243	226	12	9	.964
1964—Pittsburgh		Nat.	OF-1B	117	421	53	115	19	7	21	78	.273	565	24	10	.983
1965—Pittsburgh		Nat.	OF-1B	144	533	68	145	25	8	27	107	.272	268	14	8	.972
1966—Pittsburgh		Nat.	OF-1B	140	485	84	153	30	0	33	102	.315	300	13	11	.966
1967—Pittsburgh		Nat.	OF-1B	134	462	54	125	18	6	20	73	.271	447	27	11	.977
1968—Pittsburgh		Nat.	OF-1B	128	435	57	103	15	1	24	67	.237	254	19	9	.968
1969—Pittsburgh		Nat.	OF-1B	145	522	89	160	31	6	29	92	.307	314	14	7	.980
1970—Pittsburgh		Nat.	*OF-1B	136	474	70	125	18	3	31	85	.264	184	*17	5	.976
1971—Pittsburgh		Nat.	OF	141	511	104	151	26	0	*48	125	.295	237	8	4	.984
1972—Pittsburgh		Nat.	*1B-OF	138	495	75	145	28	2	33	112	.293	931	41	*17	.983
1973—Pittsburgh		Nat.	OF	148	522	106	156	*43	3	*44	*119	.299	261	14	7	.975
1974—Pittsburgh		Nat.	OF-1B	140	508	90	153	37	4	25	96	.301	256	8	9	.967
1975—Pittsburgh		Nat.	1B	124	461	71	136	32	2	22	90	.295	1121	54	10	.992
1976—Pittsburgh		Nat.	1B	117	428	54	110	20	3	20	65	.257	1037	53	13	.988
1977—Pittsburgh†		Nat.	1B	63	186	29	51	12	0	13	35	.274	449	27	7	.986
1978—Pittsburgh		Nat.	1B	122	390	60	115	18	2	28	97	.295	875	57	6	.994
1979—Pittsburgh		Nat.	1B	126	424	60	119	19	0	32	82	.281	949	47	3	*.997
1980—Pittsburgh‡		Nat.	1B	67	202	28	53	10	1	11	38	.262	460	33	4	.992
Major League Totals				2248	7794	1187	2198	415	55	472	1514	.282	9165	483	151	.985

Signed as free agent by Pittsburgh Pirates' organization, August 7, 1958.
†On supplemental disabled list, April 11 to April 26, and August 4 to October 18, 1977.
‡On supplemental disabled list, July 7 to July 29 and August 18 to October 8, 1980.

CHAMPIONSHIP SERIES RECORD

Established Championship Series record for highest slugging percentage, three-game Series (1.182), 1979.
Tied Championship Series records for most series played, one club (6); most games, total Series, one club (22); most strikeouts, four-game Series (6), 1971.
Tied National League Championship Series record for most series played, all games (6).

Year	Club	League	Pos.	G.	AB.	R.	H.	2B.	3B.	HR.	RBI.	B.A.	PO.	A.	E.	F.A.
1970—Pittsburgh		Nat.	OF	3	12	0	6	1	0	0	1	.500	4	0	0	1.000
1971—Pittsburgh		Nat.	OF	4	14	1	0	0	0	0	0	.000	6	0	0	1.000
1972—Pittsburgh		Nat.	1B-OF	5	16	1	1	1	0	0	1	.063	32	3	0	1.000
1974—Pittsburgh		Nat.	OF	4	15	3	6	0	0	2	4	.400	13	0	0	1.000
1975—Pittsburgh		Nat.	1B	3	11	1	2	1	0	0	0	.182	15	0	0	1.000
1979—Pittsburgh		Nat.	1B	3	11	2	5	2	0	2	6	.455	32	2	0	1.000
Championship Series Totals				22	79	8	20	5	0	4	12	.253	102	5	0	1.000

Established World Series records for most total bases, seven-game Series (25), 1979; most long hits, seven-game Series (7), 1979.

Tied World Series record for most hits, game (4), October 17, 1979.

Year Club	League	Pos.	G.	AB.	R.	H.	2B.	3B.	HR.	RBI.	B.A.	PO.	A.	E.	F.A.
1971—Pittsburgh	Nat.	OF	7	24	3	5	1	0	0	1	.208	11	1	0	1.000
1979—Pittsburgh	Nat.	1B	7	30	7	12	4	0	3	7	.400	59	2	2	.968
World Series Totals			14	54	10	17	5	0	3	8	.315	70	3	2	.973

ALL-STAR GAME RECORD

Year League	Pos.	AB.	R.	H.	2B.	3B.	HR.	RBI.	B.A.	PO.	A.	E.	F.A.
1964—National	PH	1	0	0	0	0	0	0	.000	0	0	0	.000
1965—National	OF	3	2	2	0	0	1	2	.667	1	0	0	1.000
1966—National	PH	1	0	0	0	0	0	0	.000	0	0	0	.000
1971—National	OF	2	1	0	0	0	0	0	.000	2	0	0	1.000
1972—National	OF	1	0	0	0	0	0	0	.000	0	0	0	.000
1973—National	PH-OF	1	0	0	0	0	0	0	.000	1	0	0	1.000
1978—National	PH	1	0	0	0	0	0	0	.000	0	0	0	1.000
All-Star Game Totals		10	3	2	0	0	1	2	.200	4	0	0	1.000

DANIEL JOSEPH STAUB
(Rusty)

(Named by nurses in hospital of birth for his hair.)

Born April 1, 1944, at New Orleans, La.
Height, 6.02. Weight, 215.
Throws right and bats lefthanded.
Hobbies—Golf, coin and stamp collecting.

Tied major league record for most seasons, consecutive, leading league, grounded into double plays (2).
Tied for National League lead in double plays by outfielders with 5 in 1971, with 5 in 1973 and with 5 in 1974.
Led Carolina League first basemen in double plays with 123 in 1962.
Named Rookie of the Year and Player of the Year in Carolina League, 1962.
Named designated hitter on THE SPORTING NEWS American League All-Star Team, 1978.
Received reported $100,000 bonus to sign with Houston Astros, 1961.

Year Club	League	Pos.	G.	AB.	R.	H.	2B.	3B.	HR.	RBI.	B.A.	PO.	A.	E.	F.A.
1962—Durham	Carol.	1B	•140	509	•115	149	20	4	23	93	.293	•1247	•76	•20	.985
1963—Houston	Nat.	1B-OF	150	513	43	115	17	4	6	45	.224	963	63	11	.989
1964—Houston	Nat.	1B-OF	89	292	26	63	10	2	8	35	.216	512	30	9	.984
1964—Oklahoma City	P.C.	OF-1B	71	226	55	71	13	1	20	45	.314	306	22	5	.985
1965—Houston	Nat.	OF-1B	131	410	43	105	20	1	14	63	.256	203	12	11	.951
1966—Houston	Nat.	OF-1B	153	554	60	155	28	3	13	81	.280	291	15	12	.962
1967—Houston	Nat.	OF	149	546	71	182	•44	1	10	74	.333	269	10	11	.962
1968—Houston†	Nat.	1B-OF	161	591	54	172	37	1	6	72	.291	1336	94	13	.991
1969—Montreal	Nat.	OF	158	549	89	166	26	5	29	79	.302	265	•16	10	.966
1970—Montreal	Nat.	OF	160	569	98	156	23	7	30	94	.274	308	14	5	.985
1971—Montreal‡	Nat.	OF	•162	599	94	186	34	6	19	97	.311	290	•20	•18	.945
1972—New York§	Nat.	OF	66	239	32	70	11	0	9	38	.293	108	4	2	.982
1973—New York	Nat.	OF	152	585	77	163	36	1	15	76	.279	297	17	7	.978
1974—New York	Nat.	OF	151	561	65	145	22	2	19	78	.258	262	•19	5	.983
1975—New York x	Nat.	OF	155	574	93	162	30	4	19	105	.282	267	•15	4	.986
1976—Detroit	Amer.	OF	161	589	73	176	28	3	15	96	.299	218	8	7	.970
1977—Detroit	Amer.	DH	158	623	84	173	34	3	22	101	.278	0	0	0	.000
1978—Detroit	Amer.	DH	162	642	75	175	30	1	24	121	.273	0	0	0	.000
1979—Detroit yz	Amer.	DH	68	246	32	58	12	1	9	40	.236	0	0	0	.000
1979—Montreal a	Nat.	1B-OF	38	86	9	23	3	0	3	14	.267	156	7	1	.994
1980—Texas bc	Amer.	1B-OF	109	340	42	102	23	2	9	55	.300	262	14	6	.979
American League Totals			658	2440	306	684	127	10	79	413	.280	480	22	13	.975
National League Totals			1875	6668	854	1863	341	37	200	951	.279	5527	336	119	.980
Major League Totals			2533	9108	1160	2547	468	47	279	1364	.280	6007	358	132	.980

Signed as free agent by Houston Astros' organization, September 11, 1961.
†Traded to Montreal Expos for First Baseman Donn Clendenon and Outfielder Jesus Alou, January 22, 1969. Clendenon refused to report to Houston; Pitchers John Billingham and Drannon (Skip) Guinn and cash sent to Houston to complete deal, April 8, 1969.
‡Traded to New York Mets for Outfielder Ken Singleton, First Baseman Mike Jorgensen and Infielder Tim Foli, April 6, 1972.
§On disabled list, July 21 to September 1, 1972.
xTraded with Pitcher Bill Laxton to Detroit Tigers for Pitcher Mickey Lolich and Outfielder Billy Baldwin, December 12, 1975.
yOn disqualified list, April 5 to May 1, 1979.
zSold to Montreal Expos, July 20, 1979.
aTraded to Texas Rangers for Second Baseman LaRue Washington and Third Baseman Chris Smith, March 31, 1980.
bOn supplemental disabled list, May 1 to June 5, 1980.
cGranted free agency, October 23, 1980; signed by New York Mets, December 16, 1980.

CHAMPIONSHIP SERIES RECORD

Established Championship Series records for most home runs, five-game Series (3), 1973; most home runs, two consecutive innings (2), October 8, 1973 (first and second innings).

Established National League Championship Series records for highest slugging average, five-game Series (.800), 1973; most runs batted in, five-game Series (5), 1973.

Year Club	League	Pos.	G.	AB.	R.	H.	2B.	3B.	HR.	RBI.	B.A.	PO.	A.	E.	F.A.
1973—New York..........Nat.		OF	4	15	4	3	0	0	3	5	.200	10	0	0	1.000

WORLD SERIES RECORD

Tied World Series records for most times reached first base safely, game (batting 1.000) (5), October 4, 1973; most hits game (4), October 4, 1973.

Year Club	League	Pos.	G.	AB.	R.	H.	2B.	3B.	HR.	RBI.	B.A.	PO.	A.	E.	F.A.
1973—New York..........Nat.		OF-PH	7	26	1	11	2	0	1	6	.423	5	0	0	1.000

ALL-STAR GAME RECORD

Year League	Pos.	AB.	R.	H.	2B.	3B.	HR.	RBI.	B.A.	PO.	A.	E.	F.A.
1967—National.............................	PH	1	0	1	0	0	0	0	1.000	0	0	0	.000
1968—National.............................	PH	1	0	0	0	0	0	0	.000	0	0	0	.000
1970—National.............................	PH	1	0	0	0	0	0	0	.000	0	0	0	.000
1976—American.............................	OF	2	0	2	0	0	0	0	1.000	1	0	0	1.000
All-Star Game Totals		5	0	3	0	0	0	0	.600	1	0	0	1.000

Member of National League All-Star Team for 1969 and 1971 games; did not play.

JOHN HARDIN STEARNS

Born August 21, 1951, at Denver, Colo.
Height, 6.00. Weight, 185.
Throws and bats righthanded.
Hobby—Listening to music.
Attended University of Colorado, Boulder, Colo.
Brother of Bill Stearns, catcher in New York Yankees' organization.

Established modern National League record for most stolen bases by catcher, season (25), 1978.
Tied for Carolina League lead in double plays by catchers with 9 in 1974.

Year Club	League	Pos.	G.	AB.	R.	H.	2B.	3B.	HR.	RBI.	B.A.	PO.	A.	E.	F.A.
1973—Reading ....East.		C-O-3-1	67	166	28	40	7	4	3	24	.241	232	33	4	.985
1974—Rocky Mount.....Carol.		C-O-1	62	230	41	79	16	4	4	38	.343	400	62	13	.973
1974—Toledo...............Int.		C-3B	77	278	34	74	9	2	3	28	.266	414	49	5	.989
1974—Philadelphia† ....Nat.		C	1	2	0	1	0	0	0	0	.500	1	0	0	1.000
1975—New York..........Nat.		C	59	169	25	32	5	1	3	10	.189	297	40	2	.994
1976—New York..........Nat.		C	32	103	13	27	6	0	2	10	.262	200	20	3	.987
1976—Tidewater ....Int.		C-3B	102	332	64	103	17	2	10	45	.310	416	100	14	.974
1977—New York..........Nat.		C-1B	139	431	52	108	25	1	12	55	.251	772	79	19	.978
1978—New York ....Nat.		C-3B	143	477	65	126	24	1	15	73	.264	711	84	12	.985
1979—New York..........Nat.		C-1-3-O	155	538	58	131	29	2	9	66	.243	754	107	16	.982
1980—New York‡........Nat.		C-1-3	91	319	42	91	25	1	0	45	.285	552	61	8	.987
Major League Totals			620	2039	255	516	114	6	41	259	.253	3287	391	60	.984

Selected by Oakland A's organization in 17th round of free-agent draft, June 5, 1969.
Selected by Philadelphia Phillies' organization in 1st round (second player selected) of free-agent draft, June 5, 1973.
†Traded with Outfielder Del Unser and Pitcher Mac Scarce to New York Mets for Pitcher Tug McGraw and Outfielders Don Hahn and Dave Schneck, December 3, 1974.
‡On supplemental disabled list, July 27, 1980; transferred to disabled list, August 20 to October 14, 1980.

ALL-STAR GAME RECORD

Year League	Pos.	AB.	R.	H.	2B.	3B.	HR.	RBI.	B.A.	PO.	A.	E.	F.A.
1977—National.............................	C	0	0	0	0	0	0	0	.000	2	0	0	1.000
1980—National.............................	C	1	0	0	0	0	0	0	.000	5	0	0	1.000
All-Star Game Totals		1	0	0	0	0	0	0	.000	7	0	0	1.000

Member of National League All-Star Team for 1979 game; did not play.

DAVID MICHAEL STEFFEN
(Dave)

Born December 17, 1958, at Dearborn, Mich.
Height, 6.03. Weight, 220.
Throws and bats righthanded.

Year Club	League	G.	IP.	W.	L.	Pct.	H.	R.	ER.	SO.	BB.	ERA.
1977—Bristol ....Ap'lachian		9	49	6	2	.750	38	21	19	29	20	3.49
1978—Lakeland†............................Florida St.		32	62	9	4	.692	35	14	6	35	28	0.87
1978—Montgomery ....Southern		11	18	0	0	.000	24	9	8	10	9	4.00
1979—Montgomery ....Southern		16	90	5	5	.500	100	59	51	83	45	5.10
1979—Evansville ....Am. Assoc.		19	44	2	4	.333	51	27	19	28	18	3.88
1980—Evansville‡............................Am. Assoc.		4	7	0	0	.000	11	13	13	3	9	16.71

Selected by Detroit Tigers' organization in 6th round of free-agent draft, June 7, 1977.
†On disabled list, April 11 to April 21, 1978.
‡On disabled list, April 11 to May 2, May 5 to July 2 and July 17 to August 30, 1980.

DAVID WILLIAM STEGMAN
(Dave)

Born January 30, 1954, at Inglewood, Calif.
Height, 5.11. Weight, 190.
Throws and bats righthanded.
Attended University of Arizona, Tucson, Ariz.; received Bachelor of
Science degree in Engineering and Math.

Year Club League	Pos.	G.	AB.	R.	H.	2B.	3B.	HR.	RBI.	B.A.	PO.	A.	E.	F.A.
1976—Montgomery......South.	OF	61	188	31	50	8	0	0	20	.266	105	2	3	.973
1977—Montgomery......South.	OF	67	226	55	78	19	5	11	59	.345	132	6	1	.993
1977—Evansville........A.A.	OF	50	153	25	34	12	0	6	18	.222	99	4	6	.945
1978—Evansville ........A.A.	★OF-C	●135	462	95	122	30	1	14	67	.264	299	8	3	★.990
1978—Detroit.............Amer.	OF	8	14	3	4	2	0	1	3	.286	11	0	0	1.000
1979—Evansville........A.A.	OF	133	506	95	153	33	2	11	60	.302	★322	12	5	.985
1979—Detroit.............Amer.	OF	12	31	6	6	0	0	3	5	.194	35	0	0	1.000
1980—Evansville ........A.A.	OF	18	59	11	12	2	1	1	6	.203	37	1	1	.974
1980—Detroit†...........Amer.	OF	65	130	12	23	5	0	2	9	.177	82	1	1	.988
Major League Totals		85	175	21	33	7	0	6	17	.189	128	1	1	.992

Selected by Minnesota Twins' organization in 10th round of free-agent draft, June 6, 1972.
Selected by Boston Red Sox' organization in 9th round of free-agent draft, June 4, 1975.
Selected by Atlanta Braves' organization in secondary phase of free-agent draft, January 7, 1976.
Selected by Detroit Tigers' organization in secondary phase of free-agent draft, June 8, 1976.
†Traded to San Diego Padres for Pitcher Dennis Kinney, December 12, 1980.

WILLIAM ALLEN STEIN
(Bill)

Born January 21, 1947, at Battle Creek, Mich.
Height, 5.10. Weight, 175.
Throws and bats righthanded.
Hobbies—Bowling, basketball and golf.
Attended Brevard Junior College, Cocoa, Fla., and Southern Illinois
University, Carbondale, Ill.

Led American Association in total bases with 274 in 1974.

Year Club League	Pos.	G.	AB.	R.	H.	2B.	3B.	HR.	RBI.	B.A.	PO.	A.	E.	F.A.
1969—Tulsa ....A. A.	2-3-S	62	183	24	54	11	5	1	20	.295	81	97	9	.952
1970—Arkansas...........Texas	2-O-S	114	429	56	124	21	2	8	52	.289	179	198	17	.957
1971—Tulsa†..............A. A.	O-3-2-P	103	389	50	106	22	4	8	67	.272	154	86	13	.949
1972—Tulsa ....A. A.	O-2-3-1	103	360	49	100	26	4	5	36	.278	146	52	5	.975
1972—St. Louis ....Nat.	3B-OF	14	35	2	11	0	1	2	3	.314	5	4	0	1.000
1973—St. Louis ....Nat.	OF-1-3	32	55	4	12	2	0	0	2	.218	37	1	0	1.000
1973—Tulsa‡§ ....A. A.	3B	21	81	12	23	2	1	0	8	.284	8	37	1	.978
1974—Iowa ....A. A.	3B-OF	●135	543	★107	★178	32	8	16	74	.328	89	204	13	.958
1974—Chicago...........Amer.	3B	13	43	5	12	1	0	0	5	.279	7	20	4	.871
1975—Chicago...........Amer.	2-3-O	76	226	23	61	7	1	3	21	.270	87	118	9	.958
1976—Chicago x.........Amer.	2-3-1-S-O	117	392	32	105	15	2	4	36	.268	161	243	19	.955
1977—Seattle ....Amer.	★3B-SS	151	556	53	144	26	5	13	67	.259	★146	255	15	.964
1978—Seattle ....Amer.	3B	114	403	41	105	24	4	4	37	.261	72	244	24	.929
1979—Seattle y ....Amer.	3B-2B-SS	88	250	28	62	9	2	7	27	.248	64	162	7	.970
1980—Seattle za..........Amer.	3B-2B-1B	67	198	16	53	5	1	5	27	.268	119	115	4	.983
American League Totals		626	2068	198	542	87	15	36	220	.262	656	1157	82	.957
National League Totals		46	90	6	23	2	1	2	5	.256	42	5	0	1.000
Major League Totals		672	2158	204	565	89	16	38	225	.262	698	1162	82	.958

Selected by Baltimore Orioles' organization in 33rd round of free-agent draft, June 7, 1968.
Selected by St. Louis Cardinals' organization in 27th round of free-agent draft, June 5, 1969.
†On temporary inactive list, July 1 through July 12, 1971.
‡Traded by Tulsa (St. Louis Cardinals' organization) to Salt Lake City (California Angels' organization) for Infielder Jerry DaVanon, September 25, 1973.
§Sold by California Angels to Chicago White Sox, April 3, 1974; White Sox sent Pitcher Steve Blateric to Angels, August 1, 1974, to complete deal.
xSelected by Seattle Mariners in American League expansion draft, November 5, 1976.
yOn supplemental disabled list, May 25 to June 15, 1979.
zOn supplemental disabled list, June 2, 1980; transferred to disabled list, June 12 to July 22, 1980.
aGranted free agency, October 22, 1980; signed by Texas Rangers, December 18, 1980.

PITCHING RECORD

Year Club	League	G.	IP.	W.	L.	Pct.	H.	R.	ER.	SO.	BB.	ERA.
1971—Tulsa....................Am. Assoc.		1	6	0	0	.000	8	3	3	6	0	4.50

WILLIAM RANDOLPH STEIN
(Randy)

Born March 7, 1953, at Pomona, Calif.
Height, 6.04. Weight, 210.
Throws and bats righthanded.

Year Club	League	G.	IP.	W.	L.	Pct.	H.	R.	ER.	SO.	BB.	ERA.
1971—Aberdeen ....Northern		6	40	2	3	.400	27	21	17	28	23	3.83
1972—Miami....................Florida St.		20	142	11	5	.688	111	43	28	110	60	1.77

Year Club	League	G.	IP.	W.	L.	Pct.	H.	R.	ER.	SO.	BB.	ERA.
1973—Asheville ....Southern		20	156	14	6	.700	133	66	49	73	54	2.83
1973—Rochester ....Int'national		6	36	1	2	.333	36	19	14	19	15	3.50
1974—Rochester† ....Int'national		6	34	3	1	.750	39	19	16	17	12	4.24
1975—Rochester‡..........................Int'national		21	110	8	2	.800	91	47	38	59	62	3.11
1976—Rochester§..........................Int'national		24	110	5	6	.455	120	71	67	51	58	5.48
1977—Miami..................................Florida St.		11	31	2	2	.500	21	15	12	30	15	3.48
1977—Syracuse x ....Int'national		45	73	7	2	.778	80	40	31	42	45	3.82
1978—Milwaukee ....American		31	73	3	2	.600	78	51	43	42	39	5.30
1979—Vancouver y-Spokane ....P. Coast		16	95	7	2	.778	79	35	23	59	33	2.18
1979—Seattle.................................American		23	41	2	3	.400	48	29	27	39	27	5.93
1980—Spokane z ....P. Coast		24	150	12	8	.600	170	79	65	87	51	3.90
Major League Totals...............................		54	114	5	5	.500	126	80	70	81	66	5.53

Selected by Baltimore Orioles' organization in 1st round (23rd player selected) of free-agent draft, June 8, 1971.

†On disabled list, June 7 to October 25, 1974.
‡On disabled list, May 20 to June 19, 1975.
§On disabled list, May 3 to May 23, 1976.
xGranted free agency, November 5, 1977; signed by Milwaukee Brewers, January 16, 1978.
yTraded to Seattle Mariners for Pitcher Paul Mitchell, June 7, 1979.
zOn disabled list, May 9 to May 21, 1980.

JEFFREY ALAN STEMBER
(Jeff)

Born March 2, 1958, at Elizabeth, N.J.
Height, 6.05. Weight, 220.
Throws and bats righthanded.
Hobby—Architectural drawing.

Year Club	League	G.	IP.	W.	L.	Pct.	H.	R.	ER.	SO.	BB.	ERA.
1977—Great Falls ....Pioneer		13	75	7	2	.778	62	43	31	55	54	3.72
1978—Cedar Rapids ....Midwest		27	132	5	•14	.263	118	100	•82	94	•97	5.59
1979—Cedar Rapids ....Midwest		9	56	3	3	.500	51	34	29	35	21	4.66
1979—Fresno.................................California		20	44	4	2	.667	43	38	25	41	29	5.11
1980—Shreveport..........................Texas		16	102	5	5	.500	78	39	30	61	47	2.65
1980—Phoenix...............................P. Coast		8	55	5	2	.714	48	22	21	29	29	3.44
1980—San Francisco ....National		1	3	0	0	.000	2	3	1	0	2	3.00
Major League Totals...............................		1	3	0	0	.000	2	3	1	0	2	3.00

Selected by San Francisco Giants' organization in 26th round of free-agent draft, June 8, 1976.

MICHAEL STEVEN STENHOUSE
(Mike)

Born May 29, 1960, at Pueblo, Colo.
Height, 6.01. Weight, 185.
Throws right and bats lefthanded.
Attended Harvard University, Cambridge, Mass.
Led Florida State League batters in walks with 123 in 1980.

Year Club	League	Pos.	G.	AB.	R.	H.	2B.	3B.	HR.	RBI.	B.A.	PO.	A.	E.	F.A.
1980—W. Palm Beach .Fla. St.		1B-OF	133	439	77	120	17	7	13	49	.273	912	56	12	.988
1980—Memphis...........South.		OF-1B	1	3	0	0	0	0	0	0	.000	2	0	0	1.000

Selected by Oakland A's organizaton in 1st round (26th player selected) of free-agent draft, June 5, 1979.
Selected by Montreal Expos' organization in secondary phase of free-agent draft, January 8, 1980.

RENALDO ANTONIO STENNETT
(Rennie)

Born April 5, 1951, at Colon, Panama.
Height, 5.11. Weight, 185.
Throws and bats righthanded.
Hobbies—Basketball, dancing, sports and movies.
Brother of Fernando Stennett, infielder in Pittsburgh Pirates' organization, 1973-76.

Established modern major league records for most hits, game (7), September 16, 1975; most consecutive hits, game (7), September 16, 1975; most hits, two consecutive games (10), September 16 and 17, 1975.
Tied major league record for most innings, two or more hits, game (2), September 16, 1975.
Tied modern major league records for most times reached first base safely, game, (7), September 16, 1975; most at bats, game (7), September 16, 1975.
Tied modern National League record for most hits, three consecutive games, (12), September 16 through September 18, 1975.
Major league stolen bases: 1971 (1), 1972 (4), 1973 (2), 1974 (8), 1975 (5), 1976 (18), 1977 (28), 1978 (2), 1979 (1), 1980 (4). Total—73.
Led National League second basemen in total chances with 950 in 1976.
Led Carolina League in total bases with 229 in 1970.
Led Western Carolinas League outfielders in double plays with 5 in 1969.

Year Club	League	Pos.	G.	AB.	R.	H.	2B.	3B.	HR.	RBI.	B.A.	PO.	A.	E.	F.A.
1969—Gastonia ....W. Car.		•O-3B	107	396	51	114	17	•7	3	49	.288	150	•14	8	.953
1970—Salem ....Carol.		OF	131	•540	65	•176	20	•9	5	50	•.326	201	13	10	.955
1970—Columbus..........Int.		2B	1	4	1	2	1	0	0	0	.500	5	1	1	.857

Year	Club	League	Pos.	G.	AB.	R.	H.	2B.	3B.	HR.	RBI.	B.A.	PO.	A.	E.	F.A.
1971—Charleston	Int.		2B	80	323	61	111	17	10	3	39	.344	172	224	17	.959
1971—Pittsburgh	Nat.		2B	50	153	24	54	5	4	1	15	.353	82	106	9	.954
1972—Pittsburgh	Nat.		2-O-S	109	370	43	106	14	5	3	30	.286	197	173	10	.974
1973—Pittsburgh	Nat.		2-S-O	128	466	45	113	18	3	10	55	.242	281	348	14	.978
1974—Pittsburgh	Nat.		*2B-OF	157	673	84	196	29	3	7	56	.291	*444	475	19	.980
1975—Pittsburgh	Nat.		2B	148	616	89	176	25	7	7	62	.286	379	463	18	.979
1976—Pittsburgh	Nat.		*2B-SS	157	654	59	168	31	9	2	60	.257	*432	506	19	.980
1977—Pittsburgh†	Nat.		2B	116	453	53	152	20	4	5	51	.336	269	315	11	.982
1978—Pittsburgh	Nat.		2B-3B	106	333	30	81	9	2	3	35	.243	167	215	13	.967
1979—Pittsburgh‡	Nat.		2B	108	319	31	76	13	2	0	24	.238	172	282	12	.974
1980—San Francisco	Nat.		2B	120	397	34	97	13	2	2	37	.244	244	293	15	.973
Major League Totals				1199	4434	492	1219	177	41	40	425	.275	2667	3176	140	.977

Signed as free agent by Pittsburgh Pirates' organization, February 12, 1969.
†On disabled list, August 20 through remainder of season.
‡Granted free agency, November 1, 1979; signed by San Francisco Giants, December 12, 1979.

CHAMPIONSHIP SERIES RECORD

Year	Club	League	Pos.	G.	AB.	R.	H.	2B.	3B.	HR.	RBI.	B.A.	PO.	A.	E.	F.A.
1972—Pittsburgh	Nat.		OF-2B	5	21	2	6	0	0	0	1	.286	17	1	0	1.000
1974—Pittsburgh	Nat.		2B	4	16	1	1	0	0	0	0	.063	10	10	1	.952
1975—Pittsburgh	Nat.		2B-SS	3	14	0	3	0	0	0	0	.214	3	8	0	1.000
1979—Pittsburgh	Nat.		2B	1	0	0	0	0	0	0	0	.000	0	1	0	1.000
Championship Series Totals				13	51	3	10	0	0	0	1	.196	30	20	1	.980

WORLD SERIES RECORD

Year	Club	League	Pos.	G.	AB.	R.	H.	2B.	3B.	HR.	RBI.	B.A.	PO.	A.	E.	F.A.
1979—Pittsburgh	Nat.		PH	1	1	0	1	0	0	0	0	1.000	0	0	0	.000

DAVID KEITH STEWART
(Dave)

Born February 19, 1957, at Oakland, Calif.
Height, 6.02. Weight, 200.
Throws and bats righthanded.

Tied for Midwest League lead in complete games with 15 and in shutouts with 3 in 1977.
Tied for Texas League lead in games started with 28 in 1978.
Led Pacific Coast League in games started with 29 in 1980.

Year	Club	League	G.	IP.	W.	L.	Pct.	H.	R.	ER.	SO.	BB.	ERA.
1975—Bellingham	Northwest	22	49	0	5	.000	59	46	30	37	49	5.51
1976—Danville	Midwest	4	10	0	2	.000	17	20	18	10	16	16.20
1976—Bellingham	Northwest	24	50	1	1	.500	47	35	28	53	58	5.04
1977—Clinton	Midwest	24	176	*17	4	*.810	152	52	42	144	72	2.15
1977—Albuquerque	P. Coast	1	6	1	0	1.000	4	3	3	3	6	4.50
1978—San Antonio	Texas	28	193	14	12	.538	181	99	79	130	97	3.68
1978—Los Angeles	National	1	2	0	0	.000	1	0	0	1	0	0.00
1979—Albuquerque	P. Coast	28	170	11	12	.478	198	112	99	105	81	5.24
1980—Albuquerque	P. Coast	31	*202	●15	10	.600	189	94	83	125	89	3.70
Major League Totals		1	2	0	0	.000	1	0	0	1	0	0.00

Selected by Los Angeles Dodgers' organization in 16th round of free-agent draft, June 4, 1975.

SAMUEL LEE STEWART JR.
(Sammy)

Born October 28, 1954, at Asheville, N.C.
Height, 6.03. Weight, 208.
Throws and bats righthanded.
Hobbies—Music, hunting and fishing.
Attended Montreat-Anderson Junior College, Montreat, N.C.

Established major league record for most consecutive strikeouts, first major league game (7), September 1, 1978 (second game).
Pitched seven-inning, 1-0 no-hit victory against Winter Haven, July 20, 1976.

Year	Club	League	G.	IP.	W.	L.	Pct.	H.	R.	ER.	SO.	BB.	ERA.
1975—Bluefield	Ap'lachian	18	43	3	3	.500	62	44	29	26	6.07
1976—Miami	Florida St.	23	182	12	8	.600	147	65	49	79	*86	2.42
1977—Rochester	Int'national	10	54	0	5	.000	68	41	38	28	35	6.33
1977—Charlotte	Southern	16	117	9	6	.600	93	32	27	56	45	*2.08
1978—Rochester	Int'national	27	173	13	10	.565	168	90	73	111	93	3.80
1978—Baltimore	American	2	11	1	1	.500	10	5	4	11	3	3.27
1979—Baltimore	American	31	118	8	5	.615	96	47	46	71	71	3.51
1980—Baltimore	American	33	119	7	7	.500	103	51	47	78	60	3.55
Major League Totals		66	248	16	13	.552	209	103	97	160	134	3.52

Selected by Kansas City Royals' organization in 28th round of free-agent draft, June 5, 1974.
Signed as free agent by Baltimore Orioles' organization, June 15, 1975.

WORLD SERIES RECORD

Year	Club	League	G.	IP.	W.	L.	Pct.	H.	R.	ER.	SO.	BB.	ERA.
1979—Baltimore	American	1	2⅔	0	0	.000	4	0	0	0	1	0.00

DAVID ANDREW STIEB
(Dave)

Born July 22, 1957, at Santa Ana, Calif.
Height, 6.01. Weight, 185.
Throws and bats righthanded.
Attended Santa Ana College, Santa Ana, Calif., and
Southern Illinois University, Carbondale, Ill.
Brother of Steve Stieb, catcher in Atlanta Braves' organization.

Year Club	League	G.	IP.	W.	L.	Pct.	H.	R.	ER.	SO.	BB.	ERA.
1978—Dunedin	Florida St.	4	26	2	0	1.000	23	10	6	8	1	2.08
1979—Dunedin	Florida St.	8	51	5	0	1.000	54	30	24	38	28	4.24
1979—Syracuse	Int'national	7	51	5	2	.714	39	15	12	20	14	2.12
1979—Toronto	American	18	129	8	8	.500	139	70	62	52	48	4.33
1980—Toronto	American	34	243	12	15	.444	232	108	100	108	83	3.70
Major League Totals		52	372	20	23	.465	371	178	162	160	131	3.92

Selected by Toronto Blue Jays' organization in 5th round of free-agent draft, June 6, 1978.

RECORD AS OUTFIELDER

Year Club	League	Pos.	G.	AB.	R.	H.	2B.	3B.	HR.	RBI.	B.A.	PO.	A.	E.	F.A.
1978—Dunedin	Fla. St.	OF-P	35	99	10	19	3	0	1	9	.192	85	7	3	.968

ALL-STAR GAME RECORD

Tied All-Star Game record for most wild pitches, inning and game (2), July 8, 1980 (seventh inning).

Year League	IP.	W.	L.	Pct.	H.	R.	ER.	SO.	BB.	ERA.
1980—American	1	0	0	.000	1	1	0	0	2	0.00

CRAIG STEVEN STIMAC

Born November 18, 1954, at Oak Park, Ill.
Height, 6.02. Weight, 185.
Throws and bats righthanded.
Attended University of Denver, Denver, Colo.;
received Bachelor of Science degree in Business Management.

Year Club	League	Pos.	G.	AB.	R.	H.	2B.	3B.	HR.	RBI.	B.A.	PO.	A.	E.	F.A.
1976—Reno	Calif.	OF	22	65	8	20	2	3	2	16	.308	15	0	0	1.000
1976—Amarillo	Texas	C-O-1	31	86	13	25	6	0	3	14	.291	56	7	2	.969
1977—Amarillo	Texas	O-C-3-1	127	501	61	142	22	5	14	74	.283	250	78	17	.951
1978—Hawaii	P.C.	C-3-O-1	122	472	62	126	32	4	8	70	.267	211	79	11	.963
1979—Hawaii†	P.C.	1-O-3-P	102	381	54	104	20	6	8	58	.273	564	47	8	.987
1980—Hawaii	P.C.	3-C-O-1	110	423	60	126	22	5	11	47	.298	174	193	12	.968
1980—San Diego	Nat.	C-3B	20	50	5	11	2	0	0	7	.220	51	16	2	.971
Major League Totals			20	50	5	11	2	0	0	7	.220	51	16	2	.971

Selected by San Diego Padres' organization in 9th round of free-agent draft, June 8, 1976.
†On disabled list, June 12 to July 26, 1979.

RECORD AS PITCHER

Year Club	League	G.	IP.	W.	L.	Pct.	H.	R.	ER.	SO.	BB.	ERA.
1979—Hawaii	P. Coast	1	4	0	1	.000	8	4	3	1	2	6.75

GORRELL ROBERT STINSON III
(Bob)

Born October 11, 1945, at Elkin, N. C.
Height, 5.11. Weight, 180.
Throws right and bats lefthanded.
Hobbies—Hunting, fishing and horseback riding.
Attended Miami-Dade (North) Junior College, Miami, Fla.

Tied major league record for most times reached first base on catcher's interference, season (6), 1978.
Led Pioneer League outfielders in double plays with 4 in 1966.
Tied for Pacific Coast League in passed balls with 18 in 1969.

Year Club	League	Pos.	G.	AB.	R.	H.	2B.	3B.	HR.	RBI.	B.A.	PO.	A.	E.	F.A.
1966—Santa Barbara	Calif.	OF	5	12	0	3	0	0	0	1	.250	6	0	0	1.000
1966—Ogden	Pion.	OF	56	176	34	50	7	2	5	33	.284	71	*8	*11	.878
1967—Albuquerque	Tex.	O-C-P	120	387	47	92	15	3	6	42	.238	234	6	7	.972
1968—Albuquerque	Tex.	C-O-3	96	291	37	83	10	0	4	25	.285	500	64	9	.984
1969—Spokane	P. C.	C-OF	117	349	47	98	9	5	6	54	.281	477	51	8	.985
1969—Los Angeles	Nat.	C	4	8	1	3	0	0	0	2	.375	20	0	1	.952
1970—Spokane	P. C.	*C-O-3	101	315	56	94	19	4	6	53	.298	471	47	9	*.983
1970—Los Angeles†	Nat.	C	4	3	1	0	0	0	0	0	.000	3	0	0	1.000
1971—Tulsa	A. A.	C-O-3	87	299	54	97	21	3	7	46	.324	344	42	13	.967
1971—St. Louis‡	Nat.	C-OF	17	19	3	4	1	0	0	1	.211	36	0	1	.973
1972—Houston§	Nat.	C-OF	27	35	3	6	1	0	0	2	.171	26	2	1	.966
1973—Montreal	Nat.	C-3B	48	111	12	29	6	1	3	12	.261	174	9	4	.979
1974—Montreal x y	Nat.	C	38	87	4	15	2	0	1	6	.172	122	14	0	1.000
1975—Kansas City	Amer.	C-2-O-1	63	147	18	39	9	1	1	9	.265	257	33	2	.993
1976—Kansas City z	Amer.	C	79	209	26	55	7	1	2	25	.263	304	30	7	.979
1977—Seattle	Amer.	C	105	297	27	80	11	1	8	32	.269	494	43	9	.984
1978—Seattle a	Amer.	C	124	364	46	94	14	3	11	55	.258	472	60	7	.987

Year Club League	Pos.	G.	AB.	R.	H.	2B.	3B.	HR.	RBI.	B.A.	PO.	A.	E.	F.A.
1979—Seattle .... Amer.	C	95	247	19	60	8	0	6	28	.243	376	29	9	.978
1980—Seattle b .... Amer.	C	48	107	6	23	2	0	1	8	.215	135	8	3	.979
National League Totals....................		138	263	24	57	10	1	4	23	.217	381	25	7	.983
American League Totals.................		514	1371	142	351	51	6	29	157	.256	2038	203	37	.984
Major League Totals		652	1634	166	408	61	7	33	180	.250	2419	228	44	.984

Selected by Los Angeles Dodgers' organization in special phase of free-agent draft, June, 1966.

†Traded with Infielder Ted Sizemore to St. Louis Cardinals for First Baseman Richie Allen, October 5, 1970.

‡Traded to Houston Astros for Infielder Orlando Martinez, November 3, 1971.

§Sold to Montreal Expos, March 27, 1973.

xOn supplemental disabled list from beginning of season until May 13, 1974.

ySold to Kansas City Royals, March 31, 1975; Royals sold Shortstop Rodney Scott to Expos, December 12, 1975, to complete deal.

zSelected by Seattle Mariners in American League expansion draft, November 5, 1976.

aOn supplemental disabled list, August 21 to September 7, 1978.

bReleased, August 8, 1980.

CHAMPIONSHIP SERIES RECORD

Year Club League	Pos.	G.	AB.	R.	H.	2B.	3B.	HR.	RBI.	B.A.	PO.	A.	E.	F.A.
1976—Kansas City .... Amer.	PH-C	2	1	0	0	0	0	0	0	.000	0	0	0	.000

PITCHING RECORD

Year Club	League	G.	IP.	W.	L.	Pct.	H.	R.	ER.	SO.	BB.	ERA.
1967—Albuquerque .... Texas		1	1	0	0	.000	3	4	4	0	1	36.00

ROBERT LYLE STODDARD
(Bob)

Born March 8, 1957, at Morgan Hill, Calif.
Height, 6.01. Weight, 190.
Throws and bats righthanded.
Attended Gavilan College, Gilroy, Calif., and
Fresno State University, Fresno, Calif.

Year Club	League	G.	IP.	W.	L.	Pct.	H.	R.	ER.	SO.	BB.	ERA.
1978—Stockton .... California		10	51	1	6	.143	46	36	31	47	39	5.47
1979—Stockton .... California		20	120	7	5	.583	78	45	40	104	58	3.00
1980—Spokane† .... P. Coast		21	124	4	9	.308	147	84	68	84	53	4.94

Selected by Milwaukee Brewers' organization in 19th round of free-agent draft, June 4, 1975.

Selected by Atlanta Braves' organization in secondary phase of free-agent draft, January 7, 1976.

Selected by Oakland A's organization in secondary phase of free-agent draft, June 8, 1976.

Selected by Seattle Mariners' organization in 10th round of free-agent draft, June 6, 1978.

†On disabled list, April 10 to April 24 and May 14 to May 26, 1980.

TIMOTHY PAUL STODDARD
(Tim)

Born January 24, 1953, at East Chicago, Ind.
Height, 6.07. Weight, 250.
Throws and bats righthanded.
Hobbies—Basketball and listening to music.
Attended North Carolina State University, Raleigh, N. C.

Major League saves: 1975 (0), 1978 (0), 1979 (3), 1980 (26). Total—29.
Tied for Southern League lead in wild pitches with 17 in 1977.

Year Club	League	G.	IP.	W.	L.	Pct.	H.	R.	ER.	SO.	BB.	ERA.
1975—Knoxville .... Southern		31	66	3	4	.429	66	40	31	37	43	4.23
1975—Chicago .... American		1	1	0	0	.000	2	1	1	0	0	9.00
1976—Knoxville .... Southern		20	140	9	8	.529	147	55	45	62	60	2.89
1976—Iowa† .... Am. Assoc.		12	29	0	2	.000	37	20	18	20	15	5.59
1977—Charlotte .... Southern		36	174	10	7	.588	175	75	62	94	66	3.21
1978—Rochester‡........................... Int'national		45	76	7	3	.700	80	28	22	70	32	2.61
1978—Baltimore .... American		8	18	0	1	.000	22	17	12	14	8	6.00
1979—Baltimore§........................... American		29	58	3	1	.750	44	12	11	47	19	1.71
1980—Baltimore .... American		64	86	5	3	.625	72	27	24	64	38	2.51
Major League Totals		102	163	8	5	.615	140	57	48	125	65	2.65

Selected by Texas Rangers' organization in 24th round of free-agent draft, June 5, 1974.

Selected by Chicago White Sox' organization in secondary phase of free-agent draft, January 9, 1975.

†Released, March 28, 1977; signed by Charlotte (Baltimore Orioles' organization), April 8, 1977.

‡On disabled list, June 15 to July 9, 1978.

§On disabled list, July 21 to September 1, 1979.

WORLD SERIES RECORD

Year Club	League	G.	IP.	W.	L.	Pct.	H.	R.	ER.	SO.	BB.	ERA.
1979—Baltimore .... American		4	5	1	0	1.000	6	3	3	3	1	5.40

STEVEN MICHAEL STONE
(Steve)

Born July 14, 1947, at Cleveland, O.
Height, 5.10. Weight, 178.
Throws and bats righthanded.
Hobbies—Chess, reading, sports cars and golf.
Attended Kent State University, Kent, O.; received Bachelor of
Science degree in Education.

Named righthanded pitcher on THE SPORTING NEWS American League All-Star Team, 1980.
Named American League Pitcher of the Year by THE SPORTING NEWS, 1980.
Won Cy Young Memorial Award, 1980.

Year Club	League	G.	IP.	W.	L.	Pct.	H.	R.	ER.	SO.	BB.	ERA.
1969—Fresno	California	27	167	12	•13	.480	170	82	67	184	57	3.61
1970—Amarillo	Texas	19	114	9	5	.643	103	55	50	108	59	3.95
1970—Phoenix	P. Coast	8	58	5	3	.625	46	13	11	50	23	1.71
1971—Phoenix	P. Coast	10	61	6	3	.667	60	29	27	57	23	3.98
1971—San Francisco	National	24	111	5	9	.357	110	56	51	63	55	4.14
1972—San Francisco†	National	27	124	6	8	.429	97	48	41	85	49	2.98
1973—Chicago‡	American	36	176	6	11	.353	163	87	83	138	82	4.24
1974—Chicago	National	38	170	8	6	.571	185	92	78	90	64	4.13
1975—Chicago	National	33	214	12	8	.600	198	103	94	139	80	3.95
1976—Chicago§x	National	17	75	3	6	.333	70	36	34	33	21	4.08
1977—Chicago	American	31	207	15	12	.556	228	115	104	124	80	4.52
1978—Chicago y	American	30	212	12	12	.500	196	110	103	118	84	4.37
1979—Baltimore	American	32	186	11	7	.611	173	91	78	96	73	3.77
1980—Baltimore	American	37	251	•25	7	•.781	224	103	90	149	101	3.23
National League Totals		139	694	34	37	.479	660	335	298	410	269	3.86
American League Totals		166	1032	69	49	.585	984	506	458	625	420	3.99
Major League Totals		305	1726	103	86	.545	1644	841	756	1035	689	3.94

Selected by Cleveland Indians' organization in 16th round of free-agent draft, June 7, 1968.
Selected by San Francisco Giants' organization in secondary phase of free-agent draft, February 1, 1969.
†Traded with Outfielder Ken Henderson to Chicago White Sox for Pitcher Tom Bradley, November 29, 1972.
‡Traded with Pitcher Ken Frailing, Catcher Steve Swisher and a player to be named later to Chicago Cubs for Third Baseman Ron Santo, December 11, 1973; White Sox sent Pitcher Jim Kremmel to Cubs, December 18, 1973, to complete deal.
§On disabled list, April 25 to July 2, 1976.
xGranted free agency, November 1, 1976; re-signed with Chicago White Sox, November 24, 1976.
yGranted free agency, November 2, 1978; signed by Baltimore Orioles, November 29, 1978.

WORLD SERIES RECORD

Year Club	League	G.	IP.	W.	L.	Pct.	H.	R.	ER.	SO.	BB.	ERA.
1979—Baltimore	American	1	2	0	0	.000	4	2	2	2	2	9.00

ALL-STAR GAME RECORD

Year League	IP.	W.	L.	Pct.	H.	R.	ER.	SO.	BB.	ERA.
1980—American	3	0	0	.000	0	0	0	3	0	0.00

JOSEPH A. STRAIN JR.
(Joe)

Born April 30, 1954, at Denver, Colo.
Height, 5.10. Weight, 169.
Throws and bats righthanded.
Attended University of Northern Colorado, Greeley, Colo.; received Bachelor of Arts degree in Education.

Led Pioneer League in stolen bases with 32 in 1976.
Led Pioneer League second basemen in assists with 194, in double plays with 49 and in fielding average with .953 in 1976.
Led California League second basemen in double plays with 91 in 1977.
Led Pacific Coast League second basemen in double plays with 141 in 1978.

Year Club	League	Pos.	G.	AB.	R.	H.	2B.	3B.	HR.	RBI.	B.A.	PO.	A.	E.	F.A.
1976—Great Falls	Pion.	2B-SS	•71	282	63	94	13	7	1	50	.333	153	197	17	.954
1977—Fresno	Calif.	2B	136	•556	124	•188	33	3	7	88	.338	•309	•396	24	.967
1978—Phoenix	P. C.	2B	138	561	88	171	37	4	3	52	.305	•336	•493	23	.973
1979—Phoenix	P. C.	2B	75	310	47	92	13	1	1	26	.297	169	238	15	.964
1979—San Francisco	Nat.	2B-3B	67	257	27	62	8	1	1	12	.241	147	189	6	.982
1980—San Fran.†‡	Nat.	2B-3B-SS	77	189	26	54	6	0	0	16	.286	88	113	4	.980
Major League Totals			144	446	53	116	14	1	1	28	.260	235	302	10	.982

Signed as free agent by San Francisco Giants' organization, June 14, 1976.
†On disabled list, August 1 to September 1, 1980.
‡Traded with Pitcher Phil Nastu to Chicago Cubs for Outfielders Jerry Martin and Jesus Figueroa, December 12, 1980.

DID YOU KNOW—
That the 1981 All-Star Game will be played in Cleveland?

JOHN ANTON STUPER

Born May 9, 1957, at Butler, Pa.
Height, 6.02. Weight, 200.
Throws and bats righthanded.
Attended Butler County Community College, Butler, Pa., Point Park College, Pittsburgh, Pa.
and LaRoche College, Pittsburgh, Pa.; received Bachelor of Arts degree in English.

Year	Club	League	G.	IP.	W.	L.	Pct.	H.	R.	ER.	SO.	BB.	ERA.
1978—Charleston†	W. Carol.	13	76	4	8	.333	85	59	45	36	62	5.33
1979—St. Petersburg	Florida St.	42	93	2	5	.286	84	38	28	62	54	2.71
1980—St. Petersburg	Florida St.	24	39	1	4	.200	38	12	10	28	19	2.31
1980—Arkansas	Texas	25	88	7	2	.778	77	28	24	57	40	2.45

Selected by Pittsburgh Pirates' organization in 18th round of free-agent draft, June 6, 1978.
†Traded to St. Louis Cardinals' organization for Infielder Tommy Sandt, January 25, 1979.

GUY PATRICK SULARZ

Born November 7, 1955, at Minneapolis, Minn.
Height, 5.11. Weight, 165.
Throws and bats righthanded.

Led Pacific Coast League shortstops in putouts with 229, in assists with 471, in double plays with 131 and in fielding percentage with .962 in 1978.

Year	Club	League	Pos.	G.	AB.	R.	H.	2B.	3B.	HR.	RBI.	B.A.	PO.	A.	E.	F.A.
1974—Great Falls	Pion.	OF-P-3B	47	92	24	21	3	0	1	12	.228	33	6	1	.975
1975—Fresno†	Calif.	SS-2-O	92	293	46	83	16	2	1	28	.283	116	202	32	.877
1976—Fresno	Calif.	SS-3B-2B	134	497	87	135	22	5	0	60	.272	138	269	38	.915
1977—Waterbury	East.	SS-2B	134	491	64	134	22	5	1	52	.273	201	413	33	.949
1978—Phoenix‡	P.C.	SS-3B	130	463	67	140	24	7	2	63	.302	230	477	31	.958
1979—Phoenix§	P.C.	3-2-S-O	144	521	79	153	23	4	2	68	.294	285	92	14	.964
1980—Phoenix x	P.C.	3-S-2	88	306	44	84	17	0	2	26	.275	129	234	13	.965
1980—San Francisco	Nat.	2B-3B	25	65	3	16	1	1	0	3	.246	50	79	3	.977
Major League Totals			25	65	3	16	1	1	0	3	.246	50	79	3	.977

Selected by San Francisco Giants' organization in 10th round of free-agent draft, June 5, 1974.
†On disabled list, July 3 to July 20, 1975.
‡On disabled list, June 27 to July 7, 1978.
§Drafted by Minnesota Twins from Phoenix (San Francisco Giants' organization), December 3, 1979.
xOn disabled list, May 4 to May 30, 1980.

PITCHING RECORD

Year	Club	League	G.	IP.	W.	L.	Pct.	H.	R.	ER.	SO.	BB.	ERA.
1974—Great Falls	Pioneer	3	12	0	1	.000	8	4	4	9	5	3.00

JOHN J. SUMMERS
(Champ)

Born June 15, 1948, at Bremerton, Wash.
Height, 6.02. Weight, 205.
Throws right and bats lefthanded.
Hobby—Billiards.
Attended Nicholls State University, Thibodaux, La., and Southern Illinois University at
Edwardsville, Edwardsville, Ill.

Led American Association in total bases with 307 in 1978.
Named American Association Most Valuable Player, 1978.
Named Minor League Player of the Year by THE SPORTING NEWS, 1978.

Year	Club	League	Pos.	G.	AB.	R.	H.	2B.	3B.	HR.	RBI.	B.A.	PO.	A.	E.	F.A.
1971—C. Bay-N. Bend	Northw.	OF	65	222	36	56	8	5	3	34	.252	90	6	6	.941
1972—Burlington	Midw.	OF-1B	97	273	43	84	20	0	10	54	.308	210	13	9	.961
1973—Tucson	P.C.	OF-1-3	94	288	49	96	15	5	8	45	.333	97	4	3	.971
1974—Tucson	P.C.	OF	94	334	49	88	13	6	10	59	.263	139	4	3	.979
1974—Oakland	Amer.	OF	20	24	2	3	1	0	0	3	.125	6	0	0	1.000
1975—Tucson†	P.C.	OF	17	54	5	17	0	2	0	6	.315	21	0	0	1.000
1975—Chicago	Nat.	OF	76	91	14	21	5	1	1	16	.231	16	0	2	.889
1976—Chicago‡	Nat.	OF-1B-C	83	126	11	26	2	0	3	13	.206	95	5	1	.990
1977—Cincinnati	Nat.	OF-3B	59	76	11	13	4	0	3	6	.171	24	2	0	1.000
1978—Indianapolis	A.A.	OF-1B	132	462	98	*170	25	5	*34	*124	.368	261	8	9	.968
1978—Cincinnati	Nat.	OF	13	35	4	9	2	0	1	3	.257	14	0	1	.933
1979—Cincinnati§	Nat.	OF-1B	27	60	10	12	1	1	1	11	.200	56	6	2	.969
1979—Detroit	Amer.	OF-1B	90	246	47	77	12	1	20	51	.313	110	4	1	.991
1980—Detroit	Amer.	OF-1B	120	347	61	103	19	1	17	60	.297	60	1	3	.953
National League Totals			258	388	50	81	15	2	9	49	.209	205	13	6	.973
American League Totals			230	617	110	183	32	2	37	114	.297	176	5	4	.978
Major League Totals			488	1005	160	264	47	4	46	163	.263	381	18	10	.976

Signed as free agent by Oakland A's organization, June 12, 1971.
†Traded by Oakland Athletics to Chicago Cubs, April 29, 1975, to complete deal in which Athletics obtained Pitcher Jim Todd from Cubs for a player to be named later, April 6, 1975.
‡Traded to Cincinnati Reds' organization for Outfielder Dave Schneck, February 16, 1977.
§Traded to Detroit Tigers for a player to be named later, May 25, 1979; Cincinnati acquired Pitcher Sheldon Burnside to complete deal, October 25, 1979.

JAMES HOWARD SUNDBERG
(Jim)

Born May 18, 1951, at Galesburg, Ill.
Height, 6.00. Weight, 196.
Throws and bats righthanded.
Hobby—Hunting.
Attended University of Iowa, Iowa City, Iowa.

Tied major league records for most assists by catcher, inning (3), September 3, 1976 (fifth inning); fewest errors by catcher, season (4), 1979.

Established American League records for highest fielding percentage by catcher, season (.995), 1979; most seasons leading league, assists by catchers (5).

Tied American League record for most games, catcher, season (155), 1975.

Led American League catchers in double plays with 15 in 1974 and with 11 in 1976.

Tied for American League lead among catchers in double plays with 12 in 1977 and with 14 in 1978.

Tied for American League lead in passed balls by catchers with 17 in 1980.

Named catcher on THE SPORTING NEWS American League All-Star fielding team, 1976 through 1980.

Named catcher on THE SPORTING NEWS American League All-Star Team, 1978.

Year Club League	Pos.	G.	AB.	R.	H.	2B.	3B.	HR.	RBI.	B.A.	PO.	A.	E.	F.A.
1973—Pittsfield...........East.	C	91	242	39	72	14	0	5	40	.298	449	52	3	*.994
1974—Texas................Amer.	C	132	368	45	91	13	3	3	36	.247	722	69	8	.990
1975—Texas................Amer.	C	155	472	45	94	9	0	6	36	.199	*791	*101	17	.981
1976—Texas................Amer.	C	140	448	33	102	24	2	3	34	.228	*719	*96	7	*.991
1977—Texas................Amer.	C	149	453	61	132	20	3	6	65	.291	*801	* 103	5	*.994
1978—Texas ....Amer.	C	149	518	54	144	23	6	6	58	.278	*769	*91	3	*.997
1979—Texas ....Amer.	C	150	495	50	136	23	4	5	64	.275	*754	75	4	*.995
1980—Texas ....Amer.	C	151	505	59	138	24	1	10	63	.273	*853	*76	7	.993
Major League Totals		1026	3259	347	837	136	19	39	356	.257	5409	611	51	.992

Selected by Oakland A's organization in 14th round of free-agent draft, June 5, 1969.

Selected by Texas Rangers' organization in 8th round of free-agent draft, June 6, 1972.

Selected by Texas Rangers' organization in secondary phase of free-agent draft, January 10, 1973.

ALL-STAR GAME RECORD

Year League	Pos.	AB.	R.	H.	2B.	3B.	HR.	RBI.	B.A.	PO.	A.	E.	F.A.
1978—American	C	0	0	0	0	0	0	0	.000	2	1	0	1.000

Member of American League All-Star Team in 1974 game; did not play.

RICHARD LEE SUTCLIFFE
(Rick)

Born June 21, 1956, at Independence, Mo.
Height, 6.06. Weight, 200.
Throws right and bats lefthanded.
Hobbies—Basketball and football.
Brother of Terry Sutcliffe, pitcher in Los Angeles Dodgers' organization.

Tied for Northwest League lead in shutouts with 2 in 1974.

Named National League Rookie Pitcher of the Year by THE SPORTING NEWS, 1979.

Named National League Rookie of the Year by Baseball Writers Association of America, 1979.

Received reported $80,000 bonus to sign with Los Angeles Dodgers, 1974.

Year Club League	G.	IP.	W.	L.	Pct.	H.	R.	ER.	SO.	BB.	ERA.
1974—Bellingham ....Northwest	17	95	10	3	.769	79	42	35	69	48	3.32
1975—Bakersfield ....California	*28	193	8	*16	.333	*214	*115	*89	91	68	4.15
1976—Waterbury ....Eastern	30	187	10	11	.476	*187	90	66	121	45	3.18
1976—Los Angeles ....National	1	5	0	0	.000	2	0	0	3	1	0.00
1977—Albuquerque†......................P. Coast	17	77	3	10	.231	96	67	55	48	63	6.43
1978—Albuquerque ....P. Coast	30	184	13	6	.684	179	101	91	99	92	4.45
1978—Los Angeles ....National	2	2	0	0	.000	2	0	0	1	0	0.00
1979—Los Angeles ....National	39	242	17	10	.630	217	104	93	117	97	3.46
1980—Los Angeles ....National	42	110	3	9	.250	122	73	68	59	55	5.56
Major League Totals	84	359	20	19	.513	343	177	161	179	154	4.04

Selected by Los Angeles Dodgers' organization in 1st round (21st player selected) of free-agent draft, June 5, 1974.

†On disabled list, May 3 to May 24, 1977.

LEONARDO C. SUTHERLAND
(Leo)

Born April 6, 1958, at Santiago, Cuba.
Height, 5.10. Weight, 165.
Throws and bats lefthanded.
Attended Golden West College, Huntington Beach, Calif.

Tied for Gulf Coast League lead in double plays by outfielders with 3 in 1976.

Year Club League	Pos.	G.	AB.	R.	H.	2B.	3B.	HR.	RBI.	B.A.	PO.	A.	E.	F.A.
1976—Sara. White Sox. G.C.	OF	51	199	34	48	3	3	1	18	.241	95	6	*7	.935
1977—Appleton ....Midw.	OF	125	439	66	116	13	4	0	36	.264	191	●21	14	.938
1978—Appleton ....Midw.	OF	127	471	*100	124	22	5	4	50	.263	231	6	9	.963

Year	Club	League	Pos.	G.	AB.	R.	H.	2B.	3B.	HR.	RBI.	B.A.	PO.	A.	E.	F.A.
1979—Knoxville	..........South.		OF	124	452	65	144	14	7	1	38	.319	256	11	14	.950
1980—Iowa	.................A.A.		OF	96	365	56	95	10	2	2	23	.260	223	6	4	.983
1980—Chicago	............Amer.		OF	34	89	9	23	3	0	0	5	.258	50	0	3	.943
Major League Totals	....			34	89	9	23	3	0	0	5	.258	50	0	3	.943

Selected by Cleveland Indians' organization in 16th round of free-agent draft, June 4, 1975.
Selected by Chicago White Sox' organization in secondary phase of free-agent draft, January 7, 1976.

HOWARD BRUCE SUTTER

Name pronounced Suit-er.
(Known by middle name.)

Born January 8, 1953, at Lancaster, Pa.
Height, 6.02. Weight, 190.
Throws and bats righthanded.
Hobby—Hunting.

Tied major league record for striking out side on 9 pitches, September 8, 1977 (ninth inning).
Tied National League records for most strikeouts, consecutive, relief pitcher, game, 6, September 8, 1977; most saves, season (37), 1979.
Major League saves: 1976 (10), 1977 (31), 1978 (27), 1979 (37), 1980 (28). Total—133.
Led National League in saves with 37 in 1979 and with 28 in 1980.
Tied for Texas League lead in saves with 13 in 1975.
Named National League Fireman of the Year by THE SPORTING NEWS, 1979.
Won National League Cy Young Memorial Award, 1979.

Year	Club	League	G.	IP.	W.	L.	Pct.	H.	R.	ER.	SO.	BB.	ERA.
1972—Bradenton Cubs	....................Gulf Coast		2	5	0	0	.000	3	0	0	4	0	0.00
1973—Quincy	................................Midwest		40	85	3	3	.500	94	52	39	76	27	4.13
1974—Key West†	............................Florida St.		18	40	1	5	.167	26	9	6	50	13	1.35
1974—Midland	..............................Texas		8	25	1	2	.333	22	6	4	14	6	1.44
1975—Midland	..............................Texas		41	67	5	7	.417	64	26	16	50	21	2.15
1976—Wichita	...............................Am. Assoc.		7	12	2	1	.667	9	3	2	16	4	1.50
1976—Chicago	...............................National		52	83	6	3	.667	63	27	25	73	26	2.71
1977—Chicago‡	...............................National		62	107	7	3	.700	69	21	16	129	23	1.35
1978—Chicago	...............................National		64	99	8	10	.444	82	44	35	106	34	3.18
1979—Chicago	...............................National		62	101	6	6	.500	67	29	25	110	32	2.23
1980—Chicago§	..............................National		60	102	5	8	.385	90	35	30	76	34	2.65
Major League Totals	....		300	492	32	30	.516	371	156	131	494	149	2.40

Selected by Washington Senators' organization in 21st round of free-agent draft, June 4, 1970.
Signed as free agent by Chicago Cubs' organization, September 9, 1971.
†On disabled list, May 22, to July 28, 1974.
‡On disabled list, August 2 to August 23, 1977.
§Traded to St. Louis Cardinals for Third Baseman Ken Reitz, Outfielder-First Baseman Leon Durham and a player to be named later, December 9, 1980; Third Baseman Ty Waller traded to Cubs completing deal, December 22, 1980.

ALL-STAR GAME RECORD

Year	League	IP.	W.	L.	Pct.	H.	R.	ER.	SO.	BB.	ERA.
1978—National	....	1⅔	1	0	1.000	0	0	0	2	0	0.00
1979—National	....	2	1	0	1.000	2	0	0	3	2	0.00
1980—National	....	2	0	0	.000	0	0	0	1	1	0.00
All-Star Game Totals	....	5⅔	2	0	1.000	2	0	0	6	3	0.00

Named to National League All-Star Team in 1977; replaced due to injury.

DONALD HOWARD SUTTON

(Don)

Born April 2, 1945, at Clio, Ala.
Height, 6.01. Weight, 190.
Throws and bats righthanded.
Hobbies—All other sports.
Attended Mississippi College, Clinton, Miss., and Whittier College, Whittier, Calif.

Established major league record for most consecutive games lost to one club, lifetime (13), 1966 through 1969, (vs. Chicago).
Tied National League record for most consecutive home runs allowed, inning (3), May 27, 1980 (third inning).
Tied modern National League record for most one-hit games, lifetime (5).
Led National League in shutouts with 9 in 1972.
Led National League pitchers in games started with 40 in 1974.
Named National League Rookie Pitcher of the Year by THE SPORTING NEWS, 1966.
Named righthanded pitcher on THE SPORTING NEWS National League All-Star Team, 1976.
Named Player of the Year in Texas League, 1965.

Year	Club	League	G.	IP.	W.	L.	Pct.	H.	R.	ER.	SO.	BB.	ERA.
1965—Santa Barbara	.....................California		10	84	8	1	.889	59	18	14	101	15	1.50
1965—Albuquerque	........................Texas		21	165	15	6	*.714	151	60	51	138	30	2.78
1966—Los Angeles	........................National		37	226	12	12	.500	192	82	75	209	52	2.99
1967—Los Angeles	........................National		37	233	11	15	.423	223	106	102	169	57	3.94
1968—Spokane	...............................P. Coast		2	16	1	1	.500	11	2	2	19	5	1.13

Year Club	League	G.	IP.	W.	L.	Pct.	H.	R.	ER.	SO.	BB.	ERA.
1968–Los Angeles	National	35	208	11	15	.423	179	64	60	162	59	2.60
1969–Los Angeles	National	41	293	17	18	.486	269	123	113	217	91	3.47
1970–Los Angeles	National	38	260	15	13	.536	251	127	●118	201	78	4.08
1971–Los Angeles	National	38	265	17	12	.586	231	85	75	194	55	2.55
1972–Los Angeles	National	33	273	19	9	.679	186	78	63	207	63	2.08
1973–Los Angeles	National	33	256	18	10	.643	196	78	69	200	56	2.43
1974–Los Angeles	National	40	276	19	9	.679	241	111	99	179	80	3.23
1975–Los Angeles	National	35	254	16	13	.552	202	87	81	175	62	2.87
1976–Los Angeles	National	35	268	21	10	.677	231	98	91	161	82	3.06
1977–Los Angeles	National	33	240	14	8	.636	207	93	85	150	69	3.19
1978–Los Angeles	National	34	238	15	11	.577	228	109	94	154	54	3.55
1979–Los Angeles	National	33	226	12	15	.444	201	109	96	146	61	3.82
1980–Los Angeles†	National	32	212	13	5	.722	163	56	52	128	47	*2.21
Major League Totals		534	3728	230	175	.568	3200	1406	1273	2652	966	3.07

Signed as free agent by Los Angeles Dodgers' organization, September 11, 1964.
†Granted free agency, October 23, 1980; signed by Houston Astros, December 4, 1980.

CHAMPIONSHIP SERIES RECORD

Established Championship Series records for most consecutive scoreless innings, Series (15⅔), 1974; most innings pitched, four-game Series (17), 1974; most strikeouts, four-game Series (13), 1974.
Tied Championship Series record for most games won, Series (2), 1974.
Established National League Championship Series record for most consecutive scoreless innings, total Series (15⅔).
Tied National League Championship Series records for most games won, total Series (3); most complete games, total Series (2).

Year Club	League	G.	IP.	W.	L.	Pct.	H.	R.	ER.	SO.	BB.	ERA.
1974–Los Angeles	National	2	17	2	0	1.000	7	1	1	13	2	0.53
1977–Los Angeles	National	1	9	1	0	1.000	9	1	1	4	0	1.00
1978–Los Angeles	National	1	5⅔	0	1	.000	7	7	4	0	2	6.35
Championship Series Totals		4	31⅔	3	1	.750	23	9	6	17	4	1.71

WORLD SERIES RECORD

Tied World Series records for most consecutive home runs allowed, inning (2), October 16, 1977 (eighth inning); most games lost, six-game Series (2), 1978; most runs allowed, six-game Series (10), 1978.

Year Club	League	G.	IP.	W.	L.	Pct.	H.	R.	ER.	SO.	BB.	ERA.
1974–Los Angeles	National	2	13	1	0	1.000	9	4	4	12	3	2.77
1977–Los Angeles	National	2	16	1	0	1.000	17	7	7	6	1	3.94
1978–Los Angeles	National	2	12	0	2	.000	17	10	10	8	4	7.50
World Series Totals		6	41	2	2	.500	43	21	21	26	8	4.61

ALL-STAR GAME RECORD

Year League	IP.	W.	L.	Pct.	H.	R.	ER.	SO.	BB.	ERA.
1972–National	2	0	0	.000	1	0	0	2	0	0.00
1973–National	1	0	0	.000	0	0	0	0	0	0.00
1975–National	2	0	0	.000	3	0	0	1	0	0.00
1977–National	3	1	0	1.000	1	0	0	4	1	0.00
All-Star Game Totals	8	1	0	1.000	5	0	0	7	1	0.00

CRAIG STEVEN SWAN

Born November 30, 1950, at Van Nuys, Calif.
Height, 6.03. Weight, 215.
Throws and bats righthanded.
Attended Arizona State University, Tempe, Ariz.

Led International League in complete games with 13 in 1975.
Tied for International League lead in shutouts with 4 in 1973.

Year Club	League	G.	IP.	W.	L.	Pct.	H.	R.	ER.	SO.	BB.	ERA.
1972–Memphis	Texas	14	108	7	3	.700	102	28	27	81	26	2.25
1973–Tidewater†	Int'national	16	100	7	5	.583	88	30	26	79	25	2.34
1973–New York	National	3	8	0	1	.000	16	9	8	4	2	9.00
1974–Tidewater	Int'national	9	51	2	3	.400	53	29	27	31	17	4.76
1974–New York‡	National	7	30	1	3	.250	28	19	15	10	21	4.50
1975–Tidewater	Int'national	26	165	13	7	.650	136	48	44	111	38	2.40
1975–New York	National	6	31	1	3	.250	38	22	22	19	13	6.39
1976–New York	National	23	132	6	9	.400	129	64	52	89	44	3.55
1977–New York	National	26	147	9	10	.474	153	76	69	71	56	4.22
1978–New York	National	29	207	9	6	.600	164	62	56	125	58	*2.43
1979–New York§	National	35	251	14	13	.519	241	102	92	145	57	3.30
1980–New York§x	National	27	126	5	9	.357	117	59	51	79	30	3.64
Major League Totals		156	932	45	54	.455	886	413	365	542	281	3.52

Selected by St. Louis Cardinals' organization in 8th round of free-agent draft, June 7, 1968.
Selected by New York Mets' organization in 3rd round of free-agent draft, June 6, 1972.
†On disabled list, June 5 to June 25, 1973.
‡On disabled list, June 14 to July 22, 1974.
§On disabled list, July 16 to August 16, 1980.
xOn emergency disabled list, August 29 to October 14, 1980.

RICHARD JOE SWEET
(Rick)

Born September 7, 1952, at Longview, Wash.
Height, 6.01. Weight, 200.
Throws right and bats lefthanded.
Hobbies—Stamp collecting, reading, tennis and golf.
Attended Gonzaga University, Spokane, Wash.
Led National League in total bases with 149 in 1975.
Led Pacific Coast League catchers in double plays with 11 in 1977.

Year Club	League	Pos.	G.	AB.	R.	H.	2B.	3B.	HR.	RBI.	B.A.	PO.	A.	E.	F.A.
1975—Walla Walla.......N'west		*C-1B	75	260	48	91	21	2	11	*66	*.350	471	53	11	*.979
1976—Amarillo ....Texas		*C-1-3-O	117	412	63	116	22	5	4	67	.282	627	49	*19	.973
1977—Hawaii ..............P.C.		C-1-2-3	128	452	87	146	35	4	11	67	.323	459	72	10	.982
1978—San Diego ....Nat.		C	88	226	15	50	8	0	1	11	.221	337	33	6	.984
1979—Hawaii ..............P.C.		C-1B	135	452	59	116	17	4	5	52	.257	763	72	11	.987
1980—Hawaii†‡ ..........P.C.		C-3-1	99	337	42	88	11	3	1	35	.261	376	100	16	.967
Major League Totals......................			88	226	15	50	8	0	1	11	.221	337	33	6	.984

Selected by Pittsburgh Pirates' organization in 31st round of free-agent draft, June 5, 1974.
Selected by San Diego Padres' organization in secondary phase of free-agent draft, January 9, 1975.
†On disabled list, July 12 to July 22, 1980.
‡Sold to New York Mets' organization, December 15, 1980.

WELDON SWIFT

Born February 17, 1958, at Baltimore, Md.
Height, 6.02. Weight, 200.
Throws and bats righthanded.

Year Club	League	G.	IP.	W.	L.	Pct.	H.	R.	ER.	SO.	BB.	ERA.
1978—Burlington ....Midwest		23	130	10	7	.588	93	61	42	94	93	2.91
1979—Holyoke ....Eastern		29	118	3	10	.231	144	90	76	59	61	5.80
1980—Holyoke ....Eastern		28	179	11	10	.524	148	76	67	92	97	3.37

Selected by Milwaukee Brewers' organization in 1st round (7th player selected) of free-agent draft,
January 10, 1978.

STEVEN EUGENE SWISHER
(Steve)

Born August 9, 1951, at Parkersburg, W. Va.
Height, 6.02. Weight, 205.
Throws and bats righthanded.
Attended Ohio University, Athens, O.; received Bachelor of science degree in Education.

Year Club	League	Pos.	G.	AB.	R.	H.	2B.	3B.	HR.	RBI.	B.A.	PO.	A.	E.	F.A.
1973—Knoxville ....South.		C	54	161	19	34	5	0	6	18	.211	235	25	4	.985
1973—Iowa† ....A. A.		C	6	21	1	6	0	0	1	1	.286	30	4	0	1.000
1974—Wichita ....A. A.		C	52	153	15	30	4	1	3	13	.196	284	33	●11	.966
1974—Chicago..............Nat.		C	90	280	21	60	5	0	5	27	.214	493	50	7	.987
1975—Wichita ....A. A.		C	7	21	8	6	0	0	4	9	.286	27	4	1	.969
1975—Chicago..............Nat.		C	93	254	20	54	16	2	1	22	.213	426	36	10	.979
1976—Chicago..............Nat.		C	109	377	25	89	13	3	5	42	.236	574	49	11	.983
1977—Chicago‡ ....Nat.		C	74	205	21	39	7	0	5	15	.190	327	38	9	.976
1978—St. Louis ....Nat.		C	45	115	11	32	5	1	1	10	.278	202	13	2	.991
1979—St. Louis ....Nat.		C	38	73	4	11	1	1	1	3	.151	105	6	3	.974
1980—St. Louis§.........Nat.		C	18	24	2	6	1	0	0	2	.250	21	1	1	.957
Major League Totals			467	1328	104	291	48	47	18	121	.219	2148	193	43	.982

Selected by Chicago White Sox' organization in 1st round (21st player selected) of free-agent draft, June 5,
1973.

†Traded with Pitchers Ken Frailing and Steve Stone and a player to be named later by Chicago White Sox
to Chicago Cubs for Third Baseman Ron Santo, December 11, 1973; White Sox sent Pitcher Jim Kremmel to
Cubs, December 18, 1973, to complete deal.

‡Traded with Outfielder Jerry Morales and a player to be named later to St. Louis Cardinals for Catcher
Dave Rader and Outfielder-Third Baseman Hector Cruz, December 8, 1977.

§Traded with Catcher Terry Kennedy, Pitchers John Littlefield, Kim Seaman, Al Olmsted and John Urrea
and Infielder Mike Phillips to San Diego Padres for Pitchers Rollie Fingers and Bob Shirley, Catcher-First
Baseman Gene Tenace and a player to be named later, December 8, 1980; Catcher Bob Geren traded to
Cardinals' organization completing deal, December 10, 1980.

ALL-STAR GAME RECORD
Member of National League All-Star Team in 1976; did not play.

ROBERT JOSEPH SYKES
(Bob)

Born December 11, 1954, at Neptune, N. J.
Height, 6.02. Weight, 200.
Throws left and bats left and righthanded.
Attended Miami-Dade (North) Community College, Miami, Fla.

Led Appalachian League in shutouts with 6 and complete games with 7 in 1974.
Tied for Appalachian League lead in games started with 13 in 1974.

Year	Club	League	G.	IP.	W.	L.	Pct.	H.	R.	ER.	SO.	BB.	ERA.
1974	Bristol	Ap'lachian	14	*101	*11	0	*1.000	52	18	12	96	31	*1.07
1975	Montgomery	Southern	27	191	●14	10	.583	180	63	67	88	87	3.16
1976	Evansville†	Am. Assoc.	24	118	8	11	.421	137	71	56	70	71	4.27
1977	Detroit	American	32	133	5	7	.417	141	74	65	58	50	4.40
1978	Evansville	Am. Assoc.	4	32	4	0	1.000	26	7	5	12	9	1.41
1978	Detroit‡	American	22	94	6	6	.500	99	43	41	58	34	3.93
1979	St. Louis§	National	13	67	4	3	.571	86	49	46	35	34	6.18
1979	St. Petersburg	Florida St.	4	15	0	3	.000	11	5	5	6	12	3.00
1979	Springfield	Am. Assoc.	4	5	0	0	.000	13	12	9	4	7	16.20
1980	St. Louis	National	27	126	6	10	.375	134	67	65	50	54	4.64
	American League Totals		54	227	11	13	.458	240	117	106	116	84	4.20
	National League Totals		40	193	10	13	.435	220	116	111	85	88	5.18
	Major League Totals		94	420	21	26	.447	460	233	217	201	172	4.65

Selected by Detroit Tigers' organization in 19th round of free-agent draft, June 5, 1974.
†On disabled list, June 10 to June 21, 1976.
‡Traded with Pitcher Jack Murphy to St. Louis Cardinals for Outfielder Jerry Morales and Pitcher Aurelio Lopez, December 4, 1978.
§On disabled list, June 11 to July 26, 1979.

PATRICK SEAN TABLER
(Pat)
Born February 2, 1958, at Hamilton, O.
Height, 6.03. Weight, 185.
Throws and bats righthanded.

Year	Club	League	Pos.	G.	AB.	R.	H.	2B.	3B.	HR.	RBI.	B.A.	PO.	A.	E.	F.A.
1976	Oneonta	NYP	3B-OF	65	238	27	55	3	0	1	20	.231	79	71	12	.926
1977	Ft. Lauderdale	Fla. St.	3B	110	391	35	93	7	1	1	36	.238	87	209	*35	.894
1978	Ft. Lauderdale	Fla. St.	1-3-O	138	455	56	124	9	5	5	70	.273	855	88	15	.984
1979	Ft. Lauderdale	Fla. St.	O-3-2-1	75	247	39	78	12	4	2	33	.316	102	41	11	.929
1979	West Haven	East.	2B-OF	56	190	33	57	15	3	6	36	.300	124	169	13	.958
1980	Nashville	South.	2B	136	479	82	142	38	8	16	83	.296	262	361	*27	.958

Selected by New York Yankees' organization in 1st round (16th player selected) of free-agent draft, June 8, 1976.

JOHN FELIX TAMARGO SR.
Born November 7, 1951, at Tampa, Fla.
Height, 5.10. Weight, 195.
Throws right and bats left and righthanded.
Hobbies—Golf and tennis.
Attended Miami-Dade (North) Community College, Miami, Fla., and
Georgia Southern College, Statesboro, Ga.; received Bachelor
of Arts degree in Business Administration.

Year	Club	League	Pos.	G.	AB.	R.	H.	2B.	3B.	HR.	RBI.	B.A.	PO.	A.	E.	F.A.
1973	St. Petersburg	Fla. St.	C	68	220	24	57	3	2	2	32	.259	404	32	4	.991
1974	Modesto†	Calif.	C	26	90	16	24	5	0	2	9	.267	166	15	5	.973
1974	Arkansas‡	Tex.	C	1	1	0	0	0	0	0	0	.000	4	1	0	1.000
1974	St. Petersburg§	Fla. St.	DH	8	25	5	7	1	0	1	5	.280	0	0	0	.000
1975	Arkansas	Tex.	C	39	120	20	31	7	1	1	11	.258	167	20	4	.979
1975	Tulsa	A. A.	C	53	164	27	47	12	0	5	23	.287	231	19	2	.992
1976	Tulsa	A. A.	C-1B	113	346	44	96	21	3	8	48	.277	663	45	19	.974
1976	St. Louis	Nat.	C	10	10	2	3	0	0	0	1	.300	4	0	0	1.000
1977	New Orleans	A. A.	C-3B	111	284	38	72	13	2	10	42	.254	483	38	12	.977
1977	St. Louis	Nat.	C	4	4	0	0	0	0	0	0	.000	1	0	0	1.000
1978	Springfield	A. A.	C-3B	65	222	35	67	14	1	9	43	.302	326	25	9	.975
1978	St.L. x-S.F.	Nat.	C	42	98	6	22	4	1	1	8	.224	157	9	6	.965
1979	S.F. y-Mont.	Nat.	C	42	81	7	20	5	0	2	11	.247	80	6	1	.989
1979	Denver	A.A.	C	53	187	35	60	11	2	4	29	.321	208	28	3	.989
1980	Montreal z	Nat.	C	37	51	4	14	3	0	1	13	.275	36	3	1	.975
	Major League Totals			135	244	19	59	12	1	4	33	.242	278	18	8	.974

Selected by New York Yankees' organization in 15th round of free-agent draft, June 5, 1969.
Selected by Chicago White Sox' organization in secondary phase of free-agent draft, January 17, 1970.
Selected by Milwaukee Brewers' organization in secondary phase of free-agent draft, June 4, 1970.
Selected by Boston Red Sox' organization in secondary phase of free-agent draft, January 13, 1971.
Selected by St. Louis Cardinals' organization in 6th round of free-agent draft, June 5, 1973.
†On disabled list, April 29 to June 4, 1974.
‡On disabled list, June 19 to June 30, 1974.
§On disabled list, July 1 to August 9, 1974.
xTraded to San Francisco Giants for a player to be named later, July 18, 1978; Pitcher Rob Dressler assigned from Phoenix to Springfield to complete deal, July 24, 1978.
yTraded to Montreal Expos' organization for a player to be named later, June 13, 1979; Infielder Joe Pettini traded to Giants completing deal, March 14, 1980.
zOn supplemental disabled list, July 24 to August 18, 1980.

FRANK DARYL TANANA

Last name rhymes with banana.

Born July 3, 1953, at Detroit, Mich.
Height, 6.03. Weight, 195.
Throws and bats lefthanded.
Hobbies—Golf and all physical activities.
Attended California State University at Fullerton, Calif.
Son of Frank Richard Tanana, former outfielder in Cleveland Indians' organization.

Established American League record for most balks, season (8), 1978.
Tied American League record for most consecutive hits allowed, start of game (5), May 18, 1980.
Led American League in shutouts with 7 in 1977.
Led Texas League pitchers in complete games with 15 in 1973.
Named American League Rookie Pitcher of the Year by THE SPORTING NEWS, 1974.
Named Texas League Pitcher of the Year in 1973.
Named lefthanded pitcher on THE SPORTING NEWS American League All-Star Team, 1976 and 1977.

Year	Club	League	G.	IP.	W.	L.	Pct.	H.	R.	ER.	SO.	BB.	ERA.
1971—Idaho Falls†		Pioneer	....	....	..	..	....	....	..	..	....	..	....
1972—Quad Cities		Midwest	19	129	7	2	.778	111	48	40	134	57	2.79
1973—El Paso		Texas	26	*206	16	6	.727	170	72	62	*197	63	2.71
1973—Salt Lake City		P. Coast	2	14	1	0	1.000	11	5	4	15	2	2.57
1973—California		American	4	26	2	2	.500	20	11	9	22	8	3.12
1974—California		American	39	269	14	19	.424	262	104	93	180	77	3.11
1975—California		American	34	257	16	9	.640	211	80	75	*269	73	2.63
1976—California		American	34	288	19	10	.655	212	88	78	261	73	2.44
1977—California		American	31	241	15	9	.625	201	72	68	205	61	*2.54
1978—California		American	33	239	18	12	.600	239	108	97	137	60	3.65
1979—California‡		American	18	90	7	5	.583	93	44	39	46	25	3.90
1980—California§		American	32	204	11	12	.478	223	107	94	113	45	4.15
Major League Totals			225	1614	102	78	.567	1461	614	553	1233	422	3.08

Selected by California Angels' organization in 1st round (13th player selected) of free-agent draft, June 8, 1971.

†Appeared in one game as pinch runner (did not pitch due to a sore arm).
‡On disabled list, July 9 to September 4, 1979.
§Traded with Pitcher Jim Dorsey and Outfielder Joe Rudi to Boston Red Sox for Outfielder Fred Lynn and Pitcher Steve Renko, January 23, 1981.

CHAMPIONSHIP SERIES RECORD

Year	Club	League	G.	IP.	W.	L.	Pct.	H.	R.	ER.	SO.	BB.	ERA.
1979—California		American	1	5	0	0	.000	6	2	2	3	2	3.60

ALL-STAR GAME RECORD

Year	League	IP.	W.	L.	Pct.	H.	R.	ER.	SO.	BB.	ERA.
1976—American		2	0	0	.000	3	3	3	0	1	6.00

Named to American League All-Star Team for the 1977 game; replaced due to injury.
Named to American League All-Star Team for 1978 game; did not play.

FRANKLIN TAVERAS (FABIAN)

Name pronounced Tuh-VAIR-us

(Frank)

Born December 24, 1950, at Villa Vasquez, Dominican Republic.
Height, 6.00. Weight, 170.
Throws and bats righthanded.

Established major league record for most games, two clubs, season (164), 1979.
Tied major league records for most games, season (164), 1979; most strikeouts, game (5), May 1, 1979; fewest sacrifice flies and most at bats, season (0 and 680), 1979.
Led National League in stolen bases with 70 in 1977.
Major league stolen bases: 1974 (13), 1975 (17), 1976 (58), 1977 (70), 1978 (46), 1979 (44), 1980 (32). Total—280.
Led Western Carolinas League shortstops in double plays with 56 in 1970 and International League with 96 in 1973.

Year	Club	League	Pos.	G.	AB.	R.	H.	2B.	3B.	HR.	RBI.	B.A.	PO.	A.	E.	F.A.
1968—Clinton	Midw.	2-3-S	21	58	7	12	1	0	0	5	.207	28	34	12	.838
1968—Brad'ton Pir.	Gulf C.	SS	14	50	18	17	0	2	0	8	.340	21	36	12	.826
1968—Salem	Carol.	2B-SS	14	26	4	5	0	0	0	2	.192	10	19	1	.967
1969—Salem	Carol.	2B	20	57	5	11	0	2	0	4	.193	29	46	7	.915
1969—Gastonia	W. Car.	2-S	80	308	40	63	2	3	0	15	.205	147	228	26	.935
1969—Geneva	NYP	S-2-3	13	54	9	19	1	1	0	6	.352	17	39	9	.862
1970—Gastonia	W. Car.	SS	*122	442	67	115	13	2	1	41	.260	*193	*337	37	*.935
1971—Waterbury	East.	SS	87	314	52	65	12	2	2	19	.207	112	258	25	.937
1971—Charleston	Int.	SS	48	146	19	39	2	2	0	11	.267	65	127	9	.955
1971—Pittsburgh	Nat.	PR	1	0	0	0	0	0	0	0	.000	0	0	0	.000
1972—Charleston	Int.	SS	133	455	52	112	14	3	1	46	.246	202	411	30	*.953
1972—Pittsburgh	Nat.	SS	4	3	0	0	0	0	0	0	.000	2	2	0	1.000
1973—Charleston	Int.	*S-3-O	145	462	51	112	7	3	2	44	.242	*222	*429	*43	.938
1974—Pittsburgh	Nat.	SS	126	333	33	82	4	2	0	26	.246	170	321	31	.941
1975—Pittsburgh	Nat.	SS	134	378	44	80	9	4	0	23	.212	200	369	28	.953

Year Club League	Pos.	G.	AB.	R.	H.	2B.	3B.	HR.	RBI.	B.A.	PO.	A.	E.	F.A.
1976—Pittsburgh.........Nat.	SS	144	519	76	134	8	6	0	24	.258	210	481	35	.952
1977—Pittsburgh.........Nat.	SS	147	544	72	137	20	10	1	29	.252	178	449	25	.962
1978—Pittsburgh ....Nat.	SS	157	654	81	182	31	9	0	38	.278	216	448	38	.946
1979—Pitt.†-New York Nat.	SS	*164	680	93	178	29	9	1	34	.262	287	464	28	.964
1980—New York ....Nat.	SS	141	562	65	157	27	0	0	25	.279	237	347	25	.959
Major League Totals		1018	3673	464	950	128	40	2	199	.259	1500	2881	210	.954

Signed as free agent by Pittsburgh Pirates' organization, January 8, 1968.
†Traded to New York Mets for Pitcher Greg Field and Shortstop Tim Foli, April 19, 1979.

CHAMPIONSHIP SERIES RECORD

Year Club League	Pos.	G.	AB.	R.	H.	2B.	3B.	HR.	RBI.	B.A.	PO.	A.	E.	F.A.
1974—Pittsburgh.........Nat.	SS	2	2	0	0	0	0	0	0	.000	2	1	0	1.000
1975—Pittsburgh.........Nat.	SS	3	7	0	1	0	0	0	1	.143	4	6	0	1.000
Championship Series Totals.............		5	9	0	1	0	0	0	1	.111	6	7	0	1.000

KENTON CHARLES TEKULVE

Name pronounced tuh-KULL-vee.

(Kent)

Born March 5, 1947, at Cincinnati, O.
Height, 6.04. Weight, 175.
Throws and bats righthanded.
Hobbies—Golf and bowling.
Attended Marietta College, Marietta, O.; received Bachelor of
Science degree in Physical Education.

Major League saves: 1974 (0), 1975 (5), 1976 (9), 1977 (7), 1978 (31), 1979 (31), 1980 (21). Total—104.

Year Club League	G.	IP.	W.	L.	Pct.	H.	R.	ER.	SO.	BB.	ERA.
1969—Geneva ....NYP	9	53	6	2	.750	40	15	10	60	22	1.70
1970—Salem ....Carolina	41	79	4	6	.400	68	29	17	75	51	1.94
1971—Salem ....Carolina	47	75	11	5	.688	77	36	29	62	31	3.48
1971—Waterbury ....Eastern	2	3	0	0	.000	3	0	0	0	2	0.00
1972—Sherbrooke ....Eastern	31	72	7	6	.538	61	24	21	54	22	2.63
1972—Charleston ....Int'national	9	22	2	1	.667	22	10	10	9	10	4.09
1973—Sherbrooke ....Eastern	*57	94	●12	4	*.750	70	24	16	89	35	1.53
1974—Charleston ....Int'national	35	60	6	3	.667	50	20	15	38	21	2.25
1974—Pittsburgh ....National	8	9	1	1	.500	12	6	6	6	5	6.00
1975—Charleston ....Int'national	24	71	5	4	.556	47	23	14	46	19	1.77
1975—Pittsburgh ....National	34	56	1	2	.333	43	20	14	28	23	2.25
1976—Pittsburgh ....National	64	103	5	3	.625	91	30	28	68	25	2.45
1977—Pittsburgh ....National	72	103	10	1	.909	89	41	35	59	33	3.06
1978—Pittsburgh ....National	*91	135	8	7	.533	115	44	35	77	55	2.33
1979—Pittsburgh† ....National	*94	134	10	8	.556	109	46	41	75	49	2.75
1980—Pittsburgh ....National	78	93	8	12	.400	96	39	35	47	40	3.39
Major League Totals	441	633	43	34	.558	555	226	194	360	230	2.76

Signed as free agent by Pittsburgh Pirates' organization, July 16, 1969.
†Appeared in one game as outfielder.

CHAMPIONSHIP SERIES RECORD

Year Club League	G.	IP.	W.	L.	Pct.	H.	R.	ER.	SO.	BB.	ERA.
1975—Pittsburgh ....National	2	1⅓	0	0	.000	3	1	1	2	1	6.75
1979—Pittsburgh ....National	2	2⅔	0	0	.000	2	1	1	2	2	3.38
Championship Series Totals	4	4	0	0	.000	5	2	2	4	3	4.50

WORLD SERIES RECORD

Established World Series record for most saves, seven-game Series (3), 1979.

Year Club League	G.	IP.	W.	L.	Pct.	H.	R.	ER.	SO.	BB.	ERA.
1979—Pittsburgh ....National	5	9⅓	0	1	.000	4	3	3	10	3	2.89

ALL-STAR GAME RECORD

Member of National League All-Star Team in 1980; did not play.

THOMAS JOHN TELLMANN

(Tom)

Born March 29, 1954, at Warren, Pa.
Height, 6.04. Weight, 185.
Throws and bats righthanded.
Attended Grand Canyon College, Phoenix, Ariz.; received Bachelor
of Arts degree in Physical Education.

Led California League in saves with 12 in 1977.
Led Pacific Coast League in shutouts with 4 in 1980.

Year Club League	G.	IP.	W.	L.	Pct.	H.	R.	ER.	SO.	BB.	ERA.
1976—Walla Walla ....Northwest	17	69	3	4	.429	56	37	25	46	33	3.26
1977—Reno...................................California	48	88	8	7	.533	92	50	33	82	32	3.38
1978—Amarillo ....Texas	48	76	5	6	.455	74	29	22	48	25	2.61

Year Club	League	G.	IP.	W.	L.	Pct.	H.	R.	ER.	SO.	BB.	ERA.
1979—Hawaii	P. Coast	44	83	4	8	.333	98	37	27	51	40	2.93
1979—San Diego	National	1	3	0	0	.000	7	5	5	1	0	15.00
1980—Hawaii	P. Coast	24	170	13	5	.722	155	74	61	83	58	3.23
1980—San Diego	National	6	22	3	0	1.000	23	5	4	9	8	1.64
Major League Totals		7	25	3	0	1.000	30	10	9	10	8	3.24

Selected by San Diego Padres' organization in 11th round of free-agent draft, June 8, 1976.

GARRY LEWIS TEMPLETON

Born March 24, 1956, at Lockey, Tex.
Height, 5.11. Weight, 190.
Throws right and bats left and righthanded.
Brother of Ken Templeton, former minor league outfielder for Oakland A's, 1972-74 and son of Spiavia Templeton, former infielder in the Negro Leagues.

Established major league record by collecting 100 or more hits righthanded and lefthanded, 1979.
Tied major league record for most consecutive seasons leading league, three-base hits (3), 1977 through 1979.
Tied modern major league record for most three-base hits by switch hitter, season, (19), 1979.
Major League stolen bases: 1976 (11), 1977 (28), 1978 (34), 1979 (26), 1980 (31). Total—130.
Led National League shortstops in double plays with 108 in 1978.
Tied for National League lead in double plays by shortstops with 102 in 1979.
Named shortstop on THE SPORTING NEWS National League All-Star Team, 1977, 1979 and 1980.
Named shortstop on THE SPORTING NEWS National League Silver Bat team, 1980.
Named American Association Rookie of the Year, 1976.
Received reported $40,000 bonus to sign with St. Louis Cardinals, 1974.

Year Club	League	Pos.	G.	AB.	R.	H.	2B.	3B.	HR.	RBI.	B.A.	PO.	A.	E.	F.A.
1974—Sarasota Cards	Gulf C.	SS	18	71	11	19	1	0	3	10	.268	15	41	3	.949
1974—St. Petersburg	Fla. St.	SS	23	95	3	20	1	0	0	2	.211	42	64	7	.938
1975—St. Petersburg	Fla. St.	SS	82	349	50	92	7	8	1	32	.264	130	253	29	.930
1975—Arkansas	Tex.	SS	42	177	36	71	9	4	2	20	.401	60	131	18	.914
1976—Tulsa	A.A.	*S-3-O	106	443	65	142	24	*15	6	38	.321	*178	319	34	.936
1976—St. Louis	Nat.	SS	53	213	32	62	8	2	1	17	.291	111	172	24	.922
1977—St. Louis	Nat.	SS	153	621	94	200	19	*18	8	79	.322	285	453	32	.958
1978—St. Louis	Nat.	SS	155	647	82	181	31	*13	2	47	.280	*285	523	*40	.953
1979—St. Louis	Nat.	SS	154	672	105	*211	32	*19	9	62	.314	*292	525	*34	.960
1980—St. Louis†‡	Nat.	SS	118	504	83	161	19	9	4	43	.319	223	451	*29	.959
Major League Totals			633	2657	396	815	109	61	24	248	.307	1196	2124	159	.954

Selected by St. Louis Cardinals' organization in 1st round (13th player selected) of free-agent draft, June 5, 1974.

†On disabled list, July 24 to August 14, 1980.
‡On supplemental disabled list, August 24 to September 8, 1980.

ALL-STAR GAME RECORD

Year League	Pos.	AB.	R.	H.	2B.	3B.	HR.	RBI.	B.A.	PO.	A.	E.	F.A.
1977—National	SS	1	1	1	1	0	0	0	1.000	1	2	1	.750

Named to National League All-Star Team for 1979 game; declined.

FURY GENE TENACE

Name pronounced TEN-nis.

(Known by middle name.)
Born October 10, 1946, at Russelton, Pa.
Height, 6.00. Weight, 195.
Throws and bats righthanded.
Hobby—Hunting.

Established major league records for fewest singles, season (150 or more games), 58, in 1974; fewest chances offered by first baseman, two consecutive games, 17 innings (5), August 31 and September 1, 1974.
Tied major league records for fewest chances accepted and fewest putouts, first baseman, game, 0, September 1, 1974.
Tied American League record for most chances accepted by catcher, inning (4), May 24, 1975 (fifth inning).
Led American League in bases on balls with 110 in 1974.
Led National League in bases on balls with 125 in 1977.
Led National League catchers in fielding percentage with .998 in 1979.
Led Carolina League catchers in double plays with 13 in 1968 and Southern League catchers with 7 in 1969.

Year Club	League	Pos.	G.	AB.	R.	H.	2B.	3B.	HR.	RBI.	B.A.	PO.	A.	E.	F.A.
1965—Shelby	W. Car.	OF	32	93	10	17	2	1	2	6	.183	22	2	1	.960
1966—Leesburg	Fla. St.	1-O-3-P	91	228	28	48	8	2	1	24	.211	310	23	12	.965
1967—Peninsula	Carol.	OF	3	7	0	0	0	0	0	1	.000	2	1	0	1.000
1967—Leesburg	Fla. St.	C-I-P	106	354	47	94	12	2	6	44	.266	204	14	11	.952
1968—Peninsula	Car.	C-O-3-1	132	435	78	123	20	3	21	71	.283	639	68	17	.977
1969—Birmingham	South.	C-OF-3	89	276	56	88	20	4	20	74	.319	442	51	7	.986
1969—Oakland	Amer.	C	16	38	1	6	0	0	1	2	.158	61	6	0	1.000
1970—Iowa	A.A.	C-OF	93	319	54	90	24	1	16	63	.282	534	57	9	.985
1970—Oakland	Amer.	C	38	105	19	32	6	0	7	20	.305	180	18	2	.990
1971—Oakland	Amer.	C-OF	65	179	26	49	7	0	7	25	.274	300	20	2	.994

Year Club	League	Pos.	G.	AB.	R.	H.	2B.	3B.	HR.	RBI.	B.A.	PO.	A.	E.	F.A.
1972—Oakland ....Amer.		C-O-INF	82	227	22	51	5	3	5	32	.225	329	23	7	.981
1973—Oakland ....Amer.		1-C-2	160	510	83	132	18	2	24	84	.259	1218	71	14	.989
1974—Oakland ....Amer.		1-C-2	158	484	71	102	17	1	26	73	.211	1110	83	10	.992
1975—Oakland ....Amer.		C-1B	158	498	83	127	17	0	29	87	.255	942	84	11	.989
1976—Oakland†‡ ....Amer.		1B-C	128	417	64	104	19	1	22	66	.249	840	56	8	.991
1977—San Diego.........Nat.		C-1B-3B	147	437	66	102	24	4	15	61	.233	820	112	16	.983
1978—San Diego ....Nat.		1B-C-3B	142	401	60	90	18	4	16	61	.224	944	79	8	.992
1979—San Diego ....Nat.		C-1B	151	463	61	122	16	4	20	67	.263	995	83	8	.993
1980—San Diego§ ....Nat.		C-1B	133	316	46	70	11	1	17	50	.222	540	56	11	.982
American League Totals.................			805	2458	369	603	89	7	121	389	.245	4980	361	54	.990
National League Totals...................			573	1617	233	384	69	13	68	239	.237	3299	330	43	.988
Major League Totals			1378	4075	602	987	158	20	189	628	.242	8279	691	97	.989

Selected by Kansas City A's organization in free-agent draft, June, 1965.

†On disabled list, April 30 to May 27, 1976.

‡Granted free agency, November 1, 1976; signed with San Diego Padres, December 14, 1976.

§Traded with Pitchers Rollie Fingers and Bob Shirley and a player to be named later to St. Louis Cardinals for Catchers Terry Kennedy and Steve Swisher, Pitchers John Littlefield, Al Olmsted, Kim Seaman and John Urrea and Infielder Mike Phillips, December 8, 1980; Catcher Bob Geren traded to Cardinals' organization completing deal December 10, 1980.

PITCHING RECORD

Year Club	League	G.	IP.	W.	L.	Pct.	H.	R.	ER.	SO.	BB.	ERA.
1966—Leesburg ....Florida St.		3	17	0	1	.000	24	7	4	8	6	2.12
1967—Leesburg ....Florida St.		4	8	0	0	.000	4	0	0	8	1	0.00
1968—Peninsula...........................Carolina		2	3	0	0	.000	4	1	1	0	1	3.00

CHAMPIONSHIP SERIES RECORD

Established American League Championship Series record for most bases on balls, total Series (13).

Tied American League Championship Series record for most positions played, total Series (3).

Year Club	League	Pos.	G.	AB.	R.	H.	2B.	3B.	HR.	RBI.	B.A.	PO.	A.	E.	F.A.
1971—Oakland ....Amer.		C	1	3	0	0	0	0	0	0	.000	8	0	0	1.000
1972—Oakland ....Amer.		C-2B	5	17	1	1	0	0	0	1	.059	21	5	1	.963
1973—Oakland ....Amer.		1B-C	5	17	3	4	1	0	0	0	.235	40	3	0	1.000
1974—Oakland ....Amer.		1B	4	11	1	0	0	0	0	1	.000	35	2	0	1.000
1975—Oakland ....Amer.		C-1B	3	9	0	0	0	0	0	0	.000	19	1	0	1.000
Championship Series Totals.............			18	57	5	5	1	0	0	2	.088	123	11	1	.993

WORLD SERIES RECORD

Established World Series record for slugging percentage, 7-game series, .913, 1972.

Tied World Series records for most home runs, seven-game Series (4), 1972; most bases on balls, seven-game Series (11), 1973; most double plays by first baseman, game (4), October 17, 1973.

First player to hit two home runs in first two World Series at bats, October 14, 1972.

Year Club	League	Pos.	G.	AB.	R.	H.	2B.	3B.	HR.	RBI.	B.A.	PO.	A.	E.	F.A.
1972—Oakland ....Amer.		C-1B	7	23	5	8	1	0	4	9	.348	48	5	1	.981
1973—Oakland ....Amer.		1B-C	7	19	0	3	1	0	0	3	.158	57	2	2	.967
1974—Oakland ....Amer.		1B	5	9	0	2	0	0	0	0	.222	20	1	0	1.000
World Series Totals			19	51	5	13	2	0	4	12	.255	125	8	3	.978

ALL-STAR GAME RECORD

Year League	Pos.	AB.	R.	H.	2B.	3B.	HR.	RBI.	B.A.	PO.	A.	E.	F.A.
1975—American..............................	1B-C	3	1	0	0	0	0	0	.000	4	0	1	.800

JERRY WAYNE TERRELL

Born July 13, 1946, at Elysian, Minn.

Height, 6.00. Weight, 170.

Throws and bats righthanded.

Hobbies—Numismatics and music.

Attended Mankato State College, Mankato, Minn.; received Bachelor of Arts degree in Accounting.

Led New York-Pennsylvania League second basemen in chances accepted with 350 and double plays with 48 in 1968.

Led Carolina League second basemen in double plays with 81 in 1972.

Year Club	League	Pos.	G.	AB.	R.	H.	2B.	3B.	HR.	RBI.	B.A.	PO.	A.	E.	F.A.
1968—Auburn ....NYP		2B	73	*304	65	90	●17	5	5	36	.296	*164	186	18	.951
1969—†					(In Military Service)										
1970—Lynchburg ....Carol.		2B	118	463	60	129	16	5	1	36	.279	*332	341	20	*.971
1971—Charlotte..........South.		2B	109	424	61	98	8	1	0	32	.231	267	271	15	.973
1972—Tacoma.............P. C.		2B	119	496	82	144	20	7	2	35	.290	272	321	14	.977
1973—Minnesota ....Amer.		S-3-2-O	124	438	43	116	15	2	1	32	.265	170	298	18	.963
1974—Minnesota ....Amer.		IF-OF	116	229	43	56	4	6	0	19	.245	114	179	9	.970
1975—Tacoma.............P. C.		2B-3B	45	178	35	57	13	1	2	14	.320	88	112	9	.957
1975—Minnesota ....Amer.		IF-OF	108	385	48	110	16	2	1	36	.286	267	232	14	.973
1976—Minnesota ....Amer.		2-3-S-O	89	171	29	42	3	1	0	8	.246	82	122	8	.962
1977—Minnesota‡.......Amer.		3-2-1-S-O	93	214	32	48	6	0	1	20	.224	58	129	7	.964
1978—Kansas City ......Amer.		2-3-S-1	73	133	14	27	1	0	0	8	.203	88	103	4	.979
1979—Kansas City § ....Amer.		3-2-S-P	31	40	5	12	3	0	1	2	.300	10	28	1	.974

Year	Club	League	Pos.	G.	AB.	R.	H.	2B.	3B.	HR.	RBI.	B.A.	PO.	A.	E.	F.A.
1980–Omaha...............	A.A.	O-1-3-S-2	41	163	25	47	6	0	2	21	.288	175	51	4	.983
1980–Kansas City	Amer.	O-2-1	23	16	4	1	0	0	0	0	.063	29	6	0	1.000
Major League Totals			657	1626	218	412	48	11	4	125	.253	818	1097	61	.969

PITCHING RECORD

Year	Club	League	G.	IP.	W.	L.	Pct.	H.	R.	ER.	SO.	BB.	ERA.
1979–Kansas City	American	1	1	0	0	.000	0	0	0	0	0	0.00
1980–Kansas City	American	1	1	0	0	.000	1	5	0	0	1	0.00
Major League Totals..............................		2	2	0	0	.000	1	5	0	0	1	0.00

Selected by Minnesota Twins' organization in 18th round of free-agent draft, June 7, 1968.
†On military list, May 20 through September 23, 1969.
‡Granted free agency, November 5, 1977; signed by Kansas City Royals, November 29, 1977.
§On supplemental disabled list, April 5 to May 9 and July 6 to July 21, 1979.

MARK ROBERT TEUTSCH

Born August 25, 1957, at Plainfield, N. J.
Height, 6.01. Weight, 175.
Throws and bats righthanded.

Year	Club	League	G.	IP.	W.	L.	Pct.	H.	R.	ER.	SO.	BB.	ERA.
1978–Saltillo................................	Mexican	22	95	6	6	.500	127	58	49	34	48	4.64
1979–Appleton..............................	Midwest	26	61	4	4	.500	63	34	30	50	32	4.43
1979–Knoxville	Southern	17	37	2	2	.500	40	31	29	27	13	7.05
1980–Glens Falls	Eastern	*58	119	13	6	.684	113	53	43	67	55	3.25

Signed as free agent by Chicago White Sox' organization, March 12, 1978.

DERREL OSBON THOMAS

Born January 14, 1951, at Los Angeles, Calif.
Height, 6.00. Weight, 160.
Throws right and bats right and lefthanded.
Hobbies–Singing and dancing.

Year	Club	League	Pos.	G.	AB.	R.	H.	2B.	3B.	HR.	RBI.	B.A.	PO.	A.	E.	F.A.
1969–Cocoa................	Fla. St.	SS	33	114	17	33	5	3	0	8	.289	57	75	22	.857
1969–Okla. City..........	A. A.	SS-OF	36	154	21	48	4	6	0	17	.312	50	64	11	.912
1970–Columbus	South.	SS-2B	38	156	24	38	5	4	4	12	.244	60	95	14	.917
1970–Okla. City..........	A. A.	S-2-O	75	272	39	73	5	6	4	21	.268	126	156	20	.934
1971–Okla. City..........	A. A.	*2B-SS	122	486	74	139	22	8	3	42	.286	*257	325	15	*.975
1971–Houston†	Nat.	2B	5	5	0	0	0	0	0	0	.000	3	2	0	1.000
1972–Hawaii	P. C.	OF-2B	6	27	2	4	2	0	0	3	.148	13	6	2	.905
1972–San Diego..........	Nat.	2-S-O	130	500	48	115	15	5	5	36	.230	290	357	26	.961
1973–San Diego..........	Nat.	SS-2B	113	404	41	96	7	1	0	22	.238	211	324	37	.935
1974–San Diego†	Nat.	2-3-O-S	141	523	48	129	24	6	3	41	.247	310	336	18	.973
1975–San Francisco ...	Nat.	2B-OF	144	540	99	149	21	9	6	48	.276	349	372	19	.974
1976–San Francisco§..	Nat.	2-O-3-S	81	272	38	63	5	4	2	19	.232	163	215	15	.962
1977–San Francisco x.	Nat.	O-2-3-1	148	506	75	135	13	10	8	44	.267	307	158	14	.971
1978–San Diego yz	Nat.	O-2-3-1	128	352	36	80	10	2	3	26	.227	328	168	12	.976
1979–Los Angeles	Nat.	0-3-2-S-1	141	406	47	104	15	4	5	44	.256	298	38	5	.985
1980–Los Angeles	Nat.	O-S-2-C-3	117	297	32	79	18	3	1	22	.266	203	175	14	.964
Major League Totals			1148	3805	464	950	128	44	33	402	.250	2462	2145	160	.966

Selected by Houston Astros' organization in 1st round (first player selected) of free-agent draft, February 1, 1969.
†Traded with Pitchers Bill Greif and Mark Schaeffer to San Diego Padres for Pitcher Dave Roberts, December 3, 1971.
‡Traded to San Francisco Giants for Second Baseman Tito Fuentes and Pitcher Butch Metzger, December 6, 1974.
§On disabled list, July 12 to September 15, 1976.
xTraded to San Diego Padres for Catcher-Infielder Mike Ivie, February 28, 1978.
yOn supplemental disabled list, July 3 to July 22, 1978.
zGranted free agency, November 2, 1978; signed by Los Angeles Dodgers November 14, 1978.

JAMES GORMAN THOMAS, III

(Known by middle name.)

Born December 12, 1950, at Charleston, S. C.
Height, 6.03. Weight, 200.
Throws and bats righthanded.
Hobbies–Drag racing, reading and rock music.
Attended Baptist College, Charleston, S. C.

Tied major league records for most strikeouts, two consecutive games (8), July 27 and 28, 1975; most strikeouts, three consecutive games (10), July 27 through 29, 1975; most strikeouts, season (175), 1979.
Tied American League records for most consecutive strikeouts (8), July 27 through 29, 1975; most strikeouts, season (175), 1979.
Led Texas League batters in strikeouts with 171 and tied for lead in double plays by outfielders with 4 in 1972.
Led Midwest League batters in strikeouts with 170 in 1971.
Led Pacific Coast League batters in strikeouts with 175 in 1974.
Led Pacific Coast League in total bases with 320 in 1977.

Led American League batters in strikeouts with 175 in 1979 and with 170 in 1980.
Tied for American League lead in strikeouts with 133 in 1978.

Year Club League	Pos.	G.	AB.	R.	H.	2B.	3B.	HR.	RBI.	B.A.	PO.	A.	E.	F.A.
1969–Billings ....Pion.	SS-1B	41	142	23	42	10	3	4	28	.296	94	82	27	.867
1970–Clinton† ....Midw.	S-3-2	85	297	36	63	5	4	8	39	.212	105	186	28	.912
1971–Danville ....Midw.	OF-3	121	457	82	112	20	4	*31	83	.245	195	14	10	.954
1972–San Antonio.......Texas	*O-1	135	465	70	112	22	2	*26	68	.214	*305	*24	6	*.982
1973–Evansville ....A. A.	OF	46	146	26	31	6	0	8	18	.212	66	3	4	.945
1973–Milwaukee ....Amer.	OF-3B	59	155	16	29	7	1	2	11	.187	87	1	4	.957
1974–Sacramento.......P. C.	OF	138	474	117	141	15	1	51	122	.297	302	16	10	.970
1974–Milwaukee ....Amer.	OF	17	46	10	12	4	0	2	11	.261	26	0	0	1.000
1975–Milwaukee ....Amer.	OF	121	240	34	43	12	2	10	28	.179	215	5	9	.961
1976–Milwaukee ....Amer.	OF-3B	99	227	27	45	9	2	8	36	.198	211	4	4	.982
1977–Spokane‡§ ....P. C.	OF	143	500	114	161	41	5	36	114	.322	325	13	7	*.980
1978–Milwaukee ....Amer.	OF	137	452	70	111	24	1	32	86	.246	345	5	6	.983
1979–Milwaukee ....Amer.	OF	156	557	97	136	29	0	*45	123	.244	435	4	4	.991
1980–Milwaukee ....Amer.	OF	162	628	78	150	26	3	38	105	.239	455	6	7	.985
Major League Totals		751	2305	332	526	111	9	137	400	.228	1774	25	34	.981

Selected by Seattle Pilots' organization in 1st round (21st player selected) of free-agent draft, June 5, 1969.
†On restricted list, March 4 through May 30, 1970.
‡Traded to Texas Rangers (completion of deal in which Milwaukee received Outfielder-First Baseman Ed Kirkpatrick, August 20, 1977), October 25, 1977.
§Sold to Milwaukee Brewers, February 8, 1978.

RANDALL WAYNE THOMAS
(Randy)

Born April 18, 1955, at Lynchburg, Va.
Height, 5.10. Weight, 165.
Throws and bats righthanded.
Attended Lynchburg College, Lynchburg, Va.

Year Club League	Pos.	G.	AB.	R.	H.	2B.	3B.	HR.	RBI.	B.A.	PO.	A.	E.	F.A.
1976–Johnson City .....Appal.	SS	40	158	31	43	6	1	1	10	.272	55	135	7	.964
1976–St. Petersburg...Fla. St.	SS	17	46	2	6	0	0	0	2	.130	18	46	2	.970
1977–Gastonia†.........W.Car.	SS-3B	87	258	38	52	7	1	0	26	.202	111	240	24	.936
1978–Arkansas ....Texas	SS	116	384	52	98	9	1	0	32	.255	200	371	28	.953
1979–Arkansas ....Texas	SS	111	349	42	88	11	0	2	34	.252	176	296	20	.959
1980–Springfield........A.A.	SS	93	264	25	65	5	0	2	22	.246	126	181	15	.953

Selected by St. Louis Cardinals' organization in 4th round of free-agent draft, June 8, 1976.
†On disabled list, June 3 to June 28, 1977.

ROY JUSTIN THOMAS

Born June 22, 1953, at Quantico, Va.
Height, 6.05. Weight, 215.
Throws and bats righthanded.
Hobbies—Billiards, basketball and trap shooting.
Attended University of Tampa, Tampa, Fla., and De Anza College, Cupertino, Calif.

Pitched seven-inning, 2-0 no-hit victory against West Haven, August 20, 1974 (2nd game of doubleheader).
Led Eastern League in games started by pitchers with 27 in 1974.
Led Carolina League in shutouts with 6 in 1973.
Led American Association pitchers in wild pitches with 17 in 1976.
Received reported $75,000 bonus to sign with Philadelphia Phillies, 1971.

Year Club League	G.	IP.	W.	L.	Pct.	H.	R.	ER.	SO.	BB.	ERA.
1971–Walla Walla ....Northwest	7	12	0	3	.000	19	22	14	8	16	10.50
1972–Spartanburg......................W. Carol.	24	152	11	7	.611	128	67	58	128	62	3.43
1973–Rocky Mount......................Carolina	26	169	•15	8	.652	119	53	42	*193	77	*2.24
1973–Reading ....Eastern	2	16	2	0	1.000	11	2	2	14	7	1.13
1974–Reading ....Eastern	27	•191	14	11	.560	154	77	55	*168	89	2.59
1974–Toledo ....Int'national	2	7	0	0	.000	5	3	1	5	2	1.29
1975–Toledo ....Int'national	19	119	4	9	.308	112	63	53	95	49	4.01
1975–Reading†..............................Eastern	10	67	6	3	.667	50	22	19	53	29	2.55
1976–Iowa‡§ ....Am. Assoc.	27	168	6	11	.353	167	89	70	103	72	3.75
1977–Charleston ....Int'national	44	168	11	6	.647	151	63	59	71	65	3.16
1977–Houston ....National	4	6	0	0	.000	5	2	2	4	3	3.00
1978–Charleston x ....Int'national	28	66	9	4	.692	63	28	23	40	30	3.14
1978–St. Louis ....National	16	28	1	1	.500	21	14	12	16	16	3.86
1979–Springfield....................Am. Assoc.	17	74	5	6	.455	79	55	48	85	31	5.84
1979–St. Louis ....National	26	77	3	4	.429	66	29	25	44	24	2.92
1980–St. Louis ....National	24	55	2	3	.400	59	32	29	22	25	4.75
1980–Springfield y..................Am. Assoc.	19	37	5	1	.833	34	18	14	36	18	3.41
Major League Totals	70	166	6	8	.429	151	77	68	86	68	3.69

Selected by Philadelphia Phillies' organization in 1st round (sixth player selected) of free-agent draft, June 8, 1971.

†Traded with Pitcher Dick Ruthven and Infielder-Outfielder Alan Bannister by Philadelphia Phillies to Chicago White Sox for Pitcher Jim Kaat and Shortstop Mike Buskey, December 10, 1975.
‡Selected by Seattle Mariners in American League expansion draft, November 5, 1976.
§Traded to Houston Astros for Infielder Larry Milbourne, March 30, 1977.
xSold on waivers to St. Louis Cardinals, June 23, 1978.
yDrafted by Oakland A's, December 8, 1980.

GARY LEAH THOMASSON

Name pronounced Tom-as-son.

Born July 29, 1951, at San Diego, Calif.
Height, 6.01. Weight, 180.
Throws and bats lefthanded.
Hobbies—Hunting, fishing and playing the guitar.

Tied major league record for fewest putouts by first baseman, game (0), July 31, 1977.
Tied for Midwest League lead in double plays by outfielders with 4 in 1970.

Year Club	League	Pos.	G.	AB.	R.	H.	2B.	3B.	HR.	RBI.	B.A.	PO.	A.	E.	F.A.
1969—Great Falls	Pion.	OF-1-P	49	117	25	42	7	5	0	12	.359	101	5	8	.980
1970—Decatur	Midw.	OF	115	424	76	115	18	6	8	53	.271	179	14	8	.960
1971—Amarillo	Texas	OF	126	418	57	114	14	7	6	55	.273	287	7	10	.967
1972—Phoenix	P.C.	●1B-OF	138	482	88	136	32	8	11	76	.282	865	34	●14	.985
1972—San Francisco	Nat.	1B-OF	10	27	5	9	1	1	0	1	.333	60	1	0	1.000
1973—San Francisco	Nat.	1B-OF	112	235	35	67	10	4	4	30	.285	312	15	6	.982
1974—San Francisco	Nat.	OF-1B	120	315	41	77	14	3	2	29	.244	235	17	7	.973
1975—San Francisco	Nat.	OF-1B	114	326	44	74	12	3	7	32	.227	293	18	7	.978
1976—San Francisco†	Nat.	OF-1B	103	328	45	85	20	5	8	38	.259	376	20	12	.970
1977—San Francisco‡	Nat.	OF-1B	145	446	63	114	24	6	17	71	.256	404	11	14	.967
1978—Oak.§-N.Y.x	Amer.	OF-1B	102	270	37	63	8	2	8	36	.233	212	11	7	.970
1979—Los Angeles	Nat.	OF-1B	115	315	39	78	11	1	14	45	.248	196	4	4	.980
1980—Los Angeles y	Nat.	OF-1B	80	111	6	24	3	0	1	12	.216	38	1	1	.975
National League Totals			799	2103	278	528	95	23	53	258	.251	1914	87	51	.975
American League Totals			102	270	37	63	8	2	8	36	.233	212	11	7	.970
Major League Totals			901	2373	315	591	103	25	61	294	.249	2126	98	58	.975

Selected by San Francisco Giants' organization in 25th round of free-agent draft, June 5, 1969.

†On disabled list, April 29 to June 2, 1976.

‡Traded with Catcher Gary Alexander, Pitchers Dave Heaverlo, Alan Wirth, John Johnson and Phillip Huffman, a player to be named later and cash to Oakland A's for Pitcher Vida Blue, March 15, 1978; Shortstop Mario Guerrero sent to A's to complete deal, April 10, 1978.

§Traded to New York Yankees for Outfielder Dell Alston, Infielder Mickey Klutts and $50,000, June 15, 1978.

xTraded to Los Angeles Dodgers for Catcher Brad Gulden, February 15, 1979.

ySold to Yomiuri Giants of Japanese baseball, December 22, 1980.

PITCHING RECORD

Year Club	League	G.	IP.	W.	L.	Pct.	H.	R.	ER.	SO.	BB.	ERA.
1969—Great Falls	Pioneer	1	1	0	0	.000	0	2	2	1	5	18.00

CHAMPIONSHIP SERIES RECORD

Year Club	League	Pos.	G.	AB.	R.	H.	2B.	3B.	HR.	RBI.	B.A.	PO.	A.	E.	F.A.
1978—New York	Amer.	PH-OF	3	1	0	0	0	0	0	0	.000	2	0	0	1.000

WORLD SERIES RECORD

Year Club	League	Pos.	G.	AB.	R.	H.	2B.	3B.	HR.	RBI.	B.A.	PO.	A.	E.	F.A.
1978—New York	Amer.	OF	3	4	0	1	0	0	0	0	.250	3	0	0	1.000

JASON DOLPH THOMPSON

Born July 6, 1954, at Hollywood, Calif.
Height, 6.03. Weight, 210.
Throws and bats lefthanded.
Attended California State University at Northridge, Northridge, Calif.

Led American League first basemen in total chances with 1,712 in 1977.
Led American League first basemen in double plays with 153 in 1978.

Year Club	League	Pos.	G.	AB.	R.	H.	2B.	3B.	HR.	RBI.	B.A.	PO.	A.	E.	F.A.
1975—Montgomery	South.	1B	75	222	42	72	12	1	10	38	.324	633	47	10	.986
1976—Evansville	A.A.	1B	4	16	3	5	0	0	3	6	.313	29	7	0	1.000
1976—Detroit	Amer.	1B	123	412	45	90	12	1	17	54	.218	1157	88	8	.994
1977—Detroit	Amer.	1B	158	585	87	158	24	5	31	105	.270	●1599	97	16	.991
1978—Detroit	Amer.	1B	153	589	79	169	25	3	26	96	.287	1503	92	11	.993
1979—Detroit	Amer.	1B	145	492	58	121	16	1	20	79	.246	1176	91	8	.994
1980—Det.†-Calif.	Amer.	1B	138	438	69	126	19	0	21	90	.288	679	51	0	1.000
Major League Totals			717	2516	338	664	96	10	115	424	.264	6114	419	43	.993

Selected by Los Angeles Dodgers' organization in 15th round of free-agent draft, June 6, 1972.

Selected by Detroit Tigers' organization in 4th round of free-agent draft, June 4, 1975.

†Traded to California Angels for Outfielder Al Cowens, May 27, 1980.

ALL-STAR GAME RECORD

Year League	Pos.	AB.	R.	H.	2B.	3B.	HR.	RBI.	B.A.	PO.	A.	E.	F.A.
1978—American	PH	1	0	0	0	0	0	0	.000	0	0	0	.000

Member of American League All-Star Team in 1977; did not play.

DID YOU KNOW—

That Cincinnati and Oakland will play in the Hall of Fame game in Cooperstown? The date is August 3.

VERNON SCOT THOMPSON

(Known by middle name.)

Born December 7, 1955, at Grove City, Pa.
Height, 6.03. Weight, 175.
Throws and bats lefthanded.
Hobbies—Swimming, basketball, bowling and automobiles.
Son of William K. Thompson, first baseman-outfielder in Cincinnati Reds'
organization and Milwaukee Braves' organization, 1953-1962;
brother of Joe Thompson, former minor league first baseman.

Led American Association first basemen in fielding percentage with .994 in 1977.

Year Club	League	Pos.	G.	AB.	R.	H.	2B.	3B.	HR.	RBI.	B.A.	PO.	A.	E.	F.A.
1974—Bradenton Cubs .Gulf C.		OF-1B	47	169	22	43	6	3	1	19	.254	86	7	5	.948
1975—Key West ....Fla.St.		OF-1B	123	424	40	95	6	3	3	41	.224	186	10	*12	.942
1976—Midland.............Texas		1B-OF	116	425	47	121	11	2	7	54	.285	766	50	12	.985
1977—Wichita .............A.A.		1B-OF	124	446	77	136	24	5	11	54	.305	920	62	7	.993
1978—Wichita.............A. A.		1B-OF	●135	*519	83	169	*33	7	10	64	.326	873	59	13	.986
1978—Chicago ....Nat.		OF-1B	19	36	7	15	3	0	0	2	.417	14	1	0	1.000
1979—Chicago ....Nat.		OF	128	346	36	100	13	5	2	29	.289	161	7	5	.971
1980—Chicago†..........Nat.		OF-1B	102	226	26	48	10	1	2	13	.212	149	6	4	.975
Major League Totals......................			249	608	69	163	26	6	4	44	.268	324	14	9	.974

Selected by Chicago Cubs' organization in 1st round (seventh player selected) of free-agent draft, June 5, 1974.

†On supplemental disabled list, July 10, 1980; transferred to disabled list, July 10 to August 6, 1980.

RICHARD W. THON

(Dickie)

Born June 20, 1958, at South Bend, Ind.
Height, 5.11. Weight, 150.
Throws and bats righthanded.
Grandson of Fred Thon, former player and manager in Puerto Rican Winter League;
brother of Francis Thon, second baseman in San Francisco Giants' organization.

Year Club	League	Pos.	G.	AB.	R.	H.	2B.	3B.	HR.	RBI.	B.A.	PO.	A.	E.	F.A.
1976—Quad Cities ....Midw.		SS	69	246	46	68	11	4	1	32	.276	96	193	32	.900
1977—Salinas ....Calif.		SS	56	225	48	71	13	2	4	44	.316	95	162	13	.952
1977—Salt Lake City ...P.C.		SS	77	274	47	79	9	3	8	43	.288	129	242	26	.935
1978—Salt Lake City ... P. C.		2B-SS	130	439	67	113	17	3	1	47	.257	273	380	26	.962
1979—Salt Lake City ... P. C.		SS-2B	38	162	25	47	3	1	2	21	.290	70	120	11	.945
1979—California ....Amer.		2B-SS-3B	35	56	6	19	3	0	0	8	.339	38	46	8	.913
1980—Salt Lake City ...P.C.		2B-SS	40	155	28	61	14	2	2	28	.394	81	107	12	.940
1980—California ....Amer.		S-2-3-1	80	267	32	68	12	2	0	15	.255	70	124	10	.951
Major League Totals......................			115	323	38	87	15	2	0	23	.269	108	170	18	.939

Signed as free agent by California Angels' organization, November 23, 1975.

CHAMPIONSHIP SERIES RECORD

Year Club	League	Pos.	G.	AB.	R.	H.	2B.	3B.	HR.	RBI.	B.A.	PO.	A.	E.	F.A.
1979—California ....Amer.		PR-SS	1	0	1	0	0	0	0	0	.000	0	0	0	.000

ANDRE THORNTON

Born August 13, 1949, at Tuskegee, Ala.
Height, 6.02. Weight, 205.
Throws and bats righthanded.
Hobbies—Reading and billiards.
Attended Cheyney State College, Cheyney, Pa.

Tied major league record for most assists, first baseman, inning, 3, August 22, 1975, 5th inning.
Led Northwest League first basemen in double plays with 35 in 1968.

Year Club	League	Pos.	G.	AB.	R.	H.	2B.	3B.	HR.	RBI.	B.A.	PO.	A.	E.	F.A.
1967—Huron†.............North.		3-OF	19	55	3	10	1	2	1	3	.182	7	9	10	.615
1968—Eugene‡...........Northw.		1B	56	185	27	46	9	2	5	31	.249	*427	*24	10	*.978
1969—Spartanburg‡‡ ...W. Car.		*1-3-O	90	299	56	75	13	4	13	51	.251	701	45	*20	.974
1970—Peninsula§ ....Carol.		1B	67	193	24	48	7	2	5	23	.249	499	30	5	.991
1971—Reading x...........East.		1B	116	367	67	98	18	1	26	76	.267	1006	48	15	.986
1972—Eugene y...........P.C.		1B-3B	46	141	22	45	8	2	6	29	.319	224	46	11	.961
1972—Richmond z......Int.		1B-OF	49	159	30	42	5	0	14	36	.264	379	33	6	.986
1973—Richmond a.......Int.		3-1-O	16	49	8	10	2	0	4	8	.204	67	17	5	.944
1973—Wichita .............A.A.		1B	40	135	34	39	2	0	17	45	.289	362	23	1	.997
1973—Chicago............Nat.		1B	17	35	3	7	3	0	0	2	.200	81	10	1	.989
1974—Chicago............Nat.		1B-3B	107	303	41	79	16	4	10	46	.261	760	70	7	.992
1975—Chicago b.........Nat.		1B-3B	120	372	70	109	21	4	18	60	.293	984	77	13	.988
1976—Chi c-Mont. d.....Nat.		1B-OF	96	268	28	52	11	2	11	38	.194	542	46	6	.990
1977—Cleveland..........Amer.		1B	131	433	77	114	20	5	28	70	.263	1026	71	6	.995
1978—Cleveland..........Amer.		1B	145	508	97	133	22	4	33	105	.262	1327	106	7	.995
1979—Cleveland.........Amer.		1B	143	515	89	120	31	1	26	93	.233	1089	82	7	.994
1980—Cleveland e........Amer.							Did not play								
American League Totals			419	1456	263	367	73	10	87	268	.252	3442	259	20	.995
National League Totals			340	978	142	247	51	10	39	146	.252	2367	203	27	.990
Major League Totals......................			759	2434	405	614	124	20	126	414	.252	5809	462	47	.993

Signed as free agent by Philadelphia Phillies' organization, August 6, 1967.
†On military list, December 29, 1967 through May 1, 1968.
‡On temporary inactive list, June 1 through July 2.
‡‡On temporary inactive list, June 4 through June 24.
§On temporary inactive list, June 11 through June 30.
xOn temporary inactive list, June 7 through June 26.
yReleased to Richmond (part of deal in which Philadelphia Phillies sent Pitcher Joe Hoerner to Atlanta Braves in trade for Pitchers Jim Nash and Gary Neibauer), June 15, 1972.
zOn temporary inactive list, June 28 through July 1. On disabled list, July 5 through July 16. On temporary inactive list, August 1 through August 4.
aTraded by Atlanta Braves to Chicago Cubs for First Baseman Joe Pepitone, May 19, 1973.
bOn disabled list, April 1 to May 4, 1975.
cTraded to Montreal Expos for Pitcher Steve Renko and Outfielder-First Baseman Larry Biittner, May 17, 1976.
dOn disabled list, June 10 to July 1, 1976; traded to Cleveland Indians for Pitcher Jackie Brown, December 10, 1976.
eOn disabled list, March 28 to June 9 and June 19 to October 13, 1980.

THOMAS PAUL THURBERG
(Tom)

Born October 16, 1957, at Weymouth, Mass.
Height, 6.01. Weight, 190.
Throws and bats righthanded.

Led Appalachian League batters in strikeouts with 69 in 1976.
Tied for Appalachian League lead in double plays by outfielders with 3 in 1976.

Year Club	League	G.	IP.	W.	L.	Pct.	H.	R.	ER.	SO.	BB.	ERA.
1978—Lynchburg	Carolina	25	65	2	1	.667	54	33	19	54	39	2.63
1979—Lynchburg	Carolina	34	67	7	2	.778	56	26	20	66	40	2.69
1979—Tidewater	Int'national	1	6	0	1	.000	3	2	2	4	3	3.00
1980—Jackson	Texas	31	92	7	2	.778	64	39	28	84	59	2.74

Selected by New York Mets' organization in 1st round (13th player selected) of free-agent draft, June 8, 1976.

RECORD AS OUTFIELDER-THIRD BASEMAN

Year Club	League	Pos.	G.	AB.	R.	H.	2B.	3B.	HR.	RBI.	B.A.	PO.	A.	E.	F.A.
1976—Marion	Appal.	OF	57	169	13	31	4	2	3	18	.183	94	8	7	.936
1977—Wausau	Midw.	OF	116	350	62	80	13	1	11	43	.229	163	*25	*22	.895
1977—Little Falls	NYP	OF-3B	14	47	4	8	1	0	0	1	.170	11	7	2	.900

LUIS CLEMENTE TIANT (VEGA)
Name pronounced TEE-aunt.

Born November 23, 1940, at Havana, Cuba.
Height, 5.11. Weight, 187.
Throws and bats righthanded.

Tied major league record for most strikeouts, two consecutive games (32), June 29 and July 3, 1968.
Established American League record for most strikeouts, ten-inning game (19), July 3, 1968.
Pitched 4-0 no-hit victory against Winston-Salem, May 7, 1963.
Led American League in shutouts with 7 in 1974.
Tied for American League lead in shutouts with 5 in 1966 and led with 9 in 1968.
Led Carolina League in shutouts with 6 and in complete games with 17 in 1963.
Named THE SPORTING NEWS American League Comeback Player of the Year, 1972.
Named Player of the Year in Pacific Coast League, 1964.

Year Club	League	G.	IP.	W.	L.	Pct.	H.	R.	ER.	SO.	BB.	ERA.
1959—Mexico City Tigers	Mexican	41	184	5	19	.208	214	*139	121	98	107	5.92
1960—Mexico City Tigers	Mexican	41	180	●17	7	*.708	194	115	93	107	*124	4.65
1961—Mexico City Tigers	Mexican	24	145	12	9	.571	138	77	61	141	106	3.79
1962—Jacksonville	Int'national	1	1	0	0	.000	0	0	0	0	1	0.00
1962—Charleston	Eastern	29	139	7	8	.467	141	75	56	99	72	3.63
1963—Burlington	Carolina	31	204	14	9	.609	151	68	58	*207	81	2.56
1964—Portland	P. Coast	17	137	15	1	*.938	88	37	31	154	40	2.04
1964—Cleveland	American	19	127	10	4	.714	94	41	40	105	47	2.83
1965—Cleveland	American	41	196	11	11	.500	166	88	77	152	66	3.54
1966—Cleveland	American	46	155	12	11	.522	121	50	48	145	50	2.79
1967—Cleveland	American	33	214	12	9	.571	177	76	65	219	67	2.73
1968—Cleveland	American	34	258	21	9	.700	152	53	46	264	73	*1.60
1969—Cleveland†	American	38	250	9	*20	.410	229	*123	103	156	*129	3.71
1970—Minnesota‡§	American	18	93	7	3	.700	84	36	35	50	41	3.39
1971—Richmond x-Louisville	Int'national	9	54	3	5	.375	47	27	25	48	28	4.17
1971—Boston	American	21	72	1	7	.125	73	42	39	59	32	4.88
1972—Boston	American	43	179	15	6	.714	128	45	38	123	65	*1.91
1973—Boston	American	35	272	20	13	.606	217	105	101	206	78	3.34
1974—Boston	American	38	311	22	13	.629	281	106	101	176	82	2.92
1975—Boston	American	35	260	18	14	.563	262	126	116	142	72	4.02
1976—Boston	American	38	279	21	12	.636	274	107	95	131	64	3.06
1977—Boston	American	32	189	12	8	.600	210	98	95	124	51	4.52
1978—Boston yz	American	32	212	13	8	.619	185	80	78	114	57	3.31

Year Club	League	G.	IP.	W.	L.	Pct.	H.	R.	ER.	SO.	BB.	ERA.
1979—New York	American	30	196	13	8	.619	190	94	85	104	53	3.90
1980—New York ab	American	25	136	8	9	.471	139	79	74	84	50	4.90
Major League Totals		558	3399	225	165	.577	2982	1349	1236	2354	1077	3.27

Signed as free agent by Mexico City Tigers, February 21, 1959.
†Traded with Pitcher Stan Williams to Minnesota Twins for Pitchers Dean Chance and Bob Miller, Outfielder Ted Uhlaender and Outfielder-Third Baseman Graig Nettles, December 12, 1969.
‡On disabled list June 1 through August 3.
§Unconditionally released, March 31, 1971; signed as free agent by Atlanta Braves, April 16, 1971.
xReleased by Atlanta Braves, May 15, 1971; signed as free agent by Boston Red Sox, May 17, 1971.
yOn disabled list, March 22 to April 18, 1978.
zGranted free agency, November 2, 1978; signed by New York Yankees, November 13, 1978.
aOn disabled list, June 30 to July 22, 1980.
bGranted free agency, October 27, 1980; signed by Pittsburgh Pirates' organization, February 23, 1981.

CHAMPIONSHIP SERIES RECORD

Year Club	League	G.	IP.	W.	L.	Pct.	H.	R.	ER.	SO.	BB.	ERA.
1970—Minnesota	American	1	⅔	0	0	.000	1	2	1	0	0	13.50
1975—Boston	American	1	9	1	0	1.000	3	1	0	8	3	0.00
Championship Series Totals		2	9⅔	1	0	1.000	4	3	1	8	3	0.93

WORLD SERIES RECORD

Year Club	League	G.	IP.	W.	L.	Pct.	H.	R.	ER.	SO.	BB.	ERA.
1975—Boston	American	3	25	2	0	1.000	25	10	10	12	8	3.60

ALL-STAR GAME RECORD

Tied All-Star Game record for most games lost (2).

Year League		IP.	W.	L.	Pct.	H.	R.	ER.	SO.	BB.	ERA.
1968—American		2	0	1	.000	2	1	0	2	2	0.00
1974—American		2	0	1	.000	4	3	2	0	1	9.00
1976—American		2	0	0	.000	1	0	0	1	0	.000
All-Star Game Totals		6	0	2	.000	7	4	2	3	3	3.000

RICHARD WILLIAM TIDROW
(Dick)

Born May 14, 1947, at San Francisco, Calif.
Height, 6.04. Weight, 213.
Throws and bats righthanded.
Hobbies—Music and sports in general.
Attended Chabot College, Hayward, Calif.

Named THE SPORTING NEWS American League Rookie Pitcher of the Year, 1972.

Year Club	League	G.	IP.	W.	L.	Pct.	H.	R.	ER.	SO.	BB.	ERA.
1967—Reno	California	7	19	0	1	.000	20	16	14	18	10	6.63
1967—Rock Hill	W. Carol.	4	16	0	1	.000	15	10	10	9	9	5.63
1968—Reno†	California	6	8	1	0	1.000	3	0	0	11	4	0.00
1969—Reno	California	25	187	15	6	.714	170	71	55	189	48	2.65
1970—Wichita	Am. Assoc.	18	83	3	4	.429	99	49	47	71	29	5.10
1970—Reno	California	6	35	2	2	.500	35	16	10	33	12	2.57
1971—Wichita	Am. Assoc.	20	124	8	6	.571	123	61	57	81	45	4.15
1971—Reno	California	7	38	4	0	1.000	38	16	14	29	11	3.32
1972—Cleveland	American	39	237	14	15	.483	200	83	73	123	70	2.77
1973—Cleveland	American	42	275	14	16	.467	289	150	135	138	95	4.42
1974—Cleveland‡-New York	American	37	210	12	12	.500	226	116	97	108	66	4.16
1975—New York§	American	37	69	6	3	.667	65	27	24	38	31	3.13
1976—New York	American	47	92	4	5	.444	80	29	27	65	24	2.64
1977—New York	American	49	151	11	4	.733	143	57	53	83	41	3.16
1978—New York	American	31	185	7	11	.389	191	87	79	73	53	3.84
1979—New York x	American	14	23	2	1	.667	38	20	20	7	4	7.83
1979—Chicago	National	63	103	11	5	.688	86	35	31	68	42	2.71
1980—Chicago	National	•84	116	6	5	.545	97	44	36	97	53	2.79
American League Totals		296	1242	70	67	.511	1232	569	508	635	384	3.68
National League Totals		147	219	17	10	.630	183	79	67	165	95	2.75
Major League Totals		443	1461	87	77	.530	1415	648	575	800	479	3.54

Selected by Washington Senators' organization in 22nd round of free-agent draft, June, 1965.
Selected by San Francisco Giants' organization in secondary phase of free-agent draft, January 29, 1966.
Selected by Cincinnati Reds' organization in 3rd round of free-agent draft, June, 1966.
Selected by Cleveland Indians' organization in secondary phase of free-agent draft, January 28, 1967.
†On military list from beginning of season until August 13.
‡Traded with First Baseman Chris Chambliss and Pitcher Cecil Upshaw to New York Yankees for Pitchers Fritz Peterson, Fred Beene, Steve Kline and Tom Buskey, April 26, 1974.
§On disabled list from beginning of season until April 19 and from August 19 through remainder of season.
xTraded to Chicago Cubs for Pitcher Ray Burris, May 23, 1979.

CHAMPIONSHIP SERIES RECORD

Year Club	League	G.	IP.	W.	L.	Pct.	H.	R.	ER.	SO.	BB.	ERA.
1976—New York	American	3	7⅓	1	0	1.000	6	4	3	0	4	3.68

Year Club	League	G.	IP.	W.	L.	Pct.	H.	R.	ER.	SO.	BB.	ERA.
1977—New York	American	2	7	0	0	.000	6	3	3	3	3	3.86
1978—New York	American	1	5⅔	0	0	.000	8	3	3	1	2	4.76
Championship Series Totals		6	20	1	0	1.000	20	10	9	4	9	4.05

WORLD SERIES RECORD

Year Club	League	G.	IP.	W.	L.	Pct.	H.	R.	ER.	SO.	BB.	ERA.
1976—New York	American	2	2⅓	0	0	.000	5	2	2	1	1	7.71
1977—New York	American	2	3⅔	0	0	.000	5	2	2	1	0	4.91
1978—New York	American	2	4⅔	0	0	.000	4	1	1	5	0	1.93
World Series Totals		6	10⅔	0	0	.000	14	5	5	7	1	4.22

RONALD IRVIN TINGLEY

Born May 27, 1959, at Presque Isle, Maine.
Height, 6.02. Weight, 160.
Throws and bats righthanded.

Year Club	League	Pos.	G.	AB.	R.	H.	2B.	3B.	HR.	RBI.	B.A.	PO.	A.	E.	F.A.
1977—Walla Walla	Northw.	OF	21	33	8	5	0	0	1	3	.152	5	2	0	1.000
1978—Walla Walla	Northw.	OF-C	43	140	22	29	2	0	2	21	.207	149	16	8	.954
1979—Santa Clara	Calif.	C-OF	52	143	11	29	4	1	0	17	.203	258	42	8	.974
1979—Amarillo	Texas	C-OF	30	90	16	23	4	1	1	6	.256	133	17	4	.974
1980—Reno†	Calif.	C-OF	65	204	37	61	3	3	3	35	.299	333	46	10	.974

Selected by San Diego Padres' organization in 10th round of free-agent draft, June 7, 1977.
†On disabled list, April 10 to April 29, 1980.

DAVID VANCE TOBIK

Name pronounced TOE-bick.

(Dave)

Born March 2, 1953, at Euclid, O.
Height, 6.01. Weight, 195.
Throws and bats righthanded.
Attended Ohio University, Athens, O.; received Bachelor of
Business Administration degree.

Year Club	League	G.	IP.	W.	L.	Pct.	H.	R.	ER.	SO.	BB.	ERA.
1975—Lakeland	Florida St.	5	36	1	4	.200	29	14	10	22	19	2.50
1975—Montgomery	Southern	20	99	6	9	.400	107	57	48	62	44	4.36
1976—Lakeland	Florida St.	6	42	3	1	.750	28	11	5	29	15	1.07
1976—Montgomery†	Southern	18	63	4	5	.444	56	33	26	44	32	3.71
1977—Montgomery	Southern	27	48	4	4	.500	31	17	14	42	17	2.63
1977—Evansville	Am. Assoc.	13	19	4	1	.800	19	8	7	17	9	3.32
1978—Evansville	Am. Assoc.	33	79	5	4	.556	71	43	30	70	26	3.42
1978—Detroit	American	5	12	0	0	.000	12	5	5	11	3	3.75
1979—Evansville	Am. Assoc.	19	38	4	0	1.000	24	6	2	45	13	0.47
1979—Detroit	American	37	69	3	5	.375	59	34	33	48	25	4.30
1980—Evansville	Am. Assoc.	30	48	3	3	.500	35	22	21	49	26	3.94
1980—Detroit	American	17	61	1	0	1.000	61	27	27	34	21	3.98
Major League Totals		59	142	4	5	.444	132	66	65	93	49	4.12

Selected by Montreal Expos' organization in 3rd round of free-agent draft, June 5, 1974.
Selected by Detroit Tigers' organization in secondary phase of free-agent draft, January 9, 1975.
†On disabled list, June 3 to June 24, 1976.

JACKSON A. TODD

Born November 20, 1951, at Tulsa, Okla.
Height, 6.02. Weight, 190.
Throws and bats righthanded.
Hobbies—Outdoor sports.
Attended University of Oklahoma, Norman, Okla.
Pitched 3-0 no-hit victory against Arkansas, May 14, 1974.

Year Club	League	G.	IP.	W.	L.	Pct.	H.	R.	ER.	SO.	BB.	ERA.
1973—Memphis	Texas	14	76	6	5	.545	69	29	24	57	20	2.84
1974—Victoria†	Texas	23	173	11	8	.579	165	78	62	115	43	3.23
1975—Jackson‡	Texas	13	54	3	4	.429	52	29	19	31	20	3.17
1976—Tidewater	Int'national	26	*201	13	9	.520	204	75	65	125	53	2.91
1977—Tidewater	Int'national	9	63	2	3	.400	65	34	28	47	19	4.00
1977—New York§	National	19	72	3	6	.333	78	41	38	39	20	4.75
1978—Oklahoma City xy	Am. Assoc.	16	80	3	4	.429	94	56	41	47	25	4.61
1979—Syracuse	Int'national	21	124	9	4	.692	116	48	46	59	35	3.34
1979—Toronto	American	12	32	0	1	.000	40	26	21	14	7	5.91
1980—Syracuse	Int'national	22	153	7	9	.438	135	68	58	118	63	3.41
1980—Toronto	American	12	85	5	2	.714	90	40	38	44	30	4.02
National League Totals		19	72	3	6	.333	78	41	38	39	20	4.75
American League Totals		24	117	5	3	.625	130	66	59	58	37	4.54
Major League Totals		43	189	8	9	.471	208	107	97	97	57	4.62

Selected by Chicago Cubs' organization in 11th round of free-agent draft, June 4, 1970.
Selected by New York Mets' organization in 2nd round of free-agent draft, June 5, 1973.
†Played one game at shortstop.
‡On temporary inactive list, April 10 to June 19, 1975.
§Traded to Philadelphia Phillies organization for Catcher Ed Cuervo, March 27, 1978.
xOn disabled list, June 2 to July 17, 1978.
yReleased, April 13, 1979; signed by Toronto Blue Jays' organization, April 13, 1979.

JIMMY WAYNE TOLLESON

(Known by middle name.)
Born November 22, 1959, at Spartanburg, S. C.
Height, 5.09. Weight, 160.
Throws right and bats left and righthanded.
Attended Western Carolina University, Cullowhee, N. C.

Year	Club	League	Pos.	G.	AB.	R.	H.	2B.	3B.	HR.	RBI.	B.A.	PO.	A.	E.	F.A.
1978—Asheville		W. Car.	3B-SS	70	212	35	57	4	1	0	21	.269	85	175	20	.929
1979—Tulsa		Texas	SS	130	418	43	98	9	7	1	36	.234	179	413	•41	.935
1980—Tulsa		Texas	SS	131	452	69	124	19	7	1	30	.274	161	395	31	.947

Selected by Pittsburgh Pirates' organization in 12th round of free-agent draft, June 7, 1977.
Selected by Texas Rangers' organization in 8th round of free-agent draft, June 6, 1978.

DAVID ALLEN TOMLIN
(Dave)

Born June 22, 1949, at Maysville, Ky.
Height, 6.02. Weight, 185.
Throws and bats lefthanded.
Hobbies—Hunting and horses.

Led Appalachian League pitchers in games started with 13 and tied for lead in complete games with 6 in 1967.

Year	Club	League	G.	IP.	W.	L.	Pct.	H.	R.	ER.	SO.	BB.	ERA.
1967—Wytheville		Ap'alchian	14	85	•7	6	.538	•93	55	41	47	43	4.34
1968—Tampa		Florida St.	37	56	6	3	.667	47	19	15	38	16	2.41
1969—Tampa		Florida St.	23	44	5	1	.833	34	18	14	25	22	2.86
1970—Asheville		Southern	25	139	6	10	.375	135	62	48	73	58	3.11
1971—Indianapolis		Am. Assoc.	41	61	7	4	.636	46	19	15	50	24	2.23
1972—Indianapolis		Am. Assoc.	36	90	5	6	.455	83	30	28	86	36	2.79
1972—Cincinnati		National	3	4	0	0	.000	7	4	4	2	1	9.00
1973—Indianapolis†		Am. Assoc.	25	31	1	3	.250	29	15	12	26	11	3.52
1973—Cincinnati†		National	16	28	1	2	.333	24	15	15	20	15	4.82
1974—Hawaii		P. Coast	25	48	5	1	.833	33	10	9	48	20	1.69
1974—San Diego		National	47	58	2	0	1.000	59	29	28	29	30	4.34
1975—San Diego		National	67	83	4	2	.667	87	38	30	48	31	3.25
1976—San Diego		National	49	73	0	1	.000	62	24	23	43	20	2.84
1977—San Diego†§		National	76	102	4	4	.500	98	38	34	55	32	3.00
1978—Cincinnati		National	57	62	9	1	.900	88	54	40	32	30	5.81
1979—Cincinnati		National	53	58	2	2	.500	59	29	17	30	18	2.64
1980—Cincinnati x		National	27	26	3	0	1.000	38	17	16	6	11	5.54
Major League Totals			395	494	25	12	.676	522	248	207	265	188	3.77

Selected by Cincinnati Reds' organization in 29th round of free-agent draft, June 6, 1967.
†Traded with Outfielder Bobby Tolan to San Diego Padres for Pitcher Clay Kirby, November 9, 1973.
‡Traded with $125,000 to Texas Rangers for Pitcher Gaylord Perry, February 15, 1978.
§Sold to Cincinnati Reds, March 28, 1978.
xReleased, September 2, 1980.

CHAMPIONSHIP SERIES RECORD

Year	Club	League	G.	IP.	W.	L.	Pct.	H.	R.	ER.	SO.	BB.	ERA.
1973—Cincinnati		National	1	1⅔	0	0	.000	5	3	3	1	1	16.20
1979—Cincinnati		National	3	3	0	0	.000	3	1	0	3	2	0.00
Championship Series Totals			4	4⅔	0	0	.000	8	4	3	4	3	5.79

ROSENDO TORRES JR.
(Rusty)

Born September 30, 1948, at Aguadilla, Puerto Rico.
Height, 5.11. Weight, 180.
Throws right and bats right and lefthanded.
Hobby—Repairing racing cars.

Led Carolina League outfielders in double plays with 5 in 1969.

Year	Club	League	Pos.	G.	AB.	R.	H.	2B.	3B.	HR.	RBI.	B.A.	PO.	A.	E.	F.A.
1967—Greensboro		Carol.	OF	13	15	1	3	1	0	0	0	.200	4	0	0	1.000
1967—Ft. Lauderdale†		Fla. St.	OF	6	19	1	2	0	0	0	0	.105	10	0	1	.909
1967—Oneonta		NYP	OF	8	13	5	3	0	0	0	0	.231	11	0	0	1.000
1967—Johnson City		Appal.	OF	48	127	23	35	8	0	3	22	.276	60	1	7	.897
1968—Ft. Lauderdale		Fla. St.	•OF-2B	125	340	47	78	6	•13	3	26	.229	169	29	•15	.930
1969—Kinston		Carol.	OF	139	507	•96	137	26	11	13	49	.270	319	•21	11	.969
1970—Manchester‡		East.	OF	41	127	21	31	5	0	3	16	.244	86	2	3	.967

Year Club League	Pos.	G.	AB.	R.	H.	2B.	3B.	HR.	RBI.	B.A.	PO.	A.	E.	F.A.
1971—Syracuse...........Int.	OF	133	441	91	128	25	7	19	71	.290	256	16	5	*.982
1971—New York ....Amer.	OF	9	26	5	10	3	0	2	3	.385	13	0	0	1.000
1972—Syracuse...........Int.	OF	19	57	6	19	3	1	1	3	.333	25	2	0	1.000
1972—New York§.........Amer.	OF	80	199	15	42	7	0	3	13	.211	86	4	2	.978
1973—Cleveland.........Amer.	OF	122	312	31	64	8	1	7	28	.205	191	9	5	.976
1974—Cleveland x......Amer.	OF	108	150	19	28	2	0	3	12	.187	110	8	5	.959
1975—Salt Lake C. y ...P. C.	OF	107	369	59	113	18	•9	8	64	.306	290	10	5	.984
1976—California ....Amer.	OF-3B	120	264	37	54	16	3	6	27	.205	195	5	2	.990
1977—California za.....Amer.	OF	58	77	9	12	1	1	3	10	.156	60	1	1	.984
1978—Tucson b...........P. C.	OF	30	107	32	37	7	7	7	39	.346	80	3	1	.988
1978—Iowa ....A. A.	OF	91	321	62	90	19	4	16	55	.280	233	11	7	.972
1978—Chicago ....Amer.	OF	16	44	7	14	3	0	3	6	.318	27	0	1	.964
1979—Chicago e.........Amer.	OF	90	170	26	43	5	0	8	24	.253	117	4	3	.976
1980—Omaha..............A. A.	OF	8	25	8	9	1	0	4	11	.360	9	0	0	1.000
1980—Kansas City f ....Amer.	OF	51	72	10	12	0	0	0	3	.167	67	4	2	.973
Major League Totals......................		654	1314	159	279	45	5	35	126	.212	866	35	21	.977

Selected by New York Yankees' organization in 37th round of free-agent draft, June, 1966.

†On disabled list, May 18 to June 20, 1967.

‡On disabled list, April 24 to May 12. On temporary inactive list, May 25 to August 8.

§Traded with Catcher-First Baseman John Ellis, Infielder Jerry Kenney and Outfielder Charlie Spikes to Cleveland Indians for Catcher Jerry Moses and Infielder-Outfielder Graig Nettles, November 27, 1972.

xTraded with Catcher Ken Suarez to California Angels, December 4, 1974, to complete deal in which Indians acquired Outfielder Frank Robinson on waivers from Angels, September 12, 1974.

yOn disabled list, April 10 to May 10, 1975.

zOn disabled list, March 29 to May 17, 1977.

aGranted free agency, October 25, 1977; signed by Texas Rangers' organization, March 1, 1978.

bTraded with Outfielder Claudell Washington and a player to be named later to Chicago White Sox for Outfielder Bobby Bonds, May 16, 1978.

cOn disabled list, August 27 to September 11, 1979.

dGranted free agency, November 1, 1979.

eReleased, April 2, 1980; signed by Kansas City Royals' organization, May 5, 1980.

fReleased, August 29, 1980; signed by Pittsburgh Pirates' organization, January 20, 1981.

MICHAEL AUGUSTINE TORREZ
(Mike)

Born August 28, 1946, at Topeka, Kan.
Height, 6:05. Weight, 210.
Throws and bats righthanded.
Hobbies—Hunting, fishing, billiards and entering car shows.

Received reported $20,000 bonus to sign with St. Louis Cardinals, 1965.

Year Club	League	G.	IP.	W.	L.	Pct.	H.	R.	ER.	SO.	BB.	ERA.
1965—Raleigh..............................Carolina		20	94	4	8	.333	92	66	50	81	75	4.79
1966—Rock Hill ....W. Carol.		15	90	7	4	.636	63	35	25	85	37	2.50
1966—Arkansas ....Texas		15	79	3	9	.250	73	44	23	65	42	2.62
1967—Tulsa..................................P. Coast		29	190	10	10	.500	152	82	70	155	*108	3.32
1967—St. Louis ....National		3	6	0	1	.000	5	2	2	5	1	3.00
1968—St. Louis ....National		5	19	2	1	.667	20	7	6	6	12	2.84
1968—Tulsa..................................P. Coast		16	86	8	2	.800	74	33	31	82	36	3.24
1969—St. Louis ....National		24	108	10	4	.714	96	47	43	61	62	3.58
1970—St. Louis ....National		30	179	8	10	.444	168	96	84	100	103	4.22
1971—Winnipeg ....Int'national		18	75	2	4	.333	96	72	68	45	52	8.16
1971—St. Louis†-Montreal ....National		10	39	1	2	.333	45	27	24	10	31	5.54
1972—Montreal ....National		34	243	16	12	.571	215	97	90	112	103	3.33
1973—Montreal ....National		35	208	9	12	.429	207	116	103	90	115	4.46
1974—Montreal‡ ....National		32	186	15	8	.652	184	90	74	92	84	3.58
1975—Baltimore§ ....American		36	271	20	9	*.690	238	103	92	119	*133	3.06
1976—Oakland ....American		39	266	16	12	.571	231	93	74	115	87	2.50
1977—Oakland x-New York y.........American		35	243	17	13	.567	235	113	105	102	86	3.89
1978—Boston ....American		36	250	16	13	.552	272	122	110	120	99	3.96
1979—Boston ....American		36	252	16	13	.552	254	*144	*126	125	*121	4.50
1980—Boston ....American		36	207	9	16	.360	256	124	117	97	75	5.09
American League Totals...........................		218	1489	94	76	.553	1486	699	624	678	601	3.77
National League Totals.............................		173	988	61	50	.550	940	482	426	476	511	3.88
Major League Totals................................		391	2477	155	126	.552	2426	1181	1050	1154	1112	3.82

Signed as free agent by St. Louis Cardinals' organization, September 10, 1964.

†Traded to Montreal Expos' organization for Pitcher Bob Reynolds, June 15, 1971.

‡Traded with Outfielder Ken Singleton to Baltimore Orioles for Outfielder Rich Coggins and Pitchers Dave McNally and Bill Kirkpatrick, December 4, 1974.

§Traded with Outfielder Don Baylor and Pitcher Paul Mitchell to Oakland Athletics for Outfielder Reggie Jackson and Pitchers Ken Holtzman and Bill Van Bommel, April 2, 1976.

xTraded to New York Yankees for Pitcher Dock Ellis, Infielder Marty Perez, and Outfielder Larry Murray, April 27, 1977.

yGranted free agency, October 31, 1977; signed by Boston Red Sox, November 23, 1977.

CHAMPIONSHIP SERIES RECORD

Tied American League Championship Series record for most strikeouts by relief pitcher, game (4), October 9, 1977.

Year Club	League	G.	IP.	W.	L.	Pct.	H.	R.	ER.	SO.	BB.	ERA.
1977—New York	American	2	11	0	1	.000	11	5	5	5	5	4.09

Year Club	League	G.	IP.	W.	L.	Pct.	H.	R.	ER.	SO.	BB.	ERA.
1977—New York	American	2	18	2	0	1.000	16	7	5	15	5	2.50

JAMES EDWIN TRACY
(Jim)

Born December 31, 1955, at Hamilton, O.
Height, 6.03. Weight, 193.
Throws and bats lefthanded.
Attended Marietta College, Marietta, O., and Xavier University, Cincinnati, O.
Son of Jim Tracy Sr., pitcher in Philadelphia Phillies' and
New York Giants' organizations, 1948-52.

Year Club	League	Pos.	G.	AB.	R.	H.	2B.	3B.	HR.	RBI.	B.A.	PO.	A.	E.	F.A.
1977—Pompano Beach	Fla. St.	1B-OF	93	261	27	59	13	2	4	34	.226	147	6	4	.975
1978—Pompano Beach	Fla. St.	1B-OF	78	225	42	55	7	5	6	43	.244	329	27	4	.989
1978—Midland	Texas	OF-1B	54	189	34	49	9	2	8	29	.259	174	10	2	.989
1979—Midland	Texas	1B	86	301	75	107	16	1	15	67	*.355	799	31	6	.993
1979—Wichita	A.A.	1B-OF	44	150	26	41	9	1	4	18	.273	364	20	11	.972
1980—Wichita	A.A.	O-1-3	112	406	66	130	17	6	16	63	.320	428	33	6	.987
1980—Chicago	Nat.	OF-1B	42	122	12	31	3	3	3	9	.254	44	0	2	.957
Major League Totals			42	122	12	31	3	3	3	9	.254	44	0	2	.957

Selected by Chicago Cubs' organization in 4th round of free-agent draft, January 11, 1977.

ALAN STUART TRAMMELL
Name pronounced Tram-mull.

Born February 21, 1958, at Garden Grove, Calif.
Height, 6.00. Weight, 170.
Throws and bats righthanded.
Hobby—Sports.

Major league stolen bases: 1977 (0), 1978 (3), 1979 (17), 1980 (12). Total—32.
Named shortstop on THE SPORTING NEWS American League All-Star fielding team, 1980.
Named Southern League Most Valuable Player in 1977.

Year Club	League	Pos.	G.	AB.	R.	H.	2B.	3B.	HR.	RBI.	B.A.	PO.	A.	E.	F.A.
1976—Bristol	Appal.	SS	41	140	27	38	2	2	0	7	.271	59	131	12	.941
1976—Montgomery	South.	SS	21	56	4	10	0	0	0	2	.179	40	64	2	.981
1977—Montgomery	South.	SS	134	454	78	132	9	*19	3	50	.291	188	397	27	.956
1977—Detroit	Amer.	SS	19	43	6	8	0	0	0	0	.186	15	34	2	.961
1978—Detroit	Amer.	SS	139	448	49	120	14	6	2	34	.268	239	421	14	.979
1979—Detroit	Amer.	SS	142	460	68	127	11	4	6	50	.276	245	388	26	.961
1980—Detroit	Amer.	SS	146	560	107	168	21	5	9	65	.300	225	412	13	.980
Major League Totals			446	1511	230	423	46	15	17	149	.280	724	1255	55	.973

Selected by Detroit Tigers' organization in 2nd round of free-agent draft, June 8, 1976.

Year League	Pos.	AB.	R.	H.	2B.	3B.	HR.	RBI.	B.A.	PO.	A.	E.	F.A.
1980—American	SS	0	0	0	0	0	0	0	.000	0	0	0	.000

WILLIAM EDWARD TRAVERS
(Billy)

Born October 27, 1952, at Norwood, Mass.
Height, 6:04. Weight, 187.
Throws and bats lefthanded.
Hobbies—Bowling, fishing and golf.

Pitched 16-1 no-hit victory against Quad Cities, May 30, 1971.
Tied for Pacific Coast League lead in shutouts with 3 in 1975.

Year Club	League	G.	IP.	W.	L.	Pct.	H.	R.	ER.	SO.	BB.	ERA.
1970—Clinton	Midwest	10	48	1	6	.143	53	35	30	38	26	5.63
1971—Danville	Midwest	21	137	7	8	.467	126	63	46	98	33	3.02
1972—San Antonio	Texas	17	89	3	7	.300	87	37	29	77	26	2.93
1973—Evansville†	Am. Assoc.	2	3	0	0	.000	4	3	3	3	3	9.00
1974—Sacramento	P. Coast	5	23	2	3	.400	19	22	17	16	20	6.65
1974—Milwaukee	American	23	53	2	3	.400	59	29	29	31	30	4.92
1975—Sacramento	P. Coast	12	61	3	3	.500	55	24	20	46	31	2.95
1975—Milwaukee	American	28	136	6	11	.353	130	78	65	57	60	4.30
1976—Milwaukee	American	34	240	15	16	.484	211	92	75	120	95	2.81
1977—Milwaukee‡	American	19	122	4	12	.250	140	75	71	49	57	5.24
1978—Milwaukee§	American	28	176	12	11	.522	184	93	86	66	58	4.40
1979—Milwaukee	American	30	187	14	8	.636	196	89	81	74	45	3.90
1980—Milwaukee x	American	29	154	12	6	.667	147	76	67	62	47	3.92
Major League Totals		191	1068	65	67	.492	1067	532	474	459	392	3.99

Selected by Milwaukee Brewers' organization in 6th round of free-agent draft, June 4, 1970.

†On disabled list, April 13 to May 16 and June 17 to September 4, 1973.
‡On disabled list, June 6 to July 15, 1977.
§On disabled list, March 22 to May 12, 1978.
xGranted free agency, October 22, 1980; signed by California Angels, January 26, 1981.

ALL-STAR GAME RECORD

Member of American League All-Star Team in 1976; did not play.

ALEJANDRO TREVINO (CASTRO)
(Alex)

Born August 26, 1957, at Monterrey, Mexico.
Height, 5.10. Weight, 165.
Throws and bats righthanded.
Attended University of Nuevo Leon, Monterrey, Mexico.
Brother of Bobby Trevino, former outfielder in California Angels' organization;
currently with Nuevo Laredo in Mexican League.

Led Carolina League catchers in passed balls with 18 in 1976.
Led Midwest League catchers in putouts with 847 and in assists with 102 in 1977.

Year Club	League	Pos.	G.	AB.	R.	H.	2B.	3B.	HR.	RBI.	B.A.	PO.	A.	E.	F.A.
1973—Victoria†	Mx. Cen.	C-OF	12	26	3	6	1	0	0	2	.231	26	5	1	.969
1974—Marion	Appal.	C-SS	12	16	0	1	0	0	0	1	.063	15	0	0	1.000
1975—Marion	Appal.	C-2B-OF	22	60	10	12	1	0	0	3	.200	96	8	6	.963
1976—Lynchburg	Carol.	C-3-2-S	94	284	17	57	11	2	0	31	.201	400	130	18	.967
1977—Wausau	Midw.	C-2-1-3	128	422	57	100	10	0	2	36	.237	865	110	15	.985
1978—Tidewater	Int.	C-3B	87	262	44	77	13	2	5	37	.294	303	68	11	.971
1978—New York	Nat.	C-3B	6	12	3	3	0	0	0	0	.250	12	4	0	1.000
1979—New York	Nat.	C-3B-2B	79	207	24	56	11	1	0	20	.271	229	71	9	.971
1980—New York	Nat.	C-3B-2B	106	355	26	91	11	2	0	37	.256	450	76	16	.970
Major League Totals			191	574	53	150	22	3	0	57	.261	691	151	25	.971

Signed as free agent by Victoria, May 16, 1974.
†Sold to New York Mets' organization, May 22, 1974.

JESUS MANUEL TRILLO (MARCANO)

Name pronounced TREE-yo.

(Manny)

Born December 25, 1950, at Caritito, Monagas, Venezuela.
Height, 6:01. Weight, 164.
Throws and bats righthanded.
Hobbies—Movies and all sports.
Attended Colegio Libertador Bolivar, Maturin, Monagas, Venz.

Led National League second basemen in double plays with 99 in 1978.
Led Pacific Coast League second basemen in double plays with 113 in 1973.
Named second baseman on THE SPORTING NEWS National League All-Star fielding team, 1979 and 1980.
Named second baseman on THE SPORTING NEWS National League Silver Bat team, 1980.

Year Club	League	Pos.	G.	AB.	R.	H.	2B.	3B.	HR.	RBI.	B.A.	PO.	A.	E.	F.A.
1968—Huron†	North.	S-3-C	35	92	8	24	2	1	0	4	.261	35	48	5	.943
1969—Spartanburg‡	W. Car.	3-C-S-2	83	275	41	77	18	0	1	26	.280	188	98	12	.960
1970—Birmingham	South.	3-2-S	84	241	26	63	10	1	2	19	.261	101	130	14	.943
1971—Birmingham§	South.	3B-SS	107	371	37	104	18	1	5	44	.280	110	212	31	.912
1972—Iowa	A. A.	3-2-S	133	509	67	153	27	6	9	53	.301	176	304	28	.945
1973—Tucson	P. C.	*2B-OF	135	519	76	162	25	7	8	78	.312	*304	*373	19	*.973
1973—Oakland	Amer.	2B	17	12	0	3	2	0	0	3	.250	15	17	2	.941
1974—Tucson	P. C.	2B	85	320	31	81	19	1	2	39	.253	198	256	12	.974
1974—Oakland x	Amer.	2B	21	33	3	5	0	0	0	2	.152	31	43	4	.949
1975—Chicago	Nat.	*2B-SS	154	545	55	135	12	2	7	70	.248	350	*509	*29	.967
1976—Chicago	Nat.	*2B-SS	158	582	42	139	24	3	4	59	.239	350	*527	17	.981
1977—Chicago	Nat.	2B	152	504	51	141	18	5	7	57	.280	330	*467	*25	.970
1978—Chicago y	Nat.	2B	152	552	53	144	17	5	4	55	.261	354	*505	19	.978
1979—Philadelphia z	Nat.	2B	118	431	40	112	22	1	6	42	.260	270	368	10	.985
1980—Philadelphia a	Nat.	2B	141	531	68	155	25	9	7	43	.292	*360	467	11	.987
American League Totals			38	45	3	8	2	0	0	5	.178	46	60	6	.946
National League Totals			875	3145	309	826	118	25	35	326	.263	2014	2843	111	.978
Major League Totals			913	3190	312	834	120	25	35	331	.261	2060	2903	117	.977

Signed as free agent by Philadelphia Phillies' organization, January 26, 1968.
†On disabled list, August 16 to September 3, 1968.
‡Drafted by Birmingham (Oakland Athletics' organization) from Raleigh-Durham (Philadelphia Phillies' organization), December 1, 1969.
§On disabled list, May 1 through May 20, 1971.
xTraded with Pitchers Darold Knowles and Bob Locker to Chicago Cubs for First Baseman-Outfielder Billy Williams, October 23, 1974.
yTraded with Outfielder Greg Gross and Catcher Dave Rader to Philadelphia Phillies for Outfielder Jerry Martin, Catcher Barry Foote, Second Baseman Ted Sizemore and Pitchers Derek Botelho and Henry Mack, February 23, 1979.
zOn disabled list, May 4 to June 16, 1979.
aOn supplemental disabled list, April 20 to May 7, 1980.

Year Club	League	Pos.	G.	AB.	R.	H.	2B.	3B.	HR.	RBI.	B.A.	PO.	A.	E.	F.A.
1974–Oakland ....Amer.		PR	1	0	1	0	0	0	0	0	.000	0	0	0	.000
1980–Philadelphia......Nat.		2B	5	21	1	8	2	1	0	4	.381	18	25	1	.977
Championship Series Totals			6	21	2	8	2	1	0	4	.381	18	25	1	.977

WORLD SERIES RECORD

Tied World Series record for most chances accepted by second baseman, six-game Series (39), 1980.

Year Club	League	Pos.	G.	AB.	R.	H.	2B.	3B.	HR.	RBI.	B.A.	PO.	A.	E.	F.A.
1980–Philadelphia......Nat.		2B	6	23	4	5	2	0	0	2	.217	14	25	1	.975

ALL-STAR GAME RECORD

Year League	Pos.	AB.	R.	H.	2B.	3B.	HR.	RBI.	B.A.	PO.	A.	E.	F.A.
1977–National...............................	2B	1	0	0	0	0	0	0	.000	0	1	0	1.000

STEVEN RUSSELL TROUT
(Steve)

Born July 30, 1957, at Detroit, Mich.
Height, 6.04. Weight, 195.
Throws and bats lefthanded.
Son of Dizzy Trout, pitcher with Detroit Tigers, Boston Red Sox and
Baltimore Orioles, 1932 through 1952 and 1957.

Year Club	League	G.	IP.	W.	L.	Pct.	H.	R.	ER.	SO.	BB.	ERA.
1976–Sarasota White Sox...............G. Coast		9	38	1	3	.250	28	18	11	35	29	2.61
1977–Appleton ....Midwest		21	111	6	8	.429	113	66	50	101	66	4.05
1977–Iowa ....Am. Assoc.		5	24	0	4	.000	27	16	15	14	11	5.63
1978–Knoxville ....Southern		12	71	8	3	.727	46	16	13	48	33	1.65
1978–Iowa ....Am. Assoc.		9	55	3	4	.429	57	36	32	38	22	5.24
1978–Chicago ....American		4	22	3	0	1.000	19	10	10	11	11	4.09
1979–Iowa ....Am. Assoc.		4	27	3	1	.750	24	10	9	12	19	3.00
1979–Chicago ....American		34	155	11	8	.579	165	77	67	76	59	3.89
1980–Chicago ....American		32	200	9	16	.360	229	102	82	89	49	3.69
Major League Totals.................................		70	377	23	24	.489	413	189	159	176	119	3.80

Selected by Chicago White Sox' organization in 1st round (eighth player selected) of free-agent draft, June 8, 1976.

JOHN THOMAS TUDOR

Born February 2, 1954, at Schenectady, N.Y.
Height, 6.00. Weight, 185.
Throws and bats lefthanded.
Attended North Shore Community College, Beverly, Mass. and
Georgia Southern College, Statesboro, Ga.; received
Bachelor of Science degree in Criminal Justice.

Pitched 2-0, seven-inning, no-hit victory against Reading, June 28, 1977.

Year Club	League	G.	IP.	W.	L.	Pct.	H.	R.	ER.	SO.	BB.	ERA.
1976–Winston-Salem ....Carolina		25	82	5	2	.714	77	26	25	76	28	2.74
1977–Bristol ....Eastern		27	115	6	5	.545	113	57	45	78	35	3.52
1977–Pawtucket ....Int'national		4	4	1	1	.500	5	1	1	1	3	2.25
1978–Pawtucket ....Int'national		26	105	7	4	.636	100	46	36	83	56	3.09
1979–Pawtucket ....Int'national		25	163	10	11	.476	145	73	53	103	52	2.93
1979–Boston ....American		6	28	1	2	.333	39	23	20	11	9	6.43
1980–Pawtucket ....Int'national		12	74	4	5	.444	67	36	30	51	33	3.65
1980–Boston ....American		16	92	8	5	.615	81	35	31	45	31	3.03
Major League Totals.................................		22	120	9	7	.563	120	58	51	56	40	3.83

Selected by New York Mets' organization in 21st round of free-agent draft, June 4, 1975.
Selected by Boston Red Sox' organization in secondary phase of free-agent draft, January 7, 1976.

MICHAEL ALAN TURGEON
(Mike)

Born March 9, 1956, at New London, Conn.
Height, 6.02. Weight, 180.
Throws right and bats left and righthanded.
Attended Eastern Connecticut State College, Willimantic, Conn.

Led New York-Pennsylvania league in total bases with 156 in 1978.
Led Texas League third basemen in double plays with 37 in 1979.

Year Club	League	Pos.	G.	AB.	R.	H.	2B.	3B.	HR.	RBI.	B.A.	PO.	A.	E.	F.A.
1977–Brad. Cubs........G.C.		SS-3B	9	37	9	16	1	0	0	6	.432	11	7	1	.947
1978–Pompano Beach Fla. St.		SS	28	80	8	20	3	0	0	6	.250	26	43	4	.945
1978–Geneva ....NYP		2B	70	285	64	*98	16	6	10	48	*.344	111	152	9	.967
1979–Midland ....Texas		3B-OF	130	461	79	137	25	7	10	83	.297	103	226	25	.929
1980–Wichita.............A.A.		3B-OF	127	489	61	122	26	1	13	75	.249	125	166	19	.939

Selected by Chicago Cubs' organization in 6th round of free-agent draft, June 7, 1977.

JOHN WEBBER TURNER
(Jerry)

Born January 17, 1954, at Texarkana, Ark.
Height, 5.09. Weight, 180.
Throws and bats lefthanded.
Hobbies—Fishing and bowling.

Year Club League	Pos.	G.	AB.	R.	H.	2B.	3B.	HR.	RBI.	B.A.	PO.	A.	E.	F.A.
1972—Tri-City.............Northw.	OF	66	199	44	75	7	3	6	47	*.377	69	*10	12	.868
1973—Alexandria†.......Texas	OF	75	269	30	69	15	1	7	28	.257	103	6	8	.932
1974—Alexandria ....Texas	OF	130	472	77	154	24	5	18	68	.326	247	13	*21	.925
1974—San Diego.........Nat.	OF	17	48	4	14	1	0	0	2	.292	14	1	0	1.000
1975—Hawaii .............P.C.	OF	142	535	88	*176	27	3	11	91	.329	195	9	*16	.927
1975—San Diego.........Nat.	OF	11	22	1	6	0	0	0	0	.273	10	0	1	.909
1976—San Diego.........Nat.	OF	105	281	41	75	16	5	5	37	.267	115	6	5	.960
1977—San Diego.........Nat.	OF	118	289	43	71	16	1	10	48	.246	114	10	7	.947
1978—San Diego.........Nat.	OF	106	225	28	63	9	1	8	37	.280	91	5	3	.970
1979—San Diego ....Nat.	OF	138	448	55	111	23	2	9	61	.248	197	7	9	.958
1980—San Diego‡.......Nat.	OF	85	153	22	44	5	0	3	18	.288	44	2	0	1.000
Major League Totals		580	1466	194	384	70	9	35	203	.262	585	31	25	.961

Selected by San Diego Padres' organization in 10th round of free-agent draft, June 6, 1972.
†On disabled list, July 22 to September 7, 1973.
‡On disabled list, August 15 to October 9, 1980.

JEFFREY DEAN TWITTY
(Jeff)

Born November 10, 1957, at Lancaster, S. C.
Height, 6.02. Weight, 185.
Throws and bats lefthanded.
Attended Anderson Junior College, Anderson, S. C., and
University of South Carolina, Columbia, S. C.

Year Club League	G.	IP.	W.	L.	Pct.	H.	R.	ER.	SO.	BB.	ERA.
1979—Sara. Royal Golds................G. Coast	4	6	0	0	.000	8	2	2	4	1	3.00
1979—Ft.Myers ....Florida St.	3	5	0	0	.000	2	0	0	6	2	0.00
1979—Jacksonville.......................Southern	14	25	2	0	1.000	23	11	9	21	4	3.24
1980—Omaha.............................Am. Assoc.	31	48	6	3	.667	34	16	10	24	9	1.88
1980—Kansas City ....American	13	22	2	1	.667	33	17	15	9	7	6.14
Major League Totals.................................	13	22	2	1	.667	33	17	15	9	7	6.14

Selected by Kansas City Royals' organization in 24th round of free-agent draft, June 5, 1979.

MICHAEL RAY TYSON
(Mike)

Born January 13, 1950, at Rocky Mount, N. C.
Height, 5.09. Weight, 170.
Throws and bats righthanded.
Hobby—Golf.
Attended Indian River Community College, Ft. Pierce, Fla.

Led National League shortstops in double plays with 108 in 1974.
Led American Association second basemen in double plays with 97 in 1972.

Year Club League	Pos.	G.	AB.	R.	H.	2B.	3B.	HR.	RBI.	B.A.	PO.	A.	E.	F.A.
1970—St. Petersburg ...Fla.St.	SS-2B	109	400	47	98	10	3	4	37	.245	177	279	35	.929
1971—Modesto ....Calif.	2-S-3-O	107	326	46	78	12	1	2	26	.239	179	208	19	.953
1972—Tulsa ................A.A.	*2B-SS	132	444	39	103	14	3	3	50	.232	*319	335	13	*.981
1972—St. Louis ....Nat.	2B-SS	13	37	1	7	1	0	0	0	.189	26	36	3	.954
1973—St. Louis ....Nat.	•SS-2B	144	469	48	114	15	4	1	33	.243	239	401	•33	.951
1974—St. Louis ....Nat.	SS-2B	151	422	35	94	14	5	1	37	.223	247	434	31	.956
1975—St. Louis ....Nat.	SS-2-3	122	368	45	98	16	3	2	37	.266	184	308	15	.970
1976—St. Louis† ....Nat.	2B	76	245	26	70	12	9	3	28	.286	158	237	12	.971
1977—St. Louis ....Nat.	2B	138	418	42	103	15	2	7	57	.246	267	423	15	.979
1978—St. Louis ....Nat.	2B	125	377	26	88	16	0	3	26	.233	246	306	13	.977
1979—St. Louis‡§ ....Nat.	2B	75	190	18	42	8	2	5	20	.221	125	184	8	.975
1980—Chicago ....Nat.	2B	123	341	34	81	19	3	3	23	.238	222	329	18	.968
Major League Totals		967	2867	275	697	116	28	25	261	.243	1714	2658	148	.967

Selected by St. Louis Cardinals' organization in 3rd round of free-agent draft, January 17, 1970.
†On disabled list, April 14 to May 9 and July 18 to September 1, 1976.
‡On disabled list, August 7 to September 9, 1979.
§Traded to Chicago Cubs for Pitcher Donnie Moore, October 17, 1979.

GERALD RAYMOND UJDUR

Named pronounced you-JUR.

(Jerry)

Born March 5, 1957, at Duluth, Minn.
Height, 6.01. Weight, 195.
Throws and bats righthanded.
Attended University of Minnesota, Minneapolis, Minn.

Tied for American Association lead in shutouts with 3 in 1980.

Year Club	League	G	IP	W	L	Pct.	H	R	ER	SO	BB	ERA
1978—Lakeland	Florida St.	13	64	5	2	.714	54	22	17	23	20	2.39
1979—Montgomery†	Southern	19	37	2	5	.286	48	27	23	30	16	5.59
1980—Evansville	Am. Assoc.	29	115	9	4	.692	103	54	43	62	38	3.37
1980—Detroit	American	9	21	1	0	1.000	36	20	18	8	10	7.71
Major League Totals		9	21	1	0	1.000	36	20	18	8	10	7.71

Selected by Detroit Tigers' organization in 4th round of free-agent draft, June 6, 1978.

†On temporary inactive list, April 16 to July 9, 1979.

JAMES HAROLD UMBARGER
(Jim)

Born February 17, 1953, at Burbank, Calif.
Height, 6.06. Weight, 205.
Throws and bats lefthanded.
Hobbies—Music, all sports, reading, driving, people and traveling.
Attended Arizona State University, Tempe, Ariz.

Tied major league record for pitchers by recording an unassisted double play, August 19, 1975.
Tied for Eastern League lead in shutouts with 5 in 1974.

Year Club	League	G	IP	W	L	Pct.	H	R	ER	SO	BB	ERA
1974—Pittsfield	Eastern	14	97	7	4	.636	74	24	18	74	27	1.67
1975—Texas	American	56	131	8	7	.533	134	63	60	50	59	4.12
1976—Texas†	American	30	197	10	12	.455	208	86	69	105	54	3.15
1977—San Jose‡	P. Coast	13	56	3	5	.375	90	62	48	21	32	7.71
1977—Oakland§-Texas	American	15	57	2	6	.250	76	48	40	29	32	6.32
1978—Texas	American	32	98	5	8	.385	116	58	53	60	36	4.87
1979—Tucson	P. Coast	26	133	6	10	.375	166	85	80	73	69	5.41
1980—Charleston x	Int'national	2	6	1	0	1.000	6	3	1	2	1	1.50
1980—Tulsa y	Texas	22	32	3	1	.750	25	10	9	33	12	2.53
Major League Totals		133	483	25	33	.431	534	255	222	244	181	4.14

Selected by Cleveland Indians' organization in 2nd round of free-agent draft, June 8, 1971.
Selected by Texas Rangers' organization in 15th round of free-agent draft, June 5, 1974.

†Traded with Infielder Rodney Scott and cash estimated at $100,000 to Oakland A's for Outfielder Claudell Washington, March 26, 1977.

‡On disabled list, July 5 to July 18, 1977.

§Sold to Texas Rangers, August 25, 1977.

xOn disabled list, April 23 to July 11, 1980.

yGranted free agency, November 1, 1980; signed by Baltimore Orioles' organization, February 10, 1981.

PATRICK JOHN UNDERWOOD
(Pat)

Born February 9, 1957, at Kokomo, Ind.
Height, 6.00. Weight, 175.
Throws and bats lefthanded.
Brother of Tom Underwood, pitcher with New York Yankees; son of John Underwood,
former minor leaguer in Philadelphia Phillies' organization.

Year Club	League	G	IP	W	L	Pct.	H	R	ER	SO	BB	ERA
1976—Lakeland	Florida St.	12	77	6	2	.750	63	26	19	45	32	2.22
1977—Montgomery	Southern	14	104	9	2	.818	82	46	39	64	37	3.38
1977—Evansville	Am. Assoc.	16	50	3	5	.375	57	39	29	37	22	5.22
1978—Evansville†	Am. Assoc.	20	104	5	5	.500	116	57	48	73	31	4.15
1979—Evansville	Am. Assoc.	7	48	2	3	.400	41	20	15	35	17	2.81
1979—Detroit	American	27	122	6	4	.600	126	64	62	83	29	4.57
1980—Detroit	American	49	113	3	6	.333	121	51	45	60	35	3.58
Major League Totals		76	235	9	10	.474	247	115	107	143	64	4.10

Selected by Detroit Tigers' organization in 1st round (second player selected) of free-agent draft, June 8, 1976.

†On disabled list, June 30 to August 12, 1978.

THOMAS GERALD UNDERWOOD
(Tom)

Born December 22, 1953, at Kokomo, Ind.
Height, 5.11. Weight, 185.
Throws left and bats righthanded.
Hobbies—Golf and hunting.
Brother of Pat Underwood, pitcher with Detroit Tigers; son of John Underwood,
former minor leaguer in Philadelphia Phillies' organization.

Named Most Valuable Pitcher in Western Carolinas League, 1973.

Year Club	League	G	IP	W	L	Pct.	H	R	ER	SO	BB	ERA
1973—Spartanburg	W. Carol.	26	193	13	6	.684	137	66	45	•187	79	•2.10
1974—Reading	Eastern	23	165	14	5	•.737	134	65	46	157	69	2.51
1974—Toledo	Int'national	3	9	0	1	.000	8	4	4	11	4	4.00
1974—Philadelphia	National	7	13	1	0	1.000	15	8	7	8	5	4.85
1975—Philadelphia	National	35	219	14	13	.519	221	110	101	123	84	4.15

Year Club	League	G.	IP.	W.	L.	Pct.	H.	R.	ER.	SO.	BB.	ERA.
1976—Philadelphia	National	33	156	10	5	.667	154	63	61	94	63	3.52
1977—Phil.†-St.L.‡	National	33	133	9	11	.450	148	82	74	86	75	5.01
1978—Toronto	American	31	198	6	14	.300	201	105	90	139	87	4.09
1979—Toronto§	American	33	227	9	16	.360	213	113	93	127	95	3.69
1980—New York	American	38	187	13	9	.591	163	85	76	116	66	3.66
National League Totals		108	521	34	29	.540	538	263	243	311	227	4.20
American League Totals		102	612	28	39	.418	577	303	259	382	248	3.81
Major League Totals		210	1133	62	68	.477	1115	566	502	693	475	3.99

Selected by Philadelphia Phillies' organization in 2nd round of free-agent draft, June 6, 1972.

†Traded with First Baseman Dane Iorg and Outfielder Rick Bosetti to St. Louis Cardinals for Pitcher Steve Waterbury and Outfielder Bake McBride, June 15, 1977.

‡Traded with Pitcher Victor Cruz to Toronto Blue Jays for Pitcher Pete Vuckovich, December 6, 1977. (Toronto sent Outfielder John Scott to Cardinals to complete deal, December 16, 1977.)

§Traded with Catcher Rick Cerone and Outfielder Ted Wilborn to New York Yankees for First Baseman Chris Chambliss, Infielder Damaso Garcia and Pitcher Paul Mirabella, November 1, 1979.

CHAMPIONSHIP SERIES RECORD

Year Club	League	G.	IP.	W.	L.	Pct.	H.	R.	ER.	SO.	BB.	ERA.
1976—Philadelphia	National	1	⅓	0	0	.000	1	0	0	0	2	0.00
1980—New York	American	2	3	0	0	.000	3	2	0	3	0	0.00
Championship Series Totals		3	3⅓	0	0	.000	4	2	0	3	2	0.00

DELBERT BERNARD UNSER
(Del)

Born December 9, 1944, at Decatur, Ill.
Height, 5.11. Weight, 180.
Throws and bats lefthanded.
Hobby—Golf.
Attended Mississippi State University, Starkville, Miss., and Eastern Illinois University, Charleston, Ill.; received Bachelor of Arts degree in Mathematics. Did post-graduate work in physical education at University of Maryland.
Son of Al Unser, major league catcher with Detroit Tigers and Cincinnati Reds, 1942 through 1945; brother of Lawrence Unser, former outfielder in Cleveland Indians' organization.

Established major league record for fewest triples, season, for league leader in triples, 8, in 1969; most home runs by pinch-hitter, consecutive plate appearances (3), June 30, July 5 and 10, 1979.
Led American League outfielders in double plays with 10 in 1968.
Tied for lead in double plays by Eastern League outfielders with 10 in 1968.
Named THE SPORTING NEWS American League Rookie Player of the Year, 1968.
Received reported $25,000 bonus to sign with Washington Senators, 1966.

Year Club	League	Pos.	G.	AB.	R.	H.	2B.	3B.	HR.	RBI.	B.A.	PO.	A.	E.	F.A.
1966—York	East.	OF	39	123	11	27	4	1	3	11	.220	58	3	5	.924
1967—York	East.	OF	138	507	56	117	14	7	6	32	.231	269	*20	8	.973
1968—Washington	Amer.	*OF-1	156	635	66	146	13	7	1	30	.230	392	*22	5	.988
1969—Washington	Amer.	OF	153	581	69	166	19	*8	7	57	.286	339	8	10	.972
1970—Washington	Amer.	OF	119	322	37	83	5	1	5	30	.258	173	8	3	.984
1971—Washington†	Amer.	OF	153	581	63	148	19	6	9	41	.255	394	10	8	.981
1972—Cleveland‡	Amer.	OF	132	383	29	91	12	0	1	17	.238	248	10	3	.989
1973—Philadelphia	Nat.	OF	136	440	64	127	20	4	11	52	.289	329	14	4	.988
1974—Philadelphia§	Nat.	OF	142	454	72	120	18	5	11	61	.264	300	13	6	.981
1975—New York	Nat.	OF	147	531	65	156	18	2	10	53	.294	362	13	5	.987
1976—N.Y. x-Mont.	Nat.	OF	146	496	57	113	19	4	12	40	.228	288	10	3	.990
1977—Montreal	Nat.	OF-1B	113	289	33	79	14	1	12	40	.273	280	13	3	.990
1978—Montreal y	1B-OF	OF	130	179	16	35	5	0	2	15	.196	232	12	2	.992
1979—Philadelphia‡	Nat.	OF-1B	95	141	26	42	8	0	6	29	.298	118	5	3	.976
1980—Philadelphia z	Nat.	OF	96	110	15	29	6	4	0	10	.264	116	13	0	1.000
American League Totals			713	2502	264	634	68	22	23	175	.253	1546	58	29	.982
National League Totals			1005	2640	348	701	108	20	64	300	.266	2025	93	26	.988
Major League Totals			1718	5142	612	1335	176	42	87	475	.260	3571	151	55	.985

Selected by Minnesota Twins' organization in 2nd round of free-agent draft, June, 1965.
Selected by Pittsburgh Pirates' organization in secondary phase of free-agent draft, January, 1966.

†Traded with Pitchers Gary Jones, Terry Ley and Dennis Riddleberger to Cleveland Indians for Pitchers Mike Paul and Rich Hand, Catcher Ken Suarez and Outfielder Roy Foster, December 2, 1971.

‡Traded with Infielder Terry Wedgewood to Philadelphia Phillies for Outfielders Oscar Gamble and Roger Freed, November 30, 1972.

§Traded with Pitcher Mac Scarce and Catcher John Stearns to New York Mets for Pitcher Tug McGraw and Outfielders Don Hahn and Dave Schneck, December 3, 1974.

xTraded with Infielder Wayne Garrett to Montreal Expos for Outfielders Jim Dwyer and Jose (Pepe) Mangual, July 21, 1976.

yGranted free agency, November 2, 1978; signed by Philadelphia Phillies, March 29, 1979.

zGranted free agency, November 4, 1980; re-signed by Phillies, December 22, 1980.

CHAMPIONSHIP SERIES RECORD

Year Club	League	Pos.	G.	AB.	R.	H.	2B.	3B.	HR.	RBI.	B.A.	PO.	A.	E.	F.A.
1980—Philadelphia	Nat.	OF-PH	5	5	2	2	1	0	0	1	.400	2	0	0	1.000

WORLD SERIES RECORD

Year Club	League	Pos.	G.	AB.	R.	H.	2B.	3B.	HR.	RBI.	B.A.	PO.	A.	E.	F.A.
1980—Philadelphia	Nat.	PH-OF	3	6	2	3	2	0	0	2	.500	1	0	0	1.000

WILLIE CLAY UPSHAW

Born April 27, 1957, at Blanco, Tex.
Height, 6.00. Weight, 185.
Throws and bats lefthanded.
Hobby—Off-season sports.
First-Cousin of Gene Upshaw, guard for Oakland Raiders and Marvin Upshaw,
former lineman with Cleveland Browns, Kansas City Chiefs and St. Louis Cardinals.

Year Club	League	Pos.	G	AB	R	H	2B	3B	HR	RBI	B.A.	PO	A	E	F.A.
1975—Oneonta	NYP	OF	29	91	8	8	1	0	0	4	.088	7	1	0	1.000
1976—Ft. Lauderdale	Fla.St.	OF	84	263	20	60	6	0	3	22	.228	22	0	0	1.000
1977—Ft. Lauderdale	Fla.St.	1B-OF	87	335	38	92	13	7	3	29	.275	358	31	14	.965
1977—West Haven†	East.	OF-1B	41	157	20	47	5	2	4	22	.299	40	0	4	.909
1978—Toronto	Amer.	OF-1B	95	224	26	53	8	2	1	17	.237	131	4	7	.951
1979—Syracuse	Int.	OF-1B	140	526	71	131	25	8	12	68	.249	544	24	14	.976
1980—Syracuse	Int.	OF-1B	100	358	55	91	13	7	9	52	.254	355	19	7	.982
1980—Toronto	Amer.	1B-OF	34	61	10	13	3	1	1	5	.213	51	7	1	.983
Major League Totals			129	285	36	66	11	3	2	22	.232	182	11	8	.960

Selected by New York Yankees' organization in 5th round of free-agent draft, June 4, 1975.
†Drafted by Toronto Blue Jays, December 5, 1977.

JOHN GODOY URREA

Name pronounced yur-REE-uh.

Born February 9, 1955, at Los Angeles, Calif.
Height, 6.03. Weight, 205.
Throws and bats righthanded.
Attended Rio Hondo Junior College, Whittier, Calif.
Tied for American Association lead in shutouts with 3 in 1980.

Year Club	League	G	IP	W	L	Pct.	H	R	ER	SO	BB	ERA.
1974—St. Petersburg	Florida St.	1	2	0	0	.000	2	0	0	0	2	0.00
1974—Sarasota Cardinals	Gulf C.	6	26	2	1	.667	21	5	4	15	6	1.38
1975—St. Petersburg	Florida St.	23	175	●14	8	.636	138	61	41	108	60	2.11
1976—Arkansas	Texas	24	151	11	8	.579	167	71	63	113	45	3.75
1977—St. Louis	National	41	140	7	6	.538	126	56	49	81	35	3.15
1978—Springfield	Am. Assoc.	14	45	2	1	.667	48	32	29	39	22	5.80
1978—St. Louis	National	27	99	4	9	.308	108	75	59	61	47	5.36
1979—Springfield†	Am. Assoc.	20	128	8	5	.615	115	60	50	64	58	3.52
1979—St. Louis	National	3	11	0	0	.000	13	7	5	5	9	4.09
1980—Springfield§	Am. Assoc.	14	92	5	4	.556	77	47	36	44	42	3.52
1980—St. Louis‡	National	30	65	4	1	.800	57	28	25	36	41	3.46
Major League Totals		101	315	15	16	.484	304	166	138	183	132	3.94

Selected by St. Louis Cardinals' organization in 1st round (14th player selected) of free-agent draft, January 9, 1974.
†On disabled list, April 30 to May 27, 1979.
‡Traded with Pitchers John Littlefield, Kim Seaman and Al Olmsted, Catchers Terry Kennedy and Steve Swisher and Infielder Mike Phillips to San Diego Padres for Pitchers Rollie Fingers and Bob Shirley, Catcher-First Baseman Gene Tenace and a player to be named later, December 8, 1980; Catcher Bob Geren traded to Cardinals' organization completing deal, December 10, 1980.

MICHAEL LEWIS VAIL
(Mike)

Born November 10, 1951, at San Francisco, Calif.
Height, 6.00. Weight, 185.
Throws and bats righthanded.
Hobbies—Collecting stamps and coins and breeding Persian cats.
Attended De Anza College, Cupertino, Calif.

Tied major league record for most strikeouts, doubleheader (7), September 26, 1975 (24 innings).
Tied modern National League record for most consecutive games, one or more hits, rookie season (23), August 22 through September 15, 1975.
Tied for California League lead in double plays by outfielders with 3 in 1973.
Named Player of the Year and Rookie of the Year in International League, 1975.

Year Club	League	Pos.	G	AB	R	H	2B	3B	HR	RBI	B.A.	PO	A	E	F.A.
1971—Sarasota Cards	Gulf C.	3B-2B	35	95	6	24	4	1	0	17	.253	18	53	5	.934
1972—Modesto	Calif.	3B	42	136	15	32	5	0	4	17	.235	30	57	15	.853
1972—Cedar Rapids	Midw.	3B-OF	61	202	19	49	7	1	7	37	.243	48	50	14	.875
1972—Arkansas	Texas	3B-OF	19	65	4	12	6	0	1	7	.185	23	14	1	.974
1973—Modesto	Calif.	*OF-3B	134	479	81	133	●31	9	15	80	.278	150	*23	12	.935
1974—Modesto	Calif.	OF	62	221	37	79	15	3	7	41	.357	113	2	6	.950
1974—Arkansas†	Texas	OF	73	261	31	82	7	4	8	35	.314	116	6	4	.968
1975—Tidewater	Int.	OF	115	409	53	140	23	*9	7	79	*.342	182	9	2	.990
1975—New York	Nat.	OF	38	162	17	49	8	1	3	17	.302	92	9	3	.971
1976—New York‡	Nat.	OF	53	143	8	31	5	1	0	9	.217	63	1	4	.941
1977—New York§	Nat.	OF	108	279	29	73	12	1	8	35	.262	159	5	6	.965
1978—Portland	P.C.	OF	14	56	10	22	2	0	4	19	.393	14	1	0	1.000
1978—Cleveland x	Amer.	OF	14	34	2	8	2	1	0	2	.235	18	0	0	1.000

Year Club League	Pos.	G.	AB.	R.	H.	2B.	3B.	HR.	RBI.	B.A.	PO.	A.	E.	F.A.
1978—Chicago ....Nat.	OF-3B	74	180	15	60	6	2	4	33	.333	50	1	1	.981
1979—Chicago ....Nat.	OF-3B	87	179	28	60	8	2	7	35	.335	51	4	2	.965
1980—Chicago y.........Nat.	OF	114	312	30	93	17	2	6	47	.298	126	5	5	.963
National League Totals		474	1255	127	366	56	9	28	176	.292	541	25	21	.964
American League Totals		14	34	2	8	2	1	0	2	.235	18	0	0	1.000
Major League Totals		488	1289	129	374	58	10	28	178	.290	559	25	21	.965

Selected by Los Angeles Dodgers' organization in 10th round of free-agent draft, June 4, 1970.
Selected by St. Louis Cardinals' organization in secondary phase of free-agent draft, January 13, 1971.
†Traded with Infielder Jack Heidemann by St. Louis Cardinals to New York Mets for Infielder Teddy Martinez, December 11, 1974.
‡On disabled list, April 1 to June 15, 1976.
§Sold on waivers to Cleveland Indians, March 25, 1978.
xTraded to Chicago Cubs for Outfielder Joe Wallis, June 15, 1978.
yTraded to Cincinnati Reds for Outfielder Hector Cruz, December 12, 1980.

JULIO JULIAN VALDEZ

Born July 3, 1956, at Nizao de Peravia, Dominican Republic.
Height, 6.02. Weight, 150.
Throws right and bats left and righthanded.

Led Carolina League in sacrifice hits with 15 in 1977.
Led Carolina League shortstops in putouts with 237 and in double plays with 76 in 1977.

Year Club League	Pos.	G.	AB.	R.	H.	2B.	3B.	HR.	RBI.	B.A.	PO.	A.	E.	F.A.
1976—Winter Haven....Fla. St.	SS-3B	76	185	12	25	3	1	0	10	.135	78	142	20	.917
1977—Winston-Salem ..Carol.	*SS-2B	132	451	66	112	19	4	8	47	.248	239	*368	*45	*.931
1978—Bristol ....East.	SS	124	396	50	105	13	3	8	56	.265	*213	285	39	.927
1979—Pawtucket† ....Int.	OF	103	370	43	82	12	6	5	31	.222	178	305	*34	.934
1980—Pawtucket ....Int.	SS	101	279	22	61	10	3	4	27	.219	164	288	29	.940
1980—Boston ....Amer.	SS	8	19	4	5	1	0	1	4	.263	17	26	3	.935
Major League Totals......................		8	19	4	5	1	0	1	4	.263	17	26	3	.935

Signed as free agent by Boston Red Sox' organization, December 12, 1975.
†On disabled list, May 29 to July 2, 1979.

ELLIS CLARENCE VALENTINE

Born July 30, 1954, at Helena, Ark.
Height, 6.04. Weight, 218.
Throws and bats righthanded.
Hobbies—Music, billiards and chess.

Major league stolen bases: 1975 (0), 1976 (14), 1977 (13), 1978 (13), 1979 (11), 1980 (5). Total—56.
Led International League in total bases with 226 in 1975.
Led Eastern League outfielders in double plays with 5 in 1974.
Named outfielder on THE SPORTING NEWS National League All-Star fielding team, 1978.

Year Club League	Pos.	G.	AB.	R.	H.	2B.	3B.	HR.	RBI.	B.A.	PO.	A.	E.	F.A.
1972—Cocoa Expos......Fl. E.C.	OF	53	177	24	47	8	0	1	18	.266	76	4	1	.988
1973—W. Palm Beach..Fla. St.	OF	119	403	59	124	18	4	8	61	.308	169	11	5	.973
1974—Quebec City.......East.	OF	130	426	46	112	11	7	5	50	.263	204	*20	10	.957
1975—Memphis..........Int.	OF-1B	139	494	*87	*151	●30	3	13	66	.306	266	12	6	.979
1975—Montreal ....Nat.	OF	12	33	2	12	4	0	1	3	.364	12	1	2	.867
1976—Denver..............A.A.	OF	57	204	31	63	9	1	7	32	.309	122	8	2	.985
1976—Montreal ....Nat.	OF	94	305	36	85	15	2	7	39	.279	162	12	5	.972
1977—Montreal ....Nat.	OF	127	508	63	149	28	2	25	76	.293	232	9	7	.972
1978—Montreal† ....Nat.	OF	151	570	75	165	35	2	25	76	.289	296	●24	10	.970
1979—Montreal ....Nat.	OF	146	548	73	151	29	3	21	82	.276	281	10	5	.983
1980—Montreal‡ ....Nat.	OF	86	311	40	98	22	2	13	67	.315	154	6	5	.970
Major League Totals		616	2275	289	660	133	11	92	343	.290	1137	62	34	.972

Selected by Montreal Expos' organization in 2nd round of free-agent draft, June 6, 1972.
†On suspended list, September 20 to September 22, 1978.
‡On disabled list, May 31 to July 6, 1980.

ALL-STAR GAME RECORD

Year League	Pos.	AB.	R.	H.	2B.	3B.	HR.	RBI.	B.A.	PO.	A.	E.	F.A.
1977—National................................	OF	1	0	0	0	0	0	0	.000	0	0	0	.000

FERNANDO VALENZUELA (ANGUAMEA)

Born November 1, 1960, at Navajoa, Sonora, Mexico
Height, 5.11. Weight, 180.
Throws and bats lefthanded.

Led Mexican Center League in wild pitches with 13 in 1978.

Year Club League	G.	IP.	W.	L.	Pct.	H.	R.	ER.	SO.	BB.	ERA.
1978—Guanajuato ....Mex. Cen.	16	93	5	6	.455	88	46	23	*91	46	2.23
1979—Yucatan† ....Mexican	26	181	10	12	.455	157	68	50	141	70	2.49
1979—Lodi ....California	3	24	1	2	.333	21	10	3	18	3	1.13
1980—San Antonio ....Texas	27	174	13	9	.591	156	70	60	*162	70	3.10
1980—Los Angeles ....National	10	18	2	0	1.000	8	2	0	16	5	0.00
Major League Totals................................	10	18	2	0	1.000	8	2	0	16	5	0.00

†Sold to Los Angeles Dodgers' organization, July 6, 1979.

DAVID VALLE
(Dave)

Born October 30, 1960, at Bayside, N. Y.
Height, 6.02. Weight, 200.
Throws and bats righthanded.
Brother of John Valle, outfielder in Baltimore Orioles' organization.
Led Northwest League catchers in double plays with 8 and tied for lead in passed balls with 23 in 1978.

Year Club	League	Pos.	G.	AB.	R.	H.	2B.	3B.	HR.	RBI.	B.A.	PO.	A.	E.	F.A.
1978—Bellingham	Northw.	C	57	167	12	34	2	0	2	21	.204	*338	65	10	.976
1979—Alexandria†	Carol.	C	58	169	17	36	5	0	6	25	.213	290	44	11	.968
1980—San Jose	Calif.	C	119	430	81	126	14	0	12	70	.293	570	*102	17	.975

Selected by Seattle Mariners' organization in 2nd round of free-agent draft, June 6, 1978.
†On disabled list, July 26 to August 25, 1979.

DAVID THOMAS VAN GORDER
(Dave)

Born March 27, 1957, at Los Angeles, Calif.
Height, 6.02. Weight, 205.
Throws and bats righthanded.
Attended University of Southern California, Los Angeles, Calif.
Led American Association catchers in fielding average with .992 in 1980.

Year Club	League	Pos.	G.	AB.	R.	H.	2B.	3B.	HR.	RBI.	B.A.	PO.	A.	E.	F.A.
1978—Nashville	South.	C	73	217	23	57	10	0	1	25	.263	396	38	5	.989
1979—Nashville	South.	C	137	461	58	131	27	1	6	64	.284	*726	*74	6	*.993
1980—Indianapolis†	A.A.	C-1B	71	253	11	57	12	1	3	26	.225	442	45	4	.992

Selected by Philadelphia Phillies' organization in 9th round of free-agent draft, June 4, 1975.
Selected by Cincinnati Reds' organization in 2nd round of free-agent draft, June 6, 1978.
†On disabled list, July 10 to September 30, 1980.

HEDIBERTO VARGAS (RODRIGUEZ)

Born February 23, 1959, at Guanica, Puerto Rico.
Height, 6.04. Weight, 205.
Throws and bats righthanded.
Led Eastern League in total bases with 242 in 1980.
Led Eastern League first basemen in double plays with 115 in 1980.
Tied for Gulf Coast League lead in double plays by first basemen with 8 in 1977.

Year Club	League	Pos.	G.	AB.	R.	H.	2B.	3B.	HR.	RBI.	B.A.	PO.	A.	E.	F.A.
1977—Brad. Pirates	G. C.	1B-OF	47	165	21	52	5	6	2	18	.315	300	14	9	.972
1978—Charleston	W. Car.	1B-OF	56	189	18	46	12	1	3	18	.243	109	6	7	.943
1978—Niagara Falls	NYP	1B-OF	57	205	35	47	11	1	4	23	.229	472	25	14	.973
1979—Shelby	W. Car.	1B-OF	126	440	76	124	23	5	*31	78	.282	868	49	11	.988
1980—Buffalo	East.	1B	133	509	78	138	28	2	24	87	.271	*1268	85	●15	.989

Signed as free agent by Pittsburgh Pirates' organization, January 17, 1977.

RAFAEL SANTIAGO VASQUEZ

Born June 28, 1958, at La Romana, Dominican Republic.
Height, 6.00. Weight, 160.
Throws and bats righthanded.
Tied for Carolina League lead in complete games with 11 in 1977.
Led Texas League in complete games with 13 in 1978.

Year Club	League	G.	IP.	W.	L.	Pct.	H.	R.	ER.	SO.	BB.	ERA.
1976—Bradenton Pirates	G. Coast	9	53	3	5	.375	56	35	20	30	14	3.40
1976—Charleston	W. Carol.	4	22	2	2	.500	19	5	4	13	2	1.64
1977—Salem	Carolina	26	175	14	6	.700	*218	*111	*91	114	46	4.68
1978—Columbus	Int'national	1	2	0	1	.000	6	4	4	2	0	18.00
1978—Shreveport†	Texas	27	*184	14	9	.609	174	91	66	150	54	3.23
1979—Seattle	American	9	16	1	0	1.000	23	9	9	9	6	5.06
1979—Spokane‡	P. Coast	22	126	8	11	.421	153	90	75	63	50	5.36
1980—Tacoma§	P. Coast	32	139	8	10	.444	170	99	83	55	67	5.37
Major League Totals		9	16	1	0	1.000	23	9	9	9	6	5.06

Signed as free agent by Pittsburgh Pirates' organization, December 4, 1975.
†Traded with Pitcher Odell Jones and Shortstop Mario Mendoza to Seattle Mariners for Pitchers Enrique Romo and Rick Jones and Shortstop Tom McMillan, December 5, 1978.
‡Traded with Pitcher Rob Pietroburgo and a player to be named later to Cleveland Indians for Infielder Ted Cox, December 6, 1979; Pitcher Bud Anderson traded to Indians' organization completing deal, March 29, 1980.
§Traded with Pitchers Bob Owchinko and Victor Cruz and Catcher Gary Alexander to Pittsburgh Pirates for Pitcher Bert Blyleven and Catcher Manny Sanguillen, December 9, 1980.

JESUS ANTHONY VEGA

Born October 14, 1955, at Bayamon, Puerto Rico
Height, 6.01. Weight, 190.
Throws and bats righthanded.

Year Club	League	Pos.	G.	AB.	R.	H.	2B.	3B.	HR.	RBI.	B.A.	PO.	A.	E.	F.A.
1975—Newark	NYP	OF-1B	52	188	26	58	7	4	1	27	.309	160	10	4	.977
1976—Newark	NYP	OF	45	169	25	53	12	3	4	36	.314	80	5	4	.955
1977—Burlington†	Midw.	1B	*139	496	80	*155	21	2	23	91	.313	*1169	68	*30	.976
1978—Orlando‡	South.	1B-3B	73	269	36	80	11	1	8	49	.297	646	46	14	.980
1979—Toledo	Int.	1B-OF	129	450	62	132	24	3	13	72	.293	895	53	8	.992
1979—Minnesota	Amer.	DH	4	7	0	0	0	0	0	0	.000	0	0	0	.000
1980—Toledo	Int.	1B	126	459	63	139	26	2	14	79	.303	971	66	*17	.984
1980—Minnesota	Amer.	1B	12	30	3	5	0	0	0	4	.167	1	1	0	1.000
Major League Totals			16	37	3	5	0	0	0	4	.135	1	1	0	1.000

Signed as free agent by Milwaukee Brewers' organization, March 3, 1975.
†Drafted by Tacoma (Minnesota Twins' organization) from Holyoke (Milwaukee Brewers' organization), December 6, 1977.
‡On disabled list, July 6 to September 11, 1978.

OTONIEL VELEZ (FRANCESCHI)
(Otto)

Born November 29, 1950, at Ponce, Puerto Rico.
Height, 6.00. Weight, 195.
Throws and bats righthanded.

Tied American League records for most home runs, 10-inning game (3), May 4, 1980; most home runs, doubleheader, home run in each game (4), May 4, 1980.
Hit three home runs in one game, vs. Cleveland Indians, May 4, 1980.
Led International League hitters in bases on balls with 130 in 1973 and with 87 in 1975.
Named Appalachian League Player of the Year in 1970.
Named International League Rookie of the Year, 1973.

Year Club	League	Pos.	G.	AB.	R.	H.	2B.	3B.	HR.	RBI.	B.A.	PO.	A.	E.	F.A.
1970—FT. Lauderdale†	Fla.St.	OF	20	54	7	9	0	1	0	4	.167	27	2	2	.935
1970—Johnson City	Appal.	3-2-OF	53	176	*49	65	10	4	7	●44	*.369	61	83	15	.906
1971—Kinston	Carol.	3B	113	384	82	119	21	4	16	73	.310	68	172	25	.906
1972—West Haven	East.	3-OF-1	122	409	64	102	17	1	13	68	.249	102	211	28	.918
1973—Syracuse	Int.	OF-3B	138	409	92	110	19	7	29	98	.269	177	11	10	.949
1973—New York	Amer.	OF	23	77	9	15	4	0	2	7	.195	45	2	2	.959
1974—Syracuse	Int.	1-2-3	65	200	44	62	13	0	13	35	.310	474	39	13	.975
1974—New York	Amer.	1-OF-3	27	67	9	14	1	1	2	10	.209	140	8	3	.980
1975—Syracuse‡	Int.	3B-1B	81	244	56	61	18	2	10	35	.250	302	90	19	.954
1975—New York	Amer.	1B	6	8	0	2	0	0	0	1	.250	11	0	0	1.000
1976—New York§	Amer.	OF-1-3	49	94	11	25	6	0	2	10	.266	89	2	2	.978
1977—Toronto	Amer.	OF	120	360	50	92	19	3	16	62	.256	140	5	4	.973
1978—Toronto	Amer.	OF-1B	91	248	29	66	14	2	9	38	.266	161	12	3	.983
1979—Toronto	Amer.	OF-1B	99	274	45	79	21	0	15	48	.288	159	5	4	.976
1980—Toronto x..........	Amer.	1B	104	357	54	96	12	3	20	62	.269	36	3	1	.975
Major League Totals			519	1485	207	389	77	9	66	238	.262	781	37	19	.977

Signed as free agent by New York Yankees' organization, December 23, 1969.
†On disabled list, May 19 to June 6, 1970.
‡On disabled list, June 10 to August 2, 1975.
§Selected by Toronto Blue Jays in American League expansion draft, November 5, 1976.
xOn disabled list, August 29 to October 8, 1980.

CHAMPIONSHIP SERIES RECORD

Year Club	League	Pos.	G.	AB.	R.	H.	2B.	3B.	HR.	RBI.	B.A.	PO.	A.	E.	F.A.
1976—New York..........	Amer.	PH	1	1	0	0	0	0	0	0	.000	0	0	0	.000

WORLD SERIES RECORD

Tied World Series record for most strikeouts by pinch-hitter, Series (3), 1976.

Year Club	League	Pos.	G.	AB.	R.	H.	2B.	3B.	HR.	RBI.	B.A.	PO.	A.	E.	F.A.
1976—New York..........	Amer.	PH	3	3	0	0	0	0	0	0	.000	0	0	0	.000

WILLIAM McKINLEY VENABLE JR.
(Max)

Born June 6, 1957, at Phoenix, Ariz.
Height, 5.10. Weight, 185.
Throws right and bats lefthanded.

Year Club	League	Pos.	G.	AB.	R.	H.	2B.	3B.	HR.	RBI.	B.A.	PO.	A.	E.	F.A.
1976—Bellingham†	N'west	OF	51	162	25	35	2	0	1	16	.216	·58	4	8	.886
1977—Clinton	Midw.	OF-2B	125	425	72	115	19	4	9	63	.271	149	13	13	.926
1978—Lodi‡	Calif.	OF	140	566	134	180	30	9	17	101	.318	220	8	8	.966
1979—San Francisco ...	Nat.	OF	55	85	12	14	1	1	0	3	.165	25	30	2	.914
1979—Shreveport	Texas	OF	18	69	11	16	1	2	0	3	.232	28	2	1	.968
1979—Phoenix	P. C.	OF	38	150	27	46	5	4	0	11	.307	96	4	3	.971

Year Club League	Pos.	G.	AB.	R.	H.	2B.	3B.	HR.	RBI.	B.A.	PO.	A.	E.	F.A.
1980—Phoenix ....P. C.	OF	78	312	52	89	10	10	5	40	.285	179	7	4	.979
1980—San Francisco ...Nat.	OF	64	138	13	37	5	0	0	10	.268	61	0	0	1.000
Major League Totals.......................		119	223	25	51	6	1	0	13	.229	86	30	2	.983

Selected by Los Angeles Dodgers' organization in 3rd round of free-agent draft, June 8, 1976.
†On disabled list, June 26 to July 10, 1976.
‡Drafted from Los Angeles Dodgers' organziation by San Francisco Giants, December 4, 1978.

JOHN C. VERHOEVEN
Name pronounced Vur-WHO-ven.

Born July 3, 1953, at Long Beach, Calif.
Height, 6.05. Weight, 207.
Throws and bats righthanded.
Attended Westmont College, Santa Barbara, Calif., and La Verne College,
La Verne, Calif.; received Bachelor of Arts Degree in Physical Education.

Year Club League	G.	IP.	W.	L.	Pct.	H.	R.	ER.	SO.	BB.	ERA.
1974—Quad Cities ....Midwest	27	43	1	0	1.000	37	19	15	52	17	3.14
1975—El Paso.............................Texas	31	56	4	0	1.000	45	18	10	46	26	1.61
1975—Salt Lake City ....P. Coast	18	26	3	1	.750	24	15	13	9	18	4.50
1976—Salt Lake City ....P. Coast	28	60	7	2	.778	53	19	15	56	18	2.25
1976—California ....Amer.	21	37	0	2	.000	35	15	14	23	14	3.41
1977—Salt Lake City ....P. Coast	19	33	4	1	.800	47	20	18	26	19	4.91
1977—Iowa.................................Am. Assoc.	30	44	2	5	.286	46	18	14	35	21	2.86
1977—California†-Chicago ....American	9	15	0	2	.000	13	6	5	9	6	3.00
1978—Iowa‡ ....Am. Assoc.	44	82	6	7	.462	94	49	44	53	25	4.83
1979—Toledo ....Int'national	50	100	6	6	.500	96	42	33	51	33	2.97
1980—Minnesota...........................American	44	100	3	4	.429	109	53	44	42	29	3.96
Major League Totals	74	152	3	8	.273	157	74	63	74	49	3.73

Selected by California Angels' organization in 12th round of free-agent draft, June 5, 1974.
†Traded with Pitcher Don Kirkwood and Infielder John Flannery to Chicago White Sox for Pitcher Ken Brett, June 15, 1977.
‡Sold to Minnesota Twins' organization, April 2, 1979.

THOMAS MARTIN VERYZER
Name pronounced Vuh-RISE-er.

(Tom)

Born February 11, 1953, at Islip, N.Y.
Height, 6.01. Weight, 185.
Throws and bats righthanded.
Hobbies—Music and basketball.

Tied for Southern League lead in sacrifice flies with 7 in 1972.
Shared Appalachian League Player of the Year, 1971.

Year Club League	Pos.	G.	AB.	R.	H.	2B.	3B.	HR.	RBI.	B.A.	PO.	A.	E.	F.A.
1971—Bristol ....Appal.	SS	51	169	27	38	7	4	4	20	.225	68	137	19	*.915
1972—Montgomery† ....South.	SS	111	381	36	84	20	4	8	49	.220	166	358	26	.953
1973—Toledo...............Int.	SS	94	284	32	71	11	5	3	26	.250	155	239	28	.934
1973—Detroit ....Amer.	SS	18	20	1	6	0	1	0	2	.300	6	12	3	.857
1974—Evansville‡ .......A.A.	SS	67	223	36	66	7	1	11	36	.296	109	207	15	.955
1974—Detroit ....Amer.	SS	22	55	4	13	2	0	2	9	.236	18	33	4	.927
1975—Detroit ....Amer.	SS	128	404	37	102	13	1	5	48	.252	215	358	24	.960
1976—Detroit§ ....Amer.	SS	97	354	31	83	8	2	1	25	.234	164	313	17	.966
1977—Detroit x ....Amer.	SS	125	350	31	69	12	1	2	28	.197	185	377	18	.969
1978—Cleveland.........Amer.	SS	130	421	48	114	18	4	1	32	.271	177	375	21	.963
1979—Cleveland.........Amer.	SS	149	449	41	99	9	3	0	34	.220	238	446	18	.974
1980—Cleveland.........Amer.	SS	109	358	28	97	12	0	2	28	.271	169	331	15	.971
Major League Totals		778	2411	221	583	74	12	13	206	.242	1172	2245	120	.966

Selected by Detroit Tigers' organization in 1st round (11th player selected) of free-agent draft, June 8, 1971.
†On disabled list, April 11 to April 28, 1972.
‡On disabled list, June 5 to July 6, 1974.
§On disabled list, August 19 to October 4, 1976.
xTraded to Cleveland Indians for Outfielder Charlie Spikes, December 9, 1977.

ROBERT MICHAEL VESELIC
Name pronounced Vuh-SELL-ik.

(Bob)

Born September 27, 1955, at Pittsburgh, Pa.
Height, 6.00. Weight, 182.
Throws and bats righthanded.
Attended Mount San Antonio College, Walnut, Calif.

Led International League in shutouts with 4 in 1980.
Tied for California League lead in games started with 28 in 1978.
Tied for Southern League lead in games started with 28 in 1979.

Year	Club	League	G.	IP.	W.	L.	Pct.	H.	R.	ER.	SO.	BB.	ERA.
1976—Reno		California	7	19	1	1	.500	22	22	22	16	21	10.42
1977—Wisconsin Rapids†		Midwest	16	98	8	5	.615	90	58	46	81	56	4.22
1978—Visalia		California	29	*215	●18	8	.692	214	102	80	160	98	3.35
1979—Orlando		Southern	28	201	11	10	.524	*220	101	80	*151	71	3.58
1980—Toledo		Int'national	27	174	11	8	.579	162	73	65	105	55	3.36
1980—Minnesota		American	1	4	0	0	.000	3	2	2	2	1	4.50
Major League Totals			1	4	0	0	.000	3	2	2	2	1	4.50

Selected by Minnesota Twins' organization in 1st round (ninth player selected) of free-agent draft, January 7, 1976.

†On disabled list, May 20 to July 13, 1977.

OSVALDO JOSE VIRGIL JR.
(Ozzie)

Born December 7, 1956, at Mayaguez, P. R.
Height, 6.01. Weight, 195.
Throws and bats righthanded.
Son of Ozzie Virgil, coach with Montreal Expos and former major league infielder and catcher.
Led Carolina League in total bases with 234 in 1978.
Named Carolina League Most Valuable Player, 1978.

Year	Club	League	Pos.	G.	AB.	R.	H.	2B.	3B.	HR.	RBI.	B.A.	PO.	A.	E.	F.A.
1976—Auburn		NYP	C	39	113	10	16	1	2	1	10	.142	153	14	5	.971
1977—Spartanburg		W. Car.	C	107	365	53	103	21	1	14	54	.282	502	*68	18	.969
1978—Peninsula		Carol.	C	126	409	79	124	21	1	*29	*98	.303	581	45	8	.987
1979—Reading		East.	C	128	429	57	99	17	1	8	66	.231	532	64	12	.980
1980—Reading		East.	C-1B	135	456	92	123	15	2	28	*104	.270	592	62	16	.976
1980—Philadelphia		Nat.	C	1	5	1	1	1	0	0	0	.200	4	0	0	1.000
Major League Totals				1	5	1	1	1	0	0	0	.200	4	0	0	1.000

Selected by Philadelphia Phillies' organization in 6th round of free-agent draft, June 8, 1976.

STEVEN ANTHONY VISKAS

Born November 8, 1959, at San Diego, Calif.
Height, 6.02. Weight, 185.
Throws and bats righthanded.
Tied for Midwest League lead in shutouts with 3 in 1979.

Year	Club	League	G.	IP.	W.	L.	Pct.	H.	R.	ER.	SO.	BB.	ERA.
1978—Pompano Beach		Florida St.	19	99	7	5	.583	102	56	43	51	58	3.91
1979—Quad Cities		Midwest	25	161	14	6	.700	120	59	49	135	66	2.74
1980—Midland		Texas	8	55	4	2	.667	58	30	27	36	15	4.42
1980—Wichita		Am. Assoc.	14	78	3	5	.375	84	46	42	30	34	4.85

Signed as free agent by Chicago Cubs' organization, December 16, 1977.

DAVID VON OHLEN

Born October 25, 1958, at Flushing, N. Y.
Height, 6.02. Weight, 200.
Throws and bats lefthanded.

Year	Club	League	G.	IP.	W.	L.	Pct.	H.	R.	ER.	SO.	BB.	ERA.
1976—Marion		Appal.	5	20	1	0	1.000	11	5	3	12	6	1.35
1976—Wausau		Midwest	9	31	1	4	.200	42	27	16	18	21	4.65
1977—Lynchburg		Carolina	37	65	6	3	.667	75	39	34	49	28	4.71
1978—Lynchburg		Carolina	34	72	6	7	.462	62	28	23	54	22	2.88
1979—Jackson		Texas	37	34	4	1	.800	28	11	7	26	10	1.85
1980—Tidewater		Int'national	45	87	5	4	.556	88	40	31	44	27	3.21

Selected by New York Mets' organization in 17th round of free-agent draft, June 8, 1976.

PETER DENNIS VUCKOVICH

Name pronounced VOO-Ko-vitch.

(Pete)

Born October 27, 1952, at Johnstown, Pa.
Height, 6.04. Weight, 220.
Throws and bats righthanded.
Attended Clarion State College, Clarion, Pa.

Year	Club	League	G.	IP.	W.	L.	Pct.	H.	R.	ER.	SO.	BB.	ERA.
1974—Appleton		Midwest	5	15	1	0	1.000	10	2	2	22	3	1.20
1974—Knoxville		Southern	13	47	2	5	.286	50	32	22	42	29	4.21
1975—Denver		Am. Assoc.	19	116	11	4	.733	103	63	56	86	54	4.34
1975—Chicago		American	4	10	0	1	.000	17	15	15	5	7	13.50
1976—Chicago†		American	33	110	7	4	.636	122	59	57	62	60	4.66
1977—Toronto‡		American	53	148	7	7	.500	143	64	57	123	59	3.47
1978—St. Louis		National	45	198	12	12	.500	187	65	56	149	59	2.55
1979—St. Louis		National	34	233	15	10	.600	229	108	93	145	64	3.59
1980—St. Louis§		National	32	222	12	9	.571	203	96	84	132	68	3.41
American League Totals			90	268	14	12	.538	282	138	129	190	126	4.33
National League Totals			111	653	39	31	.557	619	269	233	426	191	3.21
Major League Totals			201	921	53	43	.552	901	407	362	616	317	3.54

Selected by Chicago White Sox' organization in 3rd round of free-agent draft, June 5, 1974.

†Selected by Toronto Blue Jays in American League expansion draft, November 5, 1976.

‡Traded to St. Louis Cardinals for Pitchers Tom Underwood and Victor Cruz, December 6, 1977. (Toronto sent Outfielder John Scott to St. Louis, December 16, 1977.)

§Traded with Pitcher Rollie Fingers and Catcher Ted Simmons to Milwaukee Brewers for Outfielders Sixto Lezcano and David Green and Pitchers Lary Sorensen and Dave LaPoint, December 12, 1980.

GEORGE STEPHEN VUKOVICH

Born June 24, 1956, at Chicago, Ill.
Height, 6.00. Weight, 198.
Throws right and bats lefthanded.
Attended Southern Illinois University, Carbondale, Ill.

Led Eastern League in sacrifice flies with 14 in 1979.
Tied for Eastern League in double plays by outfielders with 3 in 1979.

Year Club League	Pos.	G.	AB.	R.	H.	2B.	3B.	HR.	RBI.	B.A.	PO.	A.	E.	F.A.
1977—Auburn ....NYP	DH	1	2	0	1	0	0	0	0	.500	0	0	0	.000
1978—Peninsula ....Carol.	OF-1B	135	453	*94	141	26	•9	10	69	.311	208	14	10	.957
1979—Reading ....East.	OF	138	501	80	147	14	10	13	88	.293	238	13	8	.969
1980—Philadelphia......Nat.	OF	78	58	6	13	1	1	0	8	.224	14	0	1	.933
Major League Totals.......................		78	58	6	13	1	1	0	8	.224	14	0	1	.933

Selected by Philadelphia Phillies' organization in 4th round of free-agent draft, June 7, 1977.

CHAMPIONSHIP SERIES RECORD

Year Club League	Pos.	G.	AB.	R.	H.	2B.	3B.	HR.	RBI.	B.A.	PO.	A.	E.	F.A.
1980—Philadelphia......Nat.	OF-PH	4	3	0	0	0	0	0	0	.000	0	0	0	.000

JOHN CHRISTOPHER VUKOVICH

Name pronounced VOO-koe-vich.

Born July 31, 1947, at Sacramento, Calif.
Height, 6.01. Weight, 190.
Throws and bats righthanded.
Hobbies—Hunting and fishing.
Attended American River College, Sacramento, Calif.

Led Pacific Coast League third basemen in double plays with 29 in 1970 and tied for lead with 24 in 1972.
Led American Association shortstops in fielding percentage with .948 in 1978 and with .960 in 1979.
Led American Association shortstops in putouts with 104 in 1978.
Tied for American Association lead in double plays by shortstops with 25 in 1978.

Year Club League	Pos.	G.	AB.	R.	H.	2B.	3B.	HR.	RBI.	B.A.	PO.	A.	E.	F.A.
1966—Huron ....North.	SS	67	241	30	62	5	2	2	35	.257	56	103	12	*.930
1967—Spartanburg†.....W. Car.	3B	74	261	35	66	12	1	4	40	.253	50	120	16	.914
1968—Spartanburg ......W. Car.	3B	37	134	23	42	11	0	3	20	.313	37	78	5	.958
1968—Tidewater ....Carol.	3B-2B	66	225	23	65	12	0	4	34	.280	69	99	9	.949
1969—Reading ....East.	3B	110	372	39	94	9	4	6	45	.253	114	187	15	*.953
1970—Eugene .............P.C.	*3B-1B	138	520	58	143	21	3	22	96	.275	*124	*334	22	*.954
1970—Philadelphia......Nat.	SS-3B	3	8	1	1	0	0	0	0	.125	4	8	2	.857
1971—Eugene .............P.C.	3B	58	221	31	68	16	2	5	35	.308	55	104	14	.919
1971—Philadelphia......Nat.	3B	74	217	11	36	5	0	0	14	.166	58	137	9	.956
1972—Eugene‡............P.C.	3-2-SS	139	539	84	141	32	2	13	68	.262	194	364	19	.967
1973—Milwaukee ....Amer.	3-1-SS	55	128	10	16	3	0	2	9	.125	66	67	5	.968
1974—Milwaukee§ ......Amer.	S-3-2-1	38	80	5	15	1	0	3	11	.188	46	68	5	.958
1975—Cincinnati x ....Nat.	3B	31	38	4	8	3	0	0	2	.211	12	37	4	.925
1975—Indianapolis x....A.A.	INF-OF	49	152	6	21	7	0	0	12	.138	89	88	6	.967
1975—Toledo...............Int.	3B-OF	26	97	6	22	5	0	0	10	.227	26	49	2	.974
1976—Reading y..........East.	2-SS-3	47	171	15	41	9	0	5	16	.240	68	140	8	.963
1976—Philadelphia......Nat.	3B-1B	4	8	2	1	0	0	1	2	.125	6	2	0	1.000
1977—Reading z ....East.	3B-1B	80	303	30	86	16	1	8	52	.284	96	148	13	.949
1977—Philadelphia......Nat.	PH	2	2	0	0	0	0	0	0	.000	0	0	0	.000
1978—Oklahoma City ..A. A.	3-2-S-1	126	429	49	90	16	1	7	47	.210	119	253	20	.949
1979—Oklahoma City aA. A.	3B-1B	101	382	38	111	20	1	12	66	.291	84	183	12	.957
1979—Philadelphia......Nat.	3B-2B	10	15	0	3	1	0	0	1	.200	2	13	0	1.000
1980—Philadelphia......Nat.	3-2-S-1	49	62	4	10	1	1	0	5	.161	18	35	2	.964
National League Totals..................		173	350	22	59	10	1	1	24	.169	100	232	17	.951
American League Totals.................		93	208	15	31	4	0	5	20	.149	132	135	10	.964
Major League Totals		266	558	37	90	14	1	6	44	.161	232	367	27	.957

Selected by Philadelphia Phillies' organization in free-agent draft, June, 1966.

†On temporary inactive list, June 17 to June 28. On military list, July 29, 1967 to February 6, 1968.

‡Traded by Philadelphia Phillies with Pitcher Billy Champion and Infielder Don Money to Milwaukee Brewers for Pitchers Jim Lonborg, Ken Brett, Ken Sanders and Earl Stephenson, October 31, 1972.

§Traded to Cincinnati Reds for Pitcher Pat Osburn, October 22, 1974.

xTraded by Cincinnati Reds to Philadelphia Phillies for Outfielder Dave Schneck, August 5, 1975.

yOn suspended list (on Oklahoma City roster), April 16 to June 29, 1976; on disabled list, August 1 to August 12, 1976.

zOn disabled list, June 23 to July 17, 1977.

aOn disabled list, April 20 to April 30, 1979.

MARK DUANE WAGNER

Born March 4, 1954, at Conneaut, O.
Height, 6.01. Weight, 175.
Throws and bats righthanded.
Hobbies—Basketball, handball and playing the guitar.

Year Club League	Pos.	G.	AB.	R.	H.	2B.	3B.	HR.	RBI.	B.A.	PO.	A.	E.	F.A.
1972—Bristol ....Appal.	2-S-3	56	196	35	40	5	2	2	13	.204	106	142	19	.929
1973—Clinton.............Midw.	SS	122	451	51	125	16	1	1	48	.277	169	*348	34	.938
1974—Lakeland† ....Fla. St.	SS	23	77	12	21	1	1	0	10	.273	27	70	9	.915
1975—Clinton.............Midw.	SS	119	436	52	111	11	4	1	50	.255	*175	339	31	*.943
1976—Evansville........A. A.	SS	107	304	32	79	9	5	1	22	.260	148	297	*36	.925
1976—Detroit.............Amer.	SS	39	115	9	30	2	3	0	12	.261	60	135	11	.947
1977—Evansville........A. A.	SS	64	222	33	68	12	6	3	27	.306	97	189	13	.957
1977—Detroit.............Amer.	SS-2B	22	48	4	7	0	1	1	3	.146	15	58	6	.924
1978—Detroit.............Amer.	SS-2B	39	109	10	26	1	2	0	6	.239	57	81	5	.965
1979—Detroit.............Amer.	SS-2B-3B	75	146	16	40	3	0	1	13	.274	88	146	8	.967
1980—Detroit‡§..........Amer.	S-3-2	45	72	5	17	1	0	0	3	.236	43	61	7	.937
Major League Totals		220	490	44	120	7	6	2	37	.245	263	481	37	.953

Selected by Detroit Tigers' organization in 19th round of free-agent draft, June 6, 1972.
†On disabled list, May 10 through remainder of season.
‡On supplemental disabled list, May 28 to June 18, 1980.
§Traded to Texas Rangers for Pitcher Kevin Saucier, December 10, 1980.

MICHAEL RICHARD WAITS
(Rick)

Born May 15, 1952, at Atlanta, Ga.
Height, 6.03. Weight, 195.
Throws left and bats left and righthanded.
Hobbies—Singing, writing, reading and golf.
Attended Clayton Junior College and Atlanta Baptist College, Chamblee, Ga.

Year Club League	G.	IP.	W.	L.	Pct.	H.	R.	ER.	SO.	BB.	ERA.
1970—Anderson ....W. Carol.	9	42	2	3	.400	27	25	22	37	33	4.71
1971—Pittsfield...............Eastern	25	139	5	9	.357	123	65	50	98	82	3.24
1972—Pittsfield...............Eastern	25	116	8	8	.500	104	66	40	84	82	3.10
1973—Spokane...............P. Coast	28	154	14	7	.667	153	96	67	99	103	3.92
1973—Texas ....American	1	1	0	0	.000	1	1	1	0	1	9.00
1974—Spokane...............P. Coast	26	153	12	6	.667	152	98	75	90	95	4.41
1975—Spokane†...............P. Coast	11	67	5	4	.556	76	46	36	38	37	4.84
1975—Oklahoma City ......Am. Assoc.	9	53	1	5	.167	55	29	26	31	27	4.42
1975—Cleveland...............American	16	70	6	2	.750	57	25	23	34	25	2.96
1976—Cleveland‡...............American	26	124	7	9	.438	143	60	55	65	54	3.99
1977—Cleveland...............American	37	135	9	7	.563	132	67	60	62	64	4.00
1978—Cleveland...............American	34	230	13	15	.464	206	97	82	97	86	3.21
1979—Cleveland...............American	34	231	16	13	.552	230	123	114	91	91	4.44
1980—Cleveland...............American	33	224	13	14	.481	231	118	111	109	82	4.46
Major League Totals	181	1015	64	60	.516	1000	491	446	458	403	3.95

Selected by Washington Senators' organization in 5th round of free-agent draft, June 4, 1970.
†Traded with Pitchers Jim Bibby and Jackie Brown and an estimated $100,000 by Texas Rangers to Cleveland Indians for Pitcher Gaylord Perry, June 12, 1975.
‡On disabled list, April 30 to May 29, 1976.

ROBERT VERNON WALK
(Bob)

Born November 26, 1956, at Van Nuys, Calif.
Height, 6.03. Weight, 200.
Throws and bats righthanded.
Attended College of the Canyons, Valencia, Calif.

Year Club League	G.	IP.	W.	L.	Pct.	H.	R.	ER.	SO.	BB.	ERA.
1977—Spartanburg........................W. Carol.	15	99	6	9	.400	90	55	40	66	46	3.64
1977—Peninsula ....Carolina	8	36	0	2	.000	44	31	17	23	20	4.25
1978—Peninsula ....Carolina	26	187	13	8	.619	147	58	44	150	64	2.12
1979—Reading ....Eastern	24	185	12	7	.632	156	62	46	*135	77	*2.24
1980—Oklahoma City ....Am. Assoc.	8	49	5	1	.833	39	21	16	36	17	2.94
1980—Philadelphia.......................National	27	152	11	7	.611	163	82	77	94	71	4.56
Major League Totals.................................	27	152	11	7	.611	163	82	77	94	71	4.56

Selected by California Angels' organization in 5th round of free-agent draft, January 9, 1975.
Selected by Philadelphia Phillies' organization in 5th round of free-agent draft, January 7, 1976.
Selected by Philadelphia Phillies' organization in secondary phase of free-agent draft, June 8, 1976.

WORLD SERIES RECORD

Year Club League	G.	IP.	W.	L.	Pct.	H.	R.	ER.	SO.	BB.	ERA.
1980—Philadelphia.......................National	1	7	1	0	1.000	8	6	6	3	3	7.71

CLEOTHA WALKER
(Chico)

Born November 25, 1957, at Jackson, Miss.
Height, 5.09. Weight, 170.
Throws right and bats left and righthanded.

Tied for International League lead in double plays by second basemen with 74 in 1980.

Year Club	League	Pos.	G.	AB.	R.	H.	2B.	3B.	HR.	RBI.	B.A.	PO.	A.	E.	F.A.
1976—Elmira	NYP	2B	22	28	9	5	1	2	0	1	.179	9	18	3	.900
1977—Elmira	NYP	2B-SS	64	227	26	50	4	3	1	14	.220	122	196	15	.955
1978—Winter Haven	Fla. St.	S-3-2	133	480	66	134	10	6	3	52	.279	172	380	42	.929
1979—Bristol†	East.	2B	123	498	75	132	19	*12	8	57	.265	252	357	23	.964
1980—Pawtucket	Int.	2B	139	536	59	146	18	7	8	52	.272	252	*394	*21	.969
1980—Boston	Amer.	2B	19	57	3	12	0	0	1	5	.211	15	31	2	.958
Major League Totals			19	57	3	12	0	0	1	5	.211	15	31	2	.958

Selected by Boston Red Sox' organization in 22nd round of free-agent draft, June 8, 1976.
†On disabled list, August 22 to September 19, 1979.

DUANE ALLEN WALKER

Born March 13, 1957, at Pasadena, Tex.
Height, 6.00. Weight, 180.
Throws and bats lefthanded.
Attended San Jacinto College, Pasadena, Tex.

Year Club	League	Pos.	G.	AB.	R.	H.	2B.	3B.	HR.	RBI.	B.A.	PO.	A.	E.	F.A.
1976—Tampa	Fla. St.	OF	29	91	9	19	1	0	0	3	.209	36	5	2	.953
1976—Eugene	N'west.	OF	46	172	41	49	11	5	10	24	.285	51	5	3	.949
1977—Tampa	Fla. St.	OF	122	466	67	116	13	7	2	37	.249	180	12	3	.985
1978—Nashville	South.	OF	103	288	38	69	15	3	2	31	.240	133	7	5	.966
1979—Nashville	South.	OF	143	545	97	165	28	*15	9	57	.303	237	9	12	.953
1980—Indianapolis	A.A.	OF	109	351	41	87	16	4	6	30	.248	169	14	9	.953

Selected by San Francisco Giants' organization in 34th round of free-agent draft, June 4, 1975.
Selected by Cincinnati Reds' organization in secondary phase of free-agent draft, January 7, 1976.

JOHN KEVIN WALKER
(Johnnie)

Born May 7, 1958, at Sacramento, Calif.
Height, 5.11. Weight, 165.
Throws right and bats left and righthanded.

Led Pioneer League shortstops in double plays with 36 in 1976.
Led International League in sacrifice hits with 24 in 1980.

Year Club	League	Pos.	G.	AB.	R.	H.	2B.	3B.	HR.	RBI.	B.A.	PO.	A.	E.	F.A.
1976—Lethbridge	Pion.	SS	68	*290	46	78	7	3	0	29	.269	●95	*212	26	.922
1977—W. Palm Beach	Fla. St.	2-S-3	47	105	15	26	1	0	0	7	.248	65	95	19	.894
1977—Jamestown	NYP	2B	63	216	21	39	7	0	1	18	.181	145	156	14	.956
1978—W. Palm Beach	Fla. St.	3-2-S	55	177	11	40	6	1	0	11	.226	57	117	14	.926
1978—Memphis†	South.	3B	3	3	1	0	0	0	0	0	.000	1	6	0	1.000
1978—Lodi	Calif.	SS-2B	17	43	11	7	0	0	2	4	.163	19	56	4	.949
1979—Lodi‡	Calif.	SS-2B	121	449	82	135	15	5	0	47	.301	179	288	26	.947
1980—Toledo	Int.	SS	128	487	67	124	19	4	1	48	.255	*224	368	30	.952

Selected by Montreal Expos' organization in 7th round of free-agent draft, June 8, 1976.
†Released, June 30, 1978; signed by Los Angeles Dodgers' organization, July 5, 1978.
‡Drafted by Minnesota Twins' organization, December 4, 1979.

TIMOTHY CHARLES WALLACH
(Tim)

Born September 14, 1957, at Huntington Park, Calif.
Height, 6.03. Weight, 220.
Throws and bats righthanded.
Attended Saddleback Junior College, Mission Viejo, Calif., and
California State University at Fullerton, Fullerton, Calif.

Tied major league record by hitting home run in first major league at-bat, September 6, 1980.
Led American Association in total bases with 295 and tied for lead in sacrifice flies with 9 in 1980.
Named THE SPORTING NEWS College Player of the Year, 1979.

Year Club	League	Pos.	G.	AB.	R.	H.	2B.	3B.	HR.	RBI.	B.A.	PO.	A.	E.	F.A.
1979—Memphis	South.	1B-3B	75	257	50	84	16	4	18	51	.327	290	35	4	.988
1980—Denver	A.A.	3-O-1	134	512	103	144	29	7	36	124	.281	222	147	21	.946
1980—Montreal	Nat.	OF-1B	5	11	1	2	0	0	1	2	.182	12	0	0	1.000
Major League Totals			5	11	1	2	0	0	1	2	.182	12	0	0	1.000

Selected by California Angels' organization in 8th round of free-agent draft, June 6, 1978.
Selected by Montreal Expos' organization in 1st round (10th player selected) of free-agent draft, June 5, 1979.

ELLIOTT TYRONE WALLER
(Ty)

Born March 14, 1957, at Fresno, Calif.
Height, 6.00. Weight, 180.
Throws and bats righthanded.
Attended San Diego City College, San Diego, Calif.

Led Pioneer League third basemen in putouts with 72, in assists with 142 and in double plays with 17 in 1977.

Led Florida State League third basemen in putouts with 123, in assists with 269, in double plays with 23 and in fielding percentage with .958 in 1978.

Year	Club	League	Pos.	G.	AB.	R.	H.	2B.	3B.	HR.	RBI.	B.A.	PO.	A.	E.	F.A.
1977–Calgary		Pion.	3B-SS	●70	*300	*77	*96	15	3	8	●77	.320	74	146	27	.891
1978–St. Petersburg		Fla. St.	3B-2B	137	474	43	123	19	2	2	56	.259	124	270	17	.959
1979–Arkansas		Texas	3B	126	432	48	122	29	4	6	54	.282	*105	*275	*26	*.936
1980–Springfield		A.A.	3B	123	420	55	110	14	7	6	53	.262	81	215	22	.931
1980–St. Louis†		Nat.	3B	5	12	3	1	0	0	0	0	.083	1	2	0	1.000
Major League Totals				5	12	3	1	0	0	0	0	.083	1	2	0	1.000

Selected by San Francisco Giants' organization in 33rd round of free-agent draft, June 4, 1975.
Selected by St. Louis Cardinals' organization in 4th round of free-agent draft, January 11, 1977.
†Traded to Chicago Cubs, December 22, 1980, completing deal in which Cubs traded Pitcher Bruce Sutter to St. Louis Cardinals for Third Baseman Ken Reitz and Outfielder-First Baseman Leon Durham, December 9, 1980.

DENNIS MARTIN WALLING
(Denny)

Born April 17, 1954, at Neptune, N. J.
Height, 6.01. Weight, 185.
Throws right and bats lefthanded.
Hobby–Hunting.
Attended Brookdale Community College, Lincroft, N. J., and
Clemson University, Clemson, S. C.
Brother of Gregory Walling, outfielder-first baseman in Houston
Astros' organization, 1967.

Year	Club	League	Pos.	G.	AB.	R.	H.	2B.	3B.	HR.	RBI.	B.A.	PO.	A.	E.	F.A.
1975–Oakland		Amer.	OF	6	8	0	1	1	0	0	2	.125	3	0	0	1.000
1976–Chattanooga		South.	OF	115	369	48	95	15	5	9	42	.257	241	8	2	*.992
1976–Oakland		Amer.	OF	3	11	1	3	0	0	0	0	.273	8	0	1	.889
1977–San Jose†‡		P.C.	OF	3	10	1	3	0	0	0	4	.300	8	0	0	1.000
1977–Charleston		Int.	OF	29	89	17	31	4	1	4	14	.348	66	0	0	1.000
1977–Houston		Nat.	OF	6	21	1	6	0	1	0	6	.286	14	0	0	1.000
1978–Houston		Nat.	OF	120	247	30	62	11	3	3	36	.251	140	4	3	.980
1979–Houston		Nat.	OF	82	147	21	48	8	4	3	31	.327	65	2	1	.985
1980–Houston		Nat.	1B-OF	100	284	30	85	6	5	3	29	.299	525	31	6	.989
American League Totals				9	19	1	4	1	0	0	2	.210	11	0	1	.917
National League Totals				308	699	82	201	25	13	9	102	.288	744	37	10	.987
Major League Totals				317	718	83	205	26	13	9	104	.286	755	37	11	.986

Selected by San Francisco Giants' organization in 8th round of free-agent draft, June 5, 1974.
Selected by Oakland A's organization in secondary phase of free-agent draft, June 4, 1975.
†On disabled list, April 18 to June 15, 1977.
‡Traded with cash to Houston Astros' organization for Willie Crawford, June 15, 1977.

CHAMPIONSHIP SERIES RECORD

Year	Club	League	Pos.	G.	AB.	R.	H.	2B.	3B.	HR.	RBI.	B.A.	PO.	A.	E.	F.A.
1980–Houston		Nat.	1-O-PH	3	9	2	1	0	0	0	2	.111	6	0	0	1.000

DANIEL JAMES WALTON
(Danny)

Born July 14, 1947, at Los Angeles, Calif.
Height, 6.00. Weight, 195
Throws right and bats left and righthanded.
Hobbies–Hunting, shooting and skiing.

Named THE SPORTING NEWS Minor League Player of the Year, 1969.

Year	Club	League	Pos.	G.	AB.	R.	H.	2B.	3B.	HR.	RBI.	B.A.	PO.	A.	E.	F.A.
1965–Brad. Astros		Fla. Rk.	C-OF	11	21	0	0	0	0	0	1	.000	27	7	1	.971
1965–Cocoa		Fla. St.	OF-C	14	30	3	6	1	0	0	2	.200	8	0	0	1.000
1966–Salisbury		W. Car.	OF	111	425	82	136	26	5	20	80	.320	186	13	*19	.913
1966–Amarillo		Texas	OF	11	33	2	3	1	0	0	0	.091	16	0	2	.889
1967–Asheville		Carol.	OF	120	411	76	124	14	3	25	78	.302	154	10	6	.965
1968–Dall.-Ft. Worth		Texas	OF	78	279	32	69	7	4	9	41	.247	110	6	5	.959
1968–Houston		Nat.	PH	2	2	0	0	0	0	0	0	.000	0	0	0	.000
1968–Oklahoma City		P.C.	OF	6	10	1	3	0	0	0	0	.300	2	0	0	1.000
1969–Oklahoma City†		A.A.	OF	132	482	74	160	34	7	*25	*119	.332	204	7	11	.950
1969–Seattle		Amer.	OF	23	92	12	20	1	2	3	10	.217	40	0	1	.976
1970–Milwaukee		Amer.	OF	117	397	32	102	20	1	17	66	.257	162	4	6	.965

Year Club League	Pos.	G.	AB.	R.	H.	2B.	3B.	HR.	RBI.	B.A.	PO.	A.	E.	F.A.
1971–Milw.‡–N.Y. ......Amer.	OF-3B	35	83	6	16	3	0	3	11	.193	28	0	2	.933
1971–Syracuse...........Int.	OF	61	157	21	38	7	0	8	25	.242	78	3	3	.964
1972–Syracuse§.........Int.	OF-1-3	137	410	63	111	20	0	23	88	.271	449	22	11	.977
1973–Minnesota.........Amer.	OF-3B	37	96	13	17	1	1	4	8	.177	18	3	0	1.000
1974–Tacoma ...........P.C.	DH	139	520	86	137	29	3	35	109	.263	0	0	0	.000
1975–Tacoma ............P.C.	C	49	157	27	48	6	0	13	38	.306	8	2	0	1.000
1975–Minnesota x ......Amer.	1B-C	42	63	4	11	2	0	1	8	.175	27	1	1	.966
1976–Los Angeles ......Nat.	PH	18	15	0	2	0	0	0	2	.133	0	0	0	.000
1976–Albuquerque .....P.C.	3B-OF	60	219	40	64	13	2	8	45	.292	20	35	9	.859
1977–Albuquerque y ..P.C.	OF-1B	136	492	*117	142	25	0	*42	*122	.289	15	0	2	.882
1977–Houston z.........Nat.	1B	13	21	0	4	0	0	0	1	.190	41	2	2	.994
1978						(Did not play)								
1979–Spokane a.........P.C.	1B	146	522	71	135	*39	0	15	81	.259	3	0	0	1.000
1980–Charleston ....Int.	DH	104	341	42	77	13	0	15	54	.226	0	0	0	.000
1980–Texas b............Amer.	DH	10	10	2	2	0	0	0	1	.200	0	0	0	.000
National League Totals		33	38	0	6	0	0	0	3	.158	41	2	2	.994
American League Totals		264	741	69	168	27	4	28	104	.227	275	8	10	.966
Major League Totals......................		297	779	69	174	27	4	28	107	.223	316	10	12	.964

Selected by Houston Astros' organization in 51st round of free-agent draft, June 10, 1965.
†Traded with Outfielder Sandy Valdespino to Seattle Pilots for Outfielder Tommy Davis, August 31, 1969.
‡Traded to New York Yankees for Outfielder Bob Mitchell and First Baseman-Outfielder Frank Tepedino, June 7, 1971.
§Traded to Minnesota Twins for Catcher Rick Dempsey, October 27, 1972.
xTraded to Los Angeles Dodgers for Second Baseman Bob Randall, December 23, 1975.
ySold to Houston Astros' organization, September 6, 1977.
zReleased, March 27, 1978; signed by Seattle Mariners' organization, March 30, 1979.
aReleased, March 25, 1980; signed by Texas Rangers' organization, April 6, 1980.
bTraded to Cincinnati Reds' organization for Pitcher Greg Hughes, February 15, 1981.

REGINALD SHERARD WALTON
(Reggie)

Born October 24, 1952, at Kansas City, Mo.
Height, 6.03. Weight, 205.
Throws and bats righthanded.
Attended Compton Community College, Compton, Calif.
Tied for Texas League lead in double plays by outfielders with 4 in 1975.

Year Club League	Pos.	G.	AB.	R.	H.	2B.	3B.	HR.	RBI.	B.A.	PO.	A.	E.	F.A.
1972–Great Falls ......Pioneer	OF-1B	62	208	36	67	10	3	1	28	.322	127	1	6	.955
1973–Decatur ....Midw.	OF-1B	118	404	48	90	15	5	6	50	.223	189	10	15	.930
1974–Fresno ....Calif.	OF	137	494	85	154	20	9	4	54	.312	171	13	8	.958
1975–Lafayette ....Texas	OF-1B	124	452	77	140	23	5	8	78	.310	449	24	13	.973
1976–Lafayette† ....Texas	OF	132	471	52	119	21	5	6	50	.253	153	8	12	.931
1977–Monterrey‡§ .....Mex.	OF	45	152	16	39	7	3	1	9	.257	60	2	1	.984
1978–Coahuila x ....Mex.	OF	103	368	42	110	16	2	3	49	.299	191	6	8	.961
1979–Spokane...........P. C.	OF	122	463	79	149	31	7	11	76	.322	298	7	9	.971
1980–Spokane............P.C.	OF	91	340	50	103	17	6	10	57	.303	125	2	6	.955
1980–Seattle..............Amer.	OF	31	83	8	23	6	0	2	9	.277	26	0	2	.929
Major League Totals......................		31	83	8	23	6	0	2	9	.277	26	0	2	.929

Selected by San Francisco Giants' organization in 14th round of free-agent draft, January 12, 1972.
†Released by San Francisco Giants' organization, April 6, 1977; signed by Monterrey, April 25, 1977.
‡Released by Monterrey, June 9, 1977; signed by Seattle Mariners' organization, December 11, 1977.
§Released, April 13, 1978; signed by Coahuila, April 25, 1978.
xSold to Seattle Mariners' organization, October 2, 1978.

GARY LAMELL WARD

Born December 6, 1953, at Los Angeles, Calif.
Height, 6.02. Weight, 207.
Throws and bats righthanded.
Hit for the cycle vs. Milwaukee Brewers, September 18, 1980.
Led New York-Pennsylvania League first basemen in double plays with 12 in 1973.
Tied for Midwest League lead among outfielders in assists with 18 in 1974.

Year Club League	Pos.	G.	AB.	R.	H.	2B.	3B.	HR.	RBI.	B.A.	PO.	A.	E.	F.A.
1973–Geneva ....NYP	1-O-3	61	211	36	57	13	1	10	38	.270	336	20	14	.962
1974–Wis. Rapids.......Midw.	*OF-1B	126	*467	*104	122	12	5	26	78	.261	184	19	*11	.949
1975–Orlando ....South.	OF-C	124	438	45	117	18	5	8	71	.267	204	10	4	.982
1976–Orlando ....South.	OF	132	475	50	119	17	2	9	65	.251	235	●16	●10	.962
1977–Tacoma .............P.C.	OF-3B	125	413	62	97	15	8	8	43	.235	212	34	10	.961
1978–Toledo ....Int.	*O-1-3	139	511	82	150	20	12	14	79	.294	260	6	*13	.953
1979–Toledo ....Int.	OF	134	506	75	133	16	9	13	67	.263	323	12	●11	.968
1979–Minnesota........Amer.	DH-PH	10	14	2	4	0	0	0	1	.286	0	0	0	.000
1980–Toledo†............Int.	OF-1B	128	496	82	140	22	8	13	66	.282	269	14	8	.973
1980–Minnesota........Amer.	OF	13	41	11	19	6	2	1	10	.463	14	0	0	1.000
Major League Totals......................		23	55	13	23	6	2	1	11	.418	14	0	0	1.000

Signed as free agent by Minnesota Twins' organization, August 29, 1972.
†On disabled list, April 16 to April 26, 1980.

CLAUDELL WASHINGTON

Born August 31, 1954, at Los Angeles, Calif.
Height, 6.00. Weight, 190.
Throws and bats lefthanded.
Brother of Don Washington, outfielder in Los Angeles Dodgers' organization.

Hit three home runs in one game, vs. Detroit Tigers, July 14, 1979 and vs. Los Angeles Dodgers, June 22, 1980.
Major league stolen bases: 1974 (6), 1975 (40), 1976 (37), 1977 (21), 1978 (5), 1979 (19), 1980 (21). Total—149.
Led Midwest League in total bases with 218 in 1973.

Year Club	League	Pos.	G.	AB.	R.	H.	2B.	3B.	HR.	RBI.	B.A.	PO.	A.	E.	F.A.
1972—C's Bay-N. Bend	Northw.	OF	33	111	13	31	3	2	2	15	.279	37	1	6	.864
1973—Burlington.........	Midw.	OF	108	447	*92	144	25	5	13	81	.322	149	10	*15	.914
1974—Birmingham......	South.	OF	74	294	64	106	23	3	11	55	.361	116	5	13	.903
1974—Oakland	Amer.	OF	73	221	16	63	10	5	0	19	.285	63	2	1	.985
1975—Oakland	Amer.	OF	148	590	86	182	24	7	10	77	.308	305	8	7	.978
1976—Oakland†	Amer.	OF-DH	134	490	65	126	20	6	5	53	.257	276	10	●11	.963
1977—Texas‡	Amer.	OF	129	521	63	148	31	2	12	68	.284	255	11	6	.978
1978—Tex.§-Chi. x	Amer.	OF	98	356	34	90	16	5	6	33	.253	170	6	8	.957
1979—Chicago	Amer.	OF	131	471	79	132	33	5	13	66	.280	256	7	7	.974
1980—Chicago y	Amer.	OF	32	90	15	26	4	2	1	12	.289	41	1	3	.933
1980—New York z.......	Nat.	OF	79	284	38	78	16	4	10	42	.275	123	12	3	.978
American League Totals..................			745	2739	358	767	138	32	47	328	.280	1366	45	43	.970
National League Totals			79	284	38	78	16	4	10	42	.275	123	12	3	.978
Major League Totals.......................			824	3023	396	845	154	36	57	370	.280	1489	57	46	.971

Signed as free agent by Oakland A's organization, July 7, 1972.
†On disabled list, August 16 through September 1, 1976; traded to Texas Rangers for Pitcher Jim Umbarger, Infielder Rodney Scott and cash estimated at $100,000, March 26, 1977.
‡On supplemental disabled list, May 27 to June 11, 1977.
§Traded with Outfielder Rusty Torres and a player to be named later to Chicago White Sox for Outfielder Bobby Bonds, May 16, 1978.
xOn supplemental disabled list, May 22 to June 16, 1978.
yTraded to New York Mets for Pitcher Jesse Anderson, June 7, 1980.
zGranted free agency, October 31, 1980; signed by Atlanta Braves, November 15, 1980.

CHAMPIONSHIP SERIES RECORD

Year Club	League	Pos.	G.	AB.	R.	H.	2B.	3B.	HR.	RBI.	B.A.	PO.	A.	E.	F.A.
1974—Oakland	Amer.	OF-PH	4	11	1	3	1	0	0	0	.273	11	0	0	1.000
1975—Oakland	Amer.	OF-DH	3	12	1	3	1	0	0	1	.250	1	0	2	.333
Championship Series Totals.............			7	23	2	6	2	0	0	1	.261	12	0	2	.857

WORLD SERIES RECORD

Tied World Series record for most positions played, Series (3), 1974 (all three outfield positions).

Year Club	League	Pos.	G.	AB.	R.	H.	2B.	3B.	HR.	RBI.	B.A.	PO.	A.	E.	F.A.
1974—Oakland	Amer.	OF-PH	5	7	1	4	0	0	0	0	.571	3	0	0	1.000

ALL-STAR GAME RECORD

Year League	Pos.	AB.	R.	H.	2B.	3B.	HR.	RBI.	B.A.	PO.	A.	E.	F.A.
1975—American............................	PR-OF	1	0	1	0	0	0	0	1.000	1	0	0	1.000

U. L. WASHINGTON

Born October 27, 1953, at Atoka, Okla.
Height, 5.11. Weight, 175.
Throws right and bats lefthanded.
Attended Murray State College, Tishomingo, Okla.

Switch-hit home runs in one game, vs. Oakland A's, September 21, 1979.
Led American Association batters in strikeouts with 145 in 1975.
Led Appalachian League shortstops in double plays with 29 in 1973.
Led Appalachian League in sacrifice flies with 8 in 1973.

Year Club	League	Pos.	G.	AB.	R.	H.	2B.	3B.	HR.	RBI.	B.A.	PO.	A.	E.	F.A.
1973—Kingsport	Appal.	SS	68	244	47	69	14	4	5	51	.283	89	176	36	.880
1974—San Jose...........	Calif.	SS-2B	68	245	38	61	9	2	6	21	.249	81	201	34	.892
1974—Jacksonville	South.	SS	47	167	29	43	11	1	2	20	.257	71	172	17	.935
1975—Omaha.............	A.A.	SS	128	475	60	113	11	8	5	37	.238	195	367	*46	.924
1976—Omaha†	A.A.	SS	30	120	20	30	3	2	4	16	.250	48	102	15	.909
1977—Omaha.............	A.A.	*SS-2B	131	*514	82	131	13	10	2	37	.255	218	391	*48	.927
1977—Kansas City.......	Amer.	SS	10	20	4	4	1	1	0	1	.200	13	21	5	.872
1978—Kansas City	Amer.	SS-2B	69	129	10	34	2	1	0	9	.264	79	92	9	.950
1979—Kansas City	Amer.	SS-2B-3B	101	268	32	68	12	5	2	25	.254	174	243	18	.959
1980—Kansas City	Amer.	SS	153	549	79	150	16	11	6	53	.273	237	467	32	.957
Major League Totals			333	966	121	256	31	18	8	88	.265	503	823	64	.954

Signed as free agent by Kansas City Royals' organization, August 4, 1972.
†On disabled list, May 21 to September 6, 1976.

CHAMPIONSHIP SERIES RECORD

Year Club	League	Pos.	G.	AB.	R.	H.	2B.	3B.	HR.	RBI.	B.A.	PO.	A.	E.	F.A.
1980—Kansas City	Amer.	SS	3	11	1	4	1	0	0	1	.364	5	7	0	1.000

Year	Club	League	Pos.	G.	AB.	R.	H.	2B.	3B.	HR.	RBI.	B.A.	PO.	A.	E.	F.A.
1980–Kansas City		Amer.	SS	6	22	1	6	0	0	0	2	.273	8	20	1	.966

RONALD WASHINGTON
(Ron)
Born April 29, 1952, at New Orleans, La.
Height, 5.11. Weight, 160.
Throws and bats righthanded.
Attended Manatee Junior College, Bradenton, Fla.

Year	Club	League	Pos.	G.	AB.	R.	H.	2B.	3B.	HR.	RBI.	B.A.	PO.	A.	E.	F.A.
1971–Sara. Royals†		Gulf C.	C	38	127	29	37	2	•6	1	23	.291	★213	23	3	★.987
1972–Waterloo		Midw.	C-O-3	76	241	37	55	3	1	1	30	.228	424	48	8	.983
1973–Waterloo		Midw.	SS	85	289	35	80	13	5	6	34	.277	130	198	29	.919
1974–San José‡		Calif.	2-S-C	109	425	49	104	16	3	2	41	.245	233	266	33	.938
1975–Jacksonville§		South.	2-3-S-1	96	267	22	61	7	1	0	20	.228	133	199	22	.938
1976–Waterbury x		East.	3B-SS	115	436	61	128	9	10	4	32	.294	170	249	26	.942
1977–San Antonio y		Texas	SS	39	158	24	44	8	4	0	13	.278	78	92	12	.934
1977–Albuquerque		P. C.	SS	85	359	71	116	17	8	8	59	.323	204	250	★33	.932
1977–Los Angeles		Nat.	SS	10	19	4	7	0	0	0	1	.368	4	14	3	.857
1978–Albuquerque z		P.C.	3B	31	122	26	42	10	3	5	32	.344	23	58	8	.910
1979–Aguila		Mex.	3B	42	165	22	43	3	3	0	14	.261	35	96	10	.929
1979–Tidewater a		Int.	3B-SS	83	273	18	72	13	4	1	26	.264	77	157	13	.947
1980–Toledo		Int.	3B-2B-SS	114	407	62	117	•31	5	3	36	.287	131	268	30	.930
Major League Totals				10	19	4	7	0	0	0	1	.368	4	14	3	.857

Signed as free agent by Kansas City Royals' organization, July 17, 1970.
†On military list, September 30, 1971, to March 3, 1972.
‡On temporary inactive list, July 4 to July 25, 1974.
§On disabled list, June 19 to June 30, 1975.
xTraded to Los Angeles Dodgers' organization for Catcher Steve Patchin, November 2, 1976.
yOn temporary inactive list, April 12 to April 22, 1977.
zOn disabled list, May 12 to June 26 and July 17 to September 10, 1978.
aTraded to Minnesota Twins' organization for Infielder Wayne Caughery, March 26, 1980.

JOHN DAVID WATHAN
Born October 4, 1949, at Cedar Rapids, Ia.
Height, 6.02. Weight, 205.
Throws and bats righthanded.
Hobbies–Reading, flying and all sports.
Attended University of San Diego, San Diego, Calif., and
Mount Mercy College, Cedar Rapids, Ia.

Year	Club	League	Pos.	G.	AB.	R.	H.	2B.	3B.	HR.	RBI.	B.A.	PO.	A.	E.	F.A.
1971–San Jose		Calif.	C-OF	64	215	37	56	11	2	1	29	.260	438	31	14	.971
1971–Waterloo		Midw.	C-O-1	43	147	31	41	4	4	3	21	.279	282	18	1	.997
1972–San José†		Calif.	C-1-3	48	148	25	40	8	0	4	15	.270	324	31	3	.992
1972–Omaha		A. A.	C	18	51	8	15	1	1	0	2	.294	94	5	1	.990
1972–Jacksonville		South.	C	16	54	6	17	3	1	0	3	.315	111	7	4	.967
1973–Jacksonville‡		South.	C-1-3	65	233	20	58	8	3	5	34	.249	294	28	4	.988
1974–Jacksonville		South.	1-O-C	120	428	63	105	14	2	7	47	.245	760	50	7	.991
1975–Omaha		A. A.	C-OF	104	360	42	109	14	4	8	46	.303	532	45	10	.983
1976–Omaha§		A. A.	C-OF	24	84	4	13	5	0	0	6	.155	128	14	4	.973
1976–Kansas City		Amer.	C-1B	27	42	5	12	1	0	0	5	.286	63	4	1	.985
1977–Kansas City		Amer.	C-1B	55	119	18	39	5	3	2	21	.328	156	9	2	.988
1978–Kansas City x		Amer.	1B-C	67	190	19	57	10	1	2	28	.300	385	28	2	.995
1979–Kansas City		Amer.	1B-C-OF	90	199	26	41	7	3	2	28	.206	336	24	3	.992
1980–Kansas City		Amer.	C-OF-1B	126	453	57	138	14	7	6	58	.305	472	33	8	.984
Major League Totals				365	1003	125	287	37	14	12	140	.286	1412	98	16	.990

Selected by Kansas City Royals' organization in 4th round of free-agent draft, January 13, 1971.
†On disabled list, May 5 to May 30, 1972.
‡On disabled list, May 25 to June 28, 1973.
§On disabled list, July 29 to September 1, 1976.
xOn supplemental disabled list, June 16 to June 29; on disabled list, June 29 to July 7, 1978.

CHAMPIONSHIP SERIES RECORD

Year	Club	League	Pos.	G.	AB.	R.	H.	2B.	3B.	HR.	RBI.	B.A.	PO.	A.	E.	F.A.
1976–Kansas City		Amer.	C	1	0	0	0	0	0	0	0	.000	0	0	0	.000
1977–Kansas City		Amer.	C-1-D-PH	4	6	0	0	0	0	0	0	.000	19	0	0	1.000
1978–Kansas City		Amer.	1B	1	3	0	0	0	0	0	0	.000	7	0	0	1.000
1980–Kansas City		Amer.	OF-PH	3	6	1	0	0	0	0	0	.000	7	0	0	1.000
Championship Series Totals				9	15	1	0	0	0	0	0	.000	33	0	0	1.000

WORLD SERIES RECORD

Year	Club	League	Pos.	G.	AB.	R.	H.	2B.	3B.	HR.	RBI.	B.A.	PO.	A.	E.	F.A.
1980–Kansas City		Amer.	PH-OF-C	3	7	1	2	0	0	0	1	.286	7	1	0	1.000

ROBERT JOSE WATSON
(Bob)

Born April 10, 1946, at Los Angeles, Calif.
Height, 6.02. Weight, 212.
Throws and bats righthanded.
Attended Los Angeles Harbor College, Wilmington, Calif.

Established major league record by hitting for the cycle in both leagues, June 24, 1977, and September 15, 1979.
Tied major league record for fewest times caught stealing, season, 150 or more games (0), 1977.
Hit for the cycle, vs. Los Angeles Dodgers, June 24, 1977.
Hit for the cycle, vs. Baltimore Orioles, September 15, 1979.
Led Florida State League catchers in double plays with 14 in 1966.

Year Club	League	Pos.	G.	AB.	R.	H.	2B.	3B.	HR.	RBI.	B.A.	PO.	A.	E.	F.A.
1965—Salisbury	W. Car.	C	80	309	51	88	20	3	12	55	.285	476	25	15	.971
1966—Cocoa	Fla. St.	C-OF	105	348	56	105	21	8	10	55	.302	529	36	13	.978
1966—Houston	Nat.	PH	1	1	0	0	0	0	0	0	.000	0	0	0	.000
1967—Amarillo	Texas	*1B-OF	96	351	73	98	14	5	14	60	.279	778	41	*17	.980
1967—Oklahoma City	P. C.	OF-1B	41	148	18	39	4	2	5	15	.264	64	3	3	.957
1967—Houston	Nat.	1B	6	14	1	3	0	0	1	2	.214	21	2	1	.958
1968—Oklahoma City	P. C.	OF	20	76	14	30	7	2	5	16	.395	34	0	2	.944
1968—Houston†	Nat.	OF	45	140	13	32	7	0	2	8	.229	46	0	6	.885
1969—Savannah	South.	C-1B	26	96	19	25	4	0	4	10	.260	178	12	5	.974
1969—Oklahoma City	A. A.	C-1-O-2	61	223	41	91	14	4	7	48	.408	369	25	9	.978
1969—Houston	Nat.	O-1-C	20	40	3	11	3	0	0	3	.275	46	3	0	1.000
1970—Houston‡	Nat.	1-C-OF	97	327	48	89	19	2	11	61	.272	707	40	6	.992
1971—Houston§	Nat.	OF-1B	129	468	49	135	17	3	9	67	.288	470	18	7	.986
1972—Houston	Nat.	OF-1B	147	548	74	171	27	4	16	86	.312	231	7	5	.979
1973—Houston	Nat.	OF-1-C	158	573	97	179	24	3	16	94	.312	433	11	12	.974
1974—Houston	Nat.	OF-1B	150	524	69	156	19	4	11	67	.298	237	12	4	.984
1975—Houston	Nat.	1B-OF	132	485	67	157	27	1	18	85	.324	1089	70	8	.993
1976—Houston	Nat.	1B	157	585	76	183	31	3	16	102	.313	1395	96	15	.990
1977—Houston	Nat.	1B	151	554	77	160	38	6	22	110	.289	1331	*118	9	.994
1978—Houston	Nat.	1B	139	461	51	133	25	4	14	79	.289	974	95	9	.992
1979—Houston x	Nat.	1B	49	163	15	39	4	0	3	18	.239	371	33	3	.993
1979—Boston y	Amer.	1B	84	312	48	105	19	4	13	53	.337	525	47	7	.988
1980—New York	Amer.	1B	130	469	62	144	25	3	13	68	.307	851	63	9	.990
National League Totals			1381	4883	640	1448	241	30	139	782	.297	7351	505	85	.989
American League Totals			214	781	110	249	44	7	26	121	.319	1376	110	16	.989
Major League Totals			1595	5664	750	1697	285	37	165	903	.300	8727	615	101	.989

Signed as free agent by Houston Astros' organization, January 31, 1965.
†Suffered broken ankle July 31; on disabled list from August 3 through end of season.
‡On military list, August 8 to August 24, 1970.
§On military list, July 17 to August 2, 1971.
xTraded to Boston Red Sox for Pitcher Pete Ladd and a player to be named later, June 13, 1979; Pitcher Bob Sprowl assigned to Houston to complete deal, June 19, 1979.
yGranted free agency, November 1, 1979; signed by New York Yankees, November 8, 1979.

CHAMPIONSHIP SERIES RECORD

Tied Championship Series record for most two-base hits, three-game Series (3), 1980.
Established American League Championship Series record for most long hits, three-game Series (4), 1980.
Tied American League Championship Series record for highest slugging average, three-game Series (.917), 1980.

Year Club	League	Pos.	G.	AB.	R.	H.	2B.	3B.	HR.	RBI.	B.A.	PO.	A.	E.	F.A.
1980—New York	Amer.	1B	3	12	0	6	3	1	0	0	.500	28	5	1	.971

ALL-STAR GAME RECORD

Year League	Pos.	AB.	R.	H.	2B.	3B.	HR.	RBI.	B.A.	PO.	A.	E.	F.A.
1973—National	OF	0	0	0	0	0	0	0	.000	0	0	0	.000
1975—National	PH	1	0	0	0	0	0	0	.000	0	0	0	.000
All-Star Game Totals		1	0	0	0	0	0	0	.000	0	0	0	.000

ROGER EDWARD WEAVER

Born October 6, 1954, at Amsterdam, N.Y.
Height, 6.03. Weight, 200.
Throws and bats righthanded.
Attended New York State University at Oneonta, Oneonta, N.Y.;
received Bachelor of Arts degree in American history.

Led Florida State League in saves with 22 in 1977.

Year Club	League	G.	IP.	W.	L.	Pct.	H.	R.	ER.	SO.	BB.	ERA.
1976—Bristol	Ap'lachian	13	82	6	2	.750	53	22	13	67	21	*1.43
1977—Lakeland	Florida St.	*52	97	10	5	.667	65	20	17	84	43	1.58
1978—Montgomery†‡	Southern	7	12	1	0	1.000	12	2	2	4	3	1.50
1979—Evansville‡	Am. Assoc.	29	99	8	2	.800	102	43	41	63	47	3.73
1980—Evansville	Am. Assoc.	10	37	3	3	.500	29	16	13	21	17	3.16
1980—Detroit§	American	19	64	3	4	.429	56	32	29	42	34	4.08
Major League Totals		19	64	3	4	.429	56	32	29	42	34	4.08

Selected by Detroit Tigers' organization in 13th round of free-agent draft, June 8, 1976.
†On Evansville disabled list, April 14 to April 26, 1978.
‡On disabled list, June 5 to July 15 and August 8 to September 30, 1978.
‡On disabled list, April 13 to April 25, 1979.
§On disabled list, August 17 to September 7, 1980.

DAVID THOMAS WEHRMEISTER

Name pronounced WAIR-my-stur.

(Dave)

Born November 9, 1952, at Berwyn, Ill.
Height, 6.04. Weight, 190.
Throws and bats righthanded.
Hobby—Golf.
Attended Northeast Missouri State College, Kirksville, Mo.

Year—Club	League	G.	IP.	W.	L.	Pct.	H.	R.	ER.	SO.	BB.	ERA.
1973—Alexandria	Texas	23	137	8	12	.400	110	64	49	84	60	3.22
1974—Hawaii	P. Coast	4	12	0	3	.000	17	13	12	7	9	9.00
1974—Alexandria	Texas	18	130	5	10	.333	119	73	59	90	65	4.08
1975—Alexandria†	Texas	17	105	5	8	.385	103	54	40	58	36	3.43
1975—Hawaii	P. Coast	10	52	3	5	.375	63	37	37	31	24	6.40
1976—San Diego	National	7	19	0	4	.000	27	17	16	10	11	7.58
1976—Hawaii	P. Coast	23	112	6	11	.353	137	85	72	61	54	5.79
1977—Hawaii	P. Coast	5	39	2	2	.500	34	14	11	23	8	2.54
1977—San Diego	National	30	70	1	3	.250	81	53	47	32	44	6.04
1978—Hawaii	P. Coast	21	129	2	11	.154	140	89	81	61	64	5.65
1978—San Diego	National	4	7	1	0	1.000	8	5	5	2	5	6.43
1979—Hawaii‡	P. Coast	13	96	8	5	.615	70	24	20	56	24	1.88
1979—Columbus	Int'national	17	75	2	8	.200	84	43	41	54	28	4.92
1980—Columbus§	Int'national	39	86	3	4	.429	66	30	27	67	36	2.83
Major League Totals		41	96	2	7	.222	116	75	68	44	60	6.38

Selected by San Diego Padres' organization in 1st round (third player selected) of free-agent draft, January 10, 1973.
†On disabled list, May 2 to May 17, 1975.
‡Traded to New York Yankees' organization for Outfielder Jay Johnstone, June 15, 1979.
§Drafted by Kansas City Royals, December 8, 1980.

GARY LEE WEISS

Born December 27, 1955, at Brenham, Tex.
Height, 5.10. Weight, 170.
Throws right and bats lefthanded.
Attended Blinn Junior College, Brenham, Tex., and University of Houston, Houston, Tex.

Year—Club	League	Pos.	G.	AB.	R.	H.	2B.	3B.	HR.	RBI.	B.A.	PO.	A.	E.	F.A.
1978—Clinton	Midw.	2B-SS	68	231	33	65	14	0	2	26	.281	139	145	5	.983
1979—San Antonio	Texas	SS	125	455	82	146	27	4	8	66	.321	220	410	35	.947
1980—Albuquerque	P.C.	SS	130	423	71	123	16	8	6	51	.291	182	378	26	.956
1980—Los Angeles	Nat.	PR	8	0	2	0	0	0	0	0	.000	0	0	0	.000
Major League Totals			8	0	2	0	0	0	0	0	.000	0	0	0	.000

Selected by Montreal Expos' organization in 5th round of free-agent draft, January 7, 1976.
Selected by San Diego Padres' organization in 23rd round of free-agent draft, June 7, 1977.
Selected by Los Angeles Dodgers' organization in 19th round of free-agent draft, June 6, 1978.

ROBERT LYNN WELCH

(Bob)

Born November 3, 1956, at Detroit, Mich.
Height, 6.03. Weight, 190.
Throws and bats righthanded.
Attended Eastern Michigan University, Ypsilanti, Mich.

Year—Club	League	G.	IP.	W.	L.	Pct.	H.	R.	ER.	SO.	BB.	ERA.
1977—San Antonio	Texas	14	71	4	5	.444	94	44	35	56	17	4.44
1978—Albuquerque	P. Coast	11	69	5	1	.833	72	33	29	53	19	3.78
1978—Los Angeles	National	23	111	7	4	.636	92	28	25	66	26	2.03
1979—Los Angeles	National	25	81	5	6	.455	82	42	36	64	32	4.00
1980—Los Angeles	National	32	214	14	9	.609	190	85	78	141	79	3.28
Major League Totals		80	406	26	19	.578	364	155	139	271	137	3.08

Selected by Chicago Cubs' organization in 14th round of free-agent draft, June 5, 1974.
Selected by Los Angeles Dodgers' organization in 1st round (20th player selected) of free-agent draft, June 7, 1977.

CHAMPIONSHIP SERIES RECORD

Year—Club	League	G.	IP.	W.	L.	Pct.	H.	R.	ER.	SO.	BB.	ERA.
1978—Los Angeles	National	1	4⅓	1	0	1.000	2	1	1	5	0	2.08

WORLD SERIES RECORD

Year—Club	League	G.	IP.	W.	L.	Pct.	H.	R.	ER.	SO.	BB.	ERA.
1978—Los Angeles	National	3	4⅓	0	1	.000	4	3	3	6	2	6.23

Year League	IP.	W.	L.	Pct.	H.	R.	ER.	SO.	BB.	ERA.
1980—National	3	0	0	.000	5	2	2	4	1	6.00

CHRISTOPHER CHARLES WELSH
(Chris)

Born April 14, 1955, at Wilmington, Del.
Height, 6.02. Weight, 185.
Throws and bats lefthanded.
Attended University of South Florida, Tampa, Fla.; received
Bachelor of Arts degree in Marketing.

Led New York-Pennsylvania League in complete games with 12 and in shutouts with 4 and tied for lead in games started with 14 in 1977.
Tied for Eastern League lead in wild pitches with 18 in 1978.

Year—Club	League	G.	IP.	W.	L.	Pct.	H.	R.	ER.	SO.	BB.	ERA.
1977—Oneonta	NYP	14	*112	8	5	.615	77	40	31	*125	54	2.49
1978—Ft. Lauderdale	Florida St.	2	15	1	1	.500	5	5	1	13	10	0.60
1978—West Haven	Eastern	24	164	11	9	.550	159	88	63	115	68	3.46
1979—Columbus	Int'national	36	114	8	4	.667	120	67	59	79	48	4.70
1980—Columbus	Int'national	29	158	9	12	.429	134	78	48	84	68	2.73

Selected by New York Yankees' organization in 24th round of free-agent draft, June 8, 1976.
Selected by New York Yankees' organization in 21st round of free-agent draft, June 7, 1977.

DONALD PAUL WERNER
(Don)

Born March 8, 1953, at Appleton, Wis.
Height, 6.01. Weight, 180.
Throws and bats righthanded.

Year—Club	League	Pos.	G.	AB.	R.	H.	2B.	3B.	HR.	RBI.	B.A.	PO.	A.	E.	F.A.
1971—Brad'ton Reds	Gulf C.	C-3B	10	21	7	7	1	1	0	5	.333	45	2	1	.979
1971—Tampa	Fla. St.	C	36	122	10	21	3	1	0	16	.172	186	22	1	.995
1972—Tampa	Fla. St.	C	116	377	42	97	8	1	1	31	.257	736	75	15	.982
1973—Three Rivers	East.	C-OF	110	284	31	57	9	1	5	34	.201	452	47	11	.978
1974—Tampa	Fla. St.	C	120	397	44	92	13	1	2	38	.232	580	71	3	*.995
1975—Indianapolis	A. A.	C	86	228	39	64	11	5	9	34	.281	423	51	7	*.985
1975—Cincinnati	Nat.	C	7	8	0	1	0	0	0	0	.125	10	2	1	.923
1976—Indianapolis	A. A.	C-1B	38	112	14	23	4	1	1	12	.205	208	28	6	.975
1976—Richmond	Int.	C-OF	49	151	19	40	1	1	2	21	.265	215	22	5	.979
1976—Cincinnati	Nat.	C	3	4	0	2	1	0	0	1	.500	7	2	0	1.000
1977—Indianapolis†	A. A.	C-1B	34	94	12	20	5	1	5	13	.213	182	23	4	.981
1977—Cincinnati	Nat.	C	10	23	3	4	0	0	2	4	.174	40	4	0	1.000
1978—Indianapolis	A. A.	C	40	125	14	30	6	1	3	22	.240	202	24	7	.970
1978—Cincinnati	Nat.	C	50	113	7	17	2	1	0	11	.150	214	21	3	.987
1979—Indianapolis	A. A.	C-1B-OF	99	260	35	66	18	3	7	36	.254	476	57	12	.978
1980—Cincinnati	Nat.	C	24	64	2	11	2	0	0	5	.172	119	6	5	.962
1980—Indianapolis	A. A.	C-1B-3B	65	219	32	60	10	2	6	35	.274	355	25	8	.979
Major League Totals			94	212	12	35	5	1	2	21	.165	390	35	9	.979

Selected by Cincinnati Reds' organization in 5th round of free-agent draft, June 8, 1971.
†On disabled list, May 3 to July 27, 1977.

DENNIS DEAN WERTH
(Denny)

Born December 29, 1952, at Lincoln, Ill.
Height, 6.01. Weight, 201.
Throws and bats righthanded.
Attended Lincoln College, Lincoln, Ill., and
Southern Illinois University at Edwardsville, Edwardsville, Ill.

Led New York-Pennsylvania League in total bases with 127 and in sacrifice flies with 10 in 1974.
Led International League in sacrifice flies with 10 in 1979.

Year—Club	League	Pos.	G.	AB.	R.	H.	2B.	3B.	HR.	RBI.	B.A.	PO.	A.	E.	F.A.
1974—Oneonta	NYP	C-1B	64	238	42	80	*23	6	4	*61	.336	357	16	8	.979
1975—Ft. Lauderdale	Fla. St.	1B-C-OF	121	381	63	101	18	5	9	54	.265	664	48	11	.985
1976—West Haven	East.	1B-C	125	386	56	91	20	1	17	57	.236	656	61	7	.990
1977—Syracuse†	Int.	1B-3B	104	312	55	83	20	5	9	43	.266	817	80	13	.986
1978—Tacoma	P.C.	1B	93	285	57	95	19	4	11	58	.333	794	57	6	*.993
1979—Columbus	Int.	1B-C	133	421	69	126	27	3	17	74	.299	1189	73	9	.993
1979—New York	Amer.	1B	3	4	1	1	0	0	0	0	.250	5	1	0	1.000
1980—Columbus	Int.	O-3-2	32	91	16	20	5	0	3	15	.220	33	7	4	.952
1980—New York	Amer.	OF-1-2-C	39	65	15	20	3	0	3	12	.308	82	3	2	.977
Major League Totals			42	69	16	21	3	0	3	12	.304	87	4	2	.978

Selected by New York Yankees' organization in 19th round of free-agent draft, June 5, 1974.
†On disabled list, August 10 to August 22, 1977.

GARY RICHARD WHEELOCK

Born November 29, 1951, at Bakersfield, Calif.
Height, 6.03. Weight, 205.
Throws and bats righthanded.
Attended Fullerton College, Fullerton, Calif., and University of California at Irvine,
Irvine, Calif.; received Bachelor of Arts degree in Social Science.

Year Club	League	G.	IP.	W.	L.	Pct.	H.	R.	ER.	SO.	BB.	ERA.
1974—Salinas	California	2	3	0	0	.000	3	0	0	3	1	0.00
1974—Quad Cities	Midwest	25	68	3	3	.500	57	25	18	79	15	2.38
1975—Salt Lake City	P. Coast	31	120	7	6	.538	113	56	41	68	47	3.08
1976—Salt Lake City†	P. Coast	27	201	•15	8	.652	206	100	85	•138	154	3.81
1976—California‡	American	2	2	0	0	.000	6	6	6	2	1	27.00
1977—Seattle§	American	17	88	6	9	.400	94	58	48	47	26	4.91
1978—San Jose x	P. Coast	21	116	1	12	.077	170	102	90	32	43	6.98
1979—Spokane y	P. Coast	18	97	7	5	.583	118	53	47	19	30	4.36
1980—Seattle	American	1	3	0	0	.000	4	2	2	1	1	6.00
1980—Spokane z	P. Coast	17	99	4	3	.308	117	60	53	23	37	4.82
Major League Totals		20	93	6	9	.400	104	66	56	50	28	5.42

Selected by California Angels' organization in 6th round of free-agent draft, June 5, 1974.
†On disabled list, June 15 to June 28, 1976.
‡Selected by Seattle Mariners in American League expansion draft, November 5, 1976.
§On disabled list, May 2 to June 17 and August 22 to October 4, 1977.
xOn disabled list, April 14 to April 16, 1978.
yOn disabled list, April 26 to June 1, 1979.
zOn disabled list, May 16, to June 17, 1980.

LOUIS RODMAN WHITAKER
(Lou)

Born May 12, 1957, at Brooklyn, N.Y.
Height, 5.11. Weight, 160.
Throws right and bats lefthanded.
Named Florida State League Most Valuable Player, 1976.
Named American League Rookie of the Year by Baseball Writers Association of America, 1978.

Year Club	League	Pos.	G.	AB.	R.	H.	2B.	3B.	HR.	RBI.	B.A.	PO.	A.	E.	F.A.
1975—Bristol	Appal.	3B-SS	42	114	17	27	6	1	1	17	.237	38	82	16	.882
1976—Lakeland	Fla.St.	3B	124	434	*70	129	12	5	1	62	.297	*99	*267	*30	*.924
1977—Montgomery†	South.	2B	107	396	*81	111	13	4	3	48	.280	208	285	15	.970
1977—Detroit	Amer.	2B	11	32	5	8	1	0	0	2	.250	17	18	0	1.000
1978—Detroit	Amer.	2B	139	484	71	138	12	7	3	58	.285	301	458	17	.978
1979—Detroit‡	Amer.	2B	127	423	75	121	14	8	3	42	.286	280	369	9	.986
1980—Detroit	Amer.	2B	145	477	68	111	19	1	1	45	.233	340	428	12	.985
Major League Totals			422	1416	219	378	46	16	7	147	.267	738	1273	38	.981

Selected by Detroit Tigers' organization in 5th round of free-agent draft, June 4, 1975.
†On disabled list, May 3 to May 14, 1977.
‡On disabled list, June 13 to June 28, 1979.

FRANK WHITE JR.

Born September 4, 1950, at Greenville, Miss.
Height, 5.11. Weight, 170.
Throws and bats righthanded.
Hobbies—Hunting and listening to music.
Hit for the cycle, vs. California Angels, September 26, 1979.
Led Gulf Coast League in stolen bases with 18 and led shortstops in double plays with 27 in 1971.
Named second baseman on THE SPORTING NEWS American League All-Star fielding team, 1977 through 1980.
Named second baseman on THE SPORTING NEWS American League All-Star Team, 1978.

Year Club	League	Pos.	G.	AB.	R.	H.	2B.	3B.	HR.	RBI.	B.A.	PO.	A.	E.	F.A.
1971—Sara. Royals	Gulf C.	SS	50	158	31	39	6	3	1	21	.247	70	*149	17	*.928
1972—San Jose	Calif.	SS	49	187	44	55	7	2	10	26	.294	77	138	14	.939
1972—Jacksonville	South.	SS	91	333	34	84	12	2	2	23	.252	124	306	31	.933
1973—Omaha	A. A.	2B-SS	86	348	49	92	19	2	4	32	.264	163	221	21	.948
1973—Kansas City	Amer.	SS-2B	51	139	20	31	6	1	0	5	.223	71	121	12	.941
1974—Kansas City	Amer.	2-S-3	99	204	19	45	6	3	1	18	.221	119	189	12	.963
1975—Kansas City	Amer.	2-S-3-C	111	304	43	76	10	2	7	36	.250	182	275	12	.974
1976—Kansas City	Amer.	2B-SS	152	446	39	102	17	6	2	46	.229	296	479	23	.971
1977—Kansas City	Amer.	*2B-SS	152	474	59	116	21	5	5	20	.245	310	437	8	*.989
1978—Kansas City	Amer.	2B	143	461	66	127	24	6	7	50	.275	325	385	16	.978
1979—Kansas City†	Amer.	2B	127	467	73	124	26	4	10	48	.266	317	332	12	.982
1980—Kansas City	Amer.	2B	154	560	70	148	23	4	7	60	.264	395	448	10	.988
Major League Totals			989	3055	389	769	133	31	39	313	.252	2015	2666	105	.978

Signed as free agent by Kansas City Royals' organization, July 2, 1970.
†On disabled list, May 9 to June 11, 1979.

Year	Club	League	Pos.	G.	AB.	R.	H.	2B.	3B.	HR.	RBI.	B.A.	PO.	A.	E.	F.A.
1976–Kansas City		Amer.	2B-PR	4	8	2	1	0	0	0	0	.125	6	11	0	1.000
1977–Kansas City		Amer.	2B	5	18	1	5	1	0	0	2	.278	13	16	0	1.000
1978–Kansas City		Amer.	2B	4	13	1	3	0	0	0	2	.231	9	12	0	1.000
1980–Kansas City		Amer.	2B	3	11	3	6	1	0	1	3	.545	9	10	1	.950
Championship Series Totals				16	50	7	15	2	0	1	7	.300	37	49	1	.989

WORLD SERIES RECORD

Tied World Series records for fewest runs, Series (0), 1980; most at-bats, nine-inning game, no hits (5), October 18, 1980; most unassisted double plays by second baseman, game (1), October 17, 1980.

Year	Club	League	Pos.	G.	AB.	R.	H.	2B.	3B.	HR.	RBI.	B.A.	PO.	A.	E.	F.A.
1980–Kansas City		Amer.	2B	6	25	0	2	0	0	0	0	.080	13	21	2	.944

ALL-STAR GAME RECORD

Year	League	Pos.	AB.	R.	H.	2B.	3B.	HR.	RBI.	B.A.	PO.	A.	E.	F.A.
1978–American		2B	1	0	0	0	0	0	0	.000	1	2	0	1.000
1979–American		2B	2	0	0	0	0	0	0	.000	2	2	0	1.000
All-Star Game Totals			3	0	0	0	0	0	0	.000	3	4	0	1.000

JEROME CARDELL WHITE
(Jerry)

Born August 23, 1952, at Shirley, Mass.
Height, 5.11. Weight, 172.
Throws right and bats left and righthanded.
Hobbies–Football, ping pong and basketball.
Attended City College of San Francisco, San Francisco, Calif.

Year	Club	League	Pos.	G.	AB.	R.	H.	2B.	3B.	HR.	RBI.	B.A.	PO.	A.	E.	F.A.
1970–Brad'ton Expos	Gulf C.	OF	55	201	32	58	10	2	1	16	.289	102	5	5	.955
1971–W. Palm Beach	Fla. St.	OF	130	505	71	132	17	4	2	32	.261	222	4	●13	.946
1972–Quebec City†	East.	OF	26	56	4	13	1	0	0	2	.232	46	1	0	1.000
1972–W. Palm Beach	Fla. St.	OF	27	96	13	28	1	1	1	13	.292	63	1	2	.970
1973–Peninsula‡	Int.	OF	112	360	50	99	10	6	1	30	.275	182	7	5	.974
1974–Quebec City	East.	OF	21	69	13	17	2	2	0	5	.246	35	2	1	.974
1974–Memphis	Int.	OF	77	175	28	45	6	2	3	17	.257	87	5	1	.989
1974–Montreal	Nat.	OF	9	10	0	4	1	1	0	2	.400	6	0	0	1.000
1975–Memphis	Int.	OF	98	354	44	105	16	5	10	45	.297	223	6	6	.974
1975–Montreal	Nat.	OF	39	97	14	29	4	1	2	7	.299	81	1	2	.976
1976–Montreal	Nat.	OF	114	278	32	68	11	1	2	21	.245	157	4	3	.982
1977–Denver	A.A.	OF-1B	123	463	92	145	32	9	14	57	.313	235	7	6	.976
1977–Montreal	Nat.	OF	16	21	4	4	0	0	1	1	.190	5	0	0	1.000
1978–Denver	A. A.	OF	27	100	22	29	4	0	5	19	.290	53	0	1	.981
1978–Chi.§-Mtl.x	Nat.	OF	77	146	24	39	6	0	1	10	.267	102	4	2	.981
1979–Montreal	Nat.	OF	88	138	30	41	7	1	3	18	.297	55	2	1	.983
1980–Montreal	Nat.	OF	110	214	22	56	9	3	7	23	.262	101	5	6	.946
Major League Totals				453	902	126	241	38	7	15	82	.267	507	16	14	.974

Selected by Montreal Expos' organization in 14th round of free-agent draft, June 4, 1970.
†On temporary inactive list, April 22 to June 24, 1972.
‡On temporary inactive list, July 28 to August 14, 1973.
§Sent to Chicago Cubs, June 23, 1978, to complete deal in which Montreal acquired Pitcher Woodie Fryman, June 9, 1978.
xTraded with Infielder-Outfielder Rodney Scott to Montreal Expos for Outfielder Sam Mejias, December 14, 1978.

LEONARD JOSEPH WHITEHOUSE
(Len)

Born September 10, 1957, at Burlington, Vt.
Height, 5.11. Weight, 175.
Throws and bats lefthanded.

Year	Club	League	G.	IP.	W.	L.	Pct.	H.	R.	ER.	SO.	BB.	ERA.
1977–Asheville		W. Carol.	5	7	0	2	.000	15	15	7	3	6	9.00
1977–Sarasota Rangers		G. Coast	11	40	3	3	.500	45	30	20	27	21	4.50
1978–Asheville		W. Carol.	32	92	6	6	.500	89	60	44	79	57	4.30
1979–Tulsa		Texas	25	102	5	7	.417	126	75	64	79	45	5.65
1980–Tulsa		Texas	10	48	3	2	.600	52	35	29	38	22	5.44
1980–Charleston		Int'national	18	99	8	9	.471	110	62	47	64	37	4.27

Signed as free agent by Texas Rangers' organization, December 25, 1976.

TERRY BERTLAND WHITFIELD

Born January 12, 1953, at Blythe, Calif.
Height, 6.01. Weight, 200.
Throws right and bats lefthanded.
Hobbies–Assembling toys and working puzzles.
Tied for International League lead in double plays by outfielders with 3 in 1976.

Led International League batters in strikeouts with 129 in 1974.
Led Appalachian League in total bases with 125 in 1971.
Led Carolina League in total bases with 234 in 1973.
Named Carolina League Player of the Year in 1973.
Shared Appalachian League Player of the Year in 1971.

Year Club League	Pos.	G.	AB.	R.	H.	2B.	3B.	HR.	RBI.	B.A.	PO.	A.	E.	F.A.
1971–Johnson City .....Appal.	OF	67	252	42	73	14	4	*10	*43	.290	104	6	•9	.924
1972–Ft. Lauderdale ..Fla.St.	OF	49	153	21	25	3	5	1	15	.163	57	4	5	.924
1972–Oneonta ....NYP	OF	•70	256	*65	70	6	•11	7	47	.273	120	7	3	.977
1973–Kinston ....Carol.	OF	129	451	94	151	25	2	•18	81	*.335	197	9	11	.949
1974–Syracuse ....Int.	OF	140	499	71	129	25	4	17	71	.259	*345	12	5	.986
1974–New York.........Amer.	OF	2	5	0	1	0	0	0	0	.200	0	0	0	.000
1975–Syracuse ....Int.	OF	111	390	47	106	24	4	11	69	.272	208	10	10	.956
1975–New York.........Amer.	OF	28	81	9	22	1	1	0	7	.272	42	3	1	.978
1976–Syracuse ....Int.	OF	•138	*525	81	152	25	6	16	89	.290	208	13	15	.936
1976–New York†........Amer.	OF	1	0	0	0	0	0	0	0	.000	0	0	0	.000
1977–San Francisco ...Nat.	OF	114	326	41	93	21	3	7	36	.285	167	4	5	.972
1978–San Francisco ...Nat.	OF	149	488	70	141	20	2	10	32	.289	249	7	3	.988
1979–San Francisco ...Nat.	OF	133	394	52	113	20	4	5	44	.287	167	10	8	.957
1980–San Francisco ...Nat.	OF	118	321	38	95	16	2	4	26	.296	140	11	2	.987
American League Totals		31	86	9	23	1	1	0	7	.267	42	3	1	.978
National League Totals		514	1529	201	442	77	11	26	138	.289	723	32	18	.977
Major League Totals		545	1615	210	465	78	12	26	145	.288	765	35	19	.977

Selected by New York Yankees' organization in 21st round of free-agent draft, June 8, 1971.
†Traded to San Francisco Giants for Second Baseman Marty Perez, March 14, 1977.

DANIEL C. WHITMER
(Dan)

Born November 23, 1955, at Redlands, Calif.
Height, 6.03. Weight, 200.
Throws and bats righthanded.
Attended California State University at Fullerton.

Year Club League	Pos.	G.	AB.	R.	H.	2B.	3B.	HR.	RBI.	B.A.	PO.	A.	E.	F.A.
1978–Salinas ....Calif.	C	76	247	33	62	9	1	7	36	.251	377	52	11	.975
1979–El Paso............Texas	C-1B	43	148	25	50	11	1	8	29	.338	122	20	4	.973
1979–Salt Lake City ...P.C.	C	66	210	25	48	8	0	4	31	.229	251	41	4	.986
1980–California ....Amer.	C	48	87	8	21	3	0	0	7	.241	190	12	0	1.000
1980–Salt Lake City†..P.C.	C	59	183	24	41	6	0	3	27	.224	240	42	10	.966
Major League Totals		48	87	8	21	3	0	0	7	.241	190	12	0	1.000

Selected by California Angels' organization in 14th round of free-agent draft, June 6, 1978.
†Drafted by Toronto Blue Jays, December 8, 1980.

EDDIE LEE WHITSON

Born May 19, 1955, at Johnson City, Tenn.
Height, 6.03. Weight, 200.
Throws and bats righthanded.

Year Club League	G.	IP.	W.	L.	Pct.	H.	R.	ER.	SO.	BB.	ERA.
1974–Bradenton Pirates ....Gulf Coast	8	44	1	4	.200	45	28	21	25	15	4.30
1975–Charleston ....W. Carol.	24	142	8	*15	.348	140	*96	*80	120	99	5.07
1976–Salem ....Carolina	26	*203	•15	9	.625	168	75	57	*186	65	2.53
1977–Columbus...........................Int'national	26	175	8	13	.381	175	74	65	120	68	3.34
1977–Pittsburgh ....National	5	16	1	0	1.000	11	6	6	10	9	3.38
1978–Columbus...........................Int'national	7	51	2	2	.500	56	25	21	55	10	3.71
1978–Pittsburgh ....National	43	74	5	6	.455	66	31	27	64	37	3.28
1979–Pittsburgh†-San Francisco....National	37	158	7	11	.389	151	83	72	93	75	4.10
1980–San Francisco ....National	34	212	11	13	.458	222	88	73	90	56	3.10
Major League Totals	119	460	24	30	.444	450	208	178	257	177	3.48

Selected by Pittsburgh Pirates' organization in 6th round of free-agent draft, June 5, 1974.
†Traded with Pitchers Fred Breining and Al Holland to San Francisco Giants for Infielders Bill Madlock and Lenny Randle and Pitcher Dave Roberts, June 28, 1979.

ALL-STAR GAME RECORD

Member of National League All-Star Team in 1980; did not play.

LEO ERNEST WHITT
(Ernie)

Born June 13, 1952, at Detroit, Mich.
Height, 6.02. Weight, 200.
Throws right and bats lefthanded.
Hobbies—Hunting and fishing.
Attended Macomb County Community College, Warren, Mich.

Led International League catchers in passed balls with 16 in 1978.
Led International League catchers in fielding percentage with .995 in 1979.

Year Club	League	Pos.	G.	AB.	R.	H.	2B.	3B.	HR.	RBI.	B.A.	PO.	A.	E.	F.A.
1972—Williamsport	NYP	1B	1	4	1	2	1	0	0	0	.500	8	1	0	1.000
1972—Winter Haven	Fla.St.	C-1B-OF	31	82	3	15	1	1	0	7	.183	151	14	5	.971
1973—Winston-Salem	Carol.	C-OF-1B	130	424	63	123	23	3	1	50	.290	686	70	15	.980
1974—Bristol	East.	C-OF-1B	111	385	55	96	10	1	9	56	.249	557	50	6	.990
1975—Bristol†	East.	C-OF	82	252	29	64	9	1	2	19	.254	357	36	7	.982
1976—Bristol	East.	C	26	87	12	19	2	3	1	10	.218	127	25	1	.993
1976—Rhode Island	Int.	C-1-OF-3	90	304	33	81	16	2	7	42	.266	487	59	9	.984
1976—Boston‡	Amer.	C	8	18	4	4	2	0	1	3	.222	24	0	0	1.000
1977—Charleston	Int.	C-3B	29	94	12	24	6	0	0	7	.255	129	28	7	.957
1977—Toronto§	Amer.	C	23	41	4	7	3	0	0	6	.171	62	4	0	1.000
1978—Syracuse	Int.	C-1B-OF	121	399	50	98	16	3	12	53	.246	673	79	7	.991
1978—Toronto	Amer.	C	2	4	0	0	0	0	0	0	.000	7	1	0	1.000
1979—Syracuse	Int.	C-OF-3B	114	382	32	95	18	4	7	43	.249	494	69	3	.995
1980—Toronto	Amer.	C	106	295	23	70	12	2	6	34	.237	436	56	7	.986
Major League Totals			139	358	31	81	17	2	7	43	.226	529	61	7	.988

Selected by Boston Red Sox' organization in 15th round of free-agent draft, June 6, 1972.
†On disabled list, April 11 to June 13, 1975.
‡Selected by Toronto Blue Jays in American League expansion draft, November 5, 1976.
§On supplemental disabled list, August 17 to September 27, 1977.

THOMAS JOHN WIEDENBAUER
(Tom)

Born November 5, 1958, at Menomonie, Wis.
Height, 6.01. Weight, 175.
Throws and bats righthanded.

Year Club	League	Pos.	G.	AB.	R.	H.	2B.	3B.	HR.	RBI.	B.A.	PO.	A.	E.	F.A.
1976—Covington	Appal.	OF	55	193	21	40	8	1	0	14	.207	70	6	7	.916
1977—Cocoa	Fla. St.	OF	124	435	47	122	9	1	2	34	.280	275	19	10	.967
1978—Columbus†	South.	OF	27	93	10	25	2	0	0	6	.269	64	4	0	1.000
1979—Columbus	South.	OF	141	554	68	147	31	4	3	64	.265	•345	•22	6	.984
1979—Houston	Nat.	OF	4	6	0	4	1	0	0	2	.667	3	0	0	1.000
1980—Tucson‡	P.C.	OF	108	384	45	98	15	1	0	33	.255	264	6	9	.968
Major League Totals			4	6	0	4	1	0	0	2	.667	3	0	0	1.000

Selected by Houston Astros' organization in 7th round of free-agent draft, June 8, 1976.
†On disabled list, April 17 to May 10 and June 14 to September 4, 1978.
‡On disabled list, July 12 to August 9, 1980.

THOMAS ROBERT WIEGHAUS

Name pronounced WIG-house

(Tom)

Born February 1, 1957, at Chicago Heights, Ill.
Height, 6.00. Weight, 195.
Throws and bats righthanded.
Attended Illinois State University, Normal, Ill.

Led New York-Pennsylvania League catchers in double plays with 7 in 1978.
Led Florida State League catchers in double plays with 10 in 1979.

Year Club	League	Pos.	G.	AB.	R.	H.	2B.	3B.	HR.	RBI.	B.A.	PO.	A.	E.	F.A.
1978—Jamestown	NYP	C	63	202	28	49	10	2	0	19	.243	•438	•54	8	.984
1979—W. Palm Beach	Fla. St.	C	121	382	41	83	15	0	2	35	.217	•742	95	11	•.987
1980—Memphis	South.	C	120	371	44	101	13	1	4	44	.272	•678	•82	9	.988

Selected by Oakland A's organization in 10th round of free-agent draft, June 4, 1975.
Selected by Montreal Expos' organization in 10th round of free-agent draft, June 6, 1978.

ALAN ANTHONY WIGGINS
(Al)

Born February 17, 1958, at Los Angeles, Calif.
Height, 6.02. Weight, 160.
Throws right and bats left and righthanded.
Attended Pasadena City College, Pasadena, Calif.

Led California League in stolen bases with 120 in 1980.

Year Club	League	Pos.	G.	AB.	R.	H.	2B.	3B.	HR.	RBI.	B.A.	PO.	A.	E.	F.A.
1977—Idaho Falls	Pion.	2B	63	225	64	61	3	1	1	23	.271	137	163	28	.915
1978—Quad Cities†‡	Midw.	2B	49	169	30	34	3	0	1	12	.201	96	130	12	.950
1979—Clinton	Midw.	S-O-1-2-3	95	296	57	76	3	1	0	27	.257	196	198	32	.925
1980—Lodi §	Calif.	O-2-1-S	135	513	108	148	10	5	0	35	.288	365	76	23	.950

Selected by California Angels' organization in 1st round (7th player selected) of free-agent draft, January 11, 1977.
†On suspended list, June 8 to June 10, 1978.
‡Released, June 10, 1978; signed by Los Angeles Dodgers' organization, January 26, 1979.
§Drafted by San Diego Padres, December 8, 1980.

ALEXANDER AMES WIHTOL
Name pronounced Wit-tall
(Sandy)

Born June 1, 1955, at Palo Alto, Calif.
Height, 6.02. Weight, 190.
Throws and bats righthanded.
Hobbies—Golf, water skiing, hunting and sports cars.
Attended De Anza Junior College, Cupertino, Calif. and Washington State University, Pullman, Wash.
Brother of Al Wihtol, once a member of New York Mets' organization.

Led Midwest League in saves with 15 in 1977.

Year—Club	League	G.	IP.	W.	L.	Pct.	H.	R.	ER.	SO.	BB.	ERA.
1975—San Jose	California	15	58	1	7	.125	74	46	38	43	30	5.90
1975—Sarasota Indians	G. Coast	7	38	3	1	.750	44	26	18	44	18	4.26
1976—San Jose	California	51	101	1	6	.143	120	58	52	99	60	4.63
1977—Waterloo	Midwest	48	87	9	4	.692	50	22	21	85	47	2.17
1977—Jersey City	Eastern	1	1	0	0	.000	1	1	1	2	0	9.00
1978—Portland†	P. Coast	31	84	6	5	.545	107	47	38	64	39	4.07
1979—Tacoma	P. Coast	49	85	5	5	.500	73	24	23	73	38	2.44
1979—Cleveland	American	5	11	0	0	.000	10	4	4	6	3	3.27
1980—Tacoma	P. Coast	36	58	4	9	.308	52	28	23	38	30	3.57
1980—Cleveland	American	17	35	1	0	1.000	35	18	14	20	14	3.60
Major League Totals		22	46	1	0	1.000	45	22	18	26	17	3.52

Selected by Kansas City Royals' organization in 13th round of free-agent draft, June 5, 1973.
Selected by Cleveland Indians' organization in secondary phase of free-agent draft, June 5, 1974.
†On disabled list, August 11 to September 5, 1978.

THADDEAUS IGLEHART WILBORN
(Ted)

Born December 16, 1958, at Waco, Tex.
Height, 6.00. Weight, 170.
Throws right and bats right and lefthanded.

Led New York-Pennsylvania League in stolen bases with 57 in 1978.
Led New York-Pennsylvania League outfielders in double plays with 3 in 1978.

Year—Club	League	Pos.	G.	AB.	R.	H.	2B.	3B.	HR.	RBI.	B.A.	PO.	A.	E.	F.A.
1976—Oneonta	NYP	OF	28	85	8	16	3	0	0	4	.188	48	3	2	.962
1977—Ft. Lauderdale	Fla. St.	OF	84	223	39	48	8	2	0	10	.215	168	7	3	.983
1978—Ft. Lauderdale	Fla. St.	OF	41	70	10	13	1	0	0	3	.186	41	2	3	.935
1978—Oneonta†	NYP	OF	65	220	63	68	5	2	5	29	.309	*138	6	*4	.973
1979—Toronto	Amer.	OF	22	12	3	0	0	0	0	0	.000	7	0	1	.875
1979—Syracuse‡	Int.	OF	61	227	28	56	5	1	1	10	.247	168	8	0	1.000
1980—Nashville§	South.	OF	121	455	70	123	15	14	6	63	.270	210	7	7	.969
1980—New York	Amer.	OF	8	8	2	2	0	0	0	1	.250	6	1	0	1.000
Major League Totals			30	20	5	2	0	0	0	1	.100	13	1	1	.933

Selected by New York Yankees' organization in 4th round of free-agent draft, June 8, 1976.
†Drafted from New York Yankees' organization by Toronto Blue Jays, December 4, 1978.
‡Traded with Catcher Rick Cerone and Pitcher Tom Underwood to New York Yankees for First Baseman Chris Chambliss, Infielder Damaso Garcia and Pitcher Paul Mirabella, November 1, 1979.
§On disabled list, April 11 to April 21, 1980.

MILTON EDWARD WILCOX
(Milt)

Born April 20, 1950, at Honolulu, Hawaii.
Height, 6.02. Weight, 215.
Throws and bats righthanded.
Hobby—Bowling.

Pitched seven-inning, 2-0 no-hit victory against Evansville, July 4, 1970.
Led American Association in shutouts with 5 in 1970 and tied for lead with 3 in 1971.
Named American Association Pitcher of the Year, 1970.

Year—Club	League	G.	IP.	W.	L.	Pct.	H.	R.	ER.	SO.	BB.	ERA.
1968—Tampa	Florida St.	8	47	3	3	.500	28	11	7	48	18	1.34
1968—Sarasota Reds	Gulf Coast	6	33	3	2	.600	24	10	4	33	11	1.09
1969—Tampa†	Florida St.	15	46	4	1	.800	53	30	28	38	29	5.48
1970—Indianapolis	Am. Assoc.	28	168	12	10	.545	144	58	53	110	53	2.84
1970—Cincinnati	National	5	22	3	1	.750	19	6	6	13	7	2.45
1971—Indianapolis	Am. Assoc.	16	102	8	5	.615	84	29	25	62	22	2.20
1971—Cincinnati‡	National	18	43	2	2	.500	43	22	16	21	17	3.35
1972—Cleveland	American	32	156	7	14	.333	145	67	59	90	72	3.40
1973—Cleveland§	American	26	134	8	10	.444	143	90	87	82	68	5.84
1974—Cleveland x	American	41	71	2	2	.500	74	42	37	33	24	4.69
1975—Wichita	Am. Assoc.	8	48	4	3	.571	56	31	23	18	15	4.31
1975—Chicago	National	25	38	0	1	1.000	50	27	24	21	17	5.68
1976—Wichita y-Evansville	Am. Assoc.	27	130	6	7	.462	141	72	55	94	63	3.81
1977—Evansville	Am. Assoc.	14	107	9	4	.692	89	38	29	69	40	2.44

Year Club	League	G.	IP.	W.	L.	Pct.	H.	R.	ER.	SO.	BB.	ERA.
1977–Detroit..............................	American	20	106	6	2	.750	96	46	43	82	37	3.65
1978–Detroit..............................	American	29	215	13	12	.520	208	94	90	132	68	3.77
1979–Detroit..............................	American	33	196	12	10	.545	201	105	95	109	73	4.36
1980–Detroit..............................	American	32	199	13	11	.542	201	112	99	97	68	4.48
National League Totals......................		48	103	5	4	.556	112	55	46	55	41	4.02
American League Totals......................		213	1077	61	61	.500	1068	556	510	625	410	4.26
Major League Totals		261	1180	66	65	.504	1180	611	556	680	451	4.24

Selected by Cincinnati Reds' organization in 2nd round of free-agent draft, June 7, 1968.
†On military list, April 16 to May 9; on temporary inactive list, June 11 to July 1, 1969.
‡Traded to Cleveland Indians for Outfielder Ted Uhlaender, December 6, 1971.
§On military list, June 16 to June 30; on disabled list, July 24 to August 15, 1973.
xOn military list, July 20 to August 4, 1974. Traded to Chicago Cubs for Pitcher Dave LaRoche and Outfielder Brock Davis, February 28, 1975.
ySold to Detroit Tigers, June 10, 1976.

CHAMPIONSHIP SERIES RECORD

Year Club	League	G.	IP.	W.	L.	Pct.	H.	R.	ER.	SO.	BB.	ERA.
1970–Cincinnati ....National		1	3	1	0	1.000	1	0	0	5	2	0.00

WORLD SERIES RECORD

Year Club	League	G.	IP.	W.	L.	Pct.	H.	R.	ER.	SO.	BB.	ERA.
1970–Cincinnati ....National		2	2	0	1	.000	3	2	2	2	0	9.00

ROBERT DONALD WILFONG
(Rob)

Born September 1, 1953, at Pasadena, Calif.
Height, 6.01. Weight, 185.
Throws right and bats lefthanded.
Hobbies—Hunting, fishing and golf.
Attended Mount San Antonio Junior College, Walnut, Calif.
Brother of James Wilfong, outfielder in Detroit Tigers' organization.

Established American League record for highest fielding average by second baseman, season, 100 or more games (.99481), 1980.
Led American League in sacrifice hits with 25 in 1979.
Led American League second basemen in fielding average with .995 in 1980.

Year Club	League	Pos.	G.	AB.	R.	H.	2B.	3B.	HR.	RBI.	B.A.	PO.	A.	E.	F.A.
1972–Charlotte†	W. Car.	2B	102	363	64	107	18	2	2	35	.295	212	224	16	.965
1973–Lynchburg	Carol.	2B	131	520	94	143	13	9	7	37	.275	∗323	326	18	.973
1974–Orlando	South.	2B	109	403	58	99	7	4	3	23	.246	249	303	8	∗.986
1975–Orlando	South.	2B	125	403	54	99	14	1	4	37	.246	274	347	16	.975
1976–Tacoma	P.C.	2B	69	220	41	67	8	3	3	16	.305	163	191	6	.983
1977–Tacoma	P.C.	2B	34	123	26	40	8	1	2	17	.325	83	101	8	.958
1977–Minnesota	Amer.	2B	73	171	22	42	1	1	1	13	.246	114	164	12	.959
1978–Minnesota‡	Amer.	2B	92	199	23	53	8	0	1	11	.266	152	196	5	.986
1979–Minnesota	Amer.	2B-OF	140	419	71	131	22	6	9	59	.313	287	379	14	.979
1980–Minnesota	Amer.	2B-OF	131	416	55	103	16	5	8	45	.248	245	338	4	.993
Major League Totals......................			436	1205	171	329	47	12	19	128	.273	798	1077	35	.982

Selected by Minnesota Twins' organization in 13th round of free-agent draft, June 8, 1971.
†On disabled list, May 22 to June 2, 1972.
‡On supplemental disabled list, March 22 to April 7, 1978.

ERIC LAMOINE WILKINS

Born December 9, 1956, at St. Louis, Mo.
Height, 6.01. Weight, 180.
Throws and bats righthanded.
Attended Washington State University, Pullman, Wash.

Year Club	League	G.	IP.	W.	L.	Pct.	H.	R.	ER.	SO.	BB.	ERA.
1977–Waterloo....................Midwest		11	75	9	1	.900	54	27	23	71	32	2.76
1978–Portland ....P. Coast		26	156	∗15	5	.750	145	94	79	126	85	4.56
1979–Cleveland.....................American		16	70	2	4	.333	77	41	34	52	38	4.37
1980–Tacoma‡.....................P. Coast		17	101	7	4	.636	108	59	44	72	66	3.92
Major League Totals......................		16	70	2	4	.333	77	41	34	52	38	4.37

Selected by Cleveland Indians' organization in 6th round of free-agent draft, June 7, 1977.
†On disabled list, July 24 to September 4, 1979.
‡On disabled list, July 14 to August 27, 1980.

ALBERTO WILLIAMS (DeSOUZA)
(Al)

Born May 7, 1954, at Maiguetio, Venezuela
Height, 6.04. Weight, 190.
Throws and bats righthanded.

Year Club	League	G.	IP.	W.	L.	Pct.	H.	R.	ER.	SO.	BB.	ERA.
1975—Charleston	W. Car.	29	148	4	12	.250	148	94	63	115	65	3.83
1976—Charleston†	W. Car.	26	46	4	1	.800	39	25	24	49	22	4.70
1979—Panama-Caracas‡	Inter-Am.	17	76	1	7	.125	79	40	32	52	27	3.79
1980—Toledo	Int'national	15	107	9	3	.750	85	34	25	59	32	2.10
1980—Minnesota	Amer.	18	77	6	2	.750	73	33	30	35	30	3.51
Major League Totals		18	77	6	2	.750	73	33	30	35	30	3.51

Signed as free agent by Pittsburgh Pirates' organization, February 20, 1975.

†Released, July 2, 1976; signed as free agent by Panama of the Inter-American League, April 11, 1979.

‡Declared free agent when Inter-American League folded, June 30, 1979; signed by Minnesota Twins' organization, January 6, 1980.

DALLAS McKINLEY WILLIAMS JR.

Born February 28, 1958, at Brooklyn, N. Y.
Height, 5.11. Weight, 165.
Throws and bats lefthanded.

Led Florida State League outfielders in double plays with 5 in 1977.

Year Club	League	Pos.	G.	AB.	R.	H.	2B.	3B.	HR.	RBI.	B.A.	PO.	A.	E.	F.A.
1976—Bluefield	Appal.	OF	69	256	26	69	8	1	3	30	.270	*161	*11	7	.961
1977—Miami	Fla. St.	OF	125	464	56	126	17	4	2	50	.272	295	10	*16	.950
1978—Charlotte	South.	OF	139	*549	52	145	17	4	2	35	.264	315	18	10	.971
1979—Charlotte	South.	OF	133	519	68	144	25	2	12	52	.277	319	16	10	.971
1980—Rochester	Int.	OF	137	529	63	143	21	2	11	54	.270	330	11	5	.986

Selected by Baltimore Orioles' organization in 1st round (20th player selected) of free-agent draft, June 8, 1976.

EARL CRAIG WILLIAMS JR.

Born July 14, 1948, at Newark, N. J.
Height, 6.03. Weight, 225.
Throws and bats righthanded.
Hobbies—Reading an listening to phonograph records.
Attended Ithaca College, Ithaca, N. Y.

Led National League in passed balls with 28 in 1972.
Led Western Carolinas League in total bases with 252 in 1969.
Named by THE SPORTING NEWS as National League Rookie Player of the Year, 1971.
Named by the Baseball Writers' Association as National League Rookie of the Year, 1971.
Named Western Carolinas League Most Valuable Player in 1969.

Year Club	League	Pos.	G.	AB.	R.	H.	2B.	3B.	HR.	RBI.	B.A.	PO.	A.	E.	F.A.
1966—Sarasota Braves	Gulf C.	1B-P	31	90	8	19	4	0	1	10	.211	153	19	2	.989
1967—W.Palm B'ch	Fla. St.	OF-1B	85	287	33	72	6	3	7	27	.251	376	21	4	.990
1968—Greenwood†	W. Car.	OF	8	29	5	8	0	0	1	3	.276	6	2	2	.800
1968—W. Palm B'ch	Fla. St.	1B-OF	50	144	14	34	8	0	0	12	.236	309	22	6	.982
1969—Greenwood	W. Car.	1B	103	382	83	130	19	2	*33	107	*.340	*1002	54	15	.986
1970—Shreveport	Texas	3-1-S	89	330	53	105	21	2	19	63	.318	151	122	21	.929
1970—Richmond	Int.	OF-3-1	22	68	10	18	1	0	5	15	.265	27	17	2	.957
1970—Atlanta	Nat.	1B-3B	10	19	4	7	4	0	0	5	.368	23	8	0	1.000
1971—Atlanta	Nat.	C-3-1	145	497	64	129	14	1	33	87	.260	596	117	18	.975
1972—Atlanta‡	Nat.	C-3-1	151	565	82	146	24	2	28	87	.258	620	219	31	.964
1973—Baltimore	Amer.	C-1B	132	459	58	109	18	1	22	83	.237	733	52	8	.990
1974—Baltimore§	Amer.	C-1B	118	413	47	105	16	0	14	52	.254	707	50	8	.990
1975—Atlanta	Nat.	1B-C	111	383	42	92	13	0	11	50	.240	896	56	12	.988
1976—Atl. x-Mont. y	Nat.	1B-C	122	374	35	84	13	2	17	55	.225	715	64	9	.988
1977—Oakland z	Amer.	C-1B	100	348	39	84	13	0	13	38	.241	305	26	3	.991
1978—Oakland ab							Did not play								
1979—Durango c	Mex.	1B	134	505	69	173	25	2	20	*112	.343	1163	69	11	.991
1980—Campeche d	Mex.	1B	47	175	18	35	6	0	6	22	.200	400	27	4	.991
National League Totals			539	1838	217	458	68	5	89	284	.249	2850	464	70	.979
American League Totals			350	1220	144	298	47	1	49	173	.244	1745	128	19	.990
Major League Totals			889	3058	361	756	115	6	138	457	.247	4595	592	89	.983

Selected by Milwaukee Braves' organization in free-agent draft, June 10, 1965.

†On restricted list, April 4 to June 12, 1968.

‡Traded with Infielder Taylor Duncan to Baltimore Orioles for Pitchers Pat Dobson and Roric Harrison, Catcher Johnny Oates and Infielder Dave Johnson, November 30, 1972.

§Traded to Atlanta Braves for Pitcher Jimmy Freeman and an estimated $75,000, April 17, 1975.

xSold to Montreal Expos, July 2, 1976.

yReleased, March 26, 1977; signed by Oakland A's, April 3, 1977.

zOn supplemental disabled list, July 27, 1977; transferred to disabled list, August 5 to August 26, 1977.

aOn disabled list, March 25 to May 17, 1978.

bReleased, May 17, 1978; signed by Durango, March 9, 1979.

cSold to Campeche, March 13, 1980.

dReleased, June 1, 1980; signed by Pittsburgh Pirates' organization, December 19, 1980.

PITCHING RECORD

Year Club	League	G.	IP.	W.	L.	Pct.	H.	R.	ER.	SO.	BB.	ERA.
1966—Sarasota Braves	Gulf Coast	11	61	1	0	1.000	60	26	21	32	22	3.10

Year Club	League	Pos.	G.	AB.	R.	H.	2B.	3B.	HR.	RBI.	B.A.	PO.	A.	E.	F.A.
1973—Baltimore ....Amer.		1B-C	5	18	2	5	2	0	1	4	.278	43	2	0	1.000
1974—Baltimore ....Amer.		1B	2	6	0	0	0	0	0	0	.000	16	1	1	.944
Championship Series Totals			7°	24	2	5	2	0	1	4	.208	59	3	1	.984

RICHARD ALLEN WILLIAMS
(Rick)

Born November 9, 1952, at Merced, Calif.
Height, 6.01. Weight, 180.
Throws and bats righthanded.
Attended Merced College, Merced, Calif.

Year Club	League	G.	IP.	W.	L.	Pct.	H.	R.	ER.	SO.	BB.	ERA.
1972—Cocoa Astros......................Florida E.C.		8	58	3	5	.375	52	23	12	37	23	1.86
1973—Cedar Rapids ....Midwest		23	117	7	6	.538	135	52	43	93	36	3.31
1974—Columbus ....Southern		32	105	8	3	.727	115	65	46	45	40	3.94
1975—Columbus ....Southern		22	118	8	7	.533	111	46	35	46	35	2.67
1975—Iowa ....Am. Assoc.		4	7	1	0	1.000	15	14	11	2	6	14.14
1976—Columbus ....Southern		24	146	7	7	.500	134	49	43	53	46	2.65
1977—Charleston ....Int'national		29	206	9	11	.450	188	94	69	59	59	3.01
1978—Charleston ....Int'national		11	80	8	1	.889	69	28	21	31	18	2.36
1978—Houston ....National		17	35	1	2	.333	43	19	18	17	10	4.63
1979—Charleston ....Int'national		2	10	0	1	.000	15	6	2	5	6	1.80
1979—Houston ....National		31	121	4	7	.364	122	45	44	37	30	3.27
1980—Tucson† ....P. Coast		28	188	14	11	.560	*240	*123	105	85	69	5.03
Major League Totals.................................		48	156	5	9	.357	165	64	62	54	40	3.58

Signed as free agent by Houston Astros' organization, May 21, 1972.
†Sold to Minnesota Twins' organization, February 5, 1981.

MICHAEL HENRY WILLIS
(Mike)

Born December 26, 1950, at Oklahoma City, Okla.
Height, 6.02. Weight, 200.
Throws and bats lefthanded.
Hobbies—Fishing and golf.
Attended Vanderbilt University, Nashville, Tenn.

Pitched 4-0 no-hit victory against Pulaski, June 28, 1972.
Tied for International League lead in shutouts with 4 in 1974.

Year Club	League	G.	IP.	W.	L.	Pct.	H.	R.	ER.	SO.	BB.	ERA.
1972—Bluefield.............................Ap'achian		12	86	7	4	.636	67	42	29	98	33	3.03
1973—Miami.................................Florida St.		18	125	9	6	.600	88	36	27	87	34	1.94
1973—Asheville ....Southern		9	69	5	3	.625	68	30	26	30	18	3.39
1974—Asheville ....Southern		7	36	3	0	1.000	34	16	12	18	11	3.00
1974—Rochester ....Int'national		21	143	9	4	.692	117	49	42	74	42	2.64
1975—Rochester ....Int'national		32	175	●14	8	.636	151	71	50	84	54	2.57
1976—Rochester† ....Int'national		27	156	12	6	.667	161	81	73	80	39	4.21
1977—Toronto...............................American		43	107	2	6	.250	105	48	47	59	38	3.95
1978—Toronto...............................American		44	101	3	7	.300	104	55	51	52	39	4.54
1979—Toronto...............................American		17	27	0	3	.000	35	27	25	8	16	8.33
1979—Syracuse.............................Int'national		20	34	1	3	.250	36	21	20	28	10	5.29
1980—Syracuse.............................Int'national		44	69	7	4	.636	44	24	19	48	35	2.48
1980—Toronto ....American		20	26	2	1	.667	25	6	5	14	11	1.73
Major League Totals		124	261	7	19	.269	269	136	128	133	104	4.41

Selected by Cincinnati Reds' organization in 25th round of free-agent draft, June 7, 1968.
Selected by Baltimore Orioles' organization in 20th round of free-agent draft, June 6, 1972.
†Selected by Toronto Blue Jays in American League expansion draft, November 5, 1976.

ELLIOTT TAYLOR WILLS
(Bump)
(Nicknamed by father after Bump Elliott.)

Born July 27, 1952, at Washington, D. C.
Height, 5.09. Weight, 177.
Throws right and bats left and righthanded.
Hobby—Playing the guitar.
Attended Arizona State University, Tempe, Ariz.
Son of Maury Wills, manager of Seattle Mariners.

Major League stolen bases: 1977 (28), 1978 (52), 1979 (35), 1980 (34). Total—149.

Year Club	League	Pos.	G.	AB.	R.	H.	2B.	3B.	HR.	RBI.	B.A.	PO.	A.	E.	F.A.
1975—Pittsfield.............East.		2B-SS	122	456	72	*140	23	2	9	49	.307	223	304	26	.953
1976—Sacramento.......P. C.		2B	117	432	91	140	20	6	26	95	.324	297	350	19	.971
1977—Texas................Amer.		*2-1-S	152	541	87	155	28	6	9	62	.287	321	*492	15	.982

Year	Club	League	Pos.	G.	AB.	R.	H.	2B.	3B.	HR.	RBI.	B.A.	PO.	A.	E.	F.A.
1978–Texas	....	Amer.	2B	157	539	78	135	17	4	9	57	.250	*350	*526	17	.981
1979–Texas†	....	Amer.	2B	146	543	90	148	21	3	5	46	.273	337	468	20	.976
1980–Texas‡	....	Amer.	2B	146	578	102	152	31	5	5	58	.263	340	473	13	.984
Major League Totals	....			601	2201	357	590	97	18	28	223	.268	1348	1959	65	.981

Selected by San Diego Padres' organization in 12th round of free-agent draft, June 5, 1974.
Selected by Texas Rangers' organization in secondary phase of free-agent draft, January 9, 1975.
†On disabled list, July 28 to August 11, 1979.
‡On supplemental disabled list, August 30 to September 15, 1980.

WILLIAM HAYWARD WILSON
(Mookie)

Born February 9, 1956, at Bamberg, S. C.
Height, 5.10. Weight, 170.
Throws and bats righthanded.
Attended Spartanburg Methodist College, Spartanburg, S. C.,
and University of South Carolina, Columbia, S. C.
Named International League Rookie of the Year, 1979.

Year	Club	League	Pos.	G.	AB.	R.	H.	2B.	3B.	HR.	RBI.	B.A.	PO.	A.	E.	F.A.
1977–Wausau	....	Midw.	OF	68	245	50	71	10	2	6	32	.290	150	8	9	.946
1978–Jackson	....	Texas	OF	132	497	72	145	13	*15	7	72	.292	282	10	7	.977
1979–Tidewater	....	Int.	OF	*141	529	84	141	22	10	5	36	.267	317	11	7	.979
1980–Tidewater	....	Int.	OF	132	515	*92	*152	11	*14	4	44	.295	*350	11	7	.981
1980–New York	....	Nat.	OF	27	105	16	26	5	3	0	4	.248	72	1	2	.973
Major League Totals	....			27	105	16	26	5	3	0	4	.248	72	1	2	.973

Selected by Los Angeles Dodgers' organization in 4th round of free-agent draft, January 7, 1976.
Selected by New York Mets' organization in 2nd round of free-agent draft, June 7, 1977.

WILLIE JAMES WILSON

Born July 9, 1955, at Montgomery, Ala.
Height, 6.03. Weight, 187.
Throws right and bats left and righthanded.

Established major league records for most at bats season (705), 1980; most at bats by switch-hitter, season (705), 1980.
Tied major league record for most hits by switch-hitter, season (230), 1980.
Established American League records for fewest times, grounded into double play, season (1), 1979; most one-base hits by switch-hitter, season (184), 1980; most consecutive stolen bases with no caught stealing (32).
Tied American League record for most three-base hits by switch-hitter, season (15), 1980.
Major League stolen bases: 1976 (2), 1977 (6), 1978 (46), 1979 (83), 1980 (79). Total–216.
Switch-hit home runs in one game, vs. Milwaukee Brewers, June 15, 1979.
Led Gulf Coast League in stolen bases with 24 in 1974.
Led Midwest League in stolen bases with 76 in 1975.
Led American League in stolen bases with 83 in 1979.
Named as outfielder on THE SPORTING NEWS American League All-Star fielding team, 1980.
Named Midwest League Most Valuable Player in 1975.
Received reported $90,000 bonus to sign with Kansas City Royals, 1974.

Year	Club	League	Pos.	G.	AB.	R.	H.	2B.	3B.	HR.	RBI.	B.A.	PO.	A.	E.	F.A.
1974–Sarasota Royals.		Gulf C.	OF	47	155	30	39	3	5	1	14	.252	92	8	4	.962
1975–Waterloo	....	Midw.	OF	127	486	92	*132	18	4	8	73	.272	249	●117	*17	.940
1976–Jacksonville	......	South.	OF	107	388	54	98	13	6	1	35	.253	273	5	8	.972
1976–Kansas City	......	Amer.	OF	12	6	0	1	0	0	0	0	.167	6	1	1	.875
1977–Omaha	....	A.A.	OF	132	495	67	139	10	6	4	47	.281	*278	7	11	.963
1977–Kansas City	......	Amer.	OF	13	34	10	11	2	0	0	1	.324	24	0	1	.960
1978–Kansas City	......	Amer.	OF	127	198	43	43	8	2	0	16	.217	171	6	4	.978
1979–Kansas City	......	Amer.	OF	154	588	113	185	18	13	6	49	.315	384	12	6	.985
1980–Kansas City	......	Amer.	OF	161	705	*133	*230	28	●15	3	49	.326	482	9	6	.988
Major League Totals	....			467	1531	299	470	56	30	9	115	.307	1067	28	18	.984

Selected by Kansas City Royals' organization in 1st round (18th player selected) of free-agent draft, June 5, 1974.

CHAMPIONSHIP SERIES RECORD

Year	Club	League	Pos.	G.	AB.	R.	H.	2B.	3B.	HR.	RBI.	B.A.	PO.	A.	E.	F.A.
1978–Kansas City	......	Amer.	PR-OF	3	4	0	1	0	0	0	0	.250	2	0	0	1.000
1980–Kansas City	......	Amer.	OF	3	13	2	4	2	1	0	4	.308	6	1	0	1.000
Championship Series Totals	....			6	17	2	5	2	1	0	4	.294	8	1	0	1.000

WORLD SERIES RECORD

Established World Series record for most strikeouts, six-game and any length Series (12), 1980.
Tied World Series record for most at bats, inning (2), October 18, 1980 (first inning).

Year	Club	League	Pos.	G.	AB.	R.	H.	2B.	3B.	HR.	RBI.	B.A.	PO.	A.	E.	F.A.
1980–Kansas City	......	Amer.	OF	6	26	3	4	1	0	0	0	.154	15	1	0	1.000

DAVID MARK WINFIELD
(Dave)

Born October 3, 1951, at St. Paul, Minn.
Height, 6.06. Weight, 220.
Throws and bats righthanded.
Hobbies—Reading, art and fashion.
Attended University of Minnesota, Minneapolis, Minn.

Major League stolen bases: 1973 (0), 1974 (9), 1975 (23), 1976 (26), 1977 (16), 1978 (21), 1979 (15), 1980 (23).
Total—133.
Led National League in total bases with 333 in 1979.
Named outfielder on THE SPORTING NEWS National League All-Star Team, 1979 and 1980.
Named right fielder on THE SPORTING NEWS National League All-Star Team, 1979.
Received reported $100,000 bonus to sign with San Diego Padres, 1973.

Year Club League	Pos.	G.	AB.	R.	H.	2B.	3B.	HR.	RBI.	B.A.	PO.	A.	E.	F.A.
1973—San Diego..........Nat.	OF-1B	56	141	9	39	4	1	3	12	.277	65	1	3	.957
1974—San Diego..........Nat.	OF	145	498	57	132	18	4	20	75	.265	276	11	•12	.960
1975—San Diego..........Nat.	OF	143	509	74	136	20	2	15	76	.267	302	9	9	.972
1976—San Diego..........Nat.	OF	137	492	81	139	26	4	13	69	.283	304	*15	6	.982
1977—San Diego..........Nat.	OF	157	615	104	169	29	7	25	92	.275	368	15	11	.972
1978—San Diego..........Nat.	OF-1B	158	587	88	181	30	5	24	97	.308	328	8	7	.980
1979—San Diego ....Nat.	OF	159	597	97	184	27	10	34	•118	.308	344	14	5	.986
1980—San Diego† ....Nat.	OF	162	558	89	.154	25	6	20	87	.276	273	20	4	.987
Major League Totals		1087	3997	599	1134	179	39	154	626	.284	2260	93	57	.976

Selected by Baltimore Orioles' organization in 40th round of free-agent draft, June 5, 1969.
Selected by San Diego Padres' organization in 1st round (fourth player selected) of free-agent draft, June 5, 1973.
†Granted free agency, October 22, 1980; signed by New York Yankees, December 15, 1980.

ALL-STAR GAME RECORD

Tied All-Star Game record for most at bats, game (5), July 17, 1979.

Year League	Pos.	AB.	R.	H.	2B.	3B.	HR.	RBI.	B.A.	PO.	A.	E.	F.A.
1977—National..............................	OF	2	0	2	1	0	0	2	1.000	1	0	0	1.000
1978—National..............................	OF	2	1	1	0	0	0	0	.500	1	0	0	1.000
1979—National..............................	OF	5	1	1	1	0	0	1	.200	3	0	0	1.000
1980—National..............................	OF	2	0	0	0	0	0	1	.000	2	0	0	1.000
All-Star Game Totals		11	2	4	2	0	0	3	.364	7	0	0	1.000

ALAN LEE WIRTH

Born December 8, 1956, at Mesa, Ariz.
Height, 6.05. Weight, 190.
Throws and bats righthanded.

Led Pioneer League in games started with 14 in 1975.
Led Eastern League in wild pitches with 16 in 1977.
Tied for Pioneer League lead in complete games with 7 in 1975.
Tied for California League lead in complete games with 12 in 1976.
Tied for Eastern League lead in complete games with 15 in 1977.

Year Club League	G.	IP.	W.	L.	Pct.	H.	R.	ER.	SO.	BB.	ERA.
1974—Great Falls ....Pioneer	9	43	1	3	.250	33	14	10	23	26	2.09
1975—Great Falls ....Pioneer	14	*105	8	5	.615	*96	44	36	*90	39	3.09
1976—Fresno...............................California	28	181	11	12	.478	*227	*125	94	114	76	4.67
1977—Waterbury†.........................Eastern	27	*210	15	5	.750	180	87	67	*149	77	2.87
1978—Vancouver‡.........................P. Coast	12	73	4	2	.667	87	45	34	43	31	4.19
1978—Oakland..............................American	16	81	5	6	.455	72	39	31	31	34	3.44
1979—Oakland..............................American	5	12	1	0	1.000	14	8	8	7	8	6.00
1979—Ogden................................P. Coast	23	155	6	15	.286	170	101	88	112	85	5.11
1980—Ogden................................P. Coast	20	111	6	9	.400	129	95	78	45	73	6.32
1980—Oakland..............................American	2	2	0	0	.000	3	1	1	1	0	4.50
Major League Totals	23	95	6	6	.500	89	48	40	39	42	3.79

Selected by New York Yankees' organization in 16th round of free-agent draft, June 4, 1970.
Selected by Montreal Expos' organization in secondary phase of free-agent draft, January 13, 1971.
Selected by San Francisco Giants' organization in 3rd round of free-agent draft, June 5, 1974.
†Traded with Outfielder Gary Thomasson, Catcher Gary Alexander, Pitchers Dave Heaverlo, John Johnson and Phillip Huffman, a player to be named later and cash to Oakland A's for Pitcher Vida Blue, March 15, 1978; Shortstop Mario Guerrero sent to A's to complete deal, April 10, 1978.
‡On disabled list, June 20 to July 7 and July 15 to July 25, 1978.

RICHARD CHARLES WISE
(Rick)

Born September 13, 1945, at Jackson, Mich.
Height, 6.02. Weight, 195.
Throws and bats righthanded.
Hobbies—Hunting and fishing.
Brother of Tom Wise, former infielder in Houston Astros' organization, 1970-75.

Tied major league records for most games, two or more home runs by a pitcher in a season (2), 1971; most putouts, game, pitcher, 5, May 15, 1973.

Pitched 4-0 no-hit victory against Cincinnati Reds, June 23, 1971.

Year Club	League	G.	IP.	W.	L.	Pct.	H.	R.	ER.	SO.	BB.	ERA.
1963—Bakersfield ....California	12	65	6	3	.667	47	26	19	98	23	2.63
1964—Philadelphia ....National	25	69	5	3	.625	78	41	31	39	25	4.04
1965—Arkansas ....P. Coast	30	194	8	*16	.333	195	107	96	148	84	4.45
1966—San Diego ....P. Coast	12	55	3	1	.750	44	16	14	26	9	2.29
1966—Philadelphia ....National	22	99	5	6	.455	100	50	41	58	23	3.73
1967—Philadelphia ....National	36	181	11	11	.500	177	69	66	111	45	3.28
1968—Philadelphia ....National	30	182	9	15	.375	210	100	*92	97	37	4.55
1969—Philadelphia ....National	33	220	15	13	.536	215	100	79	144	61	3.23
1970—Philadelphia ....National	35	220	13	14	.481	253	115	102	113	65	4.17
1971—Philadelphia† ....National	38	272	17	14	.548	261	110	87	155	70	2.88
1972—St. Louis ....National	35	269	16	16	.500	250	98	93	142	71	3.11
1973—St. Louis‡ ....National	35	259	16	12	.571	259	113	97	144	59	3.37
1974—Boston§ ....American	9	49	3	4	.429	47	23	21	25	16	3.86
1975—Boston ....American	35	255	19	12	.613	262	126	112	141	72	3.95
1976—Boston ....American	34	224	14	11	.560	218	100	88	93	48	3.54
1977—Boston x ....American	26	128	11	5	.688	151	68	68	85	28	4.78
1978—Cleveland......................American	33	212	9	19	.321	226	116	102	106	59	4.33
1979—Cleveland y ....American	34	232	15	10	.600	229	111	96	108	68	3.72
1979—San Diego z ....National	27	154	6	8	.429	172	69	63	59	37	3.68
American League Totals	171	1100	71	61	.538	1133	544	487	558	291	3.98
National League Totals	316	1925	113	112	.502	1975	865	751	1062	494	3.51
Major League Totals.................................	487	3025	184	173	.515	3108	1409	1238	1620	785	3.68

Signed as free agent by Philadelphia Phillies' organization, June 16, 1963.
†Traded to St. Louis Cardinals for Pitcher Steve Carlton, February 25, 1972.
‡Traded with Outfielder Bernie Carbo to Boston Red Sox for Outfielder Reggie Smith and Pitcher Ken Tatum, October 26, 1973.
§On disabled list, August 7 to September 1, 1974.
xTraded with Pitcher Mike Paxton, Third Baseman Ted Cox and Catcher Bo Diaz to Cleveland Indians for Pitcher Dennis Eckersley and Catcher Fred Kendall, March 30, 1978.
yGranted free agency, November 1, 1979; signed by San Diego Padres, November 19, 1979.
zOn disabled list, June 16 to July 12, 1980.

CHAMPIONSHIP SERIES RECORD

Year Club	League	G.	IP.	W.	L.	Pct.	H.	R.	ER.	SO.	BB.	ERA.
1975—Boston ....American	1	7⅓	1	0	1.000	6	3	2	2	3	2.45

WORLD SERIES RECORD

Tied World Series record for most consecutive home runs allowed, inning (2), October 14, 1975 (fifth inning).

Year Club	League	G.	IP.	W.	L.	Pct.	H.	R.	ER.	SO.	BB.	ERA.
1975—Boston ....American	2	5⅓	1	0	1.000	6	5	5	2	2	8.44

ALL-STAR GAME RECORD

Year League		IP.	W.	L.	Pct.	H.	R.	ER.	SO.	BB.	ERA.
1973—National		2	1	0	1.000	2	1	1	1	0	4.50

Member of National League All-Star Team in 1971 game; did not play.

MICHAEL ATWATER WITT
(Mike)

Born July 20, 1960, at Fullerton, Calif.
Height, 6.07. Weight, 185.
Throws and bats righthanded.
Attending Cypress Junior College, Cypress, Calif.

Year Club	League	G.	IP.	W.	L.	Pct.	H.	R.	ER.	SO.	BB.	ERA.
1978—Idaho Falls ....Pioneer	13	86	7	1	.875	88	45	34	79	26	3.56
1979—Salinas ....California	30	141	8	10	.444	156	96	80	94	70	5.11
1980—Salinas ....California	13	90	7	3	.700	85	30	21	76	35	2.10
1980—El Paso................................Texas	12	70	5	5	.500	72	53	45	64	39	5.79

Selected by California Angels' organization in 4th round of free-agent draft, June 6, 1978.

JOHNNY BILTON WOCKENFUSS
Name pronounced WAHK-en-fuss.

(John)

Born February 27, 1949, at Welch, W. Va.
Height, 6.00. Weight, 180.
Throws and bats righthanded.
Hobbies—Hunting and fishing.

Tied major league record for most unassisted double plays by catcher, game (1), June 21, 1975.
Led American Association in passed balls with 10 in 1974.
Tied for Eastern League lead in passed balls with 24 in 1972.

Year Club	League	Pos.	G.	AB.	R.	H.	2B.	3B.	HR.	RBI.	B.A.	PO.	A.	E.	F.A.
1967—Geneva	NYP	OF	3	7	0	1	0	0	0	1	.143	0	0	1	.000
1968—Geneva	NYP	OF-3B	39	132	13	26	1	1	4	17	.197	50	5	7	.887
1969—Burlington........	Carol.	OF	62	197	23	33	7	1	4	15	.168	110	4	4	.966
1969—Shelby..............	W. Car.	OF	39	157	26	51	12	0	7	29	.325	77	7	4	.955
1970—Pittsfield..........	East.	*O-3-2	123	429	65	106	11	6	15	47	.247	219	11	4	*.983
1971—Pittsfield..........	East.	OF-C	103	331	37	77	11	1	9	41	.233	182	5	3	.984
1972—Pittsfield..........	East.	*C-OF	125	410	57	118	20	2	9	60	.288	*772	*68	7	.992
1973—Spokane†..........	P.C.	C-OF	20	54	6	11	2	0	1	6	.204	64	4	3	.953
1973—Tulsa‡..............	A.A.	C-OF	60	184	22	49	12	1	2	22	.266	298	32	5	.985
1974—Evansville........	A.A.	C	84	233	40	64	11	2	10	43	.275	412	41	10	.978
1974—Detroit	Amer.	C	13	29	1	4	1	0	0	2	.138	45	10	4	.932
1975—Evansville........	A.A.	C-OF	43	142	20	41	11	0	6	28	.289	174	26	3	.985
1975—Detroit	Amer.	C	35	118	15	27	6	3	4	13	.229	195	23	4	.982
1976—Detroit	Amer.	C	60	144	18	32	7	2	3	10	.222	221	19	15	.941
1977—Detroit	Amer.	C-OF	53	164	26	45	8	1	9	25	.274	181	20	3	.985
1978—Detroit	Amer.	OF	71	187	23	53	5	0	7	22	.283	89	2	2	.978
1979—Detroit	Amer.	1B-C-OF	87	231	27	61	9	1	15	46	.264	318	26	3	.991
1980—Detroit	Amer.	1B-OF-C	126	372	56	102	13	2	16	65	.274	575	47	11	.983
Major League Totals			445	1245	166	324	49	9	54	183	.260	1624	147	44	.976

Selected by Washington Senators' organization in 42nd round of free-agent draft, June 6, 1967.

†Traded with Pitcher Mike Nagy by Texas Rangers to St. Louis Cardinals for Pitcher Jim Bibby, June 6, 1973.

‡Traded by St. Louis Cardinals to Detroit Tigers for Infielder Larry Elliott, December 3, 1973.

JAMES EUGENE WOHLFORD
(Jim)

Born February 28, 1951, at Visalia, Calif.
Height, 5.11. Weight, 175.
Throws and bats righthanded.
Hobbies—Golf and playing phonograph records.
Attended College of the Sequoias, Visalia, Calif.

Led Pioneer League in stolen bases with 32 in 1970.

Year Club	League	Pos.	G.	AB.	R.	H.	2B.	3B.	HR.	RBI.	B.A.	PO.	A.	E.	F.A.
1970—Billings	Pion.	SS-2-3	62	221	42	68	7	2	3	37	.308	72	158	*36	.865
1971—San Jose...........	Calif.	2B-SS	120	491	82	149	27	6	11	41	.303	193	327	30	.945
1972—Omaha..............	A.A.	*2-3-O	132	475	75	138	13	10	7	47	.291	247	292	*32	.944
1972—Kansas City.......	Amer.	2B	15	25	3	6	1	0	0	0	.240	7	12	1	.950
1973—Omaha..............	A.A.	OF	65	246	30	76	9	4	3	30	.309	91	5	2	.980
1973—Kansas City.......	Amer.	OF	45	109	21	29	1	3	2	10	.266	31	2	0	1.000
1974—Kansas City.......	Amer.	OF	143	501	55	136	16	7	2	44	.271	273	7	5	.982
1975—Kansas City.......	Amer.	OF	116	353	45	90	10	5	0	30	.255	175	9	9	.953
1976—Kansas City†.....	Amer.	OF-2B	107	293	47	73	10	2	1	24	.249	190	8	5	.975
1977—Milwaukee........	Amer.	OF-2B	129	391	41	97	16	3	2	36	.248	246	7	5	.981
1978—Milwaukee........	Amer.	OF	46	118	16	35	7	2	1	19	.297	52	2	1	.982
1979—Milwaukee‡	Amer.	OF	63	175	19	46	13	1	1	17	.263	126	0	4	.969
1980—San Francisco ...	Nat.	OF-3B	91	193	17	54	6	4	1	24	.280	89	3	2	.979
American League Totals.................			664	1965	247	512	74	23	9	190	.261	1100	47	30	.975
National League Totals			91	193	17	54	6	4	1	24	.280	89	3	2	.979
Major League Totals......................			755	2158	264	566	80	27	10	214	.262	1189	50	32	.975

Selected by California Angels' organization in 11th round of free-agent draft, June 5, 1969.

Selected by Kansas City Royals' organization in secondary phase of free-agent draft, January 17, 1970.

†Traded with Infielder Jamie Quirk and a player to be named later to Milwaukee Brewers for Pitcher Jim Colborn and Catcher Darrell Porter, December 6, 1976; Pitcher Bob McClure was sent to Milwaukee to complete deal, March 15, 1977.

‡Granted free agency, November 1, 1979; signed by San Francisco Giants, November 28, 1979.

CHAMPIONSHIP SERIES RECORD

Year Club	League	Pos.	G.	AB.	R.	H.	2B.	3B.	HR.	RBI.	B.A.	PO.	A.	E.	F.A.
1976—Kansas City.......	Amer.	OF-PH	5	11	3	2	0	0	0	0	.182	7	0	0	1.000

LAURENCE MARCY WOLFE
(Larry)

Born March 2, 1953, at Melbourne, Fla.
Height, 5.11. Weight, 170.
Throws and bats righthanded.
Hobbies—Basketball, football, golf and tennis.
Attended Sacramento City Junior College, Sacramento, Calif.

Led Midwest League third basemen in double plays with 25 in 1974.
Led Southern League in sacrifice flies with 13 in 1976.
Tied for International League lead among third basemen in double plays with 29 in 1977.

Year Club	League	Pos.	G.	AB.	R.	H.	2B.	3B.	HR.	RBI.	B.A.	PO.	A.	E.	F.A.
1973—Geneva	NYP	SS-2B	29	104	19	34	6	0	2	19	.327	32	75	19	.849
1973—Wis. Rapids	Midwest	3B	26	82	9	17	1	0	1	5	.207	18	51	5	.932
1974—Wis. Rapids	Midwest	3B	*127	462	67	140	23	1	14	77	.303	*114	*310	18	*.959

— 495 —

Year Club League	Pos.	G.	AB.	R.	H.	2B.	3B.	HR.	RBI.	B.A.	PO.	A.	E.	F.A.
1975—Orlando............South.	3B	*138	436	46	109	6	0	4	42	.250	*101	*266	15	.961
1976—Orlando............South.	3B	136	476	67	126	24	5	11	61	.265	87	231	19	.944
1977—Charleston ....Int.	3B	134	467	71	142	•33	6	9	77	.304	*117	*258	27	.933
1977—Minnesota ....Amer.	3B	8	25	3	6	1	0	0	6	.240	9	13	0	1.000
1978—Minnesota† ....Amer.	3B-SS	88	235	25	55	10	1	3	25	.234	66	163	12	.950
1979—Boston ....Amer.	2-3-S-C-1	47	78	12	19	4	0	3	15	.244	48	70	5	.959
1980—Pawtucket ....Int.	3B	78	247	24	56	11	0	7	35	.227	59	145	15	.932
1980—Boston ....Amer.	3B	18	23	3	3	1	0	1	4	.130	3	—8	—0	1.000
Major League Totals		161	361	43	83	16	1	7	50	.230	126	254	17	.957

Selected by Los Angeles Dodgers' organization in 21st round of free-agent draft, June 8, 1971.
Selected by New York Yankees' organization in secondary phase of free-agent draft, January 12, 1972.
Selected by Minnesota Twins' organization in 9th round of free-agent draft, June 5, 1973.
†Traded to Boston Red Sox for Outfielder Dave Coleman, February 12, 1979.

ALVIS WOODS
(Al)

Born August 8, 1953, at Oakland, Calif.
Height, 6.03. Weight, 200.
Throws and bats lefthanded.
Hobbies—Listening to music, the outdoors and crafts.
Attended Laney Junior College, Oakland, Calif.
Hit home run as pinch-hitter first at bat in major leagues, April 7, 1977.

Year Club League	Pos.	G.	AB.	R.	H.	2B.	3B.	HR.	RBI.	B.A.	PO.	A.	E.	F.A.
1973—Geneva ....NYP	OF	35	116	17	35	6	1	2	10	.302	47	3	5	.909
1974—Wis. Rapids ....Midw.	OF	111	405	87	126	17	5	18	77	.311	207	6	5	.977
1975—Orlando† ....South.	OF	123	411	55	108	11	4	6	50	.263	248	9	4	.985
1976—Tacoma‡ ....P. C.	OF	121	416	60	118	15	4	6	74	.284	219	11	9	.962
1977—Toronto............Amer.	OF	122	440	58	125	17	4	6	35	.284	215	6	7	.969
1978—Syracuse...........Int.	OF	81	287	47	89	13	1	11	49	.310	145	7	4	.974
1978—Toronto ....Amer.	OF	62	220	19	53	12	3	3	25	.241	131	2	3	.978
1979—Toronto ....Amer.	OF	132	436	57	121	24	4	5	36	.278	251	10	9	.967
1980—Toronto ....Amer.	OF	109	373	54	112	18	2	15	47	.300	205	5	2	.991
Major League Totals		425	1469	188	411	71	13	29	143	.280	802	23	21	.975

Selected by Montreal Expos' organization in 32nd round of free-agent draft, June 8, 1971.
Selected by Minnesota Twins' organization in secondary phase of free-agent draft, June 6, 1972.
†On disabled list, May 29 to June 8, 1975.
‡On disabled list, April 17 to April 27, 1976; selected by Toronto Blue Jays in American League expansion draft, November 5, 1976.

GARY LEE WOODS

Born July 20, 1954, at Santa Barbara, Calif.
Height, 6.02. Weight, 190.
Throws and bats righthanded.
Attended Santa Barbara City Junior College, Santa Barbara, Calif.
Led Pacific Coast League outfielders in putouts with 354 in 1976.

Year Club League	Pos.	G.	AB.	R.	H.	2B.	3B.	HR.	RBI.	B.A.	PO.	A.	E.	F.A.
1973—Lewiston...........Northw.	OF	63	220	23	45	7	3	2	15	.205	87	2	7	.927
1974—Burlington ....Midw.	OF	117	405	68	115	*30	3	11	59	.284	228	4	8	.967
1975—Birmingham .....South.	OF	134	484	76	126	15	6	1	43	.260	*366	*20	7	.982
1976—Tucson .............P.C.	OF-3B	137	526	79	162	22	6	8	67	.308	355	14	13	.966
1976—Oakland† ....Amer.	OF	6	8	0	1	0	0	0	0	.125	7	0	0	1.000
1977—Toronto ....Amer.	OF	60	227	21	49	9	1	0	17	.216	154	4	1	.994
1977—Toledo ....Int.	OF	89	313	46	85	17	4	4	33	.272	231	5	6	.975
1978—Syracuse...........Int.	OF	133	504	74	136	*33	6	13	45	.270	*316	8	11	.967
1978—Toronto‡ ....Amer.	OF	8	19	1	3	1	0	0	0	.158	12	0	0	1.000
1979—Charleston§.......Int.	OF	97	338	46	90	25	1	6	49	.266	253	7	9	.967
1980—Tucson .............P.C.	OF	140	517	102	162	*42	6	8	86	.313	264	13	5	.982
1980—Houston ....Nat.	OF	19	53	8	20	5	0	2	15	.377	19	1	0	1.000
American League Totals		74	254	22	53	10	1	0	17	.209	173	4	1	.994
National League Totals		19	53	8	20	5	0	2	15	.377	19	1	0	1.000
Major League Totals......................		93	307	30	73	15	1	2	32	.238	192	5	1	.995

Signed as free agent by Oakland A's organization, May 12, 1973.
†Selected by Toronto Blue Jays in American League expansion draft, November 5, 1976.
‡Traded to Houston Astros for Outfielder Don Pisker, December 5, 1978.
§On disabled list, July 14 to August 13, 1979.

CHAMPIONSHIP SERIES RECORD

Year Club League	Pos.	G.	AB.	R.	H.	2B.	3B.	HR.	RBI.	B.A.	PO.	A.	E.	F.A.
1980—Houston ....Nat.	OF-PH	4	8	0	2	0	0	0	1	.250	1	0	0	1.000

DID YOU KNOW—
That the last switch-hitter to win the American League MVP award was Vida Blue? That was in 1971.

RICHARD COOPER WORTHAM

Born October 22, 1953, at Odessa, Tex.
Height, 6.00. Weight, 185.
Throws left and bats righthanded.
Attended University of Texas, Austin, Tex.

Year Club	League	G.	IP.	W.	L.	Pct.	H.	R.	ER.	SO.	BB.	ERA.
1976−Knoxville	Southern	11	68	4	2	.667	58	33	32	56	38	4.24
1977−Iowa	Am. Assoc.	9	31	1	3	.250	54	39	30	22	20	8.71
1977−Knoxville	Southern	22	114	9	7	.563	116	62	32	80	45	2.53
1978−Iowa	Am. Assoc.	22	138	5	8	.385	136	75	61	73	54	3.98
1978−Chicago	American	8	59	3	2	.600	59	24	20	25	23	3.05
1979−Chicago	American	34	204	14	14	.500	195	126	111	119	100	4.90
1980−Chicago†	American	41	92	4	7	.364	102	73	61	45	58	5.97
Major League Totals		83	355	21	23	.477	356	223	192	189	181	4.87

Selected by Texas Rangers' organization in 5th round of free-agent draft, June 6, 1972.
Selected by New York Mets' organization in 14th round of free-agent draft, June 4, 1975.
Selected by Chicago White Sox' organization in secondary phase of free-agent draft, January 7, 1976.
†Traded to Montreal Expos for Second Baseman Tony Bernazard, December 12, 1980.

JAMES LEON WRIGHT JR.
(Jim)

Born March 3, 1955, at St. Joseph, Missouri.
Height, 6.05. Weight, 205.
Throws and bats righthanded.
Hobbies−Hunting, fishing and coin collecting.
Attends Missouri Western State College, St. Joseph, Missouri.

Named American Association pitcher of the year, 1977.
Led Western Carolinas League in complete games with 15 in 1975.
Tied for Western Carolinas League lead in shutouts with 4 in 1975.
Tied for American Association lead in complete games with 10 in 1977.

Year Club	League	G.	IP.	W.	L.	Pct.	H.	R.	ER.	SO.	BB.	ERA.
1973−Pulaski	Ap'lachian	10	72	4	5	.444	56	36	25	53	33	3.13
1974−Auburn	NYP	13	75	3	4	.429	75	46	41	42	47	4.92
1975−Spartanburg	W. Carol.	26	181	∗14	7	.667	166	83	55	127	56	2.73
1976−Reading†	Eastern	20	147	13	5	.722	124	51	39	107	56	2.39
1977−Oklahoma City‡	Am. Assoc.	22	161	14	6	.700	148	68	56	118	42	3.13
1978−Oklahoma City§	Am. Assoc.	5	20	1	1	.500	25	13	11	10	7	4.95
1979−Philadelphia x	National					(Did not pitch)						
1980−Oklahoma City y	Am.Assoc.	23	106	9	9	.500	118	71	63	46	55	5.35

Selected by Philadelphia Phillies' organization in 5th round of free-agent draft, June 5, 1973.
†On disabled list, June 29 to July 25, 1976.
‡On disabled list, August 3 to August 31, 1977.
§On disabled list, April 14 to June 22 and July 17 to September 22, 1978.
xOn disabled list, April 5 to October 4, 1979.
yDrafted by Kansas City Royals, December 18, 1980.

HAROLD DELANO WYNEGAR JR.
Name pronounced WY-nuh-ger.
(Butch)

Born March 14, 1956, at York, Pa.
Height, 6.00. Weight, 194.
Throws right and bats left and righthanded.
Hobbies−Astronomy, music and coins.

Led Appalachian League catchers in double plays with 9 in 1974.
Led California League batters in walks with 142 in 1975.
Led American League catchers in double plays with 13 in 1980.
Named American League Rookie Player of the Year by THE SPORTING NEWS, 1976.

Year Club	League	Pos.	G.	AB.	R.	H.	2B.	3B.	HR.	RBI.	B.A.	PO.	A.	E.	F.A.
1974−Elizabethton	Appal.	C	●60	191	32	66	10	0	8	51	∗.346	344	39	5	∗.987
1975−Reno	Calif.	C	●139	468	106	147	18	6	19	∗112	.314	∗734	∗99	9	∗.989
1976−Minnesota	Amer.	C	149	534	58	139	21	2	10	69	.260	650	78	∗16	.978
1977−Minnesota	Amer.	C-3B	144	532	76	139	22	3	10	79	.261	676	84	5	.993
1978−Minnesota	Amer.	C-3B	135	454	36	104	22	1	4	45	.229	582	70	8	.988
1979−Minnesota	Amer.	C	149	504	74	136	20	0	7	57	.270	653	65	6	.992
1980−Minnesota	Amer.	C	146	486	61	124	18	3	5	57	.255	670	72	9	.988
Major League Totals			823	2510	305	642	103	9	36	307	.256	3231	369	44	.988

Selected by Minnesota Twins' organization in 2nd round of free-agent draft, June 5, 1974.

ALL-STAR GAME RECORD

Year League	Pos.	AB.	R.	H.	2B.	3B.	HR.	RBI.	B.A.	PO.	A.	E.	F.A.
1976−American	PH	0	0	0	0	0	0	0	.000	0	0	0	.000
1977−American	C	2	1	1	0	0	0	0	.500	3	0	0	1.000
All-Star Game Totals		2	1	1	0	0	0	0	.500	3	0	0	1.000

CARL MICHAEL YASTRZEMSKI

Name pronounced Yah-STREM-skee.

Born August 22, 1939, at Southampton, N. Y.
Height, 5.11. Weight, 185.
Throws right and bats lefthanded.
Attended Notre Dame University, Notre Dame, Ind., and Merrimack College,
North Andover, Mass.; received Bachelor of Science degree in Business Administration.

Established major league records for lowest batting average, season, leader in batting (.301), 1968; most years leading league in assists by outfielders, 7, 1977; most times grounded into double play by lefthanded batter, season (30), 1964.

Tied major league records for fewest triples, season, 150 or more games (0), 1970; fewest double plays by outfielder, season, for leader in double plays (4), 1971; most home runs, two consecutive games (5), May 19 and 20, 1976; highest fielding average by outfielder, season, 100 or more games (1.000), 1977.

Established American League records for most intentional bases on balls, lifetime (169); most consecutive seasons, 100 or more games (20).

Tied American League record for most seasons, 100 or more games (20).

Won American League Triple Crown, 1967.

Hit three home runs in one game, vs. Detroit Tigers, May 19, 1976.

Led American League batters in walks with 95 in 1963 and 119 in 1968; led in slugging percentage with .536 in 1965, .622 in 1967 and .592 in 1970; led in total bases with 360 in 1967 and 335 in 1970; led in sacrifice flies with 9 in 1972.

Led American League outfielders in assists with 16 in 1977.

Tied for American League lead in double plays by outfielders with 4 in 1971.

Tied for American League lead in sacrifice flies with 11 in 1977.

Named Most Valuable Player in Carolina League, 1959.

Named outfielder on THE SPORTING NEWS American League All-Star Teams, 1963-65-67.

Named as outfielder on THE SPORTING NEWS American League All-Star fielding team 1963-65-67-68-69-71-77.

Named Most Valuable Player in American League, 1967.

Named American League Player of the Year by THE SPORTING NEWS, 1967.

Named Major League Player of the Year by THE SPORTING NEWS, 1967.

Received reported $100,000 bonus to sign with Boston Red Sox, 1958.

Year—Club	League	Pos.	G.	AB.	R.	H.	2B.	3B.	HR.	RBI.	B.A.	PO.	A.	E.	F.A.
1959—Raleigh	Car.	*2B-SS	120	451	87	*170	*34	6	15	100	*.377	*255	284	*45	.923
1960—Minneapolis	A. A.	OF	148	570	84	*193	36	8	7	69	.339	243	18	5	.981
1961—Boston	Amer.	OF	148	583	71	155	31	6	11	80	.266	248	12	10	.963
1962—Boston	Amer.	OF	160	646	99	191	43	6	19	94	.296	329	*15	*11	.969
1963—Boston	Amer.	OF	151	570	91	*183	*40	3	14	68	*.321	283	*18	6	.980
1964—Boston	Amer.	*OF-3B	151	567	77	164	29	9	15	67	.289	372	●24	11	.973
1965—Boston	Amer.	OF	133	494	78	154	●45	3	20	72	.312	222	11	3	.987
1966—Boston	Amer.	OF	160	594	81	165	*39	2	16	80	.278	310	*15	5	.985
1967—Boston	Amer.	OF	161	579	*112	*189	31	4	●44	*121	*.326	297	13	7	.978
1968—Boston	Amer.	OF-1B	157	539	90	162	32	2	23	74	*.301	315	13	3	.991
1969—Boston	Amer.	OF-1B	●162	603	96	154	28	2	40	111	.255	427	*38	6	.987
1970—Boston	Amer.	1B-OF	161	566	*125	186	29	0	40	102	.329	816	64	14	.984
1971—Boston	Amer.	OF	148	508	75	129	21	2	15	70	.254	281	*16	2	.993
1972—Boston†	Amer.	OF-1B	125	455	70	120	18	2	12	68	.264	498	43	8	.985
1973—Boston	Amer.	1-3-O	152	540	82	160	25	4	19	95	.296	979	119	18	.984
1974—Boston	Amer.	1B-OF	148	515	*93	155	25	2	15	79	.301	806	46	6	.993
1975—Boston	Amer.	1B-OF	149	543	91	146	30	1	14	60	.269	1217	88	5	.996
1976—Boston	Amer.	1B-OF	155	546	71	146	23	2	21	102	.267	922	55	4	.996
1977—Boston	Amer.	*OF-1B	150	558	99	165	27	3	28	102	.296	344	22	0	*1.000
1978—Boston	Amer.	OF-1B	144	523	70	145	21	2	17	81	.277	523	49	5	.991
1979—Boston	Amer.	1B-OF	147	518	69	140	28	1	21	87	.270	529	56	4	.993
1980—Boston	Amer.	OF-1B	105	364	49	100	21	1	15	50	.275	225	13	4	.983
Major League Totals			2967	10811	1689	3109	586	57	419	1663	.288	9943	730	132	.988

Signed as free agent by Boston Red Sox' organization, November 29, 1958.

†Placed on supplemental disabled list, May 10 through June 9, 1972.

CHAMPIONSHIP SERIES RECORD

Year—Club	League	Pos.	G.	AB.	R.	H.	2B.	3B.	HR.	RBI.	B.A.	PO.	A.	E.	F.A.
1975—Boston	Amer.	OF	3	11	4	5	1	0	1	2	.455	7	2	0	1.000

WORLD SERIES RECORD

Year—Club	League	Pos.	G.	AB.	R.	H.	2B.	3B.	HR.	RBI.	B.A.	PO.	A.	E.	F.A.
1967—Boston	Amer.	OF	7	25	4	10	2	0	3	5	.400	16	2	0	1.000
1975—Boston	Amer.	OF-1B	7	29	7	9	0	0	0	4	.310	35	1	0	1.000
World Series Totals			14	54	11	19	2	0	3	9	.352	51	3	0	1.000

ALL-STAR GAME RECORD

Tied All-Star Game records for most hits, game (4), July 14, 1970; most one-base hits, game (3), July 14, 1970; most home runs by pinch-hitter, game (1), July 15, 1975.

Year—League	Pos.	AB.	R.	H.	2B.	3B.	HR.	RBI.	B.A.	PO.	A.	E.	F.A.
1963—American	OF	2	0	0	0	0	0	0	.000	1	0	0	1.000
1967—American	OF	4	0	3	1	0	0	0	.750	2	0	0	1.000
1968—American	OF	4	0	0	0	0	0	0	.000	0	0	0	.000
1969—American	OF	1	0	0	0	0	0	0	.000	1	0	0	1.000
1970—American	OF-1B	6	1	4	1	0	0	1	.667	8	0	0	1.000
1971—American	OF	3	0	0	0	0	0	0	.000	0	0	0	.000
1972—American	OF	3	0	0	0	0	0	0	.000	3	0	0	1.000

Year League	Pos.	AB.	R.	H.	2B.	3B.	HR.	RBI.	B.A.	PO.	A.	E.	F.A.
1974–American	1B	1	0	0	0	0	0	0	.000	5	0	0	1.000
1975–American	PH	1	1	1	0	0	1	3	1.000	0	0	0	.000
1976–American	OF	2	0	0	0	0	0	0	.000	0	0	0	.000
1977–American	OF	2	0	0	0	0	0	0	.000	0	0	0	.000
1979–American	1B	3	0	2	0	0	0	1	.667	5	1	0	1.000
All-Star Game Totals		32	2	10	2	0	1	5	.313	25	1	0	1.000

Member of American League All-Star Team in 1966; did not play. Named to American League All-Star Teams for 1965, 1973 and 1978 games; replaced due to injury.

STEPHEN WAYNE YEAGER

Name pronounced YAY-gur.

(Steve)

Born November 24, 1948, at Huntington, W. Va.
Height, 6.00. Weight, 200.
Throws and bats righthanded.
Hobbies—Arts, hunting, fishing and auto mechanics.

Tied major league record for most putouts, extra-inning game, catcher, 22, August 8, 1972 (19 innings). Established National League record for most chances accepted, extra-inning game, catcher (24), August 8, 1972 (19 innings).

Year Club	League	Pos.	G.	AB.	R.	H.	2B.	3B.	HR.	RBI.	B.A.	PO.	A.	E.	F.A.
1967–Ogden	Pion.	C	1	0	0	0	0	0	0	0	.000	0	0	0	.000
1967–Dubuque	Midw.	C-1B	14	35	0	6	0	0	0	2	.171	67	3	3	.959
1968–Daytona Beach	Fla. St.	C	59	144	17	22	3	1	1	6	.153	314	23	9	.974
1969–Bakersfield	Calif.	C	22	65	8	10	1	0	0	2	.154	145	26	4	.977
1969–Albuquerque	Texas	PH	1	1	0	0	0	0	0	0	.000	0	0	0	.000
1970–Albuquerque	Texas	C-O-3	55	151	23	42	5	1	3	24	.278	224	29	5	.981
1971–Albuquerque	Texas	C	107	339	49	93	16	5	8	53	.274	678	84	*14	.982
1972–Albuquerque	P. C.	C	82	257	46	72	6	6	13	45	.280	494	26	9	.983
1972–Los Angeles	Nat.	C	35	106	18	29	0	1	4	15	.274	220	19	4	.984
1973–Los Angeles	Nat.	C	54	134	18	34	5	0	2	10	.254	230	24	5	.981
1974–Los Angeles	Nat.	C	94	316	41	84	16	1	12	41	.266	552	58	5	.992
1975–Los Angeles	Nat.	C	135	452	34	103	16	1	12	54	.228	*806	62	7	.992
1976–Los Angeles	Nat.	C	117	359	42	77	11	3	11	35	.214	522	*77	7	.985
1977–Los Angeles	Nat.	C	125	387	53	99	21	2	16	55	.256	690	89	*18	.977
1978–Los Angeles†	Nat.	C	94	228	19	44	7	0	4	23	.193	373	55	5	.988
1979–Los Angeles	Nat.	C	105	310	33	67	9	2	13	41	.216	513	56	9	.984
1980–Los Angeles	Nat.	C	96	227	20	48	8	0	2	20	.211	382	36	7	.984
Major League Totals			855	2519	278	585	93	10	76	294	.232	4288	476	69	.986

Selected by Los Angeles Dodgers' organization in 4th round of free-agent draft, June 6, 1967.
†On supplemental disabled list, August 8 to August 25, 1978.

CHAMPIONSHIP SERIES RECORD

Year Club	League	Pos.	G.	AB.	R.	H.	2B.	3B.	HR.	RBI.	B.A.	PO.	A.	E.	F.A.
1974–Los Angeles	Nat.	C	3	9	1	0	0	0	0	0	.000	14	1	0	1.000
1977–Los Angeles	Nat.	C	4	13	1	3	0	0	0	2	.231	22	1	0	1.000
1978–Los Angeles	Nat.	C	4	13	2	3	0	0	1	2	.231	21	2	0	1.000
Championship Series Totals			11	35	4	6	0	0	1	4	.171	57	4	0	1.000

WORLD SERIES RECORD

Year Club	League	Pos.	G.	AB.	R.	H.	2B.	3B.	HR.	RBI.	B.A.	PO.	A.	E.	F.A.
1974–Los Angeles	Nat.	C	4	11	0	4	1	0	0	1	.364	32	4	1	.973
1977–Los Angeles	Nat.	C	6	19	2	6	1	0	2	5	.316	32	6	0	1.000
1978–Los Angeles	Nat.	C	5	13	2	3	1	0	0	0	.231	23	2	0	1.000
World Series Totals			15	43	4	13	3	0	2	6	.302	87	12	1	.990

EDGAR FREDERICK YOST

(Ned)

Born August 19, 1955, at Eureka, Calif.
Height, 6.01. Weight, 185.
Throws and bats righthanded.
Hobbies—Hunting, fishing and taxidermy.
Attended Chabot Junior College, Hayward, Calif.

Led Texas League catchers in passed balls with 16 in 1976.

Year Club	League	Pos.	G.	AB.	R.	H.	2B.	3B.	HR.	RBI.	B.A.	PO.	A.	E.	F.A.
1974–Batavia	NYP	C	44	123	14	31	2	2	2	11	.252	199	21	*11	.952
1975–Wausau	Midwest	C	79	265	26	51	7	0	6	27	.192	450	42	●19	.963
1976–Jackson	Texas	C	83	266	25	53	5	0	3	25	.199	390	42	7	.984
1977–Jackson	Texas	C	30	94	7	29	9	0	1	8	.309	145	21	4	.976
1977–Tidewater†	Int.	C	60	165	27	48	8	1	12	31	.291	171	29	3	.985
1978–Spokane‡	P.C.	C	89	267	38	70	16	1	7	42	.262	367	49	15	.965
1979–Vancouver	P.C.	C	130	419	43	110	12	2	3	53	.263	604	64	10	.985
1980–Vancouver	P.C	C-1B	80	259	32	80	20	4	2	41	.309	312	34	8	.977
1980–Milwaukee	Amer.	C	15	31	0	5	0	0	0	0	.161	41	5	0	1.000
Major League Totals			15	31	0	5	0	0	0	0	.161	41	5	0	1.000

Signed as free agent by New York Mets' organization, June 11, 1974.
†Drafted from New York Mets' organization by Milwaukee Brewers, December 5, 1977.
‡On disabled list, July 10 to July 28, 1978.

JOEL RANDOLPH YOUNGBLOOD, III

Born August 28, 1951, at Houston, Tex.
Height, 5.11. Weight, 175.
Throws and bats righthanded.
Hobbies—Hunting and fishing.
Led National League outfielders in double plays with 6 in 1980.

Year Club	League	Pos.	G.	AB.	R.	H.	2B.	3B.	HR.	RBI.	B.A.	PO.	A.	E.	F.A.
1970—Tampa	Fla. St.	SS	17	54	7	12	0	0	0	3	.222	22	40	9	.873
1970—Sioux Falls	North.	2-3-S	65	236	27	53	11	1	0	17	.225	110	134	26	.904
1971—Tampa	Fla. St.	3-S-O	136	443	75	113	25	4	5	44	.255	159	207	26	.934
1972—Three Rivers	East.	OF-3B	104	366	57	106	15	5	12	60	.290	118	80	30	.868
1973—Indianapolis	A. A.	O-S-3	124	451	88	143	24	9	11	50	.317	136	112	28	.899
1974—Indianapolis†	A. A.	OF	103	316	55	90	17	4	13	49	.285	115	6	4	.968
1975—Indianapolis	A. A.	OF-2B	123	418	65	110	21	•9	6	51	.263	201	13	7	.968
1976—Cincinnati‡	Nat.	1-O-C-2	55	57	8	11	1	1	0	1	.193	15	3	1	.947
1977—St.L.§-N.Y.	Nat.	2-O-3	95	209	17	51	13	1	0	12	.244	107	94	8	.962
1978—New York	Nat.	O-2-3-S	113	266	40	67	12	8	7	30	.252	160	96	13	.952
1979—New York	Nat.	OF-2-3	158	590	90	162	37	5	16	60	.275	337	57	9	.978
1980—New York	Nat.	O-3-2	146	514	58	142	26	2	8	69	.276	318	65	13	.967
Major League Totals			567	1636	213	433	89	17	31	172	.265	937	315	44	.966

Selected by Cincinnati Reds' organization in 2nd round of free-agent draft, January 17, 1970.
†On disabled list, June 7 to June 19, 1974.
‡Traded to St. Louis Cardinals for Pitcher Bill Caudill, March 28, 1977.
§Traded to New York Mets for Shortstop Mike Phillips, June 15, 1977.

ROBIN R. YOUNT

Born September 16, 1955, at Danville, Ill.
Height, 6.00. Weight, 170.
Throws and bats righthanded.
Hobbies—Golf, fishing and motorcycles.
Brother of Larry Yount, former minor league pitcher in Houston Astros', Milwaukee Brewers' and Pittsburgh Pirates' organizations, 1968-1976.

Led American League shortstops in double plays with 104 in 1976.
Named shortstop on THE SPORTING NEWS American League All-Star Team, 1978 and 1980.
Named shortstop on THE SPORTING NEWS American League Silver Bat team, 1980.

Year Club	League	Pos.	G.	AB.	R.	H.	2B.	3B.	HR.	RBI.	B.A.	PO.	A.	E.	F.A.
1973—Newark	NYP	SS	64	242	29	69	15	3	3	25	.285	43	85	18	.877
1974—Milwaukee	Amer.	SS	107	344	48	86	14	5	3	26	.250	148	327	19	.962
1975—Milwaukee	Amer.	SS	147	558	67	149	28	2	8	52	.267	273	402	•44	.939
1976—Milwaukee	Amer.	•SS-OF	161	638	59	161	19	3	2	54	.252	•290	510	31	.963
1977—Milwaukee	Amer.	SS	154	605	66	174	34	4	4	49	.288	256	449	29	.964
1978—Milwaukee†	Amer.	SS	127	502	66	147	23	9	9	71	.293	246	453	30	.959
1979—Milwaukee	Amer.	SS	149	577	72	154	26	5	8	51	.267	267	517	25	.969
1980—Milwaukee	Amer.	SS	143	631	211	179	•49	10	23	87	.293	239	455	28	.961
Major League Totals			988	3855	589	1050	193	38	57	390	.272	1719	3113	203	.960

Selected by Milwaukee Brewers' organization in 1st round (third player selected) of free-agent draft, June 5, 1973.
†On supplemental disabled list, March 28 to May 3, 1978.

ALL-STAR GAME RECORD

Year League	Pos.	AB.	R.	H.	2B.	3B.	HR.	RBI.	B.A.	PO.	A.	E.	F.A.
1980—American	SS	2	0	0	0	0	0	0	.000	3	2	0	1.000

PATRICK PAUL ZACHRY
(Pat)

Born April 24, 1952, at Richmond, Tex.
Height, 6.05. Weight, 175.
Throws and bats righthanded.
Named National League Rookie of the Year by Baseball Writers Association of America, 1976.

Year Club	League	G.	IP.	W.	L.	Pct.	H.	R.	ER.	SO.	BB.	ERA.
1970—Bradenton Reds	Gulf Coast	9	54	1	4	.200	53	29	15	55	24	2.50
1970—Sioux Falls	Northern	3	21	2	1	.677	20	9	8	19	5	3.43
1971—Tampa†	Florida St.	22	143	12	4	.750	125	58	51	115	72	3.21
1972—Three Rivers	Eastern	25	133	7	7	.500	110	55	39	102	79	2.64
1973—Three Rivers	Eastern	42	178	•12	12	.500	158	81	65	130	•127	3.29
1974—Indianapolis	Am. Assoc.	33	151	10	7	.588	129	69	59	98	71	3.52
1975—Indianapolis	Am. Assoc.	27	159	10	7	.588	120	52	43	100	70	•2.44
1976—Cincinnati	National	38	204	14	7	.667	170	70	62	143	83	2.74

Year Club	League	G.	IP.	W.	L.	Pct.	H.	R.	ER.	SO.	BB.	ERA.
1977—Cincinnati‡-New York...........National		31	195	10	13	.435	207	104	92	99	77	4.25
1978—New York§...........................National		21	138	10	6	.625	120	57	51	78	60	3.33
1979—New York x..........................National		7	43	5	1	.833	44	19	17	17	21	3.56
1980—New York y..........................National		28	165	6	10	.375	145	65	55	88	58	3.00
Major League Totals		125	745	45	37	.549	686	315	277	425	299	3.35

Selected by Cincinnati Reds' organization in 19th round of free-agent draft, June 4, 1970.
†Appeared in one game as second baseman.
‡Traded with Infielder Doug Flynn and Outfielders Dan Norman (assigned to Tidewater) and Steve Henderson to New York Mets for Pitcher Tom Seaver, June 15, 1977.
§On disabled list, August 1 to September 7, 1978.
xOn disabled list, April 24 to May 23 and June 10 to September 27, 1979.
yOn disabled list, April 27 to May 3, 1980.

CHAMPIONSHIP SERIES RECORD

Year Club	League	G.	IP.	W.	L.	Pct.	H.	R.	ER.	SO.	BB.	ERA.
1976—Cincinnati ....National		1	5	1	0	1.000	6	2	2	3	3	3.60

WORLD SERIES RECORD

Year Club	League	G.	IP.	W.	L.	Pct.	H.	R.	ER.	SO.	BB.	ERA.
1976—Cincinnati...........................National		1	6⅔	1	0	1.000	6	2	2	6	5	2.70

ALL-STAR GAME RECORD
Member of National League All-Star Team for 1978 game; did not play.

GEOFFREY CLAYTON ZAHN
(Jeff)

Born December 19, 1946, at Baltimore, Md.
Height, 6.01. Weight, 185.
Throws and bats lefthanded.
Attended University of Michigan, Ann Arbor, Mich.; received Bachelor
of Science degree in Education.

Pitched 1-0 no-hit loss against St. Petersburg, June 30, 1968.

Year Club	League	G.	IP.	W.	L.	Pct.	H.	R.	ER.	SO.	BB.	ERA.
1968—Daytona Beach† ....Florida St.		21	138	8	9	.471	97	44	32	108	38	2.09
1969—Albuquerque‡§ ....Texas		15	98	9	3	.750	103	42	38	44	29	3.49
1970—Spokane x ....P. Coast		27	53	1	1	.500	67	41	32	22	32	5.43
1971—Albuquerque y.....................Texas		29	164	8	12	.400	155	77	39	126	50	2.14
1972—El Paso...............................Texas		9	73	7	2	.778	54	21	15	77	17	1.85
1972—Albuquerque ....P. Coast		18	109	10	1	.909	126	66	57	80	30	4.71
1973—Albuquerque z......................P. Coast		25	177	13	8	.619	185	81	60	103	66	3.05
1973—Los Angeles ....National		6	13	1	0	1.000	5	2	2	9	2	1.38
1974—Los Angeles ....National		21	80	3	5	.375	78	28	18	33	16	2.03
1975—Los Angeles a-Chicago b.......National		18	66	2	8	.200	69	40	34	22	31	4.64
1976—Wichita...............................Am. Assoc.		21	137	8	8	.500	142	81	65	66	61	4.27
1976—Chicago c............................National		3	8	0	1	.000	16	10	10	4	2	11.25
1977—Minnesota............................American		34	198	12	14	.462	234	116	103	88	66	4.68
1978—Minnesota............................American		35	252	14	14	.500	260	101	85	106	81	3.04
1979—Minnesota d ....American		26	169	13	7	.650	181	74	67	58	41	3.57
1980—Minnesota e ....American		38	223	14	18	.438	273	138	*114	96	66	4.40
American League Totals...........................		133	842	53	53	.500	948	429	369	348	254	3.94
National League Totals		48	167	6	14	.300	168	80	64	68	51	3.45
Major League Totals		181	1009	59	67	.468	1116	509	433	416	305	3.86

Selected by Chicago White Sox' organization in 28th round of free-agent draft, June, 1966.
Selected by Boston Red Sox' organization in secondary phase of free-agent draft, January 28, 1967.
Selected by Detroit Tigers' organization in secondary phase of free-agent draft, June 7, 1967.
Selected by Los Angeles Dodgers' organization in secondary phase of free-agent draft, January 27, 1968.
†On restricted list, April 11 to May 2, 1968.
‡On temporary inactive list, April 22 to June 16, 1969.
§On disabled list, June 16 to July 7, 1969.
xAppeared as first baseman.
yAppeared as an outfielder.
zOn disabled list, June 18 to June 30, 1973.
aTraded with Pitcher Eddie Solomon to Chicago Cubs for Pitcher Burt Hooton, May 2, 1975.
bOn disabled list, July 21 to September 2, 1975.
cReleased, January 17, 1977; signed with Minnesota Twins, March 18, 1977.
dOn disabled list, May 2 to June 2, 1979.
eGranted free agency, October 23, 1980; signed by California Angels, December 2, 1980.

DID YOU KNOW—

That, starting in 1972, Bill Buckner has had .300 seasons every even-numbered year, but fell short in the odd years? Here's the figures: 1971—.277, 1973—.275, 1975—.243, 1977—.284 and 1979—.284; 1972—.319, 1974—.314, 1976—.301, 1978—.323 and 1980—.324.

RICHARD WALTER ZISK
(Richie)

Born February 6, 1949, at Brooklyn, N. Y.
Height, 6.01. Weight, 205.
Throws and bats righthanded.
Hobbies—Golf, bowling and fishing.
Attended Seton Hall University, South Orange, N. J.
Brother of John Zisk, outfielder in Texas Rangers' organization.

Tied major league record for fewest times caught stealing, season, 150 or more games (0), 1976.
Led International League in total bases with 252 in 1972.
Led American League outfielders in double plays with 6 in 1979.
Named as outfielder on THE SPORTING NEWS National League All-Star Team, 1974.
Named Player of the Year in Appalachian League, 1967.

Year Club	League	Pos.	G.	AB.	R.	H.	2B.	3B.	HR.	RBI.	B.A.	PO.	A.	E.	F.A.
1967—Salem	Appal.	O-1B	56	189	41	58	9	2	*16	51	.307	97	6	9	.920
1968—Gastonia	W. Car.	OF	53	185	32	52	8	1	13	41	.281	78	7	5	.944
1969—Salem†	Carol.	OF	78	265	43	84	12	5	11	45	.317	157	7	2	.988
1970—Waterbury	East.	OF	125	450	83	133	17	6	*34	88	.296	175	10	8	.959
1971—Charleston	Int.	OF	135	424	90	123	15	1	29	*109	.290	214	6	8	.965
1971—Pittsburgh	Nat.	OF	7	15	2	3	1	0	1	2	.200	7	0	0	1.000
1972—Charleston	Int.	OF	122	441	83	136	30	4	*26	86	.308	220	16	1	.996
1972—Pittsburgh	Nat.	OF	17	37	4	7	3	0	0	4	.189	14	1	1	.938
1973—Pittsburgh	Nat.	OF	103	333	44	108	23	7	10	54	.324	139	12	2	.987
1974—Pittsburgh	Nat.	OF	149	536	75	168	30	3	17	100	.313	312	9	5	.985
1975—Pittsburgh	Nat.	OF	147	504	69	146	27	3	20	75	.290	264	7	7	.975
1976—Pittsburgh‡	Nat.	OF	155	581	91	168	35	2	21	89	.289	300	11	4	.987
1977—Chicago§	Amer.	OF	141	531	78	154	17	6	30	101	.290	210	9	4	.982
1978—Texas x.............	Amer.	OF	140	511	68	134	19	1	22	85	.262	155	6	2	.988
1979—Texas	Amer.	OF	144	503	69	132	21	1	18	64	.262	234	10	7	.972
1980—Texas y.............	Amer.	OF	135	448	48	130	17	1	19	77	.290	45	3	1	.980
American League Totals..................			560	1993	263	550	74	9	89	327	.276	644	28	14	.980
National League Totals...................			578	2006	285	600	119	15	69	324	.299	1036	40	19	.983
Major League Totals			1138	3999	548	1150	193	24	158	651	.288	1680	68	33	.981

Selected by Pittsburgh Pirates' organization in 3rd round of free-agent draft, June 6, 1967.
†On restricted list, April 2 through June 7, 1969.
‡Traded with Pitcher Silvio Martinez to Chicago White Sox for Pitchers Terry Forster and Rich Gossage, December 10, 1976.
§Granted free agency, November 2, 1977; signed by Texas Rangers, November 9, 1977.
xOn supplemental disabled list, July 21 to August 5, 1978.
yTraded with Pitchers Brian Allard, Ken Clay, Steve Finch and Jerry Gleaton and Shortstop Rick Auerbach to Seattle Mariners for Catcher Larry Cox, Pitcher Rick Honeycutt, Shortstop Mario Mendoza and Outfielders Willie Horton and Leon Roberts, December 12, 1980.

CHAMPIONSHIP SERIES RECORD

Year Club	League	Pos.	G.	AB.	R.	H.	2B.	3B.	HR.	RBI.	B.A.	PO.	A.	E.	F.A.
1974—Pittsburgh	Nat.	OF-PH	3	10	1	3	0	0	0	0	.300	2	0	0	1.000
1975—Pittsburgh	Nat.	OF	3	10	0	5	1	0	0	0	.500	8	0	0	1.000
Championship Series Totals.............			6	20	1	8	1	0	0	0	.400	10	0	0	1.000

ALL-STAR GAME RECORD

Year League		Pos.	AB.	R.	H.	2B.	3B.	HR.	RBI.	B.A.	PO.	A.	E.	F.A.
1977—American............................		OF	3	0	2	1	0	0	2	.667	0	0	0	.000
1978—American		OF	2	0	1	0	0	0	0	.500	0	0	0	.000
All-Star Game Totals			5	0	3	1	0	0	2	.600	0	0	0	.000

PLAYER MOVES

The following player deals involve players in the register with the transactions occurring after March 1, 1981 and including March 21.

BRAUN, STEVE: Signed by St. Louis Cardinals' organization, March 3, 1981.

BURROUGHS, JEFF: Traded by Atlanta Braves to Seattle Mariners for Pitcher Carlos Diaz, March 6, 1981.

FISK, CARLTON: Signed by Chicago White Sox, March 18, 1981.

GONZALEZ, ORLANDO: Released by Oakland A's, March 3, 1981.

HALICKI, ED: Released by Philadelphia Phillies, March 21, 1981.

KELLEHER, MICK: Re-signed by Chicago Cubs' organization, March 2, 1981.

KIMM, BRUCE: Placed on voluntarily retired list by Chicago White Sox' organization, March 7, 1981.

MONTAGUE, JOHN: Signed by Toronto Blue Jays' organization, March 2, 1981.

TOMLIN, DAVE: Signed by Toronto Blue Jays' organization, March 2, 1981.

WHITFIELD, TERRY: Sold by San Francisco Giants to Seibu Lions of Japanese baseball, March 4, 1981.

Major League Managers

JOHN JOSEPH AMALFITANO
Name pronounced UH-mal-fuh-TONN-oh.
(Joe)
Chicago Cubs

Born January 23, 1934, at San Pedro, Calif.
Height, 5.11. Weight, 179.
Threw and batted righthanded.
Attended Loyola University, Los Angeles, Calif., and University of
Southern California, Los Angeles, Calif.; received Bachelor
of Arts degree in Accounting.

Received reported $35,000 bonus to sign with New York Giants, 1954.

Year	Club	League	Pos.	G.	AB.	R.	H.	2B.	3B.	HR.	RBI.	B.A.	PO.	A.	E.	F.A.
1954—New York	Nat.		3B-2B	9	5	2	0	0	0	0	0	.000	2	5	0	1.000
1955—New York	Nat.		SS-3B	36	22	8	5	1	1	0	1	.227	12	19	3	.912
1956—Minneapolis	A.A.		2B	44	121	23	31	4	1	0	8	.256	76	90	6	.965
1956—Johnstown	East.		3B-SS	64	257	36	75	14	2	4	30	.292	81	144	18	.926
1957—Dallas	Texas		INF	98	359	40	105	14	6	3	27	.292	99	183	20	.934
1958—Phoenix†	P.C.		INF-OF	114	372	62	106	28	4	9	51	.285	195	207	21	.950
1959—Toronto‡	Int.		2B	115	380	62	117	19	6	7	43	.308	240	274	9	.983
1960—San Francisco	Nat.		3-2-S-O	106	328	47	91	15	3	1	27	.277	103	187	14	.954
1961—San Francisco§	Nat.		2B-3B	109	384	64	98	11	4	2	23	.255	204	236	13	.971
1962—Houston x	Nat.		2B-3B	117	380	44	90	12	5	1	27	.237	231	270	18	.965
1963—San Francisco	Nat.		2B-3B	54	137	11	24	3	0	1	7	.175	61	92	3	.981
1963—Tacoma y	P.C.		2B-SS	24	86	8	20	4	0	1	12	.233	51	64	5	.958
1964—Chicago	Nat.		2-SS-1	100	324	51	78	19	6	4	27	.241	201	254	17	.964
1965—Chicago	Nat.		2B-SS	67	96	13	26	4	0	0	8	.271	31	67	2	.980
1966—Chicago	Nat.		2-3-SS	41	38	8	6	2	0	0	3	.158	23	19	1	.977
1966—Tacoma	P.C.		SS-3B	17	66	9	16	4	0	1	4	.242	32	56	4	.957
1967—Chicago	Nat.		PH	4	1	0	0	0	0	0	0	.000	....	....	....	....
Major League Totals				643	1715	248	418	67	19	9	123	.244	868	1149	71	.966

†Assigned outright to Toronto by San Francisco Giants, December 5, 1958.
‡Drafted by San Francisco Giants, November 30, 1959.
§Selected by Houston Colts in National League expansion draft, October 10, 1961.
xTraded to San Francisco Giants for Pitcher Dick LeMay and Outfielder Manuel Mota, November 30, 1962.
ySold by San Francisco Giants to Chicago Cubs, March 29, 1964.

RECORD AS MANAGER

Year	Club	League	Position	W.	L.
1979—Chicago†	Nat.		Fifth (E)	2	5
1980—Chicago‡	Nat.		Sixth(E)	26	46
Major League Totals				28	51

†Named interim manager replacing Herman Franks (record of 78-77), September 24, 1979.
Coach, Chicago Cubs, 1967 through 1971; San Francisco Giants, 1972 through 1975; San Diego Padres, 1976 and 1977; Chicago Cubs, 1978 through 1980.
‡Replaced Preston Gomez with club in sixth place (record of 38-52) July 24, 1980.

GEORGE LEE ANDERSON
(Sparky)
Detroit Tigers

Born February 22, 1934, at Bridgewater, S. D.
Height, 5.09. Weight, 168.
Threw and batted righthanded.

Led California League shortstops in double plays with 83 in 1953.
Led Texas League second basemen in double plays with 117 in 1955, Pacific Coast League with 135 in 1957 and International League with 104 in 1958 and 89 in 1960.
Led Western League in sacrifice hits with 20 in 1954 and International League with 15 in 1960; tied for Texas League lead with 22 in 1955 and International League lead with 15 in 1960.

Year	Club	League	Pos.	G.	AB.	R.	H.	2B.	3B.	HR.	RBI.	B.A.	PO.	A.	E.	F.A.
1953—Santa Barbara	Calif.		SS	•141	•598	98	157	21	4	5	55	.263	•277	395	32	.955
1954—Pueblo	West.		2B	147	497	72	147	13	5	0	62	.296	•397	432	20	•.976
1955—Fort Worth	Texas		2B	158	594	86	158	24	1	0	42	.266	•456	•469	18	•.981
1956—Montreal	Int.		2B	140	453	65	135	17	5	0	47	.298	372	391	15	.981
1957—Los Angeles	P.C.		•2B-SS	•168	619	74	161	15	0	2	35	.260	•524	•488	•15	•.985
1958—Montreal†	Int.		2B	•155	580	78	156	35	5	2	56	.269	•387	•464	10	•.983
1959—Philadelphia	Nat.		2B	152	477	42	104	9	3	0	34	.218	343	403	12	.984
1960—Toronto	Int.		2B	148	543	67	123	11	5	5	21	.227	319	•416	12	.984
1961—Toronto	Int.		2B	97	275	30	66	17	0	0	22	.240	189	203	6	.985
1962—Toronto	Int.		2B	124	432	56	111	18	2	2	38	.257	282	327	8	•.987
1963—Toronto	Int.		2B	116	358	56	89	12	5	3	25	.249	226	256	6	•.988
Major League Totals				152	477	42	104	9	3	0	34	.218	343	403	12	.984

†Recalled by Los Angeles Dodgers; traded to Philadelphia Phillies for Pitchers Jim Golden and Gene Snyder and Outfielder Eldon (Rip) Repulski, December 23, 1958.

RECORD AS MANAGER

Year—Club	League	Position	W.	L.	Year—Club	League	Position	W.	L.
1964—Toronto	Int.	Fifth	80	72	1974—Cincinnati	Nat.	Second(W)	98	64
1965—Rock Hill	W. Carol.	Eighth	24	40	1975—Cincinnati	Nat.	First(W)	108	54
(Second Half)		†First	35	23	1976—Cincinnati	Nat.	First(W)	102	60
1966—St. Petersburg	Fla. St.	Second	42	24	1977—Cincinnati	Nat.	Second(W)	88	74
(Second Half)		‡First	49	21	1978—Cincinnati	Nat.	Second(W)	92	69
1967—Modesto	Calif.	§Second	38	32	1979—Detroit z	Amer.	Fifth(E)	56	50
(Second Half)		xFirst	41	29	1980—Detroit	Amer.	Fifth(E)	84	78
1968—Asheville	South.	First	86	54	American League Totals			140	128
1970—Cincinnati	Nat.	First(W)	102	60	National League Totals			863	586
1971—Cincinnati	Nat.	yFourth(W)	79	83	Major League Totals			1003	714
1972—Cincinnati	Nat.	First(W)	95	59					
1973—Cincinnati	Nat.	First(W)	99	63					

†Won playoff against Salisbury (First Half winner), two games to none.
‡Lost playoff against Leesburg (First Half winner), three games to two.
§Tied for position with Santa Barbara.
xLost playoff against San Jose (First Half winner), two games to none.
yTied for position with Houston Astros.
zReplaced Les Moss and interim manager Dick Tracewski with club in fifth place (record of 29-26), June 14, 1979.
Coach, San Diego Padres, 1969.
Manager, National League All-Star Team, 1971, 1973 and 1976.
Coach, National League All-Star Team, 1974.

CHAMPIONSHIP SERIES RECORD

Year—Club	League	W.	L.
1970—Cincinnati	National	3	0
1972—Cincinnati	National	3	2
1973—Cincinnati	National	2	3
1975—Cincinnati	National	3	0
1976—Cincinnati	National	3	0

WORLD SERIES RECORD

Year—Club	League	W.	L.
1970—Cincinnati	National	1	4
1972—Cincinnati	National	3	4
1975—Cincinnati	National	4	3
1976—Cincinnati	National	4	0

ROBERT JOE COX
(Bobby)
Atlanta Braves

Born May 21, 1941, at Tulsa, Okla.
Height, 6.00. Weight, 185.
Threw and batted righthanded.
Hobby—Golf.
Attended Reedley Junior College, Reedley, Calif.
Led Alabama-Florida League shortstops in double plays with 71 in 1961.
Received reported $40,000 bonus to sign with Los Angeles Dodgers, 1959.

Year—Club	League	Pos.	G.	AB.	R.	H.	2B.	3B.	HR.	RBI.	B.A.	PO.	A.	E.	F.A.
1960—Reno	Calif.	2B	125	440	99	112	20	5	13	75	.255	282	*385	*39	.945
1961—Salem	Northw.	2B	14	44	3	9	2	0	0	2	.205	25	25	2	.962
1961—Panama City	Ala.-Fl.	2B	92	335	66	102	27	4	17	73	.304	220	247	8	*.983
1962—Salem	Northw.	3-2B	*141	514	83	143	26	7	16	82	.278	174	296	28	.944
1963—Albuquerque	Texas	3B	17	53	5	15	2	0	2	5	.283	8	27	1	.972
1963—Great Falls	Pion.	3B	109	407	103	137	*31	4	19	85	.337	82	211	21	*.933
1964—Albuquerque	Texas	2B	138	523	98	152	29	13	16	91	.291	*322	*415	*28	.963
1965—Salt Lake City	P. C.	*3B-2B	136	473	58	125	32	1	12	55	.264	133	337	22	*.955
1966—Tacoma	P. C.	3B-2B	10	34	2	4	1	0	0	4	.118	23	15	0	1.000
1966—Austin	Texas	2-3B	92	339	35	77	11	1	7	30	.227	140	216	12	.967
1967—Richmond†	Int.	3B-1B	99	350	52	104	17	4	14	51	.297	84	136	8	.965
1968—New York	Amer.	3B	135	437	33	100	15	1	7	41	.229	98	279	17	.957
1969—New York	Amer.	3B-2B	85	191	17	41	7	1	2	17	.215	50	147	11	.947
1970—Syracuse‡	Int.	3-SS-2B	90	251	34	55	15	0	9	30	.219	86	163	13	.950
1971—Ft. Lauderdale§	Fla. St.	2B	4	9	1	1	0	0	0	0	.111	3	3	0	1.000
Major League Totals			220	628	50	141	22	2	9	58	.224	148	426	28	.953

†Recalled by Atlanta Braves; traded to New York Yankees for Catcher Bob Tillman and Pitcher Dale Roberts (latter transferred to Richmond), December 7, 1967.
‡On disabled list, May 28 through June 18, 1970.
§Player-manager.

PITCHING RECORD

Year—Club	League	G.	IP.	W.	L.	Pct.	H.	R.	ER.	SO.	BB.	ERA.
1971—Ft. Lauderdale	Florida St.	3	10	1	0	1.000	15	9	6	4	5	5.40

RECORD AS MANAGER

Year—Club	League	Position	W.	L.	Year—Club	League	Position	W.	L.
1971—Ft. Lauderdale	Fla. St.	Fourth(E)	71	70	1976—Syracuse	‡Int.	Second	82	57
1972—West Haven	†East.	First (A.)	84	56	1978—Atlanta	Nat.	Sixth(W)	69	93
1973—Syracuse	Int.	Third(Am.)	76	70	1979—Atlanta	Nat.	Sixth(W)	66	94
1974—Syracuse	Int.	Second(N)	74	70	1980—Atlanta	Nat.	Fourth(W)	81	80
1975—Syracuse	Int.	Third	72	64	Major League Totals			216	267

†Defeated Three Rivers in playoff, three games to none.
‡Won playoffs by defeating Memphis, three games to none; and Richmond (finals), three games to one.
Coach, New York Yankees, 1977.

JAMES LOUIS FREGOSI

Name Pronounced Free-GO-see.

(Jim)
California Angels

Born April 4, 1942, at San Francisco, Calif.
Height, 6.02. Weight, 197.
Threw and batted righthanded.
Hobbies—Golf, bowling and basketball.
Attended Menlo College, Menlo Park, Calif.

Tied major league records for most double plays started by shortstop, nine-inning game (5), May 1, 1966 (first game); fewest stolen bases, 150 or more games, season (0), 1970.
Tied American League record for most games, season, shortstop (162), 1966.
Led American League in sacrifice hits with 15 in 1965.
Led American League shortstops in double plays with 125 in 1966 and tied for lead with 92 in 1968.
Tied American Association shortstops for lead in double plays with 100 in 1961.
Named shortstop on THE SPORTING NEWS American League All-Star Teams, 1964 and 1967.
Named shortstop on THE SPORTING NEWS American League All-Star fielding team, 1967.

Year	Club	League	Pos.	G.	AB.	R.	H.	2B.	3B.	HR.	RBI.	B.A.	PO.	A.	E.	F.A.
1960—Alpine†		Soph.	IN-OF	112	404	96	108	17	7	6	58	.267	198	261	39	.922
1961—Dal-Ft. Worth		A. A.	SS	150	516	54	131	18	4	6	50	.254	247	*495	*53	.933
1961—Los Angeles		Amer.	SS	11	27	7	6	0	0	0	3	.222	12	22	2	.944
1962—Dal-Ft. Worth		A. A.	SS-OF	64	219	25	62	9	3	1	14	.283	94	164	22	.921
1962—Los Angeles		Amer.	SS	58	175	15	51	3	4	3	23	.291	96	150	15	.943
1963—Los Angeles		Amer.	SS	154	592	83	170	29	12	9	50	.287	271	446	27	.964
1964—Los Angeles		Amer.	SS	147	505	86	140	22	9	18	72	.277	225	421	23	.966
1965—California		Amer.	SS	161	602	66	167	19	7	15	64	.277	*312	481	26	.968
1966—California		Amer.	*S-1B	162	611	78	154	32	7	13	67	.252	299	*531	●35	.960
1967—California		Amer.	SS	151	590	75	171	23	6	9	56	.290	258	435	25	.965
1968—California		Amer.	SS	159	614	77	150	21	*13	9	49	.244	273	454	29	.962
1969—California		Amer.	SS	161	580	78	151	22	6	12	47	.260	255	465	21	.972
1970—California		Amer.	SS-1B	158	601	95	167	33	5	22	82	.278	313	475	20	.975
1971—California‡§		Amer.	S-1-O	107	347	31	81	15	1	5	33	.233	241	251	22	.957
1972—New York		Nat.	3-S-1	101	340	31	79	15	4	5	32	.232	91	162	15	.944
1973—New York x		Nat.	S-3-1-O	45	124	7	29	4	1	0	11	.234	47	70	9	.929
1973—Texas		Amer.	3-1-S	45	157	25	42	6	2	6	16	.268	98	53	5	.968
1974—Texas		Amer.	1B-3B	78	230	31	60	5	0	12	34	.261	331	73	5	.988
1975—Texas		Amer.	1B-3B	77	191	25	50	5	0	7	33	.262	356	35	6	.985
1976—Texas		Amer.	1B-2B	58	133	17	31	7	0	2	12	.233	183	18	2	.990
1977—Texas yz		Amer.	1B	13	28	4	7	1	0	1	5	.250	31	4	0	1.000
1977—Pittsburgh		Nat.	1B-3B	36	56	10	16	1	1	3	16	.286	99	5	2	.981
1978—Pittsburgh a		Nat.	3B-1B-2B	20	20	3	4	1	0	0	1	.200	14	4	2	.900
American League Totals				1700	5983	793	1598	243	72	143	646	.267	3554	4314	263	.968
National League Totals				202	540	51	128	21	6	8	60	.237	251	241	28	.946
Major League Totals				1902	6523	844	1726	264	78	151	706	.265	3805	4555	291	.966

†Selected by Los Angeles Angels off Boston Red Sox roster in American League expansion draft, December 14, 1960.
‡On disabled list July 12 through August 5.
§Traded to New York Mets for Pitchers Nolan Ryan and Don Rose, Outfielder Leroy Stanton and Catcher Francisco Estrada, December 10, 1971.
xTraded to Texas Rangers for a player to be named later, July 11, 1973.
yOn supplemental disabled list, April 22 through May 12, 1977.
zTraded to Pittsburgh Pirates for First Baseman-Catcher Ed Kirkpatrick, June 15, 1977.
aReleased, June 1, 1978 (in order to accept managerial position with California Angels).

ALL-STAR GAME RECORD

Year	League	Pos.	AB.	R.	H.	2B.	3B.	HR.	RBI.	B.A.	PO.	A.	E.	F.A.
1964—American		SS	4	1	1	0	0	0	1	.250	4	1	0	1.000
1966—American		SS	2	0	0	0	0	0	0	.000	0	1	0	1.000
1967—American		SS	4	0	1	0	0	0	0	.250	2	3	0	1.000
1968—American		SS	3	0	1	1	0	0	0	.333	1	6	0	1.000
1969—American		SS	1	0	0	0	0	0	0	.000	0	0	0	.000
1970—American		PH	1	0	0	0	0	0	0	.000	0	0	0	.000
All Star Game Totals			15	1	3	1	0	0	1	.200	7	11	0	1.000

RECORD AS MANAGER

Year	Club	League	Position	W.	L.
1978—California†		Amer.	‡Second(W)	62	54
1979—California		Amer.	First (W)	88	74
1980—California		Amer.	Sixth(W)	65	95
Major League Totals				215	223

†Replaced Dave Garcia with club in third place (record of 25-21), June 1, 1978.
‡Tied for position.

CHAMPIONSHIP SERIES RECORD

Year	Club	League	W.	L.
1979—California		Amer.	1	3

JAMES GOTTFRIED FREY
(Jim)
Kansas City Royals

Born May 26, 1931, at Cleveland, O.
Height, 5.09. Weight, 170.
Threw and batted lefthanded.
Hobbies—Golf and bowling.
Attended Ohio State University, Columbus, O.

Led Texas League in total bases with 294 and tied for lead in stolen bases with 21 in 1957.
Named Most Valuable Player in Texas League, 1957.

Year Club	League	Pos.	G.	AB.	R.	H.	2B.	3B.	HR.	RBI.	B.A.	PO.	A.	E.	F.A.
1950—Evansville	I.I.I.				(appeared in less than 10 games; no record available)										
1950—Paducah	M.O.V.	OF	106	412	73	134	21	11	1	58	.325	180	17	6	.970
1951—Evansville	I.I.I.	OF	119	447	69	145	24	9	1	58	.324	197	18	10	.956
1952—Hartford	East.	OF	20	80	12	21	8	0	0	7	.263	23	2	0	1.000
1952—Evansville	I.I.I.	OF	90	307	66	103	25	3	2	54	.336	145	15	6	.964
1953—Jacksonville	So. Atl.	OF	117	429	64	136	25	4	2	37	.317	241	18	2	*.992
1954—Jacksonville	So. Atl.	OF	139	529	89	167	*40	4	11	65	.316	314	18	5	.985
1955—Toledo	A. A.	OF	142	486	88	137	36	0	4	54	.282	209	17	11	.954
1956—Atlanta	S. A.	OF	25	87	14	22	4	0	1	11	.253	39	5	2	.957
1956—Austin†-Ft. W.‡	Texas	OF	126	447	63	125	20	2	6	39	.280	224	7	10	.959
1957—Tulsa§	Texas	OF	*155	589	*102	*198	*50	*11	8	74	*.336	310	16	12	.964
1958—Omaha	A. A.	OF	117	420	63	119	19	7	4	45	.283	211	8	6	.973
1959—Rochester	Int.	OF	114	338	56	100	17	2	11	42	.296	157	7	4	.976
1960—Rochester x	Int.	OF	125	441	78	140	21	4	16	66	*.317	199	12	8	.963
1961—Buffalo	Int.	OF	115	354	49	93	17	1	10	47	.263	180	8	4	.979
1962—Buffalo y	Int.	OF	134	448	67	121	18	1	16	59	.270	196	17	5	.977
1963—Col.z-Atl.a	Int.	OF	62	108	11	28	3	0	2	12	.259	29	2	3	.912

†Traded by Milwaukee Braves' organization to Brooklyn Dodgers' organization for Outfielder Ray Shearer, July 4, 1956.
‡Sold by Brooklyn Dodgers' organization to Tulsa, April 12, 1957.
§Sold to St. Louis Cardinals' organization, July 31, 1957, to be announced after the season was over.
xReleased by St. Louis Cardinals' organization to Buffalo, October 5, 1960.
yReleased to Pittsburgh Pirates' organization, December 3, 1962.
zReleased by Pittsburgh Pirates' organization, May 7, 1963; signed as free agent by St. Louis Cardinals' organization, May 18, 1963.
aOn disabled list, July 8 to July 29, 1963. Released, October 15, 1963.

PITCHING RECORD

Year Club	League	G.	IP.	W.	L.	Pct.	H.	R.	ER.	SO.	BB.	ERA.
1956—Austin	Texas	1	....	0	0	.000	....	....	....	....	....	......
1957—Tulsa	Texas	4	....	0	0	.000	....	....	....	....	....	......
1960—Rochester	Int'national	1	....	0	0	.000	....	....	....	....	....	......
1961—Buffalo	Int'national	2	....	0	0	.000	....	....	....	....	....	......

RECORD AS MANAGER

Year Club	League	Position	W.	L.
1964—Bluefield	Appal.	Fourth	27	44
1965—Bluefield	Appal.	Fifth	31	38
1980—Kansas City	Amer.	First(W)	97	65
Major League Totals			97	65

CHAMPIONSHIP SERIES RECORD				WORLD SERIES RECORD			
Year Club	League	W.	L.	Year Club	League	W.	L.
1980—Kansas City	American	3	0	1980—Kansas City	American	2	4

Scout, Baltimore Orioles, 1966 through 1969; coach, Baltimore Orioles, 1970 through 1979. Coach, American League All-Star Team, 1980.

DAVID GARCIA
(Dave)
Cleveland Indians

Born September 15, 1920, at East St. Louis, Ill.
Height, 6.00. Weight, 180.
Threw and batted righthanded.

Led Wisconsin State League in total bases with 259 in 1951.

Year Club	League	Pos.	G.	AB.	R.	H.	2B.	3B.	HR.	RBI.	B.A.	PO.	A.	E.	F.A.
1939—Lake Charles†	Evan.	2B-OF	4	8	0	1	0	0	0	0	.125	2	0	0	1.000
1940—					(Out of Organized Baseball)										
1941—G.F.-E.C	North.	2B	43	143	16	32	7	0	3	25	.224	78	78	8	.951
1942—Eau Claire	North.	3B-2B	123	487	83	156	25	9	18	107	.320	89	183	33	.892
1943-44-45—					(In U. S. Army Air Corps)										
1946—Minneapolis	A. A.	3B	20	65	8	17	6	0	1	9	.262	14	37	7	.879
1946—Little Rock	S. A.	3B	20	42	5	5	0	0	0	2	.119	21	32	5	.914
1946—Wilkes-Barre	East.	3B-2B	68	216	24	46	9	1	1	20	.213	35	51	8	.915
1947—Sioux City	West.	*2B-3B	130	533	85	157	19	10	13	71	.295	325	*343	45	.937

Year	Club	League	Pos.	G.	AB.	R.	H.	2B.	3B.	HR.	RBI.	B.A.	PO.	A.	E.	F.A.
1948—Jersey City	Int.	2B-3B	7	14	1	3	2	0	0	1	.214	2	8	2	.833
1948—Knoxville	T.-S.	3-2B-P	95	347	54	98	16	3	16	59	.282	111	178	25	.920
1949—Oshkosh	W.S.	2-3B-SS	116	391	75	128	34	2	10	82	.327	310	281	32	.949
1950—Oshkosh	W.S.	2B-SS-P	119	421	89	139	20	5	22	130	.330	262	256	27	.950
1951—Oshkosh	W.S.	2B-3B	118	426	97	*157	27	3	*23	*127	*.369	226	286	28	.948
1952—Oshkosh	W.S.	2-3B-SS	117	404	82	132	30	2	15	82	.327	192	255	26	.945
1953—Oshkosh	W.S.	2B-P-OF	119	436	79	138	27	3	15	90	.317	295	277	27	.955
1954—Sioux City	West.	2B-3B	126	421	47	112	20	3	10	52	.266	322	315	24	.964
1955—Mayfield	Kitty	2B	91	237	64	112	19	2	19	81	.332	176	199	11	.972
1955—Minneapolis	A. A.	2B	5	12	2	3	1	0	0	0	.250	1	1	0	1.000
1956—Minneapolis	A. A.	2B-3B	5	3	0	1	0	0	0	0	.333	2	5	1	.875
1957—Danville	Carol.	2B	27	76	8	20	3	0	1	8	.263	22	55	3	.975

†Released by St. Louis Browns' organization, September 1939.

RECORD AS PITCHER

Year	Club	League	G.	IP.	W.	L.	Pct.	H.	R.	ER.	SO.	BB.	ERA.
1948—Knoxville	Tri-State	1	5	0	0	.000	3	1	1	2	2	1.80
1950—Oshkosh	Wis. State	4	13	1	0	1.000	15	21	19	6	17	9.69
1953—Oshkosh	Wis. State	4	5	0	0	.000	3	2	1	2	5	1.80

RECORD AS MANAGER

Year	Club	League	Position	W.	L.	Year	Club	League	Position	W.	L.
1948—Knoxville†	Tri-St.	Sixth	51	44	1967—Fresno	Calif.	Fifth	35	35
1949—Oshkosh	Wis. St.	First	72	49	(Second Half)		Sixth	32	37
1950—Oshkosh	Wis. St.	‡First	74	49	1968—Fresno	Calif.	Fourth	36	34
1951—Oshkosh	Wis. St.	Second	65	55	(Second Half)		xFirst	43	26
1952—Oshkosh	Wis. St.	Third	63	58	1969—Salt Lake City	Pion.	Fourth	37	34
1953—Oshkosh	Wis. St.	Eighth	17	38	1974—El Paso	Texas	yFirst(W)	76	61
(Second Half)		Third	40	28	1977—California z	Amer.	Fifth(W)	35	46
1954—Sioux City	West.	Fifth	78	75	1978—California a	Amer.	Third(W)	25	21
1955—Mayfield	Kitty	Second	65	43	1979—Cleveland b	Amer.	Sixth(E)	38	28
1957—Danville	Carol.	Fifth	28	39	1980—Cleveland	Amer.	Sixth(E)	79	81
(Second Half)§		Fifth	10	18	Major League Totals			177	176
1964—El Paso	Texas	Fourth	67	73					

†Replaced Dale Alexander, June 8, with club in eighth place.
‡Won playoffs by defeating Fond du Lac, three games to one and Janesville, four games to two.
§Replaced by Jack Pollitt, July 22.
xWon playoff by defeating San Jose (First Half winner), two games to one.
yLost playoff to Victoria (Eastern Division winner), three games to none.
zReplaced Norm Sherry with club in fifth place, July 11, 1977.
aReplaced by Jim Fregosi, June 1, 1978.
bReplaced Jeff Torborg with club in sixth place (record of 43-52), July 22, 1979.
Coach, Minneapolis (American Association), 1956; scout, San Francisco Giants, 1957 through 1963 and 1965 and 1966; coach, San Diego Padres, 1970 through 1973; coach, Cleveland Indians, 1975, 1976 and 1979; coach, California Angels, 1977.

JOHN ALBERT GORYL

Name pronounced GORR-ul.

Minnesota Twins

Born October 21, 1933, at Cumberland, R. I.
Height, 5.10. Weight, 170.
Threw and batted righthanded.
Hobbies—Fishing, hunting and golf.

Year	Club	League	Pos.	G.	AB.	R.	H.	2B.	3B.	HR.	RBI.	B.A.	PO.	A.	E.	F.A.
1951—Bluefield	App.	IF-OF	50	169	36	53	10	5	2	34	.314	60	60	20	.857
1952—Evansville	I.I.I.	3B	50	182	31	45	9	2	1	22	.247	52	95	24	.860
1952—Eau Claire	North.	3B	59	218	48	64	6	3	8	25	.294	45	128	17	.911
1953—Evansville	I.I.I.	3B	116	398	65	98	21	5	12	55	.246	*137	215	22	*.941
1954—Evansville	I.I.I.	3B	10	25	4	4	0	0	0	1	.160	....	....	....	....
1954—Eau Claire	North.	3B	117	465	79	146	*38	3	9	90	.314	101	232	21	*.941
1955—Wichita	West.	2B-OF	135	489	84	147	24	2	10	64	.301	260	187	18	.961
1956—Los Angeles	P. C.	3B	12	21	4	4	1	0	1	4	.190	8	9	3	.850
1956—Tulsa	Tex.	INF	69	267	36	75	9	2	7	27	.281	169	192	14	.963
1957—Memphis	South.	SS-3B	147	535	81	161	24	7	18	86	.301	242	402	40	.942
1957—Chicago	Nat.	3B	9	38	7	8	2	0	1	1	.211	6	14	1	.952
1958—Chicago	Nat.	3B-2B	83	219	27	53	9	3	4	14	.242	91	153	16	.938
1959—Chicago	Nat.	2B-3B	25	40	1	9	3	1	1	6	.188	11	31	1	.977
1959—Minneapolis†	A.A.	SS-3B	60	208	26	50	8	0	3	25	.240	62	127	13	.936
1960—St. Paul	A.A.	2B-3B	140	494	72	151	32	10	7	50	.306	240	325	16	.972
1961—Omaha‡	A.A.	3B	135	521	60	146	22	6	10	60	.280	*118	*322	*33	.930
1962—Minnesota	Amer.	2B-SS	37	26	6	5	0	1	2	2	.192	2	10	1	.923
1963—Minnesota	Amer.	INF	64	150	29	43	5	3	9	24	.287	75	92	7	.960
1964—Minnesota	Amer.	2B-3B	58	114	9	16	0	2	0	1	.140	73	70	3	.979
1965—Denver	P.C.	3-2-SS	121	361	50	107	17	4	5	48	.296	146	181	12	.965

Year	Club	League	Pos.	G.	AB.	R.	H.	2B.	3B.	HR.	RBI.	B.A.	PO.	A.	E.	F.A.
1966–	....							(Did Not Play)								
1967–Denver	.............P.C.		2-3-1B	45	116	12	33	2	1	2	13	.284	57	52	7	.940
	National League Totals	....		117	305	35	70	14	4	5	21	.230	108	198	18	.944
	American League Totals	....		159	290	44	64	5	6	11	27	.221	150	172	11	.967
	Major League Totals	....		276	595	79	134	19	10	16	48	.225	258	370	29	.956

†Recalled by Chicago Cubs, August 31, 1959; traded with Outfielder Lee Handley, Pitcher Ron Perranoski and cash to Los Angeles Dodgers' organization for Infielder Don Zimmer, April 7, 1960.

‡Drafted by Minnesota Twins from Omaha (Los Angeles Dodgers' organization), November 27, 1961.

RECORD AS MANAGER

Named Midwest League Manager of the Year, 1974.

Year	Club	League	Position	W.	L.	Year	Club	League	Position	W.	L.
1966–Orlando	.... Fla. St.		Fourth	71	68		(Second Half)		xSecond(N)	38	27
1967–Denver†	.... P.C.		Fifth(E)	48	51	1975–Wis. Rapids	.... Midw.		Third(N)	25	33
1968–Denver‡	.... P.C.		Sixth(E)	8	22		(Second Half)		Second(N)	46	25
1970–Wis. Rapids	.... Midw.		Sixth	59	60	1976–Reno	.... Calif.		Third	33	37
1971–Lynchburg	.... Carol.		Third	37	30		(Second Half)		yFirst	42	25
	(Second Half)		Fifth	31	37	1977–Orlando	.... South.		zaFirst(E)	39	30
1972–Charlotte	.... South.		Third	70	70		(Second Half)		Second(E)	37	31
1973–Wis. Rapids	.... Midw.		First	41	19	1978–Orlando	.... South.		First(E)	43	25
	(Second Half)		§Fourth	27	34		(Second Half)		bThird(E)	39	36
1974–Wis. Rapids	.... Midw.		First(N)	42	21	1980–Minnesota c	.... Amer.		Third(W)	23	13

†Replaced Cal Ermer with club in sixth place, June 9.

‡Replaced by Billy Martin with club in sixth place, May 25.

§Won Northern Division championship playoff from Clinton, two games to none; won championship playoff from Danville, two games to one.

xLost Northern Division championship playoff to Appleton, two games to none.

yWon league championship playoff from Salinas, three games to one.

zTied for position.

aLost first-half championship playoff to Savannah, one game to none.

bLost Eastern Division championship playoff to Savannah, two games to one.

cReplaced Gene Mauch with club tied for fourth place (record of 54-71), August 24, 1980.

Player-coach, Denver, Pacific Coast League, 1967 (through June 8); coach, Minnesota Twins, May 30, 1968 through 1969, 1979 and 1980.

GEORGE DALLAS GREEN JR.
(Known by middle name).
Philadelphia Phillies

Born August 4, 1934, at Newport, Del.
Height, 6.05½. Weight, 210.
Threw right and batted lefthanded.
Attended University of Delaware, Newark, Del.

Year	Club	League	G.	IP.	W.	L.	Pct.	H.	R.	ER.	SO.	BB.	ERA.
1955–Reidsville	.... Carolina		7	17	1	1	.500	25	22	19	8	16	10.06
1955–Mattoon	.... M-O. V.		11	55	4	3	.571	43	29	21	85	42	3.44
1956–Salt Lake City	.... Pioneer		33	239	17	12	.586	182	126	95	*226	*187	3.58
1957–Miami	.... Int'national		2	6	0	1	.000	6	8	7	5	4	10.50
1957–High Point-Thomasville	.... Carolina		25	159	12	9	.571	143	84	71	147	92	4.02
1958–Miami	.... Int'national		31	159	7	10	.412	135	73	66	103	70	3.74
1959–Buffalo	.... Int'national		17	101	9	5	.643	94	39	33	72	28	2.94
1960–Buffalo	.... Int'national		11	75	3	4	.429	72	35	28	44	26	3.36
1960–Philadelphia	.... National		23	109	3	6	.333	100	54	49	51	44	4.05
1961–Philadelphia	.... National		42	128	2	4	.333	160	77	69	51	47	4.85
1962–Philadelphia	.... National		37	129	6	6	.500	145	58	55	58	43	3.84
1963–Philadelphia	.... National		40	120	7	5	.583	134	53	43	68	38	3.23
1964–Arkansas†	.... P. Coast		7	48	4	1	.800	46	15	14	34	9	2.63
1964–Philadelphia	.... National		25	42	2	1	.667	63	31	27	21	14	5.79
1965–Washington‡	.... American		6	14	0	0	.000	14	6	5	6	3	3.21
1965–Arkansas	.... P. Coast		23	172	12	7	.632	180	81	70	119	36	3.66
1966–San Diego§	.... P. Coast		26	184	14	9	.609	200	91	78	90	28	3.82
1966–New York x	.... National		4	5	0	0	.000	6	3	3	1	2	5.40
1967–Reading y	.... Eastern		8	66	6	2	.750	59	20	13	42	12	1.77
1967–Philadelphia z	.... National		8	15	0	0	.000	25	16	15	12	6	9.00
	National League Totals	....	179	548	20	22	.476	633	292	261	262	194	4.29
	American League Totals	....	6	14	0	0	.000	14	6	5	6	3	3.21
	Major League Totals	....	185	562	20	22	.476	647	298	266	268	197	4.26

†Sold to Washington Senators, April 11, 1965.

‡Returned to Philadelphia Phillies' organization, May 11, 1965.

§Sold to New York Mets' organization, July 22, 1966.

xReturned to Philadelphia Phillies' organization, August 10, 1966.

yPlayer-coach.

zReleased, September 22, 1967.

RECORD AS MANAGER

Year Club	League	Position	W.	L.
1968–Huron................	Northern	Fifth	26	43
1969–Pulaski..............	Appal.	First(N)	38	28
1979–Philadelphia†	Nat.	Fourth(E)	19	11
1980–Philadelphia.......	Nat.	First(E)	91	71
Major League Totals...........................			110	82

CHAMPIONSHIP SERIES RECORD

Year Club	League	W.	L.
1980–Philadelphia....... Nat.		3	2

WORLD SERIES RECORD

Year Club	League	W.	L.
1980–Philadelphia....... Nat.		4	2

†Replaced Danny Ozark, August 31, 1979, with record of 65-67 and team in fifth place.

Assistant farm director, Philadelphia Phillies, 1970 to June 2, 1972; Director of Minor Leagues, Philadelphia Phillies, June 2, 1972 to August 31, 1979.

DORREL NORMAN ELVERT HERZOG
(Relly and Whitey)

(Named "Relly" by mother from his first name; "Whitey" by Bill Speith, McAlester sportscaster, because of light hair.)

St. Louis Cardinals

Born November 9, 1931, at New Athens, Ill.
Height, 5.11½. Weight, 187.
Threw and batted lefthanded.

Year Club	League	Pos.	G.	AB.	R.	H.	2B.	3B.	HR.	RBI.	B.A.	PO.	A.	E.	F.A.
1949–McAlester.........	Soo. St.	OF	96	398	53	111	19	7	0	31	.279	222	14	0	∗1.000
1950–McAlester.........	Soo. St.	OF	132	467	107	164	36	10	4	85	.351	272	15	7	∗.976
1951–Norfolk............	Pied.	OF	5	17	5	1	0	0	0	2	.059	13	0	1	.926
1951–Joplin	W.A.	OF-1B	113	418	99	119	14	8	7	48	.285	454	19	9	.981
1952–Beaumont	Texas	OF	35	121	11	24	4	1	0	9	.198	83	3	5	.945
1952–Quincy.............	I.I.I.	OF	68	225	53	65	9	6	7	44	.289	131	9	5	.966
1952–Kansas City	A.A.	OF-1B	14	27	5	8	1	0	1	5	.296	21	1	1	.957
1953-54–....................								(In Military Service.)							
1955–Denver†............	A.A.	OF-1B	149	515	101	149	24	7	21	98	.289	324	10	4	.988
1956–Washington	Amer.	OF-1B	117	421	49	103	13	7	4	35	.245	274	10	7	.976
1957–Washington	Amer.	OF	36	78	7	13	3	0	0	4	.167	53	0	1	.981
1957–Miami...............	Int.	OF	77	257	48	70	14	5	2	25	.272	114	5	4	.967
1958–Wash.‡-K.C.	Amer.	OF-1B	96	101	11	23	1	2	0	9	.228	146	6	3	.981
1959–Kansas City	Amer.	OF-1B	38	123	25	36	7	1	1	9	.293	87	2	3	.967
1960–Kansas City§......	Amer.	OF-1B	83	252	43	67	10	2	8	38	.266	137	6	4	.973
1961–Baltimore	Amer.	OF	113	323	39	94	11	6	5	35	.291	143	2	0	1.000
1962–Baltimore x.......	Amer.	OF	99	263	34	70	13	1	7	35	.266	132	4	3	.978
1963–Detroit.............	Amer.	1B-OF	52	53	5	8	2	1	0	7	.151	44	1	1	.978
Major League Totals.......................			634	1614	213	414	60	20	25	172	.257	1016	31	22	.979

†Traded to Washington Senators with Pitcher Bob Wiesler, Catcher Lou Berberet, Second Baseman Herb Plews and Outfielder Dick Tettelbach for pitcher Maury McDermott and Shortstop Bob Kline (assigned to the Yankees' American Association farm club–Denver). Other players in deal assigned February 8, 1956; Herzog, April 2, 1956.

‡Sold to Kansas City Athletics, May 14, 1958.

§Traded to Baltimore Orioles with Outfielder Russ Snyder and a player to be named at later date, for Pitcher Jim Archer, Catcher Clint Courtney, First Baseman Bob Boyd, Infielder Wayne Causey and Outfielder Al Pilarcik, January 24, 1961; Courtney returned to the Orioles, April 15, 1961, to complete deal.

xTraded to Detroit Tigers with Catcher Gus Triandos for Catcher Dick Brown, November 26, 1962.

RECORD AS MANAGER

Year Club	League	Position	W.	L.
1973–Texas†...............	Amer.	Sixth(W)	47	91
1974–California‡.........	Amer.	Sixth(W)	2	2
1975–Kansas City§......	Amer.	Second(W)	41	25
1976–Kansas City	Amer.	First(W)	90	72
1977–Kansas City	Amer.	First(W)	102	60
1978–Kansas City	Amer.	First(W)	92	70
1979–Kansas City	Amer.	Second(W)	85	77
1980–St. Louis xy........	Nat.	Fifth(E)	38	35
National League Totals			38	35
American League Totals			459	397
Major League Totals...........................			497	432

†Replaced by interim manager Del Wilber, September 7.

‡Served as interim manager, June 27 through June 30 after Dick Williams replaced Bobby Winkles, June 26.

§Replaced Jack McKeon, July 24.

xReplaced Ken Boyer (and interim manager Jack Krol) with club in sixth place (record of 18-33), June 9, 1980.

yNamed General Manager, August 28, 1980, with Red Schoendienst serving as manager remainder of season.

Scout, Kansas City Athletics, 1964.

Coach, Kansas City Athletics, 1965; New York Mets, 1966; California Angels, 1974 and part of 1975.

Director of Player Development, New York Mets, 1967 through 1972.

Coach, American League All-Star Team, 1973, 1974 and 1978.

CHAMPIONSHIP SERIES RECORD

Year Club	League	W.	L.
1976–Kansas City	American	2	3
1977–Kansas City	American	2	3
1978–Kansas City	American	1	3

RALPH GEORGE HOUK
Boston Red Sox

Born August 9, 1919, at Lawrence, Kan.
Height, 5.11. Weight, 198.
Threw and batted righthanded.
Hobbies—Hunting and fishing.

Year Club	League	Pos.	G.	AB.	R.	H.	2B.	3B.	HR.	RBI.	B.A.	PO.	A.	E.	F.A.
1939—Neosho	Ak.Mo.	C	119	427	69	122	15	6	1	56	.286	634	*79	13	*.982
1940—Joplin	W.A.	C	110	364	53	114	18	7	0	63	.313	517	78	10	*.983
1941—Binghamton	East.	C	5	9	3	3	0	0	0	0	.333	9	1	1	.909
1941—Augusta	Sally	C	97	340	37	92	11	5	1	48	.271	542	62	12	.981
1942-45—Bing'ton	East.					(In Military Service)									
1946—Kansas City	A.A.	C	8	23	5	8	2	0	1	1	.348	28	5	0	1.000
1946—Beaumont	Tex.	C-OF	87	279	38	82	20	2	0	40	.294	297	45	9	.974
1947—New York	Amer.	C	41	92	7	25	3	1	0	12	.272	138	13	2	.987
1948—Kansas City	A.A.	*C-3B	103	364	54	110	24	5	1	49	.302	464	*72	7	.987
1948—New York	Amer.	C	14	29	3	8	2	0	0	3	.276	41	5	0	1.000
1949—New York	Amer.	C	5	7	0	4	0	0	0	1	.571	8	0	1	.889
1949—Kansas City	A.A.	C	95	313	47	86	18	1	0	36	.275	398	48	7	.985
1950—New York	Amer.	C	10	9	0	1	1	0	0	1	.111	12	1	1	.929
1951—New York	Amer.	C	3	5	0	1	0	0	0	2	.200	2	1	0	1.000
1952—New York	Amer.	C	9	6	0	2	0	0	0	0	.333	10	1	1	.917
1953—New York	Amer.	C	8	9	2	2	0	0	0	1	.222	10	0	0	1.000
1954—New York	Amer.	PH	1	1	0	0	0	0	0	0	.000	0	0	0	.000
1955—Denver	A.A.	C	15	26	1	4	3	0	0	4	.154	33	1	3	.919
1956—Denver	A.A.	C	1	4	0	0	0	0	0	0	.000	7	1	0	1.000
Major League Totals			91	158	12	43	6	1	0	20	.272	221	21	5	.980

WORLD SERIES RECORD

Year Club	League	Pos.	G.	AB.	R.	H.	2B.	3B.	HR.	RBI.	B.A.	PO.	A.	E.	F.A.
1947—New York	Amer.	PH	1	1	0	1	0	0	0	0	1.000	0	0	0	.000
1952—New York	Amer.	PH	1	1	0	0	0	0	0	0	.000	0	0	0	.000
World Series Totals			2	2	0	1	0	0	0	0	.500	0	0	0	.000

RECORD AS MANAGER

Named Major League Manager of the Year by THE SPORTING NEWS, 1961.

Year Club	League	Position	W.	L.	Year Club	League	Position	W.	L.
1955—Denver	A.A.	†Third	83	71	1970—New York	Amer.	Second(E)	93	69
1956—Denver	A.A.	Second	87	67	1971—New York	Amer.	Fourth(E)	82	80
1957—Denver	A.A.	‡Second	90	64	1972—New York	Amer.	Fourth(E)	79	76
1961—New York	Amer.	First	109	53	1973—New York	Amer.	Fourth(E)	80	82
1962—New York	Amer.	First	96	66	1974—Detroit	Amer.	Sixth(E)	72	90
1963—New York	Amer.	First	104	57	1975—Detroit	Amer.	Sixth(E)	57	102
1966—New York§	Amer.	Tenth	66	73	1976—Detroit	Amer.	Fifth(E)	74	87
1967—New York	Amer.	Ninth	72	90	1977—Detroit	Amer.	Fourth(E)	74	88
1968—New York	Amer.	Fifth	83	79	1978—Detroit	Amer.	Fifth(E)	86	76
1969—New York	Amer.	Fifth(E)	80	81	Major League Totals			1307	1249

†Tied for position.
‡Won playoffs by defeating Minneapolis, four games to none and St. Paul, four games to two; won Junior World Series against Buffalo (International League), four games to one.
§Replaced Johnny Keane, May 7.
Coach, New York Yankees, part of 1953 and 1954 seasons and 1958 through 1960; vice-president-general manager, New York Yankees, 1964 through May 6, 1966.
Manager, American League All-Star Team, 1962 and 1963.
Coach, American League All-Star Team, 1970.

WORLD SERIES RECORD

Year Club	League	W.	L.
1961—New York	American	4	1
1962—New York	American	4	3
1963—New York	American	0	4

FRANK OLIVER HOWARD
San Diego Padres

Born August 8, 1936, at Columbus, O.
Height, 6.07. Weight, 250.
Threw and batted righthanded.
Attended Ohio State University, Columbus, O.

Established following major league records: Most home runs, one week (10), May 12 through May 18, 1968; most home runs, five consecutive games, (8), May 12 through May 17, 1968 and May 14 through 18, 1968; most home runs, six consecutive games (10), May 12 through May 18, 1968.

Tied major league records for most strikeouts, game (5), September 19, 1970, first game; most strikeouts, two consecutive games and most strikeouts doubleheader (7), July 9, 1965; most unassisted putouts, first baseman, inning (3), September 9, 1972 (first inning); most intentional bases on balls, season, by righthanded batter, since 1955 (29), 1970.

Tied American League record for most home runs, four consecutive games (7), May 12 through May 16, 1968; most consecutive games, hitting home run in each game (6), 1968.

Led Three-I League in total bases with 311 and strikeouts with 129 in 1958.

Tied American League record for most consecutive games, hitting homer each game (6), 1968.

Led American League batters in strikeouts with 155 in 1967.

Led American League in total bases with 330 and slugging percentage with .552 in 1968; and led in total bases with 340 in 1969.

Led the American League in grounding into double plays, 29, in 1969.

Led American League batters in walks with 132 in 1970.

Named Minor League Player of the Year by THE SPORTING NEWS, 1959.

Named National League Rookie of the Year by the Baseball Writers' Association and THE SPORTING NEWS, 1960.

Named an outfielder on THE SPORTING NEWS American League All-Star Team, 1968-69-70.

Received reported $108,000 bonus to sign with Los Angeles Dodgers, 1958.

Year Club	League	Pos.	G.	AB.	R.	H.	2B.	3B.	HR.	RBI.	B.A.	PO.	A.	E.	F.A.
1958—Green Bay.........I.I.I.		OF-P	●129	487	104	162	34	2	∗37	∗119	.333	186	6	8	.960
1958—Los Angeles.......Nat.		OF	8	29	3	7	1	0	1	2	.241	12	1	0	1.000
1959—Victoria ....Tex.		OF-3B	63	261	59	93	13	0	27	79	.356	99	16	5	.958
1959—Spokane ............P.C.		OF-1B	76	295	43	94	19	2	16	47	.319	243	16	6	.977
1959—Los Angeles ....Nat.		OF	9	21	2	3	0	1	1	6	.143	10	0	0	1.000
1960—Spokane ............P.C.		1B	26	97	17	36	11	0	4	24	.371	233	19	8	.969
1960—Los Angeles.......Nat.		OF-1B	117	448	54	120	15	2	23	77	.268	196	11	4	.981
1961—Los Angeles.......Nat.		OF-1B	92	267	36	79	10	2	15	45	.296	122	10	8	.943
1962—Los Angeles.......Nat.		OF	141	493	80	146	25	6	31	119	.296	187	19	6	.972
1963—Los Angeles.......Nat.		OF	123	417	58	114	16	1	28	64	.273	190	4	8	.960
1964—Los Angeles†.......Nat.		OF	134	433	60	98	13	2	24	69	.226	183	2	4	.979
1965—Washington ....Amer.		OF	149	516	53	149	22	6	21	84	.289	204	5	4	.981
1966—Washington ....Amer.		OF	146	493	52	137	19	4	18	71	.278	216	5	4	.982
1967—Washington ....Amer.		OF-1B	149	519	71	133	20	2	36	89	.256	225	6	3	.987
1968—Washington ....Amer.		OF-1B	158	598	79	164	28	3	∗44	106	.274	576	52	19	.971
1969—Washington ....Amer.		OF-1B	161	592	111	175	17	2	48	111	.296	602	34	14	.978
1970—Washington ....Amer.		OF-1B	161	566	90	160	15	1	∗44	∗126	.283	601	31	11	.983
1971—Washington ....Amer.		OF-1B	153	549	60	153	25	2	26	83	.279	.555	65	5	.992
1972—Tex.‡-Det. ....Amer.		1B-OF	109	320	29	78	10	0	10	38	.244	521	32	13	.977
1973—Detroit§ ....Amer.		1B	85	227	26	58	9	1	12	29	.256	12	0	1	.923
1974—Taiheiyo x ....Pacific		OF	1	2	0	0	0	0	0	0	.000	0	0	0	.000
American League Totals..................			1271	4380	571	1207	165	21	259	737	.276	3512	230	74	.981
National League Totals....................			624	2108	293	567	80	14	123	382	.269	900	47	30	.969
Major League Totals			1895	6488	864	1774	245	35	382	1119	.273	4412	277	104	.978

†Traded to Washington Senators with Pitchers Phil Ortega and Pete Richert and Infielder Ken McMullen for Pitcher Claude Osteen, Infielder John Kennedy and cash estimated at $100,000, December 4, 1964; deal was completed with transfer of First Baseman Dick Nen to Senators, December 15, 1964.

‡Sold to Detroit Tigers, August 31, 1972.

§Unconditionally released, October 25, 1973; played professional baseball in Japan for Taiheiyo Club Lions in 1974.

xOn disabled list, knee injury.

WORLD SERIES RECORD

Year Club	League	Pos.	G.	AB.	R.	H.	2B.	3B.	HR.	RBI.	B.A.	PO.	A.	E.	F.A.
1963—Los Angeles.......Nat.		OF	3	10	2	3	1	0	1	1	.300	4	0	0	1.000

ALL-STAR GAME RECORD

Year League	Pos.	AB.	R.	H.	2B.	3B.	HR.	RBI.	B.A.	PO.	A.	E.	F.A.
1968—American............................	OF	2	0	0	0	0	0	0	.000	0	0	0	.000
1969—American............................	OF	1	1	1	0	0	1	1	1.000	0	0	1	.000
1970—American............................	OF	2	0	0	0	0	0	0	.000	0	0	0	.000
1971—American............................	PH	1	0	0	0	0	0	0	.000	0	0	0	.000
All-Star Game Totals		6	1	1	0	0	1	1	.167	0	0	1	.000

PITCHING RECORD

Year Club	League	G.	IP.	W.	L.	Pct.	H.	R.	ER.	SO.	BB.	ERA.
1958—Green Bay ...........................I.I.I.		1	1	0	0	.000	0	0	0	1	0	0.00

RECORD AS MANAGER

Year Club	League	Position	W.	L.
1976—Spokane...............P.C.		Fourth (W)	65	78

Minor League Instructor, Milwaukee Brewers, 1975; coach, Milwaukee Brewers, 1977 through 1980.

ANTHONY LaRUSSA JR.
(Tony)
Chicago White Sox

Born October 4, 1944, at Tampa, Fla.
Height, 6.00½. Weight, 185.
Threw and batted righthanded.
Attended University of Tampa, Tampa, Fla., and University of Southern Florida, Tampa, Fla.; received degree in Industrial Management.

Year Club League	Pos.	G.	AB.	R.	H.	2B.	3B.	HR.	RBI.	B.A.	PO.	A.	E.	F.A.
1962–Daytona Beach..Fla. St.	SS	64	225	37	58	7	0	1	32	.258	135	173	38	.890
1962–Binghamton ......East.	SS-2B	12	43	3	8	0	0	0	4	.186	20	27	8	.855
1963–Kansas City ......Amer.	SS-2	34	44	4	11	1	1	0	1	.250	29	25	2	.964
1964–Lewiston† ....N'west	2-SS	90	329	50	77	22	1	1	25	.234	188	218	18	.958
1965–Birmingham‡ ....South.	2B	75	259	24	50	11	2	1	18	.193	202	161	21	.945
1966–Modesto ....Calif.	2B	81	316	67	92	20	1	7	54	.291	201	212	20	.954
1966–Mobile ....South.	2B	51	170	20	50	9	4	4	26	.294	117	133	10	.962
1967–Birmingham§ ....South.	2B	41	139	12	32	6	1	5	22	.230	88	120	5	.977
1968–Oakland ....Amer.	PH	5	3	0	1	0	0	0	0	.333	0	0	0	.000
1968–Vancouver ....P. C.	2B	122	455	55	109	16	8	5	29	.240	249	321	14	∗.976
1969–Iowa ....A. A.	2B	67	235	37	72	11	1	4	27	.306	177	222	15	.964
1969–Oakland ....Amer.	PH	8	8	0	0	0	0	0	0	.000	0	0	0	.000
1970–Iowa ....A. A.	2B	22	88	13	22	5	0	2	5	.250	52	59	3	.974
1970–Oakland ....Amer.	2B	52	106	6	21	4	1	0	6	.198	67	89	5	.969
1971–Iowa ....A. A.	2-3-S-O	28	107	21	31	5	1	2	11	.290	70	85	2	.987
1971–Oakland x ....Amer.	2-S-3	23	8	3	0	0	0	0	0	.000	8	7	2	.882
1971–Atlanta ....Nat.	2B	9	7	1	2	0	0	0	0	.286	8	6	1	.933
1972–Richmond y ......Int.	2B	122	389	68	120	13	2	10	42	.308	305	289	20	.967
1973–Wichita ....A. A.	2-1-3	106	392	82	123	16	0	5	75	.314	423	213	26	.961
1973–Chicago z ....Nat.	PR	1	0	1	0	0	0	0	0	.000	0	0	0	.000
1974–Charleston a .....Int.	2B	139	457	50	119	17	1	8	35	.260	262	∗378	17	.974
1975–Denver ....A. A.	3-O-S-2	118	354	87	99	23	2	7	46	.280	95	91	10	.949
1976–Iowa bc............A. A.	INF-O-P	107	332	53	86	11	0	4	34	.259	132	160	22	.930
1977–New Orleans de.A. A.	2B-3B	50	128	17	24	2	2	3	6	.188	66	87	7	.956
American League Totals		122	169	13	33	5	2	0	7	.195	104	121	9	.962
National League Totals		10	7	2	2	0	0	0	0	.286	8	6	1	.933
Major League Totals		132	176	15	35	5	2	0	7	.199	112	127	10	.960

†On disabled list, May 9 to September 8, 1964.
‡On disabled list, June 3 to July 15, 1965.
§On disabled list, April 12 to May 6, and July 3 to September 5, 1967.
xSold to Atlanta Braves, August 14, 1971.
yTraded to Chicago Cubs (in trade which sent Pitcher Tom Phoebus from Chicago Cubs to Atlanta Braves), October 20, 1972.
zSold to Pittsburgh Pirates' organization.
aReleased, April 4, 1975; signed by Chicago White Sox' organization, April 7, 1975.
bOn disabled list, August 8 to August 18, 1976.
cSold to St. Louis Cardinals' organization, December 13, 1976.
dNamed coach, June 20, 1977.
eReleased, September 29, 1977.

PITCHING RECORD

Year Club	League	G.	IP.	W.	L.	Pct.	H.	R.	ER.	SO.	BB.	ERA.
1976–Iowa ....Am. Assoc.		3	3	0	0	.000	3	1	1	0	0	3.00

RECORD AS MANAGER

Year Club	League	Position	W.	L.
1978–Knoxville .... South.		First(W)	49	21
(Second Half)†		Third(W)	4	4
1979–Iowa‡ .... A. A.		Second(E)	54	52
1979–Chicago§ .... Amer.		Fifth(W)	27	27
1980–Chicago .... Amer.		Fifth(W)	70	90
Major League Totals...........................			97	117

†Replaced by Joe Jones, July 3, 1978.
‡Replaced by Joe Sparks, August 3, 1979.
§Replaced Don Kessinger, August 3, 1979, with record of 46-60 and team in fifth place.
Coach, Chicago White Sox, July 3 through remainder of 1978 season.

THOMAS CHARLES LASORDA
Name pronounced Luh-SORR-duh.
(Tom)
Los Angeles Dodgers
Born September 22, 1927, at Norristown, Pa.
Height, 5.09. Weight, 175.
Threw and batted lefthanded.
Hobby–Making home movies.

Tied National League record by making three wild pitches in an inning, first inning, May 5, 1955.
Struck out 25 batters while pitching a 15-inning, 6-5 victory over Amsterdam, May 31, 1948.
Led International League in complete games with 16 and tied for lead in shutouts with 5 in 1958.
Led Canadian-American League in wild pitches with 20 in 1948 and led International League with 14 in 1953.
Named International League Most Valuable Pitcher in 1958.
Named by THE SPORTING NEWS as Minor League Manager of the Year, 1970.

Year Club	League	G.	IP.	W.	L.	Pct.	H.	R.	ER.	SO.	BB.	ERA.
1945–Concord..............................N. C. St.		27	121	3	12	.200	115	84	55	91	100	4.09
1946-47–† ....E. Shore						(In Military Service)						

Year	Club	League	G.	IP.	W.	L.	Pct.	H.	R.	ER.	SO.	BB.	ERA.
1948—Schenectady‡§	Can.-Am.		32	192	9	12	.429	180	122	99	195	153	4.64
1949—Greenville	Sally		45	178	7	7	.500	141	81	58	151	138	2.93
1950—Montreal	Int.		31	146	9	4	.692	136	73	60	85	82	3.70
1951—Montreal	Int.		31	165	12	8	.600	145	75	64	80	87	3.49
1952—Montreal	Int.		33	182	14	5	.737	156	90	74	77	93	3.66
1953—Montreal	Int.		36	208	17	8	.680	171	77	65	122	94	2.81
1954—Montreal	Int.		23	154	14	5	.737	142	66	60	75	79	3.51
1954—Brooklyn	Nat.		4	9	0	0	.000	8	5	5	5	5	5.00
1955—Brooklyn	Nat.		4	4	0	0	.000	5	6	6	4	6	13.50
1955—Montreal x	Int.		22	143	9	8	.529	125	58	52	92	62	3.27
1956—Kansas City y	Amer.		18	45	0	4	.000	40	38	31	28	45	6.20
1956—Denver	A.A.		16	83	3	4	.429	94	54	46	54	34	4.99
1957—Denver z	A.A.		6	...	0	2	.000						
1957—Los Angeles	P.C.		29	132	7	10	.412	134	73	57	72	59	3.90
1958—Montreal	Int.		34	*230	*18	6	.750	191	77	64	126	76	2.50
1959—Montreal	Int.		29	188	12	8	.600	192	93	80	64	77	3.83
1960—Montreal a	Int.		12	45	2	5	.286	79	48	41	17	24	8.20
American League Totals			18	45	0	4	.000	40	38	31	28	45	6.20
National League Totals			8	13	0	0	.000	13	11	11	9	11	7.62
Major League Totals			26	58	0	4	.000	53	49	42	37	56	6.52

†On National Defense list, May 14, 1946 through February 2, 1948.
‡On disabled list, July 9 through July 19.
§Drafted by Nashua (Brooklyn Dodgers' organization) from Philadelphia Phillies' organization, November 24, 1948.
xSold by Brooklyn Dodgers' organization to Kansas City Athletics for an estimated $35,000, March 2, 1956.
yTraded to New York Yankees for Pitcher Wally Burnette and cash, July 11, 1956.
zSold by New York Yankees' organization to Brooklyn Dodgers' organization, May 26, 1957.
aReleased by Montreal, July 9, 1960.

RECORD AS MANAGER

Year	Club	League	Position	W.	L.
1966—Ogden	Pioneer		First	39	27
1967—Ogden	Pioneer		First	41	25
1968—Ogden	Pioneer		First	39	25
1969—Spokane	P.C.		Second(N)	71	73
1970—Spokane	P.C.		†First(N)	94	52
1971—Spokane	P.C.		Third(N)	69	76
1972—Albuquerque	P.C.		‡First(E)	92	56
1976—Los Angeles§	Nat.		Second(W)	2	2
1977—Los Angeles	Nat.		First(W)	98	64
1978—Los Angeles	Nat.		First(W)	95	67
1979—Los Angeles	Nat.		Third(W)	79	83
1980—Los Angeles	Nat.		Second(W)	92	71
Major League Totals				366	287

†Won championship playoff against Hawaii, four games to none.
‡Won championship playoff against Eugene, three games to one.
§Replaced retiring Walter Alston, September 30, 1976.
Scout, Los Angeles Dodgers, 1961 through 1965; manager Los Angeles farm team in Arizona Instructional League, 1969; coach, Los Angeles Dodgers, 1973 through 1976.
Manager, National League All-Star Team, 1978 and 1979.
Coach, National League All-Star Team, 1977.

CHAMPIONSHIP SERIES RECORD					
Year	Club	League		W.	L.
1977—Los Angeles	National			3	1
1978—Los Angeles	National			3	1

WORLD SERIES RECORD					
Year	Club	League		W.	L.
1977—Los Angeles	National			2	4
1978—Los Angeles	National			2	4

ALFRED MANUEL MARTIN
(Billy)
Oakland A's

Born May 16, 1928, at Berkeley, Calif.
Height, 5.11. Weight, 170.
Threw and batted righthanded.
Hobbies—Hunting and golf.

Established major league record for most hits, inning, first game in major leagues (2), April 18, 1950 (eighth inning).
Tied major league record for fewest sacrifice hits for leader in sacrifice hits, season (13), 1958.
Tied American League record for most chances accepted by second baseman, doubleheader (24), September 24, 1952.
Led American League second basemen in double plays with 121 in 1953.
Led American League in sacrifice hits with 13 in 1958.

Year	Club	League	Pos.	G.	AB.	R.	H.	2B.	3B.	HR.	RBI.	B.A.	PO.	A.	E.	F.A.
1946—Idaho Falls	Pion.		3B-2B	32	114	13	29	7	0	0	12	.254	33	55	16	.846
1947—Phoenix	Ar.-Tex.		3B	130	*586	141	*230	*48	12	9	*174	*.392	*207	*317	*55	.905
1947—Oakland	P.C.		3B-2B	15	53	3	12	3	0	0	5	.226	23	24	5	.904
1948—Oakland	P.C.		INF	132	401	60	111	28	2	3	42	.277	301	288	21	.966
1949—Oakland	P.C.		*2B-SS	172	623	90	178	27	3	12	92	.286	*454	475	*37	.962
1950—Kansas City	A.A.		2B	29	118	15	33	6	2	4	10	.280	68	80	8	.949
1950—New York	Amer.		2B-3B	34	36	10	9	1	0	1	8	.250	24	16	1	.976
1951—New York	Amer.		2-S-3-OF	51	58	10	15	1	2	0	2	.259	45	62	4	.964
1952—New York	Amer.		2B	109	363	32	97	13	3	3	33	.267	244	323	9	.984
1953—New York	Amer.		2B-SS	149	587	72	151	24	6	15	75	.257	389	409	14	.983

Year	Club	League	Pos.	G.	AB.	R.	H.	2B.	3B.	HR.	RBI.	B.A.	PO.	A.	E.	F.A.
1954—New York	..........Amer.						(In Military Service)									
1955—New York†	........Amer.		2B-SS	20	70	8	21	2	0	1	9	.300	46	50	3	.970
1956—New York	........Amer.		2B-3B	121	458	76	121	24	5	9	49	.264	253	288	15	.973
1957—N.Y.‡-K.C.§	......Amer.		2B-3B-SS	116	410	45	103	14	5	10	39	.251	220	232	13	.972
1958—Detroit x	..........Amer.		SS-3B	131	498	56	127	19	1	7	42	.255	206	288	20	.961
1959—Cleveland y	......Amer.		2B-3B	73	242	37	63	7	0	9	24	.260	150	153	2	.993
1960—Cincinnati z	......Nat.		2B	103	317	34	78	17	1	3	16	.246	228	207	11	.975
1961—Milwaukee a	.....Nat.		PH	6	6	1	0	0	0	0	0	.000	0	0	0	.000
1961—Minnesota	........Amer.		2B-SS	108	374	44	92	15	5	6	36	.246	217	224	17	.963
American League Totals				912	3096	390	799	120	27	61	317	.258	1794	2028	98	.976
National League Totals				109	323	35	78	17	1	3	16	.241	228	207	11	.975
Major League Totals				1021	3419	425	877	137	28	64	333	.257	2022	2235	109	.976

†In Military Service most of season.

‡Traded to Kansas City Athletics with Pitcher Ralph Terry and Outfielders Woodie Held and Bob Martyn for Pitcher Ryne Duren and Outfielders Jim Pisoni and Harry Simpson, June 15, 1957. Duren and Pisoni were assigned to their Denver (American Association) farm club.

§Traded to Detroit Tigers with Pitchers Maury McDermott and Tom Morgan, Catcher Tim Thompson and Outfielders Lou Skizas and Gus Zernial for Pitchers Duke Maas and John Tsitouris, Catcher Frank House, First Basemen Kent Hadley and Jim McManus and Outfielders Jim Small and Bill Tuttle. All players but Hadley and McManus transferred November 20, 1957; Hadley added January 8, 1958, and McManus, April 2.

xTraded to Cleveland Indians with Pitcher Al Cicotte for Pitchers Don Mossi and Ray Narleski and Infielder Ossie Alvarez, November 30, 1958.

yTraded to Cincinnati Reds with Pitcher Cal McLish and First Baseman Gordon Coleman for Second Baseman Johnny Temple, December 15, 1959.

zSold to Milwaukee Braves, December 3, 1960.

aTraded to Minnesota Twins for Infielder Billy Consolo (latter assigned to Vancouver) and cash, June 1, 1961.

WORLD SERIES RECORD

Established World Series record for most hits, six-game Series (12), 1953.

Tied World Series records for highest batting average six game Series (.500), 1953; one or more hits, each game, six-game Series, 1953; most three-base hits, six-game Series (2), 1953; one or more hits, each game, seven-game Series, 1956; most times caught stealing, game (2), September 28, 1955; most three-base hits batting in three runs, game (1), September 30, 1953.

Year	Club	League	Pos.	G.	AB.	R.	H.	2B.	3B.	HR.	RBI.	B.A.	PO.	A.	E.	F.A.
1951—New York	........Amer.		PR	1	0	1	0	0	0	0	0	.000	0	0	0	.000
1952—New York	........Amer.		2B	7	23	2	5	0	0	1	4	.217	16	16	1	.970
1953—New York	........Amer.		2B	6	24	5	12	1	2	2	8	.500	13	14	0	1.000
1955—New York	........Amer.		2B	7	25	2	8	1	1	0	4	.320	17	20	0	1.000
1956—New York	........Amer.		2B-3B	7	27	5	8	0	2	2	3	.296	14	20	0	1.000
World Series Totals				28	99	15	33	2	5	5	19	.333	60	70	1	.992

ALL-STAR GAME RECORD

Year	League	Pos.	AB.	R.	H.	2B.	3B.	HR.	RBI.	B.A.	PO.	A.	E.	F.A.
1956—American	....	PH	1	0	0	0	0	0	0	.000	0	0	0	.000

RECORD AS MANAGER

Tied major league record for most clubs as manager, season (2), Detroit and Texas, 1973 and Texas and New York, 1975.

Tied American League record for most clubs as manager, lifetime (5).

Year	Club	League	Position	W.	L.	Year	Club	League	Position	W.	L.
1969—Denver†	.............P.C.		Fourth(E)	65	50	1975—New York y	........Amer.		Third(E)	30	26
1969—Minnesota	..........Amer.		First(W)	97	65	1976—New York	..........Amer.		First(E)	97	62
1971—Detroit	..............Amer.		Second(E)	91	71	1977—New York	..........Amer.		First(E)	100	62
1972—Detroit	..............Amer.		First(E)	86	70	1978—New York z	........Amer.		Third(E)	52	53
1973—Detroit‡	.............Amer.		Third(E)	71	65	1979—New York a	........Amer.		Fourth(E)	55	40
1973—Texas§	................Amer.		Sixth(W)	9	14	1980—Oakland	.............Amer.		Second(W)	83	79
1974—Texas	................Amer.		Second(W)	84	76						
1975—Texas x	...............Amer.		Fourth(W)	44	51	Major League Totals	....			899	724

†Replaced John Goryl with club in sixth place, May 27.

‡Replaced by interim manager Joe Schultz, September 1.

§Replaced interim manager Del Wilber, September 8.

xReplaced by Frank Lucchesi, July 20.

yReplaced Bill Virdon with club in third place (record of 53-51), August 1, 1975.

zReplaced by Bob Lemon, July 25, 1978.

aReplaced Bob Lemon with club in fourth place (record of 34-31), June 19, 1979.

Scout, Minnesota Twins, 1962 through 1964; coach, Minnesota Twins, 1965 through May 26, 1968.

CHAMPIONSHIP SERIES RECORD

Year	Club	League	W.	L.
1969—Minnesota	..........Amer.		0	3
1972—Detroit	...............Amer.		2	3
1976—New York	..........Amer.		3	2
1977—New York	..........Amer.		3	2

WORLD SERIES RECORD

Year	Club	League	W.	L.
1976—New York	..........Amer.		0	4
1977—New York	..........Amer.		4	2

ROBERT JAMES MATTICK
(Bobby)
Toronto Blue Jays

Born December 5, 1916, at Sioux City, Ia.
Height, 5.10. Weight, 170.
Threw and batted righthanded.
Son of Walter J. Mattick, outfielder with Chicago White Sox, 1912-13.

Year—Club	League	Pos.	G.	AB.	R.	H.	2B.	3B.	HR.	RBI.	B.A.	PO.	A.	E.	F.A.
1934—Los Angeles	P. C.	SS	53	137	10	38	5	1	0	10	.277	43	108	13	.921
1935—Los Angeles	P. C.	SS	50	131	15	35	6	0	0	18	.267	44	87	9	.936
1936—Los Angeles	P. C.	SS	73	241	30	67	11	3	1	30	.278	110	207	26	.924
1937—Los Angeles	P. C.	SS	167	612	61	171	39	7	2	66	.279	264	513	39	.952
1938—Chicago	Nat.	SS	1	1	0	1	0	0	0	1	1.000	0	0	1	.000
1938—Indianapolis	A. A.	SS	29	67	6	8	3	0	0	6	.119	25	49	6	.925
1938—Syracuse	Int.	SS	5	16	1	1	1	0	0	0	.063	9	9	2	.900
1939—Milwaukee	A. A.	SS	68	273	47	78	13	3	5	16	.286	127	189	21	.938
1939—Chicago	Nat.	SS	51	178	16	51	12	1	0	23	.287	102	179	22	.927
1940—Chicago†	Nat.	SS	128	441	30	96	15	0	0	33	.218	233	431	38	.946
1941—Cincinnati	Nat.	INF	20	60	8	11	3	0	0	7	.183	28	42	1	.986
1942—Cincinnati	Nat.	SS	6	10	0	2	1	0	0	0	.200	7	6	0	1.000
Major League Totals			206	690	54	161	31	1	0	64	.233	370	658	62	.943

†Traded with Outfielder Jimmy Gleeson and cash to Cincinnati Reds for Shortstop Billy Myers, December 4, 1940.

RECORD AS MANAGER

Year—Club	League	Position	W.	L.
1948—Ogden†	Pion.	‡Fourth	32	25
1980—Toronto	Amer.	Seventh(E)	67	95
Major League Totals			67	95

†Replaced Pip Koehler, July 18, 1948, with record of 29-40 and team in sixth place.
‡Lost playoff to Twin Falls, three games to none.
Coach, Birmingham (Southern Association), 1944 and 1945; scout, New York Yankees, 1945 through 1947; scout, Cincinnati Reds, part of 1948 through 1951 and 1953 through 1960; scout, Chicago White Sox, 1952; scout, Houston Colt .45s, August 1, 1961 through 1963; scout, Cleveland Indians, 1964 through 1966; scout, Baltimore Orioles, 1967; scout, Seattle Pilots, 1968 through 1970; scout, Montreal Expos, 1972 through 1975; scout, Toronto Blue Jays, 1976 through 1979 (Director of Player Development, 1978 and 1979).

JOHN FRANCIS McNAMARA
Cincinnati Reds

Born June 4, 1932, at Sacramento, Calif.
Height, 5.10. Weight, 175.
Threw and batted righthanded.
Attended Sacramento State College, Sacramento, Calif.

Led Northwest League catchers in double plays with 15 in 1958, 10 in 1959 and 14 in 1962.
Led Northwest League in sacrifice hits with 18 in 1959.

Year—Club	League	Pos.	G.	AB.	R.	H.	2B.	3B.	HR.	RBI.	B.A.	PO.	A.	E.	F.A.
1951—Fresno	Calif.	C	60	182	20	38	2	0	0	12	.209	284	46	11	.968
1952—Houston	Texas	....	6	13	0	1	0	0	0	0	.077	....	....	....	....
1952—Lynchburg	Pied.	C	102	303	25	54	8	0	0	19	.178	489	57	8	*.986
1953—Winston-Salem	Carol.				(In Military Service)										
1954—Omaha†	West.				(In Military Service)										
1955—Lewiston	N'west	C	129	427	49	102	24	4	1	54	.239	544	*93	●15	.977
1956—Sacramento	P. C.	C	76	181	22	31	5	1	1	18	.171	256	25	0	1.000
1956—Albuquerque	West.	C	29	83	11	23	2	2	1	9	.277	191	23	1	.995
1957—Tulsa	Texas	C	19	47	5	7	2	0	0	5	.149	92	9	2	.981
1957—Amarillo	West.	C	43	93	17	26	8	0	0	21	.280	177	13	3	.984
1958—Lewiston	N'west	C	133	439	62	117	20	2	2	63	.276	*892	*76	9	*.991
1959—Lewiston	N'west	C	141	491	74	122	25	4	1	44	.248	714	*84	8	.990
1960—Lewiston	N'west	C	120	387	62	98	19	2	0	42	.253	*726	48	7	*.991
1961—Lewiston	N'west	C	77	204	28	54	6	0	0	27	.265	368	37	4	.990
1962—Lewiston	N'west	C	93	281	41	77	11	2	1	33	.274	670	74	8	*.989
1963—Binghamton	East.	C	69	199	19	45	10	1	0	24	.226	483	34	2	.996
1964—Dallas	P. C.	C-3B	13	13	1	6	0	0	0	1	.194	58	7	0	1.000
1965—Birmingham	South.				(Did Not Play)										
1966—Mobile	South.	C	8	17	3	4	0	0	0	0	.235	44	1	0	1.000
1967—Birmingham	South.	C	2	6	1	0	0	0	0	1	.000	10	1	0	1.000

†Released by St. Louis Cardinals' organization, April 16, 1955.

PITCHING RECORD

Year—Club	League	G.	IP.	W.	L.	Pct.	H.	R.	ER.	SO.	BB.	ERA.
1960—Lewiston	Northwest	5	....	0	0	.000	....	....	....	....	....	....
1961—Lewiston	Northwest	4	....	0	0	.000	....	....	....	....	....	....
1962—Lewiston	Northwest	4	9	0	0	.000	13	6	6	3	2	6.00
1963—Binghamton	Eastern	1	1	0	0	.000	0	0	0	0	0	0.00

RECORD AS MANAGER

Year Club	League	Position	W.	L.	Year Club	League	Position	W.	L.
1959–Lewiston ....N'west		Second	36	34	1967–Birmingham ....South.		First	84	55
(Second Half)		Third	39	32	1969–Oakland‡ ....Amer.		Second(W)	8	5
1960–Lewiston ....N'west		Third	38	29	1970–Oakland...............Amer.		Second(W)	89	73
(Second Half)		Third	40	34	1974–San Diego ....Nat.		Sixth(W)	60	102
1961–Lewiston ....N'west		†First	41	25	1975–San Diego ....Nat.		Fourth(W)	71	91
(Second Half)		Second	43	31	1976–San Diego ....Nat.		Fifth(W)	73	89
1962–Lewiston ....N'west		Fifth	31	38	1977–San Diego§.........Nat.		Fifth(W)	20	28
(Second Half)		Fourth	35	37	1979–Cincinnati ....Nat.		First(W)	90	71
1963–Binghamton........East.		Fourth	65	75	1980–Cincinnati ....Nat.		Third(W)	89	73
1964–Dallas ....P. C.		Sixth(E)	53	104					
1965–Birmingham ....South.		Eighth	54	85	American League Totals			97	78
1966–Mobile................South.		First	88	52	National League Totals			403	454
					Major League Totals...........................			500	532

†Won playoff by defeating Yakima (Second Half winner), four games to one.
‡Replaced Hank Bauer, September 19, 1969.
§Replaced by Alvin Dark, May 30 (Bob Skinner served as interim manager, May 29).
Coach, Oakland Athletics, 1968 and 1969; San Francisco Giants, 1971 through 1973; California Angels, 1978.
Coach, National League All-Star Team, 1976 and 1980.

CHAMPIONSHIP SERIES RECORD

Year Club	League	W.	L.
1979–Cincinnati .... Nat.		0	3

EUGENE RICHARD MICHAEL
(Gene)
New York Yankees

Born June 2, 1938, at Kent, O.
Height, 6.02. Weight, 183.
Threw right and batted left and righthanded.
Hobbies—Basketball, golf, bowling and coin collecting.
Attended Kent State University, Kent, O.; received Bachelor of Science degree
in Education

Led Northern League shortstops in double plays with 87 in 1959 and 90 in 1960; led Sophomore League with 85 in 1961 and International League with 78 in 1965.
Led International League in sacrifice hits with 16 in 1965.

Year Club	League	Pos.	G.	AB.	R.	H.	2B.	3B.	HR.	RBI.	B.A.	PO.	A.	E.	F.A.
1959–Grand Forks ..... North.		SS	124	480	54	109	11	3	1	43	.227	★225	370	★56	.914
1960–Savannah .... Sally		3B-SS	3	10	1	1	0	0	0	0	.100	1	6	1	.875
1960–Grand Forks ..... North.		SS	121	428	47	88	15	2	2	41	.206	★232	360	★55	.915
1961–Hobbs .... Soph.		SS	121	★513	121	166	25	7	5	79	.324	★195	★391	51	.920
1962–Kinston............. Carol.		SS-3B	138	474	58	102	11	3	1	36	.215	169	253	38	.917
1963–Kinston............. Carol.		S-3-2-P	125	421	73	128	17	6	1	57	.304	202	238	26	.944
1964–Columbus .... Int.		SS-2B	131	407	43	90	13	3	3	19	.221	235	343	23	.962
1965–Columbus .... Int.		SS	138	443	53	96	14	0	1	30	.217	★254	362	26	.960
1966–Columbus .... Int.		SS	78	277	38	80	9	2	3	21	.289	126	244	14	.964
1966–Pittsburgh†....... Nat.		SS-2-3B	30	33	9	5	2	1	0	2	.152	10	20	3	.909
1967–Los Angeles‡..... Nat.		SS	98	223	20	45	3	1	0	7	.202	117	204	17	.950
1968–New York .... Amer.		SS-P	61	116	8	23	3	0	1	8	.198	68	103	11	.940
1969–New York .... Amer.		SS	119	412	41	112	24	4	2	31	.272	205	365	19	.968
1970–New York .... Amer.		★S-3-2	134	435	42	93	10	1	2	38	.214	259	390	★28	.959
1971–New York .... Amer.		SS	139	456	36	102	15	0	3	35	.224	243	474	20	.973
1972–New York .... Amer.		SS	126	391	29	91	7	4	1	32	.233	218	437	21	.969
1973–New York .... Amer.		SS	129	418	30	94	11	1	3	47	.225	208	433	23	.965
1974–New York§........ Amer.		2-S-3	81	177	19	46	9	0	0	13	.260	122	170	9	.970
1975–Detroit x........... Amer.		S-2-3	56	145	15	31	2	0	3	13	.214	63	125	10	.949
1976–Boston y............ Amer.								Did Not Play							
American League Totals			845	2550	220	592	81	10	15	217	.232	1386	2497	141	.965
National League Totals			128	256	29	50	5	2	0	9	.195	127	224	20	.946
Major League Totals.......................			973	2806	249	642	86	12	15	226	.229	1513	2721	161	.963

†Traded with Third Baseman Bob Bailey to Los Angeles Dodgers for Shortstop Maury Wills, December 1, 1966.
‡Sold to New York Yankees, November 30, 1967.
§Unconditionally released, January 21, 1975; signed as free agent by Detroit Tigers, January 28, 1975.
xReleased, October 22, 1975; signed as free agent by Boston Red Sox, February 15, 1976.
yReleased, May 8, 1976.

PITCHING RECORD

Year Club	League	G.	IP.	W.	L.	Pct.	H.	R.	ER.	SO.	BB.	ERA.
1962–Kinston................Carolina		1	2	0	0	.000	0	0	0	1	0	0.00
1963–Kinston................Carolina		16	53	1	3	.250	71	47	40	48	36	6.79
1964–Columbus ....Int'national		2	4	0	0	.000	5	4	4	2	1	9.00
1968–New York ....American		1	3	0	0	.000	5	5	0	3	0	0.00
Major League Totals...............................		1	3	0	0	.000	5	5	0	3	0	0.00

Year	Club	League	Position	W.	L.
1979—Columbus	....	Int.	†First	85	54

†Won playoff against Tidewater, three games to one; won championship playoff from Syracuse, four games to three.

Coach, New York Yankees, June 4, 1976 through Jun 13, 1977 and 1978; General Manager, New York Yankees, 1980.

FRANK ROBINSON
San Francisco Giants

Born August 31, 1935, at Beaumont, Tex.
Height, 6.01. Weight, 194.
Threw and batted righthanded.
Hobbies—Movies and music.
Attended Xavier University, Cincinnati, O.

Established major league record for most consecutive seasons leading league, intentional bases on balls (4), 1961 through 1964 (tied in 1962).

Established modern major league record for most times hit by pitch, rookie season (20), 1956.

Tied major league records for most home runs, bases filled, game (2), June 26, 1970; most home runs, bases filled, two successive at bats (2), June 26, 1970; most runs batted in, two successive innings (8), June 26, 1970 (fifth and sixth innings); fewest putouts, first baseman, game (0), July 1, 1971; most home runs, rookie season (38), 1956; most years leading league, intentional bases on balls, since 1955 (4).

Hit three home runs in a game, August 22, 1959.

Won American League Triple Crown, 1966.

Led National League in slugging percentage with .595 in 1960, .611 in 1961 and .624 in 1962; led league's first basemen in double plays with 111 in 1959.

Led American League in total bases with 367 and in slugging percentage with .637 in 1966.

Named National League Rookie of the Year by the Baseball Writers' Association and THE SPORTING NEWS, 1956.

Named outfielder on THE SPORTING NEWS National League All-Star fielding team, 1958.

Named Most Valuable National League Player, 1961.

Named Outstanding National League Player by THE SPORTING NEWS, 1961.

Named as outfielder on THE SPORTING NEWS National League All-Star Team, 1961-62.

Named as outfielder on THE SPORTING NEWS American League All-Star Team, 1966-67.

Named American League Player of the Year by THE SPORTING NEWS, 1966.

Named Major League Player of the Year by THE SPORTING NEWS, 1966.

Named Most Valuable American League Player, 1966.

Year	Club	League	Pos.	G.	AB.	R.	H.	2B.	3B.	HR.	RBI.	B.A.	PO.	A.	E.	F.A.
1953—Ogden	....	Pion.	O-3B-1B	72	270	70	94	20	6	17	83	.348	105	28	18	.881
1954—Tulsa	....	Tex.	2B-3B	8	30	4	8	0	0	0	1	.267	17	15	1	.970
1954—Columbia	....	Sally	OF-3-2B	132	491	*112	165	32	9	25	110	.336	258	63	18	.947
1955—Columbia	....	Sally	OF-1B	80	243	50	64	15	7	12	52	.263	203	3	4	.981
1956—Cincinnati	....	Nat.	OF	152	572	*122	166	27	6	38	83	.290	323	5	8	.976
1957—Cincinnati	....	Nat.	OF-1B	150	611	97	197	29	5	29	75	.322	487	36	6	.989
1958—Cincinnati	....	Nat.	OF-3B	148	554	90	149	25	6	31	83	.269	314	24	6	.983
1959—Cincinnati	....	Nat.	1B-OF	146	540	106	168	31	4	36	125	.311	1049	78	18	.984
1960—Cincinnati	....	Nat.	1-OF-3	139	464	86	138	33	6	31	83	.297	775	62	10	.988
1961—Cincinnati	....	Nat.	OF-3B	153	545	117	176	32	7	37	124	.323	284	15	3	.990
1962—Cincinnati	....	Nat.	OF	162	609	*134	208	*51	2	39	136	.342	315	10	2	.994
1963—Cincinnati	....	Nat.	OF-1B	140	482	79	125	19	3	21	91	.259	238	13	4	.984
1964—Cincinnati	....	Nat.	OF	156	568	103	174	38	6	29	96	.306	279	7	4	.986
1965—Cincinnati	....	Nat.	OF	156	582	109	172	33	5	33	113	.296	282	5	3	.990
1966—Baltimore	....	Amer.	OF-1B	155	576	*122	182	34	2	*49	*122	*.316	282	6	5	.983
1967—Baltimore	....	Amer.	OF-1B	129	479	83	149	23	7	30	94	.311	207	8	2	.991
1968—Baltimore	....	Amer.	OF-1B	130	421	69	113	27	1	15	52	.268	193	5	7	.966
1969—Baltimore	....	Amer.	OF-1B	148	539	111	166	19	5	32	100	.308	367	19	5	.987
1970—Baltimore‡	....	Amer.	OF-1B	132	471	88	144	24	1	25	78	.306	262	11	4	.986
1971—Baltimore‡	.......Amer.		OF-1B	133	455	82	128	16	2	28	99	.281	449	20	11	.977
1972—Los Angeles§	....Nat.		OF	103	342	41	86	6	1	19	59	.251	168	6	6	.967
1973—California	....	Amer.	OF	147	534	85	142	29	0	30	97	.266	38	3	1	.976
1974—Calif.x-Cleve.	....Amer.		1B-OF	144	477	81	117	27	3	22	68	.245	23	0	1	.958
1975—Cleveland yz	......Amer.		DH-PH	49	118	19	28	5	0	9	24	.237	0	0	0	.000
1976—Cleveland ya	......Amer.		1B-OF	36	67	5	15	0	0	3	10	.224	11	0	0	1.000
National League Totals	....			1605	5869	1084	1759	324	51	343	1068	.300	4514	261	70	.986
American League Totals	....			1203	4137	745	1184	204	21	243	744	.286	1832	72	36	.981
Major League Totals	....			2808	10006	1829	2943	528	72	586	1812	.294	6346	333	106	.984

†Traded to Baltimore Orioles for Outfielder Dick Simpson and Pitchers Milt Pappas and Jack Baldschun, December 9, 1965.

‡Traded with Pitcher Pete Richert to Los Angeles Dodgers for Pitchers Doyle Alexander and Bob O'Brien, Catcher Sergio Robles and First Baseman-Outfielder Royle Stillman, December 2, 1971.

§Traded with Infielders Billy Grabarkewitz and Bob Valentine and Pitchers Bill Singer and Mike Strahler to California Angels for Third Baseman Ken McMullen and Pitcher Andy Messersmith, November 28, 1972.

xReleased on waivers to Cleveland Indians, September 12, 1974; Indians assigned Outfielder Rusty Torres and Catcher Ken Suarez to Angels, December 4, 1974, to complete deal.

yPlayer-manager.

zOn supplemental disabled list, July 4 to July 23, 1975.

aOn supplemental disabled list, April 4 to April 14; on disabled list, April 14 to April 26, 1976.

Tied Championship Series records for hitting home in first Championship Series at bat, October 4, 1969; most at bats, inning (2), October 3, 1970 (fourth inning).

Year Club	League	Pos.	G.	AB.	R.	H.	2B.	3B.	HR.	RBI.	B.A.	PO.	A.	E.	F.A.
1969—Baltimore	Amer.	OF	3	12	1	4	2	0	1	2	.333	2	0	1	.667
1970—Baltimore	Amer.	OF	3	10	3	2	0	0	1	2	.200	2	0	0	1.000
1971—Baltimore	Amer.	OF	3	12	2	1	1	0	0	1	.083	7	0	0	1.000
Championship Series Totals			9	34	6	7	3	0	2	5	.206	11	0	1	.917

WORLD SERIES RECORD

Tied World Series record for most times hit by pitcher, game (2), October 8, 1961; most times hit by pitch, total Series (2); most times home run won 1-0 game (1), October 9, 1966; most putouts and chances accepted game by right fielder (7), October 14, 1969.

Year Club	League	Pos.	G.	AB.	R.	H.	2B.	3B.	HR.	RBI.	B.A.	PO.	A.	E.	F.A.
1961—Cincinnati	Nat.	OF	5	15	3	3	2	0	1	4	.200	5	0	0	1.000
1966—Baltimore	Amer.	OF	4	14	4	4	0	1	2	3	.286	6	0	0	1.000
1969—Baltimore	Amer.	OF	5	16	2	3	0	0	1	1	.188	13	0	0	1.000
1970—Baltimore	Amer.	OF	5	22	5	6	0	0	2	4	.273	7	0	0	1.000
1971—Baltimore	Amer.	OF	7	25	5	7	0	0	2	2	.280	12	0	0	1.000
World Series Totals			26	92	19	23	2	1	8	14	.250	43	0	0	1.000

ALL-STAR GAME RECORD

Year League	Pos.	AB.	R.	H.	2B.	3B.	HR.	RBI.	B.A.	PO.	A.	E.	F.A.
1956—National	OF	2	0	0	0	0	0	0	.000	1	0	0	1.000
1957—National	OF	2	0	1	0	0	0	0	.500	5	0	0	1.000
1959—National (second game)	1B	3	1	3	0	0	1	1	1.000	3	0	1	.750
1961—National (first game)	OF	1	0	1	0	0	0	0	1.000	2	0	0	1.000
1962—National (second game)	OF	3	0	0	0	0	0	0	.000	1	0	0	1.000
1965—National	PH	1	0	0	0	0	0	0	.000	0	0	0	.000
1966—American	OF	4	0	0	0	0	0	0	.000	2	0	0	1.000
1969—American	OF	2	0	0	0	0	0	0	.000	0	0	0	.000
1970—American	OF	3	0	0	0	0	0	0	.000	1	0	0	1.000
1971—American	OF	2	1	1	0	1	2	0	.500	2	0	0	1.000
1974—American	PH	1	0	0	0	0	0	0	.000	0	0	0	.000
All-Star Game Totals		24	2	6	0	0	2	3	.250	17	0	1	.944

Member of National League All-Star Team in 1959 (first game) and 1961 (second game); did not play. Named to American League Team for 1967 game; replaced due to injury.

RECORD AS MANAGER

Year Club	League	Position	W.	L.
1975—Cleveland	Amer.	Fourth(E)	79	80
1976—Cleveland	Amer.	Fourth(E)	81	78
1977—Cleveland†	Amer.	Sixth(E)	26	31
1978—Rochester‡	Int.	Sixth	58	64
Major League Totals			186	189

†Replaced by Jeff Torborg, June 19, 1977.
‡Replaced interim manager Al Widmar (replacing Ken Boyer), May 8, 1978.
Coach, California Angels, July 11 through remainder of 1977 season; Coach, Baltimore Orioles, beginning of 1978 season through May 8, 1979, 1980 and 1981.
Coach, American League All-Star Team, 1980.

ROBERT LEROY RODGERS
(Bob)
Milwaukee Brewers

Born August 16, 1938, at Delaware, O.
Height, 6.01½. Weight, 190.
Threw right and batted left and righthanded.
Hobby—Golf.
Attended Ohio Wesleyan University, Delaware, O., and Ohio Northern University, Ada, O.

Established American League record for most games, by catcher, rookie season (150), 1962.
Tied American League record for fewest assists by catcher, season, 150 or more games (73), 1962.
Led American League catchers in double plays with 14 in 1962 and 14 in 1964.

Year Club	League	Pos.	G.	AB.	R.	H.	2B.	3B.	HR.	RBI.	B.A.	PO.	A.	E.	F.A.
1956—Jamestown	Pony	OF	48	153	28	36	8	1	6	26	.235	43	6	3	.942
1957—Erie	NYP	*C-OF	114	430	79	127	26	4	12	80	.295	568	*77	*25	.963
1958—Lancaster	East.	C	19	63	8	16	3	0	3	8	.254	111	11	2	.984
1958—Idaho Falls	Pion.	*C-OF	99	378	73	115	15	6	12	74	.304	524	45	*20	.966
1959—Birmingham	South.	C	3	13	1	1	0	1	0	2	.077	28	0	1	.966
1959—Knoxville	Sally	*C-OF	105	355	53	102	18	6	7	55	.287	565	60	*13	.980
1960—Denver	A. A.	C	23	84	12	20	7	1	3	12	.238	127	15	4	.973
1960—Birmingham	South.	C	93	313	36	77	14	1	5	38	.246	456	*68	7	.987
1961—Dallas-Ft. W.†	A. A.	C	124	427	55	122	22	3	3	62	.286	*595	*70	11	.984
1961—Los Angeles	Amer.	C	16	56	8	18	2	0	2	13	.321	71	11	3	.965
1962—Los Angeles	Amer.	C	155	565	65	146	34	6	6	61	.258	826	73	●10	.989
1963—Los Angeles	Amer.	C	100	300	24	70	6	0	4	23	.233	416	48	*10	.979
1964—Los Angeles	Amer.	C	148	514	38	125	18	3	4	54	.243	884	*87	*13	.987

Year	Club	League	Pos.	G.	AB.	R.	H.	2B.	3B.	HR.	RBI.	B.A.	PO.	A.	E.	F.A.
1965—California		Amer.	C	132	411	33	86	14	3	1	32	.209	682	52	7	.991
1966—California		Amer.	C	133	454	45	107	20	3	7	48	.236	662	*69	6	.992
1967—California		Amer.	*C-OF	139	429	29	94	13	3	6	41	.219	728	*73	7	.991
1968—California		Amer.	C	91	258	13	49	6	0	1	14	.190	407	50	7	.985
1969—Hawaii		P. C.	C-3B	44	145	15	37	5	0	0	12	.255	215	26	4	.984
1969—California		Amer.	C	18	49	4	9	1	0	0	2	.196	74	9	0	1.000
1975—Salinas‡		Calif.	PH	4	3	1	1	0	0	0	0	.333	0	0	0	.000
1977—El Paso§		Texas	PH	1	0	0	0	0	0	0	0	.000	0	0	0	.000
Major League Totals				932	3033	259	704	114	18	31	288	.232	4750	472	63	.988

†Selected by Los Angeles Angels from Detroit Tigers in American League expansion draft, December 14, 1960.

‡Player-manager, August 24 through September 15, 1975.

§Player-manager, July 15 through August 14, 1977.

RECORD AS MANAGER

Year	Club	League	Position	W.	L.
1975—Salinas		Calif.	Fifth	35	35
(Second Half)			Sixth	32	38
1977—El Paso		Texas	First(W)	38	24
(Second Half)			†First(W)	40	28
1980—Milwaukee‡		Amer.	Third(E)	39	31

†Lost league championship to Arkansas, two games to none.

‡Began season as interim manager for ill George Bamberger who returned June 6, 1980, with club in second place (record of 26-21); named manager when Bamberger retired with club tied for fourth place (record of 73-66), September 7, 1980.

Coach, Minnesota Twins, 1970 through 1974; San Francisco Giants, 1976; Milwaukee Brewers, 1978 through 1980.

CHARLES WILLIAM TANNER JR.
(Chuck)
Pittsburgh Pirates

Born July 4, 1929, at New Castle, Pa.
Height, 6.00. Weight, 185.
Threw and batted lefthanded.
Father of Mark Tanner, former minor league pitcher in Chicago Cubs' and
Texas Rangers' organizations, 1972-76.

Tied major league record by hitting home run in first time at bat in major leagues, eighth inning, April 12, 1955. Hit ball on first pitch, the second player in major league history to accomplish this feat. He was at bat at the time as a pinch-hitter.

Year	Club	League	Pos.	G.	AB.	R.	H.	2B.	3B.	HR.	RBI.	B.A.	PO.	A.	E.	F.A.
1946—Evansville		I.I.I.	OF	2	1	0	0	0	0	0	0	.000	0	0	1	.000
1946—Owenboro		Kitty	OF	23	80	15	20	3	1	0	7	.250	50	3	4	.930
1947—Owensboro		Kitty	OF	25	104	32	35	9	3	0	20	.337	47	3	2	.962
1947—Eau Claire		North.	OF	40	151	29	49	6	3	7	27	.325	76	3	9	.898
1948—Eau Claire		North.	OF	67	263	60	95	22	5	7	52	.361	89	4	9	.912
1948—Pawtucket		N. Eng.	OF	46	171	26	47	1	6	2	20	.275	60	6	5	.930
1949—Denver		West.	OF	124	467	92	146	32	5	5	53	.313	206	13	12	.948
1950—Denver		West.	OF	154	619	111	*195	34	9	7	86	.315	248	16	14	.950
1951—Atlanta		South.	OF	134	506	84	161	28	6	4	44	.318	286	6	4	.986
1952—Milwaukee		A.A.	OF	11	27	2	4	1	1	0	4	.148	11	1	0	1.000
1952—Atlanta		South.	OF	117	440	64	152	18	11	2	65	.345	212	9	6	.974
1953—Toledo		A.A.	OF	17	52	5	10	3	0	2	5	.192	29	2	0	1.000
1953—Atlanta		South.	OF	126	465	71	148	29	11	6	57	.318	220	8	3	.987
1954—Atlanta		South.	OF	●155	594	109	192	35	12	20	101	.323	290	21	7	.978
1955—Milwaukee		Nat.	OF	97	243	27	60	9	3	6	27	.247	101	4	2	.981
1956—Milwaukee		Nat.	OF	60	63	6	15	2	0	1	4	.238	4	0	1	.800
1957—Mil.†-Chi.		Nat.	OF	117	387	47	108	19	2	9	48	.279	191	5	2	.990
1958—Chicago‡		Nat.	OF	73	103	10	27	6	0	4	17	.262	21	0	1	.955
1959—Minneapolis§		A.A.	OF	152	549	79	175	*41	10	12	78	.319	194	5	4	.980
1959—Cleveland		Amer.	OF	14	48	6	12	2	0	1	5	.250	18	0	0	1.000
1960—Cleveland		Amer.	OF	21	25	2	7	1	0	0	4	.280	5	0	0	1.000
1960—Toronto		Int.	OF	28	92	13	27	5	2	4	14	.293	40	1	0	1.000
1961—Toronto x		Int.	OF	70	218	19	49	5	3	6	22	.225	84	7	3	.968
1961—Dallas-Ft.Worth.		A.A.	OF	48	170	28	51	12	5	1	18	.300	74	5	5	.940
1961—Los Angeles		Amer.	OF	7	8	0	1	0	0	0	0	.125	0	0	0	.000
1962—Los Angeles		Amer.	OF	7	8	0	1	0	0	0	0	.125	0	0	0	.000
1962—Dallas-Ft.Worth.		A.A.	OF	114	359	43	113	28	2	5	41	.315	181	16	8	.961
1968—El Paso		Texas	PH	1	1	0	0	0	0	0	0	.000	0	0	0	.000
American League Totals				49	89	8	21	3	0	1	9	.236	23	0	0	1.000
National League Totals				347	796	90	210	36	5	20	96	.264	317	9	6	.982
Major League Totals				396	885	98	231	39	5	21	105	.261	340	9	6	.983

†Sold on waivers to Chicago Cubs, June 8, 1957.

‡Traded to Boston Red Sox for Pitcher Robert W. Smith, March 9, 1959.

§Purchased from Boston Red Sox by Cleveland Indians, September 9, 1959.

xSold by Cleveland Indians to Los Angeles Angels, September 8, 1961.

RECORD AS MANAGER

Named THE SPORTING NEWS Major League Manager of the Year, 1972.

Year	Club	League	Position	W.	L.
1963–Quad Cities	Midwest	Fourth	29	32	
(Second Half)		Second	37	25	
1964–Quad Cities	Midwest	Eighth	24	31	
(Second Half)		Second	38	25	
1965–El Paso	Texas	Third(W)	53	87	
1966–El Paso	Texas	Fifth	62	78	
1967–Seattle	P.C.	Fifth(W)	69	79	
1968–El Paso	Texas	†First(W)	77	60	
1969–Hawaii	P.C.	Third(S)	74	72	
1970–Hawaii	P.C.	‡First(S)	98	48	
1970–Chicago§	Amer.	Sixth(W)	3	13	
1971–Chicago	Amer.	Third(W)	79	83	

Year	Club	League	Position	W.	L.
1972–Chicago	Amer.	Second(W)	87	67	
1973–Chicago	Amer.	Fifth(W)	77	85	
1974–Chicago	Amer.	Fourth(W)	80	80	
1975–Chicago	Amer.	Fifth(W)	75	86	
1976–Oakland	Amer.	Second(W)	87	74	
1977–Pittsburgh	Nat.	Second(E)	96	66	
1978–Pittsburgh	Nat.	Second(E)	88	73	
1979–Pittsburgh	Nat.	First(E)	98	64	
1980–Pittsburgh	Nat.	Third(E)	83	79	

National League Totals 365 282
American League Totals 488 488

Major League Totals 853 770

CHAMPIONSHIP SERIES RECORD

Year	Club	League	W.	L.
1979–Pittsburgh	Nat.		3	0

WORLD SERIES RECORD

Year	Club	League	W.	L.
1979–Pittsburgh	Nat.		4	3

†Won playoff by defeating Arkansas, three games to one.
‡Lost playoff to Spokane, four games to none.
§Replaced Don Gutteridge, September 14, 1970. (Billy Adair served as interim manager from September 3 until Tanner's arrival.)
Traded to Pittsburgh Pirates for Catcher Manny Sanguillen and $100,000 cash, November 5, 1976.
Manager, National League All-Star Team, 1980.
Coach, American League All-Star Team, 1973.
Coach, National League All-Star Team, 1978.

JOSEPH PAUL TORRE
(Joe)
New York Mets

Born July 18, 1940, at Brooklyn, N. Y.
Height, 6.01. Weight, 210.
Threw and batted righthanded.
Hobbies–Popular music and golf.
Brother of Frank Torre, former first baseman with Milwaukee Braves and Philadelphia Phillies.

Tied major league record for most consecutive times grounded into double play, 4, July 21, 1975.
Led National League first basemen in double plays with 144 in 1974.
Led National League catchers in double plays with 12 in 1967.
Led National League in total bases with 352 in 1971.
Hit for cycle, game (single, double, triple, home run), June 27, 1973.
Named catcher on THE SPORTING NEWS National League All-Star Teams, 1964-65-66.
Named catcher on THE SPORTING NEWS National League All-Star fielding team, 1965.
Named third baseman on THE SPORTING NEWS National League All-Star Team, 1971.
Named Major League Player of the Year by THE SPORTING NEWS, 1971.
Most Valuable Player in the National League, 1971.

Year	Club	League	Pos.	G.	AB.	R.	H.	2B.	3B.	HR.	RBI.	B.A.	PO.	A.	E.	F.A.
1960–Eau Claire	North.	C	117	369	63	127	23	3	16	74	*.344	636	64	9	.987
1960–Milwaukee	Nat.	PH	2	2	0	1	0	0	0	0	.500	0	0	0	.000
1961–Louisville	A. A.	C	27	111	18	38	8	2	3	24	.342	185	14	2	.990
1961–Milwaukee	Nat.	C	113	406	40	113	21	4	10	42	.278	494	50	10	.982
1962–Milwaukee	Nat.	C	80	220	23	62	8	1	5	26	.282	325	39	5	.986
1963–Milwaukee	Nat.	C-1-OF	142	501	57	147	19	4	14	71	.293	919	76	6	.994
1964–Milwaukee	Nat.	*C-1B	154	601	87	193	36	5	20	109	.321	1081	94	7	*.994
1965–Milwaukee	Nat.	C-1B	148	523	68	152	21	1	27	80	.291	1022	73	8	.993
1966–Atlanta	Nat.	C-1B	148	546	83	172	20	3	36	101	.315	874	87	12	.988
1967–Atlanta	Nat.	C-1B	135	477	67	132	18	1	20	68	.277	785	81	8	.991
1968–Atlanta†	Nat.	*C-1B	115	424	45	115	11	2	10	55	.271	733	48	2	*.997
1969–St. Louis	Nat.	1B-C	159	602	72	174	29	6	18	101	.289	1360	91	7	.995
1970–St. Louis	Nat.	C-3-1B	●161	624	89	203	27	9	21	100	.325	651	162	13	.984
1971–St. Louis	Nat.	3B	161	634	97	*230	34	8	24	*137	*.363	*136	271	●21	.951
1972–St. Louis	Nat.	3B-1B	149	544	71	157	26	6	11	81	.289	336	198	15	.973
1973–St. Louis	Nat.	1B-3B	141	519	67	149	17	2	13	69	.287	881	128	12	.988
1974–St. Louis‡	Nat.	*1B-3B	147	529	59	149	28	1	11	70	.282	1173	*121	14	.989
1975–New York	Nat.	3B-1B	114	361	33	89	16	3	6	35	.247	172	157	15	.956
1976–New York§	Nat.	1-3B-PH	114	310	36	95	10	3	5	31	.306	593	52	7	.989
1977–New York§	Nat.	1B-3B	26	51	2	9	3	0	1	9	.176	83	3	1	.989
Major League Totals				2209	7874	996	2342	344	59	252	1185	.297	11618	1731	163	.988

†Traded to St. Louis Cardinals for First Baseman Orlando Cepeda, March 17, 1969.
‡Traded to New York Mets for Pitchers Tommy Moore and Ray Sadecki, October 13, 1974.
§Player-manager, beginning May 31, until released as player, June 18, 1977.

ALL-STAR GAME RECORD

Year	League	Pos.	AB.	R.	H.	2B.	3B.	HR.	RBI.	B.A.	PO.	A.	E.	F.A.
1964–National		C	2	0	0	0	0	0	0	.000	5	0	0	1.000
1965–National		C	4	1	1	0	0	1	2	.250	5	1	0	1.000
1966–National		C	3	0	0	0	0	0	0	.000	5	0	0	1.000

Year League	Pos.	AB.	R.	H.	2B.	3B.	HR.	RBI.	B.A.	PO.	A.	E.	F.A.
1967—National..............................	C	2	0	0	0	0	0	0	.000	4	1	0	1.000
1970—National..............................	PH	1	0	0	0	0	0	0	.000	0	0	0	.000
1971—National..............................	3B	3	0	0	0	0	0	0	.000	1	0	0	1.000
1972—National..............................	3B	3	0	1	0	0	0	0	.333	1	2	0	1.000
1973—National..............................	1B-3B	3	0	0	0	0	0	0	.000	5	0	0	1.000
All-Star Game Totals		21	1	2	0	0	1	2	.095	26	4	0	1.000

Member of National League All-Star Team for the 1963 game; did not play.

RECORD AS MANAGER

Year Club	League	Position	W.	L.
1977—New York†	Nat.	Sixth(E)	49	68
1978—New York	Nat.	Sixth(E)	66	96
1979—New York	Nat.	Sixth(E)	63	99
1980—New York	Nat.	Fifth(E)	67	95
Major League Totals........................			245	358

†Replaced Joe Frazier, May 31, 1977.

WILLIAM CHARLES VIRDON
(Bill)
Houston Astros

Born June 9, 1931, at Royal Oak Township, Mich.
Height, 6.00. Weight, 185.
Threw right and batted lefthanded.
Hobbies—Golf and hunting.
Attended Drury College, Springfield, Mo.

Tied major league record for most clubs managed, season, 2, in 1975.
Tied major league record for most assists by an outfielder, inning (2), second inning, second game, August 10, 1958; tied National League record for fewest triples, season, for leader in triples, 10, in 1962; led National League outfielders in double plays (5), 1959.
Named National League Rookie of the Year by THE SPORTING NEWS, 1955.
Named outfielder on THE SPORTING NEWS National League All-Star fielding team, 1962.
Named Major League Manager of the Year by THE SPORTING NEWS, 1974.

Year Club	League	Pos.	G.	AB.	R.	H.	2B.	3B.	HR.	RBI.	B.A.	PO.	A.	E.	F.A.
1950—Independence ....K-O-M		OF	119	*501	82	134	29	10	6	76	.267	215	y20	12	.951
1950—Kansas City.......A.A.		OF	14	41	3	14	3	0	0	3	.341	13	1	1	.933
1951—Norfolk ....Pied.		OF	118	486	91	139	20	4	6	48	.286	297	19	10	.969
1952—Binghamton.......East.		OF	122	467	57	122	13	9	2	46	.261	300	●18	11	.967
1953—Kansas City.......A.A.		OF	95	330	51	77	13	4	6	25	.233	174	8	7	.963
1953—Birmingham† ....South.		OF	42	164	27	52	7	2	3	14	.317	96	7	4	.963
1954—Rochester ....Int.		OF	139	505	85	168	28	11	22	98	*.333	361	6	14	.963
1955—St. Louis‡.........Nat.		OF	144	534	58	150	18	6	17	68	.281	339	7	12	.966
1956—St. L.‡-Pitts......Nat.		OF	●157	580	77	185	23	10	10	46	.319	387	12	5	.988
1957—Pittsburgh.........Nat.		OF	144	561	59	141	28	11	8	50	.251	403	13	6	.986
1958—Pittsburgh.........Nat.		OF	144	604	75	161	24	11	9	46	.267	401	11	3	.993
1959—Pittsburgh.........Nat.		OF	144	519	67	132	24	2	8	41	.254	404	16	9	.979
1960—Pittsburgh.........Nat.		OF	120	409	60	108	16	9	8	40	.264	272	10	5	.983
1961—Pittsburgh.........Nat.		OF	146	599	81	156	22	8	9	58	.260	384	6	6	.985
1962—Pittsburgh.........Nat.		OF	156	663	82	164	27	●10	6	47	.247	360	11	9	.976
1963—Pittsburgh.........Nat.		OF	142	554	58	149	22	6	8	53	.269	323	6	4	.988
1964—Pittsburgh.........Nat.		OF	145	473	59	115	11	3	3	27	.243	243	5	6	.976
1965—Pittsburgh.........Nat.		OF	135	481	58	134	22	5	4	24	.279	260	3	8	.970
1966—Williamsport .....East.		OF	5	7	0	0	0	0	0	0	.000	1	0	0	1.000
1967—.........................								(Did Not Play)							
1968—Pittsburgh.........Nat.		OF	6	3	1	1	0	0	1	2	.333	1	0	0	1.000
Major League Totals			1583	5980	735	1596	237	81	91	502	.267	3777	100	73	.981

†Traded to St. Louis Cardinals by New York Yankees with Pitcher Mel Wright and Outfielder Emil Tellinger for Outfielder Enos (Country) Slaughter, April 11, 1954.
‡Traded to Pittsburgh Pirates for Pitcher Dick Littlefield and Outfielder Bobby Del Greco, May 17, 1956.

WORLD SERIES RECORD

Year Club	League	Pos.	G.	AB.	R.	H.	2B.	3B.	HR.	RBI.	B.A.	PO.	A.	E.	F.A.
1960—Pittsburgh.........Nat.		OF	7	29	2	7	3	0	0	5	.241	18	0	1	.947

RECORD AS MANAGER

Year Club	League	Position	W.	L.	Year Club	League	Position	W.	L.
1966—Williamsport.......East	Fourth	68	72		1977—Houston..............Nat.	Third(W)	81	81	
1967—Jacksonville ....Int.	Fifth	66	73		1978—Houston ....Nat.	Fifth(W)	74	88	
1972—Pittsburgh ....Nat.	First(E)	96	59		1979—Houston ....Nat.	Second(W)	89	73	
1973—Pittsburgh†.........Nat.	Third(E)	67	69		1980—Houston ....Nat.	First(W)	93	70	
1974—New York...........Amer.	Second(E)	89	73		National League Totals		597	539	
1975—New York‡.........Amer.	Third(E)	53	51		American League Totals		142	124	
1975—Houston§ ....Nat.	Sixth(W)	17	17		Major League Totals................................		739	663	
1976—Houston.............Nat.	Third(W)	80	82						

†Replaced by Danny Murtaugh with club in second place, September 7.
‡Replaced by Billy Martin, August 1.

§Replaced Preston Gomez, August 19.
Coach, Pittsburgh Pirates, 1968 through 1971.
Coach, National League All-Star Team, 1973 and 1980.

CHAMPIONSHIP SERIES RECORD

Year	Club	League	W.	L.
1972—Pittsburgh		National	2	3
1980—Houston		National	2	3

EARL SIDNEY WEAVER
Baltimore Orioles

Born August 14, 1930, at St. Louis, Mo.
Height, 5.07. Weight, 180.
Threw and batted righthanded.

Led Western League second basemen in double plays with 112 in 1953 and Southern League with 110 in 1955.
Led Western League batters in hit by pitch with 13 in 1954.
Named Most Valuable Player in Illinois State League, 1948.

Year Club	League	Pos.	G.	AB.	R.	H.	2B.	3B.	HR.	RBI.	B.A.	PO.	A.	E.	F.A.
1948—West Frankfort	Ill. St.	2B	•120	447	96	120	20	4	2	49	.268	*302	323	21	*.967
1949—St. Joseph	W. Assn	2B	138	500	80	141	22	4	2	101	.282	307	369	26	.963
1950—Winston-Salem	Carol.	2B	127	439	57	121	20	0	3	60	.276	352	345	16	*.978
1951—Houston	Texas	2B	13	43	9	10	4	0	0	2	.233	43	40	2	.976
1951—Omaha	West.	2B	142	506	81	141	35	2	0	52	.279	330	393	25	.967
1952—Houston	Texas	2B	57	201	24	44	7	1	2	21	.219	148	128	11	.962
1952—Omaha	West.	2B	97	353	63	98	15	0	0	34	.278	239	267	16	.969
1953—Omaha†	West.	2B	141	478	57	116	16	0	3	47	.243	344	389	17	*.977
1954—Denver	West.	2B	143	541	124	153	30	2	6	59	.283	325	409	18	.976
1955—New Orleans	South.	2B	119	392	77	109	19	2	6	69	.278	294	342	10	*.985
1956—New Orleans	South.	2B	26	101	11	23	4	0	0	8	.228	60	69	5	.963
1956—Mont.-Knox.	Sally	2B	113	417	47	99	10	3	4	22	.237	300	309	11	*.982
1957—Fitzgerald	Ga.-Fla.	2B	112	354	70	102	15	3	6	38	.288	321	289	19	.970
1958—Dublin	Ga.-Fla.	2B	37	85	27	25	6	0	4	21	.294	54	41	3	.969
1959—Aberdeen	North.	2B	13	35	8	7	2	0	0	3	.200	40	25	2	.970
1960—Fox Cities	I.I.I.	2-OF	28	30	3	7	1	0	0	4	.233	10	20	1	.968
1965—Elmira	East.	2B	1	0	0	0	0	0	0	0	.000	0	0	0	.000

†Released by St. Louis Cardinals' organization to Pittsburgh Pirates' organization, September 23, 1953.

PITCHING RECORD

Year Club	League	G.	IP.	W.	L.	Pct.	H.	R.	ER.	SO.	BB.	ERA.
1957—Fitzgerald	Ga.-Fla.	5	....	1	0	1.000	....	....	....	....	....	....
1958—Dublin	Ga.-Fla.	2	....	0	0	.000	....	....	....	....	....	....
1959—Aberdeen	Northern	1	....	0	0	.000	....	....	....	....	....	....

RECORD AS MANAGER

Named Major League Manager of the Year by THE SPORTING NEWS, 1977 and 1979.

Year Club	League	Position	W.	L.		Year Club	League	Position	W.	L.
1956—Knoxville†	Sally	Eighth	10	24		1968—Baltimore x	Amer.	Second	48	34
1957—Fitzgerald	Ga.-Fla.	Fourth	37	33		1969—Baltimore	Amer.	First(E)	109	53
(Second Half)		Sixth	28	41		1970—Baltimore	Amer.	First(E)	108	54
1958—Dublin	Ga.-Fla.	Third	37	28		1971—Baltimore	Amer.	First(E)	101	57
(Second Half)		Third	35	28		1972—Baltimore	Amer.	Third(E)	80	74
1959—Aberdeen	North.	Second	69	55		1973—Baltimore	Amer.	First(E)	97	65
1960—Fox Cities	I.I.I.	First	82	56		1974—Baltimore	Amer.	First (E)	91	71
1961—Fox Cities	I.I.I.	Fourth	67	62		1975—Baltimore	Amer.	Second(E)	90	69
1962—Elmira	East.	‡Second	72	68		1976—Baltimore	Amer.	Second(E)	88	74
1963—Elmira	East.	Second	76	64		1977—Baltimore	Amer.	ySecond(E)	97	64
1964—Elmira	East.	First	82	58		1978—Baltimore	Amer.	Fourth(E)	90	71
1965—Elmira	East.	Second	83	55		1979—Baltimore	Amer.	First(E)	102	57
1966—Rochester	Int.	§First	83	64		1980—Baltimore	Amer.	Second(E)	100	62
1967—Rochester	Int.	Second	80	61		Major League Totals			1201	805

†Replaced Dick Bartell, August 8.
‡Won playoffs by defeating York, two games to one and Williamsport, three games to one.
§Lost in playoffs to Richmond, three games to one.
xReplaced Hank Bauer with club in third place, July 11.
yTied for position.
Coach, Baltimore Orioles, 1968 (through July 10).

CHAMPIONSHIP SERIES RECORD

Year Club	League	W.	L.
1969—Baltimore	Amer.	3	0
1970—Baltimore	Amer.	3	0
1971—Baltimore	Amer.	3	0
1973—Baltimore	Amer.	2	3
1974—Baltimore	Amer.	1	3
1979—Baltimore	Amer.	3	1

WORLD SERIES RECORD

Year Club	League	W.	L.
1969—Baltimore	Amer.	1	4
1970—Baltimore	Amer.	4	1
1971—Baltimore	Amer.	3	4
1979—Baltimore	Amer.	3	4

Manager, American League All-Star Team, 1970 through 1972 and 1980.
Coach, American League All-Star Team, 1969 and 1974.

RICHARD HIRSHFELD WILLIAMS
(Dick)
Montreal Expos

Born May 7, 1929, at St. Louis, Mo.
Height, 6.00. Weight, 190.
Threw and batted righthanded.
Hobby—Golf.
Attended Pasadena City College, Pasadena, Calif.
Father of Ricky Williams, pitcher in Montreal Expos' organization.

Year Club	League	Pos.	G.	AB.	R.	H.	2B.	3B.	HR.	RBI.	B.A.	PO.	A.	E.	F.A.
1947—Santa Barbara	Calif.	OF-3B	79	313	47	77	20	2	4	50	.246	165	36	5	.976
1948—Santa Barbara	Calif.	OF	97	385	82	129	29	2	16	90	.335	245	19	9	.967
1948—Fort Worth	Tex.	OF-3B	41	140	16	29	1	0	4	16	.207	60	2	1	.984
1949—Fort Worth	Tex.	*OF-2-3B	154	562	109	174	30	6	23	114	.310	*446	18	8	.983
1950—Fort Worth	Tex.	OF	144	510	69	153	30	1	11	72	.300	401	20	6	.986
1951—Brooklyn†	Nat.	OF	23	60	5	12	3	1	1	5	.200	21	1	0	1.000
1952—Brooklyn	Nat.	OF-1-3B	36	68	13	21	4	1	0	11	.309	51	3	0	1.000
1953—Brooklyn	Nat.	OF	30	55	4	12	2	0	2	5	.218	24	0	2	.923
1953—Montreal	Int.	OF	66	230	28	64	12	1	2	33	.278	111	3	2	.983
1954—Brooklyn	Nat.	OF	16	34	5	5	0	0	1	2	.147	12	0	0	1.000
1954—St. Paul	A.A.	OF-1B	49	162	23	40	8	0	6	18	.247	212	15	3	.987
1955—Fort Worth	Tex.	OF-1B	153	596	82	189	29	4	24	91	.317	580	22	7	.989
1956—Brooklyn	Nat.	PH	7	7	0	2	0	0	0	0	.286	0	0	0	.000
1956—Montreal‡	Int.	1B	13	50	3	13	3	0	0	6	.260	106	17	4	.969
1956—Baltimore	Am.	O-1-2-3	87	353	45	101	18	4	11	37	.286	249	17	4	.985
1957—Balt.§-Cleve.x	Am.	O-3-1B	114	372	49	97	17	2	7	34	.261	244	72	8	.975
1958—Baltimore y	Am.	O-3-1-2	128	409	36	113	17	0	4	32	.276	359	61	8	.981
1959—Kansas City	Am.	3-1-O-2	130	488	72	130	33	1	16	75	.266	349	181	13	.976
1960—Kansas City z	Am.	3-1B-OF	127	420	47	121	31	0	12	65	.288	376	131	11	.979
1961—Baltimore	Am.	O-1-3B	103	310	37	64	15	2	8	24	.206	209	16	3	.987
1962—Baltimore a b	Am.	OF-1-3B	82	178	20	44	7	1	1	18	.247	180	13	0	1.000
1963—Boston	Am.	3-1B-OF	79	136	15	35	8	0	2	12	.257	64	28	1	.989
1964—Boston	Am.	1-3-OF	61	69	10	11	2	0	5	11	.159	50	21	1	.986
American League Totals			911	2735	331	716	148	10	66	308	.262	2080	540	49	.982
National League Totals			112	224	27	52	9	2	4	23	.232	108	4	2	.982
Major League Totals			1023	2959	358	768	157	12	70	331	.260	2188	544	51	.982

†On National Defense Service List, February 7 to May 29, 1951.
‡Recalled by Brooklyn Dodgers and sold to Baltimore Orioles, June 25, 1956.
§Traded to Cleveland Indians for Outfielder Jim Busby, June 13, 1957.
xTraded with Pitcher Bud Daley and Outfielder Gene Woodling to Baltimore Orioles for Pitcher Don Ferrarese and Outfielder Larry Doby, April 1, 1958.
yTraded to Kansas City Athletics for Shortstop Chico Carrasquel, October 2, 1958.
zTraded with Pitcher Dick Hall to Baltimore Orioles for Pitcher Jerry Walker and Outfielder Chuck Essegian, April 13, 1961.
aSold to Houston Colts, October 12, 1962.
bTraded by Houston Colts to Boston Red Sox for Outfielder Carroll Hardy, December 10, 1962.

WORLD SERIES RECORD

Year Club	League	Pos.	G.	AB.	R.	H.	2B.	3B.	HR.	RBI.	B.A.	PO.	A.	E.	F.A.
1953—Brooklyn	Nat.	PH	3	2	0	1	0	0	0	0	.500	0	0	0	.000

RECORD AS MANAGER

Named Major League Manager of the Year by THE SPORTING NEWS, 1967.

Year Club	League	Position	W.	L.	Year Club	League	Position	W.	L.
1965—Toronto	Int.	†Third	81	64	1976—California z	Amer.	Fourth(W)	39	57
1966—Toronto	Int.	‡Second	82	65	1977—Montreal	Nat.	Fifth(E)	75	87
1967—Boston	Amer.	First	92	70	1978—Montreal	Nat.	Fourth(E)	76	86
1968—Boston	Amer.	Fourth	86	76	1979—Montreal	Nat.	Second(E)	95	65
1969—Boston§	Amer.	Third(E)	82	71	1980—Montreal	Nat.	Second(E)	90	72
1971—Oakland	Amer.	First(W)	101	60	National League Totals			336	310
1972—Oakland	Amer.	First(W)	93	62	American League Totals			695	601
1973—Oakland x	Amer.	First(W)	94	68	Major League Totals			1031	911
1974—California y	Amer.	Sixth(W)	36	48					
1975—California	Amer.	Sixth(W)	72	89					

†Won playoffs by defeating Atlanta, four games to none and Columbus, four games to one.
‡Tied for position during regular season. Won playoffs by defeating Columbus, three games to two and Richmond, four games to one.
§Replaced by interim manager Eddie Popowski, September 23, 1969.
xQuit as manager of the Oakland Athletics following 1973 World Series. Signed contract to manage New York Yankees but American League President Joe Cronin ruled that Williams must honor the two years remaining on his Oakland contract.
yReplaced Bobby Winkles as manager, June 26, 1974. (Whitey Herzog served as interim manager, June 27 through June 30.)
zReplaced by Norm Sherry, July 23, 1976.
Coach, Montreal Expos, 1970.
Manager, American League All-Star Team, 1968, 1973 and 1974.
Coach, American League All-Star Team, 1972.

Year Club League	W.	L.	Year Club League	W.	L.
1971—Oakland............Amer.	0	3	1967—Boston...............Amer.	3	4
1972—Oakland............Amer.	3	2	1972—Oakland............Amer.	4	3
1973—Oakland............Amer.	3	2	1973—Oakland............Amer.	4	3

MAURICE MORNING WILLS
(Maury)
Seattle Mariners

Born October 2, 1932, at Washington, D.C.
Height, 5.10. Weight, 165.
Threw right and batted left and righthanded.

Established major league record for most games played, 162-game season (165), 1962.
Established National League record for most consecutive seasons leading in stolen bases (6), 1965.
Tied National League records for most years leading league, singles (4), 1967; most at-bats, season (695), 1962.
Led Pony League in stolen bases with 54 in 1952; Western League with 34 in 1956 and National League with 50 in 1960, 35 in 1961, 104 in 1962, 40 in 1963; 53 in 1964 and 94 in 1965.
Named Major League Player of the Year by THE SPORTING NEWS, 1962.
Named National League Player of the Year by THE SPORTING NEWS, 1962.
Named Most Valuable National League Player, 1962.
Named as shortstop on THE SPORTING NEWS National League All-Star Team, 1961, 1962 and 1965.
Named shortstop on THE SPORTING NEWS National League All-Star fielding team, 1961 and 1962.

Year Club	League	Pos.	G.	AB.	R.	H.	2B.	3B.	HR.	RBI.	B.A.	PO.	A.	E.	F.A.
1951—Hornell	Pony	INF-P	123	461	94	129	16	6	4	51	.280	235	210	28	.941
1952—Hornell	Pony	2B-SS	125	*533	*108	*160	34	4	4	58	.300	330	292	19	.970
1953—Pueblo	West.	2B	18	63	17	18	2	0	0	8	.286	39	53	7	.929
1953—Miami	Fla. I.	IN-C-P	93	343	71	98	16	5	6	31	.286	205	256	30	.939
1954—Pueblo	West.	*S-3-2-O	145	552	89	154	17	10	6	53	.279	261	420	*60	.919
1955—Fort Worth	Tex.	S-2-OF	123	326	44	66	11	0	7	39	.202	177	287	38	.924
1956—Pueblo	West.	SS	134	540	110	163	33	8	10	54	.302	*265	*361	42	.937
1957—Seattle	P. C.	INF	147	491	67	131	23	6	0	33	.267	265	428	51	.931
1958—Spokane	P. C.	SS	144	534	69	135	20	7	2	37	.253	245	426	33	.953
1959—Spokane	P. C.	SS	49	192	42	60	6	3	1	18	.313	68	161	12	.950
1959—Los Angeles	Nat.	SS	83	242	27	63	5	2	0	7	.260	121	220	12	.966
1960—Los Angeles	Nat.	SS	148	516	75	152	15	2	0	27	.295	260	431	*40	.945
1961—Los Angeles	Nat.	SS	148	*613	105	173	12	10	1	31	.282	253	428	29	.959
1962—Los Angeles	Nat.	SS	*165	*695	130	208	13	●10	6	48	.299	295	493	36	.956
1963—Los Angeles	Nat.	SS-3B	134	527	83	159	19	3	0	34	.302	197	381	26	.957
1964—Los Angeles	Nat.	SS-3B	158	630	81	173	15	5	2	34	.275	275	428	27	.963
1965—Los Angeles	Nat.	SS	158	650	92	186	14	7	0	33	.286	267	*535	25	.970
1966—Los Angeles†	Nat.	SS-3B	143	594	60	162	14	2	1	39	.273	231	460	23	.968
1967—Pittsburgh	Nat.	3B-SS	149	616	92	186	12	9	3	45	.302	102	346	24	.949
1968—Pittsburgh	Nat.	3B-SS	153	627	76	174	12	6	0	31	.278	115	308	18	.959
1969—Montreal§-L.A.	Nat.	SS	151	623	80	171	10	8	4	47	.274	240	496	28	.963
1970—Los Angeles	Nat.	SS-3B	132	522	77	141	19	3	0	34	.270	171	397	24	.959
1971—Los Angeles	Nat.	SS-3B	149	601	73	169	14	3	3	44	.281	220	486	17	.976
1972—Los Angeles x	Nat.	SS-3B	71	132	16	17	3	1	0	4	.129	39	103	2	.986
Major League Totals			1942	7588	1067	2134	177	71	20	458	.281	2786	5512	331	.962

†Traded to Pittsburgh Pirates for Shortstop Gene Michael and Third Baseman-Outfielder Bob Bailey, December 1, 1966.
‡Selected by Montreal Expos from Pittsburgh Pirates in expansion draft, October 14, 1968.
§Traded with Outfielder Manny Mota to Los Angeles Dodgers for Outfielder-First Baseman Ron Fairly and Infielder Paul Popovich, June 11, 1969.
xReleased October 24, 1972.

PITCHING RECORD

Year Club	League	G.	IP.	W.	L.	Pct.	H.	R.	ER.	SO.	BB.	ERA.
1951—Hornell	Pony	1	7	0	0	.000	5	2	2	1	1	2.57
1953—Miami	Fla. Int.	1	4	0	0	.000	3	0	0	0	2	0.00

WORLD SERIES RECORD

Tied World Series records for most hits, game (4), October 11, 1965; most double plays started, seven-game series, shortstop (4), 1965; most double plays started, game, nine innings, shortstop (3), October 11, 1965.

Year Club	League	Pos.	G.	AB.	R.	H.	2B.	3B.	HR.	RBI.	B.A.	PO.	A.	E.	F.A.
1959—Los Angeles	Nat.	SS	6	20	2	5	0	0	0	1	.250	10	21	1	.969
1963—Los Angeles	Nat.	SS	4	15	1	2	0	0	0	0	.133	5	10	1	.938
1965—Los Angeles	Nat.	SS	7	30	3	11	3	0	0	3	.367	14	26	0	1.000
1966—Los Angeles	Nat.	SS	4	13	0	1	0	0	0	0	.077	12	15	0	1.000
World Series Totals			21	78	6	19	3	0	0	4	.244	41	72	2	.983

ALL-STAR GAME RECORD

Year League	Pos.	AB.	R.	H.	2B.	3B.	HR.	RBI.	B.A.	PO.	A.	E.	F.A.
1961—National (both games)	SS	7	2	2	0	0	0	0	.286	1	3	0	1.000
1962—National (both games)	SS	2	2	1	0	0	0	0	.500	1	2	0	1.000
1965—National	SS	4	0	1	0	0	0	0	.250	2	3	0	1.000
1966—National	SS	1	0	1	0	0	0	1	1.000	1	1	0	1.000
All-Star Game Totals		14	2	5	0	0	0	1	.357	5	9	0	1.000

Member of National League All-Star team in 1963; did not play.

RECORD AS MANAGER

Year	Club	League	Position	W.	L.
1980—Seattle†		Amer.	Seventh(W)	20	38

†Replaced Darrell Johnson with club tied for sixth place (record of 39-65), August 3, 1980.
Instructor, Los Angeles Dodgers, 1977.

DONALD WILLIAM ZIMMER
(Don)
Texas Rangers

Born January 17, 1931, at Cincinnati, O.
Height, 5.09½. Weight, 188.
Threw and batted righthanded.
Hobbies—Golf and fishing.
Father of Tom Zimmer, manager of Wisconsin Rapids (Minnesota Twins' organization).
Named American Association Rookie of the Year, 1953.

Year Club	League	Pos.	G.	AB.	R.	H.	2B.	3B.	HR.	RBI.	B.A.	PO.	A.	E.	F.A.
1949—Cambridge	E. Shore	SS	71	304	56	69	14	3	4	30	.227	162	171	27	.925
1950—Hornell	Pony	*SS-3B	123	518	*146	163	34	5	*23	122	.315	*269	*367	45	*.934
1951—Elmira	East.	SS	137	546	94	149	28	2	9	70	.273	*326	414	38	*.951
1952—Mobile	South.	SS	153	613	107	190	32	7	17	91	.310	*355	*517	*52	.944
1953—St. Paul†	A.A.	SS	81	320	57	96	14	4	23	63	.300	165	264	21	.953
1954—St. Paul	A.A.	SS	73	268	54	78	9	6	17	53	.291	152	200	16	.957
1954—Brooklyn	Nat.	SS	24	33	3	6	0	1	0	0	.182	14	32	3	.939
1955—Brooklyn	Nat.	2-S-3	88	280	38	67	10	1	15	50	.239	184	207	12	.970
1956—Brooklyn‡	Nat.	S-3-2	17	20	4	6	1	0	0	2	.300	10	11	1	.955
1957—Brooklyn	Nat.	3-S-2	84	269	23	59	9	1	6	19	.219	114	186	15	.952
1958—Los Angeles	Nat.	S-3-2-O	127	455	52	119	15	2	17	60	.262	281	395	26	.963
1959—Los Angeles x	Nat.	S-3-2	97	249	21	41	7	1	4	28	.165	120	240	10	.973
1960—Chicago	Nat.	2-3-S-O	132	368	37	95	16	7	6	35	.258	211	274	16	.968
1961—Chicago y	Nat.	2-3-OF	128	477	57	120	25	4	13	40	.252	284	332	20	.969
1962—N.Y. z-Cinn. a	Nat.	3-2-S	77	244	19	52	12	2	2	17	.213	77	129	11	.949
1963—Los Angeles b	Nat.	3-2-S	22	23	4	5	1	0	1	2	.217	3	14	2	.895
1963—Washington	Am.	3B-2B	83	298	37	74	12	1	13	44	.248	90	177	18	.937
1964—Washington	Am.	3-OF-C-2	121	341	38	84	16	2	12	38	.246	72	144	10	.956
1965—Washington c	Am.	C-3-2	95	226	20	45	6	0	2	17	.199	181	81	12	.956
1966—Toei	Pacific	3B-SS	87	203	14	37	2	0	9	20	.182	101	143	11	.957
1967—Knoxville	So.	P-3-1-C	25	49	2	10	3	0	0	5	.204	21	12	6	.846
1967—Buffalo	Int.	3B-OF	16	33	2	6	2	0	1	2	.182	4	9	3	.813
American League Totals			299	865	95	203	34	3	27	99	.235	343	402	40	.949
National League Totals			796	2418	258	570	96	19	64	253	.236	1298	1820	116	.964
Major League Totals			1095	3283	353	773	130	22	91	352	.235	1641	2222	156	.961

†Was leading American Association in home runs and runs batted in July 7, 1953, when he was struck in the head by Pitcher Jim Kirk of Columbus; out of action for rest of season.

‡Suffered cheek bone fracture when he was struck by a pitch from Hal Jeffcoat of Cincinnati Redlegs, June 23, 1956; out of action for rest of season.

xTraded to Chicago Cubs for Pitcher Ron Perranoski, Infielder John Goryl, Outfielder Lee Handley and reported $25,000, April 8, 1960; players acquired by Dodgers were from the Cubs' farm system and assigned by Los Angeles to minor league clubs.

ySelected by New York Mets in Expansion Draft, October 10, 1961.

zTraded to Cincinnati Reds for Pitcher Robert G. Miller and Third Baseman Cliff Cook May 6, 1962.

aTraded to Los Angeles Dodgers for Pitcher Scott Breeden, January 24, 1963.

bSold to Washington Senators, June 24, 1963.

cReleased, November 19, 1965; went on to play one year of professional baseball in Japan with Toei Flyers.

PITCHING RECORD

Year Club	League	G.	IP.	W.	L.	Pct.	H.	R.	ER.	SO.	BB.	ERA.
1967—Knoxville	Southern	12	27	0	0	.000	33	15	14	8	7	4.67

WORLD SERIES RECORD

Year Club	League	Pos.	G.	AB.	R.	H.	2B.	3B.	HR.	RBI.	B.A.	PO.	A.	E.	F.A.
1955—Brooklyn	Nat.	2B	4	9	0	2	0	0	0	2	.222	4	8	2	.857
1959—Los Angeles	Nat.	SS	1	1	0	0	0	0	0	0	.000	0	1	0	1.000
World Series Totals			5	10	0	2	0	0	0	2	.200	4	9	2	.867

ALL-STAR GAME RECORD

Year League	Pos.	AB.	R.	H.	2B.	3B.	HR.	RBI.	B.A.	PO.	A.	E.	F.A.
1961—National (first game)	2B	1	0	0	0	0	0	0	.000	0	0	1	.000

RECORD AS MANAGER

Year	Club	League	Position	W.	L.
1967—Knoxville	South.	†Sixth	26	46	
1967—Buffalo	Int.	Seventh	33	40	
1968—Indianapolis	P.C.	Fifth(E)	66	78	
1969—Key West	Fla. St.	‡Third(S)	67	63	
1972—San Diego§	Nat.	Sixth(W)	54	88	
1973—San Diego	Nat.	Sixth(W)	60	102	
1976—Boston x	Amer.	Third(E)	42	34	
1977—Boston	Amer.	ySecond(E)	97	64	
1978—Boston	Amer.	Second(E)	99	64	
1979—Boston	Amer.	Third (E)	91	69	
1980—Boston z	Amer.	yThird(E)	82	73	
American League Totals				411	304
National League Totals				114	190
Major League Totals				525	494

†Transferred by Cincinnati Reds' Organization from Knoxville to Buffalo, July 5.
‡Tied for position with Pompano Beach.
§Replaced Preston Gomez, April 27, 1972.
xReplaced Darrell Johnson, July 19, 1976.
yTied for position.
zReplaced by interim manager Johnny Pesky, October 1, 1980.
Coach, Montreal Expos, 1971; San Diego Padres, 1972; Boston Red Sox, 1974 to July, 1976.
Coach, American League All-Star Team, 1978.

Major League Coaches

TOMMIE LEE AARON
Atlanta Braves

Born August 5, 1939, at Mobile, Ala.
Height, 6.01. Weight, 200.
Threw and batted righthanded.
Hobbies—Music and movies.

Brother of Henry Aaron, former outfielder with Milwaukee Braves, Atlanta Braves and Milwaukee Brewers; currently vice president and Director of Player Development with Atlanta Braves.

Tied major league record for most double plays by first baseman, game (3), May 27, 1962.
Led Three-I League first basemen in double plays with 115 in 1960.

Year	Club	League	Pos.	G.	AB.	R.	H.	2B.	3B.	HR.	RBI.	B.A.	PO.	A.	E.	F.A.
1958—Eau Claire	North.	OF-SS	66	237	32	65	10	0	3	33	.274	90	75	14	.922
1959—Eau Claire	North.	2B	123	472	88	121	16	3	26	80	.256	*361	330	28	.961
1960—Jacksonville	Sally	1B	6	19	3	4	0	0	1	4	.211	50	7	1	.983
1960—Cedar Rapids	I.I.I.	1B	137	515	93	154	26	7	20	88	.299	*1123	77	23	.981
1960—Louisville	A. A.	PH	1	1	0	0	0	0	0	0	.000	0	0	0	.000
1961—Austin	Tex.	1B	138	528	77	158	26	3	15	70	.299	1236	88	12	*.991
1962—Milwaukee	Nat.	IN-OF	141	334	54	77	20	2	8	38	.231	572	48	10	.984
1963—Milwaukee	Nat.	IN-OF	72	135	6	27	6	1	1	15	.200	221	18	1	.996
1963—Denver	P. C.	INF	66	252	46	78	12	2	10	36	.310	266	114	6	.984
1964—Denver	P. C.	*1-2-O-3	152	553	*103	153	28	11	21	86	.277	1068	106	10	*.992
1965—Milwaukee	Nat.	1B	8	16	1	3	0	0	0	1	.188	45	4	2	.961
1965—Atlanta	Int.	2-1-O-3	114	402	41	114	19	2	4	36	.284	296	188	12	.976
1966—Richmond	Int.	1-O-3B	110	320	41	86	14	4	11	49	.269	373	44	7	.983
1967—Richmond	Int.	O-1-2B	119	424	45	131	17	0	11	56	.309	465	71	10	.982
1968—Atlanta	Nat.	O-1-3B	98	283	21	69	10	3	1	25	.244	287	20	5	.984
1969—Atlanta	Nat.	1B-OF	49	60	13	15	2	0	1	5	.250	65	2	0	1.000
1970—Atlanta	Nat.	1B-OF	44	63	3	13	2	0	2	7	.206	53	2	2	.966
1971—Richmond	Int.	3B-1B-O	96	355	55	113	19	3	12	54	.318	198	122	17	.950
1971—Atlanta	Nat.	1B-3B	25	53	4	12	2	0	0	3	.226	74	19	2	.979
1972—Richmond	Int.	1B-3B-O	106	337	36	91	15	0	1	39	.270	479	91	14	.976
1973—Savannah†	South.	1B	105	374	51	98	22	1	13	47	.262	770	42	4	.995
Major League Totals			437	944	102	216	42	6	13	94	.229	1317	113	22	.985

†Player-manager.

CHAMPIONSHIP SERIES RECORD

Year	Club	League	Pos.	G.	AB.	R.	H.	2B.	3B.	HR.	RBI.	B.A.	PO.	A.	E.	F.A.
1969—Atlanta	Nat.	PH	1	1	0	0	0	0	0	0	.000	0	0	0	.000

RECORD AS MANAGER

Year	Club	League	Position	W.	L.
1973—Savannah†	South.	Second(E)	37	45
1974—Savannah	South.	Third(E)	73	65
1975—Savannah	South.	Second(E)	70	64
1976—Savannah	South.	Third(E)	69	71
1977—Richmond	Int.	‡Fourth	71	69
1978—Richmond	Int.	§Fourth	71	68

†Replaced Clint Courtney, June 16, 1973.
‡Lost playoff semifinals to Pawtucket, three games to one.
§Won playoff semifinals from Charleston, three games to one; won championship playoff from Pawtucket, four games to three.
Coach, Atlanta Braves, 1979 through 1981.

DID YOU KNOW—

That the Giants pulled an All-rookie triple play in 1980? On October 3 against San Diego, Dave Cash hit a looping drive that was caught by second baseman Guy Sularz. Sularz tossed to rookie shortstop Joe Pettini, doubling Luis Salazar at second. Salazar then threw to first baseman Rich Murray, catching Gene Tenace to complete the triple play.

JOSEPH SALVATORE ALTOBELLI
(Joe)
New York Yankees

Born May 26, 1932, at Detroit, Mich.
Height, 6.00. Weight, 180.
Threw and batted lefthanded.
Hobby—Hunting.

Led American Association first basemen in double plays with 146 in 1954, with 126 in 1955, and with 160 in 1962.

Led International League first basemen in double plays with 143 in 1960.

Year Club	League	Pos.	G.	AB.	R.	H.	2B.	3B.	HR.	RBI.	B.A.	PO.	A.	E.	F.A.
1951—Daytona Beach..Fla. St.		1B	•140	598	118	204	∗40	19	8	101	.341	∗1259	∗90	∗45	.967
1952—Reading	East.	1B	128	436	49	118	9	7	2	37	.271	1036	63	∗20	.982
1953—Reading	East.	1B	148	528	76	155	28	9	4	65	.294	1092	∗83	19	.984
1954—Indianapolis	A.A.	1B	149	551	73	158	31	10	6	79	.287	1120	84	12	.990
1955—Indianapolis	A.A.	1B	98	395	58	107	24	1	7	53	.271	322	61	14	.984
1955—Cleveland	Amer.	1B	42	75	8	15	3	0	2	5	.200	224	11	2	.992
1956—Indianapolis	A.A.	1B	145	528	69	134	18	10	19	81	.254	1181	100	15	.988
1957—Cleveland	Amer.	1B-OF	83	87	9	18	3	2	0	9	.207	158	9	1	.994
1957—Columbus	Int.	1B	22	77	16	18	5	1	2	10	.234	176	20	3	.985
1958—Indianapolis†	A.A.	∗1B-OF	133	463	60	133	24	4	12	74	.287	1012	83	14	∗.987
1959—Toronto‡	Int.	1B	148	518	71	131	17	6	17	61	.253	1244	87	13	.990
1960—Montreal	Int.	1B	154	552	79	141	25	5	∗31	∗105	.255	∗1401	101	14	.991
1961—Syracuse	Int.	1B-OF	96	351	50	90	11	4	10	47	.256	396	31	13	.968
1961—Minnesota§	Amer.	OF-1B	41	95	10	21	2	1	3	14	.221	54	1	2	.965
1962—Omaha	A.A.	1B	141	502	81	136	23	7	13	67	.271	∗1247	∗89	12	.991
1963—Rochester x	Int.	1B-OF	97	315	45	77	13	0	15	44	.244	361	31	4	.990
1964—Rochester	Int.	1B	122	345	35	86	11	1	11	52	.249	680	51	3	.996
1965—Rochester y	Int.	1B	117	393	51	116	11	3	20	59	.295	884	74	15	.985
1966—Rochester y	Int.	OF	25	60	5	14	5	0	1	5	.233	24	1	0	1.000
1967—Elmira	East.	1B	3	7	0	1	0	0	0	2	.143	17	2	0	1.000
1970—Dal.-Ft. Worth	Tex.	1B-P	11	11	1	4	0	0	0	3	.364	17	1	2	.917
Major League Totals			166	257	27	54	8	3	5	28	.210	436	21	5	.989

RECORD AS PITCHER

Year Club	League	G.	IP.	W.	L.	Pct.	H.	R.	ER.	SO.	BB.	ERA.
1970—Dallas-Ft. Worth	Texas	2	4	0	0	.000	5	8	6	1	3	13.50

†Sold by Cleveland Indians' organization to Toronto (International) for a reported $20,000, January 13, 1959.

‡Traded to Los Angeles Dodgers' organization for Third Baseman Clyde Parris, April 1, 1960.

§Released outright by Minnesota Twins' organization to Los Angeles Dodgers' organization, October 12, 1961.

xOn disabled list, May 13 to May 29 and July 19 to August 14, 1963.

yPlayer-coach.

RECORD AS MANAGER

Named by THE SPORTING NEWS as Minor League Manager of the Year, 1974.
Named Appalachian League Manager of the Year, 1967.
Named International League Manager of the Year, 1971, 1974 and 1980.

Year Club	League	Position	W.	L.	Year Club	League	Position	W.	L.
1966—Bluefield	Appal.	Third	38	33	1974—Rochester	Int.	§First(N)	88	56
1967—Bluefield	Appal.	First	42	25	1975—Rochester	Int.	Second	85	56
1968—Stockton	Calif.	Seventh	29	41	1976—Rochester	Int.	xFirst	88	50
(Second Half)		Second	38	32	1977—San Francisco	Nat.	Fourth(W)	75	87
1969—Dallas-Ft. Worth	Texas	Second(W)	75	58	1978—San Francisco	Nat.	Third(W)	89	73
1970—Dallas-Ft. Worth	Texas	Third(W)	63	73	1979—San Francisco y	Nat.	Fourth(W)	61	79
1971—Rochester	Int.	†First	86	54	1980—Columbus	Int.	zFirst	83	57
1972—Rochester	Int.	Fourth	76	68	Major League Totals			225	239
1973—Rochester	Int.	‡First(A)	79	67					

†Won playoffs by defeating Syracuse, three games to one and Tidewater, three games to two; won Junior World Series against Denver (American Association), four games to three.

‡Lost championship playoff to Charleston, three games to none.

§Won Governor's Cup by defeating Syracuse, four games to three, won League Championship by defeating Memphis, four games to two.

xLost semifinal playoff series to Richmond, three games to one.

yReplaced by Dave Bristol, September 5, 1979.

zWon playoffs from Richmond, three games to two; won championship series from Toledo, four games to one.

Coach, New York Yankees, 1981.

RUBEN AMARO (MORA)
Name pronounced Uh-MARR-oh.
Philadelphia Phillies

Born January 7, 1936, at Monterrey, Nuevo Leon, Mex.
Height 5.10½. Weight, 165.
Threw and batted righthanded.
Attended University of Veracruz, Veracruz, Mex.

Led Arizona-Mexico League shortstops in double plays with 112 in 1955.
Led International League shortstops in double plays with 84 in 1959.
Named shortstop on THE SPORTING NEWS National League All-Star fielding team, 1964.

Year-Club	League	Pos.	G.	AB.	R.	H.	2B.	3B.	HR.	RBI.	B.A.	PO.	A.	E.	F.A.
1954—Mexicali	A.-Mex.	SS-3B	93	319	55	91	17	4	5	47	.285	161	278	42	.913
1955—Mexicali	A.-Mex.	SS	140	583	•140	180	29	6	18	66	.309	*303	*490	*67	.922
1956—Houston	Tex.	SS	152	533	53	142	15	2	2	64	.266	*257	*471	42	.945
1957—Houston	Tex.	SS	142	451	50	100	17	0	3	46	.222	243	430	35	.951
1958—Rochester	Int.	SS	92	275	30	55	9	2	1	20	.200	171	243	20	.954
1958—St. Louis†	Nat.	SS-2B	40	76	8	17	2	1	0	0	.224	45	66	6	.949
1959—Buffalo	Int.	SS-3B	119	423	59	109	18	3	3	31	.258	207	389	28	.955
1960—Indianapolis	A. A.	SS	45	176	24	38	5	1	1	16	.216	95	173	9	.968
1960—Philadelphia	Nat.	SS	92	264	25	61	9	1	0	16	.231	153	230	14	.965
1961—Philadelphia	Nat.	SS-1-2B	135	381	34	98	14	9	1	32	.257	254	380	19	.971
1962—Philadelphia‡	Nat.	SS-1B	79	226	24	55	10	0	0	19	.243	144	224	12	.968
1963—Philadelphia	Nat.	SS-3-1B	115	217	25	47	9	2	2	19	.217	111	169	13	.956
1964—Philadelphia	Nat.	IN-OF	129	299	31	79	11	0	4	34	.264	298	203	11	.979
1965—Philadelphia§	Nat.	SS-1-2B	118	184	26	39	7	0	0	15	.212	187	134	11	.967
1966—New York x	Amer.	SS	14	23	0	5	0	0	0	3	.217	17	25	1	.977
1967—New York	Amer.	S-3-1B	130	417	31	93	12	0	1	17	.223	228	379	18	.971
1968—New York y	Amer.	SS-1B	47	41	3	5	1	0	0	0	.122	54	37	2	.978
1969—California z	Amer.	1-2-S-3	41	27	4	6	0	0	0	1	.222	41	17	1	.983
1970—Eugene a	P. C.	SS-1B	106	310	54	72	11	3	2	17	.232	143	300	26	.945
1971—Reading	East.	SS-2B	11	35	2	5	2	0	0	3	.143	25	44	2	.972
1971—Eugene bc	P. C.	3B-2B-SS	17	54	11	19	4	1	0	7	.352	15	25	1	.976
American League Totals			232	508	38	109	13	0	1	21	.215	340	458	22	.973
National League Totals			708	1647	173	396	62	13	7	135	.240	1192	1406	86	.968
Major League Totals			940	2155	211	505	75	13	8	156	.234	1532	1864	108	.969

†Traded to Philadelphia Phillies for Outfielder Charles Essegian, December 3, 1958.
‡In Military Service part of season.
§Traded to New York Yankees for Infielder Phil Linz, November 29, 1965.
xOn disabled list, April 18 to August 29, 1966.
ySold to California Angels, November 6, 1968.
zReleased, October 22, 1969; signed by Philadelphia Phillies' organization, April 13, 1970.
aOn disabled list, July 15 to July 25, 1970.
bOn disabled list, June 30 to August 7, 1971.
cReleased, March 1, 1972.

RECORD AS MANAGER

Year	Club	League	Position	W.	L.
1977—Auburn	NYP	Fifth(E)	17	53

Scout, Philadelphia Phillies, 1972, 1973 and 1979; Coach, Philadelphia Phillies, 1980 and 1981.

LOREN ROLLAND BABE
Chicago White Sox

Born January 11, 1928, at Pisgah, Ia.
Height, 5.10. Weight, 175.
Threw and batted righthanded.

Year-Club	League	Pos.	G.	AB.	R.	H.	2B.	3B.	HR.	RBI.	B.A.	PO.	A.	E.	F.A.
1945—Kansas City	A.A.	3B	5	8	2	3	0	0	0	0	.375	2	2	0	1.000
1945—Binghamton	East.	3B-2B	34	118	13	33	4	1	0	7	.280	50	54	13	.889
1945—Norfolk	Pied.	3B	69	282	47	93	10	1	1	27	.330	77	150	20	.919
1946—Kansas City	A.A.						(In Military Service)								
1947—Denver	West.	2B-3B	52	209	37	62	6	7	0	20	.297	115	122	35	.871
1948—Beaumont	Tex.	3B	133	464	51	106	9	5	1	41	.228	*162	*291	*43	.913
1949—Binghamton	East.	2B-3B	102	375	53	103	11	5	3	27	.275	186	230	22	.950
1950—Beaumont	Tex.	SS-OF	12	13	3	3	0	0	0	3	.231	1	1	2	.500
1950—Muskegon	Cent.	2B	117	448	75	150	27	4	10	68	.335	310	315	19	•.970
1951—Syracuse	Int.	3B-SS	153	595	88	162	32	1	8	56	.272	169	355	37	.934
1952—Syracuse	Int.	3B	130	498	67	152	19	6	11	73	.305	139	250	*30	.928
1952—New York	Amer.	3B	12	21	1	2	1	0	0	0	.095	4	16	2	.909
1953—N.Y.†-Phila.	Amer.	3B-SS	108	361	36	83	17	2	2	26	.230	122	207	18	.948
1954—Toronto	Int.	3B-2B	151	582	99	168	27	4	19	73	.289	143	316	33	.933
1955—Toronto	Int.	3B	142	528	87	151	22	7	11	64	.286	102	277	20	.950
1956—Toronto	Int.	3B	133	454	55	119	21	4	5	54	.262	121	209	23	.935
1957—Toronto	Int.	3-2B-OF	101	328	39	85	10	2	4	32	.259	119	159	7	.975
1958—Seattle	P.C.	3B	19	49	2	10	2	0	0	4	.204	23	29	1	.980
1958—Rochester	Int.	3B	89	311	25	83	11	1	3	30	.267	44	134	15	.922
1959-60						(Out of Organized Ball)										
1961—Auburn	NYP	PH	1	1	0	0	0	0	0	0	.000	0	0	0	.000
Major League Totals			120	382	37	85	18	2	2	26	.223	126	223	20	.946

†Sold to Philadephia Athletics, April 27, 1953.

RECORD AS MANAGER

Year	Club	League	Position	W.	L.	Year	Club	League	Position	W.	L.
1961—Auburn	NYP		Eighth	52	73	1963—Idaho Falls	Pion.		First	40	17
1962—Idaho Falls	Pion.		Sixth	20	40	(Second Half)			Third	37	32
(Second Half)			Fifth	32	38	1964—Greensboro	Carol.		Second(W)	76	61

Year Club	League	Position	W.	L.	Year Club	League	Position	W.	L.
1965—Columbus	South.	First	79	59	1975—Denver	A.A.	‡First(W)	81	55
1966—Toledo	Int.	Sixth	71	75	1976—Iowa	A.A.	§Second(E)	68	68
1971—Syracuse	Int.	†Fourth	73	67					

†Lost playoff to Rochester, three games to one.
‡Lost championship playoff to Evansville, four games to two.
§One tie.
Coach, New York Yankees, 1967; scout, New York Yankees, 1968 through 1970 and 1972 through 1974; special assignment scout, Chicago White Sox, 1977 through 1979; coach, Chicago White Sox, 1980 and 1981.

ROMANUS BASGALL
(Monty)
Los Angeles Dodgers

Born, February 8, 1923, at Pfeifer, Kan.
Height, 5.10½. Weight, 185.
Threw and batted righthanded.
Hobbies—Hunting and fishing.
Attended Sterling College, Sterling, Kan.

Led Pacific Coast League in sacrifice hits with 27 in 1952.

Year Club	League	Pos.	G.	AB.	R.	H.	2B.	3B.	HR.	RBI.	B.A.	PO.	A.	E.	F.A.
1942—Valdosta............	Ga.-Fla.	2B	126	502	71	127	14	7	1	65	.253	427	502	35	.964
1943-44-45—Durham	Pied.				(In Military Service)										
1946—Fort Worth........	Texas	2B-P	155	545	60	123	22	2	1	45	.226	432	457	41	.956
1947—Fort Worth†	Texas	2B-SS	153	599	75	163	30	5	3	71	.272	460	422	30	.967
1948—Pittsburgh...........	Nat.	2B	38	51	12	11	1	0	2	6	.216	37	35	0	1.000
1948—New Orleans	South.	2B	23	94	25	34	9	1	1	12	.362	51	66	2	.983
1949—Pittsburgh.........	Nat.	2B-3B	107	308	25	67	9	1	2	26	.218	224	225	13	.972
1950—Indianapolis	A.A.	2B	133	462	63	130	29	4	13	58	.281	331	286	25	.961
1951—Pittsburgh.........	Nat.	2B	55	153	15	32	5	2	0	9	.209	140	144	9	.969
1951—Indianapolis	A.A.	SS	37	106	15	27	5	1	1	13	.255	42	73	11	.913
1952—Hollywood	P.C.	2B	149	578	89	161	22	0	8	63	.279	379	345	24	.968
1953—Hollywood	P.C.	2B	162	578	63	144	28	4	10	77	.249	417	429	*31	.965
1954—Hollywood	P.C.	2B	145	457	57	115	18	1	4	59	.252	356	16	.977	
1955—Seattle‡...........	P.C.	2B-3B	132	420	59	103	25	1	8	42	.245	266	297	25	.957
1956—Waco§	Big St.	2B	54	154	20	50	8	0	4	24	.325	86	94	12	.938
1957—Beaumont§........	Big St.	2B	36	80	10	27	4	1	0	17	.338	55	52	3	.973
1958—Lincoln§............	West.	INF	6	10	1	2	1	0	0	2	.200	figures unavailable			
Major League Totals			200	512	52	110	15	3	4	41	.215	401	404	22	.973

†Drafted from Montreal (Brooklyn Dodgers' organization) by Pittsburgh Pirates, December 3, 1947.
‡Released, September 19, 1955.
§Player-manager.

RECORD AS PITCHER

Year Club	League	G.	IP.	W.	L.	Pct.	H.	R.	ER.	SO.	BB.	ERA.
1946—Fort Worth.........................Texas		1	1	0	0	.000	3	4	2	1	1	18.00

RECORD AS MANAGER

Year Club	League	Position	W.	L.	Year Club	League	Position	W.	L.
1956—Waco..................	Big St.	†Second	78	62	1958—Lincoln...............	West.	Third	75	71
1957—Beaumont...........	Big St.	Fourth	31	33	1971—Albuquerque	Tex.	Third(W)	67	75
(Second Half)		Second	30	30	1972—El Paso‡	Tex.	Second(W)	33	31

†Tied for position with Port Arthur.
‡Replaced by Stan Wasiak, June 22, 1972.
Scout, Los Angeles Dodgers, 1959 through 1970, and from July 20, 1972 through the end of the season; coach, Los Angeles Dodgers, 1973 through 1981.

LAWRENCE PETER BERRA SR.
(Yogi)

(Named by boyhood pals on The Hill, the heavily-populated Italian section of St. Louis. A Yogi was considered an odd character— later in life the term grew to one of affection.)

New York Yankees

Born May 12, 1925, at St. Louis, Mo.
Height, 5.08. Weight, 191.
Threw right and batted lefthanded.
Hobby—Sports.
Father of Larry Berra, Jr., former catcher in New York Mets' organization, Tim Berra, former wide receiver with New York Giants and Baltimore Colts, and Dale Berra, third baseman in Pittsburgh Pirates' organization.

Established major league records for most years leading league in games as catcher (8); most years leading league in chances accepted by catcher (8); most consecutive errorless games, catcher (148) and most consecutive chances accepted, no errors (950), July 28, 1957 (second game), to May 10, 1959 (second game).

Tied major league record for most years leading league in double plays, catcher (6); most unassisted double plays by catcher, lifetime (2).

Established American League record for most home runs by catcher, lifetime (313).

Tied American League record for most home runs by catcher, season (30), 1952 and 1956.

Led American League catchers in double plays with 18 in 1949, 16 in 1950, 25 in 1951, 10 in 1952, 14 in 1954 and 15 in 1956.

Led American League catchers in passed balls with 7 in 1950.

Named American League Most Valuable Player, 1951-54-55.

Named catcher on THE SPORTING NEWS Major League All-Star Teams, 1950-52-54-56.

Elected to Hall of Fame, 1972.

Year Club	League	Pos.	G.	AB.	R.	H.	2B.	3B.	HR.	RBI.	B.A.	PO.	A.	E.	F.A.
1943–Norfolk	Pied.	C	111	376	52	95	17	8	7	56	.253	*480	75	*16	.972
1944-45–Kansas City	A. A.						(In Military Service)								
1946–Newark	Int.	C-OF	77	277	41	87	14	1	15	59	.314	344	45	11	.973
1946–New York	Amer.	C	7	22	3	8	1	0	2	4	.364	28	6	0	1.000
1947–New York	Amer.	C-OF	83	293	41	82	15	3	11	54	.280	307	18	9	.973
1948–New York	Amer.	C-OF	125	469	70	143	24	10	14	98	.305	390	40	9	.979
1949–New York	Amer.	C	116	415	59	115	20	2	20	91	.277	544	60	7	.989
1950–New York	Amer.	C	151	597	116	192	30	6	28	124	.322	*777	•64	13	.985
1951–New York	Amer.	C	141	547	92	161	19	4	27	88	.294	*693	*82	•13	.984
1952–New York	Amer.	C	142	534	97	146	17	1	30	98	.273	*700	*73	6	.992
1953–New York	Amer.	C	137	503	80	149	23	5	27	108	.296	566	64	9	.986
1954–New York	Amer.	*C-3B	151	584	88	179	28	6	22	125	.307	*718	64	8	.990
1955–New York	Amer.	C	147	541	84	147	20	3	27	108	.272	*721	54	*13	.984
1956–New York	Amer.	*C-OF	140	521	93	155	29	2	30	105	.298	*733	57	*11	.986
1957–New York	Amer.	*C-OF	134	482	74	121	14	2	24	82	.251	*707	61	4	*.995
1958–New York	Amer.	*C-OF-1	122	433	60	115	17	3	22	90	.266	558	44	2	*.997
1959–New York	Amer.	*C-OF	131	472	64	134	25	1	19	69	.284	*706	62	4	*.995
1960–New York	Amer.	C-OF	120	359	46	99	14	1	15	62	.276	312	24	5	.985
1961–New York	Amer.	OF-C	119	395	62	107	11	0	22	61	.271	237	15	2	.992
1962–New York	Amer.	C-OF	86	232	25	52	8	0	10	35	.224	238	17	6	.977
1963–New York†	Amer.	C	64	147	20	43	6	0	8	28	.293	244	13	3	.988
1964–New York‡	Amer.					(Did not play–served as manager.)									
1965–New York	Nat.	C	4	9	1	2	0	0	0	0	.222	15	1	1	.941
American League Totals			2116	7546	1174	2148	321	49	358	1430	.285	9179	818	124	.988
National League Totals			4	9	1	2	0	0	0	0	.222	15	1	1	.941
Major League Totals			2120	7555	1175	2150	321	49	358	1430	.285	9194	819	125	.988

†Player-coach.

‡Released by New York Yankees, October 16, 1964; signed as coach with New York Mets, November 17, 1964.

WORLD SERIES RECORD

Established World Series records for most Series played (14); most Series played, one club (14); most games (75); most games one club (75); most times on winning team (10); most at bats, total Series (259); most hits, total Series (71); most hits, total Series, one club (71); most one-base hits, total Series (49); most Series, one or more runs batted in (11); most Series, one or more runs (12); most Series, one or more bases on balls (13); most Series played by catcher (12); most games caught, total Series (63); most consecutive errorless games by catcher (30); most putouts by catcher, total Series (421); most assists by catcher, total Series (36); most chances accepted by catcher, total Series (457).

Tied World Series records for most consecutive Series played (5), 1949 through 1953; most Series, one or more hits (12); most Series, one or more home runs (9); most times hit by pitch, total Series (3); most double plays by catcher, total Series (6); most two-base hits, total Series (10); one or more hits, each game of seven-game Series, 1955; most positions played, Series (3), 1960 (left field, right field and catcher); most home runs as pinch-hitter, game (1), October 2, 1947 (first player to hit pinch-hit home run); most times hit by pitch, game (2), October 2, 1953; most home runs with bases filled, game (1), October 5, 1956; most runs batted in, inning (4), October 5, 1956; fewest putouts by catcher, game (1), October 3, 1952 and October 10, 1956.

Year Club	League	Pos.	G.	AB.	R.	H.	2B.	3B.	HR.	RBI.	B.A.	PO.	A.	E.	F.A.
1947–New York	Amer.	C-OF	6	19	2	3	0	0	1	2	.158	21	2	2	.920
1949–New York	Amer.	C	4	16	2	1	0	0	0	1	.063	37	3	0	1.000
1950–New York	Amer.	C	4	15	2	3	0	0	1	2	.200	30	1	0	1.000
1951–New York	Amer.	C	6	23	4	6	1	0	0	0	.261	27	3	1	.968
1952–New York	Amer.	C	7	28	2	6	1	0	2	3	.214	59	7	1	.985
1953–New York	Amer.	C	6	21	3	9	1	0	1	4	.429	36	3	0	1.000
1955–New York	Amer.	C	7	24	5	10	1	0	1	2	.417	40	4	0	1.000
1956–New York	Amer.	C	7	25	5	9	2	0	3	10	.360	50	3	0	1.000
1957–New York	Amer.	C	7	25	5	8	1	0	1	2	.320	44	2	1	.979
1958–New York	Amer.	C	7	27	3	6	3	0	0	2	.222	60	6	0	1.000
1960–New York	Amer.	C-OF-PH	7	22	6	7	0	0	1	8	.318	18	1	0	1.000
1961–New York	Amer.	OF	4	11	2	3	0	0	1	3	.273	11	0	1	.917
1962–New York	Amer.	C	2	2	0	0	0	0	0	0	.000	6	1	0	1.000
1963–New York	Amer.	PH	1	1	0	0	0	0	0	0	.000	0	0	0	.000
World Series Totals			75	259	41	71	10	0	12	39	.274	439	36	6	.988

ALL-STAR GAME RECORD

Established All-Star Game records for most games played by catcher (14); most putouts by catcher, total games (61); most assists by catcher, total games (7); most chances accepted by catcher, total games (68).

Tied All-Star Game records for most putouts by catcher, game (10), July 10, 1956; most assists by catcher, game (2), July 10, 1951 and July 12, 1955 (11 innings); most chances accepted by catcher, game (11), July 10, 1956.

Year League	Pos.	AB	R	H	2B	3B	HR	RBI	B.A.	PO	A	E	F.A.
1949—American	C	3	0	0	0	0	0	0	.000	2	1	0	1.000
1950—American	C	2	0	0	0	0	0	0	.000	2	0	0	1.000
1951—American	C	4	1	1	0	0	0	0	.250	4	2	1	.857
1952—American	C	2	0	0	0	0	0	0	.000	6	0	0	1.000
1953—American	C	4	0	0	0	0	0	0	.000	4	0	0	1.000
1954—American	C	4	2	2	0	0	0	0	.500	5	0	0	1.000
1955—American	C	6	1	1	0	0	0	0	.167	8	2	0	1.000
1956—American	C	2	0	2	0	0	0	0	1.000	10	1	0	1.000
1957—American	C	3	0	1	0	0	0	1	.333	6	0	0	1.000
1958—American	C	2	0	0	0	0	0	0	.000	3	0	0	1.000
1959—American (second game)	C	3	1	1	0	0	1	2	.333	2	0	0	1.000
1960—American (both games)	C	4	0	0	0	0	0	0	.000	9	1	0	1.000
1961—American (first game)	C	1	0	0	0	0	0	0	.000	0	0	0	.000
1962—American (second game)	PH	1	0	0	0	0	0	0	.000	0	0	0	.000
All-Star Game Totals		41	5	8	0	0	1	3	.195	61	7	1	.986

Member of American League All-Star Team in 1948, 1959 (first game) and 1961 (second game); did not play.

RECORD AS MANAGER

One of three managers to represent both leagues as manager in World Series, New York (American), 1964 and New York (National), 1973.

Year Club	League	Position	W.	L.
1964—New York	Amer.	First	99	63
1972—New York	Nat.	Third(E)	83	73
1973—New York	Nat.	First(E)	82	79
1974—New York	Nat.	Fifth(E)	71	91
1975—New York†	Nat.	Third (E)	56	53
American League Totals			99	63
National League Totals			292	296
Major League Totals			391	359

†Replaced by Roy McMillan, August 5.
Coach, New York Mets, 1965 through 1971; New York Yankees, 1976 through 1981.
Manager, National League All-Star Team, 1974.

CHAMPIONSHIP SERIES RECORD					WORLD SERIES RECORD				
Year Club	League		W.	L.	Year Club	League		W.	L.
1973—New York	National		3	2	1964—New York	American		3	4
					1973—New York	National		3	4

CLETIS LE ROY BOYER
(Clete)
Oakland A's

Born February 9, 1937, at Cassville, Mo.
Height, 6.00. Weight, 183.
Threw and batted righthanded.
Brother of Cloyd Boyer, coach with Atlanta Braves and Ken Boyer, scout with St. Louis Cardinals.

Named third baseman on THE SPORTING NEWS National League All-Star fielding team, 1969.
Led American League third basemen in double plays with 41 in 1962 and with 46 in 1965.

Year Club	League	Pos.	G.	AB.	R.	H.	2B.	3B.	HR.	RBI.	B.A.	PO.	A.	E.	F.A.
1955—Kansas City	Amer.	INF	47	79	3	19	1	0	0	6	.241	32	41	3	.961
1956—Kansas City	Amer.	2B-3B	67	129	15	28	3	1	1	4	.217	100	124	6	.974
1957—Kansas City†	Amer.	2B-3B	10	0	0	0	0	0	0	0	.000	0	0	0	.000
1957—Binghamton	East.	SS	93	325	44	79	15	2	12	48	.243	191	249	21	.954
1958—Richmond	Int.	SS	132	500	82	142	25	7	22	71	.284	*222	*371	28	.955
1959—Richmond	Int.	SS-3B	64	228	31	51	6	1	12	36	.224	102	201	17	.947
1959—New York	Amer.	SS-3B	47	114	4	20	2	0	0	3	.175	49	90	2	.986
1960—New York	Amer.	3B-SS	124	393	54	95	20	1	14	46	.242	157	297	17	.964
1961—New York	Amer.	*3-S-O	148	504	61	113	19	5	11	55	.224	170	*373	17	.970
1962—New York	Amer.	3B	158	566	85	154	24	1	18	68	.272	*187	*396	22	.964
1963—New York	Amer.	INF	152	557	59	140	20	3	12	54	.251	184	344	25	.955
1964—New York	Amer.	3B-SS	147	510	43	111	10	5	8	52	.218	164	339	16	.969
1965—New York	Amer.	*3B-SS	148	514	69	129	23	6	18	58	.251	137	*354	16	.968
1966—New York‡	Amer.	3B-SS	144	500	59	120	22	4	14	57	.240	201	396	18	.971
1967—Atlanta	Nat.	*3B-SS	154	572	63	140	18	3	26	96	.245	177	309	15	*.970
1968—Atlanta	Nat.	3B	71	273	19	62	7	2	4	17	.227	74	135	4	.981
1969—Atlanta	Nat.	3B	144	496	57	124	16	1	14	57	.250	139	275	15	*.965
1970—Atlanta	Nat.	3B-SS	134	475	44	117	14	1	16	62	.246	113	278	19	.954
1971—Atlanta§	Nat.	3B-SS	30	98	10	24	1	0	6	19	.245	18	57	3	.962
American League Totals			1192	3866	452	929	144	26	96	403	.240	1381	2754	142	.967
National League Totals			533	1914	193	467	56	7	66	251	.244	521	1054	56	.966
Major League Totals			1725	5780	645	1396	200	33	162	654	.242	1902	3808	198	.966

†Traded to New York Yankees with Pitchers Art Ditmar, Bobby Shantz and Jack McMahan and First Baseman Wayne Belardi for Pitchers Walter (Rip) Coleman, Tom Morgan and Maury McDermott, Shortstop Billy Hunter, Second Baseman Milt Graff and Outfielder Irv Noren. Boyer included in deal, February 19, 1957—but voided by Commissioner Ford Frick, who ruled he must complete his bonus term with Athletics. Cletis transferred to Yanks, June 4, 1957, and assigned to Binghamton (Eastern League) farm club.

‡Traded with player to be named later to Atlanta Braves for Outfielder Bill Robinson and Pitcher Chi-Chi Olivo (transferred from Richmond to Syracuse), November 29, 1966.
§Released, December 30, 1971.
Minor league instructor, Atlanta Braves, 1978 and 1979; coach Oakland A's, 1980 and 1981.

CHAMPIONSHIP SERIES RECORD

Year Club	League	Pos.	G.	AB.	R.	H.	2B.	3B.	HR.	RBI.	B.A.	PO.	A.	E.	F.A.
1969—Atlanta	Nat.	3B	3	9	0	1	0	0	0	3	.111	4	8	1	.923

WORLD SERIES RECORD

Established World Series record for most assists by third baseman, total Series (65).
Tied World Series records for most double plays started, game, third baseman (2), October 12, 1960; most times at bat, nine-inning game (6), October 12, 1960.

Year Club	League	Pos.	G.	AB.	R.	H.	2B.	3B.	HR.	RBI.	B.A.	PO.	A.	E.	F.A.
1960—New York	Amer.	3B-SS	4	12	1	3	2	1	0	1	.250	0	8	0	1.000
1961—New York	Amer.	3B	5	15	0	4	2	0	0	3	.267	6	12	1	.947
1962—New York	Amer.	3B	7	22	2	7	1	0	1	4	.318	9	16	2	.926
1963—New York	Amer.	3B	4	13	0	1	0	0	0	0	.077	2	8	0	1.000
1964—New York	Amer.	3B	7	24	2	5	1	0	1	3	.208	5	22	2	.931
World Series Totals........................			27	86	5	20	6	1	2	11	.233	22	66	5	.946

CLOYD VICTOR BOYER
Atlanta Braves

Born September 1, 1927, at Alba, Mo.
Height, 6.01. Weight, 188.
Threw and batted righthanded.
Hobbies—Hunting and fishing.
Brother of Ken Boyer, scout with St. Louis Cardinals, and Clete Boyer, former third baseman with Kansas City, New York Yankees, and Atlanta, 1955-71 and coach with Oakland A's.

Year Club	League	G.	IP.	W.	L.	Pct.	H.	R.	ER.	SO.	BB.	ERA.
1945—Lynchburg	Piedmont	2	2	0	0	.000	6	7	7	2	7	31.50
1945—Johnson City	Ap'alachian	13	72	4	7	.364	70	56	40	55	49	5.00
1945-46—Johnson City	Ap'alachian					(In Military Service)						
1946—Carthage	K-O-M	5	26	3	1	.750	25	....	12	35	24	4.15
1947—Duluth	Northern	32	∗228	16	9	.640	199	89	62	∗239	106	2.45
1948—Houston	Texas	30	223	16	10	.615	191	97	78	∗188	126	3.15
1949—Rochester	Int'national	31	190	15	10	.600	147	77	66	143	110	3.13
1949—St. Louis	National	4	3	0	0	.000	5	4	4	0	7	12.00
1950—St. Louis	National	36	120	7	7	.500	105	52	47	82	49	3.53
1951—Columbus...........................	Am. Assoc.	5	40	2	3	.400	29	12	9	44	22	2.03
1951—St. Louis	National	19	63	2	5	.286	68	42	37	40	46	5.29
1952—St. Louis	National	23	110	6	6	.500	108	56	52	44	47	4.25
1953—Houston	Texas	28	65	4	2	.667	64	26	20	31	3	2.77
1954—Rochester	Int'national	12	30	0	0	.000	....	....	....	21	24	4.50
1954—Columbus†	Am. Assoc.	10	39	2	3	.400	41	18	16	20	20	3.69
1955—Kansas City	American	30	98	5	5	.500	107	81	68	32	66	6.24
1956—Sacramento	P. Coast	26	164	10	9	.526	173	91	72	64	77	3.95
1957—Sacramento‡.......................	P. Coast	11	42	1	4	.200	53	36	25	18	24	5.31
1957—Indianapolis	Am. Assoc.	26	90	6	4	.600	93	42	37	35	41	3.70
1958—Indianapolis	Am. Assoc.	28	182	13	8	.619	171	79	60	83	67	2.97
1959—Indianapolis	Am. Assoc.	34	202	10	14	.417	186	95	74	85	59	3.30
1960—Indianapolis	Am. Assoc.	32	209	12	8	.600	215	100	90	78	65	3.88
1961—Indianapolis	Am. Assoc.	29	61	3	5	.375	83	59	46	17	36	6.79
National League Totals.....................		82	296	15	18	.454	286	154	140	166	149	4.26
American League Totals.....................		30	98	5	5	.500	107	81	68	32	66	6.24
Major League Totals		112	394	20	23	.465	393	235	208	198	215	4.75

†Drafted by Kansas City A's, November 22, 1954.
‡Sold to Indianapolis (Chicago White Sox' organization), June 6, 1957.

RECORD AS MANAGER

Year Club	League	Position	W.	L.	Year Club	League	Position	W.	L.
1962—Shelby†	W. Carol.	Third	21	30	1968—Binghamton§	East.	Fourth	67	72
1963—Ft. Lauderdale‡ ..	Fla. St.	Third	31	28					

†Replaced Joe Abernethy for second half of season, June 26, 1962.
‡Replaced Steve Souchock for second half of season, June 30, 1963.
§Replaced Frank Verdi, June 14, 1968.
Coach, Richmond (New York Yankees' organization), 1962; New York Yankees' minor league pitching coach, 1963-64, 74-76; Scout, New York Yankees, 1964-74; Coach, New York Yankees, 1977; Atlanta Braves, 1978 through 1981.

EDWIN ALBERT BRINKMAN
(Ed)
San Diego Padres

Born December 8, 1941, at Cincinnati, O.
Height, 6.00. Weight, 171.
Threw and batted righthanded.
Hobby—Sports.

Attended University of Cincinnati, Cincinnati, O.
Brother of Chuck Brinkman, catcher in Pittsburgh Pirates' organization.

Established major league records for fewest errors, shortstop, season, 150 or more games (7), 1972; most consecutive errorless games, shortstop, season (72), May 21 through August 4, 1972; most consecutive chances accepted, no errors, shortstop, season (331), 1972.

Tied major league records for fewest stolen bases, season, 150 or more games (0), 1972; fewest caught stealing, season, 150 or more games (0), 1972.

Established American League records for fewest total bases, season, 150 or more games (114), 1965; fewest hits, season, 150 or more games (82), 1965; highest fielding average, shortstop, season (.990), 1972.

Tied American League record for most games, season, shortstop (162), 1973.

Led American League shortstops in double plays with 97 in 1963 and with 103 in 1970.

Named shortstop on THE SPORTING NEWS American League All-Star fielding team, 1972.

Received reported $65,000 bonus to sign with Washington Senators, 1961.

Year	Club	League	Pos.	G.	AB.	R.	H.	2B.	3B.	HR.	RBI.	B.A.	PO.	A.	E.	F.A.
1961—Pensacola		Al.-Fla.	3B-2B	53	210	32	61	14	2	2	26	.290	92	127	7	.969
1961—Middlesboro		Appal.	SS-3B	7	26	12	13	3	1	3	8	.500	9	19	2	.933
1961—Washington		Amer.	3B	4	11	0	1	0	0	0	0	.091	2	6	1	.889
1962—Raleigh		Carol.	SS-3B	58	222	49	72	14	7	6	45	.324	81	153	20	.921
1962—Washington		Amer.	SS-3B	54	133	8	22	7	1	0	4	.165	71	96	9	.949
1963—Washington		Amer.	SS	145	514	44	117	20	3	7	45	.228	241	462	*37	.950
1964—Washington		Amer.	SS	132	447	54	100	20	3	8	34	.224	234	364	19	.969
1965—Washington		Amer.	SS	154	444	35	82	13	2	5	35	.185	292	369	25	.964
1966—Washington		Amer.	SS	158	582	42	133	18	9	7	48	.229	263	501	28	.965
1967—Washington		Amer.	SS	109	320	21	60	9	2	1	18	.188	160	309	10	*.979
1968—Washington		Amer.	SS-2-OF	77	193	12	36	3	0	0	6	.187	97	198	11	.964
1969—Washington		Amer.	SS	151	576	71	153	18	5	2	43	.266	248	511	19	.976
1970—Washington		Amer.	SS	158	625	63	164	17	2	1	40	.262	*301	*569	23	.974
1971—Detroit		Amer.	SS	159	527	40	120	18	2	1	37	.228	235	*513	15	.980
1972—Detroit		Amer.	SS	*156	516	42	105	19	1	6	49	.203	233	495	7	•.990
1973—Detroit		Amer.	SS	•162	515	55	122	16	4	7	40	.237	249	480	24	.968
1974—Detroit‡§		Amer.	SS-3B	153	502	55	111	15	3	14	54	.221	239	498	21	.972
1975—St. Louis x		Nat.	SS	28	75	6	18	4	0	1	6	.240	40	69	6	.948
1975—Tex.y-N.Y.z		Amer.	SS-3-2	45	65	2	11	4	1	0	2	.169	31	60	6	.938
American League Totals				1817	5970	544	1337	197	38	59	455	.224	2896	5431	255	.970
National League Totals				28	75	6	18	4	0	1	6	.240	40	69	6	.948
Major League Totals				1845	6045	550	1355	201	38	60	461	.224	2936	5500	261	.970

†Traded with Third Baseman Aurelio Rodriguez and Pitchers Joe Coleman and Jim Hannan to Detroit Tigers for Pitchers Denny McLain and Norm McRae, Third Baseman Don Wert and Infielder-Outfielder Elliott Maddox, October 9, 1970.

‡Traded with Outfielder Dick Sharon and Pitcher Bob Strampe to San Diego Padres for First Baseman Nate Colbert, November 18, 1974.

§Traded with a player to be named later by San Diego Padres to St. Louis Cardinals for Pitchers Rich Folkers, Alan Foster and Sonny Siebert, November 18, 1974; Padres assigned Catcher Denny Breeden to Cardinals, December 10, 1974, to complete deal.

xTraded with Pitcher Tommy Moore to Texas Rangers for Outfielder Willie Davis, June 4, 1975.

ySold to New York Yankees, June 13, 1975.

zReleased, March 29, 1976.

CHAMPIONSHIP SERIES RECORD

Year	Club	League	Pos.	G.	AB.	R.	H.	2B.	3B.	HR.	RBI.	B.A.	PO.	A.	E.	F.A.
1972—Detroit		Amer.	SS	1	4	0	1	1	0	0	0	.250	1	2	0	1.000

ALL-STAR GAME RECORD

Year	League	Pos.	AB.	R.	H.	2B.	3B.	HR.	RBI.	B.A.	PO.	A.	E.	F.A.
1973—American		SS	1	0	0	0	0	0	0	.000	1	1	0	1.000

RECORD AS MANAGER

Year	Club	League	Position	W.	L.
1977—Montgomery		South	First(W)	45	22
(Second Half)			†First(W)	41	29
1978—Montgomery		South.	Third(W)	32	36
(Second Half)			Fifth	35	41
1980—Lakeland		Fla. St.	Fifth(N)	56	77

†Won Championship Playoffs from Jacksonville, two games to none.
Detroit minor league instructor, 1976; coach, Detroit Tigers, 1979; coach, San Diego Padres, 1981.

JACKIE GENE BROWN
Texas Rangers

Born May 31, 1943 at Holdenville, Okla.
Height, 6.02. Weight, 190.
Threw and batted righthanded.
Hobbies—Golf, fishing and hunting.
Brother of Paul Brown, pitcher for Philadelphia Phillies, 1961 through 1963 and 1968.

Led California League pitchers in games started with 32 in 1965.
Led Pacific Coast League in games started with 28 in 1978.

Year	Club	League	G.	IP.	W.	L.	Pct.	H.	R.	ER.	SO.	BB.	ERA.
1962—Miami†		Florida St.	7	10	0	1	.000	13	10	7	12	8	6.30
1963—Spartanburg‡		W. Carol.	19	101	5	10	.333	109	66	52	100	47	4.63

Year Club	League	G.	IP.	W.	L.	Pct.	H.	R.	ER.	SO.	BB.	ERA.
1964–Bakersfield ....California	6	26	1	1	.500	33	23	19	17	13	6.58
1964–Miami..................................Florida St.	23	152	8	10	.444	118	55	34	124	61	2.01
1965–Bakersfield ....California	33	236	15	11	.577	*228	117	96	214	110	3.66
1966–Macon ....Southern	24	95	3	5	.375	87	60	51	91	63	4.83
1967–Tidewater§........................Carolina	17	73	5	5	.500	62	33	31	53	26	3.82
1968–Tidewater x-Burlington........Carolina	24	61	2	4	.333	55	34	27	79	34	3.98
1968–Savannah ....Southern	5	21	3	1	.750	19	11	8	19	8	3.43
1969–Savannah ....Southern	24	142	9	7	.563	119	50	41	103	70	2.60
1970–Denver ....Am. Assoc.	12	71	6	1	.857	68	24	20	56	27	2.54
1970–Washington ....American	24	57	2	2	.500	49	28	25	47	37	3.95
1971–Denver ....Am. Assoc.	14	91	6	4	.600	90	47	40	85	40	3.96
1971–Washington ....American	14	47	3	4	.429	60	34	31	21	27	5.94
1972–Denver ....Am. Assoc.	32	165	6	*17	.261	*212	*120	*101	128	60	5.51
1973–Spokane............................P. Coast	19	96	10	1	.909	76	28	25	84	44	2.34
1973–Texas ....American	25	67	5	5	.500	82	31	29	45	25	3.90
1974–Texas y..............................American	35	217	13	12	.520	219	97	86	134	74	3.57
1975–Texas z-Cleveland ....American	42	140	6	7	.462	142	77	66	76	64	4.24
1976–Cleveland ....American	32	180	9	11	.450	193	94	85	104	55	4.25
1977–Montreal b ....National	42	186	9	12	.429	189	99	93	89	71	4.50
1978–Tucson ....P. Coast	29	*203	12	10	.545	*256	*140	115	103	74	5.10
American League Totals............................	172	708	38	41	.481	745	361	322	427	282	4.09
National League Totals..............................	42	186	9	12	.429	189	99	93	89	71	4.50
Major League Totals	214	894	47	53	.470	934	460	415	516	353	4.18

†On temporary inactive list, May 25 to August 7, 1962.
‡On disabled list, June 11 to July 18, 1963.
§On disabled list, May 5 to May 31; on temporary inactive list, July 15 to July 28, 1967.
xReleased by Philadelphia Phillies' organization, May 16, 1968; signed as free agent by Washington Senators' organization, May 17, 1968.
yOn temporary inactive list from beginning of season until April 29, 1974.
zTraded with Pitchers Jim Bibby and Rick Waits and an estimated $100,000 to Cleveland Indians for Pitcher Gaylord Perry, June 12, 1975.
aTraded to Montreal Expos for First Baseman Andre Thornton, December 10, 1976.
bReleased, January 27, 1978; signed by Tucson (Texas Rangers' organization), March 1, 1978.
Coach, Texas Rangers, 1979 through 1981.

WILLIAM JAMES BROWN
(Gates)
Detroit Tigers

Born May 2, 1939, at Crestline, O.
Height, 5.11. Weight, 220.
Threw right and batted lefthanded.
Hobby–Sports in general.

Tied major league record for most home runs, consecutive at bats, pinch-hitter (2), August 9 and 11, 1968.
Established American League records for most hits, pinch-hitter, lifetime (107); most home runs by pinch-hitter, lifetime (16).
Hit home run as pinch-hitter first time at bat in majors, June 19, 1963.

Year Club League	Pos.	G.	AB.	R.	H.	2B.	3B.	HR.	RBI.	B.A.	PO.	A.	E.	F.A.
1960–Duluth-Superior.North.	OF	121	461	104	135	14	*13	10	68	.293	196	12	*15	.933
1961–Knoxville ....Sally	OF	26	96	15	24	4	1	2	19	.250	35	1	0	1.000
1961–Durham ....Carol.	OF	113	432	84	140	33	3	15	72	*.324	144	16	11	.936
1962–Denver..............A.A.	OF	139	523	73	157	25	*14	3	50	.300	197	7	7	.967
1963–Syracuse ....Int.	OF	60	221	38	57	11	2	13	43	.258	101	4	6	.946
1963–Detroit ....Amer.	OF	55	82	16	22	3	1	2	14	.268	35	3	0	1.000
1964–Detroit ....Amer.	OF	123	426	65	116	22	6	15	54	.272	205	4	4	.981
1965–Detroit ....Amer.	OF	96	227	33	58	14	2	10	43	.256	108	1	3	.973
1966–Detroit ....Amer.	OF	88	169	27	45	5	1	7	27	.266	46	4	1	.980
1967–Detroit† ....Amer.	OF	51	91	17	17	1	1	2	9	.187	22	1	0	1.000
1968–Detroit ....Amer.	OF-1B	67	92	15	34	7	2	6	15	.370	21	1	0	1.000
1969–Detroit ....Amer.	OF	60	93	13	19	1	2	1	6	.204	28	1	3	.906
1970–Detroit ....Amer.	OF	81	124	18	28	3	0	3	24	.226	37	1	2	.950
1971–Detroit‡ ....Amer.	OF	82	195	37	66	2	3	11	29	.338	68	2	1	.986
1972–Detroit ....Amer.	OF	103	252	33	58	5	0	10	31	.230	122	5	3	.977
1973–Detroit ....Amer.	OF	125	377	48	89	11	1	12	50	.236	1	0	0	1.000
1974–Detroit ....Amer.	DH	73	99	7	24	2	0	4	17	.242	0	0	0	.000
1975–Detroit§ ....Amer.	PH	47	35	1	6	2	0	1	3	.171	0	0	0	.000
Major League Totals	1051	2262	330	582	78	19	84	322	.257	693	23	17	.977

†Dislocated left wrist crashing into wall; on disabled list from June 30 through August 31, 1967.
‡On disabled list, June 30 through July 24, 1971.
§Placed on voluntarily retired list, October 10, 1975.
Scout, Detroit Tigers, 1976 and 1977; Coach, Detroit Tigers, 1978 through 1981.

CHAMPIONSHIP SERIES RECORD

Year Club League	Pos.	G.	AB.	R.	H.	2B.	3B.	HR.	RBI.	B.A.	PO.	A.	E.	F.A.
1972–Detroit ....Amer.	PH	3	2	1	0	0	0	0	0	.000	0	0	0	.000

WORLD SERIES RECORD

Year Club League	Pos.	G.	AB.	R.	H.	2B.	3B.	HR.	RBI.	B.A.	PO.	A.	E.	F.A.
1968–Detroit ....Amer.	PH	1	1	0	0	0	0	0	0	.000	0	0	0	.000

DONALD ALVIN BUFORD
(Don)
San Francisco Giants

Born February 2, 1937, at Linden, Tex.
Height, 5.07. Weight, 165.
Threw right and batted right and lefthanded.
Hobbies—Chess, reading, home movies.
Attended Los Angeles City College, Los Angeles, Calif., and
University of Southern California, Los Angeles, Calif.

Tied major league record for most strikeouts, nine inning game (5), August 26, 1971.
Tied for Sally League lead in double plays by outfielders with 5 in 1962.
Led International League in stolen bases with 42 in 1963.
Led American League in sacrifice hits with 17 in 1966.
Named Minor League Player of the Year by THE SPORTING NEWS, 1963.

Year—Club	League	Pos.	G.	AB.	R.	H.	2B.	3B.	HR.	RBI.	B.A.	PO.	A.	E.	F.A.
1960—San Diego	P. C.	OF	18	41	6	11	1	0	0	5	.268	18	2	3	.870
1960—Lincoln	I.I.I.	OF	120	433	83	125	21	8	7	53	.289	241	9	12	.954
1961—Charleston	Sally	OF	132	496	76	117	18	7	7	27	.236	284	•19	7	.977
1962—Indianapolis	A. A.	3B-OF	12	27	2	3	1	0	0	1	.111	9	10	0	1.000
1962—Savannah	Sally	OF-3B	111	418	100	135	22	5	6	43	.323	171	79	18	.933
1963—Indianapolis	Int.	•3-IN-O	152	•613	•114	•206	•41	3	9	53	•.336	130	•311	20	.957
1963—Chicago	Amer.	3B-2B	12	42	9	12	1	2	0	5	.286	13	12	2	.926
1964—Chicago	Amer.	2B-3B	135	442	62	116	14	6	4	30	.262	226	261	16	.968
1965—Chicago	Amer.	2B-3B	155	586	93	166	22	5	10	47	.283	339	416	14	.982
1966—Chicago	Amer.	•3-2-OF	•163	607	85	148	26	7	8	52	.244	199	383	•34	.945
1967—Chicago†	Amer.	3-2-OF	156	535	61	129	10	9	4	32	.241	198	349	27	.953
1968—Baltimore	Amer.	OF-2-3B	130	426	65	120	13	4	15	46	.282	239	111	8	.978
1969—Baltimore	Amer.	OF-2-3B	144	554	99	161	31	3	11	64	.291	255	38	6	.979
1970—Baltimore	Amer.	OF-2-3B	144	504	99	137	15	2	17	66	.272	224	19	4	.984
1971—Baltimore	Amer.	OF	122	449	•99	130	19	4	19	54	.290	217	6	3	.987
1972—Baltimore‡	Amer.	OF	125	408	46	84	6	2	5	22	.206	173	6	2	.989
Major League Totals			1286	4553	718	1203	157	44	93	418	.264	2083	1601	116	.969

†Traded with Pitchers Bruce Howard and Roger Nelson to Baltimore Orioles for First Baseman-Outfielder John Matias, Outfielder Russ Snyder and Shortstop Luis Aparicio, November 29, 1967.
‡Sold by Baltimore Orioles to Fukuoka Lions of the Japanese Baseball Association, February 1, 1973.
Coach, San Francisco Giants, 1981.

CHAMPIONSHIP SERIES RECORD

Year—Club	League	Pos.	G.	AB.	R.	H.	2B.	3B.	HR.	RBI.	B.A.	PO.	A.	E.	F.A.
1969—Baltimore	Amer.	OF	3	14	3	4	1	0	0	1	.286	8	0	0	1.000
1970—Baltimore	Amer.	OF	2	7	2	3	1	0	1	3	.429	2	0	0	1.000
1971—Baltimore	Amer.	OF	2	7	1	3	0	1	0	0	.429	1	0	0	1.000
Championship Series Totals			7	28	6	10	2	1	1	4	.357	11	0	0	1.000

WORLD SERIES RECORD

Year—Club	League	Pos.	G.	AB.	R.	H.	2B.	3B.	HR.	RBI.	B.A.	PO.	A.	E.	F.A.
1969—Baltimore	Amer.	OF	5	20	1	2	1	0	2	2	.100	8	0	0	1.000
1970—Baltimore	Amer.	OF	4	15	3	4	0	0	1	1	.267	6	0	0	1.000
1971—Baltimore	Amer.	OF	6	23	3	6	1	0	2	4	.261	13	1	0	1.000
World Series Totals			15	58	7	12	2	0	4	7	.207	27	1	0	1.000

ALL-STAR GAME RECORD

Year—League	Pos.	AB.	R.	H.	2B.	3B.	HR.	RBI.	B.A.	PO.	A.	E.	F.A.
1971—American	PH	1	0	0	0	0	0	0	.000	0	0	0	.000

GALEN BERNARD CISCO
Name pronounced SIS-coe.
Montreal Expos

Born March 7, 1937, at St. Marys, Ohio.
Height, 6.00. Weight, 197.
Threw and batted righthanded.
Hobbies—Hunting and fishing.
Attended Ohio State University, Columbus, O.; received Bachelor
of Science degree in Education.

Led International League in shutouts with 6 in 1968.

Year—Club	League	G.	IP.	W.	L.	Pct.	H.	R.	ER.	SO.	BB.	ERA.
1958—Raleigh	Carolina	14	29	2	2	.500	23	16	14	27	20	4.34
1958—Corning	NYP	18	122	4	10	.286	124	71	53	100	64	3.91
1959—Allentown	Eastern	2	1	0	1	.000	3	2	2	0	1	18.00
1959—Raleigh	Carolina	5	23	2	2	.500	22	17	12	16	18	4.70
1959—Waterloo	Midwest	23	182	15	7	.682	142	63	45	165	62	•2.23
1960—Minneapolis	Am. Assoc.	33	138	3	7	.300	122	54	45	70	45	2.93
1961—Seattle	P. Coast	9	70	6	1	.857	55	20	12	37	20	1.54
1961—Boston	American	17	52	2	4	.333	67	40	39	26	28	6.75
1962—Boston†	American	23	83	4	7	.364	95	66	62	43	50	6.72
1962—New York	National	4	19	1	1	.500	15	7	7	13	11	3.32

Year	Club	League	G.	IP.	W.	L.	Pct.	H.	R.	ER.	SO.	BB.	ERA.
1963—New York		National	51	156	7	15	.318	165	88	75	81	64	4.33
1964—New York		National	36	192	6	19	.240	182	85	77	78	54	3.61
1965—New York		National	35	112	4	8	.333	119	63	56	58	51	4.50
1966—Jacksonville‡-Toronto		Int'national	30	140	11	6	.647	157	71	64	98	40	4.11
1967—Boston		American	11	22	0	1	.000	21	10	9	8	8	3.68
1967—Pittsfield		Eastern	4	11	0	0	.000	5	3	1	7	1	0.82
1967—Toronto		Int'national	10	65	3	5	.375	63	20	15	46	13	2.08
1968—Louisville§		Int'national	29	204	11	12	.478	157	58	50	157	60	*2.21
1969—Omaha		Am. Assoc.	10	63	3	4	.429	77	40	35	42	15	5.00
1969—Kansas City		American	15	22	1	1	.500	17	11	9	18	15	3.68
1970—Omaha		Am. Assoc.	24	76	6	3	.667	63	25	21	49	17	2.49
American League Totals			66	179	7	13	.350	200	127	119	95	101	5.98
National League Totals			126	479	18	43	.295	481	243	215	230	180	4.04
Major League Totals			192	658	25	56	.309	681	370	334	325	281	4.57

†Sold to New York Mets, September 7, 1962.
‡Sold by New York Mets' organization to Boston Red Sox' organization, June 6, 1966.
§Sold by Boston Red Sox' organization to Kansas City Royals' organization, August 14, 1968.
Coach, Kansas City Royals, 1971 through 1979; coach, Montreal Expos, 1980 and 1981.

ELWOOD ROBERT CLEAR
(Bob)
California Angels
Born December 14, 1927, Denver, Colo.

Height, 5.10. Weight, 170.
Threw and batted righthanded.
Hobbies—Fishing and hunting.
Father of John Clear, former outfielder-first baseman in California Angels' organization;
uncle of Mark Clear, pitcher with Boston Red Sox.

Led Far West League Pitchers in complete games with 23 in 1948.
Led Western League in shutouts with 4 in 1950.
Tied for Arizona-Mexico League lead in games started with 31 in 1957.
Led Arizona-Mexico League in complete games with 28 in 1957 and with 22 in 1958.
Tied for Northern League lead in games started with 27 and shutouts with 3 in 1960.
Lead Northern League in complete games with 23 in 1960.

Year	Club	League	G.	IP.	W.	L.	Pct.	H.	R.	ER.	SO.	BB.	ERA.
1946—Bakersfield		California	2	11	1	0	1.000	5	3	....	7	9	......
1948—Fresno		California	3	11	0	1	.000	....	....	....	7	6	......
1948—Willows		Far West	36	*219	17	12	.586	190	125	84	143	102	3.45
1949—Lynchburg		Piedmont	5	12	0	1	.000	....	....	....	4	10	......
1949—Pocatello		Pioneer	24	151	11	6	.647	183	116	98	108	103	5.84
1950—Omaha		Western	31	224	16	7	.696	182	102	84	129	119	3.38
1951—Rochester		Int'national	4	5	0	1	.000	....	....	....	2	4	0.00
1951—Columbus		Am. Assoc.	11	22	0	4	.000	....	....	24	15	23	9.82
1951—Houston		Texas	9	31	1	2	.333	....	....	28	11	18	8.13
1952—Houston		Texas	35	193	9	12	.429	177	86	74	84	102	3.44
1953—Houston		Texas	40	113	4	6	.400	100	53	42	79	69	3.35
1954—Omaha		Western	39	267	*20	11	.645	236	107	87	145	114	2.93
1955—Omaha		Am. Assoc.	27	57	1	10	.091	51	34	28	39	33	4.42
1956—Omaha		Am. Assoc.	3	7	0	0	.000	....	....	....	....	....	6.00
1956—Sioux City§		Western	22	78	5	4	.556	95	56	52	60	44	6.00
1957—Douglas§		Ariz.-Mex.	37	268	●20	11	.645	251	133	108	228	83	3.63
1958—Douglas§		Ariz.-Mex.	30	216	18	8	*.692	227	132	106	193	84	4.42
1959—Idaho Falls§		Pioneer	26	176	13	8	.619	156	82	55	189	45	2.81
1960—Grand Forks§x		Northern	27	*216	*21	6	.778	*193	83	60	●183	64	2.50
1961—Grand Forks§		Northern	12	66	4	5	.444	81	60	37	50	35	5.05
1967—Clinton§		Midwest	2	11	1	0	1.000	6	2	2	12	2	1.64

RECORD AS INFIELDER

Year	Club	League	Pos.	G.	AB.	R.	H.	2B.	3B.	HR.	RBI.	B.A.	PO.	A.	E.	F.A.
1945—Batavia		Pony	SS-3B	119	472	80	105	27	2	0	46	.222	184	367	70	.887
1946—Bakersfield†		Calif.	3B	66	218	31	58	13	0	0	20	.266	58	118	34	.838
1947—Decatur‡		I.I.I.	3B-2B	64	231	24	48	7	1	5	30	.208	47	108	16	.906
1947—Lynchburg		Pied.		16	45	3	9	1	1	0	8	.200	....	....	....	......
1965—Kinston§		Carol.	....	2	3	0	1	0	0	0	1	.333	....	....	....	......

†On temporary inactive list, June through September, 1946.
‡On disabled list, July 22 through July 31, 1947.
§Player-manager.
xOn disabled list, July 2 through July 12, 1960.

RECORD AS MANAGER

Year	Club	League	Position	W.	L.	Year	Club	League	Position	W.	L.
1956—Sioux City†		Western	Eighth	18	36	1959—Idaho Falls		Pioneer	Third	64	65
	(Second Half)		Eighth	27	43	1960—Grand Forks		Northern	Fifth	61	62
1957—Douglas		Ariz.-Mex.	Fourth	32	36	1961—Grand Forks		Northern	Fourth	60	66
	(Second Half)		Third	36	33	1962—Batavia		N.Y.P.	Fifth	51	67
1958—Douglas		Ariz.-Mex.	First	68	52	1963—Gastonia		‡W. Carol.	Second	31	26
							(Second Half)		Second	42	26

Year	Club	League	Position	W.	L.
1964—Gastonia............	W. Carol.	Eighth	24	39
(Second Half)§			Third	8	7
1964—Asheville	Southern	Eighth	24	33
1965—Kinston	Carolina	Third(E)	72	71
1966—Gastonia............	W. Carol.	Fifth	34	31
(Second Half)			Third	33	26
1967—Clinton	Midwest	xSixth	27	31
(Second Half)			Tenth	24	38
1968—Clinton	Midwest	Sixth	28	32
(Second Half)			xEighth	26	35
1969—Geneva...............	N.Y.P.	Eighth	27	46
1970—Idaho Falls	Pioneer	First	44	26
1971—Idaho Falls	Pioneer	Third	36	34
1972—Idaho Falls	Pioneer	Fourth	27	45
1973—Idaho Falls	Pioneer	Fourth	23	48

†Replaced Harold Olt, May 16, 1956.
‡Lost playoff to Greenville, two games to none.
§Promoted to Asheville, July 9, 1964.
xTied for position.
Scout, California Angels, 1969 through 1975; coach, California Angels, July 23, 1976 through 1981.

EUGENE ANTHONY CLINES
(Gene)
Chicago Cubs

Born October 6, 1946, at San Pablo, Calif.
Height, 5.09. Weight, 170.
Threw and batted righthanded.
Hobby—Collecting records.

Led Eastern League in stolen bases with 63 in 1969 and 32 in 1970.

Year Club	League	Pos.	G.	AB.	R.	H.	2B.	3B.	HR.	RBI.	B.A.	PO.	A.	E.	F.A.
1966—Salem	Appal.	OF-3	52	176	37	*63	6	●4	1	28	.358	47	30	10	.885
1967—Raleigh†	Carol.	O-3-2B	83	290	34	75	7	4	4	29	.259	111	102	20	.914
1968—York	East.	*OF-3B	137	*494	46	119	12	2	4	33	.241	209	*31	10	.960
1969—York	East.	*3B-2-O	135	470	86	126	10	8	5	47	.268	*153	*224	39	.906
1970—Waterbury........	East.	OF	95	371	62	115	19	3	6	42	.310	233	●15	5	.980
1970—Pittsburgh........	Nat.	OF	31	37	4	15	2	0	0	3	.405	4	0	0	1.000
1971—Pittsburgh........	Nat.	OF	97	273	52	84	12	4	1	24	.308	146	8	3	.981
1972—Pittsburgh........	Nat.	OF	107	311	52	104	15	6	0	17	.334	131	7	6	.958
1973—Pittsburgh‡	Nat.	OF	110	304	42	80	11	3	1	23	.263	145	6	5	.968
1974—Pittsburgh§	Nat.	OF	107	276	29	62	5	1	0	14	.225	177	6	2	.989
1975—New York x	Nat.	OF	82	203	25	46	6	3	0	10	.227	98	9	2	.982
1976—Texas y	Amer.	OF	116	446	52	123	12	3	0	38	.276	215	9	3	.987
1977—Chicago z	Nat.	OF	101	239	27	70	12	2	3	41	.293	68	3	1	.986
1978—Chicago	Nat.	OF	109	229	31	59	10	2	0	17	.258	84	6	2	.978
1979—Chicago a..........	Nat.	PH	10	10	0	2	0	0	0	0	.200	0	0	0	.000
American League Totals..................			116	446	52	123	12	3	0	38	.276	215	9	3	.987
National League Totals...................			754	1882	262	522	73	21	5	149	.277	853	45	21	.977
Major League Totals			870	2328	314	645	85	24	5	187	.277	1068	54	24	.979

†On temporary inactive list, May 2 to June 10, 1967.
‡On disabled list, July 11 to August 1, 1973.
§Traded to New York Mets for Catcher Duffy Dyer, October 21, 1974.
xTraded to Texas Rangers for Outfielder Joe Lovitto, December 12, 1975.
yTraded with cash to Chicago Cubs for Pitcher Darold Knowles, February 5, 1977.
zOn supplemental disabled list, July 5 to July 25, 1977.
aReleased, May 11, 1979.
Coach, Chicago Cubs, May 18, 1979 through 1981.

PITCHING RECORD

Year Club	League	G.	IP.	W.	L.	Pct.	H.	R.	ER.	SO.	BB.	ERA.
1969—York.....................................	Eastern	1	2	0	0	.000	2	1	0	0	0	0.00

CHAMPIONSHIP SERIES RECORD

Year Club	League	Pos.	G.	AB.	R.	H.	2B.	3B.	HR.	RBI.	B.A.	PO.	A.	E.	F.A.
1971—Pittsburgh........	Nat.	OF	1	3	1	1	0	0	1	1	.333	1	0	0	1.000
1972—Pittsburgh........	Nat.	PH-PR	3	2	1	0	0	0	0	0	.000	0	0	0	.000
1974—Pittsburgh........	Nat.	OF-PR	2	1	1	0	0	0	0	0	.000	0	0	0	.000
Championship Series Totals.............			6	6	3	1	0	0	1	1	.167	1	0	0	1.000

WORLD SERIES RECORD

Year Club	League	Pos.	G.	AB.	R.	H.	2B.	3B.	HR.	RBI.	B.A.	PO.	A.	E.	F.A.
1971—Pittsburgh........	Nat.	OF	3	11	2	1	0	1	0	0	.091	6	0	0	1.000

WILLIAM JOSEPH CONNORS III
(Bill)
Kansas City Royals

Born November 2, 1941, at Schenectady, N. Y.
Height, 6.00. Weight, 185.
Threw and batted righthanded.
Attended Syracuse University, Syracuse, N. Y.

Received reported $35,000 bonus to sign with Chicago Cubs, 1961.

Year Club	League	G.	IP.	W.	L.	Pct.	H.	R.	ER.	SO.	BB.	ERA.
1961–Wenatchee	Northwest	2	6	0	0	.000	6	5	4	2	4	6.00
1961–Carlsbad	Sophomore	4	23	1	0	1.000	28	12	9	16	4	3.52
1962–Palatka	Florida St.	11	64	3	4	.429	50	31	18	48	29	2.53
1963–Wenatchee	Northwest	30	187	12	11	.522	173	87	67	138	71	3.22
1964–Fort Worth	Texas	35	198	7	14	.333	216	113	88	106	43	4.00
1965–Dallas-Fort Worth	Texas	8	26	2	0	1.000	38	19	17	14	13	5.88
1965–Wenatchee	Northwest	9	56	7	1	.875	45	15	13	41	8	2.09
1965–Salt Lake City	P. Coast	16	108	8	3	.727	122	45	44	42	22	3.67
1966–Tacoma	P. Coast	26	159	8	11	.421	139	59	46	90	41	2.60
1966–Chicago	National	11	16	0	1	.000	20	13	13	3	7	7.31
1967–Tacoma†‡	P. Coast	27	177	9	9	.500	180	76	60	105	60	3.05
1967–New York	National	6	13	0	0	.000	8	9	9	13	5	6.23
1968–Jacksonville	Int'national	23	112	8	5	.615	101	49	37	63	31	2.97
1968–New York	National	9	14	0	1	.000	21	14	14	8	7	9.00
1969–Tidewater	Int'national	33	140	7	●13	.350	148	90	74	68	72	4.76
1970–Pompano Beach§	Florida St.	24	43	4	3	.571	43	27	19	38	22	3.98
Major League Totals		26	43	0	2	.000	49	36	36	24	19	7.53

†On disabled list, May 27 to June 11, 1967.
‡Sold to New York Mets, August 20, 1967.
§Released, August 1, 1970.

RECORD AS INFIELDER-OUTFIELDER

Year Club	League	Pos.	G.	AB.	R.	H.	2B.	3B.	HR.	RBI.	B.A.	PO.	A.	E.	F.A.
1961–Wenatchee	N'west	2B-P	32	111	9	25	4	1	0	17	.225	65	66	14	.903
1961–Carlsbad	Soph.	2B-P	29	97	13	22	3	1	0	15	.227	59	57	9	.928
1962–Palatka	Fla. St.	O-C-P	100	280	31	83	11	0	2	35	.296	228	33	8	.970

RECORD AS MANAGER

Year Club	League	Position	W.	L.
1975–Marion†	Appal.	First(N)	16	19
1977–Oklahoma City‡	A. A.	....	0	1

†Replaced Chuck Hiller, July 26, 1975, with record of 19-14 and team in first place.
‡Interim manager between Cal Emery and Mike Ryan, July 11, 1977.
Member of front office, New York Mets, 1971 and 1972; minor league pitching instructor, New York Mets, 1973 through 1976; minor league coach, Philadelphia Phillies, 1977 and 1978; coach, Kansas City Royals, 1980 and 1981.

WILLIAM ANGELO CONSOLO
(Billy)
Detroit Tigers

Born August 18, 1934, at Cleveland, O.
Height, 5.11. Weight, 180.
Threw and batted righthanded.
Attended Los Angeles City College, Los Angeles, Calif.
Received reported bonus of $60,000 to sign with Boston Red Sox, 1953.

Year Club	League	Pos.	G.	AB.	R.	H.	2B.	3B.	HR.	RBI.	B.A.	PO.	A.	E.	F.A.
1953–Boston	Amer.	3B-2B	47	65	9	14	2	1	1	6	.215	26	47	6	.924
1954–Boston	Amer.	INF	91	242	23	55	7	1	1	11	.227	113	184	15	.952
1955–Oakland	P. C.	*2B-SS	159	590	93	163	33	8	14	68	.276	366	433	*29	.965
1955–Boston	Amer.	2B	8	18	4	4	0	0	0	0	.222	11	5	2	.889
1956–Boston	Amer.	2B	48	11	13	2	0	0	0	1	.182	9	14	2	.920
1957–Boston	Amer.	INF	68	196	26	53	6	1	4	19	.270	92	189	16	.946
1958–Boston	Amer.	INF	46	72	13	9	2	1	0	5	.125	37	55	5	.948
1959–Bos.†-Wash.	Amer.	SS-2B	89	216	28	46	6	3	0	10	.213	126	242	19	.951
1960–Washington	Amer.	INF	100	174	23	36	4	2	3	15	.207	97	183	18	.940
1961–Minnesota‡	Amer.	INF	11	5	1	0	0	0	0	0	.000	5	1	0	1.000
1961–Vancouver§	P. C.	INF	99	389	63	110	10	7	4	40	.283	209	261	11	.977
1962–Philadelphia x	Nat.	3B	13	5	3	2	0	0	0	0	.400	0	0	0	.000
1962–L.A.y-K.C.z	Amer.	SS-3B-2B	82	174	15	39	4	2	0	16	.224	78	140	13	.944
American League Totals			590	1173	155	258	31	11	9	83	.220	594	1060	96	.945
National League Totals			13	5	3	2	0	0	0	0	.400	0	0	0	.000
Major League Totals			603	1178	158	260	31	11	9	83	.221	594	1060	96	.945

†Traded to Washington Senators with Pitcher Murray Wall for Pitcher Dick Hayes and Infielder Herb Plews, June 11, 1959; when it was charged by Red Sox Hayes had arm trouble, and was returned to Washington, Senators shipped Wall back to Sox, June 14, 1959.
‡Traded to Milwaukee Braves with cash for Second Baseman Billy Martin, June 1, 1961.
§Drafted by Philadelphia Phillies, November 27, 1961.
xSold to Los Angeles Angels, May 9, 1962.
ySold on waivers to Kansas City A's, June 26, 1962.
zReleased, November 2, 1962.
Coach, Detroit Tigers, June 14, 1979 through 1981.

DID YOU KNOW—
That Frank Robinson is the only player in All-Star game history to hit homers for each league?

CHARLES KEITH COTTIER
Name pronounced "Cot-TEE-er"
(Chuck)
New York Mets

Born January 8, 1936, at Delta, Colo.
Height, 5.11½. Weight, 178.
Threw and batted righthanded.
Hobby—Golf.

Led Georgia-Florida League second basemen in double plays with 76 in 1954.
Led Evangeline League second basemen in double plays with 106 in 1955.
Led Western League second basemen in double plays with 130 in 1957.
Tied for Pacific Coast League lead in sacrifice hits with 11 in 1967.

Year Club	League	Pos.	G.	AB.	R.	H.	2B.	3B.	HR.	RBI.	B.A.	PO.	A.	E.	F.A.
1954—Ameri's-Cordele Ga.-Fla.		2B	138	507	71	127	22	9	2	49	.250	*370	*398	*46	.943
1955—New Iberia........Evang.		2B	139	521	63	132	20	0	3	52	.253	361	*401	38	.953
1956—Jacksonville†....Sally		2B	4	11	0	2	1	0	0	0	.182	5	0	0	1.000
1956—Topeka............West.		2B	29	102	13	22	2	1	3	14	.216	71	77	5	.967
1956—Baton Rouge.....Evang.		2B	42	155	32	40	8	3	5	14	.258	125	109	4	.983
1957—Topeka............West.		2B	151	603	95	158	29	4	20	79	.262	389	*479	●30	.967
1958—Atlanta‡............South.		2B	153	583	32	157	29	8	8	62	.269	*414	*455	31	.966
1959—Milwaukee........Nat.		2B	10	24	1	3	1	0	0	1	.125	18	22	1	.976
1959—Louisville..........A. A.		2B	122	425	54	96	22	6	4	40	.226	290	339	21	.968
1960—Louisville..........A. A.		2B	46	181	24	56	11	3	4	19	.309	132	108	11	.956
1960—Milwaukee§......Nat.		2B	95	229	29	52	8	0	3	19	.227	180	214	13	.968
1961—Det. x-Wash.......Amer.		2B-SS	111	344	39	81	14	4	2	35	.235	242	323	11	.981
1962—Washington.......Amer.		2B	136	443	50	107	14	6	6	40	.242	368	354	14	.981
1963—Washington.......Amer.		2-S-3B	113	337	30	69	16	4	5	21	.205	233	286	25	.954
1964—Washington.......Amer.		2-3-SS	73	137	16	23	6	2	3	10	.168	110	115	5	.978
1965—Hawaii y..........P. C.		2B-SS	93	309	38	64	11	1	3	27	.207	201	270	9	.981
1965—Washington.......Amer.		PH-PR	7	1	1	0	0	0	0	0	.000	0	0	0	.000
1966—Hawaii z..........P. C.		2B	97	321	39	82	20	1	4	39	.255	199	266	16	.967
1967—Seattle.............P. C.		2B	140	482	50	119	29	2	5	61	.247	313	400	15	.979
1968—Sea.-Portland a .P. C.		2B	88	294	33	65	7	4	7	31	.221	216	241	14	.970
1968—California..........Amer.		3B-2B	33	67	2	13	4	1	0	1	.194	15	45	2	.968
1969—California b.......Amer.		2B	2	2	0	0	0	0	0	0	.000	1	1	0	1.000
1969—Hawaii cd..........P. C.							(Did not play)								
American League Totals.................			475	1331	138	293	54	17	16	107	.220	969	1124	57	.973
National League Totals			105	253	30	55	9	0	3	20	.217	198	236	14	.969
Major League Totals.......................			580	1584	168	348	63	17	19	127	.220	1167	1360	71	.973

†On disabled list May 21 to May 31, 1956.
‡On military list, September 24, 1958 to April 2, 1959.
§Traded with Pitcher Terry Fox, Catcher Dick Brown and Outfielder Billy Bruton to Detroit Tigers for Second Baseman Frank Bolling and Outfielder Neil Chrisley, December 7, 1960.
xTraded to Washington Senators for Pitcher Hal Woodeshick, June 5, 1961.
yOn disabled list, August 17 to August 30, 1965.
zSold to California Angels' organization, February 16, 1967.
aOn disabled list, June 15 to June 25, 1968.
bOn disabled list, April 8 to April 30, 1969.
cOn disabled list, May 13 through remainder of 1969 season.
dReleased, April 6, 1970.

RECORD AS MANAGER

Year Club	League	Position	W.	L.	Year Club	League	Position	W.	L.
1971—Niagara Falls† ...NYP		Second	8	3	1977—Quad Cities .... Midw.		Third(S)	41	29
1972—Niagara Falls.....NYP		First	48	22	(Second Half)		Third(S)	34	35
1973—Charleston ....W. Carol.		Second	35	25	1978—Salinas .... Calif.		Second(S)	42	28
(Second Half)		Second	37	27	(Second Half)		Second(S)	42	28

†Replaced due to injury by Dick Cole, July 3, 1971.
Coach, New York Mets, 1979 through 1981.

ROGER LEE CRAIG
Detroit Tigers

Born February 17, 1931, at Durham, N. C.
Height, 6.04. Weight, 196.
Threw and batted righthanded.
Hobby—Sports.
Attended North Carolina State College, Raleigh, N. C.

Tied major league record for most 1-0 games lost, season (5), 1963; tied National League mark for most consecutive losses, season (18), May 4 through August 4, 1963, inclusive.
Tied for National League lead in shutouts with 4 in 1959.

Year Club	League	G.	IP.	W.	L.	Pct.	H.	R.	ER.	SO.	BB.	ERA.
1950—Newport News....................Piedmont		6	19	0	1	.000	22	17	15	7	23	7.11
1950—Valdosta ....Ga.-Fla.		23	167	14	7	.667	136	86	58	152	150	3.13
1951—Newport News....................Piedmont		38	21	14	11	.560	175	109	90	119	*175	3.67
1952-53—Elmira............................Eastern						(In Military Service)						
1954—Elmira................................Eastern		3	2	0	0	.000	4	6	2	1	2	9.00

Year	Club	League	G.	IP.	W.	L.	Pct.	H.	R.	ER.	SO.	BB.	ERA.
1954—Pueblo	Western		6	14	1	1	.500	14	17	15	8	19	9.64
1954—Newport News	Piedmont		20	125	8	3	.727	107	44	35	108	56	2.50
1955—Montreal	Int'national		22	117	10	2	.833	105	48	46	68	64	3.54
1955—Brooklyn	National		21	91	5	3	.625	81	37	28	48	43	2.77
1956—Brooklyn	National		35	199	12	11	.522	169	90	82	109	87	3.71
1957—Brooklyn	National		32	111	6	9	.400	102	58	57	69	47	4.62
1958—Los Angeles	National		9	32	2	1	.667	30	20	16	16	12	4.50
1958—St. Paul	Am. Assoc.		28	182	5	•17	.227	180	100	79	119	77	3.91
1959—Spokane	P. Coast		14	96	6	7	.462	86	39	34	46	26	3.19
1959—Los Angeles	National		29	153	11	5	.688	122	49	35	76	45	2.06
1960—Los Angeles	National		21	116	8	3	.727	99	48	42	69	43	3.26
1961—Los Angeles†	National		40	113	5	6	.455	130	87	77	63	52	6.13
1962—New York	National		42	233	10	•24	.294	261	133	117	118	70	4.52
1963—New York‡	National		46	236	5	•22	.185	249	117	99	108	58	3.78
1964—St. Louis§	National		39	166	7	9	.438	180	76	60	84	35	3.25
1965—Cincinnati x	National		40	64	1	4	.200	74	33	26	30	25	3.66
1966—Philadelphia	National		14	23	2	1	.667	31	15	14	13	5	5.48
1966—Seattle	P. Coast		6	22	0	1	.000	15	11	6	11	9	2.45
1968—Albuquerque	Texas		1	4	0	0	.000	3	0	0	2	2	0.00
Major League Totals			368	1537	74	98	.430	1528	763	653	803	522	3.82

†Selected by New York Mets in National League expansion draft, October 10, 1961.

‡Traded to St. Louis Cardinals for Pitcher Bill Wakefield and Outfielder George Altman, November 4, 1963.

§Traded to Cincinnati Reds with Outfielder Charlie James for Pitcher Bob Purkey and a player to be named later, December 14, 1964.

xReleased by Cincinnati Reds and signed by Philadelphia Phillies, April 11, 1966.

WORLD SERIES RECORD

Year	Club	League	G.	IP.	W.	L.	Pct.	H.	R.	ER.	SO.	BB.	ERA.
1955—Brooklyn	National		1	6	1	0	1.000	4	2	2	4	5	3.00
1956—Brooklyn	National		2	6	0	1	.000	10	8	8	4	3	12.00
1959—Los Angeles	National		2	9⅓	0	1	.000	15	9	9	8	5	8.68
1964—St. Louis	National		2	5	1	0	1.000	2	0	0	9	3	0.00
World Series Totals			7	26⅓	2	2	.500	31	19	19	25	16	6.49

RECORD AS MANAGER

Year	Club	League	Position	W.	L.
1968—Albuquerque	Texas		Second(W)	70	69
1978—San Diego	Nat.		Fourth(W)	84	78
1979—San Diego	Nat.		Fifth(W)	68	93
Major League Totals				152	171

Scout, Los Angeles Dodgers, 1967; coach, San Diego Padres, 1969 through 1972; minor league pitching instructor, Los Angeles Dodgers, 1973; coach, Houston Astros, 1974 and 1975; coach, San Diego Padres, 1976 and 1977; named manager of Padres (replacing Alvin Dark), March 21, 1978; coach, Detroit Tigers, 1980 and 1981.

MARK EMERY CRESSE
Los Angeles Dodgers

Born September 21, 1951, at St. Albans, N. Y.
Height, 6.03. Weight, 220.
Threw and batted righthanded.
Attended California State University at Long Beach and Golden West College, Huntington Beach, Calif.

Year	Club	League	Pos.	G.	AB.	R.	H.	2B.	3B.	HR.	RBI.	B.A.	PO.	A.	E.	F.A.
1971—Sara. Cardinals	G. C.		C	7	17	2	3	2	0	0	2	.176	34	5	0	1.000
1971—Modesto†	Calif.		C	11	16	1	2	1	0	0	2	.125	34	0	1	.971
1972—Sara. Cards-RB	G. C.		C	8	24	1	5	1	1	0	2	.208	46	6	5	.912
1972—Cedar Rapids	Midw.		C	2	8	0	2	0	0	0	1	.250	15	2	2	.895
1972—St. Petersburg	Fla. St.		C	2	4	0	1	0	0	0	0	.250	6	4	0	1.000
1973—St. Petersburg‡	Fla. St.		C-OF	22	73	10	13	3	1	0	9	.178	141	15	3	.981
1973—Modesto§x	Calif.		C	31	80	9	14	2	0	2	8	.175	142	10	5	.968

†On temporary inactive list, April 14 to June 8, 1972.

‡Released by St. Louis Cardinals' organization, May 17, 1973; re-signed by Cardinals' organization, May 26, 1973.

§On temporary inactive list, June 13 to June 29, 1973.

xReleased, September 20, 1973.

Bullpen catcher and batting practice pitcher, Los Angeles Dodgers, 1974 through 1976; coach, Los Angeles Dodgers, 1977 through 1981.

JAMES HOUSTON DAVENPORT
(Jim)
San Francisco Giants

Born August 17, 1933, at Siluria, Ala.
Height, 5.11. Weight, 183.
Threw and batted righthanded.
Hobbies—Hunting, fishing and golf.
Attended Mississippi Southern College, Hattiesburg, Miss.

Established major league record for most consecutive errorless games by third baseman, league, 97, July 29, 1966 through April 28, 1968 (209 chances accepted—played other positions during streak).

Established National League record for most consecutive errorless games by third baseman, season, 64, May 22 through September 30, 1967, first game (137 chances accepted—played other positions during streak).

Tied for National League lead in sacrifice hits with 17 in 1958.

Led Cotton States League in total bases with 239 in 1955.

Received Gold Glove award as outstanding fielding third baseman in National League, 1962.

Year	Club	League	Pos.	G.	AB.	R.	H.	2B.	3B.	HR.	RBI.	B.A.	PO.	A.	E.	F.A.
1955—El Dorado	.........Cot. St.	3B	105	405	102	•147	29	6	17	76	★.363	★113	★190	23	.929
1956—Dallas	...............Tex.	3B-SS	154	577	97	154	28	6	14	74	.267	125	349	24	.952
1957—Minneapolis	.......A. A.	3B-SS	148	529	68	154	28	3	10	53	.291	123	252	15	.962
1958—San Francisco	...Nat.	3B-SS	134	434	70	111	22	3	12	41	.256	96	232	14	.959
1959—San Francisco	...Nat.	★3B-SS	123	469	65	121	16	3	6	38	.258	91	222	7	★.978
1960—San Francisco	...Nat.	★3B-SS	112	363	43	91	15	3	6	38	.251	83	178	10	★.963
1961—San Francisco	...Nat.	3B	137	436	64	121	28	4	12	65	.278	119	235	13	★.965
1962—San Francisco	...Nat.	3B	144	485	83	144	25	5	14	58	.297	125	256	19	.953
1963—San Francisco	...Nat.	3-2-S	147	460	40	116	19	3	4	36	.252	152	230	13	.967
1964—San Francisco	...Nat.	S-3-2	116	297	24	70	10	6	2	26	.236	138	237	11	.972
1965—San Francisco	...Nat.	3-SS-2	106	271	29	68	14	3	4	31	.251	97	147	14	.950
1966—San Francisco	...Nat.	S-3-2-1	111	305	42	76	6	2	9	30	.249	107	201	14	.957
1967—San Francisco	...Nat.	3-S-2B	124	295	42	81	10	3	5	30	.275	83	192	4	.986
1968—San Francisco	...Nat.	3-SS-2	113	272	27	61	1	1	1	17	.224	57	137	8	.961
1969—San Francisco	...Nat.	3-1-O-S	112	303	20	73	10	1	2	42	.241	84	158	8	.968
1970—San Francisco	...Nat.	3B	22	37	3	9	1	0	0	4	.243	7	7	0	1.000
Major League Totals	....		1501	4427	552	1142	177	37	77	456	.258	1314	2432	135	.965

WORLD SERIES RECORD

Established World Series records for most double plays, third baseman, 7-game Series (4), 1962, and most double plays started, third baseman, 7-game Series (4), 1962.

Tied World Series record for most double plays by third baseman, total Series (4).

Year	Club	League	Pos.	G.	AB.	R.	H.	2B.	3B.	HR.	RBI.	B.A.	PO.	A.	E.	F.A.
1962—San Francisco	...Nat.	3B	7	22	1	3	1	0	0	1	.136	6	12	3	.857

ALL-STAR GAME RECORD

Year	League	Pos.	AB.	R.	H.	2B.	3B.	HR.	RBI.	B.A.	PO.	A.	E.	F.A.
1962—National (first game)	....	3B	1	0	1	0	0	0	0	1.000	0	1	0	1.000

Member of National League All-Star Team in 1962 (second game); did not play.

RECORD AS MANAGER

Year	Club	League	Position	W.	L.
1971—Phoenix	.............P. C.	Second(S)	74	70
1972—Phoenix	.............P. C.	Second(E)	81	67
1973—Phoenix	.............P. C.	Third(E)	70	73

Coach, San Francisco Giants, July 13, 1970 to close of season; coach, San Diego Padres, 1974 and 1975; coach, San Francisco Giants, 1976 through 1981.

HERMAN THOMAS DAVIS JR.
(Tommy)
Seattle Mariners

Born March 21, 1939, at Brooklyn, N. Y.
Height, 6.02. Weight, 200.
Threw and batted righthanded.
Hobby—Modern jazz recordings.

Tied major league record for fewest triples, season (150 or more games), 0, 1967.

Tied modern major league record for most clubs, lifetime (10).

Led Midwest League in total bases with 271 and in stolen bases with 68 in 1957.

Led Pacific Coast League in total bases with 315 in 1959.

Named outfielder on THE SPORTING NEWS National League All-Star Team, 1962 and 1963.

Named designated hitter on THE SPORTING NEWS American League All-Star Team, 1974.

Year	Club	League	Pos.	G.	AB.	R.	H.	2B.	3B.	HR.	RBI.	B.A.	PO.	A.	E.	F.A.
1956—Hornell	.............Pony	OF	43	154	14	50	5	1	0	26	.325	49	7	4	.933
1957—Kokomo	............Midw.	OF-3B	127	★518	★115	★185	23	6	17	104	★.357	179	32	19	.917
1958—Victoria	............Tex.	OF-1B	122	461	74	140	21	10	13	66	.304	261	17	7	.975
1958—Montreal	..........Int.	OF-2-3B	14	26	3	8	0	1	1	7	.308	6	0	1	.857
1959—Spokane	............P.C.	OF	★153	★612	90	★211	32	9	18	78	★.345	★414	15	●10	.977
1959—Los Angeles	......Nat.	PH	1	1	0	0	0	0	0	0	.000	0	0	0	.000
1960—Los Angeles	......Nat.	OF-3B	110	352	43	97	18	1	11	44	.276	153	17	4	.977
1961—Los Angeles	......Nat.	OF-3B	132	460	60	128	13	2	15	58	.278	173	91	17	.940
1962—Los Angeles	......Nat.	OF-3B	163	665	120	★230	27	9	27	★153	.346	269	60	20	.943
1963—Los Angeles	......Nat.	OF-3B	146	556	69	181	19	3	16	88	★.326	204	67	15	.948
1964—Los Angeles	......Nat.	OF	152	592	70	163	20	5	14	86	.275	264	9	5	.982
1965—Los Angeles†	......Nat.	OF	17	60	3	15	1	1	0	9	.250	21	1	0	1.000
1966—Los Angeles‡	......Nat.	OF-3B	100	313	27	98	11	1	3	27	.313	99	9	3	.973
1967—New York§	........Nat.	OF-1B	154	577	72	174	32	0	16	73	.302	236	7	7	.972
1968—Chicago x	..........Amer.	OF-1B	132	456	30	122	5	3	8	50	.268	211	9	8	.965
1969—Seattle y	..........Amer.	OF-1B	123	454	52	123	29	1	6	80	.271	183	3	7	.964

Year — Club	League	Pos.	G.	AB.	R.	H.	2B.	3B.	HR.	RBI.	B.A.	PO.	A.	E.	F.A.
1969—Houston	Nat.	OF	24	79	2	19	3	0	1	9	.241	27	1	0	1.000
1970—Hou.a-Chi	Nat.	OF	68	255	28	71	14	2	5	38	.278	86	4	5	.947
1970—Oakland b	Amer.	OF-1B	66	200	17	58	9	1	1	27	.290	110	4	4	.966
1971—Oakland c	Amer.	1-O-2-3	79	219	26	71	8	1	3	42	.324	275	37	5	.984
1972—Chicago de	Nat.	1B-OF	15	26	3	7	1	0	0	6	.269	31	1	1	.970
1972—Baltimore	Amer.	OF-1B	26	82	9	21	3	0	0	6	.256	51	4	0	1.000
1973—Baltimore	Amer.	1B	137	552	53	169	20	3	7	89	.306	32	2	1	.971
1974—Baltimore f	Amer.	DH	158	626	67	181	20	1	11	84	.289	0	0	0	.000
1975—Baltimore f	Amer.	DH	116	460	43	130	14	1	6	57	.283	0	0	0	.000
1976—Calif.g-K.C.h	Amer.	DH-1B	80	238	17	63	5	0	3	26	.265	4	0	0	1.000
American League Totals			917	3287	314	938	113	11	45	461	.285	866	59	25	.974
National League Totals			1082	3936	497	1183	159	24	108	591	.301	1563	267	77	.960
Major League Totals			1999	7223	811	2121	272	35	153	1052	.294	2429	326	102	.964

†Suffered broken ankle against San Francisco Giants, May 1; on disabled list from May 3 through September 22.

‡Traded with Outfielder-Infielder Derrell Griffith to New York Mets for Second Baseman Ron Hunt and Outfielder-Infielder Jim Hickman, November 29, 1966.

§Traded with Pitchers Jack Fisher and Billy Wynne to Chicago White Sox for Outfielder Tommie Agee and Infielder Al Weiss, December 15, 1967. White Sox purchased Catcher Dick Booker from Jacksonville as part of deal.

xSelected by Seattle Pilots from Chicago White Sox in expansion draft, October 15, 1968.

yTraded to Houston Astros for Outfielders Hilario Valdespino and Dan Walton, August 31, 1969.

aSold to Oakland Athletics, June 22, 1970.

bSold to Chicago Cubs, September 16, 1970. Released by Chicago Cubs, December 28, 1970, and signed as free agent by Oakland Athletics, March 29, 1971.

cOn disabled list, August 31 through September 15.

dReleased by Oakland A's, March 30, 1972, and signed as free agent by Chicago Cubs, July 6, 1972.

eTraded to Baltimore Orioles for Catcher Ellie Hendricks, August 18, 1972.

fReleased, February 12, 1976; signed as free agent by New York Yankees, February 20, 1976. Released by New York Yankees, April 6, 1976.

gSigned as free agent by California Angels, June 2, 1976; sold to Kansas City Royals, September 20, 1976.

hReleased, February 8, 1977.

Coach, Seattle Mariners, 1981.

CHAMPIONSHIP SERIES RECORD

Year — Club	League	Pos.	G.	AB.	R.	H.	2B.	3B.	HR.	RBI.	B.A.	PO.	A.	E.	F.A.
1971—Oakland	Amer.	PH-1B	3	8	1	3	1	0	0	0	.375	8	0	0	1.000
1973—Baltimore	Amer.	DH	5	21	1	6	1	0	0	2	.286	0	0	0	.000
1974—Baltimore	Amer.	DH	4	15	0	4	0	0	0	1	.267	0	0	0	.000
Championship Series Totals			12	44	2	13	2	0	0	3	.295	8	0	0	1.000

WORLD SERIES RECORD

Tied World Series records for most three-base hits, game (2), October 3, 1963; most three-base hits, four-game Series (2), 1963; most putouts, game, by left fielder (6), October 3, 1963—and in same game most putouts by outfielder, inning (3), seventh inning.

Year — Club	League	Pos.	G.	AB.	R.	H.	2B.	3B.	HR.	RBI.	B.A.	PO.	A.	E.	F.A.
1963—Los Angeles	Nat.	OF	4	15	0	6	0	2	0	2	.400	6	0	0	1.000
1966—Los Angeles	Nat.	OF	4	8	0	2	0	0	0	0	.250	3	0	0	1.000
World Series Totals			8	23	0	8	0	2	0	2	.348	9	0	0	1.000

ALL-STAR GAME RECORD

Year — League	Pos.	AB.	R.	H.	2B.	3B.	HR.	RBI.	B.A.	PO.	A.	E.	F.A.
1962—National (both games)	OF	5	0	0	0	0	0	0	.000	2	1	1	.750
1963—National	OF	3	1	1	0	0	0	0	.333	2	1	0	1.000
All-Star Game Totals		8	1	1	0	0	0	0	.125	4	2	1	.857

WILLIAM LESTER DeMARS
(Billy)
Philadelphia Phillies

Born August 26, 1925, at Brooklyn, N. Y.
Height, 5.10. Weight, 170.
Threw and batted righthanded.

Year — Club	League	Pos.	G.	AB.	R.	H.	2B.	3B.	HR.	RBI.	B.A.	PO.	A.	E.	F.A.
1943—Olean	Pony	SS	50	189	27	51	12	1	0	29	.270	88	131	16	.932
1943—Lancaster..........	Int.-St.	SS	21	82	13	19	2	1	0	6	.232	42	73	7	.943
1944-45—Durham	Pied.	(In Military Service)													
1946—Nashua	N. Eng.	SS	98	321	43	76	9	8	1	42	.237	170	275	38	.921
1947—Asheville†	Tri-St.	SS	112	427	85	140	21	4	5	88	.328	203	321	33	.941
1948—Philadelphia	Amer.	S-3-2B	18	29	3	5	0	0	1	.172	18	25	3	.935
1949—Buffalo‡	Int.	SS	109	378	49	105	18	1	6	56	.278	228	329	28	.952
1950—St. Louis	Amer.	SS-3B	61	178	25	44	5	1	0	13	.247	118	129	19	.929
1951—San Antonio.......	Texas	SS	129	408	46	100	14	2	3	30	.245	251	254	30	.944
1951—St. Louis	Amer.	SS	1	4	1	1	0	0	0	0	.250	1	4	0	1.000
1952—Toronto.............	Int.	3B-SS	141	524	70	148	23	6	4	45	.282	174	283	21	.956
1953—Toronto.............	Int.	*SS-3B	148	545	69	142	23	3	3	52	.261	272	400	24	*.966

Year	Club	League	Pos.	G.	AB.	R.	H.	2B.	3B.	HR.	RBI.	B.A.	PO.	A.	E.	F.A.
1954—Toronto	............Int.		SS	40	134	17	40	9	2	0	9	.299	62	84	7	.954
1955—Toronto	............Int.		2B-SS	67	184	24	52	10	0	3	17	.283	115	123	7	.971
1956—Buffalo	..............Int.		SS	104	320	26	78	9	0	1	22	.244	153	244	12	.971
1957—Portland	.............P. C.		3-S-2B	137	356	35	86	16	1	3	34	.242	136	281	10	.977
1958—Port.-Vancouver	P. C.		PH	2	1	0	0	0	0	0	0	.000	0	0	0	.000
1958—Aberdeen	..........No.		S-3-OF	81	240	28	62	5	0	4	30	.258	78	158	13	.948
1959—Stockton	............Calif.		3B-P	2	5	0	1	0	0	0	1	.200	0	1	0	1.000
1960—Stockton	............Calif.		3B-P	7	14	3	3	0	0	0	1	.214	1	3	0	1.000
Major League Totals	....			80	211	29	50	5	1	0	14	.237	137	158	22	.931

†Drafted by Philadelphia Athletics from Mobile (Brooklyn Dodgers' organization), November 10, 1947.

‡Recalled by Philadelphia Athletics; traded with Third Baseman Frank Gustine, Outfielders Ray Coleman and Rocky Ippolito and $100,000 to St. Louis Browns for Third Baseman Bob Dillinger and Outfielder Paul Lehner, December 13, 1949.

PITCHING RECORD

Year	Club	League	G.	IP.	W.	L.	Pct.	H.	R.	ER.	SO.	BB.	ERA.
1959—Stockton	............................California		1	....	1	0	1.000	....	....	....	....	....	....
1960—Stockton	............................California		3	....	0	0	.000	....	....	....	....	....	....

RECORD AS MANAGER

Year	Club	League	Position	W.	L.	Year	Club	League	Position	W.	L.
1958—Aberdeen†	..........North.		Eighth	37	63	1964—Fox Cities	...........Midwest		Second	39	22
1959—Stockton	.............Calif.		Fourth	35	34	(Second Half)			First	42	21
(Second Half)			Third	41	29	1965—Fox Cities	...........Midwest		Eighth	25	35
1960—Stockton	.............Calif.		Sixth	27	43	(Second Half)			Fifth	30	28
(Second Half)			Second	39	31	1966—Miami	................Fla. St.		Seventh	31	36
1961—Leesburg‡	...........Fla. St.		Seventh	15	41	(Second Half)			Third	44	27
1961—Tri-Cities§	..........Northw.		Sixth	9	18	1967—Elmira	...............East.		xFirst(W)	74	65
(Second Half)			Sixth	27	42	1968—Rochester	...........Int.		Third	77	69
1962—Aberdeen	............North.		Fourth	64	60						
1963—Fox Cities	...........Midwest		Fifth	28	32						
(Second Half)			Eighth	27	33						

†Replaced Bernie Lutz with club in eighth place, May 25.
‡Replaced by Cal Ripken, June 7.
§Replaced Whitey McDowell with club in sixth place, June 10.
xLost playoff to Binghamton (Eastern Division winner), three games to one.
Coach, Philadelphia Phillies, 1969 through 1981.

ROBERT W. DEWS
(Bobby)
Atlanta Braves

Born March 23, 1938, at Clinton, Iowa.
Height, 6.01. Weight, 175.
Threw and batted righthanded.
Attended Mercer University, Atlanta, Ga. and Georgia Tech, Atlanta, Ga.

Year	Club	League	Pos.	G.	AB.	R.	H.	2B.	3B.	HR.	RBI.	B.A.	PO.	A.	E.	F.A.
1960—Daytona Beach	..Fla. St.		SS	82	342	51	93	7	2	1	29	.272	132	204	25	.931
1961—Billings	..............Pion.		SS	47	211	33	59	10	3	1	19	.280	86	140	16	.934
1961—Tulsa†	..............Texas		....	7	27	1	9	1	0	0	3	.333	....	....	....	.....
1961—Lancaster	.........East.		....	6	22	0	5	0	0	0	0	.227	....	....	....	.....
1962—Portsmouth‡	.....S. Atl.		SS	117	417	48	103	12	0	1	24	.247	172	306	33	.935
1963—Winnipeg§	.........North.		OF-SS	98	399	61	103	11	5	1	31	.258	203	107	21	.937
1964—Tulsa	...............Texas		SS-O-2	134	499	67	138	10	5	0	40	.277	211	287	19	.963
1965—Jacksonville x	...Int.		SS-2-O	89	281	26	58	3	5	2	17	.206	161	239	5	.988
1966—Tulsa	..................P. C.		SS	43	113	8	24	2	1	0	8	.212	52	93	4	.979
1966—Arkansas y	.......Texas		SS-2-3	64	206	24	60	5	1	1	20	.291	58	104	7	.959
1967—Tulsa z	..............P. C.		SS-1B	10	16	1	6	0	0	0	2	.375	8	3	3	.786
1967—Arkansas a	.......Texas		3B-2-S	95	347	43	86	11	3	0	18	.248	84	183	12	.957
1968—Arkansas b	.......Texas		INF-O-C	65	146	16	34	1	0	0	8	.233	67	35	8	.927
1970—St. Petersburg c	Fla. St.		2B-SS	15	31	5	10	1	0	0	3	.323	26	19	0	1.000

†On disabled list, June 22 through August 3, 1961.
‡On disabled list, May 25 through June 4, 1962.
§On disabled list, August 9 through August 20, 1963.
xOn disabled list, May 5 through June 19, 1965.
yOn restricted list, February 27 through March 14, 1967.
zPlayer-Coach.
aOn temporary inactive list, August 20 through September 4, 1967.
bReleased, January 18, 1969.
cReleased, May 24, 1970.

PITCHING RECORD

Year	Club	League	G.	IP.	W.	L.	Pct.	H.	R.	ER.	SO.	BB.	ERA.
1966—Arkansas	............................Texas		1	1	0	0	.000	1	0	0	0	0	.00

RECORD AS MANAGER

Year Club	League	Position	W.	L.
1969—Lewiston............	N'west	Fourth	30	49
1971—Cedar Rapids	Midw.	Second(N)	32	26
(Second Half)		†Second(N)	35	27
1972—Sara. Cards........	G. Coast	Fifth	27	32
1973—Modesto............	Calif.	Sixth	31	39
(Second Half)		Eighth	29	41
1974—Sara. Cards‡	G. Coast	Fifth	27	21
1975—Greenwood	W. Car.	Fourth	25	46
(Second Half)		Second	37	33
1976—Kingsport...........	Appal.	Fourth(S)	25	42
1977—Greenwood	W. Car.	First	39	31
(Second Half)		§Third	36	33
1978—Savannah...........	South.	Fifth(E)	33	39
(Second Half)		xFirst(E)	39	33

†Tied for position.

‡Co-manager with Tom Burgess.

§Lost Championship Playoffs to Gastonia, three games to one.

xWon Eastern Division Championship from Orlando, two games to one; Lost Championship Playoffs to Knoxville, two games to one.

Coach, Atlanta Braves, 1979 through 1981.

ROBERT PERSHING DOERR
(Bobby)
Toronto Blue Jays

Born April 7, 1918, at Los Angeles, Calif.
Height, 5.11. Weight, 185.
Threw and batted righthanded.
Hobbies—Hunting and fishing.

Established modern major league record for most chances accepted by second baseman, two consecutive games (28), May 30 and June 3, 1946.

Tied major league record for most double plays by second baseman, doubleheader (8), June 25, 1950.

Tied American League record for most seasons leading league in double plays by second baseman (5).

Led American League second basemen in double plays with 118 in 1938, 118 in 1940, 132 in 1943, 129 in 1946 and 118 in 1947.

Named Most Valuable Player in the American League by THE SPORTING NEWS, 1944.

Named as second baseman on the major league All-Star Team by THE SPORTING NEWS, 1944.

Year Club	League	Pos.	G.	AB.	R.	H.	2B.	3B.	HR.	RBI.	B.A.	PO.	A.	E.	F.A.
1934—Hollywood	P.C.	2B	67	210	12	52	6	0	0	11	.259	135	164	14	.955
1935—Hollywood	P.C.	2B	172	647	87	205	22	8	4	74	.317	444	466	38	.960
1936—San Diego.........	P.C.	2B	175	695	100	*238	37	12	2	77	.342	399	*504	33	.965
1937—Boston	Amer.	2B	55	147	22	33	5	1	2	14	.224	94	124	6	.973
1938—Boston	Amer.	2B	145	509	70	147	26	7	5	80	.289	372	420	26	.968
1939—Boston	Amer.	2B	127	525	75	167	28	2	12	73	.318	336	431	19	.976
1940—Boston	Amer.	2B	151	595	87	173	37	10	22	105	.291	*401	480	21	●.977
1941—Boston	Amer.	2B	132	500	74	141	28	4	16	93	.282	290	389	20	.971
1942—Boston	Amer.	2B	144	545	71	158	35	5	15	102	.290	376	453	21	*.975
1943—Boston	Amer.	2B	●155	604	78	163	32	3	16	75	.270	*415	●490	9	*.990
1944—Boston	Amer.	2B	125	468	95	152	30	10	15	81	.325	341	363	17	.976
1945—Boston							(In Military Service)								
1946—Boston	Amer.	2B	151	583	95	158	34	9	18	116	.271	*420	*483	13	*.986
1947—Boston	Amer.	2B	146	561	79	145	23	10	17	95	.258	376	●466	16	.981
1948—Boston	Amer.	2B	140	527	94	150	23	6	27	111	.285	366	430	6	●.993
1949—Boston	Amer.	2B	139	541	91	167	30	9	18	109	.309	395	439	17	.980
1950—Boston	Amer.	2B	149	586	103	172	29	●11	27	120	.294	*443	431	11	*.988
1951—Boston	Amer.	2B	106	402	60	116	21	2	13	73	.289	303	311	12	.981
Major League Totals			1865	7093	1094	2042	381	89	223	1247	.288	4928	5710	214	.980

WORLD SERIES RECORD

Established World Series records for highest fielding average by second baseman, seven-game Series (1.000 and 49 chances), 1946; most assists by second baseman, seven-game Series (31), 1946.

Tied World Series record for most assists by second baseman, game (8), October 9, 1946.

Year Club	League	Pos.	G.	AB.	R.	H.	2B.	3B.	HR.	RBI.	B.A.	PO.	A.	E.	F.A.
1946—Boston	Amer.	2B	6	22	1	9	1	0	1	3	.409	18	31	0	1.000

ALL-STAR GAME RECORD

Year League	Pos.	AB.	R.	H.	2B.	3B.	HR.	RBI.	B.A.	PO.	A.	E.	F.A.
1941—American...........................	2B	3	0	0	0	0	0	0	.000	0	0	0	.000
1943—American...........................	2B	4	1	2	0	0	1	3	.500	3	3	0	1.000
1944—American...........................	2B	3	0	0	0	0	0	0	.000	4	1	1	.833
1946—American...........................	2B	2	0	0	0	0	0	0	.000	1	1	0	1.000
1947—American...........................	2B	2	1	1	0	0	0	0	.500	0	2	0	1.000
1948—American...........................	2B	2	0	0	0	0	0	0	.000	0	3	0	1.000
1950—American...........................	2B	3	0	0	0	0	0	0	.000	1	4	0	1.000
1951—American...........................	2B	1	0	1	0	0	0	0	1.000	1	0	0	1.000
All-Star Game Totals.......................		20	2	4	0	0	1	3	.200	10	14	1	.960

Member of American League All-Star team in 1942; did not play.

Scout, Boston Red Sox, 1957 through 1966; coach, Boston Red Sox, 1967 through 1969; coach, Toronto Blue Jays, 1977 through 1981.

DAVID EDWIN DUNCAN
(Dave)
Cleveland Indians

Born September 26, 1945, at Dallas, Tex.
Height, 6.02. Weight, 195.
Throws and bats righthanded.
Hobbies—Hunting, fishing, water skiing and golf.

Tied following major league records: unassisted double play, catcher, game, June 21, 1972; most doubles and most consecutive doubles, game, 4, June 30, 1975 (2nd game of doubleheader).
Tied for Southern League lead in double plays by catchers with 8 in 1967.
Named Most Valuable Player in California League, 1966.
Received reported $65,000 bonus to sign with Kansas City Athletics, 1963.

Year	Club	League	Pos.	G.	AB.	R.	H.	2B.	3B.	HR.	RBI.	B.A.	PO.	A.	E.	F.A.
1963—Daytona Beach	..Fla. St.	C	47	152	16	22	2	1	4	10	.145	250	23	12	.958
1964—Kansas City	.......Amer.	C	25	53	2	9	0	1	1	5	.170	99	7	2	.981
1965—Birmingham	......South.	C	61	192	20	40	11	2	6	20	.208	405	31	9	.980
1965—Lewiston	...........N'west	C	55	188	30	52	9	1	9	35	.277	426	28	7	.985
1966—Modesto	............Calif.	C-OF	121	439	103	119	8	2	*46	112	.271	807	61	14	.984
1967—Birmingham	......South.	C	95	323	40	78	14	1	13	48	.241	552	50	13	.979
1967—Kansas City	.......Amer.	C	34	101	9	19	4	0	5	11	.188	176	13	4	.979
1968—Vancouver	.........P. C.	C	35	114	21	36	4	2	6	21	.316	177	20	1	.995
1968—Oakland	.........Amer.	C	82	246	15	47	4	0	7	28	.191	474	41	7	.987
1969—Oakland	...........Amer.	C	58	127	11	16	3	0	3	22	.126	209	15	4	.982
1970—Oakland†	...........Amer.	C	86	232	21	60	7	0	10	29	.259	373	28	9	.978
1971—Oakland‡	...........Amer.	C	103	363	39	92	13	1	15	40	.253	678	41	*12	.984
1972—Oakland§	...........Amer.	C	121	403	39	88	13	0	19	59	.218	661	43	5	.993
1973—Cleveland x	.......Amer.	C	95	344	43	80	11	1	17	43	.233	533	41	7	.988
1974—Cleveland y	.......Amer.	C-1B	136	425	45	85	10	1	16	46	.200	564	48	15	.976
1975—Baltimore	.........Amer.	C	96	307	30	63	7	0	12	41	.205	397	41	8	.982
1976—Baltimore z	.........Amer.	C	93	284	20	58	7	0	4	17	.204	371	35	6	.985
Major League Totals	....		929	2885	274	617	79	4	109	441	.214	4535	353	79	.984

†On military list August 7 through August 24.
‡On military list July 23 through August 9.
§Traded with Outfielder George Hendrick to Cleveland Indians for Catcher Ray Fosse and Infielder Jack Heidemann, March 24, 1973.
xOn disabled list, July 2 to August 18, 1973.
yTraded with Outfielder Alvin McGrew to Baltimore Orioles for First Baseman Boog Powell and Pitcher Don Hood, February 25, 1975.
zTraded to Chicago White Sox for Outfielder Pat Kelly, November 18, 1976; released, March 30, 1977.
Coach, Cleveland Indians, 1978 through 1981.

CHAMPIONSHIP SERIES RECORD

Year	Club	League	Pos.	G.	AB.	R.	H.	2B.	3B.	HR.	RBI.	B.A.	PO.	A.	E.	F.A.
1971—Oakland	.............Amer.	C	2	6	0	3	1	0	0	2	.500	15	0	0	1.000
1972—Oakland	.............Amer.	PH-C	2	2	0	0	0	0	0	0	.000	5	1	0	1.000
Championship Series Totals	....		4	8	0	3	1	0	0	2	.375	20	1	0	1.000

WORLD SERIES RECORD

Year	Club	League	Pos.	G.	AB.	R.	H.	2B.	3B.	HR.	RBI.	B.A.	PO.	A.	E.	F.A.
1972—Oakland	............Amer.	PH-C	3	5	0	1	0	0	0	0	.200	5	1	0	1.000

ALL-STAR GAME RECORD

Member of American League All-Star Team for 1971 game; did not play.

HARRY ALEXANDER DUNLOP
Cincinnati Reds

Born September 6, 1933, at Sacramento, Calif.
Height, 6.03. Weight, 200.
Threw right and batted lefthanded.

Led Northwest League catchers in double plays with 9 in 1960 and tied for California League lead with 13 in 1961.

Year	Club	League	Pos.	G.	AB.	R.	H.	2B.	3B.	HR.	RBI.	B.A.	PO.	A.	E.	F.A.
1952—Bristol	.............Appal.	C	16	55	4	14	4	0	0	8	.255	187	12	5	.975
1952—Burlington	........Carol.	C	70	223	19	53	9	0	1	3	.238	299	43	13	.963
1953-54—Burlington	.....Carol.					(In Military Service)									
1955—Lincoln	.............West.	C	84	250	28	58	8	0	1	29	.232	477	53	8	.985
1956—New Orleans	.....South.	....	9	26	....	6	....	....	....	....	.231	....	....	....	....
1956—Williamsport	.....East.	C	96	296	22	74	14	0	2	36	.250	425	37	5	.989
1957—Lincoln†	..........West.	C	87	252	22	50	5	2	1	15	.198	421	42	7	.988
1958—Tucson	.......Az.-Mx.	C	112	427	70	149	26	8	4	77	.349	*806	*81	7	*.992
1959—Tri-Cities	.........N'west	C	134	453	58	119	22	0	3	60	.263	*730	60	6	*.992
1960—Tri-Cities	.........N'west	C	119	387	58	129	22	0	2	68	.333	596	52	8	.988
1961—Stockton	.........Calif.	C	103	348	47	110	9	0	1	37	.287	689	*90	9	*.989
1962—Stockton	...........Calif.	1B-C	78	201	22	50	9	1	1	16	.249	360	28	8	.980
1963—Stockton	...........Calif.	C	19	48	9	17	4	0	2	8	.354	68	5	1	.986
1964—Stockton	...........Calif.	C	28	69	7	17	0	0	2	6	.246	129	6	3	.978

Year	Club	League	Pos.	G.	AB.	R.	H.	2B.	3B.	HR.	RBI.	B.A.	PO.	A.	E.	F.A.
1965—Quad Cities		Midw.	C-3B	15	36	4	11	2	1	0	3	.306	47	5	2	.963
1966—Quad Cities		Midw.	P-3-C	9	14	1	6	2	0	0	1	.429	5	6	3	.786
1968—Seattle		P.C.	PH	1	1	0	0	0	0	0	0	.000	0	0	0	.000

†Released by Pittsburgh Pirates' organization, January 28, 1958.

PITCHNG RECORD

Year	Club	League	G.	IP.	W.	L.	Pct.	H.	R.	ER.	SO.	BB.	ERA.
1957—Lincoln	Western	2	....	0	0	.000	....	....	....	....	....	....
1958—Tucson	Ariz.-Mex.	1	....	0	0	.000	....	....	....	....	....	....
1959—Tri-Cities	Northwest	1	....	0	0	.000	....	....	....	....	....	....
1961—Stockton	California	2	....	0	0	.000	....	....	....	....	....	....
1962—Stockton	California	9	19	2	0	1.000	29	10	8	12	1	3.79
1963—Stockton	California	3	6	0	0	.000	8	3	3	2	2	4.50
1964—Stockton	California	3	5	0	0	.000	2	0	0	5	0	0.00
1965—Quad Cities	Midwest	2	5	0	0	.000	8	4	3	3	0	5.40
1966—Quad Cities	Midwest	3	16	1	1	.500	17	8	6	8	3	3.38

RECORD AS MANAGER

Named California League Manager of the Year, 1963.

Year	Club	League	Position	W.	L.	Year	Club	League	Position	W.	L.
1958—Tucson	Arz.-Mx.	Second	66	54	1965—Quad Cities	Midwest	Ninth	25	37
1961—Stockton	Calif.	Sixth	21	46	(Second Half)		Seventh	28	33
(Second Half)		Third	33	36	1966—Quad Cities	Midwest	Sixth	30	31
1962—Stockton	Calif.	Sixth	33	38	(Second Half)		Fourth	33	30
(Second Half)		Third	37	30	1967—San Jose	Calif.	‡First	46	22
1963—Stockton	Calif.	Second	41	31	(Second Half)		Second	40	30
(Second Half)		†First	46	21	1977—Wichita	A.A.	Second(W)	68	64
1964—Stockton	Calif.	Fourth	34	35	1978—Wichita	A.A.	Fourth(W)	58	77
(Second Half)		Sixth	35	35					

†Won playoff against Modesto (First Half winner), two games to none.
‡Won playoff against Modesto (Second Half winner), two games to none.
Coach, Seattle (Pacific Coast League), 1968; coach, Kansas City Royals, 1969 through 1975; coach, Chicago Cubs, 1976; coach, Cincinnati Reds, 1979 through 1981.

LEE CONSTANTINE ELIA

Name pronounced Eel-e-ya.

Philadelphia Phillies

Born July 16, 1937, at Philadelphia, Pa.
Height, 5.11 Weight, 184.
Threw and batted righthanded.
Attended University of Delaware, Newark, Del.

Year	Club	League	Pos.	G.	AB.	R.	H.	2B.	3B.	HR.	RBI.	B.A.	PO.	A.	E.	F.A.
1959—Elmira	NYP	3B-SS	98	374	103	111	18	1	8	66	.297	164	213	30	.926
1960—Williamsport	East.	3-S-1	124	421	51	98	11	0	10	59	.233	172	223	39	.910
1961—Chattanooga	South.	SS	148	523	83	139	33	3	4	56	.266	243	359	42	.935
1962—Buffalo	Int.	SS-OF-3B	125	382	51	90	10	3	16	50	.236	204	321	34	.939
1963—Arkansas	Int.	SS	147	487	59	128	19	8	18	73	.263	240	418	•41	.941
1964—Arkansas	P. C.	1B-SS	139	442	58	116	24	4	16	57	.262	248	365	37	.943
1965—Indianapolis	P. C.	SS	137	487	77	127	20	2	29	75	.261	196	418	29	.955
1966—Chicago	Amer.	SS	80	195	16	40	5	2	3	22	.205	103	186	14	.954
1966—Indianapolis	P. C.	SS	21	85	16	21	5	1	4	14	.247	41	62	6	.945
1967—Indplst-Tacoma	P. C.	SS	128	457	58	122	24	2	14	59	.267	229	357	36	.942
1968—Tacoma	P. C.	SS-3B	13	43	4	10	2	0	3	8	.233	15	27	4	.913
1968—Chicago	Nat.	SS-3B-2B	15	17	1	3	0	0	0	3	.176	3	2	0	1.000
1969—Tacoma‡§x	P. C.	SS	3	13	1	2	1	0	0	0	.154	7	9	0	1.000
1969—Syracuse	Int.	2B-SS	17	53	3	15	3	0	1	5	.283	19	21	2	.952
1970-72—y								(Did not play)								
1973—Eugene z	P. C.	SS-3B	16	35	6	10	2	0	1	4	.286	12	25	2	.949
American League Totals			80	195	16	40	5	2	3	22	.205	103	186	14	.954
National League Totals			15	17	1	3	0	0	0	3	.176	3	2	0	1.000
Major League Totals			95	212	17	43	5	2	3	25	.203	106	188	14	.955

†Sold to Chicago Cubs' organization, May 23, 1967.
‡Loaned to New York Yankees' organization, April 19, 1969; returned, May 25, 1969.
§On disabled list, May 24 to September 15, 1969.
xOn voluntarily retired list, February 18, 1970, to December 9, 1971.
yReleased, January 3, 1972; signed by Philadelphia Phillies' organization, January 30, 1973.
zPlayer-coach.

RECORD AS MANAGER

Named Western Carolinas League Manager of the Year, 1975.
Named Eastern League Manager of the Year, 1978.

Year	Club	League	Position	W.	L.	Year	Club	League	Position	W.	L.
1975—Spartanburg	W. Car.	First	38	32	1977—Reading	East.	Third(CA)	63	75
(Second Half)		First	43	27	1978—Reading	East.	Third	36	33
1976—Spartanburg	W. Car.	Third	33	36	(Second Half)		†First	43	24
(Second Half)		Fourth	26	44	1979—Oklahoma City	A. A.	‡First(W)	72	63

†Lost championship playoff to Bristol, two games to none.
‡Lost championship playoff to Evansville, four games to two.
Minor league coach, Philadelphia Phillies, 1974; coach, Philadelphia Phillies, 1980 and 1981.

CHARLES LEONARD ESTRADA
Name pronounced Ess-TRAH-duh.
(Chuck)
San Diego Padres

Born February 15, 1938, at San Luis Obispo, Calif.
Height, 6.01. Weight, 185.
Threw and batted righthanded.

Year	Club	League	G.	IP.	W.	L.	Pct.	H.	R.	ER.	SO.	BB.	ERA.
1957—Salinas	California	39	223	17	11	.607	180	106	90	230	136	3.63
1958—Knoxville	Sally	39	217	15	11	.577	177	99	•87	•181	•153	3.61
1959—Vancouver	P. Coast	37	183	14	6	.700	133	74	58	178	77	2.85
1960—Baltimore	American	36	209	•18	11	.621	162	87	83	144	101	3.57
1961—Baltimore	American	33	212	15	9	.625	159	91	87	160	•132	3.69
1962—Baltimore	American	34	223	9	•17	.346	199	112	95	165	121	3.83
1963—Baltimore†	American	8	31	3	2	.600	26	17	16	16	19	4.65
1964—Baltimore‡	American	17	55	3	2	.600	62	34	32	32	21	5.24
1965—Rochester	Int'national	30	166	7	•14	.333	145	93	82	108	•91	4.45
1966—Chicago x	National	9	12	1	1	.500	16	12	10	3	5	7.50
1966—Seattle-Tacoma§	P. Coast	23	132	6	8	.429	108	62	54	81	75	3.68
1967—New York	National	9	22	1	2	.333	28	24	23	15	17	9.41
1967—Jacksonville	Int'national	15	81	6	8	.429	68	34	28	53	36	3.11
1968—Jacksonville y	Int'national	21	58	1	7	.125	64	59	52	27	34	8.07
1969—Visalia z	California	14	88	9	3	.750	96	60	40	54	30	4.09
American League Totals		128	730	48	41	.539	608	341	313	517	394	3.86
National League Totals		18	34	2	3	.400	44	36	33	18	22	8.74
Major League Totals		146	764	50	44	.532	652	377	346	535	416	4.08

†On disabled list with sore elbow from June 8 through September 15, 1963.
‡On disabled list with sore elbow from July 22 through August 31, 1964.
§Seattle (7 games)—Tacoma (16 games).
xReleased to Tacoma on June 23, 1966.
yOn disabled list from May 10 through May 20 and on temporary inactive list, September 5 through September 20, 1968.
zReleased July 13, 1969.

ALL-STAR GAME RECORD

Year	League	IP.	W.	L.	Pct.	H.	R.	ER.	SO.	BB.	ERA.
1960—American (first game)		1	0	0	.000	4	1	1	1	0	9.00

Minor League Instructor, New York Mets, 1970 through 1972; Coach, Texas Rangers, 1973; Minor League Instructor, Atlanta Braves, 1974; California Angels, 1975 through 1977; Coach, San Diego Padres, 1978 through 1981 (named pitching coach, March 21, 1978, after Roger Craig replaced Alvin Dark as manager).

JOHN FREDERICK FELSKE
Toronto Blue Jays

Born May 30, 1942, at Chicago, Ill.
Height, 6.03. Weight, 205.
Threw and batted righthanded.
Attended University of Illinois, Urbana, Ill.

Led Northern League catchers in passed balls with 19 in 1963.
Led Florida State League catchers in double plays with 9 in 1962.
Led Texas League catchers in double plays with 14 in 1964 and tied for lead with 8 in 1966.
Led American Association catchers in double plays with 12 in 1971.

Year	Club	League	Pos.	G.	AB.	R.	H.	2B.	3B.	HR.	RBI.	B.A.	PO.	A.	E.	F.A.
1962—Palatka	Fla. St.	C	94	269	29	50	12	1	5	32	.186	546	60	11	•.982
1962—St. Cloud	North.	C	5	9	0	0	0	0	0	1	.000	22	2	0	1.000
1963—St. Cloud	North.	C	117	396	52	99	22	2	12	58	.250	656	•86	8	.989
1964—Fort Worth	Texas	C	108	319	28	58	15	1	6	28	.182	528	•86	11	.982
1965—Salt Lake City	P. C.	C	41	124	10	23	4	0	3	11	.185	226	21	0	1.000
1965—Dallas-Ft.Worth	Texas	C	74	231	21	51	8	1	2	18	.221	383	41	7	.984
1966—Tacoma	P. C.	C	2	5	1	0	0	0	0	0	.000	0	0	0	.000
1966—Dallas-Ft. Worth	Texas	C	73	220	18	44	10	0	6	24	.200	456	49	7	.986
1967—Dallas-Ft. W.†	Texas	C-OF	68	203	18	53	3	1	3	20	.261	352	31	7	.982
1968—Tacoma	P. C.	C-OF	84	249	19	53	9	1	7	29	.213	388	41	7	.984
1968—Chicago	Nat.	C	4	2	0	0	0	0	0	0	.000	5	0	1	.833
1969—San Antonio	Texas	C-1-O	91	265	25	72	14	1	9	44	.272	438	48	7	.986
1970—Portland	P. C.	•C-1B	131	432	70	136	25	2	18	75	.315	•778	60	•10	.988
1971—Evansville	A. A.	1-C-O-3	119	402	54	118	20	4	14	68	.294	802	92	9	.990
1972—Evansville	A. A.	C-1B	33	113	14	27	5	2	1	16	.239	211	20	1	.996
1972—Milwaukee	Amer.	C-1B	37	80	6	11	3	0	1	5	.138	124	9	3	.978
1973—Milwaukee‡	Amer.	C-1B	13	22	1	3	0	1	0	4	.136	41	4	0	1.000
National League Totals			4	2	0	0	0	0	0	0	.000	5	0	1	.833
American League Totals			50	102	7	14	3	1	1	9	.137	165	13	3	.983
Major League Totals			54	104	7	14	3	1	1	9	.135	170	13	4	.979

†On disabled list, August 22 to September 4, 1967.
‡Released, October 23, 1973.

RECORD AS MANAGER

Year Club	League	Position	W.	L.
1974–Newark .... NYP		†Fifth	30	36
1975–Thetford Mines .. East.		Fifth	28	35
(Second Half)		Eighth	31	45
1976–Berkshire .... East.		Third(N)	68	68

Year Club	League	Position	W.	L.
1977–Spokane............. P. C.		Second(W)	75	69
1978–Spokane............. P. C.		Fourth(W)	64	75
1979–Vancouver .... P. C.		Third(N)	39	36
(Second Half)		‡First(N)	40	32

†One tie.
‡Lost playoff to Hawaii, two games to one.
Coach, Toronto Blue Jays, 1980 and 1981.

MICHAEL DENNIS FERRARO
(Mike)
New York Yankees

Born August 18, 1944, at Kingston, N. Y.
Height, 5.11. Weight, 175.
Threw and batted righthanded.
Attended Orange County Community College, Middletown, N. Y.

Tied major league record for most assists by third baseman, game (11), September 14, 1968.
Led Florida State League in total bases with 200 in 1964.
Named Most Valuable Player in Florida State League, 1964.
Led International League third basemen in double plays with 32 in 1966 and with 20 in 1971.

Year—Club	League	Pos.	G.	AB.	R.	H.	2B.	3B.	HR.	RBI.	B.A.	PO.	A.	E.	F.A.
1962–Ft. Lauderdale†	Fla. St.	SS	18	50	4	10	3	1	0	3	.200	23	36	8	.881
1963–Shelby	W. Car.	SS-3B	122	447	59	111	16	10	8	64	.248	95	134	46	.833
1964–Ft. Lauderdale ..	Fla. St.	3B	139	498	60	∗158	19	10	1	∗77	∗.317	∗130	∗273	22	.948
1965–Columbus	South.	3B	124	451	48	114	18	2	4	54	.253	91	215	●23	.930
1966–Toledo	Int.	∗3-2-SS	143	525	54	129	14	5	9	50	.246	∗101	∗274	∗16	.959
1966–New York	Amer.	3B	10	28	4	5	0	0	0	0	.179	4	21	2	.926
1967–Syracuse...........	Int.	3B	84	304	26	73	15	1	5	36	.240	59	157	6	.973
1967–Spokane...........	P. C.	3B	53	192	20	56	12	4	1	23	.292	54	75	7	.949
1968–New York	Amer.	3B	23	87	5	14	0	1	0	1	.161	16	61	2	.975
1968–Syracuse‡	Int.	3B-SS	118	440	58	129	20	2	4	41	.293	108	242	20	.946
1969–Rochester§........	Int.	3-2-S	115	438	66	122	19	5	4	40	.279	116	195	14	.957
1969–Seattle	Amer.	PH	5	4	0	0	0	0	0	0	.000	0	0	0	.000
1970–Rochester	Int.	3B	135	474	57	144	29	1	6	70	.304	∗99	∗267	∗27	.931
1971–Rochester x	Int.	∗3B-2B	120	408	59	111	20	5	7	65	.272	∗90	∗199	5	∗.983
1972–Milwaukee y	Amer.	3B-SS	124	381	19	97	18	1	2	29	.255	94	174	14	.950
1973–Tacoma z...........	P. C.	2B-3B	12	45	3	6	1	0	0	4	.133	5	16	1	.955
1973–Syracuse a	Int.	3B-OF-P	69	204	17	45	7	2	1	23	.221	37	99	6	.958
Major League Totals.......................			162	500	28	116	18	2	2	30	.232	114	256	18	.954

†On disabled list, June 27 to July 13 and July 25 to August 7, 1962.
‡Selected from New York Yankees' organization by Seattle Pilots, October 15, 1968; traded by Pilots' organization with Pitcher Gerry Scheon to Baltimore Orioles' organization for Pitchers Tom Fisher, John O'Donoghue and Lloyd Fourroux, April 30, 1969.
§On suspended list, May 1 to May 15, 1969.
xSold to Milwaukee Brewers, October 22, 1971.
yTraded to Minnesota Twins for Pitcher Ken Reynolds, March 27, 1973.
zReleased, May 2, 1973; Signed by Syracuse (New York Yankees' organization), May 7, 1973.
aReleased, April 10, 1974.

PITCHING RECORD

Year Club	League	G.	IP.	W.	L.	Pct.	H.	R.	ER.	SO.	BB.	ERA.
1973–Syracuse............................Int'national		1	2	0	0	.000	1	1	1	0	2	4.50

RECORD AS MANAGER

Year Club	League	Position	W.	L.
1974–Oneonta .... NYP		First	53	16
1975–Oneonta .... NYP		Third	35	34
1976–Ft. Lauderdale ... Fla. St.		†Second(S)	77	62

Year Club	League	Position	W.	L.
1977–West Haven........ East.		‡First(NE)	86	52
1978–Tacoma .... P. C.		§First(W)	80	57

†Lost playoff semifinals to Tampa, two games to none.
‡Won championship playoffs from Three Rivers, three games to none.
§Tacoma-Portland series tied, two to two, when series was ended due to continuing rain and wet grounds. Tacoma and Albuquerque ruled co-champions.
Coach, New York Yankees, 1979 through 1981.

WILLIAM CHARLES FISCHER
(Bill)
Cincinnati Reds

Born October 11, 1930, at Wausau, Wis.
Height, 6.00. Weight, 195.
Threw and batted righthanded.
Hobbies—Hunting and fishing.
Brother of Tom Fischer, Pitcher in Chicago White Sox' organization, 1958 through 1960 and Gary Fischer, pitcher in Los Angeles Dodgers' and California Angels' organizations, 1964 through 1968.

Established major league record for most consecutive innings, no bases on balls (84⅓), 1962.

Year Club	League	G.	IP.	W.	L.	Pct.	H.	R.	ER.	SO.	BB.	ERA.
1948–Wisconsin Rapids	Wis. St.	19	147	14	3	*.824	131	66	43	118	47	2.63
1949–Hot Springs	Cotton St.	34	227	16	15	.516	*272	148	98	140	94	3.89
1950–Memphis	Southern	5	14	1	1	.500	17	9	9	9	10	5.79
1950–Waterloo	I.I.I.	25	177	11	7	.611	155	97	81	138	93	4.12
1951–Waterloo	I.I.I.	24	124	5	10	.333	121	66	52	63	63	3.77
1951–Colorado Springs	Western	16	65	3	6	.333	82	63	59	46	46	8.17
1952-53–Memphis	Southern						(In Military Service)					
1954–Memphis	Southern	35	203	14	12	.538	207	107	87	92	73	3.86
1955–Memphis	Southern	34	204	5	15	.250	213	123	110	73	82	4.85
1956–Chicago	American	3	2	0	0	.000	6	4	4	2	1	18.00
1956–Toronto	Int'national	13	64	5	3	.625	68	22	22	24	14	3.09
1956–Vancouver	P. Coast	16	97	6	8	.429	125	54	50	40	26	4.66
1957–Chicago	American	33	124	7	8	.467	139	50	48	48	35	3.48
1958–Chi.†-Det.‡-Washington	American	42	88	4	10	.286	113	71	62	42	31	6.34
1959–Washington	American	34	187	9	11	.450	211	98	89	62	43	4.28
1960–Washington§-Detroit	American	40	132	8	8	.500	135	68	63	55	35	4.30
1961–Detroit x-Kansas City	American	41	68	4	2	.667	80	37	35	30	23	4.63
1962–Portland	P. Coast	13	36	2	2	.500	23	8	4	26	7	1.00
1962–Kansas City	American	34	128	4	12	.250	150	61	56	38	8	3.94
1963–Kansas City y	American	45	96	9	6	.600	86	44	38	34	29	3.56
1964–Minnesota za	American	9	7	0	1	.000	16	6	6	2	5	7.71
1965–Indianapolis	P. Coast	30	163	11	10	.524	158	76	61	91	18	3.37
1966–Indianapolis	P. Coast	37	165	11	6	.647	144	50	43	110	23	2.35
1967–Indianapolis b	P. Coast	24	118	12	4	.750	123	47	31	55	12	2.36
1968–Hawaii bc	P. Coast	24	139	8	9	.471	137	57	48	46	15	3.11
Major League Totals		281	832	45	58	.437	936	439	401	313	210	4.34

†Traded to Detroit Tigers with Outfielder Tito Francona for Pitcher Bob Shaw and Infielder Ray Boone, June 15, 1958.

‡Released to Washington Senators on waivers, September 11, 1958.

§Traded to Detroit Tigers in waiver deal for Pitcher Tom Morgan, July 22, 1960.

xTraded to Kansas City Athletics with Infielder Ozzie Virgil for Pitcher Gerry Staley and Indielder Reno Bertoia. Transaction started with shift of Fischer to A's, July 31, 1961 and transfer of other players August 2, 1961.

yDrafted from Portland roster by Minnesota Twins, December 2, 1963.

zOn voluntarily retired list, May 26, 1964 to January 14, 1965.

aReleased, January 21, 1965. Signed by Indianapolis (Chicago White Sox' organization), January 26, 1965.

bPlayer-coach.

cOn disabled list, May 4 to September 8, 1968. Released, September 25, 1968.

Scout, Minnesota Twins, part of 1964; Scout, Kansas City Royals, 1969 through 1974; Kansas City Royals minor league pitching instructor, 1975 through 1978; Coach, Cincinnati Reds, 1979 through 1981.

JOHN ARTHUR FOWLER
(Art)
Oakland A's

Born July 3, 1922, at Converse, S.C.
Height, 5.11. Weight, 180.
Threw and batted righthanded.

Year Club	League	G.	IP.	W.	L.	Pct.	H.	R.	ER.	SO.	BB.	ERA.
1944–Bristol	Ap'lachian	26	169	13	6	.684	187	77	52	108	40	2.77
1945–Danville	Carolina	30	253	*23	6	.793	221	109	72	177	81	2.56
1946–Jersey City	Int'national	31	118	4	8	.333	140	82	73	55	65	5.57
1947–Minneapolis	Am. Assoc.	2	3	0	0	.000	5	5	4	1	3	12.00
1947–Jacksonville	Sally	36	210	11	14	.440	233	123	84	107	87	3.60
1948–Jacksonville	Sally	37	234	19	10	.655	221	101	88	124	92	3.38
1949–Atlanta	Southern	42	113	7	6	.538	120	59	50	66	55	3.98
1950–Atlanta	Southern	41	241	19	12	.613	242	111	92	129	101	3.44
1951–Milwaukee	Am. Assoc.	17	78	4	7	.364	101	48	46	51	27	5.31
1951–Atlanta	Southern	18	95	6	5	.545	104	52	45	58	41	4.26
1952–Atlanta	Southern	38	236	16	10	.615	224	100	88	130	96	3.36
1953–Atlanta†	Southern	*54	*261	16	10	.643	*273	102	88	149	80	*3.03
1954–Cincinnati	National	40	228	12	10	.545	256	112	97	93	85	3.83
1955–Cincinnati	National	46	208	11	10	.524	198	96	90	94	63	3.89
1956–Cincinnati	National	45	178	11	11	.500	191	92	80	86	35	4.04
1957–Cincinnati	National	33	88	3	0	1.000	111	65	63	45	24	6.44
1958–Seattle‡-Spokane	P. Coast	38	249	16	13	.552	225	93	83	136	51	3.00
1959–Los Angeles	National	36	61	3	4	.429	70	39	36	47	23	5.31
1959–Spokane	P. Coast	8	44	4	2	.667	52	32	29	23	7	5.93
1960–St. Paul	Am. Assoc.	36	187	13	10	.565	208	70	61	109	38	2.94
1961–Omaha§	Am. Assoc.	10	55	5	3	.625	61	33	30	33	21	4.91
1961–Los Angeles	American	53	89	5	8	.385	68	42	36	78	29	3.64
1962–Los Angeles	American	48	77	4	3	.571	67	25	24	38	25	2.81
1963–Los Angeles	American	57	89	5	3	.625	70	26	24	53	19	2.43
1964–Los Angeles x	American	4	7	0	2	.000	8	8	8	5	5	10.29
1965–Denver	P. Coast	53	82	4	4	.500	96	43	36	55	25	3.95
1966–Denver	P. Coast	46	70	8	2	.800	62	18	18	47	16	2.31
1967–Denver	P. Coast	39	52	5	3	.625	52	22	19	30	12	3.29

Year Club	League	G.	IP.	W.	L.	Pct.	H.	R.	ER.	SO.	BB.	ERA.
1968—Denver y	P. Coast	28	56	1	1	.500	45	14	12	43	11	1.93
1970—Denver z	Am. Assoc.	45	68	9	5	.643	67	22	12	30	16	1.59
National League Totals		200	763	40	35	.533	826	404	366	365	230	4.32
American League Totals		162	262	14	16	.467	213	101	92	174	78	3.16
Major League Totals		362	1025	54	51	.514	1039	505	458	539	308	4.02

†Conditionally released by Milwaukee Braves to Cincinnati Reds, October 6, 1953.

‡Assigned by Cincinnati Reds to Spokane (Los Angeles Dodgers' organization), June 23, 1958, to complete deal in which Reds obtained Pitcher Don Newcombe from Dodgers for Pitcher Johnny Klippstein, First Baseman Steve Bilko and cash, plus transfer on option of Pitcher Charley Rabe from Seattle to Montreal, June 15, 1958.

§Sold by Los Angeles Dodgers to Los Angeles Angels, May 27, 1961.

xUnconditionally released, May 15, 1964; signed as free agent by Denver (Minnesota Twins' organization), February 15, 1965.

yOn disabled list, April 16 to May 16; on temporary inactive list, May 16 to May 28, 1968.

zPlayer-coach.

Coach, Los Angeles Angels, 1964; Minnesota Twins, 1969; Denver (American Association), 1970; Detroit Tigers, 1971 through 1973; Texas Rangers, 1974 and 1975; New York Yankees, part of 1977, 1978 and 1979; Oakland A's, 1980 and 1981.

FRANKLIN RAY FUNK
(Frank)
Seattle Mariners

Born August 30, 1935, at Washington, D. C.
Height, 6.00. Weight, 180.
Threw and batted righthanded.
Attended Shepherd College, Shepherdstown, W. Va., Montgomery College,
Takoma Park, Md., University of Maryland, College Park, Md.,
and American University, Washington, D. C.
Pitched seven-inning, 1-0 perfect game against Superior, July 27, 1955.
Pitched seven-inning, 1-0 no-hitter against Havana, June 16, 1960.
Tied for Kitty League lead in complete games with 17 in 1954.

Year Club	League	G.	IP.	W.	L.	Pct.	H.	R.	ER.	SO.	BB.	ERA.
1954—Mayfield	Kitty	26	200	14	11	.560	200	116	86	140	85	3.87
1955—St. Cloud	Northern	32	205	*18	7	.720	192	83	76	128	77	3.34
1956—Johnstown	Eastern	4	6	0	1	.000	14	10	6	2	1	9.00
1956—Danville	Carolina	8	25	0	3	.000	31	20	20	18	10	7.20
1956—St. Cloud	Northern	24	141	10	6	.625	102	55	42	92	44	2.68
1957—Sioux City	Western	5	7	0	2	.000	9	5	2	6	5	2.57
1957—Danville	Carolina	22	129	6	9	.400	120	74	47	102	46	3.28
1958—Corpus Christi	Texas	48	149	14	7	.667	113	52	43	105	59	2.60
1958—Phoenix†	P. C.	8	12	0	2	.000	18	9	9	9	3	6.75
1959—Toronto	Int'national	46	119	6	10	.375	115	57	49	80	39	3.71
1960—Toronto	Int'national	32	90	6	3	.667	72	23	21	73	24	2.10
1960—Cleveland	American	9	32	4	2	.667	27	8	7	18	9	1.97
1961—Cleveland	American	56	92	11	11	.500	79	35	34	64	31	3.33
1962—Cleveland	American	47	81	2	1	.667	62	35	29	49	32	3.22
1962—Salt Lake City‡	P. Coast	15	28	2	0	1.000	24	11	6	31	7	1.93
1963—Milwaukee	National	25	44	3	3	.500	42	14	13	19	13	2.66
1964—Denver	P. Coast	24	53	3	4	.429	43	28	26	48	15	4.42
1964—Toronto	Int'national	33	71	4	6	.400	68	25	22	55	20	2.79
1965—Atlanta	Int'national	14	82	4	3	.571	93	37	35	51	12	3.84
1965—Tacoma	P. Coast	26	49	2	4	.333	59	33	29	34	11	5.33
1966—Richmond	Int'national	3	7	0	0	.000	6	1	1	3	1	1.29
1966—Austin	Texas	30	151	11	9	.550	150	63	53	94	29	3.16
1967—Richmond§	Int'national	12	35	1	3	.250	51	31	24	27	10	6.17
American League Totals		112	205	17	14	.548	168	78	70	131	72	3.07
National League Totals		25	44	3	3	.500	42	14	13	19	13	2.66
Major League Totals		137	249	20	17	.541	210	92	83	150	85	3.00

†Sold by San Francisco Giants' organization to Cleveland Indians' organization, April 6, 1959.

‡Finished season with Cleveland Indians; traded to Milwaukee Braves with Outfielder Don Dillard for Pitcher Jack Curtis and First Baseman Joe Adcock, November 27, 1962; Braves promised added player in deal—Outfielder Ty Cline transferred March 18, 1963.

§Player-coach.

RECORD AS MANAGER

Year Club	League	Position	W.	L.
1969—Decatur	Midwest	Eighth	14	35
(Second Half)		Third	39	31
1970—Decatur	Midwest	Sixth	27	29
(Second Half)		First	36	26
1971—Decatur	Midwest	Fifth(S)	20	42
(Second Half)		†Third(S)	34	28

Year Club	League	Position	W.	L.
1972—Fresno	Calif.	Fourth	34	34
(Second Half)		†Second	40	30
1973—Fresno	Calif.	Fifth	34	36
(Second Half)		†Fourth	35	35

†Tied for position.

‡Lost to Quad Cities 8-5 on September 1 in playoff for second-half championship.

Minor League Pitching Instructor, San Francisco Giants, 1975, 1977 and 1978; coach, San Francisco Giants, 1976; minor league pitching instructor, Philadelphia Phillies, 1979 and 1980; coach, Seattle Mariners, August 15, 1980 through 1981.

WILLIAM FREDERICK GARDNER
(Billy)
Minnesota Twins

Born July 19, 1927, at New London, Conn.
Height, 6.00. Weight, 180.
Threw and batted righthanded.
Hobbies—Fishing, hunting and basketball.

Established major league record for fewest assists by second baseman, season, 150 or more games (350), 1958.

Tied American League record for most putouts by second baseman, extra-inning game (12), May 21, 1957 (16 innings).

Led American League second basemen in double plays, 1959.

Year	Club	League	Pos.	G.	AB.	R.	H.	2B.	3B.	HR.	RBI.	B.A.	PO.	A.	E.	F.A.
1945—Bristol	Appal.	3B	74	304	67	100	16	6	5	56	.329	*107	*132	11	*.956
1945—Jersey City	Int.	3B-OF	49	172	16	47	4	2	1	20	.273	55	75	8	.942
1946—Jersey City	Int.						(In Military Service)								
1947—Jacksonville	Sally	3B-SS	110	423	55	111	18	5	1	41	.262	129	191	32	.909
1948—Jacksonville	Sally	3B	•154	548	66	140	26	4	3	66	.255	*150	262	*36	.920
1949—Minneapolis	A.A.	3B	17	28	7	5	0	0	2	6	.179	5	16	4	.840
1949—Jersey City	Int.	3B	17	45	6	11	1	0	0	1	.244	18	25	4	.915
1950—Sioux City	West.	3B	154	581	96	176	32	7	22	118	.303	*159	*335	*48	.911
1951—Ottawa	Int.	3B	150	555	56	128	19	6	3	37	.231	•182	279	*36	.928
1952—Minneapolis	A.A.	INF-OF	93	224	29	58	15	1	1	15	.259	109	165	23	.923
1953—Nashville	Sou.	*SS-3B	153	591	88	182	•42	5	10	71	.308	255	444	*42	.943
1954—New York	Nat.	INF	62	108	10	23	5	0	1	7	.213	42	82	2	.984
1955—New York	Nat.	INF	59	187	26	38	10	1	3	17	.203	76	139	13	.943
1955—Minneapolis†	A.A.	INF	73	290	55	90	15	1	17	48	.310	161	210	17	.956
1956—Baltimore	Amer.	INF	144	515	53	119	16	2	11	50	.231	301	386	18	.974
1957—Baltimore	Amer.	*2B-SS	154	*644	79	169	*36	3	6	55	.262	406	450	12	*.986
1958—Baltimore	Amer.	2B-SS	151	560	32	126	28	2	3	33	.225	354	356	11	.985
1959—Baltimore†	Amer.	*2-SS-3	140	401	34	87	13	2	6	27	.217	334	393	*18	.976
1960—Washington	Amer.	*2B-SS	145	592	71	152	26	5	9	56	.257	360	418	*21	.974
1961—Minn.§-N.Y.	Amer.	2B-3B	86	253	24	57	14	0	2	13	.225	121	160	11	.962
1962—N.Y.x-Boston	Amer.	INF	57	200	23	54	9	2	0	12	.270	80	125	10	.953
1963—Boston y	Amer.	2B-3B	36	84	4	16	2	1	0	1	.190	37	59	1	.990
1964—Seattle z	P.C.	2B	101	308	23	69	8	4	1	28	.224	173	226	11	.973
1967—Pittsfield a	East.	3B	2	2	0	0	0	0	0	0	.000	1	0	0	1.000
1969—Pittsfield a	East.	2B	2	3	1	1	0	0	0	0	.333	3	2	0	1.000
1971—Pawtucket a	East.	PH	1	1	0	0	0	0	0	0	.000	0	0	0	.000
American League Totals			913	3249	320	780	144	17	37	247	.240	1993	2347	102	.997
National League Totals			121	295	36	61	15	1	4	24	.207	118	221	15	.958
Major League Totals			1034	3544	356	841	159	18	41	271	.237	2111	2568	117	.976

†Started 1956 season with New York Giants; sold to Baltimore Orioles for reported $20,000, April 21, 1956.

‡Traded to Washington Senators for Catcher Clint Courtney and Infielder Ron Samford, April, 1960.

§Traded to New York Yankees for Pitcher Danny McDevitt, June 14, 1961.

xTraded to Boston Red Sox for cash and transfer of Outfielder Tom Umphlett from Seattle, Pacific Coast League, to Richmond, International League, June 21, 1962.

yReleased by Boston Red Sox, October 2, 1963.

zPlayer-coach.

aPlayer-manager.

WORLD SERIES RECORD

Year	Club	League	Pos.	G.	AB.	R.	H.	2B.	3B.	HR.	RBI.	B.A.	PO.	A.	E.	F.A.
1961—New York	Amer.	PH	1	1	0	0	0	0	0	0	.000	0	0	0	.000

RECORD AS MANAGER

Named American Association Manager of the Year, 1980.

Year	Club	League	Position	W.	L.	Year	Club	League	Position	W.	L.
1967—Pittsfield	East.	Second(E)	75	62	1974—Jacksonville	South.	§First(E)	78	60
1968—Pittsfield	East.	†First	84	55	1975—Omaha	A.A.	Third(E)	67	69
1969—Pittsfield	East.	Fourth	68	72	1976—Omaha	A.A.	xFirst(E)	78	58
1970—Louisville	Int.	Sixth	69	71	1979—Memphis	South.	yzFirst(W)	36	34
1971—Pawtucket	East.	Third(Am.)	63	76	(Second Half)			Second(W)	46	28
1972—Jacksonville	South.	Fourth(E)	64	75	1980—Denver	A.A.	aFirst(W)	92	44
1973—Jacksonville	South.	‡First(E)	76	60						

†Lost playoff to Reading, three games to one.

‡Lost playoff to Montgomery, three games to one.

§Lost playoff to Knoxville, three games to two.

xLost playoff to Denver, four games to one.

yTied for position and won one-game first-half playoff from Montgomery.

zLost playoff to Nashville, two games to one.

aLost championship playoffs to Springfield, four games to one.

Coach, Boston Red Sox' organization, October 1964 through 1966; coach, Montreal Expos, 1977 and 1978; coach, Minnesota Twins, 1981.

DID YOU KNOW—
That the San Diego Padres had three players steal 50 or more bases in 1980? That ties a major league record.

ROBERT GIBSON
(Bob)
New York Mets

Born November 9, 1935, at Omaha, Neb.
Height, 6.01. Weight, 193.
Threw and batted righthanded.
Attended Creighton University, Omaha, Neb.

To be inducted into Baseball Hall of Fame, August 2, 1981.

Established major league records for lowest earned-run average, season, 300 or more innings (1.12), 1968; most seasons, 200 or more strikeouts (9), 1972; most consecutive games, starting pitcher, 303, August 31, 1965 through May 31, 1975.

Tied major league record for most strikeouts, inning (3), June 7, 1966 (fourth inning); struck out three batters on nine pitched balls, May 12, 1969 (seventh inning).

Established National League records for lowest earned-run average, season, 200 or more innings (1.12), 1968; most strikeouts, lifetime, right-handed pitcher (3,117), 1975; most clubs shut out (won or tied), season, 8 in 1968 (all clubs except Los Angeles); and most sacrifice flies allowed, lifetime, 95, 1975.

Tied National League record for most shutout games won or tied, one month, June 1968.

Pitched 11-0 no-hit victory against Pittsburgh Pirates, August 14, 1971.

Led National League in shutouts with 13 in 1968.

Led National League pitchers in complete games with 28 in 1969.

Tied for National League lead in shutouts with 5 in 1962, 5 in 1966 and 5 in 1971.

Named National League Most Valuable Player, 1968.

Won National League Cy Young Memorial Award, 1968-70.

Named as pitcher on THE SPORTING NEWS National League All-Star Team, 1968 and 1970.

Named THE SPORTING NEWS National League Pitcher of the Year, 1968 and 1970.

Named pitcher on THE SPORTING NEWS National League All-Star fielding teams, 1965 through 1973.

Year Club	League	G.	IP.	W.	L.	Pct.	H.	R.	ER.	SO.	BB.	ERA.
1957—Omaha	A.A.	10	42	2	1	.667	46	26	20	25	27	4.29
1957—Columbus	Sally	8	43	4	3	.571	36	26	18	24	34	3.77
1958—Omaha	A.A.	13	87	3	4	.429	79	45	32	47	39	3.31
1958—Rochester	Int.	20	103	5	5	.500	88	35	28	75	54	2.45
1959—Omaha	A.A.	24	135	9	9	.500	128	59	46	98	70	3.07
1959—St. Louis	Nat.	13	76	3	5	.375	77	35	28	48	39	3.32
1960—St. Louis	Nat.	27	87	3	6	.333	97	61	54	69	48	5.59
1960—Rochester	Int.	6	41	2	3	.400	33	15	13	36	17	2.85
1961—St. Louis	Nat.	35	211	13	12	.520	186	91	76	166	*119	3.24
1962—St. Louis	Nat.	32	234	15	13	.536	174	84	74	208	95	2.85
1963—St. Louis	Nat.	36	255	18	9	.667	224	110	96	204	96	3.39
1964—St. Louis	Nat.	40	287	19	12	.613	250	106	96	245	86	3.01
1965—St. Louis	Nat.	38	299	20	12	.625	243	110	102	270	103	3.07
1966—St. Louis	Nat.	35	280	21	12	.636	210	90	76	225	78	2.44
1967—St. Louis†	Nat.	24	175	13	7	.650	151	62	58	147	40	2.98
1968—St. Louis	Nat.	34	305	22	9	.710	198	49	38	*268	62	*1.12
1969—St. Louis	Nat.	35	314	20	13	.606	251	84	76	269	95	2.18
1970—St. Louis	Nat.	34	294	•23	7	.767	262	111	102	274	88	3.12
1971—St. Louis‡	Nat.	31	246	16	13	.552	215	96	83	185	76	3.04
1972—St. Louis	Nat.	34	278	19	11	.633	226	83	76	208	88	2.46
1973—St. Louis§	Nat.	25	195	12	10	.545	159	71	60	142	57	2.77
1974—St. Louis	Nat.	33	240	11	13	.458	236	111	102	129	104	3.83
1975—St. Louis x	Nat.	22	109	3	10	.231	120	66	61	60	62	5.04
Major League Totals		528	3885	251	174	.591	3279	1420	1258	3117	1336	2.91

†Suffered broken leg when hit by line drive, July 15; on disabled list through August 31.
‡On disabled list from May 30 to June 19.
§On disabled list, August 5 to September 17, 1973.
xPlaced on voluntarily retired list, September 29, 1975.
Coach, New York Mets, 1981.

WORLD SERIES RECORD

Established following World Series records: Most consecutive games won, total Series (7); most consecutive complete games won, total Series (7); most consecutive complete games, total Series (8); most strikeouts, game (17), October 2, 1968; most strikeouts, Series (35), 1968; most games, 10 or more strikeouts, total Series (5).

Tied following World Series records: Most games won, seven-game Series (3), 1967; most games won, no losses, seven-game Series (3), 1967; most complete games, seven-game Series (3), 1967 and 1968; most innings, one or more strikeouts, game, (9), October 2, 1968.

Year Club	League	G.	IP.	W.	L.	Pct.	H.	R.	ER.	SO.	BB.	ERA.
1964—St. Louis	Nat.	3	27	2	1	.667	23	11	9	31	8	3.00
1967—St. Louis	Nat.	3	27	3	0	1.000	14	3	3	26	5	1.00
1968—St. Louis	Nat.	3	27	2	1	.667	18	5	5	35	4	1.67
World Series Totals		9	81	7	2	.778	55	19	17	92	17	1.89

ALL-STAR GAME RECORD

Year League		IP.	W.	L.	Pct.	H.	R.	ER.	SO.	BB.	ERA.
1962—National (second game)		2	0	0	.000	1	1	1	1	2	4.50
1965—National		2	0	0	.000	2	0	0	3	1	0.00
1967—National		2	0	0	.000	2	0	0	2	0	0.00
1969—National		1	0	0	.000	2	1	1	2	1	9.00
1970—National		2	0	0	.000	3	2	2	2	1	9.00
1972—National		2	0	0	.000	1	0	0	0	0	0.00
All-Star Game Totals		11	0	0	.000	11	4	4	10	5	3.27

Member of National League All-Star Team in 1962 (first game) and 1968; did not play. Named to National League All-Star Team for 1966 game; replaced due to injury.

PEDRO W. GOMEZ (MARTINEZ)
(Preston)
California Angels

Born April 20, 1923, at Central Preston, Oriente, Cuba.
Height, 5.11. Weight, 185.
Threw and batted righthanded.
Hobbies—Fishing and golf.
Attended Mexico City College, Mexico City, Mexico, and Florida Southern, Lakeland, Fla.

Year Club	League	Pos.	G.	AB.	R.	H.	2B.	3B.	HR.	RBI.	B.A.	PO.	A.	E.	F.A.
1944—Washington†	Amer.	2B-SS	8	7	2	2	1	0	0	2	.286	4	1	1	.833
1945—Buffalo	Int.	SS	108	375	52	101	19	2	3	23	.269	202	288	43	.919
1946—Vicksburg	So'east	SS	22	76	3	8	1	0	0	3	.105	26	69	8	.922
1947—Vicksburg	So'east	SS	14	48	5	14	1	1	1	11	.292	17	37	5	.915
1947—New London	Col.	SS	90	332	53	95	8	3	9	55	.286	133	246	56	.871
1948—Florence	Tri-St.	SS	51	187	21	34	9	0	1	15	.182	68	147	24	.900
1949—Saginaw	Cent.	SS	105	358	42	76	17	3	3	42	.212	174	258	35	.925
1950—Saginaw	Cent.			(On voluntary retired list)											
1951—Three Rivers	Prov.	SS	125	448	58	120	21	1	9	58	.268	175	348	41	.927
1952—Tol.-Charleston	A.A.	SS	18	52	4	10	1	0	0	5	.192	20	37	5	.919
1952—Havana	Fla. Int.	SS	9	33	3	6	1	0	0	4	.182	11	18	3	.906
1953—				(Out of Organized Baseball)											
1954—Yakima	W. Int.		12	27	3	5	0	0	1	2	.185	6	28	3	.906
Major League Totals			8	7	2	2	1	0	0	2	.286	4	1	1	.833

†Released, March 1945.

RECORD AS MANAGER

Year Club	League	Position	W.	L.	Year Club	League	Position	W.	L.
1957—Fresnillo	Cen. Mex.	Second	6	4	1964—Richmond	Int.	Seventh	65	88
1957—Mex. C. Reds†	Mexican	Second	59	50	1969—San Diego	Nat.	Sixth (W)	52	110
1958—Mex. C. Reds‡	Mexican	Second	48	43	1970—San Diego	Nat.	Sixth (W)	63	99
1959—Havana	Int.	§Third	80	73	1971—San Diego	Nat.	Sixth (W)	61	100
1960—Spokane	P.C.	First	92	61	1972—San Diego y	Nat.	Fourth (W)	4	7
1961—Spokane	P.C.	xSixth	68	86	1974—Houston	Nat.	Fourth(W)	81	81
1962—Spokane	P.C.	Eighth	58	96	1975—Houston z	Nat.	Sixth(W)	47	80
1963—Richmond	Int.	Fifth	66	81	1980—Chicago	Nat.	Sixth(E)	38	52
					Major League Totals			346	529

†Replaced Lazaro Salazar following latter's death with Reds in first place, May 1, 1957. Won playoffs by defeating Monterrey, four games to none and Mexico City Tigers, four games to three.
‡Replaced by Molinero Montes de Oca, August 1, 1958.
§Won playoffs by defeating Columbus in semifinals, four games to none and defeating Richmond in finals, four games to two. Won Junior World Series by defeating Minneapolis of American Association, four games to three.
xTied for position with Hawaii.
yReplaced by Don Zimmer, April 27.
zReplaced by Bill Virdon, August 18.
aReplaced by Joey Amalfitano, July 24, 1980.
Coach, Los Angeles Dodgers, 1965 through 1968 and 1977 through 1979; coach, Houston Astros, 1973; coach, St. Louis Cardinals, 1976; coach, California Angels, 1981.
Coach, American League All-Star Team, 1973.

ALEXANDER PETER GRAMMAS
Name pronounced GRAMM-uss.
(Alex)
Detroit Tigers

Born April 3, 1927, at Birmingham, Ala.
Height, 6.00. Weight, 176.
Threw and batted righthanded.
Hobby—Fishing.
Attended Mississippi State University, State College, Miss.;
received Bachelor of Science degree in Business.
Tied for American Association lead in double plays by shortstops with 96 in 1953.

Year Club	League	Pos.	G.	AB.	R.	H.	2B.	3B.	HR.	RBI.	B.A.	PO.	A.	E.	F.A.
1949—Muskegon	Cent.	3B	87	294	42	96	12	3	0	30	.327	120	217	24	.934
1950—Memphis	South.	*SS-3B	135	457	49	102	16	6	1	41	.223	247	381	24	*.963
1951—Memphis	South.	3B	52	185	35	47	6	1	2	16	.254	54	88	12	.922
1951—Tulsa	Tex.	SS-3B	88	302	29	83	10	3	2	32	.275	146	256	27	.937
1952—Tulsa	Tex.	SS-2B	158	602	80	146	28	9	2	51	.243	314	536	37	.958
1953—Kansas City†	A.A.	SS	140	584	93	179	29	3	2	62	.307	*262	*438	24	.967
1954—St. Louis	Nat.	SS-3B	142	401	57	106	17	4	2	29	.264	253	432	24	.966
1955—St. Louis	Nat.	SS	128	366	32	88	19	2	3	25	.240	235	340	19	.968
1956—St. L.‡-Cinn.	Nat.	3-S-2	83	152	18	37	11	0	0	17	.243	60	105	5	.971

Year Club	League	Pos.	G.	AB.	R.	H.	2B.	3B.	HR.	RBI.	B.A.	PO.	A.	E.	F.A.
1957—Cincinnati ....Nat.		S-2-3	73	99	14	30	4	0	0	8	.303	60	75	3	.978
1958—Cincinnati§.......Nat.		S-3-2	105	216	25	47	8	0	0	12	.218	125	174	6	.980
1959—St. Louis ....Nat.		SS	131	368	43	99	14	2	3	30	.269	216	373	22	.964
1960—St. Louis ....Nat.		S-2-3	102	196	20	48	4	1	4	17	.245	102	171	9	.968
1961—St. Louis ....Nat.		S-2-3	89	170	23	36	10	1	0	21	.212	112	182	10	.967
1962—St. L.x-Chi.......Nat.		S-2-3	44	78	3	16	3	0	0	4	.205	34	66	2	.980
1963—Chicago............Nat.		SS	16	27	1	5	0	0	0	0	.185	8	13	1	.955
Major League Totals			913	2073	236	512	90	10	12	163	.247	1206	1931	101	.969

†On option to Kansas City by Cincinnati Reds; Traded to St. Louis Cardinals for Pitcher Jack Crimian and reported $100,000, December 2, 1953.

‡Traded to Cincinnati Redlegs with Outfielder Joe Frazier for Infielder Chuck Harmon, May 16, 1956.

§Traded to St. Louis Cardinals with Pitcher Alex Kellner and First Baseman George Crowe for Pitcher Bobby Mabe, Shortstop Eddie Kasko and Outfielder Del Ennis, October 3, 1958.

xTraded to Chicago Cubs with Outfielder Don Landrum for Infielder Daryl Robertson and Outfielder Bobby Gene Smith, June 5, 1962.

RECORD AS MANAGER

Year Club	League	Position	W.	L.
1964—Ft. Worth ....Texas		Sixth	51	89
1969—Pittsburgh†.........Nat.		Third(E)	4	1
1976—Milwaukee..........Amer.		Sixth(E)	66	95
1977—Milwaukee..........Amer.		Sixth(E)	67	95
National League Totals			4	1
American League Totals			133	190
Major League Totals.............................			137	191

†Replaced Larry Shepard, September 26.

Coach, Pittsburgh Pirates, 1965 through 1969; Cincinnati Reds, 1970 through 1975, 1978; Atlanta Braves, 1979; Detroit Tigers, 1980 and 1981.

Coach, American League All-Star Team, 1977.

HARVEY HADDIX JR.
Pittsburgh Pirates

Born September 18, 1925, at Medway, O.
Height, 5.09. Weight, 161.
Threw and batted lefthanded.
Hobbies—Hunting and fishing.
Brother of Ben Haddix, former catcher in New York Giants' organization and
Fred Haddix, former pitcher in Boston Red Sox' organization.

Established major league record for most consecutive batters retired, game (36), May 26, 1959, against Milwaukee Braves. Lost, 1-0, in thirteenth inning.
Tied National League record for most wild pitches, inning (3), sixth inning, August 21, 1963.
Led National League in shutouts with 6 in 1953.
Led American Association pitchers in complete games with 17 in 1950.
Named Carolina League Most Valuable Player, 1947.
Named pitcher on THE SPORTING NEWS National League All-Star fielding team, 1958-59-60.

Year Club	League	G.	IP.	W.	L.	Pct.	H.	R.	ER.	SO.	BB.	ERA.
1947—Winston-Salem ....Carolina		27	204	19	5	*.792	144	62	43	268	70	*1.90
1948—Columbus.............................Am. Assoc.		32	186	11	9	.550	199	109	99	144	67	4.79
1949—Columbus.............................Am. Assoc.		35	219	13	13	.500	206	98	85	177	94	3.49
1950—Columbus.............................Am. Assoc.		30	217	*18	6	.750	192	76	65	*160	59	*2.70
1951—St. Louis ....National						(In Military Service)						
1952—St. Louis ....National		7	42	2	2	.500	31	18	13	31	10	2.79
1953—St. Louis ....National		36	253	20	9	.690	220	97	86	163	69	3.06
1954—St. Louis ....National		43	260	18	13	.581	247	114	103	184	77	3.57
1955—St. Louis ....National		37	208	12	16	.429	216	111	103	150	62	4.46
1956—St. Louis†-Philadelphia ....National		35	230	13	8	.619	224	113	97	170	65	3.68
1957—Philadelphia‡ ....National		27	171	10	13	.435	176	84	77	136	39	4.05
1958—Cincinnati§ ....National		29	184	8	7	.533	191	79	72	110	43	3.52
1959—Pittsburgh ....National		31	224	12	12	.500	189	88	78	149	49	3.13
1960—Pittsburgh ....National		29	172	11	10	.524	189	87	76	101	38	3.98
1961—Pittsburgh ....National		29	156	10	6	.625	159	72	71	99	41	4.10
1962—Pittsburgh ....National		28	141	9	6	.600	146	74	66	101	42	4.21
1963—Pittsburgh x ....National		49	70	3	4	.429	67	27	26	70	20	3.34
1964—Baltimore ....American		49	90	5	5	.500	68	26	23	90	23	2.30
1965—Baltimore ....American		24	34	3	2	.600	31	22	13	21	23	3.44
American League Totals............................		73	124	8	7	.533	99	48	36	111	46	2.61
National League Totals..............................		380	2111	128	106	.547	2055	964	865	1464	555	3.69
Major League Totals		453	2235	136	113	.546	2154	1012	901	1575	601	3.63

†Traded to Philadelphia Phillies with Pitchers Ben Flowers and Stu Miller for Pitchers Murry Dickson and Herman Wehmeier, May 11, 1956.

‡Traded to Cincinnati Redlegs for Outfielder Wally Post, December 6, 1957.

§Traded to Pittsburgh Pirates with Catcher Forrest (Smoky) Burgess and Third Baseman Don Hoak for Pitcher Charles (Whammy) Douglas, Infielders-Outfielders Jim Pendleton and Frank Thomas and Outfielder Johnny Powers, January 31, 1959.

xTraded to Baltimore Orioles for Shortstop Dick Yencha and cash, December 14, 1963.

Year	Club	League	G.	IP.	W.	L.	Pct.	H.	R.	ER.	SO.	BB.	ERA.
1960–Pittsburgh		National	2	7⅓	2	0	1.000	6	2	2	6	2	2.45

ALL-STAR GAME RECORD

Year	League	IP.	W.	L.	Pct.	H.	R.	ER.	SO.	BB.	ERA.
1955–National		3	0	0	.000	3	1	1	2	0	3.00

Member of National League All-Star Team in 1953 and 1954; did not play in 1953 and replaced due to injury in 1954.

Coach, New York Mets, 1966 and 1967; coach, Cincinnati Reds, 1969; minor league pitching coach, Pittsburgh Pirates, 1968 and 1970; coach, Boston Red Sox, 1971; coach, Cleveland Indians, 1975 through 1978; coach, Pittsburgh Pirates, 1979 through 1981.

WALLACE LARRY HANEY
(Known by middle name.)
Milwaukee Brewers

Born November 19, 1942, at Charlottesville, Va.
Height, 6.02. Weight, 195.
Throws and bats righthanded.
Hobby–Golf.
Brother of George Haney, pitcher in New York Yankees' organization, 1959 through 1963.
Led California League catchers in double plays with 18 and in passed balls with 38 in 1962.
Led Eastern League catchers in double plays with 17 in 1963.
Received reported $60,000 bonus to sign with Baltimore Orioles, 1961.

Year	Club	League	Pos.	G.	AB.	R.	H.	2B.	3B.	HR.	RBI.	B.A.	PO.	A.	E.	F.A.
1961–Bluefield	Appal.	C	47	145	24	37	6	0	6	26	.255	356	20	6	.984	
1962–Stockton	Calif.	*C-1B	123	425	77	109	17	9	18	77	.256	966	*99	17	*.984	
1963–Elmira	East.	C	120	404	41	98	19	1	8	40	.243	894	85	8	.992	
1964–Elmira†	East.	C	3	7	0	2	1	0	0	1	.286	14	0	0	1.000	
1965–Elmira‡	East.	C	76	252	23	64	12	3	3	21	.254	574	39	9	.986	
1966–Rochester	Int.	C	63	197	18	42	6	1	7	25	.213	407	27	3	.993	
1966–Baltimore	Amer.	C	20	56	3	9	1	0	1	3	.161	123	6	2	.985	
1967–Baltimore	Amer.	C	58	164	13	44	11	0	3	20	.268	311	31	3	.991	
1968–Baltimore‡‡	Amer.	C	38	89	5	21	3	1	1	5	.236	149	18	1	.994	
1969–Seattle§-Oak.	Amer.	C	75	145	11	28	7	0	4	19	.193	255	24	6	.979	
1970–Winnipeg	Int.	C-1-3	81	251	21	55	8	2	3	26	.219	459	44	8	.984	
1970–Oakland	Amer.	C	2	2	2	0	0	0	0	0	.000	6	0	0	1.000	
1971–Iowa	A.A.	C-3-OF	102	354	36	95	15	0	10	53	.268	528	43	6	.990	
1972–Hawaii y	P.C.	C-3-1	55	155	22	38	7	1	3	15	.245	289	18	0	1.000	
1972–Oakland x	Amer.	C-2B	5	4	0	0	0	0	0	0	.000	4	0	1	.800	
1973–Tucson	P.C.	C-3B	75	265	39	76	12	1	2	44	.287	370	46	6	.966	
1973–Oakland z	Amer.	C	2	2	0	1	0	0	0	0	.500	3	0	0	1.000	
1973–St. Louis a	Nat.	C	2	1	0	0	0	0	0	0	.000	2	0	0	1.000	
1974–Oakland	Amer.	C-3-1	76	121	12	20	4	0	2	3	.165	219	21	3	.968	
1975–Oakland	Amer.	C-3B	47	26	3	5	0	0	1	2	.192	70	4	0	1.000	
1976–Oakland b	Amer.	C	88	177	12	40	2	0	0	10	.226	290	45	9	.974	
1977–Milwaukee c	Amer.	C	63	127	7	29	2	0	0	10	.244	223	32	4	.985	
1978–Milwaukee d	Amer.	C	4	5	0	1	0	0	0	1	.200	6	0	0	1.000	
American League Totals			478	918	68	198	30	1	12	73	.216	1659	181	29	.984	
National League Totals			2	1	0	0	0	0	0	0	.000	2	0	0	1.000	
Major League Totals			480	919	68	198	30	1	12	73	.215	1661	181	29	.985	

†On temporary inactive list, May 25 through June 6. In military service most of the season, was taken off military list, February 24, 1965.

‡On disabled list, July 20 through August 10.

‡‡Selected by Seattle Pilots from Baltimore Orioles in expansion draft, October 15, 1968.

§Traded to Oakland Athletics for Infielder John Donaldson, June 13, 1969.

xSold to San Diego Padres' organization, May 30, 1972.

yRecalled by San Diego Padres, September 1, 1972. Sold by San Diego Padres to Oakland A's, September 6, 1972.

zPurchased by St. Louis Cardinals, September 1, 1973.

aSold to Oakland Athletics, March 26, 1974.

bSold to Milwaukee Brewers, December 6, 1976.

cReleased, March 30, 1978.

dPlayer-coach.

Coach, Milwaukee Brewers, part of 1978 through 1981.

WORLD SERIES RECORD

Year	Club	League	Pos.	G.	AB.	R.	H.	2B.	3B.	HR.	RBI.	B.A.	PO.	A.	E.	F.A.
1974–Oakland	Amer.	C	2	0	0	0	0	0	0	0	.000	6	0	0	1.000	

RONALD LA VERN HANSEN
(Ron)
Milwaukee Brewers

Born April 5, 1938, at Oxford, Neb.
Height, 6.03. Weight, 200.
Threw and batted righthanded.

Tied major league records for fewest stolen bases, season, 150 or more games (0), 1967; fewest three-base hits, season, 150 or more games (0), 1967.

Established major league record for most chances accepted by shortstop, doubleheader (28), August 29, 1965 (23 innings).

Tied American League record for most chances accepted by shortstop in extra-inning game (18), August 29, 1965 (first game).

Led Pacific Coast League shortstops in double plays with 96 in 1959.

Made unassisted triple play, July 30, 1968, for Washington Senators against Cleveland Indians (night game). With runners on first and second he caught Jose Azcue's line drive, stepped on second to double Dave Nelson who had broke for third and tagged Russ Snyder going into second base.

Led American League shortstops in double plays with 110 in 1961 with 105 in 1964 and with 91 in 1967.

Named American League Rookie of the Year by Baseball Writers' Association and THE SPORTING NEWS, 1960.

Year	Club	League	Pos.	G.	AB.	R.	H.	2B.	3B.	HR.	RBI.	B.A.	PO.	A.	E.	F.A.
1956–Stockton		Calif.	3B-SS	•140	494	86	143	20	9	8	84	.289	192	446	47	.931
1957–Baltimore†		P. C.					(On Disabled List)									
1958–Baltimore		Amer.	SS	12	19	1	0	0	0	0	1	.000	10	23	2	.943
1958–Knoxville‡		Sally	SS	90	301	30	65	7	1	6	36	.216	177	254	26	.943
1959–Vancouver		P. C.	SS	147	508	61	130	17	5	18	61	.256	*321	*496	•40	.953
1959–Baltimore		Amer.	SS	2	4	0	0	0	0	0	0	.000	2	6	1	.889
1960–Baltimore		Amer.	SS	153	530	72	135	22	5	22	86	.255	*325	456	29	.964
1961–Baltimore§		Amer.	SS-2B	155	533	51	132	13	2	12	51	.248	272	460	31	.959
1962–Baltimore xy		Amer.	SS	71	196	12	34	7	0	3	17	.173	114	159	10	.965
1963–Chicago		Amer.	SS	144	482	55	109	17	2	13	67	.226	247	*483	13	.983
1964–Chicago		Amer.	SS	158	575	85	150	25	3	20	68	.261	*292	*514	21	.975
1965–Chicago		Amer.	*SS-2	•162	587	61	138	23	4	11	66	.235	287	*527	26	.969
1966–Chicago z		Amer.	SS	23	74	3	13	1	0	0	4	.176	49	73	7	.946
1967–Chicago a		Amer.	SS	157	498	35	116	20	0	8	51	.233	243	*482	27	.964
1968–Wash.b-Chicago		Amer.	SS-3-2	126	362	35	71	15	0	9	32	.196	170	336	21	.960
1969–Chicago c		Amer.	INF	85	185	15	48	6	1	2	22	.259	216	83	8	.974
1970–New York d		Amer.	SS-3-2	59	91	13	27	4	0	4	14	.297	25	57	1	.986
1971–New York e		Amer.	3-2-SS	61	145	6	30	3	0	2	20	.207	52	72	8	.939
1972–Kansas City f		Amer.	SS-3-2	16	30	2	4	0	0	0	2	.133	5	28	1	.971
Major League Totals				1384	4311	446	1007	156	17	106	501	.234	2309	3759	206	.967

†On disabled list, April 11 to September 25, 1957.

‡On disabled list, May 14 to June 11, 1958.

§On military list, November 2, 1961, to April 20, 1962.

xOn disabled list, August 24 to September 23, 1962.

yTraded to Chicago White Sox with Pitcher Hoyt Wilhelm, Third Baseman Pete Ward and Outfielder Dave Nicholson for Shortstop Luis Aparicio and Outfielder-Third Baseman Al Smith, January 14, 1963.

zOn disabled list, May 26 to October 17, 1966.

aTraded with Pitchers Dennis Higgins and Steve Jones to Washington Senators for Pitchers Bob Priddy and Les Narum and Infielder Tim Cullen, February 13, 1968.

bTraded to Chicago White Sox for Infield Tim Cullen, August 2, 1968.

cSold to New York Yankees, March 1, 1970.

dOn disabled list, August 7 to September 1, 1970.

eReleased, February 15, 1972; signed by Kansas City Royals, April 5, 1972.

Coach, Milwaukee Brewers, 1981.

ALL-STAR GAME RECORD

Year	League	Pos.	AB.	R.	H.	2B.	3B.	HR.	RBI.	B.A.	PO.	A.	E.	F.A.
1960–American (both games)		SS	6	0	3	0	0	0	0	.500	2	4	0	1.000

TOMMY HARPER
Boston Red Sox

Born October 14, 1940, at Oak Grove, La.
Height, 5.09. Weight, 160.
Threw and batted righthanded.
Attended San Francisco State College, San Francisco, Calif., and
Santa Rosa Junior College, Santa Rosa, Calif.

One of five players in major league history to hit 30 home runs and steal 30 bases in the same season (31 home runs and 38 stolen bases in 1970).

Led American League in stolen bases with 73 in 1969 and with 54 in 1973.

Major League stolen bases: 1962 (1), 1963 (12), 1964 (24), 1965 (35), 1966 (29), 1967 (23), 1968 (11), 1969 (73), 1970 (38), 1971 (25), 1972 (25), 1973 (54), 1974 (28), 1975 (26), 1976 (4). Total—408.

Led Three I League in stolen bases with 31 in 1961.

Led Three I League batters in walks with 136 in 1961 and Pacific Coast League batters with 105 in 1962.

Named Most Valuable Player in Three I League, 1961.

Year	Club	League	Pos.	G.	AB.	R.	H.	2B.	3B.	HR.	RBI.	B.A.	PO.	A.	E.	F.A.
1960–Topeka†		I.I.I.	2B	79	252	65	64	14	3	5	36	.254	162	203	28	.929
1961–Topeka		I.I.I.	2B	124	426	*131	138	27	*11	15	65	.324	285	315	23	*.963
1962–Cincinnati		Nat.	3B	6	23	1	4	0	0	0	1	.174	6	7	1	.929
1962–San Diego		P. C.	3B-OF	144	499	*120	166	24	8	26	84	.333	106	233	34	.909
1963–Cincinnati		Nat.	OF-3B	129	408	67	106	12	3	10	37	.260	224	7	4	.983
1964–Cincinnati		Nat.	OF-3B	102	317	42	77	5	2	4	22	.243	149	6	1	.994
1965–Cincinnati		Nat.	OF-3-2B	159	646	*126	166	28	3	18	64	.257	279	10	5	.983
1966–Cincinnati		Nat.	OF	149	553	85	154	22	5	5	31	.278	257	5	1	.996
1967–Cincinnati‡§		Nat.	OF	103	365	55	82	17	3	7	22	.225	208	6	1	.995

Year Club League	Pos.	G.	AB.	R.	H.	2B.	3B.	HR.	RBI.	B.A.	PO.	A.	E.	F.A.
1968–Cleveland x.......Amer.	OF-2B	130	235	26	51	15	2	6	26	.217	121	1	2	.984
1969–Seattle.............Amer.	2-3-OF	148	537	78	126	10	2	9	41	.235	232	268	22	.958
1970–Milwaukee.......Amer.	*3-2-OF	154	604	104	179	35	4	31	82	.296	192	330	*28	.949
1971–Milwaukee y.....Amer.	O-3-2	152	585	79	151	26	3	14	52	.258	227	118	18	.950
1972–Boston.............Amer.	OF	144	556	92	141	29	2	14	49	.254	321	4	5	.985
1973–Boston.............Amer.	OF	147	566	92	159	23	3	17	71	.281	251	13	4	.985
1974–Boston z...........Amer.	OF	118	443	66	105	15	3	5	24	.237	105	2	2	.982
1975–Calif.a-Oak.b.....Amer.	1-O-3	123	354	51	90	14	1	5	38	.254	249	10	6	.977
1976–Baltimore c.......Amer.	1B-OF	46	77	8	18	5	0	1	7	.234	2	0	0	1.000
National League Totals..................		648	2312	376	589	84	16	44	177	.255	1123	41	13	.989
American League Totals.................		1162	3957	596	1020	172	20	102	390	.258	1700	746	87	.966
Major League Totals.......................		1810	6269	972	1609	256	36	146	567	.257	2823	787	100	.973

†On temporary inactive list, May 28 to June 16, 1960.
‡On disabled list, May 28 to July 26, 1967.
§Traded to Cleveland Indians for First Baseman Fred Whitfield and Pitcher George Culver, November 21, 1967. Outfielder Bob Raudman was assigned from Chicago Cubs to Reds as part of deal.
xSelected by Seattle Pilots from Cleveland Indians in expansion draft, October 15, 1968.
yTraded with Pitchers Marty Pattin and Lew Krausse and Outfielder Pat Skrable to Boston Red Sox for Catcher Don Pavletich, Pitchers Ken Brett and Jim Lonborg, First Baseman George Scott and Outfielders Billy Conigliaro and Joe Lahoud, October 11, 1971.
zTraded to California Angels for Infielder Bob Heise, December 2, 1974.
aSold to Oakland Athletics, August 13, 1975.
bReleased, November 20, 1975; signed as free agent by Baltimore Orioles, April 9, 1976.
cReleased, December 17, 1976.

CHAMPIONSHIP SERIES RECORD

Year Club League	Pos.	G.	AB.	R.	H.	2B.	3B.	HR.	RBI.	B.A.	PO.	A.	E.	F.A.
1975–Oakland.............Amer.	PH	1	0	0	0	0	0	0	0	.000	0	0	0	.000

ALL-STAR GAME RECORD

Year League	Pos.	AB.	R.	H.	2B.	3B.	HR.	RBI.	B.A.	PO.	A.	E.	F.A.
1970–American	PR	0	0	0	0	0	0	0	.000	0	0	0	.000

Minor league coach, New York Yankees, 1977; scout, New York Yankees, 1978; public relations officer, Boston Red Sox, 1979; coach, Boston Red Sox, 1980 and 1981.

TOMMY VANN HELMS
Texas Rangers

Born May 5, 1941, at Charlotte, N. C.
Height, 5.10. Weight, 173.
Threw and batted righthanded.
Hobbies–Music and golf.

Led National League second basemen in double plays with 107 in 1970, 130 in 1971 and 115 in 1972.
Led Florida State League shortstops in double plays with 93 in 1960 and led Sally League shortstops with 102 in 1962.
Led Three I League in sacrifice hits with 19 in 1961 and Sally League with 18 in 1962.
Named National League Rookie of the Year by the Baseball Writers' Association, 1966.
Named National League Rookie Player of the Year by THE SPORTING NEWS, 1966.
Named second baseman on THE SPORTING NEWS National League All-Star Team, 1968.
Named second baseman on THE SPORTING NEWS National League All-Star Fielding Team, 1970 and 1971.

Year Club League	Pos.	G.	AB.	R.	H.	2B.	3B.	HR.	RBI.	B.A.	PO.	A.	E.	F.A.
1959–Palatka.............Fla. St.	SS	56	210	37	53	3	1	0	16	.252	75	151	26	.897
1960–Palatka.............Fla. St.	SS	•137	*586	*119	*171	*33	5	3	69	.292	217	*423	*57	.918
1961–Topeka.............I.I.I.	SS	121	484	86	134	13	10	2	57	.277	178	378	*38	.936
1962–Macon ....Sally	SS	139	*573	102	*195	*38	7	1	50	.340	245	*452	*34	.953
1963–San Diego .........P.C.	SS-2B	138	471	40	106	21	3	2	39	.225	231	395	28	.957
1964–San Diego .........P.C.	SS-2B	142	543	57	168	25	9	7	69	.309	212	466	32	.955
1964–Cincinnati ....Nat.	PH	2	1	0	0	0	0	0	0	.000	0	0	0	.000
1965–Cincinnati ....Nat.	SS-3-2B	21	42	4	16	2	2	0	6	.381	17	22	1	.975
1965–San Diego .........P.C.	SS	96	382	48	122	23	3	6	51	.319	167	297	13	.973
1966–Cincinnati ....Nat.	3B-2B	138	542	72	154	23	1	9	49	.284	155	258	13	.969
1967–Cincinnati ....Nat.	2B-SS	137	497	40	136	27	4	2	35	.274	264	347	21	.967
1968–Cincinnati ....Nat.	2-SS-3B	127	507	35	146	28	2	2	47	.288	322	372	15	.979
1969–Cincinnati ....Nat.	2B-SS	126	480	38	129	18	1	1	40	.269	325	347	17	.975
1970–Cincinnati ....Nat.	*2B-SS	150	575	42	136	21	1	1	45	.237	353	412	13	*.983
1971–Cincinnati† ......Nat.	2B	150	547	40	141	26	1	3	52	.258	*395	468	9	*.990
1972–Houston ....Nat.	2B	139	518	45	134	20	5	5	60	.259	353	*441	17	.979
1973–Houston ....Nat.	2B	146	543	44	156	28	2	4	61	.287	325	438	9	.988
1974–Houston ....Nat.	2B	137	452	32	126	21	1	5	50	.279	308	360	10	*.985
1975–Houston‡§ ....Nat.	2-3-SS	64	135	7	28	2	0	0	14	.207	58	109	2	.988
1976–Pittsburgh x......Nat.	3-2-SS	62	87	10	24	5	1	1	13	.276	30	46	3	.962
1977–Pittsburgh y......Nat.	PH	15	12	0	0	0	0	0	0	.000	0	0	0	.000
1977–Boston z...........Amer.	2B-3B	21	59	5	16	2	0	1	5	.271	4	4	0	1.000
National League Totals..................		1414	4938	409	1326	221	21	33	472	.269	2905	3620	130	.980
American League Totals.................		21	59	5	16	2	0	1	5	.271	4	4	0	1.000
Major League Totals.......................		1435	4997	414	1342	223	21	34	477	.269	2909	3624	130	.980

†Traded with First Baseman Lee May and Outfielder Jim Stewart to Houston Astros for Infielder Denis Menke, Second Baseman Joe Morgan, Pitcher Jack Billingham and Outfielders Cesar Geronimo and Ed

Armbrister (latter assigned from Oklahoma City to Indianapolis), November 29, 1971.
‡On disabled list, March 24 to April 30, 1975.
§Traded to Pittsburgh Pirates for a player to be named later, December 12, 1975; Pirates sent Infielder Art Howe to Astros, January 6, 1976, to complete deal.
xSold to Oakland A's, November 5, 1976; traded with Second Baseman Phil Garner and Pitcher Chris Batton to Pittsburgh Pirates for Pitchers Doc Medich, Dave Giusti, Rick Langford and Doug Bair, Outfielders Mitchell Page and Tony Armas, March 15, 1977.
yReleased, June 14, 1977; signed as free agent by Boston Red Sox, June 21, 1977.
zReleased, March 25, 1978.
Coach, Texas Rangers, 1981.

CHAMPIONSHIP SERIES RECORD

Year Club	League	Pos.	G.	AB.	R.	H.	2B.	3B.	HR.	RBI.	B.A.	PO.	A.	E.	F.A.
1970—Cincinnati	Nat.	2B	3	11	0	3	0	0	0	0	.273	11	12	0	1.000

WORLD SERIES RECORD

Year Club	League	Pos.	G.	AB.	R.	H.	2B.	3B.	HR.	RBI.	B.A.	PO.	A.	E.	F.A.
1970—Cincinnati	Nat.	2B	5	18	1	4	0	0	0	0	.222	10	13	0	1.000

ALL-STAR GAME RECORD

Year League	Pos.	AB.	R.	H.	2B.	3B.	HR.	RBI.	B.A.	PO.	A.	E.	F.A.
1967—National	PH	1	0	0	0	0	0	0	.000	0	0	0	.000
1968—National	2B	3	0	1	1	0	0	0	.333	1	2	0	1.000
All-Star Game Totals		4	0	1	1	0	0	0	.250	1	2	0	1.000

ELROD JEROME HENDRICKS
(Ellie)
Baltimore Orioles

Born December 22, 1940, at St. Thomas, Virgin Islands.
Height, 6.01½. Weight, 175.
Threw right and batted lefthanded.
Hobby—Water color painting.

Tied National League record for most bases on balls, game, since 1900 (5), September 16, 1972.
Led Mexican League catchers in double plays with 19 in 1967.
Tied Mexican League catchers for lead in double plays with 9 in 1965.

Year Club	League	Pos.	G.	AB.	R.	H.	2B.	3B.	HR.	RBI.	B.A.	PO.	A.	E.	F.A.
1959—McCook	Neb. St.	C	25	34	6	8	1	0	0	3	.235	91	7	2	.980
1960—Wellsville†	NYP	C	73	217	36	51	8	1	11	36	.235	372	36	15	.965
1961—							(Out of Organized Ball)								
1962—Winnipeg	North.	C	69	213	25	45	7	2	3	22	.211	415	43	11	.977
1963—Winnipeg‡	North.	C	22	50	10	14	0	0	3	12	.280	95	11	2	.981
1964—Jalisco	Mex.	C-OF	67	202	43	59	8	4	10	45	.292	214	23	9	.963
1965—Jalisco	Mex.	C	128	411	100	117	14	8	35	98	.285	556	•65	6	.990
1966—Jalisco	Mex.	C	122	386	78	116	19	2	23	87	.301	555	64	6	.990
1966—El Paso	Tex.	C	18	56	6	15	2	0	3	12	.268	119	12	0	1.000
1967—Jalisco	Mex.	C	131	434	•124	137	18	4	•41	112	.316	613	63	7	.990
1967—Seattle§	P. C.	C	13	36	3	8	1	0	2	4	.222	59	3	0	1.000
1968—Baltimore	Amer.	C	79	183	19	37	8	1	7	23	.202	303	21	3	.991
1969—Baltimore	Amer.	*C-1B	105	295	36	72	5	0	12	38	.244	488	41	1	*.998
1970—Baltimore	Amer.	C	106	322	32	78	9	0	12	41	.242	509	35	8	.986
1971—Baltimore	Amer.	C-1B	101	316	33	79	14	1	9	42	.250	453	34	7	.986
1972—Baltimore x	Amer.	C	33	84	6	13	4	0	4	4	.155	130	15	2	.986
1972—Chicago y	Nat.	C	17	43	7	5	1	0	2	6	.116	83	7	2	.978
1973—Baltimore	Amer.	C	41	101	9	18	5	1	3	15	.178	148	9	1	.994
1974—Baltimore	Amer.	C-1B	66	159	18	33	8	2	3	8	.208	194	13	0	1.000
1975—Baltimore	Amer.	C	85	223	32	48	8	2	8	38	.215	332	36	2	.995
1976—Balt.z-N.Y.	Amer.	C	54	132	8	23	2	0	4	9	.174	147	17	3	.982
1977—Syracuse	Int.	C	56	135	30	38	9	0	11	37	.281	114	4	4	.967
1977—New York a	Amer.	C	10	11	1	3	1	0	1	2	.273	11	0	0	1.000
1978—Baltimore b	Amer.	C	13	18	4	6	1	0	1	1	.333	19	2	1	.955
1979—Baltimore c	Amer.	C	1	1	0	0	0	0	0	0	.000	1	0	1	.500
American League Totals			694	1845	198	410	65	7	60	224	.222	2735	223	29	.990
National League Totals			17	43	7	5	1	0	2	6	.116	83	7	2	.978
Major League Totals			711	1888	205	415	66	7	62	230	.220	2818	230	31	.990

†Released by Milwaukee Braves' organization, September 21, 1960; signed as free agent by Tulsa (St. Louis Cardinals' organization), November 21, 1961.
‡Released by St. Louis Cardinals' organization, June 13, 1963.
§Drafted by Baltimore Orioles from Seattle (California Angels' organization), November 28, 1967.
xTraded to Chicago Cubs for Outfielder H. Thomas Davis, August 18, 1972.
yTraded to Baltimore Orioles for Catcher Francisco Estrada, October 27, 1972.
zTraded with Pitchers Ken Holtzman, Doyle Alexander, Grant Jackson and Jimmy Freeman, latter assigned from Rochester to Syracuse, to New York Yankees for Pitchers Rudy May, Tippy Martinez, Dave Pagan and Scott McGregor, and Catcher Rick Dempsey, June 15, 1976.
aGranted free agency, October 20, 1977; signed by Baltimore Orioles as coach, November 23, 1977.
bActivated, May 18, 1978; released, March 26, 1979.
cPlayer-coach, September 1 through remainder of 1979 season.
Coach, Baltimore Orioles, 1978 through 1980.

PITCHING RECORD

Year Club	League	G.	IP.	W.	L.	Pct.	H.	R.	ER.	SO.	BB.	ERA.
1978—Baltimore	American	1	2	0	0	.000	1	0	0	0	1	0.00

CHAMPIONSHIP SERIES RECORD

Year Club	League	Pos.	G.	AB.	R.	H.	2B.	3B.	HR.	RBI.	B.A.	PO.	A.	E.	F.A.
1969—Baltimore	Amer.	C	3	8	2	2	2	0	0	3	.250	18	0	0	1.000
1970—Baltimore	Amer.	C	1	5	2	2	0	0	0	0	.400	5	0	0	1.000
1971—Baltimore	Amer.	C	2	4	1	2	0	0	1	2	.500	6	0	0	1.000
1974—Baltimore	Amer.	C	3	6	1	1	0	0	0	0	.167	11	1	0	1.000
1976—New York	Amer.	PH	1	1	0	1	0	0	0	0	1.000	0	0	0	.000
Championship Series Totals			10	24	6	8	2	0	1	5	.333	40	1	0	1.000

WORLD SERIES RECORD

Year Club	League	Pos.	G.	AB.	R.	H.	2B.	3B.	HR.	RBI.	B.A.	PO.	A.	E.	F.A.
1969—Baltimore	Amer.	C	3	10	1	1	0	0	0	0	.100	21	1	0	1.000
1970—Baltimore	Amer.	C	3	11	1	4	1	0	1	4	.364	17	2	1	.950
1971—Baltimore	Amer.	C	6	19	3	5	1	0	0	1	.263	40	4	1	.978
1976—Baltimore	Amer.	PH	2	2	0	0	0	0	0	0	.000	0	0	0	.000
World Series Totals			14	42	5	10	2	0	1	5	.238	78	7	2	.977

Coach, Baltimore Orioles, 1978 through 1981.

JACK E. HIATT

Named pronounced HY-ut.

Chicago Cubs

Born July 27, 1942, at Bakersfield, Calif.
Threw and batted righthanded.
Attended Pierce Junior College, Woodland Hills, Calif.

Led Western Carolinas League catchers in double plays with 6 in 1961.

Year Club	League	Pos.	G.	AB.	R.	H.	2B.	3B.	HR.	RBI.	B.A.	PO.	A.	E.	F.A.
1961—Statesville	W.C.	*C-1-O-2	96	332	63	108	20	4	3	69	.325	*609	76	14	*.980
1962—San Jose	Calif.	C	106	314	51	99	21	2	2	32	.315	711	61	17	.978
1963—Tri-City	N'w't	C-OF	85	261	30	83	10	0	2	36	.318	566	32	8	.987
1963—Hawaii	P. C.	C	4	5	0	0	0	0	0	0	.000	5	0	0	1.000
1964—Hawaii	P. C.	C-OF	125	406	71	125	20	6	23	83	.308	434	36	9	.981
1964—Los Angeles†	Amer.	C-1B	9	16	2	6	0	0	0	2	.375	17	2	1	.950
1965—San Francisco	Nat.	C-1B	40	67	5	19	4	0	1	7	.284	119	10	3	.977
1965—Tacoma	P. C.	C-1B	33	102	14	29	8	0	2	15	.284	217	10	5	.978
1966—San Francisco	Nat.	1B	18	23	2	7	2	0	0	1	.304	49	6	1	.982
1966—Phoenix	P. C.	1B-C	106	337	62	91	18	3	13	68	.270	868	61	10	.989
1967—San Francisco	Nat.	1-C-OF	73	153	24	42	6	0	6	26	.275	303	18	4	.988
1968—San Francisco	Nat.	C-1B	90	224	14	52	10	2	4	34	.232	387	37	2	.995
1969—San Francisco‡	Nat.	C-1B	69	194	18	38	4	0	7	34	.196	359	30	3	.992
1970—Mont.§-Chi. x	Nat.	C-1B	83	221	23	57	14	1	2	29	.258	466	24	7	.986
1971—Houston	Nat.	C-1B	69	174	16	48	8	1	1	16	.276	329	20	3	.991
1972—Houston yz	Nat.	C	100	25	2	5	3	0	0	0	.200	36	4	0	1.000
1972—California a	Amer.	C	22	45	4	13	0	1	1	5	.289	48	4	0	1.000
1973—Hawaii b	P. C.	C	103	314	48	91	22	0	10	39	.290	587	44	10	.984
1974—Wichita c	A. A.	C-1B	85	215	38	58	9	0	6	38	.270	431	25	5	.989
1975—Wichita c	A. A.	C	1	2	0	0	0	0	0	0	.000	3	0	0	1.000
National League Totals			452	1081	104	268	51	4	21	147	.248	2048	149	23	.990
American League Totals			31	61	6	19	0	1	1	7	.311	65	6	1	.986
Major League Totals			483	1142	110	287	51	5	22	154	.251	2113	155	24	.990

†Traded to San Francisco Giants for Outfielder Jose Cardenal, November 21, 1964.
‡Sold to Montreal Expos, April 6, 1970.
§Traded to Chicago Cubs for Outfielder Charles (Boots) Day, May 11, 1970.
xSold to Houston Astros, December 1, 1970.
yOn disabled list, May 29 to July 21, 1972.
zTraded to California Angels for cash and a player to be named at a later date, July 29, 1972.
aReleased, March 27, 1973; signed by San Diego Padres' organization, April 13, 1973.
bReleased, October 1, 1973.
cPlayer-coach.

RECORD AS MANAGER

Year Club	League	Position	W.	L.
1975—Brad. Cubs	G. C.	Third	30	24
1976—Pompano Beach	Fla. St.	Fourth(S)	56	85
1979—Wichita	A. A.	Fourth(W)	57	79
1980—Wichita	A. A.	Fourth(W)	61	74

Minor league coach, Chicago Cubs' organization, 1974 tnrough June 15, 1975; minor league instructor, Chicago Cubs, 1977 and 1978; coach, Chicago Cubs, 1981.

DID YOU KNOW—

That Eddie Collins and Lou Brock are the only players in major league history to collect 3,000 hits yet never win a batting title?

CHARLES JOSEPH HILLER
(Chuck)
St. Louis Cardinals

Born October 1, 1935, at Johnsburg, Ill.
Height, 5.11. Weight, 172.
Threw right and batted lefthanded.
Hobbies—Bowling and all other sports.
Attended St. Thomas College, St. Paul, Minn.; received Bachelor of Arts degree in Business Administration.
Led Northwest League second basemen in double plays with 102 in 1959.
Named Texas League Most Valuable Player, 1960.

Year Club	League	Pos.	G.	AB.	R.	H.	2B.	3B.	HR.	RBI.	B.A.	PO.	A.	E.	F.A.
1957—Cocoa ....Fla.St.		2B-SS	133	505	99	148	21	9	11	51	.293	252	370	46	.931
1958—Minot† ....North.		2B	120	455	89	128	23	12	8	58	.281	*339	308	26	.961
1959—Eugene ....Northw.		2B	139	487	92	*166	24	•9	13	99	.341	*309	*395	3	*.970
1960—Rio Grande Val. Texas		2B	144	560	89	*187	*47	4	3	74	*.334	*365	*438	16	*.980
1961—San Francisco...Nat.		2B	70	240	38	57	12	1	2	12	.238	133	158	8	.973
1961—Tacoma ...........P.C.		2B	73	281	54	91	15	3	5	32	.324	163	188	14	.962
1962—San Francisco...Nat.		2B	161	602	94	166	22	2	3	48	.276	367	417	*29	.964
1963—San Francisco...Nat.		2B	111	417	44	93	10	2	6	33	.223	224	277	19	.963
1964—San Francisco...Nat.		2B-3B	80	208	21	37	8	1	1	17	.180	113	145	7	.974
1965—S.F.‡-New York.Nat.		2-OF-3	107	293	25	69	11	1	6	22	.235	151	183	14	.960
1966—New York ....Nat.		2-3-OF	108	254	25	71	8	2	2	14	.280	110	153	5	.981
1967—N.Y.§x-Phila.y ..Nat.		2B	56	97	4	18	4	0	0	5	.186	33	46	3	.963
1968—Pittsburgh ....Nat.		2B	11	13	2	5	1	0	0	1	.385	4	2	1	.857
1968—Columbus z.......Int.		3-2-1-OF	84	273	33	75	10	2	3	36	.275	208	142	10	.972
Major League Totals......................			704	2121	253	516	76	9	20	152	.243	1135	1381	86	.967

†Drafted from Cleveland Indians' organization by Eugene (San Francisco Giants' organization), December 2, 1958.
‡Sold to New York Mets, May 12, 1965.
§Suffered fractured finger when hit by a line drive, May 3; on disabled list through June 11.
xTraded to Philadelphia Phillies for Infielder Phil Linz, May 11, 1967.
yDrafted by Pittsburgh Pirates from San Diego (Philadelphia Phillies' organization), November 28, 1967.
zReleased by Pittsburgh Pirates' organization, December 20, 1968.

WORLD SERIES RECORD

Tied World Series record by hitting a home run with the bases full, seventh inning, October 8, 1962—giving him a tie for most runs batted in, inning (4).

Year Club	League	Pos.	G.	AB.	R.	H.	2B.	3B.	HR.	RBI.	B.A.	PO.	A.	E.	F.A.
1962—San Francisco...Nat.		2B	7	26	4	7	3	0	1	5	.269	16	22	1	.974

RECORD AS MANAGER

Year Club	League	Position	W.	L.	Year Club	League	Position	W.	L.
1969—Salem ....Carol.		†First(W)	78	66	1974—Marion ....Appal.		Second(N)	33	35
1970—Tidewater ....Int.		Fourth	74	66	1975—Marion ....Appal.		First(N)	35	33
1971—Marion ....Appal.		Second(S)	33	35	1980—Kingsport...........Appal.		Third	36	34
1972—Marion ....Appal.		Fourth(S)	22	45					

†Lost playoff semifinals to Burlington, two games to none after defeating High Point-Thomasville in quarterfinals, two games to none.
Coach, Texas Rangers, 1973; coach, Kansas City Royals, 1976 through 1979; coach, St. Louis Cardinals, 1981.

WALTER JOHN HRINIAK

Name pronounced RIN-ee-ack.

(Walt)
Boston Red Sox

Born May 2, 1943, at Natick, Mass.
Height, 5.11. Weight, 180.
Threw right and batted lefthanded.
Hobbies—Hunting, fishing and golf.
Led Texas League catchers in passed balls with 16 in 1968.
Led Texas League shortstops in double plays with 67 in 1966.
Received reported $50,000 bonus to sign with Milwaukee Braves, 1961.

Year Club	League	Pos.	G.	AB.	R.	H.	2B.	3B.	HR.	RBI.	B.A.	PO.	A.	E.	F.A.
1961—Eau Claire........North.		SS	76	267	35	83	14	1	2	50	.311	120	216	22	.939
1962—Yakima ....Northw.		SS	139	444	64	133	21	7	2	54	.300	*204	*352	30	.949
1963—Austin ....Tex.		2B	117	370	47	98	11	4	3	45	.265	233	295	17	.969
1964—Austin† ....Tex.		3B-2B	52	175	19	41	5	1	0	11	.234	63	95	10	.940
1965—Austin ....Tex.		2B-3B	10	28	5	3	1	0	0	0	.107	18	18	2	.947
1965—Yakima ....Northw.		S-2B	116	390	60	100	17	4	10	57	.256	190	303	26	.950
1966—Austin ....Tex.		SS	134	455	48	107	16	3	0	38	.235	230	*388	20	*.969
1967—Austin ....Tex.		2-3-S-C	83	282	50	76	11	3	8	40	.270	140	172	12	.963
1967—Richmond ....Int.		2B-C	24	40	4	11	1	1	0	7	.275	34	14	2	.960
1968—Shreveport ....Tex.		C-3-O-2	107	345	40	108	11	1	6	47	.313	453	100	8	.986
1968—Atlanta.............Nat.		C	9	26	0	9	0	0	0	3	.346	57	1	2	.967
1969—Atl.‡-San Diego..Nat.		C	38	73	4	16	0	0	0	1	.219	105	7	2	.982

Year Club League	Pos.	G.	AB.	R.	H.	2B.	3B.	HR.	RBI.	B.A.	PO.	A.	E.	F.A.
1970—Salt Lake City§..P. C.	2B-C	121	410	49	101	21	4	2	35	.246	285	330	19	.970
1971—Savannah xy......So.	3-C-2-P	48	114	8	16	0	0	0	5	.140	93	38	6	.956
1971—Winnipeg...........Int.	C-2-3-O	9	23	3	7	3	0	1	5	.304	25	6	3	.912
1972—Quebec City z ....East.	1-3-C-2	36	88	10	29	5	2	0	15	.330	183	14	4	.980
1973—Peninsula z ....Int.	3B	17	50	2	7	0	0	0	2	.140	4	10	1	.933
Major League Totals		47	99	4	25	0	0	0	4	.253	162	8	4	.977

†On disabled list from May 22 through August 3 after suffering injuries in auto accident which killed teammate Jerry Hummitzsch.

‡On disabled list, April 7 to April 28, 1969. Traded with Outfielder Andy Finlay and Infielder Van Kelly to San Diego Padres for Outfielder Tony Gonzalez, June 13, 1969.

§Traded by San Diego Padres to Atlanta Braves for Pitcher Rick Wilson, April 3, 1971.

xOn disabled list, June 7 to June 30, 1971.

yUnconditionally released by Atlanta Braves' organization, July 23, 1971; signed as free agent by Montreal Expos' organization, August 24, 1971.

zSelected by Montreal Expos' organization to manage Jamestown (New York-Pennsylvania League).

PITCHING RECORD

Year Club League	G.	IP.	W.	L.	Pct.	H.	R.	ER.	SO.	BB.	ERA.
1971—Savannah...........................Southern	1	1	0	0	.000	2	1	1	0	0	9.00

RECORD AS MANAGER

Year Club League	Position	W.	L.
1972—Jamestown ....NYP	Third	42	28
1973—Jamestown ....NYP	Third	41	28

Player-coach, Quebec City (Montreal Expos' organization), part of 1972; coach, Montreal Expos, 1974 and 1975; minor league coach and instructor, Montreal Expos, 1976; coach, Boston Red Sox, 1977 through 1981.

DARRELL DEAN JOHNSON
Texas Rangers

Born August 25, 1927, at Ord, Neb.
Height, 6.01. Weight, 190.
Threw and batted righthanded.
Hobbies—Hunting and golf.

Tied for American Association lead in double plays by catchers with 11 in 1956 and tied for International League lead with 11 in 1959.

Named Major League Manager of the Year by THE SPORTING NEWS, 1975.

Year Club League	Pos.	G.	AB.	R.	H.	2B.	3B.	HR.	RBI.	B.A.	PO.	A.	E.	F.A.
1949—Redding ....F. West	C-O	88	322	60	89	19	1	9	58	.276	589	60	17	.974
1950—Marshall ....E. Tex.	*C-O	131	493	77	162	●36	9	13	105	.329	*608	79	15	*.979
1951—San Antonio......Tex.	C-OF	49	169	23	45	8	1	3	24	.266	200	32	4	.983
1951—Wichita Falls.....Big St.	C-OF	71	288	47	89	11	2	2	38	.309	275	62	10	.971
1952—San Antonio.......Tex.	C-OF	24	83	9	27	3	0	3	15	.325	106	12	2	.983
1952—St. Louis†-Chi....Amer.	C	51	115	12	26	2	1	0	10	.226	161	23	5	.974
1953—Memphis‡ ....South.	C	113	370	50	92	15	1	4	44	.249	506	61	12	.979
1954—Richmond§........Int.	C	90	291	32	76	10	0	6	37	.261	377	54	6	.986
1955—Denver.............A.A.	C	152	555	56	170	26	4	4	49	.306	*822	*87	12	.987
1956—Denver.............A.A.	●C-3-O	107	367	61	117	20	3	7	48	.319	561	46	●14	.977
1957—New York.........Amer.	C	21	46	4	10	1	0	1	8	.217	75	8	0	1.000
1958—New York.........Amer.	C	5	16	1	4	0	0	0	0	.250	22	3	0	1.000
1959—Richmond x.......Int.	C	94	316	22	69	8	0	4	28	.218	502	56	11	.981
1960—St. Louis ....Nat.	C	8	2	0	0	0	0	0	0	.000	10	1	0	1.000
1961—Phila.y-Cinn......Nat.	C	41	115	7	31	3	0	1	9	.270	198	23	2	.991
1962—Cincinnati z.......Nat.	C	2	4	0	0	0	0	0	0	.000	16	2	0	1.000
1962—Baltimore.........Amer.	C	6	22	0	4	0	0	0	1	.182	30	2	0	1.000
American League Totals..................		83	199	17	44	3	1	1	19	.221	288	36	5	.985
National League Totals...................		51	121	7	31	3	0	1	9	.256	224	26	2	.992
Major League Totals		134	320	24	75	6	1	2	28	.234	512	62	7	.988

†Sold with Outfielder Jim Rivera to Chicago White Sox; St. Louis purchased Outfielder Ray Coleman from Chicago and Outfielder-Catcher J. W. Porter from Colorado Springs in same deal, July 28, 1952.

‡Traded with Pitcher Lou Kretlow and $75,000 to St. Louis Browns for Pitcher Virgil Trucks and Third Baseman Bob Elliott, June 13, 1953. Johnson reported at close of season, others transferred on date of trade.

§Recalled by Baltimore Orioles and traded with Pitchers Mike Blyzka, Don Larsen and Bob Turley, First Baseman Dick Kryhoski, Shortstop Billy Hunter and Outfielders Ted del Guercio and Jim Fridley to New York Yankees for Pitchers Harry Byrd, Jim McDonald and Bill Miller, Catchers Hal Smith and Gus Triandos, Second Baseman Don Leppert, Third Baseman Kal Segrist, Shortstop Willie Miranda and Outfielder Gene Woodling. Yankees assigned Blyzka, del Guercio, Johnson and Fridley to minor league teams. Byrd, McDonald, Smith, Triandos, Miranda, Woodling, Larsen, Turley and Hunter transferred November 18; others on December 3, 1954.

xDrafted by St. Louis Cardinals from Richmond (New York Yankees' organization), November 30, 1959.

yStarted season as St. Louis Cardinals' coach, released July 8, 1961; signed as player by Philadelphia Phillies, July 9, 1961; sold to Cincinnati Reds, August 14, 1961.

zReleased by Cincinnati Reds; signed as player-coach by Baltimore Orioles, April 24, 1962; released as player by Baltimore, June 12, 1962.

WORLD SERIES RECORD

Year Club League	Pos.	G.	AB.	R.	H.	2B.	3B.	HR.	RBI.	B.A.	PO.	A.	E.	F.A.
1961—Cincinnati ....Nat.	C	2	4	0	2	0	0	0	0	.500	8	1	0	1.000

RECORD AS MANAGER

Year Club	League	Position	W.	L.
1963—Rochester..........Int.	Third(N)	75	76
1964—Rochester..........Int.	†Fourth	82	72
1965—Rochester..........Int.	Fifth	73	74
1966—Elmira ....East.	First	88	51
1971—Louisville ....Int.	Fifth	71	69
1972—Louisville ....Int.	‡First	81	63
1973—Pawtucket..........Int.	§Second(A)	78	68
1974—Boston...............Amer.	Third(E)	84	78

Year Club	League	Position	W.	L.
1975—Boston................Amer.	First(E)	95	65
1976—Boston x ....Amer.	Third(E)	41	45
1977—Seattle................Amer.	Sixth(W)	64	98
1978—Seattle .... Amer.	Seventh(W)	56	104
1979—Seattle .... Amer.	Sixth(W)	67	95
1980—Seattle y .... Amer.	z Sixth(W)	39	65
Major League Totals............................		446	550

†Won playoffs by defeating Jacksonville, four games to none and Syracuse, four games to two.

‡Lost playoff final series to Tidewater, three games to two after defeating Rochester in semifinals, two games to one.

§Won playoffs by defeating Tidewater, three games to two and Charleston, three games to two; won Junior World Series against Tulsa (American Association), four games to one.

xReplaced by Don Zimmer, July 19, 1976.

yReplaced by Maury Wills, August 3, 1980.

zTied for position.

Coach, St. Louis Cardinals, August 5, 1960 through July 8, 1961; coach, Baltimore Orioles, 1962; scout, New York Yankees, 1967; coach, Boston Red Sox, 1968 and 1969; instructor and special assignment scout, Boston Red Sox, 1970.

Manager, American League All-Star Team, 1976.

Coach, American League All-Star Team, 1979.

CHAMPIONSHIP SERIES RECORD

Year Club	League	W.	L.
1975—Boston................American	3	0

WORLD SERIES RECORD

Year Club	League	W.	L.
1975—Boston................American	3	4

DERON ROGER JOHNSON
New York Mets

Born July 17, 1938, at San Diego, Calif.
Height, 6.02. Weight, 209.
Threw and batted righthanded.
Hobbies—Golf and bowling.

Established major league record for fewest chances accepted by first baseman, season, 150 or more games (1251), 1970.

Tied major league records for most home runs, consecutive plate appearances (4), July 10 and 11, 1971; fewest triples, season, 150 or more games (0), 1971; most strikeouts, inning (2), September 23, 1973 (fifth inning).

Hit three home runs in a game, July 11, 1971.

Led Nebraska State League in total bases with 167 in 1956 and Eastern League with 279 in 1957.

Tied for Nebraska State League lead in double plays by outfielders with 4 in 1956.

Named as third baseman on THE SPORTING NEWS National League All-Star Team, 1965.

Year Club	League	Pos.	G.	AB.	R.	H.	2B.	3B.	HR.	RBI.	B.A.	PO.	A.	E.	F.A.
1956—Kearney...........Neb. St.	OF	63	243	*70	80	9	3	*24	*78	.329	104	9	4	.966
1957—Binghamton.......East.	OF	137	501	*103	152	23	13	*26	102	.303	253	13	6	.978
1958—Richmond ....Int.	OF-3B	154	570	79	148	27	5	27	103	.260	248	33	7	.976
1959—Richmond ....Int.	OF-3B	154	556	85	155	23	6	25	90	.279	195	153	18	.951
1960—New York..........Am.	3B	6	4	0	2	1	0	0	0	.500	0	3	1	.750
1960—Richmond ....Int.	3B-OF	151	552	79	135	23	6	27	92	.245	172	249	15	.966
1961—N. Y.†‡-K. C.........Am.	O-3-1B	96	302	32	63	11	3	8	44	.209	134	66	9	.957
1962—Kansas City‡§....Am.	1-3B-O	17	19	1	2	1	0	0	0	.105	5	1	1	.857
1963—San Diego..........P. C.	OF-IN	129	481	85	133	22	3	*33	91	.277	360	55	14	.967
1964—Cincinnati ....Nat.	1B-O-3B	140	477	63	130	24	4	21	79	.273	952	84	10	.990
1965—Cincinnati ....Nat.	3B	159	616	92	177	30	7	32	*130	.287	132	266	22	.948
1966—Cincinnati ....Nat.	OF-1-3	142	505	75	130	25	3	24	81	.257	339	36	5	.987
1967—Cincinnati x.......Nat.	1B-3B	108	361	39	81	18	1	13	53	.224	606	73	4	.994
1968—Atlanta y...........Nat.	1B-3B	127	342	29	71	11	1	8	33	.208	759	78	4	.995
1969—Philadelphia .....Nat.	OF-3-1B	138	475	51	121	19	4	17	80	.255	250	99	11	.969
1970—Philadelphia .....Nat.	1B-3B	159	574	66	147	28	3	27	93	.256	1180	74	6	.995
1971—Philadelphia .....Nat.	1B-3B	158	582	74	154	29	0	34	95	.265	1233	123	12	.991
1972—Philadelphia z ..Nat.	1B	96	230	19	49	4	1	9	31	.213	479	24	9	.982
1973—Philadelphia a ..Nat.	1B	12	36	3	6	2	0	1	5	.167	77	6	2	.976
1973—Oakland ....Am.	1B	131	464	61	114	14	2	19	81	.246	167	6	1	.994
1974—Oa.b-Mil.c-Bo.d .Am.	1B	110	351	30	60	4	2	13	43	.171	220	10	4	.983
1975—Chi. e-Boston.....Am.	1B	151	565	68	135	25	1	19	75	.239	475	24	3	.994
1976—Boston f ....Am.	1B	15	38	3	5	1	1	0	0	.132	30	1	0	1.000
American League Totals.................		526	1743	195	381	57	9	54	243	.219	1031	111	19	.984
National League Totals..................		1239	4198	511	1066	190	24	186	680	.254	6007	863	85	.988
Major League Totals		1765	5941	706	1447	247	33	245	923	.244	7038	974	104	.987

†Traded to Kansas City Athletics with Pitcher Art Ditmar for Pitcher Bud Daley, June 14, 1961.

‡Sold to Cincinnati Reds' organization, April 5, 1963.

§On military list through July 31.

xTraded to Atlanta Braves for Outfielder Mack Jones, Pitcher Jay Ritchie and First Baseman Jim Beauchamp, October 10, 1967. Ritchie and Beauchamp assigned to Buffalo.

ySold to Philadelphia Phillies, December 3, 1968.

zOn supplemental disabled list, June 15 through July 1.

aTraded to Oakland Athletics for Third Baseman-Outfielder Jack Bastable (assigned from Birmingham to Rocky Mount), May 2, 1973.

bOn supplemental disabled list, April 11 to April 26, 1974. Released on waivers to Milwaukee Brewers, June 24, 1974; Brewers assigned Pitcher Bill Parsons to Athletics, July 1, 1974, to complete deal.

cSold to Boston Red Sox, September 7, 1974.

dReleased, October 25, 1974; signed as free agent by Chicago White Sox, April 5, 1975.

eTraded to Boston Red Sox for cash and a player to be named later, September 21, 1975; Red Sox sent Catcher Chuck Erickson to White Sox, October 21, 1975, to complete deal.

fReleased, June 4, 1976.

CHAMPIONSHIP SERIES RECORD

Year Club	League	Pos.	G.	AB.	R.	H.	2B.	3B.	HR.	RBI.	B.A.	PO.	A.	E.	F.A.
1973—Oakland ....Am.		DH	4	10	0	1	0	0	0	0	.100	0	0	0	.000

WORLD SERIES RECORD

Year Club	League	Pos.	G.	AB.	R.	H.	2B.	3B.	HR.	RBI.	B.A.	PO.	A.	E.	F.A.
1973—Oakland ....Am.		PH-1B	6	10	0	3	1	0	0	0	.300	8	1	0	1.000

RECORD AS MANAGER

Year Club	League	Position	W.	L.
1978—Salt Lake City .... P.C.	†Second(E)		72	65

†Lost playoff semifinals to Albuquerque, three games to none.

Coach, California Angels, 1979 and 1980; coach, New York Mets, 1981.

GROVER WILLIAM JONES JR.
(Deacon)

(Father was Deacon in Union Baptist Church—named for this association.)

Houston Astros

Born April 18, 1934, at White Plains, N. Y.
Height, 5.10. Weight, 190.
Threw right and batted lefthanded.
Hobby—Singing.
Attended Ithaca College, Ithaca, N. Y.; received Bachelor of Science
degree in Physiotherapy.

Led Sally League in sacrifice flies with 13 in 1962.
Led Sally League first basemen in double plays with 103 in 1962.

Year Club	League	Pos.	G.	AB.	R.	H.	2B.	3B.	HR.	RBI.	B.A.	PO.	A.	E.	F.A.
1955—Waterloo ...........I.I.I.		2B	78	267	64	85	11	7	9	58	.318	194	219	18	.958
1956—Dubuque ....Midw.		•2-1B	100	330	105	135	25	6	26	•120	•.409	308	209	16	•.970
1956—Waterloo ...........I.I.I.		3B-2B	18	50	12	12	1	2	0	6	.240	28	30	7	.982
1957-58—Colo. Springs .West.					(In Military Service)										
1959—Lincoln .............I.I.I.		1B-2B	122	428	92	128	31	2	11	76	.299	802	91	18	.980
1960—San Diego† ........P.C.		IF-OF	80	144	25	43	2	4	5	27	.299	127	53	7	.963
1961—Charleston ....Sally		1B	132	427	81	121	19	5	13	78	.283	1106	48	16	.986
1962—Savannah ....Sally		1B	136	499	119	159	30	5	26	•101	.319	•1145	•73	10	•.992
1962—Chicago............Amer.		1B	18	28	3	9	2	0	0	8	.321	46	4	2	.962
1963—Chicago............Amer.		1B	17	16	4	3	0	1	1	2	.183	6	1	0	1.000
1963—Indianapolis ......Int.		1B	97	338	64	116	17	3	19	73	.343	766	44	7	.991
1964—Indianapolis ......Int.		1B	49	163	26	31	7	2	3	17	.190	387	33	2	.995
1964—Lynchburg ....South.		1B	86	311	53	93	20	2	11	62	.299	768	52	8	.990
1965—Sarasota‡ ....Fla. St.		1B-2B	100	320	48	104	15	8	8	59	.325	527	128	12	.981
1966—Fox Cities§ ....Midw.		1B-OF	114	368	77	130	•36	4	18	•80	•.353	554	53	12	.981
1966—Chicago............Amer.		PH	5	5	0	2	0	0	0	0	.400	....	....	....	....
1967—Appleton§x ....Midw.		OF-1B	45	122	31	43	13	0	5	20	.352	89	9	0	1.000
Major League Totals			40	49	7	14	2	1	1	10	.286	52	5	2	.966

†On disabled list, July 4 to July 16, 1960.

‡On disabled list, July 6 to July 27, 1965.

§Player-coach.

xOn disabled list, June 20 to July 14, 1967. Released by Chicago White Sox' organization, September 30, 1967.

RECORD AS MANAGER

Year Club	League	Position	W.	L.
1973—Appleton............Midwest	Fifth(N)		17	41
(Second Half)	Fifth(N)		27	35

Scout and minor league instructor, Chicago White Sox, 1968 through 1972, 1974 and 1975; coach, Houston Astros, 1976 through 1981.

HUBERT MILTON KITTLE
(Hub)

St. Louis Cardinals

Born February 19, 1917, at Los Angeles, Calif.
Height, 6.01. Weight, 195.
Threw and batted righthanded.
Attended San Diego State College, San Diego, Calif.

Year Club	League	G.	IP.	W.	L.	Pct.	H.	R.	ER.	SO.	BB.	ERA.
1937—Ponca City ....W. Assoc.		47	214	9	15	.375	250	158	126	155	119	5.30
1938—Ponca City ....W. Assoc.		37	209	18	8	.692	200	113	74	150	123	3.19

Year Club	League	G.	IP.	W.	L.	Pct.	H.	R.	ER.	SO.	BB.	ERA.
1939–Yakima	W. Int.	32	238	*20	10	.667	207	104	91	156	95	3.44
1940–Yakima	W. Int.	17	119	9	5	.643	129	52	39	63	28	2.95
1940–San Francisco	P. Coast	17	55	3	3	.500	56	33	32	15	26	5.24
1941–San Francisco	P. Coast	20	44	2	2	.500	....	....	....	....	....	....
1942–Oklahoma City	Texas	8	40	1	4	.200	39	20	14	20	13	3.15
1942–Spokane	W. Int.	35	229	15	14	.517	233	107	85	99	83	3.34
1943–Oakland	P. Coast	14	59	2	1	.667	56	30	18	30	22	2.74
1944-45–						(In Military Service)						
1946–Bremerton	W. Int.	32	216	15	10	.600	187	96	89	138	103	3.71
1947–Bremerton	W. Int.	35	216	13	14	.481	192	84	67	130	60	2.79
1948–Yakima	W. Int.	38	223	7	18	.280	127	108	85	115	85	4.76
1949–Klamath Falls	Far West	17	78	7	2	.778	77	41	32	85	22	3.69
1950–Klamath Falls	Far West	24	55	10	0	1.000	48	26	24	59	23	3.93
1951–Salt Lake City	Pioneer	22	45	4	2	.667	36	20	9	46	12	1.80
1952–Salt Lake City	Pioneer	36	79	6	6	.500	64	31	17	35	25	1.94
1953–Terre Haute	Three-I	14	27	2	1	.667	27	11	5	20	9	1.67
1954–Terre Haute	Three-I	7	17	1	0	1.000	18	10	10	7	7	5.29
1955–Yakima	Northwest	1	1	0	0	.000	6	6	3	1	1	27.00
1958–Yakima	Northwest	1	2	0	0	.000	0	0	0	1	1	0.00
1966–Austin	Texas	1	1	0	0	.000	1	0	0	0	1	0.00
1969–Savannah	Southern	1	1	0	0	.000	4	3	2	1	1	9.00
1980–Springfield†	Am. Assoc.	1	1	0	0	.000	0	0	0	0	0	0.00

†Activated as player, August 27, 1980; released, August 28, 1980.

RECORD AS MANAGER

Named by THE SPORTING NEWS as Minor League Executive of the Year for 1960.

Year Club	League	Position	W.	L.
1948–Yakima†	W. Int.	Eighth	26	63
1949–Klamath Falls	Far West	Second	78	46
1950–Klamath Falls	Far West	‡First	87	52
1951–Salt Lake City	Pioneer	§First	84	52
1952–Salt Lake City	Pioneer	Sixth	60	71
1953–Terre Haute	Three-I	xFirst	76	52
1954–Terre Haute	Three-I	Seventh	60	76
1955–Yakima	N'west	Fifth	28	35
(Second Half)		Fifth	31	34
1956–Yakima	N'west	First	47	21
(Second Half)		First	39	24
1957–Yakima	N'west	Second	39	29
(Second Half)		Fifth	30	37
1958–Yakima	N'west	Third	35	32
(Second Half)		yFirst	41	28

Year Club	League	Position	W.	L.
1959–Yakima	N'west	Fifth	30	38
(Second Half)		zFirst	40	31
1964–Yakima	N'west	Sixth	28	40
(Second Half)		aFirst	44	28
1965–Yakima	N'west	Fifth	29	40
(Second Half)		Fourth	33	37
1966–Austin	Texas	bFourth	67	73
1967–Austin	Texas	Fourth	69	71
1968–Dallas-Ft. W	Texas	Fourth(E)	60	79
1969–Savannah	South.	Sixth	59	76
1970–Okla. City	A.A.	Third(W)	68	71
1977–St. Pete.c	Fla. St.	Second (N)	d83	56

†Replaced Vernon Johnson, July 2, 1948.
‡Lost playoff finals to Redding, three games to one after defeating Reno in semifinals, three games to two.
§Lost playoff semifinal series to Great Falls, two games to none.
xLost playoff semifinal series to Evansville, three games to two.
yWon playoff against Lewiston (First Half winner), four games to one.
zWon playoff against Salem (First Half winner), four games to one.
aWon playoff against Eugene (First Half winner), three games to none.
bWon playoffs by defeating Arkansas, two games to one and Albuquerque, one game to none (final series cut short because of rainouts).
cWon playoffs from West Palm Beach, two games to one; lost championship playoff to Lakeland, three games to one.
dOne tie game.

General manager, Yakima, Northwest League, 1960-61; general manager, Hawaii, Pacific Coast League, 1962; general manager, Portland, Pacific Coast League, 1963; coach, Houston Astros 1971 through 1975; minor league instructor, St. Louis Cardinals, 1976 and 1978 through 1980; coach, St. Louis Cardinals, 1981.

ROBERT FRANK KNOOP

Name pronounced K-NOP.

(Bobby)
California Angels

Born October 18, 1938, at Sioux City, Ia.
Height, 6.01. Weight, 183.
Threw and batted righthanded.
Hobby–Golf.

Established major league records for most double plays, game, 9 innings, second baseman (6), May 1, 1966, and most putouts, 9 innings, second baseman (12), August 30, 1966.

Tied major league record for most double plays, second baseman, double-header (8), May 1, 1966, (first game).

Tied major league record for most games, rookie season (162), 1964.

Led Texas League second basemen in double plays with 128 in 1959 and Pacific Coast League second basemen with 97 in 1963.

Led American League second basemen in double plays with 123 in 1964, 135 in 1966, 91 in 1967 and 94 in 1968.

Named second baseman on THE SPORTING NEWS American League All-Star fielding teams, 1966-67-68.

Year Club	League	Pos.	G.	AB.	R.	H.	2B.	3B.	HR.	RBI.	B.A.	PO.	A.	E.	F.A.
1956—Leesburg...........Fla. St.		2B	42	137	12	26	6	1	1	9	.190	78	83	10	.942
1957—Lawton ....Soo. St.		2B	125	471	61	123	22	4	11	67	.261	*321	*324	26	*.961
1958—Cedar Rapids.....I.I.I.		2B	121	417	63	114	22	1	7	61	.273	265	269	24	*.957
1959—Austin................Tex.		2B	●146	549	44	145	23	7	3	72	.264	*395	*390	*30	.963
1960—Louisville..........A. A.		2B	19	72	5	17	2	1	0	2	.236	33	50	1	.988
1960—Austin† ....Tex.		2B	88	332	47	93	17	2	5	35	.280	209	243	14	.970
1961—San Diego-Van...P. C.		IN-OF	114	290	27	58	14	2	4	23	.200	211	205	13	.970
1962—Toronto.............Int.		PH	7	7	0	0	0	0	0	0	.000	0	0	0	.000
1962—Hawaii ....P. C.		2B	95	320	41	84	12	1	11	43	.263	212	238	12	.974
1963—Hawaii‡...........P. C.		*2B-SS	146	555	72	157	19	1	20	67	.283	331	*449	*29	.952
1964—Los Angeles.......Amer.		2B	162	486	42	105	8	1	7	38	.216	357	*522	*20	.978
1965—California.........Amer.		2B	142	465	47	125	24	4	7	43	.269	331	402	*22	.971
1966—California.........Amer.		2B	161	590	54	137	18	*11	17	72	.232	*381	*488	17	*.981
1967—California.........Amer.		2B	159	511	51	125	18	5	9	38	.245	*376	392	11	.986
1968—California.........Amer.		2B	152	494	48	123	20	4	3	39	.249	350	425	15	.981
1969—Calif.§-Chi........Amer.		2B	131	416	39	93	15	1	7	47	.224	335	386	12	.984
1970—Chicago x.........Amer.		2B	130	402	34	92	13	2	5	36	.229	276	403	11	.984
1971—Kansas City y....Amer.		2B-3B	72	161	14	33	8	1	1	11	.205	89	120	7	.968
1972—Kansas City.......Amer.		2B-3B	44	97	8	23	5	0	0	7	.237	61	80	4	.972
Major League Totals			1153	3622	337	856	129	29	56	331	.236	2556	3218	119	.980

†Pitched in one game with no decision.

‡Drafted by Los Angeles Angels from Denver (Milwaukee Braves' organization), December 2, 1963.

§Traded to Chicago White Sox for Infielder Sandy Alomar and Pitcher Bob Priddy, May 14, 1969.

xSold to Kansas City Royals, March 24, 1971.

yReleased by Kansas City Royals' organization, October 5, 1972.

ALL-STAR GAME RECORD

Year League	Pos.	AB.	R.	H.	2B.	3B.	HR.	RBI.	B.A.	PO.	A.	E.	F.A.
1966—American............................	2B	2	0	0	0	0	0	0	.000	3	1	0	1.000

RECORD AS MANAGER

Year Club	League	Position	W.	L.
1975—Quad Cities.........Midwest		First(S)	35	25
(Second Half)		†First(S)	43	22
1976—El Paso ....Texas		Second(W)	77	56

†Lost playoff for League Championship to Waterloo, two games to none.

Minor League Instructor, California Angels, part of 1975; coach, Chicago White Sox, 1977 and 1978; coach, California Angels, 1979 through 1981.

FRED CARL KOENIG
Name pronounced CAIN-eg.
Texas Rangers
Born April 27, 1931, at St. Louis, Mo.
Height, 6.03. Weight, 200.
Threw and batted righthanded.
Attended University of Illinois, Champaign, Ill.

Led Eastern League first basemen in double plays with 124 in 1954.
Led Carolina League in sacrifice flies with 8 in 1957.

Year Club	League	Pos.	G.	AB.	R.	H.	2B.	3B.	HR.	RBI.	B.A.	PO.	A.	E.	F.A.
1951—Hamilton...........Pony		1B	67	235	31	60	14	2	5	39	.255	365	19	12	.967
1951—Paducah...........Kitty		1B	29	111	14	29	8	2	2	14	.261	199	6	6	.972
1952—Allentown.........Inter. St.		1B	15	50	8	12	2	0	0	11	.240	126	2	1	.992
1952—Paducah...........Kitty		1B	92	358	81	103	24	7	15	90	.288	695	41	11	.985
1953—St. Joseph ....W. A.		1B	136	486	81	134	32	11	5	81	.276	1102	69	19	.984
1954—Allentown.........East.		1B	136	484	68	139	28	4	11	83	.287	*1193	78	20	.985
1954—Columbus.........A. A.		...	...	15	...	2	...	...	...	...	.133	...	...	...	...
1955—Omaha ....A. A.		1B-OF	32	89	14	22	5	0	3	21	.247	107	2	2	.982
1955—Columbus.........Sally		1B	80	295	38	85	11	1	11	36	.288	630	50	13	.981
1956—Allentown.........East.		3B-OF	112	389	47	93	14	5	11	62	.239	99	103	25	.900
1957—Winston-Salem ..Carol.		O-3-1	78	266	49	66	20	4	5	42	.248	234	52	9	.969
1957—Columbus.........Sally		3B	62	221	41	58	12	2	6	44	.262	55	101	16	.907
1958—York ....East.		3-O-1	102	334	42	100	14	5	9	58	.299	199	75	11	.961
1959—Omaha ....A. A.		3B	16	49	4	10	2	0	1	10	.204	9	20	3	.906
1959—Tulsa ....Texas		IF-OF	19	66	5	16	1	0	1	5	.242	....	....	....	......
1959—York ....East.		1-O-3	72	264	42	71	14	4	8	26	.269	305	55	18	.952
1960—Tulsa ....Tex.		O-1-3	101	271	53	80	18	0	10	31	.295	181	33	8	.964
1961—Tulsa†...............Texas		IF-OF	90	275	41	74	18	5	12	45	.260	212	99	15	.954
1962—Winnipeg† ....North.		1B	44	98	25	36	10	3	4	23	.367	78	6	1	.988
1963—Winnipeg‡ ....North.		....	10	14	3	4	0	0	0	2	.286	....	....	....	......

†Released by St. Louis Cardinals' organization, December 9, 1961.

‡Player-manager.

PITCHING RECORD

Year Club	League	G.	IP.	W.	L.	Pct.	H.	R.	ER.	SO.	BB.	ERA.
1959—York....................Eastern		1	...	0	0	.000	...	...	...	...	...	......
1960—Tulsa ....Texas		8	...	0	0	.000	...	...	...	...	...	......

Year	Club	League	G.	IP.	W.	L.	Pct.	H.	R.	ER.	SO.	BB.	ERA.
1961–Tulsa	Texas	1	...	0	0	.000	...	...	...	...	...	...
1962–Winnipeg	Northern	5	10	0	0	.000	4	2	1	3	5	0.90
1963–Winnipeg	Northern	4	5	0	0	.000	2	0	0	4	1	0.00

RECORD AS MANAGER

Year Club	League	Position	W.	L.	Year Club	League	Position	W.	L.
1962–Winnipeg	Northern	Seventh	59	63	1968–Quad Cities	Midwest	†First	35	19
1963–Winnipeg	Northern	Fourth	55	64	(Second Half)		‡Sixth	30	31
1964–Sarasota Cards	Rookie	Second	30	30	1969–Quad Cities	Midwest	‡§First	35	19
1965–Idaho Falls	Pioneer	Fourth	31	35	(Second Half)		Seventh	29	38
1967–Quad Cities	Midwest	Third	35	23	1972–Arkansas	Texas	Third(E)	65	74
(Second Half)		Third	34	28	1975–Sarasota Cards	G. C.	Seventh	17	35

†Won playoff against Decatur (Second Half winner), two games to one.
‡Tied for position.
§Appleton defeated Quad Cities in regularly-scheduled game of July 16 and was declared First Half champion by league president.
Coach, California Angels, 1970 and 1971; Director of Player Development, St. Louis Cardinals, 1973 and 1974; coach, St. Louis Cardinals, 1976; Texas Rangers, 1977 through 1981.

JOHN THOMAS KROL
(Jack)
San Diego Padres

Born July 5, 1936, at Chicago, Ill.
Height, 5.11. Weight, 175.
Threw and batted righthanded.

Year	Club	League	Pos.	G.	AB.	R.	H.	2B.	3B.	HR.	RBI.	B.A.	PO.	A.	E.	F.A.
1954–Ardmore	Soo. St.	3B	139	578	131	162	22	5	16	92	.280	141	292	*56	.886
1955–Ardmore	Soo. St.	SS-3B	140	534	104	147	31	5	19	77	.275	218	305	56	.903
1956–Fresno	Calif.	SS	131	503	97	144	24	7	8	79	.286	191	368	*72	.886
1957–Winston-Salem	Carol.	SS	133	503	64	139	28	1	15	72	.276	*249	345	*59	.910
1958–York	East.	2B-SS	127	458	65	111	17	9	12	62	.242	279	314	30	.952
1959–York	East.	2-3-S	119	453	65	121	18	5	11	49	.267	235	278	28	.948
1960–Memphis	S. A.	3-2-S	122	362	51	103	25	2	3	43	.285	148	174	33	.910
1961–Lancaster	East.	2B	109	369	55	92	23	4	12	50	.249	216	213	●23	.949
1962–Portsmouth†	S. Atl.	2B-3B	120	401	54	99	20	0	13	55	.247	218	247	*27	.945
1963–Charlotte‡	S. Atl.	2B-1B	101	342	45	84	13	1	11	55	.246	220	172	15	.963
1964–York§	East.	2B	99	320	49	79	12	1	13	45	.247	270	235	19	.964
1965–Burlington x	Carol.	2B	133	446	70	123	22	0	12	54	.276	*332	332	22	.968
1966–Rock Hill y	W. Car.	PH	1	2	2	2	1	0	0	1	1.000	....	....	....	......

†Released, December 4, 1962; signed as free agent by Minnesota Twins' organization, April 17, 1963.
‡Released, April 13, 1964; signed as free agent by Washington Senators' organization, April 22, 1964.
§On disabled list, August 17 through September 28, 1964.
xUnconditionally released, January 24, 1976.
yPlayer-manager.

RECORD AS MANAGER

Year Club	League	Position	W.	L.	Year Club	League	Position	W.	L.
1966–Rock Hill	W. Carol.	Third	42	24	1971–Arkansas	Texas	‡First(C)	75	64
(Second Half)		Eighth	16	44	1972–Tulsa	A. A.	Second(W)	78	62
1967–Cedar Rapids	Midwest	†Sixth	27	31	1973–Tulsa	A. A.	§First(W)	68	67
(Second Half)		Ninth	26	36	1974–Little Rock	Texas	Second(E)	75	59
1968–Cedar Rapids	Midwest	Second	32	22	1975–St. Petersburg	Fla. St.	xFirst(N)	88	47
(Second Half)		Fifth	31	31	1976–Little Rock	Texas	Fourth(E)	59	76
1969–St. Petersburg	Fla. St.	Sixth(C)	54	76	1978–St. Louis y	Nat.	Sixth(E)	1	1
1970–Modesto	Calif.	†Third	38	32	1980–St. Louis z	Nat.	Sixth(E)	0	1
(Second Half)		Fourth	38	32					

†Tied for position.
‡Lost Dixie Series to Charlotte, 3 games to none.
§Won playoff by defeating Iowa, four games to three.
xWon semi-final playoff by defeating Key West, two games to one; won playoff by defeating Tampa, three games to two.
yServed as interim manager for fired Vern Rapp, April 26 through 28, 1978.
zServed as interim manager for fired Ken Boyer, second game of doubleheader, June 8, 1980.
Minor league instructor, St. Louis Cardinals, 1966 through 1976; coach, St. Louis Cardinals, 1977 through 1980; coach, San Diego Padres, 1981.

KARL OTTO KUEHL
Name pronounced KEEL.
Minnesota Twins

Born September 5, 1937, at Monterey Park, Calif.
Height, 5.11. Weight, 175.
Threw and batted lefthanded.
Led Northwest League first basemen in double plays with 102 in 1957.
Led New York-Pennsylvania League first basemen in double plays with 84 in 1961.

Year Club	League	Pos.	G.	AB.	R.	H.	2B.	3B.	HR.	RBI.	B.A.	PO.	A.	E.	F.A.
1955—Ogden†	Pion.	1B	76	310	67	106	16	2	4	37	.342	679	31	12	.983
1956—H.P.-Tho'ville	Carol.	OF-1B	•154	*613	103	178	27	2	10	45	.290	736	42	27	.966
1957—Salem	Northw.	1B	129	435	93	151	•31	6	3	86	*.347	1024	48	14	.987
1957—Seattle	P. C.	....	10	19	2	5	1	0	0	2	.263	figures unavailable			
1958—Savannah	Sally	....	18	29	6	7	1	0	1	9	.241	figures unavailable			
1958—Albuquerque	West.	1B	113	390	76	106	6	10	1	25	.272	945	65	19	.982
1959—Salem§	Northw.	*1-O-P	128	411	77	110	18	•9	3	34	.268	883	38	12	*.987
1960—Salem§x	Northw.	1-O-P	113	332	65	114	14	4	6	56	.343	589	35	7	.989
1961—Geneva§y	NYP	*1B-P	97	270	80	85	12	4	19	83	.315	687	40	7	*.990
1962—Geneva§z	NYP	1B	22	67	18	18	3	2	2	10	.269	88	5	2	.979

†On disabled list, August 1 through remainder of season.
‡Released by Cincinnati Reds' organization, March 6, 1959.
§Player-manager.
xOn temporary inactive list, April 30 to May 10, 1960. On disabled list, May 20 to May 30, 1960.
yOn disabled list, May 28 to June 23, 1961.
zOn disabled list, May 27 to August 31, 1962.

PITCHING RECORD

Year Club	League	G.	IP.	W.	L.	Pct.	H.	R.	ER.	SO.	BB.	ERA.
1959—Salem§	Northwest	2	....	0	0	.000	....	....	....	....	....	......
1960—Salem§x	Northwest	6	....	0	0	.000	....	....	....	....	....	......
1961—Geneva§y	NYP	4	....	0	0	.000	....	....	....	....	....	......

RECORD AS MANAGER

Year Club	League	Position	W.	L.	Year Club	League	Position	W.	L.
1959—Salem	Northwest	†First	43	26	1970—Clinton	Midwest	xNinth	26	37
(Second Half)		Sixth	30	41	1972—Quebec City	Eastern	Third(N)	75	64
1960—Salem	Northwest	Fifth	22	44	1973—Quebec City	Eastern	Fourth(N)	65	72
(Second Half)		Fifth	34	42	1974—Memphis	Int.	yFirst(S)	87	55
1961—Geneva	NYP	‡First	77	48	1975—Memphis	Int.	Fifth	65	75
1962—Geneva	NYP	Sixth	44	74	1976—Montreal z	National	Sixth(E)	43	85
1969—Clinton	Midwest	§Second	42	28					

†Lost playoff to Yakima (Second Half Winner), four games to one.
‡Lost playoff semifinal series to Olean, two games to one.
§Replaced Sibby Sisti, August 2. Replaced by Tom Giordano, August 25. Record is for complete Second Half of season.
xReplaced Earl Torgeson at close of First Half of season.
yLost league championship playoff to Rochester, four games to two.
zReplaced by Charlie Fox, September 4, 1976.

Scout, Houston Colt .45s and Houston Astros, 1963 through part of 1968; scout, Seattle-Milwaukee franchise, part of 1968 through part of 1971; scout, Montreal Expos, part of 1971; coach, Minnesota Twins, 1977 through 1981.

HARVEY EDWARD KUENN

Name pronounced Keen.

Milwaukee Brewers

Born December 4, 1930, at West Allis, Wis.
Height, 6.02. Weight, 200.
Threw and batted righthanded.
Hobby—Bowling.
Attended Luther College, Decorah, Ia. and University of Wisconsin, Madison, Wis.
Father of Harvey Kuenn, Jr., outfielder in Montreal Expos' organization.

Established major league record for most at bats, rookie season (679), 1953.
Tied major league record for most doubles, inning (2), July 20, 1954 and July 24, 1964.
Tied modern major league record for most long hits, inning (2), July 20, 1954 and July 24, 1964.
Established American League records for most singles, rookie season (167), 1953; most at bats, season, 154-game schedule (679), 1953.
Tied American League league record for most games, rookie season, 154-game schedule (155), 1953.
One of 12 players to make 200 or more hits in rookie season, 1953.
Named American League Rookie of the Year by the Baseball Writers' Association and THE SPORTING NEWS, 1953.
Named as shortstop on THE SPORTING NEWS All-Star Major League Team, 1956.
Received reported $55,000 bonus to sign with Detroit Tigers, 1952.

Year Club	League	Pos.	G.	AB.	R.	H.	2B.	3B.	HR.	RBI.	B.A.	PO.	A.	E.	F.A.
1952—Davenport	I.I.I.	SS	63	256	46	87	17	3	1	40	.340	114	194	26	.922
1952—Detroit	Amer.	SS	19	80	2	26	2	2	0	8	.325	44	57	4	.962
1953—Detroit	Amer.	SS	155	*679	94	*209	33	7	2	48	.308	*308	441	21	.973
1954—Detroit	Amer.	SS	•155	*656	81	•201	28	6	5	48	.306	*294	*496	28	.966
1955—Detroit	Amer.	SS	145	620	101	190	*38	5	8	62	.306	253	378	29	.956
1956—Detroit	Amer.	*SS-O	146	591	96	*196	32	7	12	88	.332	219	388	20	*.968
1957—Detroit	Amer.	*S-3-1B	151	624	74	173	30	6	9	44	.277	251	387	*30	.955
1958—Detroit	Amer.	OF	139	561	73	179	*39	3	8	54	.319	*358	9	6	.984
1959—Detroit†	Amer.	OF	139	561	99	*198	*42	7	9	71	*.353	247	6	3	.988
1960—Cleveland‡	Amer.	OF-3B	126	474	65	146	24	0	9	54	.308	222	13	9	.963
1961—San Francisco ...	Nat.	O-3-S	131	471	60	125	22	4	5	46	.265	190	43	10	.959
1962—San Francisco ...	Nat.	OF-3B	130	487	73	148	23	5	10	68	.304	180	47	6	.966
1963—San Francisco ...	Nat.	OF-3B	120	417	61	121	13	2	6	31	.290	115	60	13	.931

Year	Club	League	Pos.	G.	AB.	R.	H.	2B.	3B.	HR.	RBI.	B.A.	PO.	A.	E.	F.A.
1964–San Francisco	...Nat.		OF-1-3	111	351	42	92	16	2	4	22	.262	136	9	6	.960
1965–S.F.§-Chicago	...Nat.		OF-1B	77	179	15	40	5	0	0	12	.223	81	8	3	.967
1966–Chi. x-Phila. y	...Nat.		OF-1-3	89	162	15	48	9	0	0	15	.296	130	3	1	.993
American League Totals				1175	4846	685	1518	268	43	62	477	.313	2196	2175	150	.967
National League Totals				658	2067	266	574	88	13	25	194	.278	832	170	41	.961
Major League Totals				1833	6913	951	2092	356	56	87	671	.303	3028	2345	191	.966

†Traded to Cleveland Indians for Outfielder Rocky Colavito, April 17, 1960.

‡Traded to San Francisco Giants for Pitcher Johnny Antonelli and Outfielder Willie Kirkland, December 3, 1960.

§Traded with Catcher Ed Bailey and Pitcher Bob Hendley to Chicago Cubs for Catcher Dick Bertell and First Baseman-Outfielder Len Gabrielson, May 29, 1965.

xSold to Philadelphia Phillies, April 23, 1966.

yReleased by Philadelphia Phillies, October 7, 1966.

WORLD SERIES RECORD

Year	Club	League	Pos.	G.	AB.	R.	H.	2B.	3B.	HR.	RBI.	B.A.	PO.	A.	E.	F.A.
1962–San Francisco	...Nat.		OF	4	12	1	1	0	0	0	0	.083	11	0	0	1.000

ALL-STAR GAME RECORD

Tied All-Star Game record for most at bats, nine-inning game (5), July 10, 1956.

Year	League	Pos.	AB.	R.	H.	2B.	3B.	HR.	RBI.	B.A.	PO.	A.	E.	F.A.
1953–American		PH	1	0	0	0	0	0	0	.000	0	0	0	.000
1955–American		SS	3	1	1	0	0	0	0	.333	1	0	0	1.000
1956–American		SS	5	0	1	0	0	0	0	.200	2	3	0	1.000
1957–American		SS	2	0	0	0	0	0	1	.000	0	1	0	1.000
1959–American (first game)		OF	1	1	0	0	0	0	0	.000	0	0	0	.000
1960–American (both games)		OF-PH	4	1	1	0	0	0	0	.250	1	0	0	1.000
All-Star Game Totals			16	3	3	0	0	0	1	.188	4	4	0	1.000

RECORD AS MANAGER

Year	Club	League	Position	W.	L.
1975–Milwaukee†	........Amer.		Fifth(E)	1	0

†Served as interim manager the final game of season after Del Crandall was fired.

Coach, Milwaukee Brewers, 1971 through 1981.

ARTHUR WILLIAM KUSNYER
Pronounced Kushner.
(Art)
Chicago White Sox

Born December 19, 1945, at Akron, O.
Height, 6.02. Weight, 198.
Throws and bats righthanded.
Attended Kent State University, Kent, O.

Led Pacific Coast League in sacrifice flies with 11 in 1971.

Led Pacific Coast League catchers in double plays with 14 in 1971 and with 20 in 1974.

Led Midwest League in passed balls with 29 in 1968, led Carolina League with 24 in 1969 and tied for Southern League lead with 14 in 1970.

Year	Club	League	Pos.	G.	AB.	R.	H.	2B.	3B.	HR.	RBI.	B.A.	PO.	A.	E.	F.A.
1966–Sar. W. Sox	.......Gulf C.		C	11	20	3	6	2	0	0	0	.300	....	....	....	....
1967–Appleton	..........Midw.		O-C-1	81	292	41	73	8	3	7	37	.250	206	16	12	.949
1968–Appleton	..........Midw.		C	99	330	40	82	15	1	5	38	.248	*705	*62	*18	.977
1969–Lynchburg	.......Carol.		*C-O	129	435	58	108	19	7	13	66	.248	*793	*87	*25	.972
1970–Mobile	...............South.		C	122	396	43	99	14	2	12	49	.250	650	*88	13	.983
1970–Chicago†	..........Amer.		C	4	10	0	1	0	0	0	0	.100	12	4	1	.941
1971–Salt Lake City	...P. C.		C	129	456	73	144	27	3	10	75	.316	*764	*76	12	.986
1971–California	..........Amer.		C	6	13	0	2	0	0	0	0	.154	19	4	1	.958
1972–California	.........Amer.		C	64	179	13	37	2	1	2	13	.207	362	33	10	.975
1973–Salt Lake City	...P. C.		C	5	15	1	3	0	0	0	0	.200	12	0	1	.923
1973–California‡	..........Amer.		C	41	64	5	8	2	0	0	3	.125	130	13	3	.979
1974–Sacramento	.......P. C.		C	128	440	64	107	10	0	17	63	.243	*624	60	*28	.961
1975–Spokane	..........P. C.		C	128	448	62	118	10	2	25	76	.263	*720	55	6	*.992
1976–Spokane	..........P. C.		C	55	203	40	66	9	2	11	45	.325	182	14	6	.970
1976–Milwaukee	........Amer.		C	15	34	2	4	1	0	0	3	.118	41	4	3	.938
1977–Spokane§	...........P. C.		C	90	293	42	68	15	2	7	40	.232	402	65	14	.971
1978–Omaha	...............A.A.		C-1B	61	214	26	50	9	0	5	26	.234	164	23	4	.979
1978–Kansas City x	....Amer.		C	9	13	1	3	1	0	1	2	.231	32	3	2	.946
1979–Iowa y	...............A.A.		C-1B-P	48	123	15	25	4	0	2	10	.203	194	28	3	.987
Major League Totals				139	313	21	55	6	1	3	21	.176	596	61	20	.970

†Traded to California Angels for Pitcher Steve Kealey and Catcher Dave Adlesh, March 15, 1971.

‡Traded with Pitchers Clyde Wright and Steve Barber, Outfielder Ken Berry and a player to be named later to Milwaukee Brewers for Outfielders Ollie Brown and Joe Lahoud, Pitchers Skip Lockwood and Gary Ryerson and Catcher Ellie Rodriguez, October 22, 1973.

§Traded from Milwaukee Brewers' organization to Kansas City Royals for Pitcher Lynn McKinney, February 22, 1978.

PITCHING RECORD

Year Club	League	G.	IP.	W.	L.	Pct.	H.	R.	ER.	SO.	BB.	ERA.
1979—Iowa	Am. Assoc.	2	3	0	0	.000	2	3	3	1	1	9.00

HAROLD CLIFTON LANIER
(Hal)
St. Louis Cardinals

Born July 4, 1942, at Denton, N.C.
Height, 6.02. Weight, 186.
Threw and batted righthanded.
Son of Max Lanier, former major league pitcher.

Led Eastern League second basemen in double plays with 85 in 1963.
Received reported $50,000 bonus to sign with San Francisco Giants, 1961.

Year Club	League	Pos.	G.	AB.	R.	H.	2B.	3B.	HR.	RBI.	B.A.	PO.	A.	E.	F.A.
1961—Quincy	Midwest	SS	73	295	61	93	7	5	1	25	.315	112	204	18	.946
1962—Fresno	Calif.	2B	133	555	89	173	20	4	5	49	.312	*358	*321	23	*.967
1963—Springfield	East.	2B	138	*577	77	*163	27	9	6	49	.282	*359	*379	18	*.976
1964—Tacoma	P.C.	2B-SS	61	254	33	83	17	1	4	28	.327	140	152	9	.970
1964—San Francisco	Nat.	2B-SS	98	383	40	105	16	3	2	28	.274	226	298	11	.979
1965—San Francisco	Nat.	2B-SS	159	522	41	118	15	9	0	39	.226	294	445	18	.976
1966—San Francisco	Nat.	2B-SS	149	459	37	106	14	2	3	37	.231	303	423	13	.982
1967—San Francisco	Nat.	2B-SS	151	525	37	112	16	3	0	42	.213	253	519	20	.975
1968—San Francisco	Nat.	SS	151	486	37	100	14	1	0	27	.206	*282	496	17	*.979
1969—San Francisco	Nat.	SS	150	495	37	113	9	1	0	35	.228	252	530	25	.969
1970—San Francisco	Nat.	SS-2-1	134	438	33	101	13	1	2	41	.231	263	399	22	.968
1971—San Francisco†	Nat.	3-2-S-1	109	206	21	48	8	0	1	13	.233	91	130	6	.974
1972—New York	Amer.	3-S-2	60	103	5	22	3	0	0	6	.214	32	87	4	.967
1973—New York‡	Amer.	S-2-3	35	86	9	18	3	0	0	5	.209	45	81	4	.969
1974—Tulsa	A.A.	2-3-S	103	357	45	96	15	0	1	32	.269	158	203	10	.973
1975—Tulsa§x	A.A.	3B-2B	21	74	11	15	1	1	1	7	.203	26	50	0	1.000
1979—Springfield	A.A.	SS	1	2	0	1	0	0	0	0	.500	3	1	0	1.000
National League Totals			1101	3514	283	803	105	20	8	262	.229	1964	3240	132	.975
American League Totals			95	189	14	40	6	0	0	11	.212	77	168	8	.968
Major League Totals			1196	3703	297	843	111	20	8	273	.228	2041	3408	140	.975

†Sold to New York Yankees, February 2, 1972.
‡Released, December 10, 1973; signed by St. Louis Cardinals' organization, April 8, 1974.
§On disabled list, June 7 to August 13, 1975.
xReleased, September 19, 1975.

CHAMPIONSHIP SERIES RECORD

Year Club	League	Pos.	G.	AB.	R.	H.	2B.	3B.	HR.	RBI.	B.A.	PO.	A.	E.	F.A.
1971—San Francisco	Nat.	3B	1	1	0	0	0	0	0	0	.000	1	0	0	1.000

RECORD AS MANAGER

Named Western Carolinas League Manager of the Year, 1977.

Year Club	League	Position	W.	L.
1976—St. Petersburg	Fla. St.	Third(N)	70	71
1977—Gastonia†	W.Car.	‡Second	37	32
(Second Half)		First	45	25
1978—St. Petersburg§	Fla. St.	First(N)	41	25
(Second Half)		Second(N)	x43	31
1979—Springfield	A.A.	Second(E)	73	63
1980—Springfield y	A.A.	First(E)	75	61

†Won championship playoff from Greenwood, three games to one.
‡Tied for postion.
§Lost playoff to Lakeland, one game to none.
xOne tie game.
yLost championship playoff to Denver, four games to one.
Coach, St. Louis Cardinals, 1981.

CHARLES RICHARD LAU
Last name rhymes with "how."
(Charley)
New York Yankees

Born April 12, 1933, at Romulus, Mich.
Height, 6.00. Weight, 193.
Threw right and batted lefthanded.
Hobbies—Hunting and spear-fishing.

Tied major league record for most doubles, game (4), July 13, 1962.
Tied American League record for most passed balls, inning (3), June 14, 1962, eighth inning.

Led Carolina League catchers in double plays with 15 in 1955.
Led American Association in passed balls with 18 in 1959.

Year Club	League	Pos.	G.	AB.	R.	H.	2B.	3B.	HR.	RBI.	B.A.	PO.	A.	E.	F.A.
1952–Jamestown	Pony	C-OF	92	295	53	98	27	5	7	58	.332	406	58	10	.979
1953-54–Buffalo	Int.				(In Military Service)										
1955–Durham	Carol.	C	127	396	69	116	18	5	18	75	.293	732	77	21	.975
1956–Charleston	A. A.	C-3B	110	322	32	83	11	4	12	53	.258	475	57	10	.982
1956–Detroit	Amer.	C	3	9	1	2	0	0	0	0	.222	17	0	0	1.000
1957–Charleston	A. A.	C	70	202	23	49	14	1	8	25	.243	310	36	6	.983
1958–Charleston	A. A.	C	39	115	10	33	5	0	3	14	.287	156	23	3	.984
1958–Detroit	Amer.	C	30	68	8	10	1	2	0	6	.147	120	10	2	.985
1959–Detroit	Amer.	C	2	6	0	1	0	0	0	0	.167	11	1	0	1.000
1959–Charles.-Louis.†	A. A.	C	121	390	55	114	29	2	20	79	.292	609	46	5	.992
1960–Milwaukee	Nat.	C	21	53	4	10	2	0	0	2	.189	94	11	0	1.000
1961–Milwaukee	Nat.	C	28	82	3	17	5	0	0	5	.207	114	7	4	.968
1961–Vancouver‡	P. C.	C-O-1	45	143	22	42	7	1	6	22	.294	227	14	4	.984
1961–Baltimore	Amer.	C	17	47	3	8	0	0	1	4	.170	90	6	1	.990
1962–Baltimore	Amer.	C	81	197	21	58	11	2	6	37	.294	269	15	1	.996
1963–Balt.§-Kan. C.	Amer.	C	91	235	19	64	13	0	3	32	.272	306	20	7	.979
1964–K. C.x-Balt.	Amer.	C	105	276	27	73	22	2	3	23	.264	422	25	4	.991
1965–Baltimore	Amer.	C	68	132	15	39	5	2	2	18	.295	165	9	2	.989
1966–Baltimore y	Amer.	PH	18	12	1	6	2	1	0	5	.500	0	0	0	.000
1967–Baltimore z	Amer.	PH	11	8	0	1	1	0	0	3	.125	0	0	0	.000
1967–Atlanta	Nat.	PH	52	45	3	9	1	0	1	5	.200	0	0	0	.000
American League Totals			426	990	95	262	55	9	15	128	.265	1400	86	17	.989
National League Totals			101	180	10	36	8	0	1	12	.200	208	18	4	.983
Major League Totals			527	1170	105	298	63	9	16	140	.255	1608	104	21	.988

†Traded to Milwaukee Braves by Detroit Tigers with Pitcher Don Lee for Pitcher Don Kaiser, Catcher Mike Roarke and Infielder Casey Wise, October 15, 1959. Kaiser and Roarke were transferred from Louisville to Charleston, American Association, and Lee from Charleston to Louisville. Wise was assigned to Detroit and Lau to Milwaukee.

‡Sold by Milwaukee Braves to Baltimore Orioles, August 21, 1961.

§Sold to Kansas City Athletics for a reported $20,000, July 1, 1963.

xTraded to Baltimore Orioles for Pitcher Wes Stock, June 15, 1964.

yOn disabled list from May 11 through September 1; underwent surgery for removal of scar tissue on right elbow.

zSold to Atlanta Braves, May 31, 1967.

RECORD AS MANAGER

Year Club	League	Position	W.	L.
1968–Shreveport	Texas	Second(E)	78	62

Coach, Baltimore Orioles, 1969; coach, Oakland Athletics, 1970; coach, Kansas City Royals, 1971 through 1974; minor league instructor, Kansas City Royals, part of 1975; coach, Kansas City Royals, part of 1975 through 1978; coach, New York Yankees, 1979 through 1981.

JAMES KENNETH LEFEBVRE

Name pronounced "luh-FEE-ver."

(Jim)

San Francisco Giants

Born January 7, 1943, at Inglewood, Calif.
Height, 5.11. Weight, 180.
Threw right and batted right and lefthanded.

Tied modern National League record for most errors by third baseman, inning (3), April 25, 1967 (fourth inning).

Led California League second basemen in double plays with 79 in 1962, and Northwest League with 109 in 1963.

Named National League Rookie of the Year by Baseball Writers' Association of America, 1965.

Year Club	League	Pos.	G.	AB.	R.	H.	2B.	3B.	HR.	RBI.	B.A.	PO.	A.	E.	F.A.
1962–Reno	Calif.	2B	138	541	139	177	33	4	39	130	.327	345	313	27	.961
1963–Salem	N'west	2B	139	474	82	134	29	9	17	92	.283	•316	327	•35	.948
1964–Spokane†	P.C.	2B	55	200	26	53	10	1	6	31	.265	123	126	8	.969
1965–Los Angeles	Nat.	2B	157	544	57	136	21	4	12	69	.250	349	429	24	.970
1966–Los Angeles	Nat.	2B-3B	152	544	69	149	23	3	24	74	.274	268	389	16	.976
1967–Los Angeles	Nat.	3-2-1B	136	494	51	129	18	5	8	50	.261	173	321	18	.965
1968–Los Angeles	Nat.	2-3-O-1	84	286	23	69	12	1	5	31	.241	179	161	8	.977
1969–Los Angeles	Nat.	3-2-1B	95	275	29	65	15	2	4	44	.236	154	185	6	.983
1970–Los Angeles	Nat.	2-3-1B	109	314	33	79	15	1	4	44	.252	168	212	6	.984
1971–Los Angeles	Nat.	2B-3B	119	388	40	95	14	2	12	68	.245	247	274	9	.983
1972–Los Angeles‡	Nat.	2B-3B	70	169	11	34	8	0	5	24	.201	70	99	4	.977
1973–Lotte	Pac.	1-2-3-O	111	400	50	106	12	2	29	63	.265	763	77	7	.992
1974–Lotte	Pac.	1B-3B	82	279	37	79	12	2	14	52	.283	580	32	4	.994
1975–Lotte	Pac.	1B	47	151	13	39	5	0	9	24	.258	252	13	0	1.000
1976–Lotte	Pac.	1B	90	268	22	65	8	0	8	37	.243	506	32	3	.994
Major League Totals			922	3014	313	756	126	18	74	404	.251	1608	2070	91	.976

†On military list, March 15 to July 18, 1964.

‡Released, November 27, 1972; signed four-year contract with Lotte Orions of Japanese Baseball League.

WORLD SERIES RECORD

Year	Club	League	Pos.	G.	AB.	R.	H.	2B.	3B.	HR.	RBI.	B.A.	PO.	A.	E.	F.A.
1965—Los Angeles		Nat.	2B	3	10	2	4	0	0	0	0	.400	3	7	1	.909
1966—Los Angeles		Nat.	2B	4	12	1	2	0	0	1	1	.167	10	10	0	1.000
World Series Totals				7	22	3	6	0	0	1	1	.273	13	17	1	.968

ALL-STAR GAME RECORD

Year	League	Pos.	AB.	R.	H.	2B.	3B.	HR.	RBI.	B.A.	PO.	A.	E.	F.A.
1966—National		2B	2	0	0	0	0	0	0	.000	2	0	0	1.000

RECORD AS MANAGER

Year	Club	League	Position	W.	L.
1978—Lethbridge		Pion.	Fifth	33	35

Coach, Lotte Orions, 1977; coach, Los Angeles Dodgers, September 24 through remainder of 1978 season and 1979; San Francisco Giants, 1980 and 1981.

DONALD GEORGE LEPPERT
(Don)
Houston Astros

Born October 19, 1932, at Indianapolis, Ind.
Height, 6.02. Weight, 215.
Threw and batted righthanded.
Hobbies—Hunting and fishing.
Attended Wabash College, Crawfordsville, Ind.

Hit home run in first time at bat in major leagues, June 18, 1961.
Hit three home runs in a game, April 11, 1963.

Year	Club	League	Pos.	G.	AB.	R.	H.	2B.	3B.	HR.	RBI.	B.A.	PO.	A.	E.	F.A.
1955—Evansville		I.I.I.	C	19	43	11	15	4	0	3	10	.349	53	6	2	.967
1955—Corpus Christi		Big St.	C	58	184	29	44	9	2	10	32	.239	250	20	6	.978
1956—Wichita		A. A.	C	70	165	19	38	8	0	8	21	.230	268	20	6	.980
1957—Austin		Tex.	C	119	403	45	94	16	1	20	59	.233	521	45	*17	.971
1958—Austin		Tex.	C-OF	85	240	25	55	4	0	11	28	.229	331	25	9	.975
1959—Austin		Tex.	C	5	13	2	4	0	0	0	1	.308	28	2	0	1.000
1959—Dallas		A. A.	C	132	404	45	109	17	1	13	66	.270	479	45	9	.983
1960—Dal.-Ft. Worth		A. A.	C	118	363	41	93	18	0	17	63	.256	506	51	19	.967
1961—Columbus		Int.	C	39	114	18	44	4	1	6	30	.386	217	14	3	.987
1961—Pittsburgh		Nat.	C	22	60	6	16	2	1	3	5	.267	80	11	3	.968
1962—Pittsburgh†		Nat.	C	45	139	14	37	6	1	3	18	.266	243	23	3	.989
1963—Washington		Amer.	C	73	211	20	50	11	0	6	24	.237	281	20	5	.984
1964—Washington		Amer.	C	50	122	6	19	3	0	3	12	.156	191	14	2	.990
1965—Hawaii		P. C.	C	61	148	13	50	5	0	5	19	.338	195	22	3	.986
1966—Columbus		Int.	C	66	140	9	32	0	0	3	13	.229	206	18	4	.982
American League Totals				123	333	26	69	14	0	9	36	.207	472	34	7	.986
National League Totals				67	199	20	53	8	2	6	23	.266	323	34	6	.983
Major League Totals				190	532	46	122	22	2	15	59	.229	795	68	13	.985

†Traded to Washington Senators for Pitcher Ron Honeycutt and cash, December 15, 1962.

ALL-STAR GAME RECORD

Member of American League All-Star team in 1963; did not play.

RECORD AS MANAGER

Year	Club	League	Position	W.	L.
1967—Gastonia		W. Carol.	Second	61	59

Coach, Pittsburgh Pirates, 1968 through 1976; coach, Toronto Blue Jays, 1977 through 1979; coach, Houston Astros, 1980 and 1981.

ROBERT PERRY LILLIS
(Bob)
Houston Astros

Born June 2, 1930, at Altadena, Calif.
Height, 5.11. Weight, 168.
Threw and batted righthanded.
Hobbies—Hunting and fishing.
Attended University of Southern California, Los Angeles, Calif.

Year	Club	League	Pos.	G.	AB.	R.	H.	2B.	3B.	HR.	RBI.	B.A.	PO.	A.	E.	F.A.
1951—Pueblo		West.	SS	37	141	17	34	6	3	0	13	.241	80	104	12	.939
1951—Newport News		Pied.	SS	39	136	16	28	1	3	0	12	.206	59	110	10	.944
1952—Elmira		East.	SS	76	310	35	63	15	1	0	18	.203	147	221	18	.953
1953—Newport News		Pied.	SS	129	523	*102	152	25	6	3	60	.291	*311	*443	*40	.950
1954-55—Mobile		South.					(In Military Service)									
1956—St. Paul		A. A.	SS	144	*590	96	157	33	2	18	65	.266	*304	395	27	*.963
1957—St. Paul		A. A.	SS	*154	*598	72	155	26	5	2	49	.259	*323	477	30	●.964
1958—St. Paul		A. A.	SS	67	272	42	74	10	6	3	17	.272	136	193	17	.951

Year	Club	League	Pos.	G.	AB.	R.	H.	2B.	3B.	HR.	RBI.	B.A.	PO.	A.	E.	F.A.
1958—Los Angeles	Nat.		SS	20	69	10	27	3	1	1	5	.391	29	52	3	.964
1959—Los Angeles	Nat.		SS	30	48	7	11	2	0	0	2	.229	27	52	7	.919
1959—Spokane	P. C.		SS	103	406	50	116	17	6	3	27	.286	206	352	17	*.970
1960—Los Angeles	Nat.		SS-3-2	48	60	6	16	4	0	0	6	.267	40	52	1	.989
1961—L. A.†-St. L.‡	Nat.		SS-2-3	105	239	24	51	4	0	0	22	.213	123	201	19	.945
1962—Houston	Nat.		SS-2-3	129	457	38	114	12	4	1	30	.249	223	378	15	.976
1963—Houston	Nat.		SS-2-3	147	469	31	93	13	1	1	19	.198	249	375	26	.960
1964—Houston	Nat.		2-SS-3	109	332	31	89	11	2	0	17	.268	169	236	10	.976
1965—Houston	Nat.		SS-3-2	124	408	34	90	12	1	0	20	.221	206	304	16	.970
1966—Houston	Nat.		2-SS-3	68	164	14	38	6	0	0	11	.232	99	109	10	.954
1967—Houston	Nat.		SS-2-3	37	82	3	20	1	0	0	5	.244	27	66	7	.930
Major League Totals				817	2328	198	549	68	9	3	137	.236	1192	1825	114	.964

†Traded to St. Louis Cardinals with Outfielder Carl Warwick for Infielder Daryl Spencer, May 30, 1961.
‡Selected by Houston Colts in National League expansion draft, October 10, 1961.
Scout, Houston Astros, 1968 through 1970; Director of Minor League Instruction, Houston Astros, 1972; coach, Houston Astros, part of 1967 and 1973 through 1981.

JOSEPH PAUL LONNETT
Name pronounced Lon-NETT.
(Joe)
Pittsburgh Pirates
Born February 7, 1927, at Beaver Falls, Pa.
Height, 5.10½. Weight, 185.
Threw and batted righthanded.
Hobby—Photography.

Year	Club	League	Pos.	G.	AB.	R.	H.	2B.	3B.	HR.	RBI.	B.A.	PO.	A.	E.	F.A.
1947—Lockport	Pony		OF	78	253	45	56	11	4	5	43	.221	164	10	7	.961
1948—Bradford	Pony		C	124	445	102	138	22	9	11	82	.310	579	*79	*14	.979
1949—Vandergrift	Mid. Atl.		C	104	398	105	122	33	8	20	93	.307	498	59	11	.981
1949—Utica	East.		C	36	120	14	25	6	1	3	15	.208	134	19	9	.944
1950—Terre Haute	I.I.I.		C	109	343	62	102	21	7	11	61	.297	*779	55	●13	*.985
1951-52—Philadelphia	Nat.							(In Military Service)								
1953—Batimore	Int.		C-O-1-2	77	162	27	25	3	0	11	25	.154	277	27	2	.993
1954—Syracuse	Int.		C	98	295	63	79	16	1	21	63	.268	476	45	9	.983
1955—Syracuse	Int.		C	26	60	8	17	1	1	2	8	.283	94	4	0	1.000
1956—Philadelphia	Nat.		C	16	22	2	4	0	0	0	0	.182	24	2	0	1.000
1957—Philadelphia	Nat.		C	67	160	12	27	5	0	5	15	.169	305	16	1	.997
1958—Philadelphia	Nat.		C	17	50	0	7	2	0	0	2	.140	78	7	1	.988
1958—Wichita	A.A.		C	52	140	20	28	5	0	2	18	.200	261	21	2	.993
1959—Louisville	A.A.		C	32	86	12	25	4	1	4	14	.291	135	10	0	1.000
1959—Buffalo	Int.		C	16	50	8	15	5	0	3	8	.300	96	7	2	.981
1959—Philadelphia	Nat.		C	43	93	8	16	1	0	1	10	.172	171	4	3	.983
1960—Buffalo	Int.		C	82	257	38	63	4	0	10	34	.245	423	37	9	.981
1961—Buffalo†	Int.		C	3	5	0	2	1	0	0	0	.400	figures unavailable			
1962—Buff.-Rochester	Int.		C	69	176	18	32	5	1	6	24	.182	317	15	5	.985
1963—Little Rock	Int.		C	5	17	2	4	1	0	1	5	.235	figures unavailable			
Major League Totals				143	325	22	54	8	0	6	27	.166	578	29	5	.992

†On disabled list, May 1 to September 28.

RECORD AS MANAGER

Year	Club	League	Position	W.	L.
1966—Huron		North.	Third	32	35
1967—Huron		North.	Sixth	27	40

Scout, Philadelphia Phillies, 1963 through 1965 and 1968 through 1970; coach, Chicago White Sox, 1971 through 1975; coach, Oakland Athletics, 1976; coach, Pittsburgh Pirates, 1977 through 1981.

HARRY LEE LOWREY
(Peanuts)
Chicago Cubs
Born August 27, 1918, at Los Angeles, Calif.
Height, 5.08½. Weight, 170.
Threw and batted righthanded
Hobbies—Golf, movies, hunting and fishing.

Year	Club	League	Pos.	G.	AB.	R.	H.	2B.	3B.	HR.	RBI.	B.A.	PO.	A.	E.	F.A.
1937—Moline	I.I.I.		SS-2B	45	181	34	55	6	2	3	....	.304	73	108	21	.896
1938—Ponca City	W.A.		SS	123	479	105	128	35	5	5	63	.267	204	358	63	.899
1939—St. Joseph	W.A.		SS	137	517	122	178	39	7	15	108	.344	*244	367	*72	.895
1940—Tulsa	Texas		3B	32	110	24	33	10	0	2	14	.300	26	53	7	.919
1940—Los Angeles	P.C.		SS-3B	70	216	36	54	7	1	1	12	.250	84	142	16	.934
1941—Los Angeles	P.C.		OF-3B	164	653	110	203	39	4	6	69	.311	354	103	27	.944
1942—Chicago	Nat.		OF	27	58	4	11	0	0	1	4	.190	43	2	1	.978
1942—Milwaukee	A.A.		OF	9	32	5	9	0	0	0	0	.281	17	1	0	1.000
1942—Los Angeles	P.C.		OF	96	393	64	101	17	0	5	39	.257	211	13	6	.974

Year Club	League	Pos.	G.	AB.	R.	H.	2B.	3B.	HR.	RBI.	B.A.	PO.	A.	E.	F.A.
1943—Chicago	Nat.	OF-INF	130	480	59	140	25	12	1	63	.292	341	62	10	.976
1944—Chicago	Nat.					(In Military Service)									
1945—Chicago	Nat.	OF-SS	143	523	72	148	22	7	7	89	.283	281	19	5	.984
1946—Chicago	Nat.	OF-3B	144	540	75	139	24	5	4	54	.257	330	49	12	.969
1947—Chicago	Nat.	3-2-OF	115	448	56	126	17	5	5	37	.281	138	200	17	.952
1948—Chicago	Nat.	OF-INF	129	435	47	128	12	3	2	54	.294	238	29	5	.982
1949—Chi.†-Cincinnati	Nat.	OF-3B	127	420	66	115	21	2	4	35	.274	259	9	4	.985
1950—Cin.‡-St. Louis	Nat.	OF-2-3	108	320	44	75	14	0	2	15	.234	184	36	4	.982
1951—St. Louis	Nat.	OF-3-2	114	370	52	112	19	5	5	40	.303	230	25	9	.966
1952—St. Louis	Nat.	OF-3B	132	374	48	107	18	2	1	48	.286	176	20	7	.966
1953—St. Louis	Nat.	OF-2-3	104	182	26	49	9	2	5	27	.269	64	20	3	.966
1954—St. Louis§	Nat.	OF	74	61	6	7	1	2	0	5	.115	5	0	0	1.000
1955—Philadelphia x	Nat.	O-PH-1	54	106	9	20	4	0	0	8	.189	42	2	1	.978
1956—Buffalo	Int.	OF	117	352	41	97	12	1	4	33	.276	146	10	1	.994
1957—New Orleans	South.	OF	73	169	38	61	7	1	0	12	.361	97	2	1	.990
1958—Austin	Texas	OF	46	103	13	31	3	2	2	13	.301	24	1	0	1.000
1959—Seattle	P.C.	OF-INF	36	79	10	14	4	0	0	6	.177	35	30	7	.903
Major League Totals			1401	4317	564	1177	186	45	37	479	.273	2331	473	78	.973

†Traded to Cincinnati Reds with Outfielder Harry Walker for Outfielders Henry Sauer and Frank Baumholtz, June 15, 1949.

‡Released to St. Louis Cardinals on waivers, September 7, 1950.

§Unconditionally released by St. Louis Cardinals, October 12, 1954; signed by Philadelphia Phillies, February 10, 1955.

xReleased by Philadelphia Phillies, October 3, 1955.

WORLD SERIES RECORD

Year Club	League	Pos.	G.	AB.	R.	H.	2B.	3B.	HR.	RBI.	B.A.	PO.	A.	E.	F.A.
1945—Chicago	Nat.	OF	7	29	4	9	1	0	0	0	.310	21	1	0	1.000

ALL-STAR RECORD

Year League	Pos.	AB.	R.	H.	2B.	3B.	HR.	RBI.	B.A.	PO.	A.	E.	F.A.
1946—National	OF	2	0	1	0	0	0	0	.500	3	0	0	1.000

RECORD AS MANAGER

Year Club	League	Position	W.	L.
1957—New Orleans	South.	Eighth	60	94
1958—Austin	Texas	Fourth	77	76
1960—Idaho Falls†	Pion.	Second	24	15

†Succeeded by George Noga, June 1.

Coach, Philadelphia Phillies, June 1, 1960 through 1966; San Francisco Giants, 1967-68; Montreal Expos 1969; Chicago Cubs, 1970, 1971, 1977 through 1979 and 1981; California Angels, 1972.

HENRY GORDON MacKENZIE
(Gordy)
Kansas City Royals

Born July 9, 1937, at St. Petersburg, Fla.
Height, 5.11. Weight, 185.
Threw and batted righthanded.
Attended University of Florida, Gainesville, Fla.
Brother of Mrs. Murle MacKenzie Breer, former professional golfer.

Year Club	League	Pos.	G.	AB.	R.	H.	2B.	3B.	HR.	RBI.	B.A.	PO.	A.	E.	F.A.
1956—Abilene	Big St.	SS	22	85	12	21	6	0	2	9	.247	29	57	13	.869
1956—Pocatello	Pioneer	SS	106	410	48	102	14	10	4	57	.249	134	264	33	.923
1957—Crowley	Evang.	3B	110	406	88	125	*28	4	6	63	.308	*103	*204	*33	.903
1957—Little Rock	South.	3B	19	61	7	16	0	3	0	5	.262	27	33	4	.938
1958—Little Rock	South.	3B	14	43	8	6	3	1	0	6	.140	18	31	5	.907
1958—Winona	I.I.I.	3B	11	40	2	11	2	0	2	8	.275	11	22	1	.971
1958—Albany	East.	3B	105	358	41	81	13	3	4	32	.226	86	184	22	.925
1959—Albany†	East.	C	82	222	21	61	10	3	5	28	.275	358	20	7	.982
1960—Binghamton	East.	C	34	97	13	30	5	1	0	18	.309	157	11	2	.988
1960—Sioux City	I.I.I.	C	50	154	14	26	5	1	3	16	.169	362	26	7	.982
1961—Shreveport	South.	C	116	381	44	103	15	3	6	45	.270	672	56	15	.980
1961—Kansas City	Amer.	C	11	24	1	3	0	0	0	1	.125	22	3	0	1.000
1962—Portland	P.C.	C	87	243	30	52	9	1	7	26	.214	390	33	8	.981
1963—Portland	P.C.	C	61	182	23	34	5	1	5	14	.187	369	22	6	.985
1963—Lewiston‡	N'west.	C	25	72	8	20	5	0	2	12	.278	155	9	2	.988
1964—Spokane	P.C.	C	78	178	23	43	7	0	6	18	.242	314	26	8	.977
1965—Spokane§x	P.C.	C	68	208	20	46	11	1	2	21	.221	371	31	11	.973
1966—Geneva y	NYP	PH	2	2	0	0	0	0	0	0	.000	0	0	0	.000
Major League Totals			11	24	1	3	0	0	0	1	.125	22	3	0	1.000

†Loaned by Kansas City A's organization to New York Yankees' organization, April 14, 1960; returned, June 30.

‡Drafted by Los Angeles Dodgers' organization, December 2, 1963.

§On temporary inactive list, August 15 to October 15, 1965.

xOn voluntarily retired list, October 15, 1965, to February 24, 1966.

yPlayer-manager.

Named Florida State League Manager of the Year, 1972 and 1974.

Year Club	League	Position	W.	L.
1966–Geneva .... NYP	Sixth	18	42
(Second Half)	Sixth	16	48
1967–Geneva .... NYP	Fifth	37	42
1970–Pompano Beach . Fla. St.	Fourth(E)	58	70
1971–Pompano Beach . Fla. St.	Third(E)	70	69
1972–Pompano Beach . Fla. St.	†Second(E)	73	59
1973–Pompano Beach . Fla. St.	Fifth(S)	61	80
1974–W. Palm Beach .. Fla. St.	‡§Sec.(S)	79	53
1975–W. Palm Beach .. Fla. St.	xFour.(S)	58	77
1976–W. Palm Beach .. Fla. St.	Third(S)	63	79
1977–Jacksonville .... South.	Fourth(E)	31	36
(Second Half)	yFirst(E)	41	30
1978–Jacksonville .... South.	Third(E)	31	33
(Second Half)	Second(E)	42	36
1979–Omaha .... A. A.	Second(W)	65	71

†Lost playoff to Daytona Beach, two games to none.
‡One tie.
§Won playoff from Tampa, two games to none; won playoff championship from Ft. Lauderdale, two games to one.
xTwo ties.
yWon playoff from Savannah, two games to one; lost championship playoff to Montgomery, two games to none.
Scout, Washington Senators, 1968; scout, Los Angeles Dodgers, 1969; coach, Kansas City Royals, 1980 and 1981.

JOSE MARTINEZ (AZCUIZ)
Kansas City Royals

Born July 26, 1942, at Cardenas, Cuba.
Height, 6.00. Weight, 180.
Threw and batted righthanded.
Hobby—Music.

Led Northern League in stolen bases with 40 in 1961.

Year Club	League	Pos.	G.	AB.	R.	H.	2B.	3B.	HR.	RBI.	B.A.	PO.	A.	E.	F.A.
1960–Dubuque .... Midw.	SS-3B	101	366	65	104	16	4	8	53	.284	137	179	38	.893
1961–Grand Forks ..... North.	SS	122	460	74	129	13	5	4	36	.280	*219	313	*51	.913
1962–Asheville .... Sally	SS	119	403	49	98	17	6	4	39	.243	210	316	29	.948
1963–Kinston .... Carol.	SS	53	171	26	33	6	2	1	20	.193	69	117	14	.930
1963–Batavia .... NYP	2B	69	273	59	85	17	6	14	44	.311	137	175	16	.951
1964–Asheville .... South.	2-SS-3	119	403	65	110	18	4	20	78	.273	182	276	25	.948
1965–Columbus .... Int.	3-SS-2	96	294	42	68	8	1	7	26	.231	87	172	15	.945
1966–Columbus .... Int.	SS-3B	111	347	39	74	9	6	6	23	.213	104	265	27	.932
1967–Columbus .... Int.				(On Inactive List)										
1968–York .... East.	*3-O-1-2	125	383	28	100	9	1	1	31	.261	98	*212	21	.937
1969–Columbus .... Int.	2B-SS	6	20	3	9	1	2	0	1	.450	8	11	2	.905
1969–Pittsburgh .... Nat.	2-SS-3	77	168	20	45	6	0	1	16	.268	85	132	6	.973
1970–Columbus .... Int.	2-SS-3	91	333	52	103	18	5	4	51	.309	182	250	13	.971
1970–Pittsburgh .... Nat.	3-2-SS	19	20	1	1	0	0	0	0	.050	12	17	3	.906
1971–Charleston†‡ ..... Int.	3-2-SS	60	177	31	52	7	0	2	24	.294	59	104	4	.976
1972–Omaha .... A.A.	3-SS-2	102	337	28	85	11	1	4	38	.252	97	182	14	.952
1973–Omaha .... A.A.	2-3-SS	56	194	24	55	6	1	6	32	.284	98	119	11	.952
1974–Omaha§ .... A.A.	3-SS-2	73	207	24	47	5	2	5	31	.227	55	104	15	.914
Major League Totals		96	188	21	46	6	0	1	16	.245	97	149	9	.965

†On disabled list, April 16 to May 31 and June 28 to July 8, 1971.
‡Sold to Kansas City Royals' organization, March 15, 1972.
§Released, April 7, 1975.

RECORD AS MANAGER

Year Club	League	Position	W.	L.
1976–Sara. Royals ...... G.C.	Third	29	25
1977–Daytona Beach... Fla. St.	Fifth(N)	57	77
1978–Sara. Royals ...... G.C.	Second	31	24
1979–Sara. Roy. (Gold)G.C.	Third	29	23

Coach, Kansas City Royals, 1980 and 1981.

TOMMY LEE McCRAW
(Tom)
Cleveland Indians

Born November 21, 1940, at Malvern, Ark.
Height, 6.00. Weight, 193.
Threw and batted lefthanded.
Hobbies—Basketball and fishing.
Attended Santa Monica City College, Santa Monica, Calif.

Established major league record for fewest at bats, season, 150 or more games, 389, in 1966.
Tied major league record for most errors, inning, first baseman (3), third inning, May 3, 1968.
Hit three home runs in game, May 24, 1967.
Led American League first basemen in double plays with 103 in 1968.

Year Club	League	Pos.	G.	AB.	R.	H.	2B.	3B.	HR.	RBI.	B.A.	PO.	A.	E.	F.A.
1960–Clinton .... Midwest	1B	116	413	72	118	16	12	9	79	.286	797	52	20	.977
1961–Idaho Falls .... Pion.	1B	115	446	84	146	27	10	11	96	.327	841	48	22	.976
1962–Indianapolis ...... A. A.	1B	140	525	93	171	29	11	7	59	*.326	1193	84	11	.991
1963–Indianapolis ...... Int.	1B	53	195	27	55	9	3	4	17	.282	460	24	4	.992

Year Club League	Pos.	G.	AB.	R.	H.	2B.	3B.	HR.	RBI.	B.A.	PO.	A.	E.	F.A.
1963—Chicago ....Amer.	1B	102	280	38	71	11	3	6	33	.254	673	47	5	.993
1964—Chicago ....Amer.	1B-OF	125	368	47	96	11	5	6	36	.261	637	41	7	.990
1965—Chicago ....Amer.	1B-OF	133	273	38	65	12	1	5	21	.238	336	24	4	.989
1966—Chicago ....Amer.	1B-OF	151	389	49	89	16	4	5	48	.229	893	68	9	.991
1967—Chicago ....Amer.	1B-OF	125	453	55	107	18	3	11	45	.236	1177	110	11	.992
1968—Chicago ....Amer.	1B	136	477	51	112	16	12	9	44	.235	1285	*93	*20	.986
1969—Chicago ....Amer.	1B-OF	93	240	21	62	12	2	2	25	.258	302	15	3	.991
1970—Chicago† ....Amer.	1B-OF	129	332	39	73	11	2	6	31	.220	427	35	9	.981
1971—Washington‡ .....Amer.	OF-1B	122	207	33	44	6	4	7	25	.213	134	2	5	.965
1972—Cleveland§ ....Amer.	OF-1B	129	391	43	101	13	5	7	33	.258	504	28	3	.994
1973—California ....Amer.	OF-1B	99	264	25	70	7	0	3	24	.265	268	25	1	.997
1974—Calif. x-Cleve. ...Amer.	1B-OF	101	231	38	68	16	0	6	34	.294	448	38	3	.994
1975—Cleveland y ....Amer.	1B-OF	23	51	7	14	1	1	2	5	.275	113	8	0	1.000
Major League Totals......................		1468	3956	484	972	150	42	75	404	.246	7197	534	80	.990

†Traded to Washington Senators for Outfielder Ed Stroud, March 29, 1971.

‡Traded with Outfielder Roy Foster to Cleveland Indians for Outfielder Ted Ford, April 3, 1972.

§Traded with Second baseman Bob Marcano (assigned from Oklahoma City to Salt Lake City) to California Angels for Shortstop Leo Cardenas, April 2, 1973.

xSold to Cleveland Indians, July 17, 1974.

yPlayer-coach; released as player, June 30, 1975.

Coach, Cleveland Indians, 1975, and July 26, 1979 through 1981; minor league instructor, Cleveland Indians, 1976 through 1978.

CALVIN COOLIDGE JULIUS CEASAR TUSKAHOMA McLISH
(Cal)
Milwaukee Brewers

Born December 1, 1925, at Anadarko, Okla.
Height, 6.01. Weight, 204.
Threw right and batted left and righthanded.
Hobby—Golf.
Father of Tom McLish, pitcher in St. Louis Cardinals' organization.

Tied major league records for most home runs allowed, inning (4), May 22, 1957; most games lost to one club, season (7), 1960 (vs. Pittsburgh).

Led American League in wild pitches with 8 in 1957.

Year Club	League	G.	IP.	W.	L.	Pct.	H.	R.	ER.	SO.	BB.	ERA.
1944—Brooklyn.............................National		23	84	3	10	.231	110	81	73	24	48	7.82
1945—Brooklyn.............................National						(In Military Service)						
1946—Brooklyn†‡.........................National		1	⅓	0	0	.000	1	2	2	0	0	54.00
1947—Pittsburgh ....National		1	1	0	0	.000	2	2	2	0	0	18.00
1947—Kansas City ....Am. Assoc.		16	92	6	7	.462	104	55	45	40	42	4.40
1948—Pittsburgh ....National		2	5	0	0	.000	8	5	5	1	2	9.00
1948—Indianapolis§......................Am. Assoc.		29	172	12	9	.571	199	100	79	71	57	4.13
1949—Chicago ....National		8	23	1	1	.500	31	21	15	6	12	5.87
1949—Los Angeles ....P. Coast		29	150	8	11	.421	164	95	96	68	107	5.76
1950—Los Angeles ....P. Coast		42	260	20	11	.645	243	119	104	129	104	3.60
1951—Chicago ....National		30	146	4	10	.286	159	76	72	46	52	4.44
1952—Los Angeles ....P. Coast		34	212	10	15	.400	215	106	89	84	60	3.78
1953—Los Angeles ....P. Coast		35	235	16	11	.593	239	108	97	114	60	3.71
1954—Los Angeles ....P. Coast		37	245	13	15	.464	261	102	96	120	74	3.53
1955—Los Angeles x-San Diego y ...P. Coast		35	233	17	12	.586	230	88	80	116	69	3.09
1956—Cleveland.............................American		37	62	2	4	.333	67	36	34	27	32	4.94
1957—Cleveland.............................American		42	144	9	7	.563	118	55	44	88	67	2.75
1958—Cleveland.............................American		39	226	16	8	.667	214	92	75	97	70	2.99
1959—Cleveland z ....American		35	235	19	8	.704	*253	110	95	113	72	3.64
1960—Cincinnati a ....National		37	151	4	14	.222	170	85	70	56	48	4.17
1961—Chicago b ....American		31	162	10	13	.435	178	87	79	80	47	4.39
1962—Philadelphia.........................National		32	155	11	5	.688	184	84	73	71	45	4.24
1963—Philadelphia.........................National		32	210	13	11	.542	184	85	76	98	56	3.26
1964—Philadelphia c ....National		2	5	0	1	.000	6	3	2	6	1	3.60
American League Totals......................		184	829	56	40	.583	830	380	327	405	288	3.55
National League Totals............................		168	780	36	52	.409	855	444	390	308	264	4.50
Major League Totals		352	1609	92	92	.500	1685	824	717	713	552	4.01

†In military service most of season.

‡Traded to Pittsburgh Pirates with Pitcher Kirby Higbe, Catcher Homer Howell and Shortstop Gene Mauch for Outfielder Al Gionfriddo and reported $100,000, May 3, 1947.

§Traded to Chicago Cubs by Pittsburgh Pirates with Third Baseman Frank Gustine for Pitcher Cliff Chambers and Catcher Clyde McCullough, December 8, 1948.

xSold by Chicago Cubs' organization to San Diego, April 27, 1955.

yConditionally released to Cleveland Indians, October 15, 1955.

zTraded to Cincinnati Reds with First Baseman Gordon Coleman and Second Baseman Billy Martin for Second Baseman Johnny Temple, December 15, 1959.

aTraded to Chicago White Sox with Pitcher Juan Pizarro for Third Baseman Gene Freese, December 15, 1960.

bSent to Philadelphia Phillies as replacement for Third Baseman Andy Carey who refused to report to Phils in trade made December 15, 1961; Sox traded Pitcher Frank Barnes and Carey for Pitcher Taylor Phillips and Infielder Bob Sadowski. McLish assigned to Phillies, March 24, 1962.

cPlaced on disabled list with sore arm, April 13; returned to active list, June 29, 1964, and released, July 31, 1964.

Year League	IP.	W.	L.	Pct.	H.	R.	ER.	SO.	BB.	ERA.
1959—American (second game)	2	0	0	.000	1	0	0	2	1	0.00

Coach, Philadelphia Phillies, 1965 and 1966; scout, Philadelphia Phillies, 1967 and 1968; coach, Montreal Expos, 1969 through 1975; coach, Milwaukee Brewers, 1976 through 1981.

DONALD JOHN McMAHON
(Don)
San Francisco Giants

Born January 4, 1930, at Brooklyn, N.Y.
Height, 6.02. Weight, 210.
Threw and batted righthanded.
Hobby—Photography.

Year Club	League	G.	IP.	W.	L.	Pct.	H.	R.	ER.	SO.	BB.	ERA.
1950—Owensboro..........................	Kitty	33	218	*20	9	.690	•211	104	66	*143	119	*2.72
1951—Denver†	Western	4	16	1	0	1.000	10	5	4	15	8	2.25
1952—Milwaukee..........................	Am. Assoc.					(In Military Service)						
1953—Evansville†	I.I.I.	26	114	6	5	.545	113	69	57	91	77	4.50
1954—Atlanta	Southern	46	91	8	5	.615	87	39	36	90	64	3.56
1955—Toledo	Am. Assoc.	42	142	2	13	.133	149	88	79	93	95	5.01
1956—Atlanta	Southern	14	36	4	2	.667	23	9	8	34	17	2.00
1956—Wichita	Am. Assoc.	40	89	4	4	.500	86	48	43	78	40	4.35
1957—Wichita..........................	Am. Assoc.	21	71	6	2	.750	59	25	23	65	38	2.92
1957—Milwaukee	National	32	47	2	3	.400	33	13	8	46	29	1.53
1958—Milwaukee	National	39	59	7	2	.778	50	25	24	37	29	3.66
1959—Milwaukee	National	60	81	5	3	.625	81	26	23	55	37	2.56
1960—Milwaukee	National	48	64	3	6	.333	66	48	42	50	32	5.91
1961—Milwaukee	National	53	92	6	4	.600	84	35	29	55	51	2.84
1962—Milwaukee‡-Houston	National	53	80	5	6	.455	56	16	15	72	33	1.69
1963—Houston§..........................	National	49	80	1	5	.167	83	38	36	51	26	4.05
1964—Cleveland..........................	American	70	101	6	4	.600	67	31	27	92	52	2.41
1965—Cleveland..........................	American	58	85	3	3	.500	79	36	31	60	37	3.28
1966—Cleveland x-Boston	American	61	90	9	8	.529	73	33	27	62	44	2.70
1967—Boston y-Chicago	American	63	109	6	2	.750	68	29	24	84	40	1.98
1968—Chicago z-Detroit	American	45	82	5	2	.714	53	18	18	65	30	1.98
1969—Detroit a	American	34	37	3	5	.375	25	17	16	38	18	3.89
1969—San Francisco	National	13	24	3	1	.750	13	9	8	21	9	3.00
1970—San Francisco	National	61	94	9	5	.643	70	32	31	74	45	2.97
1971—San Francisco	National	61	82	10	6	.625	73	40	37	71	37	4.06
1972—San Francisco b	National	44	63	3	3	.500	46	26	26	45	21	3.71
1973—San Francisco c	National	22	30	4	0	1.000	21	5	5	20	7	1.50
1974—San Francisco d	National	9	12	0	0	.000	13	5	4	5	2	3.00
National League Totals		543	808	58	44	.569	689	318	288	602	358	3.21
American League Totals		331	504	32	24	.571	365	164	143	401	221	2.55
Major League Totals................................		874	1312	90	68	.570	1054	482	431	1003	579	2.96

†On military list from May 30, 1951, through May 17, 1953.
‡Sold to Houston Colt .45s, May 9, 1962.
§Sold to Cleveland Indians, September 30, 1963.
xTraded with Pitcher Lee Stange to Boston Red Sox for Pitcher Dick Radatz, June 2, 1966.
yTraded with Pitcher Bob Snow (transferred from Pittsfield to Evansville) to Chicago White Sox for Infielder Jerry Adair, June 2, 1967.
zTraded to Detroit Tigers for Pitcher Dennis Ribant, July 26, 1968.
aSold to San Francisco Giants, August 9, 1969.
bReleased, October 10, 1972.
cPlaced on active roster, June 25, 1973; released, October 9, 1973.
dPlaced on active roster, May 21, 1974; released, July 3, 1974.

Coach, San Francisco Giants, 1973 through 1975; coach, Minnesota Twins, 1976 and 1977; coach, San Francisco Giants, 1980 and 1981.

CHAMPIONSHIP SERIES RECORD

Year Club	League	G.	IP.	W.	L.	Pct.	H.	R.	ER.	SO.	BB.	ERA.
1971—San Francisco	National	2	3	0	0	.000	0	0	0	3	0	0.00

WORLD SERIES RECORD

Year Club	League	G.	IP.	W.	L.	Pct.	H.	R.	ER.	SO.	BB.	ERA.
1957—Milwaukee	National	3	5	0	0	.000	3	0	0	5	3	0.00
1958—Milwaukee	National	3	3⅓	0	0	.000	3	2	2	5	3	5.40
1968—Detroit..........................	American	2	2	0	0	.000	4	3	3	1	0	13.50
World Series Totals................................		8	10⅓	0	0	.000	10	5	5	11	6	4.35

ALL-STAR GAME RECORD
Member of National League All-Star Team in 1958 game; did not play.

DID YOU KNOW—
That when Mike Squires caught two games in 1980, he was the first lefthanded catcher since 1958?

DENIS JOHN MENKE
Toronto Blue Jays

Born July 21, 1940, at Bancroft, Ia.
Height, 6.00. Weight, 189.
Threw and batted righthanded.
Hobbies—Basketball, music and attending sports events.

Tied Major League record for most double plays by shortstop, game (5), May 4, 1969.
Tied National League record for most intentional bases on balls, game (3), May 23, 1964.
Received reported $125,000 bonus to sign with Milwaukee Braves, 1958.

Year	Club	League	Pos.	G.	AB.	R.	H.	2B.	3B.	HR.	RBI.	B.A.	PO.	A.	E.	F.A.
1958—Cedar Rapids	....	I.I.I.	SS	13	45	9	12	2	0	1	6	.267	17	23	7	.851
1958—Midland†	....	Soph.	SS	66	246	71	70	10	2	8	54	.285	72	168	26	.902
1959—Cedar Rapids‡	...	I.I.I.	SS	89	301	36	76	13	1	8	25	.252	144	239	37	.912
1960—Yakima	....	N.W.	*SS-3-2	140	473	114	159	26	7	28	103	.336	216	337	*58	.905
1961—Vancouver	....	P.C.	INF	137	434	75	127	23	6	15	73	.293	222	366	26	.958
1962—Milwaukee	....	Nat.	INF-OF	50	146	12	28	3	1	2	16	.192	87	109	8	.961
1962—Toronto‡‡	....	Int.	INF	79	263	45	71	15	2	10	46	.270	550	75	6	.990
1963—Milwaukee	....	Nat.	INF-OF	146	518	58	121	16	4	11	50	.234	234	398	24	.963
1964—Milwaukee	....	Nat.	SS-2-3	151	505	79	143	29	5	20	65	.283	283	455	27	.965
1965—Milwaukee§	......	Nat.	SS-1-3	71	181	16	44	13	1	4	18	.243	110	146	9	.966
1966—Atlanta	....	Nat.	SS-3-1	138	454	55	114	20	4	15	60	.251	228	341	24	.960
1967—Atlanta x	....	Nat.	SS-3B	129	418	37	95	14	3	7	39	.227	183	350	19	.966
1968—Houston	....	Nat.	INF	150	542	56	135	23	6	6	56	.249	346	384	15	.980
1969—Houston	....	Nat.	INF	154	553	72	149	25	5	10	90	.269	257	414	27	.961
1970—Houston	....	Nat.	*S-INF-O	154	562	82	171	26	6	13	92	.304	262	460	*30	.960
1971—Houston y	....	Nat.	INF	146	475	57	117	26	3	1	43	.246	892	151	10	.991
1972—Cincinnati	....	Nat.	3B-1B	140	447	41	104	19	2	9	50	.233	125	260	16	.955
1973—Cincinnati z	......	Nat.	INF	139	241	38	46	10	0	3	26	.191	80	197	9	.969
1974—Houston	....	Nat.	3-2-SS	30	29	2	3	1	0	0	1	.103	3	22	0	1.000
Major League Totals	....			1598	5071	605	1270	225	40	101	606	.250	3090	3687	218	.969

†On temporary inactive list, May 27 through June 6.
‡On disabled list, June 13 through July 12.
‡‡On National Defense List, October 7, 1962 through March 22, 1963.
§On disabled list May 13 through June 17.
xTraded with Pitcher Denny LeMaster to Houston for Shortstop Roland (Sonny) Jackson and First Baseman Charles Harrison (latter assigned to Richmond), October 8, 1967.
yTraded with Second Baseman Joe Morgan, Pitcher Jack Billingham and Outfielders Cesar Geronimo and Ed Armbrister, latter on Columbus, Ga., roster, to Cincinnati Reds for First Baseman Lee May, Second Baseman Tommy Helms and Outfielder Jim Stewart, November 29, 1971.
zTraded to Houston Astros for Pitcher Pat Darcy and a player to be named later, February 18, 1974; deal settled with cash.

CHAMPIONSHIP SERIES RECORD

Year	Club	League	Pos.	G.	AB.	R.	H.	2B.	3B.	HR.	RBI.	B.A.	PO.	A.	E.	F.A.
1972—Cincinnati	....	Nat.	3B	5	16	1	4	1	0	0	0	.250	3	11	0	1.000
1973—Cincinnati	....	Nat.	3-SS-PH	3	9	1	2	0	0	1	1	.222	0	4	0	1.000
Championship Series Totals	....			8	25	2	6	1	0	1	1	.240	3	15	0	1.000

WORLD SERIES RECORD

Year	Club	League	Pos.	G.	AB.	R.	H.	2B.	3B.	HR.	RBI.	B.A.	PO.	A.	E.	F.A.
1972—Cincinnati	....	Nat.	3B	7	24	1	2	0	0	1	2	.083	6	23	0	1.000

ALL-STAR GAME RECORD

Year	League	Pos.	AB.	R.	H.	2B.	3B.	HR.	RBI.	B.A.	PO.	A.	E.	F.A.
1969—National	....	SS	1	0	0	0	0	0	0	.000	1	0	0	1.000
1970—National	....	2B	0	0	0	0	0	0	0	.000	2	1	0	1.000
All-Star Game Totals	....		1	0	0	0	0	0	0	.000	3	1	0	1.000

RECORD AS MANAGER

Year	Club	League	Position	W.	L.	Year	Club	League	Position	W.	L.
1977—Burlington	....	Midw.	†Fourth(S)	28	42		(Second Half)		Fourth(N)	30	40
	(Second Half)		‡First(S)	43	26	1979—Dunedin	....	Fla. St.	Third(N)	36	34
1978—Dunedin	....	Fla. St.	Fifth(N)	29	43		(Second Half)		Third(N)	32	35

†One tie.
‡Won playoff from Cedar Rapids, one game to none; won championship playoff from Waterloo, two games to none.
Coach, Toronto Blue Jays, 1980 and 1981.

RAYMOND ROGER MILLER
(Razor)
Baltimore Orioles

Born April 30, 1945, at Takoma Park, Md.
Height, 6.03. Weight, 215.
Threw and batted righthanded.
Hobbies—Golf, bowling and hunting.

Pitched eight-inning 0-0 tie (rain) no-hit game against Statesville, August 3, 1964.

Led Western Carolinas League in shutouts with 5 in 1964.
Led Midwest League in hit batsmen with 16 in 1965 and led California League with 12 in 1966 and 13 in 1968.

Year Club	League	G.	IP.	W.	L.	Pct.	H.	R.	ER.	SO.	BB.	ERA.
1964—Lexington	W. Carol.	36	159	9	•11	.450	97	64	33	195	•109	1.87
1965—Salinas	California	3	6	0	1	.000	3	4	4	5	8	6.00
1965—Dubuque†	Midwest	30	122	7	9	.438	97	66	51	147	78	3.76
1966—Pawtucket	Eastern	1	2	0	0	.000	3	2	2	2	1	9.00
1966—Reno‡	California	24	93	5	7	.417	87	75	66	94	55	6.39
1967—Reno§	California	34	60	1	3	.250	50	40	33	49	41	4.95
1968—Reno x	California	29	193	16	8	.667	170	86	69	206	81	3.22
1969—Portland	P. Coast	45	112	5	11	.313	107	51	42	73	56	3.38
1970—Wichita y	Am. Assoc.	•56	98	6	6	.500	94	49	40	87	46	3.67
1971—Wichita	Am. Assoc.	8	11	0	1	.000	12	3	3	10	5	2.45
1971—Rochester	Int'national	44	57	3	2	.600	49	26	20	48	28	3.16
1972—Rochester	Int'national	47	73	7	5	.583	66	31	26	61	38	3.21
1973—Rochester z	Int'national	14	26	1	1	.500	13	8	4	15	4	1.38

†On disabled list, June 24 through July 8, 1965.
‡On disabled list, June 28 through July 24, 1966.
§On temporary inactive list, June 17 through July 4, 1967.
xOn temporary inactive list, June 13 through July 1, 1968; appeared in one game as outfielder.
yOn temporary inactive list, May 15 through May 18, 1970.
zPlayer-coach.
Minor league pitching instructor, Baltimore Orioles, 1974 through 1977; named pitching coach of Texas Rangers, November 21, 1977; Released from contract to become pitching coach of Baltimore Orioles, January, 1978; coach, Baltimore Orioles, 1978 through 1981.

SATURNINO ORESTES ARRIETA MINOSO (ARMAS)
(Minnie)
Chicago White Sox

Born November 29, 1922, at Pefico, Matanzas, Cuba.
Height, 5.11. Weight, 175.
Threw and batted righthanded.
Father of Orestes Minoso, Jr., outfielder in Kansas City Royals' organization,
1971 through 1974, now playing in Mexican League.

Established major league records for most consecutive years, leading league, hit by pitcher (6), 1956 through 1961; and most years leading league in hit by pitcher (10), 1961.
Established American League record for most times hit by pitch, career, 189, 1949 through 1964 (except 1950 and 1962).
Led American League in stolen bases (31) 1951, (22) 1952 and (25) 1953.
Led American League in total bases with 304 in 1954.
Named by THE SPORTING NEWS as American League Rookie of the Year, 1951.
Named as outfielder on THE SPORTING NEWS All-Star Major League Teams 1959-60.
Received Gold Glove award as outstanding major league fielder in left field, 1957; received award as outstanding American League fielder in left field, 1959-60.

Year Club	League	Pos.	G.	AB.	R.	H.	2B.	3B.	HR.	RBI.	B.A.	PO.	A.	E.	F.A.
1948—Dayton	Cent.	3B-2B	11	40	14	21	7	1	1	8	.525	6	26	0	1.000
1949—Cleveland	Amer.	OF	9	16	2	3	0	0	1	1	.188	11	0	0	1.000
1949—San Diego	P.C.	OF	137	532	99	158	19	7	22	75	.297	309	10	12	.964
1950—San Diego	P.C.	•3-OF-SS	169	599	130	203	40	10	20	115	.339	290	290	•33	.938
1951—Cleve.†-Chicago	Amer.	O-3-1-S	146	530	112	173	34	•14	10	76	.326	264	130	22	.947
1952—Chicago	Amer.	OF-2-SS	147	569	96	160	24	9	13	61	.281	323	22	7	.980
1953—Chicago	Amer.	•OF-3B	151	556	104	174	24	8	15	104	.313	282	29	•12	.963
1954—Chicago	Amer.	OF-3B	153	568	119	182	29	•18	19	116	.320	347	25	9	.976
1955—Chicago	Amer.	OF-3B	139	517	79	149	26	7	10	70	.288	289	21	9	.972
1956—Chicago	Amer.	OF-3-1	151	545	106	172	29	•11	21	88	.316	287	16	10	.968
1957—Chicago‡	Amer.	OF-3B	153	568	96	176	•36	5	12	103	.310	293	9	5	.984
1958—Cleveland	Amer.	OF-3B	149	556	94	168	25	2	24	80	.302	301	13	8	.975
1959—Cleveland§	Amer.	OF	148	570	92	170	32	0	21	92	.302	314	14	5	.985
1960—Chicago	Amer.	OF	•154	591	89	•184	32	4	20	105	.311	282	14	6	.980
1961—Chicago x	Amer.	OF	152	540	91	151	28	3	14	82	.280	273	10	13	.956
1962—St. Louis yz	Nat.	OF	39	97	14	19	5	0	1	10	.196	33	2	1	.972
1963—Washington a	Amer.	OF-3B	109	315	38	72	12	2	4	30	.229	108	26	5	.964
1964—Chicago b	Amer.	OF	30	31	4	7	0	0	1	5	.226	9	0	0	1.000
1964—Indianapolis	P.C.	OF-3B	52	178	22	47	11	0	4	26	.264	50	36	9	.905
1965—Jalisco	Mex.	OF-3B	134	469	•106	169	•35	10	14	82	.360	478	19	11	.978
1966—Jalisco c	Mex.	1B	107	376	70	131	18	1	6	45	.348	922	48	•19	.981
1967—Orizaba d	Mex. SE.	OF-3-1	36	100	20	35	7	3	5	19	.350	76	13	7	.927
1967—Jalisco	Mex.	1B-OF	13	37	5	9	1	2	0	3	.243	78	2	0	1.000
1968—Puerto Mex.d	Mex.SE.	1-OF-3	56	145	30	53	17	2	4	23	.366	181	9	8	.960
1968—Jalisco	Mex.	OF-1B	22	54	9	15	5	1	2	13	.296	24	2	0	1.000
1969—Puerto Mex.d	Mex.SE.	1B-OF	74	193	33	58	10	2	2	32	.301	448	10	9	.981
1969—Jalisco	Mex.	1-OF-3	36	103	18	33	3	1	2	14	.320	214	11	2	.991
1970—Gomez Palacio	Mex.	1B-OF	40	47	6	22	6	0	2	17	.468	25	1	1	.963
1971—Gomez Palacio	Mex.	1B-2B	112	336	37	106	15	2	6	57	.315	807	29	11	.987
1972—Gomez Palacio	Mex.	1B	121	425	48	121	24	1	12	63	.285	1015	36	10	.991
1973—Gomez Palacio	Mex.	1B-OF	120	407	50	108	15	1	12	83	.265	852	29	10	.989

Year	Club	League	Pos.	G.	AB.	R.	H.	2B.	3B.	HR.	RBI.	B.A.	PO.	A.	E.	F.A.
1976—Chicago		Amer.	PH-DH	3	8	0	1	0	0	0	0	.125	0	0	0	.000
1980—Chicago e		Amer.	PH	2	2	0	0	0	0	0	0	.000	0	0	0	.000
American League Totals				1796	6482	1122	1944	331	83	185	1013	.300	3383	329	111	.971
National League Totals				39	97	14	19	5	0	1	10	.196	33	2	1	.972
Major League Totals				1835	6579	1136	1963	336	83	186	1023	.298	3416	331	112	.971

†Traded to Chicago White Sox as part of three-club deal in which Indians also shipped Pitcher Sam Zoldak and Catcher Ray Murray to Philadelphia Athletics; Cleveland received Pitcher Lou Brissie from Athletics for their share of the players. Athletics also sent Outfielder Paul Lehner to the White Sox and added Outfielder Dave Philley and Gus Zernial from White Sox, April 30, 1951.

‡Traded to Cleveland Indians with Infielder Fred Hatfield for Pitcher Early Wynn and Outfielder Al Smith, December 4, 1957.

§Traded to Chicago White Sox with Pitchers Don Ferrarese and Jake Striker and Catcher Dick Brown for Catcher John Romano, First Baseman Norm Cash and Third Baseman-Outfielder Bubba Phillips, December 6, 1959.

xTraded to St. Louis Cardinals for First Baseman-Outfielder Joe Cunningham, November 27, 1961.

ySuffered skull fracture and broken right wrist chasing line drive, May 11, 1962; returned to active list, July 19—used sparingly for remainder of season.

zTraded to Washington Senators for an estimated $30,000 and minor league player to be named later, April 2, 1963.

aReleased, October 14, 1963; signed as free agent by Chicago White Sox, April 8, 1964.

bReleased, July 17, 1964.

cOn disabled list, May 21 to June 20, 1966.

dPlayer-manager.

eSigned by Chicago White Sox, October 3, 1980; released, October 6, 1980.

ALL-STAR GAME RECORD

Year	League	Pos.	AB.	R.	H.	2B.	3B.	HR.	RBI.	B.A.	PO.	A.	E.	F.A.
1951—American		OF	2	0	0	0	0	0	0	.000	2	0	0	1.000
1952—American		OF	1	1	1	1	0	0	0	1.000	0	0	0	.000
1953—American		OF	2	0	2	0	0	0	1	1.000	0	0	0	.000
1954—American		OF	4	1	2	0	0	0	0	.500	1	0	1	.500
1957—American		OF	1	0	1	1	0	0	1	1.000	1	1	0	1.000
1959—American (first game)		OF	5	0	0	0	0	0	0	.000	0	1	0	1.000
1960—American (both games)		OF	5	0	0	0	0	0	0	.000	1	0	0	1.000
All-Star Game Totals			20	2	6	2	0	0	2	.300	5	2	1	.875

RECORD AS MANAGER

Year	Club	League	Position	W.	L.	Year	Club	League	Position	W.	L.
1967—Orizaba		Mex.SE	Seventh	40	66	1970—Gomez Palacio		Mexican	Third(N)	68	82
1968—Puerto Mexico		Mex.SE	Third	57	36	1971—Gomez Palacio		Mex.	Fourth(N)	72	76
1969—Puerto Mexico		Mex.SE	Fourth	56	59	1975—Leon		Mex.C.	Sixth	28	39

Coach, Chicago White Sox, 1976 through July 3, 1978 and 1981.

GEORGE EUGENE MITTERWALD
Oakland A's

Born June 7, 1945, at Berkeley, Calif.
Height, 6.02. Weight, 205.
Threw and batted righthanded.
Attended Chabot College, Hayward, Calif.

Hit three home runs in a game, April 17, 1974, against Pittsburgh Pirates.
Led Southern League in passed balls with 20 in 1967.
Tied for Northern League lead in passed balls with 10 in 1965.

Year	Club	League	Pos.	G.	AB.	R.	H.	2B.	3B.	HR.	RBI.	B.A.	PO.	A.	E.	F.A.
1965—Wis. Rapids		Midw.	C	1	3	0	1	1	0	0	0	.333	5	0	0	1.000
1965—St. Cloud		North.	C	37	126	17	41	6	2	3	20	.325	273	24	7	.977
1966—Wilson		Carol.	C	86	313	35	83	18	2	6	48	.265	522	59	13	.978
1966—St. Cloud		North.	C	4	15	2	2	0	0	0	0	.133	42	1	0	1.000
1966—Minnesota		Amer.	C	3	5	1	1	0	0	0	0	.200	13	0	0	1.000
1967—Charlotte†		South.	C	104	347	43	84	19	1	8	44	.242	550	•65	9	.986
1968—Denver		P.C.	•C-OF	99	341	50	91	25	4	9	56	.267	412	51	•12	.975
1968—Wis. Rapids		Midw.	C	5	16	2	2	0	0	1	3	.125	38	10	0	1.000
1968—Minnesota		Amer.	C	11	34	1	7	1	0	0	1	.206	69	4	3	.961
1969—Minnesota‡		Amer.	C-OF	69	187	18	48	8	0	5	13	.257	340	33	5	.987
1970—Minnesota		Amer.	C	117	369	36	82	12	2	15	46	.222	740	62	3	.996
1971—Minnesota		Amer.	C	125	388	38	97	13	1	13	44	.250	656	53	10	.986
1972—Minnesota		Amer.	C	64	163	12	30	4	1	1	8	.184	272	33	5	.984
1973—Minnesota§		Amer.	C	125	432	50	112	15	0	16	64	.259	676	59	6	.992
1974—Chicago		Nat.	C	78	215	17	54	7	0	7	28	.251	335	40	10	.974
1975—Chicago		Nat.	C-1B	84	200	19	44	4	3	5	26	.220	315	38	8	.978
1976—Chicago		Nat.	C-1B	101	303	19	65	7	0	5	28	.215	512	23	4	.992
1977—Chicago x		Nat.	C-1B	110	349	40	83	22	0	9	43	.238	623	78	8	.989
1978—San Jose yza		P.C.	C	21	68	8	11	1	0	1	7	.162	48	3	2	.962
American League Totals				514	1578	156	377	53	4	50	176	.239	2766	244	32	.989
National League Totals				373	1067	95	246	40	3	26	125	.231	1785	179	30	.985
Major League Totals				887	2645	251	623	93	7	76	301	.236	4551	423	62	.988

‡On military list, August 1 to August 17, 1969.
§Traded to Chicago Cubs for Catcher Randy Hundley, December 6, 1973.
xGranted free agency, October 20, 1977; signed by Seattle Mariners' organization, February 27, 1978.
yReleased, May 6, 1978; signed by Miami of Inter-American League, January 3, 1979.
zSold to Oakland A's organization, March 4, 1979.
aActivated as player while Oakland coach, June 20 through June 25, 1979; did not play.
Batting practice pitcher and catcher, Chicago Cubs, May 27 through remainder of 1978 season; coach, Oakland A's, 1979 through 1981.

CHAMPIONSHIP SERIES RECORD

Year Club	League	Pos.	G.	AB.	R.	H.	2B.	3B.	HR.	RBI.	B.A.	PO.	A.	E.	F.A.
1969—Minnesota	Amer.	C	2	7	0	1	0	0	0	0	.143	10	4	0	1.000
1970—Minnesota	Amer.	C	2	8	2	4	1	0	0	2	.500	16	1	0	1.000
Championship Series Totals			4	15	2	5	1	0	0	2	.333	26	5	0	1.000

ALEX MONCHAK
(Al)
Pittsburgh Pirates

Born December 22, 1919, at Bayonne, N. J.
Height, 6.00. Weight, 180.
Threw right and batted right and lefthanded.

Led Longhorn League in stolen bases with 36 in 1949 and 48 in 1950.
Led Longhorn League second basemen in double plays with 109 in 1949, 140 in 1950 and 128 in 1951.

Year Club	League	Pos.	G.	AB.	R.	H.	2B.	3B.	HR.	RBI.	B.A.	PO.	A.	E.	F.A.
1937—Knoxville	South.	......	1	3	0	1	0	0	0	0	.333	....	....	....	....
1937—Albany	NYP	INF	(Appeared in less than 10 games; no figures available.)												
1937—Clarksdale	Cot.St.	SS	45	167	25	41	6	1	2	16	.246	91	111	19	.914
1937—Baltimore	Int.	INF	14	34	4	6	1	0	0	0	.176	....	....	....	....
1938—Dover	E.Shore	SS	95	390	86	118	21	7	10	46	.303	204	314	31	.944
1939—Dover	E.Shore	SS-3B	104	389	88	131	22	6	15	73	.337	229	291	32	.977
1939—Baltimore	Int.	INF	3	6		1					.167	....	....	....	....
1940—Philadelphia	Nat.	INF	19	14	1	2	0	0	0		.143	....	....	....	....
1940—Portsmouth	Pied.	SS	43	142	26	38	11	2	4	18	.268	80	137	11	.952
1941—Elmira	East.	SS	92	287	40	61	9	0	3	17	.212	154	222	22	.945
1942—Elmira	East.	2B-SS	50	176	21	43	4	2	0	10	.244	139	144	16	.947
1943-44-45—			(In Military Service)												
1946—Hartford	East.	2B	63	215	37	38	5	0	2	15	.177	144	185	10	.971
1947—			(Out of Organized Baseball)												
1948—Austin	Big St.	2B	120	446	84	129	20	9	1	64	.289	361	364	22	*.971
1949—Odessa	Long.	2B	137	522	*147	175	37	6	*35	125	.335	*402	*455	23	.974
1950—Odessa	Long.	2B	134	488	126	147	37	5	19	108	.301	*450	*388	27	*.969
1951—Roswell	Long.	2B	140	565	113	176	41	5	22	123	.311	*409	*394	25	*.970
1952—Roswell	Long.	2B	113	417	80	110	23	3	10	62	.264	326	*335	21	*.970
1953—Lexington	Tar Heel	2B	112	388	61	90	18	5	7	43	.232	*313	*327	20	*.970
1954—Portsmouth	Pied.	2B	79	274	23	72	8	5	3	41	.265	197	178	11	.972
1954—Keokuk	I.I.I.	2B	34	123	17	27	3	1	2	17	.220	84	95	7	.962
1955—Wellsville	PONY	2B	100	319	50	76	20	1	7	64	.238	248	212	11	*.977
1956—Wellsville	PONY	2B	35	99	9	21	3	0	2	12	.212	18	25	0	1.000
1957—Wellsville	NYP	INF	4	13	0	0	0	0	0	0	.000	....	....	....	....
Major League Totals			19	14	1	2	0	0	0		.143	....	....	....	....

PITCHING RECORD

Year Club	League	G.	IP.	W.	L.	Pct.	H.	R.	ER.	SO.	BB.	ERA.
1954—Portsmouth	Piedmont	1	....	0	0	.000	....	....	....	....	....	....
1956—Wellsville	PONY	1	....	0	1	.000	....	....	....	....	....	....

RECORD AS MANAGER

Year Club	League	Position	W.	L.	Year Club	League	Position	W.	L.
1949—Odessa	Long.	Fifth	66	74	1957—Wellsville	NYP	zFirst	74	43
1950—Odessa	Long.	†First	97	55	1958—Cedar Rapids	I.I.I.	Fourth	28	40
1951—Roswell	Long.	Third	79	61	(Second Half)		aFirst	49	23
1952—Roswell	Long.	‡Fifth	65	75	1959—Cedar Rapids	I.I.I.	Fifth	30	30
1953—Lexington	Tar Heel	§Fourth	59	54	(Second Half)		Eighth	23	43
1954—Portsmouth x	Pied.	Third	50	47	1960—Austin	Texas	Fifth	73	71
1955—Wellsville	PONY	Fourth	68	58	1961—Davenport	Midw.	Fourth	32	30
1956—Wellsville	PONY	yFirst	74	46	(Second Half)		Second	36	26

†Won playoffs by defeating Vernon, four games to one and Big Spring, four games to three.
‡Tied for position with San Angelo.
§Won playoffs by defeating Rutherford County, four games to two and Marion, four games to two.
xReplaced August 1 by Pepper Martin.
yWon playoffs by defeating Hornell, two games to one and Olean, three games to two.
zLost playoff semifinal series to Batavia, two games to one.
aWon playoff by defeating Davenport (First Half winner), three games to two.

Scout and farm system instructor, California Angels, 1962 through 1970; coach, Chicago White Sox, 1971 through 1975; coach, Oakland Athletics, 1976; coach, Pittsburgh Pirates, 1977 through 1981.

JACKIE SPENCER MOORE
Oakland A's

Born February 19, 1939, at Jay, Fla.
Height, 6.00, Weight, 181.
Threw and batted righthanded.
Hobbies—Hunting, fishing and golf.

Year Club	League	Pos.	G.	AB.	R.	H.	2B.	3B.	HR.	RBI.	B.A.	PO.	A.	E.	F.A.
1957—Montgomery	Al.-Fla.	O-C	71	263	36	62	6	1	7	35	.236	237	18	10	.962
1958—Valdosta	Ga.-Fla.	C-3	87	333	61	100	20	3	9	78	.300	445	75	11	.979
1958—Augusta	Sally	C-OF	13	35	4	8	1	1	1	12	.229	31	3	0	1.000
1959—Durham	Carol.	C-OF	94	305	43	79	18	2	8	55	.259	407	33	8	.982
1960—Knoxville	Sally	C	97	314	40	85	15	3	10	40	.271	541	46	10	.983
1961—Knoxville	Sally	C-2-3B	43	151	14	45	6	3	0	30	.298	248	22	2	.993
1961—Denver	A. A.	C	43	134	8	32	3	0	0	8	.239	218	26	3	.988
1962—Denver†	A. A.	C-OF	32	98	10	25	3	0	0	14	.255	164	10	3	.983
1962—Toronto	Int.	C	12	29	3	4	0	0	0	2	.138	56	6	1	.984
1963—Syracuse‡	Int.	C	73	213	23	63	5	1	7	37	.296	371	30	4	.990
1964—Syracuse	Int.	C	99	286	34	68	8	1	1	31	.238	449	35	6	.988
1965—Detroit	Amer.	C	21	53	2	5	0	0	0	2	.094	128	6	2	.985
1965—Syracuse§	Int.	C	17	50	3	9	2	0	0	4	.100	80	4	1	.988
1966—Syracuse x	Int.	C	89	290	24	60	11	2	2	17	.207	429	37	4	∗.991
1967—Toronto y	Int.	C	100	307	21	61	4	0	3	30	.199	∗643	40	4	∗.994
Major League Totals			21	53	2	5	0	0	0	2	.094	128	6	2	.985

JOn disabled list, June 19 to August 2, 1962.

‡Conditionally released by Detroit Tigers' organization to Los Angeles Angels, October 11, 1963; returned by Angels to Tigers, March 27, 1964.

§On disabled list, July 31 through August 14, 1965.

xAssigned by Detroit Tigers to Boston Red Sox, October 13, 1966, to complete deal in which Tigers obtained Pitcher Bill Monbouquette from Red Sox for Outfielder George Thomas and Infielder George Smith, October 4, 1965.

yReleased by Boston Red Sox' organization, February 21, 1968.

RECORD AS MANAGER

Year Club	League	Position	W.	L.
1968—Jamestown	NYP	Seventh	31	44
1969—Jamestown	NYP	Sixth	33	41
1975—Pittsfield	Eastern	Fourth	27	32
(Second Half)†			13	8

†Replaced by Orlando Martinez, July 24.

Coach, Milwaukee Brewers, 1970 through 1972; coach, Texas Rangers, 1973 and 1974, part of 1975, 1976 and 1980; coach, Toronto Blue Jays, 1977 through 1979; coach, Oakland A's, 1981.

THOMAS STEPHEN MORGAN
(Tom)
California Angels

Born May 20, 1930, at San Pedro, Calif.
Height, 6.02. Weight, 205.
Threw and batted righthanded.

Tied major league records for most hit batsmen, inning (3), June 30, 1954; most putouts by pitcher, game (5), June 16, 1957.

Year Club	League	G.	IP.	W.	L.	Pct.	H.	R.	ER.	SO.	BB.	ERA.
1949—Ventura	Calif.	33	200	12	9	.571	197	108	83	125	72	3.74
1950—Binghamton	East.	29	203	17	8	.680	182	92	80	114	55	3.55
1951—Kansas City	A. A.	4	20	2	1	.667	14	6	5	11	2	2.25
1951—New York	Amer.	27	125	9	3	.750	119	56	51	57	36	3.67
1952—New York	Amer.	16	94	5	4	.556	86	34	32	35	33	3.06
1953—New York	Amer.				(In U. S. Army)							
1954—New York	Amer.	32	143	11	5	.688	149	58	53	34	40	3.34
1955—New York	Amer.	40	72	7	3	.700	72	29	26	17	24	3.25
1956—New York†	Amer.	41	71	6	7	.462	74	41	33	20	27	4.18
1957—Kansas City‡	Amer.	46	144	9	7	.563	160	76	74	32	61	4.63
1958—Detroit	Amer.	39	63	2	5	.286	70	28	22	32	4	3.14
1959—Detroit	Amer.	46	93	1	4	.200	94	48	41	39	18	3.97
1960—Det.§-Wash. x	Amer.	36	53	4	5	.444	69	32	25	23	15	4.25
1961—Los Angeles	Amer.	59	92	8	2	.800	74	31	24	39	17	2.35
1962—Los Angeles	Amer.	48	59	5	2	.714	53	23	19	29	19	2.90
1963—Los Angeles	Amer.	13	16	0	0	.000	20	11	10	7	6	5.63
1963—Hawaii	P. C.	32	52	4	2	.667	41	15	15	28	10	2.60
Major League Totals		443	1025	67	47	.588	1040	467	410	364	300	3.60

†Traded in deal involving 13 players to Kansas City Athletics, February 19, 1957.

‡Traded in deal involving 13 players to Detroit Tigers, November 20, 1957.

§Traded to Washington Senators for Pitcher Bill Fischer, July 23, 1960.

xSold to Los Angeles Angels, January 31, 1961.

WORLD SERIES RECORD

Year Club	League	G.	IP.	W.	L.	Pct.	H.	R.	ER.	SO.	BB.	ERA.
1951—New York	Amer.	1	2	0	0	.000	2	0	0	3	1	0.00

Year Club	League	G.	IP.	W.	L.	Pct.	H.	R.	ER.	SO.	BB.	ERA.
1955–New York ....Amer.		2	3⅔	0	0	.000	3	2	2	1	3	4.91
1956–New York ....Amer.		2	4	0	1	.000	6	4	4	3	4	9.00
World Series Totals.................................		5	9⅔	0	1	.000	11	6	6	7	8	5.59

RECORD AS MANAGER

Year Club	League	Position	W.	L.
1966–Idaho Falls .... Pion.		†Third	29	37
1969–San Jose .... Calif.		‡Seventh	30	40
(Second Half)		Fourth	38	32

†Replaced by Alex Monchak, July 14.
‡Replaced by Eddie Bressoud, June 14.

Minor League Pitching Instructor, Los Angeles Angels, 1964 and 1965, California Angels, 1967 and 1968; scout, New York Yankees, 1971; coach, California Angels, 1972 through 1974 and 1981; San Diego Padres, 1975; scout, Atlanta Braves, 1976 through 1978; coach, New York Yankees, beginning of season through June 19, 1979; scout, New York Yankees, June 19, 1979 through 1980.

JOHN LESTER MOSS
(Les)
Chicago Cubs

Born May 14, 1925, at Tulsa, Okla.
Height, 5.11. Weight, 195.
Threw and batted righthanded.
Hobbies—Hunting and fishing.

Led Eastern League catchers in passed balls with 22 in 1943.
Tied for American Association lead among catchers in double plays with 12 in 1946.

Year Club	League	Pos.	G.	AB.	R.	H.	2B.	3B.	HR.	RBI.	B.A.	PO.	A.	E.	F.A.
1942–Americus..........Ga.-Fla.		C	109	391	46	117	23	2	3	58	.299	502	46	14	.975
1943–Elmira..............East.		C	96	279	50	86	18	3	3	45	.308	●461	52	10	.981
1944-45–Toledo...........A.A.		(In Merchant Marine)													
1946–Toledo ...............A.A.		C	121	390	44	116	21	1	13	54	.297	*590	70	*24	.965
1946–St. Louis ....Amer.		C	12	35	4	13	3	0	0	5	.371	55	5	2	.968
1947–St. Louis ....Amer.		C	96	274	17	43	5	2	6	27	.157	362	43	7	.983
1948–St. Louis ....Amer.		C	107	335	35	86	12	1	14	46	.257	357	52	5	.988
1949–St. Louis ....Amer.		C	97	278	28	81	11	0	10	39	.291	283	41	10	.970
1950–St. Louis ....Amer.		C	84	222	24	59	6	0	8	34	.266	204	20	10	.957
1951–St.L.†-Boston‡...Amer.		C	87	249	23	48	8	0	4	33	.193	335	36	7	.981
1952–St. Louis ....Amer.		C	52	118	11	29	3	0	3	12	.246	118	17	6	.957
1953–St. Louis ....Amer.		C	78	239	21	66	14	1	2	28	.276	296	21	7	.978
1954–Baltimore ....Amer.		C	50	126	7	31	3	0	0	5	.246	159	16	5	.972
1955–Balt.§–Chicago..Amer.		C	61	115	10	34	3	0	4	13	.296	156	10	1	.994
1956–Chicago ....Amer.		C	56	127	20	31	4	0	10	22	.244	149	10	1	.994
1957–Chicago ....Amer.		C	42	115	10	31	3	0	2	12	.270	138	8	3	.980
1958–Chicago ....Amer.		PH	2	1	0	0	0	0	0	0	.000	0	0	0	.000
1959–Indianapolis ......A.A.		C	43	94	9	21	2	0	0	12	.223	127	5	0	1.000
1960–San Diego .........P.C.		PH	3	3	0	1	0	0	0	0	.333	0	0	0	.000
Major League Totals......................			824	2234	210	552	75	4	63	276	.247	2612	279	64	.978

†Traded to Boston Red Sox for Pitcher Jim Suchecki, Catcher Matt Batts, player to be named later and $100,000, May 17, 1951; deal was completed with transfer of Pitcher Jim McDonald from Louisville American Association roster to St. Louis Browns, July 18, 1951.
‡Traded with Outfielder Tom Wright to St. Louis Browns for Catcher Gus Niarhos and Outfielder Ken Wood, November 28, 1951.
§Traded to Chicago White Sox for Pitcher Harry Dorish, June 6, 1955.

RECORD AS MANAGER

Named Minor League Manager of the Year by THE SPORTING NEWS, 1978.

Year Club	League	Position	W.	L.	Year Club	League	Position	W.	L.
1962–Savannah........... Sally		First	92	47	1973–Salt Lake City .... P.C.		Second(E)	‡79	65
1963–Lynchburg .... Sally		Sixth	32	37	1975–Montgomery ...... South.		§First(W)	73	61
(Second Half)		First	47	24	1976–Montgomery ...... South.		xFirst(W)	81	56
1964–Indianapolis ...... P.C.		Second(E)	89	69	1977–Evansville .... A.A.		Third(E)	65	68
1966–Indianapolis .... P.C.		Third(E)	80	68	1978–Evansville .... A.A.		Second	78	58
1968–Chicago†............ Amer.		....	12	24	1979–Detroit y........... Amer.		Fifth(E)	27	26
1971–Shreveport......... Dixie		‡69	73	1980–Midland z.......... Texas		....	10	2
1972–Salt Lake City .... P.C.		Third(E)	80	68					

†Served as acting manager for hospitalized Al Lopez.
‡Record includes one tie.
§Won Championship Playoff from Orlando, three games to none.
xWon Western Division Championship from Chattanooga, one game to none; won Championship Playoff from Orlando, three games to none.
yReplaced by Sparky Anderson (and interim manager Dick Tracewski), June 11, 1979.
zServed as acting manager for ill Randy Hundley, June 17 to June 30, 1980.
Batting practice catcher, Chicago White Sox, May 1, 1960, through end of season; scout, Chicago White Sox, 1961, 1965 and 1969; coach, Chicago White Sox, 1967, 1968 and 1970; scout California Angels, 1974; minor league pitching coach, Chicago Cubs, July 6, 1979 to June 17, 1980 and June 30 through remainder of 1980 season; coach, Chicago Cubs, 1981.

MANUEL R. MOTA (GERONIMO)
Name pronounced MOH-tuh.
(Manny)
Los Angeles Dodgers

Born February 18, 1938, at Santo Domingo, Dominican Republic.
Height, 5.11. Weight, 168.
Throws and bats righthanded.
Hobby—Golf.
Attended Escuela Salesiana, Don Bosco, Dominican Republic.
Established major league record for most hits by pinch-hitter, lifetime (150).

Year Club League	Pos.	G.	AB.	R.	H.	2B.	3B.	HR.	RBI.	B.A.	PO.	A.	E.	F.A.
1957—Michigan City....Midw.	OF	126	471	82	148	23	2	7	91	.314	217	20	13	.948
1958—Danville ....Carol.	OF	103	385	63	116	20	5	8	55	.301	167	•18	7	.964
1959—Phoenix.............P. C.	OF	21	44	9	11	2	1	1	7	.250	22	0	2	.917
1959—Springfield ....East.	OF-2B	65	245	39	77	10	7	3	28	.314	118	34	5	.968
1960—Rio Grande Val..Tex.	•OF-3	141	541	76	166	18	10	4	79	.307	316	•21	9	.974
1961—Tacoma.............P. C.	OF-1B	142	484	64	140	13	4	3	43	.289	248	17	4	.985
1962—San Francisco ...Nat.	O-3-2B	47	74	9	13	1	0	0	9	.176	38	18	2	.966
1962—El Paso†‡..........Tex.	OF	30	109	26	38	9	3	3	7	.349	51	1	1	.981
1963—Columbus..........Int.	OF-2B	75	294	46	86	9	3	5	20	.293	150	61	4	.981
1963—Pittsburgh.........Nat.	OF-2B	59	126	20	34	2	3	0	7	.270	40	1	2	.953
1964—Pittsburgh.........Nat.	OF-2B-C	115	271	43	75	8	3	5	32	.277	122	5	5	.962
1965—Pittsburgh.........Nat.	OF	121	294	47	82	7	6	4	29	.279	127	5	2	.985
1966—Pittsburgh.........Nat.	OF-3B	116	322	54	107	16	7	5	46	.332	152	4	1	.994
1967—Pittsburgh.........Nat.	OF-3B	120	349	53	112	14	8	4	56	.321	156	14	2	.988
1968—Pittsburgh§ ....Nat.	OF-2-3	111	331	35	93	10	2	1	33	.281	150	8	3	.981
1969—Mont.x-L. A......Nat.	OF	116	383	41	123	7	5	3	30	.321	157	8	8	.954
1970—Los Angeles......Nat.	OF-3B	124	417	63	127	12	6	3	37	.305	172	9	5	.973
1971—Los Angeles......Nat.	OF	91	269	24	84	13	5	0	34	.312	108	3	4	.965
1972—Los Angeles......Nat.	OF	118	371	57	120	16	5	5	48	.323	141	3	1	.993
1973—Los Angeles......Nat.	OF	89	293	33	92	11	2	0	23	.314	96	4	0	1.000
1974—Los Angeles......Nat.	OF	66	57	5	16	2	0	0	16	.281	1	0	0	1.000
1975—Los Angeles......Nat.	OF	52	49	3	13	1	0	0	10	.265	9	0	0	1.000
1976—Los Angeles......Nat.	OF	50	52	1	15	3	0	0	13	.288	11	1	0	1.000
1977—Los Angeles......Nat.	OF	49	38	5	15	1	0	1	4	.395	1	0	0	1.000
1978—Los Angeles ......Nat.	PH	37	33	2	10	1	0	0	6	.303	0	0	0	.000
1979—Los Angeles y ...Nat.	OF	47	42	1	15	0	0	0	3	.357	0	0	0	.000
1980—Los Angeles z....Nat.	PH	7	7	0	3	0	0	0	2	.429	0	0	0	.000
Major League Totals		1535	3778	496	1149	125	52	31	438	.304	1481	83	35	.978

Signed as free agent by San Francisco Giants' organization, February 21, 1957.
†Recalled by San Francisco Giants; Traded to Houston Colts with Pitcher Dick LeMay for Second Baseman Joe Amalfitano, November 30, 1962.
‡Traded to Pittsburgh Pirates with cash for Outfielder Howie Goss, April 2, 1963.
§Selected by Montreal Expos from Pittsburgh Pirates in expansion draft, October 14, 1968.
xTraded with Shortstop Maury Wills to Los Angeles Dodgers for Outfielder-First Baseman Ron Fairly and Infielder Paul Popovich, June 11, 1969.
yReleased, October 1, 1979.
zActivated, August 29, 1980; released, October 8, 1980
Coach, Los Angeles Dodgers, 1980 and 1981.

CHAMPIONSHIP SERIES RECORD

Year Club League	Pos.	G.	AB.	R.	H.	2B.	3B.	HR.	RBI.	B.A.	PO.	A.	E.	F.A.
1974—Los Angeles.......Nat.	PH-OF	3	3	0	1	0	0	0	1	.333	1	0	0	1.000
1977—Los Angeles.......Nat.	PH	1	1	1	1	1	0	0	0	1.000	0	0	0	.000
1978—Los Angeles ......Nat.	PH	2	1	0	1	1	0	0	0	1.000	0	0	0	.000
Championship Series Totals.............		6	5	1	3	2	0	0	1	.600	1	0	0	1.000

WORLD SERIES RECORD

Year Club League	Pos.	G.	AB.	R.	H.	2B.	3B.	HR.	RBI.	B.A.	PO.	A.	E.	F.A.
1977—Los Angeles.......Nat.	PH	3	3	0	0	0	0	0	0	.000	0	0	0	.000
1978—Los Angeles ......Nat.	PH	1	0	0	0	0	0	0	0	.000	0	0	0	.000
World Series Totals........................		4	3	0	0	0	0	0	0	.000	0	0	0	.000

ALL-STAR GAME RECORD

Year League	Pos.	AB.	R.	H.	2B.	3B.	HR.	RBI.	B.A.	PO.	A.	E.	F.A.
1973—National.............................	PH	1	0	0	0	0	0	0	.000	0	0	0	.000

PATRICK JOSEPH MULLIN
(Pat)
Montreal Expos

Born November 1, 1917, at Trotter, Pa.
Height, 6.02. Weight, 190.
Threw right and batted lefthanded.

Hit three home runs in a game, July 26, 1949.

Year Club	League	Pos.	G.	AB.	R.	H.	2B.	3B.	HR.	RBI.	B.A.	PO.	A.	E.	F.A.
1937—Beaumont	Tex.	OF	9	22	4	7	1	2	0	1	.318	11	2	1	.929
1937—Lake Charles	Evang.	OF	105	407	109	156	29	17	16	89	.383	213	20	14	.943
1938—Beaumont	Tex.	OF	154	612	94	168	30	11	5	67	.275	216	17	6	.975
1939—Beaumont	Tex.	OF	140	547	68	152	33	7	3	61	.278	300	17	14	.958
1940—Buffalo	Int.	OF	157	594	85	162	25	11	15	61	.273	362	15	11	.972
1940—Detroit..............	Amer.	OF	4	4	0	0	0	0	0	0	.000	0	0	0	.000
1941—Buffalo	Int.	OF	16	56	7	20	5	1	2	6	.357	25	0	2	.926
1941—Detroit..............	Amer.	OF	54	220	42	76	11	5	5	23	.345	117	2	7	.944
1942-43-44-45—Detroit..	Amer.					(In Military Service)									
1946—Detroit..............	Amer.	OF	93	276	34	68	13	4	3	35	.246	121	10	7	.949
1947—Detroit..............	Amer.	OF	116	398	62	102	28	6	15	62	.256	229	8	3	.988
1948—Detroit..............	Amer.	OF	138	496	91	143	16	11	23	80	.288	274	7	8	.972
1949—Detroit..............	Amer.	OF	104	310	55	83	8	6	12	59	.268	169	4	2	.989
1950—Detroit..............	Amer.	OF	69	142	16	31	5	0	6	23	.218	62	4	0	1.000
1951—Detroit..............	Amer.	OF	110	295	41	83	11	6	12	51	.281	151	4	10	.939
1952—Detroit..............	Amer.	OF	97	255	29	64	13	5	7	35	.251	131	6	3	.979
1953—Detroit..............	Amer.	OF	79	97	11	26	1	0	4	17	.268	16	1	1	.944
1954—Buffalo	Int.	OF	57	142	27	41	7	1	7	23	.289	49	3	2	.963
1954—Little Rock	South.	OF	45	140	16	35	3	1	4	12	.250	96	2	3	.970
1955—Idaho Falls	Pion.	OF-1B	128	386	97	115	21	6	23	75	.298	411	19	12	.973
1956—Jamestown	Pony	OF	34	78	16	26	3	1	1	16	.333	46	4	3	.943
Major League Totals......................			864	2493	381	676	106	43	87	385	.271	1270	46	41	.970

ALL-STAR GAME RECORD

Year League	Pos.	AB.	R.	H.	2B.	3B.	HR.	RBI.	B.A.	PO.	A.	E.	F.A.
1948—American	OF	1	0	0	0	0	0	0	.000	0	0	0	.000

RECORD AS MANAGER

Year Club	League	Position	W.	L.
1954—Little Rock†	South.	Sixth	20	31
1955—Idaho Falls	Pion.	Seventh	60	72
1956—Jamestown‡	Pony	Sixth	23	33

†Replaced Stubby Overmire, July 17, club in sixth place.
‡Replaced by Don Lund, July 7.
Scout, Detroit Tigers, 1957 through June 17, 1963; Coach, Detroit Tigers, June 18, 1963, through 1966; Coach, Cleveland Indians, 1967; Scout, Cleveland Indians, 1968; Scout, Montreal Expos, 1969 through 1972 and 1976; Minor League Instructor, Montreal Expos, 1973 through 1975, 1977 and 1978; Coach, Montreal Expos, 1979 through 1981.

RUSSELL EUGENE NIXON
(Russ)
Cincinnati Reds

Born February 19, 1935, at Cleves, O.
Height, 6.01. Weight, 190.
Threw right and batted lefthanded.
Hobby—Hunting.
Attended Univeristy of Cincinnati, Cincinnati, O.
Twin brother of Roy Nixon, former first baseman in Cleveland Indians' organization.

Led Florida State League catchers in double plays with 14 and passed balls with 23 in 1954.

Year Club	League	Pos.	G.	AB.	R.	H.	2B.	3B.	HR.	RBI.	B.A.	PO.	A.	E.	F.A.
1953—Green Bay.........	Wis. St.	C-OF	43	137	17	46	6	5	0	30	.336	213	22	6	.975
1954—Jack'ville Beach	Fla. St.	C	125	465	114	180	*36	12	6	96	*.387	*821	*95	22	.977
1955—Keokuk	I.I.I.	C	94	358	66	138	29	2	5	77	*.385	*718	47	10	●.987
1956—Indianapolis	A. A.	C	105	320	38	102	19	5	4	44	.319	402	37	9	.980
1957—Cleveland..........	Amer.	C	62	185	15	52	7	1	2	18	.281	268	31	5	.984
1958—Cleveland..........	Amer.	C	113	376	42	113	17	4	9	46	.301	499	31	5	.991
1959—Cleveland..........	Amer.	C	82	258	23	62	10	3	1	29	.240	374	31	6	.985
1960—Clev.†-Boston ...	Amer.	C	105	354	30	101	22	3	6	39	.285	488	34	6	.989
1961—Boston	Amer.	C	87	242	24	70	12	2	1	19	.289	330	21	9	.975
1962—Boston	Amer.	C	65	151	11	42	7	2	1	19	.278	201	7	0	1.000
1963—Boston	Amer.	C	98	287	27	77	18	1	5	30	.268	483	22	4	.992
1964—Boston	Amer.	C	81	163	10	38	7	0	1	20	.233	211	13	3	.990
1965—Boston	Amer.	C	59	137	11	37	5	1	0	11	.270	200	10	4	.981
1965—Toronto‡	Int.	C	31	93	10	30	3	2	0	14	.323	195	11	3	.986
1966—Minnesota	Amer.	C	51	90	5	25	2	1	0	7	.260	137	5	2	.986
1967—Minnesota§........	Amer.	C	74	170	16	40	6	1	1	22	.235	306	26	2	.994
1968—Pittsfield...........	East.	C-OF	41	137	15	29	3	2	0	13	.212	214	23	3	.988
1968—Boston x...........	Amer.	C	29	85	1	13	2	0	0	6	.153	147	6	1	.994
Major League Totals			906	2504	215	670	115	19	27	266	.268	3708	238	47	.988

†Traded with Outfielder Carroll Hardy to Boston Red Sox for Pitcher Ted Bowsfield and Outfielder Marty Keough, June 13, 1960. (Indians had traded Nixon to Red Sox for First Baseman Jim Marshall and Catcher Stan White, March 16, 1960, but deal was cancelled by Commissioner Ford Frick on March 25 because of White's request for voluntary retirement.)

‡Recalled by Boston Red Sox and traded with Infielder Chuck Schilling to Minnesota Twins for Pitcher Dick Stigman and a player to be named later, April 6, 1966; First Baseman Jose Calero assigned to Winston-Salem to complete deal, April 17, 1966.

§Released April 8, 1968, and signed as free agent by Boston Red Sox.

xDrafted from Louisville (Boston Red Sox' organization) by Chicago White Sox, December 2, 1968. Released by Chicago White Sox, April 5, 1969.

RECORD AS MANAGER

Year	Club	League	Position	W.	L.	Year	Club	League	Position	W.	L.
1970	Sioux Falls	Northern	Sixth	24	46	1973	Tampa	Fla. St.	Fourth(N)	73	71
1971	Tampa	Fla. St.	Second(W)	79	61	1974	Tampa	Fla. St.	†First(N)	68	64
1972	Tampa	Fla. St.	Second(W)	66	64	1975	Tampa	Fla. St.	Second(N)	72	59

†Lost semifinal playoff series to West Palm Beach, two games to none.

Coach, Cincinnati Reds, 1976 through 1981.

JOSEPH RUDOLPH NOSSEK

Name pronounced NAH-sek.

(Joe)

Cleveland Indians

Born November 8, 1940, at Cleveland, O.
Height, 6.00. Weight, 175.
Threw and batted righthanded.
Hobbies—Bowling, archery and collecting recordings.
Attended Ohio University, Athens, O.

Led Pacific Coast League outfielders in double plays with 7 in 1968.

Year	Club	League	Pos.	G.	AB.	R.	H.	2B.	3B.	HR.	RBI.	B.A.	PO.	A.	E.	F.A.
1961	Charlotte	Sally	OF-3B	80	303	24	83	9	3	0	27	.274	162	33	10	.951
1962	Charlotte	Sally	O-3-2B	134	521	58	144	17	4	3	56	.276	297	25	14	.958
1963	Dal.-Ft. Worth	P. C.	OF-3B	128	447	38	131	22	2	4	52	.293	276	15	9	.970
1964	Atlanta	Int.	O-3-2B	113	424	47	101	11	2	8	29	.238	303	29	12	.965
1964	Minnesota	Amer.	OF	7	1	1	0	0	0	0	0	.000	0	0	0	.000
1965	Minnesota	Amer.	OF-3B	87	170	19	37	9	0	2	16	.218	72	26	4	.961
1966	Minn.†-K. C.	Amer.	OF-3B	91	230	13	60	10	3	1	27	.261	161	8	3	.983
1967	Kansas City	Amer.	OF	87	166	12	34	6	1	0	10	.205	105	2	2	.982
1968	Vancouver	P. C.	*O-3-P	146	539	53	133	15	3	3	36	.247	*374	*39	11	.974
1969	Oakland	Amer.	OF	13	6	0	0	0	0	0	0	.000	7	0	0	1.000
1969	Iowa‡-Tulsa	A. A.	OF-3B	50	195	26	66	8	0	3	27	.338	99	6	5	.955
1969	St. Louis	Nat.	OF	9	5	2	1	0	0	0	0	.200	2	0	0	1.000
1970	Tulsa	A. A.	O-3-2-1	116	356	35	81	11	1	2	30	.228	165	40	6	.972
1970	St. Louis§	Nat.	PH	1	1	0	0	0	0	0	0	.000	0	0	0	.000
1971	Evansville x	A. A.	O-S-3-P-2	67	157	17	35	4	0	1	17	.223	79	16	6	.941
	American League Totals			285	573	45	131	25	4	3	53	.229	345	36	9	.977
	National League Totals			10	6	2	1	0	0	0	0	.167	2	0	0	1.000
	Major League Totals			295	579	47	132	25	4	3	53	.228	347	36	9	.977

†Sold to Kansas City Athletics, May 11, 1966.

‡Released to Tulsa (St. Louis Cardinals' organization), July 12, 1969, in traded which sent Infielder Robert W. Johnson from St. Louis Cardinals to Oakland A's.

§Sold to Milwaukee Brewers, February 4, 1971.

xPlayer-coach.

WORLD SERIES RECORD

Year	Club	League	Pos.	G.	AB.	R.	H.	2B.	3B.	HR.	RBI.	B.A.	PO.	A.	E.	F.A.
1965	Minnesota	Amer.	OF-PH	6	20	0	4	0	0	0	0	.200	13	0	0	1.000

PITCHING RECORD

Year	Club	League	G.	IP.	W.	L.	Pct.	H.	R.	ER.	SO.	BB.	ERA.
1968	Vancouver	P. Coast	7	7	1	0	1.000	6	1	1	2	0	1.29
1971	Evansville	Am. Assoc.	1	2	0	0	.000	1	1	1	0	3	4.50

RECORD AS MANAGER

Year	Club	League	Position	W.	L.
1972	Danville	Midwest	†First(S)	73	52

†Won championship playoff against Appleton, two games to none.

Coach, Milwaukee Brewers, 1973 through 1975; coach, Minnesota Twins, 1976; coach, Cleveland Indians, 1977 through 1981.

DANIEL LEONARD OZARK

(Danny)

Los Angeles Dodgers

Born November 26, 1923, at Buffalo, N.Y.
Height, 6.03. Weight, 210.
Threw and batted righthanded.
Hobbies—Taking movies and carpentry.
Brother of Norm Ozark, former infielder in Brooklyn Dodger and Milwaukee Brave organizations.

Led Texas League first basemen in double plays with 141 in 1953.

Year Club	League	Pos.	G.	AB.	R.	H.	2B.	3B.	HR.	RBI.	B.A.	PO.	A.	E.	F.A.
1942—Olean	Pony	2B	103	369	72	91	19	6	6	45	.247	208	281	31	.940
1943-44-45						(In Military Service)									
1946—Abilene	WT-NM	1B	133	526	133	171	34	6	31	142	.325	1193	*70	18	.986
1947—Fort Worth	Tex.	1B-3B	131	436	58	107	18	0	14	58	.245	637	142	40	.951
1948—St. Paul	A.A.	1B	23	62	13	14	1	0	5	12	.226	106	8	4	.966
1948—Newport News	Pied.	1B	116	414	64	124	25	2	15	78	.300	996	91	21	.981
1949—St. Paul	A.A.	1B	92	277	53	85	14	2	13	48	.307	559	68	15	.977
1950—St. Paul	A.A.	1B	24	54	9	10	0	0	1	6	.185	82	8	2	.978
1950—Elmira	East.	1B	94	328	67	101	19	4	6	46	.308	736	83	21	.975
1951—St. Paul	A.A.	1B	125	376	64	98	21	1	15	74	.261	867	92	15	.985
1952—St. Paul	A.A.	1B	112	334	58	77	18	0	17	62	.231	720	76	11	.986
1953—St. Paul	A.A.	PH	2	1	0	1	0	0	0	0	1.000	0	0	0	.000
1953—Fort Worth	Texas	1B	134	494	90	148	25	2	23	89	.300	1016	85	10	.991
1954—Fort Worth	Tex.	1B-3B	121	428	85	114	22	3	23	73	.266	617	123	19	.975
1955—Fort Worth	Texas	1B	140	447	69	121	24	2	18	79	.271	1069	85	10	.991
1956—Wichita Falls	Big St.	1B	113	386	92	135	23	3	•32	101	.350	761	85	25	.971
1957—Cedar Rapids	I.I.I.	1B	95	290	49	77	13	1	19	64	.266	526	49	12	.980
1958—Macon	Sally	PH	17	18	0	2	0	0	0	1	.111	0	0	0	.000
1959—Macon	Sally	1B-3B	8	16	0	5	2	0	0	1	.313	5	7	3	.800
1960—St. Paul	A.A.	PH	1	1	0	0	0	0	0	0	.000	0	0	0	.000
1961—Omaha	A.A.	PH	1	0	0	0	0	0	0	0	.000	0	0	0	.000
1963—Spokane	P.C.		3	4	0	1	0	0	0	0	.250	....	....	....	....

PITCHING RECORD

Year Club	League	G.	IP.	W.	L.	Pct.	H.	R.	ER.	SO.	BB.	ERA.
1957—Cedar Rapids	I.I.I.	3	....	0	0	.000	....	....	....	....	....	....
1958—Macon	Sally	1	....	0	0	.000	....	....	....	....	....	....

RECORD AS MANAGER

Named American Association Co-Manager of the Year, 1962.
Named Pacific Coast League Manager of the Year in 1963.
Named Major League Manager of the Year by THE SPORTING NEWS, 1976.

Year Club	League	Position	W.	L.	Year Club	League	Position	W.	L.
1956—Wichita Falls	Big State	Fourth	76	64	1973—Philadelphia	Nat.	Sixth(E)	71	91
1957—Cedar Rapids	I.I.I.	Sixth	49	79	1974—Philadelphia	Nat.	Third(E)	80	82
1958—Macon	Sally	†Third	70	70	1975—Philadelphia	Nat.	Second(E)	86	76
1959—Macon	Sally	Eighth	63	76	1976—Philadelphia	Nat.	First(E)	101	61
1960—St. Paul	A.A.	‡Third	83	71	1977—Philadelphia	Nat.	First (E)	101	61
1961—Omaha	A.A.	Sixth	62	87	1978—Philadelphia	Nat.	First(E)	90	72
1962—Omaha	A.A.	Second	79	68	1979—Philadelphia x	Nat.	Fifth(E)	65	67
1963—Spokane	P.C.	§First(N)	98	60	Major League Totals			594	510
1964—Spokane	P.C.	Third(W)	85	73					

†Won playoffs by defeating Augusta, one game to none and Jacksonville, two games to none.
‡Tied for position.
§Lost playoff to Oklahoma City, four games to three.
xReplaced by Dallas Green, August 31, 1979.
Coach, Los Angeles Dodgers, 1965 through 1972, 1980 and 1981.
Coach, National League All-Star Team, 1976 through 1978.

CHAMPIONSHIP SERIES RECORD

Year Club	League	W.	L.
1976—Philadelphia	National	0	3
1977—Philadelphia	National	1	3
1978—Philadelphia	National	1	3

RONALD PETER PERRANOSKI
(Ron)
Los Angeles Dodgers

Born April 1, 1937, at Paterson, N. J.
Height, 6.00. Weight, 185.
Threw and batted lefthanded.
Attended Michigan State University, East Lansing, Mich.

Tied National League record for most consecutive strikeouts, relief pitcher (6), September 12, 1966 (fifth and sixth innings).
Named THE SPORTING NEWS American League Fireman of the Year 1969 and 1970.
Received reported $21,000 bonus to sign with Chicago Cubs, 1958.

Year Club	League	G.	IP.	W.	L.	Pct.	H.	R.	ER.	SO.	BB.	ERA.
1958—Fort Worth	Texas	2	4	0	0	.000	9	4	4	3	0	9.00
1958—Burlington	I.I.I.	18	84	5	9	.357	99	70	60	92	47	6.43
1959—San Antonio†	Texas	37	199	11	10	.524	188	89	69	139	85	3.12
1960—Montreal	Int'national	47	138	9	8	.529	135	51	44	81	53	2.87
1960—St. Paul	Am. Assoc.	10	40	3	3	.500	33	13	7	33	10	1.58
1961—Los Angeles	National	53	92	7	5	.583	82	31	27	56	41	2.64
1962—Los Angeles	National	*70	107	6	6	.500	103	40	34	68	36	2.86
1963—Los Angeles	National	*69	129	16	3	*.842	112	30	24	75	43	1.67
1964—Los Angeles	National	72	125	5	7	.417	128	62	43	79	46	3.10
1965—Los Angeles	National	59	105	6	6	.500	85	28	26	53	40	2.23

Year Club	League	G.	IP.	W.	L.	Pct.	H.	R.	ER.	SO.	BB.	ERA.
1966—Los Angeles	National	55	82	6	7	.462	82	32	29	50	31	3.18
1967—Los Angeles‡	National	•70	110	6	7	.462	97	36	30	75	45	2.45
1968—Minnesota	American	66	87	8	7	.533	86	36	30	65	38	3.10
1969—Minnesota	American	75	120	9	10	.474	85	32	28	62	52	2.10
1970—Minnesota	American	67	111	7	8	.467	108	38	30	55	42	2.43
1971—Minn.§-Det.	American	47	61	1	5	.167	76	48	37	29	31	5.46
1972—Detroit x	American	17	19	0	1	.000	23	16	16	10	8	7.58
1972—Los Angeles y	National	9	17	2	0	1.000	19	8	5	5	8	2.65
1973—California za	American	8	11	0	2	.000	11	5	5	5	7	4.09
American League Totals		280	409	25	33	.431	389	175	146	226	178	3.21
National League Totals		457	767	54	41	.568	708	267	218	561	290	2.56
Major League Totals		737	1176	79	74	.516	1097	442	364	787	468	2.79

†Traded to Los Angeles Dodgers by Chicago Cubs with Infielder John Goryl, Outfielder Lee Handley and reported $25,000 for Infielder Don Zimmer, April 8, 1960; all players assigned to Dodgers sent to minor league farm clubs.

‡Traded with Catcher John Roseboro and Pitcher Bob Miller to Minnesota Twins for Pitcher Jim Grant and Shortstop Zoilo Versalles, November 28, 1967.

Sold on waivers to Detroit Tigers, July 30, 1971.

xReleased, July 31, 1972; signed by Los Angeles Dodgers, August 7, 1972.

yReleased, October 19, 1972; signed by California Angels, April 6, 1973.

zOn disabled list, June 22 to September 4, 1973.

aReleased, October 4, 1973.

Minor league pitching instructor, Los Angeles Dodgers, 1975 through 1980; coach, Los Angeles Dodgers, 1981.

CHAMPIONSHIP SERIES RECORD

Year Club	League	G.	IP.	W.	L.	Pct.	H.	R.	ER.	SO.	BB.	ERA.
1969—Minnesota	American	3	4⅔	0	1	.000	8	3	2	2	0	5.79
1970—Minnesota	American	2	2⅓	0	0	.000	5	5	5	3	1	19.29
Championship Series Totals		5	7	0	1	.000	13	8	7	5	1	9.00

WORLD SERIES RECORD

Year Club	League	G.	IP.	W.	L.	Pct.	H.	R.	ER.	SO.	BB.	ERA.
1963—Los Angeles	National	1	⅔	0	0	.000	1	0	0	1	0	0.00
1965—Los Angeles	National	2	3⅔	0	0	.000	3	3	3	1	4	7.36
1966—Los Angeles	National	2	3⅓	0	0	.000	4	2	2	2	1	5.40
World Series Totals		5	7⅔	0	0	.000	8	5	5	4	5	5.87

JOHN MICHAEL PESKY

(Christened John Paveskovich; legalized to Pesky.)

(Johnny)
Boston Red Sox

Born September 27, 1919, at Portland, Ore.
Height, 5.09. Weight, 175.
Threw right and batted lefthanded.

Tied major league record for most consecutive seasons leading league in hits (3), 1942, 1946 and 1947 (in military from 1943 through 1945).

Tied modern major league records for most runs scored, game (6), May 8, 1946; most at bats, game (7), June 8, 1950.

One of 12 players to have 200 or more hits in rookie season, 1942.

Led American League third basemen in double plays with 35 in 1948 and 48 in 1949.

Led Piedmont League shortstops in double plays with 95 in 1940.

Named as shortstop on THE SPORTING NEWS All-Star Major League Teams, 1942 and 1946.

Named American Association Most Valuable Player in 1941.

Year Club	League	Pos.	G.	AB.	R.	H.	2B.	3B.	HR.	RBI.	B.A.	PO.	A.	E.	F.A.
1940—Rocky Mount	Pied.	SS	136	•576	114	•187	28	•16	4	55	.325	257	435	44	.940
1941—Louisville	A. A.	SS	146	600	93	•195	25	5	1	48	.325	•308	411	32	.957
1942—Boston	Amer.	SS	147	620	105	•205	29	9	2	51	.331	320	•465	37	.955
1943-44-45—Boston	Amer.					(In Military Service)									
1946—Boston	Amer.	SS	153	•621	115	•208	43	4	2	55	.335	296	479	25	.969
1947—Boston	Amer.	SS-3B	155	•638	106	•207	27	8	0	39	.324	276	429	17	.976
1948—Boston	Amer.	3B	143	565	124	159	26	6	3	55	.281	121	303	22	.951
1949—Boston	Amer.	3B	148	604	111	185	27	7	2	69	.306	•184	•333	16	.970
1950—Boston	Amer.	3B-SS	127	490	112	153	22	6	1	49	.312	183	289	13	.973
1951—Boston	Amer.	S-3-2	131	480	93	150	20	6	3	41	.313	223	370	26	.958
1952—Boston†-Detroit	Amer.	S-2-3	94	244	36	55	6	0	1	11	.225	126	172	15	.952
1953—Detroit†	Amer.	2B	103	308	43	90	22	1	2	24	.292	166	224	3	.992
1954—Det.‡-Wash.§	Amer.	2B-SS	69	175	22	43	4	3	1	10	.246	92	91	4	.979
1955—Denver	A. A.	3B	66	137	32	47	7	2	1	18	.343	22	45	7	.905
1956—Durham x	Carol.	2B	17	35	2	6	2	0	0	1	.171	26	31	2	.966
Major League Totals			1270	4745	867	1455	226	50	17	404	.307	1987	3155	178	.967

†Traded to Detroit Tigers with Pitcher Bill Wight, First Baseman Walt Dropo, Third Baseman Fred Hatfield and Outfielder Don Lenhardt for Pitcher Paul (Dizzy) Trout, Third Baseman George Kell, Shortstop Johnny Lipon and Outfielder Walter (Hoot) Evers, June 3, 1952.

‡Traded to Washington Senators for Infielder Mel Hoderlein, June 14, 1954.

§Unconditionally released by Washington Senators, November 10, 1954; signed with Baltimore Orioles, December 21, 1954 and released, April 14, 1955.

xPlayer-manager.

Year	Club	League	Pos.	G.	AB.	R.	H.	2B.	3B.	HR.	RBI.	B.A.	PO.	A.	E.	F.A.
1946—Boston	....	Amer.	SS	7	30	2	7	0	0	0	0	.233	13	16	4	.879

ALL-STAR GAME RECORD

Year	League	Pos.	AB.	R.	H.	2B.	3B.	HR.	RBI.	B.A.	PO.	A.	E.	F.A.
1946—American	....	SS	2	0	0	0	0	0	0	.000	1	0	1	.500

RECORD AS MANAGER

Year	Club	League	Position	W.	L.	Year	Club	League	Position	W.	L.
1956—Durham	....	Carol.	Second	84	69	1962—Seattle	....	P. C.	Fourth	76	74
1957—Birmingham	....	South.	Sixth	74	79	1963—Boston	....	Amer.	Seventh	76	85
1958—Lancaster	....	East.	Third(S)	37	33	1964—Boston§	....	Amer.	Eighth	71	89
(Second Half)			†First(S)	38	24	1968—Columbus	....	Int.	Second	82	64
1959—Knoxville	....	Sally	‡First	78	62	1980—Boston x	....	Amer.	Fourth(E)	1	4
1960—Victoria	....	Texas	Fourth	77	69	Major League Totals	....			148	178
1961—Seattle	....	P. C.	Third	86	68						

†Lost playoff finals to Binghamton, three games to two.
‡Lost playoff semifinal series to Charleston, three games to two.
§Replaced by Billy Herman, October 3, 1964.
xServed as interim manager for fired Don Zimmer, October 1 through October 5, 1980.
Coach, Pittsburgh Pirates, 1965 through 1967; Boston Red Sox, 1975 through 1981.
Coach, American League All-Star team, 1963.

JOSEPH BENJAMIN PIGNATANO
Named pronounced Pig-na-TAWN-o.
(Joe)
New York Mets
Born August 4, 1929, at Brooklyn, N. Y.
Height, 5.10. Weight, 180.
Threw and batted righthanded.
Second cousin of Pete Falcone, pitcher with St. Louis Cardinals.

Year	Club	League	Pos.	G.	AB.	R.	H.	2B.	3B.	HR.	RBI.	B.A.	PO.	A.	E.	F.A.
1948—Cairo	....	Kitty	C	3	8	2	3	1	0	0	2	.375	14	2	4	.800
1949—Cambridge	....	E. Shore	C	87	268	51	62	7	4	0	24	.231	491	66	23	.960
1950—Valdosta	....	Ga.-Fla.	C-O	127	424	102	121	17	17	4	77	.285	732	80	18	.978
1951-52—N'port News	..	Pied.					(In Military Service)									
1953—Asheville	....	Tri St.	*C-OF	121	433	92	137	24	*13	6	82	.316	*580	63	*26	.961
1954—Elmira	....	East.	C	118	335	47	83	10	9	2	51	.248	485	*78	14	.983
1955—Fort Worth	....	Tex.	C-OF	125	381	49	76	11	5	5	41	.199	548	53	10	.984
1956—St. Paul	....	A. A.	C	81	224	37	66	11	1	5	29	.295	380	35	3	.993
1957—Brooklyn	....	Nat.	C	8	14	0	3	1	0	0	1	.214	36	1	0	1.000
1957—Montreal	....	Int.	C	70	211	32	63	7	2	1	17	.299	287	32	1	.997
1958—Los Angeles	......	Nat.	C	63	142	18	31	4	0	9	17	.218	286	18	0	1.000
1959—Los Angeles	......	Nat.	C	52	139	17	33	4	1	1	11	.237	322	17	1	.997
1960—Los Angeles†	.....	Nat.	C	58	90	11	21	4	0	2	9	.233	131	21	4	.984
1961—Kansas City‡	.....	Amer.	C-3B	92	243	31	59	10	3	4	22	.243	380	35	9	.979
1962—S.F.§-N. York	....	Nat.	C	34	61	4	14	2	0	0	2	.230	107	13	1	.992
1963—Buff.-Rochester	.	Int.	C	86	236	37	56	13	2	3	27	.237	454	37	5	.990
1964—Rochester	....	Int.	C	88	237	19	48	7	1	4	19	.203	508	23	3	*.994
American League Totals	....			92	243	31	59	10	3	4	22	.243	380	35	9	.979
National League Totals	....			215	446	50	102	15	1	12	40	.229	982	92	6	.994
Major League Totals	....			307	689	81	161	25	4	16	62	.234	1362	127	15	.990

†Sold to Kansas City Athletics, January 31, 1961.
‡Traded to San Francisco Giants for Outfielder Jose Tartabull, December 15, 1961.
§Sold to New York Mets, July 13, 1962.

WORLD SERIES RECORD

Year	Club	League	Pos.	G.	AB.	R.	H.	2B.	3B.	HR.	RBI.	B.A.	PO.	A.	E.	F.A.
1959—Los Angeles	....	Nat.	C	1	0	0	0	0	0	0	0	.000	1	0	0	1.000

Coach, Washington Senators, 1965 through 1967; New York Mets, 1968 through 1981.

VADA EDWARD PINSON JR.
Chicago White Sox
Born August 11, 1938, at Memphis, Tenn.
Height, 5.11. Weight, 187.
Threw and batted lefthanded.
One of 12 players to make 200 or more hits in rookie season (205), 1959.
Major League stolen bases: 1958 (2), 1959 (21), 1960 (32), 1961 (23), 1962 (26), 1963 (27), 1964 (8), 1965 (21), 1966 (18), 1967 (26), 1968 (17), 1969 (4), 1970 (7), 1971 (25), 1972 (17), 1973 (5), 1974 (21), 1975 (5). Total—305.
Led California League in total bases with 349 in 1957.
Led Pacific Coast League in stolen bases with 37 in 1958.
Named outfielder on THE SPORTING NEWS National League All-Star fielding team, 1961.

Year Club League	Pos.	G.	AB.	R.	H.	2B.	3B.	HR.	RBI.	B.A.	PO.	A.	E.	F.A.
1956—Wausau ....North.	1B	75	277	35	77	11	5	2	23	.278	626	28	12	.982
1957—Visalia ....Cal.	*OF-1B	135	569	*165	*209	*40	*20	20	97	.367	260	*30	16	.948
1958—Cincinnati ....Nat.	OF	27	96	20	26	7	0	1	8	.271	50	4	0	1.000
1958—Seattle .............P.C.	*OF-1	124	475	92	163	28	8	11	77	.343	385	13	*15	.964
1959—Cincinnati ....Nat.	OF	154	*648	*131	205	*47	9	20	84	.316	*423	11	7	.984
1960—Cincinnati ....Nat.	OF	154	*652	107	187	*37	12	20	61	.287	*401	11	8	.981
1961—Cincinnati ....Nat.	OF	154	607	101	*208	34	8	16	87	.343	*391	19	10	.976
1962—Cincinnati ....Nat.	OF	155	619	107	181	31	7	23	100	.292	344	13	4	.989
1963—Cincinnati ....Nat.	OF	●162	652	96	*204	37	*14	22	106	.313	357	9	8	.979
1964—Cincinnati ....Nat.	OF	156	625	99	166	23	11	23	84	.266	299	14	9	.972
1965—Cincinnati ....Nat.	OF	159	669	97	204	34	10	22	94	.305	354	9	3	*.992
1966—Cincinnati ....Nat.	OF	156	618	70	178	35	6	16	76	.288	344	9	13	.964
1967—Cincinnati ....Nat.	OF	158	650	90	187	28	*13	18	66	.288	341	4	5	.986
1968—Cincinnati†.......Nat.	OF	130	499	60	135	29	6	5	48	.271	258	7	6	.978
1969—St. Louis‡.........Nat.	OF	132	495	58	126	22	6	10	70	.255	218	6	1	*.996
1970—Cleveland..........Amer.	OF-1B	148	574	74	164	28	6	24	82	.286	284	9	5	.983
1971—Cleveland§ ....Amer.	OF-1B	146	566	60	149	23	4	11	35	.263	315	11	7	.979
1972—California.........Amer.	OF-1B	136	484	56	133	24	2	7	49	.275	207	11	2	.991
1973—California x......Amer.	OF	124	466	56	121	14	6	8	57	.260	210	11	8	.965
1974—Kansas City......Amer.	OF-1B	115	406	46	112	18	2	6	41	.276	198	9	4	.981
1975—Kansas City y ...Amer.	OF-1B	103	319	38	71	14	5	4	22	.223	151	6	1	.994
American League Totals.................		772	2815	330	750	121	25	60	286	.266	1365	57	27	.981
National League Totals..................		1697	6830	1036	2007	364	102	196	884	.294	3780	116	74	.981
Major League Totals		2469	9645	1366	2757	485	127	256	1170	.286	5145	173	101	.981

†Traded to St. Louis Cardinals for Outfielder Bob Tolan and Pitcher Wayne Granger, October 11, 1968.
‡Traded to Cleveland Indians for Outfielder Jose Cardenal, November 20, 1969.
§Traded with Outfielder Frank Baker and Pitcher Alan Foster to California Angels for Catcher Jerry Moses and Outfielder Alex Johnson, October 5, 1971.
xTraded to Kansas City Royals for Pitcher Barry Raziano and cash, February 23, 1974.
yReleased, December 17, 1975; signed as free agent by Milwaukee Brewers, January 14, 1976. Released by Milwaukee Brewers, April 4, 1976.
Coach, Seattle Mariners, 1977 through 1980; coach, Chicago White Sox, 1981.

PITCHING RECORD

Year Club	League	G.	IP.	W.	L.	Pct.	H.	R.	ER.	SO.	BB.	ERA.
1956—Wausau.................................Northern		2	....	0	0	.000	....	....	....	....	....	....
1957—Visalia...............................California		1	....	0	0	.000	....	....	....	....	....	....

WORLD SERIES RECORD

Year Club League	Pos.	G.	AB.	R.	H.	2B.	3B.	HR.	RBI.	B.A.	PO.	A.	E.	F.A.
1961—Cincinnati ....Nat.	OF	5	22	0	2	1	0	0	0	.091	18	1	1	.950

ALL-STAR GAME RECORD

Year League	Pos.	AB.	R.	H.	2B.	3B.	HR.	RBI.	B.A.	PO.	A.	E.	F.A.
1959—National (second game)........	PR	0	0	0	0	0	0	0	.000	0	0	0	.000
1960—National (both games)..........	OF	1	0	0	0	0	0	0	.000	1	0	0	1.000
All-Star Game Totals		1	0	0	0	0	0	0	.000	1	0	0	1.000

Member of National League All-Star Team in 1959 (first game); did not play.

RONALD CHARLES PLAZA
(Ron)
Cincinnati Reds

Born August 24, 1934 at Passaic, N.J.
Height, 6.00. Weight, 180.
Threw right and batted lefthanded.

Year Club League	Pos.	G.	AB.	R.	H.	2B.	3B.	HR.	RBI.	B.A.	PO.	A.	E.	F.A.
1951—Johnson City .....Appal.	3B	56	212	45	64	16	2	4	34	.302	57	127	20	.902
1952—Albany ....Ga.-Fla.	3B	135	497	75	105	11	3	9	47	.211	167	260	28	.938
1953—Hamilton...........Pony	3B	123	455	85	124	*37	7	6	106	.273	*165	233	*37	.915
1954—Allentown.........Eastern	3B	137	485	58	126	19	11	6	67	.260	119	282	26	.939
1955—Allentown.........Eastern	3B	119	423	66	120	19	9	8	79	.284	106	*290	18	*.957
1956—Rochester ....Int.	2B	121	417	69	124	23	1	5	30	.297	239	261	14	.973
1957—Rochester ....Int.	2B	144	467	54	103	17	5	14	49	.221	307	400	17	●.977
1958—Omaha ..............A.A.	2B-3B	145	478	59	114	21	7	3	36	.238	279	335	18	.971
1959—Omaha ..............A.A.	2B	133	472	55	116	20	6	4	48	.246	328	308	*24	.964
1960—Memphis...........S.A.					(Restricted)									
1961—S. Juan-Ch'ston .Int.	2-SS-3B	98	274	32	67	16	1	5	36	.245	129	215	13	.963
1962—Atlanta†............Int.	SS-3-2B	100	230	24	44	6	2	1	23	.191	96	135	13	.947

†Released by St. Louis Cardinals' organization, October 3, 1962.

DID YOU KNOW—

That there are five pitchers in major league history to hurl two no-hitters in the same season? Johnny Vander Meer (1938) Allie Reynolds (1951), Virgil Trucks (1952), Jim Maloney (1965) and Nolan Ryan (1973) all turned the trick.

Year Club League	Position	W.	L.	Year Club League	Position	W.	L.
1963–Billings.............Pioneer	†Third	28	30	1967–St. Petersburg....Fla. St.	First(W)	50	22
(Second Half)	Fourth	33	36	(Second Half)	§First(W)	46	21
1964–Winnipeg...........Northern	Fourth	52	65	1968–St. Petersburg....Fla. St.	xSec'd(W)	80	63
1965–Cedar Rapids......Midwest	Sixth	28	29	1970–Cincinnati..........Gulf C.	Sixth	25	35
(Second Half)	Second	34	23	1971–Cincinnati..........Gulf C.	Fourth	23	29
1966–Cedar Rapids......Midwest	Third	33	25	1972–Cincinnati..........Gulf C.	Eighth	21	39
(Second Half)	‡First	48	15	1973–Cincinnati..........Gulf C.	Eighth	20	32

†Tied for position.
‡Lost playoff to Fox Cities, two games to one.
§Won playoff against Orlando, three games to one.
xLost playoff semifinal series to Miami, two games to one.
Coach, Seattle Pilots, 1969; minor league instructor, Cincinnati Reds 1974 through 1977; coach, Cincinnati Reds, 1978 through 1981.

JOHN JOSEPH PODRES
(Johnny)
Minnesota Twins

Born September 30, 1932, at Witherbee, N.Y.
Height, 5.11. Weight, 185.
Threw and batted lefthanded.
Hobbies–Hunting and fishing.

Led National League in shutouts with 6 in 1957.

Year Club	League	G.	IP.	W.	L.	Pct.	H.	R.	ER.	SO.	BB.	ERA.
1951–Newport News ....Piedmont		7	17	0	2	.000	18	12	11	16	13	5.82
1951–Hazard ....Mtn. St.		26	200	21	3	*.875	139	55	37	*228	85	*1.67
1952–Montreal...........................Int'national		24	88	5	5	.500	76	37	32	47	39	3.27
1953–Brooklyn...........................National		33	115	9	4	.692	126	62	54	82	64	4.23
1954–Brooklyn† ....National		29	152	11	7	.611	147	77	72	79	53	4.26
1955–Brooklyn...........................National		27	159	9	10	.474	160	80	70	114	57	3.96
1956–Brooklyn‡ ....National						(In Military Service)						
1957–Brooklyn...........................National		31	196	12	9	.571	168	64	58	109	44	*2.66
1958–Los Angeles ....National		39	210	13	15	.464	208	96	87	143	78	3.73
1959–Los Angeles ....National		34	195	14	9	.609	192	93	89	145	74	4.11
1960–Los Angeles ....National		34	228	14	12	.538	217	88	78	159	71	3.08
1961–Los Angeles ....National		32	183	18	5	*.783	192	81	76	124	51	3.74
1962–Los Angeles ....National		40	255	15	13	.536	270	121	108	178	71	3.81
1963–Los Angeles ....National		37	198	14	12	.538	196	91	78	134	64	3.55
1964–Los Angeles§ ....National		2	3	0	2	.000	5	5	5	0	3	15.00
1965–Los Angeles ....National		27	134	7	6	.538	126	57	51	63	39	3.43
1966–Los Angeles x ....National		1	2	0	0	.000	2	0	0	1	1	0.00
1966–Detroit...............................American		36	108	4	5	.444	106	48	41	53	34	3.42
1967–Detroit y ....American		21	63	3	1	.750	58	29	27	34	11	3.86
1968–						Out of Organized Baseball						
1969–San Diego z ....National		17	65	5	6	.455	66	34	31	17	28	4.29
American League Totals		57	171	7	6	.538	164	77	68	87	45	3.58
National League Totals		383	2095	141	110	.562	2075	949	857	1348	698	3.68
Major League Totals.................................		440	2266	148	116	.561	2239	1026	925	1435	743	3.67

†On disabled list, June 23 to July 23, 1954.
‡On National Defense Service list, March 19 to November 15, 1956.
§On disabled list, June 9 to June 13, 1964.
xSold to Detroit Tigers, May 10, 1966.
yOn disabled list, August 10 to September 1, 1967. Released October 20, 1967.
zSigned as free agent by San Diego Padres, March 21, 1969. Placed on voluntarily retired list, June 27, 1969 through 1972.

Coach, San Diego Padres, 1973; coach, Boston Red Sox, 1980; coach, Minnesota Twins, 1981.

WORLD SERIES RECORD

Year Club	League	G.	IP.	W.	L.	Pct.	H.	R.	ER.	SO.	BB.	ERA.
1953–Brooklyn..............................National		1	2⅔	0	1	.000	1	5	1	0	2	3.38
1955–Brooklyn..............................National		2	18	2	0	1.000	15	3	2	10	4	1.00
1959–Los Angeles ....National		2	9⅓	1	0	1.000	7	5	5	4	6	4.82
1963–Los Angeles ....National		1	8⅓	1	0	1.000	6	1	1	4	1	1.08
World Series Totals.................		6	38⅓	4	1	.800	29	14	9	18	13	2.11

ALL-STAR GAME RECORD

Year League	IP.	W.	L.	Pct.	H.	R.	ER.	SO.	BB.	ERA.
1960–National (second game)................................	2	0	0	.000	1	0	0	1	3	0.00
1962–National (second game)................................	2	0	0	.000	2	0	0	2	0	0.00
All-Star Game Totals	4	0	0	.000	3	0	0	3	3	0.00

DID YOU KNOW—

That Garry Maddox has the longest current streak of winning a Gold Glove? He's done it six straight seasons.

VERNON FRED RAPP
(Vern)
Montreal Expos

Born May 11, 1928, at St. Louis, Mo.
Height, 6.00. Weight, 195.
Threw and batted righthanded.
Hobbies—Hunting and fishing.

Named by THE SPORTING NEWS as Minor League Manager of the Year, 1976.

Year	Club	League	Pos.	G.	AB.	R.	H.	2B.	3B.	HR.	RBI.	B.A.	PO.	A.	E.	F.A.
1946—Marion	Ohio St.	C-OF	115	375	86	118	16	8	14	89	.315	452	73	30	.946
1947—St. Joseph	W.A.	C	101	365	59	103	21	9	6	81	.282	532	76	15	.976
1948—Omaha	West.	C	56	186	30	61	12	1	9	31	.328	298	40	15	.958
1948—Columbus	A.A.	C	7	19	6	7	0	0	1	3	.368	....	....	....	......
1949—Columbus	A.A.	C	77	249	30	64	14	5	6	29	.257	313	40	14	.962
1950—Houston	Texas	C	72	186	19	35	5	4	4	21	.188	217	25	8	.968
1951-52—Columbus	A.A.	(In Military Service)													
1953—Rochester†	Int.	C	97	282	35	71	15	9	1	30	.252	290	33	6	.982
1954—Kansas City‡	A.A.	C	28	66	9	17	3	0	1	9	.258	128	10	0	1.000
1955—Charleston§x	A.A.	C	70	192	17	46	5	1	7	19	.240	171	26	6	.970
1956—Minneapolis y	A.A.	C	85	205	28	62	8	2	11	32	.302	263	26	9	.970
1957—Louisville z	A.A.	C	77	246	58	13	1	4	4	31	.236	514	42	7	.988
1958—Denver a	A.A.	1B-C	93	274	48	78	12	2	14	55	.285	436	39	10	.979
1959—Denver a	A.A.	C	89	212	18	53	10	3	4	31	.250	194	30	4	.982
1960—Denver ab	A.A.	C	36	99	9	14	4	0	2	12	.141	146	12	2	.988
1961—Modesto§	Calif.	PH	3	1	0	1	0	0	0	0	1.000	....	....	....	......
1966—Little Rock§	Tex.	PH	1	1	0	1	1	0	0	0	1.000	....	....	....	......
1976—Denver§	A.A.	C	1	1	0	1	0	0	0	1	1.000	0	0	0	.000

†Loaned by St. Louis Cardinals' organization to New York Yankees' organization, May 24, 1954.

‡Returned by Yankees' organization to Cardinals' organization, July 26, 1954. On disabled list, August 12 to September 30, 1954. Released by St. Louis Cardinals' organization, September 30, 1954; signed as free agent by Charleston, December 11, 1954.

§Player-manager.

xReleased, December 14, 1955; signed as free agent by New York Giants' organization, January 10, 1956.

yReleased by New York Giants' organization to Louisville, January 12, 1957.

zReleased to Denver (N.Y. Yankees' organization), April 2, 1958.

aPlayer-coach.

bReleased to Detroit Tigers' organization, October 12, 1960.

PITCHING RECORD

Year	Club	League	G.	IP.	W.	L.	Pct.	H.	R.	ER.	SO.	BB.	ERA.
1959—Denver†	Am. Assoc.	5	...	0	0	.000	...	...	...	...	...	......
1961—Modesto‡	California	2	...	0	0	.000	...	...	...	...	...	......
1966—Arkansas‡	Texas	1	2	0	0	.000	0	0	0	2	0	0.00

†Player-coach.

‡Player-manager.

RECORD AS MANAGER

Year	Club	League	Position	W.	L.	Year	Club	League	Position	W.	L.
1955—Charleston†	A.A.	Eighth	19	40	1971—Indianapolis	A.A.	zFirst(E)	84	55
1961—Modesto	Calif.	Fourth	30	39	1972—Indianapolis	A.A.	Fourth(E)	61	79
(Second Half)		Sixth	27	43	1973—Indianapolis	A.A.	Second(E)	74	62
1962—Greensboro‡	Carol.	Fifth	65	75	1974—Indianapolis	A.A.	aFirst(E)	78	57
1965—Tulsa	Texas	§First(E)	81	60	1975—Indianapolis	A.A.	Second(E)	71	64
1966—Arkansas	Texas	xFirst	81	59	1976—Denver	A.A.	bFirst	86	50
1967—Arkansas	Texas	Fifth	63	77	1977—St. Louis	Nat.	Third(E)	83	79
1968—Arkansas	Texas	yFirst(E)	82	58	1978—St. Louis c	Nat.	Sixth(E)	6	10
1969—Indianapolis	A.A.	Third	74	66	Major League Totals			89	89
1970—Indianapolis	A.A.	Third(E)	71	69					

†Replaced Danny Murtaugh, July 16, 1955.

‡Replaced by Steven Souchock, August 11, 1962.

§Lost playoff to Albuquerque, three games to one.

xLost playoff to Austin, two games to one.

yLost playoff to El Paso, three games to one.

zLost playoff to Denver, four games to three.

aLost playoff to Tulsa, four games to three.

bWon playoff by defeating Omaha, four games to two.

cReplaced by interim manager Jack Krol, April 25, 1978.

Coach, Montreal Expos, 1979 through 1981.

JAMES HARRISON REESE
(Jimmie)
California Angels

Born October 1, 1905, at New York, N. Y.
Height, 6.00. Weight, 170.
Threw right and batted lefthanded.
Hobby—Woodworking.

Led Pacific Coast League second basemen in total chances accepted with 1273 in 1927, 1189 in 1929, and 1125 in 1934.

Year Club	League	Pos.	G.	AB.	R.	H.	2B.	3B.	HR.	RBI.	B.A.	PO.	A.	E.	F.A.
1924—Oakland ............P.C.	INF	8	32	8	6	2	0	0	....	.188	figures unavailable			
1925—Oakland ............P.C.	2B-SS	136	463	63	115	24	2	0	37	.248	342	367	26	.965
1926—Oakland ............P.C.	2B	183	709	113	189	32	11	4	48	.267	*563	586	36	.970
1927—Oakland† ..........P.C.	2B	191	722	113	213	34	17	2	83	.295	*621	652	21	*.984
1928—Oakland ............P.C.	2B	132	478	60	118	10	5	1	35	.247	406	459	21	.976
1929—Oakland ............P.C.	2B	190	766	142	258	33	9	1	56	.337	*622	567	25	*.979
1930—New York ....Amer.	2B	77	188	44	65	14	2	3	18	.346	86	99	5	.974
1931—New York ....Amer.	2B	65	245	41	59	10	2	3	26	.241	173	168	10	.972
1932—St. Paul‡ ..........A.A.	2B	25	61	10	12	2	2	1	5	.197	39	61	2	.980
1932—St. Louis§ ....Nat.	2B	90	309	38	82	15	0	2	26	.265	209	220	9	.979
1933—Los Angeles......P.C.	2B	104	393	85	130	23	6	5	38	.330	258	298	18	.969
1934—Los Angeles......P.C.	2B	180	733	123	228	31	12	3	85	.311	*541	584	32	*.972
1935—Los Angeles......P.C.	2B	155	576	79	171	28	8	1	66	.297	448	489	36	.963
1936—Los Angeles......P.C.	2B	146	515	57	139	21	3	0	54	.270	385	422	26	.969
1937—San Diego.........P.C.	2B	138	506	59	159	23	7	2	78	.314	333	442	27	.966
1938—San Diego.........P.C.	2B	108	349	41	81	11	1	0	28	.233	284	286	15	.974
1939—Bellingham-Spo. W. Int.	INF	22	39	3	7	1	0	0	4	.179	figures unavailable			
1940—Los Angeles......P.C.	2B	2	5	0	0	0	0	0	0	.000	7	6	0	1.000
American League Totals................		142	433	85	124	24	4	6	44	.286	259	267	15	.972
National League Totals...................		90	309	38	82	15	0	2	26	.265	209	220	9	.979
Major League Totals		232	742	123	206	39	4	8	70	.278	468	487	24	.975

†Sold with Shortstop Lyn Lary to New York Yankees for an estimated $100,000, January, 1928. Reese wasn't to be delivered until 1930.

‡Sold to St. Louis Cardinals, May, 1932.

§Sold to Los Angeles, February, 1933.

RECORD AS MANAGER

Year Club	League	Position	W.	L.
1939—Bellingham.........West. Int.	†Sixth	24	44	
1960—San Diego...........P.C.	‡Fourth	34	18	
1961—San Diego...........P.C.	§Fifth	39	44	

†Replaced Ken Penner, June 8, team in sixth place; released August 17.

‡Replaced George Metkovich, July 23, with team in seventh place. Tied for position.

§Resigned July 6.

Batboy, Los Angeles Angels, 1917 through 1923; coach, Los Angeles Angels, 1940 through 1942; manager, Army service team at Camp Campbell, Kentucky, 1942; scout, Boston Braves, 1945 through 1946; coach, San Diego, 1948 through 1960; coach, Hawaii, 1963 through 1964 and 1969; coach, Seattle, 1965 through 1968; coach, Portland, 1970; scout, Montreal Expos, 1971 through 1972; coach, California Angels, 1973 through 1981.

WARREN RICHARD RENICK
(Rick)
Kansas City Royals

Born March 16, 1944, at London, O.
Threw and batted righthanded.
Attended Ohio State University, Columbus, O.

Hit home run first time at bat in major leagues, July 11, 1968.

Year Club	League	Pos.	G.	AB.	R.	H.	2B.	3B.	HR.	RBI.	B.A.	PO.	A.	E.	F.A.
1965—Orlando ....Fla.St.	SS	119	404	54	98	•21	8	6	56	.243	188	258	46	.907
1966—Denver ....P. C.	SS-2B	32	94	15	18	3	1	2	9	.191	46	73	10	.922
1966—Charlotte ....South.	SS	88	307	35	62	9	2	5	34	.202	157	237	21	.949
1967—Wilson ....Carol.	SS	128	463	65	118	20	1	20	78	.255	246	350	33	.948
1968—Denver ....P. C.	SS-OF	75	279	41	69	12	1	10	28	.247	127	231	18	.952
1968—Minnesota ....Amer.	SS	42	97	16	21	5	2	3	13	.216	50	91	8	.946
1969—Denver ....A. A.	SS-OF	6	25	9	9	2	1	0	3	.360	5	5	1	.909
1969—Minnesota ....Amer.	3-S-OF	71	139	21	34	3	0	5	17	.245	34	59	10	.902
1970—Minnesota ....Amer.	3-O-S	81	179	20	41	8	0	7	25	.229	52	54	2	.981
1971—Minnesota ....Amer.	3B-OF	27	45	4	10	2	0	1	8	.222	11	8	2	.905
1972—Minnesota ....Amer.	O-1-3-S	55	93	10	16	2	0	4	8	.172	39	10	1	.980
1973—Tacoma ....P. C.	2-3-S	119	439	67	110	15	7	19	75	.251	217	323	27	.952
1974—Tacoma ....P. C.	3-1-2-S	114	392	74	98	10	4	24	64	.250	115	246	20	.948
1975—Tacoma§x ....P. C.	3B-1B	76	259	42	70	9	2	12	38	.270	37	89	8	.940
1976—Tacoma yz ....P. C.	2B-3B	77	255	50	80	5	1	17	50	.314	117	177	15	.951
1977—Denver a...........A. A.	3B-OF	70	178	34	50	3	1	14	42	.281	35	71	9	.922
1978—Denver bcd ....A. A.	3B-1B	43	145	25	33	3	0	11	36	.228	39	35	4	.949
Major League Totals......................		276	553	71	122	20	2	20	71	.221	186	222	23	.947

†On disabled list, April 8 to April 29, 1969.

‡On disabled list, June 28 to September 1, 1971.

§Player-coach.

xOn disabled list, June 9 to July 1, 1975.

yOn disabled list, April 17 to May 20 and June 4 to June 14, 1976.

zReleased, April 8, 1977; signed by Montreal Expos' organization, April 8, 1977.

aOn disabled list, June 6 to July 14 and July 30 to August 13, 1977.

bOn disabled list, June 5 to June 23, 1978.

cOn temporary inactive list, July 8 to August 13, 1978.

dReleased, September 8, 1978.

Minor league batting instructor, Kansas City Royals, 1979 and 1980; coach, Kansas City Royals, 1981.

MERVIN WELDON RETTENMUND
(Merv)
California Angels

Born June 6, 1943, at Flint, Mich.
Height, 5.11. Weight, 195.
Throws and bats righthanded.
Hobbies—Badminton, music and reading.
Attended Ball State University, Muncie, Ind.; received Bachelor of Science degree in Education.

Established major league record for most games, pinch-hitter, season (86), 1977.
Tied major league records for most bases on balls, inning (2), June 22, 1970 (ninth inning); fewest double plays by outfielders, season, for leader in most double plays (4), 1971.
Established National League record for most bases on balls, pinch-hitter, season (16), 1977.
Tied for American League lead in double plays by outfielders with 4 in 1971.
Led California League outfielders in double plays with 6 in 1965.
Led Eastern League batters in walks with 90 in 1967.
Led International League batters in walks with 85 in 1968.
Named International League Most Valuable Player and Rookie of the Year, 1968.
Named THE SPORTING NEWS Minor League Player of the Year, 1968.
Named as outfielder on THE SPORTING NEWS American League All-Star Team, 1971.

Year	Club	League	Pos.	G.	AB.	R.	H.	2B.	3B.	HR.	RBI.	B.A.	PO.	A.	E.	F.A.
1965—Stockton	Calif.		OF	129	361	85	88	13	3	11	38	.244	212	16	5	.979
1966—Stockton	Calif.		OF	127	440	85	135	16	6	21	69	.307	∗280	6	7	.976
1967—Elmira	East.		OF	131	423	67	121	17	3	4	51	.286	246	10	7	.973
1968—Baltimore	Amer.		OF	31	64	10	19	5	0	2	7	.297	29	1	0	1.000
1968—Rochester	Int.		OF	114	393	∗104	130	25	5	22	59	∗.331	251	11	4	.985
1969—Baltimore	Amer.		OF	95	190	27	47	10	3	4	25	.247	107	3	1	.991
1970—Baltimore	Amer.		OF	106	338	60	109	17	2	18	58	.322	201	6	5	.976
1971—Baltimore	Amer.		OF	141	491	81	156	23	4	11	75	.318	292	7	7	.977
1972—Baltimore†	Amer.		OF	102	301	40	70	10	2	6	21	.233	174	6	2	.989
1973—Baltimore‡	Amer.		OF	95	321	59	84	17	2	9	44	.262	196	4	3	.985
1974—Cincinnati	Nat.		OF	80	208	30	45	6	0	6	28	.216	103	3	0	1.000
1975—Cincinnati§	Nat.		OF-3B	93	188	24	45	6	1	2	19	.239	99	2	0	1.000
1976—San Diego	Nat.		OF-PH	86	140	16	32	7	0	2	11	.229	79	6	2	.977
1977—San Diego x	Nat.		OF-3B	107	126	23	36	6	1	4	17	.286	30	0	0	1.000
1978—California	Amer.		OF	50	108	16	29	5	1	1	14	.269	30	0	1	.968
1979—California y	Amer.		OF	35	76	7	20	2	0	1	10	.263	6	0	0	1.000
1980—California	Amer.		DH	2	4	0	1	0	0	0	0	.250	0	0	0	.000
American League Totals				657	1893	300	535	89	14	52	254	.283	1035	27	19	.982
National League Totals				366	662	93	158	25	2	14	75	.239	311	11	2	.994
Major League Totals				1023	2555	393	693	114	16	66	329	.271	1346	38	21	.985

Signed as free agent by Baltimore Orioles' organization, November 28, 1964.
†On supplemental disabled list, August 25 through September 9.
‡Traded with Infielder Junior Kennedy and Catcher Bill Wood to Cincinnati Reds for Pitcher Ross Grimsley and Catcher Wally Williams, December 4, 1973.
§Traded to San Diego Padres for Infielder Rudy Meoli and cash, April 5, 1976.
xGranted free agency, November 2, 1977; signed by California Angels, March 25, 1978.
yGranted free agency, November 1, 1979.
Coach, California Angels, 1980 and 1981.

CHAMPIONSHIP SERIES RECORD

Tied Championship Series records for most clubs total Series (3); most at bats, inning (2), October 6, 1973 (first inning).
Tied American League Championship Series record for most positions played, total Series (3).

Year	Club	League	Pos.	G.	AB.	R.	H.	2B.	3B.	HR.	RBI.	B.A.	PO.	A.	E.	F.A.
1969—Baltimore	Amer.		PH	1	0	0	0	0	0	0	0	.000	0	0	0	.000
1970—Baltimore	Amer.		OF	1	3	1	1	0	0	0	1	.333	3	1	0	1.000
1971—Baltimore	Amer.		PR-OF	3	8	0	2	1	0	0	1	.250	7	0	0	1.000
1973—Baltimore	Amer.		OF	3	11	1	1	0	0	0	0	.091	3	0	0	1.000
1975—Cincinnati	Nat.		PH	2	1	1	0	0	0	0	0	.000	0	0	0	.000
1979—California	Amer.		PH-DH	2	2	0	0	0	0	0	0	.000	0	0	0	.000
Championship Series Totals				12	25	3	4	1	0	0	2	.160	13	1	0	1.000

WORLD SERIES RECORD

Tied World Series records for most hits, inning, and most singles, inning (2), October 11, 1971; most positions played, Series (3), 1960 (all three outfield positions).

Year	Club	League	Pos.	G.	AB.	R.	H.	2B.	3B.	HR.	RBI.	B.A.	PO.	A.	E.	F.A.
1969—Baltimore	Amer.		PR	1	0	0	0	0	0	0	0	.000	0	0	0	.000
1970—Baltimore	Amer.		PH-OF	2	5	2	2	0	0	1	2	.400	3	0	0	1.000
1971—Baltimore	Amer.		PH-OF	7	27	3	5	0	0	1	4	.185	17	0	0	1.000
1975—Cincinnati	Nat.		PH	3	3	0	0	0	0	0	0	.000	0	0	0	.000
World Series Totals				13	35	5	7	0	0	2	6	.200	20	0	0	1.000

DID YOU KNOW—

That Terry Puhl was the toughest batter to double up in 1980? He grounded into just three DPs in 535 at-bats.

BENJAMIN REYES (CHAVEZ)
(Cananea)
Seattle Mariners

Born February 18, 1937, at Nacosria, Sonora, Mexico
Height, 5.10. Weight, 180.
Threw and batted righthanded.

Year Club	League	Pos.	G.	AB.	R.	H.	2B.	3B.	HR.	RBI.	B.A.	PO.	A.	E.	F.A.
1963–San Luis Indians	Mx. Cn.	....	20	76	13	24	4	2	1	11	.316	....	....	....	....
1964–Campeche........	Mx. SE	O-3-2-P	84	316	51	88	18	2	2	33	.278	172	84	20	.928
1965–Jalisco.............	Mex.	OF-3B-P	117	364	67	96	13	5	3	26	.239	150	69	17	.928
1966–Jalisco.............	Mex.	OF-P	107	288	30	65	13	1	1	16	.226	114	8	4	.968
1967–Jalisco†	Mex.	O-INF.-P	98	95	16	13	2	2	0	7	.137	49	10	2	.967
1968–Fresnillo‡	Mx. Cn.	2-1-O-3-P	21	43	9	16	4	3	1	12	.372	20	7	5	.844
1969–San Luis Pot.‡..	Mx. Cn.	O-3-2-P-1	23	62	11	18	3	2	1	12	.290	23	22	4	.918
1970–Puerto Mexico ..	Mx. SE	P-OF	17	20	0	6	1	0	0	0	.300	4	1	0	1.000
1971–Jalisco‡	Mex.	O-2-1-P	20	27	4	1	3	0	0	3	.259	7	4	0	1.000
1972–Jalisco‡	Mex.	OF	1	4	0	0	0	0	0	0	.000	1	0	1	.500
1973–Juarez‡............	Mex.	OF-1B-P	6	14	3	4	0	0	1	2	.286	8	0	1	.889

†Released, September 29, 1967.
‡Player-manager.

RECORD AS PITCHER

Year Club	League	G.	IP.	W.	L.	Pct.	H.	R.	ER.	SO.	BB.	ERA.
1964–Campeche...........................	Mex. SE	2	7	0	0	.000	3	2	1	0	2	1.29
1965–Jalisco...............................	Mexican	1	2	0	0	.000	1	0	0	0	2	0.00
1966–Jalisco...............................	Mexican	1	1	0	0	.000	4	5	5	0	3	45.00
1967–Jalisco...............................	Mexican	6	10	0	0	.000	3	1	1	1	7	0.90
1968–Fresnillo.............................	Mex. Center	8	22	0	1	.000	36	24	16	13	9	6.54
1969–San Luis Potosi	Mex. Center	3	8	0	1	.000	10	6	6	6	8	6.75
1970–Puerto Mexico	Mex. SE	8	22	0	3	.000	31	18	13	8	9	5.32
1971–Jalisco...............................	Mexican	1	1	0	0	.000	2	0	0	0	2	0.00
1973–Juarez	Mexican	1	1	0	0	.000	0	0	0	0	0	0.00

RECORD AS MANAGER
Named Mexican League Manager of the Year, 1974.

Year Club	League	Position	W.	L.	Year Club	League	Position	W.	L.
1968–Fresnillo............ Mx.Cn.		Sixth	†55	70	1974–Mex. C. Reds a... Mex.		First(E)	z75	61
1969–San Luis Pot.‡.... Mx.Cn.		First	§43	18	1975–Mex. C. Reds b... Mex.		Second(E)	z80	57
(Second Half)		Second	38	27	1976–Mex. C. Reds c... Mex.		Second(E)	75	63
1970–San Luis Pot. ..... Mx.Cn.		Fifth	36	34	1977–Mex. C. Reds d... Mex.		First(E)	§94	57
(Second Half)		Fourth	30	26	1978–Mex. C. Reds e... Mex.		Second(E)	†70	76
1971–Jalisco x .... Mex.		First(S)	y82	65	1979–Mex. C. Reds ..... Mex.		Third(E)	74	64
1972–Jalisco.............. Mex.		Third(N)	§77	60	1980–Mex. C. Reds ..... Mex.		Third(E)	†52	30
1973–Juarez .... Mex.		Third(W)	z55	78					

†Three tie games.
‡Won championship playoff from Zacatecas, four games to one.
§One tie game.
xWon championship playoff from Saltillo, four games to three.
yFour tie games.
zTwo tie games.
aWon playoff from Pueblo, four games to two; won playoff from Jalisco, four games to two; won championship playoff from Gomez Palacio, four games to none.
bWon playoff from Puebla, four games to two; lost playoff to Cordoba, four games to three.
cWon playoff from Puebla, four games to two; won playoff from Cordoba, four games to two; won championship playoff from Union Laguna, four games to two.
dWon playoff from Durango, four games to one; won playoff from Cordoba, four games to none; lost championship playoff to Nuevo Laredo, four games to one.
eLost playoff to Aguascalientes, four games to two.

DAVID WILLIAM RICKETTS
(Dave)
St. Louis Cardinals

Born, July 12, 1935, at Pottstown, Pa.
Height, 6.02. Weight, 190.
Threw right and batted right and lefthanded.
Attended Duquesne University, Pittsburgh, Pa.; received Bachelor of
Arts degree in Education.
Brother of Dick Ricketts, former pitcher with St. Louis Cardinals.

Led Pacific Coast League catchers in double plays with 12 in 1963.
Led International League catchers in double plays with 11 and in passed balls with 20 in 1963.
Tied for International League lead in passed balls with 17 in 1964.

Year Club	League	Pos.	G.	AB.	R.	H.	2B.	3B.	HR.	RBI.	B.A.	PO.	A.	E.	F.A.
1957–Rochester	Int.	C	73	229	16	70	15	3	0	29	.306	291	23	7	.978
1958-59–Rochester .....Int.					(In Military Service)										
1960–Rochester ....Int.		C	29	66	4	6	0	0	0	1	.091	103	14	2	.983
1960–Lancaster..........East.		C-OF	84	283	44	94	16	3	2	27	.332	382	35	6	.986

Year	Club	League	Pos.	G.	AB.	R.	H.	2B.	3B.	HR.	RBI.	B.A.	PO.	A.	E.	F.A.
1961—Tulsa ....Tex.			C	53	174	15	43	7	0	0	10	.247	271	34	4	.987
1961—Portland............P.C.			3B-C	85	326	51	98	15	2	2	37	.301	82	144	20	.919
1962—Portland............P.C.			C	110	358	49	106	22	4	4	41	.296	568	50	8	.987
1963—Atlanta.............Int.			C	132	424	34	118	16	1	5	36	.278	*778	59	9	.989
1963—St. Louis ....Nat.			C	3	8	0	2	0	0	0	0	.250	14	0	0	1.000
1964—Jacksonville ......Int.			*C-1B	134	417	20	106	21	1	1	28	.254	*773	49	5	.994
1965—St. Louis ....Nat.			C	11	29	1	7	0	0	0	0	.241	41	2	1	.977
1965—Tol.-J'ville........Int.			C	54	154	7	37	5	0	1	19	.240	253	26	3	.989
1965—Indianapolis ......P.C.			C	16	45	2	9	2	0	0	3	.200	90	7	2	.980
1966—Tulsa ................P.C.			C	116	376	44	123	15	4	2	31	.327	607	53	5	.992
1967—St. Louis ....Nat.			C	52	99	11	27	8	0	1	14	.273	111	10	0	1.000
1968—St. Louis ....Nat.			C	20	22	1	3	0	0	0	1	.136	5	0	0	1.000
1969—St. Louis† ....Nat.			C	30	44	2	12	1	0	0	5	.273	57	1	1	.983
1970—Pittsburgh.........Nat.			C	14	11	0	2	0	0	0	0	.182	8	2	1	.909
Major League Totals				130	213	15	53	9	0	1	20	.249	236	15	3	.988

†Traded with Pitcher Dave Giusti to Pittsburgh Pirates for First Baseman-Outfielder Carl Taylor and Outfielder Frank Vanzin (later transferred from York to Tulsa), October 21, 1969.

WORLD SERIES RECORD

Year	Club	League	Pos.	G.	AB.	R.	H.	2B.	3B.	HR.	RBI.	B.A.	PO.	A.	E.	F.A.
1967—St. Louis ....Nat.			PH	3	3	0	0	0	0	0	0	.000	0	0	0	.000
1968—St. Louis ....Nat.			PH	1	1	0	1	0	0	0	0	1.000	0	0	0	.000
World Series Totals				4	4	0	1	0	0	0	0	.250	0	0	0	.000

RECORD AS MANAGER

Year	Club	League	Position	W.	L.
1976—Sarasota Cards ...G. Coast			Fourth	27	24
1977—Johnson City.......Appal.			Third	37	33

Coach, Pittsburgh Pirates, 1971 through 1973; St. Louis Cardinals, 1974, 1975 and 1978 through 1981.

CALVIN EDWIN RIPKEN SR.
(Cal)
Baltimore Orioles

Born December 17, 1935, at Aberdeen, Md.
Height, 6.00. Weight, 175.
Threw and batted righthanded.
Hobby—Golf.
Brother of Bill Ripken, former outfielder in Brooklyn Dodgers' organization; father of Cal Ripken, third baseman in Baltimore Orioles' organization.

Year	Club	League	Pos.	G.	AB.	R.	H.	2B.	3B.	HR.	RBI.	B.A.	PO.	A.	E.	F.A.
1957—Phoenix.............Ar.-Mx.			O-C-3	112	398	68	109	15	6	7	60	.274	220	54	17	.942
1958—Wilson† ....Carol.			*C-O-3	118	393	40	85	20	2	4	38	.216	655	*72	5	.993
1959—Pensacola ....Al.-Fla.			C-P	61	219	36	64	14	3	2	35	.292	378	31	6	.986
1959—Amarillo ....Tex.			C	30	69	6	14	2	0	0	3	.203	111	10	0	1.000
1960—Fox Cities .........I.I.I.			*C-OF	107	356	59	100	20	4	9	74	.281	619	34	7	*.989
1961—Little Rock........South.			C	32	81	6	15	2	1	1	8	.185	120	12	0	1.000
1961—Leesburg‡ ....Fla. St.			C-P	52	127	20	30	3	0	1	13	.236	286	32	1	.997
1961—Rochester ....Int.			C	11	24	2	2	0	0	1	2	.083	36	0	0	1.000
1962—Fox Cities‡ ....Midw.			C-P	58	143	25	39	9	0	4	36	.273	311	20	4	.988
1963—Aberdeen§........North.			(Did Not Play)													
1964—Aberdeen‡........North.				2	1	0	0	0	0	0	0	.000	....	....	....	....

†Released by Baltimore Orioles' organization, April 20, 1959; re-signed by Baltimore Orioles' organization, April 25, 1959.
‡Player-manager.
§On disabled list, April 27 to September 17, 1963.

PITCHING RECORD

Year	Club	League	G.	IP.	W.	L.	Pct.	H.	R.	ER.	SO.	BB.	ERA.
1959—Pensacola ....Ala.-Fla.			1	....	0	0	.000	....	....	....	....	....	....
1961—Leesburg‡...........................Florida St.			2	....	0	0	.000	....	....	....	....	....	....
1962—Fox Cities‡.......................Midwest			3	15	0	0	.000	22	15	11	3	7	6.60

RECORD AS MANAGER

Year	Club	League	Position	W.	L.	Year	Club	League	Position	W.	L.
1961—Leesburg†..........Fla. St.			Seventh	8	5	1967—Miami ....Fla. St.			Third(E)	31	39
(Second Half)‡			Third	30	31	(Second Half)			Second(E)	34	37
1962—Fox Cities..........Midwest			Ninth	25	36	1968—Elmira ....Eastern			Third	77	63
(Second Half)			Third	36	27	1969—Rochester...........Int.			Fifth	71	69
1963—Aberdeen...........Northern			Second	65	55	1970—Rochester...........Int.			Third	76	64
1964—Aberdeen...........Northern			§First	80	37	1971—Dallas-Ft.W. ....Texas			Second(W)	82	59
1965—Tri-City.............Northwest			Fourth	34	36	1972—Asheville ....South.			yFirst(W)	81	58
(Second Half)			xFirst	47	22	1973—Asheville ....South.			Second(W)	71	69
1966—Aberdeen...........Northern			Second	47	22	1974—Asheville ....South.			Second(W)	70	67

†Replaced Billy DeMars, June 7.
‡Assigned to Rochester as a player, August 17.
§Won Baukol Playoff (based on last 30 days of regular season) with record of 19 wins, 10 losses, 1 tie.

OCTAVIO ROJAS (RIVAS)

Name Pronounced ROW-hass.

(Cookie)
Chicago Cubs

Born March 6, 1939, at Havana, Cuba.
Height, 5.10. Weight, 171.
Threw and batted righthanded.
Hobby—Movies.

Tied major league record for fewest triples, season, 500 or more at bats (0), 1968.
Led National League in sacrifice hits with 16 in 1967.
Led National League second basemen in double plays with 110 in 1968.
Led International League second basemen in double plays with 89 in 1961.
Named second baseman on THE SPORTING NEWS American League All-Star Team, 1971.

Year	Club	League	Pos.	G.	AB.	R.	H.	2B.	3B.	HR.	RBI.	B.A.	PO.	A.	E.	F.A.
1956–W. Palm Beach	. Fla. St.		2B	129	476	75	131	19	6	1	43	.275	297	344	34	.950
1958–Savannah	Sally		INF	134	527	74	134	24	2	10	44	.254	343	335	26	.963
1959–Havana	Int.		2B	99	318	30	74	12	1	3	13	.233	212	176	13	.968
1960–Hav.-Jer. City	Int.		2B	110	276	19	62	8	1	1	24	.225	213	211	●18	.959
1961–Jersey City	Int.		2B	150	567	62	150	25	6	1	44	.265	★.350	★382	★24	★.968
1962–Cincinnati†	Nat.		2B-3B	39	86	9	19	2	0	0	6	.221	60	52	6	.949
1963–Philadelphia	Nat.		2B-OF	64	77	18	17	0	1	1	2	.221	43	68	1	.991
1964–Philadelphia	Nat.		OF-SS-C	109	340	58	99	19	5	2	31	.291	164	76	7	.972
1965–Philadelphia	Nat.		2B-OF-SS	142	521	78	158	25	3	3	42	.303	270	253	9	.983
1966–Philadelphia	Nat.		2B-OF-SS	156	626	77	168	18	1	6	55	.268	319	295	13	.979
1967–Philadelphia	Nat.		I-O-C-P	147	528	60	137	21	2	4	45	.259	297	360	15	.978
1968–Philadelphia	Nat.		★2B-C	152	621	53	144	19	0	9	48	.232	★365	424	10	★.987
1969–Philadelphia‡	Nat.		2B-OF	110	391	35	89	11	1	4	30	.228	260	229	11	.978
1970–St. Louis§	Nat.		2B-OF-SS	23	47	2	5	0	0	0	2	.106	24	30	0	1.000
1970–Kansas City	Amer.		2B	98	384	36	100	13	3	2	28	.260	217	283	9	.982
1971–Kansas City x	Amer.		★2-SS-OF	115	414	56	124	22	2	6	59	.300	254	293	5	★.991
1972–Kansas City	Amer.		2B-3B-SS	137	487	49	127	25	0	3	53	.261	265	368	9	.986
1973–Kansas City	Amer.		2B	139	551	78	152	29	3	6	69	.276	302	424	13	.982
1974–Kansas City	Amer.		2B	144	542	52	147	17	1	6	60	.271	292	368	9	★.987
1975–Kansas City	Amer.		2B	120	406	34	103	18	2	2	37	.254	233	303	11	.980
1976–Kansas City	Amer.		2B-3B-1B	63	132	11	32	6	0	0	16	.242	53	52	1	.990
1977–Kansas City y	Amer.		3B-2B	64	156	8	39	9	1	0	10	.250	49	80	5	.963
American League Totals				880	3072	324	824	139	12	25	332	.268	1665	2171	62	.984
National League Totals				942	3237	390	836	115	13	29	261	.258	1806	1789	72	.980
Major League Totals				1822	6309	714	1660	254	25	54	593	.263	3471	3960	134	.982

†Recalled by Cincinnati Reds; traded to Philadelphia Phillies for Pitcher Jim Owens, November 27, 1962.
‡Traded with First Baseman-Outfielder Richie Allen and Pitcher Jerry Johnson to St. Louis Cardinals for Catcher Tim McCarver, Outfielders Curt Flood and Byron Browne and Pitcher Joe Hoerner, October 7, 1969. Flood refused to report and the Cardinals sent First Baseman Willie Montanez and a player to be named later to Philadelphia to complete the deal, April 7, 1970. (Pitcher Robert Browning was sent from St. Louis to Philadelphia as "the player to be named later.")
§Traded to Kansas City Royals for Outfielder Fred Rico (assigned from Omaha to Tulsa), June 13, 1970.
xOn disabled list, August 22 to September 13, 1971.
yReleased, October 10, 1977.
Coach, Chicago Cubs, 1978 through 1981.

PITCHING RECORD

Year	Club	League	G.	IP.	W.	L.	Pct.	H.	R.	ER.	SO.	BB.	ERA.
1967–Philadelphia		National	1	1	0	0	.000	1	0	0	0	0	0.00

CHAMPIONSHIP SERIES RECORD

Year	Club	League	Pos.	G.	AB.	R.	H.	2B.	3B.	HR.	RBI.	B.A.	PO.	A.	E.	F.A.
1976–Kansas City	Amer.		PH-2B	4	9	2	3	0	0	0	1	.333	4	6	0	1.000
1977–Kansas City	Amer.		DH	1	4	0	1	0	0	0	0	.250	0	0	0	.000
Championship Series Totals				5	13	2	4	0	0	0	1	.308	4	6	0	1.000

ALL-STAR GAME RECORD

Tied All-Star Game record for most home runs by pinch-hitter, game (1), July 25, 1972.

Year	League	Pos.	AB.	R.	H.	2B.	3B.	HR.	RBI.	B.A.	PO.	A.	E.	F.A.
1965–National		PH	1	0	0	0	0	0	0	.000	0	0	0	.000
1971–American		2B	1	0	0	0	0	0	0	.000	1	1	0	1.000
1972–American		PH-2B	1	1	1	0	0	1	2	1.000	3	1	0	1.000
1973–American		2B	0	0	0	0	0	0	0	.000	1	1	0	1.000
All-Star Game Totals			3	1	1	0	0	1	2	.333	5	3	0	1.000

Member of American League All-Star Team in 1974 game; did not play.

RALPH EMANUEL ROWE
Baltimore Orioles

Born July 14, 1924, at Newberry, S. C.
Height 5.06. Weight, 160.
Threw right and batted lefthanded.
Graduate of Newberry College, Newberry, S. C.

Year	Club	League	Pos.	G	AB	R	H	2B	3B	HR	RBI	B.A.	PO	A	E	F.A.
1942—Thomasville		W. C.S.	OF	46	182	44	65	16	0	5	22	.357	71	8	4	.952
1943-44-45—W.-Barre	East.							(In Military Service)								
1946—Wilkes-Barre	East.							(Did not play)								
1947—Rock Hill		Tri-St.	OF	135	513	92	157	26	9	9	73	.306	218	7	11	.953
1948—Rock Hill		Tri-St.	OF	147	534	108	192	*44	15	7	123	.360	312	24	11	.968
1949—Los Angeles		P. C.	OF	14	33	9	8	2	0	0	1	.242	....	...	...	......
1949—Macon		So. Atl.	OF	120	435	72	122	19	5	8	68	.280	218	13	8	.967
1950—Rock Hill		Tri-St.	OF	139	491	79	140	21	6	10	97	.285	281	12	6	*.980
1951—Nashville		So. Assn.	OF	121	392	65	128	17	6	12	71	.327	191	12	1	*.995
1952—Springfield		Int.	OF	50	128	9	22	1	2	1	14	.172	93	4	3	.970
1952—Memphis		So. Assn.	OF	48	150	26	43	7	4	4	21	.287	70	3	4	.948
1953—Memphis		So. Assn.	OF	93	314	64	97	11	4	6	34	.309	144	9	2	.987
1954—Memphis		So. Assn.	OF	127	376	58	103	20	5	5	60	.274	196	4	5	.976
1955—Mobile		Sc. Assn.	OF	124	360	47	99	21	0	7	49	.275	194	18	10	.955
1956—Mobile		So. Assn.						(Did not play)								
1957—Mobile		So. Assn.	OF	107	301	38	78	14	0	4	43	.259	137	2	5	.965
1958—Charlotte		So. Atl.	OF	115	358	52	96	18	1	8	56	.268	182	1	5	.973
1959—Missoula		Pion.	OF	28	74	13	25	4	0	3	12	.338	39	7	2	.958
1960—Ft. Walton Bch.		Ala.-Fla.	OF	5	6	0	1	0	0	0	1	.167	....	...	...	....
1961—Charlotte		So. Atl.	OF	8	7	0	1	0	0	0	1	.143	....	...	...	....

PITCHING RECORD

Year	Club	League	G	IP.	W.	L.	Pct.	H.	R.	ER.	SO.	BB.	ERA.
1959—Missoula		Pioneer	1	....	0	0	.000	....	...	...	...	...	......

RECORD AS MANAGER

Year	Club	League	Position	W.	L.	Year	Club	League	Position	W.	L.
1959—Missoula	Pion.		Sixth	56	73	1966—Thomasville		W.Carol.	Third	71	52
1960—Ft.Walton Bch.	Al.-Fla.		Fourth	56	60	1967—Orlando		Fla. St.	First(E)	88	50
1961—Ft.Walton Bch.	Al.-Fla.		Second	58	61	1968—Orlando		Fla. St.	‡First(W)	81	59
1963—Wilson†	Carol.		Second(E)	77	67	1969—Charlotte		A.A.	§Fourth(E)	67	71
1964—Wilson	Carol.		Fifth	57	82	1970—Evansville		Southern	First	81	59
1965—Thomasville	W.Carol.		Second	73	52						

†Defeated Kinston, three games to none, and Greensboro, two games to none, in playoffs for championship.

‡Defeated Cocoa, two games to none, and Miami, two games to one, for championship.

Coach, Minnesota Twins, 1972 through 1975; minor league instructor, Minnesota Twins, 1976; minor league instructor, Baltimore Orioles, 1977 through 1980; coach, Baltimore Orioles, 1981.

MICHAEL JAMES RYAN
(Mike)
Philadelphia Phillies

Born November 25, 1941, at Haverhill, Mass.
Height, 6.02. Weight, 210.
Threw and batted righthanded.
Led Eastern League catchers in double plays with 12 in 1964.
Tied for Midwest League lead in double plays by catchers with 8 in 1962.

Year	Club	League	Pos.	G	AB	R	H	2B	3B	HR	RBI	B.A.	PO	A	E	F.A.
1961—Olean		NYP	C	45	119	21	22	3	0	3	16	.185	281	17	3	.990
1962—Waterloo		Midw.	C	117	368	56	79	13	3	10	49	.215	*875	*93	11	.989
1963—Reading		East.	C	121	388	39	89	11	0	10	45	.229	830	83	19	.980
1964—Reading		East.	C	110	343	38	85	10	0	5	34	.248	680	47	7	*.990
1964—Boston		Amer.	C	1	3	0	1	0	0	0	2	.333	5	0	0	1.000
1965—Boston		Amer.	C	33	107	7	17	0	1	3	9	.159	194	18	4	.981
1965—Toronto		Int.	C	51	161	18	38	7	2	4	19	.236	329	34	5	.986
1966—Boston		Amer.	C	116	369	27	79	15	3	2	32	.214	685	50	6	.992
1967—Boston†		Amer.	C	79	226	21	45	4	2	2	27	.199	473	34	6	.988
1968—Philadelphia		Nat.	C	96	296	12	53	6	1	1	15	.179	501	62	5	.991
1969—Philadelphia		Nat.	C	133	446	41	91	17	2	12	44	.204	769	●79	8	.991
1970—Philadelphia‡		Nat.	C	46	134	14	24	8	0	2	11	.179	238	15	2	.992
1971—Philadelphia		Nat.	C	43	134	9	22	5	1	3	6	.164	222	30	0	1.000
1972—Philadelphia		Nat.	C	46	106	6	19	4	0	2	10	.179	216	21	2	.992
1973—Philadelphia§		Nat.	C	28	69	7	16	1	2	1	5	.232	121	9	1	.992
1974—Pittsburgh xy		Nat.	C	15	30	2	3	0	0	0	0	.100	49	7	0	1.000
1976—Charleston z		W. Car.	DH	3	12	0	2	0	0	0	0	.167	0	0	0	.000
American League Totals				229	705	55	142	19	6	7	70	.201	1357	102	16	.989
National League Totals				407	1215	91	228	41	6	21	91	.188	2116	223	18	.992
Major League Totals				636	1920	146	370	60	12	28	161	.193	3473	325	34	.991

†Traded with cash to Philadelphia Phillies for Pitcher Dick Ellsworth and Catcher-First Baseman Gene Oliver (assigned to Louisville), December 15, 1967.

‡On disabled list March 29 to April 19, May 2 to July 6 and August 15 to September 5, 1970.
§Traded to Pittsburgh Pirates for Shortstop Jackie Hernandez, January 31, 1974.
xOn supplemental disabled list, July 9 to August 6, 1974.
yReleased, October 23, 1974.
zPlayer-manager.

PITCHING RECORD

Year Club	League	G.	IP.	W.	L.	Pct.	H.	R.	ER.	SO.	BB.	ERA.
1975–Charleston z.........................W. Caro.		2	5	0	0	.000	7	3	3	0	3	5.40

RECORD AS MANAGER

Year Club	League	Position	W.	L.
1975–Charleston .... W. Caro.		Third	29	40
(Second Half)		Fourth	16	56
1976–Charleston .... W. Caro.		Fourth	30	39
(Second Half)		Third	29	41
1977–Oklahoma City†.. A.A.		Third(W)	28	26
1978–Oklahoma City ... A.A.		Third(W)	62	74

†Replaced Cal Emery (and interim Manager Billy Connors), July 12, 1977, with record of 42-40 and team in second place.
Minor league instructor, Philadelphia Phillies, part of 1977 and 1979; coach, Philadelphia Phillies, 1980 and 1981.

JIMMIE RONALD SCHAFFER
(Jim)
Kansas City Royals

Born April 5, 1936, at Limeport, Pa.
Height, 5.08. Weight, 166.
Threw and batted righthanded.
Hobbies–Hunting and golf.
Cousin of Robert Schaffer, pitcher in St. Louis Cardinals' organization, 1952 through 1956.

Played all nine positions in one game, 1955.
Led Northern League catchers in double plays with 11 in 1958.
Led Pacific Coast League catchers in runners caught stealing with 38 in 1966.
Named Most Valuable Player in Northern League, 1958.

Year Club	League	Pos.	G.	AB.	R.	H.	2B.	3B.	HR.	RBI.	B.A.	PO.	A.	E.	F.A.
1955–Decatur.............M-O. V.		C-OF-3	106	370	53	97	14	2	2	32	.262	326	50	13	.967
1956–Decatur.............M-O. V.		C	59	207	40	60	12	2	3	36	.290	329	46	11	.972
1957–Winston-Salem ..Carolina		★C-SS-O	99	294	37	68	13	1	5	34	.231	441	64	★13	.975
1958–Winnipeg...........North.		●C-3B	109	404	85	125	26	2	19	87	.309	554	●89	12	.982
1959–Omaha..............A. A.		C	27	73	10	17	1	2	1	5	.233	130	6	1	.993
1959–Tulsa ....Texas		C	87	272	35	72	14	2	8	46	.255	374	44	8	.981
1960–Tulsa ....Texas		C	120	378	66	94	22	1	21	69	.249	★604	★66	9	.987
1961–Portland............P. C.		C	18	58	9	22	4	1	4	14	.379	84	8	3	.968
1961–St. Louis ....Nat.		C	68	153	15	39	7	0	1	16	.255	244	23	1	.996
1962–St. Louis† ....Nat.		C	70	66	7	16	2	1	0	6	.242	134	10	1	.993
1963–Chicago.............Nat.		C	57	142	17	34	7	0	7	19	.239	231	23	1	.996
1964–Chicago‡ ....Nat.		C	54	122	9	25	6	1	2	9	.205	143	19	5	.970
1965–Chicago§ ....Amer.		C	17	31	2	6	3	1	0	1	.194	50	7	0	1.000
1965–New York x ....Nat.		C	24	37	0	5	2	0	0	0	.135	60	1	2	.968
1966–San Diego.........P. C.		C	111	356	51	98	24	3	12	57	.275	608	68	11	.984
1966–Philadelphia ......Nat.		C	8	15	2	2	1	0	1	4	.133	17	3	1	.952
1967–San Diego.........P. C.		★C-3B	127	408	46	89	14	1	13	47	.218	736	★79	4	★.995
1967–Philadelphia y ...Nat.		C	2	2	1	0	0	0	0	0	.000	5	0	0	1.000
1968–Cincinnati z.......Nat.		C	4	6	0	1	0	0	0	1	.167	4	0	0	1.000
1968–Indianapolis ......P. C.		C-3B	47	149	13	39	7	1	3	18	.262	265	23	6	.980
1969–Spokane a ....P. C.		C	107	274	42	83	17	1	6	39	.303	413	37	6	.987
1970–Rochester b.......Int.		C	118	376	52	95	21	1	13	48	.253	607	48	4	★.994
National League Totals...................			287	543	51	122	25	2	11	55	.225	838	79	11	.988
American League Totals.................			17	31	2	6	3	1	0	1	.194	50	7	0	1.000
Major League Totals			304	574	53	128	28	3	11	56	.223	888	86	11	.989

†Traded to Chicago Cubs with Pitchers Larry Jackson and Lindy McDaniel for Pitcher Don Cardwell, Catcher Moe Thacker and Outfielder George Altman, October 17, 1962.
‡Traded to Chicago White Sox for Pitcher Frank Baumann, December 1, 1964.
§Sent to New York Mets, July 26, 1965, to complete deal in which Chicago White Sox received Pitcher Frank Lary, July 8, 1965.
xTraded with Infielders Bobby Klaus and Wayne Graham to Philadelphia Phillies' organization for First Baseman Dick Stuart, February 22, 1966.
yDrafted by Cincinnati Reds from San Diego (Philadelphia Phillies' organization), November 28, 1967.
zTraded to Los Angeles Dodgers for Outfielder Ted Savage, March 30, 1969.
aSold to Rochester, April 9, 1970.
bReleased, September 20, 1970.

PITCHING RECORD

Year Club	League	G.	IP.	W.	L.	Pct.	H.	R.	ER.	SO.	BB.	ERA.
1955–Decatur ...............M.-O. V.		1	1	0	0	.000	0	0	0	1	0	0.00

Year	Club	League	Position	W.	L.	Year	Club	League	Position	W.	L.
1971–Bluefield	Appal.	†First(N)	42	27		1975–Asheville	South.	Fourth(W)	63	75	
1972–Lodi	Calif.	Third	38	32		1976–Charlotte	South.	§xFirst(E)	37	28	
(Second Half)		Sixth	29	41		(Second Half)		Third(E)	37	38	
1973–Lodi	Calif.	‡First	46	24		1977–Charlotte	South.	Third(E)	34	35	
		Seventh	31	39		(Second Half)		Fourth(E)	35	36	
1974–Lodi	Calif.	Eighth	21	49		1979–Tulsa	Texas	Fourth(E)	25	35	
(Second Half)		Second	40	30		(Second Half)		Fourth(E)	33	40	

†Declared league champion, based on highest won-lost percentage.
‡Won playoff against Bakersfield (Second Half winner), two games to none.
§Lost playoff against Orlando (Second Half winner), one game to none.
xOne tie.
Coach, Texas Rangers, 1977 and 1978; coach, Kansas City Royals, 1980 and 1981.

ALBERT FRED SCHOENDIENST
Named pronounced SCHAIN-deenst.
(Red)
(Nicknamed because of color of hair.)
St. Louis Cardinals
Born February 2, 1923, at Germantown, Ill.
Height, 6.01. Weight, 192.
Threw right and batted right and lefthanded.
Hobbies—Hunting, fishing and bowling.
Father of Kevin Schoendienst, second baseman in Chicago Cubs' organization.

Established major league records for most doubles, three consecutive games (8), June 5 and 6 (doubleheader), 1948; most long hits, three consecutive games (9), June 5 and 6 (doubleheader), 1948; most consecutive games batted safely by switch-hitter, season (54), 1954.

Tied major league records for most doubles, two consecutive games (6) and most long hits, two consecutive games (7), June 5 and 6 (first game), 1948; most long hits, doubleheader (6), June 6, 1948; most at bats, doubleheader (more than 18 innings), no hits (12), June 9, 1947 (24 innings).

Established National League records for most years by second baseman, league (18); most seasons leading league in fielding average by second baseman, 100 or more games (7).

Tied National League records for most doubles, doubleheader (5), June 6, 1948; most double plays started by second baseman, game (4), August 20, 1954.

Switch-hit home runs in one game, July 8, 1951.

Led National League in stolen bases with 26 in 1945.

Led National League second basemen in double plays with 109 in ✝953 and 137 in 1954.

Named second baseman on THE SPORTING NEWS Major League All-Star teams, 1953 and 1957.

Named International League Most Valuable Player, 1943.

Year	Club	League	Pos.	G.	AB.	R.	H.	2B.	3B.	HR.	RBI.	B.A.	PO.	A.	E.	F.A.
1942–Union City	Kitty	2B	6	27	4	11	3	0	0	4	.407	16	20	2	.947
1942–Albany	Ga.-Fla.	S-2B	68	264	41	71	7	5	1	28	.269	155	209	27	.931
1943–Lynchburg	Pied.	SS	9	36	8	17	2	0	0	5	.472	18	36	3	.947
1943–Rochester	Int.	SS	136	555	81	∗187	21	5	6	37	∗.337	∗339	∗438	48	.942
1944–Rochester†	Int.	SS	25	102	26	38	3	2	2	14	.373	50	84	17	.887
1945–St. Louis	Nat.	OF-S-2	137	565	89	157	22	6	1	47	.278	302	30	10	.971
1946–St. Louis	Nat.	∗2-3-SS	142	606	94	170	28	5	0	34	.281	363	379	13	∗.983
1947–St. Louis	Nat.	2-3-OF	151	∗659	91	167	25	9	3	48	.253	364	417	19	.976
1948–St. Louis	Nat.	2B	119	408	64	111	21	4	4	36	.272	230	269	10	.980
1949–St. Louis	Nat.	∗2-S3-O	151	640	102	190	25	2	3	54	.297	∗428	∗471	15	.984
1950–St. Louis	Nat.	2-O-3	153	∗642	81	177	∗43	9	7	63	.276	425	437	14	.984
1951–St. Louis	Nat.	2B-SS	135	553	88	160	32	7	6	54	.289	354	419	10	.987
1952–St. Louis	Nat.	∗2-3-SS	152	620	91	188	40	7	7	67	.303	∗417	460	20	.978
1953–St. Louis	Nat.	2B	146	564	107	193	35	5	15	79	.342	∗365	∗430	14	∗.983
1954–St. Louis	Nat.	2B	148	610	98	192	38	8	5	79	.315	394	∗477	18	.980
1955–St. Louis	Nat.	2B	145	553	68	148	21	3	11	51	.268	296	381	10	∗.985
1956–St. L.‡-N. Y.	Nat.	2B	132	487	61	147	21	3	2	29	.302	298	308	4	∗.993
1957–N. Y.§-Milw.	Nat.	●2B-OF	150	648	91	∗200	31	8	15	65	.309	379	448	12	●.986
1958–Milwaukee	Nat.	2B	106	427	47	112	23	1	1	24	.262	233	301	7	.987
1959–Milwaukee x	Nat.	2B	5	3	0	0	0	0	0	0	.000	1	1	1	.667
1960–Milwaukee y	Nat.	2B	68	226	21	58	9	1	1	19	.257	120	148	10	.964
1961–St. Louis	Nat.	2B	72	120	9	36	9	0	1	12	.300	43	42	4	.955
1962–St. Louis	Nat.	2B-3B	98	143	21	43	4	0	2	12	.301	33	48	1	.988
1963–St. Louis	Nat.	PH	6	5	0	0	0	0	0	0	.000	0	0	0	.000
Major League Totals			2216	8479	1223	2449	427	78	84	773	.289	5045	5466	192	.982

†Entered Military Service in May.

‡Traded to New York Giants with Pitchers Gordon Jones and Dick Littlefield, Catcher Bill Sarni and Outfielder Jack Brandt for Pitcher Don Liddle, Catcher Ray Katt, Shortstop Al Dark and Outfielder-First Baseman Whitey Lockman. All players but Jones exchanged clubs June 14, 1956–Jones being assigned to Giants, October 1, 1956.

§Traded to Milwaukee Braves for Pitcher Ray Crone, Second Baseman Danny O'Connell and Outfielder Bobby Thomson, June 15, 1957.

xOn disabled list with tuberculosis most of season.

yReleased by Milwaukee Braves, October 14, 1960; signed by St. Louis Cardinals, March 15, 1961.

WORLD SERIES RECORD
Tied World Series records for most at bats, game (6), October 10, 1946; fewest runs batted in, Series (0), 1958.

Year Club	League	Pos.	G.	AB.	R.	H.	2B.	3B.	HR.	RBI.	B.A.	PO.	A.	E.	F.A.
1946—St. Louis ....Nat.		2B	7	30	3	7	1	0	0	1	.233	17	21	1	.974
1957—Milwaukee ....Nat.		2B	5	18	0	5	1	0	0	2	.278	5	10	0	1.000
1958—Milwaukee ....Nat.		2B	7	30	5	9	3	1	0	0	.300	18	19	1	.974
World Series Totals			19	78	8	21	5	1	0	3	.269	40	50	2	.978

ALL-STAR GAME RECORD

Year League	Pos.	AB.	R.	H.	2B.	3B.	HR.	RBI.	B.A.	PO.	A.	E.	F.A.
1946—National..............................	2B	2	0	0	0	0	0	0	.000	0	2	0	1.000
1948—National..............................	2B	4	0	0	0	0	0	0	.000	0	1	0	1.000
1949—National..............................	PH	1	0	1	0	0	0	0	1.000	0	0	0	.000
1950—National..............................	2B	1	1	1	0	0	1	1	1.000	1	1	0	1.000
1951—National..............................	2B	0	0	0	0	0	0	0	.000	0	0	0	.000
1953—National..............................	2B	3	0	0	0	0	0	0	.000	0	3	0	1.000
1954—National..............................	2B	2	0	0	0	0	0	0	.000	1	0	0	1.000
1955—National..............................	2B	6	0	2	0	0	0	0	.333	3	2	0	1.000
1957—National..............................	2B	2	0	0	0	0	0	0	.000	0	0	1	.000
All-Star Game Totals		21	1	4	0	0	1	1	.190	5	9	1	.933

Member of National League All-Star Team in 1952; did not play.

RECORD AS MANAGER

Year Club	League	Position	W.	L.	Year Club	League	Position	W.	L.
1965—St. Louis.............Nat.		Seventh	80	81	1972—St. Louis.............Nat.		Fourth(E)	75	81
1966—St. Louis.............Nat.		Sixth	83	79	1973—St. Louis.............Nat.		Second(E)	81	81
1967—St. Louis.............Nat.		First	101	60	1974—St. Louis.............Nat.		Second(E)	86	75
1968—St. Louis.............Nat.		First	97	65	1975—St. Louis.............Nat.		†Third(E)	82	80
1969—St. Louis.............Nat.		Fourth(E)	87	75	1976—St. Louis.............Nat.		Fifth(E)	72	90
1970—St. Louis.............Nat.		Fourth(E)	76	86	1980—St. Louis‡ ....Nat.		Fourth(E)	18	19
1971—St. Louis.............Nat.		Second(E)	90	72	Major League Totals...............................1028 944				

†Tied for position.

‡Served as interim manager when Whitey Herzog named general manager, August 28 through October 5, 1980.

Coach, St. Louis Cardinals, 1963, 1964, and 1979 through 1981; Oakland A's, 1977 and 1978.

WORLD SERIES RECORD

Year Club	League	W.	L.
1967—St. Louis.............National		4	3
1968—St. Louis.............National		3	4

RONALD RICHARD SCHUELER

Name pronounced SHOO-lur.

(Ron)

Chicago White Sox

Born April 18, 1948, at Hays, Kan.
Height, 6.04. Weight, 205.
Throws and bats righthanded.
Attended Fort Hays State College, Hays, Kan.

Pitched 2-0 no-hit victory against San Antonio, September 7, 1970.

Year Club	League	G.	IP.	W.	L.	Pct.	H.	R.	ER.	SO.	BB.	ERA.
1967—Kinston...............................Carolina		23	137	9	9	.500	152	90	82	87	63	5.39
1968—Greenwood...........................W. Carol.		11	31	1	3	.250	36	21	17	30	25	4.94
1968—Richmond ....Int'national		2	14	1	1	.500	13	4	4	3	2	2.57
1968—Shreveport ....Texas		18	59	5	3	.625	73	47	39	37	21	5.95
1969—Shreveport† ....Texas		134	95	5	7	.417	70	35	33	71	57	3.13
1970—Shreveport ....Texas		26	115	6	10	.375	112	66	57	93	61	4.46
1971—Savannah ....Southern		13	80	5	6	.455	78	32	29	68	17	3.26
1971—Richmond ....Int'national		13	74	4	4	.500	54	31	23	49	32	2.80
1972—Atlanta ....National		37	145	5	8	.385	124	68	59	96	60	3.66
1973—Atlanta‡..............................National		39	186	8	7	.533	179	91	80	124	66	3.87
1974—Philadelphia..........................National		44	203	11	16	.407	202	91	84	109	98	3.72
1975—Philadelphia..........................National		46	93	4	4	.500	88	55	54	69	40	5.23
1976—Philadelphia§.........................National		35	50	1	0	1.000	44	18	16	43	16	2.88
1977—Minnesota x ....American		52	135	8	7	.533	131	74	66	77	61	4.40
1978—Chicago ....American		30	82	3	5	.375	76	50	39	39	39	4.28
1979—Chicago yz ....American		8	20	0	1	.000	19	16	16	6	13	7.20
American League Totals............................		90	237	11	13	.458	226	140	121	122	113	4.59
National League Totals.............................		201	677	29	35	.453	635	323	293	441	280	3.90
Major League Totals		291	914	40	48	.455	861	463	414	563	393	4.08

Selected by Pittsburgh Pirates' organization in 12th round of free-agent draft, June, 1966.

Selected by Atlanta Braves' organization in 3rd round of free-agent draft, January, 1967.

†Played one game in outfield.

‡Traded to Philadelphia Phillies for Pitcher Barry Lersch and Shortstop Craig Robinson, December 3, 1973; Phillies traded First Baseman-Outfielder Bob Beall to Braves for Infielder Gil Garrido, December 10, 1973, to complete deal.

xGranted free agency, November 2, 1977; signed by Chicago White Sox, December 3, 1977.
yPlayer-coach.
zOn disabled list, May 25 to June 24 and July 10 to September 1, 1979.
Coach, Chicago White Sox, 1979 through 1981.

NORMAN BURT SHERRY
(Norm)
Montreal Expos

Born July 16, 1931, at New York, N.Y.
Height, 5.11. Weight, 180.
Threw and batted righthanded.
Brother of Larry Sherry, coach with California Angels and
George Sherry, pitcher in Pittsburgh Pirates' organization, 1951.

Year Club	League	Pos.	G.	AB.	R.	H.	2B.	3B.	HR.	RBI.	B.A.	PO.	A.	E.	F.A.
1950—Santa Barbara	Calif.	C-OF	96	294	35	71	12	1	4	32	.241	394	43	23	.950
1951—Fort Worth	Tex.	C	25	65	1	5	2	0	0	3	.077	90	14	12	.897
1951—Newport News	Pied.	C	72	214	41	50	2	0	2	22	.234	292	33	14	.959
1952-53—Fort Worth	Tex.					(In Military Service)									
1954—Fort Worth	Tex.	C	5	5	3	2	0	0	0	0	.400	14	1	1	.938
1954—Newport News	Pied.	C-P	122	382	56	98	13	3	12	47	.257	★727	63	21	★.974
1955—Fort Worth	Tex.	C	67	165	28	43	10	1	4	26	.261	221	18	5	.980
1956—Fort Worth†	Tex.	C	2	4	0	0	0	0	0	0	.000	7	0	0	1.000
1956—Buffalo	Int.	C-OF	64	181	14	39	5	0	2	7	.215	244	16	7	.974
1957—St. Paul‡	A.A.	C-1-O	60	193	18	47	9	3	2	29	.244	303	25	4	.988
1958—Spokane	P.C.	C	131	417	34	116	27	2	2	41	.278	551	★75	●10	.984
1959—Los Angeles	Nat.	C	2	3	0	1	0	0	0	2	.333	4	0	0	1.000
1959—Spokane	P.C.	C	108	332	35	84	15	1	7	47	.253	433	52	9	.982
1960—Los Angeles	Nat.	C	47	138	22	39	4	1	8	19	.283	282	15	2	.993
1961—Los Angeles§	Nat.	C	47	121	10	31	2	0	5	21	.256	253	16	2	.993
1962—Los Angeles x	Nat.	C	35	88	7	16	2	0	3	16	.182	221	13	2	.992
1963—New York y	Nat.	C	63	147	6	20	1	0	2	11	.136	265	26	3	.981
1964—Buffalo	Int.	C	100	289	34	67	13	0	7	43	.232	447	38	7	.986
1965—Santa Barbara z	Calif.	C	33	86	7	23	4	0	2	15	.267	154	9	4	.976
1966—Santa Barbara z	Calif.	PH	2	2	0	2	0	0	0	0	1.000	....	....	....	......
1967—Santa Barbara z	Calif.	C	15	34	2	5	3	0	0	4	.147	53	2	1	.982
1972—Shreveport z	Tex.	C	4	9	2	3	3	0	0	3	.333	23	1	0	1.000
Major League Totals			194	497	45	107	9	1	18	69	.215	525	70	9	.985

†On disabled list, April 13 to May 22 and May 26 to June 13, 1956.
‡On disabled list, May 21 to July 24, 1957.
§On disabled list, July 12 to August 14, 1961.
xSold to New York Mets, October 11, 1962.
yReleased by New York Mets' organization, October 15, 1964.
zPlayer-manager.

PITCHING RECORD

Year Club	League	G.	IP.	W.	L.	Pct.	H.	R.	ER.	SO.	BB.	ERA.
1954—Newport News	Piedmont	1	⅓	0	0	.000	1	0	0	0	0	0.00
1965—Spokane	P. Coast	1	...	0	0	.000	..	...	...	...	...	...

RECORD AS MANAGER

Year Club	League	Position	W.	L.	Year Club	League	Position	W.	L.
1965—Santa Barbara	Calif.	Sixth	30	40	1972—Shreveport	Tex.	Fourth(E)	64	76
(Second Half)		†Fifth	31	39	1973—El Paso	Tex.	Second(W)	69	71
1966—Santa Barbara	Calif.	Fifth	35	35	1974—Salt Lake City	P.C.	Third(E)	69	73
(Second Half)		†Fifth	34	36	1975—Salt Lake City	P.C.	‡First(E)	80	64
1967—Santa Barbara	Calif.	†Second	38	32	1976—California§	Amer.	Fourth(W)	37	29
(Second Half)		Third	39	31	1977—California x	Amer.	Fifth(W)	39	42
1969—Idaho Falls	Pioneer	Sixth	30	42	Major League Totals			76	71

†Tied for position.
‡Lost playoff to Hawaii, four games to two.
§Replaced Dick Williams, July 23, 1976.
xReplaced by Dave Garcia, July 11, 1977.
Scout, New York Yankees, 1968; coach, California Angels, 1970, 1971 and 1976; coach, Montreal Expos, 1978 through 1981.

ROBERT RALPH SKINNER
(Bob)
Pittsburgh Pirates

Born October 3, 1931, at LaJolla, Calif.
Height, 6.04½. Weight, 205.
Threw and batted lefthanded.
Hobby—Automobiles.

Named THE SPORTING NEWS Minor League Manager of the Year, 1967.

Year Club	League	Pos.	G.	AB.	R.	H.	2B.	3B.	HR.	RBI.	B.A.	PO.	A.	E.	F.A.
1951—Waco	Big St.	1B	98	367	67	104	22	3	9	58	.283	679	52	★35	.954
1951—Mayfield	Kitty	1B	29	106	40	50	9	4	6	29	.472	164	10	8	.956

Year Club League	Pos.	G.	AB.	R.	H.	2B.	3B.	HR.	RBI.	B.A.	PO.	A.	E.	F.A.
1952-53—Burlington.....Carol.				(In Military Service)										
1954—Pittsburgh.........Nat.	1B-OF	132	470	67	117	15	9	8	46	.249	1026	84	16	.986
1955—New Orleans .....South.	1B	86	321	62	111	24	6	8	62	.346	724	52	16	.980
1956—Pittsburgh.........Nat.	O-1-3	113	233	29	47	8	3	5	29	.202	217	8	2	.991
1957—Pittsburgh.........Nat.	O-1-3	126	387	58	118	12	6	13	45	.305	232	17	8	.969
1958—Pittsburgh.........Nat.	OF	144	529	93	170	33	9	13	70	.321	232	19	6	.977
1959—Pittsburgh.........Nat.	OF-1B	143	547	78	153	18	4	13	61	.280	285	9	11	.964
1960—Pittsburgh.........Nat.	OF	145	571	83	156	33	6	15	86	.273	250	13	5	.981
1961—Pittsburgh.........Nat.	OF	119	381	61	102	20	3	3	42	.268	175	5	5	.973
1962—Pittsburgh.........Nat.	OF	144	510	87	154	29	7	20	75	.302	210	6	9	.960
1963—Pitt.†-Cin. ....Nat.	OF	106	316	43	82	15	7	3	25	.259	131	4	1	.993
1964—Cin.‡-St. Louis .Nat.	OF	80	177	16	45	8	0	4	21	.254	62	4	5	.930
1965—St. Louis ....Nat.	OF	80	152	25	47	5	4	5	26	.309	43	0	3	.935
1966—St. Louis ....Nat.	PH	49	45	2	7	1	0	1	5	.156	0	0	0	.000
Major League Totals		1381	4318	642	1198	197	58	103	531	.277	2863	169	71	.977

†Traded to Cincinnati Reds for Outfielder Jerry Lynch, May 23, 1963.
‡Traded to St. Louis Cardinals for cash and Catcher Jim Saul, June 13, 1964; Saul was transferred from Jacksonville to San Diego.

WORLD SERIES RECORD

Year Club League	Pos.	G.	AB.	R.	H.	2B.	3B.	HR.	RBI.	B.A.	PO.	A.	E.	F.A.
1960—Pittsburgh.........Nat.	OF	2	5	2	1	0	0	0	1	.200	4	1	0	1.000
1964—St. Louis ....Nat.	PH	4	3	0	2	1	0	0	1	.667	0	0	0	.000
World Series Totals		6	8	2	3	1	0	0	2	.375	4	1	0	1.000

ALL-STAR GAME RECORD

Year League	Pos.	AB.	R.	H.	2B.	3B.	HR.	RBI.	B.A.	PO.	A.	E.	F.A.
1958—National............................	OF	3	0	1	0	0	0	1	.333	2	0	0	1.000
1960—National (both games)	OF	7	1	2	0	0	0	1	.286	3	0	0	1.000
All-Star Game Totals		10	1	3	0	0	0	2	.300	5	0	0	1.000

RECORD AS MANAGER

Year Club League	Position	W.	L.
1967—San Diego ....P. C.	†First(E)	85	63
1968—San Diego‡..........P. C.	Fourth(E)	31	28
1968—Philadelphia§......Nat.	xSeventh	48	59
1969—Philadelphia y.....Nat.	Fifth(E)	44	64
1977—San Diego z.........Nat.	Fourth(W)	1	0
Major League Totals...............................		93	123

†Defeated Spokane in championship playoff, four games to two.
‡Promoted to Philadelphia Phillies, June 15.
§Replaced Gene Mauch with club in fifth place, June 16.
xTied for position with Los Angeles Dodgers.
yReplaced by George Myatt, August 7.
zServed as interim manager, May 29, replacing John McNamara with club in fifth place.
Coach, San Diego Padres, 1970 through 1973; Pittsburgh Pirates, 1974 through 1976; coach, San Diego Padres, 1977; coach, California Angels, 1978; coach, Pittsburgh Pirates, 1979 through 1981.

DENNIS JAMES SOMMERS
(Denny)
Cleveland Indians

Born July 12, 1940, at Hortonville, Wis.
Height, 6.02. Weight, 197.
Threw right and batted lefthanded.
Hobbies—Basketball and movies.
Attended Wisconsin State University, Oshkosh, Wis.

Year Club League	Pos.	G.	AB.	R.	H.	2B.	3B.	HR.	RBI.	B.A.	PO.	A.	E.	F.A.
1958—Michigan City....Midw.	OF	37	102	11	17	1	0	1	14	.167	44	1	3	.938
1959—Michigan City....Midw.	C-OF	122	406	54	87	14	2	7	47	.214	604	51	12	.982
1960—Eugene ....Northw.	C	108	306	27	75	11	3	3	47	.245	515	32	12	.979
1961—Vic.-R.G.V. ....Texas	C	67	198	18	47	3	1	1	19	.237	370	33	1	.998
1962—Springfield ....East.	C	78	218	17	52	6	1	0	21	.239	392	15	8	.981
1963—Springfield ....East.	C	140	464	33	93	12	0	3	47	.200	*934	50	7	.993
1964—Springfield ....East.	C	123	401	27	86	15	0	1	35	.214	*795	•55	10	.988
1965—Springfield ....East.	C	88	281	28	68	9	0	1	21	.242	616	36	7	.989
1965—Tacoma ....P. C.	C	24	79	8	16	2	0	0	7	.203	137	11	4	.974
1966—Phoenix...............P. C.	C	52	101	8	23	7	0	0	12	.228	117	7	0	1.000
1966—Lexington†..........W. Car.	PH	8	7	0	1	1	0	0	2	.143	....	....	....	......
1967—Decatur†.............Midw.	PH	9	7	0	1	1	0	0	1	.143	....	....	....	......

†Player-manager.

DID YOU KNOW—
That the THE SPORTING NEWS was first published on March 17, 1886.

Year	Club	League	Position	W.	L.	Year	Club	League	Position	W.	L.
1966–Lexington		W. Carol.†	Seventh	15	28	1971–Fresno		Calif.	§First	42	28
1967–Decatur		Midwest	Fifth	27	30	(Second Half)			Seventh	28	42
(Second Half)			Second	35	28	1972–Amarillo		Texas	Second(W)	71	68
1968–Decatur		Midwest	Fifth	29	27	1973–Amarillo		Texas	Fourth(W)	64	75
(Second Half)			‡First	40	21	1974–Amarillo		Texas	Second(W)	69	62
1969–Fresno		California	Second	38	32	1975–Lafayette		Texas	xFirst(E)	72	57
(Second Half)			Fifth	34	36	1976–Midland		Texas	Fourth(W)	62	74
1970–Fresno		California	Fifth	36	33	1979–Montgomery		South.	yFirst(W)	36	34
(Second Half)			Fifth	35	35	(Second Half)			Fifth	26	47

†Replaced Alex Cosmidis, July 8, 1966.
‡Lost playoff to Quad Cities, two games to one.
§Lost playoff to Visalia, two games to one.
xMidland and Lafayette each won two games in playoff; rain prevented completion of series, and Midland and Lafayette were declared co-champions by league president.
yTied for position with Memphis; lost playoff for first-half championship to Memphis, one game to none.
Coach, New York Mets, 1977 and 1978; coach, Cleveland Indians, 1980 and 1981.

ALBERT LEE STANGE

Name pronounced STANG.

(Known by middle name.)

Boston Red Sox

Born October 27, 1936, at Chicago, Ill.
Height, 5.10. Weight, 170.
Threw and batted righthanded.
Hobbies–Bowling and golf.
Attended Drake University, Des Moines, Ia.

Tied major league record for most strikeouts in one inning by a pitcher (4), seventh inning, September 2, 1964.
Led Carolina League in games started with 35 and complete games with 20 and tied for lead in shutouts with 3 in 1960.

Year	Club	League	G.	IP.	W.	L.	Pct.	H.	R.	ER.	SO.	BB.	ERA.
1957–Fort Walton Beach		Ala.-Fla.	22	95	5	6	.455	89	64	57	62	74	5.40
1958–Fort Walton Beach		Ala.-Fla.	32	217	13	12	.520	192	100	81	171	120	3.36
1959–Fox Cities		I.I.I.	34	79	4	6	.400	96	62	52	72	53	5.92
1960–Wilson		Carolina	39	*251	*20	*13	606	*235	*125	*100	196	92	3.59
1961–Minnesota		American	7	12	1	0	1.000	15	6	4	10	10	3.00
1961–Syracuse		Int'national	56	112	7	12	.368	102	56	47	90	47	3.78
1962–Minnesota		American	44	95	4	3	.571	98	57	47	70	39	4.45
1963–Dallas-Fort Worth		P. Coast	9	66	7	1	.875	53	15	15	74	8	2.05
1963–Minnesota		American	32	165	12	5	.706	145	53	48	100	43	2.62
1964–Minnesota†-Cleveland		American	37	171	7	14	.333	176	92	84	132	50	4.42
1965–Cleveland		American	41	132	8	4	.667	122	50	49	80	26	3.34
1966–Cleveland‡-Boston		American	36	169	8	9	.471	157	70	62	85	46	3.30
1967–Boston		American	35	182	8	10	.444	171	64	56	101	32	2.77
1968–Boston		American	50	103	5	5	.500	89	54	45	53	25	3.93
1969–Boston		American	41	137	6	9	.400	137	70	56	59	56	3.68
1970–Boston§-Chicago x		American	36	50	3	2	.600	62	37	30	28	17	5.40
Major League Totals			359	1216	62	61	.504	1172	553	481	718	344	3.56

†Traded to Cleveland Indians with Outfielder George Banks for Pitcher Jim Grant, June 15, 1964.
‡Traded with Pitcher Don McMahon to Boston Red Sox for Pitcher Dick Radatz, June 2, 1966.
§Sold to Chicago White Sox, June 29, 1970.
xUnconditionally released by Chicago White Sox, December 12, 1970.

WORLD SERIES RECORD

Year	Club	League	G.	IP.	W.	L.	Pct.	H.	R.	ER.	SO.	BB.	ERA.
1967–Boston		American	1	2	0	0	.000	3	1	0	0	0	0.00

RECORD AS MANAGER

Year	Club	League	Position	W.	L.
1976–Tucson†		P.C.	Fourth(E)	15	20

†Replaced Harry Bright with club in fourth place (record of 39-68), July 31, 1976.
Coach, Boston Red Sox, 1972 through 1974 and 1981; coach, Minnesota Twins, 1975; minor league instructor, Oakland A's, 1976; coach, Oakland A's, 1977 through 1979; scout, Boston Red Sox, 1980.

HERMAN PAUL STARRETTE

Name pronounced Stah-RET.

(Herm)

Philadelphia Phillies

Born November 20, 1938, at Statesville, N. C.
Height, 6.01. Weight, 185.
Threw and batted righthanded.
Hobbies–Hunting and fishing.
Attended Lenoir Rhyne College, Hickory, N. C.

Year Club	League	G.	IP.	W.	L.	Pct.	H.	R.	ER.	SO.	BB.	ERA.
1958—Aberdeen	Northern	21	144	7	9	.438	136	70	56	103	58	3.50
1959—Aberdeen	Northern	32	196	17	7	.708	208	94	76	154	54	3.49
1960—Vancouver	P. Coast	11	27	0	2	.000	35	21	20	10	13	6.67
1960—Stockton	California	24	142	9	7	.563	159	66	54	91	31	3.42
1961—Fox Cities	I.I.I.	35	146	11	7	.611	153	64	59	128	54	3.64
1962—Elmira	Eastern	•61	163	14	10	.583	155	61	48	133	29	2.65
1963—Rochester	Int'national	24	48	6	2	.750	40	11	6	28	14	1.13
1963—Baltimore	American	18	26	0	1	.000	26	10	10	13	7	3.46
1964—Rochester	Int'national	30	55	5	2	.714	46	14	12	46	11	1.96
1964—Baltimore	American	5	11	1	0	1.000	9	3	2	5	6	1.64
1965—Rochester	Int'national	44	78	3	3	.500	79	29	25	43	14	2.88
1965—Baltimore	American	4	9	0	0	.000	8	3	1	3	3	1.00
1966—Rochester	Int'national	14	21	0	1	.000	36	23	20	8	5	8.57
Major League Totals		27	46	1	1	.500	43	16	13	21	16	2.54

Coach, Rochester (International League), 1967; Minor League Pitching Instructor, Baltimore Orioles, 1968 through 1973; coach, Atlanta Braves, 1974 through 1976; coach, San Francisco Giants, 1977 and 1978; coach, Philadelphia Phillies, 1979 through 1981.

RICHARD FRANCIS STELMASZEK

Name pronounced Stel-may-zik.

(Rick)

Minnesota Twins

Born October 8, 1948, at Chicago, Ill.
Height, 6.01. Weight, 200.
Threw right and batted lefthanded.
Attended DePaul University, Chicago, Ill.
Son of Ray Stelmack, former pitcher-outfielder in New York Yankees' organization.

Led New York-Pennsylvania League catchers in passed balls with 16 and tied for league lead in double plays with 4 in 1968.

Tied for Eastern League lead in double plays by catchers with 8 in 1970.

Year Club	League	Pos.	G.	AB.	R.	H.	2B.	3B.	HR.	RBI.	B.A.	PO.	A.	E.	F.A.
1968—Salisbury	W. Car.	C-3	55	153	15	30	2	3	2	16	.196	296	37	10	.971
1968—Geneva	NYP	C	46	127	15	35	5	2	3	21	.276	386	18	6	.985
1969—Shelby	W.C.	•C-O	115	358	54	103	16	5	5	58	.288	•548	54	14	.977
1970—Pittsfield	East.	C	128	386	50	95	11	4	4	47	.246	•782	•67	•17	.980
1971—Denver	A.A.	C	73	194	27	48	1	1	1	25	.247	402	28	3	.993
1971—Washington	Amer.	C	6	9	0	0	0	0	0	0	.000	4	1	0	1.000
1972—Hawaii	P.C.	C	5	10	0	0	0	0	0	2	.000	20	4	0	1.000
1972—Denver-Ind.	A.A.	C	94	246	22	56	6	2	1	34	.228	527	38	12	.979
1973—Salt Lake City	P.C.	C	43	106	17	25	7	1	0	8	.236	214	32	2	.992
1973—Tex.†-Calif.	Amer.	C	29	35	2	5	1	0	0	3	.143	71	5	0	1.000
1974—Salt Lake City‡	P.C.	C	83	260	39	70	12	3	6	40	.269	333	25	7	.981
1974—Chicago	Nat.	C	25	44	2	10	2	0	1	7	.227	55	2	1	.983
1975—Wichita§	A.A.	C-OF	106	336	40	89	14	3	6	47	.265	474	35	11	.979
1976—Syracuse x	Int.	C	74	214	30	47	10	0	2	23	.220	306	35	6	.983
1977—Tucson y	P.C.	C	83	240	27	68	9	1	2	35	.283	434	48	10	.980
American League Totals			35	44	2	5	1	0	0	3	.114	75	6	0	1.000
National League Totals			25	44	2	10	2	0	1	7	.227	55	2	1	.983
Major League Totals			60	88	4	15	3	0	1	10	.170	130	8	1	.993

†Traded with First Baseman Mike Epstein and Pitcher Rich Hand to California Angels for First Baseman Jim Spencer and Pitcher Lloyd Allen, May 20, 1973.

‡Traded to Chicago Cubs for Pitcher Horacio Pina, July 27, 1974.

§Traded to New York Yankees for Pitcher Gerry Pirtle, January 23, 1976.

xSold to Texas Rangers' organization, March 28, 1977.

yGranted free agency, October 20, 1977.

RECORD AS MANAGER

Named Midwest League Manager of the Year, 1980.

Year Club	League	Position	W.	L.	Year Club	League	Position	W.	L.
1978—Wis. Rapids	Mid.	Fourth(N)	†29	39			Third(N)	†34	31
(Second Half)		Third(N)	33	37	1980—Wis. Rapids‡	Mid.	Fourth(N)	32	39
1979—Wis. Rapids	Mid.	Fourth(N)	26	41	(Second Half)		First(N)	45	25

†One tie game.

‡Lost playoff to Waterloo, two games to one.

Coach, Minnesota Twins, 1981.

WESLEY GAY STOCK

(Wes)

Seattle Mariners

Born April 10, 1934, at Longview, Wash.
Height, 6.01½. Weight, 182.
Threw and batted righthanded.
Hobbies—Hunting and golf.
Attended Washington State College, Pullman, Wash.
Father of Jeff Stock, player with Seattle Sounders of North American Soccer League.

Year Club	League	G.	IP.	W.	L.	Pct.	H.	R.	ER.	SO.	BB.	ERA.
1956—Aberdeen	Northern	30	181	14	6	●.700	169	90	67	★182	109	3.33
1957-58—Knoxville	Sally					(In Military Service)						
1959—Baltimore	American	7	13	0	0	.000	16	6	5	8	2	3.46
1959—Miami	Int'national	6	15	0	1	.000	21	19	15	9	13	9.00
1959—Vancouver	P. Coast	22	98	6	6	.500	87	41	37	59	40	3.40
1960—Miami	Int'national	21	128	8	6	.571	102	41	32	102	34	2.25
1960—Baltimore	American	17	34	2	2	.500	26	11	11	23	14	2.91
1961—Baltimore	American	35	72	5	0	1.000	58	24	24	47	27	3.00
1962—Baltimore	American	53	65	3	2	.600	50	33	32	34	36	4.43
1963—Baltimore	American	47	75	7	0	1.000	69	41	33	55	31	3.96
1964—Baltimore†-K.C.	American	64	114	8	3	.727	86	30	29	115	42	2.29
1965—Kansas City	American	62	100	0	4	.000	96	62	58	52	40	5.22
1966—Vancouver	P. Coast	1	1	0	0	.000	0	0	0	1	0	0.00
1966—Kansas City	American	35	44	2	2	.500	30	15	13	31	31	2.66
1967—Kansas City	American	1	1	0	0	.000	3	2	2	0	2	18.00
Major League Totals		321	518	27	13	.675	434	224	207	365	215	3.60

†Traded to Kansas City Athletics for Catcher Charlie Lau, June 15, 1964.

Coach, Kansas City Athletics, 1967; Minor League Pitching Instructor, New York Mets, 1968 and 1969; coach, Milwaukee Brewers, 1970 through 1972; Oakland Athletics, 1973 through 1976; Seattle Mariners, 1977 through 1981.

JOHN PETER SULLIVAN
Atlanta Braves

Born January 3, 1941, at Somerville, N. J.
Height, 6.00. Weight, 197.
Threw right and batted lefthanded.
Hobbies—Hunting and golf.

Year Club	League	Pos.	G.	AB.	R.	H.	2B.	3B.	HR.	RBI.	B.A.	PO.	A.	E.	F.A.
1959—Erie	N.Y.-P.	C	110	348	69	112	29	1	13	58	.322	★604	73	11	★.984
1960—Durham	Carol.	C	125	419	59	117	18	4	11	71	.279	813	★116	22	.977
1961—Birmingham	South.	C	126	415	47	95	14	2	8	57	.229	★732	51	7	.991
1962—Knoxville	Sally	C	117	389	50	104	18	2	6	36	.267	★685	★66	7	★.991
1963—Syracuse	Int.	C	106	323	35	85	14	1	6	35	.263	617	★67	6	.991
1963—Detroit	Amer.	C	3	5	0	0	0	0	0	0	.000	9	·1	0	1.000
1964—Syracuse	Int.	C-1B	93	264	29	58	9	4	6	27	.220	421	43	4	.991
1964—Detroit	Amer.	C	2	3	0	0	0	0	0	0	.000	2	2	0	1.000
1965—Detroit	Amer.	C	34	86	5	23	0	0	2	11	.267	163	14	1	.994
1965—Syracuse	Int.	C	29	77	10	13	2	0	2	8	.169	150	12	2	.988
1966—Vancouver†	P. C.	C	83	238	34	78	12	2	5	34	.328	466	37	4	.992
1967—New York‡	Nat.	C	65	147	4	32	5	0	0	6	.218	201	17	2	.991
1968—San Diego	P. C.	C	83	256	18	63	11	0	1	23	.246	417	37	3	★.993
1968—Philadelphia§	Nat.	C	12	18	0	4	0	0	0	1	.222	26	3	1	.967
1969—Rochester x	Int.	C	95	293	26	74	17	0	4	44	.253	★509	41	8	.986
1970—Omaha	A. A.	C	64	160	10	41	12	0	1	20	.256	287	31	2	.994
1971—Omaha	A. A.	C	82	215	22	71	14	2	4	40	.330	430	37	2	.996
1972—Jacksonville y	South.	C-1B-P	88	220	19	56	11	0	3	32	.255	392	31	4	.991
Major League Totals			116	259	9	59	5	0	2	18	.228	401	37	4	.991

†Drafted by New York Mets from Syracuse (Detroit Tigers' organization), November 28, 1966.
‡Sold to Philadelphia Phillies' organization, February 19, 1968.
§Sold to Baltimore Orioles' organization, April 8, 1969.
xSold to Kansas City Royals' organization, April 13, 1970.
yPlayer-coach.

PITCHING RECORD

Year Club	League	G.	IP.	W.	L.	Pct.	H.	R.	ER.	SO.	BB.	ERA.
1972—Jacksonville	Southern	1	2	0	0	.000	0	0	0	0	0	0.00

RECORD AS MANAGER

Year Club	League	Position	W.	L.	Year Club	League	Position	W.	L.
1973—Kingsport	Appal.	First	†53	17	1976—Waterloo	Midw.	First(N)	38	24
1974—Waterloo	Midw.	Second(N)	39	22	(Second Half)		‡First(N)	40	28
(Second Half)		Third(N)	29	34	1977—Omaha	A. A.	First(E)	76	59
1975—Waterloo	Midw.	First(N)	†49	13	1978—Omaha	A. A.	xFirst(W)	66	79
(Second Half)		First(N)	44	22					

†Record includes one tie.
‡Won championship playoffs from Quad Cities, two games to none.
§Lost championship playoffs to Denver, four games to two.
xWon championship playoffs from Indianapolis, four games to one.
Coach, Kansas City Royals, 1979; coach, Atlanta Braves, 1980 and 1981.

WILLARD WAYNE TERWILLIGER
(Known by middle name.)
Texas Rangers

Born June 27, 1925, at Clare, Mich.
Height, 5.11½. Weight, 170.
Threw and batted righthanded.

Attended Western Michigan University, Kalamazoo, Mich., received
Bachelor of Science degree in Physical Education.
Led American Association in stolen bases in 1958 with 24.

Year Club	League	Pos.	G.	AB.	R.	H.	2B.	3B.	HR.	RBI.	B.A.	PO.	A.	E.	F.A.
1948—Des Moines ....West.		2B	18	46	10	9	2	0	0	4	.196	30	47	2	.975
1949—Los Angeles ......P. C.		2B	115	432	80	119	28	2	8	46	.275	297	329	18	.972
1949—Chicago ....Nat.		2B	36	112	11	25	2	1	2	10	.223	77	103	4	.978
1950—Chicago ....Nat.		INF.-OF	133	480	63	116	22	3	10	32	.242	314	380	24	.967
1951—Chicago†-Brook. Nat.		2B-3B	87	242	37	55	7	0	0	14	.227	167	187	9	.965
1952—St. Paul‡ ....A. A.		INF.-O	77	125	32	39	6	0	4	17	.312	61	82	9	.941
1953—Washington ....Amer.		2B	134	464	62	117	24	4	4	46	.252	333	395	13	982
1954—Washington ....Amer.		2-3-S	106	337	42	70	10	1	3	24	.208	227	274	16	.969
1955—Minneapolis ......A. A.		2B	72	276	51	82	22	0	4	28	.297	153	172	7	.979
1955—New York ....Nat.		2-3-SS	80	257	29	66	16	1	1	18	.257	212	240	7	.985
1956—New York ....Nat.		2B	14	18	0	4	1	0	0	0	.222	14	9	1	.958
1956—Minneapolis ......A. A.		2B	90	290	39	71	14	3	2	27	.245	203	231	16	.964
1957—Minneapolis ......A. A.		2B	144	508	84	137	35	4	7	50	.270	359	365	9	*.988
1958—Charleston§ ......A. A.		2B	146	535	103	144	23	2	2	38	.269	*361	397	9	*.988
1959—Kansas City ......Amer.		2-S-3	74	180	27	48	11	0	2	18	.267	144	167	9	.972
1960—Kansas City ......Amer.		2B	2	1	0	0	0	0	0	0	.000	1	1	0	1.000
1960—Richmond ....Int.		2B	92	277	41	57	9	0	4	20	.206	179	259	7	.984
1961—Greensboro ....Carol.		PH	1	1	0	0	0	0	0	0	.000	0	0	0	.000
1962-63......................						(Did not play)									
1964—Geneva ....NYP		PH	1	0	0	0	0	0	0	0	.000	0	0	0	.000
1965-66......................						(Did not play)									
1967—Hawaii ....P. C.		2B	7	5	2	0	0	0	0	0	.000	3	5	0	1.000
1968—Buffalo ....Int.		3B	2	6	1	1	1	0	0	0	.167	3	4	2	.778
National League Totals			350	1109	140	266	48	5	13	74	.240	784	919	49	.972
American League Totals			316	982	131	235	45	5	9	88	.239	705	837	38	.976
Major League Totals......................			666	2091	271	501	93	10	22	162	.204	1489	1756	87	.974

†Traded with Pitcher Johnny Schmitz, Catcher Al (Rube) Walker and Outfielder Andy Pafko to Brooklyn
Dodgers for Pitcher Joe Hatton, Catcher Bruce Edwards, Second Baseman Eddie Miksis and Outfielder Gene
Hermanski, June 15, 1951.
‡Recalled by Brooklyn Dodgers; sold to Washington Senators, September 23, 1952.
§Drafted by Kansas City Athletics from Charleston (Detroit Tigers' organization), December 1, 1958.

RECORD AS MANAGER

Year Club	League	Position	W.	L.	Year Club	League	Position	W.	L.
1961—Greensboro .... Carol.		Third	34	35	1975—Lynchburg .... Carol.		Fourth	30	36
(Second Half)		Third	36	33	(Second Half)		Fourth	30	42
1962—Pensacola .... Ala.-Fla.		First	79	38	1976—Asheville‡.......... W. Car.		First	37	31
1963—Wis. Rapids........ Midwest		Eighth	25	34	(Second Half)		Second	39	31
(Second Half)		Fourth	33	28	1977—Asheville .... W. Car.		Second	37	32
1964—Geneva .... NYP		Second	79	51	(Second Half)		Second	44	26
1965—Geneva .... NYP		Fourth	32	31	1978—Asheville .... W. Car.		Third	37	33
(Second Half)		Third	33	30	(Second Half)		Fourth	36	34
1966—Burlington .... Carol.		Second(W)	76	62	1979—Asheville .... W. Car.		Third	36	32
1967—Hawaii............... P. C.		Sixth(W)	60	87	(Second Half)		Third	†39	31
1968—Buffalo .... Int.		Seventh	66	81	1980—Tulsa .... Texas		Second(E)	40	27
1973—Columbus .... South.		Third(E)	†69	70	(Second Half)		Third(E)	35	34

†One tie game.
‡Lost championship playoff to Greenwood, three games to one.
Coach, Washington Senators, 1969 through 1971; coach, Texas Rangers, 1972 and 1981.

ROBERT TOLAN
(Bobby)
San Diego Padres

Born November 19, 1945, at Los Angeles, Calif.
Height, 5.11. Weight, 180.
Throws and bats lefthanded.
Hobby—Basketball.

Major League stolen bases: 1965 (2), 1966 (1), 1967 (12), 1968 (9), 1969 (26), 1970 (57), 1972 (42), 1973 (15),
1974 (7), 1975 (11), 1976 (10), 1977 (1), 1979 (0). Total—193.
Led National League in stolen bases with 57 in 1970.
Led National League outfielders in total chances with 414 in 1972.
Named outfielder on THE SPORTING NEWS National League All-Star team, 1970.
Named THE SPORTING NEWS National League Comeback Player of the Year, 1972.

Year Club	League	Pos.	G.	AB.	R.	H.	2B.	3B.	HR.	RBI.	B.A.	PO.	A.	E.	F.A.
1963—Reno† ....Calif.		1B-OF	75	299	63	81	12	5	8	42	.271	564	27	11	.982
1964—Tulsa ....Texas		*OF-1B	130	475	74	141	27	10	9	68	.297	241	19	*10	.963
1965—Jacksonville ......Int.		OF-1B	145	*558	86	162	25	●10	8	48	.290	320	10	8	.976
1965—St. Louis ....Nat.		OF	17	69	8	13	2	0	0	6	.188	32	0	1	.970
1966—Tulsa ....P. C.		1B-OF	44	171	28	57	6	3	4	26	.333	260	9	7	.975
1966—St. Louis‡..........Nat.		OF-1B	43	93	10	16	5	1	1	6	.172	41	1	2	.955
1967—St. Louis ....Nat.		OF-1B	110	265	35	67	7	3	6	32	.253	225	9	1	.996
1968—St. Louis§..........Nat.		OF-1B	92	278	28	64	12	1	5	17	.230	199	12	4	.981
1969—Cincinnati ....Nat.		OF	152	637	104	194	25	10	21	93	.305	●362	6	10	.974

— 606 —

Year Club	League	Pos.	G.	AB.	R.	H.	2B.	3B.	HR.	RBI.	B.A.	PO.	A.	E.	F.A.
1970—Cincinnati ....Nat.		OF	152	589	112	186	34	6	16	80	.316	349	7	8	.978
1971—Cincinnati x.......Nat.						(Injured; did not play.)									
1972—Cincinnati ....Nat.		OF	149	604	88	171	28	5	8	82	.283	*401	9	4	.990
1973—Cincinnati y.......Nat.		OF	129	457	42	94	14	2	9	51	.206	279	9	10	.966
1974—San Diego z ....Nat.		OF	95	357	45	95	16	1	8	40	.266	161	5	5	.971
1975—San Diego a ....Nat.		OF-1B	147	506	58	129	19	4	5	43	.255	336	20	7	.981
1976—Philadelphia .....Nat.		1B-OF	110	272	32	71	7	0	5	35	.261	395	14	5	.988
1977—Phil.b-Pitts.c .....Nat.		1B-OF	64	90	8	17	4	0	2	10	.189	125	7	1	.992
1978—Nankai d ....Pac.		1B-OF	98	360	31	96	10	1	6	36	.267	210	5	2	.991
1979—Puerto Rico e ...Int-Am.		....	30	109	7	31	6	0	2	11	.284	....			
1979—San Diego f ....Nat.		1B-OF	22	21	2	4	0	1	0	2	.190	10	2	0	1.000
Major League Totals			1282	4238	572	1121	173	34	86	497	.265	2910	101	58	.981

†Drafted by St. Louis Cardinals from Columbus (Pittsburgh Pirates' organization), December 2, 1963.
‡On military list, August 29 through December 28.
§Traded with Pitcher Wayne Granger to Cincinnati Reds for Outfielder Vada Pinson, October 11, 1968.
xOn disabled list, March 21, 1971 through April 15, 1972.
yTraded with Pitcher Dave Tomlin to San Diego Padres for Pitcher Clay Kirby, November 9, 1973.
zOn disabled list, July 19 to September 15, 1974.
aReleased, February 12, 1976; signed as a free agent by Philadelphia Phillies, March 22, 1976.
bReleased May 25, 1977; signed as free agent by Pittsburgh Pirates, June 10, 1977.
cGranted free agency, October 25, 1977; signed by Nankai Hawks of Japanese Baseball League, 1978.
dSigned by Puerto Rico, April 21, 1979.
eReleased June 1, 1979; signed by San Diego Padres, July 5, 1979.
fReleased, October 19, 1979.
Coach, San Diego Padres, June 20, 1980 through 1981.

CHAMPIONSHIP SERIES RECORD

Year Club	League	Pos.	G.	AB.	R.	H.	2B.	3B.	HR.	RBI.	B.A.	PO.	A.	E.	F.A.
1970—Cincinnati ....Nat.		OF	3	12	3	5	0	0	1	2	.417	5	0	0	1.000
1972—Cincinnati ....Nat.		OF	5	21	3	5	1	1	0	4	.238	13	0	0	1.000
1976—Philadelphia ......Nat.		PH-OF-1	3	2	0	0	0	0	0	0	.000	1	0	0	1.000
Championship Series Totals............			11	35	6	10	1	1	1	6	.286	19	0	0	1.000

WORLD SERIES RECORD

Year Club	League	Pos.	G.	AB.	R.	H.	2B.	3B.	HR.	RBI.	B.A.	PO.	A.	E.	F.A.
1967—St. Louis ....Nat.		PH	3	2	1	0	0	0	0	0	.000	0	0	0	.000
1968—St. Louis ....Nat.		PH	1	1	0	0	0	0	0	0	.000	0	0	0	.000
1970—Cincinnati ....Nat.		OF	5	19	5	4	1	0	1	1	.211	4	0	1	.800
1972—Cincinnati ....Nat.		OF	7	26	2	7	1	0	0	6	.269	11	0	1	.917
World Series Totals			16	48	8	11	2	0	1	7	.229	15	0	2	.882

JEFFREY ALLEN TORBORG
(Jeff)
New York Yankees

Born November 26, 1941, at Westfield, N. J.
Height, 6.00½. Weight, 195.
Threw and batted righthanded.
Hobby—Sports.
Attended Rutgers University, New Brunswick, N. J.; received Bachelor of Science degree in Education. Did graduate studies at Montclair State College, Montclair, N. J.; earned Master's degree in Athletic Administration.
Received reported $100,000 bonus to sign with Los Angeles Dodgers, 1963.

Year Club	League	Pos.	G.	AB.	R.	H.	2B.	3B.	HR.	RBI.	B.A.	PO.	A.	E.	F.A.
1963—Albuquerque......Texas		C	64	184	19	41	10	3	1	18	.223	349	27	6	.984
1964—Los Angeles.......Nat.		C	28	43	4	10	1	1	0	4	.233	80	4	2	.977
1965—Los Angeles.......Nat.		C	56	150	8	36	5	1	3	13	.240	300	19	3	.991
1966—Los Angeles.......Nat.		C	46	120	4	27	3	0	1	13	.225	269	17	4	.986
1967—Los Angeles.......Nat.		C	76	196	11	42	4	1	2	12	.214	413	30	5	.989
1968—Los Angeles.......Nat.		C	37	93	2	15	2	0	0	4	.161	206	20	2	.991
1969—Los Angeles.......Nat.		C	51	124	7	23	4	0	0	7	.185	251	26	1	.996
1970—Los Angeles†.....Nat.		C	64	134	11	31	8	0	1	17	.231	275	16	5	.983
1971—California‡........Amer.		C	55	123	6	25	5	0	0	5	.203	208	17	3	.987
1972—California‡‡......Amer.		C	59	153	5	32	3	0	0	8	.209	383	28	1	.998
1973—California§ x......Amer.		C	102	255	20	56	7	0	1	18	.220	611	37	6	.991
National League Totals....................			358	860	47	184	27	3	7	70	.214	1794	132	22	.989
American League Totals.................			216	531	31	113	15	0	1	31	.213	1202	82	10	.990
Major League Totals			574	1391	78	297	42	3	8	101	.214	2996	214	32	.990

†Sold to California Angels, March 13, 1971.
‡On disabled list, June 25 through July 27.
‡‡On disabled list, May 21 through June 13.
§On disabled list, July 13 to August 10, 1973.
xTraded to St. Louis Cardinals for Pitcher John Andrews, December 6, 1973; released by St. Louis, March 25, 1974.

RECORD AS MANAGER

Year	Club	League	Position	W.	L.
1977—Cleveland†	Amer.	Fifth(E)	45	59
1978—Cleveland	Amer.	Sixth(E)	69	90
1979—Cleveland‡	Amer.	Sixth(E)	43	52
Major League Totals				157	201

†Replaced Frank Robinson with club in sixth place, June 19, 1977.
‡Replaced by Dave Garcia, July 23, 1979.

Coach, Cleveland Indians, 1975 to June, 1977; coach, New York Yankees, 1980 and 1981.

RICHARD JOSEPH TRACEWSKI

Name pronounced Truh-ZOO-skee.

(Dick)
Detroit Tigers

Born February 3, 1935, at Eynon, Pa.
Height, 5.11. Weight, 170.
Threw and batted righthanded.
Hobbies—Bowling, golf and hunting.

Led Tri-State League shortstops in double plays with 83 in 1955.

Year	Club	League	Pos.	G.	AB.	R.	H.	2B.	3B.	HR.	RBI.	B.A.	PO.	A.	E.	F.A.
1953—Sheboygan	Wis. St.	SS	50	193	57	46	3	3	0	34	.238	72	157	36	.864
1954—Bakersfield	Calif.	SS	25	87	10	19	1	2	0	8	.218	41	67	18	.857
1954—Hornell	Pony	SS	18	65	16	18	1	1	0	7	.277	29	34	10	.863
1954—Thomasville	Ga.-Fla.	SS	72	274	36	76	7	4	3	32	.277	138	191	28	.922
1955—Asheville	Tri-St.	SS	117	443	78	111	15	7	0	45	.251	*240	*356	*47	.927
1956—Fort Worth	Texas	SS	66	194	30	46	5	2	0	20	.237	115	184	27	.917
1956—Cedar Rapids	I.I.I.	SS	55	212	32	55	9	3	2	15	.259	109	174	27	.913
1957—Pueblo	West.	SS	151	570	93	170	26	●14	4	69	.298	285	*446	47	.940
1958-59—Montreal	Int.						(In Military Service)								
1960—Atlanta	A. A.	SS	149	582	91	152	13	7	1	42	.261	*269	436	43	.943
1961—Omaha	South.	SS	150	532	107	153	22	8	2	58	.288	300	389	40	.945
1962—Los Angeles	Nat.	SS	15	2	3	0	0	0	0	0	.000	1	4	0	1.000
1962—Spokane	P. C.	SS-2B	121	467	62	114	25	2	3	28	.244	213	346	35	.941
1963—Los Angeles	Nat.	SS-2B	104	217	23	49	2	1	1	10	.226	105	216	4	.958
1964—Los Angeles	Nat.	2-3B-SS	106	304	31	75	13	4	1	26	.247	152	218	15	.961
1965—Los Angeles†	Nat.	3-2B-SS	78	186	17	40	6	0	1	20	.215	51	132	12	.938
1966—Detroit	Amer.	2B-SS	81	124	15	24	1	1	0	7	.194	71	100	10	.945
1967—Detroit	Amer.	SS-2-3B	74	107	19	30	4	2	1	9	.280	54	90	3	.980
1968—Detroit	Amer.	S-3-2	90	212	30	33	3	1	4	15	.156	82	157	5	.980
1969—Detroit	Amer.	SS-2-3	66	79	10	11	2	0	0	4	.139	59	87	5	.967
National League Totals			303	709	74	164	21	5	3	56	.231	309	570	41	.955
American League Totals			311	522	74	98	10	4	5	35	.188	266	434	23	.968
Major League Totals			614	1231	148	262	31	9	8	91	.213	575	1004	64	.961

†Traded to Detroit Tigers for Pitcher Phil Regan, December 15, 1965.

WORLD SERIES RECORD

Year	Club	League	Pos.	G.	AB.	R.	H.	2B.	3B.	HR.	RBI.	B.A.	PO.	A.	E.	F.A.
1963—Los Angeles	Nat.	2B	4	13	1	2	0	0	0	0	.154	7	7	1	.933
1965—Los Angels	Nat.	PH-2B	6	17	0	2	0	0	0	0	.118	11	11	1	.957
1968—Detroit	Am.	3B-PR	2	0	1	0	0	0	0	0	.000	0	0	0	.000
World Series Totals			12	30	2	4	0	0	0	0	.133	18	18	2	.947

RECORD AS MANAGER

Named Florida State League Manager of the Year, 1970.

Year	Club	League	Position	W.	L.
1970—Lakeland	Fla. St.	Sec'd(W)	69	64
1971—Montgomery	South.	Third(E)	73	69
1979—Detroit†	Amer.	Fifth(E)	2	0

†Named interim manager replacing Les Moss (record of 27-26), June 12, 1979.
Coach, Detroit Tigers, 1972 through 1981.

JOHN CLAYTON VAN ORNUM
San Francisco Giants

Born October 20, 1939, at Pasadena, Calif.
Height, 5.11. Weight, 175.
Threw and batted righthanded.
Attended Orange Coast College, Costa Mesa, Calif.
and Fresno State College, Fresno, Calif.; received Bachelor of Arts degree in Education.

Year	Club	League	Pos.	G.	AB.	R.	H.	2B.	3B.	HR.	RBI.	B.A.	PO.	A.	E.	F.A.
1959—Odessa	Soph.	SS-3B	119	416	83	110	22	8	11	73	.264	154	322	54	.898
1960—Reno	Calif.	C-1B	116	362	62	103	16	5	7	62	.285	713	50	8	.990
1961—Great Falls	Pion.	C-OF	95	320	48	96	20	6	10	51	.300	504	27	11	.980
1962—Greenville†‡§	So. Atl.	C-SS	34	92	7	16	0	1	0	8	.174	120	33	6	.962
1963—Reynosa x	Mex.	C	95	271	33	69	13	2	5	33	.255	388	35	5	.988
1964—San Jose y	Calif.	C	115	369	58	91	16	5	8	43	.247	744	44	*16	.98~

Signed by Los Angeles Dodgers' organization, June 1, 1958.
†On disabled list, April 25 to May 7, 1962.
‡Released, July 14, 1962; signed by Los Angeles Angels' organization, December 26, 1962.
§Loaned to Reynosa, March 22, 1963; returned, September 26, 1963.
xOn disabled list, April 30 to May 18, 1963.
yReleased, January 13, 1965.

RECORD AS MANAGER

Named California League Manager of the Year, 1974.

Year Club	League	Position	W.	L.	Year Club	League	Position	W.	L.
1973—Decatur†	Mid.	Third(S)	28	32	1976—Lafayette	Texas	Fourth(E)	58	76
(Second Half)		First(S)	35	30	1977—Fresno	Calif.	Second	41	29
1974—Fresno‡	Calif.	First	48	22	(Second Half)		Second	42	28
(Second Half)		Fourth	37	33	1978—Fresno	Calif.	Third(S)	32	37
1975—Fresno	Calif.	§Second	37	33	(Second Half)		Fourth(S)	27	43
(Second Half)		Third	37	33					

†Lost playoff to Danville, two games to none.
‡Won championship playoff from San Jose, three games to two.
§Tied for position.
Scout, San Francisco Giants, 1979; minor league pitching instructor, San Francisco Giants, 1980; coach, San Francisco Giants, 1981.

OSVALDO JOSE VIRGIL
(Ozzie)
Montreal Expos

Born May 7, 1933, at Monte Christi, Dominican Republic.
Height, 6.00. Weight, 185.
Threw and batted righthanded.
Hobbies—Hunting, fishing and golf.
Father of Ozzie Virgil Jr., catcher in Philadelphia Phillies' organization.

Led American Association third basemen in double plays with 39 in 1956 and International League third basemen with 28 in 1963.

Year Club	League	Pos.	G.	AB.	R.	H.	2B.	3B.	HR.	RBI.	B.A.	PO.	A.	E.	F.A.
1953—St. Cloud	North.	3B	118	433	63	112	13	4	7	60	.259	117	∗258	∗41	.901
1954—Danville	Car.	∗3B-SS	137	530	78	154	34	7	9	68	.291	∗201	287	23	.955
1955—Dallas	Tex.	∗3-2-SS	159	614	86	181	31	5	17	79	.295	178	368	16	∗.972
1956—Minneapolis	A. A.	∗3B-OF	152	525	66	139	28	4	10	67	.265	∗180	∗334	●23	.957
1956—New York	Nat.	3B	3	12	2	5	1	1	0	2	.417	3	1	1	.800
1957—New York†	Nat.	3-O-S	96	226	26	53	0	2	4	24	.235	63	111	12	.936
1958—Charleston	A. A.	3B	47	184	23	54	9	5	4	34	.293	54	102	7	.957
1958—Detroit	Amer.	3B	49	193	19	47	10	2	3	19	.244	55	101	3	.981
1959—Charleston	A. A.	IN-O-C	154	554	57	149	19	2	8	49	.269	341	252	25	.960
1960—Denver	A. A.	OF-IF	59	202	37	77	11	3	9	55	.381	75	53	4	.970
1960—Detroit	Amer.	3-2-S-C	62	132	16	30	4	2	3	13	.227	52	85	4	.972
1961—Detroit‡-K. C.§	Amer.	3-C-S-2	31	51	2	7	0	0	1	1	.137	23	17	3	.930
1962—Baltimore	Amer.	PH	1	0	0	0	0	0	0	0	.000	0	0	0	.000
1962—Rochester	Int.	3B-SS-C	104	365	60	98	14	3	2	58	.268	86	172	9	.966
1963—Rochester x	Int.	3B	149	584	71	179	23	7	11	75	.307	∗140	290	19	.958
1964—Toronto y z	Int.	3B	150	∗604	80	164	29	5	11	48	.270	∗137	∗311	23	.951
1965—Pittsburgh a	Nat.	C-3-2	39	49	3	13	2	0	1	5	.265	36	17	1	.981
1966—Phoenix	P. C.	3B-1B-C	39	153	20	44	10	0	4	26	.288	54	61	5	.958
1966—San Francisco	Nat.	C-3-1-2-O	42	89	7	19	2	0	2	9	.213	120	28	3	.980
1967—Phoenix	P. C.	2-C-3-1B	117	392	58	125	19	3	4	61	.319	400	157	17	.970
1968—Phoenix	P. C.	C-1-3-2B	106	326	26	84	10	2	0	30	.258	407	60	5	.989
1969—San Francisco	Nat.	PH	1	1	0	0	0	0	0	0	.000	0	0	0	.000
American League Totals			143	376	38	84	14	4	7	33	.221	130	203	10	.971
National League Totals			181	377	38	90	5	3	7	40	.239	222	157	17	.957
Major League Totals			324	753	75	174	19	7	14	73	.231	352	360	27	.963

†Traded to Detroit Tigers with First Baseman Gail Harris for Third Baseman Jim Finigan and estimated $25,000, January 28, 1958.
‡Traded to Kansas City Athletics with Pitcher Bill Fischer for Pitcher Gerry Staley and Infielder Reno Bertoia, August 2, 1961.
§Assigned to Portland, October 11, 1961, and drafted by Baltimore Orioles, November 27, 1961.
xTraded by Baltimore Orioles' organization to Milwaukee Braves' organization for Infielder Ted Kazanski, December 13, 1963.
yReleased by Milwaukee Braves' organization to York (Washington Senators' organization), October 13, 1964.
zDrafted from Washington Senators' organization by Columbus (Pittsburgh Pirates' organization), November 30, 1964.
aTraded with Pitcher Joe Gibbon to San Francisco Giants for Outfielder Matty Alou and player to be named later, December 1, 1965.
Coach, San Francisco Giants, 1969 through 1972; scout, 1973; coach, 1974 and 1975; coach, Montreal Expos, 1976 through 1981.

DID YOU KNOW—
That Tom Brookens was 5-for-5 and started a triple play in the same 1980 game?

ALBERT BLUFORD WALKER, JR.
(Rube)
New York Mets

Born May 16, 1926, at Lenior, N. C.
Height, 6.01. Weight, 200.
Threw right and batted lefthanded.
Hobbies—Hunting and fishing.
Brother of Verlon Walker, late Chicago Cubs' coach.

Year	Club	League	Pos.	G.	AB.	R.	H.	2B.	3B.	HR.	RBI.	B.A.	PO.	A.	E.	F.A.
1944—Erwin		Appal.	C	55	182	26	48	4	4	1	28	.264	304	18	13	.961
1945—Nashville		South.	C	20	51	3	11	1	2	0	6	.216	46	9	4	.932
1945—Portsmouth		Pied.	C	71	225	31	58	14	1	7	27	.258	332	27	15	.960
1946—Davenport		I.I.I.	C	96	356	53	126	18	6	13	85	*354	468	55	11	*.979
1947—Nashville		South.	C	128	435	67	144	20	1	22	105	.331	435	36	*17	.965
1948—Chicago		Nat.	C	79	171	17	47	8	0	5	26	.275	178	22	4	.980
1949—Chicago		Nat.	C	56	172	11	42	4	1	3	22	.244	166	23	7	.964
1950—Chicago		Nat.	C	74	213	19	49	7	1	6	16	.230	240	34	7	.975
1951—Chi.†-Brooklyn		Nat.	C	73	181	15	43	8	0	4	14	.238	173	23	6	.970
1952—Brooklyn		Nat.	C	46	139	9	36	8	0	1	19	.259	217	16	3	.987
1953—Brooklyn		Nat.	C	43	95	5	23	6	0	3	9	.242	120	12	3	.978
1954—Brooklyn		Nat.	C	50	155	12	28	7	0	5	23	.181	259	19	1	.996
1955—Brooklyn		Nat.	C	48	103	6	26	5	0	2	13	.252	147	10	2	.987
1956—Brooklyn		Nat.	C	54	146	5	31	6	1	3	20	.212	184	20	3	.986
1957—Brooklyn		Nat.	C	60	166	12	30	8	0	2	23	.181	230	20	2	.992
1958—Los Angeles		Nat.	C	25	44	3	5	2	0	1	7	.114	62	5	1	.985
1959—Hous.-St. Paul		A. A.	C	103	280	26	75	10	0	5	36	.268	338	41	3	.992
1960—Atlanta		South.	C	62	147	22	37	3	0	5	29	.252	221	11	4	.983
Major League Totals				608	1585	114	360	69	3	35	192	.227	1976	204	39	.982

†Traded to Brooklyn Dodgers with Pitcher Johnny Schmitz, Second Baseman Wayne Terwilliger and Outfielder Andy Pafko for Pitcher Joe Hatten, Catcher Bruce Edwards, Second Baseman Eddie Miksis and Outfielder Gene Hermanski, June 15, 1951.

WORLD SERIES RECORD

Year	Club	League	Pos.	G.	AB.	R.	H.	2B.	3B.	HR.	RBI.	B.A.	PO.	A.	E.	F.A.
1956—Brooklyn		Nat.	PH	2	2	0	0	0	0	0	0	.000	0	0	0	.000

RECORD AS MANAGER

Year	Club	League	Position	W.	L.	Year	Club	League	Position	W.	L.
1959—Houston†		A.A.	Fifth	29	41	1963—Augusta		Sally	§First	41	21
1960—Atlanta		Southern	‡First	87	67		(Second Half)		Fifth	34	42
1961—Atlanta		Southern	Fourth	77	74	1964—Columbus		Southern	Seventh	65	74
1962—Amarillo		Texas	Sixth	56	84						

†Replaced by Del Wilber, June 21.
‡Lost playoff semifinal series to Birmingham, three games to two.
§Won playoff against Lynchburg (Second Half winner), three games to two.
Coach, Los Angeles Dodgers, June 24, 1958, to end of season; coach, Washington Senators, 1965 through 1967; New York Mets, 1968 through 1981.

RAYMOND LEE WALLS JR.
(Known by middle name)
Oakland A's

Born January 6, 1933, at San Diego, Calif.
Height, 6.03. Weight, 195.
Threw and batted righthanded.
Hobbies—Golf and fishing.
Attended Pasadena City College, Pasadena, Calif.

Hit three home runs in a game, April 24, 1958.

Year	Club	League	Pos.	G.	AB.	R.	H.	2B.	3B.	HR.	RBI.	B.A.	PO.	A.	E.	F.A.
1951—Modesto		Calif.	INF-O	135	541	100	185	23	*16	14	109	.342	174	182	34	.913
1952—Waco		B. St.	O-3B-SS	80	312	46	96	26	5	10	59	.308	144	74	23	.905
1952—Pittsburgh		Nat.	OF	32	80	6	15	0	1	2	5	.188	44	2	0	1.000
1953—Hollywood		P.C.	OF-3B	178	593	91	159	15	5	10	83	.268	327	55	12	.970
1954—Hollywood		P.C.	OF-2B	162	601	88	174	23	5	16	93	.290	317	41	9	.975
1955—Hollywood		P.C.	OF-1B	160	568	81	161	21	3	24	99	.283	316	19	10	.971
1956—Pittsburgh		Nat.	OF-3B	143	474	72	130	20	11	11	54	.274	284	11	11	.964
1957—Pitts.†-Chicago		Nat.	OF-3B	125	388	45	92	11	5	6	33	.237	188	7	3	.985
1958—Chicago		Nat.	OF	136	513	80	156	19	3	24	72	.304	241	10	2	.992
1959—Chicago‡		Nat.	OF	120	354	43	91	18	3	8	33	.257	203	1	7	.967
1960—Cinn.§-Phila.		Nat.	O-3B-1B	94	265	31	59	9	3	4	26	.223	130	51	8	.958
1961—Philadelphia xy		Nat.	1B-3B-O	91	261	32	73	6	4	8	30	.280	247	59	8	.975
1962—Los Angeles		Nat.	O-1B-3B	60	109	9	29	3	1	0	17	.266	98	12	2	.982
1963—Los Angeles		Nat.	O-1B-3B	64	86	12	20	1	0	3	11	.233	55	12	1	.985
1964—Los Angeles z		Nat.	OF	37	28	1	5	1	0	0	3	.179	1	0	0	1.000
Major League Totals				902	2558	331	670	88	31	66	284	.262	1491	165	42	.975

†Traded to Chicago Cubs with First Baseman Dale Long for Infielder Gene Baker and First Baseman Dee Fondy, May 1, 1957.

‡Traded to Cincinnati Reds with Pitcher Bill Henry and Outfielder Lou Jackson for Outfielder-Third Baseman Frank Thomas, December 6, 1959.

§Traded to Philadelphia Phillies with Outfielder Tony Gonzalez for First Baseman Fred Hopke and Outfielders Harry Anderson and Wally Post, June 15, 1960.

xSelected by New York Mets, October 10, 1961.

yTraded to Los Angeles Dodgers with reported $100,000 for Second Baseman Charley Neal and players to be named later, December 15, 1961.

zReleased, October 14, 1964.

Coach, Oakland A's, 1979 through 1981.

HARRY CLINTON WARNER
Milwaukee Brewers

Born December 11, 1928, at Reeders, Pa.
Height, 6.02. Weight, 215.
Threw right and batted lefthanded.
Hobbies—Hunting and fishing.
Attended Muhlenberg College, Allentown, Pa.

Tied for South Atlantic League lead in double plays with 114 in 1957.
Led South Atlantic League in bases on balls with 96 in 1958 and 106 in 1959.

Year	Club	League	Pos.	G.	AB.	R.	H.	2B.	3B.	HR.	RBI.	B.A.	PO.	A.	E.	F.A.
1946—Stroudsburg		N. Atl.	2B	24	55	7	14	2	1	2	14	.255	30	15	2	.956
1947—Stroudsburg		N. Atl.	OF	60	244	40	71	8	3	2	36	.291	90	2	1	•.989
1948—Stroudsburg		N. Atl.	1B	104	392	71	117	22	8	10	94	.298	899	41	13	.986
1949—Stroudsburg		N. Atl.	1B	127	495	122	172	28	13	17	125	.347	1160	69	15	.988
1950—Eau Claire†		North.	1B	112	424	97	121	20	7	12	90	.285	1026	73	20	.982
1951—Evansville		I.I.I.	1B	110	392	66	93	14	9	5	54	.237	982	65	7	.993
1952—Evansville		I.I.I.	1B	117	418	87	111	25	11	11	69	.266	•1126	•75	8	•.993
1953—Jacksonville		S. Atl.	3B-1B	92	263	35	68	16	4	4	48	.259	202	89	13	.957
1954—Salem		West. I.	1B	126	432	88	136	32	6	17	87	.315	957	•92	8	•.992
1955—Jacksonville		S. Atl.	1B	126	427	58	117	21	6	8	61	.274	948	•88	14	.987
1956—Austin		Texas	1B	29	97	24	26	8	1	4	14	.268	239	22	2	.992
1956—Charlotte		S. Atl.	1B	99	330	67	89	12	8	8	50	.270	931	67	13	.987
1957—Charlotte		S. Atl.	1B	145	520	65	124	20	6	6	70	.238	1160	101	11	•.992
1958—Charlotte		S. Atl.	1B	140	506	81	145	22	10	13	•88	.287	1170	81	12	.990
1959—Charlotte		S. Atl.	1B	138	463	•94	121	6	14	14	64	.261	•1214	76	11	.991
1960—Erie‡		N.Y.-Pa.	1B	98	323	79	85	16	4	14	64	.263	812	•87	6	•.993
1961—Erie‡		N.Y.-Pa.	PH	11	9	1	1	0	0	0	2	.111	....	....	....	......
1962—Wilson‡		Carol.	PH	10	12	1	5	0	0	0	3	.417	....	....	....	......

†On inactive list, July 13 to July 24, 1950.
‡Player-manager.

RECORD AS MANAGER

Year	Club	League	Position	W.	L.	Year	Club	League	Position	W.	L.
1960—Erie	N.Y.-Pa.	†First	83	46		1969—Orlando	Fla. St.	‡First(C)	80	52	
1961—Erie	N.Y.-Pa.	Second	68	57		1970—Charlotte	Southern	Sixth	66	73	
1962—Wilson	Carol.	Fifth(tie)	65	75		1971—Charlotte	Southern	§First(E)	92	50	
1963—Orlando	Fla. St.	Fourth	31	31		1972—Tacoma	P. C.	Third(W)	65	83	
(Second Half)		Second	33	28		1973—Orlando	Fla. St.	Fourth(E)	65	70	
1964—Orlando	Fla. St.	Eighth	22	47		1974—Lynchburg	Carol.	Second	40	30	
(Second Half)		Second	38	31		(Second Half)		Third	38	32	
1965—Orlando	Fla. St.	Fourth	34	31		1975—Reno	Calif.	First	43	27	
(Second Half)		Second	43	26		(Second Half)			43	27	
1966—Charlotte	Southern	Sixth	64	74		1976—Tacoma	P. C.	Second(W)	76	69	
1967—Charlotte	Southern	Fourth	75	65		1980—Syracuse	Int.	Eighth	58	81	
1968—Charlotte	Southern	Third	72	68							

†Won playoff by defeating Corning, two games to none, lost championship series to Wellsville, two games to one in best-of-five finals when series was ended because of rain, with Wellsville declared champion.

‡Lost playoff to Miami, four games to one.

§Won playoff by defeating Asheville, two games to one; won Dixie Association Championship by defeating Arkansas, three games to none.

Coach, Toronto Blue Jays, 1977 through 1979; coach, Milwaukee Brewers, 1981.

ALBERT JOSEPH WIDMAR
(Al)
Toronto Blue Jays

Born March 20, 1925, at Cleveland, O.
Height, 6.04. Weight, 195.
Threw and batted righthanded.

Year	Club	League	G.	IP.	W.	L.	Pct.	H.	R.	ER.	SO.	BB.	ERA.
1942—Canton	Mid. Atl.	14	94	6	2	.750	77	42	30	34	43	2.87
1943—Scranton	Eastern	18	142	15	5	.667	114	52	35	43	39	2.22
1944—Louisville	Am. Assoc.	31	174	12	11	.522	181	105	90	59	78	4.66
1945—Louisville	Am. Assoc.	33	153	10	8	.556	160	101	81	64	94	4.76
1946—Louisville	Am. Assoc.	30	185	12	9	.571	156	64	50	73	94	•2.43
1947—Boston	American	2	1	0	0	.000	1	2	2	1	2	18.00
1947—Louisville†	Am. Assoc.	29	126	8	8	.500	130	77	69	44	63	4.93

Year Club	League	G.	IP.	W.	L.	Pct.	H.	R.	ER.	SO.	BB.	ERA.
1948—St. Louis	American	49	83	2	6	.250	88	42	41	34	48	4.45
1949—Baltimore	Int'national	45	•294	•22	15	.595	245	120	99	173	98	3.03
1950—St. Louis	American	36	195	7	15	.318	211	115	103	78	74	4.75
1951—St. Louis‡	American	26	108	4	9	.308	157	84	78	28	52	6.50
1952—Chicago	American	1	2	0	0	.000	4	1	1	2	0	4.50
1952—Seattle	P. Coast	38	246	20	12	.625	228	73	63	106	67	2.30
1953—Seattle	P. Coast	46	272	20	14	.588	283	121	112	83	108	3.70
1954—Seattle	P. Coast	40	178	8	13	.381	215	105	94	63	60	4.75
1955—Seattle	P. Coast	8	9	1	0	1.000	5	3	1	3	6	1.00
1955—Tulsa	Texas	53	152	18	8	.692	141	55	53	66	26	3.14
1956—Tulsa	Texas	36	117	11	11	.500	196	90	80	79	59	4.07
1957—Tulsa	Texas	35	192	9	12	.429	210	83	73	56	25	3.42
1958—Tulsa	Texas	11	37	2	2	.500	42	25	23	17	7	5.59
Major League Totals		114	389	13	30	.302	461	244	225	143	176	5.21

†Recalled by Boston Red Sox and traded to St. Louis Browns with Pitchers Joe Ostrowski and Jim Wilson, Catcher Roy Partee, Shortstop Eddie Pellagrini, Outfielder Pete Layden and reported $310,000 for Pitcher Jack Kramer and Shortstop Vern Stephens, November 17, 1947.

‡Traded to Chicago White Sox with Catcher Sherm Lollar and Shortstop Tommy Upton for Pitcher Dick Littlefield, Catcher Gus Niarhos, First Baseman Gordon Goldsberry, Shortstop Joe DeMaestri and Outfielder Jim Rivera, November 27, 1951.

RECORD AS MANAGER

Year Club	League	Position	W.	L.
1956—Tulsa	Texas	Fourth	77	77
1957—Tulsa	Texas	Fourth	75	79
1958—Tulsa†	Texas	Seventh	45	54
1971—Newark	NYP	Fourth	35	35
1972—San Antonio‡§	Texas	Fourth(W)	5	6

†Replaced by Jim Fanning, July 20.

‡Named interim manager replacing Mike Roarke, June 5, 1972.

§Replaced by Jim Walton, June 16.

Minor league pitching instructor, Philadelphia Phillies, 1960 and 1961; coach, Philadelphia Phillies, 1962 through 1964; minor league pitching instructor, Philadelphia Phillies, 1965 through 1967; coach, Philadelphia Phillies, 1968 and 1969; minor league pitching instructor, Seattle Pilots, 1970; minor league pitching instructor, Milwaukee Brewers, 1971 and 1972; director of player development, Milwaukee Brewers, part of 1973 and 1975; coach, Milwaukee Brewers, July 16, 1973 through 1974; director of minor league instruction, Milwaukee Brewers, 1976 and 1977; minor league instructor, Baltimore Orioles, 1978 and 1979; coach, Toronto Blue Jays, 1980 and 1981.

BILLY LEO WILLIAMS
Chicago Cubs

Born June 15, 1938, at Whistler, Ala.
Height, 6.01½. Weight, 170.
Threw and batted lefthanded.
Hobbies—Football, fishing, hunting and swimming.

Tied major league records for most home runs two consecutive games (5), September 8 and 10, 1968; most consecutive doubles, game (4), April 9, 1969; most times, four long hits, game, season (2), April 9 and September 5, 1969.

Established National League records for most games played consecutive, league (1,117), September 22, 1963 through September 2, 1970; most games by outfielder, season (164), 1965.

Tied National League record for most consecutive years, 600 or more at-bats (9), 1970.

Hit three home runs in game, September 10, 1968.

Led National League in total bases with 321 in 1968, with 373 in 1970 and with 348 in 1972.

Led National League in slugging percentage with .606 in 1972.

Named National League Rookie Player of the Year by THE SPORTING NEWS and National League Rookie of the Year by the Baseball Writers' Association, 1961.

Named THE SPORTING NEWS Major League Player of the Year, 1972.

Named THE SPORTING NEWS National League Player of the Year, 1972.

Named outfielder on THE SPORTING NEWS National League All-Star Team, 1964-68-70-72.

Year Club	League	Pos.	G.	AB.	R.	H.	2B.	3B.	HR.	RBI.	B.A.	PO.	A.	E.	F.A.
1956—Ponca City†	Soo. St.	OF	13	17	4	4	0	0	0	4	.235	6	0	1	.857
1957—Ponca City	Soo. St.	OF	•126	451	87	140	•40	3	17	95	.310	211	21	•25	.903
1958—Pueblo‡	West.	OF	21	80	9	20	2	1	2	11	.250	30	1	2	.939
1958—Burlington	I.I.I.	OF	61	214	38	65	7	0	10	38	.304	93	4	4	.960
1959—San Antonio	Tex.	1B-OF	94	371	57	118	22	7	10	79	.318	578	54	21	.968
1959—Fort Worth	A.A.	OF	5	21	7	10	4	1	1	5	.476	10	2	1	.923
1959—Chicago§	Nat.	OF	18	33	0	5	0	1	0	2	.152	18	0	0	1.000
1960—Houston§	A.A.	OF	126	473	74	153	28	3	26	80	.323	207	7	7	.968
1960—Chicago	Nat.	OF	12	47	4	13	0	2	2	7	.277	25	0	1	.962
1961—Chicago	Nat.	OF	146	529	75	147	20	7	25	86	.278	220	9	•11	.954
1962—Chicago	Nat.	OF	159	618	94	184	22	8	22	92	.298	273	18	10	.967
1963—Chicago	Nat.	OF	161	612	87	175	36	9	25	95	.286	298	13	4	.987
1964—Chicago	Nat.	OF	162	645	100	201	39	2	33	98	.312	233	14	13	.950
1965—Chicago	Nat.	OF	•164	645	115	203	39	6	34	108	.315	296	10	10	.968
1966—Chicago	Nat.	OF	•162	648	100	179	23	5	29	91	.276	319	9	8	.976
1967—Chicago	Nat.	OF	162	634	92	176	21	12	28	84	.278	271	3	3	.989
1968—Chicago	Nat.	OF	•163	642	91	185	30	8	30	98	.288	261	4	9	.967
1969—Chicago	Nat.	OF	•163	642	103	188	33	10	21	95	.293	250	15	12	.957

Year	Club	League	Pos.	G.	AB.	R.	H.	2B.	3B.	HR.	RBI.	B.A.	PO.	A.	E.	F.A.
1970–Chicago	Nat.		OF	●161	636	★137	●205	34	4	42	129	.322	259	13	3	.989
1971–Chicago	Nat.		OF	157	594	86	179	27	5	28	93	.301	284	8	7	.977
1972–Chicago	Nat.		OF-1B	150	574	95	191	34	6	37	122	★.333	275	13	4	.986
1973–Chicago	Nat.		OF-1B	156	576	72	166	22	2	20	86	.288	420	34	6	.987
1974–Chicago xy	Nat.		1B-OF	117	404	55	113	22	0	16	68	.280	635	53	11	.984
1975–Oakland	Amer.		1B	155	520	68	127	20	1	23	81	.244	30	3	1	.971
1976–Oakland z	Amer.		OF	120	351	36	74	12	0	11	41	.211	0	0	0	.000
National League Totals				2213	8479	1306	2510	402	87	392	1354	.296	4337	216	112	.976
American League Totals				275	871	104	201	32	1	34	122	.231	30	3	1	.971
Major League Totals				2488	9350	1410	2711	434	88	426	1476	.290	4367	219	113	.976

†On disabled list, July 17 to August 18, 1956.
‡On temporary inactive list, June 7 to July 2, 1958.
§On disabled list, August 8 to September 5, 1960.
xOn supplemental disabled list, August 19 to September 3, 1974.
yTraded to Oakland Athletics for Pitchers Darold Knowles and Bob Locker and Second Baseman Manny Trillo, October 23, 1974.
zReleased, November 9, 1976.
Batting instructor, Chicago Cubs, 1978 and 1979; coach, Chicago Cubs, 1980 and 1981.

CHAMPIONSHIP RECORD

Year	Club	League	Pos.	G.	AB.	R.	H.	2B.	3B.	HR.	RBI.	B.A.	PO.	A.	E.	F.A.
1975–Oakland	Amer.		DH-PH	3	8	0	0	0	0	0	0	.000	0	0	0	.000

ALL-STAR GAME RECORD

Year	League	Pos.	AB.	R.	H.	2B.	3B.	HR.	RBI.	B.A.	PO.	A.	E.	F.A.
1962–National (second game)		OF	1	0	0	0	0	0	1	.000	2	0	0	1.000
1964–National		OF	4	1	1	0	0	1	1	.250	1	0	0	1.000
1965–National		PH	1	0	0	0	0	0	0	.000	0	0	0	.000
1968–National		PH	1	0	0	0	0	0	0	.000	0	0	0	.000
1972–National		OF	2	1	1	0	0	0	0	.500	0	0	0	.000
1973–National		OF	2	0	1	0	0	0	0	.500	0	0	0	.000
All-Star Game Totals			11	2	3	0	0	1	2	.273	3	0	0	1.000

JAMES BERNARD WILLIAMS
(Jimmy)
Baltimore Orioles

Born May 15, 1927, at Toronto, Ontario, Canada.
Height, 5.10. Weight, 180.
Threw and batted righthanded.

Led Western League in stolen bases with 42 in 1949.
Led Southern Association outfielders in fielding average with .990 in 1954.
Led International League outfielders in fielding average with .991 in 1955.
Tied for Pacific Coast League lead in sacrifice hits with 12 in 1958.

Year	Club	League	Pos.	G.	AB.	R.	H.	2B.	3B.	HR.	RBI.	B.A.	PO.	A.	E.	F.A.
1947–Kingston	No. Atl.		....	20	74	23	25	2	4	1	11	.338	....	....	....	.....
1947–Sheboygan	Wis. St.		OF-3B	86	325	84	125	25	10	9	105	.385	124	43	14	.923
1947–Three Rivers	Can-Am		OF	11	45	8	13	0	1	2	5	.289	13	1	0	1.000
1948–Danville	I.I.I.		OF	120	443	65	111	21	16	5	73	.251	180	10	★20	.905
1949–Pueblo	West.		3B-OF	136	565	★126	163	23	18	11	81	.288	204	136	28	.924
1950–Mobile	So. Assn.		OF	127	414	52	103	13	8	3	38	.249	242	9	5	.980
1951–Mobile	So. Assn.		OF	72	218	39	58	12	1	3	15	.266	146	5	7	.956
1951–Elmira	East.		OF	45	128	23	33	5	2	1	14	.258	52	0	2	.963
1952–Mobile	So. Assn.		OF	124	314	46	80	16	6	2	42	.255	186	8	6	.970
1953–Mobile	So. Assn.		....	2	....	....	....	....	....	....	....	.250	....	....	....	.....
1953–Elmira	East.		OF-1B	140	509	61	159	21	5	6	64	.312	306	19	8	.976
1954–Mobile	So. Assn.		OF-3B	148	505	73	149	22	4	8	61	.295	208	53	4	.985
1955–Montreal	Int.		OF-3B	143	519	93	171	33	8	13	63	.329	220	25	6	.976
1956–Montreal	Int.		OF	146	550	96	164	27	9	8	55	.298	341	5	11	.969
1957–Montreal	Int.		O-2-3	136	441	62	116	18	4	4	37	.263	216	133	15	.959
1958–Spokane	P.C.		OF	142	493	59	149	21	3	12	64	.302	252	8	8	.970
1959–St. Paul	A.A.		OF	47	144	12	28	4	0	0	12	.194	54	2	1	.982
1959–Victoria	Texas		O-3-1	78	266	46	83	9	2	8	46	.312	174	59	5	.979
1960–Atlanta	So. Assn.		OF	142	524	100	140	37	0	17	81	.267	284	6	7	.976
1961–Atlanta	So. Assn.		OF	105	352	52	98	22	2	9	66	.278	136	5	6	.959
1962–Omaha†‡	A.A.		OF	47	96	19	27	2	1	3	20	.281	28	2	1	.968
1963–Santa Barbara§x	Calif.		OF	31	64	9	21	5	0	1	11	.328	20	0	3	.870
1964–Grand Forks§y	North.		....	6	4	0	0	0	0	0	0	.000	....	....	....	.....

†Player-coach.
‡On disabled list, May 19 to June 7, 1962.
§Player-manager.
xOn disabled list, July 6 to July 17 and July 19 to August 7, 1963.
yOn disabled list, May 25 to June 13 and July 5 to October 14, 1964.

DID YOU KNOW—

That Bob Walk was the first rookie pitcher since 1952 to start the first game of the World Series?

Named Southern League Manager of the Year, 1970.

Year	Club	League	Position	W.	L.	Year	Club	League	Position	W.	L.
1963–Santa Barbara....	Calif.	Fifth	†35	37		1972–Cocoa	Fla. St.	Fifth(E)	†56	72
(Second Half)		Fifth	32	35		1973–Denver	A.A.	Fourth(W)	61	75
1964–Grand Forks	North.	Second	69	50		1974–Columbus	South.	Fourth(E)	65	73
1965–Shelby‡.............	W. Carol.	Sixth	16	25		1976–Lodi...................	Calif.	Fifth	30	39
(Second Half)		Sixth	26	32		(Second Half)		Fifth	34	37
1966–Leesburg§..........	Fla. St.	First	50	14		1977–Albuquerque	P.C.	Fourth(E)	60	78
(Second Half)		Fifth	†37	30		1978–Miami z.............	Fla. St.	Second(S)	38	35
1967–Leesburg	Fla. St.	Fourth(W)	28	40		(Second Half)		First(S)	38	30
(Second Half)		Third(W)	†36	31		1979–Charlotte a........	South.	First(S)	†41	25
1968–Peninsula x........	Carol.	Third(E)	†75	65		(Second Half)		Third(E)	32	44
1969–Iowa	A.A.	yFourth	62	78		1980–Charlotte b........	South.	First(E)	38	33
1970–Columbus	South.	First	78	59		(Second Half)		Fourth(E)	34	39
1971–Oklahoma City ...	A.A.	Second(W)	71	69						

†One tie game.

‡Replaced Wes Ferrell with club in fourth place (record of 13-11), May 17, 1965.

§Won championship playoff from St. Petersburg, three games to two.

xLost playoff to Raleigh-Durham, one game to none.

yTied for position.

zWon playoff from Ft. Myers, one game to none; won championship playoff from Lakeland, two games to one.

aLost playoff to Columbus, two games to none.

bWon playoff from Savannah, three games to none; won championship playoff from Memphis, three games to one.

Minor league instructor, Houston Astros, 1975; coach, Baltimore Orioles, 1981.

JAMES FRANCIS WILLIAMS
(Jimy)
Toronto Blue Jays

Born October 4, 1943, at Santa Maria, Calif.
Height, 5.11. Weight, 175.
Threw and batted righthanded.
Hobbies–Hunting and fishing.
Attended Fresno State College, Fresno, Calif.

Year	Club	League	Pos.	G.	AB.	R.	H.	2B.	3B.	HR.	RBI.	B.A.	PO.	A.	E.	F.A.
1965–Waterloo†	....	Midwest	SS	115	435	64	125	19	3	2	31	.287	173	312	26	.949
1966–St. Louis‡	....	Nat.	SS-2B	13	11	1	3	0	0	0	1	.273	2	5	0	1.000
1967–Arkansas	....	Texas	SS	28	101	8	21	1	1	0	8	.208	49	80	2	.985
1967–Tulsa	....	P.C.	SS	61	164	18	37	2	0	1	21	.226	87	156	26	.903
1967–St. Louis§	....	Nat.	SS	1	2	0	0	0	0	0	0	.000	6	1	0	1.000
1968–Indianapolis x ...		P.C.	SS-2B	120	403	38	91	19	5	2	34	.226	198	323	27	.951
1969–Vancouver y		P.C.	3B-OF-SS	35	66	7	17	1	1	0	9	.258	17	23	2	.952
1970–Buff. z-Winn......		Int.	SS-2B-3B	109	361	49	83	15	0	3	18	.230	178	244	30	.934
1971–Winn. ab-Tide. c		Int.	SS-3B-2B	105	327	40	84	7	4	5	31	.257	120	219	22	.939
1975–El Paso de	....	Texas	DH	6	17	3	2	0	0	0	2	.118	0	0	0	.000
Major League Totals	....			14	13	1	3	0	0	0	1	.231	8	6	0	1.000

†Drafted by St. Louis Cardinals from Toronto (Boston Red Sox' organization), November 29, 1965.

‡In military service from July 24 through end of season.

§Traded with Catcher Pat Corrales (assigned to Indianapolis) to Cincinnati Reds for Catcher John Edwards, February 8, 1968.

xRecalled by Cincinnati Reds; selected by Montreal Expos from Cincinnati in expansion draft, October 14, 1968.

yOn disabled list, May 13 to May 30 and June 24 to September 2, 1969.

zFranchise transferred from Buffalo to Winnipeg, June 4, 1970.

aOn suspended list, June 7 to June 16, 1971.

bSold to New York Mets' organization, June 16, 1971.

cOn temporary inactive list, August 12 to August 16, 1971.

dPlayer-manager.

eOn disabled list, May 15 to July 17 and July 29 to August 20, 1975.

RECORD AS MANAGER
Named Pacific Coast League Manager of the Year, 1976 and 1979.

Year	Club	League	Position	W.	L.	Year	Club	League	Position	W.	L.
1974–Quad Cities	Midw.	First(S)	33	26		1977–Salt Lake City	P.C.	Second(E)	74	65
(Second Half)		†Third(S)	32	32		1978–Springfield.........	A.A.	Third(E)	70	66
1975–El Paso..............	Texas	Third(W)	62	71		1979–Salt Lake City	P.C.	Fourth(S)	34	40
1976–Salt Lake City	P.C.	‡First(E)	90	54		(Second Half)		§First(S)	46	28

†Lost playoff to Danville, two games to one.

‡Lost championship playoff to Hawaii, three games to two.

§Won playoff from Albuquerque, two games to none; won championship playoff from Hawaii, three games to none.

Coach, Toronto Blue Jays, 1980 and 1981.

STANLEY WILSON WILLIAMS
(Stan)
New York Yankees

Born September 14, 1936, at Enfield, N. J.
Height, 6.04. Weight, 225.
Threw and batted righthanded.

Pitched seven-inning, 9-0 no-hit victory against Quebec City, June 29, 1974 (2nd game of doubleheader). Led Piedmont League pitchers in games started with 30, complete games with 18 and hit batsmen with 16 in 1955.

Led American Association pitchers in games started with 34 and hit batsmen with 14 and tied for lead in wild pitches with 11 in 1957.

Year—Club	League	G.	IP.	W.	L.	Pct.	H.	R.	ER.	SO.	BB.	ERA.
1954—Shawnee	Soo. St.	15	61	3	5	.375	56	47	31	77	50	4.57
1955—Newport News	Piedmont	31	*242	18	7	.720	160	77	65	*301	*158	*2.42
1956—Fort Worth	Texas	9	45	2	2	.500	40	33	26	46	32	5.20
1956—St. Paul	Am. Assoc.	24	127	9	7	.563	124	76	64	95	70	4.54
1957—St. Paul	Am. Assoc.	35	246	19	7	.731	188	92	83	*223	*148	3.04
1958—St. Paul	Am. Assoc.	8	64	2	3	.400	43	22	20	44	28	2.81
1958—Los Angeles	National	27	119	9	7	.563	99	58	53	80	65	4.01
1959—Los Angeles	National	35	125	5	5	.500	102	64	55	89	86	3.96
1960—Los Angeles	National	38	207	14	10	.583	162	84	69	175	72	3.00
1961—Los Angeles	National	41	235	15	12	.556	213	114	102	205	108	3.91
1962—Los Angeles†	National	40	186	14	12	.538	184	104	92	108	98	4.45
1963—New York	American	29	146	9	8	.529	137	59	52	98	57	3.21
1964—New York‡	American	21	82	1	5	.167	76	39	35	54	38	3.84
1965—Cleveland	American	3	4	0	0	.000	6	4	3	1	3	6.75
1965—Seattle	P. Coast	34	134	6	6	.500	115	53	49	106	49	3.29
1966—Spokane§	P. Coast	31	60	4	2	.667	52	13	11	39	30	1.65
1967—Portland	P. Coast	31	98	7	6	.538	105	53	43	70	30	3.95
1967—Cleveland	American	16	79	6	4	.600	64	26	23	75	24	2.62
1968—Cleveland	American	44	194	13	11	.542	163	64	54	147	51	2.51
1969—Cleveland x	American	61	178	6	14	.300	155	86	78	139	67	3.94
1970—Minnesota	American	68	113	10	1	.909	85	34	25	76	32	1.99
1971—Minnesota y	American	46	78	4	5	.444	63	44	36	47	44	4.15
1971—St. Louis z	National	10	13	3	0	1.000	13	2	2	8	2	1.38
1972—Salt Lake City a	P. Coast	12	29	2	2	.500	33	20	15	13	14	4.66
1972—Louisville	Int'national	26	56	2	3	.400	39	18	17	43	19	2.73
1972—Boston b	American	3	4	0	0	.000	5	3	3	3	1	6.75
1974—Bristol c	Eastern	5	19	2	0	1.000	9	1	1	14	4	0.47
American League Totals		291	878	49	48	.505	754	359	309	640	317	3.17
National League Totals		191	885	60	46	.566	773	426	373	665	431	3.79
Major League Totals		482	1763	109	94	.537	1527	785	682	1305	748	3.48

†Traded to New York Yankees for First Baseman Bill Skowron, November 26, 1962.
‡Sold to Cleveland Indians, March 30, 1965.
§On temporary inactive list, April 21 to June 6, 1966.
xTraded to Minnesota Twins with Pitcher Luis Tiant for Pitchers Dean Chance and Robert L. Miller, Outfielder Ted Uhlaender and Outfielder-Third Baseman Graig Nettles, December 11, 1969.
yTraded to St. Louis Cardinals for two players to be named later, September 1, 1971; Cardinals assigned Outfielder Fred Rico and Pitcher Dan Ford to Twins, September 14, 1971, to complete deal.
zReleased by St. Louis Cardinals, April 9, 1972. Signed as free agent by Salt Lake City (California Angels' organization), April 24, 1972.
aReleased by California Angels' organization, June 1, 1972. Signed as free agent by Louisville (Boston Red Sox' organization), June 13, 1972.
bReleased by Boston Red Sox, September 23, 1972.
cPlayer-manager.

CHAMPIONSHIP SERIES RECORD

Year—Club	League	G.	IP.	W.	L.	Pct.	H.	R.	ER.	SO.	BB.	ERA.
1970—Minnesota	American	2	6	0	0	.000	2	0	0	2	1	0.00

WORLD SERIES RECORD

Year—Club	League	G.	IP.	W.	L.	Pct.	H.	R.	ER.	SO.	BB.	ERA.
1959—Los Angeles	National	1	2	0	0	.000	0	0	0	1	2	0.00
1963—New York	American	1	3	0	0	.000	1	0	0	5	0	0.00
World Series Totals		2	5	0	0	.000	1	0	0	6	2	0.00

ALL-STAR GAME RECORD

Year—League	IP.	W.	L.	Pct.	H.	R.	ER.	SO.	BB.	ERA.
1960—National (second game)	2	0	0	.000	2	0	0	2	1	0.00

RECORD AS MANAGER

Year—Club	League	Position	W.	L.
1974—Bristol	Eastern	†First(A)	74	61

†Lost playoff semifinal series to Thetford Mines, two games to none.
Coach, Boston Red Sox, 1975 and 1976; Chicago White Sox, 1977 and 1978; minor league pitching coach, New York Yankees, 1979; coach, New York Yankees, 1980 and 1981.

ROBERT PAUL WINE
(Bobby)
Philadelphia Phillies

Born September 17, 1938, at Bronx, N. Y.
Height, 6.01. Weight, 190.
Threw and batted righthanded.
Hobbies—Basketball and model building.
Brother of Ed Wine, former infielder in New York Mets' organization.
Established major league record for most double plays, shortstop, season (137), 1970.
Led International League shortstops in double plays with 104 in 1960.
Named International League Rookie of the Year, 1960.
Named as shortstop on THE SPORTING NEWS National League All-Star fielding team, 1963.

Year Club	League	Pos.	G.	AB.	R.	H.	2B.	3B.	HR.	RBI.	B.A.	PO.	A.	E.	F.A.
1957—Johnson City	Appal.	SS	54	202	53	68	11	6	6	42	.337	63	131	24	.890
1958—Bakersfield	Calif.	SS	112	440	78	137	13	11	11	75	.311	207	304	26	★.952
1959—Williamsport	East.	SS	120	426	40	89	12	3	5	33	.209	216	★333	★42	.929
1960—Buffalo	Int.	SS	154	569	61	153	28	5	8	53	.269	★246	★500	★33	.958
1960—Philadelphia	Nat.	SS	4	14	1	2	0	0	0	0	.143	9	10	0	1.000
1961—Buffalo	Int.	SS	152	534	46	130	18	6	6	48	.243	★301	430	30	.961
1962—Buffalo	Int.	SS	24	95	12	23	4	0	3	12	.242	38	88	3	.977
1962—Philadelphia	Nat.	SS-3B	112	311	30	76	15	0	4	25	.244	149	263	8	.981
1963—Philadelphia	Nat.	SS-3B	142	418	29	90	14	3	6	44	.215	224	369	17	.972
1964—Philadelphia	Nat.	SS-3B	126	283	28	60	8	3	4	34	.212	159	266	15	.966
1965—Philadelphia	Nat.	SS-1B	139	394	31	90	8	1	5	33	.228	223	387	21	.967
1966—Philadelphia	Nat.	SS-OF	46	89	8	21	5	0	0	5	.236	57	91	4	.974
1967—Philadelphia	Nat.	★SS-1B	135	363	27	69	12	5	2	28	.190	206	392	12	★.980
1968—Philadelphia†§	Nat.	SS-3B	27	71	5	12	3	0	2	7	.169	37	68	3	.972
1969—Montreal	Nat.	SS-1B-3	121	370	23	74	8	1	3	25	.200	214	367	31	.949
1970—Montreal	Nat.	SS	159	501	40	116	21	3	3	51	.232	284	481	19	.976
1971—Montreal	Nat.	SS	119	340	25	68	9	0	1	16	.200	221	321	10	.982
1972—Montreal x	Nat.	3-SS-2	34	18	2	4	1	0	0	0	.222	12	15	1	.964
Major League Totals			1164	3172	249	682	104	16	30	268	.215	1795	3030	141	.972

†Suffered wrenched back June 24; on disabled list from July 19 through August 31.
‡Underwent operation for ruptured spinal disc; on disabled list from May 29 through end of season.
§Sent by Philadelphia Phillies to Montreal Expos to replace Larry Jackson, April 7, 1969. Jackson announced retirement after being taken by Montreal in expansion draft.
xReleased, July 10, 1972.
Coach, Philadelphia Phillies, July 26, 1972 through 1981.

BOBBY BROOKS WINKLES
Chicago White Sox

Born March 11, 1932, at Swifton, Ark.
Height, 5.09. Weight, 170.
Threw and batted righthanded.
Hobbies—Golf and fishing.
Attended Illinois Wesleyan University, Bloomington, Ill., and University of Colorado,
Boulder, Colo.; received Bachelor of Arts degree in Philosophy and
Master of Science degree in Physical Education.
Named by THE SPORTING NEWS as College Baseball Coach of the Year, 1965, 1967 and 1969.

Year Club	League	Pos.	G.	AB.	R.	H.	2B.	3B.	HR.	RBI.	B.A.	PO.	A.	E.	F.A.
1951—Col. Springs	West.	SS	104	405	53	118	17	4	3	44	.291	196	339	39	.932
1952—Waterloo	Ill.	SS	30	129	17	37	9	1	0	22	.287	60	113	7	.961
1953—						(In U. S. Army)									
1954—Memphis	S. A.	SS	52	182	18	41	2	1	0	20	.222	92	157	13	.950
1954—Col. Springs	West.	SS	81	314	42	92	16	1	1	38	.293	153	277	26	.943
1955—Charleston	A. A.	SS	44	142	14	35	3	2	0	10	.246	57	116	8	.956
1955—Col. Springs	West.	SS	108	409	45	117	15	1	0	33	.286	176	382	30	.949
1956—Col. Springs	West.	2-S-3	131	510	77	152	31	4	5	60	.298	248	351	33	.948
1956—Tulsa	Texas	SS	6	24	0	5	0	0	0	0	.208	figures unavailable			
1957—Tulsa	Texas	SS	154	639	89	178	18	4	2	48	.279	★303	★513	42	.951
1958—Indianapolis	A. A.	SS	84	281	30	64	11	2	1	17	.228	125	223	17	.953
1958—Tulsa	Texas	SS	64	255	30	51	8	4	0	5	.200	113	227	13	.963

RECORD AS MANAGER

Year Club	League	Position	W.	L.
1973—California	Amer.	Fourth(W)	79	83
1974—California	Amer.	Sixth(W)	30	44
1977—Oakland‡	Amer.	Seventh(W)	37	71
1978—Oakland§	Amer.	First(W)	24	15
Major League Totals			170	213

Baseball coach at Arizona State University, 1959 through 1971. Record: 524 wins, 173 losses; won NCAA championship in 1965, 1967 and 1969.
†Replaced by Dick Williams, June 26 (Whitey Herzog served as interim manager, June 27 through June 30).
‡Replaced Jack McKeon with club tied for fifth place, June 10, 1977.
§Resigned, replaced by Jack McKeon, May 23, 1978.
Coach, California Angels, 1972; Oakland Athletics, part of 1974 and 1975; San Francisco Giants, 1976 and part of 1977; Chicago White Sox, 1979 through 1981.

MELVIN JAMES WRIGHT JR.
Houston Astros

Born May 11, 1928, at Manila, Ark.
Height, 6.03. Weight, 205.
Threw and batted righthanded.
Hobbies—Hunting and fishing.
Attended Ouachita Baptist College, Arkadelphia, Ark.

Year Club	League	G.	IP.	W.	L.	Pct.	H.	R.	ER.	SO.	BB.	ERA.
1950—McAlester	Soo. St.	32	215	15	7	.682	180	87	72	130	59	3.01
1951—Joplin	W. A.	28	206	15	9	.625	199	97	84	123	77	3.67
1952—Binghamton	Eastern	*57	121	7	8	.467	95	39	26	45	56	1.93
1953—Kansas City†	Am. Assoc.	47	111	13	2	*.867	112	47	40	73	35	3.24
1954—St. Louis	National	9	10	0	0	.000	16	15	12	4	11	10.80
1954—Columbus	Am. Assoc.	28	117	8	8	.500	138	55	49	45	21	3.77
1955—Rochester	Int'national	20	49	1	1	.500	47	24	15	15	19	2.76
1955—St. Louis	National	29	36	2	2	.500	44	26	25	18	9	6.25
1956—Omaha	Am. Assoc.	15	24	0	0	.000	28	9	9	10	7	3.38
1956—Rochester	Int'national	27	56	5	6	.455	53	26	19	33	16	3.05
1957—Rochester	Int'national	46	62	5	5	.500	58	23	20	27	22	2.90
1958—Rochester	Int'national	41	47	1	2	.333	49	21	15	31	12	2.87
1959—Houston‡-Dallas	Am. Assoc.	71	117	10	8	.556	113	42	32	74	35	2.46
1960—Dallas-Fort Worth	Am. Assoc.	54	70	5	4	.556	61	31	18	60	6	2.31
1960—Chicago	National	9	16	0	1	.000	17	9	9	8	3	5.06
1961—Chicago	National	11	21	0	1	.000	42	26	25	6	4	10.71
1961—Houston	Am. Assoc.	6	12	0	1	.000	11	6	5	8	1	3.75
Major League Totals		58	83	2	4	.333	119	76	71	36	27	7.70

†Assigned to New York Yankees and traded to St. Louis Cardinals with Outfielders Emil Tellinger and Bill Virdon for Outfielder Enos Slaughter, April 11, 1954.

‡Released by St. Louis Cardinals' organization to Dallas (Chicago Cubs' organization), June 24, 1959.

RECORD AS MANAGER

Year Club	League	Position	W.	L.
1969—Huron	Northern	Fourth	31	39

Coach, Salt Lake City (Pacific Coast League), 1962; Chicago Cubs, 1963 and 1964; scout, Chicago Cubs, 1965 through 1967; coach, Tacoma (Pacific Coast League), 1968; scout, Chicago Cubs, 1970 through 1972; coach, Pittsburgh Pirates, 1973; coach, New York Yankees, 1974 and 1975; coach, Houston Astros, 1976 through 1981.

EDWARD FRED JOSEPH YOST
(Eddie)
Boston Red Sox

Born October 13, 1926, at Brooklyn, N. Y.
Height, 5.10. Weight, 182.
Threw and batted righthanded.
Hobbies—Golf and fishing.
Attended New York University, New York City, N. Y.; received Master's degree
in Physical Education.

Established major league records for most consecutive games by third baseman, lifetime (576); most years leading league in putouts by third baseman (8).

Tied American League record for most games by third baseman, season, 154-game schedule (157), 1952.

Led American League batters in walks with 141 in 1950, 129 in 1952, 123 in 1953, 151 in 1956, 135 in 1959 and 125 in 1960.

Led American League third basemen in double plays with 45 in 1950 and 31 in 1956.

Year Club	League	Pos.	G.	AB.	R.	H.	2B.	3B.	HR.	RBI.	B.A.	PO.	A.	E.	F.A.
1944—Washington	Amer.	3B-SS	7	14	3	2	0	0	0	0	.143	9	6	2	.882
1945-46—Washington	Amer.							(In Military Service)							
1946—Washington	Amer.	3B	8	25	2	2	1	0	0	1	.080	7	17	0	1.000
1947—Washington	Amer.	3B	115	428	52	102	17	3	0	14	.238	125	198	14	.958
1948—Washington	Amer.	3B	145	555	74	138	32	11	2	50	.249	*189	240	15	.966
1949—Washington	Amer.	3B	124	435	57	110	19	7	9	45	.253	158	232	19	.954
1950—Washington	Amer.	3B	155	573	114	169	26	2	11	58	.295	*205	307	*30	.945
1951—Washington	Amer.	*3B-OF	●154	568	109	161	●36	4	12	65	.283	*209	234	21	.955
1952—Washington	Amer.	3B	*157	587	92	137	32	3	12	49	.233	*212	249	18	.962
1953—Washington	Amer.	3B	152	577	107	157	30	7	9	45	.272	*190	300	18	.965
1954—Washington	Amer.	3B	●155	539	101	138	26	4	11	47	.256	●170	*347	17	.968
1955—Washington	Amer.	3B	122	375	64	91	17	5	7	48	.243	100	217	19	.943
1956—Washington	Amer.	*3B-OF	152	515	94	119	17	2	11	53	.231	*182	*303	18	.964
1957—Washington	Amer.	3B	110	414	47	104	13	5	9	38	.251	109	207	16	.952
1958—Washington†	Amer.	*3-O-1	134	406	55	91	16	0	8	37	.224	122	187	11	*.966
1959—Detroit	Amer.	3B-2B	148	521	*115	145	19	0	21	61	.278	*168	260	11	*.962
1960—Detroit‡	Amer.	3B	143	497	78	129	23	2	14	47	.260	155	208	●26	.933
1961—Los Angeles	Amer.	3B	76	213	29	43	4	0	3	15	.202	57	103	6	.964
1962—Los Angeles	Amer.	3B-1B	52	104	22	25	9	1	0	10	.240	69	48	4	.967
Major League Totals			2109	7346	1215	1863	337	56	139	683	.254	2436	3663	271	.957

†Traded to Detroit Tigers with Shortstop Rocky Bridges and Outfielder Neil Chrisley for Third Baseman Reno Bertoia, Shortstop Ron Samford and Outfielder Jim Delsing, December 6, 1958.

‡Selected by Los Angeles Angels in American League expansion draft, December 14, 1960.

Coach, Los Angeles Dodgers, part of 1962; Washington Senators, 1963 through 1967; New York Mets, 1968 through 1977; Boston Red Sox, 1978 through 1981.

BOB GIBSON in a classic pose. His record can be found on page 552.

1981 Hall of Fame Enshrinees

ANDREW FOSTER
(Rube)

Born September 17, 1879, at Calvert, Tex.
Died December 9, 1930, at Chicago, Ill.
Height, 6.04. Weight, 220.
Threw and batted righthanded.

Andrew (Rube) Foster will be inducted into the Baseball Hall of Fame August 2 in Cooperstown, N.Y. But many might be asking the question: Who was Rube Foster?

He grew up in Calvert, Tex., and "showed promise as organizer and administrator by operating a baseball team in Calvert while he was still in grade school." When he was 17, Foster began pitching in traveling black leagues and achieved managerial brilliance in a career starting in 1910 with the Chicago Giants. That team lost just six of 129 games against semi-pro and professional teams.

Foster is most remembered for his establishment of the Negro National League in 1920. Said Buck O'Neil, a former player with the Kansas City Monarchs and a member of the Veterans Committee that voted in Foster, "With understandable pride, many black-league players and fans thought Foster was a combination of Connie Mack and John McGraw, a disciple of discipline and inside baseball. But the man's greatest contribution for the young men fortunate today to be doing so well financially is that he founded the league that was the cradle of baseball by which blacks showed how much they belonged."

Honus Wagner once said of Foster and his playing ability, often overshadowed because of his ability as an organizer, "He's one of the greatest pitchers of all time. He was the smartest pitcher I have ever seen in all my years of baseball." In 1903, pitching for the Cuban X Giants, he won four of the Giants' five victories in a series against the Philadelphia Giants for the championship. The following season, Foster jumped to the Philadelphia Giants and beat his old teammates for the title. In the three-game series, Foster got credit for both of his team's wins, striking out 18 batters in the first game and hurling a two-hitter in the deciding third contest. Not to be outdone at the plate, Foster led his team with a .400 batting average in the series.

It was during these early days that Foster got the nickname "Rube." According to Robert Peterson, in the book, "Only the Ball was White," "Legend has it that his teammates began calling him Rube after he defeated George E. (Rube) Waddell and the Philadelphia Athletics, 5-2, in a game in New York." The name remained, and wrote Peterson, "on his tombstone, which he himself chose long before his death, he is A. R. (for Andrew Rube) Foster."

Said Pittsburgh Pirate coach Jewel Ens, in 1939, "Rube Foster would have been a sensation in the big leagues." Concluded Peterson, "He would indeed. Rube Foster: pitcher, manager, league president, major league in everything but name."

JOHN ROBERT (BIG CAT) MIZE

Born January 7, 1913, at Demorest, Ga.

Height, 6.02. Weight, 215.

Threw right and batted lefthanded.

To be inducted into Baseball Hall of Fame, August 2, 1981.

Hit three homers in one game six times and hit three consecutive homers in one game four times; set N.L. season record for home runs by lefthanded batsman, 51 in 1947; made four long hits, July 3, 1939.

Second player in World Series history to hit home run as a pinch-hitter, October 3, 1952.

Named as first baseman on THE SPORTING NEWS All-Star Major League Teams, 1942-47-48.

Scout, New York Giants, 1955; coach, Kansas City Athletics, 1961.

Year Club	League	Pos.	G.	AB.	R.	H.	2B.	3B.	HR.	RBI.	B.A.	PO.	A.	E.	F.A.
1930—Greensboro	Pied.	OF	12	31	5	6	3	0	0	2	.194	10	0	1	.909
1931—Greensboro	Pied.	OF	94	341	69	115	27	1	9	64	.337	130	★17	9	.942
1932—Elmira	NYP	OF-1B	106	405	60	132	20	11	8	78	.326	402	20	6	.986
1933—Greensboro	Pied.	1B	98	378	108	136	29	10	22	104	.360	860	51	25	.973
1933—Rochester	Int.	1B	42	159	27	56	11	3	8	32	.352	355	33	5	.987
1934—Rochester	Int.	1B	90	313	49	106	16	1	17	66	.339	694	72	9	.988
1935—Rochester	Int.	1B	65	252	37	80	11	1	12	44	.317	547	41	8	.987
1936—St. Louis	Nat.	1B-OF	126	414	76	136	30	8	19	93	.329	909	67	6	.994
1937—St. Louis	Nat.	1B	145	560	103	204	40	7	25	113	.364	1308	67	17	.988
1938—St. Louis	Nat.	1B	149	531	85	179	34	★16	27	102	.337	1297	93	●15	.989
1939—St. Louis	Nat.	1B	153	564	104	197	44	14	★28	108	★.349	1348	90	●19	.987
1940—St. Louis	Nat.	1B	155	579	111	182	31	13	★43	★137	.314	1376	80	14	.990
1941—St. Louis (a)	Nat.	1B	126	473	67	150	●39	8	16	100	.317	1157	82	8	.994
1942—New York	Nat.	1B	142	541	97	165	25	7	26	★110	.305	1393	74	8	★.995
1943-44-45—New York	Nat.							(In Military Service)							
1946—New York	Nat.	1B	101	377	70	127	18	3	22	70	.337	928	83	11	.989
1947—New York	Nat.	1B	154	586	★137	177	26	2	●51	★138	.302	★1381	●118	6	★.996
1948—New York	Nat.	1B	152	560	110	162	26	4	●40	125	.289	★1359	★111	13	.991
1949—New York (b)	Nat.	1B	106	388	59	102	15	0	18	62	.263	906	65	6	.994
1949—New York	Amer.	1B	13	23	4	6	1	0	1	2	.261	47	3	1	.980
1950—Kansas City	A.A.	1B	26	94	18	28	4	0	5	18	.298	205	17	0	1.000
1950—New York	Amer.	1B	90	274	43	76	12	0	25	72	.277	490	31	2	.996
1951—New York	Amer.	1B	113	332	37	86	14	1	10	49	.259	632	44	4	.994

Year	Club	League	Pos.	G.	AB.	R.	H.	2B.	3B.	HR.	RBI.	B.A.	PO.	A.	E.	F.A.
1952—New York		Amer.	1B	78	137	9	36	9	0	4	29	.263	218	18	3	.987
1953—New York		Amer.	1B	81	104	6	26	3	0	4	27	.250	113	7	0	1.000
American League Totals				375	870	99	230	39	1	44	179	.264	1500	103	10	.994
National League Totals				1509	5573	1019	1781	328	82	315	1158	.320	13362	930	123	.991
Major League Totals				1884	6443	1118	2011	367	83	359	1337	.312	14862	1033	133	.992

aTraded to New York Giants for catcher James K. O'Dea, pitcher Bill Lohrman, first baseman Johnny McCarthy (assigned to Columbus A.A. club) and $50,000, December 11, 1941. However, Commissioner Landis later upheld Indianapolis' claim to McCarthy as per a prior agreement.

bSold to New York Yankees for $40,000, August 22, 1949.

WORLD SERIES RECORD

Year	Club	League	Pos.	G.	AB.	R.	H.	2B.	3B.	HR.	RBI.	B.A.	PO.	A.	E.	F.A.
1949—New York		Amer.	PH	2	2	0	2	0	0	0	2	1.000	0	0	0	.000
1950—New York		Amer.	1B	4	15	0	2	0	0	0	0	.133	27	3	0	1.000
1951—New York		Amer.	1B-PH	4	7	2	2	1	0	0	1	.286	12	0	0	1.000
1952—New York		Amer.	1B-PH	5	15	3	6	1	0	3	6	.400	25	3	0	1.000
1953—New York		Amer.	PH	3	3	0	0	0	0	0	0	.000	0	0	0	.000
World Series Totals				18	42	5	12	2	0	3	9	.286	64	6	0	1.000

JOHNNY MIZE . . . He finally made it.

NOTES

NOTES

NOTES